University Casebook Series

February, 1990

ACCOUNTING AND THE LAW, Fourth Edition (1978), with Problems Pamphlet (Successor to Dohr, Phillips, Thompson & Warren)

George C. Thompson, Professor, Columbia University Graduate School of Business.
Robert Whitman, Professor of Law, University of Connecticut.
Ellis L. Phillips, Jr., Member of the New York Bar.
William C. Warren, Professor of Law Emeritus, Columbia University.

ACCOUNTING FOR LAWYERS, MATERIALS ON (1980)

David R. Herwitz, Professor of Law, Harvard University.

ADMINISTRATIVE LAW, Eighth Edition (1987), with 1989 Case Supplement and 1983 Problems Supplement (Supplement edited in association with Paul R. Verkuil, Dean and Professor of Law, Tulane University)

Walter Gellhorn, University Professor Emeritus, Columbia University.
Clark Byse, Professor of Law, Harvard University.
Peter L. Strauss, Professor of Law, Columbia University.
Todd D. Rakoff, Professor of Law, Harvard University.
Roy A. Schotland, Professor of Law, Georgetown University.

ADMIRALTY, Third Edition (1987), with Statute and Rule Supplement

Jo Desha Lucas, Professor of Law, University of Chicago.

ADVOCACY, see also Lawyering Process

AGENCY, see also Enterprise Organization

AGENCY—PARTNERSHIPS, Fourth Edition (1987)

Abridgement from Conard, Knauss & Siegel's Enterprise Organization, Fourth Edition.

AGENCY AND PARTNERSHIPS (1987)

Melvin A. Eisenberg, Professor of Law, University of California, Berkeley.

ANTITRUST: FREE ENTERPRISE AND ECONOMIC ORGANIZATION, Sixth Edition (1983), with 1983 Problems in Antitrust Supplement and 1989 Case Supplement

Louis B. Schwartz, Professor of Law, University of Pennsylvania.
John J. Flynn, Professor of Law, University of Utah.
Harry First, Professor of Law, New York University.

BANKRUPTCY, Second Edition (1989)

Robert L. Jordan, Professor of Law, University of California, Los Angeles.
William D. Warren, Professor of Law, University of California, Los Angeles.

BANKRUPTCY AND DEBTOR–CREDITOR LAW, Second Edition (1988)

Theodore Eisenberg, Professor of Law, Cornell University.

UNIVERSITY CASEBOOK SERIES—Continued

BUSINESS CRIME (1990)

Harry First, Professor of Law, New York University.

BUSINESS ORGANIZATION, see also Enterprise Organization

BUSINESS PLANNING, Temporary Second Edition (1984)

David R. Herwitz, Professor of Law, Harvard University.

BUSINESS TORTS (1972)

Milton Handler, Professor of Law Emeritus, Columbia University.

CHILDREN IN THE LEGAL SYSTEM (1983) with 1988 Supplement

Walter Wadlington, Professor of Law, University of Virginia.
Charles H. Whitebread, Professor of Law, University of Southern California.
Samuel Davis, Professor of Law, University of Georgia.

CIVIL PROCEDURE, see Procedure

CIVIL RIGHTS ACTIONS (1988), with 1989 Supplement

Peter W. Low, Professor of Law, University of Virginia.
John C. Jeffries, Jr., Professor of Law, University of Virginia.

CLINIC, see also Lawyering Process

COMMERCIAL AND DEBTOR–CREDITOR LAW: SELECTED STATUTES, 1989 EDITION

COMMERCIAL LAW, Second Edition (1987)

Robert L. Jordan, Professor of Law, University of California, Los Angeles.
William D. Warren, Professor of Law, University of California, Los Angeles.

COMMERCIAL LAW, Fourth Edition (1985)

E. Allan Farnsworth, Professor of Law, Columbia University.
John Honnold, Professor of Law, University of Pennsylvania.

COMMERCIAL PAPER, Third Edition (1984)

E. Allan Farnsworth, Professor of Law, Columbia University.

COMMERCIAL PAPER, Second Edition (1987) (Reprinted from COMMERCIAL LAW, Second Edition (1987))

Robert L. Jordan, Professor of Law, University of California, Los Angeles.
William D. Warren, Professor of Law, University of California, Los Angeles.

COMMERCIAL PAPER AND BANK DEPOSITS AND COLLECTIONS (1967), with Statutory Supplement

William D. Hawkland, Professor of Law, University of Illinois.

COMMERCIAL TRANSACTIONS—Principles and Policies (1982)

Alan Schwartz, Professor of Law, University of Southern California.
Robert E. Scott, Professor of Law, University of Virginia.

COMPARATIVE LAW, Fifth Edition (1988)

Rudolf B. Schlesinger, Professor of Law, Hastings College of the Law.
Hans W. Baade, Professor of Law, University of Texas.
Mirjan P. Damaska, Professor of Law, Yale Law School.
Peter E. Herzog, Professor of Law, Syracuse University.

UNIVERSITY CASEBOOK SERIES—Continued

COMPETITIVE PROCESS, LEGAL REGULATION OF THE, Fourth Edition (1990), with 1989 Selected Statutes Supplement

Edmund W. Kitch, Professor of Law, University of Virginia.
Harvey S. Perlman, Dean of the Law School, University of Nebraska.

CONFLICT OF LAWS, Eighth Edition (1984), with 1989 Case Supplement

Willis L. M. Reese, Professor of Law, Columbia University.
Maurice Rosenberg, Professor of Law, Columbia University.

CONSTITUTIONAL LAW, Eighth Edition (1989), with 1989 Case Supplement

Edward L. Barrett, Jr., Professor of Law, University of California, Davis.
William Cohen, Professor of Law, Stanford University.
Jonathan D. Varat, Professor of Law, University of California, Los Angeles.

CONSTITUTIONAL LAW, CIVIL LIBERTY AND INDIVIDUAL RIGHTS, Second Edition (1982), with 1989 Supplement

William Cohen, Professor of Law, Stanford University.
John Kaplan, Professor of Law, Stanford University.

CONSTITUTIONAL LAW, Eleventh Edition (1985), with 1989 Supplement (Supplement edited in association with Frederick F. Schauer, Professor of Law, University of Michigan)

Gerald Gunther, Professor of Law, Stanford University.

CONSTITUTIONAL LAW, INDIVIDUAL RIGHTS IN, Fourth Edition (1986), (Reprinted from CONSTITUTIONAL LAW, Eleventh Edition), with 1989 Supplement (Supplement edited in association with Frederick F. Schauer, Professor of Law, University of Michigan)

Gerald Gunther, Professor of Law, Stanford University.

CONSUMER TRANSACTIONS (1983), with Selected Statutes and Regulations Supplement and 1987 Case Supplement

Michael M. Greenfield, Professor of Law, Washington University.

CONTRACT LAW AND ITS APPLICATION, Fourth Edition (1988)

Arthur Rosett, Professor of Law, University of California, Los Angeles.

CONTRACT LAW, STUDIES IN, Third Edition (1984)

Edward J. Murphy, Professor of Law, University of Notre Dame.
Richard E. Speidel, Professor of Law, Northwestern University.

CONTRACTS, Fifth Edition (1987)

John P. Dawson, late Professor of Law, Harvard University.
William Burnett Harvey, Professor of Law and Political Science, Boston University.
Stanley D. Henderson, Professor of Law, University of Virginia.

CONTRACTS, Fourth Edition (1988)

E. Allan Farnsworth, Professor of Law, Columbia University.
William F. Young, Professor of Law, Columbia University.

CONTRACTS, Selections on (statutory materials) (1988)

CONTRACTS, Second Edition (1978), with Statutory and Administrative Law Supplement (1978)

Ian R. Macneil, Professor of Law, Cornell University.

COPYRIGHT, PATENTS AND TRADEMARKS, see also Competitive Process; see also Selected Statutes and International Agreements

UNIVERSITY CASEBOOK SERIES—Continued

COPYRIGHT, PATENT, TRADEMARK AND RELATED STATE DOCTRINES, Second Edition (1981), with 1988 Case Supplement, 1989 Selected Statutes Supplement and 1981 Problem Supplement

Paul Goldstein, Professor of Law, Stanford University.

COPYRIGHT, Unfair Competition, and Other Topics Bearing on the Protection of Literary, Musical, and Artistic Works, Fifth Edition (1990), with 1990 Statutory Supplement

Ralph S. Brown, Jr., Professor of Law, Yale University.
Robert C. Denicola, Professor of Law, University of Nebraska.

CORPORATE ACQUISITIONS, The Law and Finance of (1986), with 1989 Supplement

Ronald J. Gilson, Professor of Law, Stanford University.

CORPORATE FINANCE, Third Edition (1987)

Victor Brudney, Professor of Law, Harvard University.
Marvin A. Chirelstein, Professor of Law, Columbia University.

CORPORATION LAW, BASIC, Third Edition (1989), with Documentary Supplement

Detlev F. Vagts, Professor of Law, Harvard University.

CORPORATIONS, see also Enterprise Organization

CORPORATIONS, Sixth Edition—Concise (1988), with Statutory Supplement (1989)

William L. Cary, late Professor of Law, Columbia University.
Melvin Aron Eisenberg, Professor of Law, University of California, Berkeley.

CORPORATIONS, Sixth Edition—Unabridged (1988), with Statutory Supplement (1989)

William L. Cary, late Professor of Law, Columbia University.
Melvin Aron Eisenberg, Professor of Law, University of California, Berkeley.

CORPORATIONS AND BUSINESS ASSOCIATIONS—STATUTES, RULES, AND FORMS (1989)

CORPORATIONS COURSE GAME PLAN (1975)

David R. Herwitz, Professor of Law, Harvard University.

CORRECTIONS, SEE SENTENCING

CREDITORS' RIGHTS, see also Debtor-Creditor Law

CRIMINAL JUSTICE ADMINISTRATION, Third Edition (1986), with 1989 Case Supplement

Frank W. Miller, Professor of Law, Washington University.
Robert O. Dawson, Professor of Law, University of Texas.
George E. Dix, Professor of Law, University of Texas.
Raymond I. Parnas, Professor of Law, University of California, Davis.

CRIMINAL LAW, Fourth Edition (1987)

Fred E. Inbau, Professor of Law Emeritus, Northwestern University.
Andre A. Moenssens, Professor of Law, University of Richmond.
James R. Thompson, Professor of Law Emeritus, Northwestern University.

CRIMINAL LAW AND APPROACHES TO THE STUDY OF LAW (1986)

John M. Brumbaugh, Professor of Law, University of Maryland.

UNIVERSITY CASEBOOK SERIES—Continued

CRIMINAL LAW, Second Edition (1986)

Peter W. Low, Professor of Law, University of Virginia.
John C. Jeffries, Jr., Professor of Law, University of Virginia.
Richard C. Bonnie, Professor of Law, University of Virginia.

CRIMINAL LAW, Fourth Edition (1986)

Lloyd L. Weinreb, Professor of Law, Harvard University.

CRIMINAL LAW AND PROCEDURE, Seventh Edition (1989)

Ronald N. Boyce, Professor of Law, University of Utah.
Rollin M. Perkins, Professor of Law Emeritus, University of California, Hastings
College of the Law.

CRIMINAL PROCEDURE, Third Edition (1987), with 1989 Supplement

James B. Haddad, Professor of Law, Northwestern University.
James B. Zagel, Chief, Criminal Justice Division, Office of Attorney General of
Illinois.
Gary L. Starkman, Assistant U. S. Attorney, Northern District of Illinois.
William J. Bauer, Chief Judge of the U.S. Court of Appeals, Seventh Circuit.

CRIMINAL PROCESS, Fourth Edition (1987), with 1989 Supplement

Lloyd L. Weinreb, Professor of Law, Harvard University.

DAMAGES, Second Edition (1952)

Charles T. McCormick, late Professor of Law, University of Texas.
William F. Fritz, late Professor of Law, University of Texas.

DECEDENTS' ESTATES AND TRUSTS, Seventh Edition (1988)

John Ritchie, late Professor of Law, University of Virginia.
Neill H. Alford, Jr., Professor of Law, University of Virginia.
Richard W. Effland, late Professor of Law, Arizona State University.

DISPUTE RESOLUTION, Processes of (1989)

John S. Murray, President and Executive Director of The Conflict Clinic, Inc.,
George Mason University.
Alan Scott Rau, Professor of Law, University of Texas.
Edward F. Sherman, Professor of Law, University of Texas.

DOMESTIC RELATIONS, see also Family Law

DOMESTIC RELATIONS, Successor Edition (1984) with 1989 Supplement

Walter Wadlington, Professor of Law, University of Virginia.

EMPLOYMENT DISCRIMINATION, Second Edition (1987), with 1989 Supplement

Joel W. Friedman, Professor of Law, Tulane University.
George M. Strickler, Professor of Law, Tulane University.

EMPLOYMENT LAW (1987), with 1987 Statutory Supplement and 1989 Case Supplement

Mark A. Rothstein, Professor of Law, University of Houston.
Andria S. Knapp, Adjunct Professor of Law, University of California, Hastings
College of Law.
Lance Liebman, Professor of Law, Harvard University.

ENERGY LAW (1983) with 1986 Case Supplement

Donald N. Zillman, Professor of Law, University of Utah.
Laurence Lattman, Dean of Mines and Engineering, University of Utah.

UNIVERSITY CASEBOOK SERIES—Continued

ENTERPRISE ORGANIZATION, Fourth Edition (1987), with 1987 Corporation and Partnership Statutes, Rules and Forms Supplement

Alfred F. Conard, Professor of Law, University of Michigan.
Robert L. Knauss, Dean of the Law School, University of Houston.
Stanley Siegel, Professor of Law, University of California, Los Angeles.

ENVIRONMENTAL POLICY LAW 1985 Edition, with 1985 Problems Supplement (Supplement in association with Ronald H. Rosenberg, Professor of Law, College of William and Mary)

Thomas J. Schoenbaum, Professor of Law, University of Georgia.

EQUITY, see also Remedies

EQUITY, RESTITUTION AND DAMAGES, Second Edition (1974)

Robert Childres, late Professor of Law, Northwestern University.
William F. Johnson, Jr., Professor of Law, New York University.

ESTATE PLANNING, Second Edition (1982), with 1985 Case, Text and Documentary Supplement

David Westfall, Professor of Law, Harvard University.

ETHICS, see Legal Profession, Professional Responsibility, and Social Responsibilities

ETHICS AND PROFESSIONAL RESPONSIBILITY (1981) (Reprinted from THE LAWYERING PROCESS)

Gary Bellow, Professor of Law, Harvard University.
Bea Moulton, Legal Services Corporation.

EVIDENCE, Sixth Edition (1988 Reprint)

John Kaplan, Professor of Law, Stanford University.
Jon R. Waltz, Professor of Law, Northwestern University.

EVIDENCE, Eighth Edition (1988), with Rules, Statute and Case Supplement (1989)

Jack B. Weinstein, Chief Judge, United States District Court.
John H. Mansfield, Professor of Law, Harvard University.
Norman Abrams, Professor of Law, University of California, Los Angeles.
Margaret Berger, Professor of Law, Brooklyn Law School.

FAMILY LAW, see also Domestic Relations

FAMILY LAW Second Edition (1985), with 1988 Supplement

Judith C. Areen, Professor of Law, Georgetown University.

FAMILY LAW AND CHILDREN IN THE LEGAL SYSTEM, STATUTORY MATERIALS (1981)

Walter Wadlington, Professor of Law, University of Virginia.

FEDERAL COURTS, Eighth Edition (1988), with 1989 Supplement

Charles T. McCormick, late Professor of Law, University of Texas.
James H. Chadbourn, late Professor of Law, Harvard University.
Charles Alan Wright, Professor of Law, University of Texas, Austin.

UNIVERSITY CASEBOOK SERIES—Continued

FEDERAL COURTS AND THE FEDERAL SYSTEM, Hart and Wechsler's Third Edition (1988), with 1989 Case Supplement, and the Judicial Code and Rules of Procedure in the Federal Courts (1989)

Paul M. Bator, Professor of Law, University of Chicago.
Daniel J. Meltzer, Professor of Law, Harvard University.
Paul J. Mishkin, Professor of Law, University of California, Berkeley.
David L. Shapiro, Professor of Law, Harvard University.

FEDERAL COURTS AND THE LAW OF FEDERAL-STATE RELATIONS, Second Edition (1989), with 1989 Supplement

Peter W. Low, Professor of Law, University of Virginia.
John C. Jeffries, Jr., Professor of Law, University of Virginia.

FEDERAL PUBLIC LAND AND RESOURCES LAW, Second Edition (1987), with 1990 Case Supplement and 1984 Statutory Supplement

George C. Coggins, Professor of Law, University of Kansas.
Charles F. Wilkinson, Professor of Law, University of Oregon.

FEDERAL RULES OF CIVIL PROCEDURE and Selected Other Procedural Provisions, 1989 Edition

FEDERAL TAXATION, see Taxation

FOOD AND DRUG LAW (1980), with Statutory Supplement

Richard A. Merrill, Dean of the School of Law, University of Virginia.
Peter Barton Hutt, Esq.

FUTURE INTERESTS (1958)

Philip Mechem, late Professor of Law Emeritus, University of Pennsylvania.

FUTURE INTERESTS (1970)

Howard R. Williams, Professor of Law, Stanford University.

FUTURE INTERESTS AND ESTATE PLANNING (1961), with 1962 Supplement

W. Barton Leach, late Professor of Law, Harvard University.
James K. Logan, formerly Dean of the Law School, University of Kansas.

GOVERNMENT CONTRACTS, FEDERAL, Successor Edition (1985), with 1989 Supplement

John W. Whelan, Professor of Law, Hastings College of the Law.

GOVERNMENT REGULATION: FREE ENTERPRISE AND ECONOMIC ORGANIZATION, Sixth Edition (1985)

Louis B. Schwartz, Professor of Law, Hastings College of the Law.
John J. Flynn, Professor of Law, University of Utah.
Harry First, Professor of Law, New York University.

HEALTH CARE LAW AND POLICY (1988)

Clark C. Havighurst, Professor of Law, Duke University.

HINCKLEY, JOHN W., JR., TRIAL OF: A Case Study of the Insanity Defense (1986)

Peter W. Low, Professor of Law, University of Virginia.
John C. Jeffries, Jr., Professor of Law, University of Virginia.
Richard C. Bonnie, Professor of Law, University of Virginia.

INJUNCTIONS, Second Edition (1984)

Owen M. Fiss, Professor of Law, Yale University.
Doug Rendleman, Professor of Law, College of William and Mary.

UNIVERSITY CASEBOOK SERIES—Continued

INSTITUTIONAL INVESTORS, (1978)

David L. Ratner, Professor of Law, Cornell University.

INSURANCE, Second Edition (1985)

William F. Young, Professor of Law, Columbia University.
Eric M. Holmes, Professor of Law, University of Georgia.

INTERNATIONAL LAW, see also Transnational Legal Problems, Transnational Business Problems, and United Nations Law

INTERNATIONAL LAW IN CONTEMPORARY PERSPECTIVE (1981), with Essay Supplement

Myres S. McDougal, Professor of Law, Yale University.
W. Michael Reisman, Professor of Law, Yale University.

INTERNATIONAL LEGAL SYSTEM, Third Edition (1988), with Documentary Supplement

Joseph Modeste Sweeney, Professor of Law, University of California, Hastings.
Covey T. Oliver, Professor of Law, University of Pennsylvania.
Noyes E. Leech, Professor of Law Emeritus, University of Pennsylvania.

INTRODUCTION TO LAW, see also Legal Method, On Law in Courts, and Dynamics of American Law

INTRODUCTION TO THE STUDY OF LAW (1970)

E. Wayne Thode, late Professor of Law, University of Utah.
Leon Lebowitz, Professor of Law, University of Texas.
Lester J. Mazor, Professor of Law, University of Utah.

JUDICIAL CODE and Rules of Procedure in the Federal Courts, Students' Edition, 1989 Revision

Daniel J. Meltzer, Professor of Law, Harvard University.
David L. Shapiro, Professor of Law, Harvard University.

JURISPRUDENCE (Temporary Edition Hardbound) (1949)

Lon L. Fuller, late Professor of Law, Harvard University.

JUVENILE, see also Children

JUVENILE JUSTICE PROCESS, Third Edition (1985)

Frank W. Miller, Professor of Law, Washington University.
Robert O. Dawson, Professor of Law, University of Texas.
George E. Dix, Professor of Law, University of Texas.
Raymond I. Parnas, Professor of Law, University of California, Davis.

LABOR LAW, Tenth Edition (1986), with 1989 Case Supplement and 1986 Statutory Supplement

Archibald Cox, Professor of Law, Harvard University.
Derek C. Bok, President, Harvard University.
Robert A. Gorman, Professor of Law, University of Pennsylvania.

LABOR LAW, Second Edition (1982), with Statutory Supplement

Clyde W. Summers, Professor of Law, University of Pennsylvania.
Harry H. Wellington, Dean of the Law School, Yale University.
Alan Hyde, Professor of Law, Rutgers University.

UNIVERSITY CASEBOOK SERIES—Continued

LAND FINANCING, Third Edition (1985)

The late Norman Penney, Professor of Law, Cornell University.
Richard F. Broude, Member of the California Bar.
Roger Cunningham, Professor of Law, University of Michigan.

LAW AND MEDICINE (1980)

Walter Wadlington, Professor of Law and Professor of Legal Medicine, University of Virginia.
Jon R. Waltz, Professor of Law, Northwestern University.
Roger B. Dworkin, Professor of Law, Indiana University, and Professor of Biomedical History, University of Washington.

LAW, LANGUAGE AND ETHICS (1972)

William R. Bishin, Professor of Law, University of Southern California.
Christopher D. Stone, Professor of Law, University of Southern California.

LAW, SCIENCE AND MEDICINE (1984), with 1989 Supplement

Judith C. Areen, Professor of Law, Georgetown University.
Patricia A. King, Professor of Law, Georgetown University.
Steven P. Goldberg, Professor of Law, Georgetown University.
Alexander M. Capron, Professor of Law, University of Southern California.

LAWYERING PROCESS (1978), with Civil Problem Supplement and Criminal Problem Supplement

Gary Bellow, Professor of Law, Harvard University.
Bea Moulton, Professor of Law, Arizona State University.

LEGAL METHOD (1980)

Harry W. Jones, Professor of Law Emeritus, Columbia University.
John M. Kernochan, Professor of Law, Columbia University.
Arthur W. Murphy, Professor of Law, Columbia University.

LEGAL METHODS (1969)

Robert N. Covington, Professor of Law, Vanderbilt University.
E. Blythe Stason, late Professor of Law, Vanderbilt University.
John W. Wade, Professor of Law, Vanderbilt University.
Elliott E. Cheatham, late Professor of Law, Vanderbilt University.
Theodore A. Smedley, Professor of Law, Vanderbilt University.

LEGAL PROFESSION, THE, Responsibility and Regulation, Second Edition (1988)

Geoffrey C. Hazard, Jr., Professor of Law, Yale University.
Deborah L. Rhode, Professor of Law, Stanford University.

LEGISLATION, Fourth Edition (1982) (by Fordham)

Horace E. Read, late Vice President, Dalhousie University.
John W. MacDonald, Professor of Law Emeritus, Cornell Law School.
Jefferson B. Fordham, Professor of Law, University of Utah.
William J. Pierce, Professor of Law, University of Michigan.

LEGISLATIVE AND ADMINISTRATIVE PROCESSES, Second Edition (1981)

Hans A. Linde, Judge, Supreme Court of Oregon.
George Bunn, Professor of Law, University of Wisconsin.
Fredericka Paff, Professor of Law, University of Wisconsin.
W. Lawrence Church, Professor of Law, University of Wisconsin.

LOCAL GOVERNMENT LAW, Second Revised Edition (1986)

Jefferson B. Fordham, Professor of Law, University of Utah.

UNIVERSITY CASEBOOK SERIES—Continued

MASS MEDIA LAW, Third Edition (1987)

Marc A. Franklin, Professor of Law, Stanford University.

MUNICIPAL CORPORATIONS, see Local Government Law

NEGOTIABLE INSTRUMENTS, see Commercial Paper

NEGOTIATION (1981) (Reprinted from THE LAWYERING PROCESS)

Gary Bellow, Professor of Law, Harvard Law School.
Bea Moulton, Legal Services Corporation.

NEW YORK PRACTICE, Fourth Edition (1978)

Herbert Peterfreund, Professor of Law, New York University.
Joseph M. McLaughlin, Dean of the Law School, Fordham University.

OIL AND GAS, Fifth Edition (1987)

Howard R. Williams, Professor of Law, Stanford University.
Richard C. Maxwell, Professor of Law, University of California, Los Angeles.
Charles J. Meyers, late Dean of the Law School, Stanford University.
Stephen F. Williams, Judge of the United States Court of Appeals.

ON LAW IN COURTS (1965)

Paul J. Mishkin, Professor of Law, University of California, Berkeley.
Clarence Morris, Professor of Law Emeritus, University of Pennsylvania.

PLEADING AND PROCEDURE, see Procedure, Civil

POLICE FUNCTION, Fourth Edition (1986), with 1989 Case Supplement

Reprint of Chapters 1–10 of Miller, Dawson, Dix and Parnas's CRIMINAL
JUSTICE ADMINISTRATION, Third Edition.

PREPARING AND PRESENTING THE CASE (1981) (Reprinted from THE LAW-YERING PROCESS)

Gary Bellow, Professor of Law, Harvard Law School.
Bea Moulton, Legal Services Corporation.

PROCEDURE (1988), with Procedure Supplement (1989)

Robert M. Cover, late Professor of Law, Yale Law School.
Owen M. Fiss, Professor of Law, Yale Law School.
Judith Resnik, Professor of Law, University of Southern California Law Center.

PROCEDURE—CIVIL PROCEDURE, Second Edition (1974), with 1979 Supplement

The late James H. Chadbourn, Professor of Law, Harvard University.
A. Leo Levin, Professor of Law, University of Pennsylvania.
Philip Shuchman, Professor of Law, Cornell University.

PROCEDURE—CIVIL PROCEDURE, Fifth Edition (1984), with 1989 Supplement

Richard H. Field, late Professor of Law, Harvard University.
Benjamin Kaplan, Professor of Law Emeritus, Harvard University.
Kevin M. Clermont, Professor of Law, Cornell University.

PROCEDURE—CIVIL PROCEDURE, Fourth Edition (1985), with 1989 Supplement

Maurice Rosenberg, Professor of Law, Columbia University.
Hans Smit, Professor of Law, Columbia University.
Harold L. Korn, Professor of Law, Columbia University.

UNIVERSITY CASEBOOK SERIES—Continued

PROCEDURE—PLEADING AND PROCEDURE: State and Federal, Sixth Edition (1989)

David W. Louisell, late Professor of Law, University of California, Berkeley.
Geoffrey C. Hazard, Jr., Professor of Law, Yale University.
Colin C. Tait, Professor of Law, University of Connecticut.

PROCEDURE—FEDERAL RULES OF CIVIL PROCEDURE, 1989 Edition

PRODUCTS LIABILITY (1980)

Marshall S. Shapo, Professor of Law, Northwestern University.

PRODUCTS LIABILITY AND SAFETY, Second Edition, (1989), with 1989 Statutory Supplement

W. Page Keeton, Professor of Law, University of Texas.
David G. Owen, Professor of Law, University of South Carolina.
John E. Montgomery, Professor of Law, University of South Carolina.
Michael D. Green, Professor of Law, University of Iowa

PROFESSIONAL RESPONSIBILITY, Fourth Edition (1987), with 1989 Selected National Standards Supplement

Thomas D. Morgan, Dean of the Law School, Emory University.
Ronald D. Rotunda, Professor of Law, University of Illinois.

PROPERTY, Fifth Edition (1984)

John E. Cribbet, Professor of Law, University of Illinois.
Corwin W. Johnson, Professor of Law, University of Texas.

PROPERTY—PERSONAL (1953)

S. Kenneth Skolfield, late Professor of Law Emeritus, Boston University.

PROPERTY—PERSONAL, Third Edition (1954)

Everett Fraser, late Dean of the Law School Emeritus, University of Minnesota.
Third Edition by Charles W. Taintor, late Professor of Law, University of Pittsburgh.

PROPERTY—INTRODUCTION, TO REAL PROPERTY, Third Edition (1954)

Everett Fraser, late Dean of the Law School Emeritus, University of Minnesota.

PROPERTY—FUNDAMENTALS OF MODERN REAL PROPERTY, Second Edition (1982), with 1985 Supplement

Edward H. Rabin, Professor of Law, University of California, Davis.

PROPERTY, REAL (1984), with 1988 Supplement

Paul Goldstein, Professor of Law, Stanford University.

PROSECUTION AND ADJUDICATION, Third Edition (1986), with 1989 Case Supplement

Reprint of Chapters 11–26 of Miller, Dawson, Dix and Parnas's CRIMINAL JUSTICE ADMINISTRATION, Third Edition.

PSYCHIATRY AND LAW, see Mental Health, see also Hinckley, Trial of

PUBLIC REGULATION OF DANGEROUS PRODUCTS (paperback) (1980)

Marshall S. Shapo, Professor of Law, Northwestern University.

PUBLIC UTILITY LAW, see Free Enterprise, also Regulated Industries

UNIVERSITY CASEBOOK SERIES—Continued

REAL ESTATE PLANNING, Third Edition (1989), with 1989 Problem and Statutory Supplement

Norton L. Steuben, Professor of Law, University of Colorado.

REAL ESTATE TRANSACTIONS, Revised Second Edition (1988), with Statute, Form and Problem Supplement (1988)

Paul Goldstein, Professor of Law, Stanford University.

RECEIVERSHIP AND CORPORATE REORGANIZATION, see Creditors' Rights

REGULATED INDUSTRIES, Second Edition, (1976)

William K. Jones, Professor of Law, Columbia University.

REMEDIES, Second Edition (1987)

Edward D. Re, Chief Judge, U. S. Court of International Trade.

REMEDIES, (1989)

Elaine W. Shoben, Professor of Law, University of Illinois.
Wm. Murray Tabb, Professor of Law, Baylor University.

SALES, Second Edition (1986)

Marion W. Benfield, Jr., Professor of Law, University of Illinois.
William D. Hawkland, Chancellor, Louisiana State Law Center.

SALES AND SALES FINANCING, Fifth Edition (1984)

John Honnold, Professor of Law, University of Pennsylvania.

SALES LAW AND THE CONTRACTING PROCESS (1982)

Reprint of Chapters 1–10 of Schwartz and Scott's Commercial Transactions.

SECURED TRANSACTIONS IN PERSONAL PROPERTY, Second Edition (1987) (Reprinted from COMMERCIAL LAW, Second Edition (1987))

Robert L. Jordan, Professor of Law, University of California, Los Angeles.
William D. Warren, Professor of Law, University of California, Los Angeles.

SECURITIES REGULATION, Sixth Edition (1987), with 1989 Selected Statutes, Rules and Forms Supplement and 1989 Cases and Releases Supplement

Richard W. Jennings, Professor of Law, University of California, Berkeley.
Harold Marsh, Jr., Member of California Bar.

SECURITIES REGULATION, Second Edition (1988), with Statute, Rule and Form Supplement (1988)

Larry D. Soderquist, Professor of Law, Vanderbilt University.

SECURITY INTERESTS IN PERSONAL PROPERTY, Second Edition (1987)

Douglas G. Baird, Professor of Law, University of Chicago.
Thomas H. Jackson, Professor of Law, Harvard University.

SECURITY INTERESTS IN PERSONAL PROPERTY (1985) (Reprinted from Sales and Sales Financing, Fifth Edition)

John Honnold, Professor of Law, University of Pennsylvania.

SOCIAL RESPONSIBILITIES OF LAWYERS, Case Studies (1988)

Philip B. Heymann, Professor of Law, Harvard University.
Lance Liebman, Professor of Law, Harvard University.

UNIVERSITY CASEBOOK SERIES—Continued

SOCIAL SCIENCE IN LAW, Second Edition (1990)

John Monahan, Professor of Law, University of Virginia.
Laurens Walker, Professor of Law, University of Virginia.

TAXATION, FEDERAL INCOME (1989)

Stephen B. Cohen, Professor of Law, Georgetown University

TAXATION, FEDERAL INCOME, Second Edition (1988), with 1989 Supplement

Michael J. Graetz, Professor of Law, Yale University.

TAXATION, FEDERAL INCOME, Sixth Edition (1987)

James J. Freeland, Professor of Law, University of Florida.
Stephen A. Lind, Professor of Law, University of Florida and University of California, Hastings.
Richard B. Stephens, late Professor of Law Emeritus, University of Florida.

TAXATION, FEDERAL INCOME, Successor Edition (1986), with 1989 Legislative Supplement

Stanley S. Surrey, late Professor of Law, Harvard University.
Paul R. McDaniel, Professor of Law, Boston College.
Hugh J. Ault, Professor of Law, Boston College.
Stanley A. Koppelman, Professor of Law, Boston University.

TAXATION, FEDERAL INCOME, VOLUME II, Taxation of Partnerships and Corporations, Second Edition (1980), with 1989 Legislative Supplement

Stanley S. Surrey, late Professor of Law, Harvard University.
William C. Warren, Professor of Law Emeritus, Columbia University.
Paul R. McDaniel, Professor of Law, Boston College.
Hugh J. Ault, Professor of Law, Boston College.

TAXATION, FEDERAL WEALTH TRANSFER, Successor Edition (1987)

Stanley S. Surrey, late Professor of Law, Harvard University.
Paul R. McDaniel, Professor of Law, Boston College.
Harry L. Gutman, Professor of Law, University of Pennsylvania.

TAXATION, FUNDAMENTALS OF CORPORATE, Second Edition (1987), with 1989 Supplement

Stephen A. Lind, Professor of Law, University of Florida and University of California, Hastings.
Stephen Schwarz, Professor of Law, University of California, Hastings.
Daniel J. Lathrope, Professor of Law, University of California, Hastings.
Joshua Rosenberg, Professor of Law, University of San Francisco.

TAXATION, FUNDAMENTALS OF PARTNERSHIP, Second Edition (1988)

Stephen A. Lind, Professor of Law, University of Florida and University of California, Hastings.
Stephen Schwarz, Professor of Law, University of California, Hastings.
Daniel J. Lathrope, Professor of Law, University of California, Hastings.
Joshua Rosenberg, Professor of Law, University of San Francisco.

TAXATION, PROBLEMS IN THE FEDERAL INCOME TAXATION OF PARTNERSHIPS AND CORPORATIONS, Second Edition (1986)

Norton L. Steuben, Professor of Law, University of Colorado.
William J. Turnier, Professor of Law, University of North Carolina.

UNIVERSITY CASEBOOK SERIES—Continued

TAXATION, PROBLEMS IN THE FUNDAMENTALS OF FEDERAL INCOME, Second Edition (1985)

Norton L. Steuben, Professor of Law, University of Colorado.
William J. Turnier, Professor of Law, University of North Carolina.

TORT LAW AND ALTERNATIVES, Fourth Edition (1987)

Marc A. Franklin, Professor of Law, Stanford University.
Robert L. Rabin, Professor of Law, Stanford University.

TORTS, Eighth Edition (1988)

William L. Prosser, late Professor of Law, University of California, Hastings.
John W. Wade, Professor of Law, Vanderbilt University.
Victor E. Schwartz, Adjunct Professor of Law, Georgetown University.

TORTS, Third Edition (1976)

Harry Shulman, late Dean of the Law School, Yale University.
Fleming James, Jr., Professor of Law Emeritus, Yale University.
Oscar S. Gray, Professor of Law, University of Maryland.

TRADE REGULATION, Second Edition (1983), with 1987 Supplement

Milton Handler, Professor of Law Emeritus, Columbia University.
Harlan M. Blake, Professor of Law, Columbia University.
Robert Pitofsky, Professor of Law, Georgetown University.
Harvey J. Goldschmid, Professor of Law, Columbia University.

TRADE REGULATION, see Antitrust

TRANSNATIONAL BUSINESS PROBLEMS (1986)

Detlev F. Vagts, Professor of Law, Harvard University.

TRANSNATIONAL LEGAL PROBLEMS, Third Edition (1986) with Documentary Supplement

Henry J. Steiner, Professor of Law, Harvard University.
Detlev F. Vagts, Professor of Law, Harvard University.

TRIAL, see also Evidence, Making the Record, Lawyering Process and Preparing and Presenting the Case

TRUSTS, Fifth Edition (1978)

George G. Bogert, late Professor of Law Emeritus, University of Chicago.
Dallin H. Oaks, President, Brigham Young University.

TRUSTS AND SUCCESSION (Palmer's), Fourth Edition (1983)

Richard V. Wellman, Professor of Law, University of Georgia.
Lawrence W. Waggoner, Professor of Law, University of Michigan.
Olin L. Browder, Jr., Professor of Law, University of Michigan.

UNFAIR COMPETITION, see Competitive Process and Business Torts

WATER RESOURCE MANAGEMENT, Third Edition (1988)

The late Charles J. Meyers, formerly Dean, Stanford University Law School.
A. Dan Tarlock, Professor of Law, II Chicago-Kent College of Law.
James N. Corbridge, Jr., Chancellor, University of Colorado at Boulder, and
    Professor of Law, University of Colorado School of Law.
David H. Getches, Professor of Law, University of Colorado School of Law.

WILLS AND ADMINISTRATION, Fifth Edition (1961)

Philip Mechem, late Professor of Law, University of Pennsylvania.
Thomas E. Atkinson, late Professor of Law, New York University.

UNIVERSITY CASEBOOK SERIES—Continued

WRITING AND ANALYSIS IN THE LAW (1989)

Helene S. Shapo, Professor of Law, Northwestern University
Marilyn R. Walter, Professor of Law, Brooklyn Law School
Elizabeth Fajans, Writing Specialist, Brooklyn Law School

University Casebook Series

EDITORIAL BOARD

DAVID L. SHAPIRO
DIRECTING EDITOR
Professor of Law, Harvard University

EDWARD L. BARRETT, Jr.
Professor of Law, University of California, Davis

ROBERT C. CLARK
Dean of the School of Law, Harvard University

OWEN M. FISS
Professor of Law, Yale Law School

JEFFERSON B. FORDHAM
Professor of Law, University of Utah

GERALD GUNTHER
Professor of Law, Stanford University

THOMAS H. JACKSON
Dean of the School of Law, University of Virginia

HARRY W. JONES
Professor of Law, Columbia University

HERMA HILL KAY
Professor of Law, University of California, Berkeley

PAGE KEETON
Professor of Law, University of Texas

ROBERT L. RABIN
Professor of Law, Stanford University

CAROL M. ROSE
Professor of Law, Yale University

SAMUEL D. THURMAN
Professor of Law, Hastings College of the Law

SECURITIES REGULATION

CASES AND MATERIALS

By

RICHARD W. JENNINGS

James W. and Isabel Coffroth Professor of Law, Emeritus
University of California, Berkeley

and

HAROLD MARSH, JR.

Of Counsel to the Firm of Brobeck, Phleger & Harrison,
Los Angeles, California

SIXTH EDITION

Mineola, New York
THE FOUNDATION PRESS, INC.
1987

COPYRIGHT © 1963, 1968, 1972, 1977, 1982 THE FOUNDATION PRESS, INC.
COPYRIGHT © 1987 By THE FOUNDATION PRESS, INC.
All rights reserved
Printed in the United States of America

Jennings & Marsh Cs.Sec.Reg. 6th Ed. UCB
3rd Reprint—1990

PREFACE TO SIXTH EDITION

This year, and the publication of this Sixth Edition, mark the Silver Anniversary of this casebook. We commented in the First Edition that our frustration in attempting to find suitable materials to teach a course in Securities Regulation led to our preparation of this book—the subject was then taught in only about half-a-dozen law schools. We also commented on the sparsity of judicial decisions in this area of the law.

Those 25 years have seen the maturity of this legal discipline. In 1962 only two Supreme Court decisions had been handed down on this subject. Twenty-eight Supreme Court decisions are included as principal cases in this edition, and a number of others are summarized in the textual notes. There were then few decisions by the courts of appeals, and most of the cases included were decisions by district judges. Over 350 circuit court decisions handed down in the four years from 1982 to 1986 were read and digested, and where appropriate cited or included, in the preparation of this new edition. District court decisions were uncounted, and perhaps uncountable, but today they are of little significance.

We would like to think that this book has contributed in some small degree to this development in the law. It has been used in over 100 law schools and has been cited over 85 times by the federal courts, including four times by the United States Supreme Court. In our view, although obviously prejudiced, considerable improvements have been made in this edition over all of the previous editions.

In the same 25 years, there have been multiple, and overlapping, revolutions in the structure and functioning of the securities industry and in the securities markets, both domestically and internationally. These changes include the advances in information technology;[1] deregulation of the financial services industry; development of new financial products and services; macroeconomic developments and policies; internationalization of the securities markets; and the restructuring of American corporations through hostile takeovers, mergers and leveraged buyouts. Moreover, the structure and regulatory framework, devised in an earlier period, with respect to commercial banking and bank holding companies on the one hand and investment banking and the securities industry on the other, is in disarray; and there is not yet any consensus as to the basic principles upon which a new structure and regulatory framework should be constructed.

On a theoretical level, the question of whether securities regulation is an effective instrument of public policy has been the subject of continuing debate. Professor Owen Fiss has written of the recent popularity of theoretical studies in American law schools and of the

[1] Langevoort, Information Technology and the Structure of Securities Regulation, 98 Harv.L.Rev. 747 (1985).

impact of two jurisprudential movements that have shaken American legal education—critical legal studies and law and economics.[2]

Although the apostles of critical legal studies have shown little interest in securities regulation as such, one can surmise that they would probably regard the entire panoply of regulatory constraints merely as a legitimating facade for finance capitalism, if not an opiate to induce the masses to believe in the integrity of the securities markets. (Cynicism seems to be the opiate of some intellectuals.)

On the other hand, the law and economics movement has had a profound effect upon the economic analysis of securities regulation. Most of this analysis has been positive, but not all. Some academics have advanced the view, largely based upon questionable statistical data, that securities regulation has substantially raised the costs of buying and selling securities without any significant benefit to shareholders and investors. The optimum solution in their view would be to repeal the securities laws and let the free market prevail. Indeed, it is argued by some that insider trading promotes market efficiency and, in the words of Professor John Coffee, that the "bad guys" are really the "good guys." Moreover, some think that the war on insider trading is "unwinnable"[3] and that any ban on such activity should be abolished. Some academics even contend that the penalties for violation of economic regulatory laws are merely a cost of noncompliance with these laws.[4]

Of course, these negative opinions were expressed before the Dennis Levine and Ivan Boesky affairs and the recent insider trading scandals at home and abroad. The sad fact is that some recent graduates of our finest business schools and law schools seem to have become infected with these ideas; and they are now convicted felons with their careers in shambles. What has been largely ignored by such persons is the impact of the computerization of the securities market on the ability of the SEC, assisted by the self-regulatory agencies, to detect and prosecute securities violations.

In this edition, we have taken a fresh look at securities regulation in the light of these developments. The first chapter introduces the reader to the institutional changes occurring in the capital markets. We describe the massive restructuring of the financial services industry coupled with the inability of a regulatory system, supposedly mandating the separation of commercial and investment banking and of finance and

[2] Fiss, The Death of the Law?, 72 Cornell L.Rev. 1 (1986). Cf. Farber, The Case Against Brilliance, 70 Minn.L.Rev. 917 (1986).

[3] See Louis, The Unwinnable War on Insider Trading, Fortune, July 13, 1981, at 72; Dooley, Enforcement of Insider Trading Restrictions, 66 Va.L.Rev. 1 (1980); Carlton & Fischel, The Regulation of Insider Trading, 35 Stan.L.Rev. 857 (1983).

[4] For example, two distinguished academicians have stated: "[M]anagers do not have an ethical duty to obey economic regulatory laws just because the laws exist. They must determine the importance of these laws. The penalties Congress names for disobedience are a measure of how much it wants firms to sacrifice in order to adhere to the rules; the idea of optimal sanctions is based on the supposition that managers not only may but also should violate the rules when it is profitable to do so." Easterbrook & Fischel, Antitrust Suits by Targets of Tender Offers, 80 Mich.L.Rev. 1155, at 1177, n. 57 (1982). But see Cooter, Prices and Sanctions, 84 Colum.L.Rev. 1523 (1984).

commerce, to cope with the regulation of commercial banks, bank holding companies, nonbank banks and investment banking.

The development of new financial products and services has also affected the securities markets. Textual material is included explaining trading in standardized stock options, index options and index futures and the various types of automated execution systems now available in the securities markets. Attention is also called to the internationalization of the securities markets, including around-the-clock global trading.

The chapter on the registration process has been enriched by the inclusion of Professor John Coffee's seminal article on "Market Failure and the Economic Case for a Mandatory Disclosure System." The article is devoted to the on-going debate as to the role government should play in regulating the financial and securities markets in the light of modern finance theory.

The chapter on Tender Offers and Issuer Repurchases has been greatly expanded and revised to show the interaction of the Williams Act and state corporate law. This is, of course, the currently most active field (and the most lucrative to lawyers) in the entire area of securities regulation.[5] In the aftermath of the *Schreiber* case (p. 1076), most of the substantive law in the area of defensive maneuvers by target companies has been relegated to state law, but Congressional action is looming on the horizon, fueled by the Wall Street scandals. We have tried to explain in simple English, so as to be understandable by persons not conversant with the jargon or mystique of this subject, the various moves and counter-moves engaged in by the contestants in these gigantic battles.

The entire Part IV on Civil Liabilities has been more extensively reorganized than any other part of the book. The new organization treats all of the express and implied liabilities together, based on a functional division relating to fault required, conduct creating liability, persons entitled to sue, persons liable, materiality, reliance and causation, defenses and procedure and remedies. An entirely new chapter has been added on Civil RICO, which threatens to make almost all of Part IV obsolete.

We make no apologies for the length of the book. Except for the omission of materials on investment companies, we have selected those topics believed to be essential to the training of a securities lawyer. The book has been prepared primarily for law school use, but we have been heartened that securities lawyers and judges have also found it valuable as a reference book. For law school purposes, the field has now exploded to the point that a two-hour course necessarily leaves vast areas of the subject that simply cannot be explored within the time allotted. As a result, some law schools have expanded to a three-unit course, and others to two courses of two semester hours each. We believe curriculum planning is tending in this direction, with the addition

---

[5] For an interesting history of the recent take-over mania in the United States, see Madrick, Taking America (Bantam Press 1987).

of special courses or seminars on mergers and acquisitions and on securities litigation. We have tried to be as comprehensive as possible in order that law professors, in the light of their curriculum constraints, may select those subjects to which they wish to devote classroom time, and omit (or assign for outside reading) those portions of the book which are less important for their purposes. We believe this furnishes the most useful teaching tool to the greatest number of users.

A word should be added as to editorial policies. In editing cases and extracts from other authors, we have preserved the numbering of the original footnotes, even though many footnotes have been omitted. In some instances, we have added to the cases and extracts our own editorial footnotes, which are lettered rather than numbered, or vice versa, and if necessary to avoid confusion are sometimes identified with the signal "[Eds.]". In some instances we have sought to update the works of others by inserting in brackets our own editorial comments. In editing the opinions, we have sometimes been forced by space limitations to prune more severely than our natural inclinations would have suggested, but in all cases we have endeavored to preserve a statement of the relevant facts and a coherent and complete explanation of the court's reasoning and decision. We do not believe that it serves a useful educational function to include what one reviewer of another book referred to as "snippets of cases."

We will be publishing along with this edition a 1987 case supplement which will contain significant Supreme Court cases expected to be decided in June after this edition had to go to press, together with the 1933 Act registration documents for the public offering of Diasonics, Inc. (See In re Diasonics Securities Litigation, 599 F.Supp. 447 (N.D.Cal.1984).) We are also publishing our annual pamphlet entitled "Selected Statutes, Rules and Forms Under the Federal Securities Laws." This pamphlet will contain the text of the 1933 Act, the 1934 Act, and the Racketeer Influenced and Corrupt Organizations Act (RICO) and the Rules under the securities acts. We are also including the Commission's Rules of Practice and the most widely-used forms under the '33 and '34 Acts. Needless to say, it is essential that the student have these statutes and rules, since they are the pegs upon which everything else hangs. At the beginning of each chapter or section we have normally listed the applicable statutes and rules so as to alert the student to the necessity of referring also to these materials. Although we have omitted the chapter on investment companies, we are continuing to include the Investment Company Act and the Investment Advisers Act and the regulations thereunder in the Statutory Supplement, since many users of this pamphlet have requested their inclusion.

We are deeply indebted to a number of persons who went out of their way to assist us in bringing this edition to fruition. We are grateful to the various authors who allowed us to reproduce excerpts from their articles; however, we are especially indebted to Professor John C. Coffee, Jr., of the Columbia Law School for allowing us to reprint his article on mandatory disclosure previously alluded to; to Carl

W. Schneider, of the Philadelphia Bar, who again with his co-authors updated his article on "Going Public," consented to the reproduction of this article and his articles on "The Elusive Definition of a Security" and "The Statutory Law of Private Placements," and again shared with us his supplementary teaching materials and ideas with respect to the treatment of various topics; to James H. Fogelson of the New York Bar and to Jesse M. Brill of the San Francisco Bar, for revising Mr. Fogelson's authoritative article on Rule 144; to Meyer Eisenberg and Harvey Rowen for their advice and assistance in connection with our discussion of the restructuring of the financial services industry; to Marc L. Berman for introducing us into the mysteries of trading in standardized stock options; and to Thomas G. Washing for enlightening us on venture capital financing. Finally, we are also indebted to the many authors who through their writings have contributed to our knowledge of securities regulation; doubtless they will detect the sources of many of our ideas.

Mr. Marsh would like to express his appreciation to Ms. Debra Orlik, who was responsible for checking all of the citations in the latter part of the book, and to his law firm for granting him a leave of absence to work on this new edition and encouraging him in this effort.

Professor Jennings wishes to express his appreciation to Dean Jesse H. Choper of Boalt Hall School of Law, University of California, Berkeley, for making various law school facilities available in the preparation of this edition; to Mr. Warren de Wied, a third-year law student at Boalt Hall, for his imaginative and dedicated research assistance; and to Ms. Liz Duke for her cheerful and efficient secretarial services in this and previous editions.

Without the valuable assistance of these persons our task would have been much harder. Finally, we wish to express our thanks to the many generations of students who have used these materials over the years for their friendly and helpful criticisms and encouragement.

RICHARD W. JENNINGS
Berkeley, California

HAROLD MARSH, JR.
Los Angeles, California

May 1, 1987

*

SUMMARY OF CONTENTS

SUMMARY OF CONTENTS

xxvi

PART III. REGULATION OF TRADING IN SECURITIES

PART IV. CIVIL LIABILITIES UNDER THE FEDERAL SECURITIES LAWS

PART V. THE RACKETEER INFLUENCED AND CORRUPT ORGANIZATIONS ACT

PART VI. SEC ENFORCEMENT ACTIONS

PART VII. TRANSNATIONAL TRANSACTIONS

PART VIII. STATE SECURITIES REGULATION

*

TABLE OF CONTENTS

TABLE OF CONTENTS

TABLE OF CONTENTS

TABLE OF CONTENTS

TABLE OF CONTENTS

xxxvii

TABLE OF CONTENTS

TABLE OF CONTENTS

TABLE OF CASES

The principal cases are in italic type. Cases cited or discussed are in roman. References are to Pages.

TABLE OF CASES

xliv

TABLE OF CASES

TABLE OF CASES

TABLE OF CASES

TABLE OF CASES

xlix

TABLE OF CASES

TABLE OF CASES

TABLE OF CASES

liv

TABLE OF CASES

TABLE OF CASES

TABLE OF CASES

*

SECURITIES REGULATION

CASES AND MATERIALS

*

Part I

THE SECURITIES MARKETS: AN OVERVIEW

Chapter 1

THE INSTITUTIONAL AND REGULATORY FRAMEWORK

SECTION 1. STRUCTURE OF THE SECURITIES MARKETS

Excerpt from:

REPORT OF SPECIAL STUDY OF SECURITIES MARKETS [a]

Securities and Exchange Commission, pt. 1, pp. 9–19 (1963).

* * *

The securities industry in the United States is a complex structure of many disparate elements. * * *

The broad term "securities markets" encompasses both the markets for distribution of securities into public hands and the markets for continuous trading in outstanding securities. Both kinds of markets are elaborate structures geared to bringing buyers and sellers together. Trading markets consist of both a limited number of organized stock exchanges and * * * [the telephone or] over-the-counter markets. Distribution markets are essentially over the counter. Since shares of corporate stock once distributed may subsequently change hands many times, the volume of trading is substantially larger than the volume of distributions. For example, the Special Study estimates that in 1961 the dollar volume of stocks traded in exchange and over-the-counter markets was almost 30 times as great as the cash proceeds received by corporations from the sale of stocks.[b] Speaking broadly, distributions are the main concern of the

a. In 1961, Congress directed the Securities and Exchange Commission (SEC) "to make a study and investigation of the adequacy, for the protection of investors, of the rules of the national securities exchanges and national securities associations, including rules for the expulsion, suspension, or disciplining of a member for conduct inconsistent with just and equitable principles of trade." 75 Stat. 465 (1961), as amended, 15 U.S.C. § 78s (1964), adding § 19(d) to the Securities Exchange Act of 1934. The investigation culminated

in the Report of Special Study of Securities Markets, H.R.Doc. No. 95, 88th Cong., 1st Sess. (1963), hereinafter cited as SEC, Report of Special Study of Securities Markets. Despite evolutionary changes in the structure of the securities markets, the report is still the most comprehensive study of the securities markets yet made.

b. In 1967, the ratio of Exchange trading in equity securities to new offerings of such securities by issuers for cash was 61.4 to 1. For similar data covering the period

1

Securities Act and trading markets are the main concern of the Exchange Act.

a. The Public Interest in the Securities Markets

Securities markets in the United States are, in contemplation of law and in fact, *public* markets. They are public both in the sense that large numbers of people are directly or indirectly involved in owning and trading securities, and in the broader sense that the performance of securities markets affects the general economy and well-being in important ways. The former sense was recently expressed, for example, by the president of the New York Stock Exchange as follows:

> The sole purpose of a modern marketplace is to provide the public with an efficient and dependable mechanism through which securities can be bought and sold.

The latter sense is expressed by section 2 of the Exchange Act, which succinctly states various reasons why securities markets are "affected with a national public interest." In the following paragraphs some of the more important impacts of securities markets on investors and the general public are very briefly noted.

First, in a capitalistic society in which the corporate form of enterprise prevails, securities are an important form of private property, constituting an integral element of the resources, and materially influencing the long-term financial security, of a large segment of the population. * * *

Potentially affecting an even larger segment of the population, private retirement and insurance programs for individuals depend considerably on investments in corporate securities. This has been historically true as to corporate bonds and in recent years has become increasingly true as to corporate stocks. * * *

Turning briefly to the general public interest in securities markets, as distinguished from the direct and indirect interest of public investors, it may first be noted that the state of the trading markets unquestionably has an important bearing on the flow of new capital into private enterprise, and thus on the country's rate of economic growth. * * *

Without doubt, original distributions of securities are facilitated by the confidence of investors that they can later dispose of their purchases in a trading market. Conversely, companies' plans to sell securities may be significantly affected by current market behavior * * *. The securities markets' vast resources for marshaling the capital of individual and institutional investors all over the world give corporate enterprise access to large sources of funds that would not otherwise be available. At the same time, by providing liquidity to investments, the markets make possible the accumulation of aggregates of capital with the assurance that they can be converted to cash or readily valued when they may be needed for planned uses or to meet maturing liabilities.

Apart from their direct bearing on the flow of savings into private enterprise through distributions of securities, the actual state of the mar-

1920 through 1967, see Disclosure to Investors: A Reappraisal of Federal Administrative Policies Under the '33 and '34 Acts, App. II–1 (1969) [An internal SEC Staff Study Group Report hereinafter referred to as "Wheat Report"].

kets and the public's attitudes toward the markets are widely believed to have important bearing on the state of the economy * * *.

Finally, surely not the least important way in which the securities markets may affect the general economy and well-being is that described in clause (4) of section 2 of the Exchange Act:

> National emergencies, which produce widespread unemployment and the dislocation of trade, transportation, and industry, and which burden interstate commerce and adversely affect the general welfare, are precipitated, intensified, and prolonged by manipulation and sudden and unreasonable fluctuations of security prices and by excessive speculation on such exchanges and markets * * *.

It is to be remembered that the Congress that made this recital had fresh in its memory the market debacle of 1929 which preceded the great depression of the 1930's.

The emphasis on the public interest in this and other clauses of section 2 is echoed repeatedly in the substantive provisions of the statute. Over and over again Congress proclaimed that the regulatory authority conferred on the Commission was to be exercised "in the public interest" and "for the protection of investors." Thus, while the private ownership of exchanges was not disturbed, the Exchange Act, in the words of the House of Representatives committee report preceding its enactment, proceeded on the theory that "the exchanges are public institutions which the public is invited to use for the purchase and sale of securities listed thereon, and are not private clubs to be conducted only in accordance with the interests of their members. The great exchanges of this country upon which millions of dollars of securities are sold are affected with a public interest in the same degree as any other great utility." Similarly, "the public interest" and "protection of investors" were established as the dominant considerations in the operation and regulation of over-the-counter markets.

    * * *

Securities traded in exchange and over-the-counter markets represent many different transferable evidences of debt or equity interests, and broker-dealers may handle a number of different types or specialize in one or a few. The securities range from those issued by the Government, including Federal, State, local, and agency bonds, to issues of corporations, including bonds, debentures, convertible issues, and common and preferred stock; in addition there are such other securities as limited partnership interests in real estate syndications and trust participation certificates. Another important category, with unique characteristics, consists of investment company shares or, in the case of contractual plans, certificates evidencing an undivided interest in such shares.

[*Options and Futures Trading.* A more recent innovation is that of trading in stock options and indices of groups of stocks. Trading in options on underlying securities began in 1973 when the Chicago Board Options Exchange (CBOE) commenced options trading on a limited number of common stocks. Since that time exchange trading in standardized options has grown to include index options, debt options on certain United States government-issued and government-guaranteed securities and foreign currency.[c]

c. See House Comm. on Interstate and Foreign Commerce, 96th Cong., 1st Sess.,   Report of the Special Study of the Options Markets to Securities and Exchange Com-

Options and futures are contracts in which one party agrees to deliver specific property to another party on a specified date, or within a specified period, in the future at a stated price. Options and futures provide a means of hedging to avoid the risk of loss arising from a drop in prices while property is being held for future sale. In the case of futures, both contracting parties are obligated to perform in accordance with the agreement. As respects options, however, only one party, the "writer" of the option, is obligated to buy or sell the asset, while the other party to the transaction has the privilege, but not the obligation, of completing the transaction. In a "call" option, the buyer pays a premium for the privilege of purchasing a specified amount of the underlying instrument at a fixed price (called the exercise or "strike" price) upon the exercise of the option. In a "put" option, the seller pays a premium for the privilege of selling the security on the option terms.

The futures and options markets may be used for speculation as well as hedging. The increased leverage aspect entailed in options trading as compared with direct investment in the underlying instrument results in a greater profit potential on the upside, and greater risk on the downside.[d]

Options can be negotiated on an individual basis, but without standardized terms, including the exercise price and expiration date, it is not possible to establish a "secondary market" in which holders or writers of options can close out their positions by offsetting sales and purchases. The securities options exchanges overcame this barrier by establishing the Options Clearing Corporation (OCC), an entity jointly owned by all of the national securities exchanges on which stock options are traded.[e]

The OCC is the issuer of all standardized put and call options traded on these exchanges. It is interposed between buyers and sellers so that there is no contractual relationship between them. An OCC call option conveys the right to buy and a put option conveys the right to sell a specified quantity of the underlying instrument within a fixed period. Although both puts and calls are traded on the same underlying instruments, they are separate and distinct investment vehicles. A call option may be bought or sold without involving a put option and the reverse is true with respect to a put. Instead, the OCC becomes the buyer to every seller and the seller to every buyer of an option. To close out a position, the buyer of an option simply makes an offsetting sale of an identical option or the writer (seller) of an option makes an offsetting purchase of an identical option.

Options and futures contracts in commodities have traditionally been traded on commodities exchanges, called "contract markets" under the

mission (Comm. Print 1978); Joint Report of Fed.Res.Bd., CFTC and SEC, A Study of the Effects on the Economy of Trading in Futures Options, submitted to Congress pursuant to Section 23(a) of the Commodity Exchange Act (Dec. 1984) (cited as Joint Agency Futures Options Study); Seligman, The Structure of the Options Market, 10 J. of Corp.L. 141 (1984); T. Russo, Regulation of the Commodities Futures and Options Market (1986 ed.).

d. The Joint Agency Futures Options Study concluded that financial futures and options markets have no measurable nega-

tive implications on capital formation and enhance rather than reduce liquidity in the underlying cash markets. c. I at I–2; Brenner, Option Pricing (1983).

e. Options are presently traded on the American Stock Exchange (AMEX), Chicago Board Options Exchange (CBOE), NASDAQ, New York Stock Exchange (NYSE), Pacific Stock Exchange (PSE) and the Philadelphia Stock Exchange (PHLX). See Options Clearing Corporation, Characteristics and Risks of Standardized Options (Sep. 1985) describing options trading on these exchanges.

Commodities Exchange Act. The differences between options and futures can be quite technical, even though in many respects they are functional equivalents. When trading in stock options, stock futures and options on stock futures was being developed, a dispute arose over the respective jurisdiction of the SEC, which traditionally has regulated trading in securities, including stock options, and the Commodities Futures Trading Commission (CFTC) which regulates trading in commodities futures on organized exchanges. The dispute arose, in part, because the sections of the securities laws expressly enumerating certain types of "securities" did not include standardized put and call options on exempted securities. The Chicago Board of Trade (CBOT), an organized commodities exchange, began futures trading in Government National Mortgage Association mortgage-backed pass-through certificates (GNMA's), which were regarded as both "commodities" and exempted "securities." Thereafter, the SEC authorized the Chicago Board Options Exchange (CBOE), a separate market from the CBOT, to trade standardized options on GNMA's. In Board of Trade of Chicago v. SEC, 677 F.2d 1137 (7th Cir.1982), the CBOT challenged the jurisdiction of the SEC to authorize the CBOE to trade in options on GNMA certificates and prevailed.

The decision, however, led to congressional action to restore SEC authority over trading in put and call options on securities; the process was initiated by an agreement (Accord) between the chairmen of the SEC and CFTC defining the agencies' respective jurisdictions. In general, the SEC was to regulate options on securities (including exempted securities such as U.S. government-issued securities and U.S. government-guaranteed securities, e.g. GNMA certificates), certificates of deposit, foreign currency and stock groups or indices traded on national securities exchanges. The CFTC was to regulate futures, and options on futures, on exempted securities (except municipal securities), certificates of deposit and indexes on securities and options on foreign currency not traded on national securities exchanges.[f] Congress implemented the Accord by amending the definition of "security" in four of the federal securities acts to make clear that an option on an underlying security is a separate security, and thereby subject to regulation, unless subject to an exemption.]

Each of these different kinds of securities is usually employed by an issuer to satisfy a particular kind of financing need. Once an issue is distributed, it may follow a pattern characteristic for its type, veering to the over-the-counter markets or to the exchanges. For example, U.S. Treasury, State, and municipal bonds are typically traded over the counter, as are the issues of [smaller] banks and insurance companies [; however, bank and insurance holding company equity securities tend to be traded on exchanges]. The shares of open-end investment companies, or mutual funds, are sold only outside the exchanges; these shares are generally redeemable at or near their net asset value and usually are offered continuously by the fund. Much of the trading in corporate bonds is over the counter. Stocks that cannot meet the listing requirements of the

---

f. For background on this jurisdictional controversy, see Joint Agency Futures Option Study, supra note c, at III–43; Joint Explanatory Statement of the Securities and Exchange Commission and Commodity Futures Trading Commission, reprinted in [1981–1982 Transfer Binder] Fed.Sec.L. Rep. (CCH) ¶ 83,096 (Feb. 2, 1982); H.R. Rep. No. 97–626 on H.R. 6156, Clarifying the Jurisdiction of the SEC and the Definition of Security, reprinted in Fed.Sec.L. Rep. (CCH) No. 973, July 7, 1982, pt. I; Board of Trade of Chicago v. SEC, 677 F.2d 1137 (7th Cir.1982).

exchanges are traded over the counter, and in a number of instances issuers elect not to list their stocks even though they meet listing standards. Moreover, a relatively small but increasing percentage of trading in listed stocks is over the counter.

* * *

The definitions of the terms "broker" and "dealer" contained in the Exchange Act are broad enough to embrace most of the individual proprietorships, partnerships, and corporations engaged in the business of effecting securities transactions with or for the investing public, whether they act as agents for others or buy and sell for their own accounts, and whether they style themselves "brokerage firms," "investment bankers," "securities dealers," or just plain "brokers." The Nation's earliest securities firms were almost exclusively brokers operating out of a single office and dealing in the limited list of bonds and shares then available to the public, but today's firms vary greatly in size and character. They range in size from the giant organization with an elaborate worldwide network of branch offices to the one-man, neighborhood office, and in type of operation from the investment banking function of bringing new issues to the public market to that of executing orders for the purchase of open-end mutual shares. In the course of trading in securities, the broker-dealer firms may perform a number of supporting services. For example, many of them arrange clearing of certificates, afford custodial facilities, grant loans and furnish investment information and advice.[g] * * *

* * *

Broker-dealers employ a variety of personnel. These include salesmen; back-office people who perform the clerical and cashier duties in connection with the transfer of securities, handling of funds, keeping of accounts, etc.; traders who buy and sell for the firms' account; order clerks who receive the customers' orders from the salesmen; researchers and analysts; and supervisory personnel. Undoubtedly, those in the securities industry who have the broadest contact with investors are the salesmen, full and part time, who are about 60 percent of all persons connected with registered broker-dealers.

* * *

Excerpt from:

SECURITIES INDUSTRY STUDY

Report of the Subcommittee on Securities, Senate Committee on Banking, Housing and Urban Affairs, 93d Cong., 1st Sess. 89–94 (Comm.Print 1973).

Recent discussion of the market structure of the future has reflected virtually unanimous sentiment in favor of a "central market system." The SEC has stated that the purpose of such a system is "to maximize the depth and liquidity of our markets, so that securities can be bought and sold at

g. There were approximately 10,000 broker-dealers and 6,000 firms in the United States in 1984 conducting a public securities business and subject to oversight by the Securities and Exchange Commission. Of these, the New York Stock Exchange had 1,366 individual members who owned "seats" and had full distributive rights in the Exchange's net assets. Some of these NYSE members had combined with other individuals to form 599 member organizations conducting a public business. There were over 6,000 offices and about 75,000 registered representatives employed by these NYSE firms. See 50 SEC Ann. Rep. 21 (1984); New York Stock Exchange Fact Book 59, 82 (1986).

reasonably continuous and stable prices, and to ensure that each investor will receive the best possible execution of his order, regardless of where it originates * * *." [1] While the various formulations of the concept differ in important respects, they have all contemplated the existence of a communication system through which (1) all orders and quotations in a particular security would have an opportunity to meet, and (2) all transactions would be reported.

* * *

The volume of trading in common stocks [in the United States] now runs in excess of [56] billion shares a year. Of this total, approximately [32.9] billion shares represent trading in issues listed on the New York Stock Exchange (NYSE), of which over [27.5] billion are reported as transactions on that exchange, while the remaining [4.5] billion are traded through regional exchanges or the over-the-counter (OTC) market. Approximately [20.7] billion shares represent trading in issues which are not listed on any exchange and are quoted and reported through the NASDAQ system, the automated quotation system for the OTC market. Approximately [2.1] billion shares represent trading in issues listed on the American Stock Exchange (AMEX), [of] which [about 1.8 billion shares] are traded * * * exclusively through the facilities of that exchange.[a]

a. The OTC Market

An estimated 20,000 or so "unlisted" securities are traded solely in the "over-the-counter" or "OTC" market. The OTC market has no physical location, and has historically been characterized by virtually complete freedom of entry. There are no formal procedures for commencing or terminating trading in a particular security. Any broker-dealer registered with the SEC can act as a dealer (buying and selling to others as principal) or broker (buying or selling for customers as their agent) or both in any OTC security. Market-making in OTC stocks ranges from sporadic activities of individual dealers in inactive local stocks to continuous competition among thirty or more dealers in the largest, most active issues.

Prior to 1971, the only formalized means of communication of quotations in the OTC market was through the publication of daily "sheets", listing the bid and asked prices of each dealer in each stock at the close of the previous day. On February 8, 1971, the National Association of Securities Dealers (NASD) put into operation an automated quotation system—NASDAQ—by which continuously updated price quotations are displayed on a real-time basis on cathode ray terminals located in subscribers' offices.

[NASDAQ originated as an interdealer quotation system in which subscribers could obtain bid and ask quotations on equity securities from market makers in a stock. After obtaining a quotation, a subscriber must consummate the transaction by telephone communication with a market maker. By 1985, there were 4,700 NASDAQ securities issued by some

---

1. SEC, Statement on the Future Structure of the Securities Markets 7 (1972) (hereinafter cited as "Market Structure Statement").

a. The numbers in brackets indicate the approximate volume of trading in these

markets during 1985. NYSE Fact Book 17, 18, 69, 74 (1986); NASDAQ Fact Book 11 (1986); Wall St. J., Jan. 2, 1986, at 1B (Year-end Review of Markets and Finance).

4,000 companies quoted on the NASDAQ system, and 500 registered market makers.

The NASDAQ quotation system offers three types of service to dealers and investors. Level I terminals are desk-top computer terminals, which continuously disseminate the best bid and offer on NASDAQ securities to registered representatives in brokers' offices. These terminals are leased to brokerage firms by market data vendor organizations, whose computers are linked to the NASDAQ System's Central Processing Complex. The NASDAQ System's main computers collect and process the information and transmit it to the vendor organizations for relay over a leased-line network to over 136,000 terminals throughout the world. Through these terminals, registered representatives can instantly give a customer the best current bid and ask prices in the interdealer market on any NASDAQ security. Level II terminals display the quotations of all market makers in NASDAQ securities, not just the highest bids and lowest offers, which appear on Level I terminals. Level II terminals are leased by financial intermediaries—banks, mutual funds and other institutional investors—to enable their trading departments to monitor the performance of NASDAQ securities and deal directly with market makers through a network of private telephone lines which allow instant communication. Level III terminals, used by NASDAQ market makers, furnish Level II information but also have an entry capability which allows the market maker to keep current its own quotations in the stocks in which it makes markets.

By building a new market in equity securities on a network of computers, NASDAQ has revolutionized the method of trading in securities. In theory, the stock exchanges are auction markets where orders meet at a central meeting place for securities trading. Orders may be placed with a broker to buy and sell securities. The broker, acting as agent, wires the order to its representative on the floor of the exchange, who takes it to the post where the stock is traded. If the order is an order to buy or sell at the market, the order is executed at the best available price. However, if the order is to buy at a price below the current bid or to sell at a price above the current offering price, the order is left with a "specialist" at the trading post. The specialist may act as sub-broker and execute the order if and when the order reaches the designated price. However, the specialist is also authorized to act as a dealer and buy and sell for its own account in order to assist in maintenance of a fair and orderly market. Thus, the specialist may buy or sell stock held by it at the limit price, thereby narrowing the spread between bids and offers in order to provide continuity and liquidity in the market. Under the specialist system, a single firm handles trading in a stock on the floor of the exchange, although there is competition with specialists on the regional exchanges and market makers who are not members of the exchange.

The specialist system is in contrast with the NASDAQ system of competing market makers where the typical stock has an average of eight or more market makers who will quote bids and offers, supported by a pool of capital which provides continuity and liquidity to the market. NASDAQ has increased access to OTC quotations, narrowed spreads between bids and offers, and stimulated investor interest in OTC stocks.

The SEC has taken further steps to enhance the attractiveness of the NASDAQ system. In 1981, the Commission designated certain NASDAQ securities as qualified for trading as a part of a national market system in accordance with the securities acts amendments of 1975.[b] NASDAQ stocks that meet Tier 1 standards as to net assets, net worth, public stock float and total market value of outstanding stock were automatically given a mandatory NMS designation. The somewhat less rigorous Tier 2 criteria permits certain additional actively traded OTC securities to become NMS securities at the election of the company. By 1985, the shares of more than 2,000 companies were traded on the NASDAQ/NMS system.

The principal effects of the NMS designation was to subject such NMS securities to last sale and firm quote requirements in accordance with the Commission's firm quotation rule.[c] As a result, the market information available on NMS securities is now more comparable with exchange trading. Market makers are required to report their trades in NMS securities within 90 seconds of execution, together with cumulative sales volumes, so as to provide current information on trading conditions. The NASDAQ/ NMS stock tables carried by newspapers report transaction information, including sales volume, high, low and last sale data, and the daily change in closing prices, rather than quotation information contained in other NASDAQ-Only tables.

In addition to the NMS tables, some newspapers publish sales volume and bid and ask quotations on NASDAQ-Only National Newspaper List Companies, comprising issuers that meet the Tier 2 criteria, but have elected not to seek the NMS designation. Finally, additional OTC bid and ask quotations are sometimes published on a third group of NASDAQ-Only companies, as to which there is significant investor interest. It must be noted, however, that since the NASDAQ system is an interdealer wholesale market, the prices reported in these tables do not include markup, markdown or commissions chargeable by dealers on retail transactions.

The NASDAQ market is still overshadowed by the New York Stock Exchange, which remains the most prestigious and dominant securities market in the world.[d] Its more than 1,500 listed companies comprise most of the largest industrial, commercial and financial enterprises in the United States. Its listing standards are significantly more rigorous than that of any other market, both quantitatively and qualitatively. Even so, the NASDAQ market has become the most technically advanced and fastest growing stock market in the world. And by 1985, annual trading volume had mushroomed to 20.7 billion shares as compared with 27.5 billion shares for the NYSE. Thus, NASDAQ is now the third largest stock market in terms of dollar value of trading, after the New York and Tokyo stock exchanges and bigger than the next six—London, Zurich, West Germany, AMEX, Toronto and Paris—combined.[e] Indeed, NASDAQ may

---

b. See Designation of National Market System Securities, Exchange Act Release No. 17549 (Feb. 17, 1981); Exchange Act Release No. 21583 (Dec. 18, 1984); Market Making and the Changing Structure of the Securities Industry (Y. Amihud, T. Ho & R. Schwartz eds. 1985).

c. 17 C.F.R. § 240.11Ac1–1.

d. On NASDAQ, see Seligman, The Future of the National Market System, 10 J. of Corp. L. 79, 96–101 (1984); NASD, From Over-The-Counter to Over-The-Computer,

Euromoney (Supp. to Euromoney, Mar. 1985), at 4. For efficiency considerations, see Hamilton, Marketplace Organization and Marketability: NASDAQ, The Stock Exchange, and the National Market System, 33 J. Fin. 487 (1978).

e. Ibid; NYSE Fact Book 17, 18 (1986); NASD Fact Book 11 (1986); N.Y. Times, May 31, 1983, § 2, at 2, col. 3; Wall St. J., Feb. 10, 1984, at 29, col. 1; id., Mar. 5, 1984, at 1, col. 6. Sec. Exchange Act Release No. 22412 (Sept. 16, 1985).

become an international securities market model. The London Stock Exchange has announced its decision to pattern its new equities trading system after the NASDAQ market and other countries have shown a similar interest. Adoption of the NASDAQ market model in financial centers around the world would facilitate the creation of a 24–hour global securities market in the coming years, thereby raising a multitude of regulatory problems at the national and international level.[f]]

b. The Exchange Market

The market for listed securities includes primarily the approximately [2300] common stocks listed on the NYSE and the * * * [824] common stocks listed on the AMEX.[g] The NYSE and AMEX are complementary, rather than competing markets.

[Upon its organization as the New York Curb Market Association in 1910, the AMEX foreswore trading in NYSE issues, and served principally as an avenue to NYSE listing for companies that did not meet the higher NYSE listing requirements. Indeed, until 1976, the AMEX was effectively prohibited from offering a competing market for NYSE stocks, since about 87% of its member firms are also members of the NYSE, and the NYSE Constitution provided for expulsion of any NYSE member who was connected with any other exchange in New York City which permitted trading in NYSE securities.[h] In 1976, however, the NYSE and AMEX, under pressure from the SEC and the Justice Department, repealed their rules prohibiting trading in the same securities. The AMEX then permitted any AMEX listed company that had decided to list its stock on the NYSE to retain its AMEX listing. A few companies did so, but there was very little trading in these issues, and by 1984 there were no issues which had a dual listing on these two exchanges.[i]]

[In addition to the 2300 NYSE issues and 940 AMEX issues listed on those exchanges, there are about 150 issues traded solely on the eight other national securities exchanges registered with the SEC. Of these regional exchanges, only five are of any significance. They are, in order of trading

f. See SEC, Report of the Securities and Exchange Commission to the House Comm. on Energy and Commerce on the Internationalization of the Securities Markets (Oct. 9, 1986), Fed.Sec.L.Rep. (CCH) (Current) ¶ 84,037.

The NASD and the London Stock Exchange have instituted a quotation sharing pilot program in which the NASDAQ system displays price quotes for 288 British and non-British stocks that are actively traded in London and the LSE automated quotation system, SEAQ, displays firm quotes on 270 NASDAQ companies. Id. at 88,294.

And see Symposium: The Internationalization of the Securities Markets, 4 B.U. Int.L.J. 1 (1986).

g. NYSE Fact Book 38 (1986); AMEX Fact Book 7 (1985).

h. NYSE Const., Art. XIV, § 8.

i. NYSE Fact Book 17 (1985). According to Professor Poser, there appear to be

three principal reasons for failure of competition to develop. First, few companies chose a dual listing; they may have concluded that the NYSE specialist would be more willing to make a good market if he saw all of the flow of orders rather than only a portion of them. Second, the AMEX was unwilling to engage in head-to-head competition with the NYSE by actively soliciting the listing of NYSE issues, or permitting unlisted trading privileges in these issues. Finally, the larger brokerage firms, most of whom are members of both exchanges, were unwilling to direct any portion of their orders on dually traded stocks to the AMEX. Their automated systems for routing orders to the exchanges make it easier, less expensive and perhaps better to route all orders to the primary market. Poser, Restructuring the Stock Markets: A Critical Look at the SEC's National Market System, 56 N.Y.U.L.Rev. 883, 892 (1981).

volume, the Midwest Stock Exchange, the Pacific Stock Exchange, the Philadelphia Stock Exchange, the Boston Stock Exchange and the Cincinnati Stock Exchange. The three other regional exchanges, the Chicago Board of Trade, the Intermountain Stock Exchange, and the Spokane Stock Exchange account for an insignificant amount of trading volume, again confined to local or regional issues.

Although a limited number of local or regional issues are traded on the five principal regional exchanges, the bulk of the trading volume occurs in NYSE-listed stocks, with some additional trading in AMEX-listed issues. NYSE-listed issues are also traded in the NASDAQ system and on Instinet—a computerized automatic execution system linking financial intermediaries, broker dealers, exchange specialists and NASDAQ market makers and enabling them to engage in direct trading among themselves on an anonymous basis. Communication is conducted via the computer, rather than by telephone; confirmations of the trades are automatically transmitted to each party and to the appropriate clearing entity for settlement.

The principal regional exchanges and NASDAQ and Instinet have become important alternate markets for NYSE-listed issues, accounting for 16% of the trading volume reported on the NYSE consolidated tape, with trading on the NYSE accounting for the remaining 84% of volume.[j] In summary, there are four markets in which NYSE-listed securities are traded: (1) the various stock exchanges where NYSE listed stocks are traded; (2) NASDAQ, where a limited number of NYSE listed stocks are traded over-the-counter; (3) the "third market" comprising nonmember firms that buy and sell NYSE-listed securities in principal transactions and which deal with financial intermediaries exclusively; and (4) the "fourth market," consisting of trading between financial intermediaries either directly or through the facilities of Instinet.]

c. *Growth of Competing Markets in NYSE-Listed Securities*

The differences in the nature of the securities listed on the NYSE and on the AMEX has in recent years led to divergence in the patterns of trading in NYSE- and AMEX-listed issues.

The AMEX, whose list consists generally of lower-priced stocks in smaller companies, has remained primarily a market for individual investors. While institutional activity in AMEX issues has shown a steady increase, individuals still accounted for 85.9% of the public (non-member) orders, 74.3% of the share volume, and 66.1% of the dollar volume in 1971. On the other hand, institutions have come to dominate the activity in NYSE-listed [and NASDAQ system stocks. The latest available figures indicate that institutional trading accounts for over 50% of the volume in these markets.] * * *

Concurrently with the increasing dominance of institutional activity in NYSE issues, there has been a steady growth in the percentage of NYSE-listed issues traded in other markets. * * * On the other hand, there has been a relatively small amount of trading in AMEX issues in other markets. * * *[k]

j. NYSE Fact Book 17, 18 (1985); N.Y. Times, Year End Review of Markets and Finance, Jan. 2, 1986, at 9B, 16B, 24B.

k. [Since the introduction of the NYSE consolidated transaction reporting system, all trades in NYSE listed securities are

* * *

* * * [A]bout one-sixth of the trading in NYSE-listed issues, and almost one-third of the trading in the most actively traded of those issues, takes place outside the NYSE.

* * *

[T]he Subcommittee approaches the question of a "central market system" not from the point of view of returning all trading in NYSE-listed stocks to the NYSE and subjecting all participants in that trading to NYSE rules and procedures, but from the point of view of preserving the competing markets that have developed, breaking down barriers to communication and competition between them, and imposing those rules—and only those rules—which are necessary to protect public investors. The objective of a "central market system" is to provide a better market, with greater liquidity and depth, to meet the present and future needs of the public—those who invest directly and those who invest through the medium of institutions.

* * *

THE DEVELOPMENT OF A NATIONAL MARKET SYSTEM

The foregoing Securities Industry Study helped spark the 1975 amendments to the Securities Exchange Act of 1934. Section 11A(a)(2) of the Act directs the SEC to facilitate the establishment of a "national market system" in conformity with certain enumerated statutory objectives. The structure of the system is not specifically defined in the Act and no blueprint was drawn up in advance for its implementation. Nevertheless, its broad outlines are beginning to emerge. The SEC envisages the term "national market system" "as a comprehensive reference to those regulatory and technological steps which the Commission and the securities industry must take in order to integrate the mechanisms for trading qualified securities and the trading behavior of investors and securities professionals in order to achieve a nationwide interactive market system." [1] In other words, rather than having a single central trading floor such as the New York Stock Exchange where all bids and offers for securities would be brought, the objective is to achieve efficient linkages between the various exchange trading floors and dealer markets conducted over-the-counter.

The Consolidated Tape. A number of steps have been taken to develop such a system. First, in 1976, a consolidated system for reporting and disseminating volume and price information for all NYSE or AMEX listed stocks was installed. [2] There is a "moving ticker" which consolidates volume and price information on all sales of NYSE securities and another tape covering AMEX securities. These computerized electronic reporting systems consolidate all transactions in NYSE or AMEX equity shares from all national securities exchanges, NASDAQ (where a limited number of NYSE securities are traded),

reported whether traded on the NYSE, a regional exchange, NASDAQ, Instinet, or in the third market. With the elimination of fixed commissions and the progress made in the development of a national market system, the share volume handled by the various exchanges has remained relatively stable, although the volume in the third market has declined. Thus in 1984, the NYSE accounted for 84% of NYSE list share volume; and the Midwest, Pacific and NASDAQ markets 6.8%, 3.2% and 2.9% respectively. NYSE Fact Book 17 (1985).

1. Securities Exchange Act Release No. 13662 (June 23, 1977), 12 SEC Dock. 947, at 952.

2. Securities Exchange Act Release No. 34–15671 (Mar. 22, 1979), [1979 Transfer Binder] (CCH) Fed.Sec.L.Rep. ¶ 82,016, at 81,563.

"Instinet" (a registered broker-dealer that operates a computerized block trading system), and the third market. Several types of desk-top terminals are available having moving tickers for the NYSE and AMEX, an information retrieval capability, and "market minders" which allow a market maker to monitor, on a dynamic basis, market data with respect to particular securities. Last sale information is available through interrogation devices on a real-time basis when there are transmission delays in the consolidated system network resulting from high volume.[3]

Consolidated Quotation System. Second, in 1978, a consolidated quotation system for all securities as to which last sale information is included in the consolidated transaction reporting system was established. A Commission rule initially required all market centers to collect and make available "firm" quotation information, including size, to securities information vendors for dissemination to market professionals and to public investors.[4] However, the adoption of this mandatory "Quote Rule" failed to achieve its objective of providing a mechanism for linking market centers so that orders could be sent and executed in the market center with the best price. Under the rule, each market center was required to establish mechanisms for collecting from exchange specialists and third market makers bids, offers and quotation sizes with respect to any reported security and make these available to quotation vendors for dissemination in other market centers. Subject to certain exceptions, the specialist or third market maker furnishing a quotation was obligated to execute any round lot order presented to it at a price at least as favorable as the bid or offer in any amount up to its published quotation size. The system failed to realize its objective because a number of regional exchange specialists and third market makers did not make available to other market centers continuous two-sided quotes throughout the trading day. Moreover, quotations, when disseminated frequently were not competitive, and on occasion, the quotations were unreliable because the broker refused to execute orders at quoted prices. The problem essentially arose with respect to stocks listed on the NYSE or the AMEX and traded on the regional exchanges or in the over-the-counter market. Since specialists on the regional exchanges and third market makers were not exposed to primary market order flow, the costs outweighed the benefits of maintaining competitive, up-to-date quotations. The solution was to have specialists in the primary market continue to be required to disseminate firm quotations. In addition, a limited number of stocks listed on the NYSE and AMEX may be traded outside of the exchanges by exchange members who act as market makers in such transactions. This permission is granted by SEC Rule 19c–3 which freed from all stock exchange off-board trading restrictions all securities which were listed on an exchange after April 26, 1979, the date when Rule 19c–3 was originally announced. The "quote" rule further provides that market makers engaging in OTC trading in "Rule 19c–3 securities" are similarly subject to the compulsory quote rule. On the other hand, the rule now permits specialists in secondary exchange markets and other OTC market makers to disseminate quotations on a voluntary, rather than a mandatory basis.[5]

---

3. SEC Rules 11Ac1–1 and 11Ac1–2. Securities Exchange Act Release No. 15671, supra note 2, at 81,563.

4. Ibid. Quotations from all market centers subject to the rule, including third market makers, other than the Cincinnati Stock Exchange (CSE) are processed by the Securities Industry Automation Corpora-

tion ("SIAC") and are made available to subscribers on computer terminals in a single consolidated data stream. And see other rules issued under Section 11A showing the pattern of regulation which is emerging.

5. Securities Exchange Act Release No. 18482 (Feb. 11, 1982).

Execution Systems Based Upon Order Size: Small Orders. Third, competition between primary and derivative markets in multiply-traded stocks has resulted in the reduction of transaction costs in processing small orders. Since a high percentage of transactions entail orders between 100 and 500 shares, the Pacific, Midwest and Philadelphia stock exchanges and NASDAQ have developed small order automated execution systems which are faster and less expensive than that available on the NYSE or AMEX. Under the Pacific Stock Exchange Security Order Routing and Execution (SCOREX) system, a broker or trading department can electronically route an order to the specialist on the floor of the PSE. The specialist must accept the order at the best price quotation available at any of the eight market centers reporting on the Consolidated Quotation System. If the specialist does not respond, after fifteen seconds, it is required to execute the order at a price equal to the best quotation in the consolidated quotation system. After the order is executed, SCOREX automatically relays the order back to the firm placing the order, sends transaction detail to the Clearing Corporation for settlement and enters the trade in the Consolidated Tape. The Midwest Automated Exchange MAX system is similar to the PSE–SCOREX system, except that SCOREX accepts orders up to 599 shares, while MAX accepts orders up to 1,099 shares.[6] The Philadelphia Stock Exchange PACE Plus system is also similar to SCOREX and accepts orders up to 599 shares.[7] The NASD has the Small Order Execution System, *SOES*, providing for rapid, automatic execution of trades up to 1,000 shares in NASDAQ/NMS issues and 500 shares in other NASDAQ issues. Customer orders can be entered into *SOES* through a NASDAQ terminal. The order is executed and confirmed automatically, by computer, in seconds, at the best quotation available. The system then automatically reports the trade to NASDAQ and sends transaction detail to the clearing corporation.[8]

The rival NYSE and the AMEX systems differ from these other systems in several respects. The NYSE Designated Order Turnaround System, known as *DOT*, or the improved SUPERDOT, is an electronic order-routing system through which member firms transmit market and limit orders directly to the post where the security is traded, thereby dispensing with the messenger services of a floor broker. Member firms can enter market orders up to 1,099 shares and limit orders up to 30,099 shares. The specialist exposes market orders to the "crowd" of floor brokers in front of the specialist's post, and the order will be executed either by a floor broker or the specialist. The limit order system electronically files orders which are then executed if a specific price is reached. SUPERDOT has the advantage of exposing orders to the auction system. This can result in better prices to the customer, but it is slower and the transaction costs exceed that of the competing systems of the regional exchanges and NASDAQ.[9] The *AMEX* Automated Post Execution Reporting System (AUTOPER) is similar to the NYSE's DOT system. It accepts market and limit orders up to 1,000 shares, directly to the Specialist on the trading floor.[10]

Block Transactions. The tremendous growth of institutional trading has put a severe strain upon the mechanism of the exchanges' auction market

6. Pacific Stock Exchange, An Introduction to SCOREX. The PSE, Pacific Automated Limit System (PALS) also automates much of procedures for limited orders that were previously conducted manually. Midwest Stock Exchange Ann. Rep. 7 (1985).

7. Philadelphia Stock Exchange Ann. Rep. 5 (1984); Securities Exchange Act Release No. 19858 (June 9, 1983); Securities Exchange Act Release No. 18742 (May 17, 1982); Securities Exchange Act Release No. 15812 (May 11, 1979).

8. NASDAQ Ann.Rep. 11 (1985).

9. NYSE Fact Book 16 (1985).

10. AMEX Fact Book 2 (1984) and Letter from AMEX, dated March 10, 1986.

system. Special methods have been devised to handle block transactions. The SEC defines these as transactions of 10,000 shares or more or involving securities having a market value of $200,000 or more.[11] Although most block transactions require special handling, two institutional computerized communication systems have been developed to facilitate block trading. Autex is simply a computerized communications system that permits brokers and dealers to advertise their interest as a buyer or seller of a block of securities at or near the current market price. Transactions are then consummated by direct communication. In contrast, the Instinet system is far more sophisticated; it permits financial intermediary subscribers to transact anonymous block trades directly through the Instinet computer facility without the interposition of a broker or dealer, thereby facilitating the Fourth market. Moreover, each Instinet terminal now provides direct access to a marketplace of broker dealers, exchange specialists, market makers and all types of institutional investors. It thus provides a capability for large block executions without affecting the quoted market price.[12]

These trading facilities for processing of small and large orders have resulted in enormous savings in time and paperwork for the broker-dealer community and freed up resources needed to improve market linkage between the various market centers.

Market Linkage. A comprehensive market linkage system has been developed which permits orders for the purchase and sale of multiply-traded securities to be routed between market centers for execution. The first phase was that of linking the various exchange markets where stocks are multiply-traded. The Intermarket Trading System (ITS) is an electronic communication network that now links the trading floors of the American, Boston, Cincinnati, Midwest, New York, Pacific and Philadelphia Stock Exchanges and the NASDAQ system. It enables any broker or market maker in any of these markets to shop all participating markets and route an order to another market center for execution whenever the nationwide Composite Quotation System shows a better price is available. The 1,160 issues eligible for trading on ITS now encompass most of the stocks traded on more than one exchange.[13] The success of ITS, however, is dependent in large part on reliable quotes. Accordingly, its value depends upon the effectiveness of the consolidated quotation system.[14]

The next stage involved the linking of the exchange markets and the over-the-counter dealer markets where the same securities were traded. The reason for the separation of these markets is historical. At the present time only a limited number of listed securities are traded in the over-the-counter market. Until 1979, NYSE Rule 390 prohibited NYSE members from engaging in off-board trading in NYSE-listed securities off the floor of the NYSE or the floor of a regional exchange where the stock had a multiple listing. As previously

11. SEC Exchange Act Release No. 19372 (Dec. 23, 1982) [1982–83 Transfer Binder] (CCH) Fed.Sec.L.Rep. ¶ 83,307 at 85,677.

12. The Instinet trading system is described in an Instinet Corporation brochure, Instinet—The Time is Now (1986).

13. Securities Exchange Act Release No. 34–15671, supra note 2, at 81,564; NYSE Fact Book 19 (1985); Pacific Stock Exchange, An Introduction to the Intermarket Trading System.

14. See SEC, A Monitoring Report on the Operation of the Intermarket Trading System 5–9 (Feb.1981). This report states that the ITS has not narrowed quotation spreads. The principal effect of ITS has been to channel orders from the regional exchanges to the NYSE (the NYSE is the "destination" market about twice as often as it is the "originating" market). ITS trading amounts to only 4.7% of the total volume in ITS stocks. Id. at 44.

For a more detailed discussion the evolution of the securities markets, see infra, at 563–594; Seligman, The Future of the National Market System, 10 J. of Corp.L. 80, 105–116 (1984).

noted, SEC Rule 19c–3 abrogated off-board trading rules with respect to stocks which were listed on an exchange after April 26, 1979. To effect a linkage of the exchange and over-the-counter markets in Rule 19c–3 securities, the NASD first developed a Computer Assisted Execution system (CAES) which permits automated executions in OTC stocks among participating members. The SEC then required ITS and the NASD to achieve an automated interface between ITS and CAES, thereby linking the various exchange trading floors with the NASDAQ system. This linkage of the exchange markets and the NASDAQ system permits orders in Rule 19c–3 securities to be efficiently routed between exchange and over-the-counter markets where multiple trading exists. It was anticipated that this linkage would broaden over-the-counter trading in Rule 19c–3 stocks. However, trading volume in Rule 19c–3 securities through the interface has been light, because several large participating firms ceased making OTC markets in those securities in 1983.[15]

The National Securities Trading System ("NSTS"). A diametrically opposite approach to linking traders was taken by the Cincinnati Stock Exchange ("CSE") which installed a multiple-dealer trading facility known as the National Securities Trading System ("NSTS"). This is a fully automated, electronic trading system which has been operated as a pilot project under SEC authorization. The CSE permits members of that exchange to participate in a market conducted under auction-type trading principles by entering bids and offers for securities in the NSTS system as principal or as agent for customers without being present on the floor of the CSE or any other exchange. Moreover, specialists on any national securities exchange may use the system to enter bids and offers with respect to any security in which that specialist is registered on another exchange. Orders are stored in the CSE's computer facilities and queued for execution on the basis of best price and, as between orders at the same price, by priority in time. Public agency orders have priority over other orders at the same price.

The NSTS system approach raised the spectre of a fully automated national market system of the future—a stock exchange without walls. However, it has not proved to be cost-effective in practice. The system requires constant monitoring. Orders have to be inserted into the system sequentially. And in connection with each order, the trader must decide whether to accept an outstanding order already in the system or negotiate a better price. As a result, the system is principally used for intra-firm executions for customers on an agency basis. And since Merrill Lynch, the principal NSTS member, withdrew in July, 1983, interest in the system has faded.[16]

A major problem in development of a national market system is the attainment of nationwide price protection for public limit orders against execution at inferior prices. A number of technological problems must be resolved before mechanisms are developed to achieve the efficient intermarket execution of orders and the gathering and display of limit order information so as to provide such price protection on public limit orders.[17] We have seen that most of the small order rapid processing systems provide for the execution of customers' orders at the best quotation in the consolidated quotation system.

15. Securities Exchange Act Release No. 17744 (Apr. 21, 1981), 22 SEC Dock. 845 (1981); Securities Exchange Act Release No. 18713 (May 6, 1981); Securities Exchange Release No. 19372 (Dec. 23, 1982); Securities Exchange Act Release No. 22412 (Sept. 16, 1985) at n. 18.

16. Wall St. J., July 13, 1983, at 2.

17. For a discussion, see Release No. 34–15671, id. at 81,565 and Release No. 34–17744, supra note 6. Other agenda items entail the establishment of a national system of clearance and settlement and the use of the improved technology in surveillance of trading in the various securities markets.

The SEC has proposed an "Order Exposure Rule" which would require intermarket exposure of customers orders in certain securities which might yield the customer the best available price, that is, a price between the bid and ask, rather than simply the best quotation. The proposed rule would cover exchange specialists, broker-dealers on the floor of an exchange, and broker-dealers trading in Rule 19c–3 securities, including off-board market makers.[18] The SEC agenda includes other steps for removing anticompetitive restraints between the exchange and over-the-counter markets. Rule 11Aa3–1 of the Exchange Act has been amended to allow a security to be designated as a NASDAQ/NMS security and also be traded on an exchange.[19] And the SEC has proposed to permit exchange trading in a limited number of NASDAQ/ NMS securities on an unlisted basis; this is consistent with the policy of permitting Rule 19c–3 securities to be traded in the NASDAQ system.[20]

The SEC believes that the development of the national market system should be an evolutionary process. Its role "is to monitor and encourage industry progress, to act as a catalyst and, when necessary, to take regulatory action to achieve a particular goal." [21] Thus, the attainment of the ultimate configuration is a joint responsibility of the SEC and the industry, with the expectation that the securities industry and the various self-regulatory organizations will assume primary responsibility for the development of facilities necessary to achieve the objectives set forth in Section 11A of the 1934 Act. The SEC issues status reports periodically which describe accomplishments, lay down an agenda, establish priorities and set forth the Commission's expectations for further progress.[22]

For discussions of the evolution of the National Market System, see Seligman, The Future of the National Market System, 10 J. of Corp. L. 79 (1984); Poser, Restructuring the Stock Markets: A Critical Look at the SEC's National Market System, 56 N.Y.U.L.Rev. 883 (1981); Werner, Adventures in the Social Control of Finance: The Market System for Securities, 75 Colum.L.Rev. 1233 (1975); Werner, The SEC as a Market Regulator, 70 Va.L.Rev. 755 (1984); Calvin, The National Market System: A Successful Adventure in Industry Self-Improvement, 70 Va.L.Rev. 785 (1984); Lipton, Best Execution: The National Market System's Missing Ingredients, 57 Notre Dame L.Rev. 449 (1982); Branson, Securities Regulation After Entering the Competitive Era: The Securities Industry, SEC Policy and the Individual Investor, 75 Nw.U.L.Rev. 857 (1978).

THE NEW ISSUES MARKET

The securities markets provide a link between investors and corporations that seek to raise long-term funds through new issues of securities in large blocks. These securities may take the form of debt instruments, such as bonds or debentures, or equity securities (shares or convertible debt securities) may be used. Under the tax laws, there are tax advantages in using debt securities instead of equity, since interest paid on debt is deductible for tax purposes,

18. Securities Exchange Act Release No. 19372 (Dec. 23, 1982). For criticism of the operation of the present system for rapid execution of small orders and proposals for reform, see Seligman, supra note 14, at 133–37.

19. Securities Exchange Act Release No. 22413 (Sept. 16, 1985).

20. Securities Exchange Act Release No. 22412 (Sept. 16, 1985).

21. Release No. 34–15671, id. at 81,682.

22. See Securities Exchange Act Release No. 13662 (June 23, 1977); Securities Exchange Act Release No. 14416 (Jan. 26, 1978); Securities Exchange Act Release No. 34–15671 (Mar. 22, 1979); Securities Exchange Act Release No. 17516 (Feb. 5, 1981); Securities Exchange Act Release No. 17744 (Apr. 27, 1981).

whereas dividends are paid out of profits remaining after taxes have been paid. The necessity for maintaining a reasonable degree of liquidity should in theory place limits upon corporate debt leveraging as a means of maintaining a growth in earnings per share. In a period of rising stock prices, however, particularly where investors become preoccupied with growth in per-share earnings and in capital gains, rather than in dividends, issuers are inclined to finance growth through retained earnings and the issue of debt securities, rather than new issues of equity securities. If the demand for equities increases faster than the supply of new shares coming to the market, the result may be a further increase in share prices. At the same time, the increase in the supply factor arising from the increased volume of debt securities tends to drive up the interest rate. In the late 1960's and early 1970's, corporate managers bent on plant expansion and modernization, tended to over-commit their corporation's resources and then turn to short-term bank loans and commercial paper to complete these programs, with a view to refinancing with long-term debt securities when market conditions and interest rates improved. This buildup of debt accompanied by increased interest payments constituted a drain on profits. A shortage in the supply of new shares arising from institutional demand was converted into an over supply as investors became disenchanted with stocks and turned to the more high-yield debt securities or withdrew altogether from the securities markets and turned to other forms of investment. As corporate profits declined, there was a need to raise funds externally and to convert short-term debt to long-term capital, despite falling stock prices. Accordingly, in such a period, notwithstanding a credit crunch, corporations may be forced to go into the equity market to try to raise funds, despite the dilution of the stockholders' equity and the depressing effect on earnings per share.[1]

On the other hand, hostile tender offers, other forms of corporate acquisitions and issuer repurchases of stock may significantly shrink the supply of outstanding equity securities. In the mid–1980's, this has occurred as corporate takeovers, leveraged buyouts and various forms of corporate restructuring, frequently financed by junk bonds and other high-leveraged, high risk investments, reached an all-time high.[2] Among the factors sparking the stock market rise of 1985–87 was the increasing institutional demand for equity securities, coupled with a decreasing supply of stocks.

The new-issue market burgeoned in the second half of the 1960's with the high-water mark being reached in 1968 when 1,026 firms went public and raised $2.6 billion.[3] Again, in 1972, 646 companies raised $3.3 billion in initial public offerings.[4] But the bubble burst in 1973 following the stock market decline, the oil embargo and the ensuing recession, and for the next six years the new issue market was stagnant.

In the meantime, however, the stock market gradually improved, despite accelerating inflation, periodic recessions and high interest rates. Moreover,

1. Metz & Gilbert, Debt, Equity Offerings Boom as Firms Seek to Repay Their Short-Term Debt, Wall St. J., Mar. 8, 1983, at 16, col. 1.

2. Congressional Research Service Report for House Comm. on Energy and The Role of High Yield Bonds [Junk Bonds] in Capital Markets and Corporate Takeovers: Public Policy Implications, 99th Cong., 1st Sess. (Comm. Print 99–20) (1985); SEC, Report on Noninvestment Grade Debt as a Source of Tender Offer Financing, Office of the Chief Economist (June 20, 1986), Fed.

Sec.L.Rep. (CCH) (Current) ¶ 84,011; Rohatyn, Junk Bonds and Other Securities Swill, Wall St. J., Apr. 18, 1985, at 30, col. 3; Williams, Takeover Tactics: How 'Junk Financings' Aid Corporate Raiders in Hostile Acquisitions, Wall St. J., Dec. 6, 1984, at 1; Mendelson, The Threat of Corporate Debt, 6 J.Comp.Bus. & Cap.Market L. 149 (1984).

3. Wall St.J., Jan. 20, 1981, at 6, col. 1.

4. Wall St.J., Oct. 17, 1980, at 26, col. 1.

the 1978 reduction in the federal capital gains taxes further encouraged investment in equities.[5] During the slump in stock prices, a two-tiered market had developed, with investment interest being centered on the corporate giants—the so-called blue chip stocks—rather than upon smaller growth companies. This was a market dominated by institutions. Later, however, this two-tiered market reversed itself as middle-range and growth companies outperformed the blue chip companies in income growth. Individual investors reacted by flocking to the AMEX (which advertises itself as "The people's market place") and to NASDAQ in increasing numbers to invest in growth, and mid-range, companies. At the same time, during the 1970's, a few regional underwriting firms began to specialize in raising venture capital for science-oriented and high technology firms in which the major underwriters appeared to show little interest. The spectacular successes of a number of these firms suddenly added to the reawakening of a dormant new issue market.[6] Thus, in 1980 the number of firms going public was the greatest since 1972 as some 237 companies raised $1.4 billion in initial public offerings. That far surpassed 1979 when 81 companies raised $506.5 million.[7] In this wave of companies going public, one young science-oriented company, Genentech, Inc. (applications of genetic research) succeeded in raising $35 million in an initial public offering only to be topped shortly thereafter by Apple Computer, Inc. (home computers) by an initial offering of over $100 million.[8]

As the new issue market heated up, the public demand for high-tech stocks seemed insatiable. Initial public offerings (IPO's) which in 1980 sold at 16 times estimated earnings were snapped up when offered at premiums in the high 30's and low 40's. In February, 1983, the Diasonics, Inc., IPO sold at $22 a share and 36.7 times estimated earnings. Even so, it soon climbed to $29 a share. Under these circumstances, it was senseless to reduce the public's offering price and transfer the premium from the issuer's coffers to the pockets of the initial purchasers of the offering. Companies rushed to the market before new product lines were adequately developed and tested. Market surveys were incomplete or inadequate. And the quality of the offerings deteriorated. The IPO market peaked in 1983 when there were a record number of new issues totaling 12.9 billion [9] but by year-end the bubble again burst.[10] As of early 1986, the new issue market was beginning to recover as the American stock market rose to new heights.

These gyrations in the new issue market add substance to the proposition that a strong primary market for the distribution of new issues of corporate securities cannot be sustained without the existence of an efficient and well-

---

5. For the argument that this has proved to be bad tax policy, see Dworsky, The Case for Raising the Capital Gains Tax (undoing the damage from venture capital), 42 Financial Analysts J. 69 (Mar.-Apr. 1986). And the Tax Reform Act of 1986 has eliminated the preferential tax treatment of capital gains.

6. Wall St.J., Dec. 2, 1980, at 25, col. 4.

7. Wall St.J., Jan. 20, 1981, at 6, col. 1. Some 300 companies went public in the first seven months of 1981, raising $2.3 billion. Wall St.J., Sept. 10, 1981, at 1, col. 4.

8. Wall St.J., Nov. 17, 1980, at 29, col. 1; S. Nazem, The Folks Who Brought You Apple, Fortune, Jan. 12, 1981, at 66.

9. Wall St. J., Feb. 21, 1986, at 25, col. 4.

Report of Congressional Research Service for Use of the House Comm. on Energy and Commerce, The Role of High Yield Bonds [Junk Bonds] in Capital Markets and Corporate Takeovers: Public Policy Implications, 99th Cong., 1st Sess. (Comm. Print 99–W 1985).

10. Flaherty, Stock Boom: Boon for Bar, 5 Nat'l L.J., Sept. 5, 1983, at 1, col. 1.

developed secondary market for securities which meets investors' strong preference for market depth and liquidity.[11]

RESTRUCTURING OF THE FINANCIAL SERVICES INDUSTRY

The Statutory Framework. The Federal Banking laws, particularly the Glass-Steagall Act [1] and the Bank Holding Company Act [2] contain prohibitions on mixing commercial banking with investment banking and commercial activities with banking. The Glass-Steagall Act consists of four sections of the Banking Act of 1933 providing for the separation of commercial and investment banking. First, Section 21 bars individuals and organizations engaging in the investment banking business from receiving deposits which are subject to withdrawal upon the depositor's request. Investment banking is defined as "the business of issuing, underwriting, selling, or distributing, at wholesale or retail, or through syndicate participation, stocks, bonds, debentures, notes, or other securities." [3] It is to be noted that section 21 applies to *all* banks, not just national banks.

The next three sections, however, apply only to *member* banks of the Federal Reserve System. Section 16 bars a member bank from dealing in securities, except purchases and sales made, "without recourse, solely upon the order, and for the account of customers," nor may the [bank] "underwrite any issue of securities." [4] Thus, member banks are prohibited from owning directly any stock in commercial enterprises. However, member banks may purchase "investment securities" for their own account, subject to regulation by the Comptroller of the Currency.

The remaining two sections implement Section 16. Section 20 prohibits member banks from using securities affiliates to circumvent the prohibitions applicable to banks; it bars member banks from affiliation with any organization *"engaged principally"* [5] in the issue, underwriting, or distribution of securities. Section 32 buttresses section 20 by prohibiting management or employees of investment banks from serving as management or employees of member banks.[6]

The Bank Holding Company Act defines a "bank holding company" as any company which has "control" over a bank.[7] The Act prohibits a bank holding company from engaging in activities other than those of banking, except for activities deemed "closely related to banking" [8] and gives the Federal Reserve Board the power to determine whether specific activities meet this test.[9] The Douglas Amendment to the Act provides that a bank holding company may not acquire a bank outside of the bank's home state unless the law of the state in which the acquired bank is located expressly

11. W. Baumol, The Stock Market and Economic Efficiency vii (1965).

1. 48 Stat. 184 (1933) §§ 16, 20, 21 and 32, 12 U.S.C. §§ 24, 377, 378 and 78 (1982).

2. 12 U.S.C. § 1841 et seq. (1982).

3. 12 U.S.C. § 378 (1982).

4. 12 U.S.C. § 24, Seventh (1982). Although section 16 applies to national banks, state member banks are made subject to the same restrictions "with respect to the purchasing, selling, underwriting and holding of investment securities and stock" as are national banks. 12 U.S.C. § 335 (1982).

5. 12 U.S.C. § 377 (1982).

6. 12 U.S.C. § 78 (1982).

7. 12 U.S.C. § 1841. Section 1841 and FRB, Reg. Y, 12 C.F.R. § 225 (1986), prescribe various tests for determining control, including the power to vote 25% or more of any class of voting securities.

8. 12 U.S.C. § 1843(c)(8) (1982).

9. The FRB has issued a list of activities which it considers meets this test. 12 C.F.R. § 225.25 (1986).

permits the acquisition.[10] A bank holding company is subject to this prohibition, however, only if it is acquiring a "bank," as that term is defined in the Bank Holding Company Act. A bank, as defined in the Act, is an institution that both accepts deposits that the depositor has a legal right to withdraw on demand, *and* that engages in the business of making commercial loans.[11] If an institution engages in one of these two activities, but not both, an institution is not a bank for purposes of the Bank Holding Company Act.

In the last decade industrial and commercial firms such as Sears and J.C. Penney have sought to enter the financial services industry and broaden their product lines by offering financial services that require a bank charter. Moreover, investment banking firms such as Merrill Lynch and insurance and investment banking firms such as Prudential also desired to engage in the banking business, but they did not want to become bank holding companies, because their core business activities do not appear on the Federal Reserve Board's list of activities deemed to be "closely related to banking."

At the same time, the big money-center bank holding companies wanted to expand their activities both functionally and geographically; they wish to broaden their product lines by engaging in securities brokerage, investment banking and insurance; and they want to do interstate banking.

This trend toward conglomeration of commercial and financial institutions has been accelerated by the instability of the economic system and by technological change. The period has been marked by volatile interest rates, changing price levels and deregulation of banking and financial services. At the same time, technological developments in electronics, computers and communications have permitted these competitors in financial services to create and package new financial products and thus enable individuals and businesses to manage their assets more effectively.[12]

The restructuring of the financial services industry has been accomplished when necessary through the creation of holding companies which conduct various commercial or financial activities through separate subsidiary corporations, thereby maintaining a formal separation between activities. In this environment, insurance companies acquired mutual funds; mutual funds introduced money market accounts, with check writing privileges; retailers acquired securities brokers, thrifts and limited-service banks, also known as "nonbank banks"; securities brokers invented cash management margin accounts featuring check writing and credit card services; and credit card companies acquired banks and securities brokers. In turn, bank holding companies acquired discount brokers, and insurance and investment company components.

Despite the restructuring of the financial services industry, Congress has been reluctant to broaden bank, or bank holding company, powers to offer new types of services, expand interstate banking, or reform the federal financial regulatory system. In the absence of a rational national policy on the regulation of financial services, the courts have become the instruments through which the players have sought to exploit "loopholes" in the existing statutory structure.

---

10. 12 U.S.C. § 1842(d) (1982). National banks are under somewhat similar restrictions on interstate banking. See Note, Interstate Banking Restrictions Under the McFadden Act, 72 Va.L.Rev. 1119 (1986).

11. 12 U.S.C. § 1841(c) (1982).

12. For a discussion of the changes occurring in banking and the financial markets in the leading industrial countries, see Corporate Finance: Topsy-turvy. A Survey, The Economist, June 7, 1986, at 64.

Several cases illustrate this process. In *Securities Industry Association v. Board of Governors of the Federal Reserve System*,[13] the Supreme Court upheld the action of the Federal Reserve Board (FRB) in authorizing a bank holding company to acquire a non-banking subsidiary engaged in retail discount securities brokerage. The services were limited to the purchase and sale of securities for the account of customers without dispensing investment advice. The Court concluded that the activity was "closely related to banking" under § 4(c)(8) of the Bank Holding Company Act. Moreover, the acquisition was not a violation of § 20 of the Glass-Steagall Act which prohibits a bank (the holding company's banking subsidiary) from engaging principally in underwriting securities. Finally, the Court concluded that the entry of the bank into securities activities of this nature would increase competition and promote efficiency without creating undue concentration of resources. Increasingly, the bank regulatory authorities are authorizing banks to engage in securities brokerage with or without dispensing investment advice.

The Nonbank Bank Loophole. When commercial or financial services companies that did not own or control a bank wanted to broaden their financial product lines by offering services that require a bank charter, it was imperative that these firms did not become bank holding companies as a result of the acquisition of a bank. The solution was to acquire a bank charter and engage either in the business of accepting deposits, withdrawable upon demand, or in the business of making commercial loans, but not both of these activities. By engaging in one of these two activities but not both, it was believed that the institution would not be a "bank" for purposes of the Bank Holding Company Act.

Accordingly, in the 1980's, a large number of insurance, securities and commercial organizations acquired limited-service or nonbank banks which accept demand deposits or make commercial loans, but do not do both. More recently, money-center bank holding companies have also sought FRB authority to operate limited-service banks in states where they were forbidden to engage in "banking," and thereby surmount the barriers against interstate banking.[14] Confronted with this situation, the FRB attempted to redefine the definition of "bank" under section 2(c) of the Bank Holding Company Act on the basis that these banks offered the functional equivalent of traditional banking services and should be regulated as "banks." In *Board of Governors of the Federal Reserve System v. Dimension Financial Corp.*,[15] the Court rejected the FRB's attempt to redefine the definition of "bank" under section 2(c) as being beyond the Congressionally mandated definition.

The nonbank bank loophole, unless closed, enables non-bank holding companies to acquire nonbank bank charters and offer various financial products and services. It also opens the door for the big bank holding companies to engage in interstate banking through the use of limited-service banks.

As this is written, Congress has refused to close this loophole in the Bank Holding Company Act. The *Dimension* case, and *Northwest Bancorp* case upholding the constitutionality of regional compacts relating to interstate banking privileges, have put pressure on the states to pass legislation which

---

13. 468 U.S. 207 (1984).

14. In Northwest Bancorp, Inc. v. Board of Governors, 472 U.S. 159 (1985), the Court sustained the constitutionality of a regional compact between New England States providing for reciprocal interstate banking privileges for each member of the compact, but excluding non-New England out-of-state bank holding companies. This has opened the way for regional interstate banking in other parts of the nation.

15. ___ U.S. ___, 106 S.Ct. 681 (1986); Note, Nonbank Banks: Who's Minding the Store?, 46 La.L.Rev. 1087 (1986).

will allow bank holding companies to cross lines and engage in interstate banking; otherwise, their "nonbank bank" competitors will have done so through limited service banks. However, as the barriers to interstate banking erode, the need for the bank holding companies to use the nonbank bank vehicle for interstate expansion will disappear.

On the other hand, non-bank holding companies which wish to expand their product lines to include banking products and services that are closely related to banking, will have to use the nonbank bank vehicle in order to continue to offer their core business non-banking products and services. There will be continuous pressure to amend the Bank Holding Company to allow holding companies to offer a broader range of services, including banking and non-banking services.[16]

The Regulatory Framework. These developments have occurred against a statutory and regulatory framework which was created in the 1930's. The banking system is regulated by multiple federal and state agencies. Seven different federal agencies regulate many, but not all, of the different types of firms providing financial services. The Federal Reserve Board regulates bank holding companies. The Comptroller of the Currency regulates national banks. State-chartered banks that are members of the Federal Reserve System are regulated by the FRB and their state regulator. "Non-member" banks are regulated by the Federal Deposit Insurance Corporation (FDIC), if they are federally insured and by their state supervisory agency. Most commercial banks are insured by the FDIC. Thrifts are regulated by the Federal Home Loan Bank Board (FHLBB) and are regulated and insured by the Federal Savings and Loan Insurance Corporation (FSLIC) as are credit unions under the National Credit Union Share Insurance Fund (NCUSIF). The business of insurance is regulated by the states, but securities products offered by insurance companies are subject to federal and state securities regulation. Investment companies are regulated by the SEC and the states, as are broker-dealers and investment advisers. Pension funds are separately regulated under ERISA.[17] Antitrust is largely the responsibility of the Justice Department.

Single Agency Regulation Versus Regulation by Function. Over the years, numerous proposals have been advanced for reorganization of the Federal agencies regulating commercial banks and other financial institutions. The latest proposal is that of the Bush Task Group on Regulation of Financial Services.[18] The Report rejects the present pattern which in some measure vests federal regulation of different types of financial institutions in a single agency, in favor of regulation by function in order to streamline unnecessary regulatory controls and provide equality of competition within the financial services industry. The specific recommendation as to regulation of securities activities is as follows:[19]

---

16. E. Gerald Corrigan, President of the Federal Reserve Bank of New York has proposed a new financial structure to reshape the financial services industry that may break the present impasse. See Ann.Rep., Federal Reserve Bank of New York (1986).

17. Employee Retirement Income Security Act of 1974, 88 Stat. 832, 29 U.S.C. § 1001 et seq.

18. Blueprint for Reform: The Report of the Task Group on Regulation of Finan-

cial Services (July 2, 1984). For a brief survey of the origins and development of the American banking system, see E. Symons & J. White, Banking Law 1–66 (2d ed. 1984). For the proposal of a new regulatory model, see Friedman & Friesen, A New Paradigm for Financial Regulation: Getting From Here to There, 43 Md.L.Rev. 413 (1984).

19. Id. at 91.

The registration requirements of the Securities Act of 1933 should be made applicable to publicly offered securities of banks and thrifts (but not deposit instruments), and administration and enforcement of disclosure and other requirements of Securities Exchange Act of 1934 for bank and thrift securities should be transferred from the bank and thrift regulatory agencies to the SEC, as is currently the case for securities of all other types of companies (including bank and thrift holding companies). The Federal Home Loan Bank Board, however, should exercise securities jurisdiction over conversions of savings and loan associations and federal savings banks from the mutual to the stock form of organization and other matters involving the safety and soundness of insured institutions or affecting the operations of the Federal Savings and Loan Insurance Corporation.

In recent years, the Federal Reserve Board,[20] the Comptroller of the Currency,[21] and the Federal Deposit Insurance Corporation [22] approved proposals permitting banks to engage in securities brokerage activities through broker-dealer affiliates or subsidiaries which were registered as broker-dealers with the SEC. Later, however, the FDIC withdrew some of its restrictions so as to permit federally insured, non-member banks to internalize their securities brokerage activities, subject to a number of restrictions.[23]

The jurisdiction of the SEC to require banks that provide securities brokerage services to the public to register as broker-dealers hinges upon an interpretation of Sections 15 and 3(a)(4) and (5) of Securities Exchange Act. Section 15 of the Exchange Act requires all brokers and dealers to register with the Commission unless an exemption is available. As defined in Sections 3(a)(4) and (5), the terms "broker" and "dealer" exclude a "bank" as defined in Section 3(a)(6). The section further provides, however, that these definitions apply "unless the context otherwise requires." Under Section 3(b) of the Exchange Act, the Commission has the authority to define terms. In order to require functional regulation of securities activities of banks, in 1985, the Commission adopted Rule 3b–9 which redefined the term "bank" as used in the definition of "broker" and "dealer" in Sections 3(a)(4) and (5) of the Exchange Act so as not to include a bank which, in effect, conducts a securities brokerage business, takes orders from customers and handles customer funds and securities without the intervention of a registered broker-dealer.[24] The Commission concluded that the "context" required that certain securities activities of banks fall outside the bank exclusion. However, Rule 3b–9 exempts from registration banks that enter into "networking" arrangements with registered-broker-dealers or underwriters for registered investment companies and banks which handle fewer than 1,000 trades a year.

The American Bankers Association, however, challenged the authority of the Commission to adopt Rule 3b–9, and in *American Bankers Association v.*

---

20. Order of the Federal Reserve System Approving the Acquisition of Charles Schwab & Co., Inc. by BankAmerica Corporation, 69 Fed.Res.Bull. 105 (1983).

21. Decision of the Comptroller of the Currency Establishing an Operating Subsidiary to be Known as Security Pacific Discount Brokerage Services, Inc. [1982 Transfer Binder] Fed.Banking L.Rep. (CCH) ¶ 99,284 (Aug. 26, 1982) (order upheld in Securities Indus. Ass'n v. Comptroller of the Currency, 577 F.Supp. 252 (D.D.C. (1983)).

22. Statement of Policy on Applicability of Glass-Steagall Act to Securities Activities of Subsidiaries of Insured Nonmember Banks, 47 Fed.Reg. 38984 (Sept. 3, 1982); Unsafe and Unsound Banking Practices, 49 Fed.Reg. 46709 (1984).

23. General Counsel's Opinion No. 6— The Legality of Discount Brokerage Services When Offered By Insured Nonmember Banks, 48 Fed.Reg. 22989 (May 23, 1983).

24. Securities Exchange Release No. 22205 (July 1, 1985).

SEC,[25] the Court of Appeals for the District of Columbia adopted the bankers' view that the Commission lacked such authority.

The fall-out from the American Bankers case and the fate of the Bush Commission proposals are uncertain. The American Bankers Association invested considerable capital in attempting to preserve single agency authority over the securities activities of banks, although it is urging Congress to expand bank powers to engage in a broader range of financial products and services. The time is overdue for Congress to undertake a reexamination of the Glass-Steagall Act, the Bank Holding Company Act and the securities laws so as to provide for rational federal regulation of the financial services area.[26] We shall take a further look at the Glass-Steagall Act and the historical barriers between commercial and investment banking as we consider investment banking and the underwriting process.

SECTION 2. INVESTMENT BANKING AND THE UNDERWRITING PROCESS

INVESTMENT BANKING, UNDERWRITING AND SYNDICATION

Investment Banking. Investment banking and the underwriting process have been shaped by the Banking Act of 1933 (known as the Glass-Steagall Act), the Securities Act of 1933 and the Securities Exchange Act of 1934. Prior to 1933, commercial banks engaged in underwriting corporate securities primarily through separately incorporated securities affiliates. By 1929, the commercial banks had achieved a competitive position which was approximately equal to the distributive capability of the private investment banks.[1]

The stock market collapse of 1929 and the ensuing drastic decline in stock market prices left most of the securities affiliates of national banks in shambles.[2] The Senate investigation of stock exchange practices developed a sordid picture of questionable practices engaged in by national banks, their securities affiliates, and bank officers and directors which affected the safety of depositors' funds and were damaging to the bank's customers and shareholders.[3] These disclosures led to the passage of the Glass-Steagall Act of 1933, which sharply curtailed the investment banking activities of commercial banks and forced them to withdraw completely from important segments of the investment banking business.[4]

The legislative history of the Act was reviewed by Mr. Justice Stewart in Investment Co. Institute v. Camp, 401 U.S. 617, 629–34 (1971). Congress foresaw three categories of hazards which might arise through the mixing of

---

25. 804 F.2d 739 (D.C.Cir.1986).

26. See Report, Restructuring Financial Markets: The Major Policy Issues, Subcomm. on Telecommunications, Consumer Protection, and Finance of the Comm. on Energy and Commerce, 99th Cong., 2d Sess. (Comm.Print 1986).

1. See E. Herman, Conflicts of Interest: Commercial Bank Trust Departments, A Report to the Twentieth Century Fund 9–25 (1975), and J. Brooks, Conflicts of Interest: Corporate Pension Fund Asset Management, A Report to the Twentieth Century Fund (1975). These studies are among a series of reports to the Twentieth Century Fund Steering Committee on Conflicts of

Interest in the Securities Markets. They have been published under the title of "Abuse on Wall Street—Conflicts of Interest in the Securities Markets—A Twentieth Century Fund Report."

2. See generally, Stock Exchange Practices, Hearings on S.Res. 84 and S.Res. 56 Before the Senate Comm. on Banking and Currency, 73rd Cong., 1st Sess. (1933).

3. For example, see Id. pts. 5–6 relating to the securities activities of the Chase National Bank and the Chase Securities Corporation.

4. 48 Stat. 162 (1933).

commercial and investment banking. First, the involvement of the bank in investment banking and securities activities might lead to the making of unsound loans and investments. Such loans might be made to companies of dubious credit standing in whose stock the securities affiliate had invested, in order to make the stock more attractive. Loans might be made to customers to facilitate the purchase of securities, thereby encouraging speculation. And loans might be made to securities affiliates that had become overextended. The Senate investigation of stock market practices had disclosed that the securities affiliates had become overextended by investing and trading in speculative securities in the rising stock market of the 1920's, only to be wiped out by the disastrous losses incurred in the ensuing bear market.[5] Second, there was thought to be a danger of loss of public confidence in the commercial bank because of its association with an entity that was engaged in the high-risk activity of investment banking. The Court noted that "pressures are created because the bank and the affiliate are closely associated in the public mind, and should the affiliate fare badly, public confidence in the bank might be impaired." Finally, the conflict between the promotional interests of the investment banker and the "obligation of the commercial banker to render disinterested investment advice" might lead to the bank's violation of its fiduciary responsibilities. Mr. Justice Stewart pointed out: "Congress had before it evidence that security affiliates might be driven to unload excessive holdings through the trust department of the sponsor bank."[6] Such fear of "unloading" was justified by the exposure of conflicts of interest and self-dealing which had been engaged in by the banks, the banks' securities affiliates and by the banks' officers and directors.[7]

National banks which had previously engaged both in commercial and deposit banking on the one hand and investment banking on the other were compelled to choose between commercial banking and investment banking. This completely eliminated the commercial banks and trust companies from this sector of the investment banking business, and the various bank affiliates were dissolved and liquidated. Under Section 16 and the Comptroller's regulations, member banks are permitted to underwrite general obligation bonds of the United States and of state and local governments, but are generally forbidden to underwrite revenue bonds of these entities.[8] Commercial banks,

---

5. Apparently most banks had decided to curtail their investment banking activities even prior to the adoption of the Glass-Steagall Act, although it is not altogether clear whether they simply were making a strategic retreat or whether their withdrawal resulted from seeing the handwriting on the wall. Thus in April, 1933, two months before the passage of the Glass-Steagall Act, the Chase National Bank and the Chase Securities Corporation jointly notified their shareholders (who held the same number of shares in each corporation) that "the experience of the past 10 years had clearly indicated the advisability of separating commercial banking from the general business of investment banking." The proposal was stated to be "in the best interests of the bank and in accord not only with sound banking policy but responsive to enlightened public opinnion." Since it appeared impossible to sell the securities business to outside interests, the governing boards recommended that the securities business be terminated and that the securities affiliate undergo an orderly liquidation. See Senate Hearings on Stock Exchange Practices, supra note 2, at 2296–2297.

6. Investment Co. Institute v. Camp, 401 U.S. 617, at 633, citing Hearings Before a Subcomm. of the Senate Comm. on Banking and Currency, 71st Cong., 3d Sess., on the Operation of National and Federal Reserve banking systems, pursuant to S.Res. 71, at 237.

7. See generally, the 1931 hearings, supra note 6, and the 1933 hearings, supra note 2. Cf. Smith, Glass-Steagall Act—A History of Its Legislative Origins and Regulatory Construction, 92 Banking L.J. 38 (1974).

8. 12 U.S.C. § 24 (1976). See Mehle, Bank Underwriting of Municipal Revenue Bonds: Preserving Free and Fair Competition, 26 Syracuse L.Rev. 1117 (1975); Note, Commercial-Bank Underwriting of Munici-

however, are still a dominant factor in the underwriting and marketing of government securities. Commercial banks also are still deeply involved in the securities markets through their trust departments, including pension fund asset management, and as long-term creditors of industry.[9]

The scope and effect of the Glass-Steagall Act has come under intense scrutiny as bank holding companies and investment banking organizations have sought to expand their securities and financial services activities (see supra at page 21) and in a series of cases the Supreme Court has narrowed its thrust. First, the Supreme Court has said that Sections 16 and 21 apply only to banks and not bank holding companies, thereby recognizing that bank holding companies may use separate affiliates to engage in securities-related activities forbidden to banks. And the Court added: "[T]he language of § 21 cannot be read to include within its prohibition separate organizations related by owner-ship with a bank, which does receive deposits."[10] Second, although a bank holding company is an "affiliate," and thereby within the reach of Section 20,[11] that section bars member banks and bank holding companies from affiliation only with organizations "engaged principally" in the issue, underwriting or distribution of securities. The section does not prohibit such affiliation when the bank is not a member of the Federal Reserve System nor an affiliation by a member bank so long as the principal activity of the affiliate is some activity other than the issuance, underwriting or distribution of securities.[12] Thus, Sections 16 and 21 apparently allow an investment banking organization to be affiliated with a non-member state bank, even though insured by the FDIC. Relying on this reading of the statute, Shearson, Loeb, Rhoades has acquired an affiliated non-member Massachusetts state bank insured by the FDIC and Merrill Lynch has acquired an affiliated non-member New Jersey state bank.

On the other hand, member banks and bank holding companies have not been entirely successful in their attempts to invade the underwriting business.[13] Traditionally, large commercial borrowers have relied on banks for their short-term funds. In recent years, however, a large commercial paper market has developed in which these borrowers have by-passed banks and sold short-term notes to sophisticated investors through the use of investment banking firms acting as underwriters. Bankers Trust Company has tried to recapture some of this business by selling third-party prime quality commercial paper in large denominations to sophisticated customers. Since the bank acted solely as an agent of the issuer in what was regarded as a private placement—not a public offering—the Federal Reserve Board granted approval on the ground that: (1) commercial paper was not a "note or other security" for the purposes of Section

pal Revenue Bonds: A Self-Regulatory Approach, 128 U.Pa.L.Rev. 1201 (1980). At the time of the adoption of the Glass-Steagall Act, the revenue-bond business was a modest portion of the municipal-securities market. Since World War II, however, revenue bonds have become a dominant factor in that market. Indeed, it is estimated that the effect of removing the restriction forbidding banks to underwrite revenue bonds would more than double the volume of securities underwritings available to them. 128 U.Pa.L.Rev. 1201, at 1203.

9. See, supra note 1.

10. Board of Governors of the Fed. Res. System v. Investment Co. Inst., 450 U.S. 46, at 58, n. 24 (1981).

11. 12 U.S.C. § 221a(b)(4) (1982).

12. The acquisition of a retail brokerage business by an affiliate of a bank holding company did not violate section 20, since the securities affiliate was not principally engaged in the issue, underwriting or distribution of securities. Securities Indus. Assn. v. Board of Governors of the Fed.Res. System, 468 U.S. 137 (1984).

13. They have, however, made substantial inroads. See Friedman & Friesen, A New Paradigm for Financial Regulation: Getting From Here to There, 43 Md.L.Rev. 413, at 436–438 (1984).

16 of Glass-Steagall, and (2) the sales on an agency basis did not entail the issuance, underwriting or distribution of securities under Section 21. The Supreme Court rejected the first contention, but on remand, the court of appeals for the District of Columbia sustained the decision of the FRB that Section 16 authorizes a commercial bank to act as agent in the private placement of commercial paper with institutional investors.[14]

Whether the constraints on the commercial banking industry imposed by Glass-Steagall should be repealed or modified have yet to be resolved by the Congress. The commercial banking industry contends that Glass-Steagall was an overreaction to stock market collapse of 1929 and the Great Depression; that the evidence is not clear that the underwriting and securities activities of banks was a major cause of the general instability and speculation in the stock market;[15] and that any supposed dangers arising from the conduct of commercial and investment banking through separate affiliates can be dealt with through regulation, rather than an outright prohibition against mixing commercial and investment banking.[16] In contrast, the securities industry rejects the arguments either that Glass-Steagall is out-dated or that it was a mistake. The industry argues that the banking system is too fragile and investor confidence too shaky to permit banks to enter into a new business as risky as the securities business; that banks are provided unique federal advantages (favorable tax treatment, credit privileges, and deposit insurance) and thus should be confined to commercial banking, and not authorized to engage in general commerce; and that the abuses which occurred during the years when banks were permitted to underwrite securities (1927–1933) would recur, although perhaps in new forms, if banks were allowed to engage in all aspects of the securities business.[17] As a fall-back, the Securities Industry Association has a ten-point program for regulation of the relations of bank holding companies and their securities affiliates designed to prevent the abuses which arose in the pre-Glass-Steagall period.[18]

The underwriting and syndication of corporate securities is conducted by a number of investment banking organizations which may or may not combine their underwriting activities with that of brokerage and money management. Although formerly these firms were privately owned, many of them now are

---

14. Securities Indus. Ass'n. v. Board of Governors of the Fed.Res. System, 468 U.S. 137 (1984); Securities Indus. Ass'n. v. Board of Governors of the Fed.Res. System, 807 F.2d 1052 (D.D.Cir.1986); Glidden, Bank Sales of Commercial Paper Under the Glass-Steagall Act: Hazards of the Bankers Trust Decisions, 42 Bus.Law. 1 (1986); Note, A Conduct-Oriented Approach to the Glass-Steagall Act, 91 Yale L.J. 102 (1981).

15. M. Friedman & A. Schwartz, A Monetary History of the United States, 1867–1960 (1963) at 299; J. Galbraith, The Great Crash, 1929 (1954) at 174; Bernanke, Nonmonetary Effects of the Financial Crisis in the Propagation of the Great Depression, 73 Am.Econ.Rev. 257 (1983).

16. J.P. Morgan & Company, Inc., Rethinking Glass-Steagall, December, 1984; T. Huertas, Vice President, Citibank, An Economic Brief Against Glass-Steagall, Autumn, 1984.

17. Securities Industry Association, Questioning Expanded Bank Powers (Sept. 1985); Di Lorenzo, Public Confidence and the Banking System: The Policy Basis for Continued Separation of Commercial and Investment Banking, 35 Am.Univ.L.Rev. 647 (1986).

18. Id. at App. C, 33–35; Note, An Alternative to Throwing Stones: A Proposal for the Reform of Glass-Steagall, 52 Brooklyn L.Rev. 281 (1986). A recent economic symposium on bank regulation reveals a surprising lack of interest in the Glass-Steagall Act as a significant public policy issue in connection with restructuring the American banking system. Symposium on Bank Regulation, 59 J. of Bus. 1–117 (1986). For a thoughtful proposal of a new regulatory model for the financial services industry, see, Friedman & Friesen, supra note 13; The Emerging Financial Industry (A. Sametz ed. 1984).

incorporated, and have substantial amounts of capital contributed by public shareholders.

Since the passage of the Securities Act of 1933, there have emerged certain standardized methods by which a corporation may float a new issue of securities, primarily in the over-the-counter market. The various types of transactions may be classified as between those in which the services of an investment banker (herein referred to as an underwriter) is used, and those in which such services are dispensed with.

Direct Offerings. Securities may be sold, without the use of an underwriter or marketing syndicate, in a direct offering by the issuer. There are five types of direct offerings: (a) a direct public offering; (b) a direct offering limited to existing shareholders, usually in the form of a "rights offering"; (c) an offer for sale by tender (or "Dutch auction"); [19] (d) an "all or none" offering; or (e) a direct private placement.

(a) *Direct Public Offering.* In a direct public offering, the issuer of a new security gambles upon its ability to sell the entire issue without the intervention of an underwriter or marketing syndicate. The issuer thus assumes the entire risk of failure to acquire the needed capital. Accordingly, the success of the offering depends greatly upon prevailing market conditions; the method is used rarely, except by an issuer with a strong credit rating and existing demand for its securities, or by a start-up company or speculative business operation either going public for the first time, or seeking to raise capital from a circle of investors with prior knowledge of the particular business enterprise.

(b) *Rights Offerings.* Another type of direct offering is that made to existing shareholders. Although shareholders may be solicited without the allocation of rights, the usual procedure is to make a "rights offering". In a rights offering, existing shareholders are offered warrants or rights to subscribe to a new class of securities of the same issuer.[20] Rights are allocated in proportion to the size of existing holdings of the issuer's securities. Shareholders are an obvious source of capital for a seasoned public company.

(c) *Dutch Auction.* The "offer for sale by tender" (or "Dutch auction") is used by issuers more frequently in the United Kingdom than in the United States. In the United Kingdom, the Dutch auction has often been used to maximize initial returns to issuers, especially those companies going public for the first time.[21] The securities are offered at a stated minimum price, subject to specified conditions. One condition is that each buyer has the option of bidding for any number of shares. The final offering price is fixed at the maximum price at which all shares can be sold pursuant to the bids. All shares will be sold at that final, maximum price. In practice, however, the offer by tender may require the investment advice of an experienced underwriter, and some kind of underwriting commitment.

19. On the "Dutch Auction" type of offer, see [1974–1975 Transfer Binder] (CCH) Fed.Sec.L.Rep. ¶ 80,046 (1974).

For a discussion of the use of offers for sale by tender in the United Kingdom, see Merrett, Howe & Newbould, Equity Issues and the London Capital Market c. 6 (1967).

20. On the logic and mechanics of rights issues, see Merrett, Howe & Newbould, id. at c. 3; Jennings & Buxbaum, Corporations 869–871 (5th ed. 1979); Cary & Eisenberg, Corporations 1087–1089 (5th ed. 1980).

21. The study of Merrett, Howe & Newbould presents data indicating that vendors of shares have suffered substantial losses through the conservative pricing of new issues in negotiated underwritings, and advances the thesis that the offer for tender is far more advantageous to the seller than a negotiated transaction. Id. 11–13, 173–79.

In the United States the offer by tender is not yet a preferred form of direct offering, and it has yet to be used in this country for any initial public offering of equity securities. In other contexts, however, the offer by tender is becoming an accepted form of direct offer. The United States Treasury Department now uses the Dutch auction as a method of marketing federal government securities. Regulated issuers, such as public utilities, are required by law in some instances to use competitive, public bids among underwriters to sell their debt offerings.[22] Finally, Exxon Corporation regularly uses the Dutch auction to sell various forms of debt securities, with or without the use of underwriters.[23] The Dutch auction has enabled Exxon to maximize its returns, eliminate or reduce underwriting commissions, and lower interest rates on new issues. On the whole, however, uncertainties regarding firm bids and the periodic resort to private placements by venture capital firms serves to provide an appropriate method of determining initial offering prices and thereby minimize the attractiveness of the Dutch auction in the United States equity market.

(d) *"All or None" Offerings.* In some situations where a minimum amount of funds are needed for a special purpose, securities may be offered by the issuer on an "all or none" basis. Thus, unless a designated number of shares are sold and paid for in full within a specified period, the offering will be terminated and all funds returned, with interest, to the subscribers. The subscribers' funds are placed "in escrow" with a designated depositary and do not become available for other disposition until the terms of the offering are met. Some State securities Administrators may require the use of an "all or none" offering under certain circumstances.[24]

(e) *Private Placements.* The last form of direct offering is a private placement. A private placement allows an issuer to sell securities to a legally restricted number of institutional and other highly sophisticated investors. The most important factors indicating a private placement of securities, either by the issuer directly or with the assistance of an underwriter, are necessity, secrecy, speed and cost.

Necessity dictates use of a private placement for some issuers. A private offering is frequently used by issuers to place new debt securities with institutional investors such as private pension plans and insurance companies. This route may be necessary where the public market may absorb only high-quality issues of well-known issuers in amounts of $50 million or more. More recently, however, the private placement has been used to market high-yield, high-risk "junk bonds." In addition, confidential matters such as sources of raw materials, executive compensation, and secret manufacturing processes may be hidden from public view. In a private placement, the small number of sophisticated investors purchasing the issue are less likely to disclose any such material, nonpublic information.

---

22. Rules requiring competitive bidding have been adopted by the Securities and Exchange Commission with respect to the sale of debt securities by public utility holding company systems, and by the Interstate Commerce Commission and the Federal Power Commission as to companies subject to their regulation. A number of states require competitive bidding for utility issues in some cases.

23. Wall St.J., Oct. 29, 1976, p. 25, ed. 5; N.Y. Times, Nov. 17, 1976, at 61, col. 2.

For the mechanics of Dutch auctions, see Exxon Corporation (Avail. April 7, 1977), Fed.Sec.L.Rep. (CCH) ¶ 81,198; Note, Auctioning New Issues of Corporate Securities, 71 Va.L.Rev. (1985).

24. See SEC v. Manor Nursing Centers, Inc., 458 F.2d 1082 (2d Cir.1972); SEC Securities Exchange Act Rules 10b–9, 15c2–4; Robbins, All-or-None Offerings, 19 Rev. of Sec. & Commodities Reg. 59 (1986); Robbins, All-or-None Offerings: An Update, 19 Rev. of Sec. & Commodities Reg. 181 (1986).

A private placement is far quicker than a public offering. The most important factor reducing the time required for a private placement is the nature of the legal documents that must be prepared for the issue. In a private placement, the issuer or underwriter contacts a restricted number of highly sophisticated purchasers to whom much of the detail required in a registration statement or statutory prospectus is unimportant. Although institutional and other sophisticated purchasers will want material investment information, it is made available to them in a different form. If an offering prospectus is necessary, frequently it will be less difficult to prepare. In addition, any written information can be supplemented by direct meetings between company officials and the prospective buyers. In dealing with sophisticated investors, the issuer (or its investment banker) can explain a highly speculative financing, or a highly technical offering, to a class of investors more likely to understand its terms than others, and to commit the funds necessary to consummate the financing.

Finally a private offering is far less costly than a public offering. Several factors increase the costs of a public offering, including legal fees, accounting costs, registration expenses, underwriters' fees and printing bills. In a private placement, it may be possible to avoid a fresh audit, and legal expenses will be substantially less. If an offering circular is required, there will be no prospectus to print. And, the transaction may be exempt from "blue sky" registration and regulatory requirements at the state level.[25]

Underwriting. The term "underwriter" was borrowed from the field of insurance. It was originally used to describe those individuals or firms that insured the issuer against any loss in connection with an offering of securities if the public investors failed to subscribe fully to the issue. This arrangement is known as a "strict underwriting." The term "underwriting," however, has long since lost this meaning, and strict underwriting is rarely, if ever, used today. The term "underwriter" now signifies a firm that specializes in the marketing of new issues of securities or secondary offerings of securities by selling shareholders. Section 2(11) of the Securities Act of 1933 broadly defines an "underwriter" to mean any person who has purchased from the issuer (or controlling persons) (1) with a view to, or (2) offers or sells for an issuer in connection with, the distribution of any security, or (3) participates in any such undertaking.

Underwriters may be used in all forms of public offerings of securities, including all-or-none offerings, as well as in private placements; they render financial advice with respect to the method of financing, the type of security to be offered, the market to be reached, the manner of offering and serve as managers of the offering.

Types of Underwritings. The most common types of underwritings, however, are three: (a) a firm commitment underwriting; (b) a "stand-by" underwriting and (c) a "best-efforts" underwriting. In a firm commitment underwriting, the underwriter (or syndicate) agree to purchase all or specific amounts of the offering for cash, subject to certain "market-outs." [26] A "stand-by" underwriting is one in which a new issue is offered only to existing shareholders. The

---

25. See Geczi, Volume of Private Debt Placement Surges to Record Levels for Variety of Reasons, Wall St. J., Mar. 8, 1976, at 14, col. 1.

26. In general, "market out" clauses in firm commitment underwriting agreements are triggered only upon the occur-

rence of "a material, adverse event affecting the issuer that materially impairs the investment quality of the offered securities." See the SEC No-Action Letter, First Boston Corporation (Available Sept. 2. 1985), Fed.Sec.L.Rep. (CCH) ¶ 78,152.

underwriters agree to "stand by" and purchase any shares not purchased by existing shareholders, at the expiration of a specified period. In a "best efforts" underwriting, the underwriter neither purchases the securities from the issuer nor resells them to the investing public; the underwriter agrees only to act as an agent of the issuer in marketing the issue to investors.[27]

In smaller issues, the investment banker may market the issue solely by the use of its own organization; in larger issues, a syndicate of other dealers of securities is organized to facilitate the distribution. In these cases, the so-called managing underwriter receives a special commission for managing the offering, and the other members of the syndicate receive a concession off the public offering price as compensation for assuming part of the underwriting risk and for services.[28] As indicated, in some cases the underwriting syndicate may make a firm commitment to the issuing company to take and pay for the securities directly and assume the risk of any wholesaler and retailer in merchandising a product. In the case of "rights offerings" to existing shareholders, the underwriting group may merely agree to act as agent in reselling the securities, but nevertheless "underwrite" the issue by agreeing to take up and pay for any securities not subscribed for by the public. It is customary to add a selling group of retailers of securities who purchase a portion of the offering at a concession off the offering price, but assume no part of the underwriting risk. Finally, the banking firm may merely agree to use its best efforts to sell the securities for the issuer, without making a firm commitment.

In actual practice, however, the members of the underwriting syndicate usually purchase the securities outright and resell them to the public. In such purchase transactions, each underwriter commits itself only for a specified portion of the offering, rather than assuming a joint liability, since under Section 11 of the Securities Act of 1933, an underwriter's overall civil liability is limited to the total public offering price of the securities underwritten by it.

In a firm commitment underwriting, the issuer will discuss its proposed offering with one or more investment banking firms which it selects to be the lead underwriter or underwriters. When the parties reach an understanding as to the type, nature and form of offering, this is usually reduced to writing, in a "letter of intent," which itself is not binding on either party.[29] The underwriter and issuer will arrive at a maximum public offering price for SEC filing fee purposes. The day before the registration statement becomes effective, the issuer and the lead underwriter will get together and reach the final terms as to price and related matters. The final terms will be based upon such factors as general market conditions and trends, and the reaction to the marketing efforts of the underwriting syndicate in receiving indications of buyer interest. At this point, the underwriters bid is firm for the entire issue, subject almost always to a "market out" if conditions change prior to effectiveness of the registration statement or an unconditional "out" prior to that time.

At an early stage of the underwriting process, the lead underwriter will prepare a syndicate list and discuss it with the issuer. The issuer will be asked

---

27. On distribution techniques in general, see 1 Securities Law Techniques ch. 18 (A.A. Sommer, Jr. ed. 1986); 1 Loss, Securities Regulation 159–172 (2d ed. 1961), Supp.1969); Merrett, Howe & Newbould, Equity Issues and the London Capital Market 511 (1967); United States v. Morgan, 118 F.Supp. 621, 635–655 (S.D.N.Y.1953).

28. For sample forms of underwriting agreements, agreements among underwrit-

ers and selling-group forms, see R. Shapiro, A. Sachs and C. Olander, Securities Regulation Forms (1983 rev., Loose-leaf); Weiss, The Underwriting Agreement—Form and Commentary, 26 Bus.Law. 647 (1971).

29. Dunhill Securities Corporation v. Microthermal Applications, Inc., 308 F.Supp. 195 (S.D.N.Y.1969).

whether there are other security dealers who have shown an interest in the issuer and should be brought into the syndicate. News of the impending underwriting may have become of general knowledge and other underwriters may contact either the lead underwriter or the issuer and request that they be made members of the syndicate. In a registered offering, during the period between the filing of the registration statement and its effectiveness (the so-called waiting period) the preliminary prospectus will be available and other underwriters will be asked to become members of the syndicate. At the same time at the signing of the underwriting agreement, the members of the syndicate will enter into an "agreement among underwriters." This agreement will designate the underwriter or underwriters who will manage the offering and fix the various terms and agreements among the members of the syndicate. The underwriting agreement is executed by the issuer and the lead underwriter, acting as agent for the other underwriters in the syndicate, who thereby also become parties to the underwriting agreement.

When the underwriting agreement is signed, the underwriters are committed for the entire issue, subject to "market outs" on certain contingencies, and it is only at this point that the issuer is assured of receiving the proceeds when the offering is completed.

If the pre-sale interest is disappointing so as to indicate that the proposed amount of the issue cannot all be sold, the underwriters will advise either that the size of the offering be cut back or that the contemplated price be reduced or that the offering be deferred until market conditions improve. If, however, the issuer and underwriters arrive at the price and related terms, the issuer will have a firm commitment from the group to purchase its securities.

A registered public offering is more complicated and time consuming than a private placement. It can take as long as two to four months to arrange the financing, allow for the underwriters to make the investigation, and to prepare the documentation for a registration statement. Depending upon the complexity of the company, and the workload of the SEC staff, it may take from three weeks to three months for the registration statement to become effective and the offering to take place. By contrast, a private placement might be completed in as little as one month. A major factor in this time differential is the nature of the documents required.

Syndication. The managing underwriter will have completed the formation of the underwriting syndicate sometime after the registration statement is filed with the Securities and Exchange Commission. During the waiting period members of the syndicate will have tested the market by distributing the preliminary prospectus among securities dealers, and received written indications of interest by prospective down the line purchasers. On the basis of this accumulation of buyer interest, the allocation of the amount of securities to be purchased by each member of the syndicate will be made, thereby separating members of the syndicates into groups based upon the size of their purchase commitments.

In the formation of the underwriting syndicate, the lead underwriter will organize a syndicate designed to give the widest possible distribution to the issue. In a large issue, the syndicate will comprise several groups of underwriters based upon the size of an underwriter's commitment. The first level will consist of "major-bracket underwriters"—a relatively small group of large investment banking firms, who bring substantial capital and prestige to the offering, in addition to their most important asset, that of distributing capability. These first-level firms will constitute the "major" group in the syndicate. A second-tier or "mezzanine" group will normally consist of a combination of

New York Stock Exchange member firms having branch offices outside of New York (called "wire houses" because the main office is connected with branch offices and correspondent brokers by private leased telephone wires), and leading regional investment banking firms around the nation. Depending upon the size of the issue, the syndicate may also include other firms located throughout the United States and, in some cases, in financial centers throughout the world. There are approximately 200 or more investment banking firms in the United States which regularly participate in underwriting; however, only approximately 10 to 100 will normally be members of the underwriting group in any given issue. A combination of large institutionally-oriented firms, large wire houses, and locally based retailers has proven to be the most effective combination for achieving a good nationwide distribution and a reasonably satisfactory pricing of the offering from the standpoint both of the issuer and the underwriter.

Over the years, there has been a definite pecking order among investment banking firms. In any syndicate, the choice spot is that of managing underwriter. A syndicate manager of an attractive issue would be subject to considerable pressure by second-tier underwriters to be elevated to a first-tier position. On the "tombstone ad" (see infra, at page 89) the managing underwriter or underwriters will receive top billing. The first level underwriters would then be listed from left to right in alphabetical order, followed by a similar listing within the various subgroups. This pecking order established a ranking of underwriters within and without the industry, and the name of the game was to be in the first level if possible, or as near the top as possible. On occasion, an underwriter would withdraw from a syndicate if its allotment was less than it felt it was entitled to, or if it felt that it had been assigned to a rank below that to which it was entitled. In a recent wave of mergers among investment banking firms, feathers occasionally became ruffled by playing games with the new firm name so as to move closer to the head of the alphabet for the purpose of ranking within any particular group.

In recent years, however, these folkways have been undergoing change. In 1979, when IBM requested that Morgan Stanley & Co., its traditional investment banker, reconsider its policy of insisting on serving as sole manager of any underwriting syndicate and share the managership of a $1 billion issue of securities with Salomon Brothers, Morgan Stanley backed out of the deal, even though it meant losing a cherished client.[30] In 1980, however, Morgan Stanley abandoned its policy and joined the regional San Francisco-based firm of Hambrecht & Quist as a co-manager of Apple Computer's first public offering of common stock. This also marked the first time that Morgan Stanley had participated in the underwriting of one of the small high-technology companies based in "Silicon Valley," California.[31] Furthermore, following the listing of the co-managers, the 133 underwriters were listed in alphabetical order, regardless of the number of shares underwritten.[32]

This practice, however, proved to be only a temporary phenomenon. Some of the big six underwriting firms (First Boston Corporation, Goldman, Sachs & Co., Merrill Lynch Capital Markets, Morgan Stanley & Co., Salomon Brothers Inc., and Shearson Lehman Brothers Inc. have since created a special or "bulge" bracket for themselves above the major bracket. In debt offerings, and

---

30. W. Guzzardi, The Bomb I.B.M. Dropped on Wall Street, Fortune, Nov. 19, 1979, at 52.

31. S. Nazem, The Folks Who Brought You Apple, Fortune, Jan. 12, 1981, at 66; Metz, Street Fighters—Morgan Stanley

Drops its Staid Image, Battles for Securities Business, Wall.St.J., July 17, 1980 at 1, col. 1.

32. Prospectus, Apple Computer, Inc., Dec. 12, 1980, at 31–32.

less frequently in equity offerings, the "bulge" bracket is followed by a "mezzanine" bracket, a sub-major bracket and a bracket for the regional firms. Some major bracket firms have refused to accept a lesser status, and Morgan Stanley has rushed to their defense. Nevertheless, institutional investors have become such a dominant factor in the new issue market that many new issues may be distributed by the "bulge" bracket underwriters by forming a small syndicate or by dispensing with a syndicate altogether.[33]

After the registration statement is filed, the syndicate manager as well as the syndicate members will test the market for the offering by making oral offers and, as we shall see later, by means of the use of the preliminary prospectus and the "tombstone ad". If the offer is in demand, other broker-dealers may seek to become members of the syndicate or become members of the "selling group." Those firms that are not included in the syndicate can be invited to become members of the "selling group," and thus will not be excluded from participating in the offering. Members of the selling group serve as retailers of the securities. Only members of the National Association of Securities Dealers, Inc., are eligible to become members of the underwriting syndicate or the selling group and receive a concession off of the offering price.[34]

Members of the syndicate may themselves deal directly with the public, or they may sell a portion of their shares to members of the "selling group." In actual practice, however, the "syndicate manager" or the lead underwriter will notify each underwriter of the amount of stock which it is to retain for sale. For example, a firm which has committed itself to take 10,000 shares may be told by the syndicate manager that it will have 5,000 shares only of the 10,000 shares for sale to its own clients. The remainder of the securities go into the syndicate account, the "pot," which is under the direct control of the syndicate manager. These securities are used to satisfy the demand of those firms which are members of the selling group, as distinguished from the underwriting group. Members of the selling group are liable solely for the amount of stock they have agreed to purchase. Securities dealers outside of the underwriting syndicate who have received indications of interest from their clients with respect to the offering will contact the syndicate manager asking to become a

---

33. Just Like Film Stars, Wall Streeters Battle to Get Top Billing, Wall St. J., Jan. 15, 1986, p. 1, col. 4.

34. In 1938 the Maloney Act added section 15A to the Securities Exchange Act of 1934 and authorized the organization of national securities associations under the supervision of the SEC. An association of brokers or dealers may register with the Commission if it meets certain statutory standards. The rules of the association must be designed to promote "just and equitable principles of trade," to prevent fraudulent and manipulative practices and to meet other statutory norms. The National Association of Securities Dealers, Inc. (NASD) registered with the Commission in 1939 and is the only association which has qualified under the act.

The vast majority of brokers or dealers in securities belong to the NASD. Thus in 1984, there were over 6,500 brokers and dealers who use the mails or interstate facilities to effect transactions in securities

in the over-the-counter markets and who had registered with the SEC under § 15 of the Securities Exchange Act of 1934. Indeed, for all practical purposes, a securities broker or dealer must be a member of the NASD in order to take part in the underwriting process as a member of the retail selling group. Under the authority prescribed in § 15A(i)(1) of the Exchange Act, an NASD rule precludes an NASD member from dealing with a nonmember broker or dealer except at the prices and on the same terms and conditions as that accorded to public investors. Accordingly, the underwriting syndicate may properly grant discounts, concessions or similar allowances below the public offering price only to those brokers or dealers who are members of the NASD. See 50 SEC Ann.Rep. 26 (1984); White, National Association of Securities Dealers, Inc., 28 Geo.Wash.L.Rev. 250 (1959); Loss, Fundamentals of Securities Regulation, 684–94 (1983); W. O. Douglas, Go East Young Man c. 18 (1974).

member of the selling group and obtain an allotment of stock. A selling group member gets compensated in the form of a selling concession, which typically amounts to 50–60% of the gross spread between the public offering price and the net amount received by the issuer.

This "gross spread" is the difference between the price to the issuer and the public offering price. It represents the compensation which is distributed among the managing underwriter, members of the underwriting syndicate and the members of the selling group—the "underwriting discounts and commissions" shown on the cover page of the prospectus or offering circular. The issuer sells the securities to the underwriting syndicate at a discount from the public offering price, usually amounting to between 6 and 15% for equity securities (the discount is much less for debt issues). If for example, the issue is to be sold to the public for $10, with $9 to the issuer, the compensation might be sliced up this way. First, the lead underwriter will receive a management fee of 20¢ per share for finding and packaging the issue, and to compensate it for managing the offering and in "running the books." The next slice would be a fee of about 30¢ a share which is called the "gross underwriting fee." This fee provides compensation to the underwriting group for their expenses, such as underwriters' counsel, "tombstone" advertising and stabilizing expenses. The rest of the 30¢ represents compensation for the use of capital and for assuming the risk in the underwriting. The remaining 50¢ of the spread goes to the underwriting firm or the selling group member that actually sells the stock at retail.

Pricing. The pricing of the issue is extremely important. If the offering relates to a security of a class which is already traded in the markets, the offering price will be related to the existing market price. If, however, the company is going public for the first time, the price of the security will be greatly affected by existing market conditions. If the issue is popular and the price is sufficiently attractive, the issue may be sold within minutes or hours after the public offering. In popular terminology it becomes a "hot issue." If the issue is priced too high so that it does not sell well, a hard sell may be needed, with the managing underwriter engaging in stabilizing transactions designed to impede any decline in the market price of the security. Various problems have arisen in connection with "hot issues" and "sticky issues". See, infra at page 642.[35]

SECURITIES EXCHANGE ACT RELEASE NO. 15807

Securities and Exchange Commission.
May 9, 1979.

PRACTICES IN FIXED PRICE OFFERINGS

[Read this release up to Part B, infra at page 599.]

---

35. On the practical aspects of underwriting, see R. Shapiro, A. Sachs and C. Olander, Securities Regulation Forms (1983 rev.); A. Jacobs, Opinion Letters in Securities Matters (1980 rev.).

SECTION 3. THE ROLE OF THE SECURITIES AND EXCHANGE COMMISSION

THE WORK OF THE SEC

October, 1986

(Published by the SEC)

INTRODUCTION

The U.S. Securities and Exchange Commission's mission is to administer Federal securities laws that seek to provide protection for investors. The purpose of these laws is to ensure that the securities markets are fair and honest and to provide the means to enforce the securities laws through sanctions where necessary. Laws administered by the Commission are the:

- Securities Act of 1933;
- Securities Exchange Act of 1934;
- Public Utility Holding Company Act of 1935;
- Trust Indenture Act of 1939;
- Investment Company Act of 1940; and
- Investment Advisers Act of 1940.

The Commission also serves as adviser to Federal courts in corporate reorganization proceedings under Chapter 11 of the Bankruptcy Reform Act of 1978 and, in cases begun prior to October 1, 1979, Chapter X of the National Bankruptcy Act. The Commission reports annually to Congress on administration of the securities laws.

Under the Securities Exchange Act of 1934, Congress created the Securities and Exchange Commission (SEC). The SEC is an independent, nonpartisan, quasi-judicial regulatory agency.

The Commission is composed of five members: a Chairman and four Commissioners. Commission members are appointed by the President, with the advice and consent of the Senate, for five-year terms. The Chairman is designated by the President. Terms are staggered; one expires on June 5th of every year. Not more than three members may be of the same political party.

Under the direction of the Chairman and Commissioners, the staff ensures that publicly held entities, broker-dealers in securities, investment companies and advisers, and other participants in the securities markets comply with Federal securities laws. These laws were designed to facilitate informed investment analyses and decisions by the investing public, primarily by ensuring adequate disclosure of material (significant) information. Conformance with Federal securities laws and regulations does not imply merit. If information essential to informed investment analysis is properly disclosed, the Commission cannot bar the sale of securities which analysis may show to be of questionable value. It is the investor, not the Commission, who must make the ultimate judgment of the worth of securities offered for sale.

The Commission's staff is composed of lawyers, accountants, financial analysts and examiners, engineers, and other professionals. The staff is divided into divisions and offices (including fourteen regional and branch offices), each directed by officials appointed by the Chairman.

* * *

SECURITIES ACT OF 1933

This "truth in securities" law has two basic objectives:

- To require that investors be provided with material information concerning securities offered for public sale; and

- To prevent misrepresentation, deceit, and other fraud in the sale of securities.

A primary means of accomplishing these objectives is disclosure of financial information by registering securities. Securities subject to registration are most corporate debt and equity securities. Government (state and Federal) and mortgage-related debt are not. Certain securities qualify for exemptions from registration provisions; these exemptions are discussed below.

PURPOSE OF REGISTRATION

Registration is intended to provide adequate and accurate disclosure of material facts concerning the company and the securities it proposes to sell. Thus, investors may make a realistic appraisal of the merits of the securities and then exercise informed judgment in determining whether or not to purchase them.

Registration requires, but does not guarantee, the accuracy of the facts represented in the registration statement and prospectus. However, the law does prohibit false and misleading statements under penalty of fine, imprisonment, or both. And, investors who purchase securities and suffer losses have important recovery rights under the law if they can prove that there was incomplete or inaccurate disclosure of material facts in the registration statement or prospectus. If such misstatements are proven, the following could be liable for investor losses sustained in the securities purchase: the issuing company, its responsible directors and officers, the underwriters, controlling interests, the sellers of the securities, and others. These rights must be asserted in an appropriate Federal or state court (not before the Commission, which has no power to award damages).

Registration of securities does not preclude the sale of stock in risky, poorly managed, or unprofitable companies. Nor does the Commission approve or disapprove securities on their merits; it is unlawful to represent otherwise in the sale of securities. The only standard which must be met when registering securities is adequate and accurate disclosure of required material facts concerning the company and the securities it proposes to sell. The fairness of the terms, the issuing company's prospects for successful operation, and other factors affecting the merits of investing in the securities (whether price, promoters' or underwriters' profits, or otherwise) have no bearing on the question of whether or not securities may be registered.

THE REGISTRATION PROCESS

To facilitate registration by different types of companies, the Commission has special forms. These vary in their disclosure requirements but generally provide essential facts while minimizing the burden and expense of complying with the law. In general, registration forms call for disclosure of information such as:

- Description of the registrant's properties and business;

- Description of the significant provisions of the security to be offered for sale and its relationship to the registrant's other capital securities;

- Information about the management of the registrant; and

- Financial statements certified by independent public accountants.

Registration statements and prospectuses on securities become public immediately upon filing with the Commission. After the registration statement is filed, securities may be offered orally or by certain summaries of the information in the registration statement as permitted by Commission rules. However, it is unlawful to sell the securities until the effective date. The act provides that most registration statements shall become effective on the 20th day after filing (or on the 20th day after filing the last amendment). At its discretion, the Commission may advance the effective date if deemed appropriate considering the interests of investors and the public, the adequacy of publicly available information, and the ease with which the facts about the new offering can be disseminated and understood.

Registration statements are examined for compliance with disclosure requirements. If a statement appears to be materially incomplete or inaccurate, the registrant usually is informed by letter and given an opportunity to file correcting or clarifying amendments. The Commission, however, has authority to refuse or suspend the effectiveness of any registration statement if it finds that material representations are misleading, inaccurate, or incomplete.

The Commission may conclude that material deficiencies in some registration statements appear to stem from a deliberate attempt to conceal or mislead, or that the deficiencies do not lend themselves to correction through the informal letter process. In these cases, the Commission may decide that it is in the public interest to conduct a hearing to develop the facts by evidence. This determines if a "stop order" should be issued to refuse or suspend effectiveness of the statement. The Commission may issue stop orders after the sale of securities has been commenced or completed. A stop order is not a permanent bar to the effectiveness of the registration statement or to the sale of the securities. If amendments are filed correcting the statement in accordance with the stop order decision, the order must be lifted and the statement declared effective.

Although losses which may have been suffered in the purchase of securities are not restored to investors by the stop order, the Commission's order precludes future public sales. Also, the decision and the evidence on which it is based may serve to notify investors of their rights and aid them in their own recovery suits.

EXEMPTIONS FROM REGISTRATION

In general, registration requirements apply to securities of both domestic and foreign issuers, and to securities of foreign governments (or their instrumentalities) sold in domestic securities markets. There are, however, certain exemptions. Among these are:

- Private offerings to a limited number of persons or institutions who have access to the kind of information that registration would disclose and who do not propose to redistribute the securities;

- Offerings restricted to residents of the state in which the issuing company is organized and doing business;

- Securities of municipal, state, Federal, and other governmental instrumentalities as well as charitable institutions, banks, and carriers subject to the Interstate Commerce Act;

- Offerings not exceeding certain specified amounts made in compliance with regulations of the Commission; and

- Offerings of "small business investment companies" made in accordance with rules and regulations of the Commission.

Whether or not the securities are exempt from registration, antifraud provisions apply to all sales of securities involving interstate commerce or the mails.

Among the special exemptions from the registration requirement, the "small issue exemption" was adopted by Congress primarily as an aid to small business. The law provides that offerings of securities under $5 million may be exempted from registration, subject to conditions the Commission prescribes to protect investors. The Commission's Regulation A permits certain domestic and Canadian companies to make exempt offerings. A similar regulation is available for offerings under $500,000 by small business investment companies licensed by the Small Business Administration. The Commission's Regulation D permits certain companies to make exempt offerings under $500,000 with only minimal Federal restrictions; more extensive disclosure requirements and other conditions apply for offerings exceeding that amount but less than $5 million.

Exemptions are available when certain specified conditions are met. These conditions include the prior filing of a notification with the appropriate SEC regional office and the use of an offering circular containing certain basic information in the sale of the securities. For a more complete discussion of these and other special provisions adopted by the Commission to facilitate capital formation by small business, please request a copy of "Q & A: Small Business and the SEC," available from the Public Reference Branch of the Commission.

SECURITIES EXCHANGE ACT OF 1934

By this act, Congress extended the "disclosure" doctrine of investor protection to securities listed and registered for public trading on our national securities exchanges. Thirty years later, the Securities Act Amendments of 1964 extended disclosure and reporting provisions to equity securities in the over-the-counter market. This included hundreds of companies with assets exceeding [$5] million and shareholders numbering 500 or more. (Today, securities of thousands of companies are traded over the counter.) The act seeks to ensure fair and orderly securities markets by prohibiting certain types of activities and by setting forth rules regarding the operation of the markets and participants.

CORPORATE REPORTING

Companies seeking to have their securities registered and listed for public trading on an exchange must file a registration application with the exchange and the SEC. If they meet the size test described above, companies whose equity securities are traded over the counter must file a similar registration form. Commission rules prescribe the nature and content of these registration statements and require certified financial statements. These are generally comparable to, but less extensive than, the disclosures required in Securities Act registration statements. Following the registration of their securities, companies must file annual and other periodic reports to update information contained in the original filing. In addition, issuers must send certain reports to requesting shareholders. Reports may be read at the Commission's public reference rooms, copied there at nominal cost, or obtained from a copying service under contract to the Commission.

PROXY SOLICITATIONS

Another provision of this law governs soliciting proxies (votes) from holders of registered securities, both listed and over-the-counter, for the election of directors and/or for approval of other corporate action. Solicitations, whether by management or minority groups, must disclose all material facts concerning matters on which holders are asked to vote. Holders also must be given an opportunity to vote "yes" or "no" on each matter. Where a contest for control of corporate management is involved, the rules require disclosure of the names and interests of all "participants" in the proxy contest. Thus, holders are enabled to vote intelligently on corporate actions requiring their approval. The Commission's rules require that proposed proxy material be filed in advance for examination by the Commission for compliance with the disclosure requirements. In addition, the rules permit shareholders to submit proposals for a vote at the annual meetings.

TENDER OFFER SOLICITATIONS

In 1968, Congress amended the Exchange Act to extend its reporting and disclosure provisions to situations where control of a company is sought through a tender offer or other planned stock acquisition of over ten percent of a company's equity securities. Commonly called the Williams Act, this amendment was further amended in 1970 to reduce the stock acquisition threshold to five percent. These amendments, and Commission rules under the act, require disclosure of pertinent information by anyone seeking to acquire over five percent of a company's securities by direct purchase or by tender offer. This disclosure is also required by anyone soliciting shareholders to accept or reject a tender offer. Thus, as with the proxy rules, public investors holding stock in these corporations may now make more informed decisions on takeover bids.

Disclosure provisions are supplemented by certain other provisions to help ensure investor protection in tender offers.

INSIDER TRADING

Insider trading prohibitions are designed to curb misuse of material confidential information not available to the general public. Examples of such misuse are buying or selling securities to make profits or avoid losses based on material non-public information—or by telling others of the information so that they may buy or sell securities—before such information is generally available to all shareholders. The Commission has brought numerous civil actions in Federal court against persons whose use of material non-public information constituted fraud under the securities laws. Additionally, the Commission supported legislation to increase the penalties that can be imposed by the courts on those found guilty of insider trading. The Insider Trading Sanctions Act, signed into law on August 10, 1984, allows imposing fines up to three times the profit gained or loss avoided by use of material non-public information.[a]

Another provision requires that all officers and directors of a company (and beneficial owners of more than ten percent of its registered equity securities) must file an initial report with the Commission, and with the exchange on which the stock may be listed, showing their holdings of each of the company's equity securities. Thereafter, they must file reports for any month during which there was any change in those holdings. In addition, the law provides that profits obtained by them from purchases and sales (or sales and purchases) of such equity securities within any six-month period may be recovered by the company or by any security holder on its behalf. This recovery right must be asserted in the appropriate U.S. District Court. Such "insiders" are also prohibited from making short sales of their company's equity securities.

MARGIN TRADING

Margin trading in securities also falls under certain provisions of the act. The Board of Governors of the Federal Reserve System is authorized to set limitations on the amount of credit which may be extended for the purpose of purchasing or carrying securities. (The Federal Reserve periodically reviews these limitations.) The objective is to restrict excessive use of the nation's credit in the securities markets. While the credit restrictions are set by the Board, investigation and enforcement is the responsibility of the SEC.

TRADING AND SALES PRACTICES

Securities trading and sales practices on the exchanges and in the over-the-counter markets are subject to provisions designed to protect the interests of investors and the public. These provisions seek to curb misrepresentations and deceit, market manipulation, and other fraudulent acts and practices. They also strive to establish and maintain just and equitable principles of trade conducive to maintaining open, fair, and orderly markets.

These provisions of the law establish the general regulatory pattern. The Commission is responsible for promulgating rules and regulations for

a. For a description of electronic surveillance of the securities markets by the stock exchanges and the NASD, see Makin,   Wall Street's Electronic Cops, 20 Institutional Investor 69 (Feb.1986).

its implementation. Thus, the Commission has adopted regulations which, among other things:

- Define acts or practices which constitute a "manipulative or deceptive device or contrivance" prohibited by the statute;

- Regulate short selling, stabilizing transactions, and similar matters;

- Regulate hypothecation (use of customers' securities as collateral for loans); and

- Provide safeguards with respect to the financial responsibility of brokers and dealers.

REGISTRATION OF EXCHANGES AND OTHERS

As amended, the 1934 Act requires registration with the Commission of:

- "National securities exchanges" (those having a substantial securities trading volume);

- Brokers and dealers who conduct securities business in interstate commerce;

- Transfer agents;

- Clearing agencies;

- Municipal brokers and dealers; and

- Securities information processors.

To obtain registration, exchanges must show that they are organized to comply with the provisions of the statute as well as the rules and regulations of the Commission. The registering exchanges must also show that their rules contain just and adequate provisions to ensure fair dealing and to protect investors.

Each exchange is a self-regulatory organization. Its rules must provide for the expulsion, suspension, or other disciplining of member broker-dealers for conduct inconsistent with just and equitable principles of trade. The law intends that exchanges shall have full opportunity to establish self-regulatory measures ensuring fair dealing and investor protection. However, it empowers the SEC (by order, rule, or regulation) to approve proposed rule changes of exchanges concerning various activities and trading practices if necessary to effect the statutory objective. Exchange rules and revisions, proposed by exchanges or by the Commission, generally reach their final form after discussions between representatives of both bodies without resort to formal proceedings.

By a 1938 amendment to the 1934 Act, Congress also provided for creation of a national securities association. The only such association, the National Association of Securities Dealers, Inc., is registered with the Commission under this provision of the law. This association is responsible for preventing fraudulent and manipulative acts and practices, and for promoting just and equitable trade principles among over-the-counter brokers and dealers. The establishment, maintenance, and enforcement of a voluntary code of business ethics is one of the principal features of this provision of the law.

BROKER–DEALER REGISTRATION

The registration of brokers and dealers engaged in soliciting and executing securities transactions is an important part of the regulatory plan of the act. Broker-dealers must apply for registration with the Commission and amend registrations to show significant changes in financial conditions or other important facts. Applications and amendments are examined by the Commission. Brokers and dealers must conform their business practices to the standards prescribed by the law and the Commission's regulations for protecting investors and to rules on fair trade practices of their association. Additionally, brokers and dealers violating these regulations risk suspension or loss of registration with the Commission (and thus the right to continue conducting an interstate securities business) or of suspension or expulsion from a self-regulatory organization.

PUBLIC UTILITY HOLDING COMPANY ACT OF 1935

Interstate holding companies engaged, through subsidiaries, in the electric utility business or in the retail distribution of natural or manufactured gas are subject to regulation under this act. Today, 13 systems are registered; 12 are active. These systems must register with the Commission and file initial and periodic reports. Detailed information concerning the organization, financial structure, and operations of the holding company and its subsidiaries is contained in these reports. (However, if a holding company or its subsidiary meets certain specifications, the Commission may exempt it from part or all of the duties and obligations otherwise imposed by statute.) Holding companies are subject to SEC regulations on matters such as structure of the system, acquisitions, combinations, and issue and sales of securities.

* * *

ISSUANCE AND SALE OF SECURITIES

Proposed security issues by any holding company must be analyzed and evaluated by the staff, and approved by the Commission, to ensure that the issues meet the following tests under prescribed standards of the law:

- The security must be reasonably adapted to the security structure of the issuer and of other companies in the same holding company system;
- The security must be reasonably adapted to the earning power of the company;
- The proposed issue must be necessary and appropriate to the economical and efficient operation of the company's business;
- The fees, commissions, and other remuneration paid in connection with the issue must not be unreasonable; and
- The terms and conditions of the issue or sale of the security must not be detrimental to the public or investor interest.

OTHER REGULATORY PROVISIONS

Other phases of the act provide for regulating dividend payments (in circumstances where payments might result in corporate abuses); intercompany loans; solicitation of proxies, consents, and other authorizations; and insider trading. "Up-stream" loans from subsidiaries to their parents and "up-stream" or "cross-stream" loans from public utility companies to any holding company in the same holding company system require Commission approval. The act also requires that all services performed for any company in a holding company system by a service company in that system be rendered at a fair and equitably allocated cost.

TRUST INDENTURE ACT OF 1939

This act applies to bonds, debentures, notes, and similar debt securities offered for public sale and issued under trust indentures with more than $1 million of securities outstanding at any one time. Even though such securities may be registered under the Securities Act, they may not be offered for sale to the public unless the trust indenture conforms to statutory standards of this act. Designed to safeguard the rights and interests of the purchasers, the act also:

- Prohibits the indenture trustee from conflicting interests which might interfere with exercising its duties on behalf of the securities purchasers;
- Requires the trustee to be a corporation with minimum combined capital and surplus;
- Imposes high standards of conduct and responsibility on the trustee;
- Precludes, in the event of default, preferential collection of certain claims owing to the trustee by the issuer;
- Provides that the issuer supply to the trustee evidence of compliance with indenture terms and conditions (such as those relating to the release or substitution of mortgaged property, issue of new securities, or satisfaction of the indenture); and
- Requires the trustee to provide reports and notices to security holders.

Other provisions of the act prohibit impairing the security holders' right to sue individually for principal and interest, except under certain circumstances. It also requires maintaining a list of security holders for their use in communicating with each other regarding their rights as security holders.

Applications for qualification of trust indentures are examined by the SEC's Division of Corporation Finance for compliance with the law and the Commission's rules.

INVESTMENT COMPANY ACT OF 1940

The Public Utility Holding Company Act of 1935 required Congress to direct the SEC to study the activities of investment companies and investment advisers. The study results were sent to Congress in a series of reports filed in 1938, 1939, and 1940, causing the creation of the Investment Advisers Act of 1940 and the Investment Company Act of 1940. The legislation was supported by both the Commission and the industry.

Activities of companies engaged primarily in investing, reinvesting, and trading in securities, and whose own securities are offered to the investing public, are subject to certain statutory prohibitions and to Commission regulation under this act. Also, public offerings of investment company securities must be registered under the Securities Act of 1933.

Investors must understand, however, that the Commission does not supervise the investment activities of these companies and that regulation by the Commission does not imply safety of investment.

In addition to the registration requirement for such companies, the law requires they disclose their financial condition and investment policies to provide investors complete information about their activities. This act also:

- Prohibits such companies from substantially changing the nature of their business or investment policies without stockholder approval;
- Bars persons guilty of security frauds from serving as officers and directors;
- Prevents underwriters, investment bankers, or brokers from constituting more than a minority of the directors of such companies;
- Requires that management contracts (and any material changes) be submitted to security holders for their approval;
- Prohibits transactions between such companies and their directors, officers, or affiliated companies or persons, except when approved by the SEC;
- Forbids such companies to issue senior securities except under specified conditions and upon specified terms; and
- Prohibits pyramiding of such companies and cross-ownership of their securities.

Other provisions of this act involve advisory fees not conforming to an adviser's fiduciary duty, sales and repurchases of securities issued by investment companies, exchange offers, and other activities of investment companies, including special provisions for periodic payment plans and face-amount certificate companies.

Regarding reorganization plans of investment companies, the Commission is authorized to institute court proceedings to prohibit plans that do not appear to be fair and equitable to security holders. The Commission may also institute court action to remove management officials who have engaged in personal misconduct constituting a breach of fiduciary duty.

Investment company securities must also be registered under the Securities Act. Investment companies must file periodic reports and are subject to the Commission's proxy and "insider" trading rules.

INVESTMENT ADVISERS ACT OF 1940

This law establishes a pattern of regulating investment advisers. In some respects, it has provisions similar to Securities Exchange Act provisions governing the conduct of brokers and dealers. With certain exceptions, this act requires that persons or firms compensated for advising others about securities investment must register with the Commission and conform to statutory standards designed to protect investors.

The Commission may deny, suspend, or revoke investment adviser registrations if, after notice and hearing, it finds that a statutory disqualification exists and that the action is in the public interest. Disqualifications include conviction for certain financial crimes or securities violations, injunctions based on such activities, conviction for violating the Mail Fraud

Statute, willfully filing false reports with the Commission, and willfully violating the Advisers Act, the Securities Act, the Securities Exchange Act, the Investment Company Act, or the rules of the Municipal Securities Rulemaking Board. In addition to the administrative sanction of denial, suspension, or revocation, the Commission may obtain injunctions prohibiting further violations of this law. The SEC may also recommend prosecution by the Department of Justice for fraudulent misconduct or willful violation of the law or Commission rules.

The law contains antifraud provisions and empowers the Commission to adopt rules defining fraudulent, deceptive, or manipulative acts and practices. It also requires that investment advisers:

- Disclose the nature of their interest in transactions executed for their clients;

- Maintain books and records according to Commission rules; and

- Make books and records available to the Commission for inspections.

CORPORATE REORGANIZATION

Reorganization proceedings in the U.S. Courts under Chapter 11 of the Bankruptcy Code are begun by a debtor, voluntarily, or by its creditors. Federal bankruptcy law allows a debtor in reorganization to continue operating under the court's protection while it attempts to rehabilitate its business and work out a plan to pay its debts. If a debtor corporation has publicly issued securities outstanding, the reorganization process may raise many issues that materially affect the rights of public investors.

Chapter 11 of the Bankruptcy Code authorizes the SEC to appear in any reorganization case and to present its views on any issue. Although Chapter 11 applies to all types of business reorganizations, the Commission generally limits its participation to proceedings involving significant public investor interest—protecting public investors holding the debtor's securities and participating in legal and policy issues of concern to public investors. The SEC also continues to address matters of traditional Commission expertise and interest relating to securities. Where appropriate, it comments on the adequacy of reorganization plan disclosure statements and participates where there is a Commission law enforcement interest.

Under Chapter 11, the debtor, official committees, and institutional creditors negotiate the terms of a reorganization plan. The court can confirm a reorganization plan if it is accepted by creditors for:

- At least two-thirds of the amounts of allowed claims;

- More than one-half the number of allowed claims; and

- At least two-thirds in amount of the allowed shareholder interest.

The principal safeguard for public investors is the requirement that a disclosure statement containing adequate information be transmitted by the debtor or plan proponent in connection with soliciting votes on the plan. In addition, reorganization plans involving publicly held debtors usually provide for issuing new securities to creditors and shareholders which may be exempt from registration under Section 5 of the Securities Act of 1933.

ORGANIZATION OF THE COMMISSION

The Commission carries out its work, in both Washington headquarters and the regional offices around the country, through divisions and offices charged with specific responsibilities under the securities laws. Additionally, there are offices responsible for the smooth and effective administration of the Commission itself. Overall responsibility for carrying out the SEC mission rests with the Commissioners.

THE COMMISSIONERS

The Securities Exchange Act of 1934 formally created the Securities and Exchange Commission on June 1, 1934. (The Securities Act of 1933 was administered by the Federal Trade Commission until creation of the SEC.) Among other provisions, this act set forth the composition of the Commission, which remains unchanged today. Five Commissioners are appointed by the President, with the advice and consent of the Senate, for five-year terms. Terms are staggered; one expires in June of every year. The Chairman is generally of the same political party as the President, but no more than three of the five Commissioners may belong to the same political party. The result is that the Commission is an independent, non-partisan agency.

A deliberative collegial body, the Commission meets numerous times monthly to debate and decide upon regulatory issues. Like other regulatory agencies, the Commission has two types of meetings. Under the Government in the Sunshine Act, meetings may be open to the public and to members of the press. However, if necessary to protect the Commission's ability to conduct investigations and/or protect the rights of individuals and entities which may be the subject of Commission inquiries, meetings may be closed.

Commission meetings are generally held to deliberate on and resolve issues the staff brings before the Commissioners. Issues may be interpretations of Federal securities laws, amendments to existing rules under the laws, new rules (often to reflect changed conditions in the marketplace), actions to enforce the laws or to discipline those subject to direct regulation, legislation to be proposed by the Commission, and matters concerning administration of the Commission itself. Matters not requiring joint deliberation may be resolved by procedures set forth in the Code of Federal Regulation.

Resolution of the issues brought before the Commission may take the form of new rules or amendments to existing ones, enforcement actions, or disciplinary actions. The most common activity is rulemaking. Rulemaking is generally the result of staff recommendations made to the Commissioners.

THE COMMISSION STAFF

The staff is organized into divisions (with subordinate offices) and major offices with specific areas of responsibility for various segments of the Federal securities laws.

For the past several years, the divisions have been Enforcement, Corporation Finance, Market Regulation, and Investment Management. The

Office of General Counsel serves as the chief legal officer for the Commission. As such, it is responsible for appellate and other litigation as well as certain other legal matters.

At present, the offices are those of Chief Accountant, Opinions and Review, Chief Economist, Administrative Law Judges, Secretary, and the Directorate of Economic and Policy Analysis.

Other offices provide administration and carry out certain necessary functions for the Commission. These include the Office of Executive Director, Comptroller, Consumer Affairs and Information Services, Personnel, Administrative Services, Applications and Reports Services, Information Systems Management, and Public Affairs.

THE DIVISIONS

The Division of Corporation Finance

Corporation Finance has the overall responsibility of ensuring that disclosure requirements are met by publicly held companies registered with the Commission. Its work includes reviewing registration statements for new securities, proxy material and annual reports the Commission requires from publicly held companies, documents concerning tender offers, and mergers and acquisitions in general.

This division renders administrative interpretations of the Securities Act of 1933 and its regulations to the public, prospective registrants, and others. It is also responsible for certain statutes and regulations pertaining to small businesses and for the Trust Indenture Act of 1939. Applications for qualification of trust indentures are examined for compliance with the applicable requirements of the law and the Commission's rules. The Division of Corporation Finance works closely with the Office of the Chief Accountant in drafting rules and regulations which prescribe requirements for financial statements.

The Division of Market Regulation

Market Regulation is responsible for oversight of activity in the secondary markets—registration and regulation of broker-dealers, oversight of the self-regulatory organizations (such as the nation's stock exchanges), and oversight of other participants in the secondary markets (such as transfer agents and clearing organizations).

Financial responsibility of these entities, trading and sales practices, policies affecting operation of the securities markets, and surveillance fall under the purview of this division. In addition, it carries out activities aimed at achieving the goal of a national market system set forth in the Securities Act Amendments of 1975. Market Regulation develops and presents market structure issues to the Commissioners for their consideration. The division also oversees the Securities Investor Protection Corporation and the Municipal Securities Rulemaking Board.

The Division of Investment Management

Investment Management has basic responsibility for the Investment Company Act of 1940 and the Investment Advisers Act of 1940. In 1985, it assumed responsibility for administering the Public Utility Holding Company Act of 1935.

The division staff ensures compliance with regulations regarding the registration, financial responsibility, sales practices, and advertising of mutual funds and of investment advisers. New products offered by these entities also are reviewed by staff in this division. They also process investment company registration statements, proxy statements, and periodic reports under the Securities Act.

The division's Office of Public Utility Regulation oversees the activities of the twelve active registered holding company systems, ensuring that their corporate structures and financings are permissible according to certain tests set up in the Holding Company Act. The staff analyze legal, financial, accounting, engineering, and other issues arising under the act. The office participates in hearings to develop the factual records where necessary, files briefs and participates in oral arguments before the Commission, and makes recommendations regarding the Commission's findings and decisions in cases which arise in administration of the law. All hearings are conducted in accordance with the Commission's Rules of Practice.

The Division of Enforcement

This division is charged with enforcing Federal securities laws. Enforcement responsibilities include investigating possible violations of Federal securities laws and recommending appropriate remedies for consideration by the Commission. Possible violations may come to light through the Enforcement Division's own inquiries, through referrals from other divisions of the Commission, from outside sources such as the self-regulatory organizations, or by other means.

When possible violations of Federal securities laws warrant further investigation by the staff, the Commission is consulted before proceeding. The Commission's decisions may result in issuing subpoenas, formal orders of investigation, or other means of proceeding with actions. At the conclusion of investigations, the Commission may authorize the staff to proceed with injunctions preventing further violative conduct, with administrative proceedings in the case of entities directly regulated by the Commission, or with other remedies as appropriate.

ACTIVITIES OF DIVISIONS

Each of the divisions, often in cooperation with an office or offices, engages in a variety of activities.

Interpretation and Guidance

On the basis of responsibilities and powers assigned under Federal securities laws, each division provides guidance and counseling to registrants, prospective registrants, the public, and others. This information is provided to help determine the application of the law and its regulations and to aid in complying with the law. For example, this advice might include an informal expression of opinion about whether the offering of a particular security is subject to the registration requirements of the law and, if so, advice on compliance with disclosure requirements of the applicable registration form. These interpretations of the rules and laws help ensure conformity on the part of the registrants. Also, most divisions occasionally issue "no action" letters which indicate they will take no action on matters regarding registrants in certain circumstances.[b]

Rulemaking

One of the most common activities engaged in by the divisions is rulemaking.

The Commission's objective of requiring regulated entities to provide effective disclosure, with a minimum of burden and expense, calls for constant review of practical operations of the rules and registration forms adopted. If experience shows that a particular requirement fails to achieve its objective, or if a rule appears unduly burdensome in relation to the resulting benefits, the staff presents the problem to the Commission. The Commission then considers modifying the rule or other requirement. Based on their particular area of expertise, the divisions and offices are often asked to contribute specific analyses.

Many suggestions for rule modification follow extensive consultation with industry representatives and others affected. The Commission normally gives advance public notice of proposals to adopt new or amended rules or registration forms and affords the opportunity for interested members of the public to comment on them.

The Commission decides, generally in open meetings, whether or not the new rules or amendments to existing rules are warranted. Proposals approved by the Commission become mandatory, usually within a specific time period after publication in the Federal Register.

The Commission's work is remedial, not punitive. Its primary activities are to ensure investor protection through full disclosure of material information and to ensure that the securities markets are fair and honest in compliance with Federal securities laws and rules under those laws. Inter-

---

b. In 1970, the SEC introduced the practice of publishing requests for no-action letters, together with the responses by the Commission staff. See SEC Securities Act Release No. 5098 [1970–1971 Transfer Binder] CCH Fed.Sec.L.Rep. ¶ 79,921 (Oct. 29, 1970), adopting Reg. § 200.81(17) CFR 200.81). These no-action requests (and responses) comprise all letters to the staff of SEC requesting interpretative advice or a statement that, on the basis of facts stated, the staff would not recommend that the Commission take any enforcement action. For the procedure applicable to requests for no-action or interpretative letters, see Securities Act Release No. 5127 (Jan. 25, 1971).

A list of all no-action letters and the statute and section to which they relate is published in the CCH Federal Securities Law Reporter and a limited number are reproduced in that service. Copies of all letters may also be purchased from the SEC, and unreported letters are available in microfilm from Commerce Clearing House, Inc. Print-outs of all letters may also be obtained by subscribers to WESTLAW, West Publishing's computer-assisted legal research system, and by subscribers to Lexis, a computer-assisted legal research system of Mead Data Central.

The proliferation of no-action letters has been the subject of controversy. Professor Louis Loss has said that "ninety percent of these letters are sheer, unadulterated, repetitious garbage." 30 Bus.Law 163, 165 (Special Issue, March, 1975). No securities lawyer should be charged with the failure to exercise due diligence in rendering legal advice to clients for failure to take note of some obscure gem hidden in this mountain of material. Moreover, complaints have been made of inconsistency of interpretation and conflicts with the applicable SEC statutes, judicial decisions and Commission releases. See Lowenfels, SEC No-Action Letters: Conflicts With Existing Statutes, Cases, and Commission Releases, 59 Va.L. Rev. 303 (1973); Lockhart, SEC No-Action Letters: Formal Advice as a Discretionary Administrative Clearance, 37 Law & Contemp.Prob. 95 (1972).

pretations, counseling, rulemaking, and similar activities are all aimed at ensuring compliance with the law.

The Commission, however, does have civil authority to enforce Federal securities laws and does so when it has reason to believe that the laws have been, or in some cases are about to be, violated. The Commission also works closely with criminal authorities in matters of mutual interest.

Investigations

Under the laws it administers, the Commission has a duty to investigate complaints and other indications of possible law violations in securities transactions. Most arise under the Securities Act of 1933 and the Securities Exchange Act of 1934. (Fraud prohibitions of the Securities Act are similar to those contained in the Securities Exchange Act of 1934.) Investigation and any subsequent enforcement work is conducted primarily by the Commission's regional offices and the Division of Enforcement.

Most of the Commission's investigations are conducted privately. Facts are developed to the fullest extent possible through informal inquiry, interviewing witnesses, examining brokerage records and other documents, reviewing and trading data, and similar means. The Commission is empowered to issue subpoenas requiring sworn testimony and the production of books, records, and other documents pertinent to the subject matter under investigation. In the event of refusal to respond to a subpoena, the Commission may apply to a Federal court for an order compelling obedience.

Inquiries and complaints by investors and the general public are primary sources of leads for detecting law violations in securities transactions. Another source is surprise inspections by regional offices and the Division of Market Regulation of the books and records of regulated persons and organizations to determine whether their business practices conform to the prescribed rules. Still another means is conducting inquiries into market fluctuations in particular stocks which don't appear to result from general market trends or from known developments affecting the issuing company.

Investigations frequently concern the sale without registration of securities subject to the registration requirement of the Securities Act. Misrepresentation or omission of material facts concerning securities offered for sale, whether or not registration is required, is another common subject of investigation. The antifraud provisions of the law also apply to the purchase of securities, whether involving outright misrepresentations or the withholding or omission of pertinent facts to which the seller was entitled. For example, it is unlawful in certain situations to purchase securities from another person while withholding material information which would indicate that the securities have a value substantially greater than that at which they are being acquired. These provisions apply not only to transactions between brokers and dealers and their customers but also to the reacquisition of securities by an issuing company or its "insiders."

Other types of inquiries relate to manipulating market prices of securities; misappropriating or illegally hypothecating customers' funds or securities; conducting a securities business while insolvent; broker-dealers buying or selling securities from or to customers, at prices not reasonably related to current market prices; and broker-dealers violating their responsibilities to treat customers fairly.

A common type of violation involves the broker-dealer who gains the customer's trust and then takes undisclosed profits in securities transactions with or for the customer over and above the agreed commission. For example, the broker-dealer may have purchased securities from customers at prices far below, or sold securities to customers at prices far above, their current market prices. In most of these cases, the broker-dealer risks no loss; the purchases from customers are made only if simultaneous sales can be made at prices substantially higher than those paid to the customers. Conversely, sales to customers are made only if simultaneous purchases can be made at prices substantially lower than those charged the customer. Another type of violation involves firms engaging in large-scale in-and-out transactions for the customer's account (called "churning") to generate increased commissions, usually without regard to any resulting benefit to the customer.

There is a fundamental distinction between a broker and a dealer. The broker serves as the customer's agent in buying or selling securities for the customer. The broker owes the customer the highest fiduciary responsibility and may charge only such agency commission as has been agreed to by the customer. On the other hand, a dealer acts as a principal and buys securities from or sells securities to customers. The dealer's profit is the difference between the prices for which the securities are bought and sold. The dealer normally will not disclose the fee or commission charged for services rendered. The law requires that the customer receive a written "confirmation" of each securities transaction. This confirmation discloses whether the securities firm is acting as a dealer (a principal for its own account) or as a broker (an agent for the customer). If the latter, the confirmation must also disclose the broker's compensation from all sources as well as other information about the transaction.

Statutory Sanctions

Commission investigations, usually conducted in private, are essentially fact-finding inquiries. The facts developed by the staff are considered by the Commission to determine whether there is valid evidence of a law violation; whether action should begin to determine if a violation actually occurred; and, if so, whether some sanction should be imposed.

When facts show possible fraud or other law violation, the laws provide several courses of action which the Commission may pursue:

- Civil injunction, where the Commission may apply to an appropriate U.S. District Court for an order prohibiting the acts or practices alleged to violate the law or Commission rules.

- Administrative remedy, where the Commission may take specific action after hearings. It may issue orders to suspend or expel members from exchanges or over-the-counter dealers association; deny, suspend, or revoke broker-dealer registrations; or censure for misconduct or bar individuals (temporarily or permanently) from employment with a registered firm.

Broker-Dealer Revocations

In the case of exchange or association members, registered brokers or dealers, or individuals who may associate with any such firm, the administrative remedy is generally invoked. In these administrative proceedings, the Commission issues an order specifying illegal acts or practices allegedly committed and directs that a hearing be held for the purpose of taking evidence. At the hearing, counsel for the Division of Enforcement (often a regional office attorney) undertakes to establish those facts supporting the charge. Respondents have full opportunity to cross-examine witnesses and to present evidence in defense. If the Commission ultimately finds that the respondents violated the law, it may take remedial action in the form of statutory sanctions as indicated above. The respondent has the right to seek judicial review of the decision by the appropriate U.S. Court of Appeals. Remedial action may effectively bar a firm from conducting a securities business in interstate commerce or on exchanges, or an individual from association with a registered firm.

The many instances in which these legal sanctions have been invoked present a formidable record. Of great significance to the investing public is the deterrent effect of the very existence of the fraud prohibitions of the law and the Commission's powers of investigation and enforcement. These provisions of the law, coupled with the disclosure requirements applicable to new security offerings and to other registered securities, tend to inhibit fraudulent stock promotions and operations. They also increase public confidence in securities as an investment medium. This facilitates financing through the public sale of securities, which contributes to the economic growth of the nation.

Administrative Proceedings

All formal administrative proceedings of the Commission follow its Rules of Practice which conform to the Administrative Procedure Act. These rules establish procedural "due process" safeguards to protect the rights and interests of parties to these proceedings. Included are requirements for timely notice of the proceeding and for a sufficient specification of the issues or charges involved to enable parties to prepare their cases adequately. All parties, including counsel for the interested SEC division or office, may appear at the hearing and present evidence and cross-examine witnesses. In addition, other interested persons may intervene or be given limited rights to participate. In some cases, the relevant facts may be stipulated instead of conducting an evidentiary hearing.

Hearings are conducted before a hearing officer, normally an administrative law judge appointed by the Commission. The hearing officer, who is independent of the interested division or office, rules on the admissibility of evidence and on other issues arising during the course of the hearing. At the conclusion of the hearing, participants may urge in writing that the hearing officer adopt specific findings of fact and conclusions of law. The hearing officer then prepares and files an initial decision (unless waived), stating conclusions to the facts established by the evidence and including an order disposing of the issues. Copies of the initial decision are served on the parties and participants, who may seek Commission review. If review is not sought and the Commission does not order review on its own motion, the initial decision becomes final and the hearing officer's order becomes effective.

If the Commission reviews the initial decision, the parties and participants may file briefs and be heard in oral argument before the Commission. On the basis of an independent review of the record, the SEC prepares and issues its own decision. The Office of Opinions and Review aids the Commission in this process. The laws provide that any person or firm aggrieved by a decision order of the Commission may seek review by the appropriate U.S. Court of Appeals. The initial decisions of hearing officers as well as the Commission decisions are made public. Ultimately, the Commission decisions (as well as initial decisions which have become final and are of precedential significance) are printed and published.

The Commission has only civil authority. However, if fraud or other willful law violation is indicated, the Commission may refer the facts to the Department of Justice with a recommendation for criminal prosecution of the offending persons. That Department, through its local U.S. Attorneys (who frequently are assisted by Commission attorneys), may present the evidence to a Federal grand jury and seek an indictment.

In its investigation and enforcement actions, the SEC cooperates closely with other Federal, state, and local law enforcement officials.

THE OFFICES

The Office of the General Counsel

The Office of General Counsel serves as the focal point for handling all appellate and other litigation brought by the Commission, either in connection with the securities laws or against the Commission or its staff. The General Counsel is the chief legal officer of the Commission.

Duties of this office include representing the Commission in judicial proceedings, handling multi-divisional legal matters, and providing advice and assistance to the Commission, its operating divisions, and regional offices. Advice concerns statutory interpretation, rulemaking, legislative matters and other legal problems, public or private investigations, and Congressional hearings and investigations. The General Counsel directs and supervises all contested civil litigation and SEC responsibilities under the Bankruptcy Code and all related litigation. It also represents the Commission in all cases in the appellate courts, filing briefs and presenting oral arguments on behalf of the Commission. In private litigation involving the statutes the Commission administers, this office represents the SEC as a friend of the court on legal issues of general importance.

The Commission's work is primarily legal in nature. Occasional questions of legality regarding the Commission's own decisions or legal decisions affecting the Federal securities laws are handled by the General Counsel.

The Commission also recommends revisions in the statutes which it administers. In addition, the SEC prepares comments on proposed legislation which might affect its work or when asked for its views by Congressional committees. The Office of the General Counsel, together with the division affected by such legislation, prepares this legislative material.

The Office of the Chief Accountant

The Chief Accountant consults with representatives of the accounting profession and the standard-setting bodies designated by the profession regarding the promulgation of new or revised accounting and auditing standards. This implements a major SEC objective to improve accounting and auditing standards and to maintain high standards of professional conduct by the independent accountants.

This office also drafts rules and regulations prescribing requirements for financial statements. Many of the accounting rules are embodied in Regulation S–X, adopted by the Commission. Regulation S–X, together with the generally accepted accounting principles promulgated by the profession's standard-setting bodies and a number of opinions issued as "Accounting Series Releases" or "Financial Reporting Releases," governs the form and content of most of the financial statements filed with the SEC.

This office administers the Commission's statutes and rules which require that accountants examining financial statements filed with the SEC be independent of their clients. This office also makes recommendations on cases arising under the Commission's Rules of Practice which specify reasons an accountant may be denied the privilege of practicing before the Commission. These reasons include lack of character or integrity, lack of qualifications to represent others, unethical or unprofessional conduct, or the willful violation of (or the willful aiding and abetting of violation of) any of the Federal securities laws, rules, or regulations. The Chief Accountant supervises the procedures followed in accounting investigations conducted by the Commission staff.

The Directorate of Economic and Policy Analysis

This group deals with the economic and empirical issues which are inextricably associated with the Commission's regulatory activities. The directorate usually works closely with the divisions responsible for rule proposals. Whether working with one of the operating divisions or serving the Commission independently, the directorate analyzes impacts and benefits of proposed regulations and conducts studies on specific rules.

More specifically, the directorate analyzes rule changes and engages in long-term research and policy planning. To accomplish this, it builds and maintains diverse computer data bases, designs programs to access data, and develops and tests alternative methodologies. The directorate assesses the impact of securities market regulations on issuers (in particular, small or high technology issuers), broker-dealers, investors, and the economy in general. One area it monitors is the emerging national market structure and regulation changes affecting the ability of small businesses to raise capital. The directorate also collects, processes, and publishes (in its SEC Monthly Statistical Review) data on the financial condition of the securities industry, registered securities issues, and trading volume and value of exchange-listed equity securities.

The Office of the Chief Economist

The Office of the Chief Economist analyzes potentially significant developments in the marketplace. Its work includes gathering and analyzing data on a wide range of market activities that may require attention by the

Commission. Examples are new types of securities, actions by publicly held entities and their impact on investors, and new or emerging trends in the securities markets.

Results of this work are used internally as part of the process to determine whether Commission action is necessary and to keep abreast of trends in the marketplace. Occasionally, subject to approval of the Commission, the research of this office is published.

The Office of Administrative Law Judges

The administrative law judges are responsible for scheduling and conducting hearings on administrative proceedings instituted by the Commission and appeals of proceedings instituted by others. Opinions and orders resulting from these hearings are prepared by the Office of Opinions and Review.

The Office of the Executive Director

The Executive Director develops and executes the overall management policies of the commission for all its operating divisions and offices. The Executive Director administers programs to implement certain statutes, regulations, and Executive Orders. Program functions include appointing program officials; reviewing and approving program policies, procedures, and regulations; authorizing and transmitting reports; and assuring appropriate resource requirements to implement the programs.

The Office of Consumer Affairs and Information Services

This office of the Commission provides direct assistance to the investing public. It reviews public complaints against entities regulated by the Commission and disseminates public information about these entities as well as Commission activities.

The office's Investor Services Branch reviews all complaints from the investing public and typically obtains written responses from firms mentioned in the complaint. Information suggesting a possible violation of Federal securities laws is referred to appropriate Commission staff. When complaints entail private disputes between parties, Commission staff attempt informally to assist the parties in resolving the problem. The Commission is not authorized to arbitrate private disputes or intercede on behalf of a private party to recover losses from the purchase or sale of securities or otherwise act as a collection agency for an individual. Investors must seek a financial judgment through civil litigation or binding arbitration. Laws which provide investors with important recovery rights if they have been defrauded can be used in private lawsuits.

Through the office's Public Reference and Freedom of Information Branches, the public may obtain a wide range of information including all public reports filed by registered entities and internal Commission information on completed investigations and official actions.

Quarterly (10Q) and annual (10K) reports, registration statements, proxy material, and other reports filed by corporations, mutual funds, or broker-dealers are available for inspection in the Public Reference Room of the Commission's headquarters office in Washington, D.C. and in the New York and Chicago Regional Offices. Registration statements (and subsequent reports) filed by companies traded over-the-counter and by those registered under the 1964 Amendments to the Exchange Act are also available in regional offices. Copies of portions or all of such public documents may be obtained for a handling charge of ten cents per page ($5.00 minimum). Estimates of the cost of copying specific documents will be provided on request to the Public Reference Branch.

BIBLIOGRAPHY

I. Securities Regulation

  A. General References.

    American Law Institute, Federal Securities Code (1980, Supp.1981).

    H. Bloomenthal, Securities and Federal Corporate Law (1985 rev.).

    A. Bromberg and L. Lowenfels, Securities Fraud and Commodities Fraud (1985 rev.).

    M. Connelly, Securities Regulation and Freedom of Information (1979).

    R. Haft & P. Fass, Tax Sheltered Investments (3d ed.1984).

    R. Haft, Key SEC No-Action Letters (1984).

    T. Hazen, The Law of Securities Regulation (1985).

    J. Hicks, Exempted Transactions Under the Securities Act of 1933 (1980 rev.).

    A. Jacobs, Litigation and Practice Under Rule 10b–5 (2d ed. 1982) (1985 rev.).

    L. Loss, Fundamentals of Securities Regulation (1983).

    L. Loss, Securities Regulation (2d ed. 1961, Supp. 1969). (The authoritative treatise in the field, although now dated).

    D. Ratner, Securities Regulation in a Nutshell (2d ed. 1982).

    R. Schapiro, A. Sachs & C. Olander, Securities Regulation Forms (1983).

    Securities Law Techniques (A.A. Sommer, Jr. ed.) (1985).

    N. Wolfson, R. Phillips & T. Russo, Regulation of Brokers, Dealers and Securities Markets (1977, Supp.1979).

  B. Services and Periodicals.

    CCH Federal Securities Law Reporter.

    CCH Blue Sky Law Reporter.

    CCH American Stock Exchange Guide.

    CCH New York Stock Exchange Guide.

    Review of Securities and Commodities Regulation (bi-weekly).

    BNA Securities Regulation Law Reports (weekly).

    SEC Docket (CCH).

    Securities Regulation Law Journal.

    The Business Lawyer (A publication of the Section of Corporation, Banking and Business Law of the American Bar Association; an excellent source of articles on a wide range of business law topics).

C. History.

J. Seligman, Transformation of Wall Street (1982) (A comprehensive history of the SEC).

M. Parrish, Securities Regulation and the New Deal (1970) (A historian examines the New Deal effort to reshape the scope and content of securities regulation).

W. Douglas, Go East, Young Man ch. 18 (1974).

SEC, A Twenty-Five Year Summary of the Activities of the Securities and Exchange Commission, 1934–1959 (1961).

Douglas, Foreword to Securities and Exchange Commission Silver Anniversary Commemorative Symposium, 28 Geo.Wash.L.Rev. 1 (1959) (Reminiscences by a former Commissioner of the formative years of the Commission's work).

Landis, The Legislative History of the Securities Act of 1933, 28 Geo.Wash.L.Rev. 29 (1959) (An account by one of the draftsmen).

D. Appraisals of Regulatory Performance.

Benston, Required Disclosure and the Stock Market: An Evaluation of the Securities Exchange Act of 1934, 63 Amer.Econ.Rev. 132 (1973) (An economist's analysis of the effects of disclosure on the character of the stock market, and his conclusion that the required disclosure of the 1934 Act has not made the stock market a "fairer game" for investors).

W. Cary, Politics and the Regulatory Agencies (1967) (Insights of a former SEC Chairman on political pressures affecting the major federal regulatory agencies).

Freedman, A Civil Libertarian Looks at Securities Regulation, 35 Ohio St.L.J. 280 (1974) (Argument that current SEC practice does not meet due process standards).

H. Kripke, The SEC and Corporate Disclosure: Regulation in Search of a Purpose (1979) (An influential SEC critic makes a harsh assessment of the Commission's disclosure policies, its failure to take into account modern economic and finance theory, and its deference to the accounting profession.)

Lowenfels, SEC Investigations: The Need for Reform, 45 St. John's L.Rev. 575 (1971).

Economic Policy and the Regulation of Corporate Securities (H. Manne ed. 1969) (The proceedings of a 1968 symposium designed to attract and focus the attention of economists on the area of securities regulation).

Ratner, The SEC: Portrait of the Agency as a Thirty-Seven Year Old, 45 St. John's L.Rev. 583 (1971) (Examination of the SEC's track record in terms of its goals and major programs).

J. Seligman, The SEC and the Future of Finance (1985).

S. Shapiro, Wayward Capitalists (1984) (An empirical study of SEC enforcement strategies and processes; one of the Yale Studies on White-Collar Crime).

Stigler, Public Regulation of the Securities Markets; Friend & Herman, The S.E.C. Through a Glass Darkly; Robbins & Werner, Professor Stigler Revisited; Stigler, Comment, 37 J.Bus. 117, 382, 406, 414 (1964) (A heated dialogue over the contribution of the SEC Special

Study to an understanding or justification of securities regulation, and over the effectiveness of the SEC).

The Report of the Advisory Committee on Corporate Disclosure to the Securities and Exchange Commission, Comm.Print 95–29, House Committee on Interstate and Foreign Commerce, 95th Cong., 1st Sess. (Nov. 3, 1977).

Wolfson, A Critique of the Securities and Exchange Commission, 30 Emory L.J. 119 (1981) (Criticism of SEC for failure to reexamine its regulatory structure in the light of modern economic analysis, empirical research and cost benefit analysis).

II. Securities Markets

  A. Basic References.

    1. Bibliography.

      Capital Markets and Finance Bibliography (Indexes by subject and author for articles in the finance and capital markets areas; prepared by the SEC Directorate of Economic and Policy Research).

    2. Dictionaries.

      J. Rudman, Handbook of the Stock Market (1970) (Prepared as a study aid for persons taking the Registered Representative exam; examples and explanations in addition to definitions).

      P. Wyckoff, The Language of Wall Street (1973) (Definitions, examples, and illustrations of usage).

    3. General.

      R. Brealy & S. Myers, Principles of Corporate Finance (2d ed. 1984).

      T. Copeland & J. Weston, Financial Theory and Corporate Policy (2d ed. 1983).

      B. Graham, D. Dodd & S. Cottle, Security Analysis (4th ed. 1962) (The classic work on fundamental analysis).

      B. Malkiel, Inflation Beater's Investment Guide: Winning Strategies for the 1980's (1980).

      R. Radcliffe, Investment Concepts, Analysis and Strategy (1982).

  B. The Markets and Their Components.

    1. Overviews and General Surveys.

      K. Garbade, Securities Markets (1982).

      M. Mendelson & S. Robbins, Investment Analysis and Securities Markets (1976) (A book by two of the leading scholars of finance.)

      J. Francis & S. Archer, Portfolio Analysis (2d ed. 1979).

      SEC, Special Study of the Securities Markets, H.R.Doc. No. 95, 88th Cong., 1st Sess. pt. 2, 797–961 (1963) (Hereinafter "Special Study").

    2. Exchange Markets.

      Special Study, pt. 2, 21–358 (1963).

      American Stock Exchange, Fact Book (published annually).

      New York Stock Exchange, Fact Book (published annually).

      S. Jaffe, Broker-Dealers and Securities Markets—A Guide to the Regulatory Process (1977, Supp.1985).

R. Sobel, N.Y.S.E. A History of the New York Stock Exchange (1975); The Curbstone Brokers (1970) (A history of the American Stock Exchange); Amex: A History of the American Stock Exchange, 1921–1971 (1972).

3. Over-the-Counter Markets.

Special Study, pt. 2, 533–678 (1963).

NASD, NASDAQ Fact Book (published annually).

4. Financial Intermediaries.

H. Bines, The Law of Investment Management (1978, Supp.1980).

T. Frankel, The Regulation of Money Managers (1978 Supp.1985).

R. Goldsmith, Financial Institutions (1968) (An explanatory text on the nature, types, functions, and growth of financial intermediaries in the United States).

M. Mayer, The Money Bazaars: Understanding the Banking Revolution Around Us (1984); M. Mayer, The Bankers (1974).

J. Van Horne, Financial Management and Policy (6th ed. 1983).

Twentieth Century Fund, Abuse on Wall Street—Conflicts of Interest in the Securities Markets (1980) (A series of studies of conflicts of interest in the securities industry: Commercial Bank Trust Departments, Real Estate Investment Trusts, Corporate Pension Fund Asset Management, State and Local Pension Fund Asset Management, Union Pension Fund Asset Management, Investment Banking, Broker-Dealer Firms, Non-profit Institutions).

SEC, Institutional Investor Study Report, H.R.Doc. No. 92–64, 92d Cong., 1st Sess. (1971).

SEC, Report on the Public Policy Implications of Investment Company Growth, H.R.Rep. No. 2337, 89th Cong., 2d Sess. (1966).

Wharton School of Finance and Commerce, A Study of Mutual Funds, H.R.Rep. No. 2274, 87th Cong., 2d Sess. (1962).

C. Economic Critiques.

E. Fama, Foundations of Finance Portfolio Decisions and Securities and Securities Prices (1976).

Fama, Efficient Capital Markets: A Review of Theory and Empirical Work, 25 J.Fin. 383 (1970).

R. Brealey, An Introduction to Risk and Return on Common Stocks (1983).

Gilson & Kraakman, The Mechanisms of Market Efficiency, 70 Va.L. Rev. 549 (1984).

J. Lorie, P. Dodd & M. Kimpton, The Stock Market: Theories and Evidence (2d ed. 1985) (A book of and about scientific research on the stock market, security analysis, and the management of investment portfolios).

B. Malkiel, A Random Walk Down Wall Street (4th ed. 1985).

R. Posner & K. Scott, Economics of Corporation Law and Securities Regulation (1980) (A collection of essays by economists and lawyer-economists).

Modern Developments in Investment Management: A Book of Readings (J. Lorie & R. Brealey eds.) (2d ed. 1978) (An excellent collection of important articles organized under the headings of Stock Market Behavior, Portfolio Management, and Valuation of Securities).

D. Recent Securities Scandals.

R. Dirks & L. Gross, The Great Wall Street Scandal—Inside Equity Funding (1974).

K. Patrick, Perpetual Jeopardy: The Texas Gulf Sulphur Affair (1972) (An account of the Texas Gulf Sulphur insider-trading episode presenting the TGS side of the story).

C. Raw, B. Page & G. Hodgson, Do You Sincerely Want to be Rich? (1971) (Story of Bernard Cornfeld and Investors Overseas Services, Ltd.).

M. Shulman, The Billion Dollar Windfall (1969) (Another account of the Texas Gulf Sulphur insider-trading episode throwing additional light upon this fascinating story and the subsequent litigation).

Part II

REGULATION OF THE DISTRIBUTION OF SECURITIES

SUBDIVISION A. THE REGISTRATION AND DISTRIBUTION PROCESS UNDER THE SECURITIES ACT OF 1933

Chapter 2

THE BASIC STRUCTURE AND PROHIBITIONS OF THE SECURITIES ACT

SECTION 1. THE STATUTORY FRAMEWORK

Statute

Securities Act, §§ 5, 17, 2, 3, 4, 6, 7, 8, 10 (and Schedule A), 11, 12, 13, 19, 20, 24, 9, 22.

Introductory Note

The Securities Act of 1933 has two basic objectives: (1) to provide investors with material financial and other information concerning new issues of securities offered for sale to the public; and (2) to prohibit fraudulent sales of securities. Its scope, however, is strictly limited, for jurisdiction is always tied to some use of the mails or of interstate facilities to accomplish a forbidden transaction. We commence our study of the 1933 Act with a guided tour through the various sections of the statute.

The basic prohibitions are found in two substantive provisions: Section 5 which prescribes the rules for compelling full disclosure and §§ 17 and 12(2) which relate to fraud or misrepresentation in interstate sales of securities. Section 17 and § 12(2) may appear to overlap to some extent, but the former provides criminal sanctions and the latter exclusively civil sanctions. Section 17 also provides a basis for enforcement by the Securities and Exchange Commission through disciplinary proceedings or by way of an injunction. It is still an open question whether a private right of action will be implied under Section 17(a).[1]

---

1. See the note on civil liability under Section 17(a), infra at page 890.

63

The key provision is § 5 around which most of the rest of the Act revolves. Its overall purpose is to require that new issues of securities offered by the use of the mails or other channels of interstate commerce shall be registered with the Commission, and that a prospectus (filed as a part of the registration statement) shall be furnished to the purchaser prior to the sale or, in some cases, at the time of the delivery of the security after sale. Section 5 can only be understood, however, by taking § 2 into account, for that section defines a number of the technical terms used in Section 5. Section 3 exempts from the operation of the Act (except for the antifraud provisions of §§ 17 and 12(2)) securities other than § 3(a)(2) securities and thus further qualifies § 5. Moreover, § 4 specifically provides that § 5 shall not apply to certain transactions and thus cuts further into the section. For example, although § 5 seemingly applies to "any person," we learn in § 4(1) that the section does not apply to transactions by anyone unless the person is "an issuer, underwriter, or dealer"— something quite different. Again, these terms are words of art which are defined in § 2.

The "registration statement" referred to in § 5 is defined in § 2(8). Sections 6 through 8 set forth the procedures for registering securities from the filing of the registration statement with the SEC until it becomes effective. Section 5 also regulates the use of the "prospectus." That term is defined in § 2(10). The information required to be set forth in the registration statement is specified in § 7 (and in Schedule A) and § 10 prescribes the contents of a prospectus.

Other sections of the act are concerned with enforcement procedures. Sections 11 and 12 give private remedies to buyers of securities. The scope of these remedies are the subject of Part V on Civil Liabilities. The private remedy sector is rounded out by § 13 which fixes a short statute of limitations for Sections 11 and 12 actions; by § 14 which invalidates any contractual provision looking toward a waiver of remedies; and by § 15 which imposes a joint and several liability upon persons in a control relationship with any person liable under §§ 11 or 12.[2]

To complete the overall picture, reference should be made to a number of miscellaneous sections. Section 18 specifically preserves state laws regulating the issuance and sale of securities instead of preempting the field of securities regulation. However, Section 19(c)(1) authorizes the SEC to cooperate with the states in securities matters for the purpose of promoting uniformity and reducing the burdens of raising capital, particularly by small business. Section 19(a) gives the Commission rule making powers, including the power to define accounting, technical and trade terms used in the Act. It also contains the important good faith provision which immunizes from any liability persons who rely upon a rule of the Commission in good faith, even though the rule is later determined to be invalid.

The government may compel compliance in various ways. Sections 19(b) and 20(a) give the SEC investigative powers. Section 20 also authorizes the Commission to seek the judicial remedies of injunction and

---

2. This, for example, would include the promoters in the case of Old Dominion Copper Mining & Smelting Co. v. Lewisohn, 210 U.S. 206 (1907), even though the securities are sold by the corporation, rather than the promoters.

mandamus.[3] However, the power to institute criminal proceedings is vested in the Attorney General; criminal penalties are specified in § 24.[4]

Court procedures are prescribed in §§ 9 and 22. Under § 9, a person aggrieved by an order of the Commission may have it reviewed in the United States Court of Appeals. Jurisdiction of "offenses and violations" is vested in the United States district courts by virtue of § 22(a), although the state and territorial courts have concurrent jurisdiction with respect to civil actions under the statute. In suits in the federal courts, venue may be laid in the district where the defendant is found, is an inhabitant, transacts business or where the offer or sale of the security occurred. Process runs throughout the world,[5] and the Court may order security for costs under § 11(e).

With this preview of the overall structure of the 1933 act, § 5 should be examined more closely. It is to be noted that the section states the ground rules for making offers and sales of securities during three distinct periods of time: (1) the pre-filing period; (2) the period between the filing of the registration statement and the effective date (the so-called waiting period); and (3) the post-effective period.

Section 5 states the rules for making offers, sales, and the manner of sales of securities in registered public offerings. Section 5(a) concerns sales of securities; § 5(b) states the prospectus requirements; and § 5(c) governs activities in the pre-filing period, although that portion of § 5(c) relating to administrative proceedings under § 8 applies only to the waiting period and the post-effective period. However, in order to understand what issuers, underwriters and dealers may or may not do in any period—pre-filing, waiting, or post-effective—one must read the entire section. None of the subsections standing alone states all the rules governing any one time period.

Problem on the Prohibitions of Section 5

Impel, Inc., incorporated in Delaware, is engaged in the business of waste management. Its principal executive offices are located in Peoria, Illinois. There are 3,000,000 shares of common stock and 2,000,000 shares

---

3. For a review of the scope of the SEC's recent enforcement efforts, see infra at Chapter 23.

4. This division of function is an important factor in the emphasis given by the Commission to non-criminal enforcement proceedings, rather than the institution of criminal proceedings. Since the staff of the Attorney General lacks expertise in securities matters, the case must be developed by the SEC enforcement staff, while the actual trial of the case is conducted by the staff of the Department of Justice. This structure provides little incentive for the SEC enforcement staff to pursue criminal remedies, except in egregious cases, and promotes delay and inertia by the Attorney General's staff.

5. Under Section 22(a), process may be served "wherever the defendant may be found." Similar language appears in Sec-

tion 27 of the 1934 Act. In Fitzsimmons v. Barton, 589 F.2d 330 (7th Cir. 1979), nationwide service under Section 27 and F.R.C.P.Rule 4(e) withstood a constitutional attack on the basis of the Due Process Clause of the Fourteenth Amendment. In Bersch v. Drexel Firestone, Inc., 389 F.Supp. 446 (S.D.N.Y.1974), rev'd in part on other grounds 519 F.2d 974 (2d Cir. 1975), service of process on a British corporation by mailing a copy of the summons and complaint pursuant to F.R.C.P.Rule 4(i)(1)(D), return receipt requested, to its office outside the United States was held sufficient, even though the envelope containing the summons and complaint was returned to the sender, marked "delivery refused". The court held defendant was "found" at its head office, despite its effort to avoid service of process merely by returning the papers.

of nonconvertible, nonparticipating 8% preferred stock outstanding. The common stock is listed on the New York Stock Exchange and is selling at about $60 a share; the preferred is unlisted and is traded over the counter. The company had net income of $3,000,000 in each of the last five fiscal years.

Impel has decided to expand into the business of radioactive waste disposal in order to meet a pressing public need in this area. The waste is to be gathered and ultimately stored in airtight containers consisting of large satellites which will be shot into outer space, presumably to stay there forever. The launch site and other installations will be located on the seashore somewhere in Texas. Impel proposes to amend its certificate of incorporation: (1) to split the common stock six-for-one in order to provide an offering price of $10.00 a share and to increase the size of the offering to provide a broader market; and (2) to make a public offering of 10,000,000 shares of common stock at a proposed price of $10.00 per share.

The problem deals with activities occurring in three time frames: (a) the pre-filing period, (b) the waiting period, and (c) the post-effective period. Part (a) (problems 1–15) should be read and answered only after reading the material in section 2; part (b) (problems 16–23) only after reading the material in section 3; and part (c) (problems 24–31) only after reading the material in section 4. The problem as posed assumes that Impel is a reporting company under the 1934 Act; as to each problem, where relevant, consider whether your answer would be different, if Impel were a non-reporting company.

(a) Assume that the securities will have to be registered under the Securities Act of 1933, but no registration statement has yet been filed. Determine the application of § 5 to the following transactions:

1. Able, the President of Impel, makes a telephone call from Peoria, Illinois to the Chicago office of Hazard & Co., investment bankers, and opens negotiations to have Hazard & Co. serve as principal underwriter of the issue.

2. Able is referred to the buying department of Hazard & Co. which is located in New York and pursues the matter further by telephoning the New York Office.

3. After further investigation by the head of the buying department of Hazard & Co. (including a tour of the plant) the corporation and Hazard & Co. reach an informal agreement that Hazard & Co. will serve as the principal underwriter of the issue and this agreement is embodied in a "letter of intent" signed by Hazard & Co. in New York and mailed to Peoria, Illinois where Able signs an acceptance on behalf of Impel and returns it to Hazard & Co. by mail. Did any of the foregoing activities result in Impel's common stock being "in registration"?

4. Impel publishes a notice announcing that it proposes to register 10,000,000 shares of common stock under the Securities Act of 1933 and make a public offering of the shares for cash at a price to be determined by market conditions at the time of the offering; that the proceeds are to be used for the purpose stated above; and that Hazard & Co. will serve as principal underwriter of the issue.

5. Assume that instead of Impel taking the action stated in question 4, Hazard & Co. distributes a press release to the New York papers and to the

principal wire services announcing the forthcoming offering of 10,000,000 common shares by Impel to be distributed through a nationwide investment banking group that it will head as managing underwriter. The release also describes the use of the proceeds, the plans of management and indicates that the offering will be at or near the market price, as adjusted for the stock-split, when a registration statement with respect to the securities has become effective.

6. Hazard & Co. telephones or writes other underwriters throughout the nation and forms an underwriting group to purchase the Impel common stock. The members then sign an "Agreement among Underwriters" in which they agree to purchase the stock on specified terms and conditions and authorize Hazard & Co. to execute the underwriting agreement with Impel on their behalf. Hazard & Co. does so and mails each underwriter a duplicate original of the underwriting agreement.

7. Hazard & Co., as managing underwriter, uses the mails and interstate facilities to contact members of the NASD and invite them to become members of the retail selling group as participants in the sale of the stock.

8. Impel mails a proxy statement to its shareholders soliciting proxies on behalf of management to be voted in favor of an amendment of the certificate of incorporation splitting the common stock and increasing the authorized common stock at a forthcoming meeting of the stockholders.

9. Assume that the common stock will first be offered to existing shareholders and the underwriters have committed themselves to "stand by" until the subscription period has expired, at which time they must take and pay for the shares not subscribed. Impel mails a notice to its common stockholders on April 1, advising them that it proposes to offer to stockholders of record on May 15 the right to subscribe to common stock on a basis of one share for each ten shares held, by means of 30-day warrants at a price of about $9.00 per share, and that the offering will be made only by means of a prospectus.

10. On his way from Peoria to New York, Able stops off at Philadelphia, Pa. and has lunch with Barton, one of Impel's largest shareholders. During lunch, Able asks Barton whether she intends to exercise her warrants in order to give Hazard & Co. some indication as to the extent of the underwriters' standby commitment.

11. A dealer in Chicago, having heard of the proposed offering, mails a letter to Hazard & Co. in New York offering to buy some of the common stock when issued.

12. A customer in Wisconsin telephones a dealer in Chicago and offers to buy some of the common stock on a when-issued basis. The dealer rejects the offer.

13. A shareholder of Impel, having been notified of the proposed rights offering, writes a dealer and offers to sell it some of the stock on a when-issued basis. The dealer accepts and mails a written confirmation of the transaction.

14. Impel's President, Able, meets in Peoria with a group of 20 security analysts and discusses the state of Impel's business and competitive conditions in the industry. The meeting was set up by Impel after the signing of the "letter of intent" referred to in question 3.

15. Impel mails an Annual Report to Shareholders as it customarily does at this time of year, which report contains its usual amount of financial and other information concerning the company's products and activities during the past year.

(b) Assume that Impel has filed a registration statement under the Securities Act of 1933 with respect to the 10,000,000 shares of common stock but that it has not yet become effective. Determine the application of § 5 to the following transactions:

16. Marjen Co., a securities dealer in Chicago, which is aware of the proposed public offering but does not intend to become a member of the underwriting syndicate or dealer group, discusses the prospects of Impel in its weekly market letter distributed to its clientele and recommends Impel common stock as a long-term investment.

17. Armitage Co., a securities dealer in Cleveland, Ohio, that intends to accept an invitation to become a member of the underwriting syndicate, in its regularly issued market letter publishes information regarding the Impel preferred stock with a recommendation of its purchase by prudent investors.

18. Armitage Co. also continues to list the Impel common stock in its monthly comprehensive list of securities currently being recommended by it as it has done for the past four years, but changes its previous "hold" recommendation to a "buy" recommendation.

19. A sales representative of Hazard & Co. in New York telephones a dealer in Chicago and offers to reserve some of the common stock for its account with a view to having it purchase the shares at a discount and reoffer them to the public as soon as the registration statement has become effective.

20. Hazard & Co. publishes a "tombstone ad" with respect to the forthcoming issue in the Wall Street Journal.

21. Hazard & Co. mails the preliminary prospectus to selected dealers throughout the nation, enclosing a card inviting them to indicate to what extent they are interested in purchasing some of the common stock from the underwriting group at a discount and reoffering it to the public as soon as the registration statement becomes effective. What, if any, restrictions are imposed upon the solicitation of indications of interest from dealers?

22. A dealer writes a letter to one of his customers, offering her Impel common stock on a when-issued basis, but does not enclose a preliminary prospectus because it knows that its customer has already received one from another source.

23. As soon as the price amendment has been filed, a dealer in Chicago telephones its customer in Wisconsin and offers to sell 100 shares of Impel common stock at the proposed offering price as set forth in the final prospectus. The customer accepts the offer. When the registration statement becomes effective, the dealer mails a confirmation to its customer who never received a preliminary or final prospectus.

(c) Assume that the Impel registration statement has become effective. Determine the application of § 5 to these transactions:

24. A dealer who is a member of the selling group writes a letter to one of its customers offering her Impel common stock. Must the dealer send a

statutory prospectus with his letter or may a Rule 431 summary prospectus be used?

25. In question 24, assume that the dealer had been told by another broker-dealer that it had previously sent a statutory prospectus to the customer, so omitted to enclose any prospectus. Although the dealer is able to prove that a prospectus was mailed to the customer, the customer can establish that she never received it.

26. In question 24, instead of writing a letter, the dealer makes an interstate telephone call to its customer and offers her the stock which the customer accepts. The dealer then mails a confirmation of the sale. Must it enclose a statutory prospectus?

27. In question 26, after the customer accepts the offer, the dealer does not mail a confirmation but puts the stock certificates in an envelope and mails them directly to the customer. Must it enclose a statutory prospectus?

28. A dealer who is a member of the selling group mails a statutory prospectus to one of his customers and also encloses a brochure, prepared by Impel's public relations department, which paints a picture of the company's future, far more optimistic than the prospectus. Copies of this sales literature were never filed with the SEC.

29. Impel, having met the conditions of Rule 431, prepared and filed a summary prospectus as a part of the registration statement that has become effective. A dealer who is a member of the selling group mails this summary prospectus to one of its customers. Is this permissible?

30. Shortly after the public offering is made, Marjen Co., which was not a member of the selling group, solicits one of its customers to buy Impel common stock on the New York Stock Exchange, and executes a buy order for the customer. The securities are delivered to the customer. Must Marjen Co. enclose a statutory prospectus?

31. Armitage & Co. failed to honor written requests from institutional investors for an Impel preliminary prospectus during the waiting period and a statutory prospectus after the effective date. What sanctions may the SEC impose against Armitage under these circumstances?

(d) Assume that the outstanding shares of Impel are not listed on any securities exchange and that the corporation was not subject, immediately prior to the time of the filing of the registration statement, to the reporting requirements of Section 13 or 15(d) of the Securities Exchange Act of 1934. What, if any, difference would this make in your answers to the foregoing questions? List those questions as to which your answer would be affected and indicate what your answer would be in each such case.

SECTION 2. THE PRE–FILING PERIOD
("GUN JUMPING")

Statutes and Regulations

Securities Act, §§ 23, 5(c), 2(10), 2(11), 2(12), 2(3), 2(4), 4(1), 7, 10, 12(1), 6; Rules 135, 137, 138, 139, 153a, 174, 430; Exchange Act Rules 15c2–8.[1]

1. Some explanation should be made as to the SEC's system of rule numbering. Since about 1940 the rules have been pub- lished in the Code of Federal Regulations, Title 17, Chapter II. The general rules and regulations under each act adminis-

PRELIMINARY NEGOTIATIONS BETWEEN ISSUER
AND UNDERWRITER

Section 5(c) in terms makes it unlawful for *any person* to make use of interstate facilities or the mails to offer to sell or to offer to buy any security, before a registration statement with respect to the security has been filed with the SEC. Even oral interstate telephone offers are proscribed for it is immaterial whether the offer is made by means of a prospectus or otherwise. (See § 2(10)). Unless the section were further qualified, it would literally prohibit normal trading transactions in outstanding securities, either on the stock exchanges or in the over-the-counter market, if the mails or interstate facilities were used. The limiting language is found in § 4(1), which excludes from § 5, transactions "by any person other than an issuer, underwriter, or dealer."

Section 4(1) is significant in two respects. On the one hand, the ordinary investor who is not engaged in the securities business, but who buys and sells securities for his or her own account, is free of any restrictions, so long as he or she does not engage in a transaction which would result in the person becoming an issuer, underwriter or dealer.[2] (See §§ 2(4), 2(11), 2(12)). On the other hand, standing alone, § 5(c) and § 4(1) would prohibit an issuer, or a controlling person, proposing to offer securities from using the mails or interstate facilities to contact a managing or lead underwriter with a view to a public issue, and preclude an underwriter from similarly approaching the issuer or controlling person, until a registration statement had been filed. Clearly, however, negotiations at this level should take place in the pre-filing period. And to prevent this cart before the horse approach, § 2(3) excludes from the definition of the terms "sell" and "offer" and the term "offer to buy" as used in § 5(c) "preliminary negotiations and agreements" between an issuer or any controlling person proposing to offer securities and any underwriter.

If as a result of negotiations between an issuer and underwriter they reach a tentative understanding that the underwriter will sponsor the issue, their mutual intention will sometimes be embodied in a "memorandum of understanding" or "letter of intent" which sets forth the amount of the issue, calls for preparation of a registration statement, and the formation of an underwriting group of which this underwriter will serve as

---

tered by the SEC appear as the following parts of Chapter II: Securities Act of 1933, part 230; Securities Exchange Act of 1934, part 240; Public Utility Holding Company Act of 1935, part 250; Trust Indenture Act of 1939, part 260; Investment Company Act of 1940, part 270; and the Investment Advisers Act of 1940, part 275. Until 1956, however, the SEC also maintained its own system of numbering. Rules under the Securities Act were not preceded by a letter, but rules under the other acts were preceded by the following letters: the Securities Exchange Act of 1934 by the letter "X"; the Public Utility Holding Company Act by the letter "U"; the Trust Indenture Act by the letter "T"; the Investment Company Act by the letter "N"; and the

Investment Advisers Act by the letter "R". Thus, Rule X–10B–5 was the fifth rule adopted under § 10(b) of the Exchange Act. This system of numbering persisted within the Commission until about 1956. See SEC Ann.Rep. for the fiscal year ended June 30, 1957, p. 20. At that time the SEC began to change over to the CFR system of numbering. Thus Rule 135 of the Securities Act may sometimes be cited as Rule 230.135, or as Rule 230.135 (17 C.F.R. § 230.135) or simply as Rule 135 where identification of the particular statute (such as the Securities Act) is obvious.

2. Morgan, Offers to Buy Under the Securities Act of 1933, 1982 Ariz.St.L.J. 809 (1982).

manager, and determines how the various expenses of the offering shall be allocated. The memorandum or letter may also indicate a proposed maximum and minimum offering price and a maximum percentage for underwriting discounts and dealer allowances, all subject, however, to market conditions. Finally, the memorandum will state that it is not intended to be a binding commitment on either party, except as to any agreement regarding the assumption of expenses should the underwriting not materialize.[3]

If the underwriter is not to take the full commitment, it will spread the risk by inducing other underwriters to join in an underwriting group in which each member will purchase a part of the offering directly from the issuer. The agreement among underwriters is the basic document which appoints the managing underwriter as the representative of the other underwriters to conclude negotiations with the issuer and defines their relationships with the manager and with each other. Typical matters covered by the agreement among underwriters are the number of shares to be purchased by each underwriter; the public offering price, the underwriting spread and the price to the issuer; and the discounts or concessions to be allowed to members of the selling group. The agreement also usually vests in the manager broad discretion to reserve from each underwriter's participation a certain number of shares to be offered to institutional investors and to selling group members and otherwise to allocate the shares so as to balance supply with demand.

From the standpoint of timing, the issuer and underwriter do not arrive at a final agreement as to price until the registration statement has been filed with the SEC and has been completely processed so as to meet any deficiencies, except for the filing of the final price amendment. Having reached this stage, the agreement among underwriters is executed by all underwriters; and the managing underwriter on their behalf then executes the underwriting agreement with the issuer. In the meantime the price amendment is prepared and filed with the SEC together with a request that the registration statement be made effective. Thus, only when the formal underwriting agreement is signed do the underwriters become firmly committed, subject even then to any "market out" clauses contained in the contract.

The exception from the term "sell" in § 2(3) extends not only to the preliminary negotiations between issuer and underwriter but to the final underwriting agreement as well. However, this contract will almost never be signed before the registration statement has been filed and, typically, it will not be executed until shortly before the registration statement becomes effective. Furthermore, the 1954 amendments made clear that the exception also extends to negotiations and agreements between a controlling person proposing to offer securities and any underwriter. The language was also enlarged to encompass negotiations and agreements among underwriters who are to be in privity of contract with an issuer or controlling person. As the Report of the Senate Committee put it: "The sole purpose of this [language] is to make clear that the usual agreement among underwriters as well as the agreement between the underwriters and the

---

3. Where a letter of intent stated that no liability was intended to be created, a prospective underwriter was denied recovery, in quantum meruit, for services performed and expenses incurred in implementation of the letter. Dunhill Securities Corp. v. Microthermal Applications, Inc., 308 F.Supp. 195 (S.D.N.Y.1969).

issuer (or controlling person, as the case may be) may be made before the registration statement has been filed." [4]

It is to be noted, however, that apart from these activities between the issuer or controlling persons and the underwriters, § 5(c) forbids any further selling effort downstream before the registration statement has been filed. This would include sales activity by the use of the mails or interstate facilities directed at dealers or any other prospective customers. A similar ban is placed upon dealers making offers to buy from the underwriters in the pre-filing period. However, as soon as a public offering is in the wind, the issuer may be inclined to shape its public relations program so as to release corporate information designed to awaken the interest of investors in the issuer and its securities. And once the underwriting contact has been made, news of the forthcoming offering travels fast in the financial world and issuers, underwriters and dealers are not easily kept under leash, despite these restraints on pre-filing selling activity.

When may the dissemination of information be regarded as a part of the normal flow of corporate information to security holders and the public, unrelated to selling effort, and when is it of a character calculated to arouse and stimulate investor and dealer interest and thus set in motion the processes of distribution? The following material sets forth the position of the Securities and Exchange Commission on the problem of "gun jumping."

SECURITIES ACT RELEASE NO. 3844
Securities and Exchange Commission.
October 8, 1957.

PUBLICATION OF INFORMATION PRIOR TO OR AFTER THE EFFECTIVE DATE OF A REGISTRATION STATEMENT

Questions frequently are presented to the Securities and Exchange Commission and its staff with respect to the impact of the registration and prospectus requirements of Section 5 of the Securities Act of 1933 on publication of information concerning an issuer and its affairs by the issuer, its management, underwriters and dealers. Some of the more common problems which have arisen in this connection and the nature of the advice given by the Commission and its staff are outlined herein for the guidance of industry, underwriters, dealers and counsel.

* * *

Absent some exemption, Section 5(c) of the Securities Act of 1933 makes it unlawful for any person directly or indirectly to make use of any means or instruments of interstate commerce or of the mails *to offer to sell* a security unless a registration statement has been filed with the Commission as to such security.

Section 5(a) of the Act makes it unlawful to *sell* a security unless a registration statement with respect to such security has become effective. Section 5(b) makes it unlawful to make use of any means or instruments of

---

4. S.Rep.No.1036, 83 Cong., 2d Sess. 11 (1954).

transportation or communication in interstate commerce or of the mails to transmit a prospectus with respect to any security as to which a registration statement has been filed unless such prospectus contains the information specified by Section 10 of the Act.

A prospectus is defined to include any notice, circular, advertisement, letter or communication, written or by radio or television, which offers any security for sale except that any communication sent after the effective date of a registration statement shall not be deemed a prospectus if, prior to or at the same time with such a communication, a written prospectus meeting the requirements of Section 10 of the Act was sent or given.

Stated otherwise, it is illegal to offer a security prior to the filing of a registration statement.[1] A security may be offered legally after filing and before the effective date of a registration statement, provided that any prospectus employed for this purpose meets the standards of Section 10 of the Act.[2] Thus, in general during this period (after the filing and before the effective date), no written communication offering a security may be transmitted through the mails or in interstate commerce other than a prospectus authorized or permitted by the statute or relevant rules thereunder. After the effective date, sales literature in addition to the prospectus may be employed legally, provided the Section 10(a) prospectus precedes or accompanies the supplemental literature.

* * *

The terms "sale," "sell," "offer to sell" and "offer for sale" are broadly defined in Section 2(3) of the Act and these definitions have been liberally construed by the Commission and the courts.

It follows from the express language and the legislative history of the Securities Act that an issuer, underwriter or dealer may not legally begin a public offering or initiate a public sales campaign prior to the filing of a registration statement. It apparently is not generally understood, however, that the publication of information and statements, and publicity efforts, generally, made in advance of a proposed financing, although not couched in terms of an express offer, may in fact contribute to conditioning the public mind or arousing public interest in the issuer or in the securities of an issuer in a manner which raises a serious question whether the publicity is not in fact part of the selling effort.

Apart from the impropriety of such publicity under the Securities Act, a collateral problem is presented by reason of the fact that the dissemination of information, other than that contained in a prospectus, prior to or during a distribution may tend to affect the market price of the issuer's securities artificially.

Instances have come to the attention of the Commission in which information of a misleading character, gross exaggeration and outright

---

1. By virtue of internal procedural standards, or agreements with stock exchanges on which securities are listed, managements wish, or are required, to advise security holders promptly of important decisions which may affect materially their interests as security holders. In recognition of the propriety of such action, Rule 230.135 permits a brief announcement, which does not "offer a security," of a forthcoming rights offering.

2. Rule 230.[430] permits the use of a "preliminary" prospectus which contains substantially all of the information in the registration statement which at this stage does not usually include the offering price, related and underwriting data. Rule 230.134 also permits a form of brief advertisement or written communication advising of the pendency of the offering and indicating where the preliminary prospectus may be obtained.

falsehood have been published by various means for the purpose of conveying to the public a message designed to stimulate an appetite for securities—a message which could not properly have been included in a statutory prospectus in conformity with the standards of integrity demanded by the statute.

Many of the cases have reflected a deliberate disregard of the provisions and purpose of the law. Others have reflected an unawareness of the problems involved or a failure to exercise a proper control over research and public relations activities in relation to the distribution of an issue of securities.[a]

* * *

THE DIVIDING LINE BETWEEN PRE–FILING SALES PUBLICITY AND TIMELY DISCLOSURES OF CORPORATE INFORMATION

Section 5(c) of the Securities Act prohibits offers to sell a security prior to the filing of a registration statement. On the other hand, issuers subject to the reporting requirements of Section 13 or 15(d) of the 1934 Act and other publicly-held companies are under a duty to make prompt disclosure under the anti-fraud provisions of the securities acts or the timely disclosure policies of self-regulatory organizations.[1] A question of fact may arise as to whether an issuer is engaged in disseminating pre-filing sales publicity or is merely complying with its obligations of timely disclosure.

In the Matter of Carl M. Loeb, Rhoades & Co. and Dominick & Dominick, 38 SEC 843 (1959), Davis, the owner of extensive real estate holdings, formed Arvida Corporation, transferred his real estate to the corporation, and sought additional capital through an offering of stock to the public. When the financing proposals reached final form, a press release, issued on the letterhead of Loeb, Rhoades, a registered broker-dealer, was distributed to the New York press and to the principal wire services. The release stated that Arvida would have assets of over one hundred million dollars, representing Mr. Davis' investment, and some $25 to $30 million of additional capital would be raised through an offering of stock to the public. The release further stated that a public offering was scheduled to be made within 60 days through a nationwide investment banking group headed by Loeb, Rhoades, and Dominick & Dominick, and that Davis would transfer to Arvida over 100,000 acres "in the area of the Gold Coast" in Florida. The release identified the principal officers of Arvida and stated that the corporation proposed to undertake a "comprehensive program of orderly development", under which some of the land would be developed immediately into residential communities and other portions would be held for investment and future development. The release attracted such buying interest from security dealers that over 100 firms contacted the proposed underwriters for inclusion in the underwriting syndicate. As a result of

---

a. The release includes a number of examples in which an issuer, a prospective underwriter, or a promoter distributes information concerning the issuer which was designed to arouse interest in the issuer and which later could be transformed into a similar interest in the contemplated financing.

1. These comprise: (a) issuers with a class of securities listed or traded on an exchange; (b) issuers having total assets exceeding $5 million and a class of equity securities held of record by 500 or more persons, and (c) issuers with outstanding securities sold pursuant to 1933 Act registration statement (§ 15(d) companies).

this pre-filing publicity, the SEC obtained a permanent injunction for violations of Section 5(c) by the proposed underwriters.[2]

Arvida subsequently filed a registration statement with respect to the proposed offering. The final prospectus disclosed that the properties were heavily mortgaged and that a substantial part of the proceeds from the financing might be required to meet mortgage indebtedness and would be unavailable to develop the property. The Commission thereupon instituted proceedings under Sections 15 and 15A of the 1934 Act to determine whether to revoke the registrations of Loeb, Rhoades, and of Dominick & Dominick, and to suspend or expel them from membership in the NASD. The Commission found willful violations of Section 5(c) of the Securities Act. However, since the Commission had taken steps to dispel the effect of the unlawful release of information and there were other mitigating factors, it concluded that public interest and protection of investors did not require the drastic action of revocation, suspension, or expulsion from membership in the NASD.

In the course of its opinion the Commission had this to say:[3]

"[W]e find that the September 19, 1958, press release and resultant publicity concerning Arvida and its securities emanated from managing underwriters contemplating a distribution of such securities in the near future as to which a registration statement had not yet been filed * * *. We further find that such release and publicity was of a character calculated, by arousing and stimulating investor and dealer interest in Arvida securities and by eliciting indications of interest from customers to dealers and from dealer to underwriters, to set in motion the processes of distribution. In fact it had such an effect * * *.

"The principal justification advanced for the September 19 release and publicity was the claim that the activities of Mr. Davis, and specifically his interests in Florida real estate, are 'news' and that accordingly Section 5(c) should not be construed to restrict the freedom of the managing underwriters to release such publicity. We reject this contention. Section 5(c) is equally applicable whether or not the issuer or the surrounding circumstances have, or by astute public relations activities may be made to appear to have, news value.

* * *

"Difficult and close questions of fact may arise as to whether a particular item of publicity by an issuer is part of a selling effort or whether it is an item of legitimate disclosure to investors unrelated to such an effort. Some of these problems are illustrated in Securities Act Release No. 3844. * * * This case, however, does not present such difficulties. Arvida was a new venture having, at the date of the September publicity, only 1 stockholder—Davis. There was no occasion to inform existing stockholders or investors in the trading markets concerning developments in its affairs in order that they might protect their interests or trade intelligently. We see no basis for concluding that the purpose of the release was different from its effect—the stimulation of investor and dealer interest as the first step in a selling effort."

It could hardly be said that a one-person company was subject to any timely disclosure obligations. A somewhat different problem was presented in Chris-Craft Industries, Inc. v. Bangor Punta Corp., 426 F.2d 569 (2d Cir. 1970). The case involved a bitter contest for the control of Piper Aircraft Corporation between Chris-Craft Industries and Bangor Punta Corporation. Chris-Craft had made a cash tender offer for Piper stock. The Piper family thereupon negotiated a competing exchange offer of a package of securities from Bangor

---

2. SEC v. Arvida Corp., 169 F.Supp. 211 (S.D.N.Y.1958).

3. Carl M. Loeb, Rhoades & Co., 38 S.E.C. 843, 851–853 (1959).

Punta Corporation under which all Piper shareholders would be entitled to exchange each share of Piper common stock held by them for Bangor Punta securities and cash "having a value in the written opinion of The First Boston Corporation, of $80 or more."

Since the Bangor Punta exchange offer entailed a public offering of securities to the Piper Aircraft shareholders, Bangor Punta prepared to file a registration statement under the 1933 Act covering the proposed exchange offer. Upon the conclusion of the agreement between them, Bangor Punta and the Piper management simultaneously issued a press release stating that Bangor Punta had "agreed to file a registration statement with the SEC covering the proposed exchange offer for any or all of the remaining outstanding shares of Piper Aircraft for a package of Bangor Punta securities to be valued in the judgment of The First Boston Corporation at not less than $80 per Piper share."

Chris-Craft sought a preliminary injunction to restrain Bangor Punta from making the exchange offer claiming that the press release violated Section 5(c) of the 1933 Act and Rule 135 promulgated thereunder. The contention was that Rule 135 exempts certain disclosures of pre-filing publicity from the definition of an "offer to sell" prohibited by Section 5(c); that the categories of information privileged under the Rule are exclusive and do not permit a disclosure of the value of the securities to be offered; and that the announcement that the package of securities to be offered by Bangor Punta would have a value of $80 overstepped the exemption and made the press release an offer to sell.

Reversing the district court's conclusion that the press release did not violate Section 5(c), the Court of Appeals for the Second Circuit stated:

"We agree with this contention. When it is announced that securities will be sold at some date in the future and, in addition, an attractive description of these securities and of the issuer is furnished, it seems clear that such an announcement provides much the same kind of information as that contained in a prospectus. See SEC v. Arvida Corp., 169 F.Supp. 211 (S.D.N.Y.1958). Doubtless the line drawn between an announcement containing sufficient information to constitute an offer and one which does not must be to some extent arbitrary. A checklist of features that may be included in an announcement which does not also constitute an offer to sell serves to guide the financial community and the courts far better than any judicially formulated 'rule of reason' as to what is or is not an offer. Rule 135 provides just such a checklist, and if the Rule is not construed as setting forth an exclusive list, then much of its value as a guide is lost.

"Moreover, it is reasonable to conclude that the assigning of a value to offered shares constitutes an offer to sell. One of the evils of a premature offer is its tendency to encourage the formation by the offeree of an opinion of the value of the securities before a registration statement and prospectus are filed. There is then no information on file at the SEC by which the Commission can check the accuracy of the information which forms the basis of the offeror's estimate of value, and any offeree, such as the reader of a press release, is encouraged to form a premature opinion of value without benefit of the full set of facts contained in a prospectus.

"Here a statement of the value of the securities Bangor Punta offered was made directly in the announcement. It is true that the value which the reader of the May 8 press releases could be expected to accept is a value based upon the opinion of a reputable financial corporation and not upon general and necessarily speculative facts about the nature of the offeror's business, as in

Arvida, supra. However, the true significance of the $80 value which Bangor Punta claimed for its securities package was nonetheless unclear. Chris-Craft charges that the figure constituted an outright misrepresentation inasmuch as most readers would construe the figure as representing the market value of the package. In fact, Chris-Craft charges, some of the securities in the package had not previously been sold on the market at all, and the market value of Piper shares never reached $80 in response to the Bangor Punta exchange offer, so that the Bangor Punta securities did not have an $80 market value and could not honestly have been thought to have such a value. * * *

"Bangor Punta and Piper argue that even prior to the filing of a registration statement an immediate disclosure of market value is compelled in cases such as this both by SEC v. Texas Gulf Sulphur Co., 401 F.2d 833 (2 Cir. 1968), cert. denied as to issues not pertinent here, sub nom. Coates v. SEC, Kline v. SEC, 394 U.S. 976 * * * (1969), and by the rules of the New York Stock Exchange. We do not agree. The only material fact in this case within the meaning of *Texas Gulf Sulphur* was Bangor Punta's commitment, to offer its securities for Piper Aircraft shares. Rule 135 provides adequately for the announcement of a material fact such as this; further disclosure would, as stated above, thwart other policies of the securities laws. Had Bangor Punta observed Rule 135 by revealing immediately its intention to make an exchange offer and by later revealing the titles of the securities it proposed to offer and the basis or ratio on which the exchange was proposed to be made as soon as these matters were decided, adequate information concerning the proposed transaction would have been placed before the public and the potentially misleading estimate of value would have been avoided. Even if we assume that knowledge of the value figure involved here might conceivably have conferred some benefit on insiders had it not been revealed, we feel that this risk of unfair advantage is outweighed by the danger that substantial numbers of investors were misled by the figure's publication. The fact that a few additional sophisticated investors could have discovered the $80 value guarantee in the description of the transaction which Bangor Punta filed with the SEC pursuant to Section 13(d) of the 1934 Act is of no moment. Such investors would almost certainly be small in number, and any arguable danger of permitting them an unfair advantage is outweighed by the stronger probability that the press release misled a large number of unsophisticated investors."

"The same principles apply to the New York Stock Exchange's requirement that insiders disclose information likely to affect the market unless such information can be restricted to a small group of top management officials. In any event, a policy of the New York Stock Exchange, although entitled to considerable respect, cannot bind the Commission or the courts. Silver v. New York Stock Exchange, 373 U.S. 341, 357 (1963). To hold that disclosure would be privileged here because the $80 value could not be kept secret and might affect the market would mean that many other companies could offer to sell securities before their registration by claiming that the terms of the proposed offer could not be kept totally secret and must therefore be disclosed in full." [4]

---

4. Compare Sheinberg v. Fluor Corp., 514 F.Supp. 133 (S.D.N.Y.1981), where a shareholder of a target corporation charged the defendant bidder corporation with "gun jumping." The bidder corporation had filed a SEC Schedule 14D–9 tender offer statement in connection with a cash tender offer for 45 percent of the target's common stock at $60 a share. The tender offer statement also stated that if the tender offer was successful, the bidder and target corporations had agreed to a merger in which 1.2 shares of common stock of the bidder would be exchanged for each outstanding common share of the target. The proposal was also publicized in press releases and in communications sent to the target shareholders. The court distinguished Bangor Punta and held that disclosure of the merger terms not only was permitted by Rules 145(b)(1) and 135(a) (4) of the 1933 Act, but was simply d

SECURITIES ACT RELEASE NO. 5009

Securities and Exchange Commission.
October 7, 1969.

PUBLICATION OF INFORMATION PRIOR TO OR AFTER THE FILING AND EFFECTIVE DATE OF A REGISTRATION STATEMENT UNDER THE SECURITIES ACT OF 1933

The Securities and Exchange Commission and its staff frequently receive inquiries concerning the impact of the registration and prospectus requirements of Section 5 of the Securities Act of 1933 ("Act") on publication of information concerning an issuer and its affairs by the issuer, its management, and by underwriters and securities dealers. Some of the more common problems which have arisen in this connection are discussed in Securities Act of 1933 Release No. 3844 (October 8, 1957).

Since the publication of that release there have been a number of developments relevant to this subject, including the broader reach of the reporting and proxy disclosure requirements through the 1964 amendments to the Securities Exchange Act of 1934 and the increased awareness of various self-regulatory organizations, corporate managements and others of the importance of timely disclosure. Moreover, in recent years the Commission and its staff also have become increasingly aware of the need for more clearly defined standards in this area. Concurrently with the publication of this release the Commission is proposing to adopt various rules which would accomplish this objective in certain respects (see Securities Act Release No. 5010). The Commission believes that a discussion of certain factors to be considered in dealing with other aspects of this subject may be of help to issuers, their advisers and professionals in the securities business.

There has been an ever increasing tendency to publicize through many media information concerning corporate affairs which goes beyond statutory requirements. This practice reflects the commendable recognition on the part of business and the investment community of the importance of informing investors and the public with respect to important business and financial developments. It has been reenforced by the policies of various self-regulatory organizations regarding timely disclosure of information which might materially affect the market for an issuer's securities.[2]

signed to inform the shareholders of the merger agreement between the bidder and target.

See Note, Preregistration Publicity in an Exchange Offer, 119 U.Pa.L.Rev. 174 (1970); Pierce, Current and Recurrent Section 5 Gun Jumping Problems, 26 Case W.Res.L.Rev. 370 (1976); Note, Prereorganization Negotiations and Securities Act Section 5(c): A Proposed Solution to the Gunjumping Problem, 24 Case W.Res.L.Rev. 731 (1973); Lovejoy, Initial Public Offerings: Prefiling and Preeffective Publicity, PLI, 13 Ann.Inst. on Sec.

Reg. 359 (1982); Mann, Initial Public Offerings: Problems in the Course of Distribution, PLI, 13 Ann.Inst. on Sec.Reg. 351 (1982).

2. See, e.g., New York Stock Exchange Company Manual, pages [2–1 through 2–6, revised June, 1983, reprinted in 3 Fed.Sec. L.Rep. (CCH) 23,514] American Stock Exchange Guide, pages 101–108[, reprinted in 3 Fed.Sec.L.Rep. (CCH) 23,124A; Brown, Corporate Communications and the Federal Securities laws, 53 Geo.Wash.L.Rev. 741, 772–82 (1985).]

As the Commission has stated:

"We realize, of course, that corporations regularly release various types of information and that a corporation in which there is wide interest may be called upon to release more information more frequently about its activities than would be expected of lesser known or privately held enterprises. In the normal conduct of its business a corporation may continue to advertise its products and services without interruption, it may send out its customary quarterly, annual and other periodic reports to security holders, and it may publish its proxy statements, send out its dividend notices and make routine announcements to the press. This flow of normal corporate news, unrelated to a selling effort for an issue of securities is natural, desirable and entirely consistent with the objectives of disclosure to the public which underlies the federal securities laws." [3]

However, the increasing obligations and incentives of corporations to make timely disclosures concerning their offerings raise a question as to a possible conflict between the obligation to make timely disclosure and the restriction on publication of information concerning an issuer which may have securities "in registration." [4] The Commission believes that such a conflict may be more apparent than real. Events resulting in a duty to make prompt disclosure under the anti-fraud provisions of the securities laws or timely disclosure policies of self-regulatory organizations at a time when a registered offering of securities is contemplated are relatively infrequent and normally may be effected in a manner which will not unduly influence the proposed offering. Disclosure of a material event would ordinarily not be subject to restrictions under Section 5 of the Securities Act if it is purely factual and does not include predictions or opinions.

The Commission recognizes that difficult and close questions will inevitably arise with respect to whether particular items of publicity are subject to restriction, and encourages issuers and their counsel to seek informal consultation with the Commission's staff which is accustomed to dealing with such questions and is usually able to give rapid and definite responses.

A number of more specific questions have been raised concerning the restrictions on circulation of information by broker-dealers, particularly during the "pre-filing" period. There appears to be some confusion as to when the restrictions on publication activities commence. Ordinarily a broker-dealer becomes subject to restrictions at any time when he commences to participate in the preparation of a registration statement or otherwise reaches an understanding with the person on whose behalf a distribution is to be made that the firm will become a managing underwriter, whether or not the terms and conditions of the underwriting have been agreed upon. Other brokers become subject to restrictions at such time as they are invited by a managing underwriter or a person on whose behalf a distribution is to be made, to participate or seeks to participate. Persons who choose to forego such underwriting in order to be free to distribute

3. Carl M. Loeb, Rhoades & Co., 38 S.E.C. 843, 853 (1959).

4. "In registration" is used herein to mean the entire process of registration, at least from the time an issuer reaches an understanding with the broker-dealer which is to act as managing underwriter until the completion of the offering and the period of 40 or 90 days during which dealers must deliver a prospectus.

such publications should not thereafter participate in the distribution as a dealer or otherwise.

Distribution of communications containing recommendations with respect to securities which have been registered for sale from time to time at prices prevailing in the market pose difficult questions. Usually no broker-dealer group has made arrangements with the selling shareholders for distribution of the securities. It does not appear that restrictions on the dissemination of such material are necessary until such time as a broker-dealer has reached an understanding that he will offer securities on behalf of the selling shareholder, whether or not he has technically accepted an order to sell the security.

After a particular security is "in registration," broker-dealers often do not know the extent to which they may follow up recommendations concerning the security made before the security was "in registration." If a broker-dealer is a participant in a proposed underwriting and material events occur during the "pre-filing" period, the broker should be able to make a brief, strictly factual report of these events to his customers.

After the registration statement is filed and until it becomes effective, written communications furnished to customers or others should be restricted to the preliminary prospectus ("red herring"), the summary prospectus described in Section 10(b), or the so-called "tombstone" announcements permitted under Section 2(10) of the Act or Rule 134 thereunder. Also, Rule 135 permits certain announcements of offerings before and after a registration statement is filed.

It should be recognized that the foregoing discussion is intended to be only a general guide for brokers in disseminating information concerning an issuer which has securities "in registration." Particular fact situations may result in different conclusions. In such situations, a broker may find consultation with the staff of the Commission helpful.

* * *

SECURITIES ACT RELEASE NO. 5101 ᵃ

Securities and Exchange Commission.
November 19, 1970.

ADOPTION OF RULES RELATING TO PUBLICATION OF INFORMATION AND DELIVERY OF PROSPECTUS BY BROKER–DEALERS PRIOR TO OR AFTER THE FILING OF A REGISTRATION STATEMENT UNDER THE SECURITIES ACT OF 1933

The Securities and Exchange Commission has adopted rules under the Securities Act of 1933 and the Securities Exchange Act of 1934 designed to establish standards for determining circumstances under which broker-dealers may publish certain information about an issuer which proposes to or has registered securities under the 1933 Act, and also to clarify a

---

a. SEC, Disclosure to Investors (Wheat Report) ch. V (1969), examined the "gun jumping" problem and recommended that more clearly defined policies should be adopted to deal with the publication of information during the time a company is "in registration." Securities Act Release 5101 stemmed from these recommendations.

dealer's obligation to deliver prospectuses under Section 4(3) of that Act, and the antifraud provisions of the 1934 Act. * * *

Information, opinions or recommendations by a broker-dealer about securities of an issuer proposing to register securities under the Securities Act of 1933 for a public offering or having securities so registered, may constitute an offer to sell such securities within the meaning of Sections 2(3) and 5 of that Act, particularly when the broker-dealer is to participate in the distribution as an underwriter or selling group member. Publishing such information may result in a violation of Section 5 of the Act.

It is the purpose of the adopted rules to provide guidance to broker-dealers and to alleviate such requirements where it appears that the purposes and policies of the Act will not be prejudiced while assuring that persons engaged in the distribution of a registered offering and their customers will be supplied with the disclosure afforded by the statutory prospectus.

Summary of Rules Adopted under the Securities Act of 1933

Rule 135. Amendments to this rule permit publishing a notice that an issuer proposes to make a cash [b] offering of securities to be registered under the 1933 Act. The requirement that such notices be sent 60 days prior to the record date or the proposed date of the initial offering has been deleted. The language of the rule has been revised and simplified.

Rule 137. This new rule is designed to clarify the status of dealers not participating in a distribution. It permits publication and distribution by a dealer in the regular course of business of information, opinions, or recommendations regarding securities of a reporting company which has filed or proposes to file a registration statement under the Act.

Rule 138. New Rule 138 permits a broker-dealer participating in an offering of non-convertible senior securities registered on [Form S–2 or F–2] to publish opinions or recommendations concerning the issuer's common stock, and vice versa.

Rule 139. New Rule 139 permits a broker-dealer participating in an offering to publish at regular intervals, as part of a comprehensive list of securities, opinions or recommendations concerning the issuer provided it is a reporting company. The opinion or recommendation, however, must not be given special prominence, and must not be more favorable than the last previous opinion distributed before the broker-dealer became a participant.

Rule 174. The amendments to this rule eliminate the prospectus delivery requirement for dealers, other than participating dealers selling any unsold participation, during the 40 or 90 day period after the effective date of the registration statement or the commencement of the offering, whichever is later, with respect to sales of securities of issuers required to file reports under the Securities Exchange Act of 1934.

Summary of Rule Adopted under the Securities Exchange Act of 1934

Rule 15c2–8. This is a new rule under the Securities Exchange Act of 1934 relating to the distribution of preliminary and final prospectuses.

---

b. The rule, as amended, apparently permits its use in non-cash offerings, and specifically in offerings entailing the exchange of securities.

The rule provides that a broker-dealer participating in a distribution must take reasonable steps to see to it that any person desiring a copy of a preliminary or final prospectus receives a copy. Each salesman who is expected to offer the securities must receive a copy of the preliminary prospectus and, if he is expected to offer the securities after the effective date of the registration statement, he must receive a copy of the final prospectus. The managing underwriter must take reasonable steps to see that broker-dealers participating in the distribution receive a sufficient number of copies of the prospectus to comply with the rule and with Section 5(b) of the Securities Act of 1933.

* * *

SECURITIES ACT RELEASE NO. 5180

Securities and Exchange Commission.
August 16, 1971.

GUIDELINES FOR THE RELEASE OF INFORMATION BY ISSUERS WHOSE SECURITIES ARE IN REGISTRATION

The Commission today took note of situations when issuers whose securities are "in registration" [1] may have refused to answer legitimate inquiries from stockholders, financial analysts, the press or other persons concerning the company or some aspect of its business. The Commission hereby emphasizes that there is no basis in the securities acts or in any policy of the Commission which would justify the practice of non-disclosure of *factual* information by a publicly held company on the grounds that it has securities in registration under the Securities Act of 1933 ("Act"). Neither a company in registration nor its representatives should instigate publicity for the purpose of facilitating the sale of securities in a proposed offering. Further, any publication of information by a company in registration other than by means of a statutory prospectus should be limited to factual information and should not include such things as predictions, projections, forecasts or opinions with respect to value.[a]

* * * It has been asserted that the increasing obligations and incentives of corporations to make timely disclosures concerning their affairs creates a possible conflict with statutory restrictions on publication of information concerning a company which has securities in registration. As the Commission has stated in previously issued releases this conflict may be more apparent than real. Disclosure of factual information in response to inquiries or resulting from a duty to make prompt disclosure under the antifraud provisions of the securities acts or the timely disclosure policies of self-regulatory organizations, at a time when a registered offering of

---

1. "In registration" is used herein to refer to the entire process of registration, at least from the time an issuer reaches an understanding with the broker-dealer which is to act as managing underwriter prior to the filing of a registration statement and the period of 40 to 90 days during which dealers must deliver a prospectus.

a. This statement expresses the SEC's former policy forbidding projections and other forms of forward-looking statements. The Commission now encourages issuers of securities to publish certain types of forward-looking and analytical information in documents filed with the Commission and otherwise, under controlled conditions. See Rule 175 and infra, at pages 169, 209.

securities is contemplated or in process, can and should be effected in a manner which will not unduly influence the proposed offering.

* * *

Guidelines

The Commission strongly suggests that all issuers establish internal procedures designed to avoid problems relating to the release of corporate information when in registration. As stated above, issuers and their representatives should not initiate publicity when in registration, but should nevertheless respond to legitimate inquiries for factual information about the company's financial condition and business operations. Further, care should be exercised so that, for example, predictions, projections, forecasts, estimates and opinions concerning value are not given with respect to such things, among others, as sales and earnings and value of the issuer's securities.[b]

It has been suggested that the Commission promulgate an all inclusive list of permissible and prohibited activities in this area. This is not feasible for the reason that determinations are based upon the particular facts of each case. However, the Commission as a matter of policy encourages the flow of factual information to shareholders and the investing public. Issuers in this regard should:

1. Continue to advertise products and services.

2. Continue to send out customary quarterly, annual and other periodic reports to stockholders.[c]

3. Continue to publish proxy statements and send out dividend notices.

4. Continue to make announcements to the press with respect to factual business and financial developments; i.e., receipt of a contract, the settlement of a strike, the opening of a plant, or similar events of interest to the community in which the business operates.

5. Answer unsolicited telephone inquiries from stockholders, financial analysts, the press and others concerning factual information.

6. Observe an "open door" policy in responding to unsolicited inquiries concerning factual matters from securities analysts, financial analysts, security holders, and participants in the communications field who have a legitimate interest in the corporation's affairs.

7. Continue to hold stockholder meetings as scheduled and to answer shareholders' inquiries at stockholder meetings relating to factual matters.

---

b. Ibid.

c. In the Harper Group (Avail. June 3, 1976), [1976–1977 Transfer Binder] (CCH) Fed.Sec.L.Rep. ¶ 80,631, the SEC Staff took a no-action posture when an issuer, a closely-held international freight company, proposed to distribute its annual report to shareholders, to customers and prospective customers, and to other persons who were closely related to the conduct of its business, including shareholders, agents, employees, air and ocean carriers and certain financial institutions as had been its custom in previous years. The annual report was of a character and content customarily published by the company and did not contain material designed to stimulate the proposed offering.

We shall see that under the present regime of integrated disclosure, annual reports are now required to contain "Management's discussion and analysis" of the audited financial statements and the company's financial condition and changes therein. Moreover, issuers are encouraged, but not required, to provide financial forecasts and other forward-looking data. The line between pre-filing sales publicity and timely disclosure has now become so blurred that the SEC should reconsider its policy on "gun-jumping."

In order to curtail problems in this area, issuers in this regard should avoid:

1. Issuance of forecasts, projections, or predictions relating but not limited to revenues, income, or earnings per share.[d]

2. Publishing opinions concerning values.[e]

In the event a company publicly releases material information concerning new corporate developments during the period that a registration statement is pending, the registration statement should be amended at or prior to the time the information is released. If this is not done and such information is publicly released through inadvertence, the pending registration statement should be promptly amended to reflect such information.

The determination of whether an item of information or publicity could be deemed to constitute an offer—a step in the selling effort—in violation of Section 5 must be made by the issuer in the light of all the facts and circumstances surrounding each case. The Commission recognizes that questions may arise from time to time with respect to the release of information by companies in registration and, while the statutory obligation always rests with the company and can never be shifted to the staff, the staff will be available for consultation concerning such questions. It is not the function of the staff to draft corporate press releases. If a company, however, desires to consult with the staff as to the application of the statutory requirements to a particular case, the staff will continue to be available, and in this regard the pertinent facts should be set forth in written form and submitted in sufficient time to allow due consideration.[f]

* * *

SECTION 3. THE WAITING PERIOD

Statutes and Regulations

Securities Act, §§ 5(a), 5(b), 2(10)(b), 10(a), 10(b); Rule 134, 135a; Regulation C, Rules 430, 431, 432, 460.

RESTRICTIONS ON OFFERS BY ISSUERS, UNDERWRITERS AND DEALERS

Issuers and Underwriters. When a registration statement is filed with respect to a security it will contain a prospectus in incomplete form, yet which will set forth most of the essential information about the company and its finances that will appear in the final prospectus. However, the final prospectus, complete with the offering price, underwriting discounts and commissions, discounts and commissions to dealers, and related data, is ordinarily not placed on file until the Commission has concluded its examination of the registration statement in this preliminary form. Then when the Commission has indicated to the registrant that the information on file is adequate to meet the full disclosure standard, except for the offering price and other missing data, the underwriting agreement is signed and a so-called price amendment is filed together with a request that the Commission declare the registration statement to be immediately effective.

d. Ibid.

e. Ibid.

f. Brown, Corporate Communications and the Federal Securities Laws, 53 Geo. Wash.L.Rev. 741, 809–17 (1985).

The final or complete prospectus, the contents of which are specified in § 10(a), is commonly called the "statutory" prospectus so as to distinguish it from the "red herring" or "preliminary" prospectus which is on file during the waiting period, before the registration statement has become effective. Once the registration statement becomes effective, however, the statutory or § 10(a) prospectus becomes available for use as a selling document and eliminates the need for the preliminary prospectus.

a. The Preliminary or "Red-Herring" Prospectus. Prior to the 1954 amendments, the theory was that during the waiting period information contained in the registration statement on file with the Commission could be disseminated among potential investors, and, indeed, should be made available at least to interested dealers. The Act, however, specifically prohibited the issuer or underwriters from using the interstate facilities or mails to solicit buyers by making offers to sell, as such. The "red herring" prospectus was devised by the Commission for the purpose of preserving the subtle distinction between "solicitation" and "dissemination," for through it material information then on file with the Commission could be distributed to potential investors in a document which specifically stated that it was not to be treated as an offer to sell.[1]

After the 1954 amendments, the "red herring" prospectus (renamed the "preliminary prospectus") was given legitimacy and a number of other avenues were opened so that issuers and underwriters can now start their sales campaign as soon as the registration statement is placed on file without having to wait for it to become effective. Thus, offers to sell by the use of the mails or interstate facilities are no longer prohibited during the waiting period but the methods for making such offers are strictly regulated. Furthermore, although offers to sell can now be made during the waiting or cooling-off period, § 5(a)(1) makes it unlawful to "sell" the securities until the registration statement has become effective, thus forbidding any acceptance of the offer until after the effective date.

Section 5(b)(1) does not prohibit *oral* offers to sell by means of interstate facilities, for example, by making an interstate telephone call. The section is aimed solely at the use of a "prospectus," a term broadly defined in § 2(10) to include any communication, written or by radio or by television, which offers a security for sale. Under § 5(b)(1), a prospectus which meets the requirements of § 10 may be used to make offers to sell during the waiting period. We have seen that the statutory prospectus referred to in § 10(a) is not yet available, since the registration statement has not become effective. But § 10(b) authorizes the Commission to issue rules allowing the use for § 5(b)(1) purposes of a prospectus which summarizes or omits a part of the information in the statutory prospectus specified in § 10(a).

Rule 430 provides that a form of prospectus filed as a part of the registration statement shall be deemed to meet the requirements of section 10 for the purpose of 5(b)(1) prior to the effective date of the registration statement, if it contains substantially the information required to meet the requirements of Section 10(a), except for the omission of information "with

---

1. See Securities Act Release No. 464 (Aug. 19, 1935). The name originated from the red ink legend disclaiming any intent to solicit offers to buy or make an offer to sell which appeared on each page of the "red herring prospectus." Lobell, Revision of the Securities Act, 48 Colum.L.Rev. 324 (1948); Dean, Twenty-Five Years of Federal Regulation by the Securities and Exchange Commission, 59 Colum.L.Rev. 697, 714–15 (1959).

respect to the offering price, underwriting discounts or commissions, discounts or commissions to dealers, amounts of proceeds, conversion rates, call prices, or other matters dependent upon the offering price." This document may be referred to as the § 10(b) prospectus to distinguish it from a § 10(a) prospectus. The red-herring tradition is carried forward in Regulation S–K, Item 501(8) which requires that any prospectus used in the waiting period carry the caption "Preliminary Prospectus" and a specifically prescribed legend which disclaims any intention to make an offer to sell or solicit an offer to buy the securities proposed to be offered.

b. The Summary Prospectus. Under Rule 431, a summary prospectus (or a Preliminary Summary Prospectus) may be prepared either by the issuer or by an independent organization, but it must be filed as a part of the registration statement. This type of prospectus is available, however, only if the registration form to be used to register the securities provides for its use. The conditions for use are prescribed by Rule 431 and by the authorizing Form. In general, a summary prospectus may be used (1) by domestic issuers that have their principal business operations in the United States; (2) are "reporting companies," that is, are issuers registered pursuant to § 12(b) of the Securities Exchange Act of 1934 or have a class of equity securities registered pursuant to section 12(g) or are required to file reports pursuant to section 15(d) of that Act; and (3) have filed reports under sections 13, 14, or 15(d) of the 1934 Act for three years prior to the filing of the 1933 Act registration statement. There are other criteria, including the absence of defaults in dividend or sinking fund obligations on preferred stock or on debt obligations.

A number of forms authorize the use of summary prospectuses. These include Forms S–1 and S–2, applicable to certain reporting companies, and Form N–1A, applicable to open-end management investment companies. A registrant that is a foreign private issuer eligible to use Form F–2 may also avail itself of a summary prospectus.

c. The "Tombstone Ad". The Act also envisages one other way for reaching potential customers—the "tombstone ad" which derives its quaint name from the starkness of its contents. Even before 1954, there was excluded from the general definition of a prospectus contained in § 2(10)—a term which must be distinguished from the § 10(a) and 10(b) prospectuses—any communication in respect of a security "if it states from whom a written prospectus meeting the requirements of Section 10 [before the 1954 amendments] may be obtained and, in addition, does no more than identify the security, state the price thereof, and state by whom orders will be executed." The use of this "tombstone ad" was not permitted until after the registration statement had become effective. In 1954, however, § 2(10) was amended: (1) to permit the use of the statutory "tombstone ad" during both the waiting period and the post-effective period, but not in the pre-filing period; and (2) to permit the Commission to issue rules authorizing this expanded "tombstone ad" or "identifying statement" to contain such additional information as it deems appropriate. The Commission has responded by the issuance of Rule 134 which permits the use of an enlarged statement, provided the conditions of the rule are met.

It should be noted that Rule 134 grants a special dispensation for investment companies that permits an expanded text to include attention-getting headlines and pictorial illustrations. Most investment companies issue redeemable securities and their securities are the subject of a continuous offering, unlike that of other issuers. The investment company exception regarding publicity reflects the fact that the distribution of investment company shares differs markedly from that of other offerings and that investment companies are subject to comprehensive regulation under the Investment Company Act of 1940. There is additional language in Rule 134 which suggests that other types of issuers may take advantage of these advertising practices. However, when real estate syndicators began to use some of the same kind of information in their advertisements as investment companies, the Commission took the position that only registered investment companies are eligible to use these special provisions.[2]

Furthermore, Rule 135a permits underwriters or sponsors of investment company securities to engage in *generic* or *institutional* advertising of investment company products. Generic advertising must be restricted to explanatory information relating to investment companies generally, the different types of funds, products and services offered, and an invitation to inquire for further information.[3] The communication must contain the name of the broker or dealer or other person sponsoring the communication, but may not refer by name to the securities of a particular company or to the investment company itself. This device for contacting the public is infrequently used, however, since issuers and underwriters may use newspapers to publish a much more attractive Rule 134 identifying statement inviting the public to telephone toll-free or write for a statutory prospectus of a particular fund in the investment fund complex.

The "tombstone ad" and "identifying statement" are not intended to serve as selling documents but serve "purely as a screening device to ascertain what persons [are] * * * sufficiently interested to warrant delivery to them of the statutory prospectus."[4] In practice, it is not customary to publish a "tombstone ad" during the waiting period and the expanded "identifying statement" is seldom used even in the post-effective period. However, an identifying statement may be used during the waiting period to test the market for the securities and attain a wider dissemination of the preliminary prospectus. There is set forth below an identifying statement for a proposed offering of common shares of Owens-Illinois Inc., which appeared in various metropolitan newspapers during the waiting period. After testing the market, the proposed offering was reduced from 2 million to 1.4 million shares. The tombstone ad which was used in the post-effective period is also set forth, to show the changes occurring in the composition of the underwriting syndicate.

2. Securities Act Release No. 6518 (Mar. 22, 1984) at n. 2; Romeo, Advertising of Real Estate Offerings, 18 Rev. of Sec. & Commodities Reg. 17 (Jan. 23, 1985).

3. Securities Act Release No. 5248 (May 9, 1972).

4. SEC Securities Act Release No. 3224, June 6, 1947, Memorandum of the Statutory Revision Committee addressed to the Commission, p. 2.

IDENTIFYING STATEMENT USED IN THE WAITING PERIOD

A registration statement relating to these securities has been filed with the Securities and Exchange Commission but has not yet become effective. These securities may not be sold nor may offers to buy be accepted prior to the time the registration statement becomes effective. This advertisement shall not constitute an offer to sell or the solicitation of an offer to buy nor shall there be any sale of these securities in any State in which such offer, solicitation or sale would be unlawful prior to registration or qualification under the securities laws of any such State.

Proposed New Issue   February 22, 1976

2,000,000
Common Shares

OWENS-ILLINOIS, INC.

($3.125 par value)

Owens-Illinois is one of the world's leading and most diversified manufacturers of packaging products. It is the world's largest manufacturer of glass containers. In addition to glass containers its products include semi-rigid plastic containers, metal and plastic closures for such containers, corrugated and solid fiber shipping containers and containerboard for such containers, metal cans, composite cans, paper and plastic bag and film products, disposable paper and plastic cups, tubs, lids and plates, and plywood. In addition, an important part of Owens-Illinois' business consists of specialized glass products, such as glass television bulbs (for color and black-and-white picture tubes), scientific and laboratory glassware, and glass tumblers and stemware for household and institutional use.

---

law's

Lazard Frères & Co.   **Goldman, Sachs & Co.**

Bache Halsey Stuart Inc.   **The First Boston Corporation**   **Blyth Eastman Dillon & Co.**
                                                                              Incorporated

Dillon, Read & Co. Inc.   **Drexel Burnham & Co.**   **Hornblower & Weeks-Hemphill, Noyes**
                                     Incorporated   Incorporated

E. F. Hutton & Company Inc.   **Kidder, Peabody & Co.**   **Kuhn, Loeb & Co.**   **Lehman Brothers**
                                          Incorporated   Incorporated

Loeb, Rhoades & Co.   **Merrill Lynch, Pierce, Fenner & Smith**   **Paine, Webber, Jackson & Curtis**
                                     Incorporated   Incorporated

Reynolds Securities Inc.   **Salomon Brothers**   **Smith Barney, Harris Upham & Co.**
                                                                   Incorporated

Wertheim & Co., Inc.   **White, Weld & Co.**   **Dean Witter & Co.**
                                   Incorporated   Incorporated

Mitchell, Hutchins Inc.   **Shearson Hayden Stone Inc.**

ABD Securities Corporation   **Basle Securities Corporation**   **Alex. Brown & Sons**

F. Eberstadt & Co., Inc.   **EuroPartners Securities Corporation**   **Robert Fleming**
                                                                                  Incorporated

Kleinwort, Benson   **Moseley, Hallgarten & Estabrook Inc.**   **New Court Securities Corporation**
   Incorporated

Oppenheimer & Co., Inc.   **Piper, Jaffray & Hopwood**
                                      Incorporated

R.W. Pressprich & Co.   **Shields Model Roland Securities**   **SoGen-Swiss International Corporation**
   Incorporated   Incorporated

Thomson & McKinnon Auchincloss Kohlmeyer Inc.   **Spencer Trask & Co.**
                                                            Incorporated

Tucker, Anthony & R. L. Day, Inc.   **UBS-DB Corporation**   **Warburg Paribas Becker Inc.**

Weeden & Co.   **William D. Witter, Inc.**   **Wood, Struthers & Winthrop Inc.**
   Incorporated

Shuman, Agnew & Co., Inc.   **Sutro & Co.**   **Birr, Wilson & Co., Inc.**
                                      Incorporated

Robertson, Colman, Siebel & Weisel   **Stone & Youngberg**

- -

Please send me a free copy of the Preliminary Prospectus of Owens-Illinois, Inc.

Name_____

Street_____City_____State_____Zip____

Telephone_____
                (business)   (residence)

A copy of the Preliminary Prospectus may be obtained by mailing or delivering this coupon to any of the above firms or to Lazard Frères & Co., One Rockefeller Plaza, New York, N.Y. 10020 or Goldman, Sachs & Co., 55 Broad Street, New York, N.Y. 10004.

TOMBSTONE AD USED IN THE POST–EFFECTIVE PERIOD

This announcement is neither an offer to sell nor a solicitation of an offer to buy any of these securities. The offer is made only by the Prospectus.

NEW ISSUE

1,400,000
Common Shares

OWENS-ILLINOIS, INC.

($3.125 par value)

Price $57.50 Per Share

Copies of the Prospectus may be obtained only from such of the underwriters, including the undersigned, as may lawfully offer these securities in this State.

Lazard Frères & Co.   Goldman, Sachs & Co.

Bache Halsey Stuart Inc.   The First Boston Corporation   Blyth Eastman Dillon & Co.
                                                                                                            Incorporated

Dillon, Read & Co. Inc.   Drexel Burnham & Co.   Hornblower & Weeks-Hemphill, Noyes
                                                             Incorporated   Incorporated

E. F. Hutton & Company Inc.   Kidder, Peabody & Co.   Kuhn, Loeb & Co.   Lehman Brothers
                                                             Incorporated   Incorporated

Loeb, Rhoades & Co.   Merrill Lynch, Pierce, Fenner & Smith   Paine, Webber, Jackson & Curtis
                                                             Incorporated   Incorporated

Reynolds Securities Inc.   Salomon Brothers   Smith Barney, Harris Upham & Co.
                                                                                                            Incorporated

Wertheim & Co., Inc.   White, Weld & Co.   Dean Witter & Co.
                                                             Incorporated   Incorporated

Mitchell, Hutchins Inc.   Shearson Hayden Stone Inc.

ABD Securities Corporation   Basle Securities Corporation   Alex. Brown & Sons

F. Eberstadt & Co., Inc.   EuroPartners Securities Corporation   Robert Fleming
                                                                                                            Incorporated

Kleinwort, Benson   Moseley, Hallgarten & Estabrook Inc.   New Court Securities Corporation
Incorporated

Oppenheimer & Co., Inc.   Piper, Jaffray & Hopwood   Prescott, Ball & Turben
                                                             Incorporated

R. W. Pressprich & Co.   Shields Model Roland Securities   SoGen-Swiss International Corporation
Incorporated   Incorporated

Thomson & McKinnon Auchincloss Kohlmeyer Inc.   Spencer Trask & Co.
                                                                                                            Incorporated

Tucker, Anthony & R. L. Day, Inc.   UBS-DB Corporation   Weeden & Co.
                                                                                                            Incorporated

William D. Witter, Inc.   Wood, Struthers & Winthrop Inc.

Bateman Eichler, Hill Richards   Crowell, Weedon & Co.   Shuman, Agnew & Co., Inc.
                         Incorporated

Sutro & Co.   Birr, Wilson & Co., Inc.   Boettcher & Company   Bosworth, Sullivan & Company
Incorporated   Incorporated

Foster & Marshall Inc.   Robertson, Colman, Siebel & Weisel   Stern, Frank, Meyer & Fox
                                                                                                            Incorporated

Stone & Youngberg   Jefferies & Company, Inc.

March 4, 1976

In summary, therefore, the 1933 Act and rules now permit issuers, underwriters and dealers to use the following methods for reaching prospective purchasers during the waiting period: (1) oral offers to sell, whether face-to-face, or by interstate telephone, although offers to buy cannot be accepted until after the effective date; (2) publication of a "tombstone" advertisement pursuant to § 2(10)(b) or an "identifying statement" pursuant to Rule 134; (3) a preliminary prospectus which meets the conditions of Rule 430; and (4) a preliminary summary prospectus prepared by the issuer or an independent organization and complying with Rule 431 and the applicable Form.

The Commission has described the limitations on the sales activities of underwriters and dealers during the waiting period in these terms: [5]

> During the period after the filing of a registration statement, the freedom of an underwriter or dealer expecting to participate in the distribution to communicate with his customers is limited only by the antifraud provisions of the Securities Act and the Securities Exchange Act, and by the fact that written offering material other than a statutory [a] prospectus or tombstone advertisement may not be used. In other words, during this period "free writing" is illegal. The dealer, therefore, can orally solicit indications of interest or offers to buy and may discuss the securities with his customers and advise them whether or not in his opinion the securities are desirable or suitable for them. In this connection a dealer proposing to discuss an issue of securities with his customers should obtain copies of the preliminary prospectus in order to have a reliable source of information. This is particularly important where he proposes to recommend the securities, or where information concerning them has not been generally available. The corollary of the dealer's obligation to secure the copy is the obligation of the issuer and managing underwriters to make it readily available. Rule 460 provides that as a condition to acceleration of the effective date of a registration statement, the Commission will consider whether the persons making the offering have taken reasonable steps to make the information contained in the registration statement available to dealers who may participate in the distribution.

> It is a principal purpose of the so-called "waiting period" between the filing date and the effective date to enable dealers and, through them, investors to become acquainted with the information contained in the registration statement and to arrive at an unhurried decision concerning the merits of the securities. Consistently with this purpose, no contracts of sale can be made during this period, the purchase price may not be paid or received and offers to buy may be cancelled.

Broker-Dealer Activities. We have seen that securities dealers are subject to specific regulation under Rules 137, 138, and 139 throughout the entire registration process. Rule 137 relaxes the rules as to dissemination of information with respect to issuers in registration under certain condi-

---

5. Securities Act Release No. 4697 (May 24, 1964).

a. For the purpose of this release, a "statutory" prospectus was defined to include the preliminary prospectus authorized in Rule 433, the predecessor of Rule 430, as well as the summary prospectuses provided for in Rules 434 and 434A, the predecessors of Rule 431. This terminology confuses the statutory prospectus specified in § 10(a) with the preliminary and summary prospectuses which the Commission may prescribe by rule pursuant to § 10(b).

tions. If the dealer is not, and does not propose to be a member of the underwriting syndicate, or dealer group, and if the issuer is a reporting company under the 1934 Act, the dealer may continue to publish and distribute information, opinions or recommendations in the regular course of its business. The privilege is destroyed, however, if any consideration is received from the issuer, directly or indirectly in connection with the publication or distribution of such information.

Moreover, some restraints have been removed with respect to a securities dealer, even if it becomes a member of the underwriting syndicate or dealer group. Under Rule 138, if the issuer meets the requirements permitting the use of Forms S–2 or F–2,[6] and is registering a nonconvertible debt security, a participating underwriter or dealer may publish and distribute information, opinions or recommendations relating solely to common stock or convertible securities of the issuer. Again, if the issuer meets the conditions for registration on Forms S–2 or F–2 and is registering common stock or a security convertible into such stock, a participating underwriter or dealer may publish or distribute information, opinions or recommendations relating solely to nonconvertible securities of the issuer, other than to nonconvertible participating preferred stock. Finally, under Rule 139, if the issuer is a reporting company, an underwriter or dealer participating in the offering may continue to publish or distribute information, opinions, or recommendations with respect to the securities to be registered, in the regular course of its business, if all of the following conditions exist: (a) the information is contained in a publication distributed with reasonable regularity by a broker or dealer who regularly publishes research with respect to the registrant or the information is contained in a publication setting forth a comprehensive list of securities which has been distributed with reasonable regularity during the last two years; (b) the information is given no greater space or prominence than that given to other securities, and does not include projections of sales or earnings beyond the issuer's current fiscal year; and (c) an opinion as favorable or more favorable was published in the last publication addressing the subject previously distributed by the dealer.

The managing underwriter need not postpone organization of the selling group until after the registration statement has become effective, as was the case before the 1954 amendments. Indeed, the managing underwriter is expected to contact prospective members of the selling group both orally and by use of preliminary prospectuses, and get indications of interest, or even offers to buy, during the waiting period.

Information regarding issues "in registration" with the SEC is broadcast in other ways. There is a financial publication, the Investment Dealers Digest, which collects current information on issues in registration. As soon as the registration statement is filed, this publication sends a card to its subscribers describing the proposed offering. A brief notice is also published in a special section of the magazine which generally includes such information as the original SEC filing date, type of securities, proposed use of the proceeds, approximate offering price, the target date for

---

6. Form S–2 is generally available to issuers incorporated, and having their principal business, in the United States which have been reporting companies for a period of at least thirty-six months and meet certain other conditions. Form F–2 is a parallel form which is available to foreign private issuers meeting somewhat similar criteria.

the offering, and the name of the managing underwriter. Interested dealers may then contact the lead underwriter directly if they wish to be included in the selling group. Furthermore, following recommendations contained in the Wheat Report [7] the Commission issued Rule 15c2–8 under the 1934 Act to assure that issuers and managing underwriters distributed the preliminary prospectus to prospective underwriters and dealers during the waiting period.

SECURITIES ACT RELEASE NO. 4968

Securities and Exchange Commission.
April 24, 1969.

PRIOR DELIVERY OF PRELIMINARY PROSPECTUS

The Commission again called attention to the continued high volume of registration statements filed under the Securities Act of 1933, and noted that the number of companies filing registration statements for the first time continues to mount, so that well over half of the filings now being made are by such companies. The Commission emphasized that the investing public should be aware that many such offerings of securities are of a highly speculative character and that the prospectus should be carefully examined before an investment decision is reached. It is characteristic of such speculative issues that the company has been recently organized, that the promoters and other selected persons have obtained a disproportionately large number of shares for a nominal price with the consequent dilution in the assets to be contributed by the investing public, and that the underwriters receive fees and other benefits which are high in relation to the proceeds to the issuer and which further dilute the investment values being offered.

The Commission has declared its policy in Rule 460 that it will not accelerate the effective date of a registration statement unless the preliminary prospectus contained in the registration statement is distributed to underwriters and dealers who it is reasonably anticipated will be invited to participate in the distribution of the security to be offered or sold. The purpose of this requirement is to afford all persons effecting the distribution a means of being informed with respect to the offering so that they can advise their customers of the investment merits of the security. Particularly in the case of a first offering by a nonreporting company, salesmen should obtain and read the current preliminary or final prospectus before offering the security to their clients.

The Commission also announced, in the exercise of its responsibilities in accelerating the effective date of a registration statement under Section 8(a) of the Securities Act of 1933, and particularly the statutory requirement that it have due regard to the adequacy of the information respecting the issuer theretofore available to the public, that it will consider whether the persons making an offering of securities of an issuer which is not subject to the reporting requirements of Section 13 or 15(d) of the Securities Exchange Act of 1934, have taken reasonable steps to furnish preliminary prospectuses to those persons who may reasonably be expected to be

---

7. Ch. IV.

purchasers of the securities. The Commission will ordinarily be satisfied by a written statement from the managing underwriter to the effect that it has been informed by participating underwriters and dealers that copies of the preliminary prospectus complying with Rule 433(a) [the predecessor of Rule 430] have been or are being distributed to all persons to whom it is then expected to mail confirmations of sale not less than 48 hours prior to the time it is expected to mail such confirmations. Such distribution should be by air mail if the confirmations will be sent by air mail, or a longer period to compensate for the difference in the method of mailing the prospectus should be provided. Of course, if the form of preliminary prospectus so distributed was inadequate or inaccurate in material respects, acceleration will be deferred until the Commission has received satisfactory assurances that appropriate correcting material (including a memorandum of changes) has been so distributed.

In view of the situation above discussed, the Commission proposes to invoke this acceleration policy immediately. When the Commission gains sufficient experience under this policy, it anticipates proposing appropriate revision of its rules.

SECTION 4. THE POST–EFFECTIVE PERIOD

Statutes and Regulations

Securities Act, §§ 4, 5, 2(3), 2(10), 10.

Rules 153, 153A, 174; Exchange Act Rule 15c2–8; Regulation C, Rules 424, 427, 431, 463; Form SR; Regulation S–K, Items 501 and 502, particularly Item 502(e).

Uniform Commercial Code § 8–319.

PROSPECTUS REQUIREMENTS IN THE POST-EFFECTIVE PERIOD

Section 5(a) concerns the "sale" of a security; it is both prohibitive and permissive. In its prohibitive aspect, § 5(a)(1) forbids the use of interstate facilities or the mails to "sell" a security by means of a prospectus or otherwise in the pre-effective period, which embraces both the pre-filing and waiting periods. Once the registration statement in respect of a security has become effective, however, the permissive aspect of § 5(a)(1) comes into play. It is no longer illegal to make use of the mails or interstate facilities to "sell" such security, a "sale" being defined in § 2(3) to include "every contract of sale or disposition of a security * * * for value."

Section 5(b) concerns prospectuses; it must be read in conjunction with § 2(10). Section 5(b)(1) prohibits the use of the mails or interstate facilities to transmit any prospectus relating to a security with respect to which a registration statement has been filed, unless such prospectus meets the requirements of § 10. A "prospectus" is defined in § 2(10) to include every written communication which "offers any security for sale or confirms the sale of any security." The "confirmation" referred to is the slip of paper which the broker or dealer sends to the buyer to confirm the transaction and thus comply with the statute of frauds and SEC regulations.[1]

We have seen that during the waiting period only those prospectuses meeting the requirements of § 10(b) may be used for § 5(b)(1) purposes. But § 5(b)(1) is so framed as to reach past the waiting period into the post-effective period, for it encompasses the entire post-filing period. Thus, after the registration statement has become effective, a § 10(a) prospectus may then be used for § 5(b)(1) purposes, but a § 10(b) summary prospectus may also be used pursuant to Rule 431 for solicitation purposes. However, under § 5(b)(2), the delivery of the security pursuant to the sale must be accompanied or preceded by a § 10(a) prospectus.

There remains one further qualification to the prohibitions of § 5(b)(1). It will be recalled that § 2(10) defines a "prospectus" to include any written communication which "offers any security for sale or confirms the sale of any security." There is then excluded from this definition any communication sent or given after the effective date (other than a § 10(b) prospectus) if it is proved that prior to or at the same time a written prospectus meeting the requirements of § 10(a) was sent or given to the person to whom the communication was directed. Section 2(10) has the effect of eliminating duplication in the furnishing of a statutory prospectus, whether given by the same or by different persons, for there is no requirement that the § 10(a) prospectus and the later communication be sent by the same person. It should be noted, however, that this exception does not apply to the use of a § 10(b) prospectus which is sent or given prior to the effective date; in this case the offeror must itself send the § 10(b) prospectus. Moreover, where such a written communication offering a security is sent, even if it is accompanied or preceded by a § 10(b) prospectus, there is a violation; such offers during the waiting period may be made only by use of the preliminary prospectus. Finally, § 2(10) permits other selling literature to be sent to a prospective buyer *after the effective date*, so long as this communication has been preceded or is accompanied by a statutory prospectus. This "free-writing" privilege is only allowed in the post-effective period.

Supplementary sales material need not be filed with the SEC with one exception. Section 24(b) of the Investment Company Act requires all investment company sales literature directed at prospective investors to be filed with the Commission. In addition, the NASD imposes substantive standards on sales literature used by its members in certain high-risk, tax-sheltered "direct participation programs," providing for flow-through tax consequences. All such advertising must be filed with the NASD and is subject to review by any NASD District Business Conduct Committee.[2]

1. U.C.C. § 8–319; Rule 10b–10; NASD Manual (CCH) ¶ 3509; M. Mendelson & S. Robbins, Investment Analysis and Securities Markets 25–86 (1976).

2. NASD Manual (CCH) Rules of Practice, Secs. 34, 35, ¶ 2191, ¶ 2192.

The SEC has proposed adoption of Reg. § 270.24b–3 under the Investment Company Act which would specify that any investment company sales literature would be deemed filed with the Commission for § 24(d) purposes upon filing with a national securities association registered under § 15A of the 1934 Act and which has adopted standards relating to investment company advertising practices and procedures to review such advertising. Only the NASD could qualify. See SEC Securities Act Release No. 6660 (Sept. 17, 1986).

As previously indicated, § 5(a) concerns sales of a security; § 5(b) concerns prospectuses. The delivery of a security for the purpose of sale or delivery after sale is dealt with in §§ 5(a)(2) and 5(b)(2). Section 5(a)(2) provides that it is unlawful to the use of the mails or interstate facilities to transport a security for the purpose of sale or for delivery after sale, unless a registration statement is in effect as to such security. The result is to prohibit such deliveries in both the pre-filing period and during the waiting period. Since oral interstate offers to sell may be made during the waiting period, so long as no actual sale is made, § 5(a)(2) forestalls the possibility of using interstate facilities or the mails to transport a security either for the purpose of sale or for delivery after sale in the pre-effective period. Furthermore, even in the case of face-to-face transactions or intrastate sales made without the use of the mails or interstate facilities, § 5(a)(2) forbids use of these media to deliver the security following the sale.

Section 5(b)(2) provides that it is unlawful to use the mails or interstate facilities to transport a security for sale or delivery after sale, unless accompanied or preceded by a § 10(a) prospectus. Thus, even if the contract of sale has been negotiated by means of an *oral* interstate telephone call made during the post-filing period, once the registration statement has become effective, the seller may not mail a written "confirmation" of the transaction, thereby closing the deal, unless the confirmation is accompanied or preceded by a statutory prospectus. Indeed, if the negotiations are conducted face-to-face, or by intrastate or interstate telephone and no written confirmation is transmitted by the use of the mails or interstate facilities, then the security may not be mailed to the buyer unless it is accompanied (or preceded) by a statutory prospectus.[3] In that event, as Lobell has put it: "the buyer in these transactions gets his prospectus more as a memento than as a vehicle of information."[4]

For how long do these § 5(b) restrictions on the methods of making offers and sales of registered securities continue? In theory, they should continue only during the period when the securities are being distributed, as the 1933 Act is concerned with the distribution process and not with trading transactions as such. The cut-off dates when issuers, underwriters and dealers are no longer subject to § 5(b) are prescribed by § 4(3). The prospectus requirements apply to the issuer so long as it is offering any of the securities to the public. § 4(2). Under § 4(3)(C) any underwriter or dealer participating in the distribution is subject to the prospectus requirements so long as it is offering an unsold allotment. Furthermore, all underwriters and dealers must comply with the prospectus requirements during a 40-day period following the effective date of the registration statement or the commencement of the public offering, whichever occurs later, whether or not they are then engaged in a distributive transaction. Under the 1964 amendment program, however, if securities of the issuer have not previously been sold pursuant to an effective registration statement under the 1933 Act, the applicable period is extended to 90 days. § 4(3(C).

---

3. A telegraphic "offer to sell" or "confirmation of the sale," standing alone, collides with § 5(b)(1) for a telegram is a written communication and thus a "prospectus" as defined in § 2(10). See Harper v. United States, 143 F.2d 795, 801 (8th Cir. 1944).

4. Lobell, Revision of the Securities Act, 48 Colum.L.Rev. 313, 323 (1948).

At the same time, the Commission was given the power, by rule or order, to prescribe a shorter period than the 40 or 90 day periods prescribed in § 4(3) for the delivery of prospectuses by dealers. Under this authority, the Commission has issued Rule 174. Irrespective of whether the 40 or 90 day period would otherwise be applicable, dealers (including an underwriter who is no longer acting as such with respect to the security) need not deliver a prospectus to the purchaser, if the issuer was subject, prior to the filing of the registration statement, to the reporting requirements of §§ 13 or 15(d) of the 1934 Act. Moreover, the obligation of a dealer to deliver a prospectus is entirely dispensed with if the registration statement is on Form F–6 (for registration of American Depositary Receipts issued against securities of foreign issuers to be deposited with an American depositary) unless registration of the deposited securities is also required. Where a registration statement relates to offerings to be made from time to time (the so-called shelf-registration to be considered at page 198) the prospectus delivery requirements are dispensed with upon the expiration of the initial prospectus delivery period specified in § 4(3) following the first bona fide offering of the securities. Regulation S–K, Item 502(e) requires that the inside front cover page or the back cover page of the prospectus contain a legend in bold-face type alerting dealers as to their prospectus delivery obligations and the date when such obligations terminate. The dealers' exemption after such 40-day or 90-day period, as well as the brokers' exemption provision (§ 4(4)), will be considered along with other exemptions in Chapter 9.

Further complications arise in the prospectus requirements when the transaction is effected on a stock exchange or in the over-the-counter market. Is it sufficient for the seller or his broker to deliver a prospectus to the buyer's broker, even though the buyer never sees it? And is the buyer's broker bound by the prospectus requirements when he confirms or delivers the securities to the buyer by use of the channels of interstate commerce or the mails? If the buyer's broker is acting as an agent rather than as a principal, delivery of a prospectus to him should be regarded as a delivery to his principal. On the other hand, the buyer's broker may himself be under an independent duty to comply with the prospectus requirements if he has solicited the buyer to purchase the security. See Section 4(4). Rule 153 relaxes the requirements for delivery of a statutory prospectus to stock exchange members where a sale is made on a national securities exchange by permitting the delivery to the Exchange upon its request of a sufficient number of copies to comply with the requests of members; it does not apply to NASDAQ or other over-the-counter transactions. However, in Hazel Bishop Inc., 40 S.E.C. 718 (1961), involving a proposed registered secondary offering to be made through brokers on the American Stock Exchange, the Commission had this to say: "The use by Hazel Bishop [the issuer] or any other participants of written communications which offer its securities will be subject to the prohibitions of Section 5(b)(1) of the Securities Act. Consequently, any such communication would be unlawful unless it were in the form of a statutory prospectus, or the communication were accompanied by or had been preceded by a statutory prospectus. Prior delivery of prospectuses to the Exchange pursuant to Rule 153 would not satisfy this requirement of Section 5(b)(1)." [5]

5. 40 S.E.C. at 736.

Finally, although the registration statement speaks only as of the effective date, registrants, underwriters and dealers must take care to see that the statutory prospectus and any supplemental sales literature is at the time of use not false and misleading under the anti-fraud provisions of the 1933 and 1934 Acts, as may be seen from the following cases. And if the offering continues over an extended period, the prospectus should be kept current under the standards of § 10(a)(3).

DISKIN v. LOMASNEY & CO.
United States Court of Appeals, Second Circuit, 1971.
452 F.2d 871.

[Plaintiff Diskin and defendant Lomasney had conversations with respect to the securities of two companies, Ski Park City West S. I. and Continental Travel Ltd. Lomasney had agreed to sell up to 60,000 common shares of the former on a "best efforts" basis and was the principal underwriter for the sale of 350,000 common shares of the latter. A registration statement with respect to the shares of Continental had been filed with the SEC, but did not become effective until February 11, 1969. In the meantime, however, on September 17, 1968, Lomasney sent Diskin a final prospectus for Ski Park City West, as to which a registration statement had become effective, together with a letter as follows:

"I am enclosing herewith, a copy of the Prospectus on SKI PARK CITY WEST. This letter will also assure you that if you take 1,000 shares of SKI PARK CITY WEST at the issue price, we will commit to you the sale at the public offering price when, as and if issued, 5,000 shares of CONTINENTAL TRAVEL, LTD."

Diskin thereupon placed an order for the 1,000 shares of Ski Park City West, received a written confirmation, and later paid for the shares.

On February 12, 1969, after the Continental Travel registration statement had become effective, Lomasney sent Diskin a confirmation of the sale of 5,000 shares of Continental Travel at $12 per share, without any further communication. Subsequently, Diskin received from Lomasney a final prospectus for these shares. Diskin thereupon paid for the shares, and received delivery. Later, he demanded rescission, and upon refusal, he brought this action, claiming that the letter, insofar as it related to the shares of Continental Travel, was a violation of § 5(b)(1) of the 1933 Act.

The district judge dismissed the complaint on the ground that the letter relating to the Continental Travel shares came within the exclusion set forth in the last sentence of § 2(3) of the 1933 Act.

FRIENDLY, CHIEF JUDGE: * * *

We have considered whether, despite the error in dismissing the complaint on this ground, the judgment could be affirmed on the basis that a registration statement concerning the Continental Travel shares had been filed prior to September 17, 1968, although it had not yet become effective. See § 5(c). However, the mere filing of a registration statement does not ensure the legality of *any* written offer made during the post-filing, pre-effective period; to be lawful, such written offers must be made by way of a "prospectus" which meets the requirements of § 10. See § 5(b)(1). * * *

We perceive no basis for disagreeing with Professor Loss' summary of the law in this respect:

> In sum there are five legal ways in which offers may be made during the waiting period even if the mails or interstate facilities are used: by means of (1) oral communication, (2) the "tombstone ad," whether the old-fashioned variety under § 2(10)(b) or the expanded type under Rule 134 (successor to the old "identifying statement"), (3) the preliminary prospectus under Rule 433 [issued pursuant to § 10(b)] (successor to the "red herring prospectus"), (4) the "buff card" type of summary prospectus independently prepared under § 10(b) and Rule 434, and (5) the summary prospectus filed as part of the registration statement under § 10(b) and Rule 434a (successor to the old "newspaper prospectus" but not limited to newspapers).[a]

I Loss, Securities Regulation 243 (2d ed. 1961). See also Jennings & Marsh, Securities Regulation 89–92 (2d ed. 1968). The letter of September 17, 1968, was none of these. Indeed, the confirmation of February 12, 1969, was a further violation unless a prospectus had been furnished, see §§ 2(10) and 5(b)(1), which the agreed statement does not say.

We pass therefore to the arguments which defendants made in their memorandum, which the district court did not reach. These were (1) that the letter was not an "offer" but was a mere expression of willingness to sell; (2) that the violation was cured by Diskin's receipt of a prospectus prior to the actual purchase; and (3) that the action was brought more than one year after the violation and was thus untimely under § 13 of the Securities Act.

Although there is a paucity of authority on these issues, we think none constituted a valid defense. The statutory language defining "offer" in § 2(3) "goes well beyond the common law concept of an offer." I Loss, supra, at 181; cf. Carl M. Loeb, Rhoades & Co., Securities Exch. Act Release No. 5870, at 7–8 (1959) * * *. Consequently, we entertain no doubt that the portion of the letter of September 17 dealing with the Continental Travel shares constituted an "offer" within § 2(3). Moreover, whether or not a dealer can lawfully "make a conditional and revocable offer to sell [without employing any of the five established procedures] if it is made clear that the offer cannot be accepted until the effective date," see I Loss, supra, at 224, the offer of September 17 did not measure up to that standard since it was not revocable. This case, where Lomasney apparently confirmed the sale without any further word from Diskin, would be a peculiarly unattractive one for endeavoring to carve out an exception to the statutory words. Indeed, as previously indicated, the confirmation, if unaccompanied by a prospectus, was itself a violation of § 5(b)(1).

On the second point, we again agree with Professor Loss that "[w]hatever doubt there may once have been as to the applicability of § 12(1) to illegal offers [followed by legal sales] was resolved when the original definition of sale was split into separate definitions of 'sale' and 'offer' in 1954, with the incidental amendment of § 12(1) to refer to any person 'who offers or sells a security in violation of section 5' so as 'to preserve the effect of the present law' by not excluding the newly permissi-

---

a. The bracketed material was inserted by the Court. In the 1982 program integrating disclosure obligations, former Rule 433 was redesignated as Rule 430 and Rule 434 was consolidated with Rule 434a and redesignated as Rule 431.

ble pre-effective offers from liabilities under § 12." III Loss, supra, at 1695–96. With respect to the one-year period of limitation, although § 13 dates this from the "violation" in cases of claims under § 12(1), it would be unreasonable to read § 13 as starting the short period for an action at a date before the action could have been brought—a construction which might lead in some extreme cases to a running of the statute of limitations before the claim had even arisen. Furthermore, the limitation argument would be wholly drained of force if, as seems likely, the confirmation of February 12, 1968, was itself a violation.

The result here reached may appear to be harsh, since Diskin had an opportunity to read the final prospectus before he paid for the shares. But the 1954 Congress quite obviously meant to allow rescission or damages in the case of illegal offers as well as of illegal sales. Very likely Congress thought that, when it had done so much to broaden the methods for making legal offers during the "waiting period" between the filing and the taking effect of a registration statement, it should make sure that still other methods were not attempted. Here all Lomasney needed to have done was to accompany the September 17, 1968 letter with any one of the three types of prospectus for the Continental shares mentioned in the extract we have quoted from Professor Loss' treatise.[b] Very likely Congress thought a better time for meaningful prospectus reading was at the time of the offer rather than in the context of confirmation and demand for payment. In any event, it made altogether clear that an offeror of a security who had failed to follow one of the allowed paths could not achieve absolution simply by returning to the road of virtue before receiving payment.

The judgment dismissing the complaint is reversed, with instructions to enter judgment for the plaintiff that, upon delivery of 5,000 shares of Continental Travel, Ltd., he shall receive $60,000 with interest from February 28, 1969, and costs.[c]

BYRNES v. FAULKNER, DAWKINS & SULLIVAN

United States Court of Appeals, Second Circuit, 1977.
550 F.2d 1303.

Before MEDINA, HAYS [*] and OAKES, CIRCUIT JUDGES.

OAKES, CIRCUIT JUDGE:

These appeals are by would-be sellers of stock from decisions granting one buyer judgment on its "second affirmative defense" to the sellers' suit for breach of contract and dismissing claims against a secondary buyer for lack of subject matter jurisdiction. * * * The principal issue on appeal is whether the * * * District Court * * * correctly upheld the affirmative defense of the appellee-buyer, a broker-dealer, that the contract for sale of stock was unenforceable because the written "comparison" sent to it by appellant sellers' agent constituted a prospectus as defined in Section 2(10) of the Securities Act * * *, did not contain the informa-

---

b. Do you agree with this statement? Suppose Lomasney had enclosed a Rule 430 preliminary prospectus with the letter. Would there be a violation of § 5(b)(1)?

c. Note, A Critique of the Delayed Offer Concept of Section 2(3) of the Securities Act of 1933 in the Light of Diskin v. Lomasney & Co., 21 J.Pub.L. 433 (1972).

* Judge Hays, owing to illness, has not formally concurred in this opinion, but we believe him to agree with the result reached.

tion required of a prospectus by Section 10 of that Act, and was therefore unlawful under Section 5(b)(1) * * *. We affirm the judgments.

Facts

Insofar as here relevant, the facts were stipulated below and are not in dispute. Byrnes, Santangelo, and their associates (hereinafter sellers or appellants) were the owners of 148,000 shares of stock of White Shield Corp. on and after September 6, 1968. This stock had been acquired from certain officers or directors of White Shield. It was not registered under the 1933 Act and therefore could not readily be sold, but appellants had acquired the right to include the stock in a registration statement filed at some future time under the Act.

In 1971 White Shield filed several registration statements under the Act. Appellants' stock was included in one that was a so-called "shelf registration" or "shelf secondary," that is, a registration statement filed on behalf of certain named owners of theretofore unregistered shares who, the statement indicates, could then sell the stock in the open market "from time to time," generally through member firms of the National Association of Securities Dealers, Inc. (NASD). The prospectus offering for sale appellants' shares and those of some 25 other selling shareholders bears the same date that the registration statement * * * "became effective": June 7, 1971. Just before June 7, appellants arranged with Tobey & Kirk, a securities broker-dealer registered with the SEC and a member firm of the NASD, to sell their stock when the registration statement became effective, and appellants delivered to Tobey & Kirk copies of a preliminary or "red herring" prospectus.

On June 7, 1971, Tobey & Kirk agreed to sell to Faulkner, Dawkins & Sullivan (hereinafter Faulkner, buyer, or appellee), at a price of $14 per share, 44,000 shares of the White Shield stock owned by appellants and included in the White Shield registration statement. At that time Faulkner was a "market-maker"[1] in White Shield stock and regularly entered bid and asked quotations in the "Pink Sheets" of the National Quotation Bureau, Inc., and in NASDAQ, the automated quotation system of the NASD. On or about June 7, 1971, Faulkner sent a written "comparison" or confirmation of the purchase to Tobey & Kirk, showing that Faulkner was a market-maker in White Shield stock, and Tobey & Kirk on the same day sent a written comparison of the sale to Faulkner. This latter comparison did not show that the stock was part of a registered distribution, and it was not preceded or accompanied by a prospectus.

Only with delivery of the stock certificates themselves on June 15, 1971, did Tobey & Kirk deliver a prospectus to Faulkner. At that time Faulkner rejected the securities and informed Tobey & Kirk that the transaction was illegal.[2] The prospectus identified the selling shareholders and said that both they and the participating members of the NASD who rendered

---

1. The term "market-maker" refers to a broker-dealer who, with respect to a particular security that is not traded on a national securities exchange (an "over-the-counter" security), "report[s] for quotation 'bid' and 'asked' prices to indicate, respectively, amounts for which it propose[s] to buy or sell the stock." * * *

2. The apparent reason for Faulkner's refusal was that it was only when the prospectus information was received that Faulkner found out that the stock it had just agreed to purchase was part of a registered secondary distribution. Because Faulkner made a market in White Shield, such a purchase was of doubtful legality.

assistance to them in connection with the sale "may be deemed to be underwriters as that term is defined in the [1933 Act]."

In respect to the counterclaim here in suit, on June 7, 1971, following the agreement with Tobey & Kirk, Faulkner agreed to sell to Singer & Mackie, Inc., a broker-dealer, 15,000 shares of White Shield at $14\frac{1}{8}$ per share for a markup of $1,875, the amount sought as compensatory damages by Faulkner in the counterclaim. That trade was cancelled without penalty when Faulkner rejected the securities proffered by Tobey & Kirk.

Appellants subsequently resold the rejected White Shield stock in the open market for considerably less than the $14 per share purchase price of the June 7, 1971, agreement. They then brought suit in the Supreme Court of New York County, alleging breach of contract and repudiation without just cause. In that suit Faulkner's answer asserted nine affirmative defenses, three alleging violations of the 1933 Act, three alleging violations of the Securities and Exchange Act of 1934, and three, relating primarily to the amount of damages, invoking state law or NASD regulations relative to resales. Appellants then filed an action in the United States District Court, seeking a declaratory judgment that the federal defenses to the state court suit were insufficient as a matter of law, but seeking no damages; the parties agreed to stay the state action pending the federal court decision. In federal court Faulkner reasserted the same nine defenses it had asserted in state court and added three counterclaims, the first for a declaratory judgment of the sufficiency of the defenses, the second charging a violation of SEC Rule 10b–6 and seeking compensatory and punitive damages, and the third charging a violation of Rule 10b–5 and seeking the identical compensatory and punitive damages. [The district court] dismissed the federal action brought by appellants for lack of subject matter jurisdiction but found that federal jurisdiction did exist over the counterclaims asserted by Faulkner under Section 17 of the 1933 Act and Section 10 of the Securities Exchange Act of 1934. [The court thereupon] granted appellants leave to answer the counterclaims and to assert as their own counterclaims the breach of contract claims that formed the basis for the original suit; the judge did so on the basis that they were cognizable in federal court as compulsory counterclaims under Fed.R.Civ.P. 13(a), a conclusion not challenged here. Thus, in the peculiar procedural posture of this case, appellants' "counterclaims" really restate their original claims as plaintiffs in federal court. The action was then heard by Judge Werker, who issued the substantive judgment appealed from here, following upon an agreed statement of certain facts and affidavits supporting cross motions for summary judgment.

The Affirmative Defense

Faulkner's "second affirmative defense," on which it prevailed by summary judgment below, was that its contract with appellants should not be enforced because Section 5(b)(1) of the 1933 Act was violated. The violation was a result, the defense runs, of Tobey & Kirk's omission to disclose the information that the Act requires to be in a prospectus when Tobey & Kirk sent its "comparison" to Faulkner. Section 5(b)(1) makes it "unlawful for

---

Compare In re Jaffee & Co., [1969–1970 Transfer Binder] Fed.Sec.L.Rep. (CCH) ¶ 77,805 (SEC 1970), with In re Collins Securities Corp., [1975–1976 Transfer Binder] Fed.Sec.L.Rep. (CCH) ¶ 80,327 (SEC 1975); see H. Bloomenthal, Securities and Federal Corporate Law § 6.17 (1975).

any person, directly or indirectly to make use of any means * * * of * * * communication in interstate commerce * * * to carry or transmit any prospectus relating to any security with respect to which a registration statement has been filed * * * unless such prospectus meets the requirements of [Section 10 of the Act]." Section 10 essentially requires the prospectus, or selling circular, to contain or be accompanied by a document that includes the information found in the registration statement itself. It is conceded that Tobey & Kirk's comparison did not satisfy the requirements of Section 10.

Appellants' first response is based upon their reading of Section 2(10) of the 1933 Act which states, however, that "unless the context otherwise requires * * * [t]he term 'prospectus' means any prospectus, notice, circular, advertisement, letter, or communication * * * which offers any security for sale *or confirms the sale of any security* * * *" (emphasis added). Appellants admit, as they must, that their comparison falls within the literal terms of Section 2(10), but they argue, relying on the caveat "unless the context otherwise requires," that a comparison should not be deemed a prospectus in the context of an interbroker confirmation. They do recognize, however, that the party seeking to avoid the explicit language of the statute has the burden of proof. * * *

Appellants direct us to the history of Section 2(10), pointing out that its original language did not specifically mention confirmations. In 1941, however, the SEC's general counsel issued an opinion to the effect that the term "prospectus" included "within its meaning an ordinary confirmation," as well as "every kind of written communication * * * which constitutes a contract of sale or disposition of a security for value." Securities Act Release No. 2623 (1941), * * * (1946). A 1954 statutory amendment incorporated this opinion in substance into the language of Section 2(10) of the 1933 Act as quoted above * * *.

Appellants attempt to avoid this consistent and straightforward history with an elaborate argument, set out in the margin,[4] directed at showing,

---

4. Appellants argue that each of the general counsel's answers to the eleven hypothetical questions making up the bulk of his 1941 opinion, Securities Act Release No. 2623 (1941) can be explained by reference to specific provisions of the 1933 Act exempting transactions from the prospectus-delivery requirements of Section 5. * * * Question and Answer 6, which state that prospectus requirements do not apply to purchase transactions executed by a broker upon the unsolicited instructions of his customer, are explained, appellants say, by Section 4(4) of the Act which exempts unsolicited brokers' transactions from Section 5's provisions. Similarly, in Question and Answer 7, involving an unsolicited sell order given by the customer to his broker, it is stated that the broker need not send a prospectus along with the confirmation of the sale.

Question and Answer 8, on which appellants most heavily rely, we reprint in full:

Question 8. Pursuant to the sell order received in Question 7, John Doe [the

broker] sells [his customer] Richard Roe's warrants to Henry Hoe, another dealer, who purchases for his own account. Must John Doe, in confirming the sale to Henry Hoe, or in delivering the warrants to him, send him a copy of the prospectus?

Answer. No. John Doe, in making the sale, is completing the execution of an unsolicited brokerage order, and therefore is exempt from the prospectus requirements. * * *

Question 9 in the 1941 opinion assumes that a broker solicits a sell order from his customer, and the answer holds that no prospectus need be delivered to the customer with the solicitation, since the broker is offering to sell for, not to, the customer. Question 10 assumes the facts of Question 9 and that the customer gives the sell order to his broker, who in turn sells the rights to a purchasing dealer. The answer to Question 10 was that the transaction, although on a brokerage basis, results from a solicitation, and consequently the pro-

through the language of the general counsel's 1941 opinion, that since a prospectus was not meant to be delivered in an inter-broker comparison situation, the confirmation is not a prospectus. To a degree, this argument confuses the definition of a prospectus with the exemptions from the prospectus delivery requirement, which will be discussed infra. On the definition of a prospectus, however, the general counsel's opinion is quite explicit. It states that *any* confirmation is a prospectus, a conclusion adopted in the 1954 statutory amendment. The general counsel's opinion, in discussing situations in which the 1933 Act provides exemptions from the prospectus delivery requirements, does have its opaque moments, see note 4 supra, but none are sufficient to help appellants meet their burden of overcoming the statutory language.

Nor is In re Collins Securities Corp., [1975–76 Transfer Binder] Fed.Sec.L.Rep. (CCH) ¶ 80,327 (SEC 1975), of any help to appellants. The SEC there held only that the Pink Sheets themselves are not prospectuses under Section 2(10) and hence do not have to contain all the information required of a prospectus to avoid a violation of Section 5, *Collins* holds, and we agree, that Section 2(10) need not literally apply if reason indicates otherwise. There the Commission was faced with the practical difficulties that would ensue if Pink Sheets were treated as prospectuses.[a] It was the perfect illustration of a situation in which "the context" required Section 2(10) not to be read literally. A sale by an underwriter through a broker to a broker-dealer is quite different. Here, the only consequence of our decision will be that the selling broker will have to accompany his first written communication to the purchasing broker with a Section 10(a) prospectus. This requirement accords with the congressional vision of the prospectus as a document to be read by the would-be purchaser before the sale becomes legally binding. See Diskin v. Lomasney & Co., 452 F.2d 871, 876 (2d Cir. 1971). Since sellers' confirmations can meet statute of frauds requirements if the purchaser does not send written objections within ten days after receipt, U.C.C. § 8–319(c), the time of delivery of the confirmation is the logical time for delivery of the prospectus.

While we therefore hold that a comparison is a prospectus for purposes of the 1933 Act, this holding is not the end of our inquiry. Section 4 of the Act provides exemptions from the prospectus delivery requirements for specified types of transactions, and appellants assert that the transaction at issue here was exempt. * * * [H]owever, we find that none of the Section 4 exemptions is applicable here.

Section 4(1) exempts "transactions by any person other than an issuer, underwriter, or dealer." While appellants argue that Tobey & Kirk was not one of these, Tobey & Kirk concededly was registered as a securities broker-dealer with the Securities and Exchange Commission and was a member firm of the NASD. "Dealer" is defined in Section 2(12) to include "any person who engages either for all or part of his time, directly or

---

spectus requirements are applicable to the broker-to-dealer sale. Appellants conclude that Answer No. 10 is wrong.

a. The "Pink Sheets" were a nat.onal daily quotation service published by the National Quotation Bureau, Inc., and disseminated among broker-dealers. It was widely used prior to the advent of NAS-

DAQ. The sheets listed the stocks traded over counter, set forth the names of the broker-dealers making markets in the stock and their wholesale or "inside" quotations. These were only available to other broker-dealers. See SEC, Report of Special Study of Securities Markets, pt. 2, at 595–610 (1963).

indirectly, as agent, broker, or principal, in the business of offering, buying, selling, or otherwise dealing or trading in securities issued by another person." Clearly Tobey & Kirk was a dealer, * * * if not also an underwriter. * * *

Section 4(2) is inapplicable on its face; it exempts "transactions by an issuer not involving any public offering." Section 4(3) exempts the usual transaction by a dealer, but not, *inter alia*, those which take place prior to the expiration of 40 days from the date the relevant registration statement becomes effective. Here, because the transaction occurred within that 40-day period, Section 4(3) does not provide an exemption.

Appellants might draw most comfort from Section 4(4), which exempts "brokers' transactions executed upon customers' orders on any exchange or in the over-the-counter market but not the solicitation of such orders," but we hold that it too is inapplicable to this sale. Appellants were themselves distributing stock in a registered offering, which makes their position quite different from that of the broker in Question No. 8 of the 1941 general counsel's opinion, on which appellants rely, see note 4 supra. As distributors of newly registered stock, appellants were subject to the requirements of Section 5 of the Securities Act, regardless whether their broker was an underwriter. See United States v. Wolfson, 405 F.2d 779, 782–83 (2d Cir. 1968), cert. denied, 394 U.S. 946 (1969). The definition of underwriter in Section 2(11) includes one who "participates or has a direct or indirect participation in any [distribution of any security by an issuer], or participates or has a participation in the direct or indirect underwriting of any such undertaking." Appellants and their associates arranged to have their stock included in one of the White Shield registration statements and were identified as putative underwriters in the White Shield prospectus. Appellants therefore became participants in the White Shield distribution and accordingly became underwriters. * * * As underwriters, appellants have no basis for arguing that they should be relieved of the consequences of Tobey & Kirk's failure to deliver a prospectus.

* * *

Appellants further suggest that a market-maker who is publishing his offers to purchase may be presumed to have a prospectus. * * * While this argument might be persuasive with regard to shares as to which a registration statement had previously become effective, or as to shares sold on an exchange where SEC Rule 153 would require that an adequate number of copies of the prospectus be available, * * * rather than over the counter as here, it does not persuade us in the instant case. Here a registration statement was filed and became effective only on the date of the over-the-counter sale. * * *

* * *

Finally, appellants argue that, even if there has been a violation of the 1933 Act, their contract with Faulkner is still enforceable. While a contract that violates the Act may not be voided if to do so would hinder the purposes of the Act, A. C. Frost & Co. v. Coeur d'Alene Mines Corp., 312 U.S. 38, 43 (1941), it is certainly voidable when the purposes of the Act are thereby furthered, Kaiser-Frazer Corp. v. Otis & Co., 195 F.2d 838, 843–44 (2d Cir.) (A. Hand, J.) (in sale by issuer to underwriters as initial step in public offering of securities, contract voided because of misleading statement in the prospectus), cert. denied, 344 U.S. 856 (1952). * * * Since Section 12(1) of the 1933 Act, gives an absolute right of rescission to an innocent purchaser of securities offered or sold in violation of the prospectus requirements, it would be anomalous to require that a buyer pay on a contract that violated those requirements and then sue under Section 12(1) to have his money returned. 3 L. Loss, supra at 1797–98 (1961); Note, Enforceability of Underwriting Contracts Illegal Under the Securities Act of 1933, 73 Harv.L.Rev. 1345, 1354 (1960). Since a violation of the prospectus requirements by Tobey & Kirk has been made out, therefore, Faulkner's contract with appellants is unenforceable.

The Counterclaims

Faulkner's counterclaims for $1,875 compensatory damages (the lost profits on the cancelled resale to Singer & Mackie, Inc.) and $1,000,000 punitive damages, at issue on the cross-appeal, were properly dismissed. Wholly apart from the merits of alleged wrongdoing, Faulkner sustained no damages cognizable under either SEC Rule 10b–6 (the Second Counterclaim) or Rule 10b–5 (the Third Counterclaim). Section 28(a) of the Securities Exchange Act of 1934, the Act under which the two rules were promulgated, denies recovery to a complainant for any amount "in excess of his actual damages on account of the act complained of." * * * This section on its face precludes recovery of punitive damages. * * * As to the loss of anticipated profits, whether or not such a loss is recoverable as an item of consequential damages, * * * it must be remembered that the sum of $1,875 was the spread on the sale of 20,000 shares out of 44,000 contracted to be bought. At no time after the cancellations on June 15, 1971, it was stipulated, was the market price of White Shield above $14 per share. If, as Faulkner's brief states, the price had declined from $14 to $12.34 at the settlement date, the loss on the unsold shares would have been $39,840, substantially offsetting the anticipated gain. Thus, far from suffering a proximate loss from the acts of appellants, * * *, Faulkner was benefited overall by them. For damages purposes under the Exchange Act, the transaction cannot be fractionated, since otherwise "actual damages on account of the act complained of" would be exceeded. * * *

Nor are the damage claims recoverable under the allegedly pendent state claim for common law fraud or a violation of New York General Business Law § 352–c. * * * [A]ny "fraud" with which appellants could be charged here would not qualify for an exemplary recovery under New York law, since the violation of Rule 10b–6 or 10b–5 is not alleged to go beyond ordinary fraud, for which punitive damages do not lie * * *.

* * *

Judgments affirmed.

———

SECURITIES AND EXCHANGE COMMISSION v. MANOR NURSING CENTERS, INC.

United States Court of Appeals, Second Circuit, 1972.
458 F.2d 1082.

[The SEC brought this action pursuant to § 22(a) of the 1933 Act, and § 27 of the 1934 Act. The complaint alleged violations of § 17(a) of the 1933 Act, and of § 10(b) and rule 10b–5 of the 1934 Act; it also alleged violation of the prospectus-delivery requirement of § 5(b)(2) of the 1933 Act.

The case stemmed from a primary offering of 350,000 shares and a secondary offering of 100,000 shares of Manor Nursing Centers, which were to be offered and sold by the underwriter on an "all or nothing" basis. This meant, according to the prospectus, that unless all of the 450,000 shares were sold and paid for within 60 days the offering would terminate and all funds would be returned, with interest, to the subscribers. The subscribers' funds were to be held "in escrow" by a designated bank and were not to be available for other use until the terms of the offering were met.

The district judge, after trial, concluded that the defendants had violated the antifraud provisions of the 1933 and 1934 Acts and the prospectus-delivery requirement of the 1933 Act. The Court permanently enjoined certain of the defendants; ordered them to disgorge any proceeds, profits and income received in connection with the sale of the common stock of Manor Nursing Centers; appointed a trustee to receive these funds and to reimburse the defrauded public investors; and ordered a freeze on the assets of all defendants until they had transferred to the trustee the proceeds received from the sale. Defendants appealed.]

TIMBERS, CIRCUIT JUDGE: * * *

The conduct of appellants in connection with the public offering of Manor shares, upon analysis, demonstrates beyond a peradventure of a doubt that they violated the antifraud provisions of the federal securities laws—§ 17(a) of the 1933 Act and § 10(b) of the 1934 Act.

The gravamen of this case is that each of the appellants participated in a continuing course of conduct whereby public investors were fraudulently induced to part with their money in the expectation that Manor and the selling stockholders would return the money if all Manor shares were not sold and all the proceeds from the sale were not received by March 8, 1970. It is undisputed that, as of March 8, Manor and the selling stockholders had not sold all the 450,000 shares and that all the proceeds expected from the sale had not been received. Moreover, it is clear that all appellants knew, or should have known, that the preconditions for their retaining the proceeds of the offering had not been satisfied. Nevertheless, rather than complying with the terms of the offering by returning the funds of public investors, appellants retained these funds for their own financial benefit.
* * *

All appellants also violated § 10(b) of the 1934 Act and Rule 10b–9 promulgated thereunder by making a misrepresentation with respect to the terms of an "all or nothing" offering. Recognizing the great potential for fraudulent conduct on the part of persons in connection with public offerings of securities on an "all or nothing" basis, the SEC in 1962 adopted Rule 10b–9, which provides in relevant part:

"It shall constitute a 'manipulative or deceptive device or contrivance,' * * * to make any representation:

(1) to the effect that the security is being offered or sold on an 'all-or-none' basis, unless the security is part of an offering or distribution being made on the condition that all or a specified amount of the consideration paid for such security will be promptly refunded to the purchaser unless (A) all of the securities being offered are sold at a specified price within a specified time, and (B) the total amount due to the seller is received by him by a specified date. * * * "

Here, it is clear, that all appellants knew that the offering was presented on an "all or nothing" basis. Moreover, the evidence established that appellants knew, or should have known, that all of the shares had not been sold and that all of the proceeds had not been received by March 8, 1970. Under the circumstances, there can be no doubt that representing that the offering would be on an "all or nothing" basis violated Rule 10b–9.

It also is clear that appellants violated the antifraud provisions of the federal securities laws by offering Manor shares when they knew, or should have known, that the Manor prospectus was misleading in several material respects. After the registration statement became effective on December 8, 1969, at least four developments occurred which made the prospectus misleading: the public's funds were not returned even though the issue was not fully subscribed; an escrow account for the proceeds of the offering was not established; shares were issued for consideration other than cash; and certain individuals received extra compensation for agreeing to participate in the offering. These developments were not disclosed to the public investors. That these developments occurred after the effective date of the registration statement did not provide a license to appellants to ignore them. Post-effective developments which materially alter the picture presented in the registration statement must be brought to the attention of public investors.[14] "The effect of the antifraud provisions of the Securities Act (§ 17(a)) and of the Exchange Act (§ 10(b) and Rule 10b–5) is to require the prospectus to reflect any post-effective changes necessary to keep the prospectus from being misleading in any material respect * * *."

III. *Violations of Prospectus-Delivery Requirement of 1933 Act*

In addition to concluding that appellants had violated the antifraud provisions of the federal securities laws, the district court also correctly held that they had violated the prospectus-delivery requirement of § 5(b)(2) of the 1933 Act.

Section 5(b)(2) prohibits the delivery of a security for the purpose of sale unless the security is accompanied or preceded by a prospectus which meets the requirements of § 10(a) of the 1933 Act * * *. To meet the requirements of § 10(a), a prospectus must contain, with specified exceptions, all "the information contained in the registration statement * * *." In turn, the registration statement, pursuant to § 7 of the 1933 Act must set forth certain information specified in Schedule A of the 1933 Act. Among the items of information which Schedule A requires the registration statement, and therefore the prospectus, to contain are the use of proceeds (item 13), the estimated net proceeds (item 15), the price at which the security will be offered to the public and any variation therefrom (item 16), and all commissions or discounts paid to underwriters, directly or indirectly (item 17).

The Manor prospectus purported to disclose the information required by the above items of Schedule A. The evidence adduced at trial showed, however, that developments subsequent to the effective date of the registration statement made this information false and misleading. Moreover,

---

14. "The way the new facts * * * are brought to the attention of offerees as a matter of mechanics is by putting a sticker on the prospectus or supplementing it otherwise, not by amending the registration statement." 1 Loss, Securities Regulation 293 (2d ed. 1961, Supp.1969). See 17 C.F.R. § 230.424(c) (1971).

Manor and its principals did not amend or supplement the prospectus to reflect the changes which had made inaccurate the information which § 10(a) required the prospectus to disclose. We hold that implicit in the statutory provision that the prospectus contain certain information is the requirement that such information be true and correct. * * *. A prospectus does not meet the requirements of § 10(a), therefore, if information required to be disclosed is materially false or misleading. Appellants violated § 5(b)(2) by delivering Manor securities for sale accompanied by a prospectus which did not meet the requirements of § 10(a) in that the prospectus contained materially false and misleading statements with respect to information required by § 10(a) to be disclosed.

Manor contends, however, that § 5(b)(2) does not require that a prospectus be amended to reflect material developments which occur subsequent to the effective date of the registration statement. This contention is premised on the assumptions that the prospectus spoke only as of the effective date of the registration statement and that the prospectus contained no false or misleading statements as of the effective date—December 8, 1969. Assuming the Manor prospectus was accurate as of December 8, 1969, appellants' claim is without merit.

In support of their argument that the prospectus need not be amended or supplemented to reflect post-effective developments, appellants cite an administrative decision in which the SEC held that it will not issue a stop order with respect to a registration statement which becomes misleading subsequent to its effective date because of material post-effective events. Funeral Directors Manufacturing and Supply Co., 39 S.E.C. 33, 34 (1959). * * * Under this line of SEC decisions, a registration statement need not be amended after its effective date to reflect post-effective developments.[23] These decisions, however, are not apposite here. Assuming that the registration statement does speak as of its effective date and that Manor did not have to amend its registration statement,[24] appellants were obliged to reflect the post-effective developments referred to above in the prospectus. Even those SEC decisions holding that the registration statement need not be amended to reflect post-effective developments recognize that the prospectus must be amended or supplemented in some manner to reflect such changes. * * *. In addition, as noted above * * *, the

---

23. The SEC has held that in some situations it may be necessary to amend the registration statement to reflect post-effective changes. As noted in * * * note 14, post-effective developments generally are brought to the attention of offerees by putting a sticker on the prospectus or otherwise supplementing it. * * * We do not reach the question whether merely supplementing the prospectus would have been adequate in the instant case.

24. As to what date the registration statement speaks, there appears to be some ambiguity in the statute. Section 11 of the 1933 Act imposes civil liability on the issuer and other persons "[i]n case any part of the registration statement, when such part became effective, contained an untrue statement * * *". On the other hand, Section 8(d) of the 1933 Act authorizes a

stop order "[i]f it appears to the Commission *at any time* that the registration statement includes any untrue statement * * *." (Emphasis added). The House Report supports the view that the SEC can require the issuer to amend the registration statement to reflect post-effective developments:

"In determining whether a stop order should issue, the Commission will naturally have regard to the facts as they then exist and will stop the further sale of securities, even though the registration statement was true when made, [and] it has become untrue or misleading by reason of subsequent developments." H.R.Rep.No.85, 73d Cong., 1st Sess. 20 (1933).

* * *

effect of the antifraud provisions of the 1933 and 1934 Acts is to require that the prospectus reflect post-effective developments which make the prospectus misleading in any material respect. There is no authority for the proposition that a prospectus speaks always as of the effective date of the registration statement.

We hold that appellants were under a duty to amend or supplement the Manor prospectus to reflect post-effective developments; that their failure to do so stripped the Manor prospectus of compliance with § 10(a); and that appellants therefore violated § 5(b)(2).[a]

[The judgment of the district court was affirmed except that portion ordering disgorgement of the profits and income earned on the proceeds of the offering; as to this, the Court reversed and remanded for modification in accordance with its opinion.]

a. Note, Truth up to the Date of Use as a Requirement for a Section 10(a) Prospectus: The Implications of SEC v. Manor Nursing Centers, Inc., 24 Case W.Res.L.Rev. 771 (1973); Note, Prospectus Liability for Failure to Disclose Post-Effective Developments: A New Duty and its Implications, 48 Ind.L.J. 464 (1973).

Was the court in Manor Nursing Centers correct in holding that a defective prospectus that did not meet the requirements of § 10 violated § 5(b)(2)? In a civil action for damages under §§ 11 or 12, should defendant be deprived of his or her defenses relating to plaintiff's knowledge or defendant's conduct? In SEC v. Blazon Corp., 609 F.2d 960, 968–69 (9th Cir. 1979), the court held that the filing of defective Regu-

lation A materials did not result in an "automatic loss of the Reg. A exemption" and thus constitute a violation of § 5. Accord, SEC v. Southwest Coal & Energy Co., 624 F.2d 1312 (5th Cir. 1980). On the other hand, in Jefferies & Co. v. Arkus-Duntov, 357 F.Supp. 1206, 1214–15 (S.D.N.Y.1973), the court held that a defective prospectus that did not meet the requirements of § 5 would give rise to a § 12(1) action based upon a violation of § 5, thereby depriving the defendant of its defenses under § 11 and § 12(2). A.L.I. Fed.Sec.Code § 1702(f) specifically rejects the novel result reached in Jeffries, which Professor Loss, the Reporter, views as "erroneously" decided.

Chapter 3

THE REGISTRATION PROCESS

Statutes and Regulations

Exchange Act Registration and Reporting Requirements

A. Registration: 12(a), 12(b), 12(g), Rule 12g–1, Form 10, Regulation S–K, Items 702, 510, 512(i).

B. Reports: 13, 14, 15(d), Regulation 12B, Rules 14a–3, 14c–3.

SECTION 1. THE SEC'S INTEGRATED DISCLOSURE SYSTEM

DISCLOSURE OBLIGATIONS UNDER THE EXCHANGE ACT AND SECURITIES ACT

a. *Exchange Act Registration and Reporting Requirements.* Originally two separate and distinct disclosure systems were established under the federal securities laws, one applicable to the Securities Act of 1933, the other to the Securities Exchange Act of 1934. The reasons for this dual disclosure system was rooted in the fact that the two statutes were supposedly designed to fulfill different needs. The Securities Act regulates public offerings of securities under a regime of full disclosure. However, the 1933 Act disclosure obligations were never triggered except when an issuer resorted to the public markets to sell its securities. The 1934 Act regulated the trading markets for securities. Disclosure obligations depended upon the issuer's status; disclosure was triggered only with respect to (1) issuers with a class of securities listed and traded on an exchange; (2) issuers having total assets exceeding $1 (now $5) million and a class of equity securities held of record by 500 or more persons (Section 12(g)(1) companies); and (3) issuers with outstanding securities sold pursuant to a 1933 Act registration (Section 15(d) companies). Under the 1934 Act, the disclosure obligations were mandated under the Sections 12 and 13 periodic reporting requirements, the Section 14 proxy rules, and the Rule 14a–3 requirement that an annual report be sent to shareholders.

This dual system spawned separate sets of registration statements, periodic reports, and proxy rules, each with its own set of instructions. The 1933 Act disclosure documents were designed primarily for companies going public for the first time. They were comprehensive documents, disclosing all material financial and non-financial information. This approach could be justified in the case of first-time 1933 Act registrants, since material information was disclosed which was not previously available. However, 1934 Act reporting companies were required to repeat company specific information already on file with the Commission or publicly available through the distribution of annual reports or proxy statements. Thus, the same financial or other information would find its way into a 1933 Act registration statement, a 1934 Act filed document (e.g. a Form 10–K Annual Report) or in a Rule 14a–3 annual report to shareholders.

Not only was the material duplicative; it was different in form and content. The financial statements included in an annual report to shareholders needed only to conform to generally accepted accounting principles (GAAP). The financials in 1933 Act registration statements and in Form 10–K's and other Exchange Act filed documents had to conform to the more stringent standards of Regulation S–X, mandating the form and content of financial statements. Again, the same type of non-financial information might be mandated in a 1933 Act or 1934 Act filed document or under the proxy rules, but a different set of instructions was applicable, frequently containing inconsistencies in form and content.

(b) Integrated Disclosure under the 1933 and 1934 Acts. The Commission instituted the integration program in order to achieve a more uniform, simplified and integrated disclosure system under the 1933 and 1934 Acts "so that investors and the marketplace are provided meaningful, non-duplicative information periodically, and when securities are sold to the public, while the costs of compliance for public companies are decreased." [1]

A first step was taken in 1977, by the adoption of Regulation S–K prescribing a single standard set of instructions for filing forms under the Securities Act and the Exchange Act. Thus, when the same type of information is mandated in the various forms under either Act, a single set of instructions applies.

More drastic surgery was performed in January, 1980 with the adoption of sweeping revisions of Form 10–K (the annual report which up-dates Form 10), Rule 14a–3 (prescribing the annual report to shareholders under the proxy rules), Regulation S–X, and the adoption of Regulation S–K (prescribing instructions for filings under the 1933 and 1934 Acts). The effect of these amendments is to prescribe uniform financial disclosure requirements for virtually all documents required to be filed under either the 1933 or 1934 Acts. This has been accomplished by mandating that the audited financial statements that must be included in annual reports to shareholders of 1934 Act reporting companies must now comply with the requirements of Regulation S–X. Moreover, Regulation S–X was amended to eliminate most of the differences between the requirements of generally accepted accounting principles and those of Regulation S–X. Under the new regime, financial disclosures need only include the basic disclosures required under GAAP (as prescribed by the pronouncements of the Financial Accounting Standards Board, and the pronouncements of predecessor bodies) and a few additional disclosures not required under GAAP that the Commission regards as essential.

The Commission explained this phase in the establishment of the SEC integrated disclosure system in the release announcing these changes. [2]

* * *

The Commission today is adopting and proposing major changes in the Securities Act and Exchange Act disclosure systems. These changes are designed to improve the disclosure made to investors and other users of financial information, to facilitate the integration of the two disclosure systems into the single disclosure system long advocated by many commentators, [3] and to reduce current impediments to combining informal security

1. Securities Act Release No. 6235 (Sept. 2, 1980), 20 SEC Dock. 1175, at 1177.

2. Securities Act Release No. 6231 (Sept. 2, 1980).

3. See generally Cohen, "Truth in Securities" Revisited, 79 Harv.L.Rev. 1340 (1968); SEC, Disclosure to Investors (Wheat Report) (1969); Report of the Advisory Committee on Corporate Disclosure to the Securities and Exchange Commission, Committee Print 95–29, House Committee on Interstate and Foreign Commerce 95th Cong., 1st Sess., November 3, 1977 ("Advisory Committee").

holder communications, such as annual reports to security holders, with official Commission filings.

* * *

The Commission's review of the purpose and utility of the Form 10–K led it to believe that there is a basic information package which most, if not all, investors expect to be furnished. Further, it has become apparent that this basic information package, which in the context of Form 10–K developed to support the current information requirements of an active trading market, is virtually identical to the similar information package independently developed in connection with the registration and sale of newly issued shares under the Securities Act. The essential content of these Form 10–K and registration statement information packages includes audited financial statements, a summary of selected financial data appropriate for trend analysis, and a meaningful description of the registrant's business and financial condition.

The restructured Form 10–K which the Commission is adopting today is specifically designed to segregate the basic information package contained in that Form from proxy related or supplemental information. In this regard, the new Form 10–K is structured in four parts. The first part retains the detailed disclosure requirements relating to business, properties, legal proceedings and beneficial ownership. Much of this information, which in the past has been required primarily in Securities Act filings and not in annual reports to security holders, has been placed in a supplemental role. The second part consists of the basic disclosure package which is common to both Securities Act and Exchange Act filings. The third part consists of the traditional proxy disclosure information relating to directors and executive officers and management remuneration. Finally, the fourth part contains requirements for financial statement schedules and * * * scaled-down requirements for exhibits.

* * *

[The] Commission [has also] amended Rules 14a–3 and 14c–3 to require that annual reports to security holders contain a variety of information, including certified financial statements, a summary of operations, a management analysis, a brief description of the issuer's business, a lines of business breakdown, an identification of the issuer's directors and executive officers, and an identification of the principal market in which the securities entitled to vote were traded.
* * *

The next phase in the evolution of integrated disclosure entailed the SEC's effort to simplify and streamline the disclosure requirements under the 1933 Act. As a part of the integrated disclosure package the Commission undertook a drastic revision of the major registration forms then in use under the 1933 Act. Forms S–1, S–2 and S–3, as adopted, establish a new three-tier system for the registration of securities under the Securities Act, other than certain specialized types of offerings.[1] Regulation S–K (the accounting regulations) was revised and expanded and the Guides for the Preparation and Filing of Registration Statements and Reports, other than the Guides relating to specific industries, were rescinded. The general tenor of these and other integrally related proposals are summarized in the following two releases. They also contain a comprehensive discussion of the theoretical foundations of the inte-

---

1. These include Form S–8 (for securities offered to employees), S–4 (for securities issued in business combinations) and Form S–18 designed to meet the special needs of small business.

gration concept and the background leading to the final adoption of the integration package: [2]

* * *

The Commission's integration program involves a comprehensive evaluation of the disclosure policies and procedures underlying the Securities Act of 1933 and the Securities Exchange Act of 1934 with a view toward integrating the information systems under those Acts so that investors and the marketplace are provided meaningful, non-duplicative information periodically and when securities are sold to the public, while the costs of compliance for public companies are decreased.

The shape of the program will be influenced by the answers to two fundamental questions:

(1) What information is material to investment decisions in the context of public offerings of securities; and

(2) Under what circumstances and in what form should such material information be disseminated and made available by companies making public offerings of securities to the various participants in the capital market system?

The task of identifying what information is material to investment and voting decisions is a continuing one in the field of securities regulation. Integration, as a concept, involves a conclusion as to equivalency between transactional (Securities Act) and periodic (Exchange Act) reporting. If a subject matter is material information (other than a description of the transaction itself), then it will be material both in the distribution of securities and to the trading markets. Moreover, requirements governing the description of such subject matters should be the same for both purposes. As an example, if a management's discussion of the financial statements is important for transactions involving distributions, then it would also be equally important for an informed trading market. Thus, both prospectuses and periodic reports should take this information into account. Also, the requirements for its content should be essentially the same. This principle of equivalency has led to the development and expansion of Regulation S–K, a technical device designed to state in one place uniform requirements which both Securities Act and Exchange Act items incorporate by reference. It also has led to increasing the quality of reports under the Exchange Act, * * *.

Integration consists, however, of more than just the notion of equivalency of reportable material information under both Acts. It involves answers to the second question posed above: Under what circumstances and to whom should this information be made available? Equivalency alone might be read to suggest that all the information contained, for example, in a Form 10–K should also be reiterated in all prospectuses.

However, the concept of integration also proceeds from the observation that information is regularly being furnished to the market through periodic reports under the Exchange Act. This information is evaluated by professional analysts and other sophisticated users, is available to the financial press and is obtainable by any other person who seeks it for free or at nominal cost. To the extent that the market accordingly acts efficiently, and this information is adequately reflected in the price of a registrant's outstanding securities, there seems little need to reiterate this information in a prospectus in the context of a distribution. The fact of market availability of information for sophisticated users also allows the exploration of other values in addition to cost reductions

2. Securities Act Release No. 6235 (Sept. 2, 1980).

afforded through non-duplication: in particular, readability and effective communication in specific contexts.

* * *

The basic issues relating to Securities Act disclosure, i.e., the type of information that should be available and the dissemination of that information, must also be considered in light of the composition of today's markets. The participants in the markets, and therefore the users of the information made available to the markets, are varied and have correspondingly varied needs. They include the professional analyst, the institutional investor, the financial press, and the individual investor.

The professional analysts, widespread throughout the country, constantly digest and synthesize market and company-specific information. These professionals use, and often implore the Commission to require, increasingly complex and sophisticated information. The influx of institutional investors, and their financial advisors, also contributes to the constituency for technical but important statistical data. To a large extent, these professionals act as essential conduits in the flow of information to the ordinary investor and as intermediaries acting on behalf of participants in collective investment media.

In addition, this country has a uniquely active and responsive financial press which facilitates the broad dissemination of highly timely and material company-oriented information to a vast readership. The information needs of the individual investor must be considered in this context, recognizing that information reaches the individual investor through both direct and indirect routes.

It is incumbent upon the Commission to consider the entire community of users of company information in developing the proposed system and its model information package and to maintain a balance between the needs of the more and less sophisticated users.

3. *Technological Advances*

The instant proposals are also evidence of * * * the increasingly easy availability of Exchange Act information through improved technological means. Computerization and electronics are progressing to such a level that information necessary to trading markets is becoming available on a timely and inexpensive basis. Additionally, a large volume of such information can be synthesized, analyzed and presented quickly and in almost any format desired by the user.

The system of public dissemination of Exchange Act information has improved dramatically in recent years. The Commission now employs an outside contractor to microfiche all filed reports. This microfiche is produced not only for the Commission's use, but also for the subscribers of private services. Such subscribers include individual and institutional investors, law firms, corporations and other specialized financial research services. * * * Should subscribers wish to extract only certain financial data or information regarding insiders or litigation, for instance, they may also subscribe to on-line computer data base systems which will provide such information. Financial research services break down this acquired information into a myriad array of informational matrices depending upon either the purposes of the users' research or the ultimate users' needs. Also developed in the last few years are magnetic tape systems which will extract numerous data items on a particular company and provide the user with a long-term historic view of such company by carrying this information back five to twenty years. The service bureaus which buy and sell Exchange Act information, either directly from the Commission's contractor or through other information providers, furnish the market with sophisticated research which is further disseminated to broker dealers and investment advisers and through them, to the public at large.[a]

PROPOSED RULEMAKING TO IMPLEMENT THE INTEGRATED DISCLOSURE SYSTEM

Securities and Exchange Commission.
Executive Summary of Securities Act Release Nos. 6331–6338 (Aug. 6, 1981).

The Commission today is publishing a group of eight releases which represent its most significant effort to date to implement an integrated corporate disclosure system, which will affect the over 9,000 public companies subject to reporting obligations under the federal securities laws. The disclosure systems under the federal securities laws are of great importance to capital raising and investor protection in the securities markets. Last year, over $600 billion in equity securities were traded on exchanges and in the over-the-counter market. There were public offerings of over $100 billion in equity and in debt securities. The continuous reporting system imposed by the Securities Exchange Act of 1934 (the "Exchange Act") and the registration system mandated by the Securities Act of 1933 (the "Securities Act") facilitate this trading activity and capital formation by assuring that investors and the market place are given the information necessary for investment decisions.

The integrated disclosure system harmonizes the two disclosure systems—which have grown up independently and on a largely piece-meal basis for the more than forty years since the statutes were enacted—into a single comprehensive disclosure system. It will perform the roles envisioned by both statutes but, at the same time, will eliminate or reduce the overlapping or duplicative corporate reporting, which was the product of two distinct systems, and will streamline corporate reporting generally.

Today's action is part of an ongoing process to integrate the disclosure systems. The foundation was laid by rulemaking actions taken over a period of more than ten years, but the most critical steps have been taken in the past two years. The Commission is publishing all eight releases as proposed rulemaking actions rather than taking any final action at this time. While this means the republication of some proposals which have already been the subject of public comment, the Commission believes that publication of the eight releases together will allow the public to see the complete system before it is adopted. This will give the Commission the benefit of public comment not only on the individual components of the system, but also on their interaction * * *.

a. The Commission is conducting a Pilot program providing for the electronic filing and dissemination of most disclosure documents with it. This Electronic Data Gathering Analysis and Retrieval system is known under the anacronym EDGAR. Temporary EDGAR rules have been adopted under the Securities Act (Rule 499), the Exchange Act (Rule 12b–37), the Trust Indenture Act, the Holding Company Act and the Investment Company Act which enable voluntary participants to use EDGAR to file disclosure documents under these Acts. For a discussion of EDGAR, see Goodman & Jayne, EDGAR: The SEC's Disclosure System, 19 Rev. of Sec. & Commodities Reg. 161 (1986); Rulemaking for Operational EDGAR System, Securities Act Release No. 6581, June 26, 1986.

Overview

The integrated disclosure system simplifies corporate reporting in three ways: (1) disclosure requirements are made uniform under the Securities Act and the Exchange Act; (2) Exchange Act periodic reporting is used to satisfy much of the disclosure necessary in Securities Act registration statements; and (3) the use of informal shareholder communications is encouraged, but not required, to satisfy formal statutory requirements under both Acts. The Commission adopted the first components of the integrated disclosure system in 1980 and early 1981. In addition, other components were proposed for comment. These outstanding proposals and the five newly developed coordinating projects being published today are as follows:

(1) Proposed Forms S-1, S-2 and S-3 to establish a new three tier system for the registration of securities under the Securities Act.

(2) Revision and expansion of Regulation S-K and rescission of the Guides for the Preparation and Filing of Registration Statements and Reports (the "Guides"), other than the Guides relating to specific industries.

(3) General revision and "sunset" review of the procedural requirements of Regulation C under the Securities Act and Regulation 12B under the Exchange Act.

(4) New Rule [415] under the Securities Act governing the registration of securities to be sold in delayed or continuous offerings. This rule was originally published as part of the general revision of Regulation S-K and the Guides in the Guides Release.

(5) New Rule 176 under the Securities Act relating to the responsibility in an integrated disclosure system of persons subject to Section 11 of the Securities Act and reproposed provisions relating to the effective date and modifying and superseding statement aspects of documents incorporated by reference. The latter provisions were previously published for comment in Securities Act Release No. 5988 (November 17, 1978) and the ABC Release.

(6) New Rule 436(g) and amendment to Rule 134(a) under the Securities Act to facilitate the Commission's decision to permit the voluntary disclosure of security ratings.

(7) Amendments to existing Securities Act registration forms to coordinate those forms with revised Regulation S-K and other aspects of the integrated disclosure system.

(8) Amendments to Exchange Act rules, forms and schedules to coordinate with revised Regulation S-K and other aspects of the integrated disclosure system; amendments to Rule [176] under the Securities Act and the corresponding safe harbor rules relating to projections under the other federal securities laws to broaden and clarify the scope of protection provided thereunder; and amendments (reproposed without change) to Schedule 14A relating to business and other relationships between a director and an issuer and the vote required for the election of directors.

Each of these releases is integrally related to the others and to the rulemaking actions taken in 1980. In the integrated disclosure system, a Securities Act registrant looks (1) to the available form for a determination of the type and amount of disclosure which must be delivered to investors, (2) to Regulation S–K for substantive disclosure requirements and (3) to Regulation C for procedural regulations. Separate releases address the role in the integrated system of security ratings, delayed or continuous offerings and Securities Act liabilities in connection with Exchange Act periodic reports incorporated by reference into Securities Act registration statements. Finally, the Commission's integration of the two existing corporate disclosure systems includes a wide ranging "sunset" review, resulting in revisions to Regulation C and in the proposed coordinating changes to rules and forms under the two systems.

The eight releases contain comprehensive discussions of the proposed actions as well as texts of the proposed rule and form provisions. *   *   *

Proposed Forms S–1, S–2 and S–3

The proposed Securities Act framework would establish three categories of registration statements. Proposed Form S–3 relies on the efficient market theory and thus allows maximum use of incorporation by reference of Exchange Act reports and requires minimal disclosure in the prospectus. In addition to being available for equity offerings by companies widely followed in the marketplace, Form S–3 could be used by most reporting companies to register investment grade debt offerings, securities offered under dividend and interest reinvestment plans and rights offerings, conversions and warrants. Companies which have been subject to the periodic reporting system of the Exchange Act for three or more years, but which are not as widely followed, would be eligible for Form S–2, which combines reliance on incorporation by reference of Exchange Act reports and presentation of streamlined information in the prospectus or in an annual report to shareholders delivered with the prospectus. Companies which have been in the Exchange Act reporting system for less than three years, and any others who choose to do so, would use Form S–1, which requires complete disclosure in the prospectus and permits no incorporation by reference.

A critical issue in Forms S–1, S–2 and S–3 has been developing criteria for determining when and by whom the abbreviated forms may be used to register securities. Since the use of abbreviated disclosure is based, to a large degree, on the theory of an efficient market, the criteria for the use of Forms S–2 and S–3 are designed to be indicative of following in the market place. The Commission believes that the standards of Exchange Act reporting experience and a minimum value of voting stock held by non-affiliates (the "float") are indicative of market place following, and thus it has moved away from registrant quality criteria (such as net income). The Commission is proposing a $150 million float test for Form S–3, which results in approximately 30% of NYSE, AMEX and NASDAQ companies being eligible to use the Form, and is also considering an alternative test involving two market factors, a $100 million float and 3 million share annual trading volume, which would address regionally followed companies.[a]

---

a. The final version of Form S–3 included the 150 million float transaction requirement and added an alternative test of 100 million float and 3 million share annual trading volume.

Revision of Regulation S–K

The revision of Regulation S–K represents the evolution of that regulation into the repository of uniform disclosure provisions relating to substantially all of the information to be set forth in registration statements under the Securities Act and in annual and other periodic reports required pursuant to the Exchange Act. Disclosure requirements are centralized in Regulation S–K in order to avoid the need to refer to multiple sources for document content requirements. Thus, certain disclosure requirements currently included in the Guides, in proposed Form A, in Regulation C and in various Securities Act registration forms and Exchange Act forms will now be moved to Regulation S–K.

The Regulation S–K release also represents the completion of the "sunset" review of the Guides. In addition to including certain substantive Guide provisions in Regulation S–K, the "sunset" review of the Guides has resulted in including certain procedural provisions in Regulation C and deleting 50% of the Guides as obsolete. The only remaining Guides will be those relating to specific industries, where greater flexibility is essential.

Revision of Regulations C and 12B

The rules comprising Regulation C and Regulation 12B were adopted to standardize the mechanics of securities registration under the Securities Act and Exchange Act, respectively. The rules implement the statutes and provide more specific instructions for registrants than are contained in the statutes. Although these regulations developed over a long period, no overall review of their provisions had been undertaken for some time.
* * *

The proposed amendments will simplify and clarify procedural requirements and conform the provisions of Regulation C and Regulation 12B to the procedures established in the integrated disclosure system. * * * The "sunset" amendments, which revise, up-date or delete provisions where appropriate, include the proposed rescission of 23% of the rules now contained in Regulation C.

Delayed or Continuous Offerings

Proposed Rule [415], which was first published in the Guides Release, would facilitate new methods of financing. For the first time, the Commission would specify by rulemaking the conditions under which registrants could register securities to be offered on a delayed or continuous basis on the market (so called "shelf registration"). * * *

Liability Issues

Some members of the financial community have expressed concerns about the integrated disclosure system because it relies on Exchange Act periodic reports to satisfy Securities Act registration disclosure requirements and allows rapid financings. These persons believe that underwriters may have diminished opportunity to conduct what would be deemed a reasonable investigation of the information incorporated by reference from Exchange Act reports into a Securities Act registration statement so as to discharge their obligations under Section 11(b) of the Securities Act. In light of these concerns, the Commission is publishing for comment several proposals addressing the questions of liability which arise in the context of the integrated disclosure system. While the proposed rules would not derogate from Section 11 with respect to the responsibilities of underwriters, they would set forth certain factors which bear on issues of liability.

First, proposed Rule 176 would codify Section 1704(g) of the draft Federal Securities Code, as modified and approved by the Commission in 1980. The proposed rule identifies certain circumstances, including incorporation by reference, which may bear upon the determination of what constitutes reasonable investigation and reasonable ground for belief as those terms are used in Section 11.

Second, the Commission is proposing to codify in Regulation C the previously proposed provisions regarding the effective date of documents incorporated by reference and the making of modifying or superseding statements. * * *

Security Ratings

The Commission traditionally has taken the view that disclosure of the security ratings assigned to classes of debt securities and preferred stock by certain professional rating organizations generally should not be permitted in filings under the Securities Act. * * * The Commission now has determined to permit the voluntary disclosure of such ratings in filings with the Commission. The security rating release sets forth the Commission's views with respect to other information that should be included with the security rating in order that such rating, standing alone, not be misleading or confusing to investors.

To facilitate this change in policy, the Commission is publishing two proposals: an exemptive rule, Rule 436(g), concerning issues of expert's consent and liability under the Securities Act; and an amendment to Rule 134 permitting the disclosure of security ratings in tombstone advertisements.[b]

    * * *

[The above proposals were implemented, with some modifications, in Securities Act Release No. 6383 (March 3, 1982). In that release, the Commission described the relationship and content of the registration and report forms under the Securities Act and the Exchange Act in the following words.]

SECURITIES ACT RELEASE NO. 6383
Securities and Exchange Commission.
March 3, 1982.

ADOPTION OF INTEGRATED DISCLOSURE SYSTEM

New Forms S–1, S–2 and S–3 provide the basic framework for the registration of securities under the Securities Act. These Forms establish three categories for registration statements. The same information will be required to be part of Securities Act registration statements in all categories, either presented in, or delivered with, the prospectus or incorporated by reference from another document. Differences among the three Forms reflect the Commission's determination as to (1) when this required information must be presented in full in the prospectus delivered to investors, (2) when certain of the delivered information may be presented on a streamlined basis and supplemented by documents incorporated by refer-

---

b. Cohen, The Integrated Disclosure System—Unfinished Business, 40 Bus.Law. 987 (1985); Greene, Integration of the Securities Act and the Exchange Act: A Case Study of Regulation in the Division of Corporation Finance of the United States Securites and Exchange Commission, 3 J. of Comp. L. & Sec.Reg. 75 (1981).

ence, and (3) when certain information may be incorporated by reference from documents in the Exchange Act continuous reporting system without delivery to investors.

Generally, it is the registrant-oriented portion of the information relating to a public offering, as opposed to the transaction-specific information, which sometimes may be satisfied otherwise than through full prospectus presentation. Much of this registrant-oriented information is the same as that which is required to be presented in annual reports to the Commission on Form 10-K and in annual reports to security holders, as well as in quarterly and current reports on Forms 10-Q and 8-K, respectively. Information about the offering, however, will not have been reported on in any other disclosure document or otherwise have been publicly disseminated and thus will be required to be presented in the prospectus in all cases.

The registration statement for the first category is Form S-1. It requires complete disclosure to be set forth in the prospectus and permits no incorporation by reference. Form S-1 is to be used by registrants in the Exchange Act reporting system for less than three years and also may be used by any registrants who choose to do so or for whom no other form is available.

The second category of registration statement is Form S-2, which combines reliance on incorporating Exchange Act reports by reference with delivery to investors of streamlined information. Registrants in the Exchange Act reporting system for three years may use this Form, which allows them to choose to either: (1) Deliver a copy of their annual report to security holders along with the prospectus describing the offering or (2) present registrant-oriented information comparable to that of the annual report in the prospectus along with the description of the offering. In either case, the more complete information in the Form 10-K is incorporated by reference into the prospectus.

Form S-3, in reliance on the efficient market theory, allows maximum use of incorporation by reference of Exchange Act reports and requires the least disclosure to be presented in the prospectus and delivered to investors. Generally, the Form S-3 prospectus will present the same transaction-specific information as will be presented in a Form S-1 or S-2 prospectus. Information concerning the registrant will be incorporated by reference from Exchange Act reports. The prospectus will not be required to present any information concerning the registrant unless there has been a material change in the registrant's affairs which has not been reported in an Exchange Act filing or the Exchange Act reports incorporated by reference do not reflect certain restated financial statements or other financial information.

* * * *

SECTION 2. PREPARATION OF THE REGISTRATION STATEMENT

Statutes and Regulations

Securities Act, §§ 6–7.

Regulation C.

Forms S–1, S–2, S–3, S–18.

Regulation S–K.

Introductory Note

The preparation of a 1933 Act registration statement, especially that of an issuer going public, is a demanding and intricate undertaking which nevertheless can challenge the imagination and ingenuity of the corporation lawyer. A great deal of expertise must be acquired in practice preferably by working with competent and experienced securities lawyers.

A study of the mechanics of preparing a registration statement should begin with an examination of the 1933 Act (particularly §§ 6–7 and Schedule A), and Regulation C which contains the general rules governing the registration process.

The Commission has prescribed a number of registration forms for use based upon the type of issuer, whether it is a reporting or non-reporting company, the form of transaction, and the extent to which the Commission believes that previously disseminated information need not be repeated in the prospectus, but may simply be incorporated therein by reference.

Regulation S–K contains standard instructions applicable to the non-financial portion of registration forms filed under the 1933 Act and registration statements, periodic reports and proxy statements filed under the 1934 Act; it was issued as a part of the Commission's integrated disclosure program.

A substantial amount of "know how" may be gained by first studying the statute and Regulation C, then moving to Form S–1 and thereafter analyzing a well-drafted prospectus in the light of the statute, rules, and form.[1] It is also helpful to prepare a cross reference sheet of the type specified in Rule 404(d) showing the location in the prospectus of the information which must be included in the prospectus in response to the various items of Form S–1. This might be followed by studying a complete registration file, including Part II relating to information not contained in the prospectus, the various amendments, and the exhibits.

There also are a few books devoted to "going public", and the mechanics of preparing a 1933 Act registration statement, written from the lawyer's point of view.[2]

The decision to "go public" is important to the future of an issuer, and should be taken only after weighing the advantages and disadvantages of becoming a public company.

In a period of rising stock prices and business expansion, the managers of private companies may be dazzled by the supposed advantages of going public, with the opportunity to cash in on the increased net worth of the company. Thus, business people who took their companies public in the 1960's suddenly wished to have it both ways by "going private" at the rock bottom stock prices of 1974–75.[3]

Carl W. Schneider, Joseph M. Manko, and Robert S. Kant members of the Philadelphia bar, have enumerated a number of advantages and

---

1. See also 2 CCH Fed.Sec.L.Rep. under the tab guide "How to Answer Form S–1," ¶ 8001 et seq.

2. See particularly, D. Goldwasser, The Underwritten Offering; L. Sonsini, Preparing the Registration Statement, 1 Securities Law Techniques ch. 18, 19 (A.A. Sommer, Jr. ed., 1985 Looseleaf); H. Bloomenthal, C. Harvey & S. Wing, 1986 Going Public Handbook; A. Jacobs, Manual of Corporate Forms for Securities Practice (1985 rev.).

3. On the "going private" phenomenon, see infra at pages 824–831.

disadvantages of going public.[4] In summary, these include: 1. To raise funds for such corporate purposes as increasing working capital, expanding plant and equipment, research and development, retiring existing debt, or for diversification of operations. 2. If a secondary offering is included, the selling shareholders may cash in on a part of their investment under favorable market conditions. 3. By going public the company may gain prestige, become better known, and obtain a wider market for its products or services, particularly if the company is engaged in distributing consumer's goods or services to the public. 4. A company with publicly traded stock is in a better position to acquire other businesses through the issuance of stock, instead of cash. 5. An existing public market for the securities permits the adoption of stock option and other employee purchase plans as a means of attracting and retaining personnel. 6. A public offering of stock will improve net worth thereby enabling the company to raise funds on more favorable terms, either in the equity markets, or privately from institutional investors. 7. The establishment of a public market may give the owners a sense of financial success and self-fulfillment as well as providing liquidity for their personal estate.

The disadvantages, which are frequently overlooked during periods of business expansion, only to be suddenly perceived at the bottom of a business cycle are: 1. The relatively high expense of maintaining a public company. 2. The full disclosure obligations of reporting companies with respect to salaries, transactions with management, conflicts-of-interest, information as to sales, profits and competitive position, all of which become available to shareholders and competitors. 3. The loss of flexibility in management arising from practical, if not legal, limitations on salaries and fringe benefits, the placing of relatives on the payroll and the necessity of acting only after approval of outside directors or shareholders. 4. Increased costs of administration, and legal, accounting and other fees associated with operating as a company subject to the reporting requirements of the Securities Exchange Act of 1934. 5. Possible loss of control over dividend policy, although frequently the company reserves the right to pay no dividends for the foreseeable future. 6. The business decisions of a public company may become affected by short-term considerations arising from management's preoccupation with day-to-day stock market price fluctuations rather than a consideration of long-term benefits. 7. If a sufficiently large proportion of the company's shares are sold to the public, the company may later become a candidate for a takeover bid, with a loss of control by the insiders. 8. Finally, the supposed advantages of an active public market for the company's shares may not develop, and the shares may actually sell at a discount substantially below the price anticipated on the basis of earnings and book values.

Set forth below are excerpts from this article describing the lawyer's role in preparing a 1933 Act registration statement for a company about to go public for the first time.

─────────

4. See Schneider, Manko and Kant, Going Public—Practice, Procedure and Consequences, 27 Vill.L.Rev. 1 (1981).

Excerpt from: Carl W. Schneider, Joseph M. Manko, and Robert
S. Kant

GOING PUBLIC: PRACTICE, PROCEDURE AND
CONSEQUENCES
27 Villanova L.Rev. 1, 1–50 (1981).[a]

Introduction

WHEN A COMPANY WISHES TO "GO PUBLIC" it faces a complex and
challenging process. It is the purpose of this article to focus on the sections
of the Securities Act of 1933 (the '33 Act) dealing with registration as it
applies to companies selling securities to the public for the first time—
"going public." The authors' aim is to cover the practice and procedure, as
well as certain important consequences, of going public. In a nutshell, the
'33 Act is designed to prohibit the public distribution of securities without
disclosure of relevant information to the investor. In this context, distribution refers to a public offering by the company itself—a "primary offering."
The '33 Act also covers certain offerings by existing security holders, who
may or may not be those persons who control the company—"secondary
offerings" or, more opprobriously, "bailouts."

During the decade of the 1970's, there were relatively few initial public
offerings compared to earlier periods. However, there has been a resur-
gence in the market for initial public offerings during certain periods
commencing in 1980, with the primary interest being in high technology
companies.

* * * *

ELIGIBILITY FOR PUBLIC FINANCING

In evaluating the advisability of going public, as well as pricing the
company's stock, the underwriters will consider the amount and trend of
the company's sales and earnings (compared with the trend in its industry),
the adequacy of its present and projected working capital and cash flow
positions, the experience, integrity and quality of its management and the
likelihood of management's being able to accept the burden of responsibility to a public shareholder group, and the growth potential of its business.
Other factors evaluated are the nature and number of its customers, its
sources of supply, its inclination and ability to diversify, and its relative
competitive position. In terms of what underwriters will require, there is
often a direct relationship between the company's sales and earnings record
and the existence of growth potential in the company's industry—the less
growth potential for the company they perceive, the more historic earnings
the underwriters will require.

During periods when investor interest in new issues is high, fads often
emerge. Investors tend to gobble up new offerings in "hot" industries, and
thereafter sometimes ascribe values to stocks which seem totally unrelated

a. Reprinted with permission from Villanova Law Review and the Authors.
©Copyright 1981 by the Authors. This
printing reflects revisions made by the authors through February, 1986. The article
covers the practice and procedure, as well
as various consequences of going public. Although only a portion is reprinted here,
the entire article is recommended. Copies
are available from Packard Press, Philadelphia, Pa. And see the companion article,
Schneider and Shargel, "Now That You
Are Publicly Owned * * *", 36
Bus.Law. 1631 (1981).

to their apparent intrinsic merits measured by more conventional criteria of valuation. Within the hot industry, some companies may survive and prosper to the point where their securities become realistically valued in the market. However, most fads spawn many ill-conceived public ventures. There is an inevitable shakedown period, with a high incidence of business failures or acquisitions of newly public companies by larger concerns, with such acquisitions tending to be merely salvage operations.

SELECTION OF AN UNDERWRITER

Once the decision has been made to go public, the parties immediately face perhaps the most important decision to be made—selecting the managing underwriter. Investment banking firms vary widely in prestige, financial strength and ability to provide the various services which the company can expect. Some underwriters are not ordinarily interested in first offerings, while others specialize in them. Some underwriters have particular stature and experience in specific industries. Underwriters may have pre-existing relationships with customers, suppliers, or competitors of a prospective company going public, which can be both an advantage and a disadvantage from varying points of view. In short, a managing underwriter appropriate for one company may be wholly inappropriate for another.

In selecting the underwriters, advice should be obtained from experienced advisers who have a background in the area of public offerings. The company's attorneys, auditors and bankers may be helpful in making the selection. Some advisers, particularly underwriters themselves, warn of dire consequences from "shopping" an offering, and suggest dealing with a single underwriter at a time. Opinions on the subject vary. There are some small and speculative offerings where the trick is to find any underwriter, and there may be little chance for selection. Additionally, among smaller underwriters, there may be a reluctance to evaluate, negotiate and otherwise develop an underwriting prospect unless the company is dealing exclusively with the particular firm at that time.

On the other hand, if the proposed offering is good enough to appeal to the larger underwriters, management may be best advised to select a few firms, possibly three to five, with which to begin preliminary discussions more or less simultaneously. If the offering has merit, the larger underwriters normally are most willing to spend time investigating the company to decide whether or not they wish to proceed, and thereafter to sell themselves and their proposal if they do wish to handle the transaction. It is important to deal in candor. Each prospective underwriter should be told that other underwriters are being considered. For offerings of genuine merit, this element of competition may well whet the appetite and stand the company in good stead. This is not to suggest, however, that a company should put itself in an auction, trying to get each bidder to top the others.

Finally, it must be stressed that price is not the sole element of comparison, nor is it necessarily advantageous for the stock to be sold for the very top dollar which any prospective underwriter will offer. If the initial offering price is set too high, the issue may have a poor reception and a weak after-market for some time to follow. Some underwriters will frankly advise the company to set the initial offering price slightly under the projected after-market price, perhaps 5 percent to 10 percent below, simply to assure a good reception for the stock. For companies with a good history and earnings record, the proper pricing of the issue often must be determined by the market conditions prevailing on the offering date. Therefore, many underwriters will indicate during the preliminary negotiations the price, or price range, at which the offering could be made if it were being made at that time, with the express reservation that final pricing will be determined by prevailing conditions on the offering date, which is normally at least a few months in the future. Thus, the managing underwriter is often selected at a time when the parties have not yet fixed the specific offering price.

*   *   *   *

Several services can be expected from the underwriters. Initially, the managing underwriter will take the lead in forming the underwriting syndicate. The underwriters are also expected to provide after-market support for the security being sold. They may serve as over-the-counter market makers which stand ready to purchase or sell the stock in the inter-dealer market; they may purchase the stock for their own account; and they may take the initiative in bringing the stock to the attention of analysts and investors, including their own customers. Ideally, the company should seek a managing underwriter which customarily makes a continuous inter-dealer market for the issues it manages, although there are some managing underwriters that do not perform this function themselves.

In addition, managing underwriters traditionally supply other investment banking services to the company following the offering. They will assist in obtaining additional financing from public or private sources as the need arises, advise the company concerning possible acquisitions and generally make available their expertise as financial institutions. In some cases, they will recommend or furnish experienced persons to become members of the company's board of directors, or to serve as officers or key employees.

*   *   *   *

STRUCTURE OF THE OFFERING

Once a company has decided to make a public offering, it must determine, in consultation with its managing underwriter, what class of securities should be offered. Most first offerings include common stock. Some first offerings consist of a package including other securities such as debentures, which may or may not be convertible into common stock, or warrants to purchase common stock. It is normally not practicable to have a publicly-traded security convertible into common stock or a publicly-traded warrant to purchase common stock unless a public market exists for the underlying common stock.

There are two other interrelated variables to consider, the number of shares offered and the offering price for the shares. It is generally felt that a minimum of 300,000 to 350,000 shares, and preferably 400,000 shares or even slightly more, is desirable in the public "float" to constitute a broad national distribution and to support an active trading market thereafter. As to price level, many of the larger investment banking firms and many investors are not particularly interested in dealing with securities offered at less than $10.   *   *   *

For an offering of $5,000,000, 500,000 shares at $10 per share would be considered in the optimum range. If the offering is below $4,000,000, a decrease in the offering price per share is recommended, rather than a reduction in the number of shares offered below 400,000. These are matters of judgment, however, which should be reviewed carefully with the underwriters in each situation. * * *

THE REGISTRATION STATEMENT

In determining the amount of public investment which can be profitably employed in the business, the underwriters will normally evaluate the company's needs for funds and the dilution in earnings per share to result from the issuance of additional stock. If the optimum level of proceeds to the company would constitute too small an offering, it may be desirable for existing shareholders to sell some of their own shares as part of the offering in order to increase its size. Sometimes the underwriters will suggest, or even insist on, a partial secondary offering with some shares to be sold by existing shareholders even though the shareholders would prefer to retain all their shares.

The registration statement is the disclosure document required to be filed with the SEC in connection with a registered offering. It consists physically of two principal parts. Part I of the registration statement is the prospectus, which is the only part that normally goes to the public offerees of the securities. It is the legal offering document. Part II of the registration statement contains supplemental information which is available for public inspection at the office of the SEC.

The registration forms, Regulation S–K, Regulation S–X and the Industry Guides [7] (when applicable) specify the information to be contained in the registration statement. Regulation S–K sets forth detailed disclosure requirements which are applicable in various contexts under the securities laws; Regulation S–X similarly sets forth financial statement requirements; and the Industry Guides require specific disclosure applicable to certain prescribed businesses such as oil and gas and banking. In addition, Regulation C sets forth certain general requirements as to the registration of securities including filing fees, the number of copies of the registration statements and amendments to be filed, signature requirements, paper and type size and other mechanical aspects of registration.

The registration forms contain a series of "items" and instructions (generally referring to the disclosure requirements contained in Regulation S–K), in response to which disclosures must be made. But they are not forms in the sense that they have blanks to be completed like a tax return. Traditionally, the prospectus describes the company's business and responds to all the disclosures required in narrative rather than item-and-answer form. It is prepared as a brochure describing the company and the securities to be offered. The usual prospectus is a fairly stylized document, and there is a customary sequence for organizing the material.

Form S–1 traditionally has been the most common registration form used. In April 1979, however, the SEC adopted a simplified Form S–18 for the registration of limited amounts of securities by certain smaller companies. Form S–18 has been used more frequently than Form S–1 by companies which satisfy the conditions to its use.

Form S–18 is available for the sale of up to $7.5 million of securities ($1.5 million of which may be for the account of other than the company) within a one year period. Form S–18 may not be used by companies which are reporting companies under the '34 Act, investment companies, or

7. See SEC Securities Act Release No. 6384 (March 3, 1982).

insurance companies. Filings on S–18 may be made at either the SEC's principal office in Washington, D.C., as is the case for Form S–1, or in the SEC Regional Office for the region in which the company conducts or intends to conduct its principal business operations.

The principal advantages of Form S–18 over Form S–1 are its somewhat less demanding requirements with respect to financial statements. Form S–18 requires a balance sheet as of the end of the company's last fiscal year (as compared to the last two fiscal years in the case of Form S–1) and statements of income, changes in financial condition and stockholders, equity for the last two fiscal years (as compared to three years in the case of the Form S–1). Form S–18 does not require financial statements to be prepared in accordance with Regulation S–X (the SEC's accounting rules), but in accordance with generally accepted accounting standards, which are somewhat less demanding in terms of details required to be disclosed. In addition, Form S–18 does not require the five year Selected Financial Data, Management's Discussion and Analysis of Financial Condition and Results of Operations, or the supporting schedules which are required by Form S–1. Form S–18 also requires a somewhat less detailed description of business, properties, and management remuneration and transactions.[b]

In the typical first public offering, the items to which it is most difficult to respond, and which require the most creative effort in preparation, deal with the description of the company's business, properties, material transactions with insiders, and use of proceeds. Other matters required to be disclosed in the prospectus deal with the details of the underwriting, the plan for distributing the securities, capitalization, pending legal proceedings, competition, description of securities being registered, identification of directors and officers and their remuneration, options to purchase securities, and principal holders of securities. There are also detailed requirements concerning financial statements and financial information concerning the company's business segments.

In Part II of the registration statement is supplemental information of a more formal type which is not required to be given to each investor. Unlike the prospectus, Part II is prepared in item-and-answer form. One requirement which is sometimes troublesome calls for disclosure of recent sales of unregistered securities and a statement of the exemption relied upon. Counsel may discover that past issuances of securities violated the '33 Act. In some such cases, the result may be that the company's financial statements must reflect a very large contingent liability under the '33 Act. In some cases, past violations may be remedied by a rescission offer. If past violations have been too flagrant, the offering may have to be deferred. Part II also contains supplemental financial schedules, as well as a list of exhibits which are filed with the registration statement. Although the information in Part II normally is not seen by individual investors, sophisticated analysts and financial services may make extensive use of it, particularly the supplemental financial schedules.

In preparing a prospectus, the applicable form is merely the beginning. The forms are quite general and apply to all types of businesses, securities and offerings except for a few industries or limited situations for which special forms have been prepared. In the course of administration over the years, the Commission has given specific content to the general disclosure

---

b. See generally, Arnold & Hopkins, Small Firm Securities Registration in the S–18 Era, Perceptions of Professionals, 8 Corp.L.Rev. 135 (1985).

requirements. It often requires disclosures on a number of points within the scope of the form but not explicitly covered by the form itself. Furthermore, in addition to the information that the form expressly requires, the company must add any information necessary to make the statements made not misleading.[10] Thus, the prospectus may not contain a half-truth—a statement which may be literally true but is misleading in context.

The Commission's views on many matters change from time to time. SEC practitioners, both lawyers and accountants, constantly exchange news of what the Commission is currently requiring as reflected in its letters of comments.

The Commission has also evolved certain principles of emphasis in highlighting disclosures of adverse facts. It cannot prohibit an offering from being made if disclosure is adequate, but its policies on disclosure can make the offering look highly unattractive. In particular, if there are sufficient adverse factors in an offering, these are required to be set forth in detail in the very beginning of the prospectus under a caption such as "Introductory Statement" or "Risk Factors of the Offering."[11] However, many new issues of going businesses do not require this treatment and counsel must make a judgment in each case. Some of the adverse factors which may be collected under such a heading include lack of business history; adverse business experience; operating losses; dependence upon particular customers, suppliers and key personnel; lack of a market for the security offered; competitive factors; certain types of transactions with insiders; a low book value for the stock compared to the offering price; potential dilution which may result from the exercise of convertible securities, options or warrants; and a small investment by the promoters compared with the public investment.

To the same end, the SEC has required that boldface reference be made to certain adverse factors on the prospectus cover page. The cover page statements must cross reference disclosures within the prospectus on such matters as high risk factors, immediate equity dilution of the public's investment and various forms of underwriting compensation beyond the normal spread.[12] To add to the brew, the Commission sometimes insists that certain factors be emphasized beyond what the attorneys working on the matter consider to be their true importance. A usual example is that prominent attention must be called to transactions between the company and its management. Often matters of relative insignificance, in terms of amounts involved, are made to appear very important by the amount of space given and placement in the prospectus.

The SEC, which reviews the registration statement, has no authority to pass on the merits of a particular offering. The SEC has no general power to prohibit an offering because it considers the investment opportunity to be a poor risk. The sole thrust of the Federal statute is disclosure of relevant information. No matter how speculative the investment, no matter how poor the risk, the offering will comply with Federal law if all the required facts are disclosed. By contrast, some state securities or "blue sky" laws, which are applicable in the jurisdictions where the distribution takes place, do regulate the merits of the securities. Typically their

---

10. SEC Rule 408 (1985).

11. See Regulation S–K, Item 503(c) (1985).

12. See Regulation S–K, Item 501 (1985).

standards are, very indefinite, often expressed in terms of offerings which are "fair, just and equitable." In practice, state administrators exercise broad discretion in determining which offerings may be sold in their states.

There are special procedures by which a registrant may obtain confidential treatment of information which is either required by the registration statement or is supplied supplementally to the Commission, but it is difficult to obtain confidential treatment as a practical matter.[13]

The prospectus is a somewhat schizophrenic document, having two purposes which often present conflicting pulls. On the one hand, it is a selling document. It is used by the principal underwriters to form the underwriting syndicate and a dealer group, and by the underwriters and dealers to sell the securities to the public. From this point of view, it is desirable to present the best possible image. On the other hand, the prospectus is a disclosure document, an insurance policy against liability. With the view toward protection against liability, there is a tendency to resolve all doubts against the company and to make things look as bleak as possible. In balancing the purposes, established underwriters and experienced counsel, guided at least in part by their knowledge of SEC staff attitudes, traditionally lean to a very conservative presentation, avoiding glowing adjectives and predictions. The layman frequently complains that all the glamor and romance have been lost. "Why can't you tell them," he says, "that we have the most aggressive and imaginative management in the industry?" It takes considerable client education before an attorney can answer this question to the client's satisfaction.

Until relatively recently, it was traditional to confine prospectuses principally to objectively verifiable statements of historic fact. It is now considered proper, and in some instances essential, to include some information in a prospectus, either favorable or adverse to the company, which is predictive or based upon opinions or subjective evaluations. However, no such "soft information" should be included in the prospectus unless it has a reasonable basis in fact and represents management's good faith judgment.

PREPARING THE REGISTRATION STATEMENT

The "quarterback" in preparing the registration statement is normally the attorney for the company.[15] Company counsel is principally responsible for preparing the non-financial parts of the registration statement.

13. SEC Securities Act Rule 406 (1985); SEC Rule of Practice 83, 17 C.F.R. § 200.83. [And see Comizio, Keeping Corporate Information Secret: Confidential Treatment under the Securities Act of 1933 and the Securities Exchange Act of 1934, 18 New Eng.L.Rev. 787 (1983).]

15. On the lawyer's role in assisting in the preparation of registration statements, see Association of the Bar of the City of New York, Report by Special Committee on Lawyers' Role in Securities Transactions, 32 Bus.Law. 1879, 1891–98 (1977), which proposes, *inter alia*, the following guidelines for practitioners:

"Guideline Four: The lawyer should assist the issuer, on the basis of information furnished to the lawyer, in reaching its decisions as to what information should be included in the registration statement, how it should be included, and to what extent its omission would raise questions under the 1933 Act—i.e., he should assist the issuer in making judgments as to materiality and compliance with the requirements of the registration form and instructions.

"Comment:

"(a) Within the confines of the agreed assignment of responsibilities and of a realistic evaluation of the extent to which a lawyer's consideration of essentially non-legal matters is useful to the client and warranted by the circumstances, the lawyer should study documents or otherwise inquire into other matters, not primarily legal in nature and not within counsel's expertise as such, in order to provide himself with a background from which better to assist the issuer in making its decisions.

Drafts are circulated to all concerned. There are normally several major

"(b) The determination of 'materiality' of a fact or its omission, or of whether there is a material inaccuracy in a statement, involves many questions of fact and judgment. Usually any legal judgment will be based on a factual analysis peculiarly within the knowledge and capability of the management of the issuer. Although a lawyer can be helpful in bringing his experience, interrogation techniques and judgment to bear on questions of materiality, he cannot—and should not—take over from the issuer or other more qualified parties the responsibility for decisions in these gray areas. There will, of course, be matters where the subject involved is primarily a legal issue, or where the facts are so clear that a positive judgment can be made based on administrative regulations or administrative or judicial precedent.

"More frequently, however, the lawyer can only give the client the benefit of an experienced judgment which he will often (as a practical matter) have to make without having knowledge of all relevant facts and which must be combined with the business judgment of the client, the underwriters, the auditors and perhaps other experts to enable the client to arrive at a final decision. This is not to say that the lawyer's advice and assistance in these matters (particularly in helping to develop the relevant considerations on which these decisions should be based) may not be extremely valuable to the client. The lawyer must not, however, claim too much for his own ability to give definitive answers to these questions nor should he insist on imposing his judgments in substitution for those of the client when he cannot, as a lawyer, say that his judgment as to materiality in the particular circumstances is clearly correct.

"(c) The lawyer should not allow the impression to be created that he will normally 'investigate' factual matters covered in a registration statement, personally examining into primary sources or data, or that he can verify the reliability of other persons providing this information. A lawyer does not search the files and records of the issuer to discover, for example, all material contracts or other documents. Except in the case of investigations into certain legal matters (such as due incorporation or valid issuance of securities) which the lawyer undertakes to perform personally rather than to rely on others, the lawyer rarely will go to primary records or other sources but will rely on interrogations of, and reports or compilations prepared by, others including other professionals such as auditors, engineers and other lawyers. Such reliance on others is entirely appropriate. Indeed, in most instances the lawyer will not have the skills and experience to work with and analyze the primary data. By questioning the issuer's officers and the other persons providing the information, the lawyer can secure an understanding of the material provided, the means by which it was prepared, and its relevance and importance, and he can, if appropriate, suggest that further investigation or inquiry be undertaken. He can also attempt to cross-check information which seems subject to doubt for some reason, or otherwise warrants such inquiry, by questioning persons who appear familiar with it. Where, because of suspicious or other unusual circumstances, the lawyer believes special investigation of a particular matter is required, he should take this up with the issuer, and a procedure for such investigation should be decided upon. Such a procedure may include the issuer's assigning specific qualified personnel or retaining outside experts to make a special investigation of underlying primary data.

"**Guideline Five:** The lawyer should assist in the drafting of the registration statement or portions thereof with the goal that, to the extent feasible, the registration statement says what the lawyer understands the issuer intends it to say, is unambiguous, and is written in a way that is designed to protect the issuer from later claims of overstatement, misleading implications, omissions or other deficiencies due to the manner in which the statements in question have been written. The lawyer should be careful, however, to dispel any impression that his assistance in drafting the registration statement can ensure that it will be free from all misleading, unclear or ambiguous statements.

"Comment:

"The lawyer's assistance in drafting the registration statement may entail preparation of initial drafts or portions thereof, and discussion and revision of drafts prepared by himself and by others. Such assistance should not be misunderstood as indicating that the lawyer has sufficient knowledge concerning the substantive content of the document that he can or does take responsibility for its accuracy or completeness. The lawyer's drafting services are significant since the manner in which the document is organized and written is of considerable importance; but the lawyer should not delude either himself or the client into regarding the lawyer's drafting or organizing abilities as also giving the lawyer the ability to determine the substantive content of the document.

"**Guideline Six:** The lawyer should avoid statements in the prospectus which could give a mistaken impression that he

revisions before sending the job to the printer and at least a few more printed drafts before the final filing. Close cooperation is required among counsel for the company, the underwriters' counsel, the accountants and the printer. Unless each knows exactly what the others expect, additional delay, expense and irritation are predictable.

It is essential for the issuer and all others involved in the financing to perceive correctly the role of company counsel. Counsel normally assists the company and its management in preparing the document and in performing their "due diligence" investigation to verify all disclosures for accuracy and completeness. Counsel often serves as the principal drafts-man of the registration statement. Counsel typically solicits information both orally and in writing from a great many people and exercises his best judgment in evaluating the information received for accuracy and consis-tency. Experience indicates that executives often overestimate their abili-ty to give accurate information from their recollections without verifica-tion. It shows no disrespect, but merely the professionally required degree of healthy skepticism, when the lawyer insists on backup documentation and asks for essentially the same information in different ways and from different sources.

A lawyer would be derelict in the discharge of his or her professional obligations if the lawyer allowed his client's registration statement to include information which the lawyer knew or believed to be inaccurate, or if the lawyer failed to pursue an investigation further in the face of factors arousing suspicions about the accuracy of the information received. On the other hand, it should be understood that a lawyer generally is not an expert in the business or financial aspects of a company's affairs. The normal scope of a professional engagement does not contemplate that the lawyer will act as the ultimate source to investigate or verify all disclosures in the registration statement or to assure that the document is accurate and complete in all respects. Indeed, in many cases the lawyer would lack the expertise to assume that responsibility. In some instances, the lawyer may lack the technical background even to frame the proper questions and must depend upon the client for education about the nature of the business. Counsel does not routinely check information received against books of original entry or source documents, as auditors do, nor does counsel generally undertake to consult sources external to the client to obtain or verify information supplied by the client.

has passed upon matters which he has not, or that he takes responsibility for the accu-racy and completeness of the prospectus.

"Comment:

"Normally, except for references to spe-cific opinions given by the lawyer on par-ticular matters which are referred to with the lawyer's consent, the only mention of the lawyer in a prospectus should be to his specific opinion as to the validity of the securities being issued. The lawyer should take care that the use of his name for express purposes is not taken as authoriza-tion to rely on it for any other purposes, expressly or impliedly. In this connection, the lawyer should consider the advisability of including the following legend wherever his name appears:

'[The lawyer/law firm] has passed on the validity of the securities being issued [or other specific matters, e.g., status of liti-gation] but purchasers of the securities offered by this Prospectus should not re-ly on [the lawyer/law firm] with respect to any other matters.'

"Such language will serve to ensure that the public does not acquire a mistaken impression as to the lawyer's responsibility for the prospectus, and inclusion of this legend may thus be a useful prophylactic measure. In no event should the lawyer permit his name to be used in connection with a registration statement if he believes the client has engaged him in order to make use of his name and reputation rath-er than for legal advice and assistance."

In the last analysis, the company and its management must assume the final responsibility to determine that the information in the registration statement is accurate and complete. Management cannot properly take a passive role and rely entirely upon counsel to identify the information to be assembled, verify the information and prepare the registration statement properly.

Clients may have, quite appropriately, a different expectation of the lawyer's role relating to those parts of the prospectus which deal with primarily "legal" matters such as descriptions of litigation, legal proceedings, tax consequences of various transactions, interpretation of contracts and descriptions of governmental requirements. To the extent that such matters are discussed, it is fair and reasonable that the company rely primarily on its counsel for the accuracy and completeness of the descriptive material in the registration statement, assuming proper disclosure of factual matters has been made to counsel. In addition, company counsel normally renders a formal opinion on the legality of the securities being registered, which is filed as an exhibit to the registration statement. In connection with a common stock offering, the opinion would state that the shares being offered are legally issued, fully paid and non-assessable.

It is typical for counsel to the company, as well as counsel to the underwriters, to be named in a prospectus, usually under a caption heading such as "Legal Opinions" or "Legal Matters." Since the naming of counsel under such a broad heading may tend to lead public investors to misconceive the lawyer's role and responsibility in the offering, it may be more appropriate for the name of the counsel to be inserted under the caption heading dealing with the description of the securities offered, along with a statement of the substance of the opinion being rendered.[16] Such presentation would emphasize that the only legal opinion being rendered relates to these formal legal matters except to the extent that the prospectus otherwise indicates in appropriate sections regarding other specific matters such as litigation or tax consequences. An engagement letter with the client, setting forth the specific terms of counsel's responsibility, also may be a helpful practice. Such a letter can contribute materially to a better understanding between lawyer and client as to their respective responsibilities.

The authors consider it essential for the lawyers, accountants and executives to be in close coordination while the prospectus is being written. It frequently occurs that the lawyers and the accountants initially have different understandings as to the structure of a transaction, or the proper characterization or effect of an event. These differences may not be apparent readily, even from a careful reading of the registration statement's narrative text together with the financial statements. Lawyers sometimes miss the full financial implication of some important matter unless the accountants are readily available to amplify upon the draft statements and supply background information. The text is often written by counsel before the financial statements are available, based upon counsel's incorrect assumptions regarding the as yet unseen financial statement treatment of a transaction.

---

16. See note 15 supra. See generally, Cheek, Counsel Named in a Prospectus, 6 Rev.Sec.Reg. 939 (1973). For the Commission's views on the responsibilities of counsel, see SEC Securities Exchange Act Release No. 17,831 (June 1, 1981); In Re Carter, SEC Securities Exchange Act Release No. 17,597 (Feb. 28, 1981); and SEC Securities Release No. 6344 (Sept. 21, 1981).

Experience indicates that the best and sometimes only way to flush out financial disclosure problems as well as inconsistencies between the narrative text and the financial statements is through the give and take of discussion as the structure of the offering is being determined and the draft registration statement is being reviewed. The accountant's participation in this process is often essential.

On the other hand, the authors are mindful of the expense involved when accounting representatives attend long and sometimes tedious meetings. An acceptable compromise is to request their attendance on a selective basis, and to focus only on the matters requiring their participation during the period of their presence. For example, it would be wasteful to have a page by page review of a draft with accountants present, and to have them sit through the discussions of management biographies or other details having no bearing on the financial presentation.

REVIEW BY THE SEC

After the registration statement is filed initially, the Commission's Division of Corporation Finance reviews it to see that it responds appropriately to the applicable form. The Division's staff almost always finds some deficiencies, which are communicated either by telephone, usually to company counsel or through the "letter of comments" or "deficiency letter." Amendments to the registration statement are then filed in response to the comments. When the comments are reflected to the satisfaction of the SEC staff, the SEC issues an order allowing the registration statement to become effective. Only after the registration statement is effective may sales to the public take place.

There are styles and trends regarding the subjects on which staff comments tend to focus. Public pronouncements by the staff indicate that subjects to receive particular attention in the review process include: the required management discussion and analysis of financial condition and results of operation, liquidity, capital resources and effects of inflation; the use of proceeds; and transactions between the issuer and related parties.

If counsel, or the accountants with respect to financial comments, believe that the staff's comments are inappropriate or should not be met for some other reason, the comments will be discussed with the examiner, usually by telephone but in person if the matter is sufficiently serious. If a point cannot be resolved to counsel's satisfaction through discussions with the examiner, it is considered appropriate to request that the matter be submitted to the Branch Chief who supervises the examiner. When a significant issue is involved, higher levels of staff review may be requested if counsel remains unsatisfied. However, review should be sought at successive levels and counsel should not leapfrog to a senior official before the subordinates have been consulted. The Commission's staff is generally reasonable in dealing with counsel's objections. However, as a practical matter, an offering cannot usually come to market unless an accommodation has been reached on all comments. Therefore, the staff usually has the last word on whether the company has adequately responded to the comments, even if the comments are not legally binding in the formal sense.

There are usually separate reviewers for the financial and non-financial portions of a filing. Typically, although not always, the accounting review of the financial portion takes longer. Some branches of the SEC staff will release whichever comments are available first, without waiting for the other set, while other branches seem to prefer issuing all comments together.

There is a practice, very frustrating for those associated with an offering, for different levels of review within the staff to take place at different times. On occasion, as part of the final review immediately before the registration statement is intended to become effective, entirely new comments and questions will be raised by the final reviewers. Even more exasperating is the situation in which the final reviewer reverses a subordinate on a point which had been discussed previously and apparently resolved to the mutual satisfaction of the company and the staff. Such last minute developments can result in unanticipated and annoying delay and expense in preparing the final prospectus.

The review process can be expedited through the use of appropriate letters or memoranda to the Commission. If the company anticipates that the staff will raise particular comments or request additional information, it may be appropriate to volunteer the information with or shortly after the filing. Since transmittal letters addressed to the Commission do not always come to the attention of all reviewers through the Commission's painfully slow internal distribution procedures, the authors recommend sending supplemental information, as well as copies of all amended filings, directly to each staff member assigned to the particular filing.

Likewise, in transmitting amendments, review can be expedited by a letter or memorandum drawing specific attention to the location in the amended filing where responses to the comments may be found and explaining why responses to other comments have been omitted. Occasionally, it is helpful to send the Commission a copy of its comment letter with various paragraphs assigned numerical references in the margin. The supplemental letter accompanying the filing, as well as the filed amendments which are marked to show changes (in accordance with the normal practice) can then use the same numerical references to relate portions of the new material to the original comment letter.

When the comment letter is received, there is a natural tendency to focus attention solely on the points raised by the Commission. However, it is most important to remember that the registration statement must be accurate as of the time it becomes effective. Accordingly, it must be reviewed carefully in its entirety just before the effective date to be sure that all statements are updated to reflect significant intervening developments, whether or not they relate to sections covered by the Commission's comments. The Commission also has a rule relating to the updating of financial statements.[17] Generally speaking, the rule requires the most recent financial statements to be as of a date within 135 days of the date the filing is expected to become effective. The rule is phrased in terms of the issuer's expectations, suggesting that financial statements may be somewhat more than 135 days old if the issuer reasonably expected the registration statement to become effective within the 135-day period, but unanticipated delays occurred. However, the staff tends to interpret the rule as a fairly inflexible requirement that financial statements be no more than 135 days stale on the effective date. Given the inherent post-balance sheet delay required to prepare the financial statements for the filing and

17. Regulation S-X, Rule 3-12, 17 C.F.R. § 210.3-12 (1985).

the further delay for SEC review, it would be prudent to anticipate that the prospectus will require financial information which is at least three months more current than the financials in the original filing.

* * * *

During the waiting period between the filing of the registration statement and its effective date, the lead underwriter may escort company executives on a tour around the country—often called a "road show" or "dog and pony show." The purpose of this tour is to attend meetings with prospective underwriters, who will be invited into the underwriting syndicate, and possibly also analysts and potential institutional investors.

THE UNDERWRITING AGREEMENT

The company often signs a "letter of intent" with its managing underwriter once the selection of the underwriter has been made. If used, the letter outlines the proposed terms of the offering and the underwriting compensation. However, it expressly states that it is not intended to bind either party, except with respect to specific matters. One typical exception is a binding provision dealing with payment of one party's expenses by the other under certain conditions if the offering aborts before the letter of intent is superceded by the formal underwriting agreement.

In a "firm commitment" underwriting agreement, the underwriters agree that they will purchase the shares being offered for the purpose of resale to the public. The underwriters must pay for and hold the shares for their own account if they are not successful in finding public purchasers. This form of underwriting is almost always used by the larger underwriters and provides the greater assurance of raising the desired funds. In the other common type of underwriting arrangement, the underwriters agree to use their "best efforts" to sell the issue as the company's agent. To the extent that purchasers cannot be found, the issue is not sold. Some best efforts agreements provide that no shares will be sold unless buyers can be found for all, while others set a lower minimum such as fifty percent. For certain special types of securities, such as tax shelter limited partnership offerings, even the major underwriters normally use the best efforts or agency underwriting relationship.

In either form of underwriting, the underwriters' obligations are usually subject to many conditions: various "outs," such as the right not to close (even if the company is not otherwise in default) in the event of certain specified adverse developments prior to the closing date; and compliance by the company with its numerous representations and warranties. The underwriters also condition their obligations upon the receipt of certain opinions of counsel and representations, sometimes called a "cold comfort letter," from the company's auditors.

The binding firm underwriting agreement normally is not signed until within twenty-four hours of the expected effective date of the registration statement—often on the morning of effectiveness. Thus, throughout the process of preparing the registration statement and during the waiting period, the company has incurred very substantial expenses with no assurance that the offering will take place. Once preparation of the registration statement has begun, however, reputable underwriters rarely refuse to complete the offering, although this can occur with some frequency, especially for small and highly speculative offerings, if there is a sharp market drop during the waiting period. However, as indicated above, the underwriters must price the offering and organize the underwriting syndicate in relationship to market conditions prevailing at the time of the offering. Thus, if market conditions have worsened materially after the letter of intent stage, the issue must either come to the market at a price below that originally contemplated, or it must be postponed until conditions improve. Furthermore, it is not uncommon for underwriters to suggest a reduction in the size of the offering if the market conditions are unfavorable. The company may find itself in a position of accepting a less than satisfactory final proposal, regarding size and pricing of the offering, as a preferable alternative to postponement or complete abandonment of the offering. On the other hand, sharply improved market conditions may result in a higher offering price than the parties originally anticipated.

Final settlement with the underwriters usually takes place seven to ten days after the registration statement has become effective, so as to allow the underwriters time to obtain the funds from their customers. At that time, the company receives the proceeds of the sale, net of the underwriting compensation.

SEC rules permit underwriters to offer and sell to the public more shares than the underwriters are obligated to purchase under the underwriting agreement—a practice known as "over-allotment." If the underwriters over-allot, they will have a "short" position, which may help to establish a better after-market for the shares following the offering, since any shares resold by original purchasers will have been placed effectively in advance through the over-allotment sales. The underwriting agreement often gives the underwriters an option to purchase additional shares from the issuer, or possibly from selling shareholders, solely for the purpose of covering over-allotments. The shares covered by the over-allotment option are purchasable on the same price terms that apply to the shares which are part of the basic offering. This option of the underwriters, often referred to as a "Green Shoe option" (based on the offering of its initial use), typically covers under present practice up to a maximum of 15% of the number of shares included in the basic offering and can only be exercised within thirty days of the offering date. To illustrate, if the basic offering is 500,000 shares, the firm commitment will obligate the underwriters to purchase and pay for 500,000 shares; the over-allotment option will entitle them to purchase up to 75,000 additional shares solely to cover over-allotments.

The NASD also reviews the underwriting arrangements in accordance with guidelines which are not fully spelled out in detail to the public. The NASD will disapprove underwriting arrangements if it considers the underwriters' compensation to be excessive under these guidelines. Occasionally an underwriter who bargains hard for a very attractive compensation package from an issuer finds that the regulatory agency will disapprove the arrangement unless some aspect of the underwriters' benefits are decreased.

PRELIMINARY PREPARATION

For the average first offering, a very substantial amount of preliminary work is required which does not relate directly to preparing the registration statement as such. To have a vehicle for the offering, the business going public normally must be conducted by a single corporation or a parent corporation with subsidiaries. In most cases, the business is not already in such a neat package when the offering project commences. It is often conducted by a number of corporations under common ownership, by partnerships or by combinations of business entities. Considerable work must be done in order to reorganize the various entities by mergers, liquidations and capital contributions. Even when there is a single corporation, a recapitalization is almost always required so that the company will have an appropriate capital structure for the public offering. A decision must be made regarding the proportion of the stock to be sold to the public. Any applicable blue sky limitations on insiders' "cheap stock" should be considered in this context, especially if the company has been organized in the relatively recent past.

Among other common projects in preparing to go public, it is often necessary to enter into, revise, or terminate employment agreements, adopt stock option plans and grant options thereunder, transfer real estate, revise leases, rewrite the corporate charter and by-laws, prepare new stock certificates, engage a transfer agent and registrar, rearrange stockholdings of insiders, draw, revise or cancel agreements among shareholders, revamp financing arrangements, prepare and order stock certificates, obtain a CUSIP number and secure a tentative ticker symbol.[c]

An increasing number of companies consider adoption of defenses against hostile takeover attempts as part of the pre-offering revision of charter, by-laws and employment arrangements. So-called "shark repellant" (or "porcupine") devices, which help to deter or defeat unwelcome tender offers, include provisions for staggered multi-year terms for directors and "supermajority" voting provisions applicable to certain types of corporate transactions (to assure that a relatively small minority can veto certain proposals which may be sponsored by the holder of a majority of the stock). Various employment devices, often referred to as "golden parachutes," may protect the status and employment benefits, or may provide very favorable severance arrangements, for executives and key employees whose positions may be adversely affected by a takeover or other abrupt change of control.

On the other hand, some underwriters may resist adoption of such devices on the ground that they appear too defensive or unattractive to investors, since investors may profit handsomely from the premium paid in a hostile tender. Furthermore, adoption of some of the more effective shark repellant devices may disqualify the offering from compliance with the blue sky laws of key states. Accordingly, many issuers omit the shark repellant provisions at the time of the initial public offering. Such issuers are free, of course, to adopt shark repellant provisions at a later date, which would normally require a majority vote of all shareholders, including the public ones. If the issuer had a fixed, preconceived plan at the time of the public offering to propose such provisions at a future date, it should consider the need to disclose such plans in the prospectus.

In preparing the registration statement, there are occasionally important threshold or interpretive problems which can have a major effect on the preparation process or, indeed, on the feasibility of the offering. It is often possible to discuss such problems with the SEC staff in a pre-filing/ conference, although some pre-filing conference requests are denied by the staff. However, decisions to request a pre-filing conference should be made

---

c. The acronym CUSIP signifies the Committee on Uniform Security Identification Procedures which was established by the American Bankers Association. The CUSIP number is an eight-digit number which is imprinted on the certificate; it is used by transfer agents to identify each issue for the purpose of identifying the issue, insuring authenticity and permitting rapid identification. See infra at page 360.

with caution. Among other considerations, once a question has been asked in advance of a filing, there may be no practical alternative other than to wait for the staff's answer, which may delay a filing considerably. Frequently, the decision is made simply to proceed with the filing, resolving the threshold issue on the basis which the company considers most appropriate, in the hope that a satisfactory resolution of the problem (either the issuer's initial solution or some other) will be achieved during the review process.

TIMETABLE

Although laymen find it difficult to believe, the average first public offering normally requires two to three months of intensive work before the registration statement can be filed. One reason so much time is required is the need to accomplish the preparatory steps just referred to at the same time the registration statement is being prepared. There are many important and often interrelated business decisions to be made and implemented and rarely are all of these questions decided definitively at the outset. Some answers must await final figures, or negotiations with underwriters, and must be held open until the last minute. In many instances, a businessman first exposed to these considerations will change his mind several times in the interim. Furthermore, drafting of the prospectus normally begins before the financial statements are available. Almost inevitably, some rewriting must be done in the non-financial parts after the financial statements are distributed in order to blend the financial and non-financial sections together. Laymen frequently have the frustrating feeling as the deadline approaches that everything is hopelessly confused. They are quite surprised to see that everything falls into place at the eleventh hour.

After the registration statement is filed with the Commission, the waiting period begins. It is during this interval that red herrings are distributed. The Commission reviews the registration statement and finally issues its letter of comments. There is a wide variation in the time required for the SEC to process a registration statement. Relevant factors include the level of the Commission's backlog of filings and the time of year. There is normally a considerable rush of filings at the end of each calendar quarter, and particularly at the end of March for filings with financial statements as of December 31.

The SEC's current policy calls for the issuance of an initial letter of comments within thirty days of the filing of a registration statement, but the delay is often longer and at times has exceeded one hundred days. A recent increased number of first-time registration statements and other filings, coupled with reductions in the number of the SEC's review personnel, raised the possibility of long delays in issuing comment letters. This occurred despite various initiatives by the SEC during the past several years including the adoption of various "short-form" registration statements for certain types of companies and transactions, increases in the dollar amount of securities which could be sold without registration and the processing of certain offerings in regional offices of the SEC.

As a result, the SEC in late 1980 announced a new procedure designed to reduce delays in the review and processing of registration statements and other documents filed with them.[28] Under the new procedure, the SEC will review offerings by public companies on a selective basis and certain registration statements of established public companies will no longer be reviewed at all. The new procedure has tended to enable the SEC to reduce time delays by concentrating its resources on certain areas, including first time public offerings which will continue to receive thorough review. The average time between the filing and the receipt of a comment letter for new offerings often is less than thirty days particularly in certain branch offices.

The overall time lapse between the beginning of preparation of a company's first registration statement and the final effective date may well exceed six months. Rarely will it be less than three months.

The SEC's requirements for unaudited financial statements for periods after the end of a company's last fiscal year represent another important ingredient in the timetable. In the case of a registration statement for a company going public for the first time, a company filing within forty-five days after its fiscal year end must include interim financial statements at least as current as the end of the third fiscal quarter of its most recently completed fiscal year as well as the required fiscal year end audited financial statements for the prior years; a company filing after forty-five days but within 134 days of the end of the company's most recent fiscal year end must include audited financial statements for its most recently completed fiscal year; and a company filing more than 134 days subsequent to the end of its most recent fiscal year must include interim financial statements within 135 days of the date of the filing as well as the required fiscal year end audited financial statements. The financial statement for the interim periods need not be audited, however, and the statements required are not as complete as those required for the audited periods. Of course, audited financial statements must be substituted once available in lieu of unaudited financial statements.

At the time the registration statement becomes effective, the unaudited interim financial statements must be as of a date within 135 days of the effective date, except that such financial statements may be as of the end of the third fiscal quarter of the most recently completed fiscal year if the registration statement becomes effective within forty-five days after the end of the most recent fiscal year. Audited financial statements for the most recently completed fiscal year must be included if the registration statement becomes effective between forty-five and ninety days after the end of such fiscal year.

EXPENSES

A major expense in going public is usually the underwriters' compensation. The underwriting cash discount or cash commission on a new issue generally ranges from 7% to 10% of the public offering price. The maximum amount of direct and indirect underwriting compensation is regulated by the National Association of Securities Dealers, Inc. (NASD), a self-regulatory agency which regulates broker-dealers. Normally, the three largest additional expenses are legal fees, accounting fees and printing costs.

---

28. See SEC News Digest, Issue Nov. 17, 1980, at 1. This new system was said to replace the procedures followed by the staff for a number of years as set forth in SEC Securities Act Release No. 5231 (Feb. 3, 1972) * * *.

Legal fees for a first offering of at least $5,000,000 generally would be between $55,000 and $115,000, with $75,000 to $100,000 being typical. This amount includes not only the preparation of the registration statement itself, but also all of the corporate work, house cleaning and other detail which is occasioned by the public offering process. Fees for smaller offerings tend to be somewhat lower. In part, this may reflect the fact that offerings for start-up companies, which tend to be smaller in size, typically require less legal work in investigating business operations, since there are none. However, start-up offerings can be more difficult in other respects— for example, risk factors are more prevalent and minor matters may require disclosure on points which would be immaterial to an established company with a history of operations. Therefore, start-up offerings occasionally are even more demanding than offerings of larger seasoned companies.

Accounting fees can vary significantly depending on the complexity of the business, whether the financial statements to be included in the registration statement have been audited in the normal course, and the extent to which the independent accountants may be involved in the development of financial and other information to be included in the registration statement. Other factors which will cause accounting fees to vary from one registration statement to another are the extent to which the independent accountants are required to participate in meetings with counsel and underwriters' representatives and the nature and extent of procedures performed at the request of the underwriters for purposes of the "comfort letter." If there have been no prior audits and new accountants are engaged at the time of the offering, fees ranging up to $65,000 and even higher would not be unusual. If the company's financial statements have been audited regularly for several years in the past, the added accounting expense for a public offering, in addition to the normal audit expense, could be much less especially if no unaudited interim statements are required. (While interim statements may be unaudited in a formal sense, the auditors are inevitably involved in some review of the interim statements, especially in connection with the comfort letter to be given to the underwriters at the closing.) Obviously, accounting expenses for start-up companies with limited past transactions can be substantially lower.

Often the total legal and accounting fees are allocated and part of the amounts are attributed directly to the public offering. This portion is included in the registration statement's list of expenses of the offering and is charged to capital for accounting and tax purposes. The balance of the professional fees for projects which are not aspects of the registration process as such, such as preparation of an employees stock option plan, is often treated as a charge for current services rather than a registration expense. For accounting and tax purposes, these non-registration charges are treated as current business expenses. The allocation, and the resulting tax and accounting treatment, should be reviewed carefully so that all parties treat the allocated expenses consistently.

Printing expenses for registration statements and various underwriting documents typically range up to $100,000, but larger charges are not unusual. Color printing, if used, can add significantly to the printing expense. If the offering involves a debt security, the printing of a trust indenture can add to the expense. Overall printing costs can be affected significantly by such factors as the length of the prospectus, the extent of updating required between the original filing and the final printing (due to staleness of financial statements, SEC comments or other intervening developments), the numbers of copies required and the extent of alterations made by the parties (which are inevitably extensive, compared to other types of commercial printing, no matter how well the registration project is planned).

For each registration statement, there is a filing fee at the rate of 0.02% of the maximum aggregate offering price of the securities, with a minimum fee of $100, which fee is non-refundable.

Among the other expenses to be borne are transfer taxes (in the event of a secondary offering), if applicable, transfer agent and registrar fees, printing of stock certificates and "blue sky" expenses. The company is generally required to reimburse the underwriter for the NASD filing fee, which is computed at the rate of $100 plus 0.01% of the maximum aggregate offering price of the securities, with a maximum fee of $5,100. Occasionally the company must pay an expense allowance (sometimes on an accountable basis and sometimes on a non-accountable basis) to the underwriters. This is a negotiated figure which can range from several thousand dollars to $100,000 or more in some cases. The company frequently pays the underwriters' counsel a special fee for compliance with applicable state securities laws (so-called "blue sky" work), which can range up to many thousand dollars, depending on the number and identity of the jurisdictions involved.

Indemnity insurance against '33 Act liability is sometimes required by the underwriters. However, it is difficult to obtain and is usually available only on the higher quality issues where it is least needed. Premiums are set on an individual basis, generally comprising about 1 percent of the amount of the coverage, which may be less than 100 percent of the total offering.

For a normal first public stock offering of several million dollars, total expenses in the $175,000 to $350,000 range would be typical, exclusive of the underwriting discount or commission but inclusive of any expense allowance (whether or not accountable) payable to the underwriters. However, it should be emphasized that there are wide variations among offerings. The estimates for aggregate as well as individual expenses given above can be too low if unusual problems or complications develop in a particular offering. Average costs have increased substantially in recent years, due to a number of factors including general inflation, the added scope and content of certain disclosure items in the forms and ever expanding notions of due diligence obligations.

Although the amount of time, effort and printing required for an offering is not necessarily related to its dollar size, smaller offerings tend to be somewhat less expensive than the larger ones. If an offering involves either debt securities or secondary sales for selling shareholders, the expenses may tend to be somewhat higher than for a simple primary offering of common stock. Other factors being equal, offerings using Form S-18 or Regulation A may be somewhat less expensive than offerings registered on Form S-1.

In addition to cash disbursements, there are other costs of going public to consider. As part of the arrangement underwriters sometimes bargain for "cheap stock"—securities which they purchase at less than the public offering price and often at a nominal price as low as a mill a share. They may insist upon receiving options or warrants exercisable over a number of years to purchase the securities being offered at a price usually equal to or above the offering price. These benefits, most typical of the smaller offerings done by the smaller underwriters, introduce an element of dilution of the security. Here again the NASD imposes limitations on the amount of cheap stock and warrants which underwriters may receive.

* * *

CONCLUSION

The process of going public is a major development in the business life of any company. It is a step which should be taken only after a thorough analysis of the advantages, disadvantages, consequences and alternative means of financing. Going public is a relatively time consuming and expensive means of raising capital, although the commensurate benefits may more than outweigh these disadvantages in the appropriate situation.

Any company considering the possibility of a public offering should begin its planning long in advance. Many of the decisions which must be made in connection with a public offering require a long period of time to implement. Therefore, a well planned public offering is a project for which the preliminary steps and long range study should begin well before the securities can be sold.[d]

SECTION 11 LIABILITY FOR DEFECTIVE REGISTRATION STATEMENTS

The underwriters' investigation in connection with the preparation of a registration statement is designed to satisfy the "due diligence" defense in case of a Section 11 action under the Securities Act alleging liability for misstatements or omissions in the registration statement. Section 11 imposes liability upon directors, the chief executive and financial officers, accountants who certify the financial statements, and underwriters, among others. Liability is imposed for material statements in the registration statement which are false or misleading, and for material omissions to state facts required to be stated, unless these designated persons can establish that they had, after reasonable investigation, reasonable grounds to believe and did believe, that the statements were accurate and complete. Moreover, the issuing corporation does not even have this "due diligence" defense. For the first thirty-five years following the enactment of the 1933 Act, a very few cases had arisen under Section 11. However, in 1968, Escott v. BarChris Construction Corp., infra at page 901, imposed Section 11 liability upon an issuer, its chief executive and financial officers, its directors, including inside and outside counsel, and the underwriters and accountants, and denied their defenses based on "due diligence". Again, in 1971 in Feit v. Leasco Data Processing Equipment Corporation, infra at page 969, Judge Weinstein imposed liability upon an issuer, its chief executive and financial officers, and its directors (including an outside director who was also company counsel), but not the underwriters, for an omission to estimate the amount of liquid assets which could be withdrawn from an insurance company (the so-called "surplus surplus") for unrestricted uses by the issuer which sought to take over the target company through an exchange offer registered under the 1933 Act. The *Feit* and *BarChris* cases and the scope of Section 11 liability for misstatements or omissions in the registration statement are considered at pages 901 and 969 respectively, as a part of an overall

d. See M. Halloran, Going Public (3d ed. Aug. 1, 1979), published by SORG Printing Company. For an inside view of the process of crafting an IPO of a high- tech company, see Uttal, Inside the Deal That Made Bill Gates $350,000,000, 114 Fortune 23 (July 21, 1986).

consideration of the interrelationships of the various civil remedies under the 1933 and 1934 Acts. Nevertheless, the possibility of crushing liabilities upon the issuer and these other persons for failure to meet the Section 11 standards of accuracy and due diligence in the preparation of the registration statement underlines the importance of an objective investigation of the material facts by the issuer's and underwriters' counsel and a fair and frank disclosure of all material facts relating to the offering in the registration statement. As Judge Weinstein said in the *Feit* case: *

> Using a [registration] statement to obscure, rather than reveal, in plain English, the critical elements of a proposed business deal cannot be countenanced under the securities regulation acts * * *. The prospective purchaser of a new issue of securities is entitled to know what the deal is all about. Given an honest and open statement, adequately warning of the possibilities of error and miscalculation and not designed for puffing, an outsider and insider are placed on more equal grounds for arms length dealing. Such equalization of bargaining power through sharing of knowledge in the securities market is a basic national policy underlying the federal securities laws.

For further implications of Section 11, see the statute and note on Section 11 Liability, infra at page 931.

INDEMNIFICATION OF OFFICERS, DIRECTORS, CONTROLLING PERSONS AND UNDERWRITERS, RIGHTS OF CONTRIBUTION, AND THE USE OF LIABILITY INSURANCE

Scope of Civil Liabilities Under Federal Securities Laws. Officers, directors, controlling persons and underwriters may be exposed to substantial potential liabilities under the Federal securities laws. These liabilities may arise under §§ 11, 12 and 17(a) of the 1933 Act as well as § 10 and Rule 10b–5 and other sections of the 1934 Act. In some cases the liability may be incurred when the person is acting in a representative capacity on behalf of the issuer; in other cases the liability may arise from activities undertaken in a nonrepresentative capacity. Section 16(b) of the Securities Exchange Act of 1934 makes officers, directors, and any beneficial owner of more than 10% of any equity security registered pursuant to Section 12 liable to the corporation for short-swing profits realized on round-trip trading within a period of less than six months. Although the liability arises because of the subject's relation to the corporation, the activity of trading in the corporation's securities entails conduct outside the individual's representative capacity.

The right of a corporate officer or director to obtain indemnification for litigation expenses or for liabilities and fines incurred either in direct or derivative actions brought on behalf of the corporation or in third party actions arising from activities undertaken in a representative capacity is generally dependent on state law. This is not the place to review the general law of indemnification of directors and officers.[1]

* Feit v. Leasco Data Processing Equipment Corp., 332 F.Supp. 544, 549 (E.D.N.Y.1971), infra at 705.

1. Jennings & Buxbaum, Corporations—Cases and Materials 746–760 (5th ed. 1979); Cary & Eisenberg, Corporations—Cases and Materials 952–970 (5th ed. 1980); Bishop, Law of Corporate Officers and Directors—Indemnification and Insurance (1983 Supp.); Bishop, Sitting Ducks and Decoy Ducks: New Trends in the Indemnification of Corporate Directors and Officers, 77 Yale L.J. 1078 (1968); Bishop, New Problems in Indemnifying and Insuring Directors, 1972 Duke L.J. 1153; Bisceglia, Practical Aspects of Directors' and Officers' Liability Insurance—Allocating and Advancing Legal Fees and the Duty to Defend, 32 UCLA L.Rev. 690 (1985); Montgomery & Thornton, Insura-

State Indemnification Statutes. A number of states have enacted director and officer indemnification statutes. Among the most expansive is Delaware Corporation Law § 145. This statute encompasses both third party actions and derivative actions brought against a director, officer, employee or agent. In both types of action, a successful defendant has an absolute right to indemnification for his or her expenses, including attorney's fees. In derivative actions, a director or officer may be indemnified against expenses, including attorney's fees, except where such person was adjudged to be liable for negligence or misconduct, but not for judgments and probably not for settlement payments.[2] On the other hand, in third party actions, a defendant may be reimbursed for all expenses, including attorney's fees, judgments and settlement payments actually and reasonably incurred. In both derivative and third-party actions, a statutory standard of conduct must be met. Thus, the defendant may be indemnified only if such individual "acted in good faith and in a manner he reasonably believed to be in or not opposed to the best interests of the corporation," and, with respect to criminal actions, only if such person had no reasonable cause to believe that the conduct was unlawful. This determination may be made by a majority of the directors who are not parties to the action, by shareholders, by independent counsel or by a court. Furthermore, the statute expressly provides that the statutory indemnification provisions shall not be deemed exclusive of any other rights conferred under any bylaw, agreement, or stockholder or director action.

Where a state indemnity statute is exclusive (New York and California) and imposes a limit on the power of the corporation to indemnify, the question still remains whether the statute should be construed to prohibit the purchase of insurance to reimburse the corporate executive for nonindemnifiable expenses.[3] Even under a nonexclusive statute, such as that in Delaware, or under the common law, it is still an open question whether it would be lawful for a corporation to insure the executive for non-indemnifiable third party claims in order to provide additional protection to third parties, or for non-indemnifiable costs and expenses in derivative suits.[4]

Indemnification and Contribution Under Federal Securities Law. The question arises as to whether an issuer may indemnify officers, directors, and underwriters for liabilities incurred under §§ 11, 12 or 17(a) of the 1933 Act or Rule 10b–5 of the 1934 Act.[5] In Globus v. Law Research Service, Inc., 418 F.2d 1276 (2d Cir. 1969), cert. denied, 397 U.S. 913 (1970) [Globus I], private actions based on § 17(a) and Rule 10b–5 were brought against LRS, the issuer, Hoppenfeld, its president, and Blair, the underwriter, alleging defects in an offering

---

bility of Losses Resulting from Liability under the Federal Securities Laws, 13 Pac.L.J. 959 (1982).

2. See Johnston, Corporate Indemnification and Liability Insurance for Directors and Officers, 33 Bus.Law. 1993, 1996, 2009 (1978).

3. Because of the doubt on this question, the California statute was amended in 1968 and the New York statute in 1969 to expressly permit the purchase by the corporation of liability insurance for the benefit of its executives. Cal.Corps.Code, § 830(h), as added by Cal.Stats.1968, ch. 400 and now found in Cal.Corps.Code § 317(i); N.Y.Bus.Corp.Law, § 727, as added by N.Y.Stats.1969, ch. 1007.

4. See the discussion in Klink, Chalif, Bishop & Arsht, Liabilities Which Can be Covered Under State Statutes and Corporate By-Laws, 27 Bus.Law. 109 (Spec. Issue, Feb. 1972); Johnston, supra note 2, at 2034–036.

5. What would be the effect of inserting a hedge clause in the offering circular to the effect that the securities are sold subject to the condition and understanding that the buyer is not relying upon the representations therein contained in purchasing the securities? See Rogen v. Ilikon Corp., 361 F.2d 260 (1st Cir. 1966), where the seller of securities disclaimed reliance upon representations or nondisclosures by the buyer. The court held such a provision ineffective under § 29(a) of the 1934 Act. Cf. § 14 of the 1933 Act.

circular used in connection with a public offering of securities under Regulation A (the small issues exemption) promulgated under § 3(b) of the 1933 Act. Blair cross-claimed against LRS pursuant to an indemnification agreement, indemnifying it for any loss arising out of defects in the offering circular, except for "wilful misfeasance, bad faith or gross negligence * * * or * * * reckless disregard of its obligations under the agreement." The court concluded that since the underwriter had *actual* knowledge of the material misstatements and omissions, it would be contrary to the public policy embodied in the federal securities laws to permit the underwriter to enforce the indemnification agreement.

In connection with its opinion the court considered the policy considerations as to indemnity under § 11 of the 1933 Act (which applies to registered securities, but not to Regulation A offerings) and expressed its views in these terms at pages 1288–1289:

"Although the 1933 Act does not deal expressly with the question before us, provisions in that Act confirm our conclusion that Blair should not be entitled to indemnity from LRS. See generally Note, Indemnification of Underwriters and § 11 of the Securities Act of 1933, 72 Yale L.J. 406. For example, § 11 of the Act, makes underwriters jointly liable with directors, experts and signers of the registration statement. And, the SEC has announced its view that indemnification of directors, officers and controlling persons for liabilities arising under the 1933 Act is against the public policy of the Act. 17 C.F.R. § 230.460.[6] If we follow the syllogism through to its conclusion, underwriters should be treated equally with controlling persons and hence prohibited from obtaining indemnity from the issuer. See 72 Yale, supra, at 411. But see 3 Loss supra, at 1834 (1961).

"Civil liability under section 11 and similar provisions was designed not so much to compensate the defrauded purchaser as to promote enforcement of the Act and to deter negligence by providing a penalty for those who fail in their duties. And Congress intended to impose a 'high standard of trusteeship' on underwriters. Kroll, [Some Reflections on Indemnification Provisions & S.E.C. Liability Insurance in the Light of BarChris and Globus, 24 Bus.Law. 685] supra, at 687. Thus, what Professor Loss terms the '*in terrorem* effect' of civil liability, 3 Loss, supra, at 1831, might well be thwarted if underwriters were free to pass their liability on to the issuer. Underwriters who knew they could be indemnified simply by showing that the issuer was 'more liable' than they (a process not too difficult when the issuer is inevitably closer to the facts) would have a tendency to be lax in their independent investigations. * * * Cases upholding indemnity for negligence in other fields are not necessarily apposite. The goal in such cases is to compensate the injured party. But the Securities Act is more concerned with prevention than cure.

"Finally, it has been suggested that indemnification of the underwriter by the issuer is particularly suspect. Although in form the underwriter is reimbursed by the issuer, the recovery ultimately comes out of the pockets of the issuer's stockholders. Many of these stockholders may be the very purchasers to whom the underwriter should have been initially liable. The 1933 Act prohibits agreements with purchasers which purport to exempt individuals from liability arising under the Act. [§ 14]. The situation before us is at least reminiscent of the evil this section was designed to avoid."[7]

Even if direct indemnification is contrary to public policy embodied in the federal securities laws, may a defendant having actual knowledge of the wrongful conduct recover contribution from the other participants arising from

---

6. [Eds.] The SEC's view now appears at SEC Regulation S–K, Item 510.

7. Accord, Heizer Corp. v. Ross, 601 F.2d 330, 334–35 (7th Cir. 1979). ALI Federal Securities Code § 1724(e) deals with the availability of indemnification and insurance in securities cases.

their joint and several liability? Moreover, may the issuer and its corporate executives obtain indirect indemnification through having the corporation purchase liability insurance protection against such exposure?

Globus I, discussed above, sets forth the SEC's position on indemnification of directors, officers and controlling persons under the 1933 and 1934 Acts. That policy is presently expressed in SEC Regulation S–K, Items 702, 510 and 512.

Item 702, where applicable, requires a statement of the general effect of any statute, provision or arrangement under which any director, officer or controlling person of the registrant is insured or indemnified against Securities Act liability. Under Item 512(i), if the registrant requests acceleration of the effectiveness of a registration statement pursuant to section 8(a) of the 1933 Act, and waivers have not been obtained, a reference to such indemnification provisions must be made in the registration statement along with a statement that in the opinion of the Commission such provisions are against public policy and will not be relied upon by any beneficiary without adjudication by a court of their validity. This statement with respect to SEC policy must substantially follow the form set forth in the Item.

Under Item 510, if acceleration of the effective date of the registration statement is not being requested so that Item 512(i) is inoperative, and if waivers have not been obtained, a description of the indemnification provisions relating to such persons and the Commission's policy on indemnification must be set forth in the registration statement. If the director, officer or controlling person of the registrant is also a member or controlling person of one of the underwriters of the issue, any applicable indemnification provisions must also be described.

These provisions do not prohibit a selling shareholder in a secondary offering from indemnifying the issuer, officers or directors, experts and underwriters from § 11 liabilities arising from his or her misstatements or omissions appearing in the registration statement. Although the registration statement is that of the issuer, registration of a selling shareholder's securities are for such shareholder's benefit and the issuer and other shareholders are entitled to indemnification. The cross-indemnifications provisions between the issuer and underwriters which are contained in the typical underwriting agreement are also permitted, provided the Item 512(i) undertaking contains a disclaimer against utilization until the validity of such provisions has been adjudicated. Finally, it is to be noted that there is no objection to insuring against § 11 liability, regardless of who pays the premiums.[8]

Globus II, below, raises the question of the right of contribution as between defendants in an implied Rule 10b–5 action, and discusses the effect of the express right of contribution provided in § 11 of the 1933 Act and §§ 9 and 18 of the 1934 Act.

GLOBUS v. LAW RESEARCH SERVICE, INC.*

United States District Court, S.D. New York, 1970.
318 F.Supp. 955.

FRANKEL, DISTRICT JUDGE. In this lawsuit, a prolific generator of nice questions, plaintiff purchasers of securities have recovered a judgment

---

8. With the problems facing insurance companies and, as a result, their customers, liability insurance is becoming more difficult to obtain and enormously expensive. In addition, insurers and courts have increasingly narrowed policy coverage. See Galante, Insurance Costs Soar; Is There Any Way Out?, Nat'l. L. J., Mar. 10, 1986, at 1; Shapiro v. American Home Assurance Company, 584 F.Supp. 1245 (D.Mass.1984).

* Aff'd per curiam, 442 F.2d 1346 (2d Cir. 1971), cert. denied sub nom. Law Research Service, Inc. v. Blair & Co., 404 U.S. 941.

under the 1933 and 1934 Securities Acts, have been paid a reduced amount allowed by a modification on appeal, and have finally gone hence. There remains a dispute as to whether one defendant, Blair & Co., Granbery, Marache, Incorporated (Blair), having paid in full the amount of the judgment, may recover contribution from the two defendants—Law Research Service, Inc. (LRS), and Ellias C. Hoppenfeld—held jointly and severally liable with it. The underlying dispute and its outcome have been fully recounted in an opinion by Judge Mansfield, which held, *inter alia*, that there could be no award of indemnity to Blair, 287 F.Supp. 188 (S.D.N.Y.1968), and an opinion of the Court of Appeals, 2 Cir., 418 F.2d 1276 (1969), affirming on that and all other subjects except punitive damages, which it ruled unavailable under § 17(a) of the 1933 Securities Act, * * * as well as under § 10(b) of the Securities Exchange Act of 1934, * * *.

[T]he judgment in its form following the appeal left Blair, LRS and Hoppenfeld jointly and severally liable to plaintiffs. The liability was for compensatory damages only. Blair, for reasons that are in part of interest now and are considered below, was held barred from recovering on its indemnity agreement with LRS. In substance and effect, while they argued before and continue to argue now about the degrees of their fault, they stood equally culpable and equally responsible.

Nevertheless, Blair alone, on May 8, 1970, paid plaintiffs the full amount of the judgment, plus interest and costs, or a total of $36,888.59, reserving any rights it might have to contribution from the others. When LRS and Hoppenfeld refused to contribute, Blair brought on the motion now before the court seeking judgment against them for one-third each of the sum paid to plaintiffs. The motion will be granted for reasons which follow.

(1) Departing from the rugged flintiness of traditional common law, the general drift of the law today is toward the allowance of contribution among joint tortfeasors. * * * See generally, Prosser, Law of Torts, § 47 (3rd Ed. 1964); Comment, Contribution Among Joint Tortfeasors, 44 Tex.L.Rev. 326, 326 n. 5 (1965) (cataloguing 24 States which have enacted statutes allowing contribution).

(2) More specifically, the securities acts underlying this case point clearly to the result Blair seeks.[2] As Judge Doyle pointed out in the *de Haas* case, supra note 2 at 815–816,

"those sections of the [securities acts] which expressly provide for civil liability contain express provisions for contribution among intentional wrongdoers. [Citing § 11 of the 1933 Act, * * * and §§ 9 and 18 of the 1934 Act. * * *] Since the specific liability provisions of the Act provide for contribution, it appears that contribution should be permitted when liability is implied under Section 10(b). III Loss, Securities Regulation 1739–40, n. 178 (1961)."

This is simply a pertinent application of the general principle that the two statutes are to be administered *in pari materia*. E.g., Globus v. Law Research Service, Inc., supra, 418 F.2d at 1286.

(3) The prior decisions of Judge Mansfield and the Court of Appeals denying Blair's claim to indemnity support Blair's position now. A central

---

2. There is no basis for doubting that the subject of contribution, like indemnity (as has been held in this case), is governed here by federal law. See, e.g., de Haas v. Empire Petroleum Company, 286 F.Supp. 809, 815–816 (D.Colo.1968).

ground for the ruling on indemnity was the judgment that allowing such means of absolution would dilute the deterrent impact of the securities laws, which seek "to encourage diligence, investigation and compliance with the requirements of the statute by exposing issuers and underwriters to the substantial hazard of liability for compensatory damages." Id. at 1289. The shoe is now on the other foot. If not identical, the mode of escape sought by LRS and Hoppenfeld is objectionable on substantially similar grounds. They may not effectively nullify their "liability for compensatory damages" by leaving the whole of the burden to the more prompt and diligent party with which they have been cast in joint and several liability.

* * * *

Blair's motion is granted. The Clerk of the Court will enter judgments for Blair against LRS and Hoppenfeld, each in the amount of $12,296.19 (the shares as computed by Blair), plus interest from May 8, 1970.[a]

SECTION 3. TRADITIONAL STANDARDS OF DISCLOSURE

Statutes and Regulations

Securities Act, § 7.

Regulation C, Rules 400–418, 421, 425, 425A, 426.

IN THE MATTER OF UNIVERSAL CAMERA CORP.

Securities and Exchange Commission, 1945.
19 S.E.C. 648.

This case comes before us on a motion to dismiss a stop order proceeding commenced with respect to a registration statement filed under the Securities Act of 1933 by Universal Camera Corporation (Universal). * * *.

That statement raised questions of general public importance concerning the character of the disclosure required by the Securities Act of 1933. Accordingly, in passing upon the motion to dismiss the proceeding we deem it appropriate to state our reasons for the action taken in this proceeding. We wish to emphasize especially (1) the nature and extent of our jurisdiction with respect to proposed securities issues subject to registration under the Act and (2) the fact that a registration statement, although it contains the essential facts, may not satisfy the disclosure requirements of the Securities Act if the facts are so stated that they do not make the

---

a. See ALI Federal Securities Code § 1724(f) (Contribution); Note, The Role of Contribution in Determining Underwriters' Liability under Section 11 of the Securities Act of 1933, 63 Va.L.Rev. 79 (1977). Other courts confronted with the question have held that contribution is available in securities cases, indemnification is not. Heizer Corp. v. Ross, 601 F.2d 330, 334 (7th Cir. 1979). Cf. Scott, Resurrecting Indemnification: Contribution Clauses in Underwriting Agreements, 61 N.Y.U.L.Rev. 223 (1986).

In Alexander & Baldwin, Inc. v. Peat, Marwick, Mitchell & Co., 385 F.Supp. 230 (S.D.N.Y.1974), a Rule 10b–5 action was brought against the seller of securities, and the accountants who certified the financial statements. Following Globus I and Globus II, the court held that settlement of the suit by the seller would not bar mutual claims for contribution as between the defendants for any amounts paid by way of settlement or judgment.

characteristics of the security clearly understandable to the ordinary investor.

On March 19, 1945, Universal filed with the Commission a registration statement under the Securities Act of 1933. The statement related to a proposed public offering of (1) 663,500 shares of a new Class A common stock of Universal and (2) warrants, expiring December 31, 1948, for the purchase of 172,700 shares of such Class A common stock. The shares called for by the warrants would also be registered under this registration statement.

Of the 663,500 Class A shares covered by the registration statement 133,000 would be offered by Universal. 530,500 would be offered by controlling stockholders of Universal.

Of the warrants for a total of 172,700 shares of Class A stock covered by the registration statement, warrants for 26,600 shares would be offered by Universal whereas warrants for 146,100 would be offered by controlling stockholders.

On April 10, 1945, prior to the effective date of the registration statement, stop order proceedings were commenced under Section 8(d) of the Securities Act of 1933 for reasons which will be stated hereafter. * * *

BACKGROUND OF THE PROPOSED OFFERING

Universal was incorporated under the laws of Delaware September 29, 1937. It succeeded a New York corporation of the same name which had been incorporated in 1933. Universal's normal peace time business is the manufacture and distribution of popular priced still and motion picture cameras, projectors, film and photographic accessories.

Early in 1942 Universal virtually discontinued making these products and since then has been engaged almost exclusively in making binoculars under prime contracts for the Army and Navy. Its resumption of the manufacture of nonwar products is dependent upon the freeing of facilities from war production requirements and a relaxation of Government regulations and restrictions imposed to meet exigencies of the current national emergency.

* * *

THE TERMS OF THE OFFERING

The registration statement covers 530,500 Class A shares to be offered to the public by Universal's present common stockholders. That is all but 1,500 of the 532,000 Class A shares which the controlling stockholders would receive (together with all of the new Class B stock and warrants for 308,400 shares of Class A stock) in exchange for the 300,000 shares of Universal's common stock which they now hold. The proceeds of sale of such Class A shares would go not to Universal but to the selling stockholders.

The registration statement covers also 133,000 Class A shares to be offered to the public by Universal itself. The proceeds of sale of such shares would go to Universal.

Of the 133,000 Class A shares to be offered by Universal, 20,000 would be offered first to Universal's employees at $4.25 a share. Subject to that offer, all of the shares to be registered, both the 530,500 to be offered by Universal's controlling stockholders and the 133,000 to be offered by

Universal itself, would be offered to the public at $5.00 a share, through an underwriter acting as an agent for the sellers.

After deducting the underwriter's commission the sellers would receive $4 a share, or a total of $2,654,000 as proceeds of the offering. Of this amount, after all selling commissions and estimated expenses are deducted, the selling stockholders, who paid $30,000 for their common stock, would receive $2,100,865 and the company would receive $524,985. The selling stockholders, through their retention of the 500,000 shares of Class B stock, would still have exclusive voting power and a 43 percent share in the earnings after preferred dividends. They would also have the 1,500 shares of Class A stock remaining unsold and warrants to purchase 162,300 shares of Class A stock. * * *

* * *

SPECULATIVE CHARACTER OF THE SHARES TO BE OFFERED

* * *

A. OMISSIONS OF MATERIAL FACTS IN RESPECT OF THE REGISTRANT'S PROPOSED FINANCIAL STRUCTURE

All of Universal's outstanding common stock was acquired by the present holders from Universal's predecessor for $30,000. As of December 31, 1944, it had a liquidating value of $279,438 according to Universal's books. On that basis the 532,000 shares of new Class A stock to be issued in exchange for the outstanding common would have a liquidating value of about 53 cents a share according to Universal's books.

The proceeds of Universal's sale of 133,000 Class A shares at $5 per share would increase the Class A stock's liquidating value to an aggregate of $804,423 for the 665,000 shares, or $1.21 per share according to Universal's books. The New Class B stock would have no asset value although it would have exclusive voting power.

Of their 532,000 shares of the new Class A stock, the selling stockholders propose to sell 530,500 shares to the public at $5 per share.

Through that sale they would realize $2,100,865 for the part which they propose to sell of the stock to be received in exchange for the common they originally purchased for $30,000. At the same time they would retain exclusive voting power and a 43 percent participation in earnings after preferred dividends by retaining all of the B stock also to be received in the exchange of their common. Beyond that they would still have the earning power and liquidating value represented by 1,500 shares of Class A stock not to be offered for sale, * * *.

The failure to state these facts in the registration statement or in the prospectus in such a way that they would be plainly evident was of extreme importance in view of Universal's past earning record. In 1942, when it was engaged almost exclusively in war work, Universal had the best earnings of its history. If it had then been capitalized as proposed in the registration statement the 1942 earnings would have amounted to about 23 cents a share of Class A and Class B stock after taxes. The earnings for 1944 would have amounted to only about 5 cents a share on the proposed new capitalization.[11]

11. The proposed offering price was therefore 21 times the 1942 earnings and 100 times the 1944 earnings.

The omission of facts disclosing plainly the contrast between the proposed offering price and the book value of the shares to be offered would have made it practically impossible for anyone but an astute and experienced security analyst to discover, from the information as it was set out in the statement, that on the basis of the company's past earning experience it would require an accumulation of many years earnings to enable an investor, buying the Class A stock and holding it, to regain through earnings, even the difference between its book value and the price at which it was offered to him.

A disclosure which makes the facts available in such form that their significance is apparent only upon searching analysis by experts does not meet the standards imposed by the Securities Act of 1933 as we understand that Act. * * *

Another aspect of the financial structure which the registration statement and prospectus did not adequately describe to the ordinary investor was the significance and effect of the proposed issuance of option warrants. Whatever may be the advantages of issuing warrants to underwriters and to purchasers, warrants do involve potentialities of disadvantage from the viewpoint of the issuing company's future financing.

Here it was proposed to issue warrants that would be effective for a period of more than 3 years beginning, as it would have happened, shortly after the war in Europe ceased. They were to be issued in an amount which, if all warrants were exercised, would bring in an amount of capital greater than the total liquidating value of the Class A stock that would be outstanding at the conclusion of the financing proposed in the registration statement.

In view of the amount of stock called for by the warrants proposed to be issued here, the critical period for which they would be outstanding and the large proportion of such warrants to be issued to others than public purchasers, we believe that for a fair and complete disclosure it would be requisite for Universal to state that for the life of the warrants, until December 31, 1948, the company might be deprived of favorable opportunities to procure additional equity capital, if it should be needed for the purpose of the business, and that at any time when the holders of such warrants might be expected to exercise them, the company would, in all likelihood, be able to obtain equity capital, if it needed capital then, by public sale of a new issue on terms more favorable than those provided for by the warrants.

B. OMISSIONS AND MISSTATEMENTS WITH RESPECT TO REGISTRANT'S BUSINESS

The original registration statement touched but lightly upon competitive conditions in the industry before the war. On the other hand it made broad general assertions concerning Universal's postwar prospects. For example, on p. 6 of the prospectus it stated:

The Company believes that its competitive position in the postwar market will be maintained by reason of the fact that it is currently designing and preparing improved and additional photographic products which should find a ready sale.

and again at p. 8 it said:

While other manufacturers have also gained skill and knowledge in the field of Optical Instruments in connection with their war work, the Company, by reason of its ability to successfully compete as to quality and price in the manufacture of binoculars, feels that it will be able to maintain its competitive position in the postwar market.

With respect to the first statement quoted the prospectus contained no disclosure of the extent of its progress in the development of what it described as "improved and additional photographic products." Nor were representatives of the company able to testify to a substantial basis for their opinions relative to sales prospects.

With respect to the second statement quoted it appears that the only competition the registrant has ever met in the sale of binoculars has been in sales to the government under war contracts. Obviously that is not the kind of competition in which it is likely to be engaged primarily after the war. Furthermore, the registration statement failed to state that the market for binoculars before the war was a relatively limited market. * * *

These and other similar deficiencies indicate not only the inadequate and the misleading character of the original prospectus, they demonstrate the deficiencies of Universal's response to Item 1 of Form S-2 which calls for a disclosure of information concerning the business done and intended to be done by the registrant.

JURISDICTION AND FUNCTIONS OF THE COMMISSION

The Securities Act of 1933 indicates with definite clarity the powers and responsibilities of the Commission with respect to registration statements that do not plainly and accurately disclose the nature of the securities to be registered.

In contrast to some of the State officials and commissions, operating under state "Blue Sky" laws that authorize them to pass upon the merits of securities registered with them, it is not this Commission's function under the Securities Act to approve or disapprove securities and the statute specifically makes it unlawful to represent that the Commission has passed upon the merits of any security, or given approval to it.
* * *

The Commission subjects all registration statements to careful and critical analysis. Many clarifying revisions are made as a consequence and we believe that the practice followed has been highly successful in detecting material errors and omissions that not infrequently occur in the statements as originally filed. It is plain, however, in view of the provisions of Section 23, that registration is not to be regarded as a finding by the Commission that the statement does not contain any material errors or omissions.

* * *

The primary remedies to forestall the offering of securities on the basis of inadequate or incorrect registration statements are provided in Section 8(b) and 8(d) of the Act. Those sections authorize the Commission after notice and opportunity for hearing to issue orders either deferring or suspending the effectiveness of registration statements found to be materially inaccurate or incomplete until they are amended in such a way as to correct their deficiencies.

It has been our practice to use sparingly the statutory authority to delay or suspend the effectiveness of deficient registration statements. Many necessary adjustments are worked out through prefiling conferences.[b] Beyond that we have adopted the practice of informing registrants, informally, by letter, of any material questions that arise during examination of the statement once it is filed. The registrant is thereby afforded opportunity to file corrective amendments without the necessity of formal proceedings.

These practices usually have resulted in prompt correction or clarification of the statement. With relatively few exceptions, amendments worked out through such informal procedures have been found to satisfy the statutory requirements and to justify acceleration of the effective date.

Occasionally, however, the deficiencies are of such character and extent that in the judgment of the Commission they cannot adequately be dealt with informally. In such cases the Commission may deem it essential to the protection of investors, in view of the policy and purposes of the Act, to take formal steps to defer or suspend the effectiveness of the statement until the facts are developed through a hearing.

This is such a case. As we have stated above, in our opinion it would have been extremely difficult, if not practically impossible on the basis of the registration statement filed in this case, for ordinary investors to form a reasonably sound judgment concerning the nature of the securities or their relationship to Universal's capital structure or the investor's rights as a holder of such securities if he should buy them. In these circumstances we deemed it requisite in the public interest and for the protection of investors that the facts be explored through a hearing to determine whether a stop order should issue. We so directed and such a hearing was commenced.

EVENTS SINCE NOTICE OF PROCEEDING

The registration statement was filed on March 19, 1945. Its effectiveness was delayed by an amendment filed on April 5 and notice of the stop order proceedings was issued April 10.

On April 23 and May 5 Universal filed material amendments designed to correct some of the deficiencies in the original statement. * * * On May 24 Universal filed an additional amendment making further material changes in the statement.

We have considered the registration statement as modified by those amendments. We are satisfied that the amendments substantially correct the deficiencies cited in the notice of this proceeding except those relating to the warrants. * * *

It appears, however, that Universal is considering some modifications in the terms of the offering and will file amendments designed to make the

---

b. The availability of the SEC staff members for pre-filing conferences depends upon the work-load at a particular time. If problems arise in preparation of the registration statement, the initial contact should be made with the Director or an assistant director of the Corporation Finance Division at the Commission's Washington, D. C. office or, if an S–18 registration is to be filed in a regional office, with the branch chief supervising the review of those filings. (See Regulation C, Rule 455.) A conference can then be arranged with a member of the staff to discuss specific problems on a limited basis. For a number of years, however the volume of work has been such that the Staff has not been able to make an examination of a registration statement before it is filed or to discuss how the statement should be prepared. The pre-filing conference is thus confined to discussing generally the problems confronting a registrant or to resolve unusual and difficult disclosure issues. It is good practice to furnish the staff with a preconference letter pinpointing the specific questions to which answers are desired. Securities Act Release No. 6276 (Dec. 23, 1980) 21 SEC Docket, 1052, 1070 (1981).

statement describe the offering as modified, including appropriate amendments relative to any warrants that may be involved.

* * *

Inasmuch as further amendments are to be filed to bring the statement up to date and into conformity with the terms of the offering ultimately to be made we make no determination at this time with respect to the effective date of the registration statement. * * *

However, in view of the corrections accomplished by the amendments already filed we see no necessity for issuing a stop order or continuing further with this proceeding. Accordingly Universal's motion to dismiss the proceeding will be granted.

———

IN THE MATTER OF FRANCHARD CORPORATION

Securities and Exchange Commission, 1964.
42 S.E.C. 163.

CARY, CHAIRMAN: These are consolidated proceedings pursuant to Sections 8(c) and 8(d) of the Securities Act of 1933 ("Securities Act") to determine whether a stop order should issue suspending the effectiveness of three registration statements filed by Franchard Corporation, formerly Glickman Corporation ("registrant"), and whether certain post-effective amendments filed by the registrant should be declared effective. * * *

I. FACTS

A. Background

Louis J. Glickman ("Glickman") has for many years been a large-scale real estate developer, operator and investor. From 1954 to 1960 he acquired control of real estate in this country and in Canada by means of "syndication" arrangements. * * * Glickman conducted some of these syndication activities and certain other phases of his real estate business through a number of wholly owned corporations, the most important of which was Glickman Corporation of Nevada, now known as Venada Corporation ("Venada").

In May of 1960, Glickman caused registrant to be formed in order to group under one entity most of the publicly owned corporations and limited partnerships under his control. Registrant was to operate on a so-called "cash flow" basis, i.e., the amount available for distribution to its stockholders was to be gauged by the excess of cash receipts over cash disbursements, without reference to such non-cash deductions from gross receipts as depreciation and leasehold amortization. Registrant's stock was divided into two classes, Class A common and Class B common, with the B stockholders given the right to elect $2/3$ of registrant's directors until 1971, when all outstanding B shares become A shares. Glickman established control of registrant by acquiring 450,000 of its 660,000 authorized B shares for $1 per share. He exercised a dominant role in the management of registrant's affairs as president at the time of its formation and later as its first chairman of the board.

The first of the three registration statements here involved ("1960 filing") became effective on October 12, 1960. * * *

The second of the three registration statements ("first 1961 filing") became effective on October 2, 1961 * * *. All of the A shares offered to the public for cash under the 1960 filing and the first 1961 filing were sold as were the A shares offered under the second 1961 filing, and the exchange offer in the 1960 filing was accepted by most of the offerees.

B. Glickman's Withdrawals and Pledges

Registrant's 1960 prospectus stated that Glickman had from time to time advanced substantial sums to the partnerships and corporations that were about to become subsidiaries of the registrant. It also said that he had advanced $211,000 to the registrant for the purpose of defraying its organization and registration costs and that this advance would be repaid without interest out of the proceeds of the public offering. On October 14, 1960—two days after the effective date of registrant's 1960 filing—Glickman began secretly to transfer funds from the registrant to Venada, his wholly owned corporation. Within two months the aggregate amount of these transfers amounted to $296,329. By October 2, 1961, the effective date of registrant's first 1961 filing, Glickman had made 45 withdrawals which amounted in the aggregate to $2,372,511. Neither the 1961 prospectuses nor any of the effective amendments to the 1960 filing referred to these transactions.

All of registrant's prospectuses stated that Glickman owned most of its B as well as a substantial block of its A stock. On the effective date of the 1960 filing Glickman's shares were unencumbered. In the following month, however, he began to pledge his shares to finance his personal real estate ventures. By August 31, 1961, all of Glickman's B and much of his A stock had been pledged to banks, finance companies, and private individuals. On the effective dates of the two 1961 filings the loans secured by these pledges aggregated about $4,250,000. The effective interest rates on these loans ran as high as 24% annually. Glickman retained the right to vote the pledged shares in the absence of a default on the loans. The two 1961 filings made no mention of Glickman's pledges or the loans they secured.

C. Action of the Board of Directors

In May 1962 the accountants who had audited the financial statements in registrant's 1960 and 1961 filings informed its directors that Glickman had from time to time diverted funds from the registrant's treasury to Venada. The directors then met with Glickman, who assured them that the withdrawals had been without wrongful intent and would not recur. Glickman agreed to repay all of the then known unauthorized withdrawals with the interest at the rate of 6%. Registrant's directors soon discovered that Glickman had made other withdrawals, and they retained former United States District Court Judge Simon H. Rifkind to determine Glickman's liability to registrant. Glickman agreed to be bound by Judge Rifkind's determination and was continued in office.

In a report submitted on August 20, 1962, Judge Rifkind found that Glickman had on many occasions withdrawn substantial sums from registrant; that Bernard Mann, who was registrant's as well as Venada's treasurer but not a member of registrant's board of directors, was the only one of registrant's officers who had known of the withdrawals and had collaborated with Glickman in effecting them; that registrant's inadequate administrative procedures had to some extent facilitated Glickman's wrongdoing; and that all of the withdrawals had been made good with 6% interest. Judge Rifkind also found that 6% was an inadequate interest rate because Glickman and Venada had been borrowing at appreciably higher interest rates from commercial finance companies and others. Accordingly, he concluded that registrant was entitled to additional interest from Glickman and from Venada in the amount of $145,279. Registrant has not thus far been able to collect any part of this sum.[10]

On November 30, 1962, registrant's directors learned that Glickman had continued to make unauthorized withdrawals after he had promised to desist from so doing and after the issuance of the Rifkind report, that Glickman and his wife had pledged all of their shares of the registrant's stock, and that Glickman and Venada were in financial straits. Glickman and Mann thereupon resigned from all of their posts with the registrant, and Glickman sold all his B stock and some of his Class A stock to a small group of investors. Monthly cash distributions to A stockholders, which registrant had made every month since its inception, were discontinued in January 1963, and registrant changed its name from Glickman Corporation to Franchard Corporation.

II. ALLEGED DEFICIENCIES—ACTIVITIES OF MANAGEMENT

A. *Glickman's Withdrawals of Registrant's Funds and Pledges of His Shares*

Of cardinal importance in any business is the quality of its management. Disclosures relevant to an evaluation of management are particularly pertinent where, as in this case, securities are sold largely on the personal reputation of a company's controlling person. The disclosures in these respects were materially deficient. The 1960 prospectus failed to reveal that Glickman intended to use substantial amounts of registrant's funds for the benefit of Venada, and the 1961 prospectuses made no reference to Glickman's continual diversion of substantial sums from the registrant. Glickman's pledges were not discussed in either the effective amendments to the 1960 filings or in the two 1961 filings.

In our view, these disclosures were highly material to an evaluation of the competence and reliability of registrant's management—in large measure, Glickman. In many respects, the development of disclosure standards adequate for informed appraisal of management's ability and integrity is a difficult task. How do you tell a "good" business manager from a "bad" one in a piece of paper? Managerial talent consists of personal attributes, essentially subjective in nature, that frequently defy meaningful analysis through the impersonal medium of a prospectus. Direct statements of opinion as to management's ability, which are not susceptible to objective verification, may well create an unwarranted appearance of reliability if placed in a prospectus. The integrity of management—its willingness to place its duty to public shareholders over personal interest—is an equally elusive factor for the application of disclosure standards.[a]

---

10. In February 1963 Glickman and Venada filed petitions in the United States District Court * * * seeking arrangements with their creditors pursuant to Chapter XI of the Bankruptcy Act. * * *

a. How realistic is it to expect that there can or will be meaningful disclosure regarding the quality of management in the prospectus? See the statement of Harold Marsh, Jr. infra at page 169. Cf. Form S-1, Item 11(j) and Reg. S-K, Item 401. This problem is also raised in an acute form in A. Solmssen, The Comfort Letter (1975), a novel centering on the preparation of a registration statement for a rising young tycoon who is gradually losing touch with reality.

Evaluation of the quality of management—to whatever extent it is possible—is an essential ingredient of informed investment decision. * * * Appraisals of competency begin with information concerning management's past business experience, which is elicited by requirements that a prospectus state the offices and positions held with the issuer by each executive officer within the last five years. With respect to established companies, management's past performance, as shown by comprehensive financial and other disclosures concerning the issuer's operations, furnish a guide to its future business performance. To permit judgments whether the corporation's affairs are likely to be conducted in the interest of public shareholders, the registration requirements elicit information as to the interests of insiders which may conflict with their duty of loyalty to the corporation. Disclosures are also required with respect to the remuneration and other benefits paid or proposed to be paid to management as well as material transactions between the corporation and its officers, directors, holders of more than 10 percent of its stock, and their associates.

Glickman's withdrawals were material transactions between registrant and its management, and the registration forms on which registrant's filings were made called for their disclosure. Registrant's argument that the withdrawals were not material because Glickman's undisclosed indebtedness to registrant never exceeded 1.5% of the gross book value of registrant's assets not only minimizes the substantial amounts of the withdrawals in relation to the stockholders' equity and the company's cash flow, but ignores the significance to prospective investors of information concerning Glickman's managerial ability and personal integrity. * * *

A description of Glickman's activities was important on several grounds. First, publication of the facts pertaining to Glickman's withdrawals of substantial funds and of his pledges of his control stock would have clearly indicated his strained financial position and his urgent need for cash in his personal real estate ventures. * * *

Second, disclosure of Glickman's continual diversion of registrant's funds to the use of Venada, his wholly owned corporation, was also germane to an evaluation of the integrity of his management. This quality is always a material factor. * * *

Third, Glickman's need for cash * * * gave him a powerful and direct motive to cause registrant to pursue policies which would permit high distribution rates and maintain a high price for registrant's A shares. * * * Investors were entitled to be apprised of these facts and such potential conflicts of interest.

Finally, the possibility of a change of control was also important to prospective investors. As we have noted, registrant's public offerings were largely predicated on Glickman's reputation as a successful real estate investor and operator. Disclosure of Glickman's secured loans, the relatively high interest rates that they bore, the secondary sources from which many of the loans were obtained, and the conditions under which lenders could declare defaults would have alerted investors to the possibility of a change in the control and management of registrant * * *.

* * *

With respect to disclosure of pledged shares, registrant is not aided by pointing out that our registration forms under the Securities Act and the reports required under the Securities Exchange Act do not call for disclosure of encumbrances on a controlling stockholder's shares, and that proposals to require such disclosures in reports filed with us under the Securities Exchange Act have not been adopted. The fact that such disclosures are not required of all issuers and their controlling persons in all cases does not negate their materiality in specific cases. The registration forms promulgated by us are guides intended to assist registrants in discharging their statutory duty of full disclosure. They are not and cannot possibly be exhaustive enumerations of each and every item material to investors in the particular circumstances relevant to a specific offering. The kaleidoscopic variety of economic life precludes any attempt at such an enumeration. The preparation of a registration statement is not satisfied, as registrant's position suggests, by a mechanical process of responding narrowly to the specific items of the applicable registration form. On the contrary, Rule 408 under the Securities Act makes clear to prospective registrants that: "In addition to the information expressly required to be included in a registration statement, there shall be added such further material information, if any, as may be necessary to make the required statements in the light of the circumstances under which they were made, not misleading."

B. *Activities of Registrant's Directors*

Another issue raised in these proceedings concerns the disclosure to be required in a prospectus regarding the adequacy of performance of managerial functions by registrant's board of directors. The Division urges that the prospectuses, by identifying the members of the board of directors, impliedly represented that they would provide oversight and direction to registrant's officers. * * *

It was obvious * * * that Glickman would exercise the dominant role in managing registrant's operations and the prospectuses contained no affirmative representations concerning the participation of the directors in registrant's affairs. Moreover, the board met regularly and received information as to registrant's affairs from Glickman and in connection with the preparation of registrant's registration statements, post-effective amendments, and periodic reports filed with us. It is clear we are not presented with a picture of total abdication of directorial responsibilities. Thus, the question posed by the Division must be whether the prospectuses were deficient in not disclosing that the directors, in overseeing the operations of the company, failed to exercise the degree of diligence which the Division believes was required of them under the circumstances in the context of the day-to-day operations of the company. We find no deficiencies in this area.

This is an issue raising fundamental considerations as to the functions of the disclosure requirements of the Securities Act. The civil liability provisions of Section 11 do establish for directors a standard of due diligence in the preparation of a registration statement—a federal rule of directors' responsibility with respect to the completeness and accuracy of the document used in the public distribution of securities. The Act does not purport, however, to define federal standards of directors' responsibility in the ordinary operations of business enterprises and nowhere empowers us to formulate administratively such regulatory standards. The diligence required of registrant's directors in overseeing its affairs is to be evaluated in the light of the standards established by state statutory and common law.

In our view, the application of these standards on a routine basis in the processing of registration statements would be basically incompatible with the philosophy and administration of the disclosure requirements of the Securities Act. Outright fraud or reckless indifference by directors might be readily identifiable and universally condemned. But activity short of that, which may give rise to legal restraints and liabilities, invokes significant uncertainty. * * * To generally require information in Securities Act prospectuses as to whether directors have performed their duties in accordance with the standards of responsibility required of them under state law would stretch disclosure beyond the limitations contemplated by the statutory scheme and necessitated by considerations of administrative practicality. * * * [T]he disclosures sought here by the staff would require evaluation of the entire conduct of a board of directors in the context of the whole business operations of a company in the light of diverse and uncertain standards. In our view, this is a function which the disclosure requirements of the Securities Act cannot effectively discharge. It would either result in self-serving generalities of little value to investors or grave uncertainties both on the part of those who must enforce and those who must comply with that Act.

* * *

V. CONCLUSIONS

The deficiencies we have found in registrant's effective filings are serious. * * * Omissions of so material a character would normally require the issuance of a stop order.

Here, however, several factors taken together lead us to conclude that the distribution of copies of this opinion to all of registrant's past and present stockholders, as registrant has proposed, will give adequate public notice of the deficiencies in registrant's effective filings, and that neither the public interest nor the protection of investors requires the issuance of a stop order. Among those factors are Glickman's departure, the transfer of his controlling B shares to a management which has made a substantial financial commitment in registrant's securities, and registrant's voluntary disclosures to our staff prior to the initiation of these proceedings. Registrant also filed post-effective amendments to its 1960 filings which, though admittedly inadequate, represented a bona fide effort to remedy the deficiencies in its effective filings. In addition, * * * unusually extensive publicity was given to the true facts affecting registrant's affairs and to the resulting deficiencies in its effective filings.

Any new post-effective amendment should conform to the views expressed in this opinion. After the Division has reviewed such amendment, it will communicate its views with respect to it to the registrant, and thereafter the matter will be submitted to us for appropriate action.

* * *

SECTION 4. NEW APPROACHES TO DISCLOSURE

FULL DISCLOSURE IN THE 1960's

The Securities Act rests upon the proposition that full disclosure holds the key to an effective system of securities regulation. As Mr. Justice Brandeis put it: "Sunlight is said to be the best of disinfectants; electric light the most efficient policeman." [1] It took the swinging sixties, described by John Brooks in "The Go-Go Years: When Prices Went Topless," to shake the faith of those who had believed that the benefits of disclosure justified the burdens. The limitations of the disclosure system during these years lent further support to those who have contended that the 1933 Act has substantially raised the costs of selling securities without significant benefit to shareholders and investors.[2] In The Go-Go Years, Mr. Brooks concluded: [3]

> Full disclosure in the nineteen sixties market was largely a failure, giving the small investor the semblance of protection without the substance. And that failure raised the question of just how much full disclosure can ever accomplish. Rules can be tightened, as many were during the decade and more will be in the future; but as surely as night follows day, the tricksters of Wall Street and its financial tributaries will be ever busy topping the new rules with new tricks, and there is no reason to doubt that the respectable institutions will again play Pied Piper by catching the quick-money fever the next time it is epidemic. As [Bernard J.] Lasker[a] said in 1972, "I can feel it coming, SEC or not, a whole new round of disastrous speculation, with all the familiar stages in order—blue-chip boom, then a fad for secondary issues, then an over-the-counter play, then another garbage market in new issues, and finally the inevitable crash. I don't know when it will come, but I can feel it coming, and, damn it, I don't know what to do about it."

During the 1960's the Congress and the Commission had sponsored the SEC Special Study of the Securities Markets, which was followed by the "Wheat Report". Both studies were aimed at improving disclosure. Through the integration of the 1933 Act and 1934 Act disclosure requirements, prospectuses have been simplified for 1934 Act reporting companies, and even shorter-form registration statements were adopted for blue-chip offerings. Indeed, we have seen that the Commission's integrated disclosure program rests upon an efficient market hypothesis that information made available to the market through periodic reports under the 1934 Act is evaluated by professional analysts, sophisticated users, the financial press and others and is thereby reflected in the price of issuers' outstanding securities. On the other hand, the hot-issue phase of the bull market of the sixties showed that the prospectus requirements had little effect on the ability of promoters to sell millions of dollars of junk securities.

As an aftermath of this experience and the criticism leveled at the ineffectiveness of the disclosure system, in the 1970's, the SEC sought to make disclosure more comprehensive, particularly with respect to high-risk and other speculative offerings.

The SEC Staff issued guides for the preparation of registration statements directed at prospectuses of initial public offerings of high risk and speculative securities. These prospectuses were to contain an "introductory statement" at the beginning of the prospectus which highlighted the risk factors and speculative features of an offering, a throwback to the *Universal Camera* case (supra at page 148). In addition to the written statement

1. L. D. Brandeis, Other People's Money 62 (1933).

2. See statement of Professor Henry G. Manne in H. Manne and E. Solomon, Wall Street in Transition 51 (1974); H. Kripke, The SEC and Corporate Disclosure—Regulation in Search of a Purpose (1979).

3. J. Brooks, The Go-Go Years, at 347 (1973). For a review of the changes occur-

ring in the securities markets and in the regulatory environment in the 1960's, see ABA Nat'l. Inst., Revolution in Securities Regulation, 29 Bus.Law. (Special Issue, Mch.1974).

a. Chairman, Board of Governors, The New York Stock Exchange, 1969–72.

of the risk factors, pie charts and bar graphs illustrating any significant disparity between the offering price to public investors and the cash cost of such securities to officers, directors and affiliates in earlier rounds of financing were mandated. The "introductory statement" was to be preceded by a "prospectus summary" "highlighting the salient features of the offering with appropriate cross reference to more detailed discussions elsewhere in the prospectus." The "use of proceeds" section must discuss any contingencies which might result in a diversion of the proceeds received on the offering from the proposed purposes as stated in the prospectus, together with a statement of the alternative use of proceeds to be followed in the event that the contingencies should arise. This statement was designed to inhibit the diversion of proceeds for uses other than those stated in the prospectus.

Although these guides were rescinded as a part of the SEC's integration program, some aspects have been reformulated and relocated in Regulation S–K. On Summary Information, see Item 503(a); Risk Factors, Item 503(c); Introductory Statement and Dilution, Items 503(a), 506; and Use of Proceeds, Item 504(7).

The following material represents an evaluation and critique of these new approaches to disclosure. You should consider to what extent the SEC should reexamine its disclosure policies with respect to smaller, unseasoned, and growing companies which have experienced difficulty in raising adequate amounts of investment capital in recent years.

Excerpts from:

NEW APPROACHES TO DISCLOSURE IN REGISTERED SECURITY OFFERINGS—A Panel Discussion *
28 Bus.Law. 505–535 (1973).ᵃ

Remarks of A. A. SOMMER, Jr.

The Securities Act of 1933 was really a "rotten egg statute." You could sell all the rotten eggs you wanted if you told people fully how rotten they were. Alas, a lot of rotten eggs were sold under this statute and you suspect that a lot of them are continuing to be sold. Disclosure has been the pervading philosophy of the SEC and of the other statutes they administer. * * *

Through the years, there have grown up certain disclosure practices, certain habits of mind, certain stereotyped habits of expression, both on the part of the Commission staff and private practitioners. You could virtually recite the typical prospectus language concerning, for instance, competition. You always said that competition in this industry is intensive and

---

* Panelists were: A. A. Sommer, Jr., Moderator, Member of the Ohio Bar, Cleveland, Ohio; Carl W. Schneider, Member of Pennsylvania Bar, Philadelphia, Pennsylvania; Warren F. Grienenberger, Member of the Illinois Bar, Chicago, Illinois; Harold Marsh, Jr., Member of the California Bar, Los Angeles, California * * *.

a. Copyright 1973. Reprinted from the January, 1973 issue of The Business Lawyer with permission of the American Bar Association and its Section of Corporations, Banking and Business Law.

characterized by a large number of competitors, many of whom have greater resources than those of the registrant, etc. Likewise wherever you had a new product that was being introduced, you resorted pretty much to standardized modes of expression: "there can be no assurance that this product will be successfully marketed and it may be that company's investment in the amount of approximately blank dollars in the development of this product may not be recovered, etc., etc., etc." You could often predict with precision what a prospectus would say about various problems.

There was always a consensus that conservatism was the safest course. If you strayed from this approach and said that your company was one of the largest producers of its product in the country, you would likely be called upon to substantiate that in spades. Conservatism and downplaying were a way of life, so much so that the first outcry of every president of a company going public for the first time when he saw the first draft of the prospectus was, "My God, what have you done to my company?" He found it incredible that the negativism and conservatism that characterized the prospectus for his company were meant to be a serious description of a security to be offered to the public. And of course opinions, projections, estimates were forbidden; only hard, demonstrable *facts* had a place in a prospectus.

So we have had stereotyped, negative, conservative habits. The acceptability of those habits is now changing under the prodding of Homer Kripke, who has written extensively on this subject, and the spur of other authors who have seen the futility of this kind of approach. They have recognized well that it was not this kind of approach that impelled people to invest, but rather it was information otherwise available which could not be expressed in prospectuses.

* * *

Remarks of CARL W. SCHNEIDER

The corporate image created by a prospectus, proxy statement or other SEC filing may be likened to a shadow—it tells something about the subject's gross outline but in a flat, lifeless and sometimes distorted form. Many commentators, including SEC Chairman Casey, have suggested that SEC disclosure filings should be a more lifelike representation, devoting greater attention to economic realities and the nitty gritty of the business, rather than boiler plate which could fit almost any filing.

Historically, certain types of highly relevant information—which I will call "soft" information—have been largely excluded from filings by the SEC. Recently, the SEC and others have shown interest in expanded use of such information in filings, and its greater use seems to be inevitable. I will try to explore some of the policy implications.

SEC filings have traditionally been confined to what may be called "hard" information, meaning statements concerning objectively verifiable historical events or situations, commonly called "facts," as distinguished from opinions, predictions or subjective evaluations. The term "soft" information implies the opposite of hard, and can be illustrated by several categories: (1) forward looking statements, such as projections, predictions and statements concerning future expectations; (2) statements when the maker lacks hard data necessary to prove its accuracy, such as information on a company's historical share of the market; (3) information based primarily on subjective evaluations; (4) statements involving qualifying words, such as "excellent," "efficient" and "imaginative," for which there are no generally accepted objective standards.

* * *

Let me offer eight general observations relative to the need for change:

1. *The increased use of soft information in filings would make the soft information now widely disseminated more responsible and reliable in the long run.* In fact, soft information is now used quite commonly in the securities markets, largely through oral selling activities which are difficult to police. Its inclusion in filings would tend to make it more cautious and conservative, and more exposed to liability if it were not supportable.

2. *The prevailing approach is counter-productive to the goal of informed investor decision.* When every situation is made to look bad, it is hard to distinguish the truly bad from the moderately bad and the genuinely good. Thus, with all statements of future plans being followed by the same pro forma disclaimer that success is not assured, and with no estimate of realistic probabilities being permitted, the value of the warning becomes completely diluted.

3. *Various types of filings present different considerations.* One may concede arguendo that highly "conservative" disclosure is appropriate when the principal users of a disclosure document will be prospective new investors, as in the case of a prospectus for a first public offering. Different standards should apply, however, with respect to periodic reports, proxy statements and, to some extent 1933 Act registration statements of companies which are already publicly owned. * * *

4. *The traditional approach underestimates investors' capabilities.* * * * I submit that investors are accustomed to dealing with soft data through the trading market and can discount it accordingly, as long as it is appropriately identified. If they are told the company earned $1.00 per share last year, projects $1.50 per share for the current year which is nine months complete, and expects $2.00 per share next year, they should be able to attach a different credibility factor to each figure.

5. *The traditional approach is inconsistent with the basic disclosure philosophy.* The general premise of the securities laws is to give investors *all* relevant information, and rely on them to make their own evaluations. In effect, the traditional view on soft information is based on the paternalistic view that certain investors may misuse such information. The result is that soft information is kept not only from the unsophisticated but also from the highly sophisticated investors who would use it effectively and properly. In effect, the system is tailored to the lowest common denominator of investor sophistication, to the detriment of all others. * * *

6. *The traditional policy discriminates against small investors.* By and large, if there is a story on economic reality which is based on soft information not appearing in the prospectus, large customers and institutions now have first preference in receiving such information as part of the routine oral selling activity. To the extent that soft information is going to be used properly in connection with selling, it should be in the prospectus where all investors have equal access to it.

7. *I suggest that different standards be required for mandatory and permissive disclosures.* We must recognize that disclosure is not, in fact, required of everything an investor would like to know, but only those items required by the specific disclosure form, plus other statements necessary to avoid half-truths. I hasten to add that the half-truths prohibition is a very potent tool for prying out additional disclosures.

* * *

To a large extent, I would rely on a vigorous application of the half-truths prohibition to force out disclosures of soft information, rather than attempt to rewrite specific disclosure forms.ᵃ

* * *

Remarks of HAROLD MARSH, Jr.

As I listened to Carl Schneider's thoughtful and constructive suggestions for the improvement of disclosure in the 1933 Act prospectus and to Warren Grienenberger's able exposition of the new requirements which have been either adopted or proposed by the Securities and Exchange Commission, I could not help wondering whether either really came to grips with the scathing criticisms to which the Securities Bar, and the Commission, have recently been subjected both from the bench and from the academic community.

In Feit v. Leasco Data Processing Equipment Corporation Judge Weinstein had the following to say about the type of disclosure contained in some prospectuses—he stopped short of asserting that this was typical of all or most prospectuses: [13]

"In at least some instances, what has developed in lieu of the open disclosure envisioned by the Congress is a literary art form calculated to communicate as little of the essential information as possible while exuding an air of total candor. Masters of this medium utilize turgid prose to enshroud the occasional critical revelation in a morass of dull, and—to all but the sophisticates—useless financial and historical data. In the face of such obfuscatory tactics the common or even the moderately well informed investor is almost as much at the mercy of the issuer as was his pre-SEC parent. He cannot by reading the prospectus discern the merit of the offering." [14]

Judge Weinstein is here talking about the document which most of the people in this room have spent the greater part of their adult lives developing.

The Commission and the Securities Bar have also come under fire from Professor Homer Kripke of New York University, who has asserted in various published articles and speeches that "the prospectus has become a

------

a. For a more complete statement of Mr. Schneider's views on how to make the prospectus more useful to investors and the difficulties entailed in the use of soft information, see Schneider, Nits, Grits, and Soft Information in SEC Filings, 121 U.Pa.L.Rev. 254 (1972).

13. However, one has to say that, when the passage is read in context, one gets the distinct feeling that Judge Weinstein wanted to say "most prospectuses," but was deterred by the thought that perhaps that was not in evidence.

14. Feit v. Leasco Data Processing Equipment Corp., 332 F.Supp. 544, 565 (E.D.N.Y.1971).

routine, meaningless document which does not serve its purpose." [15] While this judgment does not utilize the purple prose employed by Judge Weinstein, it is apparently just as absolute.   * * *

How should we reply to these sweeping indictments?   * * *

In attempting to evaluate these criticisms, it may be helpful to identify some of the specific complaints concerning the content and style of the current "literary art form."

ARE PROSPECTUSES TOO NEGATIVE?

One of Professor Kripke's major complaints about present day prospectuses is that they are too "negative." He asserts that "a prospectus loses its effect if every prospectus crys 'Wolf' all the time." [17] Of course, this has been a common complaint about Registration Statements for many years. It may, indeed, be possible to go too far in this direction. One Registration Statement presented to the Commission for filing had the following to say:

"The present directors do not foresee the possibility of the corporation ever being in a position to pay any dividends or having any assets of determinable value. The continued existence of the corporation is questionable. Bankruptcy may result at any time."

"Anyone considering purchase of this security must be prepared for immediate and total loss."

"No representation is made that the possibility exists that the corporation can continue to exist." [18]

However, the Commission thought that this was a put-on and refused to accept the document for filing on the ground that it was not a serious attempt to register the securities. One of the reasons for this may have been that the Commission had been trying to enjoin the same lawyer who had prepared this "Registration Statement" in connection with a previous offering of the same company with which he had been associated,[19] on the ground that that prospectus had been too optimistic. If it had not been for his previous problems with the Commission, it is possible that this filing would have been regarded as a little extreme, but might have been routinely accepted as more or less along the lines that the Commission had been forcing registrants to write their prospectuses for the preceding thirty years.

The lawyer who had presented the document for filing brought a mandamus action to force the Commission to accept it, but the District Court in Holmes v. Cary[20] agreed with the Commission that it was not a "bona fide attempt to qualify to sell securities." It is doubtful whether the Commission would have been so touchy if the parody had not been uncomfortably close to the manner in which most prospectuses read.

It is easy to criticize the drafting of a prospectus as being merely an "insurance policy" against potential civil liability, and there is little doubt

15. Kripke, Securities Regulation—The Myth of the Informed Layman, Addresses at Annual Meeting of Banking, Corporation and Business Law Section, N.Y.S.B.A. 19 (1972) * * *.

17. Kripke, Securities Regulation—The Myth of the Informed Layman, supra note 15, at 23.

18. Holmes v. Cary, 234 F.Supp. 23, 24 (N.D.Ga.1964).

19. See Holmes v. United States, 231 F.Supp. 971 (N.D.Ga.1964).

20. 234 F.Supp. 23, 24 (N.D.Ga.1964).

investors would probably get more meaningful disclosures if this could be changed. However, none of the proposals seeking to reverse this trend which I have seen include any proposal to eliminate or alleviate the risk against which the insurance policy is written. Certainly, so long as crushing civil liabilities exist for the slightest misstatement in a prospectus, any conscientious securities lawyer drafting a Registration Statement must try to protect his clients to the extent possible against that liability; and he is not going to change that approach merely because Professor Kripke would prefer to have the prospectus read some other way.

ARE PROSPECTUSES TOO UNIFORM?

The Securities and Exchange Commission has recently deprecated the use of standardized, boiler plate "risk factor" disclaimers in prospectuses.[21] This is also one of Professor Kripke's principal complaints. There is no hint, of course, in the SEC's Release that its Staff was the one which originated, elaborated upon, and insisted upon the absolute uniformity of these "risk factors" if the registrant hoped to have his filing processed with any expedition.

The lawyer who has copied previous filings which have become effective, with the knowledge that this would expedite his Registration Statement, must now apparently become a master of paraphrase (which in the Army we used to practice with messages before they were encoded), but there is obviously only a finite number of ways in which the same thing can be said in different words.

* * *

TO WHOM IS THE PROSPECTUS ADDRESSED?

In attempting to evaluate these condemnations of the Securities Bar and the Commission, there are several questions which need to be answered. One is obviously the question of to whom the disclosure is intended to be directed, since any communication to be effective must be tailored to the intended audience. The official position of the Commission, as reflected in the Wheat Report and echoed by Judge Weinstein, is that the prospectus must be completely informative both to the "unsophisticated investor" and to the "knowledgeable student of finance."[22] In other words, the drafter of a prospectus is enjoined to be "all things to all men." Of course, if he attempts this, he runs an extreme danger, to paraphrase the same Apostle, of "saying those things which he should have left unsaid, and leaving unsaid those things which he should have said."

On the other hand, Professor Kripke denounces what he calls the "myth of the informed layman," which he asserts has colored the Commission's concept of disclosure and rendered the prospectus useless. He asserts that the prospectus should be written solely for the "professional" or "expert."

With regard to Professor Kripke's obeisance to the so-called experts in securities investment, one can, I believe, with equal justification oppose his concept of the "myth of the informed layman" with the "myth of the 'expert' expert." It would be very interesting to have some graduate

21. SEC Securities Act Release No. 5279 (July 26, 1972).

22. Disclosure to Investors—Report of the Disclosure Policy Study, at 9–10 (1969);

Feit v. Leasco Data Processing Equipment Corp., 332 F.Supp. 544, 565–566 (E.D.N.Y.1971).

student in a business college conduct a research project to determine how much of the worthless junk securities sold by conglomerates in the last few years were bought by those self-appointed "expert money managers" advising mutual funds and other institutional investors, as compared to the percentage foisted off on the general public.

It seems to me that the only common sense approach to the question of the audience to whom the disclosure should be directed is that it should be directed to those persons who are capable of understanding the transactions being described. In my opinion, this will include only a small minority of the general public and only a small minority of the self-appointed experts. But to attempt to explain to a person who is incapable of understanding is a complete waste of time. If a physicist attempted to make "full disclosure" to me regarding the theory of relativity, his attempt would be doomed to failure, whatever his talents.

Some courts seem to have adopted this common sense approach. In Shvetz v. Industrial Rayon Corporation,[23] Judge Murphy stated:

> "While it might be true that a person of limited education or nonfamiliarity with corporate finances and legal matters would find it difficult to understand many of the facets of the proposed merger, that is not the test. The statute requires the absence of false and misleading statements, as do the S.E.C. rules. Nowhere does either require that corporate reorganizations and mergers be explained in language comprehensible to school children."

* * * However, as indicated above, Judge Weinstein adopted lock, stock and barrel the Commission view that a prospectus must be completely intelligible to everyone.

We now, of course, have the new official position that not only must prospectuses be intelligible to school children, but they must even reach down to the kindergarten set, who have not yet graduated from finger painting. Under the recent guide adopted by the Commission, the drafter of the prospectus must draw pictures to inform the person looking at the prospectus—one cannot say the "reader," since they assume he will not or cannot read—of the percentage of the equity retained by the promoters and the percentage being sold to the public.

Nowhere in the Release announcing that new artistic enterprise does the Commission even hint at what it hopes to achieve by its pie charts and graphs. It is impossible to believe that the Commission thinks that it will deter a purchaser from buying the stock by drawing him a picture, when he has not been dissuaded in the past by a statement to the same effect in plain English, especially since everyone knows that the reason he buys is because his broker has told him that it is going to be a "hot issue." To assert that the Commission believes that the issue which shows the larger slice of the "pie" going to the public is always the better buy for the investor would also be an insult to their intelligence. And I, for one, refuse to give any credence to the rumors that, shortly before the issuance of this Release, there were heavy purchases of the stock of compass and protractor manufacturers through the Washington brokerage houses. The only reasonable explanation of these new requirements, at least the only one that I

23. 212 F.Supp. 308, 310 (S.D.N.Y.1960).

have been able to think of, is that someone got access to the outgoing mail department of the SEC and smuggled in this Release as another put-on.

DISCLOSURE OF WHAT?

The lawyer approaching the task of drafting a Registration Statement starts, of course, with the specific items required by the appropriate form and has in mind the requirement of Rule 408 that he must also include any further material information which is necessary to make the required statements not misleading.   *   *   *

However, most of the present proposals do not suggest that anything may ever be subtracted, but center on the proposition that additional categories of information which Mr. Schneider has labeled "soft information" should be included. Basically, these boil down to three major categories of information, *i.e.,* projections of future earnings, appraisals of assets, and evaluation of management. Professor Kripke has championed including both future earnings projections and appraisals as a routine matter in prospectuses, and Chairman Casey has indicated that the Securities and Exchange Commission is actively considering the possibility of permitting or requiring both projections and appraisals in prospectuses.[26]

I think that the first thing that should be said concerning the matter of management projections of future operating results is that there may be a failure in some of the discussions of this subject to distinguish between "plans" and "expectations." No management of any company ever *plans* to lose money; and if it did, the entire management should be instantly discharged. This, however, does not alter the fact that a large number of businesses do, in fact, lose money every year. In other words, the so-called "projections" of management are in no sense a realistic and unbiased judgment as to what the corporation is likely to achieve in the way of earnings, but represent rather the hopes of management after discounting to a large extent all unfavorable factors.

In my opinion, the routine inclusion of such projections in prospectuses would be highly dangerous, not only from the point of view of the investor who may attach too great a significance to them, but even more importantly from the point of view of the company officials who are going to be sued when the projections turn out to be erroneous. As far as I am concerned, I would not advise any client, under any circumstances to include such projections in a prospectus unless Section 11 and Rule 10b–5 were first repealed or unless their inclusion is made mandatory by the Securities and Exchange Commission, in which event I would preface them with a statement that the Commission has forced their inclusion and that the projections are probably *wrong*.

So far as appraisals of assets are concerned, it would appear that under present law such appraisals of the assets of a business to be acquired must be included, at least under Rule 10b–5 and Section 14(a), if an acquiring corporation intends to realize any hidden values by sale or liquidation, as in the *Transamerica* case[27] and the *Gamble-Skogmo* case.[28] Presumably the same thing is true under Section 11 with respect to a tender offer prospec-

---

26. Casey, The Securities Bar and the Securities Laws, Addresses at Annual Meeting of Banking, Corporation and Business Law Section, N.Y.S.B.A. 29, at 33 (1972).

27. Speed v. Transamerica Corp., 99 F.Supp. 808 (D.Del.1951), 135 F.Supp. 176 (D.Del.1955), aff'd, 235 F.2d 369 (3d Cir. 1956).

tus where hidden values exist in the target company, as suggested by the *Leasco* case.[29]

It is quite another thing, however, to say that a registrant selling securities for cash, which has no intention of liquidating or selling its fixed assets, should be permitted or required to give appraised values of assets in excess of their book value, or estimates of ore reserves which have no firm scientific basis, as Professor Kripke advocates. Mark Twain once defined a "mine" as a "hole in the ground with a liar on top." In my opinion, wholesale abandonment of the cost basis of accounting would destroy all of the very substantial improvements which have been made in financial reporting and accountability since 1933 and return us to the unbridled excesses of the 1920's.

So far as disclosure regarding the quality of management is concerned, this would be the most important possible disclosure to a prospective investor, if it were feasible. It is elementary that the difference between a business with a high chance of success and one with little or none lies primarily in the quality of its leadership. Unfortunately, I can see no way in which such disclosure can be compelled, or even permitted, for the simple reason that the prospectus is the document of the very people whose ability needs to be appraised. While I am sure that you as well as I have often wondered whether the top officials of some of your clients ever read the proofs of the Registration Statement which you dutifully send to them, if it contains one word which might reflect upon management, you will find out very quickly that they have read *that part*. To expect any company president to say: "I am an incompetent, promoted by nepotism, and my stupidity is liable to bankrupt this company" is hardly realistic, even though you and I know that it is often true. But, if only favorable appraisals can realistically be expected, any beneficial results from this type of disclosure are impossible. Merely requiring more detail regarding the background and experience of management, while probably desirable, hardly meets the need or puts a person relying solely upon the prospectus on a par with those who can meet with and evaluate the management face to face.

* * *

SEC POLICIES ON ECONOMIC PROJECTIONS

As a result of the widespread criticism of the SEC's policy restricting the use of economic projections, in 1972 the Commission began a reassessment of its policies relating to disclosure of projections, economic forecasts and other forward-looking information. Following public hearings, relating to the use, both in Commission filings and otherwise by issuers whose securities were publicly traded, the Commission determined to reverse its long standing policy of not permitting the inclusion of projections in registration statements and reports filed with the Commission. During the next several years, the Commission issued a series of rule and form proposals with respect to projections of future economic performance and requested letters of comment on its proposals.

28. Gerstle v. Gamble-Skogmo, Inc., 298 F.Supp. 66 (E.D.N.Y.1969).

29. Feit v. Leasco Data Processing Equipment Corp., 332 F.Supp. 544, 565 (E.D.N.Y.1971).

The Commission later commented on the sequence of events which culminated in its present policies on economic projections in these terms:[1]

In its statement of general views in Release 33–5699 [April 23, 1976], the Commission indicated that it would not object to disclosure in filings with the Commission of projections which are made in good faith and have a reasonable basis, provided that they are presented in an appropriate format and accompanied by information adequate for investors to make their own judgments. The Commission also expressed its concern over the problem of selective disclosure of material non-public information regarding registrants and reminded issuers of their responsibilities under the federal securities laws in connection with the dissemination of management's assessment of a company's future performance. The Commission noted that registrant's responsibilities to make full and prompt disclosure of material facts, both favorable and unfavorable, regarding their financial condition may extend to situations where management knows its previously disclosed assessments no longer have a reasonable basis. * * *

The Commission's disclosure policy on projections and other items of soft information was among the subjects considered by the Advisory Committee on Corporate Disclosure. In its final report, issued * * * [in] 1977, the Advisory Committee * * * recommended that the Commission issue a public statement encouraging companies voluntarily to disclose management projections in their filings with the Commission and elsewhere. * * *

The Commission concurs in the Advisory Committee's recommendation and findings. As noted by the Advisory Committee, the availability of forward-looking and analytical information is important to an investor's assessment of a corporation's future earning power and may be material to informed investment decision-making. Projections and other types of forward-looking information are generally available within the investment community and are obtained and used by investors and their advisors.

In addition, a majority of the commentators * * * were in favor of a position that would permit the inclusion of projections in filings with the Commission by those issuers with the ability and willingness to make them. Accordingly, in light of the significance attached to projection information and the prevalence of projections in the corporate and investment community, the Commission has determined to follow the recommendation of the Advisory Committee and wishes to encourage companies to disclose management projections both in their filings with the Commission and in general. In order to further encourage such disclosure, the Commission has, in a separate release issued today, proposed for comment a safe-harbor rule for projection information whether or not included in Commission filings. The Commission also has determined to authorize publication of revised staff guides to assist implementation of the Advisory Committee's recommendation. * * * *

The Commission's new policy with respect to disclosure of projections was at first reflected in Staff Guides to the preparation of registration

---

1. SEC Securities Act Release No. 5992, 16 SEC Dock. 81 (1978), at 83.

statements, reports, and proxy statements. In 1982, however, in adopting the integration disclosure system, the Commission's policy on projections was embodied in Regulation S–K, Item 10(b).

The 1978 policy statement quoted above was accompanied by Securities Act Rule 175 and Exchange Act Rule 3b–6 which were designed to provide a safe harbor against liability under the 1933 and 1934 Acts for economic projections contained in disclosure documents.

1. Do Rules 175 and 3b–6 provide an adequate safe harbor against potential civil liability for economic projections made in filed documents which later prove to be false or misleading?

2. Who has the burden of proof as to the issues of "reasonable basis" and "good faith"?

3. What kinds of information are protected by the rules?

4. What categories of issuers are covered by the rules?

5. Are disclosed statements of assumptions underlying projections within the scope of the rules?

6. To what extent does an issuer have a duty to correct statements which (a) have become inaccurate as a result of subsequent events; or (b) are later discovered to have been inaccurate when made?

AMERICAN LAW INSTITUTE, FEDERAL SECURITIES CODE (1980) [a]

This Code has three principal aims: (1) simplification of an inevitably complex body of law in the light of almost a half-century of administration and litigation; (2) elimination (so far as possible) of duplicate regulation; and (3) reexamination of the entire scheme of investor protection with a view to increasing its efficiency and doing so, in President Roosevelt's words, "with the least possible interference to honest business."

THE NEED FOR CODIFICATION

Almost from the beginning—at least as far back as 1940—both the Securities and Exchange Commission and the securities industry recognized the need for integration of the six closely interrelated statutes that Congress had enacted between 1933 and 1940.[2] As the years went by, the need became more apparent. For example:

(1) Many terms are defined differently in different statutes. Even the basic term "security" does not have a single definition. The provisions on investigation, subpoenas, administrative hearings, judicial review and so on vary from statute to statute for no good reason. There are nuances in the jurisdictional references to the mails and interstate commerce that invite distinctive arguments. There is the central concept of "control," which, though frequently critical in determining the SEC's jurisdiction, is defined differently in the Holding Company, Investment Company and Investment Advisers Acts and not at all in the others. There is a variety of fraud provisions, with distinctions that create much needless complexity.

a. Copyright 1980 by the American Law Institute. Reprinted with permission of the American Law Institute.

2. See Loss, The American Law Institute's Federal Securities Code Project, 25 Bus.Law. 27 (1969). * * *

All this inconsistency—along with both gaps and overlaps that are equally illogical—is the price of the piecemeal adoption of seven related statutes, not to mention major amendments that have added to the patch-work effect. But it is not a price that society should go on paying indefinitely.

(2) A great deal of the needless complexity, as well as a major loss of efficiency in the regulatory system, is caused by the archaic centrality of S5, the registration provision of the Securities Act of 1933. When the 1933 Act was passed, its registration provision with respect to public offerings was the only disclosure device. But that is no longer true. There is a crying need for a scheme of continual disclosure that is not keyed to the fortuity of a public offering. There are more effective disclosure devices than the prospectus for the ordinary investor—the proxy statement, over which the Commission has had control since 1934, and, perhaps even more, the annual report to stockholders, over which the Commission should be given the authority that it does not now have directly but has sought to exercise indirectly through the proxy rules. Moreover, the dependence of the registration and prospectus requirements of the 1933 Act on the concept of an "offer" or "sale" has resulted in a series of overly sophistic rules whose interpretation eats up thousands of hours of both Government and private lawyers' time out of all proportion to the contribution that the rules make to the protection of investors; and this is apart from the question whether rules extending to seven or eight pages, complete with filing and prospectus-like requirements, would survive judicial scrutiny as "definitions" of "technical" or "trade" terms within S19(a).

(3) In the area of civil liability the law has become almost chaotic as a result of the judicial implication of private rights of action—a development that, however salutary, should be synchronized with the express civil liability provisions in the several statutes in a way that appropriately levels the peaks and valleys and reduces the volume of needless litigation.

These are but a few of the major problem areas. And their enumeration is not to criticize a Government agency that has justifiably enjoyed a high reputation over the years for efficiency and imaginative administration. In recent years particularly, the Commission has done a great deal toward synthesizing the filing requirements under the basic statutes of 1933 and 1934. But there is a limit to what it can do without legislative reform; indeed, some of its efforts are doomed to being counterproductive so far as the general degree of complexity of the present statutory scheme is concerned.

* * *

The Federal Securities Code was prepared under the auspices of the American Law Institute. Professor Louis Loss of the Harvard Law School served as Reporter. He was assisted by a distinguished group of Consultants and Advisers. The final product represents a decade of sustained effort by the Reporter, his consultants and Advisers with substantial impact from the American Bar Association, the securities industry and the SEC. The Official Draft was endorsed by the American Bar Association, and by the SEC, with modifications. See Appendix A of SEC Securities Act Release 6242 (Sept. 18, 1980). These modifications are also reflected in the Second Supplement to the Official Code.

Although the Code has yet to be considered by the Congress, it has had a significant influence on the SEC integration program and in rule-making with respect to transactional exemptions. The Reporter's notes and comments are a reservoir of scholarly commentary which courts and scholars have found extremely useful.

Any legislative codification and revision of this magnitude necessarily entails compromise. As Professor Loss has said, "a Code of this size cannot be expected to be perfect." Instead, "the Code must be compared with the existing state of affairs rather than some imaginary ideal."

For commentary, see Loss, Fundamentals of Securities Regulation 38–54 (1983); W. Painter, the Federal Securities Code and Corporate Disclosure (1979); Symposium: Proposed Securities Code, 1 Pace L.Rev. 279 (1981) (with Bibliography); American Law Institutes Proposed Federal Securities Code: Symposium, 32 Vand.L.Rev. 455 (1979); ALI Proposed Federal Securities Code: A Program, 34 Bus.Law. 345 (1978); Lowenfels, The Case Against the Proposed Federal Securities Code, 65 Va.L.Rev. 615 (1979); The American Law Institute Federal Securities Code: Symposium, 33 U.Miami L.Rev. 1425 (1979).

SECTION 5. THE CONTINUING DEBATE OVER THE MERITS OF MANDATORY DISCLOSURE: A STATUS REPORT

Excerpt from: John C. Coffee, Jr.*

MARKET FAILURE AND THE ECONOMIC CASE FOR A MANDATORY DISCLOSURE SYSTEM [a]

70 Virginia Law Review 717–753 (1984).

Recent academic commentary on the securities laws has much in common with the battles fought in historiography over the origins of the First World War. The same progression of phases is evident. First, there is an orthodox school, which tends to see historical events largely as a moral drama of good against evil. Next come the revisionists, debunking all and explaining that the good guys were actually the bad. Eventually, a new wave of more professional, craftsmanlike scholars arrives on the scene to correct the gross overstatements of the revisionists and produce a more balanced, if problematic, assessment.

This same cycle is evident in the recent securities law literature. Not so long ago, academic treatment of the securities laws was clearly at the first or "motherhood" stage: to criticize the SEC was tantamount to favoring fraud. Then came the revisionists—most notably Professors Stigler,[1] Benston,[2] and Manne[3]—who argued that the securities laws produced few benefits and considerable costs. According to Professor Benston, the

---

* Professor of Law, Columbia University Law School. The author wishes to acknowledge the advice and comments of Bruce Ackerman, Susan Rose-Ackerman, Ronald Gilson, and Joel Seligman. None of them bear responsibility for the views expressed herein.

a. Reprinted with permission from Virginia Law Review Association. Copyright ©1984 by Virginia Law Review Association.

1. See Stigler, Public Regulation of the Securities Markets, 37 J.Bus. 117 (1964).

2. Professor Benston's prolific writings on this topic include the following: G. Benston, Corporate Financial Disclosure in the UK and the USA (1976); Benston, The Costs and Benefits of Government-Required Disclosure: SEC and FTC Requirements, in Corporations at the Crossroads: Governance and Reform 37–69 (D. DeMott ed. 1980); Benston, Required Disclosure

passage of these statutes did not even significantly improve the quality of information provided to investors.[4] These claims provoked a flurry of critical responses, both from academic critics [5] and the SEC.[6] Commentators have charged Professor Stigler with methodological laxness;[7] a new literature on insider trading has suggested that such trading may create perverse incentives; [8] and the leading historian on the SEC has effectively rebutted Professor Benston's account of market conditions prior to the passage of the Securities Exchange Act of 1934 (the '34 Act).[9]

and the Stock Market: An Evaluation of the Securities Exchange Act of 1934, 63 Am.Econ.Rev. 132 (1973) [hereinafter cited as Benston, An Evaluation of the Securities Exchange Act of 1934]; Benston, The Value of the SEC's Accounting Disclosure Requirements, 44 Acct.Rev. 515 (1969) [hereinafter cited as Benston, The Value of the SEC's Accounting Disclosure Requirements].

3. See H. Manne, Insider Trading and the Stock Market (1966); H. Manne & E. Solomon, Wall Street in Transition: The Emerging System and its Impact on the Economy (1974). For a critique of Manne, see Schotland, Unsafe at any Price: A Reply to Manne, Insider Trading and the Stock Market, 53 Va.L.Rev. 1425 (1967).

4. Benston, An Evaluation of the Securities Exchange Act of 1934, supra note 2; Benston, The Value of the SEC's Accounting Disclosure Requirements, supra note 2.

5. See, e.g., Friend & Herman, Professor Stigler on Securities Regulation: A Further Comment, 38 J.Bus. 106 (1965) [hereinafter cited as Friend & Herman, Professor Stigler on Securities Regulation]; Friend & Herman, The SEC Through a Glass Darkly, 37 J.Bus. 382 (1964) [hereinafter cited as Friend & Herman, The SEC Through a Glass Darkly]; Friend & Westerfield, Required Disclosure and the Stock Market, 65 Am.Econ.Rev. 467 (1975); Mendelson, Economics and the Assessment of Disclosure Requirements, 1 J.Comp.Corp.L. & Sec.Reg. 49 (1978). * * * Probably the most comprehensive recent survey of these critiques is contained in Seligman, The Historical Need for a Mandatory Corporate Disclosure System, 9 J.Corp.L. 1 (1983).

6. The SEC responded in 1977 with a report prepared by a distinguished Advisory Committee. See House Comm. on Interstate and Foreign Commerce, Report of the Advisory Committee on Corporate Disclosure to the Securities and Exchange Commission, 95th Cong., 1st Sess. (Comm.Print 1977) (hereinafter cited as Advisory Committee Report). For a critique of this report, see H. Kripke, The SEC and Corporate Disclosure: Regulation in Search of a Purpose (1979).

7. See Friend & Herman, Professor Stigler on Securities Regulation, supra

note 5, at 107–09; Mendelson, supra note 5. A more recent empirical study by Professor Jarrell, while also discounting the impact of the federal securities laws, produced results in some respects strikingly at odds with Professor Stigler's findings. See Jarrell, The Economic Effects of Federal Regulation of the Market for New Security Issues, 24 J.L. & Econ. 613 (1981). For a review of the inconsistencies in results, see Friend, supra note 5.

8. See Easterbrook, Insider Trading, Secret Agents, Evidentiary Privileges, and the Production of Information, 1981 Sup. Ct.Rev. 309; Levmore, Securities and Secrets: Insider Trading and the Law of Contracts, 68 Va.L.Rev. 117 (1982); Schotland, supra note 3; Scott, Insider Trading: Rule 10(b)–5 Disclosure and Corporate Privacy, 9 J.Legal Stud. 801 (1980). For a critique from a managerial perspective, see Haft, The Effect of Insider Trading Rules on the Internal Efficiency of the Large Corporation, 80 Mich.L.Rev. 1051 (1982). [And see Cox, Insider Trading and Contracting: A Critical Response to the "Chicago School", 1986 Duke L.J. 628.]

9. See Seligman, supra note 5, at 12–18. Professor Seligman is the author of a comprehensive work regarding the history of the SEC. See J. Seligman, The Transformation of Wall Street: A History of the Securities and Exchange Commission and Modern Corporate Finance (1982). Briefly, Professor Benston studied the financial information disclosed in Moody's Manuals by 508 corporations that were traded on the New York Stock Exchange on June 1935, just before the Securities and Exchange Act took effect. Sixty-two percent of these corporations disclosed sales figures, as opposed to only 55% in 1926. Benston, The Value of the SEC's Accounting Disclosure Requirements, supra note 2, at 519. This increase, which to Professor Benston demonstrated that regulation was unnecessary, is susceptible to different interpretations. Corporations may have begun to bow before the Act's requirements as the inevitable effective date approached, or as Professor Seligman suggests, this increase may have been largely a statistical artifact caused by non-complying firms leaving the Exchange to avoid the '34 Act's coverage (as some did). Seligman, supra note 5, at

We therefore may be approaching a new stage, which can be called "post-revisionism." Among post-revisionism's defining characteristics are (1) a recognition of the Efficient Capital Market Hypothesis as, at the least, the best generalization by which to summarize the available empirical evidence;[10] (2) a clearer sense of the difficulties inherent in relying on aggregate statistical evidence either to prove or rebut any broad thesis about the impact and effects of disclosure;[11] and (3) a shift in focus from continued debate over the impact the federal securities laws had fifty years

14–15. The more significant fact actually appears to be that even on the eve of the '34 Act's effectiveness, 38% of New York Stock Exchange corporations were still not publishing sales figures. In any event, because Professor Seligman's critique of Benston's data is detailed and lengthy, it will not be summarized further here.

10. Conventionally, the Efficient Capital Market Hypothesis (ECMH) is subdivided into three distinct versions: the "weak" form, the "semi-strong," and the "strong." See Fama, Efficient Capital Markets: A Review of Theory and Empirical Work, 25 J.Fin. 383 (1970). As so often happens in the relationship between the law and social sciences, at the very moment that judicial and administrative decisions have begun to accept the ECMH, anomalies have begun to appear in the research data. These anomalies call into question either the extent of the ECMH's applicability or suggest the need for technical reformation. Research in three areas has identified fissures in the foundation of the ECMH. First, studies of the volatility of securities prices suggest that the response of securities prices may be excessive in relation to the significance of the underlying events. See, e.g., Shiller, Do Stock Prices Move Too Much to Be Justified By Subsequent Changes in Dividends?, 71 Am.Econ.Rev. 421 (1981). Second, studies demonstrate a "small firm" effect under which small firms (typically, the bottom 20% of publicly traded companies) earn abnormally high returns, even after risk adjustment. Other anomalies involving seasonal and weekly variations in stock returns and similar cyclical regularities are also recurrently documented. For an easily accessible summary of these findings, see Seligman, Can You Beat the Stock Market?, Fortune, Dec. 26, 1983, at 82, 94. For the latest data on the small firm effect, see Symposium on Size and Stock Returns, and Other Empirical Regularities, 12 J.Fin.Econ. 3 (1983). For the response of the Chicago School, see Rosett, Chicago School Bets on Inefficiency, N.Y. Times, Dec. 11, 1983, at F10, col. 3 (group of Chicago graduate students and professors formed investment company that invests solely in small firm stocks). Third, the conceptual and practical utility of beta—the measure of stock market volatility—remains in serious doubt and some

theorists are trying to replace it with a reformulated definition of non-diversifiable risk. See B. Malkiel, A Random Walk Down Wall Street 213–26 (2d ed. 1981); Black, Yes, Virginia There Is Hope: Tests of the Value Line Ranking System, Fin. Anal.J., Sept.-Oct. 1973, at 10–14; Downes & Dyckman, A Critical Look at the Efficient Market Empirical Research Literature as it Relates to Accounting Information, 48 Acct.Rev. 300 (1973); Downes & Dyckman, The Efficient Market Reconsidered 4 J. Portfolio Mgmt. 4, 4–74 (Fall 1977); Seligman, supra note 5.

Although none of these anomalies seem likely to weaken the basic point that investors cannot "beat" the market based on diligent search efforts, they do suggest that distinctions should be drawn in terms of the degree to which the ECMH is used as a justification for deregulation—particularly since very little evidence exists with respect to any market other than the New York Stock Exchange. This article will suggest that a mandatory disclosure system should focus on disclosures that assist the investor in assessing beta and better enable him to reduce diversifiable risk; greater disclosure seems also justified in the case of small firms given their apparent immunity to the predictions of the ECMH.

11. Recent studies have agreed that the variance in debt securities returns declined after the '34 Act. This decline, however, can be interpreted in various ways. Professor Friend concludes that it resulted from the prevention of fraudulent issues, which were recurrent before 1934. See Friend, supra note 5. Professor Jarrell posits that this change was the consequence of a paternalistic SEC policy that denied investors the opportunity to invest in higher risk securities having a higher return. See Jarrell, supra note 7, at 648–49. Although statistical data can often be interpreted in various ways, the usual approach of social scientists in such instances is to utilize direct observation and interview data. Here, the historical evidence compiled by Professor Seligman seems compelling in its thesis that fraud was prevalent prior to 1934. See Seligman, supra note 5, at 18–33.

ago to an examination of contemporary market structure and the needs of investors under existing conditions.[12]

In this typology of phases, the article by Professors Easterbrook and Fischel [13] seems at the threshold of "post-revisionism." This categorization may overstate the degree to which they have moved beyond the simple catechism of Professors Stigler and Benston, but at least their article recognizes that the statistical studies are not clearly dispositive [14] and that a faint possibility remains open that benefits might accrue to investors from a mandatory disclosure system.[15] On the other hand, of the possible reasons they offer for believing that issuers might underprovide information, only one—the third party effects hypothesis [16]—seems plausible.[17]

In contrast, a simpler theory can justify a mandatory disclosure system. Such a theory can also explain where a disclosure system should focus. Essentially, this response will make four claims.

First, because information has many characteristics of a public good, securities research tends to be underprovided. This underprovision means both that information provided by corporate issuers will not be optimally verified and that insufficient efforts will be made to search for material information from non-issuer sources. A mandatory disclosure system can thus be seen as a desirable cost reduction strategy through which society,

---

12. Much has changed since the 1920's. Among the most obvious differences are the following: (1) the appearance in the stock market of small investors, who were a rarity before 1934, (2) the increasing domination of trading by institutional investors, and (3) the maturation of the securities analyst into a true professional. Each of these trends really dates from after World War II (at the earliest).

These trends, however, do not necessarily point in the same direction. Institutional investors, who began to dominate trading in the 1960's, see infra note 43 and accompanying text, clearly are better able to fend for themselves than are individuals whose small holdings make investment in securities research infeasible. Conversely, the abolition of fixed rate brokerage commissions in 1975 probably has lessened the desire and ability of competing firms to provide securities advice and research to customers as a form of non-price competition. No attempt is made here to assess the net balance of these changes; rather, the point is that a series of economists, in comparing pre–1933 and post–1933 returns on securities, and even in comparing pre–1933 and 1950–era returns, have overlooked the probability that the securities markets have changed dramatically since the 1950's so as to call into question the relevance of any prior conclusions about the impact of the '34 Act.

13. Easterbrook & Fischel, Mandatory Disclosure and the Protection of Investors, 70 Va.L.Rev. 669 (1984).

14. Id. at 709–13.

15. Id. at 696–707.

16. Id. at 685–87, 697.

17. Others have also suggested that issuers might resist disclosures, particularly involving line-of-business data, for fear of informing business rivals. See Foster, Externalities and Financial Reporting, 35 J.Fin. 521, 523–25 (1980) (discussing externalities of "competitive sensitive" content to the reporting firm); Advisory Committee Report, supra note 6, at xxi (noting analysts' complaints about their difficulties in obtaining information not required for disclosure but important for investment decisions). This point has then been made before, but Professors Easterbrook and Fischel correctly elaborate on it. See Easterbrook & Fischel, supra note 13, at 685–87.

As to their interstate exploitation argument, see id. at 697–98, their discussion seems to extrapolate the problem of state anti-takeover statutes, which admittedly is a serious problem, beyond its realistic limits. No evidence is cited to support the proposition that before 1933 states placed excessive demands on corporate issuers to favor local investors. Nor did the '34 Act change anything in this regard. States continued to legislate disclosure requirements under their "Blue Sky" statutes, which were expressly not preempted by either the Securities Act of 1933 or the '34 Act. See Securities Act of 1933, ch. 38, § 18, 48 Stat. 74, 85 (codified as amended at 15 U.S.C. § 77zzz (1982)); Securities Exchange Act of 1934, ch. 404, § 28(a), 48 Stat. 881, 903 (codified as amended at 15 U.S.C. § 78bb(a) (1982)). * * * *

in effect, subsidizes search costs to secure both a greater quantity of information and a better testing of its accuracy. Although the end result of such increased efforts may not significantly affect the balance of advantage between buyers and sellers, or even the more general goal of distributive fairness, it does improve the allocative efficiency of the capital market—and this improvement in turn implies a more productive economy.

Second, a substantial basis exists for believing that greater inefficiency would exist without a mandatory disclosure system because excess social costs would be incurred by investors pursuing trading gains. Collectivization minimizes the social waste that would otherwise result from the misallocation of economic resources to this pursuit.

Third, the theory of self-induced disclosure, now popular among theorists of the firm and relied upon by Professors Easterbrook and Fischel,[18] has only a limited validity. A particular flaw in this theory is that it overlooks the significance of corporate control transactions and assumes much too facilely that manager and shareholder interests can be perfectly aligned. In fact, the very preconditions specified by these theorists as being necessary for an effective voluntary disclosure system do not seem to be satisfied. Although management can be induced through incentive contracting devices to identify its self-interest with the maximization of share value, it will still have an interest in acquiring the shareholders' ownership at a discounted price, at least so long as it can engage in insider trading or leveraged buyouts. Because the incentives for both seem likely to remain strong, instances will arise in which management can profit by giving a false signal to the market.

Fourth, even in an efficient capital market, there remains information that the rational investor needs to optimize his securities portfolio. Such information seems best provided through a mandatory disclosure system.

None of these claims is intended, however, as a complete defense of the status quo, nor will this response address the important, but distinct, question of the utility of disclosure as a form of substantive regulation of corporate behavior through the sanction of stigmatization.

I. A PUBLIC GOODS PERSPECTIVE

Easy as it is today to criticize the original premise of the federal securities laws—i.e., that mandatory disclosure would enable the small investor to identify and invest in higher quality and lower risk securities— such criticism does not take us very far because its target has shifted. The securities markets have evolved significantly since the 1930's, and one of the most important developments is the appearance of the professional securities analyst.[19] Little known in 1934 and common today, the analyst

---

18. See Easterbrook & Fischel, supra note 13, at 684–85.

19. The SEC's Advisory Committee on Corporate Disclosure found that there were some 14,646 professional securities analysts employed by financial institutions, brokerage firms, and consulting services as of 1977. See Advisory Committee Report, supra note 6, at 36. Presumably, this profession has survived because it performs a useful service. Typically, the chief source of firm-specific data used by the analyst appears to come from personal conversations with managers. Id. at 66–68. That managers do divulge information in this fashion to analysts provides some support for the theory of voluntary disclosure discussed below. See infra section II. For a refreshingly skeptical treatment of the analyst, however, see B. Malkiel, supra note 10, at 157–61.

seems likely to become the critical mechanism of market efficiency because on-line computerization of SEC-filed data makes access to such information both immediate and relatively costless to the analyst.[20]

The work of the securities analyst can be subdivided into two basic functions. First, the analyst searches for information obtainable from non-issuer sources bearing on the value of a corporate security. Often, this information is critical because the issuer's performance may be substantially dependent on exogenous factors—e.g., interest rates, the behavior of competitors, governmental actions, consumer attitudes, and demographic trends—about which the issuer has no special knowledge or the analyst has superior access. Second, the analyst verifies, tests, and compares the issuer's disclosures, both to prevent deliberate fraud and to remove the unconscious bias that usually affects all forms of information transfer.

Although individual investors could also perform these search and verification functions, the professional securities analyst typically can do so at a lower cost because there appear to be significant economies of scale and specialization associated with these tasks. As a result, most accounts explaining the stock market's efficiency assign a substantial responsibility to the competition among analysts for securities information.[22]

In principle, the information volume developed by securities analysts is determined by the usual market forces and should result in the usual equilibrium: analysts should invest in verifying and obtaining material information about corporate securities until the marginal cost of this information to them equals their marginal return. Ordinarily, this private equilibrium should also result in allocative efficiency: social resources would be devoted to information verification until the social costs rose to meet the social benefits. There is a basic flaw, however, in this simple neoclassical analysis, and it involves a recurring problem that arises whenever a public good is produced.

A. *Market Failure as a Cause of Insufficient Securities Research*

Public goods are a well-known economic concept. What has not been adequately recognized, however, is the degree to which information about corporate securities from non-issuer sources resembles (albeit imperfectly) a public good. The key characteristic of a public good is the non-excludability of users who have not paid for it; people benefit whether or not they contribute to the costs of acquiring the good, in part because consumption

---

20. For this view of the future, see Sanger, S.E.C.'s Computer Revolution: Benefits Seen for Investors, N.Y. Times, Apr. 3, 1984, at D1, col. 3. As contemplated, issuers would both file and update their reports electronically. Although the individual investor could also obtain access, the analyst and the broker would have significant economies of scale, operating in their favor.

22. The view that the competition among analysts to "ferret out and analyze information" maintains market efficiency has now received the imprimatur of the Supreme Court in Dirks v. SEC, 463 U.S. 646 (1983): "Imposing a duty to disclose or abstain solely because a person knowingly receives material nonpublic information from an insider and trades on it could have an inhibiting influence on the role of market analysts, *which the SEC itself recognizes is necessary to the preservation of a healthy market.*" Id. at 3263 (emphasis added). It needs to be emphasized that the ECMH does not imply that securities research is without value, although it does call into question the price that is often paid. See Fama, Random Walks in Stock Market Prices, Fin.Anal.J., Sept.–Oct. 1965, at 55–59; Pozen, Money Managers and Securities Research, 51 N.Y.U.L.Rev. 923, 950–53 (1976).

of the good by one user does not diminish its availability to others. The net result is that public goods tend to be underprovided.[24]

Securities information displays this key characteristic of non-excludability. It seldom can be confined to a single user because many people have a motive to leak it. When the corporate insider tips a friend of a material impending development, the information does not stop with the tippee, but tends to be passed on. In fact, it is generally in the tippee's interest, once he has traded, to inform others to create excitement and induce a market upswing. Otherwise, the tippee achieves only the dubious victory of owning an undervalued security, and as the Wall Street Traders' credo says: "A bargain that remains a bargain is no bargain." Subsequent users thus gain a largely gratuitous benefit from material information leaked to them, although the value of the benefit quickly diminishes because of the market's rapid adjustment.[25]

As applied to the securities analyst, the public goods-like character of securities research implies that the analyst cannot obtain the full economic value of his discovery, and this in turn means that he will engage in less search or verification behavior than investors collectively desire. The public goods character of securities research is illustrated by the well-known commercial: "When E.F. Hutton talks, people listen." Indeed, people do listen, but the eavesdroppers do not pay for what they receive; they are, in the parlance, "free riders." Typically, securities research is reduced to an analyst's report that is circulated among prominent institutional investors in return for expected future commissions or other investment banking business. Contracting for research in this fashion is presumably more efficient than each institutional investor employing its own analysts (which also happens) because of the economies of scale and specialization.[27] Once securities research is initially disseminated in this fashion (or any similar fashion), however, free riding is predictable: news leaks out almost immediately because the confidentiality of a circulated report cannot be protected for long and because institutional investors have an incentive (after they trade) to make the analyst's report a self-fulfilling prophecy by encouraging others to trade. Either way, those in the tippee

---

24. Professors Easterbrook and Fischel have elsewhere utilized this analysis to explain why shareholders will not resist management. See Easterbrook & Fischel, The Proper Role of a Target's Management in Responding to a Tender Offer, 94 Harv.L. Rev. 1161, 1171 (1981). Because the benefit of any resistance undertaken by a single shareholder or a group of shareholders must be shared with all shareholders, "each shareholder finds it in his self-interest to be passive." Id. This free-riding problem also applies to the analyst as well as to the shareholder, because the securities analyst cannot obtain the full economic value that his efforts created. See infra text accompanying notes 26–28.

25. The rapidity of the market's response depends, however, on whether the information is truly publicly available information (e.g., earnings reports or projections or dividend announcements) or semi-public data that is slowly being leaked

from an inside source. The facts of Dirks v. SEC, 463 U.S. 646 (1983), illustrate this. In *Dirks*, Ronald Secrist, a former officer of Equity Funding, sought without success to alert regulatory authorities and others to the existence of a classic fraud. Between March 7, 1973, when Secrist alerted both Dirks and insurance authorities and March 28th, when the SEC suspended trading, the critical information was in the hands of numerous individuals. Their reaction time was relatively slow (for a number of understandable reasons). Dirks' clients were thus able to liquidate their positions in the stock and avoid serious loss, even though the details of the fraud had been described to public authorities two weeks earlier. See also infra note 43.

27. See supra text accompanying note 22. If it were not more efficient, such an institutional structure would presumably not have survived.

chain do not compensate the analyst. As a result, securities research is likely to be undercompensated. This undercompensation implies that there is underinvestment in securities research in terms of the aggregate wealth it creates or preserves. Thus, we are back to the classic public goods problem: so long as the free riders do not have to pay, the commodity will be underprovided.

A related problem with securities research involves the difficulties inherent in contracting for it. Normally, compensation for such research is on an ex post basis because the investor cannot know its value in advance. * * * The only objective test of the advice's value is the ultimate occurrence of the predicted market reaction. Although the buyer of valuable information should be willing to compensate the provider (at least to the extent that the buyer wishes to obtain such information from him in the future), the ex post and unilateral character of the payment results in less compensation being paid than if the negotiation were on a bilateral basis.

This problem is further complicated because payment typically is not made in cash. Rather, the user directs some of its brokerage business to the firm whose analyst supplied the information. In effect, the institutional investor pays above market price for brokerage services to obtain valuable research; the investor purchases advice with nothing more than the promise of future brokerage commissions at a premium rate. This premium is evidenced by the recent appearance of discount brokers, who offer only clearing services and provide no investment advice. The cost of such brokerage is estimated to be fifty percent below that of full service brokerage firms.[30] Thus, the customer has his choice of financial services—a simple clearing service or a clearing service plus advice.

This curious institutional structure has two important implications, which the neoclassical critics of mandatory disclosure have simply ignored. First, there is clearly an incentive for the buyer to cheat on the implicit deal; he can use the investment advice provided by the full service firm and then steer the majority of his brokerage business to the discount firm. Second, the persistence of full service firms and the very survival of the securities analyst as a profession in the face of this price competition suggest that consumers do want securities advice and research, both on the individual client and institutional investor levels. Otherwise, brokerage firms would fire their analysts to cut costs. Moreover, one cannot dismiss this evident demand for securities research as an irrational preference because the consumers include the most sophisticated of institutional investors.

These contractual problems, in combination with the public goods nature of securities research, help explain how a mandatory disclosure system benefits investors. Put simply, if market forces are inadequate to produce the socially optimal supply of research, then a regulatory response may be justified. Although securities advisers are regulated only in the most minimal way by the federal securities laws,[31] they are in effect heavily

---

30. See Vartan, Those Discount Stockbrokers, N.Y. Times, Jan. 19, 1984, at D10, col. 3. * * *

31. Securities analysts may be required to register as investment advisers under the Investment Advisers Act of 1940, 15

U.S.C. § 80b–1 (1982), which contains reporting and anti-fraud provisions. No educational or other qualifications, however, are required to be an investment adviser, and the regulatory strictures appear to be relatively looser than those that apply to

subsidized by these statutes. Thus, the contemporary impact of the '34 Act may lie less in providing usable information to the ultimate investor than it does in reducing costs for the securities analyst.[32] Indeed, the detailed periodic reports that "reporting" companies file under the '34 Act are chiefly useful only to the professional analyst and not the individual trader. It is therefore no surprise that the professional investment community has long supported the continuous disclosure system of the '34 Act: to them the system implies cost savings.[34]

What do these cost savings imply for the structure and efficiency of the securities market? To the extent that mandated disclosure reduces the market professional's marginal cost of acquiring and verifying information, it increases the aggregate amount of securities research and verification provided. That is, because the analyst as a rational entrepreneur will increase his output until his marginal cost equals his marginal return, it follows axiomatically that the collectivization of securities information will produce more information. Over time, excess returns to securities analysts will induce new competitors to enter the market, which will increase the competitiveness of the industry. Casual empiricism suggests that both these predictions can be observed in the post–1934 experience of the securities industry. Certainly, the volume of securities research is much higher today than in 1934, and the very title "securities analyst" would not have been understood back then.[35]

The unresolved question is why these cost savings were not clearly reflected in stock price increases or any other observable impact immediately following the '34 Act's passage?[36] Although the one existing study of

broker dealers. For an overview, see L. Loss, Fundamentals of Securities Regulation 733–48 (1983).

32. For a similar analysis of the impact of the '34 Act, see Gilson & Kraakman, The Mechanisms of Market Efficiency, 70 Va.L.Rev. 559, 637–42 (1983). Although they see the '34 Act as "a form of special-interest relief legislation" to aid the securities industries, id., this evaluation appears to give too little attention to the benefits that flow to ordinary investors in the form of more publicly available research and a greater number of companies being closely followed by securities analysts. * * * Although this data will not enable them to "beat the market," it should benefit investors in at least two distinct ways: (1) it better enables the investor to assess the risk level of individual securities, to avoid investing in securities whose risk level exceeds his personal level of risk aversion, and (2) it should reduce the variance in returns applicable to those securities not traded on major exchanges, which otherwise analysts would not closely watch.

34. See J. Seligman, supra note 9, at 311–12, 630 n. 50 (1982) (industry welcomed 1964 amendments expanding scope of '34 Act to corporations having over 500 shareholders and defined level of assets). The industry did, however, oppose the Securities Act of 1933 bitterly and conducted

what Professor Seligman has termed a "capital strike." Id. at 71–115.

35. The term "security analysis" was popularized by Benjamin Graham and David Dodd, whose immensely influential statement of the fundamental principles of financial analysis was published, interestingly enough, in 1934. See B. Graham & D. Dodd, Security Analysis: Principles and Techniques (1st ed. 1934). Although this book had its precursors, it is as difficult to conceive of the securities analyst developing in recognizable form before its publication as it is to imagine the job description of psychoanalyst arising before Freud. For example, the New York Society of Security Analysts, the largest professional organization in this field, was not founded until the late 1930's. Telephone interview with staff official, New York Society of Security Analysts (Apr.1984). Admittedly, publications such as Moody's were published in the 19th century, and a prototype of the securities analyst can be traced back well before 1934, but the real development of the modern securities analyst had to await both the development of the theory that Graham and Dodd codified and the rise of the institutional investor, which essentially occurred in the 1960's. * * *

36. Only one study has been conducted on the effect of the '34 Act on stock prices. See Benston, An Evaluation of the Securi-

the market's reaction to the '34 Act's adoption may have been too method-ologically flawed to capture any changes that occurred, another possible answer is that all the gains were captured by informed traders and other market professionals in the form of cost reductions. Arguably, these traders received the same approximate volume of information both before and after 1934, but simply obtained this data at a lower price after the '34 Act.[37] Yet this answer seems incomplete; it ignores that the securities analyst—or his predecessor in that era—should produce more information if he has a lower marginal cost.

This argument that lower costs for the securities analyst should result in more information production takes us only so far. As Professors Easterbrook and Fischel correctly observe, it is theoretically possible that too much information is already produced, particularly because not all, or even most, investors need to be well informed for the market to be efficient.[38] Yet they stop at this point, which seems to be the threshold where close analysis should begin.

According to the SEC Advisory Committee on disclosure, only about 1,000 of the 10,000 odd "reporting" companies registered under the '34 Act are regularly followed by securities analysts.[39] In the absence of analyst monitoring and in the presence of erratic trading, there is considerable reason to doubt that the market for the other 9,000 firms is "efficient," even in some cases in the "weak" sense of that term. Although other mechanisms exist by which to achieve efficiency, their efficacy is unproven

ties Exchange Act of 1934, supra note 2. Professor Benston isolated two groups of companies for comparison: one that dis-closed their sales figures prior to the '34 Act and the other that did not. Neither group showed significant changes in its aggregate rate of return after the Act's passage. In theory, one might expect the non-disclosing companies to experience ab-normal negative returns as investors learned of adverse information that had previously been withheld by management. Nevertheless, Professor Benston concluded that the Act had no effect. Professor Ben-ston's methodology, however, has been re-currently challenged, in part because his "non-disclosure" group appears to have consisted of companies that did in fact dis-close net income, the most important vari-able for investors. See Friend & Wester-field, supra note 5, at 468–70; Seligman, supra note 5, at 17. Professors Friend and Westerfield also found that both the dis-closing and non-disclosing firms performed better in the post–1934 period. See Friend & Westerfield, supra note 5, at 468–70. But see Benston, Required Disclosure and the Stock Market: Rejoinder, 65 Am.Econ. Rev. 473 (1975). Although it is common-place for scholars to rely on Benston's find-ings without pointing out the serious meth-odological flaws in his approach (or the variable interpretations that can be placed on his data), the issue still seems to be unresolved as to whether the '34 Act had

an immediate impact on stock prices or investors.

37. This is the thesis that Professors Gilson and Kraakman advance. See Gil-son & Kraakman, supra note 32, at 636–38.

38. "The more sophisticated version of the public goods explanation is that al-though investors produce information, they produce both too much and too little." Easterbrook & Fischel, supra note 13, at 681. Although their statement appears to be correct, it only frames the problem, and does not assess the impact of the '34 Act, which encourages the analyst to produce more information, while also eliminating the need for wasteful duplication of efforts by rival analysts or rival investors. Professors Easterbrook and Fischel instead rely on the Coase Theorem, which by its own terms is inapplicable when transac-tion costs are high, as is likely the case for widely dispersed small shareholders.

39. Advisory Committee Report, supra note 6, at xviii-xix. Professor Kripke has challenged this number as too low. H. Kripke, supra note 6, at 126–28. This chal-lenge appears to be correct, but only in terms of degree. Even if the number of closely watched companies were twice as high, this figure would leave 8,000 corpora-tions with over 500 shareholders and no following within the professional financial analyst community.

and highly debatable.[40] The desirability of expending social resources to improve the efficiency of the trading in these smaller issues can also be reasonably disputed. What seems to be beyond argument, however, is the consequence of increasing the securities analysts' marginal costs for obtaining or verifying information. If we repealed the '34 Act, and thereby increased analysts' marginal costs, the number of companies regularly followed by analysts would likely decline below this 1,000 figure.[41] In short, cost reductions for analysts imply broader coverage of firms, and cost increases imply the converse. This conclusion, in turn, leads to the bottom line: the more firms that are closely followed by analysts, the greater assurance both that capital markets will be allocatively efficient and that the game will be fair with respect to such companies.

    *   *   *   *

In 1934, institutional investors represented only a small fraction of equity securities trading; the dominant figure was still the professional trader, who relied more on rumors, tips, and personal contacts than on hard data. Only with the later appearance (probably in the 1960's) of the institutional investor—and in particular, a nationwide population of institutional investors—did the institutional structure arise that could support the modern securities analyst.[43] In this light, the '34 Act becomes the logical, if premature, answer to a problem that had yet to emerge: how to increase the volume of securities research, which then was not even in demand. In 1934, any gains that the Act created may well have been fully captured by a small coterie of professional traders, but with the subsequent expansion of the industry, the cost savings that the '34 Act engendered helped to create the securities analyst as a distinct profession. That this result was serendipitous does not make it any less desirable.

B. Social Waste and the Problem of Excess Research

This hypothesis that a mandatory disclosure system reduces the costs incurred by market professionals has another important corollary: aggregate social wealth is arguably increased because the partial collectivization

---

40. Of course, some will argue that market forces are adequate to induce disclosure even if monitoring by analysts is not occurring. This theory of self-induced disclosure is examined in section II of this article, which finds it a partial truth.

41. At the margin, the securities analyst can be expected as his marginal cost increases to reduce his operations (and either follow fewer companies or investigate the same number less thoroughly). One test of this thesis might be to compare the number of companies that were closely followed prior to 1934. There is, however, no simple measure of this variable, partly because there were fewer securities analysts in this era and their techniques were more rudimentary. A cursory survey reveals that as of 1941, there were 1,210 issuers listed on the New York Stock Exchange. See 7 SEC Ann.Rep. 305 (1941). Assuming that this number constitutes the upper boundary of closely followed stocks, it still does not contrast sharply with the estimat-

ed number of closely followed stocks today. * * * This figure of 1,210, however, probably overstates the number of firms that were closely monitored; Professor Seligman has informed this author that in his view few firms prior to 1934 released enough data to be closely watched to the degree presumed by the SEC Advisory Committee in its estimate that currently analysts closely follow 1,000 firms. Another test of this thesis would be to contrast the number of full time securities analysts before and after 1934. Although the 14,646 figure given by the SEC Advisory Committee in 1977, see supra note 19, probably is greatly in excess of the pre-1934 figure, this is an illegitimate comparison because the securities analysis profession was then only in its infancy.

43. The volume of institutional trading on the New York Stock Exchange rose during the 1960's from a low of 17% to a high of 52% in 1969. See J. Seligman, supra note 9, at 351–52.

of securities information that the '34 Act mandates in effect economizes on the total amounts expended in pursuing trading gains. From a social welfare perspective, trading gains do not create additional wealth; one party's gain comes at the other party's loss, whereas the process of researching and verifying securities information consumes real resources.[44] Although securities research sometimes creates social wealth (both by perfecting the allocative efficiency of the capital markets and by facilitating the entrepreneur's ability to raise capital for wealth-creating projects), the '34 Act chiefly addresses the secondary trading market. Here, one can view the participants as engaged in pursuing trading gains that do not affect aggregate shareholder wealth. Their expenditures in pursuit of such gains therefore represent social waste, as Professor Hirschleifer long ago pointed out in a classic article.[45] In this light, a major significance of a mandatory disclosure system is that it can reduce these costs. Rival firms do not need to incur expenses to produce essentially duplicative data banks when a central securities data bank is in effect created at the SEC. Thus, rather than the '34 Act producing too much information (as Professors Easterbrook and Fischel suggest),[46] it probably reduces wasteful duplication by establishing a central information repository.

This claim that wasteful duplication is eliminated by a mandatory disclosure system may sound inconsistent with the earlier assertion that inadequate securities research occurs because of the public goods-like character of securities information. Yet there is no contradiction. Financial professionals may simultaneously expend both too little and too much resources on verifying and obtaining information. The first problem arises because too few companies are followed or are researched inadequately; the second, because investigations by one analyst are duplicated by another. Still, the existence of a central information repository in the form of the SEC is at least a partial answer to both problems.

C. Allocative Efficiency: The Public Interest in Adequate Securities Research

Which of the last two problems discussed—too much research or too little—is more serious? This question is important because the design of an optimal disclosure system depends in large part on how one answers it. Two very different perspectives are possible on the securities market. If we see it as simply a "fair game" in which securities prices are "unbiased" (that is, prices are as likely to move in the buyer's favor as the seller's), there is little cause for regulatory intervention (except possibly to prevent insider trading). Moreover, because in this light the securities market is essentially a "zero-sum game"—that is, one side's gain in every transaction is the other side's loss—society has no reason to encourage the parties to invest their resources in this nonproductive attempt to obtain wealth at the other's expense. So viewed, a mandatory disclosure system would be

---

44. See Fama & Laffer, Information and Capital Markets, 44 J.Bus. 289 (1971); Hirshleifer, The Private and Social Value of Information and the Reward to Inventive Activity, 61 Am.Econ.Rev. 561 (1971).

analysts not to engage in rival research efforts where the resources so utilized would only affect the distribution of trading gains and not increase market efficiency.

45. See Hirshleifer, supra note 44. Indeed, society might rationally decide to pay

46. See Easterbrook & Fischel, supra note 13, at 693–95.

justifiable principally as a means of minimizing the wasted resources devoted to the pursuit of trading gains.

Conversely, if we view the securities market as the principal allocative mechanism for investment capital, the behavior of securities prices is important not so much because of their distributive consequences on investors but more because of their effect on allocative efficiency. In this light, it is important not only that the game be fair, but that it be accurate—that is, that capital be correctly priced. Depending on a firm's share price, its cost for obtaining capital will be either too high or low as compared to the cost that would prevail in a perfectly efficient market. In either case, society's mechanism for allocating scarce investment capital among competing users becomes distorted, even though the game remains equally fair to buyers and sellers. From this perspective, the critical empirical question shifts from whether the federal securities laws improved the mean return to investors to whether they reduced the variance associated with these returns. That is, if the federal securities laws reduced the dispersion associated with the returns on new issues, it can reasonably be inferred that they made the market for new issues more allocatively efficient. Professor Stigler appears to acknowledge this point: "Price dispersion," he writes, "is a manifestation—and, indeed, it is a measure—of ignorance in the market." [47] The greater this variance associated with securities returns, the greater the uncertainty and heterogeneity of investor expectations, and the less the likelihood that our capital allocation mechanism is working efficiently. Yet the stock market may still appear efficient to the extent that prices move randomly and mandatory public disclosures appear not to cause price adjustments.

Once the focus is shifted to the degree of dispersion associated with securities prices in the presence or absence of a mandatory disclosure system, the empirical issue is narrowed. Every scholar who has investigated the impact of the federal securities laws—including Stigler, Bentson, Jarrell, and Friend—appears to agree that price dispersion declined after the passage of the Securities Act of 1933.[48] The most logical conclusion to draw from this evidence is that allocative efficiency was enhanced and that investors thereby benefited. The key point then is that the social benefit of

---

47. See Stigler, The Economics of Information, 69 J.Pol.Econ. 213, 214 (1961).

48. Professor Stigler's initial study found that the variance associated with the returns on new securities issues declined after the passage of the '33 Act. See Stigler, Comment, 37 J.Bus. 414, 418–19 (1964); Stigler, supra note 1, at 122. Cf. Seligman, supra note 5, at 10–11 (criticizing Stigler's conclusion that a decline in the variance of new securities' prices was not meaningful). Similar findings were reported by Friend and Herman. See Friend & Herman, The SEC Through a Glass Darkly, supra note 5. In response, Professor Benston has not contested that there was a reduction in the standard deviations associated with security issues after 1933, but has disputed this reduction's relevance. See Benston, Required Disclosure and the Stock Market: Rejoinder, 65 Am.Econ.Rev. 473 (1974). For the latest round in this debate, see

Friend, supra note 5, at 8–12. Finally, in a recent study Professor Jarrell has also found a decline in the variance in returns associated with new stock issues after 1933. See Jarrell, supra note 7. Like Benston, he also doubts that this reduction in variance is a meaningful achievement and suggests that it instead signifies excessive paternalism on the SEC's part. Their position is that because this variance reduction was not associated with an increase in the mean returns, it did not benefit investors; rather, it implies to them that the SEC discouraged attractive high risk offerings at the same rate that it discouraged fraudulent ones. Even if this were true, it is curious to interpret it as a dubious achievement. If we assume that investors are risk averse, any reduction in the variance (or risk associated with a return) that does not reduce the mean return is desirable.
* * *

the federal securities laws may exceed their benefit to investors. The beneficiaries of increased allocative efficiency include virtually all members of society, not just investors. In this light, it is myopic to view the '34 Act as simply a subsidy for investors or to denigrate its benefits as merely trading gains.

This focus on allocative efficiency should also frame future research efforts. Rather than debate endlessly the effect that the federal securities laws had a half century ago, it is time to turn to issues of greater contemporary significance. For example, has the recent trend toward deregulation in connection with the administration of the '34 Act been associated with any increase in price dispersions or market volatility? To ask this question is not to answer it. Testable hypotheses, however, can be framed: for example, one could inquire whether price dispersion has increased following the adoption of the integrated disclosure system in 1982 [50] and the expanded use of shelf registration statements.[51] If not, the cost reductions to corporate issuers associated with these regulatory reforms would seem justified.[52] Clearly, however, this question cannot be safely answered by looking only at the market's immediate reaction to these developments or only at the change, if any, in mean returns to investors. Once we recognize that there is a social interest associated with an allocatively efficient capital market, then it is an overly narrow form of social cost accounting to calculate only the costs to issuers and benefits to investors.

II. THE THEORY OF VOLUNTARY DISCLOSURE

Underlying much of the thesis advanced by Professors Easterbrook and Fischel is the view that corporate managers have strong incentives to disclose voluntarily all material information to investors; thus, a mandated system is largely superfluous.[53] This thesis derives from the work of the economic theorists of the firm—most notably the work of Jensen and Meckling on agency costs [54] and Stephen Ross on signaling theory.[55]

---

50. For an overview, see SEC Securities Act Release No. 6383, 47 Fed.Reg. 11,380 (1982), reprinted in [1937–1982 Accounting Series Releases Transfer Binder] Fed.Sec.L. Rep. (CCH) ¶ 72,328 (Mar. 3, 1982). Under integrated disclosure, some issuers may use a propectus consisting almost exclusively of references to previously filed '34 Act reports. Compare Banoff, Regulatory Subsidies, Efficient Market, and Shelf Registration: An Analysis of Rule 415, 70 Va.L. Rev. 135 (1984), with Fox, Shelf Registration, Integrated Disclosure, And Underwriter Due Diligence: An Economic Analysis 70 Va.L.Rev. 1005 (1984).

51. See SEC Rule 415 * * *. For an overview, see Ferrara & Sweeney, Shelf Registration Under SEC Temporary Rule 415, 5 Corp.L.Rev. 308 (1982).

52. A substantial debate is continuing as to whether integrated disclosure and shelf registration statements will erode the due diligence efforts of underwriters and their counsel. Because Rule 176 * * * reduces the potential liability of underwrit-

ers for data that is incorporated by reference into a prospectus, it is arguable that underwriters and their counsel have less incentive today to verify the accuracy of information under an integrated disclosure system. * * * On the positive side of the ledger, it is clear that Rule 415 has reduced underwriters' commissions by encouraging greater competition among underwriters. See Ehrbar, Upheaval in Investment Banking, Fortune, Aug. 23, 1982, at 90. The suggestion made here is that any significant decline in socially desirable "due diligence" efforts would be observable in highest stock volatility (net of overall market movement) and increased price dispersion. Until efforts are made to test this thesis, the debate is indeterminable.

53. See Easterbrook & Fischel, supra note 13, at 683–85.

54. See Jensen & Meckling, Theory of the Firm: Managerial Behavior, Agency Costs and Ownership Structure, 3 J.Fin. Econ. 305 (1976).

These theorists do not deny that the separation of ownership and control in the modern public corporation implies a conflict between the interests of management and shareholders. They argue, however, that the burden of this conflict falls on the manager. To sell the firm's securities initially or to maintain the price of the firm's stock thereafter, the manager must convince the market that all relevant disclosures are being (and will continue to be) made; otherwise, he is the primary loser. As a result, according to these theorists, managers and shareholders have mutual incentives to structure the firm so that the market will be confident that all material information is being disclosed.

The typical techniques to this end are summarized in the Easterbrook and Fischel article: firms will use auditors to give their statements credibility,[56] firms will encourage managers, through stock options, to hold a substantial portion of their portfolio in the firm's stock; and the underwriters who sell the firm's stock will also retain a substantial block of stock in their own account. The reputational interests of managers also prevent behavior that would be injurious to shareholders. Clearly, to some extent these forces should inhibit opportunistic behavior by management, constrain their consumption of perquisites, and reduce any managerial tendency to shirk. The claim that they are sufficient, however, to render irrelevant the need for a mandatory disclosure system is a far stronger assertion, for which the evidence is much weaker. Agency costs should still persist,[60] and a basic conflict of interests still remains to the extent that managers can acquire the firm from its shareholders.

A. A Critique of the Theory

The fallacy in concluding that a mandatory disclosure system is irrelevant lies not in the premise that if a manager's compensation is made a function of the firm's performance, the manager is encouraged to act only to benefit the firm, but rather with the difficulties of systematically implementing such a compensation system so as to eliminate all occasions for opportunistic behavior. Typically, some economists simply assume these problems away.

For example Stephen Ross, whose incentive signaling theory contains the fullest statement of the preconditions to a wholly voluntary disclosure system, states that managers' compensation will be limited "by the wage level they could receive in competitive jobs." In other words, "no firm will hire a manager for $1 million a year when the going wage is $100,000." As he recognizes, however, any program of restricting managerial compensation to market levels must address the problem of insider trading. Such trading offers the manager an inviting means of profiting, whether or not his firm does. Ross's argument at this critical juncture is symptomatic of the economist's disregard for the problems of implementation. He writes:

> Stockholders will not permit a $100,000–a-year manager to have the freedom to trade in the firm for his own account and make million-

---

55. See Ross, Disclosure Regulation in Financial Markets: Implications of Modern Finance Theory and Signaling Theory, *in* Issues in Financial Regulation 177 (F. Edwards ed. 1979).

56. See Easterbrook & Fischel, supra note 13, at 675.

60. See Williamson, Organizational Form, Residual Claimants and Corporate Control, 26 J.L. & Econ. 351, 363 (1983) (arguing that changes in organizational form and prevalence of takeovers have mitigated but not eliminated managerial opportunism and agency costs).

dollar gains. * * * This is not to say that managers will not have an incentive to use inside information for their own gain, but rather that stockholders are aware of such incentives and will enter into contracts that penalize such activities.

Correct as it may be that shareholders would like to prevent insider trading by their management, it does not follow that they can do so as a practical matter. Professor Ross has, in effect, "assumed the can opener," [64] rather than tackled the problems that flow from a recognition that insider trading is virtually undetectable.[65] Moreover, to the extent that insider trading can be detected, public enforcement is a far more feasible technique than any system of contractual restraints.[66] Indeed, no such contractual system has been attempted.[67] As a result, the bottom line is that insider trading will persist and the prequisites to Professor Ross's theory of voluntary disclosure are therefore not satisfied.

Although this lack of congruence between the interests of managers and shareholders may show the need for a fraud rule, it is debatable whether it demonstrates the need for a mandatory disclosure system. Because managers can trade almost instantaneously once they recognize the significance of undisclosed material information, a system of periodic quarterly filings— such as the '34 Act essentially imposes—does little to inhibit such trading. Once management has traded, it has in fact a particularly strong incentive to release the positive or adverse information to hasten the desired market response. Any delay in the information's release may thus be trivial.

Even if the traditional form of insider trading supplies little justification for a mandatory disclosure system, a new phenomenon, which essentially poses the same dilemma, does suggest the utility of mandated disclosure. Within the last few years, there has been an extraordinary increase in the frequency of "leveraged buyouts." The leveraged buyout (LBO) is a technique for the purchase of the firm by its management (with possibly a few equity investors) by mortgaging the firm's assets to secure financing for the purchase price. By some accounts, LBO's rose from twenty percent of all acquisitions in 1982 to fifty percent in 1983.[71] Although there are econom-

---

64. This refers to the standard joke about the two scientists and an economist stranded on a deserted island with only a can of beans for food, which they cannot open. The physicist develops a theory for breaking open the can, and the chemist similarly devises a plan for boiling it open, but the economist suggests the simplest plan: "Assume a can opener."

65. With respect to the difficulty of detecting insider trading, see Dooley, Enforcement of Insider Trading Restrictions, 66 Va.L.Rev. 1 (1980).

66. Economies of scale probably favor public enforcement because the New York Stock Exchange and the SEC can learn quickly of unusual trading activity and indeed already have a fixed investment in market surveillance. Moreover, that classic engine of discovery—the grand jury— can (and is) used by federal prosecutors to trace leads and develop information, which a private plaintiff cannot do as easily.

There are also other problems with private enforcement. See Coffee, Rescuing the Private Attorney General: Why the Model of the Lawyer as Bounty Hunter Is Not Working, 42 Md.L.Rev. 215 (1983).

67. This point has been made by Professors Carlton and Fischel, who argue that insider trading should be legalized. See Carlton & Fischel, The Regulation of Insider Trading, 35 Stan.L.Rev. 857 (1983). This response's point is simply that the feasibility of contractual restrictions, such as those envisioned by Professor Ross, has never been demonstrated.

71. See Hill, Buyout Boom: Leveraged Purchases of Firms Keep Gaining Despite Risks, Wall St.J., Dec. 29, 1983, at 1, col. 6 (quoting Robert Mancuso, Managing Director of Merrill Lynch Capital Markets). See also, Meyer & McGough, Where the Smart Money Wants to Go, Forbes, Dec. 19, 1983, at 38.

ic justifications for such transactions,[72] the recent popularity of LBO's seems best explained as a defensive response to the increased threat of hostile takeovers. As a result, however, the availability of the managerial buyout option greatly intensifies the conflict of interests that already exists between management and shareholders. In effect, it enables management to engage in insider trading not on a piecemeal scale in the stock market, but on the much larger scale of corporate control transactions. At present, LBO's tend to occur at high premiums, and thus some will see them as a benign and desirable phenomenon. This tendency for the buyout to be effected at a high premium, however, may be more the consequence of our existing mandatory disclosure system than proof of its irrelevance.

In the absence of a mandatory disclosure system, the popularity of the LBO would likely increase. This increase should exacerbate two distinct perverse incentives. First, the possibility of a low premium takeover might lead a management to withhold or underplay positive information to preempt the appreciation by buying the firm in an LBO. Second, this possibility might induce management to release false information of adverse developments. This second point has special relevance because the theory of voluntary disclosure as expounded by both Ross and Jensen and by Meckling posits that management must report all adverse information accurately because any suspension in the corporation's stream of disclosures released will lead the market to assume that a financial disaster had occurred. In effect, these theorists conclude that the market will overrespond unless the bad news is disclosed with full candor. Professors Easterbrook and Fischel accurately summarize this argument when they state:

> The process works for bad news as well as for good. Once the firm starts disclosing it cannot stop short of making any critical revelation, because investors always assume the worst. It must disclose the bad with the good, lest investors will assume that the bad is even worse than it is.[73]

Although this iron law will come as news to the investors in Penn Central or Equity Funding, the more basic point is that any such market response is subject to obvious manipulation. Put simply, if non-disclosure did mean disaster, management could manipulate this pattern to its own self-interested ends. It could deliberately suspend disclosure to cause an economically unjustified decline in the stock price and then buy the stock at an artificially depressed price (or even sell short prior to the suspension of disclosure). Even better, it could use silence to scare the market and then offer an LBO.

In time, investors would learn to anticipate these tactics, and they would no longer equate non-disclosure with disaster. As a result, however, there would be great uncertainty as to the meaning of a halt in the flow of disclosure, and the original premise that non-disclosure would lead the market to overcorrect would no longer be true. Hence, an incentive would again arise for management to withhold disclosure of adverse information.

---

72. Above all, LBO's reduce agency costs, which may increase the value of the firm in the hands of its shareholders. Also, more flexible compensation arrangements for managers may be possible, and certain economically desirable self-dealing transactions can be approved more quickly.

73. Easterbrook & Fischel, supra note 13, at 683.

In short, one cannot have it both ways: if non-disclosure implies disaster, this equation can be exploited by management to facilitate its acquisition of either the firm's stock or assets; if non-disclosure does not imply disaster, then management need not ordinarily disclose adverse information. How does this inconsistency in the theory of voluntary disclosure relate to the need for a mandatory disclosure system (as opposed to simply supplying a justification for an anti-fraud rule)? The answer is two-fold.

First, under a mandatory disclosure system, an LBO at an inadequate price is likely to elicit a higher counter-bid from a third party. Such a counter-bid is the ideal remedy: it is self-enforcing and costless to the investor. An anti-fraud rule alone, however, cannot achieve this result. Although a fraud rule may give the investor a cause of action, it does not ensure sufficient dissemination of information to activate the market for corporate control. Bidders need information before they will invest millions (or billions) in an acquisition. A mandatory disclosure system responds to this need and so facilitates control contests. More generally, although an anti-fraud rule compensates victims, it does not sufficiently deter the underlying misbehavior because the wrongdoer does not suffer a significant loss. Instead, the wrongdoer only has to restore the gain he converted. Yet the possibility of a higher counter-bid is likely to deter because in the aftermath of a takeover, incumbent management is likely to be removed.

Second, given the incentives for nondisclosure of adverse information (either to induce a market decline and thereby to facilitate a buyout or to postpone the timing of the market response in management's self-interest), a mandatory disclosure system is a desirable supplement to an anti-fraud rule. The law of fraud has great conceptual difficulties with non-disclosures. Nor can it easily impose the costs of the wrongdoing on the responsible management. Rather, if management does not trade but simply withholds adverse information to protect its own position, it has little litigation exposure as a practical matter. The corporate issuer may be held liable (although even this is far from certain), but corporate liability in this context may mean only that a transfer payment is made from one class of stockholders to another.

In the last analysis, the assertion that market forces will alone induce adequate disclosure rests upon the flawed premise that management should see itself as a "repeat player" that can maximize its own interests over the long run only by maintaining the market's confidence. Often, this premise is accurate. In an environment increasingly characterized both by hostile takeovers and LBO's, however, it is no longer safe to assume that management expects or intends to remain a "repeat player." If management believes a stock decline will trigger a hostile takeover that will remove it from office, it does not have the luxury of taking a long-run view and may therefore seek to delay adverse news from reaching the market. Fearing a takeover, it may also decide to undertake an LBO (even though such a transaction forces it to hold an undiversified portfolio), and thus it will suppress or downplay positive information. Only in a static (and today nonexistent) world, where management is confident that it can remain in control of its firm, should we expect it to adopt the long-run perspective of the "repeat player."

B. The Comparative Evidence

Plausibility is not the ultimate test of a theory. As a result, the seeming flaws in the theory of market induced disclosure still do not eliminate the more difficult question of whether any empirical evidence is available by which to gauge the comparative efficacy of voluntary and mandatory disclosure. The one study, by Benston, comparing pre-'34 Act and post-'34 Act stock prices has generated substantial criticism. Even if this study were redone, however, other problems would still confound any attempt to evaluate the current impact of the '34 Act based primarily on a comparison of stock returns before and after its passage.[75] Institutional investors, securities analysis, and the modern law of securities fraud did not emerge until decades after 1934. Substantial reason exists to believe, as outlined above, that the '34 Act had its principal significance only in combination with these other developments. Thus, no simple comparison of the marketplace before and after 1934 can suffice to measure the Act's impact. The large scale appearance of individual investors in the equity securities markets after World War II complicates the picture even further. Their appearance may have increased "agency costs" and thereby reduced the returns on securities.[77] Consequently, there are offsetting impacts that compromise temporal studies.

Other social science techniques exist, however, for obtaining at least an inferential understanding of the impact of mandatory disclosure. * * * [W]e can look today at the differences between the disclosure level within the public securities market subject to SEC regulation and the level that prevails within the one major securities market that is exempt from registration—the municipal bond market.

A full assessment of the practices and level of disclosure within the municipal bond market is beyond this article's scope. Still, if the recent experiences with the New York City bond offerings in the 1970's [80] and the Washington Public Power System's failure in the 1980's are indicative, critical information is not being disclosed to investors. Most observers would agree with this statement,[81] but the neoclassical theorist will respond

---

75. All statistical studies must confront the problem of multicollinearity. Whenever we attempt to measure the relationship between two variables, there is always the possibility that the seeming relationship between the independent and the dependent variable is actually the result of a different and unexamined variable. Among the other variables that may confound any before and after comparison of stock returns preceding and following the '34 Act are the following: (1) the possibility of changed investor attitudes, (2) different enforcement policies at the state level, (3) the greater reluctance of issuers to offer securities in the face of new federal antifraud rules, (4) the gradual trend among institutional investors to invest in equity securities, and (5) an increased willingness of individual investors to buy securities in reliance on federal protections.

77. If stock ownership became more dispersed after 1934, this would increase the possibility of managerial opportunism and so reduce stock prices. This conclusion follows directly from the Jensen and Meckling thesis if one assumes that some exogenous change (such as the '34 Act's passage) resulted in more dispersed stockholders with smaller holdings, because such shareholders could incur smaller monitoring expenses. See Jensen & Meckling, supra note 54.

80. For a detailed exposition of the inadequacies in the municipal bond market as revealed by the New York City fiscal crisis, see SEC, Final Report in the Matter of Transactions in the Securities of the City of New York (1979).

81. Some will disagree. Professor Kripke has argued that the low rate of municipal bond defaults lulled investors into a false sense of security. See H. Kripke, supra note 6, at 129. This seems to be, however, an economically untenable posi-

that little information need reach investors because they are protected instead by the bond rating agencies—Moody's or Standard and Poor's; these agencies digest the relevant information, which in the case of a debt security consists only of its risk level, and assign a rating to each security.

If one examines the securities markets only at a distance and through the telescope of neoclassical economic theory, this rebuttal may sound persuasive. If one examines the institutional structure more closely, however, disturbing problems begin to appear. First, in the New York City fiscal crisis, Moody's did not reduce New York's rating until the crisis was universally acknowledged.[82] Second, because the issuer pays the bond rating agency to be rated, there is a conflict of interest problem. Third, the bond rating agencies are not themselves investigating agencies. Instead, they depend on the data that the issuer gives them. Yet a recent survey by Arthur Young & Co., the auditing firm, suggests that this data's accuracy is in serious doubt.[85] In a 1983 survey of 557 municipalities, it found that fifty-four percent of the municipalities issued financial reports that were so incomplete or flawed that their independent accountants could give only qualified opinions.[86] In part, these problems may stem from the still rudimentary state of the accounting principles applicable to governmental and nonprofit bodies.[87] The bottom line, however, is that if ratings are based on poor data, they will not protect investors who desire to avoid high risk: garbage in, garbage out. This conclusion leads to a broader criticism not only of the article by Professors Easterbrook and Fischel but also of other articles in this volume: too little attention has been paid to the institutional context or to observational data not reduced to hard statistics.

Where then are we left? Notwithstanding these criticisms, the theory of voluntary disclosure does seem to have some validity as applied to initial public offerings and, to a lesser extent, to all primary distributions. This theory has far less persuasive force, however, when applied to secondary market trading, which the '34 Act chiefly governs. Here, high agency costs currently exist (as the persistence of high takeover premiums averaging between fifty percent and seventy percent in recent years arguably seems to show), thus sheltering opportunistic managerial behavior.[88] A manage-

---

tion. The default rate on the bonds of major industrial corporations was also low, but investors still presumably focused on the relative risk and demanded a higher return from higher risk securities. A lower bond rating would have meant a lower trading value for outstanding bonds. Properly informed, the investors in New York City bonds would have required a higher interest yield. They were denied the chance, however, by inadequate disclosure under an essentially voluntary system (even though an anti-fraud rule—Rule 10b–5—did apply in principle).

82. Moody's Investors Services did not lower its A-rating of New York City bonds until October 1975. See Peacock, A Review of Municipal Securities and their Status Under the Federal Securities Laws as Amended by the Securities Acts Amendments of 1975, 31 Bus.Law. 2037, 2040 n. 22 (1976). This author concludes: "Owing to the notable lack of information available

to investors concerning issuers of municipal securities, ratings have doubtless played too important a role in investors' decision making process." Id.

85. See Survey Finds Flaws in Financial Data of Cities, Counties, Wall St.J., Oct. 6, 1983, at 38, col. 3.

86. Id. Typically, the financial statement defects were due to incomplete records. Other common flaws included failure to conform to generally accepted accounting principles or to report other items such as a pending lawsuit or larger pension liabilities.

87. This difference can also be ascribed to the '34 Act, which authorized the SEC to standardize accounting principles for financial statements filed with it.

88. A 1980 study found the average premium in successful tender offers to be 49%. See Bradley, Interfirm Tender Offers and the Market for Corporate Control,

ment that will oppose a lucrative takeover offer to its shareholders is also capable of biasing its disclosures to suppress adverse information; indeed, suppressing adverse information may be the most effective defense technique available to management because by delaying the inevitable downward adjustment in stock price, it delays the moment when the corporation becomes vulnerable to a hostile takeover. A mandatory disclosure system is a partial response to these problems because it both subsidizes the search costs of bidders (thereby reinforcing the disciplinary capacity of the market for corporate control) and also activates some degree of shareholder opposition through proxy fights and other means.[89]

III. DISCLOSURE TO INVESTORS: THE CASE FOR AN INVESTOR ORIENTED DISCLOSURE SYSTEM IN AN EFFICIENT MARKET

An efficient market is often defined as one in which securities prices impact all publicly available information instantaneously.[90] Even in such a market, a case can still be made for a mandatory disclosure system that primarily seeks to provide technical information to securities analysts and market professionals on the reasonable premise that they are the motor force that principally keeps the market efficient. But what case can be made for a disclosure system oriented toward the individual investor when the market has already adjusted securities prices to reflect all available information? If it is impossible to identify undervalued securities, why should investors be given disclosure documents that seemingly have this aim?

Two sensible responses exist to these questions. Although each involves a modest claim that does not assert that investors can out-perform the market, together they suggest that much information remains relevant to the securities decisions of individual investors.

A. Disclosure as a Means to Efficient Diversification

Modern financial theory divides the risk associated with securities into two components: "alpha" and "beta."[91] "Beta" is the measure of stock volatility with respect to general market movements, and "alpha" is the measure of non-market or residual factors unique to the individual stock. In a fully diversified portfolio, the alphas by definition cancel out; thus, the only inquiry for the investor who holds a diversified portfolio is to ascertain his portfolio's beta value and adjust it according to his risk preferences.

53 J.Bus. 345 (1980). Other studies have placed the average premium even higher. See Jarrell & Bradley, The Economic Effects of Federal and State Regulation of Cash Tender Offers, 23 J.L. & Econ. 371, 373 (1980) (average takeover premium rose to over 70% in wake of state anti-takeover statutes). In effect, these studies measure the agency cost level at which an external monitor—the hostile bidder—will intervene, and they suggest that this level is quite high.

89. Although the conventional wisdom is that proxy contests are seldom successful, a recent empirical study has found this conclusion overbroad. See Dodd & Warner, On Corporate Governance: A Study of Proxy Contests, 11 J.Fin.Econ. 401 (1983). In 58% of the contests studied, the dissidents won at least one seat on the board, and typically the value of the corporation's shares rose in response to the control contest. Id. at 409. To the extent that more complete disclosure enables an insurgent to decide whether it is cost justified to undertake such a contest, economic efficiency is enhanced.

90. See Fama, Efficient Capital Markets, 25 J.Fin. 383 (1970).

91. For an accessible overview of the lore and learning about beta values, see B. Malkiel, supra note 10, at 208–32.

Because a portfolio's beta value is the product of multiple securities, the disclosures that any one issuer can make have only a marginal relevance to this inquiry. Furthermore, according to the traditional theory, historical price movements rather than basic investment data best show the beta value. As a result, the theory implies that the individual investor has little need for the basic financial disclosures required by the federal securities laws.

An initial response to this conclusion is that many, and probably most, investors do not hold fully diversified portfolios. Thus, they are interested in the beta values of individual securities. This argument, however, faces a potential counterargument: why should society or the corporate issuer subsidize the folly of investors who fail to diversify their portfolios? Indeed, it is not difficult to acquire a fully diversified portfolio because investors can purchase "index funds" from any securities dealer. Professors Easterbrook and Fischel have made essentially this argument in other contexts.[92] Yet there is a simple answer to it: for most investors, it may well be rational to fail to diversify fully their *securities* portfolio because their real goal is to hold a reasonably diversified *investment* portfolio.

Most individual investors either hold or have an expectancy in a variety of investments other than public securities: e.g., real estate, insurance, stock options, deferred compensation, or a private business. Their real need is to wrap their securities portfolio around these other investments to produce a reasonably diversified overall investment portfolio. For example, the middle or senior level manager is likely to have, or to anticipate acquiring, a substantial investment in his business. Adding a purely diversified securities portfolio to his undiversified investments would not diversify away the risk he incurs by having a significant investment in his own firm. To achieve optimal diversification, this manager must counterbalance his securities investments against his other investments. Such counterbalancing requires identifying securities that in conjunction with his locked-in investment in his own firm produce relative diversification. Modern portfolio theory holds that such an investor should seek to identify securities that are negative covariants in terms of their cyclical performance. By balancing countercyclical investments, the investor reduces the overall variance (or risk) in his portfolio.[93]

This goal justifies disclosing line-of-business data to individual investors because in this era of conglomerate structure, it is not evident which lines of business a corporation is engaged (or to what extent). Thus, even though the search for high alpha stocks is theoretically impossible in an efficient market, much of the same data remains relevant to rational investors

92. See Easterbrook & Fischel, Corporate Control Transactions, 91 Yale L.J. 698, 713 (1982).

93. For a brief explanation of covariance as it applies to modern portfolio theory, see B. Malkiel, supra note 10, at 193–94. See also V. Brudney & M. Chirelstein, Corporate Finance: Cases and Materials 1151–54 (2d ed. 1979). The classic example given by Malkiel is of an umbrella company and a resort. These two firms, which have the same dispersion of expected returns, but are counter-cyclical, can combine and thereby reduce the variance in

their expected returns without changing the mean expected return. B. Malkiel, supra note 10, at 193–94. A theoretical reply is that the individual investor may do this on his own by buying shares in both companies and so corporate combinations should not create value if their only virtue is the reduction of variance. The standard counter-rebuttal, however, is that because bankruptcy would imply a loss of value for all concerned, it is desirable that the individual firm seek to reduce the variance of its own expected returns in order to minimize bankruptcy costs.

seeking to minimize the variance in their overall investment portfolio by acquiring negatively covariant securities.

B. Risk Assessment and Portfolio Revision

A second justification for requiring detailed disclosure to the individual investor concerns the relevance of fundamental analysis to the assessment of a portfolio's risk level. To begin with, knowing that a security is efficiently priced does not tell the investor whether the security carries a risk level that is incompatible with his individual preferences. Although this in itself would require some form of an individualized system of disclosure, financial theorists have responded that diversification should protect the investor from all risks, except the systematic or "market" risk that affects all securities. Although this assertion is at the heart of the Capital Asset Pricing Model, it is becoming clear today that the financial theorists are not in agreement about how to measure or even how to define systematic risk.[94] Few accept the accuracy of individual beta predictions.[95] Moreover, even if we could reliably measure beta at the portfolio level, investors are constantly confronted with the need to revise their portfolios. Here they must estimate the impact of a new individual security upon the overall beta level of their portfolio. It is in this portfolio revision context that disclosure of basic financial data and prior stock price levels may be of particular significance to the individual investor. Although financial theorists have argued that beta is best measured by historical stock prices, the contrary view is that a portfolio's overall beta level can be best estimated by a review of "investment fundamentals"—meaning in essence the basic balance sheet and income data that traditional securities analysis has long been predicated upon.[96] Although this point can be debated at some length, a demand for data about "fundamental beta" now exists among institutional investors. Financial theorists should be cautious before they reject as irrational the market's demand for such data. In any event, this response's purpose is not to claim that this issue is resolved, but rather to

---

94. The recurrent finding that small firms earn abnormally high returns even after adjustment for risk has led a number of financial theorists to conclude that existing models misspecify the systematic risk component. See Seligman, supra note 10; Symposium on Size and Stock Returns, and other Empirical Regularities, supra note 10. Consequently, alternative models—most notably, Professor Ross's Arbitrage Pricing Theory—have been proposed that do not rely on the standard mean and variance analysis of the Capital Asset Pricing Model. In short, the topic of beta (or systematic risk) is currently causing considerable intellectual embarrassment to the field of financial theory.

95. See B. Malkiel, supra note 10, at 218–26, for a brief overview. It is generally agreed that the beta value for an individual security is unstable. There have also been recent periods when, paradoxically, prior beta values correlated negatively with stock market performance. Id. For the conclusion that the current state of theoretical research into the definition and

reliability of risk measurement variables does not justify precluding money managers from purchasing research in this area, see Pozen, supra note 22, at 950–53. If this is so, mandatory disclosure of information relevant to this inquiry is important if we wish securities professionals to calculate it for smaller firms.

96. The originator of this theory of "fundamental betas" is Barr Rosenberg, a professor at Berkeley. See B. Malkiel, supra note 10, at 223–24. To estimate "Barr's bionic beta," one must assess the basic earnings of the company relative to its size and industry position and its financial structure. See Rosenberg & Guy, Prediction of Beta from Investment Fundamentals, Fin. Analysts J., May-June 1976, at 60; Rosenberg & Guy, Prediction of Beta from Investment Fundamentals, Fin. Analysts J., July-Aug. 1976, at 62 (concluding that fundamental variables "were substantially better predictors than the historical beta in the sense that they achieved a smaller measurement error").

suggest that this is precisely the sort of narrower issue that needs to be re-assessed in the "post-revisionist" era.

In summary, at least two justifications can be asserted for the disclosure of basic financial and line-of-business data to ordinary investors: (1) the need to diversify around existing investment assets makes it important for the individual investor to seek negative covariant securities to achieve optimal diversification, and (2) even in the case of a diversified portfolio, it may be important to assess the beta values of individual securities in the portfolio revision process.

IV. CONCLUSION

In their critical review of the arguments for a mandatory disclosure system, Professors Easterbrook and Fischel consider and reject a number of fairness-based justifications; e.g., investor confidence, the protection of investors, and the deterrence of fraud. Only tangentially do they consider the issue of efficiency-based justifications, and here they limit their attention largely to the problems associated with mandated disclosure of proprietary information. This focus on fairness, rather than efficiency, is not surprising because proponents of a mandatory disclosure system have historically stressed the former over the latter.

Nonetheless, the strongest arguments for a mandatory disclosure system may be efficiency-based. Empirical data strongly suggests that the adoption of a mandatory disclosure system reduced price dispersion and thereby enhanced the allocative efficiency of our capital markets. Nor need we rely only on historical evidence. Economic logic also points to the conclusion that there will be inadequate securities research and verification in the absence of a mandatory disclosure system. In the computerized securities marketplace of the future, individual investor review of corporate disclosures will be the exception, rather than the rule,[97] and clients will increasingly rely on professional advice, both to select individual securities and to diversify their portfolios efficiently. In this world, collectivization of financial data within the SEC is best justified as a strategy for making more efficient use of securities analysts and other market professionals, both by eliminating duplication and by making it feasible for them, at the margin, to cover smaller firms.

Although substantial disclosure might be made in the absence of a mandatory disclosure system, the theories offered by Jensen and Meckling or Ross are best understood as only generalized tendencies, to which there are significant exceptions. Essentially, they ignore that managers in a corporate environment increasingly characterized by rapid control changes that they cannot effectively block have strong incentives to withhold adverse information and to undertake preemptive buyouts of their own firm, which are facilitated by withholding positive information. In short, a

---

97. Although the popularity of personal computers will enable each investor to obtain access to '34 Act data that is effectively unavailable to him today, this data has never been oriented toward the individual investor. More sophisticated computer software may enable the investor to obtain current beta values (however computed) for individual securities and even to estimate the impact of an individual security upon the beta level of his portfolio. Still, the more likely scenario is that this technological revolution will enable the broker or other adviser to compute these values for the client. Hence, the impact of this new technology may require us to reconsider and redefine the nature of the broker's fiduciary duty to his client.

mandatory disclosure system should reduce the average agency costs of corporate governance. To the extent that this reduction occurs, even fully diversified investors benefit because, in effect, we are reducing an element of the systematic risk that portfolio diversification cannot itself eliminate. Thus, properly applied, neither agency theory nor portfolio theory leads to conclusions inconsistent with the probable desirability of a mandatory disclosure system. Rather, they point to the need to refocus disclosure on precisely those areas that agency theory identifies as sensitive (basically, LBO's and takeover defenses) and those decisions that portfolio diversification cannot eliminate (i.e., the choice of risk level and the need to diversify around an existing portfolio of nonsecurities investments).

Finally, although the public goods-like character of securities research cannot justify an unlimited subsidy for securities research, no careful cost-benefit analysis has yet been conducted that recognizes the likelihood of market failure due to the special character of securities research. Other alternatives may exist by which this problem could be addressed,[98] but the known evil is often preferable to the unknown one. Before the current trend toward deregulation continues much further, closer attention should be given to the impact of deregulation on the market's allocative efficiency; in particular, such measures as price dispersion and volatility need to be more carefully monitored. Here, the interests of the public at large may transcend those of investors.

In summary, the federal securities laws ain't necessarily broke, so let's be careful about fixing them.[b]

* * *

---

98. One can imagine other ways of subsidizing market professionals to monitor firms that otherwise would not be followed. Yet in contrast to a direct public subsidy, a mandatory disclosure system taxes corporations and shareholders and thus has marginally less of an impact on noninvestor classes. In addition, a mandatory disclosure system has the by-product of establishing a mechanism through which the individual investor can acquire information on the risk level of individual securities, whereas a system solely focused on the market professional would tend not to provide information to such an investor. In the last analysis, the long-term and most fundamental issue that securities regulation must confront is whether the law should seek to induce diversification by discouraging individual investors from holding undiversified portfolios. In all likelihood, this would be the principal consequence of abolishing the '34 Act's mandatory disclosure system. Arguments about whether public policy should seek to induce investor diversification can be made on both sides, but our experience with mutual funds suggests that it would add a second level of agency cost problems to those that already exist between shareholders and management.

b. The editors regret that space does not permit the inclusion of additional material on the value and need for mandatory disclosure. To those readers whose curiosity has been aroused, we suggest that they explore the wealth of literature cited and discussed by Professor Coffee. For an introduction to ECMH, see Note, The Efficient Capital Market Hypothesis, Economic Theory and the Regulation of the Securities Industry, 29 Stan.L.Rev. 1031 (1977). For a more sophisticated treatment of market efficiency, see Gilson & Kraakman, The Mechanics of Market Efficiency, 70 Va.L.Rev. 549 (1984). Cf. Gordon & Kornhauser, Efficient Markets, Costly Information, and Securities Research, 60 N.Y.U.L. Rev. 761 (1985); Wang, Some Arguments that the Stock Market is Not Efficient, 19 U.C.Davis L.Rev. 341 (1986).

More recently, it has been proposed that the 1933 Act's registration provisions be repealed with respect to securities offerings by reporting companies under the 1934 Act while retaining 1933 Act registration for IPO's. Mandatory disclosure under the 1934 Act would be retained. See McLaughlin, 1933 Act's Registration Provisions: Is Time Ripe for Repealing Them?, Nat'l.L.J. 44 (Aug. 18, 1986).

SECTION 6. LOWERING THE BARRIERS TO SHELF REGISTRATION

"Shelf Registration"

In preparing a registration statement, a decision must be reached as to how many securities are to be registered. It would be convenient to register all of the securities which an issuer might conceivably intend to distribute at any time in the future, that is, to allow registration for the "shelf." However, Securities Act § 6(a) states: "A registration statement shall be deemed effective only as to the securities specified therein as proposed to be offered." Initially, the SEC took the view that, by reason of this language, the registration of more securities than are presently intended to be offered would be misleading.[1]

In a continuous or delayed offering information as to price and manner of distribution will probably not be available until shortly before the offering. If there were a substantial delay between registration and sale of the securities, other information contained in the prospectus might no longer be accurate.

This situation placed the SEC in a dilemma. Section 11 imposes civil liability on the registrant and other named persons with respect to misstatements and omissions in the registration statement *when it became effective.* Section 12(2) gives buyers a private action against their seller for misstatements and omissions in connection with interstate sales of securities, whether registered or not. Since the registration speaks as of the effective date, the proper procedure to correct a misstatement of fact in the registration statement is to file a post-effective amendment curing the defect in an attempt to minimize § 11 liability. On the other hand, if a statement was accurate when made, but developments after the effective date render it false, § 12(2) becomes implicated. Thus, any correction should be made by placing a sticker on the cover page of the prospectus correcting the defect. See Registration C, Rules 423, 424(c).

In spite of these apparent impediments to shelf registration, the Commission found it desirable in some instances to permit or require such offerings. These permissible offerings, now dubbed "traditional shelf offerings," evolved over the years and are described in the Shelf Registration Release which follows. The administrative device used to overcome the statutory barriers to shelf registration was simply to add a requirement that the registrant file an "undertaking" in the initial registration statement. This undertaking, in effect, constituted a commitment, by the registrant to file a post-effective amendment to the statement to reflect in the prospectus any material changes in information. This gave the Staff an opportunity to review the revised prospectus prior to its use and postponed the commencement of the limitation period prescribed in § 13 of the Securities Act with respect to § 11 actions.

When introducing the integrated disclosure system it will be recalled that registrants were divided into three categories: (1) companies which are widely followed by professional analysts; (2) companies which have been subject to the Exchange Act periodic reporting requirements for at

---

1. Shawnee Chiles Syndicate, 10 SEC 109, 113 (1941).

least three years, but are not widely followed by the analysts; and (3) companies which have been subject to the Exchange Act reporting requirements for less than three years. The first category is eligible to use a short form registration statement (Form S–3) which relies upon incorporation by reference of Exchange Act reports (see Rules 411 and 412) and permits minimal disclosure in the prospectus. The second category is eligible to use Form S–2, which combines incorporation by reference of Exchange Act reports with supplemental information contained in the prospectus or in annual reports to security holders. The third category is required to use Form S–1 which requires full disclosure.

In the integration process the Commission also considered whether the option of shelf registration should be extended to firms whose shares traded under efficient market conditions. After a period of experimentation, the Commission expanded the use of shelf-registration by the adoption of Rule 415. At the same time, the Commission added Regulation S–K, Item 512(a) (relating to the undertaking applicable to Rule 415 offerings), Rule 176 (identifying the factors bearing on the issue of due diligence under § 11 of the Securities Act) and Rule 412 (relating to the effective date of documents incorporated by reference and the use of modified or superseded statements).

Rule 415 provides procedural flexibility in timing periodic offerings of registered securities so as to take advantage of favorable "market windows." The Rule also applies to other types of "traditional shelf registrations." These will be considered in connection with various types of secondary distributions infra at page 482.

SECURITIES ACT RELEASE NO. 6499

Securities and Exchange Commission.
November 17, 1983.

Shelf Registration

SUMMARY: The Commission today announced the adoption of a revised shelf registration rule. Rule 415 relates to the registration of securities to be offered or sold on a delayed or continuous basis in the future. As revised, the Rule is available for offerings qualified to use short form registration statements and for traditional shelf offerings. These modifications reflect experience with the Rule and the views that have been expressed, particularly those relating to disclosure and due diligence.

* * *

I. Executive Summary

In the eighteen months since its adoption on a temporary basis, Rule 415 has operated efficiently and has provided registrants with important benefits in their financings, most notably cost savings. The cost savings are attributable to a number of factors, including flexibility to respond to rapidly changing markets, reduced legal, accounting, printing and other expenses and increased competition among underwriters. At the same time, however, concerns have been raised, including institutionalization of the securities markets, impact on retail distribution, increased concentration in the securities industry, effects on the secondary markets, adequacy of disclosure and due diligence.

The Commission has considered the concerns that have been expressed about Rule 415. Some relate to economic factors, such as volatile interest rates and other market forces, which exist apart from Rule 415 and thus are not appropriate bases on which to take action on the Rule. The Commission believes that the concerns about disclosure and due diligence, however, should be addressed because they may be affected by the manner in which offerings under the Rule may proceed. Accordingly, the Commission has determined to modify the Rule to limit its availability to those offerings where the benefits of shelf registration are most significant and where the disclosure and due diligence concerns are mitigated by other factors. The Commission believes that limiting the Rule to primary offerings of securities qualified to be registered on Form S–3 or F–3 and to traditional shelf offerings strikes the appropriate balance.

The integrated disclosure system recognizes that, for companies in the top tier, there is a steady stream of high quality corporate information continually furnished to the market and broadly digested, synthesized and disseminated. In addition, procedures for conducting due diligence investigations of such registrants, including continuous due diligence by means such as designated underwriters' counsel, are being adapted to the integrated disclosure system and shelf registration. The Commission believes that the widespread market following of such companies and the due diligence procedures being developed serve to address the concerns about the adequacy of disclosure and due diligence and, thus, ensure the protection of investors.

With respect to traditional shelf offerings, the Commission believes that continued use of Rule 415 also is appropriate. First, concerns have not been expressed about these offerings. Second, these offerings may not be feasible on other than a delayed or continuous offering basis.

As to other offerings by non–S–3 or F–3 registrants, however, disclosure and due diligence concerns need to be addressed. Accordingly, the Commission has determined not to allow the Rule to be used for such offerings.

As revised, Rule 415 enumerates the securities which are allowed to be offered on a continuous or delayed basis. Unless the securities fall within one of the provisions spelling out the various traditional shelf offerings, they must qualify for registration on Form S–3 or F–3. If they do not, they may not be registered for delayed or continuous offerings.

II. Background

Securities have been registered for continuous and delayed offerings for many years. Some of the instances in which shelf registration was allowed were set forth in Guide 4, which was promulgated in 1968. These included securities to be issued in continuing acquisition programs or those underlying exercisable options, warrants or rights. Administrative practice, however, accommodated traditional shelf offerings beyond those specified in the Guide. Shelf registration was permitted for such diverse offerings as limited partnership tax shelters, employee benefit plans, pools of mortgage backed pass through certificates offered from time to time, and customer purchase plans.

Rule 415 arose in connection with the development of the integrated disclosure system. As part of that effort, the Commission comprehensively reviewed all of the Guides for the Preparation and Filing of Registration

Statements and Reports and reorganized them to separate the substantive disclosure and procedural provisions. The shelf rule was the procedural rule which resulted from the reevaluation of Guide 4 and reflected current administrative practice as well as the provisions of the Guide.

The Rule was published for comment twice before being adopted on a temporary basis in March 1982. Following public hearings and further public comment, the Commission, in September 1982, extended the effective date of the Rule until December 31, 1983. In June 1983, the Commission published the shelf registration rule for comment again in order to provide all interested parties another opportunity to submit their views and experience under the Rule before the Commission made its final determination. Throughout the course of this rulemaking proceeding, the Commission has received almost 400 written and oral submissions from commentators expressing their views on shelf registration.

Two dominant themes emerged from these comments on Rule 415. The majority of commentators, mostly registrants, have been pleased with the Rule and favor its adoption on a permanent basis. Members of the securities industry, on the other hand, have expressed a wide spectrum of views and have reiterated several concerns. In the most recent comment solicitation, they emphasize concerns over the adequacy of disclosure and due diligence. While these commentators voice concerns, only a few of them believe that there should be no shelf registration rule at all. Others with concerns about the Rule recommend that it be retained, either in its present form or in modified form.

The suggested modifications of Rule 415 include: (1) Restricting eligibility for use of the Rule to (a) investment grade debt securities, (b) a combination of investment grade debt securities and limited types of equity securities or (c) registrants that are widely followed in the marketplace; (2) requiring advance notice to the marketplace of forthcoming offerings; and (3) imposing some form of "cooling off period" between the announcement and sale of securities. Some commentators also suggest providing underwriters relief from liability under the Securities Act.

III. Experience

The Commission, registrants, the securities industry, and others have had over eighteen months of experience with the shelf registration rule. During this time, the Commission has monitored the operation and impact of the Rule, has been provided information concerning actual experience with the Rule and has considered empirical data and studies related to the Rule.

From March 1982 through September 1983, almost 4,600 shelf registration statements relating to $181 billion were filed. These shelf filings represent 52% of the over 8,800 registration statements and 52% of $345 billion of securities registered during this period.

Over 85% of the shelf registrations have been traditional shelf filings. Filings for employee benefit plans and dividend or interest reinvestment plans alone account for 55% of the shelf filings and represent 26% of the $181 billion in shelf registered securities.

Most of the balance have been filings for investment grade debt securities offered and sold from time to time on a delayed basis. These 369 debt filings (registering almost $70 billion) represent 53% of the $133 billion of total debt issues filed from March 1982 through September 1983. Approximately 94% of the 369 delayed debt filings were on Form S–3. Over 35% of the filings were made by companies in the financial industry and over 20% were made by utilities.

The remaining shelf filings related to 195 delayed equity filings (registering $12.5 billion). These filings amounted to about 3% of the over 7,700 equity registration statements and 6% of the $212 billion in equity securities registered. Over half were fixed price syndicated offerings which were filed under Rule 415 largely for the procedural convenience afforded by the Rule. Of the remaining delayed equity filings, 90% were on Form S–3. Approximately 70% were for common stock and 30% were for preferred stock. Fifteen percent listed an "at the market" distribution as one of the potential distribution methods described. Eleven of these filings were for so-called "dribble-outs" by utility companies, in which common stock is offered through an underwriter into an existing trading market on a regular basis.

IV. Discussion

A. *Benefits of Shelf Registration*

Virtually all commentators state that shelf registration provides substantial benefits for corporate financings. The principal benefit cited by commentators is that of cost savings. Empirical studies on shelf registration also suggest that securities sold under Rule 415 have lower issuance costs than securities not sold under the Rule.

Cost savings and other benefits are attributed to a number of factors. Flexibility is the Rule's most frequently cited benefit, because it is the source of the greatest cost savings and provides other advantages as well. Commentators stress that flexibility is important in today's volatile markets; that the procedural flexibility afforded by the Rule enables a registrant to time its offering to avail itself of the most advantageous market conditions; that by being able to meet "market windows," registrants are able to obtain lower interest rates on debt and lower dividend rates on preferred stock, thereby benefiting their existing shareholders. The flexibility provided by the Rule also permits variation in the structure and terms of securities on short notice, enabling registrants to match securities with the current demands of the marketplace. Some commentators attributed the success of their offerings to the flexibility provided by the Rule. Empirical studies also support the importance of enhanced financing flexibility in new issue design, market timing and choice of distribution technique. While most discussion of flexibility is in the context of debt offerings, some commentators also assert that flexibility is necessary in the equity markets.

Simplification of the securities registration process also is cited as reducing costs. Legal, accounting, printing and other costs are stated to have been reduced, because only a single registration statement need be filed for a series of offerings, rather than a separate registration statement each time an offering is made. Some commentators also state that simplification of the registration process has given them more flexibility in planning their financing schedules.

Finally, some commentators stress that increased competition among underwriters has resulted in lower underwriting spreads and offering yields, which produce cost savings for registrants and their shareholders. Empirical studies of debt and equity offerings under Rule 415 found lower issuance costs and attributed this primarily to increased competition among investment bankers. Some commentators note that increased competition has spurred the innovation of new financing products.

On the basis of the benefits cited, many commentators, especially registrants, support permanent adoption of Rule 415 as proposed.

B. *Concerns*

1. *Adequacy of Disclosure.* A number of commentators, especially those from the securities industry, express concerns relating to the adequacy of disclosure. While Rule 415 has been the focal point of these concerns, these commentators question aspects of the Commission's integrated disclosure system, such as short form registration and incorporation by reference. They question the amount and quality of information available, as well as whether investors receive it in time to make investment decisions. These commentators express concern that the Rule contributes to deficiencies in the disclosure provided to investors caused, in great part, by short form registration statements.

The Commission believes that the integrated disclosure system has enhanced the level of disclosure to investors. The basis for the system was the upgrading of the continuous reporting requirements under the Securities Exchange Act of 1934 (the "Exchange Act"). This upgrading was designed to ensure that complete and current information is available to all investors on a continuous basis, not only when a registrant makes a public offering of its securities, but for the trading markets as well. This focus recognized that the secondary trading market volume dwarfs the volume of Securities Act offerings.

For Securities Act registration, the integrated disclosure system builds upon the existence of timely and accurate corporate reporting. Thus, registrants that are widely followed in the marketplace may use Forms S–3 and F–3, which allow maximum use of incorporation by reference of Exchange Act reports and generally do not require information contained in those reports to be reiterated in the prospectus and delivered to investors. Forms S–3 and F–3 recognize the applicability of the efficient market theory to those companies which provide a steady stream of high quality corporate information to the marketplace and whose corporate information is broadly disseminated. Information about these companies is constantly digested and synthesized by financial analysts, who act as essential conduits in the continuous flow of information to investors, and is broadly disseminated on a timely basis by the financial press and other participants in the marketplace. Accordingly, at the time S–3/F–3 registrants determine to make an offering of securities, a large amount of information already has been disseminated to and digested by the marketplace.

2. *Due Diligence.* Concerns expressed about the quality of disclosure also relate to underwriters' ability to conduct due diligence investigations. Commentators attribute concerns about due diligence largely to fast time schedules. Under the Rule, any underwriter may be selected to handle a particular offering. Some commentators suggest that no underwriter can afford to devote the time and expense necessary to conduct a due diligence review before knowing whether it will handle an offering and that there

may not be sufficient time to do so once it is selected. These commentators also indicate that they may not have the opportunity to apply their independent scrutiny and judgment to documents prepared by registrants many months before an offering.

On the other hand, registrants using the Rule indicate that procedures for conducting due diligence investigations have developed and are developing to enable underwriters to adapt to the integrated disclosure system and the shelf registration environment. They note the use of continuous due diligence programs, which employ a number of procedures, including designated underwriters' counsel. These registrants believe that underwriters' ability to conduct adequate due diligence investigations in this environment has not been impaired and, in some cases, has been enhanced.

The Commission recognizes that procedures for conducting due diligence investigations of large, widely followed registrants have changed and are continuing to change. Registrants and the other parties involved in their public offerings—attorneys, accountants, and underwriters—are developing procedures which allow due diligence obligations under Section 11(b) to be met in the most effective and efficient manner possible. The anticipatory and continuous due diligence programs being implemented combine a number of procedures designed both to protect investors by assuring timely and accurate disclosure of corporate information and to recognize the separate legal status of underwriters by providing them the opportunity to perform due diligence.

The trend toward appointment of a single law firm to act as underwriters' counsel is a particularly significant development. Of course, this procedure is not new. Appointing a single law firm to act as underwriters' counsel has been done traditionally by public utility holding companies and their subsidiaries subject to the competitive bid underwriting requirements of Rule 50 under the Public Utility Holding Company Act of 1935. This technique is now being followed more broadly in the shelf registration environment and represents what the Commission believes to be a sound practice because it provides for due diligence investigations to be performed continually throughout the effectiveness of the shelf registration statement. Designation of underwriters' counsel facilitates continuous due diligence by ensuring on-going access to the registrant on the underwriters' behalf. Recognizing the independent statutory basis on which underwriters perform due diligence, registrants cooperate with underwriters and designated counsel in making accommodations necessary for them to perform their due diligence investigation.

Other procedures registrants have developed complement the use of underwriters' counsel by presenting various opportunities for continuous due diligence throughout the shelf process. A number of registrants indicate that they hold Exchange Act report "drafting sessions." This affords prospective underwriters and their counsel an opportunity to participate in the drafting and review of periodic disclosure documents before they are filed.

Another practice is to hold so-called periodic due diligence sessions. Some registrants hold sessions shortly after the release of quarterly earnings to provide prospective underwriters and their counsel an opportunity to discuss with management the most recent financial results and other events of that quarter. Periodic due diligence sessions also include annual meetings with management to review financial trends and business developments. In addition, some registrants indicate that prospective underwriters and underwriters' counsel are able to schedule individual meetings with management at any time.

The Commission believes that the development of anticipatory and continuous due diligence techniques is consistent with the integrated disclosure system and will permit underwriters to perform due diligence in an orderly, efficient manner. Indeed, in adopting Rule 176 as part of that system, the Commission recognized that, just as different registration forms are appropriate for different companies, the method of due diligence investigation may not be the same for all registrants. Rule 176 sets forth a non-exclusive list of circumstances which the Commission believes bear upon the reasonableness of the investigation and the determination of what constitutes reasonable grounds for belief under Section 11(b) of the Securities Act. Circumstances which may be particularly relevant to an underwriter's due diligence investigation of registrants qualified to use short form registration include the type of registrant, reasonable reliance on management, the type of underwriting arrangement and the underwriter's role, and whether the underwriter participated in the preparation or review of documents incorporated by reference into the registration statement. The Commission expects that the techniques of conducting due diligence investigations of registrants qualified to use short form registration, where documents are incorporated by reference, would differ from due diligence investigations under other circumstances.

3. *Other Concerns.* Securities industry commentators also raise concerns relating to institutionalization of the securities markets, the impact on retail distribution, increased concentration in the securities industry and effects on the secondary markets. Specifically, these commentators believe that Rule 415 is accelerating the trends toward institutionalization of the securities markets and concentration in the securities industry. In their view, the Rule is decreasing the number of syndicated offerings in which regional securities firms participate and excluding individual investors from the new issues market.

While the Commission recognizes the existence of these trends, it believes that they reflect economic and other factors apart from shelf registration. These factors include volatile interest rates and markets, the growth of mutual and pension funds which act as intermediaries for individual investors, and the homogenization of the financial services industry. These factors are not necessarily affected by Rule 415. Rule 415 is a procedural rule which presents an optional filing technique. It does not mandate any particular method of distribution. Indeed, many offerings of debt and equity securities registered under the Rule have been sold in traditional syndicated offerings. The Commission therefore believes that these concerns transcend Rule 415.

V. Commission Action

The Commission has considered all views and suggestions with respect to Rule 415. There are several reasons why it may be appropriate to adopt the shelf registration rule in substantially its present form. During the eighteen months the Rule has been in effect, it has worked well and has provided registrants with substantial benefits in their financings. Also, most of the concerns raised transcend shelf registration. On the other hand, the Commission believes that concerns raised about the quality and timing of disclosure and due diligence are important to address because they relate to the adequacy of disclosure investors receive in connection with public offerings. Having weighed all considerations, the Commission is modifying Rule 415 to strike an appropriate balance by making it available for offerings eligible to be registered on Form S-3 or F-3 and for traditional shelf offerings.

* * *

For registrants not eligible to use short form registration, however, the Commission believes that concerns about disclosure and due diligence outweigh the benefits of Rule 415. The Commission also notes that shelf registration may not be as advantageous for such registrants because they cannot rely on subsequently filed Exchange Act reports for certain updating of the information in the shelf registration statement. Such updating requires the filing of post-effective amendments. Indeed, few non-S-3 or F-3 registrants have used Rule 415 for other than traditional shelf offerings.

VI. Operation of Revised Rule 415

* * *

A. *Offerings Permitted Under Revised Rule*

1. *Traditional Shelf Offerings.* A number of traditional shelf offerings were enumerated in former paragraphs (a)(1)(ii) through (vii). These provisions have been retained and redesignated as paragraphs (a)(1)(i) through (vi).

Other traditional shelf offerings came within former paragraph (a)(1)(i). Because the primary offerings which may be made under Rule 415 are now limited, paragraph (a)(1)(i) has been deleted. That paragraph provided that any securities not falling within one of the categories specifically enumerated in the balance of paragraph (a)(1) could be registered under the Rule, but were limited to an amount reasonably expected to be offered and sold within two years. Those traditional offerings covered by former paragraph (a)(1)(i) are now set forth in paragraphs (a)(1)(vii) through (ix).

Mortgage related securities, such as mortgage backed debt and mortgage participation or pass through certificates, are listed in paragraph (a)(1) (vii). Generally, the securities are registered and then offered from time to time as series of mortgage backed debt are established or pools of mortgages are formed. Shelf registration is essential to sale of these securities. Together with the formation of blind pools, shelf registration allows registrants to match capital demands with portfolio holdings. They can form pools of mortgages as sales of securities backed by those mortgages take place. It is not necessary for the mortgages to be purchased before the securities are priced and sold. With an effective shelf registration statement, pricing and sales can occur contemporaneously with mortgage acquisition.

Paragraph (a)(1)(viii) relates to securities to be issued in connection with business combination transactions. All other traditional shelf offerings are covered by paragraph (a)(i)(ix), which permits offerings that (1) will be commenced promptly, (2) will be made on a continuous basis and (3) may continue for a period in excess of 30 days from the date of initial effectiveness.

Examples of the traditional shelf offerings which come within paragraph (a)(1)(ix) are: customer purchaser plans; exchange, rights, subscription and rescission offers; offers to employees, consultants or independent agents; offerings on a best efforts basis; tax shelter and other limited partnership interests; commodity funds; condominium rental pools; time sharing agreements; real estate investment trusts; farmers' cooperative organizations or others making distributions on a membership basis; and continuous debt sales by finance companies to their customers.

2. *Short Form Registration Shelf Offerings.* New paragraph (a)(1)(x) relates to primary delayed or continuous offerings of securities registered, or qualified to be registered, on Form S-3 or F-3. Unless an offering falls within one of the categories of offerings specified in paragraphs (a)(1)(i) through (a)(1)(ix), it must come within paragraph (a)(1)(x) or it cannot be registered pursuant to Rule 415. Thus, only traditional shelf offerings and primary shelf offerings that qualify for short form registration may be offered or sold under the Rule.

* * *

Special Concurring Opinion of Chairman Shad:

The revised shelf rule offers significant advantages to issuers and their shareholders, and mitigates the risks to investors by limiting such offerings to S-3 and F-3 corporations, the largest, most creditworthy and widely followed corporations.

However, concepts suggested under which underwriters might conduct due diligence investigations under the shelf rule are of limited practical value. Issuers can solicit competitive bids from underwriters and effect distributions of securities on the same day. In preparation for shelf offerings, it has been suggested that prospective issuers invite groups of underwriters and their counsel to attend several meetings a year. These would include meetings following release by the companies of their quarterly and annual reports, and when they are preparing their prospectuses, proxies, annual, quarterly and other SEC filing documents.

It would be very expensive for top management executives, underwriters and their counsels to spend hundreds of thousands of hours annually attending such meetings on the speculative possibility that the individual issuer will decide to do a public offering, and that one of the underwriters attending such meetings will be the high bidder for the issue. It therefore seems likely that over time, few top management executives will attend such meetings and that investment bankers will begin sending junior observers, rather than qualified participants.

It has also been suggested that the underwriters rely on due diligence reviews by attorneys hired by the issuer. It is of course the underwriter that is liable for failure to conduct an adequate due diligence investigation, and it is the underwriter's capital and reputation that are at risk if the offering is unsuccessful or performs worse than the general market following the offering.

While due diligence reviews by issuer hired attorneys are useful in defending actions brought by investor-plaintiffs, this is not the principal purpose of such reviews. The principal purpose is to protect investors.

Assessment of the risk of adverse market performance following an offering requires a careful due diligence investigation and the judgment of an experienced underwriter. However, the accelerated time schedules of such offerings limit the opportunity for such assessments.

Issuer hired attorneys have been used in certain utility offerings. While the approach suffers the foregoing infirmities, utilities are the most predictable of corporate enterprises. They are not subject to the vagaries to which industrial and other issuers are subject.

The bulk of shelf offerings to date have occurred during the broadest and strongest stock, bond and new issue markets in history. Investors do not seek rescission or other redress, unless the security declines in price. The test of the shelf rule will come during the next bear market.

The revised shelf rule offers significant advantages to issuers and their shareholders, and mitigates the risks to investors, but the due diligence techniques suggested are of limited practical value. Other due diligence techniques should therefore be reviewed in the light of the shelf rule, as adopted, and the rapidly changing marketplace.

Commissioner Thomas, Concurring in Part and Dissenting in Part:

I respectfully dissent from that portion of the Commission's decision today to adopt Rule 415 for offerings qualified to be registered on Forms S–3 and F–3 insofar as it relates to equity securities only. Although I am gratified at the compromise adopted by the Commission and sincerely believe that such a compromise was only reached because of the strong opposition to the Rule voiced by many during the experimental period, I must continue to express my reservations about the Rule on the basis of principle.

I am convinced that the Rule as applied to equities encourages changes in our capital market system substantially in excess of those necessary to facilitate the financings for which it was fashioned. In so doing the Commission risks injuring our capital market system, which is widely regarded as one of our great national assets. As I stated before, I continue to favor, however, adoption of the praiseworthy portion of the Rule that permits major companies rapid access to the markets for the sale of their debt securities.

After studying the comment letters and conferring with issuers, representatives of the securities industry, and institutional and individual investors, I continue to believe that the Rule as applied to equity offerings (1) reduces the quality and timeliness of disclosure available to investors when making their investment decisions, and (2) jeopardizes the liquidity and stability of both our primary and secondary securities markets by encouraging greater concentration of underwriters, market-makers, and other financial intermediaries and by discouraging individual investor participation in the capital market, thereby furthering the trend toward institutionalization of securities holders.

Although I do not believe that it is possible at this time to quantify the various elements of these risks due to the exceptionally strong market we have been experiencing during most of the experimental period and the inactive market experienced at the beginning of the experimental period, I am convinced that many of these risks are real. Incurring these risks is antithetical to the statutory duty of the Commission to protect investors and to maintain the integrity of our capital markets.[a]

Academicians have debated the merits of Rule 415 in the light of economic theory. Professor Barbara Ann Banoff concludes that Rule 415 "clearly benefits issuers, investors and the economy as a whole." Moreover, she believes that some S–2 issuers should also be allowed to use shelf registration, and that the restrictions imposed on "at-the-market" equity offerings should be lifted. Banoff, Regulatory Subsidies, Efficient Markets, and Shelf Registration: An Analysis of Rule 415, 70 Va.L.Rev. 135 (1984). Feeney, The Saga of Rule 415: Registration for the Shelf, 9 Corp.L.Rev. 41 (1986) is in general agreement.

On the other hand, Professor Merritt B. Fox questions some of the assumptions underlying Professor Banoff's conclusions. He projects a broader view of the economic role which the securities market plays in the national economy. In addition to viewing the securities market in terms of its impact upon participants, he believes that the market also "monitors and structures the allocation of scarce resources in the economy." He concludes: "The improvement in the quality of information about an issuer that results from underwriter due diligence enhances efficient allocation of resources of the economy. Short form and shelf registration—the heart of the integrated disclosure program—can be expected to reduce the amount of due diligence underwriters perform, and therefore reduce the benefits to the economy that flow from that activity." Accordingly, "benefits of the traditional level of underwriter due diligence are worth their accompanying costs." Fox, Shelf Registration, Integrated Disclosure, and Underwriter Due Diligence: An Economic Analysis, 70 Va.L.Rev. 1005 (1984).

Rule 415 takes a middle position. What changes, if any, in Rule 415 would you advocate? What bearing do the various arguments vis-à-vis Rule 415 have on the costs and benefits of mandatory disclosure?

DUE DILIGENCE IN AN INTEGRATED DISCLOSURE SYSTEM: THE RULE 175 SAFE HARBOR

As indicated in the Shelf Registration release, underwriters and others were concerned as to their potential § 11 liability under the integrated disclosure system. To alleviate these concerns the Commission adopted Rule 176 which codified Section 1704(g) of the American Law Institute's proposed Federal Securities Code. The Commission stated that Rule 176 "is intended to make explicit what circumstances may bear upon the determination of what constitutes a reasonable investigation and reasonable ground for belief as these terms are used in Section 11(b) of the Securities Act." [1]

---

a. A recent study comparing shelf and traditional equity offerings found that a negative price reaction was observed both for traditional and shelf registrations; however, no statistically significant differences were observed between these types of offerings. See Moore, Peterson & Peterson, Shelf Registrations and Shareholder Wealth: A Comparison of Shelf and Traditional Equity Offerings, 41 J. Finance 451 (1986).

1. SEC Securities Act Release No. 6335 (Aug. 6, 1981), Fed.Sec.L.Rep. (CCH) No. 926, Special Rep., 2d Extra Ed. (Aug. 13, 1981), at 65.

In discussing due diligence in an integrated disclosure system, the Commission had this to say: [2]

"[T]he Securities Act imposes a high standard of conduct on specific persons, including underwriters and directors, associated with a registered public offering of securities. * * *

"The principal goal of integration is to simplify disclosure and reduce unnecessary repetition and redelivery of information which has already been provided, not to alter the roles of participants in the securities distribution process as originally contemplated by the Securities Act. The integrated disclosure system, past and proposed, is thus not designed to modify the responsibility of underwriters and others to make a reasonable investigation. Information presented in the registration statement, whether or not incorporated by reference, must be true and complete in all material respects and verified where appropriate. Likewise, nothing in the Commission's integrated disclosure system precludes conducting adequate due diligence. This point can be demonstrated by addressing the two principal concerns which have been raised.

"First, * * * commentators have expressed concern about the short time involved in document preparation. There also may be a substantial reduction in the time taken for pre-effective review at the Commission. As to the latter point, however, commentators * * * themselves noted that due diligence generally is performed prior to filing with the Commission, rendering the time in registration largely irrelevant. As to the former point, there is nothing which compels an underwriter to proceed prematurely with an offering. Although, as discussed below, he may wish to arrange his due diligence procedures over time for the purpose of avoiding last minute delays in an offering environment characterized by rapid market changes, in the final analysis the underwriter is never compelled to proceed with an offering until he has accomplished his due diligence.

"The second major concern relates to the fact that documents, prepared by others, often at a much earlier date, are incorporated by reference into the registration statement.[52] Again, it must be emphasized that due diligence requires a reasonable investigation of all the information presented therein and any information incorporated by reference. If such material contains a material misstatement, or omits a material fact, then, in order to avoid liability, a subsequent document must be filed to correct the earlier one, or the information must be restated correctly in the registration statement. Nothing in the integrated disclosure system precludes such action.

"The Commission specifically rejects the suggestion that the underwriter needs only to read the incorporated materials and discuss them with representatives of the registrant and named experts. Because the registrant would be the sole source of virtually all information, this approach would not, in and of itself, include the element of verification required by the case law and contemplated by the statute.

"Thus, verification in appropriate circumstances is still required, and if a material misstatement or omission has been made, correction by amendment or restatement must be made. For example, a major supply contract

---

2. Id. at 88–91.

52. It should be noted that Item 11 of proposed Form S–2 gives preparers the choice of either incorporating by reference specified information about the registrant from the annual report to security holders and its latest Form 10–Q or of setting forth such information directly in the registration statement.

on which the registrant is substantially dependent should be reviewed to avoid the possibility of inaccurate references to it in the prospectus. On the other hand, if the alleged misstatement in issue turns on an ambiguity or nuance in the drafted language of an incorporated document making it a close question as to whether a violation even has been committed, then the fact that a particular defendant did not participate in preparing the incorporated document, when combined with judgmental difficulties and practical concerns in making changes in prepared documents, would seem to be an appropriate factor in deciding whether "reasonable belief" in the accuracy of statements existed and thus in deciding whether to attach liability to a particular defendant's conduct.

"In sum, the Commission strongly affirms the need for due diligence and its attendant vigilance and verification. The Commission's efforts towards integration of the Securities Act and the Exchange Act relate solely to elimination of unnecessary repetition of disclosure, not to the requirements of due diligence which must accompany any offering. Yet, in view of the fact that court decisions to date have construed due diligence under factual circumstances not involving an integrated system, and in order to encourage a focus on a flexible approach to due diligence rather than a rigid adherence to past practice, the Commission believes that it would be helpful to codify its prior statements so that courts and others may fully understand the new system."

SECTION 7. PROCESSING THE REGISTRATION STATEMENT

Statutes and Regulations

Securities Act, § 8.

Regulation C, Rules 459–463, 470–479; Form SR.

POST–FILING PROCEDURES

If a security is required to be registered under the Securities Act of 1933, sales of the security are prohibited unless a registration statement as to such security [1] is "in effect." The registration statement becomes effective on "the twentieth day after the filing thereof," [2] unless it is the subject of a refusal order [3] or stop order [4] by the Commission or unless it is made effective sooner (i.e., "accelerated") by the Commission.[5]

This statutory scheme originally contemplated that in the usual case the registration statement would be filed; it would be reviewed by the Commission and information about the issue disseminated during the 20-day "waiting period"; and the Statement would become effective at the end of 20 days and the offering then commenced. This is not the way that it has worked out at all, for several reasons.

SEC Review. The statute provides that any amendment to the registration statement starts a new 20-day period running. Almost every registration statement requires at least one amendment. Over the years, a review of every registration statement was conducted by a group of examiners headed by a

1. Securities Act § 5(a).

2. Id. § 8(a).

3. Id. § 8(b).

4. Id. § 8(d).

5. Id. § 8(a).

branch chief of the Division of Corporation Finance. The group would normally include a lawyer, an accountant, a security analyst and other professionals depending on the nature and complexity of the offering. If the review by the Commission disclosed what it considered to be misleading statements or omissions in the Statement, it would not institute stop-order proceedings, unless it considered that there was evidence of willful fraud. Rather, by a technique which was worked out in the early days of the Act, it would send to the issuer through its staff what it officially called a "Letter of Comment" and what was popularly referred to as a "Deficiency Letter." This gave the issuer a chance to correct the Statement without the necessity of formal stop-order proceedings, which can be very damaging to the issuer even if they are ultimately dismissed. While this informal procedure was greatly to the advantage of the issuer, the members of the Commission staff usually felt the necessity of proving in the deficiency letter that they had read the Statement by making some comments, even if relatively trivial. This lead to what Dean Landis referred to, in his report to President Kennedy on the regulatory agencies, as "lint picking" by the Commission's staff.[6] Therefore, it was a very rare issue which did not require an amendment (called the "deficiency amendment") in response to the Letter of Comments. After such an amendment, the effective date, in the absence of acceleration, would be 20 days from the filing of the amendment.

Price Amendment and Acceleration. In the case of a firm commitment underwriting, the underwriting syndicate does not want to be committed to purchase the issue at a designated price 20 days before it can commence the resale to the public at the higher public offering price and thereby "get off the hook." Consequently, in this situation, it is customary to leave the price at which the issue will be offered blank, not only upon the original filing but also in the deficiency amendment. The price and other data dependent upon the price are inserted by amendment (called the "price amendment") which is filed after other questions pertaining to the Statement have been settled to the satisfaction of the Commission's staff. This amendment is usually prepared the day before the offering is intended to be commenced, at which time the underwriting agreement is also signed, and it is filed the next morning when the Commission's offices open. In the absence of acceleration, of course, this amendment would start another 20-day period running before the Statement became effective. However, it is expected that the Commission will by acceleration declare the Statement effective the same day the price amendment is filed, and the offering can then be commenced. Usually, the underwriting agreement contains a condition to the obligations of the underwriters (or an "out") to the effect that the Statement must become effective within a relatively short period, frequently 48 hours. Therefore, in this type of transaction, it is necessary for the issuer to obtain acceleration. This requires affirmative action by the Commission and theoretically puts the issuer more or less at the Commission's mercy; it can merely say: "We are not in the accelerating vein today." Any review of this decision, even if obtainable,[7] would probably come too late to be of any benefit to the issuer.

---

6. "There has grown up over the years a considerable tendency to indulge in lint-picking in these letters, resulting in delays and unnecessary costs." Landis, Report on Regulatory Agencies to the President-Elect 46 (Dec. 1960).

7. The case of Crooker v. Securities and Exchange Commission, 161 F.2d 944 (1st Cir. 1947), is often cited for the proposition that judicial review of an order denying acceleration is not available. However, that case did not involve an order denying acceleration, but an order *granting* acceleration, which was attempted to be challenged in the courts by a *shareholder* of the Registrant. It would seem fairly clear that such a shareholder would not have any standing to challenge the order and therefore the question whether the order is inherently nonreviewable was not really decided. As a practical matter, however,

This pattern does not exist in a best efforts underwriting, since in that case it is possible for the parties to wait out the 20 days. Nor does it necessarily exist in a firm commitment underwriting if there is no pre-existing market for the securities to be offered. The price at which the securities will be offered in that case will have been negotiated by the issuer and the managing underwriter on the basis of past earnings of the issuer and other factors which are not going to change. Therefore, the price can be inserted just as easily upon the original filing, even though the underwriting agreement has not yet been signed; and there is a very slight possibility that there will be any reason to change it unless there is an abrupt change in market conditions affecting share values generally such as the 1962 stock market plunge. The underwriting agreement itself must be filed as an exhibit to the registration statement, but there is no reason why it cannot be prepared in advance. It could even be signed at the time of the original filing with an unconditional "out" to the underwriters until the Statement has become effective. However, where there is a pre-existing market for the same class of securities as are being offered, it would be unwise to attempt to establish the public offering price 20 days before the offering date, since market fluctuations during that period should be taken into account. Furthermore, in some cases the announcement of the price that far in advance might itself have an adverse effect upon the market. It is in this type of offering that the problem of acceleration is most acute.[8]

Delaying Amendments. During the early history of the Commission, is was possible for issues as to which there were no unusual problems to become effective in the basic 20 day period or even earlier. By an amendment to the statute in 1940, the Commission was given power not only to consent to the filing of all amendments "as of" the original filing, but also to shorten this basic period.[9] Many Statements were made effective in 15 to 18 days after the original filing.

In the event that there were deficiencies in the registration statement which had not been corrected by amendment, and the 20 day period was about to expire, the Commission would generally suggest to the issuer that it file a "delaying amendment" to prevent the Statement "from becoming effective in deficient form," unless the Commission thought that the deficiencies were so serious as to warrant stop-order proceedings. Since any amendment, no matter how trivial, starts a new 20-day period running, such a delaying amendment consists merely of changing one word on the front cover of the Statement. The approximate date of the proposed public offering is required to be stated on the cover, and it is generally expressed in some such language as this: "As soon as practicable after the effective date of the Registration Statement." A delaying amendment consists, for example, of changing the word "practicable" to "possible." A second delaying amendment, if one is required, could consist of changing the word "possible" back to "practicable." Such an amendment can be filed under Rule 473 by telegram and later confirmed in writing.

---

judicial review is no answer to an issuer which has been denied acceleration.

8. In the 1950's, there was a confrontation between the securities bar and the Commission when the American Bar Association House of Delegates proposed an amendment to Section 8(a) of the Securities Act to deny the Commission discretionary authority to deny acceleration of effectiveness upon the filing of price amendments. See 83 A.B.A.Rep. 839–42 (1958); Gadsby and Garrett, "Acceleration

Under the Securities Act of 1933—A Comment on the A.B.A.'s Legislative Proposal, 13 Bus.Law. 718 (1958); Mulford, "Acceleration" Under the Securities Act of 1933—A Reply to the Securities and Exchange Commission, 14 Bus.Law. 156 (1958). A last-ditch effort to embody this proposal in the ALI Federal Securities Code § 2003(b) failed. See 2 ALI Fed.Sec.Code 1014 (1980).

9. 54 Stat. 857 (1940).

The sort of timetable discussed above has become obsolete, except in periods of a depression in the new issue market. During most of the time since the late 1950's, instead of getting the Commission's letter of comment within about 10 days after filing, which could be expected in almost all cases prior to about 1956, there has been a delay of from one to three months before the letter was forthcoming. This delay has been due to a tremendous increase in the number of filings together with the failure of Congress to provide an adequate staff to the Commission to handle the work-load. Consequently the possibility of becoming effective in the basic 20-day period originally set by Congress became practically non-existent.

SEC's Current Mode of Review. In implementing the integrated disclosure program, the Division of Corporation Finance completely reorganized its system for monitoring disclosure. Issuers were divided into industry classifications and assigned to branches. As a result of industry specialization, the Staff has become more responsive to the disclosure needs of particular industries. In addition, an entirely new mode of review was instituted.[10] See as regards 1933 Act registration statements, the Commission generally concentrates on providing a thorough review only of first-time registration statements on Form S–1 or S–18 and on registration statements of financially troubled companies. With respect to 1933 Act registration statements not reviewed, a request by the registrant for acceleration of effectiveness is treated as confirmation by the various participants in the offering of their awareness of their statutory obligations under the federal securities laws. Apparently, "going private" transaction statements receive a thorough review. (See page 827 infra). Other filings under the 1933 and 1934 Acts may be reviewed on a sample basis, and the remaining filings are handled on a post-filing review basis. In commenting upon this new mode of review, Edward F. Greene, Director of the Division of Corporation Finance, had this to say: "This type of review, which has long been applied to 1934 Act reports, tender offer materials, and certain proxy materials, places a greater burden on the issuer or the registrant since there is generally no opportunity to resolve disclosure problems prior to filing. This type of review also reduces the ability of the staff to influence the quality of a disclosure since only egregious circumstances justify reprinting and recirculating a filed document. Accordingly, we will have to reexamine the traditional ways in which the staff has commented on filed effective documents to determine whether new approaches such as interpretive releases or views of the division should be implemented." [11]

To what extent does the Commission's present policy concerning review of registration statements make 1933 Act disclosure self-regulatory as opposed to mandatory? Would you advocate the repeal of the 1933 Act's registration provisions with respect to securities offerings by reporting companies under the 1934 Act while retaining 1933 Act registration for IPOs? Should mandatory disclosure under the 1934 Act be repealed? See McLaughlin, 1933 Act's Registration Provisions: Is Time Ripe for Repealing Them?, Nat'l.L.J. 44 (Aug. 18, 1986) and note b (last paragraph) at page 197.

If the original filing is complete (i.e., the price and other information is not left to be supplied by amendment), an issuer could theoretically force a review by the Commission within the 20-day period by refusing to file a delaying amendment. The Commission will suggest that such an amend-

10. See Statement of Edward F. Greene, Director, SEC Division of Corporate Finance, The SEC and Corporate Disclosure, 36 Bus.Law. 119, 126–27 (1980); SEC News Digest, Nov. 17, 1980, Issue 80– 222, Reprinted in Fed.Sec.L.Rep. (CCH) ¶ 275.20.

11. Id. at 36 Bus.Law. 119, at 127.

ment be filed to "prevent the Statement from becoming effective in deficient form," even though no one at the Commission has yet looked at it or knows whether it is in deficient form or not. In order to eliminate the necessity of the issuer filing several of such amendments while waiting for the Commission to get around to reviewing the Statement, the Commission has adopted a rule permitting what is in effect a permanent delaying amendment to be filed along with the original Statement.[12] Probably the basic reason why issuers and underwriters have not adopted the attitude suggested above, of refusing to file such delaying amendments, is that the detailed Commission review, "lint picking" or not, is a valuable insurance policy for them. And they are willing to put up with the delay to obtain it. (There was perhaps also a lingering fear that such an intransigent attitude would invite Commission reprisal in one form or another.)

In Las Vegas Hawaiian Development Co. v. Securities and Exchange Commission, 466 F.Supp. 928 (D. Hawaii 1979), however, a registrant did refuse to file a further delaying amendment after the SEC failed to declare a registration statement to be effective. In that case, three individuals, the McDonalds, were engaged in real estate syndication through numerous corporations and partnerships. In 1977 one of these entities, LVH, filed a 1933 Act registration statement with the Commission in which another corporation, owned by the McDonalds, proposed to become the general partner of LVH. A delaying amendment was attached to this registration.

In 1971, the McDonalds, through certain other corporations had sold fractional undivided interests in 1,600 acres of undeveloped land near Las Vegas, Nevada. These interests were sold to approximately 900 public investors, most of whom were residents of Hawaii, for a total sales price of over $6 million. No registration statement had been filed as to these fractional undivided interests in undeveloped land. The registration statement filed by LVH proposed an offering of limited partnership interests to those persons who had purchased the undivided fractional interests in the Nevada land.

The Division of Corporation Finance thereupon forwarded to the registrant sixteen pages of comments regarding the registration statement. LVH filed an amended registration statement, with an attached delaying amendment. The Division forwarded a second comment letter to LVH, discussing unresolved deficiencies, and added that additional comments might be forthcoming. LVH countered by filing a second amendment to its registration statement, but this time no delaying amendment was filed. This, of course, meant that, absent Commission action, the registration statement would become effective on the twentieth day after the filing of the last amendment.

Shortly before the registration would have become effective, the Commission issued an order authorizing its staff (1) to conduct a § 8(e) examination to determine whether a stop order proceeding under § 8(d) was necessary with respect to LVH proposed public offering, and (2) to conduct a private investigation of the circumstances surrounding the proposed exchange offer, pursuant to § 20(a) of the 1933 Act and § 21(a) of the 1934 Act. This raised the spectre that the SEC might introduce the issue whether the original sale of land might have entailed the sale of a "security" subject to 1933 Act registration.

LVH filed a complaint for a declaratory judgment asserting that § 8(e) could not be used by the Commission "to delay indefinitely the sale of securities under an effective registration statement," and that an examination of a

---

12. Securities Act Release No. 4329 (Feb. 21, 1961), amending Rule 473.

registration statement could not be made a bridgehead with which to investigate prior transactions not within the scope of the registration statement.

An effect of the Commission's order to conduct an examination, pursuant to § 8(e) was to bring into operation § 5(c) of the 1933 Act which prohibits the use of interstate facilities to offer to sell securities "while the registration is the subject of * * * [prior to the effective date of the registration] any public proceeding or examination under § 8(e))." Accordingly, any sales activity concerning the registered securities was foreclosed by virtue of § 5(c).

The Commission contended that a § 8(e) examination was within the Commission's discretionary powers, that plaintiffs had not shown an abuse of discretion and that the authorization of a § 8(e) examination was not a final Commission action which was reviewable. As to these contentions, the district court had this to say at page 932:

> Defendants [members of the Commission] have oversimplified the situation by arguing that there is no present hardship to the plaintiffs if judicial review is withheld at this time. If the Commission's order authorizing a public examination pursuant to section 8(e) had been issued *after* the effective date of the second amended registration statement, section 5(c) would not have come into operation. LVH could then have proceeded with its sales program, even though a stop order could later issue. But the Commission's order issued *before* the effective date of the registration statement, section 5(c) is applicable, and the plaintiffs do feel the agency action in a concrete way. See Abbott Laboratories, Inc. v. Gardner, 387 U.S. 136 (1967).

> While the SEC is given broad powers and wide discretion, provision is made for time limits, notices, hearings, appeals, and judicial reviews of actions that affect the issuance and sale of securities. It is not a sufficient answer to say that authorizing a section 8(e) examination is not a final Commission action, or to say that no one has a right to register securities for public sale. A registrant does have a right to have the Commission follow the applicable statutes and regulations, and attempts by the Commission to circumvent statutorily imposed time limits may be attacked in a judicial proceeding. See SEC v. Sloan, 436 U.S. 103 (1978).

> Yet Congress has not placed any time limitation on the duration of a section 8(e) examination. Nor is an order authorizing such an examination reviewable under section 9 of the Act. See Stardust, Inc. v. SEC, 225 F.2d 255 (9th Cir. 1955). This leaves the registrant with whatever remedy may be had pursuant to the Administrative Procedure Act (APA).

> In my opinion, a district court may, upon the petition of a registrant under the Securities Act of 1933, compel the SEC to make a determination within a reasonable time whether to notice a hearing on the issuance of a stop order under section 8(d), where the Commission has ordered an examination under section 8(e) prior to the effective date of a registration statement and the determination whether a stop order should issue has been unreasonably delayed.

> The court may not compel the Commission to institute a section 8(d) proceeding. Crooker v. SEC, 161 F.2d 944 (1st Cir. 1947). But the clear import of 5 U.S.C. § 706 is that the court may compel the SEC to either terminate a section 8(e) examination or institute a section 8(d) proceeding in a situation where the SEC's inaction has the effect of prohibiting the sale of registered securities, and when this determination has been unreasonably withheld.

The complaint was dismissed since it was not alleged that the Commission's determination whether to institute a § 8(d) proceeding had been unreasonably delayed within the intendment of § 706 of the Administrative Procedure Act. The Court also refused to place a limit on the § 8(e) examination which would have forestalled any inquiry into the circumstances surrounding the earlier land sales; the scope of such examinations was deemed to be a matter within the discretion of the Commission.

The case has not generated an attack upon the Commission's authority with respect to delaying amendments or acceleration of the effectiveness of registration statements. It should, however, discourage unreasonable stalling tactics on the part of the enforcement division.

Follow-Up Procedures. During the waiting period between filing and effectiveness, the accuracy of the registration statement in the light of changing conditions must be kept under constant review. The chief financial officer must be advised of the necessity of keeping the accounting records of the company current, for it may be necessary to update the financial statements in accordance with Commission policy.[13] Moreover, if the managing underwriter prepares a memorandum for use in connection with the organization of the underwriting syndicate or for circulation among prospective members of the selling group, any such memorandum should be promptly furnished to the Division of Corporation Finance in compliance with Rule 418. Steps will also be taken to qualify the securities under the securities laws of those states in which it is anticipated the securities will be offered.

After an initial public offering, company counsel should educate the corporate officers as to their ongoing responsibilities as a public company under the federal securities laws, particularly the Exchange Act.

As a result of going public, an issuer becomes subject to the periodic reporting requirements of § 13 by virtue of § 15(d) of the Exchange Act. In all probability, the Company will also have to comply with the registration provisions of § 12. A registrant under the 1934 Act must comply with numerous provisions: the proxy rules (§ 14); recapture of short-swing profits (§ 16(b)); the beneficial ownership reporting requirements (§ 16(a)); restrictions on short sales (§ 16(c)); the tender offer and reporting provisions of the Williams Act (§§ 14(d) and (e) and §§ 13(d) and (e)); the Foreign Corrupt Practices Act (§ 13(b)(2)); and the obligation to furnish annual reports to shareholders (§ 14 and Rules 14a–6 and 14c–3). See Schneider and Shargel, "Now That You Are Publicly Owned * * *", 36 Bus.Law. 1631 (1981). This article has been updated by its authors as of April, 1983 and republished by Packard Press, Philadelphia, Pa. And see Mann & Halloran, Educating Corporate Officers After an Initial Public Offering, 19 The Practical Law. 15 (Feb. 1973).

DENIAL OF ACCELERATION

The decision whether to grant the request for acceleration is actually made by the Director of the Division of Corporation Finance, to whom the Commission has delegated this power. Requests for acceleration must be made in writing by the registrant, the managing underwriters of the offering, and the selling security holders, if any, in compliance with other conditions specified in

13. See Schneider, Manko & Kant, "Going Public: Practice, Procedure, and Consequences", supra page 134, at n. 17.

Rule 461. The conditions governing the granting of the acceleration are set forth in Rules 460 and 461.

In passing upon a request for acceleration, the Commission will consider whether an adequate distribution of the preliminary prospectus has been made to those underwriters and dealers who are expected to participate in the proposed offering reasonably in advance of the anticipated effective date of the statement. Rule 15c2–8 requires that all brokers or dealers participating in the distribution take reasonable steps to furnish preliminary prospectuses to those who make a written request for copies. Copies must also be made available to each associated person who is expected to solicit customers' orders during the waiting period. Rule 460 specifies the information which the registrant must furnish to the Division of Corporation Finance in order to satisfy these requirements.

A denial by the Commission of acceleration of a Registration Statement, however, is usually predicated upon a failure of complete and adequate disclosure concerning the securities to be sold. See the text of Rule 461. There has been no controversy concerning Commission action on this basis. The argument has revolved around the Commission "policy" of denying acceleration upon certain bases wholly unrelated or only remotely related to disclosure. Prior to 1957, these "policies" had never been announced in any generally available Rule, regulation or other publication. They had to be learned by experience in dealing with the Commission.

Do the grounds now listed in Rule 461 impose any substantial or unreasonable restrictions upon issuers unrelated to disclosure? Could the Commission impose any substantive requirement that it found was "for the protection of investors" as a condition to acceleration? Could it, for example, refuse acceleration because in its opinion the price at which the security was offered was unreasonably high?

REFUSAL AND STOP ORDERS

A refusal order under Section 8(b) is not generally employed by the Commission, since such an order requires the Commission to act within 10 days after the filing of the Registration Statement. At least in recent years, such quick action is not possible. Furthermore, the requirement in the case of a refusal order that the deficiencies be apparent "on the face" of the Statement might raise difficulties if the proceedings show that there are deficiencies, but there is an argument over whether they are so apparent. Since under Red Bank Oil Co., 20 S.E.C. 863 (1945), the stop order is equally available whenever a refusal order might be issued and it is not subject to either of these limitations, this is the type of proceeding normally instituted by the Commission.

The number of instances in which the Commission has found it necessary to institute stop order proceedings has been amazingly small in the light of the number of Registration Statements filed. In the 1970 fiscal year, there were 4,314 registration statements filed with the Commission; there were 28 examinations inititated under Section 8(e) to determine whether stop order proceedings should be commenced; and there were 6 stop order proceedings initiated.[1] Six stop orders were actually issued during the year. However, information is not available as to which of these were the result of proceedings initiated in the prior year, of which there were 3 pending at the beginning of the year.[2] In

---

1. 36 SEC Ann.Rep. 35 (1970).   2. Ibid.

recent years, however, formal stop order disclosure proceedings have become a rarity.[3]

This scarcity of formal stop order proceedings is both a tribute to the administrative flexibility of the Commission and a reflection of the practical necessities of the investment banking business, which cannot afford to wait upon the processes of litigation or formal administrative hearings except in rare cases.

WITHDRAWAL OF THE REGISTRATION STATEMENT

A controversy, now largely put to rest, concerns the right of a registrant voluntarily to withdraw a registration statement prior to effectiveness, despite the opposition of the Securities and Exchange Commission based upon public interest considerations. Under SEC Rule 477, a registration statement or any amendment or exhibit thereto may be withdrawn upon application of the registrant only if the Commission finds such withdrawal consistent with the public interest and the protection of investors and consents thereto. In Jones v. SEC, 298 U.S. 1 (1936), the Supreme Court, in a sharply divided decision, sustained the right of a registrant to withdraw the registration statement prior to the effective date under the predecessor of Rule 477, despite objections by the SEC. The registrant had not commenced business and there were no securities outstanding in the hands of the public; the Court therefore saw no public interest issue.

The *Jones* case has since been discredited, but has never been overruled. At the same time, the validity of Rule 477 has been sustained in a number of cases, particularly when securities of the registrant are outstanding in the hands of the public at the time of the proposal to withdraw the registration statement. See Columbia General Investment Corp. v. SEC, 265 F.2d 559 (5th Cir. 1959); Wolf Corp. v. SEC, 115 U.S.App.D.C. 75, 317 F.2d 139 (1963). In *Columbia*, however, the court also stressed the fact that as a result of the 1954 amendments to the Securities Act the registrant can now make offers of the securities after filing the registration statement and before the statement becomes effective. If the registrant is then permitted to withdraw the registration statement it would be possible later to resort to Regulation A and capitalize upon the prior sales effort, thereby defeating the investor's right to public disclosure from a registration.

---

3. For examples, see In re Synthetic Fuels, Inc., Securites Act Release No. 6319 (June 2, 1981), Fed.Sec.L.Rep. (CCH) [1981 Transfer Binder] ¶ 82,876; In re Advanced Chemical Corporation, Securities Act Release No. 6507 (Feb. 9, 1984), Fed.Sec.L. Rep. (CCH) [1983–1984 Transfer Binder] ¶ 83,499. But see Mc Lucas, Stop Order Proceedings Under the Securities Act of 1933: A Current Assessment, 40 Bus.Law. 515 (1985), indicating an increasing use of this device.

SUBDIVISION B. COVERAGE OF THE REGULATION

Chapter 4

DEFINITIONS OF "SECURITY" AND "EXEMPTED SECURITIES"

SECTION 1. WHAT IS A "SECURITY"?

Statute

Securities Act, § 2(1).

A. THE MEANING OF "INVESTMENT CONTRACT"

DEFINITION OF A "SECURITY": A STUDY IN STATUTORY INTERPRETATION

Securities Act § 2(1) and Exchange Act § 3(a)(10) each define a "security" in both specific and more general terms. Thus, there is not a single test for determining what constitutes a security; there is first a specific test, followed by a more general test. The purpose of the two-part test was "to include within the definition the many types of instruments that in our commercial world fall within the ordinary concept of a security." [1]

The list of specific instruments include any "note," "stock," "bond," and "debenture."

The general catch-all phrases include within the statutory definition instruments of a more variable character such as any "evidence of indebtedness," "certificate of interest or participation in any profit-sharing agreement," "investment contract" and any "instrument commonly known as a 'security.'"

Both the specific and the general definitions in the Securities Acts apply "unless the context otherwise requires." Thus, although an instrument may be presumed to fall into any of the statutory definitions of a security, it nevertheless may not be held to be a security under the federal securities laws if the context otherwise requires.

In Securities and Exchange Commission v. C.M. Joiner Leasing Corporation,[2] the Supreme Court for the first time considered the application of the statute to the sale of interests in oil and gas leases coupled with the promise by the seller to drill test wells so located as to discover the oil-producing possibili-

1. H.R.Rep. No. 85, 73 Cong., 1st Sess. 11 (1933).   2. 320 U.S. 344 (1943).

220

ties of the surrounding land. Justice Jackson noted that the definition was similar to that found in many state "Blue Sky" laws and considered what rules of statutory construction might serve to ascertain the legislative intent. In rejecting the argument that the Act should be strictly construed, he stated: [3]

> In the Securities Act the term "security" was defined to include by name or description many documents in which there is common trading for speculation or investment. Some, such as notes, bonds, and stocks, are pretty much standardized and the name alone carries well-settled meaning. Others are of more variable character and were necessarily designated by more descriptive terms, such as "transferable share," "investment contract," and "in general any interest or instrument commonly known as a security." We cannot read out of the statute these general descriptive designations merely because more specific ones have been used to reach some kinds of documents. Instruments may be included within any of these definitions, as a matter of law, if on their face they answer to the name or description. However, the reach of the Act does not stop with the obvious and commonplace. Novel, uncommon, or irregular devices, whatever they appear to be, are also reached if it be proved as matter of fact that they were widely offered or dealt in under terms or courses of dealing which established their character in commerce as "investment contracts," or as "any interest or instrument commonly known as a 'security.'"

In applying the two tests for the security under § 2(1) to the facts, Justice Jackson first applied the specific instruments test to determine whether the oil leasehold interests were included within the specifically designated instruments. Obviously, the list of specific instruments did not include divided interests in oil and gas. He therefore proceeded to the second test for investment contracts. Noting that the leasehold interests were sold on the condition that the purchasers would share in any appreciation in value of their lease interests if oil were discovered on adjacent land, Justice Jackson concluded that these leaseholds constituted "investment contracts," and therefore were "securities."

In recent years, some federal courts, engaging in an extreme form of judicial activism, reversed this process and began to apply the test for "investment contracts" declared by the Supreme Court in SEC v. W.J. Howey Co.,[4] to specific instruments expressly enumerated in the statutory definition of a security. These courts found that the "context otherwise requires" that certain specifically enumerated instruments should be deemed to be non-securities, thereby placing such securities outside the purview of the statute. Furthermore, these courts seized upon the "economic reality" test, a test formulated to "afford the investing public a full measure of protection," and converted it into an exception to the definition of a security, thereby narrowing the scope of the statute.[5] The result was to stand the statute on its head and deprive investors of the registration, disclosure and antifraud provisions of the Securities Acts.

This novel doctrine of statutory construction produced a flood of cases holding that "notes" and "stock" were non-securities in the particular context on the basis that "economic realities" justified ignoring the plain meaning of

---

3. Id. 350–51.

4. 328 U.S. 293 (1946), infra at page 222.

5. See e.g. Judge Posner's opinion in Sutter v. Groen, 687 F.2d 197 (7th Cir. 1982). For a criticism, see Cohen, Posnerian Jurisprudence and Economic Analysis of Law: The View from the Bench, 133 U.Pa.L.Rev. 1117, 1133–34 (1985). Compare Judge Friendly's opinion in The Exchange Nat'l. Bank of Chicago v. Touche Ross & Co., 544 F.2d 1126 (2d Cir.1976), infra at 244; Judge Gibbons opinion in Ruefenacht v. O'Halloran, 737 F.2d 320 (3d Cir.1984), aff'd 471 U.S. 701 (1985), infra at 260.

the statute. As Judge Cardamone remarked, "Like modern day beachcombers with 'finders' rods seeking treasure beneath the sand, circuit courts cull through Supreme Court decisions in search of a phrase to fortify their view of how 'security' is defined under the acts." [6] And after surveying the law in this area, Judge Hill concluded that "in the end one is left with the impression that he is dealing with an area of the law subject to wide variations, serious anomalies, and judicial disagreement, if not confusion. In short, the wealth of judicial writings on the subject has produced few discernible principles of decision." [7]

The following cases provide an interesting study in statutory interpretation.

SECURITIES & EXCHANGE COMMISSION
v. W. J. HOWEY CO.

Supreme Court of the United States, 1946.
328 U.S. 293, 66 S.Ct. 1100, 90 L.Ed.2d 1244.

Mr. Justice Murphy delivered the opinion of the Court.

This case involves the application of § 2(1) of the Securities Act of 1933 to an offering of units of a citrus grove development coupled with a contract for cultivating, marketing and remitting the net proceeds to the investor.

The Securities and Exchange Commission instituted this action to restrain the respondents from using the mails and instrumentalities of interstate commerce in the offer and sale of unregistered and non-exempt securities in violation of § 5(a) of the Act. The District Court denied the injunction, * * * and the Fifth Circuit Court of Appeals affirmed the judgment * * *. We granted certiorari * * *.

* * * The respondents, W. J. Howey Company and Howey-in-the-Hills Service, Inc., are Florida corporations under direct common control and management. The Howey Company owns large tracts of citrus acreage in Lake County, Florida. During the past several years it has planted about 500 acres annually, keeping half of the groves itself and offering the other half to the public "to help us finance additional development." Howey-in-the-Hills Service, Inc., is a service company engaged in cultivating and developing many of these groves, including the harvesting and marketing of the crops.

Each prospective customer is offered both a land sales contract and a service contract, after having been told that it is not feasible to invest in a grove unless service arrangements are made. While the purchaser is free to make arrangements with other service companies, the superiority of Howey-in-the-Hills Service, Inc., is stressed. Indeed, 85% of the acreage sold during the 3-year period ending May 31, 1943, was covered by service contracts with Howey-in-the-Hills Service, Inc.

---

6. Seagrave Corp. v. Vista Resources, 696 F.2d 227, 229 (2d Cir.1982), cert. granted 466 U.S. 970 (1984), appeal dismissed __ U.S. __, 105 S.Ct. 23 (1984); Arnold, "When is a Car a Bicycle?" and Other Riddles: The Definition of a Security Under the Federal Securities Laws, 33 Clev. St.L.Rev. 448, 483 (1984–85).

7. Van Huss v. Associated Milk Producers, Inc., 415 F.Supp. 356 (N.D.Tex.1976).

The land sales contract with the Howey Company provides for a uniform purchase price per acre or fraction thereof, varying in amount only in accordance with the number of years the particular plot has been planted with citrus trees. Upon full payment of the purchase price the land is conveyed to the purchaser by warranty deed. Purchases are usually made in narrow strips of land arranged so that an acre consists of a row of 48 trees. During the period between February 1, 1941, and May 31, 1943, 31 of the 42 persons making purchases bought less than 5 acres each. The average holding of these 31 persons was 1.33 acres and sales of as little as 0.65, 0.7 and 0.73 of an acre were made. These tracts are not separately fenced and the sole indication of several ownership is found in small land marks intelligible only through a plat book record.

The service contract, generally of a 10-year duration without option of cancellation, gives Howey-in-the-Hills Service, Inc., a leasehold interest and "full and complete" possession of the acreage. For a specified fee plus the cost of labor and materials, the company is given full discretion and authority over the cultivation of the groves and the harvest and marketing of the crops. The company is well established in the citrus business and maintains a large force of skilled personnel and a great deal of equipment, including 75 tractors, sprayer wagons, fertilizer trucks and the like. Without the consent of the company, the land owner or purchaser has no right of entry to market the crop; thus there is ordinarily no right to specific fruit. The company is accountable only for an allocation of the net profits based upon a check made at the time of picking. All the produce is pooled by the respondent companies, which do business under their own names.

The purchasers for the most part are non-residents of Florida. They are predominantly business and professional people who lack the knowledge, skill and equipment necessary for the care and cultivation of citrus trees. They are attracted by the expectation of substantial profits. * * * Many of these purchasers are patrons of a resort hotel owned and operated by the Howey Company in a scenic section adjacent to the groves. The hotel's advertising mentions the fine groves in the vicinity and the attention of the patrons is drawn to the groves as they are being escorted about the surrounding countryside. They are told that the groves are for sale; if they indicate an interest in the matter they are then given a sales talk.

It is admitted that the mails and instrumentalities of interstate commerce are used in the sale of the land and service contracts and that no registration statement or letter of notification has ever been filed with the Commission in accordance with the Securities Act of 1933 and the rules and regulations thereunder.

Section 2(1) of the Act defines the term "security" to include the commonly known documents traded for speculation or investment. This definition also includes "securities" of a more variable character, designated by such descriptive terms as "certificate of interest or participation in any profit-sharing agreement," "investment contract" and "in general, any interest or instrument commonly known as a 'security.'" The legal issue in this case turns upon a determination of whether, under the circumstances, the land sales contract, the warranty deed and the service contract together constitute an "investment contract" within the meaning of § 2(1) * * *.

The term "investment contract" is undefined by the Securities Act or by relevant legislative reports. But the term was common in many state "blue sky" laws in existence prior to the adoption of the federal statute and, although the term was also undefined by the state laws, it had been broadly construed by state courts so as to afford the investing public a full measure of protection. Form was disregarded for substance and emphasis was placed upon economic reality. An investment contract thus came to mean a contract or scheme for "the placing of capital or laying out of money in a way intended to secure income or profit from its employment." State v. Gopher Tire & Rubber Co., 146 Minn. 52, 56, 177 N.W. 937, 938. This definition was uniformly applied by state courts to a variety of situations where individuals were led to invest money in a common enterprise with the expectation that they would earn a profit solely through the efforts of the promoter or of some one other than themselves.

By including an investment contract within the scope of § 2(1) of the Securities Act, Congress was using a term the meaning of which had been crystallized by this prior judicial interpretation. It is therefore reasonable to attach that meaning to the term as used by Congress, especially since such a definition is consistent with the statutory aims. In other words, an investment contract for purposes of the Securities Act means a contract, transaction or scheme whereby a person invests his money in a common enterprise and is led to expect profits solely from the efforts of the promoter or a third party, it being immaterial whether the shares in the enterprise are evidenced by formal certificates or by nominal interests in the physical assets employed in the enterprise. Such a definition necessarily underlies this Court's decision in S.E.C. v. Joiner Corp., 320 U.S. 344, and has been enunciated and applied many times by lower federal courts. It permits the fulfillment of the statutory purpose of compelling full and fair disclosure relative to the issuance of "the many types of instruments that in our commercial world fall within the ordinary concept of a security." H.Rep. No. 85, 73d Cong., 1st Sess., p. 11. It embodies a flexible rather than a static principle, one that is capable of adaptation to meet the countless and variable schemes devised by those who seek the use of the money of others on the promise of profits.

The transactions in this case clearly involve investment contracts as so defined. The respondent companies are offering something more than fee simple interests in land, something different from a farm or orchard coupled with management services. They are offering an opportunity to contribute money and to share in the profits of a large citrus fruit enterprise managed and partly owned by respondents. They are offering this opportunity to persons who reside in distant localities and who lack the equipment and experience requisite to the cultivation, harvesting and marketing of the citrus products. Such persons have no desire to occupy the land or to develop it themselves; they are attracted solely by the prospects of a return on their investment. Indeed, individual development of the plots of land that are offered and sold would seldom be economically feasible due to their small size. Such tracts gain utility as citrus groves only when cultivated and developed as component parts of a larger area. A common enterprise managed by respondents or third parties with adequate personnel and equipment is therefore essential if the investors are to achieve their paramount aim of a return on their investments. Their respective shares in this enterprise are evidenced by land sales contracts and warranty deeds, which serve as a convenient method of determining the investors' allocable shares of the profits. The resulting transfer of rights in land is purely incidental.

Thus all the elements of a profit-seeking business venture are present here. The investors provide the capital and share in the earnings and profits; the promoters manage, control and operate the enterprise. It follows that the arrangements whereby the investors' interests are made manifest involve investment contracts, regardless of the legal terminology in which such contracts are clothed. The investment contracts in this instance take the form of land sales contracts, warranty deeds and service contracts which respondents offer to prospective investors. And respondents' failure to abide by the statutory and administrative rules in making such offerings, even though the failure result from a bona fide mistake as to the law, cannot be sanctioned under the Act.

This conclusion is unaffected by the fact that some purchasers choose not to accept the full offer of an investment contract by declining to enter into a service contract with the respondents. The Securities Act prohibits the offer as well as the sale of unregistered, non-exempt securities.[6] Hence it is enough that the respondents merely offer the essential ingredients of an investment contract.

* * *

Reversed.[a]

1. FRANCHISES

SECURITIES AND EXCHANGE COMMISSION v. KOSCOT INTERPLANETARY, INC.

United States Court of Appeals, Fifth Circuit, 1974.
497 F.2d 473.

Before RIVES, GEWIN and RONEY, CIRCUIT JUDGES.

GEWIN, CIRCUIT JUDGE: This appeal emanates from a district court order denying an injunction sought by the Securities & Exchange Commission (SEC) against Koscot Interplanetary, Inc., (Koscot) for allegedly violating the federal securities laws. Specifically, the SEC maintained that the

---

6. The registration requirements of § 5 refer to sales of securities. Section 2(3) defines "sale" to include every "attempt or offer to dispose of, or solicitation of an offer to buy," a security for value.

a. In a civil case, if there is no dispute as to the facts, the question of what constitutes a security is one of law to be determined by the court. In *Howey*, the majority treated the question as one of law. Mr. Justice Frankfurter dissented on the basis that the issue was one of fact. He thought the judgment below should be affirmed under the federal two-court rule.

In a federal criminal case, however, the issue of what constitutes a "security" is for the jury. Roe v. United States, 287 F.2d 435, 440 (5th Cir. 1961), cert. denied 368 U.S. 824 (1961); United States v. Johnson, 718 F.2d 1317 (5th Cir. 1983). It is said

that this principle rests upon the commands of the sixth amendment guaranteeing jury trial and the due process clause. In view of the courts' tendency to waffle on whether common stock is a security, perhaps there is a reasonable doubt in all cases as to whether any of the specifically enumerated instruments is a security. See Arnold, "When is a Car a Bicycle?" and Other Riddles: The Definition of a Security Under the Federal Securities Laws, 33 Clev.St.L.Rev. 449 (1984–85). In a muddled opinion, the California Supreme Court has adopted this view. People v. Figueroa, 41 Cal.3d 714, 224 Cal.Rptr. 719, 715 P.2d 680 (1986). Cf. concurring opinion of Reynoso, J.; People v. Stewart, 182 Cal.App.3d 222, 227 Cal.Rptr. 275 (1986); People v. Walden, 183 Cal.App.3d 118, 228 Cal.Rptr. 57 (1986).

pyramid promotion enterprise operated by Koscot was within the ambit of the term security, as employed by the Securities Act of 1933 and the Securities Exchange Act of 1934, that as such it had to be registered with the SEC pursuant to the '33 Act, and that the manner in which Koscot purveyed its enterprise to potential investors contravened the anti-fraud provisions of the '34 Act. In a comprehensive opinion, * * *, the district court denied the injunction holding that the Koscot Scheme did not involve the sale of a security. Because of our disagreement with the district court's reasoning, we reverse.

I

A. *The Koscot Scheme*

The procedure followed by Koscot in the promotion of its enterprise can be synoptically chronicled. A subsidiary of Glenn W. Turner Enterprises, Koscot thrives by enticing prospective investors to participate in its enterprise, holding out as a lure the expectation of galactic profits. All too often, the beguiled investors are disappointed by paltry returns.

The vehicle for the lure is a multi-level network of independent distributors, purportedly engaged in the business of selling a line of cosmetics. At the lowest level is a "beauty advisor" whose income is derived solely from retail sales of Koscot products made available at a discount, customarily of 45%. Those desirous of ascending the ladder of the Koscot enterprise may also participate on a second level, that of supervisor or retail manager. For an investment of $1,000, a supervisor receives cosmetics at a greater discount from retail price, typically 55%, to be sold either directly to the public or to be held for wholesale distribution to the beauty advisors. In addition, a supervisor who introduces a prospect to the Koscot program with whom a sale is ultimately consummated receives $600 of the $1,000 paid to Koscot. The loftiest position in the multi-level scheme is that of distributor. An investment of $5,000 with Koscot entitles a distributor to purchase cosmetics at an even greater discount, typically 65%, for distribution to supervisors and retailers. Moreover, fruitful sponsorship of either a supervisor or distributor brings $600 or $3,000 respectively to the sponsor.

The SEC does not contend that the distribution of cosmetics is amenable to regulation under the federal securities laws. Rather, it maintains that the marketing of cosmetics and the recruitment aspects of Koscot's enterprise are separable and that only the latter are within the definition of a security. * * *

The modus operandi of Koscot and its investors is as follows. Investors solicit prospects to attend Opportunity Meetings at which the latter are introduced to the Koscot scheme. Significantly, the investor is admonished not to mention the details of the business before bringing the prospect to the meeting, a technique euphemistically denominated the "curiosity approach." * * *

Thus, in the initial stage, an investor's sole task is to attract individuals to the meeting.

Once a prospect's attendance at a meeting is secured, Koscot employees, frequently in conjunction with investors, undertake to apprise prospects of the "virtues" of enlisting in the Koscot plan. The meeting is conducted in conformity with scripts prepared by Koscot. * * * The principal design of the meetings is to foster an illusion of affluence. Investors and Koscot employees are instructed to drive to meetings in expensive cars, preferably Cadillacs, to dress expensively, and to flaunt large amounts of money. It is intended that prospects will be galvanized into signing a contract by these ostentations displayed in the evangelical atmosphere of the meetings.

* * *

The final stage in the promotional scheme is the consummation of the sale. If a prospect capitulates at * * * an Opportunity Meeting * * *, an investor will not be required to expend any additional effort. Less fortuitous investors whose prospects are not as quickly enticed to invest do have to devote additional effort to consummate a sale, the amount of which is contingent upon the degree of reluctance of the prospect.

* * *

The district court rebuffed the SEC's effort to subject Koscot's promotional scheme to the federal securities laws. * * * The court refused to endorse the SEC's position that the pyramid arrangement constituted an interest "commonly known as a security" for two reasons. First, even under a traditional approach, under which the essential inquiry is how the interest is viewed in legal and financial circles, the question of whether a pyramid arrangement fell within the definition was still a polemical one; and second, the risk capital theory, which allegedly would encompass the Koscot arrangement, was of such recent vintage and had such a mixed reception with the courts that it should not be applied in lieu of the traditional definition.[7]

Of more immediate concern is the reasoning employed by the district court in rejecting the SEC's contention that Koscot sold "investment contracts," for it is our disagreement with this conclusion that prompts us to reverse. The district court correctly cited * * * language from SEC v. W. J. Howey Co., * * * as the standard controlling its disposition of the case.

* * *

This test subsumes within it three elements: first, that there is an investment of money; second, that the scheme in which an investment is made functions as a common enterprise; and third, that under the scheme, profits are derived solely from the efforts of individuals other than the investors. * * *. The district court pretermitted a consideration of the first two elements in finding that the third component of the test was not satisfied because Koscot investors expended effort in soliciting recruits to meetings, in participating in the conduct of meetings, and in attempting to consummate the sale of distributorships and subdistributorships. * * *

II

Thus, we are called upon to address that which the court below did not consider—whether the Koscot scheme satisfies the first two elements of the *Howey* test—and that which the district court did consider—whether the scheme satisfies the third component of the test. The latter inquiry entails, in the first instance, a determination of whether the "solely from

---

7. The thrust of the inquiry under the risk capital test is whether the investor has subjected his money to the risk of an enterprise over which he exercises no managerial control. See SEC v. Glenn W. Turner Enterprises, Inc., 348 F.Supp. 766, 773–774 (D.Or. 1972), aff'd, 474 F.2d 476 (9th Cir.), cert. denied, 414 U.S. 82 (1973).

the efforts of others" standard is to be literally or functionally applied. We address these issues seriatim.

A. *The First Two Elements*

Since it cannot be disputed that purchasers of supervisorships and distributorships made an investment of money, * * * our initial concern is whether the Koscot scheme functions as a common enterprise. As defined by the Ninth Circuit, "[a] common enterprise is one in which the fortunes of the investor are interwoven with and dependent upon the efforts and success of those seeking the investment or of third parties." SEC v. Glenn W. Turner Enterprises, Inc., supra at 482 n. 7. The critical factor is not the similitude or coincidence of investor input, but rather the uniformity of impact of the promoter's efforts.

[T]his definition comports with the standard applied by the Supreme Court * * * in *Howey*, supra. * * *

Similarly, here, the fact that an investor's return is independent of that of other investors in the scheme is not decisive. Rather, the requisite commonality is evidenced by the fact that the fortunes of all investors are inextricably tied to the efficacy of the Koscot meetings and guidelines on recruiting prospects and consummating a sale. * * *

B. *The Third Element—Solely from the Efforts of Others*

As was noted earlier, the critical issue in this case is whether a literal or functional approach to the "solely from the efforts of others" test should be adopted, i.e., whether the exertion of some effort by an investor is inimical to the holding that a promotional scheme falls within the definition of an investment contract. We measure the viability of the SEC's advocacy of a functional approach by its compatibility with the remedial purposes of the federal securities acts, the language employed and the derivation of the test utilized in *Howey*, and the decisions in this circuit and other federal courts.

1. *The Legal Standard*

* * *

A literal application of the *Howey* test would frustrate the remedial purposes of the Act. As the Ninth Circuit noted in SEC v. Turner Enterprises, Inc., supra at 482, "[i]t would be easy to evade [the *Howey* test] by adding a requirement that the buyer contribute a modicum of effort." The admitted salutary purposes of the Acts can only be safeguarded by a functional approach to the *Howey* test.

Moreover, a close reading of the language employed in *Howey* and the authority upon which the Court relied suggests that, contrary to the view of the district court, we need not feel compelled to follow the "solely from the efforts of others" test literally. Nowhere in the opinion does the Supreme Court characterize the nature of the "efforts" that would render a promotional scheme beyond the pale of the definition of an investment contract. Clearly the facts presented no issue of how to assess a scheme in which an investor performed mere perfunctory tasks. Indeed, * * * the Court observed that "the promoters *manage, control* and *operate* the enterprise." 328 U.S. at 300 (emphasis added).

* * *

In view of * * * our analysis of the import of the language in and the derivation of the *Howey* test, we hold that the proper standard in determining whether a scheme constitutes an investment contract is that explicated by the Ninth Circuit in SEC v. Glenn W. Turner Enterprises, Inc., supra. In that case, the court announced that the critical inquiry is "whether the efforts made by those other than the investor are the undeniably significant ones, those essential managerial efforts which affect the failure or success of the enterprise." Id. at 482.

* * *

2. Application of the Test to the Instant Facts

Having concluded that the district court misperceived the controlling standard, it becomes incumbent upon us to determine whether Koscot's scheme falls with the standard adopted.

Our task is greatly simplified by the Ninth Circuit's decision in SEC v. Glenn W. Turner Enterprises, Inc., supra. The promotional scheme confronting the Ninth Circuit is largely paralleled by that exposed before this court. * * *

As in the Koscot scheme, the initial task of a purchaser of a Dare plan was to lure prospects to meetings, denominated Adventure Meetings. These were characterized by the same overzealous and emotionally charged atmosphere at which the illusion of affluence fostered in Opportunity Meetings was created and relied upon in securing sales. The Adventure Meetings were run according to script but, as the Ninth Circuit noted, "The Dare People, not the purchaser-'salesmen', run the meetings and do the selling." 474 F.2d at 479. * * *

The recruitment role played by investors in Koscot coincides with that played by investors in Dare to be Great. That investors in the latter did not participate in Adventure Meetings while they do in the Koscot scheme is insignificant. Since Koscot's Opportunity Meetings are run according to preordained script, the deviation from which would occasion disapprobation or perhaps exclusion from the meetings, the role of investors at these meetings can be characterized as little more than a perfunctory one. Nor does the fact that Koscot investors may have devoted more time than did Dare investors to closing sales transmute the essential congruity between the two schemes. The act of consummating a sale is essentially a ministerial not managerial one, * * * one which does not alter the fact that the critical determinant of the success of the Koscot Enterprise lies with the luring effect of the opportunity meetings. As was noted earlier, investors are cautioned to employ the "curiosity approach" in attracting prospects. Once attendance is secured, the sales format devised by Koscot is thrust upon the prospect. An investor's sole contribution in following the script is a nominal one. Without the scenario created by the Opportunity Meetings and Go-Tours, an investor would invariably be powerless to realize any return on his investment.

III

We confine our holding to those schemes in which promoters retain immediate control over the essential managerial conduct of an enterprise and where the investor's realization of profits is inextricably tied to the success of the promotional scheme. Thus, we acknowledge that a conventional franchise arrangement, wherein the promoter exercises merely remote control over an enterprise and the investor operates largely unfettered by promoter mandates presents a different question than the one posed herein. But the Koscot scheme does not qualify as a conventional franchising arrangement.

* * *

Accordingly, this cause is reversed and remanded for further proceedings consistent with this opinion.[a]

---

2. COOPERATIVE APARTMENTS

UNITED HOUSING FOUNDATION, INC. v. FORMAN

Supreme Court of the United States, 1975.
421 U.S. 837, 95 S.Ct. 2051, 44 L.Ed.2d 621.

MR. JUSTICE POWELL delivered the opinion of the Court.

The issue in these cases is whether shares of stock entitling a purchaser to lease an apartment in Co-op City, a state subsidized and supervised nonprofit housing cooperative, are "securities" within the purview of the Securities Act of 1933 and the Securities Exchange Act of 1934.

I

Co-op City is a massive housing cooperative in New York City. * * * The project was organized, financed, and constructed under the New York State Private Housing Finance Law. * * * In order to encourage private developers to build low-cost cooperative housing, New York provides them with large long-term, low-interest mortgage loans and substantial tax exemptions. Receipt of such benefits is conditioned on a willingness to have the State review virtually every step in the development of the cooperative. * * * The developer also must agree to operate the facility "on a nonprofit basis," * * * and he may lease apartments only to people whose incomes fall below a certain level and who have been approved by the State.

The United Housing Foundation (UHF), a nonprofit membership corporation established for the purpose of "aiding and encouraging" the creation of "adequate, safe and sanitary housing accommodations for wage earners and other persons of low or moderate income," * * * was responsible for initiating and sponsoring the development of Co-op City. Acting under [New York law], UHF organized the Riverbay Corporation (Riverbay) to own and operate the land and buildings constituting Co-op City. Riverbay, a nonprofit cooperative housing corporation, issued the stock that is the subject of this litigation. UHF also contracted with Community Services, Inc. (CSI), its wholly owned subsidiary, to serve as the general contractor and sales agent for the project. As required by [state legislation], these decisions were approved by the State Housing Commissioner.

---

a. Cf. SEC v. Aqua-Sonic Prods. Corp., 687 F.2d 577 (2d Cir. 1982), cert. denied 459 U.S. 1086 (1982) (typical franchises are not securities); Johnson & Campbell, Securities Law and the Franchise Agreement, 1980 Utah L.Rev. 311; Jacobs, The Meaning of "Security" Under Rule 10b–5, 29 N.Y.L. Sch. L.Rev. 211, 344–46 (1984). A number of states have adopted statutes regulating the sale of franchises. See Cal. Corps.Code § 31,000 et seq.; Marsh & Volk, Practice Under the California Securities Laws ch. 40 (1985).

To acquire an apartment in Co-op City an eligible prospective purchaser must buy 18 shares of stock in Riverbay for each room desired. The cost per share is $25, making the total cost $450 per room, or $1,800 for a four-room apartment. The sole purpose of acquiring these shares is to enable the purchaser to occupy an apartment in Co-op City; in effect, their purchase is a recoverable deposit on an apartment. The shares are explicitly tied to the apartment: they cannot be transferred to a nontenant; nor can they be pledged or encumbered; and they descend, along with the apartment, only to a surviving spouse. No voting rights attach to the shares as such: participation in the affairs of the cooperative appertains to the apartment, with the residents of each apartment being entitled to one vote irrespective of the number of shares owned.

Any tenant who wants to terminate his occupancy, or who is forced to move out, must offer his stock to Riverbay at its initial selling price of $25 per share. In the extremely unlikely event that Riverbay declines to repurchase the stock, the tenant cannot sell it for more than the initial purchase price plus a fraction of the portion of the mortgage that he has paid off, and then only to a prospective tenant satisfying the statutory income eligibility requirements. * * *

In May 1965, subsequent to the completion of the initial planning, Riverbay circulated an Information Bulletin seeking to attract tenants for what would someday be apartments in Co-op City. After describing the nature and advantages of cooperative housing generally and of Co-op City in particular, the Bulletin informed prospective tenants that the total estimated cost of the project, based largely on an anticipated construction contract with CSI, was $283,695,550. Only a fraction of this sum, $32,795,550, was to be raised by the sale of shares to tenants. The remaining $250,900,000 was to be financed by a 40-year low-interest mortgage loan from the New York Private Housing Finance Agency. After construction of the project the mortgage payments and current operating expenses would be met by monthly rental charges paid by the tenants. While these rental charges were to vary, depending on the size, nature, and location of an apartment, the 1965 Bulletin estimated that the "average" monthly cost would be $23.02 per room, or $92.08 for a four-room apartment.

Several times during the construction of Co-op City, Riverbay, with the approval of the State Housing Commissioner, revised its contract with CSI to allow for increased construction costs. In addition, Riverbay incurred other expenses that had not been reflected in the 1965 Bulletin. To meet these increased expenditures, Riverbay, with the Commissioner's approval, repeatedly secured increased mortgage loans from the State Housing Agency. Ultimately the construction loan was $125 million more than the figure estimated in the 1965 Bulletin. As a result, while the initial purchasing price remained at $450 per room, the average monthly rental charges increased periodically, reaching a figure of $39.68 per room as of July 1974.

These increases in the rental charges precipitated the present lawsuit. Respondents, 57 residents of Co-op City, sued in federal court on behalf of all 15,372 apartment owners, and derivatively on behalf of Riverbay, seeking upwards of $30 million in damages, forced rental reductions, and other "appropriate" relief. * * * The heart of respondents' claim was that the 1965 Co-op City Information Bulletin falsely represented that CSI would bear all subsequent cost increases due to factors such as inflation. Respondents further alleged that they were misled in their purchases of shares since the Information Bulletin failed to disclose several critical facts. On these bases, respondents asserted two claims under the fraud provisions of the federal Securities Act of 1933, as amended, § 17(a) * * * and the Securities Exchange Act of 1934, as amended, § 10(b), * * * and * * * 10b–5. * * *

Petitioners, while denying the substance of these allegations, moved to dismiss the complaint on the ground that federal jurisdiction was lacking. They maintained that shares of stock in Riverbay were not "securities" within the definitional sections of the federal Securities Acts. * * *

The District Court granted the motion to dismiss. * * *

The Court of Appeals for the Second Circuit reversed * * *.

In view of the importance of the issues presented we granted certiorari. * * * As we conclude that the disputed transactions are not purchases of securities within the contemplation of the federal statutes, we reverse.

II

Section 2(1) of the Securities Act of 1933 defines a "security" * * *. In providing this definition Congress did not attempt to articulate the relevant economic criteria for distinguishing "securities" from "non-securities." Rather, it sought to define "the term 'security' in sufficiently broad and general terms so as to include within that definition the many types of instruments that in our commercial world fall within the ordinary concept of a security." H.R.Rep.No.85, 73d Cong., 1st Sess., 11 (1933). The task has fallen to the Securities and Exchange Commission (SEC), the body charged with administering the Securities Acts, and ultimately to the federal courts to decide which of the myriad financial transactions in our society come within the coverage of these statutes.

In making this determination in the present case we do not write on a clean slate. Well-settled principles enunciated by this Court establish that the shares purchased by respondents do not represent any of the "countless and variable schemes devised by those who seek the use of the money of others on the promise of profits," Howey, 328 U.S., at 299, and therefore do not fall within "the ordinary concept of a security."

A

We reject at the outset any suggestion that the present transaction, evidenced by the sale of shares called "stock," must be considered a security transaction simply because the statutory definition of a security includes the words "any * * * stock." Rather we adhere to the basic principle that has guided all of the Court's decisions in this area:

"[I]n searching for the meaning and scope of the word 'security' in the Act[s], form should be disregarded for substance and the emphasis should be on economic reality." Tcherepnin v. Knight, 389 U.S. 332, 336 (1967).

See also Howey, supra, at 298.

The primary purpose of the Acts of 1933 and 1934 was to eliminate serious abuses in a largely unregulated securities market. The focus of the Acts is on the capital market of the enterprise system: the sale of securities to raise capital for profit-making purposes, the exchanges on which securities are traded, and the need for regulation to prevent fraud and to protect the interest of investors. Because securities transactions are economic in character Congress intended the application of these statutes to turn on the economic realities underlying a transaction, and not on the name appended thereto. Thus, in construing these Acts against the background of their purpose, we are guided by a traditional canon of statutory construction:

"[A] thing may be within the letter of the statute and yet not within the statute, because not within its spirit, nor within the intention of its makers." Church of the Holy Trinity v. United States, 143 U.S. 457, 459 (1892).

* * *

Respondents' reliance on *Joiner* [Securities and Exchange Commission v. C. M. Joiner Leasing Corporation, 320 U.S. 344 (1943)] as support for a "literal approach" to defining a security is misplaced. The issue in *Joiner* was whether assignments of interests in oil leases, coupled with the promoters' offer to drill an exploratory well, were securities. Looking to the economic inducement provided by the proposed exploratory well, the Court concluded that these leases were securities even though "leases" as such were not included in the list of instruments mentioned in the statutory definition. In dictum the Court noted that "[i]nstruments *may* be included within [the definition of a security], as [a matter of law, if on their face they answer to the name or description." 320 U.S., at 351 (emphasis supplied). And later, again in dictum, the Court stated that a security "*might*" be shown "by proving the document itself, which on its face would be a note, a bond, or a share of stock." Id., at 355 (emphasis supplied). By using the conditional words "may" and "might" in these dicta the Court made clear that it was not establishing an inflexible rule barring inquiry into the economic realities underlying a transaction. On the contrary, the Court intended only to make the rather obvious point that, in contrast to the instrument before it which was not included within the explicit statutory terms, most instruments bearing these traditional titles are likely to be covered by the statutes.

In holding that the name given to an instrument is not dispositive, we do not suggest that the name is wholly irrelevant to the decision whether it is a security. There may be occasions when the use of a traditional name such as "stocks" or "bonds" will lead a purchaser justifiably to assume that the federal securities laws apply. This would clearly be the case when the underlying transaction embodies some of the significant characteristics typically associated with the named instrument.

In the present case respondents do not contend, nor could they, that they were misled by use of the word "stock" into believing that the federal securities laws governed their purchase. Common sense suggests that people who intend to acquire only a residential apartment in a state-subsidized cooperative, for their personal use, are not likely to believe that in reality they are purchasing investment securities simply because the transaction is evidenced by something called a share of stock. These shares have none of the characteristics "that in our commercial world fall within the ordinary concept of a security." H.R.Rep.No.85, supra, at 11.

Despite their name, they lack what the Court in *Tcherepnin* deemed the most common feature of stock: the right to receive "dividends contingent upon an apportionment of profits." 389 U.S., at 339. Nor do they possess the other characteristics traditionally associated with stock: they are not negotiable; they cannot be pledged or hypothecated; they confer no voting rights in proportion to the number of shares owned; and they cannot appreciate in value. In short, the inducement to purchase was solely to acquire subsidized low-cost living space; it was not to invest for profit.

B

The Court of Appeals, as an alternative ground for its decision, concluded that a share in Riverbay was also an "investment contract" as defined by the Securities Acts. Respondents further argue that in any event what they agreed to purchase is "commonly known as a 'security'" within the meaning of these laws. In considering these claims we again must examine the substance—the economic realities of the transaction—rather than the names that may have been employed by the parties. We perceive no distinction, for present purposes, between an "investment contract" and an "instrument commonly known as a 'security.'" In either case, the basic test for distinguishing the transaction from other commercial dealings is

"whether the scheme involves an investment of money in a common enterprise with profits to come solely from the efforts of others." *Howey*, 328 U.S., at 301.[16]

This test, in shorthand form, embodies the essential attributes that run through all of the Court's decisions defining a security. The touchstone is the presence of an investment in a common venture premised on a reasonable expectation of profits to be derived from the entrepreneurial or managerial efforts of others. By profits, the Court has meant either capital appreciation resulting from the development of the initial investment, as in *Joiner*, supra (sale of oil leases conditioned on promoters' agreement to drill exploratory well), or a participation in earnings resulting from the use of investors' funds, as in Tcherepnin v. Knight, supra (dividends on the investment based on savings and loan association's profits). In such cases the investor is "attracted solely by the prospects of a return" on his investment. *Howey*, supra, at 300. By contrast, when a purchaser is motivated by a desire to use or consume the item purchased—"to occupy the land or to develop it themselves," as the *Howey* Court put it, ibid.—the securities laws do not apply. See also *Joiner*, supra.

In the present case there can be no doubt that investors were attracted solely by the prospect of acquiring a place to live, and not by financial returns on their investments. The Information Bulletin distributed to prospective residents emphasized the fundamental nature and purpose of the undertaking * * *.

---

16. This test speaks in terms of "profits to come *solely* from the efforts of others." (Emphasis supplied.) Although the issue is not presented in this case, we note that the Court of Appeals for the Ninth Circuit has held that "the word 'solely' should not be read as a strict or literal limitation on the definition of an investment contract, but rather must be construed realistically, so as to include within the definition those schemes which involve in substance, if not form, securities." SEC v. Glenn W. Turner Enterprises, 474 F.2d 476, 482, cert. denied, 414 U.S. 821 (1973). We express no view, however, as to the holding of this case.

Nowhere does the Bulletin seek to attract investors by the prospect of profits resulting from the efforts of the promoters or third parties. On the contrary, the Bulletin repeatedly emphasizes the "non-profit" nature of the endeavor. It explains that if rental charges exceed expenses the difference will be returned as a rebate, not invested for profit. It also informs purchasers that they will be unable to resell their apartments at a profit since the apartment must first be offered back to Riverbay "at the price * * * paid for it." Id., at 163a. In short, neither of the kinds of profits traditionally associated with securities was offered to respondents.

* * *

There is no doubt that purchasers in this housing cooperative sought to obtain a decent home at an attractive price. But that type of economic interest characterizes every form of commercial dealing. What distinguishes a security transaction—and what is absent here—is an investment where one parts with his money in the hope of receiving profits from the efforts of others, and not where he purchases a commodity for personal consumption or living quarters for personal use.

* * *

Since respondents' claims are not cognizable in federal court, the District Court properly dismissed their complaint. The judgment below is therefore

Reversed.

3. CONDOMINIUMS AND REAL ESTATE DEVELOPMENTS

SECURITIES ACT RELEASE NO. 5347

Securities and Exchange Commission.
January 4, 1973.

GUIDELINES AS TO THE APPLICABILITY OF THE FEDERAL SECURITIES LAWS TO OFFERS AND SALES OF CONDOMINIUMS OR UNITS IN A REAL ESTATE DEVELOPMENT

The Securities and Exchange Commission today called attention to the applicability of the federal securities laws to the offer and sale of condominium units, or other units in a real estate development, coupled with an offer or agreement to perform or arrange certain rental or other services for the purchaser. The Commission noted that such offerings may involve the offering of a security in the form of an investment contract or a participation in a profit sharing arrangement within the meaning of the Securities Act of 1933 and the Securities Exchange Act of 1934.[1] Where this is the case any offering of any such securities must comply with the registration and prospectus delivery requirements of the Securities Act, unless an exemption therefrom is available, and must comply with the anti-fraud provisions of the Securities Act and the Securities Exchange Act and the regulations thereunder. In addition, persons engaged in the business of buying or selling investment contracts or participations in profit sharing agreements of this type as agents for others, or as principal for their own account, may be brokers or dealers within the meaning of the Securities

---

1. It should be noted that where an investment contract is present, it consists of the agreement offered and the condominium itself.

Exchange Act, and therefore may be required to be registered as such with the Commission under the provisions of Section 15 of that Act.

The Commission is aware that there is uncertainty about when offerings of condominiums and other types of similar units may be considered to be offerings of securities that should be registered pursuant to the Securities Act. The purpose of this release is to alert persons engaged in the business of building and selling condominiums and similar types of real estate developments to their responsibilities under the Securities Act and to provide guidelines for a determination of when an offering of condominiums or other units may be viewed as an offering of securities. Resort condominiums are one of the more common interests in real estate the offer of which may involve an offering of securities. However, other types of units that are part of a development or project present analogous questions under the federal securities laws. Although this release speaks in terms of condominiums, it applies to offerings of all types of units in real estate developments which have characteristics similar to those described herein.

The offer of real estate as such, without any collateral arrangements with the seller or others, does not involve the offer of a security. When the real estate is offered in conjunction with certain services, a security, in the form of an investment contract, may be present. The Supreme Court in Securities and Exchange Commission v. W. J. Howey Co., 328 U.S. 293 (1946) set forth what has become a generally accepted definition of an investment contract * * *.

The *Howey* case involved the sale and operation of orange groves. The reasoning, however, is applicable to condominiums.

* * *

The existence of various kinds of collateral arrangements may cause an offering of condominium units to involve an offering of investment contracts or interests in a profit sharing agreement. The presence of such arrangements indicates that the offeror is offering an opportunity through which the purchaser may earn a return on his investment through the managerial efforts of the promoters or a third party in their operation of the enterprise.

* * *

In any situation where collateral arrangements are coupled with the offering of condominiums, whether or not specifically of the types discussed above, the manner of offering and economic inducements held out to the prospective purchaser play an important role in determining whether the offerings involve securities. * * *

In summary, the offering of condominium units in conjunction with any one of the following will cause the offering to be viewed as an offering of securities in the form of investment contracts:

1. The condominiums, with any rental arrangement or other similar service, are offered and sold with emphasis on the economic benefits to the purchaser to be derived from the managerial efforts of the promoter, or a third party designated or arranged for by the promoter, from rental of the units.

2. The offering of participation in a rental pool arrangement; and

3. The offering of a rental or similar arrangement whereby the purchaser must hold his unit available for rental for any part of the year, must use an exclusive rental agent or is otherwise materially restricted in his occupancy or rental of his unit.

In all of the above situations, investor protection requires the application of the federal securities laws.

If the condominiums are not offered and sold with emphasis on the economic benefits to the purchaser to be derived from the managerial efforts of others, and assuming that no plan to avoid the registration requirements of the Securities Act is involved, an owner of a condominium unit may, after purchasing his unit, enter into a non-pooled rental arrangement with an agent not designated or required to be used as a condition to the purchase, whether or not such agent is affiliated with the offeror, without causing a sale of a security to be involved in the sale of the unit. Further a continuing affiliation between the developers or promoters of a project and the project by reason of maintenance arrangements does not make the unit a security.

In situations where commercial facilities are a part of the common elements of a residential project, no registration would be required under the investment contract theory where (a) the income from such facilities is used only to offset common area expenses and (b) the operation of such facilities is incidental to the project as a whole and are not established as a primary income source for the individual owners of a condominium or cooperative unit.

The Commission recognizes the need for a degree of certainty in the real estate offering area and believes that the above guidelines will be helpful in assisting persons to comply with the securities laws. It is difficult, however, to anticipate the variety of arrangements that may accompany the offering of condominium projects. The Commission, therefore, would like to remind those engaged in the offering of condominiums or other interests in real estate with similar features that there may be situations, not referred to in this release, in which the offering of the interests constitutes an offering of securities. Whether an offering of securities is involved necessarily depends on the facts and circumstances of each particular case. The staff of the Commission will be available to respond to written inquiries on such matters.[a]

* * *

---

a. Hildebrandt, Real Estate Investments as Securities, 17 Rev. of Sec. Reg. 831 (1984); Id., Regulation of Real Estate Securities, 17 Rev. of Sec. Reg. 825 (1984); Note, Regulating Vacation Timesharing: A More Effective Approach, 29 UCLA L.Rev. 907 (1982); Jacobs, The Meaning of "Security" Under Rule 10b–5, 29 N.Y.L. Sch.L. Rev. 211, 338–44 (1984).

4. EMPLOYEE PENSION PLANS

INTERNATIONAL BROTHERHOOD OF TEAMSTERS, CHAUFFEURS, WAREHOUSEMEN AND HELPERS OF AMERICA v. DANIEL

Supreme Court of the United States, 1979.
439 U.S. 551, 99 S.Ct. 790, 58 L.Ed.2d 808.

MR. JUSTICE POWELL delivered the opinion of the Court.

This case presents the question whether a noncontributory, compulsory pension plan constitutes a "security" within the meaning of the Securities Act of 1933 and the Securities Exchange Act of 1934 (Securities Acts).

I

In 1954 multiemployer collective bargaining between Local 705 of the International Brotherhood of Teamsters, Chauffeurs, Warehousemen, and Helpers of American and Chicago trucking firms produced a pension plan for employees represented by the Local. The plan was compulsory and noncontributory. Employees had no choice as to participation in the plan, and did not have the option of demanding that the employer's contribution be paid directly to them as a substitute for pension eligibility. The employees paid nothing to the plan themselves.

The collective-bargaining agreement initially set employer contributions to the Pension Trust Fund at $2 a week for each man-week of covered employment. The Board of Trustees of the Fund, a body composed of an equal number of employer and union representatives, was given sole authority to set the level of benefits but had no control over the amount of required employer contributions. Initially, eligible employees received $75 a month in benefits upon retirement. Subsequent collective-bargaining agreements called for greater employer contributions, which in turn led to higher benefit payments for retirees. At the time respondent brought suit, employers contributed $21.50 per employee man-week and pension payments ranged from $425 to $525 a month depending on age at retirement.[3] In order to receive a pension an employee was required to have 20 years of continuous service, including time worked before the start of the plan.

The meaning of "continuous service" is at the center of this dispute. Respondent began working as a truck driver in the Chicago area in 1950, and joined Local 705 the following year. When the plan first went into effect, respondent automatically received 5 years credit toward the 20-year service requirement because of his earlier work experience. He retired in 1973 and applied to the plan's administrator for a pension. The administrator determined that respondent was ineligible because of a break in service between December 1960, and July 1961.[4] Respondent appealed the decision to the trustees, who affirmed. Respondent then asked the trustees

3. Because the Fund made the same payments to each employee who qualified for a pension and retired at the same age, rather than establishing an individual account for each employee tied to the amount of employer contributions attributable to his period of service, the plan provided a "defined benefit." * * *

4. Respondent was laid off from December 1960, until April, 1961. In addition, no contributions were paid on his behalf between April and July 1961, because of embezzlement by his employer's bookkeeper. During this seven-month period respondent could have preserved his eligibility by

to waive the continuous service rule as it applied to him. After the trustees refused to waive the rule, respondent brought suit in federal court against the International Union (Teamsters), Local 705 (Local), and Louis Peick, a trustee of the fund.

Respondent's complaint alleged that the Teamsters, the Local, and Peick misrepresented and omitted to state material facts with respect to the value of a covered employee's interest in the pension plan. Count I of the complaint charged that these misstatements and omissions constituted a fraud in connection with the sale of a security in violation of § 10(b) of the Securities Exchange Act of 1934, and the Securities and Exchange Commission's Rule 10b-5. Count II charged that the same conduct amounted to a violation of § 17(a) of the Securities Act of 1933. * * * Respondent sought to proceed on behalf of all prospective beneficiaries of Teamsters pension plans and against all Teamsters pension funds.

The petitioners moved to dismiss the first two counts of the complaint on the ground that respondent had no cause of action under the Securities or Securities Exchange Acts. The District Court denied the motion. * * * It held that respondent's interest in the Pension Fund constituted a security within the meaning of § 2(1) of the Securities Act and § 3(a)(10) of the Securities Exchange Act because the plan created an "investment contract" as that term had been interpreted in SEC v. W.J. Howey Co. * * *. It also determined that there had been a "sale" of this interest to respondent within the meaning of § 2(3) of the Securities Act and § 3(a)(14) of the Securities Exchange Act. It believed respondent voluntarily gave value for his interest in the plan, because he had voted on collective-bargaining agreements that chose employer contributions to the Fund instead of other wages or benefits.

[T]he Court of Appeals for the Seventh Circuit affirmed. * * * We granted certiorari and now reverse.

II

"The starting point in every case involving the construction of a statute is the language itself." Blue Chip Stamps v. Manor Drug Stores, 421 U.S. 723, 756 (1975) (Powell, J., concurring); * * *. In spite of the substantial use of employee pension plans at the time they were enacted, neither § 2(1) of the Securities Act nor § 3(a)(10) of the Securities Exchange Act, which define the term "security" in considerable detail and with numerous examples, refers to pension plans of any type. Acknowledging this omission in the statutes, respondent contends that an employee's interest in a pension plan is an "investment contract," an instrument which is included in the statutory definitions of a security.

To determine whether a particular financial relationship constitutes an investment contract, "[t]he test is whether the scheme involves an investment of money in a common enterprise with profits to come solely from the efforts of others." Howey, supra, * * *. This test is to be applied in light of "the substance—the economic realities of the transaction—rather than the names that may have been employed by the parties." United Housing Foundation, Inc. v. Forman, 421 U.S. 837, 851–852 (1975). * * * Looking separately at each element of the Howey test, it is apparent that an

making the contributions himself, but he
failed to do so.

employee's participation in a noncontributory, compulsory pension plan such as the Teamsters' does not comport with the commonly held understanding of an investment contract.

A. Investment of Money

An employee who participates in a noncontributory, compulsory pension plan by definition makes no payment into the pension fund. He only accepts employment, one of the conditions of which is eligibility for a possible benefit on retirement. Respondent contends, however, that he has "invested" in the Pension Fund by permitting part of his compensation from his employer to take the form of a deferred pension benefit. By allowing his employer to pay money into the Fund, and by contributing his labor to his employer in return for these payments, Respondent asserts he has made the kind of investment which the Securities Acts were intended to regulate.

In order to determine whether respondent invested in the Fund by accepting and remaining in covered employment, it is necessary to look at the entire transaction through which he obtained a chance to receive pension benefits. In every decision of this Court recognizing the presence of a "security" under the Securities Acts, the person found to have been an investor chose to give up a specific consideration in return for a separable financial interest with the characteristics of a security. See * * * *Howey,* supra (money paid for purchase, maintenance, and harvesting of orange grove); SEC v. C.M. Joiner Leasing Corp., 320 U.S. 344 (1943) (money paid for land and oil exploration). * * * In every case the purchaser gave up some tangible and definable consideration in return for an interest that had substantially the characteristics of a security.

In a pension plan such as this one, by contrast, the purported investment is a relatively insignificant part of an employee's total and indivisible compensation package. No portion of an employee's compensation other than the potential pension benefits has any of the characteristics of a security, yet these noninvestment interests cannot be segregated from the possible pension benefits. Only in the most abstract sense may it be said that an employee "exchanges" some portion of his labor in return for these possible benefits.[12] He surrenders his labor as a whole, and in return receives a compensation package that is substantially devoid of aspects resembling a security. His decision to accept and retain covered employment may have only an attenuated relationship, if any, to perceived investment possibilities of a future pension. Looking at the economic realities, it seems clear that an employee is selling his labor primarily to obtain a livelihood, not making an investment.

Respondent also argues that employer contributions on his behalf constituted his investment into the Fund. But it is inaccurate to describe these payments as having been "on behalf" of any employee. The trust agreement used employee man-weeks as a convenient way to measure an employer's overall obligation to the Fund, not as a means of measuring the employer's obligation to any particular employee. Indeed, there was no fixed relationship between contributions to the Fund and an employee's

---

12. This is not to say that a person's "investment," in order to meet the definition of an investment contract, must take the form of cash only rather than of goods and services. See *Forman,* supra, 421 U.S., at 852 n. 16.

potential benefits. A pension plan with "defined benefits," such as the Local's, does not tie a qualifying employee's benefits to the time he has worked. * * * One who has engaged in covered employment for 20 years will receive the same benefits as a person who has worked for 40, even though the latter has worked twice as long and induced a substantially larger employer contribution. Again, it ignores the economic realities to equate employer contributions with an investment by the employee.

B. *Expectation of Profits From A Common Enterprise*

As we observed in *Forman,* the "touchstone" of the *Howey* test "is the presence of an investment in a common venture premised on a reasonable expectation of profits to be derived from the entrepreneurial or managerial efforts of others." 421 U.S., at 852. The Court of Appeals believed that Daniel's expectation of profit derived from the Fund's successful management and investment of its assets. To the extent pension benefits exceeded employer contributions and depended on earnings from the assets, it was thought they contained a profit element. The Fund's trustees provided the managerial efforts which produced this profit element.

As in other parts of its analysis, the court below found an expectation of profit in the pension plan only by focusing on one of its less important aspects to the exclusion of its more significant elements. It is true that the Fund, like other holders of large assets, depends to some extent on earnings from its assets. In the case of a pension fund, however, a far larger portion of its income comes from employer contributions, a source in no way dependent on the efforts of the Fund's managers. The Local 705 Fund, for example, earned a total of $31 million through investment of its assets between February 1955, and January 1977. During this same period employer contributions totaled $153 million. Not only does the greater share of a pension plan's income ordinarily come from new contributions, but unlike most entrepreneurs who manage other people's money, a plan usually can count on increased employer contributions, over which the plan itself has no control, to cover shortfalls in earnings.

The importance of asset earnings in relation to the other benefits received from employment is diminished further by the fact that where a plan has substantial preconditions to vesting, the principal barrier to an individual employee's realization of pension benefits is not the financial health of the Fund. Rather, it is his own ability to meet the Fund's eligibility requirements. Thus, even if it were proper to describe the benefits as a "profit" returned on some hypothetical investment by the employee, this profit would depend primarily on the employee's efforts to meet the vesting requirements, rather than the Fund's investment success. When viewed in light of the total compensation package an employee must receive in order to be eligible for pension benefits, it becomes clear that the possibility of participating in a plan's asset earnings "is far too speculative and insubstantial to bring the entire transaction within the Securities Acts," *Forman,* supra, at 856.

III

The court below believed that its construction of the term "security" was compelled not only by the perceived resemblance of a pension plan to an investment contract, but by various actions of Congress and the SEC with regard to the Securities Acts. In reaching this conclusion, the court gave great weight to the SEC's explanation of these events, an explanation which for the most part the SEC repeats here. Our own review of the record leads us to believe that this reliance on the SEC's interpretation of these legislative and administrative actions was not justified.

A. Actions of Congress

The SEC in its *amicus curiae* brief refers to several actions of Congress said to evidence an understanding that pension plans are securities. A close look at each instance, however, reveals only that Congress might have believed certain kinds of pension plans, radically different from the one at issue here, came within the coverage of the Securities Acts. There is no evidence that Congress at any time thought noncontributory plans similar to the one before us were subject to federal regulation as securities.

The first action cited was the rejection by Congress in 1934 of an amendment to the Securities Act that would have exempted employee stock investment and stock option plans from the Act's registration requirements. The amendment passed the Senate but was eliminated in conference. The legislative history of the defeated proposal indicates it was intended to cover plans under which employees contributed their own funds to a segregated investment account on which a return was realized. * * * In rejecting the amendment, Congress revealed a concern that certain interests having the characteristics of a security not be excluded from Securities Act protection simply because investors realized their return in the form of retirement benefits. At no time however, did Congress indicate that pension benefits in and of themselves gave a transaction the characteristics of a security.

The SEC also relies on a 1970 amendment of the Securities Act which extended § 3's exemption from registration to include "any interest or participation in a single or collective trust fund maintained by a bank * * * which interest or participation is issued in connection with (A) a stock bonus, pension, or profit-sharing plan which meets the requirements for qualification under section 401 of Title 26, * * *" § 3(a)(2) of the Securities Act, as amended. It argues that in creating a registration exemption, the amendment manifested Congress' understanding that the interests covered by the amendment otherwise were subject to the Securities Acts. It interprets "interest or participation in a single * * * trust fund * * * issued in connection with * * * a stock bonus, pension, or profit-sharing plan" as referring to a prospective beneficiary's interest in a pension fund. But this construction of the 1970 amendment ignores that measure's central purpose, which was to relieve banks and insurance companies of certain registration obligations. The amendment recognized only that a pension plan had "an interest or participation" in the fund in which its assets were held, not that prospective beneficiaries of a plan had any interest in either the plan's bank-maintained assets or the plan itself.

B. SEC Interpretation

The court below believed, and it now is argued to us, that almost from its inception the SEC has regarded pension plans as falling within the scope of the Securities Acts. We are asked to defer to what is seen as a longstanding interpretation of these statutes by the agency responsible for their administration. But there are limits, grounded in the language, purpose and history of the particular statute, on how far an agency properly may go in its interpretative role. Although these limits are not always easy to discern, it is clear here that the SEC's position is neither longstanding nor even arguably within the outer limits of its authority to interpret these Acts.[20]

As we have demonstrated above, the type of pension plan at issue in this case bears no resemblance to the kind of financial interests the Securities Acts were designed to regulate. Further, the SEC's present position is flatly contradicted by its past actions. Until the instant litigation arose, the public record reveals no evidence that the SEC had ever considered the Securities Acts to be applicable to noncontributory pension plans. In 1941, the SEC first articulated the position that voluntary, contributory plans had investment characteristics that rendered them "securities" under the Acts. At the same time, however, the SEC recognized that noncontributory plans were not covered by the Securities Acts because such plans did not involve a "sale" within the meaning of the statutes. * * *

In an attempt to reconcile these interpretations of the Securities Acts with its present stand, the SEC now augments its past position with two additional propositions. First, it is argued, noncontributory plans are "securities" even where a "sale" is not involved. Second, the previous concession that noncontributory plans do not involve a "sale" was meant to apply only to the registration and reporting requirements of the Securities Acts; for purposes of the antifraud provisions, a "sale" is involved. As for the first proposition, we observe that none of the SEC opinions, reports, or testimony cited to us address the question. As for the second, the record is unambiguously to the contrary. Both in its 1941 statements and repeatedly since then, the SEC has declared that its "no sale" position applied to the Securities Acts as a whole. * * * Congress acted on this understanding when it proceeded to develop the legislation that became ERISA. * * * As far as we are aware, at no time before this case arose did the SEC intimate that the antifraud provisions of the Securities Acts nevertheless applied to noncontributory pension plans.

IV

If any further evidence were needed to demonstrate that pension plans of the type involved are not subject to the Securities Acts, the enactment of ERISA in 1974 would put the matter to rest. Unlike the Securities Acts, ERISA deals expressly and in detail with pension plans. ERISA requires pension plans to disclose specified information to employees in a specified manner, * * * in contrast to the indefinite and uncertain disclosure obligations imposed by the antifraud provisions of the Securities Acts * * *. Further, ERISA regulates the substantive terms of pension plans,

20. It is commonplace in our jurisprudence that an administrative agency's consistent, longstanding interpretation of the statute under which it operates is entitled to considerable weight. This deference is a product both of an awareness of the practical expertise which an agency normally develops, and of a willingness to accord some measure of flexibility to such an agency as it encounters new and unforeseen problems over time. But this deference is constrained by our obligation to honor the clear meaning of a statute, as revealed by its language, purpose and history. On a number of occasions in recent years this Court has found it necessary to reject the SEC's interpretation of various provisions of the Securities Acts. [Citations omitted.]

setting standards for plan funding and limits on the eligibility requirements an employee must meet. For example, with respect to the underlying issue in this case—whether respondent served long enough to receive a pension—§ 203(a) of ERISA now sets the minimum level of benefits an employee must receive after accruing specified years of service, and § 203(b) governs continuous service requirements. Thus if Daniel had retired after § 1053 took effect, the Fund would have been required to pay him at least a partial pension. The Securities Acts, on the other hand, do not purport to set the substantive terms of financial transactions.

The existence of this comprehensive legislation governing the use and terms of employee pension plans severely undercuts all arguments for extending the Securities Acts to noncontributory, compulsory pension plans. Congress believed that it was filling a regulatory void when it enacted ERISA, a belief which the SEC actively encouraged. Not only is the extension of the Securities Acts by the court below unsupported by the language and history of those Acts, but in light of ERISA it serves no general purpose. * * * Whatever benefits employees might derive from the effect of the Securities Acts are now provided in more definite form through ERISA.

V

We hold that the Securities Acts do not apply to a noncontributory, compulsory pension plan. Because the first two counts of respondent's complaint do not provide grounds for relief in federal court, the District Court should have granted the motion to dismiss them. The judgment below is therefore

    Reversed.ª

    * * *

B. NOTES

THE EXCHANGE NATIONAL BANK OF CHICAGO v. TOUCHE ROSS & CO.

United States Court of Appeals, Second Circuit, 1976.
544 F.2d 1126.

Before FRIENDLY, MANSFIELD and MULLIGAN, CIRCUIT JUDGES.

FRIENDLY, CIRCUIT JUDGE:

This appeal raises the vexing question how far instruments bearing the form of promissory notes are securities within the anti-fraud provisions of the Securities Act of 1933 and the Securities Exchange Act of 1934. * * *

This action by The Exchange National Bank of Chicago (the Bank) [was brought] against the well-known accounting firm of Touche, Ross & Company (Touche) * * *. The complaint was in four counts. Count I alleged violation of § 17(a) of the Securities Act of 1933, § 10(b) of the Securities Exchange Act of 1934, and the SEC's Rule 10b–5 * * *.

---

    a. See Tomlinson, Section 3(a)(2) of the Securities Act After *Daniel,* 5 Del.J. of Corp.L. 391 (1980).

The transactions were between the Bank and a New York brokerage firm, Weis, Voisin & Co., Inc., later Weis Securities, Inc. (Weis), which was a member of the New York Stock Exchange (NYSE) and the American Stock Exchange. These transactions were the Bank's purchase from Weis of three unsecured subordinated notes dated July 31, 1972, in the aggregate principal amount of $1 million. The conduct was Touche's issuance on July 7, 1972, of opinions saying, among other things, that Weis' Statement of Financial Condition as of May 26, 1972 (the "Statement") and Weis' "Answers to Financial Questionnaire and Additional Information" (the Report), which Weis filed with the SEC pursuant to § 17 of the Securities Exchange Act, fairly presented the financial position of Weis and conformed to generally accepted accounting principles. The Bank alleged that it had relied on these opinions as well as the Statement and the Report, and that the latter were materially false and misleading in numerous respects as Touche knew or should have known when it issued its opinions; that when the false and misleading entries were discovered in May, 1973, Weis had already been placed in receivership and was then being liquidated; and that the notes have become worthless.

Touche moved to dismiss the complaint. * * * A memorandum accompanying the moving affidavit discussed the issue of the status of the notes. Entitled "Promissory Note," with the amount and the date, July 31, 1972, at the top, each note extended over nearly nine typewritten pages. The three notes were payable on July 31, 1973, October 31, 1973, and January 31, 1974, respectively, "upon written demand received by the Company at least six (6) months prior to such date, or upon such date thereafter as may be specified by the Lender upon written demand received by the Company at least six months prior to the payment date so specified." Interest was payable after each note's maturity date, at a rate "3% in excess of the prime commercial loan rate of the Lender then in effect for short-term borrowings, but in no event less than 9% per annum." The rights of the holder were subject and subordinate to all general creditors but were senior to all other subordinated creditors except existing obligations to Fidelity Corporation and Security National Bank. The note was prepayable on three days' written notice from the Company with the prior written approval of NYSE. * * *

As indicated, several provisions of the notes were keyed to NYSE's Rule 325, entitled "Capital Requirements for Member Organizations and Individual Members." A basic proviso of this Rule was that no member "shall permit, in the ordinary course of business as a broker, his or its Aggregate Indebtedness to exceed 2000 per centum of his or its Net Capital. * * * " "Aggregate Indebtedness" was defined to exclude, inter alia, "liabilities subordinated to general creditors pursuant to a separate agreement approved by the Exchange." Consistent with this, subordinated indebtedness appeared in Weis' balance sheet along with stockholder equity rather than as a current liability.

* * *

In the spring of 1972 Lippe was Executive Vice President and Chief Administrative Officer of the Bank and was particularly concerned with expanding the Bank's business; he was not part of the staff which handled normal commercial loans. Early in March, 1972, he was notified by the manager of the Bank's recently opened branch office in Tel Aviv, Israel, that Weis had sought approximately $1 million for the expansion of its brokerage activities both in the United States and abroad. Because the Bank was interested in developing a closer relationship between its new Tel Aviv branch and that of Weis, the only American brokerage firm then operating in Israel, and the interest rate proposed by Weis was attractive, Lippe instructed the branch manager that the Bank might be interested.

Shortly thereafter Arthur T. Levine, Weis' Chief Executive Officer, and Sol Leit, its Chief Operating Officer, came to Chicago to negotiate with Lippe. Lippe continued to be interested because of the potential for the Bank's Tel Aviv branch. Levine and Leit indicated that the Bank would be expected to purchase subordinated promissory notes, which would be listed as part of Weis' net capital pursuant to Rule 325; they presented a form of such a note which they said was in conformity with Rule 325. They also exhibited copies of the notes held by Security National Bank and Fidelity Corporation, * * *. Lippe requested the Weis representative to forward financial statements and any other documents certified by Touche; this led to the sending of the documents previously mentioned. On July 19, 1972, the Bank agreed to purchase for $890,750 three unsecured subordinated notes in the aggregate principal amount of $1 million and the transaction was consummated on August 7, 1972.

* * *

After hearing argument Judge Wyatt denied the motion to dismiss for want of subject matter jurisdiction "on the ground that the transaction seems more in the character of an investment than of a commercial loan." * * * [T]his court granted leave to appeal.

* * *

As we pointed out in Zeller v. Bogue Electric Manufacturing Corp., 476 F.2d 795, 799 (2 Cir.), cert. denied, 414 U.S. 908 (1973):

The Securities Act of 1933 and the Securities Exchange Act of 1934 differ in their method of handling short-term commercial paper. Under the 1933 Act, while § 2(1) provides that any note is a "security," § 3(a)(3) exempts from the registration and prospectus requirements "[a]ny note, draft, bill of exchange, or banker's acceptance which arises out of a current transaction or the proceeds of which have been or are to be used for current transactions, and which has a maturity at the time of issuance of not exceeding nine months, exclusive of days of grace, or any renewal thereof the maturity of which is likewise limited." However, § 17, the general anti-fraud provision, provides in subsection (c) that the exemptions of § 3 shall be inapplicable. Instead of following this model in the Securities Exchange Act, Congress defined "security," § 3(a)(10), to include "any note" but inserted in the same clause that this would not include "any note, draft, bill of exchange, or banker's acceptance which has a maturity at the time of issuance of not exceeding nine months, exclusive of days of grace, or any renewal thereof the maturity of which is likewise limited."

It should be added that the definition sections of both statutes, § 2 of the 1933 Act and § 3 of the 1934 Act, begin with the words:

When used in this title, unless the context otherwise requires—

* * *

Except for the prefatory language in § 2, the terms of the 1933 Act would thus have the result of subjecting to the anti-fraud provisions, in contrast to the registration requirements, any note, however short the term and however far the transaction was from being an investment security.

When the 1934 Act was passed there was no need for a special exemption of notes from registration, since the registration requirement was tied to transactions on a national stock exchange, § 12(a). If notes were to have special treatment beyond this, the place to accord this had therefore to be in the definition of a security. Apparently there was general agreement that something of this sort should be done. The backing and filling was on whether the exemption should contain the "current transaction" language of § 3(a)(3) of the 1933 Act; ultimately this was deleted. The author of the Chicago Law Review note seems correct in concluding:

> Since there is no legislative comment with respect to this deletion, it cannot be gainfully surmised whether the omission of the "current transactions" phrasing was an inadvertent mistake, an assumption on the part of the legislature that the clause was unnecessary, or a conscious attempt to distinguish section 3(a)(10) of the 1934 Act from section 3(a)(3) of the 1933 Act.

Except for the prefatory language in § 3 the letter of the 1934 Act would thus have the result that any note with a maturity in excess of nine months would be subject to the anti-fraud provisions whereas any note with a shorter maturity would be exempt from them.

As will be seen, courts have shrunk from a literal reading that would extend the reach of the statutes beyond what could reasonably be thought to have been intended in these two great pieces of legislation and would produce a seemingly irrational difference in the scope of their anti-fraud provisions. * * * See Comment, Commercial Notes and Definition of 'Security' under Securities Exchange Act of 1934: A Note is a Note is a Note?, 52 Nebraska L.Rev. 478, 487–88 (1973).

This court's first encounter with the problem whether notes were to be considered as securities within the 1934 Act came in Movielab, Inc. v. Berkey Photo, Inc., 452 F.2d 662 (2 Cir. 1971), * * *. There one publicly held company, the defendant Berkey, had sold assets to another, the plaintiff Movielab, allegedly through misrepresentations, for two 20-year installment 8% purchase notes, each in the amount of $5,250,000 and a shorter term note of $4,178,312. Movielab sought rescission and damages. Plainly these were not "commercial" loans. Berkey was not in the business of making these, and the transaction was not functionally different than if Movielab had issued 20-year debentures. After pointing out in somewhat of an understatement that the definition "includes some notes at the very least", this court thought there could hardly be a clearer case for inclusion than "notes issued by one publicly owned company to another publicly owned company for $10,500,000, payable over a period of 20 years, in exchange for the assets of the latter * * *."

Nevertheless, the Fifth Circuit's oft-cited dictum in Lehigh Valley Trust Co. v. Central Nat'l Bank of Jacksonville, 409 F.2d 989, 991–92 (1969), that the "definition of a security has been literally read by the judiciary to the extent that almost all notes are held to be securities," has been considerably eroded, in part by that court itself. * * *

The first blow by a court of appeals was struck in Lino v. City Investing Co., 487 F.2d 689 (3 Cir. 1973). Lino had acquired two Franchise Sales Center Licensing Agreements from Franchise International (FI), a wholly-owned subsidiary of City Investing. This purchase, for cash and promissory notes of a term unspecified in the opinion, was allegedly the result of FI's fraud. Reversing the district court, the court of appeals, after referring to the "unless the context otherwise requires" clause, said, 487 F.2d at 694–95:

The commercial context of this case requires a holding that the transaction did not involve a "purchase" of securities. These were personal promissory notes issued by a private party. There was no public offering of the notes, and the issuer was the person claiming to be defrauded. The notes were not procured for speculation or investment, and there is no indication that FI was soliciting venture capital from Lino.

* * *

* * * In C. N. S. Enterprises, Inc. v. G. & G. Enterprises, Inc., 508 F.2d 1354, cert. denied, 423 U.S. 825 (* * * 1975), the Seventh Circuit was confronted with the issue. * * * Judge Sprecher recognized the difficulties of "the commercial-investment" dichotomy, saying, 508 F.2d at 1359:

In one sense every lender of money is an investor since he places his money at risk in anticipation of a profit in the form of interest. Also in a broad sense every investor lends his money to a borrower who uses it for a price and is expected to return it one day. On the other hand, the polarized extremes are conceptually identifiable: buying shares of the common stock of a publicly-held corporation, where the impetus for the transaction comes from the person with the money, is an investment; borrowing money from a bank to finance the purchase of an automobile, where the impetus for the transaction comes from the person who needs the money, is a loan. In between is a gray area which, in the absence of further congressional indication of intent or Supreme Court construction, has been and must be in the future subjected to case-by-case treatment.

* * * The most recent court of appeals bank loan decision of which we are aware is Great Western Bank & Trust v. Kotz, 532 F.2d 1252 (9 Cir. 1976). The court held in a per curiam opinion that the note of a corporation given to a bank in exchange for a 10-month renewable line of credit was not a security within the meaning of the federal securities laws so as to sustain a suit by the bank against a controlling person for misrepresentations. In a concurring opinion * * *, Judge Eugene Wright seems to suggest that in any case where a bank receives a note in what purports to be an exercise of its lending function, the federal securities laws should not apply; * * * Judge Wright argues * * * [that] the commercial bank when negotiating a loan generally deals face-to-face with the promisor, "has a superior bargaining position and can compel wide-ranging disclosures and verification of issues material to its decision on the loan application. * * * [W]hile banks are subjected to risks of misinformation, their ability to verify representations and take supervisory and corrective actions places them in a significantly different posture than the investors sought to be protected through the securities acts."

What makes Judge Wright's approach rather appealing is that the efforts to provide meaningful criteria for decision under "the commercial-investment" dichotomy do not seem to us to carry much promise of success.

For example, we do not see much force in the test * * * "whether the funding party invested 'risk capital'." a On the one hand, the securities laws cover debt, even supposedly gilt-edged debt, as well as equity; on the other a $5,000 "character" six months' bank loan to enable an old customer to enter a new line of business would scarcely qualify as a "security" although it is surely risk capital. Frequent reference is made to the test laid down by the Supreme Court in SEC v. W. J. Howey Co. * * * in defining what constitutes an "investment contract," namely, "whether the scheme involves an investment of money in a common enterprise with profits to come solely from the efforts of others." Although the Court has recently said that this "embodies the essential attributes that run through all of the Court's decisions defining a security," United Housing Foundation, Inc. v. Forman, 421 U.S. 837, 852 (1975), the Court has not yet had the note problem before it, and the test seems to us to be of dubious value in that context. There was no "common enterprise" in *Movielab* unless a debt relationship suffices to create one; if it does, it would be hard to think of a situation where profits in the shape of interest are more dependent on the "efforts of others" than a bank's unsecured short-term personal loan to an individual, the very archetype of what the securities laws were not intended to cover. We see little relevance in a distinction between loans to an enterprise in formation and to one already established, especially if the former bear individual endorsements as they frequently do. While we could go on to develop the difficulties with other suggested "criteria" in the Nebraska Law Review comment, it suffices to observe that the authors themselves recognize that there is a good countervailing argument for nearly every one. Directing district courts to "weigh" a number of such dubious factors, without any instructions as to relative weights and with admonitions such as given by the *Great Western* per curiam, is scarcely helpful to hard-pressed district judges or to counsel. Adoption of Judge Wright's view thus would afford the hope of bringing a modicum of certainty into one large section of a field in bad need of it.

Despite this we do not find ourselves able to accept Judge Wright's suggestion that no note given to evidence a bank loan can be a "security." One reason is that * * * he seems to look at the matter solely, or at least principally, from the standpoint of a bank seeking to invoke the federal securities laws as a remedy supplementing those afforded by state laws. However, * * * often it is the borrower who asserts fraud by the lender. Judge Wright's arguments based on a bank's superior bargaining position and its special investigatory facilities would have little bearing in such a case; indeed the former would weigh in favor of holding the note to be a security. Yet we see nothing in the statutes that would justify holding that the same note was a security when a borrower from a bank invoked federal law and not a security when the bank asserted this. Even when it is the bank that invoked the federal securities laws, we would find it hard to reconcile with the statutory language a holding that where a bank or a group of banks loaned many millions of dollars to a corporation for periods

a. In Amfac Mortgage Corp. v. Arizona Mall of Tempe, Inc., 583 F.2d 426 (9th Cir. 1978), the Ninth Circuit again applied its "risk capital" test. The court stated: "Under this test the ultimate inquiry is whether [the lender] contributed 'risk capital' subject to the 'entrepreneurial or managerial efforts' of (others). * * * This approach encompasses the economic realities standard and the *Howey* test * * *." Id. at 432.

of several years, the anti-fraud provisions of the federal securities laws do not apply.   *   *   *

The foregoing discussion suggests to us that, taking full account of the anti-literalist approach of the *Forman* opinion, 421 U.S. at 848–51, the best alternative now available may lie in greater recourse to the statutory language. The 1934 Act says that the term "security" includes "any note * * * [excepting one] which has a maturity at the time of issuance of not exceeding nine months," and the 1933 Act says that the term means "any note" save for the registration exemption in § 3(a)(3). These are the plain terms of both acts, to be applied "unless the context otherwise requires." A party asserting that a note of more than nine months maturity is not within the 1934 Act (or that a note with a maturity of nine months or less is within it) or that any note is not within the anti-fraud provisions of the 1933 Act has the burden of showing that "the context otherwise *requires*." (Emphasis supplied.) One can readily think of many cases where it does—the note delivered in consumer financing, the note secured by a mortgage on a home, the short-term note secured by a lien on a small business or some of its assets, the note evidencing a "character" loan to a bank customer, short-term notes secured by an assignment of accounts receivable, or a note which simply formalizes an open-account debt incurred in the ordinary course of business (particularly if, as in the case of the customer of a broker, it is collateralized). When a note does not bear a strong family resemblance to these examples and has a maturity exceeding nine months, § 10(b) of the 1934 Act should generally be held to apply. We realize this approach does not afford complete certainty but it adheres more closely to the language of the statutes and it may be somewhat easier to apply than the weighing and balancing of recent decisions of sister circuits. A more desirable solution would be for Congress to change the exclusions to encompass "a note or other evidence of indebtedness issued in a mercantile transaction," as is proposed in the ALI's Federal Securities Code, § 297(b)(3), and complement this by a grant of power to the SEC to explicate the quoted phrase by rule much as § 216A of the ALI Code does with respect to the exemption for commercial paper, see also § 301(1). So long as the statutes remain as they have been for over forty years, courts had better not depart from their words without strong support for the conviction that, under the authority vested in them by the "context" clause, they are doing what Congress wanted when they refuse to do what it said.

If ours is the correct approach, affirmance is clearly demanded—as it doubtless also would be by the "commercial-investment" dichotomy, although not, we suppose, by Judge Wright's *Great Western* concurrence. The Weis transaction is at the opposite pole from the typical "mercantile" transactions we have mentioned. The "loan" was negotiated with the Bank's chief administrative officer, not with a lending officer. The form of the note was dictated not by the Bank but directly by the borrower and ultimately by NYSE. The notes themselves bore scant resemblance to the standard forms used in commercial lending. While the notes purported to mature at dates ranging from 12 to 18 months from issuance, collection at the stated dates or later depended on the lender's giving six months' written notice. More important of all were the subordinated character of the notes and the knowledge of both parties that the proceeds would be considered by NYSE as the equivalent of equity capital for the purpose of enabling Weis further to expand its business by borrowing sums that would permit it to extend more credit to major customers. Transferability of the notes was restricted to persons approved by NYSE and prepayment was prohibited without NYSE's consent. The notes reflected the Bank's foregoing of the usual and important rights to take as security any property of the borrower that came into its possession or to exercise a right of set-off. Finally, the Exchange National loan was no isolated transaction but a part of a large financing operation conducted by Weis' combining 19 lenders who held subordinated notes, debentures and cash agreements totalling $8,735,275, with another 24 lenders who had subordinated accounts or notes to which their accounts were subordinated. We find nothing in this "context" that would justify a failure to apply the statutory language and much that demands its application.

* * *

The order denying Touche's motion to dismiss on the ground that the notes were not "securities" within the federal securities laws is affirmed.[b]

* * *

In Chemical Bank v. Arthur Andersen & Co., 726 F.2d 930 (2d Cir.1984), the Second Circuit distinguished Exchange National Bank and held that notes evidencing loans by commercial banks for current operations were not "securities." Answering the contention that Exchange National Bank ran counter to the Supreme Court cases of *Forman,* supra at page 230 and Marine Bank v. Weaver, infra at page 256, Judge Friendly said: "[W]e do not regard *Exchange National Bank* as taking a 'literalist' or even a 'neo-literalist' approach. Its position was and is that the words of the statute are not to be disregarded, as some other approaches have done * * * but are to be given significance 'unless the context otherwise requires.' This is the same approach we have taken with respect to the 'sale of business' doctrine, where we have respectfully disagreed with the more freewheeling view of the Seventh Circuit in * * * Sutter v. Groen, 687 F.2d 197 (7th Cir.1982)." 726 F.2d at 938.

The most widely adopted test, however, is the "commercial/investment" test which has been adopted by the First, Third, Fifth, Seventh, Tenth and Eleventh Circuits. The "risk capital" test is espoused by the Sixth and Ninth Circuits and only the Second Circuit follows the more conservative "literal" approach. See Futura Development Corporation v. Centex Corporation, 761 F.2d 33 (1st Cir.1985) and SEC v. Diversified Industries, Inc., 465 F.Supp. 104 (D.D.C.1979) citing authorities.

In the Diversified Industries case, after reviewing the three approaches, Judge Richey concluded that "the Second Circuit's approach is most consistent with the language of the statute and Congressional intent and is by far the easiest test to apply." 465 F.Supp. at 110.

---

b. In Robertson v. White, 635 F.Supp. 851 (W.D.Ark.1986), demand notes through which some $10 million was raised from more than 1600 persons were held to be securities under the Arkansas Securities Act. The court expressed the view that a similar result would be reached under Federal law.

C. CERTIFICATES OF DEPOSIT

MARINE BANK v. WEAVER

Supreme Court of the United States, 1982.
455 U.S. 551, 102 S.Ct. 1220, 71 L.Ed.2d 409.

CHIEF JUSTICE BURGER delivered the opinion of the Court.

We granted certiorari to decide whether two instruments, a conventional certificate of deposit and a business agreement between two families, could be considered securities under the antifraud provisions of the federal securities laws.

I

Respondents, Sam and Alice Weaver, purchased a $50,000 certificate of deposit from petitioner, Marine Bank, on February 28, 1978. The certificate of deposit has a six year maturity and it is insured by the Federal Deposit Insurance Corporation.[1] The Weavers subsequently pledged the certificate of deposit to Marine Bank on March 17, 1978, to guarantee a $65,000 loan made by the Bank to Columbus Packing Company. Columbus was a wholesale slaughterhouse and retail meat market which owed the Bank $33,000 at that time for prior loans and was also substantially overdrawn on its checking account with the Bank.

In consideration for guaranteeing the Bank's new loan, Columbus' owners, Raymond and Barbara Piccirillo, entered into an agreement with the Weavers. Under the terms of the agreement, the Weavers were to receive 50% of Columbus' net profits and $100 per month as long as they guaranteed the loan. It was also agreed that the Weavers could use Columbus' barn and pasture at the discretion of the Piccirillos, and that they had the right to veto future borrowing by Columbus.

The Weavers allege that Bank officers told them Columbus would use the $65,000 loan as working capital but instead it was immediately applied to pay Columbus' overdue obligations. The Bank kept approximately $42,800 to satisfy its prior loans and Columbus' overdrawn checking account. All but $3,800 of the remainder was disbursed to pay overdue taxes and to satisfy other creditors; the Bank then refused to permit Columbus to overdraw its checking account. Columbus became bankrupt four months later. Although the Bank had not yet resorted to the Weavers' certificate of deposit at the time this litigation commenced, it acknowledged that its other security was inadequate and that it intended to claim the pledged certificate of deposit.

These allegations were asserted in a complaint * * * [asserting] that the Bank violated § 10(b) of the Securities Exchange Act of 1934. * * * The Weavers alleged that Bank officers actively solicited them to guarantee the $65,000 loan to Columbus while knowing, but not disclosing, Columbus' financial plight or the Bank's plans to repay itself from the new loan

---

1. The certificate of deposit pays 7½% interest and provides that, if the Bank permits early withdrawal, the depositor will earn interest at the Bank's current savings passbook rate on the amount withdrawn, except that no interest will be paid for the three months prior to withdrawal. When the Weavers purchased the certificate of deposit, it could only be insured up to $40,000 by the FDIC. The ceiling on insured deposits is now $100,000. * * *

guaranteed by the Weavers' pledged certificate of deposit. Had they known of Columbus' precarious financial condition and the Bank's plans, the Weavers allege they would not have guaranteed the loan and pledged the certificate of deposit. The District Court granted summary judgment in favor of the Bank. It concluded that if a wrong occurred it did not take place "in connection with the purchase or sale of any security," as required for liability under § 10(b). * * *

The Third Circuit Court of Appeals reversed. [It] held that a finder of fact could reasonably conclude that either the certificate of deposit or the agreement between the Weavers and the Piccirillos was a security. * * *

We granted certiorari, 452 U.S. 904 (1981), and we reverse. * * *

II

The definition of security in the Securities Exchange Act of 1934 is quite broad. The Act was adopted to restore investors' confidence in the financial markets, and the term security was meant to include "the many types of instruments that in our commercial world fall within the ordinary concept of a security." H.R.Rep. No. 85, 73d Cong., 1st Sess., 11 (1933) * * *. The statutory definition excludes only currency and notes with a maturity of less than nine months. It includes ordinary stocks and bonds, along with the "countless and variable schemes devised by those who seek the use of the money of others on the promise of profits * * *." SEC v. W.J. Howey, Inc., 328 U.S. 293, 299 (1946). Thus, the coverage of the antifraud provisions of the securities laws is not limited to instruments traded at securities exchanges and over-the-counter markets, but extends to uncommon and irregular instruments. * * * We have repeatedly held that the test "is what character the instrument is given in commerce by the terms of the offer, the plan of distribution, and the economic inducements held out to the prospect." SEC v. United Benefit Life Insurance Co., 387 U.S. 202, 211 (1967), quoting SEC v. C.M. Joiner Leasing Corp., supra, 320 U.S. at 352–353.

The broad statutory definition is preceded, however, by the statement that the terms mentioned are not to be considered securities if "the context otherwise requires * * *." Moreover, we are satisfied that Congress, in enacting the securities laws, did not intend to provide a broad federal remedy for all fraud. * * *

III

The Court of Appeals concluded that the certificate of deposit purchased by the Weavers might be a security. Examining the statutory definition, * * * the court correctly noted that the certificate of deposit is not expressly excluded from the definition since it is not currency and it has a maturity exceeding nine months. It concluded, however, that the certificate of deposit was the functional equivalent of the withdrawable capital shares of a savings and loan association held to be securities in Tcherepnin v. Knight, 389 U.S. 332 (1967). The court also reasoned that, from an investor's standpoint, a certificate of deposit is no different from any other long-term debt obligation. Unless distinguishing features were found on remand, the court concluded that the certificate of deposit should be held to be a security.

Tcherepnin is not controlling. The withdrawable capital shares found there to be securities did not pay a fixed rate of interest; instead, purchasers received dividends based on the association's profits. Purchasers also received voting rights. In short, the withdrawable capital shares in *Tcherepnin* were much more like ordinary shares of stock and "the ordinary concept of a security" than a certificate of deposit.

The Court of Appeals also concluded that a certificate of deposit is similar to any other long-term debt obligation commonly found to be a security. In our view, however, there is an important difference between a bank certificate of deposit and other long-term debt obligations. This certificate of deposit was issued by a federally regulated bank which is subject to the comprehensive set of regulations governing the banking industry. Deposits in federally regulated banks are protected by the reserve, reporting, and inspection requirements of the federal banking laws; advertising relating to the interest paid on deposits is also regulated. In addition, deposits are insured by the Federal Deposit Insurance Corporation. Since its formation in 1933, nearly all depositors in failing banks insured by the FDIC have received payment in full, even payment for the portions of their deposits above the amount insured. 1980 Annual Report of the Federal Deposit Insurance Corporation 18–21 (1981).

We see, therefore, important differences between a certificate of deposit purchased from a federally regulated bank and other long-term debt obligations. The Court of Appeals failed to give appropriate weight to the important fact that the purchaser of a certificate of deposit is virtually guaranteed payment in full, whereas the holder of an ordinary longterm debt obligation assumes the risk of the borrower's insolvency. The definition of security in the 1934 Act provides that an instrument which seems to fall within the broad sweep of the Act is not to be considered a security if the context otherwise requires. It is unnecessary to subject issuers of bank certificates of deposit to liability under the antifraud provisions of the federal securities laws since the holders of bank certificates of deposit are abundantly protected under the federal banking laws. We therefore hold that the certificate of deposit purchased by the Weavers is not a security.

IV

The Court of Appeals also held that a finder of fact could conclude that the separate agreement between the Weavers and the Piccirillos is a security. Examining the statutory language, * * * the court found that the agreement might be a "certificate of interest or participation in any profit-sharing agreement" or an "investment contract." It stressed that the agreement gave the Weavers a share in the profits of the slaughterhouse which would result from the efforts of the Piccirillos. Accordingly, in that court's view, the agreement fell within the definition of investment contract stated in *Howey*, because "the scheme involves an investment of money in a common enterprise with profits to come solely from the efforts of others." 328 U.S., at 301.

Congress intended the securities laws to cover those instruments ordinarily and commonly considered to be securities in the commercial world, but the agreement between the Weavers and the Piccirillos is not the type of instrument that comes to mind when the term security is used and does not fall within "the ordinary concept of a security." * * * The unusual instruments found to constitute securities in prior cases involved offers to a number of potential investors, not a private transaction as in this case. In *Howey,* for example, 42 persons purchased interests in a citrus grove during a four-month period. 328 U.S., at 295. In *C.M. Joiner Leasing,* offers to sell oil leases were sent to over 1,000 prospects. 320 U.S., at 346. In *C.M. Joiner Leasing,* we noted that a security is an instrument in which there is "common trading." Id., at 351. The instruments involved in *C.M. Joiner Leasing* and *Howey* had equivalent values to most persons and could have been traded publicly.

Here, in contrast, the Piccirillos distributed no prospectus to the Weavers or to other potential investors, and the unique agreement they negotiated was not designed to be traded publicly.[a] The provision that the Weavers could use the barn and pastures of the slaughterhouse at the discretion of the Piccirillos underscores the unique character of the transaction. Similarly, the provision that the Weavers could veto future loans gave them a measure of control over the operation of the slaughterhouse not characteristic of a security. Although the agreement gave the Weavers a share of the Piccirillos' profits, if any, that provision alone is not sufficient to make that agreement a security. Accordingly, we hold that this unique agreement, negotiated one-on-one by the parties, is not a security.

V

Whatever may be the consequences of these transactions, they did not occur in connection with the purchase or sale of "securities."[11] * * *

Reversed and remanded.[b]

D. REPURCHASE AGREEMENTS ("REPOS")

FIRST NATIONAL BANK OF LAS VEGAS, NEW MEXICO v. ESTATE OF RUSSELL

United States Court of Appeals, Fifth Circuit, 1981.
657 F.2d 668.

[Plaintiff Bank brought a Rule 10b–5 action against defendants claiming securities fraud by Russell, Kennedy & Hodgden, Inc., (RKH), a broker-

---

a. But see Ruefenacht v. O'Halloran, infra at page 260; Landreth Timber Company v. Landreth, infra at page 278.

11. It does not follow that a certificate of deposit or business agreement between transacting parties invariably falls outside the definition of a security as defined by the federal statutes. Each transaction must be analyzed and evaluated on the basis of the content of the instruments in question, the purposes intended to be served, and the factual setting as a whole.

b. Section 2(1) of the 1933 Act and section 3(a)(10) of the 1934 Act have since been amended. Investment Company Act section 2(a)(36) was also amended to define a security to include " * * * option * * * on any security *including* a certificate of deposit," while the corresponding language in the 1933 and 1934 Acts read

"on any security, *or* certificate of deposit." H.R.Rep. No. 97–626 on H.R. 6156, 97th Cong., 2d Sess. at 10 states that no change in current law as interpreted in *Marine Bank* was intended.

Wolf v. Banco Nacional de Mexico, S.A., 739 F2d 1458 (9th Cir.1984) (Certificate of deposit for pesos issued by a Mexican bank was not a security), Note, 26 Harv.I.L.J. 616 (1985). For a criticism of the "comparable protection" rationale applied in *Daniel* and *Marine Bank,* see Arnold, "When is a Car a Bicycle?" and Other Riddles: The Definition of a Security Under the Federal Securities Laws, 33 Clev. St.L.Rev. 449 (1984–85); Note, Curbing Preemption of Securities Act Coverage in the Absence of Clear Congressional Direction, 72 Va.L.Rev. 195 (1986).

dealer in government securities. Plaintiff alleged that RKH found its government securities business to be unprofitable. Accordingly, to cover losses and provide working capital, the firm initiated a plan to engage in repurchase transactions. A repurchase transaction entails a sale of securities coupled with a parallel agreement by the seller to repurchase securities of the same description on a later specified date.[a]

RKH entered into a number of repurchase transactions with small banks that had previously purchased or sold securities through the firm. Customers were instructed to wire their money to Bossier Bank, which presumably acted as custodian of the securities to be purchased. The customers were then to receive a safekeeping receipt by mail from Bossier Bank. Upon the acceptance of their sale and repurchase offers, RKH would mail to the customer two confirmations, one confirming the sale of the securities and one confirming the repurchase of the securities. The brokerage firm, however, did not own and never acquired the securities so confirmed and did not deliver them either to the purchasing institutions or to the Bossier Bank for safekeeping. Obligations to repurchase were generally "rolled over" by entering into a superseding repurchase agreement or RKH settled the transaction with funds obtained from a subsequent purchaser.

In the transaction in question, RKH agreed to sell U.S. Treasury Notes to Plaintiff Bank in the aggregate principal amount of $600,000. The brokerage firm also agreed to repurchase the Notes, with settlement postponed for thirty days, for a sale price of $603,141.67. The attraction of repurchase agreements was that the customers earned a higher yield on them than that payable on the Treasury Notes.

The district court denied plaintiff's motion for a summary judgment and granted defendants' motion for a summary judgment on the ground that "the notes were not securities within the meaning of the Federal Securities Act" and that the transaction did not "rise to dignity of a purchase and sale of a security for Section 10(b) purposes."]

Before COLEMAN, GARZA and SAM D. JOHNSON, CIRCUIT JUDGES.

SAM D. JOHNSON, CIRCUIT JUDGE:

Section 10(b) of the Securities Exchange Act of 1934 and Rule 10b–5 thereunder prohibit fraud in connection with the "purchase or sale" of "any security." The term "security" is broadly defined in section 3(a)(10) of the 1934 Act to encompass a wide variety of instruments including notes, bonds, and debentures. The district court stated that "[n]otes which are reflective of individual commercial transactions are generally outside the

---

a. In SEC v. Miller, 495 F.Supp. 465, 467 (S.D.N.Y.1980), the Court had stated that "[f]rom a purely economic perspective * * *, a repo [repurchase agreement] is essentially a short-term collateralized loan, and the parties to these transactions tend to perceive them as such." The Court there, however, did not decide whether a sale or collateralized loan was entailed.

In SEC v. Drysdale Securities Corporation, 785 F.2d 38, 41 (2d Cir.1986), Judge Winter pointed out that repos differ from a traditional collateralized loan: "In the latter transaction, the lender holds pledged collateral for security and may not sell it in the absence of default. In contrast, repo 'lenders' take title to the securities received and can trade, sell or pledge them. The repo merely imposes a contractual obligation to deliver identical securities on the settlement date set by the repo contract. Unlike the lender [in a collateralized loan] the 'secured lender' in a repo is free to deal with the "collateral."

purview of the Act." * * * The district court noted that the following factors have led the Fifth Circuit to conclude that a note was not a security: " 'The note was payable in fixed amounts at fixed times, repayment not being conditioned upon profit or productivity of the company. No class of investors was involved, only the lending bank. The bank anticipated no gain beyond repayment of the note with interest.' " * * * The district court found that the money paid by First National Bank "was repayable at an agreed time in fixed amounts equal to principal plus interest at the agreed rate." * * * From this, the district court concluded that "the notes were not securities within the meaning of the Federal Securities Act." Id.

It is not entirely clear exactly what notes the district court was referring to in this statement. The Treasury Notes that Russell, Kennedy & Hodgden was purporting to sell were not short-term, thirty-day obligations reflective of a private loan between Russell, Kennedy & Hodgden and First National Bank. As described by the brokerage firm, they were scheduled to mature on February 15, 1978—not thirty days after the purchase. Finally, the Notes described by the brokerage firm were offered originally to a large class of investors. Purchasers and sellers of Treasury Bonds issued by the United States Government are entitled to the protection of section 10(b). * * * The plaintiff claims that Treasury Notes, which are identical in all relevant respects to Treasury Bonds, should also fall within the definition of a security. * * * [N]o party on appeal contends that the Treasury Notes were not securities within the meaning of the 1934 Act.[16]

If the district court's finding that the "notes were not securities" was based upon an assumption that First National Bank received from Russell, Kennedy & Hodgden a thirty-day note representing the firm's repurchase obligation, then both the assumption and the fact finding were incorrect. There was no promissory note involved in this repurchase transaction. The only written instruments received by First National Bank were the two confirmations verifying the agreement to purchase and sell the securities. Whatever notes the district court was referring to in its memorandum opinion, its conclusion that the notes were not securities is incorrect.

The only remaining inquiry—and the inquiry addressed by the parties on appeal—is whether the district court properly granted summary judgment for defendants on the ground that there was no purchase or sale of a security in this transaction. Summary judgment is only proper when it appears "that there is no genuine issue as to any material fact and that the moving party is entitled to a judgment as a matter of law." Fed.R.Civ.P. 56(c). * * * In determining whether a summary judgment is appropriate, the record is reviewed in the light most favorable to the party opposing the motion, and the burden is on the moving party to show that there is no genuine issue of material fact before the court. * * *

Section 3(a)(14) of the 1934 Act defines "sale" to "include any contract to sell or otherwise dispose of" securities. Section 3(a)(13) defines "pur-

---

16. That the securities were never owned or acquired by Russell, Kennedy & Hodgden does not preclude coverage by the 1934 Act. The antifraud provisions of section 10(b) and Rule 10b–5 have been held applicable even in situations when a bro-ker-dealer purported to sell nonexistent securities or securities that were to be issued in the future. See Lincoln Nat'l Bank v. Herber, 604 F.2d 1038, 1040 (7th Cir.1979) * * *.

chase" to "include any contract to buy, purchase, or otherwise acquire" securities. This Court has noted that the terms "purchase" and "sale" are to be broadly construed to effectuate the purpose of the Act. * * * Whether a repurchase transaction is a purchase or sale is a question of first impression in this Circuit.

In this case, the record indicates that Russell, Kennedy & Hodgden, a brokerage firm that engaged in the business of selling United States Government securities, deliberately structured the repurchase transaction as a sale and repurchase of Treasury Notes. The firm solicited First National Bank to invest in the securities. The parties executed no side agreements that would suggest that a sale was not contemplated or that First National Bank would not assume ownership of the securities. Title, and all incidents of ownership, were apparently intended to pass to First National Bank. This Court has generally found section 10(b) to be applicable when there is a surrender of ownership or control of the security.

Bossier Bank contends that there was no purchase or sale in the instant case because the repurchase transactions were, in substance, loans. Defendants argue that the circumstances of the so-called sale must be examined to determine whether, in economic reality, the transaction was a sale. As a basis for this analysis, defendants rely upon the investment-commercial dichotomy that has been applied in this Circuit. This Court has applied the investment-commercial dichotomy in the context of examining whether a note falls within the definition of a security within the meaning of the securities acts. Thus, although the 1934 Act defines "security" as including *"any"* note, "judicial decisions have restricted the application of the Act to those notes that are investment in nature and have excluded notes which are only reflective of individual commercial transactions." *McClure v. First National Bank of Lubbock,* 497 F.2d 490, 492 (5th Cir.1974), *cert. denied,* 420 U.S. 930 (1975). * * * The *McClure* Court concluded that:

> On one hand, the Act covers all *investment* notes, no matter how short their maturity, because they are not encompassed by the "any note" language of the exemption. On the other hand, the Act does not cover any *commercial* notes, no matter how long their maturity, because they fall outside the "any note" definition of a security. Thus, the investment or commercial nature of a note entirely controls the applicability of the Act, depriving of all utility the exemption based on maturity-length.

497 F.2d at 494–95 (emphasis in original).[b] Defendants argue that the investment-commercial dichotomy is equally applicable to an examination of whether a transaction constitutes a sale.

To support its contention that the transaction was, in reality, a collateralized loan rather than a sale, Bossier Bank points to several factors that have generally been considered by this Court in applying the investment-commercial dichotomy. Thus, Bossier Bank notes that: (1) First National Bank was obligated to resell the securities to Russell, Kennedy & Hodgden

---

b. In Chemical Bank v. Arthur Andersen & Co., 726 F.2d 930, 939, n. 12 (2d Cir. 1984), Judge Friendly pointed out that "Judge Roney conceded that his *McClure* opinion * * * virtually wrote out of the 1934 Act the distinction—seemingly drafted with care although without explanation of the reasons—between notes of more or less than nine months maturity." McClure v. First Nat'l Bank, 497 F.2d at 494.

at a fixed principal amount plus interest. According to Bossier Bank, this indicates that First National Bank was not investing in the Treasury Notes since any gain or loss in the market value of the Notes would accrue to the brokerage firm and not to the bank. (2) The resale obligation fell due on a fixed date after a relatively short term, a factor that tends to characterize commercial lending rather than investment transactions. (3) The transaction was entered into with a lending institution and was not offered to a large class of investors. * * * (4) The bank was not investing in the brokerage firm's operations. (5) The principal amount of the transaction was the par value of the Notes, which was less than their market value. According to Bossier Bank, if Russell, Kennedy & Hodgden had intended to sell the Treasury Notes, it could have obtained a higher price on the market. (6) First National Bank was to earn interest on the Treasury Notes at a negotiated market rate that was different from the coupon rate of the Treasury Notes.

Defendants contend that these factors indicate that the transaction between First National Bank and Russell, Kennedy & Hodgden was commercial in nature and was therefore not a sale within the meaning of the 1934 Act. It is true that this Court has recognized that the "securities acts have as their fundamental purpose the protection of *investors.*" * * * In determining whether a transaction is a sale, however, this Court has examined such factors as whether the transaction affects the securities industry * * * and "whether the purposes of section 10(b) of the Exchange Act and Rule 10b–5 thereunder would be advanced by their application" to the transaction. * * * Thus, it would appear that the factors pointed out by Bossier Bank are not dispositive of the issue before this Court.

Regardless of the extent to which the factors identified by Bossier Bank relate to the question whether this repurchase transaction constituted a sale, the summary judgment rendered by the district court was improper. A fact finder could have found that the repurchase transaction in this case was a purchase or sale. Since genuine issues of material fact as to the proper characterization of this transaction did exist, summary judgment was improper.[c]

* * * *

c. See The Issuance of "Retail Repurchase Agreements" by Banks and Savings and Loan Associations, Securities Act Release No. 6351 (Sept. 25, 1981), 23 SEC Dock. 1000, setting forth the enforcement positions of the SEC Staff with respect to "retail repos" and "traditional repos."

The Staff there took the position that retail repos issued by banks and savings and loans "typically are, in economic reality, debt obligations of banks and savings and loan associations that are collateralized by an interest in a [U.S. government or a U.S. government agency security], or a pool of such securities." Offers or sales of retail repos are not regarded as subject to the registration provisions of the 1933 Act, because the underlying securities are exempt. Securities Act § 3(a)(2). Such

transactions, however, are subject to the antifraud provisions of Section 17(a) of the 1933 Act and § 10(b) and Rule 10b–5 of the 1934 Act.

Traditional repos differ from retail repos in several respects. They are usually of shorter duration (one day is not unusual), involve larger amounts, are privately negotiated rather than mass marketed and involve entire government securities rather than participations and are often delivered to the purchaser or to a depositary for safekeeping. Traditional repurchase agreements as such are not separate securities, but are deemed to involve the purchase and sale of U.S. government securities. Accordingly, those transactions are also subject to the antifraud provisions of the federal securities laws.

E. STOCK

RUEFENACHT v. O'HALLORAN

United States Court of Appeals, Third Circuit, 1984.
737 F.2d 320.

Before: GIBBONS and HUNTER, CIRCUIT JUDGES, and RAMBO, DISTRICT JUDGE.*

GIBBONS, CIRCUIT JUDGE: This appeal requires that we determine whether stock transferred to effectuate the sale of all or part of a business is a "security" within the meaning of the 1933 and 1934 Securities Acts. The district court, holding that the purchase or sale of 50 percent of the stock of a business is a security only if the transaction satisfies the "investment contract" or "economic reality" test of SEC v. W.J. Howey Co., 328 U.S. 293 (1946), entered summary judgment for the defendants. The plaintiff, and the Securities and Exchange Commission as *amicus curiae,* urge that the district court erred in applying the *Howey* test in these circumstances. The question whether the *Howey* test applies to the sale of stock having the traditional attributes of stock ownership is the subject of considerable academic commentary[2] and has produced a split of authority in the circuits.[3] Joining the Second, Fourth, Fifth and Eighth Circuits, we hold that the *Howey* test does not apply to the sale of all or part of a business effectuated by the transfer of stock bearing the traditional incidents of stock ownership. Thus we reverse.

I. Facts and Proceedings in the District Court

Continental Import & Export, Inc., is an importer of wines and spirits. Joachim Birkle is president of Continental and, until 1980, owned or

---

* Honorable Sylvia H. Rambo, United States District Judge for the Middle District of Pennsylvania, sitting by designation.

2. See, e.g., Easley, Recent Developments in the Sale-of-Business Doctrine: Toward a Transactional Context-Based Analysis for Federal Securities Jurisdiction, 39 Bus.Law. 929 (1984) [hereinafter Easley, Recent Developments in the Sale-of-Business Doctrine]; Thompson, The Shrinking Definition of A Security: Why Purchasing All of a Company's Stock is Not a Federal Security Transaction, 57 N.Y.U.L.Rev. 225 (1982); Seldin, When Stock is Not a Security: The "Sale of Business" Doctrine under the Federal Securities Laws, 37 Bus.Law. 637 (1982); Karjala, Realigning Federal and State Roles in Securities Regulation Through the Definition of a Security, 1982 U.Ill.L.Rev. 413; FitzGibbon, What is a Security?—A Redefinition Based on Eligibility to Participate in the Financial Markets, 64 Minn.L.Rev. 893 (1980); Hannan & Thomas, The Importance of Economic Reality and Risk in Defining Federal Securities, 25 Hastings L.J. 219 (1974); Long, An Attempt to Return "Investment Contracts" to the Mainstream of Securities Regulation, 24 Okla.L.Rev. 135 (1971); Cof-

fey, The Economic Realities of a "Security": Is There a More Meaningful Formula?, 18 Case W.Res.L.Rev. 367 (1967); Note, Repudiating the Sale-of-Business Doctrine, 83 Colum.L.Rev. 1718 (1983) [hereafter Note, Sale-of-Business Doctrine]; Comment, A Criticism of the Sale of Business Doctrine, 71 Calif.L.Rev. 974 (1983); Comment, Acquisition of Businesses Through Purchase of Corporate Stock: An Argument for Exclusion from Federal Securities Regulation, 8 Fla.St.U.L.Rev. 295 (1980).

3. The Second, Fourth, Fifth, and Eighth Circuits have rejected the sale-of-business doctrine. See Daily v. Morgan, 701 F.2d 496, 497–504 (5th Cir.1983); Cole v. PPG Indus., Inc., 680 F.2d 549, 555–56 (8th Cir.1982); Golden v. Garafalo, 678 F.2d 1139, 1140–47 (2d Cir.1982); Coffin v. Polishing Machs., Inc., 596 F.2d 1202, 1204 (4th Cir.), cert. denied 444 U.S. 868 (1979).

The Seventh Circuit has taken the lead in applying the doctrine to the purchase of all or part of the stock of a business. See Sutter v. Groen, 687 F.2d 197, 199–204 (7th Cir.1982) * * * The Ninth, Tenth, and Eleventh Circuits have followed the Seventh Circuit's lead. * * *

* * * *

controlled 100 percent of its stock. Ruefenacht, the plaintiff, alleges that early in 1980 he purchased 2500 shares of Continental's stock for $250,000—said to represent 50 percent of the company—in reliance on financial documents and other oral representations made by Birkle, Christopher O'Halloran, a certified public accountant, and W. George Gould, Continental's corporate counsel.

In deposition testimony, Ruefenacht asserted that the consideration for the price paid for Continental's stock included a promise by him to devote certain efforts to the firm's business. In conformance with that promise, Ruefenacht engaged in various activities on behalf of company. * * *

* * * While engaging in these activities however, Ruefenacht remained a full-time employee of another corporation. Moreover, his actions on behalf of Continental were at all times subject to the veto of Birkle.

After Ruefenacht paid $120,000 of the total $250,000 purchase price for Continental stock, he began to doubt the accuracy of certain representations made to him by Birkle and others. Soon thereafter he filed this action, alleging violations of sections 12(2) and 17(a) of the Securities Act of 1933, section 10(b) of the Securities Exchange Act of 1934, and Rule 10(b)(5). Ruefenacht charges that financial statements prepared by O'Halloran and signed by Birkle overvalued Continental's good will and licenses by $243,000; that these financial statements assigned a $400,000 value to import or contract rights with no substantial worth; that the firm reported a surplus when in actuality it maintained a deficit; and that the defendants represented that net profits on sales between 1980 and 1981 would be $848,000 under a nationwide distribution program, and $1.197 million in the New York area, when in fact Continental was not seriously negotiating contracts for nationwide distribution at all and could not reasonably project these net earnings. In reliance on these representations, Ruefenacht alleges, he had purchased 1000 shares of Continental's stock and had advanced $120,000 to Birkle. The complaint seeks rescission and restoration of the amount paid. Ruefenacht also pleads pendent state claims for fraud and breach of fiduciary duties.

The district court granted summary judgment for defendants, concluding that the stock purchased by Ruefenacht was not a "security" within the meaning of the 1933 and 1934 Acts. The court so concluded not because the instrument purchased by Ruefenacht lacked any of the indicia of stock ownership; indeed, the court conceded that the "stock which Ruefenacht received contains all the attributes mentioned by the *Forman* Court as indicating that the transaction did involve a security." App. at 220. Rather, the court held, the instrument was not a "security" because of the degree of Ruefenacht's control over Continental's business. * * * Finding no federal jurisdiction over the securities claims, the district court dismissed the complaint in its entirety.

II. History of the Sale-of-Business Doctrine

The 1933 and 1934 Securities Acts include within the definition of "security" a series of specific terms—e.g., "note," "stock," "bond," and "debenture"—and thereafter employ a number of more general phrases—e.g., "investment contract," "any interest or instrument commonly known as a 'security.'" As early as 1943 the Supreme Court held that certain novel economic transactions were encompassed within these latter, more generic terms, even though not embraced by their more specific provisions like "stock," "bond," or "note." See, SEC v. C.M. Joiner Leasing Corp., 320 U.S. 344, 348–55 (1943) (holding that leasehold interests in property adjacent to exploratory oil wells were "securities"). The Court's leading opinion on this point, SEC v. W.J. Howey Co., 328 U.S. 293 (1946), held that agreements for the sale of a citrus crop coupled with optional service contracts were "investment contracts." *Howey* propounded a definition of "investment contract" derived from descriptions widely employed in state "blue sky" laws: an investment contract, the Court held, is "a contract, transaction or scheme whereby a person invests his money in a common enterprise and is led to expect profits solely from the efforts of the promoter or a third party * * *." * * *. This definition came to be known as the "*Howey* test" and led many courts to classify a variety of novel economic schemes as "investment contracts."

While the courts were giving the term "investment contract" a broad compass, the more specific term "note" was read narrowly, so as not to embrace every instrument comporting with the Acts' terms that is technically a "note" under state law. The first appellate holding that not every such "note" is a "security" under the federal Acts is this court's decision in Lino v. City Investing Co., 487 F.2d 689 (3d Cir.1973). In *Lino,* this court held that a personal promissory note tendered as partial consideration for rights under a franchise agreement was not a "note" under the federal Acts. * * * Significantly, we did not apply the *Howey* test to the notes in question, as * * * the opinion pointedly made clear by applying the *Howey* test to the franchise agreements themselves. * * * Rather, we examined the entire context of the note transaction, declining at that time to expound "a 'test' * * * that would aid in determining whether there has been a purchase or sale of securities when a personal promissory note is involved." * * *

Following *Lino's* lead, several courts strove to define the circumstances under which a "note" should be considered a "security" under the Securities Acts. The Fifth Circuit sought to determine whether a note comprised an "investment." [9] The Ninth Circuit approached the problem on a slightly different tack, seeking to determine whether the lender supplies "risk capital" to the maker.[10] In a leading opinion written by Judge Friendly, the Second Circuit rejected both of these approaches. See Exchange National Bank of Chicago v. Touche Ross & Co., 544 F.2d 1126 (2d Cir.1976) (Friendly, J.). In part the Second Circuit feared that the "investment" and "risk capital" tests obliterated Congress' carefully drawn distinctions among those notes included within and excluded from the Acts. Congress took care to provide that any note arising out of a "current transaction" and having a maturity not exceeding nine months was excluded from the registration provisions, but included in the anti-fraud provisions, of the 1933 Act; and that any note with a maturity not exceeding nine months

---

9. In a discussion not entirely free of self-defining terms, the Fifth Circuit characterized a "note" under the federal Acts as either (1) "offered to some class of investors," (2) "acquired for speculation or investment," or (3) exchanged to "obtain investment assets, directly or indirectly." McClure v. First Nat'l Bank of Lubbock, 497 F.2d 490, 493–94 (5th Cir.1974), cert. denied 420 U.S. 930 (1975). * * *

10. Great Western Bank & Trust Co. v. Kotz, 532 F.2d 1252, 1257 (9th Cir.1976). Six factors bore on the Ninth Circuit's analysis: (1) "time," (2) "collateralization," (3) "form of the obligation," (4) "circumstances of issuance," (5) "relationship between the amount borrowed and the size of the borrower's business," and (6) "contemplated use of the proceeds." Id. at 1257–58 (emphasis omitted).

was excluded from the 1934 Act. As the Fifth Circuit candidly acknowledged, its "investment test" "virtually writes [these distinctions] out of the law." McClure v. First National Bank of Lubbock, 497 F.2d 490, 494 (5th Cir.1974), cert. denied, 420 U.S. 930 (1975). In addition, the Second Circuit expressed concern over the uncertainty that would inevitably follow from a weighing of factors "without any instructions as to [their] relative weights." Exchange National Bank, 544 F.2d at 1137. In lieu of the "investment" and "risk capital" approaches, the Second Circuit enumerated a family of note transactions presumptively excluded from the Act—all concerning consumer financing or business financing of current costs—and held that other notes not bearing the family pedigree were presumptively securities under federal law.

There matters stood when late in 1976 the Seventh Circuit held that the *Howey* test for "investment contract" applies to determine whether a "note" is a security under the Acts. Emisco Industries, Inc. v. Pro's Inc., 543 F.2d 38, 39–40 (7th Cir.1976). The extension of *Howey* into the note arena was problematical. This application of *Howey* further obliterated the special statutory distinctions drawn by Congress among notes included in and excluded from the Acts, and injected into the note area the same uncertainty that pervades litigation over the inherently vague term "investment contract." Moreover, the Seventh Circuit doctrine seemed to ignore some important statutory policies underlying the securities Acts. As the legislative history makes abundantly clear, one such policy is the protection of "investors"; and to the extent that *Howey* maps the entire set of "investors" marked for protection—not an obviously correct assumption—then that policy may be satisfied. But a second policy of the Acts is, as we observe below, the protection of the marketability of certain instruments of commerce, whether or not purchased by "investors" under the *Howey* formula. Among the favored instruments, for example, is certain commercial paper.[15] Several commentators have perceptively remarked that an application of the "investment" or "*Howey*" tests to these commercial instruments would undermine federal protection for many instruments most deserving of coverage.

Notwithstanding these concerns, in 1981 the Seventh Circuit extended the *Howey* or "economic reality" test to the purchase or sale of *stock*. Frederikson v. Poloway, 637 F.2d 1147 (7th Cir.), cert. denied, 451 U.S. 1017 (1981). While the extension of the *Howey* test to the note area had been greeted with some concern, the further extension of that doctrine to the purchase or sale of stock sparked a considerable amount of alarm.[17] While

---

15. The SEC regards commercial paper as exempt from the *registration* provisions of the 1933 Act. See § [3(a)(3)], only if the paper is:

prime quality negotiable paper of a type not ordinarily purchased by the general public, that is, paper issued to facilitate well-organized types of current operational business requirements and of a type eligible for discounting by Federal Reserve Banks.

Securities Act Release No. 4412 (1961); see 17 C.F.R. § 231.4412 (1983). Commer-

cial paper is not exempt from the *antifraud* provisions of the 1933 Act. See [§ 17(c)] * * *.

17. E.g., Daily v. Morgan, 701 F.2d 496 (5th Cir.1983); * * * Golden v. Garafalo, 678 F.2d 1139 (2d Cir.1982); * * * For incisive academic commentary, see Note, Sale-of-Business Doctrine, supra note 2, 83 Colum.L.Rev. 1718 (1983); Comment, A Criticism of the Sale of Business Doctrine, 71 Calif.L.Rev. 974 (1983).

the difficulties attending the simple extension of *Howey* to notes still applied, two other difficulties loomed even larger.

First, at least in the note area there is, as we held in *Lino,* some necessity for fine-tuning the definition of "note" to avoid sweeping within the coverage of section 10(b) of the 1934 Act every consumer and business loan financing current operational costs. But there is no such necessity in the stock area. Stock is a well-defined term, is not issued by consumers, and is not ordinarily employed by business to finance current transactions. While the importation of the *Howey* test into the note arena might be justified as an expedient—albeit an imperfect one—for limiting the definition of "note," no such expedient seems necessary for the issue of stock.

Second, because the *Howey* test turns in part on whether the purchase derives profits "from the entrepreneurial or managerial efforts of others," * * * a central aspect of the test, when applied to stock, requires a determination whether the purchaser exercises a controlling share of the corporation. A controlling share may be exercised with less than 100 percent stock ownership—indeed, at times with far less than 50 percent ownership. See Sutter v. Groen, 687 F.2d 197, 203 (7th Cir.1982). Thus an instrument might be transformed from a security into a non-security by virtue of a small increase in the number of shares traded. Instruments purchased by multiple investors might be securities as to some purchasers and non-securities as to others, or securities as to sellers but not as to purchasers. Instruments might be securities if traded in a series of small transactions but non-securities if the same transaction is effectuated in a single sale. To many judges and lawyers with up to 50 years of experience with the securities laws, these seemed extraordinary consequences.[20]

The case now before us illustrates just how far the extension of *Howey* from investment contract to note to stock may be taken. Ruefenacht is the purchaser of 50 percent of the stock of Continental. Had he purchased only 49 percent, Ruefenacht would presumably have lacked corporate control, rendering the instrument purchased (at least presumptively) a security. Had he purchased 51 percent, in contrast, the instrument would presumptively not have been a security. Both presumptions, of course—at least under the Seventh Circuit approach, see *Sutter,* 687 F.2d at 203— would have been subject to rebuttal. Because Ruefenacht purchased exactly 50 percent, a more sophisticated analysis would presumably be required—although just what that analysis should be is less than obvious.

III. The Securities Acts as Interpreted by the Supreme Court

If Congress or the Supreme Court has mandated these results, then, regardless of their deficiencies in logic, we would be bound to apply them. We turn, therefore, to the language, history, structure, and policies of the

---

20. Until recently, courts expressed little doubt that the sale of 100 percent of the stock of a business (and *a fortiori* less than 100 percent) constituted the sale of a "security" under the Acts. See Occidental Life Ins. Co. v. Pat Ryan Assocs., Inc., 496 F.2d 1255, 1261–63 (4th Cir.), cert. denied 419 U.S. 1023 (1974) * * *.

The parties appear to have assumed that the sale of 100 percent of the stock of a firm constitutes the sale of a "security" in Superintendent of Ins. v. Bankers Life & Cas. Co., 404 U.S. 6 (1971). There the Supreme Court doubted whether a non-purchaser/non-seller (Manhattan Casualty Co.) had standing to invoke the Acts, see id. at 13–14 n. 10, a question later settled in Blue Chip Stamps v. Manor Drug Stores, 421 U.S. 723 (1975). No party at any stage of the litigation, however, appears to have questioned that the stock constituted a "security."

1933 and 1934 Acts. Then we consider the impact of recent Supreme Court decisions.

A.

Statutory Language, Structure, and History

1. The definition and exemption provisions

Section 2(1) of the 1933 Act as amended provides that the term "security"

> means any note, stock, treasury stock, bond, debenture, * * * investment contract, * * * or, in general, any interest or instrument commonly known as a "security" * * *.

The legislative history to section 2(1) indicates that Congress cast the definition of security "in sufficiently broad and general terms so as to include within that definition the many types of instruments that in our commercial world fall within the ordinary concept of a security." H.R.Rep. No. 85, 73d Cong., 1st Sess. 11 (1933).

Although Congress intended that the term "security" embrace those instruments that "fall within the ordinary concept of a security," several important qualifications limit this definition. Preceding all of the definitions in the 1933 Act is the clause "unless the context otherwise requires." The significance of the so-called "context clause" is addressed in Part III A 3 infra.

In addition, section 3 of the 1933 Act defines a number of important "exempted securities." Among the defined exemptions in the 1933 Act is an exception for short-term notes. Section 3(a) provides that the Act shall not apply to:

> Any note, draft, bill of exchange, or banker's acceptance which arises out of a current transaction * * * and which has a maturity at the time of issuance of not exceeding nine months * * *.

As one commentator has observed, Congress intended the short-term note exemption to free from the Act's registration requirements prime quality commercial paper sold to knowledgeable investors. The necessity for disclosure in a registration statement to these investors was less vital than for sales of other, more speculative paper to other, less knowledgeable buyers.[21] Congress did not, however, include the "commercial paper" exception in the antifraud provisions of the 1933 Act. See [§ 17(c)].

The 1933 Act also empowers the Commission to grant additional exemptions. Section 3(b) of the Act as amended provides that:

> The Commission may from time to time by its rules and regulations, and subject to such terms and conditions as may be prescribed therein, add any class of securities to the securities exempted as provided in this section, if it finds that the enforcement of this subchapter with respect to such securities is not necessary in the public interest and for the protection of investors by reason of the small amount involved or the limited character of the public offering; but no issue of securities shall be exempted under this subsection where the aggregate amount at

---

21. See Note, Commercial Paper, supra note 15, 39 U.Chi.L.Rev. at 384. * * *

which such issue is offered to the public exceeds $5,000,000 [then $100,000].

Congress envisioned that the Commission's exemption power would be reserved for "needless registration of issues of such an insignificant character as not to call for regulation." H.R.Rep. No. 85, supra, at 15. According to the House Report, however, the Commission's exemption power was carefully limited by the prohibition on exemptions for issues larger than $100,000 (now $5,000,000), "thus safeguard[ing] against any untoward pressure to exempt issues whose distribution may carry all the unfortunate consequences that the act is designed to prevent." Id.

The definition of "security" under the 1934 Act parallels that under the 1933 Act. Section 3(a)(10) of the 1934 Act provides that " 'security' means any note, stock, treasury stock, bond, debenture, * * * investment contract, * * * or in general, any instrument commonly known as a 'security.' " One important distinction between the 1933 and 1934 Act definitions pertains to short-term notes: generally speaking, short-term notes that would be exempt from the registration provisions of the 1933 Act are exempted from the antifraud provisions of the 1934 Act. And like the 1933 Act, section 3(a)(12) of the 1934 Act authorizes the SEC to grant additional exemptions for classes of securities either unconditionally or upon specialized terms and conditions.

Nowhere in these provisions is there an exemption for the sale of a controlling share of corporate stock. This conspicuous omission is significant for two reasons. First, Congress took pains to exempt certain commercial paper from the class of "notes" covered by the registration provisions of the 1933 Act and the antifraud provisions of the 1934 Act. When Congress wished to exempt a class of instruments from some or all of the Acts' provisions, it had little trouble in doing so expressly.[25] And while it might be argued that purchasers of large blocks of stock, often in face-to-face transactions, are more knowledgeable than the average investor—and therefore often less in need of protection—the same argument applies to the commercial paper exception. Congress exempted certain commercial paper in part because it is high-grade and purchased by knowledgeable investors; accordingly, the SEC approves for exemption only that commercial paper that is "prime quality" and "of a type not ordinarily purchased by the general public." * * * These arguments persuaded Congress to exempt prime quality commercial paper expressly. Congress did not, however, exempt particular stock transactions. Moreover, while Congress may not have considered the sale of all or part of a business by means of a stock purchase under the 1933 Act—the Act is, of course, primarily addressed to "public offerings," see [§ 4(2)] (private offering exemption), and the sale of a business is frequently not effectuated by a "public offering"—the same cannot be said of the 1934 Act. It was always clear that the 1934 Act would, by its terms, apply to stock purchases comprising controlling corporate shares. Nor can it be said that Congress did not envisage face-to-face transactions; it has always been clear that the Act applies to face-to-

---

25. Cf. Blue Chip Stamps v. Manor Drug Stores, 421 U.S. 723, 733–34 (1975) (noting distinction between "*purchase* or sale" in § 10(b) of 1934 Act and "*offer* or sale" in § 17(a) of 1933 Act, and stating, "When Congress wished to provide a reme-dy to those who neither purchase nor sell securities, it had little trouble in doing so expressly."); see also Touche Ross & Co. v. Redington, 442 U.S. 560, 572 (1979). * * *

face sales of stock as well as to transactions in the recognized markets. See Marine Bank v. Weaver, 455 U.S. 551, 556 (1982); Superintendent of Insurance v. Bankers Life & Casualty Co., 404 U.S. 6, 10, 12 (1971) ("Congress meant to bar deceptive devices and contrivances in the purchase or sale of securities whether conducted in the organized markets or face to face").

Second, Congress vested in the SEC the responsibility for identifying certain securities for exemption. In addition, Congress empowered the SEC to attach conditions to any exemptions granted in order to protect the investing public. These decisions suggest that in the judgment of Congress the Commission, and not the courts, has the expertise and practical experience required to ensure that exemptions to the Act are prudently chosen, and that appropriate conditions are attached to any exemptions granted. Needless to say, the SEC has never exempted the purchase or sale of a controlling share of corporate stock from the definition of security. Thus we look on the plea that this court do so with some skepticism.

2. *Text of the definitions and early interpretations*

The definition of "security" under both Acts begins with an enumeration of specific terms—"note," "stock," "bond," "debenture"—and then proceeds to more general phrases, including "investment contract." This procession from the specific to the general did not escape the Supreme Court's attention on its first occasion to consider the definition of "security." In SEC v. C.M. Joiner Corp., 320 U.S. 344 (1943), the Court observed:

> In the Securities Act the term "security" was defined to include by name or description many documents in which there is common trading for speculation or investment. Some, such as notes, bonds, and stocks, are pretty much standardized and the name alone carries well-settled meaning. Others are of more variable character and were necessarily designated by more descriptive terms, such as "transferable share," "investment contract," and "in general any interest or instrument commonly known as a security." *We cannot read out of the statute these general descriptive designations merely because more specific ones have been used to reach some kinds of documents.* Instruments may be included within any of these definitions, as a matter of law, if on their face they answer to the name or description. However, the reach of the Act does not stop with the obvious and commonplace. Novel, uncommon, or irregular devices, whatever they appear to be, are also reached if it be proved as [a] matter of fact that they were widely offered or dealt in under terms or courses of dealing which established their character as "investment contracts," or as "any interest or instrument commonly known as a 'security.'"

320 U.S. at 351 (emphasis added). Thus, the Supreme Court recognized that instruments like "stock," "bonds," and "notes" answer "on their face * * * to the name or description." The Acts' latter phrases, intended to supplement these common instruments, were devised to capture "[n]ovel, uncommon, or irregular devices" that were not so readily classified. This construction is consistent with the fact that the terms "stock," "bond," and "note" had well-defined meanings under state corporate law that Congress obviously had incorporated by reference, and that Congress did not intend the reach of the Act to stop with these well-defined terms alone.

The Court's next bout with the definition of security confirmed that the phrase "investment contract" also drew on state law for its content. In SEC v. W.J. Howey Co., 328 U.S. 293 (1946), the Supreme Court held that in the words "investment contract" Congress had employed a term "common in many state 'blue sky' laws." Id. at 298. Despite Justice Frankfurter's position in dissent that the phrase " 'investment contract' is not a term of art," id. at 301 (Frankfurter, J., dissenting), the Court held that by "including an investment contract within the scope of [the Act], Congress was using a term the meaning of which had been crystallized by [state] judicial interpretation[s]." Id. at 298. These state definitions, the Court held, "had been broadly construed by state courts so as to afford the investing public a full measure of protection." Id.

Thus, by 1946 it was plain that the definitions in the 1933 and 1934 Act drew on state law for their content, and that in order to embrace novel or unusual investment schemes within the salutary provisions of the Acts, Congress supplemented standard state-law definitions of "stock," "note," etc., with more general phrases, including "investment contract," drawn from state law. *Joiner* and *Howey* make plain that Congress did not intend to *circumscribe* the scope of the standard terms—"stock," "note," "debenture"—to that of the more generous phrases. To the contrary, that construction would turn the history of the Acts and the state-law definitions on their heads. Congress never intended that "stock" that did not also satisfy the definition of "investment contract" would not be within the Acts' terms. Rather, Congress intended that "investment contracts" that did not also satisfy the definition of "stock" *would be* within the Acts' terms. See Tcherepnin v. Knight, 389 U.S. 332, 343 (1967) (*Joiner* "rejected the respondents' invitation to 'constrict the more general terms substantially to the specific terms which they follow' ").

The language of the definition itself makes this consideration clear. As the Second Circuit recently noted, there would have been little reason for the drafters to have employed words like "stock," "bond," and "note"— which had clear definitions under state law—if their intention had been to include only those instruments that satisfied an "economic reality" test appropriate to the latter terms. If an economic reality test appropriate to these subsequent terms were intended, "a substantial portion of each class of instrument would, in fact, not be within the definition." Golden v. Garafalo, 678 F.2d 1139, 1144 (2d Cir.1982).

To be sure, the *Howey* Court also admonished that "[f]orm was [to be] disregarded for substance" and that "emphasis was [to be] placed upon economic reality." * * * Those words were written, however, in the context of disregarding the absence of a label like "stock" or "note" when novel schemes nonetheless constitute "investments" earning profits from the labor of others. They did not direct us to ignore the presence of an instrument that, as a matter of economic reality, is "stock" simply because it is not purchased by one who also entered into an "investment contract."

In summary, neither the language, the history, the structure, nor the Acts' early interpretations suggest that the transfer of stock to effectuate the sale of all or part of a business is not the purchase or sale of a "security." And several considerations—particularly Congress' express treatment of notes and its conferral on the SEC of the power to specify exempt securities—suggest the contrary. We now consider the impact of the "context clauses" on our analysis.

3. The "context clauses"

Each of the definitional sections of the 1933 and 1934 Acts begins with the words, "When used in this [sub]chapter, unless the context otherwise requires—." These clauses, the defendants maintain, authorize us to narrow the definition of "stock" as the "economic realities" require. In considering this position, we turn to the history and function of the clauses.

Perhaps the most notable feature about the "context clauses" is that they do not appear in the paragraphs defining "security" at all. Instead, these clauses precede all fifteen definitions in the 1933 Act and all forty definitions in the 1934 Act. Plainly, the "context clauses" were not directed particularly at the definition of "security." This lack of particular application is underscored by the legislative history of the definitions of "security." In neither the House nor the Senate reports, for example, did the drafters allude to the clauses or indicate that particular kinds of stock, notes, or debentures are embraced by the Act "only when the context requires." If the drafters had indeed intended that the context clause exempted certain named securities from coverage, they certainly made no mention of it.

The legislative evolution of the 1933 Act suggests even more strongly that the context clauses had no such purport. Section 2 of the Senate version of the 1933 Act provided, "When used in this Act the following terms shall, *unless the text otherwise indicates,* include the following respective meanings." H.R. 5480, 73d Cong., 1st Sess. 39 (1933) (emphasis added) * * *. This Senate bill tracked the language of an early House bill, H.R. 4314, which had also opened with the phrase "unless the text otherwise indicates." H.R. 4314, 73d Cong., 1st Sess. 2 (1933). Early in the legislative process, however, the House Committee on Interstate and Foreign Commerce substituted the language "unless the context otherwise requires" for the phrase "unless the text otherwise indicates." See H.R. 5480, 73d Cong., 1st Sess. 1 (1933). Ultimately the Conference Committee adopted the House version. * * *

It seems evident that the drafters did not attribute particular significance to the distinction between these House and Senate phrases. The "text" to which the Senate had adverted was obviously the text of the statute itself. Similarly, the "context" to which the House referred was obviously the context in which the defined words appear in the statute itself. Both the House and Senate provisions were intended to direct that the ensuing definitions were to be used throughout the statute unless the text of the Act expressly, or another section of the statute implicitly, made then inapplicable to that section.

The defendants, however, would have us attribute a very different meaning to the "context" language. That language, they assert, refers not only to the statutory context but to the context of the *underlying factual transaction.* Thus, they argue, the House and Senate versions of the 1933 Act had very different meanings. The Senate version, of course, would not have admitted of the defendants' interpretation, for it would have authorized exceptions as "the text otherwise indicates," not as the factual circumstances seem to warrant. The House version, in contrast, as the defendants construe it, sanctioned a wide-ranging exemption power varying with the facts and circumstances. It strikes us that if the conferees had observed so considerable a distinction between the House and Senate bills and had selected the broader, House version, they would at least have remarked upon so important a subject. Moreover, a wide-ranging exemption power is inconsistent with the Act's conferral of exemption power on the SEC. Because the Act conferred a narrowly tailored exemption power on the Commission, it seems extraordinary that the conferees should not have remarked upon a decision to confer a potentially broader power through the context clause.

These considerations lead us to conclude that the context clauses themselves do not authorize judicial exclusions of securities from the scope of the Act when the "factual circumstances" seem to warrant it. Of course, we do not thereby adopt a wooden approach to statutory construction. The Supreme Court has often admonished that a "thing may be within the letter of the statute and yet not within the statute." *United Housing Foundation, Inc. v. Forman*, 421 U.S. 837, 849 (1975) * * *. We simply observe that Congress did not intend the context clause as a font of authority to narrow the compass of the term "stock" when the underlying facts may seem to warrant. If that result is to obtain, it must devolve from some other indication in the language, structure, or legislative history of the Acts. The context clause alone is no such authority.[29] As Judge Friendly has written, "[s]o long as the statutes remain as they have been for over forty years, courts had better not depart from their words without strong support for the conviction that, under the authority vested in them by the 'context' clause, they are doing what Congress wanted when they refuse to do what it said." *Exchange National Bank*, 544 F.2d at 1138.

IV.

A.

Policy Considerations

As additional guides to Congress' intent, we examine the reasons and policies that gave rise to protection of securities under the 1933 and 1934 Acts.

1. Uncertainty of application

The most prominent feature of the sale-of-business doctrine is its attendant uncertainty of application, and for that reason we address this feature first. We agree with the Seventh Circuit that corporate control may be exercised with less than 100 percent of the outstanding stock of a firm, and therefore that if the sale-of-business doctrine is to be applied, it must logically be extended to all such purchases and sales, *Sutter v. Groen*, 687 F.2d 197, 203 (7th Cir.1982). No doubt, for example, the doctrine must be applicable with equal rigor to the purchase of 15 percent of a firm's stock as to the purchase of all 100 percent. This conclusion raises the specter of examining, in every securities transaction, the niceties of corporate control.

29. See, e.g., Marine Bank v. Weaver, 455 U.S. 551 (1982), holding that a certificate of deposit was not a security under the federal securities Acts because it enjoyed sufficient protection under the banking laws. Id. at 558–59. Although the Court relied in part on the context clause, its holding was independently supported by the legislative history and structure of the banking laws and securities Acts.

Such an examination would be no small task. Control may be exercised, for example, by alliances of minority shareholder factions. One indicator of whether a minority share effectively exercises control might be whether the purchase price of the share exceeded the prevailing market price. Another might be the voting patterns of various factions. Yet another might be the extent of management involvement by the faction, including, for example, whether various management employees were appointed by or are allied with that faction. And of course, testimony might be taken on the intent of the purchasers and the realities of corporate management. Even a purchaser who acquires more than 51 percent of the stock may not control with respect to certain corporate modifications for which the certificate of incorporation or state law may require supermajorities. E.g., 8 Del.Code Ann. § 102(b)(4) (1983). One commentator urges that even a buyer of 100 percent of the stock of a firm should be accorded the protections of the Acts "[i]f this party can prove he intended to be, and thereafter remained, a passive investor." Easley, Recent Developments in the Sale-of-Business Doctrine, supra note 2, 39 Bus.Law. at 971–72. Wholly apart from the oddity of making what a security *is* depend upon these factors, they raise the prospect of a substantial hearing in many cases simply to determine whether an instrument is a "security."

The Seventh Circuit acknowledges the uncertainty that would flow from this investigation, but discounts it. To interpret the Acts as creating private rights of action in favor of "entrepreneurs," the Seventh Circuit has reasoned, "is to go awfully far for the sake of having to make some distinctions." *Sutter,* 687 F.2d at 202. We are not as placid about this prospect as is the Seventh Circuit. After all, the costs of legal rules accrue not only to the courts but to those members of the public who must structure their affairs accordingly. Counsel must be hired to predict whether the purchase of a large block of stock will render it a security or a non-security. Doubts will be created over whether registrations are necessary. All of this uncertainty has real economic costs. It is one thing, if the sale-of-business doctrine were capable of clear application, to say "caveat emptor" and let the market price reflect that the purchaser no longer has federal protection from fraudulent representations. But it is another thing if the buyer and seller are unable to predict readily whether their instruments are "securities" at all. That uncertainty raises the cost of economic transactions, inhibits the flow of capital, spawns litigation, and in general benefits neither the parties nor the courts.

2. *Marketability of instruments and necessity for protection*

A concern related to the uncertainty of application is the marketability of certain favored instruments. The Acts apply not only to the sale of stock on the nationally recognized markets, but to the sale of "notes," "bonds," "debentures," and other instruments sold in non-market transactions. * * * Certain commercial paper, for example, is illustrative. * * * In favoring these widely recognized instruments, Congress reduced the transaction costs associated with their transfer; buyers may rely on the accuracy of representations made without instituting expensive investigations into information over which the seller has knowledge and control, and without demanding a premium price to reflect the risk of fraudulent representation. This protection facilitates the ready sale of instruments in interstate commerce.

The sale of a business by means of stock is such a transaction. As the Fifth Circuit has observed,

> there are special risks involved in the sale of stock in a corporation that might justify special protection. Generally speaking, one who purchases the assets of a business is not liable for its debts and liabilities, while one who purchases the stock in a corporation—a separate legal entity—assumes ownership of a business with both assets and liabilities * * *. Liabilities, alas, are often the subject of inaccurate or incomplete disclosures.

Daily v. Morgan, 701 F.2d 496, 504 (5th Cir.1983). Of course, the buyer can reduce these risks by employing professionals to comb through the most intricate details of the seller's business. But such an investigation is costly and inefficient: the seller controls this information and is already in possession of it; and the buyer's investigation is time-consuming and expensive, thereby raising transaction costs and inhibiting the flow of capital. One of Congress' purposes in singling out the named instruments in the Act was to facilitate such transactions without the ensuing delays, duplication of effort, and expenses associated with the "caveat-stockholder" era of deregulation. See H.R.Rep. No. 1383, 73d Cong., 2d Sess. 4–5 (1934). Denial of the Acts' protection in these circumstances would undermine this Congressional policy.[32]

3. *Justifiable expectations and value of the bargain*

A third concern related to the foregoing considerations is the protection of the value of the bargain to the buyer. One of the advantages to the buyer of employing stock to effectuate the sale of a business is the buyer's justifiable reliance on the antifraud provisions of the Acts to reduce transaction costs. Accordingly, the buyer may pay a price for the business that does not reflect a premium for the cost of ensuring the accuracy of all representations made. The Supreme Court has observed that such reliance by the buyer would be reasonable when the stock purchased has the traditional attributes commonly associated with stock ownership. In United Housing Foundation, Inc. v. Forman, 421 U.S. 837 (1975), the Court reasoned:

> There may be occasions when the use of a traditional name such as "stocks" or "bonds" will lead a purchaser justifiably to assume that the federal securities laws apply. This would clearly be the case when the underlying transaction embodies some of the significant characteristics typically associated with the named instrument.

* * * In the case of stock, the Court held, those characteristics include the right to receive dividends contingent upon an apportionment of profits; negotiability; capacity for use as collateral; voting rights in proportion to the number of shares owned; and share appreciation. Id. at 851.

---

32. Thus, we are unpersuaded by the argument that a sophisticated buyer with substantial resources is in a position to detect fraud and therefore undeserving of coverage. This argument misses the point. Of course the buyer may hire accountants and attorneys to scrutinize the seller's business; however, it is more efficient for the seller to warrant the accuracy of representations made than for the buyer to expend substantial amounts of time and money unearthing facts already known to the seller. This efficiency is one of the purposes of the Acts and promotes the marketability of securities and free flow of capital.

The district court concluded that the stock purchased by Ruefenacht bears these characteristics, and we accept that conclusion for the purposes of this appeal. Consequently, Ruefenacht would have been justified in agreeing on a purchase price that did not include a premium reflecting the risk of fraud. This savings to Ruefenacht represented part of the value of the bargain; and to withhold the Acts' protection in these circumstances would be to deprive the purchaser of that part of the value of the bargain.

4. Protection of "investors"

Congress unquestionably intended that the Act protect "investors" in the national securities markets. It would, however, be a grave mistake to conclude that this single purpose exhausted Congress' intent. As we have observed, Congress acted with a number of rationales in mind, among them the facilitation of commerce in certain named instruments to reduce transaction costs and enhance the free flow of capital. Thus, we disagree with the Seventh Circuit's view that the function of the federal Acts is limited solely to the protection of "investors," however defined. *Sutter,* 687 F.2d at 201. But even insofar as the Acts address "investors," there are flaws in the sale-of-business doctrine. The distinction between an "entrepreneur" and an "investor" is hardly obvious. Many investors may elect to participate in the management of a business in order to enhance their return on investment; indeed, in our free-enterprise system that is to be expected. Just why investors who choose to engage in entrepreneurship in order to improve the performances of their investment cease to be "investors," and become instead exclusively "entrepreneurs," is something of a mystery. It seems clear to us that these persons are both investors and entrepreneurs.[34] Even were Congress exclusively concerned with "investors" and not "entrepreneurs"—an assumption with which we strongly disagree—Ruefenacht is certainly an "investor."

Moreover, nothing suggests to us that the *Howey* test for investment accurately maps the universe of investors with which Congress might have been concerned. The *Howey* test emerged from the definition of "investment contract" under state "blue sky" laws. As used by state courts and the Supreme Court, this definition was intended to supplement well-defined terms like "stock" and "note." In order to avoid sweeping into the definition of "investment contract" a vast number of joint ventures, partnerships, and other business relationships,[35] the courts confined "investment contract" to a "transaction or scheme" under which persons are led to expect profits "solely from the efforts of" others. *Howey,* 328 U.S. at 298–99. This limitation on the definition of investment contract—intended to confine the number of business relationships qualifying as securities

---

34. * * *

The Seventh Circuit acknowledges that purchasers may be both investors and entrepreneurs but assumes that investment must constitute the "purchaser's *main purpose.*" *Sutter,* 687 F.2d at 203 (emphasis added). We see no evident source in the Acts for the requirement that investment must be a "main purpose" rather than a "subsidiary" purpose. Moreover, this interpretation opens a new avenue of inquiry into gradations of the purchaser's intent; we doubt that lengthy pretrial discovery

and hearings on such subtleties as whether the purchaser's "main" or "subsidiary" intent was "investment" promotes the purposes of the Acts. Nor do we believe the inquiry a fruitful one; the purchaser obviously intends both to invest and to manage.

35. See, e.g., Goodwin v. Elkins & Co., 730 F.2d 99, 103 (3d Cir.1984); id. at 112 (Seitz, C.J., concurring); id. at 114 (Becker, J., concurring) (partnership agreement did not constitute an investment contract under the terms of the agreement).

under the Acts—had no bearing whatsoever on whether instruments like "stock" were securities. Stock, bonds, notes, and debentures were well-defined instruments; there was no need to import into the definition of such instruments limitations on business relationships that might be investment contracts. Nor would there be any logic in doing so. While Ruefenacht's stock purchase may not have constituted an "investment contract"—a term of art—because of the degree of corporate control he exercised, it certainly constituted an "investment" effectuated by means of the purchase of "stock." It is erroneous to conclude that one who does not enter into an "investment contract" is *ipso facto* not an "investor." It is doubly erroneous to reason further that such an individual is therefore unprotected by the federal securities laws even though the transaction is effectuated by the purchase of an instrument clearly bearing all the attributes of stock.

5. *Arbitrary distinctions*

An additional consequence of the sale-of-business doctrine is the welter of unusual distinctions it produces among economic transactions. The sale of all of a corporation's stock to a single buyer by a single seller, for example, is alleged not to constitute the sale of a security; but the same sale to a single buyer by several sellers, each of whom did not formerly exercise control, is alleged to be a securities transaction as to the sellers but not as to the buyer. Similarly, a series of stock sales each insufficient to transfer control from a single seller to a single buyer would presumably constitute the sale of securities; a final sale leaving the buyer with stock ownership greater than 51 percent (and therefore transferring control) may or may not constitute the sale of securities, depending on how the doctrine is applied,[37] and the very same transaction consummated in a single purchase, rather than as a series of step transactions, would presumably not constitute the sale of securities.

Such distinctions are essentially arbitrary. The possibility of fraud is neither greater nor less when the purchaser acquires 49 or 51 percent of a business. Nor is the purchaser's capacity to discover fraud greater in one circumstance or the other. The variable of "control" is largely irrelevant to the risk of and capacity to discover fraud. As the Court of Appeals for the Second Circuit has observed, more appropriate considerations might include whether the sale involves a close corporation and whether the transaction takes place over a public market or face to face. Golden v. Garafalo, 678 F.2d at 1146. But close corporations and face-to-face transactions have always been within the compass of the Acts. Superintendent of Insurance v. Bankers Life & Casualty Co., 404 U.S. 6, 10, 12 (1971) * * *.

Moreover, in focusing on terms like "stock," "bond," and "note" in the early part of the definition of security, Congress drew on well-known state-law definitions. * * * These terms had a consistency of meaning under state law that did not vary with who owned the instrument at any particular moment, and did not admit of asymmetries between buyer and

---

37. The final sale itself arguably would not constitute the sale of a security because it transferred control to the buyer. Similarly, all prior sales may not constitute sales of securities if they were effectively part of a single step transaction. On the other hand, it is plausible that each of the sales would constitute the sale of securities because each comprised less than 50 percent of the business. We hesitate to speculate on the proper application of the doctrine in these circumstances.

seller. Rather, they focused on the essential attributes of the instrument: voting rights, redemption rights, the right to participate in dividends, the right to participate in assets upon dissolution, etc. * * *. Fluctuations in the identity of the instrument were foreign to the notion of stock. The chameleon-like quality of stock under the sale-of-business doctrine is wholly arbitrary with respect to the state-law definitions that are the source of the terms in the 1933 and 1934 Acts.

Nor are we persuaded that economic affairs have magnified in complexity since the Seventy-Third Congress, thereby rendering these distinctions any less arbitrary. Of course, affairs of commerce are more sophisticated now than fifty years earlier; but the transaction at issue here is not one that the appellees seek to steer clear of the securities laws because of its peculiar sophistication, and they do not argue that the transaction was unknown in earlier days. This is the simple purchase of 50 percent of a business by means of stock, a transaction as old as the concept of stock itself and certainly known to the drafter of the 1933 and 1934 Acts. If the increased sophistication of today's markets now renders appropriate a variety of distinctions that would have been rejected by the Seventy-Third Congress—an argument whose truth is hardly self-evident—we trust that Congress will amend the Acts accordingly.

6. *Adequacy of state-law protection*

Finally, it is urged that under the sale-of-business doctrine, the purchaser or seller of a business is not without a remedy for fraud; any remedy would simply lie in a common-law fraud action. We do not believe that the prospect of common-law remedies changes the analysis. The premise that common-law remedies are necessarily adequate in the sale-of-business context is flawed. The defendant, for example, may prove to be insolvent, prompting the plaintiff to seek out solvent defendants among those parties who may be sued by virtue of the absence of privity requirements under federal law. Congress, moreover, did not confine the protection of federal law to instances in which no adequate common-law remedy could be had. The Acts, for example, confer additional benefits on parties victimized by fraud, including the absence of express defenses and certain procedural advantages. In view of the Supreme Court's frequent emphasis on the remedial character of the securities Acts,[41] we do not take these proposed limitations on remedies lightly.

In summary, we do not believe that the policies underlying the Acts support the sale-of-business doctrine. To the contrary, the doctrine significantly undermines congressional policies, enhances uncertainty, and increases the likelihood of litigation. We turn now to whether recent Supreme Court authority requires a different conclusion.

B.

Recent Supreme Court Authority

In United Housing Foundation, Inc. v. Forman, 421 U.S. 837 (1975), the Supreme Court held that "stock" held by a tenant in a cooperative apartment building is not a security under the federal Acts. The Court's

---

41. See Herman & MacLean v. Huddleston, 459 U.S. 375, 103 S.Ct. 683, 689–90 (1983) (availability of express remedy under § 11 of 1933 Act does not preclude action under § 10b of 1934 Act); * * *.

analysis of the term "stock" admonished us to attend to substance over form:

> We reject at the outset any suggestion that the present transaction, evidenced by the sale of shares called "stock," must be considered a security transaction simply because the statutory definition of a security includes the words "any * * * stock." Rather we adhere to the basic principle that has guided all of the Court's decisions in this area:
>
> "[I]n searching for the meaning and scope of the word 'security' in the Act[s], form should be disregarded for substance and the emphasis should be on economic reality." * * *

See also *Howey,* supra, at 298.

421 U.S. at 848 (footnote omitted). The instruments held by the tenants, the Court concluded, lacked the attributes commonly associated with stock: the right to participate in dividends, negotiability, capacity to serve as collateral, voting rights in proportion to the number of shares owned, and appreciation in value. Consequently, the Court concluded, as a matter of economic reality the shares in issue were not "stock" within the meaning of the Acts. * * *

The Court then addressed whether the tenants' shares constituted an "investment contract" under the *Howey* test, concluding that they did not. Id. at 851–58. In the course of its investment contract analysis, the Court observed:

> In considering these [investment contract] claims we again must examine the substance—the economic realities of the transaction—rather than the names that may have been employed by the parties. We perceive no distinction, for present purposes, between an "investment contract" and an "instrument commonly known as a 'security.'" In either case, the basic test for distinguishing the transaction from other commercial dealings is "whether the scheme involves an investment of money in a common enterprise with profits to come solely from the efforts of others." *Howey,* 328 U.S. at 301. This test, in shorthand form, embodies the essential attributes that run through all of the Court's decisions defining a security. The touchstone is the presence of an investment in a common venture premised on a reasonable expectation of profits to be derived from the entrepreneurial or managerial efforts of others.

421 U.S. at 851–52 (footnote omitted).

The defendants now maintain that the foregoing passages direct that the *Howey* test is to be applied to all of the defined terms of the Act, including the definition of stock. We do not agree. In its discussion of stock, the Court's admonition to attend to economic reality simply instructed that the label "stock" is not dispositive if the instrument lacks the traditional elements associated with stock ownership. The Court's analysis was clearly not intended to, and did not, apply the *Howey* test to stock. Nor did the Court direct that an economic reality test be applied to stock other than to determine whether, as a matter of economic reality, the instrument was in fact "stock" as that term has historically been understood. The label of the instrument may be pierced in order to determine whether it indeed bears the indicia of stock ownership. In this case the district court has done so, holding that the "stock which Ruefenacht received contains all the attributes mentioned by the *Forman* Court as indicating that the transaction did involve a security." * * *.

In the second portion of the *Forman* Court's analysis—addressing the definition of "investment contract"—the Court's reference to economic reality prefaced the application of the *Howey* test. That analysis was entirely proper: the *Howey* test has for some 40 years been the appropriate metric for gauging whether, as a matter of economic reality, a business relationship constitutes an "investment contract." In no sense was the Court instructing that the *Howey* test also be applied to stock. Had the Court intended that result, of course, it would have done so. Nor was the Court holding that the same economic reality test applies to the definitions of "stock" and "investment contract." To the contrary, in assessing the economic reality of a stock transaction, we pierce the label and look to the underlying attributes of the instrument. In evaluating an investment contract, we apply the *Howey* test. Thus, *Forman* undermines rather than supports the defendants' position.

Subsequent Supreme Court authority is also unavailing. In International Brotherhood of Teamsters v. Daniel, 439 U.S. 551 (1981), the Court held that a non-contributory, compulsory pension plan was not an investment contract. In part the Court reasoned that ERISA supplanted any necessity for coverage by the securities Acts. 439 U.S. at 569–70. The Court expanded on this theme in Marine Bank v. Weaver, 455 U.S. 551 (1982), holding that a certificate of deposit insured by the FDIC did not constitute a security. Again the Court reasoned that the FDIC supplanted any necessity for coverage under the securities laws. 455 U.S. at 558. No such regulatory schemes apply in the sale-of-business context. Nor does the language in those opinions speak in favor of applying the investment-contract test to stock. Indeed, the Court's analysis in *Weaver* paralleled that of *Forman*: the Court first ascertained that a certificate of deposit is not a "note" or "withdrawable capital share," and only then turned to whether the separate agreement was an "investment contract" under the *Howey* test. 455 U.S. at 556–60. *Weaver* therefore reinforces our interpretation of *Forman*.

VI. Conclusion

We reject the sale-of-business doctrine as applied to sales of stock. The structure and history of the Acts—particularly Congress' express treatment of short-term notes and its conferral of exemption power on the SEC—counsel against such application. In addition, the doctrine is inconsistent with several policies underlying the Acts: it exacerbates uncertainty; undermines a congressional policy protecting certain instruments in order to reduce transaction costs and facilitate commerce; denies protection to investors simply because those persons are also "entrepreneurs"; deprives purchasers and sellers of part of the value of the bargain; and introduces arbitrary distinctions in the application of the definition of "security." Moreover, the doctrine derives from a misreading of United Housing Foundation, Inc. v. Forman, supra. *Forman* instructed that we attend to economic reality, in this case whether, as a matter of economic reality, the instrument has the attributes commonly associated with stock; *Forman* did not direct the application of the *Howey* test to stock. Finally, the doctrine originated as a limitation on the breadth of the word "note." While the

Howey standard might have been an imperfect expedient in the note area— a subject on which we express no opinion—a similar limitation on stock is unnecessary. Stock is a well-defined term, is not issued by consumers, and is not employed by business to finance current operational costs.

Thus, we hold that the sale of all or part of a business effectuated by the transfer of stock bearing the traditional incidents of stock ownership is the sale of a "security" under the 1933 and 1934 Acts. The judgment of the district court will be reversed and the case remanded for further proceedings consistent with this opinion.

[The concurring opinion of Hunter, Cir.J., is omitted.] a

LANDRETH TIMBER COMPANY v. LANDRETH

Supreme Court of the United States, 1985.
471 U.S. 681, 105 S.Ct. 2297, 85 L.Ed.2d 692.

JUSTICE POWELL delivered the opinion of the Court.

This case presents the question whether the sale of all of the stock of a company is a securities transaction subject to the antifraud provisions of the federal securities laws (the Acts).

I

Respondents Ivan K. Landreth and his sons owned all of the outstanding stock of a lumber business they operated in Tonasket, Washington. The Landreth family offered their stock for sale through both Washington and out-of-state brokers. Before a purchaser was found, the company's sawmill was heavily damaged by fire. Despite the fire, the brokers continued to offer the stock for sale. Potential purchasers were advised of the damage, but were told that the mill would be completely rebuilt and modernized.

Samuel Dennis, a Massachusetts tax attorney, received a letter offering the stock for sale. On the basis of the letter's representations concerning the rebuilding plans, the predicted productivity of the mill, existing contracts, and expected profits, Dennis became interested in acquiring the stock. He talked to John Bolten, a former client who had retired to Florida, about joining him in investigating the offer. After having an audit and an inspection of the mill conducted, a stock purchase agreement was negotiated, with Dennis the purchaser of all of the common stock in the lumber company. Ivan Landreth agreed to stay on as a consultant for some time to help with the daily operations of the mill. Pursuant to the terms of the stock purchase agreement, Dennis assigned the stock he purchased to B & D Co., a corporation formed for the sole purpose of acquiring the lumber company stock. B & D then merged with the lumber company, forming petitioner Landreth Timber Co. Dennis and Bolten then acquired all of petitioner's Class A stock, representing 85% of the equity, and six other investors together owned the Class B stock, representing the remaining 15% of the equity.

After the acquisition was completed, the mill did not live up to the purchasers' expectations. Rebuilding costs exceeded earlier estimates, and new components turned out to be incompatible with existing equipment.

a. Aff'd sub nom. Gould v. Ruefenacht, 471 U.S. 701, 105 S.Ct. 2308, 85 L.Ed.2d 708 (1985).

Eventually, petitioner sold the mill at a loss and went into receivership. Petitioner then filed this suit seeking rescission of the sale of stock and $2,500,000 in damages, alleging that respondents had widely offered and then sold their stock without registering it as required by the Securities Act of 1933 (the 1933 Act). Petitioner also alleged that respondents had negligently or intentionally made misrepresentations and had failed to state material facts as to the worth and prospects of the lumber company, all in violation of the Securities Exchange Act of 1934 (the 1934 Act).

Respondents moved for summary judgment on the ground that the transaction was not covered by the Acts because under the so-called "sale of business" doctrine, petitioner had not purchased a "security" within the meaning of those Acts. The District Court granted respondents' motion and dismissed the complaint for want of federal jurisdiction. It acknowledged that the federal statutes include "stock" as one of the instruments constituting a "security," and that the stock at issue possessed all of the characteristics of conventional stock. Nonetheless, it joined what it termed the "growing majority" of courts that had held that the federal securities laws do not apply to the sale of 100% of the stock of a closely held corporation. * * * Relying on United Housing Foundation, Inc. v. Forman, 421 U.S. 837 (1975), and SEC v. W.J. Howey Co., 328 U.S. 293 (1946), the District Court ruled that the stock could not be considered a "security" unless the purchaser had entered into the transaction with the anticipation of earning profits derived from the efforts of others. Finding that managerial control of the business had passed into the hands of the purchasers, and thus, that the transaction was a commercial venture rather than a typical investment, the District Court dismissed the complaint.

The United States Court of Appeals for the Ninth Circuit affirmed the District Court's application of the sale of business doctrine. [W]e granted certiorari. We now reverse.

II

It is axiomatic that "[t]he starting point in every case involving construction of a statute is the language itself." Blue Chip Stamps v. Manor Drug Stores, 421 U.S. 723, 756 (1975) (POWELL, J., concurring); accord, Teamsters v. Daniel, 439 U.S. 551, 558 (1979). Section 2(1) of the 1933 Act * * * defines a "security" as including

> "any note, stock, treasury stock, bond, debenture, evidence of indebtedness, certificate of interest or participation in any profit-sharing agreement, collateral-trust certificate, preorganization certificate or subscription, transferable share, investment contract, voting-trust certificate, certificate of deposit for a security, fractional undivided interest in oil, gas, or other mineral rights, * * * or, in general, any interest or instrument commonly known as a 'security,' or any certificate of interest or participation in, temporary or interim certificate for, receipt for, guarantee of, or warrant or right to subscribe to or purchase, any of the foregoing." [1]

As we have observed in the past, this definition is quite broad, Marine Bank v. Weaver, 455 U.S. 551, 556 (1982), and includes both instruments

---

1. We have repeatedly ruled that the definitions of "security" in § 3(a)(10) of the 1934 Act and § 2(1) of the 1933 Act are virtually identical and will be treated as such in our decisions dealing with the scope of the term. * * *

whose names alone carry well-settled meaning, as well as instruments of "more variable character [that] were necessarily designated by more descriptive terms," such as "investment contract" and "instrument commonly known as a 'security.'" SEC v. C.M. Joiner Leasing Corp., 320 U.S. 344, 351 (1943). The face of the definition shows that "stock" is considered to be a "security" within the meaning of the Acts. As we observed in United Housing Foundation, Inc. v. Forman, 421 U.S. 837 (1975), most instruments bearing such a traditional title are likely to be covered by the definition. * * *

As we also recognized in *Forman,* the fact that instruments bear the label "stock" is not of itself sufficient to invoke the coverage of the Acts. Rather, we concluded that we must also determine whether those instruments possess "some of the significant characteristics typically associated with" stock, * * * recognizing that when an instrument is both called "stock" and bears stock's usual characteristics, "a purchaser justifiably [may] assume that the federal securities laws apply," * * * We identified those characteristics usually associated with common stock as (i) the right to receive dividends contingent upon an apportionment of profits; (ii) negotiability; (iii) the ability to be pledged or hypothecated; (iv) the conferring of voting rights in proportion to the number of shares owned; and (v) the capacity to appreciate in value.[2] * * *

Under the facts of *Forman,* we concluded that the instruments at issue there were not "securities" within the meaning of the Acts. That case involved the sale of shares of stock entitling the purchaser to lease an apartment in a housing cooperative. The stock bore none of the characteristics listed above that are usually associated with traditional stock. Moreover, we concluded that under the circumstances, there was no likelihood that the purchasers had been misled by use of the word "stock" into thinking that the federal securities laws governed their purchases. The purchasers had intended to acquire low-cost subsidized living space for their personal use; no one was likely to have believed that he was purchasing investment securities. Ibid.

In contrast, it is undisputed that the stock involved here possesses all of the characteristics we identified in *Forman* as traditionally associated with common stock. Indeed, the District Court so found. * * * Moreover, unlike in *Forman,* the context of the transaction involved here—the sale of stock in a corporation—is typical of the kind of context to which the Acts normally apply. It is thus much more likely here than in *Forman* that an investor would believe he was covered by the federal securities laws. Under the circumstances of this case, the plain meaning of the statutory definition mandates that the stock be treated as "securities" subject to the coverage of the Acts.

Reading the securities laws to apply to the sale of stock at issue here comports with Congress' remedial purpose in enacting the legislation to protect investors by "compelling full and fair disclosure relative to the issuance of 'the many types of instruments that in our commercial world fall within the ordinary concept of a security.'" SEC v. W.J. Howey Co., 328 U.S., at 299 (quoting H.R.Rep. No. 85, 73d Cong., 1st Sess., 11 (1933)).

---

2. Although we did not so specify in *Forman,* we wish to make clear here that these characteristics are those usually associated with common stock, the kind of stock often at issue in cases involving the sale of a business. Various types of preferred stock may have different characteristics and still be covered by the Acts.

Although we recognize that Congress did not intend to provide a comprehensive federal remedy for all fraud, Marine Bank v. Weaver, 455 U.S. 551, 556 (1982), we think it would improperly narrow Congress' broad definition of "security" to hold that the traditional stock at issue here falls outside the Acts' coverage.

III

Under other circumstances, we might consider the statutory analysis outlined above to be a sufficient answer compelling judgment for petitioner.[3] Respondents urge, however, that language in our previous opinions, including Forman, requires that we look beyond the label "stock" and the characteristics of the instruments involved to determine whether application of the Acts is mandated by the economic substance of the transaction. Moreover, the Court of Appeals rejected the view that the plain meaning of the definition would be sufficient to hold this stock covered, because it saw "no principled way," 731 F.2d, at 1353, to justify treating notes, bonds, and other of the definitional categories differently. We address these concerns in turn.

A

It is fair to say that our cases have not been entirely clear on the proper method of analysis for determining when an instrument is a "security." This Court has decided a number of cases in which it looked to the economic substance of the transaction, rather than just to its form, to determine whether the Acts applied. In SEC v. C.M. Joiner Leasing Corp., for example, the Court considered whether the 1933 Act applied to the sale of leasehold interests in land near a proposed oil well drilling. In holding that the leasehold interests were "securities," the Court noted that "the reach of the Act does not stop with the obvious and commonplace." 320 U.S., at 351. Rather, it ruled that unusual devices such as the leaseholds would also be covered "if it be proved as matter of fact that they were widely offered or dealt in under terms or courses of dealing which established their character in commerce as 'investment contracts,' or as any interest or instrument commonly known as a 'security.'" Ibid.

SEC v. W.J. Howey Co., supra, further elucidated the Joiner Court's suggestion that an unusual instrument could be considered a "security" if the circumstances of the transaction so dictated. At issue in that case was an offering of units of a citrus grove development coupled with a contract for cultivating and marketing the fruit and remitting the proceeds to the investors. The Court held that the offering constituted an "investment contract" within the meaning of the 1933 Act because, looking at the economic realities, the transaction "involve[d] an investment of money in a common enterprise with profits to come solely from the efforts of others." 328 U.S., at 301.

This so-called "Howey test" formed the basis for the second part of our decision in Forman, on which respondents primarily rely. As discussed above, see Part II, supra, the first part of our decision in Forman concluded that the instruments at issue, while they bore the traditional label "stock," were not "securities" because they possessed none of the usual characteris-

---

3. Professor Loss suggests that the statutory analysis is sufficient. L. Loss, Fundamentals of Securities Regulation 212 (1983). See infra, at 11–12.

tics of stock. We then went on to address the argument that the instruments were "investment contracts." Applying the *Howey* test, we concluded that the instruments likewise were not "securities" by virtue of being "investment contracts" because the economic realities of the transaction showed that the purchasers had parted with their money not for the purpose of reaping profits from the efforts of others, but for the purpose of purchasing a commodity for personal consumption. 421 U.S., at 858.

Respondents contend that *Forman* and the cases on which it was based [4] require us to reject the view that the shares of stock at issue here may be considered "securities" because of their name and characteristics. Instead, they argue that our cases require us in every instance to look to the economic substance of the transaction to determine whether the *Howey* test has been met. According to respondents, it is clear that petitioner sought not to earn profits from the efforts of others, but to buy a company that it could manage and control. Petitioner was not a passive investor of the kind Congress intended the Acts to protect, but an active entrepreneur, who sought to "use or consume" the business purchased just as the purchasers in *Forman* sought to use the apartments they acquired after purchasing shares of stock. Thus, respondents urge that the Acts do not apply.

We disagree with respondents' interpretation of our cases. First, it is important to understand the contexts within which these cases were decided. All of the cases on which respondents rely involved unusual instruments not easily characterized as "securities." See n. 3, supra. Thus, if the Acts were to apply in those cases at all, it would have to have been because the economic reality underlying the transactions indicated that the instruments were actually of a type that falls within the usual concept of a security. In the case at bar, in contrast, the instrument involved is traditional stock, plainly within the statutory definition. There is no need here, as there was in the prior cases, to look beyond the characteristics of the instrument to determine whether the Acts apply.

Contrary to respondents' implication, the Court has never foreclosed the possibility that stock could be found to be a "security" simply because it is what it purports to be. In SEC v. C.M. Joiner Leasing Corp., 320 U.S. 344 (1943), the Court noted that "we do nothing to the words of the Act; we merely accept them. * * * In some cases, [proving that the documents were securities] might be done by proving the document itself, which on its face would be a note, a bond, or a share of stock." Id., at 355. Nor does *Forman* require a different result. Respondents are correct that in *Forman* we eschewed a "literal" approach that would invoke the Acts' coverage simply because the instrument carried the label "stock." *Forman* does not,

---

4. Respondents also rely on Tcherepnin v. Knight, 389 U.S. 332 (1967), and Marine Bank v. Weaver, 455 U.S. 551 (1982), as support for their argument that we have mandated in every case a determination of whether the economic realities of a transaction call for the application of the Acts. It is sufficient to note here that these cases, like the other cases on which respondents rely, involved unusual instruments that did not fit squarely within one of the enumerated specific kinds of securities listed in the definition. *Tcherepnin* involved withdrawable capital shares in a state savings and loan association, and *Weaver* involved a certificate of deposit and a privately negotiated profit sharing agreement. See Marine Bank v. Weaver, supra, at 557, n. 5, for an explanation of why the certificate of deposit involved there did not fit within the definition's category "certificate of deposit, for a security."

however, eliminate the Court's ability to hold that an instrument is covered when its characteristics bear out the label. See supra, at [280–281].

Second, we would note that the *Howey* economic reality test was designed to determine whether a particular instrument is an "investment contract," not whether it fits within *any* of the examples listed in the statutory definition of "security." Our cases are consistent with this view.[5] Teamsters v. Daniel, 439 U.S., at 558 (appropriate to turn to the *Howey* test to "determine whether a particular financial relationship constitutes an investment contract"); United Housing Foundation, Inc. v. Forman, 421 U.S. 837 (1975); see supra, at [230]. Moreover, applying the *Howey* test to traditional stock and all other types of instruments listed in the statutory definition would make the Acts' enumeration of many types of instruments superfluous. Golden v. Garafalo, 678 F.2d 1139, 1144 (CA2 1982). See Tcherepnin v. Knight, 389 U.S. 332, 343 (1967).

Finally, we cannot agree with respondents that the Acts were intended to cover only "passive investors" and not privately negotiated transactions involving the transfer of control to "entrepreneurs." The 1934 Act contains several provisions specifically governing tender offers, disclosure of transactions by corporate officers and principal stockholders, and the recovery of short-swing profits gained by such persons. See, e.g., 1934 Act, §§ 14, 16. Eliminating from the definition of "security" instruments involved in transactions where control passed to the purchaser would contravene the purposes of these provisions. Accord, Daily v. Morgan, 701 F.2d 496, 503 (CA5 1983). Furthermore, although § 4(2) of the 1933 Act exempts transactions not involving any public offering from the Act's registration provisions, there is no comparable exemption from the antifraud provisions. Thus, the structure and language of the Acts refute respondents' position.[6]

5. In support of their contention that the Court has mandated use of the *Howey* test whenever it determines whether an instrument is a "security," respondents quote our statement in Teamsters v. Daniel, 439 U.S. 551, 558, n. 11 (1979) that the *Howey* test " 'embodies the essential attributes that run through all of the Court's decisions defining a security' " (quoting *Forman*, 421 U.S., at 852). We do not read this bit of dicta as broadly as respondents do. We made the statement in *Forman* in reference to the purchasers' argument that if the instruments at issue were not "stock" and were not "investment contracts," at least they were "instrument[s] commonly known as a 'security' " within the statutory definition. We stated, as part of our analysis of whether the instruments were "investment contracts," that we perceived "no distinction, *for present purposes,* between an 'investment contract' and an 'instrument commonly known as a "security." ' " 421 U.S., at 852 (emphasis added). This was not to say that the *Howey* test applied to any case in which an instrument was alleged to be a security, but only that once the label "stock" did not hold true, we perceived no reason to analyze the case differently whether we viewed the instruments as "investment contracts" or as falling within another similarly general category of the definition—an "instrument commonly known as a 'security.' " Under either of these general categories, the *Howey* test would apply.

6. In criticizing the sale of business doctrine, Professor Loss agrees. He considers that the doctrine "comes dangerously close to the heresy of saying that the fraud provisions do not apply to private transactions; for nobody, apparently, has had the temerity to argue that the sale of a *publicly* owned business for stock of the acquiring corporation that is distributed to the shareholders of the selling corporation as a liquidating dividend does not involve a security." L. Loss, Fundamentals of Securities Regulation 212 (1983) (emphasis in original) (footnote omitted).

B

We now turn to the Court of Appeals' concern that treating stock as a specific category of "security" provable by its characteristics means that other categories listed in the statutory definition, such as notes, must be treated the same way. Although we do not decide whether coverage of notes or other instruments may be provable by their name and characteristics, we do point out several reasons why we think stock may be distinguishable from most if not all of the other categories listed in the Acts' definition.

Instruments that bear both the name and all of the usual characteristics of stock seem to us to be the clearest case for coverage by the plain language of the definition. First, traditional stock "represents to many people, both trained and untrained in business matters, the paradigm of a security." Daily v. Morgan, supra, at 500. Thus persons trading in traditional stock likely have a high expectation that their activities are governed by the Acts. Second, as we made clear in *Forman,* "stock" is relatively easy to identify because it lends itself to consistent definition. See supra, at [280–281]. Unlike some instruments, therefore, traditional stock is more susceptible of a plain meaning approach.

Professor Loss has agreed that stock is different from the other categories of instruments. He observes that it "goes against the grain" to apply the *Howey* test for determining whether an instrument is an "investment contract" to traditional stock. L. Loss, Fundamentals of Securities Regulation 211–212 (1983). As Professor Loss explains,

"It is one thing to say that the typical cooperative apartment dweller has bought a home, not a security; or that not every installment purchase 'note' is a security; or that a person who charges a restaurant meal by signing his credit card slip is not selling a security even though his signature is an 'evidence of indebtedness.' But *stock* (except for the residential wrinkle) is so quintessentially a security as to foreclose further analysis." Id., at 212 (emphasis in original).

We recognize that in SEC v. C.M. Joiner Leasing Corp., 320 U.S. 344 (1943), the Court equated "notes" and "bonds" with "stock" as categories listed in the statutory definition that were standardized enough to rest on their names. Id., at 355. Nonetheless, in *Forman,* we characterized *Joiner's* language as dictum. 421 U.S., at 850. As we recently suggested in a different context in Securities Industry Association v. Board of Governors, 468 U.S. 137 (1984), "note" may now be viewed as a relatively broad term that encompasses instruments with widely varying characteristics, depending on whether issued in a consumer context, as commercial paper, or in some other investment context. See id., at 150. We here expressly leave until another day the question whether "notes" or "bonds" or some other category of instrument listed in the definition might be shown "by proving [only] the document itself." SEC v. C.M. Joiner Leasing Corp., supra, at 355. We hold only that "stock" may be viewed as being in a category by itself for purposes of interpreting the scope of the Acts' definition of "security."

IV

We also perceive strong policy reasons for not employing the sale of business doctrine under the circumstances of this case.[7] By respondents' own admission, application of the doctrine depends in each case on whether control has passed to the purchaser. It may be argued that on the facts of this case, the doctrine is easily applied, since the transfer of 100% of a corporation's stock normally transfers control. We think even that assertion is open to some question, however, as Dennis and Bolten had no intention of running the sawmill themselves. Ivan Landreth apparently stayed on to manage the daily affairs of the business. Some commentators who support the sale of business doctrine believe that a purchaser who has the ability to exert control but chooses not to do so may deserve the Acts' protection if he is simply a passive investor not engaged in the daily management of the business. Easley, Recent Developments in the Sale-of-Business Doctrine: Toward a Transactional Context-Based Analysis for Federal Securities Jurisdiction, 39 Bus.Law. 929, 971–972 (1984); Seldin, When Stock is Not a Security: The "Sale of Business" Doctrine Under the Federal Securities Laws; 37 Bus.Law. 637, 679 (1982). In this case, the District Court was required to undertake extensive fact-finding, and even requested supplemental facts and memoranda on the issue of control, before it was able to decide the case. * * *

More importantly, however, if applied to this case, the sale of business doctrine would also have to be applied to cases in which less than 100% of

---

7. JUSTICE STEVENS dissents on the ground ˙ ɪt Congress did not intend the antifraud provisions of the federal securities laws to apply to "the private sale of a substantial ownership interest in [a business] simply because the transaction[ ] w[as] structured as [a] sale[ ] of stock instead of assets." Post, at ___. Justice Stevens, of course, is correct in saying that it is clear from the legislative history of the Securities Acts of 1933 and 1934 that Congress was concerned primarily with transactions "in securities * * * traded in a public market." United Housing Foundation, Inc. v. Forman, 421 U.S. 837, 849 (1975). It also is true that there is no indication in the legislative history that Congress considered the type of transactions involved in this case and in Gould v. Ruefenacht, infra.

The history is simply silent—as it is with respect to other transactions to which these Acts have been applied by the Commission and judicial interpretation over the half century since this legislation was adopted. One only need mention the expansive interpretation of § 10(b) of the 1934 Act and Rule 10b–5 adopted by the Commission. What the Court said in Blue Chip Stamps v. Manor Drug Stores, 421 U.S. 723 (1975), is relevant:

"When we deal with private actions under Rule 10b–5, we deal with a judicial oak which has grown from little more than a legislative acorn. Such growth may be quite consistent with the congressional enactment and with the role of the federal judiciary in interpreting it, see J.I. Case Co. v. Borak, [377 U.S. 426 (1964)], but it would be disingenuous to suggest that either Congress in 1934 or the Securities and Exchange Commission in 1942 foreordained the present state of the law with respect to Rule 10b–5. It is therefore proper that we consider, in addition to the factors already discussed, what may be described as policy considerations when we come to flesh out the portions of the law with respect to which neither the congressional enactment nor the administrative regulations offer conclusive guidance." Id., at 737.

See also Ernst & Ernst v. Hochfelder, 425 U.S. 185, 196–197 (1976).

In this case, unlike with respect to the interpretation of § 10(b) in Blue Chip Stamps, we have the plain language of § 2(1) of the 1933 Act in support of our interpretation. In Forman, supra, we recognized that the term "stock" is to be read in accordance with the common understanding of its meaning, including the characteristics identified in Forman. See supra, at 280–281. In addition, as stated in Blue Chip Stamps, supra, it is proper for a court to consider—as we do today—policy considerations in construing terms in these Acts.

a company's stock was sold. This inevitably would lead to difficult questions of line-drawing. The Acts' coverage would in every case depend not only on the percentage of stock transferred, but also on such factors as the number of purchasers and what provisions for voting and veto rights were agreed upon by the parties. As we explain more fully in Gould v. Ruefenacht, post, at 701, decided today as a companion to this case, coverage by the Acts would in most cases be unknown and unknowable to the parties at the time the stock was sold. These uncertainties attending the applicability of the Acts would hardly be in the best interests of either party to a transaction. Cf. Marine Bank v. Weaver, 455 U.S., at 559 n. 9 (rejecting the argument that the certificate of deposit at issue there was transformed, chameleon-like, into a "security" once it was pledged). Respondents argue that adopting petitioner's approach will increase the workload of the federal courts by converting state and common law fraud claims into federal claims. We find more daunting, however, the prospect that parties to a transaction may never know whether they are covered by the Acts until they engage in extended discovery and litigation over a concept as often elusive as the passage of control. Accord, Golden v. Garafalo, 678 F.2d 1145–1146.

V

In sum, we conclude that the stock at issue here is a "security" within the definition of the Acts, and that the sale of business doctrine does not apply. The judgment of the United States Court of Appeals for the Ninth Circuit is therefore

Reversed.[a]

JUSTICE STEVENS, dissenting. [The opinion is omitted.]

F. SUMMARY AND WRAP–UP

Excerpt from: CARL W. SCHNEIDER

THE ELUSIVE DEFINITION OF A SECURITY

14 Review of Securities Regulation 981–991 (1981).[b]

I. GENERAL CONSIDERATIONS

* * *

Section 2(1) of the Securities Act defines the term "security".

* * *

See also section 3(a)(10) of the Exchange Act; section 2(36) of the Investment Company Act of 1940; section 202(18) of the Investment Advisers Act of 1940.

---

a. See Hazen, Taking Stock of Stock and the Sale of Closely Held Corporations: When is Stock Not a Security?, 61 N.C.L. Rev. 393 (1983); Rosin, Functional Exclusions from the Definition of a Security, (pts. 1–2) 28 So.Tex.L.Rev. 333, ___ (1986–1987).

b. Copyright 1981. Reprinted with permission of the author and Standard & Poor's Corp. This article has been updated. See Schneider, Developments in Defining a "Security", 16 Rev. of Sec. Reg. 985 (1983); Id., Definition of a "Security"—1983/1984 Update, 17 Rev. of Sec. Reg. 851 (1984).

All of the definitions in section 2 of the Securities Act and in the other federal securities statutes are preceded by the preamble "unless the context otherwise requires." This "rubber" clause has been of material import in a number of cases. See, e.g., Exchange National Bank of Chicago v. Touche Ross & Co., 544 F.2d 1126 (2d Cir. 1976) (Friendly, J.), where the word "requires" was stressed, and the burden of showing this "requirement" was placed upon the party asserting that the statutory language should not be followed literally.   *   *   *

*   *   *

As a practical matter, it is likely that the inadequacy of disclosure or the existence of fraud affecting the transaction will militate toward the finding of a "security." For example, fraud tainting the offering seems to have influenced courts in the context of pyramid sales and multi-level distributorship programs. One court has characterized such a program as an "egregious promotional scheme." SEC v. Koscot Interplanetary, Inc., 497 F.2d 473, 486 (5th Cir. 1974).   *   *   *

*   *   *

The courts will frequently split an overall relationship, and find that it is composed of portions at least one of which constitutes a security. Thus, a variable annuity contract, which clearly had insurance features, was also determined to be a security, even though insurance products, as such, are exempt from the registration requirements. See SEC v. United Benefit Life Insurance Co., 387 U.S. 202 (1967); SEC v. Variable Annuity Life Insurance Co. of America, 359 U.S. 65 (1959).

*   *   *

In certain borderline areas, where there was a perceived need to protect investors, separate federal and/or state legislation has been passed, modeled in some respects after the disclosure provisions of the securities laws, to address particular situations. The topics covered by separate legislation include employee benefit plans covered by the Employee Retirement Income Security Act of 1974 ("ERISA"); interests in real estate, including condominiums; and the sale of franchises. The existence of an alternate scheme of federal legislation tailored to the particular circumstance has influenced certain courts to conclude that a security was not involved. See, e.g., International Brotherhood of Teamsters v. Daniel, 439 U.S. 551 (1979) (existence of ERISA cited as one of the policy reasons not to treat an interest in a non-contributory compulsory pension plan as a security under the securities laws)   *   *   *   [; Marine Bank v. Weaver, 455 U.S. 551 (1982). (A bank certificate of deposit was not a security; the existence of federal banking regulation and FDIC insurance provided abundant regulation. For a criticism of this rationale, see Note, 72 Va.L. Rev. 195 (1986).]

Inevitably, courts seem to be result-oriented and are influenced by who is suing whom for what. For example, if a sophisticated party is trying to disaffirm his or its own commitment by invoking the securities laws, such party is less likely to prevail than where the court believes the result would favor an unsophisticated party or "victim" of an improper scheme. For example, in Drovers Bank of Chicago v. SFC Corporation, 452 F.Supp. 580 (N.D.Ill.1978), a bank that later became insolvent issued 52 large denomination certificates of deposit totalling over $15 million to intermediaries who sold participations in these certificates, not exceeding $40,000 per participant, to over 1,600 individuals and entities throughout the United States.

The pooled funds of the investors were used to purchase the certificates of deposit. The intermediaries issued "Trust Certificates/Depositors' Receipts" to the ultimate purchasers. The purpose of the scheme was to allow the participating purchasers to have the advantage of the higher interest rates that a bank could pay on certificates of deposit of $100,000 or more. The action was instituted by the bank's successor in an effort to void the obligation to pay the higher rate of interest on the certificates of deposit. While the participation interests created by the intermediaries and sold to public investors certainly looked like securities, the court reached an opposite conclusion, probably influenced by the fact that a holding that the participations were securities would apparently have enabled the bank to avoid its commitment to pay the higher rate of interest.

The sales pitch of the promoter is of great significance in determining whether the investment is a security. Where investment and economic features or tax benefits are stressed, this militates in favor of finding a security. * * *.

Where the seller attracts the buyer by offering assets or facilities for the buyer's individual use or consumption, this generally militates toward finding no security. For example, stock in an apartment co-op was held to be not a security, even though the owner could realize a gain or loss on the eventual sale of his unit, since the purchaser was motivated primarily toward obtaining housing in which to live. Grenader v. Spitz, 537 F.2d 612 (2d Cir. 1976). The balance may tip the other way, however, with respect to vacation or resort area real estate where the sales pitch is to participate in a rental arrangement so that the purchaser of the unit can generate sufficient operating income to cover costs and can occupy the property himself for a portion of the year on an essentially cost-free basis.

The motive of the buyer—which is probably determined in large part from the sales pitch of the seller—is also very important. If he is oriented toward making an investment for a financial return, this militates toward finding a security. If he is oriented toward acquiring something for his own use or consumption, or if he enters a relationship (e.g., employment) where the investment aspects are not a dominant consideration, this militates toward finding no security.

The more investors there are in a parallel situation, the more likely it is that a security will be found. However, it is clear that an investment * * * by an individual investor in a face-to-face transaction can also be a security. [Gould v. Ruefenacht, 471 U.S. 701 (1985); Landreth Timber Company v. Landreth, 471 U.S. 681 (1985).]

II. "INVESTMENT CONTRACTS" AND THE HOWEY STANDARD

Most of the cases have involved the term "investment contract." It is clear that such a contract need not be in writing to be a security. In SEC v. W. J. Howey Co. * * *, the Supreme Court defined "investment contract" in terms of four factors (although there was also other broader language in the case):

[A]n investment contract for purposes of the Securities Act means a contract, transaction or scheme whereby a person [1] invests his money [2] in a common enterprise and [3] is led to expect profits [4] solely from the efforts of the promoter or a third party. * * *

The Court in *Howey* stated that the definition of securities "embodies a flexible rather than a static principle, one that is capable of adaptation to meet the countless and variable schemes devised by those who seek the use of the money of others on the promise of profits." 328 U.S. at 299. While most of the cases continue to recite the four-prong *Howey* test, each of the factors has been eroded in at least some contexts.

A. It is quite clear that the investor need not invest *"money."* The investor may contribute a note, other securities, or assets or property of almost any nature in a transaction, and can still receive a "security" in return. * * * Probably anything constituting legal consideration in a contract law sense would suffice.

B. The *"common enterprise"* test suggests by its plain meaning a number of investors who stand in a similar relationship to a business in which they invest in common—so called "horizontal commonality," which is illustrated by multiple shareholders or debentureholders of an issuing corporation. However, the common enterprise test may be satisfied by "vertical commonality" in some, but not all, circuits. For example, cases hold that discretionary securities or commodities trading accounts are securities where a single investor may expect profit out of his individual trading positions, while the broker selling the "security," represented by the discretionary account, expects profits in the form of commissions. E.g., SEC v. Continental Commodities Corp., 497 F.2d 516 (5th Cir. 1974). Accord, SEC v. Koscot Interplanetary, Inc., 497 F.2d 473 (5th Cir. 1974) (accepting the vertical commonality approach in the pyramid sales context). The vertical commonality approach has been rejected expressly, however, by other courts. E.g., Curran v. Merrill Lynch, Pierce, Fenner & Smith, Inc., 622 F.2d 216 (6th Cir. 1980). [Note, Discretionary Commodity Accounts as Securities, 53 Fordham L.Rev. 639 (1984); Jacobs, The Meaning of "Security" Under Rule 10b–5, 29 N.Y.L. Sch. L.Rev. 221, 361–67 (1984).]

C. The "expectation of profits" need not be in the form of a normal investment return. The "profit" can be in the form of the use of recreational facilities that the investor finances, occupancy of vacation real estate, etc. The expected "profit" may also be in the form of capital appreciation when an asset, rather than an interest in an ongoing business, is sold. See Aldrich v. McCulloch Properties, Inc., 627 F.2d 1036 (10th Cir. 1980).

D. The requirement that profits be realized *"solely from the efforts of the promoter or a third party"* has been very much eroded in the pyramid sales cases, where it is clear that the investor himself is expected to contribute significantly to the profit potential. In SEC v. Glenn W. Turner Enterprises, Inc., 474 F.2d 476 (9th Cir.), cert. denied, 414 U.S. 821 (1973), the court said that the critical inquiry is "whether the efforts made by those other than the investor are the undeniably significant ones, those essential managerial efforts which affect the failure or success of the enterprise." Id. at 482. * * *.

III. SOME SPECIFICS
* * *

A. *Notes, Other Evidences of Indebtedness, and Participations Therein.* There are many cases dealing with various forms of indebtedness that may or may not be evidenced by a promissory note. While the term "note" is included in the definition of security, many of the cases have held that notes in the context of normal commercial transactions are not securities within the contemplation of the securities laws. Typically, the cases involve attempts to invoke the antifraud provisions rather than a challenge to the nonregistration of the note.

[See the discussion in Exch. Nat'l Bank of Chicago v. Touche Ross & Co., supra, at 244; Ruefenacht v. O'Halloran, supra at 260.]

* * *

Participations in a commercial note or certificate of deposit may themselves be a separate "security" issued by the first-tier creditor, who in turn divides his interest in the note or certificate among other participants. The participation may be a security even if the underlying note arises in a commercial transaction with the first-tier creditor and is not a security. Lehigh Valley Trust Co. v. Central National Bank of Jacksonville, 409 F.2d 989 (5th Cir. 1969) * * *. But participation interests in a loan were deemed not to be a security in other cases. See American Fletcher Mortgage Co. v. U.S. Steel Credit Corp., 635 F.2d 1247 (7th Cir. 1980).

* * *

B. *Pension and Employee Benefit Plans.* An interest or participation in an involuntary non-contributory pension plan pursuant to a collective bargaining agreement was held not to be a security for purposes of the antifraud provisions of the securities laws. International Brotherhood of Teamsters v. Daniel, 439 U.S. 551 (1979); Wiens v. International Brotherhood of Teamsters, CCH ¶ 96,005 (D.C.Cal. Mar. 28, 1977). In an interpretive release, however, the SEC indicated that an interest in a voluntary contributory plan would be a security. Sec. Act Rel. No. 33–6188 (1980), supplemented by Sec. Act Rel. No. 33–6281 (1981). See Black v. Payne, 591 F.2d 83 (9th Cir.), cert. denied, 444 U.S. 867 (1979) (participation in a public employees' retirement plan was not a security); Fulk v. Bagley, 88 F.R.D. 153 (M.D.N.C.1980) (factual inquiry needed to determine whether benefit plans are securities); Newkirk v. General Electric Co., CCH ¶ 97,216 (N.D.Cal. Aug. 31, 1979) (contributory non-compulsory pension plan was not a security); Tanuggi v. Grolier, Inc., 471 F.Supp. 1209 (S.D.N.Y.1979) (a voluntary shared-contribution, defined-benefit pension plan was not a security). [Coward v. Colgate-Palmolive Co., 686 F.2d 1230 (7th Cir. 1982) (interest in a voluntary contributory pension plan is not a security)].

* * *

C. *Partnership Interests and Joint Ventures.* Limited partnership interests are generally classified as securities. [People v. Graham, 163 Cal.App.3d 1159, 210 Cal.Rptr. 318 (1985). However, the Uniform Limited Partnership Act (1985), adopted by the National Conference on Uniform Laws, permits a limited partner to protect his or her investment by exercising voting and other rights with respect to certain matters, without thereby being deemed to participate in control of the business. U.L.P.A. § 303, 6 U.L.A. 290 (1986 Pocket Part). (Shareholders of closely-held corporations frequently are given similar rights.) Nevertheless, limited partnership interests in these partnerships should be deemed to be securities. It would be advisable, however, to amend the federal and state securities laws specifically to include such limited partnership interests as securities. See Uniform Securities Act (1985) § 101(16), 7B U.L.A. 19 (1986 Pocket Part); Note, Are Limited Partnership Interests Securities? A Different Conclusion Under the California Limited Partnership Act, 18 Pac.L.J. 125 (1986).]

For most purposes, a general partnership interest is not treated as a security. However, when a general partner is expected to be a passive investor who will not participate in the management of the business, it may be argued that his interest is a security. [See Goodwin v. Elkins & Co., 730 F.2d 99 (3d Cir. 1984); Williamson v. Tucker, 645 F.2d 404 (5th Cir. 1981), cert. denied 454 U.S. 897 (1982)]; *Marlin Law*, avail. June 30, 1980, 562 Sec.Reg. & L.Rep. (BNA) C–3; *Brentwood Village Apartments, Ltd.*, avail. June 20, 1980, 561 Sec.Reg. & L.Rep. (BNA) at C–1 (on reconsideration). Conversely, it might be argued that the owner of a limited partnership interest does not have a security if he is actively involved in the management of the business in fact—e.g., if he is also a general partner. See Frazier v. Manson, 651 F.2d 1078 (5th Cir. 1981). * * * Although interests in joint ventures generally are not securities, they may constitute securities in some instances. See Williamson v. Tucker, 632 F.2d 579 (5th Cir. 1980); [McLish v. Harris Farms, Inc., 507 F.Supp. 1075 (E.D.Cal.1980) (joint venture in cattle sales and feed-lot operation); Less v. Lurie, 789 F.2d 624 (8th Cir. 1986) (interest in a general partnership formed as part of scheme to defraud investors is a security)].

D. *Leaseholds and Other Interests in Minerals.* While naked leaseholds or other interests in minerals may not be securities, a security is involved where an investor is substantially dependent on a promoter as a matter of economic reality for realizing any value out of the arrangement. See SEC v. C. M. Joiner Leasing Corp., 320 U.S. 344 (1943). [Fund of Funds, Ltd. v. Arthur Andersen & Co., 545 F.Supp. 1314 (S.D.N.Y.1982)]. But see Robertson v. Humphries, CCH ¶ 97,283 (10th Cir. Sept. 7, 1978). * * *

E. *Franchises, Pyramid Sales Programs and Multi-Level Distributorships.* Conventional franchises and similar arrangements where the franchisee has an active role to play under the franchise agreement are generally held not to be securities. Martin v. T. V. Tempo, Inc., 628 F.2d 887 (5th Cir. 1980); Piambino v. Bailey, 610 F.2d 1306 (5th Cir.), cert. denied, 101 S.Ct. 568 (1980) * * * However, pyramid sales programs and multi-level distributorships, which are essentially franchises, have been held to involve securities in particular factual contexts. SEC v. Koscot Interplanetary Inc., 497 F.2d 473 (5th Cir. 1974) * * *. See generally, Johnson & Campbell, Securities Law and the Franchise Agreement, 1980 Utah L.Rev. 311; Goodwin, Franchising in the Economy: The Franchise Agreement as a Security under Securities Act, Including 10b–5 Considerations, 24 Bus.Law. 1311 (1969).

F. *Real Estate—Condominiums, Co-ops, Units in Subdivisions, etc.* Condominiums or units in a real estate development may be securities if they involve rental pools and/or are sold through marketing arrangements that stress investment potential or the ability to derive income or cost-free use of the property. See generally Sec. Act Rel. No. 33–5347 (1973).

The nature of the marketing effort, as well as the substance of the arrangement, is important. See Westchester Corp. v. Peat, Marwick, Mitchell & Co., 626 F.2d 1212 (5th Cir. 1980) (sale of developed property at fixed intervals for fixed prices did not involve the sale of a security); Cameron v. Outdoor Resorts of America, Inc., 608 F.2d 187 (5th Cir. 1979), mod. on other grounds, 611 F.2d 105 (5th Cir. 1980) (condominium campsite development units were securities).

*   *   *

The interest in a normal apartment cooperative, even if it takes the form of a share of stock, is generally not considered to be a security. United Housing Foundation, Inc. v. Forman, 421 U.S. 837 (1975). This is so even if the co-op owner may realize either a gain or a loss on the eventual sale of his co-op unit. Grenader v. Spitz, 537 F.2d 612 (2d Cir.), cert. denied, 429 U.S. 1009 (1976). The SEC will decline to take no-actions with respect to "[t]ime-sharing and other novel real estate offerings." Sec. Act Rel. No. 33–6253 (1980).

Many jurisdictions have adopted special laws, modeled in some respects after the securities laws, to protect purchasers of various types of real estate interests, including co-ops and condominiums.

G. *Leases of Real Estate.* Leases of real estate generally are not considered securities, even though the lessor may be dependent in part on the success of the lessee's business, e.g., a "percentage rental" arrangement, where rental varies with the level of the lessee's sales, Klein v. Arlen Realty & Development Corp., 410 F.Supp. 1261 (E.D.Pa.1976); or where the lessee is very dependent on lessor's management, e.g., in a large multi-store shopping center, where the lessor retains many controls, Cordas v. Specialty Restaurants, Inc., 470 F.Supp. 780 (D.Ore. 1979). *   *   *

The purchase of a life membership in a retirement health care facility that included a lifetime lease of an apartment was held not to be a security. Waldo v. Central Indiana Retirement Home, CCH ¶ 97,680 (S.D.Ind. Nov. 16, 1979). See Aschenbach v. Covenant Living Centers—North, Inc., 482 F.Supp. 1241 (E.D.Wis.1980) (residency contracts were not securities).

H. *Animal Breeding Programs.* Courts have held that programs involving the breeding and sale of animals involve securities, or at least that a factual issue is raised. Smith v. Gross, 604 F.2d 639 (9th Cir. 1979) (earthworms); Miller v. Central Chinchilla Group, Inc., 494 F.2d 414 (8th Cir. 1974) (chinchillas); Continental Marketing Corp. v. SEC, 387 F.2d 466 (10th Cir. 1967), cert. denied, 391 U.S. 905 (1968) (beavers); Boone v. GLS Livestock Management, Inc., CCH ¶ 97,174 (D.Utah, Apr. 9, 1976) (cattle); SEC v. Payne, 35 F.Supp. 873 (S.D.N.Y.1940) (silver foxes). See also Exch. Act Rel. No. 34–15345 (1978) (earthworms). *   *   *

I. *Discretionary Security or Commodities Trading Accounts.* A discretionary securities or commodities trading account may be a security. *   *   * SEC v. Continental Commodities Corp., 497 F.2d 516 (5th Cir. 1974); *   *   *. But see Curran v. Merrill Lynch, Pierce, Fenner & Smith, Inc., 622 F.2d 216 (6th Cir. 1980); Milnarik v. M–S Commodities, Inc., 457 F.2d 274 (7th Cir.), cert. denied, 409 U.S. 887 (1972) *   *   *. See generally Bromberg, Commodities Law and Securities Law—Overlaps and Preemption, 1 J. of Corp.L. 217 (1976). The pooling of funds of various investors militates in favor of finding of a security. In jurisdictions accepting the "vertical commonality" test (see section II B, supra), however, even an individual non-pooled account may be a security. [See Peloso & LaBella, Determining If Discretionary Customer Accounts Are Securities, 9 Sec.Reg.L.J. 307 (1982); Note, Discretionary Trading Accounts in Commodity Futures Are Not Securities Absent Horizontal Commonality, 60 Wash.U.L.Q. 675 (1982); Discretionary Commodity Accounts as Securities: An Application of the *Howey* Test, 53 Fordham L.Rev. 639 (1984)].

J. *Investment Programs in Personal Property.* Various types of investment programs in personal property may be securities. The following factors militate in favor of finding a security, although no one is essential:

1. The seller-promoter exercises skill in selecting items to be purchased—e.g., fine art, diamonds, etc.

2. The seller-promoter manages the asset for the production of income.

3. The seller-promoter assists the purchaser in determining when or how the assets should be sold for capital appreciation.

4. The seller-promoter undertakes, expressly or by implication, to buy the asset from the original purchaser at a future date, or to find a purchaser for the original purchaser. This factor is especially significant if the asset is of a type that the intended purchaser cannot readily sell on his own. If the seller-promoter undertakes to repurchase the asset at the original sales price, or at a price related by a formula to the original sales price—e.g., the original sales price plus the equivalent of an interest differential—the arrangement may be in substance a security in the nature of an evidence of indebtedness, and may be treated as a loan. * * *

5. The investor has an undivided interest with other investors in a pool of assets.

* * *

M. *Memberships in Recreational Facilities.* Memberships in recreational facilities may be securities, especially if they are freely transferable, *Riviera Operating Co.*, avail. April 10, 1978, 449 Sec.Reg. & L.Rep. (BNA) C–1, or if the funds of the members are used as the initial capital to create the facility. Where interests in a country club are not transferable or assignable and have to be returned upon resignation, the SEC staff has concluded that no security is involved. *Bear's Paw Country Club*, avail. July 23, 1980. [And memberships in a system of outdoor resort campgrounds which did not include the right to share in profits and entailed no ownership interest in any assets of the campgrounds operation were not "securities" under the New York blue sky law. All Seasons Resorts, Inc. v. Abrams, 68 N.Y.2d 81, 506 N.Y.S.2d 10, 497 N.E.2d 33 (1986). For a comprehensive survey of the law, see Jacobs, The Meaning of "Security" Under Rule 10b–5, 29 N.Y.L.Sch.L.Rev. 211 (1984).] * * *

SECTION 2. EXEMPTED SECURITIES: SECTIONS 3(a)(2) THROUGH 3(a)(8)

Sections 3 and 4 of the Securities Act provide certain specific exemptions from the broad registration and prospectus requirements of § 5, although the antifraud provisions of both the 1933 and 1934 Acts remain applicable. Read literally, section 3 seems to exempt the securities themselves from the operation of the Act, unless the Act elsewhere provides otherwise. On the other hand, the various clauses of § 4 clearly are transaction exemptions, rather than securities exemptions.

Section 3(a)(1) is a transition section. It exempts from the registration requirements of the Act securities which were offered to the public prior to or shortly after adoption of the Act. The exemption, however, does not apply to "any new offering" of such securities by an "issuer" or "underwriter." The purpose of this exception was to exclude redistributions of outstanding securities which might be reacquired by the issuer as well as secondary sales by controlling persons through an underwriter. The cases have recognized that § 3(a)(1) is in reality a transaction exemption rather than a securities exemption.[1]

The securities covered by §§ 3(a)(2) through 3(a)(8), inclusive, are such that they were thought to be inappropriate subjects of regulation in this Act either because already subject to regulation by another governmental authority or because of the intrinsic nature of the securities themselves. Thus, broadly speaking, these comprise: (1) securities issued or guaranteed by a domestic governmental entity or by a national or state bank [§ 3(a)(2)][2]; (2) short term notes or bills of exchange [§ 3(a)(3)]; (3) securities of nonprofit, religious, educational, fraternal or charitable institutions [§ 3(a)(4)]; (4) securities of certain savings and loan associations and farmers' cooperatives [§ 3(a)(5)]; (5) interests in railroad equipment trusts [§ 3(a)(6)]; (6) certificates of a receiver, or trustee or debtor in possession in a bankruptcy proceeding, when issued with court approval [§ 3(a)(7)]; and (7) insurance policies or annuity contracts, issued subject to the supervision of a domestic governmental authority [§ 3(a)(8)]. However, § 24(d) of the Investment Company Act makes the § 3(a)(8) exemption inapplicable to any security of which an investment company is the issuer.

In recent years a series of amendments have been made to § 3(a)(2) expanding this exemption to include: (1) certain types of industrial development bonds, the interest on which is excludable from gross income under § 103(a)(1) of the Internal Revenue Code; (2) interests and participations in the traditional forms of common trust funds maintained by banks as investment vehicles in which the bank holds the assets in a bona fide fiduciary capacity; (3) interests and participations in collective trust funds maintained by banks for funding certain stock, bonus, pension or profit-sharing plans which meet the requirements for qualification under § 401(a) of the Internal Revenue Code; and (4) any interest or participation in a "separate account" maintained by an insurance company for funding certain stock, bonus, pension or profit-sharing plans which meet the requirements for qualification under IRC § 401(a) and certain annuity plans under IRC § 404(a)(2).

The default in the bonds issued by the Washington Public Power System (WPPSS) and the near default of the bonds of New York City and other American cities has raised the question whether all municipal securities should remain completely exempt from the disclosure requirements of the 1933 Act.[3] The legislative history indicates that the exemption was based upon the lack of "recurrent demonstrated abuses" in the municipal securi-

---

1. Ira Haupt & Co., 23 S.E.C. 589 (1946); SEC v. North American Research & Development Corp., 424 F.2d 63 (2d Cir. 1970).

2. This subsection is interpreted by the Commission also to include securities issued or guaranteed by United States branches or agencies of foreign banks located in the United States if federal or state regulation of the particular branch or agency is substantially equivalent to that applicable to domestic banks doing business in the same jurisdiction. Securities Act Release 6661 (Sept. 23, 1986).

Insurance companies have asked to be placed in the same competitive footing with banks in the growing field of financial guarantees. They seek a statutory amendment exempting corporate bond issues from 1933 Act registration if they are guaranteed by an insurance company with a triple-A rating. Wall St.J., Sept. 29, 1986, at 42, col. 1.

3. See In re Washington Public Power Supply System Securities Litigation, 623 F.Supp. 1466 (W.D.Wash.1985); Labich, Guess Who's Bought Whoops Bonds, Fortune, Apr. 29, 1985, at 53; Seligman, The Municipal Bond Disclosure Debate, 9 Del.J.Corp.L. 647 (1984).

ties market.[4] Further concerns were raised when § 3(a)(2) was amended to exempt certain industrial development bonds (IDBs) not previously exempted. IDBs are a form of revenue bond used by a municipality or other governmental subdivision to attract industry, provide housing or for other commercial purposes. Typically, the municipality issues revenue bonds to finance the construction of an industrial facility for a private corporation. The corporation rents the facility on a long-term basis for an amount which covers principal and interest on the bonds. The bonds are secured solely by a pledge of the revenues and a mortgage on the facilities, so that payment of the bonds is dependent upon the credit of the private corporation, rather than the municipal issuer. Thus, IDBs actually are "private activity" bonds which are funded by an industrial or commercial enterprise and conceptually are "indistinguishable from other corporate debt securities" that are subject to the registration requirements of the 1933 Act.[5] They have been widely used by retail chain stores and other private entrepreneurs because they provided tax advantages for the bondholder, a bonanza for the industrial enterprise as compared to competitors, and an exemption from the disclosure obligations of the 1933 Act. The Tax Equity and Fiscal Responsibility Act of 1982 (TEFRA) placed restrictions on the type of facilities financed with small issue IDBs and otherwise curtailed their use.[6] And the Tax Reform Act of 1986 has further curbed the abuses of this tax bonanza for certain private sector beneficiaries.

It should also be noted that the provisions of § 3(a)(2) relating to interests in certain investment vehicles maintained by banks and insurance companies do not extend an exemption from registration to: (1) either bank collective trust funds or insurance company "separate accounts" in connection with Keogh (H.R. 10) plans complying with the Self-Employed Individuals Tax Retirement Act of 1962, and (2) interests or participations in connection with qualified corporate pension or profit-sharing plans which constitute H.R. 10 plans covering employees, some or all of whom are employees within the meaning of IRC § 401(c)(1).

The House Committee Report explained that the statute "does not exempt interests or participations issued by either bank collective trust funds or insurance company separate accounts in connection with 'H.R. 10 plans,' because of their fairly complex nature as an equity investment and because of the likelihood that they could be sold to self-employed persons,

---

4. H.R.Rep. No. 85, 83rd Cong., 1st Sess. 7 (1933).

5. The SEC sponsored the Industrial Development Bond Act of 1978 which would have subjected these bonds to the registration requirements of the 1933 Act. S. 3323, 95th Cong., 2d Sess. (1978). The bill died for lack of support. For the history of industrial development bonds and a discussion of abuses arising from their use, see Seligman, supra note 2; Hellige, Industrial Development Bonds: The Disclosure Dilemma, 6 J. of Corp.L. 291 (1981). And see Note, Municipal Bonds and the Federal Securities Laws: The Results of Forty Years of Indirect Regulations, 28 Vand.L.Rev. 561, 605–11 (1975); Comment, Federal Regulation of Municipal Securities: A Constitutional and Statutory Analysis, 1976 Duke L.J. 1261, 1278–81 (1976); Note, Industrial Development Bonds, A Proposal for Reform, 65 Minn.L.Rev. 961 (1981); Note, Municipal Bonds: Is There a Need for Mandatory Disclosure?, 58 U.Det.J.U.L. 255 (1981); Shores v. Sklar, 647 F.2d 462 (5th Cir. 1981).

6. McGee, The Impact of TEFRA and the 1984 Act on Small Issue Industrial Development Bonds, 33 Emory L.J. 779 (1984); Note, Bedtime for [Industrial Development] Bonds?: Municipal Bond Tax Legislation of the First Reagan Administration, 48 L. & Contemp.Prob. 212 (Autumn 1985); Leifer & Plump, Uses of Industrial Development Bonds, 42 N.Y.U.Ann.Inst. on Fed.Tax. 7–1 (1984).

unsophisticated in the securities field." [7]   Although the 1970 amendment grants the Commission authority to exempt these security interests from the registration provisions of the 1933 Act, the Commission did not use this power until 1976, when an exemptive order was issued with respect to participation interests in connection with the establishment of a Keogh plan by a large law partnership. For some years thereafter, the Commission proceeded to issue *ad hoc* exemptive orders to groups of professionals where the employer was organized as a partnership, rather than a corporation.[8] In 1981, however, the Commission codified this practice by adopting Rule 180 which exempts from registration Keogh tax-qualified retirement plans established by partnerships, but the exemption is confined to law firms, accounting firms, investment banking firms, and firms that have secured independent expert investment advice in connection with their plans.[9] Parallel amendments have been added to § 3(a)(12) and § 12(g)(2)(H) of the Securities Exchange Act of 1934.

In general, there has not been very much litigation concerning the scope of these exemptions. Under § 3(a)(5), however, the exemption granted to securities of savings and loan associations was denied to a Maryland association where the vast majority of the shares were sold to the public not to provide loans for members but to use the proceeds to acquire slow-moving, dubious assets from the control group or their associates. Thus, although operating in the guise of a savings and loan association, the company failed to meet the test that substantially all of its business must be confined to making loans to members.[10]

Another issue which for a time was the subject of hot dispute between two segments of the insurance industry and the regulatory authorities was the place of the so-called "variable annuity" in the scheme of insurance and securities regulation. Section 3(a)(8) exempts "insurance" and "annuity" contracts when "subject to the supervision of the insurance commissioner * * * of any State. * * *" This clearly covers the fixed annuities which insurance companies have traditionally issued under which the annuitant is offered a specified and definite amount beginning at a certain time in the future.

On the other hand, the variable annuity was invented to provide a hedge against inflation. Under these contracts, a greater portion of the premiums collected are invested in common stocks; and the periodic benefits payable to the annuitant depend on the success of the insurance company's investment policy. In a sense the annuitant's interest in the portfolio of securities is something like that of an investor in a mutual fund. Because the variable annuity "places all the investment risks on the annuitant, none on the company" and "the concept of 'insurance' involves some investment risk-taking on the part of the company," the Supreme Court held that it was not an "annuity" for purposes of the § 3(a)(8) exemption.[11]

7. H.R.Rep. No. 91–1382, 91st Cong., 2d Sess. 44 (1970).

8. Securities Act Release No. 6188 (Feb. 1, 1980), 19 SEC Docket 465, 492–93 (Feb. 19, 1980).

9. Securities Act Release 6363 (Nov. 24, 1981).

10. SEC v. American International Savings & Loan Association, 199 F.Supp. 341 (D.Md.1961).

11. SEC v. Variable Annuity Co., 359 U.S. 65 (1959). And see SEC v. United Benefit Life Insurance Co., 387 U.S. 202 (1967), holding that a "flexible fund annuity" contract did not come within the § 3(a)(8) insurance exemption of the Securi-

More recently, the insurance industry has created a modified type of annuity which provides certain guarantees of principal and interest, regardless of investment results. The SEC has now accepted this investment vehicle, generally known as a "guaranteed investment contract," as entitled to an exemption from registration under § 3(a)(8), if it is issued and marketed under certain conditions. These conditions are specified in new Rule 151 which establishes a "safe harbor" under the § 3(a)(8) exemption. To qualify, the annuity contract must (1) be issued by a corporation (the insurer) that is subject to the supervision of a state insurance commissioner or an agency performing like functions; (2) provide guarantees of principal and interest sufficient for the insurer to be deemed to assume the investment risk; and (3) not be marketed primarily as an investment. The rule thus includes single premium deferred annuities.[12]

It should be noted also that there is no exemption for insurance company stocks and securities as such; only the "insurance" and "annuity" contracts written by them are exempt. Most of the problems relating to insurance company securities activities have arisen under the Investment Company Act of 1940.

Apart from §§ 3(a)(2) to 3(a)(8) the securities falling in the other paragraphs of Section 3 possess no inherent characteristics which should make them the subjects of a permanent exemption from federal regulation. They are in fact transaction exemptions. It is therefore appropriate to consider them elsewhere.

ties Act of 1933. On "insurance hybrids," see Loss, Fundamentals of Securities Regulation 213–224 (1983).

12. See Securities Act Release No. 6645 (May 29, 1986).

SUBDIVISION C. TRANSACTION EXEMPTIONS AVAILABLE TO ISSUERS OF SECURITIES

Chapter 5

THE PRIVATE OFFERING EXEMPTIONS: SECTIONS 4(2) AND 4(6)

Statutes and Regulations

Securities Act, §§ 2(4), 2(2), 4(1).

Introductory Note

We have been using the words "issuer" and "underwriter" without paying very much attention to what they mean in terms of the Securities Act. Although § 5 broadly prohibits the use of the channels of interstate commerce or the mails to sell a security unless a registration statement is in effect, § 4(1) specifically exempts transactions "by any person other than an issuer, underwriter, or dealer * * *." These terms thus serve to separate those persons who are subject to the registration or prospectus requirements from those who may ignore them. In this chapter we explore the concept of "issuer" and the transaction exemptions that are applicable to issuers in connection with the sale of securities. In Chapter 9, we will consider the meaning of the terms "underwriter" and "dealer" and their obligation to comply with the registration and prospectus provisions of the Act.

1. *Who is an "Issuer"?* An "issuer" is defined in § 2(4). In many cases there is not much difficulty in identifying the issuer of a security, although it need not be a corporation. Indeed, the issuer may be almost any juridical "person," since that term is defined in § 2(2) to mean an individual, a partnership, any trust or other unincorporated association, and a foreign or domestic government or its political subdivisions.[1]

It is to be noted further that an "issuer" includes persons who propose to issue a security as well as those who actually follow through and complete the transaction. The act of issuing a security arises from creation of a right in some other person in the form of an investment contract, whether or not evidenced by a written instrument, such as a share of stock.

---

1. The Exchange Act has similar, but not identical definitions of "issuer" and "person." See §§ 3(a)(8) (issuer) and 3(a)(9) (person). It is to be noted that municipal issuers are subject to the 1933 and 1934 Acts, including antifraud provisions. But note §§ 12(2) and 17(c) of the 1933 Act.

Thus when a promoter proposes to take a preincorporation subscription for shares in a corporation not yet formed, he intends to issue a security in the form of a "preorganization certificate or subscription." Obviously, the corporation cannot be the issuer for it is not in existence. The contract is to be made with the promoter and he has already become an issuer although this might come as a surprise to him.

If no exemption from registration is available, it is an added burden to have to register preincorporation subscriptions, since the underlying security will also be subject to registration. In actual practice, therefore, the promoter will usually dispense with the use of preorganization subscriptions. Instead, the corporation will be formed and the securities proposed to be issued will be registered without going through the extra motions. When this procedure is not followed, however, any preorganization selling activity, except preliminary negotiations between the issuer and an underwriter, is forbidden, unless some exemption from registration is available.

In SEC v. Murphy, 626 F.2d 633 (9th Cir. 1980), the court engaged in a search to determine the "issuer" in connection with a complex promotion entailing the sale of limited partnership interests. Murphy was a founder, director and officer of Intertie, a corporation engaged in financing, construction and management of cable television systems. Intertie would promote limited partnerships to which it sold newly packaged cable TV systems. Intertie would purchase an existing television system on credit. It would then sell the system to a newly organized partnership, and lease back the system from the partnership. ISC, a brokerage firm, unaffiliated with Intertie or Murphy, sold the limited partnership interests. An ISC representative was usually the general partner of the partnership, but neither Murphy nor Intertie were partners. Murphy was the architect of this promotion by which Intertie took approximately $7.5 million from 400 investors in 30 partnerships. He participated actively in the offerings. In an SEC injunction proceeding alleging violation of the registration and antifraud provisions of the securities acts, the court held Murphy to be an issuer of the securities: "[W]hen a person organizes or sponsors the organization of limited partnerships and is primarily responsible for the success or failure of the venture for which the partnership is formed, he will be considered an issuer for purposes of determining the availability of the private offering exemption." (644).[2]

There are a number of anomalous types of securities where the "issuer" is not readily identifiable. These include certificates of deposit; voting trust certificates; certificates of interest in unincorporated associations, investment trusts and business trusts; equipment trust certificates; and fractional undivided interests in oil, gas and other mineral rights. As to these securities, § 2(4) describes in some detail the persons who shall be treated as issuer for the purposes of the Securities Act. Thus, in the case of oil, gas and mineral rights generally, the issuer is any owner of such right (whether whole or fractional) who splits up his right into fractions for the purpose of making a public offering of those interests. Designation of the issuer has a bearing on who shall sign the registration statement as well as determining possible liability under Section 11.

---

2. Accord, SEC v. Holschuh, 694 F.2d 130 (7th Cir. 1982). The court noted that § 4(1) is a transaction exemption and that one who participates in or is a "substantial factor" in the unlawful sales transaction satisfies the test for primary liability in an enforcement action for injunctive relief.

2. *The Private Offering Exemptions.* There are a number of transaction exemptions which enable an issuer to avoid the registration and prospectus requirements of the 1933 Act. One set of these exemptions is available where the transaction by the issuer does not involve any public offering of securities.

Two of the private offering exemptions are statutory: § 4(2) and § 4(6). Section 4(2), which is commonly referred to as the "private offering" exemption, excludes from registration "transactions by an issuer not involving any public offering." Such an exemption is absolutely essential for there to be a workable system of Federal securities regulation. It would be inconceivable to require that, when any business is formed and capital is obtained from anyone outside of the entrepreneurial group, federal registration would be required, unless some other exemption were available, such as Regulation A (the small issue exemption) or the intrastate offering exemption.

At one end of the spectrum is the situation in which business people about to start up a new business or expand a small, closely held business, need additional capital. Frequently, the most immediate sources of capital are members of the family, friends or business, professional and social acquaintances. So long as offerings were confined to a limited number of these persons who presumably knew the principals and were willing to make an investment in the projected enterprise, it had generally been assumed that the nonpublic offering exemption was available. The purchase, however, must be for "investment" and not with a view to resale. Frequently the "seed capital" to launch the business would be raised from these immediate sources. The result was the saving of enormous costs entailed in registration such as legal and accounting fees, underwriting expenses, printing costs and the like.

At the other end of the spectrum, well established companies were in a position to make a private placement of institutional grade securities with insurance companies, pension funds, foundations and other institutional investors. Underwriters and some banks have specialized in making these private placements, and again, it was generally assumed that the private offering exemption was available because of the sophistication of the offerees of the securities. The number of participants was not thought to be significant.

In between these types of financing, there developed a grey area as to which it was difficult for lawyers to give opinions with any confidence. Moreover, beginning in the 1950's, start-up, growth companies were organized in which more remote sources of capital were tapped, such as wealthy individuals, venture capital firms, small business investment companies, and institutional investors, including mutual funds. Sometimes a group of investors would provide the "seed capital" for the first round of financing with a view toward further participation in later rounds of financing as the business expanded.

Section 4(2) exempts "transactions by an issuer, not involving any public offering" from the registration requirements of the 1933 Act. The exemption is self-determining with the burden of proof being placed on the issuer and others relying upon the exemption. However, the statute and legislative history throw very little light on its scope. The House Committee Report contained the cryptic statement that these transactions were exempted "so as to permit an issuer to make a specific or an isolated sale of its securities to a particular person, but if a sale * * * should be made generally to the public that transaction would come within the purview of the Act." The Committee further emphasized that the bill "carefully exempts from its application transactions where there is no practical need for its application or where the public benefits are too remote.[1]

In the early years of the administration of the Act, a number of criteria were suggested for determining what constitutes a nonpublic offering.

(1) *The numerical test.* At the lower end of the spectrum, the General Counsel early expressed the view that an offering to not more than approximately twenty-five persons is not an offering to a substantial number of persons and presumably does not involve a public offering.[2] In fact, however, sales were made of large blocks of investment quality securities to institutional investors. In some cases the number approached 100, but the Commission did not raise any question as the availability of the private offering exemption if all were institutional investors such as insurance companies and pension trusts. As to these persons, numbers seemed less important.

(2) *The availability of information.* The availability of information to the offerees is a key factor in establishing the exemption—some argue it is essentially the only factor that should be considered. They stress that this appears "to be the proper approach, since disclosure is in fact all that the registration process provides by way of investor protection (apart from the antifraud provisions)".[3]

(3) *Access to Information.* The access test may be met in two ways: (1) by actually furnishing such information directly to the offeror; or (2) by the offeree having access to such information either as an employee, by virtue of a family relationship or through economic bargaining power.

(4) *Nature of the Offerees.* It is clear that the Commission and courts also took into account the financial sophistication of the investor and his or her ability to bear the economic risk of the investment.

(5) *The Manner of Offering.* The concept of a private offering precludes general advertising or general solicitation through which offers are made.

Over the years considerable uncertainty arose as to the scope of the § 4(2) exemption. In 1974, the Commission sought to provide "more objective standards" under the private offering exemption by adopting former Rule 146. The Rule provided that transactions by an issuer shall not be deemed to involve any public offering within the meaning of § 4(2) if they were part of an offering that met all of the conditions of the rule.

The adoption of Rule 146 did not stem the tide of criticism of the stringent criteria imposed by § 4(2) as interpreted by the courts. (See particularly *Doran v. Petroleum Corp.,* infra at page 308.) Although Rule 146 was described by the Commission as a "safe harbor" from the pitfalls of § 4(2), it imposed even more stringent and subjective standards upon issuers and their representatives regarding the qualifications of an offeree

---

1. H.R. No. 85, 73d Cong., 1st Sess. 16 (1933).

2. General Counsel's Opinion, Securities Act Release No. 285, Jan. 24, 1935.

3. Schneider, Section 4(2) in 12th Ann. Inst. on Sec.Reg. 295, 296 (PLI 1981).

with respect to his or her knowledge and experience in financial matters and ability to evaluate and bear the risks of a prospective investment.

In 1980, the Commission issued Rule 242 in response to complaints voiced by various commentators concerning compliance with the strictures of Rule 146.[4] Although Rule 242 was promulgated pursuant to the Commission's authority under Section 3(b), the small issues exemption, it was essentially a private offering exemption in that it prohibited public solicitation and general advertising and limited offers and sales only to specified types of persons and to a maximum number of purchasers. The rule introduced the concept of an "accredited investor", defined to include various types of institutional investors, corresponding to the list later enumerated in § 2(15) of the 1933 Act. Sales could be made of restricted securities up to $2 million within any six months period to an unlimited number of accredited investors plus thirty-five other qualified persons. Rule 242 has since been superseded by Rule 505 of Regulation D.

In the meantime, Congress had become concerned that American business, and particularly small business, had experienced difficulty in raising investment capital and that part of the problem arose from difficulties in complying with the stringent criteria imposed by Section 4(2) and former Rule 146, now superseded by Rule 506 of Regulation D.[5] Although the Commission had alleviated some of these concerns by the adoption of Rule 242, Congress took further action to aid small business through the enactment of the Small Business Incentive Act of 1980.[6] A new section 4(6) was added to the 1933 Act which provides an additional statutory exemption for offers and sales by an issuer to "accredited investors," if the offer and sale does not exceed the dollar limit allowed under Section 3(b), and where there is no advertising or public solicitation entailed in the offer. Section 4(6) thus adopts the "accredited investor" concept used in former Rule 242 and that term is defined in new section 2(15). The Commission is granted the authority to enlarge the definition to include additional purchasers as "accredited investors" based upon such factors as financial sophistication, net worth, knowledge, experience in financial matters, or amounts of assets under management. It is to be noted that under § 4(6), offers or sales may be made to an unlimited number of "accredited investors". Rule 505 of Regulation D essentially tracks § 4(6), but there are slight differences which should be checked out.

Section 4(2), Rule 506, Rule 505 and Section 4(6) are interrelated, although they contain differing conditions for their use. Persons who

---

4. See Summary of Comments Relating to Small Business Hearings and Proposed Form S–18, Division of Corporation Finance, Securities and Exchange Commission, File No. S 7–734 at 148; Securities Act Release No. 6180 (Feb. 25, 1980); Marsh, Who Killed the Private Offering Exemption? A Legal Whodunit, 71 Nw.U.L.Rev. 470 (1976); Campbell, The Plight of Small Issuers Under the Securities Act of 1933: Practical Foreclosure From the Capital Markets, 1977 Duke L.J. 1139; Heumann, Is Rule 146 Too Subjective to Provide the Needed Predictability in Private Offerings?, 55 Neb.L.Rev. 1 (1975).

5. Hearings on Small Business Access to Equity and Venture Capital. Before the Subcomm. on Capital, Investment and Business Opportunities of the House Comm. on Small Business, 95th Cong., 1st Sess. (1977): Hearings on the Economic Problems of Small Business Before the Subcomm. on Energy and Environment of the House Comm. on Small Business, 94th Cong. 2d Sess. (1977); Hearings on the Overregulation of Small Business Before the Subcomm. on Government Regulation of the Senate Select Comm. on Small Business, 94th Cong., 1st Sess. (1977).

6. Pub. Law 96–477, § 602.

acquire securities from issuers in a transaction complying with any of these exemptions acquire securities that are unregistered; they are thus deemed to be "restricted securities" and can only be reoffered or resold if registered, or pursuant to an exemption from the registration provisions of the Act. The restrictions on resales of such securities are explored in Chapter 9. We shall consider (1) Section 4(2) and the evolution of the § 4(2) statutory law; and (2) the impact of former Rule 146 on the statutory law of private placements.

Statutes and Regulations

Securities Act §§ 4(2), 4(6), 2(15), Form 4(6).

Rule 152.

SECURITIES AND EXCHANGE COMMISSION v. RALSTON PURINA CO.

Supreme Court of the United States, 1953.
346 U.S. 119, 73 S.Ct. 981, 97 L.Ed. 1494.

MR. JUSTICE CLARK delivered the opinion of the Court. Section 4(1) of the Securities Act of 1933 exempts "transactions by an issuer not involving any public offering" from the registration requirements of § 5. We must decide whether Ralston Purina's offerings of treasury stock to its "key employees" are within this exemption. On a complaint brought by the Commission under § 20(b) of the Act seeking to enjoin respondent's unregistered offerings, the District Court held the exemption applicable and dismissed the suit. The Court of Appeals affirmed. The question has arisen many times since the Act was passed; an apparent need to define the scope of the private offering exemption prompted certiorari. * * *

Ralston Purina manufactures and distributes various feed and cereal products. Its processing and distribution facilities are scattered throughout the United States and Canada, staffed by some 7,000 employees. At least since 1911 the company has had a policy of encouraging stock ownership among its employees; more particularly, since 1942 it has made authorized but unissued common shares available to some of them. Between 1947 and 1951, the period covered by the record in this case, Ralston Purina sold nearly $2,000,000 of stock to employees without registration and in so doing made use of the mails.

In each of these years, a corporate resolution authorized the sale of common stock "to employees * * * who shall, without any solicitation by the Company or its officers or employees, inquire of any of them as to how to purchase common stock of Ralston Purina Company." A memorandum sent to branch and store managers after the resolution was adopted, advised that "The only employees to whom this stock will be available will be those who take the initiative and are interested in buying stock at present market prices." Among those responding to these offers were employees with the duties of artist, bakeshop foreman, chow loading foreman, clerical assistant, copywriter, electrician, stock clerk, mill office clerk, order credit trainee, production trainee, stenographer, and veterinarian. The buyers lived in over fifty widely separated communities scattered from Garland, Texas to Nashua, New Hampshire and Visalia, California. The lowest salary bracket of those purchasing was $2,700 in 1949, $2,435 in 1950 and $3,107 in 1951. The record shows that in 1947, 243 employees bought stock, 20 in 1948, 414 in 1949, 411 in 1950, and the 1951 offer, interrupted by this litigation, produced 165 applications to purchase. No records were kept of those to whom the offers were made; the estimated number in 1951 was 500.

The company bottoms its exemption claim on the classification of all offerees as "key employees" in its organization. Its position on trial was that "A key employee * * * is not confined to an organization chart. It would include an individual who is eligible for promotion, an individual who especially influences others or who advises others, a person whom the employees look to in some special way, an individual, of course, who carries some special responsibility, who is sympathetic to management and who is ambitious and who the management feels is likely to be promoted to a greater responsibility." That an offering to all of its employees would be public is conceded.

The Securities Act nowhere defines the scope of § 4(1)'s private offering exemption. Nor is the legislative history of much help in staking out its boundaries. The problem was first dealt with in § 4(1) of the House Bill, H.R. 5480, 73d Cong., 1st Sess., which exempted "transactions by an issuer not with or through an underwriter; * * *." The bill, as reported by the House Committee, added "and not involving any public offering." H.R.Rep. No. 85, 73d Cong., 1st Sess. 1. This was thought to be one of those transactions "where there is no practical need for * * * [the bill's] application or where the public benefits are too remote." Id., at 5. The exemption as thus delimited became law. It assumed its present shape with the deletion of "not with or through an underwriter" by § 203(a) of the Securities Exchange Act of 1934, * * * a change regarded as the elimination of superfluous language. H.R.Rep. No. 1838, 73d Cong., 2d Sess. 41.

Decisions under comparable exemptions in the English Companies Acts and state "blue sky" laws, the statutory antecedents of federal securities legislation have made one thing clear—to be public, an offer need not be open to the whole world. In Securities and Exchange Comm. v. Sunbeam Gold Mines Co., 9 Cir., 1938, 95 F.2d 699, 701, this point was made in dealing with an offering to the stockholders of two corporations about to be merged. Judge Denman observed that:

"In its broadest meaning the term 'public' distinguishes the populace at large from groups of individual members of the public segregated because of some common interest or characteristic. Yet such a distinction is inadequate for practical purposes; manifestly, an offering of securities to all red-headed men, to all residents of Chicago or San Francisco, to all existing stockholders of the General Motors Corporation or the American Telephone & Telegraph Company, is no less 'public' in every realistic sense of the word, than an unrestricted offering to the world at large. Such an offering, though not open to everyone who may choose to apply, is none the less 'public' in character, for the means used to select the particular individuals to whom the offering is to be made bear no sensible relation to the purposes for which the selection is made. * * * To determine the distinction between 'public' and 'private' in any particular context, it is essential to examine the circumstances under which the distinction is sought to be established and to consider the purposes sought to be achieved by such distinction."

The courts below purported to apply this test. The District Court held, in the language of the Sunbeam decision, that "The purpose of the selection bears a 'sensible relation' to the class chosen," finding that "The sole purpose of the 'selection' is to keep part stock ownership of the business within the operating personnel of the business and to spread ownership throughout all departments and activities of the business." The Court of Appeals treated the case as involving "an offering, without solicitation, of common stock to a selected group of key employees of the issuer, most of whom are already stockholders when the offering is made, with the sole purpose of enabling them to secure a proprietary interest in the company or to increase the interest already held by them."

Exemption from the registration requirements of the Securities Act is the question. The design of the statute is to protect investors by promoting full disclosure of information thought necessary to informed investment decisions. The natural way to interpret the private offering exemption is in light of the statutory purpose. Since exempt transactions are those as to which "there is no practical need for * * * [the bill's] application," the applicability of § 4(1) should turn on whether the particular class of persons affected need the protection of the Act. An offering to those who are shown to be able to fend for themselves is a transaction "not involving any public offering."

The Commission would have us go one step further and hold that "an offering to a substantial number of the public" is not exempt under § 4(1). We are advised that "whatever the special circumstances, the Commission has consistently interpreted the exemption as being inapplicable when a large number of offerees is involved." But the statute would seem to apply to a "public offering" whether to few or many. It may well be that offerings to a substantial number of persons would rarely be exempt. Indeed nothing prevents the commission, in enforcing the statute, from using some kind of numerical test in deciding when to investigate particular exemption claims. But there is no warrant for superimposing a quantity limit on private offerings as a matter of statutory interpretation.

The exemption, as we construe it, does not deprive corporate employees, as a class, of the safeguards of the Act. We agree that some employee offerings may come within § 4(1), e.g., one made to executive personnel who because of their position have access to the same kind of information that the act would make available in the form of a registration statement. Absent such a showing of special circumstances, employees are just as much members of the investing "public" as any of their neighbors in the community. Although we do not rely on it, the rejection in 1934 of an amendment which would have specifically exempted employee stock offerings supports this conclusion. The House Managers, commenting on the Conference Report said that "the participants in employees' stock-investment plans may be in as great need of the protection afforded by availability of information concerning the issuer for which they work as are most other members of the public." H.R.Rep. No. 1838, 73d Cong., 2d Sess. 41.

Keeping in mind the broadly remedial purposes of federal securities legislation, imposition of the burden of proof on an issuer who would plead the exemption seems to us fair and reasonable. * * * Agreeing, the court below thought the burden met primarily because of the respondent's purpose in singling out its key employees for stock offerings. But once it is seen that the exemption question turns on the knowledge of the offerees, the issuer's motives, laudable though they may be, fade into irrelevance. The focus of inquiry should be on the need of the offerees for the protections afforded by registration. The employees here were not shown to have access to the kind of information which registration would disclose. The obvious opportunities for pressure and imposition make it advisable that they be entitled to compliance with § 5.

Reversed.

The CHIEF JUSTICE and MR. JUSTICE BURTON dissent.[a]

SCOPE OF THE PRIVATE OFFERING EXEMPTION: JUDICIAL INTERPRETATIONS IN THE PRE–RULE 146 PERIOD

After the *Ralston Purina* case in 1953, there were a number of cases interpreting the private offering exemption. In many of those cases the defendant foundered on the inability to meet the burden of proof as to the number of offers actually made. Then in 1971, the Fifth Circuit decided Hill York Corp. v. American International Franchises, Inc.[1] Thirteen persons had paid $5,000 each for stock in a fast-food franchising corporation. All of the purchasers were sophisticated businessmen and attorneys who planned to do business with the issuer, not the average man on the street. The rec ord, however, contained no evidence of the total number of offerees. The plaintiffs brought an action to rescind the transaction and, in a jury trial, were awarded rescission of the stock sale and damages on the basis of violations of sections 5 and 12(2) of the 1933 Act. In affirming the judgment, the court approved the trial court's jury charge "that every offeree had to have information equivalent to that which a registration statement would disclose". The court also rejected the contention that a high degree of business or legal sophistication on the part of the offerees would be enough to establish the exemption. Even if the offerees were lawyers and businessmen, if they did not possess the information required to be contained in a registration statement, "they could not bring their sophisticated knowledge of business affairs to bear in deciding whether or not to invest. * * *"[2]

Hill York was followed in the Fifth Circuit by the *Continental Tobacco* bombshell, SEC v. Continental Tobacco Co., 463 F.2d 137 (5th Cir. 1972). In *Continental Tobacco*, a written prospectus, including unaudited financial statements prepared by a Certified Public Accountant was used in the offering. Moreover the offerees who purchased signed "investment letters" acknowledging receipt of the prospectus, which was designed to give them all the information registration would have afforded. Nevertheless, the court held that even if the prospectus that was sent to the purchasers contained all the information which a registration would have disclosed, "that fact alone would not justify the exemption." Furthermore, the court emphasized that the purchasers did not have the opportunity to inspect the corporation's records or to verify the statements made in the prospectus, and that at least some of the purchasers

---

a. Notes, 48 Nw.U.L.Rev. 771 (1954); 21 U.Chi.L.Rev. 113 (1953). The opinions of the lower courts evoked comments in 66 Harv.L.Rev. 1144 (1953); 39 Va.L.Rev. 376 (1953).

1. 448 F.2d 680 (5th Cir. 1971).
2. Id. at 690.

had never met any officers of the company prior to acquiring the stock. In sum, in *Hill York* and *Continental Tobacco*, the court seemed to lay down a test that the exemption was lost unless: 1. the offer was made to a limited number of offerees; 2. who must be sophisticated purchasers having a relation to each other and to the issuer; 3. with access to all the information a registration would disclose; and 4. with an actual opportunity to inspect the company's records or otherwise verify for themselves the statements made to them as inducements for the purchase.

On the same day that *Continental Tobacco* was decided, in Henderson v. Hayden Stone Inc.,[3] the Fifth Circuit allowed a wealthy investor who had invested $180,000 in a speculative "start-up" company to rescind the transaction and get his money back, even though he was aware at the time of the transaction that the stock was not registered. The plaintiff had some six brokerage accounts and read the leading financial publications, and, admittedly, could only be described as a sophisticated investor. Although the evidence showed that sales had actually been made only to seven other individuals, the Fifth Circuit reversed the district court because defendants failed to establish how many other offers may have been made by those engaged in the selling effort.

On the basis of these decisions in the Fifth Circuit, some commentators contended that the private offering exemption had been destroyed for all practical purposes.[4] It is important to note, however, that in each of the three Fifth Circuit cases, the defendants had failed to meet the burden of proof placed upon persons claiming entitlement to the exemption. Two years later, the Commission adopted Rule 146 to provide "more objective standards" for determining when sales by an issuer would be deemed to be a transaction not involving a public offering within the meaning of Section 4(2).

In Woolf v. S. D. Cohn & Co.[5] and Doran v. Petroleum Corp.,[6] the Fifth Circuit sought to explain, if not to limit, *Continental Tobacco*. As you read *Doran*, which follows, what are your answers to the following questions: (1) How, if at all, does *Doran* limit *Continental Tobacco*? (2) What factors are relevant in determining whether an offering qualifies for the § 4(2) exemption? (3) What factors are essential to establish the exemption, even if not alone sufficient? (4) What various combinations of factors are together sufficient to establish the exemption? (5) In your opinion, are the factors (and combinations of factors) given in response to questions (3) and (4) appropriate for determining whether a transaction should qualify for the exemption? (6) When does an offeree have access? How is the existence of access to be determined? What is the relationship between access and offeree sophistication? (7) In *Doran*, the issuer was not a 1934 Act reporting company. Would access to information exist whenever the issuer is a 1934 Act reporting company? To what extent are the S–1 registration disclosures duplicated in Form 10 and Form 10–K reports and to what extent would (should) these 1934 Act reports be deemed accessible to offerees?

---

3. 461 F.2d 1069 (5th Cir. 1972).

4. See Kripke, Wrap-up, in Revolution in Securities Regulation, 29 Bus.Law. 185, 187 (Special Issue, Mar. 1974); Kripke, SEC Rule 146: A 'Major Blunder,' N.Y.L.J., July 5, 1974; S. Goldberg, Private Placements and Restricted Securities § 2.16[a] (rev. ed. 1975); Marsh, Who Killed

the Private Offering Exemption?, A Legal Whodunit, 71 Nw.U.L.Rev. 470 (1977).

5. 515 F.2d 591 (5th Cir. 1975), reh. denied 521 F.2d 225, on remand 546 F.2d 1252 (1977), cert. denied 434 U.S. 831.

6. 545 F.2d 893 (5th Cir. 1975).

DORAN v. PETROLEUM CORP.

United States Court of Appeals, Fifth Circuit, 1977.
545 F.2d 893.

Before GOLDBERG, DYER and SIMPSON, CIRCUIT JUDGES.

GOLDBERG, CIRCUIT JUDGE:

In this case a sophisticated investor who purchased a limited partnership interest in an oil drilling venture seeks to rescind. The question raised is whether the sale was part of a private offering exempted by § 4(2) of the Securities Act of 1933, from the registration requirements of that Act. * * *[1]

I. Facts

Prior to July 1970, Petroleum Management Corporation (PMC) organized a California limited partnership for the purpose of drilling and operating four wells in Wyoming. The limited partnership agreement provided for both "participants," whose capital contributions were to be used first to pay all intangible expenses incurred by the partnership, and "special participants," whose capital contributions were to be applied first to pay tangible drilling expenses.

PMC and Inter-Tech Resources, Inc., were initially the only "special participants" in the limited partnership. They were joined by four "participants." As found by the district court, PMC contacted only four other persons with respect to possible participation in the partnership. All but the plaintiff declined.

During the late summer of 1970, plaintiff William H. Doran, Jr., received a telephone call from a California securities broker previously known to him. The broker, Phillip Kendrick, advised Doran of the opportunity to become a "special participant" in the partnership. PMC then sent Doran the drilling logs and technical maps of the proposed drilling area. PMC informed Doran that two of the proposed four wells had already been completed. Doran agreed to become a "special participant" in the Wyoming drilling program. In consideration for his partnership share, Doran agreed to contribute $125,000 toward the partnership. Doran was to discharge this obligation by paying PMC $25,000 down and in addition assuming responsibility for the payment of a $113,643 note owed by PMC to Mid-Continent Supply Co. Doran's share in the production payments from the wells was to be used to make the installment payments on the Mid-Continent note.

Pursuant to this arrangement, on September 16, 1970, Doran executed a promissory note, already signed by the President and Vice President of PMC in their individual capacities, for $113,643 payable to Mid-Continent. On October 5, 1970, Doran mailed PMC a check for $25,000. He thereby became a "special participant" in the Wyoming drilling program.

* * *

1. * * * The SEC's adoption of Rule 146 * * * which establishes a sufficient set of conditions for coming within the exemption, does not bear directly on the case at bar. The transaction at issue began in 1970, and the plaintiff filed suit in 1972. Rule 146 was not adopted until 1974. It applies to offers commencing on or after June 10, 1974.

Following the cessation of production payments between November 1971 and August 1972 and the decreased yields thereafter, the Mid-Continent note upon which Doran was primarily liable went into default. Mid-Continent subsequently obtained a state court judgment against Doran, PMC, and the two signatory officers of PMC for $50,815.50 plus interest and attorney's fees.

On October 16, 1972, Doran filed this suit in federal district court seeking damages for breach of contract, rescission of the contract based on violations of the Securities Acts of 1933 and 1934, and a judgment declaring the defendants liable for payment of the state judgment obtained by Mid-Continent.

The court below found that the offer and sale of the "special participant" interest was a private offering because Doran was a sophisticated investor who did not need the protection of the Securities Acts. * * * Doran filed this appeal.

II. The Private Offering Exemption

No registration statement was filed with any federal or state regulatory body in connection with the defendants' offering of securities. Along with two other factors that we may take as established—that the defendants sold or offered to sell these securities, and that the defendants used interstate transportation or communication in connection with the sale or offer of sale—the plaintiff thus states a prima facie case for a violation of the federal securities laws. * * *

The defendants do not contest the existence of the elements of plaintiff's prima facie case but raise an affirmative defense that the relevant transactions came within the exemption from registration found in § 4(2). Specifically, they contend that the offering of securities was not a public offering. The defendants, who of course bear the burden of proving this affirmative defense, must therefore show that the offering was private. * * *

This court has in the past identified four factors relevant to whether an offering qualifies for the exemption. The consideration of these factors, along with the policies embodied in the 1933 Act, structure the inquiry. * * * The relevant factors include the number of offerees and their relationship to each other and the issuer, the number of units offered, the size of the offering, and the manner of the offering. Consideration of these factors need not exhaust the inquiry, nor is one factor's weighing heavily in favor of the private status of the offering sufficient to ensure the availability of the exemption. Rather, these factors serve as guideposts to the court in attempting to determine whether subjecting the offering to registration requirements would further the purposes of the 1933 Act.

* * *

In the case at bar, the defendants may have demonstrated the presence of the latter three factors. A small number of units offered, relatively modest financial stakes, and an offering characterized by personal contact between the issuer and offerees free of public advertising or intermediaries such as investment bankers or securities exchanges—these aspects of the instant transaction aid the defendants' search for a § 4(2) exemption.

Nevertheless, with respect to the first, most critical, and conceptually most problematic factor, the record does not permit us to agree that the defendants have proved that they are entitled to the limited sanctuary afforded by § 4(2). We must examine more closely the importance of demonstrating both the number of offerees and their relationship to the issuer in order to see why the defendants have not yet gained the § 4(2) exemption.

A. *The Number of Offerees*

Establishing the number of persons involved in an offering is important both in order to ascertain the magnitude of the offering and in order to determine the characteristics and knowledge of the persons thus identified.

The number of offerees, not the number of purchasers, is the relevant figure in considering the number of persons involved in an offering. Hill York Corp. v. American International Franchises, Inc. * * * [448 F.2d 680, at 691 (5th Cir. 1971)]. A private placement claimant's failure to adduce any evidence regarding the number of offerees will be fatal to the claim. SEC v. Continental Tobacco Co. * * * [463 F.2d 137 at 161 (5th Cir. 1972)]. The number of offerees is not itself a decisive factor in determining the availability of the private offering exemption. Just as an offering to few may be public, so an offering to many may be private. * * * Nevertheless, "the more offerees, the more likelihood that the offering is public." Hill York Corp. v. American International Franchises, Inc., supra, 448 F.2d at 688. In the case at bar, the record indicates that eight investors were offered limited partnership shares in the drilling program—a total that would be entirely consistent with a finding that the offering was private.

The defendants attempt to limit the number of offerees even further, however. They argue that Doran was the sole offeree because all others contacted by PMC were offered "participant" rather than "special participant" interests. The district court, which did not issue a finding of fact or conclusion of law with respect to this argument, appears to have assumed that there were eight offerees.

The argument is, in any event, unsupported by the record. * * * We must therefore reject the argument that Doran was the sole offeree.

In considering the number of offerees solely as indicative of the magnitude or scope of an offering, the difference between one and eight offerees is relatively unimportant. Rejecting the argument that Doran was the sole offeree is significant, however, because it means that in considering the need of the offerees for the protection that registration would have afforded we must look beyond Doran's interests to those of all his fellow offerees. Even the offeree-plaintiff's 20–20 vision with respect to the facts underlying the security would not save the exemption if any one of his fellow offerees was blind.

B. *The Offerees' Relationship to the Issuer*

Since SEC v. Ralston, supra, courts have sought to determine the need of offerees for the protections afforded by registration by focusing on the relationship between offerees and issuer and more particularly on the information available to the offerees by virtue of that relationship. * * * Once the offerees have been identified, it is possible to investigate their relationship to the issuer.

The district court concluded that the offer of a "special participant" interest to Doran was a private offering because Doran was a sophisticated investor who did not need the protections afforded by registration. It is important, in light of our rejection of the argument that Doran was the sole offeree, that the district court also found that all four "participants" and all three declining offerees were sophisticated investors with regard to oil ventures.

The need of the offerees for the protection afforded by registration is, to be sure, a question of fact dependent upon the circumstances of each case. * * * Nevertheless, the trial court's conclusion with respect to the availability of the private offering exemption may be set aside if induced by an erroneous view of the law. * * *

1. *The role of investment sophistication*

The lower court's finding that Doran was a sophisticated investor is amply supported by the record, as is the sophistication of the other offerees. Doran holds a petroleum engineering degree from Texas A&M University. His net worth is in excess of $1,000,000. His holdings of approximately twenty-six oil and gas properties are valued at $850,000.

Nevertheless, evidence of a high degree of business or legal sophistication on the part of all offerees does not suffice to bring the offering within the private placement exemption. We clearly established that proposition in Hill York Corp. v. American International Franchises, Inc., supra, 448 F.2d at 690. We reasoned that "if the plaintiffs did not possess the information requisite for a registration statement, they could not bring their sophisticated knowledge of business affairs to bear in deciding whether or not to invest * * *." Sophistication is not a substitute for access to the information that registration would disclose. * * * As we said in *Hill York*, although the evidence of the offerees' expertise "is certainly favorable to the defendants, the level of sophistication will not carry the point. In this context, the relationship between the promoters and the purchasers and the 'access to the kind of information which registration would disclose' become highly relevant factors." 448 F.2d at 690.

In short, there must be sufficient basis of accurate information upon which the sophisticated investor may exercise his skills. Just as a scientist cannot be without his specimens, so the shrewdest investor's acuity will be blunted without specifications about the issuer. For an investor to be invested with exemptive status he must have the required data for judgment.

2. *The requirement of available information*

* * *

The requirement that all offerees have available the information registration would provide has been firmly established by this court as a necessary condition of gaining the private offering exemption. * * *

More specifically, we shall require on remand that the defendants demonstrate that all offerees, whatever their expertise, had available the information a registration statement would have afforded a prospective investor in a public offering. Such a showing is not independently sufficient to establish that the offering qualified for the private placement exemption, but it is necessary to gain the exemption and is to be weighed along with the sophistication and number of the offerees, the number of units offered, and the size and manner of the offering. * * * Because in this case these latter factors weigh heavily in favor of the private offering exemption, satisfaction of the necessary condition regarding the availability of relevant information to the offerees would compel the conclusion that this offering fell within the exemption.

C. On Remand: The Issuer-Offeree Relationship

In determining on remand the extent of the information available to the offerees, the district court must keep in mind that the "availability" of information means either disclosure of or effective access to the relevant information. The relationship between issuer and offeree is most critical when the issuer relies on the latter route.

To begin with, if the defendants could prove that all offerees were actually furnished the information a registration statement would have provided, whether the offerees occupied a position of access pre-existing such disclosure would not be dispositive of the status of the offering. If disclosure were proved and if, as here, the remaining factors such as the manner of the offering and the investment sophistication of the offerees weigh heavily in favor of the private status of the offering, the absence of a privileged relationship between offeree and issuer would not preclude a finding that the offering was private. * * *

Alternatively it might be shown that the offeree had access to the files and record of the company that contained the relevant information. Such access might be afforded merely by the position of the offeree or by the issuer's promise to open appropriate files and records to the offeree as well as to answer inquiries regarding material information. In either case, the relationship between offeree and issuer now becomes critical, for it must be shown that the offeree could realistically have been expected to take advantage of his access to ascertain the relevant information.[12] Similarly the investment sophistication of the offeree assumes added importance, for it is important that he could have been expected to ask the right questions and seek out the relevant information.

* * *

1. Disclosure or access: a disjunctive requirement

That our cases sometimes fail clearly to differentiate between "access" and "disclosure" as alternative means of coming within the private offering exemption is, perhaps, not surprising. Although the Ralston Purina decision focused on whether the offerees had "access" to the required information, * * * the holding that "the exemption question turns on the knowledge of the offerees," could be construed to include possession as well as access. Such an interpretation would require disclosure as a necessary condition of obtaining a private offering notwithstanding the offerees' access to the information that registration would have provided.

Both the Second and the Fourth Circuits, however, have interpreted Ralston Purina as embodying a disjunctive requirement. * * *

The cases in this circuit are not inconsistent with this view. * * *
* * *

Although Rule 146 cannot directly control the case at bar, we think its disjunctive requirement that the private offering claimant may show either "access" or "disclosure" expresses a sound view that this court has in fact implicitly accepted. * * *

---

12. For example, the offeree's ability to compel the issuer to make good his promise may depend on the offeree's bargaining power or on his family or employment relationship to the issuer.

2. *The role of insider status*

Once the alternative means of coming within the private placement exemption are clearly separated, we can appreciate the proper role to be accorded the requirement that the offerees occupy a privileged or "insider" status relative to the issuer. That is to say, when the issuer relies on "access" absent actual disclosure, he must show that the offerees occupied a privileged position relative to the issuer that afforded them an opportunity for effective access to the information registration would otherwise provide.[18] When the issuer relies on actual disclosure to come within the exemption, he need not demonstrate that the offerees held such a privileged position. Although mere disclosure is not a sufficient condition for establishing the availability of the private offering exemption, and a court will weigh other factors such as the manner of the offering and the investment sophistication of the offerees, the "insider" status of the offerees is not a necessary condition of obtaining the exemption.

Because the line between access and disclosure has sometimes been obscured, some have interpreted this court's decision in *Continental* [supra at page 306] as limiting the § 4(2) exemption to insider transactions.[19] As we pointed out in our recent decision in *Woolf,* however, such fears are unfounded. 515 F.2d at 610.

The language from *Continental* that gave rise to those fears consists in the court's findings that "Continental did not affirmatively prove that all offerees of its securities had received both written and oral information concerning Continental, that all offerees of its securities had access to any additional information which they might have required or requested, and that all offerees of its securities had personal contacts with the officers of Continental." 463 F.2d at 160. It is possible to read this as a list of the necessary conditions for coming within the § 4(2) exemption, and therefore to infer that a private placement claimant must show the "insider" status of the offerees. Properly viewed in context, however, these statements were not clearly intended to establish necessary conditions, but only to point to the manifold weaknesses of the defendant's claim which, taken together, precluded private offering status.

In *Continental,* the court admittedly agreed with the SEC's position that even if the prospectus that Continental had sent to purchasers contained all the information registration would disclose, that fact alone would not justify the exemption. 463 F.2d at 160. That is doubtless true, since even

---

18. That all offerees are in certain respects "insiders" does not ensure that the issuer will gain the private placement exemption. An insider may be an insider with respect to fiscal matters of the company, but an outsider with respect to a particular issue of securities. He may know much about the financial structure of the company but his position may nonetheless not allow him access to a few vital facts pertaining to the transaction at issue. If Doran had effective access to all information that registration would provide, he would be a transactional insider. That is all we require regarding the availability of information. If, on the other hand, his inside knowledge was incomplete or his access ineffective, he would be a transactional outsider despite the fact that we might consider him an "insider" for other purposes.

19. For example, one commentator has written that "if Continental Tobacco represents the current state of the law regarding private placement exemption in non-Rule 146 transactions (highly doubtful), its availability is limited to insider transaction." 2 S. Goldberg, Private Placements and Restricted Securities § 2.16[e] (1975). See also Schwartz, The Private Offering Exemption—Recent Developments, 37 Ohio St.L.J. 1, 19 (1976), and cases cited therein; Rediker, The Fifth Circuit Cracks Down on Not-So Private Offerings, 25 Ala. L.Rev. 289, 311–17 (1973).

if all the purchasers of Continental's securities had received full disclosure, the defendant would not have established that all offerees had received full disclosure. Because Continental had failed to sustain its burden of demonstrating the number of offerees, moreover, even the fact that all known offerees might have received disclosure would still have been insufficient to ensure the availability of the exemption. But the court's language in *Continental* should not be read as requiring in addition to full disclosure to all offerees a demonstration of the offerees' insider status.

Rather, the court's language regarding Continental's failure to show that all offerees had access to the requisite information and that all offerees had personal contacts with Continental's officers may be read as foreclosing the possible alternative route to the § 4(2) exemption. Because the prospectus did not contain all the information registration would provide and because it was not established that all offerees received the prospectus, it was clear that Continental could not rely upon actual disclosure. The additional language in *Continental*, though admittedly subject to other interpretations, may be read as making clear that there was in that case no privileged relationship between the offerees and the issuer that might have compensated for the defendant's palpable failure to disclose.

Although the disjunctive nature of the requirement is, to be sure, not made explicit in *Continental*, it is important that the pertinent conclusion of fact held clearly erroneous in that case was that "the offerees ∗ ∗ ∗ were furnished and/or provided access to the same type of information that would have been provided in a registration statement ∗ ∗ ∗." 463 F.2d at 159. In order to hold this conclusion clearly erroneous, it was thus necessary to show that the defendant had failed to prove either disclosure or access.

In any event, absent a clear and unambiguous indication to the contrary, we do not read *Continental* as requiring insider status. We think that any such requirement would inhibit the ability of business to raise capital without the expense and delay of registration under circumstances in which the offerees did not need the protection of registration. The enactment of Rule 146 represents the SEC's recognition of this legitimate business need. We think that it would be unwise to adopt in this circuit a requirement of insider status notwithstanding disclosure or that of actual disclosure notwithstanding effective access. Such requirements would constrict the scope of the private offering exemption more narrowly than does Rule 146 and would retard necessary capital investment without a corresponding benefit to those investors who need the protection of registration.

Rule 146 offers some rays of sunlight into the limbos and uncertain depths of § 4(2). The cases cast at best a faint beacon toward the horizon of decision. While we appreciate full well that the test we have fashioned remains too fluid to enable the would-be private offering issuer to feel entirely secure, we are confident that, at long last, the safe harbor of Rule 146 will provide that security and that few private placement claimants will stray far from that harbor. Rule 146 is a serotine development. More than two decades passed after *Ralston* before the SEC sufficiently elaborated on the definitional concepts behind § 4(2). With respect to those transactions that antedate the effective date of Rule 146, this case and those preceding it in this circuit establish as the critical factor in determining whether the exemption applies to a particular offering the availability of information to all offerees. The privileged status of the offerees must be demonstrated only when it is necessary to the claimant's efforts to establish that the requisite information was in fact available.

* * *

IV. Conclusion

An examination of the record and the district court's opinion in this case leaves unanswered the central question in all cases that turn on the availability of the § 4(2) exemption. Did the offerees know or have a realistic opportunity to learn facts essential to an investment judgment? We remand so that the trial court can answer that question.[a.]

* * *

SECURITIES ACT RELEASE NO. 5487
Securities and Exchange Commission.
April 23, 1974.

NOTICE OF ADOPTION OF RULE 146 UNDER THE SECURITIES ACT OF 1933—"TRANSACTIONS BY AN ISSUER DEEMED NOT TO INVOLVE ANY PUBLIC OFFERING"

The Securities and Exchange Commission today announced the adoption of Rule 146 under the Securities Act of 1933 ("Act") * * *.

The Rule is designed to provide more objective standards for determining when offers or sales of securities by an issuer would be deemed to be transactions not involving any public offering within the meaning of Section 4(2) of the Act and thus would be exempt from the registration provisions of the Act. * * * The Rule is not, however, the exclusive basis for determining whether that exemption is available. * * *

* * *

MARY S. KRECH TRUST v. LAKES APARTMENTS
United States Court of Appeals, Fifth Circuit, 1981.
642 F.2d 98, reh. denied 645 F.2d 72.

Before HILL, FAY and HATCHETT, CIRCUIT JUDGES.

FAY, CIRCUIT JUDGE:

The first question we are asked to decide in this appeal is whether one can successfully plan and execute a private offering of a security by following the guidelines prepared by the Securities and Exchange Commission and our recent decision in Swenson v. Engelstad, 626 F.2d 421, (5th Cir., 1980). Answering that question in the affirmative, we move to the second inquiry, whether or not the evidence in the record of this case supports the jury's conclusion that such a plan was completed as designed. Again we answer in the affirmative. Recognizing the rigid requirements surrounding private offerings, we hold that here ample justification exists

---

a. The defendant had initially also pleaded the one year statute of limitations under § 13 for violation of § 12(1). On remand, it prevailed on this ground and the judgment was affirmed. Doran v. Petroleum Management Corp., 576 F.2d 91 (5th Cir. 1978).

for reasonable persons to conclude that such tests were met, and we affirm the entry of final judgment upon jury verdict.

In 1974, the original owners of The Lakes Apartments, Ltd., caught in an interest squeeze and out of construction money, contacted Envicon Development Corporation (Envicon Development), a real estate company, to determine whether syndication was possible. After an investigation, Envicon Development decided to syndicate and approached Wachovia Bank for funds. Wachovia agreed to advance construction money but required a guarantee from Erving Wolf, majority shareholder of Envicon Development.

Prior to offering any units in the Lakes limited partnership, Envicon Equities Corporation (Envicon), a subsidiary of Envicon Development, was formed to put together the syndication. Envicon undertook a formidable research project called a "due diligence" investigation which would generate the kind of information that would ordinarily go into a registration statement. The syndicators envisioned an offering of twenty limited partnership units and intended to structure their offering to meet the requirements of Rule 146. Ultimately, fifteen persons were offered units. Among the thirteen purchasers of units was appellant Mary S. Krech Trust (the Trust).

During this same time period, the Trust, acting through its trustees Chapin Krech and Dr. Shepard Krech, * * * began looking for a tax shelter investment. Chapin Krech, himself a former partner in a New York Stock Exchange brokerage firm, contacted his broker, David Williams. This contact began the chain linking the defendants-appellees to the Trust.

[The brokerage firm, Bache Halsey Stuart Shields, Inc.] brought Krech and Williams into contact with defendant Donald Gary, vice president of Envicon Development. Gary was in charge of the syndication of the Lakes.

Although it had purchased the investment primarily as a tax shelter, apparently the Trust anticipated income from positive cash flow by the end of the second quarter of 1975. When no income was realized, Chapin Krech initiated an investigation which led to the present lawsuit. [The complaint alleged violations of §§ 5, 12 and 17(a) of the 1933 Act.] Following jury trial, judgment was entered for the defendant-appellees. The jury, using special verdict forms, found that the offering was exempt from registration requirements, that there were no material misrepresentations or omissions making the sale misleading, and that there was no fraud or deceit upon the Trust in connection with the "break-even" statement.

* * *

Under Rule 146, in order to be considered a private offering, the offering must: 1) not be made by any means or form of general solicitation or advertising; 2) be made only to those persons whom the issuer has reasonable grounds to believe are of knowledge and experience which would enable them to evaluate the merits of the issue or who are financially able to bear the risk; 3) be made only to those persons who have access to the same kind of information as would be contained in a registration statement. Under this rule, the issuer must have reasonable grounds to believe, and must believe, that there are no more than thirty-five purchasers from the issuer. * * *

In the instant case, the appellees designed a multi-step procedure for making the offering. A select list of Bache brokers, experienced in tax shelters and specializing in counseling a clientele of wealthy and knowledgeable investors, was compiled by nominations from Bache branch managers. This select group was given a Project Fact Sheet containing information for their own use in determining which clients would be suitable. If a broker had a client he thought was interested, he could obtain from Envicon the Private Placement Memorandum and Project Analysis—Financial Analysis. Before he could receive these materials, however, the broker was questioned with regard to his client's suitability for the placement. The potential investor reviewed the documents, was given an opportunity to ask questions, and was then asked to fill out the offeree's questionaire requiring him to set forth his net worth and financial sophistication. These offeree questionaires were reviewed by Mr. Gary, and only those persons to whom he was willing to sell were given offers. He testified that his determination was based on whether they met the qualifications of Rule 146(d).

The details of this plan were offered through the testimony of Gary and Blank [, the head of Bache's tax shelter department]. Offeree questionaires, Project Fact Sheets, list of brokers and other documents demonstrating the general control exercised by appellees were offered into evidence at trial. The list of the fifteen offerees was received in evidence. The jury was instructed:

> The ultimate test is whether the persons to whom the offering is made are in such position with respect to the issuer that they either actually have such information as a registration itself would have disclosed, or they have access to such information.

> Stated otherwise, the ultimate test is did the offerees know or have a realistic opportunity to learn facts essential to an investment judgment.

> Now on that question, if a preponderance of the evidence establishes that the offering in this matter was exempt, then your answer to that question would be yes. If there is no such preponderance of the evidence, your answer would be no.
>
> * * *

It is clear from the record that there was sufficient evidence from which the jury could conclude that the offering was exempt. As an appellate court, we are required to accept evidence in favor of the verdict as true and to give such evidence the benefit of inferences sustaining the jury's findings. * * * This case differs from [previous decisions] in which we held that in proving the private offering defense, failure to prove the number or identity of the offerees was fatal to the defense. Here, the defendants established number and identity, in addition to financial wealth and the full information required as to all offerees.

[Judgment affirmed.] ª

---

a. In the principal case, the court states that the syndicators "intended to structure their offering to meet the requirements of Rule 146." Can you ascertain from the opinion whether the Issuer actually filed a Form 146 as the rule required for an offering of this magnitude. It was not uncommon for issuers to structure their offering to meet the requirements of Rule 146, but not file the form. Regulation D also requires the filing of Form D for offerings under Regulation D and § 4(6). Would you recommend that Form D not be filed, even though the transaction is structured to

THE VENTURE CAPITAL INDUSTRY AND RULE 146

The venture capital industry emerged in the mid–1960's. Venture capital firms consist of small business investment companies, business development companies and venture capital partnerships.[1] It is a highly cyclical industry which peaks when the equity market and the market for IPO's is strong, and the valuations of smaller growth-type companies are high. During weak equity markets, however, the industry stagnates.

The industry is also highly sensitive to government policies. In 1969, when the maximum capital gains tax was increased from 25% to 49%, it became virtually impossible to raise capital for start-up businesses and exceedingly difficult for venture capitalists to raise capital.

The industry limped along throughout most of the 1970's. Moreover, the Employment Retirement Income Security Act of 1974 (ERISA) raised concern among money managers as to their exposure when venture capital investments turned sour. However, in 1972, the SEC adopted Rule 144 (infra at page ___), making open market investment in undervalued companies more attractive. By 1978 the regulatory climate began to change. In that year, the capital gains tax was reduced to 28%. In June, 1979, the Department of Labor clarified the standard of care of money managers to exercise "prudence" in investing, thereby opening up pension investment.[2]

In the meantime, Congress became concerned over the access of small business to the equity and venture capital markets.[3] Moreover, in 1978, the SEC held public hearings exploring the effects of its rules and regulations on the ability of small business to raise capital and the impact on small business of the disclosure requirements under the 1933 Act.[4]

Congress also responded to these concerns by adopting the Small Business Investment Incentive Act of 1980.[5] The Act amended the Investment Company Act of 1940 to provide for a new form of venture capital company called a "business development company" and prescribed a regulatory system which takes into account the special needs of these companies, while preserving certain investor protections.[6] Nevertheless, the venture capital partnership still appears to be the preferred form of business organization because of the constraints on management of registered business development companies.

comply with the particular exemption, and rely on the § 4(2) exemption which requires no notice?

1. Small business investment companies (SBIC) may be organized under the Small Business Investment Act of 1958, 94 Stat. 2275 (1980). SBIC's are partly financed by the Small Business Administration and are structured to provide a medium for making equity and loan funds available to eligible small businesses. For venture capital financing under the Act, see R. Haft, Venture Capital and Small Business Financing ch. 2 (1985 rev.).

2. Dept. of Labor, Rules and Regulations for Fiduciary Responsibility; Investment of Plan Assets Under the "Prudence" Rule, adopting 29 C.F.R. § 2550.404–1, 44 Fed.Reg. 37221 (June 23, 1979).

3. Hearings on Small Business Access to Equity and Venture Capital Before the Subcomm. on Capital, Investment and Business Opportunities of the House Comm. on Small Business, 95th Cong., 1st Sess. (1977); Hearings on the Economic Problems of Small Business Before the Subcomm. on Energy and Environment of the House Comm. on Small Business, 94th Cong., 2d Sess. (1977).

4. Securities Act Release No. 5914 (Mar. 6, 1978), 14 SEC Dock. 314 (1978).

5. 94 Stat. 2276 (1980).

6. Section 2(a)(48) of the 1940 Act, in effect, defines a "business development company" as a domestic closed-end investment company that (a) invests in the securities of small developing businesses; (b) makes available significant managerial assistance to its portfolio companies and (c) has notified the Commission of its election to be subject to the provisions of §§ 55 through 65 which regulate the functions and activities of business development companies.

1981–1983 were boom years for venture capitalists, with the peak being reached when $2.8 billion was invested in 1983. By the end of 1984, however, the bubble had burst and it was back to basics for venture capitalists.[7]

Rule 146 was adopted in June, 1974 and was in effect until June, 1982, when it was replaced by Regulation D. When the rule was adopted, the venture capital market was moribund. The rule was designed primarily as a private offering exemption for use in tapping venture capital pools; it was also used extensively in real estate, oil and gas and other tax shelter offerings. The total volume of reported Rule 146 offerings increased by about $1 billion a year from $1.3 billion in 1978 to $4.2 billion in 1982.[8]

Rule 146, however, was not regarded as a success. When the rule was adopted in 1974, it was greeted with misgivings by the securities bar; commentators generally were critical,[9] and one called the rule a "major blunder." [10] In the Senate hearings on capital formation, SEC Chairman Harold Williams observed that witnesses at the SEC's 1978 small business capital formation hearings "[w]ith very few exceptions * * * indicated that Rule 146 should either be amended, or a separate rule promulgated, in order to be of benefit to small business seeking to raise capital. Compliance with the rule was described as unduly complex, costly, and subjective, with an unacceptable level of risk that the exemption may be lost inadvertently." [11]

While Rule 146 was operative, however, securities lawyers established sophisticated "due diligence" procedures in order to monitor compliance and fulfill the burden of proof that all of the conditions of the rule had been met. In the *Mary S. Krech Trust* case (supra at page 315), the court was impressed by the "formidable * * * 'due diligence' investigation" used in that offering. These procedures frequently entailed the establishment of an integrated private placement compliance system which accumulated all written material relating to the offering. This evidence was placed in a "burden of proof file" which was completed and preserved at the end of the offering, ready to be introduced in evidence should the exemption be challenged at a later date. A knowledgeable and experienced securities lawyer suggested that the components of a "Rule 146 Compliance System" should consist of: (1) a private placement master schedule, setting forth all significant events that must occur throughout the offering period to meet the conditions of the rule; (2) a private placement memoranda distribution record; (3) potential offeree identification form; (4) potential offer-

---

7. See Management Today, July, 1975, at 44; Business Week, Sept. 24, 1984, at 118; Hector, A Tough Slog for Venture Capitalists, Fortune, June 10, 1985, at 110; Neises, Adventures in Alternative Investments: Picking the Right Venture Capital Firm, Pension World, Sep. 1985, at 56; Ann. Rev. of Venture Capital (Venture Economics 1985).

For guides to raising venture capital, see Deloitte Haskins & Sells, Raising Venture Capital—An Entrepreneur's Guidebook (1982); S. Pratt, Guide to Venture Capital Sources (1981); Venture Capital Journal.

8. SEC, Directorate of Economic and Policy Analysis, Report of the Use of Rule 146 Exemption in Capital Formation (Jan. 1983).

9. Kripke, SEC Rule 146: A "Major Blunder", N.Y.L.J., July 5, 1974, at 1, col. 3.

10. For criticism of Rule 146, see Kessler, Private Placement Rules 146 and 240—Safe Harbor?, 44 Fordham L.Rev. 37 (1975); Kinderman, The Private Offering Exemption: An Examination of Its Availability Under and Outside Rule 146, 30 Bus.Law. 921 (1975); Campbell, The Plight of Small Issuers Under the Securities Act of 1933: Practical Foreclosure from the Capital Market, 1977 Duke L.J. 1139, 1143–1150 (1977); Benton & Gunderson, Venture Capital Financings and Exemptions from Registration Under the Securities Act of 1933: Section 4(2), Rule 146, and Rule 242, 21 Santa Clara L.Rev. 23, 44–47 (1981).

11. Hearings on Capital Formation Before the Select Comm. On Small Business of the U.S. Senate, 95th Cong., 2d Sess. (pt. 3) 584 (1978).

ee evaluation form; (5) offeree questionnaire; (6) offeree representative documents; and (7) final evaluation form.[12] These procedures have been further refined in connection with offerings under Rule 506 of Regulation D.

W. Grienenberger & G. Reed, 1 Securities Law Techniques, ch. 1. (A.A. Sommer, Jr. ed. 1985); Note, Revising the Private Placement Exemption, 82 Yale L.J. 1512 (1973); Note, Reforming the Initial Sale Requirements of the Private Placement Exemption, 86 Harv.L.Rev. 403 (1972); Note, SEC Rules 144 and 146: Private Placements for the Few, 59 Va.L.Rev. 886 (1973).

Excerpt from: CARL W. SCHNEIDER[a]

THE STATUTORY LAW OF PRIVATE PLACEMENTS
14 Review of Securities Regulation 869–883 (1981).[b]

APPLICATION OF STATUTORY LAW

Section 4(2) of the Securities Act of 1933 provides an exemption from that Act's registration requirements for "transactions by an issuer not involving any public offering"—so-called private placements. * * * As used herein, the term "Statutory Law" refers to the exemption provided by section 4(2) without regard to rule 146.

There are various reasons why parties may rely on Statutory Law rather than the rule 146 safe harbor. For example, inexperienced issuers or counsel may have completed a transaction or taken preliminary steps that may make the rule unavailable. Because of numerous details and mechanics required by the rule, it is unlikely that the requirements for exemption under the rule will be satisfied without an affirmative intent to do so. In contrast, many private transactions probably satisfy the requirements of Statutory Law, even though no one involved in the transaction was aware of the Act's requirements.

There may be relatively more certainty that the exemption is available in a given factual setting under Statutory Law, as compared with rule 146, because of the many subjective judgments required by the rule. * * *

As a practical matter compliance with rule 146 may also be burdensome. For example, an offeree who is rich and reasonably smart, but who still needs an offeree representative, may insist that he wants to attend a meeting of investors to learn more about the offering before incurring the

---

12. See Linda A. Wertheimer, Due Diligence in Direct Participation Program Offerings, University of California, San Diego, Eighth Ann.Sec.Reg.Inst. (Jan. 21–23, 1981) 1, at 23–26.

In Zobrist v. COAL-X, Inc., 708 F.2d 1511 (10th Cir. 1983), warnings as to the risk factors associated with the offering contained in the offering circular were imputed to an investor who admittedly did not read the prospectus, but had signed a questionnaire stating that he had done so. Cf. Kennedy v. Josephthal & Co., Inc., 635 F.Supp. 399 (D.Mass.1985).

a. This article is the author's update and revision of his 1974 presentation at the Practicing Law Institute's Sixth Annual

Institute on Securities Regulation. The original presentation was substantially similar to a report of an American Bar Association Committee, of which the author was the principal draftsman, which appeared at 31 Bus.Law. 483 (1975). A companion ABA position paper on the institutional private placement is published at 31 Bus.Law. 515 (1975). See also an ABA position paper, Resale by Institutional Investors of Debt Securities Acquired in Private Placements, 34 Bus.Law. 1927 (1979).

b. Copyright 1981. Reprinted with permission of the author and Standard and Poor's Corp.

expense of hiring a representative. The attendance at a meeting by such an offeree without his representative renders the rule unavailable by virtue of rule 146(c)(2).

In rendering opinions, many lawyers rely on Statutory Law as an alternative basis for establishing the section 4(2) exemption, or simply opine that the exemption under section 4(2) applies, without specifying in the opinion whether reliance is upon the rule or the Statutory Law.

SOURCES OF STATUTORY LAW

The early legislative history of section 4(2) referred to the application of the exemption in instances of a:

"Specific or isolated sale * * * to a particular person."

"[W]here there is no practical need for the bill's application."

"[W]here the public benefits [of the registration process are too remote."

"[U]nless the stockholders are so small in number that the sale to them does not constitute a public offering."

While none of these themes is particularly descriptive, each suggests a slightly different emphasis or approach. The legislative history, therefore, is of relatively little help in giving specific content to the Statutory Law exemption.

A 1935 opinion of the SEC General Counsel set the interpretive stage for many years. This opinion focused on the number of offerees as a prime consideration, indicating that under ordinary circumstances an offering to approximately 25 or fewer persons presumably would not involve a public offering. It went on to enumerate the following factors as also being relevant:

1) number of offerees;

2) relationship of the offerees to each other;

3) relationship of the offerees to the issuer;

4) number of units offered;

5) size of the offering; and

6) manner of the offering.

* * *

While it is customary for court opinions to repeat this list of relevant factors, or variations thereof, it is suggested that a number of these factors are of little, if any, relevance in determining the availability of the exemption. It is difficult, if not impossible, to find a case where either the number of units offered or the size of the offering, as separate factors, were of much significance in determining whether the exemption applied. The exemption applies, quite properly, to tiny financings of small companies, institutional private placements involving tens and sometimes hundreds of millions of dollars, and every size of financing in between. All other factors being equal, and assuming no public redistribution, which is an independent requirement of a proper private placement, it should make no difference in a $1 million transaction whether a million shares are sold for $1.00 each or 1,000 shares are sold for $1,000 each.

Likewise, the relationship of the offerees to each other is generally irrelevant. (Occasionally one purchaser may be qualified vicariously by the knowledge or sophistication of a closely related party who also may be, but need not necessarily be, another purchaser in the transaction.) As discussed below, the relationship of the offerees to the issuer may be relevant only with respect to the means by which information is made available to them. However, if the other criteria discussed below are satisfied, there is no requirement that the offerees have any relationship whatsoever to the issuer prior to, or independent of, the private placement as such.

JUDICIAL PRECEDENTS

An early Supreme Court interpretation, SEC v. Ralston Purina Co., focused on the offerees' need for the Act's protection. It articulated the test in terms of the offerees' ability to "fend for themselves," and their "access" to the "same kind of information that the act would make available in the form of a registration statement."

The many judicial precedents since *Ralston Purina* have typically presented egregious fact situations, often involving a massive public distribution tainted with fraud. In most cases the exemption was denied, as it should have been. In many cases, however, the courts have used extremely broad dicta that, if taken literally, would leave little viability in the exemption under the statute. On the other hand, many of the holdings, narrowly read, turn on an essentially procedural matter, the defendant's failure to offer evidence sufficient to carry the burden of proving that the exemption applied. In several cases, the defendant focused only on the sale to the plaintiff, but offered insufficient evidence regarding other crucial factors necessary to establish the exemption for the offering as a whole, such as the method by which the overall offering was made, the total number of offerees, or their qualifications. On those occasions when the party relying on the exemption has prevailed, it is clear that the courts did not require full compliance with dicta from the cases that found the exemption inapplicable.[10]

The resulting body of law was characterized by former SEC Chairman Garrett (while still a private practitioner) as:

> * * * a kind of mishmash. The issuer is now told that all of these factors have something to do with whether he has an exemption under Section 4(2), but he is never given a hint as to the proper proportions in the brew. The saving recipe is kept secret, a moving target which he can never be sure he has hit.

As the Fifth Circuit recently noted: "The cases cast at best a faint beacon toward the horizon of decision." [12]

GUIDELINES

Where does this leave us? I believe that there are only five factors of recurring significance in determining whether the exemption is available under Statutory Law. * * * The five essential factors relate to the following: (1) offeree qualification (although, as noted below, cases suggest that offeree qualification is not a significant limitation if the other factors are satisfied); (2) manner of offering; (3) availability of information to

---

10. E.g., Mary S. Krech Trust v. Lake Apartments, 642 F.2d 98 (5th Cir. 1981) * * *.

12. Doran v. Petroleum Management Corp., 545 F.2d 893, 908 (5th Cir. 1977).

offerees; (4) a limited number of offerees and purchasers; and (5) absence of redistribution. Each of these will be discussed separately.

* * *

It should be noted at the outset that there are various categories of transactions for which the registration process is usually inappropriate or unnecessary—among them, the institutional private placement, and the financing of a small business among individuals closely associated with the venture through pre-existing business (but not necessarily including lower-level employment) or family ties.

To a large extent, the discussion will focus on equity private placements, typically sold to individuals or others who are not professional investors or venture capitalists, and often involving a relatively high degree of risk. Institutional private placements have been conducted for many years in a fairly standardized pattern. Such transactions involve sophisticated institutions purchasing relatively large blocks of securities, typically debt securities but sometimes equity. No significant interpretive problems have been experienced in applying the provisions of section 4(2) to such institutional transactions, and nothing that follows is intended to cast doubt on the propriety of prevailing practices in the institutional private placement field.

OFFEREE QUALIFICATION

Many cases suggest that offerees in a private placement should be appropriately qualified, but the precise offeree qualification requirements have been difficult to define and apply. For example, may qualification be established by the offeree's ability to understand the risk or his ability to assume the risk? Is either attribute necessary; is either alone sufficient? Probably neither characteristic is necessary in all cases. Probably either is sufficient, especially if the "unsophisticated" person able to bear the risk is not totally incompetent in financial matters. Indeed, ability to bear the risk is hardly ever mentioned as a necessary, sufficient, or even relevant offeree attribute in the pre-rule 146 cases.

A close personal, family, or employment relationship should also qualify an offeree as a practical matter, even though the offeree may lack the brains or wealth that would be needed to qualify him as a participant in a stranger's offering.

What does ability to assume the risk mean? Must we judge whether the offeree is able to lose all of his money, without regard to whether all of the money is likely to be lost, or is likelihood of loss a factor to be considered as well? Is it possible that an offeree may be qualified to purchase a high-grade bond but not a high-risk equity security under otherwise identical circumstances? Probably the likelihood of loss is a factor to be considered as a practical matter. Therefore, it is appropriate to evaluate the risk of loss, as well as whether such risk can be borne. * * *

The cases often refer to offeree sophistication. The term "sophistication" may be somewhat misused in this context. * * * The relevant inquiry should be whether the investor can understand and evaluate the nature of the risk based on the information supplied to him rather than whether he is familiar with all of the latest nuances and techniques of corporate finance. To the extent that the term "sophistication" raises inquiries of the latter type, the use of the term may tend to cloud the inquiry.

It is important to recognize degrees of sophistication. The inquiry as to whether an offeree is adequately sophisticated should not be answered on a simple yes or no basis, without regard to other attributes. All those who are not sufficiently sophisticated to qualify as offerees on that basis alone, for all kinds of securities in every kind of offering, should not be lumped together. The unsophisticated range from the total incompetent in financial matters, and possibly other matters as well, to the worldly person who knows a good deal about business matters generally but who has had limited experience in investments, corporate finance, and private placements. A good many heads of companies going public are not "sophisticated" in matters of corporate finance.

In connection with offeree sophistication generally, case law recognizes the offeree representative principle embodied in rule 146—that someone else may look out for the offeree's interest. Therefore the offeree's ability to understand the risk may be established vicariously.

A determination of the offeree's ability to understand the risk may well vary with the manner and scope of the disclosure made to him. The more careful, painstaking, and detailed the disclosure, the more easily a particular offeree may be able to understand the risk. Consider any business not particularly well known to the investing public. Without appropriate information, either through having access or being supplied, most people would not be able to qualify as offerees on the basis of ability to understand the risk. On the other hand, if a carefully prepared disclosure document is submitted to them, the same group of investors might well qualify as persons who can understand the risk.

* * *

IS OFFEREE QUALIFICATION NECESSARY?

There are some strong judicial dicta and analyses supporting the conclusion that the availability of information to offerees, * * * is the key to establishing the exemption. * * *

The more recent cases recognize that the disclosure requirement can be met through either of two routes: (1) the required disclosures can be voluntarily supplied to the offeree, or (2) the offeree may have "access" to the information by virtue of a relationship to the issuer such as employment, family relationship, or economic bargaining power that effectively enables the offeree to obtain the specific information he desires.

The offeree's sophistication is not sufficient by itself to establish the exemption without the availability of information since, it is said, an offeree who does not have information has nothing on which to bring his sophistication to bear in deciding whether or not to invest. On the other hand, sophistication may not even be a necessary condition in all cases. Sophistication may be relevant only in those instances where information is made available by the "access" route, and is not supplied directly by the issuer in a composite disclosure document prepared for the offering.
* * *

Some cases support the proposition that offeree sophistication, such as rule 146 requires (directly or vicariously through an offeree representative), is not always necessary to establish the exemption, and that the key to the availability of the statutory exemption is adequate disclosure of information, without any further tests of offeree qualification. * * *

* * *

* * * [The] Fifth Circuit opinions discussed above * * * establish that the "relationship to the issuer" is a factor in determining whether the offeree has economic bargaining power. But economic bargaining power is not an essential characteristic that all offerees must possess. Rather, it is an attribute that permits the information disclosure requirement to be met without having the information supplied to the offeree in a neat disclosure package in connection with the offering itself. A reading of the cases * * * strongly suggests that if adequate disclosure is made to the offeree, Statutory Law has no additional offeree qualification requirements.

* * *

MANNER OF THE OFFERING

The second general attribute of a proper private placement under Statutory Law relates to the manner of offering. In general, the issuer and its agents should make the offer through direct communication with offerees or their representatives. All forms of general advertising and mass media circulation should be avoided. * * *

INFORMATION

The third general attribute relates to information. Indeed, as discussed above in connection with offeree qualification, some cases stress the availability of information to the offerees as the central requirement of the Statutory Law exemption. It is the better view that the offerees need not have access to information about the issuer prior to and independent of the particular transaction. The required information can be supplied to the offerees in connection with the transaction. For the normal individual offeree who is not already familiar with the issuer (for example, through current high-level employment), it is customary to supply the information to him in the form of a composite disclosure document.

Certain cases adopt the approach reflected in rule 146(e), and especially the preliminary note thereto, that that information should be furnished to offerees unless they have "access" to it. Access means a relationship, based upon such factors as employment, family ties, or economic bargaining power, that enables the offeree to obtain the information effectively. * * * *

* * *

Despite intimations in the case law to the contrary, it is not generally considered necessary that the information provided to a private placement offeree be as extensive in scope and detail as the information called for by schedule A of the Securities Act (which is the 32-item appendix to the statute itself) or even '33 form S–1. * * * [The] issuer need only provide general categories of registration statement information, rather than information precisely identical to that disclosed through the registration process.

It is probably adequate to give relevant financial statements and basic information on financing (including unusual attributes of the securities), business, property, and management. To the extent applicable for a fair understanding of the offering, information should be given on use of proceeds, special tax considerations, and risk factors (especially those that are specific to the issue and not merely self-evident macroeconomic generalities). * * *

* * *

NUMBER OF OFFEREES AND PURCHASERS

It is official dogma that the number of offerees (or purchasers) is not dispositive of the availability of the exemption. * * *

Prior to the adoption of rule 146, a generally prevailing rule of thumb recognized the propriety of approximately 25 offerees, with a substantially higher number being considered appropriate for institutional private placements. A fortiori, the limit on the number of purchasers could not exceed the limit on the number of offerees.

* * * [The] adoption of rule 146 has had an inevitable effect on the interpretation of Statutory Law. Insofar as it regulates the manner of the offering but permits an essentially unlimited number of offerees, the rule supports the analysis that Statutory Law imposes no fixed ceiling on the number of offerees. Careful practitioners, therefore, are currently somewhat less concerned with the absolute number of offerees, provided that the offering is conducted in a proper manner. It is still considered prudent to have some reasonable limit on the number of offerees and purchasers. A somewhat higher number may be appropriate when dealing with sophisticated institutions making large commitments, as contrasted with individual purchasers making smaller commitments.

ABSENCE OF REDISTRIBUTION

The availability of the exemption depends on the absence of any immediate redistribution by the first-tier purchasers that would result in the overall transaction being a public offering. * * *

Statutory Law does not require any mechanical procedures to avoid redistribution, such as legends, investment letters, or stop-transfer instructions to transfer agents. However, use of these devices is to be encouraged as a matter of good practice to assure against resales, at least in cases where the company is or is expected to become publicly owned. But as long as no redistribution occurs in fact, the absence of these procedures does not render the exemption unavailable. * * *

* * *

SUBSTANTIAL COMPLIANCE

Will substantial compliance with rule 146 qualify a transaction for exemption under Statutory Law? Probably yes, since the rule is essentially, in its broad concepts, a codification of Statutory Law.

Rule 146 differs from prior law in certain significant respects in which the rule is more permissive than prior judicial interpretations. * * *

* * * While Statutory Law may not be identical to rule 146 * * * the rule does provide a helpful analogy. We may anticipate that the liberalizations accomplished by rule 146 will be reflected in the interpretation of Statutory Law.

* * *

CONCLUSION

The private offering exemption contained in section 4(2) is a very significant one, essential to the capital formation ability of American enterprise. The exemption should not be interpreted in an unduly restrictive manner. * * *

I believe that courts should reach appropriate results by focusing on five factors: (1) offeree qualification; (2) manner of offering; (3) availability of information to offerees; (4) a limited number of offerees and purchasers; and (5) absence of redistribution. Furthermore, the better view of the recent cases suggests that offeree qualification, absent extreme circumstances, should not be a requirement of independent significance. Rather, the characteristics of the offeree should only be considered in determining the appropriate manner and scope of information disclosure. Additionally, as the interpretive law continues to evolve, we may anticipate that greater attention will be given to the manner in which the offering is made and, correspondingly, less significance will be attached to the absolute number of offerees and purchasers. Ultimately, therefore, Statutory Law may resemble [former] rule 242 without a maximum dollar limit.

On the Section 4(2) statutory law outside of Rule 146, see Alberg and Lybecker, New SEC Rules 146 and 147: The Nonpublic and Intrastate Offering Exemptions From Registration for the Sale of Securities, 74 Colum.L.Rev. 622, 623–632 (1974); Meer, The Private Offering Exemption Under the Federal Securities Act—A Study in Administrative and Judicial Contraction, 20 Sw.L.J. 503 (1966); Harrison, Thirty-eight Years Without Definition—The Private Offering Exemption, 24 Ark.L.Rev. 417 (1971); Kinderman, Private Offering Exemption: An Examination of Its Availability Under and Outside Rule 146, 30 Bus.Law. 921 (1975); McDermott, Private Offering Exemption, 59 Ia.L.Rev. 525 (1974); Garrett, The Private Offering Exemption Today, PLI Fourth Ann.Inst. on Sec.Reg. 3–34 (1973); S. Goldberg, Private Placements and Restricted Securities (rev.ed.1979); Soraghan, Private Offerings: Determining "Access," "Investment Sophistication," and "Ability to Bear Economic Risk," 8 Sec.Reg.L.J. 3 (1980).

For a statement of the availability of the nonpublic offering exemption by the Commission, see Securities Act Release No. 4552 (Nov. 6, 1962).

Chapter 6

THE LIMITED OFFERING EXEMPTIONS: SECTION 3(b), REGULATION D AND REGULATION A

Introductory Note

The Commission is authorized under Section 3(b) of the 1933 Act to exempt from the registration provisions other securities if it finds that registration of these securities is not necessary in the public interest and for the protection of investors by reason of the small amount involved or the limited character of the public offering. The section specifies a maximum aggregate offering amount which initially was $100,000. The ceiling has been repeatedly increased to counteract the ravages of inflation, and is now set at $5,000,000. Acting under this authority, the Commission has issued a number of rules and regulations, the most important of which from the standpoint of capital formation by small businesses are Regulation D and Regulation A.

Regulation D was adopted by the Commission in March, 1982. It is designed to coordinate the various limited offering exemptions previously contained in Rules 146, 240 and 242 and to streamline the requirements applicable to private offerings and sales of securities. The regulation represents an effort to remove the impediments to capital formation by small businesses to the extent that the lifting of the existing burdens are deemed consistent with the public interest and the protection of investors.

Moreover, Title V of the Small Business Investment Incentive Act of 1980 [Public L. No. 96–477 (October 21, 1980)] added § 19(c) to the Securities Act authorizing the Commission to work with state securities associations in effectuating greater uniformity in Federal-State securities matters.

As a result of this legislation, the Commission and the North American Securities Administrators Association, Inc. ("NASAA") have established ongoing procedures for coordinating state securities regulation with federal regulation. As a first step, the Commission created a Small Business section in the Division of Corporation Finance. The Associate Director in charge of that section is the focus for all small-business rule-making and interpretations and coordination with congressional committees, government agencies and other groups concerned with the problems of small business.

Section 19(c) directs the Commission to cooperate with state securities officials to develop a uniform exemption from registration for small issuers. Regulation D was designed to be the basis for such exemption and the Small Business section worked closely with a special task force of NASAA in developing that regulation. Indeed, NASAA solicited comments on Regulation D simultaneously with Commission solicitation.[1]

---

1. Mary E.T. Beach, Associate Director of SEC, Corporation Finance Division (Small Business and International Corporation Finance), Initial Rounds of Financ-ing—Unregistered Offerings of Corporate Securities, 11th Ann.Sec.Reg.Inst., Univ. of Calif., San Diego, vol. 3, at 30–32 (1984).

328

In September, 1983, NASAA adopted a Uniform Limited Offering Exemption (ULOE) for enactment at the state level. ULOE would exempt from state registration any offering if it complies with Rules 501, 502, 503, 505 and 506 of Regulation D, so long as certain additional conditions are also complied with. As of 1986, virtually every state has adopted some form of nonpublic limited offering exemption or simply dispenses with securities qualification. About 30 or 60% of the states have adopted ULOE with or without variations or dispense with securities qualification altogether, thereby eliminating duplicative regulation of small issues at the state level.[2]

Annual conferences are held between representatives of NASAA and the Commission and staff, and a number of initiatives are underway to increase coordinate federal and state securities regulation and information sharing so as to carry out the policies expressed in § 19(c). The combined effort at rationalizing the private offering exemptions and the other initiatives which are being considered, if consummated, will represent a major achievement in securities regulation in the United States.

Regulation A permits an issuer to sell securities in an unregistered public offering, up to an aggregate amount of $1.5 million in any 12-month-period, provided certain conditions are met. Qualification of a Regulation A offering requires the filing of an Offering Statement (Form 1–A) and an offering circular containing information respecting the issuer and the securities offered with the regional office of the Commission for the region in which the issuer's principal business operations are conducted.

The offering circular, which may be compared to a mini-prospectus, must be furnished at or prior to the time any written offer is made. It is to be remembered, however, that Regulation A grants an exemption from registration, rather than requiring registration. Thus, there is no § 11 liability for offerings made pursuant to Regulation A. Section 15(d) of the Exchange Act does not apply to Regulation A offerings. No reporting requirements are triggered under § 13 unless the issuer otherwise becomes subject to Section 12 of that Act; however, the express civil liability provisions of § 12(2) of the 1933 Act and the implied liability provisions of § 10 and Rule 10b–5 remain applicable.

The information called for in the offering circular is not as extensive as that required in an S–18 registration statement. For example, less detailed disclosure is required in such areas as description of business, remuneration of officers, and legal proceedings. Only financial statements for the last two years are required to be furnished, and these need not be certified unless such are otherwise filed or required to be filed with the Commission.

Along with the adoption of Regulation D, the Commission overhauled the disclosure requirements of Regulation A so as to maintain the regulation as less burdensome than an S–18 registration statement, to provide more flexibility with respect to different types of offerings, and to render the offering circular a more meaningful document.[3] The Commission also has under consideration whether the Regulation A ceiling should be further increased or whether new

---

2. See Hainsfurther, Summary of Blue Sky Exemptions Corresponding to Regulation D, 38 Sw.L.J. 989 (1984) (containing a chart summarizing the law in all states as of August 1, 1984); T. Loo, 1 Securities Law Techniques, ch. 2 (A.A. Sommer, Jr. ed. 1985) (App. 2D–1 contains chart of state adoptions of Regulation D); MacEwan, Blue Sky Regulation of Regulation D Offerings, 18 Rev. of Sec. & Commodities Reg. 103 (1985); 1 Blue Sky Law Rep. (CCH) ¶ 6251 (1983).

3. Securities Act Release 6275 (Dec. 23, 1980), 21 SEC Docket 1024 (1980), Fed.Sec.L.Rep. (CCH) No. 894, pt. II (Jan. 12, 1981), at 35; Securities Act Release No. 6340 (Aug. 7, 1981), 23 SEC Dock. 482 (1981).

exemptions tailored to offerings between $2,000,000 and $5,000,000 should be fashioned as a further aid to small business.

SECTION 1. REGULATION D: COORDINATION OF FORMER RULES 146, 240 AND 242

Statutes and Regulations

Securities Act § 3(b).

Regulation D.

SECURITIES ACT RELEASE NO. 6389

Securities and Exchange Commission.
March 8, 1982.

REGULATION D—REVISION OF CERTAIN EXEMPTIONS FROM REGISTRATION UNDER THE SECURITIES ACT OF 1933 FOR TRANSACTIONS INVOLVING LIMITED OFFERS AND SALES

The Commission announces the adoption of a new regulation governing certain offers and sales of securities without registration under the Securities Act of 1933 and a uniform notice of sales form to be used for all offerings under the regulation. The regulation replaces three exemptions and four forms, all of which are being rescinded. The new regulation is designed to simplify and clarify existing exemptions, to expand their availability, and to achieve uniformity between federal and state exemptions in order to facilitate capital formation consistent with the protection of investors.

* * *

I. Background

Regulation D is the product of the Commission's evaluation of the impact of its rules and regulations on the ability of small businesses to raise capital. This study has revealed a particular concern that the registration requirements and the exemptive scheme of the Securities Act impose disproportionate restraints on small issuers. In response to this concern, the Commission has taken a number of actions, including a relaxation of certain aspects of Regulation A, the adoption of Rule 242, and the introduction of Form S–18, a simplified registration statement for certain first time issuers.

Coincident with the Commission's small business program, Congress enacted the Small Business Investment Incentive Act of 1980 (the "Incentive Act") [94 Stat. 2275 (codified in scattered sections of 15 U.S.C.)]. The Incentive Act included three changes to the Securities Act: the addition of an exemption in Section 4(6) for offers and sales solely to accredited investors,[3] the increase in the ceiling of Section 3(b) from $2,000,000 to $5,000,000, and the addition of Section 19(c) which, among other things,

---

3. The Incentive Act also added Section 2(15) to the Securities Act which defined "accredited investor" * * *.

authorized "the development of a uniform exemption from registration for small issuers which can be agreed upon among several States or between the States and the Federal Government."

As a result of the Commission's reevaluation of the impact that its rules and regulations have on small businesses and the provisions of the Incentive Act, the Commission undertook a general examination of the exemptive scheme under the Securities Act. * * *

II. Discussion

A. Overview

Regulation D is a series of six rules, designated Rules 501–506, that establishes three exemptions from the registration requirements of the Securities Act and replaces exemptions that currently exist under Rules 146, 240, and 242. The regulation is designed to simplify existing rules and regulations, to eliminate any unnecessary restrictions that those rules and regulations place on issuers, particularly small businesses, and to achieve uniformity between state and federal exemptions in order to facilitate capital formation consistent with the protection of investors.

Rules 501–503 set forth definitions, terms, and conditions that apply generally throughout the regulation. The exemptions of Regulation D are contained in Rules 504–506. Rules 504 and 505 replaces Rules 240 and 242, respectively, and provide exemptions from registration under Section 3(b) of the Securities Act. Rule 506 succeeds Rule 146 and relates to transactions that are deemed to be exempt from registration under Section 4(2) of the Securities Act.

Rule 504 generally expands Rule 240 by increasing the amount of securities sold in a 12 month period from $100,000 to $500,000, eliminating the ceiling on the number of investors, and removing the prohibition on payment of commissions or similar remuneration. Rule 504 also removes restrictions on the manner of offering and on resale if an offering is conducted exclusively in states where it is registered and where a disclosure document is delivered under the applicable state law. Like Rule 240, Rule 504 does not prescribe specific disclosure requirements. Rule 504 is an effort by the Commission to set aside a clear and workable exemption for small offerings by small issuers to be regulated by state "Blue Sky" requirements and to be subject to federal antifraud provisions and civil liability provisions such as Section 12(2). Therefore, the exemption is not available to issuers that are subject to the reporting obligations of the Securities Exchange Act of 1934 * * * or are investment companies as defined under the Investment Company Act of 1940 * * *.

Rule 505 replaces Rule 242. Its offering limit is $5,000,000 in a 12-month period, an increase from the $2,000,000 in six months ceiling in Rule 242. Like its predecessor, Rule 505 permits sales to 35 purchasers that are not accredited investors and to an unlimited number of accredited investors. However, the class of accredited investors has now been expanded. The exemption is available to all non-investment company issuers,[8] an

---

8. Like Rule 242, Rule 505 is not available to issuers that are subject to the disqualifications of Regulation A.

NASAA is a voluntary organization composed of securities regulatory agencies of

49 states, the Commonwealth of Puerto Rico, and Guam, as well as Mexico and 13 provinces of Canada.

expansion of the restriction in Rule 242 that limited the exemption's availability to certain corporate entities. An issuer under Rule 505 may not use any general solicitation or general advertising. The informational requirements under Rule 505 are substantially similar to those in Rule 242.

Rule 506 takes the place of Rule 146. As under its predecessor, Rule 506 is available to all issuers for offerings sold to not more than 35 purchasers. Accredited investors, however, do not count towards that limit. Rule 506 requires an issuer to make a subjective determination that each purchaser meets certain sophistication standards, a provision that narrows a similar requirement as to all offerees under Rule 146. The new exemption retains the concept of the purchaser representative so that unsophisticated purchasers may participate in the offering if a purchaser representative is present. Like Rule 146, Rule 506 prohibits any general solicitation or general advertising.

B. *Uniform Federal-State Limited Offering Exemptions*

In conjunction with the proposal and adoption of Regulation D, the Commission, through its Division of Corporation Finance, has coordinated with the North American Securities Administrators Association ("NASAA"), through its Subcommittee on Small Business Financing ("NASAA Subcommittee"), under the authorization of Section 19(c)(3) of the Securities Act. The objective of this process has been to develop a basic framework of limited offering exemptions that can apply uniformly at the federal and state levels. Regulation D is intended to be the principal element of this framework. Under Rule 504, offerings below $500,000 by a non-reporting company will not be required to be registered at the federal level. Moreover, if such offerings are registered in states requiring the delivery of a disclosure document, the manner of offering limitations and the restrictions on resale will not apply. Because of the small amount of the offering and the likelihood that sales will occur in a limited geographic area, the Commission and NASAA believe that greater reliance on state securities laws is appropriate. Rules 505 and 506, and applicable definitions, terms and conditions in Rules 501–503, are intended to be uniform federal-state exemptions.

In October 1981, NASAA formally adopted a uniform limited offering exemption as an official policy guideline.[10] This exemption which had two alternatives, was based on proposed Rule 505 of Regulation D but differed from that provision in certain respects. Subsequent to the endorsement of the uniform exemption and considering the public comment received, the NASAA Subcommittee and the Division of Corporation Finance coordinated to minimize differences in the NASAA policy guideline and Regulation D. The Commission understands that, following its adoption of Regulation D, the NASAA Subcommittee will recommend adoption by NASAA of modifications to its uniform limited offering exemption to provide for a uniform exemptive system. This system will endorse Rule 505 with certain additional terms as one option, and Rules 505 and 506 with no changes as a second option.

10. An official policy guideline of NASAA represents endorsement of a principle which NASAA believes has general application. NASAA has no power to en- act legislation, promulgate regulations, or otherwise bind the legislature or administrative agencies to its members.

The additional terms that NASAA is expected to consider involve the following: (1) restriction on transaction related remuneration; (2) disqualification of issuers and other persons associated with offerings on the basis of state administrative orders or judgments; (3) qualification of investors based on the suitability of the investment; and (4) requirements for filing of the notices of sales.[a]

The Commission and NASAA do not believe that these additional terms detract from the goal of increased federal-state uniformity. Because of differences between federal and state securities regulation, complete uniformity may not be an attainable objective. Certain additional terms, for instance, relate to valid state interests of jurisdiction which are not appropriately addressed in a federal regulation. Similarly, certain additional terms relate to the mechanics of regulating limited offering exemptions at the state level which cannot be included effectively in a federal rule.

The Commission commends NASAA and the members of the NASAA Subcommittee for their cooperation and effort in the development of Regulation D and anticipates continued coordination to achieve a uniform system of federal-state limited offering exemptions that facilitates capital formation consistent with the protection of investors.

III. Synopsis

The following section-by-section discussion of the provisions of Regulation D, the significant commentary on the proposals, and the revisions made to the proposed regulation are included to assist in understanding the regulation as adopted. Attention is directed to the text of Regulation D for a more complete understanding. Attention is also directed to the chart following the synopsis which compares the provisions of Regulation D exemptions to those of predecessor exemptions.

A. *Preliminary Notes*

Regulation D contains six preliminary notes. The first preliminary note reminds issuers that Regulation D offerings, although exempt from Section 5 of the Securities Act, are not exempt from antifraud or civil liability provisions of the federal securities laws. The note also reminds issuers conducting Regulation D offerings of their obligation to furnish whatever material information may be needed to make the required disclosure not misleading.

Note 2 underscores an issuer's obligation to comply with applicable state law and highlights certain areas of anticipated differences between Regulation D at the federal and state levels. (See Section II.B. of this release for further discussion of these differences.)

Note 3 makes clear that reliance on any particular exemption in Regulation D does not act as an election. An issuer may always claim the availability of any other applicable exemption. Several commentators believed this note should address specifically the availability of an exemption under Section 4(2) of the Securities Act. The Commission has reworded the note by including language that appeared in proposed Rule 506(a) and clarified the specific availability of Section 4(2).

---

a. The final version of the NASAA uniform limited offering exemption (ULOE) was adopted in September, 1983. It contains certain disqualification provisions not present in Regulation D. The NASAA, ULOE is set forth in Jennings & Marsh, Selected Statutes, Rules and Forms Under the Federal Securities Laws.

The fourth note specifies that Regulation D is available only to the issuer of the securities and not to its affiliates or others for resales of the issuer's securities. The note further provides that Regulation D exemptions are only transactional. Several commentators pointed out that the proposed note in some respects duplicated Rule 502(d), the provision governing resale limitations. That redundancy has been eliminated.

Preliminary Note 5, which confirms the availability of Regulation D for business combinations, clarifies a question raised by commentators.

The sixth note provides that the regulation is not available for use in a plan or scheme to evade the registration requirements of the Securities Act.

B. *Rule 501—Definitions and Terms Used in Regulation D*

Rule 501 sets forth, alphabetically, definitions that apply to the entire regulation. The definitions generally represent distillations of concepts in Rules 146, 240, and 242. The definition of "accredited investor," however, is an expansion of the term "accredited person" in Rule 242.

The Commission has deleted two definitions, "predecessor" and "securities of the issuer," that appeared in the proposed regulation. The effect of these definitions was principally to expand the measurement of proceeds which would be included in the aggregate offering price of an offering under Rules 504 and 505. The expansion would have required an issuer to add to the aggregate offering price of its Regulation D offering the proceeds of certain offerings by predecessors and affiliates. As commentators observed, this would thus have included, by virtue of the "predecessor" definition, sales of securities by a substantially larger issuer from which the Regulation D issuer had acquired the major portion of its assets. Further, by virtue of the "affiliate" definition, sales by limited partnerships with the same general partners as the Regulation D issuer would have been aggregated. Although there may be instances where such results would be appropriate, the Commission has determined to address those cases through general principles of integration, rather than through specific but overly inclusive rules in the regulation. Predecessor and affiliate relationships would be relevant to any consideration of whether prior offerings should be integrated with a proposed offering under Regulation D.

1. *Accredited investor.* * * *

The following subsections review the eight categories of accredited investor in Rule 501(a).

a. Rule 501(a)(1)—Institutional Investors. Rule 501(a)(1) repeats the listing of institutional investors included in Section 2(15)(i) of the Securities Act. One such investor is an employee benefit plan within the meaning of Title I of the Employee Retirement Income Security Act of 1974 ("ERISA") [codified in scattered sections of 26, 29 U.S.C.], the investment decisions for which are made by a bank, insurance company, or registered investment adviser. The Commission recognizes, and several commentators noted, that many plans, have internalized the function of the plan fiduciary and thus could not qualify under the proposed category. For this reason the Commission believes it is appropriate to extend accredited investor status to any ERISA plan with total assets in excess of $5,000,000.

b. Rule 501(a)(2)—Private Business Development Companies. This category applies to private business development companies as defined in Section 202(a)(22) of the Investment Advisers Act of 1940. As proposed, the category referred to Sections 55(a)(1) through (3) and 2(a)(47) of the Investment Company Act. The proposal was intended to include business development companies that had not made an election under Section 2(a)(48)(C) of the Investment Company Act. Several commentators noted, however, that the intent of the category could be more accurately accomplished by referring to the definition of private business development company in Section 202(a)(22) of the Advisers Act. Although the new reference expands the class of private business development companies that may be qualified as accredited investors, it still delimits the class by the obligation of its members to provide "significant managerial assistance" as defined in Section 2(a)(47) of the Investment Company Act.[12]

c. Rule 501(a)(3)—Tax Exempt Organizations. Proposed Rule 501(a)(3) created a category of accredited investor for college or university endowment funds with assets in excess of $25 million. Upon further consideration and based on commentary the Commission has determined that this category can be expanded to all organizations that are described as exempt organizations in Section 501(c)(3) of the Internal Revenue Code. Additionally, the Commission has lowered the asset level to $5 million.

d. Rule 501(a)(4)—Directors, Executive Officers and General Partners. Rule 501(a)(4) provides that certain insiders of the issuer are accredited investors. As proposed, the category pertained only to directors and executive officers. A number of comment letters recommended that the provision be modified to cover general partners of limited partnerships. The category thus has been revised to include general partners of issuers, as well as directors, executive officers and general partners of those general partners.

e. Rule 501(a)(5)—$150,000 Purchasers. This category represents the combination of a similar category in Rule 242(a)(1)(ii), an analogous provision in Rule 146(g)(2)(i)(d), and the recommendations of many commentators. Under this provision a person is an accredited investor upon the purchase of at least $150,000 of the securities if the total purchase price does not exceed 20 percent of the investor's net worth at the time of sale. For natural persons, the joint net worth of the investor and the investor's spouse may be used in measuring the ratio of purchase to net worth. The purchase may be made by one or a combination of four specified methods: cash; marketable securities; an unconditional obligation to pay cash or marketable securities within five years of sale; or a cancellation of indebtedness.

* * *

The basic premise of proposed Rule 501(a)(5) was that a person capable of investing a large amount of capital (i.e., $100,000 or more) in an offering ought to be considered an accredited investor. However, the Commission noted that, where the purchase price was spread over an extended period of time, the present value of the investment may have been reduced to a level where the investor was no longer investing sufficient amounts to merit accredited investor status.

---

12. Section 202(a)(22) of the Advisers Act refers to Section 2(a)(48) of the Investment Company Act for the core of its meaning. Section 2(a)(48) defines a business development company as a company that, among other things, "makes available significant managerial assistance," a phrase that is defined in Section 2(a)(47) of the Investment Company Act.

In addressing the concerns of commentators, the Commission revised the rule to permit a payment period of five years with no specified collateral. In view of the extension of the installment period and in order to ensure that the investor in this category is capable of investing a sufficiently large amount of capital to warrant accredited investor status, the Commission also has increased the purchase price to $150,000 and revised the rule to provide that the total purchase price be limited to no more than 20 percent of the investor's net worth. The latter restriction does not, of course, require a commitment of 20 percent of the investor's net worth in the offering.

Lastly, in response to certain comments, the Commission has supplemented the available methods of payment with securities that have a readily available market quotation.

Various aspects of this category may be demonstrated by the following examples. An investor whose net worth at the time of sale is $750,000 and who purchases $150,000 of the offering in cash on the day of sale is accredited. The same investor maintains that status if his payment is spread out over five years, so long as on the date of purchase he enters into an unconditional obligation to pay within that period. If, however, that investor agrees to purchase $200,000 of securities in installments, $150,000 to be paid on the date of sale and the balance in four years, he will not qualify under this category of accredited investor because his total purchase of $200,000 is more than 20 percent of his $750,000 net worth. A final case involves the investor with a net worth of $900,000 who agrees to purchase $180,000 of securities over six years, the first $150,000 of that purchase coming in the first five years. That investor is accredited because he is purchasing at least $150,000 within a five-year period and because the total purchase of $180,000 does not exceed 20 percent of his net worth.

f. Rule 501(a)(6)—$1,000,000 Net Worth Test. This category extends accredited investor status to any natural person whose net worth at the time of purchase is $1,000,000. Net worth may be either the individual worth of the investor or the joint net worth of the investor and the investor's spouse. * * *

g. Rule 501(a)(7)—$200,000 Income Test. A natural person who has an income in excess of $200,000 in each of the last two years and who reasonably expects an income in excess of $200,000 in the current year is an accredited investor.

* * *

One possible method of computing income is as follows: individual adjusted gross income (assuming that had been reported on a federal tax return) increased by any deduction for long term capital gains under section 1202 of the Internal Revenue Code (the "Code"), any deduction for depletion under section 611 et seq. of the Code, any exclusion for interest under section 103 of the Code, and any losses of a partnership allocated to the individual limited partner as reported on Schedule E of Form 1040 (or any successor report).

h. Rule 501(a)(8)—Entities Made up of Certain Accredited Investors. The proposed definition of accredited investor did not take into account an entity owned entirely by accredited investors. Rule 501(a)(8) of the final regulation extends accredited investor status to entities in which all the equity owners are accredited investors under Rule 501(a)(1), (2), (3), (4), (6), or (7).

2. *Affiliate.* The definition of affiliate in Rule 501(b) is the same as that contained in Rule 405 of Regulation C.

3. *Aggregate Offering Price.* Rule 501(c) defines the method for calculating the aggregate offering price. With the exception of certain changes to add clarity, the substance of this provision is similar to that in proposed Rule 501.

4. *Business Combination.* The definition of business combination in Rule 501(d) has undergone only technical revision.

5. *Calculation of Number of Purchasers.* Rule 501(e) sets forth principles that govern the calculation of the number of purchasers in offerings under Rules 505 and 506. These principles represent a consolidation of those in Rule 146(g)(2)(i) and Rule 242(e)(2) with some modifications.

6. *Executive Officer.* The definition of executive officer in Rule 501(f) has been modified to conform with the definition of that term set forth in Rule 405 of Regulation C.

7. *Issuer.* The term "issuer", as set forth in Rule 501(g), has been revised to conform with the terminology in the Federal Bankruptcy Code [11 U.S.C. 101 et seq.].

8. *Purchaser Representative.* In response to comments, the definition of purchaser representative in Rule 501(h) has been revised in three respects. First, the introductory language to the paragraph has been reformulated. As adopted, the definition includes any person who satisfies the conditions of the term in fact, as well as any person the issuer reasonably believes falls within the category. A second change incorporated the categories set forth in Rule 501(e)(1)(ii) and (iii) into subparagraphs (ii) and (iii). Thirdly, paragraph (2) was revised to permit the purchaser representative to make the requisite evaluation of the prospective investment "with the purchaser."

(C). *Rule 502—General Conditions to be Met*

Rule 502 sets forth general conditions that relate to all offerings under Rules 504 through 506. These cover guidelines for determining whether separate offers and sales constitute part of the same offering under principles of integration, requirements as to specific disclosure requirements in Regulation D offerings, and limitations on the manner of conducting the offering and on the resale of securities acquired in the offering.

                    * * *

1. *Integration.* Rule 502(a) provides that all sales that are part of the same Regulation D offering must be integrated. The rule provides a safe harbor for all offers and sales that take place at least six months before the start of or six months after the termination of the Regulation D offering, so long as there are no offers and sales, excluding those to employee benefit plans, of the same securities within either of these six-month periods.

Along with several technical revisions, the Commission changed the word "issue" to "offering" throughout the provision. This change makes the language of the rule consistent with the principle of integration.

2. *Information Requirements.* Rule 502(b) provides when and what type of disclosure must be furnished in Regulation D offerings. If an issuer

sells securities under Rule 504 or only to accredited investors, then Regulation D does not mandate any specific disclosure. If securities are sold under Rule 505 or 506 to any investors that are not accredited, then Rule 502(b)(1)(ii) requires delivery of the information specified in Rule 502(b)(2) to all purchasers. The type of information to be furnished varies depending on the size of the offering and the nature of the issuer.

* * *

The specific disclosure requirements are as follows:

a. Non-reporting companies. Disclosure requirements for companies that are not subject to the reporting obligations of the Exchange Act are set forth in Rule 502(b)(2)(i). These requirements are keyed to the size of the offering.

In offerings up to $5,000,000 an issuer must provide the same kind of information as required in Part I of Form S–18, or, for an issuer that is not qualified to use Form S–18, the same kind of information as required in Part I of a registration form available to the issuer. The issuer need only provide two years of financial statements and only the most recent year need be audited. For issuers that are not limited partnerships, only a balance sheet dated within 120 days of the offering must be audited if obtaining an audit of the other financial statements would constitute an unreasonable effort or expense. Limited partnerships may furnish tax basis financial statements if the basic requirements are an unreasonable effort or expense.

For offerings over $5,000,000 issuers must furnish the same kind of information as specified in Part I of an available form of registration. Where the audited financials cannot be obtained without unreasonable effort or expense, the issuer is given options similar to those in offerings up to $5,000,000.

* * *

b. Reporting companies. Companies that are subject to Exchange Act reporting obligations must furnish the same kind of disclosure regardless of the size of the offering. These issuers, however, have an option as to the form that this disclosure may take. Under Rule 502(b)(2)(ii)(A), a reporting company may provide its most recent annual report to shareholders, assuming it is in accordance with Rule 14a–3 or 14c–3 under the Exchange Act, the definitive proxy statement filed in connection with that annual report, and, if requested in writing, the most recent Form 10–K. Alternatively, those issuers may elect under Rule 502(b)(2)(ii)(B) to provide the information contained in the most recent of its Form 10–K or a Form S–1 registration statement under the Securities Act or a Form 10 registration statement under the Exchange Act. Although the requirement under subparagraph (B) refers to specific forms, it does not mandate delivery of the actual reference documents. An issuer, for instance, may choose to prepare and deliver a separate document that contains the necessary information.

Regardless of the issuer's choice of disclosure in subparagraph (A) or (B), Rule 502(b)(2)(ii)(C) requires the basic information to be supplemented by information contained in certain Exchange Act reports filed after the distribution or filing of the report or registration statement in question. Further, the issuer must provide certain information regarding the offering and any material changes in the issuer's affairs that are not disclosed in the basic documents.

* * *

c. Other information requirements. The balance of Rule 502(b)(2) provides for the treatment of exhibits, the right of purchasers that are not accredited to receive information which was furnished to accredited investors, and, in offerings involving nonaccredited investors, the right of all purchasers to ask questions of the issuer concerning the offering, and a specific obligation by the issuer to disclose all material differences in terms or arrangements as between security holders in a business combination or exchange offer. * * *

3. *Manner of Offering.* Rule 502(c) prohibits the use of general solicitation or general advertising in connection with Regulation D offerings, except in certain cases under Rule 504. The prohibition follows a similar restriction in Rule 146(c), except that both as proposed and as adopted the limitation in Regulation D alters those aspects of Rule 146(c) that related to qualified offerees.

4. *Limitations on Resale.* Securities acquired in a Regulation D offering, with the exception of certain offerings under Rule 504, have the status of securities acquired in a transaction under Section 4(2) of the Securities Act. As further provided in Rule 502(d), the issuer shall exercise reasonable care to assure that purchasers of securities are not underwriters, which reasonable care will include certain inquiry as to investment purpose, disclosure of resale limitations and placement of a legend on the certificate. * * *

D. *Rule 503—Filings of Notice of Sales*

The Commission is adopting a uniform notice of sales form for use in offerings under both Regulation D and Section 4(6) of the Securities Act. The form is an adaptation of Form 242 and Form 4(6) to the Regulation D context. As with the predecessor forms, issuers will furnish information on Form D mainly by checking appropriate boxes. The form requires an indication of the exemptions being claimed.

Rule 503 sets forth the filing requirements for Form D. The notice is due 15 days after the first sale of securities in an offering under Regulation D.[27] Subsequent notices are due every six months after first sale and 30 days after the last sale. One copy of each notice must be manually signed by a person duly authorized by the issuer.

Rule 503(d) requires an undertaking in Form D to furnish the staff, upon its written request, with the information provided to purchasers that are not accredited in a Rule 505 offering. * * *

E. *Rule 504—Exemption for Offers and Sales Not Exceeding $500,000*

Rule 504, which replaces Rule 240, provides an exemption under Section 3(b) of the Securities Act for certain offers and sales not exceeding an aggregate offering price of $500,000. Rule 240 permits sales up to $100,000 to 100 investors. Proceeds from securities sold within the preceding 12 months in all transactions exempt under Section 3(b) or in violation of Section 5(a) of the Securities Act must be included in computing the

---

27. In response to commentators, the Commission notes that generally the acceptance of subscription funds into an escrow account pending receipt of minimum subscriptions would trigger the filing requirements.

aggregate offering price under Rule 504. The exemption is not available to investment companies or issuers subject to Exchange Act reporting obligations. Commissions or similar transaction related remuneration may be paid.

As under Rule 240, the exemption under Rule 504 does not mandate specific disclosure requirements. However, the issuer remains subject to the antifraud and civil liability provisions of the federal securities laws and must also comply with state requirements.

Offers and sales under Rule 504 must be made in accordance with all the general terms and conditions in Rules 501 through 503. However, if the entire offering is made exclusively in states that require registration and the delivery of a disclosure document, and if the offering is in compliance with those requirements, then the general limitations on the manner of offering and on resale will not apply.

* * *

F. *Rule 505—Exemption for Offers and Sales Not Exceeding $5,000,000*

Rule 505 replaces Rule 242. The rule provides an exemption under Section 3(b) of the Securities Act for offers and sales to no more than 35 purchasers that are not accredited where the aggregate offering price over 12 months does not exceed $5,000,000. As with Rule 504, the aggregate offering price includes proceeds from offers and sales under Section 3(b) or in violation of Section 5(a) of the Securities Act.[31] Rule 242 permits up to $2,000,000 in sales, aggregated over six months to no more than 35 purchasers that are not accredited.[32]

Rule 505 is available to any issuer that is not an investment company. This is an expansion of the availability of Rule 242 which follows the eligibility criteria of Form S–18 and is currently not available to non-corporate issuers, to foreign issuers, and to issuers engaged in oil and gas activities. * * *

Finally, Rule 505 is not available to issuers that are subject to any of the disqualification provisions contained in Rule 252(c), (d), (e) or (f) of Regulation A. * * *

---

31. Based on its experience with Rule 242, the Commission is aware that in computing the aggregate offering price issuers frequently misunderstand the interaction of the concepts of aggregation and integration as applicable under Rule 504(b)(2)(i) and 505(b)(2)(i). Aggregation is the principle by which an issuer determines the dollar worth of exempt sales available directly under Section 3(b) of the Securities Act. Integration is a principle under which an issuer determines overall characteristics of its offering. The following examples illustrate the application of these concepts. An issuer that has conducted an offering under Rule 505 in May 1982 must aggregate the proceeds from that offering with the proceeds of a Rule 505 offering conducted in December 1982. If the May offering had been under Rule 506, however, it would not need to be aggregated with the December offering. In either case, the May offering should be exempt from prin-

ciples of integration by virtue of the safe harbor provision in Rule 502(a). If a Rule 506 offering had been conducted in July 1982, the integration safe harbor would not be available as to a subsequent Rule 505 offering in December. Although the proceeds from the July 506 offering would not be added to the December 505 aggregate offering price under aggregation principles, they would have to be included if the two offerings could be integrated. Assuming the two offerings were integrated, then the issuer would have to evaluate all characteristics of the combined transactions, e.g., number of investors, aggregate offering price, etc., when determining the availability of an exemption.

32. Rule 242 does not aggregate proceeds from securities sold in violation of Section 5(a) or under Regulation A pursuant to an employee plan defined in Rule 16b–3 under the Exchange Act.

G. *Rule 506—Exemption for Offers and Sales Without Regard to Dollar Amount*

Rule 506 relates to transactions that are deemed to be exempt under Section 4(2) of the Securities Act. It modifies and replaces Rule 146. Like its predecessor, Rule 506 exempts offers and sales to no more than purchasers. Whereas Rule 146 excludes certain purchasers from the count, Rule 506 excludes accredited investors in computing the number of purchasers. More significantly, Rule 506 modifies the offeree qualification principles of Rule 146 in two ways. First, Rule 506 requires that only purchasers meet the sophistication standard. Second, the rule eliminates the economic risk test. Commentators endorsed both modifications.

The Commission has redrafted Rule 506 so that it parallels the form of Rules 504 and 505. In the process, two proposed provisions have been eliminated. One, regarding business combinations in proposed Rule 506(b)(2), has been removed on the ground that, in view of other general rules in the regulation, its principle does not require specific recitation. Another, regarding purchaser representatives in proposed Rule 506(c), has been eliminated because of overlapping coverage in the definition of purchaser representative in Rule 501(h)(4).[33]

IV. Effective Date and Operation of Regulation D

Regulation D, Rule 215, Form D, and related amendments to Rules 144 and 148 will be effective and Form 4(6) will be rescinded on April 15, 1982. Rules 146, 240, and 242 and Forms 146, 240, and 242 will be rescinded on June 30, 1982. For those offerings made in compliance with the terms of Rules 146, 240 and 242 which commence prior to the effective date of Regulation D (April 15, 1982) and which continue past June 30, 1982, the Commission takes the administrative position that no registration is required under the Securities Act.

The staff will issue interpretive letters to assist persons in complying with Regulation D, but the staff will not issue no-action letters as to whether a transaction satisfies the requirements of the regulation. With respect to resales of securities, the staff will continue its present policy of not expressing an opinion on inquiries regarding the following: (1) hypothetical situations; (2) the removal of restrictive legends from securities; (3) whether a person is an affiliate; or (4) requests for no-action positions regarding securities acquired on or after April 15, 1972, as set forth in Release No. 33–6099 (August 2, 1979).

---

33. Commentators expressed concern that this exemption was not clearly designated as a safe harbor rule under Section 4(2) of the Securities Act. Such a connection is important, they noted, for purposes of exemption from Regulation T (12 CFR 220.1–220.8) of the Federal Reserve Board, exemption from the definition of "investment company" under Section 3(c)(1) of the Investment Company Act, and exemption from registration under certain state laws. The final language of Rule 506 responds to this concern. In addition, the Commis-sion's Division of Corporation Finance has conferred with and has been assured by the staff of the Federal Reserve Board that transactions under Rule 506 will be exempt from the operation of Regulation T. Finally, the Commission regards Rule 506 transactions as non-public offerings for purposes of the definition of "investment company" in Section 3(c)(1) of the Investment Company Act and as Section 4 transactions for purposes of Section 304(b) of the Trust Indenture Act of 1939 [15 U.S.C. 77aaa et seq., as amended].

Comparative Chart of Securities Act Limited Offering Exemptions and Alternatives

Comparison Item	Rule 504	Rule 505	Rule 506	Sec. 4(6)	Reg. A
Dollar Ceiling	$500,000 (12 mos.)	$5,000,000 (12 mos.)	Unlimited	$5,000,000	$1.5 million (12 mos.) aggregate; affiliates limited to $100,000, $100,000 if securities offered by any other person (up to an aggregate of $300,000, or $500,000 for estates)
Number of Investors	Unlimited	35 plus unlimited accredited investors	35 plus those purchasing $150,000	Unlimited accredited only	Unlimited
Investor Qualification	None required	Accredited or none required	Purchaser must be sophisticated (alone or with representative). Accredited presumed to be qualified	Accredited	None required
Commissions					
Limitations on Manner of Offering	Permitted No general solicitation unless registered in states that require delivery of disclosure document	Permitted No general solicitation permitted	Permitted No general solicitation permitted	Permitted Unlimited accredited only	Permitted Unlimited
Limitations on Resale	Restricted, unless registered in states that require delivery of disclosure document	Restricted	Restricted	Restricted	No restrictions

Comparative Chart of Securities Act Limited Offering Exemptions and Alternatives—Continued

Comparison Item	Rule 504	Rule 505	Rule 506	Sec. 4(6)	Reg. A
Issuer Qualification	No reporting or investment companies	No investment companies or issuers disqualified under Reg. A	None	Accredited investors (Rule 215) including investment companies	Only U.S. and Canadian issuers. No investment companies or oil and gas rights. No issuers or underwriters disqualified under Reg. A
Notice of Sale	Form D required as condition of exemption—5 copies filed with SEC 15 days after first sale.	Same as Rule 504	Same as Rule 504	Same as Rule 504	Form 1-A: 4 copies to Regional Office 10 days before offering. Sales material—4 copies filed 5 days before use.

Information Requirements	No information specified	1. If purchased solely by accredited, no information specified
		2. If purchased by non-accredited:
		  a. Non-reporting issuers must furnish
		    i. offerings up to $5 million—information in Part I of Form S–18 or available registration statement, 2 yr. financials, 1 year audited—if undue effort or expense, issuers other than limited partnerships only balance sheet as of 120 days before offering must be audited—if limited partnership and undue effort or expense, may use tax basis financials
			Same as Rule 504	No information specified	Offering Circular—See Rule 256

Comparative Chart of Securities Act Limited Offering Exemptions and Alternatives—Continued

Comparison Item	Rule 504	Rule 505	Rule 506	Sec. 4(6)	Reg. A

		ii. Offerings over $5 million—Information in Part I of available registration statement—if undue effort or expense, issuers other than limited partnerships only balance sheet as of 120 days before offering must be audited—if limited partnership and undue effort or expense, financials may be tax basis
		
		b. Reporting issuers must furnish
		  i. Rule 14a-3 annual report to shareholders, def. proxy statement and 10-K, if requested, plus subsequent reports and other updating information, or
		
		  ii. information in more recent Form S-1 or Form 10-K plus subsequent reports and other updating information
		
		c. Issuers must make available prior to sale
		  i. exhibits
		  ii. written information given accredited investors
		  iii. opportunity to ask questions and receive answers		

Comparative Chart of Securities Act Limited Offering Exemptions and Alternatives—Continued

Comparison Item	Section 3(a)(11)	Rule 147	S-18
Dollar Ceiling	Unlimited	Unlimited	$5 million for issuers $1.5 million for resales
Number of Investors	All offerees and purchasers must be "residents" of state of issuer; no maximum number	Same as § 3(a)(11)	Unlimited as to number of offerees or purchasers
Investor Qualification	No qualifications or numerical limits other than "residence"	Same as § 3(a)(11)	Unlimited as to number of offerees or purchasers
Commissions	Permitted	Permitted	Permitted
Limitations on Manner of Offering	Advertising and general solicitation within offering state permitted	Same as § 3(a)(11)	Unlimited
Limitation on Resale	Resales permitted to in-state residents; resales by nonaffiliates to out-of-state residents permitted 12 mo. after last offer or sale	Resales permitted to in-state residents; No resales by nonaffiliates to out-of-state residents until 9 mo. after last offer or sale	Unlimited
Issuer Qualification	Issuer must be organized and doing business in state where securities sold	Issuers only (no resales); issuer must be organized and doing business in state where securities sold (at least 80% of assets, sales, etc.) and 80% of proceeds expended	Issuer and resales; no investment companies, insurance companies or 1934 Act reporting companies
Notice of Sale	None required	None required	Registration Statement
Information Requirements	None required	None required	Form S-18 registration statement

SECURITIES ACT RELEASE NO. 6455

Securities and Exchange Commission.
March 3, 1983.

Interpretive Release on Regulation D

* * * *

1. General

The definition of "accredited investor" includes any person who comes within or "who the issuer reasonably believes" comes within one of the enumerated categories "at the time of the sale of the securities to that person." What constitutes "reasonable" belief will depend on the facts of each particular case. For this reason, the staff generally will not be in a position to express views or otherwise endorse any one method for ascertaining whether an investor is accredited.

(1) *Question:* A director of a corporate issuer purchases securities offered under Rule 505. Two weeks after the purchase, and prior to completion of the offering, the director resigns due to a sudden illness. Is the former director an accredited investor?

Answer: Yes. The preliminary language to Rule 501(a) provides that an investor is accredited if he falls into one of the enumerated categories "at the time of the sale of securities to that person." One such category includes directors of the issuer. *See* Rule 501(a)(4). The investor in this case had that status at the time of the sale to him.

2. Certain Institutional Investors—Rules 501(a)(1)–(3)

(2) *Question:* A national bank purchases $100,000 of securities from a Regulation D issuer and distributes the securities equally among ten trust accounts for which it acts as trustee. Is the bank an accredited investor?

Answer: Yes. Rule 501(a)(1) accredits a bank acting in a fiduciary capacity.

(3) *Question:* An ERISA employee benefit plan will purchase $200,000 of the securities being offered. The plan has less than $5,000,000 in total assets and its investment decisions are made by a plan trustee who is not a bank, insurance company, or registered investment adviser. Does the plan qualify as an accredited investor?

Answer: Not under Rule 501(a)(1). Rule 501(a)(1) accredits an ERISA plan that has a plan fiduciary which is a bank, insurance company, or registered investment adviser or that has total assets in excess of $5,000,000. The plan, however, may be an accredited investor under Rule 501(a)(5), which accredits certain persons who purchase at least $150,000 of the securities being offered.

(4) *Question:* A state run, not-for-profit hospital has total assets in excess of $5,000,000. Because it is a state agency, the hospital is exempt from federal income taxation. Rule 501(a)(3) accredits any organization described in section 501(c)(3) of the Internal Revenue Code that has total assets in excess of $5,000,000. Is the hospital accredited under Rule 501(a)(3)?

Answer: Yes. This category does not require that the investor have received a ruling on tax status under section 501(c)(3) of the Internal Revenue Code. Rather, Rule 501(a)(3) accredits an investor that falls within the substantive description in that section.

(5) *Question:* A not-for-profit, tax exempt hospital with total assets of $3,000,000 is purchasing $100,000 of securities in a Regulation D offering. The hospital controls a subsidiary with total assets of $3,000,000. Under generally accepted accounting principles, the hospital may combine its financial statements with that of its subsidiary. Is the hospital accredited?

Answer: Yes, under Rule 501(a)(3). Where the financial statements of the subsidiary may be combined with those of the investor, the assets of the subsidiary may be added to those of the investor in computing total assets for purposes of Rule 501(a)(3).

3.   Insiders—Rule 501(a)(4)

(6) *Question:* The executive officer of a parent of the corporate general partner of the issuer is investing in the Regulation D offering. Is that individual an accredited investor?

Answer: Rule 501(a)(4) accredits only the directors and executive officers of the general partner itself. Unless the executive officer of the parent can be deemed an executive officer of the subsidiary, that individual is not an accredited investor.

4. $150,000 Purchasers—Rule 501(a)(5)

This provision accredits any person who satisfies two separate tests. To be accredited under Rule 501(a)(5), an investor must purchase at least $150,000 of the securities being offered, by one or a combination of four specific methods: cash, marketable securities, an unconditional obligation to pay cash or marketable securities over not more than five years, and cancellation of indebtedness. The rule also requires that "the total purchase price" may not exceed 20 percent of the purchaser's net worth. The two tests under Rule 501(a)(5) must be considered separately. Thus, for instance, in computing the "total purchase price" for the 20 percent of net worth limitation, the investor may have to include amounts that could not be included towards the $150,000 purchase test.

a. $150,000 Purchase

(7) *Question:* Two issuers, a general partner and its limited partnership, are selling their securities simultaneously as units consisting of common stock and limited partnership interests. The issues are part of a plan of financing made for the same general purpose. If an investor purchases $150,000 of these units, would it satisfy the $150,000 purchase element of Rule 501(a)(5)?

Answer: Yes. The issuers are affiliated and the simultaneous sale of their separate securities as units for a single plan of financing would be deemed one integrated offering. Rule 501(a)(5) applies to a purchase "of the securities being offered." The rule thus applies not to the securities of a particular issuer, but to the securities of a particular offering.

(8) *Question:* An investor will purchase securities in cash installments. Each installment payment will include amounts due on the principal as well as interest. If the total of all payments is $150,000, will the investor

have purchased "at least $150,000 of the securities being offered" for purposes of Rule 501(a)(5)?

Answer: No. Under Rule 501(a)(5), any amount constituting interest due on the unpaid purchase price is not payment for the "securities being offered."

(9) *Question:* The installment payments for interest in a limited partnership that will develop commercial real estate will be conditioned upon completion of certain phases of the project. Will the obligation to make those payments be deemed "an unconditional obligation to pay" for purposes of Rule 501(a)(5)?

Answer: Yes, as long as the only conditions relate to completion of successive stages of the development project.

(10) *Question:* An investor will purchase securities in a Regulation D offering by delivering $75,000 in cash and a letter of credit for $75,000. Will such a purchase satisfy the $150,000 element of Rule 501(a)(5)?

Answer: No. Because there is no assurance that the letter of credit will ever be drawn against, the staff does not deem it to be an unconditional obligation to pay.

(11) *Question:* In connection with the sale of limited partnership interests in an oil and gas drilling program, an investor in a Regulation D offering commits to pay subsequent assessments that are mandatory, non-contingent, and for which the investor will be personally liable. Will the commitment to pay the assessments constitute an "unconditional obligation to pay" under Rule 501(a)(5)?

Answer: Yes. The assessments are essentially installment payments for which the investor makes the investment decision at the time the limited partnership interest originally is purchased.

(12) *Question:* If the assessments in Question 11 are voluntary, contingent and non-recourse, can they be included in determining whether or not the investor has purchased $150,000 of the securities being offered?

Answer: No. Voluntary assessments of this nature are not deemed to constitute an unconditional obligation to pay.

(13) *Question:* A purchaser of interests in a limited partnership makes a partial down payment and commits unconditionally to pay the balance over five years. Formation of the partnership is conditioned upon the sale of a specified number of interests. Under Rule 501(a)(5), when must the five year period for installment payments begin to run?

Answer: Rule 501(a)(5) provides that the unconditional obligation is to be discharged "within five years of the sale of the securities to the purchaser." For ease in the administration of an offering that is conditioned on a certain minimum level of sales, the staff believes it is reasonable to compute the length of installment obligations from the same date for the investors involved in reaching that minimum. Therefore, without any bearing on when the sale of the security actually occurs, the five-year time period of the investor's obligation may be measured from the date such minimum level of sales has been reached.

b. 20 Percent of Net Worth Limitation

(14) *Question:* Where an investor makes installment payments composed of principal and interest, must the interest payments be included in computing the "total purchase price" for purposes of meeting the 20 percent of net worth limitation?

Answer: No. The interest is not part of the total purchase price but rather is an expense associated with financing the total purchase price.

(15) *Question:* A corporate investor will purchase $200,000 of the securities being offered for cash. Additionally, the investor will deliver an irrevocable letter of credit for $50,000 which the issuer will use as collateral in connection with a line of credit it will establish with a lending institution. Must the issuer include the $50,000 letter of credit when determining whether or not the purchaser's total purchase price exceeds 20 percent of its net worth under Rule 501(a)(5)?

Answer: Yes. Since the investor has committed to pay the $50,000 at the election of the issuer, that amount must be included with other forms of consideration in order to measure what percentage of the investor's net worth has been committed in the investment.

(16) *Question:* As part of the purchase of an interest in a sale and lease-back program, the purchaser will deliver "non-recourse" debt where the source of payment for the debt is limited exclusively to the income generated by the security being purchased or the assets of the entity in which the security is being purchased. Must the non-recourse debt be included in the total purchase price for purposes of the 20 percent of net worth limitation under Rule 501(a)(5)?

Answer: No. Because the investor has no personal liability for the non-recourse debt, and because no part of the investor's assets at the time of purchase is available as a source of payment for the debt, the debt should not be included as part of the purchase price.

(17) *Question:* Where the purchaser is a natural person, Rule 501(a)(5) provides that the total purchase price may be measured against the purchaser's net worth combined with that of a spouse. Would property held solely by one spouse be available for calculating the net worth of the other spouse who is making the $150,000 investment?

Answer: Yes.

(18) *Question:* An investment general partnership is purchasing securities in a Regulation D offering. The partnership was not formed for the specific purpose of acquiring the securities being offered. May the issuer consider the aggregate net worth of the general partners in calculating the net worth of the partnership?

Answer: Yes. An investment general partnership is functionally a vehicle in which profits and losses are passed through to general partners and in which the net worths of the general partners are exposed to the risk of partnership investments.

(19) *Question:* A totally held subsidiary makes a cash investment of $200,000 in a Regulation D offering. May that subsidiary use the consolidated net worth of its parent in determining whether or not its total purchase price exceeds 20 percent of its net worth?

Answer: Yes.

5. Natural Persons—Rules 501(a)(6)–(7)

Rules 501(a)(6) and (7) apply only to natural persons. Paragraph (6) accredits any natural person with a net worth at the time of purchase in excess of $1,000,000. If the investor is married, the rule permits the use of joint net worth of the couple. Paragraph (7) accredits any natural person whose income has exceeded $200,000 in each of the two most recent years and is reasonably expected to exceed $200,000 in the year of the investment.

(20) *Question:* A corporation with a net worth of $2,000,000 purchases securities in a Regulation D offering. Is the corporation an accredited investor under Rule 501(a)(6)?

Answer: No. Rule 501(a)(6) is limited to "natural" persons.

(21) *Question:* In calculating net worth for purposes of Rule 501(a)(6), may the investor include the estimated fair market value of his principal residence as an asset?

Answer: Yes. Rule 501(a)(6) does not exclude any of the purchaser's assets from the net worth needed to qualify as an accredited investor.

(22) *Question:* May a purchaser take into account income of a spouse in determining possible accreditation under Rule 501(a)(7)?

Answer: No. Rule 501(a)(7) requires "individual income" over $200,000 in order to qualify as an accredited investor.

(23) *Question:* May a purchaser include unrealized capital appreciation in calculating income for purposes of Rule 501(a)(7)?

Answer: Generally, no.

6. Entities Owned By Accredited Investors—Rule 501(a)(8)

Any entity in which each equity owner is an accredited investor under any of the qualifying categories, except that of the $150,000 purchaser, is accredited under Rule 501(a)(8).

(24) *Question:* All but one of the shareholders of a corporation are accredited investors by virtue of net worth or income. The unaccredited shareholder is a director who bought one share of stock in order to comply with a requirement that all directors be shareholders of the corporation. Is the corporation an accredited investor under Rule 501(a)(8)?

Answer: No. Rule 501(a)(8) requires "all of the equity owners" to be accredited investors. The director is an equity owner and is not accredited. Note that the director cannot be accredited under Rule 501(a)(4). That provision extends accreditation to a director of the issuer, not of the investor.

(25) *Question:* Who are the equity owners of a limited partnership?

Answer: The limited partners.

7. Trusts as Accredited Investors

(26) *Question:* May a trust qualify as an accredited investor under Rule 501(a)(1)?

Answer: Only indirectly. Although a trust standing alone cannot be accredited under Rule 501(a)(1), if a bank is its trustee and makes the investment on behalf of the trust, the trust will in effect be accredited by virtue of the provision in Rule 501(a)(1) that accredits a bank acting in a fiduciary capacity.

(27) *Question:* May a trust qualify as an accredited investor under Rule 501(a)(5)?

Answer: Yes. The Division interprets "person" in Rule 501(a)(5) to include any trust.

(28) *Question:* In qualifying a trust as an accredited investor under Rule 501(a)(5), whose net worth should be considered in determining whether the total purchase price meets the 20 percent of net worth limitation test?

Answer: The net worth of the trust.

(29) *Question:* A trustee of a trust has a net worth of $1,500,000. Is the trustee's purchase of securities for the trust that of an accredited investor under Rule 501(a)(6)?

Answer: No. Except where a bank is a trustee, the trust is deemed the purchaser, not the trustee. The trust is not a "natural" person.

(30) *Question:* May a trust be accredited under Rule 501(a)(8) if all of its beneficiaries are accredited investors?

Answer: Generally, no. Rule 501(a)(8) accredits any entity if all of its "equity owners" are accredited investors. The staff does not interpret this provision to apply to the beneficiaries of a conventional trust. The result may be different, however, in the case of certain non-conventional trusts where, as a result of powers retained by the grantors, a trust as a legal entity would be deemed not to exist. Thus, where the grantors of a revocable trust are accredited investors under Rule 501(a)(6) (*i.e.* net worth exceeds $1,000,000) and the trust may be amended or revoked at any time by the grantors, the trust is accredited because the grantors will be deemed the equity owners of the trust's assets. Similarly, where the purchase of Regulation D securities is made by an Individual Retirement Account and the participant is an accredited investor, the account would be accredited under Rule 501(a)(8).

B. Aggregate Offering Price—Rule 501(c)

The "aggregate offering price," defined in Rule 501(c), is the sum of all proceeds received by the issuer for issuance of its securities. The term is important to the operation of Rules 504 and 505, both of which impose a limitation on the aggregate offering price as a specific condition to the availability of the exemption.

(31) *Question:* The sole general partner of a real estate limited partnership contributes property to the program. Must that property be valued and included in the overall proceeds of the offering as part of the aggregate offering price?

Answer: No, assuming the property is contributed in exchange for a general partnership interest.

(33) *Question:* Where the investors pay for their securities in installments and these payments include an interest component, must the issuer include interest payments in the "aggregate offering price?"

Answer: No. The interest payments are not deemed to be consideration for the issuance of the securities.

(34) *Question:* An offering of interests in an oil and gas limited partnership provides for additional voluntary assessments. These assessments, undetermined at the time of the offering, may be called at the general partner's discretion for developmental drilling activities. Must the assessments be included in the aggregate offering price, and if so, in what amount?

Answer: Because it is unclear that the assessments will ever be called, and because if they are called, it is unclear at what level, the issuer is not required to include the assessments in the aggregate offering price. In fact, the assessments will be consideration received for the issuance of additional securities in the limited partnership. This issuance will need to be considered along with the original issuance for possible integration, or, if not integrated, must find its own exemption from registration.

(35) *Question:* In purchasing interests in an oil and gas partnership, investors agree to pay mandatory assessments. The assessments, essentially installment payments, are non-contingent and investors will be personally liable for their payment. Must the issuer include the assessments in the aggregate offering price?

* * * *

Answer: Yes.

C. Executive Officer—Rule 501(f)

The definition of executive officer in Rule 501(f) is the same as that in Rule 405 of Regulation C.

(37) *Question:* The executive officer of the parent of the Regulation D issuer performs a policy making function for its subsidiary. May that individual be deemed an "executive officer" of the subsidiary?

Answer: Yes.

D. Purchaser Representative—Rule 501(h)

A purchaser representative is any person who satisfies, or who the issuer reasonably believes satisfies, four conditions enumerated in Rule 501(h). Beyond the obligations imposed by that rule, any person acting as a purchaser representative must consider whether or not he is required to register as a broker-dealer under section 15 of the Securities Exchange Act of 1934 or as an investment adviser under section 203 of the Investment Advisers Act of 1940.

(38) *Question:* May the officer of a corporate general partner of the issuer qualify as a purchaser representative under Rule 501(h)?

Answer: Rule 501(h) provides that "an affiliate, director, officer or other employee of the issuer" may not be a purchaser representative unless the purchaser has one of three enumerated relationships with the representative. The staff is of the view that an officer or director of a corporate general partner comes within the scope of "affiliate, director, officer or other employee of the issuer."

(39) *Question:* May the issuer in a Regulation D offering pay the fees of the purchaser representative?

Answer: Yes. Nothing in Regulation D prohibits the payment by the issuer of the purchaser representative's fees. Rule 501(h)(4), however, requires disclosure of this fact.

II. *Disclosure Requirements—Rule 502(b)*

A. When Required

Rule 502(b)(1) sets forth the circumstances when disclosure of the kind specified in the regulation must be delivered to investors. The regulation requires the delivery of certain information "during the course of the offering and prior to sale" if the offering is conducted in reliance on Rule 505 or 506 and if there are unaccredited investors. If the offering is conducted in compliance with Rule 504 or if securities are sold only to accredited investors, Regulation D does not specify the information that must be disclosed to investors.

(40) *Question:* An issuer furnishes potential investors a short form offering memorandum in anticipation of actual selling activities and the delivery of an expanded disclosure document. Does Regulation D permit the delivery of disclosure in two installments?

Answer: So long as all the information is delivered prior to sale, the use of a fair and adequate summary followed by a complete disclosure document is not prohibited under Regulation D. Disclosure in such a manner, however, should not obscure material information.

(41) *Question:* An issuer commences an offering in reliance on Rule 505 in which the issuer intends to make sales only to accredited investors. The issuer delivers those investors an abbreviated disclosure document. Before the completion of the offering, the issuer changes its intentions and proposes to make sales to non-accredited investors. Would the requirement that the issuer deliver the specified information to all purchasers prior to sale if any sales are made to non-accredited investors preclude application of Rule 505 to the earlier sales to the accredited investors?

Answer: No. If the issuer delivers a complete disclosure document to the accredited investors and agrees to return their funds promptly unless they should elect to remain in the program, the issuer would not be precluded from relying on Rule 505.

B. What Required

Regulation D divides disclosure into two categories: that to be furnished by non-reporting companies and that required for reporting companies. In either case, the specified disclosure is required to the extent material to an understanding of the issuer, its business and the securities being offered.

1. Non-Reporting Issuers—Rule 502(b)(2)(i)

If the issuer is not subject to the reporting requirements of section 13 or 15(d) of the Exchange Act, it must furnish the specified information "to the extent material to an understanding of the issuer, its business and the securities being offered." For offerings up to $5,000,000, the issuer should furnish the "same kind of information" as would be contained in Part I of Form S–18, except that only the most recent year's financial statements need be certified. For offerings over $5,000,000, the issuer should furnish "the same kind of information" as would be required in Part I of an available registration statement.

(42) *Question:* When an issuer is required to deliver specific disclosure, must that disclosure be in written form?

Answer: Yes.

(43) *Question:* Form S-18 requires the issuer's audited balance sheet as of the end of its most recently completed fiscal year or within 135 days if the issuer has been in existence for a shorter time. With a limited partnership that has been formed with minimal capitalization immediately prior to a Regulation D offering, must the Regulation D disclosure document contain an audited balance sheet for the issuer?

Answer: In analyzing this or any other disclosure question under Regulation D, the issuer starts with the general rule that it is obligated to furnish the specified information "to the extent material to an understanding of the issuer, its business, and the securities being offered." Thus, in this particular case, if an audited balance sheet is not material to the investor's understanding, then the issuer may elect to present an alternative to its audited balance sheet.

(44) *Question:* Is Securities Act Industry Guide 5 applicable in a $4,000,000 Regulation D offering of interests in a real estate limited partnership?

Answer: Rule 502(b)(2)(i)(A) requires the issuer to provide the same kind of information as that required in Part I of Form S-18. Form S-18 directs the issuer's attention to the Industry Guides, noting that such guides "represent Division practices with respect to the disclosure to be provided by the affected industries in registration statements." In preparing its Regulation D offering material, therefore, an issuer of interests in a real estate limited partnership should consider Guide 5 in determining the disclosure that will be material to the investor's understanding of the issuer, its business and the securities being offered.

* * * *

2. Reporting Issuers—Rule 502(b)(2)(ii)

If the issuer is subject to the reporting requirements of section 13 or 15(d) of the Exchange Act, Regulation D sets forth two alternatives for disclosure: the issuer may deliver certain recent Exchange Act reports (the annual report, the definitive proxy statement, and, if requested, the Form 10–K) or it may provide a document containing the same information as in the Form 10–K or Form 10 under the Exchange Act or in a registration statement under the Securities Act. In either case the rule also calls for the delivery of certain supplemental information.

(50) *Question:* Rule 502(b)(2)(ii)(B) refers to the information contained "in a registration statement on Form S-1." Does this requirement envision delivery of Parts I and II of the Form S-1?

Answer: No. Rule 502(b)(2)(ii)(B) should be construed to mean Part I of Form S-1.

(51) *Question:* A reporting company with a fiscal year ending on December 31 is making a Regulation D offering in February. It does not have an annual report to shareholders, an associated definitive proxy statement, or a Form 10–K for its most recently completed fiscal year. The issuer's last registration statement was filed more than two years ago. What is the appropriate disclosure under Regulation D?

Answer: The issuer may base its disclosure on the most recently completed fiscal year for which an annual report to shareholders or Form 10–K was timely distributed or filed. The issuer should supplement the information in the report used with the information contained in any reports or documents required to be filed under sections 13(a), 14(a), 14(c) and 15(d) of the Exchange Act since the distribution or filing of that report and with a brief description of the securities being offered, the use of the proceeds from the offering, and any material changes in the issuer's affairs that are not disclosed in the documents furnished.

* * * *

III. *Operational Conditions*

A. Integration—Rule 502(a)

* * * *

(53) *Question:* An issuer conducts offering (A) under Rule 504 of Regulation D that concludes in January. Seven months later the issuer commences offering (B) under Rule 506. During that seven month period the issuer's only offers or sales of securities are under an employee benefit plan (C). Must the issuer integrate (A) and (B)?

Answer: No. Rule 502(a) specifically provides that (A) and (B) will not be integrated.

B. Calculation of the Number of Purchasers—Rule 501(e)

Rule 501(e) governs the calculation of the number of purchasers in offerings that rely either on Rule 505 or 506. Both of these rules limit the number of non-accredited investors to 35. Rule 501(e) has two parts. The first excludes certain purchasers from the calculation. The second establishes basic principles for counting of corporations, partnerships, or other entities.

(54) *Question:* One purchaser in a Rule 506 offering is an accredited investor. Another is a first cousin of that investor sharing the same principal residence. Each purchaser is making his own investment decision. How must the issuer count these purchasers for purposes of meeting the 35 purchaser limitation?

Answer: The issuer is not required to count either investor. The accredited investor may be excluded under Rule 501(e)(1)(iv), and the first cousin may then be excluded under Rule 501(e)(1)(i).

(55) *Question:* An accredited investor in a Rule 506 offering will have the securities she acquires placed in her name and that of her spouse. The spouse will not make an investment decision with respect to the acquisition. How many purchasers will be involved?

Answer: The accredited investor may be excluded from the count under Rule 501(e)(1)(iv) and the spouse may be excluded under Rule 501(e)(1)(i). The issuer may also take the position, however, that the spouse should not be deemed a purchaser at all because he did not make any investment decision, and because the placement of the securities in joint name may simply be a tax or estate planning technique.

(56) *Question:* An offering is conducted in the United States under Rule 505. At the same time certain sales are made overseas. Must the foreign investors be included in calculating the number of purchasers?

Answer: Offers and sales of securities to foreign persons made outside the United States in such a way that the securities come to rest abroad generally do not need to be registered under the Act. This basis for non-registration is separate from Regulation D and offers and sales relying on this interpretation are not required to be integrated with a coincident domestic offering. Thus, assuming the sales in this question rely on this interpretation, foreign investors would not be counted.

(57) *Question:* An investor in a Rule 506 offering is a general partnership that was not organized for the specific purpose of acquiring the securities offered. The partnership has ten partners, five of whom do not qualify as accredited investors. The partnership will make an investment of $100,000. How is the partnership counted and must the issuer make any findings as to the sophistication of the individual partners?

Answer: Rule 501(e)(2) provides that the partnership shall be counted as one purchaser. The issuer is not obligated to consider the sophistication of each individual partner.

(58) *Question:* If the partnership in Question 57 purchases $200,000 of the securities being offered and if that amount does not exceed 20 percent of the partnership's net worth, how should the partnership be counted?

Answer: Rule 501(e)(2), which provides that the partnership shall be counted as one purchaser, operates in tandem with Rule 501(e)(1). Thus, because the partnership is an accredited investor (in this case under Rule 501(a)(5)), the partnership may be excluded from the count under Rule 501(e)(2)(iv).

(59) *Question:* An investor in a Rule 506 offering is an investment partnership that is not accredited under Rule 501(a)(8). Although the partnership was organized two years earlier and has made investments in a number of offerings, not all the partners have participated in each investment. With each proposed investment by the partnership, individual partners have received a copy of the disclosure document and have made a decision whether or not to participate. How do the provisions of Regulation D apply to the partnership as an investor?

Answer: The partnership may not be treated as a single purchaser. Rule 501(e)(2) provides that if the partnership is organized for the specific purpose of acquiring the securities offered, then each beneficial owner of equity interests should be counted as a separate purchaser. Because the individual partners elect whether or not to participate in each investment, the partnership is deemed to be reorganized for the specific purpose of acquiring the securities in each investment. Thus, the issuer must look through the partnership to the partners participating in the investment. The issuer must satisfy the conditions of Rule 506 as to each partner.

C. Manner of Offering—Rule 502(c)

*   *   *   *

In analyzing what constitutes a general solicitation, the staff considered a solicitation by the general partner of a limited partnership to limited partners in other active programs sponsored by the same general partner. In determining that this did not constitute a general solicitation the Division underscored the existence and substance of the pre-existing business relationship between the general partner and those being solicited. The general partner represented that it believed each of the solicitees had such knowledge and experience in financial and business matters that he or she was capable of evaluating the merits and risks of the prospective investment.   *   *   *

In analyzing whether or not an issuer was using a general advertisement to offer or sell securities, the staff declined to express an opinion on a proposed tombstone advertisement that would announce the completion of an offering. *See* letter re *Alma Securities Corporation* dated July 2, 1982. Because the requesting letter did not describe the proposed use of the tombstone announcement and because the announcement of the completion of one offering could be an indirect solicitation for a new offering, the staff did not express a view. In a letter re *Tax Investment Information Corporation* dated January 7, 1983, the staff considered whether the publication of a circular analyzing private placement offerings, where the publisher was independent from the issuers and the offerings being analyzed, would violate Rule 502(c). Although Regulation D does not directly prohibit such a third party publication, the staff refused to agree that such a publication would be permitted under Regulation D because of its susceptibility to use by participants in an offering. Finally, in the letter re *Aspen Grove* dated November 8, 1982 the staff expressed the view that the proposed distribution of a promotional brochure to the members of the "Thoroughbred Owners and Breeders Association" and at an annual sale for horse owners and the proposed use of a magazine advertisement for an offering of interests in a limited partnership would not comply with Rule 502(c).

(60) *Question:* If a solicitation were limited to accredited investors, would it be deemed in compliance with Rule 502(c)?

Answer: The mere fact that a solicitation is directed only to accredited investors will not mean that the solicitation is in compliance with Rule 502(c). Rule 502(c) relates to the nature of the offering not the nature of the offerees.

D. Limitations on Resale—Rule 502(d)

Rule 502(d) makes it clear that Regulation D securities have limitations on transferability and requires that the issuer take certain precautions to restrict the transferability of the securities.

(61) *Question:* An investor in a Regulation D offering wishes to resell his securities within a year after the offering. The issuer has agreed to register the securities for resale. Will the proposed resale under the registration statement violate Rule 502(d)?

Answer: No. The function of Rule 502(d) is to restrict the unregistered resale of securities. Where the resale will be registered, however, such restrictions are unnecessary.

IV. *Exemptions*

A. Rule 504

Rule 504 is an exemption under section 3(b) of the Securities Act available to non-reporting and non-investment companies for offerings not in excess of $500,000.

(62) *Question:* A foreign issuer proposes to use Rule 504. The issuer is not subject to section 15(d) and its securities are exempt from registration under Rule 12g3-2. May this issuer use Rule 504?

Answer: Yes.

(63) *Question:* An issuer proposes to make an offering under Rule 504 in two states. The offering will be registered in one state and the issuer will deliver a disclosure document pursuant to the state's requirements. The offering will be made pursuant to an exemption from registration in the second state. Must the offering satisfy the limitations on the manner of offering and on resale in paragraphs (c) and (d) of Rule 502?

Answer: Yes. An offering under Rule 504 is exempted from the manner of sale and resale limitations only if it is registered in *each* state in which it is conducted and only if a disclosure document is required by state law.

(64) *Question:* The state in which the offering will take place provides for "qualification" of any offer or sale of securities. The state statute also provides that the securities commissioner may condition qualification of an offering on the delivery of a disclosure document prior to sale. Would the issuer be making its offering in a state that "provides for registration of the securities and requires the delivery of a disclosure document before sale" if its offering were qualified in this state on the condition that it deliver a disclosure document before sale to each investor?

Answer: Yes.

(65) *Question:* If an issuer is registering securities at the state level, are there any specific requirements as to resales outside of that state if the issuer is attempting to come within the provision in Rule 504 that waives the limitations on the manner of offering and on resale in Rules 502(c) and (d)?

Answer: No. The issuer, however, must intend to use Rule 504 to make bona fide sales in that state and not to evade the policy of Rule 504 by using sales in one state as a conduit for sales into another state. *See* Preliminary Note 6 to Regulation D.

B. Rule 505

Rule 505 provides an exemption under section 3(b) of the Securities Act for non-investment companies for offerings not in excess of $5,000,000.

(66) *Question:* An issuer is a broker that was censured pursuant to a Commission order. Does the censure bar the issuer from using Rule 505?

Answer: No. Rule 505 is not available to any issuer who falls within the disqualifications for the use of Regulation A. *See* Rule 505(b)(2)(iii). One such disqualification occurs when the issuer is subject to a Commission order under section 15(b) of the Exchange Act. A censure has no continuing force and thus the issuer is not subject to an order of the Commission.

C. Questions Relating to Rules 504 and 505

Both Rules 504(b)(2)(i) and 505(b)(2)(i) require that the offering not exceed a specified aggregate offering price. The allowed aggregate offering price, however, is reduced by the aggregate offering price for all securities sold within the last twelve months in reliance on section 3(b) or in violation of section 5(a) of the Securities Act.

(67) *Question:* An issuer preparing to conduct an offering of equity securities under Rule 505 raised $2,000,000 from the sale of debt instruments under Rule 505 eight months earlier. How much may the issuer raise in the proposed equity offering?

Answer: $3,000,000. A specific condition to the availability of Rule 505 for the proposed offering is that its aggregate offering price not exceed $5,000,000 less the proceeds for *all* securities sold under section 3(b) within the last 12 months.

(68) *Question:* An issuer is planning a Rule 505 offering. Ten months earlier the issuer conducted a Rule 506 offering. Must the issuer consider the previous Rule 506 offering when calculating the allowable aggregate offering price for the proposed Rule 505 offering?

Answer: No. The Commission issued Rule 506 under section 4(2), and Rule 505(b)(2)(i) requires that the aggregate offering price be reduced by previous sales under section 3(b).

(69) *Question:* Seven months before a proposed Rule 504 offering the issuer conducted a rescission offer under Rule 504. The rescission offer was for securities that were sold in violation of section 5 more than 12 months before the proposed Rule 504 offering. Must the aggregate offering price for the proposed Rule 504 offering be reduced either by the amount of the rescission offer or the earlier offering in violation of section 5?

Answer: No. The offering in violation of section 5 took place more than 12 months earlier and thus is not required to be included when satisfying the limitation in Rule 504(b)(2)(i). The staff is of the view that the rescission offer relates back to the earlier offering and therefore should not be included as an adjustment to the aggregate offering price for the proposed Rule 504 offering.

(70) *Question:* Rules 504 and 505 contain examples as to the calculation of the allowed aggregate offering price for a particular offering. Do these examples contemplate integration of the offerings described?

Answer: No. The examples have been provided to demonstrate the operation of the limitation on the aggregate offering price in the absence of any integration questions.

(71) *Question:* Note 2 to Rule 504 is not restated in Rule 505. Does the principle of the note apply to Rule 505?

Answer: Yes. Note 2 to Rule 504 sets forth a general principle to the operation of the rule on limiting the aggregate offering price which is the same for both Rules 504 and 505. It provides that if, as a result of one offering, an issuer exceeds the allowed aggregate offering price in a subsequent unintegrated offering, the exemption for the first offering will not be affected.

*   *   *   *

V. *Notice of Sale—Form D*

Rule 503 requires the issuer to file a notice of sale on Form D. The notice must be filed not later than 15 days after the first sale, every six months thereafter, and no later than 30 days after the last sale.

(87) *Question:* What is a Standard Industrial Classification ("SIC") and where is it obtained?

Answer: The SIC is a code associated with a particular economic activity. The SIC system, developed by the Bureau of the Census under the auspices of the Office of Management and Budget, is used in classification of establishments by the type of activities in which they are engaged. An issuer's SIC can be found in the Standard Industrial Classification Manual, a publication of the U.S. Government that may be obtained from the Superintendent of Documents and is generally available in public and university libraries.

(88) *Question:* Question 8 of Part A asks for the issuer's CUSIP number. What is a CUSIP number?

Answer: CUSIP[53] is the trademark for a system that identifies specific security issuers and their classes of securities. Under the CUSIP plan, a CUSIP number is permanently assigned to each class and will identify that class and no other. Generally, a CUSIP number will be assigned only to a class for which there is a secondary trading market. The operation of the CUSIP numbering system is controlled by the CUSIP Board of Trustees which awarded a contract to Standard & Poor's Corporation to function as the CUSIP Service Bureau, the operational arm of the system. Issuers relying on Regulation D that do not have a class of securities with a secondary trading market and thus do not have a CUSIP number should answer Question 8 in the negative.

INTERPRETATIONS OF "GENERAL SOLICITATION" UNDER REGULATION D

Section 502(c) limits the manner in which securities may be offered or sold pursuant to Regulation D. First, there must be a determination as to whether a communication constitutes a form of general solicitation or general advertising. Second, it must be determined whether the communication is being used by the issuer, or any person acting on its behalf, to offer to sell securities.

The Division of Corporation Finance has issued a number of interpretive letters addressing these questions. In E.F. Hutton & Company (Dec. 3, 1985), Hutton established procedures under which Regulation D offerings would be made only (1) to persons who have within the last three years invested in limited partnerships sponsored or sold by them, and (2) to persons who had satisfactorily responded to a suitability questionnaire and a new account form. A suitability questionnaire and new account form dated within 12 months of the offer which indicated that the person was presently qualified to purchase in a private placement also was required of prior customers. Offering materials were to be then sent only to a small percentage of eligible individuals.

The Division stated that the avoidance of a general solicitation depends upon the substance of prior relationships between the issuer and its agents and those persons being solicited. Although there is no requirement of a preexisting relationship, it is an important factor in showing that there is no public solicitation. On the facts presented, the Division concurred in the view that substantive relationships had been created between Hutton and the previous public and private investors, even though some offerees had not previously invested in securities offered by Hutton.

Again, in Bateman, Eichler, Hill Richards, Incorporated (Dec. 3, 1985), Bateman, Eichler (BE) set up a program in which each BE account executive would make a limited mailing to a list of not more than 50 local professionals and businessmen each month. The mailing would consist of a letter and questionnaire, neither of which would mention any particular offering.

---

53. The acronym "CUSIP" derives from the title of the American Banker's Association committee that developed the CUSIP system—Committee on Uniform Security Identification Procedures.

After a review of the responses to questionnaires, the account executive would contact those who responded with a view to obtaining additional pertinent personal and financial information. If the information elicited was positive, a respondent would be placed on a list of prospective offerees for programs for which the respondent was deemed suitable.

No person would thereafter receive an offering circular with respect to a direct participation being offered at the time of the original mailing or future programs which had been subject of an announcement at that time, and in no event until 45 days after the mailing.

Noting that the proposed solicitation would be generic in nature and that precautions would be taken to prevent the solicitation with respect to current or contemplated offerings, the Division concluded that the proposed program would not constitute an offer to sell securities. The Division nevertheless noted that the questionnaire alone would not be sufficient without a follow-up which established a substantive relationship and elicited sufficient information to permit an evaluation of the respondent's sophistication and financial circumstances.

On the other hand, in Mineral Lands Research & Marketing Corporation (Dec. 4, 1985), an issuer proposed to offer securities to 600 persons who were existing clients of an officer of the issuer, who was also an insurance broker. Although the issuer's agent in this case had a pre-existing relationship with each of the proposed offerees, that relationship would not assure that the issuer, or its agent, was informed as to financial circumstances or sophistication of the proposed offerees or that such relationship was otherwise of some substance and duration. The letter was deemed to lack sufficient facts to permit the Division to make such a factual determination.[1]

Donahue, Regulation D: A Primer for the Practitioner, 8 Del.Corp.L. 495 (1983); Warren, A Review of Regulation D: The Present Exemption Regimen for Limited Offerings Under the Securities Act of 1933, 33 Am.U.L.Rev. 355 (1984); Campbell, The Plight of Small Issuers (and Others) Under Regulation D: Those Nagging Problems That Need Attention, 74 Ky.L.J. 127 (1986); Hainsfurther, Summary of Blue Sky Exemptions Corresponding to Regulation D, 38 Sw.L.J. 989 (1984); MacEwan, Blue Sky Regulation of Reg. D Offerings, 18 Rev. of Sec. & Commodities Reg. 103 (1985); 7A J. Hicks, Exempted Transactions Under the Securities Act of 1933, ch. 8A (1986 rev.); 1 Securities Law Techniques ch. 2 (A.A. Sommer, Jr. ed. 1985). Lipson & Scharfnan, General Solicitations in Exempt Offerings, 20 Rev. of Sec. & Commodities Reg. 8 (1987); Cohn, Securities Markets for Small Issuers: The Barrier of Federal Solicitation and Advertising Prohibitions, 38 U.Fla.L.Rev. 1 (1986).

---

1. If you were planning a private offering of the type presented in the *Doran* case, supra at page 308, which of the private offering exemptions do you believe to be the most feasible, and for what reasons?

2. If you were planning a private offering of the type involved in case of *Mary S. Krech Trust*, supra at page 315, which of the private offering exemptions do you believe to be the most feasible, and for what reasons?

---

1. And see In the Matter of Kennan Corporation and Kennan Securities Corporation, Exchange Act Release No. 34–21962 (Apr. 19, 1985) where the Commission found violations of Rule 502(c) and Section 4(2) of the 1933 Act as a result of a general solicitation.

3. (a) Assume that you are asked to counsel High-Tech, Inc., a small business corporation. The organizing entrepreneurs propose to raise the initial funds from friends, relatives or business associates. Which of the private offering exemptions would you recommend?

(b) In the second stage of financing, the corporation proposes to attract capital from a number of professional venture capital investors. As a condition to providing funds, the professionals insist that the management be augmented by the corporation employing one or more executive employees who are experienced in managing aspects of a business similar to that of High Tech, Inc. In order to entice these persons to leave their present employment, it will be necessary to offer them a stake in the enterprise by way of common stock or stock options. The professional venture capital investors propose to purchase common stock and convertible debentures. Certain of the existing investors wish to make a further investment in the corporation, in order to maintain their proportionate interest in the company. The maximum amount of securities to be offered will not exceed $1.5 million. What, if anything, can be done to comply with the 1933 Act short of registration? Are any of the private offering exemptions available?

In the succeeding section, we shall explore the Section 3(b) small issues exemptions. Consider whether these exemptions provide additional flexibility in planning any of these transactions.

SECTION 2. REGULATION A OFFERINGS

Statutes and Regulations

Securities Act § 3(b).

Regulation A and Forms.

Excerpt from: Larry W. Sonsini *

REGULATION A [a]

Sections 3 and 4 of the Securities Act, as amended, exempt specific types of securities and transactions from the registration requirements of section 5 of the act. In particular, section 3(b) authorizes the SEC to adopt rules and regulations that exempt from registration securities whose total offering price does not exceed $5,000,000 if it finds that registration "is not necessary in the public interest and for the protection of investors by reason of the small amount involved or the limited character of the public offering."

Regulation A is the body of rules the SEC designed pursuant to section 3(b) to provide a general exemption for issuances of up to $1,500,000. Specifically, it exempts from registration: (i) offerings by issuers, certain estates, or affiliates up to $1,500,000, provided that the aggregate offering price of securities offered or sold on behalf of any one affiliate, other than an estate, does not exceed $100,000; and (ii) offerings by persons other than the issuer or its affiliates, up to $100,000, provided that the aggregate offering price of securities offered or sold on behalf of all such other

* LARRY W. SONSINI is a partner in the Palo Alto, California, law firm of Wilson, Sonsini, Goodrich & Rosati.

a. Copyright 1983. Reprinted with permission of the author and Standard & Poor's Corporation.

persons does not exceed $300,000. Notwithstanding the above limitations, the aggregate offering price of securities offered or sold on behalf of any estate may not exceed $500,000.[1] As with other exemptions, regulation A only provides an exemption from the registration requirements and not from the antifraud provisions of the Securities Act.[2]

Availability of Regulation A

The availability of the exemption under regulation A depends principally on the following:

Type of Securities. Although the regulation A exemption is available for most types of securities, it is not available for securities consisting of fractional undivided interests in oil or gas rights or similar interests in other mineral rights. The regulation also does not apply to securities of any investment company registered, or required to be registered, under the Investment Company Act of 1940.[3]

Issuer. Generally, the exemption is available to a corporation, an unincorporated association, or a trust that is incorporated or organized under the laws of any state or province of the U.S. or Canada and that has or proposes to have its principal business operations in the U.S. or Canada. If an individual is the issuer, the individual must be a resident of, and have or propose to have his principal business operations in any state of, or province of, the U.S. or Canada.[4]

Disqualifications. Under rule 252(c) through (e), the exemption is unavailable for certain securities if specified events have occurred involving the issuer or an underwriter, or individuals or entities having specified relationships with the issuer or an underwriter.

Rule 252(c) generally applies when there has been some judicial or administrative sanction against the issuer, its affiliates, or its predecessors. The term "affiliate" is defined in rule 251 as a person controlling, controlled by, or under common control with the issuer. An individual who controls an issuer is also an affiliate of such issuer.[5] The "control" concept is defined in rule 405 of the Securities Act. However, the provisions of rule 252(c) do not apply to an order, decree, or judgment against an affiliate of an issuer before the affiliation if the affiliated entity is not now in control of the issuer and if the affiliated entity and the issuer are not under the common control of a third party who was in control of the affiliate at the time of the decree.

The term "predecessor" is defined in rule 251 as (i) a person the major portion of whose assets has been acquired directly or indirectly by the issuer, or (ii) a person from whom the issuer acquired directly or indirectly the major portion of its assets.[6]

Rule 252(d) provides that the exemption shall not be available if any of the issuer's directors, officers, general partners, beneficial owners of 10% or more of any class of its equity securities, or promoters currently connected with it in any capacity, or any underwriter of the securities to be offered, or

---

1. Sec. Act rule 254.

2. Sec. Act rule 252(a) provides that compliance with regulation A results in an exemption from "registration."

3. Sec. Act rule 252(b).

4. Sec. Act rule 252(a).

5. Sec. Act rule 251.

6. Sec. Act rule 251.

any partner, director, or officer of any such underwriter has been convicted of certain crimes or has been subject to certain administrative sanctions.

For the purposes of rule 252(d), the terms "promoter" and "underwriter" are defined by rule 251. A "promoter" is defined as

(a) Any person who, acting alone or in conjunction with one or more persons, directly or indirectly takes the initiative in founding and organizing the business or enterprise of an issuer; (b) Any person who, in connection with the founding or organization of the business or enterprise of an issuer, directly or indirectly receives in consideration of services or property, or both services and property, 10% or more of any class of securities of the issuer or 10% or more of the proceeds from the sale of any class of securities. * * *

The term "underwriter" is defined as having the meaning given to it by section 2(11) of the Securities Act.

Rule 252(e) provides for certain disqualifications applicable only to underwriters. In addition, the exemption is not available to an issuer required to file reports with the SEC under sections 13, 14, or 15(d) of the Exchange Act unless all such reports required to have been filed in the preceding 12 months have been filed.[7]

Persons Other Than the Issuer. The exemption is usually available for secondary sales of securities. However, it is not available if the issuer (i) was incorporated or organized within one year before the date of filing and has not had a net income from operations, or (ii) was incorporated more than one year and has not had net income from operations of the character in which the issuer intends to engage for at least one of the last two fiscal years.[8]

Dollar Ceiling. At present, the absolute maximum amount of securities of any one issuer that may be offered during a 12 month period under the exemption is (i) $1,500,000 if the securities are offered or sold by the issuer, by certain estates, or by affiliates of the issuer (provided that the maximum offering price of securities offered or sold by one affiliate other than an estate does not exceed $100,000); and (ii) $100,000 if the securities are offered on behalf of any other person (up to an aggregate of $300,000, or $500,000 for estates).[9]

However, these ceilings may be lowered in the following circumstances:

1. The $1,500,000 ceiling is lowered by the value of all "securities of the issuer" (i) offered or sold pursuant to the regulation, or (ii) offered or sold within one year before the commencement of the proposed offering pursuant to any other exemption under section 3(b) of the Securities Act, or (iii) offered or sold within one year before the commencement of the proposed offering in violation of section 5(a) of the Securities Act.[10] The term "securities of the issuer" includes securities issued by (i) any of the issuer's affiliates that became affiliated within two years before the filing under consideration.[11]

2. The exemption is available to the extent of offerings in the amount of $1,500,000 annually, whether or not the offerings are continuous and are

7. Sec. Act rule 252(f).

8. Sec. Act rules 253(a)(1) and (2) and 253(d).

9. Sec. Act rule 254(a)(1).

10. Sec. Act rule 254(a)(1).

11. Sec. Act rule 254(a)(3)(i).

parts of a single integrated financing or offering. For example, offerings under employee stock option or employee stock purchase plans may be made continuously so long as the amounts do not exceed the ceiling computation per year. However, if any unsold portions of former regulation A offerings are offered as part of a new proposed regulation A offering, the amount of the unsold securities must be deducted from the ceiling available for the proposed offering. This is true even if the unsold portion was a part of an offering that had commenced more than a year before the new proposed offering. Nevertheless, since the earlier offering antedated the proposed offering by more than a year, the securities actually sold under the prior offering, no matter when sold, need not be taken into account in computing the ceiling.

3. The ceilings must be reduced by the amount of all of the following securities sold in violation of section 5(a) of the Securities Act within one year prior to the commencement of the proposed offering: securities of the issuer, of any predecessor organized within the preceding two years, and of any affiliate that became affiliated within the preceding two years. Thus, it is incumbent on the issuer to review the securities transactions of predecessors and affiliates during the one-year period. In this regard, it is important to analyze whether or not any offerings made within the one-year period are to be "integrated" with the proposed offering under the regulation. If the previous transactions are integrated, this may retroactively destroy the exemption relied on for the previous offerings, resulting in a violation of section 5 of the Securities Act. As a result, the ceiling available under regulation A would have to be accordingly reduced. The SEC has set forth the following criteria for determining whether two or more offerings of securities should be integrated: (i) Are the offerings part of a single plan of financing? (ii) Do they involve issuance of the same class of securities? (iii) Are they made at or about the same time? (iv) Is the same kind of consideration to be received? (v) Are the offerings made for the same general purpose? [12]

4. With respect to the valuation of the securities to be included in the computation, securities that have a determinable market value shall be computed on the basis of such value, or the public offering price, whichever is higher. However, the aggregate gross proceeds actually received from the public for the securities cannot exceed the established ceilings.[13]

Offerings by Unseasoned Companies. There are special provisions that apply to an offering of securities if the issuer (1) was incorporated or organized within one year before the date of filing and has not had a net income from operations; or (2) was incorporated or organized more than one year before such date and has not had net income from operations, of the kind in which the issuer intends to engage, for at least one of the last two fiscal years.[14]

If an issuer falls within one of the foregoing categories, the principal effect on availability of the exemption is in computing the amount of securities that may be offered. Unless certain escrow conditions are met, the following securities must be included in the computation of the ceiling in addition to the securities specified in rule 254: (i) all securities issued before the filing, or proposed to be issued, for a consideration consisting in

---

12. Sec. Act Rel. No. 4434 (Dec.1961).   14. Sec. Act rule 253(a).

13. Sec. Act rule 254(b).

whole or in part of assets or services and held by the person to whom issued; and (ii) all securities issued to and held by or proposed to be issued, pursuant to options or otherwise, to any director, officer, or promoter of the issuer, or to any underwriter, dealer, or security salesman.[15] The computation will encompass all of the securities in these categories, regardless of how long they have been held before the offering by the persons mentioned. However, the securities issued or proposed to be issued under the above circumstances may be excluded from the computation, if provision is made by escrow or other arrangements to ensure that (a) none of the securities will be reoffered to the public within one year after the commencement of the offering under the regulation, and (b) any reoffering of such securities will be in accordance with the applicable provisions of the Securities Act.[16] The SEC provides form 7–A for such purposes.

Offerings of securities of companies that fall within the foregoing definition of promotional or unseasoned issuers may not be available to a person other than the issuer.[17]

General Procedure

Documents to Be Filed. The regulation A process is initiated by the filing of a single document, designated the "Offering Statement," on form I–A.[18] The Offering Statement, consisting of three parts, is the basic form to be used for every offering made under the exemption.

1. Part I of the Offering Statement is the "Notification." The purpose of the notification is to present information necessary to determine the availability of the exemption. The notification consists of eight items. Every notification must contain the numbers and captions of all items, as follows:

Item 1. *Significant Parties.* Under this item, information is sought as to the names and addresses of directors, officers, general partners, 10% stockholders, promoters, predecessors, affiliates, legal counsel, managing underwriters, the underwriter's officers, the underwriter's general partners, and counsel to the underwriter.

Item 2. *Application of Rule 252(c)–(e).* This item requires disclosure as to whether any of the persons or entities identified under item 1 is subject to disqualification under rule 252(c)–(e).

Item 3. *Application of Rule 253(a) and (b).* This item requires information regarding the securities of any "unseasoned" issuer as described in rule 253.

Item 4. *Jurisdictions in Which Securities Are to Be Offered.* This item calls for a list of the states, provinces, and other jurisdictions in which the securities are proposed to be offered through underwriters, dealers, salesmen, or otherwise. One of the reasons for this listing is to assist the SEC in policing the offering.

Item 5. *Unregistered Securities Issued or Sold Within One Year.* Information is required as to unregistered securities issued within one year before filing of the notification by the issuer or any of its predecessors or affiliates. The information required includes the name of the issuer, the

---

15. Sec. Act rule 253(c)(1) and (2).

16. Sec. Act rule 253(c)(2).

17. Sec. Act rule 253(d).

18. SEC form I–A, general instruction A; Sec. Act rule 255(a).

title and amount of securities issued, the aggregate offering price or other consideration, and the names of the persons to whom the securities were issued. This same kind of information must be supplied for any unregistered securities of predecessors or affiliates of the issuer. In addition, the item requires an indication of the section of the Securities Act or SEC rule or regulation under which exemption from registration was claimed with respect to such securities, and a brief statement of the facts relied on. It is essential that facts rather than conclusions be supplied, since the SEC must determine whether or not there is a basis for the exemption.

Item 6. *Other Present or Proposed Offerings.* A statement must be made as to whether or not the issuer or any of its affiliates is currently offering or contemplates offering any securities in the United States or Canada in addition to those covered by the offering statement. If so, a full description of the present or proposed offering must be given.

Item 7. *Marketing Arrangements.* This item requires information as to any arrangement to limit or restrict the sale of other securities of the same class as those being offered or otherwise to stabilize the market.

Item 8. *Relationship with Issuer or Experts Named in Offering Statement.* This item requires certain information regarding the issuer's relationship with its experts.

2. Part II of the Offering Statement consists of the Offering Circular, which must be distributed to investors. The general instructions to part II indicate the items to which a particular issuer must respond. The disclosure requirements of the Offering Circular are derived from schedule I under the Securities Act, the basic schedule for registration statement disclosure. The disclosures of part II emphasize information on the business of the issuer, the quality of its management, potential conflicts of interest, and the use of proceeds.[19] Many of the disclosures required by the Offering Circular are more extensive than those required by schedule I, reflecting the evolution of disclosure standards. However, many of the items call for significantly less disclosure than that required by regulation S–K or a registration statement on form S–18.

The Offering Circular requires the following disclosures:

Item 1. *Cover Page.* This item specifies the disclosures required on the cover page of the circular, including name and address of issuer, date of the Offering Circular, description and amount of securities offered, the statement required by rule 259, the tables required by item 2 (see below), the name of the underwriter, and, if applicable, identification of material risk.

Item 2. *Distribution Spread.* This item calls for information regarding the tabular disclosure of the securities to be offered, price, underwriting discounts, and proceeds.

Item 3. *Summary Information, Risk Factors, and Dilution.* Where it is helpful to investors, this item requires a carefully organized series of concise paragraphs summarizing the principal factors that make the offering speculative or high risk. In addition, information with respect to "dilution" is required.

Item 4. *Plan of Distribution.* This item requires disclosure as to the plan of distribution of the securities, including discounts and commissions.

19. Sec. Act Rel. No. 6275 (Dec.1980).

Item 5. *Use of Proceeds to Issuer.* This item requires the disclosure of the principal purposes for which the net proceeds from the offering are intended to be used and the approximate amount intended for each purpose.

Item 6. *Description of Business.* This item requires a narrative description of the business, including:

(1) A description of the business done and intended to be done, including a discussion of: (a) the principal products produced and services rendered and the principal markets and method of distribution; (b) the status of a new product or service that would require the investment of a material amount of assets, if the issuer has made information about the new product or service public; (c) the estimated amount spent during each of the last two fiscal years on company-sponsored research and development, and the amounts spent on material, customer-sponsored research, and development; (d) the number of persons employed, indicating the number employed full-time; (e) the material effects of compliance with federal, state, and local environmental laws on the company.

(2) The issuer should also describe those distinctive characteristics of its operation or industry that may have a material impact on its future financial performance. Examples include dependence on one or a few major customers or suppliers, governmental regulations, material terms or expiration of labor contracts or patents, licenses, etc.

(3) As to issuers that have not received revenue from operations during each of the three fiscal years immediately before the filing of the offering statement, additional disclosure must be made relating to: (a) the issuer's plan of operation, if formulated, for the 12 months following the commencement of the offering; (b) any engineering, management, or similar reports prepared for external use by the issuer or any underwriter.

Item 7. *Description of Property.* This item requires a brief statement of the location and general character of the principal plants and other important physical properties of the issuer and its subsidiaries.

Item 8. *Directors, Executive Officers, and Significant Employees.* This item requires (a) the listing of the names, ages, terms of office, and arrangements among directors, executive officers, and significant employees; (b) the disclosure of any family relationship among directors, executive officers, and significant employees; (c) a brief account of the business experience during the past five years of each director, executive officer, and significant employee; and (d) the disclosure of involvement in legal proceedings of any director or executive officer.

Item 9. *Remuneration of Directors and Officers.* This item requires disclosure, in the tabular form indicated, of the annual remuneration of each of the three highest paid persons who are officers or directors of the issuer, and all officers and directors as a group during the issuer's last fiscal year. Information is also required as to all remuneration to be made in the future to such persons.

Item 10. *Security Ownership of Management and Certain Security Holders.* This item requires the disclosure in tabular form of information as to voting securities held of record by (i) each of the three highest paid persons who are officers and directors, (ii) all officers and directors as a group, and (iii) each 10% shareholder. Information is also required on nonvoting securities and the principal holders thereof, as well as on options, warrants, or rights to purchase securities from the issuer held by each of the individuals and groups above.

Item 11. *Interest of Management and Others in Certain Transactions.* This item requires a brief description of any transactions during the previous two years or currently proposed to which the issuer or any of its subsidiaries was or is to be a party, in which any director, officer, principal security holder, promoter, or relative or spouse of any of the foregoing persons has a direct or indirect material interest.

Item 12. *Securities Being Offered.* This item requires a description of the securities being offered.

Item 13. *Financial Statements.* This item sets forth the financial statements required in the offering statement. All financial statements must be prepared in accordance with generally accepted accounting principles (GAAP) in the U.S. or, in the case of a Canadian company, be reconciled with such principles.

If the issuer has filed or is required to file with the SEC certified financial statements, under sections 13 or 15(d) of the Exchange Act (a "reporting company"), then those for the latest fiscal year shall be certified by an independent public accountant in accordance with regulation S–X. Certified financial statements are not required for a non-reporting company. In any event, the statements filed for any period preceding the latest fiscal year need not be certified. If certified financial statements are filed by a non-reporting company, the statements need not comply with the requirements of regulation S–X except as to the qualifications and reports of the independent accountant.

Subject to the foregoing, the required financial statements include:

(a) A balance sheet dated within 90 days of the filing date; for filings made more than 90 days after the end of the issuer's most recent fiscal year, the filing shall include a balance sheet as of the end of the most recent fiscal year;

(b) Statements of income, changes in financial condition, and stockholders' equity for each of the two fiscal years preceding the date of the most recent balance sheet being filed and for any interim period between the end of the more recent of such fiscal years and the date of the most recent balance sheet being filed, or for the period of the issuer's existence if less than the period specified above. If the issuer files an unaudited income statement for an interim period, it must state that, in the opinion of management, all adjustments necessary for a fair statement of the results for the interim period have been included.

(c) Special financial statements are required with respect to the past succession of certain businesses or the proposed future succession of other businesses.

3. Part III of the offering statement requires a listing of exhibits. The regulation requires that an index to the exhibits be filed, immediately following the cover page of part III. Each exhibit must be listed in an exhibit index according to the number assigned to it. Where exhibits are incorporated by reference, reference shall be made in the index to exhibits.

The kinds of exhibits required to be filed include: the underwriting agreement; charter and bylaws; instruments defining the rights of security holders; voting and trust agreements; material contracts; material foreign patents; plans of acquisition, reorganization, arrangement, liquidation or succession; a statement concerning issuer's financing; escrow agreements; and certain consents.

Where to Make Filing. Except when the issuer has its principal business operations in Canada, the offering statement must be filed with the SEC office for the region in which the principal operations are or will be conducted. If the issuer's principal operations are in Canada, the offering statement must be filed with the regional office nearest the place of operations, unless the offering is to be made through a principal underwriter in the U.S., in which case the statement must be filed with the regional office nearest the underwriter's principal office.[20]

The Filing. The regulation provides that five copies of the offering statement be filed.[21] The manually signed original of all offering statements, reports, or other documents filed shall be numbered sequentially (in addition to any internal numbering) in handwritten, typed, printed, or other legible form from the cover page through the last page of any exhibit and the total number of pages shall be set forth on the first page of the document.[22] Each offering statement shall contain an exhibit index immediately preceding the exhibits.[23] The offering statement must be signed by the issuer and by each person other than the issuer for whose account any of the securities are to be offered. At the time of filing, a $100 fee must be paid to the SEC regional office.[24]

Offering Procedures

The Offering. Regulation A requires that the offering statement be filed at least 10 business days before the initial offering of any securities under the regulation.[25] A new 10–day waiting period begins to run each time an amendment is filed.[26]

Because the burden of proof for compliance with regulation A rests on the issuer, the lapse of the 10 business days following the filing or amendment does not necessarily create such compliance if it does not otherwise exist. Any sale occurring after the waiting period expires without benefit of SEC review puts the offering at risk of noncompliance with the exemption and could result in a violation of section 5 of the Securities Act.

The regulation provides that no *written offer* shall be made unless an offering circular containing the information specified in part II of the offering statement is concurrently given or has previously been given to the offeree.[27] In addition, no securities shall be *sold* unless the offering circular is furnished to the person to whom the securities are to be sold at least 48 hours before the mailing of the confirmation of sale. However, if the issuer is required to file reports pursuant to sections 13(a) or 15(d) of the Exchange Act, the offering circular may be furnished with or before the confirmation of sale.[28]

<table>
<tr><td>20.</td><td>Sec. Act rule 255(c).</td><td>25.</td><td>Sec. Act rule 255(a).</td></tr>
<tr><td>21.</td><td>Sec. Act rule 255(a).</td><td>26.</td><td>Sec. Act rule 255(d).</td></tr>
<tr><td>22.</td><td>Sec. Act rule 255(f).</td><td>27.</td><td>Sec. Act rule 256(a)(1).</td></tr>
<tr><td>23.</td><td>Sec. Act rule 255(g).</td><td></td><td></td></tr>
<tr><td>24.</td><td>Sec. Act rule 255(b).</td><td>28.</td><td>Sec. Act rule 256(a)(2).</td></tr>
</table>

Preliminary Offering Circular. An offering circular may be distributed before the expiration of the 10–day waiting period, accompanied or followed by offers to sell the securities, provided that the offering circular relates to a proposed public offering of securities to be sold by or through one or more underwriters who are broker-dealers registered under section 15 of the Exchange Act, each of whom has furnished a signed consent in the form prescribed by the exemption. Any offering circular distributed before the 10–day waiting period expires is referred to as a "preliminary offering circular." [29]

The preliminary offering circular must contain substantially the information required in the offering circular, except for information with respect to offering price, underwriting discounts, amount of proceeds, and other matters dependent on the offering price. For nonreporting issuers, the disclosure on the cover page should include a bona fide estimate of the range of the maximum offering price and maximum number of shares or units to be offered.[30] In addition, the outside front cover page of the preliminary offering circular shall bear the required statement set forth in rule 256(h)(2).

Rule 256 further provides that an offering circular containing all the information specified in part II of the offering statement and not designated as a preliminary offering circular must be furnished with or before delivery of the confirmation of sale to any person who has been furnished with a preliminary offering circular pursuant to rule 256(h).[31]

Tombstone Advertisement. At or after the commencement of the offering, a written advertisement or other written communication, or any radio or television broadcast that states from whom an offering circular may be obtained, and in addition contains no more than certain permitted information, may be published, distributed, or broadcast to any person before sending or giving such person a copy of the circular.[32] The only information permitted in this advertisement is the following: the name of the issuer of the securities, the title of the security, the amount being offered, the per unit offering price to the public, the identity or the general type of business of the issuer, and a brief statement as to the general character and location of its property.[33]

Sales Material. Four copies of (i) every advertisement or other communication proposed to be published in any periodical or paper, (ii) the script of every radio or TV broadcast, and (iii) every written communication proposed to be given to more than 10 persons for use in connection with the offering shall be filed with the SEC at least five days before use.[34]

Amendments. An offering circular may not be used that is false or misleading.[35] Accordingly, if the original offering circular is revised or amended, the revised or amended circular shall be filed as an amendment to the offering statement with the regional office at least 10 days before its use.[36]

Periodic Revision. If the offering is not completed within nine months from the date of the offering circular, a revised offering circular shall be

---

29. Sec. Act rule 256(h) and 256(h)(3).

30. Sec. Act rule 256(h)(1).

31. Sec. Act rule 256(h)(4).

32. Sec. Act rule 256(c).

33. Sec. Act rule 256(c)(1)–(4).

34. Sec. Act rule 258.

35. Sec. Act rule 256(d).

36. Sec. Act rule 256(e).

prepared, filed, and used in accordance with the regulation, except that in the case of offerings under stock purchase, stock option, or other employee plans, if the offering is not completed within 12 months from the date of the offering circular, a revised offering circular shall be prepared and filed.[37]

Posteffective Procedures

Reports of Sales. Within 30 days after the end of each six-month period following the date of the original offering circular, there shall be filed with the regional office four copies of a report on form 2–A.[38] A final report on form 2–A must be made on completion or termination of the offering. The form 2–A report provides the SEC with a means of policing the exemption by enabling it to determine whether variances from the representations in the offering statement exist.

Notice of Delayed Offerings. Following notice by the regional office that there are no further comments as regards the offering statement, the offering should commence. If it does not begin within three business days after the issuer has received notice that the SEC has no further comments, or if the offering or sale of securities is suspended by the issuer or any underwriter within 15 days after the issuer has received such notice, a notice of the delay or suspension, stating the reasons therefor, must be filed by the issuer or underwriter with the regional office unless such information is set forth in the offering statement. The notice must be by telegraph or airmail; if by telegraph, it should be confirmed in writing by the filing of a signed copy of the notice.[39]

Abandonment. When an offering statement has been on file with the SEC for nine months from its filing date and the offering has not commenced, the SEC may, in its discretion, invoke a procedure with respect to abandonment of the offering.[40]

Failure of Compliance

Offers and sales of securities made on the claim of exemption under regulation A are in violation of section 5 of the Securities Act if compliance with the exemption is not established. Noncompliance with regulation A serves as grounds for suspension of the exemption by the SEC. Rule 261 sets forth the basis for any such order of suspension.

Practical Aspects of Regulation A

The most practical use of regulation A is for the offer and sale of securities by nonreporting ("privately held") issuers. Such offerings usually occur under employee stock option and purchase plans. These plans typically provide for a rather broad distribution of securities among the employee group. Because the plans usually involve a continuing offering, i.e., the continuous grant of stock options or the sale of shares under stock purchase plans, sooner or later the issuer faces a greater difficulty in perfecting an exemption under the Securities Act for the transactions. As the employee group broadens and deepens within the organization to middle and lower management personnel, the issuer can no longer rely on many of the conditions that must be satisfied under the private placement

---

37. Sec. Act rule 256(d).

38. Sec. Act rule 260.

39. Sec. Act rule 263.

40. Sec. Act rule 264.

exemptions. Similarly, because many employees will reside in jurisdictions other than those where the issuer is incorporated and doing business, the intrastate offering exemption under section 3(a)(11) and rule 147 of the Securities Act will be unavailable. Also, privately held issuers will often find it inappropriate to file a registration statement under the Securities Act to cover its transactions under employee stock benefit plans. The cost of registration may be high, and the issuer may not be able to satisfy certain disclosure requirements, such as those regarding financial statements. Therefore, the exemption offered by regulation A may prove most beneficial in these employee stock benefit plans. The burden of disclosure is less than under the standard registration statement forms, particularly with respect to certified financial statements (see GENERAL PROCEDURE, part 2, item 13, above). The cost of perfecting the exemption under the regulation will usually be less than for the preparation, filing, and policing of a registration statement. In addition, the scope of the required disclosure under the offering circular may be well suited for an offering of securities to an employee group who, by definition, are familiar with the business of the issuer.

It should be noted, however, that there is no exemption from compliance with the antifraud provisions of the Securities Acts. Accordingly, notwithstanding the required disclosure under the regulation, the issuer must give consideration to the disclosure of all material information, whether or not specifically covered by an item of the notification. Therefore an issuer should refer to the disclosure items required under a registration statement to determine additional areas of materiality.

The use of regulation A for public offerings of securities other than pursuant to employee stock programs is becoming more limited. Although the amendments to the regulation that now allow the use of a preliminary offering circular have made the regulation more appropriate for a public offering, there is still concern, particularly among many underwriters, that the advantages of the limited disclosure requirements of the regulation may not be suited to a public offering of broad distribution.

The burden of establishing exemption from the registration requirements of the Securities Act rests solely on the issuer or person claiming the exemption. As a result, with respect to regulation A, the issuer must be prepared to establish that the offering comes within the regulation and that all the conditions are satisfied.

The civil liability provisions of section 11 of the Securities Act do not apply to use of the regulation, because section 11 only applies to a registration statement filed under the Securities Act. However, the provisions of section 12 of the Securities Act apply to an offering and sale of securities under regulation A.

IN THE MATTER OF SHEARSON, HAMMILL & CO.

Securities and Exchange Commission.
42 S.E.C. 811 (1965).

[The above case is printed at page 629. Read that portion of the case through the material contained in the subheading "Violations of Registration Requirements."]

PROBLEM ON EXEMPTIONS FROM SECTION 5 OF THE
SECURITIES ACT OF 1933

A, B, C and D (collectively the "Founders") organize a California corporation, Newco, Inc. ("Newco") on January 15, 1986, to engage in the production and manufacture of integrated circuits. All of the Founders reside in California.

The following securities transactions occur:

Transaction (1). On January 20, 1986, each Founder purchased shares of Newco Common Stock, at a price of $.10 per share, as follows: A 600,000 shares, B 400,000 shares, C 300,000 shares, and D 200,000 shares. Each pays for the shares with a full recourse promissory note for the amount of the purchase price. Each note is due on January 20, 1989 and is secured only by the shares purchased in the transaction.

Transaction (2). In order to obtain the funds or "seed" capital to finance the development of a business plan and to hire certain key employees, the Founders decide to raise $400,000 among "friends and acquaintances". Accordingly, on March 1, 1986 Newco issues 400,000 shares of Series A Preferred Stock, at a price of $1.00 per share. The Preferred Stock is convertible into Common Stock on a one-for-one basis, subject to antidilution protection. There are a total of 20 purchasers of the Series A Preferred. Each purchaser received a brief summary of Newco's proposed business. All of the purchasers resided in California, except one resided in Nevada and another in New York. Newco and the Founders did not use any agent in the offering and they advised, "We certainly didn't talk to more than 30 individuals, and all of the persons we talked to were at least known to us, either as a friend or as a business associate."

Transaction (3). In order to attract key employees, Newco embarked upon a stock purchase program whereby it reserved 200,000 shares of Common Stock to sell to new hires, at a price of $.20 per share. During the period of March 1, 1986 through May 30, 1986, all of these shares were sold to 20 key employees, all of whom resided in California. The shares were purchased pursuant to a Stock Restriction Agreement, the terms of which gave Newco the right to repurchase the shares, at $.20 per share, in the event of an employee's termination of employment, subject to a vesting of the shares free from this repurchase right based upon continued employment over a period of 48 months. The share certificates were held in escrow at Newco. All of the shares were purchased for cash.

Transaction (4). In June 1986, the business plan was completed and the Founders decided to raise the working capital necessary to fund business operations. To assist them in raising part of the funds, Newco retained the services of New Offerings, Inc., an investment banking firm located in Chicago. Commencing during August 1, 1986, Newco, acting through the Founders and New Offerings, commenced an offering of 2,000,000 shares of Series B Preferred Stock, at a price of $1.50 per share, for a total of $3,000,000. The Series B Preferred is convertible into Common Stock on a one-for-one basis and provides for antidilution protection. The following transactions took place with the financing closing on September 15, 1986:

1. Sales of the Series B Preferred were made to a total of 15 investors: (i) A and B, who are officers and directors of Newco, each purchased $40,000 of the shares, and B's father-in-law, who resided in New York, purchased $20,000 of the shares; (ii) one of the investors was Venture Fund Associates, which purchased $1,000,000 of the shares and is a well recognized venture capital

fund, the general partners of whom have an aggregate net worth in excess of $1,000,000; (iii) five of the investors were merchant banks located in the United Kingdom, who purchased an aggregate of $1,000,000; and (iv) the balance of the investors were wealthy individuals who were clients, from time to time, of New Offerings, Inc. Of these clients of New Offerings, Inc., two (one of whom had a net worth of $500,000 and the other a net worth of $800,000) purchased $150,000 of the shares each, and the rest (who each had a net worth in excess of $1,000,000) purchased in blocks ranging from $50,000 to $100,000 each. Each purchaser received a copy of the Business Plan.

For its role in the foregoing financing, New Offerings, Inc. received a fee of $50,000 based on the dollars raised from its clients.

Transaction (5). As a condition to the closing of the Series B financing, each holder of Series A Preferred Stock was required to convert their Preferred into Common Stock, according to the terms of the instrument. Although each Series A holder was contacted by Newco through a written communication soliciting their conversion, certain of the Series A holders were also contacted, at the request of Newco, by New Offerings, Inc. to explain to them the requirement of conversion for the financing.

Transaction (6). On December 15, 1986, Newco adopted an employee incentive stock option plan (the "Option Plan") under which it reserved 500,000 shares of Common Stock for options to be granted to employees. The options would have a term of five years and would be exercisable to the extent of 20% of the shares per year, based upon continued employment. Options were to be granted on a monthly basis as new employees were hired, and to certain recent hires. Newco was hiring approximately five new employees a month, and it expected that each of these new hires over the next several months would be granted a stock option under the Option Plan. Some of the optionees were sales persons who maintained their places of residence in cities outside of the State of California. The option prices were at $.50 per share, but Newco expected that this price would increase as the fair market value of the Common Stock was reassessed based upon progress of the company.

Transaction (7). In March 1987, C terminated his employment with Newco. C, who was Vice President of Sales, would remain as a member of the Board of Directors. C proposed to sell up to ⅓ of his holdings in Newco, and contacted New Offerings, Inc. to assist him in placing the shares. They sold his shares to six private investors, who were clients of New Offerings. New Offerings indicated that it contacted approximately 10 persons, all of whom it believed to be "sophisticated" and "accredited investors" within the meaning of Regulation D under the Securities Act of 1933. All of the purchasers represented that the shares were being acquired for their own account for investment and not with a view towards distribution. All of the shares were sold by May 15, 1987.

Transaction (8). On June 30, 1987, the Board of Directors of Newco approved the acquisition of Printed Boards, Inc. ("PBI"), a California corporation engaged in the business of assembling printed circuit boards. PBI was a privately held corporation with 2,000,000 outstanding shares held by 20 shareholders, all of whom were employees who resided in Silicon Valley, California. An Agreement of Merger was entered into between Newco and PBI under which PBI would be merged with Newco, pursuant to which each outstanding share of PBI Common Stock was converted into shares of Newco Common Stock on the basis of one share of Newco for each five shares of PBI (a total of 400,000 Newco shares). Of the outstanding PBI shares, 35% was held by E. All of the outstanding shares of PBI constitute "restricted" securities within the meaning of Rule 144.

With respect to each of the above transactions, explain what exemption from Section 5 you would recommend as most appropriate with respect to the securities offered and sold and the basis for such exemption. Where appropriate, discuss what procedures you would recommend to perfect the applicable exemption. In selecting the most appropriate exemption, keep in mind all transactions and their effect upon your decision and analysis.

Transaction (8) is to be answered in connection with the material in Chapter 8, Sections 3 and 4.

PROBLEMS UNDER REGULATION A

In the following problems, assume that at the time of the transaction the present version of Regulation A is in effect.

1. Assume three years after the SEC issues a stop order against Marjen corporation, the company desires to make a public offering of its common shares using Regulation A. Is the regulation available? Is Marjen corporation subject to a permanent disability from using the regulation?

2. Assume that in the Ralston Purina case, supra at page 303, after the decision of the Supreme Court, Ralston decides to make a Regulation A offering of a different class of stock to some of its employees in the lower echelons. Would Regulation A be available?

3. Assume that six years after the decision in the Ralston Purina case, the company wants to use Regulation A to sell securities of a market value of $1,500,000 by the use of Regulation A. Would the exemption be available?

4. Aztec Mining Co. is a Delaware corporation which has been organized to exploit a mine in Mexico. May it raise funds in the United States by the use of Regulation A?

5. Assume that A Corporation files a registration statement which has become the subject of a refusal order. Three years later, the controlling shareholders of A Corporation form the Beaucoup Oil Co. May the Beaucoup Oil Co. resort to Regulation A?

6. The Marjen corporation has issued 500,000 of its 1,000,000 authorized common shares. Of these shares, Charles Marjen, the President owns 250,001 shares and the remaining shares are owned by some 100 other shareholders residing in a number of states. The Marjen corporation proposes to issue an additional 500,000 shares and offer them pro rata to its shareholders at $5 a share. (a) May this offering be made under the terms of § 3(b) and Regulation A? (b) If Regulation A authorizes such an offering, may any of the shareholders purchasing the stock nevertheless maintain an action for rescission under § 12(1) of the Securities Act of 1933? What is the relevance of the last sentence of § 19(a)?

7. James Weatherby Morrison, a brilliant aeronautical engineer, was the founder of Morrison Aircraft Corp. some years ago. Until five years ago, Morrison owned all of the outstanding stock of the company. He has three sons who are active in the business and at that time Morrison gave each 25% of the outstanding stock, retaining the rest. The sons have gradually taken over the active management of the business leaving James more time for some of his other interests. Being well along in years, James has now decided to sell some of his stock and make a gift of the proceeds to his alma mater, Pilgrim College, a small New England college. The stock has a value of about $500,000. At the same time Morrison Aircraft Corp. desires to raise funds by the sale of enough

stock to secure $1,500,000 of working capital. James in his personal capacity and as President of the Corporation consults you and asks your advice concerning these two contemplated transactions. How would you advise him?

———

D. O'Boyle, 1 Securities Law Techniques, ch. 3 (A.A. Sommer, Jr., ed. 1985); 3A H. Bloomenthal, Securities and Federal Corporate Law, c. 5 (1981 rev.); Weiss, Regulation A Under the Securities Act of 1933—Highways and Byways, 8 N.Y. Law Forum 3 (1962); Barber, Alternative for Small Business Raising Capital Under Securities Act of 1933, 8 Pepp.L.Rev. 899 (1981); Brooks, Small Business Financing Alternatives Under the Securities Act of 1933, 13 U.C.Davis L.Rev. 543 (1980); Green & Brecher, When Making a Small Public Offering Under Regulation A (with forms), (pts. 1–2), 26 Prac.Law. 25, 41 (1980).

Chapter 7

INTRASTATE OFFERINGS: SECTION 3(a)(11) AND RULE 147

SECTION 1. THE SECTION 3(a)(11) EXEMPTION

Statutes

Securities Act § 3(a)(11). Rule 147.

SECURITIES ACT RELEASE NO. 4434
Securities and Exchange Commission.
December 6, 1961.

SECTION 3(a)(11) EXEMPTION FOR LOCAL OFFERINGS

The meaning and application of the exemption from registration provided by Section 3(a)(11) * * * have been the subject of court opinions, releases of the Securities and Exchange Commission * * * and opinions and interpretations expressed by the staff of the Commission in response to specific inquiries. This release is published to provide in convenient and up-to-date form a restatement of the principles underlying Section 3(a)(11) as so expressed over the years and to facilitate an understanding of the meaning and application of the exemption.[1]

General Nature of Exemption

Section 3(a)(11), as amended in 1954, exempts from the registration and prospectus requirements of the Act:

"Any security which is a part of an issue offered and sold only to persons resident within a single State or Territory, where the issuer of such security is a person resident and doing business within, or, if a corporation, incorporated by and doing business within, such State or Territory."

The legislative history of the Securities Act clearly shows that this exemption was designed to apply only to local financing that may practicably be consummated in its entirety within the State or Territory in which the issuer is both incorporated and doing business. As appears from the legislative history, by amendment to the Act in 1934, this exemption was removed from Section 5(c) and inserted in Section 3, relating to "Exempted Securities", in order to relieve dealers of an unintended restriction on

---

1. Since publication of the 1937 release, the Investment Company Act of 1940 was enacted, and under Section 24(d) thereof, the Section 3(a)(11) exemption for an intra- state offering is not available for an investment company registered or required to be registered under the Investment Company Act.

trading activity. This amendment was not intended to detract from its essential character as a transaction exemption.[3]

"Issue" Concept

A basic condition of the exemption is that the *entire issue* of securities be offered and sold exclusively to residents of the state in question. Consequently, an offer to a non-resident which is considered a part of the intrastate issue will render the exemption unavailable to the entire offering.

Whether an offering is "a part of an issue", that is, whether it is an integrated part of an offering previously made or proposed to be made, is a question of fact and depends essentially upon whether the offerings are a related part of a plan or program. * * * Thus, the exemption should not be relied upon in combination with another exemption for the different parts of a single issue where a part is offered or sold to non-residents.

The determination of what constitutes an "issue" is not governed by state law. Shaw v. U. S., 131 F.2d 476, 480 (C.A.9, 1942). Any one or more of the following factors may be determinative of the question of integration: (1) are the offerings part of a single plan of financing; (2) do the offerings involve issuance of the same class of security; (3) are the offerings made at or about the same time; (4) is the same type of consideration to be received, and (5) are the offerings made for the same general purpose.

Moreover, since the exemption is designed to cover only those security distributions, which, as a whole, are essentially local in character, it is clear that the phrase "sold only to persons resident" as used in Section 3(a)(11) cannot refer merely to the initial sales by the issuing corporation to its underwriters, or even the subsequent resales by the underwriters to distributing dealers. To give effect to the fundamental purpose of the exemption, it is necessary that the entire issue of securities shall be offered and sold to, and come to rest only in the hands of residents within the state. If any part of the issue is offered or sold to a non-resident, the exemption is unavailable not only for the securities so sold, but for all securities forming a part of the issue, including those sold to residents. Securities Act Release No. 201 (1934); Brooklyn Manhattan Transit Corporation; 1 S.E.C. 147 (1935); S.E.C. v. Hillsborough Investment Corp., 173 F.Supp. 86 (D.N.H.1958); Hillsborough Investment Corp. v. S.E.C., 276 F.2d 665 (C.A.1, 1960); S.E.C. v. Los Angeles Trust Deed & Mortgage Exchange, et al., 186 F.Supp. 830, 871 (S.D.Cal., 1960), aff'd 285 F.2d 162 (C.A.9, 1960). It is incumbent upon the issuer, underwriter, dealers and other persons connected with the offering to make sure that it does not become an interstate distribution through resales. It is understood to be customary for such persons to obtain assurances that purchases are not made with a view to resale to non-residents.

---

3. See Report of the Securities and Exchange Commission to the Committee on Interstate and Foreign Commerce, dated August 7, 1941, on Proposals for Amendments to the Securities Act of 1933 and the Securities Exchange Act of 1934 where in referring to Sections 3(a)(1), 3(a)(9), 3(a)(10), 3(a)(11) and 3(b) of the Securities Act of 1933, it was said: " * * * Since these are in reality transaction exemptions, the Commission proposes and representatives of the securities' industry agree that they should be redesignated as transaction exemptions and transferred to Section 4. * * * " (p. 24).

Doing Business Within the State

In view of the local character of the Section 3(a)(11) exemption, the requirement that the issuer be doing business in the state can only be satisfied by the performance of substantial operational activities in the state of incorporation. The doing business requirement is not met by functions in the particular state such as bookkeeping, stock record and similar activities or by offering securities in the state. Thus, the exemption would be unavailable to an offering by a company made in the state of its incorporation of undivided fractional oil and gas interests located in other states even though the company conducted other business in the state of its incorporation. While the person creating the fractional interests is technically the "issuer" as defined in Section 2(4) of the Act, the purchaser of such security obtains no interest in the issuer's separate business within the state. Similarly, an intrastate exemption would not be available to a "local" mortgage company offering interests in out-of-state mortgages which are sold under circumstances to constitute them investment contracts. Also, the same position has been taken of a sale of an interest, by a real estate syndicate organized in one state to the residents of that state, in property acquired under a sale and leaseback arrangement with another corporation organized and engaged in business in another state.

If the proceeds of the offering are to be used primarily for the purpose of a new business conducted outside of the state of incorporation and unrelated to some incidental business locally conducted, the exemption should not be relied upon. S.E.C. v. Truckee Showboat, Inc., 157 F.Supp. 824 (S.D.Cal.1957). So also, a Section 3(a)(11) exemption should not be relied upon for each of a series of corporations organized in different states where there is in fact and purpose a single business enterprise or financial venture whether or not it is planned to merge or consolidate the various corporations at a later date. S.E.C. v. Los Angeles Trust Deed & Mortgage Exchange et al., 186 F.Supp. 830, 871 (S.D.Cal.1960), aff'd 285 F.2d 162 (C.A.9, 1960).

Residence Within the State

Section 3(a)(11) requires that the entire issue be confined to a single state in which the issuer, the offerees and the purchasers are residents. Mere presence in the state is not sufficient to constitute residence as in the case of military personnel at a military post. * * * The mere obtaining of formal representations of residence and agreements not to resell to non-residents or agreements that sales are void if the purchaser is a non-resident should not be relied upon without more as establishing the availability of the exemption.

An offering may be so large that its success as a local offering appears doubtful from the outset. Also, reliance should not be placed on the exemption for an issue which includes warrants for the purchase of another security unless there can be assurance that the warrants will be exercised only by residents. With respect to convertible securities, a Section 3(a)(9) exemption may be available for the conversion.

A secondary offering by a controlling person in the issuer's state of incorporation may be made in reliance on a Section 3(a)(11) exemption provided the exemption would be available to the issuer for a primary offering in that state. It is not essential that the controlling person be a resident of the issuer's state of incorporation.

Resales

From these general principles it follows that if during the course of distribution any underwriter, any distributing dealer (whether or not a member of the formal selling or distributing group), or any dealer or other person purchasing securities from a distributing dealer for resale were to offer or sell such securities to a non-resident, the exemption would be defeated. In other words, Section 3(a)(11) contemplates that the exemption is applicable only if the entire issue is distributed pursuant to the statutory conditions. Consequently, any offers or sales to a non-resident in connection with the distribution of the issue would destroy the exemption as to all securities which are a part of that issue, including those sold to residents regardless of whether such sales are made directly to non-residents or indirectly through residents who as part of the distribution thereafter sell to non-residents. It would furthermore be immaterial that sales to non-residents are made without use of the mails or instruments of interstate commerce. Any such sales of part of the issue to non-residents, however few, would not be in compliance with the conditions of Section 3(a)(11), and would render the exemption unavailable for the entire offering including the sales to residents.

This is not to suggest, however, that securities which have actually come to rest in the hands of resident investors, such as persons purchasing without a view to further distribution or resale to non-residents, may not in due course be resold by such persons, whether directly or through dealers or brokers, to non-residents without in any way affecting the exemption. The relevance of any such resales consists only of the evidentiary light which they might cast upon the factual question whether the securities had in fact come to rest in the hands of resident investors. If the securities are resold but a short time after their acquisition to a non-resident this fact, although not conclusive, might support an inference that the original offering had not come to rest in the state, and that the resale therefore constituted a part of the process of primary distribution; a stronger inference would arise if the purchaser involved were a security dealer. It may be noted that the non-residence of the underwriter or dealer is not pertinent so long as the ultimate distribution is solely to residents of the state.

Use of the Mails and Facilities of Interstate Commerce

The intrastate exemption is not dependent upon non-use of the mails or instruments of interstate commerce in the distribution. Securities issued in a transaction properly exempt under this provision may be offered and sold without registration through the mails or by use of any instruments of transportation or communication in interstate commerce, may be made the subject of general newspaper advertisement (provided the advertisement is appropriately limited to indicate that offers to purchase are solicited only from, and sales will be made only to residents of the particular state involved), and may even be delivered by means of transportation and communication used in interstate commerce, to the purchasers. Similarly, securities issued in a transaction exempt under Section 3(a)(11) may be offered without compliance with the formal prospectus requirements applicable to registered securities. Exemption under Section 3(a)(11), if in fact available, removes the distribution from the operation of the registration and prospectus requirements of Section 5 of the Act. It should be emphasized, however, that the civil liability and anti-fraud provisions of Sections 12(2) and 17 of the Act nevertheless apply and may give rise to civil liabilities and to other sanctions applicable to violations of the statute.

Conclusion

In conclusion, the fact should be stressed that Section 3(a)(11) is designed to apply only to distributions genuinely local in character. From a practical point of view, the provisions of that section can exempt only issues which in reality represent local financing by local industries, carried out through local investment. Any distribution not of this type raises a serious question as to the availability of Section 3(a)(11). Consequently, any dealer proposing to participate in the distribution of an issue claimed to be exempt under Section 3(a)(11) should examine the character of the transaction and the proposed or actual manner of its execution by all persons concerned with it with the greatest care to satisfy himself that the distribution will not, or did not, exceed the limitations of the exemption. Otherwise the dealer, even though his own sales may be carefully confined to resident purchasers, may subject himself to serious risk of civil liability under Section 12(1) of the Act for selling without prior registration a security not in fact entitled to exemption from registration. In Release No. 4386, we noted that the quick commencement of trading and prompt resale of portions of the issue to non-residents raises a serious question whether the entire issue has, in fact, come to rest in the hands of investors resident in the state of the initial offering.

The Securities Act is a remedial statute, and the terms of an exemption must be strictly construed against one seeking to rely on it. * * * The courts have held that he has the burden of proving its availability. * * * a

SECURITIES AND EXCHANGE COMMISSION v. McDONALD INVESTMENT CO.

United States District Court, D. Minnesota, 1972.
343 F.Supp. 343.

MEMORANDUM OPINION

NEVILLE, DISTRICT JUDGE: The question presented to the court is whether the sale exclusively to Minnesota residents of securities, consisting of unsecured installment promissory notes of the defendant, a Minnesota corporation, whose only business office is situate in Minnesota, is exempt from the filing of a registration statement under § 3(a)(11) of the 1933 Securities Act, when the proceeds from the sale of such notes are to be used principally, if not entirely, to make loans to land developers outside of Minnesota. Though this is a close question, the court holds that such registration is required and the defendants have not satisfied their burden of proving the availability of an exemption under the Act; this despite the

a. By virtue of the intrastate exemption, local sales of securities are left to state regulation. See Securities Act, § 18.

fact that the securities have heretofore been duly registered with the Securities Commissioner of the State of Minnesota for whom this court has proper respect.

Plaintiff, the Securities and Exchange Commission, instituted this lawsuit pursuant to § 20(b) of the 1933 Securities Act. The defendants are McDonald Investment Company, a Minnesota corporation, and H. J. McDonald, the company's president, treasurer, and owner of all the company's outstanding common stock. Plaintiff requests that the defendants be permanently enjoined from offering for sale and selling securities without having complied with the registration requirements of Section 5 of the Act.

Plaintiff and defendants have stipulated to the following pertinent facts: The defendant company was organized and incorporated in the State of Minnesota on November 6, 1968. The principal and only business office from which the defendants conduct their operations is located in Rush City, Minnesota, and all books, correspondence, and other records of the company are kept there.

Prior to October 19, 1971, the defendants registered an offering for $4,000,000 of its own installment notes with the Securities Division of the State of Minnesota pursuant to Minnesota law. The prospectus offering these installment notes became effective on October 19, 1971 by a written order of the Minnesota Commissioner of Securities making the registration and prospectus effective following examination and review by the Securities Division. Sales of the installment notes, according to the amended prospectus of January 18, 1972, are to be made to Minnesota residents only. Prior to the institution of this action, the defendants were enjoined from their past practices of selling, without Securities and Exchange Commission registration, notes secured by lien land contracts and first mortgages on unimproved land located at various places in the United States, principally Arizona. The defendant company is said to have sold $12,000,000 of such to some 2,000 investors. The present plan contemplates that those purchasing defendant company's securities henceforth will have only the general unsecured debt obligation of the company, though the proceeds from the installment notes will be lent to land developers with security taken from them in the form of mortgages or other liens running to the defendant corporation. The individual installment note purchasers will not, however, have any direct ownership or participation in the mortgages or other lien security, nor in the businesses of the borrowers.

No registration statement as to the installment notes described in McDonald Investment Company's amended prospectus is in effect with the United States Securities and Exchange Commission, nor has a registration statement been filed with the Commission. Furthermore, the defendants will make use of the means and instruments of transportation and communication in interstate commerce and of the mails to sell and offer to sell the installment notes though only to residents of Minnesota.

* * *

The plaintiff predicates its claim for a permanent injunction on the ground that the defendants will be engaged in a business where the income producing operations are located outside the state in which the securities are to be offered and sold and therefore not available for the 3(a)(11) exemption. Securities and Exchange Commission v. Truckee Showboat, 157 F.Supp. 824 (S.D.Cal.1957); Chapman v. Dunn, 414 F.2d 153 (6th Cir.

1969). While neither of these cases is precisely in point on their facts, the rationale of both is clear and apposite to the case at bar.

In *Truckee* the exemption was not allowed because the proceeds of the offering were to be used primarily for the purpose of a new unrelated business in another state, i.e., a California corporation acquiring and refurbishing a hotel in Las Vegas, Nevada. Likewise, in *Dunn* the 3(a)(11) exemption was unavailable to an offering by a company in one state, Michigan, of undivided fractional oil and gas interests located in another state, Ohio. The *Dunn* court specifically stated at page 159:

"* * * in order to qualify for the exemption of § 3(a)(11), the issuer must offer and sell his securities only to persons resident within a single State and the issuer must be a resident of that same State. *In addition to this, the issuer must conduct a predominant amount of his business within this same State.* This business which the issuer must conduct within the same State refers to the income producing operations of the business in which the issuer is selling the securities * * *." [Emphasis added]

This language would seem to fit the instant case where the income producing operations of the defendant, after completion of the offering, are to consist entirely of earning interest on its loans and receivables invested outside the state of Minnesota. While the defendant will not participate in any of the land developer's operations, nor will it own or control any of the operations, the fact is that the strength of the installment notes depends perhaps not legally, but practically, to a large degree on the success or failure of land developments located outside Minnesota, such land not being subject to the jurisdiction of the Minnesota court. The investor obtains no direct interest in any business activity outside of Minnesota, but legally holds only an interest as a creditor of a Minnesota corporation, which of course would be a prior claim on the defendant's assets over the shareholder's equity, now stated to be approximately a quarter of a million dollars.

This case does not evidence the deliberate attempt to evade the Act as in the example posed by plaintiff of a national organization or syndicate which incorporates in several or many states, opens an office in each and sells securities only to residents of the particular state, intending nevertheless to use all the proceeds whenever realized in a venture beyond the boundaries of all, or at best all but one of the states. See Securities & Exchange Commission v. Los Angeles Trust Deed & Mortgage Exchange, 186 F.Supp. 830, 871 (S.D.Cal.1960), aff'd 285 F.2d 162 (9th Cir. 1960). Defendant corporation on the contrary has been in business in Minnesota for some period of time, is not a "Johnny come lately" and is not part of any syndicate or similar enterprise; yet to relieve it of the federal registration requirements where none or very little of the money realized is to be invested in Minnesota, would seem to violate the spirit if not the letter of the Act.

Persuasive language is found in the Securities and Exchange Commission Release No. 4434, December 6, 1961, relating to exemptions for local offerings:

[The court quotes that portion of the Release, supra at page 380, under the heading: "Doing Business Within the State".]

Exemptions under the Act are strictly construed, with the burden of proof on the one seeking to establish the same. Securities and Exchange Commission v. Culpepper, 270 F.2d 241, 246 (2d Cir. 1959); Securities and Exchange Commission v. Ralston Purina Co., 346 U.S. 119, 126 (1954) * * *.

Defendant notes that agreements with land developers will by their terms be construed under Minnesota law; that the income producing activities will be the earning of interest which occurs in Minnesota; that the Minnesota registration provides at close proximity all the information and protection that any investor might desire; that whether or not registered with the Securities and Exchange Commission, a securities purchaser has the protection of [Section 12] which attaches liability to the issuer whether or not registration of the securities are exempted for fraudulent or untrue statements in a prospectus or made by oral communications; that plaintiff blurs the distinction between sale of securities across state lines and the operation of an intrastate business; and that if injunction issues in this case it could issue in any case where a local corporation owns an investment out of the particular state in which it has its principal offices and does business such as accounts receivable from its customers out of state. While these arguments are worthy and perhaps somewhat more applicable to the facts of this case than to the facts of *Truckee* and *Chapman*, supra, on balance and in carrying out the spirit and intent of the Securities Act of 1933, plaintiff's request for a permanent injunction should be granted.

SECTION 2. RULE 147

SECURITIES ACT RELEASE NO. 5450

Securities and Exchange Commission.
January 7, 1974.

NOTICE OF ADOPTION OF RULE 147 UNDER THE SECURITIES ACT OF 1933

* * *

The Securities and Exchange Commission today adopted Rule 147 which defines certain terms in, and clarifies certain conditions of, Section 3(a)(11) of the Securities Act of 1933 ("the Act"). Section 3(a)(11) (the "intrastate offering exemption") exempts from the registration requirements of Section 5 of the Act, securities that are part of an issue offered and sold only to persons resident within a single state or territory, if the issuer is a person resident and doing business within that state or territory. * * * *

In developing the definitions in, and conditions of, Rule 147 the Commission has considered the legislative history and judicial interpretations of Section 3(a)(11) as well as its own administrative interpretations. The Commission believes that adoption of the rule, which codifies certain of these interpretations, is in the public interest, since it will be consistent with the protection of investors and provide, to the extent feasible, more certainty in determining when the exemption provided by that Section of the Act is available. Moreover, the Commission believes that local businesses seeking financing solely from local sources should have objective standards to facilitate compliance with Section 3(a)(11) and the registration provisions of the Act, and that the rule will enable such businesses to determine with more certainty whether they may use the exemption in offering their securities. The rule also will give more assurance that the intrastate offering exemption is used only for the purpose that Congress intended, i.e., local financing of companies primarily intrastate in character. Neither Section 3(a)(11) nor Rule 147 provides an exemption from the civil liability provisions of Section 12(2) of the Act, the anti-fraud provisions of the Act or of the Securities Exchange Act of 1934 ("Exchange Act"), the registration and periodic reporting provisions of Sections 12(g) and 13 of the Exchange Act, or any applicable state laws.

Rule 147 is another step in the Commission's continuing efforts to provide protection to investors and, where consistent with that objective, to add certainty, to the extent feasible, to the determination of when the registration provisions of the Act apply. * * *

This notice contains a general discussion of the background, purpose and general effect of the rule. A brief analysis of each section of the rule is also included. However, attention is directed to the attached text of the rule for a more complete understanding of its provisions.

Background and Purpose

Congress, in enacting the federal securities laws, created a continuous disclosure system designed to protect investors and to assure the maintenance of fair and honest securities markets. The Commission, in administering and implementing these laws, has sought to coordinate and integrate the disclosure system with the exemptive provisions provided by the laws. Rule 147 is a further effort in this direction.

Section 3(a)(11) was intended to allow issuers with localized operations to sell securities as part of a plan of local financing. Congress apparently believed that a company whose operations are restricted to one area should be able to raise money from investors in the immediate vicinity without having to register the securities with a federal agency. In theory, the investors would be protected both by their proximity to the issuer and by state regulation. Rule 147 reflects this Congressional intent and is limited in its application to transactions where state regulation will be most effective. The Commission has consistently taken the position that the exemption applies only to local financing provided by local investors for local companies.[2] To satisfy the exemption, the entire issue must be offered and sold exclusively to residents of the state in which the issuer is resident and doing business. An offer or sale of part of the issue to a single non-resident will destroy the exemption for the entire issue.

Certain basic questions have arisen in connection with interpreting Section 3(a)(11). They are:

1. what transactions does the Section cover;

2. what is "part of an issue" for purposes of the Section;

3. when is a person "resident within" a state or territory for purposes of the Section; and

4. what does "doing business within" mean in the context of the Section?

2. See e.g., Securities Act of 1933 Release No. 4434 (December 6, 1961).

The courts and the Commission have addressed themselves to these questions in the context of different fact situations, and some general guidelines have been developed. Certain guidelines were set forth by the Commission in Securities Act Release No. 4434 and, in part, are reflected in Rule 147. However, in certain respects, as pointed out below, the rule differs from past interpretations.

The Transaction Concept

Although the intrastate offering exemption is contained in Section 3 of the Act, which Section is phrased in terms of exempt "securities" rather than "transactions", the legislative history and Commission and judicial interpretations indicate that the exemption covers only specific transactions and not the securities themselves. Rule 147 reflects this interpretation.

The "Part of an Issue" Concept

The determination of what constitutes "part of an issue" for purposes of the exemption, i.e. what should be "integrated", has traditionally been dependent on the facts involved in each case. The Commission noted in Securities Act Release 4434 that "any one or more of the following factors may be determinative of the question of integration:

"1. are the offerings part of a single plan of financing;

"2. do the offerings involve issuance of the same class of security;

"3. are the offerings made at or about the same time;

"4. is the same type of consideration to be received; and

"5. are the offerings made for the same general purpose."

In this connection, the Commission generally has deemed intrastate offerings to be "integrated" with those registered or private offerings of the same class of securities made by the issuer at or about the same time.

The rule as initially proposed would have done away with the necessity for such case-by-case determination of what offerings should be integrated by providing that all securities offered or sold by the issuer, its predecessor, and its affiliates, within any consecutive six month period, would be integrated. As adopted, the rule provides in Subparagraph (b)(2) that, for purposes of the rule only, certain offers and sales of securities, discussed below, will be deemed not to be part of an issue and therefore not be integrated, but the rule does not otherwise define "part of an issue." Accordingly, as to offers and sales not within (b)(2), issuers who want to rely on Rule 147 will have to determine whether their offers and sales are part of an issue by applying the five factors cited above.

The "Person Resident Within" Concept

The object of the Section 3(a)(11) exemption, i.e., to restrict the offering to persons within the same locality as the issuer who are, by reason of their proximity, likely to be familiar with the issuer and protected by the state law governing the issuer, is best served by interpreting the residence requirement narrowly. In addition, the determination of whether all parts of the issue have been sold only to residents can be made only after the securities have "come to rest" within the state or territory. Rule 147 retains these concepts, but provides more objective standards for determining when a person is considered a resident within a state for purposes of the rule and when securities have come to rest within a state.

The "Doing Business Within" Requirement

Because the primary purpose of the intrastate exemption was to allow an essentially local business to raise money within the state where the investors would be likely to be familiar with the business and with the management, the doing business requirement has traditionally been viewed strictly. First, not only should the business be located within the state, but the principal or predominant business must be carried on there.[4] Second, substantially all of the proceeds of the offering must be put to use within the local area.[5]

Rule 147 reinforces these requirements by providing specific percentage amounts of business that must be conducted within the state, and of proceeds from the offering that must be spent in connection with such business. In addition, the rule requires that the principal office of the issuer be within the state.

Synopsis of Rule 147

1. Preliminary Notes

The first preliminary note to the rule indicates that the rule does not raise any presumption that the Section 3(a)(11) exemption would not be available for transactions which do not satisfy all of the provisions of the rule. The second note reminds issuers that the rule does not affect compliance with state law. The third preliminary note to the rule briefly explains the rule's purpose and provisions.

As initially proposed, the rule was intended not to be available for secondary transactions. In order to make this clear, the fourth preliminary note indicates that the rule is available only for transactions by an issuer and that the rule is not available for secondary transactions. However, in accordance with long standing administrative interpretations of Section 3(a)(11), the intrastate offering exemption may be available for secondary offers and sales by controlling persons of the issuer, if the exemption would have been available to the issuer.[6]

2. Transactions Covered—Rule 147(a)

Paragraph (a) of the rule provides that offers, offers to sell, offers for sale and sales of securities that meet all the conditions of the rule will be deemed to come within the exemption provided by Section 3(a)(11). Those conditions are: (1) the issuer must be resident and doing business within the state or territory in which the securities are offered and sold (Rule 147(c)); (2) the *offerees* and purchasers must be resident within such state or territory (Rule 147(d)); (3) resales for a period of 9 months after the last sale which is part of an issue must be limited as provided (Rule 147(e) and (f)). In addition, the revised rule provides that certain offers and sales of

---

4. Chapman v. Dunn, 414 F.2d 153 (C.A.6, 1969).

5. SEC v. Truckee Showboat, Inc., 157 F.Supp. 824 (S.D.Cal., 1957).

6. Securities Act of 1933 Release No. 4434 (December 6, 1961).

securities by or for the issuers will be deemed not "part of an issue" for purposes of the rule only (Rule 147(b)).

3. "Part of an Issue"—Rule 147(b)

Subparagraph (b)(1) of the rule provides that all securities of the issuer which are part of an issue must be offered, offered for sale or sold only in accordance with all of the terms of the rule. For the purposes of the rule only, subparagraph (b)(2) provides that all securities of the issuer offered, offered for sale or sold pursuant to the exemptions provided under Section 3 or 4(2) of the Act or registered pursuant to the Act, prior to or subsequent to the six month period immediately preceding or subsequent to any offer, offer to sell, offer for sale or sale pursuant to Rule 147 will be deemed not part of an issue provided that there are no offers, offers to sell or sales of securities of the same or similar class by or for the issuer during either of these six month periods. If there have been offers or sales during the six months, then in order to determine what constitutes part of an issue, reference should be made to the five traditional integration factors discussed above.

As initially proposed the rule would have deemed all securities of the issuer, its predecessors and affiliates offered or sold by the issuer, its predecessors and affiliates within any consecutive six month period to be part of the same issue. On reconsideration, the Commission believes this would be too restrictive and has revised the rule as discussed above. Since subparagraph (b)(2) does not define "part of an issue", a note has been added to paragraph (b) which refers to the discussion of the five factors to be considered in determining whether a transaction is part of an issue. These factors are discussed in the third preliminary note to the rule, and should be considered in determining whether any offers and sales falling outside the scope of subparagraph (b)(2) and offers and sales made in reliance on the rule must be integrated. Neither Section 3(a)(11) nor Rule 147 can be relied upon in combination with another exemption for different parts of a single issue where a part is offered or sold to non-residents.

As initially proposed for comment the rule provided that securities offered or sold by a person which was a business separate and distinct from the issuer and which was affiliated with the issuer solely by reason of the existence of a common general partner would be deemed not to be part of the same issue. Since paragraph (b) has been revised to no longer automatically integrate offerings of affiliates, this proviso is no longer necessary and has been deleted.

Paragraph (b), as revised, is intended to create greater certainty and to obviate in certain situations the need for a case-by-case determination of when certain intrastate offerings should be integrated with other offerings, such as those registered under the Act or made pursuant to the exemption provided by Section 3 or 4(2) of the Act.

4. Nature of the Issuer—Rule 147(c)—"Person Resident Within"—Rule 147(c)(1)

Subparagraph (c)(1) of the rule defines the situations in which issuers would be deemed to be "resident within" a state or territory. A corporation, limited partnership or business trust must be incorporated or organized pursuant to the laws of such state or territory. Section 3(a)(11) provides specifically that a corporate issuer must be incorporated in the state. A general partnership or other form of business entity that is not formed under a specific state or territorial law must have its principal office within the state or territory. The rule also provides that an individual who is deemed an issuer, e.g., a promoter issuing preincorporation certificates, will be deemed a resident if his principal residence is in the state or territory. As initially proposed, the rule provided that in a partnership, *all* the general partners must be resident within such state or territory. The Commission has reconsidered this provision in light of the provisions applicable to corporations and determined to treat all business entities in a similar manner.

5. Nature of the Issuer—Rule 147(c)—Doing Business Within—Rule 147(c)(2)

Subparagraph (c)(2) of the rule provides that the issuer will be deemed to be "doing business within" a state or territory in which the offers and sales are to be made if: (1) at least 80 percent of its gross revenues and those of its subsidiaries on a consolidated basis (a) for its most recent fiscal year (if the first offer of any part of the issue is made during the first six months of the issuer's current fiscal year) or (b) for the subsequent six month period, or for the twelve months ended with that period (if the first offer of any part of the issue is made during the last six months of the issuer's current fiscal year) were derived from the operation of a business or property located in or rendering of services within the state or territory; (2) at least 80 percent of the issuer's assets and those of its subsidiaries on a consolidated basis at the end of the most recent fiscal semi-annual period prior to the first offer of any part of the issue are located within such state or territory; (3) at least 80 percent of the net proceeds to the issuer from the sales made pursuant to the rule are intended to be and are used in connection with the operation of a business or property or the rendering of services within such state or territory; and (4) the issuer's principal office is located in the state or territory.

As proposed the issuer would have been required to meet the gross revenues and assets conditions at the end of the most recent fiscal year and its most recent fiscal quarter. That provision might have been difficult for many small businesses to satisfy and it has been revised as discussed above. Also a moving twelve month calculation is permitted in some instances for determining gross revenues in recognition of the seasonal character of some businesses. The revised rule also clarifies the Commission's previous intention to include gross revenues of subsidiaries consolidated with those of the issuer. Finally, the rule as initially proposed would have required that the issuer intended to use and used 90 percent of the proceeds of the offering in connection with the operation of a business, the purchase of real property or the rendering of services in the state. This percentage has been reduced to 80 percent in the revised rule since it appeared to be unduly restrictive. Further, this is consistent with the nature of the business reflected in the other percentage tests.

Finally, subparagraph (c)(2) of the rule provides that an issuer which has not had gross revenues from the operation of its business in excess of $5,000 during its most recent twelve month period need not satisfy the revenue test of subsection (c)(2)(i).

The provisions of paragraph (c) are intended to assure that the issuer is primarily a local business. Many comments were received requesting more elaboration with respect to the above standards. The following examples demonstrate the manner in which these standards would be interpreted:

Example 1. X corporation is incorporated in State A and has its only warehouse, only manufacturing plant and only office in that state. X's only business is selling products throughout the United States and Canada through mail order catalogs. X annually mails catalogs and order forms from its office to residents of most states and several provinces of Canada. All orders are filled at and products shipped from X's warehouse to customers throughout the United States and Canada. All the products shipped are manufactured by X at its plant in State A. These activities are X's sole source of revenues.

Question. Is X deriving more than 80 percent of its gross revenues from the "operation of a business or * * * rendering of services" within State A?

Interpretive Response. Yes, this aspect of the "doing business within" standard is satisfied.

Example 2. Assume the same facts as Example 1, except that X has no manufacturing plant and purchases the products it sells from corporations located in other states.

Question. Is X deriving more than 80 percent of its gross revenues from the "operation of a business or * * * rendering of services" within State A?

Interpretive Response. Yes, this aspect of the "doing business within" standard is satisfied.

Example 3. Y Corporation is incorporated in State B and has its only office in that state. Y's only business is selling undeveloped land located in State C and State D by means of brochures mailed from its office throughout the United States.

Question. Is Y deriving more than 80 percent of its gross revenues from the "operation of a business or of property or rendering of services" within State B?

Interpretive Response. There are not sufficient facts to respond. If Y owns an interest in the developed land, it might not satisfy the "80 percent of assets" standard as well as the "80 percent of gross revenues" standard. Moreover, Y could not use more than 20 percent of the proceeds of any offerings made pursuant to the rule in connection with the acquisition of the undeveloped land.

Example 4. Z company is a firm of engineering consultants organized under the laws of State E with its only office in that state. During any year, Z will provide consulting services for projects in other states. 75 percent of Z's work in terms of man hours will be performed at Z's offices where it employs some 50 professional and clerical personnel. Z has no employees located outside of State E. However, professional personnel visit project sites and clients' offices in other states. Approximately 50 percent of Z's revenue is derived from clients located in states other than State E.

Question. Is Z deriving more than 80 percent of its gross revenues from "rendering services" within State E?

Interpretive Response. Yes, this aspect of the "doing business within" standard is satisfied.

Example 5. The facts are the same as in Example 4. In addition, at the end of Z's most recent fiscal quarter 25 percent of its assets are represented by accounts receivable from clients in other states.

Question. Does Z satisfy the "assets" standard?

Interpretive Response. Yes, Z satisfies the "assets" standard. For purposes of the rule, accounts receivable arising from a business conducted in the state would generally be considered to be located at the principal office of the issuer.

6. Offerees and Purchasers: Persons Resident—Rule 147(d)

Paragraph (d) of the rule provides that offers and sales may be made only to persons resident within the state or territory. An individual offeree or purchaser of any part of an issue would be deemed to be a person resident within the state or territory if such person has his principal residence in the state or territory. Temporary residence, such as that of many persons in the military service, would not satisfy the provisions of paragraph (d). In addition, if a person purchases securities on behalf of other persons, the residence of those persons must satisfy paragraph (d). If the offeree or purchaser is a business organization its residence will be deemed the state or territory in which it has its principal office, unless it is an entity organized for the specific purpose of acquiring securities in the offering, in which case it will be deemed to be a resident of a state only if all of the beneficial owners of interests in such entity are residents of the state.

As initially proposed, subparagraph (d)(2) provided that an individual, in order to be deemed a resident, must have his principal residence in the state and must not have any present intention of moving his principal residence to another state. The Commission believes that it would be difficult to determine a person's intentions, and accordingly, has deleted the latter requirement. In addition, as initially proposed, the rule would have deemed the residence of a business organization to be the state in which it was incorporated or otherwise organized. The Commission believes that the location of a company's principal office is more of an indication of its local character for purposes of the offeree residence provision of the rule than is its state of incorporation. Section 3(a)(11) requires that an issuer corporation be incorporated within the state, but there is no similar requirement in the statute for a corporation that is an offeree or purchaser.

7. Limitations on Resales—Rule 147(e)

Paragraph (e) of the rule provides that during the period in which securities that are part of an issue are being offered and sold and for a period of nine months from the date of the last sale by the issuer of any part of the issue, resales of any part of the issue by any person shall be made only to persons resident within the same state or territory. This provides objective standards for determining when an issue "comes to rest." The rule as initially proposed limited both *reoffers* and resales during a twelve month period after the last sale by the issuer of any part of the issue. However, the Commission believes that it would be difficult for an issuer to prohibit or even learn of reoffers. Thus, the limitation on reoffers would be impractical because, if any purchaser made a reoffer outside of such state or territory, the issuer would lose the exemption provided by the rule. In addition, the Commission determined that a shorter period would satisfy the coming to rest test for purposes of the rule. Thus, the twelve month period has been reduced to nine months.

Persons who acquire securities from issuers in transactions complying with the rule would acquire unregistered securities that could only be reoffered and resold pursuant to an exemption from the registration provisions of the Act.

The Commission, as it indicated in Rel. 33–5349, considered alternatives to the twelve month period. The Commission has determined that it is in the public interest to adopt a specific time period, but such period has been reduced to nine months and applied to resales only, which provides the necessary protections to investors against interstate trading markets springing up before the securities have come to rest within the state. As an additional precaution, a note to paragraph (e) reminds dealers that they must satisfy the requirements of Rule 15c2–11 under the Securities Exchange Act of 1934 prior to publishing any quotation for a security, or submitting any quotation for publication in any quotation medium.

A note to the rule indicates that where convertible securities are sold pursuant to the rule, resales of either the convertible security, or if it is converted, of the underlying security, could be made during the period specified in paragraph (e) only to residents of the state. However, the conversion itself, if pursuant to Section 3(a)(9) of the Act, would not begin a new period. In the case of warrants and options, sales upon exercise, if done in reliance on the rule, would begin a new period.

8. Precautions Against Interstate Offers and Sales—Rule 147(f)

Paragraph (f) of the rule requires issuers to take steps to preserve the exemption provided by the rule, since any resale of any part of the issue before it comes to rest within the state to persons resident in another state or territory will, under the Act, be in violation of Section 5. The required steps are: (i) placing a legend on the certificate or other document evidencing the security stating that the securities have not been registered under the Act and setting forth the limitations on resale contained in paragraph (e); (ii) issuing stop transfer instructions to the issuer's transfer agent, if any, with respect to the securities, or, if the issuer transfers its own securities, making a notation in the appropriate records of the issuer; and (iii) obtaining a written representation from each purchaser as to his residence. Where persons other than the issuer are reselling securities of the issuer during the time period specified in paragraph (e) of the rule, the issuer would, if the securities are presented for transfer, be required to take steps (i) and (ii). In addition, the rule requires that the issuer disclose in writing the limitations on resale imposed by paragraph (e) and the provisions of subsections (f)(1)(i) and (ii) and subparagraph (f)(2).

Operation of Rule 147

Rule 147 will operate prospectively only. The staff will issue interpretative letters to assist persons in complying with the rule, but will consider requests for "no action" letters on transactions in reliance on Section

3(a)(11) outside the rule only on an infrequent basis and in the most compelling circumstances.

The rule is a nonexclusive rule. However, persons who choose to rely on Section 3(a)(11) without complying with all the conditions of the rule would have the burden of establishing that they have complied with the judicial and administrative interpretations of Section 3(a)(11) in effect at the time of the offering. The Commission also emphasizes that the exemption provided by Section 3(a)(11) is not an exemption from the civil liability provisions of Section 12(2) or the anti-fraud provisions of Section 17 of the Act or of Section 10(b) of the Securities Exchange Act of 1934. The Commission further emphasizes that Rule 147 is available only for transactions by issuers and is not available for secondary offerings.

In view of the objectives and policies underlying the Act, the rule would not be available to any person with respect to any offering which, although in technical compliance with the provisions of the rule, is part of a plan or scheme by such person to make interstate offers or sales of securities. In such cases, registration would be required. In addition, any plan or scheme that involves a series of offerings by affiliated organizations in various states, even if in technical compliance with the rule, may be outside the parameters of the rule and of Section 3(a)(11) if what is being financed is in effect a single business enterprise.[a]

*   *   *   *

THE SECTION 3(a)(11) EXEMPTION

The Section 3(a)(11) exemption has not been subject to very much litigation. Most of the cases before 1961 were discussed in Securities Act Release No. 4434, *supra* at page 378.

In Grenader v. Spitz,[1] a general partnership with the principal place of business in the issuing state was held to be a "resident" of that state even though one of the partners resided in another state. The contention was also made that at the time of the offer or sale several of the purchasers of the securities were or since that time had become nonresidents of the state. Although the court did not pass upon this question because of failure of proof, Rule 147 is helpful in defining "residence" of offerees and purchasers; a person who is a bona fide resident of the state at the time of the offering or the purchase should not be deemed to have destroyed the exemption by a subsequent change in residence.

The exemption has been used in California in connection with real estate syndications for projects to be located in that state. The problem of establishing proof of "residence" has been solved successfully by the use and monitoring of a form of questionnaire eliciting information with respect to voting, driver's license and other facts establishing the place of residence.

In SEC v. McDonald Investment Co., *supra* page 382, the court discusses the existing judicial authority on the "doing business" requirement. Although Rule 147 is nonexclusive, what is the likelihood that a court will take a more expansive view of the "doing business" requirement than that specified in Rule 147(c)(2)?

---

a. See Note, SEC Rule 147: Ten Years of SEC Interpretation, 38 Okla.L.Rev. 507 (1985).

1. 390 F.Supp. 1112 (S.D.N.Y.1975), rev'd on other grounds 537 F.2d 612 (2d Cir. 1976).

On Rule 147, see 7 J. Hicks, Exempted Transactions Under the Securities Act of 1933, c. 4 (1980 rev.); Note, SEC Rule 147: Ten Years of SEC Interpretation, 38 Okla.L.Rev. 507 (1985); Alberg and Lybecker, New SEC Rules 146 and 147: The Nonpublic and Intrastate Offering Exemptions from Registration For the Sale of Securities, 74 Colum.L.Rev. 622 (1974); Hicks, Intrastate Offerings Under Rule 147, 72 Mich.L.Rev. 463 (1974); Long, A Lawyer's Guide to the Intrastate Exemption and Rule 147, 24 Drake L.Rev. 471 (1975); McCauley, Intrastate Securities Transactions Under the Federal Securities Act, 107 U.Pa.L.Rev. 937 (1959); Sowards, The Twilight of the Intrastate Exemption, 25 Mercer L.Rev. 437 (1974); Cummings, Intrastate Exemption and the Shallow Harbor of Rule 147, 69 Nw.U.L.Rev. 167 (1974); Kant, SEC Rule 147—A Further Narrowing of the Intrastate Offering Exemption, 30 Bus.Law. 73 (1974); Sosin, The Intrastate Exemption: Public Offerings and the Issue Concept, 16 W.Res.L.Rev. 110 (1964); Bloomenthal, The Federal Securities Act Intra-state Exemption—Fact or Fiction?, 15 Wyo.L.J. 121 (1961); Emens & Thomas, The Intrastate Exemption of the Securities Act of 1933 in 1971, 40 U.Cin.L.Rev. 779 (1971); Note, New Approach to the Intrastate Exemption: Rule 147 vs. Section 3(a)(11), 62 Calif.L.Rev. 195 (1974).

AMERICAN LAW INSTITUTE, FEDERAL SECURITIES CODE § 514(a) [a]

SEC. 514. (a) DEFINITION. A "local distribution" is one that (1) results in sales substantially restricted to persons who are residents of or have their primary employment in a single State, or an area in contiguous States (or a State and a contiguous foreign country) as that area is defined by rule or order on consideration of its population and economic characteristics, and (2) involves securities of an issuer that has or proposes to have its principal place of business in that State or area, regardless of where it is organized. Section 514(a)(1) is not satisfied unless at least 95 percent of all the buyers holding of record at least 80 percent of the securities distributed are persons described in that section.

* * *

a. Copyright 1980. Reprinted with permission of the American Law Institute.

Chapter 8

REORGANIZATIONS AND RECAPITALIZATIONS

SECTION 1. SECTION 2(3) AND THE THEORY OF "SALE"

Statutes and Regulations

Securities Act, §§ 2(3), 5.

Introductory Note

For § 5 to become operative there must be a "sale" or "offer" of a security. Section 2(3) defines the term "sale" to include "every contract of sale or disposition of a security * * *, for value." There are various types of corporate transactions involving the issue of securities in which the question of whether there must be registration will hinge upon the finding of a "sale" as that term is used in the Securities Act.

(a) *Warrants and Conversion Privileges.* A warrant or right to subscribe to a security is itself a security by the express terms of § 2(1). And the fact that a restricted stock option is non-transferable will not in and of itself remove it from this category.[1] Nevertheless, a warrant, option or right to subscribe need not be registered unless it is to be offered or disposed of for value. Thus, in the ordinary rights offering in which transferable warrants are issued to shareholders without any consideration, the warrants themselves need not be registered. A warrant, however, if immediately exercisable, constitutes an offer to sell the security called for in the warrant and thus makes the registration requirements applicable to that security.[2] This conclusion is consistent with the implication of the last sentence of § 2(3) relating to conversion and subscription rights which are not exercisable until a future date. It also follows that the offer of a security which by its terms is immediately convertible into another security of the same issuer or another person entails an offer both of the convertible security and of the security into which it may be converted. In practice, therefore, the Commission requires the registration of the securities issuable upon conversion along with registration of the convertible securities, although the view of the Federal Trade Commission that a double registration fee must be paid has long since been abandoned.[3]

On the other hand, warrants are frequently sold to underwriters in connection with a public offering of stock of the same class. If these warrants are transferable and may be exercised immediately, the SEC staff

1. See Middle South Utilities, Inc., SEC Holding Co. Act Release No. 14,367; 1 Loss, Securities Regulation 467 (2d ed. 1961, Supp.1969).

2. SEC Securities Act Release No. 3210, April 9, 1947.

3. See SEC Securities Act Release No. 97, part 2 (1933); Throop and Lane, Some Problems of Exemption under the Securities Act of 1933, 4 Law and Contemp.Prob. 89, 100 (1937); 1 Loss, Securities Regulation 579 (2d ed. 1961).

takes the view that both the warrants and the stock subject thereto must be registered along with the stock being offered to the general public, even though, for tax or other reasons, exercise of the warrants will in fact not occur for some time after the registration statement becomes effective. Where distribution of the securities subject to the warrants is to be thus postponed, the registration statement must include an undertaking to file a post-effective amendment which shall set forth the manner and terms of the offering and shall become effective prior to any such distribution.[4]

So far we have dealt with warrants and options which are immediately exercisable. Section 2(3) provides that the issue or transfer of a right of conversion or a warrant to subscribe to another security "which * * * cannot be exercised until some future date, shall not be deemed to be an offer or sale of such other security; but the issue or transfer of such other security upon the exercise of such right * * * shall be deemed a sale of such other security." According to the House Report:[5]

This makes it unnecessary to register such a security prior to the time that it is to be offered to the public, although the conversion right or the right to subscribe must be registered. When the actual securities to which these rights appertain are offered to the public, the bill requires registration as of that time. This permits the holder of any such right of conversion or warrant to subscribe to judge whether upon all the facts it is advisable for him to exercise his rights.

The Report is ambiguous as to when a warrant or conversion right must be registered where the right to exercise is postponed to a future date. Apparently, both the warrant and the underlying security must be registered prior to the exercise date of the warrant, rather than its date of issue.

(b) *Stock Dividends*. The Conference Committee reported that it had omitted a House provision exempting stock dividends since they "are exempt without express provision as they do not constitute a sale, not being given for value."[6]

This is true as to the ordinary stock dividend. But what about a situation where a corporation proposes to declare a dividend upon its common stock, payable in cash or in common stock at the election of stockholder? When faced with this problem, the General Counsel gave this opinion:[7]

Whether or not registration is required in such a case is of course primarily dependent upon whether the offering is of such a character as to constitute it a "sale," as that term is defined in Section 2(3) of the Securities Act. As you are aware, this definition is extremely broad in its scope, and includes every "attempt or offer to dispose of * * * a security * * * for value." The term "value" is not defined in the Act, but should in my opinion be regarded as including not only such ordinary forms of consideration as the transfer of cash or property, but also the waiver or surrender of a right or claim.

However, even though under ordinary circumstances the waiver of a right would in my opinion constitute "value," I do not believe that that

---

4. Op.cit. supra note 2. See Rule 415, Regulation S–K, Item 512 and supra at page 198.

5. H.R.Rep.No.85, 73d Cong., 1st Sess. 11 (1933).

6. H.R.Rep.No.152, 73d Cong., 1st Sess. 25 (1933).

7. SEC Securities Act Release No. 929 (1936).

term should be regarded as comprehending within its meaning the action of a stockholder, to whom alternative rights have been granted without consideration, in electing to exercise one such right, even though, under the terms of the grant, such election will have the effect of causing the lapse of the right not exercised. Consequently, if a corporation, by simultaneous action of its board of directors, declares a dividend payable at the election of the stockholder in cash or in securities, neither the declaration of the dividend, nor the distribution of securities to stockholders who elect to take the dividend in that form, would in my opinion constitute a sale within the meaning of the Securities Act, and no registration of the securities so distributed would be required under that Act.

However, according to my understanding it is well settled in general law that upon the public declaration of a cash dividend out of surplus, the holders of the stock in respect of which the dividend is declared acquire immediately the rights of creditors of the corporation, and cannot be divested of these rights by subsequent action of the board of directors. If, therefore, there is declared a cash dividend payable to all stockholders, and if the board thereafter determines to grant to stockholders the opportunity to waive their pre-existing and vested right to payment of the dividend in cash, and to receive the dividend in the form of securities, the stockholders electing to take securities would in my opinion be regarded as giving value for the securities so received. Under these circumstances I believe that the securities might well be held to be the subject of a sale.

(c) *Pledge of Securities.* The Courts of Appeal were divided as to whether a pledge of securities as collateral for a loan entails a sale or disposition of a security or an interest in a security, for value, within the meaning of § 2(3) and § 17(a) of the 1933 Act. The Fifth and Seventh Circuits, relying on the "context" clause prefacing § 2, concluded that although the securities laws appear literally to apply, the economic reality of the transaction consisted merely of a transfer of possession of securities to the creditor to secure a loan and that no sale or disposition takes place until foreclosure following default on the loan.[8] The Second Circuit reached a contrary result.[9] In Rubin v. United States,[10] the Supreme Court settled the matter and affirmed a criminal conviction for fraud under § 17(a) of the 1933 Act perpetrated by defendant who pledged worthless stock to a bank as collateral for a commercial loan. The Court found the terms of the statute "unambiguous" in determining that a pledge entailed a "disposition of * * * [an] interest in a security, for value." Justice Blackmun concurred, but concluded that a pledge of stock as collateral simply constituted a "disposition" within the meaning of § 2(3), also noting the parallel provision of § 3(a)(14) of the 1934 Act. Accordingly, the transaction may also be subject to the antifraud provisions of Rule 10b–5,

---

8. National Bank of Commerce of Dallas v. All American Assurance Co., 583 F.2d 1295 (5th Cir.1978); Lincoln National Bank v. Herber, 604 F.2d 1038 (7th Cir. 1979).

9. Mallis v. FDIC, 568 F.2d 824 (2d Cir. 1977), cert. dismissed sub nom. Bankers Trust Co. v. Mallis, 435 U.S. 381 (1978).

10. 449 U.S. 424 (1981); Note, New Protection for Defrauded Pledges of Securities Under the Federal Securities Laws, 23 B.C.L.Rev. 821 (1982).

although the proscribed act must be committed with respect to the pledged securities.[11]

(d) *Exchanges of Securities.* Although the definition of "sale" does not in terms include an exchange, the courts have had no difficulty in finding an exchange of securities to be a sale. As one court put it: "[O]ne may sell a security and be paid therefor in cash, or in another security, or in any other object of value such as a house. * * *"[12] Congress obviously took this view in enacting §§ 3(a)(9) and 3(a)(10) which exempt certain types of exchanges of securities from the operation of the act. The matter seems quite clear when the security holder voluntarily surrenders the document evidencing the security and receives an entirely different security. But an exchange proposal may result in a substantial change in the rights of an outstanding security without a physical exchange of securities. Thus, in SEC v. Associated Gas & Electric Co.,[13] extension of the maturity date on a bond by stamping the outstanding certificates with a legend was held to be a new issue and sale of a security under the Public Utility Holding Company Act of 1935. The modification of the original obligation by negotiation between the holders and issuer was deemed to be equivalent to an exchange of the new security for the old. Moreover, a change in the rights of outstanding securities by way of a charter amendment or otherwise, even though authorized by the law of the state of incorporation, entails the issue and sale of a new security.[14]

Another common form of exchange arises in a corporate acquisition in which one corporation makes an offer to the shareholders of another corporation to exchange its securities for the securities of the other corporation. In all of the exchanges discussed so far each offeree is free to accept or reject the offer as an individual matter. It is this element of individual consent which differentiates these voluntary exchanges from the corporate reorganizations and recapitalizations entailing a "cram-down," in which the non-consenting security holders are bound by the vote of a majority, subject to any right of appraisal.

SECTION 2. EXEMPTED EXCHANGES OF SECURITIES BETWEEN AN ISSUER AND ITS SECURITY HOLDERS: SECTION 3(a)(9)

Statutes and Regulations

Securities Act § 3(a)(9).

Rules 149, 150.

11. Chemical Bank v. Arthur Andersen & Co., 726 F.2d 930 (2d Cir.1984); Head v. Head, 759 F.2d 1172 (4th Cir.1985); United States v. Kendrick, 692 F.2d 1262 (9th Cir. 1982), cert. denied 461 U.S. 914 (1983).

12. United States v. Riedel, 126 F.2d 81 (7th Cir. 1942); United States v. Wernes, 157 F.2d 797 (7th Cir. 1946).

13. 99 F.2d 795 (2d Cir. 1938).

14. United States v. New York, New Haven & Hartford Railroad Co., 276 F.2d 525 (2d Cir. 1960), cert. denied 362 U.S. 961 (1960); Western Air Lines v. Sobieski, 191 Cal.App.2d 399, 12 Cal.Rptr. 719 (1961); McGuigan & Aiken, Amendment of Securities, 9 Rev. of Sec.Reg. 935 (1976).

SECURITIES ACT RELEASE NO. 646

Securities and Exchange Commission.
February 3, 1936.

[Letters of General Counsel Concerning the Application of Section 3(a)(9).]

The Securities and Exchange Commission today made public two opinions of its General Counsel, John J. Burns, concerning the interpretation of Section 3(a)(9) of the Securities Act of 1933. ＊ ＊ ＊

The General Counsel's opinion indicating the inapplicability of Section 3(a)(9) to other than bona fide exchanges of securities, which was given in answer to a query concerning a proposed exchange of bonds with three noteholders, is as follows:

"Section 3(a)(9) exempts

'any security exchanged by the issuer with its existing security holders exclusively where no commission or other remuneration is paid or given directly or indirectly for soliciting such exchange'.

"I assume that no commission or other remuneration will be paid in connection with this exchange, and that the bonds will be issued only to the above-mentioned noteholders in exchange for the notes of the corporation. In such case, on the further assumption that none of the bondholders is or will be in control of your company, it seems to me likely that registration of the bonds in question will be unnecessary. However, I feel that I should point out possible limitations which I believe are inherent in Section 3(a)(9), and which might operate to prevent the applicability of the exemption of that section despite formal compliance with its conditions.

"I believe Section 3(a)(9) is applicable only to exchanges which are bona fide, in the sense that they are not effected merely as a step in a plan to evade the registration requirements of the Act. For example, Corporation A, as part of such a plan, might issue a large block of its securities to Corporation B, and might then issue new securities to Corporation B in exchange for the first-issued securities, with the understanding that such new securities are to be offered to the public by Corporation B. In my opinion, the mere fact that the exchange in such case might comply with the literal conditions of Section 3(a)(9) would not avail to defeat the necessity for registration of the securities issued in such exchange. Cf. Gregory v. Helvering, 293 U.S. 465.

"In determining whether a particular exchange had been effected merely as a step in a plan to evade the registration requirements of the Act, I believe that a court would take into account various factors such as the length of time during which the securities received by the issuer were outstanding prior to their surrender in exchange, the number of holders of the securities originally outstanding, the marketability of such securities, and also the question whether the exchange is one which was dictated by financial considerations of the issuer and not primarily in order to enable one or a few security holders to distribute their holdings to the public. ＊ ＊ ＊

The second opinion of the General Counsel was in reply to an inquiry whether securities previously received by a controlling stockholder in a bona fide exchange exempt under Section 3(a)(9) should be registered before being offered to the public through an underwriter. The relevant portion of the opinion follows:

"In order to make clear my position on this question, I must briefly review the legislative histories of the present Section 3(a)(9) and of Section 2(11) of the Securities Act of 1933.

"The last sentence of Section 2(11) reads as follows:

" 'As used in this paragraph the term "issuer" shall include, in addition to an issuer, any person directly or indirectly controlling or controlled by the issuer, or any person under direct or indirect common control with the issuer.'

"This sentence, by defining an underwriter to include a person purchasing from one in a control relation with the issuer, makes the exemption afforded by Section 4(1) inapplicable to transactions by such a person and thus necessitates registration before distribution to the public of securities acquired from a person in a control relation. The report of the House Committee, which considered the identical language in the bill then before the Committee (H.R. 5480), leaves no doubt as to the reason for this requirement:

" 'The last sentence of this definition, defining "issuer" to include not only the issuer but also affiliates or subsidiaries of the issuer and persons controlling the issuer, has two functions * * * Its second function is to bring within the provisions of the bill redistribution whether of outstanding issues or issues sold subsequently to the enactment of the bill. All the outstanding stock of a particular corporation may be owned by one individual or a select group of individuals. At some future date they may wish to dispose of their holdings and to make an offer of this stock to the public. Such a public offering may possess all the dangers attendant upon a new offering of securities. Wherever such a redistribution reaches significant proportions, the distributor would be in a position of controlling the issuer and thus able to furnish the information demanded by the bill. This being so, the distributor is treated as equivalent to the original issuer and, if he seeks to dispose of the issue through a public offering, he becomes subject to the act.' H.R. 85, 73d Cong., 1st Sess., pp. 13–14.

"Section 2(11) thus gives expression to the clear intent of Congress to subject to the registration requirements of the Act any redistribution of securities purchased from persons in a control relation with the issuer.

"Turning to the present Section 3(a)(9), I call your attention to the fact that, although this Section in terms excepts *securities* issued in certain transactions of exchange, its predecessor, Section 4(3) exempted only such *transactions* of exchange. Consequently, before the 1934 amendments, distribution by a controlling person through an underwriter of stock previously issued in a transaction exempt under form Section 4(3), was subject to the registration requirements. The reasons for the relevant amendment therefore become important.

"The question early arose whether dealers' transactions in securities exchanged in a Section 4(3) transaction were exempt from the registration requirements of the Securities Act. Section 4(1) specifically excepts from the dealers' exemption

" 'transactions within one year after the first date upon which a security was bona fide offered to the public';

but in order to effectuate the evident purpose of the Act, the Federal Trade Commission took the position that dealers' transactions in securities originally issued in a transaction exempt under Section 4(3) were exempt, even though such dealers' transactions were effected within a year of the first offering of such securities.

"That the purpose of the amendment changing Section 4(3) to Sections 3(a)(9) and 3(a)(10) was to incorporate in the Act this opinion of the Commission appears from the statement of the report of the Conference Committee which considered these amendments.

" 'The amendments adding new sections 3(a)(9), 3(a)(10), and 3(a)(11) are based upon sections 4(3) and 5(c) of the original act, which are proposed to be repealed. By placing these exemptions under Section 3 it is made clear that securities entitled to exemption on original issuance retain their exemption; if the issuer is not obliged to register in order to make the original distribution, dealers within a year are subject to no restriction against dealing in the securities. The result is in line with the Commission's interpretation of the act as it stood before, but the amendment removes all doubt as to its correctness.' H.R. 1838, 73d Cong., 2d Sess., p. 40.

"This language clearly evidences that the Congressional intent was merely to offer a more adequate statutory basis for the Commission's previous interpretation, and not to alter the fundamental requirement of Section 2(11).

"Moreover, the fact that the securities in question fall within Section 3(a) does not necessarily preclude consideration of the necessity of their registration before certain transactions therein can be effected. Sections 3(a)(2) to 3(a)(8) inclusive describe classes of securities which are of such an intrinsic nature that it is evident that Congress felt that, regardless of the character of the transaction in which they have been or are to be issued or publicly offered, their registration was not necessary for the protection of investors. On the other hand, your letter calls attention to the fact that Section 3(a)(1), the exemption of which is predicated upon the *time of issuance or offering* of securities, regardless of their intrinsic nature, excepts from this exemption 'new offerings * * * by underwriters'. As your letter further states, the basis of the exemption of Section 3(a)(9) is only *'the circumstances surrounding the * * * issue'*. This view of Section 3(a)(9) is further borne out by the report of the Committee which considered the predecessor Section 4(3). H.R. 152, 73d Cong., 1st Sess., p. 25. The analogy seems to me compelling; there is nothing in the intrinsic nature of securities falling within Section 3(a)(1) or Section 3(a)(9) which justifies their permanent exemption from registration. In the language of House Report No. 85, quoted supra, a large public offering of such securities possesses all the dangers attendant upon a new offering by their issuer.

"It seems clear that a construction of Section 3(a)(9) as permanently exempting securities offered in a transaction falling within that section, even though such securities were subsequently newly offered by persons controlling the issuer, finds no rational basis. Furthermore, the language of House Report No. 85, quoted earlier in this letter, definitely indicates that the amendment which changed Section 4(3) to Section 3(a)(9) was intended only to clarify the application of the registration requirements to dealers' transactions, and was not intended to cut into the fundamental principle embodied in Section 2(11)—that persons in control of an issuer be treated as the equivalent of the issuer.

"In view of the Congressional purpose in enacting the last sentence of Section 2(11), the legislative history of the present Section 3(a)(9), and the lack of any rational basis for the continuance of the exemption provided by Section 3(a)(9) to a later offering of securities by an underwriter, it is my opinion that securities received in a Section 3(a)(9) exchange should be registered before their public distribution through an underwriter by a person in control of their issuer."

SECURITIES ACT RELEASE NO. 2029
Securities and Exchange Commission.
August 8, 1939.

[Letter of General Counsel Relating to Sections 3(a)(9) and 4(1).]

* * *

You have requested an opinion as to the applicability of Section 3(a)(9) and the second clause of Section 4(1) of the Securities Act of 1933 in the following circumstances:

The subject company has an "open end" mortgage upon its properties, the only issue of bonds now outstanding thereunder being denoted as Series A bonds. It is proposed to create two new series of bonds under the mortgage, to be called Series B and Series C bonds respectively, for the purpose of refunding the outstanding bonds. The Series B and Series C bonds will differ substantially from each other in respect of maturity date, interest rate, redemption prices and default provisions.

The Series B bonds will be offered in exchange to the holders of the outstanding Series A bonds on the basis of an equal principal amount of Series B bonds for those of Series A, with interest adjustment. No commission or other remuneration will be paid or given, directly or indirectly, for soliciting such exchange.

The necessary funds to redeem any unexchanged Series A bonds will be raised by the sale for cash of Series C bonds. The Series C bonds will be offered and sold to not more than twelve insurance companies, which will agree to purchase for investment and without a view to distribution.

If the proposed exchange offer and the proposed cash offer were isolated transactions, it would be clear that no registration under the Securities Act would be required. The Series B bonds would be exempted as securities "exchanged by the issuer with its existing security holders exclusively where no commission or other remuneration is paid or given directly or indirectly for soliciting such exchange;" and the offering and sale of the Series C bonds would be exempted by the second clause of Section 4(1), as "transactions by an issuer not involving any public offering." The interdependence of the two offerings, however, requires a more comprehensive analysis of the Act.

Section 3(a)(9) contains no language expressly limiting the exemption to securities forming part of an issue the whole of which is sold as specified in the exempting provision. At first reading, therefore, Section 3(a)(9) appears to confer exemption upon any security exchanged with the issuer's existing security holders, even though other securities of the same class, as a part of the same plan of financing, are sold to others than existing security holders, or to existing security holders otherwise than by way of exchange. Such a construction, however, gives insufficient weight to the use of the word "exclusively," as employed both in Section 3(a)(9) and in its predecessor, former Section 4(3). In neither section is the grammatical function of the word entirely clear; but in order to avoid an interpretation which would reject the word as pure surplusage, it is necessary to adopt the view that the exemption is available only to securities constituting part of an issue which, as a whole, is exchanged in conformity with the requirements of the section.

This conclusion appears to be supported by the legislative history of Section 3(a)(9). At the time of the amendment of the Securities Act of 1933 by Title II of the Securities Exchange Act of 1934, the new Section 3(a)(9) proposed in H.R. 9323 as a substitute for the first clause of Section 4(3), provided an exemption from registration for "any security issued by a person where the issue of which it is a part is exchanged by it with its own security holders exclusively." The proposed amendment was altered in conference so as to eliminate any reference to the "issue" of which a security is a part; but it appears from the Statement of the Managers on the Part of the House in the Conference Report that the changes in the proposed Section 3(a)(9) made in conference were "intended only to clarify its meaning" (H.R. (Conf.) Rep. No. 1838, 73rd Cong., 2nd Sess., p. 40).

Interpretation of the so-called "private offering" exemption provided by the second clause of Section 4(1) presents similar considerations. You will note that the clause in question does not exempt every transaction which is not itself a public offering, but only transactions "not involving any public offering." Accordingly, I am of the opinion that the exemption is not available to securities privately offered if any other securities comprised within the same issue are made the subject of a public offering.

It appears, therefore, that both with respect to Section 3(a)(9) and with respect to Section 4(1) the necessity of registering the Series B and Series C bonds depends upon whether they should be deemed separate issues or merely parts of a single issue. I believe it unnecessary at this time to enter into any extended discussion of what constitutes an "issue" for the purposes of the Act. The opinion of the Commission in In the Matter of Unity Gold Corporation (Securities Act Release No. 1776) discusses this question as it arises under Section 3(b) of the Act. The point is also touched upon, at least inferentially, in the discussion of Section 3(a)(11) contained in Securities Act Release No. 1459. Whatever may be the precise limits of the concept of "issue" when all securities involved are of the same class, I do not believe that securities of different classes can fairly be deemed parts of a single "issue." Since on the facts submitted the Series B and Series C bonds appear to be securities of different classes, they constitute separate "issues," and may be offered and sold in the manner above described without being registered under the Securities Act.

In expressing this opinion I do not mean to imply that any difference in the incidents of two blocks of securities, however trivial, renders the blocks separate classes and consequently separate "issues" for the purposes of the

Act. In this case, however, the differences between the Series B and Series C bonds are, I believe, sufficiently substantial to warrant treating them as separate classes even though they will be issued under the same mortgage indenture.

For a discussion of a variety of uses to which § 3(a)(9) may be put, see 7 J. Hicks, Exempted Transactions Under the Securities Act of 1933, c. 2 (1986 rev.)

SECTION 3. REORGANIZATIONS AND RECLAS-SIFICATIONS: THE "NO–SALE" RULE AND ITS ABOLITION

A. RULE 133 AND THE "NO–SALE" THEORY

Excerpt from:

"DISCLOSURE TO INVESTORS"—REPORT AND RECOMMEN-DATIONS TO THE SECURITIES AND EXCHANGE COM-MISSION FROM THE DISCLOSURE POLICY STUDY, "THE WHEAT REPORT", pp. 251–278 (1969)

* * *

BUSINESS COMBINATIONS

Business combinations in which payment by the acquiring corporation is made in its own securities are effected in three standard ways: (1) a voluntary exchange of securities, (2) a statutory merger or consolidation, and (3) a sale of the assets of the acquired company in exchange for securities of the acquiring company, which are thereupon transferred to the seller's shareholders on its dissolution.

Where method (1) is used, an offer of securities of the acquiring corporation is made directly to the shareholders of the acquired corporation. In methods (2) and (3), the shareholders of the corporation to be acquired are asked to cast their individual votes for or against approval of the acquisition, or, in realistic terms, for or against a legal procedure by which their present shareholdings are exchanged for shares in another company.

Employment of method (1) subjects the transaction to the disclosure requirements of the '33 Act. Employment of methods (2) or (3) does not. The reason for this lies in the existence of a longstanding Commission rule (Rule 133) under which the submission of the acquisition transactions to the vote of shareholders is not deemed to involve a "sale" or "offer to sell" the shares of the acquiring company so far as those shareholders are concerned.

Rule 133 has led a controversial life. It seems clear to the Study that its theoretical basis—the notion that the change in the stockholdings of the shareholders of the acquired corporation occurs exclusively through "corporate action"—is, in the words of Professor Loss, "unforgivably formalistic."

* * * *

(e) *Rule 133*

The administrative practice ∗ ∗ ∗ was given the status of a Commission rule in August, 1951. The new Rule 133 expressly stated that the Commission considers mergers, consolidations and similar transactions not to involve a "sale," but only for purposes of Section 5 of the '33 Act.

Within five years, however, the Commission was persuaded that the position it had taken in the "no sale" rule should be reexamined. Notice was published in October, 1956 that the Commission had under consideration a complete reversal of Rule 133. The proposed amendment to the Rule provided affirmatively that all mergers, consolidations and similar transactions should be deemed to involve the offer and sale of securities. The Commission's release did not suggest how registration under the '33 Act was to be effected in these transactions. It was observed, however, that provision would be made so that information furnished in a '33 Act prospectus would not be "unnecessarily duplicated" in a proxy statement where the Commission's proxy rules applied.

Adverse reaction to the Commission's proposal was strong. Many of the comments observed that disclosure was needed in these transactions but that it should be provided by the furnishing of a proxy statement. The Commission was urged to seek legislation which would subject over-the-counter companies to the proxy rules. The Commission determined to defer action on the proposal pending further study.

In September, 1958, the Commission published a proposal to revise Rule 133 by specifying those persons deemed to be "underwriters" of the securities newly issued in mergers, consolidations and similar transactions. Persons controlling the acquired corporation in such transactions, although not in control of the surviving corporation, were defined as "underwriters" if they acquired their newly issued shares with a view to distribution. However, their subsequent sales were not deemed to be "distributions" requiring registration if they occurred in brokerage transactions subject to limitations identical to those contained in the Commission's Rule 154.

The accompanying release observed that the new proposal was based upon certain conclusions reached by the Commission's staff after detailed examination of all relevant statutory materials, prior Commission and staff actions, and the various arguments which had come to its attention. ∗ ∗ ∗

The ultimate conclusion of the staff was ∗ ∗ ∗ (1) that the procedural and liability provisions of the '33 Act as they affect issuers, underwriters and dealers would not operate reasonably and effectively in the types of transactions covered by Rule 133, and (2) that, despite its view that the transactions described in Rule 133 come within the definition of "sale" in Section 2(3) of the '33 Act, it would be reasonable for the Commission to declare by appropriate interpretation of statutory language that such transactions do not involve "offers" or "sales" for purposes of the registration requirements.

In July, 1959 the amendments to Rule 133 proposed in September of the previous year were adopted with modifications. No subsequent material changes have been made in the Rule.

(f) *When does Rule 133 apply?*

The July, 1959 amendments to Rule 133 reflect certain limitations on the scope of that Rule which had been articulated in two important cases. In its Great Sweet Grass opinion,[15] the Commission stated that the Rule did not mean that securities issued in a business combination of the type described in the rule are "free" securities which can thereafter be offered and sold to the general public without registration. The District Court in the Micro-Moisture case[16] held that Rule 133 provides no exemption from registration for the sale of stock received in a stock-for-assets reorganization by persons who acquired control of the issuing corporation in the transaction.

* * * *

* * * Rule 133 leaves a decided disclosure gap when the company to be acquired is publicly held but has not registered with the Commission under Section 12 of the '34 Act.

* * * *

This disclosure gap has become more acute as the number of business combinations has continued to rise.

* * * *

A renewed attempt must be made to solve the problems associated with business combinations. The following guideposts are suggested:

(a) Commission policy should recognize the fact that when a shareholder is asked to vote on the question whether or not his company should be acquired by another and, accordingly, whether or not he wishes to exchange his shares for the securities of the acquired company, an offer of a security within the meaning of the '33 Act is made to him;

(b) When the offering to such shareholders constitutes a "public offering" within the meaning of the '33 Act, Commission policy should be to give the shareholders of the company to be acquired a disclosure document containing the information essential to an intelligent choice;

(c) When the offering to such shareholders constitutes a nonpublic offering under the '33 Act, Commission policy should be to provide the shareholders of the company to be acquired with clear and appropriate guidelines as to where and how they can resell the new shares which they have received. Such guidelines should eliminate the unwarranted distinctions which presently exist between a business combination accomplished by a voluntary exchange of shares on the one hand, and one which takes the form of a statutory merger or sale of assets on the other.

* * * *

15. Great Sweet Grass Oils, Ltd., 37 S.E.C. 683 (1957), aff'd per curiam sub nom. Great Sweet Grass Oils, Ltd. v. SEC, 256 F.2d 893 (D.C.Cir.1958); Kroy Oils, Ltd., 37 S.E.C. 683 (1957), petition for review withdrawn sub nom. Kroy Oils, Ltd. v. SEC, D.C.Cir., No. 13,920, Dec. 10, 1958.

16. SEC v. Micro-Moisture Controls, Inc., 148 F.Supp. 558 (S.D.N.Y.1957) (preliminary injunction), reargument denied, CCH Fed.Sec.L.Rep. ¶ 90,805 (S.D.N.Y. 1957) final injunction, 167 F.Supp. 716 (S.D.N.Y.1958), aff'd sub nom. SEC v. Culpepper, 270 F.2d 241 (2d Cir. 1959).

B. REGISTRATION AND DISCLOSURE REQUIREMENTS IN BUSINESS COMBINATIONS UNDER RULE 145 AND FORM S-4

Statutes and Regulations

Securities Act: Rules 145, 153A and Form S-4.

Exchange Act Rules: 14a-2, 14a-6, 14a-9, 14c-5.

SECURITIES ACT RELEASE NO. 5316

Securities and Exchange Commission.
October 6, 1972.

NOTICE OF ADOPTION OF RULES 145, AND 153A, PROSPECTIVE RESCISSION OF RULE 133, AMENDMENT OF FORM S-14[a] UNDER THE SECURITIES ACT OF 1933 AND AMENDMENT OF RULES 14a-2, 14a-6 AND 14c-5 UNDER THE SECURITIES EXCHANGE ACT OF 1934

The Securities and Exchange Commission today announced the adoption of Rule 145 under the Securities Act of 1933 ("Act") and several related proposals and the prospective rescission of Rule 133 under that Act. The effect of this action will be to subject transactions involving business combinations of types described in the new rule to the registration requirements of the Act. * * *

    * * *

BACKGROUND AND PURPOSE

Congress, in enacting the federal securities statutes, created a continuous disclosure system designed to protect investors and to assure the maintenance of fair and honest securities markets. The Commission in administering and implementing the objectives of these statutes has sought to coordinate and integrate this disclosure system, and the rescission of Rule 133 and adoption of Rule 145 and related matters are further steps in this direction.

    * * *

Rule 145 is * * * intended to inhibit the creation of public markets in securities of issuers about which adequate current information is not available to the public. This approach is consistent with the philosophy underlying the Act, that a disclosure law provides the best protection for investors. If a security holder who is offered a new security in a Rule 145 business combination transaction has available to him the material facts about the transaction, he will be in a position to make an informed investment judgment. In order to provide such information in connection with public offerings of these securities, Rule 145 will require the filing of a registration statement with the Commission and the delivery to security

---

a. Form S-14 has been replaced by Form S-4, effective July 1, 1985. Securities Act Release No. 6578 (Apr. 23, 1985).

holders of a prospectus containing accurate and current information concerning the proposed business combination transaction.

EXPLANATION AND ANALYSIS

I. *Rescission of Rule 133. Definition for Purposes of Section 5 of "Sale," "Offer to Sell," and "Offer for Sale."*

Rule 133 provides that for purposes only of Section 5 of the Act, the submission to a vote of stockholders of a corporation of a proposal for certain mergers, consolidations, reclassifications of securities or transfers of assets is not deemed to involve a "sale", "offer", "offer to sell", or "offer for sale" of the securities of the new or surviving corporation to the security holders of the disappearing corporation. That rule further provides that persons who are affiliates of the constituent corporation are deemed to be underwriters within the meaning of the Section 2(11) of the Act, and except for certain limited amounts cannot sell their securities in the surviving corporation without registration.

The "no-sale" theory embodied in Rule 133 is based on the rationale that the types of transactions specified in the rule are essentially corporate acts, and the volitional act on the part of the individual stockholder required for a "sale" was absent. The basis of this theory was that the exchange or alteration of the stockholder's security occurred not because he consented thereto, but because the corporate action, authorized by a specified majority of the interests affected, converted his security into a different security.

Based on the Commission's experience in administering the provisions of the Act and Rule 133 thereunder, and having given consideration to the Disclosure Policy Study Report, to the comments received * * * [to the Commission's previous proposals to revise Rule 133 and to adopt Rule 145], the Commission is of the view that the "no-sale" approach embodied in Rule 133 overlooks the substance of the transactions specified therein and ignores the fundamental nature of the relationship between the stockholders and the corporation. The fact that such relationships are in part controlled by statutory provisions of the state of incorporation does not preclude as a matter of law the application of the broad concepts of "sale", "offer", "offer to sell", and "offer for sale" in Section 2(3) of the Act which are broader than the commercial or common law meanings of such terms.

Transactions of the type described in Rule 133 do not, in the Commission's opinion, occur solely by operation of law without the element of individual stockholder volition. A stockholder faced with a Rule 133 proposal must decide on his own volition whether or not the proposal is one in his own best interest. The basis on which the "no-sale" theory is predicated, namely, that the exchange or alteration of the stockholder's security occurs not because he consents thereto but because the corporation by authorized corporate action converts his securities, in the Commission's opinion, is at best only correct in a formalistic sense and overlooks the reality of the transaction. The corporate action, on which such great emphasis is placed, is derived from the individual consent given by each stockholder in voting on a proposal to merge or consolidate a business or reclassify a security. In voting, each consenting stockholder is expressing his voluntary and individual acceptance of the new security, and generally the disapproving stockholder is deferring his decision as to whether to accept the new security or, if he exercises his dissenter's rights, a cash payment. The corporate action in these circumstances, therefore, is not some type of independent fiat, but is only the aggregate effect of the voluntary decisions made by the individual stockholders to accept or reject the exchange. Formalism should no longer deprive investors of the disclosure to which they are entitled.

The Commission also is aware that Rule 133 has caused anomalous applications of the provisions of the securities laws. For example, transactions which are deemed not to involve "sales" for purposes of Section 5 of the Act, nevertheless are deemed to be "purchases" for purposes of Section 16 of the Exchange Act. Moreover, transactions which are not deemed to be "sales" for purposes of Section 5 of the Act, nevertheless are deemed to be "sales" for purposes of the anti-fraud provisions of the Act and Exchange Act and "sales" for purposes of the Public Utility Holding Company Act of 1935, the Trust Indenture Act of 1939, and the Investment Company Act of 1940.

In addition, the Commission has difficulty in reconciling Rule 133 with certain exemptive provisions of the Act. For example, Section 3(a)(9) of the Act exempts from the registration provisions of the Act the issuance of securities in a reclassification only where no commission or other remuneration is paid or given directly or indirectly for solicitation. Notwithstanding, Rule 133 in effect provides an exemption from registration for the issuance of securities in a reclassification even though a commission or other remuneration is paid for solicitation. Further, Section 3(a)(10) exempts from the registration provisions of the Act securities issued only in court or administratively supervised reorganizations. Yet Rule 133 in effect provides that securities issued in reorganizations of the type described therein are not subject to the registration provisions of the Act even though there is no judicial or administrative supervision.

Furthermore, the Commission is aware of situations in which companies have utilized the Rule to avoid or evade the registration provisions of the Act. This has resulted in large quantities of unregistered securities being distributed to the public and has not been in the public interest or for the protection of investors.

The Commission recognizes that the "no-sale" concept has been in existence in one form or another for a long period of time. Certain persons who commented on the ＊ ＊ ＊ [previous proposals with respect to Rule 133 and Rule 145] have cited this as a reason for retaining the present Rule 133 and others have asserted that the Commission lacks the power to revise the rule. The Commission does not agree with these comments. Administrative agencies as well as courts from time to time change their interpretation of statutory provisions in the light of reexamination, new considerations, or changing conditions which indicate that earlier interpretations are no longer in keeping with the statutory objectives. The Commission believes, after a thorough reexamination of the studies and proposals cited above, that the interpretation embodied in Rule 133 is no longer consistent with the statutory objectives of the Act. The Commission's judgment is based upon a number of factors, including the observation that Rule 133 has enabled large amounts of securities to be distributed to the public without the protections afforded by the Act's registration provisions.

In view of the above, the Commission is of the opinion that transactions covered by Rule 133 involve a "sale", "offer", "offer to sell", or "offer for sale" as those terms are defined in Section 2(3) of the Act. The Commission no longer sees any persuasive reason why, as a matter of statutory construction or policy, in light of the broad remedial purposes of the Act and of public policy which strongly supports registration, this should not be the interpretative meaning.

II. *Adoption of Rule 145. Reclassifications of Securities, Mergers, Consolidations and Acquisitions of Assets.*

* * * *

B. Rule 145(a). Transactions Within the Rule

Paragraph (a) of Rule 145 provides that the submission to a vote of security holders of a proposal for certain reclassifications of securities, mergers, consolidations, or transfers of assets, is deemed to involve an "offer", "offer to sell", "offer for sale", or "sale" of the securities to be issued in the transaction. The effect of the Rule is to require registration of the securities to be issued in connection with such transactions, unless an exemption from registration is available. * * *

In response to comments received from the public, several textual changes have been made in Rule 145(a) as proposed. As noticed for comment, the rule by its literal language only applied to business combinations involving "corporations". Rule 133 was intended to apply to business combinations involving corporations as well as other entities, such as partnerships and real estate investment trusts. Accordingly, the rule has been revised to read "corporation or other person" in order to make clear that it applies to all issuers, without distinction as to the form of business organization. Also, the phrase "certificate of incorporation" has been revised to read "certificate of incorporation or similar controlling instruments."

A number of comments focused upon the question of whether foreign issuers should be included within the scope of Rule 145. * * * The United States securities statutes were intended to protect United States investors who buy securities of foreign issuers, and the need for the protections afforded by registration is not diminished because the issuer has a foreign domicile. Accordingly, Rule 145 will apply to foreign issuers making offers or sales of securities to United States investors, unless an exemption is available under the Securities Act. While it is noted that difficulties in meeting required accounting standards may arise for foreign issuers, the Commission has authority under Regulation S–X to waive or modify accounting requirements, and, to the extent applicable, Item 15(c) under the proxy rules allows the Commission to authorize the omission or substitution of financial statements. Various other forms contain similar provisions. The staff of the Commission will be available for consultation on such matters. To clarify the applicability of Rule 145 to foreign issuers, the phrase "state of incorporation" has been changed to read "jurisdiction".

Also in response to public comments, Rule 145 has been revised to make clear that it covers transactions involving action taken upon security holder approval. The words "or consent" have been added to the word "vote" wherever it appears.

1. Rule 145(a)(1). Reclassifications.

Rule 145(a), as proposed, covered any reclassification "other than a stock split or reverse stock split which involves the substitution of a security for another security." The rule has been revised to also exclude any reclassification which involves only a change in par value.

2. Rule 145(a)(2). Mergers or Consolidations.

Rule 145(a)(2) has been revised in three respects. The first revision adds the phrase "or similar plan of acquisition" after the words "merger or consolidation" because a number of similar transactions do not fit precisely within the terms "merger or consolidation". The second revision adds the phrase "held by such security holders" to describe those securities which will become or be exchanged for other securities. This revision is designed to clarify that in a transaction of the character described in Rule 145(a), an offer occurs under the rule only as to security holders who are entitled to vote or consent to the matter, and who hold securities which become or will be exchanged for new securities. The third revision adds an exception to indicate that registration is not required where a merger or consolidation is effected solely to change an issuer's domicile.[b]

Several commentators suggested that the applicability of Rule 145 to short-form mergers should be clarified. In certain instances, state law allows a merger of a parent and its 85 to 90 percent owned subsidiary to be consummated without shareholder approval. Because Rule 145(a) is couched in terms of offers arising in connection with a submission for the vote or consent of security holders, short-form mergers not requiring such vote or consent are not within the scope of the Rule. However, if a security is to be issued in such short-form mergers, the Commission is of the opinion that the transaction involves an "offer", "offer to sell", "offer for sale" or "sale", within the meaning of Section 2(3) of the Act, and accordingly such transactions are subject to the registration provisions of the Act unless an exemption is available.

3. Rule 145(a)(3). Transfers of Assets.

Rule 145(a)(3) has been revised to clarify those conditions under which Rule 145 is applicable to a stock for assets transaction. As revised, the rule applies only if: (1) the matter voted upon provides for dissolution of the corporation receiving the securities; (2) the matter voted upon provides for a pro rata distribution by the corporation receiving the securities; (3) the directors of the corporation receiving the securities adopt resolutions relative to (1) or (2) within one year after the vote; or (4) a subsequent dissolution or distribution is part of a pre-existing plan for distribution. However, if the securities acquired in the transaction are distributed after one year, notwithstanding the absence of a plan, such securities must be registered unless a statutory exemption from registration is then available.

With regard to the third condition above, if the vote of the stockholders of the selling corporation is taken to authorize the sale, and the selling corporation thereafter decides to dissolve or distribute the securities within one year after the transaction, the sale of assets and the dissolution or

---

b. Rule 145(a)(2) has been amended to make clear that the change of domicile exception does not apply when a change in national jurisdiction is involved. Securities Act Release No. 6579 (Apr. 23, 1985).

distribution by the selling corporation are deemed to be portions of the same transaction and to involve a sale for value of the purchasing corporation's stock to the shareholders of the selling corporation. Accordingly, the transaction should be registered on Form [S–4] at the time the plan or agreement for the sale of assets is submitted to shareholders for their vote or consent if it is contemplated that the corporation receiving the securities will adopt resolutions within one year for dissolution or distribution of the securities received. If the transaction is not registered at the time of submission of the plan or agreement for the vote or consent of security holders, but a resolution for dissolution or distribution of the securities received is adopted within one year, the issuer should file a registration statement covering the dissolution or distribution of securities on the appropriate form other than Form [S–4], unless an exemption is available.

C. Rule 145(b). Communications Not Deemed to Be a "Prospectus" or "Offer to Sell"

Notice of a proposed action or of a meeting of security holders for voting on transactions of the character specified in Rule 145 is generally sent or furnished to security holders. Because the Rule will make the registration provisions of the Act applicable to these transactions, questions have been raised as to whether such notices will constitute statutory prospectuses or involve an offer for sale of a security. Paragraph (b) of Rule 145 is designed to resolve these questions by providing that any written communication which contains no more than the information specified in paragraph (b) of the Rule shall not be deemed a prospectus for purposes of Section 2(10) of the Act and shall not be deemed an "offer for sale" of the security involved for the purposes of Section 5 of the Act.

Rule 145(b) has been revised to expand the permissible information that may be included in the announcement. The revised Rule permits the identification of all parties to the transaction; a brief description of their business; a description of the basis upon which the transaction will be made; and any legend or similar statement required by federal law or state or administrative authority. Also, paragraph (b) of the Rule has been revised to indicate that the notice may take the form of a written communication "or other published statement."

D. Rule 145(c). Persons and Parties Deemed to Be Underwriters

Rule 145(c), as proposed, contained specific criteria designed to clarify the underwriter status of persons who acquire substantial amounts of securities in a business combination registered on Form [S–4], and who desire to resell such securities. The public comments on the proposal noted legal and policy arguments against any interpretation that imposes statutory underwriter status on persons solely by virtue of their receiving more than a certain amount of securities in a business combination. In addition, technical problems were cited in the application of the percentage tests in proposed Rule 145(c), and it was suggested that underwriter's liability should not be imposed on persons who may not be in a position to perform any necessary due diligence investigation. Others described the practical and regulatory problems that would arise if banks, investment companies, arbitrageurs and others enter into a Rule 145 transaction with marketable securities, but receive securities subject to trading restrictions. Because the question of the underwriter status of persons taking substantial portions of registered offerings arises in connection with all registered offerings, the Commission believes that the matter should be dealt with in a more comprehensive manner after further study, and not just in the limited context of business combinations.

Accordingly, Rule 145(c) has been revised by deleting the quantitative standards contained in the proposal and in lieu thereof criteria patterned after those now contained in Rule 133 have been substituted. Revised paragraph (c) of the Rule provides that any party to any transaction specified in Rule 145(a), other than the issuer, or any person who is an affiliate of such party at the time any such transaction is submitted for vote or consent, who offers or sells securities acquired in such transaction, shall be deemed to be engaged in a distribution and therefore an underwriter, except with respect to the limited resales permitted pursuant to paragraph (d) of Rule 145. Moreover, from a practical standpoint, because such persons usually are in a position to verify the accuracy of information set forth in the registration statement, and usually are in a position to influence the transaction, the Commission believes that this provision is not unreasonably burdensome.

Rule 145(c) includes a definition of the term "party" with respect to the phrase "any party to any transaction specified in paragraph (a) * * *" The term is defined to mean the corporations, business entities, or other persons, other than the issuer, whose assets or capital structure are affected by the transaction specified in paragraph (a).

The securities received in a Rule 145 transaction by persons who are neither affiliates of the acquired company nor of the acquiring company are registered securities without restriction on resale.

E.   Rule 145(d).   Resale Provisions For Persons and
Parties Deemed Underwriters

Rule 145(d) provides that a person or party specified in paragraph (c) shall not be deemed to be engaged in a distribution if he sells in accordance with certain provisions of Rule 144: paragraph (c) (Current Public Information); (e) (Limitation on Amount of Securities Sold); (f) (Manner of Sale); and (g) (Brokers' Transactions). This provision is designed to permit public sale by such persons or parties in ordinary trading transactions of limited quantities of securities. Such resales are permissible within successive six-month periods, but no accumulation is permitted, i.e., the person cannot skip six months and then sell an accumulated amount in the following six months.[c]

The volume limitations of Rule 144(e) for resales of securities listed on a national securities exchange may be determined by reference to the average weekly trading volume for the four weeks preceding receipt of the order by the broker to execute the transaction. It should be noted that the holding period requirement of Rule 144(d), and the requirement to file a Form 144 pursuant to Rule 144(h) are not applicable. In addition to resales

---

c. Rule 145(d) has been amended to permit a non-affiliate of the issuer who has held such securities for at least two years, where the issuer meets the reporting requirements of Rule 144(c), to make resales of the securities without restriction. A non-affiliate who has held the securities for at least three years is free to make resales without any restrictions. Securities Act Release No. 6508 (Feb. 10, 1984).

permitted by Rule 145(d), Form [S–4] may be used for the registration under the Act of distributions by persons or parties who are deemed underwriters.[d]

F. Rule 145(e). Definition of "Person"

Paragraph (e) of Rule 145 provides that the term "person" in paragraphs (c) and (d) of the rule when used with reference to a person for whose account securities are to be sold, shall have the same meaning as the definition of that term in paragraph (a)(2) of Rule 144 under the Act.

III. *Rule 153A. Definition of "Preceded by a Prospectus" as used in Section 5(b)(2) of the Act, in Relation to Certain Transactions Requiring Approval of Security Holders.*

Rule 153A defines the phrase "preceded by a prospectus" in connection with transactions of the type subject to Rule 145. The rule has been revised in two respects. First, the word "delivery" has been substituted for the word "sending" to conform the Rule to the General Instructions in [Form S–4]. Second, the Rule has been revised to apply the delivery requirement when action is taken by consent.

The persons entitled to vote on or consent to a Rule 145 transaction will usually be determined either: (1) by the fixing of a record date for shareholders so entitled or, (2) by the closing of the stock transfer records of the acquired company. The group of persons thus determined may, because of interim transfers, vary somewhat from the group of persons ultimately entitled to receive the securities issued in the transaction. Thus, Rule 153A provides that the delivery of the final prospectus to security holders entitled to vote on or consent to the transaction shall be deemed to satisfy the prospectus delivery requirements of Section 5(b)(2) of the Act.

* * *

SECURITIES ACT RELEASE NO. 5463
Securities and Exchange Commission.
February 28, 1974.

DIVISION OF CORPORATION FINANCE'S INTERPRETATIONS OF RULE 145 AND RELATED MATTERS

* * *

The following illustrations, which are intended to supplement the explanation and analysis of Rule 145 set forth in Securities Act Release No. 5316, reflect the views of the Division of Corporation Finance as of the date

---

d. Rule 145(d) permits resales pursuant to Rule 144. Rule 144(e) has been amended: (1) to reduce the six-month measuring period on volume limitations to three months; (2) revise the standard used to determine the amount of securities which may be sold within any measuring period for both unlisted and listed securities to permit the sale of the *greater* of one percent of the outstanding securities of a class, or the average weekly trading volume of the four calendar weeks preceding the sale; and (3) to permit the trading volume on unlisted securities traded on NASDAQ to be measured by NASDAQ trading volume. Securities Act Release No. 5979 (Sept. 9, 1979); Securities Act Release No. 5995 (Nov. 8, 1978); Securities Exchange Act Release No. 16589 (Feb. 19, 1980).

of this release notwithstanding any previous interpretations expressed to the contrary by the Division orally or in writing: It should be assumed in each of the following illustrations that the use of the means and instruments of interstate commerce or of the mails is involved and that no statutory exemption is applicable unless so stated.

I. *Relationship of Rule 145 to Exemptions Set Forth in Sections 3 and 4 of the Act (See generally Preliminary Note to Rule 145).*

Illustration A

Facts: X Company proposes to issue common stock in exchange for the assets of Y Company after Y Company obtains the approval of its several stockholders, as required by state law, with respect to an agreement setting forth the terms and conditions of the exchange and providing for a distribution of the X Company common stock to the Y Company stockholders. X Company has determined that the private offering exemption afforded by Section 4(2) of the Act would be available for the transaction.

Question: In light of Rule 145, may X Company choose between relying upon the private offering exemption available under Section 4(2) and registering the securities to be issued in the transaction on Form [S–4]?

Interpretative Response: Yes, X Company may choose between relying upon the private offering exemption available under Section 4(2) and registering the securities to be issued in the transaction on Form [S–4]. Rule 145 does not affect statutory exemptions which are otherwise available. However, by virtue of Rule 145(a)(3)(B), X Company may register the securities to be issued in the transaction on Form [S–4] so that an affiliate of Y Company would be able to resell immediately his securities pursuant to the registration statement, if such resales are so disclosed in the registration statement, or subject to the limitations referred to in Rule 145(d).

Illustration B

Facts: X Company, an insurance company organized and regulated under the laws of State A, intends to establish Y Company, a corporation organized under the laws of State A, and to effect a Rule 145 type transaction which would result in Y Company becoming a statutory insurance holding company and the stockholders of X Company receiving securities of Y Company in return for their holdings. Among other things, the laws of State A, in this type of situation, expressly authorize its Commissioner of Insurance to hold a hearing and to make a finding on the fairness to the stockholders of X Company of the terms and the conditions of the transaction. The Commissioner is required to give appropriate notice of the hearing, and of their right to appear, to all stockholders of X Company prior to the hearing.

Question: Assuming that the Commissioner holds such a hearing and makes the appropriate findings, may Y Company rely upon the exemption afforded by Section 3(a)(10) of the Act notwithstanding that the transaction comes within Rule 145?

Interpretative Response: Yes. Rule 145 does not affect the availability of any exemption which is otherwise available so that an issuer may rely upon the exemption afforded by Section 3(a)(10) of the Act if all of the conditions of that exemption are met. Inasmuch as Section 3(a)(10) provides an exemption for the initial issuance of securities but not for the resale of such securities, it should be noted that an issuer may choose to register the securities to be issued in the transaction on Form [S-4] or S-1 in order to be more certain of the status under the Act of public resales by underwriters of securities received in the transaction.

Illustration C

Facts: X Company, a corporation organized and existing under the laws of State A, has a class of preferred stock and a class of common stock outstanding. X Company is now considering a plan of reclassification which, if approved by the requisite majority of each class, would result in X Company having only one class of equity securities outstanding. X Company has determined that it will not utilize the services of a proxy soliciting firm.

Question: May X Company rely upon the exemption afforded by Section 3(a)(9) of the Act notwithstanding that the transaction comes within Rule 145?

Interpretative Response: Yes. Assuming that all the requirements of that exemption are met, then X Company may rely upon the exemption afforded by Section 3(a)(9) of the Act because Rule 145 does not affect the availability of any statutory exemption which is otherwise available.

* * *

II. *Application of Rule 145 to Various Types of Reclassifications and Business Combination Transactions (See Paragraph (a) of Rule 145).*

Illustration A

Facts: X Company has a class of preferred stock and a class of common stock outstanding. As required by the laws of its state of incorporation, X Company intends to submit to both classes of its stockholders a plan of recapitalization, which, if approved by the requisite majority of each class, would provide, among other things, for a three-for-one stock split with respect to the common stock and for a simultaneous exchange of eight shares of common stock for each share of preferred stock. In order to assure adoption of the plan, X Company has retained the services of P Company, a proxy soliciting firm which will actively solicit proxies for approval of the plan.

Question: Inasmuch as P Company is receiving remuneration for its services and the exemption afforded by Section 3(a)(9) of the Act is, accordingly, not available, does Rule 145 require registration of the securities to be issued in connection with the stock split and preferred stock exchange?

Interpretative Response: Yes. Because this single plan of recapitalization involves a reclassification of one class of securities in addition to a stock split of the other class of securities (which in and of itself would not have to be registered under these circumstances because of the exception set forth in Rule 145(a)(1)), the entire transaction would be considered to be a reclassification within the meaning of Rule 145(a)(1) and the securities to be issued in the transaction would have to be registered on Form [S-4] or S-1.

Illustration B

Facts: In order to change its domicile, X Company, a corporation organized and existing under the laws of State A with its only class of outstanding securities registered under the Securities Exchange Act of 1934 ("the Exchange Act"), proposes to effect a statutory merger with Y Company, its newly-created wholly-owned subsidiary which was organized under the laws of State B. Y Company's Articles of Incorporation are similar to X Company's Articles of Incorporation except that Y Company's charter contains a substantially broader corporate purpose provision and authorizes a class of preferred stock. As a result of this proposed transaction, which is subject to stockholder approval, stockholders' pre-emptive rights and cumulative voting rights would be eliminated.

Question: Does Rule 145 require the registration of the securities to be issued in this transaction?

Interpretative Response: No. While a statutory merger is deemed to involve a "sale" within the meaning of Section 2(3) of the Act, Rule 145(a)(2) provides a specific exception "where the sole purpose of the transaction is to change an issuer's domicile [solely within the United States]." Notwithstanding the inclusion of a broader corporate purpose provision and the authorization of another class of securities in the charter and notwithstanding the effects on the pre-emptive and cumulative voting rights of X Company's stockholders, the exception would be applicable. It should be noted that since X Company is a reporting company under the Exchange Act, any changes in stockholders' rights should be disclosed pursuant to the applicable proxy rules.

* * *

Illustration D

Facts: X Bank, chartered under the laws of State A, proposes to enter into an agreement and plan of reorganization which, if approved by its stockholders, will result in X Bank becoming a wholly-owned subsidiary (except for directors' qualifying shares) of a newly-formed holding company, X Bancshares, organized under the laws of State B. Following the reorganization, the former stockholders of X Bank will have the same relative equity interest in X Bancshares; the directors of X Bank will be the directors of X Bancshares; and initially the sole asset of X Bancshares will be the stock of X Bank.

Question: May this transaction be effected without registration under the Act on the basis of the change-in-domicile exception set forth in Rule 145(a)(2)?

Interpretative Response: No. Inasmuch as the transaction involves significant changes in the issuer's basic organizational structure, the exception set forth in Rule 145(a)(2) is not applicable. Accordingly, absent an applicable statutory exemption, the securities issued in the transaction are required to be registered under the Act.

Illustration E

Facts: X Company proposes to acquire at least 80% of the outstanding common stock of Y Company by offering its common stock to the stockholders of Y Company in exchange for their Y Company common stock in a transaction intended to qualify as a taxfree reorganization pursuant to Section 368(a)(1)(B) of the Internal Revenue Code of 1954, as amended.

Question: Is Rule 145 applicable to such an exchange offer so that X Company can utilize Form S–14?

Interpretative Response: No. Rule 145 and Form S–14 are not applicable to "B" type reorganizations. Absent a statutory exemption, the securities issued in the transaction would have to be registered under the Act on Form S–1 or on another form if applicable.[a]

Illustration F

Facts: The board of directors of X Company is considering an offer by Y Company whereby a significant portion (but not substantially all) of X Company's assets will be transferred to Y Company in return for shares of Y Company common stock which would be distributed to the stockholders of X Company on a pro-rata basis. Although not required to do so by state law or by X Company's certificate of incorporation or by-laws, X Company's board of directors will submit the matter to the stockholders of X Company for their authorization.

Question: Assuming that no statutory exemption is available, is Rule 145 applicable to this proposed transaction?

Interpretative Response: Yes. Rule 145(a)(3) states that:

(a) "sale" shall be deemed to be involved, within the meaning of Section 2(3) of the Act, so far as the security holders of a corporation * * * are concerned where, pursuant to statutory provisions * * * or similar controlling instruments, *or otherwise*, there is submitted for the vote or consent of such security holders a plan or agreement for * * * transfers of assets. (emphasis added)

Accordingly, inasmuch as the board of directors in its discretion determined to submit the matter to stockholders, Rule 145 is applicable and the transaction may be registered on Form [S–4] or S–1.

* * *

V. *Related Matters.*

* * *

Illustration B

Facts: X Company has been utilizing a Form S–1 "shelf registration" for the issuance of its securities, and for certain resales thereof, in connection with a series of acquisitions, each of which, in and of itself, might have been effected without registration under the Act by virtue of the intrastate or private offering exemptions afforded by Sections 3(a)(11) and 4(2) of the Act. X Company now intends to make an acquisition by means of a statutory merger subject to Rule 145 for which no other statutory exemption is available.

a. The answer to this question will now be different in light of the replacement of Form S–14 by S–4. Form S–4 is available not only for the registration of securities in connection with Rule 145 transactions but may also be availed of in connection with other mergers such as short form mergers, exchange offers and resales of securities registered on the Form. See General Instructions, paragraph A. (See infra, page 420).

Question B–1: May X Company utilize the Form S–1 shelf registration for the proposed Rule 145 transaction?

Interpretative Response: Yes. Although X Company could file a new registration statement on Form [S–4] or S–1 for the Rule 145 transaction, it can utilize the existing Form S–1 shelf registration statement if sufficient shares are registered and the financial statements and other disclosures are current.

Question B–2: If X Company elects to utilize its shelf registration for the merger, is additional information required to be included in its shelf registration statement?

Interpretative Response: Yes. The information required by Form [S–4] should be set forth in a post-effective amendment to X Company's shelf registration statement.

Illustration C

Facts: X Company intends to effect a short-form merger pursuant to state law whereby its ninety percent owned subsidiary, Y Company, would be merged into X Company without a vote or consent of Y Company's minority stockholders, who would receive common stock of X Company.

Question C–1: Is this transaction subject to the registration requirements set forth in Section 5 of the Act?

Interpretative Response: Yes. The issuance of X Company common stock to the stockholders of Y Company would involve a "sale" within the meaning of Section 2(3) of the Act and, absent a statutory exemption, registration would be required.

Question C–2: May the securities to be issued in this transaction be registered pursuant to the Act on a Form [S–4]?

Interpretative Response: Yes. Although Rule 145 is not applicable because a short-form merger does not involve a vote or consent of all the stockholders, the Division will not object to the use of Form [S–4] for the registration of the securities to be issued in this transaction.

BUSINESS COMBINATIONS AND NEW REGISTRATION FORM S–4

Although Rule 145 in terms is not available for "B" type reorganizations, new Form S–4 extends the principles underlying the integrated disclosure system to all business combination transactions, not just those enumerated in Rule 145. The philosophical underpinnings of Form S–4 are stated in the release adopting that registration form: [1]

Form S–4 provides simplified and streamlined disclosure in prospectuses for business combinations whether the transactions are effected by merger or exchange offer.

The integrated disclosure system, on which Form S–4 is based, proceeds from the premise that investors in the primary market need much the same information as investors in the trading market. Integration also specifies the manner in which information should be delivered to investors. Under Forms S–1, S–2 and S–3, transaction oriented information must be presented

1. Securities Act Release No. 6578 (Apr. 23, 1985).

in the prospectus. Company oriented information, however, may be presented in, delivered with, or incorporated by reference into the prospectus, depending on the extent to which Exchange Act reports containing the information have been disseminated and assimilated in the market. Thus, for registrants qualified to use Form S–3, the most widely followed companies, company specific information that has been included in Exchange Act reports need not be reiterated in the prospectus, but may be incorporated by reference. Registrants qualified to use Form S–2, reporting companies which are less widely followed, must present certain company information, but may do so either by delivering the annual report to security holders or reiterating that level of company information in the prospectus. Finally, S–1 registrants must present all company information in the prospectus.

The prospectus requirements of Form S–4 are divided into four sections. The first section calls for information about the transaction, which will be presented in the prospectus in all cases, and which is designed to make the presentation of the complex transactions that typify business combinations more easily understood by investors. The next two sections specify the information about the businesses involved and prescribe different levels of prospectus presentation and incorporation by reference depending upon which form under the Securities Act the company could use in making a primary offering of its securities not involving a business combination. The last section sets forth the requirements as to voting and management information. All voting information must be presented in the prospectus, while the amount of prospectus presentation for management information, like company information, depends on which form could be used in a primary offering not involving a business combination.

The use of the S–1–2–3 approach in Form S–4 reflects the premise that decisions made in the context of business combination transactions and those made otherwise in the purchase of a security in the primary or trading market are substantially similar. At the same time, the Commission recognizes that there are significant differences. In particular, business combination decisions are not of the same volitional nature as other investment decisions. Moreover, typically mergers may give rise to a change in security ownership as a consequence of inaction.

To address the differences in the nature of the investment decision, special provisions have been included in the Form. First, a specifically tailored item covering risk factors, ratio of earnings to fixed charges, certain per share data and other information must be presented in the prospectus regardless of the level of disclosure available to the companies involved. This item, as adopted, has been expanded to reflect commentators' suggestions that the item include: (1) certain additional financial data; and (2) information about regulatory approvals.

While the item highlights certain information discussed more fully elsewhere in the prospectus, or in documents incorporated by reference therein, it is not intended to be a summary of all material information concerning the transaction and the parties thereto. In the case of S–3 companies, where company and management information, including historical financial statements, is not presented in the propsectus, such information will have been furnished to security holders and widely disseminated in the market by means of the company's annual report to security holders. Therefore, this information need not be reiterated in the business combination prospectus. As to other companies, the historical financial statements and other company information will be presented in the prospectus.

Second, the Form establishes a minimum time period if incorporation by reference is used. The time period is designed to address the need for documents incorporated by reference to be delivered to security holders on a timely basis. The proposed Form would have required that, where incorporation by reference is used to take the place of presentation in the delivered document, the prospectus must either: (1) be sent at least twenty business days in advance of the date of the meeting of security holders or the date of the final investment decision; or (2) be accompanied by the documents from which information is incorporated. The proposal also would have provided that where a registrant wishes to proceed faster than the twenty day time period, it could do so by delivering to security holders, along with the prospectus, all documents incorporated by reference therein.

Commentators generally supported the concept of the twenty business day period and the adopted Form requires the prospectus to be sent prior to the proposed twenty business day period where incorporation by reference is used. Concern was expressed, however, that the alternative of delivering documents incorporated by reference could result in a cumbersome and unreadable prospectus because of the potential multiplicity of documents delivered. Accordingly, Form S–4 as adopted, provides a different alternative. Registrants still may proceed faster than the twenty business day period, but if they wish to do so, they must furnish the required information to security holders at the S–1 level. The same quantum of information will be delivered as was provided in the proposal's alternative, but the S–1 alternative provides a more readable format. In addition, the Commission has added a legend to encourage security holders to request the incorporated documents promptly and an undertaking to require the registrant to respond within one business day by first class mail or other equally prompt means.

For an analysis, of Rule 145, see Schneider & Manko, Rule 145, 5 Rev.Sec. Reg. 811 (1972), 6 Rev.Sec.Reg. 1 (1973); Schneider & Manko, Rule 145 Updated, 6 Rev.Sec.Reg. 878 (1973); Eppler, Rule 145 in Practice, 5 PLI Institute of Securities Regulation 323–353 (1974); Halligan, Shareholders After Merger: What They Can and Cannot Do Under SEC Rules 144 and 145, 15 B.C.Ind. & Com.L.Rev. 70 (1973); Heyman, Implications of Rule 145 Under the Securities Act of 1933, 53 B.U.L.Rev. 785 (1973); Cohen, Some Practical and Impractical Aspects of a "Rule 145" Transaction, 30 Bus.Law. 51 (1974).

SECTION 4. COURT AND AGENCY APPROVED REORGANIZATIONS AND OTHER EXCHANGES

Statutes

Securities Act, § 3(a)(10).

SECURITIES ACT RELEASE NO. 312
Securities and Exchange Commission.
March 15, 1935.

The Securities and Exchange Commisison made public today an excerpt from a letter of its General Counsel, John J. Burns, considering the application of the exemption in Sec. 3(a)(10) of the Securities Act of 1933 of securities issued in exchange for other securities where the terms of this issuance and exchange were to be approved by a State public utility commission. Although the excerpt concerned a proposed consolidation under the supervision of a public utility commission, the interpretation of Sec. 3(a)(10) applies to all exchanges of securities approved by State commissions or other State authorities.

The excerpt from the letter follows:

* * *

"I shall take up in order the three questions you have raised as to the interpretation of [Section 3(a)(10)].

"1. Is adequate notice to all persons to whom it is proposed to issue securities of the hearing on the fairness of their issuance necessary for an exemption under Section 3(a)(10)?

"Although the wording of Section 3(a)(10) does not demand such notice, in my opinion this requirement is to be implied from the necessity for a 'hearing * * * at which all persons to whom it is proposed to issue securities * * * shall have the right to appear'. To give substance to this express requirement, some adequate form of notice seems necessary. The usual practice of giving notice to persons who will receive securities in reorganizations, mergers and consolidations supports this view. Of course, the question of what mode of notice is adequate cannot be answered in the abstract but may vary with the facts and circumstances in each case.

"2. Is a grant of 'express authorization of law' to a state governmental authority to approve the fairness of the terms and conditions of the issuance and exchange of securities necessary for an exemption under Section 3(a)(10), or is express authorization merely to approve the terms and conditions sufficient?

"The punctuation and grammatical construction of the last clause of Section 3(a)(10) indicate that the words 'expressly authorized * * * by law' were not intended to modify 'courts or officials or agencies of the United States'. In my opinion a State governmental authority (with the possible exception of a banking or insurance commission) must possess express authority of law to approve the *fairness* of the terms and conditions of the issuance and exchange of the securities in question. This interpretation seems necessary to give meaning to the express requirement of a hearing upon the fairness of such terms and conditions, which must subsume authority in the supervisory body to pass upon the fairness from the standpoint of the investor, as well as the issuer and consumer, and to disapprove terms and conditions because unfair either to those who are to receive the securities or to other security holders of the issuer, or to the public. This requirement seems the more essential in that the whole justification for the exemption afforded by Section 3(a)(10) in that the examination and approval by the body in question of the fairness of the issue in question is a substitute for the protection afforded to the investor by the information which would otherwise be made available to him through registration. The requisite express authorization of law to approve the fairness of such terms and conditions, however, probably need not necessarily be in haec verba but, to give effect to the words 'express' and 'by law', must be granted clearly and explicitly.

"3. Does a hearing by an authority expressly authorized by law to hold such a hearing satisfy the requirement of a hearing in Section 3(a)(10), if the state law does not require a hearing?

"I believe that, as a corollary to the view expressed in my answer to the second question, supra, and in order that a hearing have legal sanction, the approving authority must be expressly authorized by law to hold the hearing; but in my opinion it is unnecessary that the hearing be mandatory under applicable state law. Therefore, if state law expressly authorizes the approving authority to hold a hearing on the fairness of the terms and conditions of the issuance and exchange of securities, and such a hearing is in fact held, this requirement of Section 3(a)(10) is satisfied. * * *"

REORGANIZATIONS AND OTHER EXCHANGES UNDER SECTION 3(a)(10)

Section 3(a)(10) provides an exemption from the registration and prospectus delivery requirements of Section 5 for securities issued in certain exchange transactions. Although the history is sparse, apparently the section was designed to exempt judicially or administratively approved reorganizations or recapitalizations on the theory that if the plans were approved as to "fairness," after a hearing at which all security holders affected could appear, there would be no need for additional regulation. The "fairness" hearing before a court or administrative agency was assumed to be "a substitute for the protection afforded * * * to the investor by the information which would otherwise be made available * * * through registration." [1]

Non-judicially Supervised Exchanges. For the exemption to be available for non-judicially supervised exchanges, implementing legislation is necessary expressly to confer upon a federal or state agency the authority to grant approval, subject to the prescribed conditions.

At the state level, only California, Ohio, Oregon and North Carolina, have state securities legislation tracking the section and authorizing the securities administrator to hold a fairness hearing in conformity with the conditions of the Section.[2] As regards regulated industries, a number of states have comparable legislation relating to insurance, public utilities, banking and other financial institutions.[3]

At the federal level, facilitating legislation sufficient to permit the use of § 3(a)(10) exists under the Public Utility Holding Company Act,[4] and the Investment Company Act of 1940.[5]

1. Securities Act Release No. 33–312 (Mar. 15, 1933). And see H.R.Rep. No. 85, 73d Cong., 1st Sess. 16 (1933): "Reorganizations carried out without such judicial supervision possess all the dangers implicit in the issuance of new securities and are, therefore, not exempt from the act. For the same reason the provision [Section 3(a)(10)] is not broad enough to include mergers or consolidations of corporation entered into without judicial supervision."

2. Ohio Securities Act, Ohio Rev. Code, Tit. 17, § 1707.04; West Ann.Cal.Corps.

Code § 25142; N.C.Gen.Stat. § 78A–30(a) (Supp.1979); Ore.Rev.Stat. § 59.095 (1979).

3. For a survey of state statutes, see Ash, Reorganizations and Other Exchanges Under Section 3(a)(10) of the Securities Act of 1933, 75 Nw.U.L.Rev. 1, 45–60 (1980).

4. 15 U.S.C. §§ 79, 79k(e) (1976 & Supp. III, 1979).

5. 15 U.S.C. §§ 80a–17(b) and 17(d) (1976 & Supp. III, 1979).

Reorganization of Financially Distressed Entities. The applicability of the § 3(a)(10) exemption in connection with the reorganization of distressed corporations was unclear prior to the adoption of the Bankruptcy Reform Act of 1978.[6] That uncertainty was eliminated by the adoption of the 1978 legislation which amended § 3(a)(10) and also §§ 3(a)(7) and 3(a)(9) to exclude from the operation of these exemptions, the issuance of securities in a bankruptcy context.[7] The securities regulation aspects of the issuance of securities of financially distressed firms under the Bankruptcy Act is the subject of a separate note, infra at page 432. We shall see that securities issued under a plan of corporate reorganization are issued subject to supervision of the bankruptcy court. Unlike Section § 3(a)(10), however, solicitation of approval of a plan of corporate reorganization must be accompanied by a disclosure statement approved by the bankruptcy court as to its adequacy.[8] The court is authorized to hold a hearing on the plan and confirmation is conditioned on a finding that the plan "does not discriminate unfairly, and is fair and equitable, with respect to each class of claims that is impaired under, and has not accepted the plan."[9] The Bankruptcy Code thus represents a significant departure from the § 3(a)(10) model.

Judicially-Supervised Exchanges Pursuant to Settlement of Litigation. With the demise of the equity receivership for the organization of financially embarrassed corporations[10] and the recent bankruptcy legislation, there would seem to be little or no role for court supervised exchanges of securities pursuant to § 3(a)(10). However, the publication since December 1, 1970 of the Commission's no-action letters issued in response to inquiries concerning the application of the federal securities laws to proposed transactions has disclosed the use of § 3(a)(10) in connection with the issuance of securities by defendants and other litigants in negotiated settlements of litigation subject to court supervision.[11] Unlike state governmental agencies, courts of the United States need not be granted express authority to approve the fairness of the terms of such securities exchanges.[12]

Professor Barbara A. Ash, after reviewing approximately sixty publicly available no-action letters relating to the use of the § 3(a)(10) exemption in the settlement of litigation, has concluded that the "staff has consistently taken a no-action position based on counsel's opinion as to the availability of section 3(a)(10) irrespective of whether the issuer was one of the defendants or a corporation, a substantial number of whose securities happened to be held by one or more of the defendants."[13]

6. 11 U.S.C. §§ 364, 1125, 1145 (1976 & Supp. III, 1979).

7. Sec. 306, 92 Stat. 2674 (1978).

8. See supra note 6, at § 1125.

9. Id., §§ 1128, 1129.

10. See Jennings, Mr. Justice Douglas: His Influence on Corporate and Securities Regulation, 73 Yale L.J. 920, 931, 935–941 (1964).

11. Despite the criticisms directed at the proliferation of no-action letters, see supra at page 51, one of their important values has been to flush out the SEC Staff's views as to the application of the federal securities laws to proposed transactions. These letters have produced an enormous amount of information which had not theretofore been available and has aided to the understanding of SEC practice. See, for example, Hicks, Recapitalizations Under Section 3(a)(9) of the Securities Act of 1933, 61 Va.L.Rev. 1020 (1975); Deaktor, Integration of Securities Offerings, 31 U.Fla.L.Rev. 465 (1979); Ash, supra note 3.

12. Securities Act Release No. 312 (Mar. 15, 1935), supra at page 326.

13. Ash, supra note 3, at 38 (footnotes omitted). For an example of the use of § 3(a)(10) in settling litigation, see Brucker v. Thyssen-Bornemisza Europe N.V., 424 F.Supp. 679, 690–91 (S.D.N.Y.1976).

As to the usefulness of § 3(a)(10) for the settlement of litigation, Professor Ash had this to say: [14]

Since section § 3(a)(10) may be relied on in connection with the settlement of litigation of almost any nature, it is of widespread utility. As noted above, the amount of litigation under the federal securities laws has become rather substantial and often lends itself to a settlement agreement involving the issuance of securities. In more than a majority of the approximately sixty no-action letters referred to above, the underlying litigation was pursuant to the Federal securities laws, frequently the antifraud provisions of the Act or the Exchange Act or the federal proxy rules, and in one case interestingly enough section 3(a)(10) itself. In addition, the no-action letters indicate that section 3(a)(10) is quite often useful to the settlement of litigation arising from various provisions of the state corporation codes and to court-supervised liquidations, distributions for the benefit of creditors, and various other insolvency-related issuances of securities not pursuant to the Federal Bankruptcy Act. Despite the seeming inconsistency between the Commission's longstanding position that section 3(a)(10) was unavailable to reorganizations under the Bankruptcy Act and its unquestioned allowance of reliance on the Exchange Exemption in the case of substantively similar court-supervised issuances of securities, there appears to be no limitation, even in the Commission's view, on the availability of the Exchange Exemption because of the nature of the litigation proposed to be settled.

In the typical non-judicially supervised reorganization before an administrative agency, the agency passes upon the "fairness" of the exchange, including the valuation of issuer's business and the value of the securities being exchanged as compared with the value of the claims of loss.

In Securities and Exchange Commission v. Blinder Robinson & Co., Inc., 511 F.Supp. 799 (D.Colo.1981), a court used § 3(a)(10) to exempt securities issued pursuant to a settlement of an enforcement action brought by the SEC. The Commission had sought injunctive and ancillary equitable relief for Securities Act violations in connection with a public offering of securities of the issuer and sought rescission of the transaction.

In order to avoid the prospect of costly litigation and possible liquidation, the defendants entered into a settlement agreement with the Commission involving the offer of common stock and promissory notes to shareholders and former shareholders of the issuer in exchange for the release of all claims by those accepting the offer.

In passing on the fairness of the settlement, the court articulated a standard to be applied in this type of case which differed from that used in non-judicially supervised reorganizations or under former Chapter X of the Bankruptcy Act, requiring a finding that the reorganization plan is fair, equitable and feasible. In contrast, the court saw the fairness hearing as "the functional equivalent of the full disclosure which would be provided in an appropriate prospectus and registration statement."

The factors considered by the court in determining the "fairness" of the offer included: (1) the recommendations of counsel; (2) the scope of the discovery record as an indicator of the adequacy of the investigation into the facts; (3) the apparent alternatives to settlement; (4) the nature and volume of responses from those receiving notice of the hearing; and (5) the opportunity for direct participation in the process of attaining full disclosure.

14. Id. at 38–39 (footnotes omitted).

The court noted that persons who did not wish to accept the offer were not foreclosed from pursuing private claims of relief. It also emphasized that the SEC had initiated the enforcement proceeding and had specifically accepted the settlement agreement.

Since the standard differs from that applied in class action settlements where the approval is given only if the settlement offered is fair, reasonable and adequate, it is not at all clear that the standard enunciated by the court would apply in other contexts.[15]

On Section 3(a)(10), see Ash, Reorganizations and Other Exchanges Under Section 3(a)(10) of the Securities Act of 1933, 75 Nw.U.L.Rev. 1 (1980); Mann, The Section 3(a)(10) Exemption: Recent Interpretations, 22 UCLA L.Rev. 1247 (1975); Glickman, The State Administrative Fairness Hearing and Section 3(a) (10) of the Securities Act—Some Questions, 45 St. John's L.Rev. 644 (1971); J. Hicks, Exempted Transactions Under the Securities Act of 1933, c. 3 (1986 rev.); 1 Securities Law Techniques, ch. 6 (A.A. Sommer, Jr. ed. 1985).

INTERPLAY BETWEEN RULE 145, THE SECTIONS 3 AND 4 TRANSACTION EXEMPTIONS AVAILABLE TO ISSUERS, AND FORM S-4

a. Rule 145 Transactions. In effecting a business combination or in other corporate reorganizations and reclassifications, there may be a choice between the use of Rule 145 or one of the transaction exemptions from registration available under §§ 3 or 4. Rule 145 applies when security holders of a corporation or other legal entity, pursuant to statutory provisions, controlling instruments, or otherwise, are asked to vote or consent to a plan or agreement for: (1) a reclassification of securities, other than stock splits, reverse stock splits, and changes in par value; (2) a merger or similar plan of acquisition, except where the sole purpose of the transaction is to change an issuer's domicile solely within the United States; and (3) certain transfers of assets for securities when followed by a subsequent distribution of such securities to those voting on the transfer of the assets.

Under state law, a reclassification of outstanding securities may sometimes be effected by the issuer making a voluntary exchange offer with its existing security holders; in that event no vote would be required and, if none is taken, the transaction would not come within Rule 145. On the other hand, an involuntary reclassification may sometimes be effected by a direct charter amendment that requires a vote of shareholders in a "cram-down" situation. This would include an amendment of the articles of incorporation to change the right to vote cumulatively for directors to a system of straight voting,[1] to reclassify preferred shares into common shares, or to eliminate preferred dividend arrearages where the charter and state law permit such action.[2] It

---

15. See 7 J. Hicks, Exempted Transactions Under the Securities Act of 1933 § 3.02[4][c] (1986 rev.); Glazer, Schiffman & Packman, Settlement of Securities Litigation Through the Issuance of Securities Without Registration: The Use of Section 3(a)(10) in SEC Enforcement Proceedings, 50 Fordham L.Rev. 533 (1982); Note, Fairness Requirement in Section 3(a)(10) of the Securities Act of 1933, 23 Wm. & Mary

L.Rev. 549 (1982); Note, Section 3(a)(10) of the Securities Act of 1933—SEC v. Blinder Robinson & Co.,—Proposed Standards for Fairness Hearings, 17 New Eng.L.Rev. 1397 (1982).

1. See Maddock v. Vorclone Corp., 17 Del.Ch. 39, 147 Atl. 255 (1929).

2. See McNulty v. W. & J. Sloane, 184 Misc. 835, 54 N.Y.S.2d 253 (Sup.Ct.1945);

would also embrace similar action accomplished through the device of a merger.[3]

In the case of a business combination, Rule 145 specifically applies to fusions brought about through a merger, consolidation, and, with some exceptions, a sale of substantially all the assets for stock or other securities, all of which require a vote of shareholders of the acquired corporation. These forms of business combination include "A" and "C" reorganizations under § 368(a)(1) of the Internal Revenue Code. On the other hand, in a "B" type reorganization, the acquiring company makes an independent offer to the shareholders of the company proposed to be acquired to exchange their shares for shares of the acquiring company—an offer which the shareholders are free to accept or reject without any stockholder vote. Accordingly, Rule 145 is not available for "B" type reorganizations and former registration Form S-14 also was unavailable.

b. *Availability of Form S-4.* We have seen, however, that new Form S-4 is now available for use in "B" type exchange reorganizations. Furthermore, Form S-4 standardizes the treatment of transactions requiring filings under the Securities Act and Exchange Act, e.g. merger reorganizations, sale-of-assets reorganizations and tender offers. Thus, in situations where shareholder approval of the transaction is required, Form S-4 may also serve as a proxy statement, thereby enabling the acquiring company and the company being acquired to file a combined registration statement/proxy statement and deliver to shareholders a single prospectus/proxy statement.

If the proxy or information material to be sent to security holders is subject to Regulation 14A or 14C under the Exchange Act, then the provisions of these regulations apply; the "wrap-around" prospectus may be in the form of a proxy or information statement, but may contain the information specified in Form S-4 in lieu of that required by Schedule 14A or 14C of Regulation 14A or 14C under the Exchange Act.[4]

If the proxy or information material to be sent to security holders is not subject to Regulation 14A or 14C, such material must nevertheless be filed as part of the Form S-4 registration statement.

If the issuer has a class of equity securities registered pursuant to § 12 of the Exchange Act and the transaction in which the securities are being registered are to be issued subject to §§ 13(e), 14(d) or 14(e) (basically tender offers, or self-tenders), the provisions of those sections apply to the transaction in addition to those of Form S-4. Accordingly, Form S-4 may also be used to satisfy the Schedule 14D-1 (Tender Offer Statement) and the Schedule 14D-9 (target company's Tender Offer Solicitation/Recommendation Statement) filing requirements, if the parties exercise this option.

c. *Alternatives to Use of Rule 145 and Form S-4.* When a relatively closely held corporation is being acquired in a "B" or exchange reorganization, the private offering exemption may be available either under Rule 506 or § 4(2) of the Act. Moreover, the issuer should consider the availability of Regulation A under the 3(b) (small issue) exemption, supra at page 362, as well as the

---

Sherman v. Pepin Pickling Co., 230 Minn. 87, 41 N.W.2d 571 (1950).

3. See Federal United Corp. v. Havender, 24 Del.Ch. 318, 11 A.2d 331 (Sup.Ct. 1940); Langfelder v. Universal Laboratories, Inc., 163 F.2d 804 (3d Cir. 1947).

4. Form S-4 consists of the facing page of the Form, the prospectus containing the

information specified in part I, and the information contained in part II. Where shareholder approval of the transaction is required, a Form S-4 facing sheet is simply wrapped around the prospectus/proxy statement, hence the term "wrap-around" prospectus.

intrastate exemption, if all of the requirements of Rule 147 or the § 3(a)(11) statutory exemption can be met.

In a "C" or transfer of assets reorganization in which Rule 145 is applicable, the private offering exemption may also be available under Rule 506, or § 4(2) of the Act. The issuer then has a choice between using the private offering exemption or Rule 145. Although Rule 145 does not affect statutory exemptions which are otherwise available, under Rule 145(a)(3), the acquiring company may wish to register the securities to be issued in the transaction on Form S–4, in order that affiliates of the acquired company may make resales either pursuant to the registration statement, subject to proper disclosure, or subject to the resale provisions of Rule 145(d).[5]   In one case, a company acquiring the assets of a corporation with a single shareholder was permitted to use Rule 145, and the sole shareholder was thus enabled to make resales under Rule 145(d) without being subject to the two-year holding period of Rule 144.[6]

If an issuer proposes to effect a corporate acquisition in a Rule 145 type transaction and the private offering exemption is not available, consideration should be given to the availability of Regulation A under § 3(b) of the Act. If Regulation A is available, the Form 1–A there prescribed must be modified so that the offering circular also discloses the type of information required by Form S–4. It must be noted, however, that the resale provisions of Rule 145(d) are only applicable to "registered securities acquired" in a Rule 145 transaction. A Regulation A offering under § 3(b) is not a registered offering; it is an exempt offering. Resales within twelve months by affiliates would therefore be subject to the limitations of § 3(b) and Rule 254.[7]

In certain exchanges and reclassifications of securities, the § 3(a)(9) exemption may be available. However, that section is restricted to exchanges of securities between a single corporation and its existing security holders exclusively. As interpreted by the Commission, the word "exclusively" modifies both "exchange" and the phrase "with its existing security holders." Accordingly, in such exchanges, the exemption is destroyed, on the one hand, if the security holder pays something in addition to the securities surrendered for the security received; or if the exchange is made with any one other than existing security holders of the issuer. Rule 149 makes an exception to the restriction against additional payment by excluding cash payments by security holders to the issuer which are necessary to effect an equitable adjustment in respect of dividends or interest payable on the securities involved in the exchange, as between security holders of the same class. The surrender by the shareholder of the right to accruals of dividends in arrears on preferred stock could be deemed to represent payment of a consideration in addition to the stock surrendered so as to bar the availability of the exemption. However, the staff has granted no-action letters permitting the use of Section 3(a)(9) in this situation.[8] It appears, therefore, that one may rely on § 3(a)(9) when using a plan under which a new prior preferred is created by charter amendment and these shares are offered to the preferred shareholders in exchange for their preferred shares plus all accrued and unpaid dividends.

5. Securities Act Release No. 5463 (Feb. 28, 1974), pt. I, Illustration A.

6. Open Road Industries, Inc. (available Feb. 5, 1973); Eppler, Rule 145 in Practice, 5 PLI Institute on Securities Regulation 326 (1974).

7. Supra note 4, at pt. I, Illustration D.

8. See Hicks, Recapitalizations Under Section 3(a)(9) of the Securities Act of 1933, 61 Va.L.Rev. 1057, 1087, at n. 110 (1975), citing Diverse-Graphics, Inc., [1972] "No Action" Letters, roll 7, frame 11465 (June 20, 1972); J. Hicks, Exempted Transactions Under the Securities Act of 1933, § 2.05, at 2–56 to 2–60 (1986 rev.).

In the second place, § 3(a)(9) prohibits the payment of any commission or remuneration for soliciting security holders to make the exchange. In those cases where it is necessary to engage outside solicitors to obtain acceptances of the exchange or to obtain votes or other consents, use of § 3(a)(9) will not be feasible. Rule 150, however, excludes from the phrase "commission or other remuneration" payments by the issuer to its security holders when part of the terms of the offer of exchange. A particularly troublesome area is that of the forced conversion of outstanding convertible securities where the market price of the underlying securities exceeds the call price. In that case the issuer sometimes protects itself against a falling market in the underlying security, which would make conversion unattractive, by entering into a standby agreement with an investment banker to bid for the convertible security at a price slightly above the redemption price. The banker then converts and sells the underlying securities in the market. However, since § 3(a)(9) is a transaction exemption, any resales must rely on an independent exemption. The commission interposes no objection to this practice, although a question has been raised whether the remuneration paid to the bankers does not destroy the exemption.[9]

Section 3(a)(10) was especially designed to exempt judicially or administratively approved reorganizations or recapitalizations on the theory that if the plans were approved as to "fairness," after a hearing at which all security holders affected could appear, there is no need for additional regulation. The section applies both to "voluntary exchanges" and to "cram downs," so long as the other conditions are met.[10]

Prior to the repeal of the no-sale rule embodied in Rule 133, § 3(a)(9) was thought to apply only to *voluntary* exchanges by an issuer with its existing security holders where other conditions of the Section were met.[11] In this situation a sale was entailed, though exempt if complying with Section 3(a)(9). Reclassifications of securities requiring "corporate action" pursuant to a vote of shareholders were subject to the no-sale rule and were thought to be outside of the § 3(a)(9) exemption.

Rule 145(a)(1) includes any reclassification of securities of an issuer, other than a stock split, reverse stock split, or change in par value, which involves the substitution of a security for another security. Thus, apparently, voluntary as well as compulsory reclassifications are made subject to the rule, if the plan is submitted to a vote of shareholders. According to interpretations of the Division of Corporation Finance, however, § 3(a)(9) remains available to all reclassifications of securities, assuming that all the requirements of that exemption are met. Thus, if an issuer has a class of preferred and a class of common stock outstanding, and proposes a plan of reclassification by charter amendment which, if approved by the requisite majority of each class, would result in the issuer having only one class of common shares outstanding, Rule

9. Lomes & Nettleton Financial Corp. (Avail. May 13, 1971), 1 Securities Law Techniques § 5.02[4] (A.A. Sommer, ed. 1985); 7 J. Hicks, Exempted Transactions Under the Securities Act of 1933, § 2.02[3][b][iii] (1986 rev.).

10. See Comment, Effect of Section 3(a) (10) of the Securities Act as a Source of Exemption for Securities Issued in Reorganizations, 45 Yale L.J. 1050, 1051 (1936); Ash, Reorganizations and Other Exchanges Under Section § 3(a)(10) of the Securities Act of 1933, 75 Nw.U.L.Rev. 1, 42–44

(1980). As to the efficacy of court or agency supervision, see Note, Protection for Shareholder Interests in Recapitalizations of Publicly Held Corporations, 58 Colum.L. Rev. 1030 (1958).

11. See H.R.Rep.No.152, 73d Cong., 1st Sess. 25 (1933). The Conference report states that the § 3(a)(9) exemption was "considered necessary to permit certain voluntary readjustment of obligations." And see 1 Loss, Securities Regulation 573 (2d ed. 1961).

145 will apply if the reclassification is submitted for the vote or consent of the security holders. If the issuer proposes to utilize the services of a proxy soliciting firm, § 3(a)(9) will be unavailable, because of the prohibition against payments for soliciting security holders to make the exchange. If, however, the company determines that it will not utilize the services of a proxy soliciting firm, Section 3(a)(9) will be available provided that all the requirements of that section are met, even though the transaction also comes within Rule 145.[12]

The § 3(a)(10) exemption is free of several of the restrictions limiting the usefulness of the § 3(a)(9) exemption; it may also be available to avoid the burdens of registration following the repeal of Rule 133 and the adoption of Rule 145. Accordingly, every proposed transaction must be analyzed to determine which of the available alternatives is the most advantageous. In fact, since the repeal of Rule 133 and the adoption of Rule 145, the § 3(a)(10) exemption takes on an added significance, for as one knowledgeable securities lawyer puts it, the exemption fulfills a "need to find a new exemption for mergers and acquisitions in situations where either the time or expense of registration is not justifiable".[13] This situation may arise in connection with mergers and acquisitions, where the availability of the Rule 506 or § 4(2) statutory private offering exemption is uncertain. The § 3(a)(10) exemption may also be useful "when a large listed corporation intends to acquire a relatively small corporation too closely held to be subject to the proxy rules, yet too large to fit within the parameters of Rule [506], in a transaction which need not be approved by the shareholders of the acquiring corporation." [14] It may also prove advantageous in a "B" reorganization under I.R.C. § 368(a)(1) where the shareholders of the corporation to be acquired are invited to exchange their stock in the acquired corporation for stock in the acquiring corporation. In all mergers and corporate acquisitions § 3(a)(9) is unavailable, for the reason that the exchange is not with the issuer's security holders. In such event, the § 3(a)(10) exemption may provide an alternative to a 1933 Act registration.

Although the § 3(a)(10) exemption has generally been overlooked by many securities lawyers,[15] under some of the state securities acts, a correlative state provision may permit [16] an application to a securities commission for approval of the fairness of the transaction. In many of these transactions, involving arm's length negotiations, where there are no cross-holdings or conflicts of interest, it may be relatively easy to establish the fairness of the plan, and thus obtain a § 3(a)(10) exemption. Aside from the "single issuer" limitation of § 3(a)(9) which is not a part of § 3(a)(10), the latter section has the further advantage that the exchange may be made not only for other securities, but also for other claims or property interests, and cash may be paid in part. This permits § 3(a)(10) to be used in various types of corporate adjustments entailing the modification of outstanding securities where § 3(a)(9) is unavailable. In these situations, however, judicial or administrative approval of the fairness may pose difficulties.[17] Finally, unlike § 3(a)(9), the § 3(a)(10) exemption is not destroyed by paying remuneration for soliciting the exchange.

12. Release No. 5463, supra note 4, pt. I, Illustration C; Pt. II, Illustration A; J. Hicks, supra note 9, at § 2.07[2][a].

13. Mann, The Section 3(a)(10) Exemption: Recent Interpretations, 22 UCLA L.Rev. 1247, at 1248 (1975).

14. Id. at 1252.

15. 1 Marsh & Volk, Practice Under the California Securities Laws § 7.11 (Rev. ed. 1975); Mann, supra note 13, at 1247–250; Ash, supra note 10, 28–45.

16. Ohio Securities Act, Ohio Rev.Code, Tit. 17, § 1707.04; e.g., West's Ann.Cal. Corp.Code § 25142; N.C.Gen.Stat. § 78A–30(a) (Supp.1979); Ore.Rev.Stats. § 59.095.

17. See, for example, The Goldfield Consolidated Mines Company, before the California Commissioner of Corporations, No. 104255 LA, June 4, 1962.

Section 3(a)(10) may also provide an alternative in other Rule 145 type transactions. For example, if X Company, incorporated in State A, intends to establish Y Company, a corporation to be organized under the laws of State A, and to effect a Rule 145 type transaction which would result in Y Company becoming a holding company and the shareholders of X Company receiving securities of Y Company in exchange for their own shares, the § 3(a)(10) exemption provides an alternative to Rule 145. However, since § 3(a)(10) is regarded as a "transaction exemption" resales by shareholders of the acquired company who would be deemed to be an "issuer, underwriter, or dealer" for the purposes of § 4(1) would have to find some other exemption. The Division of Corporation Finance has suggested that in Rule 145 type transactions, "an issuer may choose to register the securities to be issued in the transaction on Form [S–4] or S–1 in order to be more certain of the status * * * of public resales by underwriters of securities received in the transaction." [18] On resales of § 3(a)(10) securities, see infra at page 535.

SECTION 5. THE BANKRUPTCY EXEMPTIONS

REORGANIZATIONS UNDER THE FEDERAL BANKRUPTCY CODE: CHAPTER 11

Chapter 11. The Bankruptcy Reform Act of 1978 made significant substantive changes in the reorganization of financially distressed companies and in the application of the federal securities laws to the issuance of securities during reorganization and the resale of such securities. Under the prior Bankruptcy Act, reorganizations could be effected under Chapter X, arrangements under Chapter XI, and real property arrangements by persons other than corporations under Chapter XII. As originally enacted, it was contemplated that Chapter X would be used for pervasive reorganizations of publicly-owned corporations and Chapter XI would be utilized for the judicial enforcement of an arrangement in which the owners of a business, whether or not incorporated, would enter into an extension or composition of unsecured debts of the firm. As a result of the cumbersome and time-consuming procedures under Chapter X, debtor corporations (and their creditors) tended to resort to Chapter XI even though the reorganization effectuated material modifications in the rights of public investors. Critics of this dual system of reorganization argued that there were no objective standards for determining whether a reorganization belonged under Chapter X or Chapter XI.[1] The upshot was that a consolidated approach to the reorganization of distressed companies was taken in the enactment of Chapter 11. The theory behind this new approach was explained this way:[2]

* * * The new consolidated chapter 11 contains no special procedure for companies with public debt or equity security holders. Instead, factors such as the standard to be applied to solicitation of acceptances of a plan of reorganization are left to be determined by the court on a case-by-case basis. In order to insure that adequate investigation of the debtor is conducted to determine fraud or wrongdoing on the part of present management, an examiner is required to be appointed in all cases in which the debtor's fixed, liquidated, and unsecured debts, other than debts for goods, services, or taxes, or owing to an insider, exceed $5 million. This should adequately

---

18. Release No. 5463, supra note 4, pt. I, Illustration B.

1. Comments of Homer Kripke on Summary of Comments of the SEC Staff on H.R. 6, H.R.Rep. No. 95–595, 95th Cong., 1st Sess., App. II, 261 (1977).

2. 124 Cong.Rec. S 17417–19 (Oct. 6, 1978) (Remarks of Senator Dennis DeConcini).

represent the needs of public security holders in most cases. However, in addition, section 1109 of the House amendment enables both the Securities and Exchange Commission and any party in interest who is creditor, equity security holder, indenture trustee, or any committee representing creditors or equity security holders to raise and appear and be heard on any issue in a case under chapter 11. This will enable the bankruptcy court to evaluate all sides of a position and to determine the public interest. * * * The advisory role of the Securities and Exchange Commission will enable the court to balance the needs of public security holders against equally important public needs relating to the economy, such as employment and production, and other factors such as the public health and safety of the people or protection of the national interest. * * *

* * *

Disclosure Requirements in Exchanges of Securities. An integral feature of a corporate reorganization is the restructuring of the debtor's capital and debt. That process necessarily involves the exchange of new debt or equity securities for outstanding claims or interests. Without some exemption for issuers and for persons who wish to resell securities received on an exchange, funds needed to revitalize the business would be absorbed by 1933 Act registration expenses. If a plan of reorganization entails the issuance of securities in exchange for outstanding claims or interests, some disclosure obligations should be imposed upon the debtor-issuer of the securities. This problem is solved by § 1125 which supplants the disclosure obligations which otherwise would be applicable under the 1933 Act by a regime under the supervision of the bankruptcy court. The operation of these disclosure requirements has been explained in these terms: [3]

* * * This section is new. It is the heart of the consolidation of the various reorganization chapters found in current law. It requires disclosure before solicitation of acceptances of a plan of reorganization.

Subsection (a) contains two definitions. First, "adequate information" is defined to mean information of a kind, and in sufficient detail, as far as is reasonably practical in light of the nature and history of the debtor and the condition of the debtor's books and records, that would enable a hypothetical reasonable investor typical of holders of claims or interests of the relevant class to make an informed judgment about the plan. Second, "investor typical of holders of claims or interests of the relevant class" is defined to mean an investor having a claim or interest of the relevant class, having such a relationship with the debtor as the holders of other claims or interests of the relevant class have, and having such ability to obtain information from sources other than the disclosure statement as holders of claims or interests of the relevant class have. That is, the hypothetical investor against which the disclosure is measured must not be an insider if other members of the class are not insiders, and so on. In other words, the adequacy of disclosure is measured against the typical investor, not an extraordinary one.

* * * Precisely what constitutes adequate information in any particular instance will develop on a case-by-case basis. Courts will take a practical approach as to what is necessary under the circumstances of each case, such as the cost of preparation of the statements, the need for relative speed in solicitation and confirmation, and, of course, the need for investor protection.

---

3. Report of the Committee on the Judiciary, H.R.Rep. No. 95–595, 95th Cong., 1st Sess. 408–10 (1977). And see Epling & Thompson, Securities Disclosures in Bankruptcy, 39 Bus.Law. 855 (1984).

Subsection (b) is the operative subsection. It prohibits solicitation of acceptances or rejections of a plan after the commencement of the case unless, at the time of the solicitation or before, there is transmitted to the solicitee the plan or a summary of the plan, and a written disclosure statement approved by the court as containing adequate information. * * *

Subsection (d) excepts the disclosure statements from the requirements of the securities laws (such as section 14 of the 1934 Act and section 5 of the 1933 Act), and from similar State securities laws (blue sky laws, for example). The subsection permits an agency or official whose duty is to administer or enforce such laws (such as the Securities and Exchange Commission or State Corporation Commissioners) to appear and be heard on the issue of whether a disclosure statement contains adequate information, but the agencies and officials are not granted the right of appeal from an adverse determination in any capacity. They may join in an appeal by a true party in interest, however.

Subsection (e) is a safe harbor provision, and is necessary to make the exemption provided by subsection (d) effective. Without it, a creditor that solicited an acceptance or rejection in reliance on the court's approval of a disclosure statement would be potentially liable under antifraud sections designed to enforce the very sections of the securities laws from which subsection (d) excuses compliance. The subsection protects only persons that solicit in good faith and in compliance with the applicable provisions of the reorganization chapter. It provides protection from legal liability as well as from equitable liability based on an injunctive action by the SEC or other agency or official.

Exemptions From the Securities Laws. Section 1145(a) exempts from federal and state securities laws registration or licensing requirements specific types of securities a debtor, or debtor's affiliate, or debtor's successor, might issue under a reorganization plan. The Section 1145(a)(1) and (2) exemptions apply only to "exchange securities" because the new security must be exchanged: (1) solely for a claim or administrative expense claim, or an interest of the debtor; or (2) principally for such consideration and partly for cash or property. Section 1145(a)(3) exempts offers or sales of portfolio securities owned by the debtor under certain conditions.

It should be noted that these exemptions do not exempt securities offered to the public to provide fresh capital to finance a Chapter 11 plan. The offerees of an unregistered security, exempted under § 1145(a)(1) and (2), must have a preexisting claim or equity interest in the debtor. The issuance of securities to raise additional funds requires compliance with the registration or exemption provisions of the 1933 Act, except that a debtor may issue debt securities having a priority claim as provided in § 364 of the Code. Section 364 authorizes the trustee to obtain credit, or incur debt, to continue the business through the use of unregistered debt securities; but excludes the use of equity securities for this purpose.[4]

---

4. Nothing in the language of § 364(f) indicates that the term equity security was to have any meaning other than that defined in § 101(15) of the Code. Since convertible debentures do not come within the Code definition of equity security, they would seem to qualify to be issued without registration under § 364(f). Nevertheless, the legislative history accompanying § 1145 and quoted below makes reference to § 364(f) as exempting "any security that is not an equity security or convertible into an equity security." H.R.Rep. No. 95–595, 95th Cong., 1st Sess. 419 (1977). And see ALI Federal Securities Code § 302(13), Comments (1) and (2).

Sales by a Debtor in Possession or Trustee of Portfolio Securities. The debtor in possession or trustee in chapter 11 may own securities which it may wish to sell to raise cash in order to facilitate the reorganization; these are known as "portfolio securities." Section 1145(a)(3) permits the debtor or trustee to make such sales free from the registration and prospectus provisions of § 5 of the Securities Act of 1933, subject to certain conditions. The "portfolio exemption has been explained this way:

Legislative Statement of Rep. Don Edwards. * * *

* * * Section 1145(a)(3) grants a debtor in possession or trustee in chapter 11 an extremely narrow portfolio security exemption from section 5 of the Securities Act of 1933 * * * or any comparable State law. The provision was considered by Congress and adopted after much study. * * *

The Commission rule would permit a trustee or debtor in possession to distribute securities at the rate of 1 percent every 6 months. Section 1145(a)(3) permits the trustee to distribute 4 percent of the securities during the 2-year period immediately following the date of the filing of the petition [and thereafter one percent of the securities outstanding during any 180-day period following such two-year period]. In addition, the security must be of a reporting company under section 13 [or § 15(d)] of the Securities and Exchange Act of 1934 * * *, and must be in compliance with all applicable requirements for the continuing of trading in the security on the date that the trustee offers or sells the security. [Thus within a three year period following the date of the petition, a debtor or trustee may distribute portfolio securities held by it in an amount not exceeding 6 percent of the securities of the class outstanding, provided that no more than 4 percent is sold during the two year period and no more than 1 percent is sold in each of the two successive 180-day periods thereafter.].

With these safeguards the trustee or debtor in possession should be able to distribute [6] percent of the securities of a class at any time during the [3]-year period immediately following the date of the filing of the petition in the interests of expediting bankruptcy administration. The same rationale that applies in expeditiously terminating decedents' estates applies no less to an estate under title 11.

Resales of § 1145(a) Exchange Securities. The value of securities on an exchange pursuant to § 1145(a)(1) and (2) depends upon the ease with which they may be resold in the public markets. Under § 4(1) of the Securities Act of 1933, secondary sales are exempt from registration, unless the seller is an issuer, underwriter or dealer.

Most creditors will accept exchange securities with a view to reselling them for cash as soon as feasible. If they were deemed to be underwriters engaged in a distribution, registration would be required. The problem could have been solved by permitting limited resales under Rule 144, to be considered in Chapter 9, infra at page 507; however, the Congress viewed such a solution to be unsatisfactory. Section 1145(b) establishes the conditions under which exchange securities may be resold. If the holder of securities received on an exchange under § 1145(a) is not an affiliate of the issuer of such securities, he or she may freely resell the securities unless deemed to be an underwriter within the meaning of § 1145(b). The application of the section was explained this way:[5]

---

5. Committee on the Judiciary, Sen. Rep. No. 95–989, 95th Cong., 2d Sess. 131– 132 (1978); 124 Cong.Rec. H 11105 (Sept. 28, 1978) (Remarks of Rep. Don Edwards).

Subsection (b) * * * specifies the standards under which a creditor, equity security holder, or other entity acquiring securities under the plan may resell them. The Securities Act places limitations on sales by underwriters. This subsection defines who is an underwriter, and thus restricted, and who is free to resell. Paragraph (1) enumerates real underwriters that participate in a classical underwriting. A person is an underwriter if he purchases a claim against, interest in, or claim for an administrative expense in the case concerning, the debtor, with a view to distribution [of the] * * * interest. This provision covers the purchase of a certificate of indebtedness issued under proposed 11 U.S.C. 364 and purchased from the debtor, if the purchase of the certificate was with a view to distribution.

A person is also an underwriter if he offers to sell securities offered or sold under the plan for the holders of such securities, or offers to buy securities offered or sold under the plan from the holders of such securities, if the offer to buy is with a view to distribution of the securities and under an agreement made in connection with the plan, with the consummation of the plan or with the offer or sale of securities under the plan. Finally, a person is an underwriter if he is an issuer, as used in section 2(11) of the Securities Act of 1933.

* * *

Paragraph (3) specifies that if an entity is not an underwriter under the provisions of paragraph (1), as limited by paragraph (2), then the entity is not an underwriter for the purposes of the Securities Act of 1933 with respect to the covered securities, that is, those offered or sold in an exempt transaction specified in subsection (a)(2). This makes clear that the current definition of underwriter in section 2(11) of the Securities Act of 1933 does not apply to such a creditor. The definition in that section technically applies to any person that purchases securities with "a view to distribution." If literally applied, it would prevent any creditor in a bankruptcy case from selling securities received without filing a registration statement or finding another exemption.

* * *

Subsection (c) makes an offer or sale of securities under the plan in an exempt transaction (as specified in subsection (a)(2)) a public offering, in order to prevent characterization of the distribution as a "private placement" which would result in restrictions, under rule 144 of the SEC * * * on the resale of the securities.

Sales by Controlling Persons. The exemptions from the registration provisions of federal and state law under § 1145(a) do not apply to offers or sales by an underwriter. (§ 1145(b)(1)) A controlling person of the debtor-issuer is deemed to be an issuer as that term is used in § 2(11) of the 1933 Act, and § 1145(b)(1)(D) specifies that such persons are underwriters with respect to exchange securities. The test of what constitutes a controlling interest is not spelled out. Although § 101(2) of the Bankruptcy Code defines an affiliate as a person or entity with 20% ownership of the voting securities of another entity, § 1145(b)(1)(D) by reference to § 2(11) of the Securities Act would seem to envisage that the concept of control should be determined by 1933 Act standards. The House Judiciary Committee Report states that any creditor with 10% of the debtor's securities is a controlling person.[6] The 10% test may stem from the SEC's presumptive underwriter doctrine, infra at page 455, but it

6. H.R.Rep. No. 95–595, 95th Cong., 1st Sess. 238 (1977).

would seem that the 10% test would not be the exclusive method for determining whether the person is in control.[7]

It should be noted that, unlike § 2(11), § 1145(b)(1)(D) designates a controlling person as an "underwriter" rather than as an "issuer" for the purpose of determining who is an underwriter. This switch would seem to deprive a controlling person and affiliates of the § 4(1) exemption under the 1933 Act. Moreover, since subsection (c) makes an offer or sale under the plan a "public offering," Rule 144 would also seem to be unavailable. The staff has recognized this anomaly, however, and has consistently allowed such persons to rely upon Rule 144 for resales of securities received pursuant to a plan of reorganization. See Calstar Inc. no action letter (available September 30, 1985). Nor can relief be obtained under SEC Rule 148.

Rule 148 purports to regulate resales of: (1) securities which were issued in bankruptcy proceedings by a debtor or its successor; and (2) securities which were in the debtor's portfolio either at the time proceedings were commenced under the Bankruptcy Act or the Securities Investor Protection Act (SIPC) or at the time the Federal Deposit Insurance Corporation (FDIC) was appointed receiver of the debtor's assets.

Rule 148 was adopted by the Commission in 1978 during a consideration of the Bankruptcy Reform Act of 1978 (the "Bankruptcy Code," as distinguished from the "Bankruptcy Act") with a view to forestalling the adoption of § 1145 and the amendments to § 3(a)(9) and § 3(a)(10) of the Securities Act of 1933.[8] That strategy failed; § 1145 was adopted and § 3(a)(9) and § 3(a)(10) were amended, effective for bankruptcy petitions filed after October 1, 1979 under the Bankruptcy Reform Act of 1978.

Rule 148 is the counterpart of Rule 144 (to be considered in Chapter 9 at page 507) with respect to bankruptcy related securities; it provides a safe harbor for the resale of securities issued in bankruptcy proceedings, as well as securities held in the debtor's portfolio at the time bankruptcy proceedings were commenced under the Bankruptcy Act.

Since there are certain inconsistencies between § 1145(b) and Rule 148, the question arises as to how the statute interacts with Rule 148. Section 1145(b) was adopted after the promulgation of Rule 148, so to the extent that the statute and rule are conflicting, § 1145(b) prevails.

Although it seems to be assumed that Rule 148 applies to bankruptcy proceedings under both the Bankruptcy Act and the Bankruptcy Reform Act of 1978 (the Bankruptcy Code),[9] a careful reading of the rule discloses otherwise.

We have seen that Rule 148 was promulgated prior to the adoption of the Bankruptcy Code. The Rule specifically states that it applies to bankruptcy proceedings under the "Bankruptcy Act," which is defined to mean "the federal Bankruptcy Act." In 1978, prior to the effective date of the Bankruptcy Code, the Commission noted that § 1145 deals in part with some of the matters covered by Rule 148. Although the Commission indicated that it would

---

7. See Sommer, Who's "in Control?" — S.E.C., 21 Bus.Law. 559 (1966), infra, at 470.

8. Securities Act Release (Mar. 29, 1978), effective May 1, 1978; the Bankruptcy Code was enacted on November 6, 1978, effective October 1, 1979. And see 124 Cong.Rec. 17422 (1978) (remarks of Senator DeConcini).

9. See 5 Collier on Bankruptcy § 1145.01[g] (15th ed., 1985 rev.); Morgan,

Application of the Securities Laws in Chapter 11 Reorganizations Under the Bankruptcy Reform Act 1983, U.Ill.L.Rev. 861, 881–901; Securities Law Techniques § 6.05[3] (A.A. Sommer, Jr. ed. 1985).

It should be added that in the Fifth Edition of this book, the writer also overlooked the reach of Rule 148.

consider whether to modify or rescind Rule 148 in the light of the existence of § 1145,[10] it has taken no action in this regard although Rule 148 has been amended in other respects since that time.[11] It appears therefore that Rule 148 applies: (1) to resales of securities received under a plan confirmed under the Bankruptcy Act; and (2) to the sale of portfolio securities of companies involved in proceedings under the Securities Investors Protection Act (SIPC) or where the Federal Deposit Insurance Corporation (FDIC) is appointed receiver of the debtor's assets. SIPC and FDIC cases are included since they are not within the jurisdiction of the bankruptcy court.

On the other hand § 1145 applies with respect to Chapter 11 petitions filed after October 1, 1979. The fact that Rule 148 does not apply to post October 1, 1979 petitions seems unfortunate, since in several respects Rule 148 is less restrictive than § 1145. For example, Rule 148(b) is available to affiliates of debtor-issuers; however, since affiliates are deemed to be § 1145(b)(1) under-writers, they could not use Rule 148(b), even if it were available with respect to reorganization petitions filed after October 1, 1979.[12] Of course, the debtor in possession or trustee may issue and sell securities pursuant to the Securities Act § 4(2) or Regulation D exemptions. In that event Rule 144 may be available. They may also utilize the § 3(a)(11) exemption and take advantage of Rule 147 with respect to resales. Or they may resort to Regulation A.

Section 1145(b)(1) deems certain holders of § 1145(a)(1) exchange securities to be underwriters under § 2(11) of the Securities Act. These persons may not resell such securities without finding an independent exemption under the 1933 Act or complying with the registration and prospectus requirements of that Act.

Resales by Non-Affiliates. The effect of §§ 1145(b)(3) and (c) is to permit persons who are not underwriters under paragraph (b)(1) or under § 2(11) of the 1933 Act to resell § 1145(a)(1) exchange securities without volume limitations. Since offers and sales of § 1145(a)(1) securities are deemed to be public offer-ings, resales of such securities are not subject to the volume and holding period limitations of Rule 144 and therefore they may be sold immediately.

On the other hand, since §§ 1145(b)(3) and (c) apply only to securities issued pursuant to § 1145(a)(1), persons holding portfolio securities sold to them in a § 1145(a)(3) transaction must search elsewhere for an exemption when reselling securities. One possibility is the Section 4(1) exemption under the Securities Act. If the portfolio securities are acquired from the debtor or an affiliate in brokers' transactions under the leakage provisions of § 1145(a)(3)(C), the pur-chaser would hold unrestricted securities. If the securities were restricted securities in the hands of the debtor and were acquired in a private sale they would be restricted securities within the meaning of Rule 144(a)(3). Persons

---

10. Securities Act Release No. 6032 (Mar. 5, 1979), at n. 10; Securities Act Release No. 6099 (Aug. 2, 1979), 1 Fed. Sec. L.Rep. (CCH) ¶ 2705H, Q. 91, at 2820.

11. Securities Act Release No. 6389 (Mar. 8, 1982).

12. In addition, the volume limitations of Rule 148 applicable to the sale of portfo-lio securities are more generous than those of § 1145. It has been argued that al-though the § 1145(a)(3) minimum standard cannot be altered by SEC action, an in-crease in the maximum volume limits for unregistered offerings of portfolio securi-ties is permissible; however, the fact re-

mains that Rule 148 in terms does not apply to proceedings under Chapter 11 of the Bankruptcy Reform Act of 1978.

Moreover, Rule 148 is more generous than Rule 144 which is applicable to re-sales of restricted securities acquired in an exempt transaction or sales by affiliates of an issuer. Under Rule 144, affiliates are subject to a two-year holding period on the resale of "restricted" securities, whereas Rule 148 does not impose a holding period requirement on affiliates.

On the interaction of § 1145 and Rule 148, compare the authorities cited at note 9 supra.

acquiring such portfolio securities in a private sale would be subject to the holding-period requirements of Rule 144(d) and the volume limitation of Rule 144(e).

Stockbrokers' Exemption. Section 1145(a)(4) provides an exemption for re-sales of securities received in a transaction under § 1145(a)(1) or (2) through a stockbroker provided certain conditions are met. The sale must occur before the expiration of 40 days after the first date on which the security was bona fide offered to the public by the issuer or by or through an underwriter; and the issuer must furnish a disclosure statement approved under § 1125, and supplementary information, if the court so orders. The exemption is patterned on § 4(3)(A) of the Securities Act. Since § 1145(a)(4) is limited to § 1145(a)(1) or (2) securities, it has no application to resales of portfolio securities received in a § 1145(a)(3) transaction.

Relation of § 3(a)(7) of the Securities Act to § 364 of the Bankruptcy Code. Section 364(a) of the Bankruptcy Code permits a trustee who is authorized to operate the business of a debtor to issue securities in the ordinary course of business, without obtaining prior approval of the court. Under subsections (b) and (c), the trustee may issue securities not in the ordinary course of business, with approval of the court. Section 364(f) exempts from the registration provisions of Section 5 of the 1933 Act, the Trust Indenture Act, and State securities laws offers and sales of these securities, except as to a person that is an underwriter as defined in § 1145(b). Although § 364(f) is a necessary exemption from registration for securities issued in the ordinary course of business under § 364(a), it seems redundant as applied to court authorized securities which are also exempt from Section 5 registration by virtue of § 3(a) (7) of the Securities Act. With respect to any debt security issued by a trustee or the debtor in possession, § 3(a)(7) continues to apply and provide an express exemption from the § 5 registration and prospectus provisions under that Act for certificates of indebtedness issued to finance post-petition operations, with approval of the court.

The conventional view has been that § 3(a)(7) of the Securities Act is a security exemption which grants a permanent exemption from registration, rather than a transaction exemption.[13] Curiously enough, the legislative history indicates that the House Committee on the Judiciary understood § 364 and § 3(a)(7) to be transaction exemptions, not perpetual exemptions for the security.[14] Moreover, the "underwriter" limitation in § 364(f) supports the view that § 364(f) is a transaction exemption. Nevertheless, the prevailing view seems to be that § 3(a)(7) is a security exemption. This view has been accepted in ALI Federal Securities Code § 302(13), codifying § 3(a)(7) on the ground that the need for limitations against resales by a § 1145(b) underwriter "is not apparent with respect to securities issued under court approval in order to finance the receivership, bankruptcy or reorganization proceedings, and in view of the absence of similar restrictions in [§ 3(a)(7) of the Securities Act] as amended by the Reform Act, § 302(13) here follows the [§] 3(a)(7) rather than the 11 U.S.C. § 364(f) model."[15] If, however, a claim for administrative expense, represented by a certificate of indebtedness, issued pursuant to a

---

13. Thompson Ross Securities Co., 6 S.E.C. 1111, 1118 (1940); Hicks, Exempted Transactions Under the Securities Act of 1933 § 1.01 [3] 1–15 (1980 rev.); 2 Collier, Bankruptcy ¶ 364.07 (15th ed. 1980); Orlanski, Resale of Securities, 53 Am. Bankr.L.J. 327, 348 (1979). Contra, Mitchell, Securities Regulation in Bankruptcy Reorganizations, 54 Am.Bankr. L.J. 99, 108, 137 (1980).

14. H.R.Rep. No. 95–595, supra note 1, at 236–38.

15. ALI, Federal Securities Code § 302(13), Comment (3).

§ 3(a)(7) exemption, is exchanged for plan securities under § 1145(a)(1), the securities so received would not be regarded as exempt securities.

For discussions of the securities regulation aspects of Chapter 11 of the Bankruptcy Reform Act of 1978, see Epling & Thompson, Securities Disclosures in Bankruptcy, 39 Bus.Law. 855 (1984); Morgan, Application of the Securities Laws in Chapter 11 Reorganizations Under the Bankruptcy Reform Act, 1983 U.Ill.L.Rev. 861; 7 Hicks, Exempted Transactions Under the Securities Act of 1933, Ch. 3 (1986 rev.); Corotto & Picard, Business Reorganizations and the Bankruptcy Reform Act of 1978—A New Approach to Investor Protection and the Role of the SEC, 28 DePaul L.Rev. 961 (1979); King, Chapter 11 of the 1978 Bankruptcy Code, 53 Am.Bankr.L.J. 107 (1979); Mitchell, Securities Regulation in Bankruptcy Reorganization, 54 Am.Bankr.L.J. 99 (1980); Orlanski, The Resale of Securities Issued in Reorganization Proceedings and the Bankruptcy Reform Act of 1978, 53 Am.Bankr.L.J. 327 (1979); Trost, Business Reorganizations Under Chapter 11 of the New Bankruptcy Code, 34 Bus.Law. 1309 (1979); Note, 53 So.Cal.L.Rev. 1527 (1980).

SECTION 6. INTEGRATION OF EXEMPTIONS

INTEGRATED OFFERINGS

The Securities Act contains a number of discrete transaction exemptions from the registration and prospectus delivery requirements of § 5 which are available to issuers of securities. Among these are the private offering exemptions (§ 4(2), § 4(6) and Rules 506 and 505); the limited offering exemptions under § 3(b) (e.g. Regulation A and Rule 504); the intrastate exemption (§ 3(a) (11) and Rule 147); and the §§ 3(a)(9) and 3(a)(10) exemptions for certain exchange transactions.

As these sections are construed, for an exemption to be available, each transaction must satisfy all of the conditions of a single exemption. Moreover, where there are a series of offerings, every proposed unregistered offering may be linked with a prior or subsequent offering; if such linkage occurs, two or more ostensibly discrete offerings may be deemed to comprise a single transaction. The doctrine of integration entails the process of combining multiple offerings into a single offering, and the effect of such combination may be to destroy one or more of the exemptions. For example, A, B and C form X corporation in State Y and issue shares to themselves at $10 a share. A is a resident of State Z; B and C are residents of State Y. Immediately thereafter, the corporation makes a public offering of shares at the same price utilizing the § 3(a)(11) exemption, the offers and sales being restricted solely to residents of State Y. If these two offerings were integrated into a single transaction, the § 4(2) private offering exemption would be nullified by backward integration; and the § 3(a)(11) exemption would be unavailable, as a result of forward integration. Again, suppose that two years later X corporation makes another intrastate offering of common stock in strict compliance with § 3(a)(11) which is followed by a 1933 Act registered offering of common stock in which sales are made to nonresidents of State Y. If the two offerings are integrated, the § 3(a) (11) exemption would be nullified, although the registered offering would remain unaffected. In that case, the concept would result only in one-way integration. The underlying policy behind the doctrine is that issuers should not be permitted to avoid registration, by splitting what is essentially a single financing into two or more ostensibly separate and distinct transactions, each of which, if regarded as a discrete transaction, would qualify under one of the exemptions. We have encountered the integration doctrine in a number of contexts. It may be helpful at this point to bring these threads together.

The principle first emerged in connection with § 3(a)(11) which makes the intrastate exemption hinge upon the *entire issue* being offered and sold only to residents of the state in question.[1] Although the Commission has stated that whether an offering will be regarded as a part of a larger offering, and thus be integrated is a question of fact, it added:[2]

> "Any one or more of the following factors may be determinative of the question of integration: (1) are the offerings part of a single plan of financing; (2) do the offerings involve issuance of the same class of security; (3) are the offerings made at or about the same time; (4) is the same type of consideration to be received, and (5) are the offerings made for the same general purpose."

According to this formulation, it is possible that the presence of a single factor may cause two offerings to be parts of a single issue. The same linguistic formulation of the doctrine appears in Rule 147.[3] At the same time, Rule 147(b)(2) provides a safe harbor against the application of the doctrine to Rule 147 offerings of the issuer pursuant to the exemptions provided by § 3 or § 4(2) of the Act or pursuant to a 1933 Act registration statement which occurs, outside of six month "window-periods" immediately preceding or immediately following offerings made pursuant to the rule. However, offerings by the issuer of the same or similar class of securities as that offered pursuant to Rule 147 during a "window-period" causes a loss of this safe-harbor. In that event, to determine whether offerings should be integrated, reference should be made to the foregoing five-factor test as set forth in Securities Act Release No. 4434.

The "issue" concept is read into the § 4(2) private offering exemption, since that exemption, with some exceptions hereafter noted, is available only to "transactions by an issuer *not involving any* public offering." In Securities Act Release No. 4552 (Nov. 6, 1962), the Commission again stated that with respect to the § 4(2) exemption the determination of whether offerings should be integrated "depends on the particular facts or circumstances," but that the five integration factors set forth above "*should be considered.*"[4] Nothing was said as to what weight should be given to the various factors, whether a single factor might be determinative, or why the formulation differs from that under § 3(a)(11) and Rule 147. This same difference in language has been repeated in Rule 502, raising the theoretical possibility that a § 3(a)(11) transaction which is followed by a § 4(2) transaction might result in backward integration so as to destroy the § 3(a)(11) exemption, although the § 4(2) transaction might remain intact.[5] Rule 502(a) contains a safe-harbor provision against integration of offerings identical with that provided in Securities Act Release No. 4552 and former Rule 146.

The safe-harbor provisions of Rule 502(a) and Rule 147(b)(2) provide a shield for the Rule 506 or Rule 147 offering as the case may be, but neither of those

---

1. Securities Act Release No. 97 (Dec. 28, 1933), 11 Fed.Reg. 10,949 (1946).

2. Securities Act Release No. 4434 (Dec. 6, 1961) supra at page 282. For an analysis of the SEC Staff's treatment of these five components in no-action letters, during the period 1971–1979, see Deaktor, Integration of Securities Offerings, 31 U.Fla. L.Rev. 465, 525–538 (1979). The Staff ceased to render no-action letters respecting integration in 1979 but reversed itself

and resumed the practice in 1985. See Clover Financial Corporation (avail. Apr. 5, 1979); 17 BNA Sec.Reg. & L.Rep. 403 (1985).

3. Preliminary Note 3 to Rule 147.

4. Securities Act Release No. 4552 (Nov. 6, 1962).

5. Preliminary Note 3 to Rule 147; see Deaktor, supra note 2, at 503.

provisions provides a safe-harbor for the other exempt offering. Thus, if an issuer were to make a Rule 506 offering separated by more than six months from a § 3(a)(9), § 3(a)(11) or a § 4(2) offering, the latter offering could lose its exemption, if the conditions for integration under the five-factor test were applicable. The integration would be only one way, however, and the Rule 506 transaction would not be affected.

The "issue" concept is also imported into § 3(a)(9). This is accomplished by reading the word "exclusively" as modifying both "exchanged" and "security holders." Accordingly, an exchange of securities with existing security holders cannot be combined with a § 4(2) private offering of the same class of securities to institutional investors.[6] Indeed, if the exchange with the shareholders is itself a public offering,[7] the private offering exemption would also be lost. If, however, the offerings entail different "issues" of securities, the exemption is not destroyed.[8]

Section 3(b) authorizing the Commission by rule to add any class of securities to those exempted in § 3, specifies that no such issue shall be exempted "where the aggregate amount at which such issue is offered to the public exceeds $5,000,000."

The Commission has made exceptions to the doctrine of integration as applied to the § 4(2) private offering exemption and to Regulation A, presumably under the authority granted in § 19(a) to define technical terms.

First. Rule 152 provides that the § 4(2) exemption is not destroyed "although *subsequently* * * * the issuer decides to make a public offering and/or files a registration statement." On the other hand, the § 3(a)(11) exemption may be destroyed if the issuer offers the rest of an issue, even after registration, to non-residents.[9] The purpose of Rule 152 was to allow "those who have contemplated or begun to undertake a private offering to register securities without incurring any risk of liability as a consequence of having first contemplated or begun to undertake a private offering."[10] If, however, a private offering and a registered offering were planned at the same time, the rule literally would seem to offer no protection. Although the rule on its face appears to apply to any "public offering," the uniform view is that only Regulation A and registered offerings qualify.[11]

The Staff has had difficulty in applying what is essentially a subjective test. The Commission interprets the Rule to apply only where the decision to undertake the public offering is made subsequent to the private offering.[12] The only exception is to allow private financing to be used for organizational expenses. Nor does the Commission integrate public offerings with contemporaneous private offerings where the issues are for a different purpose. The most serious problem arises in connection with startup companies where it is contemplated that there will be several rounds of venture capital private placements to be followed by an initial public offering when the issuer has

6. See SEC Securities Act Release No. 2029 (Aug. 8, 1939), supra at page 403.

7. Cf. SEC v. Ralston Purina Co., 346 U.S. 119 (1953), supra at page 235.

8. See supra note 6.

9. Texas Glass Manufacturing Corp., 38 S.E.C. 630 (1958).

10. Securities Act Release No. 305 (Mar. 2, 1935), quoted in Deaktor, supra note 2, at 497 n. 206 (1979).

11. 1 L. Loss, Securities Regulation 689 n. 139; 3 H. Bloomenthal, Securities and Federal Corporate Law § 4.14 [5] [a] at 4-156.1 (1981 rev.); Deaktor, supra note 2, at 497.

12. Stevenson, Integration and Private Placements, 19 Rev. of Sec. & Commodities Reg. 49, 55 (1986).

demonstrated the capacity to produce and market a highly distinctive and attractive product.[13]

Second. Rule 254(d)(2) of Regulation A exempts from the computation of the securities to be offered, securities acquired, otherwise than for distribution, by a single holder of the majority of the outstanding voting stock of the issuer in a pro rata offering to shareholders.

Third. The Commission has relaxed the rigors of Regulation A by permitting use of the maximum amount of $1,500,000 available to issuers during any twelve-month period, year after year, even though the offerings are a part of a single plan of financing or are made for the same general purpose. The same principle has been embodied in Rule 504 exempting limited securities offerings by closely-held issuers so as to allow sales of not to exceed $500,000 within successive twelve-month periods and Rule 505 exempting offerings by an issuer not exceeding $5,000,000 within successive 12-month periods. Rules 504 and 505 of Regulation D and Regulation A were all issued pursuant to § 3(b). While a transaction may be exempt under one of these rules or regulations, the transaction may be integrated with other transactions effected in reliance on another exemptive rule. These same principles of integration were generally embodied in Regulation D which replaced former Rules 240, 242 and 146 with Rules 504, 505 and 506 respectively.[14] Rule 502(a) provides a uniform safe-harbor applicable to all three rules which is identical with those contained in Rules 146(b)(1) and 242(b), except that sales pursuant to any § 3(b) exemption during the six-month "window periods" as provided in Rule 242(b) were not put under the safe-harbor umbrella.[15]

Foreign Offerings. The Commission has also taken the position that the registration provisions of Securities Act § 5 "are primarily intended to protect American investors." Accordingly, sales of securities that "come to rest" abroad will generally not be integrated with contemporaneous sales in the United States, provided that precautions are taken to ensure that securities that come to rest abroad will not flow back into the hands of American investors.[16]

ABA Task Force Integration Proposal. Despite the adoption of additional specific safe harbor tests in SEC rules, the Commission has not provided an overall conceptual framework for dealing with the problem of integration. As the ABA task force report on Integration put it:[17]

> In view of the many changes in business practices and securities regulation during the past twenty years, the entire integration concept seriously needs rethinking. If consistently and strictly applied, the concept could cause numerous sales to be integrated (and thereby registered) when their registration would not significantly enhance investor protection and could seriously impair the issuer's capital formation and operating plans. Moreover, the integration concept currently is being invoked in many diverse circumstances involving the five transaction exemptions under the Act (and several rules thereunder) that would otherwise be available—many of which have

---

13. Id.

14. Securities Act Release No. 6339 (Aug. 7, 1981), 23 SEC Docket 446, at 456–57 (Aug. 25, 1981).

15. See Securities Act Release No. 6389 (Mar. 8, 1982) text at notes 31, 32.

16. Securities Act Release No. 4708 (1984); preliminary note 7 to Regulation D; Note to Rule 502(a). The anti-flow back

provisions and their implementation are discussed in American Bar Association, Committee on Federal Regulation of Securities, Integration of Securities Offerings: Report of the Task Force on Integration, 41 Bus.Law. 595, 640 (1986) (hereinafter cited as ABA Task Force Report on Integration).

17. See ABA Task Force Report on Integration, supra note 16.

their own means for ensuring investor protection—to which the necessity for an integration concept may vary greatly.

The problem has been particularly acute in the context of partnership offerings where offerings of different entities by affiliated sponsors may be integrated into one larger nonexempt offering. An ABA committee sought to address the confusion in this area by preparing a position paper proposing a new test for "identifying *discrete* offerings which need not be integrated with other offerings sponsored by affiliated persons." [18] Although the proposals have not been acted on by the Commission, the report has been used as a guideline by securities practitioners. More recently, an ABA Task Force on Integration has produced a more ambitious product which incorporates and integrates the Subcommittee's proposals into a more comprehensive integration analysis, together with a new Proposed Rule 152 for the integration of securities offerings.

For the purpose of analysis, the Task Force identified three categories of integration: "offering integration," "venture integration," and "issuer integration." [19] Offering integration concerns multiple offerings of a single issuer. The offerings may consist of sales of different classes of securities at the same time or the same class of securities at different times. Venture integration arises when offerings of ostensibly different issuers are integrated because the projects and issuers involved are closely related. Issuer integration occurs when related entities offerings securities have a common controlling person or persons (e.g. a franchisor or licensor) and have significant economic ties with one another or with a common entity.

The ABA Task Force Report is an excellent discussion of the origin and development of the integrated offering doctrine. The proposed revised Rule 152 to replace the present Rule 152 is set forth below. It may well serve as the basis for a restatement of the doctrine of integration of securities offering by the SEC. In the meantime, the proposal will provide guidelines for securities practitioners in planning securities transactions so as to avoid the integration pitfall.

AMERICAN BAR ASSOCIATION

Task Force Report on Integration of Securities Offerings *

PROPOSED RULE 152

Integration of Securities Offerings

(a) An offering of securities shall not be integrated with any other offering of securities if it shall satisfy any of the following tests:

(1) The offerings are made by different issuers. For the purposes of this test: securities offered by different, but affiliated, entities shall be deemed not to have been offered by the same issuer if (i) the offering

---

18. American Bar Association, Subcommittee on Partnerships, Trusts and Unincorporated Associations of the Committee on Federal Regulation of Securities, 37 Bus.Law. 1591 (1982).

19. These categories were first formulated in J. Halperin, Private Placement of Securities (1984).

* American Bar Association, Committee on Federal Regulation of Securities, Integration of Securities Offerings: Report of the Task Force on Integration, 41 Bus.Law. 595, 642 app. (1986). Copyright 1986 by the American Bar Association. All rights reserved. Reprinted with permission of the American Bar Association and its Section of Corporation, Banking and Business Law.

entities shall be separate legal entities with separate books and records and the monies received by each for their securities shall not be commingled with the funds of a common promoter or sponsor or any other entity with a common promoter or sponsor; (ii) each offering entity, at the time of its offering and as a result of its receipt of the proceeds of its offering, had an independent opportunity to meet its primary investment objectives; and (iii) no material portion of the proceeds of the offering shall be invested in properties or projects in which an entity affiliated with the offering entity shall invest or shall have invested a material portion of its gross offering proceeds.

(2) The offerings are separated by at least six months. For the purpose of this test the interim period is to be measured from the closing of the last sale of the earlier offering to the first offer of the succeeding offering, and no offering integratable with either such offering, which does not satisfy any of the safe harbors enumerated in this Rule, shall have been effected during such interim period.

(3) The offerings involve different classes of securities (other than hybrid securities) and immediately prior to the second offering the issuer does not have a negative net worth and is not a development stage company. For the purposes of this safe harbor, all securities shall be deemed to fall into the following distinct classes:

    (i) *Common Stock* shall include only equity securities with ordinary voting rights and the right to receive dividends when and if declared and to participate in the net assets of the issuer upon its liquidation only after payment of all preferences.

    (ii) *Preferred Stock* shall include all equity securities with a preference as to the payment of dividends (which shall be more than nominal) and as to the distribution of the net assets of the issuer upon its liquidation and without the right to vote for the election of directors except for the right to elect a specified number of directors upon the issuer's failure to pay dividends or other specified default for a specified period.

    (iii) *Non-Secured Debt* shall include all unsecured and non-guaranteed debt which provides for the payment (as opposed to accrual) of interest at least annually and for the repayment of the unpaid principal on or before a specified date.

    (iv) *Secured Debt* shall include all non-subordinated indebtedness which is secured by a mortgage or security interest in assets that have a value which is reasonably believed by the issuer at the time of issuance of the securities to be at least equal to the face amount of the indebtedness.

    (v) *Hybrid Securities* shall include all securities which do not come within the foregoing definitions of the remaining four classes of securities.

For the purposes of this safe harbor, convertible securities shall be deemed to be both within the class of the convertible security as well as the security into which it is convertible; and stock purchase rights, options and warrants shall be deemed to constitute the class of securities which they entitle the holder to purchase.

(4) The offerings are effected for different purposes. In applying this safe harbor test, all offerings shall be deemed to have been undertaken for one or more of the following purposes: (A) to raise capital, (B) to extinguish indebtedness through an exchange of securities, (C) to secure

human resources, or (D) to acquire business operations or assets; and in determining whether an offering is for the purpose of acquiring assets or for raising operating capital, the offering shall be deemed to be for any purpose for which the proceeds of more than 25% of the offered securities are intended to be used.

(5) The offering is effected in reliance upon, and otherwise satisfies the requirements of, Section 3(a)(10) under the Act, or, if effected by an issuer, the securities of which are registered under Section 12 of the Securities Exchange Act of 1934 and which has filed all reports required to be filed under Section 13 of the Securities Exchange Act of 1934 during the preceding twelve months, satisfies the requirements of Section 3(a)(9) under the Act.

(b) No offering of securities shall be integrated with:

(1) an offering of securities registered under the Act, or

(2) an offering of securities made outside the United States to persons who are not residents of the United States and the issuer has taken measures reasonably designed to prevent such securities from flowing-back into the United States.

(c) The safe harbors created herein are not intended to be exclusive; nor shall they in any way be deemed to increase the aggregate sales limitations imposed by Regulations A, B and F and Rules 504 and 505 of Regulation D.

See American Bar Association, Committee on Federal Regulation of Securities, Integration of Securities Offerings: Report of the Task Force on Integration, 41 Bus.Law. 595 (1986); Stevenson, Integration and Private Placements, 19 Rev. of Sec. & Commodities Reg. 49 (Mar. 5, 1986); American Bar Association, Subcommittee on Partnerships, Trusts and Unincorporated Associations, Committee on Federal Regulation of Securities, Integration of Partnership Offerings: A Proposal for Identifying a Discrete Offering, 37 Bus.Law. 1591 (1982); Fein & Jacobs, Integration of Securities Transactions, 15 Rev. of Sec.Reg. 785 (1982); Deaktor, Integration of Securities Offerings, 31 U.Fla.L.Rev. 465 (1979).

PROBLEMS ON INTEGRATED OFFERINGS

1. A corporation, incorporated in State X, proposes to offer 10,000 shares of its common stock at $10 a share to build a manufacturing plant. On June 1 it makes a public offering using the § 3(a)(11) exemption, the offering being completed on June 10. The shares were sold solely to persons residing in State X. Needing additional funds to complete the project, on December 10 the company consults you as to feasibility of making a § 4(2) private offering of additional shares of common stock at the same price and for the same purpose. What do you advise and why?

2. For a number of years, Electronics, Inc., has had a stock option plan applicable to its executive group. The plan was adopted in compliance with Rule 16b–3 of the 1934 Act and meets the conditions of paragraphs (a) through (c) of that rule. The corporation now consults you regarding a proposal to adopt a stock purchase plan and make it available to a substantial number of lower echelon employees and make annual offerings of not to exceed $2,000,000 of its common stock to them while continuing to use the § 4(2) private offering exemption to issue stock options to members of its executive group. What, if any, exemptions are available? What do you recommend, and why?

3. Armidale Corp. was recently formed to build a building and operate a bowling alley and recreation center in State X. Needing $1,700,000 to finance

the enterprise, the corporation sold $200,000 of common stock to persons all of whom resided in the State of X. The company now consults you with a view to preparing a Regulation A offering of $1,500,000 of additional common shares to complete the financing. Is the regulation available?

4. If some years later Armidale Corp. should decide to raise $1,700,000 by offering $200,000 of three-year notes to three insurance companies, all of them taking for investment, and selling the remaining $1,500,000 to the public under Regulation A, is the regulation available?

5. El Rey Electronics Corp. sold and issued 300,000 shares of its common stock to Hazzard & Co., a local investment house, at $4 a share and a Letter of Notification was filed pursuant to Regulation A 12 days ago excluding Saturdays, Sundays and holidays. The Offering Circular stated that the offering price to the public was $5 a share. During the 15 days prior to the date of filing of the Letter of Notification sales of other shares of common stock were made in the over-the-counter market at $5 per share. Two days ago Hazzard & Co. started offering the shares at $5 a share and on the first day sold 30,000 shares. On the second day, however, the security became a "hot issue" and the price jumped to $8 a share. Hazzard & Co. now consults you to ascertain at what price they may sell the remainder of the shares and what they do next. They also ask whether they may sell additional shares to the public at the market so long as the gross price received by them does not exceed $1.5 million. What is your advice? Give an opinion also as to the legality of an alternative proposal, made by Hazzard, that it offer the remaining stock in 10,000 share lots to a number of brokers-dealers with which it has close business relations at $5 per share and let them have the profit on the rising market.

6. Mr. Gotrox holds oil and gas leases on 500,000 acres of land in State A. In order to finance wildcat drilling operations on the land, he formed three corporations, the corporate officers of which were his relatives and employees. He now proposes to raise the needed capital by having each corporation use the Regulation A exemption. What do you advise and why? See United States v. McGuire, 381 F.2d 306 (2d Cir. 1967).

7. Rambler Corporation, a start-up company, proposes to raise substantial amounts of capital by sales of common stock to promoters, directors, executive officers and full-time employees. It then proposes to sell an aggregate of $500,000 of securities in the next 12-month period to "outside" investors. Is Rule 504 available? See Morrison & Foerster, (Available July 30, 1975), [1975–1976 Transfer Binder] Fed.Sec.L.Rep. (CCH) ¶ 80,265.

8. Equity Programs, Inc., is a general partner in four limited partnerships, each of which proposes to offer limited partnership interests in a different real estate development. The projects are to be located in the suburbs of four different California cities. Equity wishes to offer the various limited partnership interests concurrently. There will be no general pool of offerees from which prospective purchasers will be selected; instead, a separate pool of offerees for each project will be constructed, although it is possible that some participants may invest in more than one limited partnership. There will also be a substantial variance in the prices per limited partnership unit, the prices per-unit being $1,000, $5,000, $10,000 and $15,000. What problems do you see in this proposal? What would you advise and why?

SECTION 7. GOING PUBLIC BY THE BACK DOOR

SECURITIES AND EXCHANGE COMMISSION v. DATRONICS ENGINEERS, INC.[a]

United States Court of Appeals, Fourth Circuit, 1973.
490 F.2d 250, cert. denied 416 U.S. 937.

Before BRYAN, SENIOR CIRCUIT JUDGE, and FIELD and WIDENER, CIRCUIT JUDGES.

ALBERT V. BRYAN, SENIOR CIRCUIT JUDGE: The Securities and Exchange Commission in enforcement of the Securities Act of 1933, § 20(b), and the Securities Exchange Act of 1934, § 21(e), sought a preliminary injunction to restrain Datronics Engineers, Inc., its officers and agents, as well as related corporations, from continuing in alleged violation of the registration and antifraud provisions of the Acts. The breaches are said to have been committed in the sale of unregistered securities, § 5 of the 1933 Act, and by the employment of false representations in their sale, § 10(b) of the 1934 Act, and Rule 10b-5 of the Commission.

Summary judgment went for the defendants, and the Commission appeals. We reverse.

Specifically, the complaint charged transgressions of the statutes by Datronics, assisted by the individual defendants, in declaring, and effectuating through the use of the mails, "spin-offs" to and among its stockholders of the unregistered shares of stock owned by Datronics in other corporations. With exceptions to be noted, and since the decision on appeal rests on a motion for summary judgment, there is no substantial dispute on the facts. Datronics was engaged in the construction of communications towers. Its capital stock was held by 1000 shareholders and was actively traded on the market. All of the spin-offs occurred within a period of 13 months * * * and the spun-off stock was that of nine corporations, three of which were wholly owned subsidiaries of Datronics and six were independent corporations.

The pattern of the spin-offs in each instance was this: Without any business purpose of its own, Datronics would enter into an agreement with the principals of a private company. The agreement provided for the organization by Datronics of a new corporation, or the utilization of one of Datronics' subsidiaries, and the merger of the private company into the new or subsidiary corporation. It stipulated that the principals of the private company would receive the majority interest in the merger-corporation. The remainder of the stock of the corporation would be delivered to, or retained by, Datronics for a nominal sum per share. Part of it would be applied to the payment of the services of Datronics in the organization and administration of the proposed spin-off, and to Datronics' counsel for legal services in the transaction. Datronics was bound by each of the nine agreements to distribute among its shareholders the rest of the stock.

a. As modified on denial of rehearing and rehearing en banc. Cert. denied 416 U.S. 937 (1974).

Before such distribution, however, Datronics reserved for itself approximately one-third of the shares. Admittedly, none of the newly acquired stock was ever registered; its distribution and the dissemination of the false representations were accomplished by use of the mails.

I. Primarily, in our judgment each of these spin-offs violated § 5 of the Securities Act in that Datronics caused to be carried through the mails an unregistered security "for the purpose of sale or for delivery after sale". Datronics was actually an issuer, or at least a coissuer, and not exempted from § 5 by § 4(1) of the Act, as "any person other than an issuer".

Datronics and the other appellees contend, and the District Court concluded, that this type of transaction was not a sale. The argument is that it was no more than a dividend parceled out to stockholders from its portfolio of investments. A noteworthy difference here, however, is that each distribution was an obligation. Their contention also loses sight of the definition of "sale" contained in § 2 of the 1933 Act. As pertinent here that definition is as follows:

"When used in this subchapter, unless the context otherwise requires—

* * *

"(3) The term 'sale' or 'sell' shall include every contract of sale or *disposition* of a security or interest in a security, *for value*. The term 'offer to sell', 'offer for sale', or 'offer' shall include every attempt or offer to dispose of, or solicitation of an offer to buy, a security or interest in a security, *for value*. * * *" (Accent added.)

As the term "sale" includes a "disposition of a security", the dissemination of a new stock among Datronics' stockholders was a sale. However, the appellees urged, and the District Court held, that this disposition was not a statutory sale because it was not "for value", as demanded by the definition. Here, again, we find error. Cf. Securities and Exchange Commission v. Harwyn Industries Corp., 326 F.Supp. 943, 954 (S.D.N.Y. 1971). Value accrued to Datronics in several ways. First, a market for the stock was created by its transfer to so many new assignees—at least 1000, some of whom were stockbroker-dealers, residing in various States. Sales by them followed at once—the District Judge noting that "[i]n each instance dealing promptly began in the spun-off shares". This result redounded to the benefit not only of Datronics but, as well, to its officers and agents who had received some of the spun-off stock as compensation for legal or other services to the spin-off corporations. Likewise, the stock retained by Datronics was thereby given an added increment of value. The record discloses that in fact the stock, both that disseminated and that kept by Datronics, did appreciate substantially after the distributions.

This spurious creation of a market whether intentional or incidental constituted a breach of the securities statutes. Each of the issuers by this wide spread of its stock became a publicly held corporation. In this process and in subsequent sales the investing public was not afforded the protection intended by the statutes. Further, the market and the public character of the spun-off stock were fired and fanned by the issuance of shareholder letters announcing future spin-offs, and by information statements sent out to the shareholders.

Moreover, we think that Datronics was an underwriter within the meaning of the 1933 Act. Hence its transactions were covered by the prohibitions, and were not within the exemptions, of the Act. §§ 3(a)(1) and 4(1) of the 1933 Act. By definition, the term underwriter "means any person who has purchased from an issuer with a view to, or offers or sells for an issuer in connection with, the distribution of any security, or participates or has a direct or indirect participation in any such undertaking. * * *" § 2(11) of the 1933 Act. Clearly, in these transactions the merger-corporation was an issuer; Datronics was a purchaser as well as a co-issuer; and the purchase was made with a view to the distribution of the stock, as commanded by Datronics' preacquisition agreements. By this underwriter distribution Datronics violated § 5 of the 1933 Act—sale of unregistered securities.

II. The Commission charged a violation by Datronics and its officers of § 10(b) of the 1934 Act and of Rule 10b–5. The breach occurred through untrue factual statements incident to the spin-offs. The District Court quite justifiably found that "in certain instances misleading statements were made by" Datronics and the individual defendants. This finding was reiterated by the District Court in discussing the announcements which were made to Datronics' stockholders with each spin-off.

A common explanation of the distribution to its stockholders was that it was "impractical" for Datronics itself to run the merger-corporations. Of course, as the minority stockholder, Datronics could not do so. The District Court termed the explanation false and a "pure subterfuge".

Since, however, the District Court was of the opinion that the distribution of the stock among Datronics' shareholders was not a sale, it held that the "misleading statements" were not outlawed by § 10(b) or by Commission Rule 10b–5. These provisions condemn such misrepresentations only when they are used "in connection with the purchase or sale of any security". Inasmuch as we believe there was a sale in each spin-off, we cannot agree with the District Court's determination. * * *

This was one of the trial court's reasons for not granting an injunction. Other grounds were that there was no indication that in the future the defendants might violate the statutes in suit; that the officers and agents who formulated and executed the spin-offs were no longer connected with Datronics; and that the present officers and agents assured the District Court that no more spin-offs of this kind would be indulged in. Moreover, the Court felt that by its interpretative releases the Commission had led Datronics and its codefendants to believe that spin-offs were not proscribed by these statutes. The Court was also persuaded by the failure of the Commission to act more vigilantly. While the issuance of an injunction is discretionary, it seems to us that overall, notwithstanding these considerations, the facts in this case warranted the grant of an injunction. * * *

Finally, a summary of the activities of Datronics is conclusively convincing that they violated the statutes in question, and should now be restrained to prevent recurrences. To begin with, it is noteworthy that they were not isolated or minimal transgressions. There were, to repeat, nine sales and distributions of unregistered stocks in little more than a year. They were huge in volume, ranging from 75,000 to 900,000 shares. The distribution was not confined to a small number of recipients; nor was it incidental to Datronics' corporate functions. Concededly, none of the several distributions had a business purpose. In short, the spin-offs seemingly constituted the major operation of Datronics at the time.

We cannot read the releases or letters of the Commission or its abstention from earlier suits as evincing express or implied approval of the repeated and large-scale violations as are here. The releases do not approve or condone a campaign, such as Datronics engaged in, to develop means and opportunities to promote spin-offs. Indeed, one of Datronics' agents was a "finder" of opportunities for spin-offs.

The dismissal order of the District Court will be vacated, and the cause remanded for the entry of a judgment sustaining the appellant's motion for the preliminary injunction sought in its complaint.

WIDENER, CIRCUIT JUDGE (concurring):

I concur in the issuance of the temporary injunction　*　*　*.

I note that the opinion of the court may not be broadly enough read to cast doubt upon the legitimate business acquisition of one company by another, or the legitimate business merger of two companies, although a market for securities spun off as a consequence of the transfer may be thereby created; for, as the opinion of the court recites, the market created by Datronics' spin-offs was spurious, doubtless meaning illegitimate, however actual it might have been, and Datronics caused the consummation of the transactions complained of without any business purpose of its own.

In my own opinion, the root of this case is the pre-existing agreement between Datronics and the various companies whose stocks it spun off with no apparent purpose other than the incidental benefits of creation of a public market for the stock. If the transactions were with a view to creating a public market for the stock which the various companies could not otherwise do absent compliance with the statute, then I think Datronics may be held to be an underwriter. The value requirement of a sale, for the issuer did receive value, I think, may be satisfied by the exchange of stock of the various companies with Datronics or by the exchange of stock of the various companies for services of Datronics. See also 58 Va.L.Rev. 1451.[b]

*　*　*

SPIN OFFS AND THE SHELL GAME

The *Datronics* case raised the question of the application of the 1933 Act and the 1934 Act to spin offs of securities of inactive or shell corporations and trading in such securities in the after market. In the 1960's, a method was conceived by which it was thought that a private company could achieve the status of a public company without a 1933 Act registration by going public through the back door. A variety of patterns were used; although the techniques differed, the overall objective remained the same.

In SEC v. Harwyn Industries Corp.,[1] the SEC sought to plug this possible loophole in the 1933 Act by seeking to enjoin various forms of spin offs of a subsidiary corporation's shares to the parent's stockholders without registration, thereby converting the subsidiary into a public corporation whose unregis-

---

b. On motions to reconsider, the defendants represented to the Court that no more spin offs would be undertaken. On that basis, the Court rescinded that part of the opinion which required the trial court to award a preliminary injunction, and remanded for a determination by the District Court, consistently with the remainder of the opinion, of whether an injunction should or should not be issued restraining Datronics in respect to such transactions as the opinion of the Court declares to be impermissible. Datronics' request for a rehearing in banc was denied.

1. 326 F.Supp. 943 (S.D.N.Y.1971).

tered shares would then be actively traded on the market. The court held that the *Harwyn* spin offs "violated the spirit and purpose of the registration requirements of § 5 of the 1933 Act". Nevertheless, the court concluded that defendants' interpretation of § 2(3) and 5 was "neither frivolous nor wholly unreasonable," and was made in good faith and on the advice of counsel. The court was moved by the somewhat ambivalent attitude of the Commission both before and after the Commission's Interpretative Release No. 4982. Upon assurance by counsel for defendants that since the Commission had made known its views by the commencement of the *Harwyn* action, their clients would not engage in further distribution of the type in question without registration, the court denied the Commission's motion for a preliminary injunction.

The *Datronics* case appears to have delivered the coup de grace to the spin off and shell game, while still permitting conventional spin offs, incident to a legitimate business combination.[2] Indeed, in United States v. Rubinson,[3] defendants who persisted in engaging in spin-offs followed by the resale of worthless securities to the unsuspecting public were convicted for violation of the registration and anti-fraud provisions of the federal securities laws.

In 1971, the Commission adopted Rule 15c2–11 under the 1934 Act for the purpose of preventing a broker or dealer to initiate or resume quotations respecting a security in the absence of adequate information concerning the security and the issuer.[4] In adopting the rule, the Commission emphasized that the rule was particularly applicable in connection with the distribution of securities of "shell" corporations by means of the "spin off" device. The Commission noted, however, that a fraudulent and manipulative potential also existed whenever a broker or dealer submitted quotations concerning any infrequently-traded security in the absence of adequate information. Rule 15c2–11 illustrates the Commission's use of the anti-fraud provisions of the 1934 Act to buttress the disclosure provisions of the 1933 Act.

See Orlanski, Going Public Through the Backdoor and the Shell Game, 58 Va.L.Rev. 1451 (1972); Lorne, The Portfolio Spin-Off and Securities Registration, 52 Tex.L.Rev. 918 (1974); Long, Control of the Spin-Off Device Under the Securities Act of 1933, 25 Okla.L.Rev. 317 (1972); Bloomenthal, Market-Makers, Manipulators and Shell Games, 45 St. John's L.Rev. 597, 615–625 (1971); Jacobs, The Anatomy of a Spin-Off, 1967 Duke L.J. 1 (1967); Shapiro and Katz, "Going Public Through the Backdoor" Phenomenon—An Assessment, 29 Md.L. Rev. 320 (1969); Note, A Suggested Treatment of Spin-Off Reorganizations, 53 Cornell L.Rev. 700 (1968); Note, The Spin-Off: A Sometimes Sale, 45 N.Y.U.L. Rev. 132 (1970); Note, A Spin-Off Spins in Two Directions, 43 Notre Dame Law. 389 (1968); Note, Corporate Spin-offs as a Device for Public Distribution Without Registration, 42 U.Colo.L.Rev. 111 (1970); Note, Registration of Stock Spin-Offs Under the Securities Act of 1933, 1980 Duke L.J. 965.

---

2. Compare Allied Signal, Inc. (avail. Feb. 24, 1986), 18 BNA Sec.Reg. & L.Rep. 336 (Mar. 7, 1986) in which the Staff granted no-action relief where the business objective of the spin-off was to place some 30 of its businesses in a subsidiary and distribute 70 percent of the subsidiary's stock pro rata to the shareholders without consideration.

3. 543 F.2d 951 (2d Cir. 1976), cert. denied 429 U.S. 850.

4. Securities Exchange Act Release No. 9310. (Sept. 13, 1971).

SUBDIVISION D. THE OBLIGATION TO REGISTER ON RESALES OF SECURITIES BY PERSONS OTHER THAN THE ISSUER

Chapter 9

OFFERINGS BY UNDERWRITERS AND DEALERS

SECTION 1. THE CONCEPT OF "UNDERWRITER"

Statutes and Regulations

Securities Act, §§ 2(2), 2(11), 4(1).

Rules 140–143, 152a, 405.

Statutory and Presumptive Underwriters

Statutory Underwriters. Section 5 prohibits the use of interstate facilities or the mails to sell a security unless a registration statement has become effective. However, § 4(1) specifically exempts transactions "by any person other than an issuer, underwriter or dealer * * *." Thus, only issuers, underwriters and dealers are subject to the registration and prospectus requirements of the 1933 Act. We have already explored the meaning of the term "issuer" as used in the Securities Act. We now consider the concept of "underwriter."

The definition of "underwriter" is found in § 2(11). The term means "any person who": [1] "has purchased from an issuer [or controlling person] with a view to, or [2] offers or sells for an issuer [or a controlling person] in connection with, the distribution of any security, or [3] participates or has a direct or indirect participation in any such undertaking, or [4] participates or has a participation in the direct or indirect underwriting of any such undertaking."

The addition of the bracketed material takes account of the last sentence of the paragraph which defines the term "issuer" as used therein to include, in addition to an issuer, any person in a control relationship with the issuer.

453

The House Committee Report described the meaning of the term "underwriter" this way: [1]

The term [underwriter] is defined broadly enough to include not only the ordinary underwriter, who for a commission promises to see that an issue is disposed of at a certain price, but also includes as an underwriter the person who purchases an issue outright with the idea of then selling that issue to the public. The definition of underwriter is also broad enough to include two other groups of persons who perform functions, similar in character, in the distribution of a large issue. The first of these groups may be designated as the underwriters of the underwriter, a group who, for a commission, agree to take over pro rata the underwriting risk assumed by the first underwriter. The second group may be termed participants in the underwriting or outright purchase, who may or may not be formal parties to the underwriting contract, but who are given a certain share or interest therein.

The term "underwriter," however, is interpreted to exclude the dealer who receives only the usual distributor's or seller's commission. This limitation, however, has been so phrased as to prevent any genuine underwriter passing under the mark of a distributor or dealer. The last sentence of this definition, defining "issuer" to include not only the issuer but also affiliates or subsidiaries of the issuer and persons controlling the issuer, has two functions. The first function is to require the disclosure of any underwriting commission which, instead of being paid directly to the underwriter by the issuer, may be paid in an indirect fashion by a subsidiary or affiliate of the issuer to the underwriter. Its second function is to bring within the provisions of the bill redistribution whether of outstanding issues or issues sold subsequently to the enactment of the bill. All the outstanding stock of a particular corporation may be owned by one individual or a select group of individuals. At some future date they may wish to dispose of their holdings and to make an offer of this stock to the public. Such a public offering may possess all the dangers attendant upon a new offering of securities. Wherever such a redistribution reaches significant proportions, the distributor would be in the position of controlling the issuer and thus able to furnish the information demanded by the bill. This being so, the distributor is treated as equivalent to the original issuer and, if he seeks to dispose of the issue through a public offering, he becomes subject to the act. The concept of control herein involved is not a narrow one, depending upon a mathematical formula of 51 percent of voting power, but is broadly defined to permit the provisions of the act to become effective wherever the fact of control actually exists.

Rule 140 is aimed at the indirect distribution of securities by the use of another legal entity. Thus if the chief part of a person's business consists of the purchase of the securities of one issuer, or of two or more affiliated issuers, and the sale of its own securities to finance such purchases, it is to be regarded as engaging in a distribution of the securities so acquired within the meaning of § 2(11). In this narrow range of operation, the net effect of the rule is to compel the registration of the securities acquired

1. Report of Committee on Interstate and Foreign Commerce, H.R.Rep.No.85, 73d Cong., 1st Sess., 13–14 (1933).

from the issuer or affiliated issuers before there can be a sale of the person's own securities.

Rule 141 makes clear that the dealer's "commission" referred to in § 2(11) is the usual "spread" between the underwriter's offering price to dealers and the public offering price, provided the profit margin is usual and customary for the type and size of the offering. The rule applies whether the dealer buys outright and resells the security or whether it is acting merely as a broker.

Rule 142 also permits persons who are not affiliated with the issuer or underwriter to make a commitment with the underwriter to purchase all or a part of any unsold portion of the offering after the passage of a specified period of time following the commencement of the offering, if the securities are acquired for investment rather than for distribution. According to the General Counsel of the SEC, this rule was adopted "in recognition of the value of secondary capital in facilitating the flow of investment funds into industry, and of the fact that the owners of such secondary capital cannot practicably perform the duty of thorough analysis imposed by the Act on the underwriter proper." [2] The rule thus makes clear "that a person who does no more than agree with an underwriter to take over some or all of the undistributed portion of the issue, and who purchases for investment any securities which his commitment thus obliges him to take up, does not thereby subject himself to liability as an underwriter of the securities of the issue actually distributed to the public." [3] As a practical matter, the rule opens the way for institutional investors such as insurance and investment companies or pension funds to make an advance commitment for a block of the securities to be offered at a discount from the public offering price, without thereby incurring the liability of an underwriter. The various limitations on the scope of the rule are designed to prevent evasion of the rule by persons who actually perform a distributive function or who are in a control relationship with the issuer or a principal underwriter.

Presumptive Underwriters. In recent years, during periods of a strong new issues market, there have been instances where a wealthy investor, or an institution purchased a large block of a registered offering, presumably for investment, and thereafter resold the securities to the public without the use of a statutory prospectus. To cope with this situation, the Commission and Staff have developed the "presumptive underwriter" doctrine. The doctrine as first formulated established an administrative rule-of-thumb that any person who purchased ten percent or more of a registered offering was presumed to be an underwriter within the meaning of § 2(11) of the 1933 Act. The rule was first enunciated and applied in business combination transactions under Rule 145, see supra at page 408. The doctrine, though never officially adopted by formal action of the Commission, nevertheless is applied in practice by the Staff. A definition of the doctrine as consistent with Commission practice has been formulated in these terms:

A person may be deemed to be an underwriter, within the meaning of § 2(11) of the Securities Act, if such person purchases or acquires a

2. Opinion of General Counsel, SEC Securities Act Release No. 1862, Dec. 13, 1938.

3. Ibid.

significant percentage of the securities offered pursuant to a registered distribution, except that such purchaser is not deemed to be an underwriter if he resells such securities in limited quantities.[4]

The Staff applies the presumptive underwriter doctrine in individual cases so as to prevent unrestricted resales by purchasers of large blocks of registered offerings free of the disclosure requirements generally applicable to registered offerings. Under the doctrine, such purchases followed by a resale creates a presumption that the seller is a statutory underwriter unless the burden is rebutted through showing of a change of circumstance or other justifiable cause. The Commission's practice is gleaned from no-action letters responding to interpretive requests. In practice, the Commission generally advises that such resales will not violate the Securities Act if such resales do not exceed the quantity limitations of Rule 144 or Rule 145 to be considered later in this chapter.

The doctrine, however, should not be applied woodenly where a person or entity is not engaging in a distributive activity. Thus, the Staff gave a no-action opinion that an insurance company would not be considered an underwriter in connection with recurrent purchases of large amounts of registered securities for investment so long as the securities were acquired from the issuer or underwriter in the ordinary course of the company's business, and no arrangement existed between the insurance company and others to participate in the distribution of securities. Insurance companies and pension funds must make investments which are sufficiently liquid to meet foreseeable obligations as well as unforeseen demands. This need for portfolio liquidity requires that such institutional investors be certain when purchasing securities that they will be able to resell the securities if the need arises without being tagged as a "presumptive underwriter."[5]

For an analysis and critique of the presumptive underwriter doctrine as an instrument in securities law enforcement, see Ahrenholz and Van Valkenberg, The Presumptive Underwriter Doctrine: Statutory Underwriter Status for Investors Purchasing a Specified Portion of a Registered Offering, 1973 Utah L.Rev. 773; Nathan, Presumptive Underwriters, 8 The Review of Securities Regulation 881 (1975).

SECURITIES & EXCHANGE COMMISSION v. CHINESE CONSOLIDATED BENEVOLENT ASSOCIATION, INC.[a]

United States Circuit Court of Appeals, Second Circuit, 1941.
120 F.2d 738.

AUGUSTUS N. HAND, CIRCUIT JUDGE. The Securities and Exchange Commission seeks to enjoin the defendant from the use of any instruments of interstate commerce or of the mails in disposing, or attempting to dispose, of Chinese Government bonds for which no registration statement has ever been made.

---

4. Ahrenholz and Van Valkenberg, The Presumptive Underwriter Doctrine: Statutory Underwriter Status for Investors Purchasing a Specified Portion of a Registered Offering, 1973 Utah L.Rev. 773, 775–776.

5. American Council of Life Insurance (Avail. June 10, 1983), Fed.Sec.L.Rep. (CCH) [1983–84 Transfer Binder] ¶ 77,526.

a. Cert. denied 314 U.S. 618 (1941).

The defendant is a New York corporation organized for benevolent purposes having a membership of 25,000 Chinese. On September 1, 1937, the Republic of China authorized the issuance of $500,000,000 in 4% Liberty Bonds, and on May 1, 1938 authorized a further issue of $50,000,000 in 5% bonds. In October, 1937, the defendant set up a committee which has had no official or contractual relation with the Chinese government for the purpose of:

(a) Uniting the Chinese in aiding the Chinese people and government in their difficulties.

(b) Soliciting and receiving funds from members of Chinese communities in New York, New Jersey and Connecticut, as well as from the general public in those states, for transmission to China for general relief.

All the members of the committee were Chinese and resided in New York City. Through mass meetings, advertising in newspapers distributed through the mails, and personal appeals, the committee urged the members of Chinese communities in New York, New Jersey and Connecticut to purchase the Chinese government bonds referred to and offered to accept funds from prospective purchasers for delivery to the Bank of China in New York as agent for the purchasers. At the request of individual purchasers and for their convenience the committee received some $600,000 to be used for acquiring the bonds, and delivered the moneys to the New York agency of the Bank of China, together with written applications by the respective purchasers for the bonds which they desired to buy. The New York agency transmitted the funds to its branch in Hong Kong with instructions to make the purchases for the account of the various customers. The Hong Kong bank returned the bonds by mail to the New York branch which in turn forwarded them by mail to the purchasers at their mailing addresses, which, in some cases, were in care of the defendant at its headquarters in New York. Neither the committee, nor any of its members, has ever made a charge for their activities or received any compensation from any source. The Bank of China has acted as an agent in the transactions and has not solicited the purchase of bonds or the business involved in transmitting the funds for that purpose.

No registration statement under the Securities Act has ever been made covering any of the Chinese bonds advertised for sale. Nevertheless the defendant has been a medium through which over $600,000 has been collected from would-be purchasers and through which bonds in that amount have been sold to residents of New York, New Jersey and Connecticut.

Motions for judgment were made by both parties upon pleadings setting forth the foregoing facts. As a result the court below entered a decree denying complainant's motion, granting defendant's motion and dismissing the complaint. The Commission has taken an appeal from the decree, which, in our opinion, ought to be reversed.

It should be observed at the outset that the Commission is not engaged in preventing the solicitation of contributions to the Chinese government, or its citizens. Its effort is only to prevent the sale of Chinese securities through the mails without registry. * * *

Section 5 of the Act provides as follows.

"Sec. 5. (a) Unless a registration statement is in effect as to a security, it shall be unlawful for any person, directly or indirectly—

"(1) to make use of any means or instruments of transportation or communication in interstate commerce or of the mails to sell or offer to buy such security through the use or medium of any prospectus or otherwise; or

"(2) to carry or cause to be carried through the mails or in interstate commerce, by any means or instruments of transportation, any such security for the purpose of sale or for delivery after sale."

Section 2(2) of the Act defines a "person" as including both a private corporation and a government.

Section 2(3) of the Act defines a "sale" or "offer to sell" as including: "every contract of sale or disposition of, attempt or offer to dispose of, or solicitation of an offer to buy a security * * *, for value; except that such terms shall not include preliminary negotiations or agreements between an issuer and any underwriter."

Section 4 provides the following exemptions from the requirements of Section 5 supra:

"Sec. 4. The provisions of section 5 shall not apply to any of the following transactions:

"(1) Transactions by any person other than an issuer, underwriter, or dealer; * * *."

Under Section 2(11) an "underwriter" is defined as: "any person who has purchased from an issuer with a view to, or sells for an issuer in connection with, the distribution of any security, or participates or has a direct or indirect participation in any such undertaking; * * *".

We think that the defendant has violated Section 5(a) of the Securities Act when read in connection with Section 2(3) because it engaged in selling unregistered securities issued by the Chinese government when it solicited offers to buy the securities "for value". The solicitation of offers to buy the unregistered bonds, either with or without compensation, brought defendant's activities literally within the prohibition of the statute. Whether the Chinese government as issuer authorized the solicitation, or merely availed itself of gratuitous and even unknown acts on the part of the defendant whereby written offers to buy, and the funds collected for payment, were transmitted to the Chinese banks does not affect the meaning of the statutory provisions which are quite explicit. In either case the solicitation was equally for the benefit of the Chinese government and broadly speaking was for the issuer in connection with the distribution of the bonds.

* * *

Under Section 4(1) the defendant is not exempt from registration requirements if it is "an underwriter". The court below reasons that it is not to be regarded as an underwriter since it does not sell or solicit offers to buy "for an issuer in connection with, the distribution" of securities. In other words, it seems to have been held that only solicitation authorized by the issuer in connection with the distribution of the Chinese bonds would satisfy the definition of underwriter contained in Section 2(11) and that defendant's activities were never for the Chinese government but only for the purchasers of the bonds. Though the defendant solicited the orders, obtained the cash from the purchasers and caused both to be forwarded so as to procure the bonds, it is nevertheless contended that its acts could not have been for the Chinese government because it had no contractual arrangement or even understanding with the latter. But the aim of the Securities Act is to have information available for investors. This objective will be defeated if buying orders can be solicited which result in uninformed and improvident purchases. It can make no difference as regards the policy of the act whether an issuer has solicited orders through an agent, or has merely taken advantage of the services of a person interested for patriotic reasons in securing offers to buy. The aim of the issuer is to promote the distribution of the securities, and of the Securities Act is to protect the public by requiring that it be furnished with adequate information upon which to make investments. Accordingly the words "[sell] for an issuer in connection with the distribution of any security" ought to be read as covering continual solicitations, such as the defendant was engaged in, which normally would result in a distribution of issues of unregistered securities within the United States. Here a series of events were set in motion by the solicitation of offers to buy which culminated in a distribution that was initiated by the defendant. We hold that the defendant acted as an underwriter.

There is a further reason for holding that Section 5(a)(1) forbids the defendant's activities in soliciting offers to buy the Chinese bonds. Section 4(1) was intended to exempt only trading transactions between individual investors with relation to securities already issued and not to exempt distributions by issuers. The words of the exemption in Section 4(1) are: "Transactions by any person other than an issuer, underwriter, or dealer; * * *". The issuer in this case was the Republic of China. The complete transaction included not only solicitation by the defendant of offers to buy, but the offers themselves, the transmission of the offers and the purchase money through the banks to the Chinese government, the acceptance by that government of the offers and the delivery of the bonds to the purchaser or the defendant as his agent. Even if the defendant is not itself "an issuer, underwriter, or dealer" it was participating in a transaction with an issuer, to wit, the Chinese Government. The argument on behalf of the defendant incorrectly assumes that Section 4(1) applies to the component parts of the entire transaction we have mentioned and thus exempts defendant unless it is an underwriter for the Chinese Republic. Section 5(a)(1), however, broadly prohibits sales of securities irrespective of the character of the person making them. The exemption is limited to "transactions" by persons other than "issuers, underwriters or dealers". It does not in terms or by fair implication protect those who are engaged in steps necessary to the distribution of security issues. To give Section 4(1) the construction urged by the defendant would afford a ready method of thwarting the policy of the law and evading its provisions.

It is argued that an injunction ought not to be granted because the interests of a foreign state are involved. But the provisions for registration statements apply to issues of securities by a foreign government. (See Section 2(2) and Section 7.) Section 6(a), moreover, permits a registration relating to securities issued by a foreign government to be signed by the underwriter, which we have held the defendant to be.

* * *

The decree is reversed with directions to the District Court to deny the defendant's motion to dismiss and to issue the injunction as prayed for in the bill of complaint. * * *

* * *

SECURITIES AND EXCHANGE COMMISSION v. GUILD FILMS CO., INC.[a]

United States Court of Appeals, Second Circuit, 1960.
279 F.2d 485.

MOORE, CIRCUIT JUDGE. This is an appeal under 28 U.S.C.A. § 1292(a) from an order by the district court, * * * granting a preliminary injunction to restrain the sale of 50,000 shares of Guild Films Company, Inc. common stock by two of the appellants, the Santa Monica Bank and The Southwest Bank of Inglewood. Pending a final determination of this action, the preliminary injunction was issued "unless and until" a registration statement should be filed under the Securities Act of 1933.

Section 5 of the Act makes it unlawful for anyone, by any interstate communication or use of the mails, to sell or deliver any security unless a registration statement is in effect. Section 4 provides, however, that "the provisions of section 5 * * * shall not apply to * * * (1) Transactions by any person other than an issuer, underwriter, or dealer." The banks claim that they come within this exemption to the registration requirements. The district court rejected this claim, holding that the banks were "underwriters" within the meaning of the Act. While the issue involved can be simply stated, a rather complete discussion of the facts is necessary.

The Original Loans by the Banks and the Security Therefor

On September 17, 1958, the Santa Monica Bank and The Southwest Bank of Inglewood jointly agreed to loan Hal Roach, Jr., $120,000 represented by two notes. * * *

The loans were * * * secured * * * by 30,000 shares of [F.L. Jacobs Co.] stock. Roach had used a large part of the proceeds of the loans to purchase a substantial number of the 30,000 Jacobs shares put up as collateral.

The Jacobs Stock and the Renewal Notes

Roach was an officer, director, and the controlling shareholder of F. L. Jacobs Co. of which Alexander L. Guterma was president. This company controlled the Scranton Corp. which owned Hal Roach Studios, which in turn owned both W-R Corp. and Rabco T.V. Production, Inc.

W-R Corp. and Guild Films, Inc. had made an agreement on January 23, 1959, under which W-R Corp. was to obtain 400,000 shares of Guild Films common stock (the registration of 50,000 shares of this stock is here in dispute) and a number of promissory notes in exchange for certain film properties. The stock was not registered with the S.E.C., but Guild Films agreed to use its best efforts to obtain registration. However, seeking to

a. Cert. denied 364 U.S. 819 (1960).

come within an exemption provided in section 4 of the Securities Act, the parties provided the following in their agreement:

"Stock Taken for Investment: W-R warrants, represents and agrees that all of the said 400,000 shares of Guild's common stock being contemporaneously issued hereunder, whether registered in the name of W-R or in accordance with the instructions of W-R, are being acquired for investment only and not for the purpose or with the intention of distributing or reselling the same to others. Guild is relying on said warranty and representation in the issuance of said stock."

On February 5, 1959, for reasons discussed below, Roach directed that 100,000 shares of the Guild Films stock be issued in the name of W-R Corp. and 100,000 shares (represented by two 50,000 share certificates) in the name of Rabco. Meacham, the treasurer of Guild Films, directed that the transfer agent stamp this restriction on the stock certificates:

"The shares represented by this certificate have not been registered under the Securities Act of 1933. The shares have been acquired for investment and may not be sold, transferred, pledged or hypothecated in the absence of an effective registration statement for the shares under the Securities Act of 1933 or an opinion of counsel to the company that registration is not required under said Act." The remaining 200,000 shares were not issued as the promised film properties were never transferred.

Although the Guild Films stock was issued "for investment only," the district court found that Roach "unquestionably" purchased it in order to have it resold. * * * These findings are uncontested.

On December 9, 1958, the Santa Monica Bank learned that the Jacobs stock had been suspended from trading on the New York Stock Exchange. That bank thereupon wrote to Roach asking him to liquidate the loan before December 15, 1958, because the Jacobs stock, which was then traded over-the-counter and had dropped in value to $5 per share, was "not now considered by our Loan Committee as acceptable collateral." After a number of conversations, the Santa Monica Bank agreed to renew Roach's note for 90 days upon deposit of 10,000 additional shares of Jacobs stock, or an equivalent in value in Scranton stock or upon payment of $30,000. A renewal note dated December 18, 1958 was sent to Meacham for Roach's signature, and interest on the matured note requested. The Santa Monica Bank [sic] agreed to renew on the same conditions. The notes were signed and returned, but Meacham requested "a few days in which to make up our minds" concerning the required additional collateral. Until the end of January, 1959, both banks were in constant communication with Roach, but no further collateral was deposited. On December 31, 1958, The Southwest Bank had informed him that its renewal would not be effective until additional security was supplied, and on January 28, 1959, it wrote to Roach demanding, by February 3, 1959 payment of the November 24, 1958 note, then more than six weeks overdue. On February 3, 1959, Roach telegraphed the Santa Monica Bank that he had "deposited $75,000 Guild Films, Inc. notes to your account at Chemical Corn Bank, New York. This best I can do till I return to Los Angeles next week." On the basis of this telegram, The Southwest Bank wrote to Roach agreeing to defer action until February 10th.

The Guild Films Stock

On that date Roach wired The Southwest Bank that he had sent 50,000 shares of Guild Films stock to the Santa Monica Bank. By a divided vote the Loan Committee of The Southwest Bank decided to renew the note, making it payable "On 'Demand' if 'No Demand' then all due March 18, 1959." On February 12th, one of the 50,000 share Guild Films certificates in the name of Rabco T.V. Productions was received by the Santa Monica Bank. The restrictive legend quoted above was stamped on the face of the certificate. Upon receipt thereof, the Santa Monica Bank authorized the Chemical Corn Exchange Bank in New York to release the Guild Films notes.

Subsequent Attempts by the Banks to Sell the Guild Films Stock

On February 12th, the Santa Monica Bank and The Southwest Bank learned that the Jacobs stock had been suspended from all trading by the S.E.C. The Santa Monica Bank immediately telegraphed Roach demanding payment by February 16th, and stating that otherwise the stock would be sold to liquidate the loan. Roach failed to pay and the banks attempted to sell the securities through brokers on the American Stock Exchange.

The Guild Films transfer agent refused to transfer the stock to the banks because of the stamped restriction. The Santa Monica Bank then wired Guild Films that unless the stock was released or exchanged for unrestricted securities, the matter would be taken to the American Stock Exchange and the S.E.C. "for their assistance and release." Guild Films refused to act; it also refused an offer to exchange the 50,000 shares for 25,000 shares of unrestricted stock; and no application for registration was made to the S.E.C.

In August, 1959, the Santa Monica Bank brought an action against Guild Films in the New York Supreme Court to compel the transfer of the stock. On September 18, 1959, that court ordered the transfer of the stock to the bank. The court based its order on a referee's report which found that the stock was exempt from the Securities Act of 1933. The Santa Monica Bank thereupon ordered 9,500 shares of the Guild Films stock sold. The S.E.C. learned of the sale and notified the bank and Guild Films that the stock could not be sold without registration. The bank then sought a Commission ruling that the stock was exempt. Despite an adverse opinion by the Commission, the bank sold an additional 10,500 shares on September 24, 1959. At that point, the Commission filed this suit to restrain the delivery of these shares and the sale of the remainder of the stock. The district court granted a preliminary injunction against delivery and further sale.

The Securities Act of 1933 was primarily intended to "protect investors by requiring registration with the Commission of certain information concerning securities offered for sale." Gilligan, Will & Co. v. S.E.C., 2 Cir., 1959, 267 F.2d 461, 463. An exemption from the provisions of § 5 of the Act was provided by § 4(1) for "transactions by any person other than an issuer, underwriter or dealer" because it was felt that no protection was necessary in these situations. * * * The primary question involved in this case is: were appellants issuers, underwriters or dealers within this exemption?

An "underwriter" is defined in § 2(11) as "any person who has purchased from an issuer with a view to, or sells for an issuer in connection with, the distribution of any security, * * * or participates or has a participation in the direct or indirect underwriting of any such undertaking * * *." The burden of proof is on the one seeking an exemption. * * *

The banks cannot be exempted on the ground that they did not "purchase" within the meaning of § 2(11). The term, although not defined in the Act, should be interpreted in a manner complementary to "sale" which is defined in § 2(3) as including "every * * * disposition of * * * a security or interest in a security, for value * * *." In fact, a proposed provision of the Act which expressly exempted sales "by or for the account of a pledge holder or mortgagee selling or offering for sale or delivery in the ordinary course of business and not for the purpose of avoiding the provisions of the Act, to liquidate a bona fide debt, a security pledged in good faith as collateral for such debt," was not accepted by Congress. * * *

Nor is it a defense that the banks did not deal directly with Guild Films. This court has recently stated that "the underlying policy of the Act, that of protecting the investing public through the disclosure of adequate information, would be seriously impaired if we held that a dealer must have conventional or contractual privity with the issuer in order to be an 'underwriter'." S.E.C. v. Culpepper, 2 Cir., 1959, 270 F.2d 241, 246, following S.E.C. v. Chinese Consol. Benev. Ass'n, 2 Cir., 1941, 120 F.2d 738, * * *. It was held in these two cases that § 4(1) "does not in terms or by fair implication protect those who are engaged in steps necessary to the distribution of a security issue. To give Section 4(1) the construction urged by the defendant would afford a ready method of thwarting the policy of the law and evading its provisions." S.E.C. v. Chinese Consol. Benev. Ass'n, supra * * *.

The banks have contended that they were "bona fide pledgees" and therefore "entitled upon default to sell the stock free of restrictions." They assume that "good faith" in accepting the stock is a sufficient defense. See Loss, Securities Regulation, 346 (1951). But the statute does not impose such a "good faith" criterion. The exemption in § 4(1) was intended to permit private sales of unregistered securities to investors who are likely to have, or who are likely to obtain, such information as is ordinarily disclosed in registration statements. * * * The "good faith" of the banks is irrelevant to this purpose. It would be of little solace to purchasers of worthless stock to learn that the sellers had acted "in good faith." Regardless of good faith, the banks engaged in steps necessary to this public sale, and cannot be exempted.

Without imputing to the banks any participation in a preconceived scheme to use the pledge of these securities as a device for unlawful distribution, it may be noted that when the 50,000 shares of Guild Films stock were received on February 12, 1959, the banks knew that they had been given unregistered stock and that the issuer had specifically forbidden that the stock "be sold, transferred, pledged or hypothecated in the absence of an effective registration statement for the shares under the Securities Act of 1933 or an opinion of counsel to the company that registration is not required under said Act." Furthermore, from Roach's prior unfulfilled promises, the banks should have known that immediate sale was almost inevitable if they were to recoup their loans from the security received. On February 11, 1959, the day before the stock was received, the S.E.C. suspended trading in the Jacobs stock. And on the very day that the stock was received, appellants wired Roach that they would call the loan unless payment were made. For months the banks had threatened action but declined to act; circumstances finally required action. The banks cannot now claim that this possibility was unforeseeable. The district court properly enjoined the threatened violation.

Affirmed.[b]

SECTION 2. STATUTORY RESTRICTIONS ON DISTRIBUTIONS OF SECURITIES BY CONTROLLING PERSONS OR AFFILIATES

Statutes and Regulations

Securities Act, §§ 2(11), 3(a)(1).

Regulation C, Rule 405 (Definition of "Control").

IN THE MATTER OF IRA HAUPT & CO.
Securities and Exchange Commission, 1946.
23 S.E.C. 589.

FINDINGS AND OPINION OF THE COMMISSION

This proceeding was instituted under Sections 15(b) and 15A(l)(2) of the Securities Exchange Act of 1934 to determine whether Ira Haupt & Co. ("Respondent") willfully violated Section 5(a) of the Securities Act of 1933 and, if so, whether the revocation of its registration as a broker-dealer and its expulsion or suspension from membership in the National Association of Securities Dealers, Inc. ("NASD"), a registered securities association, would be in the public interest.

The alleged violation of Section 5(a) is based on respondent's sale, for the accounts of David A. Schulte, a controlled corporation of Schulte's, and the David A. Schulte Trust (sometimes hereinafter referred to collectively as the "Schulte interests"), of approximately 93,000 shares of the common stock of Park & Tilford, Inc., during the period November 1, 1943, to June 1, 1944. It is conceded that the Schulte interests were in control of Park & Tilford during this period, that the sales were effected by use of the mails and instrumentalities of interstate commerce, and that the stock was not covered by a registration statement under the Securities Act.

b. Notes, 48 Calif.L.Rev. 841 (1960); 60 Colum.L.Rev. 1179 (1960); 74 Harv.L.Rev. 1241 (1961); 36 N.Y.U.L.Rev. 901 (1961); 8 U.C.L.A.L.Rev. 663 (1961); 13 Stan.L.Rev. 652 (1961). And see Rice, Effects of Registration Requirements on the Disposition of Pledged Securities, 21 Stan.L.Rev. 1607 (1969); Sargent, Pledges and Foreclosure Rights Under the Securities Act of 1933, 45 Va.L.Rev. 885 (1959). Cf. Sargent, The

"Guild Films" Case: The Effect of "Good Faith" in Foreclosure Sales of Unregistered Securities Pledged as Collateral, 46 Va.L.Rev. 1573 (1960).

Cf. Rubin v. United States, 449 U.S. 424 (1981), holding that a pledge of stock as security for a loan is an "offer or sale" of a security under § 17(a) of the Securities Act.

After appropriate notice a hearing was held before a trial examiner. At the hearing a stipulation of facts was submitted in lieu of testimony. A trial examiner's report was waived, briefs and reply briefs were filed, and we heard argument.

* * *

[David A. Schulte was the president and director of Park & Tilford, Inc. The company had 243,731 shares of common stock outstanding, of which the Schulte interests owned 225,482 shares or 92 per cent, and the public 18,249 shares or 8 per cent. Schulte had been a long time customer of respondent brokerage firm. In December 1943, during the period of wartime shortages, Schulte announced that Park & Tilford was issuing a dividend in whiskey to its shareholders at cost. Ira Haupt, the senior partner of respondent, testified that Schulte called him, explained that, with the announcement of the liquor plan, it was likely that the market would become "terribly active" and placed a standing order to sell from one to three hundred shares at every quarter or half point so as "to create an orderly market." As anticipated, the trading became extremely active and in a rising market Haupt was able to dispose of some 90,000 shares at prices ranging from 58 to 96. The market was further stimulated when Park & Tilford offered to sell stockholders up to six cases of whiskey for each share of stock. At this point the wartime Office of Price Administration stepped in and limited resale prices of both the purchase rights and the whiskey, and the stock fell to 30. All told, during a six months period, respondent disposed of some 93,000 shares of stock for the Schulte interests, by use of the facilities of the New York Stock Exchange, the public's holdings thereby increasing to 115,344 shares or 46 per cent.]

* * *

It is conceded that respondent's transactions in Park & Tilford stock for the account of the Schulte interests constitute a violation of Section 5(a) unless an exemption was applicable to such transactions. Respondent contends that * * * the following [exemption] was applicable: * * * Section 4(2)ᵃ which exempts

> Brokers' transactions, excecuted upon customers' orders on any exchange or in the open or counter market, but not the solicitation of such orders.

The applicability of the foregoing [exemption] involves the following subissues:

(1) Was Respondent an "underwriter" as that term is defined in Section 2(11)?

* * *

(3) Is the brokerage exemption of Section 4(2) [the predecessor of § 4(4)] available to an underwriter who effects a distribution of an issue for the account of a controlling stockholder through the mechanism of a stock exchange?

If the violation of Section 5(a) is established, there are the further questions whether the violation was "willful" and, if so, whether it is in the public interest to revoke respondent's registration, or to expel or suspend it from the NASD.

a. The Securities Acts Amendments of 1964, 78 Stat. 565, recast Section 4 so that former § 4(2) is now § 4(4).

1. Was Respondent an "Underwriter"?

Section 2(11) defines an "underwriter" as

> any person who * * * sells for an issuer in connection with, the distribution of any security * * * As used in this paragraph the term "issuer" shall include * * * any person * * * controlling * * * the issuer * * *

The purpose of the last sentence of this definition is to require registration in connection with secondary distributions through underwriters by controlling stockholders. This purpose clearly appears in the House Report on the Bill which states that it was intended:

> to bring within the provisions of the bill redistribution whether of outstanding issues or issues sold subsequently to the enactment of the bill. All the outstanding stock of a particular corporation may be owned by one individual or a select group of individuals. At some future date they may wish to dispose of their holdings and to make an offer of this stock to the public. Such a public offering may possess all the dangers attendant upon a new offering of securities. Wherever such a redistribution reaches significant proportions, the distributor would be in the position of controlling the issuer and thus able to furnish the information demanded by the bill. This being so, the distributor is treated as equivalent to the original issuer and, if he seeks to dispose of the issue through a public offering, he becomes subject to the act.

It is conceded that the Schulte interests controlled Park & Tilford and the respondent was, therefore, "selling for" a person in control of the issuer. However, respondent denies that these sales were effected "in connection with the distribution of any security." It asserts that at no time did it intend, nor was it aware that Schulte intended, a distribution of a large block of stock. It emphasizes that, in connection with the sales by which Schulte disposed of approximately 52,000 shares over a period of 6 months, each order was entered by Schulte to maintain an orderly market and was limited to 200 to 300 shares at a specific price; that the authority to sell 73,000 shares for the Trust was dependent upon a market price of at least 80; that the total amount which would be sold was never fixed or ascertained, and that consequently it did not intend to sell in connection with a distribution.

"Distribution" is not defined in the Act. It has been held, however, to comprise "the entire process by which in the course of a public offering the block of securities is dispersed and ultimately comes to rest in the hands of the investing public." In this case, the stipulated facts show that Schulte, owning in excess of 50,000 shares, had formulated a plan to sell his stock over the exchange in 200 share blocks "at 59 and every quarter up" and that the trust, holding 165,000 shares, specifically authorized the sale over the exchange of 73,000 shares "at $80 per share or better." A total of 93,000 shares was in fact sold by respondent for the account of the Schulte interests pursuant to these authorizations. We think these facts clearly fall within the above quoted definition and constitute a "distribution." We find no validity in the argument that a predetermination of the precise number of shares which are to be publicly dispersed is an essential element of a distribution. Nor do we think that a "distribution" loses its character as such merely because the extent of the offering may depend on certain conditions such as the market price. Indeed, in the usual case of an offering at a price, there is never any certainty that all or any specified part of the issue will be sold. And where part of an issue is outstanding, the extent of a new offering is almost always directly related to variations in the market price. Such offerings are not any less a "distribution" merely because their precise extent cannot be predetermined.

Nor can we accept respondent's claim that it was not aware of the distribution intended by the Schulte interests. * * *

At the time of the first discussion with Schulte, respondent knew that the Schulte orders were to be placed after an announcement of a possible liquor dividend which was expected to create greatly increased market activity and a sharp rise in price and that the stated purpose of these orders was "to have an orderly market." Moreover, the fact that the public announcement of the possible liquor dividend was made much in advance of the date the dividend was actually declared, together with Schulte's statement as to the probable effect of the general announcement, was additional evidence that Schulte intended to distribute his holdings to the public at rising prices. The only reasonable conclusion that could have been reached by respondent was that it was intended that a large block would be sold. * * *

* * *

We conclude from the foregoing facts that respondent was selling for the Schulte interests, controlling stockholders of Park & Tilford, in connection with the distribution of their holdings in the stock and was, therefore, an "underwriter" within the meaning of the Act.

* * *

3. IS THE BROKERAGE EXEMPTION OF SECTION 4(2) AVAILABLE TO AN UNDERWRITER WHO EFFECTS A DISTRIBUTION OF AN ISSUE FOR THE ACCOUNT OF A CONTROLLING STOCKHOLDER THROUGH THE MECHANISM OF A STOCK EXCHANGE?

Respondent's final argument on this phase of the case is that, notwithstanding the inapplicability of * * * [Section] 4(1) and even though respondent may be found to be an underwriter, its transactions fall within Section 4(2) which exempts "brokers' transactions, executed upon customers' orders on any exchange * * * but not the solicitation of such orders." Counsel for the staff takes the position, first that Section 4(2) can never apply to exempt the transactions of an underwriter engaged in a distribution for a controlling stockholder and, second, that, even if Section 4(2) can apply in such a situation, its applicability in the present case is destroyed by activities of respondent which exceeded the normal functions of a broker and by the further fact that respondent engaged in the solicitation of customers' orders.

* * * [W]e must determine * * * whether the broad provisions which by their terms plainly require registration and the disclosure of pertinent information to prospective investors in the case of public distributions by controlling persons, through underwriters, are so limited by the general language of Section 4(2) as to withdraw the basic protection afforded by the Act where the securities are offered to the public in an avid market by a method which we will assume, *arguendo*, foregoes the sales effort usually considered necessary to accomplish similar distributions.

It is clear from Section 4(1), read in conjunction with Section 2(11), that public distributions by controlling persons, through underwriters, are intended generally to be subject to the registration and prospectus requirements of the Act. Section 4(1) exempts transactions "by any person other than an issuer, underwriter, or dealer," "transactions by an issuer not involving a public offering" and "transactions by a dealer" other than those "within one year after the first date upon which the security was bona fide offered to the public * * * by or through an underwriter * * *" This shows a specific intention to subject to the registration and prospectus requirements public offerings by issuers or by or through "underwriters." And, as we have seen, Section 2(11) defines "underwriter" to include any person who sells for the issuer or a person controlling the issuer in connection with the distribution of a security.

These sections, by their terms, provide that whenever anyone controlling an issuer makes a public distribution of his holdings in the controlled corporation by selling through another person acting for him in connection with the distribution, the sales by which the distribution is accomplished are transactions by an underwriter which are subject to the registration requirements. Applied to such transactions by which substantial quantities of securities are disposed of to the public, the registration requirement is consistent with and calculated to further the general purpose of the Act to provide investors with pertinent information as a means of self-protection. The legislative history of the Act strongly sustains this conclusion.

We find nothing in the language or legislative history of Section 4(2) to compel the exemption of this type of secondary distribution and the consequent overriding of the general objectives and policy of the Act. On the contrary, there are affirmative indications that Section 4(2) was meant to preserve the distinction between the "trading" and "distribution" of securities which separates the exempt and non-exempt transactions under Section 4(1). This conclusion becomes apparent on examination of the legislative comments on Sections 4(1) and 4(2).

In referring to the exemption in Section 4(1) for transactions by a person "other than an issuer, underwriter, or dealer," the House Report states:

"Paragraph (1) broadly draws the line between *distribution* of securities and trading in securities, indicating that the act is, in the main, concerned with the problem of distribution as distinguished from trading. It, therefore, exempts all transactions except by an issuer, underwriter or dealer * * *" (Emphasis added.)

And, in discussing the limited exemption for dealers in the third clause of Section 4(1), the House Report again emphasized the distinction between "trading" and "distribution":

* * * Recognizing that a dealer is often concerned not only with the *distribution* of securities but also with *trading* in securities, the dealer is exempted as to *trading* when such *trading* occurs a year after the public offering of the securities. Since before that year the dealer might easily evade the provisions of the act by a claim that the securities he was offering for sale were not acquired by him in the process of *distribution* but were acquired after such process had ended, transactions during that year are not exempted. The period of a year is arbitrarily taken because, generally speaking, the average public offering has been dis-

tributed within a year and the imposition of requirements upon the dealer so far as that year is concerned is not burdensome. (Emphasis added.)

From the foregoing, it is apparent that transactions by an issuer or underwriter and transactions by a dealer during the period of *distribution* (which period for purposes of administrative practicality is arbitrarily set at one year) must be preceded by registration and the use of a prospectus. It is likewise apparent that Congress intended that, during this period, persons other than an issuer, underwriter, or dealer should be able to *trade* in the security without use of a prospectus. Since such persons would carry on their trading largely through the use of brokers (who are included in the general definition of dealers), such trading through brokers without the use of a prospectus could be permitted during the first year after the initial offering only if there were a special exemption for dealers acting as brokers. The importance of this special exemption is emphasized in the case where a stop order might be entered against a registration statement. For, although such a stop order was intended to and would operate to stop all *distribution* activities, it would also result in stopping all *trading* by individuals through dealers acting as brokers unless a special exemption were provided for brokers. It was in recognition of this fact and to permit a dealer to act as a broker for an individual's trading transactions, while the security is being distributed and during the period of a stop order, that Section 4(2) was enacted. That this was the specific purpose of Section 4(2) is clearly seen from the comment on this provision by the House Committee which considered the legislation:

> Paragraph (2) exempts the ordinary brokerage transaction. *Individuals may thus dispose of their securities according to the method which is now customary without any restrictions imposed either upon the individual or the broker. This exemption also assures an open market for securities at all times, even though a stop order against further distribution of such securities may have been entered.* Purchasers, provided they are not dealers, may thus in the event that a stop order has been entered, cut their losses immediately, if there are losses, by disposing of the securities. *On the other hand, the entry of a stop order prevents any further distribution of the security.* (Emphasis added.)

To summarize: Section 4(2) permits individuals to sell their securities through a broker in an ordinary brokerage transaction, during the period of distribution or while a stop order is in effect, without regard to the registration and prospectus requirements of Section 5. But the process of distribution itself, however carried out, is subject to Section 5.

What we have said also disposes of Respondent's argument that Section 4(2) would be rendered meaningless if it were interpreted not to apply to an underwriter "acting as a broker." Respondent has argued that such an interpretation would confine the 4(2) exemption to an area already covered by the dealer's exemption in 4(1) and thereby render Section 4(2) surplusage. But our discussion of the legislative history indicates the fallacy of this argument. It shows that the primary purpose of Section 4(2) was that it be available for trading activities during the period of distribution and during the period when a stop order might be in effect—precisely at the time when the dealer exemption is not available. Thus, far from rendering

Section 4(2) meaningless, our interpretation gives it meaning in the situation which the legislative history shows it was intended to apply.

We conclude that Section 4(2) cannot exempt transactions by an underwriter executed over the Exchange in connection with a distribution for a controlling stockholder. * * *

WILLFULNESS

* * * We find that Respondent knew that it was effecting a distribution for a controlling person and that no registration statement was in effect for the securities being distributed. Since Respondent was fully aware of what it was doing, its violation was willful within the meaning of the Act.

PUBLIC INTEREST

Even though Respondent willfully violated the Securities Act, its registration as a broker-dealer may not be revoked, and it may not be suspended or expelled from the NASD, unless such action is found to be in the public interest.

* * *

[W]e cannot overlook the fact that respondent, in the course of a public distribution of securities, engaged in a willful violation of the Securities Act—a violation which, the evidence indicates, would have been regarded as such even under previous interpretations of Section 4(2)—and, by its failure to insist on registration and the attendant disclosure of information, made it possible for the distribution to be effected to an uninformed public which suffered heavy losses. Accordingly, we find it appropriate in the public interest and for the protection of investors to suspend Respondent from membership in the NASD for a period of 20 days.

An appropriate order will issue.[c]

Excerpt from: A. A. SOMMER, JR.

WHO'S "IN CONTROL"?—S.E.C.

21 Business Lawyer 559, 559–583 (1966).*

A basic concept running through all of the statutes administered by the Securities and Exchange Commission is that of "control". * * * Some of the statutes administered by the Securities and Exchange Commission contain definitions of "control"; the Securities Act of 1933 and the Securities Exchange Act of 1934, however, the two statutes of most significance for most businesses, and the statutes which are discussed in this paper, do not include such definitions. The absence of a definition, however, has not prevented the Commission by rule, ruling and releases from limning the

---

c. Note, 14 U.Chi.L.Rev. 307 (1943); Flanagin, The Federal Securities Act and the Locked-In Stockholder, 63 Mich.L.Rev. 1139 (1965); Note, The Controlling Persons Provisions: Conduits of Secondary Liability Under Federal Securities Laws, 19 Vill. L.Rev. 621 (1974).

* Reprinted with the permission of the Author and of the American Bar Association and its Section of Corporations, Banking, and Business Law. Copyright 1966 by the American Bar Association.

outlines of a definition and it has not mitigated the vital importance of determining the meaning of "control".

* * *

Who Is A Controlling Person?

* * * [T]he situation of a "controlling person" may be perilous—and expensive. When so much attaches to the identification of a person within that category it would be most desirable if the identification could be done with certainty and precision, as, for instance, can often be done under the Internal Revenue Code. Alas, such is rarely the case with key concepts in the structure of federal securities law, and this is particularly true in the case of the concept of "control". Like so many key notions the imprecise limits of the term have been limned through the painstaking process of rule, interpretation, judicial decision and ad hoc determinations in "no action letters". Out of these there has come no mathematical standard, no slide rule computation, no certain rule which can infallibly guide counsel and client in making this most important determination—a determination which can be costly if wrongly made. Often, of course, the answer is easily arrived at; for instance, concluding that a holder of 90% of the voting power of a corporation whose stock is unencumbered and who personally runs the affairs of the corporation is a controlling person demands no subtlety. Often, however, the problem is more complex. In those situations it has become axiomatic that in deciding who is a "controlling person" the entire situation within the corporation at the time of determination, together with some of the history of the corporation, must be considered; single factors—shareholdings, offices held, titles, conduct—are rarely determinative, at least not in the close cases (clearly that ninety percent shareholder will rarely, if ever, enjoy the luxury of being found not to be in control even if every other conceivable pointer in the direction of control is lacking).

The Securities Act itself is of little help in determining who is a controlling person. * * * The Commission through Rule 405 under the Securities Act has sought to clarify the meaning of the concept of "control":

The term "control" (including the terms "controlling," "controlled by" and "under common control with") means the possession, direct or indirect, of the power to direct or cause the direction of the management and policies of a person, whether through the ownership of voting securities, by contract, or otherwise.

This definition introduces some new notions in addition to those intimated by Section 15 of the Securities Act: control is a "power" (Section 15 speaks of one who "controls," which implies exercise of the power), it may be possessed directly or indirectly, it may exist by reason of ownership of voting securities, contract or "otherwise," and the power is the power to direct or "cause the direction of management and policies" of another person (almost always a corporation). With Section 15 of the Securities Act and Rule 405 as starters, we must look principally to reported determinations, Commission and court, supplemented by logical analysis of the concept, for further delineation of this elusive notion. The administrative and judicial determinations arise in a variety of contexts; in some cases the issue is whether a person is a controlling person, thus establishing a purchaser of his stock for distribution as an underwriter; in others the question is whether a person was a "parent" of a registrant under the 1933 or 1934 Act and hence should have been identified as such in filings with the Commission; and in some few instances the question has been the derivative liability of an alleged controlling person under Section 15 of the Securities Act or Section 20 of the Securities Exchange Act.

Some basic notions should preliminarily be recognized. The *power* to control, even if unexercised, may constitute a person a controlling person. In the Walston and Co.[16] case the principal creditor of the registrant, who was the principal source of its business, had options to acquire the interests of others in the company, and received 90% of profits, had nevertheless not actively participated in the direction of the business; the Commission nonetheless held that it had the *power* to control if it so wished and hence was a controlling person of Walston and should have been so disclosed.

Correlatively, those who exercise control by the sufferance of those with the power to control may also be controlling persons. In North Country Uranium and Minerals Ltd.,[17] the holder of only a nominal amount of stock was held to be a controlling person of the defendant company because he actively managed the enterprise, which he had been instrumental in organizing, without interference from the clearly dominant shareholder who would apparently be also considered a controlling person because of his *power* to control. Similarly, in SEC v. Franklin Atlas Corp.,[18] the president and person who actually ran the corporation was not a shareholder, but because of the actuality of his control—even though subject to termination at the whim of those who controlled the stock—he was held to be a controlling person.

Thus either *the power to control* or *the actual exercise of control*, even though by sufferance of another who possesses the ultimate power to control, is sufficient to make a person a controlling person. This duality is in a sense reducible to the single notion of power to control: the person who actually controls with the acquiescence of the one having the ultimate power is realistically exercising, one might say by terminable default, the power of the other person.

Chairman Cohen of the Commission once suggested a very practical criterion for determining the person or group in control: what individual or group has the power to cause a registration statement under the Securities Act to be signed? At least one court has also used this standard for determining the identity of controlling persons. Registration statements can only be filed by an issuer and must be signed by the registrant, a majority of the board of directors, the chief executive officer, the chief financial officer, and the chief accounting officer. Obviously the statement can only be signed by the registrant under authority from the board of directors. So it would appear that control is in the hands of whoever or whatever group can cause a majority of the board to authorize the registrant's signature on the statement. At first blush it would appear this criterion offered a simple escape from their problems for purported controlling persons: simply arrange for the board to be presented with a proposal that a registration statement be signed and filed for the shares of the ostensible controlling person and have the board refuse to permit the registrant to sign and file the statement—presto, the purported controlling person has flunked the test: he could not produce a majority vote to sign

16.　7 S.E.C. 937 (1940).　　　　　　　18.　154 F.Supp. 395 (S.D.N.Y.1957).

17.　37 S.E.C. 608 (1957).

the statement and he may therefore sell without the expense and bother of a registration statement. Needless to say, any board refusal other than a simon-pure bona fide refusal could be of no avail. Furthermore, for a refusal to be of any significance, the person proposing that the corporation file a registration statement with respect to his shares must agree to indemnify the registrant for its expenses in connection with the registration; otherwise, the board might well refuse—and probably should refuse— to authorize signing and filing on the legitimate ground that the corporation could not properly incur expenses for the benefit of a shareholder.

With these propositions as starters, it is possible to discern some further guides in Commission and court cases and logical analysis of the concept of control.

* * *

* * * The initial source of power of necessity must be ownership of voting securities, not only because of the specific mention of this in Rule 405, but because under modern corporation law the power of management is *ultimately*—in theory and law, if not in practice—in the hands of the holders of voting securities. * * *

* * *

How little stock may a person own or have the power to vote and still be considered a controlling person? This depends upon many circumstances. Principal among these are the distribution of the other shares and the other relationships the shareholder has with the corporation and with other shareholders. Initially, record or beneficial ownership of (or right to vote) 10% or more of the voting stock of a corporation has become something of a benchmark and when this is encountered a red warning flag should run up. Schedule A to the Securities Act of 1933, the proxy statement rules, and many of the registration forms promulgated by the Commission require disclosure of all persons who own of record or beneficially more than 10% of any class of stock of the issuer, and the reporting and penalty provisions of Section 16 of the Securities Exchange Act (the so-called "insider trading" provisions) apply to the beneficial owners of more than 10% of a class of equity security registered pursuant to Section 12 of that Act. While there is nothing in the statutes or the regulations or rulings by the Commission which says such a holder is *ipso facto* a controlling person, generally such degree of ownership should create caution and might be regarded as creating a rebuttable presumption of control, especially if such holdings are combined with executive office, membership on the board, or wide dispersion of the remainder of the stock.

That such a percentage of ownership or right to vote is not *conclusive* evidence of control, however, is almost self-evident. In a situation in which one person owned 89% of the voting stock and the other 11% was owned by an antagonist, it is evident the owner of the 11% is not a controlling person (barring the improbable situation where unanimous shareholder action is required): he could not cause the company to file a registration statement and he could not elect a majority of the board; in fact, unless the size of the board and cumulative voting combine to afford him board representation, he is powerless save for the rights which belong to any shareholder regardless of holdings, e.g. right to inspect books, to bring a derivative suit, to secure the fair value of his shares in certain circumstances. On the other hand, ownership of less than 10% of the voting power of a corporation does not automatically spell non-control. Apart from the circumstance that a holder of less than 10% may be a member of a group which controls, a person with less than 10% may alone be a controlling person; generally to be such his ownership would have to be combined with dominant executive office and fairly wide dispersion of the remainder of the voting power. It has been suggested that ownership of as little as 5% of a corporation's stock by an officer or director may give rise to a presumption that such a person is a member of a control group.

Obviously, the more widely dispersed voting stock is generally, the amount necessary to control is smaller. In the case of a corporation with shares widely distributed the holder of substantially less than a majority may clearly be in control, and in many instances, upon acquisition of such a percentage by a shareholder, management has recognized his control and resigned. An instance of this was the acquisition by Norton Simon of approximately 9.7% of the common stock of Wheeling Steel Corporation, resulting in a management upheaval, a recognition of Simon's effective control, and the election of officers satisfactory to him; the remainder of the stock was held by approximately 12,000 shareholders. When such minority ownership is combined with actual control of a majority on the board, control is clear. * * *

When—and why—a person who owns or has the right to vote a minority of the outstanding stock of a corporation may be considered in control is not easily answered. The holder of twenty or twenty-five percent of stock of a widely and publicly held company could be defeated in a proxy contest; if he asserts control based upon his acquisition of a substantial interest the majority of the board and the officers might defy him and deny him any board representation until the next shareholders' meeting, or accord him only representation proportionate to his holdings. Victor Muscat and his associates suffered this fate in 1962 when they purchased 29 percent of the shares of B.S.F. Co. Upon demanding control of the Board of Directors, they were rebuffed. * * * One thus rebuffed could hardly be called a controlling person. Thus in many instances more than a substantial minority stockholding, even in a corporation with widely held stock, is the prerequisite to the establishment of control; such a holding may really constitute control only when it has actually resulted in the yielding of control by those who have previously possessed it. Thus, while unencumbered ownership of more than fifty percent of the outstanding voting power of a corporation will usually constitute control even though unexercised simply because the power to control is there, ownership of substantially less than 50% of the stock may be indicative of control only if the power inherent in the voting power has in some fashion been manifested through the exercise of control, usually through the election of a favorably inclined majority of the board of directors.

Voting power may be the source of power to control apart from beneficial ownership of the voting stock. For instance, trustees of a voting trust or other fiduciaries who have the power to vote a majority of voting stock or a sufficient amount to control the corporation may be controlling persons (generally, unless there is a clear schism among them, all of the trustees—if there are more than one—will be considered to be in control). A fiduciary may have sufficient voting power to be a controlling person as the consequence of aggregating the voting power derived from a number of fiduciary roles. For instance, a bank which is the trustee of several trusts and the executor of several estates containing in the aggregate sufficient voting stock of an issuer to exercise control will be a controlling person if it has the right to vote the stock, even though the holdings in a single trust or estate would not be sufficient to control. This can have the anomalous result of securities in the estate of a very minor shareholder being restricted as to disposition just as if the estate itself were in control. Similarly, if an officer or director or shareholder who is a controlling person in his own right is the trustee or executor of a trust or estate holding securities of the corporation he controls, then the securities in the trust or estate are subject to the same restrictions as those on the trustee or executor in relation to his own holdings.

* * *

The Controlling Group

There are innumerable instances in which a single person does not appear to have actual operating control or the power to control. Then the problem is to identify the *group* which is in control and those who constitute the group. The search for the group commences when the search for the individual in control or having the power to control fails. Is there always a controlling person or a controlling group in every corporation? I would suggest that there is: someone runs the show or some group runs the show, some person has the power to run the show or some group has that power. As a beginning, it may be safely suggested that simply being a member of the board of directors, or an officer of the company, does not automatically constitute one a member of the controlling group. At least as far as the directors are concerned, this is self-evident: if the corporation is subject to cumulative voting requirements some, and perhaps one short of a majority, of the directors may be quite hostile to management and to the majority of the board; it would obviously be wrong to call them members of the controlling group. It is less obvious that principal executive officers are not *ipso facto* members of the controlling group, since they serve at the will of the board and hence it may be fairly implied they would be compliant with the will of whoever controls the board; however, even then a situation is conceivable where an officer with an employment contract may be out of step with the controlling group, but perhaps the fact of his contract alone may be sufficient to cause him to be considered a controlling person if his prerogatives are broad enough. In some instances it may be pertinent to distinguish "inside" directors (i.e. directors who are officers and involved in the active management of the corporation) from "outside" directors (i.e. those *not* a part of active management); obviously "inside" directors would be more likely to be found to be in control, but this would stem from roles and positions over and above that of being a director. In general, however, unless a person or identifiable group clearly is in control by reason of possession *and* use of voting power, all directors and policy-making officers are presumptively members of the controlling group and only compelling evidence to the contrary should remove them from the group. Generally there must be some homogeneity among individuals if they are to be regarded as members of the controlling group, some significant business characteristic or relationship or course of conduct that affords an element of unity. It is clear from the legislative history of the Securities Act, judicial decisions and releases of the Commission that some "cement", other than mere association on a board, or the circumstance that adding up the holdings of a number of people yields an actual or working majority of the voting power of the corporation, is necessary to constitute individuals a controlling group. * * *

[T]he term "associate" [as defined in Rule 405 of Regulation C of the 1933 Act] is relevant in determining membership in the control group. * * * [A]s a beginning, caution would require the conclusion that if persons bearing a relationship one to the other described in the definition of "associate" have the combined voting or other power to control the corporation, then such persons are all members of the controlling group. Thus, if a person held 15% of the voting power of a corporation he alone might well not be considered to be a controlling person; but if his wife living with him had another 10%, her brother living under their roof had 5%, a corporation in which he held beneficially 12% of the stock had 10%, and a family trust in which he had a substantial beneficial interest had 15%, in all likelihood the Commission would regard him as a controlling person. * * *

* * *

The question of control is subtle and difficult in many instances. Often, to be sure, the focus of control is simply determined. Just as often, and perhaps oftener particularly in corporations in which there is substantial public participation in ownership, the answer is clouded. Ultimately the test is briefly stated: taking into account history, family, business affiliations, shareholdings, position and all the other circumstances, what person or what group calls the day-to-day shots? The shots in major matters? What person or what group could, if it wished, call those shots? When these are identified the controlling persons and the controlling group are identified. How can a putative controlling person clear away doubt? Short of actual litigation of the issue—hardly an inviting course—the only means, and at best an inadequate and uncertain one, is by seeking from the Securities and Exchange Commission a "no action" letter. * * * However, the "no action" letter is at best a weak reed. First, the conclusion of the staff is confined to the facts stated; hence the omission of any material fact or any material inaccuracy destroys the value of the letter. Second, such staff determinations do not constitute a barrier to civil liability. While it is likely that a court would look dimly upon Commission action after its issuance of a "no action" letter if the request accurately stated all material facts, such determination would not preclude a private litigant from relief under Section 12(1) for a failure to register the securities sold by the putative controlling person. Still, limited though their value is, such letters are often and anxiously sought and usually relied upon. It would appear that where the case is a close one, however, the chances of securing a "no action" letter are slim, relegating the imperilled person to the judgment of his counsel and the vagaries of securities markets, the hostilities of shareholders and the like.

* * *

TRANSACTIONS BY DEALERS AND BROKERS

The registration and prospectus requirements of § 5 are always applicable to issuers and to underwriters who, by definition, are engaged in the process of distribution of a block of securities to the public. This is not so as to dealers despite § 4(1).

(a) *The Dealer's Exemption.* Section 4(3) exempts transactions by a dealer (including an underwriter who is no longer acting as such in respect of the security involved in such transaction) with three exceptions. These exceptions in effect fix periods during which dealers are subject to the registration and prospectus requirements of § 5. The statutory language now excludes from the exemption:

(A) transactions taking place prior to the expiration of forty days after the first date upon which the security was bona fide offered to the public by the issuer or by or through an underwriter,

(B) transactions in a security, as to which a registration statement has been filed, taking place prior to the expiration of forty days after the effective date of such registration statement or prior to the expiration of forty days after the first date upon which the security was bona fide offered to the public by the issuer or by or through an underwriter after such effective date, whichever is later (excluding in the computation of such forty days any time during which a stop order issued under section 8 is in effect as to the security), or such shorter period as the Commission may specify by rules and regulations or order, and

(C) transactions as to securities constituting the whole or a part of an unsold allotment to or subscription by such dealer as a participant in the distribution of such securities by the issuer or by or through an underwriter.

The term "dealer" is defined in § 2(12) to mean "any person who engages either for all or part of his time, directly or indirectly, as agent, broker, or principal, in the business of offering, buying, selling, or otherwise dealing or trading in securities issued by another person." It is to be noted that the definition includes a broker as well as a principal trading for his own account. According to the House Report, the sole object of this definition was "to subject brokers to the same advertising restrictions [prospectus requirements] that are imposed upon dealers, so as to prevent the broker from being used as a cloak for the sale of securities." [1] At the same time, under § 2(11), a dealer is excluded from the definition of "underwriter" even though he purchases securities from an underwriter at a price below the public offering price and resells the securities to the public so long as the "commission" or "spread" is not in excess of the usual and customary dealer's commission.

In its original form, the Securities Act imposed a period of one year during which dealers not participating in the distribution of a new issue were required to deliver prospectuses in connection with trading transactions. In the 1954 amendment program, this period was reduced to 40 days. In supporting the change the Commission had this to say: "The 1-year provision has long been recognized as unrealistic, since dealers trading in a security publicly offered within 1 year find themselves unable to obtain prospectuses. This fact has rendered compliance by dealers and enforcement by the Commission difficult." [2]

At the same time § 24(d) was added to the Investment Company Act making the exemption provided in § 4(3) of the Securities Act inapplicable to transactions in the securities of investment companies that are offered to the public on a continuous basis (the largest group here being the mutual funds) because of the special characteristics of these offerings. In place of the then existing 1 year period, § 24(d) provides that dealers not participating in the distribution

---

1. H.R.Rep. No. 85, 73d Cong., 1st Sess. 14 (1933).

2. Hearings on S. 2846 Before a Subcommittee of the Senate Committee on Banking and Currency, 83d Cong., 2d Sess. 6 (1954).

must nevertheless use the prospectus in offering any such security as long as the issuer is offering any securities of the same class.

The Senate Report explained the dealer's exemption as amended in this way: [3]

> Apart from the change to a 40-day period, the amendment is not designed to affect the nature or extent of the dealer's exemption in section 4(1). For example, in the case of an unlawful offering of unregistered securities, a dealer would not be able to trade lawfully in such securities within 40 days * * * after the date on which the unlawful distribution of such securities to the public in fact commenced. And if the dealer is a participant in any such unlawful distribution he cannot lawfully effect transactions in the unregistered securities so long as he is engaged in the distribution even though the 40-day period has expired. It is unlawful for a dealer to effect transactions in unregistered securities which are about to be registered, but he may ordinarily trade in other outstanding securities of the same class which are not being registered or involved in a registrable distribution or public offering. The amendment does not change these effects of the present provisions of the Securities Act.
>
> In the case of registered securities the dealer's exemption will not be available to any dealer participating in the distribution so long as he has an unsold allotment or subscription, but dealers who are merely trading and are not participants in the distribution will be subject to the provisions of section 5 of the Securities Act only during the 40-day period. Under the revision of section 5, the offering of a registered security may commence as soon as the registration statement has been filed, but it will continue to be within the power of the registrant or the underwriters to delay the offering until some later date in the waiting period or even to some date after the registration statement has become effective. The amendment, therefore is so worded as to make dealers subject to the provisions of section 5 for 40 days after whichever is the later of the two events; i.e., the effective date of the registration statement or the date the public offering in fact commences.

A question may arise as to when a bona fide offering of an unregistered security actually commences for § 4(3) purposes. In Kubik v. Goldfield,[4] the court held that a bona fide offer to the public dated from the time when another dealer entered quotations in the National Daily Quotations Service "pink sheets" where there was no relationship or collaboration between the dealers.[5]

In the case of registered securities, the offering date is readily ascertainable, but the issuance of a stop order under § 8 extends the period beyond the 40 days by the length of time during which the order is in effect as to the security.

The Securities Acts Amendments of 1964 [6] extended the 40 day period prescribed in § 4(3)(B) to 90 days, if the securities of the issuer have not previously been sold pursuant to an earlier effective registration statement; however, the Commission was empowered by rule or order to fix a shorter period. The Commission has since issued Rule 174 dispensing with the prospectus delivery requirements for dealers (including an underwriter no longer acting as such in respect of the security) if the issuer is subject, immediately

3. S.Rep. No. 1036, 83d Cong., 2d Sess. 14 (1954).

4. 479 F.2d 472 (3d Cir. 1973).

5. Cf. SEC v. North American Research & Development Corp., 280 F.Supp. 106, aff'd in part, 424 F.2d 63 (2d Cir. 1970).

6. Pub.L. 88–467, 78 Stat. 565. See Patterson, Delivery of Prospectuses in Exempted Dealer Transactions and the Securities Amendments of 1964, 20 Bus. Law. 303 (1965).

prior to the time of filing the registration statement, to the reporting requirements of §§ 13 or 15(d) of the 1934 Act. And where securities are registered
under the 1933 Act for an offering to be made from time to time (such as a
shelf-registration), no prospectus need be delivered after the expiration of the
initial prospectus delivery period specified in § 4(3) following the first bona fide
offering of the registered securities. Moreover, in certain other types of
registered issues, the dealer's obligation to deliver a prospectus is dispensed
with altogether.

(b) *The Broker's Exemption.* This exemption now contained in § 4(4) is
discussed at length in the *Haupt* case, supra at page 464. Its purpose is to
permit the ordinary investor to sell his securities during the period of distribution or while a stop order is in effect as to a security without being subject to
the prospectus requirements of § 5. Of course, his part of the transaction is
exempt under § 4(1). But such sales will almost always be made by the use of a
broker. And since brokers are included within the definition of dealer in
§ 2(12), the dealer's exemption may not be available to the broker. For
example, a stop order, by suspending the effectiveness of the registration
statement, closes the mails and channels of interstate commerce to further
sales of the security by issuers and underwriters and by dealers selling for their
own account. It was to keep the securities markets open to the investing public
that § 4 exempts "brokers' transactions, executed upon customers' orders on
any exchange or in the over-the-counter market, but not the solicitation of such
orders."

The narrow purpose of the exemption was explained by the Federal Trade
Commission, which administered the Securities Act for about a year before the
Securities and Exchange Commission was established: "The exemption
* * * applies only to the broker's part of a brokerage transaction. It does
not extend to the customer. Whether the customer is excused from complying
with the registration requirements of Section 5 depends upon his own status or
upon the character of the particular transaction. Thus, an issuer selling
through a broker on the stock exchange is subject to the registration requirements of this Act." [7] This statement, although accurate as far as it goes, can be
misunderstood. For the *Haupt* case teaches that a broker who sells for a
controlling person in *connection with the distribution* of a security becomes an
underwriter and thereby loses his broker's exemption. Of course, the brokers'
exemption is never available to issuers.[8]

Section 4(4) is far from clear as to the meaning of the phrase "solicitation of
such orders." In a brokerage transaction, the broker may solicit the seller's
order or the buyer's order. Furthermore, is it only the solicitation that is
prohibited, so that if interstate facilities or the mails are not used for this part
of the transaction, the exemption is not thereby destroyed? Rule 154 as
adopted in 1951 provided that the "term solicitation of such orders * * *
shall be deemed to include the solicitation of an order to buy a security, but

7. FTC Securities Act Release No. 131,
March 13, 1934.

8. Stadia Oil & Uranium Co. v. Whee-
lis, 251 F.2d 269 (10th Cir. 1957). But Rule
144, considered later, also was thought to
provide protection to the controlling shareholder if all of the conditions of the respective rule were met. "Although the rule is
expressly directed at § 4(4), it was obviously contemplated that the seller's part of
the transaction would be considered to be

exempt under § 4(1) whenever the broker's
part came within the rule." Loss, Fundamentals of Securities Regulation 406, n. 14
(1983); When Corporations Go Public 30–
31 (Israels and Duff ed. 1962); S.E.C. Problems of Controlling Stockholders and in
Underwritings 44 (Israels ed. 1962). The
Wolfson case, infra at page 480, however,
rejects this view if the controlling person
deceives his broker.

shall not be deemed to include the solicitation of an order to sell a security." By way of further amplification, the Commission said: [9]

> [I]f the broker solicits the purchaser to buy the security, Section 4(2) [now § 4(4)] does not provide an exemption *either for the solicitation itself or for the resulting transaction.* On the other hand, if the broker does not solicit the purchaser to buy, the mere fact that he may solicit the seller to sell will not destroy any exemption otherwise available to him under Section 4(2); this construction is based on the fact that the statute is designed primarily for the protection of buyers rather than for the protection of sellers. [Emphasis supplied.]

It should also be noted that the prospectus delivery requirements are not restricted to transactions between brokers and public customers; they have been held also to be applicable between two broker-dealers.[10]

UNITED STATES v. WOLFSON

United States Court of Appeals, Second Circuit, 1968.
405 F.2d 779, certiorari denied 394 U.S. 946 (1969).

Before MOORE, WOODBURY * and SMITH, CIRCUIT JUDGES.

WOODBURY, SENIOR CIRCUIT JUDGE:

It was stipulated at the trial that at all relevant times there were 2,510,000 shares of Continental Enterprises, Inc., issued and outstanding. The evidence is clear, indeed is not disputed, that of these the appellant Louis E. Wolfson himself with members of his immediate family and his right hand man and first lieutenant, the appellant Elkin B. Gerbert, owned 1,149,775 or in excess of 40%. The balance of the stock was in the hands of approximately 5,000 outside shareholders. The government's undisputed evidence at the trial was that between August 1, 1960, and January 31, 1962, Wolfson himself sold 404,150 shares of Continental through six brokerage houses, that Gerbert sold 53,000 shares through three brokerage houses and that members of the Wolfson family, including Wolfson's wife, two brothers, a sister, the Wolfson Family Foundation and four trusts for Wolfson's children sold 176,675 shares through six brokerage houses.

Gerbert was a director of Continental. Wolfson was not, nor was he an officer, but there was ample evidence that nevertheless as the largest individual shareholder he was Continental's guiding spirit in that the officers of the corporation were subject to his direction and control and that no corporate policy decisions were made without his knowledge and consent. Indeed Wolfson admitted as much on the stand. No registration statement was in effect as to Continental; its stock was traded over-the-counter.

The appellants do not dispute the foregoing basic facts. They took the position at the trial that they had no idea during the period of the alleged conspiracy, stipulated to be from January 1, 1960, to January 31, 1962, that there was any provision of law requiring registration of a security before its distribution by a controlling person to the public. On the stand in their defense they took the position that they operated at a level of corporate

---

9. SEC Securities Act Release No. 3421 Aug. 2, 1951.

10. Byrnes v. Faulkner, Dawkins & Sullivan, 550 F.2d 1303 (2d Cir. 1977), supra at page 99.

* Of the First Circuit sitting by designation.

finance far above such "details" as the securities laws; as to whether a particular stock must be registered. They asserted and their counsel argued to the jury that they were much too busy with large affairs to concern themselves with such minor matters and attributed the fault of failure to register to subordinates in the Wolfson organization and to failure of the brokers to give notice of the need. Obviously in finding the appellants guilty the jury rejected this defense, if indeed, it is any defense at all.

The appellants assert numerous claims of error. We shall dispose of the claims more or less in the order of their importance.

Section 5 of the Act in pertinent part provides: "(a) Unless a registration statement is in effect as to a security, it shall be unlawful for any person, directly or indirectly—

"(1) to make use of any means or instruments of transportation or communication in interstate commerce or of the mails to sell or offer to buy such security through the use or medium of any prospectus or otherwise; * * *."

However, § 4 of the Act exempts certain transactions from the provisions of § 5 including:

"(1) Transactions by any person other than an issuer, underwriter, or dealer."

The appellants argue that they come within this exemption for they are not issuers, underwriters or dealers. At first blush there would appear to be some merit in this argument. The immediate difficulty with it, however, is that § 4(1) by its terms exempts only "transactions," not classes of persons * * * and ignores § 2(11) of the Act which defines an "underwriter" to mean any person who has purchased from an issuer with a view to the distribution of any security, or participates directly or indirectly in such undertaking unless that person's participation is limited to the usual and customary seller's commission, and then goes on to provide:

"As used in this paragraph the term 'issuer' shall include, in addition to an issuer, any person directly or indirectly *controlling* or controlled by *the issuer*, or any person under direct or indirect common control with the 'issuer.'" (Italics supplied.)

In short, the brokers provided outlets for the stock of issuers and thus were underwriters. * * * Wherefore the stock was sold in "transactions by underwriters" which are not within the exemption of § 4(1), supra.

But the appellants contend that the brokers in this case cannot be classified as underwriters because their part in the sales transactions came within § 4(4) which exempts "brokers' transactions executed upon customers' orders on any exchange or in the over-the-counter market but not the solicitiaton of such orders." The answer to this contention is that § 4(4) was designed only to exempt the brokers' part in security transactions. * * * Control persons must find their own exemptions.

There is nothing inherently unreasonable for a broker to claim the exemption of § 4(4), supra, when he is unaware that his customer's part in the transaction is not exempt. Indeed, this is indicated by the definition of "brokers' transaction" in * * * Rule 154 [the predecessor of Rule 144, infra at page 507] which provides:

"(a) The term 'brokers' transaction' in Section 4(4) of the act shall be deemed to include transactions by a broker acting as agent for the account of any person controlling, controlled by, or under common control with, the issuer of the securities which are the subject of the transaction where:

"(4) The broker is *not aware* of circumstances indicating * * * that the transactions are part of a distribution of securities on behalf of his principal."

And there can be no doubt that appellants' sale of over 633,000 shares (25% of the outstanding shares of Continental and more than 55% of their own holdings), was a distribution rather than an ordinary brokerage transaction. See Rule 154(6) which defines "distribution" for the purpose of paragraph (a) generally as "substantial" in relation to the number of shares outstanding and specifically as a sale of 1% of the stock within six months preceding the sale if the shares are traded on a stock exchange.

Certainly if the appellants' sales, which clearly amounted to a distribution under the above definitions had been made through a broker or brokers with knowledge of the circumstances, the brokers would not be entitled to the exemption. It will hardly do for the appellants to say that because they kept the true facts from the brokers they can take advantage of the exemption the brokers gained thereby.

* * *

In conclusion it will suffice to say that full consideration of the voluminous record in this rather technical case discloses no reversible error.

Affirmed.

Registered Secondary Shelf Offerings

We have already explored Rule 415 which allows certain kinds of registered offerings for the shelf. It may be worthwhile to review the textual note on "Shelf Registrations", supra at page 198 as well as Rule 415. There are other situations which may give rise to a "shelf registration." In certain mergers or sale-of-assets reorganizations, a controlling person of a constituent corporation who receives securities in a Rule 145 transaction may not make a public sale of the securities without registration, even though this person is not in a control relationship with the surviving corporation after the reorganization is completed. See supra at page 414. Under some circumstances, Form S–4 is available for registration of securities acquired in such Rule 145 transactions. At the same time, these persons may not have any present intention of selling the securities on a stock exchange or in the over-the-counter market, but the situation may change at some later date, so that they will wish to protect themselves by making a "shelf registration" of their securities. As to securities registered under Form S–4, Item 22 specifies that for the purposes of any subsequent public offering the registrant must file the undertaking required by Item 512 of Regulation S–K to file post-effective amendments so as to bring the registration statement up-to-date. And aside from any question of resales by controlling persons of the acquired company, if an issuer is engaged in a program of acquiring other companies on a more or less continuous basis, the Commission may take the position that the acquiring company is making a continuous offering of its stock, that all transactions should be integrated into a single public offering, and that the securities should be registered for the "shelf."

Another example arises from the decision in SEC v. Guild Films Co., supra at page 460, which deals with the question whether a pledgee of control shares is to be regarded as an "underwriter" under § 2(11) so that a public sale of the securities may not be made in satisfaction of the pledge without a prior registration. At the same time, however, it is probable or at least possible that the sale may never occur. Under Rule 415 a "shelf registration" may be made, possibly as a part of the normal financing operations of the issuer, with an undertaking to file a post-effective amendment so as to keep the registration statement up-to-date in the event of the later offering.

Shelf registrations are also permitted in a registration statement filed pursuant to an offering of convertible securities and to sales of stock to employees under a stock option plan provided there is the inclusion of an undertaking in the registration statement to file a post-effective amendment. All this indicates that the SEC has found it difficult to fit these unconventional offerings into the pattern of regulation envisaged by the 1933 Act.[1]

Another situation is that typified by In the Matter of Hazel Bishop.[2] In that case, some 112 selling shareholders had purportedly acquired shares of the registrant under the § 4(2) private offering exemption. If they resold their securities to the public without registration, they would become statutory underwriters under § 2(11) and be in violation of § 5 of the 1933 Act. Instead, they proposed to register the securities and sell them from time to time on the American Stock Exchange without the use of an underwriter. Since the offering would be "at the market," they were then in danger of running afoul of Rule 10b–6 of the Exchange Act. Rule 10b–6, in effect, bars any stabilizing activity by way of purchases of securities by the sellers or their agents while the distribution is taking place.[3] Accordingly, the Commission required an undertaking from each selling shareholder that he or she would comply with Rule 10b–6. It is also customary to appoint a single broker to act as agent for all of the selling shareholders so as to conduct an orderly distribution. Otherwise, a broker employed by any of the selling shareholders could unwittingly become a participant in the distribution and subject to Rule 10b–5. Any purchase of shares while the distribution was continuing would constitute a violation of the Rule.

Over the years, the Commission has had difficulty in applying Rule 10b–6 to shareholders distributing securities in the context of a shelf-registered offering. The Commission has now issued an interpretive release which clarifies its position on the application of the rule in connection with shelf-registered offerings. The release is set forth below.

---

1. On the compliance problems of broker-dealers participating in the distribution of shelf-registered securities, see Yerkes, Shelf Registrations: The Role of the Broker-Dealer, 29 Bus.Law. 397 (1974); infra, at page 523.

2. 40 S.E.C. 718 (1961).

3. For a discussion of Rule 10b–6 and the limits of stabilizing activity, see the note at page 601 infra, particularly at page 603.

SECURITIES EXCHANGE ACT RELEASE NO. 23611
Securities and Exchange Commission.
September 11, 1986.

Application of Rule 10b–6 Under the Securities Exchange Act of 1934 to Persons Participating in Shelf Distributions

I. Introduction and Summary

This release discusses the application of Rule 10b–6 ("Rule") under the Securities Exchange Act of 1934 ("Exchange Act") in the context of shelf-registered offerings and, specifically, the application of the Rule to shareholders ("Shelf Shareholders") distributing securities pursuant to a shelf-registered offering. The Commission's staff has received numerous requests for interpretive advice and other relief in this area,[3] and the Commission believes that it is appropriate to modify the interpretation of the Rule that has been applied in this context.

This release first discusses the historical development of the application of Rule 10b–6 to shelf-registered offerings. The release then presents a revised analysis of, together with a matrix for, the application of the Rule to Shelf Shareholders that is more flexible than historical positions and is consistent with the underlying anti-manipulation and investor protection purposes of the Rule. Finally, the release discusses the impact of the revised position on broker-dealers who sell securities on behalf of Shelf Shareholders.

II. The Development of the Historical Interpretation

Rule 10b–6 is an anti-manipulation rule that, subject to certain exceptions, prohibits persons who are engaged in a distribution of securities from bidding for or purchasing, or inducing other persons to bid for or purchase, such securities, any security of the same class and series as those securities, or any right to purchase any such security ("related securities") until they have completed their participation in the distribution. The purpose of the Rule is to prevent participants in a distribution from artificially conditioning the market for the securities to facilitate the distribution. The Rule is designed to protect the integrity of the secondary trading market as an independent pricing mechanism and thereby enhance investor confidence in the marketplace.

The Rule applies to every "distribution" of securities unless an exception or exemption is available. In 1983, the Commission adopted a definition of the term "distribution."

For purposes of this section only, the term "distribution" means an offering of securities, whether or not subject to registration under the Securities Act of 1933, that is distinguished from ordinary trading transactions by the magnitude of the offering and the presence of special selling efforts and selling methods.[5]

---

3. The question frequently arises in the context of shelf offerings with a large number of Shelf Shareholders who received their shares in an unregistered distribution that was part of a merger transaction. Typically, the Shelf Shareholders have no continuing relationship with the merged entity or with each other except for their shareholdings.

5. Rule 10b–6(c)(5).

The Commission indicated that the definition was to apply in all contexts, and specifically observed that it applies to shelf-registered offerings. The Commission furthermore stated that it "continues to believe that any shelf-registered offering should be considered a single distribution for purposes of the rule." [7] If the shelf-registered offering constitutes a distribution as defined by the Rule, then all participants in the distribution will be subject to the Rule for the life of the shelf.

The Commission recognized that the single distribution position in the context of Rule 10b–6 could result in unwarranted restrictions on distribution participants. For that and other reasons, the Commission adopted Exception (xii) to the Rule and modified Exception (xi).[8] Exception (xii) permits issuers and selling shareholders engaged in a shelf distribution to bid for and purchase the securities that are the subject of the distribution up until two or nine business days prior to any offers or sales off the shelf.[9] The Commission stated:

> Persons subject to the rule as a consequence of their participation in a shelf-registered distribution therefore are only required to cease their purchasing activities with respect to the security in distribution during the applicable cooling-off period and during any period in which offers or sales are being made off the shelf.

The Commission explained that the exception was designed, in part, "to eliminate any unnecessary hardship that Rule 10b–6 may have on persons that come within the rule's prohibitions as a result of their participation in a shelf-registered distribution." In further recognition of the fact that Rule 10b–6 may impose unwarranted hardships on shelf distribution participants, the Commission stated its intention to continue to review the impact of the Rule on such persons.

Until recently, the staff has interpreted Rule 10b–6 in the context of shelf distributions to require *every* distribution participant, including every Shelf Shareholder, to comply with the applicable cooling-off period prior to *any* offers or sales off the shelf by *any* Shelf Shareholder. As a result, each Shelf Shareholder was required to coordinate his market activities with every other Shelf Shareholder so that none of them engaged in activities prohibited by the Rule during the cooling-off period or selling period of any other Shelf Shareholder.

When the number of Shelf Shareholders on a given registration statement was relatively small, compliance with the historical interpretation was not difficult or burdensome. Recently, however, the staff has been presented with situations involving a large number of Shelf Shareholders, and in many situations the majority of the Shelf Shareholders are unaffiliated with the issuer. The historical interpretation requires an unwieldy coordination effort among the Shelf Shareholders. Furthermore, an inability to formulate an effective coordination plan may jeopardize the registration of the shelf offering itself.[14]

---

7. Id. This is known as the "single distribution position."

8. Rule 10b–6(a)(3)(xi) and (xii).

9. Securities satisfying a minimum price per share and public float test qualify for the two business day cooling-off period.

Rule 10b–6(a)(3)(xii)(A). Other securities are subject to the nine business day cooling-off period. Rule 10b–6(a)(3)(xii)(C).

14. See Rules 418(a)(4) and 461(b)(7), 17 CFR 230.418(a)(4) and 230.461(b)(7), under the Securities Act, and Section III.E, infra.

The two principal sources generally cited as the basis for the historical interpretation are the Commission's decisions in *Hazel Bishop Inc.*[15] and *Jaffee & Company.*[16] *Hazel Bishop* involved a proceeding pursuant to Section 8(d) of the Securities Act to determine whether a stop order should issue with respect to a registration statement relating to an offering ostensibly by 112 shareholders of approximately 67 percent of the issuer's outstanding common stock. The issuer's largest shareholder and eight of the issuer's directors were among those listed as Shelf Shareholders. The shares were to be sold "from time to time at prices current at the time of sale through brokers on the American Stock Exchange, in the open market, or otherwise."[17] The Commission found: numerous materially misleading and false statements in the registration statement, failures to disclose sales of securities by the shareholders in violation of section 5 of the Securities Act and the failure to disclose contingent liabilities related to such sales; and that shareholders had entered into numerous undisclosed arrangements with other persons whereby the latter acquired beneficial ownership of some of the stock being registered (some of these arrangements provided for profit sharing between seller and buyer and guarantees against loss, or the shares were pledged for a loan to finance the purchase).[20]

Although the above factors provided a sufficient basis to issue the stop order, the Commission deemed it appropriate to discuss "certain aspects of the proposed offering which raise serious questions under the statutes administered by the Commission." The Commission observed: "There are at least 112 selling stockholders. Apparently no procedures for coordinating their activities or guarding against unlawful practices have been established." The Commission was concerned that the offering by a large number of shareholders was not subject to any of "the contractual safeguards designed for the protection of both buyer and seller ordinarily provided in the conventional distribution through professional underwriters and dealers. * * * "[23] This led to a concern that "this large group of sellers may not be aware that various statutory provisions and rules which govern the conduct of underwriters and dealers will apply to them and their activities for the duration of the offering of their shares to the public." The Commission specifically discussed the application of Rule 10b–6 to the offering and stated that: "Each of the selling stockholders and any broker or person acting for any of them will be subject to the provisions of this rule."[25]

---

15. 40 S.E.C. 718 (1961).

16. 44 S.E.C. 285 (1970), affirmed in part and vacated in part, Jaffee & Co. v. SEC, 446 F.2d 387 (2d Cir.1971). [infra at page 597.]

17. 40 S.E.C. at 719. The Commission noted that the offering had characteristics of both a primary offering and a secondary offering. Id. at 734.

20. Id. at 729–30. The Commission also found that, as a result of many of these "arrangements," the number of selling shareholders actually was approximately 150 rather than the 112 listed in the registration statement.

23. Id. See American Finance Co., Inc., 40 S.E.C. 1043, 1051 (1962).

25. Id. at 736. The Commission also observed:

Underlining the specific requirements referred to above is the basic principle that any representation that a security is being offered "at the market" implies the existence of a free and open market which is not made, controlled or artificially influenced by any person participating in the offering. Any activity which constitutes a violation of any of the anti-manipulative provisions mentioned or which is otherwise intended to stabilize, stimulate or condition the market would be inconsistent with the representation and would render the registration statement false and misleading.

After *Hazel Bishop*, the question remained as to how much coordination was required among the Shelf Shareholders to ensure that their activities complied with Rule 10b–6. The Commission's decision in *Jaffee* suggested that the level of required coordination was high. *Jaffee* involved a registered secondary shelf offering of approximately 28 percent of the outstanding common stock of Solitron Devices, Inc. ("Solitron") by 34 shareholders, including Wilton C. Jaffee, Jr. ("Jaffee") who registered approximately 25 percent of the shares on the shelf and who was the principal partner in Jaffee & Company, a registered broker-dealer. During periods when Jaffee was not offering and selling any of his shelf-registered shares, he purchased Solitron shares for his own account, and apparently induced another broker-dealer to enter bids for Solitron shares. Jaffee engaged in one sale of 3500 shares during the distribution. The Commission stated:

> Jaffee, having agreed to participate in [the] offering, became a participant in the distribution irrespective of any sales of his own registered shares, and his participation continued for so long as any of such shares remained unsold or until they were withdrawn from registration. Otherwise, the Rule's prophylactic purpose could be circumvented since each selling stockholder in turn could refrain from selling his shares for a certain period while engaged in buying and bidding activities serving to raise the price of the stock, and thereby benefit other selling stockholders as well as himself when sales were effected at the higher price. * * * The fact that the shareholders could control the timing of their sales in no way obviated the need for the protections of the Rule or gave rise to any exemption from it.[26]

The Second Circuit strongly endorsed the Commission's application of Rule 10b–6 to Jaffee's activities.

> The dangers of market manipulation that Rule 10b–6 was designed to eradicate * * * were continually present so long as Jaffee's purchases might have artificially inflated the price of Solitron, thereby affording him an opportunity to sell his registered stock at a price higher than he would have received if the market had been permitted to seek its own level. The Commission was clearly justified in applying the rule during a period following the registration and before Jaffee had "completed his participation" in the distribution.[27]

As a result of these decisions, the staff adopted the position that all of the Shelf Shareholders are subject to Rule 10b–6 (among other provisions) until the entire distribution is completed or abandoned.[28]

---

26. 44 S.E.C. at 288–89.

27. Jaffee & Co. v. SEC, 446 F.2d 387, 391 (2d Cir.1971) (citations omitted).

28. It should be noted that the restrictions of the Rule extend beyond the actual Shelf Shareholders since "affiliated purchasers" of selling shareholders, as defined in Rule 10b–6(c)(6), also are subject to the Rule. Combined with the adoption of Exception (xii) to the Rule, 17 CFR 240.10b–6(a)(3)(xii), in 1983, the historical interpretation required all Shelf Shareholders and their affiliated purchasers to coordinate their activities and refrain from bidding and purchasing activity from the commencement of the cooling-off period prior to offers or sales off the shelf by any Shelf Shareholders and continuing until such offers and sales have terminated. See Section III.B, infra.

Another direct result of *Hazel Bishop* was the adoption of the portions of what are presently Rules 418 and 461 under the Securities Act that deal with secondary offerings. See Section III.E, infra.

III. Analysis of the Revised Interpretation

The essential issue is: Under what circumstances should an individual Shelf Shareholder participating in a shelf-registered offering [29] be subject to the restrictions of Rule 10b–6? The resolution of the issue involves the consideration of two criteria:

(1) Whether the Shelf Shareholder is an affiliated purchaser [30] of the issuer or of any other Shelf Shareholder; and

(2) Whether the Shelf Shareholder and all of his affiliated purchasers have distributed their participation in the shelf offering.

After consideration of these criteria, the Commission believes that, unless an individual Shelf Shareholder is in a control relationship as defined in Rule 10b–6(a)(ii) with the issuer or another Shelf Shareholder, or is acting in concert with the issuer or another Shelf Shareholder,[31] the restrictions of Rule 10b–6 with respect to the individual Shelf Shareholder apply only when the individual Shelf Shareholder is offering or selling shares off the shelf. A corollary position is that the individual Shelf Shareholder who is not affiliated or directly or indirectly acting in concert with the issuer or any other Shelf Shareholder will no longer be subject to Rule 10b–6 after he has distributed all of his shares off the shelf or has withdrawn them from registration. The Commission has attached a matrix to this release to provide a concise statement of its interpretive position.

A. *Individual Shelf Shareholders*

Unless a Shelf Shareholder is an affiliated purchaser of the issuer or another Shelf Shareholder (see Section III.B, Infra), the revised interpretation greatly reduces the impact of Rule 10b–6 on an individual Shelf Shareholder. Rather than being required to coordinate his purchasing and selling activity with every other Shelf Shareholder as under the historical interpretation, the individual Shelf Shareholder will be required to observe the appropriate cooling-off period and the other Rule 10b–6 restrictions only with respect to his own offers and sales off the shelf.

The Commission believes that this interpretive position is consistent with the underlying concerns expressed in *Hazel Bishop* and *Jaffee*. *Hazel Bishop* involved an egregious fact situation that included, among other things, extensive undisclosed arrangements among approximately 150 Shelf Shareholders. It seems clear that a substantial number of the Shelf Shareholders were affiliated with each other or were acting in concert. The Rule's restrictions clearly apply to such persons affiliated or acting in concert with each other when any one of such persons is selling shares off

---

29. It will be assumed that the shelf offering constitutes a distribution as defined by the Rule. See Rule 10b–6(c)(5).

30. "Affiliated purchaser" is defined in Rule 10b–6(c)(6) as:

(i) a person acting in concert with the issuer or other person on whose behalf the distribution is being made in connection with the acquisition or distribution of the issuer's securities, or (ii) an affiliate who, directly or indirectly, controls the purchases by the issuer or other person of the issuer's securities, whose

purchases are controlled by the issuer or such other person, or whose purchases are under common control with those of the issuer or such other person.

31. Where a Shelf Shareholder acts in concert with a person other than a Shelf Shareholder in connection with bids, purchases, or sales of securities of the same class and series as those registered on the shelf, the other person's activities are imputed to the Shelf Shareholder for purposes of determining the application of the Rule. See Section III.C, infra.

the shelf. Accordingly, in order to comply with Rule 10b–6, a great deal of coordination was required among the *Hazel Bishop* Shelf Shareholders. It should be noted that the decision did not specifically address the impact of Rule 10b–6 on Shelf Shareholders who were not affiliated or acting in concert with the issuer or any other Shelf Shareholder. Therefore, although the position expressed in *Hazel Bishop* that each of the Shelf Shareholders (and persons acting in concert with them) is subject to the Rule continues to be true, the Commission does not believe that applying the full rigors of coordination and the Rule's restrictions to individual Shelf Shareholders not affiliated or acting in concert with any other Shelf Shareholder is required by that decision.

In *Jaffee*, the Commission stated that each Shelf Shareholder was subject to Rule 10b–6 so long as any of his shares remained unsold. The Commission does not believe that *Jaffee* should be read too broadly or that the revised interpretation conflicts with the prophylactic purpose of the Rule. The concern expressed in *Jaffee* that a Shelf Shareholder would engage in activity ("buying and bidding activities serving to raise the price") during periods when he was not selling off the shelf, and thereby would benefit other Shelf Shareholders and himself, essentially refers to two concerns: (1) The bids and purchases could be made with a manipulative purpose to raise the price of the security; or (2) the bids and purchases by a distribution participant would contravene the Rule's goal of permitting the market to serve as a pricing mechanism independent of the influence of those with an interest in the success of the distribution. The revised interpretation accommodates both of these concerns.

First, bidding and purchasing activity by a Shelf Shareholder for the purpose of manipulating the price of the security clearly would violate Rule 10b–6 (and other antifraud and anti-manipulative provisions) [34] under both the historical and revised interpretations. [35] With respect to an individual Shelf Shareholder, the revised interpretation assumes that there is no affiliated purchaser status with the issuer or other Shelf Shareholders, and that the individual Shelf Shareholder is not acting in concert with anyone with respect to his bidding, purchasing, or selling activity. If these assumptions are true, it is extremely unlikely that an individual Shelf Shareholder would engage in any manipulative activity to benefit other Shelf Shareholders. With respect to bidding and purchasing activity by an individual Shelf Shareholder without manipulative purpose prior to his own offers and sales off the shelf, the cooling-off periods in Exception (xii) should dissipate any ordinary market transactions by the Shelf Shareholder prior to the cooling-off period.

The Commission has recognized that shelf distributions, because of their length and the absence of continuous sales efforts, warrant special consideration under Rule 10b–6, and has relaxed certain restrictions of Rule 10b–6 since the *Jaffee* case. [36] In conjunction with the historical interpretation,

---

34. E.g., sections 9(a)(2) and 10(b) under the Exchange Act, 15 U.S.C. 78i(a)(2) and 78j(b), and Rule 10b–5, 17 CFR 240.10b–5, thereunder.

35. To the extent that the Shelf Shareholder purports to rely on Exception (xii) (or any other Rule exception) to engage in manipulative behavior in his own buying and bidding activity, the exception would not be available to him, and a violation of Rule 10b–6 would result. Securities Exchange Act Release No. 22510 (October 10, 1985), 50 FR 42716, 42722 (October 22, 1985); see Jaffee & Co. v. SEC, 446 F.2d 387, 391 (2d Cir.1971).

36. See Release 34–19565, 48 FR 10635–36.

Exception (xii) permits Shelf Shareholders to coordinate their activities during the life of the shelf and engage in bidding and purchasing activity prior to cooling-off periods preceding any offer or sale off the shelf.[37] The revised interpretation extends this approach by permitting Shelf Shareholders to be evaluated individually to determine the extent to which Rule 10b–6 will apply.[38]

B. Affiliated Purchasers

An affiliated purchaser, by definition, is any person who acts in concert with a Shelf Shareholder with respect to the acquisition or distribution of the securities that are the subject of the distribution, or an affiliate of the Shelf Shareholder whose securities purchases are directly or indirectly controlling, controlled by, or under common control with those of the Shelf Shareholder. Affiliated purchasers of a Shelf Shareholder are subject to the same Rule 10b–6 restrictions as the Shelf Shareholder.

1. Shelf Shareholders Who are Affiliated Purchasers of the Issuer

Since the interests of all affiliated purchasers of the issuer ("Issuer Affiliated Purchasers") are linked to a common source (the issuer), the Commission believes that it is appropriate to apply a joint and several cooling-off period to the issuer and to all Issuer Affiliated Purchasers. Accordingly, when *any* Issuer Affiliated Purchaser sells securities off the shelf, the issuer and *all* Issuer Affiliated Purchasers (including other Shelf Shareholders who are Issuer Affiliated Purchasers) are jointly and severally subject to the 2 or 9 business day cooling-off period and other Rule 10b–6 restrictions applicable to the Shelf Shareholder proposing to sell securities off the shelf. This position requires the same degree of purchasing and selling coordination that has been required of all Shelf Shareholders (whether or not they are Issuer Affiliated Purchasers) and the issuer under the historical position.

2. Shelf Shareholders Who Are Affiliated Purchasers of Other Shelf Shareholders (but not Issuer Affiliated Purchasers)

Since Shelf Shareholders who are affiliated purchasers with respect to each other are viewed as having common interests, the Commission believes that it is appropriate to impose a joint and several cooling-off period with respect to such Shelf Shareholders. Therefore, when any one Shelf Shareholder is distributing securities off the shelf, all other Shelf Shareholders who are affiliated purchasers of the selling Shelf Shareholder are subject to the cooling-off period and other Rule 10b–6 restrictions applicable to the selling Shelf Shareholder. This position requires the same

---

37. It should be noted, however, that the benefits of Exception (xii) are essentially unavailable under the historical position where a shelf has a large number of unrelated Shelf Shareholders who may find it impracticable to coordinate their bidding, purchasing, and selling activities.

38. The application of Rule 10b–6 in the *Jaffee* case would not change under the revised interpretation. Although Jaffee apparently personally would have been in compliance with the cooling-off periods under the revised interpretation prior to his sales of Solitron stock through a broker-dealer, he acted in concert with a broker-dealer and arranged for bids to be placed in the sheets for Solitron stock. The broker-dealer's conduct therefore is imputed to Jaffee, and Jaffee violated Rule 10b–6 under both the historical and the revised interpretations.

degree of purchasing and selling coordination as the historical position, but only among affiliated purchasers of the selling Shelf Shareholder.

C. Persons Acting in Concert With Shelf Shareholders

The revised position with respect to persons who act in concert with Shelf Shareholders does not represent any change from the historical position. Since the Rule prohibits any person covered by the Rule from "directly or indirectly" engaging in prohibited activities,[39] persons not directly covered by the Rule who act in concert with Shelf Shareholders [40] are also subject to the Rule's prohibitions, and the actions of such persons are imputed to the Shelf Shareholders with whom they act in concert. The revised position continues to follow that approach: every person who acts in concert with a Shelf Shareholder is subject to the same restrictions on his market activity that apply to the Shelf Shareholder.

D. Completion of Shelf Shareholder's Participation in a Distribution

As discussed above, there has been some uncertainty and inconsistency with respect to the point at which a Shelf Shareholder is no longer subject to Rule 10b–6. Certain language in Commission releases suggests that a Shelf Shareholder is subject to the Rule any time that offers and sales are being made off the shelf by any Shelf Shareholder, even after a Shelf Shareholder has sold all of his shares off the shelf.[41]

The Commission believes that, for the purpose of Rule 10b–6, a Shelf Shareholders' participation in a shelf distribution continues for so long as any of his and any of his affiliated purchasers' shares remain unsold or until all such shares are withdrawn from registration.[42] This is consistent with the premise that the Rule should apply in situations where a person may have an incentive to manipulate the market for the securities in order to facilitate the distribution.[43] Where neither the Shelf Shareholder nor his affiliated purchasers have shares on the shelf, the manipulative incentive is absent and under the revised position the Rule's restrictions will no longer apply to that Shelf Shareholder.

E. Impact of the Revised Position on Rules 418 and 461 Under the Securities Act

1. Rule 418

Rule 418(a)(4) provides that the Commission or the staff may request supplemental information concerning the issuer, the registration statement, the distribution of securities, market activities, and underwriters' activities, including:

> Where there is a registration of an "offering at the market," as defined in Rule 10b–7 under the [Exchange Act], of more than 10 per cent of the securities owned by officers, directors or affiliates of the registrant and where there is no underwriting agreement, information (i) concerning contractual arrangements between selling security hold-

---

39. Rule 10b–6(a)(3).

40. Of course, such a person is an affiliated purchaser of the Shelf Shareholder. See Rule 10b–6(c)(6)(i).

41. See Release 34–19565, 48 FR 10631; Jaffee & Co., 44 S.E.C. at 289.

42. See Jaffee & Co. v. SEC, 446 F.2d 387, 391 (2d Cir.1971). * * *

43. See, e.g., Collins Securities Corp., 46 S.E.C. 20, 34 (1975), reversed and remanded on other grounds, Collins Securities Corp. v. SEC, 562 F.2d (2d Cir.1977).

ers of a limited group or of several groups of related shareholders to comply with the anti-manipulation rules until the offering by all members of the group is completed and to inform the exchange, brokers and selling security holders when the distribution by the members of the group is over, or (ii) concerning the registrant's efforts to notify members of a large group of unrelated sellers of the applicable Commission rules and regulations.

Rule 418, which is designed to avoid the dangers posed by situations similar to that in *Hazel Bishop,* would be unaffected by the revised interpretation with respect to Rule 10b–6. With respect to offerings covered by Rule 418, it will continue to be appropriate for the staff to request information concerning: contractual arrangements between Shelf Shareholders to comply with Rule 10b–6, among other provisions and efforts to apprise Shelf Shareholders of the application of Rule 10b–6, among other provisions.

2. Rule 461

Paragraph (b)(7) of Rule 461 provides that the Commission may refuse to accelerate the effective date of a registration statement:

> Where, in the case of significant secondary offering at the market, the registrant, selling security holders and underwriters have not taken sufficient measures to insure compliance with Rules 10b–2, 10b–6 and 10b–7 under the [Exchange Act].

Again, this rule would be unaffected by the revised position with respect to Rule 10b–6. It should be noted that, whereas the historical interpretation required Shelf Shareholders to coordinate the purchasing and selling activities of *all* Shelf Shareholders during the life of the shelf irrespective of whether individual Shelf Shareholders were affiliated with the issuer or with each other or were acting in concert with each other, the revised interpretation requires less complicated coordination activities.

F. *Broker-Dealers Selling Securities on Behalf of Shelf Shareholders*

Another recurring issue raised by shelf registration is the extent to which the restrictions of Rule 10b–6 should apply to a broker-dealer who sells shelf-registered shares on behalf of a Shelf Shareholder. In *Hazel Bishop,* the Commission stated: "Each of the selling stockholders and any broker or other person acting for any of them will be subject to the provisions of this rule." In *Jaffee,* a market maker, Greene & Company ("G Co."), had purchased approximately 25,000 shares registered on the shelf from the exclusive selling agent broker-dealer for the Shelf Shareholders. In this context the Commission stated:

> G Co. and Horn [G Co.'s trader] should have been aware that their purchases for resale of stock that they knew was part of a registered offering did not constitute normal trading activity. Persons like G Co., engaging in market-making activities in a security which at the same time is being offered in a registered distribution must not participate in such distribution unless they have terminated their bidding and purchasing in the open market as provided in Rule 10b–6.[47]

---

47. 44 S.E.C. at 289. It should be noted that the Commission found that a Shelf Shareholder had induced G Co., through   Horn, to enter bids in the "pink sheets" during the shelf distribution, id., at 288, although the Commission permitted that

As a result, the Commission found that G Co. and Horn violated Rule 10b-6.[48]

The Commission's statement in *Jaffee,* however, was derived from its holding that "[a]n offering of stock pursuant to a registration statement by its very nature constitutes a distribution within the meaning of Rule 10b-6." This holding was explicitly overruled in *Collins Securities Corporation.*[50] In *Collins,* the Commission stated:

If the term distribution in Rule 10b-6 were to be equated with the concept of public offering or distribution in the Securities Act, this would not only extend the restrictions of Rule 10b-6 beyond their intended purpose but could result in unnecessary disruption of the trading markets, particularly where an exchange specialist or other market maker acquires registered stock in the performance of his normal functions. It would obviously make no sense to conclude that a specialist, who happens to acquire some registered stock in the course of his normal activities, has to get out of the market until after he has disposed of that stock. No one has ever thought that such a result was required, even though specialists might well purchase registered stock being sold under a so-called "shelf-registration."[51]

Accordingly, in the context of a shelf-registered secondary distribution, a broker-dealer who is asked to sell securities on behalf of a Shelf Shareholder, or who proposes to purchase securities from a Shelf Shareholder, must determine whether the broker-dealer is participating in a distribution. The determination will entail an analysis of the two components of the Rule 10b-6 definition of distribution; magnitude and selling efforts. From the broker-dealer's perspective, the magnitude would be the amount

evidence to be used only with respect to the Shelf Shareholder, id., n. 6.

48. Id. at 290. Commissioner Smith took exception to the Commission's finding of a Rule 10b-6 violation with respect to G Co. and Horn. Id. at 296-302 (Commissioner Smith, concurring in part and dissenting in part). He maintained that the Rule was not intended to apply where a broker-dealer sells shelf-registered shares through "normal trading transactions," and that there was no evidence in the record that G Co. engaged in anything other than normal trading transactions in disposing of Solitron shares. Id. at 300-02. Commissioner Smith's review of previous Commission decisions identified specific situations in which Rule 10b-6 had been applied to a broker-dealer selling distribution shares, i.e., where the broker-dealer: is "acting for" (other than simply acting in an agency capacity) the Shelf Shareholder, dominates or controls the volume or price of the security; engages in unusual sales efforts to sell the shares; or engages in a pattern of manipulative trading activity that raises the price of the security. Id. at 299-302.

50. 46 S.E.C. 20, 35 (1975), reversed and remanded on other grounds, 562 F.2d 820 (D.C.Cir.1977).

51. 46 S.E.C. at 35-36. Moreover, a Commission release in 1981 specifically addressed the interrelationship of the proposed predecessor to Rule 415 and, *inter alia,* Rule 10b-6 in the context of primary at the market offerings (i.e., offerings sold solely by or on behalf of an issuer, a subsidiary of the issuer, or a person of which the issuer is a subsidiary):

The staff takes the position that, for purposes of Rule 10b-6, a market professional who does not have any prior agreement or understanding with the issuer should not be deemed to be a participant in the issuer's distribution pursuant to a shelf registration statement solely because it purchases, in the ordinary course of its business, securities that are registered on the shelf and are offered by the issuer or a broker-dealer acting for the issuer. Nevertheless, the Commission cautions such market professionals to examine carefully the manner in which they intend to dispose of those securities once they have purchased them against the traditional indicia of a Rule 10b-6 distribution in order to determine whether their resales might constitute a separate distribution for purposes of Rule 10b-6.

of shares that he is asked to sell, or foreseeably will be asked to sell,[52] on behalf of Shelf Shareholders. The selling efforts analysis will focus upon the activities that the broker-dealer will employ in selling the securities. However, as a general proposition, the disposition of such shares by a broker-dealer in "normal trading transactions" into an independent market (i.e., one not dominated or controlled by the broker-dealer, and in which the price of the security is not manipulated by the broker-dealer or others acting in concert with the broker-dealer), will not subject the broker-dealer to the restrictions of Rule 10b–6.[53] This is consistent with the purposes of Rule 10b–6 and avoids unnecessary disruption of the trading markets.

IV. Summary of the Revised Interpretation

The revised interpretation as adopted by the Commission is that:

A.　Rule 10b–6 applies to any shelf-registered offering that, viewed as a whole, constitutes a distribution as defined in Rule 10b–6(c)(5).

B.　Rule 10b–6 applies to an individual Shelf Shareholder at a minimum during the period that he is offering or selling his shares off the shelf. Therefore, the Shelf Shareholder must be out of the market for the appropriate cooling-off period prior to his offers and sales, and until his offers and sales terminate.

C.　The Rule also applies to "affiliated purchasers" of Shelf Shareholders, as that term is defined in Rule 10b–6(c)(6). Therefore persons in control relationships with a Shelf Shareholder as specified in Rule 10b–6(c)(6)(ii), or who act in concert with a Shelf Shareholder, will be subject to the same Rule 10b–6 restrictions that apply to the Shelf Shareholder.

D.　The issuer is subject to Rule 10b–6 whenever an "affiliated purchaser" of the issuer ("Issuer Affiliated Purchaser") sells securities off the shelf. Each Shelf Shareholder who is an Issuer Affiliated Purchaser is subject to joint and several restrictions under Rule 10b–6 whenever any Issuer Affiliated Purchaser sells securities off the shelf.

E.　Rule 10b–6 is no longer applicable to a Shelf Shareholder who has sold, or has withdrawn from registration, all of his securities registered on the shelf. (This assumes that the Shelf Shareholder is not an Issuer Affiliated Purchaser or an affiliated purchaser of any Shelf Shareholder who continues to have shares on the shelf.)

F.　A broker-dealer who purchases securities as principal from a Shelf Shareholder or who sells securities as agent for a Shelf Shareholder must ascertain whether his activities constitute participation in a distribution within the meaning of Rule 10b–6(c)(5), but the disposition of such shares in normal trading transactions into an independent market will not subject the broker-dealer to the Rule.

---

52. Where a broker-dealer agrees with one or more Shelf Shareholders to act as their exclusive sales agent in connection with sales off the shelf (which constitute a distribution as defined by the Rule), the broker-dealer will be subject to the Rule.
* * *

53. The foregoing discussion assumes that the broker-dealer is not an "affiliated purchaser" of the Shelf Shareholder, as that term is defined in Rule 10b–6(c)(6). It also assumes that none of the broker-dealer's bidding or purchasing activity is for the purpose of creating actual, or apparent, active trading in or raising the price of the security. *See* n. 35 supra.

Application of Rule 10b–6 in the Context of
Secondary Shelf Distributions

[Cooling-off periods]

Seller	Shelf shareholder [2]	Issuer [3]
Shelf Shareholder A who is an Affiliated Purchaser [1] of the Issuer.	2 or 9 business days before offers or sales by A or any other Affiliated Purchaser of the Issuer.	2 or 9 business days before offers or sales by A or any other Affiliated Purchaser of the Issuer.
Shelf Shareholder B who is an Affiliated Purchaser of Shelf Shareholder C (but not an Affiliated Purchaser of the Issuer).	2 or 9 business days before offers or sales by B or C.	None.
Shelf Shareholder D who is not an Affiliated Purchaser of the Issuer or Any other Shelf Shareholder.	2 or 9 business days before offers or sales by D.	None.

1. "Affiliated Purchaser" as defined by Rule 10b–6(c)(6).
2. Includes Affiliated Purchasers of the Shelf Shareholder.
3. Includes Affiliated Purchasers of the Issuer.

SECURITIES ACT RELEASE NO. 4434

Securities and Exchange Commission.
December 6, 1961.

SALES BY CONTROLLING PERSONS UNDER § 3(a)(11)

[Read the last paragraph of this release under the rubric "Residence Within the State," supra at page 389; Rule 147, Preliminary Note 4.]

SECTION 3. STATUTORY RESTRICTIONS ON RESALES OF RESTRICTED SECURITIES BY NON-AFFILIATES IN THE PRE–RULE 144 PERIOD

UNITED STATES v. SHERWOOD

United States District Court, S.D. New York, 1959.
175 F.Supp. 480.

SUGARMAN, DISTRICT JUDGE. By order to show cause filed February 6, 1959, the United States of America moves pursuant to F.R.Crim.P. 42(b) for an order adjudging Robert Maurice Sherwood to be in criminal contempt for not obeying a final decree of permanent injunction entered against him on consent * * *.

The application for the order to show cause alleges *inter alia* that:

"1. On September 23, 1958 the Securities and Exchange Commission filed in this Court a complaint * * * This action complained of sales of the common capital stock of Canadian Javelin Limited in violations of both the registration and fraud provisions of the Securities Act of 1933 and the anti-market manipulation provisions of the Securities Exchange Act of 1934.

"2. On November 24, 1958, United States District Judge Sidney Sugarman, sitting in the Southern District of New York, issued a permanent injunction enjoining Robert Maurice Sherwood and others from, among other things, * * * violations of the registration provisions of the Securities Act of 1933, in the offer and sale of common shares of Canadian Javelin Limited.

"3. On November 24, 1958, Robert Maurice Sherwood consented to the entry of this final decree of permanent injunction. * * *"

"4. It was clearly stated both in open court and in conferences leading to the acceptance of the consent, that all of the Canadian Javelin Limited shares received by Robert Maurice Sherwood from Canadian Javelin Limited, the issuer, or from John Christopher Doyle, a control person of the issuer, were and would remain control shares in Sherwood's hands, and could not be offered and sold without full registration with the Securities and Exchange Commission or, at the very least, without a request for and receipt of a so called no action letter from the Securities and Exchange Commission, based on an acceptable change of circumstances, which letter in turn would be required to be filed with the Court as a basis for an application for modification of the permanent injunction, to release any shares covered in such no action letter.

"5. No registration statement covering shares of Canadian Javelin Limited has ever been filed with the Securities and Exchange Commission, and none has ever been in effect.

"6. * * * no request for modification of the permanent injunction was ever addressed to this Court.

"7. Since November 24, 1958 * * * Robert Maurice Sherwood has offered and sold more than 8,000 shares of Canadian Javelin Limited, by orders executed in the United States, to members of the public in the United States for about $125,000, in an almost daily marketing operation. More than 4,000 additional shares were offered and sold in Canada during this same period by the defendant Robert Maurice Sherwood.

"8. These shares were all shares received by Robert Maurice Sherwood from John Christopher Doyle who in turn received them from the issuer. * * *"

Of the quoted facts alleged in the petition herein the trial of the contempt prosecution established these: the civil action for injunction commenced by the Securities and Exchange Commission; the consent of the defendant Sherwood to a final injunction; sales of numerous shares of Canadian Javelin Limited in the United States by the defendant Sherwood without the filing of a registration statement with the Securities and Exchange Commission.

The prosecution's contentions are basically that:

(1) Sherwood, by consenting to the injunction of November 24, 1958 undertook not to sell in the United States, until a registration statement was filed, the Canadian Javelin Limited shares which he did thereafter sell.

(2) Even if the defendant's undertaking was not to sell the shares he took through Doyle unless and until a registration thereof was required and filed, such registration thereof was required and Sherwood is in contempt for selling the shares without the filing of a registration statement.

The first contention of the prosecution cannot be sustained. A reading of the language of the injunction, to which Sherwood gave his consent, in the light of all the testimony and exhibits presented showing the genesis thereof, demonstrates that in so far as is here pertinent, Sherwood undertook to refrain from selling, offering to sell, or transporting Canadian Javelin Limited shares *only if a registration statement should then be required* and not be filed as is suggested by the second contention.

     * * * *

The prosecution theory is alternatively, first, that a registration statement was required to be filed because Sherwood was a statutory underwriter when he acquired his shares because he purchased them from an issuer with a view to distribution thereof, or second, that Sherwood was required to file a registration statement because when he made the sales complained of, he was a "control person".

The evidence does not sustain the second charge that Sherwood was at the time of the sales a "control person". To the contrary, although Sherwood dominated 8% of the total issued stock, he was unable to secure a representation of the board of directors, he had had a falling-out with John Christopher Doyle, who appears to have been the dominant figure in the management of Canadian Javelin Limited, and Sherwood was unable to free the bulk of his shares for distribution until Doyle consented thereto. Furthermore, no statutory or case authority has been cited nor has any been found to sustain the prosecutor's broad contention that "the shares of Canadian Javelin, Ltd., held by the defendant, Robert Maurice Sherwood, received by him from John Christopher Doyle, an admitted control person of Canadian Javelin, Ltd., and sold by Sherwood both prior to and subsequent to the final decree of November 24, 1958, were control shares from the time of their issuance; remained in their status as control shares during the period that Sherwood and Doyle were working together 'in the interests of the company'; and remain control shares from then to this very day." The court knows of no authority for a holding that shares once owned by "control" persons retain "control" characteristics in the hands of subsequent owners.

As to the first contention, that Sherwood was a statutory underwriter, on this record I am not satisfied beyond a reasonable doubt that at the time Sherwood took his shares from the issuer through Doyle, he purchased them with a view to the distribution thereof.

Defendant points to the long period between his purchase of and the first sale from his block of Canadian Javelin Limited shares. From this, he argues that:

"From such behavior, it is impossible to infer the intention to distribute, *at the time of acquisition*, that it is necessary under the Act to qualify Sherwood as an underwriter within the meaning of the Act. His retention of the shares for a minimum of two full years after he personally had obtained physical possession of them belies any inference that he had originally acquired them 'with a view to distribution,' and is inconsistent with any such intention."

On the proof before me it appears that Sherwood took the unrestricted ownership of the block of shares out of which the post-decree sales were made in September 1955 when they were delivered to his agents, Lombard & Odier. No sales or other transactions were made out of this block until September 1957. The passage of two years before the commencement of distribution of any of these shares is an insuperable obstacle to my finding that Sherwood took these shares with a view to distribution thereof, in the absence of any relevant evidence from which I could conclude he did not take the shares for investment. No such evidence was offered at the trial.

*   *   *

This decision, of course, is not to be deemed a finding that the shares of Canadian Javelin Limited stock owned by Sherwood are not subject to registration under the Securities Act of 1933, nor is it a finding that future transfer of that stock by defendant would not constitute contempt.

This decision is merely a finding *that on this record* the prosecution has not proven, beyond a reasonable doubt, that the accused's transactions were violative of the decree of this court.

The motion to punish Robert Maurice Sherwood for contempt of this court's decree of November 24, 1958 is denied and it is so ordered.[a]

GILLIGAN, WILL & CO. v. SECURITIES AND EXCHANGE COMMISSION [a]

United States Court of Appeals, Second Circuit, 1959.
267 F.2d 461.

LUMBARD, CIRCUIT JUDGE. The question for decision is whether Gilligan, Will & Co. and its partners, James Gilligan and William Will, were underwriters with respect to the distribution of Crowell-Collier Publishing Company securities and as such wilfully violated the Securities Act of 1933, as amended, by acquiring and distributing debentures and common stock which were not registered. For reasons which are discussed below, this question turns on whether the issue was a "public offering" as those words are used in the Act.

For their activities with respect to these debentures and stock the Securities & Exchange Commission, pursuant to § 15 of the Securities Exchange Act of 1934, instituted a proceeding to determine whether the petitioners had violated the 1933 Act and whether Gilligan, Will & Co.'s

---

a. In a companion case, John Christopher Doyle, described as a "suave Canadian mining promoter" was convicted of violations of the 1933 act in connection with the sale of the unregistered stock of Canadian Javelin, Ltd. He was sentenced to three years in jail and a $5,000 fine, the jail sentence to be suspended after three months. This conviction was affirmed.

United States v. Doyle, 348 F.2d 715 (2d Cir. 1965). Rather than serving his sentence, Doyle fled to Canada where he remains a fugitive from United States justice. N.Y. Times, Sept. 24, 1966, p. 27, col. 2.

a. Cert. denied 361 U.S. 896 (1959).

registration as a broker-dealer under the 1934 Act should be revoked. The facts were stipulated, a hearing was waived, and the Commission heard oral argument. It thereafter ordered that Gilligan, Will & Co. be suspended from membership in the National Association of Securities Dealers, Inc. for five days, and found that James Gilligan and William Will were each a cause of the order.

The partnership and the partners petition for review of the Commission's order claiming that its action was arbitrary and capricious in [these] respects: (1) that its finding that petitioners were underwriters with respect to 1955 and 1956 transactions in Crowell-Collier debentures and stock was not supported by substantial evidence; (2) that the findings of wilful violation of the registration provision was unsupported by substantial evidence * * *.

We hold that there was substantial evidence to justify the findings and conclusions of the Commission that the issue was a public offering and that petitioners were underwriters, and we agree that the registrant's suspension for wilful violation was proper. * * * Accordingly, we affirm the Commission's order.

The principal and essential purpose of the 1933 Act is to protect investors by requiring registration with the Commission of certain information concerning securities offered for sale. * * * For reasons which will be developed, the crucial provisions of law in this case are § 5 of the 1933 Act which makes it unlawful for anyone, by any interstate communication or use of the mails, to sell or deliver any security unless a registration statement is in effect; and § 4(1) which exempts from this prohibition "transactions by any person other than issuer, underwriter, or dealer" and "transactions by an issuer not involving any public offering."

Since the Commission's proceeding was had on stipulated facts the only question is whether it was justified in drawing from them the inferences and conclusions of which the petitioners complain, principally that the petitioners were underwriters and that the issue was a public offering. To examine these inferences and conclusions we must state in some detail the facts concerning the issuance of the unregistered debentures and common stock of Crowell-Collier Publishing Company.

On July 6, 1955, Elliott & Company agreed with Crowell-Collier to try to sell privately, without registration, $3,000,000 of Crowell-Collier 5% debentures, convertible at any time into common stock at $5 a share, and the Elliott firm received an option on an additional $1,000,000 of debentures. Edward L. Elliott, a partner in Elliott & Company, advised Gilligan, one of the two partners of the registrant, Gilligan, Will & Co., of this agreement. He told Gilligan that Gilligan could purchase, but only for investment, as much of the $3,000,000 as he wished, with the exception of $500,000 which Elliott's wife was taking, and that the debentures not taken by Gilligan would be offered to certain friends of Elliott. Gilligan was told by Elliott that Crowell-Collier had "turned the corner" and was then operating on a profitable basis. Elliott also said that the attorneys for Crowell-Collier and his lawyers had stated that the placement was an exempt transaction. Gilligan agreed to purchase $100,000 of debentures for his own account. It does not appear that Gilligan had any information regarding Crowell-Collier and the debenture issue other than what Elliott told him as summarized above.

On August 10, 1955 the $100,000 debentures were delivered to Gilligan, Will & Co., which sent a letter to Crowell-Collier stating: "that said debentures are being purchased for investment and that the undersigned has no present intention of distributing the same."

Nevertheless, by August 10, 1955, almost half of the $100,000 of debentures had already been resold. Either on July 6 or July 7, 1955, Louis Alter, a member of the American Stock Exchange agreed to buy $45,000 of the debentures. Gilligan also offered $10,000 to a friend and when this was not accepted he sold $5,000 to Michael D. Mooney, who had previously requested that amount of debentures and had been told that none were available; the remaining $5,000 debentures were placed in the registrant's trading account. In early September, when the securities were distributed, Gilligan, Alter and Mooney each signed a statement reading: "I hereby confirm to you that said debentures are being purchased for investment and that I have no present intention of distributing the same."

In May 1956, after Gilligan noticed that the advertising in Crowell-Collier magazines was not increasing, he decided to convert his debentures into common stock and to sell the stock. He advised Alter of his plans and on May 15, 1956 the registrant, Gilligan and Alter converted their debentures into common stock. Later in May they sold the stock at a profit on the American Stock Exchange. The stock had been listed on that Exchange since October 1955, and Gilligan became the specialist in the stock.

In May 1956 Gilligan, Will & Co. also purchased and participated in the sale of additional debentures by Crowell-Collier. Elliott told Gilligan that he was surrendering to Crowell-Collier his option on the remaining $1,000,000 of debentures, and that these debentures were to be sold at 160% of par, based on the stock's price at that time of $8 per share. The proceeds of the sale, Elliott stated, were to be used by Crowell-Collier in the acquisition of certain television stations which would show a profit of $4,000,000 annually. Elliott also told Gilligan that Crowell-Collier would sell him, Elliott, 100,000 stock purchase warrants at 1 each, exercisable at $10 per share for five years. Gilligan agreed to take $150,000 face amount debentures and said he would see whether Alter was interested in taking any. After Alter indicated that he wanted $50,000 face amount, Gilligan advised Elliott that the total subscription would be $200,000. Gilligan did not inform Elliott of his and Alter's sales of stock obtained from the conversion of the debentures purchased in 1955.

On May 29, 1956 the registrant subscribed to $200,000 face amount debentures and issued to Alter a confirmation for $50,000 debentures which stated: "we have this day subscribed for your account and risk; over the counter as agents * * *" Alter immediately converted his debentures into stock. On the same day the registrant similarly confirmed $150,000 face amount debentures to a joint specialist's account maintained by it and one Lloyd E. Howard, which debentures were immediately converted into common stock.

In addition, on May 29, the registrant sent Crowell-Collier a letter signed by Will, confirming that $200,000 of debentures were purchased for investment with no present intention to distribute. Howard and Alter made similar representations on copies of the confirmations issued to them by the registrant.

Late in May 1956, Elliott informed Gilligan that $200,000 of debentures were still unsold, that it was necessary to sell these debentures to one party, and that if Gilligan could find a purchaser, Elliott would sell him 50,000 stock warrants at 1 each. Gilligan contacted Harry Harris and told him that he would split his warrants with him if he, Harris, could find a purchaser for the debentures. Harris interested Value Line Special Fund, Inc., and Gilligan told Harris to contact Elliott. On May 29, 1956, the Fund's representatives met with Crowell-Collier's president, Paul Smith, and Harris and Elliott, and the Fund later agreed to purchase $200,000 face amount debentures and 15,000 warrants. To accommodate Elliott, Gilligan, Will & Co. as principal sent a confirmation, signed by Will, covering the sale of the debentures to the Fund.

Gilligan, Will & Co. received 50,000 warrants from Elliott, some of which were sold to the Fund and some of which were given to nominees of Harris and others, the 20,000 warrants given to others being subsequently returned to Elliott at his request.

Gilligan, Will & Co. sent Crowell-Collier two investment intention letters, in the usual form, one covering the Fund's purchase of debentures and the other covering the 50,000 warrants received by registrant. The Fund, at the request of Gilligan, Will & Co. signed letters of investment intent covering the debentures and the warrants.

Petitioners assert that they were not "underwriters" within the meaning of the exemption provided by the first clause of § 4(1). Since § 2(11) defines an "underwriter" as "any person who has purchased from an issuer with a view to * * * the distribution of any security" and since a "distribution" requires a "public offering," see H.R.Rep. No. 1838, 73d Cong., 2d Sess. (1934) at p. 41, the question is whether there was a "public offering." Petitioners, disclaiming any reliance on the exemption of the second clause of § 4(1) for "transactions by an issuer not involving any public offering," assert that whether there was a "distribution" must be judged solely by their own acts and intention, and not by the acts or intention of the issuer or others. In other words they claim that whether the total offering was in fact public, their purchases and resales may be found to be exempt on the ground that they were not underwriters if their own resales did not amount to a public offering.

In the view we take of this case we need not decide whether, if the petitioners had purchased with a view to only such resales as would not amount to a distribution or public offering, their acts would be exempt even though the issue was in fact a public offering. We find that the resales contemplated and executed by petitioners were themselves a distribution or public offering as the latter term has been defined by the Supreme Court, and we therefore find that petitioners were underwriters and that their transactions were not exempt under § 4(1).

In S.E.C. v. Ralston Purina Co., 1953, 346 U.S. 119, the Supreme Court considered the exemptions provided by § 4(1). * * * [I]t held that an issuer who claims the benefit of an exemption from § 5 for the sale of an unregistered security has the burden of proving entitlement to it. The rationale of this result applies as well to a broker-dealer who claims the benefit of a similar exemption. We therefore find that the burden was upon the petitioners to establish that they were not underwriters within the meaning of § 4(1).

The Court also defined the standard to be applied in determining whether an issue is a public offering. It held that the governing fact is whether the persons to whom the offering is made are in such a position with respect to the issuer that they either actually have such information as a registration would have disclosed, or have access to such information. * * * The stipulation of facts here expressly states that the purchasers "were not supplied with material information of the scope and character contemplated by the Securities Act nor were the purchasers in such a relation to the issuer as to have access to such information concerning the company and its affairs." Such a stipulation, which from the additional stipulated facts, appears equally applicable to Gilligan, the registrant, Alter, Mooney and Mrs. Elliott, concedes the very proposition of which the petitioners had to establish the negative in order to prevail, and we therefore think it dispositive of the question whether petitioners "purchased * * * with a view to * * * distribution."

Petitioners argue, however, that the definition of the Ralston Purina case is not exclusive, and that there is an exception to the standard there announced for cases in which the number of offerees or purchasers is small. In reliance on such a standard they assert that the stipulation discloses the existence of only four specific purchasers, and that therefore the Commission was bound to determine on this record that the petitioners' transactions were exempt because the issue was not public. We do not agree.

First, we think that the Ralston Purina case clearly rejected a quantity limit on the construction of the statutory term, and adopted instead the test set out above under which this issue was a public offering. It stated that "the statute would seem to apply to a 'public offering' whether to few or many," * * * and cited with approval the dictum that "anything from two to infinity may serve: perhaps even one * * *". Second, even were this not the case, and if a numerical exemption existed despite an admitted violation of the Purina standard, the stipulation adequately discloses that Gilligan well knew that the sales to Elliott's wife and to and through the registrant were not the only sales that were contemplated. It is stipulated that "Elliott advised Gilligan that * * * Elliott was * * * going to sell as much as was left to certain of his friends" after Gilligan took what he wanted of the $2,500,000 remaining after Elliott's wife took $500,000.

Thus these petitioners, who now assert an exemption based on the small number of resales that they contemplated and made, were admittedly aware that the actual placement involved many others. At the least, to establish entitlement to any numerical exemption in such circumstances, the petitioners would have to establish a reasonable and bona fide belief that the total number involved in the placement would remain within the exemption. Otherwise although a general public placement could be effected by a series of transfers to small numbers of buyers, each distributor would be entitled to an exemption on the ground that it transferred to only a small number of buyers. The stipulation reveals that without any knowledge of the actual number of sales then consummated or contemplated the petitioners effected what they now claim to be a harmless number of resales. Such a record does not require and would not justify a finding that the petitioners had sustained their burden of proving entitlement to an exemption based on the size of the contemplated distribution.

The petitioners separately attack the finding that the registrant was an underwriter on the ground that the stipulation reveals that Gilligan agreed with Elliott that Gilligan would take the $100,000 for his own account and thus it requires the conclusion that the registrant did not participate. But the stipulation also reveals that Will received the debentures on behalf of the registrant and also on its behalf issued an investment intention letter, and that $5,000 were placed in the firm trading account. On such facts the Commission was justified in concluding that the registrant participated in the acquisition and distribution of the unregistered issue.

The Commission also found that "The sales by Gilligan and registrant of the underlying common stock on the American Stock Exchange in May 1956, clearly constituted a public distribution." Petitioners contest this conclusion on the ground that since the conversion and sales occurred more than ten months after the purchase of the debentures the Commission was bound to find that the debentures so converted had been held for investment, and that the sales were therefore exempt under § 4(1) since made by a person other than an issuer, underwriter or dealer. Petitioners concede that if such sales were intended at the time of purchase, the debentures would not then have been held as investments; but it argues that the stipulation reveals that the sales were undertaken only after a change of the issuer's circumstances as a result of which petitioners, acting as prudent investors, thought it wise to sell. The catalytic circumstances were the failure, noted by Gilligan, of Crowell-Collier to increase its advertising space as he had anticipated that it would. We agree with the Commission that in the circumstances here presented the intention to retain the debentures only if Crowell-Collier continued to operate profitably was equivalent to a "purchase * * * with a view to * * * distribution" within the statutory definition of underwriters in § 2(11). To hold otherwise would be to permit a dealer who speculatively purchases an unregistered security in the hope that the financially weak issuer had, as is stipulated here, "turned the corner," to unload on the unadvised public what he later determines to be an unsound investment without the disclosure sought by the securities laws, although it is in precisely such circumstances that disclosure is most necessary and desirable. The Commission was within its discretion in finding on this stipulation that petitioners bought "with a view to distribution" despite the ten months of holding.

It is unnecessary, in the light of our decision sustaining the findings of the Commission as to violations with regard to the 1955 debentures, separately to consider the violations of § 5 found by the Commisison as to the issue in 1956. Finally, on the stipulation there is no doubt either that the Commission was justified in finding that the petitioners' acts were "wilful" within the meaning of § 15(b) of the Securities Exchange Act of 1934, * * * 174 F.2d 969, 977, or that the penalty imposed was within the Commission's discretion * * *.

* * * *

The order of the Commission is affirmed.[b]

---

b. Notes, 72 Harv.L.Rev. 789 (1959); 45 Va.L.Rev. 1053 (1959).

FROM IRA HAUPT TO RULE 144

(a) *Sales by Controlling Persons*. Before the *Haupt* case, there was great uncertainty as to the rules governing sales of securities by controlling persons. That case entailed a massive distribution of equity securities through the facilities of the stock exchange by control persons relying upon the exemption provided in § 4(4) for broker's transactions. The *Haupt* case also cast doubt as to the quantity of shares which a controlling person might sell in brokerage transactions without thereby engaging in a "distribution" of securities. Although the sale of a few hundred shares by a controlling person over the stock exchange clearly would not amount to a distribution of securities, it was impossible to determine when additional sales might be regarded as sufficient to destroy the exemption; also, it was not clear as to what interval of time should be taken into account in determining whether a distribution had occurred.

When the 1954 amendment program was underway, the securities industry recommended an amendment to the 1933 Act to "Restore the 'broker's exemption' * * * so as to give relief from the popular interpretation" of the *Haupt* opinion.[1] The Commission recommended instead that the matter be handled by a rule, and Congress acquiesced, the Senate Committee expressing the hope that the SEC "will give favorable consideration to a rule that will deal effectively with the problem." [2] The upshot was that in 1954 the Commission revised Rule 154, the predecessor of Rule 144, to clarify and limit the scope of the brokers' exemption embodied in § 4(4) with respect to secondary sales by controlling persons in reliance on the exemption.

Rule 154 defined the term "brokers" transactions in § 4(4) of the Act to include transactions by a broker acting as an agent for a control person, provided: (1) the buy order was not solicited from purchasers; (2) the broker performed no more than the usual brokerage functions; and (3) the broker was not aware of circumstances indicating that the transaction was a part of the distribution or that the broker's principal was an underwriter. The amount of securities that could be sold within a specified period was prescribed by defining "distribution" in the negative; no "distribution" would be entailed if a transaction or series of transactions did not involve an amount of sales "substantial in relation to the number of shares of the security outstanding and the aggregate volume of trading in such security." More specifically, the rules defined the term "distribution" as not including a sale or series of sales of securities, which, together with all other sales of the same person within the preceding six months, in the case of a security traded over-the-counter, did not exceed 1% of the outstanding shares, and in the case of stock exchange transactions, did not exceed the lesser of either 1% of the outstanding shares of the class, or the largest reported volume of trading on securities exchanges during any one week within the four calendar weeks preceding the receipt of the sell order. Under these "leakage" provisions, controlling persons were permitted to make limited sales of control shares, under conditions which would not disrupt the trading market for the securities and where only normal brokerage functions were performed. However, the rule provided no avenue for the sale of securities which the control person otherwise would be unable to sell without registration, such as investment securities acquired pursuant to the private offering exemp-

---

1. Hearings on S. 2846 before a Subcommittee of the Senate Committee on Banking and Currency, 83d Cong., 2d Sess. 4 (1954).

2. S.Rep. No. 1036, 83d Cong., 2d Sess 14 (1954).

tion. Resales of such securities would constitute the controlling person an underwriter, irrespective of Rule 154.

Moreover, Rule 154, like § 4(4), exempted only the broker's part of the transaction; it provided no protection to the controlling person who might have violated the Act. And through a curious method of drafting, the Securities Act does not subject controlling persons to the registration and prospectus requirements of § 5 in specific terms. A controlling person is not an issuer as that term is used in § 4(1); and such person is defined as an issuer under § 2(11) solely for the purpose of determining who is an "underwriter." Accordingly, it could be argued that the broker who sold for the controlling person with knowledge that it was participating in a distribution would be subject to criminal penalties, whereas no specific substantive provision of the Act in terms imposes liability upon the controlling person. On the other hand, if the broker, after a reasonable investigation, reasonably believed that it was not participating in a distribution by a controlling person so that it would be exempt from liability by virtue of Rule 154, would the controlling person still be exempt from liability by virtue of the lacunae in the regulatory scheme? The *Wolfson* case, supra at page 480, gave a negative answer to this question; since Rule 154 and § 4(4) are transaction exemptions, the exemption is not available to anyone participating in the forbidden transaction.

(b) *Resales of Securities Purchased in "Private Offerings."* Alongside the problem of sales of securities by controlling persons, other than investment securities, a similar problem existed with respect to the conditions under which the holder of investment securities (whether or not a controlling person) could make resales of such securities. Persons purchasing securities in a nonpublic offering pursuant to the § 4(2) exemption must purchase for investment and not with a view to distribution of the securities, otherwise they will be deemed to be an "underwriter" as defined in § 2(11). To prove an investment intent, the practice developed of having the purchaser sign an "investment letter" asserting that he or she was taking the securities for investment, and not with a view to their later distribution. Clearly, such an investment letter was worthless, if the purchaser disproved the assertion by turning around and reselling the securities shortly after their purchase. This presented the question of how long the purchaser had to hold the securities to establish an "investment intent." Was he or she ever to be relieved of the disability against resale of the securities? We have seen that in United States v. Sherwood, supra at page 495, retention of securities for more than two years was held to be sufficient to establish a presumption of investment intent. And in the pre-Rule 144 period, on occasion, the SEC Staff would issue no-action letters advising investors that it would not look with disfavor on a resale after five years.[3]

---

3. The Commission often receives letters from Counsel, on behalf of a client, setting forth facts concerning a proposed sale of securities with an opinion of counsel to the effect that registration under the Securities Act is not required on the basis of a claimed exemption and a request that the Commission advise whether they concur in the opinion. The Commission may or may not give a no-action letter in reply to these requests. If it does so, an authorized member of the Staff will sign the letter which in substance states that, on the basis of the facts set forth in the letter, no action will be recommended to the Commission, if the proposed sales are made, in the manner described, without registration under the act, in reliance on Counsel's opinion that registration is not required. Common subjects for no-action letters in the Pre-Rule 144 period were requests concerning the question of availability of the private offering exemption or the existence of "control." Thus, a person who could be thought to be in a control relationship with an issuer but who disclaimed control might be asked by a broker to get a no-action letter prior to selling unregistered securities in a brokers' transaction. As to their utility one knowledgeable Securities law-

(c) *The Doctrine of "Change of Circumstances."* If the length of holding of the securities did not itself furnish sufficient evidence of an original "investment intent," then the doctrine evolved that one must demonstrate that the resale was made solely as a result of a "change in circumstances" between the original purchase and the subsequent resale. The Staff and holders of investment securities frequently disagreed as to whether the investor had suffered a "change in circumstances" which would negate an original intent to purchase with a view to distribution rather than for investment. In the *Gilligan, Will* case, supra at page 498, the registrant claimed that the failure of *Crowell-Collier* to continue to operate profitably resulted in a change of circumstances which would have led a prudent investor to sell. The court rejected this argument as a means of establishing an investment intent, where resales followed shortly after the purchase of the securities in a private placement. The court concluded that an intention to retain the securities only if *Crowell-Collier* operated at a profit was "equivalent to a 'purchase * * * with a view to * * * distribution' within the statutory definition of underwriters in § 2(11)." The holding period requirement and the "change of circumstance" doctrine emerged from efforts of the Commission and staff to stem the flow of securities from issuers to the public without compliance with the registration and prospectus requirements of the Act.

(d) *The Fungibility Concept.* This doctrine was also developed to preserve the integrity of the holding period concept. Suppose A buys 10,000 shares of an issuer's stock in the trading markets. One month later, A buys an additional 10,000 shares of the issuer's stock in a private placement pursuant to the § 4(2) exemption. May A now sell 5,000 shares of the unrestricted stock previously purchased without destroying the § 4(2) exemption? Under the fungibility concept as applied by the Commission's staff, A could not; the entire 20,000 shares is now locked-up and cannot be resold until the expiration of the holding period for the shares purchased in the private placement. If, however the transactions were reversed, and A made a purchase of an issuer's shares in a private placement, followed by a purchase of the issuer's shares in the trading markets, it was uncertain whether the doctrine of fungibility applied so as to restrict the sale of the after-acquired securities. Moreover, uncertainty existed when there was a series of purchases of shares from the issuer pursuant to the § 4(2) exemption. Even though the holding period may have expired with respect to an earlier purchase, it was by no means certain whether those shares were locked-in as a result of the subsequent purchases of securities or whether resales of those securities could be made without thereby destroying the § 4(2) exemption.

The "Wheat Report" identified these problems and concluded that the doctrines governing the resale of securities purchased pursuant to the § 4(2) exemption were "of uncertain application, created serious administrative burdens and produce[d] results incompatible with the policy objectives of the Act." [4] The Commission thereupon rescinded Rule 154 and adopted Rule 144 to

---

yer put it this way: "The sad truth seems to be that you get 'no-action' letters in the clear cases but have an awful time getting them—or don't even ask—in the cases where you really need them." SEC Problems of Controlling Stockholders and in Underwritings 19 (Israels ed.1962).

Beginning in 1970, the Commission commenced to make available to public inspection requests for interpretative advice and no-action letters and written responses

thereto with respect to all six Acts administered by it. Securities Act Release No. 5098 (Oct. 29, 1970), adopting 17 CFR 200.80. For the procedures applicable to requests for no-action and interpretive letters, see Securities Act Release No. 6253 (Oct. 28, 1980); Securities Act Release No. 6269 (Dec. 5, 1980).

4. SEC, "Disclosure to Investors"—Report and Recommendations to the Securities and Exchange Commission From the

solve these problems as they related to controlling and non-controlling persons. The new rule built upon Rule 154 and regulates resales of securities held by controlling persons pursuant to the § 4(4) brokerage exemption. Unlike Rule 154, however, Rule 144 also applies to resales of investment securities held by controlling persons. In addition, Rule 144 also regulates resales by non-controlling person of securities acquired in a private placement by permitting limited resales of these securities in brokerage transactions after they have been held at risk for a two-year period.

SECTION 4. RESTRICTIONS ON RESALES OF CONTROL SHARES AND RESTRICTED SECURITIES UNDER RULE 144

Statutes and Rules

Securities Act, Preliminary Note to Rule 144, Rule 144 and Form 144.

Excerpt from James H. Fogelson *

RULE 144—A SUMMARY REVIEW
37 Bus. Lawyer 1519 (1982) [a]

Rule 144 under the Securities Act of 1933, as amended (the "1933 Act") has been in effect for fifteen years. Most of the interpretative problems have been addressed. The relationships to former Rules 133 and 155, Rule 145 and certain no sale distributions have been worked out for the most part. Rule 144 has eliminated much of the previous uncertainty with respect to public sales by control persons ("affiliates") and holders of privately placed securities ("restricted securities" [1]). While there are still some annoying procedural problems in the day-to-day operation of Rule 144, there is general agreement that it has been a major success in administrative rule making. The following reviews in summary form the principal provisions and interpretations of Rule 144 as set forth in Release

---

Disclosure Policy Study, "The Wheat Report", 160–77 (1969).

* Member of the law firm of Wachtell, Lipton, Rosen & Katz, New York City. This article was prepared with the assistance of Pamela S. Seymon, a third-year law student at New York University. This article updates an article earlier appearing at 29 Bus. Law. 1183–1203 (1974) and reflects the current state of the law. The article has again been updated for the purposes of the Sixth Edition of this book by Jesse M. Brill, Editor of *The Corporate Counsel* and securities counsel for Dean Witter Reynolds Inc.

a. [Eds.] This article was originally published in the July 1974 issue of The Business Lawyer and reprinted in the Fourth Edition of this book with permission of the American Bar Association and

its Section of Corporation, Banking and Business Law. The revised article is reprinted with the permission of the Author and of the American Bar Association and its Section of Corporations, Banking and Business Law. Copyright 1974, 1982 by the American Bar Association.

1. "Restricted securities" are defined as securities that are acquired directly or indirectly from the issuer, or from an affiliate or the issuer, in a transaction or chain of transactions not involving any public offering, or securities acquired from the issuer that are subject to the resale limitations of Regulation D and are acquired in a transaction or chain of transactions not involving any public offering.

17 C.F.R. § 240.144(a)(3), as amended (effective April 15, 1982).

No. 5223 [2] which promulgated Rule 144, Release No. 5306 [3] which was the first general interpretative release by the SEC, Release No. 6099,[4] the most recent interpretative release, [and] the numerous interpretative letters that have been issued by SEC * * *.

Rule 144 applies to the sale of "control" securities or restricted securities if the following basic conditions are met:

(1) Adequate current public information with respect to the issuer is available.

(2) If the securities are restricted securities, a two-year holding period has been satisfied.[12]

(3) The amount of securities sold by an affiliate in each three-month period does not exceed the greater of (i) 1% of the outstanding securities of that class or (ii) the average weekly reported exchange volume of trading and/or reported through NASDAQ during the four-week period prior to the date of the notice referred to in (5) below or (iii) the average weekly volume of trading in that class reported through the consolidated transaction reporting system during such period. The same limitation applies with respect to sales of restricted securities by non-affiliates unless the three-year cutoff under Rule 144(k) discussed below is available, in which case there is no limit as to amount.

(4) The sales are made in either ordinary brokerage transactions or directly with a market maker.

(5) Except for small sales (not more than 500 shares or $10,000 aggregate sales price in the three-month period), the seller files a notice of sale on Form 144 with the SEC and, in the case of listed securities, the principal stock exchange, concurrently with either placing the order to sell with a broker or executing the sale directly with a market maker.[15]

Availability of Rule 144

Rule 144 may be utilized notwithstanding the fact that the holder of restricted securities (1) has contractual registration rights, (2) is discussing with the issuer registration of his restricted securities, (3) has restricted securities which were included in a pending registration statement, but which securities were withdrawn voluntarily from registration before the registration statement became effective, or (4) has restricted securities which were effectively registered, but which are withdrawn from registration when the registration statement is withdrawn or are included in a registration statement which can no longer be used because it no longer is current, whether or not the registration statement included an undertaking to file a post-effective amendment and update the prospectus prior to any offering during the "stale" period. In addition, Rule 144 is available for

2. Securities Act Release No. 5223 (Jan. 11, 1972), [1971–72 Transfer Binder] Fed. Sec. L. Rep. (CCH) ¶ 78,487.

3. Securities Act Release No. 5306 (Sept. 26, 1972), [1972–73 Transfer Binder] Fed. Sec. L. Rep. (CCH) ¶ 79,000.

4. Securities Act Release No. 6099 (Aug. 2, 1979).

12. It bears emphasis that affiliates' sales of nonrestricted securities are subject to the Rule; however, compliance with the two-year holding period is not required under such circumstances. * * *

15. Id. § 230.144(h), as amended (effective March 16, 1981). But see the discussion of the three-year exemption at [415–16] infra.

shares which are covered by an effective registration statement if (1) the registration statement expressly provides that the shares so offered may be sold either by means of the registration statement or by means of Rule 144, (2) the shares are withdrawn from a current effective registration statement, or (3) even if the shares are not withdrawn from the registration statement.[16]

Concurrent sales of registered securities pursuant to an effective registration statement or pursuant to exemptions provided by Regulation A or Section 4 of the 1933 Act and securities of the same class not included in the registration statement or within any applicable exemption pursuant to Rule 144 are permitted. This is consistent with the abandonment of fungibility for Rule 144 purposes.

* * * While the general rule is that unregistered securities received pursuant to an employee benefit plan can be resold only if such securities subsequently are registered or sold in compliance with an applicable exemption, the SEC has provided an exception to that rule for stock bonus and similar plans that are not registered.[23] A plan participant desiring to effect resales of securities may do so without compliance with Rule 144 provided the following three conditions are satisfied: (1) the issuer of the securities is subject to the periodic reporting requirements of Section 13 or 15(d) of the Securities Exchange Act of 1934 (the "1934 Act"); (2) the stock being distributed is actively traded in the open market; and (3) the number of shares being distributed is relatively small in relation to the number of shares of that class issued and outstanding.[25] Where employee stock plans are registered, Rule 144 is not applicable for resales by non-affiliates of securities received under such plans since such securities are acquired in a registered offering and therefore are not "restricted securities."[26] In the case of stock option plans registered on Form S–8, affiliates cannot rely on the Form S–8 Prospectus to resell the securities received pursuant thereto.[27]

The SEC has permitted utilization of Rule 144 by security holders whose shares were purchased in purported private placements that do not comply with the private offering exemption and therefore were sold illegally.

---

16. See Dean Witter Reynolds Inc., (avail. Jan. 17, 1986) and The Corporate Counsel, Vol. X, No. 6, at p. 7.

23. Securities Act Release No. 6188 (Feb. 1, 1980), SEC Docket, Vol. 19, No. 7, pp. 465–500. Generally, the SEC does not require registration of stock bonus plans. Such plans include ESOPs (employee stock ownership plans) and SARs (stock appreciation rights).

25. Securities Act Release No. 6188 (Feb. 11, 1980).

26. Id. Thus, non-affiliates who receive securities in such a manner may freely sell the securities. However, affiliates who receive bonus securities—although registered—can only resell such securities pursuant to an effective registration statement or pursuant to Rule 144. * * *

27. Form S–8, Instruction E, 2 Fed. Sec. L. Rep. (CCH) ¶ 7198.

The affiliate, however, may effect resales of Form S–8 securities under Rule 144 (without a holding period) or pursuant to a separate S–3 prospectus filed with the S–8 registration statement provided: (1) the issuer satisfies the requirements for utilization of Form S–3; or (2) the amount of securities to be sold by the affiliate (and any other person with whom he is acting in concert) does not exceed in any three-month period the volume limitations specified in Rule 144(e)(1). If the conditions set forth cannot be satisfied (thereby precluding utilization of Form S–3), the affiliate can sell such securities pursuant to a separate registration statement—on whichever form is applicable.

Moreover, the illegal issuance of stock (which would entitle the holder to a put back to the company) will not toll the holding period.[30]

Current Public Information

The current public information requirement is met if the issuer has (1) securities registered under either the 1933 Act or the 1934 Act, and (2) been subject to the periodic reporting requirements for a period of at least 90 days prior to the sale and (3) filed all 1934 Act reports required to be filed during the 12 months (or such shorter period that the issuer was subject to the reporting requirements) preceding the sale.

Where an issuer registers securities under the 1933 Act for the first time, the 90-day waiting period applies even though no 1934 Act reports are required to be filed during that period. The SEC generally requires prospectus disclosure of the future availability of Rule 144 sales of securities of certain registrants, especially first-time registrants, and the present intention of insiders with respect thereto. Where an issuer registers securities under the 1934 Act for the first time, the 90-day waiting period commences on the effective date of the 1934 Act registration statement which is normally 60 days after filing; therefore, in such cases Rule 144 will become available 150 days after the date on which the 1934 Act registration statement was filed.

The 1934 Act report forms require issuers to state whether they have been subject to the reporting requirements for the past 90 days and have met the reporting requirements for the past 12 months (or such shorter period to which the issuer has been subject thereto). Unless he knows or has reason to believe that the issuer has not complied with the reporting requirements, the Rule 144 seller is entitled to rely on the issuer's statement in the latest of such reports or on a written statement from the issuer that the reports have been filed. An issuer that has received an extension of time to file a 1934 Act report has not filed all required reports for Rule 144 purposes, but will be deemed current when the filing is made.

* * *

Small companies that are not subject to the Section 12(g) registration requirements of the 1934 Act (less than 500 shareholders or $5 million or less in assets) may voluntarily register, and, thus, make Rule 144 available to their shareholders. Accordingly, in addition to the usual 1934 Act registration covenants, purchasers in private placements, in order to assure the availability of Rule 144, should consider obtaining the covenant of the issuer to register and maintain registration under the 1934 Act and file timely the requisite periodic reports.[41] Rule 144 is available for sales of securities of an issuer which has been required under Section 15(d) of the 1934 Act to file reports but is no longer so obligated because it has less than 300 shareholders of record as of the first day of its fiscal year, if the issuer voluntarily continues to make periodic filings under the 1934 Act.

As an alternative to voluntarily registering under Section 12(g), under Rule 144(c)(2), the information requirement can be met by nonreporting companies if the information required by Rule 15c2–11 to permit a broker

30. Hadron, Inc., (letter available July 31, 1981), [1981–82 Transfer Binder] Fed. Sec. L. Rep. (CCH) ¶ 77,041.

41. See Miller, Venture Capital: Techniques for Increasing Liquidity with a

View Toward Rule 144, 29 Bus. Law. 461 (Jan. 1974).

to quote an over-the-counter security is available publicly. This provision does not apply to a reporting company; therefore, it does not enable Rule 144 sales of securities of a delinquent reporting company. If a 1933 Act registration statement is filed by a 15c2–11 issuer, the availability of 15c2–11 information can no longer be relied on and Rule 144 is not available until 90 days after the registration statement has become effective.

Compliance with the publicly available information provision is a factual question to be decided on a case by case basis. The Staff of the SEC will respond to interpretive letter requests from issuers concerning satisfaction of the Rule 144(c)(2) public availability requirement. The SEC has ruled that information about a nonreporting company is publicly available for Rule 144 purposes if the company has distributed reports containing the 15c2–11 information to its shareholders, brokers, market makers and any other interested persons and information about the company is published in a recognized financial reporting service.[47] It is not sufficient that the company has furnished the 15c2–11 information to the broker through which the Rule 144 sale is to be made.[48]

* * *

Holding Period

A major policy predicate of Rule 144 is that the acquirer of restricted securities must take the full economic risk of a two-year holding period. Thus, restricted securities must be fully paid for and held for two years before they can be sold under Rule 144.

If securities are purchased from the issuer with notes or other obligations, they are not considered fully paid unless (1) the notes or other obligations are with full recourse, (2) the note or obligation is paid in full before the sale and (3) there is adequate collateral, other than the purchased securities, the fair market value of which is throughout the two-year period equal to the unpaid portion of the purchase price. The holding period is tolled for any periods during which the fair market value of the collateral falls below the unpaid portion of the purchase price. Excess collateral may be withdrawn without affecting the holding period.

Shares of stock issuable upon exercise of options at a stated price are not fully paid until the option has been exercised and the exercise price has been fully paid.

If restricted securities are purchased on an installment basis, the holding period commences on a staggered basis. The holding period is tolled only as to those securities which do not meet the full-recourse or collateralization requirements.

The staff of the SEC has taken the position that where money is borrowed from a third party non-affiliate lender (e.g., a bank) to purchase restricted securities, the loan is not guaranteed, directly or indirectly, by the issuer and the restricted securities are pledged as the only collateral for a normal full-recourse loan, the restricted securities are considered fully paid and the holding period is deemed to have commenced upon purchase of the restricted securities.

* * *

---

47. Securities Act Release No. 6099, supra note 4, at Question 20.

48. Id. at Illustration to Question 20.

Fungibility does not apply to Rule 144 situations. The acquisition of restricted securities will not restart the holding period on previously acquired restricted securities. * * * Likewise, fungibility does not apply in non-Rule 144 situations. The acquisition of restricted securities does not taint unrestricted securities previously acquired.[65] The holder merely must be able to trace the securities to their purchase dates. * * *

The two-year holding period is suspended for any period that the holder of the restricted securities has a short position in (including short sales against the box covered by later open market purchases), or a put or option to sell, securities of the same class (or convertible into the same class). However, the holding period is tolled only as to those securities which were actually subject to the short position, put or option and not as to all restricted securities held by such person. Short sales or acquisitions of puts after the two-year holding period has been satisfied do not affect the availability of Rule 144. Customary close corporation put and buy-back arrangements do not constitute the type of sell option that tolls the holding period for Rule 144 purposes.

A private sale of restricted or control securities pursuant to the "Section $4(1\frac{1}{2})$ exemption" will start a new two-year holding period. The holding of the previous private placee cannot be tacked to the holding of the subsequent placee.

Partners who receive restricted securities as distributions by their partnership may tack their holding periods to that of the partnership,[73] but all of the partners receiving such securities must aggregate their sales for the purpose of the volume limitation discussed below if they tack the holding periods. However, if the unlimited resale provision of paragraph (k) applies by reason of the partner not being an affiliate of the issuing corporation and the combined holding period exceeds 3 years, aggregation is inapplicable. During any period the partners are unable to utilize the unlimited resale provisions (and up to two years after the distribution), the partners are required to aggregate. In the case of a closely-held corporation, the same analysis applies.

Tacking is permitted for stock dividends and stock splits, recapitalizations (including recapitalizations resulting in changes in par values), reincorporations that do not result in changes in the business or management, conversions of convertible securities (provided the security is convertible into securities of the same issuer), warrants (provided that the only consideration surrendered upon exercise of the warrant consists of other securities of the same issuer) and securities acquired as contingent payments in business combinations. In each of these situations, for Rule 144 purposes, the subsequently acquired securities are deemed to have been acquired at the time the related restricted securities were acquired.

Stock dividends on restricted securities are restricted securities for Rule 144 purposes; however, the holding period for securities acquired as a

---

65. See Borden and Fleischman, The Continuing Development of Rule 144: Significant SEC Staff Interpretations, Eighth Annual Institute on Securities Regulation 91, 126–27 (1977) (hereinafter "The Continuing Development of Rule 144").

73. It should be noted that tacking is permitted only if the distribution does not require the distributee to furnish additional consideration as, for example, when his partnership interest is being redeemed. Securities Act Release No. 6099, supra note 4, at Question 34 n.11.

dividend is deemed to have commenced as of the date the securities on which the dividend was paid were acquired.

Tacking is permitted for bona fide pledgees, donees of gifts and trusts. However, if the settlor of a trust sells rather than donates the restricted securities to the trust, tacking is not permitted.[83] Restricted securities are deemed to have been acquired when they were acquired by the pledgor, donor or settlor. * * * The SEC has taken the position that multiple donees or beneficiaries need not aggregate horizontally provided that they do not otherwise act in concert.

Where an estate is an affiliate, tacking is permitted, and the volume limitations apply. Moreover, where a beneficiary who is an affiliate receives restricted securities from the estate, tacking is permitted of both the decedent and the estate holding periods. If the affiliated beneficiary is trustee or executor under the instrument as well, the trust or estate is deemed to be an affiliate and thus the volume limitations apply. Where the estate is not an affiliate or the securities are sold by a beneficiary who is not an affiliate, no holding period is required, and the volume limitations and the manner of sale requirement do not apply even if one or more beneficiaries (other than the trustee as discussed immediately above) are affiliates, but the other conditions of Rule 144 as to current information and notice of sale do apply. However, where the trustee or executor is an affiliate (even though the securities are non-restricted securities in the hands of the non-affiliated trust or estate), the trustee or executor must aggregate his personal sales with those of the trust or estate. Conversely, the non-affiliated trust or estate need not aggregate its sales with those of the trustee or executor for purposes of the volume limitation. The special provisions for an estate apply only to restricted securities acquired by the estate from the decedent, not to restricted securities acquired otherwise, such as by exchange of securities owned by the decedent, to which Rule 144 applies fully.

Tacking of holding periods that have been broken by transfers of restricted securities from one entity to another within a "person", as defined in Rule 144, is not permitted unless the transfer is of a type included in the Rule 144(d)(4) tacking provisions for pledges, gifts, trusts and estates.

Limitation on Amount of Securities Sold

The limitation on the amount of securities which may be sold pursuant to the Rule in any three-month period is the greater of 1% of the outstanding securities of the class being sold or the average weekly volume of that class on all exchanges or reported through the consolidated transaction reporting system for the four weeks prior to the date of the notice of sale. Sales pursuant to registered offerings and pursuant to exemptions provided by Regulation A and Section 4 of the 1933 Act are not aggregated with Rule 144 sales in determining the amount permitted to be sold under the Rule. Where a stock is traded on a national securities exchange and

---

83. Securities Act Release No. 6099, supra note 4, at Question 31.

Furthermore, where a beneficiary of a trust sells restricted securities to the trust, a new holding period begins. The SEC rejected the theory that beneficial ownership continues in the beneficiary taking the position that such a transaction transfers beneficial ownership to the trustee. Schlumberger, Ltd., (letter available Feb. 11, 1980), [1980 Transfer Binder] Fed. Sec. L. Rep. (CCH) ¶ 76,394.

NASDAQ, the NASDAQ volume may be used in lieu of the national securities exchange volume or the two may be combined. Where securities are unlisted the NASDAQ volume alone may be used.

There is no prohibition on sales in successive three-month periods, but carry-forward and accumulation are not permitted.

Both restricted and unrestricted securities are aggregated for determining the volume limitation for sales by affiliates. Only restricted securities are considered in determining the limitation on sales by non-affiliates.

* * * *

Sales by persons acting in concert are aggregated. The mere fact that several affiliates sell at the same time will not in and of itself be considered acting in concert, but it does give rise to a situation which must be considered carefully. Where investors have agreed not to sell more than a specified percentage of their securities during a specified period, the SEC staff in the past has taken the position that this constitutes an agreement to act in concert. The treatment for aggregation purposes of several funds or other accounts under the same investment management is not covered specifically in the Rule. The SEC staff has indicated that in the case of two trusts managed by the same bank it would treat each trust as a separate person, notwithstanding common trustees so long as the trusts are not administered in a manner that results in their acting in concert. But the SEC has stated that aggregation would be required if the bank made a common decision to sell securities for more than one trust—even where such decision was required due to its fiduciary duty. However, the bank must aggregate its own sales with the various trusts or estates it administers.

"Person" is defined in Rule 144 to include relatives of the seller who share a permanent home with the seller, trusts and estates in which the seller and such relatives collectively own a 10% or greater beneficial interest or which any of them serve as trustee or executor, and corporations or other entities in which the seller, such relatives and such trusts and estates together have a 10% equity interest or own 10% of a class of equity securities. Generally, sales by all those included in the definition of person are aggregated for the purpose of Rule 144. But aggregation is not required by a non-affiliated trust or estate that wishes to dispose of non-restricted securities—even though the trustee, executor or beneficiary is an affiliate. The trustee or executor, however, would be required to aggregate his personal sales with those of the trust or estate under such circumstances. An institutional investor or other person who owns 10% or more of any class of equity securities of a company is considered one person with such company for the purpose of Rule 144, and, therefore, the institutional investor would have to inquire of all companies in which it holds a 10% interest to determine if any of them had or planned transactions in a restricted security the institution wishes to sell under Rule 144. Directors of charitable foundations are not deemed to act in a capacity similar to that of a trustee or executor for the purpose of Rule 144; thus, aggregation is not required. In the pledge, gift and trust contexts there is aggregation with sales by the pledgor, donor or settlor. Such aggregation terminates two years after the original transfer to the pledgee, donee or trust, or upon completion of the Rule 144(k) three-year holding period, whichever occurs first. Pledgees should therefore consider restricting the pledgor by contract or escrow in order to ensure the availability of Rule 144 in the event of default. There is no volume limitation for estates and beneficiaries which are not affiliates even though the beneficiary (other than a beneficiary who is also a trustee) is an affiliate.

Section (e)(3)(i) of the Rule is a rather confusingly drafted provision which provides that where both a convertible and the underlying security are being sold, the amount of the underlying security for which the convertible being sold may be converted is aggregated with sales of the underlying security in determining the aggregate amount of both securities allowed to be sold. Thus, the volume limitations of Paragraph (e) cannot be circumvented by selling an amount of the underlying security in compliance with those limits, while at the same time selling an amount of the convertible security which would meet volume limitations for the convertible if it were looked at separately, but which would have resulted in an excessive sale of the underlying security if the convertible had first been converted and the sale of both blocks of securities had taken place.

Where an over-the-counter company subsequently lists on an exchange, the listed security volume limitation becomes applicable four weeks after listing and all sales in the preceding three months are considered in determining the volume limitation.

The number of shares to be sold under Rule 144 may be adjusted for stock splits or major stock dividends paid after the Form 144 has been filed. Form 144 can be amended to change the designation of the broker who has been given the sale order. No notice on Form 144 is required if the amount of securities to be sold during any three months does not exceed 500 shares or units and the aggregate sales price does not exceed $10,000.

Manner of Sale

Sales under the Rule can be made in either brokers' transactions within the meaning of Section 4(4) of the 1933 Act or transactions directly with "a market maker" as defined in the 1934 Act. The seller cannot solicit or arrange for the solicitation of buy orders or make any payment in connection with the sale other than usual commissions to the broker who executes the order.

A "market maker" is defined in Section 3(a)(38) of the 1934 Act as, either (1) a specialist who is permitted to act as a dealer, (2) a dealer who acts as a block positioner or (3) a dealer who holds himself out as willing to buy and sell a particular security for his own account on a regular or continuous basis.

A market maker is precluded from specifically soliciting buy orders for securities he wishes to buy in a Rule 144 transaction. However, a solicitation will not be implied from the fact that he continues to engage in his normal market making activities. All that is required is that the market maker not engage in a special campaign to solicit buyers for the shares he proposes to purchase pursuant to Rule 144. However, once the market maker consummates a purchase of securities in a Rule 144 transaction, the securities are freed of their restrictive character. The market maker may then solicit buy orders for such shares.

The staff has recognized that the Rule's prohibition of prior solicitations may impose particular hardships on block positioners. Due to the risks incident to block positioning, the block positioner often will attempt to cover his block in part by soliciting buyers prior to committing himself to purchase the block. Because the exchanges limit the ability of member block positioners to trade off-board securities which are listed or admitted to unlisted trading privileges on an exchange, the block positioner's purchase will not be consummated until its execution on the exchange. According to the Rule, the block positioner technically cannot solicit buy orders until this time. However, in recognition of the fact that the block positioner will have made a firm commitment to purchase the block prior in time to the execution on the exchange (at the time of accepting an order from a seller), the staff has indicated that under such circumstances the block positioner can solicit buy orders prior to the consummation of the purchase on the exchange but subsequent to the acceptance of the order.

Brokers' transactions are defined as those in which the broker (1) does no more than execute a sell order as agent for the usual commission and (2) does not solicit buy orders. The broker may inquire of other brokers who have indicated an interest within the preceding 60 days. Such inquiry may also be made of clients, institutional and non-institutional, who are bona fide and unsolicited and indicate an interest in the preceding 10 days. Brokers should maintain written records of such indications in order to substantiate the bona fide nature thereof.

Brokers can continue to make a two-way market in a security for which they have a Rule 144 sale order, if prior to receipt of the order they were making such market and published quotes 12 out of the preceding 30 calendar days with no more than four business days in succession without such two-way quotations.

Where a broker effects a cross of securities sold in a Rule 144 transaction, he may collect commissions from both buyer and seller provided such commissions are usual and customary. Where negotiated commissions are applicable they are permitted under Rule 144 if "negotiated in the usual and customary manner."

The SEC has outlined criteria for determining when Rule 144 sales may be deemed distributions for purposes of Rule 10b–6. The SEC has somewhat altered its position espoused in 1975 (when Rule 144 sales were computed on the basis of a six-month rather than a three-month time period) where it indicated that transactions pursuant to Rule 144 automatically would not be Rule 10b–6 distributions. While that view remains in effect for sales within the pre-September 1978 volume limitations, when sales are outside those volume limitations sellers must consider (1) the magnitude of the offering, (2) selling efforts and (3) selling methods used in determining whether they are engaging in a distribution prohibited by Rule 10b–6.

Rule 144 provides that the broker should obtain and retain a copy of the notice of sale and make a reasonable inquiry to ascertain whether the seller is engaged in a distribution. Reasonable inquiry should include the following:

(1) The length of time the securities have been held by the person for whose account they are to be sold. If practicable, the inquiry should include physical inspection of the securities;

(2) The nature of the transaction in which the securities were acquired by such person;

(3) The amount of securities of the same class sold during the past three months by all persons whose sales are required to be aggregated;

(4) Whether such person intends to sell additional securities of the same class through any other means;

(5) Whether such person has solicited or made any arrangement for the solicitation of buy orders in connection with the proposed sale of securities;

(6) Whether such person has made any payment to any other person in connection with the proposed sale of the securities; and

(7) The number of shares or other units of the class outstanding, or the relevant trading volume.

In addition to the foregoing, the broker should also obtain and retain a copy of the 1934 Act filing or the written statement of the issuer on which the Rule 144 seller is predicating satisfaction of the availability of current information requirements and a representation letter from the seller.[151]

Short sales may be effected under Rule 144 provided the specific securities to be used to cover the short sale are eligible for sale under Rule 144 at the time of the short sale, the seller delivers such securities to the broker at the time of the short sale and those specific securities are eventually used to cover the short sale. All of the requirements of the Rule, including the filing of Form 144, must be met at the time of the short sale, not when the short position is covered.

Rule 144 is available for short sales against the box as well provided all conditions of the Rule are satisfied. The sale is deemed to involve a broker's transaction on the date the short sale is executed rather than the date the seller's securities are replaced for the borrowed securities. To assure the availability of Rule 144 for short sales against the box, the non-affiliate initially must place his restricted securities in the box—he cannot sell securities short and then use his restricted securities to cover his short position. [Note: Section 16(c) effectively prevents officers, directors and ten-percent owners from engaging in short sales.]

Call options may be written by both affiliates and non-affiliates. To utilize Rule 144, the affiliate must comply with the Rule's requirements at the time of writing the options; the non-affiliate, on the other hand, may not become subject to Rule 144 by the mere writing of options. It is only when he either (1) covers his option position with restricted securities, (2) uses restricted securities to meet margin obligations, or (3) uses restricted securities for delivery upon exercise of an option that all the Rule 144 conditions must be met. As option transactions are fraught with potential § 16(b) and Rule 10b–5 exposure, officers, directors and ten-percent share-holders should generally be counseled against engaging in such transac-tions.[152]

Notice of Proposed Sale

Concurrently with either the placing of the sell order with the broker or the execution of the sale directly with a market maker, the seller must

---

151. There are a number of different forms in current use. Appendix A is a representation letter that is short and cov-ers the main points of concern. * * *

152. See The Corporate Counsel, Vol. III, No. 1, at p. 3.

transmit (place in the mail) to the SEC in Washington three copies of a notice of sale on Form 144 signed by the seller and one copy to the principal exchange on which the security is listed if the transaction requires that a notice be filed. The same notice requirements apply to all amended notices which may be filed.

Form 144 cannot specify an amount of listed securities to be sold in excess of the amount limitation determined as of the date of filing the Form 144. If thereafter the average trading increases, the seller may recompute the volume limitation (excluding sales by him during the new period) and file an amended Form 144 whereupon he can sell up to the new volume limitation, but in no event can sales in a three-month period exceed the greater of the 1% overall limit or the average weekly volume for the four weeks prior to the date of the amended notice of sale. If the number of outstanding shares of an issuer increases subsequent to the filing of a Form 144, an amended Form 144 may be filed to permit sales based on the increase in the number of outstanding shares, provided the information regarding the increase has been published by the issuer.

The security holder who files the Form 144 must have a bona fide intention to sell the securities referred to therein within a reasonable time after filing.]

Rule 144(k)—No Restrictions After Three Years

Rule 144(k), as amended effective October 31, 1983, now provides that restricted securities that have been held for at least three years may be sold without complying with any of the requirements of Rule 144, provided the holder is not an affiliate and has not been an affiliate for three months prior to the sale. Thus there is now a complete cutoff from the requirements of Rule 144 once a non-affiliate has held restricted securities for three years. At that time all legends and transfer restrictions should be removed from the securities.[169]

A holder who sells restricted securities pursuant to the Rule 144(k) unlimited resale provision may concurrently sell other restricted securities as to which the volume limitation applies. The former securities are stripped of all volume restrictions and thus are not aggregated with restricted securities which must be sold in compliance with the volume limitation.

Tacking is permitted to satisfy the three-year holding period. A shareholder of a close corporation or a partner who receives restricted securities of another issuer as a distribution from a corporation or partnership can immediately sell the securities so received pursuant to the unlimited resale provision—even if the partnership or corporation is an affiliate of the issuer—if the seller is not and has not been an affiliate of the issuer for three months preceding the sale and the combined holding periods of the corporation or partnership and the distributee equal three years. During the time in which the distributee is subject to the amount limitation (up to a maximum of two years from the date he or she acquired the restricted securities), sales must be aggregated.[170]

The above analysis also applies to the pledge, gift and trust situations. Even where the donor (pledgor) is an affiliate and the securities involved

169. See The Corporate Counsel, Vol. 8, No. 5.

170. See The Corporate Counsel, Vol. X, No. 3, at p. 7.

are non-restricted securities, donees (pledgees) may rely on Rule 144(k) and sell without restriction, even though the affiliate donor (pledgor) would have to sell under Rule 144. Availability of the Rule 144(k) unlimited resale provision will depend upon the satisfaction of two elements—namely the donee (pledgee) must not be an affiliate at the time of the sale and (2) the donor (pledgor) and donee (pledgee) must have a combined holding period of three years.[171] Moreover, the Staff is no longer taking the position that the donor must aggregate his or her sales with the donee for two years subsequent to the gift where the donee sells under Rule 144(k).

Where two or more individuals share the same household and are thus deemed to be a "person" within the meaning of the Rule, the unlimited resale provision is unavailable to any of them if one of them is an affiliate.

Exclusivity and Operation of Rule 144

The SEC by amendment in 1979 inserted new paragraph (j) to Rule 144. This paragraph provides that Rule 144 is not exclusive with respect to non-affiliates' sales of restricted stock nor with respect to affiliates' sales, whether they are selling restricted or unrestricted securities. The affiliate or non-affiliate may also effect such sales pursuant to (1) a registration statement, (2) an exempt transaction or (3) Regulation A. However, the affiliate who desires to effect sales pursuant to the individual exemption provided in Section 4(1) of the 1933 Act can only sell in reliance on Rule 144. In other words, reliance on Section 4(1) by an affiliate can only be predicated on Rule 144. On the other hand, Rule 144 is purely a non-exclusive safe harbor for non-affiliates' sales of restricted securities.

Now that Rule 144(k) provides a complete cutoff after three years, the need for legal opinions in reliance on Section 4(1) has been greatly reduced. Such opinions are, however, commonly rendered to avoid the Rule 144(k) three month wait for former affiliates who have held restricted securities for three years.[172]

* * * The SEC staff has withdrawn its former position that a non-affiliate holder of restricted securities who elects to sell a portion of such restricted securities under Rule 144 is bound as to the balance of such restricted securities which under the previous position could thereafter only be sold under Rule 144.

The staff of the SEC has abandoned the "float doctrine"—a policy previously adopted to limit sales of restricted securities acquired prior to April 15, 1972 outside of Rule 144.[178] Essentially, sales in excess of the volume limitations of Rule 144 were deemed to be distributions and therefore required registration.

* * * *

Rule 144 is not available where there is technical compliance, but the Rule 144 sales are part of a plan to effect a distribution.[181] Rule 144 does not exempt sales from the antifraud, civil liability or short-swing profits

---

171. See David D. Wexler, avail. July 23, 1981 and see The Corporate Counsel, Vol. VI, No. 4, at 7.

172. See The Corporate Counsel, Vol. VIII, No. 5.

178. The Sale of Restricted Securities, supra note 172, at 139–40.

181. Securities Act Release No. 5223, supra note 2, at 81,061. The SEC staff, however, has indicated that Rule 144 provides a safe harbor for sale of restricted securities even where sales pursuant to the Rule would seriously impact the trading market for the issuing company's shares. WCS Int'l, (letter available Jan. 12, 1979).

provisions of the securities laws. The SEC position is that the Rule is to be strictly construed and persons selling under the Rule have the burden of proving its availability.

* * * *

Relationship with Other Rules

* * * *

C. Private-Placement Business Combinations

Rule 144 is available for resale of securities received in business combinations where the facts are such (all shareholders sophisticated or represented by a sophisticated negotiator, access to information, etc.) as to establish a non-public offering by the acquiring company. Tacking of the period of ownership of the securities of the acquiring and acquired company is not permitted.[192]

* * * *

Exhibit A

RULE 144 REPRESENTATION LETTER

Date _____

Dear Sirs:

In connection with my order to sell _____ shares of [*name of issuer*] permitted by Rule 144 under the Securities Act of 1933, I advise you as follows:

1. I obtained the aforesaid securities in the following manner: [*date, number of shares and from or through whom acquired*].

2. I have not made, either directly or indirectly, any sales, gifts, pledges or donations within the preceding three months other than as follows: [*if none, indicate "none"*] [*date, number of shares*].

---

192. Securities Act Release No. 5316, supra note 186, at 82,204. However, if the acquisition transaction is exempt by reason of Section 3(a)(10) of the 1933 Act, tacking of the acquiring and acquired companies securities is permitted. See, e.g., Guaranty Corp. (letter available Sept. 5, 1978). See Rule 506 (one of the six rules contained in new Regulation D) which exempts from the registration requirements offers and sales without regard to dollar amount provided the issuer satisfies the following conditions: (1) the issuer must reasonably believe that there are not more than 35 purchasers other than "accredited investors" (as defined in Rule 501(a)(1)–(8)), (2) immediately prior to making any sale, the issuer must reasonably believe that each purchaser who is not an "accredited investor" has, either alone or with his purchaser representative(s), such knowledge and experience in financial matters that he is capable of evaluating the merits and risks of the prospective investment, and (3) the issuer must comply with Rule 502. 17 C.F.R.

§ 230.506 (effective April 15, 1982); Securities Act Release No. 6389, supra note 10. Rule 506 (as well as Rules 504 and 505 which exempt offers and sales in limited dollar amounts) may be the vehicle for sale of securities issued in business combinations that involve sales by virtue of Rule 145(a) (covering certain reclassifications, mergers, consolidations and asset transfers) or otherwise. See Preliminary Note 5 to Regulation D, 17 C.F.R. §§ 230.501–506. Rule 506 replaces former Rule 146 which has been rescinded effective June 30, 1982.

Rule 144(k) would be available to permit sales after three years. In the context of acquisition transactions where the acquiring company's securities are issued in reliance upon the exemption contained in Section 3(a)(10) of the 1933 Act, tacking of acquired and acquiring company securities would be permitted to satisfy the three-year holding period. E.g., BankEast Corp. (letter available Feb. 1, 1982).

3. There are no persons whose sales must be aggregated with mine in determining the amount that may be sold other than as follows: [*if none, indicate "none"*].

4. I am not and will not be acting in concert with any other person for the purpose of selling securities of this company.

5. The number of shares to be sold does not exceed the greater of:

(a) 1% of such [*issuer*] security currently outstanding; or

(b) the average weekly reported volume of trading in such security on all securities exchanges during the four calendar weeks preceding my order to sell.

6. I have not made any payments to any other person in connection with your execution of my above-mentioned order, and I will not do so; nor have I solicited or arranged for the solicitation of any orders to buy in anticipation of or in connection with this proposed sale of shares.

7. I have no buy or sell orders open in any security of this company with any other broker or bank and will not place any buy or sell orders pending completion of this order.

8. I have been the owner of the securities which I have ordered sold this day, and fully paid for same, since [*date*].

9. I have filed Form 144 with the Securities and Exchange Commission and attach a copy hereto.

10. The issuer is current in its filing pursuant to Rule 144(c). The source of such information is _____.

11. I [*am*] [*am not*] an officer, director or holder of 1% or more of the outstanding equity securities of the company and [*do*] [*do not*], alone or together with any other person, exercise control over the company.

12. I shall indemnify and hold you harmless (including any legal fees and expenses reasonably incurred by you) against any liability, loss or expense incurred or suffered by you arising out of the sale and transfer of these securities.

Very truly yours,

_____   _____

[*Signature of Seller*]   [*Date*]

_____

Developments in the administration of Rule 144 are reported in The Corporate Counsel Newsletter, Jesse M. Brill, Editor. And see 7B J. Hicks, Exempted Transactions Under the Securities Act of 1933, § 10.04 (1986 rev.).

SECTION 5.   THE SECTION "4(1 1/2)" EXEMPTION

Excerpt from: Carl W. Schneider

THE SECTION "4(1½)" PHENOMENON: PRIVATE RESALES OF "RESTRICTED" SECURITIES *
34 Business Lawyer 1961–1978 (1979).[a]

INTRODUCTION

The purpose of this Report is to consider the available methods by which a person may resell privately securities initially issued in a private placement ("restricted securities") without registration under the Securities Act of 1933.   This variety of sale has become popularly known as "section 4(1½)" transactions, primarily because the SEC, in no-action letters and other pronouncements, frequently has required that such resales meet at least some of the established criteria for exemptions under both section 4(1) and section 4(2).[3]   In this Report the term "Holder" is used to refer to a person who holds restricted securities and the term "Purchaser" to refer to a person who purchases restricted securities from a Holder.

In analyzing the section 4(1½) phenomenon, we have drawn upon the legislative history of the 1933 Act, judicial interpretations of sections 4(1) and 4(2) and SEC positions on "4(1½)" resales * * *.

OVERVIEW OF THE 4(1½) PHENOMENON

* * * *

Our initial inquiry in analyzing the scope of permissible sales of Restricted Securities is to determine what subsection within section 4 is applicable.   Sections 4(3), 4(4) and 4(5) may be ruled out summarily. Because section 4(2) exempts only "transactions *by an issuer*" and a sale by a Holder is not a sale "by an issuer", a literal reading of this section makes it inapplicable as the basis for an exemption.   Of necessity, one then must turn to section 4(1), which exempts "transactions by any person other than an issuer, underwriter, or dealer."   Recognizing that the Holder, by hypothesis, is not an "issuer" (as defined in section 2(4) and assuming that he is not a "dealer", the critical inquiry is whether he or his Purchaser may be deemed an "underwriter", as defined in section 2(11) of the 1933 Act.   To avoid "underwriter" status, the Holder (i) must not have purchased the shares from the issuer "with a view to" their "distribution" and (ii) must not offer or sell the shares "for an issuer in connection with, the distribution".

The term "distribution", although central to the "underwriter" analysis, is not defined in the 1933 Act, and it is at this point that section 4(2) concepts are typically introduced and the "underwriter" analysis becomes

---

* A Report to the Committee on Federal Regulation of Securities from the Study Group on Section "4(1½)" of the Subcommittee on 1933 Act * * * .

a. Copyright 1979 by the American Bar Association.   All rights reserved.   Reproduced with the permission of the American Bar Association and its Section of Corporation, Banking and Business Law.

3. In this Report, the phrases "4(1½) transaction" or "4(1½) Sale", are used generically to describe resales of restricted securities otherwise than through holders in public markets.

confusing. Because a "distribution", in the context of section 4(1), is generally considered to be functionally equivalent to a "public offering" as used in section 4(2), it seems reasonable in defining "distribution" to borrow by analogy from judicial and administrative interpretations of the term "public offering". Moreover, in considering a resale of Restricted Securities soon after the Holder has acquired them from the issuer, the application of section 4(2) standards to the resale may be necessary to assure that the issuer's original section 4(2) exemption is not vitiated by the resale.

Separate from the line of decisions and SEC staff positions that apply section 4(2) standards in determining whether a "distribution" is involved is the theory that section 4(2) may independently provide an exemption for sales by a Holder.

Against this general background of inconsistent application of various criteria and the lack of any clear agreement on even the applicable theory of exemption, we turn first to an analysis of the legislative history of section 4.

LEGISLATIVE HISTORY

The legislative history of the 1933 Act sheds little light on any of the questions posed above. * * *

* * * James Landis, a principal draftsman of H.R. 5480, commented upon the general scope of the 1933 Act as follows:

"Public offerings" as distinguished from "private offerings" proved to be the answer [to the question what scope the 1933 Act was to have]. The sale of an issue of securities to insurance companies or to a limited group of experienced investors was certainly not a matter of concern to the federal government. That bureaucracy, untrained in these matters as it was, could hardly equal these investors for sophistication, provided only it was their own money that they were spending. And so the conception of an exemption for all sales, other than by an issuer, underwriter, or dealer came into being, replacing the concept of "isolated transactions" theretofore traditional to blue sky legislation. [14]

The precise process by which the desire to exempt a sale by an issuer to a small group of sophisticated investors as described by Landis led to an exemption for sales by a person other than an "issuer, underwriter, or dealer" is unclear. The first part of the quoted language seems more appropriately directed to validating the private offering exemption of section 4(2) than the exemption of section 4(1). * * *

* * *

There is some support for the theory that section 4(1) was designed to cover resales in much the same fashion as section 4(2) was aimed at delineating the scope of the exemption for sales by an issuer. One House Report on this legislation reflects a primary intention to distinguish be-

14. Landis, The Legislative History of the Securities Act of 1933, 28 Geo.Wash.L. Rev. 29, 37 (1959).

tween regular trading and distributions (whether made by the issuer, affiliates or nonaffiliates).

[The Bill] does not affect the ordinary redistribution of securities unless such redistribution takes on the characteristics of a new offering by reason of the control of the issuer possessed by those responsible for the offering.[19]

Paragraph (1) broadly draws the line between distribution of securities and trading in securities, indicating that the act is, in the main, concerned with the problem of distribution as distinguished from trading. It, therefore, exempts all transactions except by an issuer, underwriter, or dealer. Again, it exempts transactions by an issuer unless made by or through an underwriter so as to permit an issuer to make a specific or isolated sale of its securities to a particular person but insisting that if a sale of the issuer's securities should be made generally to the public that that transaction shall come within the purview of the act.[20]

The Report also indicates that the regulation of sales of control securities was intended to be effected by shaping the definition of "underwriter" in section 2(11) and incorporating that term in the section 4(1) exemption:

The last sentence of this definition [of "underwriter"], defining "issuer" to include not only the issuer but also affiliates or subsidiaries of the issuer and persons controlling the issuer, has two functions. * * * Its second function is to bring within the provisions of the bill redistribution whether of outstanding issues or issues sold subsequently to the enactment of the bill. All the outstanding stock of a particular corporation may be owned by one individual or a select group of individuals. At some future date they may wish to dispose of their holdings and to make an offer of this stock to the public. Such a public offering may possess all the dangers attendant upon a new offering of securities. Whenever such a redistribution reaches significant proportions, the distributor would be in the position of controlling the issuer and thus able to furnish the information demanded by the bill. This being so, the distributor is treated as equivalent to the original issuer and, if he seeks to dispose of the issue through a public offering, he becomes subject to the act.[21]

From this passage one may draw some support for the notions that section 4(2) is properly addressed solely to issuers and that section 4(1) above should govern all resales, including sales of both Restricted Securities and securities held by controlling persons. * * *

---

19. House of Representatives Report No. 85, at 5 (May 4, 1933) (hereinafter cited as "H.Rep. 85").

20. Id. at 15–16.

21. Id. at 13–14. See also, Landis, supra n. 14, at 37–38:

There was also the problem of secondary distributions, which had to be split as between distributions by controlling and noncontrolling persons. The former was the only transaction that could be controlled through registration requirements except for dealer transactions in the latter category during the time when the information on file was still current and accessible. The definition of "underwriter" in § 2(11) of the act proved to afford a solution to this problem.

JUDICIAL INTERPRETATIONS

Judicial efforts to identify the statutory provision to be applied to sales of restricted securities and to define the parameters of the appropriate exemption have been far more successful than legislative endeavors and generally support the view that section 4(1) is the provision to be applied.

The earliest such cases were United States v. Sherwood [22] and Gilligan, Will & Co. v. SEC.[23] In *Sherwood*, criminal contempt proceedings were brought against Sherwood, the holder of 8 percent of a company's stock, for violating an injunction prohibiting sales of the company's stock absent registration or the availability of an exemption. The stock in question had been acquired by Sherwood from one Doyle, who had received the stock from the issuer. The court found that Sherwood was not a control person, had not acquired the stock with a view to distribution, and therefore was not an "underwriter". The fact that Sherwood had held the shares two years persuaded the court of Sherwood's investment intent. Sherwood's sales of the stock were found to be exempt under section 4(1).

In *Gilligan, Will* two registered dealers had participated in the placement of $3,000,000 of convertible debentures of Crowell-Collier Publishing Co. Gilligan, a partner of Gilligan, Will & Co., purchased $100,000 of the debentures for his own account and made representations that he purchased for investment. Notwithstanding these representations, Gilligan quickly sold $45,000 of the debentures to one Louis Alter, and Gilligan also made offers to two other potential purchasers, selling $5,000 of debentures to one of them. Ten months after these sales, Gilligan, Will & Co., Gilligan and Alter converted their debentures into common stock and sold the stock at a profit on the American Stock Exchange.

Gilligan and Alter later subscribed to an additional $200,000 of debentures which they similarly converted to common stock. Gilligan, Will & Co. also was active in selling $200,000 of the debentures to a mutual fund, and as a result of this transaction, other parties received warrants to purchase Crowell-Collier stock.

In a subsequent SEC enforcement action, Gilligan, Will attempted to have its own acts viewed in isolation, claiming that they were not "underwriters" because the transactions effected by them, viewed alone, did not constitute a "public offering." Similar transactions had been effected by another dealer contemporaneously with Gilligan, Will's transactions. Taken together, however, the total number of offerees was quite small. In addition to Gilligan and Alter, only two other offerees were involved. The defendants stipulated that none of the four offerees had access to the kind of information made available by registration. The court found that, even though the number of offerees was small, the offering could not be viewed as a "private" one, under the criteria established for the section 4(2) exemption, in the *Ralston-Purina* case. Accordingly, Gilligan, Will was held to be an "underwriter", having purchased with a view to public distribution.

Although the result in *Gilligan, Will* is not surprising, the court's analysis of the defendants' claims of exemption is instructive. The court focused on the section 4(1) exemption, and determined that the initial

---

22. 175 F.Supp. 480 (S.D.N.Y.1959). [Supra at page 495.]   **23.** 267 F.2d 461 (2d Cir.1959). [Supra at page 498.]

inquiry was whether a "distribution" was involved. In determining the existence of a "distribution" the court noted that the term was equivalent to "public offering" [24] and turned to the *Ralston-Purina* decision for instruction on that point. Finding that the Ralston "access" requirement had not been met, the court held that a "distribution" had occurred.

The court also recognized that a person could rely on the section 4(1) exemption even if a "distribution" had occurred, provided that person's acquisition of the shares had not been with a "view" to the subsequent distribution. In this part of its analysis, the court (i) rejected the particular "change of circumstances" asserted by the defendants (without rejecting the concept) and (ii) held that a ten-month holding period was not sufficient to establish that the defendants had not acquired the stock with a "view" to distribution.[26]

* * *

A clearer analysis of the statutory exemptions is present in Value Line Income Fund, Inc. v. Marcus.[34] This case involved an attempted rescission of an agreement between a mutual fund and Marcus, the principal shareholder and president of a machinery company, in which the mutual fund agreed to purchase one-half of Marcus' shares in the company. The transaction was completed as planned, but when the stock declined drastically in price within a year, Value Line sought to rescind the agreement on the ground that Marcus had made fraudulent representations and the shares had not been registered.

The two major defendants in *Value Line* were Marcus, the "Holder", and Van Alstyne, Noel & Co. ("Vanco"), the party through whom Marcus sold his shares to Value Line. Vanco was unaware of any misrepresentations made by Marcus, and more importantly, the court found that Vanco was neither an issuer, underwriter, or dealer, and therefore the transaction was considered exempt under section 4(1). Marcus, as a control person, was an "issuer" for purposes of determining whether Vanco was an "underwriter." [35] The only offerings of Marcus' stock made by Vanco were to mutual funds, which were recognized as highly sophisticated investors with sufficient "access" for private offering purposes. The court found there was no "distribution" or "view to distribution" by Vanco, with the result that Vanco was not an "underwriter" under section 2(11) and was entitled to rely upon the section 4(1) exemption. On the same analysis, the section 4(1) exemption was found to be available to Marcus.

Like * * * *Gilligan, Will,* * * * *Value Line* recognizes that private resales may be made in reliance on section 4(1). Moreover, *Value Line* is particularly significant in its recognition that such resales may be made immediately after the shares are acquired, provided the ultimate purchasers are persons to whom the issuer could have made a valid direct sale under section 4(2).

* * *

In summary, our review of the cases dealing with the section 4(1½) phenomenon indicates the following:

1. The appropriate exemptive provision is section 4(1) and not 4(2).

---

24. Id. at 466 (citing H.R. Rep.No. 1838, 73d Cong., 2d Sess. (1934) at 41).

26. 267 F.2d at 466.

34. [1964]1966 Transfer Binder] Fed. Sec.L.Rep. (CCH) §§ 91,523, 94,953 (S.D. N.Y.1965).

35. Id. at 94,969.

2. No particular holding period is required.

3. The Purchasers' sophistication and access to information appear to have been viewed as essential in five of the six decisions.

4. The number of purchasers, viewed alone, is not dispositive of the availability of an exemption.

5. Restrictions on resales by a Purchaser generally have not been required.

6. No decision has articulated an affirmative duty on a Holder to provide registration-type information to a Purchaser.

SEC INTERPRETATIONS

The Staff No-Action Letters

General

The SEC Staff has never enunciated the statutory basis on which it has permitted private resales of Restricted Securities, and the staff letters are relatively few in number and show little consistency. On a number of occasions, the staff has implied that the section 4(2) exemption would be applicable. Yet in one letter the Staff expressly repudiated the notion that the section 4(2) exemption is available to any party other than the issuer and suggested that section 4(1) might be the appropriate theory on which to base private resales. Similarly, the most recent step in the evolution of paragraph (e)(3)(G) of rule 144 further supports the section 4(1) basis for section $4(1\frac{1}{2})$ sales by indicating that private resales can be made in reliance upon the section 4(1) exemption if the sale is one "not involving any public offering." [49] * * *

  * * *

Qualification of Purchasers

The staff letters are mixed with respect to the necessity that the purchaser be a sophisticated investor. Most staff letters make no reference to this requirement. A few, however, grant no-action requests upon the express condition that the purchaser be somewhat sophisticated. This latter category generally includes foreclosure sales by secured lenders designed to meet certain public sale requirements under the Uniform Commercial Code. On at least three occasions the staff has declined to take a no-action position, citing its own inability to determine whether the offerees require the protection of the Act. In two letters the staff went even further, requiring the purchaser to be able "to afford the risk of the highly speculative investment."

---

49. As originally promulgated, § (e)(3)(G) of rule 144 excluded from the sales to be aggregated in determining the amount that could be sold under rule 144 any "transaction exempt pursuant to § 4(2) of the Act and not involving any public offering." * * * In Securities Act Release No. 5452 (February 1, 1974), § (e)(3)(G) of the rule was amended to exclude from the volume computations shares sold in "a transaction exempt pursuant to § 4 of the Act and not involving any public offering."

The change, according to the Release, "reflects the Commission's original intent in adopting the Rule, as well as subsequent staff interpretations." This change is more appropriately viewed as an effort by the SEC to recognize the possibility of making "private" resales (*viz.* § $4(1\frac{1}{2})$ sales) under § 4(1), as an alternative to rule 144 sales in the market, rather than a direct attempt by the SEC to impose § 4(2) criteria on such sales.

Access to or Furnishing of Information

The staff has grappled somewhat unsuccessfully with the question whether the Purchaser must have access to registration-type information or be supplied such information by the Holder. In one letter the staff required that "prospective purchasers * * * be limited to persons who have access to the same information about [the issuer's] stock that a registration statement would provide." In others, the staff has required that the seller advise all offerees where information regarding the issuer might be obtained, and in one letter the staff merely required the seller to disclose all information regarding the issuer that was known to the seller.

Restrictions on Purchaser's Resales

The staff letters tend uniformly to provide that Purchasers of restricted securities are deemed to have received restricted shares and may not resell them *publicly* without compliance with the registration provisions of the Act. In a few letters the staff also has required that restrictive legends and stop-transfer orders be placed upon the shares. In a number of other letters, however, the staff has denied that it has any power to require the placement or removal of restrictive legends.

GENERAL GUIDELINES: THEORY AND PRACTICE

Basis of Exemption

Initially, we conclude that the only proper statutory basis for section 4(1½) sales is section 4(1). We consider that the limiting phrase "by an issuer" in section 4(2) poses an insurmountable barrier to reliance on that exemption as an affirmative basis for the exemption of section 4(1½) sales. As discussed below, however, we consider it appropriate to apply certain section 4(2) criteria to limit the manner in which some varieties of section 4(1½) transactions may otherwise be effected.

Sales of Restricted Securities

Where a nonaffiliate proposes to sell Restricted Securities, the critical inquiries in determining his status as an "underwriter" are whether his acquisition was made "with a view to * * * distribution" and whether his sale is to be made "for an issuer in connection with" a "distribution". Because these phrases appear in the disjunctive in section 2(11), strict statutory analysis indicates that if either question is answered in the affirmative, the Holder would not be entitled to rely upon section 4(1). As discussed below, however, even a purchase made subjectively "with a view to * * * distribution" may under certain conditions be made under section 4(1). Each of these phrases in section 2(11) focuses, first, on the status of the shares in the hands of the Holder (specifically, have they "come to rest") and second, whether his sales constitute a "distribution".

Under the traditional (prerule 144) approach, the prevailing view of securities law practitioners was that once restricted securities had "come to rest" (in the sense that the resales would not be a further step in the issuer's distributive process), there should be no restriction on the manner of resale. Analytically, such resales by definition would not vitiate the issuer's 4(2) exemption and would be sufficiently removed from the original placement that (i) the Holder's resale would not be deemed "for" the issuer and (ii) the Holder's original purchase would not be deemed to have been made with the proscribed "view". We think that this traditional approach has continuing validity and that the section 4(1) exemption should be available if the Holder can demonstrate (i) that he did not acquire the restricted securities from the issuer or an affiliate "with a view to" distribution *and* (ii) that the resale is not being made "for an issuer" (or in the case of the resale of restricted securities acquired from an affiliate, for the affiliate). The best objective evidence on these questions will be the length of time the Holder has owned the securities. If he has established a sufficiently long holding period,[69] this alone should demonstrate conclusively that (i) his original acquisition was not "with a view" to distribution and (ii) that the resale is not being made "for the issuer". With respect to each of these standards, the mere length of the holding period should be sufficient. In this regard, we suggest that a Holder who subjectively intended when he acquired the Restricted Securities, to "distribute" them, may nevertheless thereafter resell them in reliance on section 4(1) if his actual retention of them has been consistent with the opposite intent.

In the case of restricted securities that have not "come to rest", the Holder may nevertheless sell them if the sale does not constitute a "distribution" (unless, as discussed below, the sale may be considered part of the original placement). In determining whether a "distribution" will result from the Holder's sale, we consider the better view to be that only the manner of sale and the number of purchasers are relevant. In short, only the quantitative aspects of the term "distribution" should be considered. We find no basis in the language or legislative history of the 1933 Act to impose the requirements that the Purchaser be sophisticated or have access to registration-type information. Accordingly, a Holder should be able to dispose of restricted securities provided there are few purchasers and the securities are not offered by means of mass communications. Nor, analytically, should there be any particular limit on the amount that may be sold. Obviously, some reasonable limitations must be observed on these points but there are no hard and fast rules. Similarly, the use of a broker to locate a few purchasers should not be ruled out, provided reasonable restrictions are placed on the breadth of the broker's solicitation efforts. Thus, even if the restricted securities have not "come to rest" at the time of resale, if under this second step of the "underwriter" analysis, one determines that no "distribution" will result, section 4(1) will be available.

If the restricted securities have been acquired from the issuer under circumstances in which it cannot be concluded that the shares have come to rest after their sale in the section 4(2) transaction, it is appropriate for section 4(2) requirements of offeree sophistication and access to be applied to the Holder resales. But this is appropriate only for the purpose of

---

69. Although any particular specification of a minimum holding period would be arbitrary, we agree with Professor Loss that a three-year holding period is "well-nigh conclusive" evidence of both the Holder's nondistribution intent and the lack of any connection between his original acquisition and his resale. 1 Loss, Securities Regulation 672 (1961). In many situations, counsel may consider a holding period of less than three years to be sufficient. By

comparison, we note the SEC has approved holding periods of two years and of nine months under rules 144 and 147, respectively, for the limited resales that may be made under those rules, and recently has removed the volume limitations on rule 144 sales by nonaffiliates who have held for three years (in the case of listed or NASDAQ stocks) or four years (in the case of other reporting companies).

assuring that the issuer's original section 4(2) exemption for its sale to the Holder is not lost.

Status of Securities in the Purchaser's Hands

As a theoretical matter, a Purchaser of restricted securities can resell immediately so long as he adheres to the standards discussed above for the Holder's sale (i.e., "privately") and his resales (and all others occurring around the same time) do not result in a "distribution" or otherwise vitiate the issuer's original section 4(2) exemption. The Purchaser thus is essentially in the same position as the Holder and should be able to make resales in the same fashion described herein for Holders.

One typical situation merits special mention. In considering generally the right of the Purchaser of Restricted Securities to resell, special considerations may arise if counsel concludes that the Holder has stock that, at the time of the Holder's sale to the Purchaser, is free to be sold publicly. For example, if the Holder is a noncontrolling person who purchased his stock in a private placement 20 years earlier, we think that most securities lawyers would agree that the Holder may resell the stock publicly, free of any 1933 Act limitations. But the Holder may decide to sell his shares in a directly negotiated private transaction (e.g., because the amount he desires to sell may be more than the trading market would absorb in routine sales). In this situation, the Purchaser should not be in a worse position legally than his predecessor, the Holder. If the Holder has free stock, the Purchaser should have free stock as well, even if the transaction between them is structured as a private, negotiated transaction. We conclude, on these hypothetical facts, that the Purchaser received free stock because the Holder had free stock at the time of the Holder's sale to the Purchaser, even though the stock would be within the literal definition of "restricted securities" as defined in rule 144 because it can be traced back to the issuer 20 years ago through two private transactions.

Alternatives for Dispositions of Restricted Securities

Although a thorough discussion of alternatives available to a Holder for disposing of restricted securities is beyond the scope of this Report, we note that such sales may be made under (i) SEC rule 237, (ii) Regulation A, (iii) in the case of restricted securities held by a controlling person, perhaps under the intrastate exemption contained in section 3(a)(11), and (iv) SEC Rule 144. The recent liberalizing amendments of Rule 144 make resales under that rule a particularly significant alternative for the disposition of restricted securities of reporting companies. In addition, although this Report focuses primarily on the availability of section 4(1) for essentially "private" sales of restricted securities, we recognize that section 4(1) also affords an exempt basis for "public" sales of such securities outside of Rule 144.[b]

b. See also, ABA Committee on Developments in Business Financing, ABA Section of Corporation, Banking and Business Law, Resale by Institutional Investors of Debt Securities Acquired in Private Placements, 34 Bus.Law. 1927 (1979).

SECTION 6. RESTRICTIONS ON RESALES OF SECURITIES ISSUED IN REORGANIZATIONS AND RECAPITALIZATIONS AND UNDER THE BANKRUPTCY CODE

The Section 3 Transaction Exemptions: Sections 3(a)(9) through 3(a)(11). Section 3 purports to exempt from the registration and prospectus requirements of Section 5 various classes of securities. However, only the securities falling under §§ 3(a)(2) through 3(a)(8) possess inherent characteristics which make them appropriate subjects of a permanent exemption from federal regulation.

In Securities Act Release No. 646 (page 400) the SEC General Counsel took the position that § 3(a)(9) merely exempts the transaction of exchange and not the securities themselves. Otherwise, § 3(a)(9) literally would allow a group in control of a corporation to engineer a voluntary recapitalization for the purpose of liberating the control shares from the registration and prospectus requirements of § 5.

The General Counsel's position has been adopted by the Commission. In Thompson Ross Securities Co.[1], the Commission spiked an attempt to use a stock split to secure for control shares a permanent immunity from registration, by reading Section 3 this way:[2]

Unlike securities which fall within Sections 3(a)(2) to 3(a)(8), inclusive, of the Act, there is nothing in the intrinsic nature of the securities falling within Section 3(a)(9) which justifies their permanent exemption from registration. The basis of the exemption under Section 3(a)(9) is merely the circumstances surrounding the issuance of securities.

The sale to the public of a large block of securities previously exempted from registration when they were exchanged for other securities possesses all the dangers attendant upon a new offering of securities to the public by the issuer. Section 3(a)(9) does not, therefore, permanently exempt securities offered in a transaction of exchange. This view is confirmed by the legislative history of the Act.

On this basis, the same principles are regarded as applicable to securities issued in a judicially or administratively approved exchange under § 3(a)(10); to securities issued under the intrastate exemption of § 3(a)(11); and to securities exempted from registration by Commission rule issued under §§ 3(b) and (c). Indeed, since these exemptions are regarded as transaction exemptions, from the standpoint of good drafting, they properly belong in § 4. In the abortive 1941 amendment program, which was interrupted by World War II, the House Committee Print of a SEC Report on proposals for amendments of the Securities Act had this to say:[3]

The act exempts certain securities not because of their inherent attributes but because of the circumstances surrounding their issuance. These exemptions are contained in sections 3(a)(1), 3(a)(9), 3(a)(10), 3(a)(11), and 3(b) of the act. Since these are in reality transaction exemptions rather than security exemptions, the Commission proposes and representatives of the securities

---

1. 6 S.E.C. 1111 (1940).

2. Id. at 1118.

3. SEC, Report on Proposals for Amendments to the Securities Act of 1933 and the Securities Exchange Act of 1934, submitted by the SEC on August 7, 1941 during the Hearings Before the Committee on Interstate and Foreign Commerce of the House of Representatives, 77th Cong., 1st Sess. 24 (Comm.Print 1941).

industry agree that they should be redesignated as transaction exemptions and transferred to section 4.

This remains the generally accepted view both within and without the Commission, even though the transfer has never occurred.

Resales of Section 3(a)(9) Securities. Since § 3(a)(9) is a transaction exemption, the normal rules for the sale of unregistered securities should be applicable. Nonaffiliates of the issuer who exchange unrestricted stock for securities in a § 3(a)(9) exchange, should be able to rely upon the § 4(1) exemption on the basis that the transaction is by a person other than an issuer, underwriter, or dealer. If, however, a nonaffiliated person exchanges restricted securities as defined in Rule 144(a)(3), resales may be made only pursuant to registration or in accordance with Rule 144. However, the tacking provisions of 144(d)(4)(A) or (B) will apply. These sections provide that securities acquired in stock splits, recapitalizations and conversions shall be deemed to have been acquired at the same time as the securities surrendered on the exchange.

If an affiliated person acquires restricted securities in a § 3(a)(9) exchange, tacking will also be allowed to reduce the two-year holding period as in the case of nonaffiliates.[4] Presumably, an affiliated person who engages in a § 3(a)(9) transaction would retain that status after the exchange, although that would not necessarily be the case in, for example, a preferred stock bail-out. In that event, would the recipient still be locked-in and be subject to the registration provisions or Rule 144 in connection with subsequent resales?

Even though an exchange of securities would seem to qualify for an exemption under both § 3(a)(9) and § 4(2), the Commission has sometimes sought to deny the § 3(a)(9) exemption and assert that since the exchange resembles a private placement, the securities so received in the exchange are restricted securities, and subject to the two-year holding period of Rule 144(d) or that the transaction is a "negotiated" exchange, rather than a "recapitalization" within the meaning of Rule 144(d)(4)(A).[5] This position does not seem to have been tested in the courts and appears extremely doubtful, provided all of the conditions of § 3(a)(9) have been met.[6]

Resales of Registered Securities Issued Pursuant to Rule 145. Rule 145 provides that certain transactions involving mergers and sale-of-assets reorganizations are subject to the registration requirements of the 1933 Act. Furthermore, in paragraphs (c) and (d), the rule states that persons who are affiliates of target companies which are acquired in a Rule 145 transaction shall be deemed to be engaged in a distribution and therefore underwriters of the securities received by them in such transactions. Resales of the 145 securities outside of registration may only be made in accordance with the conditions, other than the holding period and notice requirements, of Rule 144. Thus, in a mini-acquisition, a person who controlled a target corporation, but was not in a control relationship with the acquiring company, would be subject to the information, volume and manner of sale provisions of Rule 144, even though the person owned an insubstantial amount of securities. Because Rule 145 is an exclusive rule, unlike Rule 144, it forecloses reliance on the § 4(1) exemption for the resale of securities.[7] On the other hand, if the transaction is structured as a registered stock-for-stock exchange reorganization with an S-4 registration,

---

4. See Hicks, Recapitalizations Under Section 3(a)(9) of the Securities Act of 1933, 61 Va.L.Rev. 1057, 1102–1106 (1975).

5. Ibid.

6. See generally, 7 J. Hicks, Exempted Transactions Under the Securities Act of

1933, § 2.08 (1986 rev.); 1 Securities Law Techniques § 5.04 (A.A. Sommer, Jr. ed. 1985).

7. Securities Act Release No. 5932 (May 15, 1978).

nonaffiliates of the acquiring corporation may resell their securities without restrictions, unless they propose to make resales in sufficient quantities to trigger the presumptive underwriter doctrine.[8]

The Commission ultimately recognized that, in a Rule 145 transaction, to stigmatize such nonaffiliated persons as underwriters for an indefinite period was unduly burdensome and unnecessary for the protection of investors. In 1978, paragraph (d) of Rule 145 was amended to provide that a recipient of Rule 145 securities from the issuer may resell such securities without any limitations after they have been held for two years, provided that the holder is not affiliated with the issuer and that certain other conditions relating to the issuer are met.[9] These conditions require that the issuer of the Rule 145 securities have been subject to the periodic reporting requirements of §§ 13 or 15(d) of the 1934 Act for the preceding 12 months and have filed such reports during that period of time. Persons who were not affiliates of either the target corporation or the acquiring corporation are not deemed to be underwriters as defined in paragraph (c) of Rule 145. Accordingly, they may resell their Rule 145 securities, subject to the provisions of § 4(1). And, apparently, the Staff does not apply the presumptive underwriter doctrine in this context, as is done in traditional registered offerings.[10] Finally, even though restricted stock is exchanged for Rule 145 securities, a nonaffiliated person would be immediately free to resell publicly all of the securities which were acquired in the transaction.[11]

SECURITIES ACT RELEASE NO. 5316

Securities and Exchange Commission.
October 6, 1972.

NOTICE OF ADOPTION OF RULES 145 AND 153A, PROSPECTIVE RESCISSION OF RULE 133, AMENDMENT OF FORM S–14 UNDER THE SECURITIES ACT OF 1933 AND AMENDMENT OF RULES 14a–2, 14a–6 and 14c–5 UNDER THE SECURITIES EXCHANGE ACT OF 1934

[Read that portion of the above release contained in part II, D and E, supra at pages 413–415 and Rule 145(c), (d) and (e).]

---

8. See supra, at page 455.

9. Supra note 7.

10. Cyprus Mines Corp., SEC No-Action Letter (Mar. 2, 1978) (Lexis); Ash, Reorganizations and Other Exchanges Under Sec-

tion 3(a)(10) of the Securities Act of 1933, 75 Sw.U.L.Rev. 1, 81 at note 423 (1980).

11. Securities Act Release 5463 (Feb. 28, 1974), at IV, Illus. A, Q. A–4, infra at page 436.

SECURITIES ACT RELEASE NO. 5463

Securities and Exchange Commission.
February 28, 1974.

DIVISION OF CORPORATION FINANCE'S INTERPRETATIONS OF RULE 145 AND RELATED MATTERS

* * *

IV. *Resales of Securities Acquired in Rule 145 Transactions (See Paragraphs (c), (d) and (e) of Rule 145).*

Illustration A

Facts: X Company filed a registration statement on Form S–1 covering the proposed issuance of its common stock (but not covering the resale thereof) in connection with a proposed acquisition of Y Company in a Rule 145 type statutory merger which, if approved by Y Company's stockholders, would result in Y Company's stockholders receiving common stock of X Company. X Company's registration statement indicates that, for accounting purposes, the acquisition will be treated as a purchase.

Question A–1: Assuming for the purposes of this question only that A is a controlling person of X Company and also owns common stock of Y Company, would his resales of the X Company common stock which he receives in this transaction be subject to the limitations of Rule 145(d)?

Interpretative Response: No. Inasmuch as A controls X Company, he is already deemed to be an affiliate of X Company and is subject to the provisions of Rule 144. Accordingly, the resale of any additional shares of X Company common stock, which he acquires in a Rule 145 transaction or otherwise, is subject to the provisions of Rule 144.

Question A–2: Assuming for the purposes of this question only that B does not own any common stock of X Company but is a controlling person of Y Company and that after the merger he will become a controlling person of X Company, would his resales of the X Company common stock which he receives in this transaction be subject to the limitations of Rule 145(d).

Interpretative Response: No. Inasmuch as B will become a controlling person of X Company, he would be deemed to be an affiliate of X Company. By virtue of his becoming an affiliate of X Company, B would become subject to Rule 144 and the resale of all of his X Company common stock would be subject to the provisions of Rule 144.

Question A–3: Assuming for the purposes of this question only that C is an affiliate of Y Company but not of X Company; what restrictions are imposed by Rule 145(d) on C's public resale of the X Company common stock which he receives in the Rule 145 transaction?

[Under Rule 145(d)(2), C may resell such Rule 145 securities without any limitation after they have been held for two years provided that the issuer meets the qualifications of 145(d)(2).]

* * *

Question A–4: Assuming for the purposes of this question only that D is not an affiliate of X Company or of Y Company and that his only relationship to the transaction is that he owns Y Company common stock, some of which was purchased previously in a private offering, would D be immediately free to resell publicly all of the X Company common stock which he receives in the transaction?

Interpretative Response: Yes. Since D is not an affiliate of X Company or Y Company then he is not deemed to be an underwriter with respect to the securities he receives in the Rule 145 transaction. Accordingly, D is immediately free to resell publicly all of the X Company common stock which he receives in the transaction regardless of whether some of his Y Company common stock was restricted.

Question A–5: If X Company's registration statement disclosed that, for accounting purposes, the acquisition would be treated as a pooling-of-interests, would this have any effect upon the resale of X Company stock acquired in the transaction?

Interpretative Response: Yes. Although a pooling-of-interests accounting treatment would not affect the operation of Rule 145, in order to preserve such accounting treatment, the Commission's Accounting Series Release Nos. 130 (September 29, 1972) and 135 (January 5, 1973) states that the requisite risk sharing will have occurred if the affiliates of X Company and Y Company do not publicly or privately resell any of the X Company securities received in the transaction until such time as financial results covering at least 30 days of post merger combined operations have been published.

RESALES OF SECTION 3(a)(10) SECURITIES

Since Section 3(a)(10) is a transaction exemption, affiliates of the acquiring corporation are subject to the usual restrictions applicable to persons in a control relationship with the issuer of the securities. In the absence of registration, they may resell in a private sale pursuant to the Section "4(1½)" exemption or in accordance with all of the conditions of Rule 144, except for the two-year holding period. If the securities exchanged for the § 3(a)(10) securities had been acquired in a private placement and qualified as restricted securities under Rule 144(a)(3), the two-year holding period would be applicable; however the holder may tack his or her holding period of the exchanged securities in computing the two-year holding period under Rule 144(d).

In *NWS Enterprises, Inc.*,[1] the Staff issued a no-action letter which laid down rules with respect to resales of securities in transactions governed by Rule 145 of the 1933 Act, but where registration is not required because of compliance with the § 3(a)(10) exemption. These rules, as announced, however, apply only where: (1) all of the parties to the transaction are registered under § 12 of the 1934 Act and are required to comply with the proxy solicitation requirements of § 14 of that Act; and (2) the issuer will be subject to the § 13 or § 15(d) reporting requirements after the transaction is consummated.

First, securities of an issuer received in a business combination exempt from registration under § 3(a)(10) are not deemed to be "restricted" if issued in exchange for securities that are not restricted.

Second, as previously stated, securities acquired in exchange for "restricted securities" in a Section 3(a)(10) transaction continue to be "restricted," but the

---

1. (avail. Oct. 30, 1980), [1981 Transfer Binder] Fed.Sec.L.Rep. (CCH) ¶ 76,780.

holder may tack the holding period of the exchanged securities in computing the two-year holding requirement of Rule 144(d).

Third, persons who are not affiliates of any party to the business combination and who are not affiliates of the surviving issuer may freely resell securities received on a § 3(a)(10) transaction in exchange for their unrestricted securities pursuant to the exemption from registration specified in § 4(1) of the 1933 Act, provided that the issuer meets the information and reporting requirements of Rule 144(c).

Since all parties to the reorganization are subject to the periodic reporting requirements of § 13(d) and the proxy solicitation requirements of § 14 of the 1934 Act, there would generally be available adequate information both at the time of issuance of the securities as well as after the transaction. Accordingly, in this situation, the Staff waived the condition generally imposed in § 3(a)(10) transactions that if a nonaffiliate receives an amount of securities in the transaction that are "substantial" in amount as compared to the total amount of securities issued in the transaction, resales must be made in compliance with paragraphs (c), (e), (f) and (g) of Rule 144. The staff appears to regard an amount which exceeds one percent of the total amount of securities issued in the transaction as being substantial for this purpose. This condition represents an application of the "presumptive underwriter" doctrine. See supra at page 455.

Fourth, by analogy to Rule 145, affiliates of an acquired company, who are not affiliates of the acquiring company will be deemed to be engaged in a distribution and therefore underwriters of the securities received by them in the transaction. However, resales may be made pursuant to the leakage provisions of Rule 145(d) and such persons are given the benefit of the two-year cutoff provision of Rule 145(d)(2).

Fifth, persons who become affiliates of the issuer in connection with a § 3(a)(10) transaction may sell securities acquired in such transaction pursuant to Rule 144, except that the two-year holding period is applicable only to the extent that it applied to the securities exchanged in the transaction.[2]

RESTRICTIONS ON RESALES OF SECURITIES UNDER THE BANKRUPTCY CODE

[See supra, at pages 436–439]

---

2. 1 Securities Law Techniques § 6.04[2] (A.A. Sommer, Jr. ed. 1985); 7 J. Hicks, Exempted Transactions Under the Securities Act of 1933, § 3.06 (1986 ed.).

SECTION 7. RESTRICTIONS ON RESALES OF SECURITIES UNDER REGULATION A, RULE 254

SECURITIES ACT RELEASE NO. 5225

Securities and Exchange Commission.
January 10, 1972.

ADOPTION OF AMENDMENTS TO REGULATION A

The Securities and Exchange Commission has adopted certain amendments to its Regulation A under the Securities Act of 1933. Regulation A provides an exemption from registration under the Act for limited amounts of securities of certain issuers which meet the terms and conditions of the regulation. The regulation requires, among other things, the filing of a notification with the appropriate regional office of the Commission and the filing and use of an offering circular furnishing specified information in regard to the issuer and the securities offered.

Rule 254 of Regulation A has been amended with respect to the amount of securities which may be offered thereunder. The amounts in the aggregate which may be offered by various persons during any 12-month period are as follows: the issuer, an estate of a deceased person within two years after the death of such person, and affiliates of the issuer may offer in the aggregate [$1,500,000] [a]; except that any one affiliate (i.e., a person in a control relationship with the issuer) may offer only $100,000; and persons other than the issuer and its affiliates may offer $100,000 each, but the aggregate amount offered by all such other persons may not exceed $300,000 and would not be included in computing the $500,000 ceiling. Securities issued by predecessors and certain affiliates of the issuer which were sold during the same 12-month period by the person making the current offering would have to be included in determining the amount of the offering.

Item 11 of Schedule I to Form 1–A, the notification form, has been amended to provide that where the notification is filed by an issuer which has filed or is required to file with the Commission certified financial statements for its last fiscal year, the financial statements required to be included in the offering circular for such fiscal year shall be certified.

Two changes have been made in the rule as published for comment in Securities Act Release No. 5188. The first is that the definition of person has been conformed to that used in Rule 144. The second is that the rule has been revised to incorporate therein the limitations in the existing rule on the aggregate offering price of securities offered or sold by or on behalf of the estate of a deceased person within two years after the death of such person and by or on behalf of affiliates of the issuer. The purpose of the proposed amendments was to assist small businesses, to provide relief for non-affiliates who wish to sell restricted securities, and not to otherwise materially change the provisions of the existing rule.

* * *

a. SEC Securities Act Release No. 6340 (Aug. 7, 1981) amended Rule 254 to raise the ceiling in (a)(1)(i) from $500,000 to $1,500,000.

SECTION 8. RESTRICTIONS ON RESALES OF SECURITIES RECEIVED IN AN INTRASTATE OFFERING UNDER SECTION 3(a)(11) AND RULE 147

SECURITIES ACT RELEASE NO. 5450
Securities and Exchange Commission.
January 7, 1974.

NOTICE OF ADOPTION OF RULE 147 UNDER THE SECURITIES ACT OF 1933

[Read Parts 7 and 8 of this release, supra, at pages 392–393 and Rule 147(e) and (f).]

SECURITIES ACT RELEASE NO. 4434
Securities and Exchange Commission.
December 6, 1961.

RESALES BY CONTROLLING PERSONS UNDER § 3(a)(11)

[Read the last paragraph of this release under the rubric "Residence Within the State," supra at page 389; Rule 147, Preliminary Note 4.]

Part III

REGULATION OF TRADING IN SECURITIES

THE SECURITIES EXCHANGE ACT OF 1934: AN OVERVIEW

The Securities Act of 1933 is a more or less coherent and unified statute directed almost entirely to two fundamental objectives: full disclosure in connection with the distribution of securities and the prevention of fraud in the sale of securities. The Securities Exchange Act of 1934, on the other hand, is something of a hodge-podge of different provisions, some of which are largely unrelated to others.

One set of provisions relates to the regulation of the affairs of issuers which either have securities listed on a national securities exchange or meet certain asset and public ownership tests. Section 12 requires the registration of such securities under the 1934 Act (this should not be confused with a "registration" under the 1933 Act). Section 13 requires certain periodic reports to keep current the information supplied in the initial registration. Section 14, and Regulation 14A which implements it, regulate the solicitation of proxies by registered corporations. Section 16 provides for the recapture of certain short-swing profits made in the securities of their companies by officers, directors and 10% stockholders of registered corporations.

These various regulations prior to 1964 applied only to corporations with securities listed on a national securities exchange. The Securities Acts Amendments of 1964[1] extended their application to certain publicly-held corporations whose securities are traded over-the-counter. The tests established to determine the applicability of such provisions with respect to non-listed corporations were described by the Commission[2] as follows:

"The 1964 Amendments will extend the registration, periodic reporting, proxy solicitation and insider reporting and trading provisions of the Exchange Act to issuers with total assets in excess of $1,000,000 and a class of equity security which is held of record by 750 or more persons, if the issuer is engaged in interstate commerce or in a business affecting inter-state commerce, or its securities are traded by use of the mails or any means or instrumentality of interstate commerce. After July 1, 1966, these requirements will be applicable to issuers with total assets in excess of $1,000,000 [increased to $5,000,000, effective August 15, 1986] and a class of equity securities held of record by 500 or more persons.

"A number of exemptions from the new registration requirements are available. These include exemptions for securities listed and registered on a national securities exchange; securities issued by registered investment companies; securities (other than stock generally representing non-with-drawable capital) of savings and loan associations and similar institutions; securities of certain non-profit organizations operated exclusively for reli-

1. Act of August 20, 1964, Public Law 88–467.   2. Securities Exchange Act Release No. 7425, Sept. 15, 1964.

539

gious, educational, benevolent, fraternal, charitable or reformatory purposes; securities of certain agricultural marketing cooperatives; securities of certain non-profit mutual or cooperative organizations which supply a commodity or service primarily to members; [bank collective trust funds and insurance company "separate accounts" issued in connection with pension or profit-sharing plans qualifying under Internal Revenue Code § 401, or annuity plans qualifying under § 404(a)(2) of such Code;] and direct obligations issued or guaranteed by the United States or any State or political subdivision thereof.

"Insurance companies are exempt from the new registration requirements which are contained in new section 12(g) of the Exchange Act, provided the insurance company is regulated by its state of incorporation in all three of the following respects:

"(1) It is required to and does file annual reports with a state official or agency substantially in accordance with the requirements prescribed by the National Association of Insurance Commissioners;

"(2) It is regulated in the solicitation of proxies in accordance with the requirements prescribed by the National Association of Insurance Commissioners; and

"(3) After July 1, 1966, the purchase and sale of securities issued by the insurance company by beneficial owners, directors or officers of the company are subject to regulation (including reporting) substantially in the manner provided in section 16 of the Exchange Act.

The periodic reporting requirements of section 15(d) of the Exchange Act will continue to be applicable to insurance companies as in the past, and to insurance companies which file Securities Act registration statements in the future. Insurance companies registered on a national securities exchange, or which register under new section 12(g), will be subject to the periodic reporting, proxy solicitation and insider reporting and trading provisions of the Exchange Act.

"Although the Exchange Act applies to all banks, the registration, periodic reporting, proxy solicitation, and insider reporting and trading provisions with respect to bank securities, whether listed or unlisted, will now be administered and enforced by the Federal bank regulatory agencies; the Comptroller of the Currency with respect to securities issued by national and District of Columbia banks; the Board of Governors of the Federal Reserve System with respect to state banks which are members of the Federal Reserve System; and the Federal Deposit Insurance Corporation with respect to all other insured banks. Banks which are not subject to regulation by a Federal bank regulatory agency will be required to comply with these requirements as administered by this Commission. Banks, insurance companies and interested investors, therefore, may wish to contact the appropriate regulatory agency to determine the nature of the obligation and the procedure to be followed with respect to these requirements."

[The registration, periodic reporting, proxy solicitation, and insider reporting and trading provisions with respect to institutions the accounts of which are insured by the Federal Savings and Loan Insurance Corporation (FSLIC) are administered and enforced by the Federal Home Loan Bank Board.]

* * *

"The 1964 Amendments [and SEC rules] provide that an issuer may terminate registration of a class of securities registered under section 12(g) by filing a certification with the Commission that the securities are held of record by less than 300 persons [or less than 500 persons where the total assets of the issuer do not exceed $5 million.[a]]. Registration will be terminated 90 days after an issuer files the certification or within such shorter period as the Commission may direct, unless the Commission determines, after notice and opportunity for hearing, that the certification is untrue.

"An issuer with securities registered under section 12(g) will continue to be subject to the periodic reporting, proxy solicitation and insider trading provisions of the Exchange Act until registration has been terminated for each class of its registered equity securities. Any class of securities for which registration has been terminated thereafter will be subject to registration if on the last day of any fiscal year the class of securities are held of record by the requisite number of persons and the issuer has total assets in excess of [$5 million]."

Sections 7 and 8(a) of the 1934 Act deal with the regulation of margin requirements in the purchase of securities and borrowings by broker-dealers. These sections are implemented by regulations issued by the Federal Reserve Board, rather than the Securities and Exchange Commission (although the Commission has certain enforcement powers). They are concerned more with broad national economic policy than the other provisions of the Act. The current regulations issued by the Board are designated Regulation G, Regulation T, Regulation U and Regulation X. The balance of Section 8 deals with the net capital requirements for broker-dealers and with the hypothecation of their customers' securities by broker-dealers. These portions of Section 8 are administered entirely by the Commission.

Certain sections of the Act may be said to deal more specifically with regulation of the securities markets (not merely the exchange markets, as the title of the Act implies). Section 15 requires the registration with the Commission of all broker-dealers, except those whose business is exclusively intrastate and those whose business is exclusively in exempted securities, commercial paper, bankers' acceptances or commercial bills. Sections 5 and 6 require the registration with the Commission of securities exchanges and Section 15A (added by the Maloney Act of 1938) permits the registration with the Commission of associations of over-the-counter broker-dealers. Only one such association, the National Association of Security Dealers, Inc. ("NASD") has in fact registered with the Commission and includes in its membership practically all active broker-dealers conducting a general securities business in the country.[3] The exchanges and the NASD are authorized by the statute to regulate and discipline their own members, and each exchange and the NASD has an elaborate set of rules governing their conduct. The SEC has certain supervisory power both over the rules and over the disciplinary action of these quasi-official bodies. Thus the great bulk of the regulation of the securities industry is self-regulation under the supervision of a governmental agency.[4]

---

a. See SEC Rule 12g–4 under the Exchange Act.

3. See Loss, Fundamentals of Securities Regulation 689–94 (1983).

4. See Jennings, Self-Regulation in the Securities Industry: The Role of the Securities and Exchange Commission, 29 Law & Contemp.Prob. 663 (1964).

However, the original proposal of the Commission that all broker-dealers be required to join the NASD was not adopted in the Securities Act Amendments of 1964 primarily because of the opposition of the large investment management companies with their own sales forces, whose salesmen had never belonged to the NASD and who considered general broker-dealers as their competitors. Rather, the 1964 amendments adding new § 15(b)(8) and (9) provided that the Commission could impose upon non-members of the NASD regulation similar to that imposed by the NASD upon its members.

These sections established the "SECO program" for the regulation of broker-dealers who were not members of the NASD or a national securities exchange and who engaged in an over-the-counter securities business. The acronym was derived from the fact that SECO broker-dealers were subject to "SEC only" regulation.

Section 15(b)(8) and (9) granted the Commission broad powers to impose direct regulation on SECO broker-dealers and for persons associated with them. The SEC did not welcome this gratuitous authority and generally established rules which paralleled those of the NASD. In some instances, these proved to be more onerous than the comparable NASD rule. As a result, many of the SECO broker-dealer community ultimately found it in their interest to join the NASD, and by 1982, the SECO broker-dealer population had dwindled to 12 percent of broker-dealers engaged in over-the-counter trading. Thus, after almost twenty years of dual regulation, in 1983, Congress and the Commission decided to phase out the program. Section 15(b)(8) and (9) was amended to eliminate the SECO program and persons continuing to do over-the-counter trading now must become members of the NASD, unless they are a member of a national securities exchange and are only minimally involved in over-the-counter securities trading.[5] The SEC then rescinded the SECO rules and terminated the program, effective December 6, 1983.[6]

The 1975 amendments added two other self-regulatory organizations in addition to the national securities exchanges and the NASD—registered clearing agencies[7] and the Municipal Securities Rule Making Board.[8]

In 1968 the so-called Williams Act[9] (named after its sponsor, Senator Harrison A. Williams) was enacted to add Subsections (d) and (e) to Section 13 and Subsections (d), (e) and (f) to Section 14 of the Securities Exchange Act of 1934. These provisions regulate tender offers for, open market purchases of, and repurchases by the issuing corporation of securities which are either listed on a National Securities Exchange or registered under Section 12(g) of the Securities Exchange Act.

5. See 97 Stat. 205, P.L. 98–38 (1983); West's U.S.Code Cong. & Adm.News, 98th Cong., 1st Sess. 597, vol. 2 (1984); SEC Rule 15b9–1.

6. SEC Exchange Act Release No. 20409 (Nov. 22, 1983).

7. Securities Exchange Act § 17A. These agencies are engaged in the clearance and settlement of securities transactions and the safeguarding of securities and funds in their custody.

8. Securities Exchange Act § 15B. All municipal securities dealers, including banks, must register with the SEC. The Municipal Securities Rulemaking Board is composed of fifteen members appointed by the SEC. The Board is authorized to make rules regulating the conduct of municipal securities brokers and dealers with respect to transactions in municipal securities.

For a discussion of the status and functions of the various self-regulatory organizations provided in the Securities Exchange Act, see Loss, Fundamentals of Securities Regulation 689–703 (1983).

9. Act of July 29, 1968, 82 Stat. 456.

Section 14(d) requires the filing with the Commission and transmittal to the offerees of certain information regarding the maker of a tender offer and its intentions concerning the so-called "target corporation," i.e., the issuer of the securities that are the subject of the tender offer, which the maker of the tender offer ordinarily expects to control if the offer is successful. The bill as originally introduced required the filing of such a statement in advance of the making of the tender offer, but because of objections that this would give an unfair advantage to an incumbent management who wanted to resist the take-over attempt, the bill as finally enacted only required such filing simultaneously with the transmittal of the offer to the holders of the securities.

The phrase "tender offer" is nowhere defined in the new provisions; however, it is commonly understood to mean a public offer to purchase securities made otherwise than in an organized securities market (except for a "special bid" to purchase equity securities through stock exchange facilities),[10] i.e., by communication of such offer directly to all of the existing holders of the securities which are desired to be purchased.

In 1970, Section 14(d) was amended[11] to eliminate the exemption for insurance companies, which existed under the original Act because of the fact that their securities are not registered under Section 12(g) if the company is subjected to certain state regulation, as explained above. At the same time, an exemption in the original statute for exchange offers pursuant to a registration under the Securities Act of 1933 was eliminated. Where the offeror is offering to exchange its own securities (rather than cash) for the securities being acquired, then it normally must register the securities to be issued in exchange under the 1933 Act and it was originally thought that there was no need to impose additional regulation under the Williams Act. However, because the Williams Act, in addition to disclosure, imposes certain substantive regulations upon such transactions, this exemption was eliminated.

In addition to the disclosures required of a tender offeror by the Williams Act, there are a number of substantive requirements imposed upon the terms of such transactions, either by statute or SEC rule. For example, § 14(d)(5) provides that persons who deposit securities pursuant to the tender offer have the right to withdraw their deposit during the first seven business days that the offer is outstanding and after the expiration of sixty days from the time of the original offer. The SEC, under the authority to prescribe rules varying these conditions, has since extended the withdrawal right to embrace the entire offering period (Rule 14d-7). The purpose of this provision is to permit a security holder who has deposited early to change his mind if a competing offer, which is more attractive, is made soon after the first tender offer; and to prevent the tender offeror from tying up the securities in escrow indefinitely where the offer has been only partially successful and the offeror continues in his attempt to acquire a minimum percentage of the stock, without which he does not intend to accept any of the securities tendered.

The Act also requires that where the offer is for less than all of the outstanding securities of the class and a greater number are tendered within ten days after the commencement of the offer than will be accepted

---

10. Securities Exchange Act Release No. 8392 (Aug. 30, 1968).

11. Act of December 22, 1970, 84 Stat. 1497.

by the tender offeror, it must accept the ones tendered within that ten day period pro rata and cannot, as was frequently done prior to this amendment, make the offer on a first-come, first-served basis (Rule 14d–8).

In 1986, the Commission adopted the "all-holders" requirement and the "best price" provision to require that third party tender offers be open to all holders of the class of securities sought and all tendering shareholders be paid the highest price paid to any tendering shareholder (Rule 14d–10).

Section 13(d) as added by the Williams Act required a filing of certain information by any person acquiring securities in the open market which are registered under the Securities Exchange Act, if as a result of such acquisition the person would become the owner of more than 10% of the outstanding securities of that class. In the amendments to these provisions enacted in 1970, this percentage figure was reduced from 10% to 5%.[12] However, the statute exempts from this filing requirement any acquisition of 2% or less of the outstanding securities of the class during any twelve months' period. The exemption for insurance company securities, which was originally contained in this section as well as Section 14(d), was also eliminated in 1970. The information required to be filed with the Commission (and sent to the issuer and each Exchange on which the security is traded) by the acquirer within ten days after the acquisition is similar to the information required to be disclosed by a tender offeror.

Section 13(e), as added by the Williams Act, authorizes the Commission to adopt rules and regulations regulating the purchase by an issuer of its own securities. The Commission has adopted rules similar to those applicable to third party tender offers so as to provide equality of treatment among shareholders and to prevent terms in an offer which are deemed unfair (Rule 13e–4). Section 14(f) also requires that where any persons are elected or designated as directors of an issuer by a person acquiring securities in a Section 14(d) or Section 13(d) transaction, and where such persons will constitute a majority of the directors, the issuer must file with the Commission and transmit to its security holders information regarding the new directors prior to the time that they take office.

The Securities Acts Amendments of 1975 constituted the first comprehensive revision of the 1934 Act with respect to its provisions relating to the regulation of the securities markets. The 1964 Amendments had dealt primarily with the registration and reporting requirements for companies whose securities are traded, although they also introduced the SECO regulation for broker-dealers who did not choose to join the NASD. (As noted above, the SECO regulations have been phased out and broker-dealers engaged in over-the-counter trading now must become members of the NASD.) The 1968 Amendments dealt exclusively with the regulation and reporting of certain transactions by persons in the securities markets, and not with market structure or the regulation of market organizations.

In contrast, the 1975 Amendments had as their primary purpose the establishment of a framework, by an extensive rewriting of the Act, for a so-called "national market system" or "central market system." The principal changes made in order to accomplish this objective were as

---

12. Ibid. The percentage figure in Section 14(d) was also reduced by the same amendment from 10% to 5%. Neither figure in *that* section was or is very significant, since a general tender offer to acquire less than 10% of the outstanding securities of a class is virtually, if not completely, unknown.

follows: (1) New Section 11A establishes the Congressional goal of promoting a "national market system" and directs the creation of a National Market Advisory Board. (2) "Securities information processors", i.e., persons distributing information about securities quotations or transactions, are subjected to registration and regulation. (3) "Clearing agencies", i.e., transfer agents, clearing houses and other persons concerned with the mechanical completion of a securities trade, are subjected to registration and regulation by a new Section 17A. (4) The exemption for municipal broker-dealers was eliminated, and a new Section 15B provides for their registration and regulation and the creation of a Municipal Securities Rulemaking Board. (5) The supervision and oversight responsibility of the Securities and Exchange Commission with respect to the rulemaking and adjudicatory functions of the self-regulatory agencies is made consistent and plenary, and it is given authority to initiate as well as review actions by such agencies. (§ 19) (6) Certain restrictive practices of the securities exchanges, such as rate fixing and prohibition of off-board trading, are either prohibited or the authority given to the Securities and Exchange Commission to prohibit them, with a clear Congressional mandate that it act speedily to do so unless other considerations clearly override the objective of maximum competition between broker-dealers and between competing markets. (§ 19) (7) Reporting requirements regarding their holdings and transactions were imposed upon "institutional investment managers" managing assets of a certain amount ($100,000,000 or such lesser amount, but not less than $10,000,000 as the Commission by rule determines) by a new Section 13(f). (8) Transactions by a broker-dealer for his own account or for an account with respect to which he exercises investment discretion, other than an individual discretionary account, are prohibited on a national securities exchange after May 1, 1978 except as otherwise permitted by the Commission. Such prohibited transactions include those for any pooled investment funds, such as a mutual fund, for which the broker-dealer acts as investment manager. This effectively prohibits all floor trading by members and all so-called "institutional membership" on exchanges except as may be sanctioned by the Commission. (§ 11)

These are only the highlights of the changes effected by the 1975 Amendments. Nevertheless, as extensive as they were, they did not effect any startling or immediate changes in the functioning of the securities markets. "May Day", the date on which fixed commission rates were abolished on the exchanges, had already come and gone before the President signed the bill. Rather, they set a framework and a goal which the industry was directed to achieve over a period of years under the guidance of the Securities and Exchange Commission.

The Government Securities Act of 1986 eliminated the exemption for government securities brokers and dealers. A new § 15C of the Exchange Act provides for their registration and regulation. Registered securities brokers and dealers under § 15 and municipal securities dealers under § 15B that also act as government securities brokers and dealers must notify their appropriate regulatory government agencies that they are a government securities broker or dealer. The Federal Reserve Board, the Secretary of the Treasury and the SEC now share regulatory authority over government securities brokers and dealers.

As a result of the manner in which the 1934 Act has grown by accretion over a period of more than 40 years, it has become close to incomprehensible. This situation was greatly aggravated in the 1975 Amendments by the bureaucratic fight over who was going to regulate the banks, which came under the Act for the first time in their capacities as transfer agents and as municipal securities dealers (although they were included as reporting companies in the 1964 Amendments), with the inevitable compromise, under which as many as three different agencies may be involved in a single administrative action. The proposed new Federal Securities Code, if and when adopted, will hopefully reduce this morass to more intelligible form.

Finally, there are certain specific sections of the Act dealing with prohibited practices in the securities markets. Section 9 deals with the manipulation of security prices in the exchange markets. Section 10 deals with manipulative and deceptive devices in both the exchange markets and the over-the-counter markets, and also gives the Commission the authority to regulate short sales and stop-loss orders in the exchange markets. The latter authority has not been implemented to any great extent.[13] Section 11 deals with the segregation of the functions of brokers and dealers and the regulation of floor traders and specialists. Section 15(c) enumerates various fraudulent and prohibited practices on the part of broker-dealers. Apart from Section 16(b), the sections mentioned above in this paragraph are the ones under which most of the civil litigation has arisen under the 1934 Act, although since the Borak case[14] Section 14(a) has become more important in that respect. Also, Section 14(e), which was a part of the Williams Act, prohibits any fraudulent, deceptive or manipulative act or practice in connection with any tender offer or any solicitation in opposition to a tender offer. This section also has become more important in the civil liability area.

For discussion of the Securities Acts Amendments of 1964, see Phillips and Shipman, Analysis of the Securities Acts Amendments of 1964, 1964 Duke L.J. 706; Sowards, Securities Acts Amendments of 1964; New Registration and Reporting Requirements, 19 U.Miami L.Rev. 33 (1964); Sargent, The Securities Acts Amendments of 1964: Background, Effect and Practicalities, 20 Sw.L.J. 434 (1966); Symposium—Securities Acts Amendments of 1964, 20 Bus.Law. 265 (1965).

For discussion of the Williams Act, see 3 Securities Law Techniques chs. 70–71 (A.A. Sommer, Jr. ed. 1986); M. Lipton & E. Steinberger, Takeovers & Freezeouts ch. 2 (1986 rev.).

---

13. There are no SEC rules regulating stop-loss orders. Rules 10a–1 and 10a–2 regulate short sales to some extent. A "short sale" is defined in Rule 3b–3. Rule 10a–1(b) requires that all sell orders be marked "long" or "short"; and Rule 10a–1(a) prohibits a short sale below the last sale price, regular way, or at such last sale price unless it was above the next preceding different sale price, regular way. These rules are intended to prevent "bear raids." Short sales have not otherwise been significantly regulated. See Loss, Fundamentals of Securities Regulation 711–17 (1983); Pollack, Short-Sale Regulation of NASDAQ Securities (NASD, Inc. 1986).

14. J. I. Case Co. v. Borak, 377 U.S. 426 (1964).

Chapter 10

REGULATION OF THE SECURITIES MARKETS

Statutes and Regulations

Securities Exchange Act of 1934, §§ 5, 6, 7, 11, 11A, 15, 15A, 15B, 17, 17A, 19.

Exchange Act Rules 11a–1; 11a1–1(T); 11a1–2; 11a2–2(T); 11Aa2–1; 11Aa3–1; 11Ac1–1; 11Ac1–2; 19b–3; 19c–1; 19c–3.

GORDON v. NEW YORK STOCK EXCHANGE

United States Supreme Court, 1975.
422 U.S. 659, 95 S.Ct. 2598, 45 L.Ed.2d 463.

Mr. JUSTICE BLACKMUN delivered the opinion of the Court.

This case presents the problem of reconciliation of the antitrust laws with a federal regulatory scheme in the particular context of the practice of the securities exchanges and their members of using fixed rates of commission. The United States District Court for the Southern District of New York and the United States Court of Appeals for the Second Circuit concluded that fixed commission rates were immunized from antitrust attack because of the Securities and Exchange Commission's authority to approve or disapprove exchange commission rates and its exercise of that power.

I

In early 1971 petitioner Richard A. Gordon, individually and on behalf of an asserted class of small investors, filed this suit against the New York Stock Exchange, Inc. (NYSE), the American Stock Exchange, Inc. (Amex), and two member firms of the exchanges. The complaint challenged a variety of exchange rules and practices and, in particular, claimed that the system of fixed commission rates, utilized by the exchanges at that time for transactions less than $500,000, violated §§ 1 and 2 of the Sherman Act, 15 U.S.C.A. §§ 1 and 2. Other challenges in the complaint focused on (1) the volume discount on trades over 1,000 shares, and the presence of negotiated rather than fixed rates for transactions in excess of $500,000; (2) the rules limiting the number of exchange memberships; and (3) the rules denying discounted commission rates to nonmembers using exchange facilities.

Respondents moved for summary judgment on the ground that the challenged actions were subject to the overriding supervision of the Securities and Exchange Commission (SEC) under § 19(b) of the Securities Exchange Act of 1934, and, therefore, were not subject to the strictures of the antitrust laws. The District Court granted respondents' motion as to all claims * * *. Dismissing the exchange membership limitation and the Robinson-Patman Act contentions as without merit, the court focused on the relationship between the fixed commission rates and the Sherman Act mandates. It utilized the framework for analysis of antitrust immunity in

547

the regulated securities area that was established a decade ago in Silver v. New York Stock Exchange, 373 U.S. 341 (1963). Since § 19(b)(9) of the Exchange Act authorized the SEC to supervise the exchanges "in respect of such matters as * * * the fixing of reasonable rates of commission," the court held applicable the antitrust immunity reserved in *Silver* for those cases where "review of exchange self-regulation [is] provided through a vehicle other than the antitrust laws." 373 U.S., at 360. It further noted that the practice of fixed commission rates had continued without substantial challenge after the enactment of the 1934 Act, and that the SEC had been engaged in detailed study of the rate structure for a decade, culminating in the requirement for abolition of fixed rates as of May 1, 1975.

On appeal, the Second Circuit affirmed. Characterizing petitioner's other challenges as frivolous, the appellate court devoted its opinion to the problem of antitrust immunity. It, too, used *Silver* as a basis for its analysis. Because the SEC, by § 19(b)(9), was given specific review power over the fixing of commission rates, because of the language, legislative history, and policy of the Exchange Act, and because of the SEC's actual exercise of its supervisory power, the Court of Appeals determined that this case differed from *Silver*, and that antitrust immunity was proper.

By his petition for certiorari, petitioner sought review only of the determination that fixed commission rates are beyond the reach of the antitrust laws. Because of the vital importance of the question, and at the urging of all the parties, we granted certiorari.

II

Resolution of the issue of antitrust immunity for fixed commission rates may be made adequately only upon a thorough investigation of the practice in the light of statutory restrictions and decided cases. We begin with a brief review of the history of commission rates in the securities industry.

Commission rates for transactions on the stock exchanges have been set by agreement since the establishment of the first exchange in this country. The New York Stock Exchange was formed with the Buttonwood Tree Agreement of 1792, and from the beginning minimum fees were set and observed by the members. That Agreement itself stated:

"We the Subscribers, Brokers for the Purchase and Sale of Public Stock, do hereby solemnly promise and pledge ourselves to each other, that we will not buy or sell from this day for any person whatsoever, any kind of Public Stock at a less rate than one-quarter percent Commission on the Specie value, and that we will give a preference to each other in our negotiations." F. Eames, The New York Stock Exchange 14 (1968 ed.).

See generally, R. Doede, The Monopoly Power of the New York Stock Exchange, reprinted in Hearings on S. 3169 before the Subcomm. on Securities of the Senate Comm. on Banking, Housing and Urban Affairs, 92d Cong., 2d Sess., 405, 412–427 (1972). Successive constitutions of the NYSE have carried forward this basic provision. Similarly, when Amex emerged in 1908–1910, a pattern of fixed commission rates was adopted there.

These fixed rate policies were not unnoticed by responsible congressional bodies. For example, the House Committee on Banking and Currency, in a general review of the stock exchanges undertaken in 1913, reported that the fixed commission rate rules were "rigidly enforced" in order "to prevent competition amongst the members." H.R.Rep. No. 1593, 62d Cong., 3d Sess., 39 (1913). The report, known as the Pujo Report, did not recommend any change in this policy, for the Committee believed

"the present rates to be reasonable, except as to stocks, say, of $25 or less in value, and that the exchange should be protected in this respect by the law under which it shall be incorporated against a kind of competition between members that would lower the service and threaten the responsibility of members. A very low or competitive commission rate would also promote speculation and destroy the value of membership." Id., at 115–116.

Despite the monopoly power of the few exchanges, exhibited not only in the area of commission rates but in a wide variety of other aspects, the exchanges remained essentially self-regulating and without significant supervision until the adoption of the Securities Exchange Act of 1934. At the lengthy hearings before adoption of that Act, some attention was given to the fixed commission rate practice and to its anticompetitive features. See Hearings before the Senate Comm. on Banking and Currency on S.Res. 84 (72d Cong.) and S.Res. 56 and 97 (73d Cong.), 73d Cong., 1st and 2d Sess., 6075, 6080, 6868, and 7705 (1934) (Senate Hearings). See also Hearings on S.Res. 84 before the Senate Comm. on Banking and Currency, 72d Cong., 1st Sess., 85 (1932); Hearings on H.R. 7852 and 8720 before the House Comm. on Interstate and Foreign Commerce, 73d Cong., 2d Sess., 320–321, 423 (1934).

Perhaps the most pertinent testimony in the hearings preparatory to enactment of the Exchange Act was proffered by Samuel Untermyer formerly Chief Counsel to the committee that drafted the Pujo Report. In commenting on proposed S. 2693, Mr. Untermyer noted that although the bill would provide the federal supervisory commission with

"the right to prescribe uniform rates of commission, it does not otherwise authorize the Commission to fix rates, which it seems to me it should do and would do by striking out the word 'uniform.' That would permit the Commission to fix rates.

"The volume of the business transacted on the exchange has increased manyfold. Great fortunes have been made by brokers through this monopoly. The public has no access to the exchange by way of membership except by buying a seat and paying a very large sum for it. Therefore it is a monopoly. Probably it has to be something of a monopoly. But after all it is essentially a public institution. It is the greatest financial agency in the world, and should be not only controlled by the public but it seems to me its membership and the commissions charged should either be fixed by some governmental authority or be supervised by such authority. As matters now stand, the exchange can charge all that the traffic will bear, and that is a burden upon commerce." Senate Hearings 7705.

As finally enacted, the Exchange Act apparently reflected the Untermyer suggestion for it gave the SEC the power to fix and insure "reasonable" rates. Section 19(b) provided:

"(b) *The Commission is further authorized, if* after making appropriate request in writing to a national securities exchange that such exchange effect on its own behalf specified changes in its rules and practices, and after appropriate notice and opportunity for hearing, *the Commission determines* that such exchange has not made the changes so requested, and that *such changes are necessary or appropriate for the protection of investors or to insure fair dealing in securities traded in* upon such exchange or to insure fair administration of such exchange, by rules or regulations or by order *to alter or supplement the rules of such exchange* (insofar as necessary or appropriate to effect such changes) *in respect of such matters as* ∗ ∗ ∗ (9) *the fixing of reasonable rates of commission*, interest, listing, and other charges." (Emphasis added.)

This provision conformed to the Act's general policy of self-regulation by the exchanges coupled with oversight by the SEC. It is to be noted that the ninth category is one of 12 specifically enumerated. In Merrill Lynch, Pierce, Fenner & Smith v. Ware, 414 U.S. 117, 127–128 (1973), we observed:

"Two types of regulation are reflected in the Act. Some provisions impose direct requirements and prohibitions. Among these are mandatory exchange registration, restrictions on broker and dealer borrowing, and the prohibition of manipulative or deceptive practices. Other provisions are flexible and rely on the technique of self-regulation to achieve their objectives. ∗ ∗ ∗ Supervised self-regulation, although consonant with the traditional private governance of exchanges, allows the Government to monitor exchange business in the public interest."

The congressional reports confirm that while the development of rules for the governing of exchanges, as enumerated in § 19(b), was left to the exchanges themselves in the first instance, the SEC could compel adoption of those changes it felt were necessary to insure fair dealing and protection of the public. See H.R.Rep. No. 1383, 73d Cong., 2d Sess., 15 (1934); S.Rep. No. 792, 73d Cong., 2d Sess., 13 (1934). The latter report, at 15, noted that registered exchanges were required to provide the SEC with "complete information" regarding its rules.

III

With this legislative history in mind, we turn to the actual post-1934 experience of commission rates on the NYSE and Amex. After these two exchanges had registered in 1934 under § 6 of the Exchange Act, both proceeded to prescribe minimum commission rates just as they had prior to the Act. ∗ ∗ ∗ These rates were changed periodically by the exchanges, after their submission to the SEC pursuant to § 6(a)(4) and SEC Rule 17a–8. Although several rate changes appear to have been effectuated without comment by the SEC, in other instances the SEC thoroughly exercised its supervisory powers. Thus, for example, as early as 1958 a study of the NYSE commission rates to determine whether the rates were "reasonable and in accordance with the standards contemplated by applicable provisions of the Securities Exchange Act of 1934," was announced by the SEC. SEC Exchange Act Release No. 5678, April 14, 1958. ∗ ∗ ∗ This study resulted in an agreement by the NYSE to reduce commission rates in certain transactions, to engage in further study of the rate structure by the NYSE in collaboration with the SEC, and to provide the SEC with greater advance notice of proposed rate changes. SEC Exchange Act Release No. 5889, February 20, 1959. ∗ ∗ ∗ The SEC specifically stated that it had undertaken the study "in view of the responsibilities and duties imposed upon the Commission by Section 19(b) * * * with respect to the rules of national securities exchanges, including rules relating to the fixing of commission rates." Ibid.

Under subsection (d) of § 19 of the Act (which subsection was added in 1961) * * * the SEC was directed to investigate the adequacy of exchange rules for the protection of investors. Accordingly, the SEC began a detailed study of exchange rules in that year. In 1963 it released its conclusions in a six-volume study. SEC Report of Special Study of Securities Markets, H.Doc. No. 95, 88th Cong., 1st Sess. The Study, among other things, focused on problems of the structure of commission rates and procedures, and standards for setting and reviewing rate levels. Id., pt. 5, at 102. The SEC found that the rigid commission rate structure based on value of the round lot was causing a variety of "questionable consequences," such as "give-ups" and the providing of special services for certain large, usually institutional, customers. These attempts indirectly to achieve rate alterations made more difficult the administration of the rate structure and clouded the cost data used as the basis for determination of rates. These effects were believed by the SEC to necessitate a complete study of the structure. Moreover, the SEC concluded that methods for determining the reasonableness of rates were in need of overhaul. Not only was there a need for more complete information about the economics of the securities business and commission rates in particular, but also for a determination and articulation of the criteria important in arriving at a reasonable rate structure. Hence, while the Study did not produce any major immediate changes in commission rate structure or levels, it did constitute a careful articulation of the problems in the structure and of the need for further studies that would be essential as a basis for future changes.

Meanwhile, the NYSE began an investigation of its own into the particular aspect of volume discounts from the fixed commission rates. * * * This study determined that a volume discount and various other changes were needed, and so recommended to the SEC. The Commission responded in basic agreement. Letter dated December 22, 1965, from SEC Chairman Cohen to NYSE President Funston. * * * The NYSE study continued over the next few years and final conclusions were presented to the SEC in early 1968. * * *

In 1968, the SEC, while continuing the study started earlier in the decade, began to submit a series of specific proposals for change and to require their implementation by the exchanges. Through its Exchange Act Release No. 8324, May 28, 1968, the SEC requested the NYSE to revise its commission rate schedule, including a reduction of rates for orders for round lots in excess of 400 shares or, alternatively, the elimination of minimum rate requirements for orders in excess of $50,000. These changes were viewed by the SEC as interim measures, to be pending further consideration "in the context of the Commission's responsibilities to consider the national policies embodied both in the securities laws and in the antitrust laws." Letter of May 28, 1968, from SEC Chairman Cohen to NYSE President Haack. App. A284, A285. In response to these communications, the NYSE (and Amex) eventually adopted a volume discount for orders exceeding 1,000 shares, as well as other alterations in rates, all approved by the SEC. See, e.g., letter of August 30, 1968, from Chairman

Cohen to President Haack, App. A310; memorandum dated September 20, 1968, Amex Subcommittee on Commission Structure, App. A104.

Members of the securities exchanges faced substantial declines in profits in the late 1960's and early 1970. These were attributed by the NYSE to be due, at least in part, to the fact that general commission rates had not been increased since 1958. Statement of February 13, 1970, by President Haack to SEC. App. A313. The NYSE determined that a service charge of at least the lesser of $15 or 50% of the required minimum commission on orders less than 1,000 shares should be imposed as an interim measure to restore financial health by bringing rates in line with costs. NYSE Proposed Rule 383, App. A331. See also letter dated March 19, 1970, from President Haack to members of the NYSE. App. A327. This proposal, submitted to the SEC pursuant to its Rule 17a–8, was permitted by the SEC to be placed into operation on a 90-day interim basis. Letter dated April 2, 1970, from SEC Chairman Budge to President Haack. App. A333. Continuation of the interim measure was thereafter permitted pending further rate structure hearings undertaken by the SEC. SEC Exchange Act Release No. 8923, July 2, 1970. The interim rates remained in effect until the rate structure change of March 1972.

In 1971 the SEC concluded its hearings begun in 1968. Finding that "minimum commissions on institutional size orders are neither necessary nor appropriate," the SEC announced that it would not object to competitive rates on portions of orders above a stated level. 'Letter of February 3, 1971, from SEC Commissioner Smith to President Haack. App. A353. See also SEC Exchange Act Release No. 9007, October 22, 1970. Although at first supporting a $100,000 order as the cutoff below which fixed rates would be allowed, ibid., the SEC later decided to permit use of $500,000 as the breakpoint. After a year's use of this figure, the SEC required the exchanges to reduce the cutoff point to $300,000 in April 1972. Statement of the SEC on the Future Structure of the Securities Markets, February 2, 1972. * * * (Policy Study).

The 1972 Policy Study emphasized the problems of the securities markets, and attributed as a major cause of those problems the prevailing commission rate structure. The Policy Study noted:

"Our concern with the fixed minimum commission * * * is not only with the level of the rate structure but with its side effects as well. Of these, perhaps the most important are the following:

"(a) Dispersion of trading in listed securities.

"(b) Reciprocal practices of various kinds.

"(c) Increasing pressure for exchange membership by institutions." Id., at A385.

Since commission rates had been fixed for a long period of time, however, and since it was possible that revenue would decline if hasty changes were made, the SEC believed that there should be no rush to impose competitive rates. Rather, the effect of switching to competition should be gauged on a step-by-step basis, and changes should be made "at a measured, deliberate pace." Id., at A387. The result of the introduction of competitive rates for orders exceeding $500,000 was found to be a substantial reduction in commissions, with the rate depending on the size of the order. In view of this result, the SEC determined to institute competition in the $300,000–$500,000 range as well.

Further reduction followed relatively quickly. On January 16, 1973, the SEC announced it was considering requiring the reduction of the breakpoint on competitive rates to orders in excess of $100,000. SEC Exchange Act Release No. 9950. In June, the SEC began hearings on the rate schedules, stimulated in part by a request by the NYSE to permit an increase of 15% of the current rate on all orders from $5,000 to $300,000, and to permit a minimum commission on small orders (below $5,000) as well. SEC Exchange Act Release No. 10206, June 6, 1973. * * * Three months later, after completion of the hearings, the SEC determined that it would allow the increases. SEC Exchange Act Release No. 10383, September 11, 1973. * * * The SEC also announced, however: "It will act promptly to terminate the fixing of commission rates by stock exchanges after April 30, 1975, if the stock exchanges do not adopt rule changes achieving that result." Id., at 28.

Elaboration of the SEC's rationale for this phasing out of fixed commission rates was soon forthcoming. In December 1973, SEC Chairman Garrett noted that the temporary increase in fixed rates (through April 1975) was permitted because of the inflation in the cost of operating the exchanges, the decline in the volume of transactions on the exchanges, and the consequently severe financial losses for the members. SEC Exchange Act Release No. 10560, December 14, 1973. * * * Indeed, without the rate increase, "the continued deterioration in the capital positions of many member firms was foreseeable, with significant capital impairment and indirect, but consequential, harm to investors the likely result." Id., at 36. The rate increase also would forestall the possibility that the industry would be impaired during transition to competitive rates and other requirements. This view conformed to the suggestion of Senator Williams, Chairman of the Subcommittee on Securities of the Senate Committee on Banking, Housing and Urban Affairs. See statement dated July 27, 1973, of Senator Williams submitted to the SEC, cited in Exchange Act Release No. 10560 n. 12. Although not purporting to elucidate fully its reasons for abolishing fixed rates, the SEC did suggest several considerations basic to its decision: the heterogeneous nature of the brokerage industry; the desirability of insuring trading on, rather than off, the exchanges; doubt that small investors are subsidized by large institutional investors under the fixed rate system; and doubt that small firms would be forced out of business if competitive rates were required.

In response to a request by the NYSE, the SEC permitted amendment to allow competitive rates on non-member orders below $2,000. SEC Exchange Act Release No. 10670, March 7, 1974. * * * Hearings on intramember commission rates began in April 1974. SEC Exchange Act Release No. 10751, April 23, 1974. * * * The SEC concluded that intramember rates should not be fixed beyond April 30, 1975. SEC Exchange Act Release No. 11019, September 19, 1974. * * * At this time the SEC stated:

"[I]t presently appears to the Commission that it is necessary and appropriate (1) for the protection of investors, (2) to insure fair dealing in securities traded in upon national securities exchanges, and (3) to insure the fair administration of such exchanges, that the rules and practices of such exchanges that require, or have the effect of requiring, exchange members to charge any persons fixed minimum rates of commission, should be eliminated." Id., at 63.

The SEC formally requested the exchanges to make the appropriate changes in their rules. When negative responses were received from the NYSE and others, the SEC released for public comment proposed Securities Exchange Act Rules 19b–3 and 10b–22. Proposed Rule 19b–3, applicable to intra- and nonmember rates effective May 1, 1975, would prohibit the exchanges from using or compelling their members to use fixed rates of commission. It also would require the exchanges to provide explicitly in their rules that nothing therein requires or permits arrangements or agreements to fix rates. Proposed Rule 10b–22 would prohibit agreements with respect to the fixing of commission rates by brokers, dealers, or members of the exchanges. See SEC Exchange Act Release No. 11073, October 24, 1974. * * *.

Upon the conclusion of hearings on the proposed rules, the SEC determined to adopt Rule 19b–3, but not Rule 10b–22. SEC Exchange Act Release No. 11203, January 23, 1975. * * * Effective May 1, 1975 competitive rates were to be utilized by exchange members in transactions of all sizes for persons other than members of the exchanges. Effective May 1, 1976, competitive rates were to be mandatory in transactions for members as well, i.e., floor brokerage rates. Competition in floor brokerage rates was so deferred until 1976 in order to permit an orderly transition. * * *

During this period of concentrated study and action by the SEC, lasting more than a decade, various congressional committees undertook their own consideration of the matter of commission rates. Early in 1972, the Senate Subcommittee on Securities concluded that fixed commission rates must be eliminated on institutional-sized transactions, and that lower fees should be permitted for small transactions, with "unbundled" services, than those having the full range of brokerage services. Report of the Subcomm. on Securities of the Senate Comm. on Banking, Housing and Urban Affairs (For the Period Ended February 4, 1972), 92d Cong., 2d Sess., 4 (1972). The Subcommittee objected particularly to the failure of the fixed rate system to produce "fair and economic" rates, id., at 59, and to distortion in the rate structure in favor of the institutionally oriented firms.

* * *

The House Committee on Interstate and Foreign Commerce, in a report issued only six months after the Senate Report, supra, concluded that fixed rates of commission were not in the public interest and should be replaced by competitively determined rates for transactions of all sizes. Such action should occur "without excessive delay." Securities Industry Study, Report of the Subcomm. on Commerce and Finance of the House Comm. on Interstate and Foreign Commerce. H.R.Rep.No.1519, 92d Cong., 2d Sess., xiv, 141, 144–145, 146 (1972). * * *

In 1975 both Houses of the Congress did in fact enact legislation dealing directly with commission rates. Although the bills initially passed by each chamber differed somewhat, the Conference Committee compromised the differences. Compare H.R. 4111, § 6(p), as discussed in H.R.Rep.No.94–123, 94th Cong., 1st Sess., 51–53, 67–68 (1975), with S.249, § 6(e), as discussed in

S.Rep.No.94–75, 94th Cong., 1st Sess., 71–72, 98 (1975). The measure, as so compromised, was signed by the President on June 5, 1975.

The new legislation amends § 19(b) of the Securities Exchange Act to substitute for the heretofore existing provision a scheme for SEC review of proposed rules and rule changes of the various self-regulatory organizations. Reference to commission rates is now found in the new § 6(e), generally providing that after the date of enactment "no national securities exchange may impose any schedule or fix rates of commissions, allowances, discounts, or other fees to be charged by its members." An exception is made for floor brokerage rates which may be fixed by the exchanges until May 1, 1976. Further exceptions from the ban against fixed commissions are provided if approved by the SEC after certain findings: prior to November 1, 1976, the Commission may allow the exchanges to fix commissions if it finds this to be "in the public interest," § 6(e)(1)(A); after November 1, 1976, the exchanges may be permitted by the SEC to fix rates of commission if the SEC finds (1) the rates are reasonable in relation to costs of service (to be determined pursuant to standards of reasonableness published by the SEC), and (2) if the rates "do not impose any burden on competition not necessary or appropriate in furtherance of the purposes of this title, taking into consideration the competitive effects of permitting such schedule or fixed rates weighed against the competitive effects of other lawful actions which the Commission is authorized to take under this title." § 6(e)(1)(B)(ii). The statute specifically provides that even if the SEC does permit the fixing of rates pursuant to one of these exceptions, the SEC by rule may abrogate such practice if it finds that the fixed rates "are no longer reasonable, in the public interest, or necessary to accomplish the purposes of this title." § 6(e)(2).

* * *

As of May 1, 1975, pursuant to order of the SEC, fixed commission rates were eliminated and competitive rates effectuated. Although it is still too soon to determine the total effect of this alteration, there have been no reports of disastrous effects for the public, investors, the industry, or the markets.

* * *

IV

This Court has considered the issue of implied repeal of the antitrust laws in the context of a variety of regulatory schemes and procedures. Certain axioms of construction are now clearly established. Repeal of the antitrust laws by implication is not favored and not casually to be allowed. Only where there is a "plain repugnancy between the antitrust and regulatory provisions" will repeal be implied. * * *

The starting point for our consideration of the particular issue presented by this case, viz., whether the antitrust laws are impliedly repealed or replaced as a result of the statutory provisions and administrative and congressional experience concerning fixed commission rates, of course, is our decision in *Silver*. There the Court considered the relationship between the antitrust laws and the Securities Exchange Act, and did so specifically with respect to the action of an exchange in ordering its members to remove private direct telephone connections with the offices of a nonmember. Such action, absent any immunity derived from the regulatory laws, would be a *per se* violation of § 1 of the Sherman Act. 373 U.S., at 347. Concluding that the proper approach to the problem was to reconcile the operation of the antitrust laws with regulatory scheme, the Court established a "guiding principle" for the achievement of this reconciliation. Under this principle, "[r]epeal is to be regarded as implied only if necessary to make the Securities Exchange Act work, and even then only to the minimum extent necessary." Id., at 357.

In *Silver*, the Court concluded that there was no implied repeal of the antitrust laws in that factual context because the Exchange Act did not provide for SEC jurisdiction or review of particular applications of rules enacted by the exchanges. It noted:

"Although the Act gives to the Securities and Exchange Commission the power to request exchanges to make changes in their rules, § 19(b), and impliedly, therefore, to disapprove any rules adopted by an exchange, see also § 6(a)(4), it does not give the Commission jurisdiction to review particular instances of enforcement of exchange rules." Ibid.

At the time *Silver* was decided, both the rules and constitution of the NYSE provided that the exchange could require discontinuance of wire service between the office of a member and a nonmember at any time. There was no provision for notice or statement of reasons. While these rules were permissible under the general power of the exchanges to adopt rules regulating relationships between members and nonmembers, and the SEC could disapprove the rules, the SEC could not forbid or regulate any particular application of the rules. Hence, the regulatory agency could not prevent application of the rules that would have undesirable anticompetitive effects; there was no governmental oversight of the exchange's self-regulatory action, and no method of insuring that some attention at least was given to the public interest in competition.

The Court, therefore, concluded that the absence in *Silver* of regulatory supervision over the application of the exchange rules prevented any conflict arising between the regulatory scheme and the antitrust laws. * * * The Court in *Silver* cautioned, however, that "[s]hould review of exchange self-regulation be provided through a vehicle other than the antitrust laws, a different case as to antitrust exemption would be presented." 373 U.S., at 360. It amplified this statement in a footnote:

"Were there Commission jurisdiction and ensuing judicial review for scrutiny of a particular exchange ruling * * * a different case would arise concerning exemption from the operation of laws designed to prevent anticompetitive activity, an issue we do not decide today." 373 U.S., at 358 n. 12.

It is patent that the case presently at bar is, indeed, that "different case" to which the Court in *Silver* referred. In contrast to the circumstances of *Silver*, § 19(b) gave the SEC direct regulatory power over exchange rules and practices with respect to "the fixing of reasonable rates of commission." Not only was the SEC authorized to disapprove rules and practices concerning commission rates, but the agency also was permitted to require alteration or supplementation of the rules and practices when "necessary or appropriate for the protection of investors or to insure fair dealings in securities traded in upon such exchange." Since 1934 all rate changes have been brought to the attention of the SEC, and it has taken an active role in review of proposed rate changes during the last 15 years.[a] Thus, rather than presenting a case of SEC impotence to affect application of exchange rules in particular circumstances, this case involves explicit statutory authorization for SEC review of all exchange rules and practices dealing with rates of commission and resultant SEC continuing activity.

Having determined that this case is, in fact, the "different case," we must then make inquiry as to the proper reconciliation of the regulatory and antitrust statutes involved here, keeping in mind the principle that repeal of the antitrust laws will be "implied only if necessary to make the Securities Exchange Act work, and even then only to the minimum extent necessary." Id., at 357. We hold that these requirements for implied repeal are clearly satisfied here. To permit operation of the antitrust laws with respect to commission rates, as urged by petitioner Gordon and the United States as *amicus curiae*, would unduly interfere, in our view, with the operation of the Securities Exchange Act.

* * *

Our disposition of this case differs from that of the Seventh Circuit in Thill Securities Corp. v. New York Stock Exchange, 433 F.2d 264 (1970), cert. denied, 401 U.S. 994 (1971), where antitrust immunity for the NYSE's antirebate rule was claimed and denied. The Court of Appeals reversed a grant of summary judgment in favor of the NYSE, and remanded for further evidence regarding the effects of the antirebate rule on competition, the degree of actual review by the SEC, and the extent to which the rule was necessary to make the Exchange Act work. 433 F.2d, at 270. This ruling is persuasively distinguishable on at least two grounds from the case at bar: First, there was no evidence presented regarding the extent of SEC review of the challenged rule. Second, the antirebate practice differs from fixed commission rates in that (1) it was not among the items specifically listed in § 19b, although the practice might reasonably be thought to be related to the fixing of commission rates, and (2) it does not necessarily apply uniformly, and may be applied in a discriminatory manner. We do not believe it necessary, in the circumstances of this case, to take further evidence concerning the competitive effects of fixed rates, or the necessity of fixed rates as a keystone of the operation of exchanges under the Exchange Act. To the extent that the Court of Appeals in *Thill* viewed the question of implied repeal as a question of fact, concerning whether the particular rule itself is necessary to make the Act work, we decline to follow that lead.

* * *

In sum, the statutory provision authorizing regulation, § 19(b)(9), the long regulatory practice, and the continued congressional approval illustrated by the new legislation, point to one, and only one, conclusion. The Securities Exchange Act was intended by the Congress to leave the supervision of the fixing of reasonable rates of commission to the SEC. Interposition of the antitrust laws, which would bar fixed commission rates as *per se* violations of the Sherman Act, in the face of positive SEC action, would preclude and prevent the operation of the Exchange Act as intended by Congress and as effectuated through SEC regulatory activity. Implied

---

a. For a different reading of history relating to SEC exercise of its § 19(b)(9) authority over commission rates, see Werner, Adventure in Social Control of Finance: The National Market System for Securities, 75 Colum.L.Rev. 1233, 1289–1292 (1975).

repeal of the antitrust laws is, in fact, necessary to make the Exchange Act work as it was intended; failure to imply repeal would render nugatory the legislative provision for regulatory agency supervision of exchange commission rates.

Affirmed.

[JUSTICES DOUGLAS and STEWART each wrote concurring opinions.]

In Chapter I we described the present structure of the securities markets and the efforts to develop the National Market System without describing the historical background which led to the enactment of the Securities Act's Amendments of 1975. Gordon v. New York Stock Exchange, supra at page 547, and the following material describe the forces which moved Congress to enact the 1975 Amendments. These amendments to the 1934 Act were designed "to remove impediments to and perfect the mechanism of a national market system for securities" and direct the Commission to "facilitate the establishment" of that system. The Note, "The Development of a National Market System," supra at page 12, describes the structure of that system as of 1986 and should be reviewed after you study the following material. For the history of the development of the National Market System from the SEC point of view, see Development of a National Market System, Securities Exchange Act Release No. 14416 (Jan. 26, 1978); Securities Exchange Act Release No. 15671 (Mar. 22, 1979).

THE HISTORICAL BACKGROUND OF PRESENT MARKET STRUCTURE PROBLEMS

Any consideration of the securities markets on registered exchanges must center on the New York Stock Exchange, since it accounts for 80% to 90% of the dollar volume on all such exchanges.[1] The operation of the New York Stock Exchange was historically based upon four interrelated principles or rules, all of them designed to protect the economic position of the members of that exchange (i.e., all of them in "restraint of trade" to some extent).

(1) *Limited membership and exclusive dealing.* The Constitution of the Exchange limits the number of regular members to a fixed number of persons, currently 1,366.[2] However, this number includes many specialists, floor traders, odd-lot brokers and "two-dollar" brokers,[3] so that the actual number of commission houses doing business with the public is much less. There were

---

1. Figures compiled by the Special Study of the Securities Markets showed that the dollar volume of transactions on the New York Stock Exchange as a percentage of transactions on all exchanges during the period from 1935 through 1962 ranged from a high of 89.24% in 1938 to a low of 82.44% in 1961. H.Doc.No.95, 88th Cong., 1st Sess., Pt. 2, Table VIII–64 (pp. 1076–1077) (1963). More recent figures show that the NYSE percentage of such volume had increased to 85.3% in 1985, and the NYSE proportion of consolidated trades in NYSE securities amounted to 83.4%. NYSE Fact Book 17, 74 (1986).

2. N. Y. Stock Exchange Constitution, Art. II, Sec. 1, 2 NYSE Guide (CCH) ¶ 1051; NYSE Fact Book 59, 60, 82 (1986).

3. A discussion of these various categories of members of the exchange can be found in Report of Special Study of the Securities Markets, H.Doc.No.95, 88th Cong., 1st Sess., Pt. 2, pp. 45–48 (1963). The so-called "two-dollar" broker or "floor broker" is a member of the exchange who does not himself have public customers but merely acts as a sub-broker in executing transactions on the floor on behalf of the wire houses. The name comes from the fact that at one time his share of the

only 666 active *members* of the Exchange as of the end of 1962 not falling in one of these special categories,[4] and since many commission houses have multiple memberships there were probably less than that number of firms doing business with the public.[5] Since only a member of the Exchange was entitled to transact business on the floor of the Exchange,[6] these firms had a monopoly of the trading on that floor in NYSE listed securities.

(2) *The prohibition against members executing trades in listed securities off the board.* Subject to very limited exceptions, the Exchange rules prohibited its members from executing a trade in listed securities except on the floor of the Exchange.[7]

(3) *The minimum commission schedule.* The rules of the Exchange prior to 1971 prescribed minimum commissions to be charged by its members in executing all transactions for all non-members, including other broker-dealers who were not members of the New York Stock Exchange.

(4) *The uniform commission schedule for all transactions, regardless of size.* The commission schedule of the Exchange was based upon the dollar amount involved in one round-lot trade (i.e., the purchase or sale of a number of shares equal to the unit of trading in the particular stock, usually 100 shares). The odd-lot differential payable with respect to the purchase or sale of a number of shares less than the unit of trading established a kind of a volume discount up to the unit of trading. However, with respect to any trade in excess of the unit of trading there was prior to 1968 no volume discount in the commission rate structure: on a purchase of 10,000 shares exactly 100 times as much commission was payable as upon the purchase of 100 shares.

The Constitution of the New York Stock Exchange required that the minimum commissions established by the Exchange be "net and free from any rebate, return, discount or allowance made in any shape or manner, or by any method or arrangement direct or indirect." [8] The increasing power of institutional investors combined with the competition among New York Stock Exchange member firms for their business to make a mockery of this provision. There did in fact exist a volume discount available to sufficiently powerful investors through various "methods and arrangements."

Customer Directed "Give-ups". Members of the New York Stock Exchange and of other exchanges were permitted to share the commissions earned on a transaction with other members of the same exchange. In the ordinary course this is done among different members who are responsible for part of the work in connection with a trade. For example, a wire house may entrust a customer's order to a floor broker for execution and pay him a portion of the commission for handling this part of the transaction.[9] Or a member firm which has no clearing facilities in New York and no member regularly on the floor of the exchange may entrust an order to another member firm with these facilities for both execution and clearance in New York. However, the rules

---

commission was $2, although in 1963 it was about $3.50 per hundred shares. Ibid.

4. Report of Special Study of the Securities Markets, H.Doc.No.95, 88th Cong., 1st Sess., Pt. 1, Table I–4 (p. 29) (1963).

5. At the end of 1985 there were 1469 members, including regular members, associated with 599 member organizations. Of these member firms, only 381 were qualified to conduct a public business. This included odd-lot firms (which have large numbers of members) and specialist firms

as well as commission houses. No figures are given for the average number of members per commission house.

6. Rule 54, 2 NYSE Guide (CCH) ¶ 2054.

7. See discussion pp. 569–570, infra.

8. N.Y.S.E. Constitution, Art. XV, Sec. 1. (rescinded; see text, infra at note 31).

9. Report of Special Study of the Securities Markets, H.Doc.No.95, 88th Cong., 1st Sess., Pt. 2, 295–297 (1963).

formerly permitted such a sharing of the commission with another member firm which had nothing whatever to do with the transaction, at the direction of the customer. This permitted the large mutual funds to reward other brokers for such things as selling the fund shares or furnishing statistical or advisory services to the fund manager through the dispensation of this "disposable brokerage" by the "customer directed give-up." [10]

Reciprocity. If a broker-dealer who was not a member of the New York Stock Exchange received an order from a customer to buy or sell an NYSE listed stock which he forwarded to a member firm to execute on that exchange, the member firm had to charge him the same commission as it would charge any member of the public. Therefore, the non-member made nothing whatever on the transaction since as a practical matter he was precluded from charging the customer more than a competitive broker-dealer which had a seat on the Exchange. If he was a member of a regional exchange on which the stock was also traded he might be able to execute the order there and retain the entire commission; but if the stock was not traded on any regional exchange of which he was a member, or he was not a member of any exchange, then he had to execute the order for nothing. However, it had long been the practice for the member firm to "reciprocate" for business forwarded to it in this manner by directing other business (which it could execute itself) to its correspondent for execution on the regional exchange of which he was a member or in the over-the-counter market. "This reciprocal commission business * * * [was] generally placed under arrangements involving 'reciprocal ratios' of 2 to 1, 3 to 1 or similar ratios; that is, the NYSE member * * * [would] direct \$1 in commissions to the nonmember for each * * * \$2, or \$3 of commissions received. The ratio always favor[ed] the NYSE member." [11] That is, the nonmember was given in effect a $33\frac{1}{3}\%$ to 50% discount on the NYSE commission, minus the cost of executing the reciprocal business.

With the growth of the institutional investors, this device was also employed to evade the minimum commission schedule for the benefit of the customer. Since a firm which was not a member of the New York Stock Exchange could not receive "give-ups", such a firm which the customer wanted to benefit would be given "customer-directed reciprocity" in regional traded or over-the-counter securities. Again, this kind of benefit would be doled out to broker-dealers in return for services of various kinds rendered to the customer directing the reciprocity.[12]

The End Run.[13] These two devices had the disadvantages that "give-ups" were only permitted to other members of the New York Stock Exchange and that "reciprocity" might involve entrusting execution of their customers' orders to firms about which the member firm might know nothing. These disadvantages were eliminated by the invention of the "end run." Under this scheme, a customer with "disposable brokerage" would pay the full commission to the NYSE member firm on its own transaction. However, either that order or another order from an unrelated customer would be executed on a regional exchange of which the NYSE member firm was also a member and of which the broker-dealer who was the customer-directed recipient of the "disposable brokerage" was a member. The NYSE member firm could then "give-up" part of the brokerage on the transaction executed on the regional exchange to another

---

10. Public Policy Implications of Investment Company Growth, H.Rep.No.2337, 89th Cong., 2d Sess., 169–170 (1966).

11. Report of Special Study of the Securities Markets, H.Doc.No.95, 88th Cong., 1st Sess., Pt. 2, at 302 (1963).

12. Public Policy Implications of Investment Company Growth, H.Rep.No.2337, 89th Cong., 2d Sess., pp. 167–169 (1966).

13. See Wall Street Journal, July 23, 1964, p. 1, col. 6.

member of such regional exchange.[14] Since this still left over-the-counter broker-dealers who were not members of any exchange out in the cold, all of the regional exchanges amended their rules to permit "give-ups" in connection with transactions executed on those exchanges not only to their own members but also to any member of the NASD,[15] and one exchange even permitted such "give-ups" to any broker-dealer registered with the Securities and Exchange Commission although not a member of the NASD.[16]

These practices were one source of a great increase in volume on the regional exchanges. Most of such transactions were what are known as "crosses." That is, the broker for the seller of a relatively large block of stock had already found the buyer or vice versa, and the price had already been agreed upon, and the broker went onto the floor of the exchange to yield priority, parity, and precedence to limit orders on the specialist's book and to record the transaction and charge the minimum commission to both parties, part of which could then be directed by the customer who had "disposable brokerage."

The Incorporated Give-up Pocket. All of these devices involved as the final step some sort of service or benefit conferred by the final broker-dealer recipient of the "give-ups" or "reciprocity" upon the customer who was directing their distribution. In the case of banks, for example, which had a large volume of stock transactions in their trust departments, the benefits might be rental of space in the bank building or the maintenance of large demand deposits in the bank.[17] In the case of mutual funds, the most common basis of the distributions was the sale of the fund shares by the broker-dealers receiving the "disposable brokerage", but also included the furnishing of other types of services to the fund managers.[18]

Eventually, the manager of a large mutual fund complex devised the final step of arranging for the "disposable brokerage" to come directly back into its own pocket. It incorporated a subsidiary which was registered as a broker-dealer and which obtained a membership on the Pacific Coast Stock Exchange.[19] As such a member, it could and did receive the "give-ups" resulting from the "end run", although it was not intended to and did not engage in any brokerage business, or indeed in any business at all. From this nonoperation it earned $3,100,000 in one year.[20] Two other mutual funds followed suit, and it has been estimated that 20% of all the commissions earned in 1967 on the Pacific Coast Stock Exchange were paid to the brokerage affiliates of these three mutual funds.[21]

Other persons were not long in seeing the possibilities inherent in this set-up. One of the largest brokerage houses in England applied for and obtained membership on the Pacific Coast Stock Exchange so that it could obtain a volume discount for its customers on transactions which it executed for them *on*

---

14. Public Policy Implications of Investment Company Growth, H.Rep.No.2337, 89th Cong., 2d Sess., at 171–172 (1966).

15. Id. at 171; Wall Street Journal, Nov. 3, 1965, p. 29, col. 2.

16. Securities Exchange Act Release No. 8239, at 3 (SEC Jan. 26, 1968).

17. Report of Special Study of the Securities Markets, H.Doc.No.95, 88th Cong., 1st Sess., Pt. 2, at 859–861 (1963).

18. Public Policy Implications of Investment Company Growth, H.Rep.No.2337, 89th Cong., 2d Sess., at 163–167 (1966).

19. See Wall Street Journal, Feb. 2, 1966, 6:2; May 18, 1966, 3:2.

20. Securities Exchange Act Release No. 8239, p. 4 (SEC Jan. 26, 1968).

21. Speech by Commissioner Francis M. Wheat of the Securities and Exchange Commission, at the University of Southern California Corporate Law Finance Institute, Dec. 8, 1967.

the New York Stock Exchange.[22] Two other English brokerage houses immediately applied for membership.[23]

The Abolition of "Give-Ups" and Fixed Rates of Commission. Under intense and increasing pressure from the SEC,[24] the New York Stock Exchange published on January 2, 1968,[25] a proposal designed to deal with the commission rate structure and the various practices outlined above which had made a shambles of it. This proposal supported a continuation of the practice of customer directed give-ups, but with a limitation on the percentage amount which might be given up, the incorporation of a volume discount in the commission rate schedule, the nature and amount to be subsequently determined, and the institution of a discount for nonmember broker dealers. The proposal was described as being "offered as a package." All of the details were left to be spelled out after agreement upon the principles.

The Commission shortly thereafter published a proposed Rule 10b–10 under the Securities Exchange Act which would have required that all mutual fund managers direct to the fund or credit upon their management or advisory fees all "disposable brokerage" generated by portfolio transactions of the fund, rather than capturing such payments themselves in whole or in part or using them to stimulate sales of the fund's shares.[26]

The United States Department of Justice in April, 1968, filed a brief with the SEC in which it criticized both the NYSE and the SEC proposals as inadequate and proposed that the SEC prohibit all minimum commission rate fixing by the Exchange, at least on large transactions.[27]

In May, 1968, the SEC ordered public hearings on the entire problem.[28] However, before the hearings commenced the NYSE and the Amex in June, 1968, publicly abandoned their support of the practice of "give-ups" in a move which was described as an attempt to save the minimum commission rate structure.[29] In the Fall of 1968 an interim solution to the problem was adopted by the Exchange, with the approval of the SEC, which abolished the practice of give-ups, instituted some quantity discounts in the Exchange's commission rate schedule and authorized a discount to non-member broker-dealers.[30]

22. Wall Street Journal, Nov. 2, 1967, p. 14, col. 3.

23. Wall Street Journal, Nov. 28, 1967, 29:4.

24. Wall Street Journal, Sept. 13, 1965, 3:1; Sept. 22, 1965, 3:2; Jan. 3, 1966, 4:1; Jan. 23, 1967, 2:3; Feb. 2, 1967, 4:3; Feb. 6, 1967, 6:3; May 5, 1967, 28:2; Nov. 22, 1967, 4:3; Nov. 30, 1967, 4:3; Jan. 3, 1968, 3:2.

25. The text of the proposal is set forth as an appendix to Securities Exchange Act Release No. 8239 (SEC Jan. 26, 1968).

26. The Commission stated that "while the New York Stock Exchange proposal and proposed Rule 10b–10 are not mutually exclusive on all points, the New York Stock Exchange proposal is, to a significant extent, an alternative approach." Securities Exchange Act Release No. 8239, p. 10 (SEC Jan. 26, 1968). Of the mutual fund managers with captive sales forces who had employed brokerage affiliates to receive give-ups, some had credited 100% of the earnings of the brokerage affiliate to the fund, others 50% and some had kept all of such earnings for themselves. Id. at

p. 4. The managers of mutual funds which are sold through general broker-dealers had by and large felt that they were forced by competition to continue using the give-ups to reward such broker-dealers who sell the fund's shares so that they went neither to the manager nor to the fund. This practice would also have been prohibited by the proposed rule unless the manager was willing to cut his fees by an amount equal to the give-ups directed to broker-dealers.

27. See CCH, Selected Comments on SEC Proposed Rule on Give-Ups and NYSE Proposal on Commission Rates (1968) (this publication contains the text not only of the Justice Department brief but also of the comments of other interested parties).

28. Wall Street Journal, May 29, 1968, 3:1.

29. Wall Street Journal, June 11, 1968, 3:2; June 28, 1968, 3:1.

30. Wall Street Journal, Sept. 5, 1968, 3:1; Oct. 11, 1968, 3:2; Oct. 25, 1968, 2:3; Nov. 26, 1968, 27:1.

During the next three years the Securities and Exchange Commission, the Department of Justice and the New York Stock Exchange wrestled with this problem, and with each other, particularly over the question of negotiated rates which were still vehemently championed by the Department of Justice and certain members of Congress. One reason for the failure of the Commission to insist upon an earlier resolution of the controversy was undoubtedly the severe financial crisis which existed in the securities industry during the years 1969–1971 and which made any tampering with the rate schedule appear hazardous. However, the Commission finally lost patience in the Spring of 1971 and ordered the Exchange to institute negotiated commissions on trades in excess of $500,000, to be effective on April 5, 1971.[31] The subsequent history, including the progressive lowering of the "breakpoint" for negotiated rates to $100,000 and the ultimate elimination of fixed rates on May 1, 1975 ("May Day") by the SEC acting under Congressional threat to do the job legislatively if the Commission did not act, is detailed by Justice Blackmun in the Gordon case.

The Impact of Block Trading. Two competing markets have combined in recent years to erode the Exchange monopoly of trading in the securities listed on the New York Stock Exchange. Both of these alternative markets have always been present to some extent, but the considerable increase of trading off the Big Board in the last few years has been due to the interaction of two factors: the rapid growth of institutional trading by mutual funds, pension and profit-sharing funds and other fiduciaries[32] and the rigid commission structure of the New York Stock Exchange.

The Third Market. It has of course always been possible for a broker-dealer who is not a member of the New York Stock Exchange to make an over-the-counter market in listed securities without being subject to the commission schedule of the Exchange. Since this market is a negotiated market, the broker-dealer engaging in it is free to offer such volume discounts for block transactions as he may choose. Because of the great increase in institutional trading and block transactions, this market at one time became a serious threat to the practical monopoly of the Exchange in trading in listed securities. The Special Study noted that from 1955 to 1961 over-the-counter trading in New York Stock Exchange listed securities increased 185% whereas the increase in volume on the Exchange during the same period was only 60%.[33] This trend undoubtedly continued and even accelerated in subsequent years prior to the abolition of fixed commission rates. The elimination of fixed commission rates, however, destroyed the competitive advantage of persons operating in the "third market" and the Commission has stated that following such elimination in 1975, "the competitive significance of the third market has been reduced to *de minimis* levels."[34]

Dual Trading. Many of the securities listed on the New York Stock Exchange are also listed or admitted to trading on one or more regional exchanges, and may be traded there by members of such exchanges who are not members of the New York Stock Exchange as well as by those firms which have memberships both on such regional exchange and on the New York Stock Exchange. Since the commission rate structure of the regional exchanges was in the past modeled upon that of the New York Stock Exchange, such dual

31. Wall Street Journal, Feb. 12, 1971, 3:1; Mar. 9, 1971, 2:3; Mar. 12, 1971, 2:3; April 5, 1971, 6:2; April 16, 1971, 2:3.

32. See discussion page 564, infra.

33. Report of Special Study of the Securities Market, H.Doc.No.95, 88th Cong., 1st Sess., Pt. 2, p. 874 (1963).

34. In re American Stock Exchange, Securities Exchange Act Release No.17744, April 21, 1981, note 13; CCH Fed.Sec.Law Rptr. ¶ 82,866 (1981).

trading did not furnish serious competition to the monopoly of the Big Board over trading in NYSE listed securities until the reciprocity and "give-up" practices (described above) developed in connection with the assault on the Exchange's commission structure. After these practices developed, there was a dramatic increase in the volume of trading on the regional stock exchanges, from $4.4 billion in 1961 to $10.3 billion in 1966 and from 6.8% of the total volume on all exchanges to 8.4% during the same period.[35] "Substantially all of the regional exchange volume consists of trading in securities also traded on the New York Stock Exchange." [36]

The economic model upon which the rules of the New York Stock Exchange were based in the past contemplates a continuous central auction market where all buyers and sellers will congregate and arrive at the price of a particular security through the free competition of bids and offers. Since it has never been true that prospective buyers are always present whenever a seller appears in the crowd, or vice versa, the specialist system was developed as an essential lubricant to maintain continuity of the market and to prevent extreme, momentary fluctuations in the price of a particular security which are unrelated to basic supply and demand. However, the transactions by the specialist unit for its own account were considered in this economic model to be the exception rather than the rule and it was never required to have sufficient capital to assume very large positions in the stocks in which it specialized; [37] in fact, the rules of the Exchange have discouraged the specialist from becoming a dominant factor in the market.

In the ten years from 1965 to 1975, as a result of the growth of institutional trading by organizations which combined vast amounts of individual savings to invest in the stock market and the consequent increase in the number of transactions involving very large blocks of a security, this economic model increasingly no longer corresponded to the facts. Consequently, severe strains were put upon the market mechanism. The growth of institutional trading was phenomenal. As a percentage of total volume on the Big Board itself, it increased from 25.4% in March, 1956 to 33.8% in September, 1961 to 39.3% in March, 1965 to 42.9% in October, 1966 [38] to over 50% in September, 1968.[39] Concomitantly with this increase in the relative importance of institutional trading, there was a corresponding increase in the number of transactions involving large blocks of stock. The number of trades on the Exchange involving 10,000 shares or more increased from 2,171 in 1965 to 6,685 in 1967 [40] to 15,132 in 1969 and 11,597 in the first three quarters of 1970.[41] Such block transactions increased from 2.1% of total dollar volume in the fourth quarter of 1964 to 14.8% in the third quarter of 1970; and in absolute terms from $298,000,000 to $3,288,000,000 in those respective quarters.[42] The growth in large block activity reached an all-time high in 1985; there were 539,039 large block transactions constituting 51.7% of NYSE reported volume.[43]

35. Securities Exchange Act Release No. 8239, p. 4, n. 2 (SEC Jan. 26, 1968).

36. Ibid.

37. The minimum capital requirements of specialists have been successively raised from 4 trading units of each common stock in which he is registered as a specialist to 12 trading units (March 1, 1966) to 20 trading units (April 3, 1967) to 50 trading units (June 1, 1971). Even so, these minimum requirements are not very impressive in terms of a 20,000 share or 30,000 share block (200 or 300 trading units).

38. Securities Exchange Act Release No. 8239, p. 2 (SEC Jan. 26, 1968).

39. Wall Street Journal, Sept. 12, 1968, 12:3.

40. See Note 38, supra.

41. 4 Institutional Investor Study Report 1546 (SEC 1971), H.R.Doc.No.92–64, Part 4, p. 1546, 92d Cong., 1st Sess.

42. Id. at 1541.

43. NYSE Fact Book 12, 71 (1986).

The result of this development was that alternative techniques had to be devised in order to handle the volume of these types of transactions, with which the classic market mechanism could not cope. The capitalization of the specialist firms on the Exchange, even though the required minimum capital was increased several times,[43] was inadequate to withstand these demands. Such block transactions were of course impossible to execute immediately in the auction market,[44] since it is unlikely that there will be buyers already in the crowd to bid for 15,000 or 25,000 shares of a particular stock.

The Exchange developed certain techniques in an attempt to facilitate the handling of such orders on the floor of the Exchange. A Special Offer or Special Bid may be made, pursuant to which the seller or buyer may offer an extra commission to brokers who find the other side of the market.[45] Such Special Offer or Special Bid must remain open for a minimum period of fifteen minutes. Also, a so-called Exchange Distribution or Exchange Acquisition may be made, which is somewhat similar to an underwritten public offering, although the transactions are effected on the floor of the Exchange rather than in the over-the-counter market.[46] In these transactions, other member firms are solicited to form what is in effect an underwriting syndicate. The person initiating the transaction may pay them a special commission and they in turn may pay extra compensation to their registered representatives to place the shares being sold or to find the shares which are desired to be purchased.

However, these techniques were insufficient to solve the problem and as a result many or most of such block transactions were in fact conducted as negotiated sales or purchases, which were merely recorded on the floor of the Exchange, but were not in fact a part of the auction market process. In these negotiated trades, the other side of the market typically will be found from one or more of four types of investors.[47] The specialist may be willing to take some or all of the stock offered or supply some or all of the stock bid for. Other member firms of the New York Stock Exchange ("positioners") may take a position by purchasing or supplying some or all of the stock, including the member firm which has the order to execute and which would then deal with its customer as a principal. Another institution may be found which is interested in the other side of the market and which is willing to purchase or sell the quantity of stock involved. Or a broker-dealer who is not a member of the New York Stock Exchange but who engages in trading as a principal in New York Stock Exchange listed securities (a so-called "market maker") may buy or sell some or all of the stock involved in the transaction. Frequently, more than one of these types of investors are involved on the other side of the block transaction,[48] as illustrated by the discussion in the SEC Staff Study on New York Stock Exchange Rule 394 (Sept. 14, 1965).

Where the last two types of investors are involved in such a block transaction, the prohibitions of former Rule 394 (later renumbered Rule 390) came into play. The New York Stock Exchange member which had a sell order to execute for his customer could not go directly to another institution and sell the

---

43. See Note 37, supra.

44. The SEC has in fact defined a block transaction as one "in which a member firm * * * reasonably concludes that it is in the interest of the customer to search and negotiate for a matching interest on the other side of the market * * * rather than to accept or submit a bid or offer in the ordinary course of the auction market." SEC Sec.Exch.Act Rel.No.8791, p. 4 (Dec. 31, 1969).

45. 2 NYSE Guide (CCH) ¶ 2391 (Rule 391).

46. Id. at ¶ 2392 (Rule 392).

47. See 4 Institutional Investor Study Report 1587–1614 (SEC 1971, H.R.Doc.No. 92–64, Part 4, pp. 1587–1614, 92nd Cong., 1st Sess.

48. Id. at 1589–1590.

stock in a negotiated trade off the floor of the Exchange. Nor could such a member prior to November 7, 1966, go directly to a market maker and execute such a transaction off the floor of the Exchange, except with respect to a so-called "exempt list" of preferred and guaranteed stocks or in certain other narrowly defined circumstances.[49] On that date an amendment to the Exchange's former Rule 394 was put in effect which permitted a member under certain broadened circumstances to effect a transaction with an off-floor market maker in any listed stock. The member had to first make a diligent effort to explore the feasibility of obtaining a satisfactory execution of the order on the floor of the Exchange and report the facts concerning the proposed transaction to a Floor Governor. Also the member had to ask other members in the crowd whether they had orders to execute at the same price and on the same side of the market, and the bid or offer of the non-member market maker might be displaced in whole or in part by such orders, or by bids or offers on the specialist's book, or by the specialist himself if he advised the member attempting to execute the transaction off the board of the extent of his interest at an indicated price or prices prior to the solicitation of the non-member market maker. These provisions were criticized as inadequate at the time they were issued by persons active in the third market,[50] and apparently were not used very extensively.[51]

The fact that the member firm was prohibited from dealing off-board with another institution or with a market maker does not mean that these investors could not be brought into such a block transaction, which they frequently were. What it did mean was that the member firm had to execute the transaction as a "cross" on the floor of the Exchange and charge two commissions, one to his original customer and the other to the non-member who was assuming all or a part of the other side of the transaction. The inevitable consequence was that the non-member asked more for, or offered less for, the stock which he was selling or buying, by the amount of the commission which he was required to pay; so that the economic burden of the two commissions clearly fell on the original customer of the member firm. The process, however, did provide protection for public limit orders on the specialist's book which were given priority, parity and precedence in execution of the block trade.

Finally, in the Committee Reports on the 1975 Amendments to the Securities Exchange Act, Congress singled out former Rule 394 for some of its harshest criticism and specifically directed the Commission to make a report on its "anti-competitive" aspects by September, 1975. There followed the predictable action of the SEC in abrogating former Rule 394 with respect to agency transactions as of March 31, 1976 by the adoption of Rule 19c–1.[52] Securities Exchange Act Release No. 11942 (Dec. 19, 1975).

The Specialist System. The specialist system has been the heart of the exchange markets as previously conducted. It was designed to solve two

---

49. Rule 394. As noted above, this rule was relaxed to some extent in 1966. Prior to that time, trading by members in listed securities off the floor was generally prohibited without the permission of a Floor Governor, except with respect to an "exempt list" of preferred and guaranteed stocks. See Wall Street Journal, March 3, 1965, p. 8, col. 2; July 11, 1966, 32:1.

50. Wall Street Journal, Oct. 18, 1966, p. 18, col. 2.

51. Wall Street Journal, Feb. 14, 1967, p. 2, col. 3 ("SEC Checking Light Use of Big Board Rule Letting Members Trade with Non-Members"). This article stated that it had been estimated that only about 50 third-market trades had been executed under the new rule in the first 67 trading sessions after it went into effect. In contrast, the exchange had been averaging about 20 trades *per day* of 10,000 or more shares on the floor.

52. Securities Exchange Release No. 11942 (Dec. 19, 1975). Rule 390 was amended to conform to SEC Rule 19c–1. 2 CCH NYSE Guide ¶ 2390.

problems of the auction market: to provide a mechanism for handling "away from the market" orders, and to provide continuity and liquidity in the market and reduce random price fluctuations.

If a customer gives a brokerage firm an order to sell whenever the price reaches $32, at a time when the price is currently at $30, the broker obviously cannot wait at the "post" for that particular stock until the price reaches the designated level, since it may wait forever. Therefore, it gives the order to the "specialist" (who remains permanently at one "post") as a sub-broker to execute for it if and when the order can be executed at the specified price.

Also, if there are nothing but limit orders in the hands of brokers, and the highest bid price is $49 and the lowest asked price is $50, the market would come to a temporary stand-still until a bid and offer met, and this would be true even if the difference were only $1/8$th of a point. More importantly, if the above situation prevailed and a broker came into the crowd with an order to sell "at market", it would have to accept $49; however, if five minutes later a broker came into the crowd with an order to buy "at market", it would have to pay $50. Therefore, in the case of a relatively inactive stock the price could gyrate back and forth in this manner without any change whatever in the underlying supply and demand situation, unless there is someone present who is willing both to buy and to sell at narrower spreads. The specialist firm is supposed to fulfill this function. It might, for example, purchase for its own account in the first transaction for $49\frac{1}{2}$ and sell in the second transaction at $49\frac{5}{8}$. It will have made $1/8$th point on the "turn", but both the seller and the buyer will have benefitted.

The limit orders which are given to the specialist are entered in its "book", so that it and it alone knows what the buying interest is below the current market and what the selling interest is above the current market. It is this unique access to information plus the combination of the functions of broker and dealer which have caused the debate about the specialist system over the years. For a fuller description of the specialist system, see Report on the Feasibility and Advisability of the Complete Segregation of the Functions of Dealer and Broker (SEC 1936).

When the Securities Exchange Act of 1934 was debated in Congress, early drafts of that act would have abolished the specialist system by prohibiting the combination of the functions of broker and dealer.[53] As it was finally passed, however, that act merely instructed the SEC to make a study of the "feasibility and advisability" of a complete segregation of such functions,[54] and the Report of the SEC in 1936 referred to above was the result of that Congressional direction. The Report concluded that "The Commission is of the opinion that it is not advisable for the Congress at this time to enact legislation requiring the complete segregation of the functions of dealer and broker."[55]

Thereafter, the question was relatively quiescent for a period of about 24 years until the activities of a firm of specialists on the American Stock Exchange touched off an investigation of the affairs of that Exchange by the SEC and a shake-up in its governing bodies. See Re, Re & Sagarese, Sec.Exch. Act Rel.No.6264 (1960); Re, Re & Sagarese, Sec.Exch.Act Rel.No.6551 (1961); Staff Report on Organization, Management, and Regulation of Conduct of Members of the American Stock Exchange (SEC 1962). This investigation in

---

53. Report of Special Study of the Securities Markets, H.Doc.No.95, 88th Cong., 1st Sess., Pt. 2, pp. 48–50 (1963).

54. Securities Exchange Act, § 11(e).

55. Report on the Feasibility and Advisability of the Complete Segregation of the Functions of Dealer and Broker, p. 109 (SEC 1936).

turn broadened into the general investigation of the securities markets which resulted in the Report of Special Study of the Securities Markets (1963).

The Staff Report mentioned above was severely critical of a number of activities of specialists on the American Stock Exchange (such as their relationships with corporate insiders of the corporations in whose stock they specialized, participation in illegal distributions, financing arrangements, disclosure of the specialist's book in secondary distributions, etc.). The Report concluded that "Specialists are at the heart of the problems of organization, management and disciplinary procedures of the [American Stock] Exchange. Their dominance of the administration of the Exchange, their overriding concern for expansion of business through new listings, the misuse of their fundamental role in the operation of a fair and orderly auction market, and the breakdown of regulatory and disciplinary controls over them—all are part of a complex pattern of interlocking causes and effects." [56]

While this investigation was going on, there was considerable speculation that some fundamental change in the specialist system might be recommended by the SEC as a result of the Special Study.[57] However, a number of changes were subsequently made in the rules and organization of the American Stock Exchange and the Special Study failed to find evidence of similar widespread abuses on the New York Stock Exchange.[58] Its basic conclusion, which was quoted and adopted by the Commission in Securities Exchange Act Release No. 7432,[59] was that the system "appears to be an essential mechanism for maintaining continuous auction markets and in broad terms appears to be serving its purposes satisfactorily." [60]

It would be impossible to dispute the conclusion of the Special Study that both of the functions of the specialist (that of a dealer ready to buy and sell for his own account in order to narrow the spreads between bid and asked prices and to maintain continuity in the market, and that of a broker remaining at one post to execute "away from the market" orders) are "[two] essential mechanism[s] for maintaining continuous auction markets." However, the Special Study hardly reconsidered the old arguments over whether these two functions should be separated, just as the Commission itself has heretofore been unwilling to face the prospect of attempting to force such a fundamental change in their methods of doing business upon the exchanges. But the "basic dilemma" has always been "whether the specialist's contribution to an 'orderly' market outweighs in importance the fact that he may possess 'unfair' advantages for profiting as a dealer." [61] A new Rule 11b–1 of the SEC adopted in 1964[62] and the revision of the exchange rules pursuant thereto attempted to minimize this conflict as much as possible. They might be paraphrased as telling the specialist: "Don't participate in the market too little; but, on the other hand, don't participate in the market too much." [63]

56. Staff Report on Organization, Management, and Regulation of Conduct of Members of the American Stock Exchange, p. 39 (SEC 1962).

57. See New York Times, April 29, 1961, 26:5; Wall Street Journal (Pac.Coast Ed.), May 16, 1961, 3:1; July 11, 1961, 1:1; Sept. 25, 1961, 1:1; Ralph and Estelle James, Disputed Role of the Stock Exchange Specialist, 40 Harv.Bus.Rev. 133 (May-June, 1962).

58. Report of Special Study of the Securities Markets, H.Doc.No.95, 88th Cong., 1st Sess., Pt. 2, p. 161 (1963); "The Special Study's examination of the NYSE special-

ist system has disclosed no widespread abuses or patterns of illegality."

59. SEC, Sept. 24, 1964.

60. Report of Special Study of the Securities Markets, supra note 56, at p. 167.

61. 2 Loss, Securities Regulation 1204 (2d ed. 1961); Poser, Restructuring the Stock Markets: A Critical Look at the SEC's National Market System, 56 N.Y.U.L.Rev. 883, 951-57 (1981).

62. Securities Exchange Act Release No. 7432 (SEC Sept. 24, 1964).

63. For descriptions of the specialist system, see Report on the Feasibility and

Off-Board Trading Restrictions. One of the most bitterly fought battles in connection with the movement towards a national securities market has been over the question of whether all remaining restrictions on the ability of NYSE member firms to execute transactions off the board should be removed. As indicated above, almost immediately after the enactment of the Securities Acts Amendments of 1975, the Commission adopted Rule 19b–1 [64] which eliminated such restrictions with respect to all agency transactions, other than transactions where the member firm is acting as agent for both the buyer and the seller. This rule permits any NYSE member to deal directly in the over-the-counter market with any market maker or any nonmember broker-dealer acting as agent for his customer, so long as the NYSE member is not acting as principal for its own account. (The *Multiple Trading Case* [65] had very early invalidated an attempt by the NYSE to prohibit its members from trading NYSE listed securities on the regional exchanges of which they were also members.) The release which adopted Rule 19b–1 indicated rather clearly that the Commission also intended to abolish the off-board trading restrictions with respect to principal transactions by member firms in the near future.

Two concerns have delayed, however, apparently indefinitely, the adoption by the Commission of any rule lifting all of the off-board trading restrictions. The most important of these concerns is the fear of what is called "internalization." The Commission has defined this term as meaning "the withholding of retail orders from other market centers for the purpose of executing them 'in-house' as principal, without exposing those orders to buying and selling interests in those other market centers [or any market center]." [66] It also encompasses what are known as "in-house crosses", where the broker-dealer acts as agent for both the seller and the buyer and simply matches orders received by the same firm from retail customers on opposite sides of the market. Both of these things are presently prohibited by the stock exchange rules and were excluded from the lifting of the restrictions on off-board trading at the time of the adoption of Rule 19b–1. The fear is that the large, nationwide wire houses, if permitted to trade in this fashion, would withdraw a large quantity of the retail trading in securities from the exchanges (and the other markets) and would, in effect, create their own in-house stock exchanges, thus leading to a much greater fragmentation of the market.

The other concern is with what is referred to as "overreaching" on the part of a broker-dealer which is thus permitted to internalize its operations. Obviously, where the broker-dealer is dealing with his customers as principal or is acting as agent for both the seller and the buyer, there is much greater opportunity for actions which are detrimental to the customer. The Commission has said that this term "refers to the possibility that broker-dealer firms may take advantage of their customers by executing retail transactions as principal at prices less favorable to those customers than could have been obtained had those firms acted as agent [for only one side of the transaction]." [67]

Despite these concerns, the Commission proposed in 1977 to abolish all of the restrictions on off-board trading by member firms under a proposed Rule 19b–2 [68] and at the same time proposed a series of rules regarding the conduct

---

Advisability of the Complete Segregation of the Functions of Dealer and Broker (SEC 1936); Staff Report on Organization, Management, and Regulation of Conduct of Members of the American Stock Exchange (SEC 1962).

64. Sec.Exch.Act Rel. No. 11942, Dec. 19, 1975.

65. In re Rules of the New York Stock Exchange, 10 S.E.C. 270 (1941).

66. Sec.Exch.Act Rel. No. 16888, note 31, June 11, 1980; Fed.Sec.L.Rptr. (CCH) ¶ 82,608 (1980).

67. Id. at note 33.

68. Sec.Exch. Act Rel. No. 13662, June 23, 1977.

of such trading to deal with the problem of "overreaching." [69] However, the Commission abandoned this proposal and withdrew proposed Rule 19b-2 on June 11, 1980.[70] At that time, the Commission announced that it had no intention of reviving this across-the-board abolition of such restrictions in the "near future." Instead, the Commission adopted Rule 19b-3 [71] which removes such restrictions only with respect to securities which were listed for the first time after April 26, 1979 (the date of the original announcement of the proposed new rule). The Commission indicated that this action was an experiment, permitting off-board principal trading in this limited number of securities in order to attempt to determine whether the deleterious effects which were asserted to be likely as a result of such action did, in fact, develop. The securities which have thus been freed from all off-board trading restrictions are generally referred to as "Rule 19b-3 securities."

Institutional Membership. The debate over institutional membership on the stock exchanges has largely died out in recent years following the abolition of "give-ups" and fixed rates of commissions on the exchanges, since the principal reasons that institutions desired such memberships were to receive give-ups or to be able (as a practical matter) to negotiate their commission rates. The Congress in any event made the issue moot in the Securities Acts Amendments of 1975, unless the Commission acts to provide otherwise by rule, by amending Section 11(a) of the 1934 Act to prohibit any member of a national securities exchange from effecting any transaction on the exchange "for its own account, the account of an associated person, or an account with respect to which it or an associated person thereof exercises investment discretion," after February 1, 1979.[72] This means, for example, that the investment adviser to a mutual fund, even if it could obtain or already has a membership on the NYSE, cannot execute transactions for its affiliated mutual fund. While the Commission is given authority by that section to exempt any transactions from this prohibition, the Commission by the adoption of temporary Rule 11a2-2(T) has required that such transactions be executed through another member firm by the member firm which is the affiliate of the mutual fund.

At the time the structure of the national market system was being considered by the SEC and the Congress, a proposal was advanced under the sponsorship of the New York Stock Exchange.[73] The concept was to "create a national market system essentially by modifying the existing 'primary' markets, particularly the NYSE, so that substantially all orders would interact

---

69. Alternative proposed Rules 15c5-1[A], 15c5-1[B], 15c5-1[C] and 15c5-1[D], Ibid.

70. Sec.Exch. Act Rel. No. 16889, June 11, 1980, CCH Fed.Sec. Law Rptr. ¶ 82,609 (1980).

71. Sec.Exch. Act Rel. No. 16888, June 11, 1980, Fed.Sec. Law Rptr. (CCH) ¶ 82,608 (1980).

72. This date was originally May 1, 1978, but was postponed to February 1, 1979, by an amendment to the statute in 1978. P.L. No. 95-283, 95th Cong., 2d Sess., § 18, 92 Stat. 249 (May 21, 1978).

73. This proposal was based upon a report of W.M. Martin, Jr., The Securities Markets, A Report With Recommendations, Submitted to the Board of Governors of the New York Stock Exchange (Aug. 5, 1971). Mr. Martin was a former Chairman of the NYSE and the Federal Reserve Board. The report called for a creation of a national system of stock exchanges with the NYSE at the center; recommended that financial institutions be barred from access to such system; and asked for exemption of the system from the antitrust laws.

A group of 19 prominent economists led by James H. Lorie of the University of Chicago, as well as the United States Department of Justice, urged Congress to reject the Martin Report. Wall St. J. Dec. 28, 1971, p. 41, col. 3; Statement of James H. Lorie before the Securities and Exchange Commission, Nov. 23, 1971; J. Lorie, Public Policy for American Capital Markets, prepared for submission to the Secretary and Deputy Secretary of the Treasury, Feb. 7, 1974; Statement of the United States Department of Justice, SEC, Hearings on the Structure, Operation and Regulation of the Securities Markets, File No. 4-147, Dec. 1, 1971.

through the mechanisms of, or on the floor of, the 'primary' market and all qualified broker-dealers, perhaps together with certain other organizations, would have access to that market on a non-discriminatory basis." [74] The Commission did not pursue this alternative because it regarded it to be "inconsistent with the concept of the national market system contemplated by Congress in the 1975 Amendments." [75]

In summary, the following seems to have been accomplished in the twelve years since the enactment of the Securities Acts Amendments of 1975 in the way of restructuring the securities markets: (1) The design and installation of the consolidated tape and the consolidated quotation reporting system; (2) the "linkage" of all of the principal exchange markets, although the "universal order routing switch" which the Commission has talked about, whereby a broker-dealer could direct an order to any of the exchange markets from a computer terminal in his office, apparently has been abandoned; (3) a relatively modest elimination of the off-board trading restrictions so far as principal transactions are concerned with respect to a limited number of securities; and (4) a "linkage" of the NASDAQ system and ITS with respect to a limited number of securities. The efforts to achieve linkage are described supra at page 15.

Some observers assert that "the basic national market system is in place and functioning efficiently in the best interests of the investing public." [76] Other critics claim that the efforts to link the stock markets in a national market system will not achieve meaningful competition between the specialists in the primary exchange markets and third market makers and is not likely to "provide the markets with substantial additional liquidity as trading volume continues to increase and financial institutions account for an even greater share of the volume." In short, they assert that the Commission is ill-equipped to provide the leadership in restructuring the securities markets. [77] A more optimistic view is that considerable progress has been made toward facilitating a national market system, but recommends that the SEC introduce further measures to enhance direct competition between specialists and third market makers. [78]

The Congress has been constantly prodding the Commission to make faster progress toward Congress' goal, [79] even though it does not know what that goal is, and the Commission has consistently defended its record on the basis that an "evolutionary" approach to any restructuring of the markets is essential in order to avoid undue disruption. For the present status of the "National

74. Sec.Exch.Act Rel.No. 14416, Jan. 26, 1978, [1978 Transfer Binder] Fed.Sec.L.Rep. (CCH) ¶ 81,502, at page 80,038.

75. Id.

76. Calvin, The National Market System: A Successful Adventure in Industry Self-Improvement, 70 Va.L.Rev. 785, 787 (1984).

77. Poser, Restructuring the Stock Markets: A Critical Look at the SEC's National Market System, 56 N.Y.U.L.Rev. 883, 951–58 (1981); Werner, The SEC as a Market Regulator, 70 Va.L.Rev. 755 (1984); Werner, Adventure in Social Control of Finance: The National Market System for Securities, 75 Colum.L.Rev. 1233 (1975).

78. Seligman, The Future of the National Market System, 10 J.Corp.L. 79, 133–39 (1984).

79. See, e.g., Report on Oversight of the Functioning and Administration of the Securities Acts Amendments of 1975, Subcommittee on Oversight and Investigations and Subcommittee on Consumer Protection and Finance, House Committee on Interstate and Foreign Commerce, Comm.Print 95–27, 95th Cong., 1st Sess. (1977); National Market System: Five-Year Status Report, Committee on Oversight and Investigations, House Committee on Interstate and Foreign Commerce, Comm.Print 96–IFC 56, 96th Cong., 2d Sess. (1980); Improvements Needed in the Securities and Exchange Commission's Efforts to Establish a National Market System, Report to Congress by the Comptroller General of the United States (FGMSD–79–59, Sept. 19, 1979).

Market System," see the note on "The Development of a National Market System", supra at page 12.

For discussions of the problems considered above, see Poser, Restructuring The Stock Markets: A Critical Look at the SEC'S National Market System, 56 N.Y.U.L.Rev. 883 (1981); Cohen, The National Market System—A Modest Proposal, 46 Geo.Wash.L.Rev. 743 (1978); Werner, Adventure in Social Control of Finance: The National Market System, 75 Colum.L.Rev. 1233 (1975); Calvin, The National Market System: A Successful Adventure in Industry Self-Improvement, 70 Va.L.Rev. 785 (1984); Werner, The SEC as a Market Regulator, 70 Va.L.Rev. 755 (1984); Seligman, The Future of the National Market System, 10 J.Corp.L. 79 (1984); Symposium, Revolution in Securities Regulation, 29 Bus. Law. (Special Issue), March, 1974; Folk, Restructuring the Securities Markets— The Martin Report: A Critique, 57 Va.L.Rev. 1315 (1971); Weeden, Competition—Key to Market Structure: A Third Market View of the Martin Report, 110 Tr. & Est. 937 (1971); Baxter, New York Stock Exchange Fixed Commission Rates: A Private Cartel Goes Public, 22 Stan.L.Rev. 675 (1970); Ginsburg, Antitrust and Stock Exchange Minimum Commissions: A Jurisdictional Analysis, 24 U.Miami L.Rev. 732 (1970); McLaren, Antitrust and the Securities Industry, 11 B.C.Ind. & Com.L.Rev. 187 (1970); Wolff, Comparative Federal Regulation of the Commodities Exchanges and the National Securities Exchanges, 38 Geo.Wash.L.Rev. 223 (1969); Crossland and Sehr, Gods of the Marketplace: An Examination of the Regulation of the Securities Business, 48 B.U.L.Rev. 515 (1968); Bicks, Antitrust and the New York Stock Exchange, 21 Bus.Law. 129 (1965); Jennings, The New York Stock Exchange and the Commission Rate Struggle, 53 Calif.L.Rev. 1119 (1965).

For discussion of the questions raised by public ownership of member firms, see Monaghan, Taking a New York Stock Exchange Member Firm Public, 26 Bus.Law. 667 (1971); Note, Public Ownership of Stock Exchange Firms: Antitrust and Other Problems, 70 Colum.L.Rev. 102 (1970).

For discussion of the specialist system and the third market, see Wolfson and Russo, Stock Exchange Specialist: An Economic and Legal Analysis, 1970 Duke L.J. 707; Fiske, Can the Specialist System Cope with the Age of Block Trading?, 1970 Sec.L.Rev. 599.

MERRITT, VICKERS, INC. v. SECURITIES AND EXCHANGE COMMISSION

United States Court of Appeals, Second Circuit, 1965.
353 F.2d 293.

MOORE, CIRCUIT JUDGE: In 1962, the National Association of Security Dealers' (NASD) District Business Conduct Committee of District No. 12 found that Merritt, Vickers, Inc., a registered broker-dealer, had executed 120 retail sales of securities as principal between February 8, 1960, and October 10, 1960, at unfair prices not reasonably related to current market prices in violation of Sections 1 and 4 of Art. III of the NASD Rules of Fair Procedure, as interpreted by its mark-up policy.[3] The prices computed by

---

3. § 4 of Article III of the NASD Rules of Fair Practice provides in relevant part that "In 'over-the-counter' transactions, whether in 'listed' or 'unlisted' securities, if a member buys for his own account from his customer, or sells for his own account to his customer, he shall buy or sell at a price which is fair, taking into consideration all relevant circumstances, including market conditions with respect to such security at the time of the transaction, the

the NASD ranged from 10.5% to 125% over prevailing market prices. In 47 of the transactions, the mark-ups were computed on the basis of the price paid by Merritt, Vickers, Inc. in same-day purchases and averaged 40.5%. The mark-ups in the remaining 73 transactions, which were effected on days when Merritt, Vickers, Inc. did not make any purchases of the securities sold, were computed on the basis of ask quotations published in the quotation sheets of the National Daily Quotations Bureau (sheets), which the NASD considered representative of the market price. The mark-ups in these transactions ranged from 12.5% to 113% and averaged 30.1%. In addition, the NASD found that Merritt, Vickers, Inc. (a) violated Section 1 of Article III by improperly extending credit in 72 transactions effected between July 10, 1959, and August 11, 1960, in violation of Regulation T of the Board of Governors of the Federal Reserve System;[4] (b) violated Sections 1 and 21 of Article III by failing to maintain its books and records in conformity with SEC requirements set forth in 17 C.F.R. § 240.17a–3 and (c) violated Sections 1 and 12 by failing to disclose to customers on two occasions where it acted as agent for both the sellers and buyers of the same securities its dual agency role and the double commission it received.

The NASD expelled Merritt, Vickers, Inc. from membership, found that Merritt and Vickers as officers were responsible for the above violations, and revoked their registration as registered representatives of Merritt, Vickers, Inc. These findings and penalties were upheld by the Board of Governors of the NASD after a hearing.

Pursuant to Section 15A(g) of the Securities Exchange Act of 1934 (the Act), Merritt, Vickers, Inc. and Merritt and Vickers applied to the SEC for review of the NASD action and in their application requested permission to adduce before the SEC additional evidence, consisting of books and records of other broker-dealers showing prices charged by such broker-dealers for securities which allegedly Merritt, Vickers, Inc. had over-priced. The request was denied on the ground that they had failed to comply with 17 C.F.R. § 240.15ag–1(e), which permits introduction of additional evidence upon a showing that it is material and that there were reasonable grounds for failure to adduce such evidence in hearings before the NASD. On review, Merritt, Vickers, Inc. challenged the NASD mark-up computations, alleging (1) that reliance by the NASD on a member's costs resulted in equating mark-ups to profits on the transactions contrary to an NASD regulation stating that the amount of profit attributable to market appreciation should not ordinarily enter into a determination of a mark-up's fairness, and (2) that ask quotations were not a proper basis for computing mark-ups. The SEC concluded that it was proper for the NASD to utilize a

---

expense involved, and the fact that he is entitled to a profit * * *"

A mark-up of 5% or less over the current market is considered fair. The history and rationale of the 5% policy is set forth in NASD Manual, G–1 to G–6. See also National Association of Security Dealers, Inc., 17 S.E.C. 459 (1944) wherein the SEC appraises the policy.

4. § 4(c)(2) of Regulation T of the Board of Governors of the Federal Reserve System provides that:

"In case a customer purchases a security (other than an exempted security) in the special cash account and does not make full cash payment for the security within 7 days after the date on which the security is so purchased, the creditor shall, except as provided in the succeeding subdivisions of the section 4(c), promptly cancel or otherwise liquidate the transaction or the unsettled portion thereof."

member's contemporaneous cost to compute mark-ups in retail transactions; that, in the absence of such data, reliance could be placed on quotations in the sheets as reflective of current market price; and, that the NASD did not unfairly select quotations used in its computations. In addition, it sustained the findings of additional violations of NASD rules. With respect to the failure to comply with SEC records requirements, Merritt, Vickers, Inc. conceded that it failed to post its general ledger from June 1st to September 14th, 1960, but denied the existence of any other deficiencies. However, the SEC, crediting the uncontradicted testimony of the NASD examiner, found that Merritt, Vickers, Inc. had failed to record or identify as such cancellations of various customers' transactions; had failed to post its security position record; and had failed to keep adequate monthly trial balances. With respect to Regulation T, the SEC noted that the record showed that Merritt, Vickers, Inc. had not received payment in 62 transactions and had not cancelled accounts in 10 transactions within the seven-day period permitted. Additionally, although acknowledging that the customers involved in the dual agency transactions may have had actual knowledge of Merritt, Vickers, Inc.'s role and the double commissions, the SEC pointed out that Section 12 of Article III of the NASD rules requires that notice appear in the written confirmation of each transaction and that the documents in evidence contained no such written disclosure. Finally, the SEC concluded that the penalties imposed on Merritt, Vickers, Inc. and on Merritt and Vickers were not excessive in view of the numerous violations committed by the broker-dealer and the experience of Merritt and Vickers in the securities business.

Merritt, Vickers, Inc. and Merritt and Vickers (petitioners) seek review of the SEC order pursuant to Section 25(a) of the Act and urge at the outset that it was improper to rely on the ask quotations in the sheets in computing mark-ups. Generally, the petitioners allege that sheet quotations are not representative of current market prices since they do not constitute unconditional offers to buy or sell securities at the indicated price and, thus, fail to reflect changes in the market between the time the quotes are supplied and the transactions occur. In addition, it is claimed that the NASD should not be permitted to rely on sheet quotations in assessing the fairness of mark-ups unless it assumes the burden of showing that no special circumstances justified the mark-ups. This court is in agreement with the SEC that, although the quotations in the sheets are not firm offers for a fixed number of securities, and final prices are subject to change, they constitute sufficient proof of prevailing market prices "in the absence of evidence to the contrary." Charles Hughes & Co. v. SEC, 139 F.2d 434, 438 (2d Cir. 1943), cert. denied, 321 U.S. 786 (1944); see Weber v. SEC, 222 F.2d 822 (2d Cir. 1955); General Investing Corp., Securities Exchange Act Release No. 7316 (May 15, 1964); Midland Securities, Inc., 40 S.E.C. 333, 337 (1960); Managed Investment Programs, 37 S.E.C. 783, 786–87 (1957); Mitchell Securities Inc., 37 S.E.C. 178, 182 (1956); II Loss, Securities Regulation, at 1280 & n. 9 (1961 ed.). Thus, quotations in the sheets are treated as prima facie evidence of current market prices and the burden is on the broker-dealer to come forward with evidence of special circumstances to justify excessive mark-ups. The quotations relied on by the SEC and NASD here were supplied by dealers on the same day that Merritt, Vickers, Inc.'s transactions occurred and no attempt was made to adduce evidence in the NASD hearings to show that the dealer's quotations were not bona fide or were in fact at variance with prevailing prices.

The first indication that petitioners desired to present evidence to challenge the reliability of the quotations was in their application for review before the SEC. Petitioners contend that the SEC's refusal to receive the evidence was arbitrary and that this court should order the SEC to take additional evidence on the computation issue. The request is denied since we find that the SEC action was justified and did not constitute an abuse of discretion.

The SEC is authorized to grant leave to adduce additional evidence where it is shown that the evidence is material and reasonable grounds exist for failure to present the evidence at hearings before the NASD. Rule 15ag–1(e). The considerations underlying this rule were set forth by the SEC in Herrick, Waddell & Co., 23 S.E.C. 301 (1946), where it stated that it is generally desirable to present

"All evidence before the Association [NASD] at the original hearing prior to review before the Commission. The experience of our judicial system has demonstrated that, to the extent that review is limited to the record before the lower tribunal, there is more complete preparation by the parties, a clearer delineation of issues, and substantial simplification in the task of review. Moreover, fairness to the original tribunal requires that it be given the opportunity to consider all available evidence in making its decision."

Id. at 303. See Gerald M. Greenberg, 39 S.E.C. 601 (1959) and generally II Loss, Securities Regulation at 1374–80 (1961 ed.). Petitioners concede that they did not request production of broker-dealers' books and records or suggest that such evidence was material to their cause either before the NASD District Committee or the Board of Governors. However, it is asserted that such inaction was justifiable because a request would have been futile in view of the NASD's lack of power to subpoena documents. This is not persuasive. The SEC has held that the NASD's inability to subpoena documents does not itself justify the SEC's taking additional evidence or excuse a failure to attempt to produce all relevant evidence in proceedings before the NASD. See Richard A. Holman, 40 S.E.C. 870 (1961). While broker-dealers in general may be reluctant to voluntarily permit inspection of their books and records due to the possibility of provoking a NASD investigation or revealing confidential information to competitors, there is nothing in the record to demonstrate that process would have been required to obtain the desired information. Mere speculation cannot serve as an excuse for failure to produce relevant evidence before the NASD.

In sum, the SEC refusal to permit the introduction of the broker-dealer records was warranted in view of the petitioners' failure to alert the NASD to their existence or materiality. Due to the similarity in the standards governing the SEC and this court with respect to the propriety of permitting the introduction of additional evidence, we consider the reasons for upholding the SEC's rejection of petitioners' application equally persuasive reasons for denying their request for an order compelling the SEC to hear further evidence on the computation issue.

With respect to the other violations of NASD rules, we affirm the findings below on the strength of the SEC opinion which amply demonstrates that they are supported by substantial record evidence.

Petitioners' final contention is that the penalties imposed, i.e., expulsion of Merritt, Vickers, Inc. and revocation of Merritt's and Vickers' registration as registered representatives, were excessive and inconsistent with decisions imposing lesser sanctions for allegedly similar offenses. The question of whether NASD disciplinary action is excessive is determined by the SEC, pursuant to 15 U.S.C. § 78o–3(h), upon examination of the facts of each case with due regard to the public interest involved. Despite Merritt's and Vickers' allegations that they did not participate in Merritt, Vickers, Inc.'s business in a managerial capacity, and the fact that Merritt was engaged only part-time in the securities business, the SEC concluded that Merritt and Vickers were responsible for the numerous violations committed by Merritt, Vickers, Inc. and were experienced in the securities business. Merritt and Vickers were the principal stockholders (each owned between 40% to 45% of its stock) and officers of the member. Moreover, Merritt testified that both were active operating heads of the firm. Merritt's experience consisted of working as a salesman and trader for three years prior to the organization of Merritt, Vickers, Inc. in 1959, while Vickers had worked as a salesman and principal in other securities firms for nine years prior to 1959. In addition, the SEC noted that both were employed as salesmen for Vickers Bros., a firm entirely separate from Merritt, Vickers, Inc., in April, 1959, when the SEC revoked its broker-dealer registration. The substantial association of Merritt and Vickers with the securities business, coupled with their responsibility for the serious violations of NASD rules committed by Merritt, Vickers, Inc., led the SEC to reject the claim that the penalties were excessive. Moreover, contrary to petitioners' allegations, the penalties imposed were comparable to those imposed for similar violations. See Gerald M. Greenberg, 40 S.E.C. 133 (1960) (expulsion of member and representative for selling at unfair prices; unsuitable recommendations to customers; and violation of Regulation T); Midland Securities Inc., 40 S.E.C. 333 (1960) (expulsion of member and representative for selling at unfair prices and failing to maintain records). Upon the record, "we cannot say that the Commission exceeded its discretion in upholding the NASD's assessment." Nassau Securities Service v. SEC, 348 F.2d 133, 136 (2d Cir. 1965).

Affirmed.

SECURITIES EXCHANGE ACT RELEASE NO. 15807

Securities and Exchange Commission.
May 9, 1979.

PRACTICES IN FIXED PRICE OFFERINGS

* * *

* * * Pursuant to Section 19(b) of the Securities Exchange Act of 1934 ("Act"), the National Association of Securities Dealers, Inc. ("NASD") has filed a proposed rule change concerning the giving and receiving of selling concessions, discounts or other allowances in connection with fixed price offerings of securities. Notice of the proposed rule change was given by Commission release published in the Federal Register during August 1978.[1] The proposed rule change is briefly summarized below, and the full text of the proposed rule change is attached as an appendix to this release.

The purpose of this release is to solicit additional written submissions of data, views and arguments from interested persons concerning certain issues raised by the proposed rule change and to announce public hearings with respect to those issues. The Commission has received 43 comment letters on the proposed rule change, including 17 letters requesting that the Commission hold hearings. Because of the importance and complexity of these issues, the Commission considers it appropriate to hold public hearings to explore more fully the matters discussed in this release and other issues raised by the proposed rule change.   *   *   *

I. INTRODUCTION AND BACKGROUND

A. *Firm Commitment Fixed Price Offerings*

In order to establish the basic terminology used in this release, there follows a general description of the underwriting process in a typical firm commitment offering of corporate debt or equity securities, as well as a description of certain sales practices employed by broker-dealers in selling securities in fixed price offerings to institutional customers. In commenting on the issues raised in this release, interested persons should indicate when their analysis is based on circumstances that depart materially from the description provided below.

In a typical firm commitment offering of corporate securities, one or more investment banking firms organize an underwriting syndicate to purchase the securities from the issuer for resale at a specified public offering price established through negotiation with the issuer or competitive bidding. Each member of the syndicate executes an "agreement among underwriters" that designates one or more managing underwriters and fixes the obligations among the members of the syndicate. The syndicate members, through the managing underwriter, also enter into an underwriting agreement with the issuer that sets forth the terms and conditions of the offering and the amount of securities that each member is committed to underwrite.

Syndicate members are compensated for their services by receiving an underwriting discount, or "spread," which is the difference between the price paid to the issuer by the syndicate for the securities and the "initial public offering price" appearing on the cover page of the prospectus. Depending on a number of factors, including the characteristics of the security being distributed, the degree of underwriting risk, the amount of selling effort required and costs associated with the distribution of the securities, the underwriting discount for a particular offering may range from a fraction of 1% to 10% or more of the public offering price. The gross spread is composed of (i) the underwriting compensation, which includes a management fee for the lead underwriter(s), and (ii) the selling

---

1. Securities Exchange Act Release No. 15020 (August 2, 1978), 43 FR 35446 (1978). The issues associated with the proposed rule change are commonly identified by reference to a judicial decision, Papilsky v. Berndt [1976–1977 Transfer Binder] Fed. Sec.L.Rep. (CCH) ¶ 95,627 (S.D.N.Y.1976), discussed at text accompanying n. 18, infra. Accordingly, the complete NASD filing with the Commission containing the proposed rule change is referred to in this release as the "Papilsky filing."

concession. The relative size of these components is determined by the syndicate in light of the particular characteristics of the offering. The selling concession in recent years has grown as a percentage of the gross spread, apparently reflecting the increased importance of selling effort to a successful underwriting. To assist the syndicate in distributing the offering, the managing underwriter may select additional dealers to form a selling group. Members of the selling group (which may also include syndicate members) receive the selling concession for such securities as they actually sell and customarily enter into a "selected dealer agreement" setting forth their rights and obligations with respect to the offering.

In addition to the dealers selected by the managing underwriter to form the selling group, other dealers may be included in the selling group at the request of prospective purchasers seeking to place orders with, or designate orders for allocation to particular firms. "Designated orders" are usually orders for larger amounts of securities placed by institutions with the managing underwriter, with direction that the sale be credited to the account of one or more dealers that are syndicate or selling group members. A designated order is customarily confirmed, and the securities directly delivered, by the managing underwriter. A dealer designated to receive such credit on an order may be added to the selling group where that firm was not a member at the time the order was placed.

As described above, the amount of securities for which a syndicate member is responsible is fixed by agreement. Typically, however, each syndicate member retains control over and directly places only a portion of the securities it has agreed to underwrite, usually referred to as his "retention." The remainder is reserved and placed in a general syndicate account, usually referred to as the "pot," under the control of the managing underwriter. Securities in this account are then allocated and reallocated by the managing underwriter during the offering period among syndicate and selling group members for a variety of reasons, particularly the demonstrated capacity of those members to place the securities with investors. In addition to the public offering conducted directly by the members of the underwriting syndicate and the selling group, underwriting agreements often authorize these members to sell the securities being distributed to other dealers, at a specified discount (a percentage of the selling concession) referred to as the "reallowance," for resale to the public.

In connection with a particular fixed price offering, the underwriters may elect to "stabilize" the market for the offered security during the distribution period. To commence stabilizing, the managing underwriter places a syndicate bid in the primary market for the security to purchase securities offered at that bid price, usually set at or just under the public offering price. The purpose of stabilizing purchases is to facilitate an orderly distribution of the offered securities by preventing or retarding a decline in the market price for such securities during the offering.

The growth of institutional participation in the securities markets has exerted increasing pressure on the fixed price offering system. In connection with distributions, a number of practices have developed which may have the economic effect of granting to institutional and other large purchasers a rebate of some portion of the gross spread in fixed price offerings. Such practices include both direct discounting techniques, such as "overtrading" in swap transactions and certain types of underwriting fee recapture, and indirect compensation arrangements, such as the provision of goods and services in return for so-called "syndicate soft dollars."

In swap transactions, securities are taken in trade from a customer, in lieu of cash, in exchange for the offered securities. A discount from the fixed offering price may be granted to the purchaser of the offered securities where the syndicate member purchases the securities taken in trade at a price exceeding their market value. This "overtrade" is economically equivalent to paying less than the stated offering price for the securities being distributed.

A customer may seek to recapture underwriting fees by designating a broker-dealer affiliate to be included in the selling group. The customer may then purchase the offered security through its affiliate, thereby recapturing the selling concession. Such concession payments to an affiliate enable the customer to obtain direct discounts from the fixed offering price.

A broker-dealer providing research or other services to a customer may be compensated for those services, at least in part, through purchases by the customer in a fixed price offering. The customer can either purchase the securities directly through the broker-dealer or can contact the managing underwriter and "designate" the dealer to receive credit for the order. In these instances, the dealer is compensated indirectly by receiving "soft dollar" concessions for the research or other services it has provided.

B. *Background of the Proposed Rule Change*

Since the registration of the NASD in 1939 pursuant to the Maloney Act, the NASD has regulated, particularly under Article III, Section 24 of its Rules of Fair Practice, the circumstances in which concessions, discounts or other allowances may be given in fixed price offerings. Section 24, which until filing of the proposed rule change had not been the subject of revision during the 40 years of its existence, provides that:

> [s]elling concessions, discounts, or other allowances, as such, shall be allowed only as consideration for services rendered in distribution and in no event shall be allowed to anyone other than a broker or dealer actually engaged in the investment banking or securities business; provided, however, that nothing in this rule shall prevent any member from selling any security owned by him to any person at any net price which may be fixed by him unless prevented therefrom by agreement.

During this period, Section 24 has received little interpretive attention from the courts or the Commission. In 1941, the NASD imposed sanctions on several member firms that violated the terms of a fixed price underwriting agreement by selling debt securities of Public Service Company of Indiana during the distribution at prices below the public offering price. The NASD charged those members with a violation of Article III, Section 1 of its Rules of Fair Practice, which requires members to "observe high standards of commercial honor and just and equitable principles of trade." In reviewing those sanctions, the Commission held, in National Association of Securities Dealers, Inc. ("*PSI*"),[12] that Section 15A(b)(7) of the Act [15 U.S.C. 78o–3(b)(7)] [13] did not permit the NASD to use its disciplinary

---

12. 19 S.E.C 424 (1945).

13. This provision was amended in certain respects by the Securities Acts

Amendments of 1975   Pub.L.No.94–29 (1975), and was redesignated as Section 15A(b)(6) of the Act.

authority to enforce contracts "designed to restrict a free and open market, even though such contracts may under given conditions fall within an exception to the general public policy against restraints on commerce."[14] In *PSI*, the Commission rejected the NASD's argument that Section 24 supported its interpretation of Article III, Section 1, but noted that the meaning and validity of Section 24 were not directly at issue.[15]

The Commission, however, also expressly rejected any implication that, by invalidating the NASD's rule interpretation, it would similarly seek as a general matter to invalidate or otherwise question the private enforceability of customary underwriting agreements to make fixed price offerings. To the contrary, the Commission in *PSI* concluded:

> Thus, if in this case we were faced with the question whether we should or should not prohibit the use of the price-maintenance provisions in question, we would reach the same conclusion that we did with respect to stabilization, *i.e.*, that we should not prohibit such provisions. But the question here is whether the statute permits the NASD, by an interpretation of its rule of fair practice, to add to these familiar restraints and impediments a new form of compulsion—to the end that a member who breaks the price-maintenance agreement shall be subject not only to whatever legal and practical remedies the syndicate manager and members have at their disposal but also to a fine or possible suspension or even expulsion from the NASD.
>
> * * *
>
> We emphasize that all we are holding is that the NASD erroneously construed its rule as authorization for the disciplining of members for violating price-maintenance agreements. *We are not taking any action calculated to upset the use of such agreements, and we think the fears expressed by the NASD are without substance.* Price-maintenance agreements were in use prior to the creation of this Commission and long before the registration of the NASD. Our present conclusion subtracts nothing from any sanctions which might previously have been legally imposed to enforce these agreements. No showing is made that the use of the NASD as an added instrumentality for enforcing price-maintenance agreements is necessary to preserve the present system.

Neither the Commission nor the courts has been called upon to deal directly with the proper interpretation and general applicability of Section 24, until recently. A number of cases in the last few years have considered the recapture of commissions by investment companies in a variety of contexts. One of these cases, Papilsky v. Berndt ("*Papilsky*"),[18] dealt

---

14. 19 S.E.C at 444. The Commission's conclusion, in *dictum*, that agreements among underwriters to fix the price at which an offering is to be distributed do not generally violate the Sherman Act, 15 U.S.C. 1, was later judicially confirmed in U. S. v. Morgan, 118 F.Supp. 621 (S.D.N.Y. 1953).

15. 19 S.E.C. at 445–446.

18. [1976–1977 Transfer Binder] FED. SEC.L.REP. (CCH) ¶ 95,627 (S.D.N.Y.1976). The holding in *Papilsky* was that the adviser/underwriter of an investment company will be liable for unrecaptured commis-

sions or fees unless it establishes that it fully disclosed to the independent directors that recapture was a possible alternative to other uses of the commissions or fees, and those directors had decided as a matter of reasonable business judgment, not to seek recapture. See also Moses v. Burgin, 445 F.2d 369 (1st Cir.1971) cert. denied, 404 U.S. 994 (1971); Fogel v. Chestnutt, 533 F.2d 731 (2d Cir.1975), cert. denied, 429 U.S. 824 (1976); and Tannenbaum v. Zeller, 552 F.2d 402 (2d Cir. 1977), rev'g 399 F.Supp. 945 (S.D.N.Y.1975). In Moses v. Burgin, 316 F.Supp. 31, 47 (D.Mass.

directly with the recapture of underwriting discounts. In *Papilsky*, a shareholder derivative action was brought against an investment company and its adviser/underwriter for failure to seek such recapture. The court concluded that, in the absence of a contrary ruling from the Commission or the NASD, underwriting recapture was available and legal under Section 24.

As a result of the *Papilsky* decision, several requests were made to the NASD on behalf of investment advisers and investment companies for a ruling on the propriety of recapture under Section 24.[20] The NASD responded to these requests, in November and December 1976, by stating that, in its opinion, Section 24 prohibits underwriting recapture. The Commission, however, wrote to the NASD, in February 1977, stating that the NASD "interpretation" of Section 24 raised important issues of general applicability with regard to the public interest, the protection of investors and the appropriateness of burdens on competition, and that prior Commission decisions, including *PSI*, cast doubt on the NASD's authority to adopt a rule having the effect the NASD interpretation would give to Section 24. For those reasons, the Commission stated that the NASD interpretation should be filed as a proposed rule change. After a public meeting with the Commission on May 26, 1977, the NASD agreed to prepare and file the proposed rule change. In July 1978, the NASD made the Papilsky filing following circulation of two exposure drafts to its membership. Pursuant to Section 19(b) of the Act, the proposed rule change cannot become effective unless approved by the Commission after affirmatively finding that it is consistent with the requirements of the Act and Commission rules thereunder applicable to the NASD.

C. *Principal Provisions of the Proposed Rule Change*

The proposed rule change would amend the NASD's Rules of Fair Practice governing member practices in fixed price offerings. In particular, the proposed rule change would address underwriting recapture, designated orders and swap transactions through amendments to several NASD rules and interpretations.

1. *Article II, Section 1(m).*

The term "fixed price offering" would be defined to include any securities offering in the United States at a stated public offering price or prices. The definition would exclude offerings of municipal securities and other "exempted securities," as defined in Section 3(a)(12) of the Act, offerings of mutual fund securities and wholly foreign offerings.

1970), the District Court rejected, on the basis of Section 24, a cause of action relating to underwriting recapture similar to that advanced in *Papilsky*. That decision, however, was reversed on other grounds by the First Circuit.

20. In addition, a number of investment companies and their advisers applied to the Commission for certain exemptions from the Investment Company Act of 1940, including Section 17(a) thereof, which restricts securities dealings between registered investment companies and their investment advisers. See, e.g., Application of Congress Street Fund, Inc., et al., August 27, 1976 (File No. 812-3092); Application of Lord, Abbett & Co., et al., August 23, 1976 (File No. 812-4018); and Application of Fidelity High Yield Municipals, et al., May 8, 1978 (File No. 812-4306).

2. *Article III, Section 24.*

Section 24 now provides, in substance, that selling concessions, discounts or other allowances ("concessions"), as such, can only be given to NASD members actually engaged in the investment banking or securities business as consideration for services rendered in distribution. A proviso to Section 24, however, effectively limits its operation to situations where a member is contractually bound to sell a security at a fixed price.

The NASD asserts in the Papilsky filing that the proposed rule change is "not intended to alter substantially the present scope and application of Section 24." However, the NASD goes on to state that the proposed rule change does

> clarify that Section 24 applies only to the offering of securities by members at a fixed public offering price and that certain forms of indirect concessions are treated no differently than direct concessions. Thus, the interpretation of section 24 makes very clear that members who agree to offer securities at a stated public offering price cannot devise indirect means to provide select customers with the securities at prices not available to other public investors. The indirect granting of a concession by a device like that contemplated in *Papilsky* has the additional vice of creating a misleading record of the transaction, since the sale is confirmed and recorded at the fixed price while the sharing of the concession—the rebate—is accomplished through other means.

The NASD's authority to regulate member performance of the contractual terms and conditions of fixed price offerings of securities in the manner contemplated by the proposed rule change, whether or not the Papilsky filing reflects only a codification of an existing Section 24 interpretation, constitutes the core legal issue presented by the Papilsky filing.

* * *

In addition, several significant implementing rules and definitions are contained in the proposed interpretation under Section 24. The interpretation would provide that "services in distribution" may be rendered by a broker-dealer either by bearing an underwriting risk or by engaging in a selling effort (which must include direct selling contact). The interpretation would also provide that a broker-dealer is deemed to be improperly granting a concession if the broker-dealer furnishes a purchaser of securities with services or products that are commercially available or that are supplied for cash or other agreed upon consideration, unless the broker-dealer receives full consideration for those services or products from sources other than concessions in the fixed price offering.

Certain terms are also defined in the proposed interpretation. A product or service would be "commercially available" if it, or a substantially identical item, is generally available on a commercial basis. A product or service would be considered to be provided "for cash or other agreed upon consideration" if there is an express or implied agreement calling for the customer to compensate the broker-dealer for the product or service. "Full consideration" may be shown by identification of the arrangement for receipt of the consideration, including its source and amount. The broker-dealer would not be required to demonstrate that the agreed upon price represented the fair market price unless the amount of consideration appears on its face to be unreasonably low.

3. *Article III, Section 8.*

The proposed rule change would retain the requirement in existing Section 8 that broker-dealers must purchase securities taken in trade at a fair market price or act as agent in the sale of such securities, but would specify the circumstances in which those requirements would be deemed to have been violated. A definition of the term "taken in trade" would make proposed Section 8 applicable whenever an agreement or understanding existed to engage in a swap transaction in connection with a fixed price offering. "Fair market price" would be defined as a price not higher than the lowest independent offer for securities taken in trade for which offer quotations are readily available or, if quotations are not readily available, a price determined by comparison with other securities having similar characteristics. In "an exceptional or unusual case," a price higher than the lowest independent offer would be acceptable if the broker-dealer could demonstrate, taking all relevant factors into consideration, that the price was justified. Section 8 would also be amended to require that a "normal commission" be charged in swap transactions in which a broker-dealer acts as agent in the sale of securities taken in trade.

4. *Article III, Section 36.*

Proposed Section 36 would expressly prohibit a member participating in fixed price offerings from selling the securities to (or placing them with) a related person. A "related person" is defined to mean a person or account having a common ownership relationship with the member. Proposed Section 36 would, for example, preclude an institutional purchaser, such as an insurance company, from using an NASD member affiliate to purchase securities in a fixed price offering, thereby enabling it to recapture the concession. Proposed Section 36 would not apply to any related person which is itself subject to that section or which is a non-member foreign broker-dealer agreeing to comply with that section. In addition, the new section would not apply after the termination of a fixed price offering, so long as the member or related person had initially made a *bona fide* public offering of the securities.

* * *

By the Commission.

THE NASD MARK–UP POLICY

Perhaps the most controversial of the rules and interpretations of the NASD has been its so-called "5% mark-up philosophy." In an effort to clarify to some extent just what this policy means, the NASD Board of Governors has issued the following Interpretation: [1]

"The question of fair mark-ups or spreads is one which has been raised from the earliest days of the Association. No definitive answer can be given and no interpretation can be all-inclusive for the obvious reason that what might be considered fair in one transaction could be unfair in another transaction because of different circumstances.

1. CCH NASD Securities Dealers Manual (CCH) ¶ 2154 (pp. 2055–2059).

"However, it was recognized that the amount of mark-up was at least a starting point from which an answer to the question could be sought and that progress might be made if the general practice of the business on mark-ups could be established. To find this out, the Association, in 1943, made a membership-wide questionnaire examination of mark-ups in retail or customer transactions. Questionnaires were filed by 82 per cent of the membership covering transactions which varied widely with respect to price, dollar amount, type of security, and degree of market activity. They included both listed and unlisted securities, with the latter, however, in the substantial majority. This information revealed that 47 per cent of the transactions computed were made at mark-ups of 3 per cent or less and 71 per cent of the transactions were effected at mark-ups of 5 per cent or less.

"In a letter to the membership on October 25, 1943, the Board of Governors made known the results of its survey and expressed its philosophy on what constitutes a fair spread or profit. The Board stated that it would be impractical and unwise, if not impossible, to define specifically what constitutes a fair spread on each and every transaction because the fairness of a mark-up can be determined only after considering all of the relevant factors. Under certain conditions a mark-up in excess of 5 per cent may be justified, but on the other hand, 5 per cent or even a lower rate is by no means always justified. The Board instructed District Business Conduct Committees to enforce Section 1 of Article III of the Rules of Fair Practice with respect to mark-ups, keeping in mind that 71 per cent of the transactions computed from the questionnaires were effected at a mark-up of 5 per cent or less. The philosophy which the Board expressed has since been referred to as the '5% Policy.'

"The Policy has been reviewed by the Board of Governors on numerous occasions and each time the Board has reaffirmed the philosophy expressed in the letter to members of October 25, 1943. The Board is aware, however, of the need for continually re-examining the mark-up policy and its application in the light of current economic conditions and with the benefit of experience gained from enforcement of the existing Policy. The Board has carefully considered the Policy adopted in 1943 and subsequent interpretations with respect thereto. It can find no justification for a change in the basic Policy. However, it recognizes that any clarification will materially aid members in complying with the Policy and the various committees in fulfilling their responsibility to exercise judgment in determining the fairness of mark-ups.

"Based upon its review of the entire matter, the Board has adopted the interpretation set forth below.

THE INTERPRETATION

* * *

"In accordance with Article VII, Section 3(a) of the By-Laws, the following interpretation under Article III, Sections 1 and 4 of the Rules of Fair Practice has been adopted by the Board:

It shall be deemed conduct inconsistent with just and equitable principles of trade for a member to enter into any transaction with a customer in any security at any price not reasonably related to the current market price of the security or to charge a commission which is not reasonable.

A. General Considerations

"Since the adoption of the '5% Policy' the Board has determined that:

1. The '5% Policy' is a guide—not a rule.

2. A member may not justify mark-ups on the basis of expenses which are excessive.

3. The mark-up over the prevailing market price is the significant spread from the point of view of fairness of dealings with customers in principal transactions. In the absence of other bona fide evidence of the prevailing market, a member's own contemporaneous cost is the best indication of the prevailing market price of a security.

4. A mark-up pattern of 5% or even less may be considered unfair or unreasonable under the '5% Policy.'

5. Determination of the fairness of mark-ups must be based on a consideration of all the relevant factors, of which the percentage of mark-up is only one.

B. Relevant Factors

"Some of the factors which the Board believes that members and the Association's committees should take into consideration in determining the fairness of a mark-up are as follows:

1. *The type of security involved.* Some securities customarily carry a higher mark-up than others. For example, a higher percentage of mark-up customarily applies to a common stock transaction than to a bond transaction of the same size. Likewise, a higher percentage applies to sales of units of direct participation programs and condominium securities than to sales of common stock.

2. *The availability of the security in the market.* In the case of an inactive security the effort and cost of buying or selling the security, or any other unusual circumstances connected with its acquisition or sale, may have a bearing on the amount of mark-up justified.

3. *The price of the security.* While there is no direct correlation, the percentage of mark-up or rate of commission, generally increases as the price of the security decreases. Even where the amount of money is substantial, transactions in lower priced securities may require more handling and expense and may warrant a wider spread.

4. *The amount of money involved in a transaction.* A transaction which involves a small amount of money may warrant a higher percentage of mark-up to cover the expenses of handling.

5. *Disclosure.* Any disclosure to the customer, before the transaction is effected, of information which would indicate (a) the amount of commission charged in an agency transaction or (b) mark-up made in a principal transaction is a factor to be considered. Disclosure itself, however, does not justify a commission or mark-up which is unfair or excessive in the light of all other relevant circumstances.

6. *The pattern of mark-ups.* While each transaction must meet the test of fairness, the Board believes that particular attention should be given to the pattern of a member's mark-ups.

7. *The nature of the member's business.* The Board is aware of the differences in the services and facilities which are needed by, and provided for, customers of members. If not excessive, the cost of providing such services and facilities, particularly when they are of a continuing nature, may properly be considered in determining the fairness of a member's mark-ups.

C. Transactions to which the Policy is applicable

"The Policy applies to all securities handled in the over-the-counter market, whether oil royalties or any other security, in the following types of transactions:

1. *A transaction in which a member buys a security to fill an order for the same security previously received from a customer.* This transaction would include the so-called "riskless" or "simultaneous" transaction.

2. *A transaction in which a member sells a security to a customer from inventory.* In such case the amount of the mark-up should be determined on the basis of the mark-up over the bona fide representative current market. The amount of profit or loss to the member from market appreciation or depreciation before, or after, the date of the transaction with the customer would not ordinarily enter into the determination of the amount or fairness of the mark-up.

3. *A transaction in which a member purchases a security from a customer.* The price paid to the customer or the mark-down applied by the member must be reasonably related to the prevailing market price of the security.

4. *A transaction in which the member acts as agent.* In such a case, the commission charged the customer must be fair in light of all relevant circumstances.

5. *Transactions wherein a customer sells securities to, or through, a broker/dealer, the proceeds from which are utilized to pay for other securities purchased from, or through, the broker/dealer at or about the same time.* In such instances, the mark-up shall be computed in the same way as if the customer had purchased for cash and in computing the mark-up there shall be included any profit or commission realized by the dealer on the securities being liquidated, the proceeds of which are used to pay for securities being purchased.

D. Transactions to which the Policy is not applicable

"To the sale of securities where a prospectus or offering circular is required to be delivered and the securities are sold at the specific public offering price.

"This interpretation does no more than express what is clearly implied in Sections 1 and 4 of Article III of the Rules of Fair Practice. The interpretation is made, however, in order to emphasize the obligation which is assumed by every member of this Association in every transaction with a customer."

See Ratner, Regulation of the Compensation of Securities Dealers, 55 Cornell L.Rev. 348 (1970); Note, Regulation of Over-the-Counter Markups: A Reappraisal of Present Policy, 1 Loyola L.Rev. (L.A.) 128 (1968).

NASD REVIEW OF UNDERWRITERS' COMPENSATION

The securities acts of a number of states authorize the securities administrator to limit the maximum amount of compensation which underwriters may receive, and for a number of years some of these states have regulated options and warrants issued to underwriters in connection with a public offering. As a practical matter this problem arises generally in the case of an unseasoned company that desires to go into the public market and finds it difficult to obtain an underwriter. Over the years some underwriting firms have attempted to supplement their cash compensation by taking stock at a price below the market or by taking "compensation stock" or "compensation warrants" with the hope of obtaining capital gain tax treatment for a portion of their profit.[1]

In the bull market which ended on May 28, 1962 there had been an acceleration in the use of cheap stock, options and warrants as a means of compensating underwriters. As a result, on December 26, 1961 the Board of Governors of the NASD advised all of its members of its intention to review members' offerings of unseasoned companies to determine whether the underwriting arrangements were fair and reasonable, under all the circumstances of the offering. The announcement advised members of a newly appointed Committee on Underwriting Arrangements and of the newly established review procedure in these terms: [2]

> The Board of Governors of the Association is concerned with the arrangements between issuers and underwriters in connection with the offering of securities of unseasoned companies. A recent study by the Association of prospectuses and offering circulars indicates that in some of these arrangements the compensation received by underwriters for marketing these securities was unfair and unreasonable. Members are cautioned that their responsibilities as underwriters go beyond the mere successful distribution of securities. In arranging compensation for their services of distribution, members should be careful to avoid over-reaching, and these arrangements should not be unfair or unconscionable under all the circumstances of the offering.

> The Board of Governors intends to review the offerings of issues of unseasoned companies to determine whether the arrangements entered into by members in connection with the offerings are fair and consistent with just and equitable principles of trade under Article III, Section 1 of the Rules of Fair Practice. * * *

> A Special Committee of the Board of Governors known as the Committee on Underwriting Arrangements [later renamed the Committee on Corporate Financing and the membership of which is secret—Eds.] has been appointed to review offerings in the general category described above, and to furnish guidance to the Executive Office with respect to the matter for transmittal to members and their counsel.

Mr. Allen E. Throop of the New York bar, in discussing the NASD review procedure at an American Bar Association Section of Corporation, Banking and Business Law panel discussion, made these comments: [3]

> If the terms of a particular underwriting program appear unfavorable and unreasonable to the Committee on Underwriting Arrangements, apparently it is normal for the managing underwriter to be so advised and to be given one other chance to propose a different deal. He will receive advice if it is the view of the Committee that the compensation is still unreasonable. I believe that if he gets no comment, he is in good shape.

> As a matter of history, in the period from January 15th to July 25th [1962] there were about 1,100 issues filed with the N.A.S.D. office in Washington, of which some 320 were excluded as not involving unseasoned issues. There was then a processing of the remaining 780 issues, out of

1. Fleischer and Meyer, Tax Treatment of Securities Compensation: Problems of Underwriters, 16 Tax L.Rev. 119 (1960).

2. Notice of National Association of Securities Dealers, Inc., December 26, 1961, Re: Issues of Unseasoned Companies—Underwriting Compensation—Withholding. See Wall Street Journal, Dec. 28, 1961, p. 2, col. 2 (Pacific Coast ed.).

3. Current Problems of Securities Underwriters and Dealers, 18 Bus.Lawyer 27, at 45–48 (1962).

which 138 initial adverse determinations were made. Out of these, there were 39 resubmissions, of which 17 were still deemed unfair. The net result was that out of 780 unseasoned issues, about 115 were ultimately deemed to involve excessive compensation.

I believe that the procedure initiated by the N.A.S.D. in December represented a major departure from existing practice, in that for the first time the N.A.S.D. considered in advance the specific terms of a proposed transaction or series of transactions, instead of announcing a general standard, by rule or interpretation, and then dealing with specific instances in which departures from that standard may have occurred. * * *

My understanding is that, although no maximum limits on compensation have been established, the N.A.S.D.'s policy at the present time is to regard as in a questionable area and subject to careful scrutiny underwriters' compensation which exceeds 18% to 20% of the gross dollar amount received by the issuer from the securities which are being offered. This is a percentage which would be applicable to the smaller offerings of new common stock. * * *

The NASD has set forth in the following Interpretation[4] the guidelines which will be followed by the committee in passing upon underwriting arrangements and compensation:

Interpretation

"It shall be deemed conduct inconsistent with high standards of commercial honor and just and equitable principles of trade and a violation of Article III, Section 1 of the Rules of Fair Practice:

(1) for a member to participate in any way in the public distribution of an issue of securities in which the underwriting or other arrangements in connection with or related to the distribution, or the terms or conditions relating thereto, when taking into consideration all elements of compensation and all of the surrounding circumstances and relevant factors, are unfair or unreasonable;

(2) for a member who is a managing underwriter, or the equivalent thereof, of a public offering of an issue of securities to fail to timely file with the Association the documents and other information required by the Filing Requirements hereof;

(3) for a member to participate in an advisory, distributing or other capacity with an issuer, or its bona fide officers or employees, in the public distribution of a non-underwritten issue of securities if:

(a) the issuer hires persons primarily for the purpose of distributing or assisting in the distribution of the issue, or for the purpose of assisting in any way in connection with the underwriting; or

(b) the documents and other information required by the Filing Requirements hereof have not been filed with the Association and reviewed by it prior to the effective date thereof.

* * *

Guidelines

"The following guidelines shall be utilized by the Committee on Corporate Financing in making its determinations, and by District Committees and the

Board of Governors in making findings of violation of this Interpretation and of Article III, Section 1 of the Rules of Fair Practice. They should also be followed by members in their preparation of the arrangements, terms and conditions of a public issue of securities which they intend to underwrite or in reviewing an issue in the distribution of which they intend to participate or give any assistance whatsoever in the distribution or preparatory process. These guidelines should not, however, be considered exhaustive or all-inclusive since all surrounding circumstances and relevant factors whatever they may be are important to a proper and accurate determination by the appropriate Association committees and the Board of Governors regardless of whether they are delineated herein in detail.

* * *

General

"In reaching a determination of fairness or reasonableness the following factors, as well as any other relevant factors and circumstances, shall be taken into consideration: the size of the offering; whether it is being underwritten; if so, the type of commitment, i.e., whether it is being sold on a firm commitment, best efforts, or best efforts all or none basis; the type of securities being offered; the existence of restrictions, or the lack thereof, on stock, warrants, options or convertible securities received or to be received in connection with or related to the offering by the underwriter and related persons and the amount of such stock, warrants, options, or convertible securities; the nature and the amount of overall compensation received or to be received by the underwriter and related persons; the underwriter's relationship to the issuer, or its parent, subsidiary or affiliate, including whether a member of the Association is underwriting an issue of its own securities or of its parent, subsidiary or affiliate; and whether a lack of arm's-length bargaining or a conflict of interest exists in connection with the offering.

Arrangement Factors

Restrictions on Securities Received or to be Received:

"It shall be the policy of the Committee on Corporate Financing to examine closely the circumstances surrounding the purchase of securities by an underwriter and related persons and other broker/dealers and persons associated with and related to them during the twelve (12) month period prior to the filing of the registration statement or offering circular. Normally, but not necessarily in all instances, purchases made by such persons within six months prior to such filings will be considered part of the offering package and will be considered to have been acquired in connection with or in relation to the offering. A more flexible policy will be followed, however, in connection with purchases in the six to twelve-month period prior to such filing. Factors to be considered in determining whether any of such prior acquired securities were acquired in connection with or in relation to the offering shall be pricing, i.e., disparity between the price paid by the recipient and the public offering price; timing, i.e., date of acquisition of the shares by the recipient in relation to the date of filing of the registration statement; number of securities purchased; their relationship to other purchases by other purchasers and to the contemplated offering; relationship of earlier purchases to the proposed financing; the risk factors involved; the presence or absence of arm's-length bargaining and the existence of a potential or actual conflict of interest. Purchases of securities prior to an offering of a public issue of securities is an area of great concern to the Association and, therefore, under appropriate circumstances, purchases made even prior to the previous twelve month period by the aforementioned persons may be reviewed in accordance with the above criteria particularly, but not only, when questions relating to arm's-length bargaining or conflicts of interest are present.

"The transfer or assignment of stock or convertible securities, or the exercise of options and warrants or the resale, transfer and assignment of the shares underlying the options, warrants or debt securities, acquired by an underwriter and related persons, whether such was acquired prior to, at the time of, or after, but which is determined to be in connection with or related to the offering shall be restricted for a minimum period of one year from the effective date of the registration statement or definitive offering circular. Generally where the purchase of stock has been or is to be made on installment terms or in some method of payment other than cash in full, such restrictions shall apply to the transfer and assignment of the stock during the period of installment payment and for a minimum of one year from date of final payment provided, however, the installment terms themselves are reasonable.

* * *

Stock Numerical Limitations on Securities Received or to be Received:

"Shares of stock underlying warrants, options or convertible securities and/ or all stock acquired directly by an underwriter and related persons whether acquired prior to, at the time of, or after, but which is determined to be in connection with or related to, the offering shall not in the aggregate be more than ten (10%) percent of the total number of shares being offered in the proposed offering. The maximum limitation in the case of "best efforts" underwritings or participation shall be on the basis of no more than one (1) share received for every ten (10) shares actually sold. For purposes of this paragraph:

(1) Over-allotment shares and shares underlying warrants, options, or convertible securities which are part of the proposed offering are not to be counted as part of the aggregate number of shares being offered against which the 10% limitation is to be applied.

(2) In an exceptional or unusual case involving an offering of convertible securities of a company whose stock already has a public market and where the circumstances require, taking into consideration the conversion terms of the publicly offered securities and the terms of the securities to be received by the above persons, the receipt of underlying shares by such persons aggregating the above referred to 10% limitation may be considered improper and a lesser amount considered more appropriate.

(3) In an exceptional or unusual case, where a large number of shares of a company are already outstanding and/or the purchase price of the securities, risk involved or the time factor as to acquisition or other circumstances justify, a variation from the above limitations may be permitted but in all such cases the burden of demonstrating justification for such shall be upon the person seeking the variation.

"Any purchase or receipt of securities by an underwriter and related persons, or a member of the selling or distribution group which are excessive in nature must be returned to the company, or the source from which they were originally received at the original cost. The arrangements, terms and conditions of the distribution shall be considered unfair and unreasonable if this is not done. Only in exceptional and unusual circumstances upon good cause shown, will a different arrangement or procedure be considered acceptable. In all such cases the burden of demonstrating that exceptional and unusual circumstances exist shall be upon the person advocating such.

* * *

Compensation Factors

"The following items are included in determining underwriter's compensation: the gross amount of the underwriter's discount; total expenses payable by the issuer, whether accountable or non-accountable, to or on behalf of the underwriter which normally would be paid by the underwriter; underwriter's counsel's fees and expenses; finder's fees; financial consulting and advisory fees, and any other items of value accruing to the underwriter and related persons. Such other items of value include, but are not necessarily limited to, stock, options, warrants, and convertible and other debt securities, when deemed to have been received in connection with or in relation to the proposed offering, and when given by or acquired from the issuer, seller or persons in control or in common control of the issuer, or related parties of the issuer or such other persons. Expenses normally borne by the issuer, such as printing costs, registration fees, blue sky fees, and accountant's fees, are excluded from compensation even if paid through the underwriter.

"The standard of appropriate overall allowable compensation that is applied to initial offerings of a company is not necessarily the same standard that is applied to other than initial offerings.

"Stock acquired or to be acquired by an underwriter and related persons, any other broker/dealer participating in the financing, and persons associated with such broker/dealers, which has been acquired in connection with or related to or in relation to the proposed offering (hence, part of the compensation paid in connection therewith) shall be valued for compensation purposes by taking into consideration the differences between the cost of such stock and the proposed public offering price or, in the case of securities with a bona fide independent market, the cost of such stock and price of the stock on the market on the date of purchase, and other relevant factors. If, however, there is a binding obligation to hold such stock for a substantial period of time, an adjustment in such valuation is usually made.

"Options or warrants acquired or to be acquired by an underwriter and related persons, any other broker/dealer participating in the financing, and persons associated with or related to such broker/dealers, which have been acquired in connection with or in relation to the proposed offering (hence, part of the compensation paid in connection therewith) shall be valued for compensation purposes by taking into account the number and the terms of the warrants; the cost of acquiring such; their lowest exercise price; the date at which they become exercisable, assignable or transferable, and other relevant factors. However, if such options or warrants are for terms in excess of five (5) years or are exercisable below the initial public offering price, such will constitute an unfair or unreasonable underwriting arrangement. In cases where the exercise price is above the public offering price or where the exercise of the options or warrants or the sale, assignment or transfer of the underlying stock are restricted for an extended period of time in excess of the provisions outlined above, a lesser value will generally result.

"Convertible securities acquired or to be acquired by an underwriter and related persons, any other broker/dealer participating in the financing, and persons associated with or related to such broker/dealers, which have been acquired in connection with or in relation to the proposed offering (hence, part of the compensation paid in connection therewith) shall be valued for compensation purposes on the basis of the spread between the conversion price and the proposed offering price or, in the case of securities with a bona fide independent market, the conversion price and the price of the stock on the market on the date of purchase, and other relevant factors.

*   *   *

Venture Capital Restrictions

When a member participates in the initial public offering of an issuer's securities, such member or any officer, director, general partner, controlling shareholder or subsidiary of the member or subsidiary of such controlling shareholder or a member of the immediate family * of such persons, who beneficially owns any securities of said issuer at the time of filing of the offering, shall not sell such securities during the offering or sell, transfer, assign or hypothecate such securities for ninety days following the effective date of the offering unless:

(1) the price at which the issue is to be distributed to the public is established at a price no higher than that recommended by a qualified independent underwriter, as defined in Section 2(k) of Schedule E to Article VII, Section 1(a)(4) of the By-Laws, who does not beneficially own securities of the issuer, who shall also participate in the preparation of the registration statement and the prospectus, offering circular, or similar document and who shall exercise the usual standards of "due diligence" in respect thereto; or

(2) the sale of such securities by such member or related person would not exceed one percent of the securities being offered.

Conclusion

The aforementioned Guidelines are intended to serve only as a measure of guidance for members of the Association, its Committees, and the Board of Governors. As noted above, they should not be considered binding rules nor should they be considered exhaustive in scope since each issue must be reviewed on its own merits and a determination made in respect thereto taking into consideration all surrounding circumstances and relevant factors regardless of whether they are delineated herein in detail.

*   *   *

Interpretations of the NASD in the past have prohibited "self underwriting," i.e. the underwriting of an issue of its own stock or that of an affiliate by a broker-dealer. However, this rule could not survive the desire of Merrill Lynch to underwrite the issue of its own stock in the Summer of 1971 and was tacitly abandoned. In May, 1971 the NASD issued a proposed amendment to its by-laws and interpretations [5] which would have permitted such self underwriting, subject to certain requirements. The principal ones were that two qualified independent underwriters, while not necessarily participating in the distribution, must establish the price at which the issue is sold and must participate in the preparation of the registration statement and be represented by independent legal counsel in connection with such participation. Also, it was provided that the broker-dealer whose securities were being marketed must have been actively engaged in the investment banking and securities business for at least

---

* See, definition of "immediate family", Interpretation of the Board of Governors— "Free Riding and Withholding", Article III, Section 1 of the NASD Rules of Fair Practice.

5. NASD Circular (Proposed Amendments to By-Laws and Rules of Fair Practice [Interpretations] Governing the Distribution of Securities of Members), May 8, 1971.

five years and that the last three of such five years must have been "profitable." However, because of the delay in the adoption of these new rules occasioned by the controversy over the tax shelter programs, referred to below, the interpretation prohibiting self underwriting has not been formally rescinded, although it is now being ignored.

The main problem that has arisen recently concerning the amount of underwriting compensation has related to so-called "tax shelter programs," i.e. oil and gas drilling programs and real estate syndicates (with occasional exotic variations involving cattle, chickens or other assorted livestock). These programs are organized as limited partnerships either to explore for oil and gas (usually on a wildcat basis) or to invest in real property. Their principal attractiveness to investors lies in the pass-through to the limited partners of the deductions for intangible drilling costs in the case of the oil programs and the prepaid interest, investment tax credit and accelerated depreciation in the case of the real estate programs. Such programs are organized by persons known as the "sponsors" or "syndicators," who also act as the managers of the operation, either directly or through an affiliate, and who act in the case of the real estate programs as the real estate broker which sells the property to the limited partnership. For these services, the sponsors or syndicators receive fees.

In the case of the oil programs, such fees include overhead costs of the management company conducting the exploration as well as the actual cost of drilling the wells, all of which is usually paid by the limited partners' contributions. In addition, the sponsors receive certain royalties and overrides in the production, if and when any oil is ever discovered. In the case of the real estate programs, the real estate brokerage commission is ostensibly paid by the vendor of the property, but it obviously affects the price at which the partnership purchases the property and is always based upon the gross selling price. Because of the highly leveraged nature of most of these investments, a 5% real estate commission may amount to a very large percentage of the actual investment by the limited partners. For example, if property is purchased for a gross price of $1,000,000 which has a $900,000 first mortgage on it, a 5% real estate commission would amount to $50,000, which is paid indirectly by the investors in the $100,000 limited partnership offering.

The controversy which has arisen revolves around the question whether these profits accruing to affiliates of the broker-dealer marketing the limited partnership interests should be included as underwriting compensation in determining the maximum amount of the underwriting commission. If they are, then obviously almost all of these programs would violate the guidelines of the NASD, except those marketed through broker-dealers who are entirely independent of the sponsors of the program.

After extended study of the problem, in 1982, the NASD adopted Section 34 of the Rules of Fair Practice which establishes the terms and conditions under which members of the Association, and associated persons, may participate in public offerings of so-called "direct participation programs." [6] A direct participation program is defined as one which provides for flow-through tax consequences such as oil and gas, real estate and agricultural programs, condominium securities, Subchapter S corporate offerings and other programs of similar nature. Section 34 is designed to provide safeguards against unreasonable compensation and prescribe standards of fairness and reasonableness for these tax shelter programs. The rule regulates the terms and conditions relating to

6. NASD Securities Dealers Manual (CCH) ¶ 2191.

underwriting and sales compensation as well as the operating structure and management of such programs in which a member or affiliate is a sponsor.

Section 34 is concerned with rights of participants in the program, conflicts of interest, the financial condition of sponsors, sponsor's compensation, suitability standards for investors, and sales practices. Each program must establish standards of suitability for investment in the program, and these standards must be fully disclosed to prospective participants. In making investment recommendations, the member or associate must have reasonable grounds to believe that the participant will derive significant tax benefits, if tax savings are an inducement for investment; that the participant has the financial liability to bear the risk inherent in the investment; and that the program is otherwise suitable. The member is required to maintain files disclosing the basis for these judgments.

The member must also determine that all material facts are adequately and accurately disclosed in the offering circular, including the facts concerning compensation, physical properties, tax aspects, financial stability and experience of the sponsor, conflicts of interest, and appraisals. Finally, guidelines have been established (1) for underwriting compensation of ten percent of proceeds received, plus a maximum of 0.5% for reimbursement of due diligence expenses, and (2) for organization and offering expenses of 15 percent of proceeds.

The NASD regulations of public tax shelter syndicate offerings are an interesting experiment in industry self-regulation. They are, however, considerably less rigorous than the North American Securities Administrators Association, Inc. (NASAA) Statements of Policy regarding various forms of tax shelter programs [7] to which approximately thirty-three of the fifty NASAA member states subscribe. Moreover, California securities regulation has been in the forefront in establishing standards with respect to specific types and amounts of sponsor compensation and has extended a significant influence on developments in other states and upon the NASD guidelines.[8] Nevertheless, the NASD guidelines are applicable in every state and thus supplement state regulation in this field.

The Tax Reform Act of 1986 is expected to diminish the attractiveness of direct participation programs as a device for sheltering ordinary income and encourage investment in programs based primarily upon economic considerations.

RESALE PRICE MAINTENANCE AND THE "PAPILSKY RULES"

The typical underwriting agreement and selling group agreement require all underwriters and members of the selling group to adhere to the public offering price as stated in the Prospectus. In In the Matter of National Association of Securities Dealers, Inc.[1] some of the underwriters cut the price of some of the securities subject to such an agreement and were disciplined by the NASD for this breach of contract. Upon appeal the SEC held (a) that such an agreement did not violate the Sherman Act, but (b) that its attempted enforcement by the NASD did violate Section 15A(b)(8) [now Section 15A(b)(6)] of the Securities

7. See NASAA Reports (CCH), Statement of Policy on Real Estate Programs (at page 301); Oil and Gas Programs (at page 1501); and Cattle-Feeding Programs (at page 501).

8. See Lanctot, Powers & Harris, Recent Developments in State Regulation of Public Real Estate Syndication Offerings, 40 Bus.Law. 745, 753 (1985).

1. 19 S.E.C. 424 (1945).

Exchange Act requiring that the rules of the NASD not be designed "to fix minimum profits, to impose any schedule of prices, or to impose any schedule or fix minimum rates of commissions, allowances, discounts, or other charges." Thus the Commission left open the possibility of the enforcement of such an agreement in the courts, but denied the right to have it enforced through the administrative machinery. In the Morgan case, Judge Medina agreed with the majority of the Commission that resale price maintenance in securities distributions was not per se illegal under the Sherman Act.[2]

The practical problem under the Securities Act of 1933 arises from the fact that the offering price must be stated in the Prospectus (on the front cover), and any sales by underwriters below that price makes the Prospectus false and misleading (unless it is amended or supplemented) and subjects all of the underwriters to liability under Section 11 of the Act. Therefore, it is impossible to carry out a fixed-price distribution without some sort of agreement, formal or informal, among all of the underwriters that they will adhere to the stated public offering price. If one reads the Securities Act of 1933, it is inconceivable that Congress thought that fixed-price distributions were illegal when it enacted that statute.

This issue resurfaced again in 1976 as a result of the decision by Judge Frankel in the case of Papilsky v. Berndt,[3] which was one of the "recapture" suits against investment advisers to mutual funds. In that case, the plaintiff alleged that the investment adviser to a mutual fund, which was a member of the NASD, could have interposed itself as a selling group member in connection with the fund's purchases of new issues; and that it could thereby have recaptured the "concession" from the underwriting discount given to selling group members, which it should then have credited against its advisory fee. This would have amounted, of course, to a *de facto* discount from the public offering price to that particular purchaser. Judge Frankel held that since there was nothing in the NASD rules which prevented such a practice, the investment adviser was liable for not having pursued that avenue of obtaining a benefit for the mutual fund. The NASD promptly denied publicly that its rules permitted any such evasion of the maintenance of the public offering price in a fixed price distribution.

This controversy, however, caused to surface practices which had been engaged in by underwriting syndicates and selling group members in connection with such fixed price distributions and which were alleged to amount in fact to discounts to large institutional purchasers. These were the practices of "overtrading" and "designated sales" which are discussed in the SEC Release reprinted, in part, at page 576. The NASD then proposed to prohibit those practices by amendments to its rules and the Commission initiated a proceeding for a public hearing to determine whether or not it should approve such rule changes.

After the public hearing, the Commission required the NASD, as a condition to obtaining Commission approval, to make two changes in the rules it had initially proposed.[4] One of these changes was to eliminate the proposed prohibition of the use of "designated sales" to buy research with the use of "soft dollars", but instead to *permit* that practice provided it complies with the requirements of Section 28(e) of the 1934 Act regarding the use of brokerage for the same purpose.[5] The other change required by the SEC was to amend the

2. United States v. Morgan, 118 F.Supp. 621, 699 (S.D.N.Y.1953).

3. Fed.Sec.L.Rep. (CCH) ¶ 95,627 (S.D. N.Y.1976).

4. Sec.Exch.Act Rel. No. 16956, July 3, 1980, Fed.Sec.L.Rep. (CCH) ¶ 82,621 (1980).

5. Jorden, "Paying Up" For Research: A Regulatory and Legislative Analysis, 1975 Duke L.J. 1103; Burgunder & Hartmann, Soft Dollars and Section 28(e) of the Securities Exchange Act of 1934: A 1985 Perspective, 24 Am.Bus.L.J. 139 (1986);

provisions of the proposed rule relating to the calculation of a "fair price" in connection with "swaps."

In In the Matter of The National Association of Securities Dealers, Inc.,[6] the Commission approved the final rules as so amended and overruled its own decision thirty-five years earlier that the Securities Exchange Act of 1934 prohibited the NASD from enforcing resale price maintenance. This time the Commission held that NASD action to enforce voluntary agreements regarding the maintenance of a fixed offering price in connection with a new issue did *not* amount to any attempt to "impose any schedule of prices, or to impose any schedule or fix minimum rates of commissions, allowances, discounts, or other charges." The Commission pointed out that the underwriting discount and selling group concessions were separately negotiated with respect to each new public issue and that the NASD was not attempting by its action to fix those discounts or concessions, but simply to enforce the voluntary agreement of the underwriters and selling group members to adhere to them, until the managing underwriter released the group from those restrictions.

The Commission weakly attempted to distinguish its prior decision on the basis of the interim enactment in 1975 of Section 15A(b)(9) of the 1934 Act directing the Commission to "weigh" the anti-competitive effects of the rules of self-regulatory agencies in deciding whether or not to approve such rules. However, the Commission stated: "The Commission does not believe Section 15A(b)(6) requires it to conclude that the NASD would fix minimum prices or impose a schedule of discounts or fees by prohibiting discounts from the public offering price of a security to be distributed in a fixed price underwriting where the participating broker-dealer members negotiate a lawful contract to distribute the security at a fixed price." This is, of course, precisely what the Commission concluded in 1945, and that statutory language had not been significantly changed in the interval. It also stated that it was not prepared to conclude that Congress in enacting that prohibition intended "to prevent NASD disciplinary action against its members for granting discounts from the public offering price in an offering that is publicly represented to be at a fixed price."

For discussions of the NASD case and the Morgan case, see Note, Price Maintenance in the Distribution of Securities, 56 Yale L.J. 333 (1947); Note, The Investment Bankers Case, 63 Yale L.J. 399 (1954); Steffen, The Investment Bankers' Case: Some Observations, 64 Yale L.J. 169 (1954); Whitney, The Investment Bankers' Case—Including a Reply to Professor Steffen, 64 Yale L.J. 319 (1955).

For discussions of the National Association of Securities Dealers, Inc. and this phase of the regulation of the securities markets, see Cary, Self-Regulation in the Securities Industry, 49 A.B.A.J. 244 (1963); Jennings, Self-Regulation in the Securities Industry: The Role of the Securities and Exchange Commission, 29 Law & Contemp.Prob. 663 (1964): Note, The NASD—An Unique Experiment in Cooperative Regulation, 46 Va.L.Rev. 1586 (1960); Loss, Fundamentals of Securities Regulation 689–694 (1983); 2 Loss, Securities Regulation 1359–1391 (2d ed. 1961); 3 id. at 1493–1497; Hammerman & Mandel, Self-Regulatory Organization Proceedings, in 5 Securities Regulation Techniques ch. 117 (A.A. Sommer, Jr. ed. 1986); Pickard & Djinis, NASD Disciplinary Proceedings: Practice and Procedure, 37 Bus.Law. 1213 (1982).

Myers, Directed Brokerage and "Soft Dollars" Under ERISA: New Concerns for Plan Beneficiaries, 42 Bus.Law. 553 (1987).

6. Sec.Exch.Act Rel. No. 17371, Dec. 12, 1980, Fed.Sec.L.Rep. (CCH) ¶ 82,705 (1980).

Chapter 11

REGULATION OF TRADING ACTIVITIES OF BROKER–DEALERS

Statutes and Regulations

Securities Exchange Act, §§ 9, 10, 15(c).

Rules 10b–3; 10b–5; 10b–6; 10b–7; 10b–8; 10b–10; 10b–16; 15c1–1 thru 15c1–9.

———

JAFFEE & CO. v. SECURITIES AND EXCHANGE COMMISSION

United States Court of Appeals, Second Circuit, 1971.
446 F.2d 387.

Before: KAUFMAN, ANDERSON and MANSFIELD,* CIRCUIT JUDGES.

KAUFMAN, CIRCUIT JUDGE: Respondents Jaffee and Jaffee & Co., a registered broker-dealer, petition for review of an order of the Securities and Exchange Commission, dated April 20, 1970, prescribing that each petitioner be disciplined on account of Jaffee's violations of Rule 10b–6, * * *, promulgated under Section 10(b) of the Securities Exchange Act of 1934 * * *. We affirm the order with respect to Jaffee but hold that Jaffee & Co. was afforded inadequate notice that it would be disciplined derivatively on account of Jaffee's violations, rather than because of violations attributable directly to the Company, and hence set aside the order disciplining Jaffee & Co.

I.

None of the essential facts is in dispute. This proceeding was initiated by order of the Commission dated March 24, 1966, which directed a hearing into alleged violations of several provisions of the securities acts by several named respondents, including petitioners here.[1] All of the alleged infractions related to transactions between June 1963 and March 1964 in connection with a secondary offering of common stock in Solitron Devices, Inc., a designer and manufacturer of electronic products. Following a hearing extending for 10 days, the hearing examiner found that Jaffee, while he was the dominant partner in the since defunct partnership and broker-dealer of Jaffee & Leverton, had violated Rule 10b–6 as well as Section 5(b) of the 1933 Act and various anti-fraud provisions of both the 1933 and 1934

---

* Of the United States District Court for the Southern District of New York, sitting by designation, at time of submission.

1. Besides petitioners, other respondents named in the order instituting the proceedings included Greene & Co., a registered broker-dealer through whom Jaffee conducted much of the trading found by the Commission to have been illegal; Greene & Co.'s general partners, Robert Topol and Irving Greene; Bernard Horn, at the relevant times a trader for Greene & Co.; and M. L. Lee & Co., a registered broker-dealer, and its president and director, Martin L. Levy. The Commission ultimately ordered that Greene & Co. and M. L. Lee & Co. be censured and that Bernard Horn be suspended from associating with a broker or dealer for thirty days.

597

Acts. The examiner recommended that Jaffee be suspended for thirty days but dismissed the proceedings against Jaffee & Co. on the grounds that as a successor and not a mere continuation of the Leverton firm, it could not be held accountable for any of that firm's wrongdoings, and second, that Jaffee & Co. had insufficient notice to permit the imposition of derivative sanctions under Section 15(b)(5) of the Exchange Act * * *, the provision ultimately relied upon by the Commission.

The Commission granted the petitions for review which were filed by all respondents. Jaffee & Co., in light of the Examiner's favorable decision, did not petition for review. After oral argument, the S.E.C. absolved Jaffee of all but the Rule 10b–6 violations and, rejecting the hearing examiner's finding of insufficient notice, disciplined Jaffee & Co. under Section 15(b)(5) of the 1934 Act on the sole ground that at the time the proceedings were instituted and during the hearings, Jaffee's interest in the firm exceeded 90%, even though the firm had not been in existence at the time Jaffee was found to have violated Rule 10b–6. * * * The Commission ordered that Jaffee be suspended from association with a broker or dealer and that Jaffee & Co.'s registration be suspended, each suspension to run for concurrent periods of twenty days. By order of the Commission the suspensions have been stayed pending the determination of this petition.

II.

We find no merit to Jaffee's primary arguments that he did not violate Rule 10b–6 because there was no "distribution" within the meaning of that provision in progress at the time he made several purchases of stock in Solitron; or, assuming there was a distribution, that the Commission did not show that his purchases were intentionally or actually manipulative. A registration statement for a secondary offering of 107,700 shares held by thirty-four holders of common stock in Solitron (or about 28% of the then outstanding common stock) was filed under Section 6 of the 1933 Act, * * *, and became effective on October 11, 1962. The largest block of this stock, consisting of 27,500 shares, was Jaffee's. The prospectus announced that the selling stockholders intended to offer the stock for sale on the over-the-counter market "in the proximate future" and appointed Lee & Co., a New York broker-dealer, "exclusive agent" for the offering. Among other things, each shareholder agreed to "comply with the provisions of Rule 10b–6."

Jaffee's liability was premised on his purchases of ten shares of Solitron on August 19, 1963 and an additional 7,600 shares at various times between December 26, 1963 and February 13, 1964. Jaffee's only sale of registered stock during this period was of a single block of 3,500 shares on October 30, 1963. As early as May, 1963, however, Lee & Co. had disposed of 16,300 shares owned by other participants in the offering and by March of the following year the total of registered stock sold had risen to 75,100 shares, or almost 75% of the total registered offering. Shortly thereafter, between October 20 and December 30, 1964, Jaffee sold an additional 16,900 shares of his registered stock.

These facts make out a clear violation of Rule 10b–6, which in relevant part prohibits any "person on whose behalf * * * a distribution is being made" or any person "who has agreed to participate or is participating in * * * a distribution * * * to bid for or purchase * * * any security which is the subject of such distribution * * * until after he has completed his participation in such distribution * * *." There are several exceptions to this prohibition, none of which Jaffee invokes to justify his purchases of Solitron. Jaffee does not dispute that had he been actively promoting the sale and had he in fact sold substantial blocks of his registered stock immediately following his purchases, he would have violated Rule 10b–6. See J. H. Goddard & Co., Securities Exchange Act Release No. 7618 (1965). Rather, Jaffee characterizes his offering under the prospectus and registration as a "shelf registration" because—whatever the intent of other participants may have been—Jaffee himself had no present intent to publicly distribute his registered stock immediately. Jaffee seeks to excuse the 3500 shares sold in October, 1963, as an "unsolicited transaction." His related argument—related because each approach would erode the prophylactic value of the rule—is that the Commission has not shown that Jaffee intended to manipulate the market, or did in fact manipulate it, or did in fact defraud any buyer or seller through his purchases and sales.

Difficult questions may arise with respect to an underwriter's purchase of registered stock where he claims a bona fide intent to "shelve" or keep for investment some portion of it. See Whitney, Rule 10b–6: The Special Study's Rediscovered Rule, 62 Mich.L.Rev. 567 (1964); Report of Special Study of Securities Markets of the SEC, H.R.Doc.No.95, 88th Cong., 1st Sess., pt. I at 545–46 (1963). Similarly, Rule 10b–6(c)(3) provides that a person "shall be deemed * * * to have distributed securities acquired by him for investment" (at which point Rule 10b–6 ceases to apply), a provision which gives rise to close questions with respect to when an underwriter, for example, decides to "shelve" a "sour" issue, see 3 Loss, Securities Regulation 1595 (2d ed. 1961). But Jaffee does not and, on this record, could not successfully contend that at any time following the effective date of the registration statement he was holding his registered stock "for investment." His very registration of shares owned by him implied an intention to sell or distribute rather than to hold them for investment. Moreover, Rule 10b–6(a)(3)(xi) provides that for the purpose of determining the liability of an underwriter and others who purchase securities within a brief specified period before the commencement of a distribution, "the distribution shall not be deemed to commence * * * prior to the effective date of the registration statement," where the securities are registered under the 1933 Act, as here. Although the last-quoted provision does not refer to participants in a distribution generally, see Note, The SEC's Rule 10b–6: Preserving a Competitive Market During Distribution, 1967 Duke L.J. 809, 848–49 (1967), the use of the "effective" date of the registration statement to define the operative period of the rule is instructive here. The dangers of market manipulation that Rule 10b–6 was designed to eradicate, see Chris Craft Industries, Inc. v. Bangor Punta Corp., 426 F.2d 569, 577 (2d Cir. 1970) (en banc), were continually present so long as Jaffee's purchases might have artificially inflated the price of Solitron, thereby affording him an opportunity to sell his registered stock at a price higher than he would have received if the market had been permitted to seek its own level. The Commission was clearly justified in applying the rule during a period following the registration and before Jaffee had "completed his participation" in the distribution. See R. A. Holman & Co., Inc. v. Securities and Exchange Commission, 366 F.2d 446, 449 (2d Cir. 1966).

For similar reasons, and contrary to Jaffee's assertion, the Commission need not have shown that Jaffee actually intended to defraud the marketplace through his purchases. The rule proscribes and clearly defines a *practice* which had, prior to the adoption of the rule in 1955, been used fraudulently to distort the over-the-counter market. Where the rule applies, its prohibition is absolute. See Note, 1967 Duke L.J., supra, at 817–18. Apart from the plain language of the rule itself, a further internal index to the rule's prophylactic intent appears in its subdivision (a)(3)(xi), which excepts from the exemption there defined, purchases otherwise within the exemption which "are for the purpose of creating actual, or apparent, active trading in or raising the price of" the security in question. Jaffee in effect would have us emasculate the rule by reading similar language into the broad prohibition of the rule, itself, although the Commission's clear intent is to require actual manipulation or the like only to draw within the rule's ambit activity that would otherwise be exempted from it.[2]

Finally, Jaffee contends that there is no substantial evidence to support the Commission's finding either that his violation was "willful," a necessary precondition for his suspension, [Securities Exchange Act, § 15(b)(5)] (1964), or that the purchases involved the use of the mails or an instrumentality of interstate commerce, 17 C.F.R. § 240.10b–5(a)(3). But as our recitation of the undisputed facts shows, Jaffee clearly intended to commit "the act which constitutes the violation," Tager v. Securities and Exchange Commission, 344 F.2d 5 (1965), which is all that is required in this context. And most of Jaffee's purchases were effected through the broker-dealer Greene & Co., see note 2, supra, which at Jaffee's instance placed bids for Solitron stock in the "pink sheets" distributed in interstate commerce by the National Daily Quotations Bureau. The insertion of bids in the sheets is sufficient support for the SEC's jurisdiction. "The use of the mails * * * may be entirely incidental" to the scheme that is the basis for liability, United States v. Cashin, 281 F.2d 669, 673 (2d Cir. 1960), and the use here is better described as integral to the scheme than as merely incidental.

III.

This brings us to the telling argument urged by Jaffee & Co. Jaffee & Co. was disciplined, as we have already indicated, pursuant to Section 15(b) (5) of the Securities and Exchange Act, * * *. This section permits the Commission, in relevant part, to suspend the registration of a broker or dealer if it finds that the suspension "is in the public interest" and that a "person associated" with the broker or dealer, "whether prior or subsequent to becoming so associated," willfully violated any provisions of

---

2. Moreover, there is substantial evidence in the record to support the Commission's finding that the broker-dealer Greene & Co., which effected the bulk of Jaffee's purchases, was engaged in market-making activities in Solitron throughout the relevant period. During this same period, Greene & Co. purchased as principal through Bernard Horn, a trader for Greene & Co., 25,000 shares of registered Solitron stock for its own account. Jaffee admitted that prior to the period during which he was making purchases of Solitron, but after the effective date of the registration, he asked Horn to "go into" the "pink sheets" distributed by the National Quotation Bureau, Inc. Thereafter Greene & Co. continuously did insert bids in the quotation sheets. These facts amply refute the core of Jaffee's theory, which is that the dangers Rule 10b–6 were designed to avert were not inherent in Jaffee's activities.

various securities laws, including the 1934 Act, or "any rule or regulation under such statutes." Id. [§ 15(b)(5)(D)]. As we have held, Jaffee was properly found to have willfully violated Rule 10b–6. Furthermore, Jaffee was clearly a person "associated" with Jaffee & Co., as that term is defined in 15 U.S.C. § 78c(a)(18) to include both "partners" and "controlling" persons, by virtue of the firm's partnership agreement dated December 23, 1964 and effective January 1, 1965. * * *

A precondition to revocation, however, was that Jaffee & Co. be afforded "appropriate notice and opportunity for hearing," [§ 15(b)(5)]; see also 5 U.S.C. § 554(b). We conclude that with respect to Jaffee & Co.'s derivative § 15(b)(5) liability, neither condition was met in the proceedings before the Commission.

* * *

Accordingly, the order of the Commission is affirmed with respect to Jaffee but so much of the order as suspends the registration of Jaffee & Co. is vacated.

STABILIZATION

Section 9(a)(6) of the Securities Exchange Act of 1934 prohibits transactions for the purpose of "pegging, fixing, or stabilizing" the price of a security only when they are "in contravention of such rules and regulations as the Commission may prescribe as necessary or appropriate in the public interest or for the protection of investors." In 1940 in its Statement of Policy on the Pegging, Fixing and Stabilizing of Security Prices,[1] the majority of the Commission, over the dissent of Commissioner Healy, interpreted this provision as a mandate to the Commission to *regulate* rather than *prohibit* stabilizing transactions by an underwriting syndicate to facilitate a distribution of securities. It decided at that time to experiment with rules designed to eliminate the "vicious and unsocial aspects" of stabilization and issued a rule regulating initially only offerings "at the market."

The present rules developed as a result of this experimentation consist of a general prohibition in Rule 10b–6 against any person "who has agreed to participate or is participating" in a distribution from bidding for or purchasing the security being distributed or any security of the same class, with exceptions for, among other things, any stabilizing transactions carried out in conformity with Rules 10b–7 and 10b–8. Although Commissioner Healy lost the war, he eventually won the battle, since the present rules completely prohibit stabilizing in connection with an offering "at the market",[2] to which he particularly objected.

The issue of stabilizing in connection with a distribution has become less acute in recent years. In the 1956–62 bull market, and again in 1982–86, the market was apparently prepared to absorb almost any amount of new securities, the more speculative the better.[3] After the market crash of May, 1962, the

---

1. Sec.Exch.Act Rel. No. 2446 (SEC 1940).

2. Rule 10b–7(g). An offering "at the market" is defined as an offering in which it is contemplated that the offering price "set in any calendar day will be increased more than once during such day." Rule 10b–7(b)(1).

3. "The likelihood that a new issue offered to the public during the years 1959 to 1961 would go to a premium is seen from the statistical material. Of the total of 1,671 unseasoned common stock issues publicly offered during this period for which later prices are available, 1,327 (or 79 percent) sold at a premium immediately after the offering and 1,103 (or 66 percent)

market for new issues largely dried up for a time; but in the succeeding bull market of 1966–69 the phenomenon repeated itself.[4] As a result, during these periods, while the underwriters always reserved the right to stabilize in connection with a fixed-price offering where there was a preexisting market, they actually had to do very little of it. Even during the intervening mild bear markets, while there have of course been some "sticky issues", offerings which take any appreciable period of time to sell (other than rights offerings) seem to have been largely eliminated. Perhaps this is because the underwriters have become more skillful in reducing the amount or price of the issue, if necessary, immediately before the effective date of the Registration Statement so that it will all go "out the window." Whatever the reason, extensive stabilizing operations do not seem to have been common in recent years, except in connection with rights offerings where the underwriters are necessarily "on the hook" for a considerable period.

Stabilizing Otherwise Than to Facilitate a Distribution. The Commission's stabilizing rules[5] specifically apply only to the regulation of stabilizing in connection with a distribution of securities, and stabilizing is prohibited by Section 9(a)(6) of the Securities Exchange Act only to the extent that the Commission has adopted rules thereunder. Therefore, stabilizing for some purpose other than to facilitate a distribution of securities is apparently still lawful without any public notice or reports to the Commission. "For example, there have been situations in which persons who have borrowed substantial amounts of money on loans collateralized by stock, and who, when they find that the collateral is becoming inadequate because of a decline in the price of the stock, purchase the security in the open market to 'stabilize' the price of the stock and to maintain the value of their collateral. There have been other situations in which issuers or other persons not contemplating any distribution, but interested in 'improving' or 'stimulating' or 'stabilizing' the existing market for a particular security, undertake to make open market purchases of the security. Persons bidding for or purchasing a security for the purpose of affecting the price, otherwise than to facilitate a distribution, may contend that their activities constitute stabilization which is not prohibited in the absence of a Commission rule, rather than illegal manipulation."[6]

In 1959 the Commission issued a proposed amendment to Rule 10b–7 which would have prohibited all stabilizing except to facilitate a particular distribution,[7] but for some reason the amendment was never adopted.

For discussions of stabilizing, see Klein, Stabilizing Securities Prices, 5 Securities Reg.L.J. 13 (1977); Wolfson, Rule 10b–6: The Illusory Search for Certainty, 25 Stan.L.Rev. 809 (1973); Whitney, Rule 10b–6: The Special Study's Rediscovered Rule, 62 Mich.L.Rev. 567 (1964); Foshay, Market Activities of Participants in Securities Distributions, 45 Va.L.Rev. 907 (1959); Parlin and Everett, The Stabilization of Security Prices, 49 Colum.L.Rev. 607 (1949); Note, SEC's Rule 10b–6: Preserving a Competitive Market During Distributions, 1967 Duke L.J. 809; 3 Loss, Securities Regulation 1571–1614 (2d ed. 1961).

---

sold at a premium 1 month after the offering. * * *

"In 1959 and 1961, 89 percent, and in 1960, 83 percent, of issues of electronic and electrical equipment manufacturing companies, which formed the largest group of 'hot' issues, went to immediate premiums." Report of Special Study of Securities Markets, H.Doc. No. 95, 88th Cong., 1st Sess., Pt. 1, pp. 516–17 (1963).

4. See Wall Street Journal, April 27, 1966, p. 1, col. 6 (" 'Hot' Issue Rerun—Many New Stocks Soar Above Offering Prices in Manner of 1961–62").

5. Rules 10b–6, 10b–7 and 10b–8.

6. SEC Securities Exchange Act Release No. 6127 (1959).

7. Ibid.

THE LIMITS OF STABILIZING ACTIVITY

Commencement of the Prohibitions. Rule 10b–6 prohibits any issuer, underwriter, prospective underwriter or dealer from bidding for or purchasing any security which is the subject of a distribution or any security of the same class or series, if he is a participant in such distribution, except in conformity with the stabilizing rules in Rules 10b–7 and 10b–8. Proviso (11) to Rule 10b–6(a) determines the time when this prohibition commences. That proviso exempts "purchases or bids by an underwriter, prospective underwriter or dealer otherwise than on a securities exchange, 10 or more business days prior to the proposed commencement of such distribution (or 5 or more business days in the case of unsolicited purchases), if none of such purchases or bids are for the purpose of creating actual, or apparent, active trading in or raising the price of such security." This means that in the case of an over-the-counter security a prospective underwriter must "get out of the sheets" (i.e., withdraw any bid which he has been circulating in the National Daily Quotation Service) 10 days before the commencement of the offering and must "get out of the market" (i.e., cease purchasing entirely) 5 days before the commencement of the offering. (The phrase "unsolicited purchases" is not a happy one, but obviously means "purchases pursuant to unsolicited offers.") Purchases on an exchange (except unsolicited brokerage transactions) are prohibited entirely, presumably from the time a person becomes a "prospective underwriter."

The dealers in the selling group are not subject to as rigid restrictions, since the rule only covers a dealer "who has agreed to participate or is participating" in the distribution, and not a "prospective" dealer as in the case of underwriters.

The foregoing does not mean that stabilizing must be postponed until the offering date, but only that *unregulated* bids and purchases must cease at the times mentioned above. Stabilizing bids and purchases in conformity with Rule 10b–7 may be made even before the offering commences. However, this is not very frequently done, since in the typical case the underwriter is not committed to a price until the day before the offering (and even then frequently subject to a "market out"). Therefore, any stabilizing which he did before that date would be almost entirely for the benefit of the issuer. The issuer usually does not have the necessary expertise to carry out a stabilizing operation, and the debacle suffered by Kaiser-Frazer Corporation in 1948 when it tried to effect a pre-offering stabilization has been a warning to other issuers.[8]

Termination of the Prohibitions. The prohibition against bids and purchases, other than stabilizing bids and purchases under the rules, lasts as to a particular underwriter or dealer "until after he has completed his participation in such distribution." Rule 10b–6(a). This time is more definitely specified in Rule 10b–6(c)(3). With respect to an underwriter, it is when "he has distributed his participation * * * *and* any stabilization arrangements and trading restrictions with respect to such distribution to which he is a party have been terminated." The use of the conjunctive here means that a particular underwriter is subject to these restrictions until he receives notice from the syndicate manager that the syndicate has been terminated, even though he has previously sold all of his own allotment. With respect to a dealer, however, the restrictions terminate whenever "he has distributed his [own] participation." The restrictions on the issuer continue until the "distribution is completed."

---

8. For an account of this bizarre episode, see The Kaiser-Eaton Feud, 38 Fortune 88 (Oct. 1948). And see 3 Loss, Securities Regulation 1594 (2d ed. 1961).

However, in Securities and Exchange Commission v. Resch-Cassin & Co., Inc.[9] Judge Tenney held that a member of the selling group was not free to make a market in the stock being distributed even after it had distributed its own allotment, where it acted at the instigation of the underwriter knowing that the underwriter was having trouble disposing of the entire issue and where it effected transactions for the account of the underwriter. The court said: "While it is true that Nagler-Weissman [the selling group member] had disposed of its allotment of 17,500 shares prior to its commencement of trading Africa [the stock being distributed] on October 27, 1970, it also is undisputed that it entered quotes in the pink sheets and became the prime market-maker at the specific request of Resch-Cassin [the underwriter] which was engaged in a distribution of the stock and which itself could not have legally entered the pink sheets. Accordingly, Nagler-Weissman was aiding and abetting a violation of Rule 10b–6. Moreover, Forster [the trader for Nagler-Weissman] actually purchased stock on behalf of Resch-Cassin while the latter was still conducting its underwriting of Africa and at a time when Nagler, Forster and Weissman knew, or should have known, that the issue was not closed and that all was not well. Such conduct on their part was at least aiding and abetting Resch-Cassin in violation of Rule 10b–6." [10]

Stabilizing Levels. Rule 10b–7 basically prohibits the commencement of stabilizing at a price "higher than the highest current independent bid price" [Rule 10b–7(j)(1)] or "above the price at which such security is currently being distributed" [Rule 10b–7(j)(5)]. It also prohibits anyone from raising the price at which he is stabilizing [Rule 10b–7(j)(1)]. In other words, the stabilizer can follow the market down but not up [Rule 10b–7(j)(4)]. These rules are subject to numerous qualifications and exceptions.

Publicity. The fact that the underwriters "may be" stabilizing must be disclosed to a purchaser of the security at or before the completion of the transaction; whether they are or not doesn't have to be [Rule 10b–7(k)]. This obligation is routinely fulfilled by a legend on the inside front cover of the Prospectus.[11] In addition, the stabilizer must report on his actual stabilizing transactions *to the Commission.* (Rule 17a–2) These reports are open to public inspection, but only after the offering is completed [Rule 17a–2(f)], and it is doubtful if anyone ever sees them except employees of the Commission. No one makes any practice of publicly reporting or digesting these reports.

Rights Offerings. In connection with a "rights offering" to existing shareholders, the problem of stabilizing is more complex, and it is covered by Rule 10b–8.

Continuous Offerings. There were two types of situations which posed extreme dangers of a violation of Rule 10b–6, because they involve offerings which continue over a long period of time and participants who are nonprofessionals with little understanding of the highly technical stabilizing rules.

One is the situation of an issuer which has outstanding in the hands of the public either a warrant issue or a convertible issue. Typically, the warrant or the convertible has been sold in a registered public offering and the underwrit-

---

9. 362 F.Supp. 964 (S.D.N.Y.1973).

10. 362 F.Supp. at 980–81. See, also, Securities and Exchange Commission v. Blinder, Robinson & Co., CCH Fed.Sec. Law Rptr. ¶ 99,491 (10th Cir.1983).

11. Regulation C, Rule 426. However, the seller might be subject to civil liability to the buyer if the market price has been influenced by stabilizing activities and this fact is not communicated to the buyer. The legend that there "may be" stabilizing conceivably might not be a sufficient disclosure. Loss states that " * * * in practice the fact that there has been stabilization (not the amount) is usually announced in the confirmation." 3 Loss, Securities Regulation 1575, n. 24 (2d ed. 1961).

ing has been terminated. However, the issuer itself is making a continuous offering of the security purchasable upon exercise of the warrant and must maintain a current prospectus available for delivery to persons who exercise the warrants so long as they are outstanding. With respect to a convertible, both the underlying security and the convertible are considered to have been sold at the time of the sale of the convertible for the purposes of the 1933 Act, and no up-dating of the prospectus is required; nevertheless, the staff of the Commission took the position that for the purposes of Rule 10b–6 the offering continued so long as the convertible was outstanding. Therefore, in both of these situations it was the Commission's position that any purchase of the underlying stock by an issuer violated Rule 10b–6, unless it complied with the stabilization rules (which it would not except by accident) or unless an exemption was obtained. And this rule applies not only to the issuer itself but also to any pension or profit-sharing trust of the issuer, unless an independent trustee has sole investment discretion. However, the Commission, in connection with Rule 10b–18 regulating repurchases by an issuer of its own securities (see Chapter 12, p. 808, infra), has exempted from Rule 10b–6 any purchases if they would be prohibited only because the issuer has outstanding a security *convertible* into the security purchased. This action leaves the prohibition in effect where the issuer has outstanding warrants to purchase the security involved.

The other situation is that typified by the *Jaffee* case involving a so-called "shelf registration" or "Hazel Bishop type offering" (from the *Hazel Bishop* case, supra, Chapter 9, p. 483). This situation involves a registered secondary offering without an underwriter, where the selling stockholders propose to sell from time to time on the stock exchange in regular-way transactions. Since the offering is "at the market", any stabilizing is completely prohibited. Frequently, there are large numbers of selling stockholders (there were 36 in the *Jaffee* case and 112 in *Hazel Bishop*). The Commission requires an undertaking from each selling stockholder that he will comply with Rule 10b–6 (as was given in the *Jaffee* case), but, while Mr. Jaffee was a professional and should have known better, many of the participants in such distributions are incapable of understanding Rule 10b–6 or what they have "undertaken." Also, it is customary (as was done in the *Jaffee* case) to appoint a single broker as the selling agent for all of the selling stockholders, since otherwise a broker employed by any one of them would be a participant in the distribution and become subject to Rule 10b–6 (perhaps without even knowing it). However, all of these precautions do not necessarily ensure that no violation of Rule 10b–6 will occur, as is evident from the *Jaffee* case.[12]

IN THE MATTER OF SHEARSON, HAMMILL & CO.

Securities and Exchange Commission.
42 S.E.C. 811 (1965).

Findings and Opinion of the Commission

These were private proceedings pursuant to Sections 15(b), 15A and 19(a)(3) of the Securities Exchange Act of 1934 ("Exchange Act") and Section 203(d) of the Investment Advisers Act of 1940 ("Advisers Act") to determine whether to take certain remedial action with respect to Shear-

---

12. For a discussion of trading and stabilizing in distributions, particularly Rule 10b–6, see Klein, Stabilizing Securities Prices, 5 Securities Reg.L.J. 13 (1977); S.E.C. Problems of Controlling Stockholders and in Underwritings 230–251 (Israels ed. 1961).

son, Hammill & Co. ("registrant"), a partnership, and its successor, Shearson, Hammill & Co. Incorporated, registered broker-dealers and investment advisers; Murray D. Safanie, Robert C. Van Tuyl, Walter Maynard, H. Stanley Krusen, and William J. Denman, partners in registrant's principal office in New York City and members of its executive committee; and certain personnel in registrant's branch office in Los Angeles, consisting of John B. Dunbar, regional partner in charge of registrant's branch offices in California and Arizona, Richard J. Teweles, manager and later resident partner, James C. Brum, head of the trading department, and William Troutman, Robert D. Hickson, Barry Kaye, Munro J. Silver, Gerard H. Wayne and Robert H. Wechter, salesmen.

The order for proceedings alleges, among other things, that between October 1, 1960 and November 30, 1961, in the offer, sale and delivery of common stock of United States Automatic Merchandising Company ("USAMCO"), registrant, together with or aided and abetted by the individual respondents, willfully violated the registration provisions of the Securities Act of 1933 and anti-fraud provisions of that Act, the Exchange Act, and the Advisers Act and applicable rules thereunder. It is further alleged that between January 1, 1960 and July 16, 1964, registrant willfully violated anti-fraud provisions of those Acts and rules thereunder in that, among other things, it induced excessive trading in the accounts of customers, effected unauthorized transactions in such accounts, switched securities of mutual funds in the accounts of customers contrary to their best interest, and sold securities of mutual funds to customers without due regard for break points.

Following hearings, in the course of which extensive stipulations of facts and testimony were entered into by all parties except Kaye, a recommended decision by the hearing examiner was waived and proposed findings and briefs were filed by the stipulating parties. We heard oral argument. Our findings are based upon an independent review of the record.

USAMCO TRANSACTIONS

USAMCO

USAMCO was organized in California in July 1960 to engage in the automatic vending business by officials of United States Chemical Milling Corporation ("USCM"), which had expanded its operations late in 1959 to include the manufacture of vending machines. Richard S. Stevens, USCM's manager of market development, who was 30 years of age with little experience in the vending industry, was elected president, treasurer and chairman of the board. Registrant was making a principal market in USCM stock, and Dunbar was asked by the promoters and agreed to serve as a director of USAMCO and to assist it in raising $1,000,000. He advised the sale of $700,000 of convertible notes and a public offering of $300,000 of common stock pursuant to a Regulation A exemption from registration under the Securities Act.

On September 30, 1960, USAMCO sold to ten individuals $700,000 of notes convertible at the end of one year to 700,000 shares of common stock. Seven of these individuals were associated with USCM or related to its president. The other three were customers of Dunbar who purchased

$300,000 of the notes at his solicitation. USAMCO paid registrant a $7,000 fee for its assistance and advice in placing the notes.

USAMCO commenced a Regulation A offering of 290,000 shares of its common stock at $1 per share about November 8, 1960. Six days later, as more fully discussed below, registrant's Los Angeles office began trading in the stock and made the principal or sole market in it.

USAMCO's initial plan of operation, called the "USAMCO Plan," was to place vending machines (initially purchased from USCM at $875 per machine) with small vending machine operators without charge in return for the operators' agreement to purchase vendible products from USAMCO. Revenues from the sale of vendibles were expected to amortize the cost of the machines and produce a profit for USAMCO. Vending machines were placed with operators beginning in October, 1960. However, because of high administrative costs and insufficient financing, among other reasons, the USAMCO Plan proved unprofitable by April 1961 and was abandoned by June 1961, except to fulfill a few existing contracts.

USAMCO also undertook to sell and lease vending machines to operators, but its inability to discount its leases and conditional sales contracts with financial institutions resulted in the tying up of considerable working capital. Moreover, competition and the existence of manufacturing defects in some of the machines hindered USAMCO's sales and many of the machines were ultimately sold at a loss. A program to provide vending machine service to Los Angeles schools beginning in December 1960 was discontinued after the first two machines installed were vandalized.

Beginning early in 1961, USAMCO itself became a vending operator by acquiring seven vending operating companies in exchange for 35,315 shares of USAMCO stock valued at the prevailing sale prices of from $7 to $13.50 per share, $79,500 in cash, and the assumption of liabilities totalling $170,326. Two of the companies had been operating at a loss, and one, which was acquired for 8,500 shares of USAMCO stock priced at $10 per share and the assumption of $105,000 in liabilities, had shown a net profit of only $61.47 for 1960 and its liabilities exceeded its assets. All the acquired companies proved to be unprofitable and, in July 1961, USAMCO began to liquidate them.

In April 1961, USAMCO contracted to acquire all the assets of the vending machine manufacturing division of USCM, which had discontinued its unsuccessful operation of that division, in exchange for 75,000 shares of USAMCO stock priced at $10 per share. As with all other acquisitions involving the issuance of USAMCO stock, application was made to the California Commissioner of Corporations for a permit to issue such stock. After an investigation and hearing, the Commissioner approved the exchange as fair to both parties and granted the permit in August 1961. USAMCO never contemplated manufacturing vending machines, and leased and ultimately sold the manufacturing equipment to another company. One of the principal reasons given for the acquisition was to insure a supply of parts for the machines owned by USAMCO.

* * *

Internal unaudited financial statements reflect that USAMCO operated at substantial losses. By the end of March 1961, after six months of operations, USAMCO's cumulative deficit was $157,193, and by the end of April 1961 was $187,424. This was purportedly reduced by about $32,000 in May due to the inclusion in that month's income of $31,720, consisting of $7,320 then due and $24,400 not yet due on the leases of the manufacturing equipment acquired from USCM. Following a $7,177 loss in June, the deficit was reduced in July by $20,402, with much of the reduction resulting from a non-recurring profit from the sale of items acquired from USCM. An independent audit for the first fiscal year ended August 31, 1961 showed an operating loss of $495,486 and a "net loss and special items" figure of $608,893, including about $125,000 attributable to a write-down of USAMCO's acquired assets.[2]

Violations of Registration Requirements

USAMCO's initial Regulation A notification, dated September 30, 1960, stated that USAMCO did not have an underwriter but that dealers, including registrant, who might sell the securities might be statutory underwriters. Dunbar had previously been advised by Krusen, registrant's partner in charge of syndication and secondary markets and a member of its executive committee, and then by the executive committee, that it was contrary to firm policy to underwrite Regulation A offerings of new companies. Dunbar was accordingly directed to have the unauthorized reference to registrant in the notification removed. Indeed, if registrant were to be named or were to act as underwriter of the offering a Regulation A exemption would be unavailable for the offering because registrant was disqualified from acting in that capacity under Rule 252(e)(1) of the Regulation.[3] Dunbar subsequently inquired of the New York partners of registrant whether they wished to seek an exemption from the disqualification, but they declined to do so.

A revised notification dated October 20, 1960 stated that USAMCO would sell the issue itself without an underwriter, and the definitive offering circular dated November 8, 1960 stated that its officers and directors, including Dunbar who was disclosed to be a partner of registrant as well as a director of USAMCO, would make the offering for the company without receiving any remuneration therefor "other than their regular salaries." As disclosed elsewhere in the offering circular, only Stevens was to receive a salary from USAMCO in 1961.

USAMCO allocated the 290,000-share offering to 178 persons who were named on lists submitted by two officers and directors of USAMCO, including Stevens, by USCM's president, and by Troutman, after discussions with Dunbar. Dunbar was listed by Stevens. Troutman's list allocated 194,600 shares to 118 persons, including a resident partner of registrant in another branch office in California, Teweles, Troutman, Brum, Wayne, Silver, and other employees of registrant, seventy-five customers of registrant and twenty-five individuals who did not maintain accounts with registrant but had asked Troutman or Dunbar for shares. Dunbar pur-

---

2. Although not relevant to the disposition of these proceedings, it may be noted that USAMCO sustained an even larger net loss, $665,153 (uncertified), for the following fiscal year, and its cumulative deficit reached $1,274,046. In early 1964 it had only one part-time employee and was seeking sale and merger prospects.

3. Registrant had been a member of an underwriting group with respect to an is-

sue as to which a stop order under Section 8(d) of the Securities Act had been issued within the previous five years, and had been named underwriter of another issue which was then the subject of an examination under Section 8(e) of that Act. It does not appear that any question was raised in either of those matters as to any culpability on the part of registrant.

chased 10,000 shares, the resident partner, 1,000 shares, and Troutman, 5,000 shares. These purchases, together with those by registrant's employees, accounted for 36,200 shares, or about 13% of the issue, and the seventy-five customers of registrant, all but one of whom were customers of Dunbar and Troutman, acquired 133,300 shares, or about 46% of the issue. Some of the persons who advised USAMCO that they wished to subscribe were not allocated any shares and their checks were returned. Five persons on the original lists did not subscribe. During the period from November 14, 1960, when registrant's Los Angeles office, at Dunbar's direction, commenced trading in USAMCO stock, to November 28, 1960, allocations were changed to allow four additional persons to subscribe, with the allocations to three of the subscribers being reduced at Dunbar's direction, and six more new subscribers were added. Neither registrant nor any partner or employee of registrant received any commission or fee from the Regulation A offering.

We are of the opinion that registrant was the *de facto* but undisclosed principal underwriter of USAMCO's Regulation A offering. Most of the shares in the offering were sold to registrant's customers, the two partners, and the employees. Dunbar and Troutman solicited 40 customers of registrant and two persons who were not then customers to purchase such shares. As a result of such solicitation, Dunbar sold 31,000 shares and Troutman 59,100 shares. While Dunbar asserts that he was acting as a director of USAMCO in soliciting purchases of the offering, it is clear that he made substantial use of the facilities of registrant in connection with his activities in distributing the offering. Troutman, whose sales to the 27 persons he solicited accounted for more than one-fifth of the entire offering, was in no way associated with USAMCO.

The extensive solicitation by Troutman and Dunbar, when voluntary subscribers were simultaneously being turned away by the issuer, and the allocation of a clear majority of the issue to customers, partners and employees of registrant selected by Dunbar and Troutman, make it clear that registrant, through them, effected a substantial portion of the distribution. When a registered representative like Troutman, associated with a firm prominent in underwritings, solicits customers of the firm to purchase shares of a new issue, his activities cannot be brushed aside, as counsel for registrant attempts to do, as "largely of a clerical and ministerial nature," or as assertedly "consistent" with his prior activities as an assistant to Dunbar in his work as a director of numerous other corporations. Under the circumstances, registrant was a statutory underwriter of the offering, and the Regulation A exemption was unavailable because of registrant's Rule 252(e)(1) disqualification. The fact that registrant did not receive any commissions or fees from USAMCO for the services of Dunbar and Troutman and the use of its facilities in distributing the Regulation A offering did not, in our opinion, change its status as an underwriter. Nor did the refusal of registrant's New York partners to underwrite the offering affect such status, although it is a factor to be considered in determining the extent of any sanctions to be imposed in the public interest.

Moreover, it is clear that the distribution of the Regulation A offering was not completed when registrant commenced trading in the stock on November 14, 1960, but rather continued until at least June 1961. Not only were new subscriptions accepted between November 14 and 28, 1960, but partners and employees of registrant and insiders of USAMCO and

USCM sold their Regulation A shares at prices substantially above the offering price through the first half of 1961. As a result of such sales of stock, the $300,000 limitation under Regulation A was exceeded. During the first eight days beginning on November 14, 1960, Dunbar's secretary sold 200 shares through registrant at 5, Brum sold 1,500 shares at the same price through an account opened with another broker-dealer, Stevens' mother and stepfather sold 1,900 shares through registrant and Dunbar at 4 and 5, and an officer of USCM sold 500 shares through registrant at 4.

Thereafter, during the first half of 1961, partners and employees of registrant liquidated all or large portions of their Regulation A shares at substantial profits. Brum sold 3,000 shares to registrant through another broker-dealer, for a total profit on all his Regulation A shares of $37,119. One of his assistants sold 100 shares through registrant at 13 in February 1961, and another assistant sold 100 shares through registrant at 17 in May 1961. Dunbar, who testified that he followed the practice of selling enough of his holdings of a speculative security to recover his cost plus a profit when the market price reached a sufficiently high level, sold 3,300 of his 10,000 Regulation A shares for a profit on those shares of $49,479 in May 1961, when the stock became "long-term," i.e., when only a portion of any capital gain would be taxable. Similarly, Troutman sold 2,000 of his 5,000 shares in May for a profit on those shares of $31,349, the manager of a branch office in California sold 800 shares in May and June at $14\frac{7}{8}$ to $15\frac{7}{8}$, Teweles, who had become a partner of registrant on January 1, 1961, sold 6,000 shares, including 4,500 Regulation A shares, in February and June at 12 to 16, and Wayne sold 1,000 shares in June at 15. Other sales of such shares during the period by registrant's personnel included a sale of 1,000 shares by the manager of another California branch office for a profit of $8,321.

In addition, Stevens in December 1960, sold 1,000 shares of his Regulation A stock through registrant and Dunbar when the market price was at least 5, and another officer of USAMCO in February 1961 sold 3,000 shares of Regulation A stock, or stock which had been subject to the escrow agreement previously noted, through registrant and Dunbar at between 12 and $12\frac{1}{2}$. Also, officers of USCM, including the president as well as a member of his family, had sold by the end of the summer of 1961 about 30,000 shares, consisting principally of Regulation A stock, through registrant and Dunbar, and over 10,000 of such shares were sold from March to May 1961 at 14 to 18.

A distribution of securities comprises "the entire process by which in the course of a public offering a block of securities is dispersed and ultimately comes to rest in the hands of the investing public." Since a large portion of the Regulation A offering acquired by partners and employees of registrant and insiders of USAMCO and USCM was resold to the public by registrant, which was in fact effecting a substantial part of the distribution, within a relatively short period after the offering was treated as completed, such resales must be integrated with the distribution under Regulation A and the excess of the resale prices over the stated offering price included in the computation of the aggregate offering price. When so computed, the $300,000 limitation under Regulation A was exceeded by a substantial amount.

No exemption under Regulation A being available and no registration statement having been filed or being in effect with respect to the USAMCO offering, we conclude that in the offer, sale and delivery of USAMCO stock registrant, as well as Dunbar, Troutman, Teweles, Brum and Wayne, willfully violated Sections 5(a) and (c) of the Securities Act. Registrant's assertion that Dunbar was advised by counsel that it was proper for registrant to open a trading market in USAMCO stock, and believed in good faith that the offering was completed prior to the opening of such market, provides no basis for holding that the violations were not willful. Even aside from the fact that an opinion of counsel does not preclude a finding of willfulness, it was stipulated that counsel was not aware at the time he rendered his opinion that certain persons to whom shares had been allocated had not yet returned their subscription agreements or paid for the shares. It also does not appear that counsel was advised that Dunbar and other personnel of registrant did not intend to hold their Regulation A shares for investment.[a]

Fraud in USAMCO Transactions

1. *Bids For and Purchases of Stock During Distribution*

The order for proceedings alleges violations of Section 10(b) of the Exchange Act and Rule 17 CFR 240.10b–6 thereunder in the period from November 14, to December 15, 1960. That rule prohibits an underwriter or broker-dealer who is participating in a distribution of securities from bidding for or purchasing such securities in the course of the distribution. As we have seen, the public distribution of the Regulation A shares continued throughout the period alleged.

At Dunbar's direction, Brum opened a trading market on November 14, 1960, and during the period in question registrant entered daily bids for the stock in the sheets published by National Quotation Bureau, Inc. and purchased such shares for inventory. We have already discussed and found without merit Dunbar's asserted reliance upon the opinion of registrant's counsel that registrant could lawfully open a trading market in USAMCO stock, as well as registrant's contentions that the Regulation A distribution had been completed prior thereto. As we have seen, Dunbar handled the sale of 1,900 Regulation A shares by Stevens' mother and stepfather shortly after the trading was begun. Troutman must have known that the Los Angeles office was bidding for and purchasing USAMCO stock at the time changes were being made in the Dunbar-Troutman list of subscribers and in the allocations, and that certain subscribers on the list had not yet sent in their subscriptions. Brum sold part of his allotment to registrant through another broker-dealer after he opened the trading market and began purchasing USAMCO stock for registrant's account. We conclude

---

a. And see Mutual Employees Trademart, Inc., 40 S.E.C. 1092 (1962); Strathmore Securities, Inc., 43 S.E.C. 575 (1967).

In Koss v. SEC, 364 F.Supp. 1321 (S.D. N.Y.1973), an underwriter for Regulation A offerings sought to enjoin the Commission from directing several issuers to include in their offering circulars statements that the underwriter was a respondent in a pending administrative proceeding before the Commission, including a summary of the Commission's allegations. The court denied relief on the ground that the case was not ripe for judicial review; however, it observed that the Commission and staff acted within its authority in requiring the disclosure of these facts as being material to the offering.

that registrant, aided and abetted by Dunbar, Troutman and Brum, willfully violated Rule 10b–6 under Section 10(b) of the Exchange Act.

2. *Domination and Control of Market, and Operation of "Work-Out" Market*

Registrant's opening bid for USAMCO stock in the sheets on November 14, 1960, was 3. Thereafter, throughout the remainder of 1960 and the first half of 1961, registrant entered daily quotations in the sheets at generally increasing prices. On November 18, it quoted the stock at 5 bid–$5\frac{1}{2}$ asked, on December 15, at $5\frac{3}{4}$–$6\frac{1}{4}$, on December 30 at 7–$7\frac{1}{2}$, on January 31, 1961 at 12–13, and on March 3 at 14–15. On March 30 registrant's quotes were $16\frac{1}{2}$–$17\frac{1}{2}$, although no other broker-dealers had been entering quotations in the sheets since March 23, when registrant's bid was 15. The high of 18 bid–19 asked was reached in April, and sales were made at prices as high as $19\frac{7}{8}$. During May and June 1961, when the profits on the Regulation A shares became long-term for tax purposes, and Dunbar and Teweles liquidated portions of their holdings, registrant maintained its quotations at slightly below the April highs and sold the stock at 15 and 16. At the end of June, the price of the stock declined to about 10 and remained at about that level until September 11, when registrant was selling it to customers at 11. On that day, registrant's New York partners ordered the firm's registered representatives to discontinue the solicitation of USAMCO stock buy orders from customers. The market in the stock then collapsed and by December 11, its bid was $\frac{1}{4}$, after which registrant ceased making a market in the stock.

From November 14, 1960 until the end of 1961, registrant made the principal or sole market in USAMCO stock. Through November 30, 1961 registrant as principal sold 312,449 shares, including 76,098 shares to dealers, and purchased 311,117 shares, including 104,291 shares from dealers. As agent for customers registrant purchased 66,312 shares and sold 83,910 shares.

Although other broker-dealers published quotations in the sheets from time to time during the period, the role of such firms was in general not significant. One firm, which traded in USAMCO stock for its own account, appeared in the sheets daily from November 14, 1960 until March 22, 1961, and during such period purchased 15,606 shares and sold the same number. This must be compared with registrant's activities during the same period when it made principal sales of 147,701 shares and principal purchases of 147,269 shares together with agency purchases of 40,470 shares and agency sales of about the same number of shares. For a period of about $2\frac{1}{2}$ weeks, from November 14 to December 2, 1960, another firm entered quotations in the sheets, but its trades were inconsequential. A third firm entered daily quotations from July 7 to August 16, 1961, but sold only 1,340 shares compared to 56,764 shares sold by registrant during the same period. Other dealers entering occasional quotations had virtually no trades in the stock—one purchased 50 shares and another sold 50 and purchased 1,250 shares. Two other firms entered price quotations on only one day.

Registrant was both the primary wholesale and retail dealer in USAMCO stock, and the market for that stock was dependent upon registrant's continued sales efforts. From March 23, to June 29, 1961, and on most of the trading days until November 2, 1961, registrant alone entered quotations in the sheets. During the period to June 29 registrant sold over 94,000 shares at prices ranging from 15 to the high of $19\frac{7}{8}$ on April 19.

On June 12, 1961, Brum reported to Dunbar that he feared that the demand for USAMCO stock was insufficient to cover anticipated orders to sell such stock. On the following day, Dunbar authorized Brum to establish a "work-out" market, in which no sell orders from customers were to be accepted or executed by registrant unless offsetting buy orders for at least an equal number of shares were on hand.[22] During the period of the work-out market, registrant continued to enter both bid and ask quotations and was the only broker-dealer quoting the stock in the sheets. Registrant solicited customers to buy USAMCO stock but, with the exception of one order to sell 100 shares, did not accept or execute customers' sell orders in the absence of an off-setting buy order. The registered representatives who solicited buy orders from customers quoted the market to their customers in the ordinary manner and generally did not disclose that the market was work-out. Registrant sold 8,782 shares during this period, of which 3,500 shares were purchased from Teweles and 90 from his secretary, 3,000 shares were purchased from Wayne, 1,982 shares came from registrant's own inventory, and only 210 shares were purchased from customers. It did not execute any agency transactions nor purchase USAMCO stock from broker-dealers.

During the work-out market, at least two open sell orders from another California branch office were cancelled at the request of the Los Angeles office, one of them at Teweles' request on June 14. Some customer sell orders were returned by Brum to the salesmen, with the notation that there were no buyers for the stock. Several salesmen thereafter refused to accept orders from customers to sell. Nevertheless, registrant purchased the 6,500 shares from Teweles and Wayne, all at 15 except for 200 shares from Teweles at $14\frac{1}{2}$, even though on each of the six days when these purchases were effected, a prior order or orders from customers to sell USAMCO stock remained open and unexecuted. Several of such orders had been entered at prices lower than those which registrant paid Teweles and Wayne for their shares. While Teweles and Wayne were selling their shares at 15 and $14\frac{1}{2}$, they induced customers to purchase shares at between $15\frac{1}{4}$ and 16, and advised customers not to sell, without disclosing to such customers that registrant was maintaining a work-out market and that they were selling their shares on a work-out basis. Wayne in fact stressed that he personally held such stock. Brum permitted Teweles and Wayne to sell such shares for their own accounts because they generated the buy orders from their customers to match their own sales.

Other registered representatives including Silver and Wechter, also induced customers to purchase USAMCO stock at between $13\frac{3}{4}$ and 16 without disclosing, as they knew that the work-out market was in effect. Since registrant was making the only market in USAMCO stock at this time, there was no other outlet through which customers could sell their stock and they were thus "locked in" for the duration of the work-out. After the work-out market was terminated at Dunbar's direction, many of

---

22. A work-out market has been described as one in which the trader acts essentially as broker and attempts to find interest on the other side of the market. S.E.C. Special Study of Securities Markets, 88th Cong., 1st Sess., House Doc. No. 95, Part 2, p. 572 (July 17, 1963).

the customers, whose sell orders were not accepted or remained unexecuted because of the preference given to Teweles and Wayne, sold their shares at below 12.

Since registrant was the principal market maker and, as shown, dominated and controlled the market in USAMCO stock, the commencement of the work-out market created a situation which not only was potentially subject to abuse but was in fact used to conduct a one-sided market at an artificial level for the benefit of registrant and its employees while it was through its quotations giving the false appearance of maintaining a normal two-sided market. In view of the fact that registrant had no intention of purchasing USAMCO stock from broker-dealers during the work-out market it is clear that its bid quotations in the sheets during the work-out were not *bona fide* and constituted a manipulative and deceptive device and fraudulent course of business.[27] Dunbar admitted that the work-out market conducted by the Los Angeles office was not a true market, and according to Brum, in a "normal" market the price during that month would have dropped rapidly to about 10, at which price there was some demand for the stock. As noted, after the salesmen were instructed in September 1961 to cease soliciting buy orders from customers, the market in the stock collapsed. Moreover, registrant's failure to execute customers' sell orders that it had accepted, while effecting the purchases from its own employees which as noted were at prices higher than those the customers had asked, constituted a violation of the duty to deal fairly with customers that inheres in the broker-dealer relationship.

On these facts, it is clear, and we find, that registrant, aided and abetted by Dunbar, Teweles, Kaye, Wayne, Silver, Wechter and Hickson, as well as by the members of registrant's executive committee who, as discussed below, failed to exercise adequate supervision, employed manipulative, deceptive and fraudulent devices in willful violation of Rule 17 CFR 240.15c1–8 under Section 15(c)(1) of the Exchange Act, in that it represented to customers that USAMCO stock was being offered to them at or about the market price although it knew or had reasonable grounds to believe, particularly during the work-out market, that no market for the stock existed other than that made, created or controlled by it.

We further find that in its activities in the work-out market registrant, together with or aided and abetted by Brum, Teweles, Wayne, Silver, Wechter, and the members of the executive committee, willfully violated the anti-fraud provisions of Section 17(a) of the Securities Act, Sections 10(b) and 15(c)(1) of the Exchange Act and Rules 10b–5 and 15c1–2 thereunder, and Sections 206(1) and (2) of the Advisers Act. We cannot accept Brum's assertion that, as a subordinate, he had to carry out Teweles' desires because Teweles, in Dunbar's absence was in charge of the office, and that Teweles did not instruct him to refuse to execute Wayne's order tickets. According to one of the New York partners, Brum should have looked to a designated New York partner for guidance, not to Teweles.

27. See NASD Rules of Fair Practice, Article III, Section 5. See also the NASD's recently adopted policy with respect to firmness of quotations. NASD Manual, G–56. The NASD has stated that "to advertise a two-way market when one has an interest in only one side of the market" constitutes a flagrant violation of the code of ethical conduct between members. Over-the-Counter Trading Handbook, pp. 2, 3 (1960).

3. Fraudulent Representations

For years, research has been the main motif of registrant's nationwide advertising. Its slogan is "The Firm that Research Built." Its brochures and other advertisements represented that the firm considers sound research to be an indispensable instrument in evaluating investment situations. Yet, despite the substantial activity of the Los Angeles and other California offices in USAMCO stock, the stock was never analyzed or evaluated by the firm's New York research department or its west coast research associate stationed in Los Angeles to examine west coast issues.

About February 9, 1961, Kaye, with Teweles' knowledge, distributed to his customers several hundred copies of a report which he had written on the vending industry, and he and other registered representatives used the report in soliciting customers to invest in USAMCO stock. This report evaluated six of the largest manufacturers or operators of vending machines and USAMCO, and contained materially false and misleading statements with respect to USAMCO.

The report stated that USAMCO had purchased the assets of profitable operating companies or had entered into special contracts with operators which had proven to be highly profitable and that several joint ventures entered into in January 1961 would result in a gross income well in excess of $1 million in the next 12 months.[34] In fact, at the time the report was prepared, USAMCO had completed only one acquisition, and during late 1960 and early 1961, it was operating at a sizeable deficit and had incurred a loss during each month from the inception of operations. And as of the time the report was distributed, USAMCO had entered into only one joint venture which produced little revenue, resulted in a loss to USAMCO of $18,600, and was soon abandoned.

* * *

Untrue earnings projections and reports for USAMCO, as well as other optimistic reports, were also disseminated among the registered representatives and used to solicit purchases. Late in 1960 or early in January 1961, Stevens mentioned to registrant's west coast research associate that he expected USAMCO to earn $1 per share during its first year. This projection was disseminated among the registered representatives by the research associate without any investigation and despite the fact that USAMCO had barely commenced operations, had only a few employees, had not completed any acquisitions, had virtually no income, and had a large deficit.

* * *

Publicity and press releases, which were prepared from information supplied by Stevens and approved by Dunbar before distribution, and upon which newspaper articles were based described USAMCO as a new, vigorous, imaginative and expanding member of the vending machine industry. Those releases and the articles based thereon contained false and mislead-

---

34. These representations were based on a promotional pamphlet which was distributed by USAMCO in January 1961 and which Kaye also sent to his customers. The pamphlet, which contained such exaggerations as "USAMCO proposes to become the 'Sears Roebuck' for the vending industry," and "Basically, the company is a giant commodity broker to the vending industry," was hardly a reliable source on which to base a report sent to customers to induce purchases.

ing statements and were used by registered representatives, including Hickson, Kaye, Silver, Wayne and Wechter, to sell USAMCO stock.

* * *

In addition, upon the basis of our examination of the record, we find that registrant's registered representatives, including Teweles, Hickson, Kaye, Silver, Wayne and Wechter, made flamboyant predictions and other fraudulent representations to customers in the offer and sale of USAMCO stock.

* * *

The predictions of substantial price rises had no reasonable basis and, considering the unseasoned and speculative nature of USAMCO stock, could not possibly be justified whether couched in terms of opinion or fact.

* * *

Silver testified that on one occasion Stevens advised him that USAMCO "was taking money in so fast that it couldn't count it," and that Stevens informed him, when the market price of USAMCO stock was 10, that the company was contemplating a new public offering when the market price reached 20. Silver admits, however, that he had no idea of how much money, if any, USAMCO was actually earning, that he did not examine USAMCO's financial statements, and that when he asked Dunbar whether a new issue was coming out at 20, Dunbar merely shrugged and did not answer.

* * *

The record also contains glaring examples of recommendations to invest in USAMCO stock made to customers contrary to their investment needs. Kaye recommended to a 13-year-old boy, who had asked to purchase Smith-Corona stock, that he buy instead 25 shares of USAMCO stock at $18\frac{1}{2}$, pointing out that favorable developments regarding USAMCO were imminent which he was not then at liberty to disclose. The boy agreed to buy the stock and the trade was later entered in the name of the mother who consented because of her son's insistence. In addition, Kaye, without inquiring into a 70-year-old widow's finances or investment objectives, induced her to invest $1,250 in USAMCO stock although she had limited financial means, earned a weekly salary of $65, and wanted safety of principal and some dividend income. Another widow, who as Kaye knew had limited means and wanted high quality securities with good dividends, was induced by him to invest $1,650 in USAMCO stock after he falsely told her that registrant's research department had recommended it.

* * *

We conclude that registrant, together with or aided and abetted by Dunbar, Teweles, Hickson, Kaye, Silver, Wayne, Wechter, and, as shown below, the members of the executive committee, willfully violated the antifraud provisions of Section 17(a) of the Securities Act, Sections 10(b) and 15(c)(1) of the Exchange Act and Rules 17 CFR 240.10b–5, and 15c1–2 thereunder, and Sections 206(1), (2) and (4) of the Advisers Act and Rule 206(4)–1 thereunder.

* * *

Inadequate Supervision by Executive Committee

Registrant contends that its supervisory procedures and system for applying them during the period involved could reasonably be expected to prevent and detect securities violations and that the executive committee carried out its responsibilities in implementing those procedures. It points to the "prompt" action taken by the committee, "when it first became apparent in September 1961 that USAMCO might be in difficulty," in barring further solicitations in USAMCO stock, prohibiting transactions for the accounts of the firm's personnel, and urging USAMCO to inform the public as to its financial condition.

Whatever the merits of registrant's supervisory procedures and the experience and background of Dunbar and Teweles upon whom the committee strongly relied, we think the record demonstrates that there was a significant breakdown in the committee's implementation of those procedures. Registrant was on notice much earlier than September 1961 that an investigation of USAMCO as well as the Los Angeles office was in order. It was lax in assessing the realities of the situation and in taking appropriate action.

    * * *

The failure of the executive committee diligently to enforce registrant's system of internal control resulted in the perpetration of fraud upon many customers. " * * * [S]uch failure constitutes participation in such misconduct, and willful violations are committed not only by the person who performed the misconduct but also by those who did not properly perform their duty to prevent it."

Accordingly, we conclude that Safanie, Van Tuyl, Krusen, Maynard and Denman, individually or as members of the executive committee, engaged in a course of business which operated as a fraud upon customers, in willful violation of Section 10(b) of the Exchange Act and Rule 10b–5 thereunder, and, as we have found, aided and abetted the willful violations of Section 17(a) of the Securities Act, Sections 10(b) and 15(c)(1) of the Exchange Act and Rules 10b–5, 15c1–2 and 15c1–8 thereunder, and Sections 206(1), (2) and (4) of the Advisers Act and Rule 206(4)–1 thereunder.

    * * * *

PUBLIC INTEREST

Registrant urges that if any sanction is required in the public interest no more than a censure of the firm would be warranted. It stresses that the events that are the subject of these proceedings directly involved only a few people in a few California branch offices who, except for Troutman, Wechter and Silver, are no longer employed by it; that it has already suffered severely as a result of them; and that since their occurrence registrant has installed additional supervisory procedures and controls designed to prevent any future violations.

    * * *

In our opinion, the willful violations established by the record were so grave and extensive as to warrant the imposition of substantial sanctions. Registrant's argument that its questioned activities involved only a small part of its over-all securities business overlooks the nature of its obligations to the public. In our view, what is significant is that a recognized leader in the business should tolerate a system in its branch offices which would permit these offenses to occur at all.

We have carefully considered the mitigative factors presented, including the facts that the termination of the employment of most of the respondents who directly participated in the violations and the enlarged internal controls adopted by registrant have reduced the risk of any recurrence of injury to investors of the type found and that the impact of further sanctions against registrant would fall in large part upon many innocent persons. In view of those factors, we would be inclined to withhold the imposition of a sanction against registrant if the members of the executive committee, who by their failure to exercise their managerial obligations must bear a heavy responsibility for the violations, were disassociated from registrant for an appropriate period.

Accordingly we will withhold the issuance of an order for 30 days so as to afford registrant an opportunity to submit a proposal providing for the effective separation of the members of the executive committee from registrant and its corporate successor for a period of 60 days, beginning no later than 30 days after the issuance of our order approving such a proposal or any modification thereof, with such periods of separation to be concurrent or consecutive as registrant chooses. The proposal should further provide that no member of the executive committee shall engage in any securities activities on behalf of registrant and its successor nor receive, directly or indirectly, any compensation or share of the profits or dividends attributable to the period of his separation, although interest payable with respect to such period on any capital of such member held by registrant or its successor may be paid to him. If an acceptable proposal is submitted, our order approving it will reserve jurisdiction to take appropriate action in the event the proposal is not fully and effectively carried out. If an acceptable proposal is not submitted, we will issue an order imposing appropriate sanctions and making "cause" findings with respect to the individual respondents.

* * *

By the Commission (CHAIRMAN COHEN and COMMISSIONERS WOODSIDE and OWENS), COMMISSIONER BUDGE filing a separate statement concurring in part and dissenting in part, and COMMISSIONER WHEAT not participating.

COMMISSIONER BUDGE, concurring in part and dissenting in part:

Sanction should be imposed upon the registrant and its partners which is of the same nature and achieves the same result as that which the Commission has imposed in similar and in less flagrant cases. Generally, the means in other cases has been revocation, and the result the closing of the brokerage house where the illegal activity took place.

Unlike a registrant with a single office, it is not here indicated nor does the public interest require revocation of the registrant or sanction affecting its nearly fifty nationwide offices. The branch offices in southern California primarily involved, constituting as they did the "locus of infection," should be closed and registrant proscribed from doing business in that area. Such a sanction and its result would be consistent with prior decisions. It would reach each partner, yet would make clear that the Commission's action is specifically directed against the offending branch offices. It would also more clearly emphasize that the Commission's intent is not to cast adverse reflection upon the other offices of the firm.

Such an approach has previously been suggested and reflects the spirit of the 1964 amendments in that it would permit the Commission to pinpoint and take action against a segment of the registrant without condemning it in its entirety.

Otherwise, I am in agreement with the majority.

HOT ISSUES

In 1959, only a year prior to the organization of USAMCO, the Commission had already issued a warning against the practices involved in that case in a Preliminary Report on Practices in Distribution of "Hot Issues." [1] That Release stated:

"The practices in question involve a combination of some or all of the following elements:

"1. In addition to allotments of the offered securities to his own customers and to selling group dealers, if any, the underwriter may allot a portion of the offering at the public offering price to trading firms active in the over-the-counter market. These firms are expected to commence making a market in such securities at or immediately after the start of the public offering. Some of these firms sell their allotments at prices substantially in excess of the public offering price stated in the prospectus, and in some cases bid for and purchase the security while they are distributing their allotments. The inquiry also discloses that such distributions may be made by these firms without any use of a prospectus.

"In one recent offering, which almost doubled in price on the first day of trading, over thirteen percent of the entire offering was sold by the underwriters at the public offering price to four broker-dealers and one of these broker-dealers sold out its entire allotment in the course of trading activities within three weeks of the offering date at substantially higher prices. In another 'hot issue' offering the principal underwriter sold substantial amounts of its participation at the public offering price of $3 per share to several broker-dealers and on the first day of trading, six of these firms appeared in the 'sheets' of the National Daily Quotation Service with bids and offers ranging from $5\frac{3}{4}$ to $7\frac{1}{4}$.

"2. Underwriters and selling group dealers may allot a substantial portion of the securities acquired by them to partners, officers, employees or relatives of such persons ('insiders'), to other broker-dealers with whom they may have reciprocal arrangements or to 'insiders' of such other broker-dealers. Such allotments are made notwithstanding the fact that customers of such firms are unable to obtain a part of the original distribution and therefore could only purchase the securities in the market at the higher price.

"In one recent offering, which more than doubled in price on the offering date, the selling group allotted over twenty-eight percent of its total participation to 'insiders'. One member of that selling group diverted to 'insiders' over seventy-five percent of its 3,000 share allotment of the 100,000 share offering, and another sold almost fifty percent of its 5,000 share allotment to 'insiders'. Underwriters have indulged in the same practice. The underwriters in a recent offering of an electronics stock diverted almost twenty-two percent of the entire offering to 'insider' accounts. In another offering one of the underwriters diverted over eighty-seven percent of its participation to 'insider' accounts and another sold forty-seven percent to such accounts."

The Commission pointed out that these practices might involve violations of various provisions of the securities laws:

---

1. Sec. Act Rel. No. 4150 (SEC 1959).

1. The description of the plan of distribution and marketing arrangements in the prospectus or offering circular might be materially misleading, in violation of Sections 11 and 12(2) of the 1933 Act or Rule 10b–5.

2. The trading firms might be *de facto* "underwriters" and the failure to identify them as such would violate the above anti-fraud provisions. Any failure by them to deliver a prospectus to a buyer, even after the 40-day period then specified in Section 4(1) of the 1933 Act, would violate Section 5(b) of that Act.

3. The restriction of the supply, while leading the public to believe that the issue has been heavily over-subscribed, may violate the anti-fraud provisions of the securities laws.

4. The activities of the trading firms, as participants in the distribution, may violate Rule 10b–6.

5. If a broker-dealer involved represents that the security is being sold "at the market," this may constitute a violation of Rule 15c1–8 in that no bona fide market exists other than one controlled by him and persons with whom he is associated.

6. If the issue is qualified under Regulation A, sales by the "free riders" may cause the total public offering price to exceed the maximum dollar figure permissible under Section 3(b) and thereby cause all sales to be in violation of Section 5 of the 1933 Act.

Following this SEC Release, the NASD issued the following Interpretation with respect to 'Free-Riding and Withholding.'[2]

FREE–RIDING AND WITHHOLDING

Introduction

*   *   *

"In accordance with Article VII, Section 3(a) of the By-Laws, the following interpretation under Article III, Section 1 of the Rules of Fair Practice is adopted by the Board of Governors and will be applicable to all transactions.

"Members have an obligation to make a bona fide public offering, at the public offering price, of securities acquired by a participation in any distribution, whether acquired as an underwriter, a selling group member, or from a member participating in the distribution as an underwriter or selling group member. The failure to make a bona fide public offering when there is a great demand for an issue can be a factor in artificially raising the price. Not only is such failure in contravention of ethical practices, but it impairs public confidence in the fairness of the securities business.

"A member is in a position of trust, when it has information with respect to a particular security, the indicated demand, and other factors bearing on its future price not generally known to the public. To take unfair advantage of such a position as a participant in an offering indicates a lack of commercial honor.

*   *   *

Interpretation

"Except as provided herein, if a member either has unfilled orders from the public or has failed to make a bona fide public offering of the securities acquired as described above, it would be a violation of Article III, Section 1 of

2. CCH NASD Manual ¶ 2151.02.

the Rules of Fair Practice for a member directly or indirectly to sell any of its participation in the manner proscribed by categories (1) to (5) below.

"Further, sales of any of the securities so acquired to the accounts of banks, trust companies or other conduits for undisclosed principals shall not relieve a member of its responsibility to insure that the ultimate purchaser is not an account which is within the purview of the provisions of categories (2), (3) or (4) below. Specifically, a member shall not directly or indirectly:

"(1) Continue to hold any of the securities in the member's accounts;

"(2) Sell any of the securities to any officer, director, partner, employee, or agent of the member or of any other member or to a member of the immediate family of any such person;

"(3) Sell any of the securities to any senior officer of a bank, of an insurance company or of any other institutional type account; or to any person in the securities department of, or whose activities involve or are related to the function of buying or selling securities for a bank, insurance company, or other institutional type account; or to a member of the immediate family of such persons;

"(4) Sell any of the securities to any account in which any person specified under (1), (2) or (3) has a beneficial interest;

"A member may withhold for its own account, or sell to persons in categories (2), (3) or (4) part of its participation in an offering acquired as described above if the member is prepared to demonstrate that the securities were withheld for bona fide investment in accordance with the member's normal investment practice, or were sold to such other persons for bona fide investment in accordance with their normal investment practice with the member, and that the aggregate of the securities so withheld and sold is insubstantial and not disproportionate in amount as compared to sales to members of the public.

"(5) Sell any of the securities, at or above the public offering price, to any other broker or dealer.

"A member may sell part of the securities to another member if the latter represents to the selling member and is prepared to demonstrate that such purchase was made to fill orders, as an accommodation and without compensation, for bona fide public customers at the public offering price. If such accommodation order is filled for any person in categories (2), (3) or (4) above, the member who fills the order for such person must represent to the selling member and be prepared to demonstrate that such sale was for bona fide investment in accordance with the normal investment practice of such person with the member.

Definitions

* * *

Distribution

"The term 'distribution' includes all distributions of securities whether registered, unregistered or exempt from registration under the Securities Act of 1933, or whether primary or secondary distributions, including intrastate offerings and Regulation 'A' issues. This interpretation does not apply to exempted securities as defined in Section 3(a)(12) of the Securities Exchange Act of 1934.

Immediate Family

"The term 'immediate family' shall include parents, mother-in-law or father-in-law, husband or wife, brothers or sisters, children, or any relative to whose support the member, person associated with the member, or other person in categories (2) and (3) above contributes directly or indirectly.

Normal Investment Practice

" 'Normal investment practice' shall mean the history of investment in an account with the member. If such history discloses a practice of purchasing mainly 'hot issues,' such record would not constitute a 'normal investment practice' as used in this interpretation. If the account involved is that of the member, such account must be clearly an investment account as distinct from a regular inventory or trading account."

The problem of "hot issues" is the converse of the problems of stabilization and resale price maintenance. In a run-away bull market, neither of the latter are significant. But just as an over-priced security particularly requires stabilization and resale price maintenance in order to effect its distribution, an under-priced security holds forth the prospect of trading profits which in some cases is too much temptation to the underwriters. (This refers to "under-priced" in the light of market conditions, not with respect to the intrinsic value of the securities.) For example, if certain "glamour" stocks are selling in the market at 40 times earnings, and a new issue of a corporation in the same line is brought out at 18 times earnings, the underwriters can anticipate that, unless market conditions change, the price of the securities in the market may double over the offering price within a relatively short period of time. However, frequently the Blue Sky officials where the securities must be qualified will not permit the corporation to issue its securities at any higher price.[3] In this situation, if the underwriters sell all of the issue at the public offering price, they will make perhaps a 10% "spread" or commission. If they hold back say ⅓ of the issue until the market rise, they may make 110% on that portion. The resulting restriction of the supply helps to insure that the market rise will occur.

Both the SEC Release referred to above and the *Shearson, Hammill* case indicate that the activities of participants in "hot issues" almost invariably violated numerous provisions of the securities laws and regulations, and that it was the lack of enforcement rather than the lack of restraints which permitted the practices described.[4] Consistently with this interpretation, the Special Study of Securities Markets' recommendations in this area[5] were almost entirely devoted to increased surveillance and enforcement of existing regulations by the Commission and the NASD. The one specific recommendation was that the 40-day period during which the delivery of Prospectuses is required by dealers after a registered issue under the 1933 Act be extended to 90 days in

---

3. Since this type of regulation merely results in the "free riders" rather than the issuing corporation getting the difference between the initial offering price and the market price at which the securities sell shortly thereafter, the California Corporate Securities Law of 1968 withdraws any jurisdiction from the Commissioner of Corporations to refuse to qualify an issue on the basis that the price is not fair, just or equitable in any case "where the security is being publicly offered for cash pursuant to a registration statement under the Securities Act of 1933 and the offering is the subject of a firm commitment underwriting by an underwriter or syndicate of underwriters all of whom are registered under the Securities Exchange Act of 1934." West's Ann.Cal.Corp.Code, § 25140(d).

4. For a discussion of the wide range of problems generated by hot issues, see S.E.C. Problems of Controlling Stockholders and in Underwritings 252–83 (Israels ed. 1962).

5. H.Doc.No.95, 88th Cong., 1st Sess., pt. 1, Ch. IV, at 557–59 (1963).

the case of companies going public for the first time; and this recommendation was adopted in the Securities Acts Amendments of 1964.[6] Since the Study also showed [7] that many dealers were unaware of the 40-day requirement and most of them ignored it, it would seem that here also merely extending the 40 days to 90 is not going to do much good in the absence of more enforcement.

Perhaps these admonitions from the regulatory authorities tended to deter underwriters from committing the specific violations to which attention was called; at least, there has been no published indication that the rules were again widely flouted in the latest "hot issue" splurge. However, it is certain that neither public warnings nor increased surveillance prevented the revival of the "hot issue" phenomenon during the speculative frenzy of 1966-69, with fried chicken and computers substituted for uranium and electronics. In the Fall of 1971 the Commission announced a new study of "hot issues" to determine whether additional rules or legislation are needed; [8] possibly some-one should finance a study by a medical school to develop a vaccine against investor insanity. Or, as suggested by Judge Masterson, perhaps the solution is the appointment by the judiciary of involuntary guardians for investors: "The question brought to mind by the evidence in this case is, should the broker permit a compulsive investor to continue to trade through its facilities when it has become clear that his speculative activity has crossed the line between intelligent risk taking and irrational gambling? We are reminded of the established body of law which limits the bartender's discretion in selling to an obviously inebriated alcoholic." [9]

For discussions, see Grienenberger, "Hot Issue" Amendments and New Disclosure Guides, 5 Inst.Sec.Reg. 77 (1974); Sowards and Mofsky, The "Hot Issue": Possible Hidden Causes, 45 St. John's L.Rev. 802 (1971); Prifti, Hot Issue, 24 Bus.Law. 311 (1968); Rotberg, The "Hot Issue", 17 Bus.Law. 360 (1962).

MANIPULATION

Section 9 of the Securities Exchange Act of 1934 is designed to prohibit manipulation of the securities markets. It has been termed by the SEC the "very heart of the act." [10] Section 9 itself applies only to listed securities, but the prohibitions in that section have been held to be incorporated into Sections 10(b) and 15(c)(1) which prohibit "manipulative" devices with respect to over-the-counter securities also.[11] In addition to various specific provisions aimed at the more notorious practices of the "pools" of the 1920's, such as wash sales, matched orders, tipster sheets, etc., Section 9(a)(2) contains a general prohibi-tion against effecting "a series of transactions * * * creating actual or

6. Pub.Law 88–467, § 12 (1964), amend-ing § 4(3) of the Securities Act of 1933.

7. H.Doc.No.95, 88th Cong., 1st Sess., pt. 1, at 549–50 (1963).

8. SEC Sec. Act Rel. No. 5204, SEC Exch. Act Rel. No. 9374 (Oct. 21, 1971). As a result, in part, of these hearings the SEC issued a series of amendments to Rules and Guides in 1972 and another group in 1973. The amendments are summarized in Sec. Act Rel. No. 5274 (July 26, 1972) and Sec. Act Rel. No. 5395 (June 1, 1973). They are discussed in Schneider, Grienenberger, Marsh and Levenson, New Approaches to

Disclosure in Registered Security Offer-ings, 28 Bus.Law. 505 (1973); and Grienenberger, "Hot Issue" Amendments and New Disclosure Guides, 5 Inst.Sec.Reg. 77 (1974).

9. Powers v. Francis I. DuPont and Co., 344 F.Supp. 429, at 433 (E.D.Pa.1972).

10. See 3 Loss, Securities Regulation 1549 (2d ed. 1961).

11. Securities and Exchange Commis-sion v. Resch-Cassin & Co., Inc., 362 F.Supp. 964 (S.D.N.Y.1973).

apparent active trading in * * * or raising or depressing the price of" a security *"for the purpose of inducing the purchase or sale of such security by others."* The first part of the requirement of this section would be met by almost any conceivable market activity, other than a single purchase or sale. *Any* series of transactions would almost inevitably create actual or apparent trading or raise or depress the price of the security dealt in. The crucial question is the *purpose* for which the transactions are effected. If the activity is engaged in for the purpose of inducing the purchase or sale of such security by others, then it is unlawful. However, as the Commission stated in the *Halsey, Stuart* [12] case: "There is not here (as indeed there rarely is) any subjective evidence of such a purpose. If found, it must, as in most cases, be inferred from the circumstances of the case."

The *Shearson, Hammill* case presents an almost classic illustration of market manipulation (although without some of its cruder techniques), where insiders with some access to the market mechanism run up the price of a security before unloading their own holdings, and then "pull the plug" and let the public suffer the consequences of the following disastrous decline. There was of course no proof that the market activities of the Los Angeles office of Shearson, Hammill were undertaken for that purpose ("as indeed there rarely is"), but it is normally presumed that men intend the natural consequences of their own actions. Nevertheless, the Commission did not charge simple market manipulation in that case, and it has in fact brought almost no cases under Section 9 (or the prohibitions of that section as embodied in Rule 10b–5). This is probably a sound conservation of energy in cases where other, more arbitrary rules have been violated but it is understood that the Commission staff feel that the proof of purpose or intent under Section 9 is "too difficult." It is hard to see how they know this when they have never really tried.

In Crane Company v. Westinghouse Air Brake Company [13] the Second Circuit had no difficulty in determining that the purchases by American Standard of the Westinghouse Air Brake stock were made for the purpose of manipulating the market in that stock and defeating the Crane tender offer. It is true that that was a particularly aggravated case, since the purchases on the floor of the exchange were accompanied by off-board sales at a loss. However, the Court stated that "When a person who has a 'substantial, direct pecuniary interest in the success of a proposed offering takes active steps to effect a rise in the market' in the security, we think that a finding of manipulative purpose is prima facie established." [14]

In Securities and Exchange Commission v. Resch-Cassin & Co., Inc.[15] a brokerage firm, which was the principal market maker in a security following a public offering, ran the price up in thirty-four minutes on one day from $11 to $16 and in another 20 day period from $13 to $17½; but in less than two months after the issue came out at $10, the price was down to $4. The court said:

"Of course, once it is established that a price rise occurred, it becomes necessary to show that defendants caused it. There are various factors which characterize attempts by manipulators to raise the price of an over-the-counter security: (a) price leadership by the manipulator; (b) dominion and control of the market for the security; (c) reduction in the floating supply of the security; and (d) the collapse of the market for the security when the manipulator ceases his activity. As already discussed herein, the tactic of inserting successively

12. In the Matter of Halsey, Stuart & Co., Inc., 30 S.E.C. 106, 123–24 (1949).

13. 419 F.2d 787 (2d Cir. 1969).

14. 419 F.2d at 795.

15. 362 F.Supp. 964 (S.D.N.Y.1973).

higher bids in the pink sheets has the effect of giving an appearance of activity. However, it also has the effect of causing a price rise. Similarly, the use of actual purchases and sales at successively higher prices not only has the effect of giving an appearance of activity, it raises the price of the over-the-counter security. * * *

"It is true, of course, that § 9(a)(2) of the Exchange Act requires that any manipulation be 'for the purpose of inducing the purchase or sale of such security by others'. Although defendants claim they were engaged in 'normal trading', it seems clear that their transactions in Africa stock were designed to induce others to purchase the security. Here they were engaged in the distribution of the stock and obviously had the purpose of inducing the purchase of the security by others. They had an obvious incentive to artificially influence the market price of the security in order to facilitate its distribution or increase its profitability. Here the defendants used the manipulated after-market to sell the Africa stock to the public." [16]

For general discussions, see Bloomenthal, Market-Makers, Manipulators and Shell Games, 45 St. John's L.Rev. 597 (1971); Martin, Broker-Dealer Manipulation of the Over the Counter Market, 25 Bus.Law. 1463 (1970); Note, Manipulation of the Stock Markets Under the Securities Laws, 99 U.Pa.L.Rev. 651 (1951).

THE GENERAL FRAUD SECTIONS AS APPLIED TO BROKER–DEALERS

Section 17(a) of the Securities Act of 1933, Section 10(b) (as implemented by Rule 10b–5) of the Securities Exchange Act and Section 15(c)(1) of the Securities Exchange Act all prohibit manipulative, deceptive and fraudulent actions in the securities markets. Section 17(a) outlaws (1) any device, scheme, or artifice to defraud, (2) any untrue statement of a material fact or any omission to state a material fact necessary to make the statements made not misleading, and (3) any transaction, practice, or course of business which operates or would operate as a fraud or deceit. Section 10(b) itself refers only to "any manipulative or deceptive device or contrivance", but Rule 10b–5 has copied the language of the three subdivisions of Section 17(a). Section 15(c)(1) refers to "any manipulative, deceptive, *or other fraudulent* device or contrivance." But again Rule 15c1–2 has incorporated into this section the substance of the three subdivisions of Section 17(a).

The major differences between these three sections and the rules implementing them are that Section 17(a) applies only to *sales,* whereas Sections 10(b) and 15(c)(1) apply to both purchases and sales and that Section 15(c)(1) applies only to a "broker or dealer", whereas Sections 17(a) and 10(b) apply to "any person." There are other minor variations in language, which are not too significant. In connection with a revocation proceeding against a broker-dealer involving allegedly fraudulent sales of securities, the Commission uniformly cites all three sections (and their related rules).

The "Shingle Theory." The "shingle theory" was evolved by the Commission as a basis for a finding of statutory fraud under these sections in a case where no intentional misstatement or omission on the part of the broker-dealer could be established. In brief, the theory is that when a broker-dealer goes into business (hangs out his "shingle") he impliedly represents that he will deal fairly and competently with his customers and that he will have an adequate basis for any statements or recommendations which he makes concerning

16. 362 F.Supp. at 976–77.

securities. In Kahn v. Securities and Exchange Commission [1] Judge Clark, in a concurring opinion, stated that under this theory the broker-dealer "implicitly *warrants* the soundness of statements of stock value." This unquestionably goes much too far. Certainly the broker-dealer is not liable for *unavoidable* errors of fact, much less of analysis and opinion. The Hughes case [2] was the initial judicial opinion upholding this theory of the Commission. The charge in that case, as in most of the early cases involving this theory, was that the broker-dealer sold securities to his customers at prices greatly in excess of their market value and without disclosure of the market value, thus making false his implied representation that he would deal with them fairly and at prices reasonably related to market value. By the same token, if the broker-dealer makes optimistic statements to his customers about a security without any factual basis therefor, this violates his implied representation that he will have a reasonably adequate basis for any such statements.[3]

Boiler Rooms. A "boiler room" operation is a high-pressure selling campaign for a particular block of securities of a single issuer (frequently intrinsically worthless [4]), usually carried out by long-distance telephone. The name comes from the fact that sometimes 10 to 20 telephones will be connected in a single room, at each of which a salesman will sit telephoning prospective buyers whose names have been obtained from a "sucker list."

In Kahn v. Securities and Exchange Commission [5] and Berko v. Securities and Exchange Commission,[6] which involved an appeal from orders of the Commission disciplining salesmen who were allegedly involved in a "boiler room" operation, the Second Circuit worried that the Commission was attempting to fashion a "*per se* rule" to the effect that any such telephone solicitation of purchasers was illegal, and the court remanded the cases to the Commission for further findings. When the Commission reaffirmed its former action and there was a second appeal to the Second Circuit in Berko v. Securities and Exchange Commission,[7] the court then upheld the action of the Commission and stated that the Commission was "fully justified * * * in holding Berko, a 'boiler-room' salesman, chargeable with knowledge of the contents of the brochures [furnished to him by the broker-dealer relating to the company whose stock was being sold] and with responsibility for allowing customers to rely upon them. * * * The Commission acted well within its mandate in concluding that the 'public interest' requires that a salesman working out of a 'boiler-room' be held to a higher duty to prospective customers than a salesman working out of a legitimate sales operation, and in concluding that a 'boiler-room' salesman does not meet his obligation when he has no knowledge other than opinions and brochures furnished by the broker, 'without any checking, investigation, or determination of the correctness of the same before putting

---

1. 297 F.2d 112 (2d Cir. 1961).

2. Charles Hughes & Co. v. S. E. C., 139 F.2d 434 (2d Cir. 1943), cert. denied 321 U.S. 786 (1944).

3. See In re Alexander Reid & Co., Inc., SEC Securities Exchange Act Release No. 6727 (1962); SEC Securities Exchange Act Release No. 6721 (1962).

4. This was not true of the stock of Sports Arenas (Delaware) Inc. which was being sold by Kahn and Berko in the cases referred to in the next paragraph. In the fiscal year ended June 30, 1961, the corporation had in operation 29 bowling arenas with a total of 936 lanes, it grossed $5,159,458, and it had a net profit of

$287,158 equal to 27.8 per share. SEC Securities Exchange Act Release No. 6846, note 36 (1962). While these accomplishments are far short of Kahn's prediction to customers that earnings would reach a level of $1.18 per share by the end of the calendar year 1958, they do show that this was a substantial business operation. On the other hand, the typical corporation whose stock is being promoted in a "boiler room" operation is a uranium company which has no mine or an electronics company which has no plant.

5. 297 F.2d 112 (2d Cir. 1961).

6. 297 F.2d 116 (2d Cir. 1961).

7. 316 F.2d 137 (2d Cir. 1963).

them out to the public.'" The court also stated in a footnote that the Commission's second opinion had made it clear that it was "not attempting to fashion a *per se* rule to be applied indiscriminately in all 'boiler-room' cases."

The only action of the Commission which was appealed to the Court of Appeals in these cases was its declaration that Kahn and Berko were each a "cause" of the Commission's revocation of their employer's registration as a broker-dealer. The significance of this action was that it would prevent a person who is the subject of such a determination from continuing to be employed by any member of the NASD, except with the approval of the Commission. Since some of these "pitch men" have considerable expertise and are in rather widespread demand,[8] such administrative action by the Commission might be thought to have a dampening effect on other "boiler room" operations. However, prior to the 1964 amendments, such action would not bar the person from being employed by a non-member of the NASD, and it is doubtful whether most "boiler room" operators had any interest in joining the NASD.[9] Another difficulty was that prior to those amendments the SEC could only proceed against an employee of a broker-dealer through a disciplinary proceeding against his employer and this finding of "cause." While perhaps not true of "boiler rooms", in other types of cases the SEC might be hesitant to invoke any sanction against the employer where the fault lay primarily with the subordinate. Under the present statute as amended in 1964 the SEC can proceed directly against the employee for a violation of the securities laws [10] and can bar him in the future from being "associated with" any registered broker-dealer.[11]

To Per Se or Not to Per Se. In the *Kahn* and *Berko* cases, the Commission stated in its first opinion with respect to Kahn[12] that he asserted that he was "only 29 years old, [and] that his association with [this broker-dealer] was his first experience in the securities business. * * *" While his prediction that the earnings would go to $1.18 per share was inaccurate, they did equal 27.8¢ per share in the fiscal year ended June 30, 1961.[13] With respect to Berko, the Second Circuit pointed out in its first opinion that the only misrepresentation charged to him was a prediction that the price would go to $15 per share within a year and (a fact carefully omitted from the second opinion) that it actually *did* go to $15 per share within a year.[14] However, upon remand from the

---

8. For a catalogue of the successive employments of one "boiler room" salesman by three different operators, whose registrations were successively revoked, see In the Matter of B. Fennekohl & Co., SEC Securities Exchange Act Release No. 6898, note 10 (September 18, 1962).

9. What forced most broker-dealers conducting a general securities business to become members of the NASD is the fact that otherwise no member can deal with them except upon the same terms as such member deals with the general public, i.e., can offer them no discounts, concessions or allowances. However, the typical "boiler room" operator deals only with the public on his "sucker lists", and he does not expect to participate in underwritings or have other dealings with other broker-dealers. However, under the 1964 amendments to the Securities Exchange Act of 1934, nonmembers of the NASD were subjected to equivalent regulation directly by the Commission itself (the so-called "SECO

regulations"), and all registered broker-dealers are now required to belong to the NASD or a national securities exchange under the 1983 amendments.

10. Securities Exchange Act of 1934, § 15(b)(6).

11. "* * * it shall be unlawful for any broker or dealer to permit such a person to become, or remain, a person associated with him without the consent of the Commission, if such broker or dealer knew, or in the exercise of reasonable care, should have known, of such order" barring him from being "associated with" a broker or dealer. Ibid.

12. Securities Exchange Act Release No. 6498 (SEC March 16, 1961).

13. See Note 4, supra.

14. Berko v. Securities and Exchange Commission, 297 F.2d 116, at 117 (2d Cir. 1961).

Second Circuit the Commission, without taking any additional evidence, reaffirmed its former determination and made the following finding: [15] "It is clear from their own admissions that Petitioners [Kahn and Berko] knew a high-pressure telephone sales operation—a boiler room—was in progress. They were hired for the purpose of engaging in a major effort with respect to the sale of Sports stock and were aware of, and assisted in, the wide distribution of sales materials which as we have shown, were materially misleading. Their own representations served only to aggravate the misleading statements found in the brochures." In the opinion on remand, the Commission expressly disclaimed any intention of laying down a rule with respect to the right of a salesman "to rely on information provided by his employer, where securities of an established issuer are being recommended to customers by a broker-dealer who is not engaged in misleading and deceptive high-pressure selling practices. * * *"

Is it "clear", as the Second Circuit says, that the Commission was "not attempting to fashion a *per se* rule to be applied indiscriminately in all 'boiler-room' cases"? [16] On August 16, 1962, the SEC did indeed propose to adopt a "per se" rule with respect to "boiler rooms" by proposing a new rule making it a "fraudulent, deceptive or manipulative act or practice" for any broker or dealer to offer or sell any equity security at $10 or less by telephone to a person unknown to him, with some exceptions. [17] Exclusions would have included sales to other broker-dealers, institutional investors, or to a "regular customer" as defined in the rule. The rule would also have excepted "isolated transactions not a part of any concentrated sales efforts" and stocks of companies in which financial information was publicly available either in reports filed with the SEC or in a "recognized financial manual." However, this proposed rule for some reason was never adopted. Instead, the NASD adopted a prohibition against a broker-dealer recommending "speculative low-priced securities" to customers "without knowledge of or attempt to obtain information concerning the customers' other securities holdings, their financial situation and other necessary data." [18] And the SEC adopted its "know thy customer" rule with respect to all SECO brokers. [19] These requirements made the legal operation of a "boiler room" in the classic sense impossible.

Application of the Expanded "Shingle Theory" to Other Broker-Dealers. Despite the disclaimer by the Commission in the Kahn and Berko cases that it

---

15. Securities Exchange Act Release No. 6846 (SEC July 11, 1962).

16. In Old Colony Bondholders v. New York, New Haven & Hartford Railroad Co., 161 F.2d 413, at 450 (2d Cir. 1947), referred to by Judge Clark in the Kahn case, Jerome Frank stated, regarding certain findings of the ICC, that "it would be desirable to abandon the word 'valuation'—since that word misleadingly connotes some moderately rational judgment—and to substitute some neutral term, devoid of misleading associations, such as 'aluation,' or, perhaps better still, 'woosh-woosh.' The pertinent doctrine would then be this: 'When the I.C.C. has ceremonially woosh-wooshed, judicial scrutiny is barred.'" Did the SEC do more than "woosh-woosh" on the remand of these cases?

In the Matter of Hamilton Waters & Co., Inc., Securities Exchange Act Release No. 7725 (SEC Oct. 18, 1965), the Commission stated: "It is clear that registrant and the named individuals, in the sale of a speculative security of an unseasoned company by means of a high-pressure sales compaign which involved the loading and reloading of customers, the solicitation of the same customers by more than one salesman, and the recurring use of the same basic fraudulent representations and predictions, engaged in a scheme to defraud. * * *" What are the key words here?

17. Securities Exchange Act Release No. 6885 (SEC Aug. 16, 1962). See Note, Symptomatic Approach to Securities Fraud: The SEC's Proposed Rule 15c2–6 and the Boiler Room, 72 Yale L.J. 1411 (1963).

18. CCH NASD Manual ¶ 2152.

19. Rule 15b10–3, effective Oct. 2, 1967 (Securities Exchange Act Release No. 8135).

intended to deny a salesman of a reputable broker-dealer the right to rely upon information furnished to him by his employer regarding an "established issuer", it has nowhere suggested that it will not apply to all broker-dealers the requirement that there be an "adequate basis" for any statements made to customers.[20] The opinion was expressed by Mr. W. McNeil Kennedy in 1962 that the Commission had thus taken a "giant step forward in the imposition of disclosure responsibilities upon both brokers and dealers" which "may very well mark the beginning of a change in methods of doing business heretofore regarded by persons in the industry as ethical, legal and in the public interest." [21]

In Hanly v. Securities and Exchange Commission, 415 F.2d 589 (2d Cir. 1969), the Court of Appeals for the Second Circuit upheld this position of the Commission regarding the duty of investigation by a broker-dealer and stated the duties of a securities salesman, when making recommendations to his customers, as follows:

"The Commission found that the sophistication of the customers or prior relationships which many of them had enjoyed with the respective petitioners were irrelevant. It held that the absence of a boiler room did not justify affirmative misrepresentations or a failure to disclose adverse financial information. The relevance of a customer's nonloss of money or a salesman's speculation in the stock likewise was discounted.

* * *

"When a securities salesman fraudulently violates the high standards with which he is charged, he subjects himself to a variety of punitive, compensatory and remedial sanctions. In the instant proceedings petitioners have not been criminally charged, nor have they been sued for damages by their customers arising from the alleged misrepresentations. Instead, in private proceedings initiated by the Commission, each petitioner's *privilege* of being employed in the securities industry has been revoked. It is in this context that the issues before the Court must be considered.

* * *

"Brokers and salesmen are 'under a duty to investigate, and their violation of that duty brings them within the term 'willful' in the Exchange Act.[22] Thus, a salesman cannot deliberately ignore that which he has a duty to know and recklessly state facts about matters of which he is ignorant. He must analyze sales literature and must not blindly accept recommendations made therein. The fact that his customers may be sophisticated and knowledgeable does not warrant a less stringent standard. Even where the purchaser follows the market activity of the stock and does not rely upon the salesman's statements, remedial sanctions may be imposed since reliance is not an element of fraudulent misrepresentation in this context.[23]

---

20. See Securities Exchange Act Release No. 6721; In re Alexander Reid & Co., Inc., both supra Note 2. The SEC reiterated its position in In the Matter of B. Fennekohl & Co., Securities Exchange Act Release No. 6898 (SEC Sept. 18, 1962), and In the Matter of Hamilton Waters & Co., Inc., Securities Exchange Act Release No. 7725 (SEC Oct. 18, 1965).

21. Current Problems of Securities Underwriters and Dealers, 18 Bus.Lawyer 27, at 71–76 (1962). Mr. Kennedy regarded the "shingle theory" as theretofore essentially limited to pricing.

22. [Ftnote by the court] Dlugash v. SEC, 373 F.2d 107, 109 (2 Cir. 1967). See also Tager v. SEC, 344 F.2d 5, 8 (2 Cir. 1965) (" 'willfully' * * * means intentionally committing the act which constitutes the violation * * *. [A]ctual knowledge is not necessary.")

23. [Ftnote by the court] N. Sims Organ & Co., Inc. v. SEC, 293 F.2d 78 (2 Cir. 1961), cert. denied 368 U.S. 968 (1962). See also Commonwealth Securities Corporation, Securities Exchange Act Release No. 8360, p. 5 (July 23, 1968): "It is irrelevant that customers to whom fraudulent representa-

"A securities dealer occupies a special relationship to a buyer of securities in that by his position he implicitly represents he has an adequate basis for the opinions he renders. While this implied warranty may not be as rigidly enforced in a civil action where an investor seeks damages for losses allegedly caused by reliance upon his unfounded representations, its applicability in the instant proceedings cannot be questioned.[24]

* * *

"In summary, the standards by which the actions of each petitioner must be judged are strict. He cannot recommend a security unless there is an adequate and reasonable basis for such recommendation. He must disclose facts which he knows and those which are reasonably ascertainable. By his recommendation he implies that a reasonable investigation has been made and that his recommendation rests on the conclusions based on such investigation. Where the salesman lacks essential information about a security, he should disclose this as well as the risks which arise from his lack of information.

"A salesman may not rely blindly upon the issuer for information concerning a company, although the degree of independent investigation which must be made by a securities dealer will vary in each case. Securities issued by smaller companies of recent origin obviously require more thorough investigation." [25]

See Langevoort, Fraud and Deception by Securities Professionals, 61 Tex.L.Rev. 1247 (1983); Nichols, Broker's Duty to his Customer Under Evolving Federal Fiduciary and Suitability Standards, 26 Buffalo L.Rev. 435 (1977); Note, Conflicting Duties of Brokerage Firms, 88 Harv.L.Rev. 396 (1974); Brudney, Origins and Limited Applicability of the "Reasonable Basis" or "Know Your Merchandise" Doctrine, 4 Inst.Sec.Reg. 239 (1973); Jacobs, Impact of Securities Exchange Act Rule 10b–5 on Broker-Dealers, 57 Cornell L.Rev. 869 (1972); Note, New and Comprehensive Duties of Securities Sellers to Investigate, Disclose, and Have an "Adequate Basis" for Representations, 62 Mich.L. Rev. 880 (1964).

tions are made are aware of the speculative nature of the security they are induced to buy, or do not rely on such representations."

Reliance may be an element of fraudulent misrepresentation in other situations, see discussion in Vine v. Beneficial Finance Co., 374 F.2d 627, 635 (2 Cir.), cert. denied 389 U.S. 970 (1967); see also Mutual Shares Corp. v. Genesco Inc., 384 F.2d 540, 544 (2 Cir. 1967), but it is not an element in a case such as this.

24. [Ftnote by the court] Petitioners argue that their activities are to be distinguished from those of a "boiler room" and that, absent a finding of boiler room operations here, the Commission's strict standards should not be applied against petitioners.

A boiler room usually is a temporary operation established to sell a specific speculative security. Solicitation is by telephone to new customers, the salesman conveying favorable earnings projections, predictions of price rises and other optimistic prospects without a factual basis. The prospective buyer is not informed of known

or readily ascertainable adverse information; he is not cautioned about the risks inherent in purchasing a speculative security; and he is left with a deliberately created expectation of gain without risk. Berko v. SEC, 316 F.2d 137, 139 n. 3 (2 Cir. 1963). See also R. A. Holman & Co., Inc., v. SEC, 366 F.2d 446 (2 Cir. 1966), modified on other grounds 377 F.2d 665 (2 Cir.) (per curiam), cert. denied 389 U.S. 991 (1967); Harold Grill, 41 S.E.C. 321 (1963).

Salesmen in a boiler room are held to a high duty of truthfulness which is not met by a claim of lack of knowledge. The Commission having previously refused to condone misrepresentation in the absence of a boiler room, see Charles P. Lawrence, Securities Exchange Act Release No. 8213, p. 3, (December 19, 1967), aff'd 398 F.2d 176 (1 Cir. 1968), cited in Armstrong Jones and Co., Securities Exchange Act Release No. 8420, p. 9 (October 3, 1968), we specifically reject petitioners' argument that absence of boiler room operations here is a defense to a charge of misrepresentation.

25. 415 F.2d at 595–597.

$LL-159$

HECHT v. HARRIS, UPHAM & CO.
United States Court of Appeals, Ninth Circuit, 1970.
430 F.2d 1202.

Before MERRILL and DUNIWAY, CIRCUIT JUDGES, and POWELL, DISTRICT JUDGE.*

POWELL,** DISTRICT JUDGE. The cross appeals by Harris, Upham & Co., Harris, Upham & Co., Inc. (appellants), and Mrs. Bertha Hecht (appellee) are from a judgment of the District Court awarding appellee $504,391.02. The opinion of the District Court is reported at 283 F.Supp. 417 (1968). The basic facts of the case are set forth there.

In January 1955 Mr. Hecht died leaving an estate of securities to his wife, the appellee, of a net value of $508,532.00. Shortly after Mr. Hecht's death, but before distribution of the estate, a close business and social relationship was formed between Mrs. Hecht and an investment broker, Mr. Asa Wilder (co-defendant below). Mrs. Hecht transferred her separate securities account (net value $42,000) from Walston & Co. to Hooker & Fay, with whom Wilder was then employed. When her husband's estate was distributed to Mrs. Hecht it was likewise placed with Hooker & Fay. In May 1957 Wilder left Hooker & Fay to become a Representative and Commodities Manager of Harris, Upham & Co. at their San Francisco office. The Hecht account, valued at about $533,161.00, was then transferred to appellants.

The account remained with Harris, Upham & Co. until March 1964 when Mrs. Hecht's tax consultants advised her that the account was substantially depleted. At that time the account had a net value of about $251,308.00. Suit was later commenced in District Court against Wilder and Harris, Upham & Co. and others for alleged violations of Section 17(a) of the Securities Act of 1933 * * *; Section 10(b) of the Securities Exchange Act of 1934 * * *; Rule 10b-5 promulgated by the Commission; * * * and the Commodity Exchange Act of 1936 (7 U.S.C.A. § 1 et seq.). Appellee also alleged violations of the Rules of the National Association of Securities Dealers and the common law of the State of California. Liability of Harris, Upham & Co. was alleged under Section 20(a) of the Securities Exchange Act * * *.

Appellee advanced three theories for recovery, (1) the account was fraudulently converted from a blue chip investment account to a low grade speculative securities and commodity trading account, (2) Wilder excessively traded the account for the purpose of generating commissions, and (3) Wilder defrauded appellee by self-dealing in two securities transactions designated as Colonial and Itek. Damages were alleged to be in excess of $1,109,000.

The District Court ruled that Mrs. Hecht was guilty of laches, had waived certain of her rights and was estopped from asserting the wrongful conversion of her account. On the issue of excessive trading, referred to as

---

* The Honorable Charles L. Powell, United States District Judge for the Eastern District of Washington, sitting by designation.

** Disagreement has developed in the Court upon the issue of damages necessi-

tating a separate opinion for the Court upon that subject which follows the opinion of Judge Powell. The Court is in agreement upon Judge Powell's opinion.

account churning, the District Court held appellee was entitled to recover all commissions deducted from her account during the period it was with Harris, Upham & Co. and all interest charged to her. Appellee was also awarded damages for the alleged fraud in the Colonial and Itek transactions. A summary of damages awarded is set forth in the District Court's opinion, 283 F.Supp. at p. 444.

JURISDICTION

A District Court has jurisdiction of a private civil action for damages based upon violations of Section 10(b) and Rule 10b–5. * * *

The District Court held that churning [1] was a violation of Section 10(b) and Rule 10b–5. One of the principal Congressional purposes of the Securities Exchange Act is to protect the investor in a highly sophisticated field. With knowledge of this objective " * * * it is the duty of the courts to be alert to provide such remedies as are necessary to make effective the congressional purpose." J. I. Case Co. v. Borak, 377 U.S. 426, 433 and 435 * * * (1964); Deckert v. Independence Shares Corporation, 311 U.S. 282, 288 * * * (1940).

* * * Abuse of the confidence of the customer for personal gain by a broker by frequent and numerous transactions disproportionate to the size and nature of the account, has been held a violation of Rule 10b–5. Lorenz v. Watson, 258 F.Supp. 724 (E.D.Pa.1966) (extensive trading and churning of a discretionary investment account disproportionate to its size and character); Newkirk v. Hayden, Stone & Co., CCH Fed.Sec.L.Rep. para. 91,621 (S.D.Cal.1965) (churning of a discretionary trading account with an equity of $8,439.65 by a broker who earned $2,722.55 in commissions during a three month period). Cf. Carr v. Warner, 137 F.Supp. 611 (D.Mass.1955) and its companion case Nash v. J. Arthur Warner & Co., 137 F.Supp. 615 (D.Mass.1955) (purchase and sale of securities excessive in size and frequency in view of the financial resources and character of the investors' accounts). On occasion this court has sustained the Commission's finding of churning. Irish v. SEC, 367 F.2d 637 (9th Cir. 1966) (broker advancing his own interests to the detriment of his customers by making excessive trades in their accounts). See, also, Stevens v. Abbott, Proctor & Paine, 288 F.Supp. 836 (E.D.Virginia 1968) (excessive trading of an account by a broker to derive profits for himself without regard for the interests of his customer); Moscarelli v. Stamm, 288 F.Supp. 453, 457–458 (E.D.N.Y.1968) (alleged unauthorized excessive trading of securities account through broker misrepresentation).

We conclude that the issue of account churning was correctly before the District Court under Section 10(b) and Rule 10b–5.

1. The SEC has provided a definition of churning in the regulation under 15 U.S. C.A. § 78o(c)(1). See 17 C.F.R. 240.15c1–7(a). The definition reads:

"The term 'manipulative, deceptive, or other fraudulent device or contrivance,' as used in section 15(c) of the act, is hereby defined to include any act of any broker or dealer designed to effect with or for any customer's account in respect to which such broker or dealer or his agent or employee is vested with any discretionary power any transactions of purchase or sale which are excessive in size or frequency in view of the financial resources and character of such account."

This was relied upon in Lorenz v. Watson, 258 F.Supp. 724, 730 (E.D.Pa.1966). See Churning by Securities Dealers, 80 Harv.L.Rev. 869 (1967).

WAIVER, LACHES AND ESTOPPEL

This Court held in Royal Air Properties, Inc. v. Smith, 312 F.2d 210 (9th Cir. 1962) that since civil liability was judicially implied from violations of Section 10(b), estoppel, waiver and laches should be applicable. It was there stated that "[t]he purpose of the Securities Exchange Act is to protect the innocent investor, not one who loses his innocence and then waits to see how his investment turns out before he decides to invoke the provisions of the Act." 312 F.2d 213–214.

The District Court in the instant case found that:

"All during the course of the account, plaintiff regularly received from Harris, Upham the customary confirmation slips showing each security or commodity transaction as made and requesting immediate notice of any error. She also received from Harris, Upham the customary monthly statements of her account.

"It was the practice of Wilder to be in contact with plaintiff by telephone concerning her account almost every morning of the business week, and also to visit her at her home at least weekly and sometimes several times a week. Also, plaintiff would often telephone Wilder at his office during the day.

"It was the practice of plaintiff to put her confirmation slips on a table in her home, 'separating the buys from the sells', in order to discuss them with Wilder. After the discussions Wilder would gather up the confirmation slips and statements and take them to his home—although he had duplicates for his own use at the office.

"During the period of the account plaintiff had her own income tax accountants with whom she consulted concerning her personal tax deductions. Wilder supplied schedules to these income tax accountants, which indicated plaintiff's capital gains and losses arising out of her securities transactions. Plaintiff was also represented on occasion by attorneys—including representation by able and reputable counsel, recommended by Wilder in connection with the distribution of her husband's estate." 283 F.Supp. at p. 426.

With these facts in mind the court later concluded:

"Having, with this knowledge and understanding, permitted Wilder and his firm to continue handling the account on this basis in reliance upon her apparent acquiescence for nearly seven years, the Court finds that plaintiff's conduct is such that she is barred by estoppel, laches and waiver (within the meaning of the second appeal in Royal Air Properties, Inc. v. Smith, 9 Cir., 333 F.2d 568 (1964)) from suddenly taking the position that such trading of the account in securities and commodities was unsuitable for her needs and objectives, contrary to her instructions and should never have occurred." 283 F.Supp. at pp. 429–430.

The requirements of estoppel are set out in Hampton v. Paramount Pictures Corp., 9 Cir., 279 F.2d 100, 104 (1960):

"Four elements must be present to establish the defense of estoppel: (1) The party to be estopped must know the facts; (2) he must intend that his conduct shall be acted on or must so act that the party asserting the estoppel has a right to believe it is so intended; (3) the latter must be ignorant of the true facts; and (4) he must rely on the former's conduct to his injury." (citations omitted.)

To invoke laches as a defense there must be (1) a lack of diligence by the party against whom the defense is asserted, and (2) prejudice to the party asserting the defense. Costello v. United States, 365 U.S. 265, 282 * * * (1961). Where these elements are present, the damage to the party asserting the defense is caused by his detrimental reliance on his adversary's conduct. Royal Air Properties, Inc. v. Smith, 333 F.2d 568, 570 (9th Cir. 1964).

The waiver of a legal right is "the voluntary or intentional relinquishment of a known right. It emphasizes the mental attitude of the actor." Matsuo Yoshida v. Liberty Mut. Ins. Co., 240 F.2d 824, 829 (9th Cir. 1957).

Although the trial court's opinion does not specifically conclude that plaintiff intentionally relinquished a known right, it is apparent that the portion of the opinion above contains findings necessary for the application of estoppel and laches to the facts of this case.

To have these findings upset on appeal it must be shown that they are "clearly erroneous" within the meaning of Rule 52(a), Fed.R.Civ.P. In Clostermann v. Gates Rubber Company, 394 F.2d 794, 796 (9th Cir. 1968), it is stated:

"A finding is 'clearly erroneous' when although there is evidence to support it, the reviewing court, on the entire evidence, is left with the definite and firm conviction that a mistake has been committed." (citations omitted)

A review of the record does not disclose that the findings are "clearly erroneous". They will not be disturbed on this appeal.

SUITABILITY UNDER RULE N.A.S.D.

Appellee claims the District Court erred in not holding that the National Association of Securities Dealers (N.A.S.D.), "suitability" rule (Art. III, Sec. 2,) gives rise to civil liability. Unlike the fraud requirement of the Securities Exchange Act, the N.A.S.D. "suitability" rule would, if applicable, allow recovery against a member who did not have "reasonable grounds" to believe his investment recommendation was suitable for the customer. This rule has received varied consideration from the courts. Compare Colonial Realty Corp. v. Bache & Co., 358 F.2d 178 (2nd Cir. 1966), with Avern Trust v. Clarke, 415 F.2d 1238, 1242 (7th Cir. 1969). The District Court might have entertained pendent jurisdiction over the common-law claims in which violations of Art. III, Sec. 2, might have been admissible, Mercury Investment Co. v. A. G. Edwards & Sons, 295 F.Supp. 1160 (S.D.Texas 1969), however it did not reach that question.

"In any event, we have found on the evidence in this case that plaintiff is barred by estoppel and waiver from proceeding merely upon the theory that her account, as handled by defendants was 'unsuitable' to her needs and objectives." 293 F.Supp. at p. 431.

Having affirmed the lower court's ruling on estoppel we need not decide this issue.

EXCESSIVE TRADING

Although we have held that Mrs. Hecht is estopped to deny knowledge of the nature of the transactions in her account, we cannot say as a matter of law that she is also estopped from claiming lack of knowledge that her account was excessively traded. As viewed by the trial judge below:

"Although plaintiff had enough experience to tell from the confirmations slips and monthly statements, that she was paying commissions and interest on transactions in her account [of which she had knowledge], she just did not have the sufficient competence to understand whether the frequency and volume of the transactions might be 'excessive.'" 283 F.Supp. at p. 434.

Nor does the fact the account was a trading account mean it could not be excessively traded. Newkirk v. Hayden, Stone & Co., CCH Fed.Sec.L.Rep. para. 91,621 (S.D.Cal.1965); See, Stevens v. Abbott, Proctor & Paine, 288 F.Supp. 836 (E.D.Virginia 1968).

The gist of an allegation of churning is fraud in law and differs from common law fraud. Proof of a specific intent to defraud is unnecessary. Securities & Exchange Commission v. Texas Gulf Sulphur Co., 401 F.2d 833, 854–855 (2nd Cir. 1968); R. H. Johnson & Co. v. S.E.C., 97 U.S.App. D.C. 364, 231 F.2d 523 (1956), cert. denied 352 U.S. 844 * * *; Norris & Hirshberg, Inc. v. S.E.C., 85 U.S.App.D.C. 268, 177 F.2d 228 (1949). Appellee had the burden of establishing churning by a "preponderance of the evidence".

The record before us supports the finding of the District Court that this burden was met. Many facts and circumstances disclose churning. We note only two, (1) during the period the account was with appellant there were over 10,000 trades with a gross dollar volume of approximately $100,000,000, (2) Mrs. Hecht paid commissions and markups on these transactions of about $189,000 plus interest on her margin account of about $43,000. These figures represent 4.7% of the total income of the San Francisco office of Harris, Upham & Co., on an account of less than $\frac{1}{10}$th of 1% of all accounts in that office.

When, as in this case, a single fraudulent scheme involves both securities and commodities a District Court is entitled to award damages for the entire loss. Errion v. Connell, 236 F.2d 447, 454 (9th Cir. 1956); Goodman v. H. Hentz & Co., 265 F.Supp. 440, 445 (N.D.Ill.1967); Sinva, Inc. v. Merrill Lynch, Pierce, Fenner & Smith, Inc., 253 F.Supp. 359 (S.D.N.Y.1966).

The District Court held Harris, Upham & Co. liable for the churning of Mrs. Hecht's account on the grounds that it did not maintain an adequate system of internal control and that in failing to be diligent, even with the system then in force, it did not act in good faith. Liability was imposed under Section 20(a) of the Act (15 U.S.C.A. § 78t(a)).

In Kamen v. Paul H. Aschkar & Company, 382 F.2d 689, 697 (9th Cir. 1967) this Court said the test of liability under Section 20(a) is that the controlling person " * * * must have acted in bad faith and directly or indirectly induced the conduct constituting a violation or cause of action." In that case the manner of supervision of the activities of the employees was held sufficient to establish liability.

There is substantial authority imposing Section 20(a) liability under circumstances similar to those which were before the trial court in this case. Lorenz v. Watson, 258 F.Supp. 724 (E.D.Pa.1966); Goodman v. H. Hentz & Co., 265 F.Supp. 440 (N.D.Ill.1967); See, also, Moscarelli v. Stamm, 288 F.Supp. 453, 460 (E.D.N.Y.1968); Anderson v. Francis I. duPont & Co., 291 F.Supp. 705, 710 (D.Minn.1968); Myzel v. Fields, 386 F.2d 718, 738 (8th Cir. 1967), cert. denied 390 U.S. 951 * * * (1968). We affirm the court's finding of liability for churning under Section 20(a).

* * *

MERRILL, CIRCUIT JUDGE:

DAMAGES

The District Court, 283 F.Supp. at 444, by schedule specified damages awarded in the sum of $439,520. This included the sum of $64,250 covering the Itek and Colonial transactions. The balance was broken down as follows:

Actual damages due to churning:	
Commissions and interest paid by plaintiff	$232,000
Other damages due to churning	143,000
	$375,000

We have trouble with the $143,000 item of "other damages due to churning".

This sum includes $78,000 net loss suffered by the commodities account and $65,000 for dividend income loss attributable to the fact that money was diverted from the securities account to the commodities account.

Allowance of these items of damage seems to us to be inconsistent with the court's findings of waiver and estoppel (as quoted earlier in Judge Powell's opinion), and its denial on that ground of damages for loss of value in the *securities* account.

The court's reasoning in allowing these items of damage, notwithstanding its ruling on waiver and estoppel, was that Wilder's purpose in guiding Mrs. Hecht into the commodities market was solely to provide an additional opportunity to generate commissions and that "the commodity account may be regarded as a mere device for churning the securities account * * *." 283 F.Supp. at 437. Therefore, "Since the commodity account was 'a mere device for churning the securities account', the commodity losses of plaintiff, although not recoverable by plaintiff *as such,* are nevertheless, recoverable insofar as they proximately resulted from this means of churning the securities account." 283 F.Supp. at 440.

We find no error in the District Court's holding that the relationship between the securities account and the commodities account was such as to make commodities churning a fraud on the securities account and damages for that churning recoverable in this case. We do, however, have difficulty with the conclusion that loss of value in the commodities account and loss of dividend income were proximately caused by churning. The fact that the commodities account was initiated for the purpose of diversifying opportunities for churning does not to us support that conclusion if we accept the court's determination that Mrs. Hecht cannot otherwise be heard to say that commodity futures were an unsuitable subject for trading. If loss of value in the account occurred (beyond the cost of commissions), it would seem to be due not to the number of transactions engaged in but to the unfortunate choice of risk those transactions entailed. If loss in dividend income was suffered it was due not to the fact of overtrading, but to the fact that Mrs. Hecht was in commodities. These, however, are complaints Mrs. Hecht has been held estopped to assert. This would not, of course, preclude recovery were the loss attributable to Wilder's disregard of Mrs. Hecht's interests in profits or limitation of losses. However, a preoccupation with commissions to the point of churning does not compel an inference that such was the case and the court has not found to that effect.

We conclude that judgment in these respects is not supported by the findings of the District Court. Consequently the total award of damages, $439,520, must be reduced by the amount of $143,000.

Judgment, as modified, is for plaintiff-appellee in the sum of $296,520 plus interest at the rate of 7 per cent per annum on the sum of $232,000 (the portion of judgment specified by the District Court as subject to interest). In all other respects the judgment of the District Court, including its judgment against Wilder, is affirmed. No costs are allowed to either party.

POWELL, DISTRICT JUDGE (dissenting in part).

I dissent from the separate opinion on damages.

By taking $143,000 of the judgment away from the plaintiff the Court is adopting the formula for measure of recovery set forth in Newkirk v. Hayden, Stone & Co., CCH Fed.Sec.L.Rep. para. 91,621 (S.D.Calif.1965). There the court said: "Damages should be limited to the amount of the commissions because this is the only element of damage which was proximately caused by defendants." In narrowing recovery for churning solely to commissions earned (plus interest on the margin account) the Majority overlooks the fact that the dealer in his zeal to earn commissions may have caused damage unrelated in amount to what he earned in commissions.[1]

* * *

PROPOSED FEDERAL SECURITIES CODE *

American Law Institute.
May 19, 1978.

TRADING PRACTICES: GENERAL

SEC. 913. It is unlawful for a broker, dealer, municipal broker, or municipal dealer to engage in any of the following practices:

(1) PROMPT EXECUTION. To fail to execute a customer's order as promptly after its acceptance as is practicable under the circumstances.

SOURCE: New.

---

1. Churning by Securities Dealers, 80 Harv.L.Rev. 869, 883 (1967). See e.g. Stevens v. Abbott, Proctor & Paine, 288 F.Supp. 836, 851 (E.D.Va.1968) where the court in addition to awarding commissions charged in the amount of $59,689.99, also

awarded $35,831.78 for capital gains taxes incurred.

* Copyright 1980, American Law Institute. Reprinted by permission.

(2) DISCLOSURE OF CONTROL. To effect a purchase or sale of a security unless, at or before completion of the transaction, he discloses to the customer in writing that he controls, is controlled by, or is under common control with, the issuer when that is the fact ("control" being defined for purposes of section 913(2) as if section 202(29)(A) referred to a company or an issuer of a municipal security).

SOURCE: X Rule 15c1-5.

(3) UNAUTHORIZED EXECUTIONS. To effect a purchase or a sale of a security as agent for a customer without express or implied authority.

SOURCE: New.

(4) UNREASONABLE SPREADS. To effect a purchase or sale of a security as dealer or municipal dealer if the difference between the purchase or sale price and any current market price is excessive under the circumstances (unless the customer is an institutional investor that knows or is informed of the amount of the difference).

SOURCE: New.

TRADING AND INVESTMENT ADVISORY PRACTICES: RULEMAKING AUTHORITY

SEC. 915. (a) SPECIFIC AREAS. It is unlawful for a broker, dealer, municipal broker, or municipal dealer, in contravention of the rules of the Commission—

(1) to effect a purchase or sale of a security without disclosing (A) that he is a marketmaker in the security, or an underwriter, participant, or otherwise financially interested in a current distribution of the security, or (B) that he, his spouse or minor child, any other relative designated by rule, or a related trust has a long or short position in the security that is substantial in relation to that person's (or trust's) total assets or normal investment or trading practices (but not the amount of any such position);

(2) to recommend a transaction in a security unless the issuer is a registrant or reasonable information with respect to the issuer and the security is otherwise available; or

(3) to recommend a transaction in a security unless he reasonably believes that it is not unsuitable for the customer on the basis of (A) information furnished by the customer on reasonable inquiry with respect to his investment objectives, financial situation, and needs, and (B) any other information known by the broker, dealer, municipal broker, or municipal dealer.

(b) GENERAL RULEMAKING AUTHORITY. The Commission, by rule, may define in a manner not inconsistent with the conditions and restrictions of sections 913, 914, and 915(a), and prescribe means reasonably designed to prevent, any conduct by a broker, dealer, municipal broker, municipal dealer, or investment adviser that is made unlawful by those sections or any similar conduct that constitutes unfair dealing with a customer or client. It is unlawful for such a person to violate such a rule.

SOURCE: § 915(a)(1)(A): X Rules 10b-10(a)(5)(ii), 15c1-6. § 915(a)(2): X Rule 15c2-11. § 915(a)(3): cf. X Rule 15b10-3. Remainder: new.

CHURNING

SEC. 1606. It is unlawful for a broker, dealer, municipal broker, or municipal dealer to effect with or for a customer with respect to whose account he or his agent exercises investment discretion, or is in a position to determine the volume and frequency of transactions by reason of the customer's willingness to follow his or his agent's suggestions, transactions that are excessive in volume or frequency in light of the amount of profits or commissions of the broker, dealer, municipal broker, municipal dealer, or his agent in relation to the size of the account and such other factors as the character of the account, the needs and objectives of the customer as ascertained on reasonable inquiry, and the pattern of trading in the account.

SOURCE: X Rule 15c1–7(a).

* * *

CHURNING LITIGATION

Rule 15c1–7, which is quoted in footnote 1 of the opinion in the Hecht case, prohibits what is generally known as "churning", i.e., excessive trading by a broker for an account in which he holds discretionary powers, for the purpose of collecting his commissions. In In the Matter of Norris & Hirshberg, Inc., 21 S.E.C. 865 (1949),[1] the Commission stated that while the Rule itself specifically applies only to cases where the broker or dealer has been "vested" with discretionary powers, either orally or in writing, "the handling of a customer's account may become fraudulent whenever the broker or dealer is in a position to determine the volume and frequency of transactions by reason of the customer's willingness to follow the suggestions of the broker or dealer and he abuses the customer's confidence by overtrading." [2]

In the lower court opinion in the Hecht case [3] the court defined "churning" as follows: "Churning cannot be, and need not be, established by any one precise rule or formula. The essential question of fact for determination is whether the volume and frequency of transactions, considered in the light of the nature of the account and the situation, needs and objectives of the customer, have been so 'excessive' as to indicate a purpose of the broker to derive profit for himself while disregarding the interests of the customer."

In Fey v. Walston & Co., Inc.,[4] the Court of Appeals for the Seventh Circuit reversed a judgment for a plaintiff in a churning case on the ground that the lower court's instruction on the definition of "churning" was erroneous:

"Most of the court's instructions on the issue of liability, extracted largely from Hecht v. Harris, Upham & Co., * * * were quite proper. Somewhat buried in the charge, however, was reference to the element recognized in *Hecht* that the salesman failed to conform to the customer's objectives * * *. This was an important point, for if a salesman does only what the customer independently has in mind as an objective, has authority so to do, and fulfills any fiduciary duty to furnish fair advice, the additional motive of the salesman to earn commissions does not convert the transactions into a deceptive or

---

1. Aff'd 177 F.2d 228 (D.C.Cir.1949).

2. 21 S.E.C. at 890.

3. Hecht v. Harris, Upham & Co., 283 F.Supp. 417, at 435 (N.D.Cal.1968).

4. 493 F.2d 1036 (7th Cir. 1974).

manipulative device in violation of Section 10(b). Plaintiff seems to accept these qualifications by her argument that her requested instructions * * * as given by the court, 'properly instructed the jury that the needs and objectives of the plaintiff * * * were to be considered in determining whether excessive trading occurred.' " [5]

In Hatrock v. Edward D. Jones & Co.[6] the Ninth Circuit set forth the definition of "churning" which has been generally accepted in the other cases: "To establish a claim of churning, a plaintiff must show (1) that the trading in his account was excessive in light of his investment objectives; (2) that the broker in question exercised control over the trading in the account; and (3) that the broker acted with intent to defraud or with willful and reckless disregard for the interests of his client." [7] In Arceneaux v. Merrill Lynch, Pierce, Fenner & Smith, Inc.[8] the Eleventh Circuit stated that, in connection with this definition of churning, expert testimony that a broker had turned an investor's account eight times on an annualized basis was sufficient evidence for a jury to find excessive trading; and expert testimony that the velocity of trading in the account made no sense other than to generate commissions could support a finding of scienter.

In Costello v. Oppenheimer Co., Inc.[9] the Seventh Circuit appeared to hold that a churning violation may be established merely by showing that the broker-dealer violated the specific written instructions of the client as to the parameters within which trades should be executed in the account. "There was testimony showing that [the customer and the broker-dealer] * * * reached a specific understanding concerning the handling of the account, * * * and that nevertheless some of the trades * * * did not comply with these criteria. The jury was entitled to conclude that the non-conforming trades constituted excessive activity * * *. Considered as a whole, plaintiff's evidence, thin though it was, created a jury issue whether there had been churning." [10]

The cases generally have allowed the recovery by the plaintiff in a case of "churning" of the total amount of the commissions paid, but not any loss in the market value of the portfolio, in accord with the Hecht case. No deduction is allowed of the commissions which might have been earned by a "normal" volume of trading. The lower court in the Hecht case stated: "Theoretically, any recovery of commissions and interest should be limited to such as are attributable to 'excessive' transactions as distinguished from those transactions which would not have been excessive under the circumstances. But, the difficulty of making such a distinction is obvious." [11]

However, in Fey v. Walston & Co., Inc.[12] the Seventh Circuit stated that it agreed with the dissenting judge in the Hecht case regarding the proper measure of damages. While holding that the jury had been permitted to

---

5. 493 F.2d at 1047–48.

6. 750 F.2d 767 (9th Cir.1984).

7. 750 F.2d at 775. In the following two cases a churning claim failed because it was shown that the customer remained in control of the trades executed in his account. Follansbee v. Davis, Skaggs & Company, Inc., 681 F.2d 673 (9th Cir.1982); M & B Contracting Corporation v. Dale, 795 F.2d 531 (6th Cir.1986), CCH Fed.Sec. Law Rptr. ¶ 92,846.

8. 767 F.2d 1498 (11th Cir.1985).

9. 711 F.2d 1361 (7th Cir.1983).

10. 711 F.2d at 1370. See, also, Erdos v. Securities and Exchange Commission, 742 F.2d 507 (9th Cir.1984).

11. 283 F.Supp. at 440 (N.D.Cal.1968).

12. 493 F.2d 1036 (7th Cir. 1974).

improperly include in the recovery losses on transactions independently initiated by the plaintiff herself, the court said:

"Defendants assert that the court erred in its instructions on the measure of damages, having charged without qualification that market losses as well as lost profits by way of interest were recoverable if a verdict was returned in plaintiff's favor. * * *

"Plaintiff would have the damage instruction sustained on the basic premise that churning is a unified offense to be established and recompensed not on evidence of individual transactions but by the extended course of operations. The court's adoption of the 'out-of-pocket theory', she says, was in keeping with the modern enlightened view, citing 'Churning by Securities Dealers', 80 Harvard Law Review, 869, 884 (1967), * * *, and its thesis that the amount of commissions only may bear no relationship to the amount of losses suffered by a customer from churning.

"In an uncomplicated churning case, where a general, discretionary power is abused merely to generate commissions, or where through breach of fiduciary duty a broker induces a trusting customer to generally overtrade, we think the plaintiff's position may be the sounder one. A broker's zeal to make commissions undeniably may cause damage unrelated in amount to what he earned as commissions. Hecht v. Harris, Upham & Co., 430 F.2d 1202, supra, dissenting opinion, 1212–13; * * *. The difficulty here, already adverted to in another connection, is that uncontradicted testimony from plaintiff herself indicated that certain transactions which patently were considered in the jury verdict and which furnished the basis of a considerable portion of plaintiff's loss calculations, were independently instigated by the plaintiff." [13]

There would seem to be little, if any, logical connection between the mere rate of portfolio turnover and the investment risk and resulting losses of principal from decline in market values. An account could theoretically be "churned" entirely in blue chips, with AT & T sold this week to buy GM and GM sold next week to buy DuPont. Or one could construct a scenario of an investment manager putting his client into the most speculative of stocks then favored by the "gun slingers" in the early 1960's, repeatedly shifting into more conservative stocks, then into bonds and finally into CD's and T-bills by the end of the decade, with the most fantastic results by the middle 1970's in the investment community. The fact that few, if any, investment advisers compiled such a record—and the fact that the customer would not then be suing the broker-dealer for "churning"—does not alter the logic. However, churning seems to take place almost invariably in highly volatile securities, for the obvious reason that there must be some plausible reason for taking the customer out of one security and putting him into the next one. Should this aspect be considered an essential ingredient of the offense of "churning", as the Seventh Circuit seemed to think, or as a separate, independent violation based upon the "suitability" rules, as was held by the Ninth Circuit?

See Slonim, Customer Sophistication and a Plaintiff's Duty of Due Diligence: A Proposed Framework for Churning Actions in Non-Discretionary Accounts Under SEC Rule 10b–5, 54 Fordham L.Rev. 1101 (1986); Markham and Bergin, Customer Rights Under the Commodity Exchange Act, 37 Vand.L.Rev. 1299 (1984); Hyman, Churning in Securities: Full Compensation for the Investor, 9 U.Dayton L.Rev. 1 (1983); Brodsky, Measuring Damages in Churning and Suitability Cases, 6 Securities Reg.L.J. 157 (1978); Note, Churning by Securities

___

13.   493 F.2d at 1054–55.

Dealers, 80 Harv.L.Rev. 869 (1967); Rosenman, Discretionary Accounts and Manipulative Trading Practices, 5 Inst.Sec.Rev. 245 (1974).

SUITABILITY

The rules of the NASD require that the broker-dealer in recommending to a customer the purchase or sale of a security must have "reasonable grounds for believing that the recommendation is suitable for such customer upon the basis of the facts, if any, disclosed by such customer as to his other security holdings and as to his financial situation and needs." [14] While this rule does not in terms impose any duty of inquiry upon the broker-dealer, a policy statement of the Board of Governors of the NASD prohibits the broker-dealer from: [15]

"1. Recommending speculative low-priced securities to customers without knowledge of or attempt to obtain information concerning the customers' other securities holdings, their financial situation and other necessary data. The principle here is that this practice, by its very nature, involves a high probability that the recommendation will not be suitable for at least some of the persons solicited. This has particular application to high pressure telephonic sales campaigns.

    *   *   *

"3. Trading in mutual fund shares, particularly on a short-term basis. It is clear that normally these securities are not proper trading vehicles and such activity on its face may raise the question of rule violation.

    *   *   *

"5. Recommending the purchase of securities or the continuing purchase of securities in amounts which are inconsistent with the reasonable expectation that the customer has the financial ability to meet such a commitment."

The SECO rule,[16] on the other hand, which was applicable to those broker-dealers who were not members of the NASD, clearly imposed a duty of inquiry in all cases in order to determine the suitability of recommendations:

"Every nonmember broker or dealer and every associated person who recommends to a customer the purchase, sale or exchange of any security shall have reasonable grounds to believe that the recommendation is not unsuitable for such customer on the basis of information furnished by such customer *after reasonable inquiry* concerning the customer's investment objectives, financial

---

14. Art. III, Sec. 2, NASD Rules of Fair Practice, CCH NASD Manual ¶ 2152. See In the Matter of Boren & Co., Sec.Exch.Act Rel. No. 6367 (SEC 1960). Compare Rule 15c2–5 (adopted in SEC Sec.Exch.Act Rel. No. 6851, July 17, 1962) which deals with the so-called "equity funding" of the purchase of mutual fund shares, i.e., the purchase of such shares together with a policy of life insurance, the premiums on which are paid by money borrowed on the shares. The Rule provides that it is a fraudulent practice for a broker-dealer to sell a customer such a "package" unless, among other things, the broker-dealer "obtains from such person information concerning his financial situation and needs, reasonably de-

termines that the entire transaction, including the loan arrangement, is suitable for such person, and delivers to such person a written statement setting forth the basis upon which the broker or dealer made such determination."

15. Ibid.

16. The SECO (SEC only) rules were those authorized by the Securities Acts Amendments of 1964 with respect to those broker-dealers who did not choose to join the NASD. They were primarily applicable to the "captive sales forces" of mutual fund organizations. Since the 1983 amendments, all broker-dealers have been required to join the NASD.

situation and needs, and any other information known by such broker or dealer or associated person." [17]

The New York Stock Exchange rule, on the other hand, is phrased in terms of a duty of inquiry without any express prescription of what action is supposed to follow on the basis of the facts discovered. It requires that a member broker "use due diligence to learn the essential facts relative to every customer" [18] (sometimes known as the "Know Thy Customer Rule"). Obviously implicit in this injunction, though, is the requirement that the broker's recommendations be responsibly related to the investment objectives and financial situation of the customer discovered by the investigation.

While it is clear that disciplinary action may be taken against any broker-dealer who violates any one of these rules to which he is subject, the existence of any private right of action based upon their violation, and its extent if it exists, are still unresolved. See Chapter 13, infra. In the *Hecht* case the court held that the plaintiff was estopped from relying on this theory of recovery; and in the *Fey* case it was not asserted as an independent ground for relief, although the court seemed to regard it as somehow wrapped up in a general theory of "churning."

See Cohen, Suitability Doctrine: Defining Stockbrokers' Professional Responsibilities, 3 J.Corp.L. 533 (1978); Roach, Suitability Obligations of Brokers, 29 Hastings L.J. 1067 (1978); Note, "Know Your Customer" Rule of the NYSE, 1973 Duke L.J. 489; Rossbach, Client "Suitability", 111 Trusts & Est. 442 (1972); Bloomenthal, Market Makers, Manipulators and Shell Games, 45 St. John's L.Rev. (1971); Cohen, The Suitability Rule and Economic Theory, 80 Yale L.J. 1604 (1971); Fishman, Broker-dealer Obligations to Customers—The NASD Suitability Rule, 51 Minn.L.Rev. 233 (1966); Mundheim, Professional Responsibilities of Broker-dealers: The Suitability Doctrine, 1965 Duke L.J. 445.

QUOTATIONS

In 1971 the SEC adopted a new Rule 15c2–11 [19] regulating the submission of quotations by broker-dealers on over-the-counter securities to any interdealer quotation system, as well as any other "publication" of such quotations, which imposes a duty of investigation and disclosure as a prerequisite to any such submission of quotations. The Rule basically prohibits a broker-dealer from quoting an over-the-counter security which has not previously been the subject of continuous quotations, unless either (1) the issuer has registered under the 1933 Act or the 1934 Act (or is an exempt insurance company under Section 12(g) of the 1934 Act) and is current in the filing of its periodic reports under the 1934 Act; or (2) the broker-dealer has obtained and makes available to any person upon request certain basic financial and other information relating to the issuer. The information required to be collected by the broker-dealer includes a balance sheet of the issuer as of a date within 16 months of the date of submission of the quotation and income statements to a date within 6 months of such submission and financial statements for the two years prior to the date of the most recent balance sheet. In addition, there are fourteen other items of information required to be collected and preserved by the broker-dealer.

---

17. Rule 15b10–3, adopted by Securities Exchange Act Release No. 8135, effective Oct. 2, 1967 (Italics added).

18. NYSE Rule 405, CCH New York Stock Exchange Manual ¶ 2405.

19. SEC Sec.Exch.Act Rel. No. 9310 (Sept. 13, 1971).

The Rule requires that the broker-dealer must have "no reasonable basis for believing [that the information] is not true and correct or reasonably current" and that it must be "obtained by him from sources which he has a reasonable basis for believing are reliable." While this does not make the broker-dealer a guarantor of the accuracy of the information, and at least literally does not impose upon him any duty of investigation or "due diligence" beyond going to what he reasonably believes are reliable sources, the possible exposure to civil liability of a broker-dealer quoting a non-registered security is obvious. The Rule was adopted primarily for the purpose of attempting to stop the "shell game" (see Chapter 8, supra at p. 451), but it is not limited in its application to public corporations which are created by the spin-off of a shell corporation. See Note, Effects of SEC Rule 15c2–11 on the Sale of Spin Off Securities, 19 UCLA L.Rev. 487 (1972).

CHASINS v. SMITH, BARNEY & CO., INC.

United States Court of Appeals, Second Circuit, 1971.
438 F.2d 1167.

Before: SMITH, KAUFMAN and HAYS, CIRCUIT JUDGES.

SMITH, CIRCUIT JUDGE: On petition for rehearing, the opinion filed July 7, 1970 is withdrawn and the following opinion substituted therefor. The petition for rehearing is otherwise denied.

* * *

SMITH, CIRCUIT JUDGE: This is an appeal by Smith, Barney & Co., Inc., a stock brokerage firm [hereinafter "Smith, Barney"] from a judgment for damages on a determination by Judge Dudley B. Bonsal in the United States District Court for the Southern District of New York that Smith, Barney had violated Rules 10b–5 and 15c1–4 (17 C.F.R. §§ 240.10b–5 and 240.15c1–4), promulgated under the Securities Exchange Act, 15 U.S.C. §§ 78j(b) and 78o(c), in not disclosing to appellee (Chasins) that it was making a market in the securities it sold Chasins in the over-the-counter market. Chasins has cross-appealed the district court's ruling that appellant had not violated its common law fiduciary duty to Chasins by the manner it handled the transactions between the two. We find no error and affirm the judgment.

This action brought by Chasins in the district court under the Securities Act of 1933, 15 U.S.C. § 77a et seq., and the Securities Exchange Act of 1934, 15 U.S.C. § 78a et seq., for damages resulting from Smith, Barney's alleged violations of the Acts, and pendent common law violations, in handling Chasins' securities brokerage account was tried to the court without a jury. At the time the four transactions in question in his appeal occurred,[3] Chasins was the musical director of radio station WQXR in New

---

3. The four securities transactions involved in this appeal were sales of securities by Smith, Barney to Chasins in the over-the-counter market as follows:

Date	Number of Shares	Company
7/19/61	200	Welch Scientific Company
7/19/61	200	Tex-Star Oil and Gas Corp.
7/19/61	200	Howard Johnson Company
8/22/61	200	Welch Scientific Company

Total cost of the securities to Chasins was $34,950; he subsequently sold these securities on June 28, 1962 for $16,333.36.

* * *

York City and was the commentator on a musical program sponsored by Smith, Barney. According to Chasins it was due to this relationship that he opened his brokerage account with Smith, Barney by orally retaining it to act as his stockbroker. Smith, Barney acted in at least two capacities in these transactions, namely as Chasin's stockbroker and as principal, i.e., the owner of the security being sold to Chasins. In all four transactions Smith, Barney sold the securities to Chasins in the over-the-counter market, and although it revealed in the confirmation slips that it was acting as principal and for its own account in selling to Chasins, Smith, Barney did not reveal that it was "making a market" in the securities involved as was the fact. Nor did Smith, Barney disclose how much it had paid for the securities sold as principal to Chasins or that it had acted as an "underwriter" as defined by the Securities Act of 1933 in connection with the distribution of securities of Welch Scientific Company and Howard Johnson Company, two of the companies whose securities Smith, Barney sold to Chasins.

Preceding the four sales of July and August, 1961, Smith, Barney sent Chasins a written analysis of his then current security holdings and its recommendations in regard to his objective of aggressive growth of his holdings. The recommendations included strong purchase recommendations for securities of Welch Scientific, Tex-Star Oil and Gas Corp., and Howard Johnson Company. Chasins and Thomas N. Delaney, Jr., an authorized agent of Smith, Barney had various telephone conversations prior to the transactions in question. Delaney testified that at least at the times of the four transactions in question Smith, Barney was "making a market" in those securities, i.e., it was maintaining a position in the stocks on its own account by participating in over-the-counter trading in them; Smith, Barney's records indicated that at least from June 30, 1961, it had been trading in those stocks and had held positions in them during the times Chasins purchased the securities from it. There was no testimony that Chasins had any knowledge or notice that Smith, Barney was "making a market" in the securities of the three companies.

The decision of the district court was based on conflicting evidence as to whether Chasins had a "discretionary account" with Smith, Barney and on the four transactions above. Although the court ruled that Smith, Barney had not violated any common law fiduciary duty to Chasins, Smith, Barney was found to have violated Rules 10b–5 and 15c1–4 (the latter in a supplemental opinion) in not disclosing its market making (or dealer) status in the securities that it recommended Chasins purchase, when Chasins followed that advice and purchased the securities and Smith, Barney was the other principal in the sales. Damages were awarded to Chasins in the amount of $18,616.64, with interest, which constituted the difference between the price at which Chasins purchased the securities from Smith, Barney and the price at which he later sold them (prior to discovering Smith, Barney's market making in the securities).

I.

VIOLATIONS OF RULES

10b–5 and 15c1–4

Smith, Barney's major contention in attacking the district court's finding of a violation of Rules 10b–5 and 15c1–4 is that failure to disclose its "market making" role in the securities exchanged over the counter was not failure to disclose a material fact. Appellant contends that the district court's holding went farther than any other decision in this area and that no court had ever found failure to disclose a "market making" role by a stock brokerage firm to a client-purchaser to be a violation of Rule 10b–5. Smith, Barney also asserts that all brokerage firms had followed the same practice and had never thought such disclosure was required; moreover, the SEC had never prosecuted any firm for this violation. However, even where a defendant is successful in showing that it has followed a customary course in the industry, the first litigation of such a practice is a proper occasion for its outlawry if it is in fact in violation. See Opper v. Hancock Securities Corp., 250 F.Supp. 668, 676 (S.D.N.Y.1966), aff'd 367 F.2d 157 (2d Cir. 1966). In any event, it cannot fairly be said that no one in the trade had ever considered such nondisclosure to be significant. Appellant's own customers man (Delaney) testified that at the time (1961) he was disclosing to retail clients the firm's role as a market maker in a given security whenever he was aware of it.

Appellant also points to the fact that in over-the-counter trading, a market maker with an inventory in a stock is considered the best source of the security (the best available market); thus, the SEC has even punished a brokerage firm for not going directly to a firm with an inventory in a stock, i.e., interposing another firm between them. See e.g., In re Thomson & McKinnon, CCH Fed.Sec.L.Rep. ¶ 77,572, p. 83,203 (1967–69 SEC Rulings). However, the fact that dealing with a market maker should be considered by some desirable for some purposes does not mean that the failure to disclose Smith, Barney's market-making role is not under the circumstances of this case a failure to disclose a material fact. The question here is not whether Smith, Barney sold to Chasins at a fair price but whether disclosure of Smith, Barney's being a market maker in the Welch Scientific, Tex-Star Oil and Gas and Howard Johnson securities might have influenced Chasins' decision to buy the stock. See SEC v. Texas Gulf Sulphur Co., 401 F.2d 833, 849 (2d Cir. 1968) (en banc), cert. denied sub nom. Coates v. SEC, 394 U.S. 976 (1969); List v. Fashion Park, Inc., 340 F.2d 457 (2d Cir. 1965), cert. denied, 382 U.S. 811 (1965). The test of materiality " * * * is whether a reasonable man would attach importance * * * in determining his choice of action in the transaction in question. * * *" List v. Fashion Park, Inc., supra, at 340 F.2d 462; SEC v. Texas Gulf Sulphur Co., supra, at 401 F.2d 849; i.e., a material fact is one " * * * which in reasonable and objective contemplation might affect the value of the corporation's stock or securities. * * *" Kohler v. Kohler Co., 319 F.2d 634, 642 (7 Cir. 1963); List v. Fashion Park, Inc., supra, at 340 F.2d 462; SEC v. Texas Gulf Sulphur Co., supra, at 401 F.2d 849. See also Mills v. Electric Auto-Lite Co., 396 U.S. 375 (1970). In applying that test in this case, the question of materiality becomes whether a reasonable man in Chasins' position might well have acted otherwise than to purchase if he had been informed of Smith, Barney's market making role in the three stocks in addition to the fact that Smith, Barney was the other principal in the transaction. The broker-dealer, Smith, Barney, had undertaken to make a written evaluation of Chasins' securities holdings and had strongly recommended sales of some of his holdings and purchases of these three stocks in which Smith, Barney was dealing as a principal.

Knowledge of the additional fact of market making by Smith, Barney in the three securities recommended could well influence the decision of a client in Chasins' position, depending on the broker-dealer's undertaking to analyze and advise, whether to follow its recommendation to buy the securities; disclosure of the fact would indicate the possibility of adverse interests which might be reflected in Smith, Barney's recommendations. Smith, Barney could well be caught in either a "short" position or a "long" position in a security, because of erroneous judgment of supply and demand at given levels. If over supplied, it may be to the interest of a market maker to attempt to unload the securities on his retail clients. Here, Smith, Barney's strong recommendations of the three securities Chasins purchased could have been motivated by its own market position rather than the intrinsic desirability of the securities for Chasins. An investor who is at least informed of the possibility of such adverse interests, due to his broker's market making in the securities recommended, can question the reasons for the recommendations. The investor, such as Chasins, must be permitted to evaluate overlapping motivations through appropriate disclosures, especially where one motivation is economic self-interest. See SEC v. Capital Gains Research Bureau, Inc., 375 U.S. 180 at 196 (1963).

In the case at bar, the broker-dealer had undertaken at its customer's request to make a written evaluation of his securities holdings and recommendations for further purchases and sales knowing that the customer, who was, as pointed out above, musical director of a radio station and commentator on a musical program sponsored by Smith, Barney, would rely on its report to him. In this situation failure to inform the customer fully of its possible conflict of interest, in that it was a market maker in the securities which it strongly recommended for purchase by him, was an omission of material fact in violation of Rule 10b–5, 17 C.F.R. 240.10b–5.

The Securities and Exchange Commission is presently engaged in consideration of the advisability of rules on disclosure of the fact of market making, to delineate the extent and time of disclosure to be required, and whether distinctions should be made as for instance between situations where the particular broker-dealer is the sole or dominant market maker and situations where it is one of a number of market makers and the price is competitive with quotes of other market makers. Such rules and similar rules of the self-regulatory agencies may well promote full and fair disclosure, while, in the words of the SEC "furthering customer protection." We do not attempt to address ourselves to the question of the best mechanics for disclosure. We here go so far only as to hold that under the particular circumstances proved in this case the court was correct in holding that the failure to disclose was the omission of a material fact.

* * *

In view of our agreement with the finding of violation of Rule 10b–5 we need not determine whether this failure to disclose market-making or dealer status also violated Rule 15c1–4 as found by Judge Bonsal in his supplemental memorandum of decision.

* * *

II.

CHASINS' CROSS–APPEAL

In his cross-appeal Chasins contends that the district court erred in finding no violation of a common law fiduciary duty to Chasins by Smith, Barney in the way Chasins' account was handled. The cross-appeal is not pressed, however, unless the judgment in plaintiff's favor is reversed in whole or in part. We therefore do not reach it here. Affirmed.

Before: LUMBARD, CHIEF JUDGE, WATERMAN, MOORE, FRIENDLY, SMITH, KAUFMAN, HAYS, ANDERSON and FEINBERG, CIRCUIT JUDGES.

A petition for rehearing containing a suggestion that the action be reheard *in banc* having been filed herein by counsel for the appellant, and the panel having determined to withdraw its opinion, slip sheet p. 3711, filed July 7, 1970, and to file a new opinion in substitution.

It is ordered that said petition be and it hereby is denied, LUMBARD, CHIEF JUDGE, MOORE and FRIENDLY, CIRCUIT JUDGES, dissenting from such denial in an opinion by JUDGE FRIENDLY which follows, and FEINBERG, CIRCUIT JUDGE, taking no part in the consideration or decision of this petition.

J. EDWARD LUMBARD,
CHIEF JUDGE.

FRIENDLY, CIRCUIT JUDGE with whom LUMBARD, CHIEF JUDGE, and MOORE, CIRCUIT JUDGE, join (dissenting from the denial of reconsideration *in banc*):

Although the narrowing of the opinion to the particular constellation of facts here presented substantially lessens its impact, we are nevertheless constrained to voice our dissent from the refusal to grant *in banc* reconsideration.

* * *

The district court initially found that the confirmations here, which disclosed that Smith, Barney was selling "as principal for our own account," were in full compliance with the rule. Although Rule 17a–9(f) defines "market-maker," this is in a reporting requirement; it is conceded that in 1961 no rule of the SEC (other than, allegedly, the inevitable Rule 10b–5), the NASD or the New York Stock Exchange required disclosure of that fact to a customer.

The complaint nowhere asserted that Smith, Barney was under a duty to tell Mr. Chasins it was a "market-maker" in the three over-the-counter stocks that he bought. It alleged rather that defendant did not disclose the "best price" at which these and other securities could have been bought or sold in the open market, or the prices it had paid or received, and that plaintiff was deceived by Smith, Barney's failure to disclose "the material fact of its adverse interest, the extent of which is today still unknown to and not determinable by plaintiff." The plaintiff, a noted musicologist, said nothing about market-making in his testimony. The closest he came to making the claim now sustained was that, despite his alleged inability to comprehend financial matters, he would have understood if told that the stock reflected by the confirmations was owned by the defendant, since "if you have a great picture, for example, and you know that the picture is going to be worth a lot more the next year or five years or ten, I don't think you would be anxious to dispose of it." Although this is hardly convincing, since great pictures are constantly being sold and bought under exactly such circumstances, Mr. Chasins had been plainly told of defendant's ownership by the confirmation slips. In addition, the Smith, Barney research report he had received on Tex-Star contained the legend in common use at the time:

> We point out that in the course of our regular business we may be long or short of any of the above securities at any time,

and the prospectus he received of Welch Scientific company disclosed that Smith, Barney was one of the underwriters of that stock, which had only recently been placed on the market. All that the trial record contained about non-disclosure of market making was a statement by Delaney, a registered representative of Smith, Barney, that he normally would bring this fact to the attention of clients if he knew it; that he did know Smith, Barney was making a market in the three stocks; and that he couldn't recall whether or not he had brought this to Mr. Chasins' attention.

The issue of market making first assumed importance as a result of the opinion of the district judge. After finding against the plaintiff on all the contentions that had been advanced in the complaint and aired at the trial, he opined that information with respect to market making "was material to the plaintiff in considering the price at which he purchased the securities, and to what extent the price was based on defendant's own market activities," and therefore plaintiff should recover his entire market loss. Smith, Barney then made a motion pointing out there was no basis for the "therefore," since on the judge's theory the only recoverable damage would be any excessive price obtained as a result of Smith, Barney's being a market-maker. On that issue it submitted proof by way of affidavit that the prices charged the plaintiff for the three stocks were entirely fair, indeed less than he would have paid if he had bought the stocks from a person acting solely as broker. It also submitted the opinion of the experienced manager of its trading department that

> From the point of view of the knowledgeable investor, disclosure to him that he would be purchasing from a market maker would only have encouraged him in his decision to buy.

Unwilling to hear evidence on the issue first raised by its opinion, the district court took a new tack. It held, in seeming contradiction of the initial opinion, that the confirmations, in a form widely used, did not comply with Rule 15c1–4 since they conveyed "the impression that defendant had purchased a block of the securities and was selling part of it to plaintiff at the then prevailing market prices, when, in fact, defendant was acting as a dealer for its own account." We are unable to follow this, especially in light of the definition of "dealer" in § 3(a)(5), and the court wisely does not base its decision upon it. Evidently lacking confidence in that holding, the judge then went on to conclude, without semblance of an evidentiary basis, that disclosure of market making might have led Mr. Chasins not to purchase the stocks at all.

The conclusions on the materiality of disclosure of market making by the district court and in this court's opinion are predicated on an essential misconception of the role of the market maker in over-the-counter transactions. When a reputable house like Smith, Barney acts as one of several market makers, as was the case here, it serves a highly desirable purpose in reducing the spreads characteristic of over-the-counter trading. It has been widely recognized that the "best price" can be obtained by dealing directly with market makers, for one reason because a commission to an intermediary is avoided. See Thomson & McKinnon, CCH Fed.Sec.L.Rep. ¶ 77,572 (1968); Delaware Management Co., CCH Fed.Sec.L.Rep. ¶ 77,458 (1967); H. C. Keister & Co., CCH Fed.Sec.L.Rep. ¶ 77,414 (1966); Report of the SEC on the Public Policy Implications of Investment Company Growth, H.R.Rep.No.2337, 89th Cong. 2d Sess., at 179 (1966). The district judge's fears concerning the ability of a market maker to set an arbitrary price are inapplicable when as here there were several market makers, as Smith, Barney pointed out in its post-trial motion and the SEC now confirms in its letter to us as *amicus curiae*. Moreover Smith, Barney offered to prove that in fact Mr. Chasins bought at the lowest available price. So far as concerns the fears of ulterior motives voiced by the district judge and now by the court, the market maker, who buys as well as sells, is *less* likely to be interested in palming off a stock than a dealer with only a long position. Yet the confirmation here would plainly have been adequate for such a dealer, and we held only recently, in a case curiously not cited, that a dealer need not make the additional disclosure that it had originally acquired the stock for investment and not with a view towards distribution, something considerably more material than being one of several market makers. SEC v. R. A. Holman & Co., 366 F.2d 456, 457 (1966). At the very least the materiality of market making to an investment decision was an issue on which Smith, Barney was entitled to submit proofs. It never had had a fair opportunity to do this, although we read the court's opinion as leaving this open to defendants in future cases.

* * * Although the opinion is now limited to the peculiar facts of this case, we fear it will encourage many suits by other speculators who have suffered losses. At minimum, Smith, Barney is entitled to a new trial where the issues of materiality and reliance raised by the district court's opinion can be fairly litigated.

MARKET MAKING AND DOMINATION OF THE MARKET

A "market maker" is a broker-dealer who publishes, in the "pink sheets" or more recently in NASDAQ, bona fide "two-way" quotations with respect to an over-the-counter security. This means that he is quoting both a bid and asked price, as distinguished from quoting a bid price only or an asked price only or perhaps quoting "OW" (offer wanted) or "BW" (bid wanted). Obviously, this requires that he stand ready either to buy or to sell as principal in reasonable quantities, with resulting long or short positions, and as pointed out in the *Shearson* case, supra, p. 605, the NASD rules insist upon this readiness as an obligation of the market maker. The broker-dealer may also engage in what are called "riskless" or "simultaneous" transactions whereby he buys from one customer and sells to another in virtually simultaneous transactions. The Commission originally took the position that a broker-dealer engaging in non-position trading of this type was required to confirm the transaction as "broker" and to reveal the amount of his profit as a "commission"; [1] although the SEC later abandoned this position,[2] such a transaction is subject to the NASD "mark-up policy" limiting the amount of the mark-up or "spread" which the dealer may charge. (See Chapter 10, supra).

Rule 15c1–8 makes it unlawful for a broker-dealer participating in a distribution of securities to represent that such security is being offered "at the market" unless he knows or has reasonable grounds to believe that a market exists "other than that made, created, or controlled by him, or by any person for whom he is acting or with whom he is associated in such distribution". However, this principle is not limited, as the rule is by its terms, to "distributions." As the Commission stated in In the Matter of Norris & Hirshberg, Inc.: "As to sales made on the express representation that they are 'at market' we have repeatedly held that such a representation is false where in fact the 'market' has been subject to artificial influences or where no true market existed." [3] And under the "shingle theory" every sale by a broker-dealer carries with it the implied representation that the price is "reasonably related to that prevailing in an open market." For an excellent analysis of the problems which these principles pose to a dealer making an over-the-counter market, see Bloomenthal, The Case of the Subtle Motive and the Delicate Art— Control and Domination in Over-The-Counter Securities Markets, 1960 Duke L.J. 196.

This principle has always presented a perhaps insoluble problem of disclosure to any broker-dealer who is the only one "in the sheets" with respect to a particular over-the-counter stock. On any realistic test, such a broker-dealer "controls" or "dominates" the market in that stock, although it is doubtful if very many take steps to make effective disclosure to their customers of this fact. However, until the bombshell exploded by the District Court opinion in the *Chasins* case, no one thought that a broker-dealer who was one of several making a market in a stock and who did not execute a predominant portion of the trades in that stock had to make any disclosure to his customer other than to confirm the transaction as "principal." Coming at the end of a bear market, that decision appeared to impose a liability approaching the size of the National debt on an industry already teetering on the edge of insolvency. (Although all customers of market makers could apparently recover all of their losses in unlisted securities over some indefinite period in the past, no one suggested that they would have to refund their profits.)

To what extent has this result been modified, if at all, by the second opinion of the Court of Appeals? In that opinion, the panel backed down to some extent from its original opinion affirming the District Judge, apparently to avoid a reversal by the *en banc* court, and the dissenting judges say that the decision is now confined "to its peculiar facts." What facts? Does the ruling now apply only when the broker-dealer has solicited the trust and reliance of the customer and undertaken to act as his investment adviser? [4] Or does it

1. In the Matter of Oxford Co., Inc., 21 S.E.C. 21 (1946); In the Matter of Norris & Hirshberg, Inc., 21 S.E.C. 865 (1946), aff'd 177 F.2d 228 (D.C.Cir. 1949).

2. See 3 Loss, Securities Regulation 1506–1507 (2d ed. 1961).

3. 21 S.E.C. 865, at 882 (1946), aff'd 177 F.2d 228 (D.C.Cir. 1949).

4. The Fifth Circuit seemed to so interpret the Chasins case in Simon v. Merrill Lynch, Pierce, Fenner and Smith, Inc., 482 F.2d 880 (5th Cir. 1973), reh. denied 485 F.2d 687, in which it said: "Nor does *Chasins*, supra, provide him [the plaintiff] with support because the Second Circuit limited that opinion to the fact situation where the defendant 'had strongly recommended sales of [plaintiff's] holding and purchases of * * * stocks in which [defendant] was dealing as a principal' and the plaintiff relied upon defendant's recommendations of the purchase." 485 F.2d at 885.

only apply where the customer is a noted musicologist who is the commentator on the broker-dealer's radio program?

A subsidiary question is the required timing of the disclosure, assuming in a particular case that some disclosure must be made. Is it sufficient to make it in the confirmation, or must it be done at the time the order is placed by the customer? In general, it would seem to be clear that disclosure, to be adequate, must be made in time for the other party to consider it in deciding whether to enter into the transaction. However, in this case, where the broker-dealer deals with the customer as a principal, the customer is given ten days after receipt of the written confirmation to repudiate the transaction, by the provisions of the Uniform Commercial Code.[5] Therefore, it can be argued that a disclosure in the confirmation should be sufficient if it is made in a manner which is reasonably calculated to bring it to the attention of the customer.

CONFIRMATIONS; FIDUCIARY STATUS OF THE BROKER–DEALER

Rule 10b–10 (the successor to Rule 15c1–4 referred to in the *Chasins* case) requires a broker-dealer to disclose to the customer in a written confirmation of each transaction "Whether he is acting as agent for such customer, as agent for some other person, as agent for both such customer and some other person, or as principal for his own account" and, if he is acting as agent for such customer or for some other person or both, to disclose, among other things, "The amount of any remuneration received or to be received by him from such customer in connection with the transaction." If he is acting as principal for his own account, in that case he must disclose the amount of any mark-up or mark-down with respect to a simultaneous or "riskless" transaction and, with respect to a transaction in an equity security, "whether he is a market maker in that security." With the proliferation of the amount of information which must be included on the confirmation slip, and the necessity for having them printed by computer in order to manage the "back office" problems of the brokerage industry, the practice has developed of having code numbers printed on the front of the confirmation slip to refer to certain statements contained on the back of the form, including the fact, if it is true, that the broker-dealer was acting as principal in the transaction.

The difficult problems under this rule arise in connection with determining when the broker-dealer *must* act as an agent for the customer because he has acquired a fiduciary status and cannot deal with him as principal without his informed consent in advance. In In the Matter of Norris & Hirshberg, Inc.,[6] the Commission held that the broker-dealer violated his fiduciary duty in purporting to trade with his customers as principal, under the following circumstances:

"Norris and Hirshberg maintained personal friendly relations with many customers and were highly successful in procuring the trust and confidence of their customers. Because of the great reliance of many customers on respon-

---

5. Uniform Commercial Code, § 8–319(c). This assumes that there is no adequate writing evidencing the transaction signed by the customer prior to his receipt of the confirmation, as there normally would not be. This section has been held to require a writing only where the broker-dealer acts as principal, and not where he acts as an agent. Stott v. Greengos, 95 N.J.Super. 96, 230 A.2d 154 (1967); Lindsey v. Stein Brothers & Boyce, Inc., 222 Tenn. 149, 433 S.W.2d 669 (1968). This point was made explicit in the California version of the Code. West's Ann.Cal. Comm.Code, § 8–319(2).

6. Supra, Note 1.

dent it had an unusual amount of control over their trading, its power ranging from formal written and oral discretion specifically vested in it by certain customers to an ability to initiate and suggest trading with almost complete assurance of the acceptance of the trades. Notwithstanding the nature of its relations with customers, the precise terms of its discretionary powers, or the legal character of customers' orders, respondent without sufficient disclosure, purported to deal with these customers almost universally as a dealer at a profit. Its power over accounts was augmented by the fact that many of them were margin accounts. Consequently, respondent had physical possession and the powers of a creditor and pledgee over the securities in margin accounts. Margin trading also permitted respondent to effect a larger volume of business with customers than would have been possible on the basis of cash trading alone.

"As a result of this combination of factors, respondent was able to acquire large portions of the available trading supplies of the securities in which it specialized, sell those securities to customers, buy them back, sell them again to the same and to other customers, turn over its inventories again and again at kited prices unilaterally fixed by respondent in a market consisting almost wholly of itself and its customers, to a great degree unaffected by normal bargaining influences." [7]

The result in the *Chasins* case, it would seem, might have been based upon the doctrine that the broker-dealer, having solicited the trust and confidence of the customer, could not, as in *Norris & Hirshberg*, deal with the customer as a principal without his informed consent in advance. However, the Second Circuit refused to consider the question of a violation of former Rule 15c1–4 and the District Court did not base its holding that there was a violation of this Rule on this principle, but upon an incomprehensible distinction between a broker-dealer quoting both sides of the market and one merely selling out an inventory (even, presumably, if he is in the sheets with an asked price only). Whatever may be true of Rule 10b–5, there was not a syllable in former Rule 15c1–4 which required any more or different disclosure of one than the other. And to say that more disclosure *should* be required of a broker-dealer who is making a bona fide two-way market than of one who is engaged in a "work-out market", merely trying to unload his own holdings on the public, would seem to be an indefensible position. As noted above, the new Rule 10b–10 now does require that the broker-dealer disclose the fact, if it is a fact, that he is acting as a market maker in an equity security which is the subject of the transaction. What the customer is expected to do with this tidbit of information, among the flood of information required to be included on the confirmation slip, is not apparent.

In Cant v. A. G. Becker & Co., Inc.,[8] the Federal District Court for the Northern District of Illinois gave another shock to the brokerage industry by holding that the coded confirmation slips referred to above are insufficient disclosure and therefore a violation of former Rule 15c1–4, if the customer testifies that he did not understand them and they were not explained to him, at least in the circumstances of that case. However, this case also might perhaps be better explained on the basis that the broker-dealer had acquired a fiduciary status and was not entitled to deal with the customer as principal. The court said: "Further, the defendant's disclosure by means of the confirmation slips was not sufficient given the plaintiff's long-standing reliance upon defendant's investment advice, and the failure of Mr. Wieczorowski to inform and educate the plaintiff on the code and the terminology, and the fact that the

---

7. 21 S.E.C. at 867.   8. 374 F.Supp. 36 (N.D.Ill.1974).

plaintiff apparently did not understand the code or the terminology or that the defendant was acting as a principal and not a broker.

"The defendant A. G. Becker predicates its position on the case of Batchelor v. Legy & Co., 52 F.R.D. 553 (D.Md.1971). However, the *Batchelor* case does not involve the same type of special customer relationship and reliance that existed in the instant action. Cf. Chasins v. Smith Barney & Co., 438 F.2d 1167 (2nd Cir. 1971). This Court is not holding that a broker is liable in every instance where the broker is acting as a principal and this change in status is not expressly, clearly and painstakingly explained to the investor. Rather, this Court is holding that where there is, as in the case at bar, a special relationship of confidence between the investor and broker and the broker fails to adequately and clearly inform or educate the investor as to the change in the broker's status, the broker will be liable because the investor due to this failure to disclose cannot make a properly informed investment decision." [9]

"Wooden orders" and "stuffed pigs." In In the Matter of Palombi Securities Co., Inc.,[10] the Commission affirmed disciplinary action taken by the District Business Conduct Committee of the NASD with respect to a broker-dealer, in connection with sales of the stock of a particular company with respect to which there had been during a three-month period forty-nine cancellations out of eighty-seven alleged sales. The cashier of the broker-dealer told the SEC investigator that he normally cancelled sales where confirmations had been sent and the money had not been received by the day after the settlement date, since he assumed that they represented "stuffed pigs." The District Business Conduct Committee stated: "The overly aggressive sales technique in question is well recognized by a certain element in the industry and in their jargon it is referred to as the use of 'wooden orders.' * * * We are all experienced in the business and we have some knowledge of the reaction of the public to a solicitation and the extent to which they fulfill their commitments on a proper sales presentation. In the light of this background, it is inconceivable to us that in ordinary circumstances there would be a record of over 50% of reneges." The regulations of the NASD expressly prohibit "Causing the execution of transactions which are unauthorized by customers or the sending of confirmations in order to cause customers to accept transactions not actually agreed upon." [11] There would seem to be little doubt that such conduct would violate the general fraud rules even in the absence of a specific prohibition.

See Loss, the SEC and the Broker-Dealer, 1 Vand.L.Rev. 516 (1948); Note, Disclosure Requirements in Over the Counter Trading, 57 Yale L.J. 1316 (1948); 3 Loss, Securities Regulation 1500–1508 (2d ed. 1961). The Chasins case is noted in 71 Colum.L.Rev. 495 (1971); 45 Tul.L.Rev. 668 (1971); 19 Kan.L.Rev. 339 (1971).

MARGIN REQUIREMENTS

There are large numbers of NASD and SEC disciplinary actions based upon brokers' violations of the margin requirements of the Federal Reserve Board issued under the authority of Section 7 of the Securities Exchange Act. Although the FRB has the authority to promulgate the regulations and to fix from time to time the margin level (currently 50%), the securities regulatory agencies are charged with the responsibility of enforcing the margin rules with

9. 374 F.Supp. at 46–47.

10. Sec.Exch.Act Rel. No. 6961 (SEC Nov. 30, 1962).

11. CCH NASD Manual ¶ 2152.

respect to broker-dealers. The current regulation governing lending on securities by broker-dealers is designated Regulation T. There is a similar, but by no means identical, regulation governing loans by banks secured directly or indirectly by margin stock "for the purpose * * * of buying or carrying margin stock," [12] which is designated Regulation U, and relatively new regulations governing lending by persons other than broker-dealers and banks, who engage in the business of making loans for the purpose of buying or carrying margin securities (Regulation G) [13] and governing borrowing by persons in the United States from either domestic or foreign lenders (Regulation X). [14]

Regulation T formerly prohibited a broker-dealer from lending for the purpose of purchasing or carrying any securities other than those which are either registered on a national securities exchange or are widely traded over-the-counter stocks on a list of "OTC Margin Stocks" issued by the FRB or are "exempted securities" as defined in the Securities Exchange Act (primarily governments). By an amendment to Regulation T adopted on June 30, 1984, however, this prohibition was eliminated, but the required margin for a purchase of other over-the-counter securities is 100%; [15] therefore, such a loan does not substantially assist the customer in the purchase of such securities since he must deposit (or already have on deposit) in his margin account the entire purchase price of the securities. Such securities held in a margin account do, however, have a loan value in the margin account and may assist in avoiding a margin call if the market value has increased to an amount in excess of the initial purchase price (i.e., the amount of the original loan), and, conversely, will increase the chances of a margin call in conection with future transactions if they have declined in value. [16]

12. For a discussion of the differences between the regulation of lending on securities by broker-dealers, on the one hand, and by banks, on the other, prior to 1968, see Report of Special Study of the Securities Markets, H.Doc.No.95, 88th Cong., 1st Sess., Pt. 4 at 15–25 (1963).

The primary difference prior to that time was that broker-dealers could not lend at all on over-the-counter securities, whereas lending by banks on such securities was completely unregulated. By Act of July 29, 1968, 82 Stat. 452, Section 7 of the Securities Exchange Act was amended to give the FRB the authority to regulate credit on OTC securities and to eliminate the prohibition against broker-dealers lending on such securities. While the current Regulation T permits lending by broker-dealers on any securities, the required margin is 100% with respect to over-the-counter securities which are neither exempted securities nor on the list of "OTC Margin Stocks" issued by the FRB. On the other hand, a bank may lend on any such securities without regard to the margin requirement, and may assign a loan value to such collateral of any amount (not exceeding 100% of current market) upon the basis of which "a bank, excercising sound banking judgment, would lend, without regard to the customer's other assets held as collateral in connection with unrelated transactions." 12 C.F.R. §§ 220.4(b), 220.18(f), 221.2(f), 221.3(a), 221.8(b).

13. 12 C.F.R. Part 207 (§ 207.0 et seq.) effective March 11, 1968. This regulation in general conforms to Regulation U applicable to banks.

14. 12 C.F.R. Part 224 (§ 224.1 et seq.). This regulation was authorized by Act of October 26, 1970, P.L. 91–508, 84 Stat. 1124, adding subsection (f) to Section 7 of the Securities Exchange Act. While primarily intended to stop the practice of United States persons borrowing from foreign lenders in order to evade the margin requirements, the statute and Regulation X originally applied to any borrowing, whether domestic or foreign, and thus for the first time made the borrower as well as the lender guilty of an offense when there is a violation of the margin rules. On January 23, 1984, Regulation X was revised to apply to a domestic borrowing *only* if "the borrower willfully causes the credit to be extended in contravention of Regulations G, T, or U." Basically, Regulation X simply says that the borrower is prohibited from borrowing if the lender is prohibited from lending by Regulation T, U, or G or, in the case of a foreign lender, if he would have been prohibited from lending by Regulation G had he been subject to it.

15. 12 C.F.R. § 220.18(f).

16. For the different provisions relating to banks, see Note 12, supra.

Basically, Regulation T provides for two types of accounts which may be maintained for a customer by a broker-dealer: a "margin account" and a "cash account" (i.e., an account which is not subject to the margin requirements).

In a margin account the loan value of the account must be maintained at the current required level, i.e., under the currently required 50% "margin" the debit balance of an account cannot be permitted to exceed 50% of the current market value of the securities held as collateral in the account in connection with any additional purchase of securities.[17] (Although the FRB has authority to require maintenance levels of margin as well as initial levels, it has never done so; therefore, Regulation T never requires "margin calls" if no new securities are purchased.[18] This is a matter regulated entirely by the rules of the stock exchanges and the contract between the customer and the broker-dealer.) [19] If a purchase of additional securities would cause the debit balance to exceed this figure, or increases any such excess, then the broker-dealer must obtain, "a deposit of cash, margin securities, exempted securities, or any combination thereof" within "7 business days after the margin deficiency was created or increased." [20] A margin call, therefore, cannot be satisfied by the deposit of nonmargin, non-exempted securities.

On the other hand, a broker-dealer may in fact extend short-term credit on any securities in any amount in a "cash account" if he accepts "in good faith the customer's agreement that the customer will promptly make full cash payment for the security and does not contemplate selling it prior to making such payment." [21] If the customer "has not made full cash payment" for the security within 7 business days after the date on which the security is so purchased, the "creditor shall promptly cancel or otherwise liquidate" the transaction or the unsettled portion thereof. [22] If the customer sells a security within the 7 day period without previously having paid for it, then a 90-day "freeze" is put on the account during which time the broker-dealer may not purchase any securities for that customer without having cash deposited in advance to cover the full purchase price.[23] This led to what were called "clearance loans" whereby an "unregulated lender" [24] would make a 1-day loan to the customer of the purchase price so that he could deposit it with the broker-dealer prior to making the sale and thereby avoid the 90-day freeze.[25] Effective March 11, 1968, the FRB's Regulation G brought such previously unregulated lenders under the margin rules and both banks and Regulation G

---

17. 12 C.F.R. §§ 220.4, 220.18.

18. The withdrawal of cash or securities from a margin account is not permitted, however, even though no new securities are being purchased, if thereafter the adjusted debit balance of the account would exceed the maximum loan value of the securities remaining, with certain exceptions. 12 C.F.R. § 220.4(e).

19. Report of Special Study of the Securities Markets, H.Doc.No.95, 88th Cong., 1st Sess. Pt. 4, pp. 5–6 (1963); 12 C.F.R. § 220.3(c).

20. 12 C.F.R. § 220.4(c). The previous four day period in this regulation was changed to five by amendment effective February 5, 1968, and to 7 business days by the revision of Regulation T effective June 30, 1984.

21. 12 C.F.R. § 220.8(a)(1).

22. 12 C.F.R. § 220.8(b)(4).

23. 12 C.F.R. § 220.8(c).

24. Prior to March 11, 1968, only broker-dealers and banks had been subjected to the lending restrictions of the FRB's margin rules. For a discussion of the unregulated lenders, sometimes called "factors", see Report of Special Study of the Securities Markets, H.Doc.No.95, 88th Cong., 1st Sess., Pt. 4, pp. 25–35 (1963).

25. The customer was sometimes charged a minimum of 1 month's interest for such a loan, at a rate which was already 12% to 24% per annum. Report of Special Study of the Securities Markets, H.Doc.No.95, 88th Cong., 1st Sess., Pt. 4, at 27 (1963).

lenders are now prohibited from making "clearance loans" except in compliance with the margin rules applicable to those lenders.[26]

For discussions of the margin rules, see Note, Proposed Rule 3a12–5—A High Price for an Exemption from Regulation T for Condominium Securities, 29 U.Miami L.Rev. 89 (1974); Note, Margin Requirements—Installment Purchase of Tax-sheltered Programs, 24 Case W.Res.L.Rev. 391 (1973); Lipton, Some Recent Innovations to Avoid the Margin Regulations, 46 N.Y.U.L.Rev. 1 (1971); Solomon and Hart, Recent Developments in the Regulation of Securities Credit, 20 J.Pub.L. 167 (1971); Karmel, The Investment Banker and the Credit Regulations, 45 N.Y.U.L.Rev. 59 (1970); Kelly and Webb, Credit and Securities, 24 Bus.Law. 1153 (1969); Friedman, Financing of Employee Stock Purchase Plans under New Regulation G, 23 Bus.Law. 947 (1968).

26. 12 C.F.R. §§ 221.3, 207.3.

Chapter 12

TENDER OFFERS AND ISSUER REPURCHASES

Statutes and Regulations

Securities Exchange Act, §§ 13(d) and (e), 14(d), (e) and (f).

Rules 10b–4; 10b–13; 10b–18; Regulation 13D–G; Rules 13e–1; 13e–4; Regulation 14D.

SECURITIES AND EXCHANGE COMMISSION v. CARTER HAWLEY HALE STORES, INC.

United States Court of Appeals, Ninth Circuit, 1985.
760 F.2d 945.

Before: GOODWIN, SNEED, and SKOPIL, CIRCUIT JUDGES.

SKOPIL, CIRCUIT JUDGE:

The issue in this case arises out of an attempt by The Limited ("Limited"), an Ohio corporation, to take over Carter Hawley Hale Stores, Inc. ("CHH"), a publicly-held Los Angeles corporation. The SEC commenced the present action for injunctive relief to restrain CHH from repurchasing its own stock in an attempt to defeat the Limited takeover attempt without complying with the tender offer regulations. The district court concluded CHH's repurchase program was not a tender offer. The SEC appeals from the district court's denial of its motion for a preliminary injunction. We affirm.

FACTS AND PROCEEDINGS BELOW

On April 4, 1984 Limited commenced a cash tender offer for 20.3 million shares of CHH common stock, representing approximately 55% of the total shares outstanding, at $30 per share. Prior to the announced offer, CHH stock was trading at approximately $23.78 per share (pre-tender offer price). Limited disclosed that if its offer succeeded, it would exchange the remaining CHH shares for a fixed amount of Limited shares in a second-step merger.

In compliance with section 14(d) of the Securities Exchange Act of 1934 ("Exchange Act"), Limited filed a Schedule 14D-1 disclosing all pertinent information about its offer. The schedule stated that (1) the offer would remain open for 20 days, (2) the tendered shares could be withdrawn until April 19, 1984, and (3) in the event the offer was oversubscribed, shares would be subject to purchase on a pro rata basis.

While CHH initially took no public position on the offer, it filed an action to enjoin Limited's attempted takeover. Carter Hawley Hale Stores, Inc. v. The Limited, Inc., 587 F.Supp. 246 (C.D.Cal.1984). CHH's motion for an injunction was denied. Id. From April 4, 1984 until April 16, 1984 CHH's incumbent management discussed a response to Limited's offer.

658

During that time 14 million shares, about 40% of CHH's common stock, were traded. The price of CHH stock increased to approximately $29.25 per share. CHH shares became concentrated in the hands of risk arbitrageurs.

On April 16, 1984 CHH responded to Limited's offer. CHH issued a press release announcing its opposition to the offer because it was "inadequate and not in the best interests of CHH or its shareholders." CHH also publicly announced an agreement with General Cinema Corporation ("General Cinema"). CHH sold one million shares of convertible preferred stock to General Cinema for $300 million. The preferred shares possessed a vote equivalent to 22% of voting shares outstanding. General Cinema's shares were to be voted pursuant to CHH's Board of Directors recommendations. General Cinema was also granted an option to purchase Walden Book Company, Inc. a profitable CHH subsidiary, for approximately $285 million. Finally, CHH announced a plan to repurchase up to 15 million shares of its own common stock for an amount not to exceed $500 million. If all 15 million shares were purchased, General Cinema's shares would represent 33% of CHH's outstanding voting shares.

CHH's public announcement stated the actions taken were "to defeat the attempt by Limited to gain voting control of the company and to afford shareholders who wished to sell shares at this time an opportunity to do so." CHH's actions were revealed by press release, a letter from CHH's Chairman to shareholders, and by documents filed with the Securities and Exchange Commission ("SEC")—a Schedule 14D–9 and Rule 13e–1 transaction statement. These disclosures were reported by wire services, national financial newspapers, and newspapers of general circulation. Limited sought a temporary restraining order against CHH's repurchase of its shares. The application was denied. Limited withdrew its motion for a preliminary injunction.

CHH began to repurchase its shares on April 16, 1984. In a one-hour period CHH purchased approximately 244,000 shares at an average price of $25.25 per share. On April 17, 1984 CHH purchased approximately 6.5 million shares in a two-hour trading period at an average price of $25.88 per share. By April 22, 1984 CHH had purchased a total of 15 million shares. It then announced an increase in the number of shares authorized for purchase to 18.5 million.

On April 24, 1984, the same day Limited was permitted to close its offer and start purchasing, CHH terminated its repurchase program having purchased approximately 17.5 million shares, over 50% of the common shares outstanding. On April 25, 1984 Limited revised its offer increasing the offering price to $35.00 per share and eliminating the second-step merger. The market price for CHH then reached a high of $32.00 per share. On May 21, 1984 Limited withdrew its offer. The market price of CHH promptly fell to $20.62 per share, a price below the pre-tender offer price.

On May 2, 1984, two and one-half weeks after the repurchase program was announced and one week after its apparent completion,[1] the SEC filed

---

1. In addition to seeking to enjoin further stock purchases, the SEC sought preliminary injunctive relief requiring CHH to issue 17.9 million shares of its common stock to trustees who, pending a trial on the merits, would be required to vote such shares in the same proportion as the votes

this action for injunctive relief. The SEC alleged that CHH's repurchase program constituted a tender offer conducted in violation of section 13(e) of the Exchange Act, and Rule 13e–4. On May 5, 1984 a temporary restraining order was granted. CHH was temporarily enjoined from further stock repurchases. The district court denied SEC's motion for a preliminary injunction, finding the SEC failed to carry its burden of establishing "the reasonable likelihood of future violations * * * [or] * * * a fair chance of success on the merits' * * *." SEC v. Carter Hawley Hale Stores, Inc., 587 F.Supp. 1248, 1257 (C.D.Cal.1984) (citations omitted). The court found CHH's repurchase program was not a tender offer because the eight-factor test proposed by the SEC and adopted in Wellman v. Dickinson, 475 F.Supp. 783 (S.D.N.Y.1979), aff'd on other grounds, 682 F.2d 355 (2d Cir. 1982), cert. denied, 460 U.S. 1069 (1983), had not been satisfied. SEC v. Carter Hawley Hale Stores, Inc., 587 F.Supp. at 1255. The court also refused to adopt, at the urging of the SEC, the alternative test of what constitutes a tender offer as enunciated in S–G Securities, Inc. v. Fuqua Investment Co., 466 F.Supp. 1114 (D.Mass.1978). 587 F.Supp. at 1256–57. On May 9, 1984 the SEC filed an emergency application for an injunction pending appeal to this court. That application was denied.

DISCUSSION

The grant or denial of a preliminary injunction is reviewed to determine if the district court abused its discretion. Lopez v. Heckler, 725 F.2d 1489, 1497 (9th Cir.), rev'd on other grounds, 104 S.Ct. 10 (1984). A district court abuses its discretion if it rests its conclusion on clearly erroneous factual findings or an incorrect legal standard. Id.; Apple Computer, Inc. v. Formula International, Inc., 725 F.2d 521, 523 (9th Cir.1984).

The SEC urges two principal arguments on appeal: (1) the district court erred in concluding that CHH's repurchase program was not a tender offer under the eight-factor *Wellman* test, and (2) the district court erred in declining to apply the definition of a tender offer enunciated in *S–G Securities,* 466 F.Supp. at 1126–27. Resolution of these issues on appeal presents the difficult task of determining whether CHH's repurchase of shares during a third-party tender offer itself constituted a tender offer.

1. *The Williams Act.*

A. *Congressional Purposes*

The Williams Act amendments to the Exchange Act were enacted in response to the growing use of tender offers to achieve corporate control. Edgar v. Mite Corp., 457 U.S. 624, 632 (1982) (citing Piper v. Chris-Craft Industries, 430 U.S. 1, 22 (1977)). Prior to the passage of the Act, shareholders of target companies were often forced to act hastily on offers without the benefit of full disclosure. See H.R.Rep. No. 1711, 90th Cong., 2d Sess. (1968), reprinted in 1968 U.S.Code, Cong. & Admin.News 2811 ("House Report 1711").[2] The Williams Act was intended to ensure that

---

of unaffiliated shareholders. This matter therefore is not moot.

  2. For additional discussion of the concerns giving rise to the Williams Act amendments, see Full Disclosure of Corpo-

rate Equity Ownership and in Corporate Takeover Bids: Hearing on S. 510 Before the Subcommittee on Securities of the Senate Committee on Banking and Currency, 90th Cong., 1st Sess. (1967) ("Senate Hear-

investors responding to tender offers received full and fair disclosure, analogous to that received in proxy contests. The Act was also designed to provide shareholders an opportunity to examine all relevant facts in an effort to reach a decision without being subject to unwarranted pressure. House Report 1711.

This policy is reflected in section 14(d), which governs third-party tender offers, and which prohibits a tender offer unless shareholders are provided with certain procedural and substantive protections including: full disclosure; time in which to make an investment decision; withdrawal rights; and pro rata purchase of shares accepted in the event the offer is oversubscribed.

[handwritten margin note: Provisions of 14(d)]

There are additional congressional concerns underlying the Williams Act. In its effort to protect investors, Congress recognized the need to "avoid favoring either management or the takeover bidder." *Edgar,* 456 U.S. at 633; see also Financial General Bank Shares, Inc. v. Lance, [1978] Fed.Sec.L.Rptr. (CCH) ¶ 96,403 at 93,424–25 (D.D.C.1978) (quoting Rondeau v. Mosinee Paper Corp., 422 U.S. 49, 58 (1975)). The Supreme Court has recognized that to serve this policy it is necessary to withhold "from management or the bidder any undue advantage that could frustrate the exercise of informed choice." *Edgar,* 456 U.S. at 634. Congress was also concerned about avoiding undue interference with the free and open market in securities. City Investing Co. v. Simcox, 633 F.2d 56, 62 n. 14 (7th Cir.1980) (noting less burdensome regulations in cases involving certain open market purchases); see also 113 Cong.Rec. 856 (1968). Each of these congressional concerns is implicated in the determination of whether CHH's issuer repurchase program constituted a tender offer.

B. *Issuer Repurchases Under Section 13(e)*

Issuer repurchases and tender offers are governed in relevant part by section 13(e) of the Williams Act and Rules 13e–1 and 13e–4 promulgated thereunder.

The SEC argues that the district court erred in concluding that issuer repurchases, which had the intent and effect of defeating a third-party tender offer, are authorized by the tender offer rules and regulations. The legislative history of these provisions is unclear. Congress apparently was aware of an intent by the SEC to regulate issuer tender offers to the same extent as third-party offers. Senate Hearings 214–16, 248; Exchange Act Release No. 16,112 [1979] Fed.Sec.L.Rptr. (CCH) ¶ 82,182 at 82,205 (Aug. 16, 1979) (proposed amendments to tender offer rules). At the same time, Congress recognized issuers might engage in "substantial repurchase programs * * * inevitably affect[ing] market performance and price levels." House Hearings at 14–15; see also House Report 1711 at 2814–15. Such repurchase programs might be undertaken for any number of legitimate purposes, including with the intent "to preserve or strengthen * * * control by counteracting tender offer or other takeover attempts. * * * " House Report 1711 at 2814; House Hearings at 15. Congress neither explicitly banned nor authorized such a practice. Congress did grant the

ings"); Takeover Bids: Hearing on H.R. 14475, and S. 510 Before the Subcommittee on Commerce and Finance of the House   Committee on Interstate and Foreign Commerce, 90th Cong., 2d Sess. (1968) ("House Hearings").

SEC authority to adopt appropriate regulations to carry out congressional intent with respect to issuer repurchases. The legislative history of section 13(e) is not helpful in resolving the issues.

There is also little guidance in the SEC Rules promulgated in response to the legislative grant of authority. Rule 13e–1 prohibits an issuer from repurchasing its own stock during a third-party tender offer unless it discloses certain minimal information. The language of Rule 13e–1 is prohibitory rather than permissive. It nonetheless evidences a recognition that not all issuer repurchases during a third-party tender offer are tender offers. Id. In contrast, Rule 13e–4 recognizes that issuers, like third parties, may engage in repurchase activity amounting to a tender offer and subject to the same procedural and substantive safeguards as a third-party tender offer. The regulations do not specify when a repurchase by an issuer amounts to a tender offer governed by Rule 13e–4 rather than 13e–1.[3]

We decline to adopt either the broadest construction of Rule 13e–4, to define issuer tender offers as virtually all substantial repurchases during a third-party tender offer, or the broadest construction of Rule 13e–1, to create an exception from the tender offer requirements for issuer repurchases made during a third-party tender offer. Like the district court, we resolve the question of whether CHH's repurchase program was a tender offer by considering the eight-factor test established in *Wellman*, 587 F.Supp. at 1256–57.[4]

To serve the purposes of the Williams Act, there is a need for flexibility in fashioning a definition of a tender offer. See Smallwood v. Pearl Brewing Co., 489 F.2d 579 (5th Cir.), cert. denied 419 U.S. 873 (1974). The *Wellman* factors seem particularly well suited in determining when an issuer repurchase program during a third-party tender offer will itself constitute a tender offer. *Wellman* focuses, *inter alia,* on the manner in which the offer is conducted and whether the offer has the overall effect of pressuring shareholders into selling their stock. *Wellman,* 475 F.Supp. at 823–24. Application of the *Wellman* factors to the unique facts and circumstances surrounding issuer repurchases should serve to effect congressional concern for the needs of the shareholder, the need to avoid giving either the target or the offeror any advantage, and the need to maintain a free and open market for securities.

3. The procedural and substantive requirements that must be complied with under Rule 13e–1 differ from those under Rule 13e–1. An issuer engaged in a repurchase under Rule 13e–1 is required to file a brief statement with the SEC setting forth the amount of shares purchased; the purpose for which the purchase is made; and the source and amount of funds used in making the repurchase. CHH complied with the requirements of Rule 13e–1.

An issuer engaged in a tender offer under Rule 13e–4 must comply with more burdensome regulations. All the substantive and procedural protections for share-

holders come into play under Rule 13e–4 including: full disclosure; time in which to make investment decisions; withdrawal rights; and requirements for pro rata purchase of shares. CHH did not comply with Rule 13e–4.

4. We have followed the *Wellman* test in another context, see Polinsky v. MCA, Inc., 680 F.2d 1286, 1290–91 (9th Cir.1982) (open market purchases made in anticipation of a tender offer met none of the *Wellman* indicia), but have not addressed the question of the applicability of the *Wellman* factors to issuer repurchase programs during third-party tender offers.

2. *Application of the Wellman Factors.*

Under the *Wellman* test, the existence of a tender offer is determined by examining the following factors:

(1) Active and widespread solicitation of public shareholders for the shares of an issuer; (2) solicitation made for a substantial percentage of the issuer's stock; (3) offer to purchase made at a premium over the prevailing market price; (4) terms of the offer are firm rather than negotiable; (5) offer contingent on the tender of a fixed number of shares, often subject to a fixed maximum number to be purchased; (6) offer open only for a limited period of time; (7) offeree subjected to pressure to sell his stock; [and (8)] public announcements of a purchasing program concerning the target company precede or accompany rapid accumulation of a large amount of target company's securities.

475 F.Supp. at 823–24.

Not all factors need be present to find a tender offer; rather, they provide some guidance as to the traditional indicia of a tender offer. Id. at 824; see also Zuckerman v. Franz, 573 F.Supp. 351, 358 (S.D.Fla.1983).

The district court concluded CHH's repurchase program was not a tender offer under *Wellman* because only "two of the eight indicia" were present. 587 F.Supp. at 1255. The SEC claims the district court erred in applying *Wellman* because it gave insufficient weight to the pressure exerted on shareholders; it ignored the existence of a competitive tender offer; and it failed to consider that CHH's offer at the market price was in essence a premium because the price had already risen above pre-tender offer levels.

A. *Active and Widespread Solicitation*

The evidence was uncontroverted that there was "no direct solicitation of shareholders." 587 F.Supp. 1253. No active and widespread solicitation occurred. See Brascan Ltd. v. Edper Equities Ltd., 477 F.Supp. 773, 789 (S.D.N.Y.1979) (no tender offer where defendant "scrupulously avoided any solicitation upon the advice of his lawyers"). Nor did the publicity surrounding CHH's repurchase program result in a solicitation. 587 F.Supp. 1253–54. The only public announcements by CHH were those mandated by SEC or Exchange rules. See Ludlow Corp. v. Tyco Laboratories, 529 F.Supp. 62, 68–69 (D.Mass.1981) (schedule 13d filed by purchaser could not be characterized as forbidden publicity); Crane Co. v. Harsco Corp., 511 F.Supp. 294, 303 (D.Dela.1981) (Rule 13e–1 transaction statement and required press releases do not constitute a solicitation); but cf. S–G Securities, Inc., 466 F.Supp. at 1119–21 (tender offer present where numerous press releases publicized terms of offer).

B. *Solicitation for a Substantial Percentage of Issuer's Shares*

Because there was no active and widespread solicitation, the district court found the repurchase could not have involved a solicitation for a substantial percentage of CHH's shares. 587 F.Supp. 1253–54. It is unclear whether the proper focus of this factor is the solicitation or the percentage of stock solicited. The district court probably erred in concluding that, absent a solicitation under the first *Wellman* factor, the second factor cannot be satisfied, see Hoover Co. v. Fuqua Industries, [1979–80] Fed.Sec.L.Rptr. (CCH) ¶ 97,107 at 96,148 n. 4 (N.D.Ohio 1979) (second *Wellman* factor did not incorporate the type of solicitation described in factor one), but we need not decide that here. The solicitation and percentage of stock elements of the second factor often will be addressed adequately in an evaluation of the first *Wellman* factor, which is concerned with solicitation, and the eighth *Wellman* factor, which focuses on the amount of securities accumulated. In this case CHH did not engage in a solicitation under the first *Wellman* factor but did accumulate a large percentage of stock as defined under the eighth *Wellman* factor. An evaluation of the second *Wellman* factor does not alter the probability of finding a tender offer.

C. *Premium Over Prevailing Market Price*

The SEC contends the open market purchases made by CHH at market prices were in fact made at a premium not over market price but over the pre-tender offer price. At the time of CHH's repurchases, the market price for CHH's shares (ranging from $24.00 to $26.00 per share) had risen above the pre-tender offer price (approximately $22.00 per share). Given ordinary market dynamics, the price of a target company's stock will rise following an announced tender offer. Under the SEC's definition of a premium as a price greater than the pre-tender offer price, a premium will always exist when a target company makes open market purchases in response to a tender offer even though the increase in market price is attributable to the action of the third-party offeror and not the target company. See LTV Corp. v. Grumman Corp., 526 F.Supp. 106, 109 & n. 7 (E.D.N.Y.1981) (an increase in price due to increased demand during a tender offer does not represent a premium). The SEC definition not only eliminates consideration of this *Wellman* factor in the context of issuer repurchases during a tender offer, but also underestimates congressional concern for preserving the free and open market. The district court did not err in concluding a premium is determined not by reference to pre-tender offer price, but rather by reference to market price. This is the definition previously urged by the SEC, Exchange Act Release No. 16,385 [1979–80] Fed.Sec.L.Rptr. (CCH) ¶ 82,374 at 82,605 (Nov. 29, 1979) (footnotes omitted) (proposed amendments to tender offer rules) (premium defined as price "in excess of ＊ ＊ ＊ the current market price ＊ ＊ ＊."), and is the definition we now apply. See LTV Corp., 526 F.Supp. at 109 & n. 7.

D. *Terms of Offer Not Firm*

There is no dispute that CHH engaged in a number of transactions or purchases at many different market prices. 587 F.Supp. at 1254.

E. *Offer Not Contingent on Tender of Fixed Minimum Number of Shares*

Similarly, while CHH indicated it would purchase up to 15 million shares, CHH's purchases were not contingent on the tender of a fixed minimum number of shares. 587 F.Supp. at 1254.

F. *Not Open for Only a Limited Time*

CHH's offer to repurchase was not open for only a limited period of time but rather was open "during the pendency of the tender offer of The Limited." 587 F.Supp. at 1255. The SEC argues that the offer was in fact open for only a limited time, because CHH would only repurchase stock until 15 million shares were acquired. The fact that 15 million shares were acquired in a short period of time does not translate into an issuer-imposed time limitation. The time within which the repurchases were made was a product of ordinary market forces, not the terms of CHH's repurchase program.

G–H. *Shareholder Pressure and Public Announcements Accompanying a Large Accumulation of Stock*

With regard to the seventh *Wellman* factor, following a public announcement, CHH repurchased over the period of seven trading days more than 50% of its outstanding shares. 587 F.Supp. at 1255. The eighth *Wellman* factor was met.

The district court found that while many shareholders may have felt pressured or compelled to sell their shares, CHH itself did not exert on shareholders the kind of pressure the Williams Act proscribes. Id.

While there certainly was shareholder pressure in this case, it was largely the pressure of the marketplace and not the type of untoward pressure the tender offer regulations were designed to prohibit. See Panter v. Marshall Field & Co., 646 F.2d 271, 286 (7th Cir.) (where no deadline and no premium, shareholders "were simply not subjected to the proscribed pressures the Williams Act was designed to alleviate"), cert. denied, 554 U.S. 1092 (1981); Brascan Ltd. v. Edper Equities, 477 F.Supp. at 789–92 (without high premium and threat that the offer will disappear, large purchases in short time do not represent the kind of pressure the Williams Act was designed to prevent); Kennecott Copper Corp. v. Curtis-Wright Corp., 449 F.Supp. 951, 961 (S.D.N.Y.), aff'd in relevant part, rev'd in part, 584 F.2d 1195, 1207 (2d Cir.1978) (where no deadline and no premium, no pressure, other than normal pressure of the marketplace, exerted on shareholders).

CHH's purchases were made in the open market, at market and not premium prices, without fixed terms and were not contingent upon the tender of a fixed minimum number of shares. CHH's repurchase program had none of the traditional indicia of a tender offer. See, e.g., Energy Ventures, Inc. v. Appalachian Co., 587 F.Supp. 734, 739 (D.Del.1984) (major acquisition program involving open market purchases not subject to tender offer regulation); Ludlow Corp. v. Tyco Laboratories, Inc., 529 F.Supp. at 68 (no tender offer where shareholders not pressured into making hasty ill-advised decision due to premium, fixed terms, or active solicitation); LTV Corp. v. Grumman, 526 F.Supp. at 109 (massive buying program, with attendant publicity, made with intent to defeat third-party tender offer, not itself a tender offer); Brascan Ltd. v. Edper Equities, 477 F.Supp. at 792 (the pressure the Williams Act attempts to eliminate is that caused by "a high premium with a threat that the offer will disappear within a certain time").

The shareholder pressure in this case did not result from any untoward action on the part of CHH. Rather, it resulted from market forces, the third-party offer, and the fear that at the expiration of the offer the price of CHH shares would decrease.

The district court did not abuse its discretion in concluding that under the *Wellman* eight factor test, CHH's repurchase program did not constitute a tender offer.

3. *Alternative S–G Securities Test.*

The SEC finally urges that even if the CHH repurchase program did not constitute a tender offer under the *Wellman* test, the district court erred in refusing to apply the test in *S–G Securities,* 466 F.Supp. at 1114.[5] Under the more liberal *S–G Securities* test, a tender offer is present if there are

(1) A publicly announced intention by the purchaser to acquire a block of the stock of the target company for purposes of acquiring control thereof, and (2) a subsequent rapid acquisition by the purchaser of large blocks of stock through open market and privately negotiated purchases.

Id. at 1126–27.

There are a number of sound reasons for rejecting the *S–G Securities* test. The test is vague and difficult to apply. It offers little guidance to the issuer as to when his conduct will come within the ambit of Rule 13e–4 as opposed to Rule 13e–1. SEC v. Carter Hawley Hale Stores, 587 F.Supp. at 1256–57. A determination of the existence of a tender offer under *S–G Securities* is largely subjective and made in hindsight based on an *ex post facto* evaluation of the response in the marketplace to the repurchase program. Id. at 1257. The SEC's contention that these concerns are irrelevant when the issuer's repurchases are made with the intent to defeat a third-party offer is without merit. See, e.g., LTV Corp. v. Grumman Corp., 526 F.Supp. at 109–10 (Rule 13e–1 may apply to open market purchases even when made to thwart a tender offer); Crane Co. v. Harsco Corp., 511 F.Supp. 294, 300–301 (D.Dela.1981) (same).

The SEC finds further support for its application of the two-pronged *S–G Securities* test in the overriding legislative intent "to ensure that shareholders * * * are adequately protected from pressure tactics * * * [forcing them to make] * * * ill-considered investment decisions." The *S–G Securities* test does reflect congressional concern for shareholders; however, the same can be said of the *Wellman* test. The legislative intent in the context of open market repurchases during third-party tender offers is, at best, unclear. 587 F.Supp. 1256; see pages 8–11, supra. The *S–G Securities* test, unlike the *Wellman* test, does little to reflect objectively the multiple congressional concerns underlying the Williams Act, including due regard for the free and open market in securities. See pages 7–8, supra.

We decline to abandon the *Wellman* test in favor of the vague standard enunciated in *S–G Securities.* The district court did not err in declining to

---

5. Some courts have opted for the broader *S–G Securities* definition of a tender offer, see, e.g., Panter v. Marshall Field & Co., 646 F.2d at 286 (also citing *Wellman*); Hoover Co. v. Fuqua Industries, [1979–80] Fed.Sec.L.Rptr. (CCH) ¶ 97,107 at 96,146–149 (also citing *Wellman*); Nachman Corp. v. Halfred, Inc., [1973–74] Fed. Sec.L.Rptr. (CCH) ¶ 94,455 at 95,590 (N.D. Ill.1973); Cattlemen's Investment Co. v. Fears, 345 F.Supp. 1248, 1251 (W.D.Okla. 1972), vacated per stipulation, No. 75–152 (W.D.Okla. May 8, 1972), while other courts have rejected this broad test in favor of the eight-factor *Wellman* test. See, e.g., Kennecott Copper Corp. v. Curtis-Wright Corp., 584 F.2d at 1207; LTV Corp. v. Grumman Corp., 527 F.Supp. at 109; Brascan Ltd. v. Edper Equities Ltd., 477 F.Supp. at 791; D–Z Investment Co. v. Holloway, [1974–75] Fed.Sec.L.Rep. (CCH) ¶ 94,771 at 96,562–63 (S.D.N.Y.1974). There is no one factor other than the result which distinguishes these cases although the greater weight of authority seems to have accepted the *Wellman* test.

apply the *S–G Securities* test or in finding CHH's repurchases were not a tender offer under *Wellman.*

Affirmed.

———

HANSON TRUST PLC v. SCM CORPORATION

United States Court of Appeals, Second Circuit, 1985.
774 F.2d 47.

Before MANSFIELD, PIERCE and PRATT, CIRCUIT JUDGES.

MANSFIELD, CIRCUIT JUDGE:

Hanson Trust PLC, HSCM Industries, Inc., and Hanson Holdings Netherlands B.V. (hereinafter sometimes referred to collectively as "Hanson") appeal from an order of the Southern District of New York, 617 F.Supp. 832 (1985), Shirley Wohl Kram, Judge, granting SCM Corporation's motion for a preliminary injunction restraining them, their officers, agents, employees and any persons acting in concert with them, from acquiring any shares of SCM and from exercising any voting rights with respect to 3.1 million SCM shares acquired by them on September 11, 1985. The injunction was granted on the ground that Hanson's September 11 acquisition of the SCM stock through five private and one open market purchases amounted to a "tender offer" for more than 5% of SCM's outstanding shares, which violated §§ 14(d) (1) and (6) of the Williams Act and rules promulgated by the Securities and Exchange Commission (SEC) thereunder. See 17 C.F.R. §§ 240.14(e)(1) and 240.14d–7. We reverse.

The setting is the familiar one of a fast-moving bidding contest for control of a large public corporation: first, a cash tender offer of $60 per share by Hanson, an outsider, addressed to SCM stockholders; next, a counterproposal by an "insider" group consisting of certain SCM managers and their "White Knight," Merrill Lynch Capital Markets (Merrill), for a "leveraged buyout" at a higher price ($70 per share); then an increase by Hanson of its cash offer to $72 per share, followed by a revised SCM-Merrill leveraged buyout offer of $74 per share with a "crown jewel" irrevocable lock-up option to Merrill designed to discourage Hanson from seeking control by providing that if any other party (in this case Hanson) should acquire more than one-third of SCM's outstanding shares ($66\frac{2}{3}\%$ being needed under N.Y.Bus.L. § 903(a)(2) to effectuate a merger), Merrill would have the right to buy SCM's two most profitable businesses (consumer foods and pigments) at prices characterized by some as "bargain basement." The final act in this scenario was the decision of Hanson, having been deterred by the SCM-Merrill option (colloquially described in the market as a "poison pill"), to terminate its cash tender offer and then to make private purchases, amounting to 25% of SCM's outstanding shares, leading SCM to seek and obtain the preliminary injunction from which this appeal is taken. A more detailed history of relevant events follows.

SCM is a New York corporation with its principal place of business in New York City. Its shares, of which at all relevant times at least 9.9 million were outstanding and 2.3 million were subject to issuance upon conversion of other outstanding securities, are traded on the New York Stock Exchange (NYSE) and Pacific Stock Exchange. Hanson Trust PLC is an English company with its principal place of business in London. HSCM, a Delaware corporation, and Hanson Holdings Netherlands B.V., a Netherlands limited liability company, are indirect wholly-owned subsidiaries of Hanson Trust PLC.

On August 21, 1985, Hanson publicly announced its intention to make a cash tender offer of $60 per share for any and all outstanding SCM shares. Five days later it filed the tender offer documents required by § 14(d)(1) of the Williams Act and regulations issued thereunder. The offer provided that it would remain open until September 23, unless extended, that no shares would be accepted until September 10, and that

> "Whether or not the Purchasers [Hanson] purchase Shares pursuant to the Offer, the Purchasers may thereafter determine, subject to the availability of Shares at favorable prices and the availability of financing, to purchase additional Shares in the open market, in privately negotiated transactions, through another tender offer or otherwise. Any such purchases of additional Shares might be on terms which are the same as, or more or less favorable than, those of this Offer. The Purchasers also reserve the right to dispose of any or all Shares acquired by them." *Offer to Purchase For Cash Any and All Outstanding Shares of Common Stock of SCM Corporation* (Aug. 26, 1985) at 21.

On August 30, 1985, SCM, having recommended to SCM's stockholders that they not accept Hanson's tender offer, announced a preliminary agreement with Merrill under which a new entity, formed by SCM and Merrill, would acquire all SCM shares at $70 per share in a leveraged buyout sponsored by Merrill. Under the agreement, which was executed on September 3, the new entity would make a $70 per share cash tender offer for approximately 85% of SCM's shares. If more than two-thirds of SCM's shares were acquired under the offer the remaining SCM shares would be acquired in exchange for debentures in a new corporation to be formed as a result of the merger. On the same date, September 3, Hanson increased its tender offer from $60 to $72 cash per share. However, it expressly reserved the right to terminate its offer if SCM granted to anyone any option to purchase SCM assets on terms that Hanson believed to constitute a "lock-up" device. *Supplement Dated September 5, 1985, to Offer to Purchase*, at 4.

The next development in the escalating bidding contest for control of SCM occurred on September 10, 1985, when SCM entered into a new leveraged buyout agreement with its "White Knight," Merrill. The agreement provided for a two-step acquisition of SCM stock by Merrill at $74 per share. The first proposed step was to be the acquisition of approximately 82% of SCM's outstanding stock for cash. Following a merger (which required acquisition of at least $66 2/3\%$), debentures would be issued for the remaining SCM shares. If any investor or group other than Merrill acquired more than one-third of SCM's outstanding shares, Merrill would have the option to buy SCM's two most profitable businesses, pigments and consumer foods, for $350 and $80 million respectively, prices which Hanson believed to be below their market value.

Hanson, faced with what it considered to be a "poison pill," concluded that even if it increased its cash tender offer to $74 per share it would end up with control of a substantially depleted and damaged company. Accordingly, it announced on the Dow Jones Broad Tape at 12:38 P.M. on

September 11 that it was terminating its cash tender offer. A few minutes later, Hanson issued a press release, carried on the Broad Tape, to the effect that "all SCM shares tendered will be promptly returned to the tendering shareholders."

At some time in the late forenoon or early afternoon of September 11 Hanson decided to make cash purchases of a substantial percentage of SCM stock in the open market or through privately negotiated transactions. Under British law Hanson could not acquire more than 49% of SCM's shares in this fashion without obtaining certain clearances, but acquisition of such a large percentage was not necessary to stymie the SCM-Merrill merger proposal. If Hanson could acquire slightly less than one-third of SCM's outstanding shares it would be able to block the $74 per share SCM-Merrill offer of a leveraged buyout. This might induce the latter to work out an agreement with Hanson, something Hanson had unsuccessfully sought on several occasions since its first cash tender offer.

Within a period of two hours on the afternoon of September 11 Hanson made five privately-negotiated cash purchases of SCM stock and one open-market purchase, acquiring 3.1 million shares or 25% of SCM's outstanding stock. The price of SCM stock on the NYSE on September 11 ranged from a high of $73.50 per share to a low of $72.50 per share. Hanson's initial private purchase, 387,700 shares from Mutual Shares, was not solicited by Hanson but by a Mutual Shares official, Michael Price, who, in a conversation with Robert Pirie of Rothschild, Inc., Hanson's financial advisor, on the morning of September 11 (before Hanson had decided to make any private cash purchases), had stated that he was interested in selling Mutual's Shares' SCM stock to Hanson. Once Hanson's decision to buy privately had been made, Pirie took Price up on his offer. The parties negotiated a sale at $73.50 per share after Pirie refused Price's asking prices, first of $75 per share and, later, of $74.50 per share. This transaction, but not the identity of the parties, was automatically reported pursuant to NYSE rules on the NYSE ticker at 3:11 P.M. and reported on the Dow Jones Broad Tape at 3:29 P.M.

Pirie then telephoned Ivan Boesky, an arbitrageur who had a few weeks earlier disclosed in a Schedule 13D statement filed with the SEC that he owned approximately 12.7% of SCM's outstanding shares. Pirie negotiated a Hanson purchase of these shares at $73.50 per share after rejecting Boesky's initial demand of $74 per share. At the same time Rothschild purchased for Hanson's account 600,000 SCM shares in the open market at $73.50 per share. An attempt by Pirie next to negotiate the cash purchase of another large block of SCM stock (some 780,000 shares) from Slifka & Company fell through because of the latter's inability to make delivery of the shares on September 12.

Following the NYSE ticker and Broad Tape reports of the first two large anonymous transactions in SCM stock, some professional investors surmised that the buyer might be Hanson. Rothschild then received telephone calls from (1) Mr. Mulhearn of Jamie & Co. offering to sell between 200,000 and 350,000 shares at $73.50 per share, (2) David Gottesman, an arbitrageur at Oppenheimer & Co. offering 89,000 shares at $73.50, and (3) Boyd Jeffries of Jeffries & Co., offering approximately 700,000 to 800,000 shares at $74.00. Pirie purchased the three blocks for Hanson at $73.50

per share. The last of Hanson's cash purchases was completed by 4:35 P.M. on September 11, 1985.

In the early evening of September 11 SCM successfully applied to Judge Kram in the present lawsuit for a restraining order barring Hanson from acquiring more SCM, stock for 24 hours. On September 12 and 13 the TRO was extended by consent pending the district court's decision on SCM's application for a preliminary injunction. Judge Kram held an evidentiary hearing on September 12–13, at which various witnesses testified, including Sir Gordon White, Hanson's United States Chairman, two Rothschild representatives (Pirie and Gerald Goldsmith) and stock market risk-arbitrage professionals (Robert Freeman of Goldman, Sachs & Co., Kenneth Miller of Merrill Lynch, and Danial Burch of D.F. King & Co.). Sir Gordon White testified that on September 11, 1985, after learning of the $74 per share SCM-Merrill leveraged buyout tender offer with its "crown jewel" irrevocable "lock-up" option to Merrill, he instructed Pirie to terminate Hanson's $72 per share tender offer, and that only thereafter did he discuss the possibility of Hanson making market purchases of SCM stock. Pirie testified that the question of buying stock may have been discussed in the late forenoon of September 11 and that he had told White that he was having Hanson's New York counsel look into whether such cash purchases were legally permissible.

SCM argued before Judge Kram (and argues here) that Hanson's cash purchases immediately following its termination of its $72 per share tender offer amounted to a *de facto* continuation of Hanson's tender offer, designed to avoid the strictures of § 14(d) of the Williams Act, and that unless a preliminary injunction issued SCM and its shareholders would be irreparably injured because Hanson would acquire enough shares to defeat the SCM-Merrill offer. Judge Kram found that the relevant underlying facts (which we have outlined) were not in dispute, Memorandum Opinion and Order, at 6 (Sept. 14, 1985), and concluded that "[W]ithout deciding what test should ultimately be applied to determine whether Hanson's conduct constitutes a 'tender offer' within the meaning of the Williams Act * * * SCM has demonstrated a likelihood of success on the merits of its contention that Hanson has engaged in a tender offer which violates Section 14(d) of the Williams Act." Id. at 7. The district court, characterizing Hanson's stock purchases as "a deliberate attempt to do an 'end run' around the requirements of the Williams Act," id. at 8, made no finding on the question of whether Hanson had decided to make the purchases of SCM before or after it dropped its tender offer but concluded that even if the decision had been made after it terminated its offer preliminary injunctive relief should issue. From this decision Hanson appeals.

DISCUSSION

A preliminary injunction will be overturned only when the district court abuses its discretion. * * *

Since, as the district court correctly noted, the material relevant facts in the present case are not in dispute, this appeal turns on whether the district court erred as a matter of law in holding that when Hanson terminated its offer and immediately thereafter made private purchases of a substantial share of the target company's outstanding stock, the purchases became a "tender offer" within the meaning of § 14(d) of the

Williams Act. Absent any express definition of "tender offer" in the Act, the answer requires a brief review of the background and purposes of § 14(d).

* * *

The typical tender offer, as described in the Congressional debates, hearings and reports on the Williams Act, consisted of a general, publicized bid by an individual or group to buy shares of a publicly-owned company, the shares of which were traded on a national securities exchange, at a price substantially above the current market price. * * * The offer was usually accompanied by newspaper and other publicity, a time limit for tender of shares in response to it, and a provision fixing a quantity limit on the total number of shares of the target company that would be purchased.

Prior to the Williams Act a tender offeror had no obligation to disclose any information to shareholders when making a bid. The Report of the Senate Committee on Banking and Currency aptly described the situation: "by using a cash tender offer the person seeking control can operate in almost complete secrecy. At present, the law does not even require that he disclose his identity, the source of his funds, who his associates are, or what he intends to do if he gains control of the corporation."

* * *

The purpose of the Williams Act was, accordingly, to protect the shareholders from that dilemma by insuring "that public shareholders who are confronted by a cash tender offer for their stock will not be required to respond without adequate information." Piper v. Chris-Craft Industries, 430 U.S. 1, 35 (1977); Rondeau v. Mosinee Paper Corp., 422 U.S. 49, 58 (1975).

Congress took "extreme care," 113 Cong.Rec. 24664 (Senator Williams); id. at 854 (Senator Williams), however, when protecting shareholders, to avoid "tipping the balance of regulation either in favor of management or in favor of the person making the takeover bid." * * *

Congress finally settled upon a statute requiring a tender offer solicitor seeking beneficial ownership of more than 5% of the outstanding shares of any class of any equity security registered on a national securities exchange first to file with the SEC a statement containing certain information specified in § 13(d)(1) of the Act, as amplified by SEC rules and regulations. Congress' failure to define "tender offer" was deliberate. Aware of "the almost infinite variety in the terms of most tender offers" and concerned that a rigid definition would be evaded, Congress left to the court and the SEC the flexibility to define the term. * * *

Although § 14(d)(1) clearly applies to "classic" tender offers of the type described above (pp. 54–55), courts soon recognized that in the case of privately negotiated transactions or solicitations for private purchases of stock many of the conditions leading to the enactment of § 14(d) for the most part do not exist. The number and percentage of stockholders are usually far less than those involved in public offers. The solicitation involves less publicity than a public tender offer or none. The solicitees, who are frequently directors, officers or substantial stockholders of the target, are more apt to be sophisticated, inquiring or knowledgeable concerning the target's business, the solicitor's objectives, and the impact of the solicitation on the target's business prospects. In short, the solicitee in the private transaction is less likely to be pressured, confused, or ill-informed regarding the businesses and decisions at stake than solicitees who are the subjects of a public tender offer.

These differences between public and private securities transactions have led most courts to rule that private transactions or open market purchases do not qualify as a "tender offer" requiring the purchaser to meet the pre-filing strictures of § 14(d). Kennecott Copper Corp. v. Curtiss-Wright Corp., 449 F.Supp. 951, 961 (S.D.N.Y.), aff'd in relevant part, 584 F.2d 1195, 1206–07 (2d Cir.1978); Stromfeld v. Great Atlantic & Pac. Tea Co., Inc., 496 F.Supp. 1084, 1088–89 (S.D.N.Y.), aff'd mem., 646 F.2d 563 (2d Cir.1980); SEC v. Carter-Hawley Hale Stores, Inc., 760 F.2d 945, 950–53 (9th Cir.1985); Brascan Ltd. v. Edper Equities, Ltd., 477 F.Supp. 773, 791–92 (S.D.N.Y.1979); Astronics Corp. v. Protective Closures Co., 561 F.Supp. 329, 334 (W.D.N.Y.1983); LTV Corp. v. Grumman Corp., 526 F.Supp. 106, 109 (E.D.N.Y.1981); Energy Ventures, Inc. v. Appalachian Co., 587 F.Supp. 734, 739–41 (D.Del.1984); Ludlow v. Tyco Laboratories, Inc., 529 F.Supp. 62, 67 (D.Mass.1981); Chromalloy American Corp. v. Sun Chemical Corp., 474 F.Supp. 1341, 1346–47 (E.D.Mo.), aff'd, 611 F.2d 240 (8th Cir.1979). The borderline between public solicitations and privately negotiated stock purchases is not bright and it is frequently difficult to determine whether transactions falling close to the line or in a type of "no man's land" are "tender offers" or private deals. This has led some to advocate a broader interpretation of the term "tender offer" than that followed by us in Kennecott Copper Corp. v. Curtiss-Wright Corp., supra, 584 F.2d at 1207, and to adopt the eight-factor "test" of what is a tender offer, which was recommended by the SEC and applied by the district court in Wellman v. Dickinson, 475 F.Supp. 783, 823–24 (S.D.N.Y.1979), aff'd on other grounds, 682 F.2d 355 (2d Cir.1982), cert. denied, 460 U.S. 1069 (1983), and by the Ninth Circuit in SEC v. Carter-Hawley Hale Stores, Inc., supra. The eight factors are:

"(1) active and widespread solicitation of public shareholders for the shares of an issuer;

(2) solicitation made for a substantial percentage of the issuer's stock;

(3) offer to purchase made at a premium over the prevailing market price;

(4) terms of the offer are firm rather than negotiable;

(5) offer contingent on the tender of a fixed number of shares, often subject to a fixed maximum number to be purchased;

(6) offer open only for a limited period of time;

(7) offeree subjected to pressure to sell his stock;

* * * *

[(8)] public announcements of a purchasing program concerning the target company precede or accompany rapid accumulation of large amounts of the target company's securities." (475 F.Supp. at 823–24).

Although many of the above-listed factors are relevant for purposes of determining whether a given solicitation amounts to a tender offer, the elevation of such a list to a mandatory "litmus test" appears to be both unwise and unnecessary. As even the advocates of the proposed test recognize, in any given case a solicitation may constitute a tender offer even though some of the eight factors are absent or, when many factors are present, the solicitation may nevertheless not amount to a tender offer because the missing factors outweigh those present. Id., at 824; *Carter,* supra, at 950.

We prefer to be guided by the principle followed by the Supreme Court in deciding what transactions fall within the private offering exemption provided by § 4(1) of the Securities Act of 1933, and by ourselves in *Kennecott Copper* in determining whether the Williams Act applies to private transactions. That principle is simply to look to the statutory purpose. In S.E.C. v. Ralston Purina Co., 346 U.S. 119 (1953), the Court stated, "the applicability of § 4(1) should turn on whether the particular class of persons affected need the protection of the Act. An offering to those who are shown to be able to fend for themselves is a transaction 'not involving any public offering.' " Id., at 125. Similarly, since the purpose of § 14(d) is to protect the ill-informed solicitee, the question of whether a solicitation constitutes a "tender offer" within the meaning of § 14(d) turns on whether, viewing the transaction in the light of the totality of circumstances, there appears to be a likelihood that unless the pre-acquisition filing strictures of that statute are followed there will be a substantial risk that solicitees will lack information needed to make a carefully considered appraisal of the proposal put before them.

Applying this standard, we are persuaded on the undisputed facts that Hanson's September 11 negotiation of five private purchases and one open market purchase of SCM shares, totalling 25% of SCM's outstanding stock, did not under the circumstances constitute a "tender offer" within the meaning of the Williams Act. Putting aside for the moment the events preceding the purchases, there can be little doubt that the privately negotiated purchases would not, standing alone, qualify as a tender offer, for the following reasons:

(1) In a market of 22,800 SCM shareholders the number of SCM sellers here involved, six in all, was miniscule compared with the numbers involved in public solicitations of the type against which the Act was directed.

(2) At least five of the sellers were highly sophisticated professionals, knowledgeable in the market place and well aware of the essential facts needed to exercise their professional skills and to appraise Hanson's offer, including its financial condition as well as that of SCM, the likelihood that the purchases might block the SCM-Merrill bid, and the risk that if Hanson acquired more than $33\frac{1}{3}\%$ of SCM's stock the SCM-Merrill lockup of the "crown jewel" might be triggered. Indeed, by September 11 they had all had access to (1) Hanson's 27–page detailed disclosure of facts, filed on August 26, 1985, in accordance with § 14(d)(1) with respect to its $60 tender offer, (2) Hanson's 4–page amendment of that offer, dated September 5, 1985, increasing the price to $72 per share, and (3) press releases regarding the basic terms of the SCM-Merrill proposed leveraged buyout at $74 per share and of the SCM-Merrill asset option agreement under which SCM granted to Merrill the irrevocable right under certain conditions to buy SCM's consumer food business for $80 million and its pigment business for $350 million.

(3) The sellers were not "pressured" to sell their shares by any conduct that the Williams Act was designed to alleviate but by the forces of the market place. Indeed, in the case of Mutual Shares there

was no initial solicitation by Hanson; the offer to sell was initiated by Mr. Price of Mutual Shares. Although each of the Hanson purchases was made for $73.50 per share, in most instances this price was the result of private negotiations after the sellers sought higher prices and in one case price protection, demands which were refused. The $73.50 price was not fixed in advance by Hanson. Moreover, the sellers remained free to accept the $74 per share tender offer made by the SCM-Merrill group.

(4) There was no active or widespread advance publicity or public solicitation, which is one of the earmarks of a conventional tender offer. Arbitrageurs might conclude from ticker tape reports of two large anonymous transactions that Hanson must be the buyer. However, liability for solicitation may not be predicated upon disclosures mandated by Stock Exchange Rules. See S.E.C. v. Carter-Hawley Hale Stores, Inc., supra, 760 F.2d at 950.

(5) The price received by the six sellers, $73.50 per share, unlike that appearing in most tender offers, can scarcely be dignified with the label "premium." The stock market price on September 11 ranged from $72.50 to $73.50 per share. Although risk arbitrageurs sitting on large holdings might reap sizeable profits from sales to Hanson at $73.50, depending on their own purchase costs, they stood to gain even more if the SCM-Merrill offer of $74 should succeed, as it apparently would if they tendered their shares to it. Indeed, the $73.50 price, being at most $1 over market or 1.4% higher than the market price, did not meet the SEC's proposed definition of a premium, which is $2.00 per share or 5% above market price, whichever is greater. SEC Exchange Act Release No. 16,385 (11/29/79) [1979–80] Fed.Sec.L.Rep. ¶ 82,374.

(6) Unlike most tender offers, the purchases were not made contingent upon Hanson's acquiring a fixed minimum number or percentage of SCM's outstanding shares. Once an agreement with each individual seller was reached, Hanson was obligated to buy, regardless what total percentage of stock it might acquire. Indeed, it does not appear that Hanson had fixed in its mind a firm limit on the amount of SCM shares it was willing to buy.

(7) Unlike most tender offers, there was no general time limit within which Hanson would make purchases of SCM stock. Concededly, cash transactions are normally immediate but, assuming an inability on the part of a seller and Hanson to agree at once on a price, nothing prevented a resumption of negotiations by each of the parties except the arbitrageurs' speculation that once Hanson acquired $33\frac{1}{3}\%$ or an amount just short of that figure it would stop buying.

In short, the totality of circumstances that existed on September 11 did not evidence any likelihood that unless Hanson was required to comply with § 14(d)(1)'s pre-acquisition filing and waiting-period requirements there would be a substantial risk of ill-considered sales of SCM stock by ill-informed shareholders.

There remains the question whether Hanson's private purchases take on a different hue, requiring them to be treated as a "*de facto*" continuation of its earlier tender offer, when considered in the context of Hanson's earlier acknowledged tender offer, the competing offer of SCM-Merrill and

Hanson's termination of its tender offer. After reviewing all of the undisputed facts we conclude that the district court erred in so holding.

In the first place, we find no record support for the contention by SCM that Hanson's September 11 termination of its outstanding tender offer was false, fraudulent or ineffective. Hanson's termination notice was clear, unequivocal and straight-forward. Directions were given, and presumably are being followed, to return all of the tendered shares to the SCM shareholders who tendered them. Hanson also filed with the SEC a statement pursuant to § 14(d)(1) of the Williams Act terminating its tender offer. As a result, at the time when Hanson made its September 11 private purchases of SCM stock it owned no SCM stock other than those shares revealed in its § 14(d) pre-acquisition report filed with the SEC on August 26, 1985.

The reason for Hanson's termination of its tender offer is not disputed: in view of SCM's grant of what Hanson conceived to be a "poison pill" lock-up option to Merrill, Hanson, if it acquired control of SCM, would have a company denuded as the result of its sale of its consumer food and pigment businesses to Merrill at what Hanson believed to be bargain prices. Thus, Hanson's termination of its tender offer was final; there was no tender offer to be "continued." Hanson was unlikely to "shoot itself in the foot" by triggering what it believed to be a "poison pill," and it could not acquire more than 49% of SCM's shares without violating the rules of the London Stock Exchange.

Nor does the record support SCM's contention that Hanson had decided, before terminating its tender offer, to engage in cash purchases. Judge Kram referred only to evidence that "Hanson had *considered* open market purchases before it announced that the tender offer was dropped" (emphasis added) but made no finding to that effect. Absent evidence or a finding that Hanson had decided to seek control of SCM through purchases of its stock, no duty of disclosure existed under the federal securities laws.

Second, Hanson had expressly reserved the right in its August 26, 1985, pre-acquisition tender offer filing papers, whether or not tendered shares were purchased, "*thereafter* * * * to purchase additional Shares in the open market, in privately negotiated transactions, through another tender offer or otherwise." (Emphasis added). See p. 46, supra. Thus, Hanson's privately negotiated purchases could hardly have taken the market by surprise. Indeed, professional arbitrageurs and market experts rapidly concluded that it was Hanson which was making the post-termination purchases.

Last, Hanson's prior disclosures of essential facts about itself and SCM in the pre-acquisition papers it filed on August 26, 1985, with the SEC pursuant to § 14(d)(1), are wholly inconsistent with the district court's characterization of Hanson's later private purchases as "a deliberate attempt to do an 'end run' around the requirements of the Williams Act."

* * *

In the present case we conclude that since the district court erred in ruling as a matter of law that SCM had demonstrated a likelihood of success on the merits, based on the theory that Hanson's post-tender offer private purchases of SCM constituted a *de facto* tender offer, it was an abuse of discretion to issue a preliminary injunction. Indeed, we do not believe that Hanson's transactions raise serious questions going to the merits that would provide a fair ground for litigation. In view of this holding it becomes unnecessary to rule upon the district court's determination that the balance of hardships tip in favor of SCM and that absent preliminary relief it would suffer irreparable injury. However, our decision is not to be construed as an affirmance of the district court's resolution of these issues.

* * *

The order of the district court is reversed, the preliminary injunction against Hanson is vacated, and the case is remanded for further proceedings in accordance with this opinion. The mandate shall issue forthwith.

———

SECURITIES EXCHANGE ACT RELEASE NO. 16385
Securities and Exchange Commission.
November 29, 1979.

* * *

DISCUSSION

A. Proposed Rule 14d–1(b)(1): Definition of the Term "Tender Offer"

The term "tender offer" is not defined in the Williams Act. Since the passage of the Williams Act, the Commission has been continually involved in the development of the meaning of the term but has not adopted a definition.

This position has been premised upon the dynamic nature of these transactions and the need for the Williams Act to be interpreted flexibly in a manner consistent with its purposes to protect investors. Consequently, the Commission specifically declined to define the term on two prior occasions.

While there has been essential compliance with the provisions of the Williams Act when people seek shares through a public announcement and filings with the Commission, many persons have not complied with the Williams Act when they have invited tenders for shares in other ways. Many persons have deliberately structured tender offers in an effort to evade the provisions of the Williams Act. These approaches have included purported privately negotiated transactions, wide-scale solicitation of members of one family and various forms of massive open market purchase programs. In the Commission's judgment, these tender offers, however packaged, are subject to the provisions of the Williams Act and are required to be effected in accordance with its provisions. Recognizing the dynamic nature of these activities, the Commission has proposed a definition which would include within its coverage at least certain of these diverse forms of transactions. The Commission has done so because it believes that in substance many of these transactions are in reality tender offers and that the public is entitled to the benefits that would flow from their specific inclusion within the provisions of the Williams Act.

In developing the proposed definition, the Commission considered the provisions and purposes of the Williams Act, its legislative history, applicable case law, enforcement actions, administrative proceedings and positions, legal commentary and past and present tender offer practice. The proposed definition does distinguish between tender offers and transactions involving open market or privately negotiated purchases. However, not all so-called open market or privately negotiated purchases are automatically exempted from the definition simply because they occur on or off the market, and certain of these programs would be defined as tender offers.[6]

In proposing a specific delineation, the Commission is aware that the scope of the definition may include transactions which others believe ought to be excluded and may exclude transactions which others believe ought to be included. While this is a necessary consequence of any definition, the Commission invites public comment as to the scope of the term and what transactions should be excluded and included. In addition, the Commission requests specific suggestions as to the appropriate methods for taking account of such transactions.

Moreover, the scope of the proposed definition reflects the Commission's long-standing position that the term "tender offer" embraces not only tender offers formally announced by communications to shareholders but also offers accomplished by other means. This position is supported by the case law and legal commentators.

The definition in proposed Rule 14d–1(b)(1) is designed to provide guidance to members of the financial community and their advisers. The proposal is divided into two tiers which would operate independently of each other. That is, an offer is a tender offer if it meets the test in either of the two tiers.

Under the first tier, proposed Rule 14d–1(b)(1)(i), the term "tender offer" consists of four elements: (1) one or more offers to purchase or solicitations of offers to sell securities of a single class; (2) during any 45–day period; (3) directed to more than 10 persons; and (4) seeking the acquisition of more than 5% of the class of securities.

In order to be a tender offer within the meaning of proposed Rule 14d–1(b)(1)(i), all four elements must be present. Thus, an offer to purchase more than 5% of a class of securities from nine persons within a 45–day period would not constitute a tender offer. It should be noted that a block transaction which meets the four elements would be a tender offer subject to the Williams Act unless the exception, discussed below, is applicable.

The Commission recognizes that ordinary open market purchases which are part of the "free and open auction market" should not be regulated as tender offers. To say that purchases take place on the floor of a securities exchange, however, does not end the inquiry. The use of facilities of an exchange may be a mere formality to disguise what is otherwise in effect a tender offer that should be subject to the requirements of the Williams Act. While the proposal contemplates that certain open market purchasing programs meeting the four elements discussed above would be tender offers, others are excepted. The exception would be limited to offers by a

---

6. Section 14(d)(1) of the Act provides in pertinent part:

It shall be unlawful for any person, directly or indirectly, by use of the mails or by any means of instrumentality of interstate commerce *or of any facility of a national securities exchange* or otherwise, to make a tender offer (emphasis supplied).

Thus, the statute recognizes that a tender offer may be made directly or indirectly by using the facilities of a national securities exchange. For example, a special bid, *see* New York Stock Exchange Rule 391 and American Stock Exchange Rule 560, is a tender offer within the meaning of the Williams Act. See Securities Exchange Act Release No. 8392 (August 30, 1968) (33 FR 14109).

broker and its customer or by a dealer at the then current market price on a national securities exchange or in the over-the-counter market if in connection with such offers three conditions are present.

First, neither the person making the offers nor the broker or dealer solicits or arranges for the solicitation of any order to sell. With respect to offers at the then current market on a national securities exchange, a broker or dealer who merely talked to the specialist(s) or the persons in the crowd on the floor of the exchange would not in the Commission's view be making a solicitation as that term is used in the definition. However, if the person making the offers and/or the broker or dealer talked to persons off the floor of the exchange and/or arranged for them or their representatives to be present in the crowd on the floor to accept the offer, such conduct would in the Commission's judgment be a solicitation and the exception would not be available. Moreover, special bids and "assembling a block" off the floor which is then crossed on the exchange would also be viewed as solicitations. With respect to offers at the then current market price in the over-the-counter market, the mere fact that a market maker who has previously made quotes on a continuous basis in the securities being sought during the period that the offer is made should not be viewed as a solicitation by the dealer. Finally, with respect to both exchange and over-the-counter market transactions, the person making the offers to purchase will be considered to have solicited or arranged for the solicitation of sell orders if that person has, directly or indirectly, publicly announced or stated that it intends or is about to engage in a substantial purchase program.

The second condition to the availability of the exception to proposed Rule 14d–1(b)(1)(i) is that the broker or dealer performs only the customary functions of a broker or dealer. Finally, the broker or dealer can receive no more than the broker's usual and customary commission or the dealer's usual and customary mark-up for executing the trade.

If the conditions discussed above are satisfied, offers at the then current market price by a broker or dealer on a national securities exchange or in the over the counter market would be excluded for all purposes from the four elements of proposed Rule 14d–1(b)(1)(i).

As previously noted, the four elements embodied in proposed Rule 14d–1(b)(1)(i) are intended to distinguish tender offers from other transactions, including open market and privately negotiated purchases. The Commission notes that other percentage tests, time periods and numbers of solicitees have been suggested in other approaches, and specifically requests comment as to whether one of these or any other percentage tests, time periods or numbers of solicitees should be included in the first tier of the definition. The Commission also requests comment on the interrelationship of the proposed exception to the four elements generally and specifically requests comment on the following questions: (1) whether the exception is necessary in Rule 14d–1(b)(1)(i) as proposed since most ordinary open market purchase programs rarely exceed 5% within a 45–day period; (2) whether the exception would be unnecessary if other elements of proposed Rule 14d–1(b)(1)(i), such as the percentage, were increased; (3) whether the exception should be retained in any event; and, (4) if so, the proper form and scope thereof. The Commission also requests specific comment on what customary practices should be included within the meaning of customary functions of a broker or dealer.

The Commission requests specific comment from the public and from members of the brokerage community in particular concerning the extent, if any, to which a broker-dealer engages in transactions during any 45–day period which involve offers to purchase or solicitations of offers to sell in excess of 5% of a single class of securities from more than 10 persons, where such offers are not on behalf of any single person or group other than such broker-dealer acting in the ordinary course of business. In connection with this inquiry, the Commission requests that commentators provide examples of any such situations together with supporting details concerning these transactions. The Commission also inquires whether it would be appropriate to except such offers from the first tier of the proposed definition.

The second tier of the definition of tender offer is set forth in proposed Rule 14d–1(b)(1)(ii). Unlike the first tier, the second tier does not contain a specific percentage test, time period or number of solicitees. Under the second tier, one or more offers to purchase, or solicitations of offers to sell, securities of a single class would be a tender offer if three conditions are present. First, the offers to purchase or the solicitation of offers to sell must be disseminated in a widespread manner. While this requirement could be satisfied through public announcements by means of newspaper advertisements or press releases, the absence of such announcements would not be determinative. A tender offer may be widely disseminated by other means, including telephone solicitations, the use of the mails and personal visits to security holders.

Second, the price offered must represent a premium in excess of the greater of 5% of or $2 above the current market price of the securities being sought. The third condition of the second tier is that the offers do not provide for a meaningful opportunity to negotiate the price and terms. Thus, truly negotiated purchases of securities would not be regulated as a tender offer under the second tier. The Commission asks for general comment on the appropriateness of the three criteria and whether additional standards should be included.

As noted above, the two tiers of proposed Rule 14d–1(b)(1) are intended to operate independently of one another. One or more offers to purchase or solicitations of offers to sell can therefore be a tender offer under one tier of the definition even though they would not constitute a tender offer under the other tier. In view of the complexity of securities transactions, the diverse and dynamic nature of tender offers, and the need to provide adequate protection of investors within the purposes of the Williams Act, the Commission believes that the two tier approach embodied in proposed Rule 14d–1(b) is feasible, and capable of providing guidance and certainty to practitioners and their clients and would not be unduly burdensome to prospective bidders.

The issue of what constitutes a tender offer is not limited to resolving the issues of whether privately negotiated and open market purchases can be tender offers. Another question is whether an exchange of securities pursuant to a statutory merger or consolidation which is the subject of a shareholder vote is a tender offer. The Commission believes that statutory mergers and consolidations are not tender offers within the meaning of the definition proposed for comment. Under proposed Rule 14d–1(b)(1), an exchange of securities pursuant to a statutory merger or consolidation would not constitute an offer to purchase or a solicitation of an offer to sell securities. Rather, the exchange would be viewed as part of the mechanics of the merger process itself. Similarly, certain repurchases of securities by corporations which are imposed by statute would not be viewed as tender offers within the meaning of proposed Rule 14d–1(b)(1). These would include purchases in court approved bankruptcy reorganizations and repurchases by a corporation of securities owned by shareholders who dissented from a proposal to eliminate mandatory preemptive rights when such obligation is imposed by statute. The Commission requests specific comment on other repurchases which corporations are obligated by statute to make which should not be deemed offers to purchase within the meaning of the proposed definition.

* * *

D. Rule 14e–5. Prohibiting purchases not made by means of a tender offer.

The Commission is proposing to rescind Rule 10b–13 and to adopt in lieu thereof proposed Rule 14e–5. Rule 10b–13 currently prohibits purchases from being made otherwise than pursuant to a tender offer from the time the tender offer is publicly announced until the expiration of the offer. Proposed Rule 14e–5 would prohibit any person who makes a tender offer or simultaneous tender offers for one or more classes of securities issued by a single subject company from making purchases of specified securities except by means of the tender offers during the period from the public announcement of certain information or, if no announcement is made, the date on which the first of the tender offers commences through the tenth business day after the termination of the last of the tender offers to expire. Thus, tender offers for more than one class of securities would be specifically permitted under the proposal so long as purchases were not made outside of the tender offer, during the specified period.

The information which must be included in a public announcement that will trigger Rule 10b–13 is similar to that found in Rule 14d–2(c). However, proposed Rule 14e–5 would prohibit purchases from being made except by means of the tender offer after the public announcement of the information specified in Rule 14d–2(d) through the tenth business day after the termination of the tender offer. By basing the prohibition on the information contained in Rule 14d–2(d), the proposal would interrelate with and augment the protections afforded by Rule 14d–2(b).

Rule 14d–2(b) provides that a bidder's public announcement through a press release, newspaper advertisement or public statement of certain material terms of a tender offer in which the consideration consists solely of cash and/or securities exempt from registration under Section 3 of the Securities Act causes the bidder's tender offer to commence under Section 14(d). The information which will trigger Rule 14d–2(b) includes: the identity of the bidder and the subject company; a statement of the class and amount of securities being sought; and disclosure of the price or range of prices being offered therefor. The determination that Section 14(d) is applicable upon the date of such public announcement was based on the Commission's judgment that putting such information in the public domain has such a demonstrable impact on both security holders and the market as to constitute the practical commencement of the tender offer. Such public announcements cause investors to make investment decisions with respect to a tender offer on the basis of incomplete information and trigger market activity normally attendant to a tender offer, such as arbitrageur activity.

Rule 14d–2(d) does, however, permit a bidder to make a public announcement of the following information with respect to a tender offer in which the consideration consists solely of cash and/or securities exempt from registration under Section 3 of the Securities Act without deeming the tender offer to have commenced under Rule 14d–2(b): the identity of the bidder and the subject company; and a statement that the bidder intends to make a tender offer in the future for a class of equity securities of the subject company which statement does not specify the amount of securities of such class to be sought or the consideration to be offered therefor. While the Commission recognizes that the impact such statements on security holders and the market is not as significant as those in which the price to be offered and the amount of securities to be sought is specified, such statements do have a demonstrable impact and pose the same types of problems, albeit to a lesser extent, as the statements comprehended by Rule 14d–2(b).

In view of their lesser impact and the burden which would be imposed on bidders if such statements were deemed to constitute the commencement of the tender offer, the Commission has determined that such statements will not be viewed as commencing the tender offer. However, the Commission believes that a person who intends to make a tender offer should not be able to purchase securities after such public announcements have been made except by means of the tender offer. Requiring the person who intends to make a tender offer to cease purchasing after such an announcement is made will minimize, to the extent feasible, the abuses noted above. It will also reduce the likelihood of fraudulent, deceptive or manipulative acts or practices during this period. Moreover, once the specified information has been publicly announced, the proposal removes any incentive on the part of holders of substantial blocks of securities to demand from the person making the tender offer(s) a consideration greater than or different from that currently offered to unaffiliated security holders.

The Commission specifically requests comment on whether the operation of proposed Rule 14e–5(a) should be predicated on an event other than the public announcement of the information contained in Rule 14d–2(d), such as, for example, the announcement or dissemination of the information contained in Rule 14d–2(c). The latter formulation would be consistent with existing interpretations under Rule 10b–13. In addition, the Commission requests comment on the impact which proposed Rule 14e–5(a) would have on the timing of the announcement to make a tender offer.

As noted above, proposed Rule 14e–5 also differs from Rule 10b–13 in that it would prohibit purchases for a period of ten business days after the termination of the tender offer. The Commission believes that this provision may be necessary to ensure that a bidder does not take advantage of unsettled market conditions following the termination of its tender offer. The Commission specifically requests comment on whether a period of ten business days after a tender offer is sufficient to permit the impact of the offer on the market to subside before subsequent purchases can be made.

Rule 13e–4(f)(6) (§ 240.13e–4(f)(6)) prohibits purchases of securities of the same class and series which are the subject of a tender offer covered by the rule during the ten business day period subsequent to the termination of the tender offer. Commentators advocating a longer period are asked to consider whether a different period should apply to tender offers which are subject to Rule 13e–4.

Paragraph (b) of proposed Rule 14e–5 specifies the securities to which the rule applies. The securities include not only those to be sought in the bidder's tender offer but also any option, warrant or right, convertible security or other security which involves a contractual right, privilege or other provision to purchase or acquire the security which is the subject of the tender offer. It should be noted, however, that a person meeting the conditions specified in paragraph (c) of proposed Rule 14e–5 may purchase any of these securities pursuant to the exercise of options, warrants or rights, the conversion of convertible securities, or the performance of agreements to purchase such securities. The specified conditions are: that the options, warrants, rights, convertible securities, or agreements were acquired or entered into prior to the time of such public announcement or pursuant to the tender offer; and that such securities or agreements and any exercise thereof are disclosed in any applicable filings under the Williams Act. If adopted, the proposal would change the practice under Rule 10b–13 which limits purchases other than pursuant to the tender offer during the specified period to the exercise of a right of conversion or exchange of another security that is immediately convertible into or exchangeable for the security which is the subject of the tender offer if the other security is owned prior to the public announcement. Specific comment is requested as to whether the expansion of the scope of purchases which are permitted to be made under proposed Rule 14e–5(c) except by means of the tender offer during the specified period is preferable to the limitation under Rule 10b–13. Comment is also requested with respect to the impact of each of these limitations on tender offer practice given the proposed change in the type of announcement that will trigger the prohibition on purchases outside of the tender offer.

* * *

PROPOSED FEDERAL SECURITIES CODE *

American Law Institute.
May 19, 1978.

SEC. 202. For purposes of this Code—

(166) TENDER OFFER.—

(A) GENERAL. "Tender offer" means an offer to buy a security, or a solicitation of an offer to sell a security, that is directed to more than thirty-five persons, unless—

(i) it (I) is incidental to the execution of a buy order by a broker, or to a purchase by a dealer, who performs no more than the usual function of a broker or dealer, or (II) does no more than state an intention to make such an offer or solicitation; and

(ii) it satisfies any additional conditions that the Commission imposes by rule.

(B) MULTIPLE TENDER OFFERS. A tender offer is separate from any other tender offer (or from an offer to buy a security, or a solicitation of an offer to sell a security, that is directed to not more than thirty-five persons) if (i) it is for a different class of securities, or (ii) it is for additional securities of the same class but is substantially distinct on the basis of such factors as manner, time, purpose, price, and kind of consideration.

TENDER OFFERS

For many years general offers have been made to the stockholders of publicly-held corporations to acquire all or some specified majority of the outstanding shares (either for cash or in exchange for stock of the acquiring corporation in a "B" reorganization), but until the last 15 or 20 years such an offer was usually made only with the cooperation of the management of the corporation to be acquired and even then it was quite infrequently used as a method of acquisition as compared with a purchase of assets or a statutory merger. In the last 20 years, however, such offers have become increasingly frequent as a method of attempting to take over control of a corporation in opposition to its existing management. Such offers are usually referred to as "tender offers" or "takeover bids."

While such offers during the conglomerate acquisition days in the 1960's were frequently of securities of the acquiring corporation, in recent years they have usually been cash offers at a substantial premium above the current market price of the stock of the target company and have in many instances involved billions of dollars for a single acquisition. This phase of corporate law practice has become one of the most active, and certainly the most lucrative. It has spawned its own mystique and jargon, such as "Pac-Man Defense", "poisoned pill", "greenmail", "shark repellent", "bear hug" (or perhaps only a "teddybear hug"), and "white knight".

This trend has escalated in the last four or five years to the point where it is rare to see an issue of the Wall Street Journal that does not carry a story regarding some new tender offer being made for a company, whether with or without the cooperation of the management of the target company, frequently in the range of hundreds of millions or billions of dollars.[1] This development has probably been due to three interacting changes in the financial environment in the United States, which together have completely altered the financial landscape.

First, there is no longer any hesitancy on the part of any corporation or any brokerage house to engage in a hostile tender offer to take over some other corporation. At one time such activity was regarded as "ungentlemanly" on Wall Street and the early practitioners of that art were considered somewhat disreputable persons. Now, every old-line brokerage house on Wall Street has its take-over department, which is the most profitable end of its business in view of the unconscionable fees which are charged to "advise" either a corpora-

1. See Deal Mania—The Restructuring of Corporate America, Business Week, Nov. 24, 1986, p. 74.

tion engaging in a take-over bid or the management of the target company which is resisting such an attempt. The first thing that both the tender offeror and the target company do is hire an investment banker to plan their strategy; the second thing they do is to hire an attorney expert in this field of law, whose fees are modest compared to those of the investment banker, but nevertheless frequently run into millions of dollars in a single deal.[2]

Second, credit has become available to finance such transactions in a seemingly unlimited amount. This has been due to two subsidiary developments. In the first place, banks have become increasingly willing to lend money, if the interest rate is high enough, without as much concern as bankers used to have regarding such things as debt to equity ratios. This may be due, at least in part, to the bank holding company phenomenon where virtually every bank is now owned by a holding company and the shares of the holding company of any large bank are actively traded in the stock market. There was a time in the United States when banks refused to list their shares on a stock exchange because they did not want the reputation of the bank to be tied up in any way with the "volatile" activity of the stock market. As a result of this development, bankers now tend to be more concerned, as are other corporate managers, with the current year's "bottom line" and less concerned as to whether a particular loan can ever be collected. In the second place, it was discovered that the very large institutional investors in the United States will buy completely unrated bond issues (commonly referred to as "junk bonds") in amounts running to hundreds of millions or even billions of dollars if the rate of return is high enough. These bond issues are used to finance many of the large takeover bids. The brokerage house of Drexel Burnham, which was apparently the first to observe this curious syndrome, is probably the most profitable house on Wall Street today as a result of the fees earned in selling such "junk bonds." [3]

Third, it has in recent years been discovered that many of the largest corporations in the United States can be sold off piece by piece for a great deal more (sometimes twice as much) as the current aggregate market value of the shares of the parent corporation. The alleged intention of the tender offeror to do that has frequently been opprobiously referred to as intending to carry out a "bust-up merger", as though this were immoral. This situation probably arose primarily from the "conglomeration" mania of the 1960's and 1970's, when it was asserted that putting together totally different types of businesses under one corporate roof would enhance the value of the entire entity, or, in other words, that the whole was greater than the sum of its parts because of something called "synergism." While the stock market for a brief period reflected this same irrational view,[4] the "synergism" rarely worked out. Now, the sum of the parts is greater than the whole.

2. See Los Angeles Times, Aug. 13, 1986, Part IV, p. 2 ("Bankers, Lawyers, and Advisers to Reap $150 Million"). That story related to a leveraged buy-out of Safeway Stores, Inc., as a defensive maneuver to defeat a hostile takeover, and revealed that Kohlberg Kravis Roberts & Co., the firm arranging the leveraged buy-out, received $60 million in fees, Morgan Stanley, the "financial adviser" to Kohlberg Kravis, received $10 million in fees, plus an opportunity to purchase as much as $10 million in equity in the new company, and lawyers and accountants received another $10 million, "while printers will get a total of $3 million for preparing documents." Mr. Andrew C. Sigler, the Chairman of Champion International Corp., and chairman of a task force on corporate responsibility appointed by the Business Roundtable, was quoted as saying that the fee system "has gone totally out of control. It is highway robbery."

3. See *Business Week*, July 7, 1986, p. 56 ("Power on Wall Street; Drexel Burnham is Reshaping Investment Banking—and U.S. Industry"). See also, Wall Street Journal (Western Ed.), June 13, 1986, 1:6; June 18, 1986, 7:1.

4. For a contemporary analysis of this syndrome, see Marsh, Conflicts of Interest (part of ABA Institute on Conglomerates and Other Modern Merger Movements), 25

It is hardly immoral for the shareholders of a company to wish to realize upon this value, whether by way of a premium over market price offered by a tender offeror or by a program initiated by the existing management of the company. A number of corporations, most notably City Investing and W.R. Grace & Co. and, to a certain extent, Arco, have in the last year or so engaged in such a "deconglomeration" program on their own initiative without any immediate threat of a take-over bid (although they may have had it in the back of their minds that they had better do it before it was done to them).

Frequently, the lenders who furnish the funds to make such a take-over bid expect to be repaid, at least in substantial part, from the proceeds of the sale of one or more subsidiaries of the holding company. Although such a hostile take-over bid cannot technically be called a "leveraged buy-out", since the bidder is unable to give any lien on the assets of the target company before it has been acquired, in fact what the lenders are looking to as their security for repayment are the assets of the company to be taken over. If the bid fails, and therefore the assets of the target company cannot be reached, they never have to advance the money, although they receive very handsome "commitment fees" for agreeing to do so.

As a result of all of these developments, almost any insignificant corporation can dream of taking over General Motors, with at least a possibility of succeeding;[5] and the largest corporations in the country are so frightened by this prospect that they are all scrambling to adopt anti-takeover measures. It was recently reported that over 350 of the corporations on Standard & Poor's 500 stock list had already adopted such measures and that many more were going to be voted on at the annual meetings of the remaining 150 companies in 1986.

Obviously, there is a potentially serious threat to the economy involved in the massive conversion of equity into debt which these transactions usually involve,[6] and they can be applauded or deplored on economic grounds. There certainly should be a national policy formulated (although there is yet no indication that it will be) as to what, if anything, should be done by the government to influence the course of these events, based upon purely economic considerations.

Quite clearly a tender offer to purchase securities is a transaction which is subject to Rule 10b–5 and its prohibition against false or misleading statements, so that a seller of stock pursuant to such an offer could sue for damages under Rule 10b–5 if the offer violated the Rule.[7] However, there was an unresolved question as to whether a stockholder who had not tendered his shares or the corporation itself had any standing to sue to enjoin an allegedly false or misleading tender offer (since neither is a purchaser or seller and neither has relied on the false or misleading statement as the complaint alleges that they know the truth). As a practical matter only such a stockholder who is siding with the management, or the corporation under its control, is likely to be

---

Bus.Law 827, 827–831 (1970). One definition of "synergism" given by Webster's New International Dictionary (2d Ed.) is: "The Semi-Pelagian doctrine that in regeneration there is co-operation of divine grace and human activity." It would probably have taken divine grace for some of these conglomerates to work out successfully.

5. Drexel Burnham has "created a huge financing network that can raise billions overnight for almost anyone." *Business Week,* July 7, 1986, Cover.

6. See *Business Week,* Aug. 18, 1986, p. 22. The Chairman of Sony, one of the more successful Japanese companies, has stated that U.S. business executives "are moving to the 'money game'—buy a company, sell a company. If you continue this, American industry will completely deteriorate." U.S. News & World Report, Nov. 17, 1986, p. 57.

7. See Vine v. Beneficial Finance Co., 374 F.2d 627 (2d Cir.1967), cert. denied 389 U.S. 970 (1967).

available as a plaintiff in such a private injunction action. In Schoenbaum v. Firstbrook [8] Judge Cooper held that neither had any standing to bring such an action under Rule 10b–5; but Judge Connell in Moore v. Greatamerica Corp.[9] held that both did. In Symington Wayne Corp. v. Dresser Industries, Inc.[10] the Second Circuit reserved this question. The *Blue Chip* case (see Chapter 16, below) has resolved this question so far as a damage action is concerned; but not necessarily an injunction action.

As a result of the addition of Section 14(e) to the Securities Exchange Act by the Williams Act, specifically prohibiting false and misleading statements in connection with a tender offer, and the holdings that the target company has standing under that section,[11] this issue under Rule 10b–5 has perhaps become moot. It is true that the Supreme Court in Piper v. Chris-Craft Industries, Inc., infra, page 841, held that an unsuccessful tender offeror had no standing to sue the target company (and its management and investment adviser) for damages under Section 14(e), but it has been held that this ruling does not apply to an action by the tender offeror for an injunction to prevent violations,[12] and it should not be considered to have overruled those cases holding that the target company similarly has standing to sue for an injunction.

On the other hand, such an offer was not, prior to the Williams Act, subject to any of the *affirmative* disclosure requirements of the securities acts. Since it is an offer to purchase, rather than an offer to sell, securities, it is not subject to the registration requirements of the Securities Act of 1933, unless it is an exchange offer (rather than a cash purchase) involving the issuance of its own securities by the offeror as the consideration for those being acquired. And since it is an offer to purchase the stock, rather than a solicitation of a proxy, it is not subject to the disclosure requirements of Regulation 14A under the Securities Exchange Act of 1934.[13] It is true that if the management of the corporation which is subject to the takeover bid proposes a "fighting merger", communications regarding the tender offer may thereafter be deemed to be solicitations of proxies, since such communications must necessarily be opposed to the proposed merger requiring a shareholder vote.[14] A "fighting merger" is a common tactic of the management whose tenure is threatened by a takeover bid—it consists of proposing a merger with another corporation (a "white knight") whose management is friendly to the management of the victim, on terms which are allegedly superior to those offered by the "raider." [15] However, if this tactic was not used or the "white knight" also offered cash, there was prior to 1968 no statutory requirement of any disclosure by the offeror.

Senate Bill 510, which became the Williams Act, was designed to fill this "gap" [16] in the securities laws and require certain disclosures in connection

---

8. 268 F.Supp. 385 (S.D.N.Y.1967).

9. 274 F.Supp. 490 (N.D.Ohio 1967).

10. 383 F.2d 840 (2d Cir.1967).

11. Electronics Specialty Co. v. International Controls Corp., 409 F.2d 937 (2d Cir. 1969); Butler Aviation International, Inc. v. Comprehensive Designers, Inc., 425 F.2d 842 (2d Cir.1970); cf. GAF Corp. v. Milstein, infra, p. 693.

12. Humana, Inc. v. American Medicorp, Inc., 445 F.Supp. 613 (S.D.N.Y. 1977).

13. A cash tender offeror does not have to comply with the Proxy Rules, as well as the Williams Act, in connection with the tender offer merely because it proposes a merger with the target company as a subsequent, second step in the takeover. Radol v. Thomas, 772 F.2d 244 (6th Cir. 1985), cert. denied ___ U.S. ___, 106 S.Ct. 3272 (1986).

14. See Brown v. Chicago, Rock Island & Pacific Railroad Co., 328 F.2d 122 (7th Cir.1964).

15. See Schmults and Kelly, Cash Take-Over Bids—Defense Tactics, 23 Bus.Law 115 (1967).

16. Once something has been identified as a "gap", there of course remains only one thing to do—"fill" it!

with tender offers. As explained by the Senate Committee on Banking and Currency:

* * * Under this bill, the material facts concerning the identity, background, and plans of the person or group making a tender offer or acquiring a substantial amount of securities would be disclosed.

Any person or group acquiring more than 10 percent [later reduced to 5 percent] of any class of equity security registered under the Securities Exchange Act would be required to disclose the size of the holdings of the person or group involved, the source of the funds used or to be used to acquire the shares, any contracts or arrangements relating to the shares, and, if the purpose of the acquisition is to acquire control of the company, any plans to liquidate the company, sell its assets, merge it with another company, or make major changes in its business or corporate structure.

As initially introduced, the bill would have required the disclosure statement to be filed with the Securities and Exchange Commission 5 days before the tender offer was made to allow the staff of the Securities and Exchange Commission an opportunity to review the material for compliance with the applicable requirements. At the hearings it was urged that this prior review was not necessary and in some cases might delay the offer when time was of the essence. In view of the authority and responsibility of the Securities and Exchange Commission to take appropriate action in the event that inadequate or misleading information is disseminated to the public to solicit acceptance of a tender offer, the bill as approved by the committee requires only that the statement be on file with the Securities and Exchange Commission at the time the tender offer is first made to the public.

The bill as introduced would also have required that all shares deposited during the tender offer be taken upon a pro rata basis if less than all of the deposited shares were purchased. During the hearings representatives of the New York Stock Exchange testified as to their experience with an exchange policy which requires pro rata acceptance of shares offered for the first 10 days of the offer and suggested an additional 10–day period in case of an increase in price. In view of the experience of the New York Stock Exchange, your committee believes that the pro rata period can be so limited and has amended the bill accordingly.[17]

At the hearings, the committee was informed of a practice known as "short tendering," in which brokers tender securities they do not own. Tender offers commonly provide that the stock certificates need not be deposited if a bank or a member firm of a stock exchange guarantees that the certificates will be delivered on demand or at a specified time if they are accepted. This procedure was originally introduced to permit acceptance on behalf of shareholders who were out of town or otherwise not in a position to

---

17. In San Francisco Real Estate Investors v. Real Estate Investment Trust of America, 692 F.2d 814 (1st Cir.1982), the court held that the trial court's decision extending this ten day proration period, pending a decision on the merits relating to an anti-takeover bylaw adopted by the target company, was improper. The court said that the ten day deadline in the statute, "while not necessarily immutable, is certainly entitled to respect from the courts, and should not be enlarged without a significant reason." The SEC, however, has subsequently enlarged the proration period to the duration of the offer. Rule 14(d)–8. There are, therefore, no longer any multiple "proration pools."

In Pryor v. United States Steel Corp., 794 F.2d 52 (2d Cir.1986), the court held that the tender offeror could not extend the original 10–day proration period after it had expired, thus admitting shareholders who subsequently tendered into the proration pool. This decision has also been mooted by the Rule mentioned above.

deposit their certificates. It has, however, resulted in abuses. For example, if a broker estimates that only half of the shares which he actually owns will be accepted, and the number of shares purchased from other investors will be correspondingly reduced. The committee believes the Securities and Exchange Commission at present has adequate power to deal with the abuse of short tendering under the anti-fraud provisions of the Securities Exchange Act.[18]

The SEC responded to the last observation of the Committee by adopting a rule making "short tendering" illegal.[19]

The disclosure required of a tender offeror by the Williams Act relates primarily to the identity and background of the persons making the offer, the source of the funds used and the "purpose" of the transaction including any "plans" which the tender offeror may have to merge or liquidate the target company or otherwise to make any "major change" in its business or corporate structure.[20] The last requirement was the one which originally caused the most difficulty, since it in effect requires something in the nature of a prediction of the future—a type of disclosure which previously was not only not generally required, but was actually prohibited under the securities laws. It is true that the requirement is phrased in terms of a disclosure of present intention or "plans," but obviously if the "plan" doesn't materialize then the discloser is in trouble and may have to explain in court why it didn't work out. And if he is unable to do so to the satisfaction of the trier of fact, he may be found not to have had the "plan" in the first place and therefore to be liable for a misstatement of fact. However, in Susquehanna Corp. v. Pan American Sulphur Co.[21] the Fifth Circuit held that there had not been insufficient disclosure of the offeror's possible plans to merge the target company into another company even though a hearing examiner for the SEC had previously reached a contrary conclusion in the same case, which decision was later affirmed by the Commission itself.[22] The court said:

> "The person or corporation filing a Schedule 13D statement need not necessarily walk a tortuous path. He must, of course, be precise and forthright in making full and fair disclosure as to all material facts called for by the various items of the schedule. At the same time he must be careful not to delineate extravagantly or to enlarge beyond reasonable bounds. The securities market is delicately arranged and needs only slight impetus to upset it. * * * Though the offeror has an obligation fairly to disclose its plans in the event of a takeover, it is not required to make predictions of future behavior, however tentatively phrased, which may cause the offeree or the public investor to rely on them unjustifiably. * * * Target companies must not be provided the opportunity to use the future plans provision as a tool for dilatory litigation."[23]

---

18. S.Rep. No. 550 (Committee on Banking and Currency), 90th Cong., 1st Sess., pp. 4–5 (1967).

19. Rule 10b–4, as adopted in Securities Exchange Act Release No. 8321 (SEC May 28, 1968). See Oday, The Short Tendering Rule in the Sale of Securities, 21 Clev.St.L. Rev. 78 (1972); and Securities and Exchange Commission v. Weisberger, CCH Fed.Sec.Law Rptr. ¶ 95,108 (S.D.N.Y.1975), where an injunction was granted against a "short tenderer" and the sale to him on a pro rata basis was rescinded.

20. Securities Exchange Act, §§ 13(d)(1), 14(d)(1); Schedule 4D–1, Items 2, 4 and 5.

21. 423 F.2d 1075 (5th Cir.1970).

22. In the Matter of Reports of the Susquehanna Corp., Sec.Exch.Act Rel. No. 8933 (July 17, 1970).

23. 423 F.2d at 1085–86.

And the Second Circuit in Electronic Specialty Co. v. International Controls Corp.[24] stated that: "It would be as serious an infringement of these regulations to overstate the definiteness of the plans as to understate them." [25] The court also said: "Congress intended to assure basic honesty and fair dealing, not to impose an unrealistic requirement of laboratory conditions that might make the new statute a potent tool for incumbent management to protect its own interests against the desires and welfare of the stockholders." [26]

A frequent bone of contention between the target company and a prospective tender offeror arises from the requirement that a Schedule 13D (required to be filed by any person acquiring 5% or more of the stock of a registered company) contain a statement as to the "purpose" of the acquisition of the stock and whether or not the acquirer intends to try to gain control of the company. It is not infrequently stated in such a filing that the acquisition is merely for the purpose of "investment", a disclaimer which the target company usually distrusts. In Chromalloy American Corp. v. Sun Chemical Corp.,[27] the court held that a purchaser's desire substantially to influence the policies, management and actions of the issuer amounted to a purpose to control requiring disclosure in a Schedule 13D filing. This problem should be capable of solution by proper drafting of the Schedule 13D. The offeror does not, of course, usually attempt to conceal his intention to control the target company at the time of the actual making of a tender offer and the filing of a Schedule 14D–1.

After some confusion in the cases as to whether or not financial information relating to the tender offeror was required to be disclosed in connection with a cash tender offer,[28] the SEC adopted an amendment to Regulation 14D in 1977 to deal with this question.[29] The amendment did little to alleviate this confusion since it merely provided that such financial information should be disclosed if it is "material." However, the SEC did state that the facts and circumstances determining whether such financial information is material "include, but are not limited to: (1) the terms of the tender offer, particularly those terms concerning the amount of securities being sought, such as any or all, a fixed minimum with a right to accept additional shares tendered, all or none, and a fixed percentage of the outstanding; (2) whether the purpose of the tender offer is for control of the subject company; (3) the plans or proposals of the bidder described in Item 5 of the Schedule; and (4) the ability of the bidder to pay for the securities sought in the tender offer and/or to repay any loans made to the bidder or its affiliate in connection with the tender offer or otherwise." [30]

Rule 10b–13, which was adopted in Exchange Act Release No. 8712 (Oct. 8, 1969), prohibits a tender offeror from purchasing any securities which are the subject of a tender offer "alongside the offer," i.e., purchases in private transactions or on an exchange which are not subject to all of the terms and conditions of the tender offer. Even before this rule was adopted, the Commission took the position that, where the offer was an exchange offer, any purchase

---

24. 409 F.2d 937 (2d Cir.1969).

25. 409 F.2d at 948.

26. Ibid. See, also, Seaboard World Airlines, Inc. v. Tiger International, Inc., 600 F.2d 355 (2d Cir.1979); Missouri Portland Cement Co. v. Cargill, Inc., 498 F.2d 851 (2d Cir.1974), cert. denied 419 U.S. 883 (1974).

27. 611 F.2d 240 (8th Cir.1979).

28. Corenco Corp. v. Schiavone & Sons, Inc., 362 F.Supp. 939 (S.D.N.Y.1973), aff'd

488 F.2d 207 (2d Cir.1973); Alaska Interstate Co. v. McMillian, 402 F.Supp. 532 (D.Del.1975); Copperweld Corp. v. Imetal, 403 F.Supp. 579 (W.D.Pa.1975).

29. Securities Exchange Act Release No. 5844 (July 21, 1977).

30. Ibid. See Prudent Real Estate Trust v. Johncamp Realty, Inc., 599 F.2d 1140 (2d Cir.1979).

of securities of the target company by the offeror alongside the offer violated Rule 10b–6, because it was purchasing securities "convertible" (i.e., by acceptance of the exchange offer) into its own securities during the course of a distribution of the latter. This interpretation of the Commission was upheld by the Second Circuit in the Chris-Craft case,[31] but the question of the applicability of Rule 10b–6 has been made moot by the express prohibition in Rule 10b–13.

The amendments to Regulation 14D proposed by the Securities and Exchange Commission in Exchange Act Release No. 16385 set forth above would have overruled the *Hanson Trust* case by mandating a ten day "cooling off" period following the termination of a tender offer during which the offeror would be prohibited from engaging in further market purchases. As it now exists, Rule 10b–13 only prohibits a tender offeror from purchasing stock outside of the tender offer from the time of its commencement to the time of its termination. The proposed amendments have been pending since 1979 without any further action by the SEC to adopt them, but this amendment is still under consideration by the Commission.

For discussions of tender offers and the Williams Act see: Aranow and Einhorn, Tender Offers for Corporate Control (1973); Aranow, Einhorn & Berlstein, Developments in Tender Offers for Corporate Control (1977); Lipton and Steinberger, Takeovers and Freezeouts (1978); Leebron, Games Corporations Play: A Theory of Tender Offers, 61 N.Y.U.L.Rev. 153 (1986); Fogelson, Wenig and Friedman, Changing the Takeover Game: The Securities and Exchange Commission's Proposed Amendments to the Williams Act, 17 Harv.J. Legis. 409 (1980); Volk, Practical Effects of Hart-Scott-Rodino Premerger Notification on Tactics in Tender Offers and Related Transactions, 48 ABA Antitrust L.J. 1459 (1979); Axinn, Fogg, and Stoll, Contests for Corporate Control Under the New Law of Preacquisition Notification, 24 N.Y.L.S.L.Rev. 857 (1979); Tender Offer Symposium—Part 1, 23 N.Y.L.S.L.Rev. 375 (1978); Tender Offer Symposium—Part 2, 23 N.Y.L.S.L.Rev. 553 (1978); Fischel, Efficient Capital Market Theory, the Market for Corporate Control, and the Regulation of Cash Tender Offers, 57 Tex.L.Rev. 1 (1978); Disclosure Problems in Tender Offers and Freeze Outs—A Panel, 32 Bus.Law. 1365 (1977).

WHAT IS A "TENDER OFFER"?

No attempt was made in the Williams Act to define a "tender offer", presumably on the theory that the management of a company would "know it when they saw it." Its basic meaning is unmistakable: It is a general invitation to all of the shareholders of a company to purchase their shares at a specified price, sometimes subject to a minimum and/or a maximum that the offeror will accept, communicated to the shareholders by means of newspaper advertisements and sometimes by a general mailing to the entire list of shareholders.[1] While this is the typical pattern, what about an active and

---

31. Chris-Craft Industries, Inc. v. Bangor Punta Corp., 426 F.2d 569 (2d Cir.1970), rev'd on the basis that Chris-Craft lacked standing to sue for damages for the violation of Rule 10b–6, 430 U.S. 1 (1977).

1. In the revision of the tender offer Rules in 1979, the SEC included for the first time a provision, similar to that in the Proxy Rules, requiring the target company either to furnish a list of shareholders to a tender offeror or to mail for the tender

offeror the tender offer materials at his expense. Rule 14d–5. An official of the SEC has stated, however, that this rule was very rarely invoked by tender offerors during the first year of its existence. They apparently did not consider the additional dissemination of the offer worth the cost, in view of the fact that in any event most tenders are made by arbitrageurs who purchase the shares in the market during the course of the tender offer.

widespread solicitation by telephone of public shareholders to sell their shares (a sort of "boiler room" in reverse)?[2] What about a "special bid" made on the floor of the stock exchange?[3] A "special offer" or "special bid" is a technique devised by the exchanges in an attempt to lure back some of the block trades lost to the third market. It permits the buyer to offer an extra commission to the brokers who find the other side of the market, and it must remain open for a minimum of 15 minutes.[4] What about privately negotiated purchases from a half-dozen or a dozen substantial shareholders?[5] What about ordinary, "regular way" purchases on the floor of the stock exchange?[6]

The significance of this determination lies in the fact that, while under Section 13(d) a person must in any event file a Schedule 13D once he acquires 5% or more of the stock of a company within 10 days after making such acquisition, the filing under Section 14(d) must be made simultaneously with the making of the "tender offer" and must contain additional items of information not required in Section 13(d) filing. Secondly, a holding that the transaction is a "tender offer" brings into play the requirements for the proration of purchases where more is tendered than will be accepted and for the payment of equal consideration to all those who have tendered, when the price is later raised.[7]

In Hoover Co. v. Fuqua Industries, Inc.,[8] the court stated that the list of eight "factors" formulated by the SEC and discussed by the court in the *Carter Hawley Hale* case "conveniently separates the factors which enter into the determination whether an offer is a tender offer. Of course, in any particular factual context, the various factors may be entitled to different weight in the final decision." In that case, the court held that an offer made to over one hundred members of the family of the original founder of the company was a tender offer. The court stated: "The Court does not find that the family ties give the group any characteristics that would differentiate them from the rest of the public shareholders. The family group is composed of over a hundred members, their shareholdings vary greatly in size, and the majority of them have never worked for the company. Therefore, the Court finds that although Fuqua has not solicited the shares of all the Hoover Company shareholders, the solicitation of the family members is the equivalent of a solicitation of all the public shareholders."

Other cases dealing with the determination of when there is a tender offer were summarized as follows in the *Hoover Company* case:

2. See Cattlemen's Investment Co. v. Fears, 343 F.Supp. 1248 (W.D.Okl.1972); Note, 1972 Duke L.J. 1051.

3. See SEC Sec.Exch.Act Rel. No. 8392 (Aug. 30, 1968).

4. 2 CCH N.Y.S.E. Guide ¶ 2391 (Rule 391).

5. See D–Z Investment Co. v. Holloway, CCH Fed.Sec.Law Rptr. ¶ 94,771 (S.D.N.Y. 1974); Nachman Corp. v. Halfred, CCH Fed.Sec.Law Rptr. ¶ 94,455 (N.D.Ill.1973).

6. See Gulf & Western Industries, Inc. v. The Great Atlantic & Pacific Tea Co., Inc., 356 F.Supp. 1066 (S.D.N.Y.1973), aff'd 476 F.2d 687 (2d Cir.1973); Water & Wall Associates, Inc. v. American Consumer Industries, Inc., CCH Fed.Sec.Law Rptr. ¶ 93,943 (D.N.J.1973); D–Z Investment Company v. Holloway, supra Note 5. While the offeror usually takes a full page,

or two, in the newspapers to set forth all of the disclosures contained in his SEC filings, the Second Circuit in Corenco Corporation v. Schiavone & Sons, Inc., 488 F.2d 207 (2d Cir.1973), held that the mere "announcement" of a tender offer in the Wall Street Journal (apparently in the form of a "tombstone ad") was not itself a tender offer required to contain all that detail, where any shareholder had to obtain the full text of the offer and its accompanying form in order to make a tender. Such "short form" advertisements have subsequently been expressly permitted by Rules 14d–4(a)(2), 14d–6(a)(2) and 14d–6(e)(2).

7. Securities Exchange Act, § 14(d)(6) and (7).

8. CCH Fed.Sec.Law Rptr. ¶ 97,107 (N.D.Ohio 1979).

"A number of cases have found no tender offer where the purchases were made from a small group of sophisticated investors. In Brascan Limited v. Edper Equities Limited, No. 79 Civ. 2288 (S.D.N.Y.1979) (order denying preliminary injunction), the court concluded that there was no active and widespread solicitation of public shareholders because the solicitations 'were directed to only approximately 50 of Brascan's 50,000 shareholders, each of the 50 being either an institution or a sophisticated individual holder of large blocks of Brascan shares.' Id. at 51. Curtiss-Wright was accused of making an illegal tender offer when in addition to making purchases on national exchanges, it bought Kennecott stock from about a dozen institutional shareholders. The district court found 'that the off-market purchases were made largely from sophisticated institutional shareholders,' and the appeals court affirmed the ruling that there was no tender offer. Kennecott Copper Corp. v. Curtiss-Wright Corp., 584 F.2d 1195, 1206 (2d Cir.1978). *Accord,* D–Z Investment Co. v. Holloway, [1974–75 Transfer Binder] Fed.Sec. L.Rep. (CCH) ¶ 94,771 (S.D.N.Y.1974) (no tender offer when market purchases combined with four privately negotiated transactions with highly sophisticated financial institutions). A solicitation to at most 10 shareholders who held a substantial percentage of target company stock, and who were sophisticated investors, was held not to be the widespread solicitation that is characteristic of a tender offer. Financial General Bankshares, Inc. v. Lance, 80 F.R.D. 22 (D.C.D.C.1978)".

In Wellman v. Dickinson [9] Judge Carter held that the solicitation to sell stock in a target company made to thirty large institutional holders of stock and nine individuals was a tender offer, applying the eight "factors" which are discussed in the *Carter Hawley Hale* case and which were first enunciated by the Securities and Exchange Commission. The solicitation was carried out like a military operation with thirty different representatives of the brokerage firm, each sitting with a lawyer, telephoning the solicitees at 4 p.m. New York time after the close of the New York Stock Exchange and giving them only one hour to decide whether or not to accept the offer, which was at a substantial premium over market. By this operation, the offeror acquired approximately thirty-four percent of the outstanding stock of the target company. The solicitees had been alerted earlier to expect a phone call at 4 p.m. New York time, but were not given the exact price that was going to be offered until those phone calls were made after the close of the market. Judge Carter indicated that in his opinion all of the "factors" were satisfied except one, the widespread publication of the offer to the general body of shareholders. It would not appear that the *Hanson Trust* case has overruled that decision, although the court did not approve the automatic use of these "factors."

In the proposed amendment to Regulation 14D which is printed above, the SEC was attempting to bring some certainty into this area by a definition which employs mechanical or mathematical tests to determine when a tender offer has occurred. The first branch of the proposed definition by the SEC is entirely mechanical in that it focuses solely on the quantity of stock sought, the number of persons solicited and the time period within which such solicitation occurs. There is, however, an exclusion from this definition of open market purchases (subject to the restrictions which are described in the Release). The second branch of the proposed SEC definition is more like the traditional definition of a tender offer (i.e., a premium price above market, widespread dissemination of the offer and no meaningful opportunity to negotiate the terms), but it would seem to be largely superfluous if the first branch is adopted as proposed. The widespread dissemination of the offer would certainly mean

9. 475 F.Supp. 783 (S.D.N.Y.1979).

that it is communicated to more than ten people within a period of forty-five days, and provided only that the offer is for more than 5% of the outstanding stock, it would always be caught by the first branch of the definition if it satisfies this one element of the second branch. Therefore, it would appear that the second branch of the proposed definition would only additionally catch traditional tender offers for less than 5% of the outstanding stock. Since such a tender offer is virtually unknown, the second branch of the definition does not appear to have much significance.

The transactions in the *Carter Hawley Hale* case would not have been a tender offer if the SEC's proposed definition had been in effect, since that definition contains an exception for open market purchases at the then current market price, provided that neither the person making the purchases nor the broker-dealer solicits or arranges for the solicitation of any order to sell, the broker-dealer performs only the customary functions of a broker or dealer, and the broker-dealer receives no more than the customary commission or mark-up for executing the trades. All of these conditions were present in that case. Also, it would seem, as the court held, that these open market transactions were not a tender offer under the eight-factor test set forth in the *Wellman* case. Since it could not win on either of those bases, the SEC abandoned its own definition and its own eight-factor test and tried to persuade the court to hold that a different, broader definition should be adopted or that the court should rule that any market purchases by an issuer during the pendency of a hostile takeover bid were themselves a tender offer. This the court declined to do.

See Wurczinger, Toward a Definition of Tender Offer, 19 Harv.J.Legis. 191 (1982); Einhorn, What is a "Tender Offer"? 10 Inst.Securities Reg. 245 (1979); Aranow and Einhorn, Essential Ingredients of the Cash Tender Invitation, 27 Bus.Law. 415 (1972); Note, Scope of Section 14(d): What is a Tender Offer, 34 Ohio S.L.J. 375 (1973); Note, Developing Meaning of "Tender Offer" Under the Securities Exchange Act of 1934, 86 Harv.L.Rev. 1250 (1973).

GAF CORP. v. MILSTEIN
United States Court of Appeals, Second Circuit, 1971.
453 F.2d 709.

Before KAUFMAN and MANSFIELD, CIRCUIT JUDGES, and LEVET, DISTRICT JUDGE.

KAUFMAN, CIRCUIT JUDGE. This appeal involves the interpretation of Section 13(d) of the Securities Exchange Act, hitherto a largely unnoticed provision [2] added in 1968 by the Williams Act. We write, therefore, on a relatively *tabula rasa,* despite the burgeoning field of securities law. Essentially, section 13(d) requires any person, after acquiring more than 10% (now 5% [4]) of a class of registered equity security, to send to the issuer and

2. We are aware of only four other cases which considered the section. Bath Industries, Inc. v. Blot, 305 F.Supp. 526 (E.D.Wis.1969), aff'd, 427 F.2d 97 (7th Cir. 1970); Ozark Airlines, Inc. v. Cox, 326 F.Supp. 1113 (E.D.Mo.1971); Sisak v. Wings and Wheels Express, Inc., CCH Fed. Sec.L.Rep. ¶ 92,991 (S.D.N.Y. Sept. 9, 1970); Grow Chemical Corp. v. Uran, 316 F.Supp. 891 (S.D.N.Y.1970). See generally Comment, Section 13(d) and Disclosure of Corporate Equity Ownership, 119 U.Pa.L.Rev. 853 (1971).

4. As of December 22, 1970, section 13(d)(1) was amended to require filing after the acquisition of 5%. Act of December 22, 1970, Pub.L. No. 91–567, § 1, 84 Stat. 1497, amending Securities Exchange Act § 13(d)(1), 15 U.S.C. § 78m(d)(1).

the exchanges on which the security is traded and file with the Commission the statement required by the Act. Although the section has not attracted as much comment as section 14(d), also added by the Williams Act and requiring disclosure by persons engaging in tender offers, the section has potential for marked impact on holders, sellers and purchasers of securities.

GAF Corporation filed its complaint in the United States District Court for the Southern District of New York alleging that Morris Milstein, his two sons, Seymour and Paul, and his daughter, Gloria Milstein Flanzer, violated section 13(d) of the Securities Exchange Act first by failing to file the required statements and then by filing false ones. The complaint also alleged violation of section 10(b) based on the same false statements and, in addition, market manipulation of GAF stock. The Milsteins moved for dismissal under Rule 12(b)(6), F.R.Civ.P., on the ground that the complaint failed to state a claim on which relief could be granted or, in the alternative, for summary judgment under Rule 56. Judge Pollack aptly framed the issues involved:

> The ultimate issue presented by the defendants' motion to dismiss the first count is whether, organizing a group of stockholders owning more than 10% of a class of equity securities with a view to seeking control is, without more, a reportable event under Section 13(d) of the Exchange Act; and as to the second count, whether in the absence of a connected purchase or sale of securities, the target corporation claiming violation of Section 10 and Rule 10b(5), has standing to seek an injunction against a control contestant for falsity in a Schedule 13D filing. (Footnote omitted.)

324 F.Supp. 1062, 1064–1065 (S.D.N.Y.1971). Judge Pollack granted the Milsteins' motion to dismiss under Rule 12(b)(6), and GAF has appealed. We disagree with Judge Pollack's determination that GAF failed to state a claim under section 13(d) and Rule 13d–1 promulgated thereunder, and thus reverse his order in this respect, but we affirm the dismissal of the second claim of the complaint on the ground that GAF, as an issuer, has no standing under section 10(b).

Before considering the merits of the issues involved on appeal, a statement of the facts as presented in the complaint and the briefs is in order. We note also that in this posture of the proceeding we must accept as true all well pleaded allegations in the complaint.

The four Milsteins received 324,166 shares of GAF convertible preferred stock, approximately 10.25% of the preferred shares outstanding, when The Ruberoid Company, in which they had substantial holdings, was merged into GAF in May, 1967. They have not acquired any additional preferred shares since the merger.

The complaint informs us that at some time after July 29, 1968, the effective date of the Williams Act, the Milsteins "formed a conspiracy among themselves and other persons to act as a syndicate or group for the purpose of acquiring, holding, or disposing of securities of GAF with the ultimate aim of seizing control of GAF for their own personal and private purposes." It is necessary for our purposes to examine only a few of the nine overt acts GAF alleged were taken in furtherance of this conspiracy.

The complaint alleged that initially the Milsteins sought senior management and board positions for Seymour Milstein with GAF. When this sinecure was not forthcoming, the Milsteins allegedly caused Circle Floor Co., Inc., a company in their control, to reduce its otherwise substantial purchases from GAF. It also charged that the Milsteins thereafter undertook a concerted effort to disparage its management and depress the price of GAF common and preferred stock in order to facilitate the acquisition of additional shares. On May 27, 1970, the Milsteins filed a derivative action in the district court, charging the directors, *inter alia*, with waste and spoliation of corporation assets. A companion action was filed in the New York courts. GAF further alleged that these actions were filed only to disparage management, to depress the price of GAF stock and to use discovery devices to gain valuable information for their takeover conspiracy.

In the meantime, the complaint tells us, Paul and Seymour Milstein purchased respectively 62,000 and 64,000 shares of GAF common stock. When GAF contended that the Milsteins were in violation of section 13(d) because they had not filed a Schedule 13D as required by Rule 13d–1, the Milsteins, although disclaiming any legal obligation under section 13(d), filed such a schedule on September 24, 1970. In their 13D statement (appended to the complaint), the Milsteins disclosed their preferred and common holdings and stated they "at some future time [might] determine to attempt to acquire control of GAF. * * *" They also stated that they had "no present intention as to whether or not any additional securities of GAF [might] be acquired by them in the future. * * *" Indeed, within the next two months, commencing with October 2, Paul and Seymour each purchased an additional 41,650 shares of common. The Milsteins thereafter filed a Restated and Amended Schedule 13D on November 10 to reflect these new purchases.

Then, on January 27, 1971, the Milsteins filed a third Schedule 13D, disclosing their intention to wage a proxy contest at the 1971 annual meeting. Although the statement again disclaimed any present intention to acquire additional shares, Paul purchased 28,300 shares of common stock during February, 1971. These last purchases, which brought the Milsteins' total common holdings to 237,600 shares having a value in excess of $2 million and constituting 1.7% of the common shares outstanding, were reflected in a February 23 amendment to the January 27, Schedule 13D.

The last essential datum for our purposes is the proxy contest. On May 10, 1971, it was announced that GAF management had prevailed at the April 16 meeting by a margin of some 2 to 1.

GAF's complaint in this action filed on December 16, 1970, requested that the Milsteins be preliminarily and permanently enjoined from (1) acquiring or attempting to acquire additional GAF stock; (2) soliciting any proxy from a GAF shareholder to vote GAF stock; (3) voting any shares of GAF stock held or acquired during the conspiracy; and (4) otherwise acting in furtherance of the conspiracy. It asks for this relief "until the effects of the conspiracy have been fully dissipated and the unlawful acts committed pursuant to the conspiracy fully corrected. * * *"

I.

At the time the conspiracy allegedly was formed, section 13(d)(1) in relevant part provided:

Any person who, after acquiring directly or indirectly the beneficial ownership of any equity security of a class which is registered pursuant to section 12 of this title * * *, is directly or indirectly the beneficial owner of more than 10 per centum of such class shall, within ten days after such acquisition, send to the issuer of the security at its principal executive office, by registered or certified mail, send to each exchange where the security is traded, and file with the Commission, a statement. * * *

This section, however, exempts from its filing requirements any acquisition which, "together with all other acquisitions by the same person of securities of the same class during the preceding twelve months, does not exceed 2 per centum of that class." Section 13(d)(6)(B). Section 13(d)(3), which is crucial to GAF's claim, further provides that "[w]hen two or more persons act as a partnership, limited partnership, syndicate, or other group for the purpose of acquiring, holding, or disposing of securities of an issue, such syndicate or group shall be deemed a 'person' for the purposes of [section 13(d)]." On the assumption that the facts alleged in the complaint are true, we cannot conclude other than that the four Milsteins constituted a "group" and thus, as a "person," were subject to the provisions of section 13(d). We also are aware of the charge that the Milsteins agreed after July 29, 1968, to hold their GAF preferred shares for the common purpose of acquiring control of GAF. Furthermore, the individuals collectively or as a "group" held more than 10% of the outstanding preferred shares—a registered class of securities. Since the section requires a "person" to file only if he acquires more than 2% of the class of stock in a 12–month period after July 29, 1968,[12] the principal question presented to us is whether the complaint alleges as a matter of law that the Milstein *group* "acquired" the 324,166 shares of preferred stock owned by its members after that date. We conclude that it does and thus that it states a claim under section 13(d).

The statute refers to "acquiring directly or indirectly the beneficial ownership of securities." Thus, at the outset, we are not confronted with the relatively simple concept of legal title, but rather with the amorphous and occasionally obfuscated concepts of indirect and beneficial ownership which pervade the securities acts.

The Act nowhere explicitly defines the concept of "acquisition" as used in section 13(d). Although we are aware of Learned Hand's warning "not to make a fortress out of the dictionary," Cabell v. Markham, 148 F.2d 737, 739 (2d Cir.), aff'd 326 U.S. 404 (1945), some light, although dim, is shed by Webster's Third International Dictionary. It tells us that "to acquire" means "to come into possession [or] control." If the allegations in the complaint are true, then the group, which must be treated as an entity separate and distinct from its members, could have gained "beneficial control" of the voting rights of the preferred stock[13] only after its formation, which we must assume occurred after the effective date of the Williams Act. Manifestly, according to the complaint, the group when

---

12. The Milsteins concede that their group would have been required to file if the individual members had acquired additional preferred shares after the effective date of the Williams Act and within a 12–month period which amounted to more than 2% of the outstanding shares.

13. The convertible preferred stock votes share-for-share with the common stock. Each share of preferred is convertible into 1.25 shares of common stock.

formed acquired a beneficial interest in the individual holdings of its members. We find ourselves in agreement with the statement of the Court of Appeals for the Seventh Circuit in Bath Industries, Inc. v. Blot, 427 F.2d 97, 112 (7th Cir.1970), that in the context of the Williams Act, where the principal concern is focused on the battle for corporate control, "voting control of stock is the only relevant element of beneficial ownership." Thus, we hardly can agree with Judge Pollack that the language of the statute compels the conclusion that individual members must acquire shares before the group can be required to file.

We are well aware of the first catechism of statutory construction which teaches that we should begin the process of interpretation with "the language of the statute itself," see Jones v. Alfred H. Mayer Co., 392 U.S. 409, 420 (1968); that, however, is *toto caelo* from saying that the process must end there or that we are required to blind ourselves to other relevant aids to construction, particularly when dealing with a statute as complex as the one before us. The wisdom of Learned Hand guides us again: "it is one of the surest indexes of a mature and developed jurisprudence * * * to remember that statutes always have some purpose or object to accomplish, whose sympathetic and imaginative discovery is the surest guide to their meaning." Cabell v. Markham, supra, 148 F.2d at 739. See also United States v. Dickerson, 310 U.S. 554, 562 (1940). We are, therefore, totally puzzled by the experienced trial judge's conclusion that "the legislative reports should not be resorted to here since the specific statutory language is clear. * * *" 324 F.Supp. at 1067. Indeed, the statute before us is anything but a model of clarity [14] and the ritualistic approach to statutory interpretation which the district judge suggests would close off the only light available to illumine the statute.

The legislative history, as well as the purpose behind section 13(d), bear out our interpretation. Any residual doubt over its soundness is obviated by the following clear statement appearing in both the House and Senate reports accompanying the Williams Act:

"[Section 13(d)(3)] would prevent a group of persons who seek to pool their voting or other interests in the securities of any issuer from evading the provisions of the statute because no one individual owns more than 10 per cent of the securities. *The group would be deemed to have become the beneficial owner, directly or indirectly, of more than 10 percent of a class of securities at the time they agreed to act in concert. Consequently, the group would be required to file the information called for in section 13(d)(1) within 10 days after they agree to act together, whether or not any member of the group had acquired any securities at that time.*" S.Rep. No. 550, 90th Cong., 1st Sess. 8 (1967); H.R.Rep. No. 1711, 90th Cong., 2d Sess. 8–9 (1968), U.S.Code Cong. & Admin.News p. 2818 (Emphasis added.)

Indeed, Professor Loss, one of the foremost scholars of securities law, reached the same interpretation in his treatise, citing this passage. 6 L. Loss, Securities Regulation 3664 (Supp.1969).

---

14. The meaning of "acquiring" hardly could be considered plain when two district court judges recently failed to agree on whether an inheritance of stock was an "acquisition." Compare Sisak v. Wings and Wheels Express, Inc., CCH Fed.Sec.L. Rep. ¶ 92,991 (S.D.N.Y. Sept. 9, 1970), with Ozark Airlines, Inc. v. Cox, 326 F.Supp. 1113 (E.D.Mo.1971).

The Senate and House reports and the Act as finally enacted, contrary to appellees' contention,[15] are entirely consistent in our view. This conclusion is buttressed by a consideration of the purpose of the Act. The 1960's on Wall Street may best be remembered for the pyrotechnics of corporate takeovers and the phenomenon of conglomeration. Although individuals seeking control through a proxy contest were required to comply with section 14(a) of the Securities Exchange Act and the proxy rules promulgated by the SEC, and those making stock tender offers were required to comply with the applicable provisions of the Securities Act, before the enactment of the Williams Act there were no provisions regulating cash tender offers or other techniques of securing corporate control. According to the committee reports:

> "The [Williams Act] would correct the current gap in our securities laws by amending the Securities Exchange Act of 1934 to provide for full disclosure in connection with cash tender offers and other techniques for accumulating large blocks of equity securities of publicly held companies." S.Rep. No. 550 at 4; H.R.Rep. No. 1711 at 4, U.S.Code Cong. & Admin.News p. 2814.

Specifically, we were told, "the purpose of section 13(d) is to require disclosure of information by persons who have acquired a substantial interest, or increased their interest in the equity securities of a company by a substantial amount, within a relatively short period of time." S.Rep. No. 550 at 7; H.R.Rep. No. 1711 at 8 U.S.Code Cong. & Admin.News p. 2818. Otherwise, investors cannot assess the potential for changes in corporate control and adequately evaluate the company's worth. See generally Comment, Section 13(d) and Disclosure of Corporate Equity Ownership, 119 U.Pa.L.Rev. 853, 854–55, 858, 865–66 (1971).

That the purpose of section 13(d) is to alert the marketplace to every large, rapid aggregation or accumulation of securities, regardless of technique employed, which might represent a potential shift in corporate control is amply reflected in the enacted provisions. Section 13(d)(1)(C) requires the person filing to disclose any intention to acquire control. If he has such an intention, he must disclose any plans for liquidating the issuer, selling its assets, merging it with another company or changing substantially its business or corporate structure. It is of some interest, moreover, that section 13(d)(6)(D) empowers the Commission to exempt from the filing requirements "any acquisition * * * as not entered into for the purpose of, and not having the effect of, changing or influencing the control of the issuer *or otherwise* as not comprehended within the purpose of [section 13(d)]." (Emphasis added.)

The alleged conspiracy on the part of the Milsteins is one clearly intended to be encompassed within the reach of section 13(d). We have before us four shareholders who together own 10.25% of an outstanding class of securities and allegedly agreed to pool their holdings to effect a takeover of GAF. This certainly posed as great a threat to the stability of the corporate structure as the individual shareholder who buys 10.25% of the equity security in one transaction. A shift in the *loci* of corporate

---

15. Appellees in their brief "concede" that the 1968 committee reports are "against" them. Professor Loss, co-counsel for the Milsteins both in this and the lower court, informed us at the argument that the view set forth in his treatise was "a mistake" and that this passage is "diametrically opposed to the text of the statute" and the purpose and intent of the Williams Act.

power and influence is hardly dependent on an actual transfer of legal title to shares, and the statute and history are clear on this.

In light of the statutory purpose as we view it, we find ourselves in disagreement with the interpretation of *Bath Industries,* supra, that the group owning more than 10%, despite its agreement to seize control, in addition, must agree to acquire more shares before the filing requirement of section 13(d) is triggered. The history and language of section 13(d) make it clear that the statute was primarily concerned with disclosure of *potential changes* in control resulting from new aggregations of stockholdings and was not intended to be restricted to only individual stockholders who made future purchases and whose actions were, therefore, more apparent.[18] See Comment, Section 13(d) and Disclosure of Corporate Equity Ownership, 119 U.Pa.L.Rev. 853, 869–72 (1971). It hardly can be questioned that a group holding sufficient shares can effect a takeover without purchasing a single additional share of stock.

Two "policy" considerations have been advanced against our interpretation. First, the district judge warned that "[t]he inherent difficulty of ascertaining when a group was formed is akin to an attempt to grasp quicksilver." 324 F.Supp. at 1068. This supposed difficulty, however, would not be dissipated even under his view—that individual members must acquire more than 2% after July 29, 1968, before the group can be compelled to file. The court still would be required to determine whether the individuals indeed constituted a "group." But, we hardly envision this as an insuperable obstacle to stating a claim in a complaint. GAF, in order to succeed on the merits, will have to carry its burden of proof by a fair preponderance of the evidence. It will have to produce evidence establishing that the conspiracy came into being after July 29, 1968, with the purpose of seizing control. If GAF should succeed on the merits, any difficulty in pinpointing the precise date, as distinguished from an approximate time, when the conspiracy was formed and the group became subject to section 13(d) can be one of the elements considered by the district judge in fashioning appropriate equitable relief.

The Milsteins also caution us against throwing our hook into the water and catching too many fish—namely, hundreds of families and other management groups which control companies with registered securities and whose members collectively own more than 5% of a class of the company's stock. Although this problem is not part of the narrow issue we must decide, we cannot close our eyes to the implications of our decision. Upon examination, however, the argument while superficially appealing proves to be totally without substance. Management groups *per se* are not customarily formed for the purpose of "acquiring, holding, or disposing of securities of [the] issuer" and would not be required to file unless the members conspired to pool their securities interests for one of the stated purposes.[20]

---

18. Section 13(d)(3) refers to groups formed "for the purpose of acquiring, holding, *or* disposing of securities." Bath Industries would read out "holding" and "disposing."

20. The more difficult question, and a question we need not decide on this appeal, is whether management groups which expressly agree to pool their interests to fight a potential takeover are subject to section 13(d). Nor do we intimate any view on whether an insurgent group which has filed under section 13(d) and subsequently is successful in its takeover bid remains subject to the section. In any event, as we have already indicated, the Commission can forestall any untoward effects under

It is not sufficient that we merely conclude that the allegations of the complaint state a violation of section 13(d). We also must determine whether GAF has standing to assert those violations. Here, unlike in our prior discussion we write with the aid of substantial precedent.

The Milsteins do not contend, with good reason, that there is no private right of action under section 13(d). The teachings of J.I. Case Co. v. Borak, 377 U.S. 426 (1964), are part of the ABC's of securities law. Nor do the Milsteins challenge the standing of GAF as an issuer.[21]

* * *

III.

The more difficult question is whether GAF has standing under section 13(d) to seek an injunction against allegedly false and misleading filings. The Milsteins in their brief argue that "the short answer" is that false filing does not violate the section that requires the filing—i.e., section 13(d)—but rather the penal provision on false filings, section 32(a), or one of the antifraud provisions, for example, section 10(b). This response, deceptively pleasing in its simple, compartmental approach to the Securities Exchange Act, immediately brings to mind the Supreme Court's instruction that the securities acts should not be construed technically and restrictively, but "flexibly to effectuate [their] remedial purposes." S.E.C. v. Capital Gains Research Bureau, Inc., 375 U.S. 180, 195 (1963). With this teaching in mind, we conclude that the obligation to file *truthful* statements is implicit in the obligation to file with the issuer, and *a fortiori,* the issuer has standing under section 13(d) to seek relief in the event of a false filing.

The Williams Act was entitled "An Act Providing for full disclosure of corporate equity ownership of securities under the Securities Exchange Act of 1934." In particular, section 13(d) was intended to alert investors to potential changes in corporate control so that they could properly evaluate the company in which they had invested or were investing. Disclosure which is false or misleading subverts this purpose. In some instances, a false filing may be more detrimental to the informed operation of the securities markets than no filing at all. We also find support for our conclusion in section 13(d)(2) which places a continuing obligation on the person filing to amend his statements "[i]f any material change occurs in the facts set forth." Indeed, it is an argument not without force to urge that false statements immediately place those required to file in violation of Rule 13d–2 which requires "prompt" amendment.[23]

* * *

In reversing that part of Judge Pollack's order which dismissed Claim I of GAF's complaint on the ground that it failed to state a claim on which relief could be granted, we emphasize that we are not yet called upon to

the exemptive power conferred upon it by section 13(d)(6)(D).

21. Clearly, a shareholder has standing. See Grow Chemical Corp. v. Uran, 316 F.Supp. 891 (S.D.N.Y.1970).

23. GAF informs us that the Milsteins' first Schedule 13D, dated September 24, 1970, was false because it disclaimed any present intention to acquire additional stock, whereas Paul and Seymour Milstein purchased 83,800 shares of GAF common stock within the next two months. The Milsteins, however, did not amend their Schedule 13D until after these purchases were completed. Thus, even assuming that the statement filed on September 24 accurately and truthfully reflected their intentions, clearly those intentions changed when the Milsteins decided to make the additional purchases and before those purchases were actually completed.

determine whether the Milsteins have in fact violated section 13(d), or, if they have, what relief would be appropriate. That part of Judge Pollack's order dismissing Claim II of the complaint under section 10(b) is affirmed. Costs to the appellant.

"GROUP" LEGAL THERAPY

When the Williams Act was being considered by Congress, a number of academic witnesses before the Congressional Committees expressed the fear that the bill might have the result of protecting entrenched, inefficient managements of corporations from any challenge to their control. There can be no doubt that the original motive force behind the introduction of the bills which eventually resulted in the Williams Act was the panic experienced by the business "establishment" as a result of the takeover or threatened takeover of major corporations by brash young "conglomerators," particularly the attempted takeover of Chemical Bank by Leasco (which recalled the old saw about the flea on the elephant's back with rape in its mind) and the rumour (which turned out to be false) that a French syndicate was trying to acquire control of American Broadcasting Company (this was at the time that Le Grand Charles was threatening to "liberate" Quebec and Louisiana).

However, as the provisions of the Williams Act were modified to meet certain of the objections of the academic critics, they did not seem to give any particular advantage to management in a takeover battle, and the initial decisions under the Act seemed to support this conclusion.[1] During the first few years after the enactment of the statute the number of such attempts declined drastically due to general market conditions and in particular the market performance of the stock of conglomerates, which had theretofore been the most avid practitioners of the art.[2] Thereafter, the even more drastic decline in market values, with many sound companies selling at aggregate market values far below their book values and in some cases not much in excess of their cash in the bank, revived the phenomenon. When certain companies, particularly the oil companies, began accumulating so much cash that they had trouble finding anything to do with it (other than distributing it to the shareholders—which, of course, is unthinkable), the tender offer became an established part of the American scene. While some of these tender offers had been stymied by litigation under the Williams Act and under the state takeover statutes (until the SEC eliminated the latter roadblock), it appeared that the only way a determined takeover bidder could be surely defeated was by the target company finding a "white knight" who offered more in cash than the original bidder (which in the jargon of the trade is a "show stopper", although it obviously does not preserve the independence of the target company). More sophisticated techniques have recently been developed, see pages 785–803, below, to attempt to fend off unwanted takeover bids, which may be more successful; although once a corporation has been "put in play" (as the saying goes) it rarely has been able to preserve its independence.

A little noticed provision of the Williams Act, designed merely to "round out" the legislation, seemed, however, to result for a time in the worst fears of

---

1. See Susquehanna Corp. v. Pan American Sulphur Co. and Electronic Specialty Co. v. International Controls Corp., discussed supra at pp. 688–89.

2. See Symposium, Conglomerates and Other Modern Merger Movements, 25 Bus. Law. 555–881 (1970), for a discussion of the legal attacks mounted against conglomerates from every point of the compass, until the market did the job for their opponents.

the original critics being realized. Section 13(d) of the 1934 Act as originally added by the Williams Act was designed to require that a person acquiring more than 10% (or if already a 10% holder increasing his holdings) of a registered equity security otherwise than by a tender offer (i.e., by open market purchases or in private transactions) file, within ten days after such acquisition, essentially the same information as that required of a tender offeror. Since such a person was already required to file a Form 3 or Form 4 under Section 16(a), this merely required an earlier filing and additional disclosure. Furthermore, there is an exemption in Section 13(d)(6)(B) for acquisitions during any 12 months' period of two percent or less of the class, so that this additional filing requirement was triggered only by a major purchase or purchasing campaign. Even when the 10% figure was reduced to 5% by amendment in 1970, when a similar reduction was made in the tender offer section, the 2% exemption was retained in Section 13(d), although the SEC has attempted to abolish it by regulation.[3] Nevertheless, there did not seem to be any serious danger that anyone would inadvertently violate this section or that it would give any particular advantage to management.

However, this line of reasoning overlooked the definition of the word "person" in Section 13(d)(3), which has turned out to be the most important provision in the section. That definition, which is quoted in the *GAF Corporation* case, states that when two or more persons act as a "group" for the purpose of "acquiring, holding, or disposing" of securities, then the group shall be deemed a "person" for the purposes of Section 13(d). This raises a number of questions.

What is a "group?" Obviously, under the terms of the statute, any two or more persons *may* be a "group," subject only to the requirement that they form some common "purpose." Even a father and his children sitting around the dinner table, as in the *GAF Corporation* case, may be a group.

What is the proscribed "purpose?" Basically, both the *GAF Corporation* case and the *Bath Industries* case [4] (which is discussed in that opinion) say that the illegitimate purpose is that of ousting the present management, although the *Bath Industries* case requires that in addition the group must have the purpose of acquiring additional securities. It is not entirely clear from that opinion whether the court means *any* additional securities, or only securities during any 12 months' period in excess of the 2% exemption, although Judge Pollack in the lower court opinion in the *GAF Corporation* case interpreted *Bath Industries* as meaning the latter.[5]

When is the filing requirement triggered? Both the *GAF Corporation* case and the *Bath Industries* case say that the "formation" of the group requires a filing within 10 days thereafter. Bath Industries recognizes that it will be difficult to prove whether at that time the group intended to acquire additional securities, but says that any subsequent acquisition will raise a presumption that they did and make the group retroactively illegal if they haven't filed.

---

3. Rule 13d–2(a).

4. Bath Industries, Inc. v. Blot, 427 F.2d 97 (7th Cir.1970).

5. GAF Corp. v. Milstein, 324 F.Supp. 1062 (S.D.N.Y.1971). There may in fact be a "group" where there is no purpose at all, or at least none that any of the members would recognize. For example, the staff of the Commission takes the position that whenever two or more persons participate as buyers in the same private placement, they are automatically a "group" since they have combined "for the purpose of acquiring," even though they may have never met one another. Whether, and how, they can thereafter dissolve the group, or whether "once a group, always a group," is unclear. The answer to this question may depend in part on the terms of the purchase agreement.

What are the consequences of a failure to file? The court in *GAF Corporation* was not called upon to discuss the question of remedies, since that was an appeal from a dismissal of the action, but the court in *Bath Industries* enjoined the holders of "nearly 50%" of the stock of the corporation from voting that stock to oust the existing management, thus handing over the legal control of the corporation from its owners to its managers. This was done without any evidence that anyone was injured or misled by the failure to file, and the court does not clearly say when, if ever, the confiscated right of control will be returned to the owners.[6]

It is evident that if these decisions had represented the law, the exemption in the Proxy Rules for the solicitation of not to exceed ten persons by someone other than the management,[7] which was included for the express purpose of permitting a "group" to be formed in order for a proxy contest to get off the ground, was effectively destroyed. It is almost inevitable that at least two shareholders will have talked to each other about ousting the existing management more than ten days before they consult a lawyer. They might then be told that if their combined holdings exceeded 5% they were probably defeated before they could start. The case of Rondeau v. Mosinee Paper Corp.,[8] which is set forth and discussed below in chapter 20, may, however, have established a different trend.[9]

In Wellman v. Dickinson,[10] the Second Circuit held that when five target company shareholders reached an understanding to dispose of their stock in an effort to aid a third party acquisition of the target company, they were a "group" under Section 13 of the Exchange Act, thereby triggering the requirement that a Schedule 13D be filed. The court held, however, that the premium received by a director, major stockholder and former CEO of the target company when he sold his stock was not a result of the failure to file the Schedule 13D and therefore could not be recovered from him in a class action on behalf of the target company shareholders. The court stated that his position as a director "placed him under no fiduciary duty to reveal to the company's management his intention to use his Becton holdings to effectuate a third party takeover of the company, * * * or to refrain from promoting a takeover by a third party. Dickinson [the director] also had no fiduciary obligation to other Becton stockholders to refuse the premium offered by Sun [the takeover bidder] or to advise them that he was receiving a premium." [11]

---

6. The court states in a footnote that the preliminary injunction will preserve the status quo "until it is finally determined *whether defendants should be disenfranchised from voting all or any part of the stock which they now hold,* some of which they held prior to the alleged violation." 427 F.2d 97, at 113–14, n. 8 (7th Cir. 1970) (italics added).

7. Rule 14a–2(a). On the other hand, Judge Lacey held in Scott v. Multi-Amp Corp., 386 F.Supp. 44 (D.N.J.1974), that a *management* "group" is not required to file under Section 13(d). Does it depend on whether you are a "good group" or a "bad group"?

8. 422 U.S. 49 (1975).

9. See Dan River, Inc. v. Icahn, 701 F.2d 278 (4th Cir.1983). Compare, however, Securities and Exchange Commission v.

Savoy Industries, Inc., 587 F.2d 1149 (D.C. Cir.1978) cert. denied 440 U.S. 913 (1979).

10. 682 F.2d 355 (2d Cir.1982), cert. denied Dickinson v. SEC, 460 U.S. 1069 (1983).

11. In Portsmouth Square, Inc. v. Shareholders Protective Committee, 770 F.2d 866 (9th Cir.1985), the court held that a committee of shareholders who solicited funds from other shareholders by the assignment of dividends, in order to institute litigation to challenge the issuance of corporate stock which had effected a change in control of the corporation, were not a "group" under Section 13 of the 1934 Act. The court stated that their agreement to act together "invoked neither voting power nor investment power. * * * At most, they have agreed to act as a group to raise funds for litigation, and solicited corporate

CARDIFF ACQUISITIONS, INC. v. HATCH

United States Court of Appeals, Eighth Circuit, 1984.
751 F.2d 906.

Before LAY, CHIEF JUDGE, and HEANEY and FAGG, CIRCUIT JUDGES.

HEANEY, CIRCUIT JUDGE.

Cardiff Acquisitions, Inc., and Cardiff Equities Corporation (Cardiff) appeal from a district court order dismissing Cardiff's complaint requesting preliminary and permanent injunctive relief preventing the Commissioner of Commerce, the Attorney General, and the Conwed Corporation from enforcing the Minnesota Corporate Take-Overs Act, 1984 Minn.Laws ch. 488, to be codified as Minn.Stat.Ann. chs. 80B and 302A. The district court held that the Act does not violate either the commerce or the supremacy clause of the United States Constitution. It reasoned that the Minnesota Take-Overs Act does not directly regulate interstate commerce, because "its scope is limited to Minnesota shareholders of companies that have a substantial nexus with the state [and] Minnesota claims no right under the statute to suspend the effect of a tender offer with regard to shareholders outside of Minnesota." Cardiff Acquisitions, Inc. v. Hatch, 597 F.Supp. 1493, at 1497 (D.Minn.1984).

The district court recognized that the statute has indirect effects on interstate commerce, but it determined that these effects were outweighed by the state's legitimate interest in protecting local investors. Id. at 1497–1498.

The district court also held that the take-over statute does not violate the supremacy clause of the United States Constitution. It reasoned that Section 28(a) of the Securities Exchange Act of 1934 specifically permits states to enact tender offer legislation consistent with the Williams Act, 15 U.S.C. §§ 78m(d)–(e) and 78n(d)–(f) (1982). * * *

We affirm in part the district court's decision that the Minnesota Act is not facially unconstitutional because we believe the Act may be narrowly construed in a manner which 1) is substantially consistent with the Williams Act; 2) is not unduly burdensome to interstate commerce; and 3) serves the state's legitimate interest in protecting local investors. We agree that Minnesota may require disclosures in addition to those required under the Williams Act before a tender offer becomes effective within the state so long as the disclosures are purely factual and not judgmental in nature, are not inconsistent with the Williams Act and are not unduly burdensome to interstate commerce. Applying these tests, we approve, in part, the additional disclosures required by the Commissioner.

I. FACIAL CONSTITUTIONALITY OF MINNESOTA TAKE–OVERS ACT.

A. Commerce Clause.

In Edgar v. MITE Corp., 457 U.S. 624 (1982), the Supreme Court held that the Illinois Business Takeover Act, Ill.Rev.Stat. ch. 121½, ¶ 137.51–.70

dividends from other shareholders to finance the litigation. But beneficial ownership *does not* include the right to receive dividends. Indeed, the SEC squarely re- jected a proposed rule that would have defined 'beneficial owner' as one with a right to receive or direct the receipt of dividends or sale proceeds."

(1979), is unconstitutional under the commerce clause of the federal Constitution, Art. I, § 8, cl. 3. Justice White's five-part opinion considered MITE's challenges to the Illinois Act under the supremacy clause and direct and indirect commerce clause tests, but a majority only adopted Part V–B.[1] Part V–B holds that the Illinois Act violates the commerce clause under the accepted standard set forth in Pike v. Bruce Church, Inc., 397 U.S. 137, 142 (1970), because the indirect burdens on interstate commerce were excessive in relation to the putative local benefits. Justice White's opinion indicated that several provisions of the Illinois Act were particularly burdensome to interstate commerce; Part V–B, however, relied principally on the provisions of the Act which authorized the Secretary of State to suspend a tender offer even where none of the target corporation's shareholders were Illinois residents:

> While protecting local investors is plainly a legitimate state objective, the State has no legitimate interest in protecting nonresident shareholders. Insofar as the Illinois law burdens out-of-state transactions, there is nothing to be weighed in the balance to sustain the law.

Id., 457 U.S. at 644.

Justice Powell provided the vote necessary to obtain a majority with the reservation, "I join Part V–B because its Commerce Clause reasoning leaves some room for state regulation of tender offers." Id., 457 U.S. at 646.

The Minnesota Act is materially different in scope and application from the Illinois Act at issue in MITE. The Minnesota Act was revised in 1984, in light of MITE and its progeny, to reduce its burden on interstate commerce and to tighten its relation to the state's legitimate interest in protecting resident investors. MITE is distinguishable because none of the provisions of the Illinois Act[2] which the Court indicated were significant burdens on interstate commerce are present in the Minnesota Act.

1. Under the Illinois Act, a tender offeror must notify the Secretary of State and the target company of its intent to make a tender offer and the material terms of the offer twenty business days before the offer becomes effective. Ill.Rev.Stat., ch. 121½, ¶ 137.54.E (1979). During that time, the offeror may not communicate its offer to the shareholder. Meanwhile, the target company is free to disseminate information to its shareholders concerning the pending offer.

By contrast, the Minnesota Act does not provide for a precommencement filing period, and provides that the target corporation may not disseminate information to or solicit shares from its Minnesota sharehold-

---

1. Parts I and II state the facts and dispose of a mootness claim. Parts III and IV reason that the Illinois Act violates the supremacy clause because it is substantially inconsistent with the William Act. Three justices concurred in that analysis, two disagreed with it, and four did not reach the issue. Part V–A reasoned that the Illinois Act was unconstitutional as a direct regulation of interstate commerce. Four justices concurred in that analysis. Five justices agreed only on Part V–B, discussed above; with Parts I and II, it forms the opinion of the Court.

2. The commerce clause holding in National City Lines v. LLC Corp., 687 F.2d 1122, 1128 (8th Cir.1982), is also distinguishable on this basis because our holding was based on the lack of any significant distinctions between the Illinois Act considered in MITE and the Missouri Act at issue.

ers while the offer is suspended in Minnesota. 1984 Minn.Sess.Law Serv., ch. 488, § 80B.05(4) (West).

2. The Illinois Act permitted the Secretary of State to convene a hearing regarding the tender offer at any time prior to its commencement and provided that the offer could not proceed until the hearing is completed. Ill.Rev.Stat., ch. 121½, ¶ 137.57.A and B (1979). The Illinois Act required the Secretary of State to call a hearing if requested to do so by a majority of the target company's outside directors or by Illinois shareholders who own at least ten percent of the class of securities subject to the offer. ¶ 137.57.A. This provided target management with a delay period, requestable at will, during which it could oppose the takeover or mount its own tender offer. Additionally, there is no deadline for completion of the hearing and although the Secretary is required to render a decision within fifteen days, that period may be extended without limitation. ¶ 137.57.C and D.

The Minnesota Act contains no similar provisions. An offer becomes effective when the offeror files with the commissioner a registration statement disclosing the information prescribed in section 80B.03(2) & (6).[3] The Commissioner may suspend the tender offer in Minnesota within three days if the registration materials fail to apprise local investors fairly of the information required by 80B.03(2) & (6). 1984 Minn.Sess.Law Serv., ch. 488, § 80B.03(4a) (West). The suspension may be lifted once the offeror discloses the information specified in section 80B.03(2) & (6). A hearing on the suspension must be convened within ten days and a decision rendered within three days. 1984 Minn.Sess.Law Serv., ch. 488, § 80B.03(5) (West). The Minnesota Act does not contain a provision like the one in the Illinois Act which required the Commissioner to convene a hearing at the request of the target corporation. In sum, there is no delay under the Minnesota Act as there was under the Illinois Act because the Commissioner must complete the process within nineteen *calendar* days, 1984 Minn.Sess.Law Serv., ch. 488, § 80B.03(5) (West), which is prior to the expiration of the twenty *business*-day minimum offering period specified by federal law and the fifteen *business*-day period for withdrawal rights. Rules 14d–7 and 14e–1 (1984).

Cardiff argues that hearings on the suspension of the offer may be unreasonably delayed because section 80B.03(5) provides that the "commissioner may prescribe different time limits than those specified in this subdivision by rule or order." The Commissioner has not done so, however, and in this case and in Edudata Corp. v. Scientific Computers, Inc., 746 F.2d 429 (8th Cir.1984)—the only other case in which chapter 80B has been applied—the Commissioner has offered to advance the hearing date. Section 80B.03(5) does not specify that the deadlines may be extended, rather it says that different time periods may be provided. This might contemplate expedited hearings as the Commissioner offered here and in *Edudata*. In this case, review in this Court will be completed within or shortly after the twenty business day deadline under the Williams Act. Additionally, in

---

3. This scheme is substantially similar to that set forth in SEC regulations promulgated in 1980. Regulation 14d–2(b), 17 C.F.R. § 240.14d–2(b) (1984), requires that an offeror make its offer effective by disseminating specified information to shareholders and filing appropriate documents with the SEC within five days of its commencement or else withdraw it. This provision postdated the *MITE* tender offer and was not considered by the Court. 457 U.S. at 636 n. 11, 102 S.Ct. at 2638 n. 11.

this case, the Commissioner construed section 80B.05(4) to allow Conwed to mail the Cardiff offering materials to its Minnesota shareholders pending the hearing before the Commissioner. In light of this experience, we have no reason to believe the Minnesota Act will be applied in a manner which creates burdensome delay.

3. Under section 137.57.E of the Illinois law, the Secretary is required to deny registration of a takeover offer if he finds that the takeover offer is *inequitable*. There is no similar provision in the Minnesota Act.

4. The Illinois Act applies whenever ten percent of the target corporation's outstanding shares are held by Illinois residents, *MITE*, 457 U.S. at 637, or when the target corporation meets any two of the following conditions: (1) its principal executive office is in Illinois; (2) it is organized under the laws of Illinois; or (3) it has at least ten percent of its stated capital and paid-in-surplus represented in Illinois. Ill.Rev.Stat., ch. 121½, ¶ 137.52–10(2) (1979). In *MITE*, Justice White emphasized that the Illinois Act regulated offers from an out-of-state tender offeror to an out-of-state shareholder. The Act could apply even if none of the target's shareholders were Illinois residents.

By contrast, the Minnesota statute applies only when at least twenty percent of the target's shareholders are Minnesota residents and the target has "substantial assets" in the state.[4] 1984 Minn.Sess.Law Serv., ch. 488, § 80B.01(9) (West). Any suspension applies only to Minnesota residents. Thus, the *Pike* test leads to different results in this case than it did in *MITE*. In that case, Justice White held that, to the extent the Illinois Act applied even when none of the target corporation's shareholders were Illinois residents, there were no legitimate local interests to be weighed against the effects on interstate commerce. Under the Minnesota Act, however, interstate commerce is indirectly burdened only when the target company has substantial numbers of Minnesota shareholders. Thus, *MITE* is distinguishable.

Cardiff, however, argues that even though the Minnesota Act is not as burdensome as the Illinois Act at issue in *MITE*, it still violates the commerce clause because its indirect burdens on interstate commerce are excessive in relation to the putative local benefits. Cardiff points out that the Minnesota Act burdens interstate commerce because it imposes disclosure requirements beyond those of the Williams Act, because the existence, enforcement and cost of complying with the Act burden interstate commerce and because a suspension in Minnesota may discredit the tender offer nationwide. It also argues that the asserted protections to local investors are illusory because most of the disclosures required by the Minnesota Act are already required by the Williams Act, and the additional disclosures serve no valid purpose.

We join the district court in rejecting these arguments. First, the benefits to local investors are not illusory. Although the disclosure requirements of 1984 Minn.Sess.Law Serv., ch. 488, § 80B.03(2) & (6) largely

---

4. Although the precise meaning of "substantial assets" is unclear, the Commissioner has only applied the statute to target corporations which have their primary places of business in Minnesota. In this case, almost three-fourths of Conwed's employees, most of its manufacturing facilities, all of its research and testing centers, and the beneficial holders of more than twenty percent of its stock reside in Minnesota. Cardiff Acquisitions, Inc. v. Hatch, 597 F.Supp. 1493 at 1495 (D.Minn.1984); Hill Aff. ¶¶ 3–8.

parallel those set forth in the Williams Act, simultaneous enforcement of the requirements imposes little burden on offerors but ensures protection of local investors. This is particularly true in view of the fact that the SEC apparently lacks the resources to police the thousands of schedule 13(d) reports and amendments filed each year.[6] The state, on the other hand, apparently has the resources to carefully examine the reports to ensure that they in fact disclose the information required by the state statute and regulations.

We also agree with the district court that the additional disclosures required by the Minnesota Act will aid Minnesota shareholders in appraising the value of a tender offer and will not result in the shareholders receiving a mass of irrelevant information that will serve to confuse rather than enlighten. The additional disclosures are primarily concerned with the impacts of the proposed takeover on Minnesota residents, including employees and suppliers. While the state may not use the statute as a protectionist measure, it may require the offeror to inform Minnesota stockholders as to the impacts on the state or its residents of the takeover, so that they can consider these factors as an element in their decision to retain their stock or to sell it.

B. Supremacy Clause.

We now turn to Cardiff's claim that the district court erroneously held that the Minnesota Act is consistent with the purposes of the Williams Act and thus is not facially invalid under the supremacy clause of the federal Constitution.

1. *The Legal Standard.*

When Congress added the Williams Act, Sections 13(d)–(e) and 14(d)–(f) to the Securities Exchange Act of 1934, it refused to amend section 28(a) of the 1934 Act. In pertinent part, section 28(a) provides that

[n]othing in this chapter shall affect the jurisdiction of the securities commission (or any agency or officer performing like functions) of any State over any security or any person insofar as it does not conflict with the provisions of this chapter or the rules and regulations thereunder.

Thus, Congress did not explicitly or impliedly bar states from regulating tender offers. *National City Lines,* 687 F.2d at 1129. It left to the courts the determination whether a state act conflicts with the Williams Act. *MITE,* 457 U.S. at 631 (plurality opinion).

In *MITE,* Justice White, joined by Chief Justice Burger and Justice Blackmun, reasoned that three provisions of the Illinois Takeover Act violated the supremacy clause of the federal Constitution because they conflicted with the secondary purpose of the Williams Act to maintain a balance of neutrality between a tender offeror and the management of the

---

6. Cf. Gearhart Industries, Inc. v. Smith Intern, Inc., 741 F.2d 707 (5th Cir.1984) (In an amicus brief, the SEC noted that "[d]uring the 1983 fiscal year, approximately 1,700 schedule 13(d) reports and 3,700 amendments to those reports were filed pursuant to section 13(d) by persons or groups acquiring more than five percent of a class of securities. More importantly, these filings are only a small part of the many thousands of disclosure documents filed with the Commissioner each year under the federal securities laws. The Commission does not have the resources to police the truthfulness of the myriad 13(d) filings made each year." Brief of Amicus SEC at 3 n. 2.)

target corporation. (The primary purpose of the Act is to protect investors.) Justices Powell and Stevens disagreed. Justice Powell wrote:

> I agree with Justice Stevens that the Williams Act's neutrality policy does not necessarily imply a congressional intent to prohibit state legislation designed to assure—at least in some circumstances—greater protection to interests that include but often are broader than those of incumbent management.

Id., 457 U.S. at 646–47.

Because the remaining four justices did not reach the issue, the Court has not definitively resolved whether the view of Justices Powell and Stevens, the view of Justices White, Burger and Blackmun, or some other analysis should apply.

In National City Lines v. LLC Corp., 687 F.2d 1122 (8th Cir.1982), this Court held that certain provisions of the Missouri Takeover Bid Disclosure Act, Mo.Rev.Stat. 409.500 et seq. (1979), as applied to *National*, were unconstitutional under the supremacy and commerce clauses of the federal Constitution. We stated that there were no significant distinctions between the Illinois Act and the Missouri Act, and that, therefore, the issues raised under the commerce clause were controlled by the majority decision in *MITE*. 687 F.2d at 1128. We also held that the provisions of the Missouri Act relating to timetables, disclosure requirements, and substantive requirements—which were substantially identical to similar provisions of the Illinois Act were preempted—because they were "incompatible" with the Williams Act. *Id.* We now turn to Cardiff's specific arguments that certain sections or aspects of the Minnesota law are incompatible with the Williams Act.

2. *Cardiff's Arguments.*

Cardiff argues that certain provisions of the Minnesota Act are invalid under the supremacy clause analysis adopted in *National City Lines*. Initially, it asserts that the Minnesota Act conflicts with the Williams Act because it empowers the Commissioner to review the adequacy of disclosures and to stop the tender offer if he determines that there has not been "full disclosure * * * of all material information" or of "other information which would affect the shareholders' evaluation of the acquisition." 1984 Minn.Sess.Law Serv., ch. 488, § 80B.03(4a) (West). See also id. § 80B.03(6)(c) (West). Cardiff contends that these provisions are contrary to the teachings of *National City Lines*, 687 F.2d at 1132–33, because they allow the Commissioner to "second guess" the judgment of the Securities and Exchange Commission as to "what data is material to aid an investor considering a tender offer."

We join the district court in rejecting this argument. The disclosure requirements of the Missouri statutes considered in *National City Lines* were much broader and more open-ended than those of the Minnesota statute. In addition to a number of disclosure provisions not found in federal law, Mo.Rev.Stat. § 409.515 (1979) required disclosure of "such additional information as the Commissioner may require as necessary in the public interest or for the protection of investors." *National City Lines*, 687 F.2d at 1131. We noted that this open-ended provision could likely require disclosure of a "mass of irrelevant data" which could confuse rather than enlighten investors. Id.

We agree with the district court, for the reasons stated at pages 911–12, that the principal additional disclosure required by the Minnesota Act (the effect that a takeover will have on the target company's operations, its employees, suppliers and customers, and the communities in which it operates, *see* 1984 Minn.Sess.Law Serv., ch. 488, § 80B.03(6)(c) (West)), is not inconsistent with the Williams Act and serves to protect unique and legitimate interests of Minnesota shareholders. We agree with Cardiff, however, that the clause in section 80B.03(2) which authorizes the Commissioner to require "such additional information as the commissioner by rule prescribes" is unconstitutional. We also agree that a similar clause in section 80B.03(6) which also requires the offeror to disclose such "additional information the commissioner may by rule prescribe" is unconstitutional. These open-ended provisions are similar to the clause in Mo.Rev.Stat. § 409.515 (1979) which we found to be unconstitutional in *National City Lines,* 687 F.2d at 1131. These sections are unconstitutionally vague and may require the disclosure of irrelevant or confusing data and may require judgmental data that the Commissioner has no authority to require. We believe, however, that it is constitutional for the Commissioner to require disclosure of all the other factual matters set forth in 1984 Minn.Sess.Law Serv., ch. 488, § 80B.03(2) & (6), including those closely related factual matters which must be disclosed so that shareholders can adequately evaluate the information which these sections require to be disclosed.

Next, we believe that it is constitutionally permissible for the Commissioner to review the adequacy of the disclosures required by 1984 Minn. Sess.Law Serv., ch. 488, § 80B.03(2) & (6)(a)–(e) so long as he restricts himself to deciding whether sufficient facts have been disclosed to comply with the specific disclosures required by these sections. The Commissioner has no authority to suspend the effectiveness of a tender offer on the ground that the quality of the facts alleged do not satisfy him. He may not require evaluative, judgmental, or overly burdensome or irrelevant disclosures, and he may not pass on the fairness of the offer as disclosed.

Cardiff also challenges the constitutionality of section 80B.06(7) of the Minnesota Act, which provides that Minnesota residents who do not tender shares may later demand "a reasonable opportunity to dispose of the securities to the offeror upon substantially equivalent terms as provided in the earlier takeover offer." The district court did not address the validity of this provision. We also express no view on its validity because we agree with the State that Cardiff's constitutional challenge to the price protection provision does not present this Court with a case or controversy ripe for judicial resolution.

Because we find that the Act is, with a few exceptions, constitutional on its face, we must also analyze whether the Act is constitutional as applied by the Commissioner. The Commissioner's order was divided into four sections. We analyze each section in turn.

II. CONSTITUTIONALITY OF THE MINNESOTA TAKE–OVERS ACT AS APPLIED.

A. Sources of Financing and Future Plans.

* * *

The Commissioner determined that Cardiff failed to disclose with adequate specificity the source of its financing. We agree. While the Commissioner does not have the authority to decide whether the financing plan is fair, he can require that financing statements be sufficiently comprehensive so that stockholders can determine for themselves whether they should exercise their right to retain their stock or to sell it.

*　*　*

It is apparent from the record that Cardiff Acquisitions is a shell corporation without assets. It is the wholly owned subsidiary of Cardiff Equities which has a net worth of only $5 million. (The purchase price for the stock is estimated to be approximately $30.5 million.) The disclosure filing states that Leucadia National Corporation (a corporation which controls Cardiff) has agreed to advance Cardiff funds to effect the purchase agreement, but no written agreement exists and the terms of the oral agreement, if one in fact exists, have not been spelled out. The filing goes on to state that Cardiff is negotiating with several banks concerning a revolving line of credit but indicates that no bank has as yet made a commitment. *　*　*

We agree with the Commissioner that if Cardiff has an agreement with National to advance Cardiff funds to affect the purchase agreement, Conwed's Minnesota shareholders must be informed of the terms of this agreement. On the other hand, if Cardiff does not have an agreement with National, it should clearly say so.

Subsection (c) of section 80B.03(6) requires the disclosure of the offeror's plans, if any, for the target corporation if acquired, including "any plans or proposals *　*　* to liquidate the issuer [and] sell its assets *　*　*." The Commissioner noted that, in light of the financial statements of Conwed and Cardiff, it is likely that Cardiff will liquidate a substantial portion of Conwed's assets if the takeover is successful. While we believe it is improper for the Commissioner to characterize what Cardiff might do if it acquires Conwed, we agree that if Cardiff has plans to liquidate Conwed, it must disclose these plans.

B. Exposure to Lawsuits.

Subsection (c) of section 80B.03(2) requires a corporation to disclose, among other listed information, "any material pending legal or administrative proceedings in which the offeror or any of the subsidiaries is a party *　*　*." The Commissioner noted that

With regard to the various lawsuits against the parent companies, and the apparent use of their funds to finance the purchase of Conwed, the materials should disclose whether any liability or "trust" arrangement could be imposed on Conwed's assets.

This request is improper because it goes beyond a request for disclosure of facts and requests Cardiff to characterize and evaluate *potential* lawsuits or legal claims in pending suits which might be asserted in the future. Subsection (c) of section 80B.03(2) only requires a corporation to state the facts fully regarding *pending* lawsuits. Additionally, the Minnesota Act does not give the Commissioner authority to require offerors to evaluate the facts which they have disclosed.

C. Actions of Controlling Persons Vis-a-Vis Rights of Minority Shareholders.

In this section, Part B, the Commissioner determined that Cardiff's disclosure filing failed to address adequately a variety of lawsuits and corporate transactions relating to actions of controlling persons vis-a-vis rights of minority shareholders. The Commissioner requested Cardiff to discuss the "value and propriety" of these transactions and events. We believe the Minnesota Act does not authorize the Commissioner to request this information. Cardiff may be required to disclose the facts concerning pending lawsuits, but it need not evaluate these facts or discuss the "value and propriety" of its transactions. These evaluative determinations are to be made by Conwed's shareholders, not by the Commissioner or by Cardiff.

D. Two-Tier Offer.

* * *

Cardiff's tender offer filing states that a second-tier offer might not comply with [section 80B.06(7) of the Minnesota Act, referred to by the Court above]. . . . The Commissioner's order, Part A, required Cardiff to disclose that its potential two-tier offer would not comply with the above prohibition on two-tier offers. We find the Minnesota Act does not authorize the Commissioner to request that Cardiff include such a statement in its disclosure filing. The Commissioner's order requires Cardiff to evaluate what might happen if, at some point in the future, it makes a two-tier offer in violation of a new statutory section which might be unconstitutional. The statute provides other and better methods to deal with Cardiff's potential two-tier offer proposal. First, if section 80B.06(7) is constitutional, Cardiff will be prevented from making a two-tier proposal when and if it decides to try to do so. Second, Cardiff's statement might be a fraudulent and deceptive practice under Minn.Stat. § 80B.05. If so, adequate remedy for Cardiff's two-tier offer claim is available.

Affirmed in part, reversed in part, and remanded to the district court for further proceedings consistent with the opinion. Each party to this appeal shall bear its own costs.

PREEMPTION OF STATE REGULATION

Attempted state regulation of tender offers was initiated in Virginia [1] and Ohio [2] in 1968 and 1969, and there was a veritable flood of such state legislation following the adoption of state takeover statutes in New York [3] and Delaware [4] in 1976. By 1979, such legislation had been enacted in thirty-seven states.

This original state legislation typically required a "waiting period" after the initial announcement of a tender offer, postponing its commencement for a time (the most popular time period being twenty days) for the express purpose of giving the target company time to react and attempting to outlaw the "Saturday night special." In addition, in some states, as was true of the Illinois statute involved in the *Mite Corporation* case, discussed in the *Cardiff* case, the state Blue Sky official is given authority to determine whether or not the offer

1. Va.Laws 1968, Ch. 119; Va.Code Ann. §§ 13.1–528–541.

2. Ohio Rev.Code Ann. § 1707.041, as added by Ohio Laws 1969, S.B. No. 138.

3. N.Y.Bus.Corp.Law §§ 1600–1614, added by N.Y.Laws 1976, Ch. 893.

4. Del.Gen.Corp.Law § 203, added by Del.Laws 1976, Ch. 371.

is "fair, just and equitable" to the shareholders of the target company and to prevent it from proceeding on the basis of an adverse determination of this question. The statutes varied as to the bases asserted for the application of the state statute, such as incorporation in that state, the location of the principal business office in that state, the residence of a specified percentage of the shareholders in that state or other tests. Many of the statutes contained several alternative bases of jurisdiction as did the Illinois statute.

These enactments provided the occasion for another race to the courthouse by the tender offeror and the target company, the target company trying to enjoin the offer on the basis that it violated the state statute and the tender offeror attempting to enjoin the state official from enforcing the statute. The Supreme Court decision in Edgar v. Mite Corp.[5] pretty well sounded the death knell for these early state statutes. While the court was highly splintered and there were a total of six opinions filed in the case, five justices agreed that the Illinois statute imposed indirect burdens on interstate commerce that were excessive in the light of the local interests attempted to be protected. Four justices also thought that the act was a direct burden on interstate commerce, in view of the fact that it attempted to regulate entirely out-of-state transactions; and therefore was *per se* invalid without any "weighing" of the local interests against the extent of the burden on interstate commerce. Justice Blackmun agreed that the statute was preempted by the Williams Act and therefore invalid (only the Chief Justice and Justice White concurred on this point), but he did not join in the holding regarding the Commerce Clause. Three justices did not reach the merits at all because they thought that the case was moot. (Justice Powell agreed with them on that point, but joined in an opinion on the merits in order to provide the five justice majority needed to dispose of the case.) Despite the somewhat inconclusive nature of the Supreme Court's action, subsequent lower court decisions have struck down every pre-Mite state takeover statute which has come before them[6] and injunctions against the enforcement of these statutes are now routinely granted.

It seems fairly clear that merely confining the state statute to prohibiting the tender offer with respect to local residents would not avoid the Commerce Clause objection which was upheld in the *Mite* case. In Martin-Marietta Corporation v. Bendix Corporation[7] the court invalidated the pre-Mite Michigan takeover statute even though it noted that a Michigan court had construed that statute as limited to shareholders who were Michigan residents. The court said: "However, the Michigan statute, as applied, still impermissibly burdens interstate commerce. It prevents Michigan shareholders from participating in the nationwide tender offer because of provisions of the Michigan statutes. This is an indirect burden on interstate commerce in that it has the effect of defeating the tender offers of residents from other states where the tendered shares owned by Michigan residents are needed to provide sufficient tendered shares to satisfy the tender offer."[8] Neither the burdens on interstate commerce nor the local interests supposedly protected by the state statute, which the Supreme Court "weighed" and found wanting in the *Mite*

---

5. 457 U.S. 624, (1982).

6. National City Lines, Inc. v. LLC Corporation, 687 F.2d 1122 (8th Cir.1982) (Missouri); Martin-Marietta Corporation v. Bendix Corporation, 690 F.2d 558 (6th Cir. 1982) (Michigan): Telvest, Inc. v. Bradshaw, 697 F.2d 576 (4th Cir.1983) (Virginia); Mesa Petroleum Company v. Cities Service Company, 715 F.2d 1425 (10th Cir.

1983) (Oklahoma); Esmark, Inc. v. Strode, 639 S.W.2d 768 (Ky.1982) (Kentucky); Sharon Steel Corporation v. Whaland, 124 N.H. 1, 466 A.2d 919 (1983) (New Hampshire), to cite only appellate court decisions.

7. 690 F.2d 558 (6th Cir.1982).

8. 690 F.2d at 567.

case, would be appreciably altered by thus confining the operation of the statute.[9]

On December 6, 1979, the SEC adopted new regulations under the Williams Act creating a direct conflict between those regulations and almost all of the pre-Mite state takeover statutes. While only three justices of the Supreme Court were willing to base the invalidation of the Illinois statute on the ground of preemption by the Williams Act, the court noted in a footnote that these new regulations had not been in effect at the time of the events upon which that lawsuit was based. Rule 14d–2(b) now *requires* that a tender offer be commenced within five days after any public announcement of the identity of the bidder and the target company, the amount of securities being sought and the price being offered. The pre-Mite state statutes, however, typically *prohibited* the commencement of the tender offer for a period of twenty days after the disclosure of that information. Therefore, it now seems clear that these state takeover statutes are preempted by the federal regulation, unless this rule is held to be beyond the authority of the SEC to adopt under the Williams Act (which seems unlikely) or the state statutes are drastically revised so as to eliminate this conflict. See Kennecott Corp. v. Smith,[10] in which the Third Circuit held that the New Jersey take-over statute was preempted on this basis. A state takeover statute might still mandate a delay of only five days (which would result in outlawing the "Saturday night special"), provided that this shorter delay is not itself held to be in conflict with the basic purposes of the Williams Act. The SEC rule *permits* a delay of up to five days, but does not mandate any delay in the commencement of the offer from the time of its initial publication, and the reasoning of the *Mite* and *Kennecott* cases might result in a holding that any state mandated delay is not permissible.

The *Cardiff* case illustrates the fact that there may still be some room for State regulation of tender offers, provided it does not substantially interfere with the Federal timetable established under the Williams Act (i.e., the offer must be commenced within five business days after the first public announcement of certain information regarding the tender offer, the offer must remain open for a minimum of twenty business days and the offer must be consummated or the persons who have tendered be permitted to withdraw their stock at the end of sixty days from the time it is commenced) and provided that a State official is not given any authority to delay indefinitely or to prohibit completely a nationwide tender offer, based upon his judgment as to the "fairness" of the offer or other judgmental factors. In fact, most State legislation enacted since the *Mite* case has taken somewhat different approaches, probably because merely requiring additional disclosure relating to local interests is not thought

---

9. In L.P. Acquisition Company v. Tyson, 772 F.2d 201 (6th Cir.1985), a different panel of the Sixth Circuit held by a two to one vote that the very same Michigan statute was not invalid under the Commerce Clause as applied to a corporation whose shares were not registered under the 1934 Act (because it had less than 500 shareholders). This is a strange decision, since the burdens on interstate commerce and the local interests to be protected were not in any way altered by the fact that the corporation was not registered under the 1934 Act, except that the local interest in requiring disclosure was greater in view of the fact that none was mandated by the federal law. Even more strangely, the court struck down the statute as applied to that corporation because, in its opinion, the statute was preempted by the Williams Act, even though the tender offer was not subject to the regulations under the Williams Act except for the rule requiring a twenty business day minimum offering period which was issued under the anti-fraud provisions of Section 14(e) (applicable to tender offers for both registered and unregistered companies). This decision must be regarded as a sport.

10. 637 F.2d 181 (3d Cir.1980).

to give to local management the kind of protection they desire against hostile takeover bids.

Ohio has enacted a statute,[11] which has been copied in several other States, requiring that a person who wishes to acquire more than 20% of the outstanding stock of an Ohio corporation, which has its principal place of business, principal executive office or substantial assets in Ohio, must first secure the approval of the shareholders of the corporation before he can consummate that transaction. A second and possibly third approval must be obtained if he desires in subsequent transactions to exceed 33⅓% or 50% ownership of the outstanding shares. The vote required is a majority of all of the shares voting at a meeting to consider the matter and, in addition, a majority of the disinterested shares, which are defined as those not belonging either to the tender offeror or to the management of the target company. The Sixth Circuit has held that the Ohio statute is unconstitutional under the Commerce Clause and the preemption doctrine, and district court decisions have invalidated similar statutes enacted in Missouri, Minnesota and Hawaii.[12] What the Ohio statute has attempted to do is to substitute a required approval by the shareholders of the target company for the approval of a State administrative official, as required by the Illinois statute, and without any requirement that they even have a reason for refusing to approve the acquisition. It clearly could delay or prohibit a sale of stock by one non-resident shareholder to another non-resident shareholder and the Supreme Court stated in the majority opinion in the *Mite* case: "Insofar as the Illinois law burdens out-of-state transactions, there is nothing to be weighed in the balance to sustain the law."

The statute adopted in Indiana [13] is a variation on the Ohio approach. It also requires a vote of the "disinterested" shares of the corporation when a person acquires 20% or more of the outstanding stock, but the vote is on the question of whether or not the shares acquired by that person shall be disenfranchised. If the proposal to let the acquiring person be "admitted to the club" is voted down by the other shareholders (with his shares not being entitled to vote), then they are automatically converted into nonvoting shares for all purposes. If the acquiring person does not file with the corporation a statement containing specified information about his intentions and financial capacity, the corporation can redeem the shares at their "fair value * * * pursuant to the procedures adopted by the corporation." It is not clear whether this value is to be determined before or after they became nonvoting shares. In Dynamics Corporation of America v. CTS Corporation,[14] the Seventh Circuit held that this statute was unconstitutional both under the Supremacy Clause as being in conflict with the Williams Act and under the Commerce Clause as substantially interfering with interstate commerce.

Pennsylvania has adopted a different approach which would prohibit all partial offers and all front-end loaded, two-tier offers by amending its corporation law to provide that if a person acquires 30% or more of the stock of a corporation, all of the shareholders who did not tender can force him to purchase their shares at an appraised value.[15] This statute would also substantially deter a person from making an "any or all offer" because the offeror

---

11. Ohio Rev.Code § 1701.01.

12. Fleet Aerospace Corporation v. Holderman, 796 F.2d 135 (6th Cir.1986); Icahn v. Blunt, 612 F.Supp. 1400 (W.D.Mo. 1985); APL v. Van Dusen Air, Inc., 622 F.Supp. 1216 (D.Minn.1985); Terry v. Yamashita, 643 F.Supp. 161 (D.Hawaii 1986).

13. West's Ann.Ind.Code 23–1–42–1 et seq.

14. 794 F.2d 250 (7th Cir.1986), CCH Fed.Sec.Law Rptr. ¶ 92,768.

15. Pa.Bus.Corp.Laws, §§ 408–409.1, 910.

cannot calculate his total cost. The determination in the appraisal of the "fair value" of the shares of those shareholders who do not tender may produce a figure in excess of the amount which he paid to those who were willing to tender at whatever premium he has offered. Consequently, the offeror might have to insist upon a very high percentage of the shares being tendered as a condition of the offer, and he may not consider that it is feasible to obtain such a high percentage of the shares. The Williams Act, of course, contains no prohibition against partial offers or front-end loaded offers. The Pennsylvania statute would also seem to be subject to serious constitutional objections, since it obviously attempts to prohibit certain types of tender offers made on a nation-wide basis with respect to Pennsylvania corporations.

A third approach has been taken by Maryland and a number of other states following its lead, which basically tries only to combat the front-end loaded offer. It enacts as a matter of local corporation law certain charter provisions which have been adopted by hundreds of corporations relating to the second step in an acquisition, in which the shareholders who have not tendered are cashed out in a merger. Since this statute is closely related to charter or bylaw provisions adopted by corporations that believe they may be potential targets of a hostile takeover bid, it is discussed below under the heading "Shark Repellents" (see page 804, below).

See Shafer, The Virginia Take-Over-Bid Disclosure Act after Edgar v. Mite, 12 Hastings Const. L.Q. 347 (1985); Lowenstein, Tender Offer Litigation and State Law, 63 N.C.L.Rev. 493 (1985); Brody, The Demise of State Takeover Regulation, 11 N.Ky.L.Rev. 613 (1984); Wolff, Toward a Constitutional State Tender Offer Statute, 7 U.Ark.Little Rock L.J. 83 (1984); Sell, A Critical Analysis of a New Approach to State Takeover Legislation after MITE, 23 Washburn L.J. 473 (1984); Graves, A Failed Experiment: State Takeover Regulation after Edgar v. Mite Corp., 1983 U.Ill.L.Rev. 457 (1983); Kreider, Fortress Without Foundation? Ohio Takeover Act II, 52 U.Cin.L.Rev. 108 (1983); McCauliff, Federalism and the Constitutionality of State Takeover Statutes, 67 Va.L.Rev. 295 (1981); Dickinson, Exclusive Federal Jurisdiction and the Role of the States in Securities Regulation, 65 Iowa L.Rev. 1201 (1980); Boehm, State Interests and Interstate Commerce: A Look at the Theoretical Underpinnings of Takeover Legislation, 36 Wash. & Lee L.Rev. 733 (1979); Wilner and Landy, Tender Trap: State Takeover Statutes and Their Constitutionality, 45 Fordham L.Rev. 1 (1976).

GENERAL HOST CORP. v. TRIUMPH AMERICAN, INC.

United States District Court, S.D.N.Y., 1973.
359 F.Supp. 749.

PIERCE, DISTRICT JUDGE.

In an action filed in this Court on March 19, 1973, General Host Corp. (hereinafter Host) alleged various violations of federal law in connection with a cash tender offer for Host common stock announced on March 16, 1973 by Triumph American, Inc. (hereinafter Triumph). By order to show cause dated March 19, 1973, Host sought a preliminary injunction restraining Triumph from further solicitation of Host shares, and from consummating the tender offer, and from voting or utilizing in any way Host shares previously acquired by Triumph.

For the reasons set forth below, this Court has determined that Host has met its burden of showing probable success on the merits of at least two of the alleged violations of Section 14(e) of the Securities Exchange Act of

1934. The Court further finds that the balance of the equities favors Host; and enjoins Triumph from consummating the tender offer pending final determination of the issues at trial.

The factual background

The plaintiff Host is a New York corporation whose stock is listed on the New York Stock Exchange and is registered pursuant to Section 12 of the Securities Exchange Act of 1934. Through its various divisions and subsidiaries Host manufactures and sells baked goods, convenience foods, and owns and operates convenience food stores, inns, lodges, vessels, restaurants and recreational facilities in two national parks. Host's sales for the year ending December 31, 1972, totalled $55,484,000; its total assets exceed $213,000,000, including about $35,000,000 in cash and marketable securities.

Defendant Triumph is a Delaware corporation organized in November of 1970. In December of 1970 it acquired 95% of the outstanding common stock of Resolute Insurance Company (hereinafter Resolute), its major asset. Triumph's revenues for the year ending March 31, 1972, were $25,795,905; its total assets at that time were $39,455,625.

Eighty-two percent of Triumph's outstanding common stock is owned by defendant Triumph Investment Trust Ltd. (hereinafter Triumph Investment), an English corporation principally engaged in merchant banking, insurance underwriting, investments and securities, international metal trading and real estate investment.

On March 14, 1973, Triumph borrowed $20,000,000 from defendant Lloyds-Bolsa International Bank, Ltd. (hereinafter Lloyds-Bolsa), an English corporation, for the purpose of financing a tender offer for Host shares; and on March 14, 1973, Triumph Investment, having received permission from the United Kingdom Treasury, guaranteed the loan. On March 15, 1973, Triumph filed with the Securities and Exchange Commission (hereinafter SEC) a Schedule 13D with respect to its proposal to purchase 1,075,000 shares of Host common stock at $18.50 per share. The public announcement of the cash tender offer was made the following day, March 16, 1973, in several publications including The New York Times and The Wall Street Journal. The offer stated that it would expire at 5 p.m., March 30, 1973, with Triumph reserving the option to extend it from time to time. Triumph reserved the right to purchase less than 1,075,000 shares, if less were tendered, and the right to purchase more, if more were tendered. Coupled with its prior holdings of Host stock, acquisition of the 1,075,000 shares would give Triumph fifty-one percent of Host's outstanding common stock. Triumph stated in its tender offer that its intention was to gain control of Host.

As noted above, Host then filed this action against Triumph's tender offer on the following Monday, March 19, 1973. This Court granted Host's motion for accelerated discovery and scheduled a hearing on the motion for a preliminary injunction to commence Friday, March 23, 1973. * * *

The issues

Host's allegations regarding Triumph's tender offer can be divided into three categories:

(1) Claimed violations of the federal shipping and communications laws.

Among Host's holdings are two wholly owned subsidiaries, Yellowstone Park Co. and Everglades Park Co., Inc., which operate concessions in the named parks pursuant to U.S. Department of Interior contracts. Among the assets owned by Everglades are two tourist vessels, the Bald Eagle and the Pelican, which ply the waters of that park. Host asserts that the transfer of fifty-one percent of its outstanding common stock to a foreign controlled company such as Triumph, without prior permission of the U.S. Secretary of Commerce, will result in violations of the Shipping Act, 46 U.S.C.A. §§ 808 and 835, and could lead to forfeiture of the boats and forfeiture of Triumph's acquired interest in Host to the U.S. Government.

Similarly, Host asserts that the transfer of fifty-one percent of its shares may result in revocation by the Federal Communications Commission of the licenses for its radio stations which are used in both parks for communications from ship to shore, and in Yellowstone, from snow coaches to base. Host cites the Communications Act (47 U.S.C.A. § 310), which states that any transfer of an FCC license must be first approved by that Commission.

Host claims that loss of the two vessels and the radio licenses would result in substantial impairment of these park operations and cause uncertainty among Host shareholders as to the viability of these two subsidiaries. The gross sales of these two companies combined represented about two percent of Host's total gross revenue in 1972.

(2) Claimed violation of the margin requirements of securities law.

Host asserts that Triumph Investment's guarantee of the $20,000,000 loan to Triumph from Lloyds-Bolsa to finance the tender offer is an indirect extension of credit which far exceeds the maximum allowed by Section 7 of the Securities Exchange Act of 1934, thereby subjecting Host and its shareholders to participation in an illegal transaction which is contrary to the intent of Congress and the public interest.

(3) Claimed violations of the disclosure requirements of securities law.

Finally, Host asserts several misrepresentations and omissions of material fact in Triumph's tender offer which, it is alleged, violate Section 14(e) of the Securities Exchange Act of 1934:

(a) Failure to disclose the possibility that the tender offer violates the Shipping Act, the Communications Act, and the margin requirements of the Securities Exchange Act of 1934; and failure to disclose the possible consequences of such violations.

(b) Failure to disclose Triumph's alleged Investment Company status, or potential Investment Company status, and the fact that Triumph has not registered as an Investment Company pursuant to 15 U.S.C. §§ 80a–1 to 80a–52; and failure to disclose the possible consequences of such violation.

(c) Failure to disclose foreign government controls.

(d) Failure to disclose intentions with regard to Host's liquid assets.

(e) Failure to disclose the adverse consequences under Office of Foreign Direct Investment rules if, through Triumph's acquisition of Triumph Insurance Company, an English corporation, Host becomes a direct foreign investor and is forced to repatriate approximately $28,000,000 in liquid assets currently invested abroad, where it obtains a higher return.

(f) Failure to disclose that there is a group behind the tender offer, consisting of Triumph, Triumph Investment, possibly Lloyds-Bolsa, and others unknown; and failure to file a Schedule 13D as a group.

The preliminary injunction

At this juncture in this action, this Court is required only to decide if the plaintiff Host has carried its burden of demonstrating either a combination of probable success on the merits and the possibility of irreparable injury, or that it has raised serious questions going to the merits and that the balance of hardship is tipped sharply in its favor. See Gulf & Western Industries, Inc. v. Great Atlantic & Pacific Tea Company, Inc., 476 F.2d 687, at 692, 2 Cir., March 12, 1973, quoting Stark v. New York Stock Exchange, 466 F.2d 743, 744 (2 Cir.1972).

Given the time-frame in which this controversy has arisen and must be decided, the Court has proceeded on the premise that relief should issue if Host has borne its burden on at least one of the issues raised. This Court, at this time, has selected for determination of probability of success on the merits two of the issues which commend themselves for immediate consideration, leaving for trial those issues which, however substantial, are not critical to the determination of this motion.

Thus, in the main this opinion will address the alleged violations of Section 14(e), and more specifically, the allegations of failure to disclose the matters relating to Triumph's plans for Host's liquid assets, and the matter of foreign control. The Court will first turn to the consideration of the substantiality of these alleged violations of the securities law, and the probability of Host's success on the merits of such claims at a trial. Thereafter, the Court will consider the balance of equities as between the parties.

The probability of success on the merits

Section 14(e) of the Securities Exchange Act of 1934 has been held to track the language of Rule 10b–5, the difference being that the relatively new Section 14(e) applies to tender offers and 10b–5 applies to the purchase or sale of securities. Therefore, with respect to each of the two alleged violations of Section 14(e) which the Court has selected as dispositive of the motion before it, the determinative question at a trial on the merits is: Was the omission or misrepresentation of fact material?

* * *

(a) Failure to disclose intentions with regard to Host's liquid assets.

Host contends that Triumph failed to meet the requirements of Section 14(e) by not disclosing in its tender offer published March 16, 1973, its intention to convert certain of Host's assets into cash. Host offers the following evidence in support of its contention as to Triumph's intentions.

On February 28, 1873, G. Thomas Whyte, Chairman of the Board of Triumph and Chief Executive officer of Triumph Investment, wrote to Philip Saul, Vice President of Triumph and Assistant Managing Director of Triumph Investment, stating:

* * * The subsidiary companies of General Host could (depending on results of future studies and analyses) each be converted into cash. Further information is being made available to Alan [Alan Gruber is

President of Triumph] in the next few days but present indications from our informants confirm that if everything was sold, the net equity would come out at over $20 per GH share and the total cash that would be available would amount to $150 million.

Plaintiff's Exh. I–KK, p. 5.

On March 8, 1973, Stephen H. Crane, Assistant to the President of Triumph, sent to Whyte a written communication in which he stated:

* * * More important to Triumph American would be the growth potential inherent in GH's large capital resources and borrowing power, as well as the possibility of making further acquisitions with presently held cash. Also, future plans might include decisions to cause GH to sell assets not deemed essential to efficient operations, and proceeds therefrom could be used to augment the cash resources available for acquisitions.

* * *

Triumph American would intend to finance the proposed tender offer with a two-year bank loan of 20 million dollars, to be guaranteed by Triumph Investment Trust, and would plan to repay the loan through one of the following possibilities or a combination thereof:

1. A public offering of stock by Triumph American for a major portion of the amount of the loan.

2. *A merger of Triumph American into GH, and repayment of the loan with the latter's financial resources.*

3. The refinancing of part or all of the debt with institutional lenders. * * *

Plaintiff's Exh. I–MM, pp. 3–5; See also Plaintiff's Exh. I–OO, pp. 3–4. (Emphasis added)

In a communication dated March 12, 1973, from Whyte to Alan Gruber, President of Triumph, which apparently pertains to Triumph's interest in Host, the following is stated: " * * * [T]he attraction of the transaction lies in the use of approximately $100 million of gearings [Eds.—In American, "leverage."] that comes with the company." Plaintiff's Exh. I–NN, p. 3.

Clearly a tender offeror is not required to share with prospective tenderers every matter that was discussed or considered in anticipation of making its offer. Any number of strategic fiscal and investment possibilities and combinations necessarily must be considered in undertakings such as these where the aim is to achieve control of a major target company. Thus, there is nothing unusual about the fact that these exchanges occurred and ordinarily there would be no need to consider divulging them to shareholders.[4]

However, there are important additional facts here which must be considered in assessing Host's assertions that Triumph violated Section 14(e) by its failure to disclose to Host shareholders in its tender offer that Triumph was in all likelihood planning the conversion of certain of Host assets into cash.

---

4. In fact it could be as serious an infringement of Section 14(e) to overstate the definiteness of plans as to understate them. Electronic Specialty Co. v. International Controls Corp., 409 F.2d 937, 948 (2 Cir.1969).

The evidence shows that Triumph was organized under the laws of Delaware in 1970 and has been engaged primarily in the insurance business through its subsidiary, Resolute. Resolute was acquired on December 29, 1970, by Triumph for cash at a cost of approximately $14,033,000. Most of the cash used in making acquisition was borrowed from Lloyds-Bolsa and from Triumph Investment. In its prospectus dated April 28, 1972, offering 125,000 shares of common stock, Triumph stated:

> Dividends: Resolute paid no cash dividends prior to its acquisition by the Company [Triumph] in December, 1970. In 1971 a dividend of $2,098,252 was paid by Resolute to the Company, which dividend was used to repay in part a loan incurred in financing the acquisition. * * * In February 1972 Resolute paid the Company a $1,600,000 dividend.

Plaintiff's Exh. I–K, pp. 9–10.

Host asserts, and it is not controverted by Triumph, that less than thirty days after Triumph acquired Resolute, its nominees were elected to Resolute's Board of Directors, and four days later Resolute's Board, which had never declared a cash dividend previously, voted a $3,000,000 cash dividend.

Host contends that in the instant case, predicated upon this course of conduct undertaken by Triumph once it took over Resolute, and upon the statements of Triumph's officers and directors, supra, it is clearly reasonable to conclude that it is Triumph's intention, if it gains control of Host, a cash-rich company,[6] to convert certain of Host's assets in order to repay the cost of acquiring Host shares—in other words, that Host is to be purchased, in effect, by Triumph using Host's own cash. Host contends that this is a material fact which pursuant to Section 14(e) should have been disclosed to Host shareholders.

This Court agrees. The sole major transaction of Triumph from the time it was organized in 1970 until the present time has been its acquisition of Resolute, and, thus, Triumph's history of dealings with Resolute must be considered in conjunction with the pre-tender offer dialogue which occurred among Triumph officers and directors. As noted above, this history includes Triumph causing Resolute (with equity of $14,822,000) to declare a $3,000,000 dividend within one month after Triumph took over Resolute.

The Court finds that Triumph failed to meet its burden of fully, frankly and honestly revealing in its tender offer sufficient information from which prospective tenderers might draw their own conclusions regarding the likelihood of Triumph converting Host assets into cash. In short, had the prototype shareholder known that Triumph was seriously discussing the conversion into cash of certain Host assets, coupled with the knowledge of what Triumph had done in this regard in its sole prior acquisition, he might well have not tendered his shares.

---

6. Following an unsuccessful cash tender offer to gain control of Armour & Co., in late 1968, Host negotiated the sale of its 54% of Armour for cash, notes, warrants, and convertible preferred shares valued at $211,000,000, and later converted this package to cash. Since then it has made several investments utilizing these liquid funds, but it still has approximately $35,000,000 in cash and marketable securities. See Plaintiff's Exh. I–BBB, p. 4.

Triumph has argued that even should it be successful in acquiring fifty-one percent of Host shares it still would not have "control" of Host due to the difficulties presented by Host's by-laws which have apparently been adopted in order to be highly protective of Host's present structure and management. The difficulties posed by Host's by-laws in this respect notwithstanding, Triumph *"is offering to purchase General Host common stock with a view to control of General Host."* Plaintiff's Exh. I–A, p. 4 (Emphasis added). Further, Triumph fully expected, upon advice of counsel, that these "defenses against a take-over bid * * * will not prove effective to the management of General Host if Triumph American obtains 51% of General Host." Plaintiff's Exh. I–BBB.

The Court notes that Triumph's tender offer states that it has borrowed $20,000,000, on an unsecured basis, at high interest rates, in order to make the offer and that the loan is repayable in approximately two years. Since Triumph reports assets of only $15,000,000, further credence is lent to Host's contention that Triumph, if successful in its take-over bid, plans to convert Host assets into cash, just as it did when it took over Resolute, and will use this cash to repay the loan.

Triumph did see fit to state in its prospectus of April 28, 1972, the fact that after Triumph acquired Resolute it declared its first cash dividend and paid Triumph over $2,000,000 in dividends which was used to repay in part a loan incurred in financing the acquisition. Plaintiff's Exh. I–K, p. 9. While this disclosure was no doubt intended to make Triumph's stock offering attractive to prospective purchasers, it also revealed material facts concerning Triumph's history. These facts, under the circumstances of the instant case, were no less material and should have been disclosed in Triumph's tender offer for Host shares, thereby enabling Host shareholders to determine with knowledge of this history whether they wished to tender their shares.

The Court is aware that Triumph states in its tender offer that it "does not presently have any plan or proposal to liquidate General Host, to sell its assets * * * " and that "it also may evaluate General Host's operations to determine whether there should be any disposition of assets." This statement is found to be insufficient to meet the requirements of Section 14(e) under the circumstances of this case. The Court does not at this time pass upon the question of whether Triumph made an untrue statement of material facts, but rather finds, for the purposes of this proceeding, that it omitted to state material facts necessary in order to make the statements made, in the light of the circumstances under which they are made, not misleading.

(b) Failure to disclose the applicability of foreign government controls.

In the Statute Law of England, there are at least two provisions which assert authority over corporate residents (such as Triumph Investment) and companies not residents of England over which corporate residents have direct or indirect control (such as Triumph).

The British Exchange Control Act 1947, confers power on the United Kingdom Treasury (hereinafter Treasury) to compel Triumph Investment to cause its non-resident companies to declare and pay dividends specified by the Treasury; [10] and to compel Triumph Investment to cause its non-

---

10. Under Exchange Control Regulations currently in force, the Treasury usu-   ally expects remittances to the United Kingdom amounting to two-thirds of the

resident companies to realize any of their assets as directed by the Treasury.

The Income and Corporation Taxes Act 1970, requires the consent of the Treasury before Triumph Investment can permit any of its non-resident companies to issue any shares or debentures.

There is no serious disagreement between the parties that should the tender offer for Host shares be successful, Host will be a non-resident company indirectly controlled by Triumph Investment, and the laws cited above will be applicable.

The contention centers on whether or not these laws will ever be invoked by the Treasury in a way adverse to Host's operations and business in the United States, and to the foreign minority shareholders (i.e., Host shareholders who do not tender and who become foreign minority shareholders by virtue of Triumph's acquisition of fifty-one percent of the outstanding shares).

From the evidence hastily assembled for the hearing on this motion it is impossible for the Court to assess the probabilities with respect to the use of these laws, now or in the future. However, some of the exhibits reveal that the laws are not dead letters, although they are apparently applied in a very low key manner, at the present time.

* * *

Triumph itself felt that the existence of these laws was significant enough to set them forth in some detail in its prospectus dated April 28, 1972 (Plaintiff's Exh. I–K, p. 28) announcing the issuance of Triumph shares. Triumph has argued that SEC regulations are more stringent with respect to disclosure where the prospect is being encouraged to buy (stock offers) rather than to sell (tender offers). That may have some technical validity, but we are not dealing here solely with SEC minimum standards.

In the Court's view, both the existence of the Treasury authority to manipulate the operations and business decisions of a company such as Host, *and* a factually based opinion as to the probability or lack of probability of adverse consequences, are facts which the reasonable investor should have in order to make an informed decision to tender or not to tender, or to tender some and withhold some shares. Triumph, by revealing that Triumph Investment is an English company and that it owns eighty-two percent of Triumph, and that it sought control of Host, put the Host shareowning public on notice that a foreign parent was in the picture. But the facts omitted with respect to British law are not facts which the reasonable investor is apt to know himself, or could be expected to find out on his own. Foreign controls, particularly when they differ in extent and kind from controls the U.S. investor has come to expect from the U.S. government in relation to domestic corporations, are matters which should be called to the attention of shareholders in a tender offer.

consolidated net foreign earnings after aggregating all foreign earnings of all the foreign companies controlled by the United Kingdom corporate resident. Plaintiff's Exh. I–VV, p. 2, ¶ 6. However, at least for Triumph, Triumph Investment has obtained assurances from the Bank of England that the Treasury will not require Triumph Investment, for the time being to cause Triumph to remit to the United Kingdom. Plaintiff's Exh. I–K, p. 40.

Balancing the equities

Defendant Triumph asserts that if a preliminary injunction is granted it will be irreparably injured in that: other tender offers might be made while awaiting the case being tried on the merits, resulting in shareholders tendering to others while Triumph is enjoined; Host will have the advantage of a lengthy period of time to place obstacles in the way of Triumph; Host shareholders would lose confidence in Triumph and would not tender; and arbitrageurs would hesitate to continue to buy Host stock with a view to tendering.

The principal harm which Triumph will suffer should the application for a preliminary injunction be granted is that it will be unable to consummate its tender offer at such time as it deems ripe and profitable. This Court has determined that there is the probability that there has been an unlawful tender offer in that Host shareholders have not been honestly and fairly informed by Triumph. Triumph has no inherent right to proceed with an unlawful tender offer. "A requirement of lawfulness is included by implication in every tender offer." Gulf & Western Industries, Inc. v. Great Atlantic & Pacific Tea Co., supra, 473 F.2d at 698. Further, also as in the *Gulf & Western* case, if this Court permitted the tender offer to be consummated and at some later date was to find the violations charged by Host were valid, " * * * it would be almost impossible to unravel the situation." Id. at 698, quoting Gulf & Western Industries, Inc. v. Great Atlantic & Pacific Tea Company, Inc., 356 F.Supp. 1066, 1074 (S.D. N.Y., 1973).

If after a trial on the merits Triumph is vindicated, it will not be foreclosed from renewing its offer.

Remedies

In view of the serious possible consequences which can result from the granting of preliminary injunctive relief in matters such as these, this Court must consider the various forms of relief which might be invoked in order to: protect the public interest; protect shareholders so that they might be fully informed of all material facts; avoid, where possible, frustrating the desires of those who may wish to tender when all the facts are known, should the tender offer be extended. See Butler Aviation International, Inc. v. Comprehensive Designers, Inc., 425 F.2d 842, 844–845 (2 Cir.1970). While an assessment of certain 14(e) issues for the purpose of making a determination of this motion has been made, the Court remains confronted with issues raised by claimed violations of the Shipping Act, the Communications Act and several alleged failures to disclose material facts under the securities law, including Triumph's alleged investment company status, the possible adverse consequences of direct investment abroad, and the alleged group source of the tender offer. Further, there is an alleged violation of the margin requirements of the securities law which presents serious questions going to the merits and requires a complete record upon a trial in order that findings of fact essential to a determination of the issue may be made.

While the 14(e) issues preliminarily determined in this opinion directly affect the parties to the action and the Host shareholders, some of these remaining issues affect the public interest as well.

Corrective relief requiring rescission and disclosure of those facts which the Court has determined should have been revealed by Triumph might avoid frustrating the desires of those who wish to tender when all the facts are known, but it will not suffice to protect the interests of the public should it be determined upon trial that Host's allegations, such as the claimed margin requirement violation, have been sustained. By then, the situation indeed would be almost impossible to unravel.

The Court concludes that the opportunity for doing equity is considerably better now than later and that the balance of hardships tips sharply in favor of granting preliminary injunctive relief which enjoins consummation of the tender offer, thereby maintaining the status quo. See Electronic Specialty Co. v. International Controls Corp., 409 F.2d 937, 947 (2 Cir.1969).

* * * *

NORLIN CORPORATION v. ROONEY, PACE, INC.

United States Court of Appeals, Second Circuit, 1984.
744 F.2d 255.

Before FEINBERG, CHIEF JUDGE, KAUFMAN and PIERCE, CIRCUIT JUDGES.

IRVING R. KAUFMAN, CIRCUIT JUDGE.

Contests for corporate control have become ever more frequent phenomena on the American business scene. Waged with the intensity of military campaigns and the weaponry of seemingly bottomless bankrolls, these battles determine the destinies of large and small corporations alike. Elaborate strategies and ingenious tactics have been developed both to facilitate takeover attempts and to defend against them. Skirmishes are fought in company boardrooms, in shareholders' meetings, and, with increasing regularity, in the courts.

The efforts of targeted management to resist acquisitive moves, and the means they employ, have been alternatively praised and damned. Proponents of corporate "free trade" argue that defensive techniques permit managers to entrench themselves and thus avoid accountability for their performance, at the expense of shareholders who are denied the opportunity to maximize their investment in sought-after corporations.[1] Opponents contend that takeover struggles squander enormous capital resources which could better be spent to improve industrial productivity and to develop and commercialize new technologies.[2]

When these battles for corporate dominance spawn legal controversies, the judicial role is neither to displace the judgment of the participants nor to predetermine the outcome. Rather, the responsibility of the court is to insure that rules designed to safeguard the fairness of the takeover process be enforced. Our most important duty is to protect the fundamental structure of corporate governance. While the day-to-day affairs of a company are to be managed by its officers under the supervision of

---

1. See, e.g., Easterbrook and Fischel, "The Proper Role of a Target's Management in Responding to a Tender Offer," 94 Harv.L.Rev. 1161 (1981); Gelfond and Sebastian, "Reevaluating the Duties of Target Management in a Hostile Tender Offer," 60 B.U.L.Rev. 403 (1980).

2. See, e.g., Lipton, "Takeover Bids in the Target's Boardroom," 35 Bus.Law. 101 (1979); Steinbrink, "Management's Response to the Takeover Attempt," 28 Case W.L.Rev. 882 (1978).

directors, decisions affecting a corporation's ultimate destiny are for the shareholders to make in accordance with democratic procedures.

The instant case involves defensive action taken by a company that feared it might soon be the target of a takeover attempt. The first salvo in this battle was fired by appellee Piezo Electric Products, Inc., which in conjunction with Rooney, Pace Inc., began buying up large blocks of stock of appellant Norlin Corporation. In response, the board of directors of Norlin issued new common and voting preferred stock to a wholly-owned subsidiary and a newly-created employee stock option plan. Since Norlin would control the voting of the newly-issued stock, the effect of the transactions was to concentrate greater voting control in the hands of its board of directors, and thus to ward off any acquisitive moves that might be made against the company. Piezo sought and the district court granted a preliminary injunction barring the board from voting the stock in question. The judge found that any vote resulting from these transfers would likely be illegal, and that a possible consequence of the stock transfer—delisting from the New York Stock Exchange—would cause irreparable injury to Norlin's shareholders. We hold that the district court's findings were not erroneous, and therefore affirm. Before analyzing the legal issues presented, we shall describe the events that gave rise to the present dispute.

I

Appellant Norlin Corporation ("Norlin") is a diversified company whose principal lines of business are the manufacture of musical instruments and financial printing. Norlin is incorporated in the Republic of Panama, but has no significant operations in that country. The company's principal place of business and executive offices are located in White Plains, New York, and its shareholder and directors' meetings take place in New York as well.

Appellee Piezo Electric Products, Inc. ("Piezo") is primarily engaged in the research, development, manufacture and sale of piezoelectric and thermistor products. It is a Delaware corporation with its principal place of business in Cambridge, Massachusetts. On the two trading days of January 6 and 12, 1984, and in conjunction with the investment banking firm Rooney, Pace Inc., Piezo purchased some 32% of Norlin's common stock in a number of separate transactions. Fearful that a takeover attempt was imminent, Norlin filed suit on January 13, alleging various violations of the federal securities laws. The company sought to enjoin appellees from acquiring any additional Norlin stock, to force divestiture of stock already purchased, and to bar voting of Norlin stock owned by them. After hearing oral argument, Judge Edelstein denied Norlin's motions for a temporary restraining order and expedited discovery, finding that the company had not demonstrated irreparable harm stemming from the stock purchases.

Having failed to secure protection in the courts, Norlin immediately took defensive measures on its own. On January 20, 1984, the same day the judge ruled on its motions, Norlin's board transferred 28,395 shares of common stock to Andean Enterprises, Inc. ("Andean"), a wholly-owned subsidiary of Norlin also incorporated in Panama. The transfer was purportedly made in consideration for Andean's cancellation of a Norlin promissory note in the amount of $965,454. Three days later, on January

23, Norlin announced it had "retained the investment banking firm of Dillon, Read & Co., Inc. to explore various opportunities which may be available to Norlin, including the merger or sale of Norlin, the repurchase of shares of Norlin Common Stock or the sale or issuance of shares or other securities of Norlin."

On January 25, Norlin's board approved two additional transfers of large blocks of stock. The board conveyed 800,000 shares of authorized but unissued preferred stock, which would vote on a share for share basis with Norlin common, to Andean in exchange for a $20 million interest-bearing note. On the same day, the board created the Norlin Industries, Inc. Employee Stock Option Plan and Trust ("ESOP"), and appointed three Norlin board members as trustees. The board immediately transferred 185,000 common shares to the ESOP in consideration for a promissory note in the principal amount of $6,824,945. In filings with the Securities and Exchange Commission, Norlin acknowledged that it would be the beneficial owner of all of the transferred shares. Moreover, it is undisputed that the board retained voting control of the shares conveyed to Andean and to the ESOP. Together with shares already under the board's control, the January 20 and 25 transactions resulted in the Norlin directors controlling the votes of 49% of the corporation's outstanding stock.

Also on January 25, Norlin's Chairman and Chief Executive Officer, Norton Stevens, and President, Gilbert A. Simpkins, wrote to the company's shareholders explaining these actions. Their letter mentioned the Piezo and Rooney, Pace acquisitions, and asserted that "[t]he Board of Directors and management are strongly opposed to the stated purposes of Rooney, Pace and Piezo and are taking all steps deemed necessary or appropriate to protect Norlin's shareholders and the value of their investment in the Company." The letter offered no justification for the stock transfers to Andean and the ESOP other than to ward off a prospective attempt to obtain control of Norlin.

Norlin's directors concede that prior to taking the steps described above, they were warned by their financial advisers that absent shareholder approval, the stock transactions violated the rules of the New York Stock Exchange ("NYSE") and might result in the delisting of Norlin common stock. On March 15, the NYSE did in fact suspend trading in Norlin common, and indicated its intention to delist the stock. A release announcing the move explained:

The Exchange said it deems [the stock issuances to Andean and to the ESOP] to have resulted in a change in control of the company.

The Exchange said its policy requires that a company obtain shareholder approval in such circumstances and it said its decision to delist the Norlin securities results from the fact that Norlin didn't seek shareholder approval of the issuance.

In addition Norlin is presently below the Big Board's continued listing criteria relating to the number of publicly held shares—at least 600,000 shares—and the number of holders of 100 shares or more—at least 1,200—the Exchange said.

On February 9, some time before the NYSE announcement was issued, Piezo filed the counterclaim that is the basis of the instant action. Its complaint alleged that the Norlin stock transfers violated Panama and New York law in addition to several provisions of the federal securities laws. Piezo contended that the transactions had no valid business purposes, and were intended solely "to further entrench management by placing additional shares of voting stock at management's disposal." To forestall delisting from the NYSE, as well as other alleged harms to Piezo in its capacity as a Norlin shareholder, the counterclaimant sought to have the issuance of shares to Andean and the ESOP declared void, and to bar Norlin from voting those shares for any purpose.

Piezo subsequently moved for preliminary relief, and Judge Edelstein heard argument on the motion. In a written order entered April 16, the judge granted Piezo's application for a preliminary injunction. He stated that Panamanian law barred Norlin from voting the shares transferred to its wholly-owned subsidiary, and that the issuance of the ESOP shares was "clearly part of the same management scheme to entrench itself in power. * * *" His order also concluded that Piezo had met its burden of demonstrating irreparable harm, "because the delisting of the common stock together with the inability of purchasers generally to acquire over-the-counter shares on margin seriously limits the liquidity of such shares; and further, the delisting of securities generally is a serious loss of prestige and has a chilling effect on prospective buyers. * * *" Based upon these determinations, the judge barred Norlin from voting the contested shares pending further proceedings, and ordered Norlin to take "all reasonable steps necessary and desirable" to prevent delisting from the NYSE.

On appeal, Norlin takes issue with every one of Judge Edelstein's findings and conclusions, arguing that its actions were well within the board's discretion once it determined that Piezo's designs were not in the company's best interest. Before we turn to the merits of Norlin's arguments, we must dispose of several preliminary issues which provide the context for our discussion.

II

* * *

Norlin initially raises a procedural barrier which, it contends, prevents Piezo from asserting any claim for relief arising from the stock transfers. Norlin argues that New York courts subscribe to the "internal affairs rule," under which the law of the jurisdiction of incorporation governs internal corporate matters, including the existence and extent of corporate fiduciary obligations. Because Norlin is a Panamanian corporation, it contends, a New York court under this doctrine would apply Panama law to determine whether Norlin's shareholders have a cause of action against its directors for breach of their fiduciary duty. According to the affidavits of Panamanian lawyers submitted on Norlin's behalf, however, Panama law conditions the existence of a cause of action by shareholders against directors upon the passage of a resolution authorizing the lawsuit at a general meeting of shareholders. Neither party suggests that such a resolution has been proposed or adopted. Hence, Norlin asserts, Piezo has failed to state a claim for relief.

We need not discuss the fidelity of New York courts to the internal affairs rule at this juncture, although we shall return to that issue infra. We find it unnecessary to adopt the choice of law ruling Norlin urges, because the New York legislature has expressly decided to apply certain provisions of the state's business law to any corporation doing business in the state, regardless of its domicile. Thus, under New York Business Corporation Law ("NYBCL") § 1319, a foreign corporation operating within New York is subject, *inter alia,* to the provisions of the state's own substantive law that control shareholder actions to vindicate the rights of the corporation. NYBCL § 626, made applicable to foreign corporations by § 1319, permits a shareholder to bring an action to redress harm to the corporation, including injury wrought by the directors themselves. See Barr v. Wackman, 36 N.Y.2d 371, 368 N.Y.S.2d 497, 329 N.E.2d 180 (1975).

* * *

III

Piezo asserts, and the district court appropriately found, that the illegality of voting the stock transferred to Andean and the ESOP had been demonstrated with sufficient certainty to warrant injunctive relief. As we will explain, the right of a wholly-owned subsidiary to vote shares of a parent company's stock is controlled by statute. The propriety of an issuance of stock to an ESOP in the context of a contest for corporate control has not been legislatively resolved, and so must be assessed in relation to fiduciary principles governing the conduct of officers and directors. Thus, we must analyze the two issues separately.

A. *Voting of Andean's shares.*

Both New York and Panamanian law expressly prohibit a subsidiary that is controlled by its parent corporation from voting shares of the parent's stock. * * * Both statutes seek to safeguard minority shareholders from management attempts at self-perpetuation. If cross-ownership and cross-voting of stock between parents and subsidiaries were unregulated, officers and directors could easily entrench themselves by exchanging a sufficient number of shares to block any challenge to their autonomy. See Hornstein, Corporate Law and Practice § 311, at 410 (1959).

Norlin, however, contends that neither New York nor Panama law should be applied to bar Andean from voting the Norlin shares it owns. New York, Norlin argues, applies the internal affairs rule * * * to issues of corporate governance. Thus, a New York court would look to the law of Panama, as the state of incorporation, to decide whether Andean can vote its shares. But under Article 37 of the above-mentioned Panamanian Cabinet Decree, the prohibition contained in Article 35 is applicable only "to corporations registered at the National Securities Commission [of Panama] and to such corporations whose shares are sold in the market, although such corporations do not offer their own shares to the public." In other words, unless a corporation undertakes to list its shares for sale in Panama, or its shares are in fact sold in that country, the proscription contained in Article 35 does not govern.

The district judge appears to have accepted the argument that Panama law is controlling. He found, based upon an affidavit offered by Piezo, that a purchase of Norlin stock had been made through a branch office of Merrill Lynch, Pierce, Fenner & Smith located in Panama City. Thus, while Norlin shares concededly are not registered at the Securities Commission, the judge determined that they were "sold in the market," and so governed by Article 35. On appeal, however, appellants have brought to our attention a recent opinion by the General Attorney of Panama, dated May 2, 1984, which interprets the requirement that shares be "sold in the market," the alternative predicate to the application of Article 35. The opinion states that a company's shares are not deemed to be "sold in the market" if it "sell[s] shares in a private manner to a number of persons of no mre [sic] than 10 per year." Because Piezo has only documented a single sale of Norlin stock, Norlin urges, Piezo has not demonstrated that Panama law should govern the voting of shares owned by Andean.

We accept the initial premise of Norlin's argument—that a federal court adjudicating a state law claim must apply the choice of law principles of the forum state. Klaxon Co. v. Stentor Electric Manufacturing Co., Inc., 313 U.S. 487, 496 (1941). We are not so certain, however, that a New York court would apply the internal affairs rule and decide this case by reference to Panama law. In Greenspun v. Lindley, 36 N.Y.2d 473, 369 N.Y.S.2d 123, 330 N.E.2d 79 (1975), the Court of Appeals confronted the question whether New York or Massachusetts law should govern a shareholder's derivative action brought in a New York court against the trustees of a business trust organized under laws of Massachusetts. Although holding that Massachusetts law controlled, the court rejected "any automatic application of the so-called 'internal affairs' choice-of-law rule. . . ." 36 N.Y.2d at 478, 369 N.Y.S.2d at 126, 330 N.E.2d at 81. * * *

Norlin's contacts with the State of New York are far from insubstantial. The company's principal place of business is located within the state, and its board of directors meets here. The resolution approving the contested stock issuances were adopted in this state, and the company stock has been traded on the NYSE. Whether these contacts are sufficient for a New York court to apply New York law is, in our view, a question that does not lend itself to a simple answer. We need not, however, grapple with it to resolve the present inquiry. The principles compelling a forum state to apply foreign law come into play only when a legitimate and substantial interest of another state would thereby be served. * * *

In this case, Panama apparently would refrain from applying its own law to the transactions under scrutiny, because appellant does not meet the criteria of Article 37, as interpreted by the General Attorney. In essence, Panama has made a determination that its interest in Norlin's affairs is insufficient to warrant the application of Panamanian law to this dispute. New York, as the forum state, has a more than adequate number of contacts with Norlin to give it a legitimate interest in regulating these corporate actions.

Moreover, it is of interest to note that the relevant rules of law in New York and Panama are identical on this point: A wholly-owned subsidiary may not vote shares of its parent's stock. In these circumstances, it would be an absurd result indeed if neither jurisdiction could apply its law, and the public policy of both should be frustrated. See Leflar, American Conflicts Law § 93, at 188 (3d ed. 1977). We therefore conclude that whatever choice of law principles would be applied, Piezo has made an adequate showing on these facts that the voting of Andean's shares would be unlawful.

B. *Voting of shares held by the ESOP.*

We now turn to the district court's conclusion that appellee had demonstrated probable illegality stemming from the voting of Norlin shares held by the ESOP. This is a somewhat more difficult problem, for we have little statutory authority to guide us in our quest. We must look instead to those fiduciary principles of state common law which constrain the actions of corporate officers and directors.

A board member's obligation to a corporation and its shareholders has two prongs, generally characterized as the duty of care and the duty of loyalty. The duty of care refers to the responsibility of a corporate fiduciary to exercise, in the performance of his tasks, the care that a reasonably prudent person in a similar position would use under similar circumstances. See NYBCL § 717. In evaluating a manager's compliance with the duty of care, New York courts adhere to the business judgment rule, which "bars judicial inquiry into actions of corporate directors taken in good faith and in the exercise of honest judgment in the lawful and legitimate furtherance of corporate purposes." Auerbach v. Bennett, 47 N.Y.2d 619, 629, 419 N.Y.S.2d 920, 926, 393 N.E.2d 994 (1979).

The second restriction traditionally imposed, the duty of loyalty, derives from the prohibition against self-dealing that inheres in the fiduciary relationship. See Pepper v. Litton, 308 U.S. 295, 306–07 (1939). Once a prima facie showing is made that directors have a self-interest in a particular corporate transaction, the burden shifts to them to demonstrate that the transaction is fair and serves the best interests of the corporation and its shareholders. See NYBCL § 713(a)(3); Schwartz v. Marien, 37 N.Y.2d 487, 493, 373 N.Y.S.2d 122, 127, 335 N.E.2d 334 (1975); Limmer v. Medallion Group, Inc., 75 A.D.2d 299, 428 N.Y.S.2d 961, 963 (1980); see also Marsh, Are Directors Trustees?, 22 Bus.Law. 35, 43–48 (1966).

In applying these principles in the context of battles for corporate control, we begin with the business judgment rule, which affords directors wide latitude in devising strategies to resist unfriendly advances. See, e.g., Treadway Companies, Inc. v. Care Corp., 638 F.2d 357, 380–84 (2d Cir.1980); Crouse-Hinds Co. v. Internorth, Inc., 634 F.2d 690, 701–04 (2d Cir.1980). As Judge Kearse made clear in those cases, however, the business judgment rule governs only where the directors are not shown to have a self-interest in the transaction at issue. *Treadway,* 638 F.2d at 382. Once self-dealing or bad faith is demonstrated, the duty of loyalty supersedes the duty of care, and the burden shifts to the directors to "prove that the transaction was fair and reasonable to the corporation." Id.; *Crouse-Hinds,* 634 F.2d at 702; Panter v. Marshall Field & Co., 646 F.2d 271, 301 (7th Cir.1981) (Cudahy, J., concurring and dissenting), cert. denied, 454 U.S. 1092, 102 S.Ct. 658, 70 L.Ed.2d 631 (1981); Johnson v. Trueblood, 629 F.2d 287, 300 (3d Cir.1980) (Rosenn, J., concurring and dissenting), cert. denied, 450 U.S. 999 (1981); see Klaus v. Hi-Shear Corp., 528 F.2d 225, 233–34 (9th Cir.1975); Mobil Corp. v. Marathon Oil Co., [1981 Transfer Binder] Fed.Sec.L.Rep. (CCH) ¶ 98,375 (S.D.Ohio), rev'd on other grounds, 669 F.2d 366 (6th Cir. 1981); cf. Bennett v. Propp, 41 Del.Ch. 14, 187 A.2d 405, 409 (1962).

In this case, the evidence adduced was more than adequate to constitute a prima facie showing of self-interest on the board's part. All of the stock transferred to Andean and the ESOP was to be voted by the directors; indeed, members of the board were appointed trustees of the ESOP. The precipitous timing of the share issuances, and the fact that the ESOP was created the very same day that stock was issued to it, give rise to a strong inference that the purpose of the transaction was not to benefit the employees but rather to solidify management's control of the company. This is buttressed by the fact that the board offered its shareholders no rationale for the transfers other than its determination to oppose, at all costs, the threat to the company that Piezo's acquisitions ostensibly represented. Where, as here, directors amass voting control of close to a majority of a corporation's shares in their own hands by complex, convoluted and deliberate maneuvers, it strains credulity to suggest that the retention of control over corporate affairs played no part in their plans.[7]

We reject the view, propounded by Norlin, that once it concludes that an actual or anticipated takeover attempt is not in the best interests of the company, a board of directors may take any action necessary to forestall acquisitive moves. The business judgment rule does indeed require the board to analyze carefully any perceived threat to the corporation, and to act appropriately when it decides that the interests of the company and its shareholders might be jeopardized. As we have explained, however, the duty of loyalty requires the board to demonstrate that any actions it does take are fair and reasonable. We conclude that Norlin has failed to make that showing.

    *   *   *

    *   *   * When an ESOP is set up in the context of a contest for control, however, it devolves upon the board to show that the plan was in fact

---

7. We do not think our conclusion on this point is inconsistent with the findings in *Treadway* and *Crouse-Hinds* that no prima facie showing of conflict of interest had been made. The facts in this case differ in significant respects. *Treadway* involved the sale of 230,000 shares of Treadway Companies, Inc. stock to Fair Lanes, Inc., preparatory to a merger between the two companies. The agreement to sell the shares was reached sometime after a third party, Care Corporation, had acquired a large block of Treadway stock. Care claimed that Treadway's board had approved the sale to Fair Lanes for the improper purpose of perpetuating its control over the corporation. Judge Kearse, writing for this court, found that Care had failed to establish a conflict of interest on the part of Treadway's board. Her opinion specifically noted evidence that Fair Lanes had been interested in merging with Treadway for a number of years, that all of Treadway's directors but one anticipated losing their positions if the merger with Fair Lanes were consummated, and that the merger was not merely a "sham or a pretext," but rather a viable business proposition. *Treadway*, 638 F.2d at 383. No analogous facts are present here.

Crouse-Hinds also involved a three-way competition for corporate control. In that case, Crouse-Hinds Co. and Belden Corporation entered into an agreement whereby Belden would be merged into a Crouse-Hinds subsidiary. Four days *after* the agreement was reached, Internorth, Inc. made a tender offer for Crouse-Hinds' shares, intending to follow that action with a merger of the two companies. Subsequent to the tender offer, Crouse-Hinds and Belden announced an Exchange Agreement permitting Belden shareholders to tender their shares in exchange for Crouse-Hinds stock, at the same ratio of 1.24 Crouse-Hinds shares to 1 Belden share which was contemplated in the original merger agreement. Internorth challenged the Exchange Agreement as a device by the Crouse-Hinds board to retain control. In holding that board self-interest had not been demonstrated, Judge Kearse noted that the Crouse-Hinds board had no indication that Internorth would make a tender offer at the time the merger agreement was entered into. Because the Exchange Agreement was a reasonable means of facilitating a merger which was itself legitimate, no showing of bad faith had been made. *Crouse-Hinds*, 634 F.2d at 703–04. Again, these facts are at considerable variance with those in the instant case.

created to benefit the employees, and not simply to further the aim of managerial entrenchment. In applying that distinction, courts have looked to factors such as the timing of the ESOP's establishment, the financial impact on the company, the identity of the trustees, and the voting control of the ESOP shares. See Note, Employee Stock Ownership Plans and Corporate Takeovers: Restraints on the Use of ESOPs by Corporate Officers and Directors to Avert Hostile Takeovers, 10 Pepperdine L.Rev. 731, 744 (1983).

In this case, an examination of each of these factors indicates that the ESOP was created solely as a tool of management self-perpetuation. It was created a mere five days after the district court refused to enjoin further stock purchases by Piezo, and at a time when Norlin's officers were clearly casting about for strategies to deter a challenge to their control.[10] No real consideration was received from the ESOP for the shares. The three trustees appointed to oversee the ESOP were all members of Norlin's board, and voting control of all of the ESOP shares was retained by the directors.[12] We therefore conclude that the record supports the finding that the transfer of stock to the ESOP was part of a management entrenchment effort.

* * *

Norlin's final justification, and one emphasized at oral argument, was that the board needed to consolidate control to "buy" time to explore financial alternatives to a Piezo takeover. The company asserts that the shareholders will benefit if the directors are insulated from challenges to their control, for an interim period of unspecified duration, so that all of Norlin's future operations can be considered with professional guidance. This argument stands our prior cases on their heads. It is true that in conformity with the duty of care, we have required corporate managers to examine carefully the merits of a proposed change in control. We have also urged consultation with investment specialists in undertaking such analysis. See, e.g., *Treadway,* 638 F.2d at 384. The purpose of this exercise, however, is to insure a reasoned examination of the situation *before* action is taken, not afterwards. We have never given the slightest indication that we would sanction a board decision to lock up voting power by any means, for as long as the directors deem necessary, prior to making the decisions that will determine a corporation's destiny. Were we to countenance that, we would in effect be approving a wholesale wresting of

---

10. Other courts have noted that the issuance of shares to an ESOP shortly after a challenge to corporate control gives rise to an inference of improper motive. See, e.g., Klaus v. Hi-Shear Corp., supra, 528 F.2d at 231–33; Podesta v. Calumet Industries, Inc., [1978 Transfer Binder] Fed.Sec. L.Rep. (CCH) ¶ 96,433 (N.D.Ill.1978). Norlin also argues that the ESOP had been under consideration for some time, even though it was not created until a threat to the company emerged. No more support for that assertion exists here than in *Hi-Shear Corp.,* 528 F.2d at 233, or *Calumet Industries,* ¶ 96,433 at 93,556.

12. Norlin argues that "Piezo's burden under the business judgment rule is all the

heavier because the Norlin board that approved [the stock issuances] was overwhelmingly composed of independent 'outside' directors." We are not persuaded that a different test applies to "independent" as opposed to "inside" directors under the business judgment rule. See, e.g., Zapata Corp. v. Maldonado, 430 A.2d 779 (Del.1981); Note, "The Misapplication of the Business Judgment Rule in Contests for Corporate Control," 76 Nw.U.L.Rev. 980, 1001–03 (1982) and authorities cited therein. In any event, once a collective conflict of interest underlying the board's action is shown, any such distinction has no bearing on the fairness and reasonableness of the action taken.

corporate power from the hands of the shareholders, to whom it is entrusted by statute, and into the hands of the officers and directors.

We thus find that Piezo has succeeded in demonstrating the likelihood of success on the merits, with regard to the share issuances to both Andean and the ESOP. We move on to the other requirement for the issuance of a preliminary injunction: a showing of irreparable harm.

IV

Judge Edelstein based his finding of irreparable harm upon the probability that Norlin common stock would be delisted from the NYSE if shareholder approval were not obtained for the stock transfers. In prior cases, we have noted the importance of NYSE listing to a corporation and its shareholders. Listing on the "Big Board" protects the liquidity of shares, and reassures shareholders and potential purchasers that the extensive NYSE listing requirements are being met. See Sonesta Int'l Hotels Corp. v. Wellington Associates, 483 F.2d 247, 254 (2d Cir.1973). Moreover, as we noted in Van Gemert v. Boeing Co., 520 F.2d 1373 (2d Cir. 1975), cert. denied, 423 U.S. 947 (1975), the investing public places great stock in these protections:

> * * * [L]isting on the New York Stock Exchange carries with it implicit guarantees of trustworthiness. The public generally understands that a company must meet certain qualifications of financial stability, prestige, and fair disclosure, in order to be accepted for that listing, which is in turn so helpful to the sale of the company's securities. Similarly it is held out to the investing public that by dealing in securities listed on the New York Stock Exchange the investor will be dealt with fairly and pursuant to law.

Id. at 1381. Cf. United Funds, Inc. v. Carter Products, Inc., [1961–64 Transfer Binder] Fed.Sec.L.Rep. (CCH) ¶ 91,288 (Balt.Cir.Ct. May 16, 1963) (enjoining stock issuance that would lead to loss of NYSE listing, which constituted "valuable corporate asset").

Norlin makes two attacks on the district judge's finding of irreparable harm. First, the company argues that its stock will suffer no loss of liquidity from NYSE delisting, because the shares are and will continue to be traded on NASDAQ, which Norlin asserts is a comparable market in all respects. At best, this undercuts only one of the three reasons for maintaining NYSE listing. It does not respond to the point that investors rely heavily upon the rules of the NYSE to insure fair dealing in corporate matters. Indeed, the fact that Norlin stock continues to be traded on NASDAQ even while it is suspended on the NYSE suggests that this investor confidence may be well placed. In addition, Norlin's assertion does not contradict Judge Edelstein's finding that "delisting of securities generally is a serious loss of prestige and has a chilling effect on prospective buyers. * * *"

* * *

V

In analyzing the issues presented to us, we have been mindful of the preliminary stage at which this litigation stands. Developments in corporate control contests often proceed swiftly, and timing may have a crucial impact on the outcome. A more complete record will also be required to reach a final adjudication of the merits of Norlin's and Piezo's competing claims. We would therefore urge the district judge to proceed expeditiously to a trial on the important issues raised by the parties.

This case well illustrates the increasing complexity and bitterness of the tactics employed by contestants vying for corporate dominion. As here, each new offensive may be met with a counter-offensive intended, in turn, to weaken the aggressor. When these maneuvers fail, the courts themselves are too often drawn into the fray.

Although we are cognizant that takeover fights, potentially involving billions of dollars, profoundly affect our society and economy, it is not for us to make the policy choices that will determine whether this style of corporate warfare will escalate or diminish. Our holding here is not intended to reflect a more general view of the contests being played out on this and other corporate battlefields. We do, however, believe that a preliminary injunction was warranted in this case. Whatever denouement may flow from the events that have transpired, the rules of fairness we have outlined must govern the actions taken by both sides. Because Piezo has succeeded in demonstrating probable illegality in the issuance of shares to Andean and the ESOP, as well as irreparable harm therefrom, we agree that the voting of those shares should, pending further proceedings, be enjoined. Accordingly, the order of the district court is affirmed.

MORAN v. HOUSEHOLD INTERNATIONAL, INC.

Supreme Court of Delaware, 1985.
500 A.2d 1346.

Before MCNEILLY, MOORE and CHRISTIE, JUSTICES.

MCNEILLY, JUSTICE:

This case presents to this Court for review the most recent defensive mechanism in the arsenal of corporate takeover weaponry—the Preferred Share Purchase Rights Plan ("Rights Plan" or "Plan"). The validity of this mechanism has attracted national attention. *Amici curiae* briefs have been filed in support of appellants by the Securities and Exchange Commission ("SEC")[1] and the Investment Company Institute. An *amicus curiae* brief has been filed in support of appellees ("Household") by the United Food and Commercial Workers International Union.

In a detailed opinion, the Court of Chancery upheld the Rights Plan as a legitimate exercise of business judgment by Household. Moran v. Household International, Inc., Del.Ch., 490 A.2d 1059 (1985). We agree, and therefore, affirm the judgment below.

I

The facts giving rise to this case have been carefully delineated in the Court of Chancery's opinion. Id. at 1064–69. A review of the basic facts is necessary for a complete understanding of the issues.

---

1. The SEC split 3–2 on whether to intervene in this case. The two dissenting Commissioners have publicly disagreed with the other three as to the merits of the Rights Plan. 17 Securities Regulation & Law Report 400; The Wall Street Journal, March 20, 1985, at 6.

On August 14, 1984, the Board of Directors of Household International, Inc. adopted the Rights Plan by a fourteen to two vote.[2] The intricacies of the Rights Plan are contained in a 48–page document entitled "Rights Agreement". Basically, the Plan provides that Household common stockholders are entitled to the issuance of one Right per common share under certain triggering conditions. There are two triggering events that can activate the Rights. The first is the announcement of a tender offer for 30 percent of Household's shares ("30% trigger") and the second is the acquisition of 20 percent of Household's shares by any single entity or group ("20% trigger").

If an announcement of a tender offer for 30 percent of Household's shares is made, the Rights are issued and are immediately exercisable to purchase $\frac{1}{100}$ share of new preferred stock for $100 and are redeemable by the Board for $.50 per Right. If 20 percent of Household's shares are acquired by anyone, the Rights are issued and become non-redeemable and are exercisable to purchase $\frac{1}{100}$ of a share of preferred. If a Right is not exercised for preferred, and thereafter, a merger or consolidation occurs, the Rights holder can exercise each Right to purchase $200 of the common stock of the tender offeror for $100. This "flip-over" provision of the Rights Plan is at the heart of this controversy.

Household is a diversified holding company with its principal subsidiaries engaged in financial services, transportation and merchandising. HFC, National Car Rental and Vons Grocery are three of its wholly-owned entities.

Household did not adopt its Rights Plan during a battle with a corporate raider, but as a preventive mechanism to ward off future advances. The Vice-Chancellor found that as early as February 1984, Household's management became concerned about the company's vulnerability as a takeover target and began considering amending its charter to render a takeover more difficult. After considering the matter, Household decided not to pursue a fair price amendment.[3]

In the meantime, appellant Moran, one of Household's own Directors and also Chairman of the Dyson-Kissner-Moran Corporation, ("D–K–M") which is the largest single stockholder of Household, began discussions concerning a possible leveraged buy-out of Household by D–K–M. D–K–M's financial studies showed that Household's stock was significantly undervalued in relation to the company's break-up value. It is uncontradicted that Moran's suggestion of a leveraged buy-out never progressed beyond the discussion stage.

Concerned about Household's vulnerability to a raider in light of the current takeover climate, Household secured the services of Wachtell, Lipton, Rosen and Katz ("Wachtell, Lipton") and Goldman, Sachs & Co. ("Goldman, Sachs") to formulate a takeover policy for recommendation to the Household Board at its August 14 meeting. After a July 31 meeting

---

2. Household's Board has ten outside directors and six who are members of management. Messrs. Moran (appellant) and Whitehead voted against the Plan. The record reflects that Whitehead voted against the Plan not on its substance but because he thought it was novel and would bring unwanted publicity to Household.

3. A fair price amendment to a corporate charter generally requires supermajority approval for certain business combinations and sets minimum price criteria for mergers. *Moran*, 490 A.2d at 1064, n.I.

with a Household Board member and a pre-meeting distribution of material on the potential takeover problem and the proposed Rights Plan, the Board met on August 14, 1984.

Representatives of Wachtell, Lipton and Goldman, Sachs attended the August 14 meeting. The minutes reflect that Mr. Lipton explained to the Board that his recommendation of the Plan was based on his understanding that the Board was concerned about the increasing frequency of "bust-up"[4] takeovers, the increasing takeover activity in the financial service industry, such as Leucadia's attempt to take over Avco, and the possible adverse effect this type of activity could have on employees and others concerned with and vital to the continuing successful operation of Household even in the absence of any actual bust-up takeover attempt. Against this factual background, the Plan was approved.

Thereafter, Moran and the company of which he is Chairman, D–K–M, filed this suit. On the eve of trial, Gretl Golter, the holder of 500 shares of Household, was permitted to intervene as an additional plaintiff. The trial was held and the Court of Chancery ruled in favor of Household. Appellants now appeal from that ruling to this Court.

II

The primary issue here is the applicability of the business judgment rule as the standard by which the adoption of the Rights Plan should be reviewed. Much of this issue has been decided by our recent decision in Unocal Corp. v. Mesa Petroleum Co., Del.Supr., 493 A.2d 946 (1985). In *Unocal,* we applied the business judgment rule to analyze Unocal's discriminatory self-tender. We explained:

> When a board addresses a pending takeover bid it has an obligation to determine whether the offer is in the best interests of the corporation and its shareholders. In that respect a board's duty is no different from any other responsibility it shoulders, and its decisions should be no less entitled to the respect they otherwise would be accorded in the realm of business judgment.

Id. at 954 (citation and footnote omitted).

Other jurisdictions have also applied the business judgment rule to actions by which target companies have sought to forestall takeover activity they considered undesirable. See Gearhart Industries, Inc. v. Smith International, 5th Cir., 741 F.2d 707 (1984) (sale of discounted subordinate debentures containing springing warrants); Treco, Inc. v. Land of Lincoln Savings and Loan, 7th Cir., 749 F.2d 374 (1984) (amendment to by-laws); Panter v. Marshall Field, 7th Cir., 646 F.2d 271 (1981) (acquisitions to create antitrust problems); Johnson v. Trueblood, 3d Cir., 629 F.2d 287 (1980), cert. denied, 450 U.S. 999 (1981) (refusal to tender); Crouse-Hinds Co. v. InterNorth, Inc., 2d Cir., 634 F.2d 690 (1980) (sale of stock to favored party); Treadway v. Cane Corp., 2d Cir., 638 F.2d 357 (1980) (sale to White Knight), Enterra Corp. v. SGS Associates, E.D.Pa., 600 F.Supp. 678 (1985) (standstill agreement); Buffalo Forge Co. v. Ogden Corp., W.D.N.Y., 555 F.Supp. 892, aff'd, 717 F.2d 757, cert. denied, 104 S.Ct. 550 (1983) (sale of treasury shares and grant of stock option to White Knight); Whittaker

---

4. "Bust-up" takeover generally refers to a situation in which one seeks to finance an acquisition by selling off pieces of the acquired company.

Corp. v. Edgar, N.D.Ill., 535 F.Supp. 933 (1982) (disposal of valuable assets); Martin Marietta Corp. v. Bendix Corp., D.Md., 549 F.Supp. 623 (1982) (Pac-Man defense).[6]

This case is distinguishable from the ones cited, since here we have a defensive mechanism adopted to ward off possible future advances and not a mechanism adopted in reaction to a specific threat. This distinguishing factor does not result in the Directors losing the protection of the business judgment rule. To the contrary, pre-planning for the contingency of a hostile takeover might reduce the risk that, under the pressure of a takeover bid, management will fail to exercise reasonable judgment. Therefore, in reviewing a pre-planned defensive mechanism it seems even more appropriate to apply the business judgment rule. See Warner Communications v. Murdoch, D.Del., 581 F.Supp. 1482, 1491 (1984).

Of course, the business judgment rule can only sustain corporate decision making or transactions that are within the power or authority of the Board. Therefore, before the business judgment rule can be applied it must be determined whether the Directors were authorized to adopt the Rights Plan.

III

Appellants vehemently contend that the Board of Directors was unauthorized to adopt the Rights Plan. First, appellants contend that no provision of the Delaware General Corporation Law authorizes the issuance of such Rights. Secondly, appellants, along with the SEC, contend that the Board is unauthorized to usurp stockholders' rights to receive hostile tender offers. Third, appellants and the SEC also contend that the Board is unauthorized to fundamentally restrict stockholders' rights to conduct a proxy contest. We address each of these contentions in turn.

A.

While appellants contend that no provision of the Delaware General Corporation Law authorizes the Rights Plan, Household contends that the Rights Plan was issued pursuant to 8 Del.C. §§ 151(g) and 157. It explains that the Rights are authorized by § 157 and the issue of preferred stock underlying the Rights is authorized by § 151. Appellants respond by making several attacks upon the authority to issue the Rights pursuant to § 157.

Appellants begin by contending that § 157 cannot authorize the Rights Plan since § 157 has never served the purpose of authorizing a takeover defense. Appellants contend that § 157 is a corporate financing statute, and that nothing in its legislative history suggests a purpose that has anything to do with corporate control or a takeover defense. Appellants are unable to demonstrate that the legislature, in its adoption of § 157, meant to limit the applicability of § 157 to only the issuance of Rights for the purposes of corporate financing. Without such affirmative evidence, we decline to impose such a limitation upon the section that the legislature has not. Compare Providence & Worchester Co. v. Baker, Del.Supr., 378

---

6. The "Pac-Man" defense is generally a target company countering an unwanted tender offer by making its own tender offer for stock of the would-be acquirer. Block & Miller, The Responsibilities and Obligations of Corporate Directors in Takeover Contests, 11 Sec.Reg.L.J. 44, 64 (1983).

A.2d 121, 124 (1977) (refusal to read a bar to protective voting provisions into 8 Del.C. § 212(a)).

As we noted in *Unocal:*

> [O]ur corporate law is not static. It must grow and develop in response to, indeed in anticipation of, evolving concepts and needs. Merely because the General Corporation Law is silent as to a specific matter does not mean that it is prohibited.

493 A.2d at 957. See also Cheff v. Mathes, Del.Supr., 199 A.2d 548 (1964).

Secondly, appellants contend that § 157 does not authorize the issuance of sham rights such as the Rights Plan. They contend that the Rights were designed never to be exercised, and that the Plan has no economic value. In addition, they contend the preferred stock made subject to the Rights is also illusory, citing Telvest, Inc. v. Olson, Del.Ch., C.A. No. 5798, Brown, V.C. (March 8, 1979).

Appellants' sham contention fails in both regards. As to the Rights, they can and will be exercised upon the happening of a triggering mechanism, as we have observed during the current struggle of Sir James Goldsmith to take control of Crown Zellerbach. See Wall Street Journal, July 26, 1985, at 3, 12. As to the preferred shares, we agree with the Court of Chancery that they are distinguishable from sham securities invalidated in *Telvest,* supra. The Household preferred, issuable upon the happening of a triggering event, have superior dividend and liquidation rights.

Third, appellants contend that § 157 authorizes the issuance of Rights "entitling holders thereof to purchase from the corporation any shares of *its* capital stock of any class * * *" (emphasis added). Therefore, their contention continues, the plain language of the statute does not authorize Household to issue rights to purchase another's capital stock upon a merger or consolidation.

Household contends, *inter alia,* that the Rights Plan is analogous to "anti-destruction" or "anti-dilution" provisions which are customary features of a wide variety of corporate securities. While appellants seem to concede that "anti-destruction" provisions are valid under Delaware corporate law, they seek to distinguish the Rights Plan as not being incidental, as are most "anti-destruction" provisions, to a corporation's statutory power to finance itself. We find no merit to such a distinction. We have already rejected appellants' similar contention that § 157 could only be used for financing purposes. We also reject that distinction here.

"Anti-destruction" clauses generally ensure holders of certain securities of the protection of their right of conversion in the event of a merger by giving them the right to convert their securities into whatever securities are to replace the stock of their company. See Broad v. Rockwell International Corp., 5th Cir., 642 F.2d 929, 946, cert. denied, 454 U.S. 965 (1981); Wood v. Coastal States Gas Corp., Del.Supr., 401 A.2d 932, 937–39 (1979); B.S.F. Co. v. Philadelphia National Bank, Del.Supr., 204 A.2d 746, 750–51 (1964). The fact that the rights here have as their purpose the prevention of coercive two-tier tender offers does not invalidate them.

* * *

B.

Appellants contend that the Board is unauthorized to usurp stockholders' rights to receive tender offers by changing Household's fundamental structure. We conclude that the Rights Plan does not prevent stockholders from receiving tender offers, and that the change of Household's structure was less than that which results from the implementation of other defensive mechanisms upheld by various courts.

Appellants' contention that stockholders will lose their right to receive and accept tender offers seems to be premised upon an understanding of the Rights Plan which is illustrated by the SEC *amicus* brief which states: "The Chancery Court's decision seriously understates the impact of this plan. In fact, as we discuss below, the Rights Plan will deter not only two-tier offers, but virtually all hostile tender offers."

The fallacy of that contention is apparent when we look at the recent takeover of Crown Zellerbach, which has a similar Rights Plan, by Sir James Goldsmith. Wall Street Journal, July 26, 1985, at 3, 12. The evidence at trial also evidenced many methods around the Plan ranging from tendering with a condition that the Board redeem the Rights, tendering with a high minimum condition of shares and Rights, tendering and soliciting consents to remove the Board and redeem the Rights, to acquiring 50% of the shares and causing Household to self-tender for the Rights. One could also form a group of up to 19.9% and solicit proxies for consents to remove the Board and redeem the Rights. These are but a few of the methods by which Household can still be acquired by a hostile tender offer.

In addition, the Rights Plan is not absolute. When the Household Board of Directors is faced with a tender offer and a request to redeem the Rights, they will not be able to arbitrarily reject the offer. They will be held to the same fiduciary standards any other board of directors would be held to in deciding to adopt a defensive mechanism, the same standard as they were held to in originally approving the Rights Plan. See Unocal, 493 A.2d at 954–55, 958.

In addition, appellants contend that the deterence of tender offers will be accomplished by what they label "a fundamental transfer of power from the stockholders to the directors." They contend that this transfer of power, in itself, is unauthorized.

The Rights Plan will result in no more of a structural change than any other defensive mechanism adopted by a board of directors. The Rights Plan does not destroy the assets of the corporation. The implementation of the Plan neither results in any outflow of money from the corporation nor impairs its financial flexibility. It does not dilute earnings per share and does not have any adverse tax consequences for the corporation or its stockholders. The Plan has not adversely affected the market price of Household's stock.

Comparing the Rights Plan with other defensive mechanisms, it does less harm to the value structure of the corporation than do the other mechanisms. Other mechanisms result in increased debt of the corporation. See Whittaker Corp. v. Edgar, supra (sale of "prize asset"), Cheff v. Mathes, supra, (paying greenmail to eliminate a threat), Unocal Corp. v. Mesa Petroleum Co., supra, (discriminatory self-tender).

There is little change in the governance structure as a result of the adoption of the Rights Plan. The Board does not now have unfettered discretion in refusing to redeem the Rights. The Board has no more discretion in refusing to redeem the Rights than it does in enacting any defensive mechanism.

The contention that the Rights Plan alters the structure more than do other defensive mechanisms because it is so effective as to make the corporation completely safe from hostile tender offers is likewise without merit. As explained above, there are numerous methods to successfully launch a hostile tender offer.

C.

Appellants' third contention is that the Board was unauthorized to fundamentally restrict stockholders' rights to conduct a proxy contest. Appellants contend that the "20% trigger" effectively prevents any stockholder from first acquiring 20% or more shares before conducting a proxy contest and further, it prevents stockholders from banding together into a group to solicit proxies if, collectively, they own 20% or more of the stock.[12] In addition, at trial, appellants contended that read literally, the Rights Agreement triggers the Rights upon the mere acquisition of the right to vote 20% or more of the shares through a proxy solicitation, and thereby precludes any proxy contest from being waged.[13]

Appellants seem to have conceded this last contention in light of Household's response that the receipt of a proxy does not make the recipient the "beneficial owner" of the shares involved which would trigger the Rights. In essence, the Rights Agreement provides that the Rights are triggered when someone becomes the "beneficial owner" of 20% or more of Household stock. Although a literal reading of the Rights Agreement definition of "beneficial owner" would seem to include those shares which one has the right to vote, it has long been recognized that the relationship between grantor and recipient of a proxy is one of agency, and the agency is revocable by the grantor at any time. Henn, Corporations § 196, at 518. Therefore, the holder of a proxy is not the "beneficial owner" of the stock. As a result, the mere acquisition of the right to vote 20% of the shares does not trigger the Rights.

The issue, then, is whether the restriction upon individuals or groups from first acquiring 20% of shares before waging a proxy contest fundamentally restricts stockholders' right to conduct a proxy contest. Regarding this issue the Court of Chancery found:

> Thus, while the Rights Plan does deter the formation of proxy efforts of a certain magnitude, it does not limit the voting power of individual shares. On the evidence presented it is highly conjectural to assume that a particular effort to assert shareholder views in the election of directors or revisions of corporate policy will be frustrated by the proxy feature of the Plan. Household's witnesses, Troubh and Higgins de-

---

12. Appellants explain that the acquisition of 20% of the shares trigger the Rights, making them non-redeemable, and thereby would prevent even a future friendly offer for the ten-year life of the Rights.

13. The SEC still contends that the mere acquisition of the right to vote 20% of the shares through a proxy solicitation triggers the Rights. We do not interpret the Rights Agreement in that manner.

scribed recent corporate takeover battles in which insurgents holding less than 10% stock ownership were able to secure corporate control through a proxy contest or the threat of one.

Moran, 490 A.2d at 1080.

We conclude that there was sufficient evidence at trial to support the Vice-Chancellor's finding that the effect upon proxy contests will be minimal. Evidence at trial established that many proxy contests are won with an insurgent ownership of less than 20%, and that very large holdings are no guarantee of success. There was also testimony that the key variable in proxy contest success is the merit of an insurgent's issues, not the size of his holdings.

IV

Having concluded that the adoption of the Rights Plan was within the authority of the Directors, we now look to whether the Directors have met their burden under the business judgment rule.

The business judgment rule is a "presumption that in making a business decision the directors of a corporation acted on an informed basis, in good faith and in the honest belief that the action taken was in the best interests of the company." Aronson v. Lewis, Del.Supr., 473 A.2d 805, 812 (1984) (citations omitted). Notwithstanding, in *Unocal* we held that when the business judgment rule applies to adoption of a defensive mechanism, the initial burden will lie with the directors. The "directors must show that they had reasonable grounds for believing that a danger to corporate policy and effectiveness existed. * * * [T]hey satisfy that burden 'by showing good faith and reasonable investigation * * *.'" *Unocal,* 493 A.2d at 955 (citing Cheff v. Mathes, 199 A.2d at 554–55). In addition, the directors must show that the defensive mechanism was "reasonable in relation to the threat posed." *Unocal,* 493 A.2d at 955. Moreover, that proof is materially enhanced, as we noted in *Unocal,* where, as here, a majority of the board favoring the proposal consisted of outside independent directors who have acted in accordance with the foregoing standards. *Unocal,* 493 A.2d at 955; *Aronson,* 473 A.2d at 815. Then, the burden shifts back to the plaintiffs who have the ultimate burden of persuasion to show a breach of the directors' fiduciary duties. *Unocal,* 493 A.2d at 958.

There are no allegations here of any bad faith on the part of the Directors' action in the adoption of the Rights Plan. There is no allegation that the Directors' action was taken for entrenchment purposes. Household has adequately demonstrated, as explained above, that the adoption of the Rights Plan was in reaction to what it perceived to be the threat in the market place of coercive two-tier tender offers. Appellants do contend, however, that the Board did not exercise informed business judgment in its adoption of the Plan.

Appellants contend that the Household Board was uninformed since they were *inter alia,* told the Plan would not inhibit a proxy contest, were not told the plan would preclude all hostile acquisitions of Household, and were told that Delaware counsel opined that the plan was within the business judgment of the Board.

As to the first two contentions, as we explained above, the Rights Plan will not have a severe impact upon proxy contests and it will not preclude all hostile acquisitions of Household. Therefore, the Directors were not misinformed or uninformed on these facts.

Appellants contend the Delaware counsel did not express an opinion on the flip-over provision of the Rights, rather only that the Rights would constitute validly issued and outstanding rights to subscribe to the preferred stock of the company.

To determine whether a business judgment reached by a board of directors was an informed one, we determine whether the directors were grossly negligent. Smith v. Van Gorkom, Del.Supr., 488 A.2d 858, 873 (1985). Upon a review of this record, we conclude the Directors were not grossly negligent. The information supplied to the Board on August 14 provided the essentials of the Plan. The Directors were given beforehand a notebook which included a three-page summary of the Plan along with articles on the current takeover environment. The extended discussion between the Board and representatives of Wachtell, Lipton and Goldman, Sachs before approval of the Plan reflected a full and candid evaluation of the Plan. Moran's expression of his views at the meeting served to place before the Board a knowledgeable critique of the Plan. The factual happenings here are clearly distinguishable from the actions of the directors of Trans Union Corporation who displayed gross negligence in approving a cash-out merger. Id.

In addition, to meet their burden, the Directors must show that the defensive mechanism was "reasonable in relation to the threat posed". The record reflects a concern on the part of the Directors over the increasing frequency in the financial services industry of "boot-strap" and "bust-up" takeovers. The Directors were also concerned that such takeovers may take the form of two-tier offers.[14] In addition, on August 14, the Household Board was aware of Moran's overture on behalf of D–K–M. In sum, the Directors reasonably believed Household was vulnerable to coercive acquisition techniques and adopted a reasonable defensive mechanism to protect itself.

V

In conclusion, the Household Directors receive the benefit of the business judgment rule in their adoption of the Rights Plan.

The Directors adopted the Plan pursuant to statutory authority in 8 Del. C. §§ 141, 151, 157. We reject appellants' contentions that the Rights Plan strips stockholders of their rights to receive tender offers, and that the Rights Plan fundamentally restricts proxy contests.

The Directors adopted the Plan in the good faith belief that it was necessary to protect Household from coercive acquisition techniques. The Board was informed as to the details of the Plan. In addition, Household has demonstrated that the Plan is reasonable in relation to the threat posed. Appellants, on the other hand, have failed to convince us that the Directors breached any fiduciary duty in their adoption of the Rights Plan.

While we conclude for present purposes that the Household Directors are protected by the business judgment rule, that does not end the matter.

---

14. We have discussed the coercive nature of two-tier tender offers in *Unocal*, 493 A.2d at 956, n. 12. We explained in *Unocal* that a discriminatory self-tender was reasonably related to the threat of two-tier tender offers and possible greenmail.

The ultimate response to an actual takeover bid must be judged by the Directors' actions at that time, and nothing we say here relieves them of their basic fundamental duties to the corporation and its stockholders. *Unocal*, 493 A.2d at 954–55, 958; Smith v. Van Gorkom, 488 A.2d at 872–73; *Aronson*, 473 A.2d at 812–13; Pogostin v. Rice, Del.Supr., 480 A.2d 619, 627 (1984). Their use of the Plan will be evaluated when and if the issue arises.

Affirmed.

DYNAMICS CORPORATION OF AMERICA v. CTS CORPORATION *

United States Court of Appeals, Seventh Circuit, 1986.
794 F.2d 250.

Before: BAUER, CUDAHY, and POSNER, CIRCUIT JUDGES.

POSNER, CIRCUIT JUDGE.

On March 10 of this year Dynamics Corporation of America, which already owned 9.6 percent of the common stock of CTS Corporation, made a tender offer for another million shares. The offer if accepted would bring its stock holdings up to 27.5 percent of the company. On the same day, Dynamics filed this suit in the federal district court in Chicago; as later amended, the suit sought to enjoin the enforcement of Indiana's statute regulating takeovers, on the ground that the statute violates the supremacy and commerce clauses of the federal Constitution. When CTS "opted in" to a new Indiana statute on the subject, the Control Share Acquisition Chapter as it is called, Ind.Code §§ 23–1–42–1 et seq., Dynamics further amended its complaint to challenge the new statute on the same grounds. A pendent count in the complaint sought to enjoin CTS from enforcing a recently adopted shareholders' rights plan ("poison pill"), on the ground that it violated the fiduciary obligations of CTS's management toward its shareholders. CTS counterclaimed against Dynamics, seeking an injunction against the tender offer on the grounds that it would result in a violation of section 8 of the Clayton Act, 15 U.S.C. § 19 (interlocking directorates), and that it failed to disclose material information. There are some individual parties, but as they are not important to the legal issues we shall ignore them.

Both Dynamics and CTS moved for preliminary injunctions. After a month of frantic pretrial discovery a one-day evidentiary hearing was held before the district judge, who in a series of orders then ruled that the poison pill plan violated Indiana law, that the Indiana statute violated both the supremacy and commerce clauses of the federal Constitution, and that CTS was not entitled to a preliminary injunction. She therefore granted the preliminary injunction requested by Dynamics. CTS, joined by the Attorney General of Indiana, who has intervened in the case to defend his state's statute, appeals under 28 U.S.C. § 1292(a)(1), which allows an

---

* The district court, subsequent to this decision, denied an injunction against a second "poisoned pill" adopted by CTS, 635 F.Supp. 1174, 638 F.Supp. 802 (N.D.Ill. 1986), which decision was affirmed in part and reversed in part by the court of appeals, 805 F.2d 705 (7th Cir. 1986). The Supreme Court has noted probable jurisdiction in an appeal by the State of Indiana from the decision printed above. ___ U.S. ___, 107 S.Ct. 258, 93 L.Ed.2d 17 (1986).

immediate appeal from an order granting or denying a preliminary injunction. We accelerated our consideration of the appeal because Dynamics had only till April 24 to decide whether to buy the shares tendered in response to its offer. We heard argument on April 23 and later that day affirmed the district judge's orders, with a notation that an opinion explaining the grounds of our decision would follow.

The main issues we must address are the lawfulness of CTS's poison pill scheme, the district court's compliance with a federal statute requiring that a state's attorney general be notified that the constitutionality of a statute of his state is being challenged, the constitutionality of the new Indiana takeover statute under the supremacy clause and also under the commerce clause, the significance of the potential violation of the Clayton Act, and the adequacy of the disclosures made in the tender offer.

Before taking up these issues we shall comment briefly on the procedural posture of the case in this court, an appeal from orders granting and denying requests for preliminary injunctions. As emphasized in our recent opinions, in different but compatible formulations, the task for a district judge asked to grant a preliminary injunction is to compare the irreparable harm to the plaintiff if the injunction is denied, weighted by the likelihood that the denial would be erroneous because the plaintiff will prevail in the plenary trial, with the irreparable harm to the defendant if the injunction is granted, weighted by the likelihood that the grant would be erroneous because the defendant, not the plaintiff, will prevail in the trial. See Lawson Products, Inc. v. Avnet, Inc., 782 F.2d 1429, 1433–34 (7th Cir.1986); American Hospital Supply Corp. v. Hospital Products Ltd., 780 F.2d 589, 593 (7th Cir.1986); Roland Machinery Co. v. Dresser Industries, Inc., 749 F.2d 380, 387–88 (7th Cir.1984). So, for example, the greater the probability that the plaintiff will win the case in the end, the less irreparable harm he need show relative to the defendant in order to get the preliminary injunction. If both parties are likely to suffer the same amount of irreparable harm, so far as estimation is possible, then likelihood of success becomes decisive. See American Hospital Supply Corp. v. Hospital Products Ltd., supra, 780 F.2d at 598. That seems a reasonable description of the present case; the fact that both parties sought preliminary injunctions does not affect the analysis.

* * *

Against this background we first ask whether the district court was right to conclude that the adoption of the poison pill violated the fiduciary obligations of CTS's management to its shareholders. The parties agree both that the question is governed by the common law of Indiana and that Indiana takes its cues in matters of corporation law from the Delaware courts, which are more experienced in such matters since such a large fraction of major corporations is incorporated in Delaware and such a small fraction in Indiana.

The whole issue of permissible defensive tactics in the face of a tender offer is immensely contentious, and it is no business of ours, whose duty on this branch of the appeal is only to predict how the Indiana courts would evaluate CTS's poison pill maneuver, to choose sides. There are two polar positions in the debate. One views hostile takeovers as a bad thing, on a variety of grounds such as that they make managers of companies that are potential targets of takeover bids worry too much about short-term financial results and that they promote absentee ownership and control. See, e.g., Scherer, Takeovers: Present and Future Dangers, Brookings Rev. (winter-spring 1986), at 15; Herman, Corporate Control, Corporate Power 100–01 (1981). Whether or not Dynamics ever merges CTS into it, the parties seem agreed that if the tender offer succeeds, Dynamics, as by far the largest shareholder of CTS, will probably be able to elect a majority of the board of directors. Dynamics is a New York corporation with head-quarters in Connecticut, CTS an Indiana corporation with headquarters in Indiana. The record is not clear on where the firms' assets and employees are concentrated, and indeed reveals little about the companies except that CTS is a manufacturer of electronic and electromechanical components and Dynamics a diversified manufacturer of consumer and industrial products and that both are large companies whose stock is traded on the New York Stock Exchange.

The other pole is that all resistance to takeover attempts is bad. See, e.g., Easterbrook & Fischel, The Proper Role of a Target's Management in Responding to a Tender Offer, 94 Harv.L.Rev. 1161 (1981); Gilson, A Structural Approach to Corporations: The Case Against Defensive Tactics in Tender Offers, 33 Stan.L.Rev. 819 (1981); cf. SEC Office of Chief Economist, A Study on the Economics of Poison Pills, Fed.Sec.L.Rep. (CCH) ¶ 83,971 (March 5, 1986). The market price of publicly traded stock impounds all available information about the value of the stock, and anyone who offers a higher price (Dynamics' tender offer price was $43, and when the offer was made CTS's stock was trading at $36) thereby offers an unequivocal benefit to the shareholders of the target firm, which management if it is really a fiduciary of the shareholders should embrace rather than oppose. In that way the market for corporate control will be kept fluid and corporate assets will be transferred, with a minimum of friction, to those who value them the most, as measured by the prices they offer. See also Ginsburg & Robinson, The Case Against Federal Intervention in the Market for Corporate Control, Brookings Rev. (winter-spring 1986), at 9.

It is a safe prediction that the Indiana courts would reject the polar views, as the Delaware courts have done. To allow management to use its control of the board of directors to frustrate all hostile takeovers would nullify an important protection for shareholders. The threat of hostile takeover plays a vital role in keeping management on its toes. CTS has been a troubled firm of late; a major acquisition (which Dynamics, long a major shareholder, opposed) soured, and was written off at a large loss. If CTS's management is allowed to insulate the company from any change of control to which management does not agree, the shareholders may be unable to realize the potential value of their investment. Maybe under different control, specifically Dynamics' control, CTS would be a more valuable company; then its shareholders would benefit from a takeover, hostile or otherwise. It is only human for CTS's officers and directors to doubt that a company which, if it takes control of CTS, will fire them can actually do a better job of running "their" company. But it is not their company; at least it is not supposed to be. It is supposed to be the shareholders' company, for it is they who are entitled to all the income that the company generates after paying off all contractually or otherwise obligated expenses. The officers and directors are the agents and fiduciaries of the shareholders and owe a duty of complete loyalty which is inconsistent with erecting insuperable barriers to hostile takeovers.

But it does not follow that loyalty requires passivity. See, e.g., Bebchuk, The Case for Facilitating Competing Tender Offers, 95 Harv.L.Rev. 1028 (1982). If someone stops you on the street and says, "Say, that's a beautiful watch you're wearing—I'll give you $250 for it," you won't necessarily agree to the sale even if the watch is worth only $100 to you (apart from any sale value it may have). You may want to see whether you can sell it for even more than $250, now that you have an inkling of what its market value may be. Likewise the first tender offer may not be the best. It is true that each shareholder can decide for himself whether he is likely to do better by holding out for a better offer, and if enough decide this way the offer will fail and maybe the offeror, or some other investor, will offer more. But many shareholders are passive investors. They know little about the companies in which they invest or about the market for corporate control. They want to be told whether they should sell their shares now or wait for a better offer to come along. Better yet—for it is difficult to absorb information about a subject you don't know much about—they want management to create a process that will maximize the value of their shares in a takeover situation. That may require the use of some defensive tactics.

One defensive tactic that is permitted and indeed required by federal law is, as we shall see, to have a cooling off period between the announcement and the consummation of a tender offer. Such a period gives the shareholders time to do some shopping around. This is not an unmixed blessing. It reduces the expected gain to the first maker of a tender offer, for now he may have to compete with other offerors and may have to raise his price—a possibility that will reduce the likelihood of a tender offer's being made in the first place. On the other hand, the waiting period creates an opportunity for other investors to make competing offers, and thus encourages an auction of the firm's assets with more than one bidder. Maybe the second effect dominates the first. To take another example, if a corporation offers its key managers "golden parachutes" (generous severance pay in the event they lose their jobs because of a takeover), this may make them resist takeovers less; and the benefits to shareholders may exceed the costs of the golden parachutes themselves as well as the effect of the parachutes in making the takeover more costly to the acquiring firm.

Conceivably even the "poison pill" may, if it is not actually lethal, benefit shareholders of the target firm. This wonderfully vivid term refers to a family of shareholder rights agreements which, upon some triggering event such as the acquisition by a tender offeror of a certain percentage of the target corporation's common stock, entitle the remaining shareholders to receive additional shares of common stock (or other securities) at bargain prices. Suppose that the tender offeror makes an offer for 51 percent of the stock of the target firm, knowing that if the offer succeeds he can then force out the minority shareholders by voting his shares for a swap of the target's assets for cash (a cash merger). Although minority shareholders who are squeezed out in this fashion have a legal right to receive the fair value of their shares, that value may be less than either the tender offer price or the value that their shares would command in the market had there been no tender offer. A poison pill triggered by the acquisition of a majority stock interest gives the remaining shareholders more shares. This both improves their position if the tender offer succeeds and makes all shareholders less frantic to tender. Without the poison pill, shareholders will compete to tender their shares because if they do not they may miss out on an opportunity to sell their shares at a premium price and thus to escape the fate of the minority shareholder. But at the same time, by making a tender offer less certain to succeed and more costly to the offeror, the poison pill may reduce the number of tender offers and the price of each offer, thus hurting all shareholders ex ante.

The tradeoffs obviously are complex, so it is no surprise to find that the evidence on whether particular defensive tactics enhance or reduce shareholder welfare is mixed. See Jensen & Ruback, The Market for Corporate Control: The Scientific Evidence, 11 J. Financial Econ. 5, 29–40 (1983). An intriguing recent finding is that targets that resist tender offers yet are later acquired do better, at least in the short run, in maximizing shareholder wealth than targets that do not resist. The qualification is vital; if, as seems likely, defensive tactics reduce the number of tender offers, then shareholders may lose in the long run. Moreover, the study finds that if the target resists so stubbornly that it is not acquired later, its shareholders are made unequivocally worse off. See Jarrell, The Wealth Effects of Litigation by Targets: Do Interests Diverge in a Merge?, 28 J. Law & Econ. 151 (1985). But maybe, even with the risk that resistance will be too successful or that defensive tactics may eventually weaken the market for corporate control and hurt all shareholders, some resistance is the optimal strategy for managements perfectly loyal to their shareholders to follow. If so, the adoption of some defensive measures, perhaps even some poison pills, may be in the interest of all the corporation's shareholders, though we are not aware of any rigorous study which finds that poison pills help shareholders.

Personally we are rather skeptical about the arguments for defensive measures. They strike us as giving too little weight to the effect of "defensive" measures in rendering shareholders defenseless against their own managements. (The shareholders of CTS were not asked to approve the poison pill.) We are especially skeptical about the arguments used to defend poison pills. If the present case is representative, the poison pill seems (as we shall see) more a reflex device of a management determined to hold on to power at all costs than a considered measure for maximizing shareholder wealth. Unlike a fair price amendment, which requires the tender offeror to pay the same price to the nontendering as to the tendering shareholders in order to head off a stampede to tender that may reduce the price of the tender offer, the poison pill can (in this case did) substantially dilute the tender offeror's shares, thereby defeating the object of the offer, which is to take over the company in the hope of squeezing more profit out of its assets. Depending on its terms the poison pill may also make each shareholder think himself better off not tendering, hoping instead to get the goodies that nontendering shareholders receive by virtue of the poison pill. But of course if no one tenders, no tender offer can succeed.

So we have grave doubts about poison pills. But our personal views on a matter committed to the authority of the states are not terribly important; and given the complexity of the issue it is understandable why state courts would hesitate to condemn all defensive measures (even all poison pills) as breaches of fiduciary duty, on the basis of the present incomplete evidence of the actual effects of these measures.

Indeed, the Delaware courts have been quite emphatic that defensive measures in general and poison pills in particular are within the power of the board of directors of a target corporation. E.g., Revlon, Inc. v. MacAndrews & Forbes Holdings, Inc., 506 A.2d 173, 180 (Del.1986). But at the same time these courts have insisted that the measures be plausibly related to the goal of stockholder wealth maximization. See id. ("when a board implements anti-takeover measures, * * * [the] potential for conflict [of interest] places upon the directors the burden of proving that they had reasonable grounds for believing there was a danger to corporate policy and effectiveness, a burden satisfied by a showing of good faith and reasonable investigation"); Moran v. Household Int'l, Inc., 500 A.2d 1346, 1356 (Del. 1985) ("when the business judgment rule applies to adoption of a defensive mechanism, the initial burden [of proving that the directors acted on an informed basis, in good faith, and in the honest belief that the action taken was in the best interests of the company] will lie with the directors"); Unocal Corp. v. Mesa Petroleum Co., 493 A.2d 946, 954 (Del.1985) ("Because of the omnipresent specter that a board may be acting primarily in its own interests, rather than those of the corporation and its shareholders, there is an enhanced duty which calls for judicial examination at the threshold before the protections of the business judgment rule may be conferred"). The shifting of burdens adopted in these decisions was anticipated by Judge Cudahy's dissenting opinion in Panter v. Marshall Field & Co., 646 F.2d 271, 299–304 (7th Cir.1981). See also Hanson Trust PLC v. ML SCM Acquisition Inc., 781 F.2d 264, 273 (2d Cir.1986) (dictum).

Thus the Delaware courts have not, as CTS argues, written targets' management a blank check endorsed with "business judgment rule." This rule expresses a sensible policy of judicial noninterference with business decisions made in circumstances free from serious conflicts of interest between management, which makes the decisions, and the corporation's shareholders. Not only do businessmen know more about business than judges do, but competition in the product and labor markets and in the market for corporate control provides sufficient punishment for businessmen who commit more than their share of business mistakes. When however there is a serious conflict of interest, and in particular when management is making decisions that may thwart the operation of the market in corporate control, the judicial role (under Delaware law, and we assume Indiana law as well) is less deferential. When managers are busy erecting obstacles to the taking over of the corporation by an investor who is likely to fire them if the takeover attempt succeeds, they have a clear conflict of interest, and it is not cured by vesting the power of decision in a board of directors in which insiders are a minority (five of CTS's eight directors are outsiders). No one likes to be fired, whether he is just a director or also an officer. The so-called outsiders moreover are often friends of the insiders. And since they spend only part of their time on the affairs of the corporation, their knowledge of those affairs is much less than that of the insiders, to whom they are likely therefore to defer.

These problems have seemed serious enough to warrant a more searching judicial review of corporate decisions concerning defensive measures to takeovers than of decisions concerning ordinary business decisions. Such review is not without its costs. It makes directors overcautious, makes people reluctant to serve as directors, drives up directors' fees and officers' and directors' liability insurance rates, and leads boards of directors to adopt ponderous, court-like procedures. But the price is one the courts have been willing to pay.

From these general reflections we turn at last to the particulars of this case. Since the present management of CTS took over the company in 1981, a year after Dynamics first became a major shareholder, CTS's rate of return has declined substantially, in part because of a series of acquisitions to which Dynamics objected and which indeed turned out to be flops. Dynamics therefore coupled its March 10 announcement of the tender offer with a declaration that it would field a slate of candidates for the board of directors election scheduled for April 24 (since postponed). On the very same day (March 10, which was also the day this lawsuit was filed) CTS's management announced its opposition to Dynamics' actions—without having studied their business and financial implications or even having consulted CTS's outside directors. The next day CTS retained as its investment advisor Smith Barney under a contract whereby the advisor would receive a bonus if Dynamics lost the proxy fight. The following day the board met to discuss the matter. Without consulting the board, CTS's chairman wrote the shareholders the next day urging them not to vote for Dynamics' slate. On March 22 Smith Barney presented its poison pill proposal to the board, with an accompanying "fairness opinion" in which it opined that Dynamics' tender offer was unfair. The board did not discuss price either, but did at that very meeting unanimously adopt the poison pill.

The tender offer was not evaluated in a cool, dispassionate, and thorough fashion. We do not mean to suggest that the board was obliged to accord due process to Dynamics; we have no desire to judicialize board of directors meetings. But it is apparent that the insiders on the board, in particular the chairman, decided from the start to block the tender offer, before its ramifications for shareholder welfare were considered; judgment first, trial later, as the Queen of Hearts said in *Alice in Wonderland.* Smith Barney held itself out as a blocker, and would have lost its $75,000 bonus if it had advised the board that the tender offer was fair and if the end result of this advice had been Dynamics' wresting control of the board from the existing directors. How the fairness of the tender offer could be determined without any consideration of the fairness of the offer price is mystifying. CTS argues that not all the shareholders could get the tender offer price, because Dynamics was seeking tenders of only 17.9 percent of the shares. This is doubly misleading. Every fifth shareholder (.179 divided by .904—the other 9.6 percent of the shares being owned by Dynamics already—is .198) would get that price. More important, all the shareholders benefited ex ante. Upon announcement of the tender offer the price of CTS stock rose from below $36 to above $40 (a much bigger percentage leap than the NYSE Composite, S & P 500, or Dow Jones indexes took that day). Those shareholders who did not expect to be in the lucky one-fifth to sell to Dynamics at $43 could sell the day the offer was announced for $40. (Of course some stockholders would not have known about the movement in the price and some who did know would adhere to a buy-and-hold strategy, and so not sell.) It is worth noting that the price of CTS shares dropped substantially the day after the poison pill was announced, and rose again when the district judge's order invalidating the poison pill was released.

CTS argues that it did not need to investigate the tender offer in order to know it was bad, for there was a long history of bad blood between it and Dynamics. Dynamics had been a very restive, unhappy shareholder. There had been litigation between the companies. CTS's management had formed the judgment that the companies had incompatible philosophies, with CTS focusing on the long term and hence making substantial capital investments and Dynamics going for the quick buck. It *knew* a takeover of CTS by Dynamics would be bad. But given CTS's disappointing performance in recent years and the fact that Dynamics seemed to have been vindicated in its opposition to CTS's acquisitions by CTS having written off the largest one as a loss, CTS's management could not be so confident that a takeover by Dynamics would reduce shareholder wealth. The friction between the companies required, if anything, more than the usual amount of care by CTS's board of directors in evaluating the proposal, to make sure that personal feelings would not be allowed to interfere with the board's fiduciary obligations.

All this might be of little moment if the particular poison pill which Smith Barney sold CTS's board were a plausible measure for maximizing shareholder wealth, for as we have said we have no desire to force boards of directors into a judicialized mode of proceeding and we recognize the time pressure under which the board was operating, with the stockholders' meeting scheduled for April 24 and the starting gun for selling stock to Dynamics in response to its tender offer due to go off only 28 days after the announcement of the offer. So let us look at the terms of the poison pill. As soon as one shareholder had 15 percent or more of CTS's stock, all the others would get the right to buy a securities package, consisting of stock and a debenture, for 25 percent of the then market price of the package. The right would thus be triggered if the tender offer went through, and presumably would be exercised since the terms are so advantageous to the shareholder (illustrating our earlier point that poison pills discourage acceptance of tender offers). Assuming that all rights were exercised, the effect of the additional shares that would be issued to the existing shareholders would be to reduce Dynamics' holdings from 27.5 percent of CTS's common stock to 20.7 percent. Not only would this reduce Dynamics' voting power in the election for the board of directors but it would inflict a substantial capital loss on Dynamics. CTS would be worth no more just because, the "poison pill" having taken effect, the company had more shares outstanding than it did previously. Therefore 20.7 percent of the company would be worth less than the 27.5 percent Dynamics thought it was getting: $24 million less, assuming a $40 price for CTS shares.

In addition, the total amount of debentures to be issued to the shareholders as part of the poison pill would burden CTS with a new, long-term fixed debt of $80 million at a high interest rate (13 percent), further reducing the value of Dynamics' holdings. This large debt, for which CTS would not receive commensurate value in exchange, would reduce CTS's net profits. It could, indeed, imperil its financial health very seriously; for the taking on of such a large debt would entitle some existing creditors of CTS to treat CTS as having thereby defaulted on their loans to it, and these creditors would therefore be entitled to call the loans—and the whole house of cards might collapse. At the very least, the new debt would increase the volatility of CTS's earnings by increasing the fraction of fixed costs in the company's financial structure. This in turn would reduce the value of the stock quite apart from the effect of lower earnings, simply because most investors are risk averse. See, e.g., Lorie & Hamilton, The Stock Market: Theories and Evidence, chs. 11–12 (1973).

We do not want to paint too bleak a picture. Unless the debentures so weighted down CTS with debt that they forced the company into bankruptcy, the shareholders—other than Dynamics, of course—would be getting something of value out of the transaction: the debentures. Their investment in CTS would be converted from an all-equity investment to a package consisting of a riskier equity investment and a debt investment. Indeed, putting aside the effect on Dynamics, the immediate effect of issuing the debentures would just be to raise CTS's debt-equity ratio; and if the ratio was too low before, the shareholders might be made better off. But there is no indication that it was too low before; and if a company's debt-equity ratio is too high, the risk of bankruptcy may become very great.

All this *Sturm und Drang* seems a high price to pay for fending off a change of corporate control that may, for all that appears, benefit the shareholders greatly, though it will be a humiliation to the present officers and directors. It is defended as necessary to protect minority shareholders from a disadvantageous "backend" transaction. But even after Dynamics obtains 27.5 percent of CTS's stock, it will not be a majority shareholder, and will therefore not be able to squeeze out the remaining shareholders. To be able to do that it will have to buy up another 22.5–plus percent of the shares. CTS's poison pill is thus to be administered prematurely. If the rationale is to protect minority shareholders, it should be triggered by a transaction that creates a majority shareholder or that attempts to squeeze out the minority shareholders, and it should give the minority the same price per share as the majority—not a higher price calculated to kill off the tender, indeed to kill off any tender. CTS's shareholder rights agreement is triggered much earlier, and at a higher price. It effectively precludes a hostile takeover, and thus allows management to take the shareholders hostage. To buy CTS, you must buy out its management.

CTS argues that once Dynamics controls the board of directors and hence the proxy machinery, it will be able to gull the remaining shareholders into selling their shares to it for too low a price. Setting aside the legal remedies against abuse of the proxy machinery, CTS's argument if correct underscores the importance of not impeding tender offers too much, since the premise of the argument is that management cannot be trusted to protect the interests of the shareholders.

We conclude that the poison pill was properly enjoined, and move on to the cluster of issues concerning the distinct takeover obstacle erected by the Indiana control-share acquisition statute, which if valid would thwart Dynamics' tender offer. [Discussion of the Indiana statute omitted; see p. 715, above.]

     *   *   *

The last issue is whether the tender offer should have been enjoined because of a failure to disclose material facts. As the district judge correctly found, most of these facts were not material. One was. The tender-offer materials do not disclose Dynamics' intention to oust the present management of CTS if the tender offer succeeds and enables Dynamics to elect a new board of directors. The district judge held that this omission was cured by the distribution to all shareholders, two weeks before the end of the tender-offer period, of Dynamics' proxy materials, in which it urges the shareholders to elect Dynamics' slate of directors. CTS argues that this was not good enough, because some shareholders may not have paid attention to the proxy solicitation. But such shareholders might have paid equally little attention to the same disclosure in the tender offer. In truth Dynamics' desire to oust the present board was broadcast loudly and widely.

Even if exclusion from the tender offer could not be cured by inclusion in the proxy materials—an arcane question of federal securities law on which CTS's briefs cast little light—it would not follow that enjoining the tender offer was a proper remedy. The fashioning of remedies is largely within the discretion of the district judge and that discretion was not abused in this case.

Affirmed.

———

REVLON, INC. v. MacANDREWS & FORBES HOLDINGS, INC.

Supreme Court of Delaware, 1986.
506 A.2d 173.

Before McNEILLY and MOORE, JJ., and BALICK, JUDGE (Sitting by designation pursuant to Del. Const., Art. IV, § 12.).

MOORE, JUSTICE:

In this battle for corporate control of Revlon, Inc. (Revlon), the Court of Chancery enjoined certain transactions designed to thwart the efforts of Pantry Pride, Inc. (Pantry Pride) to acquire Revlon.[1] The defendants are Revlon, its board of directors, and Forstmann Little & Co. and the latter's affiliated limited partnership (collectively, Forstmann). The injunction barred consummation of an option granted Forstmann to purchase certain Revlon assets (the lock-up option), a promise by Revlon to deal exclusively with Forstmann in the face of a takeover (the no-shop provision), and the payment of a $25 million cancellation fee to Forstmann if the transaction was aborted. The Court of Chancery found that the Revlon directors had breached their duty of care by entering into the foregoing transactions and effectively ending an active auction for the company. The trial court ruled that such arrangements are not illegal per se under Delaware law, but that their use under the circumstances here was impermissible. We agree. See MacAndrews & Forbes Holdings, Inc. v. Revlon, Inc., Del.Ch., 501 A.2d 1239 (1985). Thus, we granted this expedited interlocutory appeal to consider for the first time the validity of such defensive measures in the face of an active bidding contest for corporate control. Additionally, we address for the first time the extent to which a corporation may consider the impact of a takeover threat on constituencies other than shareholders. See Unocal Corp. v. Mesa Petroleum Co., Del.Supr., 493 A.2d 946, 955 (1985).

In our view, lock-ups and related agreements are permitted under Delaware law where their adoption is untainted by director interest or

1. The nominal plaintiff, MacAndrews & Forbes Holdings, Inc., is the controlling stockholder of Pantry Pride. For all practical purposes their interests in this litigation are virtually identical, and we hereafter will refer to Pantry Pride as the plaintiff.

other breaches of fiduciary duty. The actions taken by the Revlon directors, however, did not meet this standard. Moreover, while concern for various corporate constituencies is proper when addressing a takeover threat, that principle is limited by the requirement that there be some rationally related benefit accruing to the stockholders. We find no such benefit here.

Thus, under all the circumstances we must agree with the Court of Chancery that the enjoined Revlon defensive measures were inconsistent with the directors' duties to the stockholders. Accordingly, we affirm.

I.

The somewhat complex maneuvers of the parties necessitate a rather detailed examination of the facts. The prelude to this controversy began in June 1985, when Ronald O. Perelman, chairman of the board and chief executive officer of Pantry Pride, met with his counterpart at Revlon, Michel C. Bergerac, to discuss a friendly acquisition of Revlon by Pantry Pride. Perelman suggested a price in the range of $40–50 per share, but the meeting ended with Bergerac dismissing those figures as considerably below Revlon's intrinsic value. All subsequent Pantry Pride overtures were rebuffed, perhaps in part based on Mr. Bergerac's strong personal antipathy to Mr. Perelman.

Thus, on August 14, Pantry Pride's board authorized Perelman to acquire Revlon, either through negotiation in the $42–$43 per share range, or by making a hostile tender offer at $45. Perelman then met with Bergerac and outlined Pantry Pride's alternate approaches. Bergerac remained adamantly opposed to such schemes and conditioned any further discussions of the matter on Pantry Pride executing a standstill agreement prohibiting it from acquiring Revlon without the latter's prior approval.

On August 19, the Revlon board met specially to consider the impending threat of a hostile bid by Pantry Pride.[3] At the meeting, Lazard Freres, Revlon's investment banker, advised the directors that $45 per share was a grossly inadequate price for the company. Felix Rohatyn and William Loomis of Lazard Freres explained to the board that Pantry Pride's financial strategy for acquiring Revlon would be through "junk bond" financing followed by a break-up of Revlon and the disposition of its assets. With proper timing, according to the experts, such transactions could produce a return to Pantry Pride of $60 to $70 per share, while a sale of the company as a whole would be in the "mid 50" dollar range. Martin Lipton, special counsel for Revlon, recommended two defensive measures: first, that the company repurchase up to 5 million of its nearly 30 million outstanding shares; and second, that it adopt a Note Purchase Rights Plan. Under this plan, each Revlon shareholder would receive as a dividend one

---

3. There were 14 directors on the Revlon board. Six of them held senior management positions with the company, and two others held significant blocks of its stock. Four of the remaining six directors were associated at some point with entities that had various business relationships with Revlon. On the basis of this limited record, however, we cannot conclude that this board is entitled to certain presumptions that generally attach to the decisions of a board whose majority consists of truly outside independent directors. See Polk v. Good & Texaco, Del.Supr., 507 A.2d 531, ___ (1986); Moran v. Household International, Inc., Del.Supr., 500 A.2d 1346, 1356 (1985); Unocal Corp. v. Mesa Petroleum Co., Del.Supr., 493 A.2d 946, 955 (1985); Aronson v. Lewis, Del.Supr., 473 A.2d 805, 812, 815 (1984); Puma v. Marriott, Del.Ch., 283 A.2d 693, 695 (1971).

Note Purchase Right (the Rights) for each share of common stock, with the Rights entitling the holder to exchange one common share for a $65 principal Revlon note at 12% interest with a one-year maturity. The Rights would become effective whenever anyone acquired beneficial ownership of 20% or more of Revlon's shares, unless the purchaser acquired all the company's stock for cash at $65 or more per share. In addition, the Rights would not be available to the acquiror, and prior to the 20% triggering event the Revlon board could redeem the rights for 10 cents each. Both proposals were unanimously adopted.

Pantry Pride made its first hostile move on August 23 with a cash tender offer for any and all shares of Revlon at $47.50 per common share and $26.67 per preferred share, subject to (1) Pantry Pride's obtaining financing for the purchase, and (2) the Rights being redeemed, rescinded or voided.

The Revlon board met again on August 26. The directors advised the stockholders to reject the offer. Further defensive measures also were planned. On August 29, Revlon commenced its own offer for up to 10 million shares, exchanging for each share of common stock tendered one Senior Subordinated Note (the Notes) of $47.50 principal at 11.75% interest, due 1995, and one-tenth of a share of $9.00 Cumulative Convertible Exchangeable Preferred Stock valued at $100 per share. Lazard Freres opined that the notes would trade at their face value on a fully distributed basis. Revlon stockholders tendered 87 percent of the outstanding shares (approximately 33 million), and the company accepted the full 10 million shares on a pro rata basis. The new Notes contained covenants which limited Revlon's ability to incur additional debt, sell assets, or pay dividends unless otherwise approved by the "independent" (nonmanagement) members of the board.

At this point, both the Rights and the Note covenants stymied Pantry Pride's attempted takeover. The next move came on September 16, when Pantry Pride announced a new tender offer at $42 per share, conditioned upon receiving at least 90% of the outstanding stock. Pantry Pride also indicated that it would consider buying less than 90% , and at an increased price, if Revlon removed the impeding Rights. While this offer was lower on its face than the earlier $47.50 proposal, Revlon's investment banker, Lazard Freres, described the two bids as essentially equal in view of the completed exchange offer.

The Revlon board held a regularly scheduled meeting on September 24. The directors rejected the latest Pantry Pride offer and authorized management to negotiate with other parties interested in acquiring Revlon. Pantry Pride remained determined in its efforts and continued to make cash bids for the company, offering $50 per share on September 27, and raising its bid to $53 on October 1, and then to $56.25 on October 7.

In the meantime, Revlon's negotiations with Forstmann and the investment group Adler & Shaykin had produced results. The Revlon directors met on October 3 to consider Pantry Pride's $53 bid and to examine possible alternatives to the offer. Both Forstmann and Adler & Shaykin made certain proposals to the board. As a result, the directors unanimously agreed to a leveraged buyout by Forstmann. The terms of this accord were as follows: each stockholder would get $56 cash per share; management would purchase stock in the new company by the exercise of their

Revlon "golden parachutes";[5] Forstmann would assume Revlon's $475 million debt incurred by the issuance of the Notes; and Revlon would redeem the Rights and waive the Notes covenants for Forstmann or in connection with any other offer superior to Forstmann's. The board did not actually remove the covenants at the October 3 meeting, because Forstmann then lacked a firm commitment on its financing, but accepted the Forstmann capital structure, and indicated that the outside directors would waive the covenants in due course. Part of Forstmann's plan was to sell Revlon's Norcliff Thayer and Reheis divisions to American Home Products for $335 million. Before the merger, Revlon was to sell its cosmetics and fragrance division to Adler & Shaykin for $905 million. These transactions would facilitate the purchase by Forstmann or any other acquiror of Revlon.

When the merger, and thus the waiver of the Notes covenants, was announced, the market value of these securities began to fall. The Notes, which originally traded near par, around 100, dropped to 87.50 by October 8. One director later reported (at the October 12 meeting) a "deluge" of telephone calls from irate noteholders, and on October 10 the Wall Street Journal reported threats of litigation by these creditors.

Pantry Pride countered with a new proposal on October 7, raising its $53 offer to $56.25, subject to nullification of the Rights, a waiver of the Notes covenants, and the election of three Pantry Pride directors to the Revlon board. On October 9, representatives of Pantry Pride, Forstmann and Revlon conferred in an attempt to negotiate the fate of Revlon, but could not reach agreement. At this meeting Pantry Pride announced that it would engage in fractional bidding and top any Forstmann offer by a slightly higher one. It is also significant that Forstmann, to Pantry Pride's exclusion, had been made privy to certain Revlon financial data. Thus, the parties were not negotiating on equal terms.

Again privately armed with Revlon data, Forstmann met on October 11 with Revlon's special counsel and investment banker. On October 12, Forstmann made a new $57.25 per share offer, based on several conditions. The principal demand was a lock-up option to purchase Revlon's Vision Care and National Health Laboratories divisions for $525 million, some $100–$175 million below the value ascribed to them by Lazard Freres, if another acquiror got 40% of Revlon's shares. Revlon also was required to accept a no-shop provision. The Rights and Notes covenants had to be removed as in the October 3 agreement. There would be a $25 million cancellation fee to be placed in escrow, and released to Forstmann if the new agreement terminated or if another acquiror got more than 19.9% of Revlon's stock. Finally, there would be no participation by Revlon management in the merger. In return, Forstmann agreed to support the par value of the Notes, which had faltered in the market, by an exchange of new notes. Forstmann also demanded immediate acceptance of its offer, or it would be withdrawn. The board unanimously approved Forstmann's proposal because: (1) it was for a higher price than the Pantry Pride bid, (2) it protected the noteholders, and (3) Forstmann's financing was firmly in place.[7] The board further agreed to redeem the rights and waive the

---

5. In the takeover context "golden parachutes" generally are understood to be termination agreements providing substantial bonuses and other benefits for manag-

ers and certain directors upon a change in control of a company.

7. Actually, at this time about $400 million of Forstmann's funding was still

covenants on the preferred stock in response to any offer above $57 cash per share. The covenants were waived, contingent upon receipt of an investment banking opinion that the Notes would trade near par value once the offer was consummated.

Pantry Pride, which had initially sought injunctive relief from the Rights Plan on August 22, filed an amended complaint on October 14 challenging the lock-up, the cancellation fee, and the exercise of the Rights and the Notes covenants. Pantry Pride also sought a temporary restraining order to prevent Revlon from placing any assets in escrow or transferring them to Forstmann. Moreover, on October 22, Pantry Pride again raised its bid, with a cash offer of $58 per share conditioned upon nullification of the Rights, waiver of the covenants, and an injunction of the Forstmann lock-up.

On October 15, the Court of Chancery prohibited the further transfer of assets, and eight days later enjoined the lock-up, no-shop, and cancellation fee provisions of the agreement. The trial court concluded that the Revlon directors had breached their duty of loyalty by making concessions to Forstmann, out of concern for their liability to the noteholders, rather than maximizing the sale price of the company for the stockholders' benefit. MacAndrews & Forbes Holdings, Inc. v. Revlon, Inc., 501 A.2d at 1249-50.

II.

To obtain a preliminary injunction, a plaintiff must demonstrate both a reasonable probability of success on the merits and some irreparable harm which will occur absent the injunction. Gimbel v. Signal Companies, Del. Ch., 316 A.2d 599, 602 (1974) aff'd, Del.Supr., 316 A.2d 619 (1974). Additionally, the Court shall balance the conveniences of and possible injuries to the parties. Id.

A.

We turn first to Pantry Pride's probability of success on the merits. The ultimate responsibility for managing the business and affairs of a corporation falls on its board of directors. 8 Del.C. § 141(a). In discharging this function the directors owe fiduciary duties of care and loyalty to the corporation and its shareholders. Guth v. Loft, Inc., 23 Del.Supr. 255, 5 A.2d 503, 510 (1939); Aronson v. Lewis, Del.Supr. 473 A.2d 805, 811 (1984). These principles apply with equal force when a board approves a corporate merger pursuant to 8 Del.C. § 251(b); Smith v. Van Gorkom, Del.Supr., 488 A.2d 858, 873 (1985); and of course they are the bedrock of our law regarding corporate takeover issues. Pogostin v. Rice, Del.Supr., 480 A.2d 619, 624 (1984); Unocal Corp. v. Mesa Petroleum Co., Del.Supr., 493 A.2d 946, 953, 955 (1985); Moran v. Household International, Inc., Del.Supr., 500 A.2d 1346, 1350 (1985). While the business judgment rule may be applicable to the actions of corporate directors responding to takeover threats, the

subject to two investment banks using their "best efforts" to organize a syndicate to provide the balance. Pantry Pride's entire financing was not firmly committed at this point either, although Pantry Pride represented in an October 11 letter to La-

zard Freres that its investment banker, Drexel Burnham Lambert, was highly confident of its ability to raise the balance of $350 million. Drexel Burnham had a firm commitment for this sum by October 18.

principles upon which it is founded—care, loyalty and independence—must first be satisfied.[10]   Aronson v. Lewis, 473 A.2d at 812.

If the business judgment rule applies, there is a "presumption that in making a business decision the directors of a corporation acted on an informed basis, in good faith and in the honest belief that the action taken was in the best interests of the company."   Aronson v. Lewis, 473 A.2d at 812.   However, when a board implements anti-takeover measures there arises "the omnipresent specter that a board may be acting primarily in its own interests, rather than those of the corporation and its shareholders * * *"   Unocal Corp. v. Mesa Petroleum Co., 493 A.2d at 954.   This potential for conflict places upon the directors the burden of proving that they had reasonable grounds for believing there was a danger to corporate policy and effectiveness, a burden satisfied by a showing of good faith and reasonable investigation.   Id. at 955.   In addition, the directors must analyze the nature of the takeover and its effect on the corporation in order to ensure balance—that the responsive action taken is reasonable in relation to the threat posed.   Id.

B.

The first relevant defensive measure adopted by the Revlon board was the Rights Plan, which would be considered a "poison pill" in the current language of corporate takeovers—a plan by which shareholders receive the right to be bought out by the corporation at a substantial premium on the occurrence of a stated triggering event.   See generally Moran v. Household International, Inc., Del.Supr., 500 A.2d 1346 (1985).   By 8 Del.C. §§ 141 and 157, the board clearly had the power to adopt the measure.   See Moran v. Household International, Inc., 500 A.2d at 1351.   Thus, the focus becomes one of reasonableness and purpose.

The Revlon board approved the Rights Plan in the face of an impending hostile takeover bid by Pantry Pride at $45 per share, a price which Revlon reasonably concluded was grossly inadequate.   Lazard Freres had so advised the directors, and had also informed them that Pantry Pride was a small, highly leveraged company bent on a "bust-up" takeover by using "junk bond" financing to buy Revlon cheaply, sell the acquired assets to pay the debts incurred, and retain the profit for itself.[12]   In adopting the Plan, the board protected the shareholders from a hostile takeover at a

---

10. One eminent corporate commentator has drawn a distinction between the business judgment rule, which insulates directors and management from personal liability for their business decisions, and the business judgment doctrine, which protects the decision itself from attack.   The principles upon which the rule and doctrine operate are identical, while the objects of their protection are different.   See Hinsey, Business Judgment and the American Law Institute's Corporate Governance Project: The Rule, the Doctrine and the Reality, 52 Geo.Wash.L.Rev. 6909, 611–13 (1984).   In the transactional justification cases, where the doctrine is said to apply, our decisions have not observed the distinction in such terminology.   See Polk v. Good & Texaco, Del.Supr., ___ A.2d ___, ___ (1986); Moran

v. Household International, Inc., Del.Supr., 500 A.2d 1346, 1356 (1985); Unocal Corp. v. Mesa Petroleum Co., Del.Supr., 493 A.2d 946, 953–55 (1985); Rosenblatt v. Getty Oil Co., Del.Supr., 493 A.2d 929, 943 (1985). Under the circumstances we do not alter our earlier practice of referring only to the business judgment rule, although in transactional justification matters such reference may be understood to embrace the concept of the doctrine.

12. As we noted in *Moran,* a "bust-up" takeover generally refers to a situation in which one seeks to finance an acquisition by selling off pieces of the acquired company, presumably at a substantial profit. *See Moran,* 500 A.2d at 1349, n. 4.

price below the company's intrinsic value, while retaining sufficient flexibility to address any proposal deemed to be in the stockholders' best interests.

To that extent the board acted in good faith and upon reasonable investigation. Under the circumstances it cannot be said that the Rights Plan as employed was unreasonable, considering the threat posed. Indeed, the Plan was a factor in causing Pantry Pride to raise its bids from a low of $42 to an eventual high of $58. At the time of its adoption the Rights Plan afforded a measure of protection consistent with the directors' fiduciary duty in facing a takeover threat perceived as detrimental to corporate interests. *Unocal,* 493 A.2d at 954–55. Far from being a "show-stopper," as the plaintiffs had contended in *Moran,* the measure spurred the bidding to new heights, a proper result of its implementation. See *Moran,* 500 A.2d at 1354, 1356–67.

Although we consider adoption of the Plan to have been valid under the circumstances, its continued usefulness was rendered moot by the directors' actions on October 3 and October 12. At the October 3 meeting the board redeemed the Rights conditioned upon consummation of a merger with Forstmann, but further acknowledged that they would also be redeemed to facilitate any more favorable offer. On October 12, the board unanimously passed a resolution redeeming the Rights in connection with any cash proposal of $57.25 or more per share. Because all the pertinent offers eventually equalled or surpassed that amount, the Rights clearly were no longer any impediment in the contest for Revlon. This mooted any question of their propriety under *Moran* or *Unocal.*

C.

The second defensive measure adopted by Revlon to thwart a Pantry Pride takeover was the company's own exchange offer for 10 million of its shares. The directors' general broad powers to manage the business and affairs of the corporation are augmented by the specific authority conferred under 8 Del.C. § 160(a), permitting the company to deal in its own stock. *Unocal,* 493 A.2d at 953–54; Cheff v. Mathes, 41 Del.Supr. 494, 199 A.2d 548, 554 (1964); Kors v. Carey, 39 Del.Ch. 47, 158 A.2d 136, 140 (1960). However, when exercising that power in an effort to forestall a hostile takeover, the board's actions are strictly held to the fiduciary standards outlined in *Unocal.* These standards require the directors to determine the best interests of the corporation and its stockholders, and impose an enhanced duty to abjure any action that is motivated by considerations other than a good faith concern for such interests. *Unocal,* 493 A.2d at 954–55; see Bennett v. Propp, 41 Del.Supr. 14, 187 A.2d 405, 409 (1962).

The Revlon directors concluded that Pantry Pride's $47.50 offer was grossly inadequate. In that regard the board acted in good faith, and on an informed basis, with reasonable grounds to believe that there existed a harmful threat to the corporate enterprise. The adoption of a defensive measure, reasonable in relation to the threat posed, was proper and fully accorded with the powers, duties, and responsibilities conferred upon directors under our law. *Unocal,* 493 A.2d at 954; Pogostin v. Rice, 480 A.2d at 627.

D.

However, when Pantry Pride increased its offer to $50 per share, and then to $53, it became apparent to all that the break-up of the company was inevitable. The Revlon board's authorization permitting management to negotiate a merger or buyout with a third party was a recognition that the company was for sale. The duty of the board had thus changed from the preservation of Revlon as a corporate entity to the maximization of the company's value at a sale for the stockholders' benefit. This significantly altered the board's responsibilities under the *Unocal* standards. It no longer faced threats to corporate policy and effectiveness, or to the stockholders' interests, from a grossly inadequate bid. The whole question of defensive measures became moot. The directors' role changed from defenders of the corporate bastion to auctioneers charged with getting the best price for the stockholders at a sale of the company.

III.

This brings us to the lock-up with Forstmann and its emphasis on shoring up the sagging market value of the Notes in the face of threatened litigation by their holders. Such a focus was inconsistent with the changed concept of the directors' responsibilities at this stage of the developments. The impending waiver of the Notes covenants had caused the value of the Notes to fall, and the board was aware of the noteholders' ire as well as their subsequent threats of suit. The directors thus made support of the Notes an integral part of the company's dealings with Forstmann, even though their primary responsibility at this stage was to the equity owners.

The original threat posed by Pantry Pride—the break-up of the company—had become a reality which even the directors embraced. Selective dealing to fend off a hostile but determined bidder was no longer a proper objective. Instead, obtaining the highest price for the benefit of the stockholders should have been the central theme guiding director action. Thus, the Revlon board could not make the requisite showing of good faith by preferring the noteholders and ignoring its duty of loyalty to the shareholders. The rights of the former already were fixed by contract. Wolfensohn v. Madison Fund, Inc., Del.Supr., 253 A.2d 72, 75 (1969); Harff v. Kerkorian, Del.Ch., 324 A.2d 215 (1974). The noteholders required no further protection, and when the Revlon board entered into an auction-ending lock-up agreement with Forstmann on the basis of impermissible considerations at the expense of the shareholders, the directors breached their primary duty of loyalty.

The Revlon board argued that it acted in good faith in protecting the noteholders because *Unocal* permits consideration of other corporate constituencies. Although such considerations may be permissible, there are fundamental limitations upon that prerogative. A board may have regard for various constituencies in discharging its responsibilities, provided there are rationally related benefits accruing to the stockholders. *Unocal*, 493 A.2d at 955. However, such concern for non-stockholder interests is inappropriate when an auction among active bidders is in progress, and the object no longer is to protect or maintain the corporate enterprise but to sell it to the highest bidder.

Revlon also contended that by Gilbert v. El Paso Co., Del.Ch., 490 A.2d 1050, 1054-55 (1984), it had contractual and good faith obligations to consider the noteholders. However, any such duties are limited to the principle that one may not interfere with contractual relationships by improper actions. Here, the rights of the noteholders were fixed by agreement, and there is nothing of substance to suggest that any of those terms were violated. The Notes covenants specifically contemplated a waiver to permit sale of the company at a fair price. The Notes were accepted by the holders on that basis, including the risk of an adverse market effect stemming from a waiver. Thus, nothing remained for Revlon to legitimately protect, and no rationally related benefit thereby accrued to the stockholders. Under such circumstances we must conclude that the merger agreement with Forstmann was unreasonable in relation to the threat posed.

A lock-up is not *per se* illegal under Delaware law. Its use has been approved in an earlier case. Thompson v. Enstar Corp., Del.Ch. (1984). Such options can entice other bidders to enter a contest for control of the corporation, creating an auction for the company and maximizing shareholder profit. Current economic conditions in the takeover market are such that a "white knight" like Forstmann might only enter the bidding for the target company if it receives some form of compensation to cover the risks and costs involved. Note, Corporations-Mergers—"Lock-up" Enjoined Under Section 14(e) of Securities Exchange Act—Mobil Corp. v. Marathon Oil Co., 669 F.2d 366 (6th Cir.1981), 12 Seton Hall L.Rev. 881, 892 (1982). However, while those lock-ups which draw bidders into the battle benefit shareholders, similar measures which end an active auction and foreclose further bidding operate to the shareholders' detriment. Note, Lock-up Options: Toward a State Law Standard, 96 Harv.L.Rev. 1068, 1081 (1983).

Recently, the United States Court of Appeals for the Second Circuit invalidated a lock-up on fiduciary duty grounds similar to those here.[15] Hanson Trust PLC, et al. v. ML SCM Acquisition Inc., et al., 781 F.2d 264 (2nd Cir.1986). Citing Thompson v. Enstar Corp., supra, with approval, the court stated:

> In this regard, we are especially mindful that some lock-up options may be beneficial to the shareholders, such as those that induce a bidder to compete for control of a corporation, while others may be harmful, such as those that effectively preclude bidders from competing with the optionee bidder. 781 F.2d at 274.

In *Hanson Trust*, the bidder, Hanson, sought control of SCM by a hostile cash tender offer. SCM management joined with Merrill Lynch to propose a leveraged buy-out of the company at a higher price, and Hanson in turn increased its offer. Then despite very little improvement in its subsequent bid, the management group sought a lock-up option to purchase SCM's two main assets at a substantial discount. The SCM directors granted the lock-

---

15. The federal courts generally have declined to enjoin lock-up options despite arguments that lock-ups constitute impermissible "manipulative" conduct forbidden by Section 14(e) of the Williams, Act [15 U.S.C. § 78n(e)]. See Buffalo Forge Co. v. Ogden Corp., 717 F.2d 757 (2nd Cir.1983), cert. denied, 464 U.S. 1018, 104 S.Ct. 550, 78 L.Ed.2d 724 (1983); Data Probe Acquisition Crop. v. Datatab, Inc., 772 F.2d 1 (2nd Cir.1983); cert. denied 465 U.S. 1052, 104 S.Ct. 1326, 79 L.Ed.2d 722 (1984); but see Mobil Corp. v. Marathon Oil Co., 669 F.2d 366 (6th Cir.1981). The cases are all federal in nature and were not decided on state law grounds.

up without adequate information as to the size of the discount or the effect the transaction would have on the company. Their action effectively ended a competitive bidding situation. The Hanson Court invalidated the lock-up because the directors failed to fully inform themselves about the value of a transaction in which management had a strong self-interest. "In short, the Board appears to have failed to ensure that negotiations for alternative bids were conducted by those whose only loyalty was to the shareholders." Id. at 277.

The Forstmann option has a similar destructive effect on the auction process. Forstmann had already been drawn into the contest on a preferred basis, so the result of the lock-up was not to foster bidding, but to destroy it. The board's stated reasons for approving the transactions were: (1) better financing, (2) noteholder protection, and (3) higher price. As the Court of Chancery found, and we agree, any distinctions between the rival bidders' methods of financing the proposal were nominal at best, and such a consideration has little or no significance in a cash offer for any and all shares. The principal object, contrary to the board's duty of care, appears to have been protection of the noteholders over the shareholders' interests.

While Forstmann's $57.25 offer was objectively higher than Pantry Pride's $56.25 bid, the margin of superiority is less when the Forstmann price is adjusted for the time value of money. In reality, the Revlon board ended the auction in return for very little actual improvement in the final bid. The principal benefit went to the directors, who avoided personal liability to a class of creditors to whom the board owed no further duty under the circumstances. Thus, when a board ends an intense bidding contest on an insubstantial basis, and where a significant by-product of that action is to protect the directors against a perceived threat of personal liability for consequences stemming from the adoption of previous defensive measures, the action cannot withstand the enhanced scrutiny which *Unocal* requires of director conduct. See Unocal, 498 A.2d at 954–55.

In addition to the lock-up option, the Court of Chancery enjoined the no-shop provision as part of the attempt to foreclose further bidding by Pantry Pride. MacAndrews & Forbes Holdings, Inc. v. Revlon, Inc., 501 A.2d at 1251. The no-shop provision, like the lock-up option, while not *per se* illegal, is impermissible under the *Unocal* standards when a board's primary duty becomes that of an auctioneer responsible for selling the company to the highest bidder. The agreement to negotiate only with Forstmann ended rather than intensified the board's involvement in the bidding contest.

It is ironic that the parties even considered a no-shop agreement when Revlon had dealt preferentially, and almost exclusively, with Forstmann throughout the contest. After the directors authorized management to negotiate with other parties, Forstmann was given every negotiating advantage that Pantry Pride had been denied: cooperation from management, access to financial data, and the exclusive opportunity to present merger proposals directly to the board of directors. Favoritism for a white knight to the total exclusion of a hostile bidder might be justifiable when the latter's offer adversely affects shareholder interests, but when bidders make relatively similar offers, or dissolution of the company becomes inevitable, the directors cannot fulfill their enhanced *Unocal* duties by playing favorites with the contending factions. Market forces must be allowed to operate freely to bring the target's shareholders the best price available for their equity. Thus, as the trial court ruled, the shareholders' interests necessitated that the board remain free to negotiate in the fulfillment of that duty.

The court below similarly enjoined the payment of the cancellation fee, pending a resolution of the merits, because the fee was part of the overall plan to thwart Pantry Pride's efforts. We find no abuse of discretion in that ruling.

IV.

Having concluded that Pantry Pride has shown a reasonable probability of success on the merits, we address the issue of irreparable harm. The Court of Chancery ruled that unless the lock-up and other aspects of the agreement were enjoined, Pantry Pride's opportunity to bid for Revlon was lost. The court also held that the need for both bidders to compete in the marketplace outweighed any injury to Forstmann. Given the complexity of the proposed transaction between Revlon and Forstmann, the obstacles to Pantry Pride obtaining a meaningful legal remedy are immense. We are satisfied that the plaintiff has shown the need for an injunction to protect it from irreparable harm, which need outweighs any harm to the defendants.

V.

In conclusion, the Revlon board was confronted with a situation not uncommon in the current wave of corporate takeovers. A hostile and determined bidder sought the company at a price the board was convinced was inadequate. The initial defensive tactics worked to the benefit of the shareholders, and thus the board was able to sustain its *Unocal* burdens in justifying those measures. However, in granting an asset option lock-up to Forstmann, we must conclude that under all the circumstances the directors allowed considerations other than the maximization of shareholder profit to affect their judgment, and followed a course that ended the auction for Revlon, absent court intervention, to the ultimate detriment of its shareholders. No such defensive measure can be sustained when it represents a breach of the directors' fundamental duty of care. See Smith v. Van Gorkom, Del.Supr., 488 A.2d 858, 874 (1985). In that context the board's action is not entitled to the deference accorded it by the business judgment rule. The measures were properly enjoined. The decision of the Court of Chancery, therefore, is

Affirmed.

HECKMANN v. AHMANSON

Court of Appeal, Second District, 1985.
168 Cal.App.3d 119, 214 Cal.Rptr. 177.

JOHNSON, ASSOCIATE JUSTICE.

Plaintiffs, stockholders in Walt Disney Productions, are suing to recover the payoff in the greenmailing [1] of Disney. Defendants are the Disney

---

1. A greenmailer creates the threat of a corporate takeover by purchasing a significant amount of the company's stock. He then sells the shares back to the company at a premium when its executives, in fear of their jobs, agree to buy him out. For

directors who paid the greenmail and the "Steinberg Group"[2] to whom the money, approximately $325 million, was paid.

Plaintiffs obtained a preliminary injunction which, in effect, imposes a trust on the profit from the Disney-Steinberg transaction, approximately $60 million, and requires the Steinberg Group to render periodic accountings of the disposition of the entire proceeds. The Steinberg Group appeals from this preliminary injunction. We affirm.

As will be discussed more fully below, if plaintiffs prove the Steinberg Group breached a fiduciary duty to the corporation and its shareholders in the sale of stock to the corporation the plaintiffs would be entitled to a constructive trust upon the profits of that sale. Plaintiffs have established a reasonable probability of proving breach of fiduciary duties by the Steinberg Group. The trial court could reasonably conclude from the evidence a preliminary injunction was necessary to prevent the dissipation or disappearance of the profit during the pendency of the action and the balance of hardships involved in granting or denying the injunction incline in plaintiffs' favor.

FACTS AND PROCEEDINGS BELOW

In March 1984 the Steinberg Group purchased more than two million shares of Disney stock. Probably interpreting this as the opening shot in a takeover war, the Disney directors countered with an announcement Disney would acquire Arvida Corporation for $200 million in newly-issued Disney stock and assume Arvida's $190 million debt.[3] The Steinberg Group countered this move with a stockholders' derivative action in federal court to block the Arvida transaction. Nonetheless, on June 6, 1984, the Arvida transaction was consummated.

Undeterred by its failure to halt Disney's purchase of Arvida, the Steinberg Group proceeded to acquire some two million additional shares of Disney stock, increasing its ownership position to approximately 12 percent of the outstanding Disney shares. On June 8, 1984, the Steinberg Group advised Disney's directors of its intention to make a tender offer for 49 percent of the outstanding shares at $67.50 a share and its intention to later tender for the balance at $72.50 a share. The directors' response was swift. On the evening of the same day, the directors proposed Disney repurchase all the stock held by the Steinberg Group. Agreement was reached on June 11.

further discussion of greenmail see, Lowenstein, Pruning Deadwood In Hostile Takeovers: A Proposal For Legislation, (1983) 83 Colum.L.Rev. 249, 311 & fn. 249; Greene & Junewicz, A Reappraisal Of Current Regulations Of Mergers And Acquisitions (1984) 132 U. of Penn.L.Rev. 647, 706–707.

2. The "Steinberg Group" consists of defendants, Saul P. Steinberg, Reliance Financial Services Corp., Reliance Group, Inc., Reliance Group Holdings, Inc., Reliance Insurance Co., Reliance Insurance Co. of New York, United Pacific Insurance Co., United Pacific Life Insurance Co., and United Pacific Insurance Company of New York.

3. Like the puff fish, a corporate delicacy will often attempt to avoid being swallowed up by making itself appear less attractive to a potential predator. See, Lowenstein, supra, at p. 313; Nathan & Sobel, Corporate Stock Repurchases In The Context Of Unsolicited Takeover Bids (1980) 35 Bus.Lawyer 1545, 1547 & fn. 2; Rosenzweig, The Legality Of "Lock-Ups" [etc.] (1983) 10 Sec.Reg.Law J., 291, 299; Prentice, Target Board Abuse Of Defensive Tactics [etc.] (1983) J. of Corp.Law 337, 341, 343; Greene & Junewicz, supra, at p. 702.

Under the agreement with the Steinberg Group, Disney purchased all the stock held by the group for $297.4 million and reimbursed the estimated costs incurred in preparing the tender offer, $28 million, for a total of $325.4 million, or about $77 per share. The Steinberg Group garnered a profit of about $60 million. In return, the Steinberg Group agreed not to purchase Disney stock and to dismiss its individual causes of action in the Arvida litigation. It did not dismiss the derivative claims.

Disney borrowed the entire sum necessary to repurchase its shares. This transaction, coupled with the debt assumed in the Arvida purchase, increased Disney's total indebtedness to $866 million, two-thirds of Disney's entire shareholder equity. Upon the announcement of its agreement with the Steinberg Group, the price of Disney stock dropped below $50 per share. Thus, the Steinberg Group received a price 50 percent above the market price following the transaction.

The gravamen of the action against the Steinberg Group is that it used its tender offer and the Arvida litigation to obtain a premium price for its shares in violation of its fiduciary duties to Disney and the other shareholders. The complaint seeks, among other things, rescission of Disney's repurchase agreement with the Steinberg Group, an accounting and a constructive trust upon all funds the Steinberg Group received from Disney.

After due notice and hearing, the trial court issued a preliminary injunction enjoining the Steinberg Group from transferring, investing or disposing of the profit [4] from its sale of Disney stock except in accordance with the standards applicable to a prudent trustee under Civil Code section 2261. The injunction also requires the Steinberg Group to notify plaintiffs and the court of every change in the form or vehicle of investment of the entire proceeds of the repurchase agreement. The injunction became effective upon plaintiffs' posting an undertaking in the sum of $1 million.

DISCUSSION

I. SCOPE OF REVIEW.

Trial courts consider two interrelated questions in deciding whether to issue a preliminary injunction: "1) are the plaintiffs likely to suffer greater injury from a denial of the injunction than the defendants are likely to suffer from its grant; and 2) is there a reasonable probability that the plaintiffs will prevail on the merits * * *.

" '[By] balancing the respective equities of the parties, [the court] concludes that, pending a trial on the merits, the defendant should or that he should not be restrained from exercising the right claimed by him.' [Citations omitted.]" (Robbins v. Superior Court, (1985) 38 Cal.3d 199, 206, 211 Cal.Rptr. 398, 695 P.2d 695.) The grant or refusal of a preliminary injunction is, generally speaking, within the discretion of the trial court and its order may be reversed on appeal only if abuse of discretion is shown. (Gosney v. State of California (1970) 10 Cal.App.3d 921, 924, 89 Cal.

---

4. The profit, for purposes of the preliminary injunction, was defined as the difference paid by defendants for the stock, approximately $63.25 per share, and the total amount received under the repur- chase agreement, approximately $77.50 per share, together with income earned on that amount from the date of receipt. This totals approximately $60 million.

Rptr. 390.) Discretion is abused in the legal sense " 'whenever it may be fairly said that in its exercise the court * * * exceeded the bounds of reason or contravened the uncontradicted evidence.' " [Citations omitted.] (Continental Baking Co. v. Katz (1968) 68 Cal.2d 512, 527, 67 Cal.Rptr. 761, 439 P.2d 889.)

In the case before us, the Steinberg Group contends plaintiffs failed to demonstrate a likelihood of success on the issue of its liability or that they would be harmed in any way if the Steinberg Group maintained unfettered control over the proceeds and profits of the stock sale pending a final decision on the merits. As we review these contentions we bear in mind our inquiry is a limited one:

> " 'The granting or denial of a preliminary injunction does not amount to an adjudication of the ultimate rights in controversy. It merely determines that the court, balancing the respective equities of the parties, concludes that, pending a trial on the merits, the defendant should or that he should not be restrained from exercising the right claimed by him.' " [Citations omitted.] (Continental Baking Co. v. Katz, supra, 68 Cal.2d at p. 528, 67 Cal.Rptr. 761, 439 P.2d 889.)

II. PLAINTIFFS DEMONSTRATED A REASONABLE PROBABILITY OF SUCCESS ON THE MERITS ENTITLING THEM TO A CONSTRUCTIVE TRUST UPON THE PROFITS THE STEINBERG GROUP RECEIVED FROM ITS SALE OF DISNEY STOCK.

A. *Liability of the Steinberg Group as an Aider and Abettor of the Disney Directors' Breach of Fiduciary Duty.*

Although we have found no case in which a greenmailer was ordered to return his ill-gotten gains, precedent for such a judgment exists in California law.

In Jones v. H.F. Ahmanson & Co. (1969) 1 Cal.3d 93, 108–109, 81 Cal. Rptr. 592, 460 P.2d 464, our Supreme Court adopted the shareholders' Magna Carta set forth in Pepper v. Litton (1939) 308 U.S. 295:

> " ' A director is a fiduciary. * * * So is a dominant or controlling stockholder or group of stockholders. * * * Their powers are powers of trust. * * * ' He who is in such a fiduciary position cannot serve himself first and his *cestuis* second. He cannot manipulate the affairs of his corporation to their detriment and in disregard of the standards of common decency and honesty. * * * He cannot use his power for his personal advantage and to the detriment of the stockholders. * * * For that power is at all times subject to the equitable limitation that it may not be exercised for the aggrandizement, preference, or advantage of the fiduciary to the exclusion or detriment of the *cestuis*. Where there is a violation of these principles, equity will undo the wrong or intervene to prevent its consummation."

The ultimate question "is whether or not under all the circumstances the transaction carries the earmarks of an arm's length bargain." (Id., at pp. 306–307.)

Ahmanson involved a scheme in which the majority stockholders set up a holding company in a manner which made the minority shares unmar ketable. (1 Cal.3d at p. 114, 81 Cal.Rptr. 592, 460 P.2d 464.) The court held the facts alleged in the complaint stated a cause of action for breach of fiduciary duty. "[D]efendants chose a course of action in which they used their control of the Association to obtain an advantage not made available to all stockholders. They did so without regard to the resulting detriment to the minority stockholders and in the absence of any compelling business purpose." (1 Cal.3d at p. 114, 81 Cal.Rptr. 592, 460 P.2d 464.)

While there may be many valid reasons why corporate directors would purchase another company or repurchase the corporation's shares, the naked desire to retain their positions of power and control over the corporation is not one of them.[5] (See Andersen v. Albert & J.M. Anderson Mfg. Co. (1950) 325 Mass. 343, 90 N.E.2d 541, 544; Bennett v. Propp (1962) 41 Del.Ch. 14, 187 A.2d 405, 408; Schilling v. Belcher (5th Cir.1978) 582 F.2d 995, 1003–1005 [Florida law]; 1 Ballantine & Sterling, Cal. Corporation Laws (4th ed.1984) § 143.02, subd. (d), pp. 8–58–59; Lynch & Steinberg, The Legitimacy of Defensive Tactics In Tender Offers (1979) 64 Cornell L.Rev. 901, 914–915.)

If the Disney directors breached their fiduciary duty to the stockholders, the Steinberg Group could be held jointly liable as an aider and abettor. The Steinberg Group knew it was reselling its stock at a price considerably above market value to enable the Disney directors to retain control of the corporation. It knew or should have known Disney was borrowing the $325 million purchase price. From its previous dealings with Disney, including the Arvida transaction, it knew the increased debt load would adversely affect Disney's credit rating and the price of its stock. If it were an active participant in the breach of duty and reaped the benefit, it cannot disclaim the burden. (Gray v. Sutherland, (1954) 124 Cal.App.2d 280, 290, 268 P.2d 754; Bancroft-Whitney Co. v. Glen (1966) 64 Cal.2d 327, 353, 49 Cal.Rptr. 825, 411 P.2d 921.) "Where there is a common plan or design to commit a tort, all who participate are jointly liable whether or not they do the wrongful acts." (Certified Grocers of California, Ltd. v. San Gabriel Valley Bank (1983) 150 Cal.App.3d 281, 289, 197 Cal.Rptr. 710.)

The Steinberg Group contends there was no evidence presented to the trial court that the repurchase agreement was motivated by the Disney directors' desire to perpetuate their own control instead of a good faith belief the corporate interest would be served thereby. (See Fairchild v. Bank of America (1961) 192 Cal.App.2d 252, 256, 13 Cal.Rptr. 491; compare Klaus v. Hi-Shear Corporation (9th Cir.1975) 528 F.2d 225, 233 with Kors v. Carey (1960) 39 Del.Ch. 47, 158 A.2d 136 and Cheff v. Mathes (1964) 41 Del. Ch. 494, 199 A.2d 548.)

At this point in the litigation, it is not necessary the court be presented with a "smoking gun." We believe the evidence presented to the court was sufficient to demonstrate a probability of success on the merits. The acts of the Disney directors—and particularly their timing—are difficult to understand except as defensive strategies against a hostile takeover. The Steinberg Group began acquiring Disney stock in March 1984. In May 1984 the Disney directors announced Disney would acquire Arvida and its $190 million debt. Trying to make the target company appear less attractive is

---

5. We recognize the Disney directors were not parties to the proceedings on the preliminary injunction nor this appeal and have not had the opportunity to tell their side of the story.

a well-recognized defensive tactic by a board seeking to retain control. (See fn. 3, supra.) Furthermore, the Steinberg Group announced its tender offer for 49 percent of the outstanding Disney shares on June 8, 1984. Immediately following this announcement, the Disney directors began negotiations to repurchase the Steinberg Group's stock and reached an agreement on the repurchase two days later. (Cf. Joseph E. Seagram & Sons, Inc. v. Abrams (S.D.N.Y.1981) 510 F.Supp. 860, 861–862.)

Once it is shown a director received a personal benefit from the transaction, which appears to be the case here, the burden shifts to the director to demonstrate not only the transaction was entered in good faith, but also to show its inherent fairness from the viewpoint of the corporation and those interested therein. (Lynch v. Cook (1983) 148 Cal.App.3d 1072, 1082, 196 Cal.Rptr. 544; and see, Rosenzweig, supra, at p. 294.) The only evidence presented by the Disney directors was the conclusory statement of one of its attorneys that "[t]he Disney objective in purchasing [the] stock was to avoid the damage to Disney and its shareholders which would have been the result of [the] announced tender offer." This vague assertion falls short of evidence of good faith and inherent fairness. (Cf. Schilling v. Belcher, supra, 582 A.2d at p. 1004; Klaus v. Hi-Shear Corporation, supra, 528 F.2d at p. 233.)

B. *Liability of the Steinberg Group for Breach of Fiduciary Duty to the Disney Shareholders.*

When the Steinberg Group filed suit against Disney to block Disney's purchase of Arvida it assumed a fiduciary duty to the other shareholders with respect to the derivative claims.

"A stockholder who institutes [a derivative suit] sues purely as a trustee to redress corporate injuries. He has the unquestioned right to sue, but it is in no sense his duty to sue * * *. He is a trustee pure and simple, seeking in the name of another a recovery for wrongs that have been committed against that other. His position in the litigation is in every legal sense the precise equivalent of that of the guardian ad litem." (Whitten v. Dabney (1915) 171 Cal. 621, 629, 630–631, 154 P. 312.)

The United States Supreme Court set forth in strong terms the strict obligations of a plaintiff in a derivative suit:

"[A] stockholder who brings suit on a cause of action derived from the corporation assumes a position, not technically as a trustee perhaps, but one of a fiduciary character. He sues, not for himself alone, but as representative of a class comprising all who are similarly situated. The interests of all in the redress of the wrongs are taken into his hands, dependent upon his diligence, wisdom and integrity. And while the stockholders have chosen the corporate director or manager, they have no such election as to a plaintiff who steps forward to represent them. He is a self-chosen representative and a volunteer champion." (Cohen v. Beneficial Loan Corp. (1949) 337 U.S. 541, 549.)

One who assumes such a fiduciary role cannot abandon it for personal aggrandizement. (Young v. Higbee (1945) 324 U.S. 204, 213; Lemer v. Boise Cascade, Inc. (1980) 107 Cal.App.3d 1, 7, 165 Cal.Rptr. 555.) In the case before us plaintiffs have demonstrated a reasonable probability the

Steinberg Group breached its fiduciary duty to the other shareholders by abandoning the Arvida litigation.

In its verified complaint in federal district court, Reliance Insurance Company, part of the Steinberg Group, alleged, among other things, that Disney's purchase of Arvida was contrary to sound business judgment and a waste of corporate assets since the purchase price was excessive, the purchase would erode Disney's profitability, substantially increase its debt load and make it more difficult and expensive for Disney to acquire the capital necessary to complete its current projects. It also claimed the Arvida purchase would depress the value of Disney common stock. In bringing the action, Reliance alleged it would fairly and adequately represent the interests of Disney and all other stockholders who were similarly situated.

Despite its dire warnings about the Arvida acquisition and its promise to fairly and adequately represent the interests of Disney and its shareholders, the Steinberg Group abandoned the federal litigation just two weeks after it was filed. The Steinberg Group sold all of its Disney shares to Disney at a $60 million profit, dismissed its individual claims in the Arvida litigation and promised not to oppose any motion to dismiss the derivative claims.

A trier of fact could reasonably find the Steinberg Group did not fairly and adequately represent the Disney shareholders but, instead, used its position as class representative for its own financial advantage.

The Steinberg Group abandoned its derivative claims when it sold its stock back to the corporation. Once a derivative plaintiff sells its stock, it no longer has standing to prosecute the derivative claims on behalf of the remaining shareholders. (See Lewis v. Knutson (5th Cir.1983) 699 F.2d 230, 238 and cases cited therein; 7A Wright & Miller, Federal Practice and Procedure (1972) § 1839, p. 437.)

It is argued the Steinberg Group breached no fiduciary duty in merely dismissing its individual claims and selling its stock. It did not dismiss the derivative claims; and the sale of stock, even though to the defendants in the action, is not a "compromise" within the meaning of rule 23.1 of the Federal Rules of Civil Procedure. (See Malcolm v. Cities Service Co. (D.Del. 1942) 2 F.R.D. 405, 407.) A current shareholder would appear to have the right to intervene in the derivative claims under rule 24 subdivision (a)(2). (*Malcolm,* ibid.)

The foregoing argument avoids the issue. The Steinberg Group could not have unilaterally dismissed or compromised the derivative claims even if it wanted to. (See rule 23.1, supra.) Therefore, the fact it did not do so is not dispositive of plaintiffs' claim of breach of fiduciary duty. In Shelton v. Pargo, Inc. (4th Cir.1978) 582 F.2d 1298, the court recognized settlement of the class representative's *individual* claims may indeed affect the fulfillment of the fiduciary duty owed the class.

> "The parties, who are settling their individual claims, are not merely members of a putative class; they are the representative parties, without whose presence as plaintiffs the case could not proceed as a class action. Had the appellees been other than the representative parties, there would be no objection to a voluntary settlement of their claim. But, by asserting a representative role on behalf of the alleged class, these appellees voluntarily accepted a fiduciary obligation towards the

members of the putative class they thus have undertaken to represent. They may not abandon the fiduciary role they assumed at will or by agreement with the [defendant], *if prejudice to the members of the class they claimed to represent would result or if they have improperly used the class action procedure for their personal aggrandizement.*" (Id., at p. 1305; fns. omitted; italics added.)

The court cited as authority, among other cases, Cohen v. Beneficial Loan Corp., supra, and Young v. Higbee Co., supra. (See also Rothenberg v. Security Management Co., Inc. (11th Cir.1982) 667 F.2d 958, 961; Blum v. Morgan Guaranty Trust Co. of New York (5th Cir.1976) 539 F.2d 1388, 1390; and G.A. Enterprises, Inc. v. Leisure Living Commun., Inc. (1st Cir. 1975) 517 F.2d 24, 27.) These cases hold a plaintiff breaches the duty to fairly and adequately represent the other shareholders when he uses the derivative action as leverage to achieve his own personal objectives.

* * *

In filing its derivative suit, the Steinberg Group volunteered to prevent Disney from acquiring the large debt associated with Arvida "which," it alleged, "could materially diminish Disney earnings and * * * threaten its long-term profitability." Instead of preventing the Arvida acquisition, the Steinberg Group bailed out of the lawsuit, and out of Disney, with $325 million of Disney's money. According to plaintiffs, Disney borrowed the entire amount used to buy off the Steinberg Group. This loan together with the $190 million Arvida debt increased Disney's total indebtedness to about $830 million compared to about $585 million before the Steinberg Group came on the scene. This increased debt load resulted in a lowering of Disney's credit rating and a plunge of 16 points in the price of Disney stock from $65\frac{1}{8}$, the trading day before the repurchase agreement, to $49\frac{1}{2}$ a week later.

Thus, it can be argued, with a reasonable probability of success, the Disney shareholders are worse off after the intervention of their "volunteer champion" than they were before. They are like the citizens of a town whose volunteer fire department quits fighting the fire and sells its equipment to the arsonist who set it (who obtains the purchase price by setting fire to the building next door).

We conclude, therefore, plaintiffs have established a reasonable probability of success on the claim the Steinberg Group breached its fiduciary duty as a plaintiff in the stockholders' derivative action.

* * *

III. THE TRIAL COURT REASONABLY CONCLUDED INJUNCTIVE RELIEF WAS NECESSARY TO PREVENT THE DISSIPATION OR DISAPPEARANCE OF THE PROCEEDS AND PROFITS OF THE TRANSACTION.

Code of Civil Procedure section 526, subdivision 3 authorizes a preliminary injunction "[w]hen it appears, during the litigation, that a party to the action is doing, or threatens, or is about to do, * * * some act in violation of the rights of another party to the action respecting the subject of the action, and tending to render the judgment ineffectual; * * *."

An injunction against disposing of property is proper if disposal would render the final judgment ineffectual. (Wilkins v. Oken (1958) 157 Cal. App.2d 603, 606–607, 321 P.2d 876.) Thus, in a case similar to the one before us, a preliminary injunction was granted to restrain the disposal of property pending the result of an accounting. (Raisch v. Warren (1912) 18 Cal.App. 655, 667, 124 p. 95.) To paraphrase Justice Cardozo, if "[a] constructive trust is the [voice] through which the conscience of equity finds expression",[9] then a court can surely prevent the stifling of that voice before it has a chance to be heard.

In order to create a constructive trust there must be an existing res (property or some interest in the property). (Calistoga Civic Club v. City of Calistoga (1983) 143 Cal.App.3d 111, 116, 191 Cal.Rptr. 571; see also Elliott v. Elliott, supra, 231 Cal.App.2d at p. 209, 41 Cal.Rptr. 686; Angelus Securities Corp. v. Luton, supra, 47 Cal.App.2d at p. 268, 117 P.2d 741.) Clearly, the equitable remedy of constructive trust would be ineffectual if the trustee were permitted to defeat recovery by wrongfully permitting the res to be dissipated. Similarly, the remedy of constructive trust is defeated if plaintiffs are unable to trace the trust property into its succeeding transfigurements. (Walsh v. Majors (1935) 4 Cal.2d 384, 399, 49 P.2d 598; Efron v. Kalmanovitz, supra, 249 Cal.App.2d at pp. 195–196, 57 Cal.Rptr. 248; 5 Scott on Trusts, supra, § 521.3, pp. 3657–3659.)

The purpose of the injunction in this case was not to lessen the difficulty of determining damages. (Cf. Voorhies v. Greene (1983) 139 Cal.App.3d 989, 997, 189 Cal.Rptr. 132.) Its purpose was to restrain the Steinberg Group from dissipating the profit from the sale of Disney stock and, thereby, destroying plaintiffs' equitable remedy of constructive trust. (Cf. Steinmeyer v. Warner Cons. Corp. (1974) 42 Cal.App.3d 515, 520, 116 Cal. Rptr. 57.) As discussed below, the trial court had sufficient evidence to believe dissipation of the profit was already occurring. Thus, absent injunctive relief, plaintiffs would be left with a "naked claim for damages * * * to be obtained through an action at law." (Lathrop v. Bampton (1866) 31 Cal. 17, 23.) Instead of obtaining the income the fund could have earned if invested, plaintiffs would be entitled only to simple interest at the legal rate of 7 percent per annum. (See Civ.Code § 2262: "If a trustee omits to invest trust moneys * * * he must pay simple interest thereon, if such omission is negligent merely, and compound interest if it is willful."; and see Lynch v. John M. Redfield Foundation (1970) 9 Cal.App.3d 293, 302, 88 Cal.Rptr. 86.)[10]

* * *

DISPOSITION

The array of law and facts advanced by plaintiffs evaluated against defendants' counter-contentions demonstrates a reasonable probability that plaintiffs will be successful although, we stress, the final decision must await trial and a trial might well produce a different result. As to hardship, we believe the trial court reasonably concluded detriment to the plaintiffs if the proceeds and profits are dissipated or untraceable exceeds

---

9. Beatty v. Guggenheim Exploration Co. (1919) 225 N.Y. 380, 122 N.E. 378, 380.

10. The court in *Lynch* noted some treatise support for a more liberal standard than the legal rate of interest, e.g. the usual rate of return on trust investments. (Ibid.; but see Civ.Code § 2262, supra.) We have found no California case law hold-

ing the trustee liable for the amount of income the trust res reasonably could have earned had it not been dissipated. Furthermore, the Steinberg Group, while urging the plaintiffs have an adequate remedy at law, refused to stipulate to this standard of damages at oral argument.

any hardship to the Steinberg Group in complying with the investment and accounting provisions of the preliminary injunction.

The order granting a preliminary injunction is affirmed.

THOMPSON, Acting P.J., and HARRIS, J.,* concur.

SECURITIES AND EXCHANGE COMMISSION

Securities Act Release No. 33–6653; Exchange Act Release No. 34–23421.
July 11, 1986.

SUMMARY: The Securities and Exchange Commission ("Commission") today announced the adoption of amendments to its issuer and third-party tender offer rules. The amendments provide that a bidder's or issuer's tender offer must be open to all holders of the class of securities subject to the tender offer and that any security holder must be paid the highest consideration paid to any other security holder during the tender offer. In addition, the Commission is amending existing rules concerning minimum offering periods and withdrawal rights. With respect to minimum offering periods, a tender offer would be required to remain open for ten business days upon the announcement of an increase or decrease in (i) the percentage of securities being sought or (ii) the consideration offered by the offeror. With respect to withdrawal rights, the amendments provide that withdrawal rights extend throughout the offering period and that the extension of withdrawal rights upon commencement of a competing bid is eliminated.

* * *

I. *Executive Summary*

In July 1985, the Commission proposed a new rule to require a bidder making a tender offer under Section 14(d) of the Securities Exchange Act of 1934 ("Exchange Act") [4]: (1) to extend the offer to all security holders who own shares of the class of securities subject to the offer ("all-holders requirement"); and (2) to pay every tendering security holder the highest consideration offered to any other security holder at any time during the tender offer ("best-price provision").[5] At that same time, the Commission proposed corresponding amendments to Rule 13e–4 which made the all-holders requirement and best-price provision applicable to issuer tender offers.[6]

The Commission also proposed to require that both third-party and issuer tender offers remain open for at least ten business days from the announcement of an increase in the amount of securities being sought by the offeror. The Commission proposed that such amended offers remain open for the same period of time currently required for increases in the

---

* Assigned by the Chairperson of the Judicial Council.

4. 15 U.S.C. 78n(d).

5. Release No. 33–6595 (July 1, 1985) [50 FR 27976].

6. Release No. 33–6596 (July 1, 1985) [50 FR 28210]. This release also included proposed amendments to the applicable time periods for issuer tender offers in

order to bring the provisions governing the conduct of issuer tender offers into conformity with third-party tender offers, to eliminate the advantages afforded defensive issuer tender offers, and to alleviate the confusion that may arise from disparate time periods. On January 9, 1986, the Commission adopted these amendments. See Release No. 33–6618 (January 14, 1986) [51 FR 3031].

consideration offered or the dealer's soliciting fee in order to allow time for security holders to consider the offer as amended.

* * *

With respect to the best-price provision, three commentators suggested revising the best-price proposal to require that all security holders to whom a tender offer is made must be paid the highest consideration paid, rather than offered, to any other security holder. This would permit a bidder to reduce the consideration offered without having to terminate the initial offer and commence a new offer, as has previously been required. The Commission agreed with the suggested reformulation of the best-price provision and in January 1986 proposed, *inter alia*, a revised best-price provision.[8]

The revised best-price proposal also necessitated the proposal of amendments to extend withdrawal rights and to require the offering period to remain open for ten business days upon an increase or decrease in the amount of securities sought or consideration offered.

Specifically, the Commission proposed to amend Rules 13e–4(f)(1)(ii) and 14e–1(b) to provide that a tender offer must remain open for ten business days upon the announcement of an increase or decrease in the percentage of securities being sought or in the consideration offered by the offeror. The Commission proposed two alternatives to extend withdrawal rights. Under the first alternative, additional withdrawal rights would attach for ten business days upon the announcement of a decrease in the percentage of securities being sought or consideration offered. The second alternative provided that withdrawal rights would extend throughout the offer, and that the current requirement to extend withdrawal rights upon the commencement of a competing bid would be eliminated.

* * *

The Commission continues to believe that it has the requisite rulemaking authority to adopt the all-holders requirement and best-price provision and, accordingly, is adopting those amendments substantially as proposed. In addition, the Commission is adopting, substantially as proposed, the amendments to Rules 13e–4(f)(1)(ii) and 14e–1(b) regarding the extension of the offering period for changes in the consideration offered or the amount of securities sought. Finally, the Commission is adopting the amendments to Rules 13e–4(f)(2) and 14d–7 to provide that withdrawal rights extend until the expiration of the offering period. These amendments also eliminate the extension of withdrawal rights upon the commencement of a competing bid.

II. *Authority*

* * *

The all-holders and best-price rules are "necessary or appropriate" to implement the Williams Act. They expressly preclude bidders from discriminating among holders of the class of securities that is the subject of the offer, either by exclusion from the offer or by payment of different consideration. Without the all-holders and best-price requirements, the

---

8. Release No. 33–6619 (January 14, 1986) [51 FR 3186].

investor protection purposes of the Williams Act would not be fully achieved because tender offers could be extended to some security holders but not to others. Such discriminatory tender offers could result in the abuses inherent in "Saturday Night Specials," "First-Come First-Served" offers and unconventional tender offers since security holders who are excluded from the offer may be pressured to sell to those in the included class in order to participate, at all, in the premium offered. These excluded security holders would not receive the information required by the Williams Act, would have their shares taken upon a first-come first-served basis and would have no withdrawal rights. There is nothing in the Williams Act or its legislative history to suggest that Congress intended to permit such selective protection of target company security holders.

Consistent with the disclosure objectives of the Williams Act, Section 14(d) is "designed to make the relevant facts known so that shareholders have a fair opportunity to make their [investment] decision" to tender, sell or hold their securities. Specifically, Section 14(d)(1) requires bidders at the time a tender offer is made to provide investors, as well as the Commission, with information concerning, among other things, the terms of the offer and the bidder's plans or proposals with respect to the target company. In addition, Section 14(d)(1) specifically grants to the Commission the authority to prescribe other disclosure requirements for bidders "as [may be] necessary or appropriate in the public interest or for the protection of investors." Congress also provided the Commission with this same broad grant of rulemaking authority in Section 14(d)(4) which authorizes the Commission to specify "as necessary or appropriate in the public interest or for the protection of investors" the information to be included in any recommendation by the management or others in favor of or in opposition to a tender offer.

Consistent with that intent, the Commission has used its rulemaking authority to promulgate regulations designed to ensure that security holders have adequate information about a tender offer. For example, Rule 14d–2 provides that a tender offer will commence upon publication or public announcement of the tender offer. That rule does not contemplate that notification of the tender offer will be made to only certain security holders, but rather operates on the assumption that all holders will be adequately informed about the tender offer. Similarly, Rule 14d–4 provides for dissemination of tender offer materials to all security holders.

The all-holders requirement complements these rules and serves as a means of effecting the purposes of the Williams Act. The all-holders requirement would realize the disclosure purposes of the Williams Act by ensuring that all members of the class subject to the tender offer receive information necessary to make an informed decision regarding the merits of the tender offer. If tender offer disclosure is given to all holders, but some are barred from participating in the offer, the Williams Act disclosure objectives would be ineffective.

Further, the specific language of the Williams Act contemplates tender offers made for a "class" of equity security. That language reflects Congress' understanding that all security holders were to have the opportunity to participate in a tender offer for a target's securities. In addition to Section 14(d)(1)'s references to tender offers for "any class of any equity security," Section 14(d)(6), which governs proration of securities tendered, discusses tender offers "for less than all the outstanding equity securities of a class." By using the term "class" of equity security,[25] it can be inferred that Congress intended that, when a tender offer is made, it will be made to all holders of the outstanding securities of such class.

The substantive provisions of the Williams Act also support the Commission's rulemaking authority to require that all security holders subject to a tender offer be treated alike. For example, in promulgating both the pro rata and equal price provisions of Sections 14(d)(6) and (d)(7), Congress intended, *inter alia,* to assure fair treatment among security holders who may desire to tender their shares. The pro rata provisions of Section 14(d)(6) were promulgated in order to give all security holders an equal opportunity to participate in a tender offer for less than all the outstanding shares of the target.[26] Specifically, that section provides that where a greater number of securities are deposited than the offeror is bound or willing to take up, the securities deposited must be taken up pro rata according to the number of securities deposited by each person. Although Section 14(d)(6) recognizes that a tender offeror may accept less than all the securities of a particular class, that section does not authorize tender offers to be made to less than all security holders of the particular class of securities sought.

Similarly, Section 14(d)(7) assures equality of treatment among all security holders who tender their shares by requiring that any increase in consideration offered to security holders be paid to all security holders whose shares are taken up during the offer. One of Congress' purposes in promulgating the provision was "to assure equality of treatment among all shareholders who tender their shares."[27] These substantive provisions assume that offers will be made to all security holders and not just to a select few, and that offers will not be made to security holders at varying prices. Without the all-holders requirement and best-price provision, the specific protections provided by Sections 14(d)(6) and (d)(7) would be vitiated because an offeror could simply address its offer either to a privileged group of security holders who hold the desired number of shares or to all security holders but for different considerations. The all-holders requirement and best-price provision both are consistent with Congressional intent and complement the pro rata and equal price protections of the Williams Act.

That the substantive provisions of the Williams Act are intended to assure equal treatment of tendering security holders does not detract from the fact that the Williams Act is designed to protect all security holders regardless of whether they tender their shares. Courts and commentators alike have stated that "nontendering shareholders are within the class for whose protection the Williams Act was specifically designed."[28] The all-

---

25. Pursuant to the authority vested in it by Sections 3(b) and 23(a) to define terms, the Commission, by promulgating the all-holders provision, is defining the term "class" of equity security.

26. S.Rep. No. 550, supra, at 10; H.R. Rep. No. 1711, supra, at 11.

27. Id.

28. Hundahl v. United Benefit Life Insurance Co., 465 F.Supp. 1349, 1368 (N.D.

Tex.1979); see also Plaine v. McCabe, [Current] Fed.Sec.L.Rep. (CCH) ¶ 92,749 (9th Cir.1986); Wellman v. Dickinson, 475 F.Supp. 783, 817 (S.D.N.Y.1979), aff'd on other grounds, 682 F.2d 355 (2d Cir.1982), cert. denied, 469 U.S. 1069 (1983); In re Com Oil/Tesoro Petroleum Corp. Sec. Litig., 467 F.Supp. 227, 241–43 (W.D.Tex. 1979); A. Bromberg, Securities Law: Fraud § 6.3 (1974).

holders and best-price amendments implement the purpose of the Williams Act to protect all tendering and non-tendering security holders.

Thus, under Sections 14(d) and 23(a) of the Exchange Act, the Commission has the requisite authority to promulgate the all-holders requirement and best-price provision for third-party tender offers. Section 13(e) of the Exchange Act provides additional authority for the all-holders and best-price requirements in connection with issuer tender offers.[29]

When it adopted Section 13(e), Congress determined that, notwithstanding that share repurchases by an issuer were regulated by state corporation law, there was a need for federal regulation. Those who argue that adoption of the all-holders rule would preempt state corporation law fail to recognize that Congress made that decision when it enacted Section 13(e). Regulation of issuer tender offers in the same manner as third-party tender offers is entirely consistent with Congressional intent.

In addition, many commentators have asserted that the Commission's authority under this provision is limited to regulating disclosure. It is clear, however, that in adopting the Williams Act, Congress granted to the Commission broad rulemaking authority in Section 13(e) to determine the most appropriate regulatory scheme for issuer tender offers, and that the exercise of this authority could include adoption of substantive regulations.[30] For example, the Commission stated during Congressional consideration that the rulemaking authority in Section 13(e) could be used to apply the substantive provisions of Section 14(d) to issuer tender offers: "If the Commission is given rulemaking power with respect to issuers' purchases as provided in the bill, it could, and presumably would, provide separately for tender offers by issuers following provisions of [Section 14(d)] to the extent appropriate." [31]

In conformity with this mandate, the Commission adopted Rule 13e–4 to regulate issuer tender offers. Rule 13e–4 extends to issuer tender offers many of the protections in the Williams Act pertaining to third party offers, including disclosure (Rule 13e–4(d)), withdrawal (Rule 13e–4(f)(2)), proration (Rule 13e–4(f)(3)), and equal price (Rule 13e–4(f)(4)). Thus, it is entirely appropriate that the all-holders requirement and best-price provision apply equally to issuers and third-parties.

While Section 14(d) is only applicable to third-party tender offers, Congress nevertheless intended that the Williams Act's statutory purpose of investor protection was to be accomplished in a neutral manner. In implementing this policy of neutrality, the Commission has avoided favoring either management or the takeover bidder. There is no reason to provide different treatment for issuers with respect to the all-holders and best-price amendments. A tender offer, whether made by a bidder that is a third party or an issuer, puts the same pressure on target company security holders. Security holders have no less need in an issuer tender offer for the protections provided by the disclosure requirements and the substan-

---

29. Section 13(e)(1) authorizes the Commission "(A) to define acts and practices which are fraudulent, deceptive, or manipulative, and (B) to prescribe means reasonably designed to prevent such acts and practices * * *."

30. See Schreiber v. Burlington Northern, Inc., 105 S.Ct. 2458, 2463 n. 8 (1985).

31. Senate Hearings, at 202 (Supplemental Memorandum of the Securities and Exchange Commission with Respect to Certain Comments on S.510). Others at the Senate Hearings also noted that the substantive provisions in Section 14(d) "should be equally applicable to issuers' offers." Id. at 248 (statement by Milton Cohen).

tive protections of proration and withdrawal. Similarly, Congress' intent to ensure equal treatment of holders of the same class of securities is equally applicable. Consistent with that policy, the all-holders requirement and best-price provision must be applied equally to issuer and third-party tender offers to avoid tipping the balance in favor of either party.[32]

Further, Sections 13(e) and 23(a) of the Exchange Act provide ample statutory authority for the Commission to promulgate the all-holders requirement and best-price provision for issuer tender offers. Indeed, the Commission believes that ensuring that the fundamental policy of neutrality in the Williams Act is implemented through an equivalent all-holders requirement and best-price provision for issuer tender offers is the kind of use for which the general rulemaking authority in Section 23(a) is appropriate.

* * *

In Release No. 33–6596, the Commission indicated that it may be appropriate to except modified "dutch auction" issuer tender offers from application of the best-price provision.[64] The revised best-price provision would require that all security holders whose securities are accepted in a modified dutch auction issuer tender offer be paid the highest consideration paid to any other security holder whose securities are accepted. Accordingly, there would no longer be any need to except these transactions from the operation of the best-price provision.

The Commission proposed to except, under Rule 13e–4, issuer rescission offers from the all-holders and best-price provisions. Under that exception, issuers would be permitted to offer to repurchase securities only from certain security holders whose securities may have been issued in violation of state law or the registration provisions of the Securities Act of 1933 ("Securities Act"). The offer to purchase may be made at varying prices equal to the price paid by each such security holder plus legal interest. In most cases, issuers would not make rescission offers if they were required to extend the offer to all holders of the class of securities that is the subject of the rescission offer, or if they were required to pay to every security holder the highest consideration paid to any other security holder pursuant to the rescission offer. Accordingly, the Commission is adopting that exception under Rule 13e–4(g)(6) as proposed.

* * *

---

32. See, e.g., S.Rep. No. 550, supra, at 3; H.R.Rep. No. 1711, supra, at 4.

64. Under current staff interpretation, issuers have been permitted to make modified "dutch auction" issuer tender offers, although pure issuer "dutch auction" tender offers currently are not permitted under Rule 13e–4. In a pure dutch auction cash tender offer, the bidder invites security holders to tender securities to it at a price to be specified by the tendering security holder, rather than at a price specified by the bidder. Securities are accepted, beginning with those for which the lowest price has been specified, until the bidder has purchased the desired number of securi-

ties. Modified issuer dutch auction tender offers have been permitted under Rule 13e–4 subject to several conditions: (i) disclosure in the tender offer materials of the minimum and maximum consideration to be paid; (ii) pro rata acceptance throughout the offer with all securities purchased participating equally in prorationing; (iii) withdrawal rights throughout the offer; (iv) prompt announcement of the purchase price, if determined prior to the expiration of the offer; and (v) purchase of all accepted securities at the highest price paid to any security holder under the offer. The staff has not addressed defensive modified issuer dutch auction tender offers.

D. *Minimum Offering Period*

Rules 14e–1(b) and 13e–4(f)(1)(ii) currently provide that a tender offer must remain open for ten business days upon an increase in the offered consideration or the dealer's soliciting fee.[69] In Release Nos. 33–6595 and 6596, the Commission proposed to add, as an additional trigger for the ten business day period, an increase in the amount of securities sought pursuant to a tender offer.

In Release No. 33–6619, the Commission proposed to further revise Rules 14e–1(b) and 13e–4(f)(1)(ii) to provide that a decrease in consideration offered or amount of securities sought would also trigger the ten business day extension. These proposed amendments were intended to ensure that security holders receive information pertaining to the amended offer and have additional time to analyze that offer and withdraw tendered shares.

In addition, the Commission proposed to revise the language in Rules 14e–1(b) and 13e–4(f)(1)(ii) from "amount of securities sought" to "percentage of securities sought." This proposed revision recognized those circumstances where an increase in the number of shares sought does not increase the percentage of shares ultimately sought. This situation may occur in a partial tender offer where a bidder, in the face of an issuance of securities by the issuer, continues to offer for the same desired percentage of outstanding securities even though the total number of securities sought increases.[70]

The ten business day time period will only be triggered as a result of changes in the offer effected by the bidder. Thus, if the target company increases the number of shares outstanding and the bidder does nothing, the ten business day time period will not be triggered despite the fact that the percentage of securities sought by the bidder has decreased. Only if the bidder's own actions cause a decrease or increase in the consideration offered or percentage of securities sought will the ten business day time period be triggered.

The majority of commentators who addressed these proposed amendments supported them, and, accordingly, the Commission is adopting them

---

69. In this regard, the Commission notes that in a recent tender offer the bidder publicly announced that it was prepared to increase the consideration offered if a specified number of shares were tendered prior to the expiration of the offer. In the Commission's view, such a public announcement constitutes an increase in the consideration offered, requiring the filing of an amendment to the Schedule 14D–1 and the extension of the offering period for ten business days.

70. The minimum period during which an offer must remain open following material changes in the terms of the offer or information concerning the offer, other than a change in price or percentage of securities sought, will depend on the facts and circumstances, including the relative materiality of the terms or information. As a general rule, the Commission is of the view that, to allow dissemination to shareholders "in a manner reasonably designed to inform [them] of such change" (17 CFR 240.14d–4(c)), the offer should remain open for a minimum of five business days from the date that the material change is first published, sent or given to security holders. If material changes are made with respect to information that approaches the significance of price and share levels, a minimum period of ten business days may be required to allow for adequate dissemination and investor response. Moreover, the five business day period may not be sufficient where revised or additional materials are required because disclosure disseminated to security holders is found to be materially deficient. Similarly, a particular form of dissemination may be required. For example, amended disclosure material designed to correct materially deficient material previously delivered to security holders would have to be delivered rather than disseminated by publication.

substantially as proposed. Other commentators suggested that the Commission clarify whether *de minimis* purchases of securities in addition to the amount initially sought would trigger the additional time period. The Commission agrees that such a clarification is necessary and has amended Rules 13e–4(f)(1)(ii) and 14e–1(b) to provide that if at the expiration of the offer, the offeror accepts for payment an additional amount of securities that is less than two percent of the class of securities that is the subject of the tender offer [71] the tender offer will not be required to remain open for an additional time period. For example, under Rule 13e–4(f)(1)(ii) and 14e–1(b), if an offer were made for 51% of the class and 52.9% were tendered in response to that offer, the offeror could purchase the entire amount tendered without triggering the requirement to extend the offering period for ten business days. Conversely, the exercise of a reservation of a right to acquire an additional amount of securities tendered that is greater than two percent of the amount outstanding will trigger the requirement.

E. *Withdrawal Rights*

In Release No. 33–6619, the Commission proposed amending Rules 13e–4(f)(2) and 14d–7 in one of two alternate ways. The first alternative would provide for additional withdrawal rights for ten business days from the date that notice of a decrease in the consideration offered or percentage of securities sought is first communicated to security holders.[72] This proposal was intended to ensure that security holders who tendered prior to the decrease have the ability to reconsider their tender in light of the disclosure.

The Commission also proposed, as a second alternative, a broader approach to withdrawal rights. In light of the existing offering period framework, the Commission, as an alternative proposal, sought comment on a rule amendment that would extend withdrawal rights until the expiration of the tender offer. This proposal would protect security holders through a system that provides for prorationing and withdrawal throughout the offering period.[73] In this connection, the Commission pointed out that if the proposal to extend withdrawal rights throughout the offer is adopted no additional withdrawal rights will attach in the event of the commencement of a competing offer.[74]

* * *

The amendments also have the advantage of significantly simplifying the process. As a result of these amendments, security holders will have only one date to be concerned with—the expiration date. Proration and

---

71. The standard of less than two percent is consistent with the exemptions provided by Sections 13(d)(6) and 14(d)(8) of the Exchange Act. For purposes of Rules 13e–4(f)(1)(ii) and 14e–1(b), the percentage of a class of securities will be calculated in accordance with Section 14(d)(3) of the Exchange Act.

72. See 17 CFR 240.13e–4(e) and 240.14d–4(c).

73. The Commission has previously expressed a view that there should be coextensive withdrawal periods. See, e.g., Statement of John S.R. Shad, Chairman of the Securities and Exchange Commission,

before the House Subcommittee on Telecommunications, Consumer Protection, and Finance, March 28, 1984.

74. See Report of Recommendations of Advisory Committee on Tender Offers at 28–29 (July 8, 1983). The Advisory Committee's recommendation to eliminate the extension of withdrawal rights upon commencement of a competing bid was premised on the idea "that each bidder should control its own bid" and that the other recommendations concerning withdrawal periods "provide[ ] shareholders protections comparable to those under the current system." Id. at 29.

withdrawal rights will exist throughout the offer. A bidder will be the master of its own bid; timing will not be altered by actions of a competing bidder. This should reduce the potential for gamesmanship in commencing competing bids. Accordingly, the Commission is adopting, as proposed, the alternative requiring withdrawal rights to extend throughout the offer. By requiring withdrawal rights to extend throughout the offer, there is no longer a need to require under paragraph (f)(7) of Rule 13e–4 that the computation of withdrawal rights be done on a concurrent as opposed to a consecutive basis. Accordingly, paragraph (f)(7) of Rule 13e–4 has been amended to delete any references to withdrawal rights.

* * *

By the Commission, Commissioners Peters and Fleischman dissenting in part. The separate written views of any individual Commissioner will be published forthwith in Release Nos. 33–6653 A, 34–23421 A and IC–15199 A.

TARGET COMPANY RESPONSES TO TAKEOVER BIDS

A corporate management whose tenure is threatened by a takeover bid may recommend to the shareholders that they accept the offer or, without actively supporting it, may simply acquiesce in the takeover attempt. However, human nature being what it is, a management in that position is usually able to persuade itself that the success of the offer would be detrimental not only to themselves, but to the shareholders as well. If the management of the target company desires to recommend that the shareholders not accept the tender offer, it is required by Section 14(d)(4) and Rule 14d–9 implementing that section to file a statement with the Commission containing the information specified in Schedule 14D–9 at the time such communication is first sent to the security holders. However, under Rule 14d–9(e) no filing is required with respect to a communication which does no more than state that the management is studying the matter and will make a recommendation not later than ten business days after the commencement of the offer and to request that the security holders defer making any decision until receipt of the management's recommendation. (In any event, the target company must advise its shareholders under Rule 14e–2 that it recommends acceptance or rejection or is remaining neutral or is unable to take a position, with its reasons.)

The cases have generally held that a decision by the board of directors of the target company as to what response will be made to a tender offer is protected by the so-called "business judgment rule", under which a decision by the board of directors of a business corporation is immunized from being overturned by a court, and the directors are immunized from being liable for having made it, if (1) the decision was made after a reasonable investigation and due consideration by the board regarding the matter presented, (2) the directors making the decision are not interested in the transaction and are free of any conflict of interest (which could be shown in this context by demonstrating that the directors acted solely or primarily to perpetuate their control of the corporation), and (3) the action is taken in good faith, that is, with an honest belief that the action is in the best interest of the corporation and in furtherance of a rational business purpose. It is also generally held that the person attacking the validity or legality of a decision of the board of directors has the burden at least of coming forward with evidence to show that one or more of these elements was absent in order to make the business judgment rule inapplicable to the particular transaction.

There has been a dispute as to whether the business judgment rule should be applied in the context of defensive measures adopted in an attempt to ward off an unwelcome tender offer. Some dissenting judges [1] and some of the decisions (although a small minority) [2] have adopted the view that there is an "inherent" conflict of interest involved on the part of the directors where there is a threat to their continued control of the corporation, and therefore the business judgment rule should not be applied in this situation. A different basis for objecting to the application of the business judgment rule in such situations might be that the adoption of a defensive measure to prevent an unwelcome takeover of the company is not a "business" decision at all, that is, a decision relating to the conduct of the business of the corporation, but rather an attempt by the corporation to interfere with the freedom of the shareholders to sell their stock to whomever they choose. It is doubtful if most shareholders consider that they have entrusted that decision to the board of directors.

The Delaware Supreme Court in the case of Unocal Corp. v. Mesa Petroleum Co.,[3] while affirming the basic application of the business judgment rule to decisions taken by the directors in response to a takeover bid, expressly recognized that there may be some inherent conflict of interest involved in making such a decision. Therefore, the court imposed a fourth requirement of the applicability of the business judgment rule to this situation; that is, that any defensive measure approved be "reasonable in relation to the threat posed." Under this additional requirement for the application of the business judgment rule in Delaware, the directors must in good faith perceive a threat to the corporation from the success of the tender offer (exactly what such a "threat" may be is not elucidated with any precision in the opinion), and what the directors do must be a "reasonable" response to that perceived threat. The court said that the directors do not have "unbridled discretion to defeat any perceived threat by any Draconian means available." Similarly, the court in the *Norlin* case stated that "even if a board concludes that a takeover attempt is not in the best interest of the company, it does not hold a blank check to use all possible strategies to forestall the acquisition moves." Normally, the business judgment rule would preclude a court from inquiring into the reasonableness or unreasonableness of the decisions made by the board of directors (that is indeed its primary purpose), at least if they could have *any* rational basis.

Obviously, the directors of a target company must walk a fine line, and it is not entirely clear what constituencies they may take into account in deciding to try to prevent a hostile takeover. While most of the cases have indicated that they may consider other interested groups (for example, the employees and the community) in addition to the stockholders, the court in the *Revlon* case held that the directors could not take action merely for the benefit of noteholders without considering the stockholders, at least where a sale of the company had become "inevitable" and the directors had a conflict of interest in that they had been threatened with suit by the noteholders. (Compare the *Cardiff* case, above, regarding the disclosure which might be required by state legislation regarding the impact of the takeover on these other constituencies). The dangers are illustrated by the case of Panter v. Marshall Field & Co.,[4] which is discussed below, where the directors of Marshall Field, having defeated a

1. Panter v. Marshall Field & Co., 646 F.2d 271, 299 (7th Cir.1981) (Cudahy, J., dissenting), cert. denied 454 U.S. 1092 (1981); Johnson v. Trueblood, 629 F.2d 287, 300 (3d Cir.1980) (Rosenn, J., dissenting).

2. Minstar Acquiring Corp. v. AMF, Inc., 621 F.Supp. 1252 (S.D.N.Y.1985); the *Heckmann* case, above.

3. 493 A.2d 946 (Del.1985).

4. 646 F.2d 271 (7th Cir.1981), cert. denied 454 U.S. 1092 (1981).

takeover bid, only escaped being held liable for the more than $200,000,000 that the aggregate price of the stock of the company declined thereafter by a two-to-one vote in the Seventh Circuit Court of Appeals.

The simplest and most direct response which the management of the target company may make is to recruit a rival bidder, who is willing to pay more than the hostile tender offeror and who is expected to retain the present management of the company (or has expressly agreed to do so by an employment contract). This tactic has the greatest chance of success, although it frequently leads to a bidding war and the original tender offeror may top the highest bid that the "White Knight" is willing to make. It is also the least underhanded and purports to get the shareholders a better deal, and only incidentally to maintain the management's perquisites. If the competing offer is of securities of another corporation, there is frequently room for argument as to whether it is or is not a "better deal." The offer by the White Knight obviously must comply with the disclosure requirements: if a sale of assets or statutory merger, with the Proxy Rules; if an exchange offer, with the Securities Act of 1933; and if a rival cash tender offer, with the Williams Act.

Sometimes the White Knight is a syndicate organized by the management of the target company in cooperation with a brokerage firm specializing in this type of transaction to conduct a "leveraged buy-out" of the company, as in the *Revlon* case. Such a transaction is financed primarily with bank debt which is secured by a lien on the assets of the company (hence the phrase "leveraged buy-out"), but also with additional equity investment by a group of private investors. The existing management is almost always given a piece of the action in terms of an equity participation in the continuing business (although the existing management was excluded in the second offer made by the White Knight in the *Revlon* case), and its tenure in office is expected to continue. The existing management is almost always in a minority position in the continuing enterprise, however, and it may be replaced by the other investors if its future performance does not meet their expectations. This type of transaction is a form of "going private" (discussed below) and is frequently engaged in prior to any hostile tender offer emerging, although it may be motivated in part by an anticipation that such an offer is likely to occur; it may be difficult to put together on the spur of the moment after a tender offer has been made by another party, although that response is increasingly being made.

In Edelman v. Fruehauf Corporation [5] the court enjoined the implementation of a leveraged buy-out by the management of the target company when it concluded that the Board of Directors "unreasonably preferred incumbent management in the bidding process—acting without objectivity and requisite loyalty to the corporation." The court stated that "the Board made it appear that the management proposal was the best bid obtainable after giving Edelman [the hostile tender offeror] a reasonable opportunity to top the bid. In fact the Board accepted the leverage buy-out proposal of the management and Merrill Lynch without giving Edelman an opportunity to bid further and then rejected out of hand Edelman's offer a couple of days later to acquire the company on the same terms as management but at a higher price. While refusing to talk to Edelman or promote an open bidding process, the Board agreed to pay well over $30 million in corporate funds to Merrill Lynch as financing and advisory fees so that the management buyout could be consummated. (Over half of this amount would be paid even if another bidder

5. 798 F.2d 882 (6th Cir.1986).

prevailed.) The Board also made available $100 million of corporate funds for management's use in the purchase of shares and entered into an agreement severely limiting the Board's ability to negotiate another offer."

See Black, Barton & Radin, The Business Judgment Rule (1987); Fleischer, Tender Offers: Defenses, Responses, and Planning (2d ed. 1983); Lipton, Mirvis and Brownstein, Takeover Defenses and Directors' Liabilities (ALI–ABA 1986); Leebron, Games Corporations Play: A Theory of Tender Offers, 61 N.Y.U.L.Rev. 153 (1986); Gordon & Kornhauser, Takeover Defense Tactics: A Comment on Two Models, 96 Yale L.J. 295 (1986); Macey, Takeover Defense Tactics and Legal Scholarship, 96 Yale L.J. 342 (1986); Wander and Le Coque, Corporate Control Transactions and Today's Business Judgment Rule, 42 Bus. Law. 29 (1986); Gerke, The Business Judgment Rule and Potential Liability for Defensive Takeover Maneuvers by the Board of Directors, 53 U.M.K.C.L.Rev. 646 (1985); Siegel, Tender Offer Defensive Tactics: A Proposal for Reform, 36 Hastings L.J. 377 (1985); Oesterle, Target Managers as Negotiating Agents for Target Shareholders in Tender Offers, 71 Corn.L.Rev. 53 (1985); Coffee, Regulating the Market for Corporate Control, 84 Colum.L.Rev. 1145 (1984); Sommer, The Norlin Case and the Business Judgment Rule, 17 Rev.Sec.Reg. 799 (1984); Greene and Junewicz, A Reappraisal of Current Regulation of Mergers and Acquisitions, 132 U.Pa.L.Rev. 647 (1984); Harrington, The Legal Propriety of Defenses Against Hostile Takeover Bids, 34 Syracuse L.Rev. 977 (1983); Gutman, Tender Offer Defensive Tactics and the Business Judgment Rule, 58 N.Y. U.L.Rev. 621 (1983); Gilson, Seeking Competitive Bids Versus Pure Passivity in Tender Offer Defense, 35 Stan.L.Rev. 51 (1982); Easterbrook and Fischel, The Proper Role of a Target's Management in Responding to a Tender Offer, 94 Harv.L.Rev. 1161 (1981); Easterbrook and Fischel, Takeover Bids, Defensive Tactics, and Shareholders' Welfare, 36 Bus.Law. 1733 (1981); Lipton, Takeover Bids in the Target's Boardroom: An Update after One Year, 36 Bus.Law. 1017 (1981); Gelfond and Sebastian, Reevaluating the Duties of Target Management in a Hostile Tender Offer, 60 B.U.L.Rev. 403 (1980); Lipton, Takeover Bids in the Target's Boardroom, 35 Bus.Law. 101 (1979); McIntyre, Shareholders' Recourse Under Federal Securities Law Against Management for Opposing Advantageous Tender Offers, 34 Bus.Law. 1283 (1979); Lynch and Steinberg, Legitimacy of Defensive Tactics in Tender Offers, 64 Cornell L.Rev. 901 (1979).

"SUE THE BASTARDS!"

Despite the initial rebuff experienced by corporate management attempting to enjoin takeover bids for alleged failure to describe sufficiently the offeror's "plans", as noted above, this setback was soon overcome by the ingenuity of counsel. Almost without exception, any announcement of a takeover bid is now instantly [6] followed by an injunction action filed by the corporate management charging the "raider" with most of the crimes in the Decalogue, but usually stopping short of statutory rape. This is almost always followed by counterclaims filed against the corporation and its management making similar allegations. The Williams Act has become a "lawyers' paradise." [7] In Texasgulf, Inc. v. Canada Development Corp.[8] Judge Seals stated that the attorney

6. In reading some of the cases, one has the feeling that the complaint may have been drafted in advance with the name of the defendant left blank, to be filled in as the occasion may require.

7. This was the phrase used by Sir Harry Fisher, the Chairman of the Company Law Committee of the City, at a securities law seminar in London in April, 1975, to describe the American securities laws in general and in particular Rule 10b–5 and Section 16(b).

8. 366 F.Supp. 374 (S.D.Tex.1973). In this case it was alleged that the acquisition

for Texasgulf had described the tender offer as a "Pearl Harbor like" attack made "with the avowed purpose of stunning Texasgulf and overwhelming them." But he went on to observe that Texasgulf "was not so surprised, stunned or overwhelmed as to cause the management to hesitate or falter." The injunction action was filed three days after the announcement of the tender offer. And in the *General Host* case, where the offer was announced on a Friday, the complaint was filed on the following Monday, painting the pitiful picture, among others, of a ship lost forever on the Everglades because its ship-to-shore radio had been disconnected by the FCC.[9]

In D–Z Investment Company v. Holloway [10] Judge Wyatt stated regarding such a contest:

"It seems clear that there is a struggle here between two groups over the control of NJB [the target company] and that each group has attempted to use this Court to further its objective. DZ [the offeror] moved to restrain management and Judge Cannella (wisely, in my view) denied the motion. Now management moves to restrain DZ; it seems clear that this motion should also be denied. Management is simply trying to protect its entrenched position and, while its attackers must obey the securities laws, enforcement of those laws is, with rare exceptions, best left to the SEC or to the stockholders of NJB." [11]

This attitude on the part of the courts was rare in the early days under the Williams Act,[12] with the result that in some cases the predilections of a federal district judge (and perhaps the appellate court) were substituted as the arbiter of whether the tender offer would succeed for the informed decision of the shareholders.[13] The attitude of the courts has shifted in recent years, however, and now most courts are inclined to subscribe to Judge Wyatt's view. As Judge Winter said in a recent case: "The disclosure required by the Act is not a rite of confession or exercise in common law pleading." [14] Generally, all that a litigant can hope to accomplish is to secure an injunction prohibiting further action by the other side until some additional disclosure is made, at which time the battle shifts back to the market place. Nevertheless, the flood of litigation has continued unabated, since it may secure tactical advantages or temporary

of control of Texasgulf, most of the properties of which are located in Canada, by a corporation owned by the Canadian government would (1) violate the U.S. antitrust laws, (2) create a conflict of interest in favor of Canadian shareholders, (3) result in a cancellation of the corporate charter under a Texas statute, (4) result in the loss of eligibility to participate in the Overseas Investment Corporation's program to stimulate investment in have-not nations, (5) violate the Federal Communications Act by transferring broadcasting licenses to an alien government and without prior application to the FCC, and (6) result in the loss of Australian mining properties.

9. The peculiar restrictions in the Federal Communications Act on takeovers, which resulted from a rumour that a French syndicate was about to try to take control of ABC, have made it advisable for companies which feel themselves to be potential targets for a take-over bid to acquire some kind of a broadcasting license. Also, acquiring a small insurance company can be very helpful because of the regula-

tory road-blocks which can then be thrown up, no matter how insignificant a part of the business it may represent.

10. CCH Fed.Sec.Law Rptr. ¶ 94,771 (S.D.N.Y.1974).

11. Ibid.

12. See Gulf & Western Industries, Inc. v. The Great Atlantic & Pacific Tea Co., Inc., 476 F.2d 687 (2d Cir.1973); Sonesta International Hotels Corp. v. Wellington Associates, 483 F.2d 247 (2d Cir.1973); Corenco Corp. v. Schiavone & Sons, Inc., 488 F.2d 207 (2d Cir.1973).

13. One court held that, even though the offeror had been enjoined, he could still be sued by a person tendering stock for non-performance of the contract when there was no "litigation out" in the offer. Lowenschuss v. Kane, 520 F.2d 255 (2d Cir. 1975), on remand 72 F.R.D. 498 (S.D.N.Y. 1976).

14. Data Probe Acquisition Corporation v. Datatab, Inc., 722 F.2d 1, 5–6 (2d Cir. 1983), cert. denied 465 U.S. 1052 (1984).

delays in the tender offer which can be beneficial to one of the litigants. But it is recognized today that litigation alone is not going to defeat a tender offer.

The *General Host* case is a classic case of man bites dog (or, perhaps some would say, dog bites dog). The exchange offer by General Host of debentures and warrants for the stock of Armour & Co. at about the time of the passage of the Williams Act resulted in the same kind of frantic maneuvering by the target company and led to the introduction in the Illinois Legislature of a takeover bill.[15] Armour brought in Greyhound as a rival suitor and, although General Host acquired more than 50% of the stock, Greyhound acquired more than one third and was in a position to block any merger of General Host and Armour. Such a merger was essential to General Host in order for it to meet the interest payments on the debentures it had issued in the acquisition. The result was that General Host eventually sold out to Greyhound at an enormous profit, which in turn made it a prime takeover candidate. See Burke, Availability of Injunctive Relief to Private Litigants for Violation of Section 13(d) of the Securities Exchange Act of 1934, 15 U.S.F.L.Rev. 399 (1981); Johnson, Disclosure in Tender Offer Transactions: The Dice are Still Loaded, 42 U.Pitt. L.Rev. 1 (1980); Young, Judicial Enforcement of the Williams Amendments: The Need to Separate the Questions of Violation and Relief, 27 Bus.Law. 391 (1972); Note, The Courts and the Williams Act: Try a Little Tenderness, 48 N.Y.U.L.Rev. 991 (1973).

ACQUISITIONS AND OTHER ISSUANCES OF ADDITIONAL SHARES

The management of the target company may issue additional authorized and unissued shares, either to itself or to persons believed to be friendly. This increases the total number of shares outstanding and thereby "raises the ante" for the tender offeror since he will have to acquire more stock in order to have a majority. The executives may exercise their stock options (perhaps with money lent to them by the corporation) or acquisitions may be made in private transactions which create additional blocks of stock in the hands of persons who have explicitly or implicitly agreed not to tender and to vote with the management. Obviously, the management is not exactly in a favorable position at this point to negotiate the best deal for the company. The action of the board of directors in approving such an acquisition would be subject to the business judgment rule discussed above and their action has generally been sustained by the courts in the absence of very egregious circumstances.[16] The recipient of

---

15. See Aranow and Einhorn, Tender Offers for Corporate Control 153, n. 3, 168–69 (1973). The court in the General Host case printed above is mistaken in saying in Note 6 that the Host offer for Armour was a cash tender offer.

16. In addition to the *Carter Halley Hale* case and the *Heckmann* case above, see Treadway Companies, Inc. v. Care Corp., 638 F.2d 357 (2d Cir.1980); Chris-Craft Industries, Inc. v. Piper Aircraft Corp., 480 F.2d 341 (2d Cir.1973); Oscar Gruss & Son v. Natomas Co., CCH Fed.Sec.Law Rptr. ¶ 96,258 (N.D.Cal.1976); Klaus v. Hi-Shear Corp., 528 F.2d 225 (9th Cir. 1975); Seagrave Corp. v. Mount, 212 F.2d 389 (6th Cir. 1954); Cummings v. United Artists Theatre Circuit, Inc., 237

Md. 1, 204 A.2d 795 (1964); Marsh, Are Directors Trustees?, 22 Bus.Law. 35, 62–63 (1966).

This maneuver brings to mind the story of the fight for control of the Erie Railroad between Daniel Drew and Cornelius Vanderbilt, which was supposedly the cause of the New York Stock Exchange's requirement that every listed company have a "registrar" to prevent any "overissuances" of stock. Drew allegedly saw that he was losing the battle and decided that, since he then had control of the company and its printing presses for producing stock certificates, if Vanderbilt wanted to buy Erie stock he (Drew) would give him a surfeit of it. Vanderbilt might have been in danger of ending up owning considerably over

the shares issued in such an acquisition has been referred to, in the proliferation of the jargon relating to this branch of the law, as a "White Squire" (as contrasted with a "White Knight" to whom the entire target company is sold in order to defeat the "raider".)

Another method of getting more shares into friendly hands which has recently become popular is to issue additional shares to the Company's Employee Stock Ownership Plan, either one already in place or one newly created. The fact that members of the management of the corporation are typically the trustees of such an ESOP assures that the newly issued shares will not be tendered and will be voted as the management desires. See, however, Donovan v. Bierwirth,[17] in which the court held that the trustees of a corporate pension plan had violated their fiduciary duties under ERISA by failing to give adequate consideration as to whether to tender the shares of the company owned by the pension plan to a takeover bidder and by going into the market and purchasing additional stock of the company for an aggregate of $44,000,000 during the pendency of the tender offer, and by generally siding with the management of the corporation, which included two of the trustees.

The most extreme example of this tactic was the proposed issuance by Continental Airline to an ESOP of an amount of additional stock exceeding 100% of the presently outstanding stock, so that absolute control of the corporation would have been vested in the trustees of the ESOP, who were members of the management of the company. The stock was to be purchased by the ESOP from the company with money lent by banks, and the money was to be used by the company to repay its existing bank loans. The company would guarantee the new loans to the ESOP, which were to be repaid by annual cash contributions to the ESOP in future years. This had the effect of permitting the bank loans to be paid with pre-tax dollars, since the contributions would be deductible. This would have had the effect of handing over control of the corporation to the management of the company for nothing (the ostensible payment by the ESOP to the corporation was illusory since the debt was guaranteed by the corporation and could only be repaid through the annual contributions by the corporation to the ESOP). Continental refused to obtain a shareholders' vote on this transaction as required by the rules of the New York Stock Exchange in the case of any issuance of more than $18\frac{1}{2}\%$ of the presently outstanding shares (it knew that it could not obtain such a vote because Texas International Airlines, the tender offeror, had already acquired 49% of the then outstanding stock). The NYSE thereupon delisted the shares of Continental; this had the effect of eliminating the exemption for the issuance of the shares under the California Corporate Securities Law of 1968 and the California Commissioner of Corporations refused to issue a permit to authorize the transaction. Therefore, this tactic ultimately failed in that particular case; but a federal district judge in Los Angeles had refused to enjoin the transaction and the California Corporate Securities Law was subsequently amended to exempt from the Commissioner's jurisdiction any such issuance of shares to an ESOP.[18]

100% of all of the issued and outstanding stock. See Mott, Between the Ocean and the Lakes—the Story of the Erie 147–160 (1899). (Subsequently, James Fisk and Jay Gould did substantially the same thing to Drew.) This may have been the occasion for the Commodore's famous aphorism: "He who sells what isn't his'n, must buy it back or go to prison."

17. 680 F.2d 263 (2d Cir.1982), cert. denied 459 U.S. 1069 (1982).

18. Cal.Stats.1982, ch. 1524, adding § 25102(m) to the Cal.Corp.Code. See 1 Marsh & Volk, Practice Under the California Securities Laws (Rev. ed. 1985) § 4.06[1][b]. See also, in addition to the *Norlin* case, Klaus v. Hi-Shear Corporation, 528 F.2d 225 (9th Cir.1975); Frantz

The management may also make acquisitions of other companies (whether for cash or stock) which create or exascerbate antitrust problems for the tender offeror with respect to the acquisition or which create regulatory roadblocks because the acquired company is in a regulated industry and, therefore, the acquisition by the tender offeror will require the approval of some regulatory agency which will delay and perhaps prevent the acquisition. In Panter v. Marshall Field & Co.[19] the target company, Marshall Field & Company, accelerated plans laid in advance (on the advice of a tender offer specialist) to acquire a company in the Pacific Northwest with five stores and to open a new store in Houston, both in direct competition with Carter Hawley Hale, the tender offeror, which operated a national retail chain of stores including The Broadway and Neiman-Marcus. Marshall Field also authorized the filing of an antitrust action to enjoin the proposed tender offer. As a result of these maneuvers, the offer was withdrawn before it was ever formally communicated to the shareholders of Marshall Field. In an action on behalf of the shareholders of Marshall Field to recover damages of the difference between the amount offered ($42.00 per share in cash and stock) and the price to which the stock of Marshall Field declined after the withdrawal of the tender offer ($19.76), amounting in the aggregate to more than $200,000,000, the Seventh Circuit held that the actions taken by the Board of Directors of Marshall Field were within the protection of the "business judgment rule" under state law and that there had been no misrepresentations upon which to base a claim under the federal securities laws. Judge Cudahy, in a somewhat bitter dissent, stated that the majority "has moved one giant step closer to shredding whatever constraints still remain upon the ability of corporate directors to place self-interest before shareholders' interest in resisting a hostile tender offer for control of the corporation." [20]

See McLean, Employee Stock Ownership Plans and Corporate Takeovers, 10 Pepperdine L.Rev. 731 (1983); Brecher, Lazarus and Gray, The Function of Employee Retirement Plans as an Impediment to Takeovers, 38 Bus.Law. 503 (1983); Sidak, Antitrust Preliminary Injunctions in Hostile Tender Offers, 30 U.Kan.L.Rev. 491 (1982).

THE PAC–MAN DEFENSE

The target company may turn upon its pursuer, particularly if the original tender offeror is much smaller than the target, and itself make a tender offer for the shares of the initial offeror. (This was dubbed the "Pac-Man Defense" after the then popular video game where a little round character with a very large mouth would turn upon its pursuers and gobble them up.) This tactic received widespread publicity during the notorious fight between Bendix Corpo-

Manufacturing Company v. EAC Industries, 501 A.2d 401 (Del.1985) (the issuance of stock to an ESOP *after* control had already passed to an acquiring company was not protected by the business judgment rule because of its "retrospective" nature). Cf. Manbourne, Inc. v. Conrad, 796 F.2d 884 (7th Cir.1986).

19. 646 F.2d 271 (7th Cir.1981).

20. Compare Royal Industries, Inc. v. Monogram Industries, Inc., CCH Fed.Sec. Law Rptr. ¶ 95,863 (C.D.Cal.1976). In that case Judge Real enjoined a proposed acquisition by the target company of a corpora-

tion in competition with the tender offeror, which he found was made for the express purpose of creating an antitrust "block" to the proposed takeover. Judge Real stated: "Since the attempted acquisition of Sar [the other corporation] by Royal [the target] was made solely to thwart Monogram's proposed tender offer, it serves no proper corporate purpose, is a waste of Royal's corporate assets, is calculated to serve the interest of Royal's management to the exclusion or detriment of Royal shareholders, and should, therefore, be enjoined."

ration and Martin-Marietta Corporation in 1982.[21] In that contest, each corporation acquired more than 50% of the stock of the other, and the joke on Wall Street was that each might acquire 100% ownership of the other corporation, thereby creating a "black hole" with nothing left but a strong gravitational field. While each one was racing to try to depose the board of directors of the opponent, that was not in fact accomplished because of various maneuvers by the other corporation. It would appear, under most corporation statutes, that once each had acquired more than 50% ownership of the other, none of the shares could be voted by either side, since those statutes prohibit the voting of shares of a parent corporation held by a majority-owned subsidiary.[22] At that point, each had become a majority-owned subsidiary of the other, and the control of both corporations reverted to the remaining public shareholders. This would have been an ironic result of such a monumental fight, but perhaps would have been poetic justice. In fact, the affair was then settled out of court, with the two corporations remaining separate and independent.

This tactic requires that the target company have sufficient cash or borrowing capacity to make the counter-tender and it is very expensive compared to other available defenses. While rather popular for a period of time in 1982 and 1983, it seems recently to have lost its novelty and fallen out of favor as a defense in view of the emergence of more recent fads.

See DeMott, Pac-Man Tender Offers, 1983 Duke L.J. 116.

REPURCHASE OF ITS SHARES BY THE TARGET CORPORATION

Another tactic used by the management of a target company is to have the target corporation repurchase large quantities of its own stock in competition with the tender offeror, either through market transactions (whether on or off the board), as in the *Carter Hawley Hale* case, or by a tender offer for its own stock (a "self-tender"), as in the *Unocal* case. Any such repurchases by the target corporation must, of course, be of something less than all of the outstanding shares, which the tender offeror may be seeking, since if that were done the corporation would then be owned by no one.

On its face, this tactic would seem to be self defeating, since the stock reacquired by the corporation cannot be voted, and the result is simply that the aggregate amount of stock necessary to be acquired by the tender offeror to constitute an absolute majority of the voting power is thereby reduced. However, the collateral effects of such a transaction by the target company may substantially deter or defeat the hostile tender offer.

(1) In the first place, the market purchases by the target company or the self tender at a higher price than that offered by the hostile bidder may cause the market price of the stock to increase to a level above the amount that is being offered by the tender offeror, which will result in no further tenders being made, since a shareholder can simply call his broker and sell his stock in the market for more than he will receive by tendering to the hostile bidder.

(2) If the target corporation has a large amount of idle cash, which is thought to be what is attracting the takeover bid, it can in this manner dispose of the idle cash and thereby possibly remove the honey that is attracting the bees. Such idle

---

21. See Martin-Marietta Corporation v. Bendix Corporation, 549 F.Supp. 623 (D.Md.1982). For the history of this affair, see Rowan and Moore, Behind the Lines in the Bendix War, *Fortune,* Oct. 18, 1982, p. 157.

22. Del.Gen.Corp.Law, § 160(c); N.Y.— McKinney's Bus.Corp.Law § 612(b); Cal. Gen.Corp.Law, § 703(b).

cash is not generally reflected in the market price of the stock since the market looks almost entirely to earnings rather than assets in determining the price of an equity security. The tender offeror may be intending to use this cash to pay a large portion of its acquisition cost, and without that incentive may no longer have any desire to own the target corporation. A repurchase of shares rather than a dividend of the cash is made because a dividend would be ordinary income for tax purposes; if the proposal in the current tax bill pending in Congress is passed, eliminating any distinction between ordinary income and capital gains, it will be simpler and faster and less expensive to declare a dividend of the cash, if getting rid of it is the only objective.

(3) If the corporation does not have available cash to make the massive repurchases of its own stock, then it will, of course, have to borrow money in order to pay for the stock. The result may be that the corporation is so loaded with debt that it is no longer an attractive target to the tender offeror or his financing falls out of bed. As indicated above, in very many of these takeover battles, the tender offeror intends to repay the debt which it has incurred to make the tender offer from the assets of the acquired corporation. That corporation may not be able to survive with both the massive debt incurred by the management and the additional debt incurred by the tender offeror which he expects to be assumed or repaid by the target company. The CEO of Unocal has publicly worried about whether the company will ever be able to repay the $4 billion in debt which the company incurred in its self-tender to defeat T. Boone Pickens and to buy his stock (let alone the debt which Pickens hoped to saddle on it). Consequently, the banks and "junk bond" purchasers who are financing the tender offer may withdraw their support, particularly if the debt incurred by the target company is secured by a lien on some or all of the assets of the corporation, which would give that debt priority over the loans that they are making.

If the target company goes into the market to purchase its own stock, there are few legal restrictions applicable to those transactions other than the anti-manipulation rules. The State corporation law cases do not condemn the use of corporate funds for this purpose during a hostile takeover attempt, except perhaps in an aggravated situation.[23]

Rule 10b–13, which prohibits market purchases by the offeror "alongside the offer" does not apply to the issuing corporation which is the target company. While Exchange Act Release No. 8712 adopting Rule 10b–13 states that one reason for the adoption of the rule was that purchases outside the tender offer "could defeat the tender offer, either by driving the market price above the offer price or by otherwise reducing the number of shares tendered below the stated minimum," the Rule does not apply to anyone who could possibly have any motive to defeat the tender offer.[24] Nor does the proposed revision of Rule 10b–13 in Exchange Act Release No. 16385 apply to any such persons. The Securities and Exchange Commission wanted the Ninth Circuit in the *Carter Hawley Hale* case in effect to hold that Rule 10b–13 was applicable to the target company as well as the tender offeror, but the court declined to do that since the SEC had not done so itself.

---

23. Martin v. American Potash & Chemical Corp., 33 Del.Ch. 234, 92 A.2d 295 (1952); Kors v. Carey, 39 Del.Ch. 47, 158 A.2d 136 (1960); Cheff v. Mathes, 41 Del.Ch. 494, 199 A.2d 548 (1964); Lawrence v. Decca Records, Inc., 20 Misc.2d 424, 195 N.Y.S.2d 431 (Sup.Ct.1959); but cf. Propp v. Sadacca, 40 Del.Ch. 113, 175 A.2d 33 (1961). See Marsh, Are Directors Trustees?, 22 Bus.Law. 35, at 60–63 (1966).

24. Rule 13e–1 does require that the issuer file a notice with the Commission and transmit the information therein to its equity security holders before making such purchases.

Rule 10b–18 (discussed below, page 821 imposes strict limitations on the price, volume and timing of market purchases by an issuer, in order for the "safe harbor" rule immunizing the corporation from liability under Rule 10b–5 to be applicable; but that rule does not brand as "manipulative" transactions which do not comply with those requirements (in contrast to the previously proposed Rule 13e–2 which was "pending" for about fifteen years before it was finally abandoned in favor of the "safe harbor rule" in Rule 10b–18).

Such market purchases by the target company are facilitated by the fact that huge quantities of stock of a target company are accumulated by arbitrageurs; frequently, more than a majority of the outstanding stock of the target company is concentrated in the hands of a few such arbitrageurs. An "arbitrageur" is a market professional who purchases stock of the target company in the hope of making a substantial profit by tendering the stock to the tender offeror or any White Knight who outbids the original offeror. The profits can be enormous, in contrast to the classical arbitrageur who makes a tiny profit by purchasing a security and immediately reselling an equivalent security (such as one into which the first security is convertible); but correspondingly the risks may be extremely high: when the price of the stock of Marshall Field in the case discussed above (page 787) dropped from $42 per share to $19.76 per share when the tender offer was withdrawn, the arbitrageurs who had accumulated a large position took a bath. The arbitrageurs are like jackals circling around a lion's kill, but they take the chance that they may be bitten by the lion.

The restrictions in Rule 10b–18 could not generally be complied with in a program by the target company to acquire a large quantity of stock, were it not for the fact that the volume limitations in that rule do not apply to a "block transaction." A block transaction is defined as one involving a purchase price of not less than $50,000 and, if the purchase price is less than $200,000, a number of shares that is not less than 5,000. The requirements regarding the price (not higher than the last sale price or the highest current independent bid) and timing of the purchases could perhaps be met, particularly if the arbitrageurs are nervous regarding the success of the offer and wish to cash in their already built-in profit due to the market increase. It is not clear whether Carter Hawley Hale complied with the requirements of Rule 10b–18, although the court states that its purchases were made "at market." Since Carter Hawley Hale managed to purchase more than 50% of the outstanding stock in only six trading days, most of its purchases must have been large block purchases from the arbitrageurs.

Any such program of market purchases by the target company necessarily incurs some risk that it may be held to be manipulative in violation of Section 9(a)(2) of the 1934 Act or of Rule 10b–5. For example, in Crane Co. v. Westinghouse Air Brake Co.[25] the court held that such purchases by a rival merger candidate, when accompanied by off-board sales at less than the purchaser was simultaneously paying on the exchange, constituted illegal manipulation in violation of Section 9(a)(2) of the Exchange Act. The court described the situation as follows:

"The facts surrounding the manipulation of Air Brake stock by Standard are substantially free from dispute. The critical day in the takeover battle was April 19, the day Crane's tender offer for Air Brake stock was to expire. The holders of Air Brake stock could be expected to delay until the last

---

25. 419 F.2d 787 (2d Cir.1969), cert. denied 400 U.S. 822 (1970). This decision was reversed on a subsequent appeal on the basis that Crane Company had not purchased or sold any securities at a price affected by the illegal manipulation. Crane Co. v. American Standard, Inc., 603 F.2d 244 (2d Cir.1979).

moment in order to make a decision based on the latest market information, i.e., to compare the value of the tender offer, here not more than $50, with the market price on the day the offer was to expire. In fact, 85 percent of the shares tendered to Crane by the 19th were offered on that day. See Schmults and Kelly, Cash Take-Over Bids—Defense Tactics, 23 Bus.Lawyer 115, 124 (1967). On April 19, Air Brake opened at $45\frac{1}{4}$ on the New York Stock Exchange, giving Crane's tender offer a good prospect of success. The surest way to defeat the Crane offer was to run the price up to $50. The tape did quickly reach $50 on April 19, and Crane's tender offer failed. Crane's claim that this was the result of extraordinary transactions by Standard is supported by the record.

"At the close of trading on the 18th, Standard's net accumulation of Air Brake totalled 367,000 shares. Standard had a self-imposed limit of 460,000 shares, or 10 percent of Air Brake's outstanding stock, allegedly to avoid problems of pooling-of-interest accounting treatment and liability under section 16(b) of the Exchange Act. Only 92,600 shares remained to be purchased to reach Standard's self-imposed limit. On Friday, the 19th, Standard proceeded to purchase in a series of transactions, ranging in size from 100 to 9700 shares, a total of 170,200 Air Brake shares, at an average price of $49.08 per share, and a total price of approximately $8.4 million. The net result of this buying was to represent to the public, whose primary source of information is the tape, that there was a great demand for Air Brake at an increased value. It is reasonable to conclude that many Air Brake stockholders who might otherwise have chosen to tender to Crane chose not to do so because their own holdings in Air Brake looked better as the price went up.

"The fact was, however, that not only was Standard creating this extraordinary demand for Air Brake stock, but only 50,000 of the 170,000 shares represented an actual increase in Standard's holding in Air Brake. Before the opening of the market on Friday, Mr. Ledbetter of IDS agreed to purchase from Standard 100,000 shares of Air Brake at $44\frac{1}{2}$. This transaction did not affect the dramatic 5 point climb of the 'tape' price of Air Brake since Standard made no public announcement of the private sale. The sale to IDS was secret; Standard's telegram to IDS confirming the sale was marked 'HIGHLY CONFIDENTIAL.' Shortly after the opening Standard sold another 20,000 Air Brake shares to Dillon Read at $44\frac{7}{8}$, at the same time that it was buying on the exchange. At the close of trading on Friday the 19th, Standard held a total of 417,000 Air Brake shares. It had sold 120,000 shares at a price of just above $44\frac{1}{2}$, and purchased 170,000 shares at an average price of $49.08, for a net trading loss exceeding one-half million dollars. Standard had 'painted the tape' in Air Brake stock. It appears that of the 26,300 shares of Air Brake traded at 50 that day, all but 100 were bought by Standard. This course of conduct was certain to raise the price of Air Brake stock suddenly and dramatically." [26]

If the market purchases are proposed to be made by a rival tender offeror or exchange offeror, that person would be subject to Rule 10b–13 because of the pendency of his own offer and a rival merger candidate, under the rationale of the *Chris-Craft* case,[27] would probably be subject to Rule 10b–6, since the merger is a "distribution" of the securities of the acquiring corporation and the securities of the merged corporation are "convertible" into the ones being distributed.

---

26. 419 F.2d at 793.

27. Chris-Craft Industries, Inc. v. Bangor Punta Corp., 426 F.2d 569 (2d Cir.1970), rev'd on other grounds 430 U.S. 1 (1977).

If the takeover bid takes the form of an exchange offer rather than a cash tender offer, acceptance of it may be deterred not only by driving up the price of the target company's shares but by driving down the price of the offeror's shares, since the "package" of securities offered, if not consisting of common stock, usually contains a convertible or a warrant the value of which depends upon the market price of the common stock of the offeror. The success of such an offer typically depends upon the activity of the arbitrageurs, and it has been said that the surest way to defeat an exchange offer is: "Frighten the arbitrageurs!"[28] However, any "bear raid" on the stock of the offeror would obviously present the same dangers of being held to be in violation of Section 9(a)(2) or Rule 10b–5 as would purchases of the target company's stock, if undertaken by anyone with a motive for defeating the exchange offer.

If the purchases of its own stock by the target company take the form of a self tender which is extended to all of the shareholders of the company, this may permit the hostile bidder to make a quick profit by tendering the shares which he has previously accumulated into the company's offer, which would be at a higher price than he is offering and probably substantially in excess of what he has paid for his prior market accumulations. In Unocal Corp. v. Mesa Petroleum Co.[29] however, the Delaware Supreme Court held, to the surprise of many, that the target company could exclude the hostile tender offeror from being eligible to tender to the company. The Securities and Exchange Commission acted quickly to counteract the decision in the *Unocal* case by adopting the "All Holders" rule, which had been kicking around in different "proposed" forms for almost ten years without having previously moved forward, in the Release reprinted above (page 772).[30] This rule requires that any tender offer, whether by a third party bidder or by the issuer, be open to all holders of securities of any class to which it is extended (as well as a requirement that the highest consideration being paid to any tendering shareholder be paid to all shareholders who tender under companion rules adopted at the same time). Some people contend that the SEC has no authority to adopt rules regulating the substantive terms of a tender offer contrary to the rules applicable under state corporation law, but the SEC vigorously defended its authority in the above-mentioned Release, and it seems rather unlikely the courts will hold that these rules are invalid. If they are upheld, then an issuer self-tender, as a defensive measure against a takeover bid, may become passé.

Another disadvantage of the self tender is that it may simply result in the hostile bidder raising his offer to top that of the target company, which obviously has to be made at a price in excess of that already offered by the hostile bidder. While this would certainly be a benefit to the shareholders of the target company, it may not be what the management wants.

See Rosenzweig, Defensive Stock Repurchases, 99 Harv.L.Rev. 1378 (1986); Bradley & Rosenzweig, Defensive Stock Repurchases and the Appraisal Remedy, 96 Yale L.J. 322 (1986); Atkins, Lyons and Feder, Stock Repurchases in Tender Offers, 17 Rev.Sec.Reg. 787 (1984); De La Mater, Target Defensive Tactics as Manipulative Under Section 14(e), 84 Colum.L.Rev. 228 (1984); Weiss, Defensive Responses to Tender Offers and the Williams Act's Prohibition Against Manipulation, 35 Vand.L.Rev. 1087 (1982); Nathan and Sobel, Corporate Stock Repurchases in the Context of Unsolicited Takeover Bids, 35 Bus.

---

28. O'Boyle, Changing Tactics in Tender Offers, 25 Bus.Law. 863, at 865 (1970).

30. Rule 14d–10; Rule 13e–4.

29. 493 A.2d 946 (Del.1985).

Law. 1545 (1980); Burack, When Buying Rights is Wrong: Purchases of Target Company Stock During Exchange Offers and Mergers, 33 Bus.Law. 605 (1978).

POISONED PILLS

The so-called "poisoned pill" defense to a takeover was invented by Martin Lipton, perhaps the leading takeover attorney in the United States (although Joseph Flom would disagree with that statement). While the different permutations of this tactic are extremely complicated, the essence of the defense is that "rights" are issued to all of the shareholders of the company which is a target or potential target (1) entitling them to purchase additional shares of common stock of the company at a price that is only a fraction of the market price (frequently one-half) upon the happening of certain events (the "triggering events") and (2) entitling them to purchase stock of the tender offeror at the same discount after there has been a merger accomplished of the target company into the tender offeror or its subsidiary (the "flip-over provision").

The triggering events are typically the acquisition by any person of shares of the target company in excess of a specified percentage of the outstanding stock (ranging from 20% to 35%) or the making of a tender offer by any person for stock of the company in excess of the percentage specified, with perhaps the expiration of a period of time, such as ten days, to give the management time to negotiate with the third party before the rights are triggered. Also, the rights are generally not triggered if the tender offeror promptly announces, and accomplishes by a cash-out merger within 120 days, the acquisition of all of the remaining stock of the target company at a specified minimum price. This triggering of the rights is sometimes referred to as the "flip-in provision." The rights attached to any shares acquired by the person responsible for the triggering event become invalid and cannot be exercised by him.

There is a question under any applicable state corporations code as to whether that type of discrimination against a specified shareholder is permissible simply on the basis that he has acquired a certain position in the stock of the company. The Delaware Supreme Court in the *Moran* case of course held that this type of provision was permissible under Delaware corporate law, but Judge Broderick of the Southern District of New York held in Amalgamated Sugar Company v. NL Industries [31] that it was not permissible under the New Jersey corporate law. It may not be feasible to adopt a particular type of plan if the hostile bidder has to be given the ability, along with the other shareholders, to exercise the rights which are issued to the shareholders.

The flip-over provision is designed to prevent the tender offeror from defeating this maneuver by acquiring a majority of the outstanding stock of the target company (with their attached rights) and then having a cash-out merger of the target company which wipes out the remaining rights. The rights are made redeemable by the board of directors of the company at a nominal figure at any time before the happening of a triggering event or usually for a period of time thereafter. The board therefore can wipe out the rights and remove this obstacle to any friendly acquisition which it has negotiated, as was done in the *Revlon* case.

In its original form as conceived by Mr. Lipton, this plan involved the issuance as a dividend to the shareholders of a new issue of preferred stock; and the "rights" were a right to convert that preferred stock into stock of the target company or to buy stock of the surviving company after a merger under

---

31. 644 F.Supp. 1229 (S.D.N.Y.1986).

the flip-over provision.[32] Also, the holder of the preferred stock was given a right to "put" that stock back to the corporation for a price in cash equal to a specified amount. It was soon realized, however, that the preferred stock feature of this plan was not essential to its fundamental operation and resulted in a permanent change in the capital structure of the corporation once the preferred dividend had been issued to the shareholders. Since that feature of the plan was a non-essential complicating factor, it has now generally been dispensed with in the new plans that are being adopted, and pure "rights" are being issued to the shareholders which are irrevocably attached to their common shares and subject to the conditions described above.

There was considerable doubt as to the validity as a matter of corporate law of the flip-over provision and there still may be in States other than Delaware. Many people thought that Corporation A could not give an option to its shareholders to purchase shares of Corporation B which would be binding upon that corporation. The validity of the flip-over provision was not actually involved in the *Moran* case, since that issue could only be raised directly by a tender offeror completing a hostile takeover in the face of a poisoned pill in effect and then resisting the attempt of the shareholders who were cashed out in the second step to exercise their purported rights to purchase stock of the acquiror at half its market price. So far, no tender offeror has been willing to take that chance. Nevertheless, the *Moran* case has been accepted as settling the law of Delaware in favor of the validity of this provision, even if the discussion in that case was arguably only *dictum*, and hundreds of Delaware corporations have adopted this type of plan.

It was originally asserted that the poisoned pill plan was designed only to deter or prevent partial offers and front-end loaded offers. This was probably true of such a plan in its pristine form; but it is only true if the rights are only triggered by the failure of the person acquiring the specified percentage of the outstanding stock of the corporation to complete the acquisition of 100% of the outstanding stock within a specified period of time at the same price that he paid to acquire his initial position. That was in fact what was recommended by Mr. Lipton in his original description of the plan; the cash price for which the preferred stockholder could "put" the stock back to the corporation and the market value of the stock into which the preferred could be converted after a merger was merely the highest price paid for any of the stock acquired by the tender offeror.[33] Therefore, the plan only guaranteed that all shareholders would receive the same premium initially offered by the tender offeror and it would not deter an "any or all offer" where there is an announced intention to cash out the remaining shareholders at the same price.

In fact, such plans now typically include a "fair price" provision which triggers the rights unless the shareholders who are cashed out in the second step of the acquisition (which is almost always intended, whether or not the offer was a partial offer or was front-end loaded) receive a specified minimum price for their shares; for example, a figure equal to double the market price of the stock prior to the announcement of the tender offer or a dollar figure or a price based upon some formula, which in either case represents the "intrinsic value" of the company in the eyes of its management.

No tender offeror is willing to offer that kind of a premium, of course, since it would mean that he would have no hope of making a profit out of the transaction. Therefore, whether any tender offeror would be willing to make

32. Wachtell, Lipton, Rosen & Katz, "To Our Clients—Takeovers: Convertible Preferred Stock Dividend Plan", dated August 17, 1983.

33. Ibid.

any kind of offer would depend on the percentage of stock which he hopes to acquire in the first step; if he could acquire, say, 90% or 95% of the stock at the premium he is willing to pay, he might be willing to stand the additional cost of cashing out the remaining shareholders at the greater premium established by the fair price provision in the poisoned pill plan. In the *Moran* case there was conflicting testimony of "experts" as to whether a tender offer conditioned upon such a high percentage of the stock being tendered could ever succeed, and the court accepted the opinion of one set of experts that it could; but it is contrary to common sense to expect that such a high percentage of shareholders would tender when they knew that if they held out (and a sufficient number of other shareholders tendered), they would ultimately receive substantially more than they would by accepting the offer. One expert stated that he had never heard of a "back-end loaded" offer succeeding.[34]

The plan adopted by Household International in the *Moran* case was atypical, probably because of the situation of that particular corporation with respect to its authorized and unissued stock. The rights issued to the shareholders were rights to purchase preferred stock which was in fact only a disguised common stock in that the preferred was "participating" and entitled to receive, for each $1/100$th of a share of preferred stock, the same dividend and liquidation rights as a share of common stock, with only an insignificant cumulative preferred dividend and liquidation right as a minimum. (The reason this was related to $1/100$th of a share, rather than issuing 100 times as many shares of the preferred stock was presumably the fact that the corporation did not have that many shares authorized of its blank preferred stock. It is easier to understand the mechanics if one assumes that in fact 100 times as many shares had been issued and each share was equivalent to one share of common stock.) The purchase price for a share of preferred stock on the basis of that assumption was $100 per share, but the market price of the common stock to which it was substantially equivalent was only in the range of $30 to $33 per share. Therefore, the rights were "deep in the money" and would never be exercised unless the price of the common stock rose above $100 per share some years down the road. It was thus deliberately intended that the rights to purchase preferred stock of the target company would never be exercised. However, upon the merger of the target company in the second step of an acquisition, the rights became rights to purchase common stock of the acquiring corporation at 50% of their market value, and the Delaware Supreme Court correctly viewed this aspect of the rights as the only significant feature of them. This plan, therefore, had no "bite" until the second step was taken, and if a tender offeror was willing to simply acquire control and let the minority shareholders sit there for a considerable period of time, until they got tired of that and were themselves willing to tender, the plan would not increase the cost to the acquiring corporation.

In view of the limited nature of the plan involved in that decision, it is strange that the bar seems generally to have assumed that that decision validated all rights plans under the law of Delaware. The Delaware Supreme Court itself seems to have made that assumption in the *Revlon* case, despite the fact that the plan in that case was quite different. While noting that the issue of the validity of the rights plan was moot because the rights had been redeemed, the Court said: "Under the circumstances it cannot be said that the Rights Plan as employed was unreasonable, considering the threat posed," without any analysis whatever of the differences between that plan and the one involved in *Moran*.

---

34. See the opinion of Vice Chancellor Walsh in the *Moran* case in the lower court, Moran v. Household International, Inc., 490 A.2d 1059, at 1068 (Del.Ch.1985).

The court's discussion in that case of whether the poisoned pill plan was a "show stopper",[35] that is, a defensive tactic that makes inevitable the retirement of the hostile bidder from the field of battle, is rather unconvincing. For example, the court said that one method by which the hostile bidder could succeed would be to persuade the board of directors to redeem the rights; if it did that, of course, the bid would no longer be a hostile bid.

A rights plan has the possible disadvantage that it requires a cash investment by the shareholders, even though there is an instant built-in profit; and they may not be anxious immediately to cash in that profit by reselling the stock which they have acquired, because of possible adverse tax consequences. A variation on the pure rights plan is to give the shareholders of the target company a right to turn in their common stock as payment for a debt security to be issued by the target company, which has a face amount that is equal to the "intrinsic" value of the corporation in the eyes of its management. The shareholders, other than the person responsible for the trigerring event, are thus all able to convert themselves from equity owners to creditors of the corporation. This was the type of plan adopted by Revlon, although never implemented. The Revlon shareholders were able to turn in a share of common stock and receive a $65 note due in one year, which was $20 more than the market price of the stock when the plan was adopted. That price ($45⅝) was already substantially inflated due to the announced tender offer—it increased from $42 to $45⅝ on that very day.

Under such a plan, if it is triggered by a person acquiring 21% of the outstanding stock, who does not desire to own any more, all the other stockholders can turn themselves into creditors, leaving him as the sole owner of a corporation which is probably headed for bankruptcy because of the immense load of additional debt which has been saddled on it. Such a threat by the corporation to commit hara-kiri if anyone acquires such a position in its stock should be sufficient to deter most people from doing so. It is true that the tender offeror in the *Revlon* case persisted, and ultimately prevailed, in its efforts to take over Revlon; but all of its offers were conditioned upon the board of directors redeeming these rights so that the debt securities would never be issued.

Is the decision in the *Dynamics Corporation of America* case consistent with the decisions in *Moran* and *Revlon?* Judge Posner purports to be applying Delaware law because he believes that Indiana would do so in the absence of any controlling decision by the Indiana courts. Certainly, the Indiana courts would not be less solicitous of the desires of the managements of Indiana-based corporations than would the Delaware Supreme Court. Judge Posner, however, does not engage in any analysis of the plans involved in those cases nor of the language of the Delaware Court in its opinions in those cases. Are the differences in the respective plans sufficient to distinguish *Dynamics Corporation of America* from those Delaware decisions? Is the fact of any significance that the person threatening to trigger the rights in *Dynamics Corporation of America* was not seeking to "take over" the corporation in the sense of acquiring 100% ownership, but merely to get in a position to wage a proxy fight to oust the existing management? Is the fact of any significance that that person was previously the largest shareholder of the corporation, rather than a "raider"?

The Delaware Supreme Court in the *Moran* case emphasized that, although it was upholding the action of the board of directors in putting into effect a

---

35. Incidentally, Judge Waterman was, understandably, confused by the proliferating jargon in this field of law when he referred, in the *Hanson Trust* case, to a "lockup option" as a "poisoned pill", rather than a "show stopper."

rights plan before any hostile tender offer was made, the directors would have to observe their fiduciary duties to the shareholders at a time in the future when a potential acquiror requested that they redeem the rights in order to permit his offer to proceed. Therefore, by refusing to redeem the rights pursuant to such a request, the directors may expose themselves to liability to the shareholders for breach of their fiduciary duty if the proposed offering price pursuant to an all-or-any offer is at a very substantial premium over market, and their refusal causes the withdrawal of the offer. If the proposed premium is substantial, the damages claimed by the shareholders could be enormous. Presumably, the business judgment rule, which is discussed above, would be applicable to the action of the board of directors in making that decision, but perhaps these takeover battles have stretched the business judgment rule almost to the breaking point. The Revlon board, in the final analysis, did not have the *chutzpa* actually to implement that rights plan.

A recent variation on the "poisoned pill" is what has been called the "value assurance plan." As an example, this plan might consist of issuing to the shareholders a promissory note payable in two years or upon an acquisition of the company within that time, with a variable amount payable on the note depending on whether the acquisition is by a hostile tender offer or is a transaction negotiated with the management or a leveraged buy-out by the management. If the acquisition is by a hostile tender offer at less than $33 per share (as an example), the principal amount payable on the note is the difference between the amount offered and $33. If there is a negotiated acquisition or a leveraged buy-out for at least $30 per share, the board can redeem the notes at 5¢ a note; but if the price is less than $30 per share, the notes are payable as in the case of a hostile tender offer. In addition, if there has been no acquisition during the two year term of the notes, a principal amount is payable on the notes equal to the difference between the then current market price of the stock, if less than $30, and $30. The plan thus guarantees to every shareholder (not merely those who are cashed out in a second step) a minimum price for his stock and market protection against a failure of the stock to reach the specified minimum level in two years if the management has failed to arrange a deal with as favorable a premium to the shareholders.

The figures which have been used are of course not an inherent element of this plan, but were those actually used in the plan adopted by Mayflower Group Inc., which was the first to adopt this type of plan.[36] These figures would have to be related to the market price of the common stock and to the premium which is being offered by an unfriendly suitor if the plan is adopted after the company has actually been approached with such an offer. The stock of Mayflower Group Inc. has been selling in the neighborhood of $25 in the market after this plan proved to be a "show stopper", causing the withdrawal of a hostile offer (the tender offeror had offered $29¼ and was unwilling to pay $33).

This plan effectively establishes an absolute floor for any tender offer, since any difference between the offer and the price specified is simply taken from the company in cash and paid to the shareholders, thereby increasing the cost to the tender offeror to the minimum figure specified. Unlike the plan in the *Revlon* case, this plan does not threaten to saddle the company with an astronomical amount of debt, unless the price protection provision is unrealistically high. There is a strong incentive not to make the difference too great between the floor price for an unfriendly takeover and that for a friendly

36. Business Week, July 7, 1986, p. 36.

acquisition (including an LBO in which management participates), since if this were very large the management would appear to be positioning itself to rip off the shareholders. The price protection feature of this plan could be eliminated and the term of the notes changed without materially altering its fundamental effect of establishing a minimum price which any unfriendly suitor must pay while the notes are outstanding in order to acquire the company. A disadvantage of this plan is that once the notes have been issued, it becomes irrevocable regardless of any subsequent change in circumstances, which is a reason for not making the term of the notes too long. No management wants to advertise a minimum price for the company for the indefinite future, since that may invite offers at that price after their expectations have increased.

See Dawson, Pence and Stone, Poison Pill Defensive Measures, 42 Bus.Law. 423 (1987); Chittur, Wall Street's Teddy Bear: The Poison Pill as a Takeover Defense, 11 J.Corp.L. 25 (1985); Reskin, Poison Pill Tactic Passes First Legal Test, 71 A.B.A.J. 122 (1985); Protecting Shareholders Against Partial and Two-Tiered Takeovers: the "Poison Pill" Preferred, 97 Harv.L.Rev. 1964 (1984); Finkelstein, Antitakeover Protection Against Two-Tier and Partial Tender Offers, 11 Sec.Reg.L.J. 291 (1984).

LOCK–UPS AND SCORCHED EARTH

A "lock-up option" refers to an option granted to a favored bidder by the target corporation to ensure the success of his bid and the defeat of the bid of any hostile bidder. It has been used in two different circumstances: (1) one is in connection with a negotiated friendly acquisition, to prevent any third party from disrupting the deal which has been worked out with the management of the corporation by making a competitive bid, and thereby to prevent any bidding from ever developing; (2) the other is in connection with a deal made with a White Knight in the course of a takeover battle, as in the *Revlon* case, to attempt to guarantee that the White Knight will win over the initial takeover offeror and that there can be no further escalation of the price through the bidding war. It also may take two different forms: (1) the first is an option to purchase authorized and unissued stock of the corporation at a discount from market and with a substantial differential between the option price and the price negotiated in the sale of the corporation; (2) the second is an option to purchase one or more of the divisions or subsidiaries of the target company at a bargain price, which are usually the most profitable of the business segments owned by the target company or which are thought to be the attraction to the hostile bidder.

The simplest, but least effective, of lock-up devices is merely an agreement by the target corporation with the friendly suitor that it will not solicit competing bids from the time of the execution of the agreement until the shareholder vote on whether to approve that acquisition. This is referred to as a "no-shop provision." Sometimes it is coupled with an agreement by the board of directors that they will not support, or will oppose, any such competing bid; but a board which is advised by a conservative lawyer will usually refuse to sign that agreement because of the fear that they may be sued by the shareholders for having abdicated in advance their fiduciary duty to be concerned only with the best interests of the shareholders.

The Ninth Circuit recently held that a no-shop provision in a merger agreement was valid and enforceable, and that the corporation to be acquired was liable in damages for having violated it.[37]   This decision, if generally followed, would certainly deter other bidders solicited by the management from making any competitive bid, since a judgment against the acquired corporation would ultimately come out of the rival bidder's pocket if its bid were successful. This provision, however, is not very effective since once the proposed acquisition by the friendly suitor is announced, and it is known that the corporation is for sale, other bidders may appear who are not solicited by the corporation or its management.   If an offer is made before the shareholder vote to pay an amount in cash greater than that being received by the shareholders pursuant to the agreement with the friendly acquiror, it is highly likely that the shareholders will vote down the original proposal, whether it is supported or opposed by the management of the corporation.   If a tender offer is made during the period before the holding of the shareholders' meeting and the competitive bidder acquires more than a majority of the stock, then of course he can vote down the original proposal all by himself.

Another type of lock-up used in connection with friendly acquisitions, where the insiders of the acquired corporation hold a majority or even a substantial minority (such as 40% or 45%) of the stock of the corporation to be acquired, is for the acquiring corporation to insist upon the granting of an option by those shareholders to it to purchase their shares for the same price that is being offered to all shareholders in the merger, which is exercisable whether or not the merger is approved by the shareholders.   This provision makes impossible the success of any competitive bid.   The inside shareholders obviously cannot be accused of any breach of fiduciary duty to the other shareholders, since they are willing to accept the price negotiated and they have the greatest interest in securing the highest price possible for the corporation, unless the facts indicate that they are benefiting in some other way from the sale to the friendly suitor.

The third level of escalation of this type of lock-up is for the corporation to grant an option to the friendly suitor to purchase authorized and unissued shares of the corporation at a price which is less than that being paid pursuant to the merger agreement.   This technique would only be necessary in cases where there is not a sufficient concentration of stock in the hands of the insiders to make a lock-up of that stock alone effective.   If the option is to purchase an additional amount of stock in excess of the presently outstanding number of shares, this effectively prevents any competitive bid, since even if the rival bidder acquired all of the presently outstanding stock, the original acquiror could defeat that bid by simply exercising its option and outvoting the rival bidder.   If the option is for less than that amount of stock, it nevertheless substantially deters anyone from making a rival bid since the original acquiror, by exercising its option and then tendering that stock to the rival bidder or surrendering it in a merger proposal with that corporation, would realize an instant profit, at the expense of the rival bidder, of the differential between the option price and the amount being paid by that bidder.

All of the foregoing techniques are typically used in a friendly acquisition where there is no evidence that there will be any competitive bid, but the acquiror does not want a bidding war to develop before the transaction is consummated.   They can, however, also be used in connection with a transaction with a White Knight in the midst of a bidding war between two rival suitors.   The no-shop provision, as remarked by the court in the *Revlon* case, is rather irrelevant in that circumstance, since the target company has already selected its favorite.

37.   Jewel Companies, Inc. v. Pay Less Drug Stores Northwest, Inc., 741 F.2d 1555 (9th Cir.1984).

The other type of lock-up option which has been employed is the granting of an option to purchase a division or subsidiary of the target corporation, frequently at a sacrifice price, if the hostile tender offer succeeds. Such an option may relate to the business segment of the corporation which is the most profitable (sometimes referred to as the "Crown Jewel Option") or to only that portion of the business which it is believed the hostile tender offeror primarily wants to acquire because it is in the same line of business as that of the offeror. In the latter situation, it is expected that the tender offeror would sell off the remaining portions of the business, and if they are all that would be left, he will lose interest in the takeover. The option is usually granted to a White Knight that has been recruited by the corporation, although sometimes it is simply given to another corporation interested in acquiring that segment of the business, even though it is not in the bidding war.

In Hanson Trust PLC v. ML SCM Acquisition Inc.,[38] the Second Circuit (over the dissent of Judge Kearse) enjoined the the enforcement of a lock-up option granted to a White Knight in a transaction very similar to that involved in the *Revlon* case. The court held that the directors had failed to conduct an adequate inquiry into the value of the assets optioned to the White Knight. It stated that the plaintiff "produced substantial evidence at the eight-day hearing that the optioning of the 'crown jewels' demonstrates that the directors failed to meet their duty of inquiry and had an inadequate basis for concluding one way or the other that the prices were 'within the range of fair value.' "[39] The court also said: "SCM's second attempt at justification is to argue that the purpose of the lock-up option is to achieve a better bid for the shareholders. Primary purpose analysis is undoubtedly a sound theory of lock-up option justification, and is tested in pertinent part according to whether the lock-up option objectively benefits shareholders. * * * Whatever good intentions the directors might have had, they have pointed to little or no evidence to rebut the evidence discussed above that suggested that they failed to ensure that their acts would redound to the benefit of SCM and its shareholders. Indeed, the district court found that the directors 'knew or should have known' that the lockup option would end the bidding. * * * The directors thus face the difficult task of justifying a lock-up option that is suspect for foreclosing bidding, * * * and for thereby impinging upon shareholder decisional rights regarding corporate governance * * *."[40]

The courts have repeatedly suggested that a lock-up option of this type might be justified by showing that it was necessary in order to bring in another bidder who was willing to top the last offer of the hostile tender offeror. Such a bidder may hesitate to spend the millions of dollars that it may cost to make a rival bid, without any hope of recouping that expenditure in the event that its bid fails. It would seem, however, that there are other, less drastic means to entice such a rival bidder into the fray. For example, the corporation might simply agree to pay all of its expenses incurred in connection with making the rival bid (which, it might be noted, amounted to $28,000,000 in the *Heckmann* case). It is true that the court in the *Revlon* case enjoined the payment of a $25,000,000 "cancellation fee" to the White Knight if its bid was unsuccessful, but it did so without any discussion only because this was part and parcel "of the overall plan to thwart Pantry Pride's efforts." This cancellation fee may have reflected in large part the extortionate fee which the White Knight had agreed to pay to its investment banker, and which it could not pay itself because it was a newly formed entity that had no assets. In connection with the enforcement of an agreement by the target company to pay the expenses of

38. 781 F.2d 264 (2d Cir.1986).　　　　　　**40.** 781 F.2d at 281.

39. 781 F.2d at 279.

the White Knight, the court hopefully might find some way to review the reasonableness of these "fees."

The phrase "scorched earth" was invented to refer to the tactic of a target company in selling off its most valuable assets so as to make it no longer an attractive target for the hostile bidder, from the tactic used by the Russians in retreating before the invasion of Napoleon's army. The Crown Jewel Option discussed above achieves the same objective and is usually triggered only by the success of the hostile bidder's offer; therefore, the corporation is not left denuded of its most valuable assets if the original tender offer fails. Consequently, the "scorched earth" tactic is no longer used very frequently in its pure form, although the phrase is still used sometimes to refer to a Crown Jewel Option.

See Maxa, The Legality of Lock-Ups Under Section 14(e) of the Williams Act, 26 Wm. and Mary L.Rev. 115 (1984); Finkelstein, Lock-Ups in Contested Takeovers, 17 Rev.Sec.Reg. 866 (1984); Lewis, Section 14(e) of the Williams Act: Formulated Lock-Ups Are not Manipulative Acts in Conjunction With a Tender Offer, 24 Santa Clara L.Rev. 155 (1984); French, Tender Offers, Lock-Ups and The Williams Act, 21 Duq.L.Rev. 669 (1983); Lock-Up Options: Toward a State Law Standard, 96 Harv.L.Rev. 1068 (1983).

NON–VOTING AND SUPER–VOTING STOCK

The ultimate "lock-up" is simply to issue to the public a stock which has no vote, retaining in the hands of the insiders or family group controlling the corporation a different class of stock which is voting, or to issue to the public a stock which is a voting stock but the vote of which is meaningless. The so-called Anglo-Dutch "combines", such as Royal Dutch-Shell and Unilever, were giant industrial organizations which were structured so that the English company owned a majority of the shares of the Dutch company and the Dutch company owned a majority of the shares of the English company. Therefore, each board of directors could elect the other in perpetuity, and the ostensible vote enjoyed by the public shareholders of each company was meaningless. Prudential Insurance Company (when it was a stock company at the turn of the century rather than a mutual insurance company) proposed to set up the same kind of structure by issuing a majority of its shares to a small New Jersey bank in exchange for a majority of the shares of the bank, thereby creating such a circular ownership. The New Jersey Chancellor enjoined that transaction [41] and modern corporation statutes, as noted above, would make this arrangement ineffective because the shares owned by each of the corporations would lose their votes.

The other method of accomplishing this result, which was developed in the United States, was simply to create two classes of common stock, one of which was voting and the other nonvoting common stock, and to sell to the public only the nonvoting stock. This method of ensuring control by the insiders was used extensively in the early 1920's when public ownership of corporations burgeoned for the first time in the United States, but it virtually died out after the Depression because of two legal developments. In 1926 the New York Stock Exchange adopted a rule under which it refused to list any nonvoting stock or any shares of common stock which did not have an equal vote with all other shares of common stock (the so-called "one share—one vote" rule).[42]   The

---

41. Robotham v. Prudential Insurance Company of America, 64 N.J.Eq. 673, 53 A. 842 (Ch.1903).

42. For the history of these developments, see Seligman, Equal Protection in Shareholder Voting Rights: The One Com-

NYSE was then the only viable market for the stock of large national corporations and the adoption of this policy by the NYSE effectively prevented any further employment of this device by those corporations. Also, the State Blue Sky Laws which were enacted in the early 1920's were used by the administrators of those laws to prohibit the sale to the public of any nonvoting stock in many States. In those States, this interpretation of the Blue Sky Laws effectively prevented the use of this device with respect to smaller corporations which were not eligible for listing on the New York Stock Exchange.

The American Stock Exchange, which until 1972 permitted the listing of nonvoting common stock, adopted in that year a compromise position which banned the listing of completely nonvoting common stock, but which permitted a corporation to issue two classes of stock that elected different classes of directors or the issuance of two classes of stock, one of which had greater voting rights than the other. However, one class of common stock could not elect more than 75% of the directors and then only if it represented at least $12\frac{1}{2}\%$ of the equity of the corporation, and the disparity in votes between two classes of common stock could not exceed 10 to 1.[43] Under these rules, the management of a corporation could retain absolute control over the composition of the board of directors so long as it owned stock representing at least $12\frac{1}{2}\%$ of the equity of the corporation or at least 10% of the outstanding shares of voting common stock, provided that the public shareholders voting separately as a class were always entitled to elect at least 25% of the members of the board of directors. These minimum rights of the public shareholders are not, of course, anything that a "raider" would want to buy from them at any price. Most very large industrial corporations, however, do not have that great a concentration of ownership in the hands of the management (even 10% of the outstanding stock can amount to billions of dollars in market value).

The development of the NASDAQ market system in the last few years has thrown a time bomb into this situation. The NASDAQ market system is now a viable alternative (to all except perhaps the very largest corporations) to listing on the NYSE or the AMEX to provide liquidity for the shareholders. The NASD has no rules whatever restricting the creation of different classes of common stock or the issuance of nonvoting common stock, and it has thus far refused to adopt any.

Therefore, the exchanges are threatened with the desertion of a large number of their listed companies, the managements of which want to be free to go back to the "good old days" when the public shareholders could be completely disenfranchised. None of the modern state corporation laws impose any restrictions whatever on the creation of different classes of common stock or the voting rights which they are given; for over 50 years, legislators and regulators have relied upon the NYSE rule as the method of preventing that sort of development.

The issue came to a head for the NYSE when General Motors acquired EDS; and in connection with that huge acquisition issued a separate class of common stock entitled to different voting and dividends rights than the "old" General Motors shares. This structure did not comply with the NYSE "one share—one vote" rule and the question was presented to the Exchange as to whether it was going to delist the stock of General Motors. It of course did not do that, but appointed a "blue ribbon committee" to study the matter and make a report.

mon Share, One Vote Controversy, 54 Geo. Wash.L.Rev. 687 (1986). See, also, Dent, Dual Class Capitalization: A Reply to Professor Seligman, 54 Geo.Wash.L.Rev. 725 (1986).

43. See the discussion in Seligman, supra note 42, 54 Geo.Wash.L.Rev. at 704–705.

The committee made its report in January, 1985, which essentially recommended that the NYSE adopt a new rule along the lines of the AMEX rule, permitting a disparity in voting rights of no greater than 10 to 1.[44] This recommendation found no favor in the exchange community and has been abandoned. On July 7, 1986, the NYSE announced its decision [45] that it would adopt a rule change abandoning any restrictions on dual-voting stock, subject only to a requirement that the shareholders approve the creation of such stock. An earlier report that the Big Board would require a two-thirds vote of the shareholders to approve the issuance of dual-voting stock turned out to be incorrect, and only a simple majority is required by the proposal as finally announced. This rule change must be approved by the Securities and Exchange Commission, and such approval is by no means certain; a spokesman for the Commission has indicated that it will hold public hearings on the question. If the rule change is approved as proposed, this type of "lock-up" may become the darling of corporate managers, perhaps making unnecessary any of the tactics described above.

There is, however, one last obstacle to the major corporations in the United States adopting this type of corporate structure, and that is the vastly increased concentration of ownership of the stock of major corporations in the hands of institutional investors and their recent inclination to oppose management proposals which they view as inimical to their interest as shareholders or to their future prospects of receiving a large premium over market price from a tender offeror. Whether the managements of corporations could obtain a favorable vote of the shareholders for such a self-disenfranchisement, even with their control of the proxy machinery, especially if a two-thirds vote is required, is a question that is very much in doubt, although it probably would not have been 20 or 30 years ago.

GREENMAIL

The tactic which has been dubbed the payment of "greenmail" consists of buying off the tender offeror by agreeing to repurchase all of the shares which he has acquired, usually at a substantial premium over the current market price, and the execution of what is called a "standstill agreement" whereby the tender offeror agrees that he will not acquire any more shares of the corporation for a period of time, usually five to ten years. Sometimes this merely attracts another bidder, who is not a party to the standstill agreement and who would like to share in the same largesse, as Disney successively attracted Saul Steinberg and Irwin Jacobs. This consequence is sometimes referred to as "double dipping."

The *Heckmann* case is so far the only case which has condemned a transaction of this sort. In Polk v. Good [46] the Delaware Supreme Court upheld the payment by Texaco of approximately $650,000,000 in cash and 12.6 million shares of a voting preferred stock to repurchase the stock of Texaco held by the Bass brothers, who had acquired about 9.9% of Texaco's outstanding shares and were hinting at a takeover bid. The facts of that case, however, were vastly different from those of the *Heckmann* case. The premium over market paid to the Bass brothers was only approximately 3% or $1⅝ per share. Furthermore, the justifications offered by the directors of Texaco as to why such a takeover

---

44. Initial Report of the Subcommittee on Shareholder Participation and Qualitative Listing Standards, Dual Class Capitalization (N.Y.S.E. Jan. 3, 1985).

45. Wall Street Journal, July 7, 1986, 2:2.

46. 507 A.2d 531 (Del.1986).

bid would be highly disruptive to the business of Texaco (which was in the process of trying to assimilate the Getty Oil Company, recently acquired for $10 billion) were much more plausible and persuasive than those offered for the action by Disney in the *Heckmann* case. Nevertheless, the perfervid definition of greenmail which is set out by the *Heckmann* court in footnote 1, and which assumes that the directors always engage in such a transaction "in fear of their jobs", should be contrasted with the calm description of it by the Delaware Court as "the practice of buying out a take-over bidder's or dissident's stock at a premium that is not available to other shareholders." [47]

The *Heckmann* decision can be interpreted as holding that the business judgment rule is not applicable to such a transaction and that the directors have the burden of showing "its inherent fairness from the viewpoint of the corporation and those interested therein." The Delaware Supreme Court, on the other hand, stated in the *Polk* case: "Unless the primary or sole purpose was to perpetuate the directors in office, such an acquisition will be sustained if, after reasonable investigation, a board has a justifiable belief that there was a reasonable threat to the corporate enterprise." [48]

See Macey and McChesney, A Theoretical Analysis of Corporate Greenmail, 95 Yale L.J. 13 (1985); Dennis, Two Tiered Tender Offers and Greenmail: Is New Legislation Needed?, 19 Ga.L.Rev. 281 (1985); Kanter and Baroff, Deductibility of Green Mail Payments, 63 J.Tax 63 (1985) and More on Deductibility of Green Mail Payments, 63 J.Tax 199 (1985); Wilson, Loynd, Pickens and Le Baron, How To Handle the Greenmailer, 9 Direct. & Boards 6 (1984); Greenmail: Targeted Stock Repurchases and the Management-Entrenchment Hypothesis, 98 Harv.L.Rev. 1045 (1985).

SHARK REPELLENTS

The phrase "shark repellents" refers to provisions inserted in the articles or bylaws of a corporation in advance of any takeover threat, which are thought to be an impediment to a hostile bidder's achieving immediate control of the target company or carrying out the second step of a planned acquisition of 100% of the outstanding stock by a squeeze-out merger of the shareholders who do not tender in the original offer. Such provisions have become very popular in recent years, but the general opinion of experts in this field is that they do not constitute any real deterrence for a determined and well financed tender offeror.

The most elementary of these provisions is the adoption of a staggered board of directors, i.e., a board only one-third of whose members are elected each year, so that it might take even a majority shareholder three years or more to elect a majority of the board of directors, particularly if it is coupled with a provision for cumulative voting and the management retains a very substantial percentage of the shares, even though a minority. To be effective, such a provision for a staggered board must be coupled with a provision prohibiting the removal of directors by the shareholders except for cause (although that rule applies in Delaware merely as a result of creating a staggered board).[49] It is unlikely, however, that in the usual situation there is going to be any director who is willing to stay around for three years fighting a hopeless battle against a

---

47. 507 A.2d at 537.

48. 507 A.2d at 536–537.

49. Del.Gen.Corp.Law, § 141(k) (i). Such a provision cannot legally be adopted

in California, but neither can a staggered board. Cal.Gen.Corp.Law, §§ 301, 303.

person who has acquired 80% or 90% of the stock of the corporation; more likely, they will all simply resign once the outcome is inevitable.

Another popular provision is designed to prevent an unfair merger in the second step of a planned acquisition by a tender offeror, whether or not the initial offer is a partial offer or front-end loaded. This provision requires a super-majority vote of the shareholders (say 85% of the outstanding shares) to approve a merger with an "interested person", which is defined as a shareholder of the corporation holding in excess of a specified percentage of the outstanding shares, such as 20%. Since even that requirement may not be an obstacle if the tender offeror acquires a percentage in excess of the vote required, this requirement is sometimes accompanied by a requirement for a majority vote of the disinterested shares (or even a super-majority vote). The "disinterested shares" are defined as those not owned by the other party to the merger transaction or its affiliates.

Since these provisions alone might present a serious obstacle to a friendly acquisition negotiated by the management or to bringing in a White Knight in the face of a hostile tender offer, they are usually accompanied by a provision which eliminates these special voting requirements if the proposed transaction is approved by a super-majority of the board of directors or a majority or super-majority of the "continuing directors." The continuing directors are defined as those elected to office before the other party to the transaction acquired the percentage interest in the stock of the corporation which makes it an interested party. This provision will prevent a hostile tender offeror from avoiding these special voting requirements even if he succeeds in ousting all of the members of the previous board of directors, since then there are *no* continuing directors and the special voting requirements will apply.

On the other hand, where a White Knight acquires by a rival tender offer a sufficient stock interest to itself become an interested party, usually the members of the previous board of the target company continue in office, at least until the second step of the transaction is carried out, and by their vote they can eliminate the special voting requirements regarding a merger with the White Knight or its subsidiary. It is in connection with provisions such as these that the staggered board of directors assumes greater importance, since the previous members of the board whose terms have not expired and who cannot be ousted without cause may be willing to stay around long enough to fight for the minority shareholders and secure for them a negotiated fair price when they are cashed out.

Another provision frequently included in such charter amendments is what is called a "fair price provision." This provision operates similarly to the fair price provision which is included in poisoned pills as discussed above. It eliminates the super-majority voting requirements and the requirements regarding the vote of the board of directors if the price being offered by the interested party in the merger is at least equal to a "fair price" as defined in the charter provision. As indicated in the discussion above, this provision is designed primarily to protect against the partial or front-end loaded offer, but it may also set a floor under the amount which can be offered by the hostile bidder in the initial tender offer.

Maryland has adopted an amendment to its corporation law in response to the *Mite* case,[50] which in essence establishes a fair price provision as a matter of statutory law, similar to the charter provisions adopted by many corpora-

---

50. Md.Corps & Ass'ns. Code Ann., § 3–601 et seq.

tions.[51] Under this statute, any merger of a Maryland corporation with an "interested stockholder" requires an 80% vote of all of the outstanding shares of the corporation and a two-thirds vote of all the shares owned by stockholders other than the interested stockholder, unless the price meets a "fair price" definition in the statute. An interested stockholder is defined as any person who owns directly or indirectly 10% or more of the outstanding voting stock, which is lower than the percentage usually inserted in a similar charter amendment. The "fair price" which will make these voting requirements inapplicable may be summarized as the highest of the price paid for any of the stock by the interested stockholder, the market value, or the price shareholders would be paid for the stock in the event of liquidation or dissolution of the corporation. There is an exclusion from the statutory provisions of any corporation which had an interested stockholder as of July 1, 1983 (although such a corporation can "opt in" the statute by a shareholder vote), and there is a provision that any other corporation can "opt out" of the statute by the same vote required for a merger with an interested stockholder. This statute will only protect against the two tier, front-end loaded offer.

This Maryland statute probably has a good chance of surviving any constitutional challenge, since the States have historically regulated the vote required for any merger or other business combination with respect to corporations which are incorporated in that State. Indeed, it has been argued that it is unconstitutional under the Full Faith and Credit Clause and the Commerce Clause for any other State to attempt to do so.[52] At one time, almost all States required a two-thirds vote (or even higher vote) for any merger, although that has generally been reduced to a simple majority; no one ever suggested that these voting requirements were an impermissible burden on interstate commerce, regardless of the residences of the shareholders or the location of the business operations of the corporation.

It may be possible, however, for the raider to avoid these provisions after it has acquired control of the corporation by reincorporating it in Delaware. The merger of the target company into a shell corporation incorporated in Delaware to accomplish that reincorporation would not appear to be a merger with an interested shareholder or its affiliate which is regulated by the statute.

In some cases, as a "shark repellent", an incumbent management has even amended the corporation's loan agreement to provide for an automatic default on the loans if the management is replaced (which, if it ever actually happened, would seem to make them clearly liable to the shareholders for a breach of their fiduciary duty). This and other similar maneuvers not only give the appearance of panic, but may be of dubious legality. They may, however, persuade some potential "raiders" to seek less vicious prey.

See Palmer, Corporate Takeover Battles—Shark-Repellent Charter and By-law Provisions That Deter Hostile Tender Offers or Other Acquisitions, 27 Howard L.J. 1683 (1984); Lautzenhiser, State and Federal Regulation of Shark Repellent Provisions, 11 N.Ky.L.Rev. 481 (1984); Hudson, The Use of Shark Repellent Charter Provisions to Forestall Hostile Takeover Bids, 62 Mich.B.J. 522 (1983); Gilson, The Case Against Shark Repellent Amendments, 34 Stan.L. Rev. 775 (1982); Black and Smith, Antitakeover Charter Provisions, 36 Wash.

51. Virginia has adopted a similar statute. Va.Code 1985, §§ 13.1–725 to 13.1–728.

52. For discussions, see Reese and Kaufman, The Law Governing Corporate Affairs: Choice of Law and the Scope of Full Faith and Credit, 58 Colum.L.Rev.

1118 (1958); Horowitz, The Commerce Clause as a Limitation on State Choice-of-Law Doctrine, 84 Harv.L.Rev. 806 (1971); Halloran & Hammer, Section 2115 of the New California General Corporation Law, 23 U.C.L.A.L.Rev. 1282 (1976).

and Lee L.Rev. 699 (1979); Mullaney, Guarding Against Takeovers—Defensive Charter Provisions, 25 Bus.Law. 1441 (1970); Scriggins and Clarke, Takeovers and the 1983 Maryland Fair Price Legislation, 43 Md.L.Rev. 266 (1984); Second Generation State Takeover Legislation: Maryland Takes a New Tack, 83 Mich. L.Rev. 433 (1984).

GOLDEN PARACHUTES

A "golden parachute" is the name given to a contract made by the target company with one or more of its senior executives to pay them large severance bonuses if they resign or are fired after a change in control of the corporation. This is not a defensive measure, since the amount is not significant enough in relation to the total price being paid that the hostile bidder would be deterred by having to add that to his cost. He may, in any event, intend to litigate the validity of the contract and thereby delay having to pay the amount for a number of years (although the executive may obtain an escrow of the money, as the White Knight did of the "cancellation fee" in the *Revlon* case). Such an arrangement is merely a way for the executive to say to the shareholders: Heads, I win; tails, I win.

After Pantry Pride won the battle against Revlon following the enjoining by the Delaware Court of the lock-up option granted to the White Knight, the CEO of Revlon, Mr. Michel C. Bergerac, walked away with $35,000,000 in cash, which *Business Week* headlined as the "biggest ever" golden parachute.[53] This headline was somewhat misleading, since (as the details of the story reveal) the $35,000,000 included a $15,000,000 profit on his previously granted stock options and restricted stock (although the major portion of this profit was undoubtedly due to the astronomical increase in the price of Revlon stock as a result of the bidding war) and "deferred compensation" retirement benefits, which had been approved years before and were payable regardless of any change in control of the corporation, with a present value of $7,000,000. The remaining $15,000,000 was a true Golden Parachute, which was adopted in anticipation of a takeover attempt, although a couple years before Pantry Pride appeared on the scene.

Mr. Bergerac argued to *Business Week* that he was worth this amount because his actions caused Pantry Pride to raise its price paid to the shareholders of Revlon from an initial $1.9 billion to $2.7 billion. It is certainly true that Mr. Bergerac fought tooth and claw, using every trick known to man (or to lawyer) to try to fend off Pantry Pride, but he could hardly have been inspired to do that by the knowledge that if he *lost* he would receive a consolation prize of $35,000,000. A former Revlon executive was quoted as saying: "No one is worth that much money unless they walk on water." There were also Golden Parachutes for two other Revlon senior executives aggregating $4,600,000.

Sometimes a compensation arrangement is made by the acquiring corporation with the senior executives of the target company which has the opposite effect to that of a golden parachute, i.e., it is an attempt to induce them to remain with the target company after it has been acquired. For example, new employment contracts may be offered at a substantially increased salary (perhaps twice the amount of their previous salaries) for a period of five to ten years, but they have to remain with the corporation in order to earn this increased compensation. This arrangement has acquired the name of a "Silver Belt Buckle."

---

53. Business Week, May 5, 1986, p. 56.

See Chapoton, Golden Parachutes and Corporate Shareholders, 29 Tax Notes 278 (1985); Hutton, Unreasonable Compensation and Golden Parachutes, 8 Corp.L.Rev. 153 (1985); Royer, Testing the Flight of the Golden Parachute: Judicial Smooth Sailing or Turbulence Ahead, 11 N.Ky.L.Rev. 519 (1984); Haggerty, Golden Parachute Agreements, 57 St. John's L.Rev. 516 (1983); Riger, On Golden Parachutes—Ripcords or Ripoffs?, 3 Pace L.Rev. 15 (1982).

PURCHASE OF CERTAIN EQUITY SECURITIES BY THE ISSUER AND OTHERS

SECURITIES AND EXCHANGE COMMISSION

Securities Exchange Act Release No. 19244.
November 17, 1982.

I. INTRODUCTION

The Commission has considered on several occasions since 1967 the issue whether to regulate an issuer's repurchases of its own securities.[1] The predicates for this effort have been twofold: first, investors and particularly the issuer's shareholders should be able to rely on a market that is set by independent market forces and not influenced in any manipulative manner by the issuer or persons closely related to the issuer. Second, since the general language of the anti-manipulative provisions of the federal securities laws offers little guidance with respect to the scope of permissible issuer market behavior, certainty with respect to the potential liabilities for issuers engaged in repurchase programs has seemed desirable.

The most recent phase of this proceeding is proposed Rule 13e–2 which was published for public comment on October 17, 1980.[2] This rule would have imposed disclosure requirements and substantive purchasing limitations on an issuer's repurchases of its common and preferred stock. These restrictions, which generally would have limited the time, price, and volume of purchases, also would have been imposed on certain persons whose purchases could be deemed to be attributable to the issuer. In addition, the issuer, its affiliates, and certain other persons would have been subject to a general antifraud provision in connection with their purchases of the issuer's common and preferred stock.

The Commission has recognized that issuer repurchase programs are seldom undertaken with improper intent, may frequently be of substantial economic benefit to investors, and, that, in any event, undue restriction of these programs is not in the interest of investors, issuers, or the marketplace. Issuers generally engage in repurchase programs for legitimate

---

1. Before its most recent release in October, 1980, issuer repurchases had been the subject of three public rule proposals. The first was a Commission draft of a proposed Rule 10b–10 published in 1967 by the United States Senate in connection with hearings on proposed legislation that became the Williams Act Amendments of 1968. Pub.L.No. 90–439, 82 Stat. 454 (July 29, 1968). Proposed Rule 10b–10 was reprinted in Hearings on S. 510 before the Subcommittee on Securities of the Senate Committee on Banking and Currency, 90th Cong., 1st Sess. 214–216 (1967). The Commission then published Rule 13e–2 for comment in 1970 and in 1973. Securities Exchange Act Release Nos. 8930 (July 13, 1970), 35 FR 11410 (1970) and 10539 (December 6, 1973), 38 FR 34341 (1973).

2. Securities Exchange Act Release No. 17222 (October 17, 1980), 45 FR 70890 (1980) ("October Release").

business reasons and any rule in this area must not be overly intrusive. Accordingly, the Commission has endeavored to achieve an appropriate balance between the goals described above and the need to avoid complex and costly restrictions that impinge on the operation of issuer repurchase programs.

In light of these considerations, and based on the extensive public files developed in this proceeding, the Commission has determined that it is not necessary to adopt a mandatory rule to regulate issuer repurchases. Accordingly, the Commission has today withdrawn proposed Rule 13e–2, and, as discussed in this release, is amending Rule 10b–6 to eliminate most issuer repurchase regulation under that rule. In lieu of direct regulation under Rule 10b–6 and proposed Rule 13e–2, the Commission has determined that a safe harbor is the appropriate regulatory approach to offer guidance concerning the applicability of the anti-manipulative provisions of Rule 10b–5 and Section 9(a)(2) to issuer repurchase programs. New Rule 10b–18 reflects this determination.

The Commission wishes to stress, however, that the safe harbor is not mandatory nor the exclusive means of effecting issuer purchases without manipulating the market. As a safe harbor, new Rule 10b–18 will provide clarity and certainty for issuers and broker-dealers who assist issuers in their repurchase programs. If an issuer effects its repurchases in compliance with the conditions of the rule, it will avoid what might otherwise be substantial and unpredictable risks of liability under the general antimanipulative provisions of the federal securities laws. Moreover, since Rule 10b–18 is a safe harbor rather than a *per se* rule, the Commission believes that the safe harbor should be available to all issuers and their affiliated purchasers and should not be limited in its application to any particular class of issuers, such as those defined in the October Release as "Section 13(e) issuers."

The Commission emphasizes that no affirmative inference should be drawn that bids for or purchases of an issuer's stock by persons to which the safe harbor is not explicitly available, or with respect to securities other than the issuer's common stock, should be made in accordance with the safe harbor. The safe harbor is not intended to define the appropriate limits to be observed by those persons not covered by the safe harbor nor the appropriate limits to be observed by anyone when purchasing securities other than common stock. In addition, the safe harbor is not the exclusive means by which issuers and their affiliated purchasers may effect purchases of the issuer's stock in the marketplace. Given the greatly varying characteristics of the markets for the stock of different issuers, there may be circumstances under which an issuer could effect repurchases outside the guidelines that would not raise manipulative concerns. This is especially the case in the context of the uniform volume guidelines, which cannot easily reflect those varying market characteristics. As discussed more fully below, the Commission wishes to continue to receive the views of any interested persons on whether additional disclosure by the issuer concerning the repurchase program should affect the percentage level of purchases that would be covered under the safe harbor. In order to make it clear that Rule 10b–18 is not the exclusive means to effect issuer repurchases, paragraph (c) of the rule provides that no presumption shall arise that an issuer or affiliated purchaser has violated Section 9(a)(2) or Rule 10b–5 if the purchases do not meet the conditions of paragraph (b).

The remaining parts of the release describe Rule 10b–18 and the amendments to Rule 10b–6 and contrast those provisions to the proposals in the October Release. Interested persons should refer to the October Release for a more detailed discussion of the general background of the Commission's consideration of issuer repurchase programs. In addition, interested persons may wish to refer to a release that the Commission recently issued proposing for comment several amendments to its trading practices rules, including Rule 10b–6.

II. SAFE HARBOR RULE 10b–18

A. *Coverage of Rule 10b–18*

The safe harbor of paragraph (b) is available for any bid or purchase that constitutes a "Rule 10b–18 bid" or a "Rule 10b–18 purchase," as defined in the rule. Paragraph (a)(3) defines a Rule 10b–18 purchase as a purchase of common stock of an issuer by or for the issuer or any affiliated purchaser of the issuer. Paragraph (a)(4) defines a Rule 10b–18 bid as a bid for securities that, if accepted, or a limit order to purchase securities that, if executed, would result in a Rule 10b–18 purchase.

B. *General Antifraud Provision*

Under paragraph (b) of proposed Rule 13e–2, a class of issuers defined as "Section 13(e) issuers," their affiliates, affiliated purchasers, and any broker, dealer, or other person acting on behalf of these issuers, affiliates, or affiliated purchasers would have been subject to a broad general antifraud and anti-manipulative prohibition in connection with any bids or purchases or any equity security of the issuer. The commentators that addressed this provision opposed its adoption for essentially two reasons. First, they argued that it was unnecessary in view of existing provisions of the Act such as Section 9(a)(2) and Section 10(b) and Rule 10b–5 thereunder. Second, they argued that the general nature of paragraph (b) would detract from the certainty otherwise provided by the rule.

The Commission has reconsidered the question of whether a general antifraud provision is necessary in this context and has concluded that it is not. The sole purpose of the rule as adopted is to provide a safe harbor from liability under the anti-manipulative provisions of the Act. For that reason, the Commission has determined not to include a general antifraud provision in Rule 10b–18.

C. *Disclosure*

Proposed Rule 13e–2 would have required issuers and affiliated purchasers that sought to repurchase more than two percent of the issuer's stock during any twelve-month period publicly to disclose certain specified information prior to effecting any purchases of the issuer's stock. In addition, those persons would have been required to disclose the specified information to any exchange on which the stock was listed for trading or to the NASD if the stock was authorized for quotation in NASDAQ.

Most of the commentators that addressed the issue suggested that the disclosure provisions were not necessary in view of the existing requirements of other provisions of the federal securities laws (e.g., Section 10(b) and Rule 10b–5). Other commentators stated that disclosure obligations should depend on the particular facts and circumstances involved. Accordingly, they suggested that *per se* disclosure requirements were not appropriate, and, indeed, might cause persons subject thereto to believe that disclosure of other information was unnecessary. Finally, commentators cited practical compliance problems that might arise, such as determining at the beginning of any twelve-month period whether the issuer would need to purchase more than two percent of its stock to satisfy corporate needs, and the need to periodically update disclosure to reflect material changes.

The proposed disclosure requirements were not intended to be coextensive with other disclosure obligations. Nevertheless, the Commission is persuaded that the obligation to disclose information concerning repurchases of an issuer's stock should depend on whether the information is material under the circumstances, regardless of whether such purchases are made as part of a program authorized by a company's board of directors or otherwise. The Commission has therefore determined not to adopt the specific disclosure requirements contained in paragraph (d) of proposed Rule 13e–2, even as a safe harbor. Other relevant provisions of the federal securities laws and existing policies and procedures of the various self-regulatory organizations impose disclosure responsibilities that appear to be sufficient to ensure that investors and the marketplace in general receive adequate information concerning issuer repurchases. The Commission emphasizes its belief that timely disclosure of all material information is the context of issuer repurchases may significantly facilitate the maintenance of an orderly market for the issuer's stock.

D. *Definitions*

Affiliated purchaser. Rule 10b–18 contains a definition of the term "affiliated purchaser" that differs somewhat from the definition of that term as contained in proposed Rule 13e–2. As proposed in Rule 13e–2, the definition of affiliated purchaser would have included natural persons acting with the issuer for the purpose of acquiring the issuer's securities, as well as persons who controlled the issuer's purchases, or whose purchases were controlled by, or were under common control with, the issuer's purchases. Commentators were critical of the use of the terms "acting with" and "control" because, in their view, those terms are imprecise. Some commentators noted that the use of those terms suggested that all directors and officers of the issuer would be deemed to be affiliated purchasers and therefore covered by the rule notwithstanding the Commission's stated intent to the contrary. In particular, they stated that the "control" standard articulated in paragraph (a)(2)(ii) of proposed Rule 13e–2 could be interpreted to be the same as the historical affiliation standard and therefore would encompass more than the control of actual purchasing activity that the Commission intended the rule to cover.

The commentators suggested that the "acting with" standard should be changed to an "acting in concert" standard since the latter has particular legal significance. Commentators also suggested that the class of persons defined in proposed paragraph (a)(2)(ii) as affiliated purchasers should be limited to persons that have day-to-day responsibility for the issuer's purchases. In addition, commentators recommended the addition of a proviso in the definition that would specifically except purchases by officers or directors unless they otherwise were an affiliated purchaser.

The Commission agrees with the commentators that the concept of "acting in concert" provides more legal certainty than the standard proposed in the October Release. Accordingly, the first part of the definition of affiliated purchaser has been modified to include the "acting in concert" standard instead of the "acting with" standard. The Commission believes that the "acting in concert" standard will cover the same persons as proposed Rule 13e–2 was intended to cover, including persons acting with the issuer in purchasing the issuer's securities, regardless of whether the purchases are made for the account of the issuer itself.

As adopted, the second clause of the definition of affiliated purchaser covers any affiliate that, directly or indirectly, controls the issuer's Rule 10b–18 purchases, or whose purchases are controlled by, or are under common control with, those of the issuer. Under this formulation, a person would not be considered to be an affiliated purchaser unless the person is an affiliate and one of the three control standards is met.

Finally, to provide further guidance in the definition of affiliated purchaser, the Commission has added a proviso that states, in part, that an officer or director that participates in a decision to authorize the issuer to make or effect Rule 10b–18 bids or purchases will not be considered to be an affiliated purchaser on that basis alone.

The definition of affiliated purchaser as proposed in Rule 13e–2 also would have included affiliates who controlled the issuer by means of ownership of the issuer's securities and affiliates that were not natural persons. The commentators were critical of the application of the rule to these affiliates in the absence of any evidence of concerted activity or control over the issuer's purchases of its securities. The Commission agrees that paragraphs (a)(2)(iii) and (iv) as proposed could be overly broad, in the context of a safe harbor or mandatory rule, in light of the rationale underlying the affiliated purchaser concept. Accordingly, it has determined not to include in Rule 10b–18 paragraphs (a)(2)(iii) and (iv).

Trading Volume. The term trading volume has been adopted in paragraph (a)(11) of Rule 10b–18 with some modification from the term as proposed in Rule 13e–2. Generally, the term defines trading volume as the average daily trading volume over the preceding four weeks. This calculation would then be used in the context of the volume provisions of the Rule, which provide a safe harbor for daily purchase of up to 25% of the trading volume.

Proposed Rule 13e–2 would have required that the issuer subtract from the trading volume figure all "Rule 13e–2" purchases by or for the issuer or any affiliated purchaser. The rationale for the exclusion was to assure that the trading volume figures used to calculate the permissible volume of issuer purchases reflected only transactions effected by persons other than issuers or affiliated purchasers. Some commentators stated that the computations required to determine the amounts to be excluded would impose a substantial compliance burden on issuers, affiliated purchasers and broker-dealers that would be disproportionate to the benefits sought to be achieved by requiring the exclusion. In addition, commentators argued that, because of the volume limits, the permissible volume of Rule 13e–2 purchases would not be increased significantly if Rule 13e–2 purchases were included in the calculation of the average trading volume figure.

The Commission generally agrees that compliance with the volume conditions would prevent any significant increase in the permissible volume of purchases that could result from including Rule 10b–18 purchases in less than block size in the trading volume figure. The inclusion of block purchases by the issuer, however, in calculating trading volume could significantly increase the amount of stock that could be purchased within the volume limitations of the safe harbor. Accordingly, the definition of trading volume as adopted in Rule 10b–18 would require the issuer or affiliated purchaser to subtract block purchases that are made by or for the issuer or affiliated purchaser from the trading volume figure.

Block. The Commission has considered two alternative definitions of the term "block." The significance of the term is that purchases of blocks are excepted from the volume conditions. Thus, an issuer that chooses to comply with those conditions may purchase up to 25% of the trading volume, and, in addition, may purchase one or more blocks, as defined. The amount of securities purchased in block size need not be included in determining whether the 25% limitation has been reached. The Commission has adopted the simpler of the two definitions. Paragraph (a)(14) of Rule 10b–18 defines a block as that amount of stock that has an aggregate purchase price of not less than $50,000 and, if the aggregate purchase price is less than $200,000, a number of shares that is not less than 5,000.

The Commission has considered whether to require the issuer to exclude, in calculating the amount of securities that would constitute a block (i) any amount of securities that a broker or dealer had assembled or accumulated for the purpose of sale or resale to the issuer or to any affiliated purchaser, and (ii) any amount that a broker-dealer had sold short to the issuer or to an affiliated purchaser if the issuer or affiliated purchaser knew or had reason to know that the sale was a short sale.

Some commentators suggested that the issuer should be required to exclude from a block only those shares that a broker or dealer had accumulated as principal with the purpose of sale or resale to the issuer or affiliated purchaser. In their view, a broader exclusion would impede normal block trading practices, since a broker could not assemble a block on an agency basis and then cross it as such on an exchange. The commentators suggested that this kind of transaction would not have adverse market impact, or present the opportunity for circumvention of the volume limitations, that led the Commission to propose this part of the block definition. The Commission agrees with the commentators that these concerns arise only where broker-dealers accumulate blocks as principal for the purpose of sale or resale to the issuer or affiliated purchasers, and the definition of the term block reflects that judgment.

Certain commentators also suggested that the "know or have reason to know" standard that was proposed to apply in determining whether to exclude from an amount of securities that otherwise would constitute a block broker-dealer's short sales to the issuer should also apply in determining whether to exclude shares accumulated for the purpose of resale to the issuer. The Commission has modified the proviso accordingly.

E. *Purchasing Conditions*

In order to take advantage of the safe harbor provided by Rule 10b–18, an issuer or affiliated purchaser would have to comply with all of the conditions of paragraph (b) of the rule.

1. Timing Conditions

The conditions that relate to the timing of purchases have been adopted, for purposes of the Rule 10b–18 safe harbor, substantially as they were proposed in Rule 13e–2. For a transaction in a NASDAQ security, otherwise than on an exchange, there need only be an independent bid currently reported in Level 2 of NASDAQ. For exchange traded securities, if the Rule 10b–18 purchase is to be effected on an exchange, the transaction cannot be the opening transaction for the security on such exchange, and the transactions cannot be effected during the one-half hour before the scheduled close of trading on that exchange.

For transactions in reported securities, the Rule 10b–18 purchase cannot constitute the opening transaction reported on the consolidated tape. Other time restrictions, as proposed in Rule 13e–2, applicable to trading in reported securities have been modified. Proposed Rule 13e–2 would have prohibited persons subject to the time limitations from purchasing a reported security for which the principal market was a national securities exchange during the period commencing one-half hour before the scheduled close of trading in the principal market for the security and ending with the termination of the period in which last sale prices were reported in the consolidated system. Some commentators argued that this limitation might have anti-competitive effects because it would prohibit trading by the issuer and any affiliated purchaser on other exchanges and in the over-the-counter markets for a substantial period of time. Some commentators suggested as an alternative that the trading prohibition should be only in the period within one-half hour of the scheduled close of trading in the market where the transaction was proposed to be effected. Another commentator suggested that trading should be prohibited only during the one-half hour before the termination of the period in which last sale prices are reported in the consolidated system.

The timing conditions in Rule 10b–18 provide that an issuer or an affiliated purchaser may effect, consistent with the safe harbor provisions of the rule, a transaction in a reported security (i) if the principal market for such security is an exchange, at a time other than during the one-half hour before the scheduled close of trading on the principal market, or (ii) if the transaction is to be effected on an exchange, at a time other than during the one-half hour before the scheduled close of trading on the exchange on which the transaction is to be effected, or (iii) if the transaction is to be effected otherwise than on an exchange, at a time other than during the one-half hour before the termination of the period in which last sale prices are reported in the consolidated system. The Commission believes that these limitations, as modified, appropriately resolve the commentators' concerns while achieving the objectives of the time limitations.

2. Price Conditions

The price conditions have been adopted as published in proposed Rule 13e–2. The price limit for purchases of reported securities would be the higher of the last sale price reported in the consolidated system or the highest independent published bid, as defined in Rule 11Ac1–1(a)(9) under the Act, regardless of the market reporting that figure. The price limit applicable to purchases of exchange traded securities in transactions on an exchange is the higher of the highest current independent bid quotation or the last sale price on such exchange.

The pricing conditions of Rule 10b–18 provide that purchases of a NASDAQ security otherwise than on an exchange may be made at a net price no higher than the lowest current independent offer quotation reported in Level 2 of NASDAQ. Purchases of securities that are neither NASDAQ securities nor reported securities otherwise than on an exchange may be made at the lowest current independent offer quotation ascertained on the basis of reasonable inquiry. In both cases, the purchase price would include any commission equivalent, mark-up, or differential paid to a dealer.

3. Single Broker-Dealer Limitation

A condition that the issuer or affiliated purchaser make purchases from or through not more than one broker or dealer on any day has been adopted as proposed. Purchases may be made from any number of broker-dealers in transactions that are not solicited by the issuer or affiliated purchaser. Some commentators suggested that the Commission should define what would constitute a solicitation for purposes of the rule. Whether a transaction has been solicited necessarily depends on the facts and circumstances of each case and must be determined by those who wish to rely on the rule's safe harbor. Although the Commission does not believe it should define the term solicitation, disclosure and announcement of a repurchase program would not necessarily cause all subsequent purchases to be deemed solicited.

4. Volume Conditions

The volume conditions to the safe harbor, are more liberal than those set forth in the October Release. Under Rule 10b–18, an issuer is permitted to purchase up to 25% of the average daily trading volume over the preceding four calendar weeks. Under Rule 13e–2, that number was 15%. The Commission has concluded that a 25% purchasing condition is appropriate in that Commission cases concerning manipulation in the context of issuer repurchases have historically involved conduct outside the conditions of Rule 10b–18, including a volume limitation of 25%. The Commission also recognizes that establishing a uniform condition might be thought to suggest that purchases in excess of the limitations are *per se* manipulative. Accordingly, the Commission has provided in paragraph (c) of the rule that no presumption shall arise that purchases not in conformity with the limitations of the safe harbor violate the anti-manipulative provisions of the securities laws. The rule operates to impose *per se* volume prohibition on issuer repurchases, and there may be circumstances in which an issuer would be justified in exceeding the volume conditions. Repurchases outside of the safe harbor that are manipulative, of course, continue to be actionable under the securities laws.

F. *Purchases on Behalf of Employee and Shareholder Plans*

The definition of a Rule 10b–18 purchase contained in paragraph (a) of the rule excludes any purchase effected by or for an issuer plan if the transaction is effected by an agent independent of the issuer. Those purchases are not considered to be attributable to the issuer and, therefore, are not intended to be addressed by the rule. The criteria contained in paragraph (a)(6) of the rule that are used to determine whether the purchasing agent is independent of the issuer are designed to insulate the market in the issuer's securities from influence by the issuer or an affiliate.

Two changes, however, have been made in paragraph (a)(6) as published in proposed Rule 13e–2. First, to avoid the possible need for various amendments to existing issuer plans, the commentators suggested that both paragraph (a)(6), and the proviso to it, should be drafted in terms of actual use or exercise of control over the agent by the issuer or affiliate rather than the retention of the power to use or exercise such control. The Commission has adopted this suggestion.

The second change to paragraph (a)(6) incorporates a new clause in the proviso. Certain commentators noted that in many issuer plans, particularly those which the issuer administers or allocates shares purchased for the plan to the participants' accounts, the issuer instructs the agent with respect to the amount of shares it is to purchase over a prescribed period of time. The amount to be purchased is determined by a formula set forth in the plan that generally is based on the amount of contributions and the average market price of the security over a prescribed period of time. The new clause in the proviso will permit the issuer to use such a formula to determine the amount of shares to be purchased by the agent without compromising the independence of the agent so long as the issuer or affiliate does not revise the formula more than once in any three-month period.

Certain commentators also suggested incorporating into the rule various interpretive positions concerning independent agents. For example, the Commission stated in the October Release that neither a common directorship between the issuer and the agent nor the issuer's right to remove the agent would by itself constitute control over the agent. In addition, restrictions imposed on the agent otherwise than by the issuer, or which are required by other statutes, would not preclude a determination that the agent was independent. Commentators also suggested incorporating into the rule a provision that would permit the imposition of certain controls if done in "good faith" and without manipulative intent.

As the Commission noted in the October Release, the determination of whether a control relationship exists between the issuer and the agent is a factual one to be made by the issuer. It is not possible to incorporate in the rule or in a release every possible interpretive position concerning independent agents, since the issue of whether a control relationship exists necessarily will depend on the particular facts and circumstances. Accordingly, the Commission has determined not to attempt to further delineate that relationship in Rule 10b–18. Nevertheless, the Commission reaffirms the interpretive positions expressed in the October Release with respect to independent agents.

III. SOLICITATION OF VIEWS: CONTINUING REVIEW OF ISSUER REPURCHASES AND RULE 10b–18

The Commission intends to monitor the operation of issuer repurchase programs to determine the effects of Rule 10b–18 on those programs and the market for an issuer's securities. In view of the Commission's ongoing interest in this area, it continues to solicit the advice and views of all interested persons on the effects of Rule 10b–18 and whether the rule can be improved. It has been suggested, for example, that an issuer should have the benefit of a safe harbor where purchases exceed the percentage volume limitation of Rule 10b–18 and additional disclosure is made concerning the repurchases. The Commission is interested in whether dissemination of additional information by an issuer during its repurchase program, perhaps on a daily basis, should affect the availability of the safe harbor. Such information might include a further statement of the purpose and expected duration of the repurchase program, the amount of shares acquired or to be acquired on a particular day and the time of day or time period during the day the purchase or purchases are made or are proposed to be made. Commentators are invited to address the question of whether, if this (or other) information is disseminated in a full and timely fashion, the issuer should be afforded the protections of the safe harbor notwithstanding the fact that its purchases exceed the current twenty-five percent limitation. In this regard, the following additional questions may be relevant:

1. When should the information be disclosed (i.e., before or after the shares are acquired)?

2. How should the information be disclosed (e.g., by press release and notification to the exchange on which the securities are registered and listed for trading and to the NASD if the securities are authorized for quotation in NASDAQ)?

3. Would daily disclosure of such information add to or detract from the maintenance of a fair and orderly market for the issuer's stock?

4. Could the information be disseminated in a full and timely fashion that would protect the markets and investors?

5. Can a disclosure requirement be devised, in the context of a rule like Rule 10b–18, that would assure that manipulative practices do not occur or that those who engage in such practices are not insulated from liability?

IV. AMENDMENTS TO RULE 10b–6

As reproposed for comment in the October Release, an amendment to Rule 10b–6 would have provided an exception from that rule for purchases of securities that were the subject of a "technical" distribution (i.e., the issuer had outstanding securities immediately convertible into or exchangeable for the security to be purchased), provided that the purchases were made in compliance with Rule 13e–2.

The Commission has adopted the amendment with modifications. Paragraph (f) of Rule 10b–6 now provides that the rule shall not apply to bids for or purchase of any security, any security of the same class and series as such security, or any security that is convertible into, or exchangeable or exercisable for, such security, solely because the issuer or a subsidiary of the issuer has outstanding securities that are immediately convertible into or, exchangeable or exercisable for, that equity security. The effect of the amendment is to eliminate the need for an issuer or any person whose purchases would be attributable to the issuer to seek specific exemptive or interpretive relief from Rule 10b–6 to permit purchases of any class of the issuer's stock solely because the issuer is engaged in a technical distribution. Rule 10b–6 continues to apply, however, to purchases of any security that is the subject of any other kind of distribution, any security of the same class and series as that security, or any right to purchase any such security.

The Commission has adopted the second amendment to Rule 10b–6 proposed in the October Release concerning purchases by independent agents. Paragraph (g) now provides that a bid for or purchase of any security made or effected by or for a plan shall be deemed to be a purchase by the issuer unless the bid is made, or the purchase is effected, by an agent independent of the issuer, as that term is defined in Rule 10b–18(a) (6).

* * *

By the Commission.

———————

PURCHASES BY A CORPORATION OF ITS OWN SHARES

Purchases by an issuing corporation of its own shares normally are accomplished either by means of a general tender offer to all of the existing shareholders, or by means of ordinary market transactions effected through a broker-dealer. The former is normally utilized when it is desired to reacquire a large quantity of shares, since attempting to acquire the shares in the market would tend to raise the price to an unacceptable level if accomplished within a relatively short period of time. Such a tender offer, however, must be made at some premium over the current market price or the shareholders have no incentive to tender their shares rather than simply disposing of them in the market at the same price.

In Vaughn v. Teledyne, Inc.,[1] Teledyne made, in the period from September 1972 to February 1976, four cash tender offers for its own shares and two exchange offers to issue subordinated debentures in exchange for outstanding common stock. These offers were made at varying prices during this period approximating the market price of the Teledyne common stock. As a result, an aggregate of 22,000,000 shares were reacquired by the company; and the total number of shares outstanding was reduced from 38,000,000 to 11,000,000. As a result of both this reduction in the number of shares outstanding and an increase in the total net income of the corporation during the same period, from $56.2 million to $115.3 million, the net income per share increased from $1.48 in 1971 to $10.48 in 1976. The plaintiffs in this case had sold stock of Teledyne in the market and to the corporation in one or more of the tender offers during the same period; they alleged that the defendant directors had conspired to increase their proportionate control of Teledyne and their earnings from the common stock owned by them as a result of these transactions in violation of Rule 10b–5 and Section 14(e) of the 1934 Act.

The court affirmed the granting of a summary judgment in favor of the defendants on the basis that there were no material issues of fact as to whether there was actually such a conspiracy or whether the defendants had violated any duty by failing to disclose certain divisional operational plans and projections in connection with the tender offers. The court said:

> "Any tender offer or acquisition by a company of its own stock obviously would reduce the number of outstanding shares and increase the proportionate control and earnings of all shareholders who retained their stock (not just the control and earnings of the directors). It is not a violation of any securities law to fail to disclose a result that is obvious even to a person with

1. 628 F.2d 1214 (9th Cir.1980).

only an elementary understanding of the stock market. * * * Nor is it necessarily a violation of the securities law to have a plan to make a stock acquisition with such a result, unless the plan includes practices that are intended to mislead or to defraud investors. * * *

"The undisputed facts in this case establish that there was a series of six major stock acquisitions in less than four years, that more than twenty-two million shares of Teledyne common stock were purchased by the corporation, and that those shareholders retaining their stock have acquired a greater proportion of control of the corporation as well as higher per share earnings (a result that is obvious given the first two facts). Even if these facts alone were sufficient to raise an inference that appellants had a long-range plan, they do not raise the slightest inference that the plan was unlawful or in any way intended to defraud investors." [2]

The court also said, regarding the failure to disclose the operational plans and projections which were made semiannually by the operating divisions of Teledyne: "It is just good general business practice to make such projections for internal corporate use. There is no evidence, however, that the estimates were made with such reasonable certainty even to *allow* them to be disclosed to the public." [3]

Tender offers by issuers were left unregulated by the Williams Act so far as the statute is concerned, since they were exempted from the statutory requirements relating to ordinary tender offers, but the Commission was given authority in Section 13(e) to adopt rules relating to tender offers by issuers, which it finally did in 1979 pursuant to Exchange Act Release No. 16112. Even prior to the adoption of those rules, issuers generally complied with the substantive requirements relating to tender offers by third parties, such as the minimum period during which the offer would remain open, withdrawal rights and pro rata acceptance where more securities were tendered than the maximum to be accepted. In fact, the Commission generally imposed those requirements with respect to the offer where the issuer found it necessary to obtain a no-action letter or an order of the Commission to exempt it from Rule 10b–6 because it had outstanding an issue of warrants or convertible securities and therefore was prohibited from purchasing its own securities by Rule 10b–6 without an exemption.

In 1979 the Securities and Exchange Commission adopted Rule 13e–4 which imposed requirements on an issuer tender offer similar to those applicable to tender offers by third parties, except for the time periods specified. The offer had to remain open for at least fifteen business days; and securities might be withdrawn by the person tendering at any time until the expiration of ten business days from the date of commencement. The issuer had to accept the securities tendered within the first ten business days pro rata, calculated from the date of commencement or the date of a notice of an increase in the consideration. Purchases by the issuer alongside the offer were prohibited during the pendency of the offer and for a period of ten days following the date of its termination. The Commission with respect to issuer tender offers thus implemented the ten-day "cooling off" period after the termination of a tender offer, which it had failed to do with respect to third-party tender offers in the *Hanson Trust* case. The Commission has now conformed these time periods to those specified for third-party offers in Release No. 33–6618 (January 14, 1986) and Release No. 33–3653 (July 11, 1986) (printed above). The duration of the offer is a minimum of twenty business days in both cases and the proration period and withdrawal period of each run for the duration of the offer. The

2. 628 F.2d at 1220.   3. 628 F.2d at 1221.

periods are extended in the event of a change in the consideration offered or in the percentage of securities sought by the offeror. The information required to be filed and disseminated to the security holders is generally similar to that required with respect to third-party tender offers.

Even when there was no express requirement relating to disclosure with respect to such an offer, issuers generally provided financial statements to the shareholders, including pro forma calculations of the effect of the tender offer on the net worth and earnings per share of the shares remaining outstanding which were not tendered. Item 7 of Schedule 13E–4 now requires the furnishing of financial statements for the issuer's two most recent fiscal years plus the interim statements required to be included in the issuer's most recent 10–Q Report, and including pro forma data relating to the effect of the tender offer on the issuer's balance sheet and earnings per share "if material", which such pro forma information normally would be.

The item of disclosure in Schedule 13E–4 which is likely to cause the most difficulty in drafting the tender offer material is that contained in Item 3 which requires that the issuer "state the purpose or purposes of the tender offer." The effect of a repurchase by the issuer of a sizeable block of its own outstanding shares is always and inevitably to increase the earnings per share of those shares which remain outstanding, if the aggregate of the net income remains the same or increases. (Similarly, a loss will be magnified on a per share basis; and if the earnings decline, the magnification of the earnings per share may not offset the reduction caused by the decline in the aggregate net income.) If money is borrowed to pay for the shares purchased, then, of course, the interest cost must be taken into account in calculating the pro forma effect of the transaction on earnings per share.

These inevitable consequences of a reduction in the number of outstanding shares are what the Ninth Circuit said in the *Vaughn* case any damn fool ought to know without being told. Typically, the officers and directors and any controlling shareholders announce in the tender offer that they are not going to tender their own shares, which obviously indicates that they prefer to gamble on the future of the company rather than accept a premium over market at the present time. They usually also think that earnings are going to increase, although they may or may not have any reliable basis for that institutional optimism.

In the light of these considerations, how should the drafting of a disclosure statement relating to the purpose or purposes of the tender offer be approached? If this regulation had been in effect at the time of the Teledyne tender offers in the Vaughn case, and the Schedule 13E–4 and the tender offer materials had merely stated that the purpose of the tender offer was "to reduce the number of outstanding shares and thereby increase the earnings (or loss) per share," would the result of that case have been the same? If not, what more would you have said to avoid any liability?

With respect to ordinary market purchases by a corporation of its own shares, in the early days under the Securities Acts, before Rule 10b–5 became a hobgoblin, these were frequently made by a corporation for the purpose of "supporting" or "maintaining" the price of its shares in the market, on the theory that this did not violate Section 9(a)(2) of the 1934 Act because they were not made for the purpose of "raising or depressing" the price of the security. In an injunction action against Georgia-Pacific Corporation in 1966,[4] the

---

4. Complaint in Securities and Exchange Commission v. Georgia-Pacific Corp., CCH Fed.Sec.L.Rptr. ¶ 91,680 (1966). The injunctive action filed by the SEC resulted in private civil suits being filed against Georgia-Pacific. See Richland v.

Commission charged that Georgia-Pacific "intentionally caused GP common stock to be bid for and purchased for * * * [its] Stock Bonus Plan and for the GP treasury on the NYSE in a manner which would and did * * * cause the price of GP common stock * * * to rise in order that GP's obligation to issue additional shares of its common stock in return for the interest in other corporations would be avoided or reduced [under a contingent share provision in the acquisition agreements guaranteeing the price of the stock at a future date]." A similar charge was made against Genesco, Inc. in connection with a 1933 Act registration.[5] The statutory provision and regulations then and now prohibit such purchases as being manipulative *per se* only when the corporation or some affiliated person is making a distribution of securities at a time within reasonable proximity to the date of purchase, so as to make Rule 10b–6 applicable.

With the addition of Section 13(e) to the 1934 Act by the Williams Act, however, the Commission was given authority to adopt additional restrictions with respect to such purchases. The Senate Committee report accompanying the bill which became the Williams Act indicated that "Corporate repurchases of their own stock have become increasingly important. According to a recent study, corporations listed on the New York Stock Exchange repurchased more than 26,600,000 of their own shares in 1963, at a cost of more than $1.3 billion. The number of shares purchased in this manner in 1954 was 5,800,000 at a cost of $274 million." [6]

The Commission in July, 1970, moved to implement this grant of authority by issuing proposed Rule 13e–2,[7] which was extensively amended on December 6, 1973,[8] and again on October 17, 1980.[9] That "proposed" Rule was never adopted. The staff of the Commission, however, treated the provisions of the proposed Rule 13e–2 as though they were already in effect, which is not unusual; and corporations generally adhered to the restrictions contained therein in making such market purchases. While corporations were able as a practical matter to rely upon the guidelines in the proposed Rule in effecting such market purchases, the failure to amend Rule 10b–6 required during this period that corporations with outstanding warrants or convertibles apply for a specific exemption by the SEC in order to effect any market purchases. However, the Commission did adopt in 1980 an exemption from Rule 10b–6 for issuer *tender offers*, where that rule was applicable only because the corporation had outstanding convertibles.[10]

In 1982 the Commission in Exchange Act Release No. 19244 (reprinted above) abandoned the proposed Rule 13e–2 and adopted instead Rule 10b–18. The restrictions upon market purchases of its own stock by an issuer in Rule 10b–18 are generally similar to those previously proposed by Rule 13e–2, with the only major change being that the volume limitation upon such purchases was increased from 15% of the average daily trading volume for the preceding four weeks to 25%. The major difference, however, between the new rule and the previously proposed rule is that proposed Rule 13e–2 imposed mandatory restrictions upon such market transactions by an issuer, which made such

Cheatham, 272 F.Supp. 148 (S.D.N.Y.1967), where Judge Ryan refused to permit these actions to be maintained as representative actions.

5. Genesco, Inc. Prospectus, dated May 10, 1966; see Baker, Purchases by a Corporation of its Own Shares for Employee Benefit Plans, 22 Bus.Law. 439, 445–46 (1967).

6. S.Rep. No. 550, 90th Cong., 1st Sess., p. 5 (August 29, 1967).

7. Sec.Exch.Act Rel. No. 8930 (July 13, 1970).

8. Sec.Exch.Act Rel. No. 10539 (Dec. 6, 1973).

9. Exch.Act Release No. 17222 (Oct. 17, 1980), 45 Fed.Reg. 70890 (1980).

10. See Exch.Act Rel. No. 16645, Mar. 13, 1980, CCH Fed.Sec.L.Rptr. ¶ 82,479 (1980).

trar.sactions illegal unless the restrictions were observed. The new Rule 10b–18 has been adopted only as a "safe harbor provision" and the Release emphasizes that transactions by an issuer which do not comply with the rule are not *per se* manipulative.

What the rule does is to immunize the issuer from being held liable under Section 9(a)(2) of the 1934 Act or Rule 10b–5 if the market transactions are carried out in compliance with the provisions of the rule. The Commission also adopted at the same time an amendment to Rule 10b–6 which exempts from the provisions of that rule purchases by an issuer that are subject to Rule 10b–6 only because the issuer is engaged in a technical "distribution" as a result of having outstanding a class of securities which are convertible into the security being purchased.

Neither in this amendment to Rule 10b–6 nor in the amendment to Rule 10b–6 relating to issuer *tender offers* mentioned above is there any exemption granted for purchases made during a time when the issuer has outstanding a warrant entitling the holder to purchase stock of the issuer for cash. If that is the situation, then the issuer must still obtain a specific exemption from the Commission in order to engage in any tender offer or repurchase program; otherwise, any purchases would be *per se* manipulative under Rule 10b–6. Why a broader exemption was not granted covering this situation also is difficult to understand, since Section 9(a)(2) and Rule 10b–5 should be sufficient to prevent any purchases made with actual manipulative intent while the issuer has such warrants outstanding. The sale by an issuer, for example, of debentures with detachable warrants (rather than a convertible debenture) is merely an alternative financing technique without any real difference in substance; frequently, the debentures can be surrendered to pay the exercise price under the warrants.

The securities acts problems involved in corporate repurchases are discussed in Swanson, Federal Regulation of Issuer Tender Offers, 12 Pacific L.J. 659 (1981); Bator, Repurchase by Issuers and "Cash Option Mergers": The Impact of Rules 10b–6 and 10b–13, 9 Inst.Securities Reg. 247 (1978); Stone, Corporation's Repurchase of its Own Shares, 49 L.A.Bar Bull. 106 (1974); Malley, Corporate Repurchases of Stock and the SEC Rules: An Overview, 29 Bus.Law. 117 (1973); Baker, Purchases by a Corporation of its Own Shares for Employee Benefit Plans, 22 Bus.Law. 439 (1967); The SEC's Rule 10b–6: Preserving a Competitive Market During Distributions, 1967 Duke L.J. 809; 48 U.Chi.L.Rev. 372 (1981); 15 Calif.Western L.Rev. 264 (1979); 51 N.Y.U.L.Rev. 217, 914 (1976); 62 Ia.L.Rev. 236 (1976).

————

TENDER OFFERS BY THE ISSUER

The legal issues involved in the phenomenon known as "going private" have unfortunately been obscured, if not totally forgotten, because of the misleading phrase which has been employed to describe it. The phrase "going private" describes only an incidental result *in some cases* of a broader category of transactions engaged in for other reasons.

The essence of one type of transaction which has raised this so-called issue of "going private" is that cash (either excess cash on hand or cash raised by borrowing) or debt securities of the issuer are used to retire a large block of the publicly-held stock of the issuer in a tender offer or an exchange offer. The basic result of this type of transaction is that it increases the leverage of the issuer (even if idle cash on hand is used, this is a form of negative leverage which is eliminated by the transaction). The reason the transactions are entered into is that somebody expects to make a profit from the deal, and usually both parties since that is what makes a horse trade—not some momentary irritation over the regulations of the SEC. Whether the people who retain their stock will profit from greater leverage will depend on whether the profits go up or down—greater leverage will enhance the profits per share if the profits remain the same or go up; it will also (as some REIT's discovered) multiply the losses per share if losses are incurred.

In order to isolate the legal issues inherent in this type of transaction, it may be helpful to consider two apparently similar, but legally quite different, cases and several variations of the second case:

Case No. 1: Corporation A has an outstanding common stock listed and traded on the New York Stock Exchange and held by 10,000 shareholders, none of whom hold more than $\frac{1}{2}$ of 1%. The stock is selling for $5 per share. The Board of Directors (none of whom own any stock) believe that the market has grossly undervalued the "real worth" of the company, as corporate executives are fond of saying at shareholders' meetings. They also estimate that approximately 50% of the shareholders would be delighted to "cash out" at a fair price, and that the other 50% would like to stay along for the ride. They determine that $10 per share is a fair price for the stock of the company and that the company, which now has no debt at all, can easily borrow an amount equal to $10 times one-half the number of outstanding shares. It arranges for such borrowing and the corporation makes a tender offer to acquire up to 50% of the total number of outstanding shares. Exactly 50% are tendered and accepted.

Case No. 2: Exactly the same as Case No. 1, except that the 50% not tendered are all owned by one person, who announced in advance that he would not tender.

Variation No. 1: Case No. 2 except that the controlling shareholder and the Board are advised by the company's investment banker that a 20% premium over current market will bring in all of the public shares and therefore the offering price is $6 per share rather than $10, but all of the public shareholders accept.

Variation No. 2: Case No. 2, Variation No. 1, except that 1,000 shareholders holding 5% of the outstanding stock do not accept, but the stock of the corporation is nevertheless delisted on the New York Stock Exchange because the corporation no longer meets its listing requirements. However, an over-the-counter market is still made in the stock by several market makers.

Variation No. 3: Case No. 2, Variation No. 1, except that 310 shareholders holding 2% of the outstanding stock do not accept. The stock of the corporation is thereupon delisted on the New York Stock Exchange and no viable over-the-counter market is created, although one broker-dealer occasionally quotes the stock in the sheets.

Is the crucial difference between these cases the fact that the corporation has "gone private" in Case No. 2 and Case No. 2(1), but not in any of the others?

Case No. 1 would not seem to raise any legal issues except perhaps a question of business judgment (which the courts have traditionally said is reserved to the Board of Directors) and the question of whether the risks and benefits of electing to abandon the ship or to stay aboard were adequately explained to the shareholders.

Does Case No. 2 raise any other legal issues? These are suggested by the variations. In Case No. 1 the Board of Directors has no motive to favor the non-tendering over the tendering shareholders, but the controlling shareholder obviously has such a motive in Case No. 2 and the Board of Directors selected by him may with some reason be suspected of sharing his objectives. Since the money being used is that of the corporation, and therefore half that of the public shareholders, it would seem that the Board has an obligation to offer a "fair" price, whatever that may mean. Does full disclosure of all of the aspects of the transaction cure any failure to offer what a court may deem to be a "fair" price? In answering this question, what effect should be given to the coercive effect of the possibility that Variation No. 2 or Variation No. 3 may be the consequence of the transaction, so that a non-tendering shareholder may have the liquidity of his investment seriously curtailed or virtually eliminated? What effect should be given to an announcement by the corporation that it will discontinue the future payment of dividends after the tender offer, regardless of how many shares are tendered? Is the public shareholder realistically offered a free choice in these circumstances, regardless of how much "disclosure" is made to him?

On the other hand, if we assume a Case No. 3 where the issuer is offering to exchange a 10% Sinking Fund Debenture for not more than 20% of its total outstanding stock, which will not result in any delisting of its shares, but will give an income security to a certain number of its shareholders (or all of them on a pro rata basis, if all of them elect to tender), whereas the corporation has historically never paid a dividend on its common stock, what does this transaction have in common with any of the previous hypothetical cases? The dangers of excessive generalization would seem to be obvious.

Finally, whatever answers may be given to these questions, there remain two fundamental issues: to what extent should these problems be resolved by Federal as opposed to State law, and to what extent should they be resolved by the Congress rather than an administrative agency without a clearcut mandate to enter into this field of substantive regulation?

So far as the existing authority is concerned, it is clear that a tender offer by the issuer is a "tender offer" subject to the anti-fraud provisions of Section 14(e) [11] and it may be enjoined, as held in Broder v. Dane,[12] for failure to disclose a material fact necessary in order to make the statements made not misleading. Such an omission could include, if true, the fact that when the corporation "went public" it intended later to "go private", as held in Dreier v. The Music Makers Group, Inc.,[13] but there is no judicial support for the proposition once advanced by certain members of the SEC staff that when any corporation goes public it promises by operation of law to remain public forever.

SQUEEZE–OUTS

The question whether under Rule 10b–5 there must be some "deception" in connection with the purchase or sale transaction has been presented in an aggravated form in the recent cases like the *Santa Fe Industries* case, infra, p.

---

11. The specific exemption of an issuer tender offer from the provisions of Section 14(d) indicates quite clearly that it nevertheless is a "tender offer" and subject to Section 14(e), since that subsection contains no similar exemptive language.

12. 384 F.Supp. 1312 (S.D.N.Y.1974).

13. CCH Fed.Sec.Law Rptr. ¶ 94,406 (S.D.N.Y.1974). Judge Gagliardi made it clear in his opinion that he had no confi-

dence in the ability of the plaintiff to prove such an allegation. He said: "Recognizing both the novelty of plaintiff's claim and the clear problems of proof, we cannot say that the allegations are so clearly beyond the broad scope of § 10b and Rule 10b–5 as to compel the dismissal of this claim. However, it is clear that a more definite statement is required by both Rule 12(e) and Rule 9(b) Fed.R.Civ.P."

1059, which are one aspect of the so-called "going private" phenomenon. The essential complaint in those cases is that it is inherently "unfair" to cash out the minority shareholders in a depressed market using corporate cash, whether or not they have a right to demand an independent appraisal of the cash price being offered. While the plaintiff challenging such a transaction may or may not be able to identify or construct some alleged misrepresentation or nondisclosure in connection with the transaction, full disclosure would not really have done him any good; his essential complaint would remain.

Most of the important State corporation laws today permit the differing treatment of shareholders of a single class in connection with any merger transaction. For example, if Corporation A merges into Corporation B and Corporation A has outstanding a single class of common stock, 80% of which is held by X and the other 20% by any number of other shareholders, it is permissible to provide that X will receive one type of consideration in the merger (e.g., common stock of Corporation B) and the other holders of common stock of A will receive something different (e.g., cash). At one time such a "cash out" of a group of shareholders was permitted only in a so-called "short form" parent-subsidiary merger where the parent already owned 90% or 95% of the stock of the subsidiary. When the general merger statutes were amended to permit cash to be used as consideration in any merger transaction and to permit some members of a class of shareholders to be treated differently from other members of the same class (although some might possibly be read as requiring all members of a class to be treated equally), the only remaining difference between the two types of transactions was the elimination of any requirement for a shareholders' vote in a "short form" merger.[14] But if the controlling persons of the corporation own, for example, 80% of the outstanding stock, a shareholders' vote is a formality since no State requires the approval of more than two-thirds of the outstanding stock to effectuate a merger.

In this type of transaction, of course, legal coercion is substituted for the practical coercion which may exist in the issuer tender offer situation, subject to whatever equitable limitations may be imposed by the state courts and whatever effect the federal securities laws may have. Only a small minority of these cases, however, involve "going private" as a result of the merger transaction itself. The squeeze-out may follow a tender by an outside party who thereafter eliminates the remaining shareholders of the target company who did not tender by a "short form" merger,[15] or, as in Greenberg v. Institutional Investor Systems, Inc.,[16] the merger transaction for the same purpose may follow a tender offer by the issuer.[17] Or the squeeze-out may be of one shareholder or a small group of shareholders in a closely held corporation who are feuding with the majority, in a case where the corporation never was public.[18]

14. California, however, does not permit the cash-out of minority shareholders in a merger unless the parent corporation owns at least 90% of the outstanding shares of each class, Cal.Corp.Code § 1101 (last paragraph), or unless the transaction is approved by a public official as provided in Cal.Corp.Code § 1101.1.

15. Green v. Santa Fe Industries, Inc., infra, p. 1059; Grimes v. Donaldson, Lufkin & Jenrette, Inc., 392 F.Supp. 1393 (N.D.Fla.1974).

16. CCH Fed.Sec.Law Rptr. ¶ 95,231 (S.D.N.Y.1975).

17. The reason a regular merger transaction had to be employed in the Greenberg case was that the tender offer had increased the majority's holdings only to 85%, and 95% ownership is required in New York for a "short form" merger. However, the company had already reduced the number of shareholders to less than 300 and had de-registered under the 1934 Act; therefore, it had already "gone private" under the SEC's definition.

18. Bryan v. Brock & Blevins Co., Inc., 343 F.Supp. 1062 (N.D.Ga.1972), aff'd 490 F.2d 563, 493 F.2d 664 (5th Cir.1973), cert. denied 419 U.S. 844 (1974); Levine v. Bid-

On the other hand, such a transaction may be used as the initial and only step to completely eliminate all of the public shareholders, as in Albright v. Bergendahl.[19] In that case Judge Ritter said: "The Court further finds that this merger was a 'freeze out' wherein defendants * * * were to receive capital stock of Body Contour, Inc. [the surviving corporation in the merger] while the public stockholders of International Service Industries, Inc. were to receive 18 cents per share cash only, with no opportunity to receive Body Contour, Inc. stock as the said defendants granted to themselves. The Court holds that such a transaction, under these facts and these circumstances, constituted a 'device, scheme or artifice to defraud' or an 'act, practice or course of business which operates or would operate as a fraud or deceit' upon the public minority stockholders of International Service Industries, Inc." [20] This decision would seem clearly to have been overruled by the *Santa Fe Industries* case (see p. 1059, below).

The issues involved here seem to be fairly easy to identify:

Should the majority shareholders ever be permitted to force the minority to take cash for their interest, while the majority retains the assets and goodwill of the business?

If so, should this be permitted only to some specified very large majority, as in the "short form" merger statutes?

Should it be required that the transaction have some "valid corporate purpose" other than the mere desire to eliminate the minority? If so, what would be an example of such a "corporate purpose"?

Should the courts interfere on the basis of the "unfairness" of the amount of cash offered, (a) if the minority shareholders have the right under state law to demand an appraisal by the state court and the payment of the appraised value of their shares in lieu of what was offered, or (b) if such right of appraisal does not exist? (Note that in the *Green* case there was a right to an appraisal under state law, but in Marshel v. AFW Fabric Corp.[21] there was not.)

The Delaware Supreme Court in the last ten years, in addressing these questions, has prescribed a virtual 360° circle (or at least 340°). Prior to 1977, it was considered to be established Delaware law under the case of Stauffer v. Standard Brands, Inc.[22] that the appraisal remedy was the exclusive remedy for a minority shareholder who was dissatisfied with a cash-out merger, in the absence of illegality or fraud (which is the formulation in the Model Business Corporation Act [23] that was believed to codify prior law, including that of Delaware).

In 1977, the Delaware Supreme Court decided the case of Singer v. Magnavox Co.,[24] in which it overruled the *Stauffer* case and held that a minority shareholder could bring an action to enjoin a cash-out merger or to recover damages after it had been accomplished, unless there was a "valid corporate purpose" for the merger. What such a valid corporate purpose might be was a question with which the subsequent decisions in Delaware and in

---

dle Sawyer Corp., 383 F.Supp. 618 (S.D. N.Y.1974).

19. 391 F.Supp. 754 (D.Utah 1974).

20. 391 F.Supp. at 756. In the case of Bryan v. Brock & Blevins Co., Inc., supra, Note 18, the District Judge held that there was a violation of both state and federal law, but the Fifth Circuit preferred to rest its affirmance on state law alone. In the Levine case, supra, Note 18, Judge Bonsal held that the complaint stated a cause of

action under Federal law because it alleged material misstatements and omissions.

21. 533 F.2d 1277 (2d Cir.1976), reh. denied 533 F.2d 1309, on remand 552 F.2d 471, 441 F.Supp. 299, 441 F.Supp. 300 (S.D. N.Y.1977).

22. 41 Del. Ch. 7, 187 A.2d 78 (1962).

23. 2 Model Bus. Corp. Act Ann. § 13.02(b) (1985).

24. 380 A.2d 969 (Del.1977).

other jurisdictions adopting this approach struggled, without ever reaching any clear resolution, although the subsequent case of Tanzer v. International General Industries, Inc.[25] held that it might be a business purpose of the *parent corporation* even though not one of the merged subsidiary. In the vast majority of such transactions, the purpose is merely to do what the transaction accomplishes, i.e., to get rid of the minority shareholders. While this will save the corporation money previously spent on preparing proxy statements and 8K, 10Q and 10K Reports to the SEC, and defending "nuisance suits" by minority shareholders, that is true in every case and can hardly have been the "corporate purpose" the court had in mind. Other alleged corporate purposes were usually invented by lawyers after a suit was filed; a corporation doesn't care (or shouldn't care) who owns it, with rare exceptions such as legal disabilities arising from foreign ownership.

In 1983 the Delaware Supreme Court in Weinberger v. UOP, Inc.[26] overruled the *Singer* case and all of its progeny and reinstated the *Stauffer* case as the governing authority in Delaware, based primarily upon the fact that the appraisal procedure had been "liberalized" in Delaware as a result of amendments to the Delaware General Corporation Law and court decisions, including the decision in that case. The court nevertheless held in the *Weinberger* case that the plaintiff there was not relegated to an appraisal remedy because the parent corporation in that case had breached its duty of "entire candor" to the minority shareholders and to the independent directors of the subsidiary by withholding material information relating to the merger transaction. The court also said that the appraisal remedy "may not be adequate in certain cases, particularly where fraud, misrepresentation, self-dealing, deliberate waste of corporate assets, or gross and palpable overreaching are involved."[27] While this stops short of making the appraisal remedy exclusive except where illegality or fraud is shown, the requirement of a "valid corporate purpose" for a cash-out merger of the minority shareholders is dead in Delaware, at least for the time being.

Should the answers to the previous questions be a matter of state law or a matter of federal law under Rule 10b–5? See Symposium—An In-Depth Analysis of the Federal and State Roles in Regulating Corporate Management, 31 Bus.Law. (Special Issue, Feb.1976).

THE SEC'S "GOING PRIVATE" RULES

In 1975[28] and again in 1977,[29] the Commission issued for comment proposed rules under Section 13(e) of the 1934 Act to regulate a "going private" transaction as defined in proposed Rule 13e–3. These proposed rules would have authorized the Commission to prohibit going private transactions which were deemed to be "unfair." However, when the final rule was adopted in 1979,[30] the Commission backed off from this assertion of substantive jurisdiction to approve or disapprove transactions, in the face of an avalanche of criticism asserting that the Commission had no statutory authority to engage in that type of regulation. The new Rule 13e–3 as finally adopted purports to require only "disclosure" with respect to such a transaction.

25. 379 A.2d 1121 (Del.1977) (although it appears in an earlier volume of the Atlantic Reporter, this case was decided a month after the *Singer* case).

26. 457 A.2d 701 (Del.1983).

27. 458 A.2d at 714.

28. Sec.Exch.Act Rel. No. 11231 (Feb. 6, 1975).

29. Sec.Exch.Act Rel. No. 14185 (Nov. 17, 1977).

30. Sec.Exch.Act Rel. No. 16075 (Aug. 2, 1979).

The Commission attempted indirectly, however, to achieve much the same result by mandating that an issuer engaged in such a transaction state whether it believes that the transaction is "fair or unfair" to the minority shareholders and the basis for such belief. The Commission obviously thought that no one would say to the minority shareholders, "I believe that this transaction is unfair to you"; and that the shareholders could bring an action under the rule [31] if the issuer said, "I believe this transaction to be fair" and, in fact, it is not, on the theory that the issuer didn't really believe it. The Commission explained the scope and effect of the revised rule as adopted in part as follows: [32]

"Most of the commentators were opposed to the requirement in the 1977 proposals that a Rule 13e–3 transaction must be both substantively and procedurally fair to unaffiliated security holders. A number of these commentators expressed the view that the Commission does not have the authority to adopt such a requirement. They also maintained that, in the absence of an explicit legislative mandate to regulate the fairness of going private transactions, the Commission should, as a matter of policy, refrain from doing so because substantive regulation of corporate affairs is, in their view, a subject for state and not federal cognizance. It was noted in this regard that recent decisions by state courts indicate that state law provides protection to unaffiliated security holders if control persons act unfairly when taking a company private. The imposition of a federal fairness requirement was also criticized because it would, in their view, result in the staff making decisions concerning the fairness of a proposed transaction in connection with its review of registration statements, preliminary proxy materials and tender offer documents relating to going private transactions. These commentators believe that the staff would not have the resources and expertise to handle such a role.

"The Commission believes that the question of regulation of the fairness of going private transactions should be deferred until there is an opportunity to determine the efficacy of the provisions of Rule 13e–3. Further developments in the remedies provided by state law for unfairness in going private transactions will also be important in this regard. In the interim, the Commission believes that the protection of investors will be enhanced substantially by the more meaningful disclosure, particularly with respect to the fairness of going private transactions, and the other protections afforded by Rule 13e–3.

"Several commentators criticized the application of the 1977 proposals to transactions which in their view do not involve the potential for abuse and overreaching associated with the normal going private transaction. Thus, they were of the view that the following types of transactions, among others, should not be covered: (i) mergers following an any and all tender offer by a bidder who, as a result of the tender offer, becomes an affiliate if the same price were being paid in each transaction; (ii) exchange offers to holders of non-redeemable preferred stock or convertible debentures; (iii) transactions structured to create a holding company or reincorporate the entity in a new jurisdiction; and (iv) mergers with and exchange offers by affiliates in which unaffiliated security holders would receive common stock of the surviving entity. In response to these comments, exceptions for such transactions are now provided by paragraphs (g)(1) and (g)(2) of Rule 13e–3, assuming that the other conditions of those provisions are satisfied.

---

31. The Commission asserted that a private right of action would arise under the rule in the 1977 Release and reiterated this position in Note 3 to the 1979 Release despite the decision of the Supreme Court in Touche Ross & Co. v. Redington (infra, p. 849) in the interim.

32. Sec.Exch.Act Rel. No. 16075 (Aug. 2, 1979).

*   *   *

"A Rule 13e–3 transaction is defined to mean any transaction or series of transactions involving one or more of the transactions specified in paragraph (a)(4)(i) which has either a reasonable likelihood or purpose of producing, directly or indirectly, any of the effects specified in paragraph (a)(4)(ii). The specified transactions are: (a) a purchase of any equity security by the issuer of such security or by an affiliate of such issuer; (b) a tender offer or request or invitation for tenders of any equity security made by the issuer of such class of securities or by an affiliate of such issuer; or (c) a solicitation or distribution subject to Regulation 14A [§§ 240.14c–1 to 14c–101] in connection with certain corporate events. The corporate events include a merger, consolidation, reclassification, recapitalization, reorganization or similar corporate transaction by an issuer or between an issuer (or its subsidiaries) and its affiliates; a sale by the issuer of substantially all of its assets to its affiliate; or a reverse stock split of any class of equity securities of the issuer involving the purchase of fractional interests.

"As proposed, the effects selected to trigger the application of Rule 13e–3 were entirely in the disjunctive. As noted by the commentators, this produced the unintended result of applying Rule 13e–3 to specified transactions which had the reasonable likelihood or purpose of causing, for example, a class of equity securities of the issuer to be subject to delisting from an exchange, even though the securities would have continued to be authorized to be quoted on an inter-dealer quotation system of a registered national securities association. As revised, Rule 13e–3 is triggered by a specified transaction which has either the reasonable likelihood or purpose of causing either (i) the termination of reporting obligations under the Exchange Act, by virtue of the class of securities being held of record by less than 300 persons, or (ii) the securities to be neither listed on an exchange nor authorized to be quoted on an inter-dealer quotation system of any registered national securities association. Accordingly, in the above illustration, delisting of a class of equity securities from an exchange would not trigger the application of Rule 13e–3 if the securities were nevertheless authorized to be quoted on an interdealer quotation system of a registered national securities association.

*   *   *

"If the Rule 13e–3 transaction is a purchase as described in Rule 13e–3(a)(3) (i)(A) or a vote, consent or authorization or distribution of information statements, as described in proposed Rule 13e–3(a)(3)(i)(C), Rule 13e–3(f)(1) would apply. While the disclosure would be disseminated in accordance with the provisions of applicable Federal or state law, in no event would such dissemination occur later than 20 days prior to: any such purchase; any such vote, consent or authorization; or with respect to the distribution of information statements, the meeting date; or if corporate action is to be taken by means of the written authorization or consent of security holders, the earliest date on which corporate action may be taken. Thus, Rule 13e–3(f)(1)(i)(A) would provide for a 20–day waiting period during which a Rule 13e–3 transaction could not be effected. Moreover, Rule 13e–3(f)(1)(i)(B) requires that the disclosure be disseminated to persons who are record holders as of a date not more than 20 days prior to the date of dissemination. For example, if the vote on a Rule 13e–3 transaction will occur on August 30, the disclosure would be disseminated no later than August 10. If August 10 is the date of dissemination, the disclosure would be transmitted to persons who are listed as record holders as of a date not earlier than July 21.

*   *   *

"The most significant change in the items of the Schedule is with respect to disclosure of the fairness of the transaction. Item 8 requires the issuer or affiliate to state whether it reasonably believes the Rule 13e–3 transaction is fair or unfair to unaffiliated security holders. The issuer or affiliate is also required to provide a detailed discussion of the material factors upon which that belief is based. This discussion is required to address the extent to which the following factors were taken into account: (1) whether the transaction is structured so that approval of at least a majority of unaffiliated security holders is required; (2) whether the consideration offered to unaffiliated security holders constitutes fair value; (3) whether the majority of nonemployee directors has retained an unaffiliated representative to act solely on behalf of unaffiliated security holders for the purposes of negotiating the terms of the transaction and/or preparing a report concerning the fairness of the transaction; (4) whether the Rule 13e–3 transaction was approved by a majority of the directors of the issuer who are not employees of the issuer; and (5) whether a report, opinion or appraisal of the type described in Item 9 of the Schedule was obtained. In order to minimize meaningless, boilerplate responses an instruction specifies that conclusory statements are not considered sufficient disclosure in responding to this requirement.

"These factors are based to a large extent on the considerations set forth in the Note to proposed Rule 13e–3(b) which rule would have required that the transaction be fair to unaffiliated security holders. The commentators were concerned that the factors chosen would conflict with the standards under state law for determining fairness. Since a substantive fairness requirement is not being adopted at this time, this concern is now inapplicable. Moreover, Instruction 1 to Item 8(b) of Schedule 13E–3 indicates that the factors which are important in determining the fairness of a transaction to unaffiliated security holders, and the weight which should be given to them in a particular context, will vary. The context in which this determination is made, of course, includes the applicable state law. Accordingly, accommodation with those requirements is assured.

"In any event, the Commission believes that increased discussion of factors bearing upon fairness to unaffiliated security holders is necessary in view of the potential for abuse which exists in a Rule 13e–3 transaction. The absence of arms-length negotiations which is characteristic of going private transactions requires that unaffiliated security holders be furnished with detailed information so that they can determine whether their rights have been adequately protected."

The intense national debate over the "going private" phenomenon and the legal requirements which should be imposed upon such a transaction by the courts and the Commission has virtually disappeared in the last few years. This may be due, in part, to the greater legal certainty which has resulted from the adoption of Rule 13e–3 by the Securities and Exchange Commission and the decision in the *Weinberger* case in Delaware, and also perhaps in part from the fact that the greater disclosure required by both the state and federal law with respect to such a transaction has deterred some people from engaging in transactions which are grossly unfair to the minority shareholders. There is no doubt, however, that this result is due primarily, or perhaps solely, to the fact that market conditions no longer make such transactions attractive to the majority shareholders of most corporations.

These transactions originated during a period when the market prices of the stock of most corporations were at such a depressed level that the majority shareholders saw an opportunity to make a substantial profit by cashing out the minority at the current market price or even a slight premium above that price. In the last two or three years, the rampaging bull market[33] has generally removed this essential precondition to the desirability of a going private transaction from the point of view of the management and the controlling shareholders and consequently they have virtually ceased. As is not unusual, market forces may have solved a problem which the regulators were not able to solve.

For discussions of the "going private" phenomenon, see Borden, Going Private—Old Tort, New Tort or No Tort? 49 N.Y.U.L.Rev. 987 (1974); Brudney, Note on "Going Private", 61 Va.L.Rev. 1019 (1975); Note, Going Private, 84 Yale L.Rev. 903 (1975); Note, Federal Regulation of the Going Private Phenomenon, 6 Cumb.L.Rev. 141 (1975); 80 Colum.L.Rev. 782 (1980); 58 Wash. U.L.Q. 883 (1980); 28 Emory L.J. 111 (1979); 58 B.U.L.Rev. 792 (1978). For discussions of "squeeze-outs", see McClure, Are Freeze-Outs Thawing in Going Private Transactions?, 15 Houston L.Rev. 907 (1978); Lederman, Two-Step Acquisitions and Minority Squeeze Outs—The Securities Law Aspects, 36 N.Y.U.Inst.Fed.Taxation 941 (1978); Minority Stockholder Freezeouts and Going Private Transactions—A Panel, 32 Bus.Law. 1489 (1977); O'Neal and Janke, Utilizing Rule 10b–5 for Remedying Squeeze-Outs or Oppression of Minority Shareholders, 16 B.C.Ind. & Com.L.Rev. 327 (1975); Kessler, Elimination of Minority Interests by Cash Merger: Two Recent Cases, 30 Bus.Law. 699 (1975).

33. The Dow-Jones Industrial Average increased from 776.92 in August, 1982, to over 1,000 in February, 1983, to over 1,900 on July 1, 1986. Los Angeles Times, July 2, 1986, IV:1:2. Since July 1986, that average has broken the 2,200 level.

Part IV

CIVIL LIABILITIES UNDER THE FEDERAL SECURITIES LAWS

Chapter 13

IMPLICATION OF A PRIVATE RIGHT OF ACTION

Statutes and Regulations

Securities Act of 1933, §§ 11, 12, 17(a).

Securities Exchange Act of 1934, §§ 7, 9, 10(b), 13(d), 13(e), 14(a), 14(d), 14(e), 18.

Rules 10b-5 and 10b-16.

Regulations T, U, G and X.

EXPRESS AND IMPLIED ACTIONS UNDER THE 1933 AND 1934 ACTS

There are in each of the 1933 Act and the 1934 Act two sections creating civil liability in favor of persons injured by violation of those sections (putting to one side Section 16(b) of the 1934 Act, which is *sui generis,* and under which the judgment runs in favor of the corporation and not in favor of other private parties). These sections are Sections 11 and 12 of the 1933 Act and Sections 9 and 18 of the 1934 Act.

Section 11 of the 1933 Act. Stated in the simplest terms, Section 11 imposes liability upon certain designated persons for material statements in a registration statement which are false or misleading, and for material omissions to state facts required to be stated, unless they can establish that they had, after reasonable investigation, reasonable grounds to believe, and did believe, that the statements were accurate and complete (except that the issuing corporation does not have this defense). The most important aspects of any litigation under Section 11 are the questions of the "materiality" of the alleged misstatement or omission and of whether the defendants have established their so-called "due diligence defense" (i.e., the reasonableness of their investigation and the reasonableness of their belief in the accuracy and completeness of the registration statement).

Section 12 of the 1933 Act. The two express civil liability provisions in the 1933 Act, aside from Section 11, are contained in Section 12(1) which deals with a sale of securities in violation of the registration and prospectus delivery requirements of that Act and Section 12(2) which deals with civil liability for false or misleading statements in connection with a sale (although not a purchase) of a security. Under both of these sections, the plaintiff must first establish that what has been sold is a "security" (as is true of all of the express and implied liabilities under the securities laws).

832

This question has been considered above in Chapter 4. In addition, the defendant may escape liability under Section 12(1), of course, if he can show that the security or the transaction was exempted from the registration and prospectus delivery requirements, since then there could not be shown to have been any violation of Section 5. See the discussion in Byrnes v. Faulkner, Dawkins & Sullivan.[1] These exemption questions have been considered above in Chapters 5 through 8. On the other hand, Section 12(2) expressly applies with respect to a security "whether or not exempted by the provisions of section 3" (other than bank securities and governments). While the section does not expressly say that it applies whether or not the transaction was exempted by the provisions of *Section 4*, the general understanding of the Bar has been that Section 12(2) applies regardless of any exemptions from registration, except for the two mentioned.

Section 12(1) imposes civil liability for sale of a security in violation of Section 5 of the Act. The liability is absolute, there being no defense except to show that the sale was not in violation of Section 5. Even if a prospectus were prepared truthfully containing all of the information required by the Act and were delivered to the vendee, this fact would be immaterial in an action under Section 12(1), unless it were part of an effective registration statement. Thus, Section 12(1) gives the vendee of a security sold in violation of Section 5 an unqualified "put" of the security back to the vendor within the period of the statute of limitations at the purchase price.

It should be noted that Section 5 covers more than the sale of an unregistered security which is required to be registered. It prohibits the sale of a registered security without delivery of a prospectus or by use of a prospectus not meeting the requirements of Section 10 [e.g., a prospectus which is not current under Section 10(a)(3)]. In this connection, it is important to distinguish between a "prospectus" as defined in Section 2(10) of the 1933 Act and a "statutory prospectus", i.e., one meeting the requirements of Section 10, which means that it must include most of the information contained in the registration statement. The confirmation of the sale delivered in the *Byrnes* case was by definition a "prospectus", but it was not, of course, a "statutory prospectus." Therefore, it had to be accompanied or preceded by a statutory prospectus; and, since it was not, there was a violation of Section 5 and consequently liability under Section 12(1). Section 5 also prohibits an *offer* of sale prior to the *filing* of the registration statement (i.e., "gun jumping")[2] or while a refusal or stop order is in effect or after a notice of stop order proceedings has been given before the effective date.

Contrary to some popular misconceptions, however, the fact that a security required to be registered has been sold without registration does not impose any "taint" upon the security. (This wholly inaccurate word has even been used in some judicial opinions.) A registration under the Securities Act of 1933 is not like a dog license which must be obtained for a security in order for it not to be "tainted." The prohibitions of Section 5 must be applied to each individual transaction. For example, if an issuer

1. 550 F.2d 1303 (2d Cir.1977).

2. Cf. Diskin v. Lomasney & Co., 452 F.2d 871 (2d Cir.1971).

sells unregistered securities to numerous persons in violation of Section 5, and none of these persons is in a control relationship with the issuer or is a dealer or underwriter as defined in Section 2(11), these purchasers are perfectly free to resell the securities to others without violating Section 5 since their transactions are exempt by the provisions of Section 4(2). Thus they would incur no liability in such resales under Section 12(1) and their vendees could not sue the issuer for the original violation since there is no privity between them.

See, generally, 3 Loss, Securities Regulation 1692–1998 (2d ed. 1961, Supp.1969).

Section 12(2) is a broad anti-fraud provision which is not directly related to the registration requirements of that statute. It applies to any sale of a security using the jurisdictional means "whether or not [the security is] exempted" from the registration requirements (except for bank securities and governmental securities) and also by necessary inference whether or not the security is in fact registered. Therefore, the purchaser of a registered security may have an action under Section 12(2) as well as Section 11. In one important respect he could only have an action under Section 12(2), and that is the case where false statements were made to him *orally* or in written selling literature not a part of the statutory prospectus. Section 12(2) covers an "oral communication" containing a false or misleading statement, as well as a "prospectus" in the sense of any written communication; whereas, Section 11 only refers to a false or misleading statement *in the registration statement*. On the other hand, if the purchaser is not in privity with the persons named in Section 11, he could not also sue them under Section 12(2) since that Section provides that a seller is liable only to "the person purchasing such security from him." If a purchaser *is* in privity with the defendant, but the defendant is not named in Section 11 (e.g., a dealer in the selling group), the purchaser could sue him *only* under Section 12(2).

The remedy given to the buyer of a security under Section 12(2) is in some respects broader and in other respects narrower than an equitable action for rescission based upon misrepresentation. For an analysis, see 3 Loss, Securities Regulation 1700–1705 (2d ed. 1961, Supp.1969).

Section 9 of the 1934 Act. Section 9 deals with the manipulation of the price of a listed security on a national securities exchange and subdivision (e) provides that any person who "willfully participates" in any act or transaction in violation of that section "shall be liable to any person who shall purchase or sell any security at a price which was affected by such act or transaction." This action is subject to a number of restrictions which have in the past made it unattractive to plaintiffs. The court is given discretion in this section to require an undertaking for costs, including attorneys' fees, against either party litigant. There is a relatively short statute of limitations contained within subdivision (e) itself, which requires that the action be brought "within one year after the discovery of the facts constituting the violation and within three years after such violation." In addition, the requirement of "willfulness" on the part of the defendant at one time seemed to make an action under Rule 10b–5 more favorable to the plaintiff, at least in some circuits. The section is also limited to listed securities and does not prohibit similar actions in the over-the-counter market, although it would seem that Rule 10b–5, even after its recent paring back by the Supreme Court, would clearly cover similar activity in the over-the-counter market to that described in Section 9.

Section 18 of the 1934 Act. Section 18 provides for civil liability with respect to any false or misleading statement contained in any application, report or other document filed with the Commission pursuant to the 1934 Act or any rule or regulation thereunder. This liability runs only in favor of a person who "purchased or sold a security at a price which was affected by such statement" and only if the plaintiff acted "in reliance upon such statement." The defendant is not liable under that section if he "acted in good faith and had no knowledge that such statement was false or misleading", but the burden of proving those facts is imposed upon the defendant. Section 18 also contains provisions for security for costs and a one-year and three-year statute of limitations, identical to the provisions in Section 9.

These sections will be further considered below, in connection with the discussion of the question of whether an implied cause of action can arise under Rule 10b–5 in a situation where one of these express liability provisions is apparently applicable to the transaction, although the plaintiff may not be able to win the lawsuit under one of them because of the restrictions to which they were subjected by Congress.

Implied Rights of Action Under Other Sections or Rules. While the foregoing provisions are an impressive array of damage actions created in favor of private parties by the 1933 and 1934 Acts, Congress did not (presumably deliberately) attempt to cover in the civil liability provisions the entire universe of securities transactions nor all of the conduct which was regulated in some fashion or proscribed by other provisions of those statutes. For example, Section 11 dealt only with sales of securities by an issuer (or a control person) pursuant to a registered offering, because those were the only persons required to register a sale of securities under the 1933 Act. Section 12(1) dealt only with a failure to register an offering where that was required by the 1933 Act. Section 12(2), while broader than Section 11, dealt only with sales of securities, not purchases, and apparently restricted the right of action created to a person who was in direct privity as a purchaser with the defendant-seller. Section 9 was limited to listed securities and did not cover any transactions in the over-the-counter market nor any private transactions not on any organized securities market. It was also limited to specific, enumerated types of "manipulation" which had occurred in trading on the stock exchanges but did not have particular relevance to transactions not carried out on any organized securities market. Section 18 dealt only with false or misleading statements in a filed document, and therefore did not cover any oral or written misrepresentations otherwise made in connection with a securities transaction. It also required reliance by the plaintiff on the misrepresentation in the filed document, which it would be impossible to show if he had never seen it and perhaps was unaware of its existence (as would frequently be the case, unless the document, such as a proxy statement, were required both to be filed and to be disseminated to shareholders).

One judicial reaction to this state of the legislation might have been to say: Congress created certain limited private rights of action under the securities laws; if it had intended to create any others, it would have said so, since it obviously knew how to do that; and that is the end of the matter. If that had in fact been the original and consistent attitude of the courts, then this Chapter and most of this Part of this book would have been completely unnecessary.

The other attitude which might have been adopted (and which originally was adopted) by the courts was to say: Any wilful violation of any provision of the statutes, or of any rule or regulation of the SEC issued thereunder, is made a crime by Section 24 of the 1933 Act and Section 32 of the 1934 Act, and under general principles of tort law the violation of a criminal statute is also a tort which can be the basis for a damage action by a person who was intended to be protected by the statute and who was injured by the violation. There is little cogent evidence that Congress considered this issue in any way when it passed the 1933 Act and the 1934 Act.[3] Therefore, the courts were initially free to adopt either of these approaches regarding implied civil liability under other sections of the statutes and the rules adopted by the SEC.

The fountainhead of the approach initially adopted was the case of Kardon v. National Gypsum Co., 69 F.Supp. 512 (E.D.Pa.1946), where the court in a very brief opinion by Judge Kirkpatrick held that there was a private right of action under Rule 10b–5, basing this result upon the general principle stated in the Restatement of Torts. The court said:

"It is not, and cannot be, questioned that the complaint sets forth conduct on the part of the * * * [defendants] directly in violation of the provisions of Sec. 10(b) of the Act and of Rule X–10B–5 which implements it. It is also true that there is no provision in Sec. 10 or elsewhere expressly allowing civil suits by persons injured as a result of violation of Sec. 10 or of the Rule. However, 'The violation of a legislative enactment by doing a prohibited act, or by failing to do a required act, makes the actor liable for an invasion of an interest of another if; (a) the intent of the enactment is exclusively or in part to protect an interest of the other as an individual; and (b) the interest invaded is one which the enactment is intended to protect. * * *' Restatement, Torts, Vol. 2, Sec. 286. This rule is more than merely a canon of statutory interpretation. The disregard of the command of a statute is a wrongful act and a tort. As was said in Texas & Pacific R. Co. v. Rigsby, 241 U.S. 33, 39, 484 (1916), 'This is but an application of the maxim, *Ubi jus ibi remedium.*'

"Of course, the legislature may withhold from parties injured the right to recover damages arising by reason of violation of a statute but the right is so fundamental and so deeply ingrained in the law that where it is not expressly denied *the intention to withhold it should appear very clearly and plainly.* The defendants argue that such intention can be deduced from the fact that three other sections of the statute (Sections 9, 16 and 18) each declaring certain types of conduct illegal, all expressly provide for a civil action by a person injured and for incidents and limitations of it, whereas Sec. 10 does not. The argument is not without force. Were the whole question one of statutory interpretation it might be convincing, but the question is only partly such. *It is whether an intention can be implied to deny a remedy and to wipe out a liability which, normally, by virtue of basic principles of tort law*

---

3. Cf. Ruder, Civil Liability Under Rule 10b–5: Judicial Revision of the Legislative Intent?, 57 Nw.U.L.Rev. 627 (1963); Jo- seph, Civil Liability Under Rule 10b–5: A Reply, 59 Nw.U.L.Rev. 171 (1964).

uccompanies the doing of the prohibited act. Where, as here, the whole statute discloses a broad purpose to regulate securities transactions of all kinds and, as a part of such regulation, the specific section in question provides for the elimination of all manipulative or deceptive methods in such transactions, the construction contended for by the defendants may not be adopted. In other words, in view of the general purpose of the Act, the mere omission of an express provision for civil liability is not sufficient to negative what the general law implies." [4] [Italics added.]

Under this approach, of course, any violation of any section of the statutes or of any rule of the Commission would seem to create a cause of action in favor of any one injured by such violation, since the statutes were repeatedly stated in Congress and in the very text of the statutes themselves to be for the protection of investors and the rules of the Commission must be issued "for the protection of investors" in order for the Commission to have any authority to issue them. Therefore, all that a plaintiff need do was to identify himself as an "investor", which would presumably include every purchaser and every seller of securities—in the *Kardon* case itself, the plaintiff was a seller of securities rather than a purchaser, but the court said that he was an "investor" before he sold and that was good enough. The mere fact that the plaintiff was injured by the violation would seem to be sufficient to show that he was the type of investor which the statute or rule was intended to protect.

The further development of this issue since 1946 is explored in the cases and notes which follow in this Chapter.

J.I. CASE CO. v. BORAK
United States Supreme Court, 1964.
377 U.S. 426, 84 S.Ct. 1555, 12 L.Ed.2d 423.

MR. JUSTICE CLARK delivered the opinion of the Court.

This is a civil action brought by respondent, a stockholder of petitioner J.I. Case Company, charging deprivation of the pre-emptive rights of respondent and other shareholders by reason of a merger between Case and the American Tractor Corporation. It is alleged that the merger was effected through the circulation of a false and misleading proxy statement by those proposing the merger. The complaint was in two counts, the first based on diversity and claiming a breach of the directors' fiduciary duty to the stockholders. The second count alleged a violation of § 14(a) of the Securities Exchange Act of 1934 with reference to the proxy solicitation material. The trial court held that as to this count it had no power to redress the alleged violations of the Act but was limited solely to the granting of declaratory relief thereon under § 27 of the Act. The court held Wis.Stat.1961, § 180.405(4), which requires posting security for expenses in derivative actions, applicable to both counts, except that portion of Count 2 requesting declaratory relief. It ordered the respondent to furnish a bond in the amount of $75,000 thereunder and, upon his failure to do so, dismissed the complaint, save that part of Count 2 seeking a declaratory judgment. On interlocutory appeal the Court of Appeals reversed on both counts, holding that the District Court had the power to

4. 69 F.Supp. at 513–514.

grant remedial relief and that the Wisconsin statute was not applicable. 317 F.2d 838. We granted certiorari. 375 U.S. 901. We consider only the question of whether § 27 of the Act authorizes a federal cause of action for rescission or damages to a corporate stockholder with respect to a consummated merger which was authorized pursuant to the use of a proxy statement alleged to contain false and misleading statements violative of § 14(a) of the Act. This being the sole question raised by petitioners in their petition for certiorari, we will not consider other questions subsequently presented. See Supreme Court Rule 40(1)(d)(2); Local 1976, United Brotherhood of Carpenters v. Labor Board, 357 U.S. 93, 96 (1958); Irvine v. California, 347 U.S. 128, 129–130 (1954).

I.

Respondent, the owner of 2,000 shares of common stock of Case acquired prior to the merger, brought this suit based on diversity jurisdiction seeking to enjoin a proposed merger between Case and the American Tractor Corporation (ATC) on various grounds, including breach of the fiduciary duties of the Case directors, self-dealing among the management of Case and ATC and misrepresentations contained in the material circulated to obtain proxies. The injunction was denied and the merger was thereafter consummated. Subsequently successive amended complaints were filed and the case was heard on the aforesaid two-count complaint. The claims pertinent to the asserted violation of the Securities Exchange Act were predicated on diversity jurisdiction as well as on § 27 of the Act. They alleged: that petitioners, or their predecessors, solicited or permitted their names to be used in the solicitation of proxies of Case stockholders for use at a special stockholders' meeting at which the proposed merger with ATC was to be voted upon; that the proxy solicitation material so circulated was false and misleading in violation of § 14(a) of the Act and Rule 14a–9 which the Commission had promulgated thereunder; that the merger was approved at the meeting by a small margin of votes and was thereafter consummated; that the merger would not have been approved but for the false and misleading statements in the proxy solicitation material; and that Case stockholders were damaged thereby. The respondent sought judgment holding the merger void and damages for himself and all other stockholders similarly situated, as well as such further relief "as equity shall require." The District Court ruled that the Wisconsin security for expenses statute did not apply to Count 2 since it arose under federal law. However, the court found that its jurisdiction was limited to declaratory relief in a private, as opposed to a government, suit alleging violation of § 14(a) of the Act. Since the additional equitable relief and damages prayed for by the respondent would, therefore, be available only under state law, it ruled those claims subject to the security for expenses statute. After setting the amount of security at $75,000 and upon the representation of counsel that the security would not be posted, the court dismissed the complaint, save that portion of Count 2 seeking a declaration that the proxy solicitation material was false and misleading and that the proxies and, hence, the merger were void.

II.

It appears clear that private parties have a right under § 27 to bring suit for violation of § 14(a) of the Act. Indeed, this section specifically grants the appropriate District Courts jurisdiction over "all suits in equity and actions at law brought to enforce any liability or duty created" under the Act. The petitioners make no concessions, however, emphasizing that Congress made no specific reference to a private right of action in § 14(a); that, in any event, the right would not extend to derivative suits and should be limited to prospective relief only. In addition, some of the petitioners argue that the merger can be dissolved only if it was fraudulent or nonbeneficial, issues upon which the proxy material would not bear. But the causal relationship of the proxy material and the merger are questions of fact to be resolved at trial, not here. We therefore do not discuss this point further.

III.

While the respondent contends that his Count 2 claim is not a derivative one, we need not embrace that view, for we believe that a right of action exists as to both derivative and direct causes.

The purpose of § 14(a) is to prevent management or others from obtaining authorization for corporate action by means of deceptive or inadequate disclosure in proxy solicitation. The section stemmed from the congressional belief that "[f]air corporate suffrage is an important right that should attach to every equity security bought on a public exchange." H.R.Rep. No. 1383, 73d Cong., 2d Sess., 13. It was intended to "control the conditions under which proxies may be solicited with a view to preventing the recurrence of abuses which * * * [had] frustrated the free exercise of the voting rights of stockholders." Id., at 14. "Too often proxies are solicited without explanation to the stockholder of the real nature of the questions for which authority to cast his vote is sought." S.Rep. No. 792, 73d Cong., 2d Sess., 12. These broad remedial purposes are evidenced in the language of the section which makes it "unlawful for any person * * * to solicit or to permit the use of his name to solicit any proxy or consent or authorization in respect of any security * * * registered on any national securities exchange in contravention of such rules and regulations as the Commission may prescribe as necessary or appropriate in the public interest *or for the protection of investors.*" (Italics supplied.) While this language makes no specific reference to a private right of action, among its chief purposes is "the protection of investors," which certainly implies the availability of judicial relief where necessary to achieve that result.

The injury which a stockholder suffers from corporate action pursuant to a deceptive proxy solicitation ordinarily flows from the damage done the corporation, rather than from the damage inflicted directly upon the stockholder. The damage suffered results not from the deceit practiced on him alone but rather from the deceit practiced on the stockholders as a group. To hold that derivative actions are not within the sweep of the section would therefore be tantamount to a denial of private relief. Private enforcement of the proxy rules provides a necessary supplement to Commission action. As in anti-trust treble damage litigation, the possibility of civil damages or injunctive relief serves as a most effective weapon in the enforcement of the proxy requirements. The Commission advises that it examines over 2,000 proxy statements annually and each of them must necessarily be expedited. Time does not permit an independent examinatior. of the facts set out in the proxy material and this results in the Commission acceptance of the representations contained therein at their face value, unless contrary to other material on file with it. Indeed, on the allegations of respondent's complaint, the proxy material failed to disclose alleged unlawful market manipulation of the stock of ATC, and this unlawful manipulation would not have been apparent to the Commission until after the merger.

We, therefore, believe that under the circumstances here it is the duty of the courts to be alert to provide such remedies as are necessary to make effective the congressional purpose. * * *

* * *

Nor do we find merit in the contention that such remedies are limited to prospective relief. This was the position taken in Dann v. Studebaker-Packard Corp., 288 F.2d 201, where it was held that the "preponderance of questions of state law which would have to be interpreted and applied in order to grant the relief sought * * * is so great that the federal question involved * * * is really negligible in comparison." At 214. But we believe that the overriding federal law applicable here would, where the facts required, control the appropriateness of redress despite the provisions of state corporation law, for it "is not uncommon for federal courts to fashion federal law where federal rights are concerned." Textile Workers v. Lincoln Mills, 353 U.S. 448, 457 (1957). In addition, the fact that questions of state law must be decided does not change the character of the right; it remains federal. As Chief Justice Marshall said in Osborn v. Bank of the United States, 9 Wheat. 738 (1824):

"If this were sufficient to withdraw a case from the jurisdiction of the federal Courts, almost every case, although involving the construction of a law, would be withdrawn * * *." At 819–820, 6 L.Ed. 223, 224.

Moreover, if federal jurisdiction were limited to the granting of declaratory relief, victims of deceptive proxy statements would be obliged to go into state courts for remedial relief. And if the law of the State happened to attach no responsibility to the use of misleading proxy statements, the whole purpose of the section might be frustrated. Furthermore, the hurdles that the victim might face (such as separate suits, as contemplated by Dann v. Studebaker-Packard Corp. supra, security for expenses statutes, bringing in all parties necessary for complete relief, etc.) might well prove insuperable to effective relief.

IV.

Our finding that federal courts have the power to grant all necessary remedial relief is not to be construed as any indication of what we believe to be the necessary and appropriate relief in this case. We are concerned here only with a determination that federal jurisdiction for this purpose does exist. Whatever remedy is necessary must await the trial on the merits.

The other contentions of the petitioners are denied.

Affirmed.[a]

---

a. [Eds.] The J.I. Case Co. case is noted in 64 Colum.L.Rev. 1336 (1964); 50 Corn. L.Q. 370 (1965); 59 Nw.U.L.Rev. 809 (1965); 1964 U.Ill.L.F. 838 (1964); 18 Vand.L.Rev. 275 (1964).

PIPER v. CHRIS–CRAFT INDUSTRIES, INC.
Supreme Court of the United States, 1977.
430 U.S. 1, 97 S.Ct. 926, 51 L.Ed.2d 124.

MR. CHIEF JUSTICE BURGER delivered the opinion of the Court.

We granted certiorari in these cases to consider, among other issues, whether an unsuccessful tender offeror in a contest for control of a corporation has an implied cause of action for damages under § 14(e) of the Securities Exchange Act of 1934, as amended by the Williams Act of 1968, or under Rule 10b–6, based on alleged antifraud violations by the successful competitor, its investment adviser, and individuals comprising the management of the target corporation.

I

Background

The factual background of this complex contest for control, including the protracted litigation culminating in the case now before us, is essential to a full understanding of the contending parties' claims.

The three petitions present questions of first impression, arising out of a "sophisticated and hard fought contest" for control of Piper Aircraft Corporation, a Pennsylvania-based manufacturer of light aircraft. Piper's management consisted principally of members of the Piper family, who owned 31% of Piper's outstanding stock. Chris-Craft Industries, Inc., a diversified manufacturer of recreational products, attempted to secure voting control of Piper through cash and exchange tender offers for Piper common stock. Chris-Craft's takeover attempt failed, and Bangor Punta Corporation, with the support of the Piper family, obtained control of Piper in September 1969. Chris-Craft brought suit under § 14(e) of the Securities Exchange Act of 1934 and Rule 10b–6, alleging that Bangor Punta achieved control of the target corporation as a result of violations of the federal securities laws by the Piper family, Bangor Punta, and Bangor Punta's underwriter, First Boston Corporation, who together had successfully repelled Chris-Craft's takeover attempt.

The struggle for control of Piper began in December 1968. At that time, Chris-Craft began making cash purchases of Piper common stock. By January 22, 1969, Chris-Craft had acquired 203,700 shares, or approximately 13% of Piper's 1,644,790 outstanding shares. On the next day, following unsuccessful preliminary overtures to Piper by Chris-Craft's president, Herbert Siegel, Chris-Craft publicly announced a cash tender offer for up to 300,000 Piper shares at $65 per share, which was approximately $12 above the then current market price. Responding promptly to Chris-Craft's bid, Piper's management met on the same day with the company's investment banker, First Boston, and other advisers. On January 24, the Piper family decided to oppose Chris-Craft's tender offer. As part of its resistance to Chris-Craft's takeover campaign, Piper management sent several letters to the company's stockholders between January 25–27, arguing against acceptance of Chris-Craft's offer. On January 27, a letter to shareholders from W.T. Piper, Jr., president of the company, stated that the Piper Board "has carefully studied this offer and is convinced that it is inadequate and not in the best interests of Piper's shareholders."

In addition to communicating with shareholders, Piper entered into an agreement with Grumman Aircraft Corporation on January 29, whereby Grumman agreed to purchase 300,000 authorized but unissued Piper shares at $65 per share. The agreement increased the amount of stock necessary for Chris-Craft to secure control and thus rendered Piper less vulnerable to Chris-Craft's attack. A Piper press release and letter to shareholders announced the Grumman transaction but failed to state either that Grumman had a "put" or option to sell the shares back to Piper at cost, plus interest, or that Piper was required to maintain the proceeds of the transaction in a separate fund free from liens.

Despite Piper's opposition, Chris-Craft succeeded in acquiring 304,606 shares by the time its cash tender offer expired on February 3. To obtain the additional 17% of Piper stock needed for control, Chris-Craft decided to make an exchange offer of Chris-Craft securities for Piper stock. Although Chris-Craft filed a registration statement and preliminary prospectus with the SEC in late February 1969, the exchange offer did not go into effect until May 15, 1969.

In the meantime, Chris-Craft made cash purchases of Piper stock on the open market until Mr. Siegel, the company's president, was expressly warned by SEC officials that such purchases, when made during the pendency of an exchange offer, violated SEC Rule 10b–6. At Mr. Siegel's direction, Chris-Craft immediately complied with the SEC's directive and canceled all outstanding orders for purchases of Piper stock.

While Chris-Craft's exchange offer was in registration, Piper in March 1969 terminated the agreement with Grumman and entered into negotiations with Bangor Punta. Bangor had initially been contacted by First Boston about the possibility of a Piper takeover in the wake of Chris-Craft's initial cash tender offer in January. With Grumman out of the picture, the Piper family agreed on May 8, 1969, to exchange their 31% stockholdings in Piper for Bangor Punta securities. Bangor also agreed to use its best efforts to achieve control of Piper by means of an exchange offer of Bangor securities for Piper common stock. A press release issued the same day announced the terms of the agreement, including a provision that the forthcoming exchange offer would involve Bangor securities to be valued, in the judgment of First Boston, "at not less than $80 per Piper share."

While awaiting the effective date of its exchange offer, Bangor in mid-May 1969 purchased 120,200 shares of Piper stock in privately negotiated, off-exchange transactions from three large institutional investors. All three purchases were made after the SEC's issuance of a release on May 5 announcing proposed Rule 10b–13, a provision which, upon becoming effective in November 1969, would expressly prohibit a tender offeror from making purchases of the target company's stock during the pendency of an exchange offer. The SEC release stated that the proposed rule was "in effect, a codification of existing interpretations under Rule 10b–6," the provision invoked by SEC officials against Mr. Siegel of Chris-Craft a month earlier. Bangor officials, although aware of the release at the time of the three off-exchange purchases, made no attempt to secure an exemption for the transactions from the SEC, as provided by Rule 10b–6(f). The

Commission, however, took no action concerning these purchases as it had with respect to Chris-Craft's open market transactions.

With these three block purchases, amounting to 7% of Piper stock, Bangor Punta in mid-May took the lead in the takeover contest. The contest then centered upon the competing exchange offers. Chris-Craft's first exchange offer, which began in mid-May 1969, failed to produce tenders of the specified minimum number of Piper shares (80,000). Meanwhile, Bangor Punta's exchange offer, which had been announced on May 8, became effective on July 18. The registration materials which Bangor filed with the SEC in connection with the exchange offer included financial statements, reviewed by First Boston, representing that one of Bangor's subsidiaries, the Bangor and Aroostock Railroad (BAR), had a value of $18.4 million. This valuation was based upon a 1965 appraisal by investment bankers after a proposed sale of the BAR failed to materialize. The financial statements did not indicate that Bangor was considering the sale of BAR or that an offer to purchase the railroad for $5 million had been received.

In the final phase of the see-saw of competing offers, Chris-Craft modified the terms of its previously unsuccessful exchange offer to make it more attractive. The revised offer succeeded in attracting 112,089 additional Piper shares, while Bangor's exchange offer, which terminated on July 29, resulted in the tendering of 110,802 shares. By August 4, 1969, at the conclusion of both offers, Bangor Punta owned a total of 44.5%, while Chris-Craft owned 40.6% of Piper stock. The remainder of Piper stock, 14.9%, remained in the hands of the public.

After completion of their respective exchange offers, both companies renewed market purchases of Piper stock, but Chris-Craft, after purchasing 29,200 shares for cash in mid-August, withdrew from competition. Bangor Punta continued making cash purchases until September 5, by which time it had acquired a majority interest in Piper. The final tally in the nine-month takeover battle showed that Bangor Punta held over 50% and Chris-Craft held 42% of Piper stock.

II

Before either side had achieved control, the contest moved from the marketplace to the courts. Then began more than seven years of complex litigation growing out of the contest for control of Piper Aircraft.

* * *

III

The Williams Act

* * *

Besides requiring disclosure and providing specific benefits for tendering shareholders, the Williams Act also contains a broad antifraud prohibition, which is the basis of Chris-Craft's claim. Section 14(e) of the Act provides:

"It shall be unlawful for any person to make any untrue statement of a material fact or omit to state any material fact necessary in order to make the statements made, in the light of the circumstances under which they are made, not misleading, or to engage in any fraudulent, deceptive, or manipulative acts or practices, in connection with any tender offer or request or invitation for tenders, or any solicitation of security holders in opposition to or in favor of any such offer, request, or invitation."

This provision was expressly directed at the conduct of a broad range of persons, including those engaged in making or opposing tender offers or otherwise seeking to influence the decision of investors or the outcome of the tender offer. Senate Report, at 11.

The threshold issue in these cases is whether tender offerors such as Chris-Craft, whose activities are regulated by the Williams Act, have a cause of action for damages against other regulated parties under the statute on a claim that antifraud violations by other parties have frustrated the bidder's efforts to obtain control of the target corporation. Without reading such a cause of action into the Act, none of the other issues need be reached.

IV

Our analysis begins, of course, with the statute itself. Section 14(e), like § 10(b), makes no provision whatever for a private cause of action, such as those explicitly provided in other sections of the 1933 and 1934 Acts. E.g., §§ 11, 12, 15 of the 1933 Act, §§ 9, 16, 18, 20 of the 1934 Act. This Court has nonetheless held that in some circumstances a private cause of action can be implied with respect to the 1934 Act's antifraud provisions, even though the relevant provisions are silent as to remedies. J.I. Case Co. v. Borak, 377 U.S. 426 (1964) (§ 14(a)); Superintendent of Insurance v. Bankers Life & Cas. Co., 404 U.S. 6, 13 n. 9 (1971) (§ 10(b)).

The reasoning of these holdings is that, where congressional purposes are likely to be undermined absent private enforcement, private remedies may be implied in favor of the particular class intended to be protected by the statute. * * *

Against this background we must consider whether § 14(e), which is entirely silent as to private remedies, permits this Court to read into the statute a damages remedy for unsuccessful tender offerors. To resolve that question we turn to the legislative history to discern the congressional purpose underlying the specific statutory prohibition in § 14(e). Once we identify the legislative purpose, we must then determine whether the creation by judicial interpretation of the implied cause of action asserted by Chris-Craft is necessary to effectuate Congress' goals.

A

Reliance on legislative history in divining the intent of Congress is, as has often been observed, a step to be taken cautiously. Department of Air Force v. Rose, 425 U.S. 352, 388–389 (1976) (Blackmun, J., dissenting); United States v. Public Utilities Comm'n, 345 U.S. 295, 319 (1953) (Jackson, J., concurring); Scripps-Howard Radio v. FCC, 316 U.S. 4, 11 (1942). In this case both sides press legislative history on the Court not so much to explain the meaning of the language of a statute as to explain the absence of any express provision for a private cause of action for damages. As Mr. Justice Frankfurter reminded us, "We must be wary against interpolating our notions of policy in the interstices of legislative provisions." Scripps-

Howard Radio v. FCC, 316 U.S., at 11. With that caveat, we turn to the legislative history of the Williams Act.

In introducing the legislation on the Senate floor, the sponsor, Senator Williams stated:

"This legislation will close a significant gap in *investor protection* under the Federal securities laws by requiring the disclosure of pertinent information *to stockholders* when persons seek to obtain control of a corporation by a cash tender offer or through open market or privately negotiated purchases of securities." 113 Cong.Rec. 854 (1967) (remarks of Sen. Williams). (Emphasis supplied.)

* * *

The legislative history thus shows that Congress was intent upon regulating takeover bidders, theretofore operating covertly, in order to protect the shareholders of target companies. That tender offerors were not the intended beneficiaries of the bill was graphically illustrated by the statements of Senator Kuchel, co-sponsor of the legislation, in support of requiring takeover bidders whom he described as "corporate raiders" and "takeover pirates," to disclose their activities.

* * *

The sponsors of this legislation were plainly sensitive to the suggestion that the measure would favor one side or the other in control contests; however, they made it clear that the legislation was designed solely to get needed information to the investor, the constant focal point of the committee hearings. Senator Williams articulated this singularity of purpose, even while advocating neutrality:

"We have taken extreme care to avoid tipping the scales either in favor of management or in favor of the person making the takeover bid. *S. 510 is designed solely to require full and fair disclosure for the benefit of investors.*" 113 Cong.Rec. 24664 (Aug. 30, 1967) (remarks of Sen. Williams). (Emphasis supplied.)

Accordingly, the congressional policy of "even-handedness" is nonprobative of the quite disparate proposition that the Williams Act was intended to confer rights for money damages upon an injured takeover bidder.

Besides the policy of even-handedness, Chris-Craft emphasizes that the matter of implied private causes of action was raised in written submissions to the Senate Subcommittee. Specifically, Chris-Craft points to the written statements of Professors Israels and Painter, who made reference to J.I. Case v. Borak, supra. Chris-Craft contends, therefore, that Congress was aware that private actions were implicit in § 14(e).

But this conclusion places more freight on the passing reference to *Borak* than can reasonably be carried. Even accepting the value of written statements received without comment by the committee and without cross-examination, the statements do not refer to implied private actions by *offeror-bidders.* * * *

* * *

The legislative history thus shows that the sole purpose of the Williams Act was the protection of investors who are confronted with a tender offer. As we stated in Rondeau v. Mosinee Paper Corp., 422 U.S., at 58, "[t]he purpose of the Williams Act is to insure that public shareholders who are confronted by a cash tender offer for their stock will not be required to respond without adequate information * * *." We find no hint in the legislative history, on which respondent so heavily relies, that Congress contemplated a private cause of action for damages by one of several contending offerors against a successful bidder or by a losing contender against the target corporation.

* * *

B

Our conclusion as to the legislative history is confirmed by the analysis in Cort v. Ash, 422 U.S. 66 (1975). There, the Court identified four factors as "relevant" in determining whether a private remedy is implicit in a statute not expressly providing one. The first is whether the plaintiff is " 'one of the class for whose *especial* benefit the statute was enacted * * *.' " Id., at 78. (Emphasis in original.) As previously indicated, examination of the statute and its genesis shows that Chris-Craft is not an intended beneficiary of the Williams Act, and surely is not one "for whose *especial* benefit the statute was enacted." Id., at 78. To the contrary, Chris-Craft is a member of the class whose activities Congress intended to regulate for the protection and benefit of an entirely distinct class, shareholders-offerees. As a party whose previously unregulated conduct was purposefully brought under federal control by the statute, Chris-Craft can scarcely lay claim to the status of "beneficiary" whom Congress considered in need of protection.

Second, in Cort v. Ash we inquired whether there is "any indication of legislative intent, explicit or implicit, either to create such a remedy or to deny one?" Id., at 78. Although the historical materials are barren of any express intent to deny a damages remedy to tender offerors as a class, there is, as we have noted, no indication that Congress intended to create a damages remedy in favor of the loser in a contest for control. Fairly read, we think the legislative documents evince the narrow intent to curb the unregulated activities of tender offerors. The expression of this purpose, which pervades the legislative history, negates the claim that tender offerors were intended to have additional weapons in the form of an implied cause of action for damages, particularly if a private damages action confers no advantage on the expressly protected class of shareholders-offerees, a matter we discuss later. Infra, at 948.

Chris-Craft argues, however, that Congress intended standing under § 14(e) to encompass tender offerors since the statute, unlike § 10(b), does not contain the limiting language, "in connection with the purchase or sale" of securities. Instead, in § 14(e), Congress broadly proscribed fraudulent activities "in connection with any tender offer * * * or any solicitation * * * in opposition to or in favor of any such offer * * *."

The omission of the purchaser-seller requirement does not mean, however, that Chris-Craft has standing to sue for damages under § 14(e) in its capacity as a takeover bidder. It may well be that Congress desired to protect, among others, shareholders-offerees who decided not to tender their stock due to fraudulent misrepresentations by persons opposed to a takeover attempt. See generally 1 A. Bromberg, supra, § 6.3(101b), at 122.17. See also Senate Report, at 2; House Report, at 3. These shareholders, who might not enjoy the protection of § 10(b) under Blue Chip Stamps v. Manor Drug Stores, supra, could perhaps state a claim under

§ 14(e), even though they did not tender their securities.[25] But increased protection, if any, conferred upon the class of shareholders-offerees by the elimination of the purchaser-seller restriction can scarcely be interpreted as giving protection to the entirely separate and unrelated class of persons whose conduct the statute is designed to regulate.

Third, Cort v. Ash tells us that we must ascertain whether it is "consistent with the underlying purposes of the legislative scheme to imply such a remedy for the plaintiff." Ibid. We conclude that it is not. As a disclosure mechanism aimed especially at protecting shareholders of target corporations, the Williams Act cannot consistently be interpreted as conferring a monetary remedy upon regulated parties, particularly where the award would not redound to the direct benefit of the protected class. Although it is correct to say that the $36 million damage award indirectly benefits those Piper shareholders who became Chris-Craft shareholders when they accepted Chris-Craft's exchange offer, it is equally true that the damage award injures those Piper shareholders who exchanged their shares for Bangor Punta's stock and who, as Bangor Punta shareholders, would necessarily bear a large part of the burden of any judgment against Bangor Punta. The class sought to be protected by the Williams Act are the shareholders of the *target* corporation; hence it can hardly be said that their interests as a class are served by a judgment in favor of Chris-Craft and against Bangor Punta. Moreover, the damages are awarded to the very party whose activities Congress intended to curb; Chris-Craft did not sue in the capacity of an injured Piper shareholder, but as a defeated tender offeror.

Nor can we agree that an ever-present threat of damages against a successful contestant in a battle for control will provide significant additional protection for shareholders in general. The deterrent value, if any, of such awards can never be ascertained with precision. More likely, however, is the prospect that shareholders may be prejudiced because some tender offers may never be made if there is a possibility of massive damages claims for what courts subsequently hold to be an actionable violation of § 14(e).[26] Even a contestant who "wins the battle" for control may well wind up exposed to a costly "war" in a later and successful defense of its victory. Or at worst—on Chris-Craft's damage theory—the victorious tender offeror or the target corporation might be subject to a large substantive judgment, plus high costs of litigation.

In short, we conclude that shareholder protection, if enhanced at all by damages awards such as Chris-Craft contends for, can more directly be

---

25. This case, of course, does not present that issue, and we express no view on it.

26. The liability of the Piper family petitioners is instructive in this regard. Several able federal judges, including District Judges Tenney and Pollack and Chief Judge Lumbard of the Second Circuit, have expressly concluded that the Piper defendants did *not* violate the securities laws in their efforts to defeat Chris-Craft's bid. Judge Mansfield, while of the view that the Pipers had violated § 14(e), was convinced that their violation has not caused injury to Chris-Craft. The legal uncertainties that inevitably pervade this area of the law call into question whether "deterrence" of § 14(e) violations is a meaningful goal, except possibly with respect to the most flagrant sort of violations which no reasonable person could consider lawful. Such cases of flagrant misconduct, however, are not apt to occur with frequency, and to the extent that the violations are obvious and serious, injunctive relief at an earlier stage of the contest is apt to be the most efficacious form of remedy.

achieved with other, less drastic means more closely tailored to the precise congressional goal underlying the Williams Act.

Fourth, under the Cort v. Ash analysis, we must decide whether "the cause of action [is] one traditionally relegated to state law * * *." Ibid. Despite the pervasiveness of federal securities regulation, the Court of Appeals concluded in this case that Chris-Craft's complaint would give rise to a cause of action under common-law principles of interference with a prospective commercial advantage. Although Congress is, of course, free to create a remedial scheme in favor of contestants in tender offers, we conclude, as we did in Cort v. Ash, that "it is entirely appropriate in this instance to relegate [the offeror-bidder] and others in [that] situation to whatever remedy is created by state law," at least to the extent that the offeror seeks damages for having been wrongfully denied a "fair opportunity" to compete for control of another corporation.

C

What we have said thus far suggests that, unlike J.I. Case v. Borak, supra, judicially creating a damages action in favor of Chris-Craft is unnecessary to ensure the fulfillment of Congress' purposes in adopting the Williams Act. Even though the SEC operates in this context under the same practical restraints recognized by the Court in *Borak*, institutional limitations alone do not lead to the conclusion that any party interested in a tender offer should have a cause of action for damages against a competing bidder. First, as Judge Friendly observed in Electronic Specialty Co. v. International Controls Corp., 409 F.2d 937, 947 (C.A.2 1969), in corporate control contests the stage of preliminary injunctive relief, rather than post-contest lawsuits, "is the time when relief can best be given." Furthermore, awarding damages to parties other than the protected class of shareholders has only a remote, if any, bearing upon implementing the congressional policy of protecting shareholders who must decide whether to tender or retain their stock.[28] Indeed, as we suggested earlier, a damages award of this nature may well be inconsistent with the interests of many members of the protected class and of only indirect value to shareholders who accepted the exchange offer of the defeated takeover contestant.

We therefore conclude that Chris-Craft, as a defeated tender offeror, has no implied cause of action for damages under § 14(e).

* * *

[The Court's discussion of liability under Rule 10b–6 is omitted.—Eds.]

VI

Our resolution of these issues makes it unnecessary to address the other questions raised by the parties in their petitions for certiorari. Since we

---

28. Our holding is a limited one. Whether shareholders-offerees, the class protected by § 14(e), have an implied cause of action under § 14(e) is not before us, and we intimate no view on the matter. Nor is the target corporation's standing to sue in issue in this case. We hold only that a tender offeror, suing in its capacity as a takeover bidder, does not have standing to sue for damages under the Williams Act.

Our precise holding disposes of many observations made in dissent. Thus, the argument with respect to the "exclusion" from standing for "persons most interested in effective enforcement," infra, at 62, is simply unwarranted in light of today's narrow holding.

have concluded that Chris-Craft cannot avail itself of § 14(e) or Rule 10b–6 in its suit for damages, it is unnecessary to consider the Court of Appeals' holdings with respect to scienter, causation, the calculation of damages, the imposition of joint and several liability, the liability of underwriters in § 14(e) damages actions, and the award of prejudgment interest.

* * *

Accordingly, the judgment of the Court of Appeals is Reversed.

MR. JUSTICE BLACKMUN, concurring in the judgment.

I concur in the judgment. For the reasons set out in MR. JUSTICE STEVENS' dissenting opinion, post, 955, I am willing to begin with the premise that respondent Chris-Craft had "standing" in the sense that it possessed an implied right to sue under § 14(e) of the Securities Exchange Act of 1934. Unlike the dissenters, however, I do not conclude, from this, that the Court of Appeals' judgment as to liability is to be affirmed. Since I am of the opinion that respondent failed to prove that petitioners' violations of the securities laws caused its injury, I agree with the Court that the judgment below should be reversed.

* * *

MR. JUSTICE STEVENS, with whom MR. JUSTICE BRENNAN joins, dissenting.

* * *

TOUCHE ROSS & CO. v. REDINGTON

Supreme Court of the United States, 1979.
442 U.S. 560, 99 S.Ct. 2479, 61 L.Ed.2d 82.

MR. JUSTICE REHNQUIST delivered the opinion of the Court.

Once again, we are called upon to decide whether a private remedy is implicit in a statute not expressly providing one. During this Term alone, we have been asked to undertake this task no less than five times in cases in which we have granted certiorari.[1] Here we decide whether customers of securities brokerage firms that are required to file certain financial reports with regulatory authorities by § 17(a) of the Securities Exchange Act of 1934 (1934 Act) have an implied cause of action for damages under § 17(a) against accountants who audit such reports based on misstatements contained in the reports.

I

Petitioner Touche Ross & Co. is a firm of certified public accountants. Weis Securities, Inc. (Weis), a securities brokerage firm registered as a broker-dealer with the Securities and Exchange Commission (Commission) and a member of the New York Stock Exchange (Exchange), retained Touche Ross to serve as Weis' independent certified public accountant from 1969 to 1973. In this capacity Touche Ross conducted audits of Weis' books and records and prepared for filing with the Commission the annual reports of financial condition required by § 17(a) of the 1934 Act, and the

1. See Chrysler Corp. v. Brown, 441 U.S. 281 (1979); Cannon v. University of Chicago, 441 U.S. 677 (1979); Southeastern Community College v. Davis, 442 U.S. 397 (1979); Transamerica Mortgage Advisors, Inc. v. Lewis, No. 77–1645, cert. granted, 439 U.S. 952 (1978); Touche Ross & Co. v. Redington, No. 78–309, cert. granted, 439 U.S. 979 (1978).

rules and regulations adopted thereunder. Touche Ross also prepared for Weis responses to financial questionnaires required by the Exchange of its member firms.

This case arises out of the insolvency and liquidation of Weis. In 1973, the Commission and the Exchange learned of Weis' precarious financial condition and of possible violations of the 1934 Act by Weis and its officers. In May 1973, the Commission sought and was granted an injunction barring Weis and five of its officers from conducting business in violation of the 1934 Act.[4] At the same time, the Securities Investor Protection Corporation (SIPC), pursuant to statutory authority, applied in the United States District Court for the Southern District of New York for a decree adjudging that Weis' customers were in need of the protection afforded by the Securities Investor Protection Act (SIPA), 84 Stat. 1636, 15 U.S.C. § 78aaa et seq. The District Court granted the requested decree and appointed respondent Redington (Trustee) to act as trustee in the liquidation of the Weis business under SIPA.

During the liquidation, Weis' cash and securities on hand appeared to be insufficient to make whole those customers who had left assets or deposits with Weis. Accordingly, pursuant to SIPA, SIPC advanced the Trustee $14 million to satisfy, up to specified statutory limits, the claims of the approximately 34,000 Weis customers and certain other creditors of Weis. Despite the advance of $14 million by SIPC, there apparently remain several million dollars of unsatisfied customer claims.

In 1976, SIPC and the Trustee filed this action for damages against Touche Ross in the District Court for the Southern District of New York. The "common allegations" of the complaint, which at this stage of the case we must accept as true, aver that certain of Weis' officers conspired to conceal substantial operating losses during its 1972 fiscal year by falsifying financial reports required to be filed with regulatory authorities pursuant to § 17(a) of the 1934 Act. App. 8. SIPC and the Trustee seek to impose liability upon Touche Ross by reason of its allegedly improper audit and certification of the 1972 Weis financial statements and preparation of answers to the Exchange financial questionnaire. Id., at 15–19. The complaint alleges that because of its improper conduct, Touche Ross breached duties that it owed SIPC, the Trustee and others under the common law, § 17(a) and the regulations thereunder and that Touche Ross' alleged dereliction prevented Weis' true financial condition from becoming known until it was too late to take remedial action to forestall liquidation or to lessen the adverse financial consequences of such a liquidation to the Weis customers. Id., at 8–9. The trustee seeks to recover $51 million on behalf of Weis in its own right and on behalf of the customers of Weis whose property the Trustee was unable to return. SIPC claims $14 million, either as subrogee of Weis' customers whose claims it has paid under SIPA or in its own right. The federal claims are based on § 17(a) of the 1934 Act; the complaint also alleges several state common-law causes of action

---

4. Some months later several of Weis' officers were indicted, in part, for a conspiracy to violate and a number of substantive violations of the recordkeeping and reporting regulations adopted by the Commission under § 17(a). United States v. Arthur Levine, et al., 73 Crim. 693, SDNY; see United States v. Solomon, 509 F.2d 863, 865 (C.A.2 1975). Four of the defendants pleaded guilty to at least one substantive count; the other was found guilty of one substantive count. Ibid.

based on accountants' negligence, breach of contract and breach of warranty.

The District Court dismissed the complaint, holding that no claim for relief was stated because no private cause of action could be implied from § 17(a). 428 F.Supp. 483 (1977). A divided panel of the Second Circuit reversed. Nos. 77–7183, 77–7186, Apr. 21, 1978 * * *. The court first found that § 17(a) imposes a duty on accountants. * * * It next concluded, based on the factors set forth in Cort v. Ash, 422 U.S. 66, 78 (1975), that an accountant's breach of his § 17(a) duty gives rise to an implied private right of action for damages in favor of a broker-dealer's customers, even though it acknowledged that the "legislative history of the section is mute on the issue." * * * The court held that SIPC and the Trustee could assert this implied cause of action on behalf of the Weis customers. We granted certiorari, 439 U.S. 979 (1978), and we now reverse.

II

The question of the existence of a statutory cause of action is, of course, one of statutory construction. Cannon v. University of Chicago, 441 U.S. 677, 688 (1979); see National Railroad Passenger Corp. v. National Association of Railroad Passengers, 414 U.S. 453, 458 (1974) (hereinafter *Amtrak*). SIPC's argument in favor of implication of a private right of action based on tort principles, therefore, is entirely misplaced. Brief for SIPC 22–23. As we recently have emphasized, "the fact that a federal statute has been violated and some person harmed does not automatically give rise to a private cause of action in favor of that person." Cannon v. University of Chicago, supra, at 688. Instead, our task is limited solely to determining whether Congress intended to create the private right of action asserted by SIPC and the Trustee. And as with any case involving the interpretation of a statute, our analysis must begin with the language of the statute itself. Cannon v. University of Chicago, supra, at 689; Teamsters v. Daniel, 439 U.S. 551, 558 (1979); Santa Fe Indus., Inc. v. Green, 430 U.S. 462, 472 (1977); Piper v. Chris-Craft Indus., Inc., 430 U.S. 1, 24 (1977); Ernst & Ernst v. Hochfelder, 425 U.S. 185, 197 (1976).

At the time pertinent to the case before us, § 17(a) read, in relevant part as follows:

> "Every national securities exchange, every member thereof * * * and every broker or dealer registered pursuant to * * * this title, shall make, keep and preserve for such periods, such accounts, correspondence * * * and other records, and make such reports, as the Commission by its rules and regulations may prescribe as necessary or appropriate in the public interest or for the protection of investors."

In terms, § 17(a) simply requires broker-dealers and others to keep such records and file such reports as the Commission may prescribe. It does not, by its terms, purport to create a private cause of action in favor of anyone. It is true that in the past our cases have held that in certain circumstances a private right of action may be implied in a statute not expressly providing one. But in those cases finding such implied private remedies, the statute in question at least prohibited certain conduct or created federal rights in favor of private parties. E.g., Cannon v. University of Chicago, supra (20 U.S.C. § 1681); Johnson v. Railway Express Agency,

Inc., 421 U.S. 454 (1975) (42 U.S.C. § 1981); Superintendent of Ins. v. Bankers Life & Cas. Co., 404 U.S. 6 (1971) (15 U.S.C. § 78j(b)); Sullivan v. Little Hunting Park, Inc., 396 U.S. 229 (1969) (42 U.S.C. § 1982); Allen v. State Board of Elections, 393 U.S. 544 (1969) (42 U.S.C. § 1973c); Jones v. Alfred H. Mayer Co., 392 U.S. 409 (1968) (42 U.S.C. § 1982); J.I. Case Co. v. Borak, 377 U.S. 426 (1964) (15 U.S.C. § 78n(a)). By contrast, § 17(a) neither confers rights on private parties nor proscribes any conduct as unlawful.

The intent of § 17(a) is evident from its face. Section 17(a) is like provisions in countless other statutes that simply require certain regulated businesses to keep records and file periodic reports to enable the relevant governmental authorities to perform their regulatory functions. The reports and records provide the regulatory authorities with the necessary information to oversee compliance with and enforce the various statutes and regulations with which they are concerned. In this case, the § 17(a) reports, along with inspections and other information, enable the Commission and the Exchange to ensure compliance with the "net capital rule," the principal regulatory tool by which the Commission and the Exchange monitor the financial health of brokerage firms and protect customers from the risks involved in leaving their cash and securities with broker-dealers. The information contained in the § 17(a) reports is intended to provide the Commission, the Exchange and other authorities with a sufficiently early warning to enable them to take appropriate action to protect investors before the financial collapse of the particular broker-dealer involved. But § 17(a) does not by any stretch of its language purport to confer private damage rights or, indeed, any remedy in the event the regulatory authorities are unsuccessful in achieving their objectives and the broker becomes insolvent before corrective steps can be taken. By its terms, § 17(a) is forward-looking, not retrospective; it seeks to forestall insolvency, not to provide recompense after it has occurred. In short, there is no basis in the language of § 17(a) for inferring that a civil cause of action for damages lay in favor of anyone. Cort v. Ash, 422 U.S., at 79.

As the Court of Appeals recognized, the legislative history of the 1934 Act is entirely silent on the question whether a private right of action for damages should or should not be available under § 17(a) in the circumstances of this case. * * * SIPC and the Trustee nevertheless argue that because Congress did not express an intent to deny a private cause of action under § 17(a), this Court should infer one. But implying a private right of action on the basis of congressional silence is a hazardous enterprise, at best. See Santa Clara Pueblo v. Martinez, 436 U.S. 49, 64 (1978). And where, as here, the plain language of the provision weighs against implication of a private remedy, the fact that there is no suggestion whatsoever in the legislative history that § 17(a) may give rise to suits for damages reinforces our decision not to find such a right of action implicit within the section. See Cort v. Ash, supra, at 82–84; cf. Securities Investor Protection Corp. v. Barbour, supra; *Amtrak,* supra; T.I.M.E., Inc. v. United States, 359 U.S. 464 (1959).[11]

---

11. What legislative history there is of § 17(a) simply confirms our belief that § 17(a) was intended solely to be an integral part of a system of preventative reporting and monitoring, and not to provide remedies to customers for losses after liquidation. S.Rep. No. 792, 73d Cong., 2d Sess. 13, 21 (1934); H.R.Rep. No. 1383, 73d Cong., 2d Sess., 25 (1934); Hearings before the House Interstate and Foreign Com-

Further justification for our decision not to imply the private remedy that SIPC and the Trustee seek to establish may be found in the statutory scheme of which § 17(a) is a part. First, § 17(a) is flanked by provisions of the 1934 Act that explicitly grant private causes of action. § 16(b), § 18(a). Section 9(e) of the 1934 Act also expressly provides a private right of action. See also § 20. Obviously, then, when Congress wished to provide a private damage remedy, it knew how to do so and did so expressly. Blue Chip Stamps v. Manor Drug Stores, 421 U.S. 723, 734 (1975); see *Amtrak,* 414 U.S., at 458; T.I.M.E., Inc. v. United States, supra, at 471.

Second, § 18(a) creates a private cause of action against persons, such as accountants, who "make or cause to be made" materially misleading statements in any reports or other documents filed with the Commission, although the cause of action is limited to persons who, in reliance on the statements, purchased or sold a security whose price was affected by the statements. * * * see Ernst & Ernst v. Hochfelder, 425 U.S., at 211 n. 31; Blue Chip Stamps v. Manor Drug Stores, supra, at 736. Since SIPC and the Trustee do not allege that the Weis customers purchased or sold securities in reliance on the § 17(a) reports at issue, they cannot sue Touche Ross under § 18(a).[13] Instead, their claim is that the Weis customers did not get the enforcement action they would have received if the § 17(a) reports had been accurate. SIPC and the Trustee argue that § 18(a) cannot provide the exclusive remedy for misstatements made in § 17(a) reports because the cause of action created by § 18(a) is expressly limited to purchasers and sellers. They assert that Congress could not have intended in § 18(a) to deprive customers, such as those whom they seek to represent, of a cause of action for misstatements contained in § 17(a) reports.

There is evidence to support the view that § 18(a) was intended to provide the exclusive remedy for misstatements contained in any reports filed with the Commission, including those filed pursuant to § 17(a). Certainly, SIPC and the Trustee have pointed to no evidence of a legislative intent to except § 17(a) reports from § 18(a)'s purview. Cf. Securities Investor Protection Corp., 421 U.S., at 419–420; *Amtrak,* 414 U.S., at 458. But we need not decide whether Congress expressly intended § 18(a) to provide the exclusive remedy for misstatements contained in § 17(a) reports. For where the principal express civil remedy for misstatements in reports created by Congress contemporaneously with the passage of § 17(a) is by its terms limited to purchasers and sellers of securities, we are extremely reluctant to imply a cause of action in § 17(a) that is significantly broader than the remedy that Congress chose to provide. Blue Chip

merce Committee on H.R. 7852 and H.R. 8720, 73d Cong., 2d Sess., 22, 225–226 (1934). See also S.Rep. No. 94–75, 94th Cong., 1st Sess., 119 (1975) (legislative history of the 1975 amendments to § 17).

13. In another action arising out of the Weis financial collapse, the District Court has sustained a § 18(a) claim against Touche Ross by a bank that allegedly purchased securities of Weis in reliance upon the § 17(a) reports involved in this case. Exchange National Bank v. Touche Ross & Co., 75 Civ. 916 (S.D.N.Y.); see Redington v. Touche Ross & Co., App. 215 n. 5 (Mulli-

gan, J., dissenting). And in a case related to the instant case, the customers of Weis brought a class action against Touche Ross under § 18(a), claiming, *inter alia,* that Touche Ross violated Commission Rule 17a–5. The District Court in that case dismissed the complaint on the ground that the plaintiffs did not meet the purchaser-seller requirement of § 18(a) and thus could not maintain an action under that section. Rich v. Touche Ross & Co., 415 F.Supp. 95, 102–104 (S.D.N.Y.1976). We express no view as to the correctness of either of these rulings.

Stamps v. Manor Drug Stores, supra, at 735–736; see Ernst & Ernst v. Hochfelder, supra, at 210; Securities Investor Protection Corp. v. Barbour, supra, at 421–423; *Amtrak,* supra, at 458; cf. T.I.M.E., Inc. v. United States, 359 U.S., at 471.

SIPC and the Trustee urge, and the Court of Appeals agreed, that the analysis should not stop here. Relying on the factors set forth in Cort v. Ash, 422 U.S., at 78, they assert that we also must consider whether an implied private remedy is necessary to "effectuate the purpose of the section" and whether the cause of action is one traditionally relegated to state law. SIPC and the Trustee contend that implication of a private remedy is essential to the goals of § 17(a) and that enforcement of § 17(a) is properly a matter of federal, not state, concern. Brief for Trustee 30–35; Brief for SIPC 42–52. We need not reach the merits of the arguments concerning the "necessity" of implying a private remedy and the proper forum for enforcement of the rights asserted by SIPC and the Trustee, for we believe such inquiries have little relevance to the decision of this case. It is true that in Cort v. Ash, supra, the Court set forth four factors that it considered "relevant" in determining whether a private remedy is implicit in a statute not expressly providing one. But the Court did not decide that each of these factors is entitled to equal weight. The central inquiry remains whether Congress intended to create, either expressly or by implication, a private cause of action. Indeed, the first three factors discussed in *Cort*—the language and focus of the statute, its legislative history, and its purpose, see 422 U.S., at 78—are ones traditionally relied upon in determining legislative intent. Here, the statute by its terms grants no private rights to any identifiable class and proscribes no conduct as unlawful. And the parties as well as the Court of Appeals agree that the legislative history of the 1934 Act simply does not speak to the issue of private remedies under § 17(a). At least in such a case as this, the inquiry ends there. The question whether Congress, either expressly or by implication, intended to create a private right of action, has been definitely answered in the negative.

Finally, SIPC and the Trustee argue that our decision in J.I. Case v. Borak, supra, requires implication of a private cause of action under § 17(a). In *Borak,* the Court found in § 14(a) of the 1934 Act an implied cause of action for damages in favor of shareholders for losses resulting from deceptive proxy solicitations in violation of § 14(a). SIPC and the Trustee emphasize language in *Borak* that discusses the remedial purposes of the 1934 Act and § 27 of the Act, which inter alia, grants to federal district courts the exclusive jurisdiction of violations of the Act and suits to enforce any liability or duty created by the Act or the rules and regulations thereunder. They argue that Touche Ross has breached its duties under § 17(a) and the rules adopted thereunder and that in view of § 27 and of the remedial purposes of the 1934 Act, federal courts should provide a damage remedy for the breach.[18]

---

18. SIPC and the Trustee also appear to suggest that the rules adopted under § 17(a) can themselves provide the source of an implied damage remedy even if § 17(a) itself cannot. See Brief for SIPC 27–31; Brief for Trustee 25–35; n. 3, supra. It suffices to say, however, that the language of the statute and not the rules must control. Ernst & Ernst v. Hochfelder, 425 U.S., at 214; Santa Fe Indus. v. Green, 430 U.S., at 472.

The reliance of SIPC and the Trustee on § 27 is misplaced. Section 27 grants jurisdiction to the federal courts and provides for venue and service of process. It creates no cause of action of its own force and effect; it imposes no liabilities. The source of plaintiffs' rights must be found, if at all, in the substantive provisions of the 1934 Act which they seek to enforce, not in the jurisdictional provision. See Securities Investors Protection Corp. v. Barbour, 421 U.S., at 424. The Court in *Borak* found a private cause of action implicit in § 14(a). See Cannon v. University of Chicago, supra, at 690–693 n. 13; Piper v. Chris-Craft Indus., Inc., 430 U.S., at 25; Allen v. State Bd. of Elections, 393 U.S., at 557. We do not now question the actual holding of that case, but we decline to read the opinion so broadly that virtually every provision of the securities acts gives rise to an implied private cause of action. E.g., Piper v. Chris-Craft Indus., Inc., supra.[19]

The invocation of the "remedial purposes" of the 1934 Act is similarly unavailing. Only last Term, we emphasized that generalized references to the "remedial purposes" of the 1934 Act will not justify reading a provision "more broadly than its language and the statutory scheme reasonably permit." Securities and Exchange Commission v. Sloan, 436 U.S. 103, 116 (1978); see Ernst & Ernst v. Hochfelder, 425 U.S., at 200. Certainly, the mere fact that § 17(a) was designed to provide protection for brokers' customers does not require the implication of a private damage action in their behalf. Cannon v. University of Chicago, supra, at 688 n. 9; Securities Investor Protection Corp. v. Barbour, supra, at 421. To the extent our analysis in today's decision differs from that of the Court in *Borak*, it suffices to say that in a series of cases since *Borak* we have adhered to a stricter standard for the implication of private causes of action, and we follow that stricter standard today. Cannon v. University of Chicago, 441 U.S. at 688–709. The ultimate question is one of congressional intent, not one of whether this Court thinks that it can improve upon the statutory scheme that Congress enacted into law.

III

SIPC and the Trustee contend that the result we reach sanctions injustice. But even if that were the case, the argument is made in the wrong forum, for we are not at liberty to legislate. If there is to be a federal damage remedy under these circumstances, Congress must provide it. "[I]t is not for us to fill any *hiatus* Congress has left in this area." Wheeldin v. Wheeler, 373 U.S. 647, 652 (1963). Obviously, nothing we have said prevents Congress from creating a private right of action on behalf of brokerage firm customers for losses arising from misstatements contained

---

19. We also have found implicit within § 10(b) of the 1934 Act a private cause of action for damages. See Superintendent of Ins. v. Bankers Life & Cas. Co., 404 U.S., at 13 n. 9. But we recently have stated that in *Superintendent* this Court simply explicitly acquiesced in the 25–year-old acceptance by the lower federal courts of an implied action under § 10(b). Cannon v. University of Chicago, supra, at 690–693, n. 13; see Ernst & Ernst v. Hochfelder, supra, at 196; Blue Chip Stamps v. Manor Drug Stores, Inc., 421 U.S., at 730. There is no similar history of longstanding lower court interpretation in this case. Indeed, only one other court in the 45–year history of the 1934 Act has held that a private cause of action for damages is available under § 17(a). Hawkins v. Merrill Lynch, Pierce, Fenner & Beane, 85 F.Supp. 104, 124 (WD Ark.1949). * * *

in § 17(a) reports. But if Congress intends those customers to have such a federal right of action, it is well aware of how it may effectuate that intent.

The judgment of the Court of Appeals is reversed and the case is remanded for further proceedings consistent with this opinion.

It is so ordered.

MR. JUSTICE POWELL took no part in the consideration or decision of this case.

MR. JUSTICE BRENNAN, concurring.

I join the Court's opinion. The Court of Appeals implied a cause of action for damages under § 17(a) of the Securities Exchange Act of 1934 in favor of respondents, who purport to represent customers of a bankrupt brokerage firm, against petitioner accountants, who allegedly injured those customers by improperly preparing and certifying the reports on the brokerage firm required by § 17(a) and the rules promulgated thereunder. Under the tests established in our prior cases, no cause of action should be implied for respondents under § 17(a). Although analyses of the several factors outlined in Cort v. Ash, 422 U.S. 66 (1975), may often overlap, I agree that when, as here, a statute clearly does not "create a federal right in favor of the plaintiff," id., at 78, i.e., when the plaintiff is not " 'one of the class for whose *especial* benefit the statute was enacted,' " ibid., quoting Texas & Pacific R. Co. v. Rigsby, 241 U.S. 33, 39 (1916), and when there is also in the legislative history no "indication of legislative intent, explicit or implicit ∗ ∗ ∗ to create such a remedy," 422 U.S., at 78, the remaining two *Cort* factors cannot by themselves be a basis for implying a right of action.

MR. JUSTICE MARSHALL, dissenting.

In determining whether to imply a private cause of action for damages under a statute that does not expressly authorize such a remedy, this Court has considered four factors:

> "First, is the plaintiff 'one of the class for whose *especial* benefit the statute was enacted,' that is, does the statute create a federal right in favor of the plaintiff? Second, is there any indication of legislative intent, explicit or implicit, either to create such a remedy or to deny one? Third, is it consistent with the underlying purposes of the legislative scheme to imply such a remedy for the plaintiff? And finally, is the cause of action one traditionally relegated to state law, in an area basically the concern of the States, so that it would be inappropriate to infer a cause of action based solely on federal law?" Cort v. Ash, 422 U.S. 66, 78 (1975) (citations omitted).

Applying these factors, I believe respondents are entitled to bring an action against accountants who have allegedly breached duties imposed under § 17(a) of the Securities Exchange Act of 1934.

∗ ∗ ∗

MERRILL LYNCH, PIERCE, FENNER & SMITH, INC. v. CURRAN

Supreme Court of the United States, 1982.
456 U.S. 353, 102 S.Ct. 1825, 72 L.Ed.2d 182.

JUSTICE STEVENS delivered the opinion of the Court.

The Commodity Exchange Act (CEA), 7 U.S.C. § 1 et seq. (1976 ed. and Supp. IV), has been aptly characterized as "a comprehensive regulatory structure to oversee the volatile and esoteric futures trading complex." The central question presented by these cases is whether a private party may maintain an action for damages caused by a violation of the CEA. The United States Court of Appeals for the Sixth Circuit answered that question affirmatively, holding that an investor may maintain an action against his broker for violation of an antifraud provision of the CEA.[3] The Court of Appeals for the Second Circuit gave the same answer to the question in actions brought by investors claiming damages resulting from unlawful price manipulation that allegedly could have been prevented by the New York Mercantile Exchange's enforcement of its own rules.[4]

We granted certiorari to resolve a conflict between these decisions and a subsequent decision of the Court of Appeals for the Fifth Circuit,[5] and we now affirm. Prefatorily, we describe some aspects of the futures trading business, summarize the statutory scheme, and outline the essential facts of the separate cases.

I

Prior to the advent of futures trading, agricultural products generally were sold at central markets. When an entire crop was harvested and marketed within a short time-span, dramatic price fluctuations sometimes created severe hardship for farmers or for processors. Some of these risks were alleviated by the adoption of quality standards, improvements in storage and transportation facilities, and the practice of "forward contracting"—the use of executory contracts fixing the terms of sale in advance of the time of delivery.

When buyers and sellers entered into contracts for the future delivery of an agricultural product, they arrived at an agreed price on the basis of their judgment about expected market conditions at the time of delivery. Because the weather and other imponderables affected supply and demand, normally the market price would fluctuate before the contract was performed. A declining market meant that the executory agreement was more valuable to the seller than the commodity covered by the contract; conversely, in a rising market the executory contract had a special value for the buyer, who not only was assured of delivery of the commodity but also could derive a profit from the price increase.

The opportunity to make a profit as a result of fluctuations in the market price of commodities covered by contracts for future delivery motivated speculators to engage in the practice of buying and selling "futures contracts." A speculator who owned no present interest in a commodity but anticipated a price decline might agree to a future sale at the current market price, intending to purchase the commodity at a reduced price on or before the delivery date. A "short" sale of that kind would result in a loss if the price went up instead of down. On the other hand, a price increase

---

3. 622 F.2d 216 (1980). Accord, Merrill Lynch, Pierce, Fenner & Smith, Inc. v. Goldman, 593 F.2d 129, 133, n. 7 (CA8) (dictum), cert. denied, 444 U.S. 838, 100 S.Ct. 76, 62 L.Ed.2d 50 (1979); Hirk v. Agri-Research Council, Inc., 561 F.2d 96, 103, n. 8 (CA7 1977). See also Master Commodities, Inc. v. Texas Cattle Management Co., 586 F.2d 1352, 1355 (CA10 1978) (assuming that a private right of action exists).

4. Leist v. Simplot, 638 F.2d 283 (1980).

5. Rivers v. Rosenthal & Co., 634 F.2d 774 (1980), cert. pending, No. 80–1542.

would produce a gain for a "long" speculator who had acquired a contract to purchase the same commodity with no intent to take delivery but merely for the purpose of reselling the futures contract at an enhanced price.

* * *

II

Because Congress has recognized the potential hazards as well as the benefits of futures trading, it has authorized the regulation of commodity futures exchanges for over 60 years. In 1921 it enacted the Futures Trading Act, 42 Stat. 187, which imposed a prohibitive tax on grain futures transactions that were not consummated on an exchange designated as a "contract market" by the Secretary of Agriculture. The 1921 statute was held unconstitutional as an improper exercise of the taxing power in Hill v. Wallace, 259 U.S. 44 (1922), but its regulatory provisions were promptly re-enacted in the Grain Futures Act, 42 Stat. 998, and upheld under the commerce power in Chicago Board of Trade v. Olsen, 262 U.S. 1 (1923). Under the original legislation, the principal function of the Secretary was to require the governors of a privately organized exchange to supervise the operation of the market. Two of the conditions for designation were that the governing board of the contract market prevent its members from disseminating misleading market information and prevent the "manipulation of prices or the cornering of any grain by the dealers or operators upon such board." The requirement that designated contract markets police themselves and the prohibitions against disseminating misleading information and manipulating prices have been part of our law ever since.

In 1936 Congress changed the name of the statute to the Commodity Exchange Act, enlarged its coverage to include other agricultural commodities, and added detailed provisions regulating trading in futures contracts. Commodity Exchange Act, ch. 545, 49 Stat. 1491. Among the significant new provisions was § 4b, prohibiting any member of a contract market from defrauding any person in connection with the making of a futures contract, and § 4a, authorizing a commission composed of the Secretary of Agriculture, the Secretary of Commerce, and the Attorney General to fix limits on the amount of permissible speculative trading in a futures contract. The legislation also required registration of futures commission merchants and floor brokers.

In 1968 the CEA again was amended to enlarge its coverage and to give the Secretary additional enforcement authority. Act of Feb. 19, 1968, 82 Stat. 26. The Secretary was authorized to disapprove exchange rules that were inconsistent with the statute, and the contract markets were required to enforce their rules; the Secretary was authorized to suspend a contract market or to issue a cease-and-desist order upon a showing that the contract market's rules were not being enforced. In addition, the criminal sanctions for price manipulation were increased significantly, and any person engaged in price manipulation was subjected to the Secretary's authority to issue cease-and-desist orders for violations of the CEA and implementing regulations.

In 1974, after extensive hearings and deliberation, Congress enacted the Commodity Futures Trading Commission Act of 1974. 88 Stat. 1389. Like the 1936 and the 1968 legislation, the 1974 enactment was an amendment to the existing statute that broadened its coverage and increased the penalties for violation of its provisions. The Commission was authorized to seek injunctive relief, to alter or supplement a contract market's rules, and to direct a contract market to take whatever action deemed necessary by the Commission in an emergency. The 1974 legislation retained the basic statutory prohibitions against fraudulent practices and price manipulation, as well as the authority to prescribe trading limits. The 1974 amendments, however, did make substantial changes in the statutory scheme; Congress authorized a newly created Commodities Futures Trading Commission to assume the powers previously exercised by the Secretary of Agriculture, as well as certain additional powers. The enactment also added two new remedial provisions for the protection of individual traders. The newly enacted § 5a(11) required every contract market to provide an arbitration procedure for the settlement of traders' claims of no more than $15,000. And the newly enacted § 14 authorized the Commission to grant reparations to any person complaining of any violation of the CEA, or its implementing regulations, committed by any futures commission merchant or any associate thereof, floor broker, commodity trading adviser, or commodity pool operator. This section authorized the Commission to investigate complaints and, "if in its opinion the facts warrant such action," to afford a hearing before an administrative law judge. Reparations orders entered by the Commission are subject to judicial review.

The latest amendments to the CEA, the Futures Trading Act of 1978, 92 Stat. 865, again increased the penalties for violations of the statute. The enactment also authorized the States to bring *parens patriae* actions, seeking injunctive or monetary relief for certain violations of the CEA, implementing regulations, or Commission orders.

Like the previous enactments, as well as the 1978 amendments, the Commodity Futures Trading Commission Act of 1974 is silent on the subject of private judicial remedies for persons injured by a violation of the CEA.

III

In the four cases before us, the allegations in the complaints filed by respondents are assumed to be true. The first involves a complaint by customers against their broker. The other three arise out of a malfunction of the contract market for futures contracts covering the delivery of Maine potatoes in May 1976, " 'when the sellers of almost 1,000 contracts failed to deliver approximately 50,000,000 pounds of potatoes, resulting in the largest default in the history of commodities futures trading in this country.' "

No. 80–203

Respondents in No. 80–203 were customers of petitioner, a futures commission merchant registered with the Commission. In 1973, they authorized petitioner to trade in commodity futures on their behalf and deposited $100,000 with petitioner to finance such trading. The trading initially was profitable, but substantial losses subsequently were suffered and the account ultimately was closed.

In 1976, the respondents commenced this action in the United States District Court for the Eastern District of Michigan. They alleged that petitioner had mismanaged the account, had made material misrepresentations in connection with the opening and the management of the account, had made a large number of trades for the sole purpose of generating commissions, and had refused to follow their instructions. Respondents claimed that petitioner had violated the CEA, the federal securities laws, and state statutory and common law.

* * *

Nos. 80–757, 80–895, and 80–936

One of the futures contracts traded on the New York Mercantile Exchange provided for the delivery of a railroad car lot of 50,000 pounds of Maine potatoes at a designated place on the Bangor and Aroostook Railroad during the period between May 7, 1976, and May 25, 1976. Trading in this contract commenced early in 1975 and terminated on May 7, 1976. On two occasions during this trading period the Department of Agriculture issued reports containing estimates that total potato stocks, and particularly Maine potato stocks, were substantially down from the previous year. This information had the understandable consequences of inducing investors to purchase May Maine potato futures contracts (on the expectation that they would profit from a shortage of potatoes in May) and farmers to demand a higher price for their potatoes on the cash market.

To counteract the anticipated price increases, a group of entrepreneurs described in the complaints as the "short sellers" formed a conspiracy to depress the price of the May Maine potato futures contract. The principal participants in this "short conspiracy" were large processors of potatoes who then were negotiating with a large potato growers association on the cash market. The conspirators agreed to accumulate an abnormally large short position in the May contract, to make no offsetting purchases of long contracts at a price in excess of a fixed maximum, and to default, if necessary, on their short commitments. They also agreed to flood the Maine cash markets with unsold potatoes. This multifaceted strategy was designed to give the growers association the impression that the supply of Maine potatoes would be plentiful. On the final trading day the short sellers had accumulated a net short position of almost 1,900 contracts, notwithstanding a Commission regulation limiting their lawful net position to 150 contracts. They did, in fact, default.

The trading limit also was violated by a separate group described as the "long conspirators." Aware of the short conspiracy, they determined that they not only could counteract its effects but also could enhance the price the short conspirators would have to pay to liquidate their short positions by accumulating an abnormally large long position—at the close of trading they controlled 911 long contracts—and by creating an artificial shortage of railroad cars during the contract delivery period. Because the long conspirators were successful in tying up railroad cars, they prevented the owners of warehoused potatoes from making deliveries to persons desiring to perform short contracts.

Respondents are speculators who invested long in Maine futures contracts. Allegedly, if there had been no price manipulation, they would have earned a significant profit by reason of the price increase that free market forces would have produced.

Petitioners in No. 80–757 are the New York Mercantile Exchange and its officials. Respondents' complaints alleged that the Exchange knew, or should have known, of both the short and the long conspiracies but failed to perform its statutory duties to report these violations to the Commission and to prevent manipulation of the contract market. The Exchange allegedly had the authority under its rules to declare an emergency, to require the shorts and the longs to participate in an orderly liquidation, and to authorize truck deliveries and other measures that would have prevented or mitigated the consequences of the massive defaults.

Petitioners in No. 80–895 and No. 80–936 are the firms of futures commission merchants that the short conspirators used to accumulate their net short position. The complaint alleged that petitioners knowingly participated in the conspiracy to accumulate the net short position, and in doing so violated position and trading limits imposed by the Commission and Exchange rules requiring liquidation of contracts that obviously could not be performed. Moreover, the complaint alleged that petitioners violated their statutory duty to report violations of the CEA to the Commission.

* * *

IV

* * *

Our approach to the task of determining whether Congress intended to authorize a private cause of action has changed significantly, much as the quality and quantity of federal legislation has undergone significant change. When federal statutes were less comprehensive, the Court applied a relatively simple test to determine the availability of an implied private remedy. If a statute was enacted for the benefit of a special class, the judiciary normally recognized a remedy for members of that class. Texas & Pacific R. Co. v. Rigsby, 241 U.S. 33 (1916). Under this approach, federal courts, following a common-law tradition, regarded the denial of a remedy as the exception rather than the rule.

Because the *Rigsby* approach prevailed throughout most of our history, there is no merit to the argument advanced by petitioners that the judicial recognition of an implied private remedy violates the separation-of-powers doctrine. * * *

During the years prior to 1975, the Court occasionally refused to recognize an implied remedy, either because the statute in question was a general regulatory prohibition enacted for the benefit of the public at large, or because there was evidence that Congress intended an express remedy to provide the exclusive method of enforcement. While the *Rigsby* approach prevailed, however, congressional silence or ambiguity was an insufficient reason for the denial of a remedy for a member of the class a statute was enacted to protect.

In 1975 the Court unanimously decided to modify its approach to the question whether a federal statute includes a private right of action. In Cort v. Ash, 422 U.S. 66 (1975), the Court confronted a claim that a private litigant could recover damages for violation of a criminal statute that had never before been thought to include a private remedy. In rejecting that claim the Court outlined criteria that primarily focused on the intent of Congress in enacting the statute under review. The increased complexity of federal legislation and the increased volume of federal litigation strongly supported the desirability of a more careful scrutiny of legislative intent than *Rigsby* had required. Our cases subsequent to *Cort v. Ash* have plainly stated that our focus must be on "the intent of Congress." Texas Industries, Inc. v. Radcliff Materials, Inc., 451 U.S. 630, 639 (1981). "The key to the inquiry is the intent of the Legislature." Middlesex County Sewerage Auth. v. National Sea Clammers Assn., 453 U.S. 1, 13 (1981). The key to these cases is our understanding of the intent of Congress in 1974 when it comprehensively reexamined and strengthened the federal regulation of futures trading.

V

In determining whether a private cause of action is implicit in a federal statutory scheme when the statute by its terms is silent on that issue, the initial focus must be on the state of the law at the time the legislation was enacted. More precisely, we must examine Congress' perception of the law that it was shaping or reshaping. When Congress enacts new legislation, the question is whether Congress intended to create a private remedy as a supplement to the express enforcement provisions of the statute. When Congress acts in a statutory context in which an implied private remedy has already been recognized by the courts, however, the inquiry logically is different. Congress need not have intended to create a new remedy, since one already existed; the question is whether Congress intended to preserve the pre-existing remedy.

* * *

Prior to the comprehensive amendments to the CEA enacted in 1974, the federal courts routinely and consistently had recognized an implied private cause of action on behalf of plaintiffs seeking to enforce and to collect damages for violation of provisions of the CEA or rules and regulations promulgated pursuant to the statute. The routine recognition of a private remedy under the CEA prior to our decision in *Cort v. Ash* was comparable to the routine acceptance of an analogous remedy under the Securities Exchange Act of 1934. * * *

Although the consensus of opinion concerning the existence of a private cause of action under the CEA was neither as old nor as overwhelming as the consensus concerning Rule 10b–5, it was equally uniform and well understood. This Court, as did other federal courts and federal practitioners, simply assumed that the remedy was available. The point is well illustrated by this Court's opinion in Chicago Mercantile Exchange v. Deaktor, 414 U.S. 113 (1973), which disposed of two separate actions in which private litigants alleged that an exchange had violated § 9(b) of the CEA by engaging in price manipulation and § 5a by failing both to enforce its own rules and to prevent market manipulation. The Court held that the judicial proceedings should not go forward without first making an effort to invoke the jurisdiction of the Commodity Exchange Commission, but it did not question the availability of a private remedy under the CEA.

In view of the absence of any dispute about the proposition prior to the decision of *Cort v. Ash* in 1975, it is abundantly clear that an implied cause of action under the CEA was a part of the "contemporary legal context" in which Congress legislated in 1974. Cf. Cannon v. University of Chicago, 441 U.S., at 698–699. In that context, the fact that a comprehensive reexamination and significant amendment of the CEA left intact the statutory provisions under which the federal courts had implied a cause of action is itself evidence that Congress affirmatively intended to preserve that remedy. A review of the legislative history of the statute persuasively indicates that preservation of the remedy was indeed what Congress actually intended.

VI

Congress was, of course, familiar not only with the implied private remedy but also with the long history of federal regulation of commodity futures trading. From the enactment of the original federal legislation, Congress primarily has relied upon the exchanges to regulate the contract markets. The 1922 legislation required for designation as a contract market that an exchange "provide for" the making and filing of reports and records, the prevention of dissemination of false or misleading reports, the prevention of price manipulation and market cornering, and the enforcement of Commission orders. To fulfill these conditions, the exchanges promulgated rules and regulations, but they did not always enforce them. In 1968, Congress attempted to correct this flaw in the self-regulation concept by enacting § 5a(8), which requires the exchanges to enforce their own rules.

The enactment of § 5a(8), coupled with the recognition by the federal courts of an implied private remedy for violations of the CEA, gave rise to a new problem. As representatives of the exchanges complained during the hearings preceding the 1974 amendments, the exchanges were being sued for not enforcing their rules. The complaint was taken seriously because it implicated the self-regulation premise of the CEA:

> "In the few years [§ 5a(8)] has been in the present Commodity Exchange Act, there is growing evidence to indicate that, as opposed to strengthening the self-regulatory concept in present law, such a provision, coupled with only limited federal authority to require the exchanges to make and issue rules appropriate to enforcement of the Act—may actually have worked to weaken it. With inadequate enforcement personnel the Committee was informed that attorneys to several boards of trade have been advising the boards to *reduce*—not expand exchange regulations designed to insure fair trading, since there is a growing body of opinion that failure to enforce the exchange rules is a violation of the Act which will support suits by private litigants." House Report, at 46 (emphasis in original).

Congress could have removed this impediment to exchange rulemaking by eliminating the implied private remedy, but it did not follow that course. Rather, it solved the problem by authorizing the new Commodity Futures Trading Commission to supplement exchange rules. Congress thereby corrected the legal mechanism of self-regulation while preserving a significant incentive for the exchanges to obey the law. Only this course was consistent with the expressed purpose of the 1974 legislation, which was to "amend the Commodity Exchange Act to *strengthen* the regulation of futures trading."

Congress in 1974 created new procedures through which traders might seek relief for violations of the CEA, but the legislative evidence indicates that these informal procedures were intended to supplement rather than supplant the implied judicial remedy. These procedures do not substitute for the private remedy either as a means of compensating injured traders or as a means of enforcing compliance with the statute. * * * It was assumed by hearings witnesses that the informal procedures were supplementary. Indeed, it was urged that complainants be put to the choice between informal and judicial actions. A representative of one exchange urged Congress to place a dollar limit on claims arbitrable under § 5a(11) because there was an "economic impediment to Court litigation" only with small claims, and such a limit was enacted. Chairman Poage described the newly enacted informal proceedings as "new customer protection features," and Senator Talmadge, the Chairman of the Senate Committee on Agriculture and Forestry, stated that the reparations procedure was "not intended to interfere with the courts in any way," although he hoped that the burden on the courts would be "somewhat lighten[ed]" by the availability of the informal actions.

The late addition of a saving clause in § 2(a)(1) provides direct evidence of legislative intent to preserve the implied private remedy federal courts had recognized under the CEA. Along with an increase in powers, the Commission was given exclusive jurisdiction over commodity futures trading. The purpose of the exclusive-jurisdiction provision in the bill passed by the House was to separate the functions of the Commission from those of the Securities and Exchange Commission and other regulatory agencies. But the provision raised concerns that the jurisdiction of state and federal courts might be affected. Referring to the treble damages action provided in another bill that he and Senator McGovern had introduced, Senator Clark pointed out: "[T]he House bill not only does not authorize them, but section 201 of that bill may prohibit all court actions. The staff of the House Agriculture Committee has said that this was done inadvertently and they hope it can be corrected in the Senate." It was. The Senate added a saving clause to the exclusive-jurisdiction provision, providing that "[n]othing in this section shall supersede or limit the jurisdiction conferred on courts of the United States or any State." The Conference accepted the Senate amendment.

* * *

In view of our construction of the intent of the Legislature there is no need for us to "trudge through all four of the factors when the dispositive question of legislative intent has been resolved." See California v. Sierra Club, 451 U.S., at 302 (REHNQUIST, J., concurring in judgment). We hold that the private cause of action under the CEA that was previously available to investors survived the 1974 amendments.

VII

In addition to their principal argument that no private remedy is available under the CEA, petitioners also contend that respondents, as speculators, may not maintain such an action and that, in any event, they may not sue an exchange or futures commission merchants for their alleged complicity in the price manipulation effected by a group of short traders. To evaluate these contentions, we must assume the best possible case for the speculator in terms of proof of the statutory violations, the causal connection between the violations and the injury, and the amount of damages. It is argued that no matter how deliberate the defendants' conduct, no matter how flagrant the statutory violation, and no matter how direct and harmful its impact on the plaintiffs, the federal remedy that is available to some private parties does not encompass these actions.

The cause of action asserted in No. 80–203 is a claim that respondents' broker violated the prohibitions against fraudulent and deceptive conduct in § 4b. In the other three cases the respondents allege violations of several other sections of the CEA that are designed to prevent price manipulation. We are satisfied that purchasers and sellers of futures contracts have standing to assert both types of claims.

The characterization of persons who invest in futures contracts as "speculators" does not exclude them from the class of persons protected by the CEA. * * *

Although § 4b compels our holding that an investor defrauded by his broker may maintain a private cause of action for fraud, petitioners in the three manipulation cases correctly point out that the other sections of the CEA that they are accused of violating are framed in general terms and do not purport to confer special rights on any identifiable class of persons. Under Cort v. Ash, the statutory language would be insufficient to imply a private cause of action under these sections. But we are not faced with the *Cort v. Ash* inquiry. We have held that Congress intended to preserve the pre-existing remedy; to determine whether the pre-existing remedy encompasses respondents' actions, we must turn once again to the law as it existed in 1974.

Although the first case in which a federal court held that a futures trader could maintain a private action was a fraud claim based on § 4b, subsequent decisions drew no distinction between an action against a broker and an action against an exchange. When Congress acted in 1974, courts were recognizing causes of action on behalf of investors against exchanges. The *Deaktor* case, which came before this Court, is an example. Moreover, these actions against exchanges were well recognized. During the hearings on the 1974 amendments to the CEA, a complaint voiced by representatives of the exchanges was that the exchanges were being sued for not enforcing their rules. Congress responded to the complaint by authorizing the Commission to supplement exchange rules because, we have inferred, Congress wished to preserve the private cause of action as a tool for enforcement of the self-regulation concept of the CEA.

    * * *

The judgments of the Courts of Appeals are affirmed.

It is so ordered.

JUSTICE POWELL, with whom THE CHIEF JUSTICE, JUSTICE REHNQUIST, and JUSTICE O'CONNOR join, dissenting.

The Court today holds that Congress intended the federal courts to recognize implied causes of action under five separate provisions of the Commodity Exchange Act (CEA), 7 U.S.C. § 1 et seq. (1976 ed. and Supp. IV). The decision rests on two theories. First, the Court relies on fewer than a dozen cases in which the lower federal courts *erroneously* upheld private rights of action in the years prior to the 1974 amendments to the CEA. Reasoning that these mistaken decisions constituted "the law" in 1974, the Court holds that Congress must be assumed to have endorsed this path of error when it *failed to amend* certain sections of the CEA in that year. This theory is incompatible with our constitutional separation of powers, and in my view it is without support in logic or in law. Additionally—whether alternatively or cumulatively is unclear—the Court finds that Congress in 1974 "affirmatively" manifested its intent to "preserve" private rights of action by adopting particular amendments to the CEA. This finding is reached without even token deference to established tests for discerning congressional intent.

* * *

B

Despite its imaginative use of other sources, the Court neglects the only unambiguous evidence of Congress' intent respecting private actions for civil damages under the CEA. That evidence is a chart that appears in the record of Senate Committee hearings.[16] This chart compares features of four proposed bills with the "Present Commodities Exchange Act." It evidently was prepared by the expert Committee staff advising the legislators who considered the 1974 amendments.

The chart is detailed. It occupies five pages of the hearing record. Comparing the feature of "civil money penalties" between the different proposed bills, however, the chart does not list "implied damages actions" under the existing Act. Rather, it says there are "none." Neither does the chart make any reference to implied private damages actions under any of the four proposed amending bills.

Under these circumstances, the most that the Court fairly can claim to have shown is that the 1974 Congress did not disapprove *Goodman* and its progeny. There simply is no persuasive evidence of affirmative congressional intent to recognize rights through the enactment of statutory law, even under the Court's unprecedented theory of congressional ratification by silence of judicial error.

* * *

For reasons that I have expressed before, I remain convinced that "we should not condone the implication of any private right of action from a federal statute absent the most compelling evidence that Congress in fact intended such an action to exist." Cannon v. University of Chicago, 441 U.S. 677, 749 (1979) (POWELL, J., dissenting). Here the evidence falls far short of this constitutionally appropriate standard.

Accordingly, I respectfully dissent.

16. The relevant portion of this chart is attached as an Appendix to this opinion.

Appendix to Opinion of Powell J., dissenting

	HUMPHREY	McGOVERN	HART	Page 5
FEATURES	H.R. 13113	S. 2485	S. 2578	S. 2837, AS AMENDED	PRESENT COMMODITY EXCHANGE ACT
Civil money penalties.	Permits civil money penalties up to $100,000. (Sec. 212)	Permits money penalties of $1,000 to $100,000 but only for failure to comply with a Commission order to cease and desist from violating the Act. (Sec. 7)	Permits money penalties up to $100,000 and provides criteria for assessment. Civil actions may be brought by individuals for treble damages. (Sec. 16)	Civil actions may be brought by individuals for treble damages (Sec. 505) Provides for civil money penalties for violation of a final order (Sec. 504) Provides Commission with authority to directly impose a fine of up to $100,000, issue a cease and desist order, require restitution, suspend registration, and grant other relief that a court of equity would have the right to grant. (Sec. 406)	None

Commodity Futures Commission Act: Hearings on S. 2485, S. 2578, S. 2837 and H.R. 13113 before the Senate Committee on Agriculture and Forestry, 93d Cong., 2d Sess., 194 (1974).

HERMAN & MacLEAN v. HUDDLESTON

Supreme Court of the United States, 1983.
459 U.S. 375, 103 S.Ct. 683, 74 L.Ed.2d 548.

JUSTICE MARSHALL delivered the opinion of the Court.

These consolidated cases raise two unresolved questions concerning Section 10(b) of the Securities Exchange Act of 1934. The first is whether purchasers of registered securities who allege they were defrauded by misrepresentations in a registration statement may maintain an action under Section 10(b) notwithstanding the express remedy for misstatements and omissions in registration statements provided by Section 11 of the Securities Act of 1933. The second question is whether persons seeking recovery under Section 10(b) must prove their cause of action by clear and convincing evidence rather than by a preponderance of the evidence.

I

In 1969 Texas International Speedway, Inc. ("TIS"), filed a registration statement and prospectus with the Securities and Exchange Commission offering a total of $4,398,900 in securities to the public. The proceeds of the sale were to be used to finance the construction of an automobile speedway. The entire issue was sold on the offering date, October 30, 1969.

TIS did not meet with success, however, and the corporation filed a petition for bankruptcy on November 30, 1970.

In 1972 plaintiffs Huddleston and Bradley instituted a class action in the United States District Court for the Southern District of Texas on behalf of themselves and other purchasers of TIS securities. The complaint alleged violations of Section 10(b) of the Securities Exchange Act of 1934 ("the 1934 Act") and SEC Rule 10b–5 promulgated thereunder.[2] Plaintiffs sued most of the participants in the offering, including the accounting firm, Herman & MacLean, which had issued an opinion concerning certain financial statements and a pro forma balance sheet that were contained in the registration statement and prospectus. Plaintiffs claimed that the defendants had engaged in a fraudulent scheme to misrepresent or conceal material facts regarding the financial condition of TIS, including the costs incurred in building the speedway.

After a three-week trial, the District Judge submitted the case to the jury on special interrogatories relating to liability. The judge instructed the jury that liability could be found only if the defendants acted with scienter.[4] The judge also instructed the jury to determine whether plaintiffs had proven their cause of action by a preponderance of the evidence. After the jury rendered a verdict in favor of the plaintiffs on the submitted issues, the judge concluded that Herman & MacLean and others had violated Section 10(b) and Rule 10b–5 by making fraudulent misrepresentations in the TIS registration statement. The court then determined the amount of damages and entered judgment for the plaintiffs.

On appeal, the United States Court of Appeals for the Fifth Circuit held that a cause of action may be maintained under Section 10(b) of the 1934 Act for fraudulent misrepresentations and omissions even when that conduct might also be actionable under Section 11 of the Securities Act of 1933 ("the 1933 Act"). Huddleston v. Herman & MacLean, 640 F.2d 534, 540–543 (1981). However, the Court of Appeals disagreed with the District Court as to the appropriate standard of proof for an action under Section 10(b), concluding that a plaintiff must prove his case by "clear and convincing" evidence. Id., at 545–546. The Court of Appeals reversed the District Court's judgment on other grounds and remanded the case for a new trial. Id., at 547–550, 560.

We granted certiorari to consider whether an implied cause of action under Section 10(b) of the 1934 Act will lie for conduct subject to an express civil remedy under the 1933 Act, an issue we have previously reserved,[6] and to decide the standard of proof applicable to actions under Section 10(b). 456 U.S. 914 (1982). We now affirm the court of appeals' holding

---

2. Plaintiffs also alleged violations of, *inter alia*, Section 17(a) of the Securities Act of 1933. We have previously reserved decision on whether Section 17(a) affords a private remedy, International Brotherhood of Teamsters v. Daniel, 439 U.S. 551, 557, n. 9 (1979), and we do so once again. Plaintiffs have abandoned their Section 17(a) claim, Brief, at 4, n. 6, and the Court of Appeals did not address the existence of a separate cause of action under Section 17(a). Accordingly, there is no need for us to decide the issue.

4. The judge stated that reckless behavior could satisfy the scienter requirement. While this instruction reflects the prevailing view of the courts of appeals that have addressed the issue, see McLean v. Alexander, 599 F.2d 1190, 1197, and n. 12 (CA3 1979) (collecting cases), we have explicitly left open the question whether recklessness satisfies the scienter requirement. Ernst & Ernst v. Hochfelder, 425 U.S. 185, 194, n. 12 (1976).

6. See, e.g., Blue Chip Stamps v. Manor Drug Stores, 421 U.S. 723, 752 n. 15 (1975).

that plaintiffs could maintain an action under Section 10(b) of the 1934 Act, but we reverse as to the applicable standard of proof.

II

The Securities Act of 1933 and the Securities Exchange Act of 1934 "constitute interrelated components of the federal regulatory scheme governing transactions in securities." Ernst & Ernst v. Hochfelder, 425 U.S. 185, 206 (1976). The Acts created several express private rights of action, one of which is contained in Section 11 of the 1933 Act. In addition to the private actions created explicitly by the 1933 and 1934 Acts, federal courts have implied private remedies under other provisions of the two laws.[9] Most significantly for present purposes, a private right of action under Section 10(b) of the 1934 Act and Rule 10b–5 has been consistently recognized for more than 35 years.[10] The existence of this implied remedy is simply beyond peradventure.

The issue in this case is whether a party should be barred from invoking this established remedy for fraud because the allegedly fraudulent conduct would apparently also provide the basis for a damage action under Section 11 of the 1933 Act.[11] The resolution of this issue turns on the fact that the two provisions involve distinct causes of action and were intended to address different types of wrongdoing.

Section 11 of the 1933 Act allows purchasers of a registered security to sue certain enumerated parties in a registered offering when false or misleading information is included in a registration statement. The section was designed to assure compliance with the disclosure provisions of the Act by imposing a stringent standard of liability on the parties who play a

---

9. See, e.g., J.I. Case Co. v. Borak, 377 U.S. 426 (1964) (Section 14(a) of the Securities Exchange Act); Dan River, Inc. v. Unitex Ltd., 624 F.2d 1216 (CA4 1980), cert. denied, 449 U.S. 1101 (1981) (Section 13 of the Securities Exchange Act); Kirshner v. United States, 603 F.2d 234, 241 (CA2 1978), cert. denied, 442 U.S. 909 (1979) (Section 17(a) of the Securities Act). But see, e.g., Touche Ross & Co. v. Redington, 442 U.S. 560 (1979) (no implied private right of action under Section 17(a) of the Securities Exchange Act); Piper v. Chris-Craft Industries, Inc., 430 U.S. 1 (1977) (defeated tender offeror has no implied private right of action under Section 14(e) of the Securities Exchange Act).

10. The right of action was first recognized in Kardon v. National Gypsum Co., 69 F.Supp. 512 (ED Pa.1946). By 1961, four courts of appeals and several district courts in other circuits had recognized the existence of a private remedy under Section 10(b) and Rule 10b–5, and only one district court decision had reached a contrary conclusion. See III L. Loss, Securities Regulation 1763–1764 and nn. 260–263 (2d ed. 1961) (collecting cases). By 1969, the existence of a private cause of action had been recognized by ten of the eleven courts of appeals. See VI L. Loss, Securi-

ties Regulation 3871–3873 (2d ed. Supp. 1969) (collecting cases). When the question whether an implied cause of action can be brought under Section 10(b) and Rule 10b–5 was first considered in this Court, we confirmed the existence of such a cause of action without extended discussion. See Superintendent of Insurance v. Bankers Life & Cas. Co., 404 U.S. 6, 13, n. 9 (1971). We have since repeatedly reaffirmed that "the existence of a private cause of action for violations of the statute and the Rule is now well established." Ernst & Ernst v. Hochfelder, supra, 425 U.S. at 196 (citing prior cases).

11. The Court of Appeals noted that the plaintiffs "apparently did have a Section 11 remedy." 640 F.2d, at 541, n. 5. While accurate as to the two other defendants, this conclusion may be open to question with respect to Herman & MacLean. Accountants are liable under Section 11 only for those matters which purport to have been prepared or certified by them. 15 U.S.C. § 77k(a)(4). Herman & MacLean contends that it did not "expertise" at least some of the materials that were the subject of the lawsuit, Tr. of Oral Arg. at 6–8, which if true could preclude a Section 11 remedy with respect to these materials.

direct role in a registered offering. If a plaintiff purchased a security issued pursuant to a registration statement, he need only show a material misstatement or omission to establish his *prima facie* case. Liability against the issuer of a security is virtually absolute,[14] even for innocent misstatements. Other defendants bear the burden of demonstrating due diligence. See 15 U.S.C. § 77k(b).

Although limited in scope, Section 11 places a relatively minimal burden on a plaintiff. In contrast, Section 10(b) is a "catchall" antifraud provision, but it requires a plaintiff to carry a heavier burden to establish a cause of action. While a Section 11 action must be brought by a purchaser of a registered security, must be based on misstatements or omissions in a registration statement, and can only be brought against certain parties, a Section 10(b) action can be brought by a purchaser or seller of "*any* security" against "*any* person" who has used "*any* manipulative or deceptive device or contrivance" in connection with the purchase or sale of a security. 15 U.S.C. § 78j (emphasis added). However, a Section 10(b) plaintiff carries a heavier burden than a Section 11 plaintiff. Most significantly, he must prove that the defendant acted with scienter, i.e., with intent to deceive, manipulate, or defraud.

Since Section 11 and Section 10(b) address different types of wrongdoing, we see no reason to carve out an exception to Section 10(b) for fraud occurring in a registration statement just because the same conduct may also be actionable under Section 11. Exempting such conduct from liability under Section 10(b) would conflict with the basic purpose of the 1933 Act: to provide greater protection to purchasers of registered securities. It would be anomalous indeed if the special protection afforded to purchasers in a registered offering by the 1933 Act were deemed to deprive such purchasers of the protections against manipulation and deception that Section 10(b) makes available to all persons who deal in securities.

While some conduct actionable under Section 11 may also be actionable under Section 10(b), it is hardly a novel proposition that the Securities Exchange Act and the Securities Act "prohibit some of the same conduct." United States v. Naftalin, 441 U.S. 768, 778 (1979) (applying Section 17(a) of the 1933 Act to conduct also prohibited by Section 10(b) of the 1934 Act in an action by the SEC). " 'The fact that there may well be some overlap is neither unusual nor unfortunate.' " Ibid., quoting SEC v. National Securities, Inc., 393 U.S. 453, 468 (1969). In savings clauses included in the 1933 and 1934 Acts, Congress rejected the notion that the express remedies of the securities laws would preempt all other rights of action. Section 16 of the 1933 Act states unequivocally that "[t]he rights and remedies provided by this subchapter shall be in addition to any and all other rights and remedies that may exist at law or in equity." Section 28(a) of the 1934 Act contains a parallel provision. These provisions confirm that the remedies in each Act were to be supplemented by "any and all" additional remedies.

This conclusion is reinforced by our reasoning in Ernst & Ernst v. Hochfelder, supra, which held that actions under Section 10(b) require proof of scienter and do not encompass negligent conduct. In so holding, we noted that each of the express civil remedies in the 1933 Act allowing recovery for negligent conduct is subject to procedural restrictions not

---

14. See Feit v. Leasco Data Processing Equipment Corp., 332 F.Supp. 544, 575 (EDNY 1971); R. Jennings & H. Marsh, Securities Regulation 828–829 (1977).

applicable to a Section 10(b) action. 425 U.S., at 208–210. We emphasized that extension of Section 10(b) to negligent conduct would have allowed causes of action for negligence under the express remedies to be brought instead under Section 10(b), "thereby nullify[ing] the effectiveness of the carefully drawn procedural restrictions on these express actions." Id., at 210 (footnote omitted). In reasoning that scienter should be required in Section 10(b) actions in order to avoid circumvention of the procedural restrictions surrounding the express remedies, we necessarily assumed that the express remedies were not exclusive. Otherwise there would have been no danger of nullification. Conversely, because the added burden of proving scienter attaches to suits under Section 10(b), invocation of the Section 10(b) remedy will not "nullify" the procedural restrictions that apply to the express remedies.

This cumulative construction of the remedies under the 1933 and 1934 Acts is also supported by the fact that, when Congress comprehensively revised the securities laws in 1975, a consistent line of judicial decisions had permitted plaintiffs to sue under Section 10(b) regardless of the availability of express remedies. In 1975 Congress enacted the "most substantial and significant revision of this country's Federal securities laws since the passage of the Securities Exchange Act in 1934." See Securities Acts Amendments of 1975, Pub.L. No. 94–29, 89 Stat. 97. When Congress acted, federal courts had consistently and routinely permitted a plaintiff to proceed under Section 10(b) even where express remedies under Section 11 or other provisions were available. In light of this well-established judicial interpretation, Congress' decision to leave Section 10(b) intact suggests that Congress ratified the cumulative nature of the Section 10(b) action. See Merrill Lynch, Pierce, Fenner & Smith, Inc. v. Curran, 456 U.S. 353, 382 (1982); Lorillard v. Pons, 434 U.S. 575, 580–581 (1978).

A cumulative construction of the securities laws also furthers their broad remedial purposes. In enacting the 1934 Act, Congress stated that its purpose was "to impose requirements necessary to make [securities] regulation and control reasonably complete and effective." 15 U.S.C. § 78b. In furtherance of that objective, Section 10(b) makes it unlawful to use "*any* manipulative or deceptive device or contrivance" in connection with the purchase or sale of any security. The effectiveness of the broad proscription against fraud in Section 10(b) would be undermined if its scope were restricted by the existence of an express remedy under Section 11.[22] Yet we have repeatedly recognized that securities laws combating fraud should be construed "not technically and restrictively, but flexibly to effectuate [their] remedial purposes." SEC v. Capital Gains Research Bureau, 375 U.S. 180, 195 (1963). Accord: Superintendent of Insurance v. Bankers Life & Cas. Co., 404 U.S. 6, 12 (1971); Affiliated Ute Citizens v.

---

22. Moreover, certain individuals who play a part in preparing the registration statement generally cannot be reached by a Section 11 action. These include corporate officers other than those specified in 15 U.S.C. § 77k(a), lawyers not acting as "experts," and accountants with respect to parts of a registration statement which they are not named as having prepared or certified. If, as Herman & MacLean argues purchasers in registered offerings were required to rely solely on Section 11, they would have no recourse against such individuals even if the excluded parties engaged in fraudulent conduct while participating in the registration statement. The exempted individuals would be immune from federal liability for fraudulent conduct even though Section 10(b) extends to "any person" who engages in fraud in connection with a purchase or sale of securities.

United States, 406 U.S. 128, 151 (1972). We therefore reject an interpretation of the securities laws that displaces an action under Section 10(b).

Accordingly, we hold that the availability of an express remedy under Section 11 of the 1933 Act does not preclude defrauded purchasers of registered securities from maintaining an action under Section 10(b) of the 1934 Act. To this extent the judgment of the court of appeals is affirmed.

III

[The Court's discussion of the burden of proof is omitted.—Eds.]

We therefore decline to depart from the preponderance-of-the-evidence standard generally applicable in civil actions. Accordingly, the Court of Appeals' decision as to the appropriate standard of proof is reversed.

IV

The judgment of the Court of Appeals is affirmed in part and reversed in part and otherwise remanded for proceedings consistent with this opinion.

It is so ordered.

JUSTICE POWELL took no part in the decision of these cases.

LANDRY v. ALL AMERICAN ASSURANCE CO.
United States Court of Appeals, Fifth Circuit, 1982.
688 F.2d 381.

Before GARZA, POLITZ and WILLIAMS, CIRCUIT JUDGES.

GARZA, CIRCUIT JUDGE:

Below, the unsuccessful plaintiffs sought to try their case under several theories of securities law, but were permitted to proceed under only one. On this appeal it is their contention that the district court erred both in its dismissal of the other claims and the jury instructions given. With the exception of one state law issue, we find that no reversible error was committed and affirm the result below.

I. A CHANGE OF SEASONS

In the spring of 1974, appellants Bryan Zeringue, Curtis Chauvin and Dr. W.B. Landry learned—later to their detriment—that certain common stock of the St. Charles Bank and Trust Company was to be made available for sale. The circumstances surrounding the sale of that stock gave rise to the present suit. Disagreement between the parties as to the facts is minuscule.

Appellants are two businessmen and a practicing physician who live and work in St. Charles Parish, Louisiana. For years they had banked with the St. Charles Bank and Trust Company [hereinafter referred to as the Bank]. When the Bank formed an "advisory board" in the fall of 1973, appellants Zeringue and Chauvin were asked to serve on it; they accepted. In the spring of 1974, both Zeringue and Chauvin were informed at one of the board's meetings that the Bank's chairman of the board, Charest Thibaut, was thinking of retiring and was willing to sell some of his common stock. Not long thereafter, Dr. Landry was also informed, by one of his patients, that stock in the Bank was to be made available for purchase. That summer, each appellant purchased 1,500 shares of the Bank's common stock at $60 per share for a total of $90,000 apiece, or $270,000 for the total purchase price.

At first, it appeared that the money invested by the appellants was well spent—in January of 1975 a 25% stock dividend was declared, increasing the common stock ownership of each appellant from 1,500 to 1,875 shares. This feeling of euphoria, however, was unfounded. In the fall and winter of 1974, and the spring of 1975, various audits and bank examinations conducted by the Federal Deposit Insurance Corporation and the Louisiana Commissioner of Financial Institutions revealed gross inadequacies and deficiencies in the financial structure of the Bank. As a result of these examinations and actions taken by regulatory authorities, very substantial changes in the Bank's organization were brought about, including the resignation of the Bank's president, C. Therral Ransome, and the Bank's chairman of the board, Charest Thibaut. Other members of the board also resigned or were asked to resign in the spring and summer of 1975. Finally, in December of 1975, the Bank issued a proxy statement in which its precarious financial condition was set out, and in January, 1976, the Bank issued a stock offering to raise needed additional capital. At that time the Bank's common stock was valued at $4 per share—down from the $60 per share paid by appellants in the summer of 1974.

Outraged by the drastic devaluation of their investments, appellants consulted with counsel, and on January 26, 1977, filed suit in federal court alleging that All American Assurance Company, Republic Securities Corporation, Charest Thibaut, Remy F. Gross and C. Therral Ransome had violated § 10(b) of the Securities Exchange Act of 1934 and Rule 10b–5 promulgated thereunder.[3] Specifically, appellants contended that the financial statements prepared and issued by the Bank in 1973 and 1974 were inaccurate and grossly misrepresented its financial condition. Furthermore, it was asserted that representations made by the various defendants at advisory board meetings and elsewhere were affirmatively misleading, inaccurate and omitted material information.

On January 29, 1979, appellants amended their complaint so as to expand both the number of defendants and the causes of action asserted. Added to the list of defendants were the Bank, Royal American Corporation, Henry Friloux and Alcide J. Laurent. The causes of action asserted were broadened to encompass claims under § 17(a) of the Securities Act of 1933, La.Rev.Stat.Ann. § 12:91, and the Louisiana Blue Sky Law (La.Rev. Stat.Ann. § 51:701, et seq.).

Prior to trial, however, the defendants filed motions to dismiss and/or for summary judgment claiming that no private cause of action was created under either § 17(a) of the Securities Act of 1933 or La.Rev.Stat.Ann.

---

3. As earlier noted, Charest Thibaut was the chairman of the board of the Bank of St. Charles with controlling stock ownership. All American Assurance Company and Republic Securities Corporation were corporations controlled by Thibaut. Both Thibaut and the two corporations were the owners of stock purchased by appellants.

C. Therral Ransome died before the trial, but was the president of the Bank until May of 1975. Remy F. Gross, who settled his suit during the course of the trial, was a member of the Bank's board of directors, its executive committee and its loan committee.

§ 12:91. The trial court agreed and dismissed the counts. The trial court also granted defendants' motion to dismiss the Louisiana Blue Sky claim and held that the two-year statute of limitations included in the Blue Sky Law was peremptive rather than prescriptive.

Thereafter, the case went to trial. Although the jury found that the Bank, Henry Friloux and Alcide J. Laurent had knowingly or recklessly misrepresented or failed to disclose material facts to the appellants in connection with their purchases of stock, it also found that the appellants had not exercised "due diligence" in purchasing the stock and were, therefore, precluded from recovery. This appeal ensued.

II. THE DISMISSED THEORIES FOR RELIEF

(a) Implied Private Cause of Action Under § 17(a) of the Securities Act of 1933

Unquestionably, the most far reaching of the issues we resolve today is whether § 17(a) of the federal Securities Act of 1933 creates an implied private cause of action. While *res nova* in this Circuit, the controversy over this issue is by no means new. Of the circuits which have expressly addressed the issue, four have ruled that a private cause of action may be implied,[11] while one has ruled that it may not.[12] But while a clear majority view exists, few circuit court decisions have analyzed the issue in depth. In fact, as one learned commentator has observed, the existence of the § 17(a) private remedy "seems to be taken for granted." 6 L. Loss, Securities Regulation 3913 (2nd ed. Supp.1969).

Most of these cases trace their creation of a private cause of action back to Chief Judge Friendly's concurring opinion in SEC v. Texas Gulf Sulphur Co., 401 F.2d 833 (2nd Cir.1968), cert. denied, 394 U.S. 976, 404 U.S. 1005 (1969). Judge Friendly's opinion was primarily concerned with establishing that negligence in the drafting of a press release should not be the basis of civil liability under Rule 10b–5(2). In his discussion of the origins of Rule 10b–5, however, Judge Friendly stated in dicta that while he had considerable doubt as to whether a private remedy under § 17(a) was ever intended, "there seemed little practical point in denying the existence of such an action under § 17" "[o]nce it had been established * * * that an aggrieved buyer has a private action under § 10(b) of the 1934 Act." As subsequent decisions have revealed, this seed fell on very fertile ground. The lack of a clearly articulated standard, however, has resulted in the fragmentation of the district courts with respect to this issue. Nor can it be said that a general consensus exists among the commentators.[18]

---

11. Stephenson v. Calpine Conifers II, Ltd., 652 F.2d 808, 815 (9th Cir.1981); Kirshner v. United States, 603 F.2d 234, 241 (2nd Cir.1978), cert. denied, 442 U.S. 909 (1979), 444 U.S. 995 (1979); Newman v. Prior, 518 F.2d 97, 99 (4th Cir.1975); and Surowitz v. Hilton Hotels Corp., 342 F.2d 596, 604 (7th Cir.1965), rev'd on other grounds, 383 U.S. 363 (1966).

12. Greater Iowa Corp. v. McLendon, 378 F.2d 783, 789, 791 (8th Cir.1967).

18. Compare Hazen, A Look Beyond the Pruning of Rule 10b–5: Implied Remedies and Section 17(a) of the Securities Act of 1933, 64 Va.L.Rev. 641 (1978); Note, Implied Civil Remedies Under Section 17(a) of the Securities Act of 1933, 53 B.U.L.Rev. 70 (1973); Note, Section 17(a) of the Securities Act of 1933: Implication of a Private Right of Action, supra, note 10; and Note, Implied Private Rights of Action Under the Securities Act of 1933 Section 17(a), 14 U.Mich.J.L.Ref. 563 (1981) (private cause of action may be implied) with 3 L. Loss, Securities Regulation 1784–86 (2nd ed. 1961); Douglas & Bates, Federal Securities Act of 1933, 43 Yale L.J. 171, 181–82 (1933); Horton, Section 17(a) of the 1933

Perhaps the main reason for the somewhat awkward development of the law under § 17(a) of the 1933 Act is the fact that it has traditionally lived in the shadow of another area of securities law: Rule 10b–5. Rule 10b–5, adopted under § 10(b) of the Securities and Exchange Act of 1934, is substantially identical to § 17(a). When the judiciary recognized a private cause of action under Rule 10b–5 shortly after its promulgation, cases that might have fit a § 17(a) cause of action were instead decided under Rule 10b–5. This was true even when a plaintiff pleaded a cause of action under both.

In 1976, however, the Supreme Court severely limited the Rule 10b–5 cause of action in Ernst & Ernst v. Hochfelder, 425 U.S. 185 (1976). There the Court established that allegations of the defendant's scienter are an essential element of the plaintiff's cause of action under Rule 10b–5. The Court based its holding on the language of § 10(b) of the 1934 Act, asserting that the narrower language of that section constrained the reach of the broader Rule 10b–5 language.

The law under § 17(a), however, is not so distinct. In Aaron v. SEC, 446 U.S. 680 (1980), the Supreme Court was faced with the question of whether the SEC was required to establish scienter as an element of a civil enforcement action to enjoin violations of § 10(b) and Rule 10b–5 of the 1934 Act, and § 17(a) of the 1933 Act. While the Court decided that scienter was a necessary prerequisite under the 1934 Act, its response split with respect to § 17(a):

> The language of § 17(a) strongly suggests that Congress contemplated a scienter requirement under § 17(a)(1), but not under § 17(a)(2) or § 17(a)(3). The language of § 17(a)(1), which makes it unlawful "to employ any device, scheme, or artifice to defraud," plainly evinces an intent on the part of Congress to proscribe only knowing or intentional misconduct * * *.
>
> By contrast, the language of § 17(a)(2), which prohibits any person from obtaining money or property "by means of any untrue statement of a material fact," is devoid of any suggestion whatsoever of a scienter requirement * * *.
>
> Finally, the language of § 17(a)(3), under which it is unlawful for any person "to engage in any transaction, practice, or course of business which *operates* or *would operate* as a fraud or deceit," (emphasis added) quite plainly focuses upon the *effect* of particular conduct on members of the investing public, rather than upon the culpability of the person responsible * * *.
>
> It is our view, in sum, that the language of § 17(a) requires scienter under § 17(a)(1), but not under § 17(a)(2) or § 17(a)(3).

446 U.S. at 695–97. True, the court resolved the issue only with respect to SEC enforcement actions; however, it is doubtful that a different interpretation would be given if an implied private cause of action is found to exist. Given this assumption, § 17(a) suddenly becomes an attractive, viable

Securities Act—the Wrong Place for a Private Right, 68 Nw.U.L.Rev. 44 (1973); Landis, Liability Sections of Securities Act, 18 Am.Accountant 330, 331 (1933); Ruder, Civil Liability Under Rule 10b–5; Judicial Revision of Legislative Intent?, 57 Nw.U.L. Rev. 627, 656–57 (1963); and Note, Section 17(a) of the '33 Act: Defining the Scope of Antifraud Protection, 37 Wash. & Lee L.Rev. 859 (1980) (private cause of action may not be implied).

alternative to actions previously brought under Rule 10b–5, at least as to those based upon negligence. All of this, however, takes for granted that a private cause of action does indeed exist under § 17(a). After analyzing the issue in light of recent Supreme Court decisions, we conclude that it does not.

The question of whether a private cause of action should be implied under § 17(a) operates against a backdrop of long-developing and varied judicial formulations of the circumstances under which implication is appropriate. The most recent test stems from the Supreme Court's decision of Cort v. Ash, 422 U.S. 66 (1975). In *Cort,* the Supreme Court unanimously refused to imply a private cause of action for damages against corporate directors and in favor of stockholders for purported violations of a criminal statute prohibiting corporations from making certain campaign contributions. In rejecting the plaintiff's theory that implication was appropriate for violations of this criminal statute, Justice Brennan outlined the following four-part test for determining when a private remedy should be implied:

First, is the plaintiff "one of the class for whose *especial* benefit the statute was enacted,"—that is, does the statute create a federal right in favor of the plaintiff? Second, is there any indication of legislative intent, explicit or implicit, either to create such a remedy or to deny one? Third, is it consistent with the underlying purposes of the legislative scheme to imply such a remedy for the plaintiff? And finally, is the cause of action one traditionally relegated to state law, in an area basically the concern of the States, so that it would be inappropriate to infer a cause of action based solely on federal law?

(citations omitted). 422 U.S. at 78. Combined, these four factors present the relevant inquiries to pursue in resolving the question of whether an implied cause of action exists.

The test set down in *Cort* was more restrictive than any of its predecessors. Notwithstanding this, more recent cases, by their music if not their lyrics, evince a further retreat from the creation of implied causes of action. For example, in Touche Ross & Co. v. Redington, 442 U.S. 560, 568–74 (1979), the court observed that examination of the language, legislative history and purpose of a statute are the proper means for resolving the implication issue. Since the first three criteria of the *Cort* standard are the traditional indicia of legislative intent, the *Redington* Court placed special emphasis on these factors. If these three inquiries remain unsatisfied, the *Redington* court held that courts need not determine whether an implied private right is a cause of action traditionally relegated to state law. In denying private rights under § 17(a) of the 1934 Act, the court indicated for the first time that the four elements of the *Cort* test are not of equal weight; the ultimate issue is whether Congress intended to create a private cause of action. Id., at 575–77. See also California v. Sierra Club, 451 U.S. 287, 293 (1981).

This approach was echoed later that year in Transamerica Mortgage Advisors, Inc. v. Lewis, 444 U.S. 11 (1979), where the court premised its analysis of the implication issues upon basic statutory construction. There, the court declined to imply a private remedy under § 206 of the Investment Advisers Act of 1940, relying primarily on its understanding of the Act's legislative history. It noted that other sections of the Act provided for criminal penalties, civil action by the SEC, and other administrative sanctions and expressed doubt that Congress merely forgot to mention a private action it meant to confer. Thereafter, the court concluded that if neither the statutory language nor the legislative history revealed congressional intent to imply a private cause of action, the inquiry ends with a denial of private rights.

Application of the modified *Cort* test to § 17(a) of the 1933 Act leads this Court to believe that a private cause of action is not implied. As expressed by so many opinions before us, our analysis must begin with the language of the statute itself. * * * On its face, § 17(a) does not appear to satisfy the first factor of the *Cort* test, for the statutory language does not suggest a private cause of action. The statute merely represents a general censure of fraudulent practices; only subsequent provisions enable equitable and criminal causes of action.

Nor can there be said to be any indication of legislative intent, explicit or implicit, to create such a remedy. The legislative history of the 1933 Act makes no mention of civil liability under § 17(a); congressional discussion of civil liability under the Act centers on §§ 11 and 12. As one commentator has noted:

> The most reasonable view regarding Section 17(a) of the 1933 Act is that Congress intended that the *Commission* would use it to deal with flagrant cases of abuse. Evidence of this point of view appears in connection with an amendment offered by Senator Fletcher to Title II of the 1934 Act, which was an amendment to the 1933 Act. Senator Fletcher asked that section 17(a) be amended to require that groups purporting to act on behalf of stockholders comply with certain registration provisions. Section 17(a) was to be amended by adding subsections (c), (d) and (e) and renumbering section 17(c) as section 17(f). Senator Fletcher then asked to have a memorandum explaining the amendment printed in the *Congressional Record*. At the end of the memorandum the following statement appears: "It is to be noted that enforcement of the provisions of the new subsection is left to injunction, stop order, and criminal prosecution. *No civil liability attaches for any violation thereof.*"
>
> It is significant that this memorandum was offered by the Senator whose name was commonly associated with the 1934 Act. He was obviously well acquainted with the provisions of the 1934 Act and the 1933 Act. It seems clear that in Senator Fletcher's opinion no civil liability attached under Section 17 of the 1933 Act.

Ruder, Civil Liability Under Rule 10b–5: Judicial Revision of Legislative Intent?, supra note 19, at 656–57. It would, therefore, appear that the second *Cort* factor has been answered in the negative.

Under Transamerica Mortgage Advisors, Inc. v. Lewis, 444 U.S. at 23–24, our analysis could stop here. However, an examination of the remaining *Cort* factors reinforces our result. The third *Cort* factor asks whether "it is consistent with the underlying purposes of the legislative scheme to imply such a remedy for the plaintiffs?" Cort v. Ash, 422 U.S. at 78. A review of the Act indicates that the answer to this question is also no.

The Securities Act of 1933 contains two express civil liabilities for the protection of purchasers. The first of these is § 11 which prohibits falsehoods and omissions in the registration statement. The second is § 12(2) which protects purchasers from misstatements or omissions in written or oral communications. Together these sections confer specific private rights upon purchasers. Before a purchaser may successfully bring suit under either of these two sections, however, strict procedural requirements must first be satisfied. Section 17(a)(2) prohibits the same type of conduct as §§ 11 and 12, but has none of the limitations imposed by Congress. The creation of an implied cause of action § 17(a) under these circumstances would effectively frustrate the carefully laid framework of the Act.

Finally, *Cort* rejects implication of a private cause of action for matters traditionally relegated to state courts. 422 U.S. at 78. Liability for the sorts of transactions arising under § 17(a), however, is not such a matter. The congressional hearings regarding enactment of the Securities Act are replete with testimony regarding the states' inability to deal with securities fraud. In addition, the Securities Act confers concurrent jurisdiction upon federal and state courts, providing strong support for the proposition that § 17(a) matters are not solely within the state sphere.

Summarizing, then, it would appear that the *Cort* test as applied to § 17(a) of the Securities Act of 1933 points away from the implication of a private cause of action. This, together with the Supreme Court's conservative interpretation of the test in recent years, leads us to the conclusion that the district court correctly dismissed this theory of relief.

* * *

Affirmed in Part and Reversed in Part; Remanded to the court below to decide whether or not he will decide the state law claim or relegate the parties to the state courts of Louisiana.

THE DEVELOPMENT OF IMPLIED ACTIONS

For a period of almost thirty years following the decision in the *Kardon* case, the courts routinely assumed that a private right of action for damages existed under whatever section of the statute or rule of the Commission was being invoked by the plaintiff as the basis for his law suit. The courts rarely even mentioned the existence of a private right of action as an issue to be resolved, presumably because the defendants did not seriously argue to the contrary, and were solely concerned with defining the requirements for and limitations upon such an action. These had, of course, been left totally undefined by Congress since it had not created any such cause of action other than by implication.

In 1975 the case of Cort v. Ash,[1] which is discussed in the *Curran* case, was decided by the Supreme Court. In that case, the court reversed this trend regarding the implication of causes of action generally (although that case dealt with the question of an implied right of action under the Hatch Act prohibiting corporate political contributions rather than under the securities laws) and stated that four "factors" should be considered in determining whether such a private right of action exists. The court said: "In determining whether a private remedy is implicit in a statute not expressly providing one, several factors were relevant. First, is the plaintiff 'one of the class for whose *especial* benefit the statute was enacted' * * *—that is, does the statute create a federal right in favor of the plaintiff? Second, is there any indication of legislative intent, explicit or implicit, either to create such a remedy or to deny

1. 422 U.S. 66 (1975).

one?　*　*　*　Third, is it consistent with the underlying purposes of the legislative scheme to imply such a remedy for the plaintiff?　*　*　*　And finally, is the cause of action one traditionally relegated to state law, in an area basically the concern of the States, so that it would be inappropriate to infer a cause of action based solely on federal law?" [2]

In the *Redington* case, however, the court stated that it was unnecessary to go into these "factors" because there was no evidence of any legislative intent to create a private right of action for the violation of Section 17(a) of the 1934 Act. This approach is of course diametrically opposite to that of the *Kardon* case, which required affirmative evidence of an intent to *deny* a private right of action in order for one not to be implied under general principles of law. The *Redington* case was followed by that of Transamerica Mortgage Advisors, Inc. v. Lewis.[3] In that case, the Supreme Court held that no private right of action for damages exists under Section 206 of the Investment Advisers Act of 1940, the general fraud section in that statute, the language of which parallels that of Rule 10b-5. However, the court held that a party to an investment advisory contract with an investment adviser could bring an action under Section 215 of the Act, declaring "void" any contract entered into in violation of the provisions of the Act, for rescission of the contract and the return of the consideration which he had paid (i.e., the advisory fees). The court relied upon the absence of any express provision in the Act for a private right of action for damages and the absence of any indication in the legislative history that Congress intended to create such a private right of action, as well as upon the provisions of Section 214 giving the Federal courts jurisdiction only over "suits in equity" as contrasted with the provision in other Federal securities statutes, which refer both to suits in equity and "actions at law."

The court said: "Relying on the factors identified in Cort v. Ash, supra, the respondent and the Commission, as *amicus curiae,* argue that our inquiry in this case cannot stop with the intent of Congress, but must consider the utility of a private remedy, and the fact that it may be one not traditionally relegated to state law. We rejected the same contentions last Term in Touche Ross & Co. v. Redington, supra, where it was argued that these factors standing alone justified the implication of a private right of action under § 17(a) of the Securities Exchange Act of 1934." The four dissenters, in an opinion by Mr. Justice White, argued that all of the four "factors" set forth in *Cort v. Ash* pointed in this case to the implication of a private right of action for damages; that is, that the statute was enacted for the benefit of a special class of persons, the clients of investment advisers; that there was no evidence of any express or implicit legislative intent to negate a private right of action; that the existence of a private right of action was compatible with the legislative scheme and even essential to its achievement; and that the subject matter of the cause of action was not one which has traditionally been relegated to state law so as to make it inappropriate to infer a federal cause of action.

It was assumed by some as a result of the *Redington* case and the *Transamerica* case, listening as the Fifth Circuit says to the music if not the words, that no additional implied causes of action would be created in the securities law field and that those already recognized were in jeopardy. Some people even went so far as to predict that the Supreme Court would abolish any private right of action under Rule 10b-5. This euphoria of the Defendants' Bar was short-lived. The *Curran* case and the *Herman & MacLean* case seemed to evidence a partial return to the free-wheeling days of the implication of private rights of action. In the *Curran* case, Justice Stevens hoisted Justice Rehnquist

---

2.　422 U.S. at 78.　　　　　　　　**3.**　444 U.S. 11 (1979).

on his own petard by saying that we do not have to go into the *Cort v. Ash* "factors" because we have found affirmative evidence in the legislative history that Congress intended to "preserve" the private rights of action which were recognized by the courts prior to the amendment of the statute in 1974 (although these indications in the legislative history were disputed point by point by the dissenters).

What implication does this have for private rights of action under the securities laws in view of the major amendments, although not to the civil liability sections, which were enacted in 1975? In the *Curran* case, Justice Stevens stated in footnote 88 that "Congress comprehensively reexamined the CEA [Commodity Exchange Act] in 1974 and did not amend the sections under which the cause of action had been implied; no comprable legislative approval or acquiescence exists for the Rule 10b–5 remedy." Nevertheless, Justice Marshall in the opinion in the *Herman & MacLean* case relied to some extent on the 1975 amendments to the securities laws as justifying the decision in that case, without referring to this disclaimer in the prior decision. It should be noted that the *Curran* case was a five to four decision, but so was the *Lewis* case. It would appear to be impossible, in the present state of authority, to say with certainty whether a private right of action exists under any particular section or rule other than those already adjudicated by the Supreme Court.

See Conard, Securities Regulation in the Burger Court, 56 U.Colo.L.Rev. 193 (1985); Ashford, Implied Causes of Action Under Federal Laws: Calling the Court back to *Borak*, 79 Nw.U.L.Rev. 227 (1984); Mather and Mather, Statutorily Implied Federal Causes of Action After Merrill Lynch, How Sad It Is; How Simple It Could Be, 88 Dick.L.Rev. 593 (1984); Schneider, Implying Private Rights and Remedies Under the Federal Securities Acts, 62 N.C.L.Rev. 853 (1984); Steinberg, The Propriety and Scope of Cumulative Remedies Under the Federal Securities Laws, 67 Corn.L.Rev. 557 (1982); Frankel, Implied Rights of Action, 67 Va.L.Rev. 553 (1981); Maher, Implied Private Rights of Action and the Federal Securities Laws: A Historical Perspective, 37 Wash. & Lee L.Rev. 717 (1980); Hazen, Implied Private Remedies Under Federal Statutes: Neither a Death Knell Nor a Moratorium, 33 Vand.L.Rev. 1333 (1980); Steinberg, Implied Private Rights of Action Under Federal Law, 55 Notre Dame Law 33 (1979); Brooks, Rule 10b–5 in the Balance: An Analysis of the Supreme Court's Policy Perspective, 32 Hastings L.J. 403 (1980).

ACTIONS UNDER SECTION 10(b) AND RULE 10b–5 OF THE 1934 ACT

As has been indicated above, all of the early cases dealing with Rule 10b–5 held that there was a private right of action under that rule.[4] In 1971, the Supreme Court in Superintendent of Insurance v. Bankers Life and Casualty Co.[5] casually brushed aside this question in a one sentence footnote: "It is now established that a private right of action is implied under § 10(b)," and this question has now been conclusively resolved by the *Herman & MacLean* decision. It should be noted that this was a unanimous decision of the Supreme Court (although Justice Powell did not participate).

4. For early cases discussing the question, see Fischman v. Raytheon Manufacturing Co., 188 F.2d 783 (2d Cir.1951); Fratt v. Robinson, 203 F.2d 627 (9th Cir. 1953); Ellis v. Carter, 291 F.2d 270 (9th Cir.1961); Kardon v. National Gypsum Co., 69 F.Supp. 512 (E.D.Pa.1946); Speed v. Transamerica Corp., 71 F.Supp. 457 (D.Del.

1947), 99 F.Supp. 808 (D.Del.1951), aff'd 235 F.2d 369 (3d Cir.1956); Osborne v. Mallory, 86 F.Supp. 869 (S.D.N.Y.1949). Few of the hundreds of subsequent cases even bothered to mention this basic issue.

5. 404 U.S. 6 (1971).

Section 10(b) by its terms applies to "any security registered [i.e., listed] on a national securities exchange or any security not so registered", which would seem to be all inclusive. However, on the basis of the expressed intention of Congress in the 1934 Act to regulate the exchanges and the over-the-counter markets, it was once argued that the section and rule do not apply to the purchase or sale of a security which is not traded in any organized market. The cases are in accord in rejecting this argument.[6] In fact, originally the great majority of private civil suits instituted under the rule concern closely-held corporations whose securities were not actively traded in any market, although in recent years public corporations have been the primary target of these actions.

The principal rearguard action which has been fought against liability under Rule 10b–5 in recent years has been the contention that an action cannot be maintained under Rule 10b–5 where one of the express civil liability provisions of the 1933 Act or the 1934 Act is applicable.

The Alleged Conflict with Section 11 of the 1933 Act. The first two cases actually involving suits under Rule 10b–5 by purchasers of registered securities held that no such suit could be maintained [7] or that if it could it was subject to all of the defenses and qualifications of a suit under Section 11 [8] (which is the same thing as saying that it can't be maintained at all). However, in Fischman v. Raytheon Manufacturing Co.[9] Judge Jerome Frank stated in dictum that a buyer of securities could sue under Rule 10b–5 "whether or not he could maintain a suit under § 11 of the 1933 Act." He justified this result on the basis that Rule 10b–5 required proof of "fraud" and therefore, because of this greater burden on the plaintiff, did not conflict with Section 11 liability; and this rationale has now of course been adopted by the Supreme Court in the *Herman & MacLean* case.

The Alleged Conflict with Section 12(2) of the 1934 Act. In the *Fischman* case, Judge Frank stated that in the absence of an action under Rule 10b–5 the plaintiff-buyers "would have no redress whatever under the statute." [10] How-ever, he overlooked entirely Section 12(2) of the 1933 Act under which the plaintiff-buyers could have maintained an action. In the subsequent case of Ellis v. Carter,[11] where the conflict was pointed out to the court, the court held that this duplication was no reason not to imply a right of action under Rule 10b–5. An action under Section 12(2) would be subject to a defense of due care, and it would also be subject to a more stringent venue provision, and to a shorter statute of limitations. If you assume, as Judge Frank did, that proof of an intentional misstatement is required under Rule 10b–5, then it can be plausibly argued that if the plaintiff wants to assume this additional burden he should reasonably be freed of the restrictions.

In Berger v. Bishop Investment Corporation [12] the Eighth Circuit explained this rationale as follows: "Our holding that the plaintiffs are entitled to rely on Section 10(b) free of the restrictions of Section 12(2) does not nullify those procedural provisions. If the plaintiffs want the advantage of the 1933 Act's diminished burden of proof, they cannot avoid the restrictive provisions of that Act. Only when the plaintiffs have accepted the burden of proving scienter

6. Fratt v. Robinson, supra note 4; Er-rion v. Connell, 236 F.2d 447 (9th Cir.1956); Ellis v. Carter, 291 F.2d 270 (9th Cir.1961); Stevens v. Vowell, 343 F.2d 374 (10th Cir. 1965); but cf. Boone v. Baugh, 308 F.2d 711 (8th Cir.1962).

7. Montague v. Electronic Corp. of America, 76 F.Supp. 933 (S.D.N.Y.1948).

8. Rosenberg v. Globe Aircraft Corp., 80 F.Supp. 123 (E.D.Pa.1948).

9. 188 F.2d 783 (2d Cir.1951).

10. 188 F.2d at 787.

11. 291 F.2d 270 (9th Cir.1961).

12. 695 F.2d 302 (8th Cir.1982).

under Section 10(b) are defendants deprived of the benefit of the shorter statute of limitations under Section 12(2). Moreover, if the plaintiffs attempt to proceed under Section 10(b) but cannot carry their burden of proving fraud, the provisions of Section 12(2) must be applied." [13] Under this rationale, which was adopted by the Supreme Court in holding that an action under Rule 10b–5 could be maintained despite the concurrent availability of an action under Section 11, there is little doubt that the Supreme Court would similarly rule with respect to a concurrent action under Section 12(2).

The Alleged Conflict with Section 18 of the 1934 Act. Section 18 of the 1934 Act creates a private right of action in favor of both buyers and sellers of securities and, therefore, to that extent overlaps any implied right of action existing under Rule 10b–5. The cause of action under Section 18 is limited, however, in a number of important respects which have made it highly unattractive to plaintiffs, and there are virtually no cases in which plaintiffs have actually recovered under Section 18 and few in which they have even seriously tried to do so in view of the broader remedy which has been available under Rule 10b–5.

(1) The remedy under Section 18 is limited to a false or misleading statement which is contained in a document *filed* with the Commission under the provisions of the 1934 Act. Therefore, it gives no remedy whatever in connection with a transaction in the securities of a non-reporting company, since it will file nothing with the Commission. It also gives no remedy with respect to an oral or written misstatement which is made otherwise than in a filed document even if the company is a reporting company.

(2) The plaintiff must prove that he purchased or sold "in reliance upon such statement." While this may not be too difficult in the case of a document, such as a proxy statement, which is required to be circulated to the shareholders, in the case of a document which is merely filed by the reporting company and is not further disseminated proof of such reliance may be impossible. Under Rule 10b–5 the question of whether, or to what extent, the plaintiff must show reliance upon the false or misleading statement is still uncertain (see Chapter 18, below).

(3) The defendant may escape liability if he shows that "he acted in good faith and had no knowledge that such statement was false or misleading." While the requirement of "good faith" might be interpreted to impose liability if the defendant's conduct was "reckless", literally this provision would seem to impose a more stringent requirement with respect to the fault of the defendant than exists under Rule 10b–5 (although the defendant has the burden of proof of showing his state of mind). It is clearly less favorable to the plaintiff than an action under Section 12(2) of the 1933 Act which imposes liability for negligence and also puts the burden of proof of showing lack of negligence on the defendant.

(4) A short statute of limitations is imposed by the provisions of Section 18(c) upon an action under Section 18 of one year after discovery by the plaintiff of the facts or, in any event, three years after the accrual of the cause of action. By contrast, many of the borrowed state statutes of limitations applicable to an action under Rule 10b–5 (see Chapter 19, below) do not commence the running of the limitations period until discovery by the plaintiff of the facts constituting the cause of action and are frequently of three, four or five years in duration.

While the implication of a cause of action under Rule 10b–5 with respect to a false or misleading statement made otherwise than in a filed document does

---

13. 695 F.2d at 308.

not overlap to any extent with the express civil remedy contained in Section 18, the question arises as to whether such a cause of action under Rule 10b–5 should be implied if the false or misleading statement *is* contained in a filed document, and thereby permit the restrictive provisions in Section 18 to be evaded by the plaintiff. When the Supreme Court in the *Borak* case upheld a cause of action under Section 14(a) of the 1934 Act with respect to a false or misleading statement in a proxy statement, however, it did not even refer to Section 18 or discuss this possible objection to implying an action under Section 14.

In Ross v. A.H. Robins Co., Inc.,[14] the Second Circuit held that an action for damages under Rule 10b–5 is not precluded by the fact that the conduct alleged may also have constituted a violation of Section 18 of the 1934 Act since the allegedly false and misleading statements were contained in documents filed with the Securities and Exchange Commission under that Act. The court said: "To establish a § 10(b) violation, *the plaintiff must plead and prove* that the defendant acted with scienter in making a material misstatement or omission. A plaintiff seeking recovery under § 18 faces a significantly lighter burden. He must merely plead and prove that a document filed with the Commission contains a material misstatement or omission. If he can show reliance on that statement, liability is established, unless by the very terms of section 18, *the person sued shall prove that he acted in 'good faith and had no knowledge that such statement was false or misleading.'* (emphasis added). See Ernst & Ernst v. Hochfelder, supra, 425 U.S. at 211, n. 31. As is readily apparent this difference may prove critical. A plaintiff unable to allege those specific facts necessary under Fed.R.Civ.P. 9(b) which would raise a strong inference of scienter, * * * would not be able to establish a *prima facie* case under § 10(b). The very same plaintiff, however, could proceed under § 18. Moreover, the ultimate outcome of the litigation may hinge upon who bears the burden of establishing the defendant's state of mind. In our view the far more difficult task which confronts a plaintiff seeking to proceed under § 10(b) provides a rationale for dispensing with the reliance requirement inherent in § 18. Moreover, for several other reasons we are unwilling to bar plaintiffs from proceeding under § 10(b) and Rule 10b–5.

"To now hold, at this late date, that conduct is not proscribed by § 10(b) merely because it is also subject to § 18 would effectively deprive open market investors who relied on misleading market information of any remedy simply because the misinformation happened to be lodged in a form filed with the SEC. Such a result would be remarkably incongruous in view of the fact that it is the open market investor who over the years has become one of the prime beneficiaries of the protections afforded by § 10(b) and Rule 10b–5. As we have already indicated, we are not being asked to liberalize even further the recognized implied right of action under § 10(b) or judicially to create a new right in place of that provided by § 18. Cf. Touche Ross & Co. v. Redington, supra. Rather, plaintiffs only ask that we permit § 10(b) to be used, as it has in the past, to state a claim that is beyond the scope of § 18—the latter section furthering the narrow and particularized objective of encouraging use of and reliance upon records filed with the SEC, by expressly authorizing damage suits against those who make them depositaries of materially false or misleading statements. Furthermore, we can conceive of no rational purpose which would be furthered by creating a structure where liability for material misrepresentations adversely affecting investors would vary tremendously depending upon

---

14. 607 F.2d 545 (2d Cir.1979), cert. denied, 446 U.S. 946 (1980), reh. denied 448 U.S. 911.

whether the statement happened to be filed with the SEC. Accepting the existence of a private action under § 10(b) and its well established contours, see Cannon v. University of Chicago, supra, 441 U.S. at 691 n. 13 (recognizing that the very existence of the implied right of action under § 10(b) can be explained historically), we believe that we can fairly say that Congress would not approve of such a disparity. We also believe that holding that plaintiffs must proceed under the terms of § 18 because the statements were filed with the SEC would encourage corporate managers to include their misrepresentations in material filed with the SEC, for the sole purpose of insulating themselves from liability under § 10(b) and restricting the class of potential plaintiffs to the unlikely few who actually viewed and relied on the misleading information."

In Wachovia Bank & Trust Co. v. National Student Marketing Corp.[15] the District of Columbia Circuit held that the existence of the various express remedies under the 1933 Act and the 1934 Act, including Section 18 of the 1934 Act, did not prevent the implication of a private right of action under Section 10(b) and Rule 10b–5. The court stated that: "It may be reasonable to infer from these recent pronouncements [in the *Redington* case and the *Transamerica* case] that the [Supreme] Court is not favorably inclined toward expanding the doctrine of implied remedies; it is unreasonable to imply * * * that all the implied remedies that have previously been established have now been swept away. In sum, we find that under the *Cort* analysis, section 10(b) continues to lend itself to private remedies, and that neither the spirit nor the letter of any Supreme Court opinion suggests otherwise." [16] The Court also relied, in part, upon the fact that the securities laws were amended in 1975. It stated: "As we noted above, the securities laws have been addressed by Congress on numerous occasions since 1934, most recently in 1975. Obviously, if Congress had wished to disapprove the judicial implication of a private remedy under section 10(b), it had an opportunity to do so. The silence is significant." [17]

The Alleged Conflict with Section 9(e) of the 1934 Act. In Chemetron Corp. v. Business Funds, Inc.[18] the court initially held that an action could not be maintained under Rule 10b–5 where an action was available under Section 9(e) of the 1934 Act, because Section 9 only prohibited certain *wilful* misconduct; therefore, the plaintiff was not assuming a greater burden of proof by suing under Rule 10b–5 and to recognize such a right of action would nullify the procedural restrictions applicable to an action under Section 9. In fact, the court indicated that the plaintiff would have a *lesser* burden of proof under Rule 10b–5 because of the requirement that certain additional facts be proven under the express provisions of Section 9(a)(1), (2) and (6). Judge Jerre Williams dissented from this decision. The court purported to apply the same analysis which had been used in the earlier decision of the Fifth Circuit in holding that an action could be maintained under Rule 10b–5 despite the concurrent existence of an action under Section 11 of the 1933 Act,[19] a decision later affirmed by the Supreme Court in the opinion printed above.

The Supreme Court granted certiorari in this case and then vacated the judgment and remanded the case for "further consideration in light of [the Supreme Court decision in] Herman & MacLean v. Huddleston". On remand, Judge Gee, who wrote the original majority opinion, adhered to his former opinion even "in the light of" the decision in the *Herman & MacLean* case, but

15. 650 F.2d 342 (D.C.Cir.1980), cert. denied 452 U.S. 954 (1981).

16. 650 F.2d at 353.

17. 650 F.2d at 358–359.

18. 682 F.2d 1149 (5th Cir.1982), cert. denied 460 U.S. 1013 (1983).

19. Huddleston v. Herman & MacLean, 640 F.2d 534 (5th Cir.1981).

Judge Reavley changed his vote and Judge Williams wrote the new majority opinion upholding the Rule 10b–5 action despite the alleged conflict with Section 9.[20] The Fifth Circuit then granted a hearing in the case *en banc,* but the lawsuit was settled prior to that *en banc* hearing.

In the light of the *Herman & MacLean* case, which time was the Fifth Circuit panel correct in its analysis and decision of this issue?

Government Securities. Perhaps the most difficult problem of all is the question whether a buyer of government securities can maintain an action under Rule 10b–5. There is then no conflict with any other section of the 1933 or 1934 Acts, since such securities are not registered under the 1933 Act and therefore no action is maintainable under Section 11 and also no action is maintainable under Section 12(2). The latter section covers exempt securities except those exempt by Section 3(a)(2) of the 1933 Act (i.e., government and bank securities). It can be argued that the absence of any action under Sections 11 and 12(2) is the very reason for recognizing an action under Rule 10b–5.[21] On the other hand, it is difficult to believe that, after carefully excluding all Federal statutory liability for the sale of government securities in express terms in 1933, Congress impliedly included such liability by a cryptic section in 1934.[22]

For general discussions of Rule 10b–5 see Bromberg, Securities Law Fraud—SEC Rule 10b–5 (McGraw-Hill, 1977) (a 4 volume work devoted entirely to Rule 10b–5); A. Jacobs, The Impact of Rule 10b–5 (3 Vols.) (1980 rev.); Bloomenthal, Securities and Federal Corporate Law (3 vols.) (1979). In addition to the articles cited in the previous note, see Bloomenthal, Shareholder Derivative Actions Under the Securities Laws—Phoenix or Endangered Species?, 26 Ariz. L.Rev. 767 (1984); Aldave, "Neither Unusual nor Unfortunate"; The Overlap of Rule 10b–5 With the Express Liability Sections of the Securities Acts, 60 Tex.L. Rev. 719 (1982); Ruder, Civil Liability Under Rule 10b–5: Judicial Revision of the Legislative Intent?, 57 Nw.U.L.Rev. 627 (1963); Joseph, Civil Liability Under Rule 10b–5—A Reply, 59 Nw.U.L.Rev. 171 (1964).

ACTIONS UNDER SECTION 14(a) OF THE 1934 ACT

The initial actions under the Proxy Rules were actions by one contesting group of shareholders to enjoin the other group from committing alleged violations and the case of Studebaker Corp. v. Gittlin [23] held that the corporation itself had standing to sue the insurgents for such an injunction.[24] But it was considered very doubtful prior to the *Borak* case that any cause of action would lie under the Proxy Rules after the holding of the meeting and the completion of the corporate action authorized at the meeting. In fact, for a period of time the Proxy Rules themselves contained a provision that violation of them would not invalidate any action taken at the meeting.[25] This provision was later removed by the SEC, but expressions such as the following by Judge

20. Chemetron Corporation v. Business Funds, Inc., 718 F.2d 725 (5th Cir.1983).

21. Cf. Thiele v. Shields, 131 F.Supp. 416, 420 n. 5 (S.D.N.Y.1955). See, also, Trussell v. United Underwriters, Limited, 228 F.Supp. 757 (D.Colo.1964).

22. Citizens Casualty Co. v. Shields, CCH Fed.Sec.L.Rep. ¶ 90,683 (S.D.N.Y. 1954).

23. 360 F.2d 692 (2d Cir.1966). Accord, Studebaker Corp. v. Allied Products Corp., 256 F.Supp. 173 (W.D.Mich.1966).

24. The *Studebaker* case overruled the earlier case of Howard v. Furst, 238 F.2d 790 (2d Cir.1956), cert. denied, 353 U.S. 937 (1957).

25. See 2 Loss, Securities Regulation 960–61 (2d ed.1961).

Walsh in the lower court decision in Howard v. Furst [26] discouraged any belief that retroactive invalidation of corporate action would be possible under the Rules: "There is no basis in the statute or its legislative history for an implication that Congress intended to give an individual stockholder, as an incident of his protection by proxy statement regulations, the right to rescind completed corporate transactions. * * *" [27] And the case of Dann v. Studebaker-Packard Corp.,[28] which is discussed and overruled in the *Borak* decision, had held that the Federal court could only grant a declaratory judgment as to a violation of the Proxy Rules, leaving the remedy, if any, to be determined by State law in a State court.

The proxy statement alleged to be false or misleading in the *Borak* case was of course a document required to be filed with the Commission and was subject to the provisions of Section 18 providing for civil liability. However, the Supreme Court does not even bother to cite Section 18, much less discuss the question whether, Congress having provided a remedy, the courts should imply a totally different one. It is true that in that case the plaintiffs may not have had any remedy under Section 18, since they were shareholders of the acquiring corporation in a merger and, even if Rule 133 then in force did not apply to the 1934 Act,[29] they didn't exchange their shares for those of a different corporate entity in the transaction. Therefore, they may not have been considered to be purchasers or sellers under Section 18.[30] Even if this analysis had been made and this conclusion reached, there would still seem to remain the question whether Congress by excluding certain persons from the civil remedy provisions had intended just that or had intended that the courts nevertheless create one for them. But these considerations either were not recognized or were not thought worthy of mention by the Supreme Court.

It has not been questioned since the *Borak* case that a private right of action exists under Section 14(a) for a violation of the Proxy Rules, both injunction actions to prevent a violation and actions for other "appropriate remedies" which the court did not undertake to define in that decision. The reliance by the court upon Section 27 of the 1934 Act as a basis for implying a private right of action under any section of the 1934 Act was repudiated, however, by the Supreme Court in the *Redington* case. That section confers upon the federal courts exclusive jurisdiction to entertain any suits "to enforce any liability or duty" created by that act. The court said in the *Redington* case: "Section 27 grants jurisdiction to the federal courts and provides for venue and service of process. It creates no cause of action of its own force and effect; it imposes no liabilities. The source of plaintiffs' rights must be found, if at all, in the substantive provisions of the 1934 Act which they seek to enforce, not in the jurisdictional provision."

The pioneering articles relating to civil actions under the Proxy Rules were by Professor Loss, The SEC Proxy Rules in the Courts, 73 Harv.L.Rev. 1041 (1960); and The SEC Proxy Rules and State Law, 73 Harv.L.Rev. 1249 (1960), which have been substantially reprinted in 2 Loss, Securities Regulation 931–1019 (2d ed. 1961). See, also, Painter, Civil Liability Under the Federal Proxy Rules, 64 Wash.U.L.Q. 425 (1986); Kaplan, Shareholder Attacks On Mergers

26. 140 F.Supp. 507 (S.D.N.Y.1956), aff'd 238 F.2d 790 (2d Cir.1956), cert. denied 353 U.S. 937 (1957).

27. 140 F.Supp. at 513.

28. 288 F.2d 201 (6th Cir.1961).

29. Securities and Exchange Commission v. National Securities, Inc., 393 U.S. 453 (1969).

30. But see Nanfito v. Tekseed Hybrid Co., 341 F.Supp. 240 (D.Neb.1972), aff'd 473 F.2d 537 (8th Cir.1973), holding that the shareholders of the surviving corporation in a merger may sue under Rule 10b–5, despite the Birnbaum rule restricting a remedy to "purchasers or sellers."

and Acquisitions under Federal Securities Laws, 50 Chi.Bar Rec. 441 (1969); Lockwood, Corporate Acquisitions and Actions under Sections 10(b) and 14 of the Securities Exchange Act of 1934, 23 Bus.Law. 365 (1968).

ACTIONS UNDER SECTIONS 13(d), 14(d) AND 14(e) OF THE 1934 ACT

When litigation under the Williams Act came along, the initial Circuit Court decisions were all in favor of the full implication of liability under Section 14(e),[31] despite some initial misgivings expressed by some district judges.[32] The holdings of these cases that a defeated tender offeror had an implied cause of action to collect damages from the target company and its directors and officers and other persons was, however, overruled by the Supreme Court decision in the *Piper* case. The Supreme Court seems to accept the idea, although it expressly does not rule on it since the issue was not before it, that a cause of action could be asserted under Section 14(e) by the shareholders of the target company for whose "especial benefit" the Williams Act was enacted. But it is difficult to see how the shareholders of the target company could allege that they were injured in any way by having tendered as a result of false statements by the tender offeror, since the offer is usually at a substantial premium above market. As to those who fail to tender, this would hardly be the result of statements made by the tender offeror, which is attempting to induce them to accept, not reject, the offer. In any event, they are frequently cashed out at the same price as was paid in the tender offer.

It may be alleged, of course, that the market price of the stock would have gone above the tender offer price in later years if everybody had held on, but this is something that cannot be known after a successful tender offer since the market disappears. It seems doubtful that any court would award damages based upon a hypothetical subsequent market price established by sheer speculation.

In Kalmanovitz v. G. Heileman Brewing Co.[33] the Third Circuit held that an unsuccessful tender offeror who was also a shareholder of the target company did not have standing under the *Piper* case to bring a suit for damages under Section 14(e). It stated that one who occupies those dual roles may be

---

31. H.K. Porter Co., Inc. v. Nicholson File Company, 482 F.2d 421 (1st Cir.1973); Chris-Craft Industries, Inc. v. Bangor Punta Corp., 480 F.2d 341 (2d Cir.1973), cert. denied 414 U.S. 910 (this decision was, of course, reversed by the Supreme Court on a subsequent appeal, in the Chris-Craft case reprinted above). See, also, Butler Aviation International, Inc. v. Comprehensive Designers, Inc., 425 F.2d 842 (2d Cir. 1970); Electronic Specialty Co. v. International Controls Corp., 409 F.2d 937 (2d Cir. 1969); Metro-Goldwyn-Mayer Inc. v. Transamerica Corp., 303 F.Supp. 1344 (S.D.N.Y. 1969). These latter cases were injunction actions, as were the earlier cases under the Proxy Rules.

32. In Washburn v. Madison Square Garden Corp., 340 F.Supp. 504 (S.D.N.Y. 1972), the court said: "We are cited no cases holding that these filing requirements create a private right of action for a

stockholder." In Bangor Punta Corp. v. Chris-Craft Industries, Inc., 337 F.Supp. 1147 (S.D.N.Y.1971), Judge Pollack said: "This complaint, like that in the companion case, is replete with charges of breach of the requirements of securities laws and rules. Like the other, it has been brought and tried as though any such breach by a competitor automatically creates windfalls for a sophisticated and well-financed contender for corporate control. * * * The Court has here been especially challenged to maintain its footing in the realities and the equities in searching (in vain) for credible evidence establishing causal connections between alleged violations and actionable damage." However, Judge Pollack was promptly reversed by the Second Circuit. Note 31, supra. It in turn, however, was reversed by the Supreme Court.

33. 769 F.2d 152 (3d Cir.1985).

considered to be only an offeror for the purposes of judging his standing to bring claims under Section 14(e). The court also said: "In *Piper*, the Supreme Court left open the questions whether a private right of action exists under § 14(e) and, if so, whether a shareholder has standing to assert such a claim. * * * Although plaintiff's contention [that a private right of action exists in favor of a shareholder of the target company in view of the Supreme Court's explicit statement that the act was passed to protect such shareholders] arguably may be correct, our disposition of this case does not require us to decide that issue." [34]

With respect to false statements by the management and its allies in connection with such a takeover battle, in Panter v. Marshall Field & Co.[35] the Seventh Circuit held that the shareholders of the target company could not establish any cause of action under Section 14(e) in a case where the tender offer was withdrawn, since they had not "relied" on the allegedly false statements in not tendering—they had never been given an opportunity to tender. If the *Panter* case is correct, this would seem to leave only a situation where the tender offer is not withdrawn but is defeated by allegedly false statements of the management, and the price of the stock later declines, in which the shareholders of the target company might be able to state a cause of action under Section 14(e) by claiming that they had not tendered in reliance on the false statements of the management. This discussion, of course, relates to actions for damages and not for injunctive relief, which may be subject to different considerations.

Section 14(e) basically outlaws the same type of conduct as Rule 10b–5 and Rule 14a–9, i.e., false or misleading statements or (in the case of Rule 10b–5) other "fraudulent" conduct. In the lower court opinion in the Chris-Craft case [36] Judge Pollack suggests two respects in which Section 14(e) outlawing false and misleading statements in connection with a tender offer may differ from Rule 10b–5 as furnishing the basis for an action for damages. First, he quotes the section and italicizes the last sentence which was added in 1970: "The Commission shall, for the purposes of this subsection, by rules and regulations define, and prescribe means reasonably designed to prevent, such acts and practices as are fraudulent, deceptive, or manipulative." He then points out that this sentence was added after the decision in Crane Co. v. Westinghouse Air Brake Co.[37] on which the plaintiff relied. If he meant to suggest by this that after the amendment the section is not operative until the SEC adopts rules, he was clearly in error. The first sentence establishing a statutory prohibition was not changed; and it is only necessary to compare the language of Section 10(b) ("in contravention of such rules and regulations" as *may be issued* by the SEC) to realize that any such suggestion regarding Section 14(e) is untenable.

Secondly, Judge Pollack points out that there are some differences in the language of Rule 10b–5 and Section 14(e), which he says are "significant": "Section 14(e) refers to 'fraudulent or manipulative acts or practices' whereas Rule 10b–5 makes unlawful 'any act, practice or course of business which operates *or would operate* as a fraud or deceit on any person' * * * and contains a prohibition against employment of 'any device, scheme or artifice to defraud,' * * * (language not present in section 14(e))." (Judge Pollack's italics.) Aside from the fact that Judge Pollack's decision was reversed, one

34. 769 F.2d at 158–159.

35. 646 F.2d 271 (7th Cir.1981). See, also, Lewis v. McGraw, 619 F.2d 192 (2d Cir.1980), cert. denied 449 U.S. 951.

36. Chris-Craft Industries, Inc. v. Piper Aircraft Corp., 337 F.Supp. 1128 (S.D.N.Y. 1971), rev'd, 480 F.2d 341 (2d Cir.1973).

37. 419 F.2d 787 (2d Cir.1969), cert. denied 400 U.S. 822 (1970).

would have more confidence that these differences are indeed "significant" if the courts had ever indicated that they really cared which clause of Rule 10b–5 they were applying. The Commission has adopted a general fraud rule with respect to issuer tender offers [38] under Section 13(e) in the exact language of Rule 10b–5 (since Section 13(e), unlike Section 14(e), does not purport to be self-operative); and it would undoubtedly do the same with respect to Section 14(e) if the missing language noted by Judge Pollack were held to have any substantive significance.

The cases have uniformly held that an issuer has an implied private right of action under Section 13(d) to seek injunctive relief, since Congress must have intended to confer a private remedy on the issuer as the only party with the capability and incentive to pursue violations of the reporting statute. In Gearhart Industries, Inc. v. Smith International, Inc.,[39] the court stated: "[T]o conclude that such relief is available in no circumstances whatever—however flagrant—would be all but to license the filing of deliberately misleading 13(d) and 14(e) disclosure statements on pain of nothing more than a possible damage suit by sellers or intervention by the SEC—a body that assures us on amicus brief that its resources are inadequate to police the myriad of 13(d) filings made each year so as to insure truthful disclosures." [40] The court held, however, reversing the district judge, that enjoining the tender offer and the voting of the shares acquired were "too drastic" remedies and that the injunction should only hold up the tender offer until corrective statements were filed.

In Liberty National Insurance Holding Company v. Charter Company [41] the Eleventh Circuit apparently held to the contrary in ruling that there was no private right of action in favor of an issuer under Section 13(d) or Section 14(d) and (e) to require the divestment of shares acquired by a person attempting a hostile takeover of the corporation. The language of the court indicated that it did not believe that there was a private right of action of any kind in favor of an issuer under those sections. Only one year later, however, the Eleventh Circuit in Florida Commercial Banks v. Culverhouse [42] "interpreted" that decision almost out of existence by holding that it only dealt with a right of action to force divestment of the shares acquired by a tender offeror, not with an injunction merely to require corrective disclosures as in the *Culverhouse* case. Judge Fay dissented, saying that he was "unable to read *Liberty National* as narrowly as the majority" of the panel.[43]

A number of cases have held, however, that there is no private right of action for damages under Section 13(a).[44]

---

38. Rule 13e–4(b)(1); Sec.Exch.Act Release No. 16112 (Sept. 21, 1979).

39. 741 F.2d 707 (5th Cir.1984).

40. 741 F.2d at 714–715. Accord: Dan River, Inc. v. Unitex Ltd., 624 F.2d 1216 (4th Cir.1980), cert. denied 449 U.S. 1101 (1981); Chromalloy American Corp. v. Sun Chemical Corp., 611 F.2d 240 (8th Cir. 1979); Indiana National Corp. v. Rich, 712 F.2d 1180 (7th Cir.1983); General Aircraft Corp. v. Lampert, 556 F.2d 90 (1st Cir. 1977).

41. 734 F.2d 545 (11th Cir.1984).

42. 772 F.2d 1513 (11th Cir.1985).

43. In Washburn v. Madison Square Garden Corp., supra, note 32, the court held that a former shareholder of a tender offeror could not sue it for alleged violations of Sections 13(d) and 14(d) and (e), claiming damage to the shareholders of the target corporation to whom the offer was made (and of whom he was not one). The plaintiff in that case had sold his stock in the offeror corporation before he brought the action; therefore, he was in no position to bring a derivative action against the directors claiming that the corporation was damaged by its own violations; and the case is consequently not authority on the question whether such an action could be brought under the Williams Act.

44. In re Penn Central Securities Litigation, 494 F.2d 528 (3d Cir.1974); Lewis v. Elam, CCH Fed.Sec.Law Rptr. ¶ 96,013 (S.D.N.Y.1977); Meer v. United Brands Co., CCH Fed.Sec.Law Rptr. ¶ 95,648 (S.D.N.Y. 1976).

See Conard, Tender Offer Fraud: The Secret Meaning of Subsection 14(e), 40 Bus.Law. 87 (1984); Junewicz, The Appropriate Limits of Section 14(e) of the Securities Exchange Act of 1934, 62 Tex.L.Rev. 1171 (1984); Loewenstein, Section 14(e) of the Williams Act and the Rule 10b–5 Comparisons, 71 Geo.L.J. 1311 (1983); Block and Solovy, Developments Under Rules 10b–5 and 14e–3, 14 Inst. on Sec.Reg. 301 (1983); Burke, Availability of Injunctive Relief to Private Litigants for Violation of Section 13(d) of the Securities Exchange Act of 1934, 15 U.S. F.L.Rev. 399 (1981); Ross, Private Rights of Action for Damages Under Section 13(d), 32 Stan.L.R. 581 (1980); Jorden and Woodward, Appraisal of Disclosure Requirements in Contests for Control Under the Williams Act, 46 Geo.Wash.L.Rev. 817 (1978); Dugan and Fairfield, Chris-Craft Corp. v. Piper Aircraft Corp.: Liability in the Context of a Tender Offer, 35 Ohio S.L.J. 412 (1974).

ACTIONS UNDER SECTION 17(a) OF THE 1933 ACT

Section 17(a) of the 1933 Act is identical with Rule 10b–5 so far as its substantive provisions are concerned, for the simple reason that the Commission copied Section 17(a) when it adopted Rule 10b–5. However, the coverage of the two provisions is not identical because Section 17(a) applies only to an "offer or sale", whereas Rule 10b–5 applies to a "purchase or sale." Therefore, Section 17(a) applies to an *offer to sell* although Rule 10b–5 does not; and Rule 10b–5 applies to a purchase of a security by the defendant although Section 17(a) does not. On the other hand, the coverage of Section 17(a) is almost identical with the coverage of the express civil liability provision in Section 12(2) of the 1933 Act, with the sole exception that Section 17(a) covers all offers and sales which are exempt from registration by the provisions of Section 3, whereas Section 12(2) does not cover transactions in two of the exempt securities, i.e., government and bank securities.

Since the substantive provisions of sections 17(a) and 12(2) are quite different, however, to recognize a private right of action under Section 17(a) would be to assume that Congress "casually nullified" in a later section what it did in the very same Act. Nor are any of the procedural provisions relating to an action under Section 12(2), such as the express statute of limitations in Section 13, applicable to an action under Section 17(a) and the courts would have to invent such rules as they have done under Rule 10b–5.

Nevertheless, the majority of the few decided cases prior to 1971 upheld such a private right of action under Section 17(a),[45] and it was supported by a dictum of Judge Frank in the *Fischman* case and of Judge Friendly in Securities and Exchange Commission v. Texas Gulf Sulphur Co.[46] In the latter case Judge Friendly stated that "Once it had been established, however, that an aggrieved buyer has a private action under § 10(b) of the 1934 Act, there seemed little practical point in denying the existence of such an action under § 17—with the important proviso that fraud, as distinct from mere negligence, must be alleged." [47] However, this statement overlooks the fact that while the language does not appear to vary in any significant detail, what that conduct must be "in connection with" does differ significantly: only "sale" under Rule

---

45. See 3 Loss, Securities Regulation 1784–1789 (2d ed. 1961); Pfeffer v. Cressaty, 223 F.Supp. 756 (S.D.N.Y.1963); Goldstein v. Grayson, CCH Fed.Sec.Law Rptr. ¶ 92,645 (S.D.N.Y.1970).

46. 401 F.2d 833 (2d Cir.1968) (Friendly, J., concurring), cert. denied 394 U.S. 976 (1969).

47. 401 F.2d at 867.

10b–5, but *"offer or* sale" under Section 17(a).[48] See Blue Chip Stamps v. Manor Drug Stores, infra Chapter 16. In addition, the Supreme Court has now decided in the *Aaron* case, infra page 946, that while the language of Section 17(a) and Rule 10b–5 is virtually identical, the *meaning* is different with respect to the fault required to be shown on the part of the defendant.

In 1971, Judge Gignoux in Dyer v. Eastern Trust and Banking Co.[49] held in a scholarly opinion that there was no implied right of action under Section 17(a), and this sparked a renewed debate over this question, with the Eighth Circuit [50] and several lower court judges [51] and now the Fifth Circuit in the *Landry* case following the lead of Judge Gignoux, but with the Second Circuit [52] and the Fourth Circuit [53] adhering to the view that there is a private right of action under Section 17(a). More recently, however, panels of both the Ninth Circuit [54] and the Second Circuit [55] have "reserved" the question whether there exists a private right of action under Section 17(a), although those circuits are counted among the "majority" holding that such an action is available, perhaps indicating that some of the judges even in those circuits do not consider that the law has been settled in favor of their prior rulings.

On the other hand, in Mosher v. Kane [56] another panel of the Ninth Circuit expressly reaffirmed the existence of such an implied right of action, stating that it had no authority to overrule prior Ninth Circuit precedents and that: "In any event we believe that the better view is to recognize an implied private right of action [under Section 17(a)]." The court in that case also stated: "In order to bring a claim under Section 17(a), plaintiff must be a purchaser or seller." This statement is of course doubly wrong—the plaintiff cannot be a seller and the plaintiff does not necessarily need to be a purchaser, but only an offeree. The fact that the court apparently didn't understand Section 17(a) may perhaps reduce the authority of this decision, as well as the fact that the court upheld an action under Rule 10b–5 which made the decision with respect to Section 17(a) unnecessary.

In the *Blue Chip* case, infra Chapter 16, the Supreme Court reserved this question in a footnote; however, it is difficult to believe that it will cast aside all the weighty "policy" arguments which it advanced for the result of that case merely because the next plaintiff chooses to sue under Section 17(a) rather than

---

48. This observation is not intended as a criticism of Judge Friendly; he cited for this statement a prior edition of this casebook, where the authors had similarly overlooked this distinction.

49. 336 F.Supp. 890 (D.Me.1971).

50. Shull v. Dain Kalman & Quail Inc., 561 F.2d 152 (8th Cir.1977), cert. denied, 434 U.S. 1086 (1978).

51. Mendelsohn v. Capital Underwriters, Inc., 490 F.Supp. 1069 (N.D.Cal. 1979); Kulchok v. Government Employees' Insurance Co., CCH Fed.Sec.Law Rptr. ¶ 96,002 (D.D.C.1977); The Architectural League of New York v. Bartos, 404 F.Supp. 304 (S.D.N.Y.1975); Russell v. Travel Concepts Corp., 20 F.R.Serv.2d 851, CCH Fed.Sec.Law Rptr. ¶ 95,230 (M.D.Tenn.1975); cf. Dorfman v. First Boston Corp., 336 F.Supp. 1089 (E.D.Pa. 1972). See, also, the cases cited in the *Landry* case.

52. Kirshner v. United States of America, 603 F.2d 234 (2d Cir.1978), cert.

denied 444 U.S. 995 (1980). In Baron v. Commercial & Industrial Bank of Memphis, CCH Fed.Sec.Law Rptr. ¶ 96,826 (S.D. N.Y.1979), the court stated that until the Supreme Court resolves the question or the Second Circuit reverses its position, the District Court in New York is bound to adhere to the rule that there is a private right of action under Section 17(a) of the 1933 Act.

53. Newman v. Prior, 518 F.2d 97 (4th Cir.1975). In Sanders v. John Nuveen & Co., Inc., 554 F.2d 790 (7th Cir.1977), appeal after remand 619 F.2d 1222, cert. denied 450 U.S. 1005, the Seventh Circuit reserved this question.

54. Kramas v. Security Gas & Oil, Inc., 672 F.2d 766 (9th Cir.1982), cert. denied 459 U.S. 1035 (1982).

55. Zerman v. Ball, 735 F.2d 15 (2d Cir. 1984).

56. 784 F.2d 1385 (9th Cir.1986).

Rule 10b–5, on the mechanical basis that the former contains the word "offer" whereas the latter does not. It is also difficult to believe that the Supreme Court will say that a buyer (although not a seller) of securities can avoid the *scienter* requirement of the *Hochfelder* case, infra page 936, merely by suing under Section 17(a) and thereby recover on the basis of mere negligence (or perhaps on the basis of "no fault" liability) as a result of the interpretation of that section in the *Aaron* case, infra page 946.[57] The way to avoid all of these inconsistencies, of course, would be for it to say that there is no private right of action in any case under Section 17(a), in accord with the *Landry* case.

See Aiken, Availability of an Implied Civil Cause of Action Under Section 17(a) of the Securities Act of 1933, 9 N.C.J. Int'l L. & Com.Reg. 207 (1984); School and Perkowski, An Implied Right of Action Under Section 17(a): The Supreme Court Has Said "No," But is Anybody Listening?, 36 U.Miami L.Rev. 41 (1981); Implied Private Rights of Action Under the Securities Act of 1933— Section 17(a), 14 U.Mich.L.Rev. 563 (1981); Section 17(a) of the Securities Act of 1933: Implication of A Private Right of Action, 29 UCLA L.Rev. 244 (1981); Steinberg, Section 17(a) of the Securities Act of 1933 After Naftalin and Redington, 68 Geo.L.J. 163 (1979); Hazen, A Look Beyond the Pruning of Rule 10b–5; Implied Remedies and Section 17(a) of the Securities Act of 1933, 64 Va. L.Rev. 641 (1978).

VIOLATIONS OF THE MARGIN RULES

In Remar v. Clayton Securities Corp.[58] Judge Wyzanski justified the implication of a private right of action under Section 7(c) of the Securities Exchange Act as follows: "The general principle regarding civil liability for violations of prohibitory statutes has been put with precision in Restatement, Torts, § 286. Broadly stated, the rule is that where defendant's violation of a prohibitory statute has caused injury to plaintiff the latter has a right of action if one of the purposes of the enactment was to protect individual interests like the plaintiff's.

"That rule applies to the case at bar. Undoubtedly 'the main purpose' of § 7 of the Securities and [*sic*] Exchange Act was 'To give a government credit agency an effective method of reducing the aggregate amount of the nation's credit resources which can be directed by speculation into the stock market.' * * * But Congress recognized that 'protection of the small speculator by making it impossible for him to spread himself too thin * * * will be achieved as a by-product of the main purpose.' * * *

"Plaintiff's right of action is not affected by his participation as borrower in the transaction in which Clayton and the bank violated the statute. Since the statute was passed for the benefit of people like plaintiff, and since the Legislature regarded him as incapable of protecting himself, he is not disabled from suing for the injury he sustained." [59]

The *Remar* case is usually cited as the leading case establishing civil liability for violation by a broker-dealer of Regulation T, although that case

---

57. In In re Diasonics Securities Litigation, 599 F.Supp. 447 (N.D.Cal.1984), the court held that the plaintiff must prove "scienter" under Section 17(a) since there is a private right of action only under Section 17(a)(1) and not Section 17(a)(2) and (3). It is difficult to see how Section 17(a) can be fragmented in this fashion or can

mean something different because the plaintiff is a private party rather than the SEC (as in the *Aaron* case). Cf. Cleary v. Perfectune, Inc., 700 F.2d 774 (1st Cir. 1983).

58. 81 F.Supp. 1014 (D.Mass.1949).

59. 81 F.Supp. at 1017.

actually only involved the "arranging" prohibition of Section 7(c) rather than a loan by the broker himself in violation of Regulation T. That section not only makes it illegal for a broker-dealer to extend or maintain credit in violation of the margin rules issued by the Federal Reserve Board, but also for him to "arrange for the extension or maintenance of credit" in violation of such rules. In Bronner v. Goldman,[60] however, the First Circuit held that no civil liability was incurred by an unregulated factor who extended a perfectly legal loan to the plaintiff (although in excess of the amount that a broker or a bank would be permitted to lend), even though the loan was "arranged" by a broker-dealer allegedly in violation of Section 7(c). The plaintiff's theory was that the factor by making the loan "aided and abetted" the broker in the illegal "arranging" of the loan, and thereby became a participant in *the broker's* violation of Section 7(c). The court said: "The law reflects a strong policy against a broker playing a role in such a loan, not a policy of invalidating force against the credit transaction itself. We think effect should and can be given to both the policy permitting the loan itself and the policy proscribing broker participation in it. The validity of the loan can be recognized by denying the borrower as against the lender any such rescission or damages as this action seeks." [61] After noting that disciplinary, injunctive and criminal sanctions would be available against the broker, the court said: "We find it unnecessary to consider whether sufficient basis exists for giving a borrower a right to recover damages against his broker who has violated Regulation T by arranging a valid unregulated factor loan for him." [62] This question could be distinguished from that in the *Remar* case on the basis that there the loan itself was illegal as being made by a bank in violation of Regulation U. This question is unlikely to recur since the promulgation of Regulations G and X, bringing virtually all securities credit under control, but it can still arise because of the fact that the prohibitions on brokers under Regulation T are broader than those on banks and other lenders.

The highwater mark of liability of a broker-dealer or bank for violation of the margin rules was reached in the Second Circuit case of Pearlstein v. Scudder & German in 1970,[63] in which the court held (over the dissent of Judge Friendly) that a sophisticated investor who pleaded with his broker not to sell him out when he failed to post the required margin in connection with a purchase of bonds, because he was in the hospital having an operation, and the soft-hearted broker acquiesced in this request for a period of time, could nevertheless sue the broker for damages for violation of Regulation T. Thereafter, following an amendment to the statute in 1970 [64] imposing the same prohibitions on borrowers as are imposed on lenders, the Federal Reserve Board promulgated Regulation X to implement these new prohibitions.[65] While these new provisions were primarily intended to prevent the use of foreign sources of credit to avoid the margin rules, they applied to all transactions, either domestic or foreign, and made the borrower a *particeps criminis* with the lender in every violation of Regulation T, U or G. This development was held in Stern v. Merrill Lynch, Pierce, Fenner & Smith, Inc.,[66] and in the earlier Tenth Circuit case of Utah State University v. Bear Stearns & Co.,[67] which is relied on in that case, to have eliminated any implied private right of action for a violation of the margin regulations.

60. 361 F.2d 759 (1st Cir.1966), cert. denied 385 U.S. 933 (1966).

61. 361 F.2d at 763.

62. Id. at 763, n. 1.

63. 429 F.2d 1136 (2d Cir.1970), cert. denied 401 U.S. 1013 (1971).

64. Public Law 91–508, 84 Stat. 1124 (Oct. 26, 1970), adding subsection (f) to Section 7 of the Securities Exchange Act.

65. 12 C.F.R. Part 224 (§ 224.1 et seq.).

66. 603 F.2d 1073 (4th Cir.1979).

67. 549 F.2d 164 (10th Cir.1977), cert. denied 434 U.S. 890 (1977).

In the *Stern* case, the court cited four circuit court decisions decided in 1973 and 1974 [68] which the plaintiff and the SEC as amicus curiae contended had recognized a private right of action for violation of the margin rules. The court said: "What both the plaintiff and the amicus either overlook or disregard is that every circuit court case cited by them in this connection involved transactions which took place prior to the effective date of Section 7(f). Section 7(f) was by its language not to be applied retroactively. The circuit court authority cited by the plaintiff and amicus in this connection are thus not relevant." [69] The court also relied upon the decision in *Cort v. Ash* as having undermined the authority of these prior decisions. It said: "There is another development in the law—this time, judicial in character—which leaves no possible room for doubt about the absence of any such private right of action. That development is the declaration by the Supreme Court of definitive rules to halt the trend in circuit and district court decisions toward a freewheeling implication of private actions to be observed in determining whether a private remedy is to be implied." [70]

In Bennett v. United States Trust Company of New York [71] this development came full circle. In that case, the Second Circuit repudiated the *Pearlstein* case and held that there is no private right of action for a violation of the margin rules, citing three additional circuit court cases [72] since the *Stern* and *Utah State University* cases to that effect. The court said: "There is no conflict, however, among the circuit courts that have recently considered this issue. All five which have decided the question have held that no private cause of action exists under Section 7." [73]

On January 23, 1984, the Board of Governors of the Federal Reserve System substantially undermined one of the bases for all of these recent decisions, however, by amending Regulation X to provide that it does not apply to any domestic credit "unless the borrower willfully causes the credit to be extended" in violation of Regulation G, T or U. (48 F.R. 56571, Dec. 22, 1983). Therefore, unless that degree of fault on the part of the borrower can be shown, it can no longer be said that the borrower is equally guilty with the lender for a violation of those regulations. The other basis for some of these decisions, that is, that an analysis of the *Cort v. Ash* factors shows that Congress did not intend to create any private right of action for violation of the margin rules, still remains. This will undoubtedly set off a new round of litigation as to whether a private right of action for violation of the margin rules exists with respect to transactions occurring after the date of that amendment, the outcome of which is difficult to predict.

Under the cases imposing liability for a violation of the Margin Rules, it was clear that where the broker or other lender extended credit initially in excess of the amount permitted by the regulations, the borrower could recover the damages proximately resulting from this violation.[74] However, where a broker failed to close out a special cash account for non-payment by the customer

---

68. Daley v. Capitol Bank and Trust Company, 506 F.2d 1375 (1st Cir.1974); McCormick v. Esposito, 500 F.2d 620 (5th Cir. 1974), cert. denied 420 U.S. 912 (1975); Spoon v. Walston & Co., Inc., 478 F.2d 246 (6th Cir.1973); Landry v. Hemphill, Noyes & Co., 473 F.2d 365 (1st Cir.1973), cert. denied 414 U.S. 1002 (1973).

69. 603 F.2d at 1082–1083.

70. 603 F.2d at 1084–1085.

71. 770 F.2d 308 (2d Cir.1985), cert. denied ___ U.S. ___, 106 S.Ct. 800 (1986).

72. Bassler v. Central National Bank in Chicago, 715 F.2d 308 (7th Cir.1983); Walck v. American Stock Exchange, 687 F.2d 778 (3d Cir.1982), cert. denied 461 U.S. 942 (1983); Gutter v. Merrill Lynch, Pierce, Fenner & Smith, 644 F.2d 1194 (6th Cir.1981), cert. denied 455 U.S. 909 (1982).

73. 770 F.2d at 312.

74. Myer v. Shields & Co., 25 A.D.2d 126, 267 N.Y.S.2d 872 (1966).

within the 7 days allowed, but without any agreement with the customer to refrain from doing so for any period of time, the case of Billings Associates, Inc. v. Bashaw [75] in the Appellate Division of the New York Supreme Court held that this was not an "extension of credit" and did not furnish the basis for any action by the customer against the broker. However, the *Pearlstein* case was clearly contra to that decision. The latter was followed in Avery v. Merrill Lynch, Pierce, Fenner & Smith [76] in which the court held that the same rule applied to the failure of the broker to close out a margin account on default by the customer, in connection with a short sale, in depositing the additional margin required by Regulation T within the 4 day period then allowed.

See Kanouse, Rise and Fall of the Private Cause of Action for Violation of Margin Requirements, 98 Banking L.J. 133 (1981); Impact of Federal Reserve Margin Regulations on Acquisition Financing (Symposium), 35 Bus.Law. 517 (1980); Note, Regulation X: A Complexis, 50 Notre Dame Law 136 (1974); Note, Civil Liability for Margin Violations—The Effect of Section 7(f) and Regulation X, 43 Ford.L.Rev. 93 (1974).

VIOLATIONS OF THE RULES OF THE STOCK EXCHANGES AND THE NASD

Under Sections 6 and 15A of the 1934 Act, the stock exchanges and the NASD (the self-regulatory agencies or "SROs") are required to adopt rules which, among other things, "are designed to prevent fraudulent and manipulative acts and practices, to promote just and equitable principles of trade, * * * and, in general, to protect investors and the public interest. * * * " Section 19(g) requires the SROs to enforce their own rules against their members and persons associated with such members. Section 21(d) authorizes the Commission to bring an injunctive action to prevent a violation of the rules of the exchanges and the NASD, as well as the provisions of the statute and the Commission's own rules. However, Section 32(a) does not appear to make it a crime for a person to violate a rule of the SROs. Compare the reference in Section 32(a) only to "any rule or regulation thereunder [i.e., under the 1934 Act]" with the specific reference in Section 21(d) to the rules of the SROs as well as "the rules and regulations thereunder." Also, Section 27 of the 1934 Act, which confers exclusive jurisdiction on the federal courts of actions to enforce any liability or duty created by the 1934 Act refers only to such liabilities or duties created "by this title [i.e., the act itself] or the rules and regulations thereunder," and makes no mention of rules of SROs as do the other sections mentioned above.

Under this statutory scheme, is there any basis for implying a cause of action for a violation of one of the rules of the self regulatory organizations? Such a violation is of course in some sense a "prohibited act", since the offender can be disciplined by the SRO (even to the extent of revoking his license and thereby depriving him of his livelihood) and is subject to a possible injunction action by the SEC, but it is not anywhere in the statute declared to be "unlawful" and would not appear to be subject to any criminal penalty. Even

---

75. 27 A.D.2d 124, 276 N.Y.S.2d 446 (1967).

76. 328 F.Supp. 677 (D.D.C.1971). But cf. Cohen v. G.F. Rothschild & Co., Inc., CCH Fed.Sec.Law Rptr. ¶ 90,849 (S.D.N.Y. 1958). Judge Leibell there held that *the broker* could raise the violation of the 7- day requirement of Regulation T as a defense in an action against him by the customer who tendered payment after the expiration of that period, although the broker had agreed to wait a longer time for payment.

if a cause of action is created by the statute and the rules of the SROs, would the federal courts have any jurisdiction to entertain it in view of the language in Section 27?

In Colonial Realty Corp. v. Bache & Co.[77] the court, in an opinion by Judge Friendly, held that there was no cause of action for a violation of the requirement under the rules of the NYSE and the NASD that their members observe "just and equitable principles of trade." Judge Friendly refused, however, to say that there might never be an implied cause of action for violation of some of the rules of the SROs. He stated:

"What emerges is that whether the courts are to imply federal civil liability for violation of exchange or dealer association rules by a member cannot be determined on the simplistic all-or-nothing basis urged by the two parties; rather, the court must look to the nature of the particular rule and its place in the regulatory scheme, with the party urging the implication of a federal liability carrying a considerably heavier burden of persuasion than when the violation is of the statute or an SEC regulation. The case for implication would be strongest when the rule imposes an explicit duty unknown to the common law. The rules here at issue, however, are near the opposite pole. Although they do impose a duty upon members not to engage in conduct inconsistent with fair and equitable principles of trade, which the exchange or association can enforce through disciplinary proceedings, they are something of a catch-all which, in addition to satisfying the letter of the statute, preserves power to discipline members for a wide variety of misconduct, including merely unethical behavior which Congress could well not have intended to give rise to a legal claim. We find little reason to believe that by requiring exchanges and dealers' associations to include such provisions in their rules Congress meant to impose a new legal standard on members different from that long recognized by state law." [78]

Is the distinction attempted to be drawn in the *Colonial Realty Corporation* case between an "explicit duty unknown to the common law" and a "commandment vaguely adjuring * * * [a person] to behave himself" a workable one? The only example of the former given by the court—Rule 452 of the NYSE relating to the voting of street-name stock—is probably a safe one, since it is impossible to imagine how the customer could ever allege any damage resulting to him from the violation of that rule. The only example given of the latter is the rule involved in that case—the prohibition against conduct inconsistent with "just and equitable principles of trade." Where would the "suitability rule", for example, fall in this spectrum? If it is concluded that it is not "moderately specific" but only a "vague adjuration", would this mean that there could also not have been a civil action for violation of the SEC's own "suitability rule" for the former SECO brokers? [79] If it is concluded that under the Rule 10b–5 and Section 14(a) cases there was a civil action for violation of the SEC's rule, how could you have justified treating NASD and NYSE members differently?

In Buttrey v. Merrill Lynch, Pierce, Fenner & Smith, Inc.[80] the Seventh Circuit upheld a cause of action against a broker-dealer based upon his

---

77. 358 F.2d 178 (2d Cir.1966), cert. denied 385 U.S. 817 (1966).

78. 358 F.2d at 182.

79. The SECO (meaning "SEC only") brokers were those (consisting primarily of the captive sales forces for mutual funds) who formerly did not choose to join the NASD and were regulated only by the SEC. Now all broker-dealers are required to join the NASD and the SECO category has been abolished, along with the SEC rules applicable to them.

80. 410 F.2d 135 (7th Cir.1969), cert. denied 396 U.S. 838 (1969).

violation of Rule 405 of the New York Stock Exchange—the so-called "Know thy customer" rule. The court said:

" *   *   * The touchstone for determining whether or not the violation of a particular rule is actionable should properly depend upon its design 'for the direct protection of investors.' *   *   * Here one of the functions of Rule 405 is to protect the public, so that permitting a private action for its violation is entirely consistent with the purposes of the statute.

"We do not decide that an alleged violation of Rule 405 is *per se* actionable. However, Count I pertains to the defendant's acceptance of investments without regard for the bankrupt broker's defalcations of investors' funds. Such a breach of fair practice undermines the protection of investors and surely 'play[s] an integral part in SEC regulation' of Exchanges and their members. Colonial Realty Corporation v. Bache & Co., supra, at p. 182. *   *   *

"Although mere errors of judgment by defendant might not support a federal cause of action, the facts alleged here are tantamount to fraud on the bankrupt's customers, thus giving rise to a private civil damage action. See Hecht v. Harris Upham & Co., 283 F.Supp. 417, 430, 431 (N.D.Cal. 1968)." [81]

Is the *Buttrey* case consistent with the *Colonial Realty Corporation* case? Is the "Know thy customer" rule of the stock exchanges and the NASD "moderately specific" or is it only a "vague adjuration"? The court in the *Buttrey* case cites and purports to follow the *Colonial Realty Corporation* case; but it cites it for the proposition that a private action can be maintained if the particular rule of the self-regulatory agency is "for the protection of investors" and "plays an integral part in SEC regulation." Are there any rules of the self-regulatory agencies which cannot be so characterized?

In Landy v. Federal Deposit Insurance Corp.,[82] the Third Circuit found it unnecessary to decide whether a private right of action should be implied under Rule 405 of the NYSE, although it stated in a footnote that "implication of liability should be done reluctantly [with respect to stock exchange rules] for the following reasons: first, accurate evaluation of the degree to which any particular rule represents SEC policy is often difficult, if not impossible *   *   *; second, imposition of liability might chill the process of self-regulation by creating fear of damaging liability; and, finally, as appellees argue, exchange rules are not promulgated by a government body after careful deliberation and weighing of the variegated competing public interests." [83]

In Jablon v. Dean Witter & Co.[84] the Ninth Circuit held that under the *Redington* case and the *Transamerica* case there could be no implication of a

---

81. 410 F.2d at 143.

82. 486 F.2d 139 (3d Cir.1973), cert. denied 416 U.S. 960 (1974).

83. 486 F.2d at 166, n. 23. Several contemporaneous District Court cases had held that there was no cause of action for violation of Rule 405 since the violation was alleged to have been merely "negligent", distinguishing the *Buttrey* case on the ground that there "fraud" was involved. Jenny v. Shearson, Hammill & Co., Inc., CCH Fed.Sec.Law Rptr. ¶ 95,021 (S.D.N.Y.1975); McMaster Hutchinson and Co. v. Rothschild and Co., CCH Fed.Sec. Law Rptr. ¶ 93,541 (N.D.Ill.1972). Similarly, as to the NASD "suitability" rule.

Wells v. Blythe & Co., Inc., 351 F.Supp. 999 (N.D.Cal.1972). On the other hand, Judge Weinfeld held in Starkman v. Seroussi, 377 F.Supp. 518 (S.D.N.Y.1974), that there was a private right of action for violation of NYSE Rule 345.17 (prohibiting a registered representative from taking a position with his customer or guaranteeing his customer against loss) and Rule 405. Judge Weinfeld stated that these rules were "precise" and not broad, generalized rules "with vague and uncertain contours." Cf. Bush v. Bruns Nordeman & Co., CCH Fed.Sec. Law Rptr. ¶ 93,674 (S.D.N.Y.1972).

84. 614 F.2d 677 (9th Cir.1980).

private right of action for a violation of any of the rules of the SROs, and indicated that in its opinion the *Buttrey* case had been overruled by those decisions of the Supreme Court. The court stated: "The Securities Exchange Act does not expressly authorize private actions for stock exchange rule violations. Prior to *Transamerica* and *Touche Ross,* court and commentators found a statutory basis for implying private actions for exchange rule violations under §§ 6(b) and 27 of the Securities Exchange Act. Section 6(b), requiring exchanges to adopt rules promoting 'just and equitable principles of trade,' was said to create a duty. A private action was recognized in conjunction with § 27 of the Act which provides that an action may be 'brought to enforce any liability or duty created by this chapter or the rules and regulations thereunder.' This theory is no longer viable." [85]

Since the recent restrictive trend in the Supreme Court regarding the implication of liability, all of the lower court decisions deny the plaintiff any cause of action based upon the particular stock exchange or NASD rule being asserted as the basis for liability.[86] It can be argued, however, that under the rationale of the *Curran* case the extensive amendments to the 1934 Act in 1975, including major amendments to the sections dealing with the SROs, Congress intended to "preserve" the implied right of action which had been recognized prior thereto because it did not specifically negate those rulings of the courts. What would be the chances of success of such an argument? If that argument is accepted, which type of action did Congress preserve—the *Buttrey* cause of action or the *Colonial Realty* cause of action?

As has been noted in Chapter 11, supra, Regulation T applies only to initial margin requirements and never requires "margin calls." Although the Federal Reserve Board has authority to enact rules relating to so-called "maintenance margin", it has never done so; however, the stock exchange rules do require maintenance margin, and the plaintiffs in several cases have attempted to bootstrap a margin violation case out of an alleged failure by the broker-dealer to make margin calls or to sell out the plaintiff when he failed to meet them by alleging a violation of Rules 431 and 432 of the NYSE. In Golob v. Nauman, Vandervoort, Inc.,[87] the court held that Regulation T only applied to initial margin requirements and that there was no civil liability for violation of the stock exchange rules. However in McCormick v. Esposito,[88] the Fifth Circuit said: "The district court concluded that 'the violation of Rules 431 and 432 of the NYSE does not create a cause of action cognizable in a federal court.' * * * Although we are not now prepared to endorse such a universal proposition, we affirm the district court's denial of relief on the facts of this case. In * * * Gordon v. duPont Glore Forgan (5th Cir.1973) 487 F.2d 1260

---

85. 614 F.2d at 679–680.

86. Carrott v. Shearson Hayden Stone, Inc., 724 F.2d 821 (9th Cir.1984) (the NYSE "Know thy customer" rule); Thompson v. Smith Barney, Harris Upham & Co., Inc., 709 F.2d 1413 (11th Cir.1983) (the NYSE "Know thy customer" rule; NASD "suitability rule"); Jablon v. Dean Witter & Co., 614 F.2d 677 (9th Cir.1980) (NYSE Rule 405—"Know Thy Customer"); Sacks v. Reynolds Securities, Inc., 593 F.2d 1234 (D.C.Cir.1978) (NYSE Rule 412—relating to transfer of customer accounts); Musser v. Bache & Co., Inc., CCH Fed.Sec.Law Rptr. ¶ 96,183 (N.D.Cal.1977) (NASD suitability rule); Zagari v. Dean Witter & Co., Inc., CCH Fed.Sec.Law Rptr. ¶ 95,777 (N.D.Cal.

1976) (AMEX Rule 411—"Know Thy Customer"; and margin maintenance rule); Plunkett v. Dominick & Dominick, Inc., 414 F.Supp. 885 (D.Conn.1976) (NYSE and NASD suitability and supervision rules). In Sanders v. John Nuveen & Co., Inc., 554 F.2d 790 (7th Cir.1977), appeal after remand 619 F.2d 1222, cert. denied 450 U.S. 1005, the Seventh Circuit held that there was no cause of action under Rule 27 of the NASD in the absence of any allegation of "fraud", following the *Buttrey* case.

87. 353 F.Supp. 1264 (N.D.Ohio 1972).

88. 500 F.2d 620 (5th Cir.1974), cert. denied 420 U.S. 912 (1975).

* * * we held 'that under Rules 431 and 432 there is no right of action that will allow a recovery to investors who know their accounts are inadvertently undermargined, maintain their silence for a substantial period of time, and take no corrective action.' " [89]

Can the customer of a broker-dealer maintain an action against a stock exchange or the NASD for the alleged failure to enforce its own rules if he can show that this failure to enforce the particular rule was a cause of his loss in dealing with the broker-dealer? In Walck v. American Stock Exchange [90] the court held that there was no cause of action against an exchange under Sections 6 and 27 of the 1934 Act. The court analyzed the case under the four factors of Cort v. Ash and concluded that Congress did not intend to create such a cause of action against a stock exchange. The court also said that "appellant overlooks the reality that the Exchanges and not Congress promulgated the rules; and we perceive no basis for an inference that the Exchanges in their quasi-legislative capacity intended to subject themselves to damages for non-enforcement." The court held, however, that "Because all relevant events concluded in 1974, we apply the statute as it then existed and not as amended in 1975." [91]

In those 1975 amendments, Congress added Section 19(g) expressly requiring the SROs to enforce their rules. The Supreme Court in the Curran case relied upon such a requirement in the Commodity Exchange Act to hold that a commodity exchange could be sued by a customer of a broker. Therefore, the question obviously can no longer be framed in terms of whether the exchanges or the NASD intended to subject themselves to liability when they adopted the rules, but is whether Congress intended to subject them to liability when it commanded them to enforce their own rules. The answer to this question may turn upon the remarks, whether casual or calculated, of various individual Senators and Congressmen in the course of the adoption of the 1975 amendments.[92] The Walck case is therefore of only limited significance today.[93]

---

89. 500 F.2d at 627. In Zeffiro v. First Pennsylvania Banking and Trust Co., 623 F.2d 290 (3d Cir.1980), the court held that an implied private right of action exists under the Trust Indenture Act of 1939 in favor of debenture holders against an indenture trustee for breach of the indenture provisions required to be included by that Act. Several cases have held that there is no implied right of action under Section 13(a) of the 1934 Act, In re Penn Central Securities Litigation, 494 F.2d 528 (3d Cir. 1973); Lewis v. Elam, CCH Fed.Sec.Law Rptr. ¶ 96,013 (S.D.N.Y.1977); Meer v. United Brands Co., CCH Fed.Sec.Law Rptr. ¶ 95,648 (S.D.N.Y.1976); but the Fourth Circuit has held that a target company has standing to bring an equitable action under Section 13(d) to require the tender offeror to file an accurate and complete Schedule 13D. Dan River, Inc. v. Unitex Limited, 624 F.2d 1216 (4th Cir.1980), cert. denied 449 U.S. 1101 (1981). And a district court has held that there is a private right of action for violation of Rule 10b–13 prohibiting purchases alongside a tender offer. Warren v. Bokum Resources Corp., 433 F.Supp. 1360 (D.N.M.1977).

90. 687 F.2d 778 (3d Cir.1982), cert. denied 461 U.S. 942 (1983).

91. 687 F.2d at 782.

92. In England, the courts will not consider any argument regarding the interpretation of a statute based upon the Parliamentary debates; the adoption of that rule in the United States, whether or not a good thing, would certainly shorten Supreme Court opinions.

93. The Second Circuit also held that there was no liability under Section 6 of the 1934 Act of the stock exchanges to a member firm or investors in a member firm for alleged negligent failure of the exchange to enforce its own rules. Lank v. New York Stock Exchange, 548 F.2d 61 (2d Cir.1977); Arneil v. Ramsey, 550 F.2d 774 (2d Cir.1977). But cf. Hochfelder v. Midwest Stock Exchange, 503 F.2d 364 (7th Cir.1974), cert. denied 419 U.S. 875 (1974); Collins v. PBW Stock Exchange, Inc., 408 F.Supp. 1344 (E.D.Pa.1976). All of these cases are of limited authority after the 1975 amendments.

In addition to the major issues discussed above, there have been a number of cases dealing with an implied right of action under miscellaneous sections and rules. It has been held that there is a private right of action under Rule 10b–16 dealing with the disclosure of credit terms by broker-dealers.[94] There is a cause of action to rescind a contract under Section 29 of the 1934 Act if there was a violation of the act or rules thereunder in the making or enforcement of the contract.[95] This is consistent with the holding of the *Lewis* case regarding the similar provision of the Investment Advisers Act of 1940.[96] The Ninth Circuit held, however, that there is no cause of action in favor of an issuer to require the filing of reports under Section 16(a)—the issuer is limited to the express remedy provided in Section 16(b).[97]

This topic has generated a great deal of discussion in the law reviews. See Lashbrooke, Implying a Cause of Action for Damages: Rule Violations by Registered Exchanges and Associations, 48 U.Cin.L.Rev. 949 (1979); Lowenfels, Lack of Fair Procedures in the Administrative Process: Disciplinary Proceedings at the Stock Exchanges and the NASD, 64 Corn.L.Rev. 375 (1979); Wolfson and Russo, Stock Exchange Member Liability for Violation of Stock Exchange Rules, 58 Calif.L.Rev. 1120 (1970); Allen, Liability under the Securities Exchange Act for Violations of Stock Exchange Rules, 25 Bus.Law. 1493 (1970); Hoblin, Stock Broker's Implied Liability to its Customer for Violation of a Rule of a Registered Stock Exchange, 39 Ford.L.Rev. 253 (1970); Lowenfels, Implied Liabilities Based Upon Stock Exchange Rules, 66 Colum.L.Rev. 12 (1966); Lowenfels, Private Enforcement in the Over-the-Counter Securities Markets: Implied Liabilities Based on NASD Rules, 51 Corn.L.Q. 633 (1966).

94. Robertson v. Dean Witter Reynolds, Inc., 749 F.2d 530 (9th Cir.1984); Angelastro v. Prudential—Bache Securities, Inc., 764 F.2d 939 (3d Cir.1985), cert. denied —— U.S. ——, 106 S.Ct. 267 (1985).

95. Regional Properties, Inc. v. Financial and Real Estate Consulting Company, 678 F.2d 552 (5th Cir.1982). The Seventh Circuit held, however, that there is no cause of action under Section 29(b) to void a loan agreement which allegedly violated Regulation U. Bassler v. Central National Bank in Chicago, 715 F.2d 308 (7th Cir. 1983).

96. There is also a private right of action under Section 15(f) of the Investment Company Act of 1940 dealing with the sale of control of an investment adviser. Meyer v. Oppenheimer Management Corporation, 764 F.2d 76 (2d Cir.1985).

97. ScienTex Corporation v. Kay, 689 F.2d 879 (9th Cir.1982).

Chapter 14

FAULT REQUIRED

Statutes and Regulations

Securities Act of 1933, §§ 11, 12(2).

Securities Exchange Act of 1934, §§ 10(b), 14(a), 14(e), 17(a), 20(b), 21(d).

Rules 10b–5 and 14a–9.

ESCOTT v. BARCHRIS CONSTRUCTION CORP.

United States District Court, S.D., New York, 1968.
283 F.Supp. 643.

McLEAN, DISTRICT JUDGE. This is an action by purchasers of $5\frac{1}{2}$ per cent convertible subordinated fifteen year debentures of BarChris Construction Corporation (BarChris). Plaintiffs purport to sue on their own behalf and "on behalf of all other and present and former holders" of the debentures. When the action was begun on October 25, 1962, there were nine plaintiffs. Others were subsequently permitted to intervene. At the time of the trial, there were over sixty.

The action is brought under Section 11 of the Securities Act of 1933. Plaintiffs allege that the registration statement with respect to these debentures filed with the Securities and Exchange Commission, which became effective on May 16, 1961, contained material false statements and material omissions.

Defendants fall into three categories: (1) the persons who signed the registration statement; (2) the underwriters, consisting of eight investment banking firms, led by Drexel & Co. (Drexel); and (3) BarChris's auditors, Peat, Marwick, Mitchell & Co. (Peat, Marwick).

The signers, in addition to BarChris itself, were the nine directors of BarChris, plus its controller, defendant Trilling, who was not a director. Of the nine directors, five were officers of BarChris, i.e., defendants Vitolo, president; Russo, executive vice president; Pugliese, vice president; Kircher, treasurer; and Birnbaum, secretary. Of the remaining four, defendant Grant was a member of the firm of Perkins, Daniels, McCormack & Collins, BarChris's attorneys. He became a director in October 1960. Defendant Coleman, a partner in Drexel, became a director on April 17, 1961, as did the other two, Auslander and Rose, who were not otherwise connected with BarChris.

Defendants, in addition to denying that the registration statement was false, have pleaded the defenses open to them under Section 11 of the Act, plus certain additional defenses, including the statute of limitations. Defendants have also asserted cross-claims against each other, seeking to hold one another liable for any sums for which the respective defendants may be held liable to plaintiffs.

This opinion will not concern itself with the cross-claims or with issues peculiar to any particular plaintiff. These matters are reserved for later decision. On the main issue of liability, the questions to be decided are (1) did the registration statement contain false statements of fact, or did it omit to state facts which should have been stated in order to prevent it from being misleading; (2) if so, were the facts which were falsely stated or omitted "material" within the meaning of the Act; (3) if so, have defendants established their affirmative defenses?

* * *

In general, BarChris's method of operation was to enter into a contract with a customer, receive from him at that time a comparatively small down payment on the purchase price, and proceed to construct and equip the bowling alley. When the work was finished and the building delivered, the customer paid the balance of the contract price in notes, payable in installments over a period of years. BarChris discounted these notes with a factor and received part of their face amount in cash. The factor held back part as a reserve.

In 1960 BarChris began a practice which has been referred to throughout this case as the "alternative method of financing." In substance this was a sale and leaseback arrangement. It involved a distinction between the "interior" of a building and the building itself, i.e., the outer shell. In instances in which this method applied, BarChris would build and install what it referred to as the "interior package." Actually this amounted to constructing and installing the equipment in a building. When it was completed, it would sell the interior to a factor, James Talcott Inc. (Talcott), who would pay BarChris the full contract price therefor. The factor then proceeded to lease the interior either directly to BarChris's customer or back to a subsidiary of BarChris. In the latter case, the subsidiary in turn would lease it to the customer.

Under either financing method, BarChris was compelled to expend considerable sums in defraying the cost of construction before it received reimbursement.[4] As a consequence, BarChris was in constant need of cash to finance its operations, a need which grew more pressing as operations expanded.

In December 1959, BarChris sold 560,000 shares of common stock to the public at $3.00 per share. This issue was underwritten by Peter Morgan & Company, one of the present defendants.

By early 1961, BarChris needed additional working capital. The proceeds of the sale of the debentures involved in this action were to be devoted, in part at least, to fill that need.

The registration statement of the debentures, in preliminary form, was filed with the Securities and Exchange Commission on March 30, 1961. A first amendment was filed on May 11 and a second on May 16. The registration statement became effective on May 16. The closing of the financing took place on May 24. On that day BarChris received the net proceeds of the financing.

By that time BarChris was experiencing difficulties in collecting amounts due from some of its customers. Some of them were in arrears in payments due to factors on their discounted notes. As time went on those difficulties increased. Although BarChris continued to build alleys in 1961

---

4. Under the sale and leaseback arrangement, Talcott paid part of the price to BarChris as the work progressed.

and 1962, it became increasingly apparent that the industry was overbuilt. Operators of alleys, often inadequately financed, began to fail. Precisely when the tide turned is a matter of dispute, but at any rate, it was painfully apparent in 1962.

In May of that year BarChris made an abortive attempt to raise more money by the sale of common stock. It filed with the Securities and Exchange Commission a registration statement for the stock issue which it later withdrew. In October 1962 BarChris came to the end of the road. On October 29, 1962, it filed in this court a petition for an arrangement under Chapter XI of the Bankruptcy Act. BarChris defaulted in the payment of the interest due on November 1, 1962 on the debentures.

* * *

Summary

For convenience, the various falsities and omissions which I have discussed in the preceding pages are recapitulated here. They were as follows:

1. *1960 Earnings*
   - (a) *Sales*

As per prospectus	$9,165,320
Correct figure	8,511,420
Overstatement	$ 653,900

   - (b) *Net Operating Income*

As per prospectus	$1,742,801
Correct figure	1,496,196
Overstatement	$ 246,605

   - (c) *Earnings per Share*

As per prospectus	$ .75
Correct figure	.65

5. *Earnings Figures for Quarter ending March 31, 1961*
   - (a) *Sales*

As per prospectus	$2,138,455
Correct figure	1,618,645
Overstatement	$ 519,810

   - (b) *Gross Profit*

As per prospectus	$ 483,121
Correct figure	252,366
Overstatement	$ 230,755

6. *Backlog as of March 31, 1961*

As per prospectus	$6,905,000
Correct figure	2,415,000
Overstatement	$4,490,000

7. *Failure to Disclose Officers' Loans Outstanding and Unpaid on May 16, 1961* — $ 386,615

8. *Failure to Disclose Use of Proceeds in Manner not Revealed in Prospectus*

Approximately	$1,160,000

9. *Failure to Disclose Customers' Delinquencies in May 1961 and BarChris's Potential Liability with Respect Thereto* — Over $1,350,000

10. *Failure to Disclose the Fact that BarChris was Al-
      ready Engaged, and was about to be More Heavily
      Engaged, in the Operation of Bowling Alleys*

* * *

[The contingent liabilities as of December 31, 1960 arose from Bar-
Chris's selling practices. Under the first method, the corporation accepted
customers' installment notes with maturities up to seven years as part
payment for products sold or services performed. The notes were generally
discounted to financial institutions. Under the alternative method of
financing, the corporation sold the product directly to financial institutions.
Under Type A contracts used under the alternative method, BarChris sold
the bowling alley to a factor, James Talcott Inc., and Talcott leased the
property directly to a BarChris customer. BarChris guaranteed the customers' performance in an amount equal to 25% of the customers' total
obligation under the lease. In Type B contracts, also used under the
alternative method, BarChris sold the bowling alley to Talcott, who leased
back the property to a BarChris subsidiary, BarChris Leasing Corporation,
who in turn leased the property to the customer. In Type B arrangements,
BarChris was liable to the extent of 100% for the performance by its
subsidiary of its obligations under the leases.]

[With respect to the contingent liabilities for 1960, the prospectus stated
that under the second method of financing, the Company was contingently
liable in an amount equal to 25% of the customers' aggregate unexpired
rental payments under the leases. Although this was correct as to the
Type A contracts, the contingent liabilities on Type B contracts were
understated to the extent of 75% of unpaid balances under the leases.]

The "Due Diligence" Defenses

Section 11(b) of the Act provides that:

"* * * no person, other than the issuer, shall be liable * * * who
shall sustain the burden of proof—

* * *

"(3) that (A) as regards any part of the registration statement not
purporting to be made on the authority of an expert * * * he had, after
reasonable investigation, reasonable ground to believe and did believe, at
the time such part of the registration statement became effective, that the
statements therein were true and that there was no omission to state a
material fact required to be stated therein or necessary to make the
statements therein not misleading; * * * and (C) as regards any part of
the registration statement purporting to be made on the authority of an
expert (other than himself) * * * he had no reasonable ground to believe
and did not believe, at the time such part of the registration statement
became effective, that the statements therein were untrue or that there
was an omission to state a material fact required to be stated therein or
necessary to make the statements therein not misleading. * * *"

Section 11(c) defines "reasonable investigation" as follows:

"In determining, for the purpose of paragraph (3) of subsection (b) of
this section, what constitutes reasonable investigation and reasonable
ground for belief, the standard of reasonableness shall be that required
of a prudent man in the management of his own property."

Every defendant, except BarChris itself, to whom, as the issuer, these defenses are not available, and except Peat, Marwick, whose position rests on a different statutory provision, has pleaded these affirmative defenses. Each claims that (1) as to the part of the registration statement purporting to be made on the authority of an expert (which, for convenience, I shall refer to as the "expertised portion"), he had no reasonable ground to believe and did not believe that there were any untrue statements or material omissions, and (2) as to the other parts of the registration statement, he made a reasonable investigation, as a result of which he had reasonable ground to believe and did believe that the registration statement was true and that no material fact was omitted. As to each defendant, the question is whether he has sustained the burden of proving these defenses. Surprising enough, there is little or no judicial authority on this question. No decisions directly in point under Section 11 have been found.

Before considering the evidence, a preliminary matter should be disposed of. The defendants do not agree among themselves as to who the "experts" were or as to the parts of the registration statement which were expertised. Some defendants say that Peat, Marwick was the expert, others say that BarChris's attorneys, Perkins, Daniels, McCormack & Collins, and the underwriters' attorneys, Drinker, Biddle & Reath, were also the experts. On the first view, only those portions of the registration statement purporting to be made on Peat, Marwick's authority were expertised portions. On the other view everything in the registration statement was within this category, because the two law firms were responsible for the entire document.

The first view is the correct one. To say that the entire registration statement is expertised because some lawyer prepared it would be an unreasonable construction of the statute. Neither the lawyer for the company nor the lawyer for the underwriters is an expert within the meaning of Section 11. The only expert, in the statutory sense, was Peat, Marwick, and the only parts of the registration statement which purported to be made upon the authority of an expert were the portions which purported to be made on Peat, Marwick's authority.

The parties also disagree as to what those portions were. Some defendants say that it was only the 1960 figures (and the figures for prior years, which are not in controversy here). Others say in substance that it was every figure in the prospectus. The plaintiffs take a somewhat intermediate view. They do not claim that Peat, Marwick expertised every figure, but they do maintain that Peat, Marwick is responsible for a portion of the text of the prospectus, i.e., that pertaining to "Methods of Operation," because a reference to it was made in footnote 9 to the balance sheet.

Here again, the more narrow view is the correct one. The registration statement contains a report of Peat, Marwick as independent public accountants dated February 23, 1961. This relates only to the consolidated balance sheet of BarChris and consolidated subsidiaries as of December 31, 1960, and the related statement of earnings and retained earnings for the five years then ended. This is all that Peat, Marwick purported to certify. It is perfectly clear that it did not purport to certify the 1961 figures, some of which are expressly stated in the prospectus to have been unaudited.

Moreover, plaintiffs' intermediate view is also incorrect. The cross reference in footnote 9 to the "Methods of Operation" passage in the prospectus was inserted merely for the convenience of the reader. It is not a fair construction to say that it thereby imported into the balance sheet everything in that portion of the text, much of which had nothing to do with the figures in the balance sheet.

I turn now to the question of whether defendants have proved their due diligence defenses. The position of each defendant will be separately considered.

* * *

Kircher

Kircher was treasurer of BarChris and its chief financial officer. He is a certified public accountant and an intelligent man. He was thoroughly familiar with BarChris's financial affairs. He knew the terms of BarChris's agreements with Talcott. He knew of the customers' delinquency problem. He participated actively with Russo in May 1961 in the successful effort to hold Talcott off until the financing proceeds came in. He knew how the financing proceeds were to be applied and he saw to it that they were so applied. He arranged the officers' loans and he knew all the facts concerning them.

Moreover, as a member of the executive committee, Kircher was kept informed as to those branches of the business of which he did not have direct charge. He knew about the operation of alleys, present and prospective. He knew that Capitol was included in 1960 sales and that Bridge and Yonkers were included in first quarter 1961 sales despite the fact that they were not sold. Kircher knew of the infirmities in customers' contracts included in the backlog figure. Indeed, at a later date, he specifically criticized Russo's handling of the T-Bowl situation. In brief, Kircher knew all the relevant facts.

Kircher worked on the preparation of the registration statement. He conferred with Grant and on occasion with Ballard. He supplied information to them about the company's business. He had the prospectus and understood it. He knew what it said and what it did not say.

Kircher's contention is that he had never before dealt with a registration statement, that he did not know what it should contain, and that he relied wholly on Grant, Ballard and Peat, Marwick to guide him. He claims that it was their fault, not his, if there was anything wrong with it. He says that all the facts were recorded in BarChris's books where these "experts" could have seen them if they had looked. He says that he truthfully answered all their questions. In effect, he says that if they did not know enough to ask the right questions and to give him the proper instructions, that is not his responsibility.

There is an issue of credibility here. In fact, Kircher was not frank in dealing with Grant and Ballard. He withheld information from them. But even if he had told them all the facts, this would not have constituted the due diligence contemplated by the statute. Knowing the facts, Kircher had reason to believe that the expertised portion of the prospectus, i.e., the 1960 figures, was in part incorrect. He could not shut his eyes to the facts and rely on Peat, Marwick for that portion.

As to the rest of the prospectus, knowing the facts, he did not have a reasonable ground to believe it to be true. On the contrary, he must have known that in part it was untrue. Under these circumstances, he was not entitled to sit back and place the blame on the lawyers for not advising him about it.

Kircher has not proved his due diligence defenses.

* * *

Birnbaum

Birnbaum was a young lawyer, admitted to the bar in 1957, who, after brief periods of employment by two different law firms and an equally brief period of practicing in his own firm, was employed by BarChris as house counsel and assistant secretary in October 1960. Unfortunately for him, he became secretary and a director of BarChris on April 17, 1961, after the first version of the registration statement had been filed with the Securities and Exchange Commission. He signed the later amendments, thereby becoming responsible for the accuracy of the prospectus in its final form.

Although the prospectus, in its description of "management," lists Birnbaum among the "executive officers" and devotes several sentences to a recital of his career, the fact seems to be that he was not an executive officer in any real sense. He did not participate in the management of the company. As house counsel, he attended to legal matters of a routine nature. Among other things, he incorporated subsidiaries, with which BarChris was plentifully supplied. Among the subsidiaries which he incorporated were Capitol Lanes, Inc. which operated Capitol, Yonkers Lanes, Inc. which eventually operated Yonkers, and Parkway Lanes, Inc. which eventually operated Bridge. He was thus aware of that aspect of the business.

Birnbaum examined contracts. In that connection he advised BarChris that the T-Bowl contracts were not legally enforceable. He was thus aware of that fact.

One of Birnbaum's more important duties, first as assistant secretary and later as fullfledged secretary, was to keep the corporate minutes of BarChris and its subsidiaries. This necessarily informed him to a considerable extent about the company's affairs. Birnbaum was not initially a member of the executive committee, however, and did not keep its minutes at the outset. According to the minutes, the first meeting which he attended, "upon invitation of the Committee," was on March 22, 1961. He became a member shortly thereafter and kept the minutes beginning with the meeting of April 24, 1961.

It seems probable that Birnbaum did not know of many of the inaccuracies in the prospectus. He must, however, have appreciated some of them. In any case, he made no investigation and relied on the others to get it right. Unlike Trilling, he was entitled to rely upon Peat, Marwick for the 1960 figures, for as far as appears, he had no personal knowledge of the company's books of account or financial transactions. But he was not entitled to rely upon Kircher, Grant and Ballard for the other portions of the prospectus. As a lawyer, he should have known his obligations under the statute. He should have known that he was required to make a reasonable investigation of the truth of all the statements in the unexpertised portion of the document which he signed. Having failed to make such an investigation, he did not have reasonable ground to believe that all these statements were true. Birnbaum has not established his due diligence defenses except as to the audited 1960 figures.

Auslander

Auslander was an "outside" director, i.e., one who was not an officer of BarChris. He was chairman of the board of Valley Stream National Bank in Valley Stream, Long Island. In February, 1961, Vitolo asked him to become a director of BarChris. Vitolo gave him an enthusiastic account of BarChris's progress and prospects. As an inducement, Vitolo said that when BarChris received the proceeds of a forthcoming issue of securities, it would deposit $1,000,000 in Auslander's bank.

In February and early March 1961, before accepting Vitolo's invitation, Auslander made some investigation of BarChris. He obtained Dun & Bradstreet reports which contained sales and earnings figures for periods earlier than December 31, 1960. He caused inquiry to be made of certain of BarChris's banks and was advised that they regarded BarChris favorably. He was informed that inquiry of Talcott had also produced a favorable response.

On March 3, 1961, Auslander indicated his willingness to accept a place on the board. Shortly thereafter, on March 14, Kircher sent him a copy of BarChris's annual report for 1960. Auslander observed that BarChris's auditors were Peat, Marwick. They were also the auditors for the Valley Stream National Bank. He thought well of them.

Auslander was elected a director on April 17, 1961. The registration statement in its original form had already been filed, of course without his signature. On May 10, 1961, he signed a signature page for the first amendment to the registration statement which was filed on May 11, 1961. This was a separate sheet without any document attached. Auslander did not know that it was a signature page for a registration statement. He vaguely understood that it was something "for the SEC."

Auslander attended a meeting of BarChris's directors on May 15, 1961. At that meeting he, along with the other directors, signed the signature sheet for the second amendment which constituted the registration statement in its final form. Again, this was only a separate sheet without any document attached. Auslander never saw a copy of the registration statement in its final form.

At the May 15 directors' meeting, however, Auslander did realize that what he was signing was a signature sheet to a registration statement. This was the first time that he had appreciated that fact. A copy of the registration statement in its earlier form as amended on May 11, 1961, was passed around at the meeting. Auslander glanced at it briefly. He did not read it thoroughly.

At the May 15 meeting, Russo and Vitolo stated that everything was in order and that the prospectus was correct. Auslander believed this statement.

In considering Auslander's due diligence defenses, a distinction is to be drawn between the expertised and non-expertised portions of the prospectus. As to the former, Auslander knew that Peat, Marwick had audited the

1960 figures. He believed them to be correct because he had confidence in Peat, Marwick. He had no reasonable ground to believe otherwise.

As to the non-expertised portions, however, Auslander is in a different position. He seems to have been under the impression that Peat, Marwick was responsible for all the figures. This impression was not correct, as he would have realized if he had read the prospectus carefully. Auslander made no investigation of the accuracy of the prospectus. He relied on the assurance of Vitolo and Russo, and upon the information he had received in answer to his inquiries back in February and early March. These inquiries were general ones, in the nature of a credit check. The information which he received in answer to them was also general, without specific reference to the statements in the prospectus, which was not prepared until some time thereafter.

It is true that Auslander became a director on the eve of the financing. He had little opportunity to familiarize himself with the company's affairs. The question is whether, under such circumstances, Auslander did enough to establish his due diligence defense with respect to the nonexpertised portions of the prospectus.

Although there is a dearth of authority under Section 11 on this point, an English case under the analogous Companies Act is of some value. In Adams v. Thrift [1915] 1 Ch. 557, aff'd [1915] 2 Ch. 21, it was held that a director who knew nothing about the prospectus and did not even read it, but who relied on the statement of the company's managing director that it was "all right," was liable for its untrue statements.

* * *

Section 11 imposes liability in the first instance upon a director, no matter how new he is. He is presumed to know his responsibility when he becomes a director. He can escape liability only by using that reasonable care to investigate the facts which a prudent man would employ in the management of his own property. In my opinion, a prudent man would not act in an important matter without any knowledge of the relevant facts, in sole reliance upon representations of persons who are comparative strangers and upon general information which does not purport to cover the particular case. To say that such minimal conduct measures up to the statutory standard would to all intents and purposes, absolve new directors from responsibility merely because they are new. This is not a sensible construction of Section 11, when one bears in mind its fundamental purpose of requiring full and truthful disclosure for the protection of investors.

I find and conclude that Auslander has not established his due diligence defense with respect to the misstatements and omissions in those portions of the prospectus other than the audited 1960 figures.

* * *

Grant

Grant became a director of BarChris in October 1960. His law firm was counsel to BarChris in matters pertaining to the registration of securities. Grant drafted the registration statement for the stock issue in 1959 and for the warrants in January 1961. He also drafted the registration statement for the debentures. In the preliminary division of work between him and Ballard, the underwriters' counsel, Grant took initial responsibility for preparing the registration statement, while Ballard devoted his efforts in the first instance to preparing the indenture.

Grant is sued as a director and as a signer of the registration statement. This is not an action against him for malpractice in his capacity as a lawyer. Nevertheless, in considering Grant's due diligence defenses, the unique position which he occupied cannot be disregarded. As the director most directly concerned with writing the registration statement and assuring its accuracy, more was required of him in the way of reasonable investigation than could fairly be expected of a director who had no connection with this work.

There is no valid basis for plaintiffs' accusation that Grant knew that the prospectus was false in some respects and incomplete and misleading in others. Having seen him testify at length, I am satisfied as to his integrity. I find that Grant honestly believed that the registration statement was true and that no material facts had been omitted from it.

In this belief he was mistaken, and the fact is that for all his work, he never discovered any of the errors or omissions which have been recounted at length in this opinion, with the single exception of Capitol Lanes. He knew that BarChris had not sold this alley and intended to operate it, but he appears to have been under the erroneous impression that Peat, Marwick had knowingly sanctioned its inclusion in sales because of the allegedly temporary nature of the operation.

Grant contends that a finding that he did not make a reasonable investigation would be equivalent to holding that a lawyer for an issuing company, in order to show due diligence, must make an independent audit of the figures supplied to him by his client. I do not consider this to be a realistic statement of the issue. There were errors and omissions here which could have been detected without an audit. The question is whether, despite his failure to detect them, Grant made a reasonable effort to that end.

Much of this registration statement is a scissors and paste-pot job. Grant lifted large portions from the earlier prospectuses, modifying them in some instances to the extent that he considered necessary. But Bar-Chris's affairs had changed for the worse by May 1961. Statements that were accurate in January were no longer accurate in May. Grant never discovered this. He accepted the assurances of Kircher and Russo that any change which might have occurred had been for the better, rather than the contrary.

It is claimed that a lawyer is entitled to rely on the statements of his client and that to require him to verify their accuracy would set an unreasonably high standard. This is too broad a generalization. It is all a matter of degree. To require an audit would obviously be unreasonable. On the other hand, to require a check of matters easily verifiable is not unreasonable. Even honest clients can make mistakes. The statute imposes liability for untrue statements regardless of whether they are intentionally untrue. The way to prevent mistakes is to test oral information by examining the original written record.

There were things which Grant could readily have checked which he did not check. For example, he was unaware of the provisions of the agreements between BarChris and Talcott. He never read them. Thus, he did not know, although he readily could have ascertained, that BarChris's contingent liability on Type B leaseback arrangements was 100 per cent, not 25 per cent. He did not appreciate that if BarChris defaulted in repurchasing delinquent customers' notes upon Talcott's demand, Talcott could accelerate all the customer paper in its hands, which amounted to over $3,000,000.

As to the backlog figure, Grant appreciated that scheduled unfilled orders on the company's books meant firm commitments, but he never asked to see the contracts which, according to the prospectus, added up to $6,905,000. Thus, he did not know that this figure was overstated by some $4,490,000.

Grant was unaware of the fact that BarChris was about to operate Bridge and Yonkers. He did not read the minutes of those subsidiaries which would have revealed that fact to him. On the subject of minutes, Grant knew that minutes of certain meetings of the BarChris executive committee held in 1961 had not been written up. Kircher, who had acted as secretary at those meetings, had complete notes of them. Kircher told Grant that there was no point in writing up the minutes because the matters discussed at those meetings were purely routine. Grant did not insist that the minutes be written up, nor did he look at Kircher's notes. If he had, he would have learned that on February 27, 1961, there was an extended discussion in the executive committee meeting about customers' delinquencies, that on March 8, 1961 the committee had discussed the pros and cons of alley operation by BarChris, that on March 18, 1961 the committee was informed that BarChris was constructing or about to begin constructing twelve alleys for which it had no contracts, and that on May 13, 1961 Dreyfuss, one of the worst delinquents, had filed a petition in Chapter X.

Grant knew that there had been loans from officers to BarChris in the past because that subject had been mentioned in the 1959 and January 1961 prospectuses. In March Grant prepared a questionnaire to be answered by officers and directors for the purpose of obtaining information to be used in the prospectus. The questionnaire did not inquire expressly about the existence of officers' loans.[21] At approximately the same time, Grant prepared another questionnaire in order to obtain information on proxy statements for the annual stockholders' meeting. This questionnaire asked each officer to state whether he was indebted to BarChris, but it did not ask whether BarChris was indebted to him.

Despite the inadequacy of these written questionnaires, Grant did, on March 16, 1961, orally inquire as to whether any officers' loans were outstanding. He was assured by Russo, Vitolo and Pugliese that all such loans had been repaid. Grant did not ask again. He was unaware of the new loans in April. He did know, however, that, at Kircher's request, a provision was inserted in the indenture which gave loans from individuals priority over the debentures. Kircher's insistence on this clause did not arouse his suspicions.

---

21. Question 3 of this questionnaire read:

"Describe briefly and state the approximate amount of any material interest, direct or indirect, of you, or any associate of you in any material transactions during the last three years, or in any material proposed transactions, to which the Company or its subsidiaries were or are to be a party."

This involved query could hardly have been understood by men like Vitolo and Pugliese to call for information as to loans.

It is only fair to say that Grant was given to understand by Kircher that there were no new officers' loans and that there would not be any before May 16. It is still a close question, however, whether, under all the circumstances, Grant should have investigated further, perhaps by asking Peat, Marwick, in the course of its S-1 review, to look at the books on this particular point. I believe that a careful man would have checked.

There is more to the subject of due diligence than this, particularly with respect to the application of proceeds and customers' delinquencies.

The application of proceeds language in the prospectus was drafted by Kircher back in January. It may well have expressed his intent at that time, but his intent, and that of the other principal officers of BarChris, was very different in May. Grant did not appreciate that the earlier language was no longer appropriate. He never learned of the situation which the company faced in May. He knew that BarChris was short of cash, but he had no idea how short. He did not know that BarChris was withholding delivery of checks already drawn and signed because there was not enough money in the bank to pay them. He did not know that the officers of the company intended to use immediately approximately one-third of the financing proceeds in a manner not disclosed in the prospectus, including approximately $1,000,000 in paying old debts.

In this connection, mention should be made of a fact which has previously been referred to only in passing. The "negative cash balance" in BarChris's Lafayette National Bank account in May 1961, included a check dated April 10, 1961 to the order of Grant's firm, Perkins, Daniels, McCormack & Collins, in the amount of $8,711. This check was not deposited by Perkins, Daniels until June 1, after the financing proceeds had been received by BarChris. Of course, if Grant had knowingly withheld deposit of this check, until that time, he would be in a position similar to Russo, Vitolo and Pugliese. I do not believe, however, that that was the case. I find that the check was not delivered by BarChris to Perkins, Daniels until shortly before June 1.

This incident is worthy of mention, however, for another reason. The prospectus stated on page 10 that Perkins, Daniels had "received fees aggregating $13,000" from BarChris. This check for $8,711 was one of those fees. It had not been received by Perkins, Daniels prior to May 16. Grant was unaware of this. In approving this erroneous statement in the prospectus, he did not consult his own bookkeeper to ascertain whether it was correct. Kircher told him that the bill had been paid and Grant took his word for it. If he had inquired and had found that this representation was untrue, this discovery might well have led him to a realization of the true state of BarChris's finances in May 1961.

As far as customers' delinquencies are concerned, although Grant discussed this with Kircher, he again accepted the assurances of Kircher and Russo that no serious problem existed. He did not examine the records as to delinquencies, although BarChris maintained such a record. Any inquiry on his part of Talcott or an examination of BarChris's correspondence with Talcott in April and May 1961 would have apprised him of the true facts. It would have led him to appreciate that the statement in this prospectus, carried over from earlier prospectuses, to the effect that since 1955 BarChris had been required to repurchase less than one-half of one per cent of discounted customers' notes could no longer properly be made without further explanation.

Grant was entitled to rely on Peat, Marwick for the 1960 figures. He had no reasonable ground to believe them to be inaccurate. But the matters which I have mentioned were not within the expertised portion of the prospectus. As to this, Grant was obliged to make a reasonable investigation. I am forced to find that he did not make one. After making all due allowances for the fact that BarChris's officers misled him, there are too many instances in which Grant failed to make an inquiry which he could easily have made which, if pursued, would have put him on his guard. In my opinion, this finding on the evidence in this case does not establish an unreasonably high standard in other cases for company counsel who are also directors. Each case must rest on its own facts. I conclude that Grant has not established his due diligence defenses except as to the audited 1960 figures.

The Underwriters and Coleman

The underwriters other than Drexel made no investigation of the accuracy of the prospectus. One of them, Peter Morgan, had underwritten the 1959 stock issue and had been a director of BarChris. He thus had some general familiarity with its affairs, but he knew no more than the other underwriters about the debenture prospectus. They all relied upon Drexel as the "lead" underwriter.

Drexel did make an investigation. The work was in charge of Coleman, a partner of the firm, assisted by Casperson, an associate. Drexel's attorneys acted as attorneys for the entire group of underwriters. Ballard did the work, assisted by Stanton.

On April 17, 1961 Coleman became a director of BarChris. He signed the first amendment to the registration statement filed on May 11 and the second amendment constituting the registration statement in its final form, filed on May 16. He thereby assumed a responsibility as a director and signer in addition to his responsibility as an underwriter.

The facts as to the extent of the investigation that Coleman made may be briefly summarized. He was first introduced to BarChris on September 15, 1960. Thereafter he familiarized himself with general conditions in the industry, primarily by reading reports and prospectuses of the two leading bowling alley builders, American Machine & Foundry Company and Brunswick. These indicated that the industry was still growing. He also acquired general information on BarChris by reading the 1959 stock prospectus, annual reports for prior years, and an unaudited statement for the first half of 1960. He inquired about BarChris of certain of its banks and of Talcott and received favorable replies.

The purpose of this preliminary investigation was to enable Coleman to decide whether Drexel would undertake the financing. It did not have direct reference to any specific registration statement for at that time, of course, none had been prepared. Coleman was sufficiently optimistic about BarChris's prospects to buy 1,000 shares of its stock, which he did in December 1960.

On January 24, 1961, Coleman held a meeting with Ballard, Grant and Kircher, among others. By that time Coleman had about decided to go ahead with the financing, although Drexel's formal letter of intent was not delivered until February 9, 1961 (subsequently revised on March 7, 1961). At this meeting Coleman asked Kircher how BarChris intended to use the proceeds of the financing. In reply to this inquiry, Kircher wrote a letter to Coleman dated January 30, 1961 outlining BarChris's plans. This eventually formed the basis of the application of proceeds section in the prospectus.

Coleman continued his general investigation. He obtained a Dun & Bradstreet report on BarChris on March 16, 1961. He read BarChris's annual report for 1960 which was available in March.

By mid-March, Coleman was in a position to make more specific inquiries. By that time Grant had prepared a first draft of the prospectus, consisting of a marked-up copy of the January 1961 warrant prospectus. Coleman attended the meetings to discuss the prospectus with BarChris's representatives. The meetings were held at Perkins, Daniels' office on March 20, March 23 and March 24, 1961. Those present included Grant or his partner McCormack and Kircher for the company,[22] and Coleman, Casperson and Ballard for the underwriters. Logan, Peat, Marwick's manager of the 1960 audit, was present at one of the meetings.

At these discussions, which were extensive, successive proofs of the prospectus were considered and revised. At this point the 1961 figures were not available. They were put in the prospectus in May.

Coleman and Ballard asked pertinent questions and received answers which satisfied them. Among other things, the following transpired.

Logan explained some of the 1960 figures, including the reserve for bad debts, which he considered adequate.

There was a discussion of the application of proceeds section. It was not changed in any respect material here.

As to the backlog of orders on hand, Ballard said that the figure, not then available, must be "hard and fast," not "puffy." Grant and Kircher "concurred."

There was talk about the 15 to 25 per cent down payment figure. Kircher said that this was accurate.

More important for our purposes, there was a discussion of the one-half of one percent figure with respect to BarChris's past experience in repurchasing discounted customers' notes. Kircher said that this figure was "conservative." Ballard inquired whether, regardless of what past experience had been, there was "any real chance that you see of being forced to take any [alleys] back in the future?" Kircher's answer was "negative."

The alternative method of financing was explained. Kircher said that BarChris's contingent liability was only 25 percent.

There was talk about operating alleys. Kircher said that BarChris did not operate any. Coleman and Ballard inquired whether BarChris built alleys on speculation, i.e., without any customer's contract for them. Kircher said BarChris did not.

There was discussion of officers' loans. Kircher said that the $155,000 had been repaid and that no further officers' loans were contemplated.

---

22. Grant was in charge of this work for his firm, but he was out of town on March 20 and March 23, and McCormack substituted for him on those days.

Coleman said that this was wise, for loans from officers "indicated financial instability of the company."

Coleman did not participate personally in any further meetings of this sort. Casperson attended some and reported to Coleman. Ballard advised Coleman as to what he was doing.

After Coleman was elected a director on April 17, 1961, he made no further independent investigation of the accuracy of the prospectus. He assumed that Ballard was taking care of this on his behalf as well as on behalf of the underwriters.

In April 1961 Ballard instructed Stanton to examine BarChris's minutes for the past five years and also to look at "the major contracts of the company." [23] Stanton went to BarChris's office for that purpose on April 24. He asked Birnbaum for the minute books. He read the minutes of the board of directors and discovered interleaved in them a few minutes of executive committee meetings in 1960. He asked Kircher if there were any others. Kircher said that there had been other executive committee meetings but that the minutes had not been written up.

Stanton read the minutes of a few BarChris subsidiaries. His testimony was vague as to which ones. He had no recollection of seeing the minutes of Capitol Lanes, Inc. or Biel or Parkway Lanes, Inc. He did not discover that BarChris was operating Capitol or that it planned to operate Bridge and Yonkers.

As to the "major contracts," all that Stanton could remember seeing was an insurance policy. Birnbaum told him that there was no file of major contracts. Stanton did not examine the agreements with Talcott. He did not examine the contracts with customers. He did not look to see what contracts comprised the backlog figure. Stanton examined no accounting records of BarChris. His visit, which lasted one day, was devoted primarily to reading the directors' minutes.

On April 25 Ballard wrote to Grant about certain matters which Stanton had noted on his visit to BarChris the day before, none of which Ballard considered "very earth shaking." As far as relevant here, these were (1) Russo's remark as recorded in the executive committee minutes of November 3, 1960 to the effect that because of customers' defaults, BarChris might find itself in the business of operating alleys; (2) the fact that the minutes of Sanpark Realty Corporation were incomplete; and (3) the fact that minutes of the executive committee were missing.

On May 9, 1961, Ballard came to New York and conferred with Grant and Kircher. They discussed the Securities and Exchange Commission's deficiency letter of May 4, 1961 which required the inclusion in the prospectus of certain additional information, notably net sales, gross profits and net earnings figures for the first quarter of 1961. They also discussed the points raised in Ballard's letter to Grant of April 25. As to the latter, most of the conversation related to what Russo had meant by his remark on November 3, 1960. Kircher said that the delinquency problem was less severe now than it had been back in November 1960, that no alleys had been repossessed, and that although he was "worried about one alley in Harlem" (Dreyfuss), that was a "special situation." Grant reported that

---

23. Stanton was a very junior associate. He had been admitted to the bar in January 1961, some three months before. This was the first registration statement he had ever worked on.

Russo had told him that his statement on November 3, 1960 was "merely hypothetical." On the strength of this conversation, Ballard was satisfied that the one-half of one percent figure in the prospectus did not need qualification or elaboration.

As to the missing minutes, Kircher said that those of Sanpark were not significant and that the executive committee meetings for which there were no written minutes were concerned only with "routine matters."

It must be remembered that this conference took place only one week before the registration statement became effective. Ballard did nothing else in the way of checking during that intervening week.

Ballard did not insist that the executive committee minutes be written up so that he could inspect them, although he testified that he knew from experience that executive committee minutes may be extremely important. If he had insisted, he would have found the minutes highly informative, as has previously been pointed out * * *. Ballard did not ask to see BarChris's schedule of delinquencies or Talcott's notices of delinquencies, or BarChris's correspondence with Talcott.

Ballard did not examine BarChris's contracts with Talcott. He did not appreciate what Talcott's rights were under those financing agreements or how serious the effect would be upon BarChris of any exercise of those rights.

Ballard did not investigate the composition of the backlog figure to be sure that it was not "puffy." He made no inquiry after March about any new officers' loans, although he knew that Kircher had insisted on a provision in the indenture which gave loans from individuals priority over the debentures. He was unaware of the seriousness of BarChris's cash position and of how BarChris's officers intended to use a large part of the proceeds. He did not know that BarChris was operating Capitol Lanes.[24]

Like Grant, Ballard, without checking, relied on the information which he got from Kircher. He also relied on Grant who, as company counsel, presumably was familiar with its affairs.

The formal opinion which Ballard's firm rendered to the underwriters at the closing on May 24, 1961 made clear that this is what he had done. The opinion stated (italics supplied):

"In the course of the preparation of the Registration Statement and Prospectus by the Company, we had had numerous conferences with representatives of and counsel for the Company and with its auditors and we have raised many questions regarding the business of the Company. Satisfactory answers to such questions were in each case given us, and all other information and documents we requested have been supplied. We are of the opinion that the *data presented* to us are accurately reflected in the Registration Statement and Prospectus and that there has been omitted from the Registration Statement no material facts *included in such data.* Although *we have not otherwise verified* the completeness or accuracy of the information furnished to us, on the basis of the foregoing and with the exception of the financial statements and schedules (which this opinion does not pass upon), we have no

24. Stanton was also unaware of this, although there was a reference to it in the minutes of the board of directors' meeting of November 22, 1960, which he presumably read.

reason to believe that the Registration Statement or Prospectus contains any untrue statement of any material fact or omits to state a material fact required to be stated therein or necessary in order to make the statements therein not misleading."

Coleman testified that Drexel had an understanding with its attorneys that "we expect them to inspect on our behalf the corporate records of the company including, but not limited to, the minutes of the corporation, the stockholders and the committees of the board authorized to act for the board." Ballard manifested his awareness of this understanding by sending Stanton to read the minutes and the major contracts. It is difficult to square this understanding with the formal opinion of Ballard's firm which expressly disclaimed any attempt to verify information supplied by the company and its counsel.

In any event, it is clear that no effectual attempt at verification was made. The question is whether due diligence required that it be made. Stated another way, is it sufficient to ask questions, to obtain answers which, if true, would be thought satisfactory, and to let it go at that, without seeking to ascertain from the records whether the answers in fact are true and complete?

I have already held that this procedure is not sufficient in Grant's case. Are underwriters in a different position, as far as due diligence is concerned?

The underwriters say that the prospectus is the company's prospectus, not theirs. Doubtless this is the way they customarily regard it. But the Securities Act makes no such distinction. The underwriters are just as responsible as the company if the prospectus is false. And prospective investors rely upon the reputation of the underwriters in deciding whether to purchase the securities.

There is no direct authority on this question, no judicial decision defining the degree of diligence which underwriters must exercise to establish their defense under Section 11.[25]

There is some authority in New York for the proposition that a director of a corporation may rely upon information furnished him by the officers without independently verifying it.

See Litwin v. Allen, 25 N.Y.S.2d 667 (Sup.Ct.1940).

In support of that principle, the court in Litwin, (25 N.Y.S.2d at 719) quoted from the opinion of Lord Halsbury in Dovey v. Cory, [1901] App.Cas. 447, 486, in which he said:

"The business of life could not go on if people could not trust those who are put into a position of trust for the express purpose of attending to details of management."

Of course, New York law does not govern this case. The construction of the Securities Act is a matter of federal law. But the underwriters argue that *Litwin* is still in point, for they say that it establishes a standard of reasonableness for the reasonably prudent director which should be the

---

25. There are at least two decisions of the Securities and Exchange Commission which indicate that it is the Commission's view that an underwriter must go beyond and behind the representations of manage-ment. Matter of Richmond Corp., [1962–1964 Decisions] CCH Sec.L.Rep. ¶ 76,904 (1963); Matter of Charles E. Bailey & Co., 35 S.E.C. 33 (1953).

same as the standard for the reasonably prudent underwriter under the Securities Act.

In my opinion the two situations are not analogous. An underwriter has not put the company's officers "into a position of trust for the express purpose of attending to details of management." The underwriters did not select them. In a sense, the positions of the underwriter and the company's officers are adverse. It is not unlikely that statements made by company officers to an underwriter to induce him to underwrite may be self-serving. They may be unduly enthusiastic. As in this case, they may, on occasion, be deliberately false.

The purpose of Section 11 is to protect investors. To that end the underwriters are made responsible for the truth of the prospectus. If they may escape that responsibility by taking at face value representations made to them by the company's management, then the inclusion of underwriters among those liable under Section 11 affords the investors no additional protection. To effectuate the statute's purpose, the phrase "reasonable investigation" must be construed to require more effort on the part of the underwriters than the mere accurate reporting in the prospectus of "data presented" to them by the company. It should make no difference that this data is elicited by questions addressed to the company officers by the underwriters, or that the underwriters at the time believe that the company's officers are truthful and reliable. In order to make the underwriters' participation in this enterprise of any value to the investors, the underwriters must make some reasonable attempt to verify the data submitted to them. They may not rely solely on the company's officers or on the company's counsel. A prudent man in the management of his own property would not rely on them.

It is impossible to lay down a rigid rule suitable for every case defining the extent to which such verification must go. It is a question of degree, a matter of judgment in each case. In the present case, the underwriters' counsel made almost no attempt to verify management's representations. I hold that that was insufficient.

On the evidence in this case, I find that the underwriters' counsel did not make a reasonable investigation of the truth of those portions of the prospectus which were not made on the authority of Peat, Marwick as an expert. Drexel is bound by their failure. It is not a matter of relying upon counsel for legal advice. Here the attorneys were dealing with matters of fact. Drexel delegated to them, as its agent the business of examining the corporate minutes and contracts. It must bear the consequences of their failure to make an adequate examination.

The other underwriters, who did nothing and relied solely on Drexel and on the lawyers, are also bound by it. It follows that although Drexel and the other underwriters believed that those portions of the prospectus were true, they had no reasonable ground for that belief, within the meaning of the statute. Hence, they have not established their due diligence defense, except as to the 1960 audited figures.[26]

The same conclusions must apply to Coleman. Although he participated quite actively in the earlier stages of the preparation of the prospectus,

---

26. In view of this conclusion, it becomes unnecessary to decide whether the underwriters other than Drexel would have been protected if Drexel had established that as lead underwriter, it made a reasonable investigation.

and contributed questions and warnings of his own, in addition to the questions of counsel, the fact is that he stopped his participation toward the end of March 1961. He made no investigation after he became a director. When it came to verification, he relied upon his counsel to do it for him. Since counsel failed to do it, Coleman is bound by that failure. Consequently in his case also, he has not established his due diligence defense except as to the audited 1960 figures.

Peat, Marwick

Section 11(b) provides:

"Notwithstanding the provisions of subsection (a) no person * * * shall be liable as provided therein who shall sustain the burden of proof—

* * *

"(3) that * * * (B) as regards any part of the registration statement purporting to be made upon his authority as an expert * * * (i) he had, after reasonable investigation, reasonable ground to believe and did believe, at the time such part of the registration statement became effective, that the statements therein were true and that there was no omission to state a material fact required to be stated therein or necessary to make the statements therein not misleading * * *."

This defines the due diligence defense for an expert. Peat, Marwick has pleaded it.

The part of the registration statement purporting to be made upon the authority of Peat, Marwick as an expert was, as we have seen the 1960 figures. But because the statute requires the court to determine Peat, Marwick's belief, and the grounds thereof, "at the time such part of the registration statement became effective," for the purposes of this affirmative defense the matter must be viewed as of May 16, 1961, and the question is whether at that time Peat, Marwick, after reasonable investigation, had reasonable ground to believe and did believe that the 1960 figures were true and that no material fact had been omitted from the registration statement which should have been included in order to make the 1960 figures not misleading. In deciding this issue, the court must consider not only what Peat, Marwick did in its 1960 audit, but also what it did in its subsequent "S–1 review." The proper scope of that review must also be determined.

It may be noted that we are concerned at this point only with the question of Peat, Marwick's liability to plaintiffs. At the closing on May 24, 1961, Peat, Marwick delivered a so-called "comfort letter" to the underwriters. This letter stated:

"It is understood that this letter is for the information of the underwriters and is not to be quoted or referred to, in whole or in part, in the Registration Statement or Prospectus or in any literature used in connection with the sale of securities."

Plaintiffs may not take advantage of any undertakings or representations in this letter. If they exceeded the normal scope of an S–1 review (a question which I do not now decide) that is a matter which relates only to the crossclaims which defendants have asserted against each other and which I have postponed for determination at a later date.

The 1960 Audit

Peat, Marwick's work was in general charge of a member of the firm, Cummings, and more immediately in charge of Peat, Marwick's manager, Logan. Most of the actual work was performed by a senior accountant, Berardi, who had junior assistants, one of whom was Kennedy.

Berardi was then about thirty years old. He was not yet a C.P.A. He had had no previous experience with the bowling industry. This was his first job as a senior accountant. He could hardly have been given a more difficult assignment.

After obtaining a little background information on BarChris by talking to Logan and reviewing Peat, Marwick's work papers on its 1959 audit, Berardi examined the results of test checks of BarChris's accounting procedures which one of the junior accountants had made, and he prepared an "internal control questionnaire" and an "audit program." Thereafter, for a few days subsequent to December 30, 1960, he inspected BarChris's inventories and examined certain alley construction. Finally, on January 13, 1961, he began his auditing work which he carried on substantially continuously until it was completed on February 24, 1961. Toward the close of the work, Logan reviewed it and made various comments and suggestions to Berardi.

It is unnecessary to recount everything that Berardi did in the course of the audit. We are concerned only with the evidence relating to what Berardi did or did not do with respect to those items which I have found to have been incorrectly reported in the 1960 figures in the prospectus. More narrowly, we are directly concerned only with such of those items as I have found to be material.

Capitol Lanes

First and foremost is Berardi's failure to discover that Capitol Lanes had not been sold. This error affected both the sales figure and the liability side of the balance sheet. Fundamentally, the error stemmed from the fact that Berardi never realized that Heavenly Lanes and Capitol were two different names for the same alley. In the course of his audit, Berardi was shown BarChris's contract file. He examined the contracts in the file and made a list of them. The file must have included a contract with an outside purchaser for Heavenly Lanes, although no such contract was ever produced at the trial, for Berardi included Heavenly on his list. Apparently there was no contract in the file for a lane named Capitol because that name did not appear on Berardi's list.

Kircher also made a list of jobs. Heavenly was on his list. Capitol was not. Berardi compared the two lists and satisfied himself that he had the proper jobs to be taken into account. Berardi assumed that Heavenly was to be treated like any other completed job. He included it in all his computations.

The evidence is conflicting as to whether BarChris's officers expressly informed Berardi that Heavenly and Capitol were the same thing and that BarChris was operating Capitol and had not sold it. I find that they did not so inform him.

Berardi did become aware that there were references here and there in BarChris's records to something called Capitol Lanes. He also knew that there were indications that at some time BarChris might operate an alley of that name. He read the minutes of the board of directors' meeting of November 22, 1960 which recited that:

"* * * the Chairman recommended that the Corporation operate Capitol Lanes, 271 Main Street, East Haven, Connecticut, through a corporation which would be a subsidiary of Sanpark Realty Corp."

The minutes further recorded that:

"* * * it was unanimously agreed that the officers of the Corporation exercise their discretion as to operating Capitol Lanes through the aforesaid subsidiary on an experimental basis."

The junior accountant Kennedy, read the minute book of Capitol Lanes, Inc., a Connecticut corporation organized in December 1960. The book contained a certificate of incorporation which empowered the corporation, among many other things, to own and manage bowling alleys. There was no minute in the book, however, that indicated that the corporation actually did own or manage one.

Berardi knew from various BarChris records that Capitol Lanes, Inc., was paying rentals to Talcott. Also, a Peat, Marwick work paper bearing Kennedy's initials recorded that Capitol Lanes, Inc. held certain insurance policies, including a fire insurance policy on "contents," a workman's compensation and a public liability policy. Another Peat, Marwick work paper also bearing Kennedy's initials recorded that Capitol Lanes, Inc. had $1,000 in a fund in Connecticut. A note on this paper read:

"Traced to disbursements book—advanced for operation of alley—not expensed at 12/31/60."

Logan's written comments upon the audit contained an entry reading as follows:

"When talking to Ted Kircher in latter part of '60 he indicated one subsidiary is leasing alley built by BarChris—the profit on this job should be eliminated as its ownership is within the affiliated group."

Opposite this note is an entry by Berardi reading as follows:

"Properties sold to others by affiliates. Capitol Lanes is paying currently lease rentals which amount to a lease purchase plan."

This note is somewhat ambiguous. If by "others" Berardi meant outside buyers, then it would seem that he should have accounted in some way for this sale, which he did not do. Presumably, by "others" he meant "other affiliates." Hence, he regarded the transaction, whatever he thought it to have been, as an intercompany one. Apparently Logan so understood Berardi's explanation.

Berardi testified that he inquired of Russo about Capitol Lanes and that Russo told him that Capitol Lanes, Inc. was going to operate an alley some day but as yet it had no alley. Berardi testified that he understood that the alley had not been built and that he believed that the rental payments were on vacant land.

I am not satisfied with this testimony. If Berardi did hold this belief, he should not have held it. The entries as to insurance and as to "operation of alley" should have alerted him to the fact that an alley existed. He should have made further inquiry on the subject. It is apparent that Berardi did not understand this transaction.

In any case, he never identified this mysterious Capitol with the Heavenly Lanes which he had included in his sales and profit figures. The vital question is whether he failed to make a reasonable investigation which, if he had made it, would have revealed the truth.

Certain accounting records of BarChris, which Berardi testified he did not see, would have put him on inquiry. One was a job cost ledger card for job no. 6036, the job number which Berardi put on his own sheet for Heavenly Lanes. This card read "Capitol Theatre (Heavenly)." In addition, two accounts receivable cards each showed both names on the same card, Capitol and Heavenly. Berardi testified that he looked at the accounts receivable records but that he did not see these particular cards. He testified that he did not look on the job cost ledger cards because he took the costs from another record, the costs register.

The burden of proof on this issue is on Peat, Marwick. Although the question is a rather close one, I find that Peat, Marwick has not sustained that burden. Peat, Marwick has not proved that Berardi made a reasonable investigation as far as Capitol Lanes was concerned and that his ignorance of the true facts was justified.

Howard Lanes Annex

Berardi also failed to discover that this alley was not sold. Here the evidence is much scantier. Berardi saw a contract for this alley in the contract file. No one told him that it was to be leased rather than sold. There is no evidence to indicate that any record existed which would have put him on notice. I find that his investigation was reasonable as to this item.

* * *

This disposes of the inaccuracies in the 1960 sales figures. I turn now to the errors in the current assets which involve four items: cash, reserve for Federal Lanes, factors' reserves and Howard Lanes Annex, which latter I have already covered.

As to cash, Berardi properly obtained a confirmation from the bank as to BarChris's cash balance on December 31, 1960. He did not know that part of this balance had been temporarily increased by the deposit of reserves returned by Talcott to BarChris conditionally for a limited time. I do not believe that Berardi reasonably should have known this. Although Peat, Marwick's work papers record the fact that these reserves were returned, there was nothing to indicate that the payment was conditional. Russo obviously did not reveal this fact. It would not be reasonable to require Berardi to examine all of BarChris's correspondence files when he had no reason to suspect any irregularity.

* * *

As to factors' reserves, it is hard to understand how Berardi could have treated this item as entirely a current asset when it was obvious that most of the reserves would not be released within one year. If Berardi was unaware of that fact, he should have been aware of it.

The net result, as far as current assets are concerned, is that Peat, Marwick is responsible for the errors as to reserves but not for those involving the cash item and the receivable from Howard Lanes Annex.

* * *

The S–1 Review

The purpose of reviewing events subsequent to the date of a certified balance sheet (referred to as an S–1 review when made with reference to a registration statement) is to ascertain whether any material change has occurred in the company's financial position which should be disclosed in order to prevent the balance sheet figures from being misleading. The scope of such a review, under generally accepted auditing standards, is limited. It does not amount to a complete audit.

Peat, Marwick prepared a written program for such a review. I find that this program conformed to generally accepted auditing standards. Among other things, it required the following:

"1. Review minutes of stockholders, directors and committees * * *.

"2. Review latest interim financial statements and compare with corresponding statements of preceding year. Inquire regarding significant variations and changes.

* * *

"4. Review the more important financial records and inquire regarding material transactions not in the ordinary course of business and any other significant items.

* * *

"6. Inquire as to changes in material contracts * * *.

* * *

"10. Inquire as to any significant bad debts or accounts in dispute for which provisions has not been made.

* * *

"14. Inquire as to * * * newly discovered liabilities, direct or contingent * * *."

Berardi made the S–1 review in May 1961. He devoted a little over two days to it, a total of 20½ hours. He did not discover any of the errors or omissions pertaining to the state of affairs in 1961 which I have previously discussed at length, all of which were material. The question is whether, despite his failure to find out anything, his investigation was reasonable within the meaning of the statute.

What Berardi did was to look at a consolidating trial balance as of March 31, 1961 which had been prepared by BarChris, compare it with the audited December 31, 1960 figures, discuss with Trilling certain unfavorable developments which the comparison disclosed, and read certain minutes. He did not examine any "important financial records" other than the trial balance. As to minutes, he read only what minutes Birnbaum gave him, which consisted only of the board of directors' minutes of BarChris. He did not read such minutes as there were of the executive committee. He did not know that there was an executive committee, hence he did not discover that Kircher had notes of executive committee minutes which had not been written up. He did not read the minutes of any subsidiary.

In substance, what Berardi did is similar to what Grant and Ballard did. He asked questions, he got answers which he considered satisfactory, and he did nothing to verify them. For example, he obtained from Trilling a list of contracts. The list included Yonkers and Bridge. Since Berardi did not read the minutes of subsidiaries, he did not learn that Yonkers and Bridge were intercompany sales. The list also included Woonsocket and the six T–Bowl jobs, Moravia Road, Milford, Groton, North Attleboro, Odenton and Severna Park. Since Berardi did not look at any contract documents, and since he was unaware of the executive committee minutes of March 18, 1961 (at that time embodied only in Kircher's notes), he did not learn that BarChris had no contracts for these jobs. Trilling's list did not set forth contract prices for them, although it did for Yonkers, Bridge and certain others. This did not arouse Berardi's suspicion.

Berardi noticed that there had been an increase in notes payable by BarChris. Trilling admitted to him that BarChris was "a bit slow" in paying its bills. Berardi recorded in his notes of his review that BarChris was in a "tight cash position." Trilling's explanation was that BarChris was experiencing "some temporary difficulty."

Berardi had no conception of how tight the cash position was. He did not discover that BarChris was holding up checks in substantial amounts because there was no money in the bank to cover them.[27] He did not know of the loan from Manufacturers Trust Company or of the officers' loans. Since he never read the prospectus, he was not even aware that there had ever been any problem about loans from officers.

During the 1960 audit Berardi had obtained some information from factors, not sufficiently detailed even then, as to delinquent notes. He made no inquiry of factors about this in his S–1 review. Since he knew nothing about Kircher's notes of the executive committee meetings, he did not learn that the delinquency situation had grown worse. He was content with Trilling's assurance that no liability theretofore contingent had become direct.

Apparently the only BarChris officer with whom Berardi communicated was Trilling. He could not recall making any inquiries of Russo, Vitolo or Pugliese. As to Kircher, Berardi's testimony was self-contradictory. At one point he said that he had inquired of Kircher and at another he said that he could not recall making any such inquiry.

There had been a material change for the worse in BarChris's financial position. That change was sufficiently serious so that the failure to disclose it made the 1960 figures misleading. Berardi did not discover it. As far as results were concerned, his S–1 review was useless.

Accountants should not be held to a standard higher than that recognized in their profession. I do not do so here. Berardi's review did not come up to that standard. He did not take some of the steps which Peat, Marwick's written program prescribed. He did not spend an adequate amount of time on a task of this magnitude. Most important of all, he was too easily satisfied with glib answers to his inquiries.

---

27. One of these checks was a check to the order of Peat, Marwick in the amount of $3,000. It was dated April 4, 1961. It was deposited by Peat, Marwick on May 29, 1961.

This is not to say that he should have made a complete audit. But there were enough danger signals in the materials which he did examine to require some further investigation on his part. Generally accepted accounting standards required such further investigation under these circumstances. It is not always sufficient merely to ask questions.

Here again, the burden of proof is on Peat, Marwick. I find that that burden has not been satisfied. I conclude that Peat, Marwick has not established its due diligence defense.

* * *

Defendants' motions to dismiss this action, upon which decision was reserved at the trial, are denied. Motions made at various times during the trial to strike certain testimony are also denied, except in so far as such motions pertain to evidence relating to the issues still undecided.

Pursuant to Rule 52(a), this opinion constitutes the court's findings of fact and conclusions of law with respect to the issues determined herein.

So ordered.

SANDERS v. JOHN NUVEEN & CO., INC.

United States Court of Appeals, Seventh Circuit, 1980.
619 F.2d 1222, cert. denied, 450 U.S. 1005 (1981).

Before TONE and WOOD, CIRCUIT JUDGES, and DUMBAULD, SENIOR DISTRICT JUDGE.*

TONE, CIRCUIT JUDGE: The issue we decide on this appeal is whether plaintiff class members have established their claims under § 12(2) of the Securities Act of 1933, 15 U.S.C. § 77*l*(2). Holding that they have, we affirm the district court's judgment in their favor.

The case has been here three times previously. 463 F.2d 1075 (7th Cir.), cert. denied, 409 U.S. 1009 (1972) (*Sanders I*); 524 F.2d 1064 (7th Cir.1975), vacated and remanded, 425 U.S. 929 (1976) (*Sanders II*); 554 F.2d 790 (7th Cir.1977) (*Sanders III*). It is enough at this point to say that our affirmance in *Sanders II* of the judgment in plaintiffs' favor based on § 10(b) of the Securities Exchange Act of 1934, 15 U.S.C. § 78j(b), was rendered untenable by the holding of the Supreme Court in Ernst & Ernst v. Hochfelder, 425 U.S. 185 (1976), that scienter is an element of a private cause of action under § 10(b); and that in *Sanders III* we therefore remanded the case to the district court primarily for a determination of plaintiffs' claims under § 12(2) of the 1933 Act.[1] On remand that court held an evidentiary hearing and then made additional findings in favor of plaintiffs and entered judgment accordingly.

---

* The Honorable Edward Dumbauld, Senior District Judge of the United States District Court for the Western District of Pennsylvania is sitting by designation.

1. We left it to the discretion of the district court whether to allow amendment to add allegations of violation of § 12(1) of the 1933 Act. *See* 554 F.2d at 798–99. That court allowed amendment and decided the § 12(1) issue in favor of the plaintiff class. Because § 12(1) is merely an alternate ground of recovery and we hold in favor of the class on the § 12(2) issue, we do not reach the § 12(1) issue. For the same reason we need not rule on defendants' argument that the district court abused its discretion on remand in allowing plaintiffs to amend the complaint to allege violation of § 12(1).

The background facts having been stated in detail in *Sanders II* and revisited in *Sanders III*, we shall do no more here than summarize those facts that are now material.

Plaintiff class consists of forty-two purchasers of unsecured short term promissory notes aggregating $1,612,500 issued by Winter & Hirsch, Inc. (WH), a consumer finance company. The purchases were made from John Nuveen & Co., Inc. during a seven-month period immediately preceding WH's default on the notes in February 1970. The defendants other than Nuveen are corporations found to be controlling persons of Nuveen.

Nuveen was the exclusive underwriter of the WH notes, which were sold, like other commercial paper, through its branch offices throughout the United States. As the underwriter, it bought the notes from WH and resold them to customers at a profit. According to the head of Nuveen's commercial paper department, Nuveen sold commercial paper, including the notes of WH, on the basis "that there should be no question but what the paper will be paid at maturity."

Nuveen prepared and circulated to prospective customers "commercial paper reports" on the WH commercial paper that it held for sale. Three members of the plaintiff class testified to having received copies of these reports before they bought WH notes. Two other members testified to having received commercial paper reports, but could not swear to having received them before making their purchases. Nine class members, including the three who had received reports before purchasing, testified that, when they bought their WH notes, Nuveen salesmen made oral statements about the quality of the notes. There was no evidence of oral communications to any other class members. All class members received the usual written confirmations advising them that they had purchased certain described notes and that Nuveen had sold the notes as principal.

WH's default was the product of a fraud it perpetrated with the connivance of the certified public accountants who audited its financial statements and rendered opinions thereon. In summary, over a period of ten years WH continually issued financial statements in which accounts receivable were overstated and some of its indebtedness was omitted. By 1970 WH's financial statements overstated accounts receivable by some $14,000,000 and failed to reflect some $1,750,000 of indebtedness. When the notes in issue in this case were purchased by members of the plaintiff class, WH's liabilities exceeded its assets.

Nuveen was not aware of the fraud and held "the mistaken but honest belief that financial statements [of WH] prepared by certified public accountants correctly represented the condition of" WH. 524 F.2d at 1066. It accordingly proceeded to sell the WH notes and also to issue commercial paper reports thereon that reflected the false WH financial statements.

Sanders II held that Nuveen failed to make a reasonable investigation, which it was the duty of an underwriter to make under § 10(b) of the 1934 Act, and that such an investigation "would have revealed the fraud." Id. at 1071.

After WH had dishonored the notes sold to the plaintiff class members, it was taken over by its creditors. They established the WH Liquidating Trust, liquidated WH, and over a period of time distributed the proceeds of the liquidation to creditors, including members of the plaintiff class, who received through these distributions approximately two-thirds of the amounts they paid Nuveen for the notes. The judgment appealed from is for the unpaid balance of the purchase price of the notes and prejudgment interest thereon.

* * *

II.

Defendants also argue that they have established a defense under § 12(2) by sustaining their burden of proving that they "in the exercise of reasonable care could not have known" of the claimed untruth or omission. This argument is in essence a reargument of issues decided by the opinion of Mr. Justice (then Judge) Stevens in his opinion in *Sanders II.*

Proceeding on the assumption that scienter, whether in its wilful or reckless form, was not an essential element of a § 10(b) claim, *Sanders II* upheld the district court's determination that Nuveen had "breached a duty to make reasonable inquiries that would have led to the discovery of the issuer's fraud." 524 F.2d at 1066. In determining what Nuveen could reasonably have been expected to do, that opinion noted that Nuveen's status as underwriter was significant even though neither § 10(b) nor Rule 10b–5 expressly imposed a greater burden on underwriters. For instance, in response to Nuveen's argument that it needed only to discover and to disclose those facts that were "reasonably ascertainable," the standard generally applicable to broker-dealers, the court declared that,

> a greater quantity of information is "reasonably ascertainable" by an underwriter than by a mere broker, and something more than published data must be analyzed if an underwriter is to discharge his duty of investigation. In this case, the district court correctly found that Nuveen's investigation of WH was deficient and that an appropriate investigation would have revealed the fraud.

Id. at 1071. The court also took into account two arguments Nuveen repeats here—that it needed to make a lesser investigation because WH notes were short term commercial paper and not stock or long term indebtedness, and that its reliance on the credit lines extended by various banks to WH was reasonable. The court concluded that Nuveen was "under a duty to make at least some investigation directed at the question whether the ever present possibility of fraud is in fact a reality," and that Nuveen had breached that duty. Id. at 1071.

We find no reason to distinguish between the duty of reasonable care in the implied cause of action for negligence that was assumed to exist under § 10(b) in *Sanders II* and the duty of reasonable care expressly imposed by § 12(2) of the 1933 Act. Defendants attempt to distinguish *Sanders II* on the ground that while this court relied heavily in that case on decisions construing § 11, which explicitly requires a "reasonable investigation," § 12(2) requires only that defendants show exercise of "reasonable care." We find no significance in this difference in language in the case at bar.

It is not at all clear that Congress intended to impose a higher standard of care under § 11 than under § 12(2). The difference in language appeared in the House bill and was retained in the Act as agreed to by the Joint Conference Committee and as passed by both Houses. *See* H.R. 5480, 73d Cong., 1st Sess. §§ 11 & 12 (1933), reprinted at 1 Legislative History, supra, Item 1 (bill as passed by both Houses), and 3 id., Items 25 & 26 (bill as presented to the House by its Committee on Interstate and Foreign

Commerce and as originally passed by House). The Conference Committee report, in its discussion of the standard of liability imposed for a misleading registration statement, describes the standard adopted not as one of "reasonable investigation," but one of "reasonable care." H.R.Rep. No. 152, 73d Cong., 1st Sess. 26 (1933) (Conference Report), reprinted at 2 Legislative History, supra, Item 19. More specifically, Congress does not appear to have intended that a different standard apply to underwriters. Thus, the House Report draws no distinction between an underwriter's burden in the case of misleading statements in a prospectus, for which it can be liable only under § 12(2), and its § 11 duty to conduct a "reasonable investigation." H.R.Rep. No. 85, 73d Cong., 1st Sess. 9 (1933), reprinted at 2 Legislative History, supra, Item 18. The difference in language can be explained not as an attempt to impose different duties of care under §§ 11 and 12, but by the fact that § 12(2) imposes the duty on all sellers of securities, while § 11 imposes liability only on specified groups of persons having such a close relationship with the registration statement that the 1933 Act, before it was amended the following year, treated them as fiduciaries. See Securities Act of 1933, ch. 38, § 11(c), 48 Stat. 74, 83 (1933); Securities Exchange Act of 1934, ch. 404, § 206(c), 48 Stat. 881, 907 (1934). Thus the general duty of reasonable care, the specific requirements of which are determined by the circumstances of the case, was to be applied in § 11 only to persons who had a stronger connection with a registration statement than a seller necessarily has to a prospectus, so a more stringent articulation of the standard was appropriate.

In the circumstances of this case, the reasonable care standard required the reasonable investigation described in Sanders II. Since what constitutes reasonable care under § 12(2) depends upon the circumstances, we, of course, do not intimate that the duty of a seller under § 12(2) is always the same as that of an underwriter in a registration offering under § 11.

III.

Defendants argue in a footnote of their brief that plaintiffs failed to prove they did not know of the untruth or omission. In this case, however, it is fair to presume from the fact that a plaintiff purchased the notes that he did not know the issuer was hopelessly insolvent, a fact that would have been disclosed by accurate figures. Earlier in this case, Nuveen contended specifically that at least one of the forty-two plaintiffs, National Stock Yards National Bank, knew of the fraud before purchasing. That contention was disposed of in Sanders II. 524 F.2d at 1074.

Defendants argue in another footnote that the duty of reasonable care it owed its bank customers was not as great as the duty it owed to individuals, because banks were more sophisticated and had greater access to information about WH than individual customers. Section 12(2) does not establish a graduated scale of duty depending upon the sophistication and access to information of the customer. Hill York Corp. v. American International Franchises, Inc., 448 F.2d 680, 696 (5th Cir.1971). A plaintiff under § 12(2) is not required to prove due diligence. See, e.g., Gilbert v. Nixon, 429 F.2d 348, 356 (10th Cir.1970). All that is required is ignorance of the untruth or omission.

IV.

In still another footnote argument, defendants invoke the rule that a purchaser can recover under § 12(2) only from his immediate seller. See note 5 supra. Hill York Corp. v. American International Franchises, Inc., supra, 448 F.2d at 692 & n. 17, 695 & n. 24. They say this rule bars the claims of "several plaintiffs" whom they do not identify but who they assert "purchased from third parties." That assertion is supported only by a reference to an exhibit in the record that consists of a large stack of Nuveen confirmations reciting the sale of WH notes by Nuveen to various purchasers. Plaintiffs' brief ignores this footnote argument. Lacking any further guidance, we are unable to determine the basis for the assertion that several plaintiffs purchased from third parties or to say that the contrary finding implicit in the district court's judgment is erroneous.

Affirmed.

JOHN NUVEEN & CO., INC. v. SANDERS

Supreme Court of United States, 1981.
450 U.S. 1005, 101 S.Ct. 1719, 68 L.Ed.2d 210.

The petition for a writ of certiorari is denied.

JUSTICE STEVENS took no part in the consideration or decision of this petition.

JUSTICE POWELL, with whom JUSTICE REHNQUIST joins, dissenting.

* * *

Although the opinion of the Court of Appeals is not explicit, it appears to impose a duty of "reasonable investigation" rather than § 12(2)'s requirement of "reasonable care."

A

Section 11(a) of the 1933 Act imposes liability on certain persons for selling securities in a registered public offering pursuant to a materially false or misleading registration statement. A registered offering is the class of financial transactions for which Congress prescribed the most stringent regulation. The standard of care imposed on an underwriter is that it must have "had after *reasonable investigation,* reasonable grounds to believe and did believe" that the registration statement was accurate. Section 11(b)(3)(A) of the Act (emphasis added).

Liability in this case was not imposed on petitioner under § 11, but under § 12(2). Under that section, it is necessary for sellers to show only that they "did not know and in the exercise of *reasonable care* could not have known" that their statements were false or misleading. (Emphasis added.)

In providing standards of care under the 1933 Act, Congress thus used different language for different situations. "Reasonable *investigation*" is required for registered offerings under § 11, but nothing more than "mer[e] * * * 'reasonable *care*'" is required by § 12(2). W.O. Douglas & G.E. Bates, The Federal Securities Act of 1933, 43 Yale L.J. 173, 208 (1933). The difference in language is significant, because in the securities acts Congress has used its words with precision. See, e.g., Ernst & Ernst v. Hochfelder, 425 U.S. 185, 198–201 (1976); Blue Chip Stamps v. Manor Drug Stores, 421 U.S. 723, 755, 756 (1975) (Powell J., concurring). "Investigation" commands a greater undertaking than "care." See W.O. Douglas & G.E. Bates, supra, at 208, n. 205.

In a brief filed in this case with the Court of Appeals, the SEC expressly stated that the standard of care under § 12(2) is less demanding than that prescribed by § 11:

> "[I]t would be inconsistent with the statutory scheme to apply precisely the same standards to the scope of an underwriter's duty under Section 12(2) as the case law appropriately has applied to underwriters under Section 11. Because of the vital role played by an underwriter in the distribution of securities, and because the registration process is integral and important to the statutory scheme, we are of the view that a higher standard of care should be imposed on those actors who are critical to its proper operations. Since Congress has determined that registration is not necessary in certain defined situations, we believe that it would undermine the Congressional intent—that issuers and other persons should be relieved of registration—if the same degree of investigation were to be required to avoid potential liability whether or not a registration statement is required." Brief for SEC, at 69, *Sanders III*, 554 F.2d 790 (1977).

The Court of Appeals' opinion may be read as holding that petitioner's duty of "reasonable care" under § 12(2) required it independently to *investigate* the accuracy and completeness of the certified financial statements. It was customary, however—and in my view entirely reasonable—for petitioner to rely on these statements as accurately reflecting W & H's financial condition. Even under § 11 of the Act, an underwriter is explicitly absolved of the duty to investigate with respect to "any part of the registration statement purporting to be made on the authority of an expert" such as a certified accountant if "he had no reasonable ground to believe, and did not believe" that the information therein was misleading. Section 11(b)(3)(C) of the Act; see id., § 11(a)(4). This provision is in the Act because, almost by definition, it *is* reasonable to rely on financial statements certified by public accountants. Yet, in this case, the Court of Appeals nevertheless seems to have imposed the higher duty prescribed by § 11 to investigate, but denied petitioner the right to rely on "the authority of an expert" that also is provided by § 11.[5]

B

* * * My concern is that the opinion of the Court of Appeals will be read as recognizing no distinction between the standards of care applicable

---

5. Moreover, the duty to investigate imposed by the Court of Appeals rarely would uncover the type of fraud involved in this case. According to the Court of Appeals, petitioner would have learned of the fraud if it had examined W & H's minute books, the accountant's work papers, and company tax returns. *Sanders II*, 524 F.2d, at 1069. I accept this finding, but observe that this would be most unusual. What one normally finds in minute books sheds no light whatever on the accuracy of audited financial statements. Nor would it be enlightening to examine the work papers of the certified public accountants. The drafters of corporate minutes and accountants bent on fraud hardly are likely to reflect the fraud in records or papers that are easily subpoenaed. Similarly, information can be gleaned from tax returns only if they are honestly prepared. The Court of Appeals itself noted, "Experience teaches us that fraud can be skilfully hidden." *Sanders II*, 524 F.2d, at 1071.

under §§ 11 and 12(2), and particularly as casting doubt upon the reasonableness of relying upon the expertise of certified public accountants. Dealers may believe that they must undertake extensive independent financial investigations rather than rely on the accuracy of the certified financial statements. If this is so, the efficiency of the short-term financial markets will be impaired.[6] I would grant certiorari.

THE "DUE DILIGENCE" DEFENSE UNDER SECTION 11; THE "DUE CARE" DEFENSE UNDER SECTION 12(2)

How Much Diligence is Due?[1] So far as the issuer is concerned, the only defense available under Section 11, if a material misstatement or omission is shown, is to prove that the plaintiff at the time of his acquisition of the security knew of the untruth or omission, a defense which is available to all defendants. Obviously, this theoretical defense is of no practical significance in this age of class actions, since it could never be proven as to more than a handful of the numerous plaintiffs, if it can be proven as to any. All defendants other than the issuer, however, have the defense that they had, "after reasonable investigation, reasonable grounds to believe and did believe" that the statements were true and complete, which is commonly referred to as the "due diligence defense." Under this requirement, mere passive ignorance is wholly insufficient. There must be an affirmative belief based upon reasonable grounds *and upon reasonable investigation.* It was stated by the Committee report at the time of the enactment of the 1933 Act that this casts a burden of "competence as well as innocence" upon the persons involved in an issue of securities.[2]

What is the type and extent of the investigation that is necessary to fulfill this duty and establish this defense? Both the *BarChris* case and the *Feit* case, infra Chapter 15, indicate that the answer will vary depending upon the type of defendant involved and his function in the registration process.

The "Outside" Directors: This phrase is used to refer to directors who are not employed by the issuer and who normally have other full-time occupations. They have in the past universally simply relied upon the persons who are charged with the preparation of the registration statement to do the job right. Those persons are the personnel of the issuer and of the underwriter who are delegated this responsibility, the independent public accountants and counsel for both the issuer and the underwriter. However, the *BarChris* case clearly holds that, while the outside director can delegate his duty of investigation, he is liable if the persons to whom this duty is delegated do not perform it properly; in other words, he is a guarantor of the diligence of the persons upon whom he relies. Would it make any difference as to the liability of such a director if he carefully read the proofs of the registration statement and raised questions which occurred to him based upon his knowledge of the affairs of the company or suggested by apparent ambiguities or inconsistencies in the state-

---

6. Commercial paper, for example, normally is issued for periods of 30 to 90 days, and in no event more than 270 days. It is useful for borrowers with fluctuating temporary cash needs. Dealers such as petitioner buy commercial paper from issuers and resell it to investors. A dealer's compensation is the "spread" between the price at which he buys the paper from the issuer and the price charged the investor. Comment, The Commercial Paper Market and the Securities Acts, 39 U.Chi.L.Rev.

362, 367–368 (1972). The dealer's "spread" historically has been relatively small. Id., at 368; see Pet. for Cert., at 17, n. 20. The additional expense and legal exposure made necessary by the Court of Appeals' decision will increase the "spread," and hence also the cost of borrowing.

1. See 17 Kan.L.Rev. 651 (1969) from which this heading is borrowed.

2. H.R.Rep. No. 85, 73d Cong., 1st Sess., (1933) 9.

ment? In the *BarChris* case itself two of the outside directors held liable were newly elected and had no detailed knowledge of the past history of the company; therefore, it is doubtful if any meaningful questions would have occurred to them even if they had carefully read the statement (which they did not). On the other hand, anything more than this in the way of investigation by each director seems to be wholly impractical—there would be so many "investigators" falling over each other that the registration statement could never be completed.

Another two of the outside directors in *BarChris,* however, were held to a higher standard than the standard (whatever it is) applicable to the run-of-the-mill outside director. These were the partner in the law firm which was counsel for the issuer and the partner in the investment banking firm which was underwriting the issue. While the court rejected the contention that the law firm by undertaking the preparation of the registration statement thereby "expertised" the entire prospectus, and the investment banker was not liable individually as an underwriter but only in conjunction with his firm,[3] the court held that by undertaking the laboring oar in the preparation of the registration statement they made themselves liable *as directors* when their performance fell short of what the court considered proper for an attorney or investment banker engaged in that task. In other words, they were apparently judged by the standards applicable to their professions, and not by those which might be applied to a director who had no expertise in the registration process and did not undertake to oversee compliance with the requirements.[4]

"Inside" Directors and Officers: These defendants were held by the court in the *BarChris* case to a very high standard of diligence, which the court in the *Feit* case interprets as making them virtual guarantors of the accuracy of the registration statement.[5] This seems to be flatly contrary both to the express language and to the clear legislative history of Section 11.[6] Nor do the facts of either of those cases necessarily support such a rule: In the *BarChris* case the "inside" defendants were either affirmatively dishonest or incredibly lax; and the question of due diligence was not really involved in the *Feit* case— essentially that case involved a question of what should have been said on the basis of what was admittedly known.

3. A partner in an underwriting firm would be jointly and severally liable with the firm in their capacity as underwriters. However, the officers of an incorporated underwriter who work on the registration statement would presumably not be individually liable under Section 11, and most investment banking firms have now been incorporated. If such an officer were also a director of the issuer, the rules discussed in the text above would be applicable to him *in that capacity.*

4. Judge Weinstein in the *Feit* case, infra Chapter 15, held that Mr. Hodes, the outside counsel, was an "inside" director because of his intimate involvement with the affairs of the issuer. However, under the approach of the *BarChris* case he would probably have been held to pretty much the same standard of diligence even though not labelled an "inside" director.

5. The court quotes from Professor Folk's article Civil Liabilities under the

Federal Securities Laws: The BarChris Case, 55 Va.L.Rev. 1 (1969), to the effect that "Such an individual [an 'inside' director] comes close to the status of a guarantor of accuracy." 55 Va.L.Rev. at 22 (1969). However, Professor Folk made this statement only with respect to Mr. Russo in the *BarChris* case, who was chief executive officer and "familiar with all aspects of the business." Perhaps the court felt that all three of the "inside" defendants in the *Feit* case were in the same category; it may not necessarily have intended to extend this observation to all "inside" defendants in every case.

6. A proposal to make the directors guarantors of the accuracy of the prospectus was specifically considered and rejected by Congress when it enacted the 1933 Act, See Folk, Civil Liabilities under the Federal Securities Laws: The BarChris Case, 55 Va.L.Rev. 1, at 18 (1969).

Underwriters: The court in the *BarChris* case indicates that the underwriters will also be held to a very high standard of diligence, although perhaps not as great as that of the "inside" defendants, because the public looks to them for an independent, disinterested investigation of the business, and for advice regarding the issue.

The members of the underwriting syndicate other than the managing or so-called "lead" underwriter typically undertake no investigation of the issuer at all, but rely entirely upon the managing underwriter to do this for them. There should be no doubt that they are entitled to rely upon his investigation if it in fact complies with the statutory requirements; conversely, however, it is fairly inferable from the *BarChris* opinion that if his performance falls short, they are equally liable with him. Whether they might have some action over against the managing underwriter for this failure is debatable, although the typical "agreement among underwriters" attempts to negative any fiduciary relationship between the managing underwriter and the other members of the syndicate.

The lurking fear that perhaps the other members of the underwriting syndicate will not be permitted to rely upon the investigation by the managing underwriter has led to a ritual known as the "due diligence meeting." Shortly before the effective date of the registration statement, representatives of all of the underwriters gather in a room with officials of the issuer, ostensibly to question them about the company's affairs as disclosed in the registration statement. In fact, the questions are more likely to be about matters which are not disclosed in the registration statement, but which may be useful in selling the issue, such as: "What is the projection for next quarter's earnings?" It would seem that this meeting, which is frequently a pure formality, is not going to save the other underwriters if the managing underwriter has failed in his duty of investigation; on the other hand, if he has performed that duty, it would seem to be unnecessary.

Each underwriter is jointly and severally liable for any damages recovered in a Section 11 action, but because of the fears of unlimited liability voiced at the time of the enactment of the 1933 Act, in 1934 this section was amended to limit the liability of any underwriter to the amount of his participation. This does not mean that he is no longer jointly and severally liable or that he is only liable for the loss on the shares he sells. For example, if a $10,000,000 issue is brought out at $10 per share, of which a particular underwriter has a $500,000 participation, and there is later a judgment under Section 11 in favor of the purchasers for a loss of $1.00 per share or an aggregate of $1,000,000, that particular underwriter would be liable up to a maximum of $500,000 or one-half of the total judgment, even though he only underwrote one-twentieth of the total issue.

"Experts" and Liability With Respect to "Expertised Portions" of the Registration Statement: An expert is liable under Section 11 only with respect to those portions of a registration statement which are expressly stated to be made on his authority as an expert. The court in the *BarChris* case properly rejected the contentions that the accountants were liable for all of the figures in the registration statement, even those that were uncertified, and that the lawyer was liable for the entire statement because he wrote it. The investigation required of such an expert with respect to that portion for which he is responsible would certainly have to conform to the standards generally considered appropriate in his profession. The court in *BarChris* did not have to go further than this, since it found that the accountants did not meet those standards, nor indeed even comply with their own written procedures for an S–

1 review. However, the Simon case[7] in the Second Circuit held that compliance with the standards of his profession would not necessarily insulate an accountant from even criminal prosecution, if the court considered them too lax; it would seem *a fortiori* not to insulate him from liability under Section 11. Whether the judges, being lawyers themselves, will be as harsh on lawyers remains to be seen.

With respect to an "expertised portion" of the registration statement, the burden of defense of all of the other defendants, except the expert himself and the issuer, is considerably relaxed. No investigation need be shown, and the defendant must only prove that he "had no reasonable ground to believe, and did not believe," that the statements were false. Thus passive ignorance is sufficient with respect to these statements, unless the defendant had some reason to question them.[8] Therefore, all of the defendants in *BarChris* were absolved of liability for the errors in the certified financial statements, except the accountants who certified them and the insiders who knew or should have known that they were false; but this was probably of small comfort to them, since they were all held liable for misstatements in other portions of the same prospectus.

The Duty of the Defendant Under Section 12(2). Section 12(2) of the 1933 Act makes liable any person who "offers or sells a security" (for consideration of the persons that this phrase may include, see Chapter 17, below) "by means of" any false or misleading statement, oral or written. The plaintiff does not need to plead or prove any fault on the part of the defendant; however, a defendant is given a defense if he sustains the burden of proof that "he did not know, and in the exercise of reasonable care could not have known," of the untruth or omission. The use of the phrase "could not have known" in the statute might suggest that the defendant has to prove that it would have been impossible for him to have discovered the truth through any amount of investigation. This is surely, however, not what was intended. This provision should be read as saying that the defendant may escape liability if he proves that, "*if* he had exercised reasonable care, he *would* not have known." The section thus imposes liability based on simple negligence and the defendant has the burden of establishing that he was free of negligence. (Whether the same standard of conduct regarding the duty of the defendant is applicable to a person who is sued as a "participant" in the sale, rather than being the direct seller to the plaintiff, is discussed below in Chapter 17.)

There is no defense under Section 12(2), as there is in Section 11, based upon the "expertising" of certain statements. For example, if there is a misstatement in the financial statements which were "expertised" by independent accountants, a director of the issuer could defend under Section 11 on the ground that he simply accepted their figures and "had no reasonable ground to believe" that they were erroneous, as in the *BarChris* case. On the other hand, in a suit under Section 12(2), the director (who may possibly be liable as the

---

7. United States v. Simon, 425 F.2d 796 (2d Cir.1969), cert. denied, 397 U.S. 1006 (1970).

8. Professor Folk argues that, despite an amendment to Section 11 in 1934 which specifically eliminated any requirement of investigation by other defendants of any "expertised portion" of the registration statement, a requirement should still be imposed on the non-expert of some inquiry "to satisfy himself that the expertised statements are reliable." He bases this position primarily on a statement on the floor of Congress that the amendment made no change in the substance of this provision. See Folk, Civil Liabilities under the Federal Securities Acts: The BarChris Case, 55 Va.L.Rev. 1, at 19, 27–29 (1969). The Senator who made this statement either failed to exercise due diligence to find out what the amendment plainly said or failed to make full disclosure of its manifest effect.

"person who sells") is literally not given this defense. He must show that "in the exercise of reasonable care [he] could not have known" of the error.[9] Does reasonable care in this situation require any investigation by him of the figures of the independent accountants? The Seventh Circuit apparently thinks so; but Justice Powell disagrees.[10]

An underwriter may of course be liable under Section 12(2) as a "person who sells", since that is what he does, although a particular underwriter may be in privity with only a small portion of the purchasers of a public offering if there is a large underwriting syndicate and shares are sold through "selling group dealers" as well as directly by the underwriters. In order to escape liability, must the underwriter exercise "due diligence" in investigating the truth of the representations in the selling document, as under Section 11, or may he merely rely upon the fact that he had no knowledge that it was false and no reason to believe that it was false? If he must show that he exercised "due diligence", is the burden of that investigation the same or greater or less than it is under Section 11? At least with respect to the financial statements, may the underwriter assert the "expertising" defense to the effect that he merely relied upon the financial statements certified by the company's CPAs and had no reason to believe them to be false? There is an unexplained discrepancy between the statements in Justice Powell's opinion and that of the Seventh Circuit in the *Sanders* case regarding the nature of the financial statements which were furnished by the underwriters to the purchasers of the securities. Justice Powell refers to them as "certified financial statements", which of course they would have to be in order for the underwriters to have the "expertising" defense under Section 11. On the other hand, the Seventh Circuit stated that the commercial paper reports "stated that the figures were from a detailed audit when in fact the auditors' opinions stated that no detailed audit had been made." What the court meant by a "detailed audit" is uncertain; the statements were either certified on the basis of an audit or they were not; unless an auditor follows all of the procedures specified in the auditing standards issued by the AICPA, he cannot certify the figures. No audit need be any more "detailed" than that.

The Seventh Circuit in the prior decision in the Sanders case,[11] which was reversed by the Supreme Court "for further consideration in the light of Ernst

---

9. See Gould v. Tricon, Inc., 272 F.Supp. 385 (S.D.N.Y.1967).

10. In Franklin Savings Bank of New York v. Levy, 551 F.2d 521 (2d Cir.1977), involving an action against Goldman, Sachs by a purchaser from it of Penn Central commercial paper, the court said: "We have held that where a broker-dealer makes a representation as to the quality of the security he sells, he impliedly represents that he has an adequate basis in fact for the opinion he renders. Hanly v. Securities and Exchange Commission, 415 F.2d 589, 596–97 (2d Cir.1969). We see no reason why that theory is not at least equally appropriate in cases involving § 12(2) of the 1933 Act.

"Here Goldman, Sachs became an exclusive source of the Penn Central notes in issue. It was a professional vendor admittedly recommending this paper for sale to an institution authorized by statute only to invest in prime paper. Such an undertak-

ing implies that Goldman, Sachs has conducted an ongoing investigation of Penn Central's financial condition. If Goldman, Sachs failed to exercise reasonable professional care in assembling and evaluating the financial data, particularly in view of the worsening condition of Penn Central, then its representation that the paper was credit worthy and high quality was untrue in fact and misleading no matter how honestly but mistakenly held. This view does not render Goldman, Sachs an insurer as appellants claim—liable for some catastrophe beyond its control. Rather, it in fact makes the dealer responsible to Franklin if it is unable to shoulder the burden of establishing that it was not reasonable for it to have determined on March 16, 1970 that the quality of the paper it was purveying was less than that represented."

11. Sanders v. John Nuveen & Co., Inc., 524 F.2d 1064 (7th Cir.1975), vac'd and remanded 425 U.S. 929 (1976).

& Ernst v. Hochfelder," clearly answered these questions, at least in dicta, to the effect that under Rule 10b–5 the underwriter must exercise a diligence far beyond that heretofore thought to be required under Section 11 and cannot rely to any extent upon the auditing firm retained by the company, but must assume that they are crooks (as indeed they were in that case). While of course it may be argued on the facts that the underwriter exercised no diligence whatever in that case, and therefore the decision does not *hold* anything about what amount of diligence might be sufficient, the court says that the underwriter should have examined the tax returns of the company and the "working papers" of the company's auditors. Presumably it didn't mean that the underwriter should do so just to see whether pieces of paper existed with those headings at the top; in order to do that to any purpose, the underwriter would have to hire its own firm of CPAs to audit the tax returns and to audit the audit of the company's CPAs.

How far does the Seventh Circuit retreat from these requirements in its second decision in the *Sanders* case, as to which certiorari was denied by the Supreme Court? It is true that the court shifted the basis of its decision from Rule 10b–5 to Section 12(2), acknowledging that the *Ernst & Ernst* case precluded any liability under Rule 10b–5. But it seemed to impose the same duties regarding investigation of the affairs of the issuing corporation as it had in the first decision (see the opinion of Justice Powell on the denial of certiorari).

Do these requirements, if they exist, under Section 12(2) apply in the case of a registered offering subject to the express liability provisions of Section 11? It would certainly seem anomalous as a matter of policy to say that the public is entitled to greater protection in an exempt offering, with respect to which Congress deliberately decided that less protection was needed. If these dicta represent the law, then all of the express defenses in Section 11 would seem to have been repealed for underwriters, and perhaps for all other defendants, if the plaintiff can sue under Section 12(2).

In addition to the article by Folk cited above, the *BarChris* case is discussed in Symposium, The BarChris Case, 24 Bus.Law. 523 (1969) (this is the transcript of a two-day institute held by the A.B.A., attended by over a thousand lawyers); Heller, Weiss, Israels and Schwartz, BarChris: A Dialogue on a Bad Case Making Hard Law, 57 Geo.L.J. 221 (1968); Jordan, BarChris and the Registration Process, 22 Sw.L.J. 790 (1968); Wyant and Smith, BarChris: Reevaluation of Prosectus Liability?, 3 Ga.L.Rev. 122 (1968); Evans, Impact of BarChris, 21 S.C.L.Rev. 687 (1969); 921 Kurland, Accountant's Legal Liability—Ultramares to BarChris, 25 Bus.Law. 155 (1969); Davis and Brown, Developments under Federal Securities Laws—BarChris and Globus, 54 Ia.L.Rev. 1038 (1969). See, also, Nicholas, The Integrated Disclosure System and Its Impact Upon Underwriters' Due Diligence: Will Investors Be Protected?, 11 Sec.Reg.L.J. 3 (1983); Greene, Determining the Responsibilities of Underwriters Distributing Securities Within an Integrated Disclosure System, 56 Notre Dame Law. 755 (1981).

ERNST & ERNST v. HOCHFELDER

United States Supreme Court, 1976.
425 U.S. 185, 96 S.Ct. 1375, 47 L.Ed.2d 668.

MR. JUSTICE POWELL delivered the opinion of the Court.

The issue in this case is whether an action for civil damages may lie under § 10(b) of the Securities Exchange Act of 1934 (1934 Act) and

Securities and Exchange Commission Rule 10b–5, in the absence of an allegation of intent to deceive, manipulate, or defraud on the part of the defendant.

I

Petitioner, Ernst & Ernst, is an accounting firm. From 1946 through 1967 it was retained by First Securities Company of Chicago (First Securities), a small brokerage firm and member of the Midwest Stock Exchange and of the National Association of Securities Dealers, to perform periodic audits of the firm's books and records. In connection with these audits Ernst & Ernst prepared for filing with the Securities and Exchange Commission (the Commission) the annual reports required of First Securities under § 17(a) of the 1934 Act. It also prepared for First Securities responses to the financial questionnaires of the Midwest Stock Exchange (the Exchange).

Respondents were customers of First Securities who invested in a fraudulent securities scheme perpetrated by Leston B. Nay, president of the firm and owner of 92% of its stock. Nay induced the respondents to invest funds in "escrow" accounts that he represented would yield a high rate of return. Respondents did so from 1942 through 1966, with the majority of the transactions occurring in the 1950's. In fact, there were no escrow accounts as Nay converted respondents' funds to his own use immediately upon receipt. These transactions were not in the customary form of dealings between First Securities and its customers. The respondents drew their personal checks payable to Nay or a designated bank for his account. No such escrow accounts were reflected on the books and records of First Securities, and none was shown on its periodic accounting to respondents in connection with their other investments. Nor were they included in First Securities' filings with the Commission or the Exchange.

This fraud came to light in 1968 when Nay committed suicide, leaving a note that described First Securities as bankrupt and the escrow accounts as "spurious." Respondents subsequently filed this action for damages against Ernst & Ernst in the United States District Court for the Northern District of Illinois under § 10(b) of the 1934 Act. The complaint charged that Nay's escrow scheme violated § 10(b) and Commission Rule 10b–5, and that Ernst & Ernst had "aided and abetted" Nay's violations by its "failure" to conduct proper audits of First Securities. As revealed through discovery, respondents' cause of action rested on a theory of negligent nonfeasance. The premise was that Ernst & Ernst had failed to utilize "appropriate auditing procedures" in its audits of First Securities, thereby failing to discover internal practices of the firm said to prevent an effective audit. The practice principally relied on was Nay's rule that only he could open mail addressed to him at First Securities or addressed to First Securities to his attention, even if it arrived in his absence. Respondents contended that if Ernst & Ernst had conducted a proper audit, it would have discovered this "mail rule." The existence of the rule then would have been disclosed in reports to the Exchange and to the Commission by Ernst & Ernst as an irregular procedure that prevented an effective audit. This would have led to an investigation of Nay that would have revealed the fraudulent scheme. Respondents specifically disclaimed the existence of fraud or intentional misconduct on the part of Ernst & Ernst.

After extensive discovery the District Court granted Ernst & Ernst's motion for summary judgment and dismissed the action. The court rejected Ernst & Ernst's contention that a cause of action for aiding and abetting a securities fraud could not be maintained under § 10(b) and Rule 10b-5 merely on allegations of negligence. It concluded, however, that there was no genuine issue of material fact with respect to whether Ernst & Ernst had conducted its audits in accordance with generally accepted auditing standards.

The Court of Appeals for the Seventh Circuit reversed and remanded, holding that one who breaches a duty of inquiry and disclosure owed another is liable in damages for aiding and abetting a third party's violation of Rule 10b-5 if the fraud would have been discovered or prevented but for the breach. 503 F.2d 1100 (1974).[7] The court reasoned that Ernst & Ernst had a common-law and statutory duty of inquiry into the adequacy of First Securities' internal control system because it had contracted to audit First Securities and to prepare for filing with the Commission the annual report of its financial condition required under § 17 of the 1934 Act and Rule 17a-5. The Court further reasoned that respondents were beneficiaries of the statutory duty to inquire and the related duty to disclose any material irregularities that were discovered. Id., at 1105–1111. The court concluded that there were genuine issues of fact as to whether Ernst & Ernst's failure to discover and comment upon Nay's mail rule constituted a breach of its duties of inquiry and disclosure, id., at 1111, and whether inquiry and disclosure would have led to the discovery or prevention of Nay's fraud. Id., at 1115.

We granted certiorari to resolve the question whether a private cause of action for damages will lie under § 10(b) and Rule 10b-5 in the absence of any allegation of "scienter"—intent to deceive, manipulate, or defraud.[12]

---

7. In support of this holding, the Court of Appeals cited its decision in Hochfelder v. Midwest Stock Exchange, supra, where it detailed the elements necessary to establish a claim under Rule 10b-5 based on a defendant's aiding and abetting a securities fraud solely by inaction. * * *. In such a case the plaintiff must show "that the party charged with aiding and abetting had knowledge of or, but for the breach of a duty of inquiry, should have had knowledge of the fraud, and that possessing such knowledge the party failed to act due to an improper motive or breach of a duty of disclosure." * * *. The court explained in the instant case that these "elements constitute a flexible standard of liability which should be amplified according to the peculiarities of each case." 503 F.2d, at 1104. In view of our holding that an intent to deceive, manipulate, or defraud is required for civil liability under § 10(b) and Rule 10b-5, we need not consider whether civil liability for aiding and abetting is appropriate under the section and the rule, nor the elements necessary to establish such a cause of action. See, e.g., Brennan v. Midwestern United Life Ins. Co., 259 F.Supp. 673 (1966), 286 F.Supp. 702 (ND Ind.1968), aff'd, 417 F.2d 147 (CA7

1969), cert. denied, 397 U.S. 989 (1970) (defendant held liable for giving active and knowing assistance to a third party engaged in violations of the securities laws). See generally Ruder, Multiple Defendants in Securities Law Fraud Cases: Aiding and Abetting, Conspiracy, In Pari Delicto, Indemnification and Contribution, 120 U.Pa. L.Rev. 597, 620–645 (1972).

12. Although the verbal formulations of the standard to be applied have varied, several courts of appeals have held in substance that negligence alone is sufficient for civil liability under § 10(b) and Rule 10b-5. See, e.g., White v. Abrams, 495 F.2d 724, 730 (CA9 1974) ("flexible duty" standard); Myzel v. Fields, 386 F.2d 718, 735 (CA8 1967), cert. denied 390 U.S. 951 (1968) (negligence sufficient); Kohler v. Kohler Co., 319 F.2d 634 (CA7 1963) (knowledge not required). Other courts of appeals have held that some type of scienter—i.e., intent to defraud, reckless disregard for the truth, or knowing use of some practice to defraud—is necessary in such an action. See, e.g., Clegg v. Conk, 507 F.2d 1351, 1361–1362 (CA10 1974), cert. denied, 422 U.S. 1007 (1975) (an element of "scienter or conscious fault"); Lanza v.

421 U.S. 909 (1975). We conclude that it will not and therefore we reverse.[13]

II

Federal regulation of transactions in securities emerged as part of the aftermath of the market crash in 1929. The Securities Act of 1933 (1933 Act), as amended was designed to provide investors with full disclosure of material information concerning public offerings of securities in commerce, to protect investors against fraud and, through the imposition of specified civil liabilities, to promote ethical standards of honesty and fair dealing. See H.R.Rep. No. 85, 73d Cong., 1st Sess., 1–5 (1933). The 1934 Act was intended principally to protect investors against manipulation of stock prices through regulation of transactions upon securities exchanges and in over-the-counter markets, and to impose regular reporting requirements on companies whose stock is listed on national securities exchanges. See S.Rep. No. 792, 73d Cong., 2d Sess., 1–5 (1934). Although the Acts contain numerous carefully drawn express civil remedies and criminal penalties, Congress recognized that efficient regulation of securities trading could not be accomplished under a rigid statutory program. As part of the 1934 Act Congress created the Commission, which is provided with an arsenal of flexible enforcement powers. See, e.g., 1933 Act §§ 8, 19, 20; 1934 Act §§ 9, 19, 21.

* * *

Although § 10(b) does not by its terms create an express civil remedy for its violation, and there is no indication that Congress, or the Commission when adopting Rule 10b–5, contemplated such a remedy, the existence of a private cause of action for violations of the statute and the rule is now well established. Blue Chip Stamps v. Manor Drug Stores, 421 U.S. 723, 730 (1975); Affiliated Ute Citizens v. United States, 406 U.S. 128, 150–154 (1972); Superintendent of Insurance v. Bankers Life and Casualty Co., 404 U.S. 6, 13 n. 9 (1971). During the 30–year period since a private cause of

Drexel & Co., 479 F.2d 1277, 1306 (CA2 1973) ("willful or reckless disregard" of the truth). But few of the decisions announcing that some form of negligence suffices for civil liability under § 10(b) and Rule 10b–5 actually have involved only negligent conduct. Smallwood v. Pearl Brewing Co., 489 F.2d 579, 606 (CA5), cert. denied, 419 U.S. 879 (1974); Kohn v. American Metal Climax, Inc., 458 F.2d 255, 286 (CA3 1972) (Adams, J., concurring); Bucklo, Scienter and Rule 10b–5, 67 Nw.U.L.Rev. 562, 568–570 (1972).

In this opinion the term "scienter" refers to a mental state embracing intent to deceive, manipulate, or defraud. In certain areas of the law recklessness is considered to be a form of intentional conduct for purposes of imposing liability for some act. We need not address here the question whether, in some circumstances, reckless behavior is sufficient for civil liability under § 10(b) and Rule 10b–5.

Since this case concerns an action for damages we also need not consider the

question whether scienter is a necessary element in an action for injunctive relief under § 10(b) and Rule 10b–5. Cf. SEC v. Capital Gains Research Bureau, Inc., 375 U.S. 180 (1963).

13. Respondents further contend that Ernst & Ernst owed them a direct duty under § 17(a) and Rule 17a–5 of the 1934 Act to conduct a proper audit of First Securities and that they may base a private cause of action against Ernst & Ernst for violation of that duty. Respondents' cause of action, however, was premised solely on the alleged violation of § 10(b) and Rule 10b–5. During the lengthy history of this litigation they have not amended their original complaint to aver a cause of action under § 17(a) and Rule 17a–5. We therefore do not consider that a claim of liability under § 17(a) is properly before us even assuming respondents could assert such a claim independently of § 10(b).

action was first implied under § 10(b) and Rule 10b–5, a substantial body of case law and commentary has developed as to its elements. Courts and commentators long have differed with regard to whether scienter is a necessary element of such a cause of action, or whether negligent conduct alone is sufficient. In addressing this question, we turn first to the language of § 10(b), for "[t]he starting point in every case involving construction of a statute is the language itself." *Blue Chip Stamps*, supra, at 756 (Powell, J., concurring); e.g., FTC v. Bunte Brothers, Inc., 312 U.S. 349, 350 (1941).

A

Section 10(b) makes unlawful the use or employment of "any manipulative or deceptive device or contrivance" in contravention of Commission rules. The words "manipulative or deceptive" used in conjunction with "device or contrivance" strongly suggest that § 10(b) was intended to proscribe knowing or intentional misconduct. See SEC v. Texas Gulf Sulphur Co., 401 F.2d 833, 868 (CA2 1968) (Friendly, J., concurring), cert. denied sub nom., Kline v. SEC, 394 U.S. 976 (1969); Loss, Summary Remarks, 30 Bus.Lawyer 163, 165 (1975). See also Kohn v. American Metal Climax, Inc., 458 F.2d 255, 280 (CA3 1972) (Adams, J., concurring).

In its *amicus curiae* brief, however, the Commission contends that nothing in the language "manipulative or deceptive device or contrivance" limits its operation to knowing or intentional practices. In support of its view, the Commission cites the overall congressional purpose in the 1933 and 1934 Acts to protect investors against false and deceptive practices that might injure them. See Affiliated Ute Citizens v. United States, supra, at 151; Superintendent of Insurance v. Bankers Life & Casualty Co., 404 U.S., at 11–12; J.I. Case Co. v. Borak, 377 U.S. 426, 432–433 (1964). See also SEC v. Capital Gains Research Bureau, Inc., 375 U.S. 180, 195 (1963). The Commission then reasons that since the "effect" upon investors of given conduct is the same regardless of whether the conduct is negligent or intentional, Congress must have intended to bar all such practices and not just those done knowingly or intentionally. The logic of this effect-oriented approach would impose liability for wholly faultless conduct where such conduct results in harm to investors, a result the Commission would be unlikely to support. But apart from where its logic might lead, the Commission would add a gloss to the operative language of the statute quite different from its commonly accepted meaning. See, e.g., Addison v. Holly Hill Fruit Products, Inc., 322 U.S. 607, 617–618 (1944). The argument simply ignores the use of the words "manipulative," "device," and "contrivance," terms that make unmistakable a congressional intent to proscribe a type of conduct quite different from negligence. Use of the word "manipulative" is especially significant. It is and was virtually a term of art when used in connection with securities markets. It connotes intentional or willful conduct designed to deceive or defraud investors by controlling or artificially affecting the price of securities.

In addition to relying upon the Commission's argument with respect to the operative language of the statute, respondents contend that since we are dealing with "remedial legislation," Tcherepnin v. Knight, 389 U.S. 332, 336 (1967), it must be construed " 'not technically and restrictively, but flexibly to effectuate its remedial purposes.' " Affiliated Ute Citizens v.

United States, supra, at 151, quoting SEC v. Capital Gains Research Bureau, supra, at 186. They argue that the "remedial purposes" of the Acts demand a construction of § 10(b) that embraces negligence as a standard of liability. But in seeking to accomplish its broad remedial goals, Congress did not adopt uniformly a negligence standard even as to express civil remedies. In some circumstances and with respect to certain classes of defendants, Congress did create express liability predicated upon a failure to exercise reasonable care. E.g., 1933 Act § 11(b)(3)(B) (liability of "experts," such as accountants, for misleading statements in portions of registration statements for which they are responsible). But in other situations good faith is an absolute defense. 1934 Act § 18 (misleading statements in any document filed pursuant to the 1934 Act). And in still other circumstances Congress created express liability regardless of the defendant's fault, 1933 Act § 11(a) (issuer liability for misleading statements in the registration statement).

It is thus evident that Congress fashioned standards of fault in the express civil remedies in the 1933 and 1934 Acts on a particularized basis. Ascertainment of congressional intent with respect to the standard of liability created by a particular section of the Acts must therefore rest primarily on the language of that section. Where, as here, we deal with a judicially implied liability, the statutory language certainly is no less important. In view of the language of § 10(b) which so clearly connotes intentional misconduct, and mindful that the language of a statute controls when sufficiently clear in its context, United States v. Oregon, 366 U.S. 643, 648 (1961); Packard Motor Car Co. v. NLRB, 330 U.S. 485, 492 (1947), further inquiry may be unnecessary. We turn now, nevertheless, to the legislative history of the 1934 Act to ascertain whether there is support for the meaning attributed to § 10(b) by the Commission and respondents.

B

Although the extensive legislative history of the 1934 Act is bereft of any explicit explanation of Congress' intent, we think the relevant portions of that history support our conclusion that § 10(b) was addressed to practices that involve some element of scienter and cannot be read to impose liability for negligent conduct alone.

* * *

Neither the intended scope of § 10(b) nor the reasons for the changes in its operative language are revealed explicitly in the legislative history of the 1934 Act, which deals primarily with other aspects of the legislation. There is no indication, however, that § 10(b) was intended to proscribe conduct not involving scienter. The extensive hearings that preceded passage of the 1934 Act touched only briefly on § 10, and most of the discussion was devoted to the enumerated devices that the Commission is empowered to proscribe under § 10(a). The most relevant exposition of the provision that was to become § 10(b) was by Thomas G. Corcoran, a spokesman for the drafters. Corcoran indicated:

"Subsection (c) [§ 9(c) of H.R. 7852—later § 10(b)] says, 'Thou shalt not devise any other cunning devices.' * * *

"Of course subsection (c) is a catch-all clause to prevent manipulative devices. I do not think there is any objection to that kind of clause.

The Commission should have the authority to deal with new manipulative devices."

Hearings on H.R. 7852 and H.R. 8720 before the House Comm. on Interstate and Foreign Commerce, 73d Cong., 2d Sess., 115 (1934). This brief explanation of § 10(b) by a spokesman for its drafters is significant. The section was described rightly as a "catch-all" clause to enable the Commission "to deal with new manipulative [or cunning] devices." It is difficult to believe that any lawyer, legislative draftsman, or legislator would use these words if the intent was to create liability for merely negligent acts or omissions. Neither the legislative history nor the briefs supporting respondents identify any usage or authority for construing "manipulative [or cunning] devices" to include negligence.

* * *

C

The 1933 and 1934 Acts constitute interrelated components of the federal regulatory scheme governing transactions in securities. See *Blue Chip Stamps,* 421 U.S., at 727–730. As the Court indicated in SEC v. National Securities, Inc., 393 U.S. 453 (1969), "the interdependence of the various sections of the securities laws is certainly a relevant factor in any interpretation of the language Congress has chosen. * * * Recognizing this, respondents and the Commission contrast § 10(b) to other sections of the Acts to support their contention that civil liability may be imposed upon proof of negligent conduct. We think they misconceive the significance of the other provisions of the Acts.

The Commission argues that Congress has been explicit in requiring willful conduct when that was the standard of fault intended, citing § 9 of the 1934 Act, which generally proscribes manipulation of securities prices. Sections 9(a)(1) and (a)(2), for example, respectively prohibit manipulation of security prices "[f]or the purpose of creating a false or misleading appearance of actual trading in a security * * * or * * * with respect to the market for any such security," and "for the purpose of inducing the purchase or sale of such security by others." See also § 9(a)(4). Section 9(e) then imposes upon "[a]ny person who willfully participates in any act or transaction in violation of" other provisions of § 9 civil liability to anyone who purchased or sold a security at a price affected by the manipulative activities. From this the Commission concludes that since § 10(b) is not by its terms explicitly restricted to willful, knowing, or purposeful conduct, it should not be construed in all cases to require more than negligent action or inaction as a precondition for civil liability.

The structure of the Acts does not support the Commission's argument. In each instance that Congress created express civil liability in favor of purchasers or sellers of securities it clearly specified whether recovery was to be premised on knowing or intentional conduct, negligence, or entirely innocent mistake. See 1933 Act, §§ 11, 12, 15; 1934 Act §§ 9, 18, 20. For example, § 11 of the 1933 Act unambiguously creates a private action for damages when a registration statement includes untrue statements of material facts or fails to state material facts necessary to make the statements therein not misleading. Within the limits specified by § 11(e), the issuer of the securities is held absolutely liable for any damages resulting from such misstatement or omission. But experts such as accountants who have prepared portions of the registration statement are accorded a "due diligence" defense. In effect, this is a negligence standard. An expert may avoid civil liability with respect to the portions of the registration statement for which he was responsible by showing that "after reasonable investigation" he had "reasonable ground[s] to believe" that the statements for which he was responsible were true and there was no omission of a material fact.[26] § 11(b)(3)(B)(i). See, e.g., Escott v. BarChris Construction Corp., 283 F.Supp. 643, 697–703 (SDNY 1968). The express recognition of a cause of action premised on negligent behavior in § 11 stands in sharp contrast to the language of § 10(b), and significantly undercuts the Commission's argument.

We also consider it significant that each of the express civil remedies in the 1933 Act allowing recovery for negligent conduct, see §§ 11, 12(2), 15, is subject to significant procedural restrictions not applicable under § 10(b).[28] Section 11(e) of the 1933 Act, for example, authorizes the court to require a plaintiff bringing a suit under § 11, § 12(2), or § 15 thereof to post a bond for costs, including attorneys' fees and in specified circumstances to assess costs at the conclusion of the litigation. Section 13 specifies a statute of limitations of one year from the time the violation was or should have been discovered, in no event to exceed three years from the time of offer or sale, applicable to actions brought under § 11, § 12(2), or § 15. These restrictions, significantly, were imposed by amendments to the 1933 Act adopted as part of the 1934 Act. Prior to amendment § 11(e) contained no provision for payment of costs. The amendments also substantially shortened the statute of limitations provided by § 13. Compare Pub.L. No. 22, supra, § 13, 48 Stat. 84, with 15 U.S.C. § 77m. See 1934 Act, § 207, 48 Stat. 908. We think these procedural limitations indicate that the judicially created private damage remedy under § 10(b)—which has no comparable restrictions—cannot be extended, consistently with the intent of Congress, to

---

26. Other individuals who sign the registration statement, directors of the issuer, and the underwriter of the securities similarly are accorded a complete defense against civil liability based on the exercise of reasonable investigation and a reasonable belief that the registration statement was not misleading. §§ 11(b)(3)(A), (C), (D), (c). See, e.g., Feit v. Leasco Data Processing Equipment Corp., 332 F.Supp. 544, 575–583 (EDNY 1971) (underwriters, but not officer-directors, established their due diligence defense). See generally R. Jennings & H. Marsh, Securities Regulation 1018–1027 (3d ed. 1972), and sources cited therein; Folk, Civil Liabilities under the Federal Securities Acts: The BarChris Case, 55 Va.L.Rev. 199 (1969).

28. Each of the provisions of the 1934 Act that expressly create civil liability, except those directed to specific classes of individuals such as directors, officers, or 10% beneficial holders of securities, see § 16(b), Foremost-McKesson, Inc. v. Provident Securities Co., supra; Kern County Land Co. v. Occidental Petroleum Corp., 411 U.S. 582 (1973), contains a state-of-mind condition requiring something more

than negligence. Section 9 creates potential civil liability for any person who "willfully participates" in the manipulation of securities on a national exchange. § 9(e). Section 18 creates potential civil liability for misleading statements filed with the Commission, but provides the defendant with the defense that "he acted in good faith and had no knowledge that such statement was false or misleading." And § 20, which imposes liability upon "controlling persons" for violations of the Act by those they control, exculpates a defendant who "acted in good faith and did not * * * induce the act * * * constituting the violation * * *." Emphasizing the important difference between the operative language and purpose of § 14(a) of the 1934 Act as contrasted with § 10(b), however, some courts have concluded that proof of scienter is unnecessary in an action for damages by the shareholder recipients of a materially misleading proxy statement against the issuer corporation. Gerstle v. Gamble-Skogmo, Inc., 478 F.2d 1281, 1299 (CA2 1973). See also Kohn v. American Metal Climax, Inc., supra, at 289–290.

actions premised on negligent wrongdoing. Such extension would allow causes of action covered by § 11, § 12(2), and § 15 to be brought instead under § 10(b) and thereby nullify the effectiveness of the carefully drawn procedural restrictions on these express actions. See e.g., Fischman v. Raytheon Manufacturing Co., 188 F.2d 783, 786–787 (CA2 1951); SEC v. Texas Gulf Sulphur Co., 401 F.2d at 867–868 (Friendly, J., concurring); Rosenberg v. Globe Aircraft Corp., 80 F.Supp. 123, 124 (ED Pa.1948); 3 L. Loss, Securities Regulation 1787–1788 (2d ed. 1961); R. Jennings & H. Marsh, Securities Regulation 1070–1074 (3d ed. 1972). We would be unwilling to bring about this result absent substantial support in the legislative history, and there is none.[31]

D

We have addressed, to this point, primarily the language and history of § 10(b). The Commission contends, however, that subsections (2) and (3) of Rule 10b–5 are cast in language which—if standing alone—could encompass both intentional and negligent behavior. These subsections respectively provide that it is unlawful "[t]o make any untrue statement of a material fact or to omit to state a material fact necessary in order to make the statements made, in light of the circumstances under which they were made, not misleading ＊ ＊ ＊" and "to engage in any act, practice, or course of business which operates or would operate as a fraud or deceit upon any person. ＊ ＊ ＊" Viewed in isolation the language of subsection (2), and arguably that of subsection (3), could be read as proscribing, respectively, any type of material misstatement or omission, and any course of conduct, that has the effect of defrauding investors, whether the wrongdoing was intentional or not.

We note first that such a reading cannot be harmonized with the administrative history of the rule, a history making clear that when the Commission adopted the rule it was intended to apply only to activities that involved scienter. More importantly, Rule 10b–5 was adopted pursuant to authority granted the Commission under § 10(b). The rulemaking power granted to an administrative agency charged with the administration of a

---

31. Section 18 of the 1934 Act creates a private cause of action against persons, such as accountants, who "make or cause to be made" materially misleading statements in reports or other documents filed with the Commission. We need not consider the question whether a cause of action may be maintained under § 10(b) on the basis of actions that would constitute a violation of § 18. Under § 18 liability extends to persons who, in reliance on such statements, purchased or sold a security whose price was affected by the statements. Liability is limited, however, in the important respect that the defendant is accorded the defense that he acted in "good faith and had no knowledge that such statement was false or misleading." Consistent with this language, the legislative history of the section suggests something more than negligence on the part of the defendant is required for recovery. The original version of § 18(a), § 17(a) of S.

2693, H.R. 7852 and H.R. 7855, see pp. 14–15, supra, provided that the defendant would not be liable if "he acted in good faith and in the exercise of reasonable care had no ground to believe that such statement was false or misleading." The accounting profession objected to this provision on the ground that liability would be created for honest errors in judgment. See Senate Hearings on Stock Exchange Practices, supra, at 7175–7183; House Hearings on H.R. 7852 and H.R. 8720, supra, at 653. In subsequent drafts the current formulation was adopted. It is also significant that actions under § 18 are limited by a relatively short statute of limitations similar to that provided in § 13 of the 1933 Act, § 18(c). Moreover, as under § 11(e) of the 1933 Act the District Court is authorized to require the plaintiff to post a bond for costs, including attorney's fees, and to assess such costs at the conclusion of the litigation. § 18(a).

federal statute is not the power to make law. Rather, it is " 'the power to adopt regulations to carry into effect the will of Congress as expressed by the statute.' " Dixon v. United States, 381 U.S. 68, 74 (1965), quoting Manhattan General Equipment Co. v. Commissioner, 297 U.S. 129, 134 (1936). Thus, despite the broad view of the Rule advanced by the Commission in this case, its scope cannot exceed the power granted the Commission by Congress under § 10(b). For the reasons stated above, we think the Commission's original interpretation of Rule 10b–5 was compelled by the language and history of § 10(b) and related sections of the Acts. See, e.g., Gerstle v. Gamble-Skogmo, Inc., 478 F.2d 1281, 1299 (CA2 1973); Lanza v. Drexel & Co., 479 F.2d 1277, 1304–1305 (CA2 1973); SEC v. Texas Gulf Sulphur Co., supra, at 868; 3 L. Loss, supra, 1766; 6 id., at 3883–3885 (Sup. 1969). When a statute speaks so specifically in terms of manipulation and deception, and of implementing devices and contrivances—the commonly understood terminology of intentional wrongdoing—and when its history reflects no more expansive intent, we are quite unwilling to extend the scope of the statute to negligent conduct.

III

Recognizing that § 10(b) and Rule 10b–5 might be held to require proof of more than negligent nonfeasance by Ernst & Ernst as a precondition to the imposition of civil liability, respondents further contend that the case should be remanded for trial under whatever standard is adopted. Throughout the lengthy history of this case respondents have proceeded on a theory of liability premised on negligence, specifically disclaiming that Ernst & Ernst had engaged in fraud or intentional misconduct. In these circumstances, we think it inappropriate to remand the action for further proceedings.

The judgment of the Court of Appeals is Reversed.

MR. JUSTICE STEVENS took no part in the consideration or decision of this case.

MR. JUSTICE BLACKMUN, with whom MR. JUSTICE BRENNAN joins, dissenting.

Once again—see Blue Chip Stamps v. Manor Drug Stores, 421 U.S. 723, 730 (1975)—the Court interprets § 10(b) of the Securities Exchange Act of 1934 and the Securities and Exchange Commission's Rule 10b–5 restrictively and narrowly and thereby stultifies recovery for the victim. This time the Court does so by confining the statute and the Rule to situations where the defendant has "scienter," that is, the "intent to deceive, manipulate, or defraud." Sheer negligence, the Court says, is not within the reach of the statute and the Rule, and was not contemplated when the great reforms of 1933, 1934, and 1942 were effectuated by Congress and the Commission.

Perhaps the Court is right, but I doubt it. The Government and the Commission doubt it too, as is evidenced by the thrust of the brief filed by the Solicitor General on behalf of the Commission as *amicus curiae*. The Court's opinion, ante, to be sure has a certain technical consistency about it. It seems to me, however, that an investor can be victimized just as much by negligent conduct as by positive deception, and that it is not logical to drive a wedge between the two, saying that Congress clearly intended the one but certainly not the other.

No one questions the fact that the respondents here were the victims of an intentional securities fraud practiced by Leston B. Nay. What is at issue, of course, is the petitioner-accountant firm's involvement and that firm's responsibility under Rule 10b–5. The language of the Rule, making it unlawful for any person "in connection with the purchase or sale of any security"

"(b) To make any untrue statement of a material fact or to omit to state a material fact necessary in order to make the statements made, in the light of the circumstances under which they were made, not misleading, or

"(c) To engage in any act, practice, or course of business which operates or would operate as a fraud or deceit upon any person,"

seems to me, clearly and succinctly, to prohibit negligent as well as intentional conduct of the kind proscribed, to extend beyond common law fraud, and to apply to negligent omission and commission. This is consistent with Congress' intent, repeatedly recognized by the Court, that securities legislation enacted for the purpose of avoiding frauds be construed "not technically and restrictively, but flexibly to effectuate its remedial purposes." SEC v. Capital Gains Research Bureau, 375 U.S. 180, 195 (1963); Superintendent of Insurance v. Bankers Life & Casualty Co., 404 U.S. 6, 12 (1971); Affiliated Ute Citizens v. United States, 406 U.S. 128, 151 (1972).

* * *

AARON v. SECURITIES AND EXCHANGE COMMISSION

Supreme Court of the United States, 1980.
446 U.S. 680, 100 S.Ct. 1945, 64 L.Ed.2d 611.

MR. JUSTICE STEWART delivered the opinion of the Court.

The issue in this case is whether the Securities and Exchange Commission (Commission) is required to establish scienter as an element of a civil enforcement action to enjoin violations of § 17(a) of the Securities Act of 1933 (1933 Act), § 10(b) of the Securities Exchange Act of 1934 (1934 Act), and Commission Rule 10b–5 promulgated under that section of the 1934 Act.

I

When the events giving rise to this enforcement proceeding occurred, the petitioner was a managerial employee at E.L. Aaron & Co. (the firm), a registered broker-dealer with its principal office in New York City. Among other responsibilities at the firm, the petitioner was charged with supervising the sales made by its registered representatives and maintaining the so-called "due diligence" files for those securities in which the firm served as a market maker. One such security was the common stock of Lawn-A-Mat Chemical & Equipment Corp. (Lawn-A-Mat), a company engaged in the business of selling lawn care franchises and supplying its franchisees with products and equipment.

Between November 1974 and September 1975, two registered representatives of the firm, Norman Schreiber and Donald Jacobson, conducted a sales campaign in which they repeatedly made false and misleading statements in an effort to solicit orders for the purchase of Lawn-A-Mat common stock. During the course of this promotion, Schreiber and Jacobson informed prospective investors that Lawn-A-Mat was planning or in the process of manufacturing a new type of small car and tractor, and that the car would be marketed within six weeks. Lawn-A-Mat, however, had no such plans. The two registered representatives also made projections of substantial increases in the price of Lawn-A-Mat common stock and optimistic statements concerning the company's financial condition. These projections and statements were without basis in fact, since Lawn-A-Mat was losing money during the relevant period.

Upon receiving several complaints from prospective investors, an officer of Lawn-A-Mat informed Schreiber and Jacobson that their statements were false and misleading and requested them to cease making such statements. This request went unheeded.

Thereafter, Milton Kean, an attorney representing Lawn-A-Mat, communicated with the petitioner twice by telephone. In these conversations, Kean informed the petitioner that Schreiber and Jacobson were making false and misleading statements and described the substance of what they were saying. The petitioner, in addition to being so informed by Kean, had reason to know that the statements were false, since he knew that the reports in Lawn-A-Mat's due diligence file indicated a deteriorating financial condition and revealed no plans for manufacturing a new car and tractor. Although assuring Kean that the misrepresentations would cease, the petitioner took no affirmative steps to prevent their recurrence. The petitioner's only response to the telephone calls was to inform Jacobson of Kean's complaint and to direct him to communicate with Kean. Otherwise, the petitioner did nothing to prevent the two registered representatives under his direct supervision from continuing to make false and misleading statements in promoting Lawn-A-Mat common stock.

In February 1976, the Commission filed a complaint in the District Court for the Southern District of New York against the petitioner and seven other defendants in connection with the offer and sale of Lawn-A-Mat common stock. In seeking preliminary and final injunctive relief pursuant to § 20(b) of the 1933 Act and § 21(d) of the 1934 Act, the Commission alleged that the petitioner had violated and aided and abetted violations of three provisions—§ 17(a) of the 1933 Act, § 10(b) of the 1934 Act, and Commission Rule 10b–5 promulgated under that section of the 1934 Act. The gravamen of the charges against the petitioner was that he knew or had reason to know that the employees under his supervision were engaged in fraudulent practices, but failed to take adequate steps to prevent those practices from continuing. * * *

Following a bench trial, the District Court found that the petitioner had violated and aided and abetted violations of § 17(a), § 10(b), and Rule 10b–5 during the Lawn-A-Mat sales campaign and enjoined him from future violations of these provisions. The District Court's finding of past violations was based upon its factual finding that the petitioner had intentionally failed to discharge his supervisory responsibility to stop Schreiber and Jacobson from making statements to prospective investors that the petitioner knew to be false and misleading. * * *

The Court of Appeals for the Second Circuit affirmed the judgment. SEC v. Aaron, 605 F.2d 612. Declining to reach the question whether the petitioner's conduct would support a finding of scienter, the Court of Appeals held instead that when the Commission is seeking injunctive relief, "proof of negligence alone will suffice" to establish a violation of § 17(a), § 10(b), and Rule 10b–5. Id., at 619. * * *

We granted certiorari to resolve the conflict in the federal courts as to whether the Commission is required to establish scienter—an intent on the part of the defendant to deceive, manipulate, or defraud [5]—as an element of a Commission enforcement action to enjoin violations of § 17(a), § 10(b), and Rule 10b–5. * * *

II

The two substantive statutory provisions at issue here are § 17(a) of the 1933 Act and § 10(b) of the 1934 Act. Section 17(a), which applies only to sellers, provides:

* * *

Section 10(b), which applies to both buyers and sellers, makes it "unlawful for any person * * * [t]o use or employ, in connection with the purchase or sale of any security * * * any manipulative or deceptive device or contrivance in contravention of such rules and regulations as the Commission may prescribe as necessary or appropriate in the public interest or for the protection of investors." Pursuant to its rulemaking power under this section, the Commission promulgated Rule 10b–5. * * *

* * *

The civil enforcement mechanism for these provisions consists of both express and implied remedies. One express remedy is a suit by the Commission for injunctive relief. Section 20(b) of the 1933 Act provides:

"Whenever it shall appear to the Commission that any person is engaged or about to engage in any acts or practices which constitute or will constitute a violation of the provisions of this subchapter [e.g., § 17(a)], or of any rule or regulation prescribed under the authority thereof, it may in its discretion, bring an action in any district court of the United States * * * to enjoin such acts or practices, and upon a proper showing a permanent or temporary injunction or restraining order shall be granted without bond."

Similarly, § 21(d) of the 1934 Act authorizes the Commission to seek injunctive relief whenever it appears that a person "is engaged in or is about to engage in any acts or practices constituting" a violation of the 1934 Act [e.g., § 10(b)], or regulations promulgated thereunder [e.g., Rule 10b–5], and requires a district court "upon a proper showing" to grant injunctive relief.

Another facet of civil enforcement is a private cause of action for money damages. This remedy, unlike the Commission injunctive action, is not expressly authorized by statute, but rather has been judicially implied. See Ernst & Ernst v. Hochfelder, supra, 425 U.S., at 196–197. Although this Court has repeatedly assumed the existence of an implied cause of action under § 10(b) and Rule 10b–5, see Ernst & Ernst v. Hochfelder,

---

5. The term "scienter" is used throughout this opinion, as it was in Ernst & Ernst v. Hochfelder, 425 U.S. 185, at 193, n. 12, to refer to "a mental state embracing intent to deceive, manipulate, or defraud." We have no occasion here to address the question, reserved in *Hochfelder*, ibid., whether, under some circumstances, scienter may also include reckless behavior.

supra; Blue Chip Stamps v. Manor Drug Stores, 421 U.S. 723, 730; Affiliated Ute Citizens v. United States, 406 U.S. 128, 150–154; Superintendent of Insurance v. Bankers Life & Cas. Co., 404 U.S. 6, 13, n. 9, it has not had occasion to address the question whether a private cause of action exists under § 17(a). See Blue Chip Stamps v. Manor Drug Stores, supra, at 733, n. 6.

The issue here is whether the Commission in seeking injunctive relief either under § 20(b) for violations of § 17(a), or under § 21(d) for violations of § 10(b) or Rule 10b–5, is required to establish scienter. Resolution of that issue could depend upon (1) the substantive provisions of § 17(a), § 10(b), and Rule 10b–5, or (2) the statutory provisions authorizing injunctive relief "upon a proper showing," § 20(b) and § 21(d). We turn to an examination of each to determine the extent to which they may require proof of scienter.

A

In determining whether scienter is a necessary element of a violation of § 10(b) and Rule 10b–5, we do not write on a clean slate. Rather, the starting point for our inquiry is Ernst & Ernst v. Hochfelder, 425 U.S. 185, a case in which the Court concluded that a private cause of action for damages will not lie under § 10(b) and Rule 10b–5 in the absence of an allegation of scienter. Although the issue presented in the present case was expressly reserved in *Hochfelder,* id., at 193, n. 12, we nonetheless must be guided by the reasoning of that decision.

The conclusion in *Hochfelder* that allegations of simple negligence could not sustain a private cause of action for damages under § 10(b) and Rule 10b–5 rested on several grounds. The most important was the plain meaning of the language of § 10(b). It was the view of the Court that the terms "manipulative," "device," and "contrivance"—whether given their commonly accepted meaning or read as terms of art—quite clearly evinced a congressional intent to proscribe only "knowing or intentional misconduct." Id., at 197–199. This meaning, in fact, was thought to be so unambiguous as to suggest that "further inquiry may be unnecessary." Id., at 201.

The Court in *Hochfelder* nonetheless found additional support for its holding in both the legislative history of § 10(b) and the structure of the civil liability provisions in the 1933 and 1934 Acts. * * *

In our view the rationale of *Hochfelder* ineluctably leads to the conclusion that scienter is an element of a violation of § 10(b) and Rule 10b–5, regardless of the identity of the plaintiff or the nature of the relief sought. Two of the three factors relied upon in *Hochfelder* —the language of § 10(b) and its legislative history—are applicable whenever a violation of § 10(b) or Rule 10b–5 is alleged, whether in a private cause of action for damages or in a Commission injunctive action under § 21(d). In fact, since *Hochfelder* involved an implied cause of action that was not within the contemplation of the Congress that enacted § 10(b), id., at 196, it would be quite anomalous in a case like the present one, involving as it does the express remedy Congress created for § 10(b) violations, not to attach at least as much significance to the fact that the statutory language and its legislative history support a scienter requirement.

The Commission argues that *Hochfelder,* which involved a private cause of action for damages, is not a proper guide in construing § 10(b) in the present context of a Commission enforcement action for injunctive relief. We are urged instead to look to SEC v. Capital Gains Research Bureau, 375 U.S. 180. That case involved a suit by the Commission for injunctive relief to enforce the prohibition in § 206(2) of the Investment Advisers Act of 1940 against any act or practice of an investment adviser that "operates as a fraud or deceit upon any client or prospective client." The injunction sought in *Capital Gains* was to compel disclosure of a practice known as "scalping," whereby an investment adviser purchases shares of a given security for his own account shortly before recommending the security to investors as a long-term investment, and then promptly sells the shares at a profit upon the rise in their market value following the recommendation.

The issue in *Capital Gains* was whether in an action for injunctive relief for violations of § 206(2) the Commission must prove that the defendant acted with an intent to defraud. The Court held that a showing of intent was not required. This conclusion rested upon the fact that the legislative history revealed that the "Investment Advisers Act of 1940 * * * reflects a congressional recognition 'of the delicate fiduciary nature of an investment advisory relationship,' as well as a congressional intent to eliminate, or at least to expose, all conflicts of interest which might incline an investment adviser—consciously or unconsciously—to render advice which was not disinterested." 375 U.S., at 191–192 (footnote omitted). To require proof of intent, the Court reasoned, would run counter to the expressed intent of Congress.

The Court added that its conclusion was "not in derogation of the common law of fraud." Id., at 192. Although recognizing that intent to defraud was a necessary element at common law to recover money damages for fraud in an arm's-length transaction, the Court emphasized that the Commission's action was not a suit for damages, but rather a suit for an injunction in which the relief sought was the "mild prophylactic" of requiring a fiduciary to disclose his transactions in stocks he was recommending to his clients. Id., at 193. The Court observed that it was not necessary in a suit for "equitable or prophylactic relief" to establish intent, for "[f]raud has a broader meaning in equity [than at law] and intention to defraud or to misrepresent is not a necessary element." Id., quoting De Funiak, Handbook of Modern Equity 235 (2d ed. 1956). Moreover, it was not necessary, the Court said, in a suit against a fiduciary such as an investment adviser, to establish all the elements of fraud that would be required in a suit against a party to an arm's-length transaction. Finally, the Court took cognizance of a "growing recognition by common-law courts that the doctrines of fraud and deceit which developed around transactions involving land and other tangible items of wealth are ill-suited to the sale of such intangibles as advice and securities, and that, accordingly, the doctrines must be adapted to the merchandise in issue." Id., at 194. Unwilling to assume that Congress was unaware of these developments at common law, the Court concluded that they "reinforce[d]" its holding that Congress had not sought to require a showing of intent in actions to enjoin violations of § 206(2). Id., at 195.

The Commission argues that the emphasis in *Capital Gains* upon the distinction between fraud at law and in equity should guide a construction of § 10(b) in this suit for injunctive relief. We cannot, however, draw such guidance from *Capital Gains* for several reasons. First, wholly apart from its discussion of the judicial treatment of "fraud" at law and in equity, the Court in *Capital Gains* found strong support in the legislative history for its conclusion that the Commission need not demonstrate intent to enjoin practices in violation of § 206(2). By contrast, as the Court in *Hochfelder* noted, the legislative history of § 10(b) points towards a scienter requirement. Second, it is quite clear that the language in question in *Capital Gains,* "any * * * practice * * * which *operates* as a fraud or deceit," (emphasis added) focuses not on the intent of the investment adviser, but rather on the effect of a particular practice. Again, by contrast, the Court in *Hochfelder* found that the language of § 10(b)—particularly the terms "manipulative," "device," and "contrivance,"—clearly refers to "knowing or intentional misconduct." Finally, insofar as *Capital Gains* involved a statutory provision regulating the special fiduciary relationship between an investment adviser and his client, the Court there was dealing with a situation in which intent to defraud would not have been required even in a common-law action for money damages. Section 10(b), unlike the provision at issue in *Capital Gains,* applies with equal force to both fiduciary and nonfiduciary transactions in securities. It is our view, in sum, that the controlling precedent here is not *Capital Gains,* but rather *Hochfelder.* Accordingly, we conclude that scienter is a necessary element of a violation of § 10(b) and Rule 10b–5.

B

In determining whether proof of scienter is a necessary element of a violation of § 17(a), there is less precedential authority in this Court to guide us. But the controlling principles are well settled. Though cognizant that "Congress intended securities legislation enacted for the purpose of avoiding frauds to be construed 'not technically and restrictively, but flexibly to effectuate its remedial purposes,'" Affiliated Ute Citizens v. United States, supra, at 151, quoting, SEC v. Capital Gains Research Bureau, supra, at 195, the Court has also noted that "generalized references to the 'remedial purposes'" of the securities laws "will not justify reading a provision 'more broadly than its language and statutory scheme reasonably permit.'" Touche Ross & Co. v. Redington, 442 U.S. 560, 578, quoting, SEC v. Sloan, 436 U.S. 103, 116. Thus, if the language of a provision of the securities laws is sufficiently clear in its context and not at odds with the legislative history, it is unnecessary "to examine the additional considerations of 'policy' * * * that may have influenced the lawmakers in their formulation of the statute." Ernst & Ernst v. Hochfelder, supra, at 214, n. 33.

The language of § 17(a) strongly suggests that Congress contemplated a scienter requirement under § 17(a)(1), but not under § 17(a)(2) or § 17(a)(3). The language of § 17(a)(1), which makes it unlawful "to employ any device, scheme, or artifice to defraud," plainly evinces an intent on the part of Congress to proscribe only knowing or intentional misconduct. Even if it be assumed that the term "defraud" is ambiguous, given its varied meanings at law and in equity, the terms "device," "scheme," and "artifice" all connote knowing or intentional practices. Indeed, the term "device," which also appears in § 10(b), figured prominently in the Court's conclusion in *Hochfelder* that the plain meaning of § 10(b) embraces a scienter requirement. Id., at 199.

By contrast, the language of § 17(a)(2), which prohibits any person from obtaining money or property "by means of any untrue statement of a material fact or any omission to state a material fact," is devoid of any suggestion whatsoever of a scienter requirement. As a well-known commentator has noted, "[t]here is nothing on the face of Clause (2) itself which smacks of *scienter* or intent to defraud." III L. Loss, Securities Regulation 1442 (2d ed. 1961). In fact, this Court in *Hochfelder* pointed out that the similar language of Rule 10b–5(b) "could be read as proscribing * * * any type of material misstatement or omission * * * that has the effect of defrauding investors, whether the wrongdoing was intentional or not." 425 U.S., at 212.

Finally, the language of § 17(a)(3), under which it is unlawful for any person "to engage in any transaction, practice, or course of business which *operates* or *would operate* as a fraud or deceit," (emphasis added) quite plainly focuses upon the *effect* of particular conduct on members of the investing public, rather than upon the culpability of the person responsible. This reading follows directly from *Capital Gains*, which attributed to a similarly worded provision in § 206(2) of the Investment Advisers Act of 1940 a meaning that does not require a "showing [of] deliberate dishonesty as a condition precedent to protecting investors." 375 U.S., at 200.

It is our view, in sum, that the language of § 17(a) requires scienter under § 17(a)(1), but not under § 17(a)(2) or § 17(a)(3). Although the parties have urged the Court to adopt a uniform culpability requirement for the three subparagraphs of § 17(a), the language of the section is simply not amenable to such an interpretation. This is not the first time that this Court has had occasion to emphasize the distinctions among the three subparagraphs of § 17(a). In United States v. Naftalin, 441 U.S. 768, 774, the Court noted that each subparagraph of § 17(a) "proscribes a distinct category of misconduct. Each succeeding prohibition is meant to cover additional kinds of illegalities—not to narrow the reach of the prior sections." (Footnote omitted.) Indeed, since Congress drafted § 17(a) in such a manner as to compel the conclusion that scienter is required under one subparagraph but not under the other two, it would take a very clear expression in the legislative history of congressional intent to the contrary to justify the conclusion that the statute does not mean what it so plainly seems to say.

We find no such expression of congressional intent in the legislative history. * * *

* * *

* * * It seems clear, therefore, that the legislative history, albeit ambiguous, may be read in a manner entirely consistent with the plain meaning of § 17(a).[18] In the absence of a conflict between reasonably

---

18. The Commission, in further support of its view that scienter is not required under any of the subparagraphs of § 17(a), points out that § 17(a) was patterned upon New York's Martin Act, N.Y.Gen.Bus.Law §§ 352–353 (1921), and that the New York Court of Appeals had construed the Martin Act as not requiring a showing of scienter as a predicate for injunctive relief by the New York Attorney General. People v. Federated Radio Corp., 244 N.Y. 33, 154 N.E. 655 (1926). But, in the absence of any indication that Congress was even aware of the *Federated Radio* decision, much less that it approved of that decision, it cannot fairly be inferred that Congress intended not only to adopt the language of the Martin Act, but also a state judicial interpretation of that statute at odds with the plain meaning of the language Congress enacted as § 17(a)(1).

plain meaning and legislative history, the words of the statute must prevail.[19]

C

There remains to be determined whether the provisions authorizing injunctive relief, § 20(b) of the 1933 Act and § 21(d) of the 1934 Act, modify the substantive provisions at issue in this case so far as scienter is concerned.

The language and legislative history of § 20(b) and § 21(d) both indicate that Congress intended neither to add to nor detract from the requisite showing of scienter under the substantive provisions at issue. Sections 20(b) and 21(d) provide that the Commission may seek injunctive relief whenever it appears that a person "is engaged in or [is] about to engage in any acts or practices" constituting a violation of the 1933 or 1934 Acts or regulations promulgated thereunder and that, "upon a proper showing," a district court shall grant the injunction. The elements of "a proper showing" thus include, at a minimum, proof that a person is engaged in or is about to engage in a substantive violation of either one of the Acts or of the regulations promulgated thereunder. Accordingly, when scienter is an element of the substantive violation sought to be enjoined, it must be proved before an injunction may issue. But with respect to those provisions such as § 17(a)(2) and § 17(a)(3), which may be violated even in the absence of scienter, nothing on the face of § 20(b) or § 21(d) purports to impose an independent requirement of scienter. And there is nothing in the legislative history of either provision to suggest a contrary legislative intent.

This is not to say, however, that scienter has no bearing at all on whether a district court should enjoin a person violating or about to violate § 17(a)(2) or § 17(a)(3). In cases where the Commission is seeking to enjoin a person "*about* to engage in acts or practices which * * * *will* constitute" a violation of those provisions, the Commission must establish a sufficient evidentiary predicate to show that such future violation may occur. See SEC v. Commonwealth Chemical Co., 574 F.2d 90, 98–100 (CA2 1978) (Friendly, J.); III L. Loss, supra, at 1976. An important factor in this regard is the degree of intentional wrongdoing evident in a defendant's past conduct. See SEC v. Wills, 472 F.Supp. 1250, 1273–1275 (DC 1978). Moreover, as the Commission recognizes, a district court may consider scienter or lack of it as one of the aggravating or mitigating factors to be taken into account in exercising its equitable discretion in deciding whether or not to grant injunctive relief. And the proper exercise of equitable discretion is necessary to ensure a "nice adjustment and reconciliation between the public interest and private needs." Hecht Co. v. Bowles, 321 U.S. 321, 329.

III

For the reasons stated in this opinion, we hold that the Commission is required to establish scienter as an element of a civil enforcement action to enjoin violations of § 17(a)(1) of the 1933 Act, § 10(b) of the 1934 Act, and Rule 10b–5 promulgated under that section of the 1934 Act. We further

---

19. Since the language and legislative history of § 17(a) are dispositive, we have no occasion to address the "policy" arguments advanced by the parties. See Ernst & Ernst v. Hochfelder, 425 U.S. 185, 214, n. 33.

hold that the Commission need not establish scienter as an element of an action to enjoin violations of § 17(a)(2) and § 17(a)(3) of the 1933 Act. The Court of Appeals affirmed the issuance of the injunction in this case in the misapprehension that it was not necessary to find scienter in order to support an injunction under any of the provisions in question. Accordingly, the judgment of the Court of Appeals is vacated, and the case is remanded to that court for further proceedings consistent with this opinion.

It is so ordered.

MR. CHIEF JUSTICE BURGER, concurring.

I join the opinion of the Court and write separately to make three points:

(1) No matter what mental state § 10b and § 17(a) were to require, it is clear that the District Court was correct here in entering an injunction against petitioner. * * * [T]he District Court's findings (a) that petitioner "intentionally failed" to terminate the fraud and (b) that his conduct was reasonably likely to repeat itself find abundant support in the record. In my view, the Court of Appeals could well have affirmed on that ground alone.

(2) I agree that § 10b and § 17(a)(1) require scienter but that § 17(a)(2) and § 17(a)(3) do not. I recognize, of course, that this holding "drives a wedge between [sellers and buyers] and says that henceforth only the seller's negligent misrepresentations may be enjoined." Ante, at 12 (Blackmun, J., dissenting). But it is not this Court that "drives a wedge"; Congress has done that. The Court's holding is compelled in large measure by Ernst & Ernst v. Hochfelder, 425 U.S. 185 (1976), and gives effect to Congressional intent as manifested in the language of the statutes and in their histories. If, as intimated, the result is "bad" public policy, that is the concern of Congress where changes can be made.

(3) It bears mention that this dispute, though pressed vigorously by both sides, may be much ado about nothing. This is so because of the requirement in injunctive proceedings of a showing that "there is a reasonable likelihood that the wrong will be repeated." * * * To make such a showing, it will almost always be necessary for the Commission to demonstrate that the defendant's past sins have been the result of more than negligence. Because the Commission must show some likelihood of a future violation, defendants whose past actions have been in good faith are not likely to be enjoined. * * * That is as it should be. An injunction is a drastic remedy, not a mild prophylactic, and should not be obtained against one acting in good faith.

MR. JUSTICE BLACKMUN, with whom MR. JUSTICE BRENNAN and MR. JUSTICE MARSHALL join, concurring in part and dissenting in part.

I concur in the Court's judgment that §§ 17(a)(2) and (3) of the Securities Act of 1933, do not require a showing of scienter for purposes of an action for injunctive relief brought by the Securities and Exchange Commission. I dissent from the remainder of the Court's reasoning and judgment. I am of the view that neither § 17(a)(1) of the 1933 Act nor § 10(b) of the Securities Exchange Act of 1934, as elaborated by SEC Rule 10b–5, requires the Commission to prove scienter before it can obtain equitable protection against deceptive practices in securities trading. Accordingly, I would affirm the judgment of the Court of Appeals in its entirety.

* * *

THE REQUIRED CULPABILITY OF THE DEFENDANT UNDER RULE 10b–5 AND SECTION 17(a)

Sections 11 and 12(2) of the Securities Act of 1933 proscribe, in connection with the transactions covered by those sections, untrue statements of material facts and omissions of material facts necessary to make the statements made not misleading, as we have seen in Chapter 13. Rule 10b–5, like Section 17(a) of the Securities Act of 1933 from which it was copied, uses identical language in clause (2). However, Sections 11 and 12(2) provide a defense if the defendant (other than the issuer under Section 11) establishes lack of knowledge of the untruth or omission and the use of due care. No such defense is expressly recognized in Section 17(a) and Rule 10b–5. This raises the question whether the latter provisions are intended to establish absolute liability for a misstatement or omission regardless of due care or the lack thereof.

Judge Frank, in the case of Fischman v. Raytheon Manufacturing Co.,[1] in an effort to reconcile Rule 10b–5 with the express civil liability provisions of the Securities Act of 1933, assumed that "proof of fraud is required in suits under § 10(b) of the 1934 Act and Rule X–10B–5." [2] Presumably by this he meant an intentional misstatement or omission. In Securities and Exchange Commission v. Texas Gulf Sulphur Co.,[3] the Second Circuit held an injunction action under Rule 10b–5 could be based on mere negligence in the issuance of a corporate press release. However, Judge Friendly in his concurring opinion followed the *Fischman* case in asserting that negligence is insufficient to ground an action for damages, and a majority of the en banc court either expressly approved his statement or dissented even from the issuance of the injunction. This dictum was followed by the panel in Shemtob v. Shearson, Hammill & Co., Inc.,[4] in which the court said that there could be no cause of action under Rule 10b–5 "in the absence of allegation of facts amounting to *scienter,* intent to defraud, reckless disregard for the truth, or knowing use of a device, scheme or artifice to defraud. It is insufficient to allege mere negligence * * *." [5]

In Cohen v. Franchard Corp.[6] the Second Circuit approved the following charge to the jury by the District Judge as being "essentially correct": "The plaintiffs must establish that the defendant whom you are considering had knowledge and intended to defraud these plaintiffs, or that he acted in reckless disregard for the truth, or that he knowingly used a device, scheme or artifice to defraud." In Vohs v. Dickson[7] the Fifth Circuit expressly followed the *Cohen* case and stated that "some culpability beyond mere negligence is required for liability under 10b–5."

1. 188 F.2d 783 (2d Cir.1951).

2. 188 F.2d at 786.

3. 401 F.2d 833 (2d Cir.1968), cert. denied 394 U.S. 976 (1969).

4. 448 F.2d 442 (2d Cir.1971).

5. 448 F.2d at 445. Accord: Colonial Realty Corp. v. Brunswick Corp., 337 F.Supp. 546 (S.D.N.Y.1971); Trussell v. United Underwriters, Limited, 228 F.Supp. 757 (D.Colo.1964); Parker v. Baltimore Paint & Chemical Corp., 244 F.Supp. 267 (D.Colo.1965); Weber v. C.M.P. Corp., 242 F.Supp. 321 (S.D.N.Y.1965).

6. 478 F.2d 115 (2d Cir.1973), cert. denied 414 U.S. 857 (1973).

7. 495 F.2d 607 (5th Cir.1974). See, also, Smallwood v. Pearl Brewing Co., 489 F.2d 579 (5th Cir.1974); Sargent v. Genesco, Inc., 492 F.2d 750 (5th Cir.1974).

On the other hand, the Ninth Circuit in the case of Ellis v. Carter [8] rejected the contention that the plaintiff in an action under Rule 10b–5 "must allege and ultimately prove genuine fraud, as distinct from 'a mere misstatement or omission'. * * * " [9] It is difficult to see how this language requires any fault whatever on the part of the defendant, and it was so interpreted by the Federal District Judge in White v. Abrams [10] before he was reversed by the Ninth Circuit. This language was parroted by the Seventh Circuit in Jordan Building Corp. v. Doyle, O'Connor & Co. [11] and by the Tenth Circuit in Stevens v. Vowell, [12] but the Tenth Circuit explained that they didn't really mean it in Clegg v. Conk. [13]

Judge Adams in his dissenting opinion in Kohn v. American Metal Climax, Inc. [14] reviewed all of the cases on this issue up to 1972 and concluded that fraud had in fact been shown in all of the cases where the defendant had been held liable, including all of those where the language of the court purported to dispense with such a requirement.

This debate has now been resolved by the Supreme Court with respect to Rule 10b–5 in the *Ernst & Ernst* case. Note that the Supreme Court even reserved the question as to whether "reckless" behavior might be a sufficient basis of culpability to found an action under Rule 10b–5, being willing to concede in that case only that a conscious "intent to deceive, manipulate, or defraud" was sufficient. (See footnote 12 to the opinion.) Does it make any difference that that case involved a "collateral" defendant rather than the primary wrongdoer? Does the opinion suggest that the court regards this factor as of any importance? (See footnote 7.)

The Circuit Court cases since the *Ernst & Ernst* case have unanimously adopted the view that "recklessness" is a sufficient basis for liability under Rule 10b–5, the question which was there left open by the Supreme Court. [15] These cases have also almost unanimously followed the definition of "recklessness" which was first set out by the Seventh Circuit in Sundstrand Corp. v. Sun Chemical Corp., [16] as follows: "Reckless conduct may be defined as * * * highly unreasonable [conduct], involving not merely simple, or even inexcusable negligence, but an extreme departure from the standards of ordinary care, and

---

8. 291 F.2d 270 (9th Cir.1961).

9. 291 F.2d at 274.

10. 495 F.2d 724 (9th Cir.1974). The Ninth Circuit in that case established a so-called "flexible duty" standard, but it was not adopted by the Supreme Court in the *Ernst & Ernst* case.

11. 401 F.2d 47 (7th Cir.1968).

12. 343 F.2d 374 (10th Cir.1965). The Eighth Circuit cases expressly predicated liability upon negligence, while disclaiming any intention to impose liability without fault. The City National Bank of Fort Smith, Arkansas v. Vanderboom, 422 F.2d 221 (8th Cir.1970), cert. denied 399 U.S. 905 (1970); Myzel v. Fields, 386 F.2d 718 (8th Cir.1967).

13. 507 F.2d 1351 (10th Cir.1974).

14. 458 F.2d 255 (3d Cir.1972), cert. denied 409 U.S. 874 (1972).

15. Warren v. Reserve Fund, Inc., 728 F.2d 741 (5th Cir.1984); Brophy v. Redivo,

725 F.2d 1218 (9th Cir.1984); Kennedy v. Tallant, 710 F.2d 711 (11th Cir.1983); Decker v. Massey-Ferguson, Ltd., 681 F.2d 111 (2d Cir.1982); Hoffman v. Estabrook & Co., Inc., 587 F.2d 509 (1st Cir.1978); Rolf v. Blyth, Eastman, Dillon & Co., Inc., 570 F.2d 38 (2d Cir.1978), cert. denied 439 U.S. 1039, appeal after remand 637 F.2d 77; Healey v. Catalyst Recovery of Pennsylvania, Inc., 616 F.2d 641 (3d Cir.1980); McLean v. Alexander, 599 F.2d 1190 (3d Cir.1979); Coleco Industries, Inc. v. Berman, 567 F.2d 569 (3d Cir.1977), cert. denied 439 U.S. 830 (1978); Broad v. Rockwell International Corp., 614 F.2d 418 (5th Cir.1980); Mansbach v. Prescott, Ball & Turben, 598 F.2d 1017 (6th Cir.1979); The Pegasus Fund, Inc. v. Laraneta, 617 F.2d 1335 (9th Cir.1980); Keirnan v. Homeland, Inc., 611 F.2d 785 (9th Cir.1980); Nelson v. Serwold, 576 F.2d 1332 (9th Cir. 1978), cert. denied 439 U.S. 970.

16. 553 F.2d 1033 (7th Cir.1977), cert. denied 434 U.S. 875.

which presents a danger of misleading buyers or sellers that is either known to the defendant or is so obvious that the actor must have been aware of it." [17]

The courts have also frequently quoted the statement in the subsequent Seventh Circuit case of Sanders v. John Nuveen & Co.,[18] to the effect that the conduct required to meet this standard comes "closer to being a lesser form of intent [to deceive] than merely a greater degree of ordinary negligence." There are, however, decisions which seem to apply a more relaxed standard than would be suggested by this rigorous language used in the opinions.[19]

The history set out above of the courts' struggle with this question under Rule 10b–5 would now probably be irrelevant in the light of the *Ernst & Ernst* case, were it not for the decision by the Supreme Court in the *Aaron* case which construes language in Section 17(a) of the 1933 Act identical to that in Rule 10b–5 as meaning something totally different. If it should finally be decided that there is a private cause of action under Section 17(a) of the 1933 Act, the *Aaron* case again raises the specter of liability with respect to sellers for simple negligence, or perhaps even liability completely without fault. The Supreme Court says that there is no language in clause (2) of Section 17(a) which imposes any requirement of "scienter" with respect to false or misleading statements; there is also no language which imposes any requirement of negligence with respect to such a statement.

See Milich, Securities Fraud Under Section 10(b) and Rule 10b–5, 11 J.Corp. L. 179 (1986); Bunch, Aaron: The Demise of Equitable Fraud Under Section 10(b), 30 Emory L.J. 305 (1981); Steinberg and Gruenbaum, Variations of "Recklessness" After Hochfelder and Aaron, 8 Sec.Reg.L.J. 179 (1980); Walker, Accountants' Liability—The Scienter Standard Under Section 10b and Rule 10b–5 of the Securities Exchange Act of 1934, 63 Marq.L.Rev. 243 (1979); Metzger and Heintz, Hochfelder's Progeny: Implications for the Auditor, 63 Minn.L.Rev. 79 (1978); Lowenfels, Scienter or Negligence Required for SEC Injunctions Under Section 10(b) and Rule 10b–5; A Fascinating Paradox, 33 Bus.Law. 789 (1978); Cox, Ernst & Ernst v. Hochfelder: A Critique and an Evaluation of its Impact Upon the Scheme of the Federal Securities Laws, 28 Hastings L.J. 569 (1977); Haimoff, Holmes Looks at Hochfelder and 10b–5, 32 Bus.Law. 147 (1976); Branson, Statutory Securities Fraud in the Post-Hochfelder Era, 52 Tul.L.Rev. 50 (1977); Bucklo, Supreme Court Attempts to Define Scienter Under Rule 10b–5, 29 Stan.L.Rev. 213 (1977); Floor, Scienter Requirement Under Rule 10b–5 and Reliance on Advice of Counsel After Hochfelder, 12 New England L.Rev. 191 (1976).

---

17. See, generally, the cases cited supra Note 15. In the *Mansbach* case, supra Note 15, the Sixth Circuit stated: "It is not necessary for us to precisely define what constitutes reckless behavior since it is ultimately a factual determination which will necessarily vary from case to case. As a general matter, however, we express our agreement with the standard articulated in Sundstrand, supra, 553 F.2d 1045."

18. 554 F.2d 790 (7th Cir.1977). See, for example, Cook v. Avien, Inc., 573 F.2d 685, 692 (1st Cir.1978).

19. Hackbart v. Holmes, 675 F.2d 1114 (10th Cir.1982); Kehr v. Smith Barney, Harris Upham & Co., Inc., 736 F.2d 1283 (9th Cir.1984).

ADAMS v. STANDARD KNITTING MILLS

United States Court of Appeals, Sixth Circuit, 1980.
623 F.2d 422, cert. denied 449 U.S. 1067 (1981).

Before: WEICK, ENGEL, and MERRITT, CIRCUIT JUDGES.

MERRITT, CIRCUIT JUDGE, delivered the opinion of the Court in which ENGEL, CIRCUIT JUDGE, joined. WEICK, CIRCUIT JUDGE, filed a separate dissenting opinion.

MERRITT, CIRCUIT JUDGE: In this securities fraud case, Peat, Marwick, Mitchell & Co., herein referred to as "Peat," a firm of certified public accountants, appeals from a judgment of the District Court in the amount of $3.4 million, plus pre-judgment interest, plus attorneys' fees of $1.2 million. The suit is a class action based upon causes of action implied under §§ 10(b) and 14(a) of the Securities Exchange Act of 1934 and SEC Rules 10b–5 and 14a–9.[4] It is based on an allegedly false proxy solicitation issued in order to gain shareholder approval of a merger between two corporations, Chadbourn, Inc. and Standard Knitting Mills, Inc., herein referred to as "Chadbourn" and "Standard." The primary issue is whether Peat is liable for a negligent error—the failure to point out in the proxy statement sent to stockholders of the acquired corporation that certain restrictions on the payment of dividends by the acquiring corporation applied to preferred as well as common stock. We hold that in the context of this case Peat is not liable for such conduct and reverse the District Court on the issue of liability.

I. STATEMENT OF FACTS RESPECTING RESTRICTIONS ON PAYMENT OF DIVIDENDS

A. General Terms and Purpose of the Merger

In April 1970, Chadbourn, Inc., a relatively profitable North Carolina hosiery manufacturer listed on the New York Stock Exchange, acquired all of the common stock of Standard Knitting Mills, Inc., a smaller, publicly-held, Knoxville, Tennessee, textile manufacturer, whose stock traded from time to time, although infrequently, in the over-the-counter market. On April 22, 1970, Standard's stockholders at a special meeting agreed to exchange their stock for a package of Chadbourn securities. The meeting occurred after the stockholders received the proxy statement a month earlier from Standard transmitting information about the proposed merger and Chadbourn's financial condition. The proxy statement contained a recommendation by Standard's management favoring the merger as well as financial statements of Chadbourn prepared by its accountants, Peat Marwick.

---

4. (a) No solicitation subject to this regulation shall be made by means of any proxy statement, form of proxy, notice of meeting or other communication, written or oral, containing any statement which, at the time and in the light of the circumstances under which it is made, is false or misleading with respect to any material fact, or which omits to state any material fact necessary in order to make the statements therein not false or misleading or necessary to correct any statement in any earlier communication with respect to the solicitation of a proxy for the same meeting or subject matter which has become false or misleading.

17 C.F.R. § 240.14a–9(a) (1979).

Before the merger, Standard's stock traded at around $12.00 a share, although its book value was carried at approximately $21.00 a share, and Chadbourn's stock fluctuated between $8.00 and $14.00 a share. Standard's stockholders exchanged each share of Standard common for $1/10$ of a share of Chadbourn common, plus $1\frac{1}{2}$ shares of Chadbourn convertible, cumulative, preferred stock. The Chadbourn preferred was the main part of the package. According to the terms of the merger agreement, each share of Chadbourn preferred stock given in exchange was supposed to pay annual cash dividends of $.46^{2}/_{3}$ a share, and Chadbourn was supposed to redeem 20% of these preferred shares each year at $11.00 a share, beginning in 1975. Each preferred share carried a conversion privilege allowing the preferred stockholder to convert a share of preferred into $6/10$ of a share of Chadbourn common. The general purpose of the package appears to have been to give each Standard shareholder a set of Chadbourn securities with approximately the same market value as their Standard shares but with more liquidity and higher dividends.

Approximately a year after the merger, Chadbourn's sales of hosiery plummeted unexpectedly, and it suffered a loss of $17 million. This loss wiped out its retained earnings and left it with a capital deficit of $7 million. Chadbourn now was unable to redeem or pay dividends on the preferred stock. In October 1972, the former Standard stockholders sued Chadbourn, Standard, their management, their lawyers and the appellant, Peat, which was, as previously stated, the accounting firm that prepared and certified Chadbourn's financial statements in the proxy materials. Plaintiffs entered into a settlement agreement with the defendants other than Peat, under which the former Standard shareholders were awarded control of Chadbourn, renamed "Stanwood Corporation." The District Court did not take into account the value of the settlement received by the plaintiffs in determining damages against Peat. Since we reverse the findings of the District Court on liability, we need not reach questions concerning the measure of damages and the award of attorneys' fees.

B. Restrictions on the Use of Retained Earnings Contained in the Chadbourn Loan Agreements

The first restriction on retained earnings is in a 5–year term loan agreement Chadbourn made with three banks in September, 1969. Chadbourn borrowed $6 million from the banks repayable in installments over the 5–year period. In order to protect the banks, the loan agreement contained a provision which prohibited Chadbourn and its subsidiaries in any year during the term of the loan from redeeming or paying dividends "on its *capital* shares of any class" in an amount in excess of $2 million, less the amount of the repayments on the loan, plus future earnings after the 1968–1969 fiscal year.[5] These restrictions would apply to dividend payments on Chadbourn preferred shares issued to Standard shareholders

---

5. In August, 1967, at the beginning of Chadbourn's 1967–68 fiscal year, Chadbourn had retained earnings of $4.7 million. Its net earnings during the 1967–68 year were $1.6 million so that retained earnings in August, 1968, at the beginning of the fiscal year 1968–69 were approximately $6.3 million. Its net earnings during the 1968–69 fiscal year were $3.1 million so that retained earnings in August, 1969, at the beginning of the 1969–70 fiscal year were approximately $9.3 million. At this time stockholder equity, consisting of total capital of approximately $18.3 million plus these retained earnings, was $27.7 million.

(amounting annually to approximately $450,000) and would apply as well to any distributions to redeem these shares.

The second debt agreement was a little less restrictive. The second contractual restriction on paying out retained earnings is in another debt agreement which Chadbourn also entered into in 1969. Chadbourn borrowed $12.5 million in exchange for an issue of convertible, subordinated debentures. The effect of these restrictions on dividends and distributions was similar, except that under this agreement Chadbourn was free to use its 1968–69 net earnings of $3.1 million, as well as future earnings, for the payment of dividends and stock redemptions.

The net effect of both sets of restrictions on dividends and redemptions, when taken together, was that Chadbourn would either have to continue to make money or refinance its indebtedness in order to meet fully its future dividend and redemption obligations on the preferred stock issued to Standard's shareholders. As is explained above, when the bottom dropped out of its hosiery market and its retained earnings a year after the merger, it could do neither.

C. The Description of the Restrictions on Retained Earnings in the Proxy Statement

Standard's proxy statement dated March 27, 1970, contained a 35–page description of the terms of the transaction and its tax-free nature, comparative earnings and stock prices of Standard and Chadbourn and a description of their history, business, managements and properties. The text was followed by 18 pages of financial statements of both companies, including the opinions of Peat with respect to the Chadbourn financial statements and of Ernst & Ernst with respect to the Standard financial statements.

The plan for the exchange of Standard stock for Chadbourn stock was set out at pages 4–8 of the text under the heading "SUMMARY OF PLAN." Pages 6–7 of this portion of the proxy statement accurately describe the two sets of restrictions as follows:

> Under the provisions of a term loan with three banks maturing October 1, 1974, Chadbourn cannot, without the consent of such banks, [1] declare any dividend or [2] make any distribution (other than common stock dividends), or [3] acquire any of its stock if, after such action, the aggregate of all dividends (other than stock dividends), other distributions to stockholders and all amounts paid for the acquisition of its stock plus the amounts of all payments made on the term loan, would exceed $2,000,000 plus Chadbourn's consolidated net earnings since August 2, 1969. The Indenture dated as of March 15, 1969 hereinabove referred to contains certain restrictions on the payment of dividends on capital stock, however, such are less restrictive than those contained in the term loan agreement.

Chadbourn's financial statements as of August 2, 1969, and Peat's opinion, dated October 21, 1969, were published in the back of the March 27, 1970, Standard proxy statement. The liabilities and stockholders' equity side of the balance sheet was shown on page F–5 of the proxy statement. This page sets out amounts for current installments of long-term debt, and the non-current portion of long-term debt, "stockholders' equity," which referred in turn to certain notes, including footnote 7.

Footnote 7, paragraphs (c) and (d) erroneously described the two sets of restrictions as follows:

(c) As to the note payable to three banks, the Company has agreed to various restrictive provisions including those relating to maintenance of minimum stockholders' equity and working capital, the purchase, sale or encumbering of fixed assets, incurrance [sic] of indebtedness, the leasing of additional assets and the payment of dividends *on common stock* in excess of $2,000,000 plus earnings subsequent to August 2, 1969.

(d) * * * Further, the indenture has certain restrictive covenants but they are less restrictive than those contained in the note agreement with the three banks. (Emphasis added.)

The word "common" in paragraph (c) referring to the loan agreement was wrong because the relevant provision of the loan agreement restricted the use of retained earnings for the payment of dividends on "*capital* stock of any class," not just "common." Thus the restriction on retained earnings would apply to all distributions to pay dividends or redeem the preferred shares issued to Standard stockholders should they approve the merger.

D. Facts Respecting Peat's Negligence

The facts demonstrate that Peat's omissions were the result of negligence but did not arise from an intent to deceive, or *scienter,* as found by the District Court.

Peat failed to disclose fully in the financial statement the restrictive effect of the loan agreement and indenture on Chadbourn preferred stock. After each entry relating to long-term capitalization, the financial statement directs the attention of the reader to explanatory note 7. Note 7 alone pertains to Chadbourn's long-term debt. Missing from the note is any reference to limitations that the debt agreements placed on Chadbourn preferred stock.

Only in notes 7(c) and 7(d) does Peat mention the restrictive provisions. Note 7(c), which discusses the loan agreement, reports only that "the Company has agreed to various restrictive provisions including * * * the payment of dividends on common stock in excess of $2 million plus earnings subsequent to August 2, 1969." Note 7(d) describes the indenture. It says that "the indenture has certain restrictive covenants, but they are less restrictive than those contained in the [loan] agreement." Thus, there is no indication in either note that the long-term debt restrictions affected the redemption and earnings of preferred stock.

From notes 7(c) and 7(d), a reader easily could derive the following mistaken impression: The loan agreement contains certain restrictions on the payment of dividends by Chadbourn. As note 7(c) explicitly says, the loan agreement restrictions relate to the payment of dividends "on common stock." The indenture contains limitations that are "less restrictive" than those created by the loan agreement. Since the limitations of the loan agreement apply only to common stock, the reader mistakenly could reason that the "less restrictive" indenture constraints appear to have no broader sweep. What note 7 conveys to the reader is the erroneous notion that neither the loan agreement nor the indenture restrictions apply to Chadbourn preferred stock.

The remainder of the proxy solicitation does not entirely correct the misunderstanding created by the financial statement notes. Peat argues that the textual language from the body of the proxy statement, quoted above in subsection C, adequately advised Standard shareholders that long-term debt agreements restricted certain aspects of Chadbourn's preferred stock. We conclude, however, that contrary to Peat's claim, the text is equivocal.

The text states that Chadbourn cannot "declare any dividends" or "make any distributions" under certain conditions specified by the loan agreement. These phrases are placed under the heading "The Chadbourn Common Stock." It would not be irrational to conclude from the location of these statements that the restrictions applied solely to the common stock of Chadbourn. This conclusion would be confirmed by note 7(c), which explicitly states that the loan agreement restricts the payment of dividends on common stock. Moreover, under the section of the text labelled "Provisions Relating to the $.46$^{2}/_{3}$ Preferred Stock," there is no indication that any debt restrictions exist, much less that they apply to the dividends or redemption of preferred stock.

Nor does the language in the text regarding indenture restrictions correct the misleading impression of note 7(d). The text reports that the indenture contains "certain restrictions on the payment of dividends on capital stock." Like note 7(d), the text fails to mention restrictions on the redemption of Chadbourn preferred stock. The language regarding dividend payment restrictions on capital stock is found in the "Chadbourn Common Stock" section. Its location casts doubt on the argument that "capital stock," the restrictions on which are mentioned in part by the text, was meant in this context to include preferred stock. Adding to the doubt is the absence of any information about the indenture from the "Preferred Stock" section of the text. At best the textual discussion of indenture restrictions is equivocal regarding their reach.

The finding of the District Court that Peat acted with scienter in making the omissions is nevertheless clearly erroneous. We find in the record nothing to indicate that a desire to deceive, defraud or manipulate motivated Peat to omit from the financial statement information regarding the applicability of long-term debt restrictions. Indeed, Stanwood Corporation, the successor to Chadbourn controlled by the former Standard shareholders, hired and retained as vice president and treasurer the Peat associate, Hugh Freeze, who the shareholders' counsel now claim sought to defraud them. If the shareholders and their representatives really believed Freeze intended to defraud them, it seems doubtful that they would have put him in charge of the financial affairs of the corporation.

At most the evidence supports a finding that Peat acted negligently in preparing the financial statements. Peat became aware that note 7 incorrectly described the debt limitation several weeks before the merger vote occurred. The Standard proxy statement was mailed to its stockholders on March 27, 1970. Between March 23, 1970, and April 1, 1970, Chadbourn's outside counsel telephoned Freeze, the Peat manager in charge of the Chadbourn audit, and told him that a description of restrictions relating to Chadbourn's stock had been inserted in the forepart of the Standard proxy statement prior to mailing. The lawyer called to his attention the difference in the description in the proxy statement and the footnote, pointing out that the footnote said "common" rather than "capital stock of any class." In the course of this conversation, Freeze took a copy of the preliminary Standard proxy statement and noted the change by hand in note 7(c). Thereafter, footnote 7(c) was not amended, and no effort was made to call the discrepancy to the attention of Standard stockholders or officials. Freeze did not foresee that the bottom would drop out of Chadbourn's earnings and that what appeared to be a minor error at the time would become a major bone of contention.

The evidence simply suggests a mistake, an oversight, the failure to foresee a problem. We find nothing in the record indicating an intent to deceive or a motive for deception. J.B. Woolsey, Standard's vice president for financial affairs, and presumably other Standard officers, knew of the restrictions and recommended the merger anyway. No stockholder testified that he was deceived. An erroneous statement cannot *ipso facto* prove fraud, and here we find no evidence of anything other than a negligent error.

II. LIABILITY FOR NEGLIGENT MISREPRESENTATION UNDER SEC RULES 10b–5 AND 14a–9

In view of our conclusion that the District Court's findings of scienter are clearly erroneous, we reverse the imposition of liability under Rule 10b–5. In Ernst & Ernst v. Hochfelder, 425 U.S. 185 (1976), the Supreme Court settled the issue. It unequivocally held that liability under Rule 10b–5 requires "intentional misconduct." Id. at 201. The Court said that 10b–5 requires "intentional or willful conduct designed to deceive or defraud investors." Id. at 199.

We turn to the question of the standard of liability under Rule 14a–9 pertaining to statements made in proxy solicitations. There has been relatively little case law on the standard of liability following the Supreme Court decision in J.I. Case Co. v. Borak, 377 U.S. 426 (1964), which established a private right of action under 14(a) and Rule 14a–9. Two circuits have examined the issue. Both have prescribed a negligence standard for the corporation issuing the proxy statement. One held that the negligence standard also applies to outside, nonmanagement directors, Gould v. American-Hawaiian Steamship Co., 535 F.2d 761, 777–78 (3d Cir. 1976); and the other intimated in dicta, without deciding the issue, that a *scienter* standard probably should apply to outside directors and accountants, Gerstle v. Gamble-Skogmo, Inc., 478 F.2d 1281, 1300–1301 (2d Cir. 1973).

In view of the overall structure and collective legislative histories of the securities laws, as well as important policy considerations, we conclude that scienter should be an element of liability in private suits under the proxy provisions as they apply to outside accountants.

It is not simply a question of statutory interpretation. Federal courts created the private right of action under section 14, and they have a special responsibility to consider the consequences of their rulings and to mold liability fairly to reflect the circumstances of the parties. Although we are not called on in this case to decide the standard of liability of the corporate issuer of proxy material, we are influenced by the fact that the accountant here, unlike the corporate issuer, does not directly benefit from the proxy vote and is not in privity with the stockholder. Unlike the corporate issuer, the preparation of financial statements to be appended to proxies and other reports is the daily fare of accountants, and the accountant's potential liability for relatively minor mistakes would be enormous under a negligence standard. In contrast to section 12(2) of the 1933 Act which imposes liability for negligent misrepresentation in a prospectus, Rule 14a–9 does not require privity. In contrast to section 11 of the 1933 Act which imposes liability for negligent misrepresentation in registration statements, Rule 14a–9 does not require proof of actual investor reliance on the misrepresentation. Rule 14a–9, like 10b–5, substitutes the less exacting standard of materiality for reliance, TSC Ind., Inc. v. Northway, Inc., 426 U.S. 438 (1976), and in the instant case there was no proof of investor reliance on the notes to the financial statements which erroneously described the restriction on payment of dividends. We can see no reason for a different standard of liability for accountants under the proxy provisions than under 10(b).[6]

We may not end our consideration there, however. We must turn to the legislative history of the proxy provisions. Section 14(a) and Rule 14a–9 are silent regarding the proper standard of liability. The Senate Report to the 1934 Act, commonly known as the Fletcher Report, discussed the sort of proxy abuse that Congress was trying to stop, that of corporate officers using the proxy mechanism to ratify their own frauds upon the shareholders, or outsiders soliciting shareholders' approval to plunder a ripe company. The Report cited one example, * * *. The nature of each wrong deed depicted by the Report evidenced scienter.

An even more informative section of the Report is one describing the scope of 14(a):

> It is contemplated that the rules and regulations promulgated by the Commission will protect investors from *promiscuous* solicitation of their proxies, on the one hand, by irresponsible outsiders seeking to wrest control of a corporation away from honest and conscientious corporation officials; and, on the other hand, by *unscrupulous* corporate officials seeking to retain control of the management by *concealing* and *distorting* facts. (emphasis added)

Senate Committee on Banking & Currency, S.Rep. No. 1455, 73d Cong., 2d Sess. 77 (1934).

The words "unscrupulous," "concealing," and "distorting" all imply knowledge or scienter; and we interpret "promiscuous" to mean reckless. In

---

6. Indeed section 18 of the 1934 Act, dealing with misstatements in reports filed with the SEC, requires *both* scienter *and* reliance for civil liability. Section 14 is much more similar to section 18 than it is to section 11 of the 1933 Act. Under the current regulatory scheme, proxy materials must be filed in advance of the solicitation with the SEC, see 17 C.F.R. § 240.14A–6, and are therefore subject to the provisions of section 18. In contrast, proxy solicitations *per se* do not put the solicitor within the ambit of section 11.

The District Court found that the plaintiffs could not recover under section 18 because they had not shown the reliance which is required by that section. This was, of course, true. At the same time, the defendants argue that the specific remedy provided by section 18 precludes implication of a cause of action under either section 10 or section 14, when the requirements of section 18 are not met. Only one circuit has directly discussed this question, finding that inability to satisfy the requirements of section 18 does not bar a less restrictive implied action brought under section 10, Ross v. A.H. Robins Co., Inc., 607 F.2d 545 (2d Cir.1979). This question was not specifically addressed by the District Court and, because we find that in all events, the plaintiffs cannot recover under sections 10 or 14, we need not decide this question here.

addition the characterization of irresponsible outsiders trying to "wrest control * * * from *honest* * * * corporate officials," implies dishonesty—and hence scienter—on the part of the outsiders. Consequently, the Report leads us to believe that its authors contemplated that 14(a) would be applied only against the knowing or reckless wrongdoing of outsiders.

The few times the proxy section was discussed in debate paint a similar picture of the type of misconduct against which 14(a) was directed. Roosevelt's aid, Corcoran, who drafted the original version of the 1934 Act, spoke of "*unscrupulous* proxy committees" (emphasis added). See 78 Cong. Rec. 6544 (1934). Everett Dirksen, then a Representative from Illinois, stated, "[t]here is little doubt that there has been grave abuse of this authority to solicit proxies and the use of such proxies for *manipulation*" (emphasis added) 78 Cong.Rec. 7961 (1934). Further debate indicates Congress' concern that directors and officers should not be able to complete their fraud upon a company by means of a proxy solicitation that seeks ratification of their illegal acts. See 78 Cong.Rec. 7712–14 (1934). Congressman Pettengill of Indiana stated during Committee hearings exactly what he thought such undesirable activity amounted to: "larceny." See Hearings on H.R. 7852 Before the House Comm. on Interstate & Foreign Commerce, 73d Cong., 2d Sess. 480 (1934). The common denominator of all these depictions of the problem is wrongdoing with some degree of knowledge, *i.e.* scienter; and nowhere, not in the committee reports nor in the House or Senate debates, does it appear that Congress desired to protect the investor against negligence of accountants as well.

Another important consideration is Congressional intent regarding subsequent amendments that are indirectly linked to 14(a). In passing the Williams Act of 1968 governing tender offers, Congress expressed the desire that proxy statements and tender offers be governed by the *same* rules and regulations. This would logically extend to standards of liability. Because 14(e) pertaining to tender offers requires scienter, we believe there is a strong policy reason for imposing a similar standard on 14(a).

According to the House Report for the Williams Act, "[t]he cash tender offer is similar to a proxy contest, and the committee could find no reason to continue the present gap in the federal securities laws which leaves the cash tender offer exempt from disclosure provisions." H.R.Rep. No. 1711, 90th Cong., 2d Sess., reprinted in [1968] U.S.Code Cong. & Ad.News 2811, 2813. Tender offers and proxy solicitations are two alternative methods of achieving the same result, corporate control; and Congress perceived that both were subject to the same type of abuse. It therefore acted to eliminate an existing loophole in the old law so that wrongful usurpation of control would not escape securities regulation whenever one combatant chooses to seize control by tender offer rather than by proxy fight. Id.

Senator Williams of New Jersey, the sponsor of the bill, stated

What this bill would do is to provide the *same kind of disclosure requirements which now exist*, for example, *in contests through proxies* for controlling ownership in a company." (emphasis added)

113 Cong.Rec. 24665 (1967).

Senator Javits echoed this view.

The Senator [Williams] represents to the Senate, and I accept his representation fully, that this is analogous to the proxy rules. Id.

And Senator Williams repeated that "[t]his legislation is patterned on the present law and regulations which govern proxy contests." Id. Logically the above testimony implies similar standards of liability for both proxy statements and tender offers. Otherwise some misleading solicitations which would trigger liability if shaped in the form of one transaction, would be immune if shaped as the other, or *vice versa.*

The language of the Williams Act clearly demonstrates that Congress envisioned scienter to be an element of 14(e). Congress used the words "fraudulent," "deceptive," and "manipulative." This language indicates, in light of *Ernst & Ernst,* that 14(e) requires scienter. Although *Ernst & Ernst* was decided several years after the enactment of 14(e), we are bound by its holding that Congress intends scienter when it uses the above quoted language.

We conclude that 14(a) and 14(e) should be governed by the same standard of liability insofar as accountants' liability is concerned, and that an action under 14(a) requires proof of scienter. Finding no evidence of scienter, we reverse the imposition of liability under 14(a) and Rule 14a–9.

* * *

THE REQUIRED CULPABILITY OF THE DEFENDANT UNDER SECTIONS 14(a) AND 14(e)

Section 14(a) of the 1934 Act simply authorizes the Commission to adopt such rules and regulations relating to proxy solicitations as are "necessary or appropriate in the public interest or for the protection of investors." There are no substantive provisions whatever in the statute regarding the form or content of any proxy statement. Rule 14a–9, which is quoted in the *Adams* case, merely prohibits any "false or misleading" statement in a proxy statement, without any hint as to what the required culpability of a defendant must be in order for him to become liable for a violation of that rule. In Gerstle v. Gamble-Skogmo, Inc.,[1] the Second Circuit held, in an opinion by Judge Friendly, that simple negligence is a sufficient basis for liability under Rule 14a–9, at least so far as the corporate issuer of the proxy statement is concerned.[2] Judge Friendly noted the absence of any "evil-sounding language" in either Section 14(a) or Rule 14a–9 and explained the basis of the decision as follows:

"In contrast [to the language of § 10(b)], the scope of the rulemaking authority granted under section 14(a) is broad, extending to all proxy regulation 'necessary or appropriate in the public interest or for the protection of investors' and not limited by any words connoting fraud or deception. This language suggests that rather than emphasizing the prohibition of fraudulent conduct on the part of insiders to a securities transaction, as we think section 10(b) does, in section 14(a) Congress was somewhat more concerned with protection of the outsider whose proxy is being solicited. Indeed, it was this aspect of the statute that the Supreme Court emphasized in recognizing a private right of action for violation of section 14(a) in *Borak,* 377 U.S. at 431–432. We note also that while an open-ended reading of Rule 10b–5 would render the express civil liability provisions of the securities acts largely superfluous, and be inconsistent with the limitations Congress built into these sections, * * * a reading of Rule 14a–9 as imposing liability

---

1. 478 F.2d 1281 (2d Cir.1973).

2. See, also, Gould v. American Hawaiian Steamship Co., 535 F.2d 761 (3d Cir. 1976); National Home Products, Inc. v. Gray, 416 F.Supp. 1293 (D.Del.1976).

without scienter in a case like the present is completely compatible with the statutory scheme." [3]

As Judge Friendly points out, there would hardly be any difference between this standard and that of intentional misstatement if the corporation is to be charged with the knowledge of all of its officers and employees. However, he suggests, without definitively deciding the question, that perhaps the corporation would be put in the shoes of those charged with drafting the proxy statement and might be exonerated if they made no intentional misstatements and were not negligent in drafting the document. It should be noted that the *Adams* case is not necessarily inconsistent with the *Gerstle* case. Judge Friendly there limited his holding to the liability of the corporate issuer of the proxy statement and did not rule on the culpability required with respect to a collateral participant, whereas in the *Adams* case the Third Circuit limited its holding to the fault required of such a collateral participant (i.e., the accountant who had certified the financial statements included in the proxy statement). Is there a sound basis for this distinction, if it is one? The shareholders of the corporation, upon whom any loss will fall if it is held liable, would seem to be less at fault than anyone else in any way associated with the proxy statement or the transaction to which it relates.

In Shidler v. All American Life & Financial Corp.,[4] the Eighth Circuit held that there was no liability without fault in an action under Section 14(a) (the trial court had expressly found in that case that there was no negligence, although there was a material misstatement in the proxy statement). The court said: "A strict liability rule would impose liability for fully innocent misstatements. It is too blunt a tool to ferret out the kind of deceptive practices Congress sought to prevent in enacting section 14(a)." [5]

Is there any justification for a distinction between the liability of a corporation under Rule 10b–5 for issuing a misleading offering circular (in a transaction exempt from registration under the 1933 Act) and its liability for issuing a misleading proxy statement in a transaction that is functionally indistinguishable? The language of the sections may be different, as pointed out by Judge Friendly (and as relied upon exclusively by the Supreme Court in the *Aaron* case), but after all Congress didn't create any civil liability for violation of either one; the courts did that.

Section 14(e) of the 1934 Act prohibits, in connection with a tender offer, any person from "mak[ing] any [false or misleading statement], *or * * * [engaging] in any fraudulent, deceptive, or manipulative acts or practices." The court in the *Adams* case construed this language as requiring "scienter" because of the use of the words fraudulent, deceptive and manipulative. It said that, under the *Ernst & Ernst* case, Congress "intends scienter when it uses the above quoted language." Also, in Chris-Craft Industries, Inc. v. Piper Aircraft Corporation [6] (a decision later reversed on other grounds by the Supreme Court in the *Piper* case printed above in Chapter 13), the Second Circuit indicated that it would apply the "scienter" or "recklessness" standard applicable under Rule 10b–5 to an action for damages under Section 14(e). The court said: "The function of what has been called the 'scienter' requirement is to confine the imposition of liability to those whose conduct has been sufficiently culpable to justify the penalty sought to be exacted. * * * A knowing or reckless failure to discharge these obligations [of disclosure] constitutes sufficiently culpable

3. 478 F.2d at 1299.

4. 775 F.2d 917 (8th Cir.1985).

5. 775 F.2d at 927.

6. 480 F.2d 341 (2d Cir.1973), cert. denied 414 U.S. 924 (1973).

conduct to justify judgment under Rule 10b–5 or § 14(e) for damages or other appropriate relief against the wrongdoer." [7]

Both of these cases were decided, however, without the benefit of the Supreme Court's simple minded approach to the interpretation of Section 17(a) of the 1933 Act in the *Aaron* case. Section 14(e) prohibits in the *disjunctive* the making of any false or misleading statement or engaging in the "evil sounding" practices which were declared in the *Ernst & Ernst* case to connote scienter. In the *Aaron* case, the Supreme Court construed language in clauses (1) and (2) of Section 17(a), which is in substance identical to these two provisions in Section 14(e), and held that clause (1) (with the evil-sounding language) required scienter but that clause (2) did not. What state of mind the defendant must have in order for the plaintiff to sustain a damage action under Section 14(e) is therefore highly doubtful. Since virtually no actions for damages, if any, have succeeded under Section 14(e), and it is questionable whether such a cause of action even exists, such subsidiary questions may not be resolved for a considerable period of time.

See Junewicz, The Appropriate Limits of Section 14(e) of the Securities Exchange Act of 1934, 62 Tex.L.Rev. 1171 (1984); Telly, Proxies and the Modern Corporation: Scienter Under Sections 14(a) and 10(b) of the Securities Exchange Act, 19 Tulsa L.J. 491 (1984); Lowenstein, Section 14(e) of the Williams Act and Rule 10b–5 Comparisons, 71 Geo.L.Rev. 1311 (1983); Silberberg and Pollack, Are the Courts Expanding the Meaning of "Manipulation" Under Federal Securities Law?, 11 Sec.Reg.L.J. 265 (1983); Brunelle, Market Regulation: The Lost Tender Offer Opportunity and Section 14(e), 9 Sec.Reg. L.J. 285 (1981); Block and Barton, The Business Judgment Rule as Applied to Stockholder Proxy Derivative Suits Under the Securities Exchange Act, 8 Sec. Reg.L.J. 99 (1980).

7. 480 F.2d at 363.

Chapter 15

CONDUCT CREATING LIABILITY

Statutes and Regulations

Securities Act of 1933, §§ 11, 12(2), 17(a).

Securities Exchange Act of 1934, §§ 10(b), 14(a), 14(e), 21(a).

Rules 10b–5, 14a–9, 175, 3b–6.

FEIT v. LEASCO DATA PROCESSING EQUIPMENT CORP.

United States District Court, E.D., New York, 1971.
332 F.Supp. 544.

WEINSTEIN, DISTRICT JUDGE. This case raises the question of the degree of candor required of issuers of securities who offer their shares in exchange for those of other companies in take-over operations. Defendants' registration statement was, we find, misleading in a material way. While disclosing masses of facts and figures, it failed to reveal one critical consideration that weighed heavily with those responsible for the issue— the substantial possibility of being able to gain control of some hundred million dollars of assets not required for operating the business being acquired.

Using a statement to obscure, rather than reveal, in plain English, the critical elements of a proposed business deal cannot be countenanced under the securities regulation acts. The defense that no one could be certain of precisely how much was involved in the way of realizable assets is not acceptable. The prospective purchaser of a new issue of securities is entitled to know what the deal is all about. Given an honest and open statement, adequately warning of the possibilities of error and miscalculation and not designed for puffing, the outsider and the insider are placed on more equal grounds for arms length dealing. Such equalization of bargaining power through sharing of knowledge in the securities market is a basic national policy underlying the federal securities laws.

I. PROCEEDINGS

In this class action plaintiff seeks damages resulting from alleged misrepresentations and omissions in a registration statement prepared in conjunction with a 1968 offering of a "package" of preferred shares and warrants of Leasco Data Processing Equipment Corporation (Leasco) in exchange for the common stock of Reliance Insurance Company (Reliance). He is a former shareholder of Reliance who exchanged his shares for the Leasco package. Suit was commenced in October 1969 on behalf of all Reliance shareholders who accepted the exchange offer between August 19, and November 1, 1968.

It is alleged that Leasco (1) failed to disclose an approximate amount of "surplus surplus" held by Reliance and (2) failed to fully and accurately disclose its intentions with regard to reorganizing Reliance or using other

969

techniques for removing surplus surplus after it had acquired control. These failures, it is claimed, represented material misrepresentations or omissions in violation of Sections 11, 12(2), and 17(a) of the Securities Exchange Act of 1933 * * *, Sections 10(b) and 14(e) of the Securities Exchange Act of 1934 * * *, and Securities and Exchange Commission Rule X–10B–5 * * *.

Defendants are Leasco, the issuer; Saul P. Steinberg, Leasco's chief executive officer; Bernard L. Schwartz, Leasco's President; Robert B. Hodes, Leasco's general counsel and a director; and White, Weld & Co. and Lehman Brothers, the dealer-managers. In addition to denials, the answers raise a number of defenses.

II. THE EXCHANGE OFFER

During the period August 19, through November 1, 1969 Leasco offered one share of convertible preferred stock and one-half warrant of Leasco in exchange for each share of Reliance common stock tendered. The preferred shares offered carried a $2.20 annual dividend and a conversion value of $55 if converted into common stock. The warrants permitted the holder to purchase Leasco common stock for $87 per share at any time up to June 4, 1978.

Reliance common shares had a market value of approximately $30 in December of 1967. As word of an impending take-over attempt spread, the price rose gradually to a high of $99⅞ during the tender offer period. The price of Leasco common shares was also rising during this period. On August 16, 1968, the last trading day before the exchange offer was effective, Leasco common stock closed at $87⅝ while its warrants were listed at a high bid of $43. Reliance shares were then selling at $66¼.

By September 13, 1968, 3,994,042 shares of Reliance, amounting to 72% of those outstanding, had been tendered and Leasco had obtained control of Reliance. Leasco ultimately acquired 97% of Reliance's common stock by the termination of the tender offer on November 1, 1968.

III. SURPLUS SURPLUS

A. *Definition of Surplus Surplus*

Reliance's surplus surplus is the central element in this litigation. Leasco's desire to acquire it provided much of the original impetus for the exchange offer. Lack of disclosure of facts relating to the amount of surplus surplus and Leasco's intentions concerning its use, as well as the materiality of those omissions provide the basis of plaintiff's complaint. Finally, the method and difficulty of ascertaining its amount is critical to the defendants' affirmative defense. We cannot proceed without examining the concept.

Reliance is a fire and casualty insurance company subject to stringent regulation by the Insurance Commissioner of Pennsylvania. Such a company is required by the regulatory scheme to maintain sufficient surplus to guarantee the integrity of its insurance operations. Such "required surplus" cannot be separated from the insurance business of the company. That portion of surplus not required in insurance operations has been referred to as surplus surplus. In a widely relied upon report to the New York Insurance Department, the matter was summed up as follows:

"The 'required surplus' is one that will be adequate to cover for a reasonable period of time any losses and expenses larger than those predicted and any declines in asset values, including all chance variations in the crucial factors of the operation. Any surplus beyond this cover is 'surplus surplus' which, by definition, is unneeded; it may be treated quite differently in the process of regulation." State of New York Insurance Department, Report of the Special Committee on Insurance Holding Companies at 43 (Feb. 15, 1968) (hereinafter referred to as Insurance Department Report).

Simply put, surplus surplus is the highly liquid assets of an insurance company which can be utilized in non-regulated enterprises. While the importance of the concept has only recently received full recognition the idea is not new; it was previously referred to as "redundant capital."

Insurance companies are not generally permitted to engage in noninsurance business activities. If, therefore, surplus surplus is to be of any practical use it must be separated from the insurance operation with its concomitant regulatory restrictions.

In 1967 Carter, Berlind & Weill undertook a study of fire and casualty companies. The result was a report by Edward Netter submitted in August 1967. It develops the concept of "The Financial Services Holding Company," envisioning modification of the corporate structure of the typical fire and casualty company to permit more flexible utilization of its resources—particularly surplus surplus. Netter postulated a one-stop, comprehensive financial institution servicing virtually all of the consumer's financial needs. Aggressive use of capital redundancy (surplus surplus) was a critical element in Netter's analysis. He estimated Reliance's capital redundancy at $80,000,000 as of December 31, 1966.

Leasco's interest was aroused by the Netter Reports. Michael Gibbs, Leasco's Vice President for Corporate Planning, subsequently prepared a "Confidential Analysis of a Fire and Casualty Company" based "to a large extent" on Reliance. He worked from the Netter Report to illustrate the specific benefits to Leasco of increased earnings per share and leverage potential in acquiring and reorganizing a fire and casualty company with large surplus surplus. His initial idea was to establish a parent holding company to which the fire and casualty company (Reliance) could transfer its surplus surplus—freeing it from regulatory restriction—while continuing to operate as an insurance subsidiary. In his opinion such an acquisition was potentially extremely valuable to Leasco. * * *

Gibbs estimated Reliance's surplus surplus as $125,000,000 as of June 30, 1967 or $100,000,000 as of the end of 1967.

These two documents, along with the Insurance Department Report, provided the impetus for Leasco's take-over bid. Steinberg considered surplus surplus "important to Leasco" and A. Addison Roberts, Reliance's President, came away from negotiations with the impression that "one important aspect of Reliance that commended itself to Leasco was Reliance's surplus surplus." Leasco protected its interest in the surplus surplus by including a provision in an August 1, 1968 agreement with Reliance requiring its management to provide the maximum amount then available to the holding company Leasco would form.

B. *Disclosures Concerning Surplus Surplus*

The only statement in the prospectus with regard to surplus surplus appears on page five. It neither mentions the amounts that Leasco's management had in mind nor suggests the importance of Reliance's possible surplus surplus. It reads:

"The Company [Leasco] believes that this Exchange Offer is consistent with the announced intention of the Reliance management to form a holding company to become the parent of Reliance. That intention was communicated to Reliance stockholders on May 15, 1968 by A. Addison Roberts, the president of Reliance, who wrote that the holding company concept would serve the interests of Reliance and all its stockholders 'by providing more flexible operations, freedom of diversification and opportunities for more profitable utilization of financial resources.' The Company supports those objectives and intends to do all it can to promote their realization as soon as practicable. * * * Reliance will diligently pursue its previously announced intention to form a holding company which Reliance will provide with the maximum amount of funds legally available which is consistent with Reliance's present level of net premium volume. * * *"

C. *Parties' Contentions With Regard to Surplus Surplus*

Plaintiff contends that anything as important to the overall transaction as the amount of surplus surplus should have been disclosed by some sort of approximation. He asserts that such a computation could, in fact, have been made by the techniques used by Netter and Gibbs with information in Leasco's possession or that sufficient additional data could have been obtained to arrive at a reliable estimate. He further claims that while Leasco disclosed its intention to form a holding company to make use of Reliance's resources, it should also have disclosed that Leasco was considering other plans for separating surplus surplus from the insurance operation by reorganization and liquidation of Reliance or by declaration of a special dividend.

Defendants, in contrast, maintain that such omissions were not material because

"* * * the stockholders who exchanged Reliance shares for the Leasco package would not have been deterred from doing so by an estimate of surplus surplus, but rather would have been made all the more anxious to tender."

This belief stems from their perception that a large block of liquid assets in the hands of an aggressive acquisition-oriented company like Leasco would have made the Leasco package even more attractive than Reliance shares. They also assert that such an inclusion would have been "bullish" in violation of SEC standards—it would have made the prospectus a selling document.

Defendants' second principal argument is that surplus surplus could not have been calculated by Leasco because an accurate estimate required (1) access to Reliance's financial data, (2) the judgment of its management, and (3) the opinion of the insurance commissioner, all of which were denied

Leasco by the hostility of Reliance's management and its attempts to obstruct the take-over bid.

Finally, defendants contend that any other proposals for removing surplus surplus from Reliance were simply matters being considered by counsel. They never reached the level of a specific plan by Leasco during the pendency of the exchange offer.

D. *Computation of Surplus Surplus*

The problem and the variety of methods of determining surplus surplus were discussed in the New York Insurance Department Report in the context of how an insurance department should determine what is "required surplus." * * *

According to defendants, the result of this pervasive feeling of uncertainty about the accuracy of the estimates put forward by Netter and Gibbs, or any estimate, was that none of the principals in the exchange offer ever calculated surplus surplus, commissioned anyone to compute it, or even attempted to estimate it. Nor did the underwriters attempt at any time to obtain an estimate from Reliance. In fact, they did not even communicate with Reliance.

This is not to suggest that no estimate of surplus surplus was available to Leasco during the negotiations and exchange offer period—the Netter Report had estimated it at $80 million and Gibbs had indicated $100 and $125 million as his approximations. A range of $50–$125 million was discussed at meetings between Reliance and Leasco in October 1968. Leasco simply, according to defendants' testimony, considered these estimates speculative in light of their then state of knowledge of Reliance.

Nor should it be inferred that an estimate could not have been obtained at least by Roberts, who was, of course, privy to Reliance's data. He stated bluntly that he could have made such a calculation "damn quickly" if given a reason to do it. He had not calculated it because he was never presented with a specific need to do so. No one from either Leasco or the underwriters ever asked him to calculate surplus surplus during the pendency of the exchange offer, but he *could* have done so if asked. Whether he *might* or *would* have is one of the subsidiary issues in this litigation.

IV. BACKGROUND OF THE EXCHANGE OFFER

* * *

During the exchange period discussions were carried on between Hodes, Leasco's counsel, and Peter Korsan, counsel for Reliance, regarding methods of ultimately separating Reliance from its surplus surplus, and, if possible, effecting a tax savings for Leasco. Roberts was aware of these discussions. In the course of these meetings a range of $50–$125 million of surplus surplus was discussed. The figure was, however, apparently not Korsan's. During this period each of the principals was conducting an independent legal and factual investigation of reorganization schemes, holding company concepts, and tax consequences to Leasco. In at least one instance Korsan had discussions with the general counsel for the Pennsylvania Insurance Department in connection with formation of a holding company. In a memorandum to Roberts dated September 27, 1968 Korsan estimated the maximum surplus which could be distributed to a holding company by way of dividend under Pennsylvania law would be $125 million, but Leasco was not, according to defendants' testimony, made privy to this estimate.

* * *

V. THE POST EXCHANGE OFFER PERIOD

After November 1, both management teams continued their studies of alternatives for reorganizing Reliance. Korsan met with a representative of the Insurance Department on November 14 and discussed a range of surplus surplus. On December 20, 1968, however, the Insurance Department was as yet uncertain as to how determination of surplus surplus related to actuarial studies. Reliance had not obtained approval for separation of a specific amount.

A. *The January 1969 Registration Statement*

Highly significant with respect to Leasco's claims that it could give no estimate of surplus surplus was the fact that it did just that a few months after the tender period ended. It did so with no more data than it had during the exchange offer period.

Leasco filed a Form S–1 Registration Statement with the SEC on January 31, 1969 with a prospectus dated February 3, 1969. This registered various securities to be issued in the future among which were the common shares which could be obtained upon exercise of the warrants contained in the exchange package. The prospectus quite properly discussed Leasco's recently acquired insurance business and the plan for reorganizing Reliance to Leasco's benefit:

"Reliance and the Company are in the process of seeking to cause a reorganization of Reliance, subject to regulatory approvals, the effect of which will be to eliminate minority interests and to make available to the Company, for use in its various business and acquisition activities, *approximately $125,000,000 of excess surplus of Reliance. It is the opinion of Leasco that this amount represents funds which Reliance has on hand in excess of the legal requirements of its business.* No assurance can be given that such excess funds will ultimately be made available to the Company in such amount or that if so made available that such funds will be profitably utilized by the Company." (emphasis added).

This paragraph was also included in a draft of a preliminary prospectus prepared in June of 1969, but never made effective.

Barely three months after the termination of the exchange offer when Leasco sought to sell its own shares, rather than acquire Reliance's, it included the type of qualified approximation of surplus surplus which plaintiff contends was material to the August 19, 1968 exchange offer. Leasco's lawyer, Hodes, sought to justify this surprising change in position by testifying that the inclusion resulted from the development of a "decent working relationship." He further testified that this new relationship had conferred previously denied access to Reliance and the Insurance Commissioner and that both were consulted before including the estimates.

The Court has concluded, however, that Hodes' recollection is not accurate. Roberts was not consulted. He acquiesced after the paragraph on surplus surplus had been written by the same Leasco personnel who had participated in drafting the exchange offer prospectus. * * *

VI. THE DEALER MANAGERS' ROLE

* * *

Counsel for the dealer managers, Bell, Boyd, Lloyd, Haddad & Burns of Chicago, examined the corporate records of Leasco, its corporate minutes, director actions and basic contracts. Jack M. Whitney, II, a former SEC Commissioner, was the lawyer primarily in charge of the dealer manager's duties. He participated in the extensive "due diligence meetings" conducted in New York where the preliminary prospectus was examined. When the subject of Reliance's intention to form a holding company arose during these meetings Whitney became involved in a discussion of surplus surplus. He was admittedly uninformed about the concept and those present at the meeting, particularly Stone of White, Weld, undertook to edify him. Following intensive exploration of the concept and the limitations inherent in attempting to approximate it, he rendered an opinion that an estimate could not properly be included in the prospectus.

On August 13, 1968—barely six days before the registration statement became effective—Whitney received yet further confirmation of his opinion of July in the form of a copy of a letter from Wilkie, Farr & Gallagher to the SEC. It reads:

> "Certified financial statements of Reliance Insurance Company are not included in the Amendment since *that company has continued to refuse to cooperate* in the making of the Exchange Offer. Although the Reliance Insurance Company management is not actively opposing the Exchange Offer they have expressly declined to support or recommend it and have accordingly declined to furnish information in connection with this Registration Statement." (Emphasis supplied.)

On August 21 and September 18, 1969, Whitney sent a written favorable opinion to the dealer managers regarding the accuracy and completeness of the registration which became effective August 19, 1968.

The position of the dealer managers that surplus surplus should not be estimated was, the Court concludes, based upon information furnished by Leasco that Reliance continued to refuse to cooperate. This was not true. Roberts and Reliance had not been asked to confirm estimates after August 1st when the probabilities of a successful take-over became increasingly great. But the dealer managers were not aware that such cooperation was available.

* * *

VIII. DISCLOSURE

A. *Disclosure Policy*

The keystone of the Securities Act of 1933, and of the entire legislative scheme of the securities laws, is disclosure. * * *

B. *Effective Disclosure*

The ultimate goal of the Securities Act is, of course, investor protection. Effective disclosure is merely a means. The entire legislative scheme can be frustrated by technical compliance with the requirements of the Securities and Exchange Commission's Form S–1 for preparation of registration statements in the absence of any real intent to communicate. It is for this reason that the SEC, through its rule making power, has consistently required "clearly understandable" prospectuses. The Wheat Report at 78.

Unfortunately, the results have not always reflected these efforts. "[E]ven when an investor [is] presented with an accurate prospectus prior to his purchase, the presentation in most instances tend[s] to discourage reading by all but the most knowledgeable and tenacious." Knauss, A Reappraisal of the Role of Disclosure, 62 Mich.L.Rev. 607, 618–619 (1964). These documents are often drafted so as to be comprehensible to only a minute part of the investing public.

* * *

In at least some instances, what has developed in lieu of the open disclosure envisioned by the Congress is a literary art form calculated to communicate as little of the essential information as possible while exuding an air of total candor. Masters of this medium utilize turgid prose to enshroud the occasional critical revelation in a morass of dull, and—to all but the sophisticates—useless financial and historical data. In the face of such obfuscatory tactics the common or even the moderately well informed investor is almost as much at the mercy of the issuer as was his pre-SEC parent. He cannot by reading the prospectus discern the merit of the offering.

The instant case provides a useful example. Ignoring, for the moment, the alleged omissions which are the subject of the plaintiff's complaint, the passage in which Leasco's intentions with regard to surplus surplus are "disclosed" in the short excerpt set out at page 984 [972], supra. This revelation, while probably technically accurate with regard to Leasco's then intentions respecting surplus surplus, was hardly calculated to apprise the owner of shares of Reliance common stock that Reliance held a large pool of cash or near-cash assets which were legally and practically unnecessary for the efficient operation of the insurance business, and that Leasco intended to remove those assets "as soon as practicable." More important, it does not reveal Leasco's estimates of the extent of those assets. A conscientious effort by the issuer and its counsel would have produced a more direct, informative and candid paragraph about Leasco's intended reorganization of Reliance. They might have effectively disclosed, in understandable prose—as they did in January of 1969—the essence of the plan to the shareholders they were soliciting.

Disclosure to Whom?

The view that prospectuses should be intelligible to the average small investor as well as the professional analyst, immediately raises the question of what substantive standard of disclosure must be maintained. The legal standard is that all "material" facts must be accurately disclosed. But to whom must the fact have material significance?

In an industry in which there is an unmistakable "trend toward a greater measure of professionalism * * * with the accompanying demand for more information about issuers" "a pragmatic balance must be struck between the needs of the unsophisticated investor and those of the knowledgeable student of finance." The Wheat Report at 9–10. There are three distinct classes of investors who must be informed by the prospectus: (1)

the amateur who reads for only the grosser sorts of disclosures; (2) the professional advisor and manager who studies the prospectus closely and makes his decisions based on the insights he gains from it; and (3) the securities analyst who uses the prospectus as one of many sources in an independent investigation of the issuer.

The proper resolution of the various interests lies in the inclusion of a clearly written narrative statement outlining the major aspects of the offering and particularly speculative elements, as well as detailed financial information which will have meaning only to the expert. Requiring inclusion of such technical data benefits amateurs, as well as experts, because of the advice many small investors receive and the extent to which the market reflects professional judgments. The Wheat Report at 52. Such "[e]xpert sifters, distillers, and weighers are essential for an informed body of investors". Cohen, "Truth in Securities" Revisited, 79 Harv.L.Rev. 1340, 1353 (1966).

* * *

The significance of these observations is that the objectives of full disclosure can be fully achieved only by complete revelation of facts which would be material to the sophisticated investor or the securities professional not just the average common shareholder. But, at the same time, the prospectus must not slight the less experienced. They are entitled to have within the four corners of the document an intelligible description of the transaction.

* * *

IX. SECTION 11

Section 11(a) of the Securities Act of 1933 provides for civil liability for misstatements and omissions in a registration statement. * * *

A. *The Alleged Omissions*

* * *

(2) Failure to Include an Estimate of Surplus Surplus.

The failure to include an estimate of surplus surplus raises a more serious question. There is no doubt that Leasco had in its possession at least three estimates of Reliance's surplus surplus—$80,000,000 as of December 31, 1966 contained in the Netter Report and $125,000,000 or $100,000,000, at June 30th and December 31, 1967 respectively, both approximated in the Gibbs Memorandum. In addition they had available the rules of thumb for calculation contained in the New York Insurance Department Report. Leasco could have used these estimates or commissioned an independent computation based on public information. This figure could have been included with the sort of qualifying statement included in the January, 1969 prospectus. Whether the failure to do so places liability on the defendants under Section 11 is the question now presented.

B. *Materiality*

Only if the omission complained of is "material" within the meaning of Section 11 can liability be found. The SEC has defined the term by looking to what a reasonably prudent investor reasonably ought to know before buying a security. * * *

* * * It is clear, however, that facts other than the condition of the issuer bearing on the value, *qua* price, of the securities in question must be disclosed with the same scrupulousness. The issuer must disclose any fact "which in reasonable and objective contemplation *might* affect the value of the corporation's stock or securities". Kohler v. Kohler Co., 319 F.2d 634, 642 (7th Cir.1963) (emphasis added). * * * *BarChris* cannot be read as permitting exclusion of important facts merely because they involve the condition of the company being taken over rather than the issuer since these facts will bear on the relative value of the issuer's securities.

Some probability that the investor's decision would be affected by disclosure is a prerequisite to a finding of materiality. The degree of probability that it would have such an impact has been differently stated by the courts. They have focused on the effect on the reasonable purchaser, variously asking whether he "might" or "would" or "might well have been" affected by the information; they have asked whether it is "reasonably certain" that the information would have had a "substantial effect" or whether it "might" have had a "significant propensity" to affect him.
* * *

A fair summary of the rule stated in terms of probability is that a fact is proved to be material when it is more probable than not that a significant number of traders would have wanted to know it before deciding to deal in the security at the time and price in question. What is statistically significant will vary with the legal situation. Cf. Rosado v. Wyman, 322 F.Supp. 1173, 1180–1181 (E.D.N.Y.1970), aff'd 437 F.2d 619 (2d Cir.1970). Being a formal and legally required document, a prospectus must satisfy a high standard of disclosure—i.e., disclosure is required when only a relatively small percentage of traders would want to know before making a decision. Anything in the order of 10% of either the number of potential traders or those potentially making 10% of the volume of sales would seem to more than suffice.
* * *

The information with respect to the availability of tens of millions of dollars of surplus surplus is so significant that under any test proposed it is material. A substantial percentage of the reasonable persons holding shares of Reliance would want to know what Leasco's estimate and plans were respecting this asset before deciding to exchange on the terms offered. It would be unrealistic to expect an average shareholder of Reliance to know what the surplus surplus position of his company was; no proof was submitted suggesting that he would know this. Leasco did have this information as the result of its own detailed studies which had required a substantial outlay of money and executive time.
* * *

The size and availability of this resource was so important that Leasco included a clause in the August 1, 1968 contract which was intended to protect Leasco's interest in the surplus surplus after the takeover was consummated. Having relinquished control of the insurance operation for five years, Leasco simply could not afford the risk that the critical objective of the whole deal could be frustrated by a recalcitrant Reliance management.

The significance of this intense interest in surplus surplus is that by failure to disclose the size of the fund Leasco hoped to acquire, it effectively denied the Reliance shareholders knowledge of one of the principal factors underlying the transaction. This insufficiency prevented accurate evaluation of the degree of interest of Leasco. Knowledge of the intensity of demand is essential to determination of a fair price in a market economy.

*   *   *

In the absence of an estimate of surplus surplus the Leasco package may have been very attractive, offering as it did a substantial premium over the price of Reliance shares. But with full disclosure the Reliance shareholder might well have reconsidered the value of his shares. Moreover, such disclosure may have motivated the market—influenced as it is by professionals and institutional investors—to revalue the Reliance shares making the Leasco offer relatively less attractive. See Wheat Report at 52–54. The consequence of such a reevaluation would be either a refusal to exchange or an upward revision of the exchange offer package by Leasco.

*   *   *

The central point in this analysis is not whether any one of the alternatives discussed would necessarily have been adopted by the "average prudent investor," but whether they are consistent with a disclosure—however carefully qualified—of an estimate of surplus surplus. We cannot say that such an inclusion was so trivial or inconsequential that an investor would be acting manifestly illogically if he refused to exchange his Leasco shares after it was disclosed. The importance of surplus surplus to Leasco, the significant interest of the securities professionals, and the general interest in capital-rich insurance companies all combine to make estimates of surplus surplus a material fact that should have been available to the Reliance shareholders when asked to exchange their shares for the Leasco package.

*   *   *

Our finding that by failing to include an estimate-or-range-of surplus surplus in the registration statement Leasco "omitted to state a material fact required to be stated therein or necessary to make the statements therein not misleading" establishes plaintiff's cause of action. 15 U.S.C. § 77k(a). All that remains is to consider the defenses provided by Section 11 and whether the defendants have sustained their respective burdens of proof with regard to those defenses.

*   *   *

D. *Due Diligence of the Directors—Steinberg, Schwartz & Hodes*

Before analyzing the due diligence defenses presented by these defendants we must consider whether they are all properly treated together. Steinberg and Schwartz are and were, respectively, Chief Executive Officer and President of Leasco—clearly "inside" directors. Hodes is a partner in the law firm which represents Leasco; he held no management office.

The leading case of Escott v. BarChris Construction Corp., 283 F.Supp. 643 (S.D.N.Y.1968) drew a distinction between directors who were officers of BarChris and its director-lawyer, Grant, who occupied a position analogous to Hodes' at Leasco. Judge McLean treated Grant as an "outside" director despite the fact that he had been a director for eight months prior to the public offering in question and had prepared the registration statement. The court then held Grant to a very high standard of independent investigation of the registration statement because of his peculiar expertise and access to information and held him liable for failure to meet that standard. *BarChris,* supra at 689–692.

The assignment of "outside director" status to the lawyer in BarChris represented the court's conclusions on the facts peculiar to BarChris. It does not preclude a finding that "in some cases the attorney-director may be so deeply involved that he is really an insider." Folk, Civil Liabilities Under the Federal Securities Act—the *BarChris* Case, 1 Securities L.Rev. 3, 39 (1969) (reprinted from 55 Va.L.Rev. 1 (1969)). This is the case presented by Hodes.

Hodes has been a director of Leasco since 1965—three years or more at the time of this registration statement. He participated extensively in the discussions leading up to the exchange offer for Reliance shares as early as the fall of 1967 and was constantly involved in the deal throughout both the preliminary and execution stages of the transaction. He, or a representative of his law firm, attended all meetings and was consulted on all matters pertaining to this acquisition. He was directly responsible for preparation of the registration statement and initiated all of the research regarding reorganization of Reliance and separation of its surplus surplus. He kept Leasco's Schwartz, apprised of the progress on possible alternatives for Reliance. The testimony and exhibits at this trial make it clear that insofar as surplus surplus is concerned Hodes was so intimately involved in this registration process that to treat him as anything but an insider would involve a gross distortion of the realities of Leasco's management.

Section 11(b)(3)(A) provides a "due diligence" in investigation defense to all defendants but the issuer.

* * *

As already indicated, defendants' principal claim is that they considered including an estimate and decided against such action because of the uncertainties of computation. Steinberg and Hodes were both convinced, according to their testimony, that the estimates they had obtained were not reliable and that a reliable one could not be achieved with the data available. The key to all of their arguments is the unavailability of Reliance's management and the Pennsylvania Insurance Commissioner. We find that the director-defendants failed to fulfill their duty of reasonable investigation and that they had no reasonable ground to believe that an omission of an estimate of surplus surplus was not materially misleading.

* * *

Even if both of our prior conclusions regarding the lack of reasonable ground to believe in the accuracy of the registration statement were in error, these insider-defendants have nevertheless failed in their duty to reasonably investigate the accuracy of the prospectus. The uncontroverted testimony of two of the defendants themselves—Steinberg and Hodes—was that neither they nor anyone else in Leasco ever attempted to obtain a computation of surplus surplus beyond those of Leasco's Gibbs.

Surplus surplus was a crucial element of the plan to acquire Reliance. Yet, no one connected with Leasco commissioned an estimate by an insurance consultant; no one asked any Leasco employee to calculate it; Hodes never ordered one of his law firm's associates to attempt to arrive at a figure; and certainly no one made inquiry of one man who would have easily produced a figure—Roberts.

* * *

E. *Due Diligence of the Dealer-Managers—White, Weld & Co. and Lehman Brothers*

Section 11 holds underwriters to the same burden of establishing reasonable investigation and reasonable ground to believe the accuracy of the registration statement. The courts must be particularly scrupulous in examining the conduct of underwriters since they are supposed to assume an opposing posture with respect to management. The average investor probably assumes that some issuers will lie, but he probably has somewhat more confidence in the average level of morality of an underwriter who has established a reputation for fair dealing. * * *

Dealer-managers cannot, of course, be expected to possess the intimate knowledge of corporate affairs of inside directors, and their duty to investigate should be considered in light of their more limited access. Nevertheless they are expected to exercise a high decree of care in investigation and independent verification of the company's representations. Tacit reliance on management assertions is unacceptable; the underwriters must play devil's advocate. * * *

We find that the dealer-managers have just barely established that they reasonably investigated the surplus surplus concept as it related to Reliance and that they had reasonable ground to believe that omission of a specific figure was justified.

* * *

STARKMAN v. MARATHON OIL COMPANY

United States Court of Appeals, Sixth Circuit, 1985.
772 F.2d 231.

Before MERRITT and KENNEDY, CIRCUIT JUDGES, and PECK, SENIOR CIRCUIT JUDGE.

MERRITT, CIRCUIT JUDGE.

Like Radol v. Thomas, 772 F.2d 244 (6th Cir.1985), this action arises out of U.S. Steel's November, 1981 acquisition and eventual merger with Marathon Oil Company. The plaintiff here, Irving Starkman, was a Marathon shareholder until selling his shares on the open market for $78 per share on November 18, 1981, the day before U.S. Steel's tender offer for 51% of Marathon's outstanding shares at $125 per share was announced. On October 31, 1981, Mobil Oil had initiated its takeover bid for Marathon, a bid which Marathon actively resisted by urging its rejection by Marathon shareholders and by seeking and eventually finding a "white knight" or alternative, friendly merger partner-tender offeror, U.S. Steel. Starkman claims that Marathon's board violated Rule 10b–5 and its fiduciary duty to him as a Marathon shareholder by failing to disclose various items of "soft" information—information of less certainty than hard facts—in its public statements to shareholders during the period after Mobil's hostile tender offer and prior to Steel's friendly tender offer. In particular, he says that Marathon should have told shareholders that negotiations were underway with U.S. Steel prior to the consummation of those negotiations in an agreement, and that internal and externally-prepared asset appraisals and five-year earnings and cash flow projections should have been disclosed to shareholders so that they could make a fully informed choice whether to sell their shares or gamble on receiving a higher price in a possible Steel-Marathon merger.

The District Court granted summary judgment for Marathon, finding that these items of soft information had either been sufficiently disclosed or were not required to be disclosed because their nondisclosure did not render materially misleading Marathon's other affirmative public statements. For the reasons stated below, we affirm the judgment of the District Court.

I. BACKGROUND

We have discussed the background and structure of U.S. Steel's acquisition of Marathon Oil at some length in Radol v. Thomas, 772 F.2d 244 (6th Cir.1985), and our attention here will therefore be focused on the facts which are especially relevant to Starkman's Rule 10b–5 claims.

In the summer of 1981, Marathon was among a number of oil companies considered to be prime takeover targets. In this atmosphere, Marathon's top level management began preparations against a hostile takeover bid. Harold Hoopman, Marathon's president and chief executive officer, instructed the company's vice presidents to compile a catalog of assets. This document, referred to as the "Strong Report" or "internal asset evaluation," estimated the value of Marathon's transportation, refining and marketing assets, its other equipment and structures, and the value of proven, probable, and potential oil reserves as well as exploratory acreage. Hoopman and John Strong, who was responsible for combining materials received from various divisions into the final report, both testified that the Strong report was viewed as a "selling document" which placed optimistic values on Marathon's oil and gas reserves so as to attract the interest of prospective buyers and ensure that Marathon could either ward off an attempt to capture Marathon at a bargain price or obtain the best offer available.

In estimating proven, probable, and potential reserves and exploratory acreage, the Strong Report was based on information that was not available to the general public, for example in annual reports, because only the value of proven reserves was normally included in such public documents. The Strong Report defined proven reserves as those actually producing, probable reserves as reserves for properties where some production had been established and additional production was likely, and potential reserves as reserves for properties where production had not yet been established but where geologic evidence supported wildcat drilling. These reserves were valued using a discounted cash flow methodology, under which the present value of oil reserves is calculated by summing risk discounted expected net revenues from the particular field over the life of the field, and then discounted into present value by dividing by an estimated interest rate. This valuation method, a standard procedure for determining the cash value of oil and gas properties, required projections of price and cost conditions prevailing as far as 20 years into the future. For example, the Strong Report assumed that the rate of increase in oil prices would average over 9% per year from 1980–1990.

Using this methodology, the Strong Report valued Marathon's net assets at between $19 billion and $16 billion (depending on which set of interest rates was used to discount back to present value), a per share value of between \$323 and \$276. The value of oil and gas reserves made up \$14 billion of the \$19 billion estimate and \$11.5 billion of the \$16 billion estimate. A similar report using identical methodology was prepared in mid-July 1981 by the investment banking firm of First Boston, which had been hired by Marathon to assist in preparing for potential takeover bids. The First Boston Report was based only upon proven and probable oil reserves and was also intended to be used as a "presentation piece" to avoid a takeover or maximize the price obtained in a takeover. It placed Marathon's value at between \$188 and \$225 per share.

Some perspective on the values arrived at in the Strong and First Boston reports can be gained from other, publicly available appraisals of Marathon's assets prepared during 1981. The Herold Oil Industry Comparative Appraisal placed Marathon's appraised value at \$199 per share, and two other reports by securities analysts said Marathon had an appraised value of between \$200 and \$210 per share.

Marathon's market value, however, was well below these appraised values. On October 29, 1981, Marathon closed at \$63.75 per share. The next day, Mobil Oil announced its tender offer to purchase up to approximately 68% of outstanding Marathon common stock for \$85 per share in cash. Mobil proposed to follow the tender offer with a going private or freezeout merger in which the remaining shareholders of Marathon would receive sinking fund debentures worth approximately \$85 per share.

On October 31, 1981, Marathon's board of directors met in emergency session and unanimously decided that the Mobil offer was "grossly inadequate" and approved a vigorous campaign to persuade Marathon shareholders not to tender to Mobil, and to simultaneously seek a "white knight." On November 11 and 12, Marathon's Board made public statements to the shareholders recommending rejection of Mobil's bid as "grossly inadequate" and against the best interests of the company. We explore these statements in more detail below, as they are a primary focus of Starkman's claims of inadequate disclosure. However, at the time these statements to shareholders were made, Marathon representatives had already contacted all of the 30 to 35 companies who could possibly undertake an acquisition topping Mobil's bid, and, in particular, had begun negotiations with U.S. Steel on November 10. The Strong and First Boston reports were given to Steel on that same day, on the condition that they be kept confidential, and on November 12. Marathon's vice president for finance delivered five-year earnings forecasts and cash flow projections to Steel in Pittsburgh.

On November 17, Hoopman and David Roderick, Steel's president, reached agreement on the terms of Steel's purchase of Marathon, and, after Board approval, an agreement was signed on November 18, 1981. Under the terms of the agreement, Steel would make a tender offer for up to 31 million shares (about 51%) of Marathon stock for \$125 per share in cash, to be followed by a merger proposal in which each remaining Marathon shareholder would receive one \$100 face value, 12 year, $12\frac{1}{2}$ per cent guaranteed note per share of common stock. On November 19, Steel mailed its tender offer to Marathon shareholders, and Hoopman sent a letter to Marathon shareholders describing the two-stage deal and stating the opinion of Marathon's Board that the agreement was fair to Marathon shareholders. Steel's offer was successful, with over 91% of the outstanding shares tendered, and the second stage freezeout merger was approved by a two-thirds majority of the remaining shareholders in February, 1982.

II. MARATHON'S PUBLIC STATEMENTS AND DISPOSITION BELOW

There are three public statements by Marathon management at issue here. First, Marathon's November 11, 1981, press release, which states, in pertinent part, that:

Our Board of Directors has determined that Mobil Corporation's unsolicited tender offer is grossly inadequate. The offer is not in the best interests of Marathon Oil or its shareholders. It doesn't reflect current asset values and it doesn't permit the long-term investor the opportunity to participate in the potential values that have been developed.

* * * * * * * * *

We plan to do everything we possibly can to defeat this offer. We are determined to stay independent.

A. 187.

The next day, as required by Rule 14e–2, 17 C.F.R. § 240.14e–2 (1984), Marathon mailed a letter to its shareholders stating its position regarding Mobil's tender offer. The letter urged rejection of the offer, stating that Marathon's Board was "convinced that the Mobil offer is grossly inadequate and does not represent the real values of the assets underlying your investment in Marathon." A. 182. The letter described a number of alternative courses of action that were being considered by the Board, including "repurchase of Marathon shares, acquisition of all or part of another company, a business combination with another company, (and) the declaration of an extra ordinary dividend and a complete or partial liquidation of the Company," id., and concluded by again urging rejection of Mobil's attempt to "seize control of Marathon's assets at a fraction of their value," and stating that "[w]e are convinced that you and our other shareholders would be well served if Marathon remains independent." Id.

Attached to this letter was a copy of Marathon's Schedule 14D–9, filed pursuant to Rule 14d–9, 17 C.F.R. § 240.14d–9, in which the board informed the SEC that it had recommended rejection of the Mobil offer as "grossly inadequate." Item 4(b)(iv) of Marathon's Schedule 14D–9 listed as a factor supporting this recommendation the board's belief that based on current economic and market factors, "this is an extremely inopportune time to sell the Company and, in any event, that its shareholders would be better served if the Company were to remain independent." A. 92. Item 7 of this same schedule described "Certain Negotiations and Transactions" by Marathon:

At a meeting of the Board of Directors held on October 31, 1981, the Board considered and reviewed the feasibility and desirability of exploring and investigating certain types of possible transactions, including, without limitation, repurchases of Company Common Shares, the public or private sale of equity or other securities of the Company, a business combination between the Company and another company, the acquisition of a significant interest in or the entire Company or of one or more of its significant business segments by another company, a joint venture between the Company and one or more other companies, the acquisition by the Company of all or part of the business of another Company, a complete or partial liquidation of the Company or the declaration of an extraordinary dividend. After considerable discussion, the Board resolved that it was desirable and in the best interest of the Company and its shareholders to explore and investigate, with the assistance and advice of First Boston, such transactions, although the Board noted that the initiation or continuation of such activities may be dependent upon Mobil's future actions with respect to the Mobil Offer. There can be no assurance that these activities will result in any transaction being recommended to the Board of Directors or that any transaction which is recommended will be authorized or consummated.

A. 96.

Starkman argues that the failure of any of these communications to disclose the Strong and First Boston reports and the five-year earnings and cash flow projections constituted an omission of material facts which rendered these communications materially misleading, and that Marathon not only failed to adequately disclose its search for a white knight and its negotiations with Steel but actually gave the false impression that the Board was endeavoring to preserve Marathon as an independent entity. He argues that the Strong and First Boston reports, the five-year cash and earnings projections, and the fact of ongoing negotiations with U.S. Steel were all material facts because knowledge of them would have affected a reasonable shareholder's evaluation of the likelihood that Marathon would succeed in negotiating a higher price takeover, and thereby affect such a shareholder's decision to sell his shares. He contends that shareholders were not adequately informed of Marathon management's search for a "white knight" and of the negotiations with Steel, and that failure to disclose more information regarding these negotiations rendered statements suggesting that Marathon might remain independent materially misleading. Similarly, Starkman contends that if he had been told of the Strong and First Boston reports and the five-year earnings and cash flow projections, and also that Marathon management was using these figures in seeking an alternative bidder, then he would have anticipated a much higher bid than he did, and that failure to release this information rendered materially misleading the affirmative statements Marathon did make.

In his brief on this appeal, Starkman has repeatedly mischaracterized the decision of the District Court as holding that none of the information Starkman contends should have been disclosed was material. To understand the District Court's holding in this case, it is important to note at the outset that in Radol v. Thomas, 772 F.2d 244 No. 83–3598 (6th Cir.1985), the plaintiffs claimed that the same asset appraisals at issue here should have been disclosed by Steel in its tender offer and by Marathon in its statements recommending that shareholders accept Steel's offer. Judge Rubin presided over both the present suit and *Radol,* and in *Radol* he denied the defendant's motion for summary judgment on the issue of whether the asset appraisals should have been disclosed at the time of Steel's tender offer on the ground that the reports were not, as a matter of law, immaterial, and he sent the materiality of these reports to the jury. See Radol v. Thomas, 556 F.Supp. 586, 594 (S.D.Ohio 1983).

In granting summary judgment for Marathon in the present action, however, Judge Rubin found that the net asset values stated in the Strong and First Boston reports were perfectly consistent with Marathon's repeated public assertion that Mobil's bid was "grossly inadequate" in light of the true value of Marathon's assets, and that disclosure of the reports was not required under Rule 10b–5 because "disclosure of information which is consistent with other statements made is obviously not necessary in order to make those statements not misleading. Such disclosure would simply reinforce, rather than correct or modify, the statements made." A. 16. As to the claim that nondisclosure of the reports rendered misleading Marathon's statements that the best result would be for the company to remain independent, the District Court said that these statements were not misleading when placed in the context of the repeated assertion that Mobil's offer was "grossly inadequate" and that alternatives including merger into another company were under consideration. A. 17.

The District Court summarily disposed of the claim that the five-year earnings and cash flow projections should have been disclosed, concluding that disclosure of such information is simply not required under Marsh v. Armada Corp., 533 F.2d 978, 986–87 (6th Cir.1976), cert. denied, 430 U.S. 954, 97 S.Ct. 1598, 51 L.Ed.2d 803 (1977), and Arber v. Essex Wire Corp., 490 F.2d 414, 421 (6th Cir.1974), cert. denied, 419 U.S. 830, 95 S.Ct. 53, 42 L.Ed.2d 56 (1974). A. 18.

As to disclosure of the negotiations with Steel, the District Court cited Reiss v. Pan American World Airways, Inc., 711 F.2d 11, 14 (2d Cir.1983), and Staffin v. Greenberg, 672 F.2d 1196, 1206 (3d Cir.1982), in ruling that Marathon's 14D–9 disclosure that the acquisition of all or part of another company, or merger with another company, was being considered as an alternative to the Mobil offer sufficed to meet whatever disclosure obligation may have existed. A. 19–20.

III. DISCUSSION

A. Introduction

* * *

Despite occasional suggestions by commentators, see, e.g., Bauman, Rule 10b–5 and the Corporation's Affirmative Duty to Disclose, 67 Geo.L.J. 935 (1979), and the courts, Zweig v. Hearst Corp., 594 F.2d 1261, 1266 (9th Cir. 1979), that Rule 10b–5 imposes an affirmative obligation on the corporation to disclose all material information regardless of whether the corporation has made any other statements, the established view is that a "duty to speak" must exist before the disclosure of material facts is required under Rule 10b–5. See Flynn v. Bass Brothers Enterprises, Inc., 744 F.2d 978, 984 (3d Cir.1984) (citing Chiarella v. United States, 445 U.S. 222, 235, 100 S.Ct. 1108, 1118, 63 L.Ed.2d 348 (1980); Staffin v. Greenberg, 672 F.2d 1196, 1202 (3d Cir.1982)). Provided that such a duty to speak exists, a further limitation on the duty to disclose is imposed by the requirement that only misstatements of material facts and omissions of material facts necessary to make other required statements not misleading are prohibited by Rule 10b–5. The Supreme Court's definition of "material" in the context of an alleged violation of Rule 14a–9, governing disclosure requirements in proxy statements, has been adopted for cases involving Rule 10b–5 in the tender offer context. Flynn v. Bass Brothers Enterprises, 744 F.2d at 985; Staffin

v. Greenberg, 672 F.2d at 1205; Panter v. Marshall Field & Co., 646 F.2d 271, 282 (7th Cir.), cert. denied, 454 U.S. 1092, 102 S.Ct. 658, 70 L.Ed.2d 631 (1981).

* * *

In structuring the disclosure duties of a tender offer target, we begin therefore with the basic proposition that only material facts—those substantially likely to affect the deliberations of the reasonable shareholder—must be disclosed, and then *only* if the nondisclosure of the particular material facts would make misleading the affirmative statements otherwise required by the federal securities laws and SEC regulations.

Our adherence to this basic proposition ensures that target management's disclosure obligations will strike the correct balance between the competing costs and benefits of disclosure. The benefits of disclosure in ensuring that shareholders who are suddenly faced with a tender offer will not be forced to respond without adequate information are clearly recognized in Section 14(e) of the Williams Act, 15 U.S.C. § 78n(e), which somewhat broadens the reach of Rule 10b-5 to statements made "in connection with any tender offer" and which provides the statutory authority for SEC rules imposing affirmative disclosure obligations on tender offer targets. On the other hand, tender offers remain essentially contests in which participants on both sides act under the "stresses of the marketplace," and "[p]robably there will no more be a perfect tender offer than a perfect trial." Electronic Specialty Co. v. International Controls Corp., 409 F.2d 937, 948 (2d Cir.1969) (Friendly, J.). Under these conditions, imposing an "unrealistic requirement of laboratory conditions," id., would place target management under the highly unpredictable threat of huge liability for the failure to disclose, perhaps inducing the disclosure of mountains of documents and hourly reports on negotiations with potential tender offerors, a deluge of information which would be more likely to confuse than guide the reasonable lay shareholder and which could interfere with the negotiation of a higher tender offer and actually reduce the likelihood that a shareholder will benefit from a successful tender offer at a premium over the market. It is with these competing considerations in mind that we turn to the particular disclosure claims made here.

B. Assets Appraisals and Earnings Projections

We first address Starkman's contention that Marathon should have disclosed the Strong and First Boston reports and the five-year earnings projections and forecasts given to Steel. Under the authority of Section 14(e) of the Williams Act, the SEC requires a tender offer target to make two affirmative statements regarding an offer. First, Rule 14e-2 requires that the target company mail or publish a statement to its shareholders within 10 days of the tender offer stating its position (or stating it cannot take a position) and giving reasons for the position. Under Rule 14d-9, a Schedule 14D-9 must be filed with the SEC "as soon as practicable" after the recommendation letter is sent to shareholders. The information to be included in the Schedule 14D-9 is described in 17 C.F.R. § 14d-101. Significantly, although Item 4 of the Schedule 14D-9 is to contain a statement of the reasons for the target's position with respect to the offer, and Item 8 requires disclosure of any additional information as "may be necessary to make the required statements, in light of the circumstances under which they are made, not misleading" neither the shareholder recommendation letter nor the Schedule 14D–9 must contain internal asset appraisals, appraisals done by outside consultants such as First Boston, or earnings and cash flow projections.

Since there is no SEC rule specifically requiring the disclosure of this information, we must determine whether Rule 10b–5 requires its disclosure as material information, the nondisclosure of which would render misleading other statements made by Marathon. The starting point in this analysis is the underlying regulatory policy toward disclosure of such information, since regulatory rules reflect careful study of general conditions prevailing in the securities marketplace and provide guidelines upon which corporate officers and directors are entitled to rely.

The SEC's policy toward the inclusion of appraised asset valuations, projections and other "soft" information in proxy materials, tender offers and other disclosure documents has undergone a gradual evolution toward *allowing* the inclusion of such information in some special contexts, provided that the assumptions and hypotheses underlying predicted values are also disclosed.

In 1976, future earnings projections were deleted from a list of examples of potentially misleading disclosures in proxy statements in the note which followed Rule 14a–9. See Securities Act Release No. 5699, *reprinted in* [1975–76 Transfer Binder] Fed.Sec.L.Rep. (CCH) ¶ 80,461 (1976). And, effective July 30, 1979, the SEC adopted a "safe harbor" rule for projections, under which a statement containing a projection of revenues and earnings would not be considered to be a materially misleading misstatement or omission for purposes of liability under the federal securities laws provided the statement was prepared with a reasonable basis and was disclosed in good faith. See Securities Act Release No. 6084 *reprinted in* [1979 Transfer Binder] Fed.Sec.L.Rep. (CCH) ¶ 82,117, at 81,939 (June 25, 1979).

With respect to asset appraisals, Rule 13e–3, 17 C.F.R. § 240.13e–3, requires disclosure of the information called for by Items 7, 8, and 9 of Schedule 13E–3, 17 C.F.R. § 240.13e–100, in the context of freezeout mergers. Item 8 of Schedule 13E–3 requires disclosure of factors important in determining the fairness of such a transaction to unaffiliated shareholders, and these factors include liquidation value; Item 9 of that same schedule says that a summary of any outside appraisal must be furnished, with the summary including a discussion of the procedures and methods of arriving at the findings and recommendations of the appraisal. However, a 1979 SEC-proposed amendment under which an issuer would have to disclose any projection given to an appraisal furnisher was never adopted, see 2 Fed.Sec.L.Rep. (CCH) ¶ 23,706, at 17,245–21 through 21A, and, even more importantly, in Radol v. Thomas, 772 F.2d 244 No. 83–3598, (6th Cir.1985), we have rejected the position that SEC rules regarding freezeout mergers and proxies should determine the disclosure obligations of target management in the first stage of a two-tier tender offer.[6]

---

6. In addition, while the note to Rule 14a–9 lists "predictions as to specific future market values" as a potentially misleading proxy statement disclosure, the SEC in 1980 authorized disclosure of good faith appraisals made on a reasonable basis in proxy contests in which a principal issue is the disposition of the issuer's assets, provided that the valuations are accompanied by "disclosure which facilitates shareholders' understanding of the basis for and limitations on the projected realizable values." Exchange Act Release No. 34–16833, *reprinted in* 3 Fed.Sec.L.Rep. (CCH)

Finally, we note that until March, 1982, Regulation S–K, the source for disclosure obligations in annual reports, registration documents and other documents that must be filed with the SEC, provided in Instruction 2 to Item 2(b) that estimates of probable or possible oil and gas reserves should not be disclosed in any document publicly filed with the SEC. See Securities Act Release No. 6008, *reprinted in* [1978 Transfer Binder] Fed.Sec.L. Rep. (CCH) ¶ 81,768, at 81,104 (Dec. 19, 1978). The underlying reason was that "estimates of probable or possible reserves and any value thereof are not sufficiently reliable to be included * * * and may be misleading to investors." Id. In March, 1982, well after Steel's tender offer, Item 102 of Regulation S–K was amended to *allow* disclosure of "estimated" as well as proved reserves where such estimates have previously been provided to a person who is offering to acquire or merge with the subject company, see Securities Act Release No. 6383, *reprinted in* [1937–1982 Accounting Series Release Transfer Binder] Fed.Sec.L.Rep. (CCH) ¶ 72,328, at 63,003 (March 3, 1982). The Strong and First Boston reports contain estimates of probable and possible reserves, and the disclosure of this information was actually prohibited at the time of Steel's tender offer, and only *permitted* since that time.

Thus, at the time of Steel's tender offer, the SEC did not require disclosure of earnings projections in any context, and required disclosure of asset appraisals, in summary form, only in the special context of freeze-out mergers, which differs markedly from the setting of a first-stage tender offer. Although the SEC allowed disclosure of projections, provided they were prepared on a "reasonable basis" and in "good faith," and also allowed disclosure of similarly supported asset appraisals in some proxy contests, it forbade the disclosure of estimates of probable and potential oil and gas reserves, a major component of the Strong and First Boston appraisals. Absent compelling authority to the contrary, we are reluctant to impose liability on Marathon for failing to disclose asset appraisals based on hypothetical valuations which the SEC did not then permit to be disclosed in most contexts, particularly since Section 23(a) of the Securities and Exchange Act, 15 U.S.C. § 78w(a)(1) provides that no liability under the federal securities laws shall be imposed for "any act done or omitted in good faith conformity with a rule, regulation, or order of the Commission." See Gerstle v. Gamble-Skogmo, Inc., 478 F.2d 1281, 1292–94 (2d Cir.1973) (refusing, per Friendly, J., to impose liability on the basis of an ex-post modification in SEC policy for non-disclosure in 1963 merger proxy statement of asset appraisals when it was an "article of faith" among securities lawyers in 1963 that such appraisals could not be included in a proxy statement.)

Rather than suggesting a duty to disclose the Strong and First Boston reports, however, our cases firmly establish the rule that soft information such as asset appraisals and projections must be disclosed only if the reported values are virtually as certain as hard facts.

This Court has recently held that a target's failure to disclose an appraisal based on five-year cash flow and earnings projections and intended to be used as a selling document in ongoing merger discussions did not

¶ 24,117 (May 23, 1980). This same release cautioned, however, that where "valuations are so qualified and subject to material limitations and contingencies, inclusion in proxy soliciting material of specific realizable values may be unreasonable." 3 Fed.Sec.L.Rep. (CCH) at 17,621–13.

violate Rule 10b–5. Biechele v. Cedar Point, Inc., 747 F.2d 209 (6th Cir. 1984). Chief Judge Lively's opinion for the court reasoned that the report was a "selling document" which "contained projections and speculative assumptions which were little more than predictions of future business success," and valuations based on the replacement cost of assets which could be misleading to shareholders, since they varied from balance sheet information prepared according to accepted accounting principles. Id. at 216. Similarly, in James v. Gerber Products Co., 587 F.2d 324, 327 (6th Cir. 1978), we held that the failure to disclose interim earnings reports in connection with a shareholder's sale of stock back to the issuing company did not violate Rule 10b–5, because "such sales figures, projections, forecasts and the like only rise to the level of materiality when they can be calculated with substantial certainty." And in Arber v. Essex Wire Corp., 490 F.2d 414, 421 (6th Cir.), cert. denied, 419 U.S. 830, 95 S.Ct. 53, 42 L.Ed. 2d 56 (1974), another case involving a corporate stock repurchase, then Judge McCree said that while a fixed plan of future corporate activity might, under some circumstances, be viewed as a material fact, Section 10(b) and Rule 10b–5 did not require a corporate insider to disclose his educated guesses or predictions, and "[i]n short, the law mandates disclosure only of existing material facts. It does not require an insider to volunteer any economic forecast." See also Marsh v. Armada Corp., 533 F.2d 978, 987 (6th Cir.1976), cert. denied, 430 U.S. 954, 97 S.Ct. 1598, 51 L.Ed.2d 803 (1977) (failure to make a projection of future earnings in freeze-out merger proxy statement not actionable under Rule 10b–5).

Our cases fully support a rule under which a tender offer target must disclose projections and asset appraisals based upon predictions regarding future economic and corporate events only if the predictions underlying the appraisal or projection are substantially certain to hold. An example is when the predictions in fact state a fixed plan of corporate activity. If a target chooses to disclose projections and appraisals which do not rise to this level of certainty, then it must also inform the shareholders as to the basis for and limitations on the projected realizable values.[7]

The Third Circuit has enunciated a different test, under which "courts should ascertain the duty to disclose asset valuations and other soft information on a case by case basis, by weighing the potential aid such information will give the shareholder against the potential harm, such as undue reliance, if the information is released with a proper cautionary note." Flynn v. Bass Brothers Enterprises, 744 F.2d at 988. The court listed several factors the courts have considered in determining the reliability of soft information, including the qualifications of those who prepared the appraisal, the degree of certainty of the data on which it was based, and the purpose for which it was prepared. 744 F.2d at 986, 988 (compiling cases); see also Panter v. Marshall Field, 646 F.2d at 292–93.

By its very nature, however, this sort of judicial cost-benefit analysis is uncertain and unpredictable, and it moreover neglects the role of the

7. We note that this rule is fully consistent with the recent statement by the SEC Advisory Committee on Tender Offers that "current disclosures of projections and valuations given to a bidder by a target company are essentially meaningless and can be misleading without disclosure of the underlying assumptions," and with that Committee's recommendation that "[w]here the bidder discloses projections or asset valuations to target company shareholders, it must include disclosure of the principal supporting assumptions provided to the bidder by the target." See SEC Advisory Committee on Tender Offers, Report of Recommendations, at 29 (July 8, 1983).

market in providing shareholders with information regarding the target's value through competing tender offers. Our approach, which focuses on the certainty of the data underlying the appraisal or projection, ensures that the target company's shareholders will receive all essentially factual information, while preserving the target's discretion to disclose more uncertain information without the threat of liability, provided appropriate qualifications and explanations are made.

Under this standard, Marathon plainly had no duty to disclose the Strong and First Boston reports, because these reports contained estimates of the value of probable, potential and unexplored oil and gas reserves which were based on highly speculative assumptions regarding the path of oil and gas prices, recovery rates and the like over a period of thirty to fifty years. Disclosure of such estimated values could well have been misleading without an accompanying mountain of data and explanations. There is no reported case actually holding that disclosure of appraised values of oil and gas reserves is required, and several which agree with our decision that such disclosure is not required.[8]

Similarly, Marathon had no duty to disclose the five-year earnings and cash flow projections given to Steel and First Boston. This information does not rise to the level of substantial certainty triggering a duty to disclose. Biechele v. Cedar Point; James v. Gerber Products Corp., both supra.

Further, disclosure of the asset appraisals and earnings and cash flow projections was not required in order to ensure that other statements in Marathon's 14D–9 and in its letter recommending rejection of Mobil's bid were not misleading. Marathon stated that Mobil's $85 offer was "grossly inadequate" and disclosure of highly uncertain information indicating that Marathon had a net asset value of over $200 per share would only have supported this statement, and could have actually misled shareholders into thinking that the market would actually support a price of $200 per share.

C.

Starkman's contention that Marathon should have disclosed more information regarding its search for a white knight and its negotiations with Steel are equally without merit. The SEC and the courts have enunciated a firm rule regarding a tender offer target's duty to disclose ongoing negotiations: so long as merger or acquisition discussions are preliminary, general disclosure of the fact that such alternatives are being considered will suffice to adequately inform shareholders; a duty to disclose the possible terms of any transaction and the parties thereto arises only after an agreement in principle, regarding such fundamental terms as price and structure, has been reached. See Item 7 of Schedule 14D–9, 17 C.F.R. § 240.14d–101 (1984); Greenfield v. Heublein, Inc., 742 F.2d 751, 756–57 (3d Cir.1984), cert. denied, —— U.S. ——, 105 S.Ct. 1189, 84 L.Ed.2d 336 (1985)

---

8. See, e.g., Sunray DX Oil Co. v. Helmerich & Payne, Inc., 398 F.2d 447, 450–51 (10th Cir.1968) ("any statement concerning oil reserves other than in the category of 'proved' could certainly be misleading to any investor other than one who is an expert in the industry"); Caspary v. Louisiana Land and Exploration Co., 579 F.Supp. 1105 (S.D.N.Y.1983), aff'd, 725 F.2d 189 (2d Cir.1984) (no duty to disclose internal projections regarding oil recovery rates and exploration costs); Bradshaw v. Jenkins, [1983–84 Transfer Binder] Fed.Sec.L.Rep. (CCH) ¶ 99,719 (W.D.Wash. March 9, 1984) (no duty to disclose consultant's estimated value of energy loan portfolio).

(rejecting an "intent to merge" trigger standard); Staffin v. Greenberg, 672 F.2d 1196, 1207 (3d Cir.1982); Reiss v. Pan American World Airways, Inc., 711 F.2d 11, 14 (2d Cir.1983).

The rationale emerging from these cases is that when dealing with complex bargaining which may fail as well as succeed and which may succeed on terms which vary greatly from those originally anticipated, the disclosure of preliminary discussions could very easily mislead shareholders as to the prospects of success, and by making public an impending offer, push the price of the target's stock toward the expected tender price, thereby depriving shareholders of the primary inducement to tender—a premium above market price—and forcing the offeror to abandon its plans or greatly increasing the cost of the offer. See Staffin v. Greenberg, 672 F.2d at 1207.

In the instant case, Marathon's shareholder recommendation letter and its Schedule 14D–9 stated that the company was considering a number of alternatives, including a merger with another firm. These statements adequately informed the shareholders of Marathon's plans. Additional statements in these documents to the effect that Marathon's board believed the best result would be for Marathon to remain independent were not misleading when read in their full context, and at most expressed a sincere hope which the board found unrealistic under the pressure of Mobil's offer.

Finally, Starkman's claims for fraud and breach of fiduciary duty are completely unsupported by authority in his brief, and were similarly neglected in his arguments below. We therefore affirm and adopt the reasoning of the District Court finding that no claim for fraud has been made out because Marathon did not fail to disclose any information necessary to make its other public statements not misleading, and that the directors' statements, made at a time of extraordinary pressure on the board, comported in all respects with federal law and did not breach a fiduciary duty to Marathon's shareholders.

Accordingly, the judgment of the District Court is affirmed.

––––––––––

GREENFIELD v. HEUBLEIN, INC.

United States Court of Appeals, Third Circuit, 1984.
742 F.2d 751.

Before ALDISERT, CHIEF JUDGE, and HIGGINBOTHAM and ROSENN, CIRCUIT JUDGES.

ALDISERT, CHIEF JUDGE.

This appeal presents two principal questions for our consideration: (1) when does a corporation, the target of both friendly and hostile takeover activity, have a duty to disclose publicly the substance of its discussions with the suitor corporations; and (2) if the target makes a public statement, when is that statement materially misleading and under what circumstances must such a statement, if correct when issued, be updated? Here, Bruce H. Greenfield, both individually and as representative of a class of similarly situated investors, sued Heublein, Inc. (hereinafter referred to as "Heublein"), R.J. Reynolds Industries, Inc., and R.J. Reynolds Tobacco Company (hereinafter referred to jointly as "Reynolds"), claiming that they violated the federal securities laws by failing to disclose properly information related to certain merger and anti-takeover negotiations. The district court granted defendants' motion for summary judgment, 575 F.Supp. 1325, and we affirm.

I.

Beginning in mid–1981, Heublein, Inc. came to be regarded as an attractive target for a corporate takeover. One suitor, the General Cinema Corporation, pursued an aggressive approach to acquisition. It began making large, open market purchases of Heublein stock and by February 1982 owned 2.1 million shares, or about 10% of the then outstanding shares. By the end of May 1982, General Cinema's stake in Heublein had increased to 18.9%. At this point, General Cinema suspended open market purchases of Heublein stock. Although General Cinema, in its Schedule 13D filing with the Securities and Exchange Commission, described these purchases as "for investment only," Heublein regarded this activity as part of a hostile takeover attempt and responded accordingly. Early in 1982, Heublein established a high level executive strategy group to look into ways of defusing the General Cinema moves. The members of the group included Heublein President and Chief Executive Officer, Hicks Waldron, Chairman, Stuart Watson, and General Counsel, George Caspar.

By early 1982, Reynolds also became interested in acquiring Heublein. After observing the increased open market purchases by General Cinema, Reynolds began to investigate Heublein's corporate position more seriously and decided that, while Heublein was an attractive target, Reynolds could not afford to get into a bidding war and did not want to take any action that Heublein might consider hostile. Reynolds, thus, assumed the position of the white knight, waiting in the wings, ready to rescue fair Heublein from the clutches of General Cinema.

July 1982 became the decisive month. For several months Heublein had been trying to reach an agreement with General Cinema to avert an open market buy-out. Although some progress had been made, on July 8 General Cinema altered its bargaining position and issued Heublein a series of "non-negotiable" demands. Waldron and Watson of Heublein considered the demands unacceptable and responded by setting up a confidential meeting with J. Paul Sticht, Chairman of Reynolds, for July 9. At this meeting, Waldron and Watson described their problems with General Cinema, stated their desire to have Heublein remain an independent company, and inquired whether they might expect any hostile action by Reynolds. Sticht confirmed that Reynolds would make no adverse moves against Heublein and went on to describe in some detail both Reynolds' management philosophy and corporate structure. The parties also discussed how the two companies could be combined and how Heublein's upper management personnel could be integrated into Reynolds' organization. This meeting can be fairly described as a preliminary merger discussion and no formal understanding or agreement was reached.

On July 14 General Cinema told Heublein that it was considering selling one of its assets, a Florida television station, valued at approximately $150,000,000. Heublein, recognizing that a large influx of capital would give General Cinema the opportunity to resume large scale open market purchases of its stock, did not view this as good news. Also on July 14, there was a dramatic increase in trading activity in Heublein's stock on the New York Stock Exchange (NYSE) as well as a moderate rise in price.[1] Because of the volume/price increase, Patrick Conneally of the NYSE contacted Caspar at Heublein and asked for a "no corporate development" statement. It is standard procedure for the NYSE to request such statements when the activity of a listed stock changes significantly indicating that some investors may be buying or selling large numbers of shares based on information not generally known to the public at large. After consulting with several other Heublein executives, Caspar issued the following statement, which was reported by Dow Jones after the close of trading on July 14th:

> A spokesman for Heublein, Inc. said the Company was aware of no reason that would explain the activity in its stock in trading on the NYSE today.

Because of their increased concern over the actions of General Cinema, Waldron and Watson quickly organized another meeting with Sticht for the evening of July 15. Although this meeting covered much of the same territory as the July 9 meeting, the parties also discussed the July 14 public statement and the recent developments in the General Cinema situation.

Heublein still believed that it could still negotiate an amicable agreement with General Cinema. On July 23, however, General Cinema, impatient with the progress of the Heublein talks, reiterated its "non-negotiable" demands for what would constitute an acceptable agreement and openly threatened to resume its open market purchases. Heublein considered this turn of events fatal to the discussions and, sensing the seriousness of the threat, called upon its white knight for rescue. While many merger details had been discussed with Reynolds, price had never been mentioned. Therefore, at the direction of the respective corporate executives, the investment bankers for Reynolds and Heublein met on July 26 to discuss the per share purchase price. No agreement was reached. On the 27th, disappointed at the failure of the previous day's bankers meeting, Waldron and Watson met directly with Sticht and Joseph Albey, Reynolds' Vice Chairman. Late in the afternoon they agreed on a sale price of $60.00 per share.

On July 28 the NYSE again called Caspar to request that Heublein issue a "no corporate development" statement. Caspar responded that Heublein could not issue the statement, explained why, and requested that trading on Heublein stock be suspended. With the issuance of a public statement by Heublein at 1:24 p.m., trading on its stock was halted.[2] On July 29 the merger was approved by the boards of both Heublein and Reynolds and was publicly announced.

Bruce Greenfield owned some 400 shares of Heublein stock since 1977. He was generally aware of the hostile takeover action by General Cinema and watched closely the increased activity, and rises in price, of Heublein stock during July 1982. He was aware of the "no corporate development"

---

1. On July 13, 1982, in typical trading, approximately 32,500 shares of Heublein stock were traded, and the closing price was $40.25 per share. On July 14, approximately 242,500 shares were traded and the price rose to $43.00 at closing.

2. The statement read:

At Heublein's request, the New York Stock Exchange has suspended trading in the company's stock. There is a matter in the midstream of development and the company expects to have a statement tomorrow.

statement issued on July 14 and, on the basis of this information and his own knowledge, believed that Heublein's stock would be fully priced at $45.25. On July 26 he placed a "good till cancelled" order to sell his Heublein stock should it reach this price. On July 27 it reached $45.25 and Greenfield's stock was sold. On the next day, trading was suspended and on the 29th the merger was approved and announced.

Greenfield filed suit claiming that in issuing and in failing to update the July 14 statement Heublein had illegally withheld material information concerning its takeover discussions with both General Cinema and Reynolds. The complaint alleged violations of §§ 10(b) and 14(e) of the Securities Exchange Act of 1934, 15 U.S.C. §§ 78j(b) and 78n(e), Rule 10b–5, 17 C.F.R. § 240.10b–5 (1983), as well as several provisions of state law. Following discovery, the district court denied plaintiff's motion to amend his complaint, and, taking into account all of the arguments raised therein, granted defendants summary judgment on all federal counts and dismissed the pendent state law claims. Greenfield appealed.

II.

We will affirm the grant of summary judgment if there are no disputed issues of material fact and if the movant is entitled to judgment as a matter of law. Coastal States Gas Corp. v. Department of Energy, 644 F.2d 969, 978–79 (3d Cir.1981). Greenfield argues that summary judgment was error here because the district court used the wrong legal standard to determine whether an agreement in principle to merge had been reached and, if the correct principle were applied, a factual dispute as to the intent of the parties would be present. Greenfield also argues that, as a matter of law, the July 14 statement was either materially misleading when issued or became so thereafter and Heublein failed to correct it. Therefore, the resolution of this appeal turns on the scope and character of a corporation's duty to disclose information to the investing public. Our analysis will follow two steps: (1) when does a duty to disclose arise in the context of merger/anti-takeover discussions, see Staffin v. Greenberg, 672 F.2d 1196 (3d Cir.1982); and (2) when a voluntary public statement is made, under what circumstances will it be materially misleading when issued or become so on the basis of subsequent events, see Securities and Exchange Commission v. Texas Gulf Sulphur Co., 401 F.2d 833 (2d Cir.1968), cert. denied, 394 U.S. 976, 89 S.Ct. 1454, 22 L.Ed.2d 756 (1969).

III.

* * *

With specific reference to merger discussions, we have held that, so long as they are preliminary, no duty to disclose arises. *Staffin,* 672 F.2d at 1205–07. We reasoned that because disclosure of such tentative discussions may itself be misleading to shareholders, preliminary merger discussions are immaterial as a matter of law. Id. at 1206; see also Susquehanna Corp. v. Pan American Sulphur Corp., 423 F.2d 1075, 1084–85 (5th Cir. 1970). We recognized, however, that as merger discussions progress, the need to protect shareholders from the potentially misleading disclosure gives way to the right of the shareholders to have notice of corporate developments important to their investment decisions. Thus, we further held that "[w]here an agreement in principle [to merge] has been reached a duty to disclose *does* exist." *Staffin,* 672 F.2d at 1207.

A.

With respect to the Reynolds negotiations, the court below held, as a matter of law, that no agreement in principle to merge was reached, and thus no duty to disclose arose, until sometime after Greenfield sold his stock on July 27. The court stated:

> While an "agreement in principle" may exist before all of the details of a merger have been negotiated * * * it is clear that agreement on the fundamental terms of the merger must be reached before the merger negotiations become a material corporate development that must be disclosed to the investing public. Without fundamental agreement on the *price and structure* of a merger, the merger is simply too tentative to give rise to a duty of disclosure.

Memorandum opinion at 25, *reprinted in* app. at 1489a (emphasis added). As we read the district court's opinion, it stated that an agreement in principle requires agreement on the fundamental terms of the merger. The court then applied this formulation and determined that, in the case before it, an agreement in principle had not been reached until July 27 because the parties had not yet agreed on the price and structure, terms fundamental to this proposed merger. We find no error under the circumstances of this case.

Merger discussions arise in a wide variety of circumstances and the standard used to determine when disclosure of these is required must be both flexible and specific. Here the appellant takes issue with the district court's reliance on the price and structure factors and urges that we adopt a less rigid "intent of the parties to merge" standard. We find an intent standard inappropriate. Such a standard would leave both courts and corporations with insufficient guidance to determine when disclosure of merger negotiations should be made. This uncertainty, coupled with the possibility of substantial liability for tardy disclosure, would likely result in corporations issuing early public statements announcing the details of all merger talks. Not only would this have a disruptive effect on the stock markets, but, considering the delicate nature of most merger discussions, might seriously inhibit such acquisitive ventures.

Under the facts of the present case, it was more appropriate for the court below to determine that an agreement in principle to merge had been reached when the parties reached agreement on "price and structure." Although it is difficult to draw a bright line definition that will apply to all cases, these two factors are typically critical aspects of any merger. Agreement as to price and structure provides concrete evidence of a mature understanding between the negotiating corporations. They constitute a useable and definite measure for determining when disclosures need be made. Finally, with both price and structure agreed to, there is only a minimal chance that a public announcement would quash the deal or that the investing public would be misled as to likely corporate activity.

Here, most of the structural details for integrating both the Heublein product line and management team into the Reynolds corporate body had been worked out by the middle of July. But price was not discussed in detail, nor agreed to, until later. Therefore, we conclude that, because

Reynolds and Heublein did not agree on a merger price until the evening of July 27, it was not error for the district court to hold that, as a matter of law, no duty to disclose the substance of those negotiations arose prior to that time.

* * *

IV.

Although a corporation may be under no duty to disclose certain inside information, if it voluntarily chooses to make a public statement that is reasonably calculated to influence the investing public, such a statement may not be "false or misleading or * * * so incomplete as to mislead * * *." Securities and Exchange Commission v. Texas Gulf Sulphur Co., 401 F.2d 833, 862 (2d Cir.1968), cert. denied, 394 U.S. 976 (1969). Further, if a corporation voluntarily makes a public statement that is correct when issued, it has a duty to update that statement if it becomes materially misleading in light of subsequent events. Sharp v. Coopers & Lybrand, 83 F.R.D. 343, 346–47 (E.D.Pa.1979). Appellant argues: (1) that Heublein's July 14 statement, issued to the NYSE, was materially misleading when issued; and (2) that even presuming it was not materially misleading when issued, it became so in light of subsequent events and was never corrected.

A.

As noted earlier, based on unusually high trading activity in Heublein's stock on July 14, the NYSE requested, and Heublein's General Counsel, after checking with several other executives, issued, the following "no corporate development" statement:

A spokesman for Heublein, Inc. said the Company was aware of no reason that would explain the activity in its stock in trading on the NYSE today.

The court below concluded that this statement was not materially misleading. Appellant urges us to reverse this determination. Whether a statement is materially misleading is a mixed question of law and fact to which we would normally apply a mixed standard of review. Santa Fe Industries, Inc. v. Green, 430 U.S. 462, 97 S.Ct. 1292, 51 L.Ed.2d 480 (1977); Universal Minerals, Inc. v. C.A. Hughes & Co., 669 F.2d 98, 102 (3d Cir.1981). But here, because appellant argues that the district court erred in its application of legal precepts in determining that the subject statement was not misleading, our review is plenary.

The request for a "no corporate development" statement was an inquiry to try to explain the upsurge in public activity in Heublein's stock. As we have previously established, on July 14, Heublein was under no duty to disclose, and had not disclosed, the substantive elements of its discussions with either Reynolds or General Cinema. Each discussion was in a preliminary stage and no "agreement in principle," or any functional equivalent thereof, had been reached. Further, because of the confidential nature of these discussions, there was no basis for Caspar to believe, and appellant alerted the district court to no evidence which might tend to prove, that any of the details of these discussions, not previously known to the public, had been recently leaked.[6] Also, although Heublein had recently been the subject of public speculation regarding possible mergers and takeovers, see Wall St.J., Jan. 28, 1982, at 12, *reprinted in* app. at 83a, there is nothing to suggest that it started or encouraged any such rumors. Finally, with respect to General Cinema, its open market purchases were a matter of public record, see id., May 27, 1982, at 2, *reprinted in* app. at 82a, as was Heublein's resistance thereto, see Heublein Press Release of Feb. 22, 1982, *reprinted in* app. at 85a; Wall St.J., June 1, 1982, at 10, *reprinted in* app. at 199a. Therefore, when the NYSE called Caspar on July 14, he was understandably unable to explain what had caused the dramatic increase in activity in Heublein's stock that day. While he, and other Heublein executives, clearly knew of information that might have accounted for the increase in trading, there was no indication that any of this privileged information had been leaked or that they knew of, or had, information that insiders were engaged in trading. Accordingly, there is no support to the keystone of the dissent's hypothesis of the probability that this information could have been leaked, dissent at 765. Under these circumstances, we conclude that, as a matter of law, Caspar's statement that Heublein "was aware of no reason that would explain the activity in its stock ∗ ∗ ∗" was not false, inaccurate, or misleading.[7]

B.

Appellant next asserts that, even presuming the July 14 statement was correct when given, subsequent events made it materially inaccurate and Heublein breached its duty to correct it. Heublein responds that, by its own terms, the statement spoke only about the activity in its stock on July 14. The statement expired the next day and, therefore, was inapplicable to subsequent trading activity. Thus, Heublein asserts that the company was under no duty to correct the contents of the statement even if it were to become materially misleading on the basis of future events.

Although a close reading of the statement lends some support to Heublein's view, we need not concern ourselves with it further because, even presuming that the July 14 statement survived the date of issuance, as a matter of law, it never became materially misleading on the basis of subsequent events and, therefore, no duty to correct ever arose. This conclusion inescapably follows because, as previously shown, Heublein was never under a duty to disclose any of the substantive details of its discussions with either Reynolds or General Cinema prior to July 28.

∗ ∗ ∗

6. The dissent suggests that even privileged information must be disclosed because of the probability that information could have been leaked to the investing public or ascertained by the investing public, dissent at 765, that the two companies were exploring a merger. Imposing such a duty prior to July 28 runs counter to the precept that there is no duty to disclose negotiations until an agreement in principle has been reached. We know of no duty to disclose ongoing negotiations because of the possibility of a leak.

7. Although Caspar could have made any number of other statements saying substantively the same thing, this is of no consequence to our decision today. We must judge the statement made. Although Caspar might properly have responded "no comment" to the NYSE inquiry, this likewise is of no import. He did not so respond and for us to now hold that he should have would inexorably imply that the statement he actually made was legally infirm. This, as we have demonstrated, is not the case.

VI.

Accordingly, the judgment of the district court will be affirmed.

A. LEON HIGGINBOTHAM, Jr., CIRCUIT JUDGE, dissenting.

I dissent from the majority opinion because I believe that Heublein's July 14 statement was false or misleading. In my view, it is false or misleading for a corporation to *voluntarily* issue a statement that it is aware of no reason to explain increased trading in its stock when the corporation "clearly knew of information that might have accounted for the increase in trading." (Majority Opinion at 759).

I agree with the majority that a corporation is under no legal obligation to make disclosures concerning its merger activities until an agreement in principle is reached. I also agree that on July 14, when the NYSE sought a no corporate development statement from Heublein, no agreement in principle had yet been reached between Heublein and Reynolds. Moreover, I do not believe that a NYSE inquiry concerning corporate activity creates a duty to disclose. Thus, on July 14, Heublein was under no legal obligation to issue *any* statement in response to the NYSE inquiry concerning the unusually high trading activity in Heublein's stock on that day. Even though, as the majority concedes, Heublein clearly knew of information that could have accounted for the increased trading of its stock, Heublein could have remained silent in the face of the NYSE inquiry or answered "no comment."

My disagreement with the majority opinion involves Heublein's breach of its duty not to mislead. This duty applies to any corporate statement reasonably calculated to influence the investing public *whether or not* a duty to disclose exists. Once Heublein opted, however, to issue a statement that was reasonably calculated to influence the public, the July 14 statement, Heublein was obligated to ensure that its statement was not "false or misleading or * * * so incomplete as to mislead." SEC v. Texas Gulf Sulphur Co., 401 F.2d 833, 862 (2d Cir.1968), cert. denied, 394 U.S. 976 (1969). In addition, Heublein had a duty to update the July 14 statement if it became materially misleading in light of subsequent events. See Sharp v. Coopers & Lybrand, 83 F.R.D. 343, 346–47 (E.D.Pa.1979).

* * *

UNITED STATES v. MATTHEWS

United States Court of Appeals, Second Circuit, 1986.
787 F.2d 38.

Before VAN GRAAFEILAND and NEWMAN, CIRCUIT JUDGES, and WYATT, DISTRICT JUDGE.*

VAN GRAAFEILAND, CIRCUIT JUDGE:

Clark J. Matthews, II, appeals from a judgment of the United States District Court for the Eastern District of New York (Sifton, J.) convicting Matthews of violating section 14(a) of the Securities Exchange Act of 1934 and SEC's Implementing Rule 14a–9. This conviction was based on the second count of a two-count indictment. The first count charged that Matthews and S. Richmond

---

* Of the United States District Court for the Southern District of New York, sitting by designation.

Dole conspired with each other and with others to bribe members of the New York State Tax Commission in order to obtain favorable rulings on tax matters of interest to the defendants' employer, The Southland Corporation, and to file United States income tax returns for Southland which falsely listed the bribe payment as a legal fee. Both defendants were acquitted on this count.

The second count, which was against Matthews alone, charged in substance that Matthews' election to the Southland Board of Directors in 1981 was accomplished by means of a proxy statement which failed to disclose, among other things, that he was a member of the conspiracy alleged in Count I. For the reasons that follow, we reverse the judgment of conviction and remand to the district court with instructions to dismiss the indictment.

Prior to his conviction in this case, Clark Matthews had had an honorable career. He was born in Arkansas City, Kansas, but lived most of his forty-eight years in Texas. After being graduated from high school in Midland, Texas, he attended Southern Methodist University and Southern Methodist Law School. Following his admission to the bar, he worked as a staff attorney for the SEC for two years. He then served for two years as a law clerk for Judge Joe Estes of the United States District Court for the Northern District of Texas (for some years Chief Judge of that Court). Thereafter, in 1965, he became a staff attorney for the Southland Corporation, a large commercial company with headquarters in Dallas. He subsequently became Southland's General Counsel and is now its Executive Vice President and Chief Financial Officer.

In 1972 Southland became involved in litigation with the New York State Department of Taxation and Finance regarding Southland's asserted obligation to pay sales taxes owed by some of its franchised stores. Eugene DeFalco, then manager of Southland's Northeastern Division, who was the Government's principal witness and an admitted liar and thief, testified under grant of immunity that he inquired of one John Kelly, another immunized thief and liar, whether Kelly knew of anyone who could help in resolving the tax problem. Kelly arranged for DeFalco to meet with a New York attorney and City Councilman, Eugene Mastropieri.

According to DeFalco, Mastropieri informed him that the matter might require "heavy entertainment", which DeFalco took to mean a bribe. DeFalco testified that he told S. Richmond Dole, Southland's Vice President for Franchise Stores, that, in his opinion, somebody was going to be paid off. This testimony was denied by Dole. DeFalco also testified that, when Dole refused Mastropieri's request that he be paid in cash, Kelly suggested payment by way of a bill purporting to cover the lease of an airplane. This proposal brought Matthews into the picture for the first time. When Dole conveyed the lease proposal to Matthews with the explanation that Mastropieri wanted to conceal the legal fee from his law partner, Matthews telephoned DeFalco and told him that "Southland doesn't pay legal bills in the form of airplane leases [and] he did not want to see any more funny proposals coming through like the airplane lease. * * *" When DeFalco assured Matthews that the payment to Mastropieri was in fact a legal fee, Matthews replied that "if it's a legal fee, we are going to pay it as a legal fee, not as something else."

In July 1977 DeFalco sent Dole a bill from Mastropieri for legal services in the amount of $96,500, which Dole processed for payment. The bill neither was seen nor approved by Matthews. Southland's check in payment was delivered to Mastropieri by Kelly who, upon instructions from DeFalco, secured a blank check from Mastropieri in exchange, which Kelly filled out in the same amount as the Southland check. Kelly promptly deposited Mastropieri's check in a Toronto bank where "nobody would know about it". On August 8, 1977 DeFalco arranged to have $10,000 transferred from Kelly's Toronto account to DeFalco's account at The Chase Manhattan Bank. Thereafter, on August 23rd, DeFalco opened an account in his own name at the Toronto bank and had Kelly transfer $20,000 into that account. He also had five checks totalling $18,500 issued for his own personal use. On March 22, 1978 DeFalco started drawing from his Toronto account, and, by August 16, 1979, the account was closed. In all, DeFalco stole $48,500 of Southland's money. The balance of $48,000 was taken by Kelly, $20,000 on September 21, 1977 and $28,000 on July 10, 1979. Not a penny was used to bribe anyone.

While DeFalco and Kelly were in the process of stealing Southland's money, Southland, together with hundreds of other corporations, see Decker v. Massey-Ferguson, Ltd., 681 F.2d 111, 118 (2d Cir.1982); Branch and Rubright, Integrity of Management Disclosures Under the Federal Securities Laws, 37 Bus.Law. 1447, 1450 (1982), was conducting an internal questionable payments investigation, which it called the Business Ethics Review. The respected Washington law firm of Arnold and Porter had been retained as consultant for the Review, which was being handled by Southland's legal department. John Fedders, an Arnold and Porter partner with extensive experience in the field, worked closely throughout the Review with Matthews, then General Counsel, advising and assisting him in the preparation of questionnaires, the handling of interviews, the evaluation of information, and the reporting of results.

In August 1977 Matthews learned for the first time of Mastropieri's $96,500 bill. Because Matthews thought the bill was much too high, he instructed Michael Davis, a staff attorney who was assisting in the Business Ethics Review, to add Mastropieri's fee to the matters to be investigated. Accordingly, when Eugene Pender, Southland's controller, reported in his Review questionnaire that he suspected Mastropieri's bill was inflated to cover costs other than legal fees, Matthews told Davis to interview him. Following the interview, Davis reported to Matthews that "Pender did not have any specific facts which caused him to feel that way . . . he just felt that the bill appeared high."

Although DeFalco had indicated in his Review questionnaire that he had no knowledge of any wrongdoing, Matthews and Davis interviewed him together following a meeting of Division managers at a Dallas hotel on October 17, 1977. All three participants testified that at no time during this meeting did DeFalco reveal any plan to bribe a state tax official. DeFalco testified, however, that, following the meeting, he took Matthews aside in the hotel parking lot and told him that a $5,000 bribe already had been paid. Both Davis and Matthews denied that this parking lot conversation had taken place. If in fact DeFalco made the statement, it was a blatant lie. No bribe ever was paid.

Davis next interviewed Frank Kitchen, DeFalco's immediate supervisor. Kitchen told Davis that, some months before, he, John Thompson, Chairman of Southland's Board of Directors, and Dole had discussed the sales tax cases with DeFalco at a sales meeting in Hartford, Connecticut, and he formed a suspicion that an improper payment might be lurking somewhere in the background. When questioned by Davis as to the basis for this suspicion, Kitchen could point only to Mastropieri's Italian name, his high fee, the reference to entertainment expenses, and the location of the case in New York. When Matthews was informed of Kitchen's suspicions, Matthews insisted that Kitchen amend his theretofore negative responses to the Review questionnaire to incorporate his orally expressed suspicions. Matthews also interviewed both Thompson and Dole, both of whom assured him that Kitchen's suspicions were groundless.

Matthews then consulted G. Duane Vieth, another Arnold and Porter partner, concerning the advisability of interviewing Mastropieri directly. After consulting with Fedders, Vieth told Matthews to go ahead with the interview. Fedders then gave Matthews detailed instructions on how the interview should be conducted. On January 10, 1978 Matthews spoke with Mastropieri by telephone from Philadelphia, after a snowstorm prevented a scheduled face-to-face meeting in New York City. Mastropieri's responses to Matthews' questions concerning the sales tax dispute disclosed a comprehensive knowledge of the cases. In response to Matthews' questions about his fee, Mastropieri indignantly told Matthews that the amount of the fee was justified, that he had received the entire amount, and none was being paid to anyone else.

When Matthews reported the results of his interview to Fedders, Vieth, and the audit committee of Southland's Board of Directors, it was agreed that, because they had no proof of a bribe and because of the possibility of a suit for libel and slander, the matter should not be discussed in the formal Business Ethics Review report which was submitted to the Board of Directors on January 25, 1978. Nonetheless, despite Mastropieri's denial of wrongdoing, despite the fact that DeFalco and Kelly already had stolen $48,500 of Southland's money, despite the fact that not a penny had been paid to a member of the New York State Tax Commission, and despite the district court's correct charge that Matthews could not be convicted of the crime of conspiracy if all he did was to conceal its existence, the Government contends that Matthews knowingly joined an ongoing conspiracy to bribe the tax officials on January 25, 1978 when he failed to disclose the existence of the conspiracy in his report to the Board of Directors.

We are not at all surprised that the jury acquitted Matthews of the charges in Count I, and we are not completely comfortable with the Government's contention that the acquittal was based on the running of the statute of limitations. The Government argues that we must assume the jury followed the district court's instruction not to convict Matthews on Count II unless it either found him guilty of the crime charged in Count I or not guilty by reason of the statute of limitations. Although this argument states generally sound doctrine, United States v. Kaplan, 510 F.2d 606, 611 (2d Cir.1974), it comes with poor grace from a prosecution team which successfully opposed Matthews' request for a special verdict or jury interrogatory that would have precluded the making of the argument. This interrogatory, which was requested not once, but twice, would have asked the jurors to state whether, if they found a verdict of not guilty on Count I, that verdict was based on the running of the statute of limitations. It would have been quite proper for the district court to have submitted this query to the jury. * * * An affirmative answer by the jury would have eliminated any taint of inconsistency between the assumption of guilt now urged by the Government and the presumption of innocence, one of the strongest presumptions in the law * * *.

We note also that the issue of statutory time limitations virtually was ignored in the summations of counsel, and this, perhaps, was because the running of the limitation period was at best only a partial defense. The filing of Southland's allegedly fraudulent 1977 United States tax return, which was a significant part of the conspiracy alleged in Count I, took place on September 15, 1978, and the indictment against Matthews was filed on July 26, 1984, well within the statutory period of six years, see 26 U.S.C. § 6531.

Of course, the issue on this appeal is not whether the jury found Matthews guilty of conspiracy in 1985, but whether Matthews should have publicly pronounced himself guilty in 1981. We have expressed our misgivings concerning the assumed finding of guilt by the jury simply because the greater the uncertainty that exists today, the less reason there was for Matthews to confess seven years ago that he was guilty. However, regardless of the merits of the Government's contentions concerning the basis of the jury's verdict on Count I, we find no merit in the Government's argument that Matthews violated section 14a and Rule 14a–9 by not confessing that he was guilty of conspiracy three years before he was indicted on that charge.

* * *

The Commission also has promulgated rules dealing specifically with proxy statements. See Schedule 14A, 17 C.F.R. § 240.14a–101. Item 6 of this section covers statements used in the election of directors and executive officers, and incorporates the disclosure requirements of Item 401 of Regulation S–K, 17 C.F.R. § 229.401. Item 401 provides that a candidate for director must disclose whether he has been "convicted in a criminal proceeding or is a named subject of a pending criminal proceeding (excluding traffic violations and other minor offenses)" providing that the incident in question occurred during the preceding five years and disclosure is material to an evaluation of the candidate's ability or integrity. 17 C.F.R. § 229.401(f).

In November 1980 attorneys at Arnold and Porter were informed that the federal prosecutor who had been presenting evidence to a grand jury during the preceding six months concerning possible criminal activities of Councilman Mastropieri now regarded Southland and DeFalco as targets of the investigation and Matthews and Dole as subjects.[3] On January 23, 1981 four Arnold and Porter partners, including Peter Bleakley, the partner with principal responsibility for the Southland account, attended a meeting of Southland's Board of Directors and reported this change of events to them. The Board was told that this involved the same matter

---

3. There is a clear distinction between the "subject" of a grand jury investigation and the "target" of such an investigation. One about whom a grand jury seeks information in an investigation of possible wrongdoing that not yet has focused on the individual involved is a "subject" of the investigation. The Department of Justice guidelines define a "target" as a "person as to whom the prosecutor or the grand jury has substantial evidence linking him/her to the commission of a crime and who, in the judgment of the prosecutor, is a puta- tive defendant." United States Attorney's Manual § 9–11.260 (June 15, 1984); see United States v. Winter, 348 F.2d 204, 207– 08 (2d Cir.), cert. denied, 382 U.S. 955, 86 S.Ct. 429, 15 L.Ed.2d 360 (1965); People v. Steuding, 6 N.Y.2d 214, 216, 189 N.Y.S.2d 166, 160 N.E.2d 468 (1959). In accordance with longstanding practice in this Circuit, if a grand jury witness is considered to be a "target", he must be informed of that fact. United States v. Jacobs, 547 F.2d 772, 774 (2d Cir.1976), cert. dismissed, 436 U.S. 31, 98 S.Ct. 1873, 56 L.Ed.2d 53 (1978).

that Vieth and Fedders had reported three years before. The minutes of the January 28, 1981 meeting state:

Mr. Vieth then described the scope of an investigation by a Federal Grand Jury sitting in the Eastern District of New York. There followed a discussion of the investigation.

With full knowledge of Matthews' status as a "subject" of the grand jury's investigation, the Chairman of the Board nonetheless asked Matthews if he would run for election to the Board. Matthews inquired of Bleakley if, under the circumstances, he should run, and Bleakley told Matthews that there was no reason for him not to do so. Upon further inquiry by Matthews concerning disclosure, Bleakley told Matthews that Bleakley and his partners did not believe that the federal securities laws required Matthews to disclose that he was a subject of the investigation. Matthews ran and was elected.

Two years later, the grand jury returned an indictment charging Mastropieri, Dole and Southland with the same double objective conspiracy subsequently charged in the instant case, viz., the bribing of New York tax officials and the defrauding of the United States by misdescribing the bribe as a legal fee. See United States v. Southland Corp., 760 F.2d 1366 (2d Cir. 1985), cert. denied, 469 U.S. 1224 (1985). The wisdom of using special verdicts was demonstrated in that earlier case by the fact that the jury convicted Mastropieri of conspiracy to achieve both objects of the conspiracy, while Southland was found guilty of conspiring only with respect to the tax fraud objective. The jury could not agree on either charge with respect to Dole. Matthews was not indicted and did not testify. On August 2, 1984 Dole was reindicted and, in this indictment, the indictment now before us, Matthews was named as a co-conspirator. A second count, the proxy statement, securities count, was added against Matthews alone.

* * * Although "[t]raditionally, there has been a close working relationship between the Justice Department and the SEC," H.R.Rep. No. 95–650, 95th Cong., 1st Sess. 10 (September 28, 1977), quoted in United States v. Fields, 592 F.2d 638, 646 n. 19 (2d Cir.1978), cert. denied, 442 U.S. 917 (1979), in the instant case, the United States Attorney's office proceeded on its own. In fact, both the then local SEC Administrator and a former SEC General Counsel publicly questioned the wisdom of trying Matthews on the securities count. See Wall St.J., February 5, 1985, at 20, col. 1.[4] The results of proceeding without the benefit of SEC expertise are evident throughout the proceedings, beginning with the indictment itself.

The Proxy Statement upon which the Government's charges were based was for Southland's 1981 Annual Shareholders Meeting, at which eleven unopposed candidates for directorships, including Matthews, were elected. The Statement gave only basic information concerning each candidate. Insofar as Matthews was concerned, the Statement said that Matthews was

---

4. Regional Director Ira Sorkin said "I don't know of any other case where someone is accused of failing to disclose a crime they haven't been convicted of." He said that prosecutors in the instant case were pushing "an expansion of the concept" of an executive's liability in failing to disclose pertinent information and concluded "It's a new approach."

Former General Counsel Harvey L. Pitt said "To ask people to accuse themselves and indict and convict themselves is silly. So why should that be required in proxy statements?" Such a disclosure statement, he continued "runs counter to what the Fifth Amendment is all about."

forty-four years of age, that he served as Vice President and General Counsel from 1973 to 1979 and as Executive Vice President and Chief Financial Officer since 1979. The Statement also set forth Matthews' "Cash and cash-equivalent forms of remuneration" and the extent of his "Security Ownership." The Government contends that this simple recital was made false and misleading in violation of Rule 14a–9(a) because it (1) failed to disclose that Matthews had engaged in a conspiracy to bribe New York public officials and to defraud the United States by preventing the IRS from determining the true nature of the business expense deductions and (2) failed to disclose that Matthews had failed to disclose to the audit committee of the Board of Directors, Southland's independent auditors, outside tax counsel, the IRS, the SEC, the FBI and others that he was engaged in the conspiracy.

The Government argued under Count I that Matthews became a member of the conspiracy on the day he submitted his Business Ethics Review report to the Board of Directors, when, according to the prosecutor, "he held the truth and the lie in each hand and decided to give the lie to the Board of Directors." When the prosecutor thereafter turned to Count II, he argued that Matthews' failure to disclose to the shareholders that he had failed to disclose to the Board put him in violation of Rule 14a–9. We note as a preliminary matter that the evidence does not clarify precisely what facts Matthews should have told the shareholders he failed to disclose to the Board.

"Liability under Rule 14a–9 is predicated upon a showing that an allegedly omitted fact is true." Bertoglio v. Texas International Co., 488 F.Supp. 630, 649 (D.Del.1980); see Cohen v. Ayers, 449 F.Supp. 298, 317 (N.D.Ill.1978), aff'd mem., 596 F.2d 733 (7th Cir.1979). Overstatement can be as seriously misleading as understatement. Electronic Specialty Co. v. International Controls Corp., 409 F.2d 937, 948 (2d Cir.1969). Although the prosecutor managed to incorporate the words "bribe", "bribery", and "slush fund" into every possible question, and prominently displayed one or more of these words in his blown-up summary charts, DeFalco testified that he neither heard nor used any of these words until they were spoken to him in the United States Attorneys Office in 1980, some two to three years after his alleged conversations with Matthews. Moreover, although it is undisputed that not a penny of bribe money was paid to anyone, the Government, even at this late date, argues that Matthews "never even asked the Board to approve the bribe, but instead misled it into believing that no bribe had been paid." Govt.'s Brief, 58. In the light of language such as this, the Government's contention appears to be that Matthews should have misled the Board into believing that a bribe had been paid. Indeed, although DeFalco, the Government's prime witness, testified that only $20,000 of Southland's money was to be used for bribing tax officials, the Government has argued repeatedly that the "truth" which Matthews assertedly held in his hand when he reported to the Board, was that $40,000 was to be spread among the members of the Tax Commission. After four years of grand jury hearings and two lengthy trials, the Government still has failed to establish what "truth" Matthews should have disclosed to Southland's Board and shareholders concerning the payment of bribes.

Although Matthews hardly could have confessed to membership in a phantom conspiracy, the Government is equally vague concerning whom

Matthews should have identified as his co-conspirators. The SEC disapproves of attacks on character without complete and adequate supporting data, the Commission's position being that such attacks are contrary to the standards of fair disclosure unless they are in fact true. II Loss, Securities Regulation 913 (1961). In a note to Rule 14a–9, 17 C.F.R. § 240.14a–9, the Commission describes as examples of misleading statements under that section:

> Material which directly or indirectly impugns character, integrity or personal reputation, or directly or indirectly makes charges concerning improper, illegal or immoral conduct or associations, without factual foundation.

The courts agree. See, e.g., Kass v. Arden-Mayfair, Inc., 431 F.Supp. 1037, 1045 (C.D.Calif.1977) ("[A] 'puffed-up' accusation may constitute the presentation of an untrue statement.").

During the trial, the prosecutor stated categorically that Michael Davis was a co-conspirator. The district court later charged as a matter of law that Davis was not. The Government indicted and tried S. Richmond Dole for conspiracy; he was acquitted. In response to Matthews' inquiries, Mastropieri denied all wrongdoing. Should Matthews, proceeding "without factual foundation" and in complete disregard of the laws of libel and slander, have accused these men of conspiracy? The Government doesn't say. The Government likewise makes no mention of the furor that would have resulted had Matthews "impugn[ed]" the "character, integrity or personal reputation" of the members of the New York State Tax Commission by falsely stating that one of them had received a bribe of $5,000 and that $35,000 more was to be spread among the other Commission members. See Note, Disclosure of Payments to Foreign Government Officials Under the Securities Acts, 89 Harv.L.Rev. 1848, 1870 (1976) ("The State Department has warned that uncorroborated allegations that foreign officials have accepted improper payments have done grave harm to American foreign relations.").

The issue with the most far-reaching implications in the field of federal securities law, however, is not what "true" facts Matthews should have disclosed, but whether section 14a of the Exchange Act and the SEC rules enacted pursuant thereto required Matthews to state to all the world that he was guilty of the uncharged crime of conspiracy. This query, we are satisfied, must be answered in the negative.

* * *

The provisions of Item 6 of Schedule 14A, which require disclosure of only criminal convictions or pending criminal proceedings, were proposed in 1976, Securities Act Release No. 5758 [1976–77 Transfer Binder] Fed.Sec. L.Rep. (CCH) ¶ 80,783 and adopted in 1978, Securities Act Release No. 5949 [1978 Transfer Binder] Fed.Sec.L.Rep. (CCH) ¶ 81,649. In adopting the specifically articulated disclosure provisions of Item 6, the Commission said:

> Because information reflecting on management ability and integrity is, in part, subjective, it is difficult to articulate a meaningful, well-functioning objective disclosure requirement which will elicit it. The Commission believes that the categories of information about officers' and directors' involvement in litigation proposed in Release 5758 are

material to investors. They represent factual indicia of past management performance in areas of investor concern.

Securities Act Release No. 5949, supra, at p. 80,618.

It is significant that, although the Commission gave consideration to amending Schedule 14A so as to require disclosure of questionable or illegal payments, see Securities Exchange Act Release No. 13185 [1976–77 Transfer Binder] Fed.Sec.L.Rep. (CCH) ¶ 80,896 at 87,382–84, it did so knowing that this area is "difficult and complex", and it failed to adopt the proposals. See Securities Exchange Act Release No. 15570 [1979 Transfer Binder] Fed.Sec.L.Rep. (CCH) ¶ 81,959 at 81,392 n. 3.

Attempts to enlarge upon the disclosure requirements of Schedule 14A "provoked enormous disagreement * * * among respected practitioners"[5] and were described by various commentators as controversial,[6] unclear,[7] fuzzy,[8] and inconsistent.[9] This controversy and uncertainty resulted in large measure from the Commission's attempts to respond to the post-Watergate demand for complete ethical and social disclosure. After the administrative euphoria resulting from the voluntary soul-searching by over 450 companies had dissipated, the Commission again was faced with the difficult and complex problem of whether and how to compel so-called "qualitative" proxy statement disclosures concerning management ethics and integrity that were not specifically required in Schedule 14A. The Commission had not solved that problem when Southland's 1981 Proxy Statement was mailed. In 1981 the Commission itself described the law concerning disclosure of unadjudicated allegations as "unclear". See Sec. Act Rel. No. 82–19 (March 5, 1982), quoted in Integrity of Management Disclosures, supra, at 1477 n. 118. In his speech at the American Bar Association, supra, n. 6, Mr. Fedders said:

> The Commission has not promulgated specific disclosure requirements relating to all qualitative conduct, or, to the extent necessary, articulated a policy for law enforcement when information about such conduct has not been disclosed. The full extent of the obligation to disclose such information is uncertain in light of existing cases. In this limited area, there is little guidance for issuers or practitioners for resolving materiality and disclosure problems.

We deem it significant that those courts which have spoken in this area in the years following Matthews' asserted violations almost universally have rejected efforts to require that management make qualitative disclosures that were not at least implicit in the Commission's rules. In Maldonado v. Flynn, supra, 597 F.2d at 796, this Court stated that section 14(a) and Rule 14a–9 should not be used "as an avenue for access to the federal courts in order to redress alleged mismanagement or breach of fiduciary duty on the part of corporate executives." We stated further that

---

5. Speech by John M. Fedders at ABA Committee meeting on Failure to Disclose Illegal Conduct, reprinted in 14 Sec.Reg. & L.Rep. (BNA) 2057 (November 26, 1982).

6. Note, Disclosure of Corporate Payments and Practices: Conduct Regulation Through the Federal Securities Laws, 43 Brooklyn L.Rev. 681 (1977).

7. Branch and Rubright, Integrity of Management Disclosures Under the Feder-

al Securities Laws, 37 Bus.Law. 1447, 1451 n. 16 (1982).

8. Schorr, SEC's Fuzziness On What Illicit Dealings Should Be Reported Limits Disclosure, Wall St.J., March 29, 1976, at 26, col. 1.

9. Ferrara, Starr and Steinberg, Disclosure of Information Bearing on Management Integrity and Competency, 76 Nw. U.L.Rev. 555, 564 (1981).

"[e]fforts to dress up claims of the latter type in a § 14(a) suit of clothes have consistently been rejected", and we cited as illustrative Levy v. Johnson [1976–77 Transfer Binder] Fed.Sec.L.Rep. (CCH) ¶ 95,899 (S.D.N.Y. 1977) and Limmer v. GTE [1977–78 Transfer Binder] Fed.Sec.L.Rep. (CCH) ¶ 96,111 (S.D.N.Y.1977), both of which involved illegal payments. Id. We found merit in the plaintiff's claim of wrongdoing only insofar as it alleged self-dealing by the defendant directors, a matter "explicitly covered by SEC disclosure regulations." Id. See, e.g., Item 404(a)(2) of Regulation S–K, 17 C.F.R. § 229.404(a)(2).

In Weisberg v. Coastal States Gas Corp., 609 F.2d 650 (2d Cir.1979), cert. denied, 445 U.S. 951 (1980), we again recognized the danger of expanding section 14(a) to encompass allegations of corporate waste but upheld a complaint which alleged bribes and kickbacks to the defendant directors. Id. at 655. In GAF Corp. v. Heyman, supra, 724 F.2d 727, a case involving the failure to disclose a pending action against a directorship candidate in a matter that did not involve GAF, we again emphasized that the Commission's Rules do not require a candidate for election to accuse himself of antisocial or illegal activities. Id. at 740.

The Ninth Circuit is in accord. In Gaines v. Haughton, 645 F.2d 761, 779 (9th Cir.1981), cert. denied, 454 U.S. 1145 (1982), the Court stated:

> Absent credible allegations of self-dealing by the directors or dishonesty or deceit which inures to the direct, personal benefit of the directors—a fact that demonstrates a betrayal of trust to the corporation and shareholders and the director's essential unfitness for corporate stewardship—we hold that director misconduct of the type traditionally regulated by state corporate law need not be disclosed in proxy solicitations for director elections. This type of mismanagement, unadorned by self-dealing, is simply not material or otherwise within the ambit of the federal securities laws.

A number of lower courts have taken the same position. See, e.g., Amalgamated Clothing & Textile Workers Union v. J.P. Stevens & Co., 475 F.Supp. 328, 331–32 (S.D.N.Y.1979), vacated as moot, 638 F.2d 7 (2d Cir. 1980); Lewis v. Valley, 476 F.Supp. 62, 66 (S.D.N.Y.1979); Bank & Trust Co. of Old York Road v. Hankin, 552 F.Supp. 1330, 1335–36 (E.D.Pa.1982).

The Government has treated the instant case from the outset as one involving the withholding of qualitative rather than quantitative information. Government counsel conceded at oral argument that the Government had not proven that Matthews' actions had any adverse quantitative economic impact on Southland. Echoing the words of the district court, counsel contended that "[t]his was not a matter of dollars and cents, it was morality looked at through the eyeglasses of someone with economic interest." We are satisfied, however, that Matthews was not legally required to confess that he was guilty of an uncharged crime in order that Southland's shareholders could determine the morality of his conduct.

We hold that at least so long as uncharged criminal conduct is not required to be disclosed by any rule lawfully promulgated by the SEC, nondisclosure of such conduct cannot be the basis of a criminal prosecution. Our unwillingness to permit section 14(a) to be used as expansively as the Government has done in this case rests not only on the history of the Commission's approach to the problem of qualitative disclosures and the case law that has developed on this subject but also on the obvious due process implications that would arise from permitting a conviction to stand in the absence of clearer notice as to what disclosures are required in this uncertain area.

When a person of ordinary intelligence has not received fair notice that his contemplated conduct is forbidden, prosecution for such conduct deprives him of due process. United States v. Harriss, 347 U.S. 612, 617 (1954); Lanzetta v. New Jersey, 306 U.S. 451, 453 (1939). Four lawyers, including a Professor of Federal Regulation of Securities at a prominent law school, a former Chairman of the Committee on Professional Responsibility and Liability of the ABA Section on Corporation, Banking and Business Law, and a former SEC Commissioner and Chairman of the Executive Committee of the ABA Committee on Regulation of Securities, submitted affidavits in support of Matthews' pretrial motion to dismiss, asserting the lack of any precedent for the Government's theory of liability. Professor Alan R. Bromberg, an acknowledged authority in the field of securities law, filed an amicus brief with this Court in which he stated that "this case goes beyond any precedent in requiring disclosure of unadjudicated and uncharged conduct relating to 'management integrity'". See also the reaction of knowledgeable authorities to this very lawsuit quoted in footnote 4, supra. We agree with these observations. Constitutional issues aside, changes in the interpretations of the Commission's rules should not be made in such a manner. See Gerstle v. Gamble-Skogmo, Inc., 478 F.2d 1281, 1291–94 (2d Cir.1973); Flynn v. Bass Brothers Enterprises, Inc., 744 F.2d 978, 988 (3d Cir.1984).

Our rejection of criminal liability for nondisclosure of uncharged criminal conduct is also buttressed by concerns about the self-incrimination implications of accepting the Government's approach. * * *

* * * In view of the fact that a grand jury was actively investigating this very conspiracy when the proxy materials were issued, we do not understand the district court's holding that disclosure by Matthews of his participation in the conspiracy "[did] not pose a substantial possibility of incrimination", United States v. Dole, 601 F.Supp. 430, 433 (E.D.N.Y.1984). See, e.g., Grosso v. United States, 390 U.S. 62, 66–67 (1968); Carter-Wallace, Inc. v. Hartz Mountain Industries, Inc., 553 F.Supp. 45, 48–50 (S.D.N.Y. 1982).

Were we to face the issue directly, we are not certain we would find persuasive the argument that Matthews' self-incrimination privilege was not violated because he was not compelled to run for the office of director. Coercion associated with a person's livelihood, professional standing and reputation may, in some circumstances, be too powerful to ignore when Fifth Amendment rights are at issue. * * *

For all the reasons above discussed, the judgment of the district court is reversed, and the matter is remanded to the district court with instructions to dismiss the indictment.

LIABILITY FOR FALSE OR MISLEADING STATEMENTS

The basic prohibition in all of the most important statutes and rules creating liability under the federal securities laws is directed against the making of false or misleading statements. The pertinent language was originally formulated in clause (2) of Section 17(a) of the Securities Act of 1933 (which in turn echoed Section 11(a) of the same statute), proscribing "any untrue statement of a material fact or any omission to state a material fact necessary in order to make the statements made, in the light of the circumstances under which they were made, not misleading." This language was in turn substantially copied in clause (2) of Rule 10b–5; in Rule 14a–9 dealing with proxy statements (although that rule has some word changes which have no apparent significance and adds: "or necessary to correct any statement in any earlier communication with respect to the solicitation of a proxy for the same meeting or subject matter which has become false or misleading"); and in Section 14(e) of the Exchange Act dealing with a communication in connection with "any tender offer or request or invitation for tenders, or any solicitation of security holders in opposition to or in favor of any such offer."

Most of the cases alleging a violation of the Federal securities laws for the purpose of attempting to impose civil liability, and almost all of the successful ones, have been based upon a violation of this standard. These cases have considered a number of issues, among which the most important are the questions: What is a "fact"?; What is an "omission"?; and, What is "material"?

In a sense, the *Feit* case did not involve any question of materiality, but rather the question whether the alleged fact was or was not a "fact." If it had been stipulated, for example, that the so-called "surplus surplus" was a precisely determinable figure of $125,000,000, no one really argued that it was not material or that it was not required to be disclosed to the Reliance shareholders being requested to exchange their shares. The only basis for such an argument would be that the registration statement related to the securities of Leasco and therefore no disclosure was required regarding Reliance. However, the court held, it would seem properly, that in a registered exchange offer the prospectus must include material facts known to the offeror relating to the target company.

It is true that it has been held that in a cash tender offer the offeror is not required by Rule 10b–5 to disclose facts which it has deduced from published information about the target company or plans which it may have to utilize the resources of the target company, not based upon any inside information.[1] Whether or not this result would be different under the Williams Act (and it obviously would be so far as any plans of the offeror to make any major change in the business of the target company are concerned),[2] the court in the *Feit* case holds that in a registration situation the "full disclosure" policy of the 1933 Act requires the offeror to disclose material facts known to it about the target company, even though it obviously cannot be required to answer all the items in Form S–1 with respect to the target company if the management of that company refuses to cooperate (as the management of Reliance did).

The only "facts" which the Leasco management had concerning the "surplus surplus" of Reliance were its own estimates based upon published information, which it did not trust (quite rightly, it would seem, since in the event they turned out to be erroneous). Nevertheless, the court says that it should have included these estimates with an appropriate "hedge" clause. Suppose the Leasco prospectus had said: "We have estimated that the surplus surplus of Reliance may range from $80,000,000 to $125,000,000. No assurance can be given, however, that these figures are accurate or that these amounts, or any amount, of funds can be separated from the insurance business, etc., etc."

1. Mutual Shares Corp. v. Genesco, Inc., 384 F.2d 540 (2d Cir.1967); Mills v. Sarjem Corp., 133 F.Supp. 753 (D.N.J.1955).

2. See Chapter 12, supra, p. 688.

Would a buyer of the Leasco securities have a cause of action under Section 11 when the amount actually turned out to be $39,000,000? Judge Weinstein says, no; but of course that was not the case that he was adjudicating. The fear of such possible liability was obviously the other horn of the dilemma faced by the drafters of the prospectus in the *Feit* case.

The various federal securities laws and SEC rules require the disclosure of material "facts", and these were sharply distinguished by the Commission until the last ten or twelve years from anything that might be labelled "opinion" or "prediction." The latter were not only not required, but were expressly prohibited, in Commission-filed documents as being inherently misleading. For example, in Union Pacific Railroad Co. v. Chicago & North Western Railway Co.[3] the action sought to enjoin the use in proxy solicitation material of a report prepared by one Pierre R. Bretey, who was employed by Hayden, Stone & Co. and who was described as a "dean of railroad analysts." He attempted to compare the "work-out values" of the competing offers of securities by the Union Pacific and the C. & N.W. for the Rock Island, which was of course the most important ultimate fact that any stockholder would be interested in. However, under the SEC rules this was not then permitted to be told to the stockholders by anyone, no matter how expert; they were required to try and work it out for themselves from two 50 to 100 page documents crammed with statistics. The court in that case enjoined the use of such material in accordance with the SEC rules.

However, in recent years there has been a reversal of this attitude on the part of the Commission in response to considerable criticism led by Professor Homer Kripke of New York University. Professor Kripke has pointed out that what are called "facts" blend imperceptibly into opinions and predictions, and that a "statement of fact" more often than not contains elements of all three. For example, a statement on the balance sheet that a corporation has net accounts receivable of $450,000 embodies an estimate in the reserve for bad debts of the amount probably uncollectible, which is merely an opinion although possibly based in the case of an established business upon prior statistical evidence, and a prediction at a minimum that the corporation will continue as a going concern, since it is a known fact that if the corporation goes into liquidation or bankruptcy the accounts receivable will have to be drastically written down because many debtors stop paying their bills in those circumstances. In fact, all of the financial statements presented in a registration statement or proxy statement are based upon the "assumption" (or prediction) that the business will continue as a going concern since many assets shown will have to be totally written off if this assumption proves to be erroneous.[4]

Nevertheless, there is still a distinction between historical facts and bald predictions regarding future events, such as what the earnings of a business will be next year or two years from now, or mere opinions based upon nothing more than the alleged "expertise" of the opinionator, such as the "value" of an asset which is not fungible and for which there is no established market or published quotations.[5] However, with respect to so-called forward-looking information (or predictions) regarding the future prospects of the business,

---

3. 226 F.Supp. 400 (N.D.Ill.1964).

4. If the basic "going concern" assumption of the accountants is called seriously into question, the auditors are required to disclaim any opinion on the financial statements or to make their opinion "subject to" the ability of the company to continue as a going concern, depending on how serious the question is.

5. There is a standing joke in the business community that an "MAI appraisal" of real estate, which refers to one made by a Member of the Appraisal Institute, in reality stands for "made as instructed."

In reply to Professor Kripke's argument that there are no facts, one might be tempted to paraphrase Lord Byron's reply to Bishop Berkeley. He wrote: "When

Professor Kripke argues that this sort of information, particularly the evaluation of those in the best position to know—the management of the corporation, is what in fact sells securities through dissemination by salesmen orally to their customers. Anyone who has attended a so-called "due diligence" meeting, at which representatives of the members of the underwriting syndicate are supposed to probe the accuracy of the historical facts stated in the prospectus, knows that the first question, and frequently the only question, is likely to be: What is the management's projection of earnings for the next quarter or the next year? That is what the salesmen are going to use to sell the securities. Therefore, Professor Kripke argues, such projections should be brought within the scope of the formal disclosure system. But he goes much further and argues that the basic financial statements themselves are largely useless since they are based upon "historical cost" and should be replaced by what he calls "fair value accounting." The precise form this would take is not clear, although he does not discount the difficulties.

"SOFT" INFORMATION

Projections of earnings. Despite the general hostility of the SEC to projections of earnings in Commission-filed documents, there has always been an implied exception in the case of a selling document if the projection is negative or pessimistic. Prospectuses have been sprinkled with "no assurances" that the company is likely to survive for more than a week or, if it does, ever to make a profit. When American securities experts were testifying in England before the Jenkins Committee (considering a revision of English company law), they were questioned closely about the SEC prohibition of projections, since management's projection of future earnings is routinely included in all English prospectuses and the committee members had difficulty in understanding the policy basis for their exclusion. Finally, one of the committee members asked what would be the SEC's attitude if the management thought that the earnings were going to go down; and the reply was that, well, if they really thought earnings were going to go down, then they had better say that. The committee member replied: "It is rather a curious position. The trend [of earnings upward] might be continuing, in which case you would say nothing, or the directors might think it was going up in which case you would also say nothing. But if it is going down you cry stinking fish." [6]

The Commission increasingly came to realize, not only the logical inconsistency of this approach, but also the fact that, whenever there is a preexisting public trading market for the securities being sold, any disclosure document may be used as a basis for action by sellers as well as buyers. Therefore, an unwarrantedly pessimistic disclosure can harm public investors as much as an overly optimistic one. And counsel for issuers increasingly came to realize that in attempting to protect their clients from liability to the purchasers of the particular issue under Section 11 of the 1933 Act, they might be exposing them to liability under Rule 10b–5 to sellers in the market. Therefore, in 1972 the Commission announced a public rulemaking proceeding [7] relating to the use of projections of earnings in filings with it and otherwise; and on February 2, 1973, it issued a "Statement by the Commission on Disclosure of Projections of Future Economic Performance" [8] publicly abandoning its opposition to the use of projections. The Commission stated in that Release that it had "now

Bishop Berkeley said, 'There is no matter', and proved it; Twas no matter what he said."

6. Minutes of Evidence Taken Before the Company Law Committee 1031 (14th

Day, Dec. 16, 1960) (Her Majesty's Stationery Office 1961).

7. Sec.Exch.Act Rel. No. 9844 (Nov. 1, 1972).

8. Sec.Act Rel. No. 5362 (Feb. 2, 1973).

determined that changes in its present policies with regard to use of projections would assist in the protection of investors and would be in the public interest."

Despite the prohibition of projections in Commission-filed documents, earnings projections have of course been issued for many years by many companies in press releases, speeches to security analysts and otherwise. There have strangely been few suits under Rule 10b–5 based upon those which proved incorrect, perhaps because it was thought that they were not "facts" which could be alleged to have been misstated. In Marx v. Computer Sciences Corp.[9] the corporation issued on January 23, 1970, an earnings forecast for the fiscal year ending March 27, 1970 of $1 per share on 12.8 million shares outstanding. In fact, the earnings turned out to be only 41¢ per share for that period. This was due primarily to the fact that the corporation had been capitalizing the development expenses of a new computer system over a period of years and that the entire amount of these developments expenses of approximately $10,000,000 was charged off at the end of the fiscal year and the system was abandoned. There had been various warning signs that the system was not going to be successful prior to the issuance of the earnings forecast. The Ninth Circuit reversed a summary judgment which had been granted to the defendant corporation and held that there was a jury question as to whether the corporation had a reasonable basis for the forecast. The court said: "The next question is, was the forecast an 'untrue' statement. Of course in hindsight it turned out to be wrong. But at least in the case of a prediction as to the future, that in itself does not make the statement untrue when made. However, the forecast may be regarded as a representation that on January 23, 1970, CSC's [the corporation's] informed and reasonable belief was that at the end of the coming period, earnings would be approximately $1.00. That is what a reasonable investor would take the statement to mean, and we believe it would be 'untrue' when made if CSC did not then believe earnings would be in that amount or knew that there was reason to believe they would not be. In addition, because such a statement implies a reasonable method of preparation and a valid basis, we believe also that it would be 'untrue' absent such preparation or basis."[10] The court also quoted Professor Kripke as follows: "The foregoing is not intended to suggest that projections could be subjected to statutory liabilities, either express or under rule 10b–5, in the same fashion as a statement of fact about last year's sales or the ownership of a building. Rather the sole factual elements of a projection should be that it represents management's view, that it was reached in a rational fashion and that it is a sincere view. Only these elements can be subject to a statutory liability, not the eventuation of the prophecy."[11] Kripke, The SEC, The Accountants, Some Myths And Some Realities, 45 N.Y.U.L.Rev. 1151, at 1199 (1970).

In addition to the *Marx* case, another recent case dealing with liability for projections is the case of Beecher v. Able.[12] That case involved a statement in a prospectus of Douglas Aircraft issued in the middle of the fiscal year that "it is very likely that net income [of the company], if any, for fiscal 1966 will be nominal." In the light of the earnings of the company for the previous year and those announced for the earlier quarters of the current year, this was a very pessimistic statement; however, it proved not to be pessimistic enough,

---

9. 507 F.2d 485 (9th Cir.1974).

10. 507 F.2d at 489–490. See, also, Eisenberg v. Gagnon, 766 F.2d 770 (3d Cir. 1985), cert. denied 106 S.Ct. 342 (1985), citing and following the *Marx* case.

11. See Decker v. Massey-Ferguson, Limited, 681 F.2d 111 (2d Cir.1982) ("Eco-

nomic prognostication, though faulty, does not, without more, amount to fraud.")

12. 374 F.Supp. 341 (S.D.N.Y.1974); CCH Fed.Sec.Law Rptr. ¶ 95,303 (S.D.N.Y. 1975). The case was reported to have been settled for $5,000,000. BNA Sec.Reg. & L.Rep. No. 367 at A–15 (Aug. 25, 1976).

since the company actually sustained a loss of $52,000,000. The court in its first opinion dealing with liability under Section 11 of the 1933 Act [13] treated this statement as a prediction that the earnings would be substantially zero (i.e., there would be neither a profit nor a loss), and held that it was materially misleading in the light of the facts then known to the company.

The court said: "[A]n earnings forecast must be based on facts from which a reasonably prudent investor would conclude that it was highly probable that the forecast would be realized. Moreover, any assumptions underlying the projection must be disclosed if their validity is sufficiently in doubt that a reasonably prudent investor, if he knew of the underlying assumptions, might be deterred from crediting the forecast." [14] The court found that the statement quoted above would be understood by the average investor to mean, not merely that there would probably be no profit, but also that there would be no substantial loss, and that Douglas had failed to meet the high standard established by the court in the light of its knowledge at the time and had also failed to disclose its underlying assumptions which were doubtful of being realized. This finding that the statement was materially misleading disposed of the company's liability under Section 11, since the issuer is absolutely liable under that section once that finding has been made.

However, in a subsequent opinion dealing with a count under Rule 10b–5,[15] the court held that the company was not liable, since the forecast was not "intentionally" or "recklessly" false and it did have "some basis" in fact and was made in good faith.

A different question is presented when the claim of the plaintiff is, not that a published projection was misleading, but that liability arose from a failure to disclose internal projections of earnings in connection with a particular transaction. For example, in Pavlidis v. New England Patriots Football Club [16] it was claimed that the company should have disclosed, in a proxy statement for a going-private merger transaction, certain projections of future earnings made by the management. The court rejected this contention. It stated: "The federal securities laws do not require corporate management to include speculations about future profitability in proxy statements; in fact, at the time that the Patriots' proxy statement was issued, the Securities and Exchange Commission frowned on such disclosures. * * * Of course, stockholders may point to specific information in a financial projection as evidence that the management did not disclose all the material facts in its possession; but failure to disclose the projection itself does not establish a § 14(a) violation." [17]

The two most difficult questions in connection with any projection disclosure system are whether disclosure of earnings' projections made for internal purposes should be made mandatory, and what protection will be afforded, if any, to the issuer if the projections, even though made in good faith, turn out to be wrong. After years of debate, the Commission finally adopted on June 25, 1979,[18] a so-called "safe-harbor" rule designed to encourage (but not require) the disclosure of projections in documents filed with the Commission, by relieving the issuer of liability with respect to such projections under specified circumstances. These provisions, contained in Rule 175 under the 1933 Act and Rule 3b–6 under the 1934 Act, which are identical in substance, apply only to a statement made or reiterated in a document *filed* with the Commission or

13. 374 F.Supp. 341 (S.D.N.Y.1974).

14. 374 F.Supp. at 348.

15. CCH Fed.Sec.Law Rptr. ¶ 95,303 (S.D.N.Y.1975).

16. 737 F.2d 1227 (1st Cir.1984).

17. 737 F.2d at 1233.

18. Sec.Act Release No. 6084 (June 25, 1979), as amended by Sec.Act Release No. 6288 (Feb. 9, 1981) and Sec.Act Release No. 6291 (Feb. 17, 1981).

in an annual report to shareholders (which is also filed with the Commission, but is "deemed" not to be filed for the purpose of Section 18 liability) by a reporting company or in a registration statement under the 1933 Act. If the statement is initially made otherwise than in a filed document, it must be repeated in such a filed document "within a reasonable time" in order to have the protection of the rule. If the statement is initially made in a filed document, a statement "reaffirming" it made subsequently is also entitled to the protection of the rule.

A "forward-looking statement" covered by the rule is defined as including projections of revenues, income, capital expenditures, dividends, capital structure "or other financial items"; a statement of "management's plans and objectives for future operations"; and a statement of future economic performance contained in management's discussion and analysis of the results of operations. Disclosure of the assumptions underlying the projections is not specifically required, although it would be highly advisable; but if such assumptions are disclosed, they are also included within the protection of the rule.

The substantive provisions in this rule relieve the issuer from any liability under the antifraud provisions of the federal securities laws if the projection is made with a "reasonable basis" and in "good faith." This standard is necessarily somewhat vague, but it would not seem to require that it be "highly probable" that the forecast be realized; on the other hand, it may require something more than "some basis" in fact. The plaintiff, however, has the burden of proving that the projection lacked a reasonable basis or was made otherwise than in good faith.

Appraisals of assets. In Gerstle v. Gamble-Skogmo, Inc.[19] a controlling interest in the General Outdoor Advertising Company had been acquired by Gamble-Skogmo and it commenced a program to sell the outdoor advertising plants of the company at advantageous prices considerably in excess of their book value. It sold approximately 35% of the company's plants, but then suspended the sales and initiated a squeeze-out merger of the minority shareholders. The proxy statement stated that it was the intention of Gamble-Skogmo to "continue the business of General Outdoor, including the policy of considering offers for the sale to acceptable prospective purchasers of outdoor advertising branches or subsidiaries of General Outdoor." In fact, after the squeeze-out merger was accomplished, Gamble-Skogmo sold all of the remaining plants, and the court found that it intended to do this all along.

While the proxy statement was being circulated, a shareholder of General Outdoor Advertising Company complained that appraisals of the remaining plants were not included in the proxy statement and company officials consulted the Branch Chief at the SEC who was reviewing the proxy statement to determine if it should include such appraisals. The Branch Chief said, in effect, "No, that would be against the policy of the Commission not to permit any appraisals in proxy statements." In this case, ten years later, the SEC filed an *amicus* brief arguing that the defendant should be held liable because it had not included such appraisals in the proxy statement. Judge Friendly commented that this "must have been as much a surprise to the Commission's branch chief who had refused to insist on a revision of the proxy statement to include appraisals because this was contrary to Commission policy, as it was to Skogmo's counsel." [20]

The court held there was no liability for failure to disclose such appraisals, at least in the regulatory climate prevailing in 1963, although it stated, without deciding the question, that firm offers to purchase might fall into a different

19. 478 F.2d 1281 (2d Cir.1973). 20. 478 F.2d at 1292.

category. The court held the company liable, however, for failing to disclose its true intention of liquidating all of the remaining assets of General Outdoor Advertising Company after the merger.

The history of the SEC's hostility to the inclusion of appraisals, like projections, in Commission-filed documents is detailed in the *Gerstle* case. Of course, "market value", which is a form of appraisal or at least a recognition of the current value of an asset as opposed to historical cost, has always entered into the preparation of financial statements, but under the "conservative principle" of accounting only when this resulted in a write-down rather than a write-up of the recorded value of the asset; for example, in the rule that inventories are to be valued at cost or market, *whichever is lower.* And it has also been recognized that a market value which is higher than book value might have to be disclosed under the federal securities laws when the company or an insider is purchasing stock of the company. In Speed v. Transamerica Corp.,[21] one of the earliest cases under Rule 10b–5, a controlling shareholder was held liable for purchasing stock of the company without disclosing a greatly increased market value of a tobacco inventory over the cost figure at which it was shown on the financial statements of the company. However, where there is no active and widespread market for an asset, which does not consist of items that are essentially fungible (such as a tobacco inventory), then any attempt to determine current value by an "appraisal" becomes much more subjective.

The discussion by the court in the *Starkman* case of the prior Sixth Circuit decision in Radol v. Thomas [22] is somewhat confusing. It is true, as the court in the *Starkman* case says, that the trial court in that case submitted the question of the materiality of the same appraisals as were involved in the *Starkman* case to the jury. However, the circuit court stated that he should not have done that. It indicated that the error of the district court was not in the court's instructions to the jury on this issue but in submitting the issue to the jury at all; he should have ruled as a matter of law that such appraisals were not required to be disclosed as material.[23]

In Flynn v. Bass Brothers Enterprises, Inc.[24] the Third Circuit refused to hold that appraisals were immaterial as a matter of law. The court said: "Henceforth, the law is not that asset appraisals are, as a matter of law, immaterial. Rather, in appropriate cases, such information must be disclosed. Courts should ascertain the duty to disclose asset valuations and other soft information on a case by case basis, by weighing the potential aid such information will give a shareholder against the potential harm, such as undue reliance, if the information is released with a proper cautionary note. The factors a court must consider in making such a determination are: the facts upon which the information is based; the qualifications of those who prepared or compiled it; the purpose for which the information was originally intended; its relevance to the stockholders' impending decision; the degree of subjectivity or bias reflected in its preparation; the degree to which the information is unique; and the availability to the investor of other more reliable sources of information." [25] The court, however, refused to apply this "new" standard to a tender offer made in 1976 and held that there was no duty of the offeror to disclose certain asset appraisals. It did not address the question of whether the appraisals would have to be disclosed under the new standard.

21. 99 F.Supp. 808 (D.Del.1951), 135 F.Supp. 176 (D.Del.1955), aff'd 235 F.2d 369 (3d Cir.1956).

22. 772 F.2d 244 (6th Cir.1985), appeal pending, ___ U.S. ___, 106 S.Ct. 1179 (1986).

23. 772 F.2d at 253.

24. 744 F.2d 978 (3d Cir.1984).

25. 744 F.2d at 988.

The recent double-digit inflation (which has temporarily abated) has caused renewed questions as to the usefulness of financial statements based entirely upon historical cost, and has resulted in proposals either to replace or supplement the historical cost statements with additional information which recognizes the effect of inflation. These have generally taken one of two forms. One is called "current purchasing power" accounting (or CPP) and the other is called "current cost accounting" or "current value accounting."

The first would restate the financial statements upon the basis of an adjustment reflecting some price index or other index which would supposedly take account of the effects of inflation. The problem with this method is that any such general index is bound to conceal differences in the impact of inflation upon different industries and upon different companies within the same industry. For that reason, it has never been proposed that such statements replace the traditional statements, but merely that they be disclosed as supplemental information in the footnotes.

The "current cost" method would essentially restate assets on the basis of "current cost" or "replacement cost" rather than historical cost, either in the basic statements themselves or in a supplementary statement. Where this method tends to break down is when an asset would never in fact be replaced by an identical, or even very similar, asset if it were to disappear, even though it is performing its function satisfactorily for the particular business at the present time. For example, a particular machine may have been made obsolete by technological advances and may no longer even be on the market; "replacement cost" becomes then entirely a matter of opinion or an adjustment of the original price by some general "price deflator", which reintroduces the problems of the CPP method. Or if the cost of the more advanced current model is used, then that must be further adjusted to take account of the highly speculative cost savings which might or might not be realized if the company utilized the more advanced technology. These problems are of course enormously multiplied when an attempt is made to determine the "replacement cost" of an entire plant and all of its components and machines.[26] In England in September 1975 a committee appointed by the British government recommended the replacement of historical cost accounting in its entirety by a system of "current cost accounting" as outlined by the committee.

In March, 1976, the Commission adopted a rule requiring certain registrants to disclose in financial statements filed with the Commission the replacement cost of fixed assets and inventories, and to show what the cost of goods sold and depreciation expense would have been on that basis,[27] as supplemental information in a footnote to the financial statements. This requirement applied only to registrants with $100 million or more of total inventories and gross property, plant and equipment and where the total of inventories and gross property, plant and equipment was 10% or more of the total assets of the company. In September, 1979, the Financial Accounting Standards Board adopted Statement

---

26. When "replacement cost" was the criterion for determining a "rate base" in order for a public utility commission to fix the rates of a utility, before the Federal Power Commission and the Securities and Exchange Commission (under the Public Utility Holding Company Act of 1935) effectively abolished that approach, the hearings to determine the replacement cost of a particular electric power plant, for example, frequently ran for months or even years and involved tens of thousands of pages of expert testimony and exhibits. It might be a sobering experience for some of the advocates of "current value accounting" to have to read the whole of one of such records. In any event, it is obvious that something simpler will have to be devised, since no company could afford to go through that kind of a process every year merely in order to publish its financial statements.

27. SEC Accounting Series Rel. No. 190 (March 23, 1976).

of Financial Accounting Standards No. 33 requiring the reporting of certain supplemental information relating to changing prices in the financial statements. This statement became fully effective for fiscal years ending after December 25, 1980, and the SEC rule was simultaneously rescinded. The FASB requirement applies to enterprises with inventories and property, plant and equipment before depreciation amounting in the aggregate to $125 million or with total assets amounting to more than $1 billion (after deducting accumulated depreciation).

Being unable to choose definitively between current purchasing power accounting and current cost accounting,[28] the Financial Accounting Standards Board chose to require supplemental statements based on *both* of these approaches, at least as an interim measure. The former is referred to as "historical cost/constant dollar accounting" and is defined as a method of accounting "based on measures of historical prices in dollars, each of which has the same general purchasing power." The index which is to be used to adjust historical cost is the Consumer Price Index for All Urban Consumers. The second method is referred to as "current cost accounting" and is defined as a method of "measuring and reporting assets and expenses associated with the use or sale of assets, at their current cost or lower recoverable amount at the balance sheet date or at the date of use or sale." Complete income statements are required to be presented using both of these methods of adjustment of the primary statements based upon historical cost, but as supplemental information in a footnote to the primary financial statements which remain purely on an historical cost basis.

In view of the abatement of inflation in recent years, FASB rescinded Statement of Financial Accounting Standards No. 33 in December, 1986 (Statement of Financial Accounting Standards No. 89) and made such disclosures voluntary rather than mandatory for financial reports issued after December 2, 1986. The SEC has moved to conform its rules to this action by FASB, BNA Fed.Sec. and Law Rpt., Jan. 2, 1987, p. 33, while continuing to urge registrants voluntarily to furnish the previously required information (1933 Act Release No. 33–6681, Dec. 18, 1986). The return of double-digit inflation would doubtless revive this issue.

Merger Negotiations. On July 8, 1985, the Securities and Exchange Commission issued a public Release in which it expressly disagreed with the decision in the *Greenfield* case.[29] In that report of an investigation under Section 21(a) of the 1934 Act, the Commission discussed the response by a spokesman for the Carnation Company to an inquiry regarding rumors of a takeover, in which he stated that there are "no corporate developments that would account for the stock action." In fact, merger negotiations had been commenced, although unknown to the company spokesman, for an acquisition of Carnation by Nestle, S.A., a Swiss corporation. The Commission stated that in its view this response was "materially misleading" and that: "The Commission believes that *Heublein* was wrongly decided."

The Commission also stated: "When an issuer makes a public statement, information concerning preliminary acquisition discussions is material and must be disclosed if the information assumes 'actual significance in the deliberation of' and significantly alters 'the total mix of information available [to]' the

---

28. See the dissenting statements of Board members Mosso and Walters, Statement of Financial Accounting Standards No. 33 (Sept.1979), pp. 25–28. While both objected to the double-barrelled approach, they seemed to favor different ones of the two methods.

29. In the Matter of Carnation Company, 1934 Act Release No. 22214, SEC, July 8, 1985.

reasonable shareholder." It quoted from the *Texas Gulf Sulfur* case to the effect that materiality "will depend at any given time upon a balancing of both the indicated probability that the event will occur and the anticipated magnitude of the event in light of the totality of the company activities." The Commission conceded, however, that a "no comment" response might be appropriate in some circumstances to press inquiries while merger negotiations were in progress. It said: "However, an issuer that wants to prevent premature disclosure of nonpublic preliminary merger negotiations can, in appropriate circumstances, give a 'no comment' response to press inquiries concerning rumors or unusual market activity. A 'no comment' response would not be appropriate where, *inter alia*, the issuer has made a statement that has been rendered materially false or misleading as a result of subsequent events or market rumors are attributable to leaks from the issuer."

The result of these conflicting views has probably been that many corporations have adopted a rigorous "no comment" attitude to any inquiries in similar circumstances. It is to be hoped that they have also decided to keep their press spokesmen apprised of important corporate developments (the spokesman in the *Carnation* case subsequently denied that any merger negotiations, including specifically merger negotiations with Nestle, were being conducted, at a time when such negotiations were almost at the point of fruition, because he didn't know about them).

In Reiss v. Pan American World Airways, Inc.[30] the Second Circuit agreed with the Third Circuit that the preliminary merger negotiations in that case did not have to be disclosed prior to an agreement in principle. Judge Winter said: "It does not serve the underlying purposes of the securities acts to compel disclosure of merger negotiations in the not unusual circumstances before us. * * * Such negotiations are inherently fluid and the eventual outcome is shrouded in uncertainty. Disclosure may in fact be more misleading than secrecy so far as investment decisions are concerned. We are not confronted here with a failure to disclose hard facts which definitely affect a company's financial prospects. Rather, we deal with complex bargaining between two (and often more) parties which may fail as well as succeed, or may succeed on terms which vary greatly from those under consideration at the suggested time of disclosure. We have no doubt that had Pan Am disclosed the existence of negotiations on August 15th and had those negotiations failed, we would have been asked to decide a Section 10b–5 action challenging that disclosure."[31]

On the other hand, the Sixth Circuit in Levinson v. Basic, Inc.[32] specifically disagreed with the *Greenfield* case and held to the contrary in a virtually identical situation. This conflict among the circuits may have set the stage for a resolution of this issue by the Supreme Court.

In Michaels v. Michaels[33] the Seventh Circuit held that the majority shareholders in a closely-held corporation should have disclosed preliminary merger negotiations to a 14% minority shareholder whose shares were purchased, since there was no public market for the stock and the minority shareholder's options were limited to selling the stock back to the company or hoping that the company would be acquired for a higher price. The court said that the "price and structure" test of the Third Circuit was not relevant in the case of a corporation whose stock had no public market. The court stated: "We need not decide whether to adopt the Third Circuit's 'price and structure' standard of materiality because the policy underlying that standard is not

30. 711 F.2d 11 (2d Cir.1983).

31. 711 F.2d at 14.

32. 786 F.2d 741 (6th Cir.1986).

33. 767 F.2d 1185 (7th Cir.1985), cert. denied ___ U.S. ___, 106 S.Ct. 797 '1985).

applicable on the facts of this case. * * * The reasons for the 'price and structure' standard of materiality disappear when there is no public market for a shareholder's stock." [34] This decision is of course entirely consistent with a large number of early cases under Rule 10b–5 which dealt with the situation where the majority shareholders were engaged in acquisition discussions at a time when they or the corporation purchased the shares of a minority shareholder at a price considerably less than eventually realized when the acquisition in fact occurred. (See pages 1043–1053, below).

"QUALITATIVE" INFORMATION

The *Matthews* case is illustrative of a campaign which was waged by the Securities and Exchange Commission in the ten years or so preceding 1982 to require the disclosure in proxy statements of illegal, or only "questionable", conduct by corporate officials (although the Commission disavowed the vendetta which was waged by the federal prosecutors against Mr. Matthews, and which the Second Circuit also obviously regarded as "questionable" *governmental* conduct). This campaign was inspired by the surfacing of the so-called "sensitive payments" scandal regarding the conduct of certain corporations in connection with their business activities in foreign countries and, shortly thereafter, the revelations as an outgrowth of the Watergate investigation of the making of illegal political contributions by various other corporations. Following a change in the membership of the Commission and of its Enforcement Division, this campaign was publicly abandoned in the Fall of 1982. On November 19, 1982, Mr. John M. Fedders, the then new Director of the Division of Enforcement made a speech to the Federal Regulation of Securities Committee of the American Bar Association relating to the enforcement policy of the Commission in this regard and on October 18, 1982, then Commissioner Bevis Longstreth made a speech to the Investor Responsibility Research Center on the same topic. Both of these officials stressed that the current focus of the SEC is upon disclosure of what they described as information which has economic or "quantitative" materiality to an investor or shareholder and indicated that the SEC will not insist upon the disclosure of information by a corporation solely on the basis that it might have a bearing on the integrity of the management of the corporation.

Mr. Fedders indicated in his speech that the Commission would continue to institute enforcement actions in cases (1) where illegal conduct by management may have material adverse economic consequences for the company, (2) where the actions in question involve self-dealing or conflict of interest transactions, (3) where there is a failure to disclose specific items mandated by the forms or rules for proxy statements, reports or registration statements, or (4) where the failure to disclose renders misleading specific statements contained in documents filed with the Commission. Absent any of these four circumstances, Mr. Fedders stated that "the Commission generally should not utilize the antifraud provisions of the securities law for law enforcement where there is a failure to disclose conduct which may be considered *qualitatively* material. The antifraud provisions of the securities laws work well in the area of *quantitative* materiality because disclosure and enforcement decisions can be related to the bench marks of earnings, assets or liabilities."

It should be noted that this view does not require that the wrongful conduct of management have already had an adverse economic impact upon the corporation in order for its disclosure to be required, if a substantial and

---

34. 767 F.2d at 1195–1196.

material portion of the business of the company is dependent upon such conduct (for example, bribes to foreign officials) and might be jeopardized if such conduct is revealed or if it is terminated, whether voluntarily or under judicial compulsion. This situation is what then Commissioners Ray Garrett and Al Sommer described as a "Catch–22", where the disclosure may cause the very adverse impact upon a corporation, the fear of which was the basis for mandating disclosure in the first place. However, Mr. Fedders did not accept this as a sufficient reason for not making the disclosure, nor did any previous Commission despite the soul-searching of some of the Commissioners when initially faced with this problem. There were, of course, some accommodations, such as permitting the company not to reveal the names of the individuals who were being bribed (although where they were prominent people, such as the Prince Consort in Holland or the Prime Minister of Japan, their names usually got into the newspapers) or in some cases even the country or countries involved. However, the companies involved were clearly expected to cease this conduct immediately, and various corporate controls were instituted to see that they did. That of course has now been mandated by the Foreign Corrupt Practices Act.[35] It would seem that, if it were true that a material part of the business of the company was dependent upon paying bribes to foreign officials, the best way to ensure the loss of that business would be to stop paying them, although there is no evidence that such loss has occurred.

It should be emphasized that these pronouncements relate solely to the enforcement policy of the Securities and Exchange Commission and have no bearing on potential civil liability arising from a failure to disclose matters which the courts regard as mandated by the statute and the current rules and forms. The Commission has not proposed to issue any "safe harbor rule" relieving a corporation of any obligation to disclose matters which are not "quantitatively material." Therefore, the possibility of civil liability, which has probably always been the greatest incentive to disclosure, has not been changed to any appreciable extent by these new signals from the Commission.

The problem becomes most difficult where the evidence in the corporate records falls short of establishing any illegal conduct but raises serious suspicions. For example, suppose there is evidence of the payment of enormous fees to "consultants" in foreign countries for their efforts in obtaining business there, but no evidence that any of the money has been passed on to foreign officials. The executive officers of the company assert that they don't know that any of it has been (and don't want to know). Payment of foreign consultants has not been outlawed by the Foreign Corrupt Practices Act; so far as we know, no country has attempted to make "influence" illegal. But of course the facts may strongly suggest that there is something rotten in Denmark (or Holland or Japan). What is the responsibility of the lawyer for the corporation in this situation?

The decisions bearing upon this type of situation are conflicting and inconclusive. In Gaines v. Haughton[36] the Ninth Circuit apparently held that unadjudicated misconduct by management is never required to be disclosed in the absence of any conflict of interests or personal profit by the officials involved, even though it may be "quantitatively material" under the tests suggested by Mr. Fedders. The court said: "Absent credible allegations of self-dealing by the directors or dishonesty or deceit which inures to the direct, personal benefit of the directors * * *, we hold that director misconduct of the type traditionally regulated by state corporate law need not be disclosed in

---

35. Pub.L. No. 95–213, 91 Stats. 1494 (1977).

36. 645 F.2d 761 (9th Cir.1981) cert. denied 454 U.S. 1145 (1982).

proxy solicitations for director elections." [37] The SEC disagreement with this position is indicated by the fact that it filed an *amicus* brief in support of a rehearing *en banc* in an attempt to obtain a reversal or modification of that decision. On the other hand, the Second Circuit in Decker v. Massey-Ferguson, Limited [38] refused to accept this sweeping pronouncement by the Ninth Circuit, although the actual holding in that case is limited to a ruling that the complaint should not have been dismissed before any opportunity for discovery by the plaintiff.[39] The district court held in SEC v. Jos. Schlitz Brewing Company [40] that a pattern of obtaining business through commercial bribery was required to be disclosed. Another district court in Amalgamated Clothing and Textile Workers Union v. J.P. Stevens & Co., Inc.[41] held that a corporation was not required to accuse itself of having violated the National Labor Relations Act, although the complaint in that case did not actually charge any violation but only an intention to "thwart" the labor relations laws.

See Kripke, Projections and Appraisals: Analysis of the Case Law, 7 Inst. Securities Reg. 93 (1976); Note: Rule 10b–5 and the Duty to Disclose Merger Negotiations in Corporate Statements, 96 Yale L.J. 547 (1987).

THE MANNER OF DISCLOSURE

In some instances, it may be relatively easy to determine (a) that a certain fact existed, (b) that no mention of it or allusion to it was contained in a proxy statement or prospectus, and (c) that it was necessary "in order to make the statements made" not misleading. For example, if the statement should be made that a company had received a firm offer of $5,000,000 for one of its mining claims, without stating that it was made by a relative of the President, was to be evidenced by a 35-year nonrecourse promissory note and was to be payable only out of net profits from the operation of the mine; or if the statement should be made that a government official in a country where an expropriation proceeding was pending with respect to one of the company's plants had stated to the company that it would be paid $5,000,000 for the plant, without stating that the cabinet had repudiated this offer the next day and had imprisoned the official for making it; no one would have any difficulty in identifying these as "half truths."

However, it is impossible to state all of the ultimate facts, much less the evidentiary facts (to use trial terminology), regarding any business in a proxy statement or prospectus. There must be a process of summarization, which necessarily involves interpretation and omission, in order for the document to be comprehensible to anyone. And the Commission is constantly admonishing the securities bar to make these documents short and concise and "readable" (without, of course, "omitting" any "fact" which is "material"). In this context, how does the securities lawyer drafting such a document with respect to a highly complicated corporate transaction go about attempting to protect his client from a decision, made with the benefit of hindsight, that some crucial

---

37. 645 F.2d at 779. Contra: Ross v. Warner, 480 F.Supp. 268 (S.D.N.Y.1979); SEC v. American Beef Packers, Inc., CCH Fed.Sec.Law Rptr. ¶ 96,079 (D.Neb.1977). Compare GAF Corporation v. Heyman, 724 F.2d 727 (2d Cir.1983) (Proxy contestants are not required to include in their solicitation materials "allegations [against the candidates for director] * * * unrelated to the business of the subject corporation.")

38. 681 F.2d 111 (2d Cir.1982).

39. See, also, Weisberg v. Coastal States Gas Corporation, 609 F.2d 650 (2d Cir. 1979), cert. denied 445 U.S. 951 (1980).

40. 452 F.Supp. 824 (E.D.Wis.1978).

41. 475 F.Supp. 328 (S.D.N.Y.1979).

fact was omitted? In attempting to answer this question, it may be helpful to consider some of the different types of situations in which the courts have considered whether material facts were omitted or inadequately presented.

A complete omission to reveal certain facts. Where there is nothing in the statement which can plausibly be claimed to inform the shareholders of a certain alleged fact, the only questions involved are: Was it a "fact"?, and, Was it "material"? For example, in the *Gerstle* case the court held that the failure to disclose the excess of the liquidation value of General Outdoor Advertising Co.'s assets, based upon offers received from third parties, over their book value and an intention on the part of the surviving corporation to liquidate those assets, constituted material omissions.

In Berman v. Thompson [42] it was held that the fact was material that a $6,000,000 investment, stated to be in "domestic corporations", was in fact an investment of that amount in $8\frac{1}{2}\%$ of the outstanding stock of a single corporation. The corporation argued that it did not want to reveal its large position in the stock of this corporation because it was mounting a takeover campaign and did not want to alert the management of the target company prematurely. However, the court said: "If those who direct the affairs of a corporation deem it in the best interests of the corporation not to disclose certain information, then they may not solicit shareholder approval of a transaction for which that information is material." And in United States Smelting, Refining and Mining Co. v. Clevite Corp.[43] a failure to reveal a rival merger offer was held to be material in a merger proxy statement. The court said: "Certainly, * * * when shareholders are being called upon by management to approve a particular merger proposal there would appear to be no information of greater materiality to them than that relating to other definitive merger proposals available to the corporation."

On the other hand, in Sunray DX Oil Co. v. Helmerich & Payne, Inc.,[44] the Tenth Circuit held that the failure of an oil company in a merger transaction to reveal an apparently rich oil strike on an off-shore drilling tract adjacent to its own was not material, primarily on the basis that the SEC rules wouldn't have permitted it. However, this case was strongly relied upon by Texas Gulf Sulphur in Mitchell v. Texas Gulf Sulphur Co.[45] without success; while the Tenth Circuit didn't overrule it, it also didn't follow it—it simply said: That was a different case.

The manner of presentation or arrangement of the facts (the "buried facts" doctrine). In Shvetz v. Industrial Rayon Corporation [46] the court said: "Nowhere does either [the statute or the SEC rules] require that corporate reorganizations and mergers be explained in language comprehensible to school children." And this language was quoted with approval in 1968 in the case of Walpert v. Bart.[47] However, some decisions seem to be contrary to this common sense approach. In Feit v. Leasco Data Processing Equipment Corp., supra p. 969, Judge Weinstein expressly laid down the requirement that a registration statement (or presumably a proxy statement, since the exchange offer prospectus involved in that case bore more resemblance to a proxy statement than to the typical prospectus) must be completely intelligible both to the unsophisticated investor and to the professional securities analyst. And

---

42. 312 F.Supp. 1031 (N.D.Ill.1970).

43. CCH Fed.Sec.Law Rptr. ¶ 92,691 (N.D.Ohio 1968).

44. 398 F.2d 447 (10th Cir.1968).

45. 446 F.2d 90 (10th Cir.1971), cert. denied 404 U.S. 1004 (1971).

46. 212 F.Supp. 308, at 310 (S.D.N.Y. 1960).

47. 390 F.2d 877 (4th Cir.1968), aff'ing on opinion below 280 F.Supp. 1006 (D.Md. 1967).

both Gould v. American Hawaiian Steamship Co.[48] and Kohn v. American Metal Climax, Inc.[49] held that the defendants could be held liable, even if full disclosure were made, if the court considers that what it regards as the most important facts are not sufficiently "highlighted" in the statement, but are too far towards the rear or are scattered among several pages. The court in the *Kohn* case suggests that the solution to this problem is a boldface legend on the front cover of the statement, which is certainly a useful device, if one can anticipate which facts the court will consider the most important and if there is enough room on the front cover.

On the other hand, the Fifth Circuit in Smallwood v. Pearl Brewing Co.[50] stated: "We have already stated that the information required in a proxy statement is extensive. Difficult decisions must be made as to what information to place further toward the end of proxy statements, what to emphasize and what to state more blandly. It is, of course, impossible to emphasize everything, and every fact cannot be contained in the beginning. * * * We require those who draw up proxy statements to be fair and sensitive to the needs of shareholders in exercising their rights of corporate suffrage. But we do not require that the writers of proxy statements be clairvoyant. A fact essential for a shareholder decision today may become irrelevant tomorrow, and vice versa. It is enough that proxy statements be complete and not misleading in light of the circumstances existent and reasonably anticipated at the time distributed. * * *

"The doctrines of 'buried facts' and 'similar emphasis' do not compel a different result. * * * [citing cases] In each of these cases the facts held to be inadequately disclosed—predominantly concerning conflicts of interest—were apparent at the time the proxy materials were mailed, and it should have been obvious at that time that burying the facts, or giving them less than significant emphasis, would deprive the shareholders of 'full and honest disclosure' * * *."[51]

The characterization of the facts. It was formerly considered axiomatic that a corporation was under no obligation to characterize the facts presented in a registration statement or proxy statement, and especially not in a way which could be called in any sense a prediction of the future, but on the contrary was prevented from doing so by the staff of the SEC. Recent cases have raised the question whether abstaining from such characterization may not result in liability. The old theory was that the shareholder must interpret the facts himself, or have them interpreted for him by his securities adviser; some of the cases now seem to be saying that the person disseminating the proxy statement must interpret the facts revealed so that they can be understood by the most unsophisticated reader. In Robinson v. Penn Central Co.[52] the court held that a proxy statement relating to a proposed recapitalization of the debt of the parent company of the Pennsylvania Railroad (which was in reorganization under Section 77 of the Bankruptcy Act) was deficient because it did not inform the

---

48. 331 F.Supp. 981 (D.Del.1971), aff'd, 535 F.2d 761 (3d Cir.1976). The court stated: "These concepts of 'similar emphasis' and 'buried facts' are pertinent to this case. * * * The various facts listed previously which the defendants contend adequately reveal any conflict are interspersed throughout the proxy materials and could be gleaned only through a close and prolonged perusal. Under the buried facts doctrine, such disclosures are insufficient. Since the board stressed on several occasions its recommendation favoring the merger, it should have given similar emphasis to the compromised positions of Casey, Kroeger and Ludwig. The failure to do so is a material defect."

49. 322 F.Supp. 1331 (E.D.Pa.1971), aff'd 458 F.2d 255 (3d Cir.1972). Cf. Beatty v. Bright, 318 F.Supp. 169 (S.D.Iowa 1970).

50. 489 F.2d 579 (5th Cir.1974), cert. denied 419 U.S. 873 (1975).

51. 489 F.2d at pp. 602–603.

52. 336 F.Supp. 655 (E.D.Pa.1971).

stockholder that the plan might mean (as the court apparently thought it did) "a decade and a half of probable death by attrition, with insolvency and bankruptcy at the end." The court does not suggest that any facts were actually omitted; and the court itself apparently drew this conclusion solely by reading the proxy statement. But it said: "However, our concern is not the sophisticated analyst, but the reasonable stockholder and nowhere are these facts *or possible consequences* highlighted." [53]

In the *Mills* case in the Seventh Circuit [54] the material omission which was found by the court as a matter of law in the proxy statement (a decision which was not reviewed by the Supreme Court) was the failure to point out that the majority shareholder had selected and elected the directors of its subsidiary, the other party to the transaction. Who any shareholder with enough education to sign a proxy card would assume had selected the directors elected by the majority shareholder, the court didn't suggest. The court also stated that this conflict of interest had to be revealed immediately following the statement that the board of directors of the subsidiary had approved and recommended the merger. The latter holding was followed both in Gould v. American Hawaiian Steamship Co.[55] and in Kohn v. American Metal Climax, Inc.[56] One has the distinct feeling that if only the "facts" regarding the conflict of interest had been stated in whatever position and with whatever prominence, these courts still might not have been satisfied, unless the facts were accompanied by a characterization of the directors as the venal tools of the one who selected them, although Judge Friendly suggested in another context that they might not be *limited* to an "abject *peccavimus*." [57]

On the other hand, in Data Probe Acquisition Corporation v. Datatab, Inc.[58] where a target corporation granted a lock-up option to one tender offeror in a bidding contest, which had offered three-year employment contracts to the senior management of the target company, the court rejected the contentions that the proxy statement should have stated that the management of the target company preferred that bidder because of the employment guarantee and that the lock-up option would put an end to the bidding war. Judge Winter said: "We see no additional informational benefit accruing to shareholders by requiring the beneficiaries of such contracts to announce that they regard them favorably. * * * As for the failure to state that the option, if valid, brought the takeover contest to an end, that conclusion is obvious to anyone conversant with elementary mathematics. * * * The disclosure required by the Act is not a rite of confession or exercise in common law pleading." [59]

OTHER CONDUCT IN VIOLATION OF THE RULES

While almost all of the cases have involved an allegation of false or misleading statements, the question arises as to whether other types of viola-

---

53. Italics added. In fact, contrary to the court's prediction, the recapitalized Penn Central was highly successful. See, also, Colonial Realty Corp. v. Baldwin-Montrose Chemical Co., 312 F.Supp. 1296 (E.D.Pa.1970), where the court held that the failure of the corporation to characterize its 35% ownership in another corporation as "working control" made the proxy statement deficient.

54. Mills v. Electric Auto-Lite Co., 403 F.2d 429 (7th Cir.1968), rev'd on other grounds 396 U.S. 375 (1970).

55. Supra, note 48.

56. Supra, note 49.

57. In General Time Corp. v. Talley Industries, Inc., 403 F.2d at 163.

58. 722 F.2d 1 (2d Cir.1983), cert. denied 465 U.S. 1052 (1984).

59. 722 F.2d at 5–6. See, also, Morrissey v. County Tower Corp., 717 F.2d 1227 (8th Cir.1983).

tions of the rules might give rise to civil liability. Obviously, under the Securities Act of 1933 a failure to file a registration statement where the transaction is not exempt is a violation of Section 5 and gives rise to express civil liability under Section 12(1). Also, many of the cases under the Williams Act, as discussed above in Chapter 12, involved primarily a failure to file, but that Act requires a filing both with the issuer and the SEC and one of its primary purposes was stated to be to give "warning" to the issuer regarding accumulations of blocks of its stock. Therefore, arguably a failure to file may cause as much harm, or more, than a timely filing which is not entirely accurate.

However, the cases so far have indicated that a mere failure to file under Section 13(a) or Section 15(d) of the 1934 Act (aside from the Williams Act) does not give rise to an independent cause of action, since liability for violation of those sections is expressly provided in Section 18.[60] It has also been held that a violation of the filing requirements of Section 16(a) of the 1934 Act does not give rise to a civil cause of action apart from the express civil liability provisions of Section 16(b).[61] What about the Proxy Rules? For example, would a failure to file the proxy material with the SEC as required, or the mailing of the proxy material one day prior to the expiration of the 10–day period it is required to be on file, even though it admittedly contained no misleading statements, be a sufficient violation upon which to base an action for damages or rescission? In Union Pacific Railroad Co. v. Chicago & North Western Railway Co.[62] (an injunction action) the court stated that it could not excuse a failure to file as a mere "technical violation." [63] It stated: "The offense cannot be so easily dismissed. * * * A solicitor by failing to file circumvents the agency primarily responsible for protection of the investor and speculates upon the decision of the court." [64] However, the court also found in that case that the non-filed material contained misleading statements; and, of course, a court might be more willing to require a postponement of the meeting and a resolicitation with opportunity for review by the SEC on this basis than to invalidate action already taken.

For an exhaustive discussion of "soft information," see Schneider, Soft Information Disclosures: A Semi-Revolution, Fifteenth Annual Institute on Securities Regulation (1984). See also Rosenweig, The Legality of "Lock-Ups" and Other Responses of Directors to Hostile Takeover Bids or Stock Aggregations, 10 Sec.Reg.L.J. 291 (1983); Profusek, Tender Offer Manipulation: Tactics & Strategies After Marathon, 36 Sw. L.J. 975 (1982); Weiss, Defensive Responses to Tender Offers and the Williams Act's Prohibition Against Manipulation, 35 Vand.L.Rev. 1087 (1982); Kripke, The SEC and Corporate Disclosure: Regulation in Search of a Purpose (1979); Kripke, A Search for a Meaningful Securities Disclosure Policy, 31 Bus.Law. 293 (1975); Jacobs, What is a Misleading Statement or Omission under Rule 10b–5, 42 Ford.L.Rev. 243 (1973); Chalmers, Truth and Consequences—The New Game in Forecasting, 47 St. John's L.Rev. 38 (1972); Schneider, Nits, Grits, and Soft Information in SEC Filings, 121 U.Pa.L.Rev. 254 (1972); Mann, Prospectuses: Unreadable or Just

60. See In re Penn Central Securities Litigation, 494 F.2d 528 (3d Cir.1973); Lewis v. Elam, CCH Fed.Sec.Law Rptr. ¶ 96,013 (S.D.N.Y.1977); Meer v. United Brands Co., CCH Fed.Sec.Law Rptr. ¶ 95,648 (S.D.N.Y.1976).

61. Scientex Corp. v. Kay, 689 F.2d 879 (9th Cir.1982); Robbins v. Banner Industries, Inc., 285 F.Supp. 758 (S.D.N.Y.1966); Smith v. Murchison, 310 F.Supp. 1079 (S.D.

N.Y.1970). Contra: Grow Chemical Corp. v. Uran, 316 F.Supp. 891 (S.D.N.Y.1970).

62. 226 F.Supp. 400 (N.D.Ill.1964).

63. 226 F.Supp. at 408. Justice Douglas once defined a "technical" violation as one that the person accused of it could not deny having committed.

64. Ibid.

Unread?   40 Geo.Wash.L.Rev. 222 (1971); Kripke, Rule 10b–5 Liability and "Material Facts", 46 N.Y.U.L.Rev. 1061 (1971); Kripke, The SEC, the Accountants, Some Myths and Some Realities, 45 N.Y.U.L.Rev. 1151 (1970); Manne, Accounting and Administrative Law Aspects of Gerstle v. Gamble-Skogmo, Inc., 15 N.Y.L.Forum 304 (1969); Note, Fearless Forecasts, Corporate Liability for Earnings Forecasts that Miss the Mark, 16 B.C.Ind. & Com.L.Rev. 115 (1974); Note, British Profit Forecasting System: Model or Mistake for the United States, 4 Cal.West.Int.L.J. 161 (1973); Note, The Use of Appraisals in SEC Documents, 122 U.Pa.L.Rev. 138 (1973).

CHIARELLA v. UNITED STATES

Supreme Court of the United States, 1980.
445 U.S. 222, 100 S.Ct. 1108, 63 L.Ed.2d 348.

MR. JUSTICE POWELL delivered the opinion of the Court.

The question in this case is whether a person who learns from the confidential documents of one corporation that it is planning an attempt to secure control of a second corporation violates § 10(b) of the Securities Exchange Act of 1934 if he fails to disclose the impending takeover before trading in the target company's securities.

I

Petitioner is a printer by trade. In 1975 and 1976, he worked as a "markup man" in the New York composing room of Pandick Press, a financial printer. Among documents that petitioner handled were five announcements of corporate takeover bids. When these documents were delivered to the printer, the identities of the acquiring and target corporations were concealed by blank spaces or false names. The true names were sent to the printer on the night of the final printing.

The petitioner, however, was able to deduce the names of the target companies before the final printing from other information contained in the documents. Without disclosing his knowledge, petitioner purchased stock in the target companies and sold the shares immediately after the takeover attempts were made public. By this method, petitioner realized a gain of slightly more than $30,000 in the course of 14 months. Subsequently, the Securities and Exchange Commission (Commission or SEC) began an investigation of his trading activities. In May 1977, petitioner entered into a consent decree with the Commission in which he agreed to return his profits to the sellers of the shares. On the same day, he was discharged by Pandick Press.

In January 1978, petitioner was indicted on 17 counts of violating § 10(b) of the Securities Exchange Act of 1934 (1934 Act) and SEC Rule 10b–5. After petitioner unsuccessfully moved to dismiss the indictment, he was brought to trial and convicted on all counts.

The Court of Appeals for the Second Circuit affirmed petitioner's conviction. 588 F.2d 1358 (1978). We granted certiorari, 441 U.S. 942 (1979), and we now reverse.

II

Section 10(b) of the 1934 Act prohibits the use "in connection with the purchase or sale of any security * * * [of] any manipulative or deceptive device or contrivance in contravention of such rules and regulations as the Commission may prescribe." Pursuant to this section, the SEC promulgated Rule 10b–5 * * *.

This case concerns the legal effect of the petitioner's silence. The District Court's charge permitted the jury to convict the petitioner if it found that he willfully failed to inform sellers of target company securities that he knew of a forthcoming takeover bid that would make their shares more valuable. In order to decide whether silence in such circumstances violates § 10(b), it is necessary to review the language and legislative history of that statute as well as its interpretation by the Commission and the federal courts.

Although the starting point of our inquiry is the language of the statute, Ernst & Ernst v. Hochfelder, 425 U.S. 185, 197 (1976), § 10(b) does not state whether silence may constitute a manipulative or deceptive device. Section 10(b) was designed as a catchall clause to prevent fraudulent practices. Id., at 202, 206. But neither the legislative history nor the statute itself affords specific guidance for the resolution of this case. When Rule 10b–5 was promulgated in 1942, the SEC did not discuss the possibility that failure to provide information might run afoul of § 10(b).

* * *

The Federal courts have found violations of § 10(b) where corporate insiders used undisclosed information for their own benefit. E.g., SEC v. Texas Gulf Sulphur Co., 401 F.2d 833 (CA 2 1968), cert. denied, 404 U.S. 1005 (1972). The cases also have emphasized, in accordance with the common-law rule, that "[t]he party charged with failing to disclose market information must be under a duty to disclose it." Frigitemp Corp. v. Financial Dynamics Fund, Inc., 524 F.2d 275, 282 (CA 2 1975). Accordingly, a purchaser of stock who has no duty to a prospective seller because he is neither an insider nor a fiduciary has been held to have no obligation to reveal material facts. See General Time Corp. v. Talley Industries, Inc., 403 F.2d 159, 164 (CA 2 1968), cert. denied, 393 U.S. 1026 (1969).

* * *

Thus, administrative and judicial interpretations have established that silence in connection with the purchase or sale of securities may operate as a fraud actionable under § 10(b) despite the absence of statutory language or legislative history specifically addressing the legality of nondisclosure. But such liability is premised upon a duty to disclose arising from a relationship of trust and confidence between parties to a transaction. Application of a duty to disclose prior to trading guarantees that corporate insiders, who have an obligation to place the shareholder's welfare before their own, will not benefit personally through fraudulent use of material nonpublic information.[12]

---

12. "Tippees" of corporate insiders have been held liable under § 10(b) because they have a duty not to profit from the use of inside information that they know is confidential and know or should know came from a corporate insider, Shapiro v. Merrill Lynch, Pierce, Fenner & Smith, 495 F.2d 228, 237–238 (CA 2 1974). The tippee's obligation has been viewed as arising from his role as a participant after the fact in the insider's breach of a fiduciary duty. Subcommittees of American Bar

III

In this case, the petitioner was convicted of violating § 10(b) although he was not a corporate insider and he received no confidential information from the target company. Moreover, the "market information" upon which he relied did not concern the earning power or operations of the target company, but only the plans of the acquiring company.[13] Petitioner's use of that information was not a fraud under § 10(b) unless he was subject to an affirmative duty to disclose it before trading. In this case, the jury instructions failed to specify any such duty. In effect, the trial court instructed the jury that petitioner owed a duty to everyone; to all sellers, indeed, to the market as a whole. The jury simply was told to decide whether petitioner used material, nonpublic information at a time when "he knew other people trading in the securities market did not have access to the same information." Record, at 677.

The Court of Appeals affirmed the conviction by holding that "[*a*]*nyone* —corporate insider or not—who regularly receives material nonpublic information may not use that information to trade in securities without incurring an affirmative duty to disclose." 588 F.2d 1358, 1365 (CA 2 1978) (emphasis in original). Although the court said that its test would include only persons who regularly receive material nonpublic information, id., at 1366, its rationale for that limitation is unrelated to the existence of a duty to disclose. The Court of Appeals, like the trial court, failed to identify a relationship between petitioner and the sellers that could give rise to a duty. Its decision thus rested solely upon its belief that the federal securities laws have "created a system providing equal access to information necessary for reasoned and intelligent investment decisions." 588 F.2d, at 1362. The use by anyone of material information not generally available is fraudulent, this theory suggests, because such information gives certain buyers or sellers an unfair advantage over less informed buyers and sellers.

This reasoning suffers from two defects. First not every instance of financial unfairness constitutes fraudulent activity under § 10(b). See Santa Fe Industries, Inc. v. Green, 430 U.S. 462, 474-477 (1977). Second, the element required to make silence fraudulent—a duty to disclose—is absent in this case. No duty could arise from petitioner's relationship with the sellers of the target company's securities, for petitioner had no prior dealings with them. He was not their agent, he was not a fiduciary, he was not a person in whom the sellers had placed their trust and confidence. He was, in fact, a complete stranger who dealt with the sellers only through impersonal market transactions.

We cannot affirm petitioner's conviction without recognizing a general duty between all participants in market transactions to forgo actions based on material, nonpublic information. Formulation of such a broad duty, which departs radically from the established doctrine that duty arises from

Association Section of Corporation, Banking, and Business Law, Comment Letter on Material, Non-Public Information (Oct. 15, 1973) reprinted in BNA, Securities Regulation & Law Report No. 233, at D-1, D-2 (Jan. 2, 1974).

13. See Fleischer, Mundheim & Murphy, An Initial Inquiry into the Responsibility to Disclose Market Information, 121 U.Pa.L.Rev. 798, 799 (1973).

a specific relationship between two parties * * * should not be undertaken absent some explicit evidence of congressional intent.

As we have seen, no such evidence emerges from the language or legislative history of § 10(b). Moreover, neither the Congress nor the Commission ever has adopted a parity-of-information rule. Instead the problems caused by misuse of market information have been addressed by detailed and sophisticated regulation that recognizes when use of market information may not harm operation of the securities markets. For example, the Williams Act limits but does not completely prohibit a tender offeror's purchases of target corporation stock before public announcement of the offer. Congress' careful action in this and other areas contrasts, and is in some tension, with the broad rule of liability we are asked to adopt in this case.

Indeed, the theory upon which the petitioner was convicted is at odds with the Commission's view of § 10(b) as applied to activity that has the same effect on sellers as the petitioner's purchases. "Warehousing" takes place when a corporation gives advance notice of its intention to launch a tender offer to institutional investors who then are able to purchase stock in the target company before the tender offer is made public and the price of shares rises. In this case, as in warehousing, a buyer of securities purchases stock in a target corporation on the basis of market information which is unknown to the seller. In both of these situations, the seller's behavior presumably would be altered if he had the nonpublic information. Significantly, however, the Commission has acted to bar warehousing under its authority to regulate tender offers after recognizing that action under § 10(b) would rest on a "somewhat different theory" than that previously used to regulate insider trading as fraudulent activity.

We see no basis for applying such a new and different theory of liability in this case. As we have emphasized before, the 1934 Act cannot be read "'more broadly than its language and the statutory scheme reasonably permit.'" Touche Ross & Co. v. Redington, 442 U.S. 560, 578 (1979), quoting SEC v. Sloan, 436 U.S. 103, 116 (1978). Section 10(b) is aptly described as a catch-all provision, but what it catches must be fraud. When an allegation of fraud is based upon nondisclosure, there can be no fraud absent a duty to speak. We hold that a duty to disclose under § 10(b) does not arise from the mere possession of nonpublic market information. The contrary result is without support in the legislative history of § 10(b) and would be inconsistent with the careful plan that Congress has enacted for regulation of the securities markets. Cf. Santa Fe Industries Inc. v. Green, 430 U.S., at 479.

IV

In its brief to this Court the United States offers an alternative theory to support petitioner's conviction. It argues that petitioner breached a duty to the acquiring corporation when he acted upon information that he obtained by virtue of his position as an employee of a printer employed by the corporation. The breach of this duty is said to support a conviction under § 10(b) for fraud perpetrated upon both the acquiring corporation and the sellers.

We need not decide whether this theory has merit for it was not submitted to the jury. The jury was told, in the language of Rule 10b–5, that it could convict the petitioner if it concluded that he either (i) employed a device, scheme or artifice to defraud or (ii) engaged in an act, practice, or course of business which operated or would operate as a fraud or deceit upon any person. Record, at 681. The trial judge stated that a "scheme to defraud" is a plan to obtain money by trick or deceit and that "a failure by Chiarella to disclose material, non-public information in connection with his purchase of stock would constitute deceit." Id., at 683. Accordingly, the jury was instructed that the petitioner employed a scheme to defraud if he "did not disclose * * * material non-public information in connection with the purchases of the stock." Id., at 685–686.

Alternatively, the jury was instructed that it could convict if "Chiarella's alleged conduct of having purchased securities without disclosing material, nonpublic information would have or did have the effect of operating as a fraud upon a seller." Id., at 686. The judge earlier had stated that fraud "embraces all the means which human ingenuity can devise and which are resorted to by one individual to gain an advantage over another by false misrepresentation, suggestions or by suppression of the truth." Id., at 683.

The jury instructions demonstrate that petitioner was convicted merely because of his failure to disclose material, nonpublic information to sellers from whom he bought the stock of target corporations. The jury was not instructed on the nature or elements of a duty owed by petitioner to anyone other than the sellers. Because we cannot affirm a criminal conviction on the basis of a theory not presented to the jury, Rewis v. United States, 401 U.S. 808, 814 (1971), see Dunn v. United States, 442 U.S. 100, 106 (1979), we will not speculate upon whether such a duty exists, whether it has been breached, or whether such a breach constitutes a violation of § 10(b).

The judgment of the Court of Appeals is

Reversed.

MR. JUSTICE STEVENS, concurring.

* * *

MR. JUSTICE BRENNAN, concurring in the judgment.

The Court holds, correctly in my view, that "a duty to disclose under § 10(b) does not arise from the mere possession of nonpublic market information." Ante, at 1118. Prior to so holding, however, it suggests that no violation of § 10(b) could be made out absent a breach of some duty arising out of a fiduciary relationship between buyer and seller. I cannot subscribe to that suggestion. On the contrary, it seems to me that Part I of The Chief Justice's dissent, post, at 1120–1122, correctly states the applicable substantive law—a person violates § 10(b) whenever he improperly obtains or converts to his own benefit nonpublic information which he then uses in connection with the purchase or sale of securities.

While I agree with Part I of The Chief Justice's dissent, I am unable to agree with Part II. Rather, I concur in the judgment of the majority because I think it clear that the legal theory sketched by The Chief Justice is not the one presented to the jury. * * *

MR. CHIEF JUSTICE BURGER, dissenting.

I believe that the jury instructions in this case properly charged a violation of § 10(b) and Rule 10b–5, and I would affirm the conviction.

I

As a general rule, neither party to an arm's length business transaction has an obligation to disclose information to the other unless the parties stand in some confidential or fiduciary relation. See Prosser, The Law of Torts § 106. This rule permits a businessman to capitalize on his experience and skill in securing and evaluating relevant information; it provides incentive for hard work, careful analysis, and astute forecasting. But the policies that underlie the rule also should limit its scope. In particular, the rule should give way when an informational advantage is obtained, not by superior experience, foresight, or industry, but by some unlawful means. One commentator has written:

"[T]he way in which the buyer acquires the information which he conceals from the vendor should be a material circumstance. The information might have been acquired as the result of his bringing to bear a superior knowledge, intelligence, skill or technical judgment; it might have been acquired by chance; or it might be acquired by means of some tortious action on his part. * * * *Any time information is acquired by an illegal act it would seem that there should be a duty to disclose that information.*" Keeton, Fraud—Concealment and Non-Disclosure, 15 Tex.L.Rev. 1, 25–26 (1936) (emphasis added).

I would read § 10(b) and Rule 10b–5 to encompass and build on this principle: to mean that a person who has misappropriated nonpublic information has an absolute duty to disclose that information or to refrain from trading.

* * *

MR. JUSTICE BLACKMUN, with whom MR. JUSTICE MARSHALL joins, dissenting.

Although I agree with much of what is said in Part I of the dissenting opinion of The Chief Justice, ante, I write separately because, in my view, it is unnecessary to rest petitioner's conviction on a "misappropriation" theory. The fact that petitioner Chiarella purloined, or, to use The Chief Justice's word, ante, p. 1123, "stole," information concerning pending tender offers certainly is the most dramatic evidence that petitioner was guilty of fraud. He has conceded that he knew it was wrong, and he and his co-workers in the print shop were specifically warned by their employer that actions of this kind were improper and forbidden. But I also would find petitioner's conduct fraudulent within the meaning of § 10(b) of the Securities Exchange Act of 1934 and the Securities and Exchange Commission's Rule 10b–5, even if he had obtained the blessing of his employer's principals before embarking on his profiteering scheme. Indeed, I think petitioner's brand of manipulative trading, with or without such approval, lies close to the heart of what the securities laws are intended to prohibit.

* * *

DIRKS v. SECURITIES AND EXCHANGE COMMISSION

Supreme Court of the United States, 1983.
463 U.S. 646, 103 S.Ct. 3255, 77 L.Ed.2d 911.

JUSTICE POWELL delivered the opinion of the Court.

Petitioner Raymond Dirks received material nonpublic information from "insiders" of a corporation with which he had no connection. He disclosed this information to investors who relied on it in trading in the shares of the corporation. The question is whether Dirks violated the antifraud provisions of the federal securities laws by this disclosure.

I

In 1973, Dirks was an officer of a New York broker-dealer firm who specialized in providing investment analysis of insurance company securities to institutional investors. On March 6, Dirks received information from Ronald Secrist, a former officer of Equity Funding of America. Secrist alleged that the assets of Equity Funding, a diversified corporation primarily engaged in selling life insurance and mutual funds, were vastly overstated as the result of fraudulent corporate practices. Secrist also stated that various regulatory agencies had failed to act on similar charges made by Equity Funding employees. He urged Dirks to verify the fraud and disclose it publicly.

Dirks decided to investigate the allegations. He visited Equity Funding's headquarters in Los Angeles and interviewed several officers and employees of the corporation. The senior management denied any wrongdoing, but certain corporation employees corroborated the charges of fraud. Neither Dirks nor his firm owned or traded any Equity Funding stock, but throughout his investigation he openly discussed the information he had obtained with a number of clients and investors. Some of these persons sold their holdings of Equity Funding securities, including five investment advisers who liquidated holdings of more than $16 million.

While Dirks was in Los Angeles, he was in touch regularly with William Blundell, the *Wall Street Journal's* Los Angeles bureau chief. Dirks urged Blundell to write a story on the fraud allegations. Blundell did not believe, however that such a massive fraud could go undetected and declined to write the story. He feared that publishing such damaging hearsay might be libelous.

During the two-week period in which Dirks pursued his investigation and spread word of Secrist's charges, the price of Equity Funding stock fell from $26 per share to less than $15 per share. This led the New York Stock Exchange to halt trading on March 27. Shortly thereafter California insurance authorities impounded Equity Funding's records and uncovered evidence of the fraud. Only then did the Securities and Exchange Commission (SEC) file a complaint against Equity Funding and only then, on April 2, did the *Wall Street Journal* publish a front-page story based largely on information assembled by Dirks. Equity Funding immediately went into receivership.

The SEC began an investigation into Dirks' role in the exposure of the fraud. After a hearing by an administrative law judge, the SEC found that Dirks had aided and abetted violations of § 17(a) of the Securities Act of

1933, § 10(b) of the Securities Exchange Act of 1934, and SEC Rule 10b–5, by repeating the allegations of fraud to members of the investment community who later sold their Equity Funding stock. The SEC concluded: "Where 'tippees'—regardless of their motivation or occupation—come into possession of material 'information that they know is confidential and know or should know came from a corporate insider,' they must either publicly disclose that information or refrain from trading." 21 S.E.C. Docket 1401, 1407 (1981) (footnote omitted) (quoting Chiarella v. United States, 445 U.S. 222, 230 n. 12 (1980). Recognizing, however, that Dirks "played an important role in bringing [Equity Funding's] massive fraud to light," 21 S.E.C. Docket, at 1412, the SEC only censured him.

Dirks sought review in the Court of Appeals for the District of Columbia Circuit. The court entered judgment against Dirks "for the reasons stated by the Commission in its opinion." App. to Pet. for Cert. C–2. Judge Wright, a member of the panel, subsequently issued an opinion. Judge Robb concurred in the result and Judge Tamm dissented; neither filed a separate opinion. Judge Wright believed that "the obligations of corporate fiduciaries pass to all those to whom they disclose their information before it has been disseminated to the public at large." 220 U.S.App.D.C. 309, 324, 681 F.2d 824, 839 (1982). Alternatively, Judge Wright concluded that, as an employee of a broker-dealer, Dirks had violated "obligations to the SEC and to the public completely independent of any obligations he acquired" as a result of receiving the information. Id., at 325, 681 F.2d, at 840.

In view of the importance to the SEC and to the securities industry of the question presented by this case, we granted a writ of certiorari. 459 U.S. 1014 (1982). We now reverse.

II

In the seminal case of In re Cady, Roberts & Co., 40 S.E.C. 907 (1961), the SEC recognized that the common law in some jurisdictions imposes on "corporate 'insiders,' particularly officers, directors, or controlling stockholders" an "affirmative duty of disclosure * * * when dealing in securities." Id., at 911, and n. 13.[10] The SEC found that not only did breach of this common-law duty also establish the elements of a Rule 10b–5 violation, but that individuals other than corporate insiders could be obligated either to disclose material nonpublic information before trading or to abstain from trading altogether. Id., at 912. In *Chiarella*, we accepted the two elements set out in *Cady, Roberts* for establishing a Rule 10b–5 violation: "(i) the existence of a relationship affording access to inside information intended to be available only for a corporate purpose, and (ii) the unfairness of allowing a corporate insider to take advantage of that information by trading without disclosure." 445 U.S., at 227. In examining whether

10. The duty that insiders owe to the corporation's shareholders not to trade on inside information differs from the common-law duty that officers and directors also have to the corporation itself not to mismanage corporate assets, of which confidential information is one. See 3 Fletcher Cyclopedia of the Laws of Private Corporations §§ 848, 900 (1975 ed. and Supp. 1982); 3A Fletcher §§ 1168.1, 1168.2. In holding that breaches of this duty to shareholders violated the Securities Exchange Act, the *Cady, Roberts* Commission recognized, and we agree, that "[a] significant purpose of the Exchange Act was to eliminate the idea that use of inside information for personal advantage was a normal emolument of corporate office." See 40 S.E.C., at 912, n. 15.

Chiarella had an obligation to disclose or abstain, the Court found that there is no general duty to disclose before trading on material nonpublic information, and held that "a duty to disclose under § 10(b) does not arise from the mere possession of nonpublic market information." Id., at 235. Such a duty arises rather from the existence of a fiduciary relationship. See id., at 227–235.

Not "all breaches of fiduciary duty in connection with a securities transaction," however, come within the ambit of Rule 10b–5. Santa Fe Industries, Inc. v. Green, 430 U.S. 462, 472 (1977). There must also be "manipulation or deception." Id., at 473. In an inside-trading case this fraud derives from the "inherent unfairness involved where one takes advantage" of "information intended to be available only for a corporate purpose and not for the personal benefit of anyone." In re Merrill Lynch, Pierce, Fenner & Smith, Inc., 43 S.E.C. 933, 936 (1968). Thus, an insider will be liable under Rule 10b–5 for inside trading only where he fails to disclose material nonpublic information before trading on it and thus makes "secret profits." Cady, Roberts, 40 S.E.C., at 916, n. 31.

III

We were explicit in Chiarella in saying that there can be no duty to disclose where the person who has traded on inside information "was not [the corporation's] agent, * * * was not a fiduciary, [or] was not a person in whom the sellers [of the securities] had placed their trust and confidence." 445 U.S., at 232. Not to require such a fiduciary relationship, we recognized, would "depar[t] radically from the established doctrine that duty arises from a specific relationship between two parties" and would amount to "recognizing a general duty between all participants in market transactions to forgo actions based on material, nonpublic information." Id., at 232, 233. This requirement of a specific relationship between the shareholders and the individual trading on inside information has created analytical difficulties for the SEC and courts in policing tippees who trade on inside information. Unlike insiders who have independent fiduciary duties to both the corporation and its shareholders, the typical tippee has no such relationships.[14] In view of this absence, it has been unclear how a tippee acquires the Cady, Roberts duty to refrain from trading on inside information.

---

14. Under certain circumstances, such as where corporate information is revealed legitimately to an underwriter, accountant, lawyer, or consultant working for the corporation, these outsiders may become fiduciaries of the shareholders. The basis for recognizing this fiduciary duty is not simply that such persons acquired nonpublic corporate information, but rather that they have entered into a special confidential relationship in the conduct of the business of the enterprise and are given access to information solely for corporate purposes. See SEC v. Monarch Fund, 608 F.2d 938, 942 (CA2 1979); In re Investors Management Co., 44 S.E.C. 633, 645 (1971); In re Van Alystne, Noel & Co., 43 S.E.C. 1080, 1084–1085 (1969); In re Merrill Lynch, Pierce, Fenner & Smith, Inc., 43 S.E.C. 933, 937 (1968); Cady, Roberts, 40 S.E.C., at 912. When such a person breaches his fiduciary relationship, he may be treated more properly as a tipper than a tippee. See Shapiro v. Merrill Lynch, Pierce, Fenner & Smith, Inc., 495 F.2d 228, 237 (CA2 1974) (investment banker had access to material information when working on a proposed public offering for the corporation). For such a duty to be imposed, however, the corporation must expect the outsider to keep the disclosed nonpublic information confidential, and the relationship at least must imply such a duty.

A

The SEC's position, as stated in its opinion in this case, is that a tippee "inherits" the *Cady, Roberts* obligation to shareholders whenever he receives inside information from an insider. * * *

This view differs little from the view that we rejected as inconsistent with congressional intent in *Chiarella*. In that case, the Court of Appeals agreed with the SEC and affirmed Chiarella's conviction, holding that " '[*a*]*nyone* —corporate insider or not—who regularly receives material nonpublic information may not use that information to trade in securities without incurring an affirmative duty to disclose.' " United States v. Chiarella, 588 F.2d 1358, 1365 (CA 2 1978) (emphasis in original). Here, the SEC maintains that anyone who knowingly receives nonpublic material information from an insider has a fiduciary duty to disclose before trading.[15]

In effect, the SEC's theory of tippee liability in both cases appears rooted in the idea that the antifraud provisions require equal information among all traders. This conflicts with the principle set forth in *Chiarella* that only some persons, under some circumstances, will be barred from trading while in possession of material nonpublic information.[16] Judge Wright correctly read our opinion in *Chiarella* as repudiating any notion that all traders must enjoy equal information before trading: "[T]he 'information' theory is rejected. Because the disclose-or-refrain duty is extraordinary, it attaches only when a party has legal obligations other than a mere duty to comply with the general antifraud proscriptions in the federal securities laws." 220 U.S.App.D.C., at 322, 681 F.2d, at 837. See *Chiarella*, 445 U.S., at 235, n. 20. We reaffirm today that "[a] duty [to disclose] arises from the relationship between parties * * * and not

---

15. Apparently the SEC believes this case differs from *Chiarella* in that Dirks' receipt of inside information from Secrist, an insider, carried Secrist's duties with it, while Chiarella received the information without the direct involvement of an insider and thus inherited no duty to disclose or abstain. The SEC fails to explain, however, why the receipt on nonpublic information from an insider automatically carries with it the fiduciary duty of the insider. As we emphasized in *Chiarella*, mere possession of nonpublic information does not give rise to a duty to disclose or abstain; only a specific relationship does that. And we do not believe that the mere receipt of information from an insider creates such a special relationship between the tippee and the corporation's shareholders.

Apparently recognizing the weakness of its argument in light of *Chiarella*, the SEC attempts to distinguish that case factually as involving not "inside" information, but rather "market" information, i.e., "information generated within the company relating to its assets or earnings." Brief for Respondent 23. This Court drew no such distinction in *Chiarella* and, as The Chief

Justice noted, "[i]t is clear that § 10(b) and Rule 10b–5 by their terms and by their history make no such distinction." 445 U.S., at 241, n. 1 (dissenting opinion). See ALI Fed.Sec.Code § 1603, Comment (2)(j) (Proposed Official Draft 1978).

16. In *Chiarella*, we noted that formulation of an absolute equal information rule "should not be undertaken absent some explicit evidence of congressional intent." 445 U.S., at 233, 100 S.Ct., at 1117. Rather than adopting such a radical view of securities trading, Congress has expressly exempted many market professionals from the general statutory prohibition set forth in § 11(a)(1) of the Securities Exchange Act, 15 U.S.C. § 78k(a)(1), against members of a national securities exchange trading for their own account. See id., at 233, n. 16, 100 S.Ct., at 1117, n. 16. We observed in *Chiarella* that "[t]he exception is based upon Congress' recognition that [market professionals] contribute to a fair and orderly marketplace at the same time they exploit the informational advantage that comes from their possession of [nonpublic information]." Ibid.

merely from one's ability to acquire information because of his position in the market."   445 U.S., at 232–233, n. 14.

Imposing a duty to disclose or abstain solely because a person knowingly receives material nonpublic information from an insider and trades on it could have an inhibiting influence on the role of market analysts, which the SEC itself recognizes is necessary to the preservation of a healthy market.[17] It is commonplace for analysts to "ferret out and analyze information," 21 S.E.C., at 1406,[18] and this often is done by meeting with and questioning corporate officers and others who are insiders. And information that the analysts obtain normally may be the basis for judgments as to the market worth of a corporation's securities. The analyst's judgment in this respect is made available in market letters or otherwise to clients of the firm. It is the nature of this type of information, and indeed of the markets themselves, that such information cannot be made simultaneously available to all of the corporation's stockholders or the public generally.

B

The conclusion that recipients of inside information do not invariably acquire a duty to disclose or abstain does not mean that such tippees always are free to trade on the information. The need for a ban on some tippee trading is clear. Not only are insiders forbidden by their fiduciary relationship from personally using undisclosed corporate information to their advantage, but they may not give such information to an outsider for the same improper purpose of exploiting the information for their personal gain. See 15 U.S.C. § 78t(b) (making it unlawful to do indirectly "by means of any other person" any act made unlawful by the federal securities laws). Similarly, the transactions of those who knowingly participate with the fiduciary in such a breach are "as forbidden" as transactions "on behalf of the trustee himself." Mosser v. Darrow, 341 U.S. 267, 272 (1951). *   *   *

---

17. The SEC expressly recognized that "[t]he value to the entire market of [analysts'] efforts cannot be gainsaid; market efficiency in pricing is significantly enhanced by [their] initiatives to ferret out and analyze information, and thus the analyst's work redounds to the benefit of all investors." 21 S.E.C., at 1406. The SEC asserts that analysts remain free to obtain from management corporate information for purposes of "filling in the 'interstices in analysis' * * *." Brief for Respondent 42 (quoting *Investors Management Co.,* 44 S.E.C., at 646). But this rule is inherently imprecise, and imprecision prevents parties from ordering their actions in accord with legal requirements. Unless the parties have some guidance as to where the line is between permissible and impermissible disclosures and uses, neither corporate insiders nor analysts can be sure when the line is crossed. Cf. Adler v. Klawans, 267 F.2d 840, 845 (CA2 1959) (Burger, J., sitting by designation).

18. On its facts, this case is the unusual one. Dirks is an analyst in a broker-dealer firm, and he did interview management in the course of his investigation. He uncovered, however, startling information that required no analysis or exercise of judgment as to its market relevance. Nonetheless, the principle at issue here extends beyond these facts. The SEC's rule—applicable without regard to any breach by an insider—could have serious ramifications on reporting by analysts of investment views.

Despite the unusualness of Dirks' "find," the central role that he played in uncovering the fraud at Equity Funding, and that analysts in general can play in revealing information that corporations may have reason to withhold from the public, is an important one. Dirks' careful investigation brought to light a massive fraud at the corporation. And until the Equity Funding fraud was exposed, the information in the trading market was grossly inaccurate. But for Dirks' efforts, the fraud might well have gone undetected longer. * * *

As the court explained in *Mosser,* a contrary rule "would open up opportunities for devious dealings in the name of the others that the trustee could not conduct in his own." 341 U.S., at 271. See SEC v. Texas Gulf Sulphur Co., 446 F.2d 1301, 1308 (CA2), cert. denied, 404 U.S. 1005 (1971). Thus, the tippee's duty to disclose or abstain is derivative from that of the insider's duty. See Tr. of Oral Ar. 38. Cf. *Chiarella,* 445 U.S., at 246, n. 1 (Blackmun, J., dissenting). As we noted in *Chiarella,* "[t]he tippee's obligation has been viewed as arising from his role as a participant after the fact in the insider's breach of a fiduciary duty." 445 U.S., at 230, n. 12.

Thus, some tippees must assume an insider's duty to the shareholders not because they receive inside information, but rather because it has been made available to them *improperly.*[19] And for Rule 10b–5 purposes, the insider's disclosure is improper only where it would violate his *Cady, Roberts* duty. Thus, a tippee assumes a fiduciary duty to the shareholders of a corporation not to trade on material nonpublic information only when the insider has breached his fiduciary duty to the shareholders by disclosing the information to the tippee and the tippee knows or should know that there has been a breach.[20] As Commissioner Smith perceptively observed in *Investors Management Co.:* "[T]ippee responsibility must be related back to insider responsibility by a necessary finding that the tippee knew the information was given to him in breach of a duty by a person having a special relationship to the issuer not to disclose the information * * *." 44 S.E.C., at 651 (concurring in the result). Tipping thus properly is viewed only as a means of indirectly violating the *Cady, Roberts* disclose-or-abstain rule.[21]

19. The SEC itself has recognized that tippee liability properly is imposed only in circumstances where the tippee knows, or has reason to know, that the insider has disclosed improperly inside corporate information. In *Investors Management Co.,* supra, the SEC stated that one element of tippee liability is that the tippee knew or had reason to know "that [the information] was non-public and had been obtained *improperly* by selective revelation or otherwise." 44 S.E.C., at 641 (emphasis added). Commissioner Smith read this test to mean that a tippee can be held liable only if he received information in breach of an insider's duty not to disclose it. Id., at 650 (concurring in the result).

20. Professor Loss has linked tippee liability to the concept in the law of restitution that " '[w]here a fiduciary in violation of his duty to the beneficiary communicates confidential information to a third person, the third person, if he had notice of the violation of duty, holds upon a constructive trust for the beneficiary any profit which he makes through the use of such information.' " 3 L. Loss, Securities Regulation 1451 (2d ed. 1961) (quoting Restatement of Restitution § 201(2) (1937)). Other authorities likewise have expressed the view that tippee liability exists only where there has been a breach of trust by an insider of which the tippee had knowledge. * * *

21. We do not suggest that knowingly trading on inside information is ever "socially desirable or even that it is devoid of moral considerations." Dooley, Enforcement of Insider Trading Restrictions, 66 Va.L.Rev. 1, 55 (1980). Nor do we imply an absence of responsibility to disclose promptly indications of illegal actions by a corporation to the proper authorities—typically the SEC and exchange authorities in cases involving securities. Depending on the circumstances, and even where permitted by law, one's trading on material nonpublic information is behavior that may fall below ethical standards of conduct. But in a statutory area of the law such as securities regulation, where legal principles of general application must be applied, there may be "significant distinctions between actual legal obligations and ethical ideals." SEC, Report of the Special Study of Securities Markets, H.R.Doc. No. 95, 88th Cong., 1st Sess., pt. 1, pp. 237–238 (1963). The SEC recognizes this. At oral argument, the following exchange took place:

"QUESTION: So, it would not have satisfied his obligation under the law to go to the SEC first?

"[SEC's counsel]: That is correct. That an insider has to observe what has come to be known as the abstain or disclosure rule. Either the information has to be disclosed

C

In determining whether a tippee is under an obligation to disclose or abstain, it thus is necessary to determine whether the insider's "tip" constituted a breach of the insider's fiduciary duty. All disclosures of confidential corporate information are not inconsistent with the duty insiders owe to shareholders. In contrast to the extraordinary facts of this case, the more typical situation in which there will be a question whether disclosure violates the insider's *Cady, Roberts* duty is when insiders disclose information to analysts. * * * In some situations, the insider will act consistently with his fiduciary duty to shareholders, and yet release of the information may affect the market. For example, it may not be clear— either to the corporate insider or to the recipient analyst—whether the information will be viewed as material nonpublic information. Corporate officials may mistakenly think the information already has been disclosed or that it is not material enough to affect the market. Whether disclosure is a breach of duty therefore depends in large part on the purpose of the disclosure. This standard was identified by the SEC itself in *Cady, Roberts:* a purpose of the securities laws was to eliminate "use of inside information for personal advantage." 40 S.E.C., at 912, n. 15. See n. 10, supra. Thus, the test is whether the insider personally will benefit, directly or indirectly, from his disclosure. Absent some personal gain, there has been no breach of duty to stockholders. And absent a breach by the insider, there is no derivative breach. As Commissioner Smith stated in *Investors Management Co.:* "It is important in this type of case to focus on policing insiders and what they do * * * rather than on policing information *per se* and its possession. * * *" 44 S.E.C., at 648 (concurring in the result).

The SEC argues that, if inside-trading liability does not exist when the information is transmitted for a proper purpose but is used for trading, it would be a rare situation when the parties could not fabricate some ostensibly legitimate business justification for transmitting the information. We think the SEC is unduly concerned. In determining whether the insider's purpose in making a particular disclosure is fraudulent, the SEC and the courts are not required to read the parties' minds. Scienter in some cases is relevant in determining whether the tipper has violated his *Cady, Roberts* duty.[23] But to determine whether the disclosure itself "deceive[s], manipulate[s], or defraud[s]" shareholders, Aaron v. SEC, 446

---

to the market if it is inside information * * * or the insider must abstain." Tr. of Oral Arg. 27.

Thus, it is clear that Rule 10b–5 does not impose any obligation simply to tell the SEC about the fraud before trading.

23. *Scienter*—"a mental state embracing intent to deceive, manipulate, or defraud," Ernst & Ernst v. Hochfelder, 425 U.S. 185, 193, n. 12, 96 S.Ct. 1375, 1381, n. 12, 47 L.Ed.2d 668 (1976)—is an independent element of a Rule 10b–5 violation. See Aaron v. SEC, 446 U.S. 680, 695, 100 S.Ct. 1945, 1955, 64 L.Ed.2d 611 (1980). Contrary to the dissent's suggestion, see post, at p. 3271, n. 10, motivation is not irrelevant to the issue of *scienter*. It is not enough that an insider's conduct results in

harm to investors; rather, a violation may be found only where there is "intentional or willful conduct designed to deceive or defraud investors by controlling or artificially affecting the price of securities." Ernst & Ernst v. Hochfelder, supra, 425 U.S., at 199, 96 S.Ct., at 1383. The issue in this case, however, is not whether Secrist or Dirks acted with *scienter*, but rather whether there was any deceptive or fraudulent conduct at all, i.e., whether Secrist's disclosure constituted a breach of his fiduciary duty and thereby caused injury to shareholders. See n. 27, infra. Only if there was such a breach did Dirks, a tippee, acquire a fiduciary duty to disclose or abstain.

U.S. 680, 686 (1980), the initial inquiry is whether there has been a breach of duty by the insider. This requires courts to focus on objective criteria, i.e., whether the insider receives a direct or indirect personal benefit from the disclosure, such as a pecuniary gain or a reputational benefit that will translate into future earnings. Cf. 40 S.E.C., at 912, n. 15; Brudney, Insiders, Outsiders, and Informational Advantages Under the Federal Securities Laws, 93 Harv.L.Rev. 324, 348 (1979) ("The theory * * * is that the insider, by giving the information out selectively, is in effect selling the information to its recipient for cash, reciprocal information, or other things of value for himself. * * * "). There are objective facts and circumstances that often justify such an inference. For example, there may be a relationship between the insider and the recipient that suggests a *quid pro quo* from the latter, or an intention to benefit the particular recipient. The elements of fiduciary duty and exploitation of nonpublic information also exist when an insider makes a gift of confidential information to a trading relative or friend. The tip and trade resemble trading by the insider himself followed by a gift of the profits to the recipient.

Determining whether an insider personally benefits from a particular disclosure, a question of fact, will not always be easy for courts. But it is essential, we think, to have a guiding principle for those whose daily activities must be limited and instructed by the SEC's inside-trading rules, and we believe that there must be a breach of the insider's fiduciary duty before the tippee inherits the duty to disclose or abstain. In contrast, the rule adopted by the SEC in this case would have no limiting principle.

IV

Under the inside-trading and tipping rules set forth above, we find that there was no actionable violation by Dirks. It is undisputed that Dirks himself was a stranger to Equity Funding, with no pre-existing fiduciary duty to its shareholders. He took no action, directly or indirectly, that induced the shareholders or officers of Equity Funding to repose trust or confidence in him. There was no expectation by Dirks' sources that he would keep their information in confidence. Nor did Dirks misappropriate or illegally obtain the information about Equity Funding. Unless the insiders breached their *Cady, Roberts* duty to shareholders in disclosing the nonpublic information to Dirks, he breached no duty when he passed it on to investors as well as to the *Wall Street Journal.*

It is clear that neither Secrist nor the other Equity Funding employees violated their *Cady, Roberts* duty to the corporation's shareholders by providing information to Dirks.[27] The tippers received no monetary or

---

27. In this Court, the SEC appears to contend that an insider invariably violates a fiduciary duty to the corporation's shareholders by transmitting nonpublic corporate information to an outsider when he has reason to believe that the outsider may use it to the disadvantage of the shareholders. "Thus, regardless of any ultimate motive to bring to public attention the derelictions at Equity Funding, Secrist breached his duty to Equity Funding shareholders." Brief for Respondent 31. This perceived "duty" differs markedly from the one that the SEC identified in *Cady, Roberts* and

that has been the basis for federal tippee-trading rules to date. In fact, the SEC did not charge Secrist with any wrongdoing, and we do not understand the SEC to have relied on any theory of a breach of duty by Secrist in finding that Dirks breached his duty to Equity Funding's shareholders. See App. 250 (decision of administrative law judge) ("One who knows himself to be a beneficiary of non-public, selectively disclosed inside information must fully disclose or refrain from trading."); SEC's Reply to Notice of Supplemental Authority before the SEC 4 ("If Secrist was acting

personal benefit for revealing Equity Funding's secrets, nor was their purpose to make a gift of valuable information to Dirks. As the facts of this case clearly indicate, the tippers were motivated by a desire to expose the fraud. See supra, at 1–2. In the absence of a breach of duty to shareholders by the insiders, there was no derivative breach by Dirks. See n. 20, supra. Dirks therefore could not have been "a participant after the fact in [an] insider's breach of a fiduciary duty." *Chiarella,* 445 U.S., at 230, n. 12.

V

We conclude that Dirks, in the circumstances of this case, had no duty to abstain from use of the inside information that he obtained. The judgment of the Court of Appeals therefore is

Reversed.

JUSTICE BLACKMUN, with whom JUSTICE BRENNAN and JUSTICE MARSHALL join, dissenting.

The Court today takes still another step to limit the protections provided investors by § 10(b) of the Securities Exchange Act of 1934. See Chiarella v. United States, 445 U.S. 222, 246 (1980) (dissenting opinion). The device employed in this case engrafts a special motivational require-

properly, Dirks inherited a duty to [Equity Funding]'s shareholders to refrain from improper private use of the information."); Brief on behalf of the SEC in the Court of Appeals, at 47–50; id., at 51 ("[K]nowing possession of inside information by any person imposes a duty to abstain or disclose."); id., at 52–54; id., at 55 ("[T]his obligation arises not from the manner in which such information is acquired ∗ ∗ ∗."); 220 U.S.App.D.C., at 322–323, 681 F.2d, at 838 (Wright, J.).

The dissent argues that "Secrist violated his duty to Equity Funding shareholders by transmitting material nonpublic information to Dirks with the intention that Dirks would cause his clients to trade on that information." *Post,* at 3274. By perceiving a breach of fiduciary duty whenever inside information is intentionally disclosed to securities traders, the dissenting opinion effectively would achieve the same result as the SEC's theory below, i.e., mere possession of inside information while trading would be viewed as a Rule 10b–5 violation. But *Chiarella* made it explicitly clear there is no general duty to forgo market transactions "based on material, nonpublic information." 445 U.S., at 233, 100 S.Ct., at 1117. Such a duty would "depar[t] radically from the established doctrine that duty arises from a specific relationship between two parties." Ibid. See p. 3261, supra.

Moreover, to constitute a violation of Rule 10b–5, there must be fraud. See Ernst & Ernst v. Hochfelder, 425 U.S. 185, 199, 96 S.Ct. 1375, 1383, 47 L.Ed.2d 668

(1976) (statutory words "manipulative," "device," and "contrivance ∗ ∗ ∗ connot[e] intentional or willful conduct designed to *deceive or defraud* investors by controlling or artificially affecting the price of securities") (emphasis added). There is no evidence that Secrist's disclosure was intended to or did in fact "deceive or defraud" anyone. Secrist certainly intended to convey relevant information that management was unlawfully concealing, and—so far as the record shows—he believed that persuading Dirks to investigate was the best way to disclose the fraud. Other efforts had proved fruitless. Under any objective standard, Secrist received no direct or indirect personal benefit from the disclosure.

The dissenting opinion focuses on shareholder "losses," "injury," and "damages," but in many cases there may be no clear causal connection between inside trading and outsiders' losses. In one sense, as market values fluctuate and investors act on inevitably incomplete or incorrect information, there always are winners and losers; but those who have "lost" have not necessarily been defrauded. On the other hand, inside trading for personal gain is fraudulent, and is a violation of the federal securities laws. See Dooley, supra, at 39–41, 70. Thus, there is little legal significance to the dissent's argument that Secrist and Dirks created new "victims" by disclosing the information to persons who traded. In fact, they prevented the fraud from continuing and victimizing many more investors.

ment on the fiduciary duty doctrine. This innovation excuses a knowing and intentional violation of an insider's duty to shareholders if the insider does not act from a motive of personal gain. Even on the extraordinary facts of this case, such an innovation is not justified.

* * *

II

A

No one questions that Secrist himself could not trade on his inside information to the disadvantage of uninformed shareholders and purchasers of Equity Funding securities. See Brief for United States as *Amicus Curiae* 19, n. 12. Unlike the printer in *Chiarella,* Secrist stood in a fiduciary relationship with these shareholders. As the Court states, ante, at 5, corporate insiders have an affirmative duty of disclosure when trading with shareholders of the corporation. See *Chiarella,* 445 U.S., at 227. This duty extends as well to purchasers of the corporation's securities. Id., at 227, n. 8, citing Gratz v. Claughton, 187 F.2d 46, 49 (CA2), cert. denied, 341 U.S. 920 (1951).

The Court also acknowledges that Secrist could not do by proxy what he was prohibited from doing personally. Ante, at 12; Mosser v. Darrow, 341 U.S. 267, 272 (1951). But this is precisely what Secrist did. Secrist used Dirks to disseminate information to Dirks' clients, who in turn dumped stock on unknowing purchasers. Secrist thus intended Dirks to injure the purchasers of Equity Funding securities to whom Secrist had a duty to disclose. Accepting the Court's view of tippee liability, it appears that Dirk's knowledge of this breach makes him liable as a participant in the breach after the fact. Ante, at 12, 19; *Chiarella,* 445 U.S., at 230, n. 12.

B

The Court holds, however, that Dirks is not liable because Secrist did not violate his duty; according to the Court, this is so because Secrist did not have the improper purpose of personal gain. Ante, at 15–16, 18–19. In so doing, the Court imposes a new, subjective limitation on the scope of the duty owed by insiders to shareholders. The novelty of this limitation is reflected in the Court's lack of support for it.

* * *

IV

In my view, Secrist violated his duty to Equity Funding shareholders by transmitting material nonpublic information to Dirks with the intention that Dirks would cause his clients to trade on that information. Dirks, therefore, was under a duty to make the information publicly available or to refrain from actions that he knew would lead to trading. Because Dirks caused his clients to trade, he violated § 10(b) and Rule 10b–5. Any other result is a disservice to this country's attempt to provide fair and efficient capital markets. I dissent.

AFFIRMATIVE DUTY TO DISCLOSE

Rule 10b–5 does not refer specifically to an "insider" nor does it specifically require disclosure of facts known to one party to a securities transaction and unknown to the other. Clause (2) refers to omissions to state material facts only when "necessary in order to make the *statements made* * * * not misleading." In other words, it refers to half-truths, and if no statements at all are made it does not literally require any disclosure. Clause (1) prohibits a "device, scheme, or artifice to defraud" and clause (3) prohibits any "act, practice, or course of business which operates or would operate as a fraud or deceit." Neither of the latter clauses says anything specifically about disclosure.

Nevertheless, the decisions have uniformly held that, if one party to the transaction occupies a fiduciary relation to the other, the Rule imposes an affirmative duty of disclosure of any material facts known to him and unknown to the other party. This fiduciary status is usually said to arise from his being an "insider."[1] In fact, almost all of the early cases under the Rule involved such nondisclosure by insiders. Those early cases had involved face-to-face negotiations, and the Cady, Roberts[2] and Texas Gulf Sulphur[3] cases were the first to apply the same rule to stock exchange transactions. Therefore, they created a great deal of publicity,[4] although there had never been any real reason to doubt that the same rule was applicable to transactions effected on a stock exchange.

In Securities and Exchange Commission v. Texas Gulf Sulphur Co.[5] the Second Circuit held that certain corporate officers and other employees had violated Rule 10b–5 by purchasing stock of the company (or calls on such stock) and by "tipping" others who purchased, while they were in possession of certain non-public information concerning a potentially rich copper and silver strike by the company in Canada. Most of the argument in the case concerned the question at what point in the exploratory drilling by the company the probability that the discovery would be of significant value became sufficiently great that the information possessed by the insiders was "material." The court indicated that the decision of this question depends upon "a balancing of both the indicated probability that the event will occur and the anticipated magnitude of the event in the light of the totality of the company activity,"[6] and reversed the factual finding of the district court on this issue (over the bitter dissent of Judge Moore).

On the question of the substantive duty of the individual insider defendants the court said: "The essence of the Rule [10b–5] is that anyone who, trading for his own account in the securities of a corporation has 'access, directly or

---

1. Rogen v. Ilikon Corp., 361 F.2d 260 (1st Cir.1966); List v. Fashion Park, Inc., 340 F.2d 457 (2d Cir.1965), cert. denied 382 U.S. 811 (1965); Kohler v. Kohler Co., 319 F.2d 634 (7th Cir.1963); Speed v. Transamerica Corp., 99 F.Supp. 808 (D.Del.1951), 135 F.Supp. 176 (D.Del.1955), aff'd 235 F.2d 369 (3d Cir.1956); Ross v. Licht, 263 F.Supp. 395 (S.D.N.Y.1967); Northern Trust Co. v. Essaness Theatres Corp., 103 F.Supp. 954 (N.D.Ill.1952); Kardon v. National Gypsum Co., 69 F.Supp. 512 (E.D.Pa. 1946), 73 F.Supp. 798 (E.D.Pa.1947), 83 F.Supp. 613 (E.D.Pa.1947).

2. In the Matter of Cady, Roberts & Co., 40 S.E.C. 907 (1961).

3. Securities and Exchange Commission v. Texas Gulf Sulphur Co., 401 F.2d 833 (2d Cir.1968), cert. denied 394 U.S. 976 (1969); Securities and Exchange Commission v. Texas Gulf Sulphur Co., 446 F.2d 1301 (2d Cir.1971).

4. Wall Street Journal, April 20, 1965, p. 3, col. 1; April 23, 1965, p. 3, col. 1; April 27, 1965, p. 1, col. 6; Wells, SEC v. Texas Gulf Raises Sticky Questions, Life, Aug. 6, 1965, p. 29.

5. Supra, note 3.

6. 401 F.2d at p. 849.

indirectly, to information intended to be available only for a corporate purpose and not for the personal benefit of anyone' may not take 'advantage of such information knowing it is unavailable to those with whom he is dealing,' i.e., the investing public. * * * Thus, anyone in possession of material inside information must either disclose it to the investing public, or, if he is disabled from disclosing it in order to protect a corporate confidence, or he chooses not to do so, must abstain from trading in or recommending the securities concerned while such inside information remains undisclosed." [7]

The courts have not been specific as to which clause of the Rule imposes this duty, but have relied, in the words of one court, simply upon the assertion that "the rule is clear," [8] or have asserted, as the court did in List v. Fashion Park, Inc.,[9] that " * * * we fail to see that it makes any difference which clause of Rule 10b–5 is relied on. * * * " [10]

The judicial gloss thus put upon Rule 10b–5, that an insider has a duty to disclose, to the other party to a transaction in the corporation's shares, material information which is known to him but not to the other party, raises two primary questions: Who has a duty of disclosure?, and, What information is material?

WHO HAS A DUTY OF DISCLOSURE?

Insiders. It seems clear that officers and directors [11] and majority or other controlling shareholders [12] have the status of "insiders." Beyond these rather obvious categories, the identification of an "insider" becomes more difficult.

Chairman Cary in the Cady, Roberts case [13] attempts to lay down a general rule for determining when an obligation of disclosure arises as a result of the possession of inside information: " * * * the obligation rests on two principal elements; first, the existence of a relationship giving access, directly or indirectly, to information intended to be available only for a corporate purpose and not for the personal benefit of anyone, and second, the inherent unfairness involved where a party takes advantage of such information knowing it is unavailable to those with whom he is dealing."

7. 401 F.2d at p. 848.

8. Speed v. Transamerica Corp., supra note 1, 99 F.Supp. at 828. In Mitchell v. Texas Gulf Sulphur Co., 446 F.2d 90, at 96 (10th Cir.1971), the court said that "Rule 10b–5 is plain, concise and unambiguous."

9. Supra, note 1.

10. 340 F.2d at 462.

11. List v. Fashion Park, Inc.; Ross v. Licht; Northern Trust Co. v. Essaness Theatres Corp.; Kardon v. National Gypsum Co.; all supra note 1. There would also seem to be little doubt that other employees are covered by the prohibition, as was held in the Texas Gulf Sulphur case, even though they do not have an executive title. While there are no cases, the same would seem to be true of any persons regularly working for the corporation and privy to corporate information,

such as outside legal counsel or independent certified public accountants, although they may be "independent contractors" rather than "employees." Cf. Fischer v. Kletz, 266 F.Supp. 180 (S.D.N.Y.1967).

12. Rogen v. Ilikon Corp.; Speed v. Transamerica Corp.; both supra note 1; Robinson v. Difford, 92 F.Supp. 145 (E.D. Pa.1950). The issuer itself is, of course, also covered. Kohler v. Kohler Co., supra note 1. In Feldman v. Simkins Industries, Inc., 679 F.2d 1299 (9th Cir.1982), a 14% shareholder who was not represented on the issuer's board of directors and did not have access to any nonpublic corporate information was held not to be an "insider" who had any duty of disclosure to other shareholders under Rule 10b–5.

13. In the Matter of Cady, Roberts & Co., 40 S.E.C. 907 (1961).

In the Investors Management Co. case [14] Commissioner Smith in his concurring opinion summarizes the position of the majority of the Commission (while criticizing the formula to some extent) regarding the "four questions to be asked in determining the applicability of Rule 10b–5 to an inside information trading case: One, was the information material? Two, was the information non-public? Three, was the person effecting the transaction an insider or, if not an insider but a 'tippee', did he know or have reason to know that the information 'was non-public and had been obtained improperly by selective revelation or otherwise'? And four, was the information 'a factor' in the person's decision to effect the transaction?" To what extent does this test differ from that of Cady, Roberts?

Non-trading tippers. It seems now to be clear that an insider can be held liable for conveying non-public, inside information to third persons, such as relatives, friends, or mere social or business acquaintances, who in turn trade on the basis of such information before it is made public. In the Texas Gulf case an insider-tipper was held liable, at the suit of the SEC, for the profits made by his tippees. This holding was reaffirmed in the case of Shapiro v. Merrill Lynch, Pierce, Fenner & Smith, Inc.[15] In that case, Merrill Lynch was the prospective underwriter of an issue of debentures by the Douglas Aircraft Company. In that capacity, in connection with the work on the preparation of the registration statement, it was furnished information by the company regarding a drastic decline in earnings in the first half of the fiscal year. Before this decline in earnings was publicly announced, Merrill Lynch informed a number of its institutional clients who dumped their stock in Douglas Aircraft Company. Merrill Lynch was held liable to the sellers of stock in the market with respect to the transactions engaged in by its "tippees." [16] However, the court in Texas Gulf refused to hold the tipper liable with respect to transactions by tippees of tippees (or so-called "second generation" tippees), as requested by the SEC.[17]

The Supreme Court held in Bateman Eichler, Hill Richards, Inc. v. Berner [18] that the defense of *in pari delicto* is not normally available to a tipper when he is sued by a tippee claiming that the alleged inside information furnished to him, on which he acted to his detriment, was in fact false, disagreeing with earlier decisions by the Fifth and Third Circuits.[19] The court conceded that the defense of *in pari delicto* might be available to such a defendant in some

<hr/>

14. In the Matter of Investors Management Co., Inc., CCH Fed.Sec.Law Rptr. ¶ 78,163 (SEC 1971) (concurring opinion).

15. 495 F.2d 228 (2d Cir.1974).

16. Merrill Lynch, as the Douglas underwriter, could either be regarded as an "insider" or as being itself a tippee who in turn tipped certain favored customers. The former seems more reasonable, since Merrill Lynch had a duty under Section 11 to discover all material, inside information about Douglas and Douglas had a duty to reveal it; and Merrill Lynch itself did not sell. Perhaps the difference is merely one of nomenclature, if it is assumed that a tippee who does not act upon the inside information is nevertheless liable if he in turn tips others who do act upon it.

The Commission also censured Merrill Lynch and closed certain of its offices for brief periods, as well as imposing sanctions upon certain of its employees. In the Mat-

ter of Merrill Lynch, Pierce, Fenner & Smith, Inc., SEC Sec.Exch.Act Rel. No. 8459 (Nov. 25, 1968).

17. One of the derelictions charged was that Mr. Darke (the geologist for Texas Gulf) told Miss Atkinson who told Mr. Klotz who purchased calls on Texas Gulf stock; and as a result Mr. Klotz was forced out of his job as Assistant Secretary of Commerce when the publicity about the case hit the newspapers. See Wall Street Journal, April 23, 1965, p. 3, col. 2; April 27, 1965, p. 16, col. 3.

18. 472 U.S. 299 (1985).

19. Kuehnert v. Texstar Corp., 412 F.2d 700 (5th Cir.1969); Tarasi v. Pittsburg National Bank, 555 F.2d 1152 (3d Cir.1977), cert. denied 434 U.S. 965. The Supreme Court approved the reasoning of Judge Weinfeld in Nathanson v. Weis, Voisin, Cannon, Inc., 325 F.Supp. 50 (S.D.N.Y. 1971).

circumstances, but only "where (1) as a direct result of his own actions, the plaintiff bears at least substantially equal responsibility for the violations he seeks to redress, and (2) preclusion of suit would not significantly interfere with the effective enforcement of the securities laws and protection of the investing public."[20] The discussion in the opinion, however, indicates clearly that a defendant would rarely, if ever, be able to persuade the court that these requirements had been satisfied.[21] However, a stockholder cannot recover from a tipper on the basis that others were tipped but he was not and was thereby deprived of an opportunity to unload.[22] Judge Friendly stated in Levine v. Seilon, Inc.[23] that such a plaintiff was claiming "compensation for the premium [he] might have extracted from some innocent victim if [he] had known of the fraud and the buyer did not."[24] In a situation where the undisclosed information is bullish, as in Texas Gulf Sulphur, a contrary result might mean that a tipper would be liable to every person in the world for not giving him an opportunity to buy—even Rule 10b–5 cannot be stretched that far.

Trading tippees. In the *Texas Gulf* case there was no question of the liability of the tippees who traded, since they had not been sued by the SEC. However, Judge Waterman went out of his way in the majority opinion to state that their conduct was "equally reprehensible" with that of their insider-tippers.

In Ross v. Licht,[25] three of the purchasers were three dentists, one of whom (Dr. Sidney Licht) was a brother of the controlling directors and shareholders of the corporation and the other two of whom (Dr. Grapel and Dr. Bluestone) were his close personal friends. The court said: "What about Sidney [Licht], Grapel and Bluestone? Applying the test above stated, they were insiders also. National [the issuer] was controlled by the Licht family, of which Sidney was a member and in close touch with Charles and William [Licht]. Grapel and Bluestone had been close friends for some thirty years of Sidney and of Charles. Despite their denials, they must have known a great deal about National. The three—Sidney, Grapel and Bluestone—made a one year loan of $10,000 to National in 1959. * * * If Sidney, Grapel and Bluestone were not insiders, they would seem to have been 'tippees' (persons given information by insiders in breach of trust) and subject to the same duty as insiders."[26]

In the *Shapiro* case cited above, the Second Circuit agreed with the *Ross* case and held that "tipees" who traded on the basis of material, undisclosed information were liable to sellers in the market. The court said: "We are not persuaded by the selling defendants' argument that as tippees they were not able to make effective public disclosure of information about a company with which they were not associated; for the duty imposed is not a naked one to disclose, but a duty to abstain from trading unless they do disclose. Since upon the admitted facts before us the selling defendants knew or should have known of the confidential corporate source of the revised earnings information and they knew of its nonpublic nature, they were under a duty not to trade in Douglas stock without publicly disclosing such information." The Securities and Exchange Commission had earlier reached the same conclusion in an

---

20. 472 U.S. at 310–311.

21. In Rothberg v. Rosenbloom, 771 F.2d 818 (3d Cir.1985), the court remanded the case to the district court for a determination of whether these requirements were satisfied.

22. Shulof v. Merrill Lynch, Pierce, Fenner & Smith, Inc., CCH Fed.Sec.Law Rptr. ¶ 93,147 (S.D.N.Y.1971); Smachlo v. Merrill Lynch, Pierce, Fenner & Smith,

Inc., CCH Fed.Sec.Law Rptr. ¶ 93,148 (S.D.N.Y.1971) (citing three other cases against Merrill Lynch in the Southern District of New York, all reaching the same result).

23. 439 F.2d 328 (2d Cir.1971).

24. 439 F.2d at 333–334.

25. 263 F.Supp. 395 (S.D.N.Y.1967).

26. 263 F.Supp. at 409–410.

administrative proceeding under the Investment Company Act of 1940, in which it censured those trading-tippees in the *Shapiro* case that were registered investment companies.[27]

The Supreme Court in the *Dirks* case has now endorsed the proposition that trading-tipees are liable, although only in *dictum* since it was held that Mr. Dirks was not liable in that case and he did not himself trade but tipped others who did. The court, however, refused to accept the argument that a tipee simply assumes the fiduciary obligation of the insider to the shareholders of the company or that the tippee would be liable merely because he knew of the inside source of the information and the fact that it was nonpublic, as asserted in the *Shapiro* case. The court said that the insider must have breached his fidiciary duties to the shareholders in conveying the information in order for the tippee to be liable for acting on it. The court also said that the insider must have acted from a motive of "personal gain" in conveying the information in order for there to be a breach by him of his fiduciary duties, although it indicated that an intention of simply making a "gift" of the information to a person whom he desired to benefit would satisfy this requirement. It is difficult to see how a gift involves any "personal gain" to the donor, whether the subject matter of the gift is tangible property or information which can be utilized for the personal gain of the donee.

Under this test, would a person be liable for trading on the basis of material, undisclosed inside information if he merely overheard an executive of the company let slip at a party some corporate "secret" (perhaps while in his cups)? Or suppose that the corporate executive revealed an impending transaction to a friend, simply for the purpose of discussing it outside of the confines of the board room, whom he justifiably believed would not trade on the basis of this confidential information; but who did. Would the friend who traded on the basis of the information be liable as a "tippee" under the Supreme Court's test? Would the corporate executive be liable as a tipper under the holding of the *Shapiro* case? Under either test, would a person be liable for trading on the basis of information which, if true, *must* have come from an inside source and *must* have been "leaked" in violation of the fiduciary duty of someone in the company, if the defendant got the information fifth or sixth hand?

Non-trading, non-tipping issuers. In Astor v. Texas Gulf Sulphur,[28] in the Southern District of New York, the court held that Texas Gulf was not liable for non-disclosure of the ore strike because it had not traded and had a "corporate purpose" in withholding the information; whereas, the individual defendants who traded were held liable even though they presumably had the same corporate purpose (since the corporation was acting through them). This decision of course took its clue from footnote 12 in Judge Waterman's opinion in the first *Texas Gulf Sulphur* decision, in which he said that "a valuable corporate purpose was served by delaying the publication of the K–55–1 discovery" to permit the corporation to buy up the adjoining land. In other words, the legitimate corporate purpose which exculpated Texas Gulf Sulphur was the wish to do to the adjoining landowners what the individual defendants were excoriated for doing to their adjoining shareholders. The case of Dienstag v. Bronsen [29] in the same court indicates that this principle, if it is one, will not be extended to a situation where the concealment was of transactions involving

---

27. In the Matter of Investors Management Co., Inc., SEC Sec.Exch.Act Rel. No. 9267, Inv.Adv.Act Release No. 289 (July 29, 1971), CCH Fed.Sec.Law Rptr. ¶ 78,163 (1971).

28. 306 F.Supp. 1333 (S.D.N.Y.1969).

29. CCH Fed.Sec.Law Rptr. ¶ 92,274 (S.D.N.Y.1968).

It is, of course, clear that a defendant may be held liable under Rule 10b–5 for *affirmative* misrepresentations which induce purchases or sales by others, even

conflicts of interest, which the corporation would presumably have no legitimate purpose in suppressing. And in the case of Financial Industrial Fund, Inc. v. McDonnell Corp.[30] the court held that Douglas Aircraft was not liable for non-disclosure of the drastic decline in its first-half earnings because there had been no showing that there was any delay in releasing the information beyond the time necessary to issue an informative and non-misleading press release.

Neither of these cases stands for the proposition that an issuer will not be liable for a failure to release material inside information, when there is nothing that can be labelled a "corporate purpose" in withholding it and there is no need for any delay in order to obtain information for an accurate, reliable statement. The rules of the New York Stock Exchange require the prompt release of any material information concerning a listed company to the public, and an issuer might be liable for a violation of those rules if they can be used as the basis for a private right of action (see Chapter 13, above).[31] On the other hand, no case has yet held that there generally is any liability for the mere withholding of material, inside information when no one trades or tips.

Outsiders. A person who has no connection with the corporation but is making a tender offer to purchase all or some specified majority of its shares has been held not to be an insider within the meaning of this rule.[32] For example, in Mills v. Sarjem Corp.[33] a syndicate conceived the idea of purchasing all the stock of a private corporation which owned two toll bridges across the Delaware River, immediately reselling the bridges to a municipal corporation organized by them at a price roughly twice ($12,400,000) what they had paid for the stock ($6,487,500), and having the municipal corporation raise this purchase price by selling bonds to the public (which was possible because the net income from the bridges automatically doubled as a result of their becoming owned by a tax-exempt organization). A former shareholder who sold his stock to the syndicate was denied any recovery under Rule 10b-5. In other litigation,[34] the organization of the municipal corporation was held to be a fraud on the State of New Jersey, and therefore the scheme, at least as it was implemented, turned out to be illegal. Legal or illegal, however, the court said that it was not based upon any "inside information" and could have been conceived by anyone. Therefore, the defendant buyers were not liable to the plaintiff sellers for failure to reveal their plans.[35]

though he himself has not purchased or sold any securities. Heit v. Weitzen, 402 F.2d 909 (2d Cir.1968), cert. denied 395 U.S. 903 (1969); Mitchell v. Texas Gulf Sulphur Company, 446 F.2d 90 (10th Cir. 1971), cert. denied 404 U.S. 1004; Miller v. Bargain City, U.S.A., Inc., 229 F.Supp. 33 (E.D.Pa.1964). Earlier district court decisions to the contrary in the Second Circuit were overruled by the *Heit* case. This is true despite the fact that the express civil liability provision, Section 9(a)(4), would only impose such liability for false or misleading statements upon "a dealer or broker, or other person selling or offering for sale or purchasing or offering to purchase the security."

30. 474 F.2d 514 (10th Cir.1973), cert. denied 414 U.S. 874 (1973).

31. NYSE Company Manual. Section A–6.

32. Mutual Shares Corp. v. Genesco, Inc., 384 F.2d 540 (2d Cir.1967); Mills v. Sarjem Corp., 133 F.Supp. 753 (D.N.J.1955).

33. Supra, note 32.

34. Driscoll v. Burlington-Bristol Bridge Co., 8 N.J. 433, 86 A.2d 201 (1952).

35. The Williams Act would of course now require the tender offeror to reveal his plans regarding the target company. However, nothing in that act or the regulations under it requires disclosure of any information about the target company known to the offeror, which has not been obtained by him from inside sources, except as such disclosure might be necessary to complete the required disclosure concerning his future plans. Compare the *Feit* case, supra, p. 969, which held that Section 11 implicitly required such disclosure even though not specifically referred to in the forms. Does this suggest that a similar result might be reached under the Williams Act?

However, where an outside interest is obtaining control over a corporation, there is a question as to when the new controller *becomes* an insider. In the Ward La France Truck Corp. case [36] the Commission indicated that a corporation which has agreed to purchase a controlling block of stock, and which has access to information not generally available to other stockholders, is an insider for the purposes of the Rule. However, what about a person who intends to make a friendly tender offer to purchase stock of a corporation at a price in excess of the market, say at $10 per share when the stock is selling in the market at around $7, but who has no information about the corporation beyond that generally available? May he purchase stock in the market after he has formulated the plan, but before it has been submitted to the Board of Directors of the corporation to be acquired? After it has been submitted to the Board of Directors, but before they have acted upon it? After the Board has approved the offer and indicated a willingness to sell their own stock at $10, but before it has been sent out to the other shareholders? Rule 10b–13 prohibiting purchases "alongside" the offer would not apply to these time periods, since the prohibitions of that rule only become operative at the time the offer is made. In In the Matter of Hughes & Treat [37] the person making the "take-over bid" purchased stock in the market in the latter two periods, and the Commission indicated that in its mind there was a "substantial question" that he was "an 'insider' or a person having some fiduciary obligation" [38] to the corporation's stockholders. However, the opinion indicates that the acquiring corporation subsequently voluntarily paid those who sold in the market the difference between what they received and $10 per share in order "to resolve * * * any possible question that might be raised because of their not receiving the purchase price offered * * * to * * * [the] stockholders generally." [39]

In Frigitemp Corp. v. Financial Dynamics Fund, Inc.,[40] the court held that an outsider who purchased a $1,000,000 convertible debenture from a corporation was not liable to the corporation for allegedly using information obtained during the course of the negotiations to buy stock of the corporation in the market or for failure to disclose that it already owned a sizeable block of the stock. The court said: "The dealings were at arm's length. The corporate officer had the right to make the inside information available. The other party had the right to request it. We need not determine whether the buyer owed a duty to market traders to refrain from buying or selling the shares of Frigitemp based on such information, since such persons are not plaintiffs in this action. Our inquiry is limited to whether the corporation, the seller of the debenture, has a claim for relief."

Market information. Considerable speculation has occurred recently about the duty, if any, of a person to disclose so-called "market information", i.e., information about the supply of or demand for a particular security, as distinguished from "inside information" about a particular corporation or its business. For example, if a person intends to make a tender offer to take over control of a corporation and commences a buying campaign to accumulate up to 5% of the stock in the market before announcing his intentions, this is obviously information which, if revealed, would affect the market price immedi-

---

An outsider buying *in the market* is not required to make any advance disclosure at all, until he has accumulated 5% of the outstanding stock. Presumably such a buyer has no duty to inform the sellers of his analysis of published data, or even of secret information which he may have legally obtained otherwise than by "tips" from insiders.

36. In the Matter of Ward La France Truck Corp., 13 S.E.C. 373 (1943).

37. 22 S.E.C. 623 (1946).

38. 22 S.E.C. at 626, n. 2.

39. 22 S.E.C. at 628, n. 4.

40. 524 F.2d 275 (2d Cir.1975).

ately. The same situation would exist if a large bank trust department, upon the basis of a recommendation by its research division, decided to put a large number of its trusts into a particular security. If this were publicly announced before it could execute an orderly series of purchases, the price might immediately jump to a point where the recommendation would no longer be valid. It is difficult to believe that any court would hold that such persons had to frustrate their own plans by announcing in advance their own intentions. But if they are not obliged to do so, it is difficult to see why anyone else who happens to acquire the same information should not be free to act upon it, unless he is precluded by some fiduciary relationship with the person whose intentions are involved. In the Capital Gains Research Bureau case,[41] the United States Supreme Court held that an investment adviser would be liable for "scalping" his own customers, i.e., buying himself prior to making his buy recommendation to them, and then selling out after the resulting price rise but before recommending that they sell.

In the *Chiarella* case, the "majority" opinion of Justice Powell (although fully concurred in by only four of the nine justices) holds that generally there is no duty on the part of a buyer or seller in the market not to trade on the basis of material, non-public market information which is unknown to the other party to the transaction. First, the court states that because the defendant was not a "fiduciary" with respect to the persons who sold to him in the market, he had no duty to disclose the information to them or to refrain from trading. This portion of the opinion was concurred in by seven of the justices. Secondly, the court holds that whether or not the defendant violated Rule 10b–5 because he violated a duty owed to his employer, the printing company, or to its employers, the tender offerors, would not be considered because it was not properly presented to the jury and, therefore, could not be the basis for affirming a criminal conviction. Three of the justices dissented from this ruling and would have affirmed the conviction.

How do you reconcile the first holding with the liability of a trading tippee to persons who sell to him or buy from him in the market, which the court seems to accept in a footnote? The court says that the defendant had no prior dealings with the other participants in the transactions and that he was not "their agent, * * * a fiduciary, * * * [or] a person in whom the sellers had placed their trust and confidence." It also states that the defendant was, "in fact, a complete stranger who dealt with the sellers only through impersonal market transactions." Which one or ones of these assertions is not equally true with respect to the relationship of a trading tippee to the persons with whom he deals in the market? It would seem that the only possible distinction between these two situations is the type of information upon the basis of which the trading is carried out (i.e., "market" information as opposed to "inside" information), and not in the relationship of the trading defendant to those persons with whom he deals in an "impersonal market."

With respect to the second aspect of the case, which was not decided, would the fact that the defendant violated a duty owed to his employer or its employer result in liability of the defendant to the persons who traded with him in the market? It certainly would not change his relationship to those other parties in any respect. There might, possibly, be a cause of action against him in favor of the tender offerors if he were considered to have violated a secondary duty owed to them, although it is difficult to see how they could prove any damage, since they were buying, not selling, and Mr. Chiarella's transactions were

41. Securities and Exchange Commission v. Capital Gains Research Bureau, Inc., 375 U.S. 180 (1963).

certainly not large enough to have any significant effect on the market price. (Justice Stevens in his concurring opinion is clearly in error when he says that the tender offerors could not sue the defendant for damages "because they were neither purchasers nor sellers of target company securities"—a purchase of target company securities by the tender offeror is the whole purpose of the operation, and will usually have occurred in the market prior to the time of the defendant's activities and will certainly occur shortly thereafter when the tender offer is made.) What would be the result if the defendant had been told by the printing company, and the tender offeror engaging it, the name of the target company and had been authorized to make purchases as one of the "perquisites" of his job? Would such authorization have made any difference to the sellers?

This possible basis for liability under Rule 10b–5 of a person trading while in possession of material, nonpublic information which is not "inside information" is sometimes referred to as the "misappropriation theory." It was endorsed by Chief Justice Burger and three other justices in the *Chiarella* case, although Justice Brennan agreed that Mr. Chiarella could not be convicted on that basis because it wasn't presented to the jury. The Securities and Exchange Commission immediately seized upon this theory to institute a large number of prosecutions of persons with access to information regarding impending takeover attempts, such as employees of financial printers, brokerage houses and law firms.[42] The Second Circuit has fully embraced this theory as a basis for a criminal conviction.[43] In Moss v. Morgan Stanley Inc.,[44] however, the Second Circuit held that it could not be the basis for an action for damages by persons who sold in the market, since there was no fiduciary duty owed by the defendant to the plaintiffs in that case, as the court thought was required by the Supreme Court's opinion in the *Chiarella* case.

It would also seem to be true that there cannot be any Rule 10b–5 action against such persons by their employers. It can hardly be contended that the 1934 Act was intended by Congress for the "especial benefit" of financial printers, no matter how much that has been the actual result of the statute. It seems strange that a person can be convicted of a federal crime when he has not violated a federal statutory duty to anyone, although he has of course violated a common law or contractual duty to his employer. The result can be defended on the basis of policy if one regards the lack of equality of information between buyers and sellers in the market to be reprehensible, as the SEC does.

The Second Circuit has also upheld the conviction of a columnist for the Wall Street Journal who traded on the basis of information known only to

---

42. See Los Angeles Times, August 8, 1986, Part IV, 1:5. "Wall Street's insider trading travails mounted Thursday as a former Lazard Freres & Co. junior analyst was barred from the securities industry and his father, grandfather and a stockbroker agreed to give up more than $2 million in illicit profits that they are accused of having made on advance word of last year's multibillion-dollar acquisition of RCA by General Electric.

"The Securities and Exchange Commission also imposed a record $2.3 million in fines in what the watchdog agency characterized as the third-largest insider trading case in history * * *

"Both larger settlements came earlier this year. In February, eight foreign investors gave up $7.8 million in illicit profits stemming from the 1981 acquisition of Sante Fe International by the Kuwaiti government. And four months later, in a case that has deeply shaken Wall Street, investment banker Dennis B. Levine agreed to repay more than $11.5 million in profits from illicit insider trading deals."

43. Securities and Exchange Commission v. Materia, 745 F.2d 197 (2d Cir.1984), cert. denied 471 U.S. 1053 (1985); United States v. Newman, 664 F.2d 12 (2d Cir. 1981), cert. denied 464 U.S. 863 (1983), 722 F.2d 729 (2d Cir.1983) (unpublished order).

44. 719 F.2d 5 (2d Cir.1983), cert. denied 465 U.S. 1025 (1984).

himself, i.e., the companies about which he was going to write in his column "Heard On The Street." [45] It was clear that favorable discussion of a corporation in that column would probably cause the price of the stock of the corporation to rise. The columnist traded and tipped others to trade on the basis of his knowledge of what was going to appear in his future columns. The court held that he could be convicted under the "misappropriation theory" because the Journal had a policy prohibiting trading on the basis of any information obtained by its news gathering. Judge Miner dissented.

The ink was hardly dry on the *Chiarella* decision before the Commission moved to overrule the specific holding of that case by the adoption on October 14, 1980, of a new Rule 14e–3 [46] relating to transactions in the securities of target companies on the basis of non-public information with respect to the impending tender offer. Subsection (a) of that rule provides that it is a "fraudulent, deceptive or manipulative act or practice" within the meaning of Section 14(e) for any person who is in possession of material information relating to an impending tender offer which is not public to buy or sell securities of the target company, if he knows or has reason to know that the information has been acquired directly or indirectly from the tender offeror, the issuer or any officer, director, partner or employee of any other person acting on behalf of the tender offeror or of the issuer. Subsection (d) of the rule prohibits tipping of information about the proposed tender offer by the tender offeror, the issuer, or anyone acting on behalf of either, or by any other person in possession of the material non-public information about the tender offer if "he knows or has reason to know [that the information] has been acquired directly or indirectly" from any of the other persons referred to above. The tender offeror itself is exempted, however, from these prohibitions.

There is no question that the provisions of the new Rule 14e–3 directly and specifically prohibit the conduct of the defendant in the *Chiarella* case. Would there have been an implied right of action on behalf of the persons who dealt with him in the market had this rule been in effect at the time of Chiarella's market transactions? [47]

In Zweig v. Hearst Corp.,[48] the Ninth Circuit held that a financial columnist for a newspaper was liable to the plaintiff in that case under the following circumstances. The columnist had purchased stock of the company at a bargain price from the issuer at a time when he was preparing a story about the company for his column. He then published in his column an item "puffing" the stock of the company and stating information furnished to him by the officers of the company which was false and misleading. The stock thereupon experienced a sharp increase in price in the market. The plaintiffs had agreed to merge their corporation with the issuer for an amount of stock to be based upon the market price at a subsequent valuation date. The agreement preceded the publication of this information by the financial columnist, but the valuation date occurred thereafter, and the amount of stock received by the plaintiffs was drastically reduced by the artificial increase in price caused by the publication of the column. The Ninth Circuit held that under these circumstances the financial columnist was liable for the loss suffered by the owners of the merged corporation. It stated that the financial columnist violated Rule 10b–5 by publishing the column relating to the company, even if

---

45. United States v. Carpenter, Felis & Winans, 791 F.2d 1024 (2d Cir.1986).

46. Sec.Exch.Act Release No. 17120 (Sept. 4, 1980).

47. Obviously, the Commission thinks that it has provided such a remedy; but

see Note 18 to the opinion in the case of Touche Ross & Co. v. Redington, supra p. 849. Why was Mr. Chiarella not also indicted under Section 14(e)?

48. 594 F.2d 1261 (9th Cir.1979).

he did not know of the falsity of the information therein, without revealing his receipt of the bargain stock in connection with the preparation of such column. It also held that he owed a duty to the owners of the merged corporation because his actions amounted to a "fraud on the market," on the integrity of which they were relying for an honest determination of the amount of stock which they were entitled to receive. Judge Ely, in dissent, thought that it was "impossible" that any causal relationship could exist between the wrongful conduct alleged and the decision by the plaintiffs to invest in the stock of the company, since that decision preceded the wrongful conduct. The court cited in support of its decision, among other cases, the decision by the Second Circuit in the *Chiarella* case, which was reversed by the Supreme Court. Does this decision survive the Supreme Court's decision in the *Chiarella* case?

This type of information relating to market forces, i.e., supply and demand, should be distinguished from other types of information which cannot be labelled "inside" information because the corporation and its own officials may not know it, but which nevertheless relates to the business of a particular company. For example, an official of the Pentagon may know that a several hundred million dollar contract is going to be awarded the next day to a particular corporation; this is unknown at that time to the corporation itself. Or the same situation might obtain with respect to a decision by a major airline to purchase a large order of multimillion dollar planes from one of several competing aircraft manufacturers. To what extent are these persons having business relationships with the corporation in question precluded from buying or selling its securities when possessing that type of information? [49]

THE INSIDER TRADING SANCTIONS ACT

In 1984 Congress passed the Insider Trading Sanctions Act (Pub.L. 98-376, 98 Stat. 1264) providing for a penalty to be assessed at the suit of the SEC against persons violating the insider trading prohibitions of the 1934 Act of up to three times the amount of the "profit gained or loss avoided as a result" of such insider trading. In fact, this statute should have been labeled the "Outsider Trading Sanctions Act" since it was primarily inspired by the trading of persons with advance knowledge of takeover attempts or "market informa-

---

49. The first attempt to codify the doctrine of insider liability for non-disclosure is contained in the California Corporate Securities Law of 1968, which provides in Sections 25402 and 25502:

"25402. It is unlawful for an issuer or any person who is an officer, director or controlling person of an issuer or any other person whose relationship to the issuer gives him access, directly or indirectly, to material information about the issuer not generally available to the public, to purchase or sell any security of the issuer in this state at a time when he knows material information about the issuer gained from such relationship which would significantly affect the market price of that security and which is not generally available to the public, and which he knows is not intended to be so available, unless he has reason to believe that the person selling to or buying from

him is also in possession of the information.

"25502. Any person who violates Section 25402 shall be liable to the person who purchases a security from him or sells a security to him, for damages equal to the difference between the price at which such security was purchased or sold and the market value which such security would have had at the time of the purchase or sale if the information known to the defendant had been publicly disseminated prior to that time and a reasonable time had elapsed for the market to absorb the information, plus interest at the legal rate, unless the defendant proves that the plaintiff knew the information or that the plaintiff would have purchased or sold at the same price even if the information had been revealed to him."

tion", as discussed above, and not by any increase in trading by "insiders." There are a number of things that should be noted regarding the limitations of this statute.

(1) It does not change in any way the substantive law relating to liability for insider trading, so-called. The statute only applies if a person has "violated any provision * * * [of the 1934 Act] or the rules and regulations thereunder by purchasing or selling a security while in possession of material nonpublic information." Therefore, the Commission must first establish a substantive violation of the rules relating to trading on the basis of nonpublic information before it can succeed in having a court impose this penalty.

(2) It is not accurate to describe this statute as a "treble damage" provision. The statute provides that the court shall determine the penalty "in the light of the facts and circumstances" which shall not "*exceed* three times the profit gained or loss avoided as a result of such unlawful purchase or sale." The penalty does not consist of an automatic trebling of the damages recovered by a private party, as under the antitrust laws, but is *in addition to* any other liabilities which the defendant may have as a result of his conduct. Those would include any liability which he might have to any private plaintiffs, which may or may not be measured by his profit (see Chapter 20, below), or his liability for "disgorgement" of such profits in a suit by the SEC (which may be independent of any liability to private plaintiffs). Therefore, it would be more accurately described as a "quadruple damage" provision, although under the terms of the statute the court does not have to impose three times the amount of his profit as the penalty. The penalty is paid into the Treasury of the United States, not to any private parties.

(3) The penalty can only be collected if the transactions forming the basis for the assessment of the penalty were effected "through the facilities of a national securities exchange or from or through a broker or dealer." Therefore, the archetypal transactions under Rule 10b–5, by which a majority shareholder in a closely-held corporation purchased the shares of the other shareholders with knowledge of a higher offer for the company (see the *Kardon* case, discussed above in Chapter 13), would not be covered by this statute and the SEC could not collect the penalty of up to three times the amount of the defendant's profit.

(4) The statute imposes the penalty, not only upon a person who engages in "insider" trading but also upon any person "aiding and abetting the violation of such person." However, it is provided that no person shall be subject to the sanction as an aider and abetter who aids or abets "other than by communicating material nonpublic information." Therefore, this liability provision only applies to a non-trading tipper. It is also provided that no person "shall be liable under [the statute] solely by reason of employing another person who is liable." This would exclude any liability on the basis of *respondeat superior,* which might or might not be a basis for liability under the general rules relating to "insider trading." (See Chapter 17, below).

In addition to authorizing the Commission to collect this penalty for "insider trading" or "outsider trading", the statute also amended Section 20 of the 1934 Act to provide that a person trading in the options market for a security may be liable to the persons trading in the principal market for the security, if the "insider" who engaged in such trading was in possession of material, nonpublic information. This provision was apparently a reaction to the case of Laventhall v. General Dynamics Corporation [50] which held that an issuer

---

50. 704 F.2d 407 (8th Cir.1983), cert. denied 464 U.S. 846 (1983).

trading in its own stock in the principal market for such stock on the basis of alleged inside information had no duty of disclosure to a person trading in the *options market* for the same securities. The court distinguished the case of O'Connor & Associates v. Dean Witter Reynolds, Inc.,[51] wherein Judge Lasker held that an options trader had a cause of action under Rule 10b–5 against a defendant who also engaged in *options trading* with the possession of undisclosed, material inside information. The court in the *Laventhall* case said that the two markets were distinct and that a person trading in the principal market had no duty to other persons trading in the options market. It should be noted that the statute does not overrule that case. The statute deals with the reverse situation where the insider trading occurs in the options market and the plaintiffs have traded in the principal market; it was apparently feared that the principle of the *Laventhall* case would be extended to that reverse situation. In any event, that was the only situation that Congress addressed in the statute.

The recent developments regarding insider liability for nondisclosure have produced a flood of literature. Professor Manne has written a book [Insider Trading and the Stock Market (Free Press, 1966)] in which he attacks the whole concept of such liability primarily from an economic point of view. This position has not received much support in the academic journals. A 380 page book published by the Practising Law Institute consists of the edited transcript of two forum discussions on the disclosure requirements applicable to publicly-held companies and their insiders. Flom, Garfinkel and Freund, eds., Disclosure Requirements of Public Companies and Insiders (PLI 1967). This book approaches the problem from the practical rather than the theoretical point of view. Some of the articles are: Cox, Insider Trading and Contracting: A Critical Response to the "Chicago School", 1986 Duke L.J. 628; Strickler, Inside Information and Outside Traders, 73 Calif.L.Rev. 483 (1985); Schneider and Hammerman, Disclosure and Corporate Governance: A Panel, 16 Inst. on Sec. Reg. 199 (1985); Seligman, The Reformulation of Federal Securities Law Concerning Nonpublic Information, 73 Geo.L.J. 1083 (1985); Wilkinson, The Affirmative Duty to Disclose After Chiarella and Dirks, 10 J.Corp.L. 581 (1985); Wang, Dirks v. SEC: An Outsider's Guide to Insider Trading Liability Under Rule 10b–5, 22 Am.Bus.L.J. 569 (1985); Prentice, The Impact of Dirks on Outsider Trading, 13 Sec.Reg.L.J. 38 (1985); Silver, Penalizing Insider Trading: A Critical Assessment of the Insider Trading Sanctions Act of 1984, 1985 Duke L.J. 960 (1985); Blumberg, Implications of the 1984 Insider Trading Sanctions Act, 64 N.C.L.Rev. 117 (1985); Aldave, Misappropriation: A General Theory of Liability for Trading on Non-public Information, 13 Hofstra L.Rev. 101 (1984); Farley, A Current Look At the Law of Insider Trading, 39 Bus.Law 1771 (1984); Symposium on Insider Trading (Goelzer, Macey, Phillips & Zutz, Aldave), 13 Hofstra L.Rev. 1 (1984); Hiler, Dirks v. SEC—A Study in Cause and Effect, 43 Md.L.Rev. 292 (1984); Langevoort, The Insider Trading Sanctions Act of 1984 and Its Effect on Existing Law, 37 Vand.L.Rev. 1273 (1984); Poser, Misuse of Confidential Information Concerning a Tender Offer as a Securities Fraud, 49 Brooklyn L.Rev. 1265 (1983); Carlton and Fischel, The Regulation of Insider Trading, 35 Stan.L.Rev. 857 (1983); Wang, Recent Developments in the Federal Law Regulating Stock Market Insider Trading, 6 Corp.L.Rev. 291 (1983); Karjala, Statutory Regulation of Insider Trading in Impersonal Markets, 1982 Duke L.J. 627 (1982); Levmore, Securities and Secrets: Insider Trading and the Law of Contracts, 68 Va.L.Rev. 117 (1982); Langevoort, Insider Trading and the Fiduciary Principle: A Post-Chiarella Restatement, 70 Calif.L.Rev. 1 (1982); Haft, The Effect of Insider Trading Rules on Internal Efficiency of the Large

---

51. 529 F.Supp. 1179 (S.D.N.Y.1981).

Corporations, 80 Mich.L.Rev. 1051 (1982); Heller, Chiarella, SEC Rule 14e–3 and Dirks: "Fairness" versus Economic Theory, 37 Bus.Law 517 (1982); Cann, Duty to Disclose? An Analysis of Chiarella v. United States, 85 Dick.L.Rev. 249 (1981); Deutsch, Chiarella v. United States: A Study in Legal Style, 58 Tex.L. Rev. 1291 (1980); Brudney, Insiders, Outsiders, and Informational Advantages Under the Federal Securities Laws, 93 Harv.L.Rev. 322 (1979); Bauman, Rule 10b–5 and the Corporation's Affirmative Duty to Disclose, 67 Geo.L.J. 935 (1979); Allen, The Disclosure Obligation of Publicly Held Corporations in the Absence of Insider Trading, 25 Mercer L.Rev. 479 (1974); Fleischer and Mundheim, Initial Inquiry into the Responsibility to Disclose Market Information, 121 U.Pa.L.Rev. 798 (1973).

SUPERINTENDENT OF INSURANCE OF THE STATE OF NEW YORK v. BANKERS LIFE AND CASUALTY CO.

United States Supreme Court, 1971.
404 U.S. 6, 92 S.Ct. 165, 30 L.Ed.2d 128.

MR. JUSTICE DOUGLAS delivered the opinion of the Court.

Manhattan Casualty Company, now represented by petitioner, New York's Superintendent of Insurance, was, it is alleged, defrauded in the sale of certain securities in violation of the Securities Act of 1933, and of the Securities Exchange Act of 1934. The District Court dismissed the complaint, 300 F.Supp. 1083, and the Court of Appeals affirmed, by a divided bench, 430 F.2d 355. The case is here on a petition for a writ of certiorari which we granted, 401 U.S. 973.

It seems that Bankers Life, one of the respondents, agreed to sell all of Manhattan's stock to one Begole for $5,000,000. It is alleged that Begole conspired with one Bourne and others to pay for this stock, not out of their own funds, but with Manhattan's assets. They were alleged to have arranged, through Garvin, Bantel—a note brokerage firm—to obtain a $5,000,000 check from respondent Irving Trust, although they had no funds on deposit there at the time. On the same day they purchased all the stock of Manhattan from Bankers Life for $5,000,000 and as stockholders and directors, installed one Sweeny as president of Manhattan.

Manhattan then sold its United States Treasury bonds for $4,854,552.61.[1] That amount, plus enough cash to bring the total to $5,000,000, was credited to an account of Manhattan at Irving Trust and the $5,000,000 Irving Trust check was charged against it. As a result, Begole owned all the stock of Manhattan, having used $5,000,000 of Manhattan's assets to purchase it.

To complete the fraudulent scheme, Irving Trust issued a second $5,000,000 check to Manhattan which Sweeny, Manhattan's new president tendered to Belgian American Trust which issued a $5,000,000 certificate of deposit in the name of Manhattan. Sweeny endorsed the certificate of deposit over to New England Note, a company alleged to be controlled by Bourne. Bourne endorsed the certificate over to Belgian American Bank-

---

1. Manhattan's Board of Directors was allegedly deceived into authorizing this sale by the misrepresentation that the pro- ceeds would be exchanged for a certificate of deposit of equal value.

ing [2] as collateral for a $5,000,000 loan from Belgian Banking to New England. Its proceeds were paid to Irving Trust to cover the latter's second $5,000,000 check.

Though Manhattan's assets had been depleted, its books reflected only the sale of its Government bonds and the purchase of the certificate of deposit and did not show that its assets had been used to pay Begole for his purchase of Manhattan's shares or that the certificate of deposit had been assigned to New England and then pledged to Belgian Banking.

Manhattan was the seller of Treasury bonds and, it seems to us, clearly protected by § 10(b) of the Securities Exchange Act which makes it unlawful to use "in connection with the purchase or sale" of any security "any manipulative or deceptive device or contrivance" in contravention of the rules and regulations of the Securities and Exchange Commission.

There certainly was an "act" or "practice" within the meaning of Rule 10b–5 which operated as "a fraud or deceit" on Manhattan, the seller of the Government bonds. To be sure, the full market price was paid for those bonds; but the seller was duped into believing that it, the seller, would receive the proceeds. We cannot agree with the Court of Appeals that "no investor [was] injured" and that the "purity of the security transaction and the purity of the trading process were unsullied." 430 F.2d at 361.

Section 10(b) outlaws the use "in connection with the purchase or sale" of any security of "any manipulative or deceptive device or contrivance." The Act protects corporations as well as individuals who are sellers of a security. Manhattan was injured as an investor through a deceptive device which deprived it of any compensation for the sale of its valuable block of securities.

The fact that the fraud was perpetrated by an officer of Manhattan and his outside collaborators is irrelevant to our problem. For § 10(b) bans the use of any deceptive device in the "sale" of any security by "any person." And the fact that the transaction is not conducted through a securities exchange or an organized over-the-counter market is irrelevant to the coverage of § 10(b). Hooper v. Mountain States Securities Corp., 282 F.2d 195, 201. Likewise irrelevant is the fact that the proceeds of the sale that were due the seller were misappropriated. As the Court of Appeals for the Fifth Circuit said in the Hooper case, "considering the purpose of this legislation, it would be unrealistic to say that a corporation having the capacity to acquire $700,000 worth of assets for its 700,000 shares of stock has suffered no loss if what it gave up was $700,000 but what it got was zero." 282 F.2d at 203.

The Congress made clear that "disregard of trust relationships by those whom the law should regard as fiduciaries, are all a single seamless web" along with manipulation, investor's ignorance, and the like. H.R.Rep. No. 1383, 73d Cong., 2d Sess., p. 6. Since practices "constantly vary and where practices legitimate for some purposes may be turned to illegitimate and fraudulent means, broad discretionary powers" in the regulatory agency "have been found practically essential." Id., at 7. Hence we do not read § 10(b) as narrowly as the Court of Appeals; it is not "limited to preserving the integrity of the securities markets" (430 F.2d, at 361), though that

---

2. Belgian Banking at the same time made a loan to New England Note in the amount of $250,000 which was distributed in part as follows: Belgian Banking $100,000, Bourne $50,000, Begole $50,000, and Garvin, Bantel $25,000.

purpose is included. Section 10(b) must be read flexibly, not technically and restrictively. Since there was a "sale" of a security and since fraud was used "in connection with" it, there is redress under § 10(b), whatever might be available as a remedy under state law.

We agree that Congress by § 10(b) did not seek to regulate transactions which comprise no more than internal corporate mismanagement. But we read § 10(b) to mean that Congress meant to bar deceptive devices and contrivances in the purchase or sale of securities whether conducted in the organized markets or face-to-face. And the fact that creditors [8] of the defrauded corporate buyer or seller of securities may be the ultimate victims does not warrant disregard of the corporate entity. The controlling stockholder owes the corporation a fiduciary obligation—one "designed for the protection of the entire community of interests in the corporation— creditors as well as stockholders." Pepper v. Litton, 308 U.S. 295, 306–307.

The crux of the present case is that Manhattan suffered an injury as a result of deceptive practices touching its sale of securities as an investor. As stated in Shell v. Hensley, 430 F.2d 819, 827:

"When a person who is dealing with a corporation in a securities transaction denies the corporation's directors access to material information known to him, the corporation is disabled from availing itself of an informed judgment on the part of its board regarding the merits of the transaction. In this situation the private right of action recognized under Rule 10b–5 [9] is available as a remedy for the corporate disability."

The case was before the lower courts on a motion to dismiss.

Bankers Life urges that the complaint did not allege, and discovery failed to disclose, any connection between it and the fraud and that, therefore, the dismissal of the complaint as to it was correct and should be affirmed. We make no ruling on this point.

The case must be remanded for trial. We intimate no opinion on the merits, as we have dealt only with allegations and with the question of law whether a cause of action as respects the sale by Manhattan of its Treasury bonds has been charged under § 10(b).[10] We think it has been so charged and accordingly we reverse and remand for proceedings consistent with this opinion.

8. The history of the Act shows that Congress was especially concerned with the impact of frauds on creditors of corporations. See H.R.Rep. No. 1383, 73d Cong., 2d Sess., 3–4.

9. It is now established that a private right of action is implied under § 10(b). See 6 L. Loss, Securities Regulation 3869–73 (1969 Supp.); 3 L. Loss, Securities Regulation 1763 et seq. (1961). Cf. Tcherepnin v. Knight, 389 U.S. 332; J. I. Case v. Borak, 377 U.S. 426.

10. Petitioner's complaint bases his single claim for recovery alternatively on three different transactions alleged to confer jurisdiction under § 10(b): Manhattan's sale of the Treasury bonds; the sale of Manhattan stock by Bankers Life to Bourne and Begole; and the transactions involving the certificates of deposit. We only hold that the alleged fraud is cognizable under § 10(b) and Rule 10b–5 in the bond sale and we express no opinion as to Manhattan's standing under § 10(b) and Rule 10b–5 on other phases of the complaint. See Kellogg, The Inability to Obtain Analytical Precision Where Standing to Sue under Rule 10b–5 is Involved, 20 Buff.L.Rev. 93 (1970); Lowenfels, The Demise of the Birnbaum Doctrine: A New Era For Rule 10b–5, 54 Va.L.Rev. 268 (1968).

All defenses except our ruling on § 10(b) will be open on remand.
Reversed.

SANTA FE INDUSTRIES, INC. v. GREEN

Supreme Court of the United States, 1977.
430 U.S. 462, 97 S.Ct. 1292, 51 L.Ed.2d 480.

MR. JUSTICE WHITE delivered the opinion of the Court.

The issue in this case involves the reach and coverage of § 10(b) of the Securities Exchange Act of 1934 and Rule 10b–5 thereunder in the context of a Delaware short-form merger transaction used by the majority stockholder of a corporation to eliminate the minority interest.

I

In 1936 petitioner Santa Fe Industries, Inc. ("Santa Fe") acquired control of 60% of the stock of Kirby Lumber Corporation ("Kirby"), a Delaware corporation. Through a series of purchases over the succeeding years, Santa Fe increased its control of Kirby's stock to 95%; the purchase prices during the period 1968–1973 ranged from $65 to $92.50 per share. In 1974, wishing to acquire 100% ownership of Kirby, Santa Fe availed itself of § 253 of the Delaware Corporation Law, known as the "short-form merger" statute. Section 253 permits a parent corporation owning at least 90% of the stock of a subsidiary to merge with that subsidiary, upon approval by the parent's board of directors, and to make payment in cash for the shares of the minority stockholders. The statute does not require the consent of, or advance notice to, the minority stockholders. However, notice of the merger must be given within 10 days after its effective date, and any stockholder who is dissatisfied with the terms of the merger may petition the Delaware Court of Chancery for a decree ordering the surviving corporation to pay him the fair value of his shares, as determined by a court-appointed appraiser subject to review by the court. Del.Gen.Corp. Law §§ 253, 262.

Santa Fe obtained independent appraisals of the physical assets of Kirby—land, timber, buildings, and machinery—and of Kirby's oil, gas, and mineral interests. These appraisals, together with other financial information, were submitted to Morgan, Stanley & Company ("Morgan Stanley"), an investment banking firm retained to appraise the fair market value of Kirby stock. Kirby's physical assets were appraised at $320 million (amounting to $640 for each of the 500,000 shares); Kirby's stock was valued by Morgan Stanley at $125 per share. Under the terms of the merger, minority stockholders were offered $150 per share.

The provisions of the short-form merger statute were fully complied with. The minority stockholders of Kirby were notified the day after the merger became effective and were advised of their right to obtain an appraisal in Delaware court if dissatisfied with the offer of $150 per share. They also received an information statement containing, in addition to the relevant financial data about Kirby, the appraisals of the value of Kirby's assets and the Morgan Stanley appraisal concluding that the fair market value of the stock was $125 per share.

Respondents, minority stockholders of Kirby, objected to the terms of the merger, but did not pursue their appraisal remedy in the Delaware Court of Chancery. Instead, they brought this action in federal court on behalf of the corporation and other minority stockholders, seeking to set aside the merger or to recover what they claimed to be the fair value of their shares. The amended complaint asserted that, based on the fair market value of Kirby's physical assets as revealed by the appraisal included in the Information Statement sent to minority shareholders, Kirby's stock was worth at least $772 per share. The complaint alleged further that the merger took place without prior notice to minority stockholders; that the purpose of the merger was to appropriate the difference between the "conceded pro rata value of the physical assets" and the offer of $150 per share—to "freez[e] out the minority stockholders at a wholly inadequate price," app. 103a, 100a; and that Santa Fe, knowing the appraised value of the physical assets, obtained a "fraudulent appraisal" of the stock from Morgan Stanley and offered $25 above that appraisal "in order to lull the minority stockholders into erroneously believing that [Santa Fe was] generous." Id., at 103a. This course of conduct was alleged to be "a violation of Rule 10b–5 because defendants employed a 'device, scheme or artifice to defraud' and engaged in an 'act, practice or course of business which operates or would operate as a fraud or deceit upon any person, in connection with the purchase or sale of any security.'" Ibid. Morgan Stanley assertedly participated in the fraud as an accessory by submitting its appraisal of $125 per share although knowing the appraised value of the physical assets.

The District Court dismissed the complaint for failure to state a claim upon which relief could be granted. 391 F.Supp. 849 (SDNY 1975). As the District Court understood the complaint, respondents' case rested on two distinct grounds. First, federal law was assertedly violated because the merger was for the sole purpose of eliminating the minority from the company, therefore lacking any justifiable business purpose, and because the merger was undertaken without prior notice to the minority shareholders. Second, the low valuation placed on the shares in the cash exchange offer was itself said to be a fraud actionable under Rule 10b–5. In rejecting the first ground for recovery, the District Court reasoned that Delaware law required neither a business purpose for a short-form merger nor prior notice to the minority shareholders who the statute contemplated would be removed from the company, and that Rule 10b–5 did not override these provisions of state corporate law by independently placing a duty on the majority not to merge without prior notice and without a justifiable business purpose.

As for the claim that actionable fraud inhered in the allegedly gross undervaluation of the minority shares, the District Court observed that respondents valued their shares at a minimum of $772 per share, "basing this figure on the pro rata value of Kirby's physical assets." Id., at 853. Accepting this valuation for purposes of the motion to dismiss, the District Court further noted that, as revealed by the complaint, the physical asset appraisal, along with other information relevant to Morgan Stanley's valuation of the shares, had been included with the Information Statement sent to respondents within the time required by state law. It thought that if "full and fair disclosure is made, transactions eliminating minority interests are beyond the purview of Rule 10b–5," and concluded that "the complaint fail[ed] to allege an omission, misstatement or fraudulent course of conduct that would have impeded a shareholder's judgment of the value of the offer." Id., at 854. The complaint therefore failed to state a claim and was dismissed.

A divided Court of Appeals for the Second Circuit reversed. 533 F.2d 1283 (1976). It first agreed that there was a double aspect to the case: first, the claim that gross undervaluation of the minority stock itself violated Rule 10b–5; and second, that "without any misrepresentation or failure to disclose relevant facts, the merger itself constitutes a violation of Rule 10b–5" because it was accomplished without any corporate purpose and without prior notice to the minority stockholders. Id., at 1285. As to the first aspect of the case, the Court of Appeals did not disturb the District Court's conclusion that the complaint did not allege a material misrepresentation or nondisclosure with respect to the value of the stock; and the court declined to rule that a claim of gross undervaluation itself would suffice to make out a Rule 10b–5 case. With respect to the second aspect of the case, however, the court fundamentally disagreed with the District Court as to the reach and coverage of Rule 10b–5. The Court of Appeals' view was that, although the Rule plainly reached material misrepresentations and nondisclosures in connection with the purchase or sale of securities, neither misrepresentation nor nondisclosure was a necessary element of a Rule 10b–5 action; the Rule reached "breaches of fiduciary duty by a majority against minority shareholders without any charge of misrepresentation or lack of disclosure." Id., at 1287.[8] The court went on to hold that the complaint, taken as a whole, stated a cause of action under the Rule:

"We hold that a complaint alleges a claim under Rule 10b–5 when it charges, in connection with a Delaware short-form merger, that the majority has committed a breach of its fiduciary duty to deal fairly with minority shareholders by effecting the merger without any justifiable business purpose. The minority shareholders are given no prior notice of the merger, thus having no opportunity to apply for injunctive relief, and the proposed price to be paid is substantially lower than the appraised value reflected in the Information Statement." Id., at 1291.

* * *

We granted the petition for certiorari challenging this holding because of the importance of the issue involved to the administration of the federal securities laws. 429 U.S. 814 (1976). We reverse.

II

* * * The Court of Appeals' approach to the interpretation of Rule 10b–5 is inconsistent with that taken by the Court last Term in Ernst & Ernst v. Hochfelder, 425 U.S. 185 (1976).

* * *

To the extent that the Court of Appeals would rely on the use of the term "fraud" in Rule 10b–5 to bring within the ambit of the Rule all

---

8. The court concluded its discussion thus:

"Whether full disclosure has been made is not the crucial inquiry since it is the merger and the undervaluation which constituted the fraud, and not whether or not the majority determines to lay bare their real motives. If there is no valid corporate purpose for the merger, then even the most brazen disclosure of that fact to the minority shareholders in no way mitigates the fraudulent conduct." 533 F.2d at 1292.

breaches of fiduciary duty in connection with a securities transaction, its interpretation would, like the interpretation rejected by the Court in *Ernst & Ernst,* "add a gloss to the operative language of the statute quite different from its commonly accepted meaning." Id., at 199. But as the Court there held, the language of the statute must control the interpretation of the Rule: * * *[12]

The language of § 10(b) gives no indication that Congress meant to prohibit any conduct not involving manipulation or deception. Nor have we been cited to any evidence in the legislative history that would support a departure from the language of the statute. "When a statute speaks so specifically in terms of manipulation and deception, * * * and when its history reflects no more expansive intent, we are quite unwilling to extend the scope of the statute * * *." Id., at 214 (footnote omitted). Thus the claim of fraud and fiduciary breach in this complaint states a cause of action under any part of Rule 10b–5 only if the conduct alleged can be fairly viewed as "manipulative or deceptive" within the meaning of the statute.

III

It is our judgment that the transaction, if carried out as alleged in the complaint, was neither deceptive nor manipulative and therefore did not violate either § 10(b) of the Act or Rule 10b–5.

As we have indicated, the case comes to us on the premise that the complaint failed to allege a material misrepresentation or material failure to disclose. The finding of the District Court, undisturbed by the Court of Appeals, was that there was no "omission" or "misstatement" in the Information Statement accompanying the notice of merger. On the basis of the information provided, minority shareholders could either accept the price offered or reject it and seek an appraisal in the Delaware Court of Chancery. Their choice was fairly presented, and they were furnished with all relevant information on which to base their decision.[14]

12. The case for adhering to the language of the statute is even stronger here than in *Ernst & Ernst,* where the interpretation of Rule 10b–5 rejected by the Court was strongly urged by the Commission. See also Piper v. ChrisCraft Industries, Inc., ante, p. 1, and Blue Chip Stamps v. Manor Drug Stores, 421 U.S. 723 (1975) (rejecting interpretations of Rule 10b–5 urged by the SEC as *amicus curiae*). By contrast, the Commission apparently has not concluded that Rule 10b–5 should be used to reach "going private" transactions where the majority stockholder eliminates the minority at an allegedly unfair price. See SEC Securities Act Release No. 5567 (Feb. 6, 1975), CCH Fed.Sec.L.Rep. ¶ 80,104 (proposing Rules 13e–3A and 13e–3B dealing with "going private" transactions, pursuant to six sections of the 1934 Act including § 10(b), but stating that the Commission "has reached no conclusions with respect to the proposed rules"). Because we are concerned here only with § 10(b), we intimate no view as to the Commission's authority to promulgate such rules under other sections of the Act.

14. In addition to their principal argument that the complaint alleges a fraud under clauses (a) and (c) of Rule 10b–5, respondents also argue that the complaint alleges nondisclosure and misrepresentation in violation of clause (b) of the Rule. Their major contention in this respect is that the majority stockholder's failure to give the minority advance notice of the merger was a material nondisclosure, even though the Delaware short-form merger statute does not require such notice. Brief for Respondents, at 27. But respondents do not indicate how they might have acted differently had they had prior notice of the merger. Indeed, they accept the conclusion of both courts below that under Delaware law they could not have enjoined the merger because an appraisal proceeding is their sole remedy in the Delaware courts for any alleged unfairness in the terms of the merger. Thus the failure to give advance notice was not a material nondisclo-

We therefore find inapposite the cases relied upon by respondents and the court below, in which the breaches of fiduciary duty held violative of Rule 10b–5 included some element of deception.[15] Those cases forcefully reflect the principle that "[s]ection 10(b) must be read flexibly, not technically and restrictively" and that the statute provides a cause of action for any plaintiff who "suffer[s] an injury as a result of deceptive practices touching its sale [or purchase] of securities. * * *." Superintendent of Insurance v. Bankers Life & Casualty Co., 404 U.S. 6, 12–13 (1971). But the cases do not support the proposition, adopted by the Court of Appeals below and urged by respondents here, that a breach of fiduciary duty by majority stockholders, without any deception, misrepresentation, or nondisclosure, violates the statute and the Rule.

It is also readily apparent that the conduct alleged in the complaint was not "manipulative" within the meaning of the statute. Manipulation is "virtually a term of art when used in connection with securities markets." Ernst & Ernst, 425 U.S., at 199. The term refers generally to practices, such as wash sales, matched orders, or rigged prices, that are intended to mislead investors by artificially affecting market activity. See, e.g., § 9 of the 1934 Act (prohibiting specific manipulative practices); Ernst & Ernst, supra; Piper v. Chris-Craft Industries, Inc., 430 U.S., at 43 (Rule 10b–6, also

sure within the meaning of the statute or the Rule. Cf. TSC Industries, Inc. v. Northway, Inc., 426 U.S. 438 (1976).

15. The decisions of this Court relied upon by respondents all involved deceptive conduct as part of the Rule 10b–5 violation alleged. Affiliated Ute Citizens v. United States, 406 U.S. 128 (1972) (misstatements of material fact used by bank employees in position of market maker to acquire stock at less than fair value); Superintendent of Insurance v. Bankers Life & Cas. Co., 404 U.S. 6, 9 (1971) ("seller [of bonds] was duped into believing that it, the seller, would receive the proceeds"). Cf. SEC v. Capital Gains Research Bureau, 375 U.S. 180 (1963) (injunction under Investment Advisers Act of 1940 to compel registered investment adviser to disclose to his clients his own financial interest in his recommendations).

We have been cited to a large number of cases in the Courts of Appeals, all of which involved an element of deception as part of the fiduciary misconduct held to violate Rule 10b–5. E.g., Schoenbaum v. Firstbrook, 405 F.2d 215, 220 (CA2 1968) (en banc), cert. denied, 395 U.S. 906 (1969) (majority stockholder and board of directors "were guilty of deceiving" the minority stockholders); Drachman v. Harvey, 453 F.2d 722, 733, 736, 737 (CA2 1972) (en banc) (Rule 10b–5 violation alleged on facts found "indistinguishable" from Superintendent of Insurance v. Bankers Life & Cas. Co.); Schlick v. Penn-Dixie Cement Corp., 507 F.2d 374 (CA2 1974), cert. denied, 421 U.S. 976 (1975) (scheme of market manipulation and merger on unfair

terms, one aspect of which was misrepresentation); Pappas v. Moss, 393 F.2d 865, 869 (CA3 1968) ("if a 'deception' is required in the present context [of § 10(b) and Rule 10b–5], it is fairly found by viewing this fraud as though the 'independent' stockholders were standing in the place of the defrauded corporate entity," where the board of directors passed a resolution containing at least two material misrepresentations and authorizing the sale of corporate stock to the directors at a price below fair market value); Shell v. Hensley, 430 F.2d 819, 825 (CA5 1970) (derivative suit alleging that corporate officers used misleading proxy materials and other reports to deceive shareholders regarding a bogus employment contract intended to conceal improper payments to the corporation president and regarding purchases by the corporation of certain securities at excessive prices); Rekant v. Desser, 425 F.2d 872, 882 (CA5 1970) (as part of scheme to cause corporation to issue Treasury shares and a promissory note for grossly inadequate consideration, corporate officers deceived shareholders by making affirmative misrepresentations in the corporation's annual report and by failing to file any such report the next year). See Recent Cases, 89 Harv.L.Rev. 1917, 1926 (1976) (stating that no appellate decision before that of the Court of Appeals in this case and in Marshel v. AFW Fabric Corp., 533 F.2d 1277 (CA2), vacated and remanded for a determination of mootness, 429 U.S. 881 (1976), "had permitted a 10b–5 claim without some element of misrepresentation or nondisclosure") (footnote omitted).

promulgated under § 10(b), is "an antimanipulative provision designed to protect the orderliness of the securities market during distributions of stock" and "to prevent stimulative trading by an issuer in its own securities in order to create an unnatural and unwarranted appearance of market activity"); 2 A. Bromberg, Securities Law: Fraud § 7.3 (1975); 3 L. Loss, Securities Regulation 1541-70 (2d ed. 1961); 6 id., at 3755-3763 (2d ed. Supp.1969). Section 10(b)'s general prohibition of practices deemed by the SEC to be "manipulative"—in this technical sense of artificially affecting market activity in order to mislead investors—is fully consistent with the fundamental purpose of the 1934 Act "to substitute a philosophy of full disclosure for the philosophy of *caveat emptor* * * *." Affiliated Ute Citizens v. United States, 406 U.S. 128, 151 (1972), quoting SEC v. Capital Gains Research Bureau, 375 U.S. 180, 186 (1963). Indeed, nondisclosure is usually essential to the success of a manipulative scheme. 3 L. Loss, supra, at 1565. No doubt Congress meant to prohibit the full range of ingenious devices that might be used to manipulate securities prices. But we do not think it would have chosen this "term of art" if it had meant to bring within the scope of § 10(b) instances of corporate mismanagement such as this, in which the essence of the complaint is that shareholders were treated unfairly by a fiduciary.

IV

The language of the statute is, we think, "sufficiently clear in its context" to be dispositive here, Ernst & Ernst, 425 U.S., at 201; but even if it were not, there are additional considerations that weigh heavily against permitting a cause of action under Rule 10b-5 for the breach of corporate fiduciary duty alleged in this complaint. Congress did not expressly provide a private cause of action for violations of § 10(b). Although we have recognized an implied cause of action under that section in some circumstances, Superintendent of Insurance v. Bankers Life & Cas. Co., supra, 404 U.S. at 13 n. 9, we have also recognized that a private cause of action under the anti-fraud provisions of the Securities Exchange Act should not be implied where it is "unnecessary to ensure the fulfillment of Congress' purposes" in adopting the Act. Piper v. Christ-Craft Industries, 430 U.S. at 41. Cf. J.I. Case Co. v. Borak, 377 U.S. 426, 431-433 (1964). As we noted earlier, p. 1302, supra, the Court repeatedly has described the "fundamental purpose" of the Act as implementing a "philosophy of full disclosure"; once full and fair disclosure has occurred, the fairness of the terms of the transaction is at most a tangential concern of the statute. Cf. Mills v. Electric Auto-Lite Co., 396 U.S. 375, 381-385 (1970). As in Cort v. Ash, 422 U.S. 66, 78, 80 (1975), we are reluctant to recognize a cause of action here to serve what is "at best a subsidiary purpose" of the federal legislation.

A second factor in determining whether Congress intended to create a federal cause of action in these circumstances is "whether 'the cause of action [is] one traditionally relegated to state law. * * *'" Piper v. Chris-Craft Industries, Inc., 430 U.S., at 949, quoting Cort v. Ash, 422 U.S., at 78. The Delaware Legislature has supplied minority shareholders with a cause of action in the Delaware Court of Chancery to recover the fair value of shares allegedly undervalued in a short-form merger. See p. 2, supra. Of course, the existence of a particular state law remedy is not dispositive of the question whether Congress meant to provide a similar federal remedy, but as in *Piper* and *Cort,* we conclude that "it is entirely appropriate in this instance to relegate respondent and others in his situation to whatever remedy is created by state law." 422 U.S., at 84; 430 U.S., at 962.

The reasoning behind a holding that the complaint in this case alleged fraud under Rule 10b–5 could not be easily contained. It is difficult to imagine how a court could distinguish, for purposes of Rule 10b–5 fraud, between a majority stockholder's use of a short-form merger to eliminate the minority at an unfair price and the use of some other device, such as a long-form merger, tender offer, or liquidation, to achieve the same result; or indeed how a court could distinguish the alleged abuses in these going private transactions from other types of fiduciary self-dealing involving transactions in securities. The result would be to bring within the Rule a wide variety of corporate conduct traditionally left to state regulation. In addition to posing a "danger of vexatious litigation which could result from a widely expanded class of plaintiffs under Rule 10b–5," Blue Chip Stamps v. Manor Drug Stores, 421 U.S. 723, 740 (1975), this extension of the federal securities laws would overlap and quite possibly interfere with state corporate law. Federal courts applying a "federal fiduciary principle" under Rule 10b–5 could be expected to depart from state fiduciary standards at least to the extent necessary to ensure uniformity within the federal system.[16] Absent a clear indication of congressional intent, we are reluctant to federalize the substantial portion of the law of corporations that deals with transactions in securities, particularly where established state policies of corporate regulation would be overridden. As the Court stated in Cort v. Ash, supra, "Corporations are creatures of state law, and investors commit their funds to corporate directors on the understanding that, except where federal law *expressly* requires certain responsibilities of directors with respect to stockholders, state law will govern the internal affairs of the corporation." 422 U.S., at 84 (emphasis added).

We thus adhere to the position that "Congress by § 10(b) did not seek to regulate transactions which constitute no more than internal corporate mismanagement." Superintendent of Insurance v. Bankers Life & Cas. Co., 404 U.S., at 12. There may well be a need for uniform federal fiduciary standards to govern mergers such as that challenged in this complaint. But those standards should not be supplied by judicial extension of § 10(b) and Rule 10b–5 to "cover the corporate universe."

The judgment of the Court of Appeals is reversed, and the case is remanded for further proceedings consistent with this opinion.

So ordered.

---

16. For example, some States apparently require a "valid corporate purpose" for the elimination of the minority interest through a short-form merger, whereas other States do not. Compare Bryan v. Brock & Blevins Co., 490 F.2d 563 (CA5), cert. denied 419 U.S. 844 (1974) (merger arranged by controlling stockholder for no business purpose except to eliminate 15% minority stockholder violated Georgia short-form merger statute) with Stauffer v. Standard Brands, Inc., 41 Del.Ch. 7, 187 A.2d 78 (Sup.Ct.1962) (Delaware short-form merger statute allows majority stockholder to eliminate the minority interest without any corporate purpose and subject only to an appraisal remedy). Thus to the extent that Rule 10b–5 is interpreted to require a valid corporate purpose for elimination of minority shareholders as well as a fair price for their shares, it would impose a stricter standard of fiduciary duty than that required by the law of some States.

MR. JUSTICE BRENNAN dissents and would affirm for substantially the reasons stated in the majority and concurring opinions in the Court of Appeals, 2 Cir., 533 F.2d 1283 (1976).

MR. JUSTICE BLACKMUN, concurring in part.

Like Mr. Justice Stevens, I refrain from joining Part IV of the Court's opinion. I, too, regard that part as unnecessary for the decision in the instant case and, indeed, as exacerbating the concerns I expressed in my dissents in Blue Chip Stamps v. Manor Drug Stores, 421 U.S. 723, 761 (1975), and in Ernst & Ernst v. Hochfelder, 425 U.S. 185, 215 (1976). I, however, join the remainder of the Court's opinion and its judgment.

MR. JUSTICE STEVENS, concurring in part.

For the reasons stated by Mr. Justice Blackmun in his dissenting opinion in Blue Chip Stamps v. Manor Drug Stores, 421 U.S. 723, 761, and those stated in my dissent in Piper v. Chris-Craft Industries, 97 S.Ct. 926, 955 (1977), I believe both of those cases were incorrectly decided. I foresee some danger that Part IV of the Court's opinion in this case may incorrectly be read as extending the holdings of those cases. Moreover, the entire discussion in Part IV is unnecessary to the decision of this case. Accordingly, I join only Parts I, II and III of the Court's opinion. I would also add further emphasis to the fact that the controlling stockholders in this case did not breach any duty owed to the minority shareholders because (a) there was complete disclosure of the relevant facts, and (b) the minority are entitled to receive the fair value of their shares. The facts alleged in the complaint do not constitute "fraud" within the meaning of Rule 10b–5.

GOLDBERG v. MERIDOR *

United States Court of Appeals, Second Circuit, 1977.
567 F.2d 209.

Before FRIENDLY, TIMBERS and MESKILL, CIRCUIT JUDGES.

FRIENDLY, CIRCUIT JUDGE:

In this derivative action in the District Court for the Southern District of New York, David Goldberg, a stockholder of Universal Gas & Oil Company, Inc. (UGO), a Panama corporation having its principal place of business in New York City, sought to recover damages and to obtain other relief against UGO's controlling parent, Maritimecor, S.A., also a Panama corporation; Maritimecor's controlling parent, Maritime Fruit Carriers Company Ltd., an Israel corporation; a number of individuals who were directors of one or more of these companies; the investment firm of Hornblower & Weeks, Hemphill, Noyes, Inc.; and the accounting firm of Laventhal & Horwath, with respect to transactions which culminated in an agreement providing for UGO's issuance to Maritimecor of up to 4,200,000 shares of UGO stock and its assumption of all of Maritimecor's liabilities (including a debt of $7,000,000 owed to UGO) in consideration of the transfer of all of Maritimecor's assets (except 2,800,000 UGO shares already held by Maritimecor). It suffices at this point to say that the complaint, filed February 3, 1976, alleged that the contract was grossly unfair to UGO

* [Eds.] Cert. denied 434 U.S. 1069 (1978).

and violated both § 10(b) of the Securities Exchange Act and the SEC's Rule 10b–5 and common law fiduciary duties. * * * [The district court ordered plaintiff to post security for expenses under § 627 of the N.Y. Business Corporation Law or amend his complaint to eliminate all state law claims.]

Goldberg chose the latter course. The amended complaint, filed August 27, 1976, which was largely repetitive of the original complaint save for the omission of reference to state law claims, made the following principal allegations: The defendants engaged in "a conspiracy or plan" "to cause UGO to raise funds from the public by a public offering and then by various transactions hereafter set forth, including the transfer of UGO stock to Maritimecor for the latter's assets and liabilities, use the proceeds of the offering and the assets of UGO for the benefit of defendants Maritimecor and Maritime Fruit." In May 1972 defendants caused UGO to issue a prospectus offering for sale 11,000 units consisting of 363,000 shares of common stock and $11,000,000 worth of 8% convertible debentures. The prospectus stated that all the proceeds of the offering would be used to finance the construction and purchase of three tankers for the transportation of liquified gas and that UGO's business would be the transportation of such gas. In 1974 defendants caused UGO to sell the contracts for two of the vessels, for a total price of $25,000,000 of which $14,000,000 was profit. During 1974 and up to August 1975, defendants caused UGO to make loans to Maritimecor so that $7,000,000 was owed by the latter. In August 1975 defendants caused UGO to enter into the agreement described in the first paragraph of this opinion, which was later carried out at least to the extent of the transfer of Maritimecor's assets and liabilities to UGO. The "agreement and transfer was fraudulent and unfair in that the assets of Maritimecor were overpriced and of insufficient value, the liabilities of Maritimecor either exceeded the value of its assets or were so great that the net asset value was insufficient consideration, the liabilities included a $7,000,000 debt to UGO from Maritimecor, and the purpose and intent of said transaction was to cause the dissipation of the substantial assets of UGO for the benefit of defendants, Maritimecor and Maritime Fruit. [T]he defendants * * * knew at the time, or had reasonable cause to know and were negligent in not ascertaining that the agreement and transfer were a fraud and unfair to UGO, and that the net value of the assets of Maritimecor was far less than the value of the shares of UGO to be issued to Maritimecor, or that Maritimecor's liabilities exceeded its assets." Then came paragraph 19, which alleged as follows:

The issuance of the aforesaid prospectus and the foregoing transactions constituted the employment of a device, scheme or artifice to defraud, the making of untrue statements of material fact and the omission to state material facts necessary in order to make the statements made, in the light of the circumstances under which they were made, not misleading, and the engaging in acts, practices, and courses of conduct which operated as a fraud or deceit upon UGO as the seller of up to 4,200,000 shares of UGO's common stock for Maritimecor's liabilities and assets, and upon UGO's minority stockholders.

Defendants filed motions to dismiss the amended complaint for failure to state a claim under § 10(b) of the Securities Exchange Act and Rule 10b–5. In answer to defendants' argument "that deception and non-disclosure is a requirement for a 10b–5 case" which was disputed as a matter of law, plaintiff's counsel submitted an affidavit asserting that "insofar as plaintiff Goldberg, a minority shareholder is concerned, there has been no disclosure to him of the fraudulent nature of the transfer of Maritimecor assets and liabilities for stock of UGO". Counsel annexed two press releases dated August 1 and December 19, 1975, which described the agreement for and the consummation of the UGO-Maritimecor transaction. Counsel asserted that these press releases failed to disclose the facts noted in the margin [1] or "the conflicts of interest of the principals".[2] Counsel requested that he be given leave to replead should the court find any defect in the manner of pleading. In a further affidavit addressed to the question of damage, counsel averred that at the end of 1974 UGO had current assets of about $41 million and current liabilities of $2 million but that after the transfer Maritimecor's net current liabilities of $42.5 million caused UGO to wind up with a deficit of about $3.6 million of current liabilities. He also alleged that as a result of the transaction UGO had defaulted in its obligations and its ships were being seized by creditors.

On February 11, 1977, Judge Lasker filed an opinion, 426 F.Supp. 1059, that granted the motions to dismiss. He thought the case was governed by Popkin v. Bishop, 464 F.2d 714 (2 Cir.1972), rather than by our en banc decisions in Schoenbaum v. Firstbrook, 405 F.2d 215 (2 Cir.1968), cert. denied, 395 U.S. 906 (1969), and Drachman v. Harvey, 453 F.2d 722 (2 Cir. 1972), and held that Marshel v. AFW Fabric Corp., 533 F.2d 1277 (2 Cir.), vacated and remanded for consideration of mootness, 429 U.S. 881 (1976), and Green v. Santa Fe Industries, Inc., 533 F.2d 1283 (2 Cir.), which was pending before the Supreme Court on grant of certiorari, 429 U.S. 814 (1976), were limited to the situation of "going private". He denied leave to amend, as hereafter discussed. After the reversal of *Green,* 462 U.S. 430 (1977), the judge filed a memorandum adding to the opinion fn. 4 to the effect that the Supreme Court's decision rendered his analysis of our decision moot but lent substantial support to the result.

I.

Before proceeding further, we must deal with the district court's refusal to permit amendment of the complaint to include reference to the two press releases or otherwise to claim deception. * * * [The Court's discussion of this point is omitted.] We are therefore constrained to hold that the refusal of leave to amend was an abuse of discretion and to treat the cases as if an amendment, at least in the two respects noted, had been allowed.

---

1. Maritimecor, as of the end of fiscal year 1974 had current liabilities of $42.5 million dollars, and in addition Maritimecor owed UGO about $7 million dollars which apparently was being forgiven in the transaction. The shareholders' net equity in Maritimecor was $40.4 million dollars or substantially less than its current liabilities. Further, included in the assets of Maritimecor are 2.8 million shares of UGO, the value of which are substantially decreased as a result of this transaction.

2. In fact both press releases did state that Maritimecor was UGO's "parent" and the first recounted that on consummation

of the transaction Maritimecor ownership of UGO common stock "will increase from 2,800,000 (78 percent) to 7,000,000 (90 percent)" while "[a]n additional 500,000 shares and 289,100 shares of UGO common stock are now held—and will continue to be held—by a subsidiary of Panmaritime Limited S.A., a Panama corporation which controls [Maritime Fruit], and the public, respectively."

Both releases also concluded with a statement that "UGO's common stock and 8 percent Convertible Subordinated Debentures are traded over-the-counter (NAS-DAQ–UGOLF and UGOLZ, respectively)."

II.

If the complaint were thus amended, we would deem it clear that, so far as this court's decisions are concerned, the case would be governed by *Schoenbaum* rather than by *Popkin.* The August 1 press release held out an inviting picture that

> As a result of the transaction, UGO will replace Maritimecor as the principal operating subsidiary of MFC and, as such, will engage in a diversified line of shipping and shipping related activities including the sale of ships and ship-building contracts, the operation of reefers and tankers, and upon their delivery, product carriers and oil drilling rigs, and underwriting marine insurance.

when allegedly the truth was that UGO had entered into a transaction that would ensure its doom. *Popkin* was specifically rested on its special facts. The plaintiff was taken to have conceded that the complaint did not allege misrepresentation or non-disclosure and that he relied solely on the unfairness of the merger terms, see 464 F.2d at 718 & n. 9, 720. The opinion expressly noted that "[u]nquestionably this court has recognized that the Rule 10b–5 reaches beyond traditional stock transactions and into the board rooms of corporations" and that "assertions by a defendant that the misconduct complained of 'really' amounts to 'just' corporate mismanagement will not cut off a plaintiff's federal remedy." 464 F.2d at 718. The court likewise quoted with approval, 464 F.2d at 719, Judge Hays' statement in dissenting from the panel opinion in *Schoenbaum,*

> In order to establish fraud it is surely not necessary to show that the directors deceived themselves. It must be enough to show that they deceived the shareholders, the real owners of the property with which the directors were dealing. Deception of the shareholders (with the exception of the majority stockholder which was a party to the transactions) is established by showing that the directors withheld from them information that would have revealed the true value of the treasury stock.

and the statement in his opinion for the en banc court in that case,

> Moreover, Aquitaine and the directors of Banff were guilty of deceiving the stockholders of Banff (other than Aquitaine). (Footnote omitted.)

The observation in *Popkin,* 464 F.2d at 719, that "our emphasis on improper self-dealing did not eliminate nondisclosure as a key issue in the Rule 10b–5 cases" followed a statement that when, as here, state law does not demand prior shareholder approval of a transaction, "it makes sense to concentrate on the impropriety of the conduct itself rather than on the 'failure to disclose' it because full and fair disclosure in a real sense will rarely occur. It will be equally rare in the legal sense once the view is taken—as we did in *Schoenbaum* —that under federal securities law disclosure to interested insiders does not prevent a valid claim that fraud was committed upon 'outsiders' (such as minority shareholders) whatever the requirements of state corporate law may be." Id. The ruling of *Popkin* was that in the *opposite* situation, where "merger transactions * * *, under state law, must be subjected to shareholder approval * * * if federal law ensures that shareholder approval is fairly sought and freely given, the principal federal interest is at an end," 464 F.2d at 720, see also id. n. 17. Clearly that is not this case. * * *

III.

The ruling that this case is attracted by *Schoenbaum* rather than by *Popkin* by no means ends our inquiry. Rather it brings us to the serious question whether *Schoenbaum* can be here applied consistently with the Supreme Court's decision in Santa Fe Industries, Inc. v. Green, supra. We think it can be and should.

* * *

We followed *Schoenbaum* in Drachman v. Harvey, 453 F.2d 722, 736 (2 Cir.1972) (en banc), although in that case not all the directors were parties to the fraud, and in Schlick v. Penn-Dixie Cement Corp., 507 F.2d 374 (2 Cir.1974), cert. denied 421 U.S. 976 (1975). *Schoenbaum* has been generally applauded by commentators, even though it may sometimes have been read to mean more than it does or than is needed to call for a reversal here. See, e.g., Bloomenthal, From Birnbaum to Schoenbaum: The Exchange Act and Self-Aggrandizement, 15 N.Y.L.F. 332 (1969) (making the perceptive suggestion that "it is inconceivable that a court which in Texas Gulf Sulphur [401 F.2d 833 (2 Cir.1968), cert. denied 394 U.S. 976 (1969)] emphasized the disclosure purposes of the Exchange Act could have reached any different result in *Schoenbaum*"); Folk, Corporation Law Developments—1969, 56 Va.L.Rev. 755, 805–12 (1970); Comment, Schoenbaum v. Firstbrook: The "New Fraud" Expands Federal Corporation Law, 55 Va.L.Rev. 1103 (1969); Note, The Controlling Influence Standard in Rule 10b–5 Corporate Mismanagement Cases, 86 Harv.L.Rev. 1007 (1973); Note, Schlick v. Penn-Dixie Cement Corp.: Fraudulent Mismanagement Independent of Misrepresentation or Nondisclosure Violates Rule 10b–5, 63 Calif.L.Rev. 563 (1975); 41 Ford.L.Rev. 742 (1973); see also Bahlman, Rule 10b–5: The Case for its Full Acceptance as Federal Corporation Law, 37 U.Cinn.L.Rev. 727, 735–36 (1968) (criticizing the panel opinion in *Schoenbaum*); but see Note, Civil Liability Under Section 10(b) and Rule 10b–5: A Suggestion for Replacing the Doctrine of Privity, 74 Yale L.J. 658, 681–82 (1965); Comment, 47 N.Y.U.L.Rev. 1279 (1972). It likewise is viewed with approval—indeed seemingly would be adopted—by §§ 1303 and 1402(c) of the proposed ALI Federal Securities Code, Tent. Draft No. 2 (March 1973) and revised comments in Reporter's Revision of Text of Tentative Drafts Nos. 1–3, pp. 104–06 (Oct. 1, 1974), see also §§ 234D(c) and 1301. It has also found favor in other circuits. A notable instance is Shell v. Hensley, 430 F.2d 819, 827 (5 Cir.1970), where the court in a derivative suit rejected a claim that no "causal deceit" existed when the corporation's board knew all the facts, saying:

When the other party to the securities transaction controls the judgment of all the corporation's board members or conspires with them or the one controlling them to profit mutually at the expense of the corporation, the corporation is no less disabled from availing itself of an informed judgment than if the outsider had simply lied to the board. In both situations, the determination of the corporation's choice of action in the transaction in question is not made as a reasonable man would make it if possessed of the material information known to the other party to the transaction.[7]

---

7. See Superintendent of Insurance, supra, 404 U.S. 6, at 12–13, where the Court quoted the *Shell* court's description of a situation thought to be indistinguishable from the one faced in *Shell*:

See also Rekant v. Desser, 425 F.2d 872, 879–82 (5 Cir.1970); Jannes v. Microwave Communications, Inc., 461 F.2d 525, 529 (7 Cir.1972); Bailey v. Meister Brau, Inc., 535 F.2d 982, 993 (7 Cir.1976); 1 Bromberg, Securities Law: Fraud §§ 4.7(544)–(545) (collecting cases and noting, at pp. 84.51–84.52 that "[m]ost courts have now modified their views of deception to accommodate * * * (1) informational deception of a non-decision-maker who has a role or economic interest (minority director, shareholder, or creditor) or (2) non-informational deception measured by economic injury (to the company of other parties with real economic interest) equivalent to that resulting from informational deception of decision makers").

Schoenbaum, then, can rest solidly on the now widely recognized ground that there is deception of the corporation (in effect, of its minority shareholders) when the corporation is influenced by its controlling shareholder to engage in a transaction adverse to the corporation's interests (in effect, the minority shareholders' interests) and there is nondisclosure or misleading disclosures as to the material facts of the transaction. Assuming that, in light of the decision in *Green,* the existence of "controlling influence" and "wholly inadequate consideration"—an aspect of the *Schoenbaum* decision that perhaps attracted more attention, see 405 F.2d at 219–20—can no longer alone form the basis for Rule 10b–5 liability, we do not read *Green* as ruling that no action lies under Rule 10b–5 when a controlling corporation causes a partly owned subsidiary to sell its securities to the parent in a fraudulent transaction and fails to make a disclosure or, as can be alleged here, makes a misleading disclosure. The Supreme Court noted in *Green* that the court of appeals "did not disturb the District Court's conclusion that the complaint did not allege a material misrepresentation or nondisclosure with respect to the value of the stock" of Kirby; the Court's quarrel was with this court's holding that "neither misrepresentation nor nondisclosure was a necessary element of a Rule 10b–5 action", 430 U.S. at 470, and that a breach of fiduciary duty would alone suffice, see fn. 8. It was because "the complaint failed to allege a material misrepresentation or material failure to disclose" that the Court found "inapposite the cases [including *Schoenbaum*] relied upon by respondents and the court below, in which the breaches of fiduciary duty held violative of Rule 10b–5 included some element of deception", 430 U.S. at 475, see fn. 15. While appellant is wrong in saying that the Court "approved" these cases, there is no indication that the Court would have casually overturned such an impressive and unanimous body of decisions by courts of appeals. To the contrary, the Court used rather benign language about them, saying that they "forcefully reflect the principle that '[s]ection 10(b) must be read flexibly not restrictively' and that the statute provides a cause of action for any plaintiff who 'suffer[s] an injury as a result of deceptive practices touching its sale [or purchase] of securities * * *,' " citing the *Superintendent of Insurance* case, supra, 404 U.S. at 12–13. Mr. Justice White simply

---

The crux of the present case is that [the corporation] suffered an injury as a result of deceptive practices touching its sale of securities as an investor. As stated in Shell v. Hensley, 430 F.2d 819, 827:

"When a person who is dealing with a corporation in a securities transaction denies the corporation's directors access to material information known to him,

the corporation is disabled from availing itself of an informed judgment on the part of its board regarding the merits of the transaction. In this situation the private right of action recognized under Rule 10b–5 is available as a remedy for the corporate disability." (Footnote omitted.)

distinguished these cases as not supporting the position we had taken in *Green*, namely, "that a breach of fiduciary duty by majority stockholders, *without any deception, misrepresentation, or nondisclosure*, violates the statute and the Rule." (Emphasis supplied.)

Here the complaint alleged "deceit * * * upon UGO's minority shareholders" and, if amendment had been allowed as it should have been, would have alleged misrepresentation as to the UGO–Maritimecor transaction at least in the sense of failure to state material facts "necessary in order to make the statements made, in the light of the circumstances under which they were made, not misleading," Rule 10b–5(b).[8] The nub of the matter is that the conduct attacked in *Green* did not violate the "'fundamental purpose' of the Act as implementing a 'philosophy of full disclosure'", 430 U.S. at 478; the conduct here attacked does.

Defendants contend that even if all this is true, the failure to make a public disclosure or even the making of a misleading disclosure would have no effect, since no action by stockholders to approve the UGO–Maritimecor transaction was required. Along the same lines our brother Meskill invoking the opinion in *Green*, 430 U.S. at 474 n. 14, contends that the defendants' acts were not material since plaintiff has failed adequately to allege what would have been done had he known the truth.

In TSC Industries, Inc. v. Northway, Inc., 426 U.S. 438, 449, (1976), a case arising under Rule 14a–9, the Court laid down the standard of materiality as "a showing of a substantial likelihood that, under all the circumstances, the omitted fact would have assumed actual significance in the deliberations of the reasonable shareholder" or, putting the matter in another way, "a substantial likelihood that the disclosure of the omitted fact would have been viewed by the reasonable investor as having significantly altered the 'total mix' of information made available." When, as in a derivative action, the deception is alleged to have been practiced on the corporation, even though all the directors were parties to it, the test must be whether the facts that were not disclosed or were misleadingly disclosed to the shareholders "would have assumed actual significance in the deliberations" of reasonable and disinterested directors or created "a substantial likelihood" that such directors would have considered the "total mix" of information available to have been "significantly altered." That was the basis for liability in *Schoenbaum*; it was likely that a reasonable director of Banff, knowing the facts as to the oil discovery that had been withheld from minority shareholders, would not have voted to issue the shares to Aquitaine at a price below their true value. This also is the principle recognized in the passage from Judge Ainsworth's opinion in Smith v. Hensley, supra, 430 F.2d at 827, quoted above. Here there is surely a significant likelihood that if a reasonable director of UGO had known the facts alleged by plaintiff rather than the barebones of the press releases, he would not have voted for the transaction with Maritimecor.

Beyond this Goldberg and other minority shareholders would not have been without remedy if the alleged facts had been disclosed. The doubts entertained by our brother as to the existence of injunctive remedies in

---

8. We do not mean to suggest that § 10(b) or Rule 10b–5 requires insiders to characterize conflict of interest transactions with pejorative nouns or adjectives. However, if Maritimecor was in the par- lous financial condition alleged in the opposing affidavit of plaintiff's counsel, a disclosure of the acquisition of Maritimecor that omitted these *facts* would be seriously misleading.

New York, * * * are unfounded. Blumenthal v. Roosevelt Hotel, Inc., 202 Misc. 988, 115 N.Y.S.2d 52 (Sup.Ct.N.Y.Co.1952), and Williams v. Bartell, 34 Misc.2d 552, 226 N.Y.S.2d 187 (Sup.Ct.N.Y.Co.), modified, 16 A.D.2d 21, 225 N.Y.S.2d 351 (1st Dept.1962), were suits by stockholders acting in their own behalf to enjoin the sale of all corporate assets or a merger transaction as to which New York afforded dissenters the remedy of an appraisal. While the appraisal remedy was not exclusive, the existence of that remedy was held to require a plaintiff seeking an injunction to demonstrate a strong balance of equities in his favor. The UGO–Maritimecor transaction was not of the sort that would afford UGO's stockholders any right of appraisal. Where an appraisal remedy is not available, the courts of New York have displayed no hesitancy in granting injunctive relief, see e.g., Robinson v. New York & P.C.R. Co., 123 App.Div. 339, 108 N.Y.S. 91 (1st Dept.1908) (enjoining transfer of assets); * * *. The dissent also fails to take account of the liberalization of New York law by the Business Corporation Law, effective September 1, 1963. Section 720 of that statute provides:

(a) An action may be brought against one or more directors or officers of a corporation to procure a judgment for the following relief:

* * *

(3) To enjoin a proposed unlawful conveyance, assignment, or transfer of corporate assets, where there is sufficient evidence that it will be made.

(b) An action may be brought for the relief provided in this section, and in paragraph (a) of section 719 (Liability of directors in certain cases) by a corporation, or a receiver, trustee in bankruptcy, officer, director or judgment creditor thereof, or, under section 626 (Shareholders' derivative action brought in the right of the corporation to procure a judgment in its favor), by a shareholder, voting trust certificate holder, or the owner of a beneficial interest in shares thereof.

As Judge (now Chief Judge) Breitel has written, "The statute is broad and covers every form of waste of assets and violation of duty whether as a result of intention, negligence, or predatory acquisition," Rapoport v. Schneider, 29 N.Y.2d 396, 400, 328 N.Y.S.2d 431, 435, 278 N.E.2d 642, 645 (1972). Under the 1963 statute there can also be no question as to the applicability of these remedies to UGO. * * *

The availability of injunctive relief if the defendants had not lulled the minority stockholders of UGO into security by a deceptive disclosure, as they allegedly did, is in sharp contrast to *Green,* where the disclosure following the merger transaction was full and fair, and, as to the pre-merger period, respondents accepted "the conclusion of both courts below that under Delaware law they could not have enjoined the merger because an appraisal proceeding is their sole remedy in the Delaware courts for any alleged unfairness in the terms of the merger," fn. 14. Indeed, we have quite recently recognized that the availability of an injunctive action under New York law constituted a sufficient basis for distinguishing the conclusion in the *Green* footnote with respect to materiality, SEC v. Parklane Hosiery Co., Inc., 558 F.2d 1083, 1088 (2 Cir.1977). While our brother Meskill is correct in stating that *Parklane* was an enforcement action by the SEC, we do not perceive why the test of materiality should be any different; indeed this court's seminal statement with respect to materiality was made in a SEC enforcement action, SEC v. Texas Gulf Sulphur Co., 401 F.2d 833, 848–52 (2 Cir.1968), cert. denied sub nom. Coates v. SEC, 394 U.S. 976 (1969), and contained no intimation that a stricter test would be applied in a private action.

Defendants also rely on statements in Part IV of the *Green* opinion which lend them some support if taken in isolation and out of context. Thus the Court, quoting from Piper v. Chris-Craft Industries, Inc., 430 U.S. 1, 40 (1977), said that one factor in determining whether a case was covered by § 10(b) and Rule 10b–5, was "whether 'the cause of action [is] one traditionally relegated to state law * * *.' " But the Court quickly added, after referring to the Delaware appraisal statute, that "Of course, the existence of a particular state law remedy is not dispositive of the question whether Congress meant to provide a similar federal remedy," and it would be hard to think of a cause of action more "traditionally relegated to state law" than the one asserted in the *Superintendent of Insurance* case, which, as has been said, made "just plain stealing" a fraud under Rule 10b–5, on the basis that Begole failed to tell the directors "in advance that he was going to steal", Jennings & Marsh, Securities Regulation 997–98 (1977). Defendants rely also on the Court's fears of the difficulty of future line-drawing among various kinds of breach of fiduciary duty involving securities transactions. But this was said in support of drawing the line so as to require plaintiffs to make claims of nondisclosure or misleading disclosure, not as directing the lower courts to dismiss cases where it was claimed that fiduciaries had failed to disclose their self-dealing or had made a misleading disclosure, even though no disclosure was required by state law.[10] Similarly we fail to see how defendants gain from the Court's quotation of its statement in the *Superintendent of Insurance* case, 404 U.S. at 12, that "Congress by § 10(b) did not seek to regulate transactions which constitute no more than internal corporate mismanagement"—a statement that originally seemed intended only to remove *negligent* corporate misconduct from the reach of the statute. We readily agree that if all that was here alleged was that UGO had been injured by "internal corporate mismanagement", no federal claim would have been stated. But a parent's looting of a subsidiary with securities outstanding in the hands of the public in a securities transaction is a different matter; in such cases disclosure or at least the absence of misleading disclosure is required. It would be incongruous if Rule 10b–5 created liability for a casual "tip" in the bar of a country club, as we held in SEC v. Geon Industries, Inc., 531 F.2d 39 (2 Cir. 1976), but would not cover a parent's undisclosed or misleadingly disclosed

---

10. We need not now decide whether, as some commentators have suggested, in certain self-dealing situations disclosure of the fact that the transaction is to occur or has occurred is required by federal law—whether as an affirmative duty on the corporation in some circumstances to disclose under Rule 10b–5 even in the absence of its trading, Jacobs, The Impact of Rule 10b–5 § 88.04[a] (rev. ed. 1977); see, e.g., SEC v. Texas Gulf Sulphur Co., 401 F.2d 833, 850 & n. 12 (2 Cir.1968), cert. denied 394 U.S. 976 (1969); SEC v. North American Research & Development Corp., 424 F.2d 63, 79 N. 13 (2 Cir.1970); Financial Indus.

Fund, Inc. v. McDonnell Douglas Corp., 474 F.2d 514 (10 Cir.1973); Securities Act Release No. 5092 (Oct. 15, 1970), and other sources cited in Jacobs, supra; compare Electronic Specialty Co. v. International Controls Corp., 409 F.2d 937, 949 (2 Cir. 1969), or as a requirement of applicable specific reporting provisions under the 1934 Act, see, e.g., §§ 13 and 15(d); Form 10–K (Items 1 and 15); Form 8–K (Item 2), or as an obligation imposed by a national securities exchange, see e.g., NYSE Company Manual A–18; AMEX Company Guide; see also Exchange Act Rule 15c2–11.

sale of its overvalued assets for stock of a controlled subsidiary with securities in the hands of the public.

The order dismissing the complaint is reversed and the case is remanded to the district court for further proceedings, including amendment of the complaint, consistent with this opinion.

MESKILL, CIRCUIT JUDGE, concurring in part and dissenting in part:

I concur in Parts I and II of Judge Friendly's opinion, for I agree that the district judge should have allowed amendment of the complaint and that a corporation may be defrauded by some or all of its directors. I part company, however, with the majority's holding that the complaint, as "amended" in the manner suggested by Judge Friendly, to include the press releases, states a cause of action. Assuming that any deception of the minority shareholders took place, the complaint nevertheless fails to establish that the claimed deception was "material." Accordingly, I respectfully dissent from the discussion in Part III of the majority opinion concerning materiality and the impact of Santa Fe Industries, Inc. v. Green, 430 U.S. 462 (1977).

* * *

Under Panamanian law, no shareholder action was necessary to effect the UGO–Maritimecor merger. Accordingly, the burden is on the plaintiffs to demonstrate a substantial likelihood that they would have acted differently had full disclosure been made.[4]

* * *

Although the majority asserts that state remedies were available to halt the merger, the explanation of what they were is unpersuasive. The principal action suggested by the majority opinion is an injunction against the proposed merger. The theory is apparently that the shareholders, who were led down the primrose path by the misleading press releases, would have raced into court if armed with the full story. It is possible that plaintiffs could have obtained an injunction under New York's Martin Act, N.Y.Gen.Bus.Law § 352 et seq. (McKinney 1976). See American Bank & Trust Co. v. Barad Shaff Securities Corp., 335 F.Supp. 1276 (S.D.N.Y.1972). In order to prove materiality under this theory, Goldberg will have to demonstrate that he would, as a reasonable stockholder, have sought and obtained an injunction against the proposed action had the facts not been concealed. See Herzfeld v. Laventhal, Krekstein, Horwath & Horwath, 378 F.Supp. 112 (S.D.N.Y.1974), mod. on other grounds, 540 F.2d 27 (2d Cir. 1976).

Moreover, the plaintiff fails even to mention in his two complaints what course of action he contemplated taking. Under *Green*, such an allegation is required to state a claim under 10b–5. There, as here, a plaintiff who sought to recover in federal court for a breach of fiduciary duty appended a conclusory allegation of deception. * * *

---

4. The majority's heavy reliance on our *en banc* opinion in Schoenbaum v. Firstbrook, 405 F.2d 215 (2d Cir.1968), cert. denied, 395 U.S. 906 (1969), is misplaced for two reasons. First, materiality was not discussed in *Schoenbaum*, since the district court had granted summary judgment on another issue. Second, *Schoenbaum* held that a breach of fiduciary duty, there the issuance of stock for inadequate consideration, was actionable under clause (3) of Rule 10b–5. Id. at 219–20. This holding has been overruled by *Green*.

The majority suggests two other bases for a finding of materiality. The first is the artificial maintenance of the price of UGO stock through nondisclosure. While this would be relevant in an action brought by the SEC or a plaintiff suing in his individual capacity,[10] I fail to see what relevance this has in a derivative action. In his representative capacity, Goldberg may assert only the rights of UGO. It is self-evident that the artificial maintenance of a high price for its stock in no way injured UGO.[11]

The final suggested rationale of the majority is the "chastening effect" of full disclosure. The apparent theory is that those about to loot a corporation can be shamed into honesty through a requirement that they reveal their nefarious purposes.

Even the high-water mark of expansion for 10b–5, Superintendent of Insurance v. Bankers Life & Casualty Co., 404 U.S. 6 (1971), acknowledged that breaches of fiduciary obligation were governed by state, and not federal law. Id. at 12. The primary role of the states in these matters has been emphasized in a number of recent opinions of the Supreme Court. See, e.g., *Green*, supra, at 462; Piper v. Chris-Craft Industries, Inc., 430 U.S. 1 (1977); Cort v. Ash, 422 U.S. 66, 78 (1975).

Those who breach their fiduciary duties seldom disclose their intentions ahead of time. Yet under the majority's reasoning the failure to inform stockholders of a proposed defalcation gives rise to a cause of action under 10b–5. Thus, the majority has neatly undone the holdings of *Green, Piper* and *Cort* by creating a federal cause of action for a breach of fiduciary duty that will apply in all cases, save for those rare instances where the fiduciary denounces himself in advance.

If the defendants have looted UGO in the manner alleged by the plaintiffs, a full recovery should not be difficult to obtain. Under New York state law, this would be a breach of the fiduciary duty imposed upon directors. My dissent is not based upon any desire to insulate such business practices from legal redress, but upon the fact that the plaintiff has chosen the wrong forum.

* * *

SCHREIBER v. BURLINGTON NORTHERN, INC.

Supreme Court of the United States, 1985.
472 U.S. 1, 105 S.Ct. 2458, 86 L.Ed.2d 1.

CHIEF JUSTICE BURGER delivered the opinion of the Court.

We granted certiorari to resolve a conflict in the Circuits over whether misrepresentation or nondisclosure is a necessary element of a violation of § 14(e) of the Securities Exchange Act of 1934.

---

10. An individual suit by Goldberg under 10b–5 would appear to founder on the purchaser-seller requirement of Blue Chip Stamps v. Manor Drug Stores, 421 U.S. 723 (1975).

11. To the contrary, the high price of UGO stock would appear to be a benefit to the corporation. Furthermore, it is hardly fitting for Goldberg to seek equitable remedies on the ground that, properly informed,

he could have unloaded his stock on some unsuspecting third party. Of course, if Goldberg told the truth to the prospective purchaser, a sale was unlikely. Very few, except those interested in purchasing stockholder suits, would be willing to invest in a company after the controlling shareholders have announced an intention to loot it.

I

On December 21, 1982, Burlington Northern, Inc., made a hostile tender offer for El Paso Gas Co. Through a wholly owned subsidiary, Burlington proposed to purchase 25.1 million El Paso shares at $24 per share. Burlington reserved the right to terminate the offer if any of several specified events occurred. El Paso management initially opposed the takeover, but its shareholders responded favorably, fully subscribing the offer by the December 30, 1982 deadline.

Burlington did not accept those tendered shares; instead, after negotiations with El Paso management, Burlington announced on January 10, 1983, the terms of a new and friendly takeover agreement. Pursuant to the new agreement, Burlington undertook, *inter alia,* to (1) rescind the December tender offer, (2) purchase 4,166,667 shares from El Paso at $24 per share, (3) substitute a new tender offer for only 21 million shares at $24 per share, (4) provide procedural protections against a squeeze-out merger [1] of the remaining El Paso shareholders, and (5) recognize "golden parachute" [2] contracts between El Paso and four of its senior officers. By February 8, more than 40 million shares were tendered in response to Burlington's January offer, and the takeover was completed.

The rescission of the first tender offer caused a diminished payment to those shareholders who had tendered during the first offer. The January offer was greatly oversubscribed and consequently those shareholders who retendered were subject to substantial proration. Petitioner Barbara Schreiber filed suit on behalf of herself and similarly situated shareholders, alleging that Burlington, El Paso, and members of El Paso's board violated § 14(e)'s prohibition of "fraudulent, deceptive or manipulative acts or practices * * * in connection with any tender offer." 15 U.S.C. § 78n(e). She claimed that Burlington's withdrawal of the December tender offer coupled with the substitution of the January tender offer was a "manipulative" distortion of the market for El Paso stock. Schreiber also alleged that

---

1. A "squeeze-out" merger occurs when Corporation A, which holds a controlling interest in Corporation B, uses its control to merge B into itself or into a wholly owned subsidiary. The minority shareholders in Corporation B are, in effect, forced to sell their stock. The procedural protection provided in the agreement between El Paso and Burlington required the approval of non-Burlington members of El Paso's board of directors before a squeeze-out merger could proceed. Burlington eventually purchased all the remaining shares of El Paso for $12 cash and one quarter share of Burlington preferred stock per share. The parties dispute whether this consideration was equal to that paid to those tendering during the January tender offer.

2. Petitioner alleged in her complaint that respondent Burlington failed to disclose that four officers of El Paso had entered into "golden parachute" agreements with El Paso for "extended employment benefits in the event El Paso should be taken over, which benefits would give them millions of dollars of extra compensation." The term "golden parachute" refers generally to agreements between a corporation and its top officers which guarantee those officers continued employment, payment of a lump sum, or other benefits in the event of a change of corporate ownership. As described in the Schedule 14D–9 filed by El Paso with the Commission on January 12, 1983, El Paso entered into "employment agreements" with two of its officers for a period of not less than five years, and with two other officers for a period of three years. The Schedule 14D–9 also disclosed that El Paso's Deferred Compensation Plan had been amended "to provide that for the purposes of such Plan a participant shall be deemed to have retired at the instance of the Company if his duties as a director, officer or employee of the Company have been diminished or curtailed by the Company in any material respect."

Burlington violated § 14(e) by failing in the January offer to disclose the "golden parachutes" offered to four of El Paso's managers. She claims that this January nondisclosure was a deceptive act forbidden by § 14(e).

The District Court dismissed the suit for failure to state a claim. 568 F.Supp. 197 (Del.1983). The District Court reasoned that the alleged manipulation did not involve a misrepresentation, and so did not violate § 14(e). The District Court relied on the fact that in cases involving alleged violations of § 10(b) of the Securities Exchange Act, this Court has required misrepresentation for there to be a "manipulative" violation of the section. 568 F.Supp., at 202.

The Court of Appeals for the Third Circuit affirmed. 731 F.2d 163 (1984). The Court of Appeals held that the acts alleged did not violate the Williams Act, because "§ 14(e) was not intended to create a federal cause of action for all harms suffered because of the proffering or the withdrawal of tender offers." Id., at 165. The Court of Appeals reasoned that § 14(e) was "enacted principally as a disclosure statute, designed to insure that fully-informed investors could intelligently decide how to respond to a tender offer." Id., at 165–166. It concluded that the "arguable breach of contract" alleged by petitioner was not a "manipulative act" under § 14(e).

We granted certiorari to resolve the conflict,[3] 469 U.S. 815 (1984). We affirm.

II

A

We are asked in this case to interpret § 14(e) of the Securities Exchange Act. The starting point is the language of the statute. Section 14(e) provides:

"It shall be unlawful for any person to make any untrue statement of a material fact or omit to state any material fact necessary in order to make the statements made, in the light of the circumstances under which they are made, not misleading, or to engage in any fraudulent, deceptive or manipulative acts or practices, in connection with any tender offer or request or invitation for tenders, or any solicitation of security holders in opposition to or in favor of any such offer, request, or invitation. The Commission shall, for the purposes of this subsection, by rules and regulations define, and prescribe means reasonably designed to prevent, such acts and practices as are fraudulent, deceptive, or manipulative." 15 U.S.C. § 78n(e).

Petitioner relies on a construction of the phrase, "fraudulent, deceptive or manipulative acts or practices." Petitioner reads the phrase "fraudulent, deceptive or manipulative acts or practices" to include acts which, although fully disclosed, "artificially" affect the price of the takeover target's stock. Petitioner's interpretation relies on the belief that § 14(e) is

---

3. The Court of Appeals for the Sixth Circuit has held that manipulation does not always require an element of misrepresentation or nondisclosure. Mobil Corp. v. Marathon Oil Co., 669 F.2d 366 (1981), cert. denied, 455 U.S. 982 (1982). The Court of Appeals for the Second and Eighth Circuits have applied an analysis consistent with the one we apply today. Feldbaum v. Avon Products, Inc., 741 F.2d 234 (CA8 1984); Buffalo Forge Co. v. Ogden Corp., 717 F.2d 757 (CA2), cert. denied, 464 U.S. 1018 (1983); Data Probe Acquisition Corp. v. Datalab, Inc., 722 F.2d 1 (CA2 1983), cert. denied 465 U.S. 1052 (1984).

directed at purposes broader than providing full and true information to investors.

Petitioner's reading of the term "manipulative" conflicts with the normal meaning of the term. We have held in the context of an alleged violation of § 10(b) of the Securities Exchange Act:

"Use of the word 'manipulative' is especially significant. It is and was virtually a term of art when used in connection with the securities markets. It connotes intentional or willful conduct *designed to deceive or defraud* investors by controlling or artificially affecting the price of securities." Ernst & Ernst v. Hochfelder, 425 U.S. 185, 199 (1976) (emphasis added).

Other cases interpreting the term reflect its use as a general term comprising a range of misleading practices:

"The term refers generally to practices, such as wash sales, matched orders, or rigged prices, that are intended to mislead investors by artificially affecting market activity. * * * Section 10(b)'s general prohibition of practices deemed by the SEC to be 'manipulative'—in this technical sense of artifically affecting market activity in order to mislead investors—is fully consistent with the fundamental purpose of the 1934 Act ' "to substitute a philosophy of full disclosure for the philosophy of *caveat emptor* * * *." ' * * * Indeed, nondisclosure is usually essential to the success of a manipulative scheme. * * * No doubt Congress meant to prohibit the full range of ingenious devices that might be used to manipulate securities prices. But we do not think it would have chosen this 'term of art' if it had meant to bring within the scope of § 10(b) instances of corporate mismanagement such as this, in which the essence of the complaint is that shareholders were treated unfairly by a fiduciary." Santa Fe Industries, Inc. v. Green, 430 U.S. 462, 476–477 (1977).

The meaning the Court has given the term "manipulative" is consistent with the use of the term at common law,[4] and with its traditional dictionary definition.

She argues, however, that the term manipulative takes on a meaning in § 14(e) that is different from the meaning it has in § 10(b). Petitioner claims that the use of the disjunctive "or" in § 14(e) implies that acts need not be deceptive or fraudulent to be manipulative. But Congress used the phrase "manipulative or deceptive" in § 10(b) as well, and we have interpreted "manipulative" in that context to require misrepresentation. Moreover, it is a " 'familiar principle of statutory construction that words grouped in a list should be given related meaning.' " Securities Indus. Assn. v. Board of Governors, 468 U.S. 207, 218 (1984). All three species of misconduct, i.e., "fraudulent, deceptive or manipulative," listed by Congress are directed at failures to disclose. The use of the term "manipulative"

---

4. See generally, L. Loss, Securities Regulation 984–989 (3d ed. 1983). For example, the seminal English case of Scott v. Brown, Doering, McNab & Co., [1892] 2 Q.B. 724 (C.A.), which broke new ground in recognizing that manipulation could occur without the dissemination of false statements, nonetheless placed emphasis on the presence of deception. As Lord Lopes stated in that case, "I can see no substantial distinction between false rumours and false and fictitious acts." Id., at 730. See also, United States v. Brown, 5 F.Supp. 81, 85, (SDNY 1933) ("[E]ven a speculator is entitled not to have any present fact involving the subject matter of his speculative purchase or the price thereof misrepresented by word or act").

provides emphasis and guidance to those who must determine which types of acts are reached by the statute; it does not suggest a deviation from the section's facial and primary concern with disclosure or Congressional concern with disclosure which is the core of the Act.

B

Our conclusion that "manipulative" acts under § 14(e) require misrepresentation or nondisclosure is buttressed by the purpose and legislative history of the provision. Section 14(e) was originally added to the Securities Exchange Act as part of the Williams Act, 82 Stat. 457. "The purpose of the Williams Act is to insure that public shareholders who are confronted by a cash tender offer for their stock will not be required to respond without adequate information." Rondeau v. Mosinee Paper Corp., 422 U.S. 49, 58 (1975).

It is clear that Congress relied primarily on disclosure to implement the purpose of the Williams Act. Senator Williams, the Bill's Senate sponsor, stated in the debate:

"Today, the public shareholder in deciding whether to accept or reject a tender offer possess limited information. No matter what he does, he acts without adequate knowledge to enable him to decide rationally what is the best course of action. This is precisely the dilemma which our securities laws are designed to prevent." 113 Cong.Rec. 24664 (1967) (Remarks of Sen. Williams).

The expressed legislative intent was to preserve a neutral setting in which the contenders could fully present their arguments. The Senate sponsor went on to say:

"We have taken extreme care to avoid tipping the scales either in favor of management or in favor of the person making the takeover bids. S. 510 is designed solely to require full and fair disclosure for the benefit of investors. The bill will at the same time provide the offeror and management equal opportunity to present their case." Ibid.

To implement this objective, the Williams Act added §§ 13(d), 13(e), 14(d), 14(e), and 14(f) to the Securities Exchange Act. Some relate to disclosure; §§ 13(d), 14(d) and 14(f) all add specific registration and disclosure provisions. Others—§§ 13(e) and 14(d)—require or prohibit certain acts so that investors will possess additional time within which to take advantage of the disclosed information.

Section 14(e) adds a "broad antifraud prohibition," Piper v. Chris Craft Industries, 430 U.S. 1, 24 (1977), modeled on the antifraud provisions of § 10(b) of the Act and Rule 10b–5, 17 CFR § 240.10(b)–5 (1984).[10] It supplements the more precise disclosure provisions found elsewhere in the

---

10. * * *

Because of the textual similarities, it is often assumed that § 14(e) was modeled on § 10(b) and Rule 10b–5. See, e.g., Panter v. Marshall Field & Co., 646 F.2d 271, 283 (CA7), cert. denied 454 U.S. 1092 (1981). For the purpose of interpreting the term "manipulative," the most significant changes from the language of § 10(b) were the addition of the term "fraudulent," and

the reference to "acts" rather than "devices." Neither change bears in any obvious way on the meaning to be given to "manipulative."

Similar terminology is also found in § 15(c) of the Securities Exchange Act, 15 U.S.C. § 780(c), § 17(a) of the Securities Act of 1933, 15 U.S.C. § 77q, and § 206 of the Investment Advisers Act of 1940, 15 U.S.C. § 80b–6.

Williams Act, while requiring disclosure more explicitly addressed to the tender offer context than that required by § 10(b).

While legislative history specifically concerning § 14(e) is sparse, the House and Senate Reports discuss the role of § 14(e). Describing § 14(e) as regulating "fraudulent transactions," and stating the thrust of the section:

"This provision would affirm the fact that persons engaged in making or opposing tender offers or otherwise seeking to influence the decision of investors or the outcome of the tender offer are under an obligation to make *full disclosure* of material information to those with whom they deal." H.R.Rep. No. 1711, 90th Cong., 2d Sess., 11 (1968) (emphasis added); S.R.Rep. No. 550, 90th Cong., 1st Sess., 11 (1967) (emphasis added).

Nowhere in the legislative history is there the slightest suggestion that § 14(e) serves any purpose other than disclosure,[11] or that the term "manipulative" should be read as an invitation to the courts to oversee the substantive fairness of tender offers; the quality of any offer is a matter for the marketplace.

To adopt the reading of the term "manipulative" urged by petitioner would not only be unwarranted in light of the legislative purpose but would be at odds with it. Inviting judges to read the term "manipulative" with their own sense of what constitutes "unfair" or "artificial" conduct would inject uncertainty into the tender offer process. An essential piece of information—whether the court would deem the fully disclosed actions of one side or the other to be "manipulative"—would not be available until after the tender offer had closed. This uncertainty would directly contradict the expressed Congressional desire to give investors full information.

Congress' consistent emphasis on disclosure persuades us that it intended takeover contests to be addressed to shareholders. In pursuit of this goal, Congress, consistent with the core mechanism of the Securities Exchange Act, created sweeping disclosure requirements and narrow substantive safeguards. The same Congress that placed such emphasis on shareholder choice would not at the same time have required judges to oversee tender offers for substantive fairness. It is even less likely that a Congress implementing that intention would express it only through the use of a single word placed in the middle of a provision otherwise devoted to disclosure.

C

We hold that the term "manipulative" as used in § 14(e) requires misrepresentation or nondisclosure. It connotes "conduct designed to

---

11. The Act was amended in 1970, and Congress added to § 14(e) the sentence, "The Commission shall, for the purposes of this subsection, by rules and regulations define, and prescribe means reasonably designed to prevent, such acts and practices as are fraudulent, deceptive, or manipulative." Petitioner argues that this phrase would be pointless if § 14(e) was concerned with disclosure only.

We disagree. In adding the 1970 amendment, Congress simply provided a mechanism for defining and guarding against those acts and practices which involve material misrepresentation or nondisclosure. The amendment gives the Securities and Exchange Commission latitude to regulate nondeceptive activities as a "reasonably designed" means of preventing manipulative acts, without suggesting any change in the meaning of the term "manipulative" itself.

deceive or defraud investors by controlling or artificially affecting the price of securities." Ernst & Ernst v. Hochfelder, 425 U.S., at 199. Without misrepresentation or nondisclosure, § 14(e) has not been violated.

Applying that definition to this case, we hold that the actions of respondents were not manipulative. The amended complaint fails to allege that the cancellation of the first tender offer was accompanied by any misrepresentation, nondisclosure or deception. The District Court correctly found, "All activity of the defendants that could have conceivably affected the price of El Paso shares was done openly." 568 F.Supp., at 203.

Petitioner also alleges that El Paso management and Burlington entered into certain undisclosed and deceptive agreements during the making of the second tender offer. The substance of the allegations is that, in return for certain undisclosed benefits, El Paso managers agreed to support the second tender offer. But both courts noted that petitioner's complaint seeks redress only for injuries related to the cancellation of the first tender offer. Since the deceptive and misleading acts alleged by the petitioner all occurred with reference to the making of the second tender offer—when the injuries suffered by petitioner had already been sustained—these acts bear no possible causal relationship to petitioner's alleged injuries. The Court of Appeals dealt correctly with this claim.

III

The judgment of the Court of Appeals is

Affirmed.

JUSTICE POWELL took no part in the decision of this case. JUSTICE O'CONNOR took no part in the consideration or decision of this case.

RULE 10b–5 AS A REMEDY FOR MISMANAGEMENT

The currently most unsettled area with respect to Rule 10b–5 litigation is the question of the extent to which complaints essentially about mismanagement or self-dealing by the controllers of a corporation will be cognizable under Rule 10b–5. The effort of plaintiffs' counsel to bring virtually all such litigation under the Rule has engendered the confusion evidenced by the foregoing cases and many others.

Why Rule 10b–5? If the facts alleged were true, in many of the cases of this sort the shareholders of the corporation would have had an action, either direct or derivative, to redress the alleged wrongs committed by the controllers in the State court. Why were they brought under Rule 10b–5? The answer lies in the procedural advantages from the point of view of the plaintiff of an action under the Securities Exchange Act of 1934.

First, and probably most important, if the action is characterized as a derivative action, the plaintiff, as was held in McClure v. Borne Chemical Co.,[1] is not subject to a State security-for-expenses statute applicable to such actions. While the Second Circuit held in Phelps v. Burnham [2] that the bond requirement would still be applicable to any pendent state cause of action, the amount

---

1. 292 F.2d 824 (3d Cir.1961), cert. denied 368 U.S. 939 (1961). Accord, Epstein v. Solitron Devices, Inc., 388 F.2d 310 (2d Cir.1968).

2. 327 F.2d 812 (2d Cir.1964).

required would probably be influenced by the fact that the defense of the State claim would be largely duplicatory of the defense of the federal claim;[3] and in any event the pendent State cause of action is a precautionary device which can be dropped if necessary. It has also been held that the requirement of Rule 23.1 of the Federal Rules of Civil Procedure for a demand on the shareholders, "if necessary", would not apply to a derivative action based on Rule 10b–5, since the shareholders could not ratify a violation of the Federal securities laws.[4] However, the United States Supreme Court in Bangor Punta Operations, Inc. v. Bangor & Aroostook Railroad Co.[5] held that the requirement of contemporaneous ownership by the plaintiff to maintain a derivative action applies in a Rule 10b–5 action.

Second, the plaintiff has the advantage of the nationwide service of process provided for in the 1934 Act[6] and the important ability to bring the action anywhere any part of the "act or transaction" complained of occurred.[7]

Third, in the case of a non-derivative action, the Federal Rules relating to class actions may well be more liberal than under the State law and may permit the plaintiff's lawyer to attempt to represent a large number of persons who have not hired him and thereby enhance the possibility of a large fee at the end of the lawsuit.[8] Although the Federal District Judges initially attempted to impose some limits upon the availability of class actions under the revised Rule 23,[9] the appellate decisions have uniformly been in favor of the allowance of such actions in securities cases, as illustrated by Green v. Wolf Corp.[10] and by Eisen v. Carlisle & Jacquelin[11] which permitted a class action on behalf of 3,750,000 odd-lot buyers against the odd-lot dealers on the NYSE. However, the Third Circuit finally called a halt when a shareholder of four mutual funds wanted to bring a class action on behalf, not only of all the shareholders of those four funds, but

---

3. In the *Phelps* case, the Second Circuit rejected the contention that no bond whatever should be required for the pendent state claim, because it would involve the defendants in *no* additional expense, as "both wrong and self-defeating. It is wrong because the state claim broadly challenges the motivation and judgment of the directors, * * * whereas the federal claim, by necessity, is simply that the transaction * * * has not been properly disclosed. It is self-defeating because if the scope of the two claims was really the same, appellant would lose nothing by being confined to the federal one." 327 F.2d at 814. However, because of the procedural posture of the case, the court did not reach the question whether the amount of the bond required by the District Judge was excessive; and the opinion suggests that the amount of the "overlap" may be a factor to be taken into consideration.

4. Dopp v. American Electronic Laboratories, Inc., 55 F.R.D. 151 (S.D.N.Y.1972); Jannes v. Microwave Communications, Inc., 57 F.R.D. 18 (N.D.Ill.1972).

5. 417 U.S. 703 (1974).

6. § 27, Securities Exchange Act of 1934.

7. Ibid. See Zorn v. Anderson, 263 F.Supp. 745 (S.D.N.Y.1966).

8. In Polakoff v. Delaware Steeplechase & Race Association, 254 F.Supp. 574 (D.Del.1966), Judge Bartels dryly observed that "Obviously, the plaintiffs would prefer to cast their suit in the form of a true class action because such a classification would afford them an opportunity to represent a number of absent stockholders whom they might not otherwise represent." And, while a "spurious" class action may not be as desirable as a "true" class action from the plaintiff's lawyer's point of view, it is better than no class action at all.

9. See Fischer v. Kletz, 41 F.R.D. 377 (S.D.N.Y.1966); Richland v. Cheatham, 272 F.Supp. 148 (S.D.N.Y.1967); Kronenberg v. Hotel Governor Clinton, Inc., CCH Fed.Sec. Law Reptr. ¶ 92,007 (S.D.N.Y.1967); Dolgow v. Anderson, 43 F.R.D. 472, CCH (S.D. N.Y.1968).

10. 406 F.2d 291 (2d Cir.1968), cert. denied 395 U.S. 977 (1969).

11. 391 F.2d 555 (2d Cir.1968).

also of all the shareholders of 61 other funds who were allegedly "similarly situated." [12] Finally, the United States Supreme Court held in a subsequent appeal in the *Eisen* case (the so-called Eisen III decision) [13] that individual notice had to be mailed to each prospective member of the plaintiff class, rather than merely publishing notice, and that the cost of such notice had to be borne entirely by the plaintiff (as a practical matter probably by his lawyer). Although the cost of such notice in that particular case made the continuation of the litigation prohibitively expensive, it is doubtful that this additional cost to the plaintiff would be the determining factor in most cases. [14]

Fourth, the decision of the United States Supreme Court in Ross v. Bernhard [15] permits the plaintiff to demand a jury trial in a derivative action in any case in which the corporation, if it had been suing in its own right, would have been entitled to a jury. [16]

IN CONNECTION WITH THE PURCHASE OR SALE OF A SECURITY

Rule 10b–5 proscribes the various activities with which it deals only when they are employed "in connection with the purchase or sale" of securities. While many corporate mismanagement charges do not, at least on the face of things, involve any purchase or sale of securities, many others are part and parcel of a corporate transaction which involves either the issuance or the repurchase of its own securities by the corporation or the purchase or sale of the securities of another corporate entity by the corporation.

Issuance of Its Own Securities. In the leading case of Hooper v. Mountain States Securities Corp. [17] it was decided that the issuance of its own securities by a corporation was a "sale" within the meaning of Rule 10b–5 (and, of course, a "purchase" by the other party to the transaction), and this holding has been followed by all of the cases where the issue has subsequently arisen. [18]

Any acquisition by a corporation in a merger or sale of assets transaction, where the consideration is the issuance of securities by the acquiring corporation, involves a sale and a purchase. In Securities and Exchange Commission v. National Securities, Inc. [19] the United States Supreme Court held that such a

---

12. Kauffman v. The Dreyfus Fund, Inc., 434 F.2d 727 (3d Cir.1970), cert. denied 401 U.S. 974 (1971).

13. 417 U.S. 156 (1974).

14. The plaintiff's lawyer, by settling early with one or more defendants, frequently obtains a "war chest" to finance the continuation of the litigation against the remaining defendants.

15. 396 U.S. 531 (1970).

16. This decision may be a two-edged sword. We understand that some defendant's counsel, if the plaintiff's complaint survives a motion for summary judgment, immediately file a demand for a jury trial, to increase the expense to plaintiff's counsel (who is financing the litigation) and the delay until he can contemplate receiving any return. The possibility of a reasonable settlement is thought to be thereby increased. If a settlement is not achieved, they consider that their chances before a

jury are as good or better than before a Federal Judge.

17. 282 F.2d 195 (5th Cir.1960), cert. denied 365 U.S. 814 (1961).

18. Bailes v. Colonial Press, Inc., 444 F.2d 1241 (5th Cir.1971); Ruckle v. Roto American Corp., 339 F.2d 24 (2d Cir.1964); Dauphin Corp. v. Redwall Corp., 201 F.Supp. 466 (D.Del.1962); Kane v. Central American Mining & Oil, Inc., 235 F.Supp. 559 (S.D.N.Y.1964); Simon v. New Haven Board & Carton Co., 250 F.Supp. 297 (D.Conn.1966); Pappas v. Moss, 257 F.Supp. 345 (D.N.J.1966); Heilbrunn v. Hanover Equities Corp., 259 F.Supp. 936 (S.D.N.Y.1966); Stoner v. Ford, CCH Fed. Sec.Law Reptr. ¶ 94,950 (N.D.Okla.1974).

19. 393 U.S. 453 (1969). See, also, Dasho v. Susquehanna Corp., 380 F.2d 262 (7th Cir.1967), cert. denied 389 U.S. 977 (1967). Cohen v. Colvin, 266 F.Supp. 677 (S.D.N.Y.1967), held that a sale of assets

transaction was a "sale" for the purposes of Rule 10b–5 even when former Rule 133 had adopted the "no sale theory" for the purposes of determining the applicability of the registration provisions of the 1933 Act. When the consideration given to the shareholders of the acquired corporation is cash, as it typically is in the case of a "short form" merger of a subsidiary, the transaction would still involve a sale of their securities in the acquired corporation for cash. Even when the minority shareholders of a subsidiary have no choice in the matter, as in the case of a "short form merger", they will be treated as "forced sellers." [20]

Repurchase of Its Own Securities. Clearly the repurchase by a corporation of its own outstanding securities involves a purchase and sale. Cochran v. Channing Corp.[21] held that a repurchase by a corporation of its own shares could be the basis of an action under Rule 10b–5. In fact, many of the early non-disclosure cases discussed above involved a purchase of minority shares by the issuing corporation, rather than by the controlling shareholders, while there existed allegedly material, non-disclosed inside information.[22] Obviously, whether the "insiders" purchase themselves, or have the corporation purchase and thereby increase their percentage ownership, should not make any difference in that type of case.

Purchase or Sale of Portfolio Securities. As held by the Supreme Court in the *Superintendent of Insurance* case, a sale of other securities by the corporation or a purchase of such securities may be the basis for a derivative action by a shareholder on behalf of the corporation under Rule 10b–5. In Jannes v. Microwave Communications, Inc.,[23] the Seventh Circuit held that jurisdiction existed in a derivative action under Rule 10b–5 where it was alleged that a corporation fraudulently transferred assets in exchange for 25% of the stock of another corporation. And in Baylor v. Mading-Dugan Drug Co.[24] the court reached the same result where it was alleged that certain persons who gained control of an insurance company had caused it to liquidate its municipal bond portfolio and purchase over-valued stock of corporations owned or controlled by the defendants.

Sale of Control. The *Superintendent of Insurance* case involved a so-called "sale of control" question insofar as the defendant Bankers Life and Casualty Company was concerned. The typical "sale of control" case has usually involved either a claim that the seller received a "premium" which he should share with the minority shareholders or that the corporation was in some manner harmed by the conduct of the new controller, which result should have been foreseen by the seller. Most of the litigation under Rule 10b–5 in this connection has run into the obstacle of the "Birnbaum rule", now fully reaffirmed by the Supreme Court in the *Blue Chip Stamps* case (see chapter 16,

---

for stock in a "C" type reorganization, followed by a dissolution of the selling corporation and the distribution of the stock received to its shareholders, did not involve any "sale" of the stock by the corporation buying the assets to the shareholders of the selling corporation, at least where there was no commitment on the part of the selling corporation to liquidate. However, Filmways, Inc. v. Artistic Liquidating Corp., CCH Fed.Sec.Law Reptr. ¶ 92,332 (S.D.N.Y.1969), held that an issuance by a corporation of its shares is a "sale" under Rule 10b–5 and stated: "The same is true of an exchange of stock for assets, * * * and of a stock for stock exchange * * *."

The *Cohen* case would probably not be followed today.

20. Vine v. Beneficial Finance Co., Inc., 374 F.2d 627 (2d Cir.1967), cert. denied 389 U.S. 970 (1967).

21. 211 F.Supp. 239 (S.D.N.Y.1962). See, also, Mutual Shares Corp. v. Genesco, Inc., 384 F.2d 540 (2d Cir.1967) (the problem there was that the plaintiffs had not been the ones who had sold).

22. See pp. 1043–1044, supra.

23. 461 F.2d 525 (7th Cir.1972).

24. 57 F.R.D. 509 (N.D.Ill.1972).

infra).[25] While obviously there has been a sale of stock by the prior controller to the new controller, neither the minority shareholders nor the corporation have purchased or sold any stock and under the Birnbaum rule have no standing to sue under Rule 10b–5.[26]

However, the *Superintendent of Insurance* case held that there was jurisdiction under Rule 10b–5 where there was a sale of control followed by a corporate securities transaction injurious to the corporation or its shareholders (the sale of the corporation's treasury bonds with the proceeds abstracted by the new controllers to use to pay the purchase price for the stock). Of course, any securities transaction by the corporation in which there is a violation by the other party of Rule 10b–5 permits a shareholder to sue derivatively on behalf of the corporation those who were parties to the wrongful transaction. The important point here is that he may also sue the seller of control if he can legally be held responsible for subsequent conduct of the buyer. When the Supreme Court says that "we make no ruling" on the argument of Bankers Life that the complaint did not allege "any connection between it and the fraud," it must mean merely that it is not considering the substantive question of whether the subsequent conduct of the buyer was sufficiently foreseeable by the seller to render him liable—not the question whether he can be sued under Rule 10b–5. Otherwise, the court would have been refusing to rule on the only question which brought the case all the way up to it. The Second Circuit's subsequent en banc reversal of the panel's decision in Drachman v. Harvey[27] indicates that it so understands the Supreme Court's opinion.

In order for Bankers Life to be liable it would have to be shown to have some knowledge of or participation in the new controller's wrongful conduct or that such wrongful conduct was reasonably foreseeable by it when it sold control. When the case was finally settled, the Federal District Court quoted from the report of the Referee appointed by the State court to consider the reasonableness of the settlement to that effect that: "Banker's Life, Manhattan's sole stockholder, which sold its Manhattan stock to Begole for $5,000,000, consisting of an Irving Trust check, is not shown by any evidence in the voluminous depositions and exhibits to have had any knowledge of the fact that the actual source of the $5,000,000 it received

---

25. See Birnbaum v. Newport Steel Corp., 193 F.2d 461 (1952), cert. denied 343 U.S. 956; Haberman v. Murchison, 468 F.2d 1305 (2d Cir.1972); Erling v. Powell, 429 F.2d 795 (8th Cir.1970); Simmons v. Wolfson, 428 F.2d 455, cert. denied 400 U.S. 999 (6th Cir.1970); Smith v. Murchison, 310 F.Supp. 1079 (S.D.N.Y.1970).

26. The plaintiff in such a case faces the further obstacle that there is little or no authority that a mere sale of control at a "premium" confers any right upon the minority shareholders, absent allegations of a sale of corporate office or some subsequent foreseeable harm to the corporation and absent any purchase of the minority shares at a lesser price without revealing the premium paid to the control party. As Judge Pollack said in Christophides v. Porco, 289 F.Supp. 403, at 405 (S.D.N.Y. 1968), a controlling shareholder has a legal

right to a premium "which reflects merely the control potential of that stock."

27. 453 F.2d 722 (2d Cir.1972). The distinction may seem gossamer between a case where there is a sale of control and the new controller merely steals $5,000,000 from the corporate till [Cooper v. Garza, 431 F.2d 578 (5th Cir.1970); cf. Birnbaum v. Newport Steel Corp., supra, note 25] and a case where there is a sale of control and the new controller sells $5,000,000 of the corporation's securities and then steals the proceeds [the Superintendent of Insurance case], but that is where the law apparently stands at the moment. For cases in accord with the Superintendent of Insurance case, see Shell v. Hensley, 430 F.2d 819 (5th Cir. 1970); Herpich v. Wallace, 430 F.2d 792 (5th Cir.1970); Herpich v. Wilder, 430 F.2d 818 (5th Cir.1970), cert. denied 401 U.S. 947 (1971).

would be Manhattan's own assets or to have participated in or been connected with the fraud."[28]

The sale of control may also be followed by a purchase of the minority stock at a price lower than that paid for the controlling block, with or without disclosure to the other shareholders of the existence of the control premium. In Christophides v. Porco[29] Judge Pollack held that a complaint alleging that defendants paid a premium for a controlling block of stock and then made a tender offer for the remaining shares at a lesser price did not state a cause of action under Rule 10b–5. However, it would seem that the plaintiff's problem in that case was that he had no cause of action at all, since there was no allegation that the existence of the premium was not fully revealed to the other shareholders. On the other hand, it would seem equally clear that a cause of action under Rule 10b–5 would be stated against the buyer, and under some circumstances against the seller as an "aider and abettor," if it were alleged that the existence of the premium was concealed from the other sellers.

THE REQUIREMENT OF "DECEPTION" IN CONNECTION WITH THE PURCHASE OR SALE

Rule 14a–9 dealing with proxy statements outlaws statements which are false or misleading, as previously noted, and in addition requires the correction of statements contained in previous communications which have become false or misleading. Section 14(e) dealing with tender offers also prohibits false and misleading statements and contains the additional prohibition of "any fraudulent, deceptive, or manipulative acts or practices." All of these three additional phrases seem to contemplate deception of some kind, although they perhaps suggest that the victim is misled by acts rather than by oral or written communications. However, Rule 10b–5 contains the additional prohibitions in clauses (1) and (3), copied from Section 17(a) of the 1933 Act, making it unlawful for a person

"(1) to employ any device, scheme, or artifice to defraud, [or]

"(3) to engage in any act, practice, or course of business which operates or would operate as a fraud or deceit upon any person."

While these clauses multiply the synonyms used to describe the method by which the proscribed end is accomplished, they both come down to "fraud" as what is prohibited. Whatever the means used, under clause (1) it must be a means "to defraud" and under clause (3) it must result in a "fraud or deceit." Is just plain stealing "fraud"? The Superintendent of Insurance case would seem to say, yes, since the only real complaint about Mr. Begole's conduct in that case was that he stole the money received from the sale of the corporation's bond portfolio, although the court notes that the board of directors of the

---

28. Superintendent of Insurance v. Bankers Life and Casualty Co., 401 F.Supp. 640 (S.D.N.Y.1975). In the light of this fact, it is a commentary on the institution which we call a "system of justice" that Bankers Life had been forced to defend itself through over a decade of litigation all the way up to the Supreme Court, and presumably contributed something to the $1,000,000 settlement given to the plaintiff to stop further ruinous costs of litigation.

29. 289 F.Supp. 403 (S.D.N.Y.1968). The suggestion made by Judge Bonsal in Ferraioli v. Cantor, 281 F.Supp. 354 (S.D. N.Y.1967), that the fact that the seller of control offered the right to sell their shares to some other shareholders, but not to all, would confer jurisdiction under Rule 10b–5, was repudiated by the Second Circuit in Haberman v. Murchison, supra, note 25.

corporation were "allegedly deceived" because Mr. Begole didn't tell them in advance that he was going to steal. Is an allegedly "unfair" deal forced upon the minority shareholders by the controlling shareholder "fraud"? That would seem to be the issue presented by the *Santa Fe Industries* case, as it was by the earlier case of Popkin v. Bishop,[30] which seems to have been resurrected by the Supreme Court decision. The *Popkin* case had held that there must be some kind of "deception" involved in order for a transaction to violate Rule 10b–5.

Hooper v. Mountain States Securities Corp.[31] and most of the earlier cases dealing with the issuance of stock for no consideration or for inadequate consideration spoke of the corporation being "defrauded" in connection with the sale, without pausing even to consider whether anybody had made any misrepresentations to anyone else.[32] The word "defraud" was apparently used in its "modern", scientific sense of "do something bad to." In O'Neill v. Maytag [33] the court held that where its own stock was allegedly repurchased by a corporation for excessive consideration and for improper purposes, no cause of action was stated under Rule 10b–5 because the entire board of directors was allegedly implicated and therefore no "deception" was involved.[34] However, the Seventh Circuit in Dasho v. Susquehanna Corp.[35] and the Third Circuit in Pappas v. Moss [36] refused to accept this limitation. The court stated in Pappas v. Moss: "Certainly the deception of the independent stockholders is no less real because, 'formalistically,' the corporate entity was the victim of the fraud." The Second Circuit then overruled the O'Neill case in Schoenbaum v. First-brook,[37] and the Fifth Circuit has also adopted the same rule in Rekant v. Desser.[38] Therefore, it seems to be established that the entire Board of Directors may "defraud" (i.e., "do something bad to") the corporation.

Bailes v. Colonial Press, Inc.[39] case goes further and holds that even if all the existing directors *and shareholders* are implicated, a Rule 10b–5 cause of action is established if, in connection with an issuance of stock by a corporation, they intend to "defraud" *future* shareholders *or creditors* (including the ubiquitous tax collector). The District Court and the Circuit Court opinions in that

---

30. 464 F.2d 714 (2d Cir.1972).

31. Supra, note 17.

32. See, also, Dauphin Corp. v. Redwall Corp.; Kane v. Central American Mining & Oil, Inc.; Pappas v. Moss; all supra note 18. However, in Kremer v. Selheimer, 215 F.Supp. 549 (E.D.Pa.1963), it was held that the mere issuance of shares to promoters at $1 per share at the same time other shares were being sold to the public at $3 per share was not a "fraud" on the corporation under Rule 10b–5. Compare Bailes v. Colonial Press, Inc., supra note 18.

33. 339 F.2d 764 (2d Cir.1964).

34. At almost the same time as the decision in the O'Neill case, the Second Circuit (two of the three judges on the two panels were the same) held in Ruckle v. Roto American Corp., 399 F.2d 24 (2d Cir. 1964), that a cause of action was stated under Rule 10b–5 where it was alleged that a corporation issued stock for an inadequate consideration to some members of the board of directors and that a *minority* of the board was "deceived" in connection

with the transaction. See, also, Weber v. Bartle, 272 F.Supp. 201 (S.D.N.Y.1967); Condon v. Richardson, 275 F.Supp. 943 (S.D.Ill.1967), rev'd 411 F.2d 489 (7th Cir. 1969). However, this proved to be an impossible distinction to maintain; as one court said, under this theory, the greater the number of directors involved in the fraud, the less the resulting liability. Even the lower courts in the Second Circuit couldn't follow this theory. Heilbrunn v. Hanover Equities Corp., 259 F.Supp. 936 (S.D.N.Y.1966); Weitzen v. Kearns, 271 F.Supp. 616 (S.D.N.Y.1967).

35. 380 F.2d 262 (7th Cir.1967).

36. 393 F.2d 865 (3d Cir.1968).

37. 405 F.2d 215 (2d Cir.1968), cert. denied 395 U.S. 906 (1969).

38. 425 F.2d 872 (5th Cir.1970). See, also, Brummer v. Rosenberg, CCH Fed.Sec. Law Rptr. ¶ 92,341 (S.D.N.Y.1969); Bailey v. Meister Brau, Inc., 320 F.Supp. 539 (N.D. Ill.1970).

39. 444 F.2d 1241 (5th Cir.1971).

case are of course a reprise of the debate in the Lewisohn [40] and Bigelow [41] cases under state law, before there ever was a Rule 10b–5, and perhaps illustrate that the more things change, the more they remain the same.

Schoenbaum v. Firstbrook,[42] however, contains an important qualification upon the rule that the entire Board may "defraud" the corporation. That case holds that this rationale only applies if there is a conflict of interest involved and the directors, or some of them, expect to obtain some profit or benefit from the transaction personally (or are the nominees of another corporation which will profit). Therefore, the complaint was dismissed as to one of the transactions complained of, which involved a sale of stock at an allegedly inadequate price to a completely unaffiliated purchaser. This branch of the decision has been followed in two subsequent decisions in the Southern District of New York.[43]

The *Santa Fe Industries* case at first seemed drastically to undercut all of the previous decisions which are discussed above and to relegate shareholders complaining about such corporate mismanagement to an action in state court. This judgment, however, underestimated the ingenuity of the circuit courts and their determination to salvage the holdings in their previous cases. Led by Judge Friendly's opinion in the *Goldberg* case, they quickly seized upon footnote 14 in Justice White's opinion in the *Santa Fe Industries* case and treated it as though it were the entire opinion. That footnote, it will be recalled, stated that the failure to give advance notice of the short-form merger, which was alleged to be a material non-disclosure under Rule 10b–5, was irrelevant because the plaintiffs had not indicated how they could have acted any differently with such notice in view of the fact that under Delaware law "they could not have enjoined the merger because an appraisal proceeding is their sole remedy in Delaware courts for any alleged unfairness in the terms of the merger." (The Delaware Supreme Court shortly thereafter repudiated this statement as an accurate interpretation of Delaware law,[44] and then a few years later repudiated this repudiation and returned to the pre–1977 Delaware law which the Supreme Court had cited in the *Santa Fe* case.)

The circuit courts interpreted this statement as saying, by negative implication, that if the plaintiff had a cause of action to enjoin the merger under state law, then he would also have a cause of action under Rule 10b–5. As Judge Friendly stated in Mayer v. Oil Field Systems Corp.[45] (quoting from Madison Consultants v. F.D.I.C.), the courts of appeals have "unanimously" read the language of footnote 14 in the *Santa Fe* case "to mean that plaintiffs may prove the existence of a means of self-protection by showing that they could have pursued some available state remedy if they had not been deceived." [46] Having

---

40. Old Dominion Copper Mining & Smelting Co. v. Lewisohn, 210 U.S. 206 (1908).

41. Old Dominion Copper Mining & Smelting Co. v. Bigelow, 203 Mass. 159, 89 N.E. 193 (1909), aff'd 225 U.S. 111 (1912).

42. Supra, Note 37.

43. Lewis v. Spiral Metal Co., Inc., 317 F.Supp. 905 (S.D.N.Y.1970); Penn Mart Realty Co. v. Becker, 300 F.Supp. 731 (S.D. N.Y.1969).

44. Singer v. The Magnavox Co., 380 A.2d 969 (Del.1977); Tanzer v. International General Industries, Inc., 379 A.2d 1121 (Del.1977), on remand 402 A.2d 382; Roland International Corp. v. Najjar, 407

A.2d 1032 (Del.1979), all of which were in turn overruled by Weinberger v. UOP, Inc., 457 A.2d 701 (Del.1983).

45. 721 F.2d 59 (2d Cir.1983).

46. See Madison Consultants v. Federal Deposit Insurance Corporation, 710 F.2d 57 (2d Cir.1983); Lockspeiser v. Western Maryland Company, 768 F.2d 558 (4th Cir. 1985); Ray v. Karris, 780 F.2d 636 (7th Cir. 1985); and the cases cited by the Fifth Circuit in the quotation following in the text above; compare Pross v. Katz, 784 F.2d 455 (2d Cir.1986) (a failure to perform an alleged promise by the defendant to perform faithfully his fiduciary duties does not state a claim under the *Santa Fe* case).

thus removed the *Santa Fe Industries* case as any obstacle to what they wished to do, the circuit courts quickly fell into a quarrel among themselves as to whether the plaintiff needed to show only that he had a cause of action to enjoin the merger under state law or would have succeeded in doing so or would probably have succeeded in doing so or "might" have done so. In Alabama Farm Bureau Mutual Casualty Insurance Co., Inc. v. American Fidelity Life Insurance Co.,[47] the Fifth Circuit stated as follows concerning this disagreement:

"*Santa Fe Industries* leaves open the question whether, in addition to showing that he could have brought a suit in the state court, a shareholder must show that he would have prevailed in the state court action. See generally Note, Suits for Breach of Fiduciary Duty Under Rule 10b–5 After Santa Fe Industries, Inc. v. Green, 91 Harv.L.Rev. 1874, 1893–98. The Ninth Circuit has held that he must prove both, [Kidwell ex rel. Penfold v. Meikle, 597 F.2d 1273 (9th Cir.1979)], supra, 597 F.2d at 1294, and the Seventh Circuit appears to have taken a similar approach. Wright v. Heizer Corp. [560 F.2d 236 (7th Cir.1977), cert. denied 434 U.S. 1066 (1978)], supra, 560 F.2d at 250–51. However, in *Goldberg,* supra, the Second Circuit refused to dismiss a claim where a state suit would have been possible, even though there was no allegation that the shareholders would have succeeded. The court did not inquire further into the shareholder's likelihood of success in such a state action.

"We hold that all that is required to establish 10b–5 liability is a showing that state law remedies were available and that the facts shown make out a prima facie case for relief; it is not necessary to go further and prove that the state action would have been successful."

Subsequently, the Third Circuit stated in Healey v. Catalyst Recovery of Pennsylvania, Inc.,[48] that the test was whether there would have been a "reasonable probability of ultimate success" in a state court injunction action brought by the shareholder. On the other hand, the Second Circuit held in Madison Consultants v. Federal Deposit Insurance Corporation [49] that the correct test was whether the plaintiff "would have succeeded" in preventing harm had he employed the state court remedies. The court said: "This standard does not obligate a plaintiff to prove beyond a reasonable doubt or to an absolute certainty that he would have won the state court suit or otherwise prevented the injury that he in fact suffered. He needs to prove only by a fair preponderance of the evidence that he would have succeeded." [50]

This approach, of course, ignores the entire opinion in the *Santa Fe Industries* case except for one footnote, and particularly Part IV of the opinion in which six of the nine justices concurred. That portion of the opinion states that one important factor in determining whether a cause of action will lie under Rule 10b–5 is whether the matter complained of is one which is "traditionally relegated to state law." In other words, it is fair to say that a fundamental thrust of the opinion in the *Santa Fe Industries* case is the philosophy that there is no need to imply a cause of action under Rule 10b–5 with respect to complaints about corporate mismanagement if there is an

---

47. 606 F.2d 602 (5th Cir.1979), reh. denied 610 F.2d 818, cert. denied 446 U.S. 933 (1980). See, however, O'Brien v. Continental Illinois National Bank, 593 F.2d 54 (7th Cir.1979), where the court held that the failure of a trustee to make disclosures to the beneficiary with respect to purchases and sales of securities by the trust could not be the basis for an action under Rule 10b–5, even if the undisclosed information would have prompted the beneficiary to terminate the trust.

48. 616 F.2d 641 (3d Cir.1980).

49. 710 F.2d 57 (2d Cir.1983).

50. 710 F.2d at 65.

adequate remedy under state law; these cases hold that the existence of a remedy under state law *creates* a cause of action under Rule 10b–5. This would seem to be standing *Santa Fe Industries* on its head.

However, in Biesenbach v. Guenther,[51] the Third Circuit, in a case where there was a shareholder vote on the transaction, held that allegations that the statement that the transactions were "in the best interest of the shareholders" was false and that the defendants did not disclose the "true purpose" of the transactions were insufficient to avoid the ruling in *Santa Fe Industries*. The court said: "In effect, appellants are stating that the failure to disclose the breach of fiduciary duty is a misrepresentation sufficient to constitute a violation of the Act. We refuse to adopt this approach which would clearly circumvent the Supreme Court's holding in *Santa Fe*." Also, in Pross v. Katz[52] the court held that an allegation that the defendant promised to perform faithfully his fiduciary duties while secretly intending to carry out a plan to divest the plaintiff of his interest was not sufficient to allege a violation of Rule 10b–5. The court said: "Making a specific promise to perform a particular act in the future while secretly intending not to perform may violate Section 10(b) or Section 17(a) if the promise is part of the consideration for a sale of securities. * * * However, generalized promises to act as a faithful fiduciary stand on a different footing than other promises of future performance. It is clear that a breach of fiduciary duty by itself is not sufficient to make out a federal claim. Santa Fe Industries v. Green, 430 U.S. 462 (1977). Given that rule, the failure to perform a promise not to breach such a duty also does not violate federal law." [53]

With respect to Section 14(e), the courts of appeal had unanimously held, with the one exception of the Sixth Circuit in Mobil Corp. v. Marathon Oil Co. [54] (which was overruled by the Supreme Court in the *Schreiber* case), both before and after the decision in the *Schreiber* case, that an alleged breach of the fiduciary duties of the board of directors of a target company in connection with the adoption of various defensive measures did not state a claim under Section 14(e).[55] It would appear, in view of this strong current of authority prior to the *Schreiber* case, that no refined distinctions will be employed by the circuit courts to attempt to avoid the doctrine of that case, as has been done with respect to the *Santa Fe* case.

See Gelb, Rule 10b–5 and Santa Fe—Herein of Sue Facts, Shame Facts, and Other Matters, 87 W.Va.L.Rev. 189 (1984); Ferrara and Steinberg, The Interplay Between State Corporation and Federal Securities Law—Santa Fe, Singer, Burks, Maldonado, Their Progeny & Beyond, 7 Del.J.Corp.Law 1 (1982); Lashbrooke, Alternative-Action Requirement: The Derailment of Santa Fe, 1981 Duke L.J. 963 (1981); Roberts, The Status of Minority Shareholders' Remedies For Oppression After Santa Fe and Singer and the Question of "Reasonable Investment Expectation" Valuation, 6 Del.J.Corp.Law 16 (1981); Krendl, The Progeny of Sante Fe v. Green: An Analysis of the Elements of a Fiduciary Duty Claim Under Rule 10b–5 and a Case for a Federal Corporation Law, 59 No. Carolina L.Rev. 231 (1981); Brooks, Rule 10b–5 in the Balance: An Analysis of the Supreme Court's Policy Perspective, 32 Hastings L.J. 403 (1980); Ferrara

51. 588 F.2d 400 (3d Cir.1978).

52. 784 F.2d 455 (2d Cir.1986).

53. 784 F.2d at 457–458.

54. 669 F.2d 366 (6th Cir.1981).

55. Buffalo Forge Company v. Ogden Corporation, 717 F.2d 757 (2d Cir.1983), cert. denied 464 U.S. 1018 (1983); Data

Probe Acquisition Corporation v. Datatab, Inc., 722 F.2d 1 (2d Cir.1983), cert. denied 465 U.S. 1052 (1984); Feldbaum v. Avon Products, Inc., 741 F.2d 234 (8th Cir.1984); Biechele v. Cedar Point Inc., 747 F.2d 209 (6th Cir.1984); Pin v. Texaco, Inc., 793 F.2d 1448 (5th Cir.1986).

and Steinberg, Reappraisal of Santa Fe: Rule 10b–5 and the New Federalism, 129 U.Pa.L.Rev. 263 (1980); Hazen, Corporate Mismanagement and the Federal Securities Acts' Antifraud Provisions, 20 B.C.L.Rev. 819 (1979); Jacobs, Rule 10b–5 and Self Dealing by Corporate Fiduciaries: An Analysis, 48 U.Cin.L.Rev. 643 (1979); Campbell, Santa Fe Industries, Inc. v. Green, 30 Maine L.Rev. 187 (1979); Sherrard, Federal Judicial and Regulatory Responses to Santa Fe Industries, Inc. v. Green, 35 Wash. & Lee L.Rev. 695 (1978); Coffee, Beyond the Shut-Eyed Sentry, 63 Va.L.Rev. 1099 (1977); Campbell, Voluntary Recapitalizations, Fairness, and Rule 10b–5: Life Along the Trail of Santa Fe, 66 Ky.L.J. 267 (1977); Sherrard, Fiduciaries and Fairness Under Rule 10b–5, 29 Vand.L. Rev. 1385 (1976); Dyer, Essay on Federalism in Private Actions Under Rule 10b–5, 1976 Utah L.Rev. 7 (1976); Jennings, Federalization of Corporation Law: Part Way or All the Way, 31 Bus.Law. 991 (1976); Jacobs, Role of Securities Exchange Act Rule 10b–5 in the Regulation of Corporate Management, 59 Corn. L.Rev. 27 (1973).

Chapter 16

PERSONS ENTITLED TO SUE

Statutes and Regulations

Securities Act of 1933, §§ 11, 12.

Securities Exchange Act of 1934, §§ 9, 14(a), (d) and (e), 18.

Rule 10b–5.

BARNES v. OSOFSKY

United States Court of Appeals
Second Circuit, 1967.
373 F.2d 269.

Before LUMBARD, CHIEF JUDGE, and FRIENDLY and HAYS, CIRCUIT JUDGES.

FRIENDLY, CIRCUIT JUDGE.

Aileen, Inc. is engaged in the design, manufacture and sale of popular priced sports wear for girls and women. Prior to the fall of 1963 it had outstanding 1,019,574 common shares; 205,966 of these, most of them covered by a 1961 registration statement, were traded on the American Stock Exchange, and the balance, 813,608, were owned, in approximately equal proportions, by two officers and directors, Osofsky and Oberlin. Pursuant to a registration statement effective September 10, 1963, a group of underwriters offered at $23.375 per share, substantially the then market price, another 200,000 shares, also to be listed on the American Exchange; 100,000 of these were an original issue, 50,000 were Osofsky's and 50,000 were Oberlin's. The prospectus reported that "Sales volume has grown from $2,120,394 in 1956 to $15,045,826 in 1962 and reached $9,826,655 for the first six months of 1963."

A press release on October 7, 1963, and a supplement to the prospectus on the following day, announced a rift in the lute. Third quarter sales had been little more than in 1962 and the volume of orders for an important spring line had not come up to expectations. The price of the stock, which had been gradually declining since late September, declined some more, reaching $15.75 by the end of October, $14.25 at the year-end, and still lower figures thereafter.

Three class actions by purchasers against the corporation, Osofsky, Oberlin, the principal underwriters and, in one instance, other officers and directors, were brought in the District Court for the Southern District of New York on November 13 and 19, 1963 and August 17, 1964, and were subsequently consolidated. The complaints in all three set forth a claim under § 11 of the Securities Act of 1933 that the registration statement and prospectus contained material misstatements and omissions, primarily in failing to disclose danger signals of which the management was aware prior to the date when the registration statement took effect. One complaint also contained a claim based on § 10(b) of the Securities Exchange Act of 1934, Rule 10b–5 and common law fraud, but this was later

1093

withdrawn. After discovery and negotiations, a settlement was agreed upon, which the District Court approved after notice and hearing, 254 F.Supp. 721 (S.D.N.Y.1966). This provided for the deposit of a fund of $775,000, 50% of which was contributed by the corporation and the remainder by the two selling stockholders in equal amounts. After payment of approved allowances, the fund was to be distributed among persons "who beneficially acquired (in his own name or otherwise) any part of the 200,000 shares * * * which was the subject of the public offering of September 10, 1963 between September 10, 1963 and August 17, 1964" and who made timely application for participation therein. * * *

The sole objectors to the settlement were the appellants Attilio Occhi who bought 100 shares on November 22, 1963 at about $15 per share, and Fred Zilker who bought 25 shares on September 12, 1963 for $23.375 and 50 shares on December 23 for $13.50 per share. Their objection went to the provision limiting the benefits of the settlement to persons who could establish that they purchased securities issued under the 1963 registration statement, which thus eliminated those who purchased after the issuance of the allegedly incomplete prospectus but could not so trace their purchases. Although the issue has not yet been passed upon by the special master whom Judge Ryan appointed, it appears likely that Occhi will be able to trace 50 shares which were bought on the open market and Zilker can trace 25 which were bought from an underwriter, but not the balance—all purchased on the market.

We need say little as to appellants' argument that even if § 11 of the Securities Act permits recovery only by purchasers of the issue covered by the defective registration statement as the district judge held, the court on a basis of equity should have provided for participation by others who, as a practical matter, may have suffered equally. Whether or not it would have been an abuse of discretion to have diluted a settlement so as to allow recovery by persons not legally entitled thereto, as we incline to think it would have been, surely there would be none in limiting participation to those who might have recovered had the suits been fought and won. The question thus is whether the district court was right in ruling that § 11 extends only to purchases of the newly registered shares.

Section 11(a) provides that:

> "In case any part of the registration statement, when such part became effective, contained an untrue statement of a material fact or omitted to state a material fact required to be stated therein or necessary to make the statements therein not misleading, any person acquiring such security (unless it is proved that at the time of such acquisition he knew of such untruth or omission) may, either at law or in equity, in any court of competent jurisdiction, sue"

five categories of persons therein named. The key phrase is "any person acquiring such security"; the difficulty, presented when as here the registration is of shares in addition to those already being traded, is that "such" has no referent. Although the narrower reading—"acquiring a security issued pursuant to the registration statement"—would be the more natural, a broader one—"acquiring a security of the same nature as that issued pursuant to the registration statement"—would not be such a violent departure from the words that a court could not properly adopt it if there were good reason for doing so. Appellants claim there is. Starting from the seemingly correct premise that an unduly optimistic prospectus will affect the price of shares already issued to almost the same extent as those of the same class about to be issued, they say it would therefore be unreasonable to distinguish newly registered shares from those previously traded. In addition, they contend that once it is agreed that § 11 is not limited to the original purchasers, to read that section as applying only to purchasers who can trace the lineage of their shares to the new offering makes the result turn on mere accident since most trading is done through brokers who neither know nor care whether they are getting newly registered or old shares.[1] Finally, appellants argue that it is often impossible to determine whether previously traded shares are old or new, and that tracing is further complicated when stock is held in margin accounts in street names since many brokerage houses do not identify specific shares with particular accounts but instead treat the account as having an undivided interest in the house's position. Therefore, they urge that the narrower construction offends the cardinal principle of equal treatment for persons whose entitlement is not significantly different and a "golden rule" of statutory interpretation "that unreasonableness of the result produced by one among alternative possible interpretations of a statute is reason for rejecting that interpretation in favor of another which would produce a reasonable result." 2 Sutherland, Statutory Construction § 4508.1, p. 118 (Supp.1966).

Appellants' broader reading would be inconsistent with the over-all statutory scheme. The Securities Act of 1933 had two major purposes, "[t]o provide full and fair disclosure of the character of securities sold in interstate and foreign commerce and through the mails, and to prevent frauds in the sale thereof, * * *" 48 Stat. 74 (1933). These aims were "to be achieved by a general antifraud provision and by a registration provision." 1 Loss, Securities Regulation 178–79 (1961). Section 11 deals with civil liability for untrue or misleading statements or omissions in the registration statement; its stringent penalties are to insure full and accurate disclosure through registration. Since, under §§ 2(1) and 6, only individual shares are registered, it seems unlikely that the section developed to insure proper disclosure in the registration statement was meant to provide a remedy for other than the particular shares registered. In contrast both §§ 12(2) and 17, the antifraud sections of the 1933 Act, where some form of the traditional scienter requirement, dispensed with as to the issuer under § 11, is preserved, are not limited to the newly registered securities. Beyond this, the over-all limitation of § 11(g) that "In no case shall the amount recoverable under this section exceed the price at which the security was offered to the public," and the provision of § 11(e) whereby, with qualifications not here material, an underwriter's liability shall not exceed "the total price at which the securities underwritten by him and distributed to the public were offered to the public," point in the direction of limiting § 11 to purchasers of the registered shares, since

---

1. Appellants note that the impracticability of determining at the moment of purchase whether old or new shares are being acquired has led dealers to comply with the requirements of § 5(b)(2) as to the delivery of a prospectus by doing this on all sales within the period established by § 4(3), see 1 Loss, Securities Regulation 259–60 (1961). While this may enable a purchaser of shares other than those registered to rely on § 12(2) upon an appropriate showing, it does not lead to the conclusion that § 11 applies.

otherwise their recovery would be greatly diluted when the new issue was small in relation to the trading in previously outstanding shares.

* * *

While we have thought it desirable to examine the issue tendered by appellants on its merits, it is not really a new one. In Fischman v. Raytheon Mfg. Co., 9 F.R.D. 707 (S.D.N.Y.1949), rev'd on other grounds, 188 F.2d 783 (2 Cir.1951), the district court held that common stockholders could not avail themselves of a violation of § 11 in the registration of an issue of convertible preferred in the absence of an allegation that their stock resulted from conversion of the registered issue. Although this ruling was not contested on appeal, we in effect approved it, saying that an action under § 11 may be maintained "only by one who comes within a narrow class of persons, i.e. those who purchase securities that are the direct subject of the prospectus and registration statement." 188 F.2d at 786. While appellants characterize this statement as dictum, both because the point was not contested and because this court did not have to face up to the question of the rights of a purchaser of other shares of the same nature as those registered, the statement carries particular weight because of its authorship by Judge Frank, a leading member of the SEC in its early days, and it afforded a basis for the court's conclusion that allowing an action under § 10(b) of the 1934 Act would not simply duplicate a remedy already given by § 11 of the 1933 Act. Recently, in Colonial Realty Corp. v. Brunswick Corp., 257 F.Supp. 875 (S.D.N.Y.1966), Judge Edelstein reviewed the problem and concluded in favor of the traditional limited reading of § 11 on the merits as well as under the authority of *Fischman.* The leading treatise is in accord, 3 Loss, Securities Regulation 1731 fn. 160 (1961 ed.), as is the Securities and Exchange Commission in a brief as *amicus curiae* filed in response to our invitation.

Without depreciating the force of appellants' criticisms that this construction gives § 11 a rather accidental impact as between one open-market purchaser of a stock already being traded and another, we are unpersuaded that, by departing from the more natural meaning of the words, a court could come up with anything better. What appellants' argument does suggest is that the time may have come for Congress to reexamine these two remarkable pioneering statutes in the light of thirty years' experience, with a view to simplifying and coordinating their different and often overlapping remedies. See the provocative article by Milton H. Cohen, Truth in Securities Revisited, 79 Harv.L.Rev. 1340 (1966).[2]

Affirmed.

BLUE CHIP STAMPS v. MANOR DRUG STORES

Supreme Court of the United States, 1975.
421 U.S. 723, 95 S.Ct. 1917, 44 L.Ed.2d 539.

MR. JUSTICE REHNQUIST delivered the opinion of the Court.

This case requires us to consider whether the offerees of a stock offering, made pursuant to an antitrust consent decree and registered under the

---

2. While appellants contend that we should put the burden of tracing on the defendants, they have not sufficiently demonstrated the unreasonableness of leaving that burden on them, which is the more normal rule.

Securities Act of 1933, 15 U.S.C. § 77a et seq. ("the 1933 Act"), may maintain a private cause of action for money damages where they allege that the offeror has violated the provisions of Rule 10b–5 of the Securities and Exchange Commission, but where they have neither purchased nor sold any of the offered shares. See Birnbaum v. Newport Steel Corp., 193 F.2d 461 (CA2), cert. denied, 343 U.S. 956 (1952).

I

In 1963 the United States filed a civil antitrust action against Blue Chip Stamp Company ("Old Blue Chip") a company in the business of providing trading stamps to retailers, and nine retailers who owned 90% of its shares. In 1967 the action was terminated by the entry of a consent decree. United States v. Blue Chip Stamp Co., 272 F.Supp. 432 (C.D.Cal.1967), aff'd sub nom. Thrifty Shoppers Scrip Co. v. United States, 389 U.S. 580 (1968). The decree contemplated a plan of reorganization whereby Old Blue Chip was to be merged into a newly formed corporation "New Blue Chip." The holdings of the majority shareholders of Old Blue Chip were to be reduced, and New Blue Chip, one of the petitioners here, was required under the plan to offer a substantial number of its shares of common stock to retailers who had used the stamp service in the past but who were not shareholders in the old company. Under the terms of the plan, the offering to nonshareholder users was to be proportional to past stamp usage and the shares were to be offered in units consisting of common stock and debentures.

The reorganization plan was carried out, the offering was registered with the SEC as required by the 1933 Act, and a prospectus was distributed to all offerees as required by § 5 of that Act. Somewhat more than 50% of the offered units were actually purchased. In 1970, two years after the offering, respondent, a former user of the stamp service and therefore an offeree of the 1968 offering, filed this suit in the United States District Court for the Central District of California. Defendants below and petitioners here are Old and New Blue Chip, eight of the nine majority shareholders of Old Blue Chip, and the directors of New Blue Chip (collectively called "Blue Chip").

Respondent's complaint alleged, *inter alia*, that the prospectus prepared and distributed by Blue Chip in connection with the offering was materially misleading in its overly pessimistic appraisal of Blue Chip's status and future prospects. It alleged that Blue Chip intentionally made the prospectus overly pessimistic in order to discourage respondent and other members of the allegedly large class whom it represents from accepting what was intended to be a bargain offer, so that the rejected shares might later be offered to the public at a higher price. The complaint alleged that class members because of and in reliance on the false and misleading prospectus failed to purchase the offered units. Respondent therefore sought on behalf of the alleged class some $21,400,000 in damages representing the lost opportunity to purchase the units; the right to purchase the previously rejected units at the 1968 price, and in addition, it sought some $25,000,000 in exemplary damages.

The only portion of the litigation thus initiated which is before us is whether respondent may base its action on Rule 10(b)(5) of the Securities and Exchange Commission without having either bought or sold the shares described in the allegedly misleading prospectus. * * *

* * *

Despite the contrast between the provisions of Rule 10b–5 and the numerous carefully drawn express civil remedies provided in both the Acts of 1933 and 1934, it was held in 1946 by the United States District Court for the Eastern District of Pennsylvania that there was an implied private right of action under the Rule. Kardon v. National Gypsum Co., 69 F.Supp. 512 (1946). This Court had no occasion to deal with the subject until 20–odd years later, and at that time we confirmed with virtually no discussion the overwhelming consensus of the district courts and courts of appeals that such a cause of action did exist. Superintendent of Insurance v. Bankers Life and Casualty Co., 404 U.S. 6, 13 n. 9 (1971); Affiliated Ute Citizens v. United States, 406 U.S. 128, 150–154 (1972). Such a conclusion was, of course, entirely consistent with the Court's recognition in J.I. Case Co. v. Borak, 377 U.S. 426, 432 (1964), that private enforcement of Commission rules may "[provide] a necessary supplement to Commission action."

Within a few years after the seminal Kardon decision the Court of Appeals for the Second Circuit concluded that the plaintiff class for purposes of a private damage action under § 10(b) and Rule 10b–5 was limited to actual purchasers and sellers of securities. Birnbaum v. Newport Steel Corp., supra.

The Court of Appeals in this case did not repudiate Birnbaum; indeed, another panel of that court (in an opinion by Judge Ely) had but a short time earlier affirmed the rule of that case. Mount Clemens Industries v. Bell, 464 F.2d 339 (CA9 1972). But in this case a majority of the Court of Appeals found that the facts warranted an exception to the Birnbaum rule. For the reasons hereinafter stated, we are of the opinion that Birnbaum was rightly decided, and that it bars respondent from maintaining this suit under Rule 10b–5.

III

The panel which decided Birnbaum consisted of Chief Judge Swan and Judges Learned Hand and Augustus Hand: the opinion was written by the latter. Since both § 10(b) and Rule 10b–5 proscribed only fraud "in connection with the purchase or sale" of securities, and since the history of § 10(b) revealed no congressional intention to extend a private civil remedy for money damages to other than defrauded purchasers or sellers of securities in contrast to the express civil remedy provided by § 16(b) of the 1934 Act, the court concluded that the plaintiff class in a Rule 10b–5 action was limited to actual purchasers and sellers. 193 F.2d 461, 463–464.

Just as this Court had no occasion to consider the validity of the Kardon holding that there was a private cause of action under Rule 10b–5 until 20–odd years later, nearly the same period of time has gone by between the Birnbaum decision and our consideration of the case now before us. As with Kardon, virtually all lower federal courts facing the issue in the hundreds of reported cases presenting this question over the past quarter century have reaffirmed Birnbaum's conclusion that the plaintiff class for purposes of § 10(b) and Rule 10b–5 private damage action is limited to purchasers and sellers of securities. * * *

In 1957 and again in 1959, the Securities and Exchange Commission sought from Congress amendment of § 10(b) to change its wording from "in connection with the purchase of sale of any security" to "in connection with the purchase or sale of, *or any attempt to purchase or sell,* any security." (Emphasis added.) 103 Cong.Rec. 11636 (1957); SEC Legislation, Hearings before Subcom. of Sen.Com. on Banking & Currency on S. 1178–1182, 86th Cong., 1st Sess., 367–368 (1959); S. 2545, 85th Cong., 1st Sess. (1957); S. 1179, 86th Cong., 1st Sess. (1959). In the words of a memorandum submitted by the Commission to a congressional committee, the purpose of the proposed change was "to make section 10(b) also applicable to manipulative activities in connection with any attempt to purchase or sell any security." Hearings on S. 1178–1182, supra, at 331. Opposition to the amendment was based on fears of the extension of civil liability under § 10(b) that it would cause. Id., at 368. Neither change was adopted by Congress.

The longstanding acceptance by the courts, coupled with Congress' failure to reject *Birnbaum's* reasonable interpretation of the wording of § 10(b), wording which is directed towards injury suffered "in connection with the purchase or sale" of securities, argues significantly in favor of acceptance of the *Birnbaum* rule by this Court. Blau v. Lehman, 368 U.S. 403, 413 (1962).

Available extrinsic evidence from the texts of the 1933 and 1934 Acts as to the congressional scheme in this regard, though not conclusive, supports the result reached by the *Birnbaum* court. The wording of § 10(b) directed at fraud "in connection with the purchase or sale" of securities stands in contrast with the parallel antifraud provision of the 1933 Act, § 17(a)[6] reaching fraud "in the offer or sale" of securities. Cf. § 5 of the 1933 Act. When Congress wished to provide a remedy to those who neither purchase nor sell securities, it had little trouble in doing so expressly. Cf. § 16(b) of the 1934 Act, 15 U.S.C. § 78p.

Section 28(a) of the 1934 Act which limits recovery in any private damage action brought under the 1934 Act to "actual damages," likewise provides some support for the purchaser-seller rule. See, e.g., A. Bromberg, Securities Law: Fraud—SEC Rule 10b–5, § 8.8, at 221 (1968). While the damages suffered by purchasers and sellers pursuing a § 10(b) cause of action may on occasion be difficult to ascertain, Affiliated Ute Citizens v. United States, supra, 406 U.S. at 155, in the main such purchasers and sellers at least seek to base recovery on a demonstrable number of shares traded. In contrast, a putative plaintiff, who neither purchases nor sells securities, but sues instead for intangible economic injury such as loss of a noncontractual opportunity to buy or sell, is more likely to be seeking a largely conjectural and speculative recovery in which the number of shares involved will depend on the plaintiff's subjective hypothesis. Cf. Estate Counseling Service v. Merrill Lynch, Pierce, Fenner & Smith, 303 F.2d 527, 533 (CA10 1962); Levine v. Seilon, Inc., 439 F.2d 328, 335 (CA2 1971); Wolf v. Frank, 477 F.2d 467, 478 (CA5 1973).

---

6. * * * We express, of course, no opinion on whether § 17(a) in light of the express civil remedies of the 1933 Act gives rise to an implied cause of action. Compare Greater Iowa Corp. v. McLendon, 378 F.2d 783, 788, 791 (CA8 1967), with Fisch- man v. Raytheon Mfg. Corp., 188 F.2d 783, 787 (CA2 1951). See, e.g., SEC v. Texas Gulf Sulphur Co., 401 F.2d 833, 867 (CA2 1968) (Opinion of Friendly, J., concurring), cert. denied, 394 U.S. 976 (1969); 3 L. Loss, Securities Regulation 1785 (1961).

One of the justifications advanced for implication of a cause of action under § 10(b) lies in § 29(b) of the 1934 Act providing that a contract made in violation of any provision of the 1934 Act is voidable at the option of the deceived party. See e.g., Kardon v. National Gypsum Co., 69 F.Supp. 512, 514 (E.D.Pa.1946); Slavin v. Germantown Fire Insurance Co., 174 F.2d 799, 815 (CA3 1949); Fischman v. Raytheon Manufacturing Co., 188 F.2d 783, 787 n. 4 (CA2 1951); A. Bromberg, Securities Regulation: Fraud—SEC Rule 10b–5 § 2.4(1)(b) (1968). But that justification is absent when there is no actual purchase or sale of securities, or a contract to do so, affected or tainted by a violation of § 10(b). Cf. Mount Clemens Industries, Inc. v. Bell, supra.

The principal express nonderivative private civil remedies, created by Congress contemporaneously with the passage of § 10(b), for violations of various provisions of the 1933 and 1934 Acts are by their terms expressly limited to purchasers or sellers of securities. Thus § 11(a) of the 1933 Act confines the cause of action it grants to "any person acquiring the security" while the remedy granted by § 12 of that Act is limited to the "person purchasing the said security." Section 9 of the 1934 Act, prohibiting a variety of fraudulent and manipulative devices, limits the express civil remedy provided for its violation to "any person who shall purchase or sell any security" in a transaction affected by a violation of the provision. Section 18 of the 1934 Act, prohibiting false or misleading statements in reports or other documents required to be filed by the 1934 Act, limits the express remedy provided for its violation to "any person * * * who * * * shall have purchased or sold a security at a price which was affected by such statement * * *." It would indeed be anomalous to impute to Congress an intention to expand the plaintiff class for a judicially implied cause of action beyond the bounds it delineated for comparable express causes of action.

Having said all this, we would by no means be understood as suggesting that we are able to divine from the language of § 10(b) the express "intent of Congress" as to the contours of a private cause of action under Rule 10b–5. When we deal with private actions under Rule 10b–5, we deal with a judicial oak which has grown from little more than a legislative acorn. Such growth may be quite consistent with the congressional enactment and with the role of the federal judiciary in interpreting it, see J.I. Case v. Borak, supra, but it would be disingenuous to suggest that either Congress in 1934 or the Securities and Exchange Commission in 1942 foreordained the present state of the law with respect to Rule 10b–5. It is therefore proper that we consider, in addition to the factors already discussed, what may be described as policy considerations when we come to flesh out the portions of the law with respect to which neither the congressional enactment nor the administrative regulations offer conclusive guidance.

Three principal classes of potential plaintiffs are presently barred by the *Birnbaum* rule. First are potential purchasers of shares, either in a new offering or on the Nation's post-distribution trading markets, who alleged that they decided not to purchase because of an unduly gloomy representation or the omission of favorable material which made the issuer appear to be a less favorable investment vehicle than it actually was. Second are actual shareholders in the issuer who allege that they decided not to sell their shares because of an unduly rosy representation or a failure to disclose unfavorable material. Third are shareholders, creditors, and perhaps others related to an issuer who suffered loss in the value of their investment due to corporate or insider activities in connection with the purchase or sale of securities which violate Rule 10b–5. It has been held that shareholder members of the second and third of these classes may frequently be able to circumvent the *Birnbaum* limitation through bringing a derivative action on behalf of the corporate issuer if the latter is itself a purchaser or seller of securities. See, e.g., Schoenbaum v. Firstbrook, 405 F.2d 215, 219 (CA2d 1968), cert. denied sub nom. Manley v. Schoenbaum, 395 U.S. 906 (1969). But the first of these classes, of which respondent is a member, can not claim the benefit of such a rule.

A great majority of the many commentators on the issue before us have taken the view that the *Birnbaum* limitation on the plaintiff class in a Rule 10b–5 action for damages is an arbitrary restriction which unreasonably prevents some deserving plaintiffs from recovering damages which have in fact been caused by violations of Rule 10b–5. See, e.g., Lowenfels, The Demise of the *Birnbaum* Doctrine: A New Era for Rule 10b–5, 54 Va.Law Rev. 268 (1968). The Securities and Exchange Commission has filed an *amicus* brief in this case espousing that same view. We have no doubt that this is indeed a disadvantage of the *Birnbaum* rule, and if it had no countervailing advantages it would be undesirable as a matter of policy, however much it might be supported by precedent and legislative history. But we are of the opinion that there are countervailing advantages to the *Birnbaum* rule, purely as a matter of policy, although those advantages are more difficult to articulate than is the disadvantage.

There has been widespread recognition that litigation under Rule 10b–5 presents a danger of vexatiousness different in degree and in kind from that which accompanies litigation in general. This fact was recognized by Judge Browning in his opinion for the majority of the Court of Appeals in this case, 492 F.2d 141, and by Judge Hufstedler in her dissenting opinion when she said:

"The purchaser-seller rule has maintained the balances built into the congressional scheme by permitting damage actions to be brought only by those persons whose active participation in the marketing transaction promises enforcement of the statute without undue risk of abuse of the litigation process and without distorting the securities market." 492 F.2d 147.

Judge Friendly in commenting on another aspect of Rule 10b–5 litigation has referred to the possibility that unduly expansive imposition of civil liability "will lead to large judgments, payable in the last analysis by innocent investors, for the benefit of speculators and their lawyers. * * *." SEC v. Texas Gulf Sulphur Co., 401 F.2d 833, 867 (CA2 1968) (concurring opinion). See also Boone and McGowan, Standing to Sue under Rule 10b–5, 49 Tex.L.Rev. 617, 648–649 (1971).

We believe that the concern expressed for the danger of vexatious litigation which could result from a widely expanded class of plaintiffs under Rule 10b–5 is founded in something more substantial than the common complaint of the many defendants who would prefer avoiding lawsuits entirely to either settling them or trying them. These concerns have two largely separate grounds.

The first of these concerns is that in the field of federal securities laws governing disclosure of information even a complaint which by objective standards may have very little chance of success at trial has a settlement value to the plaintiff out of any proportion to its prospect of success at trial so long as he may prevent the suit from being resolved against him by dismissal or summary judgment. The very pendency of the lawsuit may frustrate or delay normal business activity of the defendant which is totally unrelated to the lawsuit. * * *

The potential for possible abuse of the liberal discovery provisions of the federal rules may likewise exist in this type of case to a greater extent than they do in other litigation. The prospect of extensive deposition of the defendant's officers and associates and the concomitant opportunity for extensive discovery of business documents, is a common occurrence in this and similar types of litigation. To the extent that this process eventually produces relevant evidence which is useful in determining the merits of the claims asserted by the parties, it bears the imprimatur of the Federal Rules of Civil Procedure and of the many cases liberally interpreting them. But to the extent that it permits a plaintiff with a largely groundless claim to simply take up the time of a number of other people, with the right to do so representing an *in terrorem* increment of the settlement value, rather than a reasonably founded hope that the process will reveal relevant evidence, it is a social cost rather than a benefit. * * *

The *Birnbaum* rule, on the other hand, permits exclusion prior to trial of those plaintiffs who were not themselves purchasers or sellers of the stock in question. The fact of purchase of stock and the fact of sale of stock are generally matters which are verifiable by documentation, and do not depend upon oral recollection, so that failure to qualify under the *Birnbaum* rule is a matter that can normally be established by the defendant either on a motion to dismiss or on a motion for summary judgment.
* * *

The second ground for fear of vexatious litigation is based on the concern that, given the generalized contours of liability, the abolition of the *Birnbaum* rule would throw open to the trier of fact many rather hazy issues of historical fact the proof of which depended almost entirely on oral testimony. We in no way disparage the worth and frequent high value of oral testimony when we say that dangers of its abuse appear to exist in this type of action to a peculiarly high degree. * * *

In considering the policy underlying the *Birnbaum* rule, it is not inappropriate to advert briefly to the tort of misrepresentation and deceit, to which a claim under § 10b–5 certainly has some relationship. Originally under the common law of England such an action was not available to one other than a party to a business transaction. That limitation was eliminated in Pasley v. Freeman, 3 Term Rep. 51, 100 Eng.Rep. 450 (1789). Under the earlier law the misrepresentation was generally required to be one of fact, rather than opinion, but that requirement, too, was gradually relaxed. Lord Bowen's famous comment in Edgington v. Fitzmaurice, that "The state of a man's mind is as much a fact as the state of his digestion," 1882, L.R. 29 Ch.Div. 359, suggests that this distinction, too, may have been somewhat arbitrary. And it has long been established in the ordinary case of deceit that a misrepresentation which leads to a refusal to purchase or to sell is actionable in just the same way as a representation which leads to the consummation of a purchase or sale. Butler v. Watkins, 13 Wall. 456 (1871). These aspects of the evolution of the tort of deceit and misrepresentation suggest a direction away from rules such as *Birnbaum*.

But the typical fact situation in which the classic tort of misrepresentation and deceit evolved was light years away from the world of commercial transactions to which Rule 10b–5 is applicable. The plaintiff in *Butler,* supra, for example, claimed that he had held off the market a patented machine for tying cotton bales which he had developed by reason of the fraudulent representations of the defendant. But the report of the case leaves no doubt that the plaintiff and defendant met with one another in New Orleans, that one presented a draft agreement to the other, and that letters were exchanged relating to that agreement. Although the claim to damages was based on an allegedly fraudulently induced decision not to put the machines on the market, the plaintiff and the defendant had concededly been engaged in the course of business dealings with one another, and would presumably have recognized one another on the street had they met.

In today's universe of transactions governed by the Securities Exchange Act of 1934, privity of dealing or even personal contact between potential defendant and potential plaintiff is the exception and not the rule. The stock of issuers is listed on financial exchanges utilized by tens of millions of investors and corporate representations reach a potential audience, encompassing not only the diligent few who peruse filed corporate reports or the sizable number of subscribers to financial journals, but the readership of the Nation's daily newspapers. Obviously neither the fact that issuers or other potential defendants under Rule 10b–5 reach a large number of potential investors, or the fact that they are required by law to make their disclosures conform to certain standards, should in any way absolve them from liability for misconduct which is proscribed by Rule 10b–5.

But in the absence of the *Birnbaum* rule, it would be sufficient for a plaintiff to prove that he had failed to purchase or sell stock by reason of a defendant's violation of Rule 10b–5. The manner in which the defendant's violation caused the plaintiff to fail to act could be as a result of the reading of a prospectus, as respondent claims here, but it could just as easily come as a result of a claimed reading of information contained in the financial pages of a local newspaper. Plaintiff's proof would not be that he purchased or sold stock, a fact which would be capable of documentary verification in most situations, but instead that he decided *not* to purchase or sell stock. Plaintiff's entire testimony could be dependent upon uncorroborated oral evidence of many of the crucial elements of his claim, and still be sufficient to go to the jury. The jury would not even have the benefit of weighing the plaintiff's version against the defendant's version, since the elements to which the plaintiff would testify would be in many cases totally unknown and unknowable to the defendant. The very real risk in permitting those in respondent's position to sue under Rule 10b–5 is that the door will be open to recovery of substantial damages on the part of one who offers only his own testimony to prove that he ever consulted a prospectus of the issuer, that he paid any attention to it, or that the representations contained in it damaged him. The virtue of the *Birnbaum* rule, simply stated, in this situation, is that it limits the class of plaintiffs to those who have at least dealt in the security to which the prospectus, representation, or omission relates. And their dealing in the security, whether by way of purchase or sale, will generally be an objectively demonstrable fact in an area of the law otherwise very much dependent upon oral testimony. In the absence of the *Birnbaum* doctrine, bystanders to the securities marketing process could await developments on the sidelines without risk, claiming that inaccuracies in disclosure caused nonselling in a falling market and that unduly pessimistic predictions by the issuer followed by a rising market caused them to allow retrospectively golden opportunities to pass.

* * *

IV

The majority of the Court of Appeals in this case expressed no disagreement with the general proposition that one asserting a claim for damages based on the violation of Rule 10b–5 must be either a purchaser or seller of securities. However, it noted that prior cases have held that persons owning contractual rights to buy or sell securities are not excluded by the *Birnbaum* rule. Relying on these cases, it concluded that respondent's status as an offeree pursuant to the terms of the consent decree served the same function, for purposes of delimiting the class of plaintiffs, as is normally performed by the requirement of a contractual relationship. 492 F.2d, at 142.

* * *

Even if we were to accept the notion that the *Birnbaum* rule could be circumvented on a case-by-case basis through particularized judicial inquiry into the facts surrounding a complaint, this respondent and the members of his alleged class would be unlikely candidates for such a judicially created exception. While the *Birnbaum* rule has been flexibly interpreted by lower federal courts, we have been unable to locate a single decided case from any court in the 20–odd years of litigation since the *Birnbaum* decision which would support the right of persons who were in the position of respondent here to bring a private suit under Rule 10b–5. Respondent was not only not a buyer or seller of any security but it was not even a shareholder of the corporate petitioners.

* * *

Beyond the difficulties evident in an extension of standing to this respondent, we do not believe that the *Birnbaum* rule is merely a short-hand judgment on the nature of a particular plaintiff's proof. As a purely practical matter, it is doubtless true that respondent and the members of its class, as offerees and recipients of the prospectus of New Blue Chip, are a smaller class of potential plaintiffs than would be all those who might conceivably assert that they obtained information violative of Rule 10b–5 and attributable to the issuer in the financial pages of their local newspaper. * * *

But respondents and the members of their class are neither "purchasers" nor "sellers," as those terms are defined in the 1934 Act, and therefore to the extent that their claim of standing to sue were recognized, it would mean that the lesser practical difficulties of corroborating at least some elements of their proof would be regarded as sufficient to avoid the *Birnbaum* rule. * * * Were we to agree with the Court of Appeals in this case, we would leave the *Birnbaum* rule open to endless case-by-case erosion depending on whether a particular group of plaintiffs were thought by the court in which the issue was being litigated to be sufficiently more discrete than the world of potential purchasers at large to justify an exception. We do not believe that such a shifting and highly fact-oriented disposition of the issue of who may bring a damage claim for violation of

Rule 10b–5 is a satisfactory basis for a rule of liability imposed on the conduct of business transactions. Nor is it as consistent as a straightforward application of the *Birnbaum* rule with the other factors which support the retention of that rule. We therefore hold that respondent was not entitled to sue for violation of Rule 10b–5, and the judgment of the Court of Appeals is reversed.

Reversed.

MR. JUSTICE POWELL, with whom MR. JUSTICE STEWART and MR. JUSTICE MARSHALL join, concurring.

* * *

Mr. Justice Blackmun's dissent charges the Court with a "preternatural solicitousness for corporate well-being and a seeming callousness toward the investing public." Our task in this case is to construe a statute. In my view, the answer is plainly compelled by the language as well as the legislative history of the Securities Acts. But even if the language is not "plain" to all, I would have thought none could doubt that the statute can be read fairly to support the result the Court reaches. Indeed, if one takes a different view—and imputes callousness to all who disagree—he must attribute a lack of legal and social perception to the scores of federal judges who have followed *Birnbaum* for two decades.

The dissenting opinion also charges the Court with paying "no heed to the unremedied wrong" arising from the type of "fraud" that may result from reaffirmance of the *Birnbaum* rule. If an issue of statutory construction is to be decided on the basis of assuring a *federal* remedy—in addition to state remedies—for every perceived fraud, at least we should strike a balance between the opportunities for fraud presented by the contending views. It may well be conceded that *Birnbaum* does allow some fraud to go unremedied under the federal Securities Acts. But the construction advocated by the dissent could result in wider opportunities for fraud. As the Court's opinion makes plain, abandoning the *Birnbaum* construction in favor of the rule urged by the dissent would invite any person who failed to purchase a newly offered security that subsequently enjoyed substantial market appreciation to file a claim alleging that the offering prospectus understated the company's potential. The number of possible plaintiffs with respect to a public offering would be virtually unlimited. As noted above * * *, an honest offeror could be confronted with subjective claims by plaintiffs who had neither purchased its securities nor seriously considered the investment. It frequently would be impossible to refute a plaintiff's assertion that he relied on the prospectus, or even that he made a decision not to buy the offered securities. A rule allowing this type of open-ended litigation would itself be an invitation to fraud.[5]

---

5. The dissent also charges that we are callous toward the "investing public"—a term it does not define. It would have been more accurate, perhaps, to have spoken of the noninvesting public, because the Court's decision does not abandon the investing public. The great majority of registered issues of securities are offered by established corporations that have shares outstanding and held by members of the investing public. The types of suits that the dissent would encourage could result in large damage claims, costly litigation, generous settlements to avoid such cost, and often—where the litigation runs its course—in large verdicts. The shareholders of the defendant corporations—the "investing public"—would ultimately bear the burden of this litigation, including the fraudulent suits that would not be screened out by the dissent's bare requirement of a "logical nexus between the alleged fraud and the sale or purchase of a security."

MR. JUSTICE BLACKMUN, with whom MR. JUSTICE DOUGLAS and MR. JUSTICE BRENNAN join, dissenting.

* * *

COWIN v. BRESLER

United States Court of Appeals, District of Columbia Circuit, 1984.
741 F.2d 410.

Before WRIGHT, WILKEY and BORK, CIRCUIT JUDGES.

BORK, CIRCUIT JUDGE:

Bresler & Reiner, Inc. is a publicly-owned company incorporated in the State of Delaware and engaged in the development and management of residential and commercial properties in the District of Columbia. In late 1980, Daniel Cowin, a Bresler & Reiner shareholder, sued the company and its directors on his own behalf. Cowin has a minority interest in the company. The individual directors-appellees, with their families, own in excess of 79% of the company's stock. Appellees Bresler and Reiner together hold more than 70% of the company's outstanding shares, and their control of the corporation is undisputed.

The thrust of Cowin's charges is that the appellees have manipulated the business for their personal profit at the expense of the minority shareholders. The complaint alleges numerous instances of corporate mismanagement, fraud, and self-dealing, all in breach of the common law fiduciary duty owed by the directors of the company to the appellant as a shareholder. Several of the challenged transactions involve deals between the company and certain limited partnerships in which the appellees, including Bresler and Reiner, have significant interests. The complaint also charges Bresler and Reiner with forcing the company to engage in a stock repurchase program at a time when the company was in default on its notes payable and having severe cash flow problems. Cowin alleges that appellees used, and are still using, the repurchase plan to "severely limit[ ] the public market for trading in Company stock"; according to appellant, their ultimate intent is to "covert[ ] the Company to a private corporation owned solely by" them for their own benefit. Brief for Plaintiff-Appellant at 14. To remedy the alleged common law violations, Cowin seeks damages for the diminished value of his stock and injunctions against the allegedly wrongful transactions. He also requests the appointment of a receiver to liquidate the company for his benefit and the benefit of the other shareholders.

The remainder of the complaint charges appellees with violations of the federal securities laws, primarily in connection with the transactions detailed above. Specifically, Cowin claims that Bresler and Reiner caused the company to "disseminate reports to the public shareholders which were materially deceptive" and concealed material information in violation of Rule 10b–5 and section 10(b) of the Securities Exchange Act of 1934 (1982). Brief for Plaintiff-Appellant at 15. The complaint also charges appellees with violating section 14(a) of the 1934 Act, by causing the company to issue deceptive proxy materials. Cowin seeks to require the disclosure of the material concealed in alleged violation of the Act and, among other things, to invalidate the elections for directors based on the alleged proxy violations.

Appellees moved promptly to dismiss the complaint. They also sought, and received from the district court, an order barring all discovery pending disposition of the motion to dismiss. As a result, no discovery was permitted during the proceedings below.

In its first order, entered December 23, 1981, the district court ruled that while Cowin could legally seek the appointment of a receiver for a solvent corporation in his individual capacity, he had failed to allege the "extreme circumstances showing imminent danger of great loss" necessary to support such drastic relief. Cowin v. Bresler, No. 80–2230, mem. op. at 3 (D.D.C. Dec. 23, 1981); Record Excerpts ("R.E.") at 32. The court then dismissed appellant's common law claims because, in its view, both federal and common law required Cowin to "bring ∗ ∗ ∗ a derivative suit to recover damages for a decline in the value of stock" due to alleged corporate mismanagement and fraud. Id. at 35. The court would "not permit [Cowin] to elevate form over substance in order to escape the requirements of a derivative suit merely by attaching an unjustified request for the appointment of a receiver ∗ ∗ ∗ to his complaint." Id. at 36.

The district court also dismissed most of appellant's Rule 10b–5 claims.[1] Relying on Santa Fe Industries, Inc. v. Green, 430 U.S. 462 (1977), the court held that the "reincorporation [into federal securities law claims] of [Cowin's] common-law claims for breaches of fiduciary duties as well as the alleged 'nondisclosures' ∗ ∗ ∗ must be dismissed as unsuccessful attempts to create a 10b–5 cause of action out of claims of corporate mismanagement." R.E. at 40. Certain other alleged securities law violations were dismissed for lack of specificity under Fed.R.Civ.P. 9(b). R.E. at 40 n. ∗, 42–43. The court did not dismiss Cowin's section 14(a) proxy disclosure claims, however, nor did it dismiss that portion of appellant's Rule 10b–5 claims that did not "integrally relate[ ] to [the] allegations of the nondisclosure of certain breaches of fiduciary duty." R.E. at 44–45.

Appellees answered those portions of the complaint that survived the lower court's order and moved for summary judgment on the section 14(a) claim. In its second order, entered April 21, 1983, the district court granted summary judgment for appellees on that claim, holding that Cowin had no standing to challenge, on an individual basis, the allegedly misleading nature of proxy solicitations because he had not personally relied on them.[2]

---

1. The court held that Cowin had standing to raise these claims. On appeal, appellees renew the argument that Cowin had no standing to sue under § 10(b) because he was neither a purchaser nor seller who had acted in reliance on the company's alleged misrepresentations. See Blue Chip Stamps v. Manor Drug Stores, 421 U.S. 723, 731–32, 737–38 (1975); Brief for Appellees at 32–36. Cowin's (and the district court's) position, on the other hand, is that the *Blue Chip* standing requirements are relaxed when a complainant seeks equitable relief and not damages. R.E. at 37–38.

2. The court ruled, alternatively, that Cowin could not demonstrate "loss causation" or economic injury and that the equitable relief appellant sought on his § 14(a) claim—the invalidation of the 1980 directors' election—would "constitute an exercise of futility" because of appellees' unquestionable control over a significant majority of votes. R.E. at 53 (citing Schlick v. Penn-Dixie Cement Corp., 507 F.2d 374, 380 (2d Cir.1974), cert. denied, 421 U.S. 976 (1975)).

With respect to that portion of Cowin's § 10(b) claim that survived the motion to dismiss, the lower court dismissed "without

This appeal followed.

I.

A.

We agree with the district court's holding that appellant's common law claims for damages and injunctive relief must be pursued, if at all, on a derivative basis. Both case law and sound policy support this conclusion. In Bokat v. Getty Oil Co., 262 A.2d 246, 249 (Del.1970), plaintiff shareholder charged that Getty Oil had, among other things, forced its wholly-owned subsidiary to purchase oil from Getty at an inflated price. Delaware's highest court characterized this claim as one "seek[ing] money damages for improper management" and held that such claims belonged to the corporation and not to its minority stockholders:

> When an injury to corporate stock *falls equally upon all stockholders,* then an individual stockholder may not recover for the injury to his stock alone, but must seek recovery derivatively in behalf of the corporation.

Id. at 249 (emphasis added). The court concluded that "[m]ismanagement which depresses the value of stock is a wrong to the corporation; i.e., the stockholders collectively, to be enforced by a derivative action." Id. See also Crane Co. v. Harsco Corp., 511 F.Supp. 294, 304 (D.Del.1981); Elster v. American Airlines, Inc., 34 Del.Ch. 94, 98–99, 100 A.2d 219, 222 (1953).

* * *

B.

Cowin's request for the appointment of a receiver to liquidate the company, as distinct from his state law claims for damages and injunctive relief, was properly before the district court in a personal action. See, e.g., Lichens Co. v. Standard Commercial Tobacco Co., 28 Del.Ch. 220, 228–32, 40 A.2d 447, 451–52 (1944); Salnita Corp. v. Walter Holding Corp., 19 Del.Ch. 426, 431, 168 A. 74, 76 (1933). The court found, however, that Cowin had failed to meet the pleading requirements necessary to support such relief. R.E. at 33. We disagree. Although a request for a court-appointed receiver "to wind up a solvent going business is rarely granted," Berwald v. Mission Development Co., 40 Del.Ch. 509, 512, 185 A.2d 480, 482 (Sup.Ct. 1962), and the court's power to do so must "always [be] exercised with great restraint," Hall v. John S. Isaacs & Sons Farms, Inc., 39 Del.Ch. 244, 253, 163 A.2d 288, 293 (Sup.Ct.1960), we believe that Cowin has sufficiently plead the requisite elements to support his claim.

* * *

II.

Appellant's federal claims raise novel questions under the Securities Exchange Act of 1934, 15 U.S.C. § 78a et seq. (1982). Although Cowin did not buy or sell his stock in connection with the allegedly misleading reports issued by the company, he relies upon section 10(b) of the Act and Rule 10b–5 in seeking to prevent appellees from "depress[ing] the value of [his] stock and . . . eliminat[ing] the public market in that stock through dissemination of deceptive statements." Reply Brief for Plaintiff-Appellant

prejudice . . . to facilitate an expeditious appeal of this action." R.E. at 55. The court based this action on what it deemed the expectations of both parties.

at 18. In short, appellant claims not that he was wrongfully induced to buy or sell stock by appellees' misrepresentations but rather that his stock was made less valuable by appellees' misrepresentations to the investing public generally. He does not seek damages but an injunction requiring an end to the alleged misrepresentations and disclosure of past misrepresentations. It is clear from Blue Chip Stamps v. Manor Drug Stores, 421 U.S. 723 (1975), that appellant could not maintain an action for damages under section 10(b) or Rule 10b–5. The question before us is whether he may bring suit for an injunction.

* * *

A.

In *Blue Chip,* the Supreme Court held that only purchasers or sellers of securities have standing to pursue private claims for damages under section 10(b) and Rule 10b–5. The only difference between that case and this is that appellant seeks only injunctive relief. The question is whether that difference means that plaintiff's action survives *Blue Chip.* We think that it does not.[11]

More than twenty years before *Blue Chip,* a distinguished panel of the Second Circuit concluded that section 10(b) was "directed solely at that type of misrepresentation or fraudulent practice usually associated with the sale or purchase of securities rather than at fraudulent mismanagement of corporate affairs. * * *" Birnbaum v. Newport Steel Corp., 193 F.2d 461, 464 (2d Cir.), cert. denied, 343 U.S. 956 (1952).[12] Relying primarily on the purpose underlying the adoption of Rule 10b–5, *Birnbaum* held that the rule extended protection "only to the defrauded purchaser or seller," 193

---

11. Our holding in this regard would also foreclose that portion of Cowin's Rule 10b–5 claim dismissed by the district court "without prejudice." R.E. at 55. We note, however, with respect to appellant's § 10(b) claims that the *Blue Chip* Court noted with apparent approval the fact that a non-selling or purchasing shareholder "who suffered loss in the value of his investment due to corporate or insider activities in connection with the purchase or sale of securities which violate Rule 10b–5 . . . . may frequently be able to circumvent the [purchaser-seller] limitation through bringing a derivative action on behalf of the corporate issuer if the latter is itself a purchaser or seller of securities." 421 U.S. at 738, 95 S.Ct. at 1926, citing Schoenbaum v. Firstbrook, 405 F.2d 215 (2d Cir.1968), cert. denied, 395 U.S. 906 (1969). See also Wright v. Heizer Corp., 411 F.Supp. 23, 32 (N.D.Ill.1975), aff'd in part and rev'd in part, 560 F.2d 236 (7th Cir.1977), cert. denied, 434 U.S. 1066 (1978). On this record, however, we cannot speculate as to the relevance of this possibility.

Cowin also based this portion of his complaint on § 13(a) of the Act, 15 U.S.C. § 78m(a) (1982). The lower court, however, found it unnecessary to decide whether Cowin could maintain his cause of action

under § 13(a), R.E. at 33, and appellant did not attempt to support his complaint on appeal by arguing that a private cause of action could be pursued under that section. The court's disposition of the § 13(a) claim in that manner puzzles us in light of the court's dismissal—based on the same factual allegations—of Cowin's Rule 10b–5 and § 10(b) claims. However, absent complete briefing and a lower court opinion on this issue, we decline to reach the question, leaving to the district court, on remand, to explore the matter further. Cf. Dan River, Inc. v. Unitex Ltd., 624 F.2d 1216 (4th Cir. 1980), cert. denied, 449 U.S. 1101 (1981) (court finds implied right of action under § 13(d) of the Act). But see In re Penn Central Securities Litigation, M.D.L. Docket No. 56, 494 F.2d 528, 539–40 (3d Cir. 1974) (no implied right of action under § 13(a) of the Act).

12. The *Birnbaum* court consisted of Chief Judge Swan, and Judges Learned Hand and Augustus N. Hand, with the last writing for a unanimous court, and was described by Justice Blackmun, dissenting in *Blue Chip,* as "a justifiably esteemed panel of that Court of Appeals regarded as the 'Mother Court' in this area of law." 421 U.S. at 762, 95 S.Ct. at 1938 (footnote omitted).

F.2d at 464, and affirmed dismissal of a complaint that failed to allege that "any of the plaintiffs fell into either class." Id.[13]

After declining an earlier opportunity to rule on *Birnbaum*'s standing requirements, *see* Superintendent of Insurance v. Bankers Life & Casualty Co., 404 U.S. 6, 13–14 n. 10 (1971), the Supreme Court in *Blue Chip* affirmed the vitality of the *Birnbaum* restriction in private damage actions under Rule 10b–5. * * *

B.

Cowin argues that the purchaser-seller limitation does not apply to actions seeking equitable relief. He points to a pre-*Blue Chip* line of cases holding that a private party who seeks only injunctive relief need not have bought or sold securities to sue under Rule 10b–5, see, e.g., Kahan v. Rosenstiel, 424 F.2d 161 (3d Cir.), cert. denied, 398 U.S. 950 (1970); Mutual Shares Corp. v. Genesco, Inc., 384 F.2d 540 (2d Cir.1967), and contends that the "exception" to the purchaser-seller rule in those cases survives *Blue Chip* because the Supreme Court limited its holding in that case to private damage actions. Brief for Plaintiff-Appellant at 19–24. We appear to be the first court of appeals squarely to address this issue,[17] and we think *Blue Chip* cannot be so limited.

It is true, as the Court in *Blue Chip* acknowledged, that the question of what constitutes the proper plaintiff class under section 10(b) and Rule 10b–5 cannot be conclusively determined by resort to the text of those enactments; as one might expect, neither the statute nor the rule speaks directly to the question of who may sue since the right to sue was created afterwards by the judiciary. See *Blue Chip,* 421 U.S. at 737. Still, in the process of implying private rights judges must take account of the statutory scheme. See generally Schneider, Implying Private Rights and Remedies Under the Federal Securities Act, 62 N.C.L.Rev. 853, 884–96 (1984); Frankel, Implied Rights of Action, 67 Va.L.Rev. 553, 559–70 (1981). No better

13. Though not apparent from the Second Circuit's opinion, *Birnbaum* was a suit in equity seeking rescission of a sale allegedly violative of Rule 10b–5 and an accounting by the defendants. See Birnbaum v. Newport Steel Corp., 98 F.Supp. 506 (S.D.N.Y.1951). The appellate court's decision, moreover, did not appear to turn on the nature of relief sought. Based on this, the Eleventh Circuit recently stated that "[i]f Birnbaum were binding on this panel it would mandate * * * dismissal of * * * [the] section 10(b) claim for injunctive relief." Liberty Nat'l Ins. Holding Co. v. Charter Co., 734 F.2d 545, 557 n. 26 (11th Cir.1984). While it is true that *Birnbaum* was an "action in equity," the nature of relief sought was essentially monetary.

17. The Eleventh Circuit recently discussed a related issue in Liberty Nat'l Ins. Holding Co. v. Charter Co., 734 F.2d 545 (1984). There the court held that the shareholder plaintiffs did not have a private cause of action under § 10(b) to force the controlling shareholder to divest itself

of its holdings, or to remove voting power from the controlling shareholder. At 558–59. In Tully v. Mott Supermarkets, Inc., 540 F.2d 187 (3d Cir.1976), the court assumed for "present purposes" only, that the "relaxed standing rule of *Kahan* retains its validity after *Blue Chip Stamps* in appropriate cases where only injunctive relief is sought to prevent incipient 10b–5 violations" but then held that the case before it did not fit into the "*Kahan* exception." Id. at 194. In Davis v. Davis, 526 F.2d 1286 (5th Cir.1976), the court, in dicta, did approve the "approach taken by the Second Circuit [in Mutual Shares Corp. v. Genesco] with regard to injunctive relief" but only after it had ruled that the plaintiff was "clearly a 'seller' under the [ ] definitional provisions of the Act." Id. at 1289–90.

The only other appellate court to reach this issue directly was a pre-*Blue Chip* case from the Eighth Circuit which adopted the view we take in this case. See Greater Iowa Corp. v. McLendon, 378 F.2d 783, 791 (8th Cir.1967).

guidance exists than the language of the relevant statute and regulation. See *Blue Chip*, 421 U.S. at 756 (Powell, J., concurring) ("The starting point in every case involving construction of a statute is the language itself.").

The relaxed standing requirement urged on us by appellant would be contrary to the rationale of section 10(b) and Rule 10b–5 as perceived by the Supreme Court in *Blue Chip*. While it may be possible to discern differences between an action for damages and a suit for an injunction, most of the Supreme Court's argument in *Blue Chip* applies quite as much to the latter as to the former. The scope of section 10(b) and Rule 10b–5 is limited to fraud "in connection with the purchase or sale of a security." Congress was asked on two different occasions to expand the jurisdictional reach of those provisions but chose not to. In contrast, Congress did choose to define the scope of other provisions in the 1933 and 1934 Acts in terms that clearly reflected a broader jurisdictional reach. Congress also limited standing in those instances where it did create express remedies under the Act to a class of persons including only purchasers or sellers. Thus, the purchaser-seller limitation is "sufficiently supported by the statutory structure of the Securities Act." The Supreme Court, 1974 Term, supra, 89 Harv.L.Rev. at 269. See also Northland Capital Corp., at 1426–27 (*Blue Chip*'s holding based primarily on the "language of the Act and its legislative history"). These features also constrain us to accept, in the context of an injunctive suit, the common meaning of the terms "purchase or sale" and reject an expansive construction of the Rule, as *Blue Chip* did for damage actions.

Attempting to fashion a different concept of standing for cases like this would involve us in distinctions altogether too awkward to be persuasive. As *Blue Chip* noted, the "wording of § 10(b) ∗ ∗ ∗ is surely badly strained when construed to provide a cause of action, not to purchasers and sellers of securities, but to the world at large." 421 U.S. at 733 n. 5. The Court also stated that it "would indeed be anomalous to impute to Congress an intention to expand the plaintiff class for a judicially implied cause of action beyond the bounds it delineated for comparable express causes of action." Id. at 737. See also id. at 755 (noting "consistency of [Birnbaum] rule with the statutes involved and their legislative history").

Our analysis might well end here. However, because *Blue Chip* went beyond statutory analysis to examine certain "policy considerations," 421 U.S. at 737, Cowin argues that relaxing the purchaser-seller requirement in his case is proper because that would not contradict the several policies relied upon by *Blue Chip*. Several lower courts, including the lower court in this case, have distinguished the Supreme Court's opinion in this fashion. See, e.g., Fuchs v. Swanton Corp., 482 F.Supp. 83, 89–90 (S.D.N.Y. 1979); Hundahl v. United Benefit Life Insurance Co., 465 F.Supp. 1349, 1357–59 (N.D.Tex.1979).

If we thought this question open, we might conclude that injunctive suits present many of the same problems of vexatiousness, "strike" suits, abuse of discovery, and the like that damage actions do. We need not decide that, however, for we think the approach appellant suggests is foreclosed by *Blue Chip* itself. There, the plaintiff had contended that two policies articulated by the Court—the difficulties in corroborating the elements of Rule 10b–5 proof and the potential for an unlimited class of plaintiffs—were simply not raised on the facts of the case. If plaintiffs were allowed to sue, the Court said, "it would mean that the lesser practical difficulties of corroborating at least some elements of their proof would be regarded as sufficient to avoid the *Birnbaum* rule." 421 U.S. at 754–55, 95 S.Ct. at 1934–35. The Court rejected this result stating that while its decision to affirm *Birnbaum* was in part based on these "practical difficulties," the consistency of the rule with "the statutes involved and their legislative history [were] likewise bases for retaining the rule." Id. at 755, 95 S.Ct. at 1934. To take such arguments into account "would leave the *Birnbaum* rule open to endless case-by-case erosion." Id. Thus, while "policy considerations" did play a role in the *Blue Chip* decision, when those policy considerations were inconsistent with the retention of a flat rule and with the other grounds on which the decision rested—the statute and its history—they were not strong enough to create an exception.

In cases of doubt, the institutional role of the Supreme Court weighs in favor of considering its rulings to be general rather than limited to the particular facts. The Supreme Court, unlike the lower federal courts, is given a largely discretionary jurisdiction which is used when areas of the law require clarification. As Judge Marshall put it in holding that *Blue Chip* forecloses injunctive suits by plaintiffs who have neither purchased nor sold securities, "[W]e must be mindful of the [Supreme] Court's function in hearing and deciding * * * cases. It does not sit to adjudicate individual disputes; that is the business of the district courts and courts of appeal. Rather it uses individual cases and controversies to shape and guide the development of the law. This is particularly true where, as here, it speaks in an area of judge made law." Wright v. Heizer Corp., 411 F.Supp. 23, 34 (N.D.Ill.1975), aff'd in part and rev'd in part, 560 F.2d 236 (7th Cir.1977), cert. denied, 434 U.S. 1066 (1978). When the Court wishes to make a narrow, fact-bound holding, typically it says so. When it does not say so, the rebuttable presumption is that a general rule has been enunciated. Here there is more than that presumption, for the Court gave every indication that it wished to speak broadly. *Blue Chip* expressly acknowledged that the rule it adopted in that case operated as a bar to Rule 10b–5 actions brought by "shareholders, creditors, and perhaps others related to an issuer who suffered loss in the value of their investment due to corporate or insider activities in connection with the purchase or sale of securities which violate Rule 10b–5." 421 U.S. at 737–38. Appellant falls directly within this group and we may not allow him to proceed on his Rule 10b–5 claims against the company.

III.

Finally, Cowin's complaint alleges that the appellees have caused the company to issue material misleading proxy statements in the years 1974 through 1979 in violation of section 14(a) of the 1934 Act and Rule 14a–9. He claims these statements artificially depressed the value of company stock by limiting the public trading market in those shares and resulted in the election of appellees as directors, thus allowing them to continue their fraudulent activities. To remedy these violations of the proxy rules, Cowin sought to have declared void the "elections of defendant directors." Reply Brief for Plaintiff-Appellant at 28.[18]

---

18. Appellees address this claim as though Cowin sought only to void the 1980 directors' elections. See Brief for Defen- dants-Appellees at 37. However, Cowin claims that the complaint alleges "that defendants are continuing to issue deceptive

The district court held that Cowin could not, under section 14(a), challenge "proxy solicitations upon which he has not relied." R.E. at 51. The court agreed with a recent Ninth Circuit decision that ruled "the policies of § 14(a) and established doctrine in analogous securities contexts supports the * * * position [that] shareholders who do not rely on allegedly misleading or deceptive proxy solicitations lack standing to assert direct (as opposed to derivative) equitable actions under § 14(a)." R.E. at 52 (quoting Gaines v. Haughton, 645 F.2d 761, 774 (9th Cir.1981), cert. denied, 454 U.S. 1145 (1982)). In response to a line of cases—relied on by Cowin—taking the contrary position, the court stated that because those cases "so preceded the Supreme Court's recent restrictions on private securities actions * * * their precedential value is dubious." R.E. at 52. On appeal, appellees rely primarily on the district court's opinion. Cowin again points to those cases holding that standing to raise section 14(a) claims does not require reliance on the allegedly deceptive proxy materials and argues that the contrary position "conflicts with the remedial purpose of Section 14(a), is unsound in logic, and is contrary to the weight of authority." Brief for Plaintiff-Appellant at 46.

Our examination of who may sue under section 14(a) follows the approach taken in part II B supra to analyze Cowin's section 10(b) claims. Regarding section 14(a), however, we find no language in the relevant statutory materials that leads us to conclude that reliance is a prerequisite to standing under that section. Nor is there any Supreme Court decision that directly controls our resolution of the question. The analysis in *Blue Chip*—heavily influenced by the statutory text—in fact supports our conclusion that Cowin does not need to show reliance to bring a section 14(a) claim.[19]

In J.I. Case Co. v. Borak, 377 U.S. 426 (1964), the Supreme Court found an implied private remedy in section 14(a) because private enforcement served that statute's purpose—"to prevent management * * * from obtaining authorization for corporate action by means of deceptive or inadequate disclosure in proxy solicitation"—and was "a necessary supplement to Commission action." Id. at 431–32. While subsequent private right cases suggest a shift in analytical focus, see, e.g., Touche Ross & Co. v. Redington, 442 U.S. 560, 577 (1979), the Supreme Court has never restricted the class of potential plaintiffs under section 14(a) as it has done under section 10(b) and Rule 10b–5.[21] In fact, the *Blue Chip* opinion stated that the implication of a private remedy under section 10(b) was "entirely

proxy statements" and that the relief he requests is not limited only to a declaration that the 1980 election is void. Reply Brief for Plaintiff-Appellant at 28. While the complaint is hardly a model of clarity on this point, we agree that it can, and should, be read in this fashion. Appellees' "mootness" argument, see Brief for Defendants-Appellees at 37, is thus rejected.

19. To the extent appellees argue that Cowin's § 14(a) claims—based primarily on self-dealing transactions in violation of the common law—are barred by Santa Fe Industries, Inc. v. Green, 430 U.S. 462 (1977), we think the district court is the proper forum for the initial determination of this

question. While the district court apparently alludes to this argument, R.E. at 40–41, the opinion on this point is undeveloped. In this regard, however, we again note our discomfort with the district court's dismissal of most of Cowin's claims without permitting any discovery on any of the issues.

21. Perhaps one reason the "delimit[ation]," *Blue Chip*, 421 U.S. at 749, has not been deemed necessary with respect to § 14(a) is that the conduct proscribed in the statute—deceptive proxy solicitations—is itself a means by which the plaintiff class is defined and restricted.

consistent with the Court's recognition in * * * *Borak* * * * that private enforcement of Commission rules may '[provide] a necessary supplement to Commission action.'" 421 U.S. at 730.

Both section 14(a) and Rule 14a–9 proscribe in clear terms a specific form of misconduct. Section 14(a) makes it unlawful to solicit proxies "in contravention of such rules and regulations as the Commission may prescribe as necessary or appropriate in the public interest or for the protection of investors * * *" Rule 14a–9 expressly prohibits false or misleading proxy solicitations:

> No solicitation subject to this regulation shall be made by means of any proxy statement * * * which, at the time and in the light of the circumstances under which it is made, is false or misleading with respect to any material fact, or which omits to state any material fact necessary in order to make the statements therein not false or misleading or necessary to correct any statement in any earlier communication with respect to the solicitation of a proxy for the same meeting or subject matter which has become false or misleading.

Unlike section 10(b) and Rule 10b–5, neither section 14(a) nor Rule 14a–9 prohibits the unlawful conduct in connection with a particular activity; deceptive proxy solicitations are unconditionally proscribed. It cannot be said then that the language of the statute and the regulation constrains us to find reliance a necessary predicate to standing under section 14(a). Cf. *Blue Chip*, 421 U.S. at 749, 95 S.Ct. at 1931. Indeed, there is much to suggest the contrary conclusion.[22]

The Act demands full and fair disclosure. Section 14(a) was enacted to prevent "management or others from obtaining authorization for corporate action by means of deceptive or inadequate disclosure in proxy solicitations." *Borak*, 377 U.S. at 431. See also T.S.C. Industries, Inc. v. Northway, Inc., 426 U.S. 438, 448 (1976). Congress sought to "ensur[e] that proxies would be solicited with 'explanation to the stockholders of the real nature of the questions for which authority to cast his vote is sought.'" Mills v. Electric Auto-Lite Co., 396 U.S. 375, 381 (1970) (quoting H.R.Rep. No. 1383, 73d Cong., 2d Sess. 14 (1934)). The goal of Congress thus seems to have been to protect a shareholder's investment from self-serving designs of those at odds with the best interest of the corporation. See, e.g., S.Rep. No. 1455, 73d Cong., 2d Sess. 77 (1934) (section 14(a) intended to protect investors from "promiscuous" proxy solicitations by "unscrupulous corporate officials seeking to retain control of the management by concealing and distorting facts"). *Borak* itself identifies the injury section 14(a) sought to prevent:

> The injury which a stockholder suffers from corporate action pursuant to a deceptive proxy solicitation ordinarily flows from the damage done the corporation, rather than from the damage inflicted directly upon the stockholder. The damage suffered results not from the deceit practiced on him alone but rather from the deceit practiced on the stockholders as a group.

377 U.S. at 432.

---

22. Like the Court in *Blue Chip*, where we must "flesh out the portions of the law with respect to which neither the congressional enactment nor the administrative regulations offer conclusive guidance," it is appropriate for us to take into account various "policy considerations." 421 U.S. at 737.

The injury Cowin alleges was not caused by his individual reliance on deceptive proxy solicitations. Rather, his claim is that other shareholders elected appellees as directors because they were misled by the proxy materials. The installation of appellees as directors and their subsequent actions has injured appellant. This injury is totally divorced from any reliance, or lack of reliance, on Cowin's part and falls precisely into the scope of injury Congress sought to protect. *Borak*, 377 U.S. at 432. Requiring reliance in these circumstances would serve no legitimate policy and we decline to do so. See Hershfang v. Knotter, 562 F.Supp. 393, 397-98 (E.D.Va.1983), aff'd mem., 725 F.2d 675 (4th Cir.1984) (plaintiff has standing under section 14(a) despite his lack of reliance because injury suffered has no connection to his individual reliance). Jones v. National Distillers & Chemical Corp., 484 F.Supp. 679, 684-85 (S.D.N.Y.1979) (same). Cf. Ash v. GAF Corp., 723 F.2d 1090, 1094-95 (3d Cir.1983) (where plaintiff's claimed injury was a violation of Rule 14a-3—requiring proxy statements to be "accompanied or preceded" by annual reports—fact that he did not vote or attempt to exercise his proxy precluded him from suing to invalidate a director's election).

We think sentiment expressed in a recent district court opinion persuasive.

It is abundantly clear that Congress' intent to protect the investing public would be seriously hampered if one who misuses the proxy process cannot be brought to task by those shareholders who have from the outset recognized his deceptions, but has only to fear that the other shareholders whom he has successfully beguiled will belatedly become enlightened and seek redress for the damage he has done them.

Lynch v. Fulks, [1981 Transfer Binder] Fed.Sec.L.Rep. (CCH) ¶ 97,831, at 90,134 (D.Kan. Dec. 12, 1980). See also Clayton v. Skelly Oil Co., [1977-1978 Transfer Binder] Fed.Sec.L.Rep. (CCH) ¶ 96,269, at 92,727 (S.D.N.Y. Dec. 30, 1977). Because the controlling statutory materials are silent on the question and because we believe a contrary rule would partially frustrate congressional policy, we find that Cowin need not prove reliance to bring a section 14(a) claim.

The district court, however, had alternative grounds for dismissing the section 14(a) claims. The court found that Cowin had failed to adequately allege an injury that was causally related to the alleged proxy violations. See R.E. at 53. Cowin claims that the misleading proxy statement damaged him by causing the market price of his stock to be artificially depressed and by reducing the available resale market for his shares.

It may be true that the appellant's alleged injury is capable of being caused by the misleading proxy statement; however, in J.I. Case Co. v. Borak, 377 U.S. 426 (1964), the Supreme Court stated that "[t]he purpose of § 14(a) is to prevent management or others from obtaining authorization for corporate action by means of deceptive or inadequate disclosure in proxy solicitation." Id. at 431, 84 S.Ct. at 1559. See also S.Rep. No. 1455, 73d Cong., 2d Sess. 77 (1934) (purpose of § 14(a) is to protect shareholders from "unscrupulous" directors and outsiders and to give a full explanation of the proposed authorizations for which shareholders' votes are sought); H.R.Rep. No. 1382, 73d Cong., 2d Sess. 14 (1934) (same). Here the appellant claims his damages are a reduction in the price and market for his shares.

This may have occurred due to a misleading proxy statement, but was not a result of a corporate action authorized by the proxy machinery.

In *Mills* the Court recognized that monetary damages may still be allowed where the misleading part of the proxy materials did not relate directly to the transaction involved (in our case the election of directors):

> Monetary relief will, of course, also be a possibility. Where the defect in the proxy solicitation relates to the specific terms of the merger, the district court might appropriately order an accounting to ensure that the shareholders receive the value that was represented as coming to them. On the other hand, where, as here, the misleading aspect of the solicitation did not relate to terms of the merger, monetary relief might be afforded to the shareholders only if the merger resulted in a reduction of the earnings or earnings potential of their holdings. In short, damages should be recoverable only to the extent that they can be shown.

Mills v. Electric Auto-Lite Co., 396 U.S. 375 at 388–89. The damages, however, that the *Mills* Court was allowing the plaintiff to show were those that resulted directly from the merger—the authorized corporate action. Allowing claims that have no direct relationship to the purpose of the proxy statement could open the court's doors to suits every time a proxy statement is alleged to have caused the market to react negatively to the stock, regardless of how difficult actual proof of damages would be. The appellant's reliance on Schlick v. Penn-Dixie Cement Corp., 507 F.2d 374 (2d Cir.1974), is likewise misplaced. There the damages alleged flowed directly from the merger authorized by the proxy statement—i.e., an unfair and disadvantageous merger ratio of shares received for those given up. Cowin's damages are not a result of the corporate action authorized by the proxy statement and therefore are not the type of damages sought to be remedied by section 14(a).

Cowin also claims that due to the misleading proxy statements the current directors were reelected and he, as a shareholder, was damaged by the continued fraudulent acts of the elected directors. The misconduct alleged here also was not a direct result of the misleading proxy statement and therefore does not meet the causation requirement of *Mills*. 396 U.S. at 385. See also Brayton v. Ostrau, 561 F.Supp. 156 (S.D.N.Y.1983); Rosenbaum v. Klein, 547 F.Supp. 586 (E.D.Pa.1982); Rosengarten v. International Telephone & Telegraph Corp., 466 F.Supp. 817 (S.D.N.Y.1979). Appellant is alleging a subsequent breach of fiduciary duty which is only an incident to the election of directors and not actionable under section 14(a). This claim is actionable, if at all, as a state law claim for breach of fiduciary duty.

Because Cowin has not claimed damages that are remediable by a section 14(a) action, the district court's dismissal of his claim was proper.

IV.

We here summarize our disposition of this appeal. We affirm the dismissal of appellant's common law and section 10(b) claims although we affirm the latter on grounds different from those relied upon by the court below. The district court's dismissal of appellant's attempt to put the company into receivership is reversed and remanded for fact-finding. Although it is unnecessary for Cowin to show reliance on the allegedly misleading proxy statements, he has not claimed injury that is remediable by a section 14(a) action. We also affirm the dismissal of Cowin's section 14(a) claims.

It is so ordered.

KALMANOVITZ v. G. HEILEMAN BREWING COMPANY, INC.

United States Court of Appeals, Third Circuit, 1985.
769 F.2d 152.

Before ADAMS and HUNTER, CIRCUIT JUDGES, and FISHER, DISTRICT JUDGE *.

ADAMS, CIRCUIT JUDGE.

This appeal, certified to us by the district court, arises in the aftermath of a bitter fight to gain control of Pabst Brewing Company. Plaintiff, a disappointed tender offeror, has sued his former partner, the successful acquiring company, and the target company, alleging violations of the federal antitrust and securities laws; in addition, plaintiff raised a variety of state law claims. Except for a breach of contract claim, the district court either dismissed or granted summary judgment to the defendants on all federal and state law causes of action. We will affirm the district court's judgment and remand the case for further proceedings on the breach of contract claim.

I.

On October 26, 1982, Paul Kalmanovitz and Irwin L. Jacobs, along with three of Jacobs' associates (the Jacobs Group),[1] signed a Memorandum of Terms. According to this memorandum, Kalmanovitz and the Jacobs Group agreed to make a tender offer for three million shares of Pabst Brewing Company at $24 per share through JMSL Acquiring Corporation. The Jacobs Group already owned more than 1.14 million shares of Pabst; acquisition of the additional three million shares would have given the parties a majority of the outstanding Pabst shares.

As part of the agreement Kalmanovitz and the Jacobs Group each were to become 50 percent shareholders in PST Acquiring Corporation, which wholly owned JMSL. On the day after JMSL accepted the three million shares on its tender offer, the Jacobs Group was to exchange its 1.14 million Pabst shares for additional shares of PST. In addition, Kalmanovitz was to contribute $26.4 million to PST in exchange for additional shares of the company. The agreement and the material accompanying the tender offer contemplated a subsequent merger of Pabst and JMSL.

On October 27, 1982, JMSL made public the terms of its tender offer. The management of Pabst opposed the offer. Thereafter, William F. Smith, Jr., Pabst's president, instituted a series of meetings with Russell G. Cleary, chief executive officer of Heileman Brewing Co., in search of a "white knight"—*i.e.*, another entity willing to make an offer more acceptable to the management of the target company. As a result of these

---

* Hon. Clarkson S. Fisher, Chief Judge, United States District Court for the District of New Jersey, sitting by designation.

1. The Jacobs Group consisted of Jacobs, Dennis Mathisen, Gerald A. Schwalbach, and Daniel T. Lindsay.

meetings, on November 10, 1982, HBC Acquisition, Inc., a wholly-owned subsidiary of Heileman, commenced a competing tender offer for 5.5 million shares of Pabst at $27.50 per share.

In the wake of Heileman's offer, Jacobs allegedly told Kalmanovitz that the Jacobs Group could not put up any additional funding to compete against the new offer. Kalmanovitz therefore agreed to obtain additional financing, and on November 18, 1982, Kalmanovitz and the Jacobs Group amended the Memorandum of Terms by letter agreement providing that JMSL would raise its offering price to $30 per share and that Kalmanovitz would increase his cash participation in the deal to $44.4 million. In a separate letter written on the same date, Jacobs promised that

> [i]n the event we decide that it is better for our group to sell our shares in Pabst, rather than continue to bid higher, you will receive fifty percent (50%) of all amounts in excess of $24.00 for all the shares in our group.

App. at 225.

On November 23, 1982, JMSL again raised its tender offer, this time to $35 per share. The new offer was made possible by Kalmanovitz' promise to increase his cash participation to $59.4 million. The next day, the district court denied cross-motions by JMSL and HBC to enjoin each others' offers. After the hearing, Heileman announced that it would reduce the number of shares sought to 4.25 million, that 3.9 million shares had already been tendered to it, and that the company would make a further announcement (presumably regarding the price offered per share) by November 26, 1982.

During the afternoon of November 24, Jacobs telephoned Cleary and expressed concern regarding the ability of the Jacobs Group to proceed further in the tender offer battle. Jacobs then informed Cleary that he would withdraw from the bidding in exchange for $7.5 million. Jacobs avers that the motivation for this decision was his attorney's advice that the HBC tender offer would probably prevail and his fear of being shut out of HBC's proration pool.

Negotiations between the Jacobs Group and Heileman ensued, and on November 26, 1982, they signed an agreement which provided that (1) HBC would make a new tender offer for 5.6 million Pabst shares at $29 per share; (2) the Jacobs Group would tender its 1.4 million shares under the new offer; (3) the parties would dismiss all outstanding non-derivative litigation; and (4) Pabst and Heileman would reimburse the Jacobs Group $7.5 million for its expenses.

Later that day, Jacobs informed Kalmanovitz of the new deal with Heileman and offered to pay plaintiff $5 million if he agreed to withdraw from the bidding. The offer was rejected. On December 2, 1982, HBC made its $29 tender offer, and JMSL withdrew its offer the following day. Not conceding defeat, Kalmanovitz then made a tender offer for 4.15 million shares at $32 per share through 21–115, Inc., a corporation wholly owned by plaintiff. Four days later, on December 10, 1982, Kalmanovitz instituted the present action in the district court in Delaware, requesting a preliminary injunction against HBC. On December 20, 1982, the district court denied the preliminary injunction, and on December 22, 1982—the withdrawal date for the HBC offer—Kalmanovitz increased his tender offer to $40 per share. On December 23, 1982, however, Heileman accepted for payment 5.6 million Pabst shares, thus ending the contest for control of the brewing company. To date plaintiff has not received any of the proceeds from the Jacobs Group's tender of its Pabst shares to HBC.

* * *

In November of 1983, the district court dismissed plaintiff's claims based on §§ 1 and 2 of the Sherman Act, 15 U.S.C. §§ 1, 2 (1982), and his tortious interference with contract claim under Fed.R.Civ.P. 12(b)(6) for failure to state a claim upon which relief could be granted. Kalmanovitz v. G. Heileman Brewing Co., 576 F.Supp. 922 (D.Del.1983). In September of 1984, the district court granted partial summary judgment to defendants with regard to the federal securities and Delaware state law claims. 595 F.Supp. 1385 (D.Del.1984). All that remains is the breach of contract claim against the Jacobs Group. Finding no just reason to delay the appeal of the claims dismissed, the district court certified its rulings under Fed.R. Civ.P. 54(b) as final for purposes of appeal. This Court accepted appellate jurisdiction under 28 U.S.C. § 1291 (1982).

* * *

[The court's discussion of the Sherman Act claims is omitted.]

III.

Kalmanovitz maintains that defendants, in connection with the HBC offer, violated §§ 13(e), 14(d), and 14(e) of the Exchange Act, 15 U.S.C. §§ 78m(e), 78n(d), 78n(e) (1982). Because it found that plaintiff did not have standing to bring a private damages suit under these provisions, the district court granted defendants' motions for summary judgment on these claims.

In Piper v. Chris-Craft Industries, 430 U.S. 1 (1977), Chris-Craft, a disappointed tender offeror, brought suit against Bangor Punta, the successful tender offeror, and Piper, the target corporation, under § 14(e) of the Exchange Act. After an exhaustive analysis of the Williams Act, the Supreme Court concluded that "the sole purpose of the Williams Act was the protection of investors who are confronted with a tender offer." 430 U.S. at 35; see also Rondeau v. Mosinee Paper Corp., 422 U.S. 49, 58 (1975). Thus the Court held that a disappointed tender offeror had no standing to bring a claim for damages under § 14(e), the general antifraud provision of the Williams Act.

Kalmanovitz recognizes that he cannot assert his claim under § 14(e) by virtue of his status as a tender offeror. Instead, he argues that his status as a Pabst shareholder gives him standing to bring suit.[11] In *Piper,* the Supreme Court left open the questions whether a private right of action exists under § 14(e) and, if so, whether a shareholder has standing to assert such a claim.

Arguing by analogy to J.I. Case v. Borak, 377 U.S. 426 (1964), in which the Supreme Court permitted a private right of action to a shareholder for a violation of § 14(a) of the Exchange Act, and by reference to the Court's explicit statements regarding the Williams Act's purpose—to protect shareholders of a target company—Kalmanovitz contends that shareholders should be permitted a private right of action for damages under § 14(e).

11. Kalmanovita owned 20 shares of Pabst stock at the time he filed his various actions.

See Note, Private Causes of Action Under SEC Rule 14e–3, 51 Geo.Wash.L. Rev. 290 (1983) (advocating a private right of action under § 14(e)). Although plaintiff's contention arguably may be correct, our disposition of this case does not require us to decide that issue.

Assuming arguendo that a shareholder may bring suit under § 14(e), Kalmanovitz still lacks standing to proceed in the present case. This Court recently noted that even though a private right of action may be implied from a particular statute or rule, not every private suit brought thereunder is proper. See Angelastro v. Prudential-Bache Securities, Inc., 764 F.2d 939, 948 n. 13 (3d Cir.1985). One such example is that in an action brought under Rule 10b–5 of the Securities and Exchange Commission, 17 C.F.R. § 240.10b–5 (1984), the plaintiff must be a purchaser or seller of securities. See Blue Chip Stamps v. Manor Drug Stores, 421 U.S. 723, 730, 95 S.Ct. 1917, 1922, 44 L.Ed.2d 539 (1975). Similarly, in *Piper,* 430 U.S. at 35, 97 S.Ct. at 946, the Court held that a disappointed tender offeror lacked standing to bring suit under § 14(e) of the Exchange Act. We now must determine whether a disappointed tender offeror who is also a nominal shareholder of the target corporation has standing to bring suit for damages.

In addition to being a disappointed offeror, the plaintiff in *Piper* was a shareholder of the target company. Although plaintiff Chris-Craft did not explicitly argue that its shareholder status gave it standing to sue under § 14(e) of the Exchange Act, the Supreme Court nevertheless rejected this contention. *Piper,* 430 U.S. at 35–37, 97 S.Ct. at 946–947. In dissent, Justice Stevens maintained that there should be a private right of action under § 14(e) and that Chris-Craft's status as a shareholder was sufficient to grant it standing to sue. Id., at 56–59, 97 S.Ct. at 956–958 (Stevens, J., dissenting). The majority did not reach the first conclusion, because it rejected the second one. It stated that the reason Chris-Craft did not assert standing as a Piper shareholder was

not hard to divine. As a tender offeror actively engaged in competing for Piper stock, Chris-Craft was not in the posture of a target shareholder confronted with the decision of whether to tender or retain its stock. Consequently, Chris-Craft could scarcely have alleged a need for the disclosures mandated by the Williams Act. In short, the fact that Chris-Craft necessarily acquired Piper stock as a means of taking over Piper adds nothing to its § 14(e) standing arguments.

Id. at 35–36, 97 S.Ct. at 946. This result is not illogical since there may well be a conflict of interest between the positions of a target shareholder and a tender offeror. It would almost be a sham to permit an individual to bring suit formally in his capacity as a shareholder, when the suit is not in the interest of the target shareholders and in fact the person's true motivation, and his only real stake in the matter, stems from his position as an offeror.

During the takeover battle in *Piper,* the disappointed plaintiff acquired several hundred thousand shares of the target; in the present case, Kalmanovitz owned 20 shares of Pabst. The market value of these shares under HBC's winning tender offer was $640; Kalmanovitz' stake in the unsuccessful JMSL tender offer eventually reached almost $60 million. Much more strongly than in *Piper,* the gravamen of Kalmanovitz' complaint was grounded in his status as a tender offeror, not as a Pabst shareholder. As the district court noted, "given this miniscule stake in any possible recovery, his assertion of standing on the basis of a shareholder is without merit." 595 F.Supp. at 1392; see also Luptak v. Central Cartage Co., [1981] Fed.Sec.L.Rep. (CCH) ¶ 98.034 (E.D.Mich.1979) (characterizing plaintiff as a competing tender offeror because his individual stake in the suit as a shareholder was minimal in comparison to his interest as an offeror), aff'd, 647 F.2d 165 (6th Cir.1981). Thus we hold that a plaintiff who occupies the dual roles of a very substantial tender offeror and merely a nominal target shareholder may be considered to be only an offeror for the purpose of judging his standing to bring the types of claims plaintiff has asserted in this case.[12] For similar reasons, we conclude that the district court did not err in dismissing plaintiff's claims under §§ 13(e) and 14(e) of the Exchange Act.

IV.

We affirm the district court's grant of summary judgment to defendants on plaintiff's claim under § 10(b) of the Exchange Act and Rule 10b–5 because Kalmanovitz was not a purchaser or seller of securities as required by Blue Chip Stamps v. Manor Drug Stores, 421 U.S. 723 (1975). And we also affirm the dismissals and/or grants of summary judgments to defendants on Kalmanovitz' various state law claims that were certified to this Court by the district court.

Accordingly, the judgments of the district court certified to us on appeal will be affirmed and the case remanded for disposition on plaintiff's breach of contract claim.

SECTION 11 ACTIONS

It is clear under the express terms of Section 11 of the 1933 Act that the plaintiff must be a purchaser of a security ("any person acquiring such security"). Also, Section 11 by its express terms eliminates any requirement of privity of contract between the plaintiff and the issuer as a defendant, as contrasted with Section 12(2). And obviously no privity of contract is required between the plaintiff and the collateral defendants made liable by Section 11, such as directors and officers. Any purchaser in the market at any time before the statute of limitations has run may sue for a violation of that section. However, as that section is interpreted in the *Barnes* case, there is still a requirement of what might be called a "semblance of privity"[1] or "linear privity." The plaintiff must show that he is a purchaser of one of the securities issued in the registered offering.[2] This makes little difference where the company has only had one public offering, since all of the securities in the market are probably traceable to that one offering. However, where there was a preexisting public market for other securities of the same class as those involved in the registered offering, or where a subsequent public offering is made of securities of the same class after the allegedly defective one, the only

---

12. We in no way mean to suggest that for an individual who is not also a tender offeror, the amount of stock he or she owns is relevant for purposes of gauging standing to bring suit.

1. With apologies to Judge Sugarman. See Joseph v. Farnsworth Radio & Televi-

sion Corp., 99 F.Supp. 701 (S.D.N.Y.1951), aff'd 198 F.2d 883 (2d Cir.1952).

2. Accord: Rudnick v. Franchard Corp., 237 F.Supp. 871 (S.D.N.Y.1965); Abbey v. Computer Memories, Inc., 634 F.Supp. 870 (N.D.Cal.1986).

potential plaintiffs under Section 11 are those who can trace the ancestry of their securities to those covered by the false or misleading registration statement.

THE "PURCHASER–SELLER" REQUIREMENT UNDER RULE 10b–5

The complete reaffirmance of the *Birnbaum* doctrine by the Supreme Court in the *Blue Chip* case has now made it clear that the plaintiff, or the corporation if he is suing derivatively, must be a purchaser or seller of securities in order for an action to be maintained under Rule 10b–5. The *Birnbaum* case itself was a so-called sale of control case. In such a case, the controlling shareholder is attempted to be held liable, either to the corporation or to the minority shareholders, for his sale of the control block to a third party. Since neither the corporation nor the other shareholders in the typical case has purchased or sold any securities, it is clear that most of such actions cannot be maintained under Rule 10b–5.[3] (But compare the discussion above in Chapter 15, under the *Superintendent of Insurance* case, where the corporation was a seller of securities in a separate transaction connected with the transfer of control.) It is also clear that a shareholder who has not tendered in a tender offer has no standing to sue the offeror or the target company under Rule 10b–5.[4] Certainly a shareholder who merely claims that the value of his stock was depreciated by acts of the defendant has no standing under Rule 10b–5 individually,[5] nor derivatively unless the wrongful acts of the defendant involved some purchase or sale of securities by the corporation.

Who is a purchaser or seller for the purpose of applying this limitation? It has been held that a trust beneficiary has standing to bring an action against the trustee alleging fraud in selling securities of the trust corpus, since the beneficial interest of the beneficiary was sold and therefore he was a "seller." [6] It has also been held that a secured party is a seller in a case where the securities were sold on foreclosure by the sheriff [7] and that the pledgor is a seller when the pledgee sells the securities on foreclosure,[8] since in both cases they have an interest in the proceeds of the sale (although the pledgor does, of

---

3. See the cases cited supra, pp. 1085–1087. See also, Northway, Inc. v. TSC Industries, Inc., 361 F.Supp. 108 (N.D.Ill. 1972).

4. See Peterson v. Federated Development Co., 387 F.Supp. 355 (S.D.N.Y.1974).

5. Sargent v. Genesco, Inc., 492 F.2d 750 (5th Cir.1974); Cooper v. Garza, 431 F.2d 578 (5th Cir.1970); Greenstein v. Paul, 400 F.2d 580 (2d Cir.1968); In re R. Hoe & Co., Inc., 508 F.2d 1126 (2d Cir. 1974); Jensen v. Voyles, 393 F.2d 131 (10th Cir.1968); Simmons v. Wolfson, 428 F.2d 455 (6th Cir.1970), cert. denied 400 U.S. 999 (1971); Edelman v. Decker, 337 F.Supp. 582 (E.D.Pa.1972); Geller v. Bohen, CCH Fed.Sec.Law Rptr. ¶ 92,429 (E.D.N.Y.1969). In Garner v. Pearson, 374 F.Supp. 591 (M.D.Fla.1974), the court held that the reduction of the assets of a bank by allegedly fraudulent transactions made the time depositors "forced sellers" of their securities because they had been "reduced to a mere claim for a portion of the remaining assets of the Bank in the liquidation proceedings." The decision in the *Sargent* case, supra, in the Fifth Circuit was handed down only six days after the *Garner* case, clearly repudiating this sort of analysis, which makes this perhaps the shortest-lived doctrine in the history of jurisprudence.

6. Norris v. Wirtz, 719 F.2d 256 (7th Cir.1983); Kirshner v. United States of America, 603 F.2d 234 (2d Cir.1978), cert. denied 444 U.S. 995 (1979); James v. Gerber Products Co., 483 F.2d 944 (6th Cir. 1973); Klamberg v. Roth, 425 F.Supp. 440 (S.D.N.Y.1976).

7. Falls v. Fickling, 621 F.2d 1362 (5th Cir.1980); Bosse v. Crowell, Collier & MacMillan, 565 F.2d 602 (9th Cir.1977); Cambridge Capital Corp. v. Northwestern National Bank of Minneapolis, 350 F.Supp. 829 (D.Minn.1972).

8. Dopp v. Franklin National Bank, 374 F.Supp. 904 (S.D.N.Y.1974).

course, only if a surplus over the amount of the debt is produced by the sale). It has also been held by the Supreme Court that a pledge of stock is itself a "sale" for the purposes of Rule 10b–5.[9]

A merger or sale of assets (whether for cash or stock) normally involves a sale by the shareholders of the acquired corporation of their shares in that corporation for whatever is received in the merger or sale of assets.[10] However, it was held in In re Penn Central Securities Litigation [11] that a merger into a shell corporation merely for the purpose of creating a holding company for Penn Central was not a purchase or sale for the purpose of Rule 10b–5, although a merger between two distinct corporations would be, since it was a mere "corporate restructuring." It has also been held that a transfer of assets to a subsidiary and the spin-off of the subsidiary's stock to the shareholders of the parent corporation did not involve any purchase or sale of securities so as to invoke the application of Rule 10b–5. The original formation of the subsidiary was a "mere transfer between corporate pockets" and the shareholders who received the stock were not "purchasers" because they gave no value.[12] Corporate law theory is that the shareholders of the surviving corporation in a merger have made no purchase or sale, since they merely retain the same securities in the same corporate entity that they had before, except perhaps in situations involving the "de facto merger doctrine" in those states which follow that doctrine. However, in Nanfito v. Tekseed Hybrid Co.[13] the court held that the shareholders of the surviving corporation in a merger would have standing to sue under Rule 10b–5 even though they have not purchased or sold, since the shareholders of the extinguished corporation have standing under prior authorities. Does this holding survive *Blue Chip?*

It has also been held that the dissolution of a partnership involves a sale by the limited partners of their limited partnership interests.[14] But a stock split is not a purchase or sale so as to invoke the provisions of Rule 10b–5.[15] The court said: "A stock split, in spite of the enthusiasm with which it is generally greeted, is simply the distribution of two or more pieces of paper for one." [16]

However, a number of exceptions and qualifications to the statement that the plaintiff must be a purchaser or seller had been established prior to the *Blue Chip* case by those courts which purported to follow the *Birnbaum*

9. Rubin v. United States, 449 U.S. 424 (1981), overruling National Bank of Commerce of Dallas v. All American Assurance Co., 583 F.2d 1295 (5th Cir.1978) and Lincoln National Bank v. Herber, 604 F.2d 1038 (7th Cir.1979). Accord: Weaver v. Marine Bank, 637 F.2d 157 (3d Cir.1980). Followed in United States v. Kendrick, 692 F.2d 1262 (9th Cir.1982), cert. denied 461 U.S. 914 (1983). Compare Chemical Bank v. Arthur Andersen & Co., 726 F.2d 930 (2d Cir.1984), cert. denied 469 U.S. 884 (1984). (While the pledge of stock of a subsidiary by a corporation to secure a loan was a "sale", the alleged fraud was not "in connection with" that sale since the plaintiff did not allege any misrepresentations by the parent corporation relating to the subsidiary.); Head v. Head, 759 F.2d 1172 (4th Cir.1985) (following the *Chemical Bank* case).

10. Dasho v. Susquehanna Corp., 380 F.2d 262 (7th Cir.1967), cert. denied 389 U.S. 977; Vine v. Beneficial Finance Co., 374 F.2d 627 (2d Cir.1967), cert. denied 389 U.S. 970.

11. 494 F.2d 528 (3d Cir.1974).

12. Rathborne v. Rathborne, 683 F.2d 914 (5th Cir.1982).

13. 341 F.Supp. 240 (D.Neb.1972), aff'd 473 F.2d 537 (8th Cir.1973).

14. Bolger v. Laventhol, Krekstein, Horwath, 381 F.Supp. 260 (S.D.N.Y.1974); Feldberg v. O'Connell, 338 F.Supp. 744 (D.Mass.1972); Houlihan v. Anderson-Stokes, Inc., 434 F.Supp. 1330 (D.D.C.1977).

15. Gurvitz v. Bregman & Co., 379 F.Supp. 1283 (S.D.N.Y.1974).

16. 379 F.Supp. at 1286. In Keys v. Wolfe, 709 F.2d 413 (5th Cir.1983), it was stated that when the terms of a security are revised, the question of whether there is a new "sale" for the purposes of Rule 10b–5 depends upon whether there has been a "fundamental change in the nature of plaintiff's investment."

doctrine. To what extent these survive the *Blue Chip* case remains to be seen. For example, in Wright v. The Heizer Corp.[17] the District Court in Illinois concluded "with some regret" that Blue Chip had overruled Eason v. General Motors Acceptance Corporation,[18] the only circuit court case which had flatly disagreed with *Birnbaum,* even though in the *Eason* case the plaintiffs would probably have qualified as sellers (guarantors of notes issued) or "forced purchasers" (of the notes which they were forced to take up upon default) under the liberal interpretations of other courts which purported to follow *Birnbaum.*

The "Forced Seller." In Vine v. Beneficial Finance Co., Inc.[19] the Second Circuit held that a minority shareholder in a corporation who was "cashed out" by the effectuation of a short-form merger of his corporation with its corporate parent was a "forced seller" and therefore entitled to sue under Rule 10b–5. This same rationale has been applied to a liquidation [20] and to an ordinary merger.[21] The *Vine* case was reaffirmed in Mayer v. Oil Field Systems Corp.,[22] in an opinion by Judge Friendly. In that case, a limited partner was forced to accept stock in a corporation in exchange for his limited partnership interest in a transaction which only had to be approved by the general partner. The court said that the fact that he had no choice in the matter, as in the *Vine* case, did not prevent him from being a "seller" under the forced seller doctrine. It would appear that he was also a "purchaser" of the stock of the corporation which he received, although the court does not analyze that side of the transaction.

The "Aborted Seller." A contract to sell securities is itself a "sale" for the purposes of the rule in the *Blue Chip* case; [23] however, parties who negotiate for the purchase and sale of securities but never arrive at any enforceable contract can not sue under Rule 10b–5.[24] In A.T. Brod & Co. v. Perlow [25] the court held that a contract of purchase entered into without the intention of paying for the securities was a "sale" within the Rule; and Commerce Reporting Company, Inc. v. Puretec [26] held that a contract of sale entered into by the defendant without any intention of performing it, but merely for the purpose of getting a better offer from a third party, was a "purchase" by the other party within the Rule. These cases have been followed in the Tenth Circuit [27] and the Seventh Circuit has held that a breach of a contract by a person who has agreed to sell securities, accompanied by "conversion" of the securities, title to which had allegedly passed to the plaintiff, amounted to "fraud" permitting an action under Rule 10b–5.[28]

---

17. 411 F.Supp. 23 (N.D.Ill.1975).

18. 490 F.2d 654 (7th Cir.1973), cert. denied 416 U.S. 960 (1974).

19. 374 F.2d 627 (2d Cir.1967), cert. denied 389 U.S. 970 (1967).

20. Alley v. Miramon, 614 F.2d 1372 (5th Cir.1980); Coffee v. Permian Corp., 434 F.2d 383 (5th Cir.1970); Dudley v. Southeastern Factor and Finance, 446 F.2d 303 (5th Cir.1971), cert. denied 404 U.S. 858 (1971).

21. Mader v. Armel, 384 F.2d 51 (6th Cir.1968).

22. 721 F.2d 59 (2d Cir.1983).

23. Mosher v. Kane, 784 F.2d 1385 (9th Cir.1986).

24. Reprosystem, B.V. v. SCM Corporation, 727 F.2d 257 (2d Cir.1984), cert. denied 469 U.S. 828 (1984); Northland Capi-

tal Corporation v. Silver, 735 F.2d 1421 (D.C.Cir.1984).

25. 375 F.2d 393 (2d Cir.1967).

26. 290 F.Supp. 715 (S.D.N.Y.1968).

27. Richardson v. MacArthur, 451 F.2d 35 (10th Cir.1971).

28. Allico National Corp. v. Amalgamated Meat Cutters and Butcher Workmen of North America, 397 F.2d 727 (7th Cir.1968). Compare, however, Keers & Co. v. American Steel & Pump Corp., 234 F.Supp. 201 (S.D.N.Y.1964), which held that a person who claimed to be an "aborted seller" could not sue under Rule 10b–5. There the other party to the contract had died and his executor refused to carry out the contract of purchase. The court said: "Surely Benkert did not defraud plaintiffs by dying."

The "Frustrated Seller." In Stockwell v. Reynolds & Co.[29] the court held that an allegation that the defendant fraudulently induced the plaintiff to *retain* securities which he owned sufficiently alleged a "purchase or sale" for the purposes of Rule 10b–5. And in the Neuman v. Electronic Specialty Co.,[30] Judge Will held that a non-tendering shareholder could sue a person who chilled the tender offer under Rule 10b–5 (as well as Section 14(e)). However, Berne Street Enterprises, Inc. v. American Export Isbrandtsen Co., Inc.[31] is contra to the Neuman decision; and Morrow v. Schapiro [32] is contra to the Stockwell decision. In addition, the case of Iroquois Industries, Inc. v. Syracuse China Corporation [33] appears to deny standing to a frustrated buyer. Under the *Blue Chip* case it seems clear that no action can be maintained under Rule 10b–5 based upon a fraudulent inducement not to buy or sell.[34]

The "Would-Be Seller." In Shulof v. Merrill Lynch, Pierce, Fenner & Smith, Inc.[35] the plaintiff's complaint was that, while Merrill Lynch was tipping certain favored customers about the drastic decline in the earnings of Douglas, he had not been tipped so he also could bail out. The court dismissed the complaint and cited four similar suits in the Southern District of New York which had been summarily dismissed.

The Injunction Plaintiff. Mutual Shares Corp. v. Genesco, Inc.[36] illustrates one situation where an exception to the rule that the plaintiff must be a purchaser or seller had clearly been established prior to the *Blue Chip* case. If the plaintiff is merely seeking an injunction against the continuance by the defendant of market manipulation or other conduct violative of Rule 10b–5, his status as a shareholder of the corporation was held to give him standing to bring such action and he need not allege that he is a purchaser or seller. This decision was followed, not only in the Southern District of New York,[37] but also by the Third Circuit [38] and the Sixth Circuit.[39] However, in Wright v. The Heizer Corp.[40] Judge Marshall stated that he did not believe that this exception

---

In Walling v. Beverly Enterprises, 476 F.2d 393 (9th Cir.1973), the court held that entering into a contract with the secret reservation not to perform it was fraud cognizable under Rule 10b–5. On the other hand, the same court held in Mount Clemens Industries, Inc. v. Bell, 464 F.2d 339 (9th Cir.1972), that a suit could not be brought under Rule 10b–5 based upon allegations that the plaintiff did not buy at a sheriff's sale because of misrepresentations of the defendant; he was neither an "aborted buyer" nor "forced buyer."

29. 252 F.Supp. 215 (S.D.N.Y.1965).

30. CCH Fed.Sec.Law Rptr. ¶ 92,591 (N.D.Ill.1969).

31. CCH Fed.Sec.Law Rptr. ¶ 92,711 (S.D.N.Y.1970).

32. 334 F.Supp. 399 (E.D.Mo.1971).

33. 417 F.2d 963 (2d Cir.1969), cert. denied, 399 U.S. 909 (1970).

See, also, Mount Clemens Industries, Inc. v. Bell, 464 F.2d 339 (9th Cir.1972). In Madison Fund, Inc. v. The Charter Co., 406 F.Supp. 749 (S.D.N.Y.1975), Judge Conner held that a breach of a covenant by the issuer to effect a shelf registration does not give standing to sue under Rule 10b–5 under the "frustrated seller" doctrine. Un-

der that doctrine "a clear indication of an alleged initial intention to sell is critical." He stated that there was no need to decide whether that doctrine is still viable under *Blue Chip.*

34. Gaudin v. KDI Corp., 576 F.2d 708 (6th Cir.1978); Tucker v. National Student Marketing Corp., CCH Fed.Sec.Law Rptr. ¶ 96,181 (S.D.N.Y.1977); Wynn v. Fields, Grant & Co., 422 F.Supp. 18 (N.D.Cal.1976); Pittsburgh Terminal Corp. v. The Baltimore & Ohio Railroad Co., 446 F.Supp. 656 (W.D.Penn.1978); Lubin v. Belco Petroleum Corp., CCH Fed.Sec.Law Rptr. ¶ 96,543 (S.D.N.Y.1978).

35. CCH Fed.Sec.Law Rptr. ¶ 93,147 (S.D.N.Y.1971).

36. 384 F.2d 540 (2d Cir.1967).

37. Puharich v. Borders Electronic Co., Inc., CCH Fed.Sec.Law Rptr. ¶ 92,141 (S.D.N.Y.1968).

38. Kahan v. Rosenstiel, 424 F.2d 161 (3d Cir.1970), cert. denied 398 U.S. 950 (1970).

39. Britt v. The Cyril Bath Co., 417 F.2d 433 (6th Cir.1969).

40. 411 F.Supp. 23 (N.D.Ill.1975).

survived the Supreme Court decision in *Blue Chip*. He said: "In this regard we note that at no point in *Blue Chip* did the Court cite, let alone discuss or disapprove a cluster of courts of appeals decisions which appear to have declined to apply the strictures of *Birnbaum* to private 10b–5 actions seeking solely equitable relief. * * * But we must be mindful of the Court's function in hearing and deciding such cases * * * it uses individual cases and controversies to shape and guide the development of the law. * * * Thus, we have concluded that we would not be justified in drawing a distinction here between an action at law and one in equity." In the *Cowin* case the District of Columbia Circuit Court of Appeals has now endorsed this conclusion of Judge Marshall.

THE QUESTION OF "PRIVITY"

All of the early cases under Rule 10b–5 involved situations where a defendant-insider purchased stock of a closely-held corporation from the plaintiff while making misrepresentations or concealing material information. This was of course the precise situation which Rule 10b–5 was adopted to cover, since as indicated above it was not subject to any of the other antifraud provisions in the federal securities laws. In that type of case, there was no question that a plaintiff-seller sold to a defendant-buyer (i.e., there was "privity of contract" between them) and there was usually no question that the plaintiff relied upon the concealment or misrepresentation. For example, if the defendant bought the plaintiff's shares at $2 per share at a time when he had a firm offer from another party to acquire the entire corporation at $5 per share,[41] the plaintiff's testimony that he would not have sold at $2, if he had known of the pending offer pursuant to which he could get $5, would obviously be accepted (in fact, the contrary would be considered inconceivable).

However, when Rule 10b–5 cases began to be brought against sellers as well as buyers with respect to transactions carried out in an organized securities market, the question immediately arose as to whether these elements were necessary in order for the action to be maintained. If, for example, the plaintiff sold 1,000 shares on a stock exchange on a given date and the defendant purchased the same number on the same date, it would only be fortuitous if their orders happen to have been executed against each other on the floor. In a situation where their respective brokers combined orders of various customers for execution, it might be impossible to determine to whom the plaintiff sold and from whom the defendant bought. Also, even though the defendant may have made a public misrepresentation, the plaintiff may never have read it or heard of it. Even in the case of a concealment, which is necessarily a concealment from everyone, it somehow seems less *personal* (and perhaps less blameworthy) in this situation, than it does when the defendant deals with the plaintiff face-to-face and necessarily makes *some* statements to him but neglects to mention the crucial fact. (This distinction is apparently what is meant to be suggested by the phrase "total non-disclosure", which is sometimes used.)

At least four different general types of situations, which are variations on the classic case, can be distinguished:

(1) The defendant buys or sells (depending on whether the fact misrepresented or concealed is bullish or bearish) and the plaintiff executes a transac-

---

41. The first reported case involving Rule 10b–5 liability, Kardon v. National   Gypsum Co., 69 F.Supp. 512 (E.D.Pa.1946), was a case similar to that.

tion on the other side of the market contemporaneously with the defendant's, but their transactions are not with each other (i.e., there is no "privity").

(2) The defendant buys or sells and the plaintiff sells or buys, but their transactions are separated by a substantial interval of time.

(3) The plaintiff sells or buys, but the defendant, whose misrepresentation or concealment has allegedly influenced the price at which the plaintiff's transaction was effected, does not engage in any market transactions.

(4) The plaintiff does not sell or buy, but claims that the value of the stock which he already owned has been depreciated by the misrepresentations, concealments or other fraudulent acts of the defendant; the defendant may or may not have himself engaged in any market transactions.

In Joseph v. Farnsworth Radio & Television Corp.[42] Judge Sugarman dealt with a case involving our situation number (2) and he denied the plaintiff a cause of action on the basis that there must be a "semblance of privity" between the plaintiff and the defendant. It is not clear what he meant by this; the court in a later case stated that it was something like being "a little bit pregnant." [43] However, later cases dealing with our situation number (3), such as Shapiro v. Merrill Lynch, Pierce, Fenner & Smith, Inc.,[44] which hold that the defendant need not have purchased or sold at all, clearly have overruled the *Joseph* case.[45]

In *Joseph* the plaintiff clearly had a cause of action on the basis of his allegations under Sections 9(a)(4) and 9(e) of the Securities Exchange Act of 1934. Section 9(a)(4) prohibits any person selling a security or offering a security for sale from making any false or misleading statement, "which he knew or had reasonable ground to believe was so false or misleading," for the "purpose of inducing the purchase or sale of such security." And a cause of action is given by Section 9(e) to any person "who shall purchase or sell *any security* at a price which was affected by such act or transaction." Clearly these sections do not require privity of contract. However, Section 9(a)(4) does require scienter, and Section 9(e) permits the court to require an undertaking for costs and establishes a short statute of limitations. The plaintiff may have been trying to escape these restrictions in *Joseph*.

If the security had been traded over-the-counter rather than a listed security, then Section 9 would not have been applicable. However, the Commission has incorporated the specific anti-manipulation provisions of Section 9 into Section 10(b), which applies to both listed and unlisted securities.[46] But Section

---

42. 99 F.Supp. 701 (S.D.N.Y.1951), aff'd 198 F.2d 883 (2d Cir.1952) (Frank, J., dissenting).

43. Miller v. Bargain City, U.S.A., Inc., 229 F.Supp. 33 (E.D.Pa.1964).

44. 495 F.2d 228 (2d Cir.1974).

45. See, also, Heit v. Weitzen, 402 F.2d 909 (2d Cir.1968), cert. denied 395 U.S. 903 (1969); Mitchell v. Texas Gulf Sulphur Co., 446 F.2d 90 (10th Cir.1971), cert. denied 404 U.S. 1004 (1971). Donovan, Inc. v. Taylor, 136 F.Supp. 552 (N.D.Cal.1955), had followed the *Joseph* case; but two cases in the Southern District of New York had refused to follow it, even before Heit v. Weitzen. Gann v. Bernzomatic Corp., 262 F.Supp. 301 (S.D.N.Y.1966); Cochran ·v. Channing Corp., 211 F.Supp. 239 (S.D.N.Y. 1962). Also, the Fifth Circuit, in Texas

Continental Life Insurance Co. v. Bankers Bond Co., Inc., 307 F.2d 242, 249 (5th Cir. 1962), had stated: "It was not necessary that there be privity between plaintiff and the defendants in the sale of the bonds." In Baretge v. Barnett, 553 F.2d 290 (2d Cir. 1977), the court stated that the holding in the *Blue Chip* case that *the plaintiff* must be a purchaser or seller "does not require that the defendant be the seller of the stock or that plaintiff have purchased the stock from defendant. The District Judge apparently resurrected the notion that in a Rule 10b–5 action, there must be 'privity' between a plaintiff and a defendant. This view is now discredited."

46. See In the Matter of Halsey, Stuart & Co., Inc., 30 S.E.C. 106 (1949).

10(b) and Rule 10b–5 do not contain any provision for security for costs or any statute of limitations. This would seem to face a court with the following choice of dilemmas: (1) To refuse to grant any private cause of action for market manipulation by the dissemination of false information in the case of over-the-counter securities. This is in effect the choice of the *Joseph* case, since few of the purchasers in the rigged market could show any privity with the disseminators of the false information. (2) To grant a cause of action under Rule 10b–5 in the case of over-the-counter securities *only*, without the restrictions in Section 9(e), despite the fact that Section 10(b) and the Rule specifically apply to "any security registered on a national securities exchange" as well as those "not so registered." This was in effect the choice of the first panel opinion in Chemetron Corp. v. Business Funds, Inc. (see page 884, supra), although that opinion was reversed in the second panel opinion opting for choice (4) below. (3) To grant a cause of action under Rule 10b–5 with respect to both listed and unlisted securities, but to read into Section 10(b) and the Rule the restrictions of Section 9(e), despite the fact that they are not there. (4) To grant a cause of action under Rule 10b–5 with respect to both listed and unlisted securities, without the restrictions in Section 9(e), thereby in effect repealing Section 9(e) since an action under the Rule would always be preferable. This is the choice of the court in the *Shapiro* case and the second panel opinion in the *Chemetron* case.

See Gevurtz, Who Represents the Corporation? In Search of a Better Method for Determining the Corporate Interest in Derivative Suits, 46 U.Pitt.L. Rev. 265 (1985); Schneider, Derivative Suit and Blue Chip Standing, 12 Conn.L. Rev. 465 (1980); Froelich and Spiegel, Standing of Federal Securities Plaintiffs—Which Way the Trend?, 24 DePaul L.Rev. 510 (1975); Whitaker, the Birnbaum Doctrine: An Assessment, 23 Ala.L.Rev. 543 (1971); Boone and McGowan, Standing to Sue under S.E.C. Rule 10b–5, 49 Tex.L.Rev. 617 (1971); Ruder, Standing to Sue under Rule 10b–5, 26 Bus.Law. 1289 (1971); Fuller, Another Demise of the Birnbaum Doctrine: "Tolls the Knell of Parting Day?", 25 Miami L.Rev. 131 (1970); Lowenfels, The Demise of the Birnbaum Doctrine: A New Era for Rule 10b–5, 54 Va.L.Rev. 268 (1968).

SECTION 12 ACTIONS

Section 12 of the 1933 Act, like Section 11, clearly and explicitly requires that the plaintiff be a purchaser of securities ("the person purchasing such security"). There is, however, a privity requirement incorporated in Section 12 which does not exist under Section 11. The person who offers or sells "shall be liable to the person purchasing such security *from him.*" While this requirement may be relaxed by the doctrine of the liability of persons other than the vendor of the security under the "participant" theory (see chapter 17, below), there still exists under any theory a requirement that the defendant be directly involved in the sale to the plaintiff.

The plaintiff would not normally have any choice as to whether to sue under Section 11 or Section 12(2) in the case of a firm commitment underwriting of a cash offering, since he would not be in privity with the issuer or any of the other defendants named in Section 11, except possibly one of the underwriter [47] (although some might be brought into a Section 12(2) action under the "participant" theory—see discussion in Chapter 17 following the *Diasonics* case). As to

---

47. Federman v. Empire Fire & Marine Insurance Co., CCH Fed.Sec.Law Rptr. ¶ 94, 822 (S.D.N.Y.1974).

those securities sold through selected dealers, the purchasers would not be in privity with any of the defendants named in Section 11. On the other hand, in a registered exchange offer, as in the *Feit* case, supra Chapter 15, all of the purchasers are in privity with the issuer and would appear to have a choice as to whether to sue the issuer under Section 11 or Section 12(2), assuming that the slightly differently worded requirements regarding materiality and lack of due diligence under the two sections are both satisfied. However, Judge Weinstein states in that case that he does not have to decide whether the plaintiffs have a cause of action under Section 12(2), because they ought to be satisfied with what he has given them in Section 11! Compare Judge Pollack's statement in Securities and Exchange Commission v. Bangor Punta Corporation,[48] in which he ordered an offer of rescission to those who had accepted an exchange offer pursuant to a defective registration statement: "Bangor Punta claims that such an offer of rescission would be an empty exercise since the Bangor Punta securities received by the Piper shareholders have a market value far in excess of the Piper shares given up by them. * * * The decision whether to rescind is nonetheless one to be made by those who took the exchange." [49]

For the discussions of Section 12(2), see O'Hara, Erosion of the Privity Requirement in Section 12(2) of the Securities Act of 1933, 31 UCLA L.Rev. 921 (1984); Silverstein, Seller Liability Under Section 12(2) of the Securities Act of 1933, 36 Vand.L.Rev. 361 (1983); Folk, Civil Liabilities under the Federal Securities Laws: The BarChris Case, 55 Va.L.Rev. 199, at 201–216 (1969); Peterson, Recent Developments in Civil Liability under Section 12(2) of the Securities Act of 1933, 5 Houston L.Rev. 274 (1967).

SECTION 14(a) ACTIONS

It seems obvious, and no court has disagreed with this proposition, that the only persons entitled to sue under Section 14(a) are the shareholders to whom the allegedly misleading proxy statement was disseminated, since the proxy rules were adopted for the "especial benefit" of those shareholders. The Circuit Court of Appeals for the District of Columbia in the *Cowin* case disagreed with the Ninth Circuit in the case of Gaines v. Haughton[50] as to whether the individual plaintiff had to allege that he personally was deceived or whether he could rely upon the fact that the body of shareholders were deceived by the misleading solicitation (the question of whether that would have to be proven or whether it will be "presumed" from the misleading nature of the proxy statement is discussed below in Chapter 18).

The holding of the court in the *Cowin* case that the plaintiff does not have to allege that he was deceived is largely undercut, however, by its further holding that any injury alleged must flow directly from the corporate action taken as a result of the proxy solicitation and that any subsequent mismanagement by the directors is too remote from the fact that they were reelected by a misleading proxy statement to form the basis for liability under Section 14(a). These rulings leave little scope for an action under Section 14(a).

Even if the court had held to the contrary, that a plaintiff-shareholder could base his action upon a general depreciation in the market value of his stock as a result of the misleading statements in the proxy statement, it would still be extremely difficult for a plaintiff to prove that those statements caused his loss. If the misleading statements are unduly optimistic (which is typical, since the

---

48. 331 F.Supp. 1154 (S.D.N.Y.1971).

49. 331 F.Supp. at 1162.

50. 645 F.2d 761 (9th Cir.1981), cert. denied 454 U.S. 1145 (1982).

management of corporations do not usually denigrate the corporation or its financial condition or future prospects), the market value of the shareholders' stock can only have been increased as a result of the misrepresentation or concealment of adverse facts. If the shareholder thereafter sells before the true facts come to light, he will only have been benefited by the misrepresentations. If he holds the stock until the truth emerges, the decrease in the price of the stock which may then occur is not the result of the misrepresentations but of the underlying facts which were previously concealed.

If, on the other hand, the underlying facts which are misrepresented or concealed are favorable, which the management does not want to acknowledge because of some special motivation (such as the desire to purchase the stock of other shareholders for themselves or the corporation), only a shareholder who received the misleading proxy statement and sold before the favorable news came out would be able to claim that his loss resulted directly from the violation of Section 14(a). This would amount to a very small number of cases in which any cause of action for damages could be successfully asserted under Section 14(a).

SECTION 14(d) AND (e) ACTIONS

In the *Piper* case (supra, Chapter 13, page 841), the Supreme Court held that a tender offeror had no implied private right of action under Section 14(e) for damages. Presumably, the issuer would similarly have no private right of action for damages under that section against the tender offeror. The court did not rule on whether any private right of action exists under Section 14(e), but it said that the statute was passed for the "especial benefit" of the target company shareholders; and therefore they would probably have such a private right of action. The court in *Kalmanovitz* said that this proposition "arguably may be correct." It seems to be accepted, however, that the target company and the tender offeror may sue each other for *injunctive* relief under that section since they are the only ones with the necessary incentive and resources to attempt to prevent future violations of that section, in view of the fact that the SEC is not able to police all of the filings under the Williams Act which are made each year (see the discussion above at pages 685–686).

The difficulties of proof by a target company shareholder in a damage action under Section 14(e) have been commented on above (pages 887–888). Perhaps the only likely situation where the target company shareholders might be able to recover would be where the issuer or a rival bidder has chilled the tender offer by misrepresentations which violate Section 14(e), and as a result the tender offer is withdrawn and any stock which had been tendered is returned to the shareholders. In that situation, the target company shareholders could fairly easily establish that the violation caused their loss of the difference between what they would have been paid if the offer had been successful and the subsequent value of the stock in the market or what they received from the rival tender offeror if he was successful. It is perfectly clear, however, from the *Schreiber* case (supra, Chapter 15) that the fact that the tender offer is defeated by defensive maneuvers of the target company, such as a poisoned pill, cannot be the basis for an action under Section 14(e) in the absence of any misrepresentation or other "deception."

See Sachs, The Relevance of Tort Law Doctrines to Rule 10b–5: Should Careless Plaintiffs be Denied Recovery, 71 Cornell L.Rev. 96 (1985); Loewenstein, Section 14(e) of the Williams Act and the Rule 10b–5 Comparisons, 71 Geo.L.J. 1311 (1983).

Chapter 17

PERSONS LIABLE

Statutes and Regulations

Securities Act of 1933, §§ 11, 12.

Securities Exchange Act of 1934, § 14(e).

Rule 10b–5.

METGE v. BAEHLER

United States Court of Appeals, Eighth Circuit, 1985.
762 F.2d 621.

Before HEANEY, BRIGHT and ROSS, CIRCUIT JUDGES.

HEANEY, CIRCUIT JUDGE.

In this securities fraud class action, the district court granted Bankers Trust Company's (BTC) motion for summary judgment. Appellant Thelma Metge appeals on behalf of herself and 635 others similarly situated, arguing that the district court erred on the facts and law regarding BTC's liability as a controlling person and as an aider and abettor, and that the district court abused its discretion in dismissing pendent state claims against BTC. We affirm on the controlling person issue, but reverse and remand on the issues of aiding and abetting and pendent jurisdiction.

I. BACKGROUND.

Investor's Equity, Inc. (IEI), is an Iowa corporation which originally was involved in the business of buying, selling, and servicing real estate contracts on low-cost homes. Fluctuating business conditions in 1969 caused IEI to form Investor's Mortgage and Finance Company (IMF) to raise capital for IEI by selling unregistered, unsecured, one-year renewable securities called thrift certificates (certificates), which resembled promissory notes. Subsequently, IEI also issued thrift certificate guaranty bonds, which unconditionally guaranteed the certificates. Initially IMF transferred proceeds from certificate sales to IEI in exchange for IEI real estate contracts; but by the end of 1970, IMF was loaning the certificate proceeds to IEI in exchange for IEI's unsecured promissory notes. Certificate sales were brisk and by mid-1974, the outstanding balance had risen to $1.5 million.

IEI invested the certificate proceeds in speculative real estate ventures which, by 1971, began to erode IEI's financial standing. Over time, certificate proceeds grew, representing a larger share of IEI's financing. Meanwhile, BTC had become heavily involved in financing IEI, and engaged in a series of banking strategies which kept IEI in business. By mid–1974, however, the State of Iowa prohibited the sale and renewal of unregistered thrift certificates. In August, 1974, IEI declared bankruptcy; as a result, certificate holders received only twelve and one-half cents on each dollar of accrued interest and no repayment of principal. BTC lost

$543,703 in principal and $107,807 in accrued interest on its loans to IEI and its subsidiaries.

The appellant class of certificate holders sued BTC and seventeen individual appellees in federal district court, alleging state common law fraud and violations of federal securities laws stemming from misrepresentations and nondisclosure of relevant facts in connection with the sale of securities. In their federal securities law count, the appellants maintained that BTC is liable for violations of section 10(b) of the Securities Exchange Act of 1934 (15 U.S.C. § 78j) and Rule 10b–5 (17 C.F.R. § 240.10b–5) on theories of aiding and abetting, conspiracy and controlling person liability. The district court granted summary judgment for appellees, and the appellants appeal on all grounds except the conspiracy theory. We consider each of these arguments in turn.

II. THE AIDING–AND–ABETTING THEORY OF LIABILITY UNDER SECTION 10(b) AND RULE 10b–5.

A. Legal Principles of Liability.

This Court has previously set forth a three-pronged test to establish aiding-and-abetting liability. These requirements include:

(1) the existence of a securities law violation by the primary party (as opposed to the aiding and abetting party);

(2) "knowledge" of the violation on the part of the aider and abettor; and

(3) "substantial assistance" by the aider and abettor in the achievement of the primary violation.

Stokes v. Lokken, 644 F.2d 779, 782–83 (8th Cir.1981). Because the theory of aiding-and-abetting liability is a matter of common law, the courts have not yet elaborated the full meaning of these factors. Nevertheless, certain aspects of the practical applications of these tests are clear. The factors—particularly the second and third—are not to be considered in isolation, but should be considered relative to one another. Id. at 784. Practically speaking, this means that "where there is a minimal showing of substantial assistance, a greater showing of scienter is required." Id., citing Woodward v. Metro Bank of Dallas, 522 F.2d 84, 95 (5th Cir.1975). Thus, the two factors vary inversely relative to one another and where, as here, the evidence of substantial assistance is slim, the requirement of knowledge or scienter is enhanced accordingly.

The common law character of this three-part test requires further elaboration of the law before we apply the legal test to the facts of this case. Regarding the first prong of the test, we note that the existence of an underlying securities law violation by the primary party is not at issue in this case. Although BTC does not concede the existence of a violation, it recognizes that the appellants adduced sufficient evidence to give rise to a question of fact, which relieves us of further inquiry on this issue.

Regarding the "substantial assistance" factor, we note that the district court properly held that the appellants had the burden of showing that the secondary party proximately caused the violation. In approving this standard, we rely on decisions in other courts that have required a showing of "substantial causal connection between the culpable conduct of the alleged aider and abettor and the harm to the plaintiff[,]" Mendelsohn v. Capital

Underwriters, Inc., 490 F.Supp. 1069, 1084 (N.D.Cal.1979), or a showing that "the encouragement or assistance is a substantial factor in causing the resulting tort[.]" Landy v. Federal Deposit Insurance Corporation, 486 F.2d 139, 163 (3d Cir.1974), cert. denied, 416 U.S. 960 (1975) (quoting Restatement of Torts § 436.)

In further examining the "substantial assistance" requirement, we note that BTC's involvement amounted to inaction rather than positive deeds of manipulation or deception. The distinction between positive action and deliberate inaction is elusive, and we do not wish to foreclose appellants' strategies on remand, but the facts suggest that we examine the standard as it relates to substantial assistance through inaction.

Although courts are by no means unanimous in treating the question of substantial assistance in a case of inaction, most seem to agree that, if the aider and abettor owes the plaintiff an independent duty to act or to disclose, inaction can be a proper basis for liability under the substantial assistance test. E.g., Cleary v. Perfectune, 700 F.2d 774, 777 (1st Cir.1983) (citing cases which impose a duty to disclose where defendant possesses insider information, where a controlling person approves fraudulent practices, or where the law imposes special obligations on a profession). We find no such duty in this case. Nevertheless, the district court properly applied an exception to this rule in deciding the case under the so-called *Woodward-Monsen* rule. In Monsen v. Consolidated Dressed Beef Co., Inc., 579 F.2d 793 (3d Cir.1978), cert. denied, 439 U.S. 930 (1979), the Third Circuit evaluated the substantial assistance requirement in a case of inaction and concluded that inaction "may provide a predicate for liability where the plaintiff demonstrates that the aider-abettor *consciously* intended to assist in the perpetration of the wrongful act." Id. at 800 (emphasis in original). The Fifth Circuit took a similar tack in Woodward v. Metro Bank of Dallas, 522 F.2d 84 (5th Cir.1975):

> When it is impossible to find any duty of disclosure, an alleged aider-abettor should be found liable only if scienter of the high "conscious intent" variety can be proved. Where some special duty of disclosure exists, then liability should be possible with a lesser degree of scienter.

Id. at 97 (footnote omitted).

Simply put, in the absence of a duty to act or disclose, an aider-abettor case predicated on inaction of the secondary party must meet a high standard of intent. As applied here, *Woodward* and *Monsen* require that the aider-abettor's inaction be accompanied by actual knowledge of the underlying fraud and intent to aid and abet a wrongful act. The requisite intent and knowledge may be shown by circumstantial evidence. *Woodward,* 522 F.2d at 96.[1]

---

1. Because the circumstances in this case dictate the high scienter standard, we leave open the question of whether other facts in another case with more substantial assistance might state a claim under a recklessness standard of scienter. See Ernst & Ernst v. Hochfelder, 425 U.S. 185, 194 n. 12 (1976). Other circuits have limited the applicability of recklessness as a scienter requirement to cases in which the secondary party owed the plaintiff a duty. Cleary v. Perfectune, 700 F.2d 774, 777 (1st Cir.1983); Edwards & Hanly v. Wells Fargo Securities Clearance Corp., 602 F.2d 478, 484 (2d Cir.1979), cert. denied, 444 U.S. 1045 (1980); *Woodward,* 522 F.2d at 97.

B. Application of the Law to the Facts.

At the outset, we note the standard governing reliance on inferences in a summary judgment motion: direct proof is not required to create a jury question, but to avoid summary judgment, "the facts and circumstances relied upon must attain the dignity of substantial evidence and not be such as merely to create a suspicion. * * * Furthermore, an inference which a jury is entitled to draw must be based upon proven facts and not upon other inferences." Impro Products, Inc. v. Herrick, 715 F.2d 1267, 1272 (8th Cir.1983), cert. denied, 465 U.S. 1026 (1984), citing Admiral Theatre Corp. v. Douglas Theatre Co., 585 F.2d 877, 884 (8th Cir.1978).

In evaluating the record under this standard, we must determine whether the bank understood that the thrift certificates were worthless and, as a result, prolonged the business lives of IEI and IMF for its own benefit at the expense of the certificate holders. Although we express no view of the outcome of this case on the merits, careful review of the record convinces us that the appellants adduced sufficient evidence to avoid a summary judgment.

To explore the question of BTC's knowledge, we initially examine the nature of the relationship between BTC and IEI. The relevant history began in 1970 when BTC acquired by foreclosure a controlling block of stock in Mid-Iowa Lakes Corporation (MIL), which developed recreational real estate outside Des Moines, Iowa. Later that year, BTC, along with an Omaha bank, loaned MIL nearly $1.5 million in an attempt "to keep everything afloat."

In February, 1971, BTC sold the MIL stock to IEI under innovative terms, which figure prominently in this litigation. The total value of the transaction was $950,000, of which IEI paid $130,000 in cash. In addition, IEI gave BTC a $575,000 collateral pledge note for the acquisition loan, 50,000 shares of IEI stock, an irrevocable proxy to vote the MIL stock (the MIL stock was registered to IEI with blank stock powers back to BTC), and a guaranty of the acquisition loan by IEI directors and officers totaling $440,000. The 50,000 shares of IEI stock (the largest block of outstanding IEI stock, amounting to seventeen to eighteen percent of total shares) were transferred to Bell and Company, which was a partnership of senior BTC officers.

The proxy held by BTC in the MIL stock was unlimited and irrevocable. It was qualified, however, in that the purchase agreement included a proviso that BTC could only vote the stock when IEI was in default on its payments under the purchase agreement. IEI was frequently behind in its payments, which gave BTC at least potential control virtually from the outset of the agreement. Because the proxy allowed BTC to vote a controlling share of MIL stock, it gave BTC potential control over the general business affairs of MIL; for instance, it could call shareholder meetings, influence the composition of the board of directors, and amend articles and by-laws.

The purchase agreement also included a provision which empowered BTC to "put" or sell IEI stock back to IEI at a rate higher than BTC had paid for the stock. Thus, BTC was protected against the vagaries of the market, for if the stock value did not increase, IEI could be compelled to repurchase it at a higher price, but if the stock's value rose, BTC could sell it in the open market at a profit.

As part of its lending relationship with IEI, BTC also arranged to receive regular financial reports on IEI and MIL. Although in 1972 they were initially receiving quarterly statements (which showed quarterly balances of outstanding thrift certificates), by 1973, BTC was also receiving unaudited financial statements which treated IEI on a separate consolidating basis and revealed large thrift certificate balances.

An account of BTC's relationship with IEI must also consider the measures that BTC undertook to perpetuate IEI's business life. Viewed separately, most of these banking transactions are unremarkable events in the turbulent economy of the early seventies; but viewed in conjunction with the other evidence we discuss, they suggest an unusual pattern of extraordinary attempts to prolong IEI's financial viability.

Under the terms of the MIL acquisition loan, IEI was obligated to make a $100,000 downpayment, followed by $23,000 quarterly payments until September, 1972, when the loan would be repaid with a large balloon payment. When the first quarterly payment came due, however, IEI's poor cash flow compelled it to default, as it also did on the second payment. After extending the deadlines several times, BTC recognized that IEI was in part hampered by its involvement in another recreational real estate project, and so to recover its quarterly payments and to secure prepayment of the third quarterly payment, BTC arranged a "take-out loan" of $200,000 for the other project and IEI made its first three payments on the original acquisition loan.

In April, 1972, BTC acted as escrow agent for IEI in an exchange of other obligations for thrift certificates and thrift certificate guaranty bonds. IEI had previously purchased the assets and liabilities of the Triple Eye Corporation, which obligated it on certain outstanding notes. Working through BTC and with the approval of BTC's president, IEI offered to exchange its thrift certificates and guaranty bonds for the notes. Two noteholders, who are members of the appellant class, accepted the offer, sent their notes to BTC and received IEI's thrift certificates and guaranty bonds from BTC in exchange. In deposition, bank officers stated that this was a standard service offered by the bank's trust department. Nevertheless, the bank's role in the exchange is relevant at least in demonstrating its awareness of IEI's reliance on the thrift certificate program in April, 1972.

In late September, 1972, after other late quarterly payments and discussion of exercising the "put" on the IEI stock and of seeking protection from the guarantors of the MIL acquisition loan, BTC agreed with IEI to renew and amend the terms of the loan agreement. Under the revised agreement, IEI was obliged to make an immediate $30,000 payment on the MIL acquisition loan, with the due date on the balance extended to October, 1974, on a new nine percent note. In addition, the bank attached an eleven percent service charge to the "put" because, according to BTC president Robert J. Sterling, the "put" represented a debt on which the bank made no interest or earnings if the "put" was not exercised. The "put" was additionally secured by stock of another IEI subsidiary and by mortgages on some IEI real estate. IEI also agreed to provide monthly, rather than quarterly, consolidating statements for itself and each of its subsidiaries, and it also agreed to refrain from borrowing more than $100,000 from any other lenders without BTC's consent.

Refinancing became necessary in May, 1973, after IEI defaulted on two more note payments and on two of the "put" service charge payments. (It also defaulted on the next six payments due on both of these obligations, through at least April, 1974.) According to Sterling, the May, 1973, refinancing plan was intended "to keep all of this thing afloat." Under this new plan, IEI borrowed an additional $71,000 from BTC, which was used to satisfy delinquent loan payments and service charges. As collateral for the loan, IEI secured a $71,000 note from MIL. In addition, BTC required IEI to pledge additional MIL stock as collateral for a $100,000 obligation which had previously been unsecured. Although the $71,000 was a "wash" transaction, the application of the loan proceeds to delinquent payments brought IEI's obligations up to date and apparently protected BTC with more collateral. Unfortunately, in real terms, the refinancing plan did little to help keep IEI "afloat." On December 31, 1973, BTC was obliged to loan IEI an additional $69,000 on an "emergency" basis to pay delinquent taxes.

Yet by March, 1974, IEI was once again in serious financial trouble which required BTC's intervention in the form of a final refinancing plan resembling the plan which went into effect ten months before. When asked if BTC was very concerned about its position on certain loans to IEI, loan officer Chris Pappas replied, "That would be an understatement." As a result, IEI was obliged to sell a $13,000 receivable note and to pledge its interest in a plastics company to secure a previously unsecured loan. In addition, MIL issued a $25,000 note to IEI, which IEI pledged to cover the balance of the $71,000 loan in May, 1973. Finally, MIL borrowed $46,000 from BTC (which was secured by receivables) which it paid to IEI which in turn paid to BTC (along with $16,000 in other funds) to bring IEI's obligations up to date. Thrift certificate sales ceased in May, 1974, and by the end of summer, IEI had filed for bankruptcy under Chapter 11.

We can only conclude from the above that several times BTC apparently rescued IEI and its subsidiaries from the brink of financial disaster with the declared objective of preserving the enterprises. The relevance of these banking decisions to the aiding-and-abetting issue becomes apparent when we review the extent to which the bank knew the extent of IEI's financial woes and of the extent to which it knew that IEI depended for cash on the sale of then-worthless thrift certificates.

In considering the financial data, the district court relied on IEI's consolidated balance sheets (which reflected the status of IMF and other subsidiaries) prepared in March, 1974, and concluded that IEI had a net worth of $975,000 at the end of fiscal 1972 and $500,000 at the end of fiscal 1973. While these figures, as far as they go, appear to be correct, a proper consideration of the existence of a jury issue on this question requires a more thorough analysis of IEI's financial outlook. When the net worth figures are considered along with certain qualifications and with other relevant figures, IEI's future looks considerably bleaker, and BTC's banking decisions are cast in a different light.

First, we review the assumptions and qualifications embodied in the net worth figures. At the deposition to which the appellees refer in their brief, the net worth figure is qualified by the assumption that the assets could be sold at the stated value and that the net worth figure is also subject to contingent liabilities cited in the balance sheets. Moreover, Coopers and

Lybrand, IEI's accountants, prepared the balance sheets on a "going concern basis" which "contemplates the realization of assets and liquidation of liabilities in the ordinary course of business. * * *_[T]he Company has not generated sufficient revenue to cover all items of expense and to liquidate liabilities in accordance with the terms of such liabilities. The Company's ability to retain the assets which are pledged as collateral for the notes which are in default and the continuation of operations depends upon achieving profitable operations and retaining additional and/or continued financing." According to Coopers and Lybrand, the figures were also subject to "(1) the Company's achieving profitable operations and obtaining additional and continued financing, and (2) any possible adjustment arising from the determination of the disputed liabilities and related litigation and final acceptance of a subsidiary utility company's rates[.]" These assumptions throw the net worth figures in considerable doubt as regards the jury issue.

Yet perhaps more important, the net worth figures contrast with other less optimistic measures of IEI's economic vitality which were included in the March, 1974, report and preceding reports. We note that IEI's net loss was $151,346 in fiscal 1971, which more than doubled to $311,611 the following fiscal year, and increased to $365,101 for fiscal 1973. In addition, the March, 1974, report noted that IEI lost its office building for failure to keep the mortgage current and that IEI lost its rights on two leases on undeveloped property due to nonpayment of rent on the land leases.

We also note that, in previous years, BTC had performed its own analysis of IEI's audited financial statements and found that IEI faced difficult economic problems. As early as February 10, 1972, BTC concluded that, for fiscal 1971, IEI exhibited an assets-to-liabilities ratio of .236 to 1 ($905,000 to $3,840,400), and a borrowing ratio of 8.70 to 1, based on liabilities of $10,933,900 and a capital structure of $1,257,300. By March, 1973, BTC's spread sheets on IEI's financial status revealed that the assets-to-liabilities ratio had improved to 1.09 to 1, but that its borrowing ratio had increased to 13.26 to 1. BTC concluded that the latter ratio showed "that the Company is under extreme pressure and Company leverage for creditors is extremely limited." Significantly, BTC loan officer Chris Pappas testified in deposition that these ratios—assets to liabilities and debt to worth—are the "most important" ratios on the spread sheets.

In evaluating these data and the relationship between BTC and IEI, we analyze finally the status of the thrift certificates to determine the likelihood that BTC had actual knowledge of their importance to IEI as its financial fortunes worsened. Careful review of the deposition testimony of BTC officers reveals that they deny all knowledge of the thrift certificates, of the fact that they were secured by real estate, and of the possibility that thrift certificate proceeds were the essential means by which IEI stayed alive and was able to make any payments on its obligations to BTC.

Due to commingling of accounts and the difficulty of tracing funds to their sources, little evidence actually documents the transfer of thrift certificate proceeds to BTC in satisfaction of IEI's obligations. Nevertheless, we find noteworthy two incidents from which a trier of fact might have inferred that BTC had actual knowledge of the existence and extent of the thrift certificate program. First is the Triple Eye Corporation's note exchange in April of 1972, which we previously discussed. BTC president

Robert J. Sterling approved the bank's role as escrow agent in handling the exchange of the Triple Eye notes for IEI thrift certificates and BTC's trust department handled the matter. Although only two members of the plaintiff class were involved in the exchange, the incident could be interpreted as confirming BTC's knowledge of the program.

The second incident involves thrift certificate proceeds received by loan officer Chris Pappas on September 30, 1972, as part of the renewed and amended loan agreement between BTC and IEI. The record reflects that Pappas received a hand-delivered $30,000 check from IMF made payable to IEI, an IEI deposit slip for the $30,000 check, and an IEI check for $30,000 payable to BTC. He signed a receipt for the deposit and personally credited the IEI account for the following business day. Although Pappas argued in deposition that he did not make the connection between the deposits and thrift certificate proceeds until he was asked about it during the deposition, we regard the evidence of the transaction as potentially probative of BTC's actual knowledge as we survey the totality of the evidence.

The other set of circumstances surrounding the thrift certificate program that we regard as important in evaluating the propriety of the summary judgment is the growth in thrift certificate sales relative to IEI's declining financial health. We believe that records available to BTC confirm that these developments were inversely correlated—the worse things got for IEI, the higher were its thrift certificate proceeds. * * *

The final inquiry we make in evaluating the relationship between BTC and IEI involves the extent to which BTC can be showed to have benefited from postponing IEI's bankruptcy. Although it is undisputed that BTC lost over $650,000 in principal and accrued interest due to IEI's insolvency, Metge v. Baehler, 577 F.Supp. 810 at 814, we believe that this figure should not be the end of the inquiry, for the loss must be placed in context. First, we note that holders of thrift certificates, who were entitled to $1.5 million of principal, received none of their principal and only twelve and one-half cents of every dollar of accrued interest. Moreover, BTC's initial exposure in its lending arrangement was $950,000, which, when compared with its loss, suggests that it received significant payments of principal and interest as well as the service charges it collected on the "put" arrangement after it renegotiated an eleven percent service charge in September, 1972. Thus, although the record is not very illuminating on the question of BTC's benefit from IEI's delayed bankruptcy, we find sufficient evidence at least to give rise to an inference that BTC may have benefited at the expense of the certificate holders from IEI's renewed lease on life.

Although the facts we have recounted here at length are unremarkable taken in isolation, we find that taken together, they present what should have been a jury issue on the question of aiding-and-abetting liability. In sum, we have remarked on an unusually favorable banking relationship between the two parties at a time when BTC knew of IEI's precarious financial position. Moreover, the evidence suggests that BTC had knowledge of the thrift certificate program and its importance to IEI's ability to repay BTC's loan to IEI. Finally, we find an inference arising from the evidence which suggests that, although BTC made no profit on its loans to IEI nor even recovered its outstanding funds by postponing IEI's demise, it may have been able to lever itself into a more favorable position than the holders of thrift certificates. We express no view of any likely outcome on the merits, but hold only that summary judgment at this stage of the proceedings appears to have been premature.

* * *

Accordingly, the judgment of the district court is affirmed on the controlling person theory of liability, but is reversed and remanded on the aiding-and-abetting theory and on the pendent state claims.

"AIDING AND ABETTING" LIABILITY UNDER RULE 10b–5

In the Rule 10b–5 area the courts, in considering the liability of persons other than the primary wrongdoer, have held that persons who assisted in the wrongful conduct in some way might be held liable as "aiders and abettors" or as "co-conspirators" with the primary defendant. These concepts were drawn from the fields of criminal law and torts.[1] For example, in relatively early cases accountants who knowingly certified false financial statements were held liable along with the corporation which persuaded them to do this and which disseminated the false information.[2] These doctrines have become of enormous importance in the last few years because of the fact that in many cases the wrongdoer is insolvent or bankrupt and because of the practice of plaintiff's counsel in suing everyone, no matter how remotely connected with the transaction, who might have the ability to pay the judgment.[3]

Banks have been the favorite target of aiding and abetting claims under Rule 10b–5 whenever a bank has been involved in any manner, no matter how peripherally, in the overall transaction in which the securities law violation occurred. The reason for this is (as Willie Sutton said, when asked why he robbed banks) "because that is where the money is." They have been followed closely as favorite targets by accountants and lawyers (who, like banks, are almost always involved in some way in a securities transaction) because such professionals have until recently had liability insurance and the insurance companies had money.[4]

The court in the *Metge* case did not seem to appreciate fully the psychology of bank loan officers. Contrary to the popular myth regarding the "hard hearted banker",[5] the last thing in the world that a bank officer wants to see

---

1. See Restatement, Torts (1933) § 876.

2. Sprayregen v. Livingston Oil Co., 295 F.Supp. 1376 (S.D.N.Y.1968); Drake v. Thor Power Tool Co., 282 F.Supp. 94 (N.D. Ill.1967).

3. For example, in Landy v. Federal Deposit Insurance Corp., 486 F.2d 139 (3d Cir.1973), cert. denied 416 U.S. 960 (1974), the president of a bank stole money from the bank, thus obviously injuring the shareholders of the bank. The plaintiff sued not only the president, as a sort of pro forma defendant, but also (1) 12 brokerage firms that had executed stock transactions for the president and 16 individuals associated with those firms, (2) the New York Stock Exchange, (3) the National State Bank of Elizabeth, New Jersey [a different bank], (4) a firm of certified public accountants, (5) the Federal Reserve Bank of New York, and (6) the Federal Deposit Insur-

ance Corporation. This is a relatively modest example of people being sued in federal securities law cases.

4. Recently, such liability coverage has become to a great extent prohibitively expensive or wholly unavailable, largely because of the vast number of Rule 10b–5 actions filed against such persons. Some lawyers and accountants have taken to forming their own captive, offshore insurance companies to try to obtain such coverage, although that is basically merely a method of self insurance by a group of potential defendants. See Wall Street Journal (Pac.Coast Ed.), August 15, 1986, page 7:1.

5. In front of the Bank of America headquarters office in San Francisco, there is a so-called "sculpture" consisting of a huge, completely formless lump of stone

happen is to be forced to declare a significant commercial loan in default, and he will go to almost any lengths to avoid this consequence. There are at least two major reasons for this attitude. The first is that bank officers tend to share the eternal optimism of the managers of the business that, if just given time, the failing business will be turned around and the loan can be paid off in full with interest. Of course, this does happen in a substantial number of cases. Even when there is no rational hope left, however, bank officials frequently refuse to recognize reality and continue lending money to the borrower which is used to pay off the past loans and increase the amount so that the business can survive a while longer, because, if the loan is not maintained as "current", it will have to be charged off in whole or in part and that will go on their records as loan officers.[6] They may also wish to strengthen the bank's position vis-a-vis the other creditors in the event of an eventual bankruptcy, perhaps by taking additional collateral as did Bankers Trust in the *Metge* case. There would seem to be nothing illegal or immoral *per se* in doing this, even if the additional collateral subsequently has to be surrendered as a preference.

The three elements of an aiding and abetting claim as stated in the *Metge* case have been concurred in by all of the courts considering this issue, although with some nuances in the formulation of the tests and some disagreements as to exactly what they mean. The existence of a primary securities law violation by the principal wrongdoer of course must be shown, but frequently cannot be denied because he has decamped with all of the money obtained as a result of the fraud.[7] The question of what degree of fault must be shown on the part of the aider and abettor has produced considerable disagreement. Under the second element, some courts have required actual "knowledge" that a securities fraud is being perpetrated by the principal wrongdoer, but others have held that "recklessness" in not knowing is sufficient to support an aiding and abetting charge, since the Supreme Court left open the question of whether *scienter* included the concept of "recklessness" in the *Hochfelder* case. Almost all courts have held that to be sufficient so far as the primary wrongdoer is concerned. (See p. 956, above.)

For example, in Woods v. Barnett Bank of Fort Lauderdale[8] the Eleventh Circuit held that a bank was liable merely because a bank officer had written a letter of recommendation regarding the promoters of the fraudulent scheme to another bank acting as escrow agent, which was alleged to have been partially responsible for the second bank releasing the funds in escrow without compliance with a requirement of the escrow agreement that all of the proceeds of the offering be deposited before any could be released. The court stated that the statements in the letter by the official of the first bank regarding the reputation and probity of the promoters were made without any basis in fact and that this constituted "recklessness" on his part, leading to liability. Whether or not his recommendation of the promoters had any foundation in fact or was made "recklessly", it would seem that this had nothing to do with the question of whether he had any "knowledge" of the fraudulent scheme or was reckless in not discovering it. The court did not discuss that question nor the question of whether he could have intended to further a fraudulent scheme of which he

embedded in the plaza. Local wags have dubbed it the "portrait of banker's heart."

6. Witness the continued lending of money to such countries as Brazil and Argentina long after any possibility that the money can ever be repaid has disappeared.

7. For example, in the cases of J. David Dominelli in San Diego and of Ronald R.

Rewald in Honolulu. The latter was given *80* years (*sic*) in the federal penitentiary by the Hawaiian district judge. In that case, the CIA was accused of "aiding and abetting" Mr. Rewald.

8. 765 F.2d 1004 (11th Cir.1985).

was ignorant. The court said that "[i]n communicating to the trustee bank, Smith [the official of the first bank] was under a duty to speak truthfully, or stated alternatively, a duty not to communicate something that he knew to be incorrect, or something for which he had little or no basis for belief. Although Smith's communication did not reach the actual investors, it was foreseeably relied upon by the trustee bank that was to hold the investors' money until the entire bond issue was purchased." [9] How could the escrow bank possibly have thought that this recommendation from another bank authorized it to violate the terms of the escrow?

On the other hand, in Decker v. Massey-Ferguson, Limited [10] the court stated that "there is some indication in this circuit" that aider and abettor liability can only be predicated upon recklessness "where the defendant owed a fiduciary duty to the plaintiff." The court went on to say:

"Assuming for the argument that recklessness on the part of a non-fiduciary accountant will satisfy *Ernst & Ernst's* requirement of scienter, such recklessness must be conduct that is 'highly unreasonable', representing 'an extreme departure from the standards of ordinary care.' . . . It must, in fact, approximate an actual intent to aid in the fraud being perpetrated by the audited company".[11]

In Woodward v. Metro Bank of Dallas,[12] where a bank was sued as an alleged aider and abettor in connection with a scheme whereby the plaintiff was fraudulently induced to a co-sign a note by which the primary wrongdoer borrowed money from the bank, the court explained the aider and abettor doctrine as follows:

"The elements of an aiding and abetting claim have not yet crystallized into a set pattern; however, we find the Sixth Circuit's analysis in SEC v. Coffey, 6 Cir.1974, 493 F.2d 1304, cert. denied 1975, 422 U.S. 1004, helpful:

Without meaning to set forth an inflexible definition of aiding and abetting, we find that a person may be held as an aider and abettor only if some other party has committed a securities law violation, if the accused party had general awareness that his role was part of an overall activity that is improper, and if the accused aider-abettor knowingly and substantially assisted the violation.

493 F.2d at 1316. The elements adopted by the Third Circuit in Landy v. Federal Deposit Insurance Corp., 3 Cir.1973, 486 F.2d 139, cert. denied 1974, 416 U.S. 960, are similar to the *Coffey* test, but *Landy* refers to 'an independent wrong' instead of a securities law violation, and knowledge of the wrong's existence instead of awareness of a role in improper activity. Finally, *Landy* omits the 'knowing' requirement for the substantial assistance aspect. The first two *Landy* elements pose a danger of over-inclusiveness and seem to lose sight of the necessary connection to the securities laws. One could know of the existence of a 'wrong' without being aware of his role in the scheme, and it is the participation that is at issue. The scienter requirement scales upward when activity is more remote; therefore, the assistance rendered should be both substantial and knowing. A remote party must not only be aware of his role, but he should also know when and to what degree he is furthering the fraud.

* * *

"The second limb of the Coffey tree calls for general awareness that one's role was part of an overall activity that is improper. In this connection, the

---

9. 765 F.2d at 1012.

10. 681 F.2d 111 (2d Cir.1982).

11. 681 F.2d at 120–121. See, also, Barker v. Henderson, Franklin, Starnes & Holt, 797 F.2d 490 (7th Cir.1986).

12. 522 F.2d 84 (5th Cir.1975).

surrounding circumstances and expectations of the parties are critical. If the alleged aider and abettor conducts what appears to be a transaction in the ordinary course of his business, more evidence of his complicity is essential. The analysis of aiding-abetting liability at this point unavoidably harks back to the nature of the security that is the object of the transaction. Transactions occur as a whole and only later are they subjected to the scalpel of the legal dissector. If the securities involved are shares of common stock and someone aids and abets a fraud perpetrated in their sale, the culprit would be hard pressed to argue innocence once his awareness of the general sales activity was shown. On the other hand, if the document is barely a security at all, like a loan, then other independent commercial assumptions come into play, and the alleged aider-abettor may be unaware of any improper activity. Still, even for facially ordinary commercial transactions, a court may be influenced by a special duty imposed by the securities acts on the particular type of party, such as an insider, a controlling person, an accountant, or a broker. Generally speaking, though, the securities acts do not impose strict liability upon all who come in contact with a security. The postman who mails a fraudulent letter is not covered by the Act, nor is the company that manufactured the paper on which the violating documents are printed. * * * Knowledge may be shown by circumstantial evidence, or by reckless conduct, but the proof must demonstrate actual awareness of the party's role in the fraudulent scheme. As Professor Ruder argued, using an example remarkably similar to the case at hand:

> If all that is required in order to impose liability for aiding and abetting is that illegal activity under the securities laws exists and that a secondary defendant, such as a bank, gave aid to that illegal activity, the act of loaning funds to the market manipulator would clearly fall within that category and would expose the bank to liability for aiding and abetting. Imposition of such liability upon banks would virtually make them insurers regarding the conduct of insiders to whom they loan money. If it is assumed that an illegal scheme existed and that the bank's loan or other activity provided assistance to that scheme, some remaining distinguishing factor must be found in order to prevent such automatic liability. The bank's knowledge of the illegal scheme at the time it loaned the money or agreed to loan the money provides that additional factor. Knowledge of wrongful purpose thus becomes a crucial element in aiding and abetting or conspiracy cases.

Ruder, [Multiple Defendants in Securities Law Fraud Cases, 120 U.Pa.L.Rev. 597 (1972)], at 630–31.

"The final requirement for aiding-abetting liability is that of knowing, substantial assistance of the violation. Most problematic in this area is the issue whether, or to what extent, silence and inaction can fulfill the requirement. This issue turns on the nature of the duty owed by the alleged aider and abettor to the other parties to the transaction. The standards courts have used for measuring culpability by silence have varied. Some declare without qualification that silence and inaction alone can create liability for aiding-abetting. * * * Other courts squarely reject the notion that inaction alone is enough, distinguishing the contrary authority. * * * The Sixth Circuit in SEC v. Coffey, supra, 493 F.2d at 1317, suggested a rule imposing liability 'only where it is shown that the silence of the accused aider and abettor was consciously intended to aid the securities law violation.' Taking a slightly different approach, the Ninth Circuit held that liability for silence or inaction arises 'only when a duty to disclose has arisen.' Strong v. France, 9 Cir.1973, 474 F.2d 747, 752." [13]

13. Ibid.

With respect to the third element of "substantial assistance", the principal disagreement among the cases, so far as their formulation of this requirement is concerned, is that some courts say that "knowing" assistance to the fraudulent scheme is required, whereas others do not use this language. It is not quite clear what is intended to be required by the statement that the defendant must have "knowingly assisted" or "knowingly participated" in the fraud. This requirement seems to blend imperceptibly into the second element that the defendant must have had "knowledge" of the primary wrongdoing; it could mean that the defendant must have consciously intended to further the fraud or merely that he knew that he was rendering substantial assistance in the securities transaction and that it involved a fraud on the part of the primary defendant. Where the defendant is accused of aiding and abetting by silence, some courts, as in the *Metge* case, have said that the intent of the defendant must be of the "high conscious variety", implying that something less is normally required.

In Zabriskie v. Lewis [14] the Tenth Circuit said that "When liability is to be imposed on participants, aiders and abettors, and co-conspirators knowing participation in the fraudulent scheme must be shown." And in Landy v. Federal Deposit Insurance Corp.[15] the Third Circuit held that where the president of a bank had stolen its funds and speculated with them in the stock market, the brokers who executed his orders were not liable as aiders and abettors in his theft. The court said:

"The *Restatement* does not define with specificity the concept of 'substantial assistance' but explains that

If the encouragement or assistance is a substantial factor in causing the resulting tort, the one giving it is himself a tortfeasor and is responsible for the consequences of the other's act.

Restatement of Torts § 436. The *Restatement* suggests that in determining if the assistance is substantial enough to make an individual liable for the act of another, the relevant factors are: (1) the amount of assistance given by the defendant; (2) his presence or absence at the time of the tort; (3) his relation to the other person; and (4) his state of mind. In this case, it would appear that the amount of assistance given by the brokers was minor. The brokers were not present at the time of the fraud. As the district court pointed out, they were not involved in any manner with the sale of the Eatontown [Bank] shares or the actual making of any misrepresentatiors. The 'state of mind' criterion would also suggest no liability. Their assistance, although necessary for the accomplishment of Schotte's [the president's] fraud, was intended to achieve another independent goal—the generation of commissions." [16]

In Cleary v. Perfectune, Inc.[17] the court held that investors in a company who allowed the promoter to list them as directors in the offering circular did not aid and abet the promoter's primary fraud since their mere inaction did not constitute the knowing and substantial assistance on which aiding and abetting liability must be based. On the other hand, in Harmsen v. Smith [18] the court held that the wife of a bank officer and director who was the primary wrongdoer was properly held liable for aiding and abetting her husband's securities frauds since she had numerous dealings with the bank, including receipt of loans at nonmarket terms and acquisition of real property at minimal

---

14. 507 F.2d 546 (10th Cir.1974).

15. Supra, note 3. See, also, Beatty v. Bright, 318 F.Supp. 169, 345 F.Supp. 1188 (S.D.Iowa 1972); Rosen v. Dick, CCH Fed. Sec.Law Rptr. ¶ 94,786 (S.D.N.Y.1974).

16. 486 F.2d at 163.

17. 700 F.2d 774 (1st Cir.1983).

18. 693 F.2d 932 (9th Cir.1982), cert. denied 464 U.S. 822 (1983). See, also, Securities and Exchange Commission v. Washington County Utility District, 676 F.2d 218 (6th Cir.1982).

cost. The court said: "There is sufficient evidence from which the jury could conclude that she knew that potential investors were being deceived by [her husband]."

May mere silence or inaction on the part of a person constitute him an aider and abettor? See the discussion of this question in the *Metge* case, which cites the relevant authorities. In Brennan v. Midwestern United Life Insurance Co.[19] the Seventh Circuit (which, like Abou Ben Adhem, then seemed to want to have its name lead all the rest in extensions of Rule 10b–5 liability) held that a corporation which should have known that a broker was manipulating the market in its stock was liable as his "aider and abettor" because it didn't do anything to stop it (such as complaining to the Indiana Securities Commissioner, whose past conduct give little indication that he would have taken any action, although he testified that he would have.)[20] And Kerbs v. Fall River Industries, Inc.[21] held that mere silence or inaction could make one an aider and abettor if it amounted to "knowing assistance of or participation in" a fraudulent scheme.[22]

The leading article on aiding and abetting and allied doctrines, which has been cited in almost all of the judicial opinions, is Dean Ruder's Multiple Defendants in Securities Law Fraud Cases: Aiding and Abetting, Conspiracy, In Pari Delicto, Indemnification, and Contribution, 120 U.Pa.L.Rev. 597 (1972). See, also, Sachs, The Relevance of Tort Law Doctrines to Rule 10b–5, 71 Cornell L.Rev. 96 (1985); McDermett, Liability for Aiding and Abetting Violations of Rule 10b–5: the Recklessness Standard in Civil Damage Actions, 62 Tex.L.Rev. 1087 (1984); Fischel, Secondary Liability Under Section 10(b) of the Securities Act of 1934, 69 Calif.L.Rev. 80 (1981); Ruder, Secondary Liability Under the Securities Acts, 8 Inst. Securities Reg. 353 (1977). Other articles dealing with particular types of collateral defendants are cited in the remainder of this chapter.

---

19. 417 F.2d 147 (7th Cir.1969), cert. denied 397 U.S. 989 (1970). See, also, Carroll v. First National Bank of Lincolnwood, 413 F.2d 353 (7th Cir.1969), cert. denied 396 U.S. 1003 (1970).

20. The Seventh Circuit purported not to be holding the defendant corporation liable for mere inaction, as had the District Judge, but the dissenting opinion makes it perfectly clear that that is what the court was doing. The court said: "The corporation's acquiescence through silence in the fraudulent acts of the broker combined with its *affirmative* acts of recommending alternatives to the reporting of the broker's violations to the state securities commission was a form of aiding and abetting." (italics added) What happened was that the broker was running a "bucket shop" and selling stock he didn't own. When a number of purchasers complained to the corporation about the non-delivery of their shares, the company contacted the broker and told him they were going to report him to the Indiana Securities Commissioner if he didn't make delivery

promptly; and he thereupon made prompt delivery to those particular customers. (This is what the court calls "recommending alternatives.") The evidence also showed that other purchasers had complained to the Indiana Securities Commissioner; and he did exactly the same thing the company did—threatened the broker, and then, when he complied, forgot about it.

21. 502 F.2d 731 (10th Cir.1974).

22. See, also, Monsen v. Consolidated Dressed Beef Co., Inc., 579 F.2d 793 (3d Cir. 1978) cert. denied 439 U.S. 930; Green v. Jonhop, Inc., 358 F.Supp. 413 (D.Ore.1973); and Odette v. Shearson, Hammill & Co., Inc., 356 F.Supp. 304 (S.D.N.Y.1975), aff'd 486 F.2d 1395 (2d Cir.1975). In Ferguson v. Omnimedia, Inc., 469 F.2d 194 (1st Cir. 1972), summary judgment in favor of the wife of another defendant, whose sole function was to record minutes at meetings and who did not know how to read a financial statement, was reversed because she "might have been" part of a "conspiracy."

DAVIS v. AVCO FINANCIAL SERVICES, INC.

United States Court of Appeals, Sixth Circuit, 1984.
739 F.2d 1057.

Before LIVELY, CHIEF JUDGE, JONES, CIRCUIT JUDGE, and BERTELSMAN, DISTRICT JUDGE.*

BERTELSMAN, DISTRICT JUDGE.

This securities case presents this court with an issue of first impression in this circuit, namely, who may be considered a "seller" under § 12(2) of the Securities Act of 1933. Other circuits have expressed diverse views regarding this issue, as have the commentators. The Supreme Court of the United States has never passed on it. Various subsidiary issues are also presented, as will be discussed below.

FACTS

This is a securities fraud class action arising out of the activities of defendants/appellants AVCO Financial Services, Inc. and defendant McCormick, the manager of Avco's Toledo, Ohio office. The plaintiffs/appellees all borrowed money from Avco in order to buy shares of a scheme called "Dare to be Great" (DTBG). DTBG was a pyramidal scheme wherein investors could buy "adventures" at Levels I, II, III or IV. Purchases of adventures Levels III (price: $2,000) and IV (price: $5,000) gave the purchasers the right to sell adventures to other purchasers, and collect a commission thereon.

The sales of DTBG were based on hard-sell tactics and promises of quick wealth by salespeople who flaunted money and expensive cars, clothing, jewelry, and the like. Because of its inherent "saturation" character, this scheme was apparently doomed to fail, and did so in 1974, causing members of the plaintiff class to lose nearly all of the money they had invested in it. DTBG marketing techniques are described in detail in S.E.C. v. Glenn W. Turner Enterprises, Inc., 474 F.2d 476 (9th Cir.), cert. denied, 414 U.S. 821, 94 S.Ct. 117, 38 L.Ed.2d 53 (1973). The evidence in this case is the same as the evidence described in the Ninth Circuit case. * * *

From about February to July, 1971, Avco provided loans, secured by promissory notes, to persons who wanted to invest in DTBG. After Avco had made some of these loans, DTBG contacted Avco's manager McCormick about further loan business. McCormick attended three meetings (two for DTBG and one for Koscot, an extremely similar venture run by identical organizers) in May through June, 1971. At these meetings, McCormick provided potential DTBG investors with blank Avco loan application forms. He also made a speech concerning obtaining financing through Avco at one of the meetings. Several members of the plaintiff class testified, and the trial court found, that McCormick represented to some plaintiffs that DTBG was a good quality investment. In July, 1971, McCormick's superior, Pok, ordered him to cease making any loans for investment in DTBG. (McCormick also attended a DTBG "go tour" after Pok put a stop to the loans.) Forty-eight people, eventually certified as a class, borrowed $2,000

---

* Hon. William O. Bertelsman, Judge, United States District Court for the East- ern District of Kentucky, sitting by designation.

or more from Avco to buy DTBG shares over an approximately six month period ending in July, 1971.

In the ensuing litigation, the trial court certified the case as a Rule 23(b) (3) class action. After trial, he ruled that both the promissory notes given by the plaintiffs for the loans and the shares of DTBG were "securities" within the meaning of the relevant federal securities statutes. He also found that Avco had solicited the plaintiffs' promissory notes and that the defendants' participation and enthusiasm in the sale of DTBG constituted a "misleading" of the plaintiffs in violation of §§ 2(3) and 12(2) of the Securities Act of 1933. He entered judgment in favor of the plaintiffs for roughly \$167,000, apportioning the judgment among the plaintiff class on the basis of money owed to Avco.

Following a bench trial, findings of fact and conclusions of law were filed in which the trial court did not find the requisite scienter by McCormick for Rule 10b–5 liability. He did conclude, however, that DTBG Adventures III and IV were securities within the meaning of the Act and that the efforts of Avco's manager in promoting their sale were sufficient to render Avco liable under § 12(2) of the Securities Act of 1933. He further found that Avco had not met its burden of showing that the representations made by its manager were made with due care. Avco is liable under the doctrine of *respondeat superior* for its manager's actions in this regard. Holloway v. Howerdd, 536 F.2d 690, 694–5 (6th Cir.1976).

This court has reviewed the entire transcript of the trial and concludes not only that the factual findings of the trial judge with regard to the actions and intentions of Avco's manager are not clearly erroneous but that it is in total agreement with them. There was abundant evidence that Avco's manager allowed himself to be duped by the DTBG promoters into facilitating their dubious pyramidal scheme up to the point of actually representing to some of the borrowers that DTBG was a sound investment.

The manager, from all that appears in the evidence, was not guilty of any fraudulent intent but rather was taken in by the DTBG hoopla. He apparently swallowed everything from the "money humming" to the thousand dollar bills in the lapel buttonholes. In fact, far from attempting clandestinely to promote a known fraudulent venture, the manager actually suggested to his superiors that Avco adopt some of the DTBG promotional methods in its own public relations. This caused the manager's superiors to make an immediate investigation. In short order, they perceived that the whole DTBG promotion was a chimera, forbade the manager to have anything further to do with it, and prohibited the making of any more loans to DTBG investors.

The fact that his supervisors so promptly perceived the inherent fallacy of the DTBG scheme indicates that its defects were obvious and that the manager, although he may have been innocent of fraudulent intent, was certainly guilty of negligence. Nor was his sincerity of any comfort to the bilked investors. One who is sold the Brooklyn Bridge by means of sincere but negligent representations is nonetheless the possessor of a worthless asset.

Since the factual findings of the trial judge were clearly supported by the evidence, he was correct in finding liability against Avco, if his conclusion that Avco was liable under § 12(2) was correct. We hold that it was and affirm his conclusion with regard to liability. The case must be remanded, however, for further proceedings on some of the issues, as hereinafter indicated.

* * *

Liability Under § 12(2) of the 1933 Act

Determining secondary liability has long been a thorny problem in implementing the securities laws.[1] Particularly is this true with regard to § 12(2). Section 10(b) of the Securities Exchange Act of 1934 and Rule 10b–5 provide a private action remedy roughly equivalent to that existing for fraud at common law. This remedy is not limited to "sellers," but applies also to persons collaterally involved in the transaction who made misrepresentations to promote the sale of securities with the requisite scienter. Ernst & Ernst v. Hochfelder, 425 U.S. 185 (1976). In this circuit recklessness may constitute the required scienter. Mansbach v. Prescott, Ball & Turben, 598 F.2d 1017, 1023 (6th Cir.1979); Ingram Industries v. Nowicki, 502 F.Supp. 1060, 1066 (E.D.Ky.1980). However, the trial judge found neither deliberate fraud nor recklessness on the part of Avco or its manager. Therefore, plaintiff's 10b–5 allegations were not supported by the evidence at trial. The trial court's findings of liability must stand or fall on § 12(2) of the 1933 Act.

Because of the variety of interpretations that have been given to § 12(2) of the 1933 Act by the various federal courts, it is incumbent upon us to examine its place in the statutory scheme Congress has provided for the protection of investors in securities. Although there is a difference of opinion whether we should limit our inquiry to the statutory language, we must at least begin there. See Touche Ross & Co. v. Redington, 442 U.S. 560, 568 (1979); Admiralty Fund v. Jones, 677 F.2d 1289, 1294 n. 3 (9th Cir. 1982); *Northwestern Comment,* supra note 1, *passim.* * * *

No definition of the term "seller" is to be found in the Act. It may be immediately discerned that the language of § 12(2)[2] on its face imposes a liability analogous to the equitable remedy of rescission only upon *sellers* of securities. If we are limited to a literal reading of the statute, it is obvious that the plaintiffs here must fail, because Avco was not in the literal sense the "seller" of DTBG securities.

Some courts have indeed held that § 12(2) may be applied only to the literal seller of a security or one in privity with him. Collins v. Signetics Corp., 605 F.2d 110 (3d Cir.1979); McFarland v. Memorex, 493 F.Supp. 631

---

1. See, generally, Kaminsky, An Analysis of Securities Litigation Under Section 12(2) and How It Compares with Rule 10b–5, 13 Hous.L.Rev. 231 (1976); Rapp, Expanded Liability Under Section 12 of the Securities Act: When Is a Seller Not a Seller? 27 Case W.Res.L.Rev. 445 (1977); Ruder, Multiple Defendants in Securities Law Fraud Cases: Aiding and Abetting, Conspiracy, In Pari Delicto, Indemnification, and Contribution, 120 U.Pa.L.Rev. 597 (1972) [hereinafter cited as *Ruder I*]; Ruder, Securities Law Secondary-Liability Theories, in Fourteenth Annual Institute on Securities Regulation 331 (1983) [hereinafter cited as *Ruder II*]; Comment, Secondary Liability under Section 12(2) of the Securities Act of 1933, 78 Nw.L.Rev. 832

(1983) [hereinafter cited as *Northwestern Comment*]; Comment, Seller Liability Under Section 12(2) of the Securities Act of 1933: A Proximate Cause-Substantial Factor Approach Limited by a Duty of Inquiry, 36 Vand.L.Rev. 361 (1983) [hereinafter cited as *Vanderbilt Comment*].

2. It has been suggested that because of the strict liability imposed in § 12(1), the definition of seller should be more narrowly applied than in § 12(2), where due care is a defense. Since we find liability here under § 12(2), we limit our analysis to it and express no opinion as to the proper interpretation of § 12(1). See Pharo v. Smith, 621 F.2d 656, 665 n. 6 (5th Cir. 1980).

(N.D.Cal.1980). These courts put great emphasis on the consideration that the securities statutes are indeed *statutes,* and not mere commissions to the federal courts to ride abroad on a great white horse like the Lone Ranger righting all wrongs. They find support in recent admonitions of the Supreme Court of the United States of like tenor. See, e.g., Touche Ross & Co. v. Redington, 442 U.S. 560, 578 (1979); Ernst & Ernst v. Hochfelder, 425 U.S. 185, 200–01 (1976). Also, the language of § 12(2) providing for recovery based on the purchase price of the security would seem to support this interpretation.

On the other hand the Supreme Court has likewise indicated that the remedial purpose of the securities laws is not to be ignored in their interpretation. Herman & MacLean v. Huddleston, 459 U.S. 375 (1983). As one commentator has aptly phrased it, the Supreme Court has called for a "flexible yet literal interpretation of the Securities Acts." *Vanderbilt Comment,* supra note 1, at 386. *But cf. Northwestern Comment,* supra note 1, *passim.*

Unfortunately, the Supreme Court has not yet synthesized these some-times antithetical considerations with regard to § 12(2). At one time some courts gave the term "seller" in § 12(2) an extremely broad reading and held that anyone who participates to any degree in the sale of a security by means of negligent misrepresentations may be considered a "seller" there-under. This view has come into disrepute, however, and has apparently been abandoned. See discussion in S.E.C. v. Murphy, 626 F.2d 633, 650 n. 18 (9th Cir.1980); *Vanderbilt Comment,* supra note 1 at 367 ff.

Still other courts have followed an aiding and abetting analysis with regard to Section 12(2) liability. See, e.g., deBruin v. Andromeda Broad-casting Systems, 465 F.Supp. 1276, 1279–80 (D.Nev.1979); In re Caesars Palace Sec. Lit., 360 F.Supp. 366 (S.D.N.Y.1973). This has been character-ized as an "extremely liberal" approach. *Vanderbilt Comment,* supra note 1 at 364. It may or may not be, inasmuch as at least in this circuit aiding and abetting requires a general awareness that a fraudulent scheme is afoot and knowing and substantial assistance toward the success of that scheme. S.E.C. v. Coffey, 493 F.2d 1304 (6th Cir.1974), cert. denied, 420 U.S. 908 (1975). Accord: S.E.C. v. Washington County Utility District, 676 F.2d 218, 226 (6th Cir.1982). It is doubtful whether these elements are present under the facts of this case. In any event the trial court, who followed the approach to § 12(2) liability next discussed, did not use an aiding and abetting analysis. Also, an aiding and abetting theory seems inconsistent with the language of § 12(2). See *Ruder II,* supra note 1 at 345–46.

Inasmuch as we uphold liability under the "proximate cause" theory employed by the trial court, we need not address the issue whether or not an aiding and abetting approach may ever be employed under § 12(2).[3] We think it appropriate to note, however, that to distinguish between an aiding and abetting theory and the other theories advanced is not a mere semantic exercise, as has been suggested by at least one court. In re Caesars Palace Sec. Lit., 360 F.Supp. 366, 380 (S.D.N.Y.1973). A case may be envisioned

---

3. Judge Lambros in a decision that primarily involved a pleading question has suggested that using the aiding and abet-ting approach under § 12 might be appro-priate. Sandusky Land Ltd. v. Uniplan Groups, Inc., 400 F.Supp. 440, 444 (N.D. Ohio 1975). But see Wright v. Schock, 571 F.Supp. 642, 658 (N.D.Cal.1983); Hokama v. E.F. Hutton Co., 566 F.Supp. 636, 642 (C.D.Cal.1983).

where there would be § 12(2) liability under a *Coffey*-type aiding and abetting approach, but not under the analysis we here adopt. We will decide that case if and when it is before us. This case presents the converse situation.

The better reasoned cases adopt a view of § 12(2) liability that transcends the strict approach (which limits liability to the literal seller or one in privity with him), which is narrower than the formerly employed broad participation approach and different—whether more conservative or more liberal is debatable—than the aiding and abetting approach.

We adopt the theory of § 12(2) liability usually referred to as the "proximate cause" theory. See *Vanderbilt Comment,* supra note 1, at 370 ff; *Ruder II,* supra note 1 at 343–45. It has a history that is particularly interesting in the context of this litigation, since it originated in the Northern District of Ohio, which is also the place of origin of this case, although the theory has never been adopted or rejected by this court.

The proximate cause theory originated in Lennerth v. Mendenhall, 234 F.Supp. 59 (N.D.Ohio 1964). * * *

Other courts, particularly the Fifth Circuit, have not only saluted the flag hoisted by the Lennerth court, but have honored it with ruffles and flourishes on many occasions. See, Hill York Corp. v. American International Franchises, Inc., 448 F.2d 680, 692–93 (5th Cir.1971); Junker v. Crory, 650 F.2d 1349, 1360 (5th Cir.1981); Croy v. Campbell, 624 F.2d 709, 713 (5th Cir.1980); Stokes v. Lokken, 644 F.2d 779, 785 (8th Cir.1981); S.E.C. v. Murphy, 626 F.2d 633, 650 (9th Cir.1980); *Vanderbilt Comment,* supra note 1, at 370 ff; *Ruder II,* supra note 1 at 343–45; *Northwestern Comment,* supra note 1 at 841–45.

For example, the Court of Appeals for the Fifth Circuit, said in Hill York Corporation v. American International Franchises, Inc., 448 F.2d 680, at 692–93:

"The law is settled that a purchaser may only recover from his immediate seller. * * * The law is not settled, however, as to who may be a seller. *It is clear that a seller is not required to be the person who passes title.* For example, a broker for the seller has been subjected to liability under Section 12(1) as a seller. See *III Loss, Securities Regulation 1713* (2d ed. 1961). This Circuit has implicitly rejected the strict privity concept on at least two prior occasions. (citations omitted). Although the term 'seller' has sometimes been accorded a broader construction under Section 12(2) than under Section 12(1), we adopt a test which we believe states a rational and workable standard for imposition of liability under either section. Its base lies between the antiquated 'strict privity' concept and the overbroad 'participation' concept which would hold all those liable who participated in the events leading up to the transaction. (citations omitted). We hold that the proper test is the one previously forged by the court in Lennerth v. Mendenhall, supra. ' * * * the line of demarcation must be drawn in terms of cause and effect: To borrow a phrase from the law of negligence, did the injury to the plaintiff flow *directly and proximately* from the actions of this particular defendant?' (citations omitted)." (emphasis added).

Later cases have broadened application of the proximate cause touchstone to include one whose efforts were a "substantial factor" in the sale of the securities. This has occurred to harmonize the securities law model with a similar development in general tort law. See Pharo v. Smith, 621 F.2d 656, 667 (5th Cir.1980); Junker v. Crory, 650 F.2d 1349, 1360 (5th Cir. 1981). See Prosser, Handbook of the Law of Torts, §§ 41, 42 at 240, 248 (4th ed. 1971). Concerning the meaning of the term "substantial factor," Restatement (Second) of Torts §§ 432, 433 state:

"§ 432. Negligent Conduct as Necessary Antecedent of Harm.

"(1) Except as stated in Subsection (2), the actor's negligent conduct is not a substantial factor in bringing about harm to another if the harm would have been sustained even if the actor had not been negligent.

"(2) If two forces are actively operating, one because of the actor's negligence, the other not because of any misconduct on his part, and each of itself is sufficient to bring about harm to another, the actor's negligence may be found to be a substantial factor in bringing it about.

* * * * * * * * *

"§ 433. Considerations Important in Determining Whether Negligent Conduct is Substantial Factor in Producing Harm.

"The following considerations are in themselves or in combination with one another important in determining whether the actor's conduct is a substantial factor in bringing about harm to another:

"(a) the number of other factors which contribute in producing the harm and the extent of the effect which they have in producing it;

"(b) whether the actor's conduct has created a force or series of forces which are in continuous and active operation up to the time of the harm, or has created a situation harmless unless acted upon by other forces for which the actor is not responsible;

(c) the lapse of time."

The Ninth Circuit has described the proximate cause—substantial factor analysis as follows:

"In assessing proximate cause, courts focus first on whether a defendant's acts were the *actual cause* of the injury, i.e., whether 'but for' the defendant's conduct, there would have been no sale. Nicewarner v. Bleavins, supra, 244 F.Supp. [261] at 266 (D.Colo.1965); see Hill York Corp. v. American International Franchises, Inc., supra, 448 F.2d at 693; Lennerth v. Mendenhall, supra, 234 F.Supp. at 65. A finding of 'but for' causation, alone, does not satisfy proximate cause, however. See Nicewarner v. Bleavins, supra, 244 F.Supp. at 266; R. Jennings & H. Marsh, Securities Regulation 1096 (4th ed. 1977); W. Prosser, Handbook of the Law of Torts 238–39, 244 (4th ed. 1971). Prior to the issuance of a security, numerous persons perform mechanical acts without which there could be no sale. For example, a printer may prepare key documents or a bank may advance cash to a customer upon the customer's presentation of any instrument and then pass the instrument to another person. Both would satisfy a 'but for' causation test, but these acts nonetheless do not render the defendants sellers. See First Trust & Savings Bank v. Fidelity-Philadelphia Trust Co., 214 F.2d 320 (3d Cir.1954); Ruder, Multiple Defendants in Securities Law Fraud Cases, 120 U.Pa.L.Rev. 597, 646 (1972). Before a person's acts can be considered the proximate cause of a sale, his acts must also be a substantial factor in bringing about the transaction. Lewis v. Walston & Co., Inc., 487 F.2d 617, 621–22 (5th Cir.1973). See Restatement (Second) of Torts § 431 (1965). Thus, a defendant will be held liable as a participant under § 12 if his acts *were both necessary to and a substantial factor in the sales transaction.* See Lewis v. Walston & Co., Inc., supra, 487 F.2d at 621–22."

S.E.C. v. Murphy, 626 F.2d at 650. (Emphasis added).

The policy question with which the courts and commentators are struggling may be stated as follows: In light of the fact that the consequence of denominating anyone a "seller" under § 12(2) is to force that person to bear the burden of persuasion in establishing his lack of negligence for representations made by him, what sort of involvement in the sale of a security should be required to justify such inclusion?

We hold that considering participants in the selling effort whose acts meet the substantial factor test as described in *Murphy,* supra, as "sellers" under § 12(2) constitutes an appropriate synthesis of the sometimes antithetical policies that the securities laws are to be construed as statutes while, at the same time, giving effect to their far-reaching remedial purpose.

This model does no violence to the statutory scheme and is not contrary to the requirement of scienter for Rule 10b–5 liability. Under Rule 10b–5 scienter is required for imposition of general damages analogous to those recoverable for fraud. Under the proximate cause approach to § 12(2), negligence is required for imposition of the more limited remedy of rescission on one who caused the sale. The approach, therefore, seems to complete the statutory scheme rather than violate it.

Some commentators fear that such an approach is too broad, imposing liability on more persons than Congress intended. *See Northwestern Comment,* supra note 1, *passim.* However, denominating a defendant a "seller" under § 12(2) does not result in automatic liability. Such a defendant may escape by showing an exercise of ordinary care.

We believe that the following considerations are pertinent to an analysis of whether a § 12(2) seller has established this affirmative defense: (1) the quantum of decisional (planning) and facilitative (promotional) participation, such as designing the deal and contacting and attempting to persuade potential purchasers, (2) access to source data against which the truth or falsity of representations can be tested, (3) relative skill in ferreting out the truth (for example, in this case Avco's manager had comparatively greater skill in evaluating judgments based on subsidiary facts, since he performed a similar function in the process of investigating the creditworthiness of borrowers), (4) pecuniary interest in the completion of the transaction, and (5) the existence of a relationship of trust and confidence between the plaintiff and the alleged "seller." These are the circumstances that determine whether a person has exercised due care in this context. See R. Coffey, Securities Regulation: An Analysis of Policy and Law 100ddd–100iii (unpublished multilith manuscript) (1981).

CONCLUSION

Although we agree with the trial court's findings of liability under § 12(2) of the 1933 Act with regard to those class members who did testify that the representations of Avco's manager were the cause of their investing in DTBG, it is necessary that findings of the existence or non-existence of such causal relationship be made with regard to each class member, inasmuch as the circumstances surrounding their individual decisions to invest differ.

We wish to make it clear that we are not introducing reliance on the part of the purchasers as a requirement of § 12(2). It is clear that scienter and reliance are not prerequisites for recovery under this section. Wigand v. Flo-Tek, Inc., 609 F.2d 1028, 1034 (2d Cir.1980). The question is the substantiality of the intrusion of Avco's manager into the selling process (that is, his presence at meetings, his making speeches, his furnishing forms, and in general his contribution to the selling momentum). However, in this case the impact of these activities varied from plaintiff to plaintiff.[4] With regard to the plaintiffs that testified, the evidence was more than sufficient to justify the finding that the manager's activities were a substantial factor in their decision to purchase DTBG securities. Avco rightly argues, however, that it has not been established that all of the members of the plaintiff class were affected by the manager's activities.

* * *

Therefore, this case is Affirmed with regard to the findings of liability of certain class members under § 12(2) and reversed and remanded for further proceedings indicated herein.

LIVELY, CHIEF JUDGE, concurring and dissenting.

* * *

In my opinion the majority has misread section 12(2) and has reached the wrong result, even if it is assumed that the district court did base its finding of liability on section 12(2). The federal securities laws are complex, but they do display a studied approach to a variety of problems. Different participants in various stages and types of securities transactions are treated individually. In this scheme section 12(2) of the 1933 Act focuses on the liability of persons who offer or sell securities using communications which contain untrue statements or which omit material facts. Only sellers and offerors of securities are reached by section 12(2). Other participants in securities transactions are treated in other provisions of the securities laws. To bring other participants within the reach of section 12(2) by invoking the broad "remedial purposes" of federal securities legislation is contrary to a consistent refusal by the Supreme Court to so construe these statutes. * * *

I agree with the construction of section 12(2) and the reasoning applied by Judge Aldisert in Collins v. Signetics Corp., 605 F.2d 110, 113 (3d Cir. 1979):

We have no difficulty in concluding that Congress intended the unambiguous language of § 12(2) to mean exactly what it says: "Any person who—* * * (2) offers or sells a security * * * shall be liable to the person purchasing from him * * *." This section is designed as a vehicle for a purchaser to claim against his immediate seller. Any broader interpretation would not only torture the plain meaning of the statutory language but would also frustrate the statutory schema be-

---

4. In many cases the contribution of the defendant to the selling effort may be so great that it may be considered a substantial factor in the sales made to all plaintiffs.

cause Congress has also provided a specific remedy for a purchaser to utilize against the issuer as distinguished from the seller of a security. Thus, § 11 gives anyone acquiring a security a specific right of action for misrepresentations against every person who signed the registration statement, or was a director or partner of the issuer or prepared a certified statement contained in the registration statement, or was an underwriter with respect to the security. 15 U.S.C. § 77k.

Ascertainment of congressional intent with respect to the standard of liability created by a particular section of the securities acts must "rest primarily on the language of that section." Ernst and Ernst v. Hochfelder, 425 U.S. 185, 200 (1976). In interpreting liability provisions of the acts, we must respect recent Supreme Court teachings that militate against excessively expansive readings. * * *

One other comment appears in order. Avco and McCormick obviously were not sellers or offerors of DTBG adventures. Yet the majority holds them liable as indirect participants whose activities were a substantial factor in the transactions between the plaintiffs and DTBG. In Ernst & Ernst v. Hochfelder, 425 U.S. 185, the Supreme Court held that secondary liability may not be imposed under section 10(b) for mere negligence; scienter is required. The majority has found that there was no scienter, and thus no Rule 10b–5 liability. By permitting recovery under section 12(2) on the basis of McCormick's failure to show that he would not have known of the fraudulent nature of the DTBG scheme even if he had exercised reasonable care, the majority permits the plaintiffs to evade the *Ernst & Ernst* requirement that secondary liability may be based only on scienter.

"PARTICIPANT" LIABILITY UNDER SECTION 12

The earliest cases involving the liability of collateral "participants" in a transaction violating the Federal securities laws concerned the question of who is liable under the express liability provisions of Section 12 of the 1933 Act. Section 12 literally imposes liability only upon a "person who offers or sells" a security. This language seems broad enough to encompass some persons other than the actual vendor of the security; for example, an agent who "offers or sells" on behalf of his principal.[1] From that, the courts progressed at an early date to the position that anyone who "participates" in the sale is liable under Section 12.

In Wonneman v. Stratford Securities Co., Inc.,[2] Judge Cashin stated that in order for the defendants to prevail on a motion for summary judgment they must "show that they did not participate in the sale and not merely that they did not actually sell the securities to plaintiff. * * * The problem is—'What constitutes "participation"?' Does one who supervises the selling operations 'participate' in an individual sale? Does one who composes advertising material 'participate' in the sale? Does a director or an officer 'participate' in a sale?" It should be noted that the word "sell" in the statute has been here replaced with "participate".

---

1. See Murphy v. Cady, 30 F.Supp. 466 (D.Me.1939) aff'd 113 F.2d 988 (1st Cir. 1940), cert. denied 311 U.S. 705 (1940); Schillner v. H. Vaughan Clarke & Co., 134 F.2d 875 (2d Cir.1943). See, also, 3 Loss, Securities Regulation 1713–1715 (2d ed. 1961, Supp.1969).

2. CCH Fed.Sec.Law Rptr. ¶ 90,923 (S.D.N.Y.1959).

However, upon the trial of the same case,[3] Judge Murphy released all of the defendants in whose favor Judge Cashin had refused to enter summary judgment, and seemed to take a quite different approach: " * * * the statutes under which plaintiff sues require an element of privity between the plaintiff-purchaser and defendants. The defendant must be, for example, the actual seller or one who negotiated the sale; the owner of the securities sold or a person who in some manner controls the seller."

On the other hand, in Zachman v. Erwin[4] the court found "sufficient allegations of * * * participation" in a Section 12 violation by members of a so-called "Advisory Board" in that "They are alleged to have wilfully or negligently cooperated with the general plan or scheme to defraud plaintiffs by *allowing their names to be used* in connection with the selling transactions. * * * "[5] Also, in the same case, the publishers of a financial service relating to insurance securities, which was alleged to have contained false and misleading statements regarding the company whose shares were sold, and who were alleged to have some unspecified "financial tie" with this particular company, were held to have "sufficiently participated" in the sale at least for the purposes of a motion for summary judgment.

In Lennerth v. Mendenhall[6] Judge Connell stated that "The hunter who seduces the prey and leads it to the trap he has set is no less guilty than the hunter whose hand springs the snare." And he stated the test of "participation" as follows: "We think that the line of demarcation must be drawn in terms of cause and effect: To borrow a phrase from the law of negligence, did the injury to the plaintiff flow directly and proximately from the actions of this particular defendant? If the answer is in the affirmative, we would hold him liable. But for the presence of the defendant Roger in the negotiations preceding the sale, could the sale have been consummated? If the answer is in the negative, and we find that the transaction could never have materialized without the efforts of that defendant, we must find him guilty."[7] Are these two statements consistent—is "proximate cause" synonymous with "but for"?

The Fifth Circuit has on several occasions reiterated its "proximate cause" test with respect to who is a "participant" under Section 12 of the 1933 Act,[8] and the Ninth Circuit had adopted substantially the same test in Securities and Exchange Commission v. Murphy.[9] On the other hand, the Third Circuit in Collins v. Signetics Corp.[10] has flatly refused to go along with this expansion of

---

3. Wonneman v. Stratford Securities Co., 23 F.R.D. 281 (S.D.N.Y.1961).

4. 186 F.Supp. 691 (S.D.Tex.1960).

5. 186 F.Supp. at 696 (S.D.Tex.1960) (Italics added).

6. 234 F.Supp. 59 (N.D.Ohio 1964).

7. 234 F.Supp. at 65. See, also, Eisenberg v. North American Leisure Corp., CCH Fed.Sec.Law Rptr. ¶ 94,434 (S.D.N.Y. 1974).

8. Pharo v. Smith, 621 F.2d 656 (5th Cir.1980); Sweenson v. Engelstad, 626 F.2d 421 (5th Cir.1980).

9. 626 F.2d 633 (9th Cir.1980). Cf. Mendelsohn v. Capital Underwriters, Inc., 490 F.Supp. 1069, (N.D.Cal.1979). In In re Caesars Palace Securities Litigation, 360 F.Supp. 366 (S.D.N.Y.1973), Judge Weiner stated: "In Katz v. Amos Treat & Co., 411 F.2d 1046 (2d Cir.1969), one of the defendants, Wofsey, an attorney for the defendant brokerage corporation and special counsel for the issuing corporation, was charged with violations of § 12 of the 1933 Act. Although Judge Friendly, in his opinion, conceded that the attorney had not taken any initiative in the offering, 'the evidence clearly warranted the inference that on both occasions in April 1961, he had not simply answered Katz' questions, but had placed Treat in a position to tackle Katz for the money'. * * * The *Katz* decision, controlling in this Circuit, appears to adopt an extremely liberal standard of privity in § 12(2) situations, essentially requiring only some indicia of participation or solicitation on the part of an individual to warrant the imposition of liability."

10. 605 F.2d 110 (3d Cir.1979).

the persons liable under Section 12. In that case the court refused to hold an issuing corporation liable under Section 12(2) with respect to a sale by an underwriter of stock of the corporation pursuant to a firm commitment underwriting. The court said: "We have no difficulty in concluding that Congress intended the unambiguous language of Section 12(2) to mean exactly what it says: 'Any person who—(2) offers or sells a security * * * shall be liable to the person purchasing from him. * * *' This section is designed as a vehicle for a purchaser to claim against his immediate seller. Any broader interpretation would not only torture the plain meaning of the statutory language but would also frustrate the statutory scheme because Congress has also provided a specific remedy for a purchaser to utilize against the issuer, as distinguished from the seller, of a security." It is, of course, difficult to imagine any greater degree of "participation" in a sale short of actually negotiating or arranging it than that of the issuer in connection with an underwritten offering of its own securities. The issuer drafts the prospectus and indemnifies the underwriter against any false or misleading statements therein; the issuer also receives all of the proceeds of the offering less only the underwriter's "discount."

The case of Foster v. Jesup and Lamont Securities Co., Inc.[11] in the Eleventh Circuit, however, agreed with this conclusion that a person who does not "participate" in the actual sales process cannot be held liable as a "participant" in the sale. In In re Diasonics Securities Litigation, 599 F.Supp. 447 (N.D.Cal. 1984), Judge Peckham similarly held that officers and directors of the issuer who only "participated" in the preparation of the Registration Statement and Prospectus could not be held liable under Section 12(2). Would this conclusion be affected by the "participation" of those persons in a typical "road show", where officials of the underwriter and issuer travel around the country during the waiting period talking about the company to securities analysts and broker-dealers? On the other hand, in Securities and Exchange Commission v. Holschuh,[12] the Seventh Circuit held that a person who "orchestrated" the issuance of the securities and the making of the related representations was liable under Section 5 of the 1933 Act (and therefore necessarily under Section 12(1)). It should be noted, however, that this was a case involving Section 12(1) rather than Section 12(2) and the court emphasized that Section 5 of the 1933 Act refers to any person who "directly or indirectly" violates that section.

In Securities and Exchange Commission v. Seaboard Corporation,[13] the court stated in a footnote that the entire concept of "participant" liability "may be in some doubt in light of recent Supreme Court cases that prescribe a strict statutory construction approach to the Securities Acts." Nevertheless, the Ninth Circuit has continued to follow this theory in subsequent cases and even in the *Seaboard* case itself. In Dahl v. Pinter[14] the court held (one judge dissenting) that a person could not be held liable under Section 12(2) as a "participant" or under Rule 10b–5 as an aider and abettor because he promoted the investment to his friends and relatives out of a desire to benefit them rather than to make any profit for himself. The court stated the novel proposition that a requirement of the "substantial factor" test is that the defendant be motivated by a desire to confer a direct or indirect benefit on someone other than the person he advises to purchase, since imposing liability on friends and family who give one another gratuitous advice on investments "unreasonably interferes with well established patterns of social discourse."

11. 759 F.2d 838 (11th Cir.1985).   13. 677 F.2d 1289 (9th Cir.1982).

12. 694 F.2d 130 (7th Cir.1982).   14. 787 F.2d 985 (5th Cir.1986).

The *Diasonics* case rejects the idea that the concept of "aiding and abetting" liability is applicable to an action under Section 12(2), as it is to an action under Rule 10b–5, and most of the cases have concurred in this conclusion. It would certainly be strange to hold that one person can "aid and abet" (a concept drawn from the criminal law) another person's mere negligence (which is all that is required for liability of the primary defendant under Section 12(2)).

Under the language of the statute, the defendant must be a "person who offers or sells" in order to be liable under Section 12(2); if he is not, under whatever interpretation of this phrase is adopted, then he cannot be liable under that section. If a particular defendant *is* a "person who sells", there is nothing in the language of the statute which suggests that the degree of fault required on his part for liability is any different than for any other "seller." Nevertheless, the Second Circuit in the recent case of Mayer v. Oil Field Systems Corporation [15] held that if a defendant is a mere "participant" in the sale rather than the direct contractual seller to the plaintiff, then the plaintiff must prove *scienter* on the part of the defendant in order to recover. It seems doubtful that the Supreme Court will ultimately approve this ruling, since there is not a word in Section 12(2) corresponding to the language in Section 10(b) which the Supreme Court relied upon to require *scienter* in an action under Rule 10b–5 in the *Hochfelder* case (see page 936, above). If this ruling is ultimately upheld, it will substantially remove any advantage to the plaintiff in suing that type of defendant under Section 12(2) rather than Rule 10b–5.

This liability of "participants" may arise under Section 12(1) of the 1933 Act for the sale of nonexempt, unregistered securities, as well as under Section 12(2) for misrepresentation. In Lewis v. Walston & Co., Inc.[16] the Fifth Circuit said: "Mrs. DeCasenave of course was not a 'seller' in the most common sense of that word, that is, she was not the party who parted with the securities sold and received the consideration given in exchange. That, however, is not conclusive under § 12(1), for the courts have recognized that other parties who participate in the negotiations of or arrangements for the sale of unregistered securities 'sell' those securities within the meaning of § 12(1). * * * Brokers have long been held liable as sellers under § 12(2), as have other parties responsible for bringing about sales of securities they themselves do not own. Hill York Corp. v. American International Franchises, Inc., 5 Cir.1971, 448 F.2d 680; Lennerth v. Mendenhall, N.D.O.1964, 234 F.Supp. 59. In Hill York, this Court announced the test applied in this Circuit to determine whether a participant in the arrangements for a sale 'sells' securities within the meaning of § 12(1). The test is whether the party is the 'proximate cause' of the sale." [17]

Most of the recent cases on this question are cited by the court in the *Davis* case.

See, also, Stokes v. Lokken, 644 F.2d 779 (8th Cir.1981), where the court held that an attorney who gave a qualified opinion that the sale of coins did not involve the sale of a "security" did not thereby become a "seller" for the purposes of Section 12(1) of the 1933 Act, and Junker v. Crory, 650 F.2d 1349 (5th Cir.1981), where the Fifth Circuit held that an attorney's participation in the transaction was sufficient to subject the attorney to liability under Section 12(2) of the 1933 Act.

See Klinges, Expanding the Liability of Managing Underwriters Under the Securities Act of 1933, 53 Fordham L.Rev. 1063 (1985); O'Hara, Erosion of the

---

15. 803 F.2d 749 (2d Cir.1986).

16. 487 F.2d 617 (5th Cir.1973).

17. 487 F.2d at 621–22. Accord: Anderson v. Aurotek, 774 F.2d 927 (9th Cir.

1985); Securities and Exchange Commission v. Holschuh, 694 F.2d 130 (7th Cir. 1982).

Privity Requirement in Section 12(2) of the Securities Act of 1933, 31 UCLA L.Rev. 921 (1984); Schneider, Section 12 of the Securities Act of 1933: The Privity Requirement in the Contemporary Securities Law Perspective, 51 Tenn. L.Rev. 235 (1984); Silverstein, Seller Liability Under Section 12(2) of the Securities Act of 1933: A Proximate Cause-Substantial Factor Approach Limited by a Duty of Inquiry, 36 Vand.L.Rev. 361 (1983).

PERSONS LIABLE UNDER SECTION 11

The text of Section 11 itself sets forth with specificity the persons who can be made defendants in an action under that section, and these are discussed in the *BarChris* case, supra page 901. These persons are: (1) the registrant, i.e., the issuing corporation which is included as a "person who signed the registration statement" since all registration statements must be signed by the issuer even when they relate to a secondary offering; (2) all directors of the issuer (including all persons who are named as "about to become" directors); (3) all other persons who sign the registration statement, i.e., the chief executive officer, the chief financial officer and the chief accounting officer of the issuer, who must sign whether or not they are also directors; (4) all underwriters of the offering; and (5) any "expert" who is named as having prepared or certified any part of the registration statement (this would always include the independent accountants who certify the financial statements and occasionally other persons who "expertize" particular statements in the registration statement, such as geologists who give opinions on mineral reserves or lawyers who give title opinions on real property or other legal matters).

No one had ever suggested that this list of persons could be expanded at the whim of the court, by such judicially invented doctrines as "aider and abettor" or "participant", as the courts have done with respect to Rule 10b–5 and Section 12, before Judge Weiner casually amended Section 11 in a sentence in the *Caesars Palace* opinion [18] by stating that a person might be liable as an "aider and abettor" of a Section 11 violation. Surely, however, this has to be wrong. The Supreme Court held in the *Herman & McClain* case that a suit could be brought for a misrepresentation in a registration statement under Rule 10b–5, including (presumably) against persons who aid and abet the violation of that rule, but only on the basis that proof of scienter by the plaintiff is required in order to maintain such an action as contrasted with the very heavy burden imposed upon all defendants under Section 11. To hold that a person might be held liable for aiding and abetting another defendant's lack of "due diligence" under Section 11 would certainly be contrary to the rationale of that Supreme Court decision.

IN RE ATLANTIC FINANCIAL MANAGEMENT, INC. SECURITIES LITIGATION

United States Court of Appeals, First Circuit, 1986.
784 F.2d 29.

Before COFFIN and BREYER, CIRCUIT JUDGES, and WYZANSKI,* SENIOR DISTRICT JUDGE.

---

18. In re Caesars Palace Securities Litigation, 360 F.Supp. 366 (S.D.N.Y.1973).

* Of the District of Massachusetts, sitting by designation.

BREYER, CIRCUIT JUDGE.

This appeal presents a certified question, 28 U.S.C. § 1292(b), arising in a Securities Act misrepresentation case. Securities Exchange Act of 1934, § 10(b); Rule 10b–5. The plaintiffs in the case claim that Maurice Strong, the chairman of AZL Resources, Inc., misrepresented certain facts as a result of which they bought AZL stock and later (when the stock's price declined) lost money. The plaintiffs want to recover damages for the misrepresentation, not only from Strong, but also from AZL, Strong's corporate employer. They assert a common law theory of agency—based on "apparent authority"—as a ground for holding the corporation "vicariously" liable for Strong's misdeeds.

The certified question concerns the relationship between a special section of the Securities Act of 1934, section 20(a), and various common law theories of vicarious liability (of which "apparent authority" is one). That section reads as follows:

> *Every person who, directly or indirectly, controls any person liable* under any provision of this chapter or of any rule or regulation thereunder *shall also be liable* jointly and severally with and to the same extent as such controlled person to any person to whom such controlled person is liable, *unless the controlling person acted in good faith and did not directly or indirectly induce the* act or acts constituting the *violation* or cause of action.

(Emphasis added.)

The significance of this section here lies in the contrast between its proviso and the common law. The proviso requires a finding of liability unless the controlling person 1) "acted in good faith" and 2) did not "induce" the violation. By way of contrast, common law agency theories may impose liability upon a principal or an employer without these two preconditions. The case before us asks whether the Securities Act means that section 20(a) is an *exclusive* remedy. That is to say, does the existence of this section foreclose holding a principal (say, a corporation) or an employer (who "controls" an agent or employee) "vicariously" liable when the proviso's two conditions are not met?

The circuits seem to be split about the proper answer to this question. The Second, Fourth, Fifth, Sixth, Seventh and Tenth Circuits have held that section 20(a) does not constitute an exclusive substitute for vicarious liability that might otherwise exist. E.g., Marbury Management, Inc. v. Kohn, 629 F.2d 705, 712–16 (2d Cir.), cert. denied, 449 U.S. 1011 (1980); Johns Hopkins University v. Hutton, 422 F.2d 1124, 1130 (4th Cir.1970), cert. denied after later appeal, 416 U.S. 916 (1974); Paul F. Newton & Co. v. Texas Commerce Bank, 630 F.2d 1111, 1118–19 (5th Cir.1980); Holloway v. Howerdd, 536 F.2d 690, 694–95 (6th Cir.1976); Fey v. Walston & Co., Inc., 493 F.2d 1036, 1051–52 (7th Cir.1974); Kerbs v. Fall River Industries, Inc., 502 F.2d 731, 740–41 (10th Cir.1974). The Ninth, and (with exceptions) the Third Circuits, have held the contrary. Zweig v. Hearst Corp., 521 F.2d 1129, 1132–33 (9th Cir.), cert. denied, 423 U.S. 1025 (1975); Sharp v. Coopers & Lybrand, 649 F.2d 175, 180–84 (3d Cir.1981), cert. denied, 455 U.S. 938 (1982); Rochez Brothers, Inc. v. Rhoades, 527 F.2d 880, 884–86 (3d Cir.1975). We have not previously considered whether, despite section 20(a), principals may be held "vicariously" liable for the "securities related" misrepresentations of their agents. But cf. Holmes v. Bateson, 583

F.2d 542, 560 (1st Cir.1978) (discussing related questions). We now consider this question; and we join the majority expressly—at least in respect to the common law "apparent authority" theory here at issue.

Because there are several different common law agency theories that may lead to "vicarious liability" and because not all courts use the same terminology in respect to each, it may help to clarify the exposition of our reasons if we divide this opinion into two parts. First, we shall explain the basis for liability that would exist in this, and similar cases, in the absence of section 20(a). Second, we shall ask whether, or when, the existence of section 20(a) might make a difference.

I

In the absence of section 20(a) a corporate principal's (or employer's) "vicarious" liability for the misrepresentations of an agent (typically an employee) must find its source in Securities Act § 10(b)—the statutory provision that makes it "unlawful for any person, directly or indirectly * * * to use * * * any manipulative or deceptive device" in connection with the purchase or sale of securities. The "majority rule" circuits have at least implicitly read these words as encompassing some kinds of vicarious liability. (See cases cited at pp. 30–31, supra.) And, the Supreme Court, while restricting the liability of *primary* actors to persons who act with "*scienter,*" Ernst & Ernst v. Hochfelder, 425 U.S. 185 (1976), has nonetheless cited with approval cases imposing "vicarious" liability upon corporations who employ those who knowingly or recklessly make misrepresentations. American Society of Mechanical Engineers, Inc. v. Hydrolevel Corp., 456 U.S. 556, 568 (1982) (hereinafter ASME), citing with approval *Holloway,* supra; *Kerbs,* supra.

These legal facts are not surprising. The common law has long imposed vicarious liability upon principals arising from torts committed by their agents. Whether broad language, such as that found in the Securities Act, embraces such principles is a matter of statutory interpretation based upon congressional intent. ASME, 456 U.S. at 569–70. And, the courts have tended to read congressional statutes that impose tort-like liability to embrace at least some of these well established common law agency principles, where language permits and doing so furthers basic statutory purposes. Id. at 568 (liability imposed upon principals for antitrust violations committed by agents). The courts must also decide *which* common law rules apply under the statutory scheme. And, it will help our exposition if, for this purpose, we divide relevant agency liability rules into three different kinds.

First, the common law typically holds principals liable when an agent's tortious representation is *actually authorized,* whether the agent's authority be express or implied. Restatement (Second) of Agency §§ 7, 257 (1958); W. Seavey, Handbook of the Law of Agency § 91 (1964). Such liability is not of great practical importance when the principal is a corporation, however, for a corporation (its charter, bylaws, directors' actions, etc.) rarely, if ever, *actually* authorizes torts. (Indeed, were it to do so, the corporation might be "directly" rather than "vicariously" liable.)

Second, a corporation's liability for an agent's misrepresentations may rest upon a theory of *"apparent authority."* Restatement (Second) of Agency § 8; cf. id. at § 8B (a related, but distinguishable theory of "estoppel"). The agent's tortious action, while not actually authorized by the corporation, appears so to those adversely affected. Vicarious "[l]iability is based upon the fact that the agent's position facilitates the consummation of the fraud, in that from the point of view of the third person the transaction seems regular on its face and the agent appears to be acting in the ordinary course of the business provided to him." ASME, 456 U.S. at 566, quoting with approval from Restatement (Second) of Agency § 261, comment a, p. 571. Courts have commonly imposed liability based on "apparent authority" upon a corporation in both state and federal "misrepresentation" cases—particularly when the person making the misrepresentation is an important corporate official. See 10 R. Eickhoff, Fletcher on Corporations § 4886 (1978 & Supp.1985).

A third basis for imposing vicarious liability consists of what commentators have called "inherent agency powers" or (in the master/servant context) "respondeat superior" or sometimes simply "the agent's position." Restatement (Second) of Agency § 8A; W. Seavey, supra, at § 8F and § 58. We shall for convenience refer to this basis of liability as "status based" (in contrast with "authority based") liability. This non-authority based vicarious liability rests upon certain important social and commercial policies. See, e.g., W. Seavey, supra, at § 58 ("[T]he business enterprise should bear the burden of the losses created by the mistakes or overzealousness of its agents [because such liability] stimulates the watchfulness of the employer in selecting and supervising the agents."); and at § 61 ("[T]he principal, [having] * * * the opportunity of investigating the agent * * * should guarantee the [agent's] honesty"). The precise scope of "status based" liability is unclear, with liability often depending upon the relationship of the social policy to the type of "principal/agent" circumstance at hand. Id. at § 8F. A "master," for example, is not held vicariously liable (on these grounds) for the torts of a "servant" where the servant does not act for the purpose of serving his master but is on a "frolic of his own." Restatement (Second) of Agency § 235 (no liability when the servant acts "with no intention to perform it as a part or incident to a service on account of which he is employed"). Yet, a principal (even though not a "master") is liable for tortious misrepresentations of an agent (even though not a "servant") even if the agent "acts entirely for his own purposes, unless the [injured person] * * * has notice of this." Id. at § 262.

The case before us is of the second kind; the *"apparent authority"* of a high corporate officer. There are strong reasons for believing that the "direct or indirect" language of the Securities Act encompasses this kind of common law agency liability. For one thing, as between the corporation that has placed the official in a position to invoke its authority (though improperly) and a victim, it seems fairer that the former bear the burden of an uncompensated loss. Further, imposing such liability will encourage corporate officials to prevent unauthorized (but "apparently authorized") misrepresentations, thereby helping to achieve an important Securities Act purpose. Moreover, both related state "misrepresentation" law (which the federal act leaves untouched, 15 U.S.C. § 78bb(a)), and federal cases (quoted by the Supreme Court with approval) apply "apparent authority" liability principles. ASME, 456 U.S. at 568 citing with approval *Holloway,* supra; *Kerbs,* supra. Thus, we have little doubt that, in the absence of section 20(a) we should read the Securities Act of 1934 as imposing vicarious liability upon a corporation for the "apparently authorized" misrepresentations of a high official.

II

We turn now to the question directly before us—whether section 20(a) precludes the imposition of this kind of vicarious liability that would otherwise exist. We think not for several reasons. First, the legislative history of section 20(a) reveals no such intent. Though the relevant written history is sparse, it is significant, for it makes clear that the section was aimed at expanding liability, rather than contracting it. Section 20(a) was modeled on section 15 of the 1933 Securities Act and it has an identical purpose. That purpose, as expressed by one of its authors, Thomas G. Corcoran, is "to prevent evasion of the [Act] * * * by organizing dummies who will undertake the actual things forbidden by the [Act]." Hearings before the Senate Comm. on Banking and Currency on S.Res. 84 (72d Cong.) and S.Res. 56 and 97 (73d Cong.), 73 Cong., 1st Sess., pt. 15, at 6571 (1934). Congress thus saw this section as *imposing* liability upon, say, a shareholder or a director who controlled a corporation engaged in misrepresentation, presumably including persons beyond the reach of ordinary common law agency liability. See id., at 6639; 2 Federal Securities Code § 793 & comment (3)(b). There is no statement of purpose suggesting that Congress saw this section as *removing* liability that the Act would otherwise impose upon a corporation that "controlled" an officer or director. Other circuits have analyzed the statute's history in some detail; and, without simply repeating their analysis of the history, we adopt their conclusions. SEC v. Management Dynamics, Inc., 515 F.2d 801, 812 (2d Cir.1975); Paul F. Newton & Co., 630 F.2d at 1115–16.

Second, the reasons, drawn from the legislative history, offered by those circuits with a different view and by appellants, do not convince us. The appellants refer to the language of the statute, noting that section 20(a) in essence says, "Every person who * * * controls any person liable * * * shall also be liable * * * unless the controlling person acted in good faith and did not directly or indirectly induce the act. * * *" Even assuming, as we do, that the word "control" includes the agency relation (*see* 15 U.S.C. § 77*o;* H.R.Rep. No. 1383, 73d Cong., 2d Sess. 26 (1934)), this language need not be read as providing an *exclusive* route for imposing liability. Section 20(a) does not *say* that it is exclusive; and its proviso ("unless * * *") is naturally read as referring to the (potentially *non* exclusive) liability which section 20(a) *itself* provides.

Appellants refer to the fact that the House and Senate differed in the versions of section 20(a) that they initially presented. The Senate wanted to impose an "insurer's liability" on controlling persons; while the House chose a "fiduciary standard" which eventually became the law. See S.Rep. No. 47, 73d Cong., 1st Sess. 5 (1933) (The Fletcher Report); H.R.Rep. No. 85, 73d Cong., 1st Sess. 5 (1933); H.R.Conf.Rep. No. 152, 73d Cong., 1st Sess. 27 (1933). Yet, this fact is not determinative once section 20(a) is seen as nonexclusive, for, in that event, the different versions refer to *liability under the section,* not to *all* liability that the statute may impose upon one who meets the definition of "controlling person." Appellants also point to statements that legislators made in 1934 when they added a proviso to section 15 of the 1933 Act, to the effect that the "mere existence of control is not made a basis for liability." H.R.Conf.Rep. No. 1838, 73d Cong., 2d Sess. 42 (1934). Yet, again, this statement in context refers to the liability *created* by section 15, not to liability that would exist anyway in its absence. To read it otherwise is to ignore the main thrust of sections 15 and 20(a).

Third, to read section 20(a) as providing the *exclusive* basis for imposing liability on one "who, directly or indirectly, controls any person liable" is to read it as having worked considerable change in existing liability assumptions. On this reading, most corporations, typically liable vicariously under state misrepresentation law for their officers' acts, would often escape liability under federal law. See 10 Fletcher on Corporations § 4886. Yet, the legislative history nowhere refers to any such important difference between state and federal law. In fact, by explicitly including corporations in its definition of "person," 15 U.S.C. § 77b(2), the statute seems to foresee that corporations will be held liable. See Management Dynamics, Inc., 515 F.2d at 812. Yet, since corporations can act only through agents, how, without principles of vicarious liability, (or twisting the meaning of "good faith") could this ordinarily be done?

Fourth, as we have previously noted, the vast majority of circuits have concluded that the "controlling person" provision of section 20(a) is not an exclusive basis for imposing secondary liability under the Securities Acts and thus that common law principles of vicarious liability are applicable to section 10(b) and Rule 10b–5 violations. See L. Loss, Fundamentals of Securities Regulations 1181 (1983) ("The Code follows the majority view, which recognizes common law liability [of a principal for the acts of its agents], so that the [section 20(a)] defenses are available only when the defendant controls as a holding company or in some other nonagency way.") We disagree with appellants' argument that the Fourth and Eighth Circuits favor their views, as we find recent cases in those circuits that ally them with the majority. Metge v. Baehler, 762 F.2d 621, 630–31 (8th Cir. 1985), aff'g 577 F.Supp. 810 (S.D.Iowa 1984), cert. denied, — U.S. —, 106 S.Ct. 798 (1986); Carras v. Burns, 516 F.2d 251, 259 (4th Cir.1975); Johns Hopkins University, 422 F.2d at 1130; Frankel v. Wyllie & Thornhill, Inc., 537 F.Supp. 730, 740–42 (W.D.Va.1982).

Moreover, we believe the persuasive force of the opinions of the Ninth and Third Circuits, in respect to the "exclusive" nature of section 20(a), is limited by the fact that the cases there in issue involved circumstances where traditional agency principles *themselves* seemed to prohibit, or caution against, liability. * * *

* * * Indeed, even the Third Circuit has denied the exclusivity of section 20(a) by accepting the imposition of vicarious liability in situations where the employer has "a duty to exercise a high standard of supervision" or where "the employee was a high level officer or director of the employer, the employer was a brokerage firm, or both." *Sharp*, 649 F.2d at 182. A flexible application of vicarious liability principles should adequately protect section 20(a)'s objectives from erosion. We do not see why reading section 20(a) as *exclusive* of all agency based liability is necessary to do so.

III

In sum, we conclude that section 20(a) does not preclude the assertion of liability—based on common law notions of "apparent authority"—against a corporation for the misrepresentations of an important corporate officer. We state this conclusion narrowly, however, for reasons that, by now, should be apparent. First, the *extent* to which a federal statute, such as the Securities Act, embraces common law agency principles, depends (as the Supreme Court stressed in the antitrust context) upon the extent to which their adoption is consistent with the statute's language and furthers its purposes. ASME, 456 U.S. at 569–70, 102 S.Ct. at 1944–45. As the Second Circuit has stated, the fact that use of common law agency concepts may be appropriate in some circumstances does not mean that we should import them where this will not further the policies of the Securities Act. *Geon Industries,* 531 F.2d at 54; *Management Dynamics,* 515 F.2d at 813. Second, the scope of the common law concepts themselves, at least at their outer perimeters, is sensitive to the basic legal policies relevant to the particular legal context. Of course, section 20(a) reflects *one* set of purposes underlying the Securities Act; and in an appropriate context (perhaps involving the use of "dummies") it could become relevant to a definition of common law vicarious liability. Yet, none of this is here at issue. The facts and theories of this case place it in the heartland of traditional agency law; and we find in section 20(a) no basis for exemption.

For these reasons, the determination of the district court is

Affirmed.

EMPLOYER AND "CONTROLLING PERSON" LIABILITY

Section 15 of the 1933 Act provides that "Every person who * * * controls any person liable under section 11 or 12, shall also be liable jointly and severally with and to the same extent as such controlled person to any person to whom such controlled person is liable, unless the controlling person had no knowledge of or reasonable grounds to believe in the existence of the facts by reason of which the liability of the controlled person is alleged to exist." Section 20(a) of the 1934 Act provides that "every person who * * * controls any person liable under any provision of this title * * * shall also be liable jointly and severally with and to the same extent as such controlled person to any person to whom such controlled person is liable, unless the controlling person acted in good faith and did not directly or indirectly induce the act or acts constituting the violation or cause of action."

The reason for this difference in language is hard to fathom, especially since Section 15 of the 1933 Act was amended in the bill which enacted the 1934 Act, and harder still to interpret. Section 15 would seem to make ignorance a complete defense; whereas, Section 20(a) requires a showing of "good faith", which would certainly include lack of knowledge of the violation but arguably might require more. In addition, Section 20(a) requires a showing that the controlling person did not "induce" the acts constituting the violation, but it is difficult to imagine a situation where the controlling person induced the act but was ignorant of it.

In Zweig v. Hearst Corp.[1] the question was whether the Hearst Corporation as the publisher of the Los Angeles Herald Examiner was liable for a violation of Rule 10b–5 committed by the financial columnist for the newspaper. The Ninth Circuit stated that there was no contention that the publisher had

1. 521 F.2d 1129 (9th Cir.1975), cert. denied 423 U.S. 1025.

"induced" the violation and therefore the only question was whether it had acted in "good faith" (since these are cumulative requirements). The court stated that the cases holding that a broker-dealer had a duty, based upon specific provisions of the 1934 Act, to "adequately supervise" its registered representatives and other employees to prevent their violation of the securities laws had no application to this case. It continued:

"Some lesser standard amounting more nearly to culpability is indicated. A newspaper which requires its reporters to report facts fairly and accurately has a right initially to expect compliance. Unless somehow placed on notice that a particular writer has violated or may violate the requirement of fairness and accuracy, the newspaper may continue to safely anticipate compliance. Where the writer is one with thirty years of service with the paper and not the subject of any complaint during that period, the continued unquestioned publication of his articles is justified. The practicalities of operating a large daily newspaper make it impossible for each item of news or reported interview to be rechecked by supervising editors. If the column or news story prepared and submitted by the columnist or reporter does not, on its face, reveal impropriety, the very nature of the newspaper business prohibits cross-checking.

"These are the factors to be taken into consideration in order to determine the issue of good faith on the part of a newspaper owner as a controlling person under Section 20(a)."

On the other hand, the Seventh Circuit in Securities and Exchange Commission v. First Securities Co. of Chicago [2] stated, without apparent qualification, although that was in fact a case involving a broker-dealer, that "good faith" under Section 20(a) requires affirmative acts on the part of the controlling person to prevent the misconduct of the controlled person.

In Burgess v. Premier Corporation [3] the court held that a director who was not involved in the day-to-day operations of a company and who did not participate in the preparation of the company's prospectus was not liable as a controlling person for alleged misrepresentations made to investors in connection with tax shelter investments and cattle herds offered by the company. In San Francisco-Oklahoma Petroleum Exploration Corporation v. Carstan Oil Company, Inc.,[4] however, the court held that a director and sole stockholder was liable as a "controlling person" in connection with the unregistered sale of fractional interest in oil and gas wells which were not exempted from registration. The defendant claimed that he was simply a figurehead, that his name was used because his son could not use his and that he did not participate in any way and made no effort to learn what the corporation was doing. The court said that even if this testimony were accepted, it demonstrated that he "must have made a conscious effort not to know."

A debate which has raged among the circuits, and even within a single circuit, is over the question whether an employer of a person who violates the securities laws while acting within the scope of his employment may be held liable upon the basis of ordinary tort principles of *respondeat superior*, even though he might not be liable under Section 15 or Section 20(a). In Securities and Exchange Commission v. Management Dynamics, Inc.[5] the court held that agency principles were fully applicable with respect to determining the liability of an employer under the securities acts, and were not limited in any respect by Section 15 of the 1933 Act and Section 20 of the 1934 Act. The court said:

---

2. 507 F.2d 417 (7th Cir.1972). See, also, Barthe v. Rizzo, 384 F.Supp. 1063 (S.D. N.Y.1974).

3. 727 F.2d 826 (9th Cir.1984).

4. 765 F.2d 962 (10th Cir.1985).

5. 515 F.2d 801 (2d Cir.1975).

"Moreover, given the pervasive applicability of agency principles elsewhere in the law, it would take clear evidence to persuade us that Congress intended to supplant such principles by enacting the 'controlling person' provisions. Not only is such evidence lacking, but the statute itself suggests otherwise. 'Person,' a key term in each act, is defined to include not only an individual or partnership, but also a corporation. Section 2 of the Securities Act of 1933; § 3(a)(9) of the Securities Exchange Act of 1934. Thus, Congress evidently intended that a corporation might be liable in some instances as a 'person'; and this can only be by virtue of agency principles, since a corporation can act only through its agents. Were §§ 15 and 20(a) the sole measures of corporate liability, * * * the inclusion of corporations under the definitions of 'person' would be not only unnecessary but also misleading.

"We find it plain, therefore, that the 'controlling person' provisions were enacted to expand, rather than restrict, the scope of liability under the securities laws. * * * Control was defined in a broad fashion, see H.R.Rep. No. 1383, 73d Cong., 2d Sess. 26 (1934), to reach prospective wrongdoers, rather than to permit the escape of those who would otherwise be responsible for the acts of their employees.

"Our conclusion is buttressed by the clear holdings of the four circuits which have applied agency principles to hold brokerage firms liable for the acts of their employees. Johns Hopkins University v. Hutton, 422 F.2d 1124, 1130 (4th Cir.1970); Lewis v. Walston & Co., 487 F.2d 617, 623–24 (5th Cir.1973); Armstrong, Jones & Co. v. SEC, 421 F.2d 359, 361–62 (6th Cir.1970), cert. denied 398 U.S. 958 (1970); Fey v. Walston & Co., 493 F.2d 1036, 1051–53 (7th Cir.1974)." [6] The ink was hardly dry on the opinion in *Management Dynamics* before a different panel of the Second Circuit "explained" that that opinion didn't mean what it apparently said. In Securities and Exchange Commission v. Geon Industries, Inc.,[7] the court noted that the SEC took the position that the broker-dealer was liable in an injunctive proceeding even though it had not failed reasonably to supervise its employees. The Court said: "That argument, however, is based on a significant extension of *Management Dynamics,* an extension which, at least in this context, we decline to make." The court also stated:

"In *Management Dynamics,* the employee held a prominent position in his firm, spoke in his firm's name, and had 'apparent authority' to do so. On those facts it was not unfair to enjoin the firm because of his acts. Here, we have only a registered representative, making no special use of his connection with his firm, and with no profit other than ordinary commissions going to it. Given the lack of balance between the need for an injunction and the hardship which it would create, we do not think that one should issue here once it has been determined that E & II [the broker-dealer] exercised reasonable supervision over Rauch [the registered representative]. However, we wish to make clear, just as did the court in *Management Dynamics,* that we intimate no view as to cases with different facts, and that situations which fall between that case and this one will have to await future resolution."

However, the Second Circuit seems finally to have come down on the side of applying the doctrine of *respondeat superior* in securities law actions against

---

6. 515 F.2d at 813. See, also, Smoky Greenhaw Cotton Co., Inc. v. Merrill Lynch, Pierce, Fenner & Smith, Inc., 785 F.2d 1274 (5th Cir.1986); AFP Imaging Corp. v. Ross, 780 F.2d 202 (2d Cir.1985), cert. denied __ U.S. __, 106 S.Ct. 3295 (1986).

7. 531 F.2d 39, at 55 (2d Cir.1976).

brokerage firms in Marbury Management Inc. v. Kohn,[8] not only in actions by the Commission such as that involved in the *Management Dynamics* case but also in private damage actions with respect to which the court reserved decision in that case.

The Ninth Circuit in Zweig v. Hearst Corp.[9] held flatly that the only basis of liability of an employer for a violation by his employee of the Federal securities laws was the "controlling person" provisions, excluding the doctrine of *respondeat superior,* and reaffirming the rule in Kamen & Co. v. Paul H. Aschkar & Co.[10] And in Rochez Brothers, Inc. v. Rhoades[11] the Third Circuit stated that "We conclude, therefore, that agency principles—*respondeat superior*—are not applicable to determine secondary liability in a securities violation case." However, it should be noted that all of the facts emphasized by the court in that case would tend to indicate that the company official was not acting within the scope of his employment in engaging in the acts constituting the violation of the securities laws, and therefore the employer corporation probably would not have been liable under traditional agency principles. The Fourth Circuit appears also to have adopted the same position in Carpenter v. Harris, Upham & Co., Inc.[12] The court said that the intent of Congress "reflected a desire to impose liability only on those who fall within its definition of control and who are in some meaningful sense culpable participants in the acts perpetrated by the controlled person. * * * The primary duty owed by a broker-dealer to the public is to supervise its employees in an adequate and reasonable fashion. While the standards of supervision may be stringent, this does not create absolute liability for every violation of the securities laws committed by a supervised individual."

On the other hand, the Seventh Circuit in Fey v. Walston & Co., Inc.[13] asserted without qualification, as did the court in *Management Dynamics,* that an employer would be liable on the basis of traditional agency principles for acts of his employees constituting a violation of the Federal securities laws, without regard to the "control" provisions of the 1933 and 1934 Acts. The Fifth,[14] Sixth[15] and Eighth[16] Circuits have agreed with the Second and Seventh in holding that the doctrine of *respondeat superior* is applicable in federal securities law cases against broker dealers.

See Fitzpatrick and Carman, Respondeat Superior and the Federal Securities Laws: A Round Peg in a Square Hole, 12 Hofstra L.Rev. 1 (1983); Lynch, Rule 10b–5—The Equivalent Scope of Liability Under Respondeat Superior and Section 20(a), 35 Vand.L.Rev. 1383 (1982); Reininger, Exclusive or Concurrent—The Role of Control and Respondeat Superior in the Imposition of Vicarious Civil Liability on Broker-Dealers, 9 Sec.Reg.L.J. 226 (1981); Bartlett and Lapatin, Status of a Creditor as a Controlling Person, 28 Mercer L.Rev. 639 (1977); Gottesman, Brokers' Derivative Liability: Does Supervision Make a Difference?, 41 Brook.L.Rev. 181 (1974); Roantree, Continuing Development of

8. 629 F.2d 705 (2d Cir.1980), cert. denied 449 U.S. 1011 (1981).

9. 521 F.2d 1129 (9th Cir.1975), cert. denied 423 U.S. 1025 (1975).

10. 382 F.2d 689 (9th Cir.1967), cert. denied 393 U.S. 801 (1968). The Ninth Circuit reiterated its position again in Christoffel v. E.F. Hutton & Co., Inc., 588 F.2d 665 (9th Cir.1978).

11. 527 F.2d 880 (3d Cir.1975).

12. 594 F.2d 388 (4th Cir.1979), cert. denied 444 U.S. 868.

13. 493 F.2d 1036 (7th Cir.1974). Compare Holloway v. Howerdd, 377 F.Supp. 754 (M.D.Tenn.1973).

14. Paul F. Newton & Co. v. Texas Commerce Bank, 630 F.2d 1111 (5th Cir. 1980), reh. denied 634 F.2d 1355.

15. Holloway v. Howerdd, 536 F.2d 690 (6th Cir.1976). See, also, Plunkett v. Dominick & Dominick, Inc., 414 F.Supp. 885 (D.Conn.1976).

16. Commerford v. Olson, 794 F.2d 1319 (8th Cir.1986).

Rule 10b-5 as a Means of Enforcing the Fiduciary Duties of Directors and Controlling Shareholders, 34 U.Pitt.L.Rev. 201 (1972); Note, Rule 10b-5 and Vicarious Liability Based on Respondeat Superior, 69 Calif.L.Rev. 1513 (1981); Note, "Controlling Persons" Liability of Broker-Dealers for Their Employees' Federal Securities Violations, 1974 Duke L.J. 824.

LANZA v. DREXEL & CO.

United States Court of Appeals, Second Circuit, 1973.
479 F.2d 1277 (en banc).

MOORE, CIRCUIT JUDGE. We sit *en banc* to decide a question important to the course of evolution of the law relating to corporate directors' liabilities largely spawned by Securities and Exchange Commission (SEC) Rule 10b-5: To what extent does a director of corporation A, (1) who does not know that officers or directors of the corporation on whose board he sits have made false representations to, or have failed to disclose the inaccuracy of material information given to, or have omitted to give material information to owners of all the shares of corporation B who are exchanging their stock for that of corporation A, and (2) who has not been a participant in the negotiation of the sale or made any representation with respect thereto or had any knowledge thereof, owe a duty to such purchaser to inquire into all statements, oral and documentary, made to the stockholders of B in connection with the transaction before voting to authorize the contract formalizing the sale?

I.

On September 16, 1971 a penal comprised of Judges Moore, Smith, and Hays heard oral argument on two appeals, both arising from a judgment entered by Judge Frankel on October 13, 1970. Before any opinion was filed disposing of the appeals, this Court, *sua sponte,* filed an order on July 5, 1972, that set plaintiffs' appeal down for reargument before all judges in active service and Judges Moore and Smith on the issue of "the effect of SEC Rule 10b-5 upon the duty of an independent director of a corporation which is about to issue securities, in connection with an acquisition." At our invitation the SEC has submitted an *amicus* brief.

II.

On December 14, 1961, Frank Lanza, Jr., Marie Lanza Sharbo, and Clara Lanza Stefano (then unmarried), son and daughters of Frank Lanza, Sr., exchanged 20,000 shares (i.e., all the stock) of Victor Billiard Company (Victor) owned by them for 20,428 shares of BarChris Construction Company. Less than one year later BarChris filed a petition in bankruptcy. After an unsuccessful effort to recover their shares in a rescission action against the trustee in bankruptcy, plaintiffs borrowed $100,000 to pay the trustee for the return of their Victor shares.

Plaintiffs then commenced this action for compensatory and punitive damages against former officers and directors of BarChris. They based their suit on Section 10(b) of the Securities Exchange Act of 1934 (1934 Act), SEC Rule 10b-5 promulgated thereunder, Section 17(a) of the Securities Act of 1933 (1933 Act), common law fraud, and a theory of prima facie tort.

After a five-week non-jury trial, Judge Frankel in a fifty-three page opinion painstakingly analyzed the facts as they related to each of the defendants and their liability or non-liability. The testimony of defendant-appellee Coleman covered 511 pages of the record. From Coleman's extended examination and cross-examination the trial judge had ample opportunity to appraise the quality of the man and his testimony. On this voluminous record Judge Frankel found: (1) that plaintiffs, through their accountant and representative Sidney Shulman, had been led by material misstatements and omissions on the part of certain officers and directors of BarChris to exchange their Victor shares for BarChris shares; (2) that plaintiffs had sustained compensable damages as a result thereof in the amount of $100,000 plus interest; (3) that defendants Christie Vitolo, president, Leonard Russo, director and vice president, and Theodore Kircher, director and treasurer, were liable to the plaintiffs under Rule 10b–5, under common law fraud, and, in the cases of Vitolo and Russo, under Section 20(a) of the 1934 Act; (4) that Leborio Pugliese, vice president, was not liable under Rule 10b–5 and, assuming him to be a control person, he had established his good faith defense; (5) that defendant John Ames Ballard, director subsequent to December 14, 1961, was not liable to the plaintiffs for allegedly conspiring with Coleman, Pugliese, and one Friedman to delay plaintiffs' appreciation of their right of rescission sometime during 1962 because in fact there had been no such conspiracy; (6) that defendant Bertram D. Coleman, director, was not liable to plaintiffs under either Rule 10b–5 or Section 20(a); and (7) that the firm of which Coleman was a partner, Drexel & Company, a Philadelphia investment and brokerage firm, was not liable on a theory of *respondeat superior* for Coleman's alleged unlawful conduct.

Plaintiffs appeal Judge Frankel's decision exonerating Coleman and Drexel & Co. * * * Our appellate task, therefore, is to review the record in order to ascertain whether there is proof sufficient to support Judge Frankel's fact-findings and conclusions. Conversely, our task is not to re-evaluate the proof but only to determine whether the fact-findings are "clearly erroneous."

Having done so, we affirm the lower court judgment in both appeals.

III.

Mindful that in construing Rule 10b–5 we deal with an area of the law "where glib generalizations and unthinking abstractions are major occupational hazards," we set out in detail the evidence as to Coleman's knowledge of, and participation in, the negotiations leading to the December 14, 1961, Victor-BarChris exchange. We note at the outset that no one disputes the finding that Kircher, aided and abetted by Vitolo, Russo, Warren Trilling, controller, and Robert Birnbaum, secretary and house counsel, violated Rule 10b–5 in making to plaintiffs untrue statements of material facts and in omitting to state material facts necessary to render the statements made, in the light of the circumstances under which they were made, not misleading. Our concern is with *Coleman's* responsibility (if any) for the fraud perpetrated by these other officers and directors, and not with whether fraud was perpetrated by such officers and directors.

As will be developed infra, neither the language nor intent of Section 10(b) or Rule 10b–5 would justify a holding (1) that a director is an insurer of the honesty of individual officers of the corporation in their negotiations which involve the purchase or sale of the corporation's stock or (2) that, although he does not conduct the negotiations, participate therein, or have knowledge thereof, he is under a duty to investigate each such transaction and to inquire as to what representations had been made, by whom and to whom, and then independently check on the truth or falsity of every statement made and document presented.

Were a contrary result to be reached it would, in effect, place an affirmative duty on Coleman (and on all other directors) to intervene personally in every transaction involving the sale or exchange of BarChris stock and would amount to a holding that a director's vote of approval for any such transaction negotiated and concluded by others, without his knowledge or participation, would be a representation to such purchasers that the director personally had inquired as to the facts upon which the negotiations were based and that he was satisfied that all representations were correct.

A. *Background*

In Escott v. BarChris Construction Corp., 283 F.Supp. 643 (S.D.N.Y. 1968), purchasers of debentures issued by BarChris sued the defendants herein and others pursuant to Section 11 of the 1933 Act. As did Judge Frankel, we adopt portions of the late Judge McLean's statement of the history of BarChris up to May 16, 1961, the date the debenture registration statement became effective:

[The statement of facts from the *BarChris* case, 283 F.Supp. 643, 653–54 (S.D.N.Y.1968) is omitted. For a condensed statement of facts, see supra, at pp. 902–904.]

Drexel & Company was the lead underwriter of the debenture offering. Coleman joined the BarChris board of directors in connection with this transaction in April of 1961, and served until March of 1962, when he resigned.

Liability was premised in *Escott* solely upon the statutory basis of Section 11, supra, which permitted any person acquiring a security issued under a registration statement containing an untrue statement of a material fact or omitting a required statement to sue "every person who signed the registration statement". Coleman had signed; hence, he was liable regardless of his knowledge of material inaccuracies. The law applicable to the case now before us is in direct contrast to the absolute liability (except for the due diligence defense) imposed by Section 11.

B. *The Negotiations Leading to the Exchange of Victor and BarChris Shares: A Chronology*

In March of 1961, Frank Lanza, Jr., an owner of Victor stock, met representatives of BarChris at a trade meeting, at which time the possibility of a Victor-BarChris exchange was first discussed. Because both Lanza and Vincent Sharbo (Marie's husband), a secretary-treasurer of Victor, had "modest academic training," and were not versed in "business theory, finance, accounting or securities trading," they relied upon their friend and accountant, Sidney Shulman, throughout the upcoming negotiations. His role was central for plaintiffs throughout the negotiations. Shulman for many years had been the accountant for the Lanzas and their enterprise. They relied upon him in the transaction here in question to study the financial papers and other data and to advise them in light of such study. His role in this respect was plain to all concerned on both sides of the deal.

[Eds.—The Court details the facts regarding the negotiations between the plaintiffs and BarChris and the fact of the non-involvement of Coleman in any of these negotiations.]

The record clearly supports Judge Frankel's finding that "Coleman neither participated in nor knew of any deception practiced upon the plaintiffs" and, as the Judge noted:

It is not suggested that Coleman himself ever communicated anything to plaintiffs or Shulman; that he ever in any sense

"withheld" anything from them; or that he was ever advised of what things had been said or left unsaid in the negotiations with them.

Thus, when the Victor-BarChris transaction first came to Coleman's attention it was already a completed transaction, approved by the board, and it had been negotiated without any knowledge or participation on Coleman's part as to any representations or omissions of material facts made by representatives of BarChris.

We turn now to the evidence relating to Coleman's conduct as a director of BarChris and to his knowledge (or, better, his lack of knowledge) of the misstatements and omissions made by Kircher et al. to the plaintiffs.

C. *Coleman's Conduct as a Director of BarChris*

We initially point out that the only documents concerning BarChris received by plaintiffs prior to the closing on December 14, 1961, were the 1960 annual report (dated March 10, 1961), the May 16, 1961, debenture prospectus, and BarChris's financial statement for the six-month period ending June 30, 1961. Shulman also read in the Wall Street Journal news of the revision of the six months' earnings from thirty to twenty cents per share. It was stipulated by the parties herein that as of May 16, 1961, the effective date of the debenture registration statement, Coleman had no knowledge of any untruth in the prospectus or of any omission of necessary fact.

Apart from Coleman's lack of knowledge of the Victor-BarChris transaction, reference should be made to his familiarity with BarChris's financial affairs and his activities as a director thereof. We begin in August of 1961 when Coleman, while on vacation, read in the Wall Street Journal that BarChris had revised its published earnings for the first six months of 1961 from thirty to twenty cents per share due to the bankruptcy of a bowling alley customer. Coleman thereafter received the financial statement reflecting the revised earnings. This was the same statement that Trilling, BarChris's controller, sent to Shulman on August 17, 1961. Coleman believed that this revised financial statement was true.

Coleman thereafter called Kircher for an explanation of the earnings revision. Kircher stated that Stratford Bowl, a customer of BarChris, had gone bankrupt and that owing to a deficiency in documentation, BarChris might be in an unsecured position. Kircher stated that BarChris hoped to be able to purchase Stratford from the bankruptcy trustee and resell the alley. Kircher explained that the bankruptcy of the alley had been caused by an incapable operator.

At a board meeting on September 13, 1961, Coleman and Grant, director and outside counsel for BarChris demanded that every effort be made to correct any deficiencies in documentation which could result in an unsecure position for BarChris on the bowling alleys of customers. At the board meeting of October 17, 1961, Birnbaum, secretary and house counsel of BarChris, reported that steps had been taken to correct such deficiencies and that BarChris's potential exposure to loss had been reduced to approximately $100,000.

* * *

At the board meeting of November 21, 1961, the Victor acquisition contract was presented and approved. Coleman was present at this meeting. Birnbaum summarized the terms of the contract, while Kircher explained the method of calculating the exchange ratio. Coleman remarked that, in his opinion, the $250,000 price for Victor seemed high, but Kircher explained that the billiard tables would be an additional recreational item to be placed in bowling alleys and would be a useful diversification for BarChris. There was no discussion of the negotiations which over the months had taken place with the plaintiffs.

* * *

1. *The point-of-crisis meeting.*

On December 6, 1961, one month after the Victor stock transaction had been approved and two weeks after the contract authorization, a special meeting of the BarChris board was called to consider the impending resignation of Vitolo as president and the installation of Russo in his place. At this meeting, attended by Coleman, Kircher read a prepared statement, endorsed by Birnbaum and Trilling, the purpose of which was to oppose the projected elevation of Russo and to expose underlying problems within the company. * * *

Coleman's conduct was summarized by Judge Frankel as follows:

Coleman was not aware or even suspicious that plaintiffs were being deceived during the negotiations with Kircher. At least until after the closing, he had no knowledge or belief that any hard figures published by BarChris were false or misleading. He knew of some negative developments—of customer defaults, declining new orders and the stringent cash situation. He came to know, too, a week or so before the closing, that there was dissension among the officers. He had no reason to suspect that Kircher had not disclosed all these facts to plaintiffs; on the contrary, after Kircher's criticisms of the corporation at the "point of crisis" meeting, Coleman might well have looked upon him as the most capable and reliable member of management. Coleman had been aware that at least one public release, in October of 1961, had contained misleadingly optimistic statements—a fact about which he complained and on which he pressed, seemingly successfully, for administrative correction at a directors' meeting on November 6, 1961. He had no reason to suspect that this was other than an isolated incident, that there was any concerted effort to mislead either the public or the plaintiffs. As other troubles became apparent to him, both before and after the October episode, he moved with other directors for corrective measures—demanding repair of loose contract practices, opposing Russo's proposed elevation to the presidency, voting for the retention of a management consultant, and resisting what he viewed as an excessive stock dividend.

* * *

The debate thus comes to this: What duty, if any, does Rule 10b–5 impose on a director in Coleman's position to insure that all material, adverse information is conveyed to prospective purchasers of the corporation's stock where the director does not know that these prospective purchasers are not receiving all such information? (The term "adverse" is used only because the claim is made in the complaint that the financial condition of BarChris was worse than as represented by Kircher, Vitolo, and Russo.) We will frequently refer to this hypothetical duty hereinafter as the "duty to convey."

We conclude that a director in his capacity as a director (a nonparticipant in the transaction) owes no duty to insure that all material, adverse information is conveyed to prospective purchasers of the stock of the corporation on whose board he sits. A director's liability to prospective purchasers under Rule 10b–5 can thus only be secondary, such as that of an aider and abettor, a conspirator, or a substantial participant in fraud perpetrated by others. Because Coleman owed no duty as a director to insure that they received information not conveyed to them by Kircher et al., and because Coleman was not an aider and abettor of, a conspirator in, or a substantial participant in the fraud perpetrated upon these plaintiffs, the complaint against Coleman and Drexel & Company was properly dismissed.

* * *

A. *A Director's Duty to Convey at Common Law*

The common law is relevant in interpreting Rule 10b–5 both because it was against a common law background that Section 10(b) was passed and because the duties of directors are still primarily defined by state and not federal law.

There was as of 1934 no common law duty upon directors to insure that all material, adverse information be conveyed to prospective purchasers. Lord Halsbury's famous opinion in Dovey v. Cory,[39] provides an apt illustration of this principle.

In *Dovey* the House of Lords affirmed a Court of Appeals decision discharging a director (Cory) of breach of duty with respect to the preparation of a fraudulent balance sheet and the payment of advances in violation of the bank's articles of association. The balance sheet allegedly fraudulently overstated profits and led to the payment of dividends impairing the bank's capital. It was admitted by the plaintiff that Cory had not been conscious of the fraud perpetrated by certain officers and other directors of the bank. Lord Halsbury analyzed Cory's liability for neglect of his duties as follows:

> The charge of neglect appears to rest on the assertion that Mr. Cory, like the other directors, did not attend to any details of business not brought before them by the general manager or the chairman, and the argument raises a serious question as to the responsibility of all persons

39. [1901] A.C. 477.

holding positions like that of directors, how far they are called upon to distrust and be on their guard against the possibility of fraud being committed by their subordinates of every degree. It is obvious if there is such a duty it must render anything like an intelligent devolution of labour impossible. Was Mr. Cory to turn himself into an auditor, a managing director, a chairman, and find out whether auditors, managing directors, and chairman were all alike deceiving him? That the letters of the auditors were kept from him is clear. That he was assured that provision had been made for bad debts, and that he believed such assurances, is involved in the admission that he was guilty of no moral fraud; so that it comes to this, that he ought to have discovered a network of conspiracy and fraud by which he was surrounded, and found out that his own brother and the managing director (who have since been made criminally responsible for frauds connected with their respective offices) were inducing him to make representation as to the prospects of the concern and the dividends properly payable which have turned out to be improper and false. I cannot think that it can be expected of a director that he should be watching either the inferior officers of the bank or verifying the calculations of the auditors himself. The business of life could not go on if people could not trust those who are put into a position of trust for the express purpose of attending to details of management. If Mr. Cory was deceived by his own officers—and the theory of his being free from moral fraud assumes under the circumstances that he was—there appears to me to be no case against him at all. The provision made for bad debts, it is well said, was inadequate; but those who assured him that it was adequate were the very persons who were to attend to that part of the business, and so of the rest.[40]

One other example should suffice. In Barnes v. Andrews [41] an outside director was sued by a receiver, *inter alia,* for the expenses of printing pamphlets and circulars used in selling shares. The receiver alleged that the circulars had contained false statements. Judge Learned Hand denied recovery:

> Second, I do not think that Andrews is to be charged with such detail of supervision as was involved in going over the circulars personally. True, I have held him accountable for not acquainting himself with the conduct of the business more intimately than he did; but there is a limit. It seems to me too much to say that he must read the circulars sent out to prospective purchasers and test them against the facts. That was a matter he might properly leave to the officers charged with that duty. He might assume that those who prepared them would not make them fraudulent. To hold otherwise is practically to charge him with detailed supervision of the business, which, consistently carried out, would have taken most of his time. If a director must go so far as that, there will be no directors.

> It is argued that he had actual notice of the circulars, because copies were sent to him, as to all other stockholders. That, indeed, gave him an opportunity to learn the facts; but it did not charge him with any

---

40. Id. at 485–86. Accord, Prefontaine v. Grenier, [1907] A.C. 101, 109–11 (P.C.1906) (Quebec).

41. 298 F. 614 (S.D.N.Y.1924).

duty which had not theretofore existed. It might prove that he did know of the frauds, but that is all. No such proof was made.[42]

At common law, then, there was no obligations upon directors to insure that all material, adverse information be conveyed to prospective purchasers of the company's stock. * * *

* * *

B. *Section 11 of the 1933 Act*

Further indication that Congress did not intend Section 10(b) of the 1934 Act to impose a duty to convey on directors is found in the legislative history of Section 11 of the 1933 Act, the one section of the securities acts squarely directed to the obligation of directors to insure that accurate information is conveyed to prospective purchasers of a company's stock.

* * *

2. *The English Companies Act.*

In enacting the Securities Act, Congress explicitly relied upon similar provisions in the English Companies Act. Section 11 was closely patterned after Section 37 of the English Companies Act, 1929. Thus cases interpreting Section 37 have relevance in construing Congressional intent concerning the obligations imposed by Section 11 upon outside directors.

In Stevens v. Hoare[55] the Court of Chancery construed Section 37 as follows:

> [T]he case has been argued on the part of the plaintiff as if the statute had required of a director not merely reasonable, but sufficient, grounds for his belief. Indeed, it was rather suggested that a director is not entitled to rely upon the assistance or advice of solicitors or clerks, but that with his own hands and eyes he must search out and read every relevant document, and with his own mind judge of its operation and legal effect, and that he is not entitled to state anything in a prospectus that he could not depose to of his own knowledge in a Court of justice. If so he would be bound to do a great deal more than the most industrious and prudent man of business could think of doing, or in most cases would be able to do, in the conduct of his own affairs.[56]

* * *

Section 11, unlike Section 37, imposes on directors an affirmative duty of reasonable investigation of the accuracy of a registration statement. The fact that Congress so changed the thrust of Section 37 buttresses the contention that Congress paid careful attention to common law doctrine concerning the duty of directors to insure that accurate information is conveyed to the purchasers of the company's stock and reinforces the conclusion therefrom that if Congress intended Section 10(b) to change common law doctrine in a similar respect it would have said so in unmistakable terms.

* * *

D. *Case Law Development of Rule 10b–5*

Rule 10b–5, however, cannot be construed solely on the basis of a close reading of legislative history. The law of the Rule has moved far from its

---

42. Id. at 620.   **56.** Id. at 409.

55. 20 T.L.R. 407 (Ch.1904).

original moorings. And we are aware that the Rule must be read flexibly, not technically and restrictively. But reading the Rule flexibly does not relieve us of the obligation to define the limits of liability imposed by the Rule and to adhere to common sense. Where a claim is made that is clearly beyond the scope of the Rule, even flexible reading will not legitimatize that claim.

The cases brought to our attention and those which our research has discovered confirm the conclusion that the Rule does not impose upon directors a duty to convey. Those cases focus, not unexpectedly, on Section 12(2) of the 1933 Act, Section 20(a) of the 1934 Act, or on secondary theories of liability such as aiding and abetting, not on Rule 10b–5.

* * *

We recognize that *participation* by a director in the dissemination of false information reasonably calculated to influence the investing public may subject such a director to liability under the Rule. But it is quite a different matter to hold a director liable in damages for failing to insure that all material, adverse information is conveyed to prospective purchasers of the company's stock absent substantial participation in the concealment or knowledge of it. Absent knowledge or substantial participation we have refused to impose such affirmative duties of disclosure upon Rule 10b–5 defendants.

* * *

Plaintiffs also insist that Coleman is liable to them even absent an affirmative duty, as a director, to scrutinize the BarChris-Victor negotiations prior to giving his approval of the sale. Coleman knew many disquieting facts about BarChris, particularly certain adverse financial developments and the making of misleading statements to the financial community by BarChris officers. Thus it is argued that it was inexcusable for Coleman, armed with such knowledge, not to ascertain whether BarChris's financial status had been fully and accurately disclosed to the prospective buyers. The plaintiffs suggest that if Coleman had inquired into the details of the BarChris-Victor negotiations, he would have discovered the fraud. In that event, Coleman could not have approved the sale of BarChris's stock to the Lanzas without incurring liability. Recognizing, however, that the record in this case cannot support a holding that Coleman's failure to inquire was in any way willful or calculated, plaintiffs, and our dissenting Brothers, urge that liability exists under Rule 10b–5 for a "negligent" omission to state material facts. * * * Although one commentator recently stated that "The question whether scienter is a required element under Rule 10b–5 * * * must be regarded as open at this time [because] [t]he circuit courts are either split or in confusion," Ruder, Multiple Defendants in Securities Law Fraud Cases: Aiding and Abetting, Conspiracy, In Pari Delicto Indemnification, and Contribution, 120 U.Pa.L.Rev. 597, 631 (1972), our recent decision in Shemtob v. Shearson, Hammill & Co., supra, eliminated any doubt that proof of scienter is required in private actions in this circuit. There, in the context of a private action for damages, we stated that no violation of Rule 10b–5 occurs "in the absence of allegation of facts amounting to *scienter,* intent to defraud, reckless disregard for the truth, or knowing use of a device, scheme, or artifice to defraud. It is insufficient to allege mere negligence." 448 F.2d at 445. Under the *Shemtob* test, a plaintiff claiming a violation of Rule 10b–5 who cannot prove that the defendant had actual knowledge of any misrepresentations and omissions must establish, in order to succeed in his action, that the defendant's failure to discover the misrepresentations and omissions amounted to a willful, deliberate, or reckless disregard for the truth that is the equivalent of knowledge.

* * *

E. *Sound Policy Supports the Conclusion that Rule 10b–5 Should Not Be Read to Impose a Duty to Convey*

As Professor Bishop has noted, "[t]here seems to be a general consensus that outside directors—i.e., directors who are not full-time employees of the corporation—are desirable." [99] A survey in 1966 of 456 manufacturing companies showed that only six had no outside directors; in two-thirds of the companies surveyed, outside directors constituted a majority of the boards of directors.[100]

The consensus as to the proper role of these non-officer directors is that they should supervise the performance of the management. Such supervision necessarily involves balancing a skepticism towards management's assessment of its performance and a trust in the integrity and competence of management.

* * *

As a practical matter, what should Coleman have done and said when the concluded Victor-BarChris stock exchange was presented to the board for approval?

Consider for a moment the practical aspects: Should Coleman have said: "Hold up all further proceedings. Disregard the closing date. I must personally examine all participants in this transaction from July to date— all Victor representatives and all BarChris representatives—as to all things said and done with respect to the exchange and no vote on my part can be made until I satisfy myself that all figures and representations are accurate." Even if he had told the Victor shareholders that BarChris' financial situation was bad and that there was dissension in the board, he might well have subjected himself to criticism. Furthermore, if this were Coleman's duty, so was it the duty of all directors to quiz all participants as to their knowledge; establishing such a duty would create an intolerable situation.

* * *

Coleman should not be forced under legal edict to hold himself out publicly as a prophet or a modern Cassandra. His own views as to the company's prospects, expressed or unexpressed, should not be made the basis for legal liability. Actually, any prophecies of doom would have misrepresented Coleman's own views and, had the Victor transaction failed because of any such misrepresentations, it could easily have resulted in suits which would have found Coleman liable to both Victor and BarChris.

In this action penalties have been visited upon those meriting them. The District Court has held liable those who made false representations. He has exonerated those who were not participants. In so doing, he has fulfilled the function of a Judge, which is to serve justice.

---

99. Bishop, Sitting Ducks and Decoy Ducks: New Trends in the Indemnification of Corporate Directors and Officers, 77 Yale L.J. 1078, 1092 (1968).

100. Id., citing J. Bacon, Corporate Directorship Practices 6 (Nat'l Indus. Conference Bd. 1967).

Congress was quite aware of the "agonizingly subtle" choices continually facing directors when it passed the securities acts. As President Roosevelt made clear in his message to Congress and as the committee reports attest, duties were to be imposed upon directors for the protection of the public "with the least possible interference to honest business."

* * *

We conclude that Coleman in his capacity as director and as a non-participant in the transaction owed no duty to insure that all material, adverse information was conveyed to prospective purchasers of BarChris stock. Because Coleman owed no duty as a director to convey to plaintiffs information not conveyed to them by Kircher et al., and because Coleman was not an aider and abettor of, a conspirator in, or a substantial participant in the fraud perpetrated upon these plaintiffs, the complaint against Coleman and Drexel & Co. was properly dismissed.

* * *

The judgment is affirmed.

HAYS, CIRCUIT JUDGE (concurring in part and dissenting in part):

* * *

I would reverse the dismissal of the complaint as to defendants Coleman and Drexel & Co.

TIMBERS, CIRCUIT JUDGE (concurring in part and dissenting in part):

I concur with the majority in affirming the denial of Kircher's motion for jury trial, but I dissent from the majority's affirmance of the dismissal of the complaint as to Coleman and Drexel & Co.

I join in Judge Hays' eminently sound opinion.

* * *

SANDERS v. JOHN NUVEEN & CO., INC.

United States Court of Appeals, Seventh Circuit, 1980.
619 F.2d 1222, cert. denied 450 U.S. 1005, 101 S.Ct. 1719, 68 L.Ed.2d 210 (1981).

[Re-read at this point the above case, which is printed at p. 925.]

OUTSIDE DIRECTORS

There is yet little authority, although a lot of literature, regarding the responsibility of directors of a corporation which commits a violation of the federal securities laws, who are not full-time employees of the corporation or actively involved in the fraud. In Mader v. Armel [1] the District Court refused to hold two "outside" directors liable for a false statement in a proxy statement and described any attempt to impose such liability for mere negligence as "frightening." The court said: "The most that can be said of them [the outside directors] is that they neglected to find out. While this Court would have no hesitancy in holding that a negligent director might well become involved in an injunction proceeding along with his more executive brothers, this Court is not prepared to say that a negligent director * * * becomes liable, simply by virtue of the fact he was a director, for damages in a 10b–5 case."

---

1. CCH Fed.Sec.Law Rptr. ¶ 93,027 (S.D.Ohio 1971).

The Sixth Circuit affirmed this judgment[2] on the basis that one of the directors was not a controlling person and that the other, while found to be a controlling person, had established his defense of "good faith." The court said:

"The District Judge ruled that, since Young was a 'controlling person' within the meaning of the Act, he had the burden of showing good faith by a preponderance of the evidence, and that he had sustained this burden; that Young served as a director without compensation; that he did nothing directly or indirectly to induce the fraudulent proxy solicitation; that 'he did not have the slightest idea anything was wrong until sometime in 1960 at the earliest;' and that 'he relied fully on the Certified Public Accountants who bore a good reputation' and upon the annual published certifications of these accountants. The District Court held that the substantial investment of Young and his family continued throughout the events which gave rise to this case and this fact 'speaks rather eloquently of his overall innocence.' The court concluded that although Young was a 'controlling person' and although his performance as a director was negligent, his actions or non-actions were in good faith."[3]

On the other hand, the court in Norte & Co. v. Huffines,[4] although it found that the defendant-directors had actual knowledge of the falsity of the proxy statement, stated that "actual knowledge is not essential." And in Gould v. American Hawaiian Steamship Co.[5] Judge Wright held the outside directors (and their corporate "principals") liable for negligence in connection with a proxy solicitation.

Has the Supreme Court's opinion in the *Ernst & Ernst* case (supra, p. 936), and its citation with approval of the *Lanza* case, resolved this conflict? Or are the cases to be distinguished because some were based on Rule 10b–5 and others on Rule 14a–9?

If a director is held liable for a willful and intentional participation in a violation of the federal securities laws, it seems clear that he would not be entitled to seek any indemnity from the corporation for the liability.[6] If he should be held liable for mere negligence, however, could he seek any indemnity from the corporation or his "more executive brothers" under the common law or under any statute or charter or bylaw provision? In a subsequent opinion in the Gould case[7] Judge Wright denied a claim for indemnity by the negligent directors against those actively engaged in the preparation of the misleading proxy material. The court said:

"This Court is aware of only one case discussing the availability of indemnity to those found liable for a violation of § 14(a) of the Securities Exchange Act. In Sherlee Land v. Commonwealth United Corp., CCH Fed.Sec.L.Rep. ¶ 93,749 (S.D.N.Y. January 16, 1973), a case involving, *inter alia,* claims under § 14(a), the court denied a motion by one of the defendants for leave to file a cross claim for indemnity stating, 'The Court, mindful of public policy embodied in Federal Securities legislation and of the public faith reposed in public accounting firms, is doubtful that third party plaintiff is entitled to indemnity.' Id. at 93,274. The extent to which this opinion rests on considerations particular to § 14(a), however, is unclear.

"Several courts have ruled on claims for indemnity for liability under other sections of the Securities Acts, particularly §§ 10(b) and 17(a), * * *. Some

---

2. Mader v. Armel, 461 F.2d 1123 (6th Cir.1972), cert. denied 409 U.S. 1023.

3. 461 F.2d at 1126.

4. 304 F.Supp. 1096 (S.D.N.Y.1968), aff'd 416 F.2d 1189 (2d Cir.1969), cert. denied 397 U.S. 989 (1970).

5. 351 F.Supp. 853 (D.Del.1972).

6. Globus v. Law Research Service, Inc., 418 F.2d 1276 (2d Cir.1969), cert. denied 397 U.S. 913 (1970).

7. Gould v. American Hawaiian Steamship Co., 387 F.Supp. 163 (D.Del.1974).

courts have held that indemnity is available to those whose participation in a fraudulent scheme has been only 'passive', 'secondary', or whose liability attaches only 'as a matter of law.' Thomas v. Duralite Co., Inc., CCH Fed.Sec.L. Rep. ¶ 94,864 (D.N.J., November 7, 1974); deHaas v. Empire Petroleum Co., 286 F.Supp. 809 (D.Colo.1968), modified on other grounds, 435 F.2d 1223 (10th Cir. 1971); Handel-Maatschappij v. Faradyne Electronics Corp., 37 F.R.D. 357 (S.D. N.Y.1964). Other courts have held that indemnity is not available to one who is guilty of 'more than ordinary negligence' or whose conduct is as culpable as that of the proposed indemnitor. Globus v. Law Research Service, Inc., 418 F.2d 1276 (2d Cir.1969), affirming 287 F.Supp. 188 (S.D.N.Y.1968), cert. denied, 397 U.S. 913 (1970); Kuehnert v. Texstar Corp., 412 F.2d 700, 705 n. 7 (5th Cir. 1969) (dictum); Herzfeld v. Laventhol, Krekstein, Horwath & Horwath, 378 F.Supp. 112 (S.D.N.Y.1974); Tucker v. Arthur Andersen & Co., CCH Fed.Sec.L. Rep. ¶ 94,955 (S.D.N.Y., April 25, 1974); State Mutual Life Assurance Co. v. Arthur Andersen & Co., CCH Fed.Sec.L.Rep. ¶ 94,543 (S.D.N.Y., September 28, 1972); State Mutual Life Assurance Co. v. Peat, Marwick, Mitchell & Co., 49 F.R.D. 202 (S.D.N.Y.1969); deHaas v. Empire Petroleum Co., supra. * * *

"In short, most of the cases on indemnity under the Securities Acts can be read to support the proposition that an unsuccessful defendant may obtain indemnity from one significantly more responsible for the injury to the plaintiff. * * * This indemnification doctrine, however, was developed in § 10(b) and § 17(a) cases, where the gravamen of the wrongdoing is fraudulent and intentional conduct, and is not necessarily applicable to indemnity under § 14(a). It may be that one joint tortfeasor whose conduct has been of limited culpability should be entitled to shift his loss to another joint tortfeasor whose conduct has been deliberately fraudulent in cases arising under sections of the Securities Acts prohibiting fraud. Shifting liability to the more culpable tortfeasor in such cases may adequately serve the deterrent purposes of those sections. But § 14(a) reaches negligent as well as deliberately deceptive conduct, 351 F.Supp. at 860, and the considerations governing indemnity thereunder are, accordingly, somewhat different.

" * * *

"Thus, the question of who pays the damages to the plaintiffs is of as great concern as the issue of whether the plaintiffs are compensated at all. To allow indemnity to those who have breached responsibilities squarely placed upon them by the statute would vitiate the remedial purposes of § 14(a). Only a realistic possibility of liability for damages will encourage due diligence by those who solicit proxies and will protect the interest of informed corporate suffrage. Consequently, even if one concurrent tortfeasor bears greater responsibility for preparation or approval of false or misleading proxy materials, a person who breaches § 14(a) duties should not thereby be entitled to indemnity."

See the Special Issue of the Business Lawyer devoted to the subject, Officers' and Directors' Responsibilities and Liabilities, 27 Bus.Law. 1 (1972); Scott, Resurrecting Indemnification: Contribution Clauses in Underwriting Agreements, 61 N.Y.U.L.Rev. 223 (1986); Cohn, Demise of the Director's Duty of Care: Judicial Avoidance of Standards and Sanctions Through the Business Judgment Rule, 62 Tex.L.Rev. 591 (1983); Sporkin, SEC Enforcement and the Corporate Board Room, 61 N.C.L.Rev. 455 (1983); Hazen, Fiduciary Obligations in the Corporate Board Room: Breaches of Fiduciary Duty and Federal Securities Laws, 61 N.C.L.Rev. 527 (1983); Golstein and Shepherd, Directors' Duties and Liabilities Under the Securities Acts and Corporation Law, 36 Wash. & Lee L.Rev. 759 (1979); Hahn and Manzoni, Monitoring Committee and Outside Directors' Evolving Duty of Care, 9 Loyola U.L.J. (Chicago) 587 (1978); Hershman, Liabilities and Responsibilities of Corporate Officers and Directors, 33 Bus.Law. 263 (1977); Sonde and Freedman, "Seagulls on the Water—Some Ships in a Storm": A Comment on Lanza v. Drexel, 49 N.Y.U.L.Rev. 270 (1974); Melchior and Chilton, Plums Turning Sour? Problems of Officers and Directors Under the Federal Securities Laws, 10 Forum 221 (1974); Goldschmid, Role of the Outside Director in Assuring Adequate Corporate Disclosure, 5 Inst.Sec. Reg. 121 (1974); Miller and Subak, Impact of Federal Securities Laws: Liabilities of Officers, Directors and Accountants, 30 Bus.Law. 387 (1975); Jacobs, Role of Securities Exchange Act Rule 10b–5 in the Regulation of Corporate Management, 59 Cornell L.Rev. 27 (1973).

UNDERWRITERS

The liability of underwriters under Section 11 and Section 12(2) of the 1933 Act has been discussed above in the *BarChris* case (page 901) and in the notes following the *Sanders* case (page 931, above). The primary difference between those two sections is that the underwriter is liable under Section 12(2) only to the persons to whom he himself sold the securities and not to any person to whom other underwriters sold or to whom the issuer itself sold in "reserved sales." [8] An underwriter can also be liable under Rule 10b–5 or Section 14(e) since both apply to "any person", but all the elements of a cause of action under those provisions would have to be established by the plaintiff. In particular, the element of "scienter" would have to be shown under both provisions, which normally would make that a less attractive alternative to a plaintiff than an action under Section 11 or Section 12(2), if the particular plaintiff can qualify to bring an action under those sections. Since the concept of "aiding and abetting" under Rule 10b–5 casts a much wider net, however, than Section 11 or Section 12(2), it may be the only alternative which the plaintiff has for suing an underwriter in a particular case.

See Fox, Shelf Regulation, Integrated Disclosure and Underwriter Due Diligence: An Economic Analysis, 70 Va.L.Rev. 1005 (1984); Weiss, Economic Analysis, Corporate Law, and the ALI Corporate Governance Project, 70 Cornell L.Rev. 1 (1984); Nicholas, Integrated Disclosure System and its Impact Upon Underwriters' Due Diligence: Will Investors be Protected?, 11 Sec.Reg. L.J. 3 (1983); Greene, Determining the Responsibilities of Underwriters Distributing Securities Within an Integrated Disclosure System, 56 Notre Dame Law 755 (1981).

----

8. Foster v. Jesup and Lamont Securities Co., Inc., 759 F.2d 838 (11th Cir.1985).

SECURITIES AND EXCHANGE COMMISSION v. ARTHUR YOUNG & COMPANY

United States Court of Appeals, Ninth Circuit, 1979.
590 F.2d 785.

Before CHOY and SNEED, CIRCUIT JUDGES, and WATERS,* DISTRICT JUDGE.

SNEED, CIRCUIT JUDGE:

This case grew out of the activities of Jack Burke, an oil and gas venture promoter, during 1964–71. In the course of these activities the appellee Arthur Young and Company (AY) performed certain audits and prepared certain financial statements in connection with some of Burke's ventures. In 1973, the Securities and Exchange Commission (SEC) brought a civil action against Burke and many of his associates charging violations of the antifraud and reporting requirements of the securities laws. The SEC joined other defendants, including the appellee and four of its auditors, charging violations of the securities acts by participating with and aiding and abetting the violations by Burke. Specifically, violations of Section 17(a) of the Securities Act, Section 10(b) of the Securities Exchange Act and Rule 10b–5 thereunder, and Sections 13(a) and 15(d) of the Securities Exchange Act, were charged.

After a thorough trial before an experienced trial judge AY and its auditors were found neither to have violated, nor to have aided and abetted the violations of, the securities laws. The trial court prepared extensive findings and conclusions of law which are printed at 426 F.Supp. 715 (N.D. Cal.1976) and which contain a complete statement of the SEC's charges and the facts that led to this appeal. The trial court also refused to enjoin AY and its auditors from future violations because "the evidence is insufficient to show a reasonable likelihood or expectation that AY would commit further violations in the future." 426 F.Supp. at 731. The SEC appealed and, because the only sanction sought to be imposed upon AY and its auditors was an injunction preventing future violations, we affirm on the ground that the trial court did not exceed the limits of its discretion in refusing to enjoin AY and its auditors.

I.

Standard of Review of Trial Court's Denial of an Injunction.

It is uniformly held that "the granting or denying of injunctive relief rests within the sound discretion of the trial court and * * * will not be disturbed unless there has been a clear abuse of it." SEC v. MacElvain, 417 F.2d 1134, 1137 (5th Cir.1969), cert. denied, 397 U.S. 972 (1970). As this court has recognized, even after a showing of a past violation of the securities laws, no *per se* rule requires that an injunction issue. SEC v. Koracorp Industries, 575 F.2d 692, 701 (9th Cir.), cert. denied, —— U.S. ——, 99 S.Ct. 348, 58 L.Ed.2d 343 (1978). See SEC v. Bausch & Lomb, Inc., 565 F.2d 8, 18 (2d Cir.1977); SEC v. Management Dynamics, Inc., 515 F.2d 801, 807 (2d Cir.1975). To succeed in its attack on the district court's exercise of discretion, the SEC must establish that there was no reasonable basis for

* Hon. Laughlin E. Waters, United States District Judge for the Central District of California, sitting by designation.

the district judge's decision. United States v. W.T. Grant Co., 345 U.S. 629, 634 (1953); SEC v. Bausch & Lomb, Inc., supra, 565 F.2d at 18.

II.

Standard of Performance Required of Auditors.

Our affirmance rests on our conviction that under the circumstances of this case the trial court did not err as a matter of law in fixing the standards of performance imposed on auditors by the securities laws. Like the trial court, we will assume, without deciding, that in a statutory enforcement proceeding such as this, negligence, rather than scienter, constitutes the standard by which an accountant's or auditor's performance must be measured. That is, we assume, without deciding, that Ernst & Ernst v. Hochfelder, 425 U.S. 185 (1976) does not require the finding of scienter in a statutory enforcement proceeding. By eliminating any significance in the distinction between scienter and negligence from that which we must review, we are only required to determine whether the trial court misconceived the standard applicable to accountants and auditors against which the existence of negligence is determined. That is, the question is did the trial court impose an insufficiently demanding standard with which accountants must comply to avoid liability under the securities laws. We hold that it did not.

We confess at the outset that our review is hampered by the fact that neither the trial court nor the parties have been pellucid in presentation of their view of what constitutes the appropriate standard. The SEC in the trial court appears to have asserted that AY and its auditors performed their work "with blinders on" and that they should have done "more" to reveal to investors the conduct of Burke and his associates that increased the financial risk of those who invested in his ventures.[1] During oral argument the SEC appeared to take the position that the proper standard is whether the accountant performed his audit functions in a manner that would have revealed to an ordinary prudent investor, who examined the accountant's audits or other financial statements, a reasonably accurate reflection of the financial risks such an investor presently bears or might bear in the future if he invested in the audited endeavor.

AY, on the other hand, contends that good faith compliance with Generally Accepted Auditing Standards (GAAS)[2] under the circumstances

---

1. Uncertainty as to what exactly the SEC contended caused the trial judge to characterize the SEC position as that AY should have done something "more" than it did. 426 F.Supp. at 759. In its brief, the SEC never clearly articulated a standard more stringent than Generally Accepted Auditing Standards (GAAS). "[B]y failing to conduct its audit in accordance with generally accepted auditing standards, AY deprived itself of any chance to discover the fraud * * *." The one concrete aspect in which the SEC asserts AY's audit was deficient was in not examining more closely the account balance and assets of Fundamental, the corporation through which the funds of all Burke oil and gas programs were channeled. The district

court, however, found that GAAS required no more than AY had done. For the reasons set out in this opinion, we find that no more was required.

2. "Auditing" is the process whereby the independent Certified Public Accountant conducts an examination of management's financial statements to determine whether the statements present fairly the financial information which they purport to convey. "Generally Accepted Auditing Standards" (GAAS) are general standards of conduct relating to the auditor's professional qualities as well as to the judgments exercised by him in the performance of his examination and issuance of his report. AICPA, Professional Standards, State-

of this case will immunize it from liability under the securities laws. The trial court did not explicitly choose between these competing standards; but a careful reading of its findings of fact and conclusions of law convinces us that it did not accept that urged by the SEC during oral argument. Its failure to do so, we hold, did not constitute error.

To accept the SEC's position would go far toward making the accountant both an insurer of his client's honesty and an enforcement arm of the SEC. We can understand why the SEC wishes to so conscript accountants. Its frequently late arrival on the scene of fraud and violations of securities laws almost always suggests that had it been there earlier *with the accountant* it would have caught the scent of wrong-doing and, after an unrelenting hunt, bagged the game. What it cannot do, the thought goes, the accountant can and should. The difficulty with this is that Congress has not enacted the conscription bill that the SEC seeks to have us fashion and fix as an interpretive gloss on existing securities laws.[3]

Under existing law we agree with Judge Pollack when, in SEC v. Republic National Life Ins. Co., 378 F.Supp. 430, 440 (S.D.N.Y.1974), he observed:

> Since an accountant is not a guarantor of the reports he prepares and is only duty bound to act honestly, in good faith and with reasonable care in the discharge of his professional obligations, the elements of fraud if charged must be pleaded with particularity to show a fraudulent breach of duty.

On the facts of this case, AY discharged its professional obligations by complying with GAAS in good faith. The trial court's findings, which are not clearly erroneous, establish beyond dispute that AY and its auditors conformed to this standard.

Moreover, it is clear that the trial court found no basis for the application of United States v. Simon, 425 F.2d 796 (2d Cir.1969), *cert. denied,* 397 U.S. 1006 (1970). *Simon* recognized that compliance with Generally Accepted Accounting Principles (GAAP)[4] would not immunize an accountant

---

ments on Auditing Standards No. 1, § 150.01.

3. As far back as 1964, the SEC was aware of the divergence of methods used to account for oil and gas operations and was concerned with protecting investors in these enterprises. Working both with the Accounting Principles Board of the Association of Independent Certified Public Accountants, and its successor, the Financial Accounting Standards Board, the SEC has sought to remedy this problem. In accordance with the directive of the Managers on the Part of the House in their statement appended to the Report of the Conference Committee on the Investment Company Amendments Act of 1970 (P.L. 91–547, approved December 14, 1970), the SEC drafted proposed legislation, the Oil and Gas Investment Act of 1972, and submitted it to Congress June 14, 1972. This legislation would have regulated oil and gas programs to prevent the type of fraud Burke was able to practice in this case.

Although Congress failed to enact the proposed legislation, the SEC has continued its efforts to gain tighter control over oil and gas programs. Recently, under its rule-making authority, the SEC issued three releases entitled, "Requirements for Financial Accounting and Reporting Practices for Oil and Gas Producing Activities," "Oil and Gas Producers-Full Cost Accounting Practices," and "Disclosure of Oil and Gas Reserves and Operations; Amendments to Regulation S–K." Releases Nos. 33–6006, 33–6007 and 33–6008 (43 Fed.Reg. 60404, 60413, 60418) (1978). Many of the substantive concerns the SEC has expressed in this case may have been at least partially removed through its own more explicit requirements.

4. "Generally Accepted Accounting Principles" (GAAP) establish guidelines relating to the process by which the transactions and events of a business entity are measured, recorded, and classified in accordance with a conventional format. GAAS

when he consciously chose not to disclose on a financial statement a known material fact. No such deliberate concealment was found by the trial court to exist in this case. Thus, although we assume *arguendo* that *Simon* strips the accountant of the protection that compliance with GAAS (*Simon*, incidentally, was concerned only with GAAP) normally affords when he fails to reveal material facts which he knows or which, but for a deliberate refusal to become informed, he should have known, there exists no basis in the trial court's findings for so applying *Simon*. We cannot say such findings in this respect are clearly erroneous.

III.

Application of Standards.

Having concluded that the trial court did not fall into error when it refused to apply the SEC's standard by which an accountant's compliance with the securities laws is to be determined and that the trial court's relevant findings of fact are not clearly erroneous, it follows that the trial court did not exceed the limits of its discretion in refusing to enjoin the AY defendants. Under such circumstances the decision that there was no reasonable likelihood that the wrong would be repeated is unassailable on appeal. Cf. SEC v. Koracorp Industries, Inc., 575 F.2d 692 (9th Cir.), cert. denied, —— U.S. ——, 99 S.Ct. 348, 58 L.Ed.2d 343 (1978) (no abuse of discretion in denying injunction against accounting firm that failed to uncover fraud through simple negligence). We would uphold the trial court's exercise of discretion in this case even if it were true that the trial court erred in one or more respects when it concluded under the standard of care it employed that the AY defendants had violated no securities law. However, we make no finding that the AY defendants have violated any securities law; we merely hold that the trial court in no respect employed an improper legal standard, that the application of *Simon* was not warranted by the facts of this case, and that the refusal to enjoin the AY defendants was within the limits of the trial court's discretion.

AFFIRMED.

SECURITIES AND EXCHANGE COMMISSION v. NATIONAL STUDENT MARKETING CORP.

District Court of the United States, District of Columbia, 1978.
457 F.Supp. 682.

BARRINGTON D. PARKER, DISTRICT JUDGE:

This opinion covers the final act in a civil proceeding brought by the Securities and Exchange Commission (Commission or SEC) seeking injunctive sanctions against numerous defendants as a result of their participation in alleged securities laws violations relating to the National Student Marketing Corporation (NSMC) securities fraud scheme. The original defendants included the corporation and certain of its officers and directors; the accounting firm of Peat, Marwick, Mitchell & Co. (Peat Marwick)

thus differs from GAAP; the former involves how an auditor goes about obtaining information, while the latter involves the format in which to present the information.

and two of its partners; several officers and directors of Interstate National Corporation (Interstate); the law firm of White & Case and one of its partners; and the law firm of Lord, Bissell & Brook (LBB) and two of its partners. The majority of these defendants are not now before the Court. As discovery progressed during the pre-trial stages of this litigation, NSMC and other principal defendants consented to the entry of final judgments of permanent injunction or otherwise reached a resolution of the charges against them. The only defendants remaining are Lord, Bissell & Brook; its two partners, Max E. Meyer and Louis F. Schauer; and Cameron Brown, a former president and director of Interstate, and presently a director of and consultant to NSMC.

The focal point of the Commission's charges against these defendants is the corporate merger of Interstate with NSMC on October 31, 1969. The principal question presented is whether the defendants violated or aided and abetted the violation of the anti-fraud provisions of the federal securities laws in two instances: (1) consummation of the NSMC merger; and (2) the immediately following sale of newly acquired NSMC stock by former Interstate principals, including certain of the defendants. These transactions are alleged to have occurred despite the prior receipt by the defendants of information which revealed that NSMC's interim financial statements, used in securing shareholder approval of the merger and available to the investing public generally, were grossly inaccurate and failed to show the true condition of the corporation. The information was included in a comfort letter prepared by NSMC's accountants. The Commission contends that these violations demonstrate a reasonable likelihood of future misconduct by the defendants, thereby justifying the requested permanent injunctive relief.

The matter was tried without a jury. After reviewing the extensive record in this case, the Court concludes, for the reasons stated below, that while each of the defendants violated the securities laws in specific instances, the Commission has not fulfilled its obligation of demonstrating a reasonable likelihood that they will do so in the future. Accordingly, the Commission's request for injunctive relief must be denied.

* * *

I. BACKGROUND

A. *The Companies*

National Student Marketing Corporation was incorporated in the District of Columbia in 1966. The company enjoyed early prosperity; it grew rapidly and experienced a steady increase in assets, sales and earnings. Its common stock, which was registered with the SEC and traded on the over-the-counter market, rose from an initial public offering [price] of $6 per share in the spring of 1968 to a high of $144 per share in mid-December 1969.[3] The financial community held the company and its potential in high regard, and in anticipation of continued high market performance, it was seen as a good "buy" prospect. Its management was considered aggressive, imaginative and capable; if there was a question of its integrity and honesty, it did not surface in the public arena until a later period. During this period, White & Case served as its outside legal counsel, with

3. The $144 per share figure is based on an adjustment for a 2-for-1 stock split in December 1968; the actual price in mid-December 1969 was $72 per share.

Marion J. Epley, III, as the partner immediately in charge of the firm's representation. Peat Marwick served as its outside accountant.

Interstate National Corporation, a Nevada corporation, was an insurance holding company. Its principal assets were several wholly-owned subsidiary insurance companies. The company's common stock was traded on the over-the-counter market and owned by approximately 1200 shareholders. Cameron Brown was president, chief executive officer, principal shareholder and a director of the company. Other Interstate principals and directors included Robert P. Tate, chairman of the board; William J. Bach, general counsel; Paul E. Allison, secretary; Louis W. Biegler; and Max E. Meyer. Between board meetings, all management authority was delegated to an executive committee composed of Brown, Tate, Bach, Allison and Biegler. Max E. Meyer, a director and shareholder was a partner in the Chicago law firm of Lord, Bissell & Brook, which had long represented Interstate and served as its outside legal counsel in all matters relating to the merger of the corporation with NSMC. Meyer, a personal friend and legal advisor to Cameron Brown, served as the contact partner for the Interstate account and was otherwise in overall charge of his firm's representation. Another partner of the firm, Louis F. Schauer, was also involved in the merger transaction due to his experience in corporate and securities law. Peat Marwick served as Interstate's outside accountant during the period in question.

B. *The Merger Negotiations*

National Student Marketing Corporation developed a reputation for having a unique and successful marketing network for selling its own and other products to college and high school students. Commencing in 1969, it undertook a highly active program to acquire companies specializing in selling goods and services to students. It was in this connection that NSMC first approached representatives of Interstate.

Initially, NSMC discussed the possibility of acquiring an Interstate subsidiary that specialized in selling insurance to students. After Interstate indicated an unwillingness to dispose of a single subsidiary, NSMC expressed interest in acquiring its entire insurance holding company operation. Cortes W. Randell, NSMC's president and chief executive officer, proposed a merger of the two corporations, offering one share of NSMC stock for every two shares of Interstate stock.

On June 10, 1969, NSMC representatives, including Randell and James F. Joy, a senior vice president and finance committee member, were invited before the Interstate directors to make a presentation concerning the proposed merger. The directors were provided with NSMC's 1968 annual report and its financial report for the first half of 1969. Randell discussed the company's acquisition program, reviewed several pending corporate acquisition commitments, and made certain earnings predictions for the fiscal year ending August 31, 1969. He also increased the earlier offer to two shares of NSMC common for every three shares of Interstate common. When certain Interstate directors expressed a desire to sell a portion of the NSMC stock which they expected to acquire in the merger, Randell responded that a registered public offering was planned for the fall of 1969, at which time the former Interstate shareholders could sell up to 25 percent of their shares.[6] Very few questions were asked by Randell or Joy about the business and financial affairs of Interstate, an aspect of the meeting which surprised several of Interstate's representatives.

This meeting resulted in an agreement in principle for the merger. Essentially identical press releases were then issued by the companies, announcing the agreed upon stock exchange ratio, the estimated value of the transaction as $37 million based on the current market value of NSMC stock, and the fact that the transaction represented approximately a 100 percent premium for the Interstate shares based on their market value at the time. Representations were also made in the releases as to NSMC's earnings for the first six months of fiscal 1969, which ended February 28, 1969.

* * *

The Agreement also provided several conditions precedent to the obligations of the two corporations to consummate the merger. One required the receipt by NSMC of an opinion letter from Interstate's counsel LBB to the effect, *inter alia*, that Interstate had taken all actions and procedures required of it by law and that all transactions in connection with the merger had been duly and validly taken, to the best knowledge of counsel, in full compliance with applicable law; a similar opinion letter was required to be delivered from NSMC's counsel to Interstate. Another condition was the receipt by each company of a "comfort letter" from the other's independent public accountants. Each letter was required to state: (1) that the accountants had no reason to believe that the unaudited interim financial statements for the company in question were not prepared in accordance with accounting principles and practices consistent with those used in the previous year-end audited financials; (2) that they had no reason to believe that any material adjustments in those financials were required in order fairly to present the results of operations of the company; and (3) that the company had experienced no material adverse change in its financial position or results of operations from the period covered by its interim financial statement up to five business days prior to the effective date of the merger. Although setting forth these specific conditions to consummation of the merger, the final paragraph of the Agreement also provided that:

> Anything herein to the contrary notwithstanding and notwithstanding any stockholder vote of approval of this Agreement and the merger provided herein, this Agreement may be terminated and abandoned by mutual consent of the Boards of Directors of NSMC and Interstate at any time prior to the Effective Date and the Board of Directors of any party may waive any of the conditions to the obligations of such party under this Agreement.

* * *

Both NSMC and Interstate utilized proxy statements and notices of special stockholder meetings to secure shareholder approval of the proposed merger. Interstate's materials included a copy of the Merger Agreement and NSMC's Proxy Statement; the latter contained NSMC's financial

---

6. Because of an accounting method in use in 1969, a company was permitted to "pool" the earnings of an acquired company with the earnings of the parent as though the companies had always operated together. However, in order for NSMC to take advantage of this retroactive pooling, no more than 25 percent of the shares received in the merger exchange could be sold during the first year.

statements for the fiscal year ended August 31, 1968, and the nine-month interim financial statement for the period ending May 31, 1969. * * *

In mid-October, Peat Marwick began drafting the comfort letter concerning NSMC's unaudited interim financials for the nine-month period ended May 31, 1969. As issued by NSMC, those financials had reflected a profit of approximately $700,000.

Soon after beginning work on the comfort letter, Peat Marwick representatives determined that certain adjustments were required with respect to the interim financials. Specifically, the accountants proposed that a $500,000 adjustment to deferred costs, a $300,000 write-off of unbilled receivables, and an $84,000 adjustment to paid-in capital be made retroactive to May 31 and be reflected in the comfort letter delivered to Interstate. Such adjustments would have caused NSMC to show a loss for the nine-month period ended May 31, 1969, and the company as it existed on May 31 would have broken even for fiscal 1969. Although Peat Marwick discussed the proposed adjustments with representatives of NSMC, neither the accountants nor NSMC informed Interstate of the adjustments prior to the closing. A draft of the comfort letter, with the adjustments, was completed on October 30 and on the next day, the morning of the closing, it was discussed among senior partners of Peat Marwick.

C. *The Closing and Receipt of the Comfort Letter*

The closing meeting for the merger was scheduled at 2 p.m. on Friday, October 31, at the New York offices of White & Case. Brown, Meyer and Schauer were present in addition to Interstate directors Bach, Allison and Tate. The representatives of NSMC included Randell, Joy, John G. Davies, their attorney Epley and other White & Case associates.

Although Schauer had had an opportunity to review most of the merger documents at White & Case on the previous day, the comfort letter had not been delivered. When he arrived at White & Case on the morning of the merger, the letter was still not available, but he was informed by a representative of the firm that it was expected to arrive at any moment.

The meeting proceeded. When the letter had not arrived by approximately 2:15 p.m., Epley telephoned Peat Marwick's Washington office to inquire about it. Anthony M. Natelli, the partner in charge, thereupon dictated to Epley's secretary a letter which provided in part:

[N]othing has come to our attention which caused us to believe that:

1. The National Student Marketing Corporation's unaudited consolidated financial statements as of and for the nine months ended May 31, 1969:

    * * *

    b. Would require any material adjustments for a fair and reasonable presentation of the information shown except with respect to consolidated financial statements of National Student Marketing Corporation and consolidated subsidiaries as they existed at May 31, 1969 and for the nine months then ended, our examination in connection with the year ended August 31, 1969 which is still in process, disclosed the following significant adjustments which in our opinion should be reflected retroactive to May 31, 1969:

1. In adjusting the amortization of deferred costs at May 31, 1969, to eliminate therefrom all costs for programs substantially completed or which commenced 12 months or more prior, an adjustment of $500,000 was required. Upon analysis of the retroactive effect of this adjustment, it appears that the entire amount could be determined applicable to the period prior to May 31, 1969.

2. In August 1969 management wrote off receivables in amounts of $300,000. It appears that the uncollectibility of these receivables could have been determined at May 31, 1969 and such charge off should have been reflected as of that date.

3. Acquisition costs in the amount of $84,000 for proposed acquisitions which the Company decided not to pursue were transferred from additional paid-in capital to general and administrative expenses. In our opinion, these should have been so transferred as of May 31, 1969.

* * *

Epley delivered one copy of the typed letter to the conference room where the closing was taking place. Epley then returned to his office.

Schauer was the first to read the unsigned letter. He then handed it to Cameron Brown, advising him to read it. Although there is some dispute as to which of the Interstate representatives actually read the letter, at least Brown and Meyer did so after Schauer. They asked Randell and Joy a number of questions relating to the nature and effect of the adjustments. The NSMC officers gave assurances that the adjustments would have no significant effect on the predicted year-end earnings of NSMC and that a substantial portion of the $500,000 adjustments to deferred costs would be recovered. Moreover, they indicated that NSMC's year-end audit for fiscal 1969 had been completed by Peat Marwick, would be published in a couple of weeks, and would demonstrate that NSMC itself had made each of the adjustments for its fourth quarter. The comfort letter, they explained, simply determined that those adjustments should be reflected in the third quarter ended May 31, 1969, rather than the final quarter of NSMC's fiscal year. Randell and Joy indicated that while NSMC disagreed with what they felt was a tightening up of its accounting practices, everything requested by Peat Marwick to "clean up" its books had been undertaken.

At the conclusion of this discussion, certain of the Interstate representatives, including at least Brown, Schauer and Meyer, conferred privately to consider their alternatives in light of the apparent nonconformity of the comfort letter with the requirements of the Merger Agreement. Although they considered the letter a serious matter and the adjustments as significant and important, they were nonetheless under some pressure to determine a course of action promptly since there was a 4 p.m. filing deadline if the closing were to be consummated as scheduled on October 31. Among the alternatives considered were: (1) delaying or postponing the closing, either to secure more information or to resolicit the shareholders with corrected financials; (2) closing the merger; or (3) calling it off completely.

The consensus of the directors was that there was no need to delay the closing. The comfort letter contained all relevant information and in light of the explanations given by Randell and Joy, they already had sufficient information upon which to make a decision. Any delay for the purpose of resoliciting the shareholders was considered impractical because it would require the use of year-end figures instead of the stale nine-month interim financials. Such a requirement would make it impossible to resolicit shareholder approval before the merger upset date of November 28, 1969, and would cause either the complete abandonment of the merger or its renegotiation on terms possibly far less favorable to Interstate. The directors also recognized that delay or abandonment of the merger would result in a decline in the stock of both companies, thereby harming the shareholders and possibly subjecting the directors to lawsuits based on their failure to close the merger. The Interstate representatives decided to proceed with the closing. They did, however, solicit and receive further assurances from the NSMC representatives that the stated adjustments were the only ones to be made to the company's financial statements and that 1969 earnings would be as predicted. When asked by Brown whether the closing could proceed on the basis of an unsigned comfort letter, Meyer responded that if a White & Case partner assured them that this was in fact the comfort letter and that a signed copy would be forthcoming from Peat Marwick, they could close. Epley gave this assurance. Meyer then announced that Interstate was prepared to proceed, the closing was consummated, and a previously arranged telephone call was made which resulted in the filing of the Articles of Merger at the Office of the Recorder of Deeds of the District of Columbia. Large packets of merger documents, including the required counsel opinion letters, were exchanged. The closing was solemnized with a toast of warm champagne.

Unknown to the Interstate group, several telephone conversations relating to the substance of the comfort letter occurred on the afternoon of the closing between Peat Marwick representatives and Epley. The accountants were concerned with the propriety of proceeding with the closing in light of the adjustments to NSMC's nine-month financials. One such conversation occurred after Epley delivered the unsigned letter to the Interstate participants but before the merger had been consummated. At that time Epley was told that an additional paragraph would be added in order to characterize the adjustments. The paragraph recited that with the noted adjustments properly made, NSMC's unaudited consolidated statement for the nine-month period would not reflect a profit as had been indicated but rather a net loss, and the consolidated operations of NSMC as they existed on May 31, 1969, would show a break-even as to net earnings for the year ended August 31, 1969. Epley had the additional paragraph typed out, but failed to inform or disclose this change to Interstate. In a second conversation, after the closing was completed and the Interstate representatives had departed, Epley was informed of still another proposed addition, namely, a paragraph urging resolicitation of both companies' shareholders and disclosure of NSMC's corrected nine-month financials prior to closing. To this, he responded that the deal was closed and the letter was not needed. Peat Marwick nonetheless advised Epley that the letter would be delivered and that its counsel was considering whether further action should be taken by the firm.

* * *

The signed letter was virtually identical to the unsigned version delivered at the closing, except for the addition of the following two paragraphs:

> Your attention is called, however, to the fact that if the aforementioned adjustments had been made at May 31, 1969 the unaudited consolidated statement of earnings of National Student Marketing Corporation

would have shown a net loss of approximately $80,000. It is presently estimated that the consolidated operations of the company as it existed at May 31, 1969 will be approximately a break-even as to net earnings for the year ended August 31, 1969.

In view of the above mentioned facts, we believe the companies should consider submitting corrected interim unaudited financial information to the shareholders prior to proceeding with the closing.

The only other change was the reduction in the write-off to receivables from $300,000 to $200,000, making total negative adjustments to NSMC's nine-month financials in the amount of $784,000.

* * *

Over the next several days the Interstate directors continued their discussion of the matter, consulting frequently with their counsel, Meyer and Shauer. As they viewed it, the available options were to attempt to undo the merger, either permanently or until the shareholders could be resolicited, or to leave things as they were. The attorneys indicated that rescission would be impractical, if not impossible, since Interstate no longer existed and NSMC had indicated that it would oppose any effort to undo the merger. Meanwhile, the market value of NSMC stock continued to increase, and the directors noted that any action on their part to undo the merger would most likely adversely affect its price. By the end of the week, the decision was made to abstain from any action. Thereafter, Brown issued a memorandum to all Interstate employees announcing completion of the merger. No effort was ever made by any of the defendants to disclose the contents of the comfort letter to the former shareholders of Interstate, the SEC or to the public in general.

D. *The Stock Sales*

Early in the negotiations the principal Interstate shareholders understood that they would be able to sell a portion of the NSMC stock received in the merger through a public offering planned for the fall of 1969. Various shareholders, including Brown, Tate, Allison, Bach and Meyer, intended to profit by this opportunity and sell up to 25 percent of their newly acquired stock. The opportunity did not materialize, however, because within several days of the merger the NSMC operating committee decided to postpone the registration. Brown was advised that the shareholders could still sell up to 25 percent of their shares in a private placement under SEC Rule 133. If they so decided, he was urged to have all use the same broker to avoid upsetting the market for the stock.

Brown then contacted Henry Meers, a personal friend and a partner in the White Weld brokerage firm, advised him of their desire to sell and inquired as to whether he could handle the transaction. Meers reported back that his firm could proceed. Brown then received the necessary authorization from the other shareholders and agreed with Meers that the sale would take place on the day of the merger closing. Meers indicated that the sale price could only be determined the day before the closing due to price fluctuations and, on October 30, the two agreed on a price of $49.50 per share.

Two matters of significance to the stock sales occurred on the day of the closing. First, certain of the Interstate principals, including Brown, were informed that the amount of NSMC shares they could sell following the merger was limited due to a restriction on their Interstate stock. As a result, Brown was limited to selling only about seven percent of his newly acquired NSMC stock instead of the 25 percent previously planned. Second, NSMC's in-house counsel Davies told Schauer that NSMC wanted an opinion from LBB in connection with the stock sales. As outlined in a memorandum prepared by White & Case for NSMC, the requested opinion was to state that LBB had made initial factual determinations as to whether the sales comported with the requirements of Rule 133(d). White & Case would then consult with NSMC and prepare its own final opinion letter as to the validity of the sales under the rule. After discussing the matter with Davies, Schauer indicated that there would be no problem delivering the letter in the form and language requested.

White Weld began processing the sales on the afternoon of October 31. It subsequently sold a total of 59,500 shares of NSMC stock. The gross received was slightly less than $3 million. Brown received approximately $500,000 for his shares and Meyer received approximately $86,000 for the shares he held, including $10,000 for shares he owned and the balance for shares he held in trust for the benefit of Brown and Brown's family. White Weld was never informed of the comfort letter adjustments before it undertook the sale as agents for the Interstate principals.

* * *

E. *Subsequent Events*

Following the acquisition of Interstate and several other companies NSMC stock rose steadily in price, reaching a peak in mid-December. However, in early 1970, after several newspaper and magazine articles appeared questioning NSMC's financial health, the value of the stock decreased drastically. Several private lawsuits were filed and the SEC initiated a wide-ranging investigation which led to the filing of this action.

* * *

Numerous charges, all of which appear to allege secondary liability, are leveled against the attorney defendants. Schauer is charged with "participating in the merger between Interstate and NSMC," apparently referring to his failure to interfere with the closing of the merger after receipt of the comfort letter. Such inaction, when alleged to facilitate a transaction, falls under the rubric of aiding and abetting. See Kerbs v. Fall River Industries, Inc., 502 F.2d 731, 739–40 (10th Cir.1974). Both Schauer and Meyer are charged with issuing false opinions in connection with the merger and stock sales, thereby facilitating each transaction, and with acquiescence in the merger after learning the contents of the signed comfort letter. The Commission contends that the attorneys should have refused to issue the opinions in view of the adjustments revealed by the unsigned comfort letter, and after receipt of the signed version, they should have withdrawn their opinion with regard to the merger and demanded resolicitation of the Interstate shareholders. If the Interstate directors refused, the attorneys should have withdrawn from the representation and informed the shareholders or the Commission. The SEC specifically characterizes the attorneys' conduct in issuing the Rule 133 opinion as aiding and abetting, and because their alleged misconduct with regard to the merger also appears sufficiently removed from the center of that transaction, it too will be considered under a charge of secondary liability. See SEC v. Coven, 581 F.2d 1020 (2d Cir.1978); SEC v. Spectrum, Ltd., 489 F.2d 535, 541 (2d Cir.

1973); 3 A. Bromberg, supra. And finally, LBB is charged with vicarious liability for the actions of Meyer and Schauer with respect to the attorneys' activities on behalf of the firm.

* * *

[Eds.—The Court's discussion of the liability of the primary defendants, Brown and Meyer, is omitted.]

Accordingly, the Court finds that Brown and Meyer violated § 10(b), Rule 10b–5, and § 17(a) through their participation in the closing of the Interstate/NSMC merger and through their sales of NSMC stock immediately following the merger, in each instance without first disclosing the material information contained in the unsigned comfort letter.

IV. AIDING AND ABETTING

The Court must now turn to the Commission's charges that the [attorney] defendants aided and abetted these two violations of the antifraud provisions. The violations themselves establish the first element of aiding and abetting liability, namely that another person has committed a securities law violation. Rolf v. Blyth, Eastman Dillon & Co., 570 F.2d at 47; Woodward v. Metro Bank of Dallas, 522 F.2d 84, 95 (5th Cir.1975); SEC v. Coffey, 493 F.2d at 1316. The remaining elements, though not set forth with any uniformity, are essentially that the alleged aider and abettor had a "general awareness that his role was part of an overall activity that is improper, and [that he] knowingly and substantially assisted the violation." SEC v. Coffey, supra. Accord, Rolf v. Blyth, Eastman Dillon & Co., 570 F.2d at 47–48; Woodward v. Metro Bank of Dallas, 522 F.2d at 94–97. See generally, Ruder, Multiple Defendants in Securities Law Fraud Cases: Aiding and Abetting, Conspiracy, In Pari Delicto, Indemnification, and Contribution, 120 U.Pa.L.Rev. 597 (1972); 3 A. Bromberg, supra at § 8.5 (530).

The Commission's allegations of aiding and abetting by the defendants * * * seem to fall into four basic categories: (1) the failure of the attorney defendants to take any action to interfere in the consummation of the merger; (2) the issuance by the attorneys of an opinion with respect to the merger; (3) the attorneys' subsequent failure to withdraw that opinion and inform the Interstate shareholders or the SEC of the inaccuracy of the nine-month financials; and (4) the issuance by the attorneys and Brown of an opinion and letter, respectively, concerning the validity of the stock sales under Rule 133. The SEC's position is that the defendants acted or failed to act with an awareness of the fraudulent conduct by the principals, and thereby substantially assisted the two violations. The Court concurs with regard to the attorneys' failure to interfere with the closing, but must conclude that the remaining actions or inaction alleged to constitute aiding and abetting did not substantially facilitate either the merger or the stock sales.

As noted, the first element of aiding and abetting liability has been established by the finding that Brown and Meyer committed primary violations of the securities laws. Support for the second element, that the defendants were generally aware of the fraudulent activity, is provided by the previous discussion concerning scienter. With the exception of LBB, which is charged with vicarious liability, each of the defendants was actually present at the closing of the merger when the comfort letter was delivered and the adjustments to the nine-month financials were revealed. Each was present at the Interstate caucus and the subsequent questioning of the NSMC representatives; each knew of the importance attributed to the adjustments by those present. They knew that the Interstate shareholders and the investing public were unaware of the adjustments and the inaccuracy of the financials. Despite the obvious materiality of the information * * * each knew that it had not been disclosed prior to the merger and stock sale transactions. Thus, this is not a situation where the aider and abettor merely failed to discover the fraud, see Rolf v. Blyth, Eastman Dillon & Co., 570 F.2d at 52 (Mansfield, J., dissenting), or reasonably believed that the victims were already aware of the withheld information, Hirsch v. du Pont, 553 F.2d 750, 759 (2d Cir.1977). The record amply demonstrates the "knowledge of the fraud, and not merely the undisclosed material facts," Hirsch v. du Pont, supra, that is required to meet this element of secondary liability. See Ruder, supra at 630–31.

The final requirement for aiding and abetting liability is that the conduct provide knowing, substantial assistance to the violation. In addressing this issue, the Court will consider each of the SEC's allegations separately. The major problem arising with regard to the Commission's contention that the attorneys failed to interfere in the closing of the merger is whether inaction or silence constitutes substantial assistance. While there is no definitive answer to this question, courts have been willing to consider inaction as a form of substantial assistance when the accused aider and abettor had a duty to disclose. Woodward v. Metro Bank of Dallas, 522 F.2d at 97; see Kerbs v. Fall River Industries, Inc., 502 F.2d at 740; Brennan v. Midwestern United Life Ins. Co., 417 F.2d 147, 154 (7th Cir.1969), cert. denied, 397 U.S. 989 (1970). Although the duty to disclose in those cases is somewhat distinguishable, in that they contemplate disclosure to an opposing party and not to one's client, they are sufficiently analogous to provide support for a duty here.

Upon receipt of the unsigned comfort letter, it became clear that the merger had been approved by the Interstate shareholders on the basis of materially misleading information. In view of the obvious materiality of the information, especially to attorneys learned in securities law, the attorneys' responsibilities to their corporate client required them to take steps to ensure that the information would be disclosed to the shareholders. However, it is unnecessary to determine the precise extent of their obligations here, since it is undisputed that they took no steps whatsoever to delay the closing pending disclosure to and resolicitation of the Interstate shareholders. But, at the very least, they were required to speak out at the closing concerning the obvious materiality of the information and the concomitant requirement that the merger not be closed until the adjustments were disclosed and approval of the merger was again obtained from the Interstate shareholders. Their silence was not only a breach of this duty to speak, but in addition lent the appearance of legitimacy to the closing, see Kerbs v. Fall River Industries, Inc., supra. The combination of these factors clearly provided substantial assistance to the closing of the merger.

Contrary to the attorney defendants' contention, imposition of such a duty will not require lawyers to go beyond their accepted role in securities transactions, nor will it compel them to "err on the side of conservatism, * * * thereby inhibiting clients' business judgments and candid attorney-client communications." Courts will not lightly overrule an attorney's determination of materiality and the need for disclosure. However, where, as here, the significance of the information clearly removes any doubt concerning the materiality of the information, attorneys cannot rest on asserted "business judgments" as justification for their failure to make a legal decision pursuant to their fiduciary responsibilities to client shareholders.

The Commission also asserts that the attorneys substantially assisted the merger violation through the issuance of an opinion that was false and misleading due to its omission of the receipt of the comfort letter and of the completion of the merger on the basis of the false and misleading nine-month financials. The defendants contend that a technical reading of the opinion demonstrates that it is not false and misleading, and that it provides accurate opinions as to Interstate's compliance with certain corporate formalities. Of concern to the Court, however, is not the truth or falsity of the opinion, but whether it substantially assisted the violation. Upon consideration of all the circumstances, see Woodward v. Metro Bank of Dallas, 522 F.2d at 97, the Court concludes that it did not.

Contrary to the implication made by the SEC, the opinion issued by the attorneys at the closing did not play a large part in the consummation of the merger. Instead, it was simply one of many conditions to the obligation of NSMC to complete the merger. It addressed a number of corporate formalities required of Interstate by the Merger Agreement, only a few of which could possibly involve compliance with the antifraud provisions of the securities laws. Moreover, the opinion was explicitly for the benefit of NSMC, which was already well aware of the adjustments contained in the comfort letter. Thus, this is not a case where an opinion of counsel addresses a specific issue and is undeniably relied on in completing the transaction. Compare SEC v. Coven, 581 F.2d 1020, at 1028; SEC v. Spectrum, Ltd., 489 F.2d 535 (2d Cir.1973). Under these circumstances, it is unreasonable to suggest that the opinion provided substantial assistance to the merger.

The SEC's contention with regard to counsel's alleged acquiescence in the merger transaction raises significant questions concerning the responsibility of counsel. The basis for the charge appears to be counsel's failure, after the merger, to withdraw their opinion, to demand resolicitation of the shareholders, to advise their clients concerning rights of rescission of the merger, and ultimately, to inform the Interstate shareholders or the SEC of the completion of the merger based on materially false and misleading financial statements. The defendants counter with the argument that their actions following the merger are not subject to the coverage of the securities laws.

The filing of the complaint in this proceeding generated significant interest and an almost overwhelming amount of comment within the legal profession on the scope of a securities lawyer's obligations to his client and to the investing public. The very initiation of this action, therefore, has provided a necessary and worthwhile impetus for the profession's recognition and assessment of its responsibilities in this area. The Court's examination, however, must be more limited. Although the complaint alleges varying instances of misconduct on the part of several attorneys and firms, the Court must narrow its focus to the present defendants and the charges against them.

Meyer, Schauer and Lord, Bissell & Brook are, in essence, here charged with failing to take any action to "undo" the merger. The Court has already concluded that counsel had a duty to the Interstate shareholders to delay the closing of the merger pending disclosure and resolicitation with corrected financials, and that the breach of that duty constituted a violation of the antifraud provisions through aiding and abetting the merger transaction. The Commission's charge, however, concerns the period following that transaction. Even if the attorneys' fiduciary responsibilities to the Interstate shareholders continued beyond the merger, the breach of such a duty would not have the requisite relationship to a securities transaction, since the merger had already been completed. It is equally obvious that such subsequent action or inaction by the attorneys could not substantially assist the merger.

The final contention of the SEC concerns the issuance by the attorneys and Brown of the Rule 133 opinion and letter, respectively. Little discussion is necessary with respect to this charge, for the Commission has clearly failed to show that these documents substantially assisted the stock sales. Neither of the documents were required by the Merger Agreement, but were requested by NSMC at the closing of the merger. The documents were not intended for the investing public, but for the sole use of NSMC and its counsel in preparing a formal, independent opinion concerning the validity of the sales under Rule 133. Further, the documents were limited to primarily factual issues relevant to the requirements of the Rule, and in no way indicated that they could be relied upon with regard to compliance with the antifraud provisions. Under the circumstances, the Court concludes that the Rule 133 documents issued by the attorneys and Brown did not substantially assist the stock sales by Interstate principals, specifically Brown and Meyer.

Thus, the Court finds that the attorney defendants aided and abetted the violation of § 10(b), Rule 10b–5, and § 17(a) through their participation in the closing of the merger.

V. APPROPRIATENESS OF INJUNCTIVE RELIEF

Although the Commission has proved past violations by the defendants, that does not end the Court's inquiry. Proof of a past violation is not a prerequisite to the grant of injunctive relief, see United States v. W.T. Grant Co., 345 U.S. 629, 633 (1953), nor by itself necessarily sufficient to justify such relief, see SEC v. Bausch & Lomb, Inc., 565 F.2d 8 (2d Cir.1977); SEC v. Management Dynamics, Inc., 515 F.2d 801, 807 (2d Cir.1975), but it may, in combination with other factors, warrant an inference of future misconduct by the charged party, SEC v. Manor Nursing Centers, Inc., 458 F.2d 1082, 1100 (2d Cir.1972). The crucial question, though, remains not whether a violation has occurred, but whether there exists a reasonable likelihood of future illegal conduct by the defendant, "something more than the mere possibility which serves to keep the case alive." United States v. W.T. Grant Co., supra. Thus, the SEC must "go beyond the mere facts of past violations and demonstrate a realistic likelihood of recurrence." SEC v. Commonwealth Chemical Securities, Inc., 574 F.2d 90, 100 (2d Cir.1978).

The factors which are relevant to such a showing have been previously stated by this Court:

> The character of the past violations, the effectiveness of the discontinuance and the bona fides of the expressed intent to comply are considered. The number and duration of past wrongs, the time which has elapsed since the last violation, the opportunity to commit further illegal acts, the novelty of the violation, and the harmful impact of the injunction on the defendant are objective factors which the courts have examined. Subjective inquiries into the wilfulness or bad faith in a defendant's prior conduct and the sincerity of his representations not to violate the law are also pertinent.

SEC v. National Student Marketing Corp., 360 F.Supp. 284, 297 (D.D.C. 1973). * * * The Court must assess these factors and determine, under the "totality of circumstances", "[w]hether the inference that the defendant is likely to repeat the wrong is properly drawn * * *." SEC v. Management Dynamics, Inc., supra. Exercising the broad discretion accorded it in making this determination, SEC v. Universal Major Industries Corp., 546 F.2d at 1048; SEC v. National Student Marketing Corp., supra, the Court concludes that in this instance injunctive relief is not warranted.

The Commission has not demonstrated that the defendants engaged in the type of repeated and persistent misconduct which usually justifies the issuance of injunctive relief. See, e.g., SEC v. Savoy Industries Inc., 190 U.S.App.D.C. 252, at 265 n. 37, 587 F.2d 1149, at 1162; SEC v. Commonwealth Chemical Securities, Inc., 574 F.2d at 100; SEC v. Shapiro, 494 F.2d 1301, 1308 (2d Cir.1974). Instead, it has shown violations which principally occurred within a period of a few hours at the closing of the merger in 1969. The Commission has not charged, or even suggested, that the defendants were involved in similar misconduct either before or after the events involved in this proceeding. Thus, the violations proved by the SEC appear to be part of an isolated incident, unlikely to recur and insufficient to warrant an injunction. See SEC v. Bausch & Lomb, Inc., 565 F.2d at 19; SEC v. Parklane Hosiery Co., 422 F.Supp. 477, 487 (S.D.N.Y.1976), aff'd, 558 F.2d 1083 (2d Cir.1977). The Commission appears to agree, for in the six years since the filing of this action, it has made no attempt to obtain interlocutory injunctive relief against these defendants. Such inaction argues strongly against the need for injunctive relief. See SEC v. Parklane Hosiery Co., supra.

Further, it is difficult to characterize the violations presented here as either "willful, blatant, and often completely outrageous," SEC v. Manor Nursing Centers, Inc., 458 F.2d at 1101, or as the "garden variety fraud" urged by the Commission, SEC Post-Trial Brief at 129. There is no evidence to suggest that these defendants knew about the comfort letter adjustments prior to the receipt of the unsigned comfort letter at the closing; and after receiving the letter, the defendants were under some pressure to determine a course of action, either to proceed with the transactions as scheduled or to abort both the merger and stock sales. Although it has now been found that they unlawfully and with scienter decided to proceed, their actions in this regard hardly resemble the deliberate and well-planned fraudulent scheme frequently found in securities fraud cases.

Finally, the Commission asserts that an injunction is necessary because the professional occupations of the defendants provide significant opportunities for further involvement in securities transactions. It notes that Brown holds positions as a director and as a consultant with NSMC, and that Meyer, Schauer and LBB continue to be involved in various corporate activities, including securities transactions, as part of their legal practice. While these opportunities distinguish the present defendants from those who, because they completely lack such opportunities, should not be subject to the threat of an injunction, see SEC v. National Student Marketing Corp., 360 F.Supp. at 300, they do not alone justify relief. In fact, various circumstances indicate that this factor is not as one-sided as the Commission suggests. Although Brown retains his positions with NSMC, he is in effect virtually retired; the likelihood of his being involved in a securities transaction, other than as an investor, seems quite small. See SEC v. Parklane Hosiery Co., supra. While the attorney defendants are more likely to be so involved, that fact is countered somewhat by their professional responsibilities as attorneys and officers of the court to conform their conduct to the dictates of the law. The Court is confident that they will take appropriate steps to ensure that their professional conduct in the future comports with the law.

After considering the "totality of circumstances" presented here, the Court concludes that the Securities and Exchange Commission has not fulfilled its statutory obligation to make a "proper showing" that injunctive relief is necessary to prevent further violations by these defendants. Accordingly, judgment will be entered for the defendants and the complaint will be dismissed.

STATEMENT OF POLICY ADOPTED BY AMERICAN BAR ASSOCIATION REGARDING RESPONSIBILITIES AND LIABILITIES OF LAWYERS IN ADVISING WITH RESPECT TO THE COMPLIANCE BY CLIENTS WITH LAWS ADMINISTERED BY THE SECURITIES AND EXCHANGE COMMISSION *

31 Bus.Law. 543 (1975).

As previously noted, the Committee on Counsel Responsibility and Liability of the Section of Corporation, Banking and Business Law of the American Bar Association has been examining the responsibilities and liabilities of lawyers engaged in securities law matters. * * * The Statement of Policy was adopted by the ABA House of Delegates on August 12, 1975 pursuant to recommendation by the Council of the Section. The specifics of how the Code of Professional Responsibility speaks to the question of disclosure by lawyers in the SEC context is examined in the Report which appeared in the July, 1975 issue of The Business Lawyer. It is recognized that the principles involved have broader application.

* * *

AMERICAN BAR ASSOCIATION REPORT TO THE HOUSE OF DELEGATES

SECTION OF CORPORATION, BANKING AND BUSINESS LAW RECOMMENDATION

The Section of Corporation, Banking and Business Law recommends adoption of the following resolution:

BE IT RESOLVED, that this Association adopts the following Statement of Policy regarding responsibilities and liabilities of lawyers in advising with respect to the compliance by clients with laws administered by the Securities and Exchange Commission ("SEC"):

1. The confidentiality of lawyer-client consultations and advice and the fiduciary loyalty of the lawyer to the client, as prescribed in the American Bar Association's Code of Professional Responsibility ("CPR"), are vital to the basic function of the lawyer as legal counselor because they enable and encourage clients to consult legal counsel freely, with assurance that counsel will respect the confidentiality of the client's communications and will advise independently and in the client's best interest without conflicting loyalties or obligations.

2. This vital confidentiality of consultation and advice would be destroyed or seriously impaired if it is accepted as a general principle that lawyers must inform the SEC or others regarding confidential information received by lawyers from their clients even though such action would not be permitted or required by the CPR. Any such compelled disclosure would seriously and adversely affect the lawyers' function as counselor, and may seriously and adversely affect the ability of lawyers as advocates to represent and defend their clients' interests.

3. In light of the foregoing considerations, it must be recognized that a lawyer cannot, consistently with his essential role as legal adviser, be regarded as a source of information concerning possible wrong-doing by clients. Accordingly, any principle of law which, except as permitted or required by the CPR, permits or obliges a lawyer to disclose to the SEC otherwise confidential information, should be established only by statute after full and careful consideration of the public interests involved, and should be resisted unless clearly mandated by law.

4. Lawyers have an obligation under the CPR to advise clients, to the best of their ability, concerning the need for or advisability of public disclosure of a broad range of events and circumstances, including the obligation of the client to make appropriate disclosures as required by various laws and regulations administered by the SEC. In appropriate circumstances, a lawyer may be permitted or required by the Disciplinary Rules under the CPR to resign his engagement if his advice concerning disclosures is disregarded by the client and, if the conduct of a client clearly establishes his prospective commission of a crime or the past or prospective perpetration of a fraud in the course of the lawyer's representation, even to make the disclosures himself. However, the lawyer has neither the obligation nor the right to make disclosure when any reasonable doubt exists concerning the client's obligation of disclosure, i.e., the client's failure to meet his obligation is not clearly established,

except to the extent that the lawyer should consider appropriate action, as required or permitted by the CPR, in cases where the lawyer's opinion is expected to be relied on by third parties and the opinion is discovered to be not correct, whether because it is based on erroneous information or otherwise.

5. Fulfillment by attorneys of their obligations to clients under the CPR best serves the public interest of assisting and furthering clients' compliance with legal requirements. Efforts by the government to impose responsibility upon lawyers to assure the quality of their clients' compliance with the law or to compel lawyers to give advice resolving all doubts in favor of regulatory restrictions would evoke serious and far-reaching disruption in the role of the lawyer as counselor, which would be detrimental to the public, clients and the legal profession. In fulfillment of their responsibility to clients under the CPR, lawyers must be free to advise clients as to the full range of their legitimately available courses of action and the relative attendant risks involved. Furthermore, it is often desirable for the lawyer to point out those factors which may suggest a decision that is morally just as well as legally permissible. However, the decision as to the course to be taken should be made by the client. The client's actions should not be improperly narrowed through the insistence of an attorney who may, perhaps unconsciously, eliminate available choices from consideration because of his concern over possible personal risks if the position is taken which, though supportable, is subject to uncertainty or contrary to a known, but perhaps erroneous, position of the SEC or a questionable lower court decision. Public policy, we strongly believe, is best served by lawyers acting in conformance with their obligations to their clients and others as prescribed under the CPR. Accordingly, liability should not be imposed upon lawyers whose conduct is in conformance with the CPR.

REPORT

I. INTRODUCTION

Lawyers are often called upon for legal advice when the answer is not clear. The statute or regulation in question may be ambiguous; judicial opinions may be in conflict or not directly in point; counsel may be of the opinion that an existing precedent is wrong and should be reversed on appeal; or the issue, in the absence of a precedent directly in point, may involve a high degree of subjective judgment, particularly when considering various central concepts deliberately imprecise in laws administered by the Securities and Exchange Commission ("SEC"). Illustrative are concepts such as "materiality," "control," "adequate disclosure," "average prudent investor," "public distribution," "care of a prudent man," "manipulative or deceptive device or contrivance," and "untrue statement of a material fact or to omit to state a material fact necessary in order to make the statements made, in light of the circumstances in which they were made, not misleading." Furthermore, there are often questions of fact presented, sometimes involving technical problems in diversified and complicated industries, regarding which clients or others are better qualified to determine than lawyers.

Various proceedings by the SEC, speeches by members and staff of the Commission, and certain statements in recent judicial opinions have caused many lawyers serious concern as to their responsibility to their clients and to the public when advising in the areas of SEC laws. Their advice is, of course, reviewed by the SEC with the benefit of "hindsight" when something has gone wrong. Must the lawyer in such matters resolve all uncertainties in favor of the law having application, e.g., if there is any question whether something may be "material" it should be treated as "material," and if the client fails to follow such advice must the lawyer report such failure to the SEC?

II. PUBLIC POLICY

It is a basic principle that the lawyer's role is essentially that of counselor to his client. The effectiveness of this role is highly dependent upon the long-accepted confidentiality of the attorney-client relationship. For this reason a role for the lawyer as investigator or informant would be a seriously inconsistent one, and the Bar should critically scrutinize any proposal, however limited, that the lawyer can be so regarded.

Whenever a proposal is made that a lawyer go beyond his fundamental role of advising his client and assume a function that could require him publicly to contradict his client or disclose possible deficiencies, on the basis of information gained in the course of his professional engagement, there is cause for concern on the part of the public as well as the Bar, since the attorney-client relationship is of fundamental importance to our legal system.

The lawyer's ability to serve his client and the public by assisting and furthering the client's compliance with legal requirements rests largely on the effectiveness of his relationship with his client. This relationship is undermined to the extent that client communications with lawyers are made with the risk that the lawyer will, if not satisfied with the client's response to his advice or if concerned over his own potential personal liabilities, report possible deficiencies to third parties. Accordingly, it has long been recognized by the Code of Professional Responsibility ("CPR") and its predecessor Canons of Ethics that only in the clearest cases of illegal or fraudulent activities by a client in the course of the lawyer's representation should the lawyer be called upon or permitted to take such action. (The text of relevant provisions of the CPR is attached).

We do not believe that the policy of disclosure as embodied in the SEC laws warrants an exception to the basic confidentiality of the attorney-client relationship. Such exceptions have to date been carefully reserved by the CPR for far more critical and limited situations. The statutes administered by the SEC give it no power to require disclosure by lawyers concerning their clients beyond what is provided in the CPR.

For the foregoing reasons we strongly urge that the American Bar Association adopt a general statement of policy concerning lawyers' responsibilities and liabilities regarding a client's failure to comply with a law administered by the SEC which will reflect the basic principles we, as lawyers, believe are essential to the preservation of the concept of the attorney-client relationship as part of our legal system.

The statement should recognize that the lawyer has a duty to advise his client candidly and responsibly as to the client's legal obligations, including the obligation to make appropriate disclosures as required by various laws and regulations administered by the SEC, and that a lawyer must take appropriate action, as required by the CPR (as adopted in his particular State), when faced with conduct of a client which clearly establishes his prospective commission of a crime, or the past or prospective perpetration of a fraud, in the course of the lawyer's representation. Similarly, the lawyer should consider appropriate action, as required or permitted by the CPR, in cases where the lawyer's opinion is expected to be relied on by third parties and the opinion is discovered to be not correct, whether because it is based on erroneous information or otherwise. The statement should also acknowledge that a lawyer need not confine his advice to purely legal considerations, but in appropriate cases should bring to the attention of the client considerations of fairness and avoidance of infliction of needless harm.

We firmly believe that such an approach will be in the long-term public interest and will provide for greater assurance of compliance with our laws, including those relating to disclosure, than would an approach requiring lawyers to disclose possible SEC violations by clients.

The Recommendation preceding this Report has been adopted by the Council of the Section of Corporation, Banking and Business Law.

IN THE MATTER OF CARTER AND JOHNSON

Securities and Exchange Commission, 1981.
Securities Exchange Act Release No. 17597.
February 28, 1981.

OPINION OF THE COMMISSION

William R. Carter and Charles J. Johnson, Jr., respondents, appeal from the initial decision of the Administrative Law Judge in this proceeding brought under Rule 2(e) of the Commission's Rules of Practice. In an opinion dated March 7, 1979, the Administrative Law Judge found that, in connection with their representation of National Telephone Company, Inc. during the period from May 1974 to May 1975, Carter and Johnson willfully violated and willfully aided and abetted violations of Sections 10(b) and 13(a) of the Securities Exchange Act of 1934 (the "Exchange Act") and Rules 10b–5, 12b–20 and 13a–11 thereunder and that they engaged in unethical and improper professional conduct. In light of these findings, the Administrative Law Judge concluded that Carter and Johnson should be suspended from appearing or practicing before the Commission for periods of one year and nine months, respectively.

For the reasons stated more fully below, we reverse the decision of the Administrative Law Judge with respect to both respondents. We have concluded that the record does not adequately support the Administrative Law Judge's findings of violative conduct by respondents. Moreover, we conclude that certain concepts of proper ethical and professional conduct were not sufficiently developed, at the time of the conduct here at issue, to permit a finding that either respondent breached applicable ethical or professional standards. In addition, we are today giving notice of an interpretation by the Commission of the term "unethical or improper professional conduct," as that term is used in Rule 2(e)(1)(ii). This interpretation will be applicable prospectively in cases of this kind.

I. JURISDICTION

Respondents challenge the Commission's authority to promulgate Rule 2(e). Because this is an issue of great significance to the bar, we issued a blanket order permitting the filing of *amicus curiae* briefs on general legal and policy issues.

We have considered the issues raised by respondents, by *amici,* and by the literature on professional responsibility generally. Although it is not an exhaustive recitation of all the issues that have been raised or that we have considered, the following fairly summarizes the arguments which have been raised regarding Rule 2(e):

1. The Commission was not given the express authority to adopt Rule 2(e), and in the comprehensive scheme of the federal securities laws it is inappropriate to imply a power not expressly given.

2. The Administrative Practice Act, 5 U.S.C. 500, precludes the adoption or exercise of powers under Rule 2(e) because that amounts to a *de facto* establishment of a specialized SEC bar, which is expressly forbidden by the statute.

3. As a matter of policy, it is inappropriate for an agency with prosecutorial responsibilities to exercise disciplinary authority over counsel who renders advice to regulated entities.

4. The implications of the Commissioner's exercise of authority under Rule 2(e) are so vast that it effectively regulates the relationship between a lawyer and his client, the public and the government; and, as an administrative body with expertise in a particular area, the Commission has neither the wisdom nor the mandate to engage in such regulation.

We have considered, in detail, each of these arguments. As set out more fully below in the discussions on Aiding and Abetting and Ethical and Professional Responsibilities, we are extremely sensitive to the role of the securities lawyer in the disclosure process and to the need to fashion a rule that is neither excessive in scope nor beyond our expertise. Nevertheless, we conclude that the enactment of Rule 2(e) and our application of that Rule in this case are clearly within our jurisdictional grant of authority and reflect an entirely appropriate discharge of our statutory mandates.
* * * [The Commission's reaffirmation of its own authority to promulgate Rule 2(e) is omitted.—Eds.]

III. RESPONDENTS' CONDUCT

* * * The conduct at issue in these proceedings occurred in connection with respondents' legal representation of National Telephone Company, Inc. ("National") during the period from mid–1974 through mid–1975. National, a Connecticut corporation with its principal offices located in East Hartford, Connecticut, was founded in 1971 to lease sophisticated telephone equipment systems to commercial customers pursuant to long-term (5- to 10–year) leases. National enjoyed an impressive growth rate in its first three years, increasing its total assets from $320,123 to $19,028,613 and its net income from $2,390 to $633,485 during this period. At the same

time, the company's backlog grew from $66,000 to $2,610,000 and the value of equipment leases written by it increased from $255,422 to $13,292,549.

The architect of National's meteoric rise was Sheldon L. Hart, one of its founders and, at all times relevant to these proceedings, its controlling stockholder. From its incorporation until his resignation on May 24, 1975, Hart was National's chief executive officer, chairman of the board of directors, president and treasurer. National's chief in-house counsel was Mark I. Lurie who, assisted by Brian Kay, was one of respondents' principal contacts with the company.

In large measure, National was a prisoner of its own success. As is commonly the case with equipment leasing companies, the greater part of National's costs in connection with a new lease, including equipment, marketing and installation expenses, was incurred well before rental payments commenced. Since rental payments were National's only significant source of revenues, the company's cash flow situation worsened with each new lease, and continued growth and operations could only be sustained through external financing. Between 1971 and 1973, National managed to obtain needed capital from an initial public offering of stock under Regulation A, short-term loans from local banks, and an offering of convertible debentures in September of 1973.

National's last successful effort to secure significant outside financing resulted in the execution, in May and June of 1974, of a $15 million credit agreement (the "Credit Agreement") with a group of five banks. Although the Credit Agreement was not closed (in amended form) until December 1974, the banks were willing to advance substantial sums to National under a variety of demand arrangements prior to the closing. In fact, by the time of the closing on December 20, 1974, these advances totaled some $16.8 million. The Credit Agreement was amended to cover this amount, plus $2.2 million for general corporate purposes and an additional $2 million available only upon the implementation of a special business plan limiting National's business growth if other sources of money could not be located. Unfortunately, funds available under the Credit Agreement, as amended, were not sufficient to finance National's expansion and operations much beyond the closing, and the pressure on National's cash flow continued.

National finally ran out of time in July of 1975, after being unable to secure sufficient external financing after the closing of the Credit Agreement. On July 2, 1975, National was forced to file a petition for an arrangement under Chapter XI of the Bankruptcy Act, 11 U.S.C. 701, et seq.; in March of 1976 this proceeding was converted into a reorganization under Chapter X of the Bankruptcy Act, 11 U.S.C. 501, et seq.

* * *

* * * Carter, an attorney admitted to practice in the State of New York, was born in 1917. He received his law degree from Harvard Law School and has been working for the law firm now known as Brown, Wood, Ivey, Mitchell & Petty ("Brown, Wood") since 1945, having become a partner of the firm in 1954. Carter's principal areas of practice have been securities, general corporate and antitrust law.

Johnson, also admitted to practice as an attorney in the State of New York, as well as in the State of Connecticut, was born in 1932. He received his legal education at Harvard Law School and joined Brown, Wood's predecessor firm in 1956, becoming a partner in 1967. Johnson's principal areas of practice have been corporate and securities law.

Kenneth M. Socha worked with Carter and Johnson on a variety of legal matters affecting National, including all of the matters which are the basis of these proceedings. Socha joined Brown, Wood as an associate in 1970 and continued in that capacity during all periods relevant to these proceedings.

* * *

During 1974 and 1975, Brown, Wood, principally through Carter, Johnson and Socha, provided a wide range of legal services to National, including the preparation of a Form S–8 registration statement, proxy materials and an annual report for the company's 1974 annual stockholders meeting, other Commission filings, press releases and communications to National's stockholders. Johnson was charged with the overall coordination of Brown, Wood's legal efforts on National's behalf and was generally kept aware of progress on all significant projects. In March of 1974, after another Brown, Wood partner left the firm, Johnson asked Carter to assist Socha in working on the Credit Agreement. Thereafter Carter assumed primary responsibility for that project.

* * *

In May and June of 1974, negotiations with a consortium of five banks, in which Carter, Johnson and Socha were all participants, culminated in the execution of the Credit Agreement, which was dated as of April 30, 1974. The Credit Agreement provided for an interim revolving loan of up to $15 million, evidenced by rolling 90–day notes, until November 29, 1974, at which time National had the option to convert the principal amount then outstanding into six-year term notes. As discussed below, the Credit Agreement (as amended) was not formally closed until December 20, 1974, in part because National was unable to satisfy the closing conditions relating to its liquidity and debt-to-net-worth ratios. Ultimately the banks agreed to waive these conditions.

Since the Credit Agreement contemplated that the loans thereunder would be secured by substantially all of National's assets, it was necessary for National to transfer these assets to Systems; a transfer which in turn required the approval of National's stockholders. In order to secure this approval, National called its annual stockholders meeting for June 27, 1974, and Brown, Wood was asked to prepare the proxy materials for this meeting. Carter and Johnson also participated in the preparation of National's 1974 Annual Report. These proxy materials, along with National's 1974 Annual Report, were sent to National's stockholders on June 17 and filed with the Commission on June 19.

In urging approval of the asset transfers necessitated by the Credit Agreement, National's proxy statement disclosed that

[t]he future growth and operations of the Company are dependent upon its ability to obtain financing such as is supplied by the Credit Agreement.

National's 1974 Annual Report contained projections of future lease installations which showed, by each quarter, a doubling of annual installations from approximately $13.3 million in fiscal 1974 to approximately $27 million in fiscal 1975. In response to a specific request from Hart, Carter advised National orally and in writing that, in light of Securities Act

Release No. 5362 (Feb. 2, 1973), a copy of which Carter sent to Hart, it was permissible to include projections in the Annual Report, but that the assumptions underlying the projections should also be disclosed. Hart ignored this advice and the Annual Report was distributed without assumptions. This incident is the first example in the record of Hart's uncooperative reaction to respondents' advice concerning the disclosure demands of the federal securities laws.

* * *

At the September 11 meeting with the banks, Hart indicated that the projected equity offering had been ruled out by National's investment bankers, due to deteriorating market conditions. He further reported that National's cash flow problems had caused the company voluntarily to institute a "wind-down" program, effective September 1. As he described it, this program, projected to last five months, was a severe retrenchment, designed to protect the banks' existing investment. Under it, National would limit its operations to the conversion of present inventory—approximately $5 million—into installed systems under new leases, phase out further marketing and installation efforts and reduce the company to a "pure maintenance organization." Hart requested an increase in the total amount of the banks' planned loan from $15 to $21 million in order to finance this wind-down program. The banks, however, hesitated, agreeing only that no decision would be made on lending National additional funds until the pending $15 million Credit Agreement was closed.

Hart, in fact, had lied to the banks. No wind-down program had then been instituted or, as it turned out, would be until almost eight months later, in May of 1975. There is, however, no evidence in the record that respondents were, or ever became, aware of Hart's September 11, 1974 deception.

* * *

In light of his presence at the July 1, August 19 and October 15 board meetings, as well as the October 18 bank meeting, Johnson was well aware of National's cash crisis, its continuing failure to obtain needed financing and its purported "wind-down" program. This, in addition to the well-known depressed state of the credit markets and the fact that National had projected, confirmed and continued to report, without obviously relevant qualifications, rapidly growing sales and earnings, undoubtedly prompted Johnson to instruct Socha to draft a disclosure letter to National's stockholders approximately two days after the October 18 bank meeting.

The proposed stockholders letter, which was reviewed by both Carter and Johnson and sent to the company in early November, was a candid summary of National's financial predicament, noting that National would "in the near future" have to obtain significant financing in addition to the Credit Agreement. It concluded:

> The Company's efforts to obtain additional financing have been adversely affected by tight credit conditions, increased interest costs, a generally unfavorable equity market and certain factors that are peculiar to its business such as the negative cash flow described above. In view of these factors the Company has determined that it would be prudent to curtail its sales operations and, therefore, to emphasize liquidity rather than growth until such time as additional debt or equity financing can be obtained.

Johnson subsequently told Lurie that this was the type of communication "that a company * * * interested in keeping its stockholders advised on a regular basis should be making." Despite this advice, National's management declined to issue the letter. Neither respondent elected to pursue the matter.

* * *

It is important to note, at this point, that both Carter and Johnson must have been aware that, if National were to implement the wind-down plan, the company would have no reasonable opportunity to meet the projections of $27 million in lease installations which were set forth in the 1974 Annual Report and indirectly reconfirmed in the company's September 12 letter to its stockholders. The wind-down plan, which Socha summarized in a December 2 memorandum to Johnson, provided that National would not be permitted to enter into any further leases. Obviously, under these circumstances, the company's sales and earnings growth would be halted—short of projected levels.

In early December, Socha received from National a draft of the company's quarterly report to its stockholders for the second fiscal quarter ended September 30, 1974. The report contained a series of graphs, illustrating the successful results of National's operations, but once again made no mention of the dire financial straits in which the company found itself in December. Such an omission was especially significant in light of the disclosure recommendations which Brown, Wood had by then made to National. When Socha inquired whether the use of the graphs had been cleared by Johnson, Lurie informed him that they had. This was not true, as Johnson noted on the copy of the draft report circulated to him by Socha. The quarterly report was mailed as proposed, and neither respondent ever spoke with the company's management about the disclosure problems it presented or about Lurie's misrepresentation to Socha.

* * *

* * * In the final days leading to the closing, National's "wind-down" plan was renegotiated somewhat and finally emerged with a new name, the lease maintenance plan ("LMP"). All the witnesses speaking to the question agreed that the term "lease maintenance plan" had no generally accepted meaning in the industry and that they had never used or heard this term before. Moreover, the terms "wind-down plan," "contingency plan," and "lease maintenance plan," were all intended to refer to the same thing.

The need to revise the original wind-down plan emerged when the consulting firm hired by National to evaluate the plan reported to the banks that, in its original form, the plan was neither feasible nor in the best interests of the banks. Rather, the independent consultants advised that the best course would be to allow National limited continuing growth, financed with additional bank borrowings, and that a wind-down should be implemented only as a last resort and only if the company were unable to obtain additional outside financing.

At a meeting held on December 11, with Carter and representatives of National and the banks present, final details of the Amendment were negotiated. A draft of the Amendment dated December 13, 1974, which was prepared by White & Case, contemplated an arrangement under which the banks would permit Systems to borrow up to $19 million at any time on or before April 30, 1975. These borrowings were to be secured by the telephone leases and equipment transferred to Systems by National and guaranteed by National. If either (1) National and/or Systems attempted to borrow in excess of $19 million from the existing bank group or (2) National failed to meet a specified liquidity test, National and Systems were required to implement the LMP. Their failure to do so in accordance with the provisions of the LMP was an event of default under the Credit Agreement, as modified by the Amendment (the "Amended Credit Agreement"), and resulted in all outstanding indebtedness under that Agreement becoming due and payable upon demand.

The December 13 draft of the Amendment for the first time contained a reference to a "lease maintenance plan" and indicated that the LMP was to be attached as an exhibit to the Amendment. The effect of the implementation of the LMP on National's operations and growth would obviously be both dramatic and devastating. Indeed, as one expert called by respondents testified, the LMP was "a sort of a holding pattern short of bankruptcy or levy by the creditors." The LMP required National to terminate all sales activities, dismiss all sales personnel, and limit its operations to those necessary to service existing leases. In effect, the company would be transformed into a mere service agency, maintaining existing leases, but writing no new ones. Moreover, the final $2 million of the funds to be provided by the banks was only available until June 30, 1975 and could only be used to implement the LMP, principally by financing the installation of equipment already in inventory to complete existing orders.

       *   *   *

On December 19, the day immediately preceding the closing under the Amended Credit Agreement, at a day-long pre-closing meeting, Hart told Carter that he did not want the terms of the LMP made public or filed with the Commission. Although Carter testified that he could not recall the reason for this request, he speculated that Hart sought not to publicize the LMP because he was concerned that the disclosure of the LMP's effects on the company's business would have a negative impact on the morale of National's sales personnel. After reading the LMP, Carter advised Hart that the LMP would have to be filed with the Commission if it were an exhibit to the Amendment, as originally had been contemplated. However, Carter added that the LMP need not be filed with the Commission or publicized if it were not an exhibit but rather merely referred to in the Amendment. Hart agreed, and the Amendment was modified to delete the LMP as an exhibit.

Also at the December 19 pre-closing conference, Carter reviewed and extensively revised a press release prepared by National announcing the closing of the Amended Credit Agreement. The revised press release was reviewed by all parties at the meeting, including the company's management. No one raised any objections to the revisions proposed by Carter.

On December 20, the Amended Credit Agreement was closed and National immediately borrowed $18 million from the banks. Of this amount, over $16.8 million was used to repay existing demand indebtedness based on advances the banks had made to National since the original Credit Agreement had been signed six months earlier. All or virtually all of the remainder was used to pay various operating expenses which National had already incurred. Even after these expenses were discharged, National was left with substantial short-term debt totalling almost

$2 million. The record is ambiguous as to the degree to which Carter was aware of this situation.

Whatever the state of Carter's knowledge concerning National's past-due obligations, the record makes it clear that Carter understood that the December 20 financing in no way extricated National from its financial dilemma. At the time of his testimony in the Commission's investigation, Carter stated that he understood that, if National did not obtain significant additional financing, it would soon be "right back in the soup."

Immediately after the closing, National issued the press release that Carter had redrafted the day before. The release stated, in its entirety:

PRESS RELEASE—FOR IMMEDIATE RELEASE

EAST HARTFORD, CONN., DECEMBER 20, 1974

National Telephone Company today announced the execution of a $6,000,000 extension of a $15,000,000 Credit Agreement with a group of banks headed by Bankers Trust Company of New York. Included in the $21 million is a contingency fund of $2 million which is available until June 30, 1975 and which may be utilized by the Company only for the purpose of funding a lease maintenance program in the event additional financing is not otherwise available.

Of the $21 million, the Company has borrowed $18 million pursuant to a seven-year term loan, of which approximately $16,500,000 was used to repay outstanding short-term loans. The balance will be used for general operating expenses. Participating in the loans are Bankers Trust Company of New York, Mellon Bank N.A. of Pittsburgh, Central National Bank of Cleveland, The Connecticut Bank and Trust Company and The Hartford National Bank and Trust Company of Hartford, Connecticut.

The press release did not discuss either of the following matters each of which was then within the knowledge of Carter and Johnson.

(1) The precise nature and effects on National's business of the LMP and the likelihood that National would be required to implement the LMP within a short period of time; and

(2) The substantial limitations placed on National's operations by the Amended Credit Agreement.

It is also apparent from the record that the press release's statement indicating that the balance of the financing remaining after the repayment of outstanding bank debt "will be used for general operating expenses" was misleading, in light of the substantial overdue obligations of National then existing.

The second major item of public disclosure concerning the closing was a stockholders' letter mailed, without respondents' knowledge, by National on or about December 23. This letter, which was issued in the face of Socha's advice to National that no further public statements should be issued concerning the Amended Credit Agreement unless such statements were cleared by Brown, Wood, contained numerous misstatements and omissions, including the following:

(1) The letter indicated that the company "was stronger now than ever before in its history" and that it had "a greater availability of

capital, expanding productivity and growing earnings" and was "looking forward to an outstanding year in calendar 1975."

(2) The letter indicated that the entire additional $6 million loan to National could be used for future operating expenses.

(3) The letter made no reference to National's repayment of existing bank loans and other pre-existing debts with the proceeds of the financing, its continuing cash needs and shortages, or the LMP.

Respondents first learned of the letter on December 27, when Brian Kay, who was aware that National had ignored Socha's advice that all public disclosure should be reviewed by them, voluntarily telephoned Socha and dictated the letter to him. Socha thought that the letter's description of the Amended Credit Agreement was "seriously inadequate" and immediately gave a copy of it to Johnson. Carter, too, was consulted. While respondents felt that the letter did not make "adequate disclosure" with respect to the Amended Credit Agreement, they concluded that, when read together with the earlier December 20 press release which Carter had revised, it was not materially false or misleading, and that no corrective action by National was therefore required. Johnson later did, however, orally express his dissatisfaction with the letter to Lurie.

* * *

* * * On January 9, 1975, National filed a current report on Form 8–K for the month of December 1974, reporting on the closing under the Amended Credit Agreement. This document was drafted by Carter, who accepted full responsibility for it.

The Amended Credit Agreement, which was attached to the Form 8–K as an exhibit, made frequent reference to the LMP. And the 8–K itself stated that $2 million of National's recent $21 million loan arrangement was "a contingency fund available until June 30, 1975 only for the purpose of financing a lease maintenance program in the event additional financing is not otherwise available." As previously requested by Hart, however, the LMP itself was not included as an exhibit to the Agreement or the filing; nor was the term "lease maintenance plan" specifically defined or the effects which it would have on the company discussed.

Between the January 9, 1975 filing of National's Form 8–K and mid-March, National's financial condition deteriorated even further, to a degree requiring the implementation of the LMP. In addition, the gap between National's public disclosure posture and its private financial condition continued to widen and National's board of directors was becoming increasingly uncomfortable with the situation. There is no indication in the record that either respondent directly or indirectly became aware of the growing seriousness of the situation until a March 17 telephone call from the banks' counsel, described below. * * *

On March 17—nearly one month after the February 20 consultants report, and over six weeks after the LMP had in fact been triggered—Brown, Wood was informed for the first time, by the *banks'* lawyers, White & Case, that events requiring implementation of the LMP had occurred. The White & Case lawyers had received a telephone call from a vice president of one of the banks informing them of this fact and reporting that no public disclosure had been made by National. The bank vice president also sought White & Case's advice on how to respond to trade creditors of National who were making inquiries to the banks about the company.

During their March 17 conversation, the White & Case lawyers advised Carter that National and its counsel, Brown, Wood, had the responsibility to determine what disclosure, if any, would be appropriate under the circumstances, and they sought assurances that, if proper disclosure were deemed necessary, it would be forthcoming. Carter, who admittedly considered the triggering of the LMP clearly material, assured White & Case that, if what they said were true, Brown, Wood would contact National and "get a statement out." The White & Case lawyers then called the bank's vice president and relayed the content of their conversation with Carter.

On the following day, March 18, Carter telephoned Lurie and informed him of the call from the White & Case lawyers. Lurie neither confirmed nor denied that the LMP had been triggered. Rather, he dissembled, stating that the situation was "tight," but adding that, "if they were careful, they would be all right." Carter advised Lurie that, if the LMP had indeed been triggered, the fact should be disclosed publicly, although he did not press Lurie for a definite answer on whether the LMP had in fact been triggered, or on whether National's management was in fact implementing the LMP as required by the Amended Credit Agreement.

* * *

On April 23, 1975 both respondents met with Hart and advised him in no uncertain terms that immediate disclosure was required. In response to Hart's protestations that National would soon obtain additional financing, respondents advised him that these hopes, as well as any negotiations for a waiver of the LMP by the banks, did not serve to excuse National's legal obligation to make prompt disclosure.

Shortly before the April 23 meeting, the vice president of one of the lending banks had written to Hart requesting, among other things, a "written response from your counsel regarding [National's] obligation to make public disclosure regarding significant transactions which may have transpired during the last several months, particularly with regard to the implementing of the lease maintenance plan." Presumably as a result of this request, Hart telephoned Johnson on April 28—only five days after having received the unambiguous and forceful advice that disclosure was required—to request that Johnson issue a legal opinion for the banks to the effect that disclosure of the triggering of the LMP was *not* necessary. Johnson testified that he replied as follows:

> I'm incredulous. I just can't believe this. You sat in my office last week and I told you as clearly and positively and precisely as I could that my advice was that you should disclose that you had gone into the lease maintenance mode.

Ultimately, Hart responded to the bank's request for an opinion of counsel with a letter from National stating that no disclosure had been made because, "in the opinion of the company," none was required.

In late April, after the telephone encounter with Hart described above, Johnson instructed Socha to draft a disclosure document for National to issue, either in its next report to the Commission or in a special letter to the stockholders. In doing so, Johnson specified that the draft should be one that would be "acceptable to a person as emotionally involved as Hart." Both respondents reviewed and approved the draft prepared by Socha and it was forwarded to Hart on or about May 1, with the suggestion that Hart call Carter or Johnson about it.

* * * National did not issue this disclosure document in any form and the record does not indicate any response to Brown, Wood's disclosure advice. Neither respondent questioned anyone at the company about management's failure to make the suggested disclosure.

On May 9, Kay called Socha to seek his approval of a draft of the company's proposed current report on Form 8–K for the month of April. Socha reiterated Brown, Wood's earlier advice that disclosure should be made concerning National's present status under the Amended Credit Agreement and of the event of default that resulted from the company's failure to implement the LMP. Although Kay agreed to include the suggested disclosure, the report actually filed with the Commission did not contain any such disclosure, because Lurie would not permit it.

* * *

Later the same day, Socha called Kay and asked for a copy of the company's April Form 8–K. Kay replied that Lurie would not permit him to mail a copy to Brown, Wood or to the Commission. The April Form 8–K was eventually filed with the Commission on May 15, 1975. Socha testified that he was required to obtain a copy of it from the Commission.

* * *

The internal and external tensions which had been developing around National came to a head on Saturday afternoon, May 24, at the special meeting of the board of directors in Hartford, Connecticut. Johnson was there, acting as secretary, having been asked to attend by Hart. Also present at the meeting was independent counsel who had been consulted by the outside directors and asked to attend the meeting in the expectation that Johnson would not be there. It was at this meeting that the outside directors learned for the first time that, for over a month, Brown, Wood had been recommending disclosure and Johnson read a draft of the letter which Brown, Wood had sent to Hart on May 1, disclosing that the LMP had been triggered and its effect on the company. One of the nonmanagement directors testified that he had no prior indication that Brown, Wood had been recommending this disclosure to Hart and that when he heard the letter read by Johnson he "was shocked to the core."

At the May 24 meeting, Hart resigned each of his corporate offices, although he remained a director of the company, Johnson prepared a press release which was unanimously approved by the Board and it was decided that Brown, Wood would continue as company counsel. Johnson, however, resigned as secretary of the company.

* * *

IV. AIDING AND ABETTING

Rule 2(e)(1)(iii) provides that the Commission may deny, temporarily or permanently, the privilege of appearing or practicing before it to any person who is found by the Commission, after notice of and opportunity for hearing, to have *willfully violated,* or *willfully aided and abetted the violation* of, any provision of the federal securities laws or the rules and regulations thereunder.

A. *The Findings Below.* The Administrative Law Judge summarized the bases for his findings that respondents had "willfully violated and aided and abetted violations" of Sections 10(b) and 13(a) of the Exchange Act and Rules 10b–5, 12b–20 and 13a–11 thereunder as follows:

(i) that the December 20, 1974 press release, revised by Carter, in describing the closing under the Amended Credit Agreement was materially false and misleading in its failure to disclose adequately the nature of the LMP and that Carter was responsible for preparing it;

(ii) that the December 23, 1974 letter which Hart sent to National's stockholders was materially false and misleading, and that neither respondent took action to correct it, or to see that adequate disclosure would be made to clear up the misperceptions created by it, after they learned of the letter on December 27;

(iii) that National's Form 8-K for December 1974 was materially false and misleading in its failure to describe adequately the nature of the LMP, and that Carter has accepted full responsibility for preparing it;

(iv) that respondents failed to communicate with the board of directors of National, or otherwise take steps to insure that adequate disclosures were made in filings with the Commission, in press releases, and in letters to stockholders, despite the optimistic information about the company which they knew had been disseminated to the marketplace; and

(v) that respondents (a) from May 1974 to May 1975, assisted National's management in its efforts to conceal material facts concerning the company's financial condition, and (b) at least from October 1974 to May 1975, failed to inform the company's board of directors concerning management's unwillingness to make required disclosures.

The initial decision makes no precise distinction between its stated conclusions as to findings of willful primary violations by respondents and its findings of secondary, that is, aiding and abetting, liability. It is clear that respondents, as individuals, could not on the instant facts be found to have directly violated Section 13(a) or Rules 13a–11 and 12b–20 because they are not an "issuer," as that term is defined in Section 3(a)(8) of the Exchange Act, the only direct object of those provisions. Moreover, given the circumstances of this case, we do not believe that respondents' involvement in the affairs or decisionmaking processes of the company was sufficient to justify a finding against them as direct, primary violators of Section 10(b) or Rule 10b–5 as a result of the antifraud violations growing out of National's statements. We therefore will consider respondents' conduct only as it may constitute willful aiding and abetting of a federal securities law violation by National.

B. *Securities Law Violations by National.* We have no doubt that National's failure to disclose the nature of the LMP in the December 20 press release and the December Form 8-K constituted a violation of Sections 10(b) and 13(a) of the Exchange Act and Rules 10b–5, 12b–20 and 13a–11 thereunder. Respondents' position to the contrary rests on the purported knowledge of the marketplace that a leasing company must have new infusions of capital to grow, and that the press release and Form 8-K adequately disclosed that the closing of the Amended Credit Agreement in December made no substantial funds available to finance new leases.

Whatever our doubts about that proposition, it is clear that the LMP involved a great deal more than merely confirming the temporary absence of funds for new leases. It required, among other things, the cessation of

all leasing activity and the termination of substantially all sales personnel.
* * *

These limiting provisions were highly unusual and their import is not conveyed by the mere repetition of the words "lease maintenance plan" in the press release and in the December Form 8–K. Nor do we find persuasive respondents' argument that the likelihood of the LMP being triggered was so remote that its provisions were not material. * * *

Respondents assert that the disclosure system deals with facts, not contingencies. But the existence of *this* contingency—the uncertainty of additional financing and its relationship to the LMP—*is itself a fact* about which investors are entitled to make their own judgments. * * *

C. *Aiding and Abetting.* Our primary concern, however, is with the respondents' relationship to these violations of the securities laws. Although "[t]he elements of an aiding and abetting claim have not yet crystallized into a set pattern," [56] we have examined the decisions of the various circuits and conclude that certain legal principles are common to all the decisions.

In the context of the federal securities laws, these principles hold generally that one may be found to have aided and abetted a violation when the following three elements are present: [57]

1. there exists an independent securities law violation committed by some other party;

2. the aider and abettor knowingly and substantially assisted the conduct that constitutes the violation; and

3. the aider and abettor was aware or knew that his role was part of an activity that was improper or illegal.

As noted above, we have no difficulty in finding that National committed numerous substantial securities law violations. The second element—substantial assistance—is generally satisfied in the context of a securities lawyer performing professional duties, for he is inevitably deeply involved in his client's disclosure activities and often participates in the drafting of the documents, as was the case with Carter. And he does so knowing that he is participating in the preparation of disclosure documents—that is his job.

In this connection, we do not distinguish between the professional advice of a lawyer given orally or in writing and similar advice which is embodied in drafting documents to be filed with the Commission. Liability in these circumstances should not turn on such artificial distinctions, particularly in light of the almost limitless range of forms which legal advice may take. Moreover, the opposite approach, which would permit a

56. Woodward v. Metro Bank of Dallas, 522 F.2d 84, 94 (C.A.5 1975).

57. S.E.C. v. Falstaff Brewing Corp., 629 F.2d 62, 72 (C.A.D.C.1980); Investors Research Corp. v. S.E.C., 628 F.2d 168, 177 (C.A.D.C.1980), cert. denied 449 U.S. 919; IIT, An International Investment Trust v. Cornfeld, 619 F.2d 909, 922 (C.A.2 1980); S.E.C. v. Coven, 581 F.2d 1020, 1028 (C.A. 2), cert. denied 440 U.S. 950 (1978); Monsen v. Consolidated Dressed Beef Company, Inc., 579 F.2d 793, 799 (C.A.3), cert. denied 439 U.S. 930 (1978); Rolf v. Blyth, Eastman Dillon & Co., Inc., 570 F.2d 38, 47–48 (C.A.2), cert. denied 439 U.S. 1039 (1978); Gould v. American-Hawaiian S.S. Co., 535 F.2d 761, 779 (C.A.3 1976); Rochez Brothers, Inc. v. Rhoades, 527 F.2d 880, 886 (C.A.3 1975); Woodward v. Metro Bank of Dallas, 522 F.2d 84, 97 (C.A.5 1975); S.E.C. v. Coffee, 493 F.2d 1304, 1316 (C.A.6 1974); Landy v. F.D.I.C., 486 F.2d 139, 162–63 (C.A.3), cert. denied 416 U.S. 960 (1974).

lawyer to avoid or reduce his liability simply by avoiding participation in the drafting process, may well have the undesirable effect of reducing the quality of the disclosure by the many to protect against the defalcations of the few.

For these reasons, the crucial inquiry in a Rule 2(e) proceeding against a lawyer inevitably tends to focus on the awareness or the intent element of the offense of aiding and abetting. It is that element which has been the source of the most disagreement among commentators and the courts. We do not seek to resolve that disagreement today. We do hold, however, that a finding of *willful aiding and abetting* within the meaning of Rule 2(e)(2)(iii) requires a showing that respondents were aware or knew that their role was part of an activity that was improper or illegal.

It is axiomatic that a lawyer will not be liable as an aider and abettor merely because his advice, followed by the client, is ultimately determined to be wrong. What is missing in that instance is a wrongful intent on the part of the lawyer. It is that element of intent which provides the basis for distinguishing between those professionals who may be appropriately considered as subjects of professional discipline and those who, acting in good faith, have merely made errors of judgment or have been careless.

Significant public benefits flow from the effective performance of the securities lawyer's role. The exercise of independent, careful and informed legal judgment on difficult issues is critical to the flow of material information to the securities markets. Moreover, we are aware of the difficulties and limitations attendant upon that role. In the course of rendering securities law advice, the lawyer is called upon to make difficult judgments, often under great pressure and in areas where the legal signposts are far apart and only faintly discernible.

If a securities lawyer is to bring his best independent judgment to bear on a disclosure problem, he must have the freedom to make innocent—or even, in certain cases, careless—mistakes without fear of legal liability or loss of the ability to practice before the Commission. Concern about his own liability may alter the balance of his judgment in one direction as surely as an unseemly obeisance to the wishes of his client can do so in the other. While one imbalance results in disclosure rather than concealment, neither is, in the end, truly in the public interest. Lawyers who are seen by their clients as being motivated by fears for their personal liability will not be consulted on difficult issues.

Although it is a close judgment, after careful review we conclude that the available evidence is insufficient to establish that either respondent acted with sufficient knowledge and awareness or recklessness to satisfy the test for willful aiding and abetting liability. Our conclusion in this regard applies to each of the Administrative Law Judge's findings as to respondents' aiding and abetting National's violations of the federal securities laws.

D. *The December Press Release and Form 8–K.* In drafting the December press release and Form 8–K, Carter advised National that the provisions of the LMP were not required to be disclosed. There is ample evidence in the record indicating both respondents' knowledge about National's financial condition and the importance of the LMP. Johnson attended the Board meetings held on July 1, August 19, and October 15, 1974 at which the directors emphasized the importance of new financing and reviewed Socha's draft shareholders' letter in October that explained the significance of a proposed informal "wind-down" phase in National's corporate life. Johnson informed Carter of these matters in connection with their joint responsibilities for the representation of National. Carter focused on the details of the LMP when he advised Hart that the document embodying the plan did not have to be filed with the Commission if it were not an exhibit to the Amended Credit Agreement. Respondents were clearly aware of the company's lack of success in raising new capital, and the increasingly critical impact of its negative cash flow.

On the other hand, the record also contains no direct evidence of Carter's knowledge that the details of the LMP were material and we decline to infer such knowledge because of facts in the record on which Carter's erroneous judgment as to its immateriality is claimed to have been based. Carter had been told by Hart and others about numerous potential sources for additional financing. For example, on October 22, 1974, National entered into a Memorandum of Intent with Iwatsu Electric Co., Ltd., one of its suppliers, providing for a sale of 800,000 shares of the company's common stock to Iwatsu for $1 million. Hart had also been developing a regional bank program, consisting of borrowings, secured by new leases, from local banks where National's sales offices were located. Donald Porter, National's financial vice president, had discussed a public offering of the company's debentures with Carter shortly before the closing and Carter was aware that Hart was often out of the country seeking foreign sources of financing and foreign merger partners. Moreover, the banks were willing to close the Amended Credit Agreement and convert their $16.8 million in demand debt to six-year notes, which suggests they did not believe that National was in serious and immediate financial difficulty.

It is also significant that the December 20 press release, while originally drafted by National's management, was entirely rewritten by Carter in longhand at the December 19 pre-closing meeting. Having thus revised the document, Carter showed it to all present at the pre-closing and no one suggested any change. In fact, the only comment recalled by Carter was to the effect of, "Boy, that's full disclosure."

In view of the foregoing, we are unable to conclude that it has been demonstrated by sufficient evidence that Carter willfully aided and abetted violations of the securities laws in connection with the December 20 press release and the December Form 8–K.[59]

E. *Subsequent Conduct.* The Administrative Law Judge found that, in addition to the violations resulting from the December 20, 1974 press release and the Form 8–K filed on January 8, 1975, National violated the federal securities laws through its continued failure to make adequate disclosures in public statements and Commission filings regarding its deteriorating cash position, its inability to meet earlier growth projections, the triggering of the LMP, and the impact the LMP would have on

---

59. The Administrative Law Judge appears to have based his findings of violation in part upon the conclusion that respondents failed to act to correct the public misperceptions created by National's December 23 stockholders letter and, perhaps, by the company's earlier growth predictions and continued optimistic public disclosure. Without deciding the precise extent of National's obligation to dispel the misleading public image of the company which it had previously created, we are unwilling to conclude that *respondents* had an affirmative obligation to do so in the context of the December press release and the December Form 8–K, or that their failure to do so itself constituted willful aiding and abetting of National's violation.

National. The Administrative Law Judge also found that respondents willfully aided and abetted these violations by failing to ensure that the required disclosures were made or to communicate to National's board of directors concerning management's refusal to make such disclosures. Our review of the record does not reveal a sufficient basis for sustaining respondents' liability as aiders and abettors of these violations.

Respondents' behavior with regard to these violations by National poses an issue that was not present in our earlier discussion of Carter's conduct. There, Carter actively assisted commission of the violations. Here, respondents' behavior was in the nature of inaction and silence.

The courts have differed with respect to the circumstances under which inaction or silence may constitute the requisite assistance to the primary wrongdoer.[60] Some cases require a showing that the alleged aider and abettor deliberately intended to assist the primary violation by his silence or inaction.[61] Other cases have held that inaction or silence may constitute "substantial assistance" when the alleged aider and abettor was under a duty to act or disclose, but failed to do so.[62]

Finally, some courts synthesize the two approaches as follows:

> When it is impossible to find any duty of disclosure, an aider and abettor should be found liable only if scienter of the high "conscious intent" variety can be found. Where some special duty of disclosure exists, then liability should be possible with a lesser degree of scienter.[63]

Accordingly, in order to sustain the law judge's finding, we must find that respondents either consciously intended to assist National's violation, or that they breached a duty to disclose or act and had some degree of scienter.

On the basis of the record before us, we think that it is a close question, but in the final analysis we are unable to infer that respondents intended to aid the violations by not acting. The level of intent required by this test is higher than that required by some courts to show the appropriate mental state for the third element of aiding and abetting. There, some courts require only that an aider and abettor be "aware" that his role was part of an illegal or improper activity. Here, the test requires a showing that he "intended" to foster the illegal activity. This is a fine distinction, but we think it is an important one.

Our review of the record, which includes respondents' periodic exhortations to Hart to improve the quality of National's disclosure, leads us to believe that respondents did not intend to assist the violations by their

---

60. We note, however, that at least one court has held that mere inaction can never give rise to liability for aiding and abetting a violation of Rule 10b–5. Wessel v. Buhler, 437 F.2d 279, 283 (C.A.9 1971).

61. Rochez Brothers, Inc. v. Rhoades, 527 F.2d 880, 889 (C.A.3 1975); * * * See also S.E.C. v. Coffee, 493 F.2d 1304, 1317 (C.A.6), cert. denied 420 U.S. 908 (1975).

62. Strong v. France, 474 F.2d 747, 752 (C.A.9 1973); Kerbs v. Fall River Industries, Inc., 502 F.2d 731, 740 (C.A.10 1974). In a factually similar situation in which the court considered whether inaction or silence constitutes substantial assistance

for the purposes of aiding and abetting, the court held that there was a duty, * * * S.E.C. v. National Student Marketing Corp., 457 F.Supp. 682, 713 (D.D.C.1978). See also Rolf v. Blyth, Eastman Dillon & Co., Inc., 570 F.2d 38, 45 (C.A.2 1978).

63. Woodward v. Metro Bank of Dallas, 522 F.2d 84, 97 (C.A.5 1975). See also IIT, An International Investment Trust v. Cornfeld, 619 F.2d 909, 922 (C.A.2 1980); Hochfelder v. Midwest Stock Exchange, 503 F.2d 364, 374 (C.A.7), cert. denied 419 U.S. 875 (1974); Woods v. Homes & Structures of Pittsburgh, Kansas, 489 F.Supp. 1270, 278 (D.Kan.1980).

inaction or silence. Rather, they seemed to be at a loss for how to deal with a difficult client.

Association of a law firm with a client lends an air of legitimacy and authority to the actions of a client. There are occasions when, but for the law firm's association, a violation could not have occurred. Under those circumstances, if the firm were cognizant of how it was being used and acquiesced, or if it gained some benefit from the violation beyond that normally obtained in a legal relationship, inaction would probably give rise to an inference of intent. This, however, is not such a case, and we find that respondents did not intend to assist the violation by their inaction.

V. ETHICAL AND PROFESSIONAL RESPONSIBILITIES

A. *The Findings of the Administrative Law Judge.* The Administrative Law Judge found that both respondents "failed to carry out their professional responsibilities with respect to appropriate disclosure to all concerned, including stockholders, directors and the investing public * * * and thus knowingly engaged in unethical and improper professional conduct, as charged in the Order." In particular, he held that respondents' failure to advise National's board of directors of Hart's refusal to disclose adequately the company's perilous financial condition was itself a violation of ethical and professional standards referred to in Rule 2(e)(1)(ii).

Respondents argue that the Commission has never promulgated standards of professional conduct for lawyers and that the Commission's application in hindsight of new standards would be fundamentally unfair. Moreover, even if it is permissible for the Commission to apply—without specific adoption or notice—generally recognized professional standards, they argue that no such standards applicable to respondents' conduct existed in 1974–75, nor do they exist today.

We agree that, in general, elemental notions of fairness dictate that the Commission should not establish new rules of conduct and impose them retroactively upon professionals who acted at the time without reason to believe that their conduct was unethical or improper. At the same time, however, we perceive no unfairness whatsoever in holding those professionals who practice before us to generally recognized norms of professional conduct, whether or not such norms had previously been explicitly adopted or endorsed by the Commission. To do so upsets no justifiable expectations, since the professional is already subject to those norms.[64]

The ethical and professional responsibilities of lawyers who become aware that their client is engaging in violations of the securities laws have not been so firmly and unambiguously established that we believe all practicing lawyers can be held to an awareness of generally recognized norms.[65] We also recognize that the Commission has never articulated or

---

64. For example, the universally recognized requirement that a lawyer refrain from acting in an area where he does not have an adequate level of preparation or care, e.g., ABA Code of Professional Responsibility, Disciplinary Rule ("ABA D.R.") 6–101.

65. We are aware that ABA D.R. 1–102(A)(4) provides that "a lawyer shall not * * * engage in conduct involving dis-

honesty, fraud, deceit or misrepresentation" and that ABA D.R. 7–102(A)(7) provides that a lawyer may not, in the course of his representation, "counsel or assist his client in conduct that the lawyer knows to be illegal or fraudulent." Although we believe the prohibitions embodied in ABA D.R. 1–102(A)(4) and 7–102(A)(7) to be of such a fundamental nature that we would not hesitate to hold that their coverage

endorsed any such standards. That being the case, we reverse the Administrative Law Judge's findings under subparagraph (ii) of Rule 2(e)(1) with respect to both respondents. Nevertheless, we believe that respondents' conduct raises serious questions about the obligations of securities lawyers, and the Commission is hereby giving notice of its interpretation of "unethical or improper professional conduct" as that term is used in Rule 2(e)(1)(ii). The Commission intends to issue a release soliciting comment from the public as to whether this interpretation should be expanded or modified.

B. *Interpretive Background.* Our concern focuses on the professional obligations of the lawyer who gives essentially correct disclosure advice to a client that does not follow that advice and as a result violates the federal securities laws. The subject of our inquiry is not a new one by any means and has received extensive scholarly treatment [66] as well as consideration by a number of local bar ethics committees and disciplinary bodies. Similar issues are also presently under consideration by the ABA's Commission on Evaluation of Professional Standards in connection with the review and proposed revision of the ABA's Code of Professional Responsibility.[68]

While precise standards have not yet emerged, it is fair to say that there exists considerable acceptance of the proposition that a lawyer must, in order to discharge his professional responsibilities, make all efforts within reason to persuade his client to avoid or terminate proposed illegal action. Such efforts could include, where appropriate, notification to the board of directors of a corporate client. In this connection, it is noteworthy that a number of commentators responding to the Commission's request, in Securities Exchange Act Release No. 16045, for written comments on a rulemaking petition concerning the disclosure of relationships between registrants and their lawyers (the "Georgetown Petition"), volunteered their beliefs that such a professional obligation already exists. This informal expression of views is, of course, not conclusive, and there continues to be a lively debate surrounding the lawyer's proper reaction to his client's wrongdoings.[72]

plainly falls within the area of conduct prohibited by Rule 2(e)(1)(ii), two factors convince us not to apply them in this case. First, it is unclear whether the operative terms used in these Disciplinary Rules are coextensive with the use of such terms in the statutory prohibitions of Section 10(b) of the Exchange Act. Second, it is not apparent that the reach of ABA D.R. 1-102(A)(4) or 7-102(A)(7) is greater or any different from the reach of Rule 2(e)(1)(ii) in the case of a lawyer who willfully aids and abets a violation of Section 10(b). Accordingly, in this opinion, we have elected to analyze respondents' actions in the context of the provisions of subparagraph (iii), as discussed above, rather than under subparagraph (ii) of Rule 2(e)(1).

66. E.g., Hoffman, On Learning of a Corporate Client's Crime or Fraud—The Lawyer's Dilemma, 33 Bus. Lawyer 1389 (1978); Association of the Bar of The City of New York, Report By Special Committee on The Lawyers' Role in Securities Transactions, 32 Bus. Lawyer 1879 (1977); Cooney, The Registration Process: The

Role of the Lawyer in Disclosure, 33 Bus. Lawyer 1329 (1978); Cutler, The Role of the Private Law Firm, 33 Bus. Lawyer 1549 (1978); Sonde, The Responsibility of Professionals under the Federal Securities Laws—Some Observations, 68 Nw.U.L.Rev. 1 (1973); New York Law Journal, "Expanding Responsibilities under the Securities Laws" (1972), 29 (remarks of Manuel F. Cohen, Esq.).

68. See ABA Commission on Evaluation of Professional Standards, Model Rules of Professional Conduct (Discussion Draft, Jan. 30, 1980), Rule 1.13.

72. See, e.g., Letter, dated December 5, 1980, from Robert J. Kutak, Chairman of the ABA Commission on Evaluation of Professional Standards, concerning the "extraordinary volume of comments" on the January 30, 1980 discussion draft of the ABA Commission's Model Rules of Professional Conduct. It is significant that, in this area, the bulk of the debate has concerned the issue of when a lawyer must disclose his client's wrongdoings to a third

We are mindful that, when a lawyer represents a corporate client, the client—and the entity to which he owes his allegiance—is the corporation itself and not management or any other individual connected with the corporation.[73] Moreover, the lawyer should try to "insure that decisions of his client are made only after the client has been informed of relevant considerations." [74] These unexceptionable principles take on a special coloration when a lawyer becomes aware that one or more specific members of a corporate client's management is deciding not to follow his disclosure advice, especially if he knows that those in control, such as the board of directors, may not have participated in or been aware of that decision. Moreover, it is well established that no lawyer, even in the most zealous pursuit of his client's interests, is privileged to assist his client in conduct the lawyer knows to be illegal.[75] The application of these recognized principles to the special role of the securities lawyer giving disclosure advice, however, is not a simple task.

The securities lawyer who is an active participant in a company's ongoing disclosure program will ordinarily draft and revise disclosure documents, comment on them and file them with the Commission. He is often involved on an intimate, day-to-day basis in the judgments that determine what will be disclosed and what will be withheld from the public markets. When a lawyer serving in such a capacity concludes that his client's disclosures are not adequate to comply with the law, and so advises his client, he is "aware," in a literal sense, of a continuing violation of the securities laws. On the other hand, the lawyer is only an adviser, and the final judgment—and, indeed, responsibility—as to what course of conduct is to be taken must lie with the client. Moreover, disclosure issues often present difficult choices between multiple shades of gray, and while a lawyer's judgment may be to draw the disclosure obligation more broadly than his client, both parties recognize the degree of uncertainty involved.

The problems of professional conduct that arise in this relationship are well-illustrated by the facts of this case. In rejecting Brown, Wood's advice to include the assumptions underlying its projections in its 1974 Annual Report, in declining to issue two draft stockholders letters offered by respondents and in ignoring the numerous more informal urgings by both respondents and Socha to make disclosure, Hart and Lurie indicated that they were inclined to resist any public pronouncements that were at odds with the rapid growth which had been projected and reported for the company.

If the record ended there, we would be hesitant to suggest that any unprofessional conduct might be involved. Hart and Lurie were, in effect, pressing the company's lawyers hard for the minimum disclosure required by law. That fact alone is not an appropriate basis for a finding that a lawyer must resign or take some extraordinary action. Such a finding would inevitably drive a wedge between reporting companies and their outside lawyers; the more sophisticated members of management would soon realize that there is nothing to gain in consulting outside lawyers.

---

party or to the public, an issue not raised in this proceeding.

73. See ABA Code of Professional Responsibility, Ethical Consideration ("ABA E.C.") 5–18.

74. ABA E.C. 7–8.

75. ABA D.R. 7–102(A)(7).

However, much more was involved in this case. In sending out a patently misleading letter to stockholders on December 23 in contravention of Socha's plain and express advice to clear all such disclosure with Brown, Wood, in deceiving respondents about Johnson's approval of the company's quarterly report to its stockholders in early December and in dissembling in response to respondents' questions about the implementation of the LMP, the company's management erected a wall between National and its outside lawyers—a wall apparently designed to keep out good legal advice in conflict with management's improper disclosure plans.

Any ambiguity in the situation plainly evaporated in late April and early May of 1975 when Hart first asked Johnson for a legal opinion flatly contrary to the express disclosure advice Johnson had given Hart only five days earlier, and when Lurie soon thereafter prohibited Kay from delivering a copy of the company's April 1975 Form 8–K to Brown, Wood.

These actions reveal a conscious desire on the part of National's management no longer to look to Brown, Wood for independent disclosure advice, but rather to embrace the firm within Hart's fraud and use it as a shield to avoid the pressures exerted by the banks toward disclosure. Such a role is a perversion of the normal lawyer-client relationship, and no lawyer may claim that, in these circumstances, he need do no more than stubbornly continue to suggest disclosure when he knows his suggestions are falling on deaf ears.

C. *"Unethical or Improper Professional Conduct."* The Commission is of the view that a lawyer engages in "unethical or improper professional conduct" under the following circumstances: When a lawyer with significant responsibilities in the effectuation of a company's compliance with the disclosure requirements of the federal securities laws becomes aware that his client is engaged in a substantial and continuing failure to satisfy those disclosure requirements, his continued participation violates professional standards unless he takes prompt steps to end the client's noncompliance. The Commission has determined that this interpretation will be applicable only to conduct occurring after the date of this opinion.

We do not imply that a lawyer is obliged, at the risk of being held to have violated Rule 2(e), to seek to correct every isolated disclosure action or inaction which he believes to be at variance with applicable disclosure standards, although there may be isolated disclosure failures that are so serious that their correction becomes a matter of primary professional concern. It is also clear, however, that a lawyer is not privileged to unthinkingly permit himself to be co-opted into an ongoing fraud and cast as a dupe or a shield for a wrongdoing client.

Initially, counselling accurate disclosure is sufficient, even if his advice is not accepted. But there comes a point at which a reasonable lawyer must conclude that his advice is not being followed, or even sought in good faith, and that his client is involved in a continuing course of violating the securities laws. At this critical juncture, the lawyer must take further, more affirmative steps in order to avoid the inference that he has been co-opted, willingly or unwillingly, into the scheme of non-disclosure.

The lawyer is in the best position to choose his next step. Resignation is one option, although we recognize that other considerations, including the protection of the client against foreseeable prejudice, must be taken into account in the case of withdrawal.[76] A direct approach to the board of directors or one or more individual directors or officers may be appropriate; or he may choose to try to enlist the aid of other members of the firm's management. What is required, in short, is some prompt action [77] that leads to the conclusion that the lawyer is engaged in efforts to correct the underlying problem, rather than having capitulated to the desires of a strong-willed, but misguided client.

Some have argued that resignation is the only permissible course when a client chooses not to comply with disclosure advice. We do not agree. Premature resignation serves neither the end of an effective lawyer-client relationship nor, in most cases, the effective administration of the securities laws. The lawyer's continued interaction with his client will ordinarily hold the greatest promise of corrective action. So long as a lawyer is acting in good faith and exerting reasonable efforts to prevent violations of the law by his client, his professional obligations have been met. In general, the best result is that which promotes the continued, strong-minded and independent participation by the lawyer.

We recognize, however, that the "best result" is not always obtainable, and that there may occur situations where the lawyer must conclude that the misconduct is so extreme or irretrievable, or the involvement of his client's management and board of directors in the misconduct is so thoroughgoing and pervasive that any action short of resignation would be futile. We would anticipate that cases where a lawyer has no choice but to resign would be rare and of an egregious nature.[78]

D. *Conclusion.* As noted above, because the Commission has never adopted or endorsed standards of professional conduct which would have applied to respondents' activities during the period here in question, and since generally accepted norms of professional conduct which existed outside the scope of Rule 2(e) did not, during the relevant time period, unambiguously cover the situation in which respondents found themselves in 1974–75, no finding of unethical or unprofessional conduct would be appropriate. That being the case, we reverse the findings of the Administrative Law Judge under Rule 2(e)(1)(ii). In future proceedings of this nature, however, the Commission will apply the interpretation of subparagraph (ii) of Rule 2(e)(1) set forth in this opinion.

An appropriate order will issue.

By the Commission (CHAIRMAN WILLIAMS and COMMISSIONERS LOOMIS and FRIEDMAN); COMMISSIONER EVANS concurring in part and dissenting in part; and COMMISSIONER THOMAS not participating.

---

76. See, e.g. ABA D.R. 2–110; ABA E.C. 2–32, 2–33.

77. In those cases where resignation is not the only alternative, should a lawyer choose not to resign, we do not believe the action taken *must be successful* to avoid the inference that the lawyer had improperly participated in his client's fraud. Rather, the acceptability of the action must be considered in the light of all relevant surrounding circumstances. Similarly, what is "prompt" in any one case depends on the situation then facing the lawyer.

78. This case does not involve, nor do we here deal with, the additional question of when a lawyer, aware of his client's intention to commit fraud or an illegal act, has a professional duty to disclose that fact either publicly or to an affected third party. Our interpretation today does not require such action at any point, although other existing standards of professional conduct might be so interpreted. See, e.g., ABA D.R. 7–102(B).

MODEL RULES OF PROFESSIONAL CONDUCT

American Bar Association, 1983.
Rules 1.6, 1.13 and 1.16.

RULE 1.6. CONFIDENTIALITY OF INFORMATION

(a) A lawyer shall not reveal information relating to representation of a client unless the client consents after consultation, except for disclosures that are impliedly authorized in order to carry out the representation, and except as stated in paragraph (b).

(b) A lawyer may reveal such information to the extent the lawyer reasonably believes necessary:

(1) to prevent the client from committing a criminal act that the lawyer believes is likely to result in imminent death or substantial bodily harm; or

(2) to establish a claim or defense on behalf of the lawyer in a controversy between the lawyer and the client, to establish a defense to a criminal charge or civil claim against the lawyer based upon conduct in which the client was involved, or to respond to allegations in any proceeding concerning the lawyer's representation of the client.

COMMENT:

The lawyer is part of a judicial system charged with upholding the law. One of the lawyer's functions is to advise clients so that they avoid any violation of the law in the proper exercise of their rights.

The observance of the ethical obligation of a lawyer to hold inviolate confidential information of the client not only facilitates the full development of facts essential to proper representation of the client but also encourages people to seek early legal assistance.

Almost without exception, clients come to lawyers in order to determine what their rights are and what is, in the maze of laws and regulations, deemed to be legal and correct. The common law recognizes that the client's confidences must be protected from disclosure. Based upon experience, lawyers know that almost all clients follow the advice given, and the law is upheld.

A fundamental principle in the client-lawyer relationship is that the lawyer maintain confidentiality of information relating to the representation. The client is thereby encouraged to communicate fully and frankly with the lawyer even as to embarrassing or legally damaging subject matter.

The principle of confidentiality is given effect in two related bodies of law, the attorney-client privilege (which includes the work product doctrine) in the law of evidence and the rule of confidentiality established in professional ethics. The attorney-client privilege applies in judicial and other proceedings in which a lawyer may be called as a witness or otherwise required to produce evidence concerning a client. The rule of client-lawyer confidentiality applies in situations other than those where evidence is sought from the lawyer through compulsion of law. The confidentiality rule applies not merely to matters communicated in confidence by the client but also to all information relating to the representation, whatever its source. A lawyer may not disclose such information except as authorized or required by the Rules of Professional Conduct or other law. * * *

The requirement of maintaining confidentiality of information relating to representation applies to government lawyers who may disagree with the policy goals that their representation is designed to advance.

Authorized Disclosure

A lawyer is impliedly authorized to make disclosures about a client when appropriate in carrying out the representation, except to the extent that the client's instructions or special circumstances limit that authority. In litigation, for example, a lawyer may disclose information by admitting a fact that cannot properly be disputed, or in negotiation by making a disclosure that facilitates a satisfactory conclusion.

Lawyers in a firm may, in the course of the firm's practice, disclose to each other information relating to a client of the firm, unless the client has instructed that particular information be confined to specified lawyers.

Disclosure Adverse to Client

The confidentiality rule is subject to limited exceptions. In becoming privy to information about a client, a lawyer may foresee that the client intends serious harm to another person. However, to the extent a lawyer is required or permitted to disclose a client's purposes, the client will be inhibited from revealing facts which would enable the lawyer to counsel against a wrongful course of action. The public is better protected if full and open communication by the client is encouraged than if it is inhibited.

Several situations must be distinguished.

First, the lawyer may not counsel or assist a client in conduct that is criminal or fraudulent. See Rule 1.2(d). Similarly, a lawyer has a duty under Rule 3.3(a)(4) not to use false evidence. This duty is essentially a special instance of the duty prescribed in Rule 1.2(d) to avoid assisting a client in criminal or fraudulent conduct.

Second, the lawyer may have been innocently involved in past conduct by the client that was criminal or fraudulent. In such a situation the lawyer has not violated Rule 1.2(d), because to "counsel or assist" criminal or fraudulent conduct requires knowing that the conduct is of that character.

Third, the lawyer may learn that a client intends prospective conduct that is criminal and likely to result in imminent death or substantial bodily harm. As stated in paragraph (b)(1), the lawyer has professional discretion to reveal information in order to prevent such consequences. The lawyer may make a disclosure in order to prevent homicide or serious bodily injury which the lawyer reasonably believes is intended by a client. It is very difficult for a lawyer to "know" when such a heinous purpose will actually be carried out, for the client may have a change of mind.

The lawyer's exercise of discretion requires consideration of such factors as the nature of the lawyer's relationship with the client and with those who might be injured by the client, the lawyer's own involvement in the transaction and factors that may extenuate the conduct in question. Where practical, the lawyer should seek to persuade the client to take suitable action. In any case, a disclosure adverse to the client's interest should be no greater than the lawyer reasonably believes necessary to the purpose. A lawyer's decision not to take preventive action permitted by paragraph (b)(1) does not violate this Rule.

Withdrawal

If the lawyer's services will be used by the client in materially furthering a course of criminal or fraudulent conduct, the lawyer must withdraw, as stated in Rule 1.16(a)(1).

After withdrawal the lawyer is required to refrain from making disclosure of the clients' confidences, except as otherwise provided in Rule 1.6. Neither this rule nor Rule 1.8(b) nor Rule 1.16(d) prevents the lawyer from giving notice of the fact of withdrawal, and the lawyer may also withdraw or disaffirm any opinion, document, affirmation, or the like.

Where the client is an organization, the lawyer may be in doubt whether contemplated conduct will actually be carried out by the organization. Where necessary to guide conduct in connection with this Rule, the lawyer may make inquiry within the organization as indicated in Rule 1.13(b).

* * *

Disclosures Otherwise Required or Authorized

The attorney-client privilege is differently defined in various jurisdictions. If a lawyer is called as a witness to give testimony concerning a client, absent waiver by the client, paragraph 1.6(a) requires the lawyer to invoke the privilege when it is applicable. The lawyer must comply with the final orders of a court or other tribunal of competent jurisdiction requiring the lawyer to give information about the client.

The Rules of Professional Conduct in various circumstances permit or require a lawyer to disclose information relating to the representation. See Rules 2.2, 2.3, 3.3 and 4.1. In addition to these provisions, a lawyer may be obligated or permitted by other provisions of law to give information about a client. Whether another provision of law supersedes Rule 1.6 is a matter of interpretation beyond the scope of these Rules, but a presumption should exist against such a supersession.

Former Client

The duty of confidentiality continues after the client-lawyer relationship has terminated.

* * *

RULE 1.13 ORGANIZATION AS CLIENT

(a) A lawyer employed or retained by an organization represents the organization acting through its duly authorized constituents.

(b) If a lawyer for an organization knows that an officer, employee or other person associated with the organization is engaged in action, intends to act or refuses to act in a matter related to the representation that is a violation of a legal obligation to the organization, or a violation of law which reasonably might be imputed to the organization, and is likely to result in substantial injury to the organization, the lawyer shall proceed as is reasonably necessary in

the best interest of the organization. In determining how to proceed, the lawyer shall give due consideration to the seriousness of the violation and its consequences, the scope and nature of the lawyer's representation, the responsibility in the organization and the apparent motivation of the person involved, the policies of the organization concerning such matters and any other relevant considerations. Any measures taken shall be designed to minimize disruption of the organization and the risk of revealing information relating to the representation to persons outside the organization. Such measures may include among others:

(1) asking reconsideration of the matter;

(2) advising that a separate legal opinion on the matter be sought for presentation to appropriate authority in the organization; and

(3) referring the matter to higher authority in the organization, including, if warranted by the seriousness of the matter, referral to the highest authority that can act in behalf of the organization as determined by applicable law.

(c) If, despite the lawyer's efforts in accordance with paragraph (b), the highest authority that can act on behalf of the organization insists upon action, or a refusal to act, that is clearly a violation of law and is likely to result in substantial injury to the organization, the lawyer may resign in accordance with Rule 1.16.

(d) In dealing with an organization's directors, officers, employees, members, shareholders or other constituents, a lawyer shall explain the identity of the client when it is apparent that the organization's interests are adverse to those of the constituents with whom the lawyer is dealing.

(e) A lawyer representing an organization may also represent any of its directors, officers, employees, members, shareholders or other constituents, subject to the provisions of Rule 1.7. If the organization's consent to the dual representation is required by Rule 1.7, the consent shall be given by an appropriate official of the organization other than the individual who is to be represented, or by the shareholders.

COMMENT:

The Entity as the Client

An organizational client is a legal entity, but it cannot act except through its officers, directors, employees, shareholders and other constituents.

Officers, directors, employees and shareholders are the constituents of the corporate organizational client. The duties defined in this Comment apply equally to unincorporated associations. "Other constituents" as used in this Comment means the positions equivalent to officers, directors, employees and shareholders held by persons acting for organizational clients that are not corporations.

When one of the constituents of an organizational client communicates with the organization's lawyer in that person's organizational capacity, the communication is protected by Rule 1.6. Thus, by way of example, if an organizational client requests its lawyer to investigate allegations of wrongdoing, interviews made in the course of that investigation between the lawyer and the client's employees or other constituents are covered by Rule 1.6. This does not mean, however that constituents of an organizational client are the clients of the lawyer. The lawyer may not disclose to such constituents information relating to the representation except for disclosures explicitly or impliedly authorized by the organizational client in order to carry out the representation or as otherwise permitted by Rule 1.6.

When constituents of the organization make decisions for it, the decisions ordinarily must be accepted by the lawyer even if their utility or prudence is doubtful. Decisions concerning policy and operations, including ones entailing serious risk, are not as such in the lawyer's province. However, different considerations arise when the lawyer knows that the organization may be substantially injured by action of a constituent that is in violation of law. In such a circumstance, it may be reasonably necessary for the lawyer to ask the constituent to reconsider the matter. If that fails, or if the matter is of sufficient seriousness and importance to the organization, it may be reasonably necessary for the lawyer to take steps to have the matter reviewed by a higher authority in the organization. Clear justification should exist for seeking review over the head of the constituent normally responsible for it. The stated policy of the organization may define circumstances and prescribe channels for such review, and a lawyer should encourage the formulation of such a policy. Even in the absence of organization policy, however, the lawyer may have an obligation to refer a matter to higher authority, depending on the seriousness of the matter and whether the constituent in question has apparent motives to act at variance with the organization's interest. Review by the chief executive officer or by the board of directors may be required when the matter is of importance commensurate with their authority. At some point it may be useful or essential to obtain an independent legal opinion.

In an extreme case, it may be reasonably necessary for the lawyer to refer the matter to the organization's highest authority. Ordinarily, that is the board of directors or similar governing body. However, applicable law may prescribe that under certain conditions highest authority reposes elsewhere; for example, in the independent directors of a corporation.

Relation to Other Rules

The authority and responsibility provided in paragraph (b) are concurrent with the authority and responsibility provided in other Rules. In particular, this Rule does not limit or expand the lawyer's responsibility under Rules 1.6, 1.8, 1.16, 3.3 and 4.1. If the lawyer's services are being used by an organization to further a crime or fraud by the organization, Rule 1.2(d) can be applicable.

* * *

Clarifying the Lawyer's Role

There are times when the organization's interest may be or become adverse to those of one or more of its constituents. In such circumstances, the lawyer should advise any constituent, whose interest the lawyer finds adverse to that of the organization of the conflict or potential conflict of interest, that the lawyer cannot represent such constituent, and that such person may wish to obtain independent representation. Care must be taken to assure that the individual understands that, when there is such adversity of interest, the lawyer for the organization cannot provide legal representation for that constituent individual, and that discussions between the lawyer for the organization and the individual may not be privileged.

Whether such a warning should be given by the lawyer for the organization to any constituent individual may turn on the facts of each case.

Dual Representation

Paragraph (e) recognizes that a lawyer for an organization may also represent a principal officer or major shareholder.

Derivative Actions

Under generally prevailing law, the shareholders or members of a corporation may bring suit to compel the directors to perform their legal obligations in the supervision of the organization. Members of unincorporated associations have essentially the same right. Such an action may be brought nominally by the organization, but usually is, in fact, a legal controversy over management of the organization.

The question can arise whether counsel for the organization may defend such an action. The proposition that the organization is the lawyer's client does not alone resolve the issue. Most derivative actions are a normal incident of an organization's affairs, to be defended by the organization's lawyer like any other suit. However, if the claim involves serious charges of wrongdoing by those in control of the organization, a conflict may arise between the lawyer's duty to the organization and the lawyer's relationship with the board. In those circumstances, Rule 1.7 governs who should represent the directors and the organization.

RULE 1.16 DECLINING OR TERMINATING REPRESENTATION

(a) Except as stated in paragraph (c), a lawyer shall not represent a client or, where representation has commenced, shall withdraw from the representation of a client if:

(1) the representation will result in violation of the rules of professional conduct or other law;

(2) the lawyer's physical or mental condition materially impairs the lawyer's ability to represent the client; or

(3) the lawyer is discharged.

(b) Except as stated in paragraph (c), a lawyer may withdraw from representing a client if withdrawal can be accomplished without material adverse effect on the interests of the client, or if:

(1) the client persists in a course of action involving the lawyer's services that the lawyer reasonably believes is criminal or fraudulent;

(2) the client has used the lawyer's services to perpetrate a crime or fraud;

(3) a client insists upon pursuing an objective that the lawyer considers repugnant or imprudent;

(4) the client fails substantially to fulfill an obligation to the lawyer regarding the lawyer's services and has been given reasonable warning that the lawyer will withdraw unless the obligation is fulfilled;

(5) the representation will result in an unreasonable financial burden on the lawyer or has been rendered unreasonably difficult by the client; or

(6) other good cause for withdrawal exists.

(c) When ordered to do so by a tribunal, a lawyer shall continue representation notwithstanding good cause for terminating the representation.

(d) Upon termination of representation, a lawyer shall take steps to the extent reasonably practicable to protect a client's interests, such as giving reasonable notice to the client, allowing time for employment of other counsel, surrendering papers and property to which the client is entitled and refunding any advance payment of fee that has not been earned. The lawyer may retain papers relating to the client to the extent permitted by other law.

COMMENT:

A lawyer should not accept representation in a matter unless it can be performed competently, promptly, without improper conflict of interest and to completion.

Mandatory Withdrawal

A lawyer ordinarily must decline or withdraw from representation if the client demands that the lawyer engage in conduct that is illegal or violates the Rules of Professional Conduct or other law. The lawyer is not obliged to decline or withdraw simply because the client suggests such a course of conduct; a client may make such a suggestion in the hope that a lawyer will not be constrained by a professional obligation.

When a lawyer has been appointed to represent a client, withdrawal ordinarily requires approval of the appointing authority. See also Rule 6.2. Difficulty may be encountered if withdrawal is based on the client's demand that the lawyer engage in unprofessional conduct. The court may wish an explanation for the withdrawal, while the lawyer may be bound to keep confidential the facts that would constitute such an explanation. The lawyer's statement that professional considerations require termination of the representation ordinarily should be accepted as sufficient.

Discharge

A client has a right to discharge a lawyer at any time, with or without cause, subject to liability for payment for the lawyer's services. Where future dispute about the withdrawal may be anticipated, it may be advisable to prepare a written statement reciting the circumstances.

* * *

If the client is mentally incompetent, the client may lack the legal capacity to discharge the lawyer, and in any event the discharge may be seriously adverse to the client's interests. The lawyer should make special effort to help the client consider the consequences and, in an extreme case, may initiate proceedings for a conservatorship or similar protection of the client. See Rule 1.14.

Optional Withdrawal

A lawyer may withdraw from representation in some circumstances. The lawyer has the option to withdraw if it can be accomplished without material adverse effect on the client's interests. Withdrawal is also justified if the client persists in a course of action that the lawyer reasonably believes is criminal or fraudulent, for a lawyer is not required to be associated with such conduct even if the lawyer does not further it. Withdrawal is also permitted if the lawyer's services were misused in the past even if that would materially prejudice the client. The lawyer also may withdraw where the client insists on a repugnant or imprudent objective.

A lawyer may withdraw if the client refuses to abide by the terms of an agreement relating to the representation, such as an agreement concerning fees or court costs or an agreement limiting the objectives of the representation.

* * *

ERNST & ERNST v. HOCHFELDER
United States Supreme Court, 1976.
425 U.S. 185, 96 S.Ct. 1375, 47 L.Ed.2d 668.

[Re-read at this point the above case which is printed at p. 936.]

ACCOUNTANTS

Accountants, like underwriters, are subject to express liability under Section 11 of the 1933 Act with respect to their involvement in a registered issue of securities. The registration statement must contain certified financial statements, and the auditing firm which certifies them is subject to liability as an "expert" with respect to those statements. The standard required of the firm in that capacity is that it "had, after reasonable investigation, reasonable ground to believe and did believe, at the time such part of the registration statement became effective, that the statements therein were true and that there was no omission to state a material fact required to be stated therein or necessary to make the statements therein not misleading." Obviously, this provision imposes liability upon the certified public accountants for negligence in the conduct of the audit or in the adequate presentation of the information in the financial statements. The liability of course runs to those purchasers of the registered securities who are specified in Section 11.

What is the extent of the liability of the accountants under Rule 10b–5 and other provisions of the Federal securities laws? The answer to this question involves the resolution of two primary issues: (1) What standard of conduct determines the duty, breach of which will give rise to liability? Is mere negligence sufficient, as under Section 11, or is something more "culpable" required? (2) What is the ambit of the duty, i.e., what persons are entitled to sue the accountants on the basis that some "connection" can be traced between the failure of the accountants to perform their duty and the loss allegedly suffered by the plaintiffs?

In considering these questions, a distinction might perhaps have been drawn (although there is no evidence in the Supreme Court opinion in *Ernst & Ernst* that it will be) between an allegation that the auditor did not discover what he should have discovered, because he omitted some procedure that he should have employed (i.e., a violation of generally accepted auditing standards), and an allegation that he did not state, or state properly, that which he knew (i.e., a violation of generally accepted accounting principles). The former are established for the profession by the American Institute of Certified Public Accountants in what are called Statements of Auditing Standards (SAS); the latter are established by the Financial Accounting Standards Board, which was recently created as the successor to the Accounting Principles Board, in what are called Statements of Financial Accounting Standards (SFAS). A violation of the former was the basis for the alleged liability in the *Ernst & Ernst* case.

It would seem that if liability is to be imposed at all for a violation of auditing standards, it would have to be premised on negligence, since it would be a rare case where it could be shown that the auditor omitted some required procedure, or deliberately conducted it improperly, because he desired not to find out what it might have revealed.

In United States v. Simon [1] the Second Circuit held that, even in a criminal case, generally accepted accounting principles were not necessarily the measure of accountants' liability for allegedly misleading statements in a footnote to the financial statements. Eight "leaders of the profession" had testified that the defendants' treatment of a particular item was in accordance with generally accepted accounting principles. The trial court refused to give a requested instruction that "would have told the jury that a defendant could be found guilty only if, *according to generally accepted accounting principles,* the financial statements as a whole did not fairly present the financial condition of" the company at the balance sheet date. The court gave a similar charge which, however, omitted the italicized language above. The Second Circuit affirmed. The court said: "We think the judge was right in refusing to make the accountants' testimony so nearly a complete defense. The critical test according to the charge was the same as that which the accountants testified was critical. We do not think the jury was also required to accept the accountants' evaluation whether a given fact was material to overall fair presentation, at least not when the accountants' testimony was not based on specific rules or prohibitions to which they could point, but only on the need for the auditor to make an honest judgment and their conclusion that nothing in the financial statements themselves negated the conclusion that an honest judgment had been made. Such evidence may be highly persuasive, but it is not conclusive, and so the trial judge correctly charged." [2]

The court in the *Simon* case also held that the admitted fact that the defendant accountants had no financial incentive whatever to falsify the financial statements of the company being audited was not necessarily a defense to a criminal charge of having done so intentionally. "Even if there were no satisfactory showing of motive, we think the Government produced sufficient evidence of criminal intent. Its burden was not to show that defendants were wicked men with designs on anyone's purse, which they obviously were not, but rather that they had certified a statement knowing it to be false." [3]

---

1. 425 F.2d 796 (2d Cir.1969), cert. denied 397 U.S. 1006 (1970).

2. 425 F.2d at 806.

3. 425 F.2d at 809.

Has the *Ernst & Ernst* decision overruled the *Simon* case?

The Ambit of the Responsibility. Assuming that the accountants have breached some legal duty with respect to the conduct of their audit or the statement of the results, to whom will they be liable? If the certified financial statements are intended to be used and are used, to the knowledge of the accountants, in the sale of securities by the company or someone else to the public, there would seem to be little question that the purchasers are persons entitled to complain of that breach of duty, even under Cardozo's opinion in the *Ultramares* case which is discussed in *Ernst & Ernst.* The decision of the Seventh Circuit in the *Ernst & Ernst* case went further and held that where the certified financial statements of a broker-dealer are required to be filed and are filed with the SEC, customers of the broker-dealer (even though they themselves never saw the financial statements) may complain that they were the victims of a fraud by the president of the broker-dealer which might have been uncovered if the audit had been conducted properly. The court reasoned that the requirement of the filing of certified statements with the SEC was expressly for the purpose of protecting the customers of the broker-dealer and if that filing had revealed the fraud, the SEC would surely have stepped in to prevent its continuance. However, in view of its holding that there was no breach of duty, the Supreme Court finds it unnecessary to decide this issue (see footnote 13 in the opinion), although it subsequently held in *Touche Ross & Co. v. Redington* that there is no private cause of action under § 17(a) of the 1934 Act.

In Competitive Associates, Inc. v. Laventhol, Krekstein, Horwath & Horwath [4] it was alleged that a firm of accountants had deliberately falsified the financial statements, and thereby the investment results, of an investment partnership conducted by an investment adviser, in order to facilitate his scheme to attract other clients to retain him as investment adviser. It was alleged that they did this "knowingly" and "with intent to defraud." Therefore, on the pleadings there was no question of breach of duty. A client who had in fact retained this investment adviser sued the accountants, although that client had never seen the certified financial statements of the investment partnership. The Second Circuit reversed a summary judgment granted to the accountants by the District Court. The court said: "The broad 'touch' test enunciated in *Bankers Life* [see p. 1056, supra] is certainly met by plaintiff's allegations that the very purpose of defendants' certification of Takara's [the investment partnership's] financial statements was to aid in placing Yamada [the investment adviser] in a position where he could manipulate securities prices and sell these securities to investors attracted by Yamada's reputation and performance." The court also found the cases relied upon by the defendants inapposite. The court said: "In each [of those] case[s], the court premised the result on a finding that the accountants involved did not know or expect their reports to be relied upon by anyone other than the members of the entity for which the reports were specifically prepared and therefore were not reasonably calculated to influence the investing public. See, e.g., Landy v. FDIC, 486 F.2d 139, 168 (3d Cir.1973), cert. denied 416 U.S. 960 (1974); Wessel v. Buhler, 437 F.2d 279, 282 (9th Cir.1971); Cf. SEC v. Texas Gulf Sulphur Co., 401 F.2d 833, 862 (2d Cir.1968), cert. denied 394 U.S. 976 (1969). In contrast, plaintiff here alleges that the accountants accepted payoffs and otherwise actively collaborated with Yamada for the specific purpose of influencing investors to authorize Yamada to carry out security transactions on its [their] behalf."

In order to fortify the independence of certified public accountants, the Commission has required that whenever the auditor for a registered company is

4. 516 F.2d 811 (2d Cir.1975).

dismissed or resigns, a report must be filed on Form 8–K of any "disagreements" between the auditor and the management of the company within the prior two years. In Securities Act Release No. 5550 (Dec. 20, 1974), the Commission explained certain changes made in this requirement (originally adopted in 1971), as follows:

"4. The item is amended to clarify the intent of the present item which was to require a description of all disagreements, including those where the disagreement was resolved to the satisfaction of the accountant. This clarification was necessary as a result of the experience gained from analyzing 8–Ks filed in which no description was given of disagreements or in which a simple statement was made that there were no unresolved disagreements and staff follow-up was required to obtain the necessary information. Some commentators on Securities Act Release No. 5534 which proposed these amendments requested clarification of whether disagreements at lower staff levels are required to be reported. Disagreements contemplated by this rule occur at the decision-making level; i.e., between personnel of the registrant responsible for presentation of its financial statements and personnel of the accounting firm responsible for rendering its report.

"5. The term 'disagreements' should be interpreted broadly in responding to this item. For example, if an accountant resigned or was dismissed after advising the registrant that he had concluded that internal controls necessary to develop reliable statements did not exist, this would constitute a reportable disagreement in the event of a change of accountants. Similarly, if an accountant were to resign or be dismissed after informing the registrant that he had discovered facts which led him no longer to be able to rely on management representations or which made him unwilling to be associated with statements prepared by management, such situations would constitute reportable disagreements."

Accountants' liability has been the topic of two special issues of law journals: Advisors to Management: Responsibilities and Liabilities of Lawyers and Accountants, 30 Bus.Law. 227 (1975); and Symposium on Accounting and the Federal Securities Laws, 28 Vand.L.Rev. 1 (1975). See, also, Note, Failure to Maintain Independence: A Proposed Cause of Action Against Accountants, 62 Tex.L.Rev. 923 (1984); Note, Disciplinary Proceedings Against Accountants: The Need for a More Ascertainable Improper Professional Conduct Standard in the SEC's Rule 2(e), 53 Fordham L.Rev. 351 (1984); Gruenbaum and Steinberg, Accountants' Liability and Responsibility, 13 Loyola U.L.Rev. 247 (1980); Walker, Accountants' Liability, 63 Marq.L.Rev. 243 (1979); Bray, Targeting Attorneys and Accountants for Prosecution and Civil Liability, 36 N.Y.U.Inst.Fed. Taxation 1235 (1978); Lessening the Legal Liability of Auditors, 32 Bus.Law. 1037 (1977); Isbell, An Overview of Accountants' Duties and Liabilities Under the Federal Securities Laws and a Closer Look at Whistle-Blowing, 35 Ohio St. L.J. 261 (1974); Chalmers, Over-accountable Accountants? A Proposal for Clarification of the Legal Responsibilities Stemming from the Audit Function, 16 W. & M.L.Rev. 71 (1974); Miller and Subak, Impact of Federal Securities Laws: Liabilities of Officers, Directors and Accountants, 30 Bus.Law. 387 (1975); Eizenstat and Speer, Accountants' Professional Liability: Expanding Exposure, 22 Fed.Ins.Coun.Q. 7 (1972).

LAWYERS

Most of the cases thus far dealing with the liability of lawyers under the federal securities laws, other than where they were sued as directors (as in the

BarChris case, supra p. 901), have dealt with liability for formal opinions rendered by the lawyer. In Securities and Exchange Commission v. Spectrum, Limited,[5] the Second Circuit held that an attorney was liable in an injunction action by the Commission for the negligent issuance of legal opinions permitting the distribution of unregistered securities in violation of the 1933 Act. The court said: "In assessing liability as an aider and abettor, however, the district judge formulated a requisite standard of culpability—actual knowledge of the improper scheme plus an intent to further that scheme—which we find to be a sharp and unjustified departure from the negligent standard which we have repeatedly held to be sufficient in the context of enforcement proceedings seeking equitable or prophylactic relief." In Securities and Exchange Commission v. Universal Major Industries Corp.[6] the court followed the *Spectrum* case in holding a lawyer liable for negligence, in an SEC injunctive action, for rendering an opinion permitting the distribution of unregistered securities, although it found that with respect to at least one of the securities issues, he knew that it was being illegally distributed. The Supreme Court in the *Aaron* case, supra page 946, has apparently confirmed the actual results of these cases, although that decision will require the Commission to proceed under Section 17(a) of the 1933 Act rather than Rule 10b–5, which it has always alleged as an alternate basis for an injunction in the past. However, in Securities and Exchange Commission v. Haswell, 654 F.2d 698 (10th Cir.1981), the Tenth Circuit affirmed a decision of the district court refusing to issue an injunction against an attorney in connection with an industrial development bond offering, despite the fact that the district court had interpreted Section 17(a) as requiring proof of scienter, contrary to the *Aaron* case, since the court held that the finding of the district court that the defendant had not acted with scienter with regard to any of the federal securities law violations charged was a sufficient basis for denying the injunction even if there had been a negligent violation of Section 17(a). The circuit court said that "the absence of scienter alone supports the denial of the injunction in this case."

In Securities and Exchange Commission v. National Student Marketing Corp.[7] the District Court in the District of Columbia held it would not grant summary judgment to a lawyer with respect to an opinion rendered by him to National Student Marketing to permit its accountants to record a transfer of a subsidiary in a certain fashion, although it also denied the motion of the SEC for summary judgment. In that case the attorney had rendered an opinion that "all of the risks and benefits of ownership" of the subsidiary had passed to the purchaser as of the end of the fiscal year, so as to permit the elimination of the subsidiary's losses on the consolidated statements of National Student Marketing, although he knew that the transaction had actually been carried out after the end of the fiscal year and ante-dated and that the transaction had no economic substance since the purchaser assumed no obligation whatever to pay the purchase price.

In the *BarChris* case the court rejected the contention that the lawyer for the issuer, in a Section 11 case, "expertised" the entire registration statement because he wrote it. The lawyer may of course expertise certain portions of a registration statement, such as an opinion regarding the title to property or the validity of patents or the tax consequences of certain transactions, but normally the only opinion given by the lawyer is that the stock being sold is validly

---

5. 489 F.2d 535 (2d Cir.1973).

6. CCH Fed.Sec.Law Rptr. ¶ 95,229 (S.D.N.Y.1975). See, also, Securities and Exchange Commission v. Coven, 581 F.2d 1020 (2d Cir.1978), cert. denied 440 U.S.

950 (1979); Securities and Exchange Commission v. Management Dynamics, Inc., 515 F.2d 801 (2d Cir.1975).

7. 402 F.Supp. 641 (D.C.D.C.1975).

issued and outstanding, fully paid and non-assessable, which is hardly likely to be wrong. Can a lawyer be held liable for a false or misleading statement in a document issued by his client, merely because he did not assume the responsibility for seeing that it was totally accurate and complete, or perhaps because, although he advised the disclosure of certain information, the client decided otherwise? All plaintiffs, since the malpractice carriers of the lawyers all have money (until such coverage is all cancelled because it has become prohibitively expensive), and apparently some SEC Commissioners favor an affirmative answer to this question, although thus far we have no judicial enlightenment. In a speech which has become famous (or infamous, depending on your point of view), then Commissioner Sommer had the following to say about this question:

"Attorneys' opinions have played other roles as well. They are customarily rendered in connection with the closing of registered public offerings, both by issuer and underwriter counsel, and in those opinions conclusions with respect to disclosure begin to emerge. In opining that a registration statement complies as to 'form' with the requirements of the Securities Act of 1933, often counsel may be saying more about the contents of the statement than he realizes and if his opinion goes to the question of the legality of the offering as distinguished from the securities, certainly clear questions concerning the adequacy of disclosure are raised.

* * *

"Another manifestation of the trends of the law with respect to the role of lawyers is, in my estimation, clearly discerned in the case which has been a consolation to many, the *BarChris* case. The outside counsel for the company was sued as a director of the company under Section 11 of the 1933 Act and the court made clear that its determination of his liability was as a director. But the discussion by the court of his liability is interesting: it all relates to his activities as lawyer in the preparation of the registration statement. For instance, the court said:

'It is claimed that a lawyer [note the court says *lawyer, not director*] is entitled to rely on the statements of his client and that to require him to verify their accuracy would set an unreasonably high standard. This is too broad a generalization. It is all a matter of degree. To require an audit would obviously be unreasonable. On the other hand, to require a check of matters easily verifiable is not unreasonable. Even honest clients make mistakes.'

"I would suggest that had this director been sued *qua* lawyer under Rule 10b–5, the court would have reached the same conclusion for the same reasons. Implicit in the language of the court is the thought that a lawyer preparing a registration statement has an obligation to do more than simply act as the blind scrivener of the thoughts of his client."[8]

In Securities Exchange Act Release No. 17831 (June 1, 1981), the Commission criticized an attorney for an underwriter in connection with an exempt offering of industrial revenue bonds for failing to make any investigation of the issuer or to protest the failure to include in the offering circular any financial statements regarding the past operations of the issuer. The attorney's opinion rendered in connection with the transaction merely went to the questions of exemptions from the 1933 Act and the Trust Indenture Act of 1939. The Commission stated, however, that, "although the opinion letter states that the signator has not independently checked or verified most of the material

---

8. Sommer, The Emerging Responsibilities of the Securities Lawyer, an address to the Banking, Corporation and Business Law Section, New York State Bar Association, Jan. 24, 1974.

statements in the offering circular, Mr. Gotten [the underwriter's counsel], who knew that the issuer was a going concern that had been in operation for a number of years, signed and issued the opinion letter without questioning the omission from the offering circular of financial statements concerning the issuer's prior operating history, reviewing any documents as to the financial status of the issuer, or making inquiry as to results of the operations of prior years. This inquiry was totally inadequate and facilitated the bond closing and the bond sales to the public."

See, also, Junker v. Crory, 650 F.2d 1349 (5th Cir.1981), Stokes v. Lokken, 644 F.2d 779 (8th Cir.1981), and Croy v. Campbell, 624 F.2d 709 (5th Cir.1980), regarding the Section 12(2) and Rule 10b–5 liability of lawyers.

The subject of lawyers' liabilities is dealt with also in the Special Issue of the Business Lawyer previously cited, Advisors to Management: Responsibilities and Liabilities of Lawyers and Accountants, 30 Bus.Law. 227 (1975). See, also, Friedman, Reflections on Carter-Johnson, 13 Inst. on Sec.Reg. 297 (1982); Robins, Policeman, Conscience or Confidant: Thoughts on the Appropriate Response of a Securities Attorney Who Suspects Client Violations of the Federal Securities Laws, 15 John Marshall L.Rev. 373 (1982); Barber, Lawyer Duties in Securities Transactions Under Rule 2(e): The Carter Opinions, 1982 BYU L.Rev. 513 (1982); Dolan, SEC Rule 2(e) After Carter-Johnson: Toward a Reconciliation of Purpose and Scope, 9 Sec.Reg. L.J. 331 (1982); Rosenfeld, Between Rights and Consequences: A Philosophical Inquiry into the Foundations of Legal Ethics in the Changing World of Securities Regulation, 49 Geo. Wash.L.Rev. 462 (1981); Patterson, Limits of the Lawyer's Discretion and the Law of Legal Ethics: National Student Marketing Revisited, 1979 Duke L.J. 1251 (1979); Gruenbaum, Corporate Securities Lawyers' Disclosure Responsibility, Liability to Investors and National Student Marketing Corp., 54 Notre Dame Law 795 (1979); Parker, Attorney Liability Under the Securities Laws After Ernst & Ernst v. Hochfelder, 10 Loyola U.L.Rev. (Los Angeles) 521 (1977); Freeman, Liability of Professionals Under Rule 10b–5, 23 Prac.Law. 45 (1977); Lowenfels, Expanding Public Responsibilities of Securities Lawyers: An Analysis of the New Trend in Standard of Care and Priorities of Duties, 74 Colum.L. Rev. 412 (1974).

THE PROFESSIONAL RESPONSIBILITIES OF SECURITIES LAWYERS

Do the professional responsibilities of lawyers to their clients, and to others, differ from those normally applicable because they are advising their clients with respect to compliance with the federal securities laws? This question has recently been the subject of an intense national debate, which was triggered by the filing by the Securities and Exchange Commission of a complaint against National Student Marketing Corporation and the prestigious New York law firm of White & Case in 1972.[9] The principal transaction attacked in that complaint was a merger of National Student Marketing Corporation with another corporation, where the accountants refused to give a "comfort letter" which was specified as a condition of the closing of the transaction. The party entitled to insist upon that condition nevertheless waived it, and the closing proceeded. The SEC asserted in the complaint that White & Case should have insisted upon a re-solicitation of the proxies for the merger and, if its client had

---

9. Complaint filed by the Commission Feb. 3, 1972, in Securities and Exchange Commission v. National Student Market- ing Corp., CCH Fed.Sec.Law Rptr. ¶ 93,360 (D.C.D.C.1972).

refused, it should have resigned *and* informed the SEC of the facts.[10] It is this final assertion, or the "snitch on your client" doctrine, which has provoked much of the controversy. The Commission seems now to have abandoned this particular assertion in the *Carter and Johnson* case.

In Barker v. Henderson, Franklin, Starnes & Holt [11] the Seventh Circuit stated as follows concerning the assertion by the plaintiff that a law firm representing a charitable foundation (and an accounting firm working for the foundation) should have "blown the whistle" on the activities of the client:

"The extent to which lawyers and accountants should reveal their clients' wrongdoing—and to whom they should reveal—is a question of great moment. There are proposals to change the rules of legal ethics and the SEC's regulations governing accountants. The professions and the regulatory agencies will debate questions raised by cases such as this one for years to come. We express no opinion on whether the Firms did what they should, whether there was malpractice under state law, or whether the rules of ethics (or other fiduciary doctrines) ought to require lawyers and accountants to blow the whistle in equivalent circumstances. We are satisfied, however, that an award of damages under the securities laws is not the way to blaze the trail toward improved ethical standards in the legal and accounting professions. Liability depends on an *existing* duty to disclose. The securities law therefore must lag behind changes in ethical and fiduciary standards. The plaintiffs have not pointed to any rule imposing on either Firm a duty to blow the whistle."

Professor Morgan Shipman has asserted [12] that the securities lawyer doesn't really have any client, but is the attorney to "the situation." This has prompted one lawyer to inquire whether he should send his bill to "the situation"; and, if he did, would the situation pay it?

Commissioner Sommer has asserted, in the speech mentioned above, that a securities lawyer has no right to be an advocate, with his only loyalty to his client, but should maintain a position of independence somewhat akin to that of the auditor. He stated:

"I would suggest that in securities matters (other than those where advocacy is clearly proper) the attorney will have to function in a manner more akin to that of the auditor than to that of the advocate. This means several things. It means he will have to exercise a measure of independence that is perhaps uncomfortable if he is also the close counselor of management in other matters, often including business decisions. It means he will have to be acutely cognizant of his responsibility to the public who engage in securities transactions that would never have come about were it not for his professional presence. It means he will have to adopt the healthy skepticism toward the representations of management which a good auditor must adopt. It means he will have to do the same thing the auditor does when confronted with an intransigent client—resign."

On the other hand, Dean Monroe Freedman asserted [13] that, even without any further development in this direction, the Securities Bar was already a

---

10. The complaint alleged that as a part of the "fraudulent scheme" White & Case and other lawyers sued "failed to insist that the financial statements be revised and shareholders be resolicited, and failing that, to cease representing their respective clients and, under the circumstances, notify the plaintiff Commission concerning the misleading nature of the nine month financial statements."

11. 797 F.2d 490 (7th Cir.1986).

12. Shipman, The Need for SEC Rules to Govern the Duties and Civil Liabilities of Attorneys Under the Federal Securities Statutes, 34 Ohio St.L.J. 231, at 257 (1973).

13. Freedman, A Civil Libertarian Looks at Securities Regulation, 35 Ohio St. L.J. 280, 285 (1974).

"wholly-owned subsidiary of the Securities and Exchange Commission." Whether this is true or not, it appeared that the SEC, or at least some of its members, at one time would have liked to make a take-over bid.

As a result of all this discussion, the American Bar Association adopted in 1975 the Statement of Policy printed above, which some staff members of the SEC promptly described as "outrageous."

After the decision of the Commission in the *Carter and Johnson* case, it followed up on its statement in the opinion that it would propose standards of conduct for lawyers under Rule 2(e) (see the discussion of Rule 2(e) in Chapter 23, below) by issuing for comment on September 21, 1981,[14] a proposal to adopt a "Standard of Conduct Constituting Unethical or Improper Professional Practice Before the Commission". That proposed standard read as follows:

"When a lawyer with significant responsibilities in the effectuation of a company's compliance with the disclosure requirements of the federal securities laws becomes aware that his client is engaged in a substantial and continuing failure to satisfy those disclosure requirements, his continued participation violates professional standards unless he takes prompt steps to end the client's uncompliance."

The Commission stated in its Release that it was not soliciting comments on the Commission's authority to adopt and administer Rule 2(e). Despite this arrogant attitude of the Commission, the proposal was greeted with withering criticism by the Bar, primarily on the issue of whether the Commission had authority to adopt any "standards of professional conduct" for lawyers practicing before it. In particular, the Section of Corporation Banking and Business Law established a special committee to prepare a letter of comment and this letter of comment was officially approved by the Board of Governors of the American Bar Association on November 20, 1981.[15] The letter of comment concluded:

"We regret that the Commission chose to publish the Proposal for public comment. We especially regret that the Commission chose to discourage comments on what we regard as the most important issue it raises. Resolution of that issue is so clearly beyond the Commission's authority, and the notion that the Commission has the power or the responsibility to become a putative bar association is such a poor approach to a complex and difficult set of problems that, in our view, it is not advisable for the Commission to adopt or further consider this or any related proposal. In our view it would be better for the Commission to direct its legal staff to continue their traditional and constructive dialogue with the ABA and other professional groups, including state bar authorities. Dialogues of this nature have served the Commission and the public interest well for nearly fifty years. This is not the time, nor is this issue the cause, to abandon that approach."

After a change in the chairmanship and other personnel of the Commission, this proposal was quietly buried and it has not been heard from since.

In 1983 the American Bar Association, after considerable debate over a draft of new rules of professional conduct produced by a special commission appointed to revise the rules, adopted the Model Rules set out above (p. 1223) emphatically repudiating any obligation of a lawyer to inform on his client unless the disclosure of confidential information received from the client is necessary to prevent the client from committing a criminal act that is "likely to result in imminent death or substantial bodily harm" to another (or necessary for the lawyer to defend himself against allegations relating to the representa-

---

14. 1933 Act Release No. 6344 (SEC Sept. 21, 1981).   **15.** 36 Bus.Law. 915 (1982).

tion). This formulation clearly does not permit a lawyer to disclose confidences received from the client merely to prevent the client from defrauding another person.

One particular aspect of the question of the professional responsibilities of securities lawyers, which created a confrontation between the legal and accounting professions lasting about five years, was raised by the demand of the accountants that the lawyers for a company describe to them in connection with their audit all "contingent liabilities" (i.e., potential lawsuits against the company) of which the lawyers had acquired knowledge in their representation of the company, so that the accountants could publish them to the SEC and to the world in the footnotes to the financial statements, and in particular to the potential plaintiffs who until then might have been unaware of their claims. This did not involve technically any violation of the attorney-client privilege, since the accountants coerced the company into requesting that the information be furnished and thereby waiving the privilege by threatening to qualify their opinion as to the "scope" of the investigation, which would make the financial statements unacceptable to the SEC.

This controversy was finally resolved in January, 1976, by a "compromise" approved by the AICPA and the American Bar Association.[16] Under this compromise, the lawyers and the accountants solved their respective professional problems by throwing all of the responsibility onto the client. Under this joint pronouncement, the lawyer is only required to comment upon so-called "loss contingencies" (the new name for "contingent liabilities") which are "specifically identified" to him by the client and which he is specifically requested to discuss. The lawyer is also required to confirm to the accountant that he understands that it might be his professional responsibility under certain (unidentified) circumstances to resign his employment if the client rejected his advice to make disclosure of a contingent liability.

Since the subjects of lawyers' liability and professional responsibility cannot be separated, all of the articles cited above, page 1236, generally have a bearing on this topic also. In addition, see Slovak, The Ethics of Corporate Lawyers: A Sociological Approach, 1981 A.B.F. Research J. 753 (1981); Pollack, The SEC Lawyer: Who Is His Client and What Are His Responsibilities, 49 Geo.Wash.L. Rev. 453 (1981); Rosenfeld, Between Rights and Consequences: A Philosophical Inquiry Into the Foundations of Legal Ethics in the Changing World of Securities Regulation, 49 Geo.Wash.L.Rev. 462 (1981); Lorne, Attorney-Client Relationships After Carter and Johnson, 3 J. of Comp.L. and Sec.Reg. 151 (1981); Evolving Problems for and Responsibilities of Attorneys under the Federal Securities Laws (Symposium), 36 Bus.Law. 1777–1885 (1981); Bloomquist, Corporate Disclosures of Relationships with Counsel: A Comment on Recent SEC Proposals, 61 Chi.B.Rec. 230 (1980); Gruenbaum, Clients' Frauds and Their Lawyers' Obligations, 68 Geo.L.J. 191 (1979); Lorne, The Corporate and Securities Adviser, the Public Interest, and Professional Ethics, 76 Mich.L. Rev. 423 (1978); Registration Process: The Role of the Lawyer in Disclosure (Symposium), 33 Bus.Law. 1329 (1978); Hoffman, On Learning of Corporate Client's Crime or Fraud—The Lawyer's Dilemma, 33 Bus.Law. 1389 (1978); Garrett, Social Responsibility of Lawyers in Their Professional Capacity, 30 U.Miami L.Rev. 879 (1976); Johnson, The Expanding Responsibilities of Attorneys in Practice Before the SEC, 25 Mercer L.Rev. 637 (1974); Freedman, A Civil Libertarian Looks at Securities Regulation, 35 Ohio St.L.J. 280 (1974);

---

16. American Bar Association, Statement of Policy Regarding Lawyers' Responses to Auditors' Requests for Information (January 15, 1976). The AICPA simultaneously issued a Statement of Auditing Standards which approved the same procedure as the ABA statement.

Small, An Attorney's Responsibilities Under Federal and State Securities Laws: Private Counselor or Public Servant?, 61 Calif.L.Rev. 1189 (1973); Sonde, The Responsibility of Professionals Under the Federal Securities Laws—Some Observations, 68 Nw.U.L.Rev. 1 (1973).

Regarding Rule 2(e), see the note commencing on p. 1560, infra, and the voluminous literature cited therein.

Chapter 18

MATERIALITY, RELIANCE AND CAUSATION

Statutes and Regulations

Securities Act of 1933, §§ 11, 12(2).

Securities Exchange Act of 1934, §§ 10(b), 14(a).

Rules 10b–5, 14a–9.

TSC INDUSTRIES, INC. v. NORTHWAY, INC.

Supreme Court of the United States, 1976.
426 U.S. 438, 96 S.Ct. 2126, 48 L.Ed.2d 757.

MR. JUSTICE MARSHALL delivered the opinion of the Court.

The proxy rules promulgated by the Securities and Exchange Commission under the Securities Exchange Act of 1934 bar the use of proxy statements that are false or misleading with respect to the presentation or omission of material facts. We are called upon to consider the definition of a material fact under those rules, and the appropriateness of resolving the question of materiality by summary judgment in this case.

I

The dispute in this case centers about the acquisition of petitioner TSC Industries, Inc. by petitioner National Industries, Inc. In February 1969 National acquired 34% of TSC's voting securities by purchase from Charles E. Schmidt and his family. Schmidt, who had been TSC's founder and principal shareholder, promptly resigned along with his son from TSC's board of directors. Thereafter, five National nominees were placed on TSC's board, Stanley R. Yarmuth, National's president and chief executive officer, became chairman of the TSC board, and Charles F. Simonelli, National's executive vice president, became chairman of the TSC executive committee. On October 16, 1969, the TSC board, with the attending National nominees abstaining, approved a proposal to liquidate and sell all of TSC's assets to National. The proposal in substance provided for the exchange of TSC Common and Series 1 Preferred Stock for National Series B Preferred Stock and Warrants. On November 12, 1969, TSC and National issued a joint proxy statement to their shareholders, recommending approval of the proposal. The proxy solicitation was successful, TSC was placed in liquidation and dissolution, and the exchange of shares was effected.

This is an action brought by respondent Northway, a TSC shareholder, against TSC and National, claiming that their joint proxy statement was incomplete and materially misleading in violation of § 14a of the Securities Exchange Act of 1934 and Rules 14a–3 and 14a–9 promulgated thereunder. * * * The basis of Northway's claim under Rule 14a–3 is that TSC and National failed to state in the proxy statement that the transfer of the Schmidt interests in TSC to National had given National control of TSC.

1241

The Rule 14a–9 claim, insofar as it concerns us, is that TSC and National omitted from the proxy statement material facts relating to the degree of National's control over TSC and the favorability of the terms of the proposal to TSC shareholders.

Northway filed its complaint in the United States District Court for the Northern District of Illinois on December 4, 1969, the day before the shareholder meeting on the proposed transaction, but while it requested injunctive relief it never so moved. In 1972 Northway amended its complaint to seek money damages, restitution, and other equitable relief. Shortly thereafter, Northway moved for summary judgment on the issue of TSC's and National's liability. The District Court denied the motion, but granted leave to appeal pursuant to 28 U.S.C. § 1292(b). The Court of Appeals for the Seventh Circuit agreed with the District Court that there existed a genuine issue of fact as to whether National's acquisition of the Schmidt interests in TSC had resulted in a change of control, and that summary judgment was therefore inappropriate on the Rule 14a–3 claim. But the Court of Appeals reversed the District Court's denial of summary judgment to Northway on its 14a–9 claims, holding that certain omissions of fact were material as a matter of law. 512 F.2d 324 (CA7 1975).

We granted certiorari because the standard applied by the Court of Appeals in resolving the question of materiality appeared to conflict with the standard applied by other courts of appeals. 423 U.S. 820 (1975). We now hold that the Court of Appeals erred in ordering that partial summary judgment be granted to Northway.

II

A

As we have noted on more than one occasion, § 14a of the Exchange Act "was intended to promote 'the free exercise of the voting rights of stockholders' by ensuring that proxies would be solicited with 'explanation to the stockholder of the real nature of the questions for which authority to cast his vote is sought.'" Mills v. Electric Auto-Lite Co., 396 U.S. 375, 381 (1970), quoting H.R.Rep. No. 1383, 73d Cong., 2d Sess., 14; S.Rep. No. 792, 73d Cong., 2d Sess., 12. See also J.I. Case Co. v. Borak, 377 U.S. 426, 431 (1964). In *Borak,* the Court held that § 14a's broad remedial purposes required recognition under § 27 of the Exchange Act of an implied private right of action for violations of the provision. And in *Mills,* we attempted to clarify to some extent the elements of a private cause of action for violation of § 14a. In a suit challenging the sufficiency under § 14a and Rule 14a–9 of a proxy statement soliciting votes in favor of a merger, we held that there was no need to demonstrate that the alleged defect in the proxy statement actually had a decisive effect on the voting. So long as the misstatement or omission was material, the causal relation between violation and injury is sufficiently established, we concluded, if "the proxy solicitation itself * * * was an essential link in the accomplishment of the transaction." 396 U.S. at 385. After *Mills,* then, the content given to the notion of materiality assumes heightened significance.[7]

---

7. Our cases have not considered, and we have no occasion in this case to consider, what showing of culpability is required to establish the liability under § 14(a) of a corporation issuing a materially misleading proxy statement, or of a person involved in the preparation of a materially misleading proxy statement. See Gerstle

B

The question of materiality, it is universally agreed, is an objective one, involving the significance of an omitted or misrepresented fact to a reasonable investor. Variations in the formulation of a general test of materiality occur in the articulation of just how significant a fact must be or, put another way, how certain it must be that the fact would affect a reasonable investor's judgment.

The Court of Appeals in this case concluded that material facts include "all facts which a reasonable shareholder *might* consider important." 512 F.2d, at 330 (emphasis added). This formulation of the test of materiality has been explicitly rejected by at least two courts as setting too low a threshold for the imposition of liability under Rule 14a-9. Gerstle v. Gamble-Skogmo, Inc., 478 F.2d 1281, 1301-1302 (CA2 1973); Smallwood v. Pearl Brewing Co., 489 F.2d 579, 603-604 (CA5 1974). In these cases, panels of the Second and Fifth Circuits opted for the conventional tort test of materiality—whether a reasonable man *would* attach importance to the fact misrepresented or omitted in determining his course of action. See Restatement (Second) of Torts § 538(2)(a) (Tent.Draft No. 10, 1964). See also ALI Federal Securities Code § 256(a) (Tent.Draft No. 2, 1973). Gerstle v. Gamble-Skogmo, supra, at 1302, also approved the following standard, which had been formulated with reference to statements issued in a contested election: "whether, taking a properly realistic view, there is a substantial likelihood that the misstatement or omission may have led a stockholder to grant a proxy to the solicitor or to withhold one from the other side, whereas in the absence of this he would have taken a contrary course." General Time Corp. v. Talley Industries, Inc., 403 F.2d 159, 162 (CA2 1968), cert. denied, 393 U.S. 1026 (1969).

In arriving at its broad definition of a material fact as one that a reasonable shareholder *might* consider important, the Court of Appeals in this case relied heavily upon language of this Court in Mills v. Electric Auto-Lite Co., supra. That reliance was misplaced. The *Mills* Court did characterize a determination of materiality as at least "embod[ying] a conclusion that the defect was of such a character that it might have been considered important by a reasonable shareholder who was in the process of deciding how to vote." 396 U.S., at 384. But if any language in *Mills* is to be read as suggesting a general notion of materiality, it can only be the opinion's subsequent reference to materiality as a "requirement that the defect have a significant *propensity* to affect the voting process." Ibid. (emphasis in original). For it was that requirement that the Court said "adequately serves the purpose of ensuring that a cause of action cannot be established by proof of a defect so trivial, or so unrelated to the transaction for which approval is sought, that correction of the defect or imposition of liability would not further the interests protected by § 14(a)." Ibid. Even this language must be read, however, with appreciation that the Court specifically declined to consider the materiality of the omissions in *Mills*. Id., at 381 n. 4. The references to materiality were simply preliminary to our consideration of the sole question in the case—whether proof of the

---

v. Gamble-Skogmo, Inc., 478 F.2d 1281, 1298-1301 (CA2 1973); Richland v. Crandall, 262 F.Supp. 538, 553 n. 12 (SDNY 1967); Jennings & Marsh, Securities Regu- lation: Cases and Materials 1358-1359 (3d ed. 1972). See also Ernst & Ernst v. Hochfelder, 425 U.S. 185 (slip op., at 23 n. 28) (Mar. 30, 1976).

materiality of an omission from a proxy statement must be supplemented by a showing that the defect actually caused the outcome of the vote. It is clear, then, that *Mills* did not intend to foreclose further inquiry into the meaning of materiality under Rule 14a–9.

C

In formulating a standard of materiality under Rule 14a–9, we are guided, of course, by the recognition in *Borak* and *Mills* of the Rule's broad remedial purpose. That purpose is not merely to ensure by judicial means that the transaction, when judged by its real terms, is fair and otherwise adequate, but to ensure disclosures by corporate management in order to enable the shareholders to make an informed choice. See *Mills,* supra, at 381. As an abstract proposition, the most desirable role for a court in a suit of this sort, coming after the consummation of the proposed transaction, would perhaps be to determine whether in fact the proposal would have been favored by the shareholders and consummated in the absence of any misstatement or omission. But as we recognized in *Mills,* supra, at 382 n. 5, such matters are not subject to determination with certainty. Doubts as to the critical nature of information misstated or omitted will be commonplace. And particularly in view of the prophylactic purpose of the Rule and the fact that the content of the proxy statement is within management's control, it is appropriate that these doubts be resolved in favor of those the statute is designed to protect. *Mills,* supra, at 385.

We are aware, however, that the disclosure policy embodied in the proxy regulations is not without limit. See id., at 384. Some information is of such dubious significance that insistance on its disclosure may accomplish more harm than good. The potential liability for a Rule 14a–9 violation can be great indeed, and if the standard of materiality is unnecessarily low, not only may the corporation and its management be subjected to liability for insignificant omissions or misstatements, but also management's fear of exposing itself to substantial liability may cause it simply to bury the shareholder in an avalanche of trivial information—a result that is hardly conducive to informed decisionmaking. Precisely these dangers are presented, we think, by the definition of a material fact adopted by the Court of Appeals in this case—a fact which a reasonable shareholder *might* consider important. We agree with Judge Friendly, speaking for the Court of Appeals in *Gerstle,* that the "might" formulation is "too suggestive of mere possibility, however unlikely." 478 F.2d, at 1302.

The general standard of materiality that we think best comports with the policies of Rule 14a–9 is as follows: an omitted fact is material if there is a substantial likelihood that a reasonable shareholder would consider it important in deciding how to vote. This standard is fully consistent with *Mills* general description of materiality as a requirement that "the defect have a significant *propensity* to affect the voting process." It does not require proof of a substantial likelihood that disclosure of the omitted fact would have caused the reasonable investor to change his vote. What the standard does contemplate is a showing of a substantial likelihood that, under all the circumstances, the omitted fact would have assumed actual significance in the deliberations of the reasonable shareholder. Put another way, there must be a substantial likelihood that the disclosure of the omitted fact would have been viewed by the reasonable investor as having significantly altered the "total mix" of information made available.

D

The issue of materiality may be characterized as a mixed question of law and fact, involving as it does the application of a legal standard to a particular set of facts. In considering whether summary judgment on the issue is appropriate, we must bear in mind that the underlying objective facts, which will often be free from dispute, are merely the starting point for the ultimate determination of materiality. The determination requires delicate assessments of the inferences a "reasonable shareholder" would draw from a given set of facts and the significance of those inferences to him, and these assessments are peculiarly ones for the trier of fact. Only if the established omissions are "so obviously important to an investor, that reasonable minds cannot differ on the question of materiality" is the ultimate issue of materiality appropriately resolved "as a matter of law" by summary judgment. John Hopkins University v. Hutton, 422 F.2d 1124, 1129 (CA4 1969). See Smallwood v. Pearl Brewing Co., 489 F.2d 579, 604 (CA5 1974); Rogen v. Ilikon Corp., 361 F.2d 260, 265–267 (CA1 1966).

III

The omissions found by the Court of Appeals to have been materially misleading as a matter of law involved two general issues—the degree of National's control over TSC at the time of the proxy solicitation, and the favorability of the terms of the proposed transaction to TSC shareholders.

A. *National's Control of TSC*

The Court of Appeals concluded that two omitted facts relating to National's potential influence, or control, over the management of TSC were material as a matter of law. First, the proxy statement failed to state that at the time the statement was issued, the chairman of the TSC board of directors was Stanley Yarmuth, National's president and chief executive officer, and the chairman of the TSC executive committee was Charles Simonelli, National's executive vice president. Second, the statement did not disclose that in filing reports required by the SEC, both TSC and National had indicated that National "may be deemed to be a 'parent' of TSC as that term is defined in the Rules and Regulations under the Securities Act of 1933." * * * App. 490, 512, 517. The Court of Appeals noted that TSC shareholders were relying on the TSC board of directors to negotiate on their behalf for the best possible rate of exchange with National. It then concluded that the omitted facts were material because they were "persuasive indicators that the TSC board was in fact under the control of National, and that National thus 'sat on both sides of the table' in setting the terms of the exchange." 512 F.2d at 333.

We do not agree that the omission of these facts, when viewed against the disclosures contained in the proxy statement, warrants the entry of summary judgment against TSC and National on this record. Our conclusion is the same whether the omissions are considered separately or together.

The proxy statement prominently displayed the facts that National owned 34% of the outstanding shares in TSC, and that no other person owned more than 10%. App. 262–263, 267. It also prominently revealed that five out of ten TSC directors were National nominees, and it recited the positions of those National nominees with National—indicating, among other things, that Stanley Yarmuth was president and a director of National, and that Charles Simonelli was executive vice president and a director of National. App. 267. These disclosures clearly revealed the nature of National's relationship with TSC and alerted the reasonable shareholder to the fact that National exercised a degree of influence over TSC. In view of these disclosures, we certainly cannot say that the additional facts that Yarmuth was chairman of the TSC board of directors and Simonelli chairman of its executive committee were, on this record, so obviously important that reasonable minds could not differ on their materiality.

Nor can we say that it was materially misleading as a matter of law for TSC and National to have omitted reference to SEC filings indicating that National "may be deemed to be a parent of TSC." As we have already noted, both the District Court and the Court of Appeals concluded, in denying summary judgment on the Rule 14a–3 claim, that there was a genuine issue of fact as to whether National actually controlled TSC at the time of the proxy solicitation. We must assume for present purposes, then, that National did not control TSC. On that assumption, TSC and National obviously had no duty to state without qualification that control did exist. If the proxy statements were to disclose the conclusory statements in the SEC filings that National "may be deemed to be a parent of TSC," then it would have been appropriate, if not necessary, for the statement to have included a disclaimer of National control over TSC or a disclaimer of knowledge as to whether National controlled TSC. The net contribution of including the contents of the SEC filings accompanied by such disclaimers is not of such obvious significance, in view of the other facts contained in the proxy statement, that their exclusion renders the statement materially misleading as a matter of law.[15]

B. *Favorability of the Terms to TSC Shareholders*

The Court of Appeals also found that the failure to disclose two sets of facts rendered the proxy statement materially deficient in its presentation of the favorability of the terms of the proposed transaction to TSC shareholders. The first omission was of information, described by the Court of Appeals as "bad news" for TSC shareholders, contained in a letter from an investment banking firm whose earlier favorable opinion of the fairness of the proposed transaction was reported in the proxy statement. The second

---

15. We emphasize that we do not intend to imply that facts suggestive of control need be disclosed only if in fact there was control. If, for example, the proxy statement in this case had failed to reveal National's 34% stock interest in TSC and the presence of five National nominees on TSC's board, these omissions would have rendered the statement materially misleading as a matter of law, regardless of whether National can be said with certainty to have been in "control" of TSC. The reasons for this are twofold. First, to the extent that the existence of control was, at the time of the proxy statement's issuance, a matter of doubt to those responsible for preparing the statement, we would be unwilling to resolve that doubt against disclosure of facts so obviously suggestive of control. Second, and perhaps more to the point, even if National did not "control" TSC, its stock ownership and position on the TSC board make it quite clear that it enjoyed some influence over TSC, which would be of obvious importance to TSC shareholders.

omission related to purchases of National common stock by National and by Madison Fund, Inc., a large mutual fund, during the two years prior to the issuance of the proxy statement.

1

The proxy statement revealed that the investment banking firm of Hornblower & Weeks-Hemphill, Noyes had rendered a favorable opinion on the fairness to TSC shareholders of the terms for the exchange of TSC shares for National securities. In that opinion, the proxy statement explained, the firm had considered, "among other things, the current market prices of the securities of both corporations, the high redemption price of the National Series B Preferred Stock, the dividend and debt service requirements of both corporations, the substantial premium over current market values represented by the securities being offered to TSC stockholders, and the increased dividend income." App. 267.

The Court of Appeals focused upon the reference to the "substantial premium over current market values represented by the securities being offered to TSC stockholders," and noted that any TSC shareholder could calculate the apparent premium by reference to the table of current market prices that appeared four pages later in the proxy statement. App. 271. On the basis of the recited closing prices for November 7, 1969, five days before the issuance of the proxy statement, the apparent premiums were as follows. Each share of TSC Series 1 Preferred, which closed at $12.00 would bring National Series B Preferred Stock and National Warrants worth $15.23—for a premium of $3.23, or 27% of the market value of the TSC Series 1 Preferred. Each share of TSC Common Stock, which closed at $13.25, would bring National Series B Preferred Stock and National Warrants worth $16.19—for a premium of $2.94, or 22% of the market value of TSC Common.

The closing price of the National Warrants on November 7, 1969, was, as indicated in the proxy statement, $5.25. The TSC shareholders were misled, the Court of Appeals concluded, by the proxy statement's failure to disclose that in a communication two weeks after its favorable opinion letter, the Hornblower firm revealed that its determination of the fairness of the offer to TSC was based on the conclusion that the value of the Warrants involved in the transaction would not be their current market price, but approximately $3.50. If the Warrants were valued at $3.50 rather than $5.25, and the other securities valued at the November 7 closing price, the Court figured, the apparent premium would be substantially reduced—from $3.23 (27%) to $1.48 (12%) in the case of the TSC Preferred, and from $2.94 (22%) to $.31 (2%) in the case of TSC Common. "In simple terms," the Court concluded, "TSC and National had received some good news and some bad news from the Hornblower firm. They chose to publish the good news and omit the bad news." 512 F.2d at 335.

It would appear, however, that the subsequent communication from the Hornblower firm, which the Court of Appeals felt contained "bad news," contained nothing new at all. At the TSC board of directors meeting held on October 16, 1969, the date of the initial Hornblower opinion letter, Blancke Noyes, a TSC director and a partner in the Hornblower firm, had pointed out the likelihood of a decline in the market price of National Warrants with the issuance of the Additional Warrants involved in the exchange, and reaffirmed his conclusion that the exchange officer was a fair one nevertheless. The subsequent Hornblower letter, signed by Mr. Noyes, purported merely to explain the basis of the calculations underlying the favorable opinion rendered in the October 16th letter. "In advising TSC as to the fairness of the offer from [National]," Mr. Noyes wrote, "we concluded that the warrants in question had a value of approximately $3.50." On its face, then, the subsequent letter from Hornblower does not appear to have contained anything to alter the favorable opinion rendered in the October 16th letter—including the conclusion that the securities being offered to TSC shareholders represented a "substantial premium over current market values."

The real question, though, is not whether the subsequent Hornblower letter contained anything that altered the Hornblower opinion in any way. It is rather whether the advice given at the October 16th meeting, and reduced to more precise terms in the subsequent Hornblower letter—that there may be a decline in the market price of the National Warrants—had to be disclosed in order to clarify the import of the proxy statement's reference to "the substantial premium over current market values represented by the securities being offered to TSC stockholders." We note initially that the proxy statement referred to the substantial premium as but one of several factors considered by Hornblower in rendering its favorable opinion of the terms of exchange. Still, we cannot assume that a TSC shareholder would focus only on the "bottom line" of the opinion to the exclusion of the considerations that produced it.

TSC and National insist that the reference to a substantial premium required no clarification or supplementation, for the reason that there was a substantial premium even if the National Warrants are assumed to have been worth $3.50. In reaching the contrary conclusion, the Court of Appeals, they contend, ignored the rise in price of TSC securities between early October 1969, when the exchange ratio was set, and November 7, 1969—a rise in price that they suggest was a result of the favorable exchange ratio's becoming public knowledge. When the proxy statement was mailed, TSC and National contend, the market price of TSC securities already reflected a portion of the premium to which Hornblower had referred in rendering its favorable opinion of the terms of exchange. Thus, they note that Hornblower assessed the fairness of the proposed transaction by reference to early October market prices of TSC Preferred, TSC Common, and National Preferred. On the basis of those prices and a $3.50 value for the National Warrants involved in the exchange, TSC and National contend that the premium was substantial. Each share of TSC Preferred, selling in early October at $11, would bring National Preferred Stock and Warrants worth $13.10—for a premium of $2.10, or 19% . And each share of TSC Common, selling in early October at $11.63, would bring National Preferred Stock and Warrants worth $13.25—for a premium of $1.62, or 14%. We certainly cannot say as a matter of law that these premiums were not substantial. And if, as we must assume in considering the appropriateness of summary judgment, the increase in price of TSC's securities from early October to November 7 reflected in large part the market's reaction to the terms of the proposed exchange, it was not materially misleading as a matter of law for the proxy statement to refer to the existence of a substantial premium.

There remains the possibility, however, that although TSC and National may be correct in urging the existence of a substantial premium based upon a $3.50 value for the National Warrants and the early October market prices of the other securities involved in the transaction, the proxy statement misled the TSC shareholder to calculate a premium substantially in excess of that premium. The premiums apparent from early October market prices and a $3.50 value for the National Warrants—19% on TSC Preferred and 14% on TSC Common—are certainly less than those that would be derived through use of the November 7 closing prices listed in the proxy statement—25% on TSC Preferred and 22% on TSC Common. But we are unwilling to sustain a grant of summary judgment to Northway on that basis. To do so we would have to conclude as a matter of law, first, that the proxy statement would have misled the TSC shareholder to calculate his premium on the basis of November 7 market prices, and second, that the difference between that premium and that which would be apparent from early October prices and a $3.50 value for the National Warrants was material. These are questions we think best left to the trier of fact.

2

The final omission that concerns us relates to purchases of National Common Stock by National and by Madison Fund, Inc., a mutual fund. Northway notes that National's board chairman was a director of Madison, and that Madison's president and chief executive, Edward Merkle, was employed by National pursuant to an agreement obligating him to provide at least one day per month for such duties as National might request. Northway contends that the proxy statement, having called the TSC shareholder's attention to the market prices of the securities involved in the proposed transaction, should have revealed substantial purchases of National Common Stock made by National and Madison during the two years prior to the issuance of the proxy statement. In particular, Northway contends that the TSC shareholders should, as a matter of law, have been informed that National and Madison purchases accounted for 8.5% of all reported transactions in National Common Stock during the period between National's acquisition of the Schmidt interests and the proxy solicitation. The theory behind Northway's contention is that disclosure of these purchases would have pointed to the existence, or at least the possible existence, of conspiratorial manipulation of the price of National Common Stock, which would have had an effect on the market price of the National Preferred Stock and Warrants involved in the proposed transaction.

Before the District Court, Northway attempted to demonstrate that the National and Madison purchases were coordinated. The District Court concluded, however, that there was a genuine issue of fact as to whether there was coordination. Finding that a showing of coordination was essential to Northway's theory, the District Court denied summary judgment.

The Court of Appeals agreed with the District Court that "collusion is not conclusively established." 512 F.2d, at 336. But observing that "it is certainly suggested," ibid., the Court concluded that the failure to disclose the purchases was materially misleading as a matter of law. The Court explained:

> "Stockholders contemplating an offer involving preferred shares convertible to common stock and warrants for the purchase of common stock must be informed of circumstances which tend to indicate that the current selling price of the common stock involved may be affected by apparent market manipulations. It was for the shareholders to determine whether the market price of the common shares was relevant to their evaluation of the convertible preferred shares and warrants, or whether the activities of Madison and National actually amounted to manipulation at all." Ibid.

In short, while the Court of Appeals viewed the purchases as significant only insofar as they suggested manipulation of the price of National securities, and acknowledged the existence of a genuine issue of fact as to whether there was any manipulation, the Court nevertheless required disclosure to enable the shareholders to decide whether there was manipulation or not.

The Court of Appeals' approach would sanction the imposition of civil liability on a theory that undisclosed information may *suggest* the existence of market manipulation, even if the responsible corporate officials knew that there was in fact no market manipulation. We do not agree that Rule 14a–9 requires such a result. Rule 14a–9 is concerned only with whether a proxy statement is misleading with respect to its presentation of material facts. If, as we must assume on a motion for summary judgment, there was no collusion or manipulation whatsoever in the National and Madison purchases—that is, if the purchases were made wholly independently for proper corporate and investment purposes, then by Northway's implicit acknowledgment they had no bearing on the soundness and reliability of the market prices listed in the proxy statement, and it cannot have been materially misleading to fail to disclose them.

That is not to say, of course, that the SEC could not enact a rule specifically requiring the disclosure of purchases such as were involved in this case, without regard to whether the purchases can be shown to have been collusive or manipulative. We simply hold that if liability is to be imposed in this case upon a theory that it was misleading to fail to disclose purchases suggestive of market manipulation, there must be some showing that there was in fact market manipulation.

IV

In summary, none of the omissions claimed to have been in violation of Rule 14a–9 were, so far as the record reveals, materially misleading as a matter of law, and Northway was not entitled to partial summary judgment. The judgment of the Court of Appeals is reversed, and the case is remanded for further proceedings consistent with this opinion.

It is so ordered.

MR. JUSTICE STEVENS took no part in the consideration or decision of this case.

WHAT FACTS ARE "MATERIAL"?

For the securities lawyer, "materiality" is the name of the game. If someone would tell him what is material, and what is immaterial, he could include all of the former and exclude all of the latter (in order to make the document "short and concise"), with no concern about the outcome. Unfortunately, the determination of this question comes down ultimately to a question of judgment, and if the judgment of the court later happens to differ from his, his client may be liable for millions of dollars in damages and he may find himself sued as an "aider and abetter" or for malpractice. The test of materiality, while perhaps easy to state in the abstract, may be extremely difficult to apply in a particular factual situation.

We have discussed above the question whether particular types of information are required to be disclosed, i.e., projections of earnings, appraisals, merger negotiations and qualitative information (see Chapter 15, pages 1012–1022, above). Those cases could be analyzed as rulings that the omitted information was not "material" as a matter of law, i.e., that a jury could not reasonably conclude that a reasonable investor would want to know that information before determining his course of action. This would seem to be a conclusion, however, that would be difficult, if not impossible, to reach in many, if not most, of those cases. Those cases are more properly viewed as rulings that the particular type of information involved is simply not required to be disclosed by the policy of the federal securities laws because the burdens and difficulties of making such disclosure outweigh any benefit which might be derived by the investor from receiving the information.

A material fact has been stated to be one "which would materially affect the judgment of the other party to the transaction," [1] or which "in reasonable and objective contemplation might affect the value of the corporation's stock or securities," [2] or to which "a reasonable man would attach importance * * * in determining his choice of action in the transaction in question." [3] In General Time Corp. v. Talley Industries, Inc.,[4] Judge Friendly stated, in the context of a proxy statement, that "The test, we suppose, is whether taking a properly realistic view, there is a substantial likelihood that the misstatement or omission may have led a stockholder to grant a proxy to the solicitor or to withhold one from the other side, whereas in the absence of this he would have taken a contrary course." [5] The *TSC Industries* case basically adopts this latter

---

1. Kardon v. National Gypsum Co., 73 F.Supp. at 800 (E.D.Pa.1947).

2. Kohler v. Kohler Co., 319 F.2d 634, at 642 (7th Cir.1963).

3. List v. Fashion Park, Inc., 340 F.2d 457, at 462 (2d Cir.1965), cert. denied 382 U.S. 811 (1965), quoting from § 538(2)(a) of the Restatement of Torts.

4. 403 F.2d 159 (2d Cir.1968), cert. denied 393 U.S. 1026 (1969).

5. 403 F.2d at 162. Judge Friendly noted that in a proxy contest situation such as involved in that case, the fact that there is a contest, with opportunity for correction by a rival solicitor, would have an important bearing on the determination of materiality.

It has been held that the following were material omissions: failure to clearly tell the shareholders in a proxy statement relating to a merger that only a record shareholder could exercise dissenter's rights, Gruss v. Curtis Publishing Co., 361 F.Supp. 58 (S.D.N.Y.1975); failure clearly to inform the holder of convertible debentures that only published notice of a call for redemption would be given to him unless he registered his debentures, Van Gemert v. The Boeing Co., 520 F.2d 1373 (2d Cir.1975); cf. Abramson v. Burroughs Corp., CCH Fed. Sec.Law Rptr. ¶ 93,456 (S.D.N.Y.1972); failure to state that three nominees for directors were defendants in a Section 16(b) action, Rafal v. Geneen, CCH Fed.Sec.Law Rptr. ¶ 93,505 (E.D.Pa.1972). However, it was held that the failure to state the intention of American Airlines to take the position that the collective bargaining agreements of Western Airlines would not survive a proposed merger with American was not a material fact which had to be

formulation of the test by Judge Friendly. This definition of "materiality" has been applied, not only in actions under Section 14(a) of the 1934 Act, but also in actions brought under Rule 10b–5,[6] Section 12(2) of the 1933 Act,[7] Section 13(d) of the 1934 Act,[8] and Sections 14(d) and 14(e) of the 1934 Act.[9] The question of materiality, as indicated in the *TSC Industries* case, is primarily a question of fact which should not be taken from the jury unless the court can rule as a matter of law that the misrepresentation or nondisclosure could not reasonably be found by a jury to have been material.[10]

The Great "Would—Might" Debate. All of the foregoing statements emphasized that a "realistic" view should be taken of what is required to be stated ("reasonable and objective contemplation"; "properly realistic view"). However, in Mills v. Electric Auto-Lite Co.[11] Justice Harlan threw out a remark that a determination of materiality "embodies a conclusion that the defect was of such a character that it might have been considered important by a reasonable shareholder who was in the process of deciding how to vote." It is perfectly clear that he did not intend by this casual remark to establish any authoritative *definition* of materiality. He had expressly noted earlier in the opinion that the question of materiality was not before the Supreme Court in that case; and he said that a determination of materiality "embodied" this conclusion— not that this conclusion established materiality. Nevertheless, in three subsequent District Court opinions[12] the courts quoted this language as a binding definition of materiality, and apparently construed it as meaning that the court should give summary judgment for the plaintiff if it can imagine any shareholder who conceivably would have wanted to know the omitted fact or have been influenced by the misstatement (i.e., it "might have been" considered important).[13]

In the *Gerstle* case Judge Friendly adopted the explanation of this language of the Supreme Court given above and stated that "a standard tending toward probability rather than toward mere possibility is more appropriate." However, other panels of the Second Circuit continued to insist upon the use of the word "might"[14] and the Seventh Circuit, in the decision reversed by the Supreme Court in the *TSC Industries* case, directly repudiated Judge Friendly's analysis. On the other hand, the Fifth Circuit in Smallwood v. Pearl Brewing Co.[15] expressly followed Judge Friendly's analysis in affirming the trial court's

disclosed. Prettner v. Aston, 339 F.Supp. 273 (D.Del.1972).

6. Huddleston v. Herman & MacLean, 640 F.2d 535 (5th Cir.1981).

7. Simpson v. Southeastern Investment Trust, 697 F.2d 1257 (5th Cir.1983); Alton Box Board Co. v. Goldman, Sachs & Co., 560 F.2d 916 (8th Cir.1977).

8. Securities and Exchange Commission v. Savoy Industries, Inc., 587 F.2d 1149 (D.C.Cir.1978), cert. denied 440 U.S. 913 (1979).

9. Seaboard World Airlines, Inc. v. Tiger International, Inc., 600 F.2d 355 (2d Cir.1979); Prudent Real Estate Trust v. Johncamp Realty, Inc., 599 F.2d 1140 (2d Cir.1979).

10. See, also, Wechsler v. Steinberg, 733 F.2d 1054 (2d Cir.1984).

11. 396 U.S. 375 (1970).

12. Gould v. American Hawaiian Steamship Co., 535 F.2d 761 (3d Cir.1976);

Berman v. Thomson, 312 F.Supp. 1031 (N.D.Ill.1970); Beatty v. Bright, 318 F.Supp. 169 (S.D.Iowa 1970).

13. The corporate defendants in these lawsuits and their securities lawyers would probably agree with Whittier that "Of all sad words of tongue or pen, The saddest are these: 'It might have been.'"

14. See for example, Shapiro v. Merrill Lynch, Pierce, Fenner & Smith, Inc., 495 F.2d 228 (2d Cir.1974); and Securities and Exchange Commission v. Shapiro [no relation], 494 F.2d 1301 (2d Cir.1974). One can imagine a scene where two judges of the Second Circuit passed each other in the corridor, and as they met one said out of the corner of his mouth: "Would!" And the other replied: "Might!"

15. 489 F.2d 579 (5th Cir.1974), cert. denied 419 U.S. 873 (1974). See, also, Rochez Brothers, Inc. v. Rhoades, 491 F.2d 402 (3d Cir.1973), where the Third Circuit

jury charge using the word "would" and the Ninth Circuit in Marx v. Computer Sciences Corp.[16] stated that, "unless clearly directed otherwise by higher authority," it would adhere "to the traditional and less speculative common law language of the objective test."

The Supreme Court has now resolved this debate in favor, neither of "would" nor "might", but of "substantial likelihood." What is a "likelihood"? Does that mean more likely than not? If so, what is a "substantial likelihood"? Does that mean considerably more than a 50% chance? Or considerably more than a 1% chance? Would a 20% chance be a "substantial likelihood"? Assuming one can answer these questions, the test enunciated by the Supreme Court does not, however, require that full disclosure of the omitted or misrepresented fact have a "substantial likelihood" of changing the decision of the voter or investor, but only that it would have had a "substantial likelihood" of assuming "actual significance" in his mind or "significantly altering" the "total mix" of information as he viewed it. The Supreme Court acknowledges its indebtedness to the Securities and Exchange Commission in arriving at this formulation. Did the "would" boys or the "might" boys win, or neither?

The cases dealing with a determination of materiality have most often been concerned with that question in the context of total non-disclosure (and are discussed below) or in the context of an omission or partial non-disclosure (which are discussed supra, at pp. 1022–1025). In any event, each case is unique since the facts being considered for disclosure and the circumstances surrounding them are never the same.

See Ratner, Recent Developments in Litigation Under the Antifraud Provisions: Materiality, Reliance and Causation, and Corporate Mismanagement, 10 Inst.Securities Reg. 445 (1979); Survey: Report of the Advisory Committee on Corporate Disclosure to the Securities and Exchange Commission (Symposium), 26 U.C.L.A.L.Rev. 48 (1978); Herzel and Hagan, Materiality and the Use of SEC Forms, 32 Bus.Law 1177 (1977); Hewitt, Developing Concepts of Materiality and Disclosure, 32 Bus.Law 887 (1977).

MATERIALITY IN THE NON–DISCLOSURE CONTEXT

The question of materiality has been discussed in general above, but arguably that issue takes on a different coloration where the complaint alleges a total non-disclosure than where the defendant is accused of a false statement or a misleading statement. Judge Waterman in the first decision in Securities and Exchange Commission v. Texas Gulf Sulphur Co.[17] adopts on the same page two wildly different tests of materiality. He first quotes Mr. Fleischer to the effect that a material fact is one which is "essentially *extraordinary in nature* and * * * [is] *reasonably certain* to have a substantial effect on the market price of the security * * *." He then states, quoting the same passage from Kohler v. Kohler Co. given above, but with an important italicization, that a material fact is "any fact ' * * * which in reasonable and objective contemplation *might* affect the value of the corporation's stock or securities * * *.' " (The italics in the first quotation are ours; those in the second are Judge Waterman's.) It seems obvious that reasonable certainty and any conceivable possibility (which the emphasis of the word "might" suggests) are not exactly the same thing.

uses the word "would" without any discussion of this dispute.

16. 507 F.2d 485 (9th Cir.1974).

17. 401 F.2d 833 (2d Cir.1968), cert. denied 394 U.S. 976 (1969).

However, in Arber v. Essex Wire Corp.[18] the Sixth Circuit expressly repudiated the application of any stricter test of materiality in a non-disclosure case than in an affirmative misstatement case (while at the same time affirming a judgment for the defendant in that case). The court said: "The district court held that the requisite 'materiality' could be demonstrated only by a showing of nondisclosure of 'special facts' such as mergers or sale of assets, not ascertainable from the books, which 'greatly appreciate' stock value. We think this test is overly restrictive of the Congressional purpose and contrary to the general interpretation of Section 10(b) in the federal courts. Whether undisclosed facts are 'material' does not depend upon whether they concern specific transactions. Nor is it necessary that the facts be of such a nature that they 'greatly appreciate' the stock's value. We adhere to the test stated by the Second Circuit Court of Appeals in the landmark *Texas Gulf Sulphur* decision: whether a reasonable man would have attached importance to the undisclosed facts in determining his choice of action in the particular transaction in question." [19]

Notwithstanding this pronouncement, it would seem that the question of materiality must be judged with some degree of difference in a non-disclosure case than in a case involving a registration statement or a proxy statement. To say that the corporation and an insider are prohibited from purchasing stock unless everything that would be in an S–1 registration statement is disclosed to the seller is to say that they may never purchase any stock (since when there *is* an effective registration statement they are prohibited from purchasing by Rule 10b–6). In fact, almost all of the cases holding insiders liable for such nondisclosure have involved situations "essentially extraordinary in nature", as stated by Mr. Fleischer and momentarily adopted by Judge Waterman.

In List v. Fashion Park, Inc.,[20] the Second Circuit undertook to distinguish between "materiality" and "reliance", stating that the former involved the question whether a "reasonable man" would have been influenced to act differently by the undisclosed fact and the latter whether this particular plaintiff would have been influenced to act differently. However, since it will not be assumed that the plaintiff is an "*unreasonable* man" and he is hardly likely to attempt to prove that, in most cases this distinction does not seem to be particularly useful.[21] It is true that in two cases the sophistication of the plaintiff seller and the particular circumstances inducing him to sell were apparently given great weight by the courts in rendering judgments for the defendants.[22] However, this is merely an illustration of the fact that "materiality" in the abstract is a meaningless concept; it can only be given content by considering the question in the context of all the circumstances of the transaction, including the identity and circumstances of the plaintiff. After carefully distinguishing the two concepts, the Second Circuit in the same case seems to have wrapped them both up in the simple statement: "The proper test is

---

18. 490 F.2d 414 (6th Cir.1974), cert. denied 419 U.S. 830 (1974).

19. 490 F.2d at 418.

20. 340 F.2d 457 (2d Cir.1965), cert. denied 382 U.S. 811 (1965).

21. There is a distinction in this connection between an affirmative misrepresentation and total nondisclosure. In the former case, the representation may be highly material and may have greatly influenced the price of the stock because of the actions of others; but it may not have been made to the plaintiff and therefore he cannot be said to have relied on it in any

direct sense. But a total nondisclosure is necessarily made to the whole world; and the question "Would he have acted differently if he had been told?" is a *hypothetical* question which can be asked of anyone.

22. List v. Fashion Park, Inc., supra note 20; Kohler v. Kohler Co., 319 F.2d 634 (7th Cir.1963). In the first case, the plaintiff was Albert List, the well-known financier and President of List Industries; in the second, he was the Governor of Wisconsin and previously had been employed by the defendant company in an executive capacity for 22 years.

whether the plaintiff would have been influenced to act differently than he did act if the defendant had disclosed to him the undisclosed fact." [23] To this there probably should be added: " * * * and the defendant should have realized that he would be so influenced."

If the other party to the transaction has no choice in the matter, then no information is "material" to him. For example, if a corporation exercises an option to purchase the stock of an employee upon the termination of his employment, nondisclosure of information by the corporation at the time of exercise is irrelevant.[24] Compare, however, the decision of the Third Circuit in Ayres v. Merrill Lynch, Pierce, Fenner & Smith, Inc.,[25] in which the court held that the decision by a former employee of Merrill Lynch to retire was also a decision by him to sell his stock back to the corporation pursuant to a stock repurchase agreement, and, therefore, he could maintain an action under Rule 10b–5 for nondisclosure of plans relating to a future public offering.

Some of the things which have been held "material," in addition to the first drill hole in *Texas Gulf Sulphur,* are: the facts that the promoters of a commuter airline had previously been involved in a "string of airline failures" and that the new venture was to fly the same route as a former bankrupt airline in which they had been involved; [26] lawsuits charging violations of federal and state securities laws against an investment holding company and its investment manager as bearing on a renewal of the advisory agreement; [27] accrual figures reflecting the true value of the business and negotiations in progress for the acquisition of the business by a third party; [28] the initial commencement of negotiations for a merger which could greatly enhance the earnings of the corporation and the preparation of a *pro forma* financial statement showing the results if the two companies were combined; [29] indications of interest from two prospective purchasers in making an offer for the company, although both of these deals later fell through after one 50% owner bought out the other, but the company was sold to a third buyer; [30] a greatly enhanced inventory value which was not revealed in the corporation's financial statements and an intention to realize on it by liquidation; [31] pending negotiations to sell all of the assets of the corporation at a price per share greatly in excess of that paid to the selling shareholder; [32] greatly enhanced earnings since the last published financial statement and an intention to liquidate; [33] the

23. List v. Fashion Park, Inc., 340 F.2d 457 at 463 (2d Cir.1965), cert. denied 382 U.S. 811 (1965).

24. Ryan v. J. Walter Thompson Co., 453 F.2d 444 (2d Cir.1971), cert. denied 406 U.S. 907 (1972); St. Louis Union Trust Co. v. Merrill Lynch, Pierce, Fenner & Smith, Inc., 562 F.2d 1040 (8th Cir.1977), cert. denied 435 U.S. 925 (1978); The Toledo Trust v. Nye, 588 F.2d 202 (6th Cir.1978); Keating v. BBDO International, Inc., 438 F.Supp. 676 (S.D.N.Y.1977); Kerrigan v. Merrill Lynch, Pierce, Fenner & Smith, Inc., 450 F.Supp. 639 (S.D.N.Y.1978).

25. 538 F.2d 532 (3d Cir.1976), cert. denied 429 U.S. 1010. In the *St. Louis Union Trust Company* case, supra note 24, the Eighth Circuit stated that it had "serious doubts about the correctness of the decision" in the *Ayres* case.

26. Securities and Exchange Commission v. Carriba Air, Inc., 681 F.2d 1318 (11th Cir.1982).

27. Zell v. Intercapital Income Securities, Inc., 675 F.2d 1041 (9th Cir.1982).

28. Holmes v. Bateson, 583 F.2d 542 (1st Cir.1978).

29. Securities and Exchange Commission v. Shapiro, 494 F.2d 1301 (2d Cir. 1974).

30. Rochez Brothers, Inc. v. Rhoades, 491 F.2d 402 (3d Cir.1973).

31. Speed v. Transamerica Corp., 99 F.Supp. 808 (D.Del.1951), 135 F.Supp. 176 (D.Del.1955), aff'd 235 F.2d 369 (3d Cir. 1956).

32. Kardon v. National Gypsum Co., 69 F.Supp. 512 (E.D.Pa.1946), 73 F.Supp. 798 (E.D.Pa.1947), 83 F.Supp. 613.

33. In the Matter of Ward La France Truck Corp., 13 S.E.C. 373 (1943).

imminence of a very profitable transaction by the corporation;[34] a firming of prices and an increasing backlog of orders to the extent that a business which had been consistently losing money could now be expected to show a profit;[35] an imminent private placement at $1.50 per share and public offering at $3 per share by the corporation, at a time when the plaintiff's shares were purchased by insiders for 60¢ per share;[36] a readjustment of reported earnings from 85¢ per share for the first five months of the fiscal year to 12¢ for the first six months.[37]

Some of the things which have been held not to be "material," are: the alleged "true motives" of the defendant directors in entering into a merger transaction when all of the material *facts* regarding the transaction were revealed in the proxy statement;[38] negotiations for the sale of a *parent corporation* as related to the purchase from minority shareholders of shares in a *subsidiary* of that corporation;[39] the failure to disclose in connection with a corporate transaction what were alleged to be the "true motives" of the management of the corporation in engaging in the transaction (not in the context of total nondisclosure, but in connection with a proxy statement which revealed all of the *facts* relating to the proposed transaction);[40] the failure to disclose in connection with a merger agreement the low tax basis of the directors' shares and negotiations for the retention of existing management;[41] a prospective 4% stock dividend;[42] a resolution by the Board of Directors to seek a purchaser for the company and an indication from the union manager for the company's employees that he knew of an undisclosed person who might be interested in buying, where the purchase of plaintiff's shares was made prior to the actual commencement of any negotiations;[43] a prospective $500,000 tax refund, the method employed by the company in accounting for past-service costs of its pension plan and the effect that this would have on earnings in future years, and a "work sheet" prepared by the defendant showing "possible" values of the company's stock based on the quoted prices of similar corporations which were publicly-held.[44] Any one of these items, of course, is not very meaningful unless it is considered in the light of all of the facts in the cited case.

---

34. Northern Trust Co. v. Essaness Theatres Corp., 103 F.Supp. 954 (N.D.Ill. 1952).

35. Janigan v. Taylor, 344 F.2d 781 (1st Cir.1965), cert. denied 382 U.S. 879 (1965). In this case the defendant was asked how things were going, and replied: "about the same." Therefore, the court purports not to decide whether there was any affirmative duty to disclose in the absence of any representations. However, if the facts were "material" in the sense that they were necessary to make the statements made not misleading (as the court held), they would seem to be equally material under the disclosure rule, since the other parties are presumably entitled to assume that things are "about the same" if *no* disclosure is made. The appellate court here obviously affirmed the judgment for the plaintiffs with great reluctance under the "clearly erroneous" rule.

36. Ross v. Licht, 263 F.Supp. 395 (S.D. N.Y.1967). (The plaintiff's shares were purchased before, and the public offering made after, a 200–for–1 split. These prices are in terms of the split shares.)

37. Financial Industrial Fund, Inc. v. McDonnell Douglas Corp., supra, p. 1048.

38. Kademian v. Ladish Co., 792 F.2d 614 (7th Cir.1986).

39. Grigsby v. CMI Corporation, 765 F.2d 1369 (9th Cir.1985).

40. Vaughn v. Teledyne, Inc., 628 F.2d 1214 (9th Cir.1980); Rodman v. The Grant Foundation, 608 F.2d 64 (2d Cir.1979); Golub v. PPD Corp., 576 F.2d 759 (8th Cir. 1978).

41. Oscar Gruss & Son v. Natomas Co., CCH Fed.Sec.Law Rptr. ¶ 96,258 (N.D.Cal. 1976).

42. Hafner v. Forest Laboratories, Inc., 345 F.2d 167 (2d Cir.1965).

43. List v. Fashion Park, Inc., supra, note 20.

44. Kohler v. Kohler Co., supra, note 22.

See Helman, Rule 10b–5 Omissions Cases and the Investment Decision, 52 Fordham L.Rev. 399 (1982); Friedman, Efficient Market Theory and Rule 10b–5 Nondisclosure Claims: A Proposal for Reconciliation, 47 Mo.L.Rev. 745 (1982).

MILLS v. ELECTRIC AUTO–LITE CO.

Supreme Court of the United States, 1970.
396 U.S. 375, 90 S.Ct. 616, 24 L.Ed.2d 593.

Mr. Justice Harlan delivered the opinion of the Court.

This case requires us to consider a basic aspect of the implied private right of action for violation of § 14(a) of the Securities Exchange Act of 1934, recognized by this Court in J.I. Case Co. v. Borak, 377 U.S. 426 (1964). As in *Borak* the asserted wrong is that a corporate merger was accomplished through the use of a proxy statement that was materially false or misleading. The question with which we deal is what causal relationship must be shown between such a statement and the merger to establish a cause of action based on the violation of the Act.

I

Petitioners were shareholders of the Electric Auto-Lite Company until 1963, when it was merged into Mergenthaler Linotype Company. They brought suit on the day before the shareholders' meeting at which the vote was to take place on the merger, against Auto-Lite, Mergenthaler, and a third company, American Manufacturing Company, Inc. The complaint sought an injunction against the voting by Auto-Lite's management of all proxies obtained by means of an allegedly misleading proxy solicitation; however, it did not seek a temporary restraining order, and the voting went ahead as scheduled the following day. Several months later petitioners filed an amended complaint, seeking to have the merger set aside and to obtain such other relief as might be proper.

In Count II of the amended complaint, which is the only count before us, petitioners predicated jurisdiction on § 27 of the 1934 Act * * *. They alleged that the proxy statement sent out by the Auto-Lite management to solicit shareholders' votes in favor of the merger was misleading, in violation of § 14(a) of the Act and SEC Rule 14a–9 thereunder. * * * Petitioners recited that before the merger Mergenthaler owned over 50% of the outstanding shares of Auto-Lite common stock, and had been in control of Auto-Lite for two years. American Manufacturing in turn owned about one-third of the outstanding shares of Mergenthaler, and for two years had been in voting control of Mergenthaler and, through it, of Auto-Lite. Petitioners charged that in light of these circumstances the proxy statement was misleading in that it told Auto-Lite shareholders that their board of directors recommended approval of the merger without also informing them that all 11 of Auto-Lite's directors were nominees of Mergenthaler and were under the "control and domination of Mergenthaler." Petitioners asserted the right to complain of this alleged violation both derivatively on behalf of Auto-Lite and as representatives of the class of all its minority shareholders.

On petitioners' motion for summary judgment with respect to Count II, the District Court for the Northern District of Illinois ruled as a matter of law that the claimed defect in the proxy statement was, in light of the circumstances in which the statement was made, a material omission. The District Court concluded, from its reading of the *Borak* opinion, that it had to hold a hearing on the issue whether there was "a causal connection between the finding that there has been a violation of the disclosure requirements of § 14(a) and the alleged injury to the plaintiffs" before it could consider what remedies would be appropriate. (Unreported opinion dated February 14, 1966.)

After holding such a hearing, the court found that under the terms of the merger agreement, an affirmative vote of two-thirds of the Auto-Lite shares was required for approval of the merger, and that the respondent companies owned and controlled about 54% of the outstanding shares. Therefore, to obtain authorization of the merger, respondents had to secure the approval of a substantial number of the minority shareholders. At the stockholders' meeting, approximately 950,000 shares, out of 1,160,000 shares outstanding, were voted in favor of the merger. This included 317,000 votes obtained by proxy from the minority shareholders, votes that were "necessary and indispensable to the approval of the merger." The District Court concluded that a causal relationship had thus been shown, and it granted an interlocutory judgment in favor of petitioners on the issue of liability, referring the case to a master for consideration of appropriate relief. (Unreported findings and conclusions dated Sept. 26, 1967; opinion reported at 281 F.Supp. 826 (1967)).

The District Court made the certification required by 28 U.S.C.A. § 1292(b), and respondents took an interlocutory appeal to the Court of Appeals for the Seventh Circuit. That court affirmed the District Court's conclusion that the proxy statement was materially deficient, but reversed on the question of causation. The court acknowledged that, if an injunction had been sought a sufficient time before the stockholders' meeting, "corrective measures would have been appropriate." 403 F.2d 429, 435 (1968). However, since this suit was brought too late for preventive action, the courts had to determine "whether the misleading statement and omission caused the submission of sufficient proxies," as a prerequisite to a determination of liability under the Act. If the respondents could show, "by a preponderance of probabilities, that the merger would have received a sufficient vote even if the proxy statement had not been misleading in the respect found," petitioners would be entitled to no relief of any kind. Id., at 436.

The Court of Appeals acknowledged that this test corresponds to the common-law fraud test of whether the injured party relied on the misrepresentation. However, rightly concluding that "[r]eliance by thousands of individuals, as here, can scarcely be inquired into" (id., at 436 n. 10), the court ruled that the issue was to be determined by proof of the fairness of the terms of the merger. If respondents could show that the merger had merit and was fair to the minority shareholders, the trial court would be justified in concluding that a sufficient number of shareholders would have approved the merger had there been no deficiency in the proxy statement. In that case respondents would be entitled to a judgment in their favor.

Claiming that the Court of Appeals has construed this Court's decision in *Borak* in a manner that frustrates the statute's policy of enforcement through private litigation, the petitioners then sought review in this Court.

We granted certiorari, * * * believing that resolution of this basic issue should be made at this stage of the litigation and not postponed until after a trial under the Court of Appeals' decision.[4]

II

As we stressed in *Borak*, § 14(a) stemmed from a congressional belief that "[f]air corporate suffrage is an important right that should attach to every equity security bought on a public exchange." H.R.Rep. No. 1383, 73d Cong., 2d Sess., 13. The provision was intended to promote "the free exercise of the voting rights of stockholders" by ensuring that proxies would be solicited with "explanation to the stockholder of the real nature of the questions for which authority to cast his vote is sought." Id., at 14; S.Rep. No. 792, 73d Cong., 2d Sess., 12; see 377 U.S., at 431. The decision below, by permitting all liability to be foreclosed on the basis of a finding that the merger was fair, would allow the stockholders to be bypassed, at least where the only legal challenge to the merger is a suit for retrospective relief after the meeting has been held. A judicial appraisal of the merger's merits could be substituted for the actual and informed vote of the stockholders.

The result would be to insulate from private redress an entire category of proxy violations—those relating to matters other than the terms of the merger. Even outrageous misrepresentations in a proxy solicitation, if they did not relate to the terms of the transaction, would give rise to no cause of action under § 14(a). Particularly if carried over to enforcement actions by the Securities and Exchange Commission itself, such a result would subvert the congressional purpose of ensuring full and fair disclosure to shareholders.

Further, recognition of the fairness of the merger as a complete defense would confront small shareholders with an additional obstacle to making a successful challenge to a proposal recommended through a defective proxy statement. The risk that they would be unable to rebut the corporation's evidence of the fairness of the proposal, and thus to establish their cause of action, would be bound to discourage such shareholders from the private enforcement of the proxy rules that "provides a necessary supplement to Commission action." J.I. Case Co. v. Borak, 377 U.S., at 432.[5]

4. Respondents ask this Court to review the conclusion of the lower courts that the proxy statement was misleading in a material respect. Petitioners naturally did not raise this question in their petition for certiorari, and respondents filed no cross-petition. Since reversal of the Court of Appeals' ruling on this question would not dictate affirmance of that court's judgment, which remanded the case for proceedings to determine causation, but rather elimination of petitioners' rights thereunder, we will not consider the question in these circumstances. * * *

5. The Court of Appeals' ruling that "causation" may be negated by proof of the fairness of the merger also rests on a dubious behavioral assumption. There is no justification for presuming that the shareholders of every corporation are willing to

accept any and every fair merger offer put before them; yet such a presumption is implicit in the opinion of the Court of Appeals. That court gave no indication of what evidence petitioners might adduce, once respondents had established that the merger proposal was equitable, in order to show that the shareholders would nevertheless have rejected it if the solicitation had not been misleading. Proof of actual reliance by thousands of individuals would, as the court acknowledged, not be feasible, see R. Jennings & H. Marsh, Securities Regulation, Cases and Materials 1001 (2d ed. 1968); and reliance on the *nondisclosure* of a fact is a particularly difficult matter to define or prove, see 3 L. Loss, Securities Regulation 1766 (2d ed. 1961). In practice, therefore, the objective fairness of the proposal would seemingly be

Such a frustration of the congressional policy is not required by anything in the wording of the statute or in our opinion in the *Borak* case. Section 14(a) declares it "unlawful" to solicit proxies in contravention of Commission rules, and SEC Rule 14a–9 prohibits solicitations "containing any statement which * * * is false or misleading with respect to any material fact, or which omits to state any material fact necessary in order to make the statements therein not false or misleading * * *." Use of a solicitation which is materially misleading is itself a violation of law, as the Court of Appeals recognized in stating that injunctive relief would be available to remedy such a defect if sought prior to the stockholders' meeting. In *Borak,* which came to this Court on a dismissal of the complaint, the Court limited its inquiry to whether a violation of § 14(a) gives rise to "a federal cause of action for rescission or damages," 377 U.S., at 428. Referring to the argument made by defendants there "that the merger can be dissolved only if it was fraudulent or non-beneficial, issues upon which the proxy material would not bear," the Court stated: "But the causal relationship of the proxy material and the merger are questions of fact to be resolved at trial, not here. We therefore do not discuss this point further." Id., at 431. In the present case there has been a hearing specifically directed to the causation problem. The question before the Court is whether the facts found on the basis of that hearing are sufficient in law to establish petitioners' cause of action, and we conclude that they are.

Where the misstatement or omission in a proxy statement has been shown to be "material," as it was found to be here, that determination itself indubitably embodies a conclusion that the defect was of such a character that it might have been considered important by a reasonable shareholder who was in the process of deciding how to vote. This requirement that the defect have a significant *propensity* to affect the voting process is found in the express terms of Rule 14a–9, and it adequately serves the purpose of ensuring that a cause of action cannot be established by proof of a defect so trivial, or so unrelated to the transaction for which approval is sought, that correction of the defect or imposition of liability would not further the interests protected by § 14(a).

There is no need to supplement this requirement, as did the Court of Appeals, with a requirement of proof of whether the defect actually had a decisive effect on the voting. Where there has been a finding of materiality, a shareholder has made a sufficient showing of causal relationship between the violation and the injury for which he seeks redress if, as here, he proves that the proxy solicitation itself, rather than the particular defect in the solicitation materials, was an essential link in the accomplishment of the transaction. This objective test will avoid the impracticalities of determining how many votes were affected, and, by resolving doubts in favor of those the statute is designed to protect, will effectuate the congressional policy of ensuring that the shareholders are able to make an informed choice when they are consulted on corporate transactions. Cf. Union Pac. R. Co. v. Chicago & N.W.R. Co., 226 F.Supp. 400, 411 (D.C.N.D.

---

determinative of liability. But, in view of the many other factors that might lead shareholders to prefer their current position to that of owners of a larger, combined enterprise, it is pure conjecture to assume that the fairness of the proposal will always be determinative of their vote. Cf. Wirtz v. Hotel, Motel & Club Employees Union, 391 U.S. 492, 508 (1968).

Ill.1964); 2 L. Loss, Securities Regulation 962 n. 411 (2d ed. 1961); 5 id., at 2929-2930 (Supp.1969).[7]

III

Our conclusion that petitioners have established their case by showing that proxies necessary to approval of the merger were obtained by means of a materially misleading solicitation implies nothing about the form of relief to which they may be entitled. We held in *Borak* that upon finding a violation the courts were "to be alert to provide such remedies as are necessary to make effective the congressional purpose," noting specifically that such remedies are not to be limited to prospective relief. 377 U.S., at 433, 434. In devising retrospective relief for violation of the proxy rules, the federal courts should consider the same factors that would govern the relief granted for any similar illegality or fraud. One important factor may be the fairness of the terms of the merger. Possible forms of relief will include setting aside the merger or granting other equitable relief, but, as the Court of Appeals below noted, nothing in the statutory policy "requires the court to unscramble a corporate transaction merely because a violation occurred." 403 F.2d, at 436. In selecting a remedy the lower courts should exercise " 'the sound discretion which guides the determinations of courts of equity,' " keeping in mind the role of equity as "the instrument for nice adjustment and reconciliation between the public interest and private needs as well as between competing private claims." Hecht Co. v. Bowles, 321 U.S. 321, 329-330 (1944), quoting from Meredith v. Winter Haven, 320 U.S. 228, 235 (1943).

* * *

For the foregoing reasons we conclude that the judgment of the Court of Appeals should be vacated and the case remanded to that court for further proceedings consistent with this opinion.

It is so ordered.

[The opinion of MR. JUSTICE BLACK, concurring in part, but dissenting as to the right of petitioners to attorneys' fees, is omitted.]

---

7. We need not decide in this case whether causation could be shown where the management controls a sufficient number of shares to approve the transaction without any votes from the minority. Even in that situation, if the management finds it necessary for legal or practical reasons to solicit proxies from minority shareholders, at least one court has held that the proxy solicitation might be sufficiently related to the merger to satisfy the causation requirement, see Laurenzano v. Einbender, 264 F.Supp. 356 (D.C.E.D.N.Y. 1966); cf. Swanson v. American Consumer Industries, Inc., 415 F.2d 1326, 1331-1332 (C.A.7th Cir.1969); Eagle v. Horvath, 241 F.Supp. 341, 344 (D.C.S.D.N.Y.1965); Globus, Inc. v. Jaroff, 271 F.Supp. 378, 381 (D.C.S.D.N.Y.1967); Comment, Shareholders' Derivative Suit to Enforce a Corporate Right of Action Against Directors Under SEC Rule 10b-5, 114 U.Pa.L.Rev. 578, 582 (1966). But see Hoover v. Allen, 241 F.Supp. 213, 231-232 (D.C.S.D.N.Y.1965); Barnett v. Anaconda Co., 238 F.Supp. 766, 770-774 (D.C.S.D.N.Y.1965); Robbins v. Banner Industries, Inc., 285 F.Supp. 758, 762-763 (D.C.S.D.N.Y.1966). See generally 5 L. Loss, Securities Regulation 2933-2938 (Supp.1969).

LIPTON v. DOCUMATION, INC.

United States Court of Appeals, Eleventh Circuit, 1984.
734 F.2d 740.

Before KRAVITCH and ANDERSON, CIRCUIT JUDGES, and TUTTLE, SENIOR CIRCUIT JUDGE.

KRAVITCH, CIRCUIT JUDGE:

The plaintiffs brought this proposed class action on behalf of themselves and other purchasers of Documation, Inc. securities, alleging violations of § 10(b) of the Securities Exchange Act of 1934 and Securities and Exchange Commission rule 10b–5. As the basis of their complaint, the plaintiffs rely on what has commonly become known as the "fraud on the market" theory. Specifically, they allege that the defendants disseminated into the marketplace financial reports and statements that falsely claimed that Documation had substantial earnings and revenue, when, in fact, the defendants knew that the company had suffered a significant net loss. The plaintiffs further allege that although they did not rely directly on these misleading documents, the documents caused the market price of Documation securities to become artificially inflated and that they detrimentally relied upon the integrity of the market prices in purchasing the securities. The plaintiffs seek recovery for the losses suffered when Documation's true financial situation came to light and the price of the securities declined.

The defendants moved to dismiss the complaint on the ground that it failed to state a claim upon which relief can be granted, because the plaintiffs had failed to allege direct reliance on the purportedly misleading documents. The district court denied the defendants' motion, concluding that the former Fifth Circuit in Shores v. Sklar, 647 F.2d 462 (5th Cir.1981) (en banc), cert. denied, 459 U.S. 1102 (1983),[2] had implicitly adopted the fraud on the market theory and, therefore, the plaintiffs did not need to prove actual reliance to recover. In a subsequent order, however, the district court granted the defendants' motion to certify pursuant to 28 U.S.C. § 1292(b) its prior order holding that this circuit recognizes the fraud on the market theory as "involv[ing] a controlling question of law as to which there is substantial ground for difference of opinion. * * *" In deciding to certify its prior order, the district court adhered to its conclusion that Shores implicitly adopted the fraud on the market theory, but recognized that Shores could be read as approving only a very narrow version of the theory. This court agreed to hear the appeal.

I.

Reliance is one of the essential elements that a plaintiff must prove to recover in a rule 10b–5 action. Dupuy v. Dupuy, 551 F.2d 1005 (5th Cir.), cert. denied, 434 U.S. 911 (1977). Requiring the plaintiff to show that he reasonably relied on the defendants' misrepresentations is a means of establishing the "causal link between the misrepresentation or omission and the injuries suffered by the private plaintiff," id. at 1016, and of ensuring that the federal securities laws do not expose defendants to limitless liability or become transformed into merely private enforcement

---

2. The Eleventh Circuit, in the en banc decision Bonner v. City of Prichard, 661 F.2d 1206, 1209 (11th Cir.1981), adopted as precedent decisions of the former Fifth Circuit rendered prior to October 1, 1981.

mechanisms. Id.; Wilson v. Comtech Telecommunications Corp., 648 F.2d 88, 92 (2d Cir.1981); List v. Fashion Park, Inc., 340 F.2d 457 (2d Cir.), cert. denied, 382 U.S. 811 (1965).

The courts have recognized, however, that in certain contexts requiring the plaintiff to prove actual reliance would effectively preclude recovery although causation in fact did exist. The Supreme Court in Affiliated Ute Citizens v. United States, 406 U.S. 128 (1972), thus held that where the plaintiff's claim is primarily one of failure to disclose,

> positive proof of reliance is not a prerequisite to recovery. All that is necessary is that the facts withheld be material in the sense that a reasonable investor might have considered them important in the making of this decision. * * * This obligation to disclose and this withholding of a material fact established the requisite element of causation in fact.

406 U.S. at 153–54, 92 S.Ct. at 1472 (citations omitted). In nondisclosure cases, therefore, a plaintiff may prove reliance through a rebuttable presumption that he relied on the undisclosed information, subject to the defendant proving that the plaintiff's decision would have been unaffected even if the omitted information had been disclosed. Rifkin v. Crow, 574 F.2d 256, 262–63 (5th Cir.1978).[3]

The Ninth Circuit in Blackie v. Barrack, 524 F.2d 891 (9th Cir.1975), extended the rationale of *Affiliated Ute* to situations where the plaintiff class alleges that deception resulted in inflated security prices on the open market. Finding that in such a context proof of direct reliance "imposes an unreasonable and irrelevant evidentiary burden," id. at 907, the court held that the burden of proof shifts to the defendant to show either that the deception was immaterial, that an insufficient number of traders relied on the misleading information to inflate the price, or that the plaintiff purchased the securities knowing of the misrepresentation or would have still purchased the securities despite the misrepresentation. Id. at 906. The court concluded that such a rebuttable presumption would further the goals of the federal securities laws without dispensing with the requirement of causation, because reliance, albeit indirect reliance on the integrity of the market price, would still exist. Id. at 906–07.

Since *Blackie,* four other circuits have adopted the fraud on the market theory to varying degrees for rule 10b–5 actions. See T.J. Raney & Sons, Inc. v. Fort Cobb, Oklahoma Irrigation Fuel Authority, 717 F.2d 1330 (10th Cir.1983), cert. denied, —— U.S. ——, 104 S.Ct. 1285, 79 L.Ed.2d 687 (1984); Panzirer v. Wolf, 663 F.2d 365 (2d Cir.1981), vacated as moot sub nom. Price Waterhouse v. Panzirer, 459 U.S. 1027 (1982); Shores v. Sklar, 647 F.2d 462 (5th Cir.1981) (en banc), cert. denied, 459 U.S. 1102 (1983). No circuit court has expressly rejected the theory, but see, Vervaecke v. Chiles, Heider & Company, Inc., 578 F.2d 713 (8th Cir.1978) (no presumption of reliance where new issues are involved and claims are based on affirmative misrepresentations), and the Supreme Court has yet to address the issue.

---

3. The Court in *Affiliated Ute* did not expressly state that a "presumption" of reliance was created or that it was rebuttable. This circuit, however, as have other courts, has treated the holding of *Affiliat-* ed *Ute* as creating a rebuttable presumption. See Note, The Reliance Requirement in Private Actions under SEC Rule 10b–5, 88 Harv.L.Rev. 584 (1975); Blackie v. Barrack, 524 F.2d 891, 906 n. 22 (9th Cir.1975).

The fraud on the market theory also has received generally favorable treatment from the commentators. See Black, Fraud on the Market: A Criticism of Dispensing with Reliance Requirements in Certain Open Market Transactions, 62 N.C.L.Rev. 435 (1984); Rapp, Rule 10b–5 and "Fraud-On-the-Market"—Heavy Seas Meet Tranquil Shores, 39 Wash. & Lee L.Rev. 861 (1982); Note, Fraud on the Market: An Emerging Theory of Recovery Under SEC Rule 10b–5, 50 Geo.W.L.Rev. 627 (1982); Note, The Fraud-on-the-Market-Theory, 95 Harv.L.Rev. 1143 (1982). The theory has been viewed as most sound where it is used in the context of class actions to eliminate the necessity of each class member proving subjective reliance and where the securities were traded on a developed and open market, so that market prices reflect available information about the corporation.[5] Black, 62 N.C.L.Rev. at 437–38. The theory, however, has been criticized when courts have applied it to undeveloped markets, see Note, 95 Harv.L. Rev. at 1156–58 (criticizing Shores v. Sklar), or used the theory to eliminate the reliance requirement entirely rather than to merely create a rebuttable presumption of reliance, see Black, 62 N.C.L.Rev. at 438–39; Rapp, 39 Wash. & Lee L.Rev. at 888–93 (criticizing Panzirer v. Wolf as using fraud on the market to extend "chain of causation" too far).

II.

It is against this background of case law and commentary that we approach the former Fifth Circuit's en banc decision in *Shores.* In *Shores,* the plaintiff had bought industrial revenue bonds and alleged under rule 10b–5 that the defendant had fraudulently marketed the bonds by, among other acts, the issuance of a misleading Offering Circular. The plaintiff admitted that he had never read the Circular and that he had bought the bonds solely on the basis of his broker's recommendation. The district court had dismissed all of the plaintiff's claims on the ground that the plaintiff could not show reliance.

The en banc court affirmed the dismissal of the plaintiff's "usual 10b–5" claim based on the Offering Circular's alleged misrepresentations and omissions, because the plaintiff had failed to show the essential element of reliance. 647 F.2d at 468. The closely divided court, however, held that the plaintiff had stated a viable claim in alleging a "broader theory [under which] it would have availed him nothing to have read the Offering Circular ∗ ∗ ∗ The securities laws allow an investor to rely on the integrity of the market to the extent that the securities it offers to him for purchase are entitled to be in the market place." Id. at 470–71.

In so holding, the majority distinguished between claims based on rule 10b–5(2) and those based on rule 10b–5(1) and (3). Reliance was necessary under 10b–5(2) because liability under that section is premised directly upon the allegedly misleading statements or omissions in the documents. With regard to 10b–5(1) and (3), however, the majority found that direct reliance on the misleading documents is not required, because the language of those sections is aimed at broader schemes of securities fraud. Accordingly, in that case, the plaintiff's "lack of reliance on the Offering Circular, only one component of the overall scheme, is not determinative. Blackie v.

---

5. The idea that securities traded on a developed market will reflect the available information on the corporation has become known as the "efficient market" thesis. Black, 62 N.C.L.Rev. at 437; see also Note, 95 Harv.L.Rev. at 1154–56.

Barrack, * * *" Id. at 469. Again citing to *Blackie,* the majority concluded that "[m]isrepresentation and omission cases under 10b–5(2) which, as we do, require reliance on the document making the misrepresentation or omitting the material fact are inapposite to a case in which the buyer relied on the integrity of the market to furnish securities which were not the product of a fraudulent scheme." Id. at 471.

Finally, the majority looked to the purpose of the reliance requirement for 10b–5 actions. Finding that reliance is a means of ensuring that causation exists between the defendant's acts and the plaintiff's harm, it reasoned that what constitutes a prima facie showing of causation varies with the factual context:

> Whenever the rule 10b–5 issue shifts from misrepresentation or omission in a document to fraud on a broader scale, the search for causation must shift also. The "reliance" that produces causation in the latter type of case cannot come from reading a document. It may arise from the duty to speak as in *Ute,* a scheme to manipulate the market at a time when a merger had forced a sale as in Schlick [v. Penn Dixie Cement Corp., 507 F.2d 374 (2nd Cir.1974), cert. denied, 421 U.S. 976 (1975)], a scheme to inflate common stock prices by misleading statements as in *Rifkin,* or a claim by a bond buyer that he relied on the market to provide securities that were not fraudulently created as we have here. The most significant common thread in all these precedents is that rule 10b–5 is not limited to a narrow right to recover for knowing fraudulent misrepresentations or omissions in disclosure documents which mislead a securities buyer. The rule is recognized also to provide the basis for a federal cause of action for more elaborate, intentional schemes which deceive or defraud purchasers of securities.

The holding in *Shores* was thus premised on two primary rationales: the expansive language of rule 10b–5(1) and (3) and the different ways in which causation may be demonstrated depending upon the nature of the alleged fraud.

Despite the apparently broad reach of the *Shores* holding and its reliance on *Blackie,* the defendants contend that the majority adopted only a very narrow version of the fraud on the market theory, limiting its operation to the context where the securities would never have been placed on the market but for the fraud. In support of their position, the defendants note that the court stated at one point that "if [the plaintiff] proves no more than that the bonds would have been offered at a lower price or a higher rate, rather than that they would never have been issued or marketed, he cannot recover." Id. at 470. In another passage, the majority similarly observed that the plaintiff's "theory is not that he bought inferior bonds, but that the bonds he bought were fraudulently marketed. The securities laws allow an investor to rely on the integrity of the market to the extent that the securities it offers him for purchase are entitled to be in the market place." Id. at 471.

We believe that much of the confusion surrounding the *Shores* opinion [7] is clarified once the unique fact setting of the case is taken into account.

---

7. The district court read *Shores* as adopting an unqualified version of the fraud on the market theory, but recognized that "there is support for [the] position that *Shores* approved only a very narrow version of the 'fraud on the market' theory." The court below is not alone in its uncertainty of how to read *Shores,* as the

Whereas the "classic" fraud on the market case arises out of transactions on an open and developed market, in *Shores* the plaintiff was buying newly issued bonds. The *Shores* court was therefore faced with the difficult task of applying a doctrine developed in one context, the open market, to the not entirely analogous setting of newly issued securities. Indeed, the *Shores* dissent objected to the majority's opinion not because the majority was adopting the fraud on the market theory, but because it saw the opinion as extending the theory in an unprecedented manner. 647 F.2d at 477–79 (Randall, J., dissenting).

The *Shores* holding was thus necessarily confined to the limited setting of newly issued securities traded on an undeveloped market and did not determine whether the fraud on the market theory should apply to the open market context. It is that question which is now before this court.

III.

Although the *Shores* court did not decide the precise issue before us, we still find that to a large degree the decision dictates that this circuit recognize the fraud on the market theory as a basis for recovery where the defendant's deception inflates open market stock prices. To hold otherwise would result in this circuit adopting the theory in a setting where its applicability has been questioned, and rejecting its use where it best advances the goals of the federal securities laws.

As noted above, the fraud on the market theory finds its greatest justification when applied to class actions alleging fraudulent misrepresentations or omissions that affected security prices on a developed open market. In such a context, it is reasonable to assume that misinformation disseminated into the marketplace will affect the market price. It is also reasonable to allow a plaintiff to allege that he relied on the integrity of the market prices in purchasing the securities and then shift the burden to the defendant to disprove actual reliance. *Blackie,* 524 F.2d at 907.

The *Shores* opinion has been criticized primarily because it extended fraud on the market to new issues in an undeveloped market. In such a setting, it is not necessarily reasonable to presume that misinformation will affect the market price, as information on an undeveloped market does not readily affect market prices and, in the case of new securities, the price will be set by the offeror and underwriters, not the market. See, Note, 95 Harv.L.Rev. at 1156–58; Black, 62 N.C.L.Rev. at 453. Moreover, the causal nexus between the misleading information and the plaintiff's decision to purchase is more direct when it affects a security's market price than when the misleading information goes merely to the legitimacy of the issuance of the securities themselves. See, Rapp, 39 Wash. & Lee L.Rev. at 886–87.

courts and commentators have also disagreed as to whether *Shores* adopted an expansive approach to the fraud on the market theory or a more restrictive version. Compare Kennedy v. Nicastro, 517 F.Supp. 1157 (N.D.Ill.1981) (*Shores* adopted limited version of fraud on the market); Note, 95 Harv.L.Rev. 1143 (1982) with T.J. Raney & Sons v. Fort Cobb Oklahoma Irrigation Fuel Authority, 717 F.2d 1330, 1333 (10th Cir.1983) (*Shores* "extends the protection of rule 10b–5"); Brunelle, The Shores Case—Expansion of the "Fraud-on-the-Market" Doctrine, 9 Sec.Regul.Law Journal 390 (1982); Rapp, 39 Wash. & Lee L.Rev. 861 (1982). See also, Black, 62 N.C.L.Rev. 435 (1984) (*Shores* represents distinct version of fraud on the market); L. Loss, "Fraud" and Civil Liability under the Federal Securities Laws (Federal Judicial Center 1983), p. 58 n. 152 (*Shores* is variation of fraud on the market).

Without impugning the ultimate soundness of the decision in *Shores*, it strikes us as untenable to adopt the fraud on the market theory in a context where its application is most questionable, while precluding its application to transactions in a developed open market, as in this case, where its operation is most justifiable. Moreover, when viewed from this perspective, the language in *Shores* disallowing recovery by a plaintiff where his claim is simply that the price of newly issued securities was adversely affected by a deficient Offering Circular, 647 F.2d at 471, becomes understandable not as a rejection of the general fraud on the market theory, but as a limitation on the theory's application to the unique context of new issue offerings. In such a setting, it is reasonable to allow recovery on the fraud on the market theory where the securities could not have been marketed but for the fraud, because there the information in the Offering Circular and other documents will affect their marketability, but not allow recovery for diminished value because the misinformation will not have an adequate causal nexus to the price. See *T.J. Raney*, 717 F.2d at 1333; Note, Geo.Wash.L.Rev. at 651; Black, 62 N.C.L.Rev. at 453.

* * *

Nor do we find, as the defendants argue, that the legislative history of the Securities Exchange Act of 1934 necessitates a different conclusion because Congress intended to make reliance on the misleading statements a prerequisite for recovery. The fraud on the market theory as articulated in *Blackie* does not eliminate the need for the plaintiff to show reliance; it simply recognizes that reliance may be presumed where securities are traded on the open market, subject to the defendant proving that the misrepresentations were not material or that the plaintiff's decision to purchase was or would have been unaffected if he had known the true facts. *Blackie*, 524 F.2d at 906. The theory thus actually facilitates Congress' intent in enacting the federal securities law by enabling a purchaser to rely on an expectation that the securities markets are free from fraud. Id. at 907.

IV.

Having concluded that the former Fifth Circuit's decision in Shores v. Sklar implicitly approved of the general fraud on the market theory, and that the theory advances the purposes of the Securities Exchange Act of 1934, the district court's order denying the defendants' motion to dismiss the complaint is AFFIRMED.

SCHLICK v. PENN-DIXIE CEMENT CORP.

United States Court of Appeals, Second Circuit, 1974.
507 F.2d 374.

Before OAKES, CIRCUIT JUDGE, and FRANKEL and KELLEHER, DISTRICT JUDGES.

OAKES, CIRCUIT JUDGE:

This appeal is from a judgment dismissing a complaint for failure to state a claim upon which relief may be granted under Fed.R.Civ.P. 12(b)(6). The action is one for damages for alleged violations of the federal securities laws, brought by a minority shareholder of Continental Steel Corporation

(Continental), an Indiana corporation listed on the New York Stock Exchange (NYSE). The alleged violations arose in connection with a merger of Continental into a wholly owned subsidiary of defendant Penn-Dixie Cement Corporation (Penn-Dixie), also listed on the NYSE.

The dismissed complaint alleges that between October, 1967, and October, 1969, Penn-Dixie acquired 1,111,514 shares or approximately 52.9 per cent of the outstanding common stock of Continental. Having thus acquired voting control over Continental, Penn-Dixie instituted management control over the corporation by placing six of its directors and officers on Continental's nine member board of directors. Appellant claims that Penn-Dixie then exercised its control of Continental so as to defraud Continental shareholders.

Generally, Penn-Dixie is said to have manipulated and depressed the market value of Continental stock in relation to that of Penn-Dixie by utilizing Continental's assets for the benefit of Penn-Dixie and to have caused Continental to enter into a merger agreement providing for an unfair exchange ratio based upon manipulated and artificial stock values of the merging parties. On March 14, 1973, the boards of directors of both companies unanimously approved an agreement of merger by which Continental shareholders would receive in exchange for each share of Continental one and one-half shares of Penn-Dixie common stock and a warrant to purchase an additional share of Penn-Dixie. In connection with the merger the complaint further alleges that Penn-Dixie issued a materially defective proxy statement which failed to disclose the manner in which Penn-Dixie had inflated the value of its shares at the expense of Continental. Damages claimed are in an indeterminate amount set at no less than $10 per Continental share, representing the difference in value between the value of the Continental shares in the actual merger and what they would have been worth but for the manipulations of Penn-Dixie.

On the basis of these general allegations, the complaint contains four claims of relief, in separate counts. The first alleges a violation of Section 10(b) of the Securities Exchange Act of 1934 and Rule 10b–5 promulgated thereunder; count two claims a violation of the proxy solicitation provision of Section 14(a) of the Securities Exchange Act of 1934 and Rule 14a–9 thereunder; the third and fourth counts of the complaint are common law counts based upon fraud and unfairness, each of which is pendent to the federal claims. Thus the whole complaint must fail unless one of the federal counts is viable. United Mine Workers v. Gibbs, 383 U.S. 715 (1966).

The district court found that the proxy count of the complaint was defective in that it failed to present "any allegation of injury which was caused by the proxy violations, aside from that claimed to flow from the unequal ratios." Schlick v. Penn-Dixie Cement Corp., No. 73, Civ. 1467 (S.D.N.Y., decided Sept. 26, 1973). In effect, the district court seemed to be saying that the appellant failed to show that the appellees' misstatements or omissions contributed to the kind of injury which the federal securities laws were intended to redress.

In reaching this conclusion, the district court relied heavily on the fact that the allegedly false and misleading proxy statement did not cause Continental minority stockholders any harm other than that caused by the unfair exchange ratio. They were not misled about their rights so as to have failed to take protective action in the form of seeking injunctive relief; rather, the court below continued, appellant chose to bring this action for damages before the merger was finalized. Nor did the complaint allege that other rights such as appraisal rights were lost as a result of appellees' action. On such a showing, the district court regarded the appellant's proxy claim as one based upon what was alleged merely to be an unfair merger. While conceding this might well state a cause of action under state law, Judge Metzner rejected the argument that a federal claim could be maintained.[7]

The dismissal by the court below of appellant's 10b–5 count was based first upon what the district court said was a concession by the appellant that if his "basic claim under the proxy rules cannot be sustained, the 10b claim must also fall for want of the necessary causal connection" and secondly upon a determination that the count was defective because it contained "only conclusory allegations without any specific allegations of fraud or deception as required to support a 10(b) claim." Segal v. Gordon, 467 F.2d 602, 607 (2d Cir.1972); O'Neill v. Maytag, 339 F.2d 764, 767–768 (2d Cir.1964). We disagree with the district court on its dismissal as to each of the federal act claims and hence reverse, for reasons stated below.

I. The Rule 10b–5 Claim.

A. *The sufficiency of the complaint.* We go first to the 10b–5 count of the complaint. That count does allege generally "the engagement in a course of business which operated as a fraud and deceit on the purchasers and holders of Continental stock." If that were all that were alleged, it would fall within this court's rule that "mere conclusory allegations to the effect that defendant's conduct was fraudulent or in violation of rule 10b–5 are insufficient." Segal v. Gordon, 467 F.2d at 607, *quoting* Shemtob v. Shearson, Hammill & Co., 448 F.2d 442, 444 (2d Cir.1971), and O'Neill v. Maytag, supra. But here the complaint contains more than conclusory allegations. Paragraph 15 specifically alleges that Continental bank accounts were utilized by Penn-Dixie as compensating balances for Penn-Dixie's own borrowings and for Penn-Dixie's benefit without compensation or benefit to Continental, thereby depriving Continental of its ability to use its own capital to expand its business and thereby obtaining a more favorable merger exchange ratio. The same paragraph specifically alleges that Continental funds were utilized by Penn-Dixie to engage in a real estate venture in Florida with a "special customer" of Penn-Dixie, for the benefit of Penn-Dixie and without compensation to Continental for the use of its funds. The complaint alleges the charging of excessive intercompany

7. In so holding, the district judge indicated that he did not have to choose between the two competing lines of cases within this circuit on the question whether causation can be shown where the management controls enough votes to approve a transaction without the assent of the minority. This question was specifically left open by the Supreme Court in Mills v. Electric Auto-Lite Co., 396 U.S. 375, 385 n. 7 (1970). It has been answered affirmatively by some district courts, headed by Laurenzano v. Einbender, 264 F.Supp. 356 (E.D.N.Y.1966), and its progeny Heyman v. Heyman, 356 F.Supp. 958, 967–968 (S.D. N.Y.1973) and Weber v. Bartle, 272 F.Supp. 201 (S.D.N.Y.1967). Other district courts have, however, found causation lacking in such a factual setting. See Barnett v. Anaconda Co., 238 F.Supp. 766 (S.D. N.Y.1965), and the cases following its line of reasoning: Hanover v. Zapata Corp., CCH Fed.Sec.L.Rep. ¶ 93,904 at 93,626 (S.D. N.Y.1973); Weiss v. Sunasco, Inc., 295 F.Supp. 824 (S.D.N.Y.1969); Adair v. Schneider, 293 F.Supp. 393 (S.D.N.Y.1968); Robbins v. Banner Industries, Inc., 285 F.Supp. 758 (S.D.N.Y.1966); Hoover v. Allen, 241 F.Supp. 213 (S.D.N.Y.1965).

costs to Continental, thus reducing Continental's income and increasing that of Penn-Dixie. It alleges an accounting change, valuing certain Continental inventories on a last-in, first-out basis rather than average cost as had been done prior to 1971, thereby incurring a $595,000 special income charge reducing Continental's earnings for the year ending December 31, 1972, the year prior to merger. The complaint also alleges an over-inflation of Penn-Dixie assets by including in Penn-Dixie book value the sum of $21,425,000 which was the excess of cost over related net assets attributed to Penn-Dixie's purchase of the common stock of Continental. Finally, it alleges that the appellees caused the Continental pension fund to purchase common stock of Penn-Dixie on the market in order to create a higher price for the shares of Penn-Dixie, which higher price was utilized to obtain an exchange ratio more favorable to Penn-Dixie. * * *

* * *

We come then to the causation question, that is, whether the scheme which appellant alleges took place brought about the injury in fact. As we have said, it is difficult to tell whether Judge Metzner felt that this element of causation was lacking in view of his finding that the proxy violations in question—the misrepresentations and omissions of the appellees—did not cause a federally remediable injury to the appellant. Having thus disposed of the proxy count, Judge Metzner seemingly regarded the 10b–5 claim to be based on precisely the same operative facts, and for that reason dismissed it as well "for want of the necessary causal connection." We disagree with these conclusions.

This is not a case where the 10b–5 claim is based solely upon material omissions or misstatements in the proxy materials. Were it so, concededly there would have to be a showing of both *loss causation*—that the misrepresentations or omissions caused the economic harm—and *transaction causation*—that the violations in question caused the appellant to engage in the transaction in question.[11] The former is demonstrated rather easily by proof of some form of economic damage, here the unfair exchange ratio, which arguably would have been fairer had the basis for valuation been disclosed. Transaction causation requires substantially more. In a misrepresentation case, to show transaction causation a plaintiff must demonstrate that he relied on the misrepresentations in question when he entered into the transaction which caused him harm. 2 Bromberg § 8.6, at 209–11. In an omission or nondisclosure case based upon Rule 10b–5, a plaintiff need not show reliance in order to show transaction causation but must still show that the facts in question were material "in the sense that a reasonable investor might have considered them important" in making his investment decisions. Affiliated Ute Citizens v. United States, 406 U.S. 128, 153–154 (1972). See Shapiro v. Merrill Lynch, Pierce, Fenner & Smith, Inc., 495 F.2d 228, 240 (2d Cir.1974).

Under the 10b–5 count, proof of transaction causation is unnecessary by virtue of the allegations as to the effectuation of a scheme to defraud which includes market manipulation and a merger on preferential terms, of which the proxy omissions and misrepresentations are only one aspect.

---

11. In terms of transaction causation, other methods of conceptualizing the same issue include the doctrines of reliance, materiality and the buyer-seller requirement. See 1 Bromberg § 4.7 (551), at 86; Shapiro v. Merrill Lynch, Pierce, Fenner & Smith, Inc., 495 F.2d 228, 238–240 (2d Cir.1974). See generally Note, Causation and Liability in Private Actions for Proxy Violations, 80 Yale L.J. 107, 123–24 (1970).

Thus appellant need only show loss causation with respect to his claim for relief under 10b–5; Judge Metzner found and we agree that this has been shown. Here the complaint clearly alleges that, as a result of the merger, appellant was forced to sell his Continental shares to Penn-Dixie on the basis of an exchange ratio that reflected adversely the manipulated market value of Continental stock, and that he sustained injury accordingly.

It is not seriously argued that there is a failure to state a claim for relief because there was no "connection" under Rule 10b–5 between the misconduct and the security transaction here involved. Nor could there be, particularly in view of the specific allegation that defendants caused the Continental pension fund to purchase the common stock of Penn-Dixie in the market in order to create a higher price for Penn-Dixie shares and thus obtain a more favorable exchange ratio. In any event, Superintendent of Insurance v. Bankers Life & Casualty Co., supra, and our own Drachman v. Harvey, 453 F.2d 736 (2d Cir.1972) (en banc), rev'g, 453 F.2d 722 (2d Cir. 1971), make it clear that the violations here alleged had a connection with the sale of Continental shares and purchase of Penn-Dixie shares effectuated by the merger. See also Vine v. Beneficial Finance Co., 374 F.2d 627, 635 (2d Cir.), cert. denied, 389 U.S. 970 (1967).

Thus, the complaint completes the showing necessary to state a claim under Rule 10b–5. It alleges a specific scheme to defraud (a scheme which includes the proxy solicitation as a part, but which included substantial collateral conduct as well); the fraud was accomplished in connection with a securities transaction; the appellant was a seller in that transaction; and as a result of the sale, appellant alleges a loss was sustained.

II. The 14a–9 Claim.

As to count two of the complaint based upon alleged proxy violations, as we have said, quite plainly appellant has alleged loss causation or economic loss in that there was an unequal, unfair and disadvantageous merger ratio, undisclosed in the proxy materials, by which he obtained fewer Penn-Dixie shares and warrants than he would have had the appellees' manipulative scheme been revealed. It is axiomatic that fewer shares are worth less on the open market than more shares, and while it is true that "damages should be recoverable only to the extent that they can be shown," Mills v. Electric Auto-Lite Co., 396 U.S. 375, 389 (1970), the complaint alleges that appellant was the holder of 2,000 shares of Continental. Depending upon what the evidence shows in terms of damages, he might well have received in excess of the 3,000 shares of Penn-Dixie which he did in fact obtain had a fair exchange ratio been adopted. Therefore, we must immediately confront the issue whether the proxy violations themselves caused the transaction in question, the exchange. Both types of causation must be shown in order to state a Section 14(a) claim: transaction causation to show a violation of the law from which an appellant may recover, and loss causation to show damages.

The premise underlying the strict view of transaction causation is that Penn-Dixie would have voted to proceed with the merger in any event, irrespective of any misstatements or omissions in the proxy. Even by dissenting to the merger minority stockholders of Continental could not have secured a higher price for their stock than the merger terms offered since under Indiana law, stockholders in a company listed on the NYSE have no appraisal rights. Burns, Ind.Stat.Ann. Title 23, art. I, ch. 5, § 7 (1972). The argument is in short that minority stockholders' votes must be viewed as meaningless since the insiders with a conflict of interest had enough votes to approve the transaction in any event.

This court has said, however, in affirming the second *Laurenzano* case, in which Judge Dooling found on the merits against the plaintiff that "[minority shareholder] approval was not meaningless; minority shareholder approval has value whether or not it is strictly essential to the power to act." Laurenzano v. Einbender, 448 F.2d 1, 5 (2d Cir.1971). See also Lewis v. Bogin, 337 F.Supp. 331, 337 (S.D.N.Y.1972). As the Seventh Circuit said in Swanson v. American Consumer Industries, Inc., 415 F.2d 1326 (7th Cir. 1969) (*Swanson I*), "[t]he power to effect a given result certainly does not negative all possibility of injury resulting from the fraudulent or manipulative use of that power." Id. at 1331–1332. While one need not go so far perhaps as Judge Sprecher, dissenting and concurring in Swanson v. American Consumer Industries, Inc., 475 F.2d 516, 522 (7th Cir.1973) (*Swanson II*), by saying that causation should be conclusively established by the mere solicitation of votes, in a very real sense the shareholders were deceived by the action of those making the corporate decision to merge. Cf. Crane Co. v. Westinghouse Air Brake Co., 419 F.2d 787, 797 (2nd Cir.1969), cert. denied 400 U.S. 822 (1970). See also Vine v. Beneficial Finance Co., 374 F.2d at 635.

We have previously said that a controlling shareholder's "ability to push through the merger—with or without any other shareholder's vote—cannot by itself defeat a claim for federal *injunctive* relief." Popkin v. Bishop, 464 F.2d at 718 (emphasis added) (but denying injunction since full disclosure was made). Again, as was recognized in Heyman v. Heyman, 356 F.Supp. 958, 967–968 (S.D.N.Y.1973), minority shareholders may "have recourse to measures other than the casting of proxies" to oppose those who have "the naked strength to consummate a fraudulent transaction." At least they are in a better position to protect their interests if they have full disclosure of the facts. Cf. Chris-Craft Industries, Inc. v. Piper Aircraft Corp., 480 F.2d 341, 375 (2d Cir.), cert. denied 414 U.S. 910 (1973); Gerstle v. Gamble-Skogmo, Inc., 478 F.2d 1281, 1302–1303 (2d Cir.1973).

* * *

Causation is a concept stemming from the law of torts, but we are here talking about the statutory purpose of the proxy rules, a purpose which, as *Mills* itself pointed out, arises from Congressional belief in "fair corporate suffrage" to obtain which "explanation to the stockholder of the real nature of the questions for which authority to cast his vote is sought." Congressional concern was specifically with conflict of interest transactions. Stock Exchange Practices, S.Rep.No. 1455, 73d Cong., 2d Sess., 74–76 (1934). See also S.Rep.No. 792, 73d Cong., 2d Sess., 12 (1934). Indeed, the addition in 1964 of Securities Exchange Act § 14(c), 15 U.S.C. § 78n(c) (1970), which operates when shareholder action is taken but proxies are not solicited, applies to the very situation when typically no minority votes are needed. That section requires dissemination to shareholders of "information substantially equivalent to the information which would be required to be transmitted if a solicitation were made * * *." Id. There has to be at least as strong a policy for accurate and complete information to the holder, such as the appellant here, whose vote is solicited but not needed. See Bromberg § 4.7(556), at 86.23 (1973). As Judge Fulham wrote in Weiss

v. Sunasco Inc., 316 F.Supp. 1197, 1205 (E.D.Pa.1970), a post-*Mills* decision, "As I understand *Mills,* the proper test is whether the proxy solicitation is 'an essential link in the accomplishment of the transaction' giving rise to the litigation, irrespective of the fact that other possibilities were available to management." The equities call for protection of the minority shareholder when he is the most helpless, as when neither disinterested director nor disinterested shareholder voting exists as a safeguard. To require strict causation would "sanction all manner of fraud and overreaching in the fortuitous circumstance that a controlling shareholder exists." Swanson v. American Consumer Industries, Inc., 415 F.2d at 1331.

* * *

The minority shareholders aside, there are two other purposes served by the disclosure requirements which make a strict causation rule—whether under a 10(b) or a 14(a) claim—antithetical to it:

1. By disclosure the *market* will be informed, so as to permit well-based decisions about buying, selling and holding the securities involved in the transaction. See generally SEC v. Texas Gulf Sulphur Co., 401 F.2d 833 (2d Cir.1968) (en banc), cert. denied, 394 U.S. 976 (1969). Thus, had there been full disclosure here, the merger ratio would have been unfair on its face and the shares of Penn-Dixie in the open market would have sold for less.

2. By virtue of the disclosure either modification or reconsideration of the terms of the merger by those in control might be effectuated. We cannot assume that even a rapacious controlling management would necessarily want to hang its dirty linen out on the line and thereby expose itself to suit or Securities Commission or other action—in terms of reputation and future takeovers. See *Swanson I,* 415 F.2d at 1332; Rosenblatt v. Northwest Airlines, Inc., 435 F.2d 1121, 1124 (2d Cir.1970); Laurenzano v. Einbender, 264 F.Supp. at 361.

In short, we refuse to adopt the narrow view of causation for which the appellees argue. Instead in the light of the *Mills* footnote, *Affiliated Ute,* supra, the Seventh Circuit's *Swanson I* and *Swanson II,* and the other cases in our own circuit above referred to, we are of the view that sufficient causation is alleged so that the complaint must not be dismissed. None of what we say, of course, goes to the merits of the case; that must await trial on the facts.

Judgment dismissing the complaint is hereby reversed and remanded.

FRANKEL, DISTRICT JUDGE (concurring):

I concur in the result and in most of the court's opinion. With all deference, however, I am unable to join completely in the opinion because of those portions which employ the concepts of "loss causation" and "transaction causation." While these terms have had some scholarly currency, as the majority shows, and while they may prove eventually to be useful, I am not convinced at this time that the Circuit ought to be committed to their employment or to their still uncertain implications.

The appeal before us arises on a bare pleading. The terminological questions explored by the majority have not been briefed or argued. It does not appear that the issues as the parties presented them require such exploration.

I am not prepared to find these labels either useful or harmful. I conclude only that, being unnecessary, they ought not to enter into an opinion on the limited questions before the court.

RELIANCE AND CAUSATION

In Affiliated Ute Citizens of Utah v. United States [1] certain Indian tribal assets had been put into a corporation and the stock distributed to the members of the Ute tribe. Two employees of a bank maintained a market in this stock in which they and other Whites assisted by them purchased from the Indians at one price and contemporaneously resold in the market conducted among Whites at the much higher price prevailing in that non-Indian market. The two employees and the employer-bank were sued by 85 Indian sellers alleging a violation of Rule 10b–5. Justice Blackmun stated for the Supreme Court:

"In the light of the congressional philosophy and purpose, so clearly emphasized by the Court, we conclude that the Court of Appeals viewed too narrowly the activities of defendants Gale and Haslem. We would agree that if the two men and the employer bank had functioned merely as a transfer agent, there would have been no duty of disclosure here. But, as the Court of Appeals itself observed, the record shows that Gale and Haslem 'were active in encouraging a market for the UDC stock among non-Indians.' 431 F.2d, at 1345. They did this by soliciting and accepting standing orders from non-Indians. They and the bank, as a result, received increased deposits because of the development of this market. The two men also received commissions and gratuities from the expectant non-Indian buyers. The men, and hence the bank, as the Court found were 'entirely familiar with the prevailing market for the shares at all material times.' 431 F.2d, at 1347. The bank itself had acknowledged, by letter to AUC in January 1958, that 'it would be our duty to see that these transfers were properly made' and that, with respect to the sale of shares, 'the bank would be acting for the individual stockholders.' The mixed-blood sellers 'considered these defendants to be familiar with the market for the shares of stock and relied upon them when they desired to sell their shares.' 431 F.2d, at 1347.

"Clearly, the Court of Appeals was right to the extent that it held that the two employees had violated Rule 10b–5; in the instances specified in that holding the record reveals a misstatement of a material fact, within the proscription of Rule 10b–5(2), namely, that the prevailing market price of the UDC shares was the figure at which their purchases were made.

"We conclude, however, that the Court of Appeals erred when it held that there was no violation of the Rule unless the record disclosed evidence of reliance on material fact misrepresentations by Gale and Haslem. 431 F.2d, at 1348. We do not read Rule 10b–5 so restrictively. To be sure, the second subparagraph of the rule specifies the making of an untrue statement of a material fact and the omission to state a material fact. The first and third subparagraphs are not so restricted. These defendants' activities, outlined above, disclosed, within the very language of one or the other of those subparagraphs, a 'course of business' or a 'device, scheme or artifice' that operated as a fraud upon the Indian sellers. Superintendent of Insurance v. Bankers Life & Casualty Co., supra. This is so because the defendants devised a plan and induced the mixed-blood holders of UDC stock to dispose of their shares without

----

1. 406 U.S. 128 (1972), reh. denied 407 U.S. 916.

disclosing to them material facts that reasonably could have been expected to influence their decisions to sell. The individual defendants, in a distinct sense, were market makers, not only for their personal purchases comprising $8\frac{1}{3}\%$ of the sales, but for the other sales their activities produced. This being so, they possessed the affirmative duty under the Rule to disclose this fact to the mixed-blood sellers. See Chasins v. Smith, Barney and Co., 438 F.2d 1167 (CA2 1970). It is no answer to urge that, as to some of the petitioners, these defendants may have made no positive representation or recommendation. The defendants may not stand mute while they facilitate the mixed-bloods' sales to those seeking to profit in the non-Indian market the defendants had developed and encouraged and with which they were fully familiar. The sellers had the right to know that the defendants were in a position to gain financially from their sales and that their shares were selling for a higher price in that market. Cf., in contrast, § 18(a) of the Act and § 11(a) of the Securities Act of 1933.

"Under the circumstances of this case, involving primarily a failure to disclose, positive proof of reliance is not a prerequisite to recovery. All that is necessary is that the facts withheld be material in the sense that a reasonable investor might have considered them important in the making of this decision. See Mills v. Electric Auto-Lite Co., 396 U.S. 375, 384 (1970); Securities & Exchange Commission v. Texas Gulf Sulphur Co., 401 F.2d 833, 849 (2d Cir. 1968), cert. denied, sub nom. Coates v. Securities & Exchange Commission, 394 U.S. 976 (1969); L. Loss, Securities Regulation, 3876–3880 (Supp.1969); A. Bromberg, Securities Law, Fraud—SEC Rule 10b–5, pts. 2.6 and 8.6 (1967). This obligation to disclose and this withholding of a material fact establish the requisite element of causation in fact. Chasins v. Smith, Barney and Co., 438 F.2d, at 1172." [2]

The *Affiliated Ute* case relied upon *Mills,* and was in turn relied upon in the *Schlick* case, as well as Shapiro v. Merrill Lynch, Pierce, Fenner & Smith, Inc.,[3] as completely eliminating any requirement of reliance in a case of non-disclosure. However, in Titan Group, Inc. v. Faggen [4] Judge Waterman rejected this interpretation of *Affiliated Ute.* He stated:

"On this appeal, Titan argues that reliance is no longer a requisite element in Rule 10b–5 actions involving omissions alleged to be material when it is shown that facts alleged to be material were not disclosed. This result derives, it is contended, from the Supreme Court's decision in Affiliated Ute Citizens v. United States, * * *.

"By this language [which is quoted above] the [Supreme] Court, rather than abolishing reliance as a prerequisite to recovery, was recognizing the frequent difficulty in *proving,* as a practical matter, that the alleged misrepresentation, allegedly relied upon, cause the injury. The parallel elements of materiality and reliance both serve to restrict the potentially limitless thrust of Rule 10b–5 to those situations in which there exists a causation in fact between the act and injury. * * * Causation remains a necessary element in a private action for damages under Rule 10b–5. Shapiro v. Merrill Lynch, Pierce, Fenner and Smith, Inc., 495 F.2d 228 (2 Cir.1974). Unlike instances of affirmative misrepresentation where it can be demonstrated that the injured party relied upon affirmative statements, in instances of total non-disclosure, as in *Affiliated Ute,* it is of course impossible to demonstrate reliance, and resort must perforce be had to materiality, i.e., whether a reasonable man would attach importance to the alleged omissions in determining his course of action." [5]

---

2. 406 U.S. at 152–54.

3. 495 F.2d 228 (2d Cir.1974).

4. 513 F.2d 234 (2d Cir.1975).

5. 513 F.2d at 238–39.

On the other hand, Judge Adams, concurring and dissenting in Kohn v. American Metal Climax, Inc.,[6] decided before *Affiliated Ute,* concluded that the true distinction based upon the "difficulty of proof" was not between misrepresentation and non-disclosure, but between an individual action and a class action. After discussing the *Mills* case, he said:

"Were *Mills* the latest word on the subject of reliance, one might contend that its broad language would be controlling, even in a 10b case. However, subsequent individual private damage cases indicate that the requirement of reliance still has vitality. See Gottlieb v. Sandia American Corp., 452 F.2d 510, 516 (3d Cir.1971); Chasins v. Smith, Barney & Co., 438 F.2d 1167 (2d Cir.1970) (test for reliance is causation in fact); City National Bank v. Vanderboom, 422 F.2d 221 (8th Cir.1970) (reliance necessary in an individual's suit). Thus, the cases seem to fall into two categories: individual damage suits requiring proof of reliance, and class or injunctive actions not requiring proof of reliance beyond the objective standard. Since the present case was brought as a class action for pecuniary relief, at the very least the objective test must be met, and recovery may not be had if reasonable men would not have relied on the material in the Explanatory Statement about which a complaint has been asserted.

"As noted in *Mills,* the objective test was primarily adopted to obviate the need to prove reliance on the part of each member of the class." [7]

The fact is that almost all of the earlier cases discussing reliance and holding that proof of reliance is required were cases of *non-disclosure* involving privately-held corporations and face-to-face dealings.[8] In Cavalier Carpets, Inc. v. Caylor [9] the court held that where there were both misstatements and omissions involved, a jury instruction stating that proof of reliance by the plaintiff was necessary was correct, because of the "practical problems" of a "dual jury instruction on reliance," which would lead to confusion.

What is one to make of all this? Thus far the courts seem to have been incapable of achieving any analytical precision in dealing with this question. In attempting any analysis of this matter it is necessary to distinguish between private transactions in stock not publicly traded and transactions in an organized market (typically giving rise to a class action); between affirmative misrepresentations and non-disclosure; between individual investment decisions and collective action taken at a stockholders' meeting; and between misrepresentations or non-disclosures and the more exotic forms of violations of Rule 10b–5 or other provisions of the securities laws.

WHAT IS RELIANCE?

In a simple case involving an affirmative misrepresentation by a defendant to a plaintiff in connection with his sale of securities to the plaintiff, or purchase of securities from the plaintiff, the concept of "reliance" by the plaintiff would seem to embody two separate questions both of which are designed to determine whether the utterances by the defendant caused the plaintiff to enter into the transaction and therefore his losses which allegedly

6. 458 F.2d 255 (3d Cir.1972), cert. denied 409 U.S. 874 (1972).

7. 458 F.2d at 290.

8. List v. Fashion Park, Inc., 340 F.2d 457 (2d Cir.1965), cert. denied 382 U.S. 811 (1965); Rogen v. Ilikon Corp., 361 F.2d 260 (1st Cir.1966); Kohler v. Kohler Co., 319 F.2d 634 (7th Cir.1963). Compare Gottlieb v. Sandia American Corp., 452 F.2d 510 (3d Cir.1971), cert. denied 404 U.S. 938 (1971).

9. 746 F.2d 749 (11th Cir.1984).

flowed from the transaction. These two questions are: Did the plaintiff believe what the defendant said?; and, was this belief the cause (or, a cause) of the plaintiff's action in entering into the transaction? (One can of course argue about the meaning of the word "cause", as lawyers are so fond of doing. For example, does it mean that "but for" this belief he would not have entered into the transaction, or only that it was a "substantial factor" or an "important factor" in his doing so?)

Obviously, if the plaintiff knew from other sources the truth about the matter allegedly misrepresented, he cannot have believed the defendant and acted upon that belief. By the same token, if the plaintiff regarded the defendant as an inveterate liar, whom he wouldn't believe on a stack of Bibles, and so admitted on the witness stand, it would be impossible to conclude that the plaintiff "relied" on the defendant's misrepresentation. It may also be true that the plaintiff was entering into the transaction for reasons having nothing to do with the matter allegedly misrepresented, and admits that if he had been told the truth rather than a falsehood about that matter, it would not have influenced his decision at all. It is of course naive to expect such admissions to be forthcoming very often in a litigated case, but the truth of the plaintiff's assertion to the contrary can be tested by cross-examination and the surrounding circumstances may be such as to permit the trier of fact to arrive at these conclusions despite any present contention to the contrary by the plaintiff.

Any statement in this situation that "reliance" is not required, but only proof of "causation in fact" is nonsensical and self-contradictory. Utterances cannot cause anything, except a small disturbance of the air, unless they are traced through the mind of the person to whom they are directed, however difficult that may be, and that of course is what the concept of reliance attempts to do.

In a case of non-disclosure, the process becomes not only subjective but hypothetical. If the concept of reliance has any meaning in that context, it must be put in the form of a hypothetical question: Would the plaintiff have acted differently *if* he had known the undisclosed fact? This is a question which can be asked of anyone who did or didn't do something during the time that the information remained undisclosed, and seems to differ little from the question of materiality, i.e., would (might?) a "reasonable person" or the "average investor" have considered the information important?

However, on closer analysis a difference does seem to appear. For example, if the plaintiff knew from other sources what the defendant did not disclose to him, then his conduct could not have been caused in any sense by the defendant's non-disclosure (although this may have been unknown to the defendant, and therefore his conduct may have been "equally reprehensible" as in a case where the plaintiff was in ignorance). And it is just as possible that the particular matter undisclosed was of no consequence to the plaintiff as in a case where he was told a lie about it.[10] Probably the difference boils down to the fact that the statistical probability of proving non-reliance is much less in a non-disclosure case than in an affirmative misrepresentation case.

Where the gravamen of the action is something other than misrepresentation or non-disclosure, then of course the question of reliance does not arise. For example, if the complaint is that the defendant sold $5,000,000 of securities

---

10. See List v. Fashion Park, Inc. and Kohler v. Kohler Co., both supra, note 8, where the courts obviously did not believe that the facts undisclosed would have been of any importance to those particular plaintiffs (Albert List, the noted financier, and Governor Kohler of Wisconsin, who previously for over 20 years had been a top executive of the defendant corporation). While the holding was framed in terms of "materiality", a different plaintiff might well have won each of those cases.

belonging to the corporation and pocketed the proceeds, or used them to pay for a controlling block of the corporation's stock, as in the *Superintendent of Insurance* case, it makes no sense to ask whether anyone relied upon anything. The complaint is about what the defendant did, not what he said or didn't say.

SHOULD RELIANCE BE REQUIRED?

The plaintiff normally need not show any reliance upon the false statement in an action under Section 11; although the defendant may establish a defense by proving that the plaintiff at the time of his acquisition of the security "knew of such untruth or omission." However, by a curious provision at the end of subsection (a), if the corporation sends out to its shareholders an earnings statement covering a period of twelve months after the effective date of the registration statement, a person thereafter acquiring the security must prove reliance in order to recover under Section 11. This may be established "without proof of the reading of the registration statement", but since at that point the prospectus need no longer be delivered to anyone (unless there is an unsold allotment), proof of such reliance would appear to be very difficult.

Under the case law, proof of reliance by the plaintiff in an action under Section 12(2) is not required, since that section makes no mention of such a requirement.[11] In the situation mentioned above where the plaintiff must prove reliance under Section 11, he would normally have no action at all under Section 12(2) against the issuer or any underwriter for a misleading statement in the prospectus for a registered offering, since the provision contemplates that he must purchase in the market more than twelve months after the public offering and he would therefore not be in privity with those persons.

All of the Rule 10b–5 cases involving face-to-face transactions, other than *Affiliated Ute*, seem to have insisted upon the element of reliance and the courts thus far have refused to accept an interpretation of that case as reading reliance entirely out of federal securities law cases.[12] If that were done, as the court said in Clegg v. Conk,[13] liability would be imposed for a misrepresentation which expended "its force entirely upon itself." Should it make a difference that the case is one of non-disclosure rather than misrepresentation? Certainly, the statement of Judge Waterman quoted above, that proof of reliance in a non-disclosure case is "impossible", is simply not true. The plaintiff can take the stand and testify that if he had been told the undisclosed fact, he would not have bought or sold; and this assertion can be tested by cross-examination. For example, if one of the Indians in *Affiliated Ute* had testified on cross-examination that he had a friend at the bank who told him that he was being

11. Alton Box Board Co. v. Goldman, Sachs and Company, 560 F.2d 916 (8th Cir. 1977); The Johns Hopkins University v. Hutton, 422 F.2d 1124 (4th Cir.1970), on remand 326 F.Supp. 250 (D.C.Md.1971), cert. denied 416 U.S. 916 (1974); Gilbert v. Nixon, 429 F.2d 348 (10th Cir.1970). However, the Eighth Circuit stated in the *Alton Box Board Company* case that "some causal relationship between the misleading representation and the sale must be shown."

12. In addition to the *Titan Group* case, supra, note 4, and Clegg v. Conk, infra, note 13, see Reeder v. Mastercraft Electronics Corp., 363 F.Supp. 574 (S.D.N.Y. 1973). In Vervaecke v. Chiles, Heider &

Co., Inc., 578 F.2d 713 (8th Cir.1978), the Eighth Circuit held that it "is not appropriate to apply the Affiliated Ute test [establishing a presumption of reliance] to this case involving primarily *misrepresentation* [as distinguished from nondisclosure] under the second subparagraph of Rule 10b–5." On the other hand, in Lake v. Kidder, Peabody & Co., Inc., CCH Fed. Sec.Law Rptr. ¶ 96,509 (N.D.Ind.1978), the court stated that the presumption of reliance under the Affiliated Ute case would not be indulged where the action is "predicated on personal, face-to-face dealings."

13. 507 F.2d 1351 (10th Cir.1974).

ripped off, and had given him all of the details, including prices and quantities, regarding shares being sold in the White market, it is difficult to believe that the Supreme Court would still have said that reliance was irrelevant in his case.[14] Perhaps all the court was really holding was that trial time should not be taken up with having all of the 85 Indians take the stand to give this type of testimony, or at least that the judgment should not be reversed because the plaintiffs' lawyer didn't do that; and that the defendant had the burden of proving non-reliance as a part of his case if he asserted that defense. (The court says that "positive" proof of reliance is not necessary; does this suggest that "negative" proof of non-reliance would be a defense?)[15] Obviously, the defendant could then call all of the 85 plaintiffs to the stand if he wished, but it would not seem that the defendant's right to constitutional due process should be abridged simply because he is sued by a lot of people.

On the other hand, where there are transactions in an organized market and a class action is brought on behalf of numerous plaintiffs who bought or sold in that market, proof of reliance becomes practically impossible. Green v. Wolf Corp.[16] suggested that there might be separate trials on the issue of reliance after determination of the common issues, but this suggestion is simply an absurdity in the typical class action, where there may be 1,000 or 10,000 or even 100,000 members of the class. In Neuman v. Electronic Specialty Co.[17] Judge Will held that actual reliance by each plaintiff on defendant's statements must be shown. However, we understand that this proof consisted, by consent of counsel on both sides, merely of unsworn answers to a questionnaire (with those who didn't reply to the questionnaire being excluded from the class). On the other hand, in Fischer v. Wolfinbarger,[18] when the defendants wanted to take interrogatories of each of the 3,000 members of the class on the issue of reliance, the District Judge prohibited it and held that each member of the class would be conclusively presumed to have relied if the named plaintiff testified that he did.[19]

In Shapiro v. Merrill Lynch, Pierce, Fenner & Smith, Inc.[20] the court simply dispenses with the element of reliance in this type of case. Obviously, that decision cannot be justified merely on the basis that we will dispense with any element of the cause of action in a class action if it would be too difficult for the plaintiffs' lawyer to prove that element as to all of his involuntary clients. Nevertheless, that decision would seem to be essentially correct because reliance is not really relevant in that type of case.

Assume that a defendant learns on June 1 of highly material inside information about a corporation which will greatly appreciate the value of its

---

14. It is difficult, of course, to imagine any reason why the Indian given this information would still have sold at the lower price. However, it is not at all difficult to imagine the plaintiff doing that in many of the litigated cases; his action would simply have demonstrated conclusively that the information was not material *to him.*

15. The Fifth Circuit has adopted this interpretation of the *Affiliated Ute* case, holding that the "presumption" of reliance established by that case in a situation involving nondisclosure may be rebutted by the defendant. Shores v. Sklar, 610 F.2d 235 (5th Cir.1980); Rifkin v. Crow, 574 F.2d 256 (5th Cir.1978). The Eighth Circuit has also ruled that the *Affiliated Ute* case establishes only a "presumption" of

reliance, which may be rebutted by the defendant. Barnes v. Resource Royalties, Inc., 795 F.2d 1359 (8th Cir.1986).

16. 406 F.2d 291 (2d Cir.1968), cert. denied 395 U.S. 977 (1969).

17. CCH Fed.Sec.Law Rptr. ¶ 92,591 (N.D.Ill.1969).

18. 55 F.R.D. 129 (W.D.Ky.1971).

19. This decision recalls Judge Moore's observation, in another context, that there "should be more constitutional methods of permitting every stockholder to be a Sir Galahad * * *." Brown v. Bullock, 294 F.2d 415, at 425 (2d Cir.1961) (dissenting opinion).

20. Supra, note 3.

stock and that, under the principles previously considered, he then has a duty to disclose it. The price of the stock has been $5 per share for the past year. He does not disclose the information until July 1, and the price of the stock immediately jumps to $10 per share. During the month of June 1,000 persons sell 100,000 shares at $5 to 1,000 other persons in the market. All of the first 1,000 sue the defendant for $500,000 (zeros can be added to this example *ad libitum*). What is the essence of their complaint? Is it that the conduct of the defendant caused them to sell, or caused them to sell during the month of June? Or is it that by not performing his duty in a timely fashion he has deprived them of $500,000 to the enrichment of the other 1,000 persons? It would seem that their basic complaint relates, not to any effect the non-disclosure had on them, but to the effect it had on other people in general and thereby on the market price. (This discussion does not, of course, deal with the question whether a person should be subject to this sort of unlimited liability for non-performance of what is frequently a highly debatable duty.)[21]

This analysis would seem to be equally applicable to a case where there are affirmative misrepresentations of a bullish nature. The buyers in the market are not really complaining that they were induced to buy, although there may be an element of that not present in the non-disclosure case, but that they paid more than they would have if the truth had been told. If there must be a showing of reliance which means that each particular plaintiff must have heard or read the statement of defendant and relied upon it in purchasing, that raises essentially the same problems as a requirement of privity, although the persons who could sue might be different and possibly more numerous. But the persons who purchased, in the words of Section 9(e) of the 1934 Act, "at a price which was affected by" the dissemination of false information would undoubtedly be much larger than those who read or heard and relied upon the specific statements of the defendant. On the other hand, if the requirement of "reliance" can be satisfied merely by the fact that the plaintiff purchased in the rigged market at a price affected by the defendant's dissemination of false information, that would seem to be equivalent to saying that reliance on the part of the plaintiff is not required at all.

It seems clear in either case, however, that the plaintiff should be required to show that the misrepresentation or non-disclosure affected the market price and to what extent.

In the proxy field the situation is somewhat different since collective action is being taken by the shareholders as a body. However, if those who voted affirmatively for the proposed transaction by the corporation did not rely in any sense on the alleged misrepresentation or omission in the proxy statement, and would have voted the same way if full disclosure had been made, then the wrongful conduct of the defendant cannot be said to have caused the transaction from which the injury is alleged to flow.[22] All of the Rule 14a-9 cases

---

21. One answer, which no one else has suggested, might be to give the defendant a class action over against the other 1,000 persons who received the benefit of that non-performance. This suggestion should not raise the vehement objections of the plaintiffs' bar which any hint of curtailing the class action does. The court could appoint a lawyer for the defendant class and *everybody* could get a fee.

22. It may, of course, be claimed that actions by the defendant other than deficiencies in the proxy statement have manipulated the market prices of two com-

panies which are merging, and thereby distorted the merger ratio. Therefore, it may be argued that absent the defendant's wrongful conduct the acquiring company would have been forced to give more to the minority shareholders of the acquired company. This argument is relied on by the court in the *Schlick* case, albeit only in a footnote. In footnote 15 to that opinion the court stated: "In this regard it might well be observed that since the merger ratio here was based upon such factors as market price and recent earnings (Joint Proxy Statement at 3) and since it is al-

have involved publicly-held corporations, since only a registered company is subject to the Proxy Rules, and the courts have given overriding weight to the difficulty of proving reliance.

In Union Pacific Railroad Co. v. Chicago & North Western Railway Co.[23] Judge Hoffman said: "To require direct proof that the votes of a critical number of shares were changed by * * * [the misleading proxy material] would raise insuperable obstacles to relief and nullify the legislative purpose. * * * The substantial probability of a different result if improper evidence had not been submitted suffices to set aside the vote of a jury. The same standard applies in reason to the stockholders' vote."[24] However, he does not refer to any evidence introduced in that case regarding either probability or certainty that the vote was affected, but apparently decides this question by pure speculation on his own part. It is difficult to see how the question could be otherwise decided in the case of a large, publicly-held corporation—it would be physically impossible to call enough stockholders to the stand, and interrogate them as to whether some additional disclosure "would" or "probably would" have influenced their vote, even to give a representative sample.

In the *Mills* case the Supreme Court settled this question (citing the foregoing passage from a prior edition of this book) by holding that if the misstatement or omission was "material", i.e., if a "reasonable" shareholder might have been influenced to vote differently, then there is no need to prove that a majority or any of the actual shareholders were in fact influenced. The court also held that the "fairness" of the transaction voted upon was not sufficient to demonstrate that the shareholders would have approved it if full disclosure had been made to them.

However, the Supreme Court in the *Mills* case left open the question whether the fact that enough shares are in the hands of the alleged wrongdoers to approve the transaction without any other votes will bar any relief under Section 14(a). The *Schlick* case answers this question in the negative, as do most of the prior cases.[25] Some of these prior cases had based this result on the fact that the shareholders had dissenters' rights and needed full and fair information in order to decide whether to demand an appraisal, even though they couldn't stop the transaction. However, the *Schlick* case says that isn't necessary. Of course, in that case there were various wrongful acts charged to the defendants, aside from lack of full disclosure, which allegedly injured the minority.

Can the decision of the Supreme Court that the fact that the transaction was "fair" doesn't matter and the decision of the Second Circuit that the fact that the defendant had the votes doesn't matter be put together, so that the

leged that those prices and earnings were manipulated by the appellees, the omissions in the proxy statement stand as a definite causal link in the transaction in question. But for the omissions and misstatements, the merger terms may have been so obviously unfair that the appellees would not have attempted the transaction on those terms."

23. 226 F.Supp. 400 (N.D.Ill.1964).

24. 226 F.Supp. at 411.

25. Most of the cases are cited in footnote 7 to the court's opinion in the *Schlick* case. To those at least leaning in the direction of *Laurenzano v. Einbender,* which found causation in this situation,

there should be added Swanson v. American Consumer Industries, Inc., 415 F.2d 1326 (7th Cir.1969); Rosenblatt v. Northwest Airlines, Inc., 435 F.2d 1121 (2d Cir. 1970); Loeb v. Whittaker Corp., 333 F.Supp. 484 (S.D.N.Y.1971); Voege v. Ackerman, 364 F.Supp. 72 (S.D.N.Y.1973); Levine v. Biddle Sawyer Corp., 383 F.Supp. 618 (S.D.N.Y.1974). In the case of Barnett v. Anaconda Co., which is the leading case taking the contrary view, the court said: "It scarcely could be said that Anaconda, the alleged villain in the piece, was misled by the claimed false and misleading statements in and omissions from the proxy material, or that the votes of its stock were influenced thereby." 228 F.Supp. at 771.

defendant would be liable for a fair merger approved by his own votes because he accidentally (see the *Gerstle* case, supra, p. 966) put an erroneous statement in the proxy statement? We would then indeed seem to have a case where liability was imposed for a misrepresentation which "expended its force entirely upon itself." [26]

THE "FRAUD ON THE MARKET" THEORY

The Ninth Circuit, in Blackie v. Barrack,[27] originated the "fraud on the market" theory which is discussed at length in the *Lipton* case and which essentially follows the same line of reasoning as that set forth above. The court in the *Blackie* case said: "A purchaser on the stock exchange * * * relies generally on the supposition that the market price is validly set and that no unsuspected manipulation has artificially inflated the price, and thus indirectly on the truth of the representations underlying the stock price— whether he is aware of it or not, the price he pays reflects material misrepresentations. Requiring direct proof from each purchaser that he relied on a particular representation when purchasing would defeat recovery by those whose reliance was indirect, despite the fact that the causational chain is broken only if the purchaser would have purchased stock even had he known of the misrepresentation."

All of the lower court decisions, as indicated in the *Lipton* case, which have considered this question have embraced the "fraud on the market" theory. In Harris v. Union Electric Co.[28] the Eighth Circuit cited and followed the *Lipton* case in applying the "fraud on the market" theory. The court said: "False or misleading information, such as that involved in this case, can actually harm investors directly—through actual reliance, or indirectly—by affecting the market upon which the investor relied and traded. * * * The plaintiffs established UE's misleading prospectus inflated the price of the bonds on the open market, which these later purchasers relied upon in making their investment decisions." [29]

In Levinson v. Basic, Inc.[30] the Sixth Circuit also adopted the "fraud on the market" theory, which it said depends on the establishment of five elements: "The plaintiff must demonstrate (1) that the defendants made public misrepresentations, * * * (2) that the misrepresentations were material, * * * (3) that the stock was traded on an efficient market, * * * (4) that the misrepresentations would induce a reasonable, relying investor to misjudge the value of the stock, * * * and (5) that the plaintiff traded in the stock between the time the misrepresentations were made and the time the truth was revealed." [31] The court stated that there could be no issue, even on rebuttal by the defendant, as to whether individual members of the class relied on the misstatement. The court also stated that a defendant could defend against this presumption of reliance in two ways: "First, of course, a defendant can rebut

---

26. It may be suggested that in this case no injury could be alleged; but that is not true. If the main plant of the acquiring company blew up uninsured two months after the acquisition, and the price of its stock plummeted, the shareholders of the acquired company might easily be able to show that the value of their stock in the acquired company would not have been affected if it had still been a separate entity; and "but for" the merger it would have been.

27. 524 F.2d 891 (9th Cir.1975), cert. denied 429 U.S. 816 (1976).

28. 787 F.2d 355 (8th Cir.1986), appeal pending.

29. 787 F.2d at 367.

30. 786 F.2d 741 (6th Cir.1986), appeal pending.

31. 786 F.2d at 750.

proof of the five elements that give rise to the presumption. Second, a defendant can disprove the presumed facts by showing that 'an insufficient number of traders relied to [distort] the price' or that 'an individual plaintiff [traded] despite knowledge of the falsity of the representation, or that he would have, had he known it.' " [32]

As a practical matter, what these cases have done is to eliminate almost completely any requirement of reliance in any case involving a publicly-held company with actively traded stock. While the courts in the *Lipton* case and the *Levinson* case suggest that the defendant might possibly "rebut" the presumption of reliance on the market by various means, none of these seem to be feasible in the vast majority of cases. This doctrine has therefore apparently restricted the requirement for the plaintiff to prove reliance primarily to a situation where there are face-to-face dealings between the parties with respect to a security which is not actively traded; and even then the plaintiff would presumably have the benefit of the "presumption" of reliance under the *Ute* case if the action is based upon an omission rather than an affirmative misrepresentation. In that type of case, however, the defendant might more easily be able to rebut the presumption of reliance (see the discussion above).

In Shores v. Sklar [33] the Fifth Circuit in an *en banc* opinion, by a vote of twelve to ten (which surely must be the strangest division on a court since the lay Lords stopped voting on appeals in the House of Lords), held that it would dispense with the requirement of reliance on the part of the plaintiff on the basis of this "fraud on the market" theory, but only in a case where it was alleged that the securities being offered were utterly worthless and that the marketing of the securities for any price was itself a fraud on the purchasers. The court said: "Throughout the opinion we refer to these Bonds as being 'fraudulently marketed.' This means the fraudulent scheme alleged by * * * [the plaintiff] was so pervasive that without it the issuer would not have issued, the dealer could not have dealt in, and the buyer could not have bought these Bonds, because they would not have been offered on the market at any price." The plaintiff in that case admitted that he had never read the Offering Circular and therefore did not rely upon any of the alleged misrepresentations or omissions contained therein.

In T.J. Raney & Sons, Inc. v. Fort Cobb, Oklahoma Irrigation Fuel Authority [34] the Tenth Circuit followed the *Shores* case in holding that the plaintiff did not need to prove reliance where there was a fraudulent issue of bonds which should never have been marketed.

This version of "fraud on the market" is of course quite different from the basic theory, as discussed at length in the *Lipton* case, since in this situation there is no pre-existing market for any fraud to be imposed upon or for the plaintiff to rely on. Whether this variation will be as widely accepted as the basic theory remains to be seen.

WHAT "CONNECTION" MUST THERE BE BETWEEN THE "FRAUD" AND THE LOSS ALLEGED?

Under *Birnbaum* and *Blue Chip* there must be a securities transaction either by the individual plaintiffs or by the corporation in order for an action to be maintained under Rule 10b–5. Under Rule 14a–9 there must be a corporate

---

32. 786 F.2d at 750.

33. 647 F.2d 462 (5th Cir.1981), cert. denied 459 U.S. 1102 (1983).

34. 717 F.2d 1330 (10th Cir.1983), cert. denied 465 U.S. 1026 (1984).

decision taken by the shareholders pursuant to a proxy statement involving some sort of corporate transaction, although not necessarily a purchase or sale of securities. For example, a suit could clearly be maintained under Rule 14a–9 complaining about a sale of assets of a corporation to an insider for cash, approval of which was procured by a misleading proxy statement. In either case, however, the securities transaction or the corporate transaction, assuming that it was caused by the defendant's wrongful conduct, must be shown to have resulted in the injury for which the plaintiff wants to be compensated by the defendant.[35] This is apparently what the *Schlick* case meant by "loss causation" as distinguished from "transaction causation."

In the typical case involving a purchase or sale of securities by an individual plaintiff (or plaintiffs), the complaint is that stock which was bought has become valueless or worth less than was paid for it, or that stock which was sold has become worth much more than was received. In that case, there would seem to be no question that the plaintiff's injury resulted from the securities transaction, since if he hadn't bought he would still have his money (or at least that will be presumed, despite the adage that "a fool and his money are soon parted") or if he hadn't sold he would still have the now more valuable stock. (The measurement of that loss is of course another matter, which is considered below.)

Despite the apparently ineluctable nature of the conclusion stated in the preceding paragraph, the Fifth Circuit in Huddleston v. Herman & MacLean [36] stated that the plaintiff, in addition to proving that he relied upon the misrepresentation or omission, must also show that the misrepresentation or omission was the "proximate cause" of the loss subsequently suffered. The court said:

"Causation requires one further step in the analysis: even if the investor would not otherwise have acted, was the misrepresented fact a *proximate* cause of the loss? * * * The plaintiff must prove not only that, had he known the truth, he would not have acted, but in addition that the untruth was in some reasonably direct, or proximate, way responsible for his loss. The causation requirement is satisfied in a Rule 10b–5 case only if the misrepresentation touches upon the reasons for the investment's decline in value. If the investment decision is induced by misstatements or omissions that are material and that were relied on by the claimant, but are not the proximate reason for his pecuniary loss, recovery under the Rule is not permitted."

The court also gave an example in a footnote of what this requirement means, as follows: "For example, an investor might purchase stock in a shipping venture involving a single vessel in reliance on a misrepresentation that the vessel had a certain capacity when in fact it had less capacity than was represented in the prospectus. However, the prospectus does disclose truthfully that the vessel will not be insured. One week after the investment the vessel sinks as a result of a casualty and the stock becomes worthless. In such circumstances, a fact-finder might conclude that the misrepresentation was material and relied upon by the investor but that it did not cause the loss."

The example given by the court necessarily asserts by implication that if the misrepresentation or omission related to the insurance coverage on the vessel, then it *would* have "caused" the loss subsequently suffered by the investor. With all due respect to the Fifth Circuit, utterances to no one can cause a ship to sink (except perhaps the sweet song of the Sirens, which Ulysses frustrated

---

35. See Bloor v. Carro, Spanbock, Londin, Rodman & Fass, 754 F.2d 57 (2d Cir.1985).

36. 640 F.2d 535 (5th Cir.1981).

by lashing himself to the mast); and representations made to an investor (true or false) relating to any subject cannot "cause" the corporation to be without hull insurance on its vessel, although misrepresentations made to the underwriter might provide a defense to an action by the corporation on a policy which it had procured.

To qualify this concept by the use of the phrase "proximate" cause, aside from the dubious nature of applying such a restriction to an intentional tort as distinguished from an action for negligence, does not eliminate this irrationality, since something that is no cause at all can be neither "proximate" nor "remote." The only logical conclusion of this line of reasoning would seem to be that a plaintiff can never recover under Rule 10b–5 because the statements made to him (or the omissions to make statements to him) *cannot* be the cause of the subsequent corporate event which, in turn, causes his loss. It would seem that Judge Frankel was properly suspicious in the *Schlick* case of the catch phrase "loss causation."

All of this is not to say, of course, that the courts cannot, if they are so inclined, impose a requirement in an action under Rule 10b–5 that the fact misrepresented or omitted have some relation to the corporate event, or the existing state of corporate affairs, which causes the decline in the price of the stock or its failure to appreciate in price to the extent anticipated. But to analyze such a requirement in terms of "causation" can only be productive of utter confusion. Why such a requirement should be imposed is, of course, highly debatable, since we are dealing with a situation where the plaintiff must already have established that the defendant engaged in a deliberate (or perhaps "reckless") misrepresentation which caused the plaintiff to be a shareholder of the corporation at the time the ship sank (either literally or metaphorically).

In Hatrock v. Edward D. Jones & Co.,[37] the court held that a plaintiff in a churning case against a broker-dealer did not have to prove "loss causation" because the plaintiff "should not have to prove loss causation where the evil is not the price the investor paid for a security, but the broker's fraudulent inducement of the investor to purchase the security." This analysis would seem to eliminate completely any requirement of "loss causation", since if the misrepresentation is about the price (value) of the security, then the so-called "loss causation" would always be present; and if it is not about that, then loss causation need not be shown.[38]

If the purchase or sale transaction involved is a corporate transaction, and the plaintiff is suing derivatively, the relationship between the transaction and the injury alleged may become much more complicated. Where stock is allegedly issued by a corporation for inadequate or no consideration, or is allegedly repurchased by a corporation for an excessive consideration, there can be no doubt that the purchase or sale is the direct and immediate cause of the alleged injury to the corporation (or more precisely to the other shareholders through the corporation). When the purchase or sale transaction are more remote from the injury complained about, the question arises as to when this connection becomes so attenuated as to snap the thread of Rule 10b–5 jurisdiction. In Dasho v. Susquehanna Corp.[39] it was held that there was a sufficient "connection" between the alleged deception of the shareholders at an annual meeting to reelect directors, at a time when such directors had the fraudulent scheme in mind, and the subsequent carrying out of the fraudulent scheme

---

37. 750 F.2d 767 (9th Cir.1984).

38. This is not intended to suggest that the elimination of this confusing concept would not be a good idea.

39. 380 F.2d 262 (7th Cir.1967), cert. denied 389 U.S. 977 (1967).

(since if the directors hadn't been reelected they wouldn't have been in a position to do it). And in Vine v. Beneficial Finance Co.[40] it was held that there was a sufficient "connection" between an alleged fraudulent tender offer and the subsequent "cashing out" of the plaintiff through a short-form merger, since the short-form merger would have been impossible without the prior acquisition of the 90% ownership.[41]

On the other hand, in Ketchum v. Green [42] the Third Circuit held, in a case where the plaintiffs alleged that the shareholders were fraudulently induced to elect directors who then voted to discharge the plaintiffs as officers, thereby triggering an obligation on their part to resell their stock in the closely-held corporation to the corporation, that the alleged fraud was not "in connection with" the sale of the securities so as to be the basis for an action under Rule 10b–5. The court characterized the action as essentially only "a dispute arising from an internal contest for control of a corporation." Mutual Shares Corp. v. Genesco, Inc.[43] holds that there is no Rule 10b–5 cause of action where an alleged fraudulent tender offer is followed by an alleged looting of the corporation, but this seems to rest more on the basis that the plaintiff shareholder was neither a purchaser nor a seller than on the basis of an insufficient connection between the purchase by the defendant and the injury alleged. Would the same result have been reached if the plaintiff had been the trustee in bankruptcy of the allegedly looted corporation? The *Superintendent of Insurance* case seems to hold that there is a sufficient connection between a sale of a controlling block of stock and a subsequent looting of the corporation *carried out by a sale of securities,* where the plaintiff was a public liquidator of the corporation.

Of course, if the thread can be stretched far enough, it is always possible to find a purchase or sale of stock of a corporation by someone at some time, if only upon its initial organization. In Voege v. American Sumatra Tobacco Corp.[44] Judge Steel held that when the plaintiff purchased her stock in the market in 1945 the corporation impliedly represented to her that if and when it ever entered into a merger it would only do so on terms that were "fair" to her; when it did enter into a merger in 1960 on terms which she alleged were "unfair", this made the representation false and gave her a cause of action under Rule 10b–5. One would have to go back at least several hundred years to find such a palpable creation of a fiction by a court to seize jurisdiction not otherwise conferred upon it. Such a theory would of course justify entertaining under Rule 10b–5 any conceivable suit by a shareholder complaining about any conceivable action by a corporation or its officers or directors. While the Second Circuit in the *Mutual Shares Corporation* case may have been somewhat disingenuous in its attempt to "distinguish" the *Voege* case, the opinion makes it quite clear that the Second Circuit doesn't subscribe to that philosophy.

In the proxy field, Hoover v. Allen [45] held that where the damage alleged had nothing to do with any action taken at the stockholders' meeting, no cause of action could be stated under Section 14(a). In that case, the "allegedly false

---

40. 374 F.2d 627 (2d Cir.1967), cert. denied 389 U.S. 970 (1967).

41. See, also, Ohashi v. Verit Industries, 536 F.2d 849 (9th Cir.1976), cert. denied 429 U.S. 1004 (1976). The Ninth Circuit there held that where the plaintiff acquired restricted stock in connection with an acquisition, fraud and market manipulation by the defendants allegedly occurring thereafter while the restrictions were still imposed were "in connection with" the original purchase by the plaintiff

under Rule 10b–5. The court characterized the contract as remaining "executory" because there was a registration covenant and a continuing obligation under California law of good faith and fair dealing on the part of the defendants.

42. 557 F.2d 1022 (3d Cir.1977) cert. denied 434 U.S. 940 (1977).

43. 384 F.2d 540 (2d Cir.1967).

44. 241 F.Supp. 369 (D.Del.1965).

45. 241 F.Supp. 213 (S.D.N.Y.1965).

and misleading statements in American-Hawaiian's 1955 proxy statement caused stockholders of American-Hawaiian, to sell their stock to defendant Ludwig or to American-Hawaiian, thus giving defendants control of American-Hawaiian, and enabling defendants to commit acts of waste." [46] The court said: "In the absence of some allegation of infringement upon corporate suffrage rights or some corporate action taken as a result of such infringement, no cause of action under Section 14(a) has been made out." [47]

Several cases in the district courts and one in a circuit court have held that an allegation that a proxy statement for the election of directors failed to reveal illegal foreign payments which had been made and "covered up" by the directors did not state a cause of action for damages against the officers and directors under Rule 14a–9, because the allegedly misleading nature of the proxy statement had no causal connection with the making of the illegal foreign payments.[48]

In Globus, Inc. v. Jaroff [49] the court indicated that in its opinion the "causal nexus" need not be as strong under Rule 10b–5 as under Section 14(a). Why there should be any such difference, if it exists, was not explained, however. The *Schlick* case seems to take the same tack, by saying that transaction causation need not be shown under the Rule 10b–5 count, but that "both types of causation" must be shown under the Section 14(a) count; but since the court then conclusively presumes without proof that transaction causation exists for the purposes of the Section 14(a) count, it is somewhat difficult to see what the distinction is.[50]

See Black, Fraud on the Market: A Criticism of Dispensing With Reliance Requirements in Certain Open Market Transactions, 62 N.C.L.Rev. 435 (1984); Grzebielski, Should the Supreme Court Recognize General Market Reliance in Private Actions Under Rule 10b–5, 36 Baylor L.Rev. 335 (1984); Heisel, Panzirer v. Wolf: An Extension of the Fraud-on-the-Market Theory of Liability Under Rule 10b–5, 32 Cath.U.L.Rev. 695 (1983); Whalen, Causation and Reliance in Private Actions Under SEC Rule 10b–5, 13 Pacific L.J. 1003 (1982); Stoll, Reliance as an Element in 10b–5 Actions, 53 Ore.L.Rev. 169 (1974); Note, Reliance Requirement in Private Actions Under SEC Rule 10b–5, 38 Harv.L. Rev. 584 (1975); Note, Nature and Scope of the Reliance Requirement in Private Actions Under SEC Rule 10b–5, 24 Cas.West.Res.L.Rev. 363 (1973); Note, Reliance Under Rule 10b–5: Is the "Reasonable Investor" Reasonable?, 72 Colum.L.Rev. 562 (1972).

46. 241 F.Supp. at 230.

47. Ibid.

48. Gaines v. Haughton, 645 F.2d (9th Cir.1981); Herman v. Beretta, 26 F.R.Serv. 2d 1237, CCH Fed.Sec.Law Rptr. ¶ 96,574 (S.D.N.Y.1978); Lewis v. Elam, CCH Fed. Sec.Law Rptr. ¶ 96,013 (S.D.N.Y.1977); Levy v. Johnson, CCH Fed.Sec.Law Rptr. ¶ 95,899 (S.D.N.Y.1977); Limmer v. General Telephone & Electronics Corp., CCH Fed.Sec.Law Rptr. ¶ 96,111 (S.D.N.Y.1977); and see Abbey v. Control Data Corp., 603 F.2d 724 (8th Cir.1979), cert. denied 444 U.S. 1017 (1980). Compare Weisberg v. Coastal States Gas Corp., 609 F.2d 650 (2d Cir.1979), cert. denied 445 U.S. 951 (1980), where the court held that an action to void an election and to appoint a receiver, as distinguished from an action for damages, could be maintained under Section 14(a) based upon alleged bribes approved by the

directors and not revealed in the proxy statement relating to the election. The court did not find that it was necessary to determine whether, in this connection, a distinction should be made between "mere" bribes and bribes coupled with kickbacks to the directors, since it stated that this went to the question of materiality, which is a factual question to be determined after trial. The Ninth Circuit in the *Gaines* case, supra, however, stated that it drew a "sharp distinction" between these two things, and that the former was "never material for § 14(a) purposes."

49. 266 F.Supp. 524 (S.D.N.Y.1967).

50. Compare Lutgert v. Vanderbilt Bank, 508 F.2d 1035 (5th Cir.1975), which seems to insist upon a rather rigorous application of the causation test in a Section 10(b) case.

Chapter 19

DEFENSES

Statutes and Regulations

Securities Act of 1933, §§ 11, 12, 13, 17(a).

Securities Exchange Act of 1934, §§ 9, 18; Rule 10b–5.

DUPUY v. DUPUY

United States Court of Appeals, Fifth Circuit, 1977.
551 F.2d 1005, cert. denied 434 U.S. 911, 98 S.Ct. 312, 54 L.Ed.2d 197 (1977).

Before JONES, WISDOM and GODBOLD, CIRCUIT JUDGES.

WISDOM, CIRCUIT JUDGE:

In this brother-against-brother case, a purchaser of stock, to depress the price, misrepresented and failed to disclose material facts regarding the value of the stock. The question presented is whether the seller of the stock will be denied recovery against the purchaser under Securities and Exchange Commission Rule 10b–5 because the seller, who could have ferreted out the facts, failed to do so until after the sale.

The case turns on the degree of diligence required of the plaintiff, Milton Dupuy, under Rule 10b–5 when the defendant, his brother Clarence, intentionally committed acts of fraud that significantly affected the plaintiff's decision to sell the stock at a price considerably below its value. This is primarily a question for the jury to decide. Here, on interrogatories submitted to the jury, the jury decided that the plaintiff had "exercised due diligence for his protection in connection with [the] sale of the stock", and awarded Milton damages of $905,000.

The trial judge granted the defendant's motion for a judgment notwithstanding the verdict. He held that there was "no evidence from which a finder of fact might have inferred any diligence on the part of the plaintiff". Alternatively, the trial judge stated that "if it were not for the Court's ability to make this finding in the fashion I have, I would feel compelled to grant a new trial, because I feel under all the circumstances of the case, the size of the verdict * * * shocks the Court's conscience and also [is] contrary to the weight [of the evidence]".

We reverse the judgment n.o.v., but remand the case for a new trial on damages.

I.

The Facts

Clarence and Milton Dupuy were raised in poverty in a poor section of New Orleans. They worked as children and as youths and always on a share and share alike basis. Until the dispute arose that generated this litigation the two brothers worked harmoniously for many years on real estate ventures. By 1971 they had accumulated certain valuable properties held by Les Freres Corporation, Argonne Corporation, Dupuy and Dupuy, a partnership, and Dupuy Construction Company, a partnership. The stock and the partnerships were divided equally between Clarence and Milton. Clarence was the older brother and dominated their personal relationships. He was an attorney, a successful politician, and an elected member of the New Orleans City Council. Milton did not finish college, but acquired firsthand knowledge of the construction business and real estate development. At one time he was appointed and served as President of the Orleans Parish Levee Board.

In late 1971 the Dupuys organized the Lori Corporation to acquire a valuable long-term lease on land bounded by Toulouse, Burgundy, Rampart, and St. Peter streets in the City of New Orleans. This property is within but on the edge of the French Quarter. The value of the land was enhanced when, prior to the Dupuys' acquisition of the lease, the City Council of New Orleans declared a moratorium on construction of hotels in the French Quarter, but excepted from the ban the premises just described.

To form Lori Corporation, each brother contributed $1,880 to the enterprise and received 47 percent of the company's stock.[6] Milton was president, Clarence Secretary-treasurer, and Mrs. Dupuy, their mother, vice-president. During 1971 and early 1972 Milton supervised the day-to-day development of this venture. He signed the lease with the landowner, met frequently with the architect, August Perez, and assembled statistics for the necessary financing. He and Clarence met with the president of the Bank of New Orleans, Lawrence Merrigan, and a mortgage banker, J.H. Harris (representing Colwell Mortgage Trust) to discuss financing the project. As compensation for these duties and his management of other jointly held properties, Milton received a monthly fee of $1,150.

At Harris's suggestion, Milton obtained an appraisal from Mr. John D. Bird, in whom Colwell had confidence. Bird valued the project initially at $7,340,000 and the market value of the lease at [$986,500.00]. Because of changes in the plans, he reduced these figures respectively to $7,100,000 and [$962,330.00].

All went well until March 30, 1972, when Clarence abruptly cut off Milton's management fee. Clarence had always controlled the checkbook. Clarence says that Milton turned his back on the project. At the time, however, Milton's monthly fees were his sole source of income; he had no substantial savings; Milton had serious kidney trouble causing increasing medical expenses; and he was supporting his present wife and child and his former wife and children. He could not borrow on his interest in the Les Freres and Argonne corporations, because he had no means of paying the debt. Milton asked Clarence to buy his interest, but Clarence offered him only a note. Milton's financial crisis forced him to find other employment. He obtained a job with Norman Brothers, real estate developers, but the work required travel to Clearwater, Florida, and to Algiers (across the Mississippi River from New Orleans). After three months, his health was so bad that he had to give up this job. He had worked for Norman Brothers from May 15 to August 18, 1972.

---

6. Their mother, Mrs. Florence Dupuy, received the remaining six percent of the stock.

After his management was terminated and having no personal contacts with the development of the Lori property, Milton had to rely on Clarence for information as to what was happening to the financing of the projected hotel. Milton testified that whenever he spoke to Clarence over the telephone Clarence told him that the Lori Hotel "was having a rough time * * * everything is going downhill"; that "it's just practically worthless".

Shortly after Clarence cut off Milton's income, Clarence began negotiations with William Monteleone, owner of a well-known and long-successful French Quarter hotel. Earlier, Clarence and Milton had discussed but had never pursued the possibility of interesting Monteleone in the venture. Milton testified that Monteleone's name came up just once and then as a possible purchaser of some of Milton's stock. The banks and mortgage brokers had conditioned financing of the construction of the Dupuy hotel on the participation of someone having larger financial resources than Clarence and Milton possessed.

Clarence's negotiations with Monteleone and his representatives were extensive. A letter to the New Monteleone Hotel from Arthur L. Ballin, an attorney who represented Monteleone, shows that instead of "everything going downhill", prospects were favorable. As early as April 21, Ballin had a four-hour conference with Monteleone and Clarence to review the "proposition of joint venture and partnership in commendum". On April 24 there was a two-hour conference by Ballin and Clarence to prepare a draft of the partnership. At that time, Monteleone was prepared to put up the necessary financing. On April 28 there was a two-hour conference by Ballin with Clarence and Monteleone, who expressed doubts about the joint venture. These doubts were later dissipated. Ballin talked with Clarence on May 1 and arranged for a meeting the next day. May 2 Ballin met with Clarence. They were in agreement as to the partnership, but Clarence wanted and obtained an option to repurchase Monteleone's interest. May 5 Ballin had several telephone conferences and a meeting with Clarence. On May 8 Ballin again met with Monteleone and Clarence. On that day Monteleone instructed Ballin to prepare papers to complete the transaction. There followed meetings by Ballin with Clarence on May 12, to discuss provisions of the partnership agreement; on May 13, to re-draft the partnership agreement; on May 15, with Monteleone as well as Clarence, to revise the agreement; on May 17, a meeting with Clarence, after Ballin had studied the tax effects of the agreement; on May 19, a long telephone conversation to discuss the tax effects; on May 22, a meeting by Ballin with Clarence and accountants to discuss tax effects of the partnership. June 2 Ballin met with Clarence to review the revised agreement. June 6 Ballin met for three hours with Clarence and accountants to review the revised partnership agreement and tax questions. Finally, on June 7, 1972, Ballin met with Clarence and reviewed the final form of the partnership and Clarence's option. The partnership agreement called for Monteleone to put up, individually, $180,000 in cash, for which he would receive a 6 percent interest, and the New Hotel Monteleone, Inc., to put up $420,000 in cash for a 14 percent interest. The Lori Corporation would receive a 40 percent interest, for its lease to the land on which the hotel was to be built. Clarence would receive a 40 percent interest. Thus, for two months before Clarence bought Milton's stock and for one month before the putative directors' meeting approving the partnership with Monteleone, Clarence knew that the Lori stock was worth a small fortune, but not Milton, although he lived in the same apartment complex with Clarence and they shared a patio.

The partnership agreement was executed on July 31, 1972, before Arthur L. Ballin, in his capacity as Notary Public. Clarence Dupuy appeared individually and as Secretary-Treasurer of Lori Corporation. William A. Monteleone appeared individually. The New Hotel Monteleone appeared through its duly authorized Executive President.

On that same day, July 31, 1972, Clarence signed a certificate as Secretary of Lori Corporation certifying as true and correct a resolution, adopted by the Board of Directors of the Corporation, authorizing Clarence to execute on behalf of Lori Corporation the partnership with Clarence Dupuy, William A. Monteleone, and New Hotel Monteleone, under the name of "Lori Corporation and Associate". The contribution of the corporation was to be the assignment of the Lori lease to the partnership. Also, on that same day Clarence certified as true and correct a resolution authorizing an option in favor of Clarence and Lori Corporation, for five years, to repurchase the interests of William A. Monteleone and the New Hotel Monteleone for $700,000.

On cross-examination, Clarence admitted that he had not notified Milton of any meeting of the Board of Directors and that no meeting had been held. Indeed, so he said, no meetings of the Board had ever been held for the Lori Corporation or for any other of their corporations. This loose practice might be understandable when the two brothers had harmonious relations. But a jury would find it hard to understand why it did not put Clarence under the unshakable duty to disclose the facts to Milton, when the effect of the meeting that did not exist was to make effective the partnership with Monteleone resulting in the successful financing of the hotel and the assignment of Lori's sole asset to the partnership.

Because of Monteleone's participation, the partnership received a construction loan of $5,000,000 from Colwell Mortgage Trust. Clarence accepted Colwell's offer on July 25, subject to certain changes. Colwell approved the changes on July 27.

Clarence revealed none of these facts to Milton. Indeed, during the time he was negotiating with Ballin and Monteleone he assured Milton that the development of the hotel had been stalled by a failure to obtain financing. Not knowing of Clarence's bright future for the hotel, never having been informed of the need for a bona fide or non-existent directors' meeting, and hard pressed financially, Milton urged Clarence to buy his stock.

Milton, more and more apprehensive about his investment, wrote letters to Clarence June 19, June 25, and July 9, 1972. These letters clearly show that Milton mistrusted his brother. By that time, however, Clarence had closed his agreement with Monteleone, except for executing final papers. He gave no inkling of this to Milton.

In early June 1972 Clarence sent Milton a statement from G.E. Conroy, their accountant, for $375, and asked him to co-sign a check of Lori Corporation for that amount, payable to Conroy. The statement did not show the nature of the services performed. The record shows that they were to consider the tax aspects of Clarence's proposed transactions with Monteleone. Milton asked for a full report on what Conroy had done to earn the $375. Clarence did not reply to this request. The jury could have inferred that a reply would have disclosed to Milton his negotiations with Monteleone.

In August, still thinking that the hotel venture was in deep trouble, Milton agreed to sell his 47 percent interest in Lori for $10,000. On August 29 Milton signed the agreement of sale. He did so without consulting the bankers, the architect, or any lawyers. He explains that he relied on Clarence's representations because, in spite of his mistrust, Clarence was his brother on whom, in spite of everything, he had always relied. Moreover, the disease prevented an independent investigation. His kidney disease, diagnosed in 1965 as incurable glomeruler nephritis, had worsened considerably by 1972. It had forced Milton to quit his job on August 18, at which time, he said, he was flat on his back. The Social Security office set the date of his complete employment disability as April 1972.

Milton argues that the true value of his 47 percent interest in Lori was at least $500,000 and perhaps $1,200,000. On January 28, 1972, Clarence had estimated the value of his 47 percent at $493,250.00. A preconstruction appraisal valued the lease alone at $1,000,000. In February 1972 the equity value of the proposed hotel was estimated at $1,810,000. And the Monteleone transaction appears to have been based on a total value of $3,000,000.

Clarence tells a different story. * * *

The brothers have different versions of the terms of the sale of the Lori stock. According to Clarence, Milton first suggested the sale and frequently pressured him through their mother for a speedy agreement on the terms. Clarence denies any direct contact with Milton except for a June meeting at which they agreed on a price of $45,000, $10,000 to be paid by check and $35,000 to be paid in cash; Clarence was to assume the corporation's note of $85,000 for interim financing. The payment on August 29, 1972, was witnessed by Milton's wife and mother. The mother testified that Clarence carried the cash to Milton's apartment in a large cardboard box. Milton denies both the June meeting and the payment of any cash, a denial corroborated by his wife.

Even though Clarence says that he paid $45,000 for Milton's interest in Lori, he insists that the stock was absolutely worthless at the time and that Milton could not have suffered any damages from the sale. Disregarding the successful financing, he argues that in August Lori owned only a lease that required annual rent payments of $50,000. There was no hotel, no income. Even if the hotel were built, substantial business risks precluded any guarantee of success. And the inherent lack of marketability of close corporation stock detracted further from the value of Milton's investment. Considering that Milton had contributed only $1,880 to the venture in 1971, Clarence argues that $45,000 was more than an adequate return in 1972. Clarence's return consisted of the value of 94 percent of Lori stock plus a 40 percent interest in the partnership.

Summarizing, Clarence bought Milton's 47 percent stock interest on August 29, 1972. A month before, July 31, Monteleone had paid $600,000 for a 20 percent interest in the partnership. By August 29 a $5,000,000 construction loan had been obtained. Two months before, on June 31, Clarence certified a resolution, on its face adopted by the Board of Directors approving the partnership and assignment of Lori's lease. At that time there could be no doubt that Milton's stock was enormously valuable.

* * * On the record before it, the jury could fairly infer that Clarence intentionally misrepresented to Milton the financial prospect for the Maison Dupuy Hotel and that he concealed material facts from his brother to depress the price of the stock.

The more difficult question is the extent to which fraud under Rule 10–b is vitiated by the victim's lack of diligence in protecting his interests.

II.

DUE DILIGENCE

A. *Judgment Notwithstanding the Verdict.*

The trial judge overturned the jury verdict because he found that the record showed no evidence that Milton had exercised due diligence to protect his own interests.

* * *

B. *The Law of Due Diligence.*

1. *Background and Approach*

The Securities and Exchange Act of 1934 did not provide expressly for a private cause of action to enforce Section 10(b). Neither the Act nor its legislative history supply the elements of such an action. When the SEC promulgated Rule 10b–5, apparently it intended to exercise its broad enforcement powers, rather than to establish a mechanism for investor compensation. Consequently, the Commission also failed to announce the prerequisites for recovery of damages by victims of stock fraud. Not until J.I. Case Co. v. Borak, 1964, 377 U.S. 426, did the Supreme Court recognize a private cause of action arising from the Acts. The burden has fallen upon the courts to define the requirements for private enforcement of the securities laws.

The courts have established that with regard to private recovery for the violation of Rule 10b–5, a properly stated cause of action must establish the scienter of the defendant, the materiality of any misrepresentation or omission by the defendant, the extent of actual reliance by the plaintiff on the defendant's statements, and the justifiability of the reliance, frequently translated into a requirement of due diligence by the plaintiff. Treatment of the last of these elements has varied substantially among the circuits. This Court established "due diligence" as a separate element in 10b–5 cases, apart from questions of materiality, reliance, or defendant's duties. Clement A. Evans & Co. v. McAlpine, 5 Cir.1970, 434 F.2d 100, cert. denied, 1971, 402 U.S. 988, rehearing denied, 404 U.S. 874; accord Bird v. Ferry, 5 Cir.1974, 497 F.2d 112, rehearing denied, 5 Cir., 503 F.2d 567; Vohs v. Dickson, 5 Cir.1974, 495 F.2d 607. By considering independently whether the carelessness of a plaintiff should preclude his recovery, the Court promotes two policies. First, general principles of equity suggest that only those who have pursued their own interests with care and good faith should qualify for the judicially created private 10b–5 remedies. See Clement A. Evans & Co. v. McAlpine, 5 Cir.1970, 434 F.2d 100, 104; City National Bank v. Vanderboom, 8 Cir.1970, 422 F.2d 221, 230 n. 10, cert. denied, 399

U.S. 905; Wheeler, Plaintiff's Duty of Due Care Under Rule 10b–5: An Implied Defense to an Implied Remedy, 70 Nw.U.L.Rev. 561, 564–68 (1976) (hereinafter cited Wheeler). Second, by requiring plaintiffs to invest carefully, the Court promotes the anti-fraud policies of the Acts and engenders stability in the markets. Wheeler, 70 Nw.U.L.Rev. at 585; Note, The Due Diligence Requirement for Plaintiffs Under Rule 10b–5, 1975 Duke L.J. 753, 760–61.

Some other circuits have used different approaches in evaluating the conduct of plaintiffs. Several courts have made the duty of defendants to disclose depend on the sophistication, status, and information of the plaintiff. White v. Abrams, 9 Cir.1974, 495 F.2d 724; Arber v. Essex Wire Corp., 6 Cir.1974, 490 F.2d 414, cert. denied, 419 U.S. 830; Kohler v. Kohler, 7 Cir. 1963, 319 F.2d 634. The First and Tenth Circuits have analyzed the facts to determine whether reliance by plaintiffs on misrepresentations was reasonable or justifiable. Holdsworth v. Strong, 10 Cir.1976, 545 F.2d 687; Rogen v. Ilikon Corp., 1 Cir.1966, 361 F.2d 260. One panel in the Second Circuit has abandoned altogether the requirements of reliance in fact and justifiable reliance in cases involving intentional misrepresentations. In Metro-Goldwyn-Mayer, Inc. v. Ross, 2 Cir.1975, 509 F.2d 930, the court held that the duty of the defendant to correct his misrepresentation is absolute, regardless of the defendant's knowledge of the misrepresentation. Accord, Competitive Associates, Inc. v. Laventhol, Krekstein, Horwath & Horwath, 2 Cir.1975, 516 F.2d 811. But see Titan Group, Inc. v. Faggen, 2 Cir.1975, 513 F.2d 234, cert. denied, 423 U.S. 840. See generally, Comment, Securities Regulation—Two Different Standards of Reliance Applied in Individual Private Damage Actions Under SEC Rule 10b–5 by the Second Circuit, 49 Temple L.Rev. 182 (1975).

These alternative approaches to the due diligence determination present several analytical problems, which cause us to retain the methodology of *McAlpine.*

First, inconsistent standards of conduct for defendants arise from analyses that vary the duty to disclose with the status of the plaintiff. Because the private 10b–5 cause of action derives from a prohibitory SEC rule, the standard of conduct for defendants logically should be the same whether the SEC or a private litigant enforces the duty. In an SEC enforcement proceeding, the due care of the victim generally does not receive consideration. SEC v. Dolnick, 7 Cir.1974, 501 F.2d 1279, 1283 (disregarding whether the victim was a knowledgable investor); Hanly v. SEC, 2 Cir.1967, 415 F.2d 589, 596 (disregarding the sophistication of the victims, as well as their previous relationships with the defendants). But see SEC v. Coffey, 6 Cir. 1974, 493 F.2d 1304, 1312–13, cert. denied, 1975, 420 U.S. 908 (on the peculiar facts of this case the defendant violated no duty because the victims possessed sufficient knowledge about a representation to avoid being misled by it). The dispositive element in these cases is that the defendant owes a duty of full and fair disclosure to the public, not to any particular investor. Whether a private plaintiff might be precluded from recovery, then, need not alter the distinct consideration whether a defendant has violated duties imposed by the Act. With a flexible duty approach, however, the defendant owes different duties depending on the status of the victim and the type of legal action. This could lead both to unnecessary confusion between public and private enforcement proceedings and to gamesmanship by defendants. See Wheeler, 70 Nw.U.L.Rev. at 591.

Second, the materiality-reliance approach of the First and Tenth Circuits also faces a problem of consistency of application. In Affiliated Ute Citizens v. United States, 1972, 406 U.S. 128, rehearing denied, 407 U.S. 916 and 408 U.S. 931, the Supreme Court held that in a 10b–5 case involving a material omission "positive proof of reliance is not a prerequisite to recovery". Id. 406 U.S. at 153. By eliminating positive proof of reliance when materiality is established, the Court relieved the plaintiffs from an almost impossible burden of proof. See Holdsworth v. Strong, 10 Cir.1976, 545 F.2d 687, 695; Jackson v. Oppenheim, S.D.N.Y.1974, 411 F.Supp. 659. *Ute Citizens* creates a distinction between affirmative misrepresentation cases, in which plaintiffs must demonstrate reliance on the assertions of defendants, and omission cases, in which such proof is not required. When due care is discussed in terms of reliance, then, the misrepresentation-omission distinction could remove from plaintiffs the responsibility of exercising due care to protect their interests in omission cases. If reliance never becomes an issue, in other words, a court will have no basis to assess the justifiability of that reliance.

The purposes of examining the diligence of a 10b–5 plaintiff, however, do not justify distinguishing between misrepresentations and omissions. As we have suggested, courts have used due diligence to limit, as a matter of equitable discretion, recoveries to those parties who have purchased securities with care and good faith. Courts have also viewed the due diligence requirement as a method to promote statutory policies encouraging investor diligence in the interest of the efficiency and stability of the securities markets. These purposes for the due diligence requirement, whatever its form, do not vanish in omissions cases. As diligence can reveal misrepresentations, it can also reveal omissions. After *Ute Citizens*, then, tying the diligence analysis to reliance can generate an improper distinction between the misrepresentation and omission causes of action.

Third, to abandon completely the consideration of reliance in fact and reasonable reliance ignores not only the above policies of due diligence but also the need for a causal link between the misrepresentation or omission and the injury suffered by the private plaintiff. The cause of action would no longer provide compensation for losses occasioned by the violation of the Act because a plaintiff could sue without relying on the fraud. This would transform the action into an enforcement mechanism. We reject this approach because of the Supreme Court's recognition of a 10b–5 private action as a device to compensate victims of stock fraud and thereby to promote the public objectives of the Act. J.I. Case Co. v. Borak, 377 U.S. at 432–35, 84 S.Ct. 1555.

As we see it, the *McAlpine* approach of treating due diligence as a separate element in private 10b–5 cases best supports the policies of the Acts and ensures proper exercise of the Court's equity powers.

2. *The Subjective Elements of the Due Diligence Consideration.*

The diligence of the plaintiff in 10b–5 cases is judged subjectively. Straub v. Vaisman & Co., 3 Cir.1976, 540 F.2d 591, 598; Clement A. Evans & Co. v. McAlpine, 5 Cir.1970, 434 F.2d 100, 102. The role model for a plaintiff, then, is an investor with the attributes of the plaintiff, rather than the average investor. For example, *McAlpine* approved a jury instruction that imposed a duty of due diligence "solely under the peculiar circumstances of each case, including existence of a fiduciary relationship, concealment of the fraud, opportunity to detect it, position in the industry, sophistication and expertise in the financial community, and knowledge of related proceedings" * * *. Several courts have also considered whether the plaintiff initiated the stock transaction or pressured for a speedy resolution. White v. Abrams, 9 Cir.1974, 495 F.2d 724; Hafner v. Forest Laboratories, Inc., 2 Cir.1965, 345 F.2d 167; Kohler v. Kohler Co., 7 Cir. 1963, 319 F.2d 634.

3. *The Standard of Care.*

This Court has announced a due diligence test that measures the plaintiff's conduct against that of a reasonable investor with the attributes of the plaintiff. It is, in effect, a negligence standard. Clement A. Evans & Co. v. McAlpine, 5 Cir.1970, 434 F.2d 100, 103, quoted with approval the test employed by the Eighth Circuit:

> With regard to misrepresentations, the question is whether a reasonable investor, in light of the facts existing at the time of the misrepresentation and in the exercise of due care, would have been entitled to rely upon the misrepresentation. * * *

McAlpine answered that question in the negative and affirmed a jury finding that the plaintiff lacked "reasonable diligence". Accord, Bird v. Ferry, 5 Cir.1974, 497 F.2d 112; Vohs v. Dickson, 5 Cir.1974, 495 F.2d 607.

Recently, however, an important reexamination has begun of the appropriateness of applying a negligence standard to the conduct of plaintiffs when the Supreme Court has forbidden a similar standard to be applied to the conduct of defendants. In Ernst & Ernst v. Hochfelder, 1976, 425 U.S. 185, the Court reversed an imposition of 10b–5 liability without proof of scienter—"intent to deceive, manipulate, or defraud". Id. at 193. * * *

Two circuits have reevaluated their due diligence standards in light of *Ernst.* In Holdsworth v. Strong, 10 Cir.1976, 545 F.2d 687, the plaintiff, Holdsworth, sold his stock in a close corporation to Strong. Although Holdsworth was a sophisticated insider with access to company books, he relied on several intentional misrepresentations by Strong about the financial health of the company. Citing *McAlpine* and Rochez Bros. v. Rhoades, 3 Cir.1974, 491 F.2d 402, the court recognized that the traditional due diligence requirement imposed a standard of negligence on plaintiffs. But it decided that *Ernst* called for a change:

> If the negligence standard were being applied it might be appropriate to allow due diligence to be exacted from the victim, but where liability of the defendant requires proof of intentional misconduct, the exaction of a due diligence standard from the plaintiff becomes irrational and unrelated.

545 F.2d at 692. Consequently, the Court held that contributory fault would bar recovery only when plaintiff exhibited "gross conduct somewhat comparable to that of defendant". Id. at 693.

In Straub v. Vaisman & Co., 3 Cir.1976, 540 F.2d 591, the Court responded to *Ernst* by reversing the burden of proof on the due diligence issue. The plaintiff, the European manager of a portfolio management company, executed an unsuccessful stock purchase on the defendant's advice. In assessing the manager's diligence, the Court noted several arguments for circumscribing the due care requirement. But it balanced the effect of *Ernst* against the general SEC policy of encouraging diligence in stock transactions. As a result, it continued to require that plaintiffs act reasonably, and it made the due care question an affirmative defense. On the facts, the American defendant did not carry his burden of proof primarily because the Europeans lacked access to information concerning the abuse of their trust.

These cases and commentary have developed several reasons for changing the due diligence standard after *Ernst*. They first draw analogies to tort theory. * * * Tort law distinguishes between intentional misrepresentations and negligent ones. Contributory negligence may bar recovery for the latter, but not for the former:

> [W]here there is an intent to mislead, [barring recovery] is clearly inconsistent with the general rule that mere negligence of the plaintiff is not a defense to an intentional tort. The better reasoned cases have rejected contributory negligence as a defense applicable to intentional deceit.

W. Prosser, Handbook of the Law of Torts § 10 at 716 (4th ed. 1971) (hereinafter cited W. Prosser). The Restatement of Torts agrees:

> The recipient in a business transaction of a fraudulent misrepresentation of fact is justified in relying on its truth, although he might have ascertained the falsity of the representation had he made an investigation.

Restatement of Torts § 540 (1938). The American Law Institute rejected any change in this rule when it considered the Restatement Second. See 42 ALI Proceedings 331 (1965), rejecting Restatement (Second) of Torts § 540 (Tent.Draft No. 11, 1965).

Two theories support the tort law dichotomy. First, the policy of deterring intentional misconduct outweighs that of deterring negligent behavior. * * * Second, comparative culpability influences the determination of who should bear any given loss. When both parties are negligent, there may be no reason for the judicial system to shift the loss from the victim. See id. at § 65. When one inflicts a loss intentionally on a negligent victim, however:

> [s]uch conduct differs from negligence not only in degree but in kind, and in the social condemnation attached to it. * * * It is in reality a rule of comparative fault which is being applied, and the court is refusing to set up the lesser fault against the greater.

Id. at § 65 at 426. * * *

* * *

Still another reason to adhere to this approach is that *Ernst* diminished substantially the need to limit the scope of the 10b–5 remedy. Before *Ernst*, tremendous liability could result from the negligent behavior of any person connected with a stock sale or purchase. For accountants, lawyers, brokers, dealers, and underwriters who handled these transactions, this potential liability posed a substantial risk to their professional existence. The principle of due diligence and other elements of the private cause of action provide mechanisms for limiting potential liability. See Clement A. Evans & Co. v. McAlpine, 5 Cir.1970, 434 F.2d 100, 104. With the scienter requirement, liability will be imposed only upon reckless or intentional wrongdoers, reducing substantially the risk on most actors in securities transactions. The need, then, for further limitation by the reasonable diligence requirement becomes questionable. Indeed, the Tenth Circuit has argued that requiring proof of both the scienter of the defendant and the reasonable diligence of the plaintiff would impermissibly limit 10b–5 recoveries to the "extraordinary" cases. Holdsworth v. Strong, 10 Cir.1976, 545 F.2d 687, 693.

The final argument for relaxing the reasonable diligence standard after *Ernst* is that most 10b–5 cases, when limited to their facts, are consistent with the distinction between intentional and negligent misrepresentation.
* * *

We consider that Ernst & Ernst v. Hochfelder prompts a change in the law of due diligence, as it is applicable in 10b–5 cases. Both tort law and federal securities policy support imposing on the plaintiff only a standard of care not exceeding that imposed on the defendant. Although the "scienter" requirement may still be unsettled, the Supreme Court has imposed on defendants a standard not stricter than recklessness. In this case, then, the question should not be whether Milton acted unreasonably by failing to investigate the condition of Lori Corporation. Instead, the Court should ask whether Milton intentionally refused to investigate "in disregard of a risk known to him or so obvious that he must be taken to have been aware of it, and so great as to make it highly probable that harm would follow." W. Prosser, § 34 at 185 (1971).

4. *The Due Diligence of Milton.*

After reviewing the voluminous trial record, we hold that a reasonable jury could find that Milton did not act recklessly when he sold his stock.

The district court's instructions were, as we view them, more favorable to Clarence than to Milton. The district court instructed the jury that to recover Milton must prove that he acted reasonably, an instruction consistent with previous holdings of this Court. The jury found that Milton had met this burden of proof—that he had acted reasonably; "with due diligence" (the language of the court's interrogatory). After *Ernst*, the jury did not have to decide whether Milton acted negligently, but only that he did not act recklessly. We reinstate the jury's verdict, then, because there is sufficient evidence in the record to support a holding that Milton did not have knowledge of the risk of Clarence's forming the partnership with Monteleone and obtaining financing for the hotel. There is also sufficient evidence to support a jury conclusion that Milton did not act in intentional disregard of whether Clarence had taken this course of action.
* * *

The alternative question posed by the recklessness standard is whether Milton acted intentionally in disregard of the probability that Clarence had organized the partnership and obtained financing. Two factors indicate that Milton intentionally sold his stock in disregard of all chances for success. First, the parties agree that the sale occurred without any independent investigation by Milton into the affairs of Lori. Although he knew Merrigan, Perez, and Harris, he did not discuss the sale with them. He relied exclusively on Clarence's representations. Second, Milton initiated the sale negotiations and exerted pressure for a quick agreement.
* * *

At least two Courts of Appeals have decided that such conduct indicates a lack of due diligence. In Kohler v. Kohler Co., 7 Cir.1963, 319 F.2d 634, the plaintiff-seller, the governor of Illinois, pressed for a speedy sale because he wanted to avoid any political problems that company labor conflict might generate. This pressure in part led the court to approve conduct by the defendant "that might not be fair if plaintiff had been a novice to stock transactions or the corporation's activities". Id. at 462.

* * *

On the facts of this case, however, a jury could find justification for Milton's conduct. First, according to his testimony, he repeatedly discussed the corporation and the stock sale with Clarence, the only other principal of Lori and the most obvious source of information about the venture. Even the cases that have required plaintiffs to refrain from negligent, rather than reckless, behavior have never required a plaintiff to launch an investigation of sources of information outside the corporation, its officers, directors, and books. See, e.g., Rogen v. Ilikon Corp., 1 Cir.1966, 361 F.2d 260; Kohler v. Kohler Co., 7 Cir.1963, 319 F.2d 634; Jackson v. Oppenheim, S.D.N.Y.1974, 411 F.Supp. 659.

Second, the time that Milton could devote to any such investigation was limited by his search for employment and later by the substantial amount of traveling required by the new job. The jury could have attributed Milton's failure to investigate fully to the financial chaos imposed on him by the abrupt cutoff of his income in March.

Third, the physical debilitation and emotional stress of Milton's kidney disease distracted him significantly during July and August. After discovering the disease in 1965, physicians notified both Milton and Clarence that it was incurable. By August 1972 it had worsened to the point that Milton was forced to quit his new job and to apply for social security. The social security office dated his complete disability from April 1972. When the jury concluded that Milton had exercised due diligence, it is not unreasonable to assume it found that Milton's condition precluded him from investigating the status of Lori. Nothing in the case law forbids or compels the jury to excuse his decision not to investigate on such a ground. Because of the subjective nature of the due diligence determination, then, Milton's ailment could have justified the jury's response to the fourth interrogatory.

* * *

IV.

CONCLUSION

We hold that a reasonable jury could have found that, in the circumstances of this case, Milton Dupuy exercised due diligence in the sale of his stock to Clarence Dupuy. The judgment notwithstanding the verdict of the district court is therefore reversed, and the district court is instructed to reinstate the verdict on Clarence Dupuy's liability. By ordering a new trial on damages, in the alternative, the trial court did not abuse its discretion. The case is therefore remanded to the district court for a new trial on damages.

Reversed in part and affirmed in part and remanded.

BATEMAN EICHLER, HILL RICHARDS, INC. v. BERNER

Supreme Court of the United States, 1985.
472 U.S. 299, 105 S.Ct. 2622, 86 L.Ed.2d 215.

JUSTICE BRENNAN delivered the opinion of the Court.

The question presented by this case is whether the common-law *in pari delicto* defense bars a private damages action under the federal securities laws against corporate insiders and broker-dealers who fraudulently induce investors to purchase securities by misrepresenting that they are conveying material nonpublic information about the issuer.

I

The respondent investors filed this action in the United States District Court for the Northern District of California, alleging that they incurred substantial trading losses as a result of a conspiracy between Charles Lazzaro, a registered securities broker employed by the petitioner Bateman Eichler, Hill Richards, Inc. (Bateman Eichler), and Leslie Neadeau, President of T.O.N.M. Oil & Gas Exploration Corporation (TONM), to induce them to purchase large quantities of TONM over-the-counter stock by divulging false and materially incomplete information about the company on the pretext that it was accurate inside information.[1] Specifically, Lazzaro is alleged to have told the respondents that he personally knew TONM insiders and had learned, *inter alia*, that (a) "[v]ast amounts of gold had been discovered in Surinam, and TONM had options on thousands of acres in gold-producing regions of Surinam"; (b) the discovery was "not publically known, but would subsequently be announced"; (c) TONM was currently engaged in negotiations with other companies to form a joint venture for mining the Surinamese gold; and (d) when this information was made public, "TONM stock, which was then selling from \$1.50 to \$3.00/share, would increase in value from \$10 to \$15/share within a short period of time, and * * * might increase to \$100/share" within a year. Complaint ¶¶ 16–17, App. 10–12. Some of the respondents aver that they contacted Neadeau and inquired whether Lazzaro's tips were accurate; Neadeau stated that the information was "not public knowledge" and "would neither confirm nor deny those claims," but allegedly advised that "Lazzaro was a very trustworthy and a good man." Id. ¶ 19, App. 12.

The respondents admitted in their complaint that they purchased TONM stock, much of it through Lazzaro, "on the premise that Lazzaro was privy to certain information not otherwise available to the general public." Id. ¶ 15, App. 10. Their shares initially increased dramatically in

---

1. The investors named Lazzaro, Neadeau, TONM, and Bateman Eichler as defendants. Complaint ¶¶ 5–8, App. 7–8. The investors charged that Neadeau and TONM had "directly and indirectly participated with, aided and abetted, and conspired with" Lazzaro in the scheme. Id. ¶ 9, App. 8; see also id. ¶ 40, App. 17. Bateman Eichler's liability was premised on its status as a "controlling person" of Lazzaro within the meaning of § 20(a) of the Securities Exchange Act of 1934. Complaint ¶¶ 5, 39, App. 7, 16–17. See n. 25, infra.

Although Lazzaro, Neadeau, and TONM also are respondents in this Court, see Sup. Ct.Rule 19.6, we shall use "respondents" to refer exclusively to the investor plaintiffs, who are defending the judgment of the Court of Appeals for the Ninth Circuit in this Court.

price, but ultimately declined to substantially below the purchase price when the joint mining venture fell through. Id. ¶¶ 22–26, App. 13–14.[4]

Lazzaro and Neadeau are alleged to have made the representations set forth above knowing that the representations "were untrue and/or contained only half-truths, material omissions of fact and falsehoods," intending that the respondents would rely thereon, and for the purpose of "influenc[ing] and manipulat[ing] the price of TONM stock" so as "to profit themselves through the taking of commissions and secret profits." Id. ¶¶ 23, 30, 38, App. 13, 15–16. The respondents contended that this scheme violated, *inter alia,* § 10(b) of the Securities Exchange Act of 1934 and SEC Rule 10b–5 promulgated thereunder (1984). They sought capital losses and lost profits, punitive damages, and costs and attorney's fees. App. 26.[9]

The District Court dismissed the complaint for failure to state a claim. The court reasoned that "trading on insider information is itself a violation of rule 10b–5" and that the allegations in the complaint demonstrated that the respondents themselves had "violated the particular statutory provision under which recovery is sought." App. to Pet. for Cert. C–2. Thus, the court concluded, the respondents were *in pari delicto* with Lazzaro and Neadeau and absolutely barred from recovery. Ibid.

The Court of Appeals for the Ninth Circuit reversed. Berner v. Lazzaro, 730 F.2d 1319 (1984). Although it assumed that the respondents had violated the federal securities laws, id., at 1324, the court nevertheless concluded that "securities professionals and corporate officers who have allegedly engaged in fraud should not be permitted to invoke the *in pari delicto* doctrine to shield themselves from the consequences of their fraudulent misrepresentation," id., at 1320. * * *

The lower courts have divided over the proper scope of the *in pari delicto* defense in securities litigation. We granted certiorari. 469 U.S. ___ (1985). We affirm.

II

The common-law defense at issue in this case derives from the Latin, *in pari delicto potior est conditio defendentis:* "In a case of equal or mutual fault * * * the position of the [defending] party * * * is the better one." The defense is grounded on two premises: first, that courts should not lend their good offices to mediating disputes among wrongdoers, and second, that denying judicial relief to an admitted wrongdoer is an effective

---

4. The respondents purchased the stock in late 1979 and early 1980 for between $1.50 and $3.00 per share, and the price of the stock rose to $7.00 per share by the fourth quarter of 1980. Id. ¶ 22, App. 13. "[S]ome or all" of the respondents claim to have told Lazzaro at this time that they wanted to sell their shares, but "Lazzaro stated that he would let the plaintiffs know when to sell the TONM stock, and that they should not sell just because the stock had reached $7.00/share because it would go higher still." Ibid. The stock then plummeted "to approximately $1.00 per share" by the end of 1980, and fell to "less than * * * $1.00 a share" early the next year. Id. ¶¶ 24–25, App. 14.

9. In addition, the respondents sought recovery pursuant to § 17(a) of the Securities Act of 1933, see Complaint ¶¶ 48–50, App. 20, which the parties and the courts below have treated as comparable to § 10(b) for purposes of applying the *in pari delicto* defense. We express no view as to whether a private right of action exists under § 17(a). Compare Keys v. Wolfe, 709 F.2d 413, 416 (CA5 1983), with Stephenson v. Calpine Conifers II, Ltd., 652 F.2d 808, 815 (CA9 1981). The respondents also alleged various other federal claims and pendent state-law claims that are not before us.

means of deterring illegality. In its classic formulation, the *in pari delicto* defense was narrowly limited to situations where the plaintiff truly bore at least substantially equal responsibility for his injury, because "in cases where both parties are in delicto, concurring in an illegal act, it does not always follow that they stand in pari delicto; for there may be, and often are, very different degrees in their guilt." 1 J. Story, Equity Jurisprudence 304–305 (13th ed. 1886) (Story). Thus there might be an "inequality of condition" between the parties, id., at 305, or "a confidential relationship between th[em]" that determined their "relative standing" before a court, 3 J. Pomeroy, Equity Jurisprudence § 942a, p. 741 (5th ed. 1941) (Pomeroy). In addition, the public policy considerations that undergirded the *in pari delicto* defense were frequently construed as precluding the defense even where the plaintiff bore substantial fault for his injury: "there may be on the part of the court itself a necessity of supporting the public interests or public policy in many cases, however reprehensible the acts of the parties may be." 1 Story 305. Notwithstanding these traditional limitations, many courts have given the *in pari delicto* defense a broad application to bar actions where plaintiffs simply have been involved generally in "the same sort of wrongdoing" as defendants. Perma Life Mufflers, Inc. v. International Parts Corp., 392 U.S., at 138.

In *Perma Life,* we emphasized "the inappropriateness of invoking broad common-law barriers to relief where a private suit serves important public purposes." Id., at 138. That case involved a treble-damages action against a Midas Muffler franchisor by several of its dealers, who alleged that the franchise agreement created a conspiracy to restrain trade in violation of the Sherman and Clayton Acts. The lower courts barred the action on the grounds that the dealers, as parties to the agreement, were *in pari delicto* with the franchisor. In reversing that determination, the opinion for this Court emphasized that there was no indication that Congress had intended to incorporate the defense into the antitrust laws, which "are best served by insuring that the private action will be an ever-present threat to deter anyone contemplating [illegal] business behavior." Id., at 139. Accordingly, the opinion concluded that "the doctrine of *in pari delicto,* with its complex scope, contents, and effects, is not to be recognized as a defense to an antitrust action." Id., at 140. The opinion reserved the question whether a plaintiff who engaged in "truly complete involvement and participation in a monopolistic scheme"—one who "aggressively support[ed] and further[ed] the monopolistic scheme as a necessary part and parcel of it"—could be barred from pursuing a damages action, finding that the muffler dealers had relatively little bargaining power and that they had been coerced by the franchisor into agreeing to many of the contract's provisions. Ibid.

* * *

Bateman Eichler argues that *Perma Life* —with its emphasis on the importance of analyzing the effects that fault-based defenses would have on the enforcement of congressional goals—is of only marginal relevance to a private damages action under the federal securities laws. Specifically, Bateman Eichler observes that Congress *expressly* provided for private antitrust actions—thereby manifesting a "desire to go beyond the common law in the antitrust statute in order to provide substantial encouragement to private enforcement and to help deter anticompetitive conduct"—whereas private rights of action under § 10(b) of the Securities Exchange Act of

1934 are merely *implied* from that provision—thereby, apparently, supporting a broader application of the *in pari delicto* defense. Brief for Petitioner 32. Bateman Eichler buttresses this argument by observing that, unlike the Sherman and Clayton Acts, the securities laws contain savings provisions directing that "[t]he rights and remedies provided by [those laws] shall be in addition to any and all other rights and remedies that may exist at law or in equity" [19]—again, apparently, supporting a broader scope for fault-based defenses than recognized in *Perma Life*.

We disagree. Nothing in *Perma Life* suggested that public policy implications should govern only where Congress expressly provides for private remedies; the classic formulation of the *in pari delicto* doctrine itself required a careful consideration of such implications before allowing the defense. See supra, at ___. Moreover, we repeatedly have emphasized that implied private actions provide "a most effective weapon in the enforcement" of the securities laws and are "a necessary supplement to Commission action." J.I. Case Co. v. Borak, 377 U.S. 426, 432 (1964); see also Blue Chip Stamps v. Manor Drug Stores, 421 U.S. 723, 730 (1975). In addition, we have eschewed rigid common-law barriers in construing the securities laws. See, e.g., Herman & MacLean v. Huddleston, 459 U.S. 375, 388–389 (1983) (common-law doctrines are sometimes of "questionable pertinence" in applying the securities laws, which were intended "to rectify perceived deficiencies in the available common-law protections by establishing higher standards of conduct in the securities industry"); A.C. Frost & Co. v. Coeur d'Alene Mines Corp., 312 U.S. 38, 43 (1941) (rejecting the unclean-hands defense on the facts of the case because it would "seriously hinder rather than aid the real purpose" of the securities laws). We therefore conclude that the views expressed in *Perma Life* apply with full force to implied causes of action under the federal securities laws. Accordingly, a private action for damages in these circumstances may be barred on the grounds of the plaintiff's own culpability only where (1) as a direct result of his own actions, the plaintiff bears at least substantially equal responsibility for the violations he seeks to redress, and (2) preclusion of suit would not significantly interfere with the effective enforcement of the securities laws and protection of the investing public.

A

The District Court and Court of Appeals proceeded on the assumption that the respondents had violated § 10(b) and Rule 10b-5, see supra, at ___—an assumption we accept for purposes of resolving the issue before us. Cf. A.C. Frost & Co. v. Coeur d'Alene Mines Co., supra, at 40–41.[21]

---

19. See § 16 of the Securities Act of 1933; § 28(a) of the Securities Exchange Act of 1934.

21. We note, however, the inappropriateness of resolving the question of the respondents' fault solely on the basis of the allegations set forth in the complaint. A tippee generally has a duty to disclose or to abstain from trading on material nonpublic information only when he knows or should know that his insider source "has breached his fiduciary duty to the shareholders by disclosing the information"—in other words, where the insider has sought

to "benefit, directly or indirectly, from his disclosure." Dirks v. SEC, 463 U.S. 646, 660, 662 (1983). Such benefit can derive from the insider's use of the information to secure a "pecuniary gain," a "reputational benefit that will translate into future earnings," or simply to confer "a gift of confidential information to a trading relative or friend." Id., at 663–664. See also id., at 655, n. 14 (alternative basis for liability where tippee has "entered into a special confidential relationship in the conduct of the business of the enterprise and [is] given access to information solely for corporate

Bateman Eichler contends that the respondents' *delictum* was substantially *par* to that of Lazzaro and Neadeau for two reasons. First, whereas many antitrust plaintiffs participate in illegal restraints of trade only "passively" or as the result of economic coercion, as was the case in *Perma Life*, the ordinary tippee acts *voluntarily* in choosing to trade on inside information. Second, § 10(b) and Rule 10b–5 apply literally to "any person" who violates their terms, and do not recognize gradations of culpability.

We agree that the typically voluntary nature of an investor's decision impermissibly to trade on an inside tip renders the investor more blameworthy than someone who is party to a contract solely by virtue of another's overweening bargaining power. We disagree, however, that an investor who engages in such trading is necessarily as blameworthy as a corporate insider or broker-dealer who discloses the information for personal gain. Notwithstanding the broad reach of § 10(b) and Rule 10b–5, there are important distinctions between the relative culpabilities of tippers, securities professionals, and tippees in these circumstances. The Court has made clear in recent Terms that a tippee's use of material nonpublic information does not violate § 10(b) and Rule 10b–5 unless the tippee owes a corresponding duty to disclose the information. Dirks v. SEC, 463 U.S. 646, 654–664 (1983); Chiarella v. United States, 445 U.S. 222, 230, n. 12 (1980). That duty typically is "derivative from * * * the insider's duty." Dirks v. SEC, supra, at 659; see also id., at 664. In other words, "[t]he tippee's obligation has been viewed as arising from his role as a participant after the fact in the insider's breach of a fiduciary duty" toward corporate shareholders. Chiarella v. United States, supra, at 230, n. 12.[22] In the

purposes"). Although the respondents certainly were aware that Lazzaro stood to gain from disclosure by the commissions he would earn, it is uncertain whether they had any basis to believe that Neadeau—the insider from whose potential breach all liability flows—had violated his fiduciary duties to TONM's shareholders by revealing the joint-venture information to Lazzaro. The respondents might well have believed that Neadeau provided the information to Lazzaro as a favor or otherwise acted against the shareholders' interests, but the complaint does not set forth sufficient facts to conclude that this was the case.

In addition, we accept the lower courts' assumption about the respondents' violations notwithstanding the uncertain character of the information the respondents traded on. The complaint rather strongly suggests that much of the information Lazzaro conveyed about the explorations and joint-venture negotiations was true, but that it was deceptive by virtue of exaggeration and the failure to include additional material information. See Complaint ¶¶ 10–12, 18, 20, 30, App. 8–9, 12–13, 15. If this was the case, and if the respondents otherwise acquired a derivative duty within the meaning of *Dirks*, there is no question that their trading on the basis of this information violated the securities laws. If the information was *entirely* false, the

SEC and Bateman Eichler contend that the respondents, by trading on what they believed was material nonpublic information, are nevertheless guilty of at least an *attempted* violation of the securities laws if they otherwise believed that Neadeau had breached his fiduciary duties. This view has drawn substantial support among the lower courts. See, e.g., Tarasi v. Pittsburgh National Bank, 555 F.2d, at 1159–1160; Kuehnert v. Texstar Corp., 412 F.2d, at 704; Grumet v. Shearson/American Express, Inc., 564 F.Supp., at 340. The respondents, on the other hand, contend that they could not have inherited any duty to disclose *false* information, and that the case is properly viewed as governed by the doctrine of legal impossibility, which would bar any liability, rather than factual impossibility, which would permit liability on an attempt theory. See also Note, The Availability of the *In Pari Delicto* Defense in Tippee-Tipper Rule 10b–5 Actions After Dirks v. SEC, 62 Wash.U.L.Q. 519, 540–542 (1984). Because this issue has not been fully briefed and was not considered by the courts below, we express no views on it and simply proceed on the assumption that the respondents' activities rendered them *in delicto*.

22. We also have noted that a tippee may be liable if he otherwise "misappropriate[s] or illegally obtain[s] the informa-

context of insider trading, we do not believe that a person whose liability is solely derivative can be said to be as culpable as one whose breach of duty gave rise to that liability in the first place.[23]

Moreover, insiders and broker-dealers who selectively disclose material nonpublic information commit a potentially broader range of violations than do tippees who trade on the basis of that information. A tippee trading on inside information will in many circumstances be guilty of fraud against individual shareholders, a violation for which the tipper shares responsibility. But the insider, in disclosing such information, also frequently breaches fiduciary duties toward the issuer itself. And in cases where the tipper intentionally conveys false or materially incomplete information to the tippee, the tipper commits an additional violation: fraud against the tippee. Such conduct is particularly egregious when committed by a securities professional, who owes a duty of honesty and fair dealing toward his clients. Cf. 3 Pomeroy § 942a, at 741. Absent other culpable actions by a tippee that can fairly be said to outweigh these violations by insiders and broker-dealers, we do not believe that the tippee properly can be characterized as being of substantially equal culpability as his tippers.

There is certainly no basis for concluding at this stage of this litigation that the respondents were *in pari delicto* with Lazzaro and Neadeau. The allegations are that Lazzaro and Neadeau masterminded this scheme to manipulate the market in TONM securities for their own personal benefit, and that they used the purchasing respondents as unwitting dupes to inflate the price of TONM stock. The respondents may well have violated the securities laws, and in any event we place no "stamp of approval" on their conduct. Chiarella v. United States, supra, at 238 (STEVENS, J., concurring). But accepting the facts set forth in the complaint as true—as we must in reviewing the District Court's dismissal on the pleadings— Lazzaro and Neadeau "awakened in [the respondents] a desire for wrongful gain that might otherwise have remained dormant, inspired in [their] mind[s] an unfounded idea that [they were] going to secure it, and then by fraud and false pretenses deprived [them] of [their] money," Stewart v. Wright, 147 F. 321, 328–329 (CA8), cert. denied, 203 U.S. 590 (1906)— actions that, if they occurred, were far more culpable under any reasonable view than the respondents' alleged conduct.[25]

---

tion." Dirks v. SEC, supra, at 665. Cf. H.R.Rep. No. 98–355, pp. 14–15 (1983).

23. Our view is reinforced by Congress' recent enactment of the Insider Trading Sanctions Act of 1984, § 2, which imposes civil penalties on nontrading tippers out of belief that, "[a]bsent the tipper's misconduct, the tippee's trading would not occur" and that a tipper is therefore "most directly culpable in a violation," H.R.Rep. No. 98–355, at 9.

25. Bateman Eichler has sought a reversal of the Ninth Circuit's judgment solely on the grounds that the investors were *in pari delicto* with its employee Lazzaro.

Amicus Securities Industry Association (SIA), however, contends that the *in pari delicto* defense should in any event bar recovery against a brokerage firm whose only role has been that of a "controlling person" of the defrauding employee, see n. 1, supra, and whose liability is therefore "vicarious" and "secondary." Brief for SIA as *Amicus Curiae* 20–24. This issue was not addressed by the Ninth Circuit, and Bateman Eichler has not raised it either in this Court or in the Ninth Circuit. We therefore express no views with respect to the liability of brokerage firms as "controlling persons" in cases such as this.

B

We also believe that denying the *in pari delicto* defense in such circumstances will best promote the primary objective of the federal securities laws—protection of the investing public and the national economy through the promotion of "a high standard of business ethics * * * in every facet of the securities industry." SEC v. Capital Gains Research Bureau, Inc., 375 U.S. 180, 186–187 (1963). Although a number of lower courts have reasoned that a broad rule of *caveat tippee* would better serve this goal, we believe the contrary position adopted by other courts represents the better view.

To begin with, barring private actions in cases such as this would inexorably result in a number of alleged fraudulent practices going undetected by the authorities and unremedied. The Securities and Exchange Commission has advised us that it "does not have the resources to police the industry sufficiently to ensure that false tipping does not occur or is consistently discovered," and that "[w]ithout the tippees' assistance, the Commission could not effectively prosecute false tipping—a difficult practice to detect." Brief for SEC as *Amicus Curiae* 25. See also H.R.Rep. No. 98–355, p. 6 (1983) ("In recent years, the securities markets have grown dramatically in size and complexity, while Commission enforcement resources have declined"). Thus it is particularly important to permit "litigation among guilty parties [that will serve] to expose their unlawful conduct and render them more easily subject to appropriate civil, administrative, and criminal penalties." Kuehnert v. Texstar Corp., 412 F.2d 700, 706, n. 3 (CA5 1969) (Godbold, J., dissenting). The *in pari delicto* defense, by denying any incentive to a defrauded tippee to bring suit against his defrauding tipper, would significantly undermine this important goal.

Moreover, we believe that deterrence of insider trading most frequently will be maximized by bringing enforcement pressures to bear on the sources of such information—corporate insiders and broker-dealers.

"The true insider or the broker-dealer is at the fountainhead of the confidential information * * *. If the prophylactic purpose of the law is to restrict the use of all material inside information until it is made available to the investing public, then the most effective means of carrying out this policy is to nip in the bud the source of the information, the tipper, by discouraging him from 'making the initial disclosure which is the first step in the chain of dissemination.' This can most readily be achieved by making unavailable to him the defense of in pari delicto when sued by his tippee upon charges based upon alleged misinformation." Nathanson v. Weis, Voisin, Cannon, Inc., 325 F.Supp. 50, 57–58 (SDNY 1971).

In addition, corporate insiders and broker-dealers will in many circumstances be more responsive to the deterrent pressure of potential sanctions; they are more likely than ordinary investors to be advised by counsel and thereby to be informed fully of the "allowable limits on their conduct." Kuehnert v. Texstar Corp., supra, at 706 (Godbold, J., dissenting). Although situations might well arise in which the relative culpabilities of the tippee and his insider source merit a different mix of deterrent incentives, we therefore conclude that in tipper-tippee situations such as the one before us the factors discussed above preclude recognition of the *in pari delicto* defense.[30]

Lower courts reaching a contrary conclusion have typically asserted that, absent a vigorous allowance of the *in pari delicto* defense, tippees would have, "in effect, an enforceable warranty that secret information is true," id., at 705, and thus no incentive *not* to trade on that information. These courts have reasoned, in other words, that tippees in such circumstances would be in "the enviable position of 'heads-I-win tails-you-lose,'" Wolfson v. Baker, 623 F.2d 1074, 1082 (CA5 1980), cert. denied, 450 U.S. 966 (1981)—if the tip is correct, the tippee will reap illicit profits, while if the tip fails to yield the expected return, he can sue to recover damages.

We believe the "enforceable warranty" theory is overstated and overlooks significant factors that serve to deter tippee trading irrespective of whether the *in pari delicto* defense is allowed. First, tippees who bring suit in an attempt to cash in on their "enforceable warranties" expose themselves to the threat of substantial civil and criminal penalties for their own potentially illegal conduct. Second, plaintiffs in litigation under § 10(b) and Rule 10b–5 may only recover against defendants who have acted with scienter. See Ernst & Ernst v. Hochfelder, 425 U.S. 185 (1976). Thus "if the tip merely fails to 'pan out' or if the information itself proves accurate but the stock fails to move in the anticipated direction, the investor stands to lose all of his investment. Only in the situation where the investor has been deliberately defrauded will he be able to maintain a private suit in an attempt to recoup his money." 730 F.2d, at 1324, n. 3.[33]

We therefore conclude that the public interest will most frequently be advanced if defrauded tippees are permitted to bring suit and to expose illegal practices by corporate insiders and broker-dealers to full public view for appropriate sanctions. As the Ninth Circuit emphasized in this case, there is no warrant to giving corporate insiders and broker-dealers "a license to defraud the investing public with little fear of prosecution." Id., at 1323.

Affirmed.

THE CHIEF JUSTICE concurs in the judgment.

JUSTICE MARSHALL took no part in the decision of this case.

---

30. Some courts have suggested that "even in a case where the fault of plaintiff and defendant were relatively equal, simultaneous and mutual, the court might still reject the [*in pari delicto*] defense if it appeared that the defendant's unlawful activities were of a sort likely to have a substantial impact on the investing public, and the primary legal responsibility for and ability to control that impact is with defendant." Woolf v. S.D. Cohn & Co., 515 F.2d, at 604; see also Mallis v. Bankers Trust Co., 615 F.2d, at 76, n. 6. Because there is no basis at this stage of the litigation for concluding that the respondents bore substantially equal responsibility for the violations they seek to redress, we need not address the circumstances in which preclusion of suit might otherwise significantly interfere with the effective enforcement of the securities laws and protection of the investing public.

33. The SEC also argues that courts should deter tippees in cases such as this by limiting potential recovery to out-of-pocket losses. The courts below did not address this issue, and we express no views on the proper measure of relief. Cf. Perma Life Mufflers, Inc. v. International Parts Corp., 392 U.S., at 140.

PLAINTIFF'S LACK OF DILIGENCE

Prior to the decision of the Supreme Court in the *Ernst & Ernst* case (supra, page 936), the courts were in the process of developing a defense to an action under Rule 10b–5 based upon the failure of the plaintiff to make any investigation of the facts relating to the corporation to protect himself in the transaction in which he claims that he was defrauded by the defendant. This defense had become known as the "due diligence defense."[1] One of the first results of the *Ernst & Ernst* case, initially considered a tremendous victory for defendants, was ironically to curtail sharply the development of this defense. In Holdsworth v. Strong,[2] the Tenth Circuit sitting en banc held that since the *Ernst & Ernst* case required "scienter" on the part of the defendant, it would be inappropriate any longer to permit a defense based upon lack of diligence by the plaintiff. The court said: "If the negligence standard were being applied it might be appropriate to allow due diligence to be exacted from the victim, but where liability of the defendant requires proof of intentional misconduct, the exaction of a due diligence standard from the plaintiff becomes irrational and unrelated." The court said, however, that reliance is required on the part of the plaintiff, at least in the case of an affirmative misrepresentation, and that "the plaintiff would not be heard to say that he relied on misrepresentations which were obviously false."

The Seventh Circuit in Teamsters Local 282 Pension Trust Fund v. Angelos[3] reached basically the same conclusion. The court stated: "A violation of Section 17(a)(1) or Rule 10b–5 is an intentional tort, requiring wilful or at least reckless misstatement. Ernst & Ernst v. Hochfelder, 425 U.S. 185 (1976); Aaron v. SEC, 446 U.S. 680 (1980). We therefore concluded in Sundstrand Corp. v. Sun Chemical Corp., 553 F.2d 1033, 1040 (7th Cir.), cert. denied 434 U.S. 875 (1977), that in a case under Rule 10b–5 the defense of the buyer's 'failure to exercise due care or diligence * * * is not available in an intentional fraud case.' See also Competitive Associates, Inc. v. Laventhol Krekstein, Horwath & Horwath, 516 F.2d 811 (2d Cir.1975); but cf. Dupuy v. Dupuy, 551 F.2d 1005, 1015 (5th Cir.1977), cert. denied 434 U.S. 911 (1977). We drew a line between fraud and negligent nondisclosure: 'In a nondisclosure case, reliance is vitiated if the plaintiff is chargeable with the omitted information. * * * But under a reckless or *Hochfelder scienter* standard, "[i]f contributory fault of plaintiff is to cancel out wanton or intentional fraud, it ought to be gross conduct somewhat comparable to that of defendant." ' Id. at 1048, quoting from Holdsworth v. Strong, 545 F.2d 687, 693 (10th Cir.1976) (en banc). See also Goodman v. Epstein, 582 F.2d 388, 405 & n. 47 (7th Cir.1978), cert. denied 440 U.S. 939 (1979), stating in dictum that in light of *Hochfelder* the victim's want of 'due diligence' is no longer a defense in actions under Rule 10b–5."[4]

The *Dupuy* case takes basically the same position, although the Fifth Circuit does concede that since "reckless conduct" has been established as a basis for liability on the part of the defendant, the plaintiff's recklessness might be a sufficient basis for denying him recovery.[5] On the other hand, in Zobrist v.

---

1. See Wheeler, Plaintiff's Duty of Due Care Under Rule 10b–5: An Implied Defense to an Implied Remedy, 70 Nw.U.L. Rev. 561 (1976).

2. 545 F.2d 687 (10th Cir.1976, cert. denied 430 U.S. 955 (1977).

3. 762 F.2d 522 (7th Cir.1985).

4. 762 F.2d at 528–529.

5. See, also, Mallis v. Bankers Trust Co., 615 F.2d 68 (2d Cir.1980, cert. denied 449 U.S. 1123 (1981). In that case the Second Circuit said that the defense of "unclean hands" will only be permitted in a Rule 10b–5 action where the plaintiff's reprehensible conduct is directly related to the subject matter in litigation and the party seeking to invoke the doctrine was

Coal-X, Inc.[6] the court held that an investor could not claim that he relied upon alleged oral misrepresentations regarding the "riskless" nature of the transaction where the offering circular delivered to him, but which he did not read, clearly spelled out the risks involved in the investment (presumably in the standard "risk factors" section). While not framed in terms of a requirement of "due diligence", this decision in effect says that the plaintiff must at least exercise enough diligence to read the written material furnished to him by the seller, or he will be charged with knowledge of it. The Seventh Circuit in the *Teamsters Local* case specifically stated that it agreed with the result reached in the *Zobrist* case.

The Third Circuit took a somewhat different tack in Straub v. Vaisman and Co.,[7] in which that court refused to abandon entirely the due diligence defense. The court said: "In Rule 10b–5 cases, where the defendant acts intentionally, the line should be drawn between the extremes of making the plaintiff's lack of diligence, regardless of degree, a complete bar or at the other limit—completely irrelevant. * * * The latter option fails to encourage investor caution and, under the former view, Rule 10b–5 would provide less assistance to the trusting or gullible than does the common law. * * * The obligation of due care must be a flexible one, dependent upon the circumstances of each case. We require only that the plaintiff act reasonably. Since the failure to meet that standard is in the nature of an affirmative defense, the burden of proof rests upon the defendant. Such matters as fiduciary relationship, opportunity to detect the fraud, sophistication of the plaintiff, the existence of long-standing business or personal relationships, and access to the relevant information, are all worthy of consideration."

If thus appears that the due diligence defense has been largely eliminated so far as any requirement that the plaintiff investigate the truth of intentional misrepresentations made to him, but it may partially survive in a requirement that the plaintiff must have "justifiably" relied upon the truth of the representation.[8]

To the extent that this defense survives, it should be applied (as it has been in the past) only in the case of face-to-face dealings between the plaintiff and the defendant, generally in the stock of corporations which are not publicly traded. It would, obviously, be inappropriate to require a person purchasing or selling stock in the organized market to launch an investigation of the corporation whose stock he is buying or of the truth of public statements made by the persons in control of the corporation.

See Slonim, Customer Sophistication and a Plaintiff's Duty of Due Diligence: A Proposed Framework for Churning Actions in Nondiscretionary Accounts Under SEC Rule 10b–5, 54 Fordham L.Rev. 1101 (1986); Sachs, The Relevance of Tort Law Doctrines to Rule 10b–5: Should Careless Plaintiffs be Denied Recovery?, 71 Cornell L.Rev. 96 (1985); Markham and Bergin, Customer Rights Under the Commodity Exchange Act, 37 Vand.L.Rev. 1299 (1984); Helman, Rule 10b–5 Omissions Cases and the Investment Decision, 51 Fordham L.Rev. 399 (1982); Marinelli, Limitations on Rule 10b–5, 80 W.Va.L.Rev. 219 (1978); Jacobs, Affirmative Defenses to Securities Exchange Act Rule 10b–5 Actions, 61

---

injured by the conduct. Also, the plaintiff must have "equal guilt" with the defendant. So far as the due diligence defense is concerned, the court said that "A plaintiff's burden is simply to negate recklessness when the defendant puts that in issue, not to establish due care."

6. 708 F.2d 1511 (10th Cir.1983).

7. 540 F.2d 591 (3d Cir.1976).

8. See Thompson v. Smith Barney, Harris Upham & Co., 709 F.2d 1413 (11th Cir. 1983).

Cornell L.Rev. 857 (1976); Wheeler, Plaintiff's Duty of Due Care Under Rule 10b–5, 70 Nw.U.L.Rev. 561 (1976).

IN PARI DELICTO

The Supreme Court held in the *Berner* case that a tippee is not ordinarily barred from suing his tipper when the information given to him turns out to be false, since the tippee's crime is less heinous than that of the tipper and the policy of the securities laws requires that the tipper be subject to suit by his tippee in order to add a further deterrent to the practice of giving such tips. The court did not, however, completely close the door to the raising of this defense in some cases where the fault of the parties is "substantially equal" and the policies of the securities laws will not be offended by permitting the defense. In Rothberg v. Rosenbloom [9] the plaintiff participated in a "joint venture" to trade on the basis of inside information and, when the supposed inside information did not turn out to be accurate and the joint venture lost $443,000, he sued to collect certain promissory notes that were given to him by the joint venture. The defendants were his "partners" in the joint venture and not the insider who furnished the information (which, it would appear, he did in good faith, and simply overestimated his influence in being able to bring about a certain corporate transaction). The defendants raised the defense of *in pari delicto*. The circuit court did not decide this question, but sent the case back to the district judge to rule on it in the light of the *Berner* case, possibly because the court was uncertain as to how it ought to be decided (it would seem that all of the facts were already in evidence). The court instructed the district judge to determine "(1) whether * * * [the plaintiff] bears at least 'substantially equal responsibility' for the violations he seeks to redress, and (2) whether preclusion of suit would 'significantly interfere' with the effective enforcement of the securities laws and protection of the investing public."

All of the cases thus far in which this doctrine has been asserted as a defense have involved insider trading situations where the "tip" turned out to be false. In the normal securities law litigation, it is unlikely that the bilked investor can be seriously alleged to have "equal fault" with the bilker.

JOY v. NORTH

United States Court of Appeals, Second Circuit, 1982.
692 F.2d 880.

Before OAKES, CARDAMONE and WINTER, CIRCUIT JUDGES.

RALPH K. WINTER, CIRCUIT JUDGE:

This is an appeal from a grant of summary judgment for defendants by the District Court for the District of Connecticut, Eginton, Judge, dismissing a derivative action against certain directors and officers of Citytrust upon a recommendation of a special litigation committee and placing that report under seal. 519 F.Supp. 1312 (D.Conn.1981).

We reverse.

---

9. 771 F.2d 818 (3d Cir.1985).

BACKGROUND

In October of 1977, Dr. Athalie Doris Joy brought this shareholder's derivative suit on behalf of Connecticut Financial Services Corporation (now Citytrust Bancorp, Inc.) against its wholly-owned banking subsidiary, Citytrust, and the officers and directors of Citytrust. Both corporations are incorporated in Connecticut. The complaint alleged diversity of citizenship, common law breach of trust and of fiduciary duty as well as violations of the National Bank Act, 12 U.S.C. § 84 (1976), which limits aggregate loans to a single person or entity to 10% of a bank's combined stockholder equity and capital. The allegations concern loans made by Citytrust to the Katz Corporation ("Katz") for construction of an office building in a redevelopment area of Norwalk, Connecticut. Plaintiff seeks a $6 million recovery plus interest and attorney's fees.

The underlying transactions need only be briefly summarized at this point. In 1967, Citytrust entered into a 20–year term lease agreement for approximately 9% of an office building which Katz was planning to build in Norwalk. Katz then a respected developer, signed a $4 million construction mortgage for a one-and-a-half year term on January 12, 1971. Although the mortgage was written through and recorded in the name of Citytrust, Chase Manhattan Bank provided the bulk of the financing, $3.5 million, with Citytrust participating to the extent of $500,000. At this time, Katz had already borrowed, largely in unsecured form, an additional $250,000 from Citytrust to finance construction of the office building. As the building neared completion in early 1972, Katz had drawn down the full value of the $4 million mortgage. At its expiration in June, 1972, the Chase mortgage was replaced by a $4.5 million mortgage by First National City Bank, with Citytrust both issuing the mortgage and participating to the extent of $90,000. Meanwhile, Katz continued to receive unsecured loans from Citytrust. By December, 1972, that unsecured debt reached $900,000, for a total of $990,000 in Citytrust loans related to the building.

In June, 1973, with the building only half rented, the First National City mortgage was extended for a year. Katz's unsecured debt to Citytrust had by now climbed to $1,840,000. In November, in conjunction with the issuance of yet another loan to Katz, Citytrust obtained a blanket second mortgage on the building and on other Katz properties to secure what was now a total loan balance of $2,140,000. Shortly thereafter, the First National City mortgage was extended to August, 1975, and Citytrust lent Katz another $300,000. Just prior to this extension of credit, the National Bank Examiners classified the Katz loans.

In April, 1975, a refinancing plan was completed with Lincoln National Life Insurance Company providing a $6 million loan to a Katz-related partnership which had taken title to the building. The loan was secured by a first mortgage on the building and was used to consolidate Katz's debt. As a condition of the new financing, Citytrust was required to take a 30–year master lease on the still largely unrented building at a rental equaling the mortgage payments to Lincoln National, in effect guaranteeing Katz's $6 million obligation to Lincoln. In addition to undertaking the master lease, Citytrust had by now extended $2,665,000 in loans to Katz.

In May, 1975, the National Bank Examiners classified $2 million of the Katz loans as doubtful and required a charge off of $665,000. On August

18, 1976, in an apparent effort to salvage what was left of its position, Citytrust's Board of Directors authorized loans which exceeded the 10% federal statutory limit. After these loans were consummated, Katz's total indebtedness to Citytrust reached $3,545,000. On October 20, 1976, Citytrust charged off the $2 million remaining on the second mortgage.

On June 13, 1977, the Katz-related partnership relinquished title to the building to Citytrust in exchange for a release from its obligation to Lincoln National and a release of personal guarantees previously assumed by members of the Katz family. Citytrust thus directly assumed the $6 million Lincoln National mortgage. In October, 1977, Second Nutmeg Financial purchased the building for $9,600,000 which consisted of its assumption of the $6 million Lincoln National mortgage and a $3,600,000 note to Citytrust secured by a second mortgage. There is an indication in the District Court record that an affiliate of Second Nutmeg which later acquired the building has defaulted and Citytrust once again owns it, along with the concurrent obligations. There is no indication that rental income is now adequate to meet those obligations, and we appear free to assume that the other Katz properties covered by the second mortgage are not of any significant value.

In October, 1977, Joy commenced this action after making an unsuccessful demand on the Directors of Citytrust. During the pendency of this case, the Supreme Court decided Burks v. Lasker, 441 U.S. 471 (1979), holding that federal courts must apply state law in determining the authority of a committee of independent directors to discontinue derivative suits even in many cases which arise under federal law. Immediately following the *Burks* decision, the Board of Directors of Citytrust and Connecticut Financial Services Corporation authorized the establishment of a Special Litigation Committee to determine whether continued prosecution of this derivative action would be in the best interests of the corporation. The Committee consisted of two Board members, Marion S. Kellogg and Ernest C. Trefz.[2] Kellogg was elected to the Board of Directors on July 21, 1976 and commenced service on September 15, 1976. Trefz was elected to the Board on December 15, 1976 and commenced service on January 3, 1977. Neither is a defendant in this action.

By resolution dated August 15, 1979, the full Board of Directors, a majority of whom were defendants, voted to delegate to the Committee the power to review, investigate and analyze the circumstances surrounding the pending derivative action. The Committee retained independent counsel, John Murtha, Esquire, to assist its investigation.

Nine months later, the Committee issued a Report recommending that the suit be discontinued as to 23 defendants, 20 of whom were outside directors of either Citytrust or Connecticut Financial Services and three of whom were either officers or directors or both. (The 23 will hereafter be referred to as the "outside defendants"). The Committee concluded there was "no reasonable possibility" that the outside defendants would be found liable. Its Report also recommended that settlement be considered with regard to seven defendants who were the senior officers most directly involved in the Katz loans. (These seven will hereafter be referred to as

---

2. Alexander L. Stott was also named to the Committee. However, he resigned on March 3, 1980.

the "inside defendants"). As to them, the Committee found there was a "possibility" that one or more might be found to have been negligent. Counsel for the Committee made it clear to the District Court, however, that the decision to pursue settlement was not necessarily a decision to press the litigation against the inside defendants. If settlement is not reached, the Committee will reconsider whether to recommend termination of that portion of the action also.

When plaintiff declined to withdraw the action as to the outside defendants, the corporation filed a motion to dismiss the case as to them. The District Court permitted discovery on the limited issue of the Committee's "*bona fides,* motivation and thoroughness." 519 F.Supp. at 1315. Portions of the Committee Report, consisting of a summary and a detailed presentation of the Committee's factual findings, supplemented by expert opinion letters and counsel's memorandum of law, were produced. These documents were put under seal pursuant to a protective order. Plaintiff was also allowed to depose a variety of persons involved in the underlying transactions and in preparation of the Report, to post interrogatories to others, and to see various documents relating to the Report.

After discovery, Judge Eginton granted the defendants' motion for summary judgment, the protective order remaining in force. Concluding that no dispositive Connecticut case or statute exists, Judge Eginton referred to the weight of authority in cases reported elsewhere. He held that Connecticut law permits the use of a *Burks* committee and that the business judgment rule limits judicial scrutiny of its recommendations to the good faith, independence and thoroughness of the Committee. 519 F.Supp. at 1325. He resolved these issues favorably to the Committee and, therefore, entered summary judgment in favor of the 23 outside defendants. Plaintiff appeals from the ruling. We reverse as to both the grant of summary judgment and the sealing of the Committee report.

DISCUSSION

The grounds of liability asserted are common law claims of negligence and breach of fiduciary duty, as well as violation of the National Bank Act. We agree with Judge Eginton for the reasons stated in his opinion that the Special Litigation Committee may seek dismissal of both the state common law and federal claims if Connecticut law authorizes it to do so. 519 F.Supp. at 1318–22; *Burks,* supra. We also agree with him that the Connecticut statutory and case law cited by the parties is not dispositive. Our task, therefore, is to predict what the Connecticut Supreme Court would do in a case such as the one before us.

Appellees assert that, since a board of directors can delegate all its powers to a committee, Conn.Gen.Stat.Ann. § 33–318(a) (West 1982), a special litigation committee of independent directors can decide whether a derivative action should be dismissed or continued. They further argue that, when an appropriate motion is made, courts must defer to the committee's recommendation under the so-called business judgment rule, even though the delegation of power is made by directors who are defendants in the action. Judge Eginton adopted that position and limited his inquiry to the Committee's good faith, independence and thoroughness. Appellees also assert that the Committee Report in question may be kept under seal, any public use being in violation of the District Court's order.

Appellant claims an absolute right to maintain a derivative action, once begun and challenges the protective order on constitutional and non-constitutional grounds.

An examination of these claims requires a discussion of some underlying principles of corporate law. Our opinion first addresses the nature and function of the business judgment rule, which played a large role in persuading the District Court to dismiss this action. It turns then to the legal oddity known as the derivative action, thought by many to be an endangered species as a consequence of the evolution of special litigation committees. See Comment, Special Litigation Committees—An Expanding and Potent Threat to Shareholder Derivative Suits, 2 Cardozo L.Rev. 169 (1980); Note, The Business Judgment Rule in Derivative Suits Against Directors, 65 Cornell L.Rev. 600 (1980); Dent, the Power of Directors to Terminate Shareholder Litigation: The Death of the Derivative Suit, 75 Northwestern L.Rev. 96 (1980). Finally, it discusses the general principles applicable to attempts by special litigation committees to terminate particular derivative actions, and their relevance to the present case.

A. The Liability of Corporate Directors and Officers and the Business Judgment Rule

While it is often stated that corporate directors and officers will be liable for negligence in carrying out their corporate duties, all seem agreed that such a statement is misleading. See generally, Lattin, Corporations, 272–75 (1971). Whereas an automobile driver who makes a mistake in judgment as to speed or distance injuring a pedestrian will likely be called upon to respond in damages, a corporate officer who makes a mistake in judgment as to economic conditions, consumer tastes or production line efficiency will rarely, if ever, be found liable for damages suffered by the corporation. See generally, Symposium, Officers' and Directors' Responsibilities and Liabilities, 27 Bus.Lawyer 1 (1971); Fever, Personal Liabilities of Corporate Officers and Directors, 28–42 (2d ed. 1974). Whatever the terminology, the fact is that liability is rarely imposed upon corporate directors or officers simply for bad judgment and this reluctance to impose liability for unsuccessful business decisions has been doctrinally labelled the business judgment rule. Although the rule has suffered under academic criticism, see, e.g., Cary, Standards of Conduct Under Common Law, Present Day Statutes and the Model Act, 27 Bus.Lawyer 61 (1972), it is not without rational basis.

First, shareholders to a very real degree voluntarily undertake the risk of bad business judgment. Investors need not buy stock, for investment markets offer an array of opportunities less vulnerable to mistakes in judgment by corporate officers. Nor need investors buy stock in particular corporations. In the exercise of what is genuinely a free choice, the quality of a firm's management is often decisive and information is available from professional advisors. Since shareholders can and do select among investments partly on the basis of management, the business judgment rule merely recognizes a certain voluntariness in undertaking the risk of bad business decisions.

Second, courts recognize that after-the-fact litigation is a most imperfect device to evaluate corporate business decisions. The circumstances surrounding a corporate decision are not easily reconstructed in a courtroom years later, since business imperatives often call for quick decisions, inevitably based on less than perfect information. The entrepreneur's function is to encounter risks and to confront uncertainty, and a reasoned decision at the time made may seem a wild hunch viewed years later against a background of perfect knowledge.

Third, because potential profit often corresponds to the potential risk, it is very much in the interest of shareholders that the law not create incentives for overly cautious corporate decisions. Some opportunities offer great profits at the risk of very substantial losses, while the alternatives offer less risk of loss but also less potential profit. Shareholders can reduce the volatility of risk by diversifying their holdings. In the case of the diversified shareholder, the seemingly more risky alternatives may well be the best choice since great losses in some stocks will over time be offset by even greater gains in others. Given mutual funds and similar forms of diversified investment, courts need not bend over backwards to give special protection to shareholders who refuse to reduce the volatility of risk by not diversifying. A rule which penalizes the choice of seemingly riskier alternatives thus may not be in the interest of shareholders generally.

Whatever its merit, however, the business judgment rule extends only as far as the reasons which justify its existence. Thus, it does not apply in cases, e.g., in which the corporate decision lacks a business purpose, see Singer v. Magnavox, 380 A.2d 969 (Del.Supr.1977), is tainted by a conflict of interest, Globe Woolen v. Utica Gas & Electric Co., 224 N.Y. 483, 121 N.E. 378 (1918), is so egregious as to amount to a no-win decision, Litwin v. Allen, 25 N.Y.S.2d 667 (N.Y.Co.Sup.Ct.1940), or results from an obvious and prolonged failure to exercise oversight or supervision, McDonnell v. American Leduc Petroleums, Ltd., 491 F.2d 380 (2d Cir.1974); Atherton v. Anderson, 99 F.2d 883 (6th Cir.1938). Other examples may occur.

B. Shareholder Derivative Actions

Whereas ordinary lenders may and will sue directly to enforce their rights and debentureholders look to indenture trustees to enforce obligations to them, direct actions by individual shareholders for injuries to the value of their investment would be an inefficient and wasteful method of enforcing management obligations. The stake of each shareholder in the likely return is usually too small to justify bringing a lawsuit and a multiplicity of such actions would result in corporate and judicial waste. Moreover, the costs of organizing a large number of geographically diverse shareholders to bring an action are usually prohibitively high. If an alternative remedy were not available, therefore, the fiduciary obligations of corporate management, however limited, might well be unenforceable. Moreover, state or federal law may impose other duties upon directors and officers which are designed to protect shareholders through procedural or other requirements, e.g. proxy rules. Enforcement of such obligations by shareholders, even where monetary recovery by the corporation is doubtful, may be desirable. J.I. Case Co. v. Borak, 377 U.S. 426 (1964); Mills v. Electric Auto-Lite, 396 U.S. 375 (1970).

The derivative action is the common law's inventive solution to the problem of actions to protect shareholder interests. In its classic form, a derivative suit involves two actions brought by an individual shareholder: (i) an action against the corporation for failing to bring a specified suit and (ii) an action on behalf of the corporation for harm to it identical to the one which the corporation failed to bring. See Ross v. Bernhard, 396 U.S. 531

(1970). The technical structure of the derivative suit is thus quite unusual. Moreover, the shareholder plaintiffs are quite often little more than a formality for purposes of the caption rather than parties with a real interest in the outcome. Since any judgment runs to the corporation, shareholder plaintiffs at best realize an appreciation in the value of their shares. The real incentive to bring derivative actions is usually not the hope of return to the corporation but the hope of handsome fees to be recovered by plaintiffs' counsel. * * *

However, there is a danger in authorizing lawyers to bring actions on behalf of unconsulted groups. Derivative suits may be brought for their nuisance value, the threat of protracted discovery and litigation forcing settlement and payment of fees even where the underlying suit has modest merit. Such suits may be harmful to shareholders because the costs offset the recovery. Thus, a continuing debate surrounding derivative actions has been over restricting their use to situations where the corporation has a reasonable chance for benefit.

C. Termination of Derivative Suits by Special Litigation Committees

In the normal course of events a decision whether to bring a lawsuit is a corporate economic decision subject to the business judgment rule. United Copper Securities Co. v. Amalgamated Copper Co., 244 U.S. 261 (1917). Thus, shareholders upset at a corporate failure to bring actions for, say, nonpayment of a debt for goods sold and delivered, may not initiate a derivative suit without first making a demand upon the directors to bring the action. Where the directors refuse, and the derivative action challenges that refusal, courts apply the business judgment rule to the action of the directors. In a demand-required case, therefore, the directors' decision will be conclusive unless bad faith is proven.

Different rules apply, however, in the cases which primarily concern us here. When there is a conflict of interest in the directors' decision not to sue because the directors themselves have profited from the transaction underlying the litigation or are named defendants, no demand need be made and shareholders can proceed directly with a derivative suit. Note, Demand on Directors and Shareholders as a Prerequisite to a Derivative Suit, 73 Harv.L.Rev. 746, 753–56 (1960). It is in demand-not-required cases that the special litigation committee plays its role.

Appellees argue that, because special litigation committees are composed of "independent" directors—usually newly-elected directors who are not defendants—courts should treat their recommendations as the equivalent of a board refusal to bring an action in demand-required cases. If that proposition were accepted, the business judgment rule would apply in full force to the recommendation, and judicial scrutiny would be limited to the good faith, independence and thoroughness of the committee, as it is in the case of everyday business decisions. Appellant argues, on the other hand, that such committees are transparent devices enabling implicated directors to avoid liability and that derivative actions in demand-not-required cases are immune from termination whatever the recommendation of special litigation committees. We disagree with both parties.

We believe Connecticut would not adopt appellees' contention that the business judgment rule should play a major role where a special litigation committee recommends termination of an action in a demand-not-required case, such as the one before us. As a practical matter, new board members are selected by incumbents. The reality is, therefore, that special litigation committees created to evaluate the merits of certain litigation are appointed by the defendants to that litigation. It is not cynical to expect that such committees will tend to view derivative actions against the other directors with skepticism. Indeed, if the involved directors expected any result other than a recommendation of termination at least as to them, they would probably never establish the committee. The conflict of interest which renders the business judgment rule inapplicable in the case of directors who are defendants is hardly eliminated by the creation of a special litigation committee.

It is here that we part company with Judge Cardamone. While he recognizes that the business judgment rule has never applied to corporate decisions tainted by a conflict of interest, he argues that the conflict in the defendants' creation of a committee to determine whether this action should be terminated is wholly cured by a judicial finding that the committee acted independently and in good faith. This view is a major departure from the traditional scrutiny courts have given to the underlying fairness of corporate decisions which benefit directors. Lattin, Corporations at 293; see also Ferris v. Polycast Technology Corp., 180 Conn. 199, 208-09, 429 A.2d 850, 854 (1980) and cases cited therein. To be sure, Judge Cardamone is correct in anticipating difficulties in judicial review of the recommendations of special litigation committees. These difficulties are not new, however, but have confronted every court which has scrutinized the fairness of corporate transactions involving a conflict of interest.

Moreover, the difficulties courts face in evaluation of business decisions are considerably less in the case of recommendations of special litigation committees. The relevant decision—whether to continue litigation—is at hand and the danger of deceptive hindsight simply does not exist. Moreover, it can hardly be argued that terminating a lawsuit is an area in which courts have no special aptitude. Citytrust's Special Litigation Committee concluded that there was "no reasonable possibility" that 23 outside defendants would be held liable. A court is not ill-equipped to review the merits of that conclusion. Even when the Committee recommendation arises from the fear of further damage to the corporation, for example, the distraction of key personnel, the cost of complying with discovery, and the possible indemnification of defendants out of the corporate treasury, courts are not on unfamiliar terrain. The rule we predict Connecticut would establish emphasizes matters such as probable liability and extent of recovery. For these reasons we hold that the wide discretion afforded directors under the business judgment rule does not apply when a special litigation committee recommends dismissal of a suit.

We think Connecticut would reject appellees' argument for a second reason. Limiting judicial scrutiny in cases such as the one before us to the good faith, thoroughness and independence of the special litigation committee would effectively eliminate the fiduciary obligation of directors and officers. As adumbrated further below, the present action involves classic allegations and substantial evidence of mismanagement and perhaps deliberate wrongdoing resulting in a loss exceeding 10% of the shareholders' capital and equity. The traditional fiduciary obligations of directors and officers under Connecticut law can hardly be said to exist if the sole enforcement method can be eliminated on a recommendation of the defendants' appointees. Other well-understood principles of corporate law would also be altered. For example, the requirement of a demand upon directors before initiating a derivative suit does not apply to a case such as the present one, where the corporate directors and officers are defendants. One reason—the other being futility—underlying the rule is that directors and officers cannot render a fair judgment on allegations of their own misconduct. Appellees would have us substantially modify this by allowing the defendants to appoint a committee to evaluate these allegations and impose their conclusions on the plaintiffs. In derivative actions, the plaintiffs have always controlled the action subject to judicial findings of adequate representation of shareholders and approval of settlements. See Conn.Gen.Stat.Ann. § 52–572j (West 1982). Appellees' view essentially vests power in defendants' appointees to bring about their dismissal.

We are aware that Auerbach v. Bennett, 47 N.Y.2d 619, 419 N.Y.S.2d 920, 393 N.E.2d 994 (1979), held that the business judgment rule limits judicial scrutiny of the recommendations of special litigation committees to their good faith, thoroughness and independence. Because we believe that test would work a major transformation of Connecticut corporate law, we predict that Connecticut would not adopt it. While the ongoing debate over the legal obligations of corporate management has spawned literature from Connecticut commentators calling for less judicial scrutiny of corporate transactions, Wolfson, A Critique of Corporate Law, 34 Miami L.Rev. 959 (1980), the special litigation committee, as envisioned in *Auerbach,* seems a rather blunt instrument to accomplish that end, since it appears to allow dismissals in actions for deliberate looting as well as in nuisance suits.

* * *

We also disagree with appellant that recommendations of special litigation committees should be ignored by courts in which derivative actions are pending. The incentives underlying derivative litigation are such that actions may well be brought which cannot be dismissed on motion but which also are unlikely to lead to net benefits to the corporation. At least where the effectuation of an overriding federal policy is not at stake, cf. Galef v. Alexander, 615 F.2d 51, 62 (2d Cir.1980) ("serious questions" whether a special litigation committee can seek dismissal of an action alleging federal proxy violations), a corporation can play a legitimate role in aiding a court to determine whether the maintenance of an action in its name is in fact in its interest. Surviving a motion to dismiss and for summary judgment establishes only that a claim for relief has been stated and that there is a scintilla of evidence to support it. It does not establish that continued prosecution of the action is actually in the corporation's interest.

* * *

We strongly disagree with the implications of the dissenting opinion that by not according the recommendations of special litigation committees conclusive weight we are somehow embarking on a new course of "stricter corporate accountability" which will lead to "more derivative lawsuits." Such committees are very recent creations. Indeed, *Auerbach,* the first decision of a state high court to address these issues, was decided only three years ago. Our failure to accord the recommendations of such committees conclusive weight can hardly be regarded as overregulation. And our holding that the recommendations of such committees may be considered by a court and provide the basis for dismissal of a derivative action will hardly lead to an increase in the number of such actions brought.

The *Auerbach* decision gives excessive weight to the recommendations of special litigation committees. In rejecting *Auerbach* and concluding that Connecticut would adopt a rule limiting the role of such committees, we are not without eminent judicial support. In Zapata Corp. v. Maldonado, 430 A.2d 779 (Del.Supr.1979), the Delaware Supreme Court, which has unique experience in the area, laid down the following rule: Where a derivative suit cannot be brought without prior demand upon the directors followed by refusal, the directors' decision will stand absent a demonstration of self-interest or bad faith; but where such a demand is excused (for reasons of futility, etc.) and a derivative action is properly brought, an independent committee of directors may obtain a dismissal only if the trial court finds both (a) that the committee was independent, acted in good faith and made a reasonable investigation; and (b) that in the court's independent business judgment as to the corporation's best interest, the action should be dismissed. We believe Connecticut would adopt a similar rule.

Independent judicial scrutiny of a special litigation committee's recommendation is apt to be difficult and in an effort to ease that task we establish some guidelines. We emphasize that what we say here applies to cases involving allegations of direct economic injury to the corporation diminishing the value of the shareholders' investment as a consequence of fraud, mismanagement or self-dealing. This is not a case involving allegations of *ultra vires* acts or acts illegal under domestic or foreign laws which do not have as a major purpose protection of the corporate shareholder's investment interest. Compare Gall v. Exxon Corp., 418 F.Supp. 508 (S.D. N.Y.1976). Nor is it a case in which the relief sought may benefit the corporation but in ways not entailing a direct financial return. Mills v. Electric Auto-Lite, supra (action for misleading proxy statement where no monetary recovery by the corporation may result); Bosch v. Meeker Cooperative Light & Power Ass'n, 257 Minn. 362, 101 N.W.2d 423 (1960) (invalidation of directors' elections). The guidelines we establish here are limited to cases involving allegations of acts resulting in direct financial harm to the corporation and a consequent diminishing of the value of shareholders' investment. We express no views on the appropriate calculus to be applied to recommendations of special litigation committees where the derivative action alleges violations of law not designed principally to protect shareholders or, which, if successful, may benefit the corporation in ways other than the recovery of compensatory damages.

In cases such as the present one, the burden is on the moving party, as in motions for summary judgment generally, to demonstrate that the action is more likely than not to be against the interests of the corporation. This showing is to be based on the underlying data developed in the course of discovery and of the committee's investigation and the committee's reasoning, not simply its naked conclusions. The weight to be given certain evidence is to be determined by conventional analysis, such as whether testimony is under oath and subject to cross-examination. Finally, the function of the court's review is to determine the balance of probabilities as to likely future benefit to the corporation, not to render a decision on the merits, fashion the appropriate legal principles or resolve issues of credibility. Where the legal rule is unclear and the likely evidence in conflict, the court need only weigh the uncertainties, not resolve them. The court's function is thus not unlike a lawyer's determining what a case is "worth" for purposes of settlement.

Where the court determines that the likely recoverable damages discounted by the probability of a finding of liability are less than the costs to the corporation in continuing the action, it should dismiss the case. The costs which may properly be taken into account are attorney's fees and other out-of-pocket expenses related to the litigation and time spent by corporate personnel preparing for and participating in the trial. The court should also weigh indemnification which is mandatory under corporate bylaws, private contract or Connecticut law, discounted of course by the probability of liability for such sums. We believe indemnification the corporation may later pay as a matter of discretion should not be taken into account since it is an avoidable cost. The existence or non-existence of insurance should not be considered in the calculation of costs, since premiums have previously been paid. The existence of insurance is relevant to the calculation of potential benefits.

Where, having completed the above analysis, the court finds a likely net return to the corporation which is not substantial in relation to shareholder equity, it may take into account two other items as costs. First, it may consider the impact of distraction of key personnel by continued litigation. Second, it may take into account potential lost profits which may result from the publicity of a trial.

Judicial scrutiny of special litigation committee recommendations should thus be limited to a comparison of the direct costs imposed upon the corporation by the litigation with the potential benefits. We are mindful that other less direct costs may be incurred, such as a negative impact on morale and upon the corporate image. Nevertheless, we believe that such factors, with the two exceptions noted, should not be taken into account. Quite apart from the elusiveness of attempting to predict such effects, they are quite likely to be directly related to the degree of wrongdoing, a spectacular fraud being generally more newsworthy and damaging to morale than a mistake in judgment as to the strength of consumer demand.

We do recognize two exceptions, however. First, where the likely net return is not substantial in relation to shareholder equity, the court can consider the degree to which key personnel may be distracted from corporate business by continuance of the litigation. We appreciate that litigation can disrupt the decision-making process and thereby impose unforeseen and undetected costs. These are not measurable and we limit consideration of them to cases where the likely return to the corporation is not great. Where that is the case and many of the key directors and officers will be heavily involved in the litigation, a court may take such potential costs into account.

Second, where the corporation deals with the general public and its level of business is dependent upon public identification and acceptance of the corporate product or service, we believe the court ought to take potential business lost as a consequence of a trial into account when the likely net return to the corporation is not substantial in relation to total shareholder equity. In such a case, there is less likelihood of a direct relationship between impact on business and degree of misconduct. Where the likely return to the corporation from the litigation is higher, however, we believe the uncertainty as to the kind of publicity which will attend a trial precludes consideration of that impact. Moreover, when potential lost profits are taken into account, the basis for calculating them must be something more solid than the conclusory opinions of alleged experts, e.g., verifiable examples in similar firms.

* * *

E. The Present Case

Given the principles outlined above, we reverse the order putting the Citytrust Committee's Report under seal and restricting its use. The showing of good cause was merely that it and the accompanying documents were protected by the attorney-client privilege and work-product immunity and involved a candid assessment of the bank's internal operations which, if made public, would adversely affect the two corporations in the banking industry and the Bridgeport community. This showing is patently inadequate. First, the submission of materials to a court in order to obtain a summary judgment utterly precludes the assertion of the attorney-client privilege or work-product immunity. Second, a naked conclusory statement that publication of the Report will injure the bank in the industry and local community falls woefully short of the kind of showing which raises even an arguable issue as to whether it may be kept under seal. The Report is no longer a private document. It is part of a court record. Since it is the basis for the adjudication, only the most compelling reasons can justify the total foreclosure of public and professional scrutiny. The potential harm asserted by the corporate defendants is in disclosure of poor management in the past. That is hardly a trade secret. * * *

* * *

Applying the standard of review set out above to the Committee's recommendation, we look first to potential liability generally without regard to which defendants are responsible. As to that liability, we find that plaintiff's chances of success are rather high. The loss to Citytrust resulted from decisions which put the bank in a classic "no win" situation. The Katz venture was risky and increasingly so. By continuing extensions of substantial amounts of credit the bank subjected the principal to those risks although its potential gain was no more than the interest it could have earned in less risky, more diversified loans. In a real sense, there was a low ceiling on profits but only a distant floor for losses. It is so similar to the classic case of Litwin v. Allen, supra (bank purchase of bonds with an option in the seller to repurchase at the original price, the bank thus bearing the entire risk of a drop in price with no hope of gain beyond the stipulated interest) that we cannot agree with the Committee's conclusion that only a "possibility of a finding of negligence" exists.

The issue as to which defendants are responsible is less clear. The Committee concluded that there is "no reasonable possibility" of the outside defendants being found liable because they had neither information nor reasonable notice of the problems raised by the Katz transactions. We note first that members of the inside defendants may contradict that version and, if so, a possibility of liability in the outside group exists. Moreover, lack of knowledge is not necessarily a defense, if it is the result of an abdication of directional responsibility. *McDonnell,* supra; *Atherton,* supra. Directors who willingly allow others to make major decisions affecting the future of the corporation wholly without supervision or oversight may not defend on their lack of knowledge, for that ignorance itself is a breach of fiduciary duty. The issue turns in large part upon how and why these defendants were left in the dark. See Graham v. Allis Chalmers Mfg. Co., 41 Del.Ch. 78, 188 A.2d 125 (1963). An individual analysis of each outside defendant's role may show that some are blameless or even that they all were justified in not acting before they did, but neither is an inexorable conclusion on the basis of the present record.

The Report concluded as to the inside defendants that there was a "possibility" of liability. This conclusion is a considerable understatement and not entirely consistent with the Report's finding as to the outside defendants. The outsiders' best defense may well be that the inside group actively concealed the Katz problem. Given the fact that exoneration of the outside defendants may show culpability of the insiders and our conclusion that the probability of liability somewhere is high, we think the exposure of the inside group is considerably more than a "possibility." Nor do we agree that "there is no evidence whatsoever" of deliberate impropriety. Not only is there the problem of North's apparently inconsistent behavior with respect to the appropriateness of his participation in the considerations of Katz transactions, but his failure to keep the Board of Directors informed may well entail more than a negligent omission.

A precise estimate of potential damages is not possible since the trier must determine at what point liability begins. We think, however, that on the present record, a trier might easily find liability extending back to early 1972 or before (assuming no statute of limitations problem), resulting in a return of several million dollars to Citytrust, or perhaps 10% or more of the shareholder equity. This far exceeds the potential cost of the litigation to the corporation.

CONCLUSION

Applying the analysis described above, we conclude that the probability of a substantial net return to the corporation is high. We reject, therefore, the recommendation of the Special Litigation Committee. The grant of summary judgment is reversed, the protective order is vacated, and the case is remanded. Since we have been unable to explain our reasoning in this opinion without extensive reference to materials under seal, the mandate shall issue forthwith as to the lifting of the protective order.

CARDAMONE, CIRCUIT JUDGE, concurring, in part,[1] and dissenting in part.

As the majority correctly concludes Connecticut law controls the question of the defendant corporation's right to terminate Joy's derivative suit. Since Connecticut's courts have not yet addressed the issue now before us, we are relegated to predicting what the Connecticut Supreme Court would decide in this case. Because it is an "iffy" business to prophesy what view a state's highest court will take in the future, and since Connecticut's Supreme Court could at any time render what we say here irrelevant, the discussion should be as simple as is possible.

I

The highest courts of only two states have addressed the question currently before us. In Auerbach v. Bennett, 47 N.Y.2d 619, 419 N.Y.S.2d

---

1. I concur with the majority insofar as it vacates the order placing the independent committee report under seal.

920, 393 N.E.2d 994 (1979), New York's Court of Appeals held that the substantive merits of an independent director committee's decision to terminate derivative litigation against defendant corporate directors are beyond judicial scrutiny and that a court's role in such cases is limited to determining whether the committee acted independently, thoroughly and in good faith. In so holding, the *Auerbach* court recognized and applied the business judgment doctrine which it stated "bars judicial inquiry into actions of corporate directors taken in good faith and in the exercise of honest judgment in the lawful and legitimate furtherance of corporate purposes." Id. at 629, 419 N.Y.S.2d 920, 393 N.E.2d 994. In Zapata Corp. v. Maldonado, 430 A.2d 779 (Del.1981), the Delaware Supreme Court expressly refused to adopt the business judgment rationale. Instead it fashioned a two-step analysis. Under the first, which mirrors *Auerbach*, the corporation seeking dismissal must establish the independence, good faith and thoroughness of the investigative efforts of the committee of the board reaching the decision to terminate the litigation. As a second step the trial court in its discretion may apply its own "independent business judgment" in determining whether to accept the board's decision to terminate the derivative suit.

Faced with these opposing views, the majority has concluded that Connecticut would not adopt the "business judgment" doctrine of *Auerbach*, but would adopt the "independent business judgment" test of *Maldonado*. In fact, the majority goes beyond *Maldonado* by requiring that the court *must* proceed to apply its own business judgment, rather than leaving the decision to resort to the second step within the trial court's discretion. I respectfully dissent from that conclusion and propose, first, to set forth briefly what I perceive to be the inherent deficiencies in *Maldonado* and the adoption of its rationale by the majority and, then, to indicate why I believe the Connecticut Supreme Court will take a position similar to *Auerbach*.

II

Under *Maldonado's* two-step analysis and the majority position unanswered questions abound. For example, reasonable inquiry could be made with regard to the following: under what circumstances can the trial court conclude that the director's decision satisfied the step one criteria, but not the "spirit" of those criteria as required by step two of *Maldonado;* will evidence be considered by the court that was not before the independent committee; in the exercise of its "business judgment" will the court consider facts not in the record; will the court need to appoint its own experts?

The majority proposes a calculus in an attempt to resolve additional issues engendered by its analysis. This calculus is so complicated, indefinite and subject to judicial caprice as to be unworkable. For example, how is a court to determine the inherently speculative costs of future attorneys' fees and expenses related to litigation, time spent by corporate personnel preparing for trial, and mandatory indemnification "discounted of course by the probability of liability for such sums." How is a court to quantify corporate goodwill, corporate morale and "the distraction of key personnel" in cases in which it "finds a likely net return to the corporation which is not substantial in relation to shareholder equity"? Should a court also take into account the potential adverse impact of continuing litigation upon the corporation's ability to finance its operations? Should future costs be discounted to present value and, if so, at what rate? Must the income tax ramifications of expected future costs be considered and, if so, how? This veritable Pandora's box of unanswered questions raises more problems than it solves.

Even more fundamentally unsound is the majority's underlying premise that judges are equipped to make business judgments. It is a truism that judges *really* are not equipped either by training or experience to make business judgments because such judgments are intuitive, geared to risk-taking and often reliant on shifting competitive and market criteria. *Auerbach,* 47 N.Y.2d at 630, 419 N.Y.S.2d 920, 393 N.E.2d 994 (courts are "ill-equipped" to make essentially business judgments). Reasons of practicality and good sense strongly suggest that business decisions be left to businessmen. Whether to pursue litigation is not a judicial decision, rather, it is a business choice. Burks v. Lasker, 441 U.S. 471, 487 (1979) (Stewart, J., concurring) ("A decision whether or not a corporation will sue an alleged wrongdoer is no different from any other corporate decision * * *."). As perceptive commentators have observed, if *Maldonado's* statement is true that "[u]nder our system of law, courts and not litigants should decide the merits of litigation," *Maldonado* at 789 n. 13 (quoting Maldonado v. Flynn, 413 A.2d 1251, 1263 (Del.Ch.1980)), then its corollary "that boards, and not courts, are entitled to exercise business judgment" is equally true. Coffee and Schwartz, The Survival of the Derivative Suit: An Evaluation and a Proposal for Legislative Reform, 81 Colum.L.Rev. 261, 329 (1981).

Public policy concerns also strongly militate against the second step of the majority's two-tiered analysis. The sudden urge for stricter corporate accountability under judicial aegis arises, one Connecticut commentator suggests, not from corporate misconduct, which he asserts is no greater now than at previous times in history but, rather, because of an anti-business bias present in our society amidst an atmosphere of pervasive government regulation. Wolfson, A Critique of Corporate Law, 34 U.Miami L.Rev. 959, 988-89 (1980). In a land weary of overregulation and the kind of judicial activism embodied in the second step of *Maldonado,* there may well be a strong inclination for business to incorporate in states more hospitable to them. See, e.g., Genzer v. Cunningham, 498 F.Supp. 682, 688 (E.D.Mich. 1980).

Moreover, when one considers that even a meritorious lawsuit can have a detrimental effect upon a company's stockholders due to the significant and rising costs of litigation, disruption of corporate work force and adverse publicity, it becomes plain how wasteful it will become for corporations not to believe it worthwhile to move to dismiss a nonmeritorious case. The Business Round Table, a group of over one hundred chief executive officers of America's largest corporations has publicly stated that a view like the one adopted by the majority will lead to more derivative lawsuits being brought, make it more difficult for corporations to have them dismissed, discourage risk-taking and make fewer candidates willing to serve on boards of directors. N.Y. Times, June 10, 1982, at D6. Such real fears overcome in large measure what the majority implicitly assumes to be the advantages of limiting directors' control over the pursuit of the derivative suit.

* * *

Our Court has been down this path before. When *Burks* was before us we took the same position that the majority now does, i.e., that directors could never be wholly disinterested in deciding whether to pursue claims against fellow directors. Lasker v. Burks, 567 F.2d 1208, 1212 (2d Cir. 1978). On appeal that view was rejected by the Supreme Court which concluded that lack of impartiality of disinterested directors is not a determination to be made as a matter of law. *Burks,* 441 U.S. at 485 n. 15.

Plainly Connecticut's Supreme Court will be influenced to some degree by the number of cases that have followed *Auerbach's* teaching that an unbiased board's power to terminate derivative litigation is essentially unreviewable.[3]

V

Applying the *Auerbach* analysis to the facts in this case, the district court correctly found that the Committee's recommendation should be adopted. The committee would be deemed "independent" under Connecticut law because none of the directors had any of the relationships prohibited under Section 33–319 of the Connecticut General Statutes. For the reasons stated in Judge Eginton's extensive opinion below, I believe that the committee acted thoroughly and in good faith when it recommended termination of the litigation against some, but not all, of the defendants. Moreover, a district judge's interpretation of the law of the state in which he sits should be accorded substantial deference.

Based upon the foregoing, I would therefore affirm the grant of summary judgment dismissing the derivative suit as to the 23 defendants and its continuance as to the others as recommended by the independent committee.

SPECIAL LITIGATION COMMITTEES

In Burks v. Lasker [1] the Supreme Court decided the issue as to whether the Investment Company Act of 1940 precluded the dismissal of a derivative action as a result of a decision by a committee of independent directors that the maintenance of the action would not be in the best interest of the investment company on whose behalf the derivative action had been instituted and whether this question should be decided as a matter of federal or state law. It held that the Investment Company Act did not preclude such a termination of a derivative action so long as the applicable state law permitted that result and

---

3. See Gaines v. Haughton, 645 F.2d 761 (9th Cir.1981); H.M. Greenspun v. Del E. Webb Corp., 634 F.2d 1204 (9th Cir. 1980); Lewis v. Anderson, 615 F.2d 778 (9th Cir.1979), cert. denied, 449 U.S. 869 (1980); Abbey v. Control Data Corp., 603 F.2d 724 (8th Cir.1979), cert. denied, 444 U.S. 1017 (1980); Joy v. North, 519 F.Supp. 1312 (D.Conn.1981); Abramowitz v. Posner, 513 F.Supp. 120 (S.D.N.Y.1981), aff'd, 672 F.2d 1025 (2d Cir.1982); Genzer v. Cunningham, 498 F.Supp. 682 (E.D.Mich.1980); Maldonado v. Flynn, 485 F.Supp. 274 (S.D.

N.Y.1980), modified, 671 F.2d 729 (2d Cir. 1982); Rosengarten v. International Telephone & Telegraph Corp., 466 F.Supp. 817 (S.D.N.Y.1979); Siegal v. Merrick, 84 F.R.D. 106 (S.D.N.Y.1979); Our own Court eschewed second-guessing by the courts of what is the responsibility of a corporate board of directors and, until today, may properly have been included in the above group. Galef v. Alexander, 615 F.2d 51 (2d Cir.1980); *Abramowitz,* supra.

1. 441 U.S. 471 (1979).

was "consistent with the policies of the Investment Company and Investment Advisers Acts." The court stated:

"In short, the structure and purpose of the Investment Company Act indicate that Congress entrusted to the independent directors of investment companies, exercising the authority granted to them by state law, the primary responsibility for looking after the interests of the funds' shareholders. There may well be situations in which the independent directors could reasonably believe that the best interests of the shareholders call for a decision not to sue—as, for example, where the costs of litigation to the corporation outweigh any potential recovery. See Note, 47 Ford.L.Rev. 568 (1979); Note, 44 U.Chi.L. Rev., at 168, 196. See, e.g., Tannenbaum v. Zeller, 552 F.2d at 418; Cramer v. General Tel. & Electronics Corp., 582 F.2d 259 (CA3 1978). In such cases, it would certainly be consistent with the Act to allow the independent directors to terminate a suit, even though not frivolous. Indeed, it would have been paradoxical for Congress to have been willing to rely largely upon 'watchdogs' to protect shareholder interests and yet, where the 'watchdogs' have done precisely that, require that they be totally muzzled.

"We hold today that federal courts should apply state law governing the authority of independent directors to discontinue derivative suits to the extent such law is consistent with the policies of the Investment Company and Investment Advisers Acts. Moreover, we hold that Congress did not require that States, or federal courts, absolutely forbid director termination of all nonfrivolous actions."

The *Burks* case has created a new defense to an action based on the federal securities laws, which defendants are asserting with great frequency and vigor, where that action is a derivative action to collect damages as a result of a purchase or sale of securities by the corporation (see pages 1084–1087, above) or a violation of the proxy rules. This defense takes the form of a motion by the corporation to have the action dismissed because there has been a determination by the board or by a committee of the board, consisting of "independent" directors, to the effect that the continuation of the litigation is not "in the best interest" of the corporation. Under the *Burks* case, the federal court must first determine whether the board or such a committee has the power under applicable state law to procure the dismissal of a derivative action on that basis and, secondly, whether permitting such dismissal would conflict with the policy of the particular federal statute being invoked as the basis for the lawsuit. If the first question is answered in the affirmative and the second in the negative, then the only function of the federal court is to determine whether the directors who purported to make the decision were, in fact, "independent" and acted in "good faith" after making a "reasonable investigation." It is not clear whether these latter questions are to be decided under the state law or under the federal law. The *Burks* case would seem to make these questions a part of the determination under state law of the first question mentioned above, but Galef v. Alexander [2] in the Second Circuit seems to hold that at least in some circumstances the "independence" of the directors will be a question of federal law.

The cases since Burks v. Lasker have generally found that this type of action is authorized under state law and that giving effect to such a decision does not conflict with the policy of either Section 14(a) of the 1934 Act or Rule 10b–5.[3] There is, of course, no legislative history with respect to the 1934 Act

---

2. 615 F.2d 51 (2d Cir.1980).

3. Abbey v. Control Data Corp., 603 F.2d 724 (8th Cir.1979), cert. denied 444

U.S. 1017 (1980); Lewis v. Anderson, 615 F.2d 778 (9th Cir.1979), cert. denied 449 U.S. 869 (1981); Maldonado v. Flynn, 485

similar to that with respect to the Investment Company Act of 1940, showing that Congress relied heavily upon "independent directors" to protect the shareholders of a mutual fund or other investment company, which was recited by the Supreme Court in the *Burks* case. The *Galef* case mentioned above held, however, that a decision by a majority of the directors who were not pecuniarily interested in the transactions at issue, but who had initially approved them and had, therefore, been named as defendants in the derivative action, would not be given effect with respect to an action under Section 14(a) even assuming that the applicable state law would permit this.

The federal cases applying Delaware law in answering the first question have been undercut by the recent decision of the Delaware Supreme Court in Zapata Corp. v. Maldonado,[4] where that court, once again, confounded the federal courts in their attempted interpretation of the Delaware law (see the discussion, above, at page 1089). In the *Zapata* case the Delaware Supreme Court held that such a "business judgment" decision by the board or a committee would not be given binding effect with respect to the dismissal of a derivative action under Delaware law, but, on the other hand, would not be considered completely irrelevant. The court held that the trial court, after determining that the committee was composed of independent directors and had acted in good faith after a reasonable investigation, should then "determine, applying its own independent business judgment, whether the motion should be granted." The court said: "The second step is intended to thwart instances where corporate actions meet the criteria of step one, but the result does not appear to satisfy its spirit, or where corporate actions would simply prematurely terminate a stockholder grievance deserving of further consideration in the corporation's interest." Compare the statement of Judge Weinfeld in Maldonado v. Flynn,[5] now, of course, overruled as a matter of Delaware law, to the effect that it is not a court's role to "parse the Committee's complicated business determination."

Currently, the principal debate in the cases is the question of whether a particular state, in the absence of controlling authority in that state, would follow the New York rule in the *Auerbach* case or the Delaware rule in the *Zapata* case, which debate is reflected in the majority and minority opinions in *Joy v. North.* In In re General Tire & Rubber Company Securities Litigation [6] the court stated that it did not find it necessary to decide whether Ohio would apply the New York rule or the Delaware rule since the district judge had dismissed the action on the basis of the "more severe *Zapata* standard" and the circuit court affirmed that decision. The court also held that dismissing the derivative action did not conflict with the policy of Section 14(a) of the 1934 Act, distinguishing the case of Galef v. Alexander referred to above on the basis that there had not been shown any connection between the challenged transactions (so-called "questionable payments" and illegal activities of management) and any corporate action taken by vote of the shareholders.

With respect to the question of what constitutes an "interest" of a director with respect to the litigation so as to disqualify him from being one of the board majority or a member of the committee making this determination, a number of different possible interests may be identified:

F.Supp. 274 (S.D.N.Y.1980); Gall v. Exxon Corp., 418 F.Supp. 508 (S.D.N.Y.1976).

6. 726 F.2d 1075 (6th Cir.1984), cert. denied 469 U.S. 858 (1984).

4. 430 A.2d 779 (Del.1981).

5. Supra, note 3. See, also, Alford v. Shaw, 318 N.C. 289, 349 S.E.2d 41 (1986).

(1) A direct pecuniary interest of the director in the transaction at issue. This is the classic case of a contract or other transaction between a director and the corporation. No case has suggested that a director who is the other party to a contract with the corporation could in any circumstances be treated as "disinterested" in that transaction within the meaning of the business judgment rule.

(2) The interest of a director in retaining his position as a director of the corporation, even though the direct pecuniary benefits in the form of compensation are not substantial enough to be thought to influence his judgment.

This class of cases, of course, involves the recently much litigated issue of actions taken by a board of directors to fend off a takeover bid. For example, in Treadway Companies, Inc. v. Care Corp.,[7] the Second Circuit held that the directors (and the corporation) were not denied the benefits of the business judgment rule because of this interest, since the action which they took in defense against the takeover bid involved a merger with a "white knight" pursuant to which they would also lose their positions with the target corporation. Therefore, the court said that it could not be presumed that the outside directors were interested within the meaning of the business judgment rule, even if the CEO was primarily interested in retaining his position. In Panter v. Marshall Field & Co.,[8] the Seventh Circuit, over the somewhat bitter dissent of one judge, also held that the directors in the situation of a threatened takeover bid were independent within the meaning of this rule, although the defensive maneuvers undertaken in that case were designed, not to merge with a "white knight", but to maintain the "independence" of the target company and, therefore, their own positions as directors at least for the time being.

(3) The interest of a director made a defendant in a derivative action because he was one of those who made the decision to approve the transaction in the first instance, although the action is primarily against other defendants who allegedly have profited from the transaction. There is, of course, a direct interest of the director in having the action dismissed since this will terminate the expense involved in his own defense of the action, which may or may not ultimately be reimbursed by the corporation and which may or may not be covered by directors' and officers' liability insurance. In the *Galef* case the Second Circuit held that this interest, when coupled with the fact that the director was one of the majority approving the transaction in the first instance, was sufficient to disqualify a director from being part of an "independent majority" which voted for dismissal of the action, at least for the purposes of Section 14(a) of the 1934 Act.

(4) The interest of a director in defending a decision which was previously made by himself, among others, even though he has not been named as a defendant in the action. There would seem to be a probable psychological reaction to the challenge by a shareholder of a decision in which that director participated, which might give him a type of interest which he did not have initially. On the other hand, it can be argued that it would be a strange rule of law that would give no weight to his decision to seek termination of the derivative action, simply because it was the second time that that director had made the same judgment.

(5) The interest of a director because he is a nominee of a majority shareholder of the corporation, whether or not he is also an executive officer of a majority shareholding corporation. The case of Weinberger v. UOP, Inc.,[9] seems to treat this as a disqualifying interest, whether or not the designees of the majority shareholder are also directors or officers of that majority share-

---

7. 638 F.2d 357 (2d Cir.1980).   9. 426 A.2d 1333 (Del.Ch.1981).
8. 646 F.2d 271 (7th Cir.1981).

holder. On the other hand, the opinion might be read as accepting the proposition that previous incumbents on the board (from a time prior to the acquisition of the majority interest by another corporation) may still be considered "independent."

(6) The interest of a director arising from the fact that he has substantial business relationships with the corporation, which presumably can be terminated by the officers (who may be the alleged wrongdoers), such as the position of outside counsel to the corporation or its regular underwriter of securities. Such persons have now been eliminated as qualifying for the category of "independent director" under the provisions of the Investment Company Act of 1940.[10] In Maldonado v. Flynn,[11] however, the Second Circuit held that the fact that a director was a partner in an outside law firm which annually received "substantial fees" from the corporation did not make him an "interested director" for the purposes of the rule relating to disclosure to an independent majority of the board of directors for the purposes of Section 14(a) or Rule 10b–5. The court said: "Unless and until board membership on the part of a corporation's outside counsel, or of anyone with a commercial relationship with the corporation, is outlawed, we cannot assume that a counsel-director acts for reasons that are against the corporation's interest, as distinguished from the private interest of its officers." In In re General Tire & Rubber Company Securities Litigation [12] the Sixth Circuit agreed with this decision. It stated: "We cannot fashion a flat rule which allows only those individuals with absolutely *no* contact with the Company to exercise independent business judgment. Such a rule would preclude virtually every outside director from involvement in the business judgment by virtue of having been nominated or selected by the corporation." [13]

(7) The possible interest of a director arising from the fact that he was selected and designated for election by the chief executive officer and the previous incumbents on the board, where the challenged transaction is with that chief executive officer or fellow directors. If this type of interest, arising inherently in any public corporation from the control of the proxy machinery by the incumbent officers and directors, is considered to be a disqualifying interest, then no transaction with the chief executive officer or other officer-directors could ever have the benefit of the business judgment rule. All of the cases cited above reject the argument that this is a disqualifying interest. In Hasan v. Clevetrust Realty Investors, Inc.,[14] however, the court stated that: "The delegation of corporate power to a special committee, the members of which are hand-picked by defendant-directors, in fact, carries with it inherent structural biases," echoing a similar statement by the Delaware Supreme Court in the *Zapata* case. The Sixth Circuit held in that case that there could be no "presumption" that the special committee acted in good faith and that it was incumbent upon the defendants to show the independence and good faith of the one-man committee which had been appointed, regardless of whether the New York or Delaware rule was to be applied.

A second highly important factor, it would seem, in evaluating the question of whether a derivative action should be dismissed on this basis, although the courts in their analyses seem largely to have ignored it, is the type of underlying transaction which is being attacked by the lawsuit. Some of these types of transactions are:

10. Investment Company Act of 1940, § 2(a)(19).

11. 597 F.2d 789 (2d Cir.1979), on remand 477 F.Supp. 1007 and 485 F.Supp. 274 (S.D.N.Y.).

12. 726 F.2d 1075 (6th Cir.1984).

13. 726 F.2d at 1084.

14. 729 F.2d 372 (6th Cir.1984).

(1) An allegation of simple negligence on the part of certain officer-directors of the corporation in which other outside "independent" directors were not involved. This type of conduct is illustrated by the *Burks* case. The charge there was that the corporation by the decision of certain officer-directors had purchased Penn Central commercial paper at the wrong time (i.e., immediately before Penn Central went into the tank). There was no allegation that the officer-directors had any interest in Penn Central or stood to profit personally in any conceivable way from the transaction. The question may be raised as to why it was necessary in that case to invoke any power of the independent directors to dismiss a derivative action, since the business judgment rule should have permitted a simple motion by all defendants to dismiss the complaint on the ground that it did not allege facts on which any relief could be granted. The answer possibly lies in the fact that the general rule is asserted to be liability for negligence, not non-liability, on the part of directors [15] and, therefore, there possibly must be a trial to determine whether the court will invoke the business judgment rule as an exception to that general rule. On the other hand, the Supreme Court seemed to accept the proposition that a decision to dismiss the derivative action might (depending on state law) preclude any court inquiry if made by the same "independent directors." In other words, their decision might be given a different effect if made subsequently than if made beforehand.

(2) An assertion that certain officer-directors of the corporation engaged in illegal conduct, which in their view was designed to benefit the corporation but in which they had no personal pecuniary interest. Because of subsequent events, however, the conduct may have caused the corporation considerable expense and public embarrassment. These are the "illegal payments" cases, involving bribes to foreign public officials.[16] The board, of course, was never asked to approve any such conduct in advance, at least in a formal manner, and, therefore, there remains a solid "independent" majority of the board to vote to dismiss any derivative action seeking to recover the amount of such payments or the subsequent expense caused to the corporation. The question may be asked: Why should there be a difference between the power of the board consisting of outside directors to approve such transactions in advance and its power to ratify them, in effect, by dismissing any action commenced against the officers responsible? The Eighth Circuit in Abbey v. Control Data Corp.[17] answered this question as follows: "The decision not to bring suit with regard to past conduct which may have been illegal is not itself a violation of law and does not result in the continuation of the alleged violation of law. Rather, it is a decision by the directors of the corporation that pursuit of a cause of action based on acts already consummated is not in the best interest of

---

15. Model Business Corporation Act, § 35; Report of Committee on Corporate Laws, 29 Bus.Law. 949, at 951 (1974). The rule of liability for negligence (failure to exercise "due care") is stated in the statute and the "business judgment rule" is relegated to a "comment" of the committee which drafted it. See 1 Marsh's California Corporation Law § 10.3 (1981). In Galef v. Alexander, supra note 2, the court stated the business judgment rule as follows: " * * * the law will not hold directors liable for honest errors, for mistakes of judgment, when they act without corrupt motive and in good faith, that is, for mistakes which may properly be classified under the head of honest mistakes. And that

is true even though the errors may be so gross that they may demonstrate the unfitness of the directors to manage the corporate affairs." This is, of course, the antithesis of liability for negligence.

16. Gaines v. Haughton, 645 F.2d 761 (9th Cir.1981); Rosengarten v. International Telegraph and Telephone Corp., 466 F.Supp. 817 (S.D.N.Y.1979); Abbey v. Control Data Corp., supra note 3; Gall v. Exxon Corporation, supra note 3.

17. 603 F.2d 724, at 730 (8th Cir.1979), cert. denied 444 U.S. 1017 (1980), quoting from Gall v. Exxon Corp., 418 F.Supp. 508, at 518 (1976).

the corporation. * * * The conclusive effect of such a judgment cannot be affected by the allegedly illegal nature of the initial action which purportedly gives rise to the cause of action."

(3) Conduct involving maneuvers to fend off a takeover bid, such as the issuance of additional shares of stock in acquisitions or to an ESOP or to a "white knight", or the acquisition of additional businesses or business locations rather obviously designated to create or exacerbate anti-trust problems for the tender offeror.[18] This type of conflict, involving defense of the control of the corporation by the existing management, has been commented on above.

(4) Transactions favoring to a significant extent other officers or directors in a pecuniary sense, but which also involve a much wider group of subordinate executives of the corporation. Typical of this class of cases are several involving the substitution of new stock options for old ones which are under water.[19] Typically, the most significant beneficiaries of such action are other officer-directors, but the action also involves a benefit to a much wider group of employees whose morale, and, therefore, the well-being of the corporation, is allegedly suffering as a result of the fact that their efforts have not produced the surge in stock prices expected when the stock options were issued.

(5) Transactions of the corporation with officer-directors which allegedly benefit only those directors. No case says that the initial approval of such a transaction by an independent majority of directors would preclude *any* judicial inquiry into the fairness of such a transaction, although the Delaware statute (copied from the former California statute)[20] seems to say that. However, the California court in Remillard Brick Co. v. Remillard Dandini[21] refused to accept this literal interpretation of the statute in connection with a shareholder approval. Should a subsequent decision to dismiss a derivative action challenging the transaction have any different effect?

Few of the questions which are raised by the foregoing analysis have been definitively answered as yet by the litigation spawned by the case of Burks v. Lasker. It is certain, however, that there will be many more decisions in this area as defendants attempt to avoid any decision on the merits.

The question may be raised as to whether all of this maneuvering is not much ado about nothing. In the *Mills* case (supra, page 1252) the Supreme Court held that a shareholder could bring an action under Section 14(a) of the 1934 Act with respect to a proxy rule violation either as a class action or as a derivative action, presumably without regard to the state law mandating one type of relief to the exclusion of the other. If the same should be held to be true with respect to Rule 10b–5 and the other substantive sections of the federal securities laws, could a plaintiff simply evade this defense by bringing his action as a class action rather than a derivative action? There has never been a suggestion by any court that a class action on behalf of shareholders could be dismissed on the basis that the defendants or any of their colleagues made a determination that the action was not in the best interest of the corporation. Proof of damages, however, might be much more difficult in a

---

18. Treadway Companies, Inc. v. Care Corp., 638 F.2d 357 (2d Cir.1980); Klaus v. Hi-Shear Corp., 528 F.2d 225 (9th Cir.1975); Panter v. Marshall Field & Co., supra note 7.

19. Lewis v. Anderson, supra note 3; Galef v. Alexander, supra note 2. Compare Zapata Corp. v. Maldonado, supra note 4, where the complaint was over the acceleration of the exercisability of options to confer a tax benefit on the employees, allegedly at the expense of the corporation by reducing its tax deduction.

20. Del.Gen.Corp.Law, § 144 (copied from former § 820 of the Cal.Corp.Code). See 1 Marsh's California Corporation Law § 10.8 (1981).

21. 109 Cal.App.2d 405, 241 P.2d 66 (1952).

class action if the conduct complained about (such as illegal payments) had no discernable effect on the price of the stock (or perhaps a favorable effect).

See Block and Barton, Business Judgment Rule as Applied to Stockholder Proxy Derivative Suits Under the Securities Exchange Act, 8 Securities Reg. L.J. 99 (1980).

STATUTES OF LIMITATIONS

Section 13 of the Securities Act of 1933 establishes a Federal statute of limitations for all civil actions under Sections 11 and 12. Under Section 12(2) the period of limitations is one year after discovery of the false statement but not more than three years after the sale.[1] Under Section 12(1) the period of limitations is one year after "the violation", i.e., the sale in violation of Section 5.[2] Under Section 11 the period of limitations is also one year after discovery of the false statement. In addition, however, for actions under Sections 12(1) and 11 the statute prescribes an over-all limitation of three years after "the security was bona fide offered to the public." This apparently means that as to a portion of an unsold allotment purchased by the plaintiff more than three years after the original public offering, his possible action under Section 12(1) (if the issue was unregistered) or under Section 11 (if the issue was registered) was barred before it accrued. While this result is ridiculous, it seems to be what the statute says. In 1954 Congress amended the Investment Company Act to eliminate this problem in connection with the sale of mutual-fund shares, where it was most acute. The Commission by the device of an "undertaking" has attempted to achieve the same result in other situations involving continuous or "shelf" registrations. See Form S–4.

The court in Straley v. Universal Uranium & Milling Corp.[3] held that "laches" is not available as a defense in an action under Section 12(1), if the statutory period has not run, but that "waiver" and "estoppel" are. What are the differences among these three concepts? How do you reconcile this holding with Section 14 of the Securities Act of 1933 which provides that any "condition, stipulation, or provision binding any person acquiring any security to waive compliance with any provision of this title * * * shall be void"? It could be argued, of course, that this refers only to a waiver at the time of purchase and not subsequently, but what is the policy of Congress as evidenced by this section?[4]

1. Cook v. Avien, Inc., 573 F.2d 685 (1st Cir.1978).

2. In Cook v. Avien, Inc., supra n. 1, the court said that "Under the explicit language of § 13, the limitations period [for an action under § 12(1)] runs from the date of violation irrespective of whether the plaintiff knew of the violation." See, also Newberg v. American Dryer Corp., 195 F.Supp. 345 (E.D.Pa.1961). Compare, however, Houlihan v. Anderson-Stokes, Inc., 434 F.Supp. 1324 (D.D.C.1977), which held that the one-year statute of limitations for an action under § 12(1) was tolled by an allegation of a fraudulent representation by the defendant sellers that no registration was required.

3. 289 F.2d 370 (9th Cir.1961).

4. Compare Pearlstein v. Scudder & German, 429 F.2d 1136 (2d Cir.1970); Cohen v. Tenney Corp., 318 F.Supp. 280 (S.D. N.Y.1970); Cohen v. Franchard Corp., 51 F.R.D. 167 (S.D.N.Y.1970). In Royal Air Properties, Inc. v. Smith, 312 F.2d 210 (9th Cir.1962) the Ninth Circuit held that not only "waiver" and "estoppel" but also "laches" would be available as defenses to an action under Rule 10b–5, since there is no Federal statute of limitations applicable to an action under Rule 10b–5. On a second appeal of the same case, the court affirmed the trial court's ruling that the defendant had failed to establish any of these defenses. Royal Air Properties, Inc. v. Smith, 333 F.2d 568 (9th Cir.1964). This opinion discusses the differences, as the court sees them, among the three concepts.

There is no period of limitations prescribed in the statute for actions under Section 10(b), as Section 13 of the Securities Act of 1933 governs the time for bringing suit under Sections 11 and 12 of that Act and Sections 9 and 18 of the 1934 Act include their own limitations periods. In the absence of any express Federal period of limitations, the courts have held that the most "analogous" state statute of limitations should be applied. Initially, this was held to be the state statute of limitations for "fraud" actions.[5] The court stated in Wachovia Bank and Trust Co. v. National Student Marketing Corp.[6] that until December, 1971, there were only two cases which had applied the state Blue Sky law limitations period to federal securities actions, whereas there had been forty-six applying the forum state's general fraud statute of limitations. However, there was for some time after that date a strong trend towards applying the state statute of limitations in its Blue Sky law to actions brought under Rule 10b-5,[7] although the Third Circuit held, over the dissent of Judge Seitz, that the New Jersey fraud statute of limitations will be applied to such an action.[8] The District of Columbia Circuit held in the *Wachovia* case that its prior decision in Forrestal Village, Inc. v. Graham[9] adopting the Blue Sky law period of limitations would not be applied retroactively to a cause of action arising in 1969. The Ninth Circuit in 1973 adhered to its prior decisions that the California fraud statute of limitations is applicable, in the case of United California Bank v. Salik.[10]

After the decision in the *Hochfelder* case, which established that an action under Rule 10b-5 is indeed an action for "fraud", the pendulum has begun once again to swing in the opposite direction.[11] The major difficulty with making any sense out of all of this welter of decisions relating to the appropriate statute of limitations to apply is that once a court has decided that a particular statute of limitations is appropriate in a particular state, it subsequently refuses to change that decision even if it has decided that a different statute of limitations is applicable in another state in the same circuit, whose statutes of limitations are completely indistinguishable from those in the first state,

5. Fratt v. Robinson, 203 F.2d 627 (9th Cir.1953); Errion v. Connell, 236 F.2d 447 (9th Cir.1956); Fischman v. Raytheon Manufacturing Co., 188 F.2d 783 (2d Cir.1951); Chiodo v. General Waterworks Corp., 380 F.2d 860 (10th Cir.1967); Azalea Meats, Inc. v. Muscat, 386 F.2d 5 (5th Cir.1967); Klein v. Auchincloss, Parker & Redpath, 436 F.2d 339 (2d Cir.1971); Sackett v. Beaman, 399 F.2d 884 (9th Cir.1968).

6. 650 F.2d 342 (D.C.Cir.1980).

7. Cahill v. Ernst & Ernst, 625 F.2d 151 (7th Cir.1980) (Wisconsin); Carothers v. Rice, 633 F.2d 7 (6th Cir.1980), cert. denied 450 U.S. 998 (1981) (Kentucky); Morris v. Stifel, Nicolaus & Co., Inc., 600 F.2d 139 (8th Cir.1979) (Missouri); O'Hara v. Kovens, 625 F.2d 15 (4th Cir.1980), cert. denied 449 U.S. 1124 (1981) (Maryland); LaRosa Building Corp. v. The Equitable Life Assurance Society of the United States, 542 F.2d 990 (7th Cir.1976) (Indiana); Hudak v. Economic Research Analysts, Inc., 499 F.2d 996 (5th Cir.1974), cert. denied 419 U.S. 1122 (1975) (Florida); Parrent v. Midwest Rug Mills, Inc., 455 F.2d 123 (7th Cir.1972) (Illinois); Vanderboom v. Sexton, 422 F.2d 1233 (8th Cir.1970), cert. denied 400 U.S. 852 (1971) (Arkansas);

Nickels v. Koehler Management Corp., 392 F.Supp. 804 (N.D.Ohio 1975) (" * * * the recent circuit decisions prefer the various Blue Sky Law limitations periods."); Kramer v. Loewi & Co., Inc., 357 F.Supp. 83 (E.D.Wis.1973); Corey v. Bache & Co., Inc., 355 F.Supp. 1123 (S.D.W.Va.1973).

8. Roberts v. Magnetic Metals Co., 611 F.2d 450 (3d Cir.1979).

9. 179 U.S.App.D.C. 225, 551 F.2d 411 (1977).

10. 481 F.2d 1012 (9th Cir.1973), cert. denied 414 U.S. 1004 (1973). See, also, Douglass v. Glenn E. Hinton Investments, Inc., 440 F.2d 912 (9th Cir.1971); Klapmeier v. Peat, Marwick, Mitchell & Co., 363 F.Supp. 1212 (D.Minn.1973).

11. Loveridge v. Dreagoux, 678 F.2d 870 (10th Cir.1982); Breen v. Centex Corporation, 695 F.2d 907 (5th Cir.1983); Armstrong v. McAlpin, 699 F.2d 79 (2d Cir. 1983); Mosesian v. Peat, Marwick, Mitchell & Co., 727 F.2d 873 (9th Cir.1984), cert. denied 469 U.S. 932, (1984); Silverberg v. Thompson McKinnon Securities, Inc., 787 F.2d 1079, CCH Fed.Sec.L.Rptr. ¶92,551 (6th Cir.1986).

because the later case was decided on a different swing of the pendulum. As a consequence, no general principle can be possibly be stated, but only that in State A this statute is applicable, in State B that statute is applicable, et cetera.

If the "fraud" statute of limitations is adopted, then it typically will not begin to run until "discovery" of the fraud. However, if the Blue Sky statute of limitations is applied and contains no such tolling provision, the cases under Rule 10b–5 have uniformly held that the general Federal equitable doctrine relating to concealment of a "fraud" will apply (even though they may have just stated that a Rule 10b–5 violation is not necessarily "fraud" as the reason for applying the Blue Sky statute).[12] This doctrine may not be as favorable to the plaintiff as the typical State "discovery" provision. As explained by the Seventh Circuit: " * * * the statute of limitations in a § 10(b) action may be tolled by the 'equitable doctrine' of fraudulent concealment. In order to invoke this doctrine, however, the plaintiff must have remained ignorant of the fraud 'without any fault or want of diligence or care on his part.' Bailey v. Glover, 88 U.S. (21 Wall.) 342, 348 (1874). It is well established that a plaintiff may not merely rely on his own unawareness of the facts or law to toll the statute. * * * The plaintiff, rather, has the burden of showing that he 'exercised reasonable care and diligence in seeking to learn the facts which would disclose fraud.' * * * The statutory period '[does] not wait appellant's leisurely discovery of the full details of the alleged scheme.' * * * "[13]

The First Circuit has indicated in Cook v. Avien, Inc.,[14] that in its view the federal equitable tolling doctrine is substantially the same as the express provision in Section 13 of the 1933 Act relating to the one-year period of limitations for an action under Section 12(2). That statute provides that the action must be brought within one year "after the discovery of the untrue statement or the omission, or after such discovery should have been made by the exercise of reasonable diligence." The court stated that in the application of the state statute of limitations to an action under Rule 10b–5, "the doctrine of fraudulent concealment operates to toll the statute of limitations 'where the party injured by the fraud remains in ignorance of it without any fault or want of diligence or care on his part * * * until the fraud is discovered, though there be no special circumstances or efforts on the part of the party committing the fraud to conceal it from the knowledge of the other party.' * * * Thus, the running of both statutes of limitations is triggered by identical considerations."

Since the one-year period specified in Section 13 of the 1933 Act for the bringing of an action under Section 12(2) is expressly postponed until the discovery by the plaintiff of the untrue statement or omission "or after such discovery should have been made by the exercise of reasonable diligence", it cannot possibly have been intended by Congress that the outside three-year limit "after the sale" should similarly be tolled by lack of knowledge of the violation by the plaintiff. In Securities and Exchange Commission v. Seaboard Corporation[15] the court said that "Though some courts have applied equitable principles to toll the [three-year] statute [specified in Section 13], * * * we believe the statutory language requires the conclusion that Congress meant the bar to be absolute." Similarly, the three-year outside limitations periods

12. Campbell v. Upjohn Company, 676 F.2d 1122 (6th Cir.1982); Trecker v. Scag, 679 F.2d 703 (7th Cir.1982) cert. denied 471 U.S. 1066 (1985); Kennedy v. Tallant, 710 F.2d 711 (11th Cir.1983).

13. Hupp v. Gray, 500 F.2d 993, 996 (7th Cir.1974). See, also, General Builders

Supply Company v. River Hill Coal Venture, 796 F.2d 8 (1st Cir.1986).

14. 573 F.2d 685 (1st Cir.1978).

15. 677 F.2d 1301 (9th Cir.1982). Accord, Cook v. Avien, supra note 1.

specified in Section 9(e) and Section 18 of the 1934 Act cannot possibly be held to be subject to any "equitable tolling principle" in the light of the statutory language.

It has also been held that a suit under Rule 10b–5, being maintainable either at law or in equity, may be barred by laches.[16] However, it would seem that the doctrine of laches should be applied only where the plaintiff asks for rescission rather than for damages.[17]

On the statute of limitations problem, see Fiebach and Doret, Quarter Century Later—The Period of Limitations for Rule 10b–5 Damage Actions in Federal Courts Sitting in Pennsylvania, 25 Vill.L.Rev. 851 (1980); Erwin, Securities Fraud and the Statute of Limitations: The Strange Case of the "Modified Uniform" Securities Act, 10 Creighton L.Rev. 324 (1976); Martin, Statutes of Limitations in 10b–5 Actions: Which State Statute is Applicable? 29 Bus.Law. 443 (1974); Einhorn and Feldman, Choosing a Statute of Limitations in Federal Securities Actions, 25 Mercer L.Rev. 497 (1974); Bateman and Keith, Statutes of Limitations Applicable to Private Actions under SEC Rule 10b–5: Complexity in Need of Reform, 39 Mo.L.Rev. 165 (1974).

16. Tobacco and Allied Stocks, Inc. v. Transamerica Corp., 143 F.Supp. 323 (D.Del.1956), aff'd 244 F.2d 902 (3d Cir. 1957); Royal Air Properties, Inc. v. Smith, 312 F.2d 210 (9th Cir.1962), 333 F.2d 568 (9th Cir.1964).

17. Baumel v. Rosen, 412 F.2d 571 (4th Cir.1969), cert. denied 396 U.S. 1037 (1970). Cf. Dottenheim v. Emerson Electric Mfg. Co., 7 F.R.D. 343 (E.D.N.Y.1947);

Arbetman v. Playford, 83 F.Supp. 335 (S.D. N.Y.1949), which held under Section 16(b) of the Securities Exchange Act that if the plaintiff did not demand a jury trial the defendant could not either, since the failure of the plaintiff to do so indicated his election to bring the suit in equity. That section, of course, expressly permits suit either "at law or in equity."

Chapter 20

PROCEDURE AND REMEDIES

Statutes and Regulations

Securities Act of 1933, §§ 5, 11, 12, 14, 20, 22.

Securities Exchange Act of 1934, §§ 21(d), 27, 29, 32.

Rules 10b–5, 14a–9.

THE "JURISDICTIONAL MEANS"; VENUE

Liability under Section 12(2) is limited to a person who offers or sells "by the use of any means or instruments of transportation or communication in interstate commerce or of the mails." Section 12(1) by incorporating the provisions of Section 5 becomes subject to the same limitation.

Almost all of the cases have held that to "sell * * * by the use of" the jurisdictional means in Section 12(2) includes any use of such means in connection with the sale, e.g., the delivery of the securities after sale or the delivery of payment after sale.[1] One case, decided by the Seventh Circuit,[2] is contra, holding that the misrepresentation must be transmitted by the jurisdictional means in order to invoke Section 12(2).

Section 5 as incorporated into Section 12(1), however, is more specific as to how the jurisdictional means must be used in order to invoke the various subdivisions of that section. According to United States v. Robertson,[3] this precludes as broad an interpretation of the language of Section 5(a)(1) as has been given the similar language in Section 12(2).

The Eighth Circuit[4] held that an *intrastate* telephone call was sufficient to give the Federal court jurisdiction under Rule 10b–5, since the same wires carried interstate messages and therefore there was a use of an "instrumentality" *of* interstate commerce.[5] Lennerth v. Mendenhall[6] states that the same is true under Section 12. However, Section 12 and Section 5 of the Securities Act of 1933 refer to the use of "any means or instruments * * * *in* interstate commerce." Although it cites the *Lennerth* case in support of its conclusion, the Eighth Circuit in a footnote seems to suggest that this difference in language may distinguish a Section 12 action from a Rule 10b–5 action with respect to an intrastate telephone call furnishing the basis of jurisdiction.[7] It

---

1. Wigand v. Flo-Tek, Inc., 609 F.2d 1028 (2d Cir.1979); Franklin Savings Bank of New York v. Levy, 551 F.2d 521 (2d Cir. 1977); Moses v. Michael, 292 F.2d 614 (5th Cir.1961); Cresswell-Keith, Inc. v. Willingham, 264 F.2d 76 (8th Cir.1959); Blackwell v. Bentsen, 203 F.2d 690 (5th Cir.1953); Schillner v. H. Vaughan Clarke & Co., 134 F.2d 875 (2d Cir.1943); United States v. Robertson, 181 F.Supp. 158 (S.D.N.Y.1959); cf. United States v. Cashin, 281 F.2d 669 (2d Cir.1960).

2. Kemper v. Lohnes, 173 F.2d 44 (7th Cir.1949).

3. Supra, Note 1.

4. Myzel v. Fields, 386 F.2d 718 (8th Cir.1967).

5. Accord, Bredehoeft v. Cornell, 260 F.Supp. 557 (D.Or.1966); Nemitz v. Cunny, 221 F.Supp. 571 (N.D.Ill.1963).

6. 234 F.Supp. 59 (N.D.Ohio 1964).

7. Myzel v. Fields, 386 F.2d 718, at 727, n. 2 (8th Cir.1967): "Despite the similarity there is a crucial omission from § 10(b) of the § 17(a) [and §§ 5 and 12–Eds.] requirement that there be a communication *in* interstate commerce; the requirement of § 10(b) is 'by the use of any means or instrumentality *of* interstate commerce.'

has generally been assumed by the bar that an intrastate telephonic offer prior to the filing of the Registration Statement would not violate Section 5(c) of the 1933 Act.

See 3 Loss, Securities Regulation 1698, 1706–1708 (2d ed. 1961, Supp.1969); 45 Va.L.Rev. 603 (1959).

In order to invoke Rule 10b–5 it is necessary that there be some use of the mails or of "a means or instrumentality of interstate commerce" or of "a facility of a national securities exchange" in connection with the purchase or sale. The same question arises here as under Section 12(2) of the Securities Act of 1933 as to whether the misstatement or omission must be transmitted by such means. The answer under the Rule has uniformly been, no: any use of the jurisdictional means in connection with the transaction is sufficient.[8] The mails need not cross a state line in order for there to be a use of the mails within the meaning of the Rule.[9] All of the recent cases have also held that an intrastate telephone call (or presumably telegram), if it is transmitted over the same wires that carry interstate messages, would be a sufficient use of an "instrumentality *of* interstate commerce." [10]

Under Section 22(a) of the 1933 Act, the jurisdiction of the federal courts over actions under that statute in the federal district courts is concurrent with jurisdiction in the state courts. If the plaintiff elects to bring the action in a state court, it cannot be removed to the federal court despite the fact that there is a federal question. On the other hand, jurisdiction of any action under the 1934 Act is exclusively in the federal district court, regardless of the amount in controversy.[11] Under the 1933 Act, venue may be laid in any district in which "the offer or sale took place, if the defendant participated therein," and under the 1934 Act in any district "wherein any act or transaction constituting the violation occurred." In addition, under both acts, venue may also be laid in any district in which the defendant is an inhabitant or transacts business or "is found." The plaintiff thus has a wide choice of venue, although the principal provision relating to the district where the offer or sale occurred or where any "act or transaction" constituting the violation occurred gives the plaintiff a much wider choice under the 1934 Act. In this case, the plaintiff may be able to bring the action in his home state if the offer or sale occurred there or any part of the transaction occurred there, which is of course a distinct advantage to the plaintiff in bringing suit against an out-of-state defendant.[12]

---

* * * 'In making the alterations in the phraseology of the similar section of the earlier act the Congress must have had some purpose.' "

8. Fratt v. Robinson, 203 F.2d 627 (9th Cir.1953); Errion v. Connell, 236 F.2d 447 (9th Cir.1956); Ellis v. Carter, 291 F.2d 270 (9th Cir.1961); Stevens v. Vowell, 343 F.2d 374 (10th Cir.1965); but cf. Boone v. Baugh, 308 F.2d 711 (8th Cir.1962).

9. Cf. Gross v. Independence Shares Corp., 36 F.Supp. 541 (E.D.Pa.1941) (Suit under § 12(2), Securities Act of 1933).

10. Loveridge v. Dreagoux, 678 F.2d 870 (10th Cir.1982); Dupuy v. Dupuy, 511 F.2d 641 (5th Cir.1975); Aquionics Acceptance Corp. v. Kollar, 503 F.2d 1225 (6th Cir. 1974); Kerbs v. Fall River Industries, Inc., 502 F.2d 731 (10th Cir.1974); Myzel v. Fields, 386 F.2d 718 (8th Cir.1967) cert.

denied 390 U.S. 951 (1968); Heyman v. Heyman, 356 F.Supp. 958 (S.D.N.Y.1973); Bredehoeft v. Cornell, 260 F.Supp. 557 (D.Or.1966); Nemitz v. Cunny, 221 F.Supp. 571 (N.D.Ill.1963); Ingraffia v. Belle Meade Hospital, Inc., 319 F.Supp. 537 (E.D.La. 1970); Jackson v. Oppenheim, CCH Fed. Sec.Law Rptr. ¶ 93,008 (S.D.N.Y.1971). The Ninth Circuit originally held to the contrary in Burke v. Triple A Machine Shop, Inc., 438 F.2d 978 (9th Cir.1971), but this case was distinguished to extinction in Spilker v. Shayne Laboratories, 520 F.2d 523 (9th Cir.1975).

11. Securities Exchange Act of 1934, § 27; Osborne v. Mallory, 86 F.Supp. 869 (S.D.N.Y.1949); Kahan v. Rosenstiel, 285 F.Supp. 61 (D.Del.1968).

12. Kardon v. National Gypsum Co., 69 F.Supp. 512 (E.D.Pa. 1946); Thiele v.

ARBITRATION OF SECURITIES LAW CLAIMS

In Wilko v. Swan [13] the United States Supreme Court held at an early date that a claim under Section 12(2) of the 1933 Act would not be sent to arbitration, despite an agreement of the parties that any dispute between them would be subject to arbitration, because this would conflict with the "non-waiver" provision in Section 14 of the 1933 Act declaring that any provision "to waive compliance with any provision of this title or of the rules and regulations of the Commission shall be void." The court reasoned that the agreement to arbitrate attempted to "waive" the right of the plaintiff to have his statutory cause of action decided exclusively by the federal court (it was, of course, always the defendant who wanted to arbitrate rather than litigate). The 1934 Act has a similar "non-waiver" provision in Section 29(a). It was thought for decades that the *Wilko* case precluded any compulsory arbitration of *any* federal security law claims.

The question arose, however, as to whether or not state law claims, whether under the common law or the state securities law, which were asserted in the same action as "pendent" to the federal securities law claims could be sent to arbitration pursuant to a valid arbitration agreement, despite the fact that the federal claims could not, thus requiring two separate proceedings probably based upon the same facts. Some of the circuit courts developed what was called the "intertwining" doctrine under which such state law claims also would not be sent to arbitration, on the basis they were so "intertwined" with the federal securities law claims that it would be too inefficient to have two separate, parallel proceedings dealing with essentially the same dispute. An approximately equal number of circuit courts refused to adopt that doctrine, although some indicated that they would stay the arbitration proceeding with respect to the state law claims until after the federal litigation was concluded.

In Dean Witter Reynolds, Inc. v. Byrd [14] the Supreme Court rejected the "intertwining doctrine" and held that state law claims which were subject to a valid arbitration agreement must be sent to arbitration by the federal court. It also held that there should be no automatic stay of the arbitration proceeding regarding the state law claims, although it seemed to leave open the possibility that such a stay could be issued in particular circumstances. Justice White, in a concurring opinion, stated that he could see no reason whatever to stay the arbitration proceeding.

Shields, 131 F.Supp. 416 (S.D.N.Y.1955); Schneider v. Sears, 265 F.Supp. 257 (S.D. N.Y.1967); Wharton v. Roth, 263 F.Supp. 922 (E.D.N.Y.1964); Trussell v. United Underwriters, Ltd., 236 F.Supp. 801 (D.Colo. 1964); United Industrial Corp. v. Nuclear Corp. of America, 237 F.Supp. 971 (D.Del. 1964). In Fitzsimmons v. Barton, 589 F.2d 330 (7th Cir.1979), the Seventh Circuit held that such nationwide service of process does not violate the due process clause nor the "fairness" doctrine of Shaffer v. Heitner, 433 U.S. 186 (1977). Robinson v. Penn Central Co., 484 F.2d 553 (3d Cir.1973), held that extraterritorial service of process under Rule 10b–5 is also sufficient to confer personal jurisdiction over the defendant for the purpose of pendent State claims, even though otherwise it would not have been possible to obtain jurisdiction over

the defendant with respect to such pendent claims. The opinion in that case cites the conflicting authorities in the lower courts regarding this point. Also, "Under the co-conspirator venue theory, where an action is brought against multiple defendants alleging a common scheme of acts or transactions in violation of securities statutes, so long as venue is established for any of the defendants in the forum district, venue is proper as to all defendants. This is true even in the absence of any contact by some of the defendants in the forum district." Securities Investor Protection Corporation v. Vigman, 764 F.2d 1309 (9th Cir.1985); Semegen v. Weidner, 780 F.2d 727 (9th Cir. 1985).

13. 346 U.S. 427 (1953).

14. 470 U.S. 213 (1985).

In a footnote in the *Byrd* case, the Supreme Court noted that it had raised the question, without deciding it, in the case of Scherk v. Alberto-Culver Co.[15] as to whether the *Wilko* rule applied to a claim under Rule 10b–5 "because the provisions of the 1933 and 1934 Acts differ, and because unlike § 12(2) of the 1933 Act, § 10(b) of the 1934 Act does not expressly give rise to a private cause of action." Although noting that "numerous" lower courts had applied the *Wilko* case to Rule 10b–5 actions, the court again expressly refused to rule on this issue. However, Justice White, in his concurring opinion, indicated rather clearly that in his view the *Wilko* case probably does not apply to an action under Rule 10b–5 since that is an "implied" cause of action and "*Wilko's* solicitude for the federal cause of action * * * is not necessarily appropriate where the cause of action is judicially implied and not so different from the common law action."

These expressions of doubt by the Supreme Court have set off another spate of litigation as to whether actions under Rule 10b–5 may not after all be subject to arbitration pursuant to a valid agreement, although previously defendants had not even bothered to make a motion to send the dispute to arbitration because of the universal acceptance of the idea that the *Wilko* case also applied to the 1934 Act. The Second, Ninth and Third Circuits have decided that the *Wilko* case *does* apply to an action under Rule 10b–5,[16] but the Eight Circuit held to the contrary in Phillips v. Merrill Lynch, Pierce, Fenner & Smith, Inc.[17]

It has been held, however, that the doctrine of the *Wilko* case does not extend to claims under the Commodities Exchange Act, which are arbitrable pursuant to an arbitration agreement.[18] It has also been held that the doctrine of that case does not extend to a dispute between two broker-dealers or between two municipal securities dealers.[19]

See Goff, Federal and State Securities Claims: Litigation or Arbitration, 61 Wash.L.Rev. 245 (1986); Bierman, Mixed Arbitrable and Nonarbitrable Claims in Securities Litigation, 34 Cath.U.L.Rev. 525 (1985); Katsoris, The Arbitration of a Public Securities Dispute, 53 Fordham L.Rev. 279 (1984).

IN RE SUBPOENAS DUCES TECUM TO FULBRIGHT & JAWORSKI AND VINSON & ELKINS

United States Court of Appeals, District of Columbia Circuit, 1984.
738 F.2d 1367.

Before WALD, MIKVA and DAVIS,* CIRCUIT JUDGES.

DAVIS, CIRCUIT JUDGE:

Appellants challenge orders of the District Court, 99 F.R.D. 582, granting appellees' motion to compel compliance with four subpoenas *duces*

15. 417 U.S. 506 (1974).

16. McMahon v. Shearson/American Express, Inc., 788 F.2d 94 (2d Cir.1986) cert. granted 550 SLW 3197 (1986); Conover v. Dean Witter Reynolds, Inc., 797 F.2d 775 (9th Cir.1986); Badart v. Merrill Lynch, Pierce, Fenner & Smith 797 F.2d 775 (9th Cir.1986); Jacobson v. Merrill Lynch, Pierce, Fenner & Smith, Inc., 797 F.2d 1197 (3d Cir.1986).

17. 795 F.2d 1393 (8th Cir.1986).

18. Smoky Greenhaw Cotton Co., Inc. v. Merrill Lynch, Pierce, Fenner & Smith, Inc., 720 F.2d 1446 (5th Cir.1983).

19. Halliburton & Associates, Inc. v. Henderson, Few & Co., 774 F.2d 441 (11th Cir.1985); Swink & Company, Inc. v. Hereth, 784 F.2d 866 (8th Cir.1986).

* Of the United States Court of Appeals for the Federal Circuit, sitting by designation pursuant to 28 U.S.C. § 291(a).

tecum on the grounds that the attorney-client and work product privileges had been waived by prior disclosure. We affirm.

I

Appellees, movants below, are seeking copies of documents which have been furnished by appellants, respondents below, to the Securities and Exchange Commission (SEC or Commission) and to a grand jury. The demand for those documents arose out of complaints filed by appellees as plaintiffs in Pennsylvania and transferred to the U.S. District Court for the Western District of Texas which involve (1) a class action brought against Tesoro Petroleum Corporation (Tesoro) and its officers and directors on behalf of Tesoro stockholders, and (2) a derivative action brought in Tesoro's name against its officers and directors. Plaintiffs allege in those complaints that defendants manipulated Tesoro stock in 1982 in order to remove enough stock from the public market to convert Tesoro from a public into a private corporation. The claim is that this contemplated corporate change was in part motivated by a desire to become free from public disclosure obligations, which obligations in turn might have caused disclosure of involvement by Tesoro in illegal payments to foreign officials before 1978. In the course of that Texas litigation, plaintiffs sought the papers now in question for use in connection with those suits. Because the documents are now in the possession, within the District of Columbia, of two law firms, Fulbright & Jaworski (Fulbright) and Vinson & Elkins (Vinson), subpoenas *duces tecum* were issued to those firms by the Clerk of the District Court, and, on their refusal to produce, a proceeding to enforce the subpoenas against them was begun in the court below.

Although neither law firm is a party to the law suits in Texas, their involvement here stems from the fact that the subpoenaed documents are the product of an investigation by Fulbright into Tesoro's alleged illegal payments to foreign officials. This came about as follows: After indications of improper corporate payments to officials, domestic and foreign, had become more frequent in the 1970's, the SEC established a "voluntary disclosure program," including independent investigations by the affected companies, and the agency made a general request to those companies to participate in the program. In re Sealed Case, 676 F.2d 793, 800-01 (D.C. Cir.1982). Following such a request to Tesoro, it hired Fulbright to perform a self-investigation on that subject and to help set up a special committee of independent directors to oversee it.[4] Tesoro disclosed the results of the investigation to the SEC under the "voluntary disclosure program." As stated by the District Court below, that program "promises wrongdoers more lenient treatment and the chance to avoid formal investigation and litigation in return for thorough self-investigation and complete disclosure of the results to the SEC." See also *Sealed Case,* supra, 676 F.2d at 801.

Made available to the SEC, under that program, were a copy of the investigation's final report and several binders which contained pertinent corporate records and documents of Tesoro, as well as the notes of the lawyers taken during the course of their investigation. The SEC filed a civil complaint against Tesoro, following the agency's receipt and considera-

---

4. The special committee later retained Vinson to advise it with regard to certain legal matters arising in conjunction with the investigation.

tion of the documents, which was resolved by entry of a consent decree. The Commission also referred some aspects of Tesoro's circumstances to the Department of Justice, which then presented the matter to a grand jury, convened in October 1978 in the District of Columbia.[5] Vinson represented Tesoro before the grand jury, and also is Tesoro's counsel in the Texas litigation. The grand jury obtained copies of the same documents through subpoenas served on the law firms.

After a hearing on the motion, the District Court ordered compliance, rejecting appellants' attorney-client and work product arguments. By Supplemental Memorandum and Order, the court denied appellants' motion for reconsideration, and confirmed its prior decision. A Revised Supplemental Memorandum corrected a reference to the clerk that issued the subpoenas. A motion for a stay pending appeal was subsequently granted by the court below.

II

The questions before us are whether the District Court correctly determined that appellants' voluntary disclosure of the documents to the SEC effected waivers of attorney-client and work product privileges with respect to the documents now sought for discovery in the Texas suits. We deal with each privilege in turn.

A. *Attorney-Client Privilege*

Attorney-client communications ordinarily are privileged, and thus are protected from discovery by a party opponent under Fed.R.Civ.P. 26(b). By allowing confidentiality of the substance of client and lawyer discussions, the privilege is held by clients as a means of encouraging their candor in discussing their circumstances with their chosen legal representatives. See Upjohn Co. v. United States, 449 U.S. 383 (1981). The privilege, however, is not absolute. As stated by this court in Permian Corp. v. United States, 665 F.2d 1214, 1219 (D.C.Cir.1981) (quoting United States v. American Telephone & Telegraph, 642 F.2d 1285, 1299 (D.C.Cir.1980)), "[a]ny voluntary disclosure by the holder of such a privilege is inconsistent with the confidential relationship and thus waives the privilege." See also *Sealed Case,* supra, 676 F.2d at 818; see generally 8 J. Wigmore, Evidence §§ 2327–28 (McNaughton rev. 1961); McCormack on Evidence § 93 (Cleary ed. 1972). There was, of course, disclosure here but appellants maintain that, although Tesoro's disclosure to the SEC was voluntary, their waiver of the attorney-client privilege with respect to those disclosures was limited to the SEC. They contend that *Permian* is compatible with a theory which allows a "limited waiver" of the attorney-client privilege (excluding disclosures to government agencies) and cite authority from other courts supporting the correctness of that rule. See, e.g., Diversified Industries, Inc. v. Meredith, 572 F.2d 596 (8th Cir.1977). We disagree, and hold that the District Court correctly interpreted and applied this court's precedent.

Contrary to appellants' assertion, the waiver theory explicated by the court in *Permian* is not limited to circumstances in which material that has been diclosed to one federal agency is sought by another federal agency. In *Permian,* Occidental Petroleum Corporation (Occidental) had allowed the

---

5. We were informed by letter prior to oral argument that the grand jury investi-   gation had been concluded with a decision not to seek a criminal prosecution.

SEC access to certain documents pursuant to an agreement by which Occidental attempted to retain its privileges. When the Department of Energy later sought access to some of the privileged materials, Occidental claimed that several of the documents were protected by the attorney-client privilege and that the prior disclosure to the SEC was a limited waiver of the privilege, i.e., it was a waiver with respect to the SEC alone.

Rejecting the limited waiver argument, this court stated: "we are aware of no congressional directive or judicially recognized priority system that places a higher value on cooperation with the SEC than on cooperation with other regulatory agencies, including the Department of Energy," *Permian,* 665 F.2d at 1221. Appellants use this quotation to urge that the *Permian* court rejected the limited waiver theory only as between federal agencies. However, such a narrow reading of that case is an incorrect characterization of its reasoning and holding. There is no need to elaborate on this court's emphatic rejection of the limited waiver doctrine in a lengthy discussion in *Permian,* see 665 F.2d 1220–1222, in which the court stated that

> The client cannot be permitted to pick and choose among his opponents, waiving the privilege for some and resurrecting the claim of confidentiality to obstruct others, or to invoke the privilege as to communications whose confidentiality he has already compromised for his own benefit * * *. The attorney-client privilege is not designed for such tactical employment.

665 F.2d at 1221.

There is no meaningful distinction in the adventitious fact that only federal agencies were involved in *Permian.* For the purposes of the attorney-client privilege, there is nothing special about another federal agency in the role of potential adversary as compared to private party litigants acting as adversaries. Like Occidental in *Permian,* Tesoro willingly sacrificed its attorney-client confidentiality by voluntarily disclosing material in an effort to convince another entity, the SEC, that a formal investigation or enforcement action was not warranted. Having done so, appellants cannot now selectively assert protection of those same documents under the attorney-client privilege. A client cannot waive that privilege in circumstances where disclosure might be beneficial while maintaining it in other circumstances where nondisclosure would be beneficial. "We believe that the attorney-client privilege should be available only at the traditional price: a litigant who wishes to assert confidentiality must maintain genuine confidentiality". *Permian,* 665 F.2d at 1222. To the same effect, see United States v. American Telephone & Telegraph, 642 F.2d 1285, 1299 (D.C.Cir.1980). Having failed to maintain genuine confidentiality, appellants are precluded from properly relying on the attorney-client privilege.

B. *Work Product Privilege*

The harder question concerns appellants' claim that the District Court erred in concluding that the disclosure effected an implied waiver of their work product privilege.[7]

---

7. Fed.R.Civ.P. 26(b)(3) provides:

   (3) Trial Preparation: Materials. Subject to the provisions of subdivision

(b)(4) of this rule, a party may obtain discovery of documents and tangible things otherwise discoverable under sub-

While the attorney-client privilege is intended to promote communication between attorney and client by protecting client confidences, the work product privilege is a broader protection, designed to balance the needs of the adversary system to promote an attorney's preparation in representing a client against society's general interest in revealing all true and material facts relevant to the resolution of a dispute. See Hickman v. Taylor, 329 U.S. 495, 509–512 (1947); see generally Cohn, The Work-Product Doctrine: Protection, Not Privilege, 71 Georgetown L.Rev. 917 (1983). As this court stated in United States v. American Telephone & Telegraph, 642 F.2d 1285, 1299 (D.C.Cir.1980), *"the work product privilege* does not exist to protect a confidential relationship, but rather *to promote the adversary system by safeguarding the fruits of an attorney's trial preparation from the discovery attempts of an opponent.* * * * A disclosure made in the pursuit of such trial preparation, and not inconsistent with maintaining secrecy against opponents, should be allowed without waiver of the privilege." (Emphasis in original.)

Recently this court decided a work product case which called upon the court to discuss the legal considerations underlying waiver of that privilege in the context of the SEC's voluntary disclosure program, In re Sealed Case, 676 F.2d 793 (D.C.Cir.1982). *Sealed Case* involved resistance to a grand jury subpoena by a multinational corporation on work product grounds (among others) for its counsel's records which had been disclosed previously to the SEC in the voluntary disclosure program. This court affirmed the district court's determination that the corporation had waived its work product privilege:

> Company entered into an arrangement with the SEC under which, as a matter of both common sense and common knowledge, Company relinquished its right to prevent the government from examining whatever documents were necessary for a fair evaluation of the final report offered to its shareholders and the SEC. Just because Company was successful in hiding crucial documents from the SEC, we need not allow Company to withhold them from a grand jury investigating possible crimes uncovered during the SEC's investigation.

Sealed Case, 676 F.2d at 817.

Although the circumstances before us differ—this is a case involving private parties, not a grand jury investigation, and appellees here are seeking the documents which were disclosed to the SEC, not those which might have been successfully hidden—and though that opinion left open the precise case before us, the general reasoning of *Sealed Case* leads us to a similar conclusion here. As Judge Wright stated, "[t]he doctrine of implied waiver allows courts to retain some discretion to ensure that specific assertions of privilege are reasonably consistent with the purposes for which a privilege was created," 676 F.2d at 817, and "[t]he question

division (b)(1) of this rule and prepared in anticipation of litigation or for trial by or for another party or by or for that other party's representative (including his attorney, consultant, surety, indemnitor, insurer, or agent) only upon a showing that the party seeking discovery has substantial need of the materials in the preparation of his case and that he is unable without undue hardship to obtain the substantial equivalent of the materials by other means. In ordering discovery of such materials when the required showing has been made, the court shall protect against disclosure of the mental impressions, conclusions, opinions, or legal theories of an attorney or other representative of a party concerning the litigation.

with respect to implied waiver is whether Wigmore's 'objective consideration' of fairness negates [the] assertion of privilege." Ibid. See also id. at 818. Obviously, the application of such a "fairness" standard is not without difficulty. However, because the underlying rationale of the work product privilege itself is also one of fairness, an analysis of whether that rationale maintains viability in particular circumstances involves of necessity the weighing of more abstract considerations within the context of those particulars.

Our present decision that there has been a waiver of the privilege rests on three main factors: (1) "the party claiming the privilege seeks to use it in a way that is not consistent with the purpose of the privilege," *Sealed Case,* 676 F.2d at 818; (2) appellants had no reasonable basis for believing that the disclosed materials would be kept confidential by the SEC; and (3) waiver of the privilege in these circumstances would not trench on any policy elements now inherent in this privilege. First, the advantage that the appellants seek from their attempt selectively to disclose their work product is greater "than the law must provide to maintain a healthy adversary system." Id. Fairness and consistency require that appellants not be allowed to gain the substantial advantages accruing to voluntary disclosure of work product to one adversary—the SEC—while being able to maintain another advantage inherent in protecting that same work product from other adversaries. See *Sealed Case,* 676 F.2d at 818–821. We are convinced that the health of the adversary system—which spawned the need for protection of an attorney's work product from discovery by an opponent—would not be well served by allowing appellants the advantages of selective disclosure to particular adversaries, a differential disclosure often spurred by considerations of self-interest.[10] "When a corporation elects to participate in a voluntary disclosure program like the SEC's, it necessarily decides that the benefits of participation outweigh the benefits of confidentiality for all files necessary to a full evaluation of its disclosures. It foregoes some of the traditional protections of the adversary system in order to avoid some of the traditional burdens that accompany adversary resolution of disputes, especially disputes with such formidable adversaries as the SEC." *Sealed Case,* 676 F.2d at 822–23 (footnote omitted).

There is no question that the SEC was an adversary to Tesoro. This was not a partnership between allies. Tesoro was not simply assisting the SEC in doing its job. Rather, Tesoro independently and voluntarily chose to participate in a thorough disclosure program, in return for which it received the *quid pro quo* of lenient punishment for any wrongdoings exposed in the process. That decision was obviously motivated by self-interest. Appellants now want work product protection for those same disclosures against different adversaries in suits centering on the very same matters disclosed to the SEC. It would be unreasonable to suppose that litigation with these other adversaries was not anticipated at the time of disclosure to the SEC. It would also be inconsistent and unfair to allow appellants to select according to their own self-interest to which adversaries they will allow access to the materials.

Second, appellants did not have any proper expectations of confidentiality which might mitigate the weight against them of such general considera-

---

10. As we show infra, the SEC did not promise confidentiality to appellants.

tions of fairness in the adversary process. Although we agree with appellants that not all voluntary disclosures effect a work product waiver, there is not here any "existence of common interests between transferor and transferee," United States v. AT & T, 642 F.2d 1285, 1299 (1980), which might establish a basis for expectations of confidentiality. Appellants contend, however, that such expectations were warranted because the materials were disclosed to the Commission pursuant to (1) SEC regulations which required their confidentiality and, (2) an understanding between Fulbright and the SEC that the materials would remain confidential.

There is a dispute between the parties whether the question of SEC regulations said to require confidentiality was raised below by appellants. We put aside this question because the regulations cited by appellants are not relevant to the circumstances before us. See 17 C.F.R. §§ 203.2, 230.122, 240.0–4 (1978). These regulations apply to formal SEC investigations—they afford no protection to documents previously disclosed under the voluntary disclosure program. Appellants maintain that "disclosure" of the materials did not occur until the formal investigation began—and thus the regulations do apply—because the SEC did not have physical possession of the materials until that time. But even before taking physical possession, the SEC unquestionably had full access to all of the documents and perused them. Contrary to appellants' argument, there is no significance to the distinction between full access and physical possession with respect to the issue of when disclosure took place. The materials were disclosed in full to the SEC prior to the institution of a formal investigation, and the regulations do not apply.

Likewise without merit is appellants' claim that the SEC had agreed by letter to maintain the confidentiality of the submitted materials. Appellants were not entirely forthcoming below on this issue. Only after the District Court held against appellants in its first memorandum did they request reconsideration of that decision based on the new submission of correspondence consisting of two letters between Fulbright and the SEC. Appellants maintain that these letters—one dated October 3, 1978 from Fulbright to the SEC and one dated October 19, 1978 from the SEC to Fulbright—demonstrate that the SEC did agree to maintain the confidentiality of the documents in question.

We are not persuaded that the District Court erred in law or fact in its assessment that "there has been no commitment by the SEC to receive and hold the documents in confidence on terms which negate the waiver of [appellants'] work product privilege effected in 1978 when they submitted the documents to the SEC." Responding to Fulbright's October 3 letter, which stated appellants' own understanding concerning disclosure of the documents, the SEC said that "[t]he Commission staff will maintain the confidentiality of any documents produced pursuant to any subpoena issued to your firm or to Tesoro, * * * as it does in connection with any other private investigation." As noted by the District Court, these documents were not "produced pursuant to any subpoena." They were provided voluntarily by Tesoro to persuade the SEC not to engage in a formal investigation of possible wrongdoings. The distinction between voluntary disclosure and disclosure by subpoena is that the latter, being involuntary, lacks the self-interest which motivates the former. As such, there may be less reason to find waiver in circumstances of involuntary disclosure.

With regard to third party access, the SEC stated:

> In the event that, during the period of investigation and thereafter, the Commission shall receive a request from any third party other than a grand jury or agencies of the federal government for access to any document submitted by your firm or Tesoro, voluntarily or pursuant to subpoena, * * * the staff of the Commission will notify Tesoro of the receipt of such a request * * *. In the further event that the Commission should determine that it is not able to grant confidential treatment consistent with the provisions of the Freedom of Information Act, the staff will immediately advise Tesoro of such decision and endeavor to afford you ten days notice prior to the release of such documents * * *.

Clearly, the SEC's assurance that Tesoro would be notified in the event of a third party request is hardly an agreement to maintain complete confidentiality. Regardless of Fulbright's attempts to extract such a promise from the SEC, neither these letters nor any other part of the record indicates any such agreement by the SEC. Indeed, the record shows that the exchange of these letters occurred *after* the SEC had already been given access to all of the documents in question. The letters were sent sometime after the beginning of a formal investigation of Tesoro by the SEC, not prior to the initial disclosure of the documents. The record shows no attempts by appellants to structure a confidentiality agreement prior to making the documents available, much less an agreement to do so by the SEC even after disclosure had been made. See *Sealed Case,* supra, 676 F.2d at 823. In short, the letters exchanged between Fulbright and the SEC warrant no expectations of confidentiality on appellants' part for the materials which were made available. The attempt to secure confidentiality occurred after the SEC had seen the voluntarily disclosed documents, and the SEC's statement concerning third party requests for documents said only that Tesoro would receive notice of any release of materials which would have been deemed appropriate by the Commission.

Appellants offer two other factors to support their expectations of confidentiality, neither of which weighs in their favor: (1) The SEC has not in fact released any of the materials, including to a private party who requested copies of the Tesoro documents under the Freedom of Information Act (FOIA), and (2) the SEC apparently will propose legislation concerning waivers of evidentiary privileges by companies involved with the SEC.

There is no significance to the fact that the SEC has not released any of the materials. The SEC denied an FOIA requestor by asserting exemption 7(A) (5 U.S.C. § 552(b)(7)(A)) because "the production of such records would * * * interfere with law enforcement proceedings," i.e., with the then on-going grand jury proceedings. However, since the grand jury proceedings have ended, the SEC has advised a requestor that the exemption will no longer be asserted and that the Commission's FOIA officer will review the Tesoro file to determine whether any material is releasable. This is a slim basis on which to claim an expectation of confidentiality.

Likewise without weight is appellants' contention that confidentiality should be accorded because the SEC has recently announced that it will propose legislation which would "provide that submission of information to the Commission does not waive the attorney-client privilege, or any other applicable evidentiary privilege, and that such information is exempt from the FOIA." This statement by the SEC hardly supports appellants' position. Rather, it seems to indicate a belief by the SEC that, under current law, submission of information to the SEC waives applicable evidentiary privileges and is not exempt from FOIA requests. We note that the SEC has not taken any public position in this case concerning judicial resolution of these problems, nor has it adopted regulations embodying the substance of its suggestion to Congress.

Finally, we believe that no policy factor now inherent in the work product privilege calls for a special exception for the SEC's voluntary disclosure program (or similar governmental enforcement projects). A healthy adversary system affords protection to an attorney's trial preparation as against actual and potential opponents. United States v. American Telephone & Telegraph, supra, 642 F.2d at 1299. But, as we have said, the privilege does not protect against the manipulation of selecting a particular opponent for selective disclosure—most probably for the discloser's own benefit. The SEC was such a potential opponent but Tesoro (and the other appellants) voluntarily and deliberately made disclosures to that agency, undoubtedly in the hope and expectation of receiving a benefit under the voluntary disclosure program. It is said that, nevertheless, such voluntary programs will be hindered unless the work product privilege covers disclosures under them. *Permian, supra,* has already rejected, for the attorney-client privilege, an exception for such disclosure, saying "we cannot see how 'the developing procedure of corporations to employ independent outside counsel to investigate and advise them' would be thwarted by telling a corporation that it cannot disclose the resulting reports to the SEC if it wishes to maintain their confidentiality." The same choice is open under the work product privilege. Or the company can insist on a promise of confidentiality before disclosure to the SEC. Cf. *Sealed Case,* 676 F.2d at 823.

If a change is to be made because it is thought that such voluntary disclosure programs are so important that they deserve special treatment, that is a policy matter for the Congress, or perhaps for the SEC (through a regulation). Courts are not the appropriate forum—for one thing, courts do not know enough—to decide on policy grounds to treat those programs (or others like them) in an exceptional way. See *Sealed Case,* supra, 676 F.2d at 824.

Affirmed.

IN RE INTERNATIONAL SYSTEMS AND CONTROLS CORPORATION SECURITIES LITIGATION

United States Court of Appeals, Fifth Circuit, 1982.
693 F.2d 1235.

Before INGRAHAM, REAVLEY and POLITZ, CIRCUIT JUDGES.

REAVLEY, CIRCUIT JUDGE.

This is an appeal of a pretrial discovery order that required production of certain documents claimed to be work product. We vacate the order, 91 F.R.D. 552, and outline how the district court should proceed if called upon to reconsider the discovery of these documents.

1. THE FACTS

Defendant International Systems and Control Corporation ("I.S.C.") is a far flung organization that conducts business throughout the Middle East. As part of this business, plaintiffs allege, I.S.C. engaged regularly in paying "commissions" or "bribes" to foreign nationals in order to secure contracts. In March 1976, the SEC sent a letter to I.S.C. requesting information regarding these "sensitive payments." In May, allegedly in an attempt to enroll in the SEC's voluntary disclosure program, I.S.C. appointed a special audit committee. This committee consisted of two independent directors who were empowered to hire the law firm of Watson, Ess, Marshall and Enggass ("W.E.") and the accounting firm of Arthur Young ("A.Y."). The committee was charged with investigating any "sensitive payments" made by I.S.C. or its subsidiaries. A.Y. was also I.S.C.'s regular auditor for the 1973–76 period. The district court found that A.Y.'s original role as an independent investigator was redefined in a letter dated May 23, 1977 as one of assisting W.E. in its investigation.

In February of 1978, the SEC served I.S.C. with a subpoena. A complaint was issued in July of that year. Ultimately a consent decree was negotiated.

As a result of the SEC subpoena and complaint, several suits against I.S.C. were filed, and then consolidated for pretrial purposes by the multidistrict panel. The suits relevant to this appeal involve Lewis and Koenig. Plaintiff Lewis filed a derivative action against the board of directors. He alleged that the defendants either (1) knowingly caused illegal payments to be made or (2) negligently failed to inquire and uncover the illegal payments. Plaintiff Koenig filed a class action against A.Y. and the directors and officers of I.S.C. Koenig alleged that A.Y. by certifying the 1976 financial statement participated in a conspiracy to defraud purchasers and sellers of I.S.C. stock.

Both Koenig and Lewis moved to compel production of A.Y.'s binders containing the information that it had developed in its special review. A.Y. was willing to produce the binders, but I.S.C. interposed claims of attorney-client privilege and work product immunity. The district court ordered that certain documents be produced and I.S.C. appeals this order.

2. THE DISTRICT COURT'S OPINION

The district court held a hearing to dispose of the privilege and work product claims. It first held that I.S.C. did not waive its claims by making certain disclosures to the SEC. This holding is not disputed. Second, the court found that all of the documents in the special review binders were within the work product immunity. This holding is clearly correct, since A.Y. was a "representative of a party," Fed.R.Civ.P. 26(b)(3), and there was a sufficient anticipation of litigation. In re Grand Jury Investigation, 599 F.2d 1224, 1228–30 (3d Cir.1979); In re Grand Jury Subpoena, 599 F.2d 504, 511 (2d Cir.1979). The district court, relying on Garner v. Wolfinbarger, 430 F.2d 1093 (5th Cir.1970), cert. denied, 401 U.S. 974 (1971) and the crime-fraud exception to the attorney-client privilege, In re Grand Jury Proceedings, 680 F.2d 1026, 1028–29 (5th Cir.1982),

order[ed] production of all material in the AY Special Review binders other than itemized documents which might reveal Watson, Ess attorney opinion or legal theories, whether such items are described as being within the attorney client privilege or as attorney work product.

Notwithstanding the ambiguity in the preceding passage, we read the district court's decision to be addressed only to the work product immunity. Earlier in its opinion, the court held that the special review binders "should be treated as work product in anticipation of litigation." This appeal therefore raises two issues for our consideration. First, should *Garner* be extended to the work product immunity. Second, should the ongoing crime-fraud exception apply to work product.

3. GARNER & WORK PRODUCT

Our decision in *Garner* dealt with the application of the attorney-client privilege in the context of corporate-shareholder litigation. The plaintiffs filed a class action alleging common-law and securities fraud. They also filed a derivative suit on behalf of the corporation against certain individual defendants. The issue on appeal was whether the corporation could assert the privilege against its shareholders. We engaged in a balancing test, holding that

> The corporation is not barred from asserting it [the privilege] merely because those demanding information enjoy the status of stockholders. But where the corporation is in suit against its stockholders on charges of acting inimically to stockholder interests, protection of those interests as well as those of the corporation and of the public require that the availability of the privilege be subject to the right of the shareholders to show cause why it should not be invoked in the particular instance.

430 F.2d at 1103–04 (footnotes omitted).

The court's reasoning was based on the nature of the corporation. Management operates the corporation for the shareholders. There is a "mutuality of interest" between shareholders and management. Id. at 1101.

In issuing the order under review the district court apparently applied *Garner* without analyzing whether the differences in work product immunity and attorney-client privilege justify a different result. Our view of *Garner* and Fed.R.Civ.P. 26(b)(3) lead us to the conclusion that *Garner* should not be so extended.

Garner's rationale indicates that it was not intended to apply to work product. *Garner* is premised upon the "mutuality of interest" between shareholder and management. This "mutuality of interest" may exist for the attorney-client privilege. But once there is sufficient anticipation of litigation to trigger the work product immunity, we think this mutuality is destroyed. To hold otherwise would be to ignore modern corporate realities. The work product privilege is based on the existence of an adversarial relationship, not the quasi-fiduciary relationship analogized to in *Garner*. The joint attorney analogy discussed by the *Garner* court also does not apply to work product. Two parties anticipating litigation against each other do not have a common interest. It is not reasonable to indulge in the fiction that counsel, hired by management, is also constructively hired by the same party counsel is expected to defend against.

The terms of disclosure of work product are spelled out in the Federal Rules. Following the discussion of Hickman v. Taylor, 329 U.S. 495 (1947),

Rule 26(b)(3) was adopted in 1970. The rule states that work product will be ordered

> *only* upon a showing that the party seeking discovery has substantial need of the materials in the preparation of his case and that he is unable without undue hardship to obtain the substantial equivalent of the materials by other means.

The plain language of the rule is inconsistent with *Garner*. In adopting the rule, a good cause standard was rejected in favor of the substantial need/ undue hardship test. 8 C. Wright & A. Miller, Federal Practice and Procedure § 2023 (1970). Since the good cause standard is the standard in *Garner*, it follows that *Garner* should not apply to work product discovery.

4. RULE 26(b)(3): SUBSTANTIAL NEED & UNDUE HARDSHIP

The district court did not make the findings of substantial need and undue hardship required by the rule. Upon remand it is still free to determine if the plaintiffs are entitled to production of the A.Y. special review binders.

The district court, of course, has broad discretion to determine whether an adequate showing has been made. We point out several factors that relate to the inquiry.

We first note that these materials are not the "mental impressions, conclusions, opinions or legal theories of an attorney." Fed.R.Civ.P. 26(b) (3). Some courts have provided an almost absolute protection for such materials. In re Murphy, 560 F.2d 326, 336 (8th Cir.1977); In re Doe, 662 F.2d 1073, 1080 (4th Cir.1981), cert. denied, 455 U.S. 1000 (1982). Since these documents are not "opinion work product," the plaintiffs do not have to make the even higher showing required.

a. Undue Hardship

I.S.C. asserts that since the information sought by plaintiffs here is available through normal discovery procedures, production of work product should be denied. This argument goes to whether the plaintiffs can demonstrate "undue hardship" in obtaining the materials from other sources.

We agree with the general proposition that discovery of work product will be denied if a party can obtain the information he seeks by deposition. 8 C. Wright & A. Miller, Federal Practice & Procedure § 2025 n. 72 (1970). We know that the work product immunity protects only the documents themselves and not the underlying facts.[7] Plaintiff may however, demonstrate undue hardship if the witness cannot recall the events in question, or is unavailable. Xerox v. I.B.M. Corp., 64 F.R.D. 367, 382 (S.D.N.Y.1974). In re Grand Jury Investigation, 599 F.2d at 1231–32. But broad unsubstantiated assertions of unavailability or faulty memory are not sufficient. See United States v. Chatham City Corp., 72 F.R.D. 640, 644 (S.D.Ga.1976). On the record before us, plaintiff has only taken one deposition. We think a more particularized showing must be made before production can be

---

7. In the deposition of Robert Teague, we note that plaintiff was prevented from questioning Teague about the facts involving the special review by I.S.C.'s assertions of privilege. This was improper. Plaintiff is entitled to learn the facts underlying the special review binders.

ordered by the district court. Xerox Corp. v. I.B.M. Corp., 79 F.R.D. 7 (S.D. N.Y.1977) (production of interview notes covering 37 employees ordered when 33 were deposed and could not remember the events of seven years earlier).

Another element that the district court may consider in determining undue hardship is expense. We agree that in the ordinary case, the cost of one or a few depositions is not enough to justify discovery of work product. *Chatham City,* 72 F.R.D. at 644. But there have been cases in which unusual expense has constituted undue hardship. Allen v. Denver-Chicago Trucking Co., 32 F.R.D. 616, 617 (W.D.Mo.1963) (decided under former good cause standard). In this case, many of the persons involved may be in Canada, England or the Middle East. Also, to evaluate A.Y.'s regular audit papers and I.S.C.'s financial information and duplicate the information contained in the special review binders could cost the plaintiffs an inordinate amount. The district court found that this investigation cost I.S.C. $1.5 million. We note, however, that plaintiff may be able to discover much of this information at much lower expense to itself, and that plaintiff is only inquiring into certain specific transactions, whereas the special review naturally covered a broader range of activities. The cost to plaintiff may be inquired into as a factor in the undue hardship analysis.

b. Substantial Need

The second prong of the Rule 26(b)(3) test is "substantial need for the materials." Some cases have found substantial need by emphasizing the importance of the documents themselves. One common justification for discovery is the claim which relates to the opposite party's knowledge that can only be shown by the documents themselves. Bird v. Penn Central Co., 61 F.R.D. 43 (E.D.Pa.1973); Kearney & Trecker Corp. v. Giddings & Lewis, Inc., 296 F.Supp. 979, 983 (E.D.Wis.1969). In *Bird,* the plaintiff insurance companies sued to rescind certain policies. Defendants interposed the defense of laches. Plaintiff responded to this with a claim of advice of counsel. The court said

Because the nature of this defense concerns knowledge, legal theories and conclusions of plaintiffs' attorneys charged with claim investigation, * * * [are] discoverable * * *.

61 F.R.D. at 47. The district court here stated that A.Y.'s certification of the 1976 financial statements was an essential element of plaintiff's fraud claims. A.Y.'s knowledge as to I.S.C.'s "sensitive payments" prior to the 1976 certification could be grounds for a finding of substantial need under these cases. Nevertheless, we think that the district court should determine if A.Y.'s knowledge can be discovered without the work product—i.e. by deposition testimony or through the regular audit information.

We note that, ultimately, these findings are part of a balancing test. The district court should weigh all the factors in deciding this issue. This balance will not be overturned absent an abuse of discretion.

5. THE CRIME-FRAUD EXCEPTION

a. Exception Applies

The second issue this appeal raises is the applicability of the ongoing crime-fraud exception to the work-product immunity. This exception is firmly entrenched in the common law of attorney-client privilege. The privilege exists to encourage full disclosure of pertinent information by clients to their attorneys. Upjohn Co. v. United States, 449 U.S. 383 (1981). Its protection extends to past criminal violations. The rationale for this is that the client, given the nature of our adversary system, has a legitimate interest in securing informed representation without fear of forced disclosure. However, the client has no legitimate interest in seeking legal advice in planning future criminal activities. The crime-fraud exception therefore comes into play if "the client consults an attorney for advice that will assist the client in carrying out a contemplated illegal or fraudulent scheme." In re Murphy, 560 F.2d at 337 (citations omitted).

Every court of appeals that has addressed the crime-fraud exception's application to work product has concluded that it does apply. E.g. In re John Doe Corp., 675 F.2d 482, 492 (2d Cir.1982); In re Grand Jury Proceedings, 604 F.2d 798, 803 (3d Cir.1979). While these cases have arisen in the grand jury context, we find them to be persuasive. The work-product immunity was first recognized in *Hickman*. Its primary purpose is to protect the "public policy underlying the orderly prosecution and defense of legal claims." 329 U.S. at 510. It protects both client and attorney's interest in preventing disclosures about the case.

> When the case being prepared involves the client's ongoing fraud, however, we see no reason to afford the client the benefit of this doctrine. It is only the "rightful interests" of the client that the work product doctrine was designed to protect.

(Citations omitted). In re Special September 1978 Grand Jury, 640 F.2d 49, 63 (7th Cir.1980). We therefore hold that the ongoing crime-fraud exception applies to work product.

b. Prima Facie Predicate

Our inquiry does not stop here. In order to invoke this exception, the party seeking to breach the walls of privilege must make out a prima facie case. In In re Grand Jury Proceedings in Matter of Fine, 641 F.2d 199, 203 (5th Cir.1981), we approved of the definition of a prima facie case contained in Black's Law Dictionary (4th ed. 1968):

> [evidence] [s]uch as will suffice until contradicted and overcome by other evidence * * * [a] case which has proceeded upon sufficient proof to that stage where it will support [a] finding if evidence to the contrary is disregarded.

The district court recognized this requirement and stated that the plaintiffs had made a prima facie case of fraud. We find nothing in the record, however, of fraud except the plaintiff's *allegations*. While the pleadings in this case are unusually detailed, they are not evidence to make a prima facie case. See In re Grand Jury Investigation, 599 F.2d at 1232 (naked assertion of a corporate cover-up insufficient to overcome work product).

The courts have evolved a two element test for a prima facie showing:

> First, there must be a *prima facie* showing of a violation sufficiently serious to defeat the work product privilege. Second, the court must find some valid relationship between the work product under subpoena and the *prima facie* violation.

(Footnotes omitted). In re Sealed Case, 676 F.2d 793, 814–15 (D.C.Cir.1982); In re Grand Jury Proceedings, 604 F.2d at 803. This test has evolved in the grand jury context.

Judge Wright, in *In re Sealed Case* explained this test in depth. He stated that it must first be shown that the client was engaged in ongoing fraudulent activity when the work product was sought or produced. 676 F.2d at 815. Then, the work product must reasonably relate to the fraudulent activity. Id.

c. Specific Intent of Client

Judge Wright, however, would dispense with proof of specific intent of the client. *In re Sealed Case* was one where the corporation withheld documents from an investigation of crime by a grand jury. The reasons given by Judge Wright for allowing discovery without a showing of specific intent, to further fraud or crime by the consultation of an attorney or preparation of a document, do not apply in the present case.

Here the plaintiffs allege fraud in the company paying bribes and failing to report them to shareholders. It seems clear that the plaintiffs will be able to show that illegal payments were made and not reported. Since this was not reported officially until 1978, it could be argued that a prima facie case of ongoing fraud was thereby established. The special review binders clearly have a reasonable relation to this ongoing fraud. Yet it may well be that the purpose in commencing the special review was entirely pure. In the modern corporate world with multiple subsidiaries and hundreds of employees, shady practices may occur without the directors' and officers' knowledge. An attempt by the management to investigate past and present questionable practices should not be discouraged by guaranteed disclosure. In the present case the court should require some proof of specific intent by management in the development of the work product documents.

The order is VACATED.

EVIDENTIARY PRIVILEGES

All of the cases thus far which have dealt with the attorney-client privilege and the work-product privilege of the securities lawyer have dealt with them, like the two cases printed above, in traditional terms of existence and waiver, except perhaps for the case of Garner v. Wolfinbarger [1] dealing with the attorney-client privilege asserted by the corporation in the context of a shareholder's suit. In that case, the Fifth Circuit held that, in connection with a lawsuit by shareholders against the corporation, the attorney-client privilege might not be available to the corporation in some circumstances with respect to advice given to it relating to the subject matter of the lawsuit, although it refused to extend the holding of the *Garner* case to the work-product privilege in the *International Systems and Controls* case.

In In re Grand Jury Proceedings [2] the Fourth Circuit held that information communicated to a securities lawyer for his use in the preparation of a proposed offering circular in connection with the sale of limited partnership

1. 430 F.2d 1093 (5th Cir.1970), cert. denied 401 U.S. 974 (1971).

2. 727 F.2d 1352 (4th Cir.1984).

interests was not privileged because it failed to meet the requirement that the communication be intended by the client to be confidential. The court held that information intended to be disclosed to others is not protected by the attorney-client privilege, and that the loss of the privilege applied not only to the particular words used in expressing the content of the communication but to the substance of the communication as well. Under this theory, courts have held that information disclosed to attorneys in connection with the preparation of tax returns or stock or partnership offering prospectuses is not privileged. The court also held it was irrelevant that no prospectus was actually issued in connection with the offering; the important factor was that the information given to the attorney was to assist in preparing a prospectus which was to be published and was not intended to be kept confidential.

In In re Sealed Case,[3] which is discussed in the *Fulbright & Jaworski* case, the Circuit Court for the District of Columbia refused to accept the "limited waiver" doctrine advanced in Diversified Industries, Inc. v. Meredith,[4] in which the Eighth Circuit held en banc that a waiver as to the Securities and Exchange Commission did not extend to a grand jury subpoena. The *Fulbright & Jaworski* case does not rule out the possibility that the waiver could be so limited if the SEC agrees to keep the information confidential. The attorney furnishing such privileged information to the SEC should obviously attempt to negotiate an agreement by the Commission that it will keep the information confidential, although the Freedom of Information Act may present an obstacle to the Commission making any such blanket commitment.

In In re Penn Central Commercial Paper Litigation[5] the court held that the testimony by an attorney in a non-public investigation by the SEC, with the consent of his client, to certain communications which would have been protected by the attorney-client privilege constituted a waiver of the privilege. In Garfinkle v. Arcata National Corp.[6] the court held that the sending of an opinion letter by company counsel to a shareholder demanding registration pursuant to a registration covenant, to the effect that his shares could be sold without registration, constituted a waiver of the attorney-client privilege regarding communications between company officials and the law firm with respect to the demand, in subsequent litigation between the shareholder and the company.

In the *Garfinkle* case the court also held that internal communications within the law firm relating to the giving of the opinion letter were not protected by the "work product" privilege since they were not prepared "in anticipation of litigation" and in any event the sending of the opinion letter would have been a waiver of that privilege. Also, in Securities and Exchange Commission v. National Student Marketing Corp.[7] the court held that White & Case was not entitled to rely upon the work product privilege with respect to material prepared to defend NSMC in connection with an SEC investigation, where NSMC had later copped out and agreed to a consent judgment in which it waived all attorney-client privileges and all work product privileges insofar as it was able, and the SEC was attempting to discover the material in connection with its continuing suit against White & Case. The court said:

"The Court is of the opinion that the policy considerations of this doctrine would not be subverted by disallowing the position of White & Case. Nor should it be overlooked that their client, NSMC, has entered into a judgment of Permanent Injunction waiving and avoiding the necessity of presenting any

---

3. 676 F.2d 793 (D.C.Cir.1982).

4. 572 F.2d 596 (8th Cir.1977).

5. 61 F.R.D. 453 (S.D.N.Y.1973).

6. 64 F.R.D. 688 (S.D.N.Y.1974).

7. CCH Fed.Sec.Law Rptr. ¶ 94,610 (D.C.D.C.1974).

defense and in so doing it agreed, *inter alia,* to make available for discovery, to any party, all material related to this litigation. Indeed, NSMC specifically waived its right to claim the attorney-client privilege which existed as of the date the suit was filed and also divested itself of any interest it might have in immunizing attorney 'work-product' from discovery.

"The Court recognizes the distinction to be drawn between the attorney-client privilege, which of course belongs to the client and is his alone to waive, and the work product doctrine. This qualified protection is designed, as Rule 26(b)(3) reflects, to foster the ability of litigants to build as strong and as robust a case as possible by protecting 'mental impressions, conclusions, opinions, or legal theories', the disclosure of which should result in, to quote Justice Murphy's majority opinion in Hickman v. Taylor, '[i]nefficiency, unfairness and sharp practices * * * in the giving of legal advice and in the preparation of cases for trial.' 329 U.S. at 511. The Court admonished that ' * * * the interests of the clients and the cause of justice would be poorly served.' Id. The Hickman rule, as well as the 1970 amendments to the Federal Rules, cannot be viewed as a means by which attorneys, based solely upon that status, are to be elevated to a preferred position when involved as parties in the litigation process. The sound basis for granting special treatment to attorney 'work-product' is the realization that, in appropriate circumstances, the adversary system of justice requires that certain activities of attorneys be sheltered from discovery. It would be difficult indeed for White & Case to now posit their reliance upon theories of work product in terms of serving or protecting the rights of a former client and codefendant who no longer has any interest in this injunctive action.

"It is highly probable that in different circumstances the material sought would be eligible for work product protection, but with White & Case as named defendants, and in light of NSMC's present posture, the Court is of the opinion that the documents do not fall under Rule 26(b)(3)'s protective umbrella."

See Block and Remz, The Confidentiality of Corporate Internal Investigations, 18 Rev. of Sec. & Comm. Reg. 61 (1985); Dorris, The Limited Waiver Rule: Creation of an SEC–Corporation Privilege, 36 Stan.L.Rev. 789 (1984); Brown, Corporate Communications and the Federal Securities Laws, 53 Geo. Wash.L.Rev. 741 (1985); Saltzburg, The Federal Rules of Evidence: Corporate and Related Attorney-Client Privilege Claims, 12 Hofstra L.Rev. 279 (1984); Sexton, A Post-Upjohn Consideration of the Corporate Attorney-Client Privilege, 57 N.Y.U.L.Rev. 443 (1982); Rosenfeld, Transformation of the Attorney-Client Privilege, 33 Hastings L.J. 495 (1982); Hubbel, Discovery of Internal Corporate Investigations, 32 Stan.L.Rev. 1193 (1980); Brodsky, The "Zone of Darkness": Special Counsel Investigations and the Attorney-Client Privilege, 8 Sec.Reg.L.J. 123 (1980); Block and Barton, Internal Corporate Investigations, 35 Bus.Law 5 (1979).

RONDEAU v. MOSINEE PAPER CORP.

United States Supreme Court, 1975.
422 U.S. 49, 95 S.Ct. 2069, 45 L.Ed.2d 12.

MR. CHIEF JUSTICE BURGER delivered the opinion of the Court.

We granted certiorari in this case to determine whether a showing of irreparable harm is necessary for a private litigant to obtain injunctive relief in a suit under § 13(d) of the Williams Act. The Court of Appeals held that it was not. We reverse.

I

Respondent Mosinee Paper Corporation is a Wisconsin company engaged in the manufacture and sale of paper, paper products, and plastics. Its principal place of business is located in Mosinee, Wisconsin, and its only class of equity security is common stock which is registered under § 12 of the Securities Exchange Act of 1934. At all times relevant to this litigation there was slightly more than 800,000 shares of such stock outstanding.

In April 1971 petitioner Francis A. Rondeau, a Mosinee businessman, began making large purchases of respondent's common stock in the over-the-counter market. Some of the purchases were in his own name; others were in the name of businesses and a foundation known to be controlled by him. By May 17, 1971, petitioner had acquired 40,413 shares of respondent's stock, which constituted more than 5% of those outstanding. He was therefore required to comply with the disclosure provisions of the Williams Act, by filing a Schedule 13D with respondent and the Securities and Exchange Commission within 10 days. That form would have disclosed, among other things, the number of shares beneficially owned by petitioner, the source of the funds used to purchase them, and petitioner's purpose in making the purchases.

Petitioner did not file a Schedule 13D but continued to purchase substantial blocks of respondent's stock; by July 30, 1971, he had acquired more than 60,000 shares. On that date the chairman of respondent's board of directors informed him by letter that his activity had "given rise to numerous rumors" and "seems to have created some problems under the Federal Securities Laws * * *" Upon receiving the letter petitioner immediately stopped placing orders for respondent's stock and consulted his attorney. On August 25, 1971, he filed a Schedule 13D which, in addition to the other required disclosures, described the "Purpose of Transaction" as follows:

"Francis A. Rondeau determined during early part of 1971 that the common stock of Issuer [respondent] was undervalued in the over-the-counter market and represented a good investment vehicle for future income and appreciation. Francis A. Rondeau and his associates presently propose to seek to acquire additional common stock of the Issuer in order to obtain effective control of the Issuer, but such investments as originally determined were and are not necessarily made with this objective in mind. Consideration is currently being given to making a public cash tender offer to the shareholders of the Issuer at a price which will reflect current quoted prices for such stock with some premium added."

Petitioner also stated that, in the event that he did obtain control of respondent, he would consider making changes in management "in an effort to provide a Board of Directors which is more representative of all of the shareholders, particularly those outside of present management. * * *" One month later petitioner amended the form to reflect more accurately the allocation of shares between himself and his companies.

On August 27 respondent sent a letter to its shareholders informing them of the disclosures in petitioner's Schedule 13D.[3] The letter stated

---

3. Respondent simultaneously issued a press release containing the same information. Almost immediately the price of its stock jumped to $19–$21 per share. A few

that by his "tardy filing" petitioner had "withheld the information to which you [the shareholders] were entitled for more than two months in violation of federal law." In addition, while agreeing that "recent market prices have not reflected the real value of your Mosinee stock," respondent's management could "see little in Mr. Rondeau's background that would qualify him to offer any meaningful guidance to a Company in the highly technical and competitive paper industry."

Six days later respondent initiated this suit in the United States District Court for the Western District of Wisconsin. Its complaint named petitioner, his companies, and two banks which had financed some of petitioner's purchases as defendants and alleged that they were engaged in a scheme to defraud respondent and its shareholders in violation of the securities laws. It alleged further that shareholders who had "sold shares without the information which defendants were required to disclose lacked information material to their decision to sell or hold," and that respondent "was unable to communicate such information to its shareholders, and to take such actions as their interest required." Respondent prayed for an injunction prohibiting petitioner and his codefendants from voting or pledging their stock and from acquiring additional shares, requiring them to divest themselves of stock which they already owned, and for damages. A motion for a preliminary injunction was filed with the complaint but later withdrawn.

After three months of pretrial proceedings petitioner moved for summary judgment. He readily conceded that he had violated the Williams Act, but contended that the violation was due to a lack of familiarity with the securities laws and that neither respondent nor its shareholders had been harmed. The District Court agreed. It found no material issues of fact to exist regarding petitioner's lack of willfulness in failing to timely file a Schedule 13D, concluding that he discovered his obligation to do so on July 30, 1971,[4] and that there was no basis in the record for disputing his claim that he first considered the possibility of obtaining control of respondent some time after that date. The District Court therefore held that petitioner and his codefendants "did not engage in intentional, covert, and conspiratorial conduct in failing to timely file the 13D Schedule."

Similarly, although accepting respondent's contention that its management and shareholders suffered anxiety as a result of petitioners' activities and that this anxiety was exacerbated by his failure to disclose his intentions until August 1971, the District Court concluded that similar anxiety "could be expected to accompany any change in management" and was "a predictable consequence of shareholder democracy." It fell far short of the irreparable harm necessary to support an injunction and no other harm was revealed by the record; as amended, petitioner's Schedule 13D disclosed all of the information to which respondent was entitled, and he had not proceeded with a tender offer. Moreover, in the view of the District

---

days later it dropped back to the prevailing price of $12.50–$14.00 per share, where it remained.

4. The District Court pointed out that prior to December 10, 1970, a Schedule 13D was not required until a person's holdings exceeded 10% of a corporation's outstanding equity securities, see Pub.L. No. 91–567, 84 Stat. 1497, and credited petitioner's testimony that he believed the 10% requirement was still in effect at the time he made his purchases. Indeed, the chairman of respondent's board of directors was not familiar with the Williams Act's filing requirement until shortly before he sent the July 30, 1971 letter.

Court even if a showing of irreparable harm were not required in all cases under the securities laws, petitioner's lack of bad faith and the absence of damage to respondent made this "a particularly inappropriate occasion to fashion equitable relief. * * *" Thus, although petitioner had committed a technical violation of the Williams Act the District Court held that respondent was entitled to no relief and entered summary judgment against it.

The Court of Appeals reversed with one judge dissenting. The majority stated that it was "giving effect" to the District Court's findings regarding the circumstances of petitioner's violation of the Williams Act, but concluded that those findings showed harm to respondent because "it was delayed in its efforts to make any necessary response to" petitioners' potential to take control of the company. In any event, the majority was of the view that respondent "need not show irreparable harm as a prerequisite to obtaining permanent injunctive relief in view of the fact that as issuer of the securities it is in the best position to assure that the filing requirements of the Williams Act are being timely and fully complied with and to obtain speedy and forceful remedial action when necessary." 500 F.2d 1011, 1016–1017. The Court of Appeals remanded the case to the District Court with instructions that it enjoin petitioner and his codefendants from further violations of the Williams Act and from voting the shares purchased between the due date of the Schedule 13D and the date of its filing for a period of five years. It considered "such an injunctive decree appropriate to neutralize [petitioner's] violation of the Act and to deny him the benefit of his wrongdoing." 500 F.2d, at 1017.

We granted certiorari to resolve an apparent conflict among the courts of appeals and because of the importance of the question presented to private actions under the Federal Securities Laws. We disagree with the Court of Appeals' conclusion that the traditional standards for extraordinary equitable relief do not apply in these circumstances, and reverse.

II

As in the District Court and the Court of Appeals, it is conceded here that petitioner's delay in filing the Schedule 13D constituted a violation of the Williams Act. The narrow issue before us is whether this record supports the grant of injunctive relief, a remedy whose basis "in the federal courts has always been irreparable harm and inadequacy of legal remedies." Beacon Theatres, Inc. v. Westover, 359 U.S. 500, 506–507 (1959).

The Court of Appeals' conclusion that respondent suffered "harm" sufficient to require sterilization of petitioner's stock need not long detain us. The purpose of the Williams Act is to insure that public shareholders who are confronted by a cash tender offer for their stock will not be required to respond without adequate information regarding the qualifications and intentions of the offering party. By requiring disclosure of information to the target corporation as well as the Securities and Exchange Commission, Congress intended to do no more than give incumbent management an opportunity to express and explain its position. The Congress expressly disclaimed an intention to provide a weapon for management to discourage takeover bids or prevent large accumulations of stock which would create the potential for such attempts. Indeed, the Act's draftsmen commented upon the "extreme care" which was taken "to avoid tipping the balance of regulation either in favor of management or in favor of the person making the take-over bid." S.Rep. No. 550, 90th Cong., 1st Sess., p. 3 (1967); H.R.Rep. No. 1711, 90th Cong., 2d Sess., p. 4 (1968). See also Electronic Specialty Co. v. International Controls Corp., 409 F.2d 937, 947 (CA2 1969).

The short of the matter is that none of the evils to which the Williams Act was directed has occurred or is threatened in this case. Petitioner has not attempted to obtain control of respondent, either by a cash tender offer or any other device. Moreover, he has now filed a proper Schedule 13D, and there has been no suggestion that he will fail to comply with the Act's requirement of reporting any material changes in the information contained therein.[9] 15 U.S.C. § 78m(d)(2); 17 CFR § 240.13d-2 (1974). On this record there is no likelihood that respondent's shareholders will be disadvantaged should petitioner make a tender offer, or that respondent will be unable to adequately place its case before them should a contest for control develop. Thus, the usual basis for injunctive relief, "that there exists some cognizable danger of recurrent violation," is not present here. United States v. W.T. Grant Co., 345 U.S. 629, 633 (1953). See also Vicksburg Waterworks Co. v. Vicksburg, 185 U.S. 65, 82 (1902).

Nor are we impressed by respondent's argument that an injunction is necessary to protect the interests of its shareholders who either sold their stock to petitioner at predisclosure prices or would not have invested had they known that a takeover bid was imminent. Brief for Respondent, at 13, 20–21. As observed, the principal object of the Williams Act is to solve the dilemma of shareholders desiring to respond to a cash tender offer, and it is not at all clear that the type of "harm" identified by respondent is redressable under its provisions. In any event, those persons who allegedly sold at an unfairly depressed price have an adequate remedy by way of an action for damages, thus negating the basis for equitable relief. See Youngstown Sheet & Tube Co. v. Sawyer, 343 U.S. 579, 595 (1952) (opinion of Frankfurter, J.). Similarly, the fact that the second group of shareholders for whom respondent expresses concern have retained the benefits of their stock and the lack of an imminent contest for control make the possibility of damage to them remote at best. See Truly v. Wanzer, 5 How. 141, 142–143 (1847).

We turn, therefore, to the Court of Appeals' conclusion that respondent's claim was not to be judged according to traditional equitable principles and that the bare fact that petitioner violated the Williams Act justified entry of an injunction against him. This position would seem to be foreclosed by Hecht Co. v. Bowles, 321 U.S. 321 (1944). There, the administrator of the Emergency Price Control Act of 1942 brought suit to redress violations of that statute. The fact of the violations was admitted, but the District Court declined to enter an injunction because they were inadvertent and the defendant had taken immediate steps to rectify them. This Court held that such an exercise of equitable discretion was proper

---

9. Because this case involves only the availability of injunctive relief to remedy a § 13(d) violation following compliance with the reporting requirements, it does not require us to decide whether or under what circumstances a corporation could obtain a decree enjoining a shareholder who is currently in violation of § 13(d) from acquiring further shares, exercising voting rights, or launching a takeover bid, pending compliance with the reporting requirements.

despite § 205(a) of the Act, which provided that an injunction or other order "shall be granted" upon a showing of violation, observing:

"We are dealing with the requirements of equity practice with a background of several hundred years of history * * *. *The historic injunctive process was designed to deter, not to punish.* The essence of equity jurisdiction has been the power of the Chancellor to do equity and to mould each decree to the necessities of the particular case. Flexibility rather than rigidity has distinguished it. The qualities of mercy and practicality have made equity the instrument for nice adjustment and reconciliation between the public interest and private needs as well as between competing private claims. We do not believe that such a major departure from that long tradition as is here proposed should be lightly implied." 321 U.S., at 329–330. (Emphasis added).

This reasoning applies *a fortiori* to actions involving only "competing private claims," and suggests that the District Court here was entirely correct in insisting that respondent satisfy the traditional prerequisites of extraordinary equitable relief by establishing irreparable harm. Moreover, the District Judge's conclusions that petitioner acted in good faith and that he promptly filed a Schedule 13D when his attention was called to this obligation support the exercise of its sound judicial discretion to deny an application for an injunction, relief which is historically "designed to deter, not to punish" and to permit the court "to mould each decree to the necessities of the particular case." 321 U.S., at 329. As Mr. Justice Douglas aptly pointed out in *Hecht Co.,* the "grant of *jurisdiction* to issue compliance orders hardly suggests an absolute duty to do so under any and all circumstances." Ibid. (emphasis by Court).

Respondent urges, however, that the "public interest" must be taken into account in considering its claim for relief and relies upon the Court of Appeals' conclusion that it is entitled to an injunction because it "is in the best position" to insure that the Williams Act is complied with by purchasers of its stock. This argument misconceives, we think, the nature of the litigation. Although neither the availability of a private suit under the Williams Act nor respondent's standing to bring it has been questioned here, this cause of action is not expressly authorized by the statute or its legislative history. Rather, respondent is asserting a so-called implied private right of action established by cases such as J.I. Case Co. v. Borak, 377 U.S. 426 (1964). Of course, we have not hesitated to recognize the power of federal courts to fashion private remedies for securities laws violations when to do so is consistent with the legislative scheme and necessary for the protection of investors as a supplement to enforcement by the Securities and Exchange Commission. Compare J.I. Case Co. v. Borak, supra, with Securities Investor Protection Corp. v. Barbour, 421 U.S. 412 (1975). However, it by no means follows that the plaintiff in such an action is relieved of the burden of establishing the traditional prerequisites of relief. Indeed, our cases hold that quite the contrary is true.

* * *

Any remaining uncertainty regarding the nature of relief available to a person asserting an implied private right of action under the Securities Laws was resolved in Mills v. Electric Auto-Lite Co., 396 U.S. 375 (1970).
* * *

Mills could not be plainer in holding that the questions of liability and relief are separate in private actions under the Securities Laws, and that the latter is to be determined according to traditional principles. Thus, the fact that respondent is pursuing a cause of action which has been generally recognized to serve the public interest provides no basis for concluding that it is relieved of showing irreparable harm and other usual prerequisites for injunctive relief. Accordingly, the judgment of the Court of Appeals is reversed and the case is remanded to it with directions to reinstate the judgment of the District Court.

So ordered.

MR. JUSTICE MARSHALL dissents.

MR. JUSTICE BRENNAN, with whom MR. JUSTICE DOUGLAS joins, dissenting.

I dissent. Judge Pell, dissenting below, correctly in my view, read the decision of the Court of Appeals to construe the Williams Act, as I also construe it, to authorize injunctive relief upon the application of the management interests "irrespective of motivation, irrespective of irreparable harm to the corporation, and irrespective of whether the purchases were detrimental to investors in the company's stock. The violation timewise is * * * all that is needed to trigger this result." 500 F.2d, at 1018. In other words, the Williams Act is a prophylactic measure conceived by Congress as necessary to effect the congressional objective "that investors and management be notified at the earliest possible moment of the potential for a shift in corporate control." 500 F.2d, at 1016. The violation itself establishes the actionable harm and no showing of other harm is necessary to secure injunctive relief. Today's holding completely undermines the congressional purpose to preclude inquiry into the results of the violation.

———

INJUNCTIVE RELIEF

The private plaintiff in a Rule 10b–5 action usually has no interest in obtaining an injunction against the alleged violation. (This is to be distinguished, of course, from a Commission enforcement action, which is considered below in Chapter 23.) In most cases, the plaintiff doesn't know what has happened to him until it is too late to stop it. Where the plaintiff claims to know in advance of the alleged violation, then he obviously would have a standing problem in bringing any action. He cannot have relied upon the false or misleading statement or omission, as he alleges that he knows the truth. In one situation, however, that involving a corporate transaction which can be carried out by a vote of a board of directors allegedly dominated by the defendant or by a vote of the shareholders where the defendant has a majority of the votes, the most efficacious form of relief would be to stop the transaction at its inception. Private plaintiffs, however, have usually not pressed for that form of relief, even where the action is filed prior to the consummation of the transaction and the complaint contains a pro forma count for injunctive relief. The reason is that if the plaintiff were successful in thus nipping the fraud in the bud, at relatively little cost and effort, his lawyer would not get a fee commensurate with that which he might obtain if he secured a judgment for damages after the fact. The same is true with respect to an action under Section 14(a) or 13(e) or 14(e) where there are not two contesting factions and the complaint is essentially about alleged derelictions of the management of the corporation.

On the other hand, in the context of a fight for control of the corporation, either in a proxy contest or with respect to a hostile tender offer, as noted above (see page 783), the favorite judicial weapon of the contestants has been an action for an injunction against the opponent, which will disrupt his timetable and, perhaps, cripple his efforts to secure proxies or tenders by the shareholders. Most of the earliest cases under the proxy rules and the tender offer rules were injunctive actions to restrain alleged violations on the part of the opposite side in the contest. Many of these cases took the position of the dissenters in the *Rondeau* case that an injunction could issue merely on the basis of the finding of a violation, in the discretion of the trial judge, without the necessity of applying the traditional principles of equity relating to such relief. In particular, these courts did not consider it necessary to find, in order to issue a *temporary* injunction, that there was a "probability of success" on the merits on the part of the plaintiff and the likelihood of "irreparable harm" to the plaintiff if the temporary injunction were not issued.

"Try a Little Tenderness." [1] Quite clearly the vigor (one is tempted to say: viciousness) with which the lower courts previously enforced the provisions of Section 13(d) will be changed by the *Rondeau* case, to what extent it is too soon to say. Certainly, the attitude (which was expressly adopted by the Seventh Circuit and the dissenting Justices in the Supreme Court) that the slightest and most inadvertent violation will trigger some punitive action against the violator—such as disenfranchisement of his shares for five years—can no longer be maintained.[2] See the discussion of the Williams Act cases above, at page 703.

The more interesting question is what effect, if any, the *Rondeau* decision will have in connection with litigation under Section 14(d) and with respect to the issuance of a *preliminary,* as opposed to a permanent, injunction. The case itself dealt only with a permanent injunction. But if a showing of irreparable harm is a prerequisite to the issuance of an injunction after a trial on the merits, it would seem to follow that a showing of the likelihood of irreparable harm should be required before an injunction is issued without a trial, especially if, as a practical matter, it is a final and conclusive determination of the litigation in favor of the plaintiff. However, the formulation in the Second Circuit has been quite different: In Stark v. New York Stock Exchange [3] the court stated that a plaintiff, in order to obtain a preliminary injunction, "assumed the burden of demonstrating *either* a combination of probable success [on the merits] and the *possibility* of irreparable injury *or* that [he] * * * had raised serious questions going to the merits and that the balance of hardships tipped sharply in [his] * * * favor." [4] All the cases under Section 14(d) in the Second Circuit have recited this formula and all of the trial judges have immediately gone into the "balancing act" which seems to be permitted to them, without bothering to find even the "possibility" of irreparable injury (or "probable" success on the merits, since it is so much easier to find "serious questions").

---

1. See Note: The Courts and the Williams Act: Try a Little Tenderness, 48 N.Y.U.L.Rev. 991 (1973).

2. Cases such as Twin Fair, Inc. v. Reger, 394 F.Supp. 156 (W.D.N.Y.1975), have obviously been overruled by *Rondeau.*

3. 466 F.2d 743 (2d Cir.1972).

4. 466 F.2d at 744 (italics added).

While the standards for the issuance of a preliminary injunction and the issuance of a permanent injunction may well differ, it will be interesting to see what effect the *Rondeau* case may have on the former attitudes of the courts with respect to the issuance of preliminary injunctions in Williams Act cases.[5]

In General Aircraft Corp. v. Lampert,[6] the First Circuit quoted and applied the *Rondeau* case in connection with the issuance of a preliminary injunction for a violation of Section 13(d). The District Court, on the basis of its finding that the defendants were late in filing their Schedule 13D and that it was materially false and misleading, had issued a temporary injunction prohibiting the defendants from soliciting proxies for the upcoming annual meeting, from acquiring any more shares of stock of the target company and from voting their own stock at the upcoming annual meeting. The Circuit Court affirmed the granting of the preliminary injunction insofar as it prohibited the solicitation of proxies or the acquisition of additional shares *"until the Schedule 13D is amended to reflect accurately"* the information called for; however, it reversed that portion of the preliminary injunction which disenfranchised the defendants with respect to the annual meeting insofar as the voting of their own shares was concerned. The court said: "In the circumstances disclosed by this record, sterilization of appellants' legally acquired shares would be punishment, not deterrence, since it would deprive appellants of previously acquired voting rights without sound reason. While it may be appropriate for the courts to enjoin the voting of shares rapidly acquired just before a contest for control following a Section 13(d) violation, * * * absent a clear showing of irreparable injury, disenfranchisement should not extend to prior holdings legally acquired."

See Steinberg, SEC and Other Permanent Injunctions—Standards for their Imposition, Modification and Dissolution, 66 Cornell L.Rev. 27 (1980); Porter, Rondeau v. Mosinee Paper Company and the Williams Act Injunction, 59 Marq. L.Rev. 743 (1976); Vandegrift, Section 13(d) Disclosure: Guidelines for Group Therapists, 16 B.C. Ind. & Com. L.R. 459 (1975); Mahoney, Schedule 13D: Wild Card in the Takeover Deck, 27 Bus.Law. 1107 (1972); Young, Section 13(d)—A New Element in the Battles for Control of Corporate Managements, 27 Bus. Law. 1107 (1972); Young, Judicial Enforcement of the Williams Amendments: The Need to Separate the Questions of Violation and Relief, 27 Bus.Law. 391 (1972); Note, The Courts and the Williams Act: Try a Little Tenderness, 48 N.Y.U.L.Rev. 991 (1973).

OSOFSKY v. ZIPF

United States Court of Appeals, Second Circuit, 1981.
645 F.2d 107.

Before: OAKES and MESKILL, CIRCUIT JUDGES, and GAGLIARDI, DISTRICT JUDGE.*

5. See Klaus v. Hi-Shear Corp., 528 F.2d 225 (9th Cir.1975).

* Of the Southern District of New York, sitting by designation.

6. 556 F.2d 90 (1st Cir.1977).

OAKES, CIRCUIT JUDGE:

This appeal presents the single narrow question whether shareholders who cede control of their company as a result of alleged misrepresentations concerning the value of the consideration they would obtain in a merger after successful completion of a tender offer have stated a claim for damages under the Securities Exchange Act of 1934 (1934 Act). This question turns on whether the term "actual damages," as used in section 28(a) of the 1934 Act, 15 U.S.C. § 78bb(a), encompasses nonspeculative, compensatory damages as measured not only by out-of-pocket loss but also by the benefit-of-the-bargain standard. The United States District Court for the Southern District of New York, John M. Cannella, Judge, held that the shareholders may not obtain the difference between what it was represented they would obtain in the merger and what they actually obtained, in the absence of allegations that the shares of the target company they gave up were actually worth more than the preferred stock package they received in exchange, and in the absence of any claim that "windfall" profits were received as a result of the allegedly misleading statements. We disagree, and reverse and remand on the issue of damages. We decline to reach the arguments of appellees as to whether appellants have stated a valid claim under section 14(a) and section 14(e) of the 1934 Act, since the district court did not rule upon these issues.

FACTS

The two cases involved in this appeal arise out of the tender offer contest in August 1977 between J. Ray McDermott & Co., Inc. (McDermott), and United Technologies Corporation (United) for control of the Babcock & Wilcox Company (B & W), in which McDermott emerged as the successful bidder. On August 4, 1977, United made a tender offer, scheduled to expire on August 25, to buy all outstanding shares of B & W common stock at $48 per share. McDermott responded, on August 14, with an offer (also scheduled to expire on August 25) to buy up to 4.3 million shares (approximately 35% of B & W's outstanding common stock) at $55 per share; the directors of B & W recommended acceptance of McDermott's offer. McDermott acknowledged that it already owned 1.2 million shares of B & W common, and conditioned its purchase of up to 4.3 million additional shares on the tender of at least 2.5 million shares by August 24, the day before the scheduled expiration date. The offer to purchase disclosed that McDermott had advised B & W that if McDermott's tender offer were successful, it would propose a combination of the two companies, and that, even though the terms of such a combination had yet to be negotiated, McDermott believed that "the consideration to be received by [B & W's] stockholders in such combination would have to approximate the price paid pursuant to this Offer."

McDermott's initial tender offer was followed by a series of offers by the two contending companies, sweetening up the deal for B & W shareholders. On August 18 United increased its offer from $48 to $55 per share. The following day McDermott increased its price to $60 per share and extended its expiration date to August 30. Three days later United increased its offer to purchase all outstanding shares of B & W to $58.50. Meanwhile the price of B & W stock was rising in response to these events. On August 24 B & W declared a special dividend of $2.50 per share payable to stockholders of record on September 14, 1977, and B & W's directors reiterated their endorsement of McDermott's tender offer. On the same day United announced that B & W shareholders who tendered to United would receive one-half of the $2.50 per share special dividend in addition to the $58.50 in cash offered. The following day, August 25, McDermott amended its offer to increase from 4.3 million to 4.8 million the number of shares it would purchase and to increase its tender price to $62.50 per share. In addition, McDermott extended its expiration date to September 3 and offered to pass on to tendering stockholders the full $2.50 special dividend. United withdrew from the bidding battle.

By September 3, 9.3 million shares of B & W common stock had been tendered to McDermott, which purchased approximately 4.8 million shares (on a pro rata basis) giving it 49% of the outstanding common stock of B & W as of September 16, 1977. McDermott and B & W issued a joint proxy statement on February 22, 1978, contemplating an effective merger date of March 31, 1978. The proposed terms of the merger were that each B & W share not owned by McDermott would be exchanged for a package of McDermott securities consisting of one share of a $2.60 cumulative preferred stock and one share of a $2.20 convertible cumulative preferred stock. The joint proxy statement quoted the language from the offer to purchase regarding the consideration believed to be required for the merger; the statement also included an opinion of B & W's financial adviser, Morgan Stanley & Co. Incorporated, that the market value of the package of McDermott preferred stock into which each share of B & W common stock would be converted upon consummation of the merger "would approximate $62.50." The stockholders approved the merger. On March 31, the effective day of the merger, the combined closing price of the McDermott stock package on the New York Stock Exchange was approximately $59.88.

Appellant Osofsky alleged that McDermott had violated section 14(e) of the 1934 Act by making a fraudulent promise in connection with a tender offer—namely, McDermott's statement that it believed that the consideration eventually to be received by B & W's shareholders with respect to the merger would have to approximate the tender offer price. Appellant Udoff's complaint contained essentially the same allegations, but in addition claimed that the joint proxy statement in connection with the merger contained materially misleading statements, in violation of section 14(a) of the 1934 Act.

Because both Osofsky and Udoff had moved for an order consolidating the two actions, as well as for class certification, the court below treated the two complaints as if all allegations were included in each. The district court did not reach the appellants' motions to consolidate and for class action status, however, but instead granted the appellees' motion for summary judgment. For purposes of the appellees' motion, the court assumed the truth of the allegations in the complaint, pursuant to Conley v. Gibson, 355 U.S. 41, 45–46 (1957). Thus, it assumed, first, that appellees misrepresented the eventual compensation to be paid in connection with the merger—because they did *not* actually believe that the compensation would "approximate the price paid pursuant to" the tender offer—and second, that reasonable shareholders relied on McDermott's misrepresentations in tendering a percentage of their shares to McDermott rather than tendering all of their shares to United. The court further assumed that at the time of issuing the proxy materials, the offeror, the target, and their respective financial advisers (who are also appellees in this case) believed that the McDermott preferred stock package would *not* have a market value of approximately $62.50, and that the shareholders who voted on the merger relied on the appellees' statements to the contrary. The court nevertheless held as a matter of law that the appellants had alleged no loss compensable under the 1934 Act, and therefore that they had failed to state a claim under the securities law.

The district court's decision was based on section 28(a) of the 1934 Act which prohibits recovery in a suit under the Act of "a total amount in excess of * * * actual damages." The court relied principally upon Levine v. Seilon, Inc., 439 F.2d 328 (2d Cir.1971), which it interpreted "as barring any recovery by a defrauded party based upon the 'benefit of the bargain' rule, that is, for 'the difference between the value of what he got and what it was represented he would be getting,' id. at 334." Because the appellants suffered no "out-of-pocket" damages, the court below held that they could not recover under the 1934 Act.

DISCUSSION

The question raised in this appeal is whether section 28(a) of the 1934 Act and relevant decisions in this circuit require the result reached by the district court, and, if not, what the proper rule of damages should be in this case. Section 28(a) speaks only in general terms, but we do not believe that its overall intent is to restrict the forms of nonspeculative, compensatory damages available to defrauded parties. The statutory language suggests that one purpose of section 28(a) is to prevent double recovery by those who assert both state and federal claims arising out of the same conduct. See 3 L. Loss, Securities Regulation 1624 & n. 5 (2d ed. 1961). In addition, section 28(a) had been construed as prohibiting the recovery of punitive, as opposed to compensatory, damages. See, e.g., Byrnes v. Faulkner, Dawkins & Sullivan, 550 F.2d 1303, 1313 (2d Cir.1977); Gould v. American-Hawaiian Steamship Co., 535 F.2d 761, 781 (3d Cir.1976); Green v. Wolf Corp., 406 F.2d 291, 302–03 (2d Cir.1968), cert. denied, 395 U.S. 977 (1969). But it is clear that the "federal courts have the power to grant all necessary remedial relief," J.I. Case Co. v. Borak, 377 U.S. 426, 435 (1964), and that the statute should be so construed as to carry out its purpose, see id. at 433; *Green,* 406 F.2d at 303. Accordingly, we believe that the purpose of section 28(a) is to compensate civil plaintiffs for economic loss suffered as a result of wrongs committed in violation of the 1934 Act, whether the measure of those compensatory damages be out-of-pocket loss, the benefit of the bargain, or some other appropriate standard.

Although the term "actual damages" is not defined in the statute itself, it had an accepted meaning when the Securities Exchange Act was enacted in 1934. As used in the patent statutes, for example, the term had been construed as requiring damages to be "given as a compensation, recompense, or satisfaction to the plaintiff, for an injury actually received." Birdsall v. Coolidge, 93 U.S. 64, 64 (1876). * * *

To be sure, this court in Levine v. Seilon, Inc., 439 F.2d 328 (2d Cir. 1971), denied benefit-of-the-bargain damages in a suit by a preferred stockholder who was promised an exchange offer of common for preferred, but whose preferred stock was subsequently redeemed by the company. That case, however, is distinguishable from the instant one. The *Levine* plaintiff alleged that the company had promised the favorable exchange offer in order to induce the preferred shareholders to give the necessary consent to new credit arrangements for the issuer, but that the issuer failed to carry out the promised exchange and instead used the newly obtained credit to redeem all the preferred stock. Levine sued under sections 10(b) and 14(e) of the 1934 Act, alleging that this fraud had misled him into retaining his preferred shares in anticipation of the exchange for common, when he could have sold the shares "at a substantially higher price than the redemption acquisition price." Id. at 331. But this court found two independent deficiencies in the plaintiff's theory: a lack of causal relation between the preferred stockholders' consent and the raising of the funds needed for the redemption, and no allegation that the preferred shares, considered apart from the exchange offer, had an investment value greater than the price at which they were redeemed. Thus the plaintiff in *Levine* was seeking to recover the benefit of the bargain that he would have obtained had he *not* been fraudulently induced to consent to the credit arrangements, and had he then sold his shares at a price that had been inflated due to the company's fraudulent exchange offer. Id. at 333–34. This is in contrast to the instant case, in which B & W stockholders were allegedly fraudulently induced to enter into the very transactions—the ceding of control of their company to McDermott and the subsequent merger—for which they now seek to recover benefit-of-the-bargain damages.

Nevertheless, the language of Judge Friendly, writing for the panel in *Levine* is quite broad. He stated in dictum that the pre-*Erie* rule in the federal courts, as well as the standard under rule 10b–5, is that a defrauded *buyer* of securities "is entitled to recover only the excess of what he paid over the value of what he got, not, as some other courts have held, the difference between the value of what he got and what it was represented he would be getting." Id. at 334. The two common law fraud cases cited for this proposition, however, Smith v. Bolles, 132 U.S. 125 (1889), and Sigafus v. Porter, 179 U.S. 116 (1900), involved situations in which the representations as to what the buyers were receiving were highly speculative. In *Smith,* the plaintiff had made a speculative investment in a silver mine, and subsequently discovered that his shares were worthless. The Court held that he could recover only the money he had actually invested, not the fraudulently represented "expected fruits of an unrealized speculation." 132 U.S. at 129–30. The Supreme Court applied the same rule in *Sigafus,* where a party was fraudulently induced to invest in a gold mine whose value had been exaggerated by the seller, the Court saying: " 'The true measure of damages * * * is the loss which he has sustained, and not the profits which he might have made by the transaction. It excludes all speculation, and is limited to compensation.' " 179 U.S. at 123 (quoting Rockefeller v. Merritt, 76 F. 909, 914 (8th Cir.1896)).

But the case of a defrauded securities buyer, whose gain was speculative, is surely different from the case of a seller who does not receive the price for which he had bargained. The distinction lies in the ability to determine the amount of damages with certainty. In fact, Judge Friendly in *Levine* contrasted the rule stated above in connection with a defrauded securities buyer with the rule in the case of a defrauded seller, who is entitled not only to "the difference between the actual value and what he received at the time of sale," but also "added profits which the buyer has realized through accretions in value subsequent thereto * * * or which the seller would have realized had he retained the stock for a reasonable period after the disclosure." 439 F.2d at 334 (citing Janigan v. Taylor, 344 F.2d 781, 786–87 (1st Cir.), cert. denied, 382 U.S. 879 (1965), and Myzel v. Fields, 386 F.2d 718, 744–47 (8th Cir.1967), cert. denied, 390 U.S. 951 (1968). Thus, at least in the case of a defrauded seller, as was the plaintiff in *Levine,* Judge Friendly's opinion fully recognized that the measure of damages could be other than simple out-of-pocket loss. Unfortunately for the plaintiff in *Levine,* the court found that, "under the unusual facts of [that] case," 439 F.2d at 334, he had received from the allegedly defrauding company as much as or more than the stock was worth, and the company had obtained no "windfall." Therefore, the defrauded seller rules were not applicable.

In another case, Zeller v. Bogue Electric Manufacturing Corp., 476 F.2d 795 (2d Cir.), cert. denied, 414 U.S. 908 (1973), Judge Friendly noted in dictum that *Levine* had repudiated benefit-of-the-bargain damages in 1934 Act suits brought by defrauded *buyers,* 476 F.2d at 801–02. But the holding in *Zeller* was that, for purposes of the equitable remedy of requiring a defrauding party to disgorge a windfall profit, the court would not differentiate between defrauded buyers and defrauded sellers, despite "the difficulty generally confronting the defrauded buyer in showing that the fraudulent seller has in fact reaped such a profit." See id. at 802 & n. 10. This difficulty in determining the amount of damages with certainty, of course, is the reason for the dictum in *Levine* to the effect that the benefit-of-the-bargain measure of damages should not be used in the case of a defrauded buyer. In the instant case, however, where allegedly defrauded sellers were not paid the price which had been agreed upon, benefit-of-the-bargain damages are not at all speculative in nature. Thus we do not view our decision as inconsistent with the statements and reasoning in either *Levine* or *Zeller.*

Indeed, we agree with Judge Weinfeld in Voege v. Ackerman, 364 F.Supp. 72 (S.D.N.Y.1973), that "[n]othing said in Zeller v. Bogue Electric Manufacturing Corp., or Levine v. Seilon, Inc., which did not involve mergers, forecloses the possibility that plaintiffs might be entitled to the value which defendants represented they would receive." Id. at 73 (footnotes omitted). In so holding Judge Weinfeld relied upon the Supreme Court's statement in Mills v. Electric Auto-Lite Co., 396 U.S. 375, 388 (1970), a case involving a materially misleading proxy statement in connection with a merger, that "[w]here the defect in the proxy solicitation relates to the specific terms of the merger, the district court might appropriately order an accounting to ensure that the shareholders receive the value that was represented as coming to them."

* * *

Thus, in the instant case, where the misleading aspect of the solicitation *does* relate to the terms of the merger, we believe, to use the language of *Mills,* 396 U.S. at 388, that "the district court might appropriately order an accounting to ensure that the shareholders receive the value that was represented as coming to them." This is precisely what then District Judge Mansfield did in Norte & Co. v. Huffines, 288 F.Supp. 855, 864 (S.D.N.Y. 1968), aff'd in relevant part, modified in part, 416 F.2d 1189, 1191 (2d Cir.

1969), cert. denied, 397 U.S. 989 (1970), and what Judge Weinfeld held could be done in Voege v. Ackerman, 364 F.Supp. 72, 73 (S.D.N.Y.1973).

Moreover, the benefit-of-the-bargain measure of compensatory damages is recognized as the preferable measure in common law fraud actions. See W. Prosser, Handbook of the Law of Torts § 110, at 733–34 (4th ed. 1971). Thus, the Restatement (Second) of Torts § 549(2) (1977) provides, in the case of a fraudulent misrepresentation in a business transaction, for the recovery of "damages sufficient to give [the recipient] the benefit of his contract with the maker, if these damages are proved with reasonable certainty." Though out-of-pocket loss may be the usual and logical form of compensatory relief in tort actions, Comment g on section 549(2) explains that this measure of damages does not always afford "just and satisfactory" compensation when the plaintiff has made a bargain based on fraudulent representations by the defendant. Therefore "the great majority of the American courts [have adopted] a broad general rule giving the plaintiff, in an action of deceit, the benefit of his bargain with the defendant in all cases, and making that the normal measure of recovery in actions of deceit." Id. Otherwise, in situations such as that involved in the instant case, "the defendant [would be] enabled to speculate on his fraud and still be assured that he [could] suffer no pecuniary loss," id. at Comment i.

We believe that the benefit-of-the-bargain rule should be applied under the 1934 Act to the limited situation involved in this case, where misrepresentation is made in the tender offer and proxy solicitation materials as to the consideration to be forthcoming upon an intended merger. But, of course, giving the plaintiff benefit-of-the-bargain damages is appropriate only when they can be established with reasonable certainty. It seems that the speculative nature of benefit-of-the-bargain damages in the fact situations involved in *Levine, Smith,* and *Sigafus* underlay the rejection of this measure of damages in those cases. In the case at bar, however, the amount of such damages—the difference between what was represented as coming to the B & W shareholders and what they actually received—can be determined with certainty.

As a matter of policy, allowing a fraudulent tender offeror or merger survivor to avoid the benefit-of-the-bargain measure in a situation such as that presented in this case would "insulate from private redress" large categories of proxy statement and tender offer violations, *Mills,* 396 U.S. at 382. Since the price paid by the successful offeror in a tender offer contest often exceeds the fair market value of the securities surrendered by the shareholders, defrauded shareholders of a target company would hardly ever, under the out-of-pocket measure of damages, have redress. Nor is it "draconian" to hold wrongdoers to the requirement of paying the consideration agreed upon in the first instance. Finally, this result furthers the purpose of sections 14(a) and 14(e) of the 1934 Act—deterrence of misrepresentations in connection with mergers and tender offers—and encourages private enforcement of the Act.

We note that the district court, as an alternative basis for its decision, concluded as a matter of law that the value of the consideration received by B & W shareholders in the merger—$59.88—was "approximately" the same as the consideration allegedly represented. But the difference between

$59.88 and $62.50 is some 4%,[6] which is not so obviously unimportant that it can be viewed as immaterial as a matter of law. The Supreme Court has held that a fact is "material" "if there is a substantial likelihood that a reasonable shareholder would consider it important in deciding how to vote." TSC Industries, Inc. v. Northway, Inc., 426 U.S. 438, 449 (1976). Here we think that whether the alleged misrepresentations were "material" is a mixed question of law and fact, see id. at 450, particularly since there were competing tender offers and the alternative courses open to B & W's shareholders were either to accept McDermott's offer extending to *less than half* of the outstanding shares at $65.00 ($62.50 plus the $2.50 special dividend), or to accept United's offer for *all* outstanding shares at $59.85 ($58.50 plus one-half of the special dividend). If B & W shareholders had been informed by McDermott that they would ultimately exchange their non-tendered or non-accepted shares for cash and securities worth only $62.38 (McDermott securities valued at $59.88 plus the special dividend), then United might not have withdrawn its tender offer, and B & W shareholders might have assessed differently the desirability of accepting United's immediate offer at $59.75 for all shares, thereby avoiding waiting for their money. Thus it would not be unreasonable for the trier of fact to find that the alleged misrepresentation here was material, and therefore this issue should not have been decided on a motion for summary judgment.

Reversed and remanded.

ELKIND v. LIGGETT & MYERS, INC.

United States Court of Appeals, Second Circuit, 1980.
635 F.2d 156.

Before: MANSFIELD and NEWMAN, CIRCUIT JUDGES.*

MANSFIELD, CIRCUIT JUDGE:

This case presents a number of issues arising out of what has become a form of corporate brinkmanship—non-public disclosure of business-related information to financial analysts. The action is a class suit by Arnold B. Elkind on behalf of certain purchasers (more fully described below) of the stock of Liggett & Myers, Inc. (Liggett) against it. They seek damages for alleged failure of its officers to disclose certain material information with respect to its earnings and operations and for their alleged wrongful tipping of inside information to certain persons who then sold Liggett shares on the open market.

After a non-jury trial Judge Constance Baker Motley held in post-trial findings and conclusions that Liggett did not violate Section 10(b) of the

---

6. We believe that the issue whether the tender offer price—and therefore the representation as to the merger consideration—was $62.50 or $65.00 (i.e., whether McDermott's offer to pass on the special dividend to tendering shareholders increased the consideration paid to those shareholders) is a question for the trier of fact, since had McDermott not passed along the dividend to tendering shareholders McDermott would have been entitled to keep it, although we recognize that the non-tendering or non-accepted shareholders of B & W also, of course, received the $2.50 special dividend. The difference between $59.88 and $65.00, of course, is even greater, amounting to some 8%.

* Pursuant to § 0.14 of the Rules of this Court, this appeal is being determined by Judges Mansfield and Newman, who are in agreement on this opinion.

Securities Exchange Act of 1934 or Rule 10b–5 promulgated thereunder by failing prior to July 18, 1972, to release figures showing a substantial downturn in earnings or to correct erroneous projections of financial analysts which it had allegedly fostered. The court found, however, that on July 10, 1972, and July 17, 1972, officers of Liggett disclosed material inside information to individual financial analysts, leading to sale of Liggett stock by investors to whom this information was conveyed. Damages were computed on the basis of the difference between the price which members of the plaintiff class (uninformed buyers of Liggett stock between the time of the first tip and subsequent public disclosure) paid and what the stock sold for after the later disclosure. See 472 F.Supp. 123 (S.D.N.Y. 1978). We affirm the dismissal of the counts alleging failure to disclose or correct. We reverse the finding of liability based on the alleged July 10, 1972, tip for want of materiality and scienter. We remand the determination of liability based on the July 17, 1972, tip for determination of damages. In all other respects the judgment is affirmed.

* * *

Liggett is a diversified company, with traditional business in the tobacco industry supplemented by acquisitions in such industries as liquor (Paddington Corp., importer of J & B Scotch), pet food (Allen Products Co. and Perk Foods Co., manufacturer of Alpo dog food), cereal, watchbands, cleansers and rugs. Its common stock is listed on the New York Stock Exchange.

In 1969 Liggett officers concluded that the company's stock was underpriced, due in part to lack of appreciation in the financial community for the breadth of its market activity. To cure this perceived deficiency, Liggett initiated an "analyst program," hiring a public relations firm and encouraging closer contact between analysts and company management. This included meetings with analysts at which Liggett officials discussed operations. Liggett also reviewed and commented on reports which the analysts were preparing, to correct errors and other misunderstandings.

Liggett had a record year in 1971, with earnings of $4.22 per share (up from $3.56 in 1970). The first quarter of 1972 was equally auspicious. On March 22, Liggett issued a press release reporting that sales of the non-tobacco lines had continued to increase in the first two months, but noting that current stockpiling of J & B Scotch by customers (in anticipation of a price increase) could affect sales. On May 3, 1972, the company released its first quarter figures, showing earnings of $1.00 per share (compared to $.81 in the first quarter of 1971).

This quarterly operations report led to considerable optimism in the financial community over Liggett's prospects. Management did nothing to deflate the enthusiasm. A number of reports containing predictions that 1972 earnings would increase about 10% over 1971 earnings were reviewed by officials of Liggett during the first five months of 1972. While company personnel corrected factual errors in these reports, they did not comment (or made noncommittal or evasive comments) on the earnings projections, according to the findings below, which are supported by the record. At group meetings with analysts in February and March, management indicated that it was making "good progress" with certain products and that it was "well-positioned" to take advantage of industry trends. At the end of March, Liggett successfully made a public offering of $50 million of debentures. At an April 25 stockholders' meeting, Liggett's Executive Vice President expressed general optimism that the company was continuing to make good progress. On May 3, the first quarter earnings were released. At a May 16 meeting with analysts in New York, officials reiterated their vague but quieting pronouncements. Similar comments, to the effect that 1972 was expected to be a "good year," were voiced at a June 5 presentation in London.

Despite the company's outward appearance of strength, Liggett's management was less sanguine intramurally. Internal budget projections called for only a two percent increase in earnings in 1972. In April and May, a full compilation of updated figures was ordered, and new projections were presented to the Board of Directors on May 15. April was marked by a sharp decline, with earnings of only $.03 per share (compared to $.30 the previous April). The 1972 earnings projection was revised downward from $4.30 to $3.95 per share. May earnings, which the Board received on June 19, rebounded somewhat to $.23 per share (compared to $.27 in May 1971 and original budget projections of $.34). At meetings with analysts during this period, Liggett officials took a more negative tone, emphasizing, for example, various cost pressures. There was no public disclosure of the adverse financial developments at this time. Beginning in late June, 1972, the price of Liggett's common stock steadily declined.

On July 17, preliminary earnings data for June and six-month totals became available to the Board of Directors. June earnings were $.20 per share (compared to $.44 in June 1971). The first half earnings for 1972 were approximately $1.46 per share, down from $1.82 the previous year. The Board decided to issue a press release the following day. That release, issued at about 2:15 P.M. on July 18, disclosed the preliminary earnings figures and attributed the decline to shortcomings in all of Liggett's product lines.

The district court found two "tips" of material inside information in the days before the July 18 press release. On July 10, analyst Peter Barry of Kuhn Loeb & Co. spoke by telephone with Daniel Provost, Liggett's Director of Corporate Communications. According to Barry's deposition testimony, apparently adopted by the court below, Provost confirmed Barry's suggestions that J & B sales were slowing due to earlier stockpiling and that a new competing dog food was affecting Alpo sales adversely. Barry asked if a projection of a 10% earnings decline would be realistic, and received what he characterized as a noncommittal response. Barry testified that Provost told him that a preliminary earnings statement would be coming out in a week or so. Since Barry knew of no prior instances in which Liggett had issued such a preliminary statement, he deduced that the figures would be lower than expected. Barry sent a wire * * * to Kuhn Loeb's offices. The information was conveyed to three clients. Two of them, holders of a total of over 600,000 shares, did not sell. A third client sold the 100 shares he owned. No other Kuhn Loeb customers sold between the time of the July 10 "tip" and the release of preliminary earnings figures on July 18; Kuhn Loeb customers bought some 5,000 shares during this period.

The second "tip" occurred on July 17, one day before the preliminary earnings figures for the first half were released. Analyst Robert Cummins of Loeb Rhoades & Co. questioned Ralph Moore, Liggett's chief financial officer, about the recent decline in price of Liggett's common stock, as well as performance of the various subsidiaries. According to Cummins' deposition, he asked Moore whether there was a good possibility that earnings would be down, and received an affirmative ("grudging") response. Moore added that this information was confidential. Cummins sent a wire to his firm, spoke with a stockbroker who promptly sold 1,800 shares of Liggett stock on behalf of his customers.

The district court held that each of these disclosures was a tip of material information in violation of Rule 10b–5, rendering Liggett liable to all persons who bought the company's stock during the period from July 11 to July 18, 1972, inclusive, without knowledge of the tipped information. However, the court rejected plaintiff's claims that Liggett was under a legal obligation to correct the analysts' earlier erroneous predictions, relying on this court's decision in Electronic Specialty Co. v. International Controls Corp., 409 F.2d 937 (2d Cir.1969). It also rejected plaintiff's claims that Liggett's earlier statements to analysts and stockholders were misrepresentations and that Liggett was under a duty to issue a preliminary earnings statement in June when it received its May figures.

In computing damages for the July 10 and 17 tips, the court attempted to award the difference between the amount plaintiff class members paid for their stock and the value they received. The latter was interpreted to be the price at which the stock would have sold had there been public disclosure of the tipped information. The court ruled that plaintiff's expert testimony on this point was speculative and unsupported by the record. Instead, following Mitchell v. Texas Gulf Sulphur Co., 446 F.2d 90 (10th Cir.), cert. denied, 404 U.S. 1004 (1971), it looked to the actual market price at the end of "a reasonable period" (eight trading days) following the July 18 release of earning figures as an approximation of what the price would have been had the tipped information been disclosed publicly. Thus damages amounted to the difference between the plaintiff class members' purchase prices (generally in the vicinity of $60 per share) and $43, the price of the stock eight trading days after disclosure. Based on the total volume of trading transactions from July 11 to July 18, the court awarded damages amounting to $740,000 on condition that any unclaimed portion would revert to Liggett. To this the court added prejudgment interest of approximately $300,000.

     * * *

4. *Damages*

This case presents a question of measurement of damages which we have previously deferred, believing that damages are best addressed in a concrete setting. See Shapiro v. Merrill Lynch, Pierce, Fenner & Smith, Inc., supra, 495 F.2d at 241–42; Heit v. Weitzen, 402 F.2d 909, 917 & n. 8 (2d Cir.1968), cert. denied, 395 U.S. 903 (1969). We ruled in *Shapiro* that defendants selling on inside information would be liable to those who bought on the open market and sustained, "substantial losses" during the period of insider trading.[23]

The district court looked to the measure of damages used in cases where a buyer was induced to purchase a company's stock by materially misleading statements or omissions. In such cases of fraud by a fiduciary intended to induce others to buy or sell stock the accepted measure of damages is the

---

23. The Sixth Circuit has since reached the opposite conclusion, Fridrich v. Brad- ford, 542 F.2d 307, 318 (6th Cir.1976), cert. denied, 429 U.S. 1053 (1977).

"out-of-pocket" measure.[24] This consists of the difference between the price paid and the "value" of the stock when brought (or when the buyer committed himself to buy, if earlier).[25] Except in rare face-to-face transactions, however, uninformed traders on an open, impersonal market are not induced by representations on the part of the tipper or tippee to buy or sell. Usually they are wholly unacquainted with and uninfluenced by the tippee's misconduct. They trade independently and voluntarily but without the benefit of information known to the trading tippee.

In determining what is the appropriate measure of damages to be awarded to the outside uninformed investor as the result of tippee-trading through use of information that is not equally available to all investors it must be remembered that investors who trade in a stock on the open market have no absolute right to know inside information. They are, however, entitled to an honest market in which those with whom they trade have no confidential corporate information. See SEC v. Texas Gulf Sulphur Co., supra, 401 F.2d at 848, 851–52.

"The primary object of the exchange is to afford facilities for trading in securities under the safest and fairest conditions attainable. In order that parties may trade on even terms they should have, as far as practicable, the same opportunities for knowledge in regard to the subject matter of the trade." H.R.Rep. No. 1383, 73d Cong., 2d Sess. 12 (1934).

It is the combination of the tip and the tippee's trading that poses the evil against which the open market investor must be protected, 2 Bromberg, Securities Law: Fraud § 7.5(3)(b), at 190.9 (1979); Cary, Insider Trading in Stocks, 21 Bus.Law 1009 (1966). The reason for the "disclose or abstain" rule is the unfairness in permitting an insider to trade for his own account on the basis of material inside information not available to others. The tipping of material information is a violation of the fiduciary's duty but no injury occurs until the information is used by the tippee. The entry into the market of a tippee with superior knowledge poses the threat that if he trades on the basis of the inside information he may profit at the expense of investors who are disadvantaged by lack of the inside information. For this both the tipper and the tippee are liable. See SEC v. Texas Gulf Sulphur Co., 312 F.Supp. 77, 95 (S.D.N.Y.1970), affd., 446 F.2d 1301, 1308 (2d Cir.1971). If the insider chooses not to trade, on the other hand, no

---

24. Affiliated Ute Citizens v. United States, 406 U.S. 128, 155 (1972); Blackie v. Barrack, 524 F.2d 890, 909 (9th Cir.1975), cert. denied 429 U.S. 816 (1976); Fershtman v. Schectman, 450 F.2d 1357, 1361 (2d Cir.1971), cert. denied 405 U.S. 1066 (1972); Note, The Measurement of Damages in Rule 10b–5 Cases Involving Actively Traded Securities, 26 Stan.L.Rev. 371, 383–84 & n. 65 (1974).

25. Some cases have suggested the availability as an alternative measure of damages of a modified rescissionary measure, consisting of the difference between the price the defrauded party paid and the price at the time he learned or should have learned the true state of affairs. The theo-

ry of this measure is to restore the plaintiff to the position where he would have been had he not been fraudulently induced to trade. See, e.g., Mitchell v. Texas Gulf Sulphur Co., 446 F.2d 90, 104–06 (10th Cir.), cert. denied 404 U.S. 1004 (1971). The soundness of this measure has been vigorously disputed in the case of open market trading. Green v. Occidental Petroleum Corp., 541 F.2d 1335, 1341–44 (9th Cir.1976) (Sneed, J., concurring). While the district court cited to Mitchell, its opinion makes clear that it was applying the out-of-pocket measure of damages. Since the district court did not apply this modified rescissionary measure, we need not pass on it here.

injury may be claimed by the outside investor, since the public has no right to the undisclosed information.

Recognizing the foregoing, we in *Shapiro* suggested that the district court must be accorded flexibility in assessing damages, after considering

"the extent of the selling defendants' trading in Douglas stock, whether such trading effectively impaired the integrity of the market, * * * what profits or other benefits were realized by defendants [and] what expenses were incurred and what losses were sustained by plaintiffs. * * * Moreover, we do not foreclose the possibility that an analysis by the district court of the nature and character of the Rule 10b–5 violations committed may require limiting the extent of liability imposed on either class of defendants." 495 F.2d at 242.

We thus gave heed to the guidance provided by the Supreme Court in Affiliated Ute Citizens v. United States, 406 U.S. 128, 151 (1972), to the effect that "Congress intended securities legislation enacted for the purpose of avoiding frauds to be construed 'not technically and restrictively, but flexibly to effectuate its remedial purposes.' Id., at 195. This was recently said once again in Superintendent of Insurance v. Bankers Life & Casualty Co., 404 U.S. 6, 12 (1971)." See also Mills v. Electric Auto-Lite Co., 396 U.S. 375, 386, 391 (1970) (1934 Act does not "circumscribe the courts' power to grant appropriate remedies").

Within the flexible framework thus authorized for determining what amounts should be recoverable by the uninformed trader from the tipper and tippee trader, several measures are possible. First, there is the traditional out-of-pocket measure used by the district court in this case. For several reasons this measure appears to be inappropriate. In the first place, as we have noted, it is directed toward compensating a person for losses directly traceable to the defendant's fraud upon him. No such fraud or inducement may be attributed to a tipper or tippee trading on an impersonal market. Aside from this the measure poses serious proof problems that may often be insurmountable in a tippee-trading case. The "value" of the stock traded during the period of nondisclosure of the tipped information (i.e., the price at which the market would have valued the stock if there had been a disclosure) is hypothetical. Expert testimony regarding that "value" may, as the district court found in the present case, be entirely speculative. This has led some courts to conclude that the drop in price of the stock after actual disclosure and after allowing a period of time to elapse for the market to absorb the news may sometimes approximate the drop which would have occurred earlier had the tip been disclosed. See Harris v. American Investment Company, 523 F.2d 220, 227 (8th Cir.1975), cert. denied, 432 U.S. 1054 (1976). The court below adopted this approach of using post-public disclosure market price as *nunc pro tunc* evidence of the "value" of the stock during the period of non-disclosure.

Whatever may be the reasonableness of the *nunc pro tunc* "value" method of calculating damages in other contexts, it has serious vulnerabilities here. It rests on the fundamental assumptions (1) that the tipped information is substantially the same as that later disclosed publicly, and (2) that one can determine how the market would have reacted to the public release of the tipped information at an earlier time by its reaction to that information at a later, proximate time. This theory depends on the parity of the "tip" and the "disclosure." When they differ, the basis of the damage calculation evaporates. One could not reasonably estimate how the public would have reacted to the news that the Titanic was near an iceberg from how it reacted to news that the ship had struck an iceberg and sunk. In the present case, the July 10 tip that preliminary earnings would be released in a week is not comparable to the later release of the estimated earnings figures on July 18. Nor was the July 17 tipped information that there was a good possibility that earnings would be down comparable to the next day's release of the estimated earnings figures.

An equally compelling reason for rejecting the theory is its potential for imposition of Draconian, exorbitant damages, out of all proportion to the wrong committed, lining the pockets of all interim investors and their counsel at the expense of innocent corporate stockholders. Logic would compel application of the theory to a case where a tippee sells only 10 shares of a heavily traded stock (e.g., IBM), which then drops substantially when the tipped information is publicly disclosed. To hold the tipper and tippee liable for the losses suffered by every open market buyer of a stock as a result of the later decline in value of the stock after the news became public would be grossly unfair. While the securities laws do occasionally allow for potentially ruinous recovery, we will not readily adopt a measure mandating "large judgments, payable in the last instance by innocent investors [here, Liggett shareholders], for the benefit of speculators and their lawyers," SEC v. Texas Gulf Sulphur Co., supra, 401 F.2d at 867 (Friendly, J., concurring); cf. Blue Chip Stamps v. Manor Drug Stores, 421 U.S. 723, 739–40 (1975), unless the statute so requires.

An alternative measure would be to permit recovery of damages caused by erosion of the market price of the security that is traceable to the tippee's wrongful trading, i.e., to compensate the uninformed investor for the loss in market value that he suffered as a direct result of the tippee's conduct. Under this measure an innocent trader who bought Liggett shares at or after a tippee sold on the basis of inside information would recover any decline in value of his shares caused by the tippee's trading. Assuming the impact of the tippee's trading on the market is measurable, this approach has the advantage of limiting the plaintiffs to the amount of damage actually caused in fact by the defendant's wrongdoing and avoiding windfall recoveries by investors at the expense of stockholders other than the tippee trader, which could happen in the present action against Liggett. The rationale is that if the market price is not affected by the tippee's trading, the uninformed investor is in the same position as he would have been had the insider abstained from trading. In such event the equilibrium of the market has not been disturbed and the outside investor has not been harmed by the informational imbalance. Only where the market has been contaminated by the wrongful conduct would damages be recoverable.

This causation-in-fact approach has some disadvantages. It allows no recovery for the tippee's violation of his duty to disclose the inside information before trading. Had he fulfilled this duty, others, including holders of the stock, could then have traded on an equal informational basis. Another disadvantage of such a measure lies in the difficult if not impossible burden it would impose on the uninformed trader of proving the time when and extent to which the integrity of the market was affected by the tippee's conduct. In some cases, such as *Mitchell,* supra, and *Shapiro,* supra, the existence of very substantial trading by the tippee, coupled with a sharp change in market price over a short period, would provide the basis for measuring a market price movement attributable to the wrongful trading. On the other hand, in a case where there was only a modest amount of tippee trading in a heavy-volume market in the stock, accompanied by other unrelated factors affecting the market price, it would be impossible as a practical matter to isolate such rise or decline in market price, if any, as was caused by the tippee's wrongful conduct. Moreover, even assuming market erosion caused by this trading to be provable and that the uninformed investor could show that it continued after his purchase, there remains the question of whether the plaintiff would not be precluded from recovery on the ground that any post-purchase decline in market price attributable to the tippee's trading would not be injury to him as a purchaser, i.e., "in connection with the purchase and sale of securities," but injury to him as a stockholder due to a breach of fiduciary duty by the company's officers, which is not actionable under § 10(b) of the 1934 Act or Rule 10b–5 promulgated thereunder. Blue Chip Stamps v. Manor Drug Stores, 421 U.S. 723 (1975); Birnbaum v. Newport Steel Corp., 193 F.2d 461 (2d Cir.), cert. denied, 343 U.S. 956 (1952). For these reasons, we reject this strict direct market-repercussion theory of damages.

A third alternative is (1) to allow any uninformed investor, where a reasonable investor would either have delayed his purchase or not purchased at all if he had had the benefit of the tipped information, to recover any post-purchase decline in market value of his shares up to a reasonable time after he learns of the tipped information or after there is a public disclosure of it but (2) limit his recovery to the amount gained by the tippee as a result of his selling at the earlier date rather than delaying his sale until the parties could trade on an equal informational basis. Under this measure if the tippee sold 5,000 shares at $50 per share on the basis of inside information and the stock thereafter declined to $40 per share within a reasonable time after public disclosure, an uninformed purchaser buying shares during the interim (e.g., at $45 per share) would recover the difference between his purchase price and the amount at which he could have sold the shares on an equal informational basis (i.e., the market price within a reasonable time after public disclosure of the tip), subject to a limit of $50,000, which is the amount gained by the tippee as a result of his trading on the inside information rather than on an equal basis. Should the intervening buyers, because of the volume and price of their purchases, claim more than the tippee's gain, their recovery (limited to that gain) would be shared *pro rata*.

This third alternative, which may be described as the disgorgement measure, has in substance been recommended by the American Law Institute in its 1978 Proposed Draft of a Federal Securities Code, §§ 1603, 1703(b), 1708(b), 1711(j). It offers several advantages. To the extent that it makes the tipper and tippees liable up to the amount gained by their misconduct, it should deter tipping of inside information and tippee-trading. On the other hand, by limiting the total recovery to the tippee's gain, the measure bars windfall recoveries of exorbitant amounts bearing no relation to the seriousness of the misconduct. It also avoids the extraordinary difficulties faced in trying to prove traditional out-of-pocket damages based on the true "value" of the shares purchased or damages claimed by reason of market erosion attributable to tippee trading. A plaintiff would simply be required to prove (1) the time, amount and price per share of his purchase, (2) that a reasonable investor would not have paid as high a price or made the purchase at all if he had had the information in the tippee's possession, and (3) the price to which the security had declined by the time he learned the tipped information or at a reasonable time after it became public, whichever event first occurred. He would then have a claim and, up to the limits of the tippee's gain, could recover the decline in market value of his shares before the information became public or known to him. In most cases the damages recoverable under the disgorgement measure would be roughly commensurate to the actual harm caused by the tippee's wrongful conduct. In a case where the tippee sold only a few shares, for instance, the likelihood of his conduct causing any substantial injury to intervening investors buying without benefit of his confidential information would be small. If, on the other hand, the tippee sold large amounts of stock, realizing substantial profits, the likelihood of injury to intervening uninformed purchasers would be greater and the amount of potential recovery thereby proportionately enlarged.

We recognize that there cannot be any perfect measure of damages caused by tippee-trading. The disgorgement measure, like others we have described, does have some disadvantages. It modifies the principle that ordinarily gain to the wrongdoer should not be a prerequisite to liability for violation of Rule 10b–5. See Myzel v. Fields, 386 F.2d 718, 750 (8th Cir. 1967); Fischer v. Kletz, 266 F.Supp. 180, 183 (S.D.N.Y.1967); Comment, Insiders' Liability Under Rule 10b–5 for the Illegal Purchase, 78 Yale L.J. 864, 876 (1969). It partially duplicates disgorgement remedies available in proceedings by the SEC or others. Under some market conditions such as where the market price is depressed by wholly unrelated causes, the tippee might be vulnerable to heavy damages, permitting some plaintiffs to recover underserved windfalls. In some instances the total claims could exceed the wrongdoer's gain, limiting each claimant to a pro rata share of the gain. In other situations, after deducting the cost of recovery, including attorneys' fees, the remainder might be inadequate to make a class action worthwhile. However, as between the various alternatives we are persuaded, after weighing the pros and cons, that the disgorgement measure, despite some disadvantages, offers the most equitable resolution of the difficult problems created by conflicting interests.

In the present case the sole Rule 10b–5 violation was the tippee-trading of 1,800 Liggett shares on the afternoon of July 17, 1972. Since the actual preliminary Liggett earnings were released publicly at 2:15 P.M. on July 18 and and were effectively disseminated in a Wall Street Journal article published on the morning of July 19, the only outside purchasers who might conceivably have been damaged by the insider-trading were those who bought Liggett shares between the afternoon of July 17 and the opening of the market on July 19. Thereafter all purchasers bought on an equal informational footing, and any outside purchaser who bought on July 17 and 18 was able to decide within a reasonable time after the July 18–19 publicity whether to hold or sell his shares in the light of the publicly-released news regarding Liggett's less favorable earnings.

The market price of Liggett stock opened on July 17, 1972, at $55\frac{5}{8}$, and remained at substantially the same price on that date, closing at $55\frac{1}{4}$. By the close of the market on July 18 the price declined to $52\frac{1}{2}$ per share. Applying the disgorgement measure, any member of the plaintiff class who bought Liggett shares during the period from the afternoon of July 17 to the close of the market on July 18 and met the reasonable investor requirement would be entitled to claim a *pro rata* portion of the tippee's gain, based on the difference between their purchase price and the price to which the market price declined within a reasonable time after the morning of July 19. By the close of the market on July 19 the market price had declined to $46\frac{3}{8}$ per share. The total recovery thus would be limited to the gain realized by the tippee from the inside information, i.e., 1,800 shares multiplied by approximately $9.35 per share.

The finding of liability based on the July 10, 1972, tip is reversed. The award of damages is also reversed and the case is remanded for a determination of damages recoverable for tippee-trading based on the July 17, 1972, tip, to be measured in accordance with the foregoing. Each party will bear its own costs.

SECURITIES AND EXCHANGE COMMISSION v. MacDONALD

United States Court of Appeals, First Circuit, 1983.
699 F.2d 47.

Before COFFIN, CHIEF JUDGE, ALDRICH, CAMPBELL, BOWNES and BREYER, CIRCUIT JUDGES.

OPINION EN BANC [1]

BAILEY ALDRICH, SENIOR CIRCUIT JUDGE.

In this proceeding brought by the Securities Exchange Commission (SEC), defendant James E. MacDonald, Jr. was ordered by the district court to disgorge profits of $53,012 realized on the purchase and subsequent sale of 9,600 shares of Realty Income Trust (RIT) stock. The court, sitting without jury, found that defendant violated the antifraud provisions of the Securities Exchange Act of 1934, section 10(b), and SEC Rule 10b–5 promulgated thereunder, by making the purchases without disclosing certain material inside information learned in his capacity as chairman of RIT's board of trustees. Defendant appeals, contending that the court erred in its findings of materiality and scienter; in excluding certain evidence, and in its measurement of the profits to be disgorged. We affirm, except as to the amount.

RIT is a real estate investment trust whose stock is traded on the American Stock Exchange. The present controversy revolves around defendant's knowledge of RIT's acquisition of the Kroger Building, a twenty-five story office building in Cincinnati, Ohio, and its likely negotiation of a profitable long-term lease of vacant space therein to Kenner Products. The basic facts, as found by the court, expressly and impliedly, are briefly as follows.

The land under the Kroger Building had been owned by RIT since 1962. Until December 1975, the building was owned and managed by City Center Development Company. Both the land and the building were subject to a first mortgage to Prudential Insurance Company. Under the terms of its ground lease, City Center was obligated to pay ground rent to RIT and

----

1. Strictly, the first portion of this opinion is the panel's. See n. 3, post.

mortgage payments to Prudential, but in 1975 it defaulted on both accounts. To protect its investment and avoid foreclosure, RIT advanced mortgage payments to Prudential, and then, on December 2, 1975, filed suit against City Center seeking reimbursement and the appointment of a receiver. The suit was publicly announced on December 4. On December 12, the case was settled by City Center's surrendering to RIT ownership of the Kroger Building. The news of the settlement was reported in a local Cincinnati paper but was not otherwise made available to the investing public. That day, however, RIT did release its quarterly financial report, which, basically, contained nothing but bad news.

Meanwhile, Kenner Products had been looking for a new home, its previous one having been acquired by the city. A tentative decision was made to move into the Kroger Building, and negotiations between City Center and Kenner ensued. After its acquisition of the building, RIT took over the negotiations. A report on the proposed terms of the lease was made to the trustees, including defendant, on December 15. The next day his wife, acting in his behalf, put in an order with her broker for the purchase of up to 20,000 shares of RIT stock at a price of $4\frac{1}{4}$. One hundred shares were purchased at that price. On December 23, defendant went personally to the broker's office and raised the purchase limit to $5 per share. This resulted in the purchase of 9,500 shares that day at $4\frac{5}{8}$.

The following day, December 24, RIT issued a press release, publicly announcing for the first time the acquisition of the Kroger Building, and referring to Kenner, that

> "the Trust expects to sign a lease almost immediately for 105,000 square feet of space in the building with a major new tenant. The lease will bring occupancy in the building up to 95%, which would indicate a market value of the building of approximately $8,500,000 which is approximately $2,000,000 more than the existing first mortgage and RIT's investment in the property."

The price of RIT stock then jumped from $4\frac{5}{8}$ to $5\frac{1}{2}$ in two days of trading—a rise of 19%—and closed the year at $5\frac{3}{4}$. Defendant held on to the stock until 1977 when it was sold at an average price of over $10 per share.

* * *

[Eds. The court's discussion of the issues relating to defendant's liability for trading on the basis of material, undisclosed inside information is omitted.]

Disgorgement [3]

The district court ordered defendant to disgorge, for restitution to defrauded shareholders, the sum of $53,012 representing the profits he realized upon reselling the 9,600 shares of stock in early 1977 at roughly $10 per share. The court noted that since the essence of defendant's inside information was made public on December 24, 1975, "any changes in the

---

3. A panel composed of Chief Judge Coffin and Judges Aldrich and Breyer, Chief Judge Coffin dissenting, decided the disgorgement issue against the Commission. The Commission's petition for rehearing en banc on this issue was thereafter granted, with briefing and argument. Only the SEC responded. The present opinion contains, for convenience, the unanimous opinion of the panel up to the present point. The rest of that opinion, and the dissent thereto, are withdrawn, and the balance of the present, viz., an en banc opinion, and dissent, substituted.

* * *

market after a fairly reasonable period of time after the 24th of December were because of other developments." But it felt that it would be "inequitable to permit the defendant to retain the benefits of a bargain that was * * * clearly illegal, and that he should be required to disgorge the entire profits." Defendant complains.

The Commission correctly states the present question to be whether, where a corporate officer fraudulently purchased company shares "while in possession of material non-public information [he should be required, in an action brought by the Commission,] to disgorge the entire profits he realized from his subsequent sale of those securities about a year later, rather than limiting disgorgement to an amount representing the increased value of the shares at a reasonable time after public dissemination of the information." We would add that there was no evidence that this subsequent increase in value was attributable to any action of the defendant, nor was there any evidence as to why defendant continued to hold the shares. In other words, there were no special circumstances affecting what should be the normal result in this situation.

While the Commission states a single question in this case, it cannot be viewed in isolation; we must consider the principles; and the entire picture to which any decision must interrelate. We accordingly put four hypotheticals, predicated on the assumption that an insider fraudulently bought shares at $4.00, and that, throughout the entire month after the undisclosed information became public, the stock sold at $5.00.

(1) Insider sold forthwith for $5.00.

(2) Stock declined thereafter and insider sold at $3.00.

(3) Stock rose a year later to $10.00, but then declined, and insider ultimately sold at $3.00.

(4) When the stock rose to $10.00, insider sold at $10.00.

The Commission would, properly, seek $1.00 in case (1). It would also seek $1.00 in case (2), its given reason being that the $1.00 profit "could have been realized." It adds, and we agree, that if the insider were to be permitted credit for the loss, he would have an investment "cushion," a "heads-I-win-tails-I-win" proposition. In case (3) the Commission concedes that it is entitled to only $1.00. In case (4) the present case, it claims the $6.00 as being "ill-gotten gains."

Before discussing the subject generally, we note two immediate seeming inconsistencies in the Commission's reasoning. If "could have been realized" is the test in case (2), equally a $6.00 profit "could have been realized" in case (3). Secondly, if the Commission does not claim the full realizable profit in case (3), as against case (4) is it not permitting the insider a "heads-I-win-tails-I-win cushion" which the Commission rejects in case (2)? We do not agree with the Commission's reasoning, or its conclusion in case (4). We also note, in passing, that inconsistencies do not bother the Commission. While it agrees with the court's result with relation to case (2) in SEC v. Shapiro, 2 Cir., 1974, 494 F.2d 1301, it rejects the court's reasoning based on avoidance of anomalies as "unnecessary to the decision."

To start at the beginning, in our earlier case of Janigan v. Taylor, 1 Cir., 1965, 344 F.2d 781, cert. denied, 382 U.S. 879, approved by the Court in Affiliated Ute Citizens of Utah v. United States, 1972, 406 U.S. 128, 155, the president of a closely held corporation, by fraudulently misrepresenting the company's prospects, bought out "virtually all" its outstanding stock for approximately $40,000. Two years later he sold it for $700,000. The increase was well beyond what could have been foreseen, on the true facts, by the fraudulent buyer. Nevertheless, we held that in the case of property,

"not bought from, but sold to the fraudulent party, future accretions not foreseeable at the time of the transfer even on the true facts, and hence speculative, are subject to another factor, viz, that they accrued to the fraudulent party. It may, as in the case at bar, be entirely speculative whether, had plaintiffs not sold, the series of fortunate occurrences would have happended in the same way, and to their same profit. However, there can be no speculation but that the defendant actually made the profit and, once it is found that he acquired the property by fraud, that the profit was the proximate consequence of the fraud, whether foreseeable or not. It is more appropriate to give the defrauded party the benefit even of windfalls than to let the fraudulent party keep them." 344 F.2d, ante, at 786.

At the same time we recognized that "[t]here are, of course, limits to this principle." Id., at 787. While not discussed there, one of the limits that has emerged in cases following *Janigan* is that where the fraudulently obtained securities are publicly traded, and hence readily available, the defrauded sellers can recover only those accretions occurring up to a reasonable time after they discovered the truth. See Baumel v. Rosen, 4 Cir., 1969, 412 F.2d 571, 576, cert. denied, 396 U.S. 1037; cf. Mitchell v. Texas Gulf Sulphur Co., 10th Cir., 1971, 446 F.2d 90, 105, cert. denied, 404 U.S. 1004. As Judge Friendly has pointed out,

"The reason for this, in the case of marketable securities, is obvious. Once the seller has discovered the fraud, he can protect against further damage by replacing the securities and should not be allowed to profit from a further appreciation, while being protected against depreciation by his right to recover at least the difference in value at the time of his sale." Gerstle v. Gamble-Skogmo, Inc., 2 Cir., 1973, 478 F.2d 1281, 1306 n. 27.

Conscious hedging aside, when a seller of publicly traded securities has learned of previously undisclosed material facts, and decides nevertheless not to replace the sold securities, he cannot later claim that his failure to obtain subsequent stock appreciation was a proximate consequence of his prior ignorance. "If he has failed to reinvest, * * * he must suffer the consequences of his own judgment." Mitchell v. Texas Gulf Sulphur Co., ante, at 105. Consistent with this position, the ALI proposed Federal Securities Code (1978 Official Draft and 1981 Supp.), which is said to codify *Janigan,* Comment (3) to section 1708(a), initially limits an insider's liability for profits in a case like the present one to "his ill-got gains," Comment 2 to section 1708(b)(4) (1981 Supp.), defined as the excess over the insider's purchase price of the "value of the security as of the end of the reasonable period after * * * the time when all material facts * * * became generally available." Sections 1708(a)(2) and 1703(h)(1)A; see sections 1703(b) and 1708(b).

When a fraudulent buyer has reached the point of his full gain from the fraud, viz., the market price a reasonable time after the undisclosed information has become public, any consequence of a subsequent decision, be it to sell or to retain the stock, is res inter alios, not causally related to the fraud. The dissent would acknowledge this reasoning as "unanswerable if we view the case as one between two private individuals, one defrauded and the other defrauding," but says the result should be different if the Commission is the plaintiff.

The Commission's rule would depart from the principle of "equal footing," SEC v. Shapiro, 494 F.2d ante, at 1309, and measure assessments by purely fortuitous circumstances. If two fraudulent insiders bought at the same time and price, but, well after public disclosure, sold at different times and prices, their assessments would be measured by their selling dates, choices they made entirely independent of the fraud. To call the additional profits made by the insider who held until the price went higher "ill-gotten gains," or "unjust enrichment," is merely to give a dog a bad name and hang him. The dissent's measure, "damage done to investor confidence and the integrity of the nation's capital markets," if a measure at all, is the same for each of the fraudulent investors hypothesized in examples 1–4, ante. Granted that it may add to the deterrent effect of the Act every time the Commission conceives of a ground for assessing greater liability, to charge one class of insiders more than others who had committed precisely the same fraudulent act does not seem to us to meet any definition of "equitable."

No case supports the Commission. In two, where the Commission sought to assess the profits acquired by the insider's reinvestment of his wrongfully obtained profits, the court held it could not do so, because these further profits were not causally related. In SEC v. Blatt, 5 Cir., 1978, 583 F.2d 1325, the court said, at 1335,

> "Disgorgement is remedial and not punitive. The court's power to order disgorgement extends only to the amount with interest by which the defendant profited from his wrongdoing. Any further sum would constitute a penalty assessment. In SEC v. Manor Nursing Centers, Inc., 458 F.3d 1082 (2d Cir.1972), the court held that the trial court erred in ordering restitution of income earned on ill-gotten profits. The court held that the defendant could be compelled only to disgorge profits and interest wrongfully obtained."

We see no legal or equitable difference, absent some special circumstances, none of which was found here, between an insider's decision to retain his original investment with the hope of profit and a decision to sell it and invest in something else. In both cases the subsequent profits are purely new matter. There should be a cut-off date, both ways, in cases where, unlike *Janigan*, the sellers have an opportunity to take remedial action.

This is essentially the approach taken in SEC v. Shapiro, ante, where the court required defendant to disgorge profits accrued from the rise in price caused by the disclosure, despite a price drop some time later, since had the price risen after the cut-off date, "he could [have kept] subsequent profits." Id. at 1309. Similarly, in the *Texas Gulf Sulphur* litigation, the insiders were required to disgorge only those profits accrued prior to the time the inside information was in general circulation among the investing public. SEC v. Texas Gulf Sulphur Co., S.D.N.Y., 1970, 312 F.Supp. 77, modified on other grounds, 2nd Cir., 1971, 446 F.2d 1301, cert. denied, 404 U.S. 1005.

The inside information in the case at bar is considerably less spectacular than that in *Texas Gulf,* and, accordingly, the reasonable period for the general dissemination, and then, digestion, of the December 24 press release could be expected to be longer than the one day period deemed sufficient there. Since, in the present case, there is no evidence of other material events during the period in question, the market itself may be the best indicator of how long it took for the investing public to learn of, and react to, the disclosed facts. The natural effect of public disclosure would be to increase the demand for, and correspondingly, the price of, RIT stock, and once investors stopped reacting to the good news, the price could be expected temporarily to level off. Therefore, upon remand, in determining what was a reasonable time after the inside information had been generally disseminated, the court should consider the volume and price at which RIT shares were traded following disclosure, insofar as they suggested the date by which the news had been fully digested and acted upon by investors. And, although we have distinguished *Janigan* on the facts, we do not depart from the principle that doubts are to be resolved against the defrauding party.

The order requiring the disgorgement of $53,012 is reversed. On remand the district court should determine a figure based upon the price of RIT stock a reasonable time after public dissemination of the inside information. Under the circumstances, assessment of pre-judgment interest on the amount to be disgorged, commencing on the valuation date chosen by the court, would be appropriate. In all other respects the judgment of the district court is affirmed.

COFFIN, CHIEF JUDGE, with whom BOWNES, CIRCUIT JUDGE, joins, dissenting in part.

* * *

RESCISSION

Section 12 of the 1933 Act expressly provides for a remedy of rescission, which is indeed the only remedy available to the plaintiff if he still owns the security. That section provides that the plaintiff may sue "to recover the consideration paid for such security with interest thereon, less the amount of any income received thereon, upon the tender of such security," and that he may, in the alternative, sue for damages only "if he no longer owns the security." On the other hand, Section 11 of the 1933 Act expressly provides only for the recovery of damages by the plaintiff. Although Section 11(e) says that the suit authorized under that section "may be" to recover damages as specified in subsection (e), the cases have not suggested that the plaintiff has any alternative to the recovery of the damages specified in that section. (Damages recoverable under Section 11 are discussed below.)

The law relating to the remedies which can be obtained by a plaintiff who establishes a cause of action under Rule 10b–5 or Rule 14a–9 or Section 14(e) is still in a formative state. However, it does appear to be fairly clear that the plaintiff may sue either for rescission or for damages. The cases are uniform in stating that one remedy which may be available to a defrauded plaintiff under Rule 10b–5 is to seek rescission of the transaction and recover his securities, if he is a seller, or recover the amount paid for the securities, if he is a buyer, upon tendering the return of what he himself received in the transaction.[1] However, there may be a number of reasons why rescission may be denied or be unavailable to a plaintiff in a particular action. Like any other equitable remedy, the right to rescission may be lost by laches on the part of the plaintiff,[2] or by waiver or estoppel.[3] On the other hand, rescission may not be possible because of events which have transpired after the original transaction. For example, if the defendant purchased securities in a transaction which violated Rule 10b–5 and has subsequently disposed of them prior to the institution of an action by the plaintiff, rescission is no longer possible as a practical matter.[4]

While there has been a great deal of discussion regarding the possibility of rescinding a completed corporate transaction such as a merger because of a securities law violation, and that remedy might well be practical with respect to closely-held corporations where the suit is based on Rule 10b–5, any notion that rescission of a completed merger can be a practical remedy with respect to a corporation with sufficient shareholders to be subject to the Proxy Rules would seem to be a fantasy. In Basch v. Talley Industries, Inc.[5] the court said: "To rescind this merger it would be necessary to trace each share of Industries [the surviving corporation] stock which was exchanged for a share of GTC [the merged corporation] stock. In all probability, innumerable transactions have occurred involving shares of Industries stock and untold numbers are now in the hands of persons who had nothing whatsoever to do with the merger. But even if this formidable task of tracing were possible, it would do little good. These new shareholders purchased, in good faith, shares they believed to be shares of Industries; they now believe, in good faith, that they are Industries shareholders. This court cannot order these persons to return their shares to those who owned them on April 13, 1970." [6]

In Swanson v. American Consumer Industries, Inc.,[7] although the Court of Appeals had held as a matter of law that the proxy statement was misleading for failure to disclose to the court's satisfaction certain conflicts of interest, the District Judge held that the transaction was fair to the minority shareholders and therefore he wouldn't order any relief at all. The court said: "To require 'unscrambling' or some payment or further issue of stock to plaintiff or anyone

1. Bowman & Bourdon, Inc. v. Rohr, 296 F.Supp. 847 (D.Mass.1969), aff'd on opinion below 417 F.2d 780 (1st Cir.); Sackett v. Beaman, 399 F.2d 884, 891 (9th Cir. 1968).

2. Baumel v. Rosen, 412 F.2d 571 (4th Cir.1969), cert. denied 396 U.S. 1037 (1970).

3. Royal Air Properties, Inc. v. Smith, 312 F.2d 210 (9th Cir.1962).

4. See Gottlieb v. Sandia American Corp., 304 F.Supp. 980 (E.D.Pa.1969), aff'd 452 F.2d 510 (3d Cir.1971), cert. denied 404 U.S. 938 where the defendant corporation had spun-off the securities acquired from the plaintiff to its shareholders prior to the suit.

In Gordon v. Burr, 506 F.2d 1080 (2d Cir. 1974), the court held that a plaintiff *purchaser* of shares was entitled to the remedy of rescission against a defendant not in privity with him, i.e., a salesman selling on behalf of his principal. However, a de-

frauded *seller* obviously could not actually obtain rescission against such a defendant, since the defendant doesn't have the stock to give back to him, although it is possible that a court in lieu thereof might apply a rescission measure of damages.

5. 53 F.R.D. 9, 14 (S.D.N.Y.1971).

6. However, in Sargent v. Genesco, Inc., 458 F.2d 9 (5th Cir.1972), in refusing to enjoin the mailing of proxy material for a sale of assets by a corporation, the court stated: "Recognizing the difficulty involved in unraveling a tangled corporate transaction after its consummation, we are nevertheless convinced that the District Court's broad equity power will be capable of fashioning an adequate remedy for any violation of the securities laws which may result if the disputed mailing of proxy materials takes place. * * * What has been done may be undone if necessary."

7. 328 F.Supp. 797 (S.D.Ill.1971).

he represents, or to his counsel, * * * would be a grave injustice to the other shareholders of ACI."

DAMAGES RECOVERABLE UNDER SECTIONS 11 AND 12(2)

In an action under Section 11 the plaintiff may recover the difference between the price he paid (not exceeding the price at which the security was offered to the public) and the value of the security at the time of the suit or the price at which he previously sold it. Thus, if there is a "hot issue" which comes out at $5.00, and the plaintiff purchases the security in the market two months later for $10.00, and it then goes back down to $5.00, he could not recover anything under Section 11 even if he could establish all the elements of a cause of action. (This assumes that there was no "free riding", which possibly might alter the "price at which the security was offered to the public.")

The plaintiff need show no causal connection between the decline in the price of the security and the false or misleading statement in the prospectus. However, if the defendant can prove that "any portion or all of such damages represents other than the depreciation in value of such security resulting from such part of the registration statement * * * not being true", he can escape liability to that extent. It had generally been assumed prior to the *Feit* case, supra page 969, that this would probably be an impossible burden for the defendant to carry. If the market generally declines following a registered issue in connection with which there are false and misleading statements, it is reasonable to suppose that some part of the decline in price of the registered security was due to general market conditions. But how can the defendant prove *exactly what part*? Judge Weinstein in the *Feit* case neatly solves this dilemma for the defendant by saying that we will arbitrarily assume that at least a portion of the decline equal to the decline in the Standard and Poor's index of 500 stocks was due to such other causes. If this approach is sound, it would clearly seem to have been more accurate in that case to use the index for conglomerates (or at least for the Dow Jones' industrials), since that would more accurately reflect the market conditions with respect to companies similar to Leasco. But this would probably have wiped out the damages altogether, and may have seemed like too much of a good thing. It remains to be seen what the appellate courts will do with respect to this theory; if it survives, Judge Weinstein, despite his animadversions against corporations and their securities lawyers, may have handed them the nicest present they have received since the first plaintiff discovered Rule 10b–5.

In Beecher v. Able [8] the Douglas Aircraft Company convertible debentures which were issued at 100 on July 12, 1966, had declined to 88 by September 26, 1966, on which date the company announced its disastrous third quarter results, which revealed the falsity of its income projections in the prospectus. The price thereafter declined further to $75\frac{1}{2}$ on October 14, the date of the filing of the law suit. The court held that all of the decline prior to September 26 was due to causes other than the falsity of the registration statement since the erroneous income projection was unknown prior to that date. It also held that all of the decline after September 26 was due to the falsity of the registration statement, but stated: "In reaching the above conclusion the court emphasizes that unlike some commentators, the court does not believe that defendant's burden of proof of 'negative causation' is 'impossible.' Compare, R. Jennings & H. Marsh, Securities Regulation, Cases and Materials, 810 (1968). [The court obviously had available only the second and not the third edition of

8.   435 F.Supp. 397 (S.D.N.Y.1977).

this book.] * * * Here, the court's conclusions are based on an assessment of all the evidence. In the court's view, the weight of the evidence clearly establishes that the depreciation in the Douglas debentures [after September 26] was due to causes directly related to the falsity of the prospectus rather than the unrelated factors urged by defendant."

However, contrary to what would appear to be the result of these holdings at first blush, the plaintiff did not recover the difference between 88 and 75½ for those class members who still held the debentures. Both the plaintiff and the defendant urged that the "value" of the debentures at the date of suit was not the market quotation, the defendant saying that it was artificially depressed by "panic selling" and did not reflect the "credit worthiness" of the company and the plaintiff saying that it was artificially high because the full extent of the debacle was still unknown. The court accepted the proposition that it should find a "value" other than the quoted market value and fixed this at 85 by projecting the decline from July 12 to September 26 forward to October 14, on the basis that the price was influenced by "panic selling." The court said that "the conclusion that 'value' is not synonymous with 'market price' seems clearly dictated by the plain language of Section 11(e) in which both 'price' (sometimes 'amount paid') and 'value' are used, apparently deliberately, to connote different concepts."

Another aspect of the damage provision in Section 11(e), which is illustrated by the *Feit* case, is that the plaintiff's filing suit stops the defendant's loss. If, one year after a registered offering at $10 per share, a suit under Section 11 is filed when the stock is selling for $8 (if $8 is determined to be the "value"), the maximum recovery is limited to $2 per share even though the price continues to plummet and the stock is only selling for $1 at the time of trial; on the other hand, if the price goes back up to $10 and a plaintiff sells for that price before judgment, he loses any recovery. However, under Section 13 the suit must be brought within one year after "the discovery of the untrue statement or the omission," so that the plaintiff dare not delay too long in filing suit to see what the market is going to do, since the statute of limitations may run on his cause of action.

The plaintiff's recovery under Section 12(2) may be quite different from his recovery under Section 11. Under Section 12(2) he may rescind and get back all of the consideration he paid, if he still owns the security. This may be quite important in a case where the price has continued to decline after the filing of suit, which, as noted above, stops the defendant's loss in an action under Section 11. If the plaintiff no longer owns the security, he may recover his "damages" under Section 12(2). The statute makes no attempt to define what these are; nor are any of the limitations on damages contained in Section 11 incorporated in this section. The damages recoverable under Section 12 would, however, presumably be a "rescissionary" measure of damages, since that section basically grants only a right of rescission. It provides for damages only when actual rescission is impossible because the plaintiff no longer owns the security. Under this measure of damages, the plaintiff could recover the amount he paid for the security less what he received when he disposed of it, and would be charged with any income thereon and credited with interest as is expressly provided where an actual rescission is ordered. In Randall v. Loftsgaarden, ___ U.S. ___, 106 S.Ct. 3143 (1986), the Supreme Court stated that in the situation where the plaintiff no longer owns the security, "we may assume that a rescissionary measure of damages will be employed [under Section 12(2)]; the plaintiff is entitled to a return of the consideration paid, reduced by the amount realized when he sold the security and by any 'income received' on the security." In that case, however, the court held that the recovery by the plaintiff should not be reduced by any "tax savings" realized by the plaintiff in connection with an investment in a "tax shelter." The court held that the tax benefits received by the investor were not "income received" within the meaning of Section 12(2).

The court also held that where a rescissionary measure of damages is applied in an action under Rule 10b–5, the same rule would be applicable. It did not, however, rule out the possibility that such tax benefits should be taken into account in an action under Rule 10b–5 where an out-of-pocket measure of damages is determined to be applicable. The court stated: "We also have no occasion in this case to decide whether, assuming that a rescissionary recovery may sometimes be proper under § 10(b), plaintiffs in such cases should invariably be free to elect a rescissionary measure of damages rather than out-of-pocket damages. Consequently, we do not consider whether courts may ever refuse to allow a rescissionary recovery under § 10(b) where the 'premium' for expected tax benefits represented a large portion of the purchase price, in which event the out-of-pocket measure might yield a significantly smaller recovery * * *. In this case, a rescissionary measure of damages was determined to be proper, and respondents have abandoned their initial challenge to that ruling." Justice Blackmun, concurring, indicated that normally "the proper measure of damages in a § 10(b) case is an investor's out-of-pocket loss," and that the tax benefits received by the investor should in that case reduce the recovery against the defendant.

DAMAGES RECOVERABLE UNDER RULE 10b–5 AND SECTION 14(e)

As to what measure of damages will be used to determine the amount recoverable by the plaintiff in an action under Rule 10b–5, the majority of the earlier cases seemed to apply the so-called "out-of-pocket" measure of damages, by which the plaintiff is awarded the difference between the value of what he gave up and the value of what he received in the transaction.[9] This so-called "out-of-pocket" rule is subject to the important qualification, as illustrated by Mitchell v. Texas Gulf Sulphur Co.,[10] that the calculation will be made with reference to a reasonable period of time after the discovery by the plaintiff of the fraud,[11] so that he is given an opportunity after all of the facts are known to repurchase where he is a defrauded seller or to dispose of the securities purchased where he is a defrauded buyer. Under this approach, the defendant is not liable for any appreciation in value of the securities after that time where he is a buyer or any depreciation in value after that time where he is a seller.

There are, however, an increasing number of cases which apply a measure of damages based upon the defendant's "profits" from the transaction,[12] rather

9. Esplin v. Hirschi, 402 F.2d 94 (10th Cir.1968), cert. denied 394 U.S. 928 (1969); Baumel v. Rosen, 412 F.2d 571 (4th Cir. 1969), cert. denied 396 U.S. 1037 (1970); Mitchell v. Texas Gulf Sulphur Co., 446 F.2d 90 (10th Cir.1971), cert. denied 404 U.S. 1004.

10. Supra, note 9. See, also Nye v. Blyth, Eastman Dillon & Co., 588 F.2d 1189 (8th Cir.1978).

11. It is interesting to note the varying periods of time selected by the District Judge in Mitchell v. Texas Gulf Sulphur

Co., supra note 9, the Tenth Circuit in that case and Judge Bonsal (who was affirmed by the Second Circuit) in Securities and Exchange Commission v. Texas Gulf Sulphur Co., 446 F.2d 1301 (2d Cir.1971), to measure the plaintiff's loss (or the defendant's profit—not necessarily the same thing), all with respect to the identical factual situation.

12. Janigan v. Taylor, 344 F.2d 781 (1st Cir.1965), cert. denied 382 U.S. 879 (1965); Gottlieb v. Sandia American Corporation, 304 F.Supp. 980 (E.D.Pa.1969), aff'd 452

than the plaintiff's loss. While the courts say in these cases that they are not applying a "benefit of the bargain" rule, as opposed to the "out-of-pocket" measure, the result appears to be much the same. The Sixth Circuit went so far as to say in Ohio Drill & Tool Co. v. Johnson [13] that the normal "standard of damages for either a defrauded seller or buyer under Rule 10b–5 is 'disgorgement of profits.' " [14] And the Second Circuit in Zeller v. Bogue Electric Manufacturing Corp.[15] held that this measure of recovery might be applied against a defendant-seller as well as a defendant-buyer in an appropriate case. The court said: "The reason why the remedy has been applied for the benefit of defrauded sellers but not of buyers is not any decisive legal difference but the difficulty generally confronting the defrauded buyer in showing that the fraudulent seller has in fact reaped such a profit." [16]

In Hackbart v. Holmes [17] the court cited and followed the *Zeller* case in holding that a benefit-of-the-bargain measure of damages should be applied to prevent unjust enrichment of the defendant. In that case the court held that the plaintiff was entitled to recover the value of his 49% interest in the corporation at the time he discovered the deception, which consisted of misrepresenting to him that the preferred stock issued to him would permit him to share in the appreciation in value of the business enterprise. And in Siebel v. Scott [18] the court held that disgorgement of the profits made by the defendant rather than the difference in value of what was paid and the fair market value of the securities at the time of the sale was the proper measure of damages. In that case the defendant had fraudulently purchased securities and subsequently resold them to another party for a profit of one million dollars. The court said: "As recently explained by a sister court: 'The early cases generally awarded the difference between the value given and the value received, but the recent trend looks to defendant's profits, rather than to plaintiff's losses, in measuring damages.' Nelson v. Serwold, 576 F.2d 1332, 1338 (9th Cir.), cert. denied, 439 U.S. 970 (1978) (citing *Janigan* and *Myzel*)."

This "rescissionary" measure of damages may even be applied in an action against a defendant-seller where it is clear that the seller in fact realized no profit at all, but the buyer is simply awarded the difference between what he paid for the security and the value of what he eventually ended up with after the fraud was discovered. In Garnatz v. Stifel Nicolaus & Co., Inc.,[19] the plaintiff purchased bonds on margin on the representation of the defendant broker that the investment was non-speculative and involved no risk whatever. The bonds had a value at the time of purchase equal to the purchase price and, therefore, there were no damages based on the "out-of-pocket" measure of damages. The Eighth Circuit, nevertheless, held that the plaintiff was entitled to recover the difference between what he paid for the bonds and what he subsequently sold them for or the market value of those still held by him. The court said: "The gravamen of the present action was not whether Garnatz bought the bonds for a fair price, but that he bought at all. Absent defendants'

F.2d 510 (3d Cir.1971), cert. denied 404 U.S. 938; Speed v. Transamerica Corp., 135 F.Supp. 176 (D.Del.1955), mod. 235 F.2d 369 (3d Cir.1956).

13. 498 F.2d 186 (6th Cir.1974).

14. However, the court said that damages under Rule 14a–9 should be limited to the "out-of-pocket" measurement. There seems to be no basis for any such distinction, particularly with respect to the same transaction. In Gould v. American Hawaiian Steamship Co., 362 F.Supp. 771 (D.Del.

1973), the court awarded a recovery of profits, even though it had been strangely stipulated that the plaintiffs had suffered no out-of-pocket loss.

15. 476 F.2d 795 (2d Cir.1973), cert. denied 414 U.S. 908.

16. 476 F.2d at 802.

17. 675 F.2d 1114 (10th Cir.1982).

18. 725 F.2d 995 (5th Cir.1984), cert. denied 467 U.S. 1242 (1984).

19. 559 F.2d 1357 (8th Cir.1977).

representations regarding the safety of the program, plaintiff's expressed disdain for speculation would undoubtedly have precluded his participation."

In Gerstle v. Gamble-Skogmo, Inc., supra page 1015, the court held that the defendant parent corporation was liable to the minority shareholders of its subsidiary which it merged into itself without disclosing its intention to sell most of the assets of the subsidiary after the merger was accomplished, as it did within a period of approximately nine months thereafter. The court held that the defendant was liable for the profit made on the sale of the assets thus disposed of, but was not liable for any appreciation in value of the stock of two subsidiaries of the merged corporation which had not been sold. The plaintiff contended that the defendant should be liable for the "highest intermediate value" of the stock of these subsidiaries between the date of the merger and the date of the judgment, but the court rejected this contention. Judge Friendly said: "We do not regard this result as allowing defendant to be unjustly enriched or to profit from its wrong. The crucial fact here is that the misrepresentations in the Proxy Statement related only to the sales of plants, as to which Skogmo's liability for profits is conceded. If the merger had been accomplished, whether in 1963 or a year later, on somewhat better terms for the GOA stockholders, adequately reflecting and disclosing the potential profits from plant sales, they would have had no conceivable claim for the post-merger appreciation of the Stedman or Claude Neon [the two subsidiaries of GAO] shares. In these circumstances, awarding plaintiffs the profits on the plant sales and the value of the unsold assets, together with pre-judgment interest at a substantial rate, amply deprives Skogmo of profit from its wrong. To go further and hold Skogmo for any appreciation in the value of Stedman or Claude Neon over the long period between the merger and the judgment below—nearly nine years—is not required by this equitable principle. The passage of time introduces so many elements—here, for example, the beneficial effects of Skogmo's management—that extreme prolongation of the period for calculating damages may be grossly unfair. Skogmo asserts that the nexus between the misrepresentations and the damage award would be too thin if this were stretched to include appreciation of the Stedman and Claude Neon shares, and much too thin if held to justify an award based on their highest intermediate value. For the reasons indicated, we agree." [20] The court in Kohn v. American Metal Climax, Inc. [21] first ordered what amounted to an offer of rescission of the transaction, but stated in a supplemental opinion that if this did not prove to be feasible then the "appropriate measure of * * * damages would appear to be the difference in value between the package of securities received as a result of the amalgamation and the actual value of the stockholders' interest in the assets of [the merged corporation]," i.e., the so-called "out-of-pocket" measure of damages. [22]

In James v. Meinke [23] the court held that even the out-of-pocket measure of damages includes any consequential or special damages which can be sufficiently established. The court said: "Such special damages may not be awarded if their relationship to the defendant is too remote; significantly, however, 'special or consequential damages are recoverable even if the plaintiff can show no general damages.'"

It would perhaps be accurate to say that the cases are in a state of some confusion as to the proper measurement of damages under Rule 10b–5 and Rule

---

20. 478 F.2d at 1306.

21. 322 F.Supp. 1331 (E.D.Pa.1971), aff'd 458 F.2d 255 (3d Cir.1972), cert. denied 409 U.S. 874 (1972).

22. Compare however, Gould v. American Hawaiian Steamship Co., supra, note 14.

23. 778 F.2d 200 (5th Cir.1985).

14a–9.[24] The recent cases, however, seem to have adopted whatever measure of damages produces the largest recovery for the plaintiff, whether the "out-of-pocket" measure of damages, the "benefit of the bargain" measure of damages or "disgorgement of profits", without giving any decisive effect to the reference in Section 28(a) of the 1934 Act to "actual damages", which some of the earlier cases thought restricted any recovery to the out-of-pocket loss by the plaintiff.

Under the Margin Rules, the Third Circuit held that where there was a violation of Regulation U, the borrower was not liable for the unpaid balance of the loan and the bank was liable to him for the decline in value of the stock pledged from the date of the pledge to the date it was sold out by the bank.[25] And the First Circuit held that a broker-dealer guilty of a violation of Regulation T was liable to the customer for his entire losses on the transaction, and not merely on that portion which made the credit excessive.[26] The court said that the customer did not have to show that he would not have made some smaller trade for which the margin would have been adequate. However, the Sixth Circuit in Goldman v. Bank of the Commonwealth [27] held that an individual who *knowingly* received loans in violation of Regulation U could not avoid repayment of the loans; the bank was entitled to recover the principal amount of the loans *without interest.*

When the court has difficulty determining the amount of the damages under any measurement, it may fall back on the "Chimney Sweeper's Case", as did the court in Chris-Craft Industries, Inc. v. Piper Aircraft Corp.[28] This case was explained by Judge Friendly in a footnote to the *Gerstle* case as follows: "Since it has now become somewhat the vogue to consider the 'Chimney Sweeper's Jewel Case,' Armory v. Delamirie, 1 Strange 505, 93 Eng.Rep. 664 (1722), as having an important bearing on issues of damages under the Securities Exchange Act, due, no doubt, to Judge L. Hand's resurrection of the case in an action under § 16(b), Gratz v. Claughton, 187 F.2d 46, 51–52 (2 Cir.), cert. denied 341 U.S. 920 (1951), it may not be amiss to add that this old decision had nothing to do with fluctuating values. The Chief Justice simply 'directed the jury, that unless the defendant did produce the jewel, and shew it not to be of the finest water, they should presume the strongest against him, and make the value of the best jewels the measure of their damages.' "

Damages for Insider Trading. The cases have held that a defendant insider who trades on the basis of material undisclosed inside information (or whose tippee trades) is liable to all the persons who trade in the market during the time that the information is undisclosed. See, for example, Shapiro v. Merrill Lynch, Pierce, Fenner & Smith, Inc.,[29] in which Judge Timbers admitted that the resulting liability might well be "Draconian", but since he was in the position of Draco in that analogy and the defendants were the citizens of Athens, this thought didn't seem to bother him too much. The court did, however, reserve in that case the question of the proper measure of damages for decision upon remand to the district court. Dean Ruder has calculated that, if liability were imposed in the *Texas Gulf Sulphur* case in favor of everyone who sold after the first drill hole in Canada showed indications of a rich ore strike,

---

24. See Note, Damages Awarded to Unsuccessful Tender Offeror Under Section 14(e) For Loss of Opportunity to Control Target Corporation, 89 Harv.L.Rev. 1239 (1976).

25. Grove v. The First National Bank of Herminie, 489 F.2d 512 (3d Cir.1973).

26. Landry v. Hemphill, Noyes & Co., 473 F.2d 365 (1st Cir.1973), cert. denied 414 U.S. 100.

27. 467 F.2d 439 (6th Cir.1972).

28. 516 F.2d 172 (2d Cir.1975).

29. 495 F.2d 228 (2d Cir.1974).

it would amount to $390 million.[30] But after the first ten or twenty million, it probably would not make much difference to the individual defendants.[31]

Is there any limitation on the extent of a defendant's liability under this doctrine? A defendant may, for example, have purchased or sold 100 shares for a price of $5,000; and he may be sued by every seller or purchaser in the market during the entire period of time that the misrepresentation or concealment allegedly affected the market price, who purchased stock with an aggregate value of $20 million and whose damages are claimed to be $5,000,000. Is he liable for this entire sum?[32] The court in Financial Industrial Fund, Inc. v. McDonnell Douglas Corp.[33] quotes Professor Bromberg in 1969 as saying that "We are a long way from holding that the TGS official who used inside information to buy 600 shares the day 440,000 traded is liable to all the sellers."

That "long way" extended only to 1971 when Mitchell v. Texas Gulf Sulphur Co.[34] held Mr. Fogarty, who had purchased 3,100 shares, for the most part months earlier, liable to *any* seller in the market after the first press release issued by Texas Gulf Sulphur Company regarding its ore strike in Canada, which the court found to be misleading. The court does suggest that Texas Gulf Sulphur should pay the judgment so Mr. Fogarty won't have to, by affirming the decision of the trial court that, if TGS paid the judgment, plaintiffs' claims against Fogarty would be "deemed paid, satisfied and discharged"; but the basis of that suggestion is difficult to understand. Mr. Fogarty, who drafted the press release, actually was primarily liable; and on the basis of the facts found by the court he could have been sued by the corporation, even if he had not been joined as a defendant by the plaintiff,

---

30. Ruder, Texas Gulf Sulphur—The Second Round, 63 Nw.U.L.Rev. 423 (1969), quoted in footnote 13 to the opinion of the Tenth Circuit in the *Mitchell* case, infra, note 32. This calculation, however, was based upon a restitution measure of damages, which the court in the *Mitchell* case rejected. Even if this figure should be reduced by, say, one-third under the *Mitchell* case approach, it would seem to make little difference to the company, which only had a net worth of $240 million, or, certainly, to the individual defendants.

Since all of the *Texas Gulf Sulphur* cases were eventually settled, there is no convenient summary of the total amount actually paid out by Texas Gulf with respect to this litigation. It would be instructive to have some graduate student prepare a dissertation on that subject, including the amounts paid to the company's lawyers, to the plaintiffs' lawyers and to the allegedly injured public. There might also be a consideration of what the *shareholders* of Texas Gulf did to deserve this.

31. A substantial question exists as to whether any judgment against the individuals can be discharged in bankruptcy. Section 523(a)(6) of the Bankruptcy Code provides that a discharge in Bankruptcy does not affect a liability for "wilful and malicious injury by the debtor * * * to the property of another." Under a finding such as that in the *Mitchell* case, infra,

note 32, that the statements made were "intentionally deceptive," the case would seem to fall within this exception to dischargeability. Even with a finding, such as that in the *Financial Industrial Fund* case, infra, note 33, that the conduct of the defendant was only "reckless," there could be a strong argument that it would not be discharged in bankruptcy; many cases have held that liability for injury caused by drunken driving is not discharged because reckless disregard of the safety of others is "equivalent to" wilfulness and maliciousness. See 1A Collier, Bankruptcy (14 ed. 1971) ¶ 17.17, pp. 1650.3–1670. Even if not discharged, it would obviously take more than a lifetime for most individual defendants to work off that kind of liability.

32. See footnote 13 to the opinion in Mitchell v. Texas Gulf Sulphur Co., 446 F.2d 90 (10th Cir.1971), cert. denied 404 U.S. 1004.

33. CCH Fed.Sec.Law Reptr. ¶ 93,004 (D.Colo.1971). This case was reversed as to McDonnell Douglas by the Tenth Circuit, Financial Industrial Fund, Inc. v. McDonald Douglas Corp., 474 F.2d 514 (10th Cir. 1973). However, Merrill Lynch did not appeal, and it was of course held liable in a class action in the *Shapiro* case, supra note 29.

34. Supra, note 32.

absent an applicable and enforceable indemnification or exculpation provision in the articles or bylaws. Even the most liberal state indemnification provisions would not seem to save Mr. Fogarty, since he was adjudged by the court to be guilty of wilful wrongdoing, and even if applicable would probably not be enforceable under the *Globus* case.[35] The only possible explanation of this statement is that the court was somewhat ashamed of what it was doing to Mr. Fogarty.

In the *Elkind* case Judge Mansfield has attempted to put a cap on the liability of a non-trading tipper (or rather the liability of his employing corporation), limiting it to an obligation to return pro rata to the public traders in the market the profits made by his tippees. The court, obviously, intended this rule to apply also to an insider who traded personally rather than tipping others, although conceivably the case might be distinguished in the future on that basis. Would it also apply in the case of an affirmative misrepresentation, as distinguished from mere non-disclosure? The liability of Mr. Fogarty in the *Mitchell* case was based upon the affirmative misrepresentation found to have been contained in the first press release issued by Texas Gulf Sulphur and drafted by him. The court in the *Shapiro* case held that it made no difference whether the basis of the action was mere non-disclosure or an affirmative misrepresentation so far as liability to all purchasers in the market was concerned.[36] Would the court that decided the *Elkind* case extend its new rule relating to limitation of damages to a person in the position of Mr. Fogarty?

In the *MacDonald* case, the court also restricted the recovery of profits from the defendant to those realized within a period of time ending when the market has had an opportunity to absorb the previously undisclosed information after it becomes public. The "disgorgement of profits" is of course the only appropriate measure of damages when that is in fact what the Commission is seeking; this holding has no necessary bearing on the measure of damages in a suit by private plaintiffs. Upon the remand of this case, the district judge found that the good news previously withheld was not fully digested by the market until three weeks after the press release disclosing it and that on this basis the amount of profit to be "disgorged" by the defendant was approximately $18,000, which was affirmed upon a second appeal.[37]

Punitive Damages. Green v. Wolf Corp.[38] held that punitive damages cannot be recovered in a suit under Rule 10b–5 and this decision was followed in deHaas v. Empire Petroleum Co.[39] in the Tenth Circuit. However, the plaintiff may be able to recover punitive damages, depending upon the particular facts and the applicable state law, pursuant to a pendent cause of action under state law joined with the action under Rule 10b–5.[40]

Indemnification and Contribution. The first decision in Globus v. Law Research Service, Inc.[41] held that an agreement by one defendant to indemnify another in connection with a transaction which violated Rule 10b–5 was unenforceable as against public policy where the person claiming indemnity had actual knowledge of the misstatements or omissions upon which the plaintiff's recovery was based. However, in the second decision in Globus v.

---

35. Globus v. Law Research Service, Inc., 418 F.2d 1276 (2d Cir.1969), cert. denied 397 U.S. 913 (1970).

36. See, also, Astor v. Texas Gulf Sulphur Co., 306 F.Supp. 1333 (S.D.N.Y. 1969).

37. Securities and Exchange Commission v. MacDonald, 725 F.2d 9 (1st Cir. 1984).

38. 406 F.2d 291 (2d Cir.1968). See, also, Pearlstein v. Scudder & German, CCH Fed.Sec.Law Rptr. ¶ 93,439 (S.D.N.Y.1971).

39. 435 F.2d 1223 (10th Cir.1970).

40. Young v. Taylor, 466 F.2d 1329 (10th Cir.1972).

41. 418 F.2d 1276 (2d Cir.1969), cert. denied 397 U.S. 913 (1970).

Law Research Service, Inc.,[42] the Court held that a defendant who had paid a judgment under Rule 10b–5 was entitled to claim contribution from another party also held liable.

See Birkeland, Securities Fraud: The Tax Benefit Offset Rule of Damages in Securities Litigation, 70 Minn.L.Rev. 1185 (1986); Scott, Resurrecting Indemnification: Contribution Clauses in Underwriting Agreements, 61 N.Y.U.L.Rev. 223 (1986); Easterbrook and Fischel, Optimal Damages in Securities Cases, 52 U.Chi.L.Rev. 611 (1985); Goldwasser and Safran, Damages in Tax Shelter Offerings, 18 Rev. of Sec. & Comm.Reg. 225 (1985); Strickler, Insider Information and Outside Traders: Corporate Recovery of the Outsider's Unfair Gain, 73 Calif.L.Rev. 483 (1985); Mira, The Measure of Disgorgement in SEC Enforcement Actions Against Insider Traders Under Rule 10b–5, 34 Cath.U.L.Rev. 445 (1985); Cheney and Sibears, A New Measure of Disgorgement in SEC Insider Trading Cases, 69 Mass.L.Rev. 180 (1984); Musslewhite, The Measure of the Disgorgement Remedy in SEC Enforcement Actions, 12 Sec.Reg.L.J. 138 (1984); Thompson, The Measure of Recovery Under Rule 10b–5: A Restitution Alternative to Tort Damages, 37 Vand.L.Rev. 349 (1984); Finkelstein, Rule 10b–5 Damage Computation: Application of Financial Theory to Determine Net Economic Loss, 51 Fordham L.Rev. 838 (1983); Sacher, Overview of the Panoply of Remedies Available to an Aggrieved Plaintiff Under SEC Rule 10b–5, 7 Cumb.L.Rev. 429 (1977); Jacobs, Measure of Damages in Rule 10b–5 Cases, 65 Geo.L.J. 1093 (1977); Mullaney, Theories of Measuring Damages in Security Cases and the Effects of Damages on Liability, 46 Fordham L.Rev. 277 (1977); Reder, Measuring Buyers' Damages in 10b–5 Cases, 31 Bus.Law. 1839 (1976); Weiskopf, Remedies under Rule 10b–5, 45 St. John's L.Rev. 733 (1971); Hirsch and Lewis, Punitive Damage Awards under the Federal Securities Acts, 47 Notre Dame Law. 72 (1971); Note, Measure of Damages in Rule 10b–5 Cases Involving Actively Traded Securities, 26 Stan.L.Rev. 371 (1974); Note, Injunctive Relief in SEC Civil Actions: The Scope of Judicial Discretion, 10 Colum.J.L. & Soc.Prob. 328 (1974); Note, Reappearance of Punitive Damages in Private Actions for Securities Fraud, 5 Tex.Tech.L.Rev. 111 (1973).

42. 442 F.2d 1346 (2d Cir.1971). See, also, Heizer Corp. v. Ross, 601 F.2d 330 (7th Cir.1979).

Chapter 21

LIABILITY FOR SHORT–SWING PROFITS—
SECTION 16(b)

Statutes and Regulations

Securities Exchange Act of 1934, § 16.

Rules 16a–2; 16a–8; 16a–10; 16b–3; 16b–6; 16b–7; 16b–9.

FEDER v. MARTIN MARIETTA CORP.

United States Court of Appeals, Second Circuit, 1969.
406 F.2d 260, cert. denied 396 U.S. 1036, 90 S.Ct. 678, 24 L.Ed.2d 681 (1970).

Before WATERMAN, SMITH and HAYS, CIRCUIT JUDGES.

WATERMAN, CIRCUIT JUDGE. Plaintiff-appellant, a stockholder of the Sperry Rand Corporation ("Sperry") after having made the requisite demand upon Sperry which was not complied with, commenced this action pursuant to § 16(b) of the Securities Exchange Act of 1934, 15 U.S.C.A. § 78p(b) (1964), to recover for Sperry "short-swing" profits realized upon Sperry stock purchases and sales by the Martin Marietta Corporation ("Martin"). Plaintiff alleged that George M. Bunker, the President and Chief Executive of Martin Marietta, was deputized by, or represented, Martin Marietta when he served as a member of the Sperry Rand Board of Directors and therefore during his membership Martin Marietta was a "director" of Sperry Rand within the meaning of Section 16(b). The United States District Court for the Southern District of New York, Cooper, J., sitting without a jury, finding no deputization, dismissed plaintiff's action. 286 F.Supp. 937 (S.D.N.Y.1968). We hold to the contrary and reverse the judgment below.

The purpose of § 16(b) as succinctly expressed in the statute itself is to prevent "unfair use of information" by insiders and thereby to protect the public and outside stockholders. The only remedy which the framers of § 16(b) deemed effective to curb insider abuse of advance information was the imposition of a liability based upon an objective measure of proof, e.g., Smolowe v. Delendo Corp., 136 F.2d 231, 235 (2 Cir.), cert. denied 320 U.S. 751 * * * (1943). Thus, application of the act is not conditional upon proof of an insider's intent to profit from unfair use of information, e.g., Blau v. Lamb, 363 F.2d 507, 515 (2 Cir.1966), cert. denied 385 U.S. 1002 * * * (1967), or upon proof that the insider was privy to any confidential information, e.g., Ferraiolo v. Newman, 259 F.2d 342, 344 (6 Cir.1958), cert. denied, 359 U.S. 927 * * * (1959). Rather, Section 16(b) liability is automatic, and liability attaches to any profit by an insider on any short-swing transaction embraced within the arbitrarily fixed time limits of the statute.

The judicial tendency, especially in this circuit, has been to interpret Section 16(b) in ways that are most consistent with the legislative purpose, even departing where necessary from the literal statutory language. See,

1395

e.g., cases cited in Blau v. Oppenheim, 250 F.Supp. 881, 884–885 (S.D.N.Y. 1966) (Weinfeld, J.). But the policy underlying the enactment of § 16(b) does not permit an expansion of the statute's scope to persons other than directors, officers, and 10% shareholders. Blau v. Lehman, 368 U.S. 403, 410–411 (1962). * * * Through the creation of a legal fiction, however, our courts have managed to remain within the limits of § 16(b)'s literal language and yet have expanded the Act's reach.

In Rattner v. Lehman, 193 F.2d 564 (2 Cir.1952), Judge Learned Hand in his concurring opinion planted the seed for a utilization of the theory of deputization upon which plaintiff here proceeds. In discussing the question whether a partnership is subject to Section 16(b) liability whenever a partner is a director of a corporation whose stock the partnership traded, Judge Hand stated:

> I agree that § 16(b) does not go so far; but I wish to say nothing as to whether, if a firm deputed a partner to represent its interests as a director on the board, the other partners would not be liable. True, they would not even then be formally "directors"; but I am not prepared to say that they could not be so considered; for some purposes the common law does treat a firm as a jural person. 193 F.2d at 567.

The Supreme Court in Blau v. Lehman, 368 U.S. 403, 408–410 (1962), affirming 286 F.2d 786 (2 Cir.1960), affirming 173 F.Supp. 590 (S.D.N.Y. 1959) more firmly established the possibility of an entity, such as a partnership or a corporation, incurring Section 16(b) liability as a "director" through the deputization theory. Though the Court refused to reverse the lower court decisions that had held no deputization, it stated:

> Although admittedly not "literally designated" as one, it is contended that Lehman is a director. No doubt Lehman Brothers, though a partnership, could for purposes of § 16 be a "director" of Tide Water and function through a deputy * * *. 368 U.S. at 409 * * *.

In Marquette Cement Mfg. Co. v. Andreas, 239 F.Supp. 962, 967 (S.D.N.Y. 1965), relying upon Blau v. Lehman, the availability of the deputization theory to impose § 16(b) liability was again recognized. * * *

In light of the above authorities, the validity of the deputization theory, presumed to be valid here by the parties and by the district court, is unquestionable. Nevertheless, the situations encompassed by its application are not as clear. The Supreme Court in Blau v. Lehman intimated that the issue of deputization is a question of fact to be settled case by case and not a conclusion of law. See 368 U.S. at 408–409. Therefore, it is not enough for appellant to show us that inferences to support appellant's contentions should have been drawn from the evidence. Id. at 409. Rather our review of the facts and inferences found by the court below is imprisoned by the "unless clearly erroneous" standard. Fed.R.Civ.P. 52(a). In the instant case, applying that standard, though there is some evidence in the record to support the trial court's finding of no deputization, we, upon considering the entire evidence, are left with the definite and firm conviction that a mistake was committed. Guzman v. Pichirilo, 369 U.S. 698, 702 (1962); United States v. United States Gypsum Co., 333 U.S. 364, 394–395 (1948). Consequently, we reverse the result reached below.

Bunker served as a director of Sperry from April 29, 1963 to August 1, 1963, when he resigned. During the period December 14, 1962 through July 24, 1963, Martin Marietta accumulated 801,300 shares of Sperry stock of which 101,300 shares were purchased during Bunker's directorship. Between August 29, 1963 and September 6, 1963, Martin Marietta sold all of its Sperry stock. Plaintiff seeks to reach, on behalf of the Sperry Rand Corporation, the profits made by Martin Marietta from the 101,300 shares of stock acquired between April 29 and August 1, all of which, of course, were sold within six months after purchase.

The district court, in determining that Bunker was not a Martin deputy, made the following findings of fact to support its decision: (1) Sperry initially invited Bunker to join its Board two and a half months before Martin began its accumulation of Sperry stock; (2) Bunker turned down a second offer by Sperry at a time when Martin already held 400,000 shares of Sperry stock; (3) Sperry, not Martin, took the initiative to encourage Bunker to accept the directorship; (4) no other Martin man was ever mentioned for the position in the event Bunker absolutely declined; and (5) Bunker's fine reputation and engineering expertise was the prime motivation for Sperry's interest in him. In addition, the testimony of the only two witnesses who testified at trial, Mr. Bunker and a Mr. Norman Frost, a Sperry director and its chief counsel, were fully believed and accepted as truthful by the court. We assume all of the foregoing findings have a basis of fact in the evidence, but we find there was additional, more germane, uncontradicted evidence, overlooked or ignored by the district court, which we are firmly convinced require us to conclude that Martin Marietta was a "director" of Sperry Rand.

First and foremost is Bunker's testimony that as chief executive of Martin Marietta he was "ultimately responsible for the total operation of the corporation" including personal approval of all the firm's financial investments, and, in particular, all of Martin's purchases of Sperry stock. As the district court aptly recognized, Bunker's control over Martin Marietta's investments, coupled with his position on the Board of Directors of Sperry Rand, placed him in a position where he could acquire inside information concerning Sperry and could utilize such data for Martin Marietta's benefit without disclosing this information to any other Martin Marietta personnel. Thus, the district court's findings that Bunker "never disclosed inside information relevant to investment decisions" and that the "information that he obtained while a director 'simply wasn't germane to that question at all'" are not significant. 286 F.Supp. at 946. Nor are these findings totally supported by the evidence. Bunker's testimony revealed that while he was a Sperry director three Sperry officials had furnished him with information relating to the "short-range outlook" at Sperry, and, in addition, Bunker admitted discussing Sperry's affairs with two officials at Martin Marietta and participating in sessions when Martin's investment in Sperry was reviewed. Moreover, an unsigned document concededly originating from the Martin Marietta files, entitled "Notes on Exploratory Investment in Sperry Rand Corporation," describing the Sperry management, evaluating their abilities, and analyzing the merit of Sperry's forecasts for the future, further indicates that Martin Marietta may have benefited, or intended to benefit, from Bunker's association with Sperry Rand.

In contrast, in Blau v. Lehman, supra, where Lehman Brothers was the alleged "director," the Lehman partner exercised no power of approval concerning the partnership's investment; was not consulted for advice; had no advance knowledge of Lehman Brothers' intention to purchase the stock of the corporation of which he was a member of the board of directors; and never discussed the operating details of that corporation's affairs with any member of Lehman Brothers. 368 U.S. at 406. Similarly, in Rattner v. Lehman, supra, the court's decision was premised on the assumption that the defendant's purchases and sales were made without any advice or concurrence from the defendant's partner sitting on the Board of the company in whose stock the defendant traded.

It appears to us that a person in Bunker's unique position could act as a deputy for Martin Marietta even in the absence of factors indicating an intention or belief on the part of both companies that he was so acting. We do not hold that, without more, Bunker's control over Martin Marietta, see Marquette Cement Mfg. Co. v. Andreas, supra at 967, or the possibility that inside information was obtained or disclosed, mandates that Bunker was Martin's deputy. However, additional evidence detailed hereafter which indicates that the managements of Sperry Rand and of Martin Marietta intended that Bunker should act as Martin's deputy on the Sperry Board, and believed he was so acting, lends valuable support to our factual conclusion.

First, in Bunker's letter of resignation to General MacArthur, the Chairman of the Board of Directors of Sperry Rand, he stated:

> When I became a member of the Board in April, it appeared to your associates that the Martin Marietta ownership of a substantial number of shares of Sperry Rand should have representation on your Board. This representation does not seem to me really necessary and I prefer not to be involved in the affairs of Sperry Rand when there are so many other demands on my time * * *.

Martin Marietta urges that we should not read this letter to mean what it so clearly says. They would have us believe that this letter was so phrased because Bunker intended "to write a gentle letter of resignation to a great (but elderly) man whom he admired, in terms that he would understand." No matter how advanced in years the Chairman of the Sperry Board may have been, we are puzzled by defendant's contention that he, and only he, of all those on the Sperry Board, considered Bunker to be representing Martin's interests. Furthermore, if, throughout Bunker's service, the Chairman of the Board misunderstood the purpose of Bunker's directorship, why Bunker upon resignation would want this misunderstanding perpetuated is even more perplexing. Certainly the more logical inference from the wording of Bunker's letter of resignation is the inference that Bunker served on the Sperry Board as a representative of Martin Marietta so as to protect Martin's investment in Sperry.

Second, the Board of Directors of Martin Marietta formally consented to and approved Bunker's directorship of Sperry prior to Bunker's acceptance of the position. While Martin's organizational policy required that Bunker secure that Board's approval of any corporate directorship he were offered, the approval was not obtained until, significantly, the Board had been informed by Bunker that Martin had a 10 million dollar investment in Sperry stock at the time. Bunker testified that he "thought the Board would draw the inference that his presence on Sperry's Board would be to Martin's interest." Indeed, as noted by the district court, "the logic behind such an inference is obvious when we stop to consider that a directorship, by its very nature, carries with it potential access to information unavailable to the ordinary investor." 286 F.Supp. at 945. Surely such conduct by the Martin Board supports an inference that it deputized Bunker to represent its interests on Sperry's Board. The trial court's finding to the contrary leaves us with the definite and firm conviction that a mistake was indeed committed.

Finally, Bunker's testimony clearly established that the Martin Marietta Corporation had representatives or deputies who served on the boards of other corporations. The only distinctions drawn by the court below to differentiate Bunker's Sperry relationship from the relationship to Martin Marietta of other Martin Marietta deputies on other corporate boards were that Bunker had no duty to report back to Martin what was going on at Sperry and there was a lesser degree of supervision over Bunker's actions than over the actions of the others. Otherwise Bunker was a typical Martin deputy. In view of Bunker's position of almost absolute authority over Martin's affairs, such differences hardly suffice to refute the evidentiary value of the similarities between the functions of Bunker and those of Martin's representatives on other corporate boards.

In summary, it is our firm conviction that the district court erred in apportioning the weight to be accorded the evidence before it. The control possessed by Bunker, his letter of resignation, the approval by the Martin Board of Bunker's directorship with Sperry, and the functional similarity between Bunker's acts as a Sperry director and the acts of Martin's representatives on other boards, as opposed to the factors relied upon by the trial court, are all definite and concrete indicatives that Bunker, in fact, was a Martin deputy, and we find that indeed he was.

The trial court's disposition of the case obviated the need for it to determine whether § 16(b) liability could attach to the corporate director's short-swing profits realized after the corporation's deputy had ceased to be a member of the board of directors of the corporation whose stock had been so profitably traded in. It was not until after Bunker's resignation from the Sperry Board had become effective that Martin Marietta sold any Sperry stock. The issue is novel and until this case no court has ever considered the question. We hold that the congressional purpose dictates that Martin must disgorge all short-swing profits made from Sperry stock purchased during its Sperry directorship and sold after the termination thereof if sold within six months of purchase.

Relying upon the congressional objectives sought to be accomplished by the passage of § 16(b), this court, in Adler v. Klawans, 267 F.2d 840 (2 Cir. 1959), held that § 16(b) imposes liability to surrender his short-swing profits upon a person who is a director at the date of sale, whether or not he was a director at the date of purchase. * * * It must be emphasized, of course, that the statute evidences a clear legislative intent to treat corporate directors and officers in one category of insiders and 10% shareholders in another. The act expressly sets forth that the liability of a 10% shareholder to surrender his short-swing profits is conditional upon his being such both at the time of purchase and at the time of sale, but there is no such limitation in the case of officers and directors. 267 F.2d at 845; Blau v. Allen, 163 F.Supp. 702, 704 (S.D.N.Y.1958). See also 2 Loss, Securities Regulation 1060 (2d ed. 1961).

Our decision in Adler, however, did not require us to consider the validity of Rule X–16A–10 of the Securities Exchange Commission, 17 C.F.R. § 240.16a–10, which reads:

Any transaction which has been or shall be exempted by the Commission from the requirements of section 16(a) shall, in so far as it is otherwise subject to the provisions of section 16(b), be likewise exempted from section 16(b).

* * *

On the form provided by the SEC for a director to file his statement of changes in stock ownership, the Commission further clarifies a director's obligation to report under § 16(a), as follows:

Form 4

1. Persons Required to File Statements.

Statements on this form are required to be filed by each of the following persons:

(a) Every person who at any time during any calendar month was (i) directly or indirectly the beneficial owner of more than 10 percent of any class of equity securities (other than exempt securities) listed and registered on a national securities exchange, or (ii) a director or officer of the company which is the issuer of such securities, and who during such month had any change in his beneficial ownership of any class of equity securities of such company * * *.

In Adler, this court read this last rule to require a director to report all "changes in his ownership" irrespective of whether the ownership was established "by a director while a director." 267 F.2d at 847. Indeed, § 16(a) itself expressly imposes its requirements on every person "who is a director" or who "becomes such * * * director." Thus, by finding that § 16(a)'s reporting rules extend to a director who became such after the acquisition of securities, we were able to avoid deciding whether Rule X–16A–10 constituted a proper exercise of the Commission's power.

Congress has vested the Commission with broad power to promulgate rules and regulations exempting transactions from the coverage of § 16(b). But, as this court has commented on a previous occasion, the promulgation of rules is not a matter solely within the expertise of the SEC and beyond the scope of judicial review. Greene v. Dietz, 247 F.2d 689, 692–693 (2 Cir. 1957). See also Perlman v. Timberlake, 172 F.Supp. 246, 254–255 (S.D.N.Y. 1959). The Commission's authority, according to the statute, is subject to the limitation that the transactions the SEC exempts are "not comprehended within the purpose" of § 16(b). We must determine, therefore, whether the Commission by exempting from § 16(b) liability any transaction not required to be reported under § 16(a) exceeded the authority delegated to it by Congress.

To be sure, the congressional belief that inside information could be abused, the belief that prompted the prophylactic enactment of § 16(b), is just as germane to the situation when a person is a director only at the time of purchase as when he is a director only at the time of sale. For, in the case of a director who resigns his directorship before the sale it is possible for both the purchase and sale to have been unfairly motivated by insider knowledge; whereas if the purchase were made prior to the directorship only the sale could be motivated by inside information. Clearly, therefore, a "short swing" sale or purchase by a resigning director must be a transaction "comprehended within the purpose of" § 16(b), and to the extent Rule X–16A–10 exempts such a transaction from § 16(b) the Rule is invalid.

* * *

Arguably, however, § 16(b) itself, as well as, arguably, the SEC regulations, limits liability to only those persons encompassed within the meaning of subsection (a), for subsection (b) applies to "such beneficial owner, director, or officer," and, when literally read, this language probably means only such beneficial owner, director, or officer as described in subsection (a). So semanticizing, it would follow that if a person has no duty to report pursuant to § 16(a) he ought not to be required to relinquish his short-swing profits under § 16(b). SEC Form 4, however, which governs the reporting provision of § 16(a) seems to extend the reporting requirement to ex-directors so as to include the calendar month during which their directorships terminate. Consequently, even if we found Rule X–16A–10 to be a valid Rule, there is no difficulty in finding that liability under § 16(b) can attach to ex-directors for transactions executed within the calendar month of their resignations. Unlike Rule X–16A–10, Form 4 is entirely consistent with and in furtherance of the legislative purpose of § 16.

While Form 4 represents a proper exercise by the Commission of its rule-making power it is arbitrarily inadequate. For example, it would permit a director of a corporation to purchase its stock within six months prior to September 3, during his directorship, resign on August 31, sell the stock on September 2, and not have any obligation to report the sales transaction, but if he had resigned on September 1 he would have had a duty to report the September 2 transaction. Such an arbitrary rule provides an unnecessary loophole in the effective operation of the statutory scheme. While we do not here determine the effect of Form 4 on the scope of § 16(a), we do point out that the Form 4 reporting requirement here mentioned extends § 16(b) putative liability to the extent of that requirement. Therefore, inasmuch as Form 4, a valid exercise of the SEC's power, has already extended § 16(b) to cover, in part, an ex-director's activities, a less arbitrarily defined reporting requirement for ex-directors is but a logical extension of § 16(b) coverage, would be a coverage in line with the congressional aims, and would afford greater assurance that the lawmakers' intent will be effectuated. In view of the foregoing, we hold that § 16(b) applies to a sale of corporate stock by a former director of that corporation if the stock were purchased by him (or purchased by any jural person that had "deputized" him) during the time he was a director and the sale was made within six months after purchase.

Under the well-established rule, profits for § 16(b) purposes are computed by arbitrarily matching purchases with sales in order to obtain the maximum amount of profits. Gratz v. Claughton, 187 F.2d 46 (2d Cir.1951); Smolowe v. Delendo Corporation, 136 F.2d 231 (2 Cir.), cert. denied 320 U.S. 751 * * * (1943). As the briefs do not agree as to the exact amount of the profits Martin Marietta made and do not give us all the relevant date for us to make a correct determination, and as, additionally, the trial court has discretion in connection with an award of interest in a § 16(b) suit, we remand the case to the district court with instructions to proceed with these determinations.

Reversed and remanded.

SECTION 16(b)—THE "RUSSIAN ROULETTE" SECTION OF THE EXCHANGE ACT

During the Congressional hearings on the Exchange Act, Section 16(b) was described as a "crude" rule-of-thumb.[1] There was never a more accurate description given of proposed legislation. Judging solely from the facts stated in the opinions in the decided cases, the function of Section 16(b) would appear to be to impose unjust liability upon entirely innocent persons.[2] However, the justification of the section lies supposedly in its *in terrorem* effect upon potential inside manipulators. It has never been demonstrated whether this principle of "Punish the innocent, in order to terrorize the guilty" works to any extent, and no one has even made an attempt to produce such evidence. It would seem clear, however, that any moderately bright manipulator should be able in many cases to string out his activities over a period of more than six months and thus escape any penalty under the section.[3] Nevertheless, the Advisers to the American Law Institute's Federal Securities Code Project were told by the Reporter that no discussion would be permitted of the policy of Section 16(b); it had to be accepted as sacred.[4]

1. "You hold the director, irrespective of any intention or expectation to sell the security within six months after, because it will be absolutely impossible to prove the existence of such intention or expectation, and you have to have this crude rule of thumb. * * *" Hearings before the Committee on Banking and Currency on S. 84, 72d Cong., 2d Sess., and S. 56 and S. 97, 73d Cong., 1st and 2d Sess., 1934, 6557, quoted in Smolowe v. Delendo Corp., 136 F.2d 231, at 235 (2d Cir.1943), cert. denied 320 U.S. 751 (1943).

In the District Court opinion in the Provident Securities Co. case, infra, p. 1409, the Judge said that to hold the defendant liable in that case would be the application "of an extremely crude rule of a most deformed and misshapen thumb." 331 F.Supp. 787, 791–92 (N.D.Cal.1971).

2. In Western Auto Supply Co. v. Gamble-Skogmo, Inc., 348 F.2d 736 (8th Cir. 1965), cert. denied 382 U.S. 987 (1966), Gamble-Skogmo purchased 25,942 shares of the stock of its subsidiary, Western Auto Supply Company at $32.35 per share, and simultaneously contributed these shares to its profit-sharing trust for the benefit of its employees. Within less than six months it sold all of its previous holdings in Western Auto, over 1,200,000 shares, to Beneficial Finance Co. for $36.00 per share. Beneficial through its new subsidiary, Western Auto, recovered from Gamble-Skogmo over $94,000 representing the "profit" obtained by matching the purchase of the 25,942 shares with the sale of that number of

shares to Beneficial. The court stated: "We * * * have noted the reference to the ethical position of Beneficial in seeking to recover, in effect, a part of the purchase price it willingly paid for the stock. The punctilios of the parties are not an issue here." 348 F.2d at 743, n. 7. Or, in other words, justice has nothing whatever to do with Section 16(b). This has been the attitude of almost all courts, following Smolowe v. Delendo Corporation, supra note 1, which held that despite the preamble to the section it establishes an absolute rule of liability, and there is no necessity to show any actual misuse of inside information. The Western Auto Supply Company case is typical of almost all reported Section 16(b) litigation. The courts themselves have employed such phrases as "Draconian" and "purposeless harshness" in connection with Section 16(b).

3. It should be noted that, while proof that there was no misuse of inside information does not avoid liability under Section 16(b), neither does proof of actual misuse of inside information establish liability, if the insider has manipulated not only the stock but also his transactions so that they fall outside the wholly arbitrary rules of that section.

4. Although refusing to permit any discussion of the basic policy of Section 16(b), on the basis that Congress would not permit any tampering with it, the Reporter unilaterally changed the language to overrule the Provident Securities Co. case (see page 1409, below) and the Reliance Electric

In recent years, following the Supreme Court opinion in the Kern County Land Co. case (p. 1418, infra), the courts have indicated that this mathematical approach to the application of Section 16(b) will not be followed with respect to so-called "unorthodox transactions" of purchase or sale (see pp. 1429–1431, infra). However, the cases have continued to insist upon the application of the "automatic" or mathematical approach to liability under the section when the transactions involved did not fall within what the courts have regarded as the Supreme Court's conception of "unorthodoxy." [5]

PROCEDURE UNDER SECTION 16(b)

Although Section 16(b) authorizes a suit under that section in "any court of competent jurisdiction," it has been held that the federal courts have exclusive jurisdiction of such suits, regardless of the amount in controversy, under the provisions of Section 27 of the Exchange Act.[6] Suit may be commenced in any district "wherein any act or transaction constituting the violation occurred," [7] as well as any district wherein the defendant is found or is an inhabitant or transacts business. If any of the sales or purchases involved was made on an exchange, the transaction on the exchange was part of the "act or transaction constituting the violation" and suit may be brought in the district where the exchange is located.[8] This is true even though only some of the purchases or sales involved occurred on that exchange and even though those particular purchases and sales produced no recoverable profit.[9] Process may be served anywhere in the world.[10] These rules permit the vast majority of Section 16(b) suits to be brought in the Southern District of New York, where the so-called "16(b) bar" is located.

The only method of enforcement of Section 16(b) provided by the statute is a suit by the issuer or, if the issuer fails or refuses to bring the suit, by "the owner of any security of the issuer in the name and in behalf of the issuer." Where a security owner brings suit on behalf of the issuer, he is entitled to an allowance for attorney's fees out of the recovery. Since such allowance will in many cases provide "the sole stimulus for the enforcement of Section 16(b)," it should not be "too niggardly." [11] Neither the fact that the plaintiff's sole motive in bringing the suit is to obtain an allowance for attorney's fees nor the fact that the conduct of the attorney in connection with the suit is champertous and criminal under state law is a defense to the action,[12] nor a bar to the allowance of attorney's fees.[13] While it was held in Fistel v. Christ-

Company case (see page 1416, below) in the United States Supreme Court. See ALI Federal Securities Code, Section 1714(d).

5. Allis-Chalmers Manufacturing Co. v. Gulf & Western Industries, Inc., 527 F.2d 335 (7th Cir.1975); Provident Securities Co. v. Foremost-McKesson, Inc., 506 F.2d 601 (9th Cir.1974), aff'd 423 U.S. 232 (1976).

6. American Distilling Co. v. Brown, 295 N.Y. 36, 64 N.E.2d 347 (1945).

7. Securities Exchange Act of 1934, § 27.

8. Gratz v. Claughton, 187 F.2d 46 (2d Cir.1951); Blau v. Mission Corp., 212 F.2d 77 (2d Cir.1954), cert. denied 347 U.S. 1016; Grossman v. Young, 70 F.Supp. 970 (S.D. N.Y.1947); Roth v. Fund of Funds, Ltd., 279 F.Supp. 935 (S.D.N.Y.1968).

9. Blau v. Lamb, 20 F.R.D. 411 (S.D. N.Y.1957). The court said: "There probably never was a more tenuous thread of jurisdiction but I think it holds." 20 F.R.D. at 414.

10. Securities Exchange Act of 1934, § 27.

11. Smolowe v. Delendo Corp., 136 F.2d 231, at 241 (2d Cir.1943), cert. denied 320 U.S. 751.

12. Magida v. Continental Can Co., Inc., 231 F.2d 843 (2d Cir.1956), cert. denied 351 U.S. 972.

13. Magida v. Continental Can Co., Inc., CCH Fed.Sec.L.Rptr. ¶ 90,777 (S.D.N.Y. 1956). Some fees which have been allowed to the plaintiff's counsel: $41,057 out of a recovery of $418,127 [Park & Tilford, Inc.

man [14] that a settlement of a Section 16(b) suit was improper when it was conditioned upon the defendant or the corporation paying a fee to counsel for the plaintiff and nothing to the corporation, Judge Palmieri in that case stated: "The parties have brought to my attention two cases in which judges in this district approved dismissals conditioned upon the defendant 'insider' paying the plaintiff's attorney a fee. Attorney for plaintiff in this case represented the plaintiff in both of those cases. In one * * * he received a $4,000 fee from the defendant 'insider.' The corporation received nothing. * * * In the other he received a $3,000 fee one-half of which was payable by the defendant 'insider' and the other half by the corporation for the benefit of which the action was brought." [15]

The requirement of Rule 23.1 that the plaintiff in a derivative action allege that he was a shareholder at the time of the transaction of which he complains or that his shares thereafter devolved on him by operation of law is not applicable to an action under Section 16(b). [16] Nor is a state security-for-expenses statute relating to the ordinary derivative action applicable to Section 16(b) litigation. [17] The plaintiff must, however, be a security holder of "the issuer"; a security holder of the parent of the issuer does not have standing to sue under Section 16(b), even though the issuer has been extinguished by merger and the surviving corporation is a wholly-owned subsidiary of a publicly-held company. [18]

Section 16(b) authorizes an action by a security holder only "if the issuer shall fail or refuse to bring such suit within sixty days after request or shall fail diligently to prosecute the same thereafter." However, such 60–day notice to the corporation is excused if it is alleged that the defendant dominates the corporation and that therefore a demand would be futile, [19] or that the statute of limitations will run on the cause of action before the elapse of the 60–day

---

v. Schulte, CCH Fed.Sec.L.Rptr. ¶ 90,413 (S.D.N.Y.1948)]; $17,000 out of a recovery of $79,635 [Levin v. Yates, CCH Fed.Sec.L. Rptr. ¶ 90,494 (S.D.N.Y.1950)]; $12,000 out of a recovery of $47,000 [Magida v. Continental Can Co., Inc., CCH Fed.Sec.L.Rptr. ¶ 90,777 (S.D.N.Y.1956)]; $3,000 out of a recovery of $18,894 [Smolowe v. Delendo Corp., 136 F.2d 231 (2d Cir.1943), cert. denied 320 U.S. 751, 64 S.Ct. 56]; $7,500 out of a recovery of $37,795.52 [Blau v. Brown and Western Nuclear, Inc., CCH Fed.Sec. Law Rptr. ¶ 92,263 (S.D.N.Y.1968)]; $1,800 out of a recovery of $9,030.97 [Blau v. Berkey and Berkey Photo, Inc., CCH Fed.Sec. Law Rptr. ¶ 92,264 (S.D.N.Y.1968)]; $35,000 out of a recovery of $407,994.08 [Bernstein v. Kennelly, 433 F.2d 10 (9th Cir.1970)]; $750,000 out of a recovery of over $8,000,000 [Newmark v. RKO General, Inc., 332 F.Supp. 161 (S.D.N.Y.1971)— counsel had asked for $2,500,000 in this case]. Even if the insider voluntarily pays the profit to the corporation without suit, a security holder who called the attention of the corporation to the liability of the insider may be entitled to an allowance for attorney's fees "if the corporation has done

nothing for a substantial period of time after the suspect transactions and its inaction is likely to continue." Blau v. Rayette-Faberge, Inc., 389 F.2d 469 (2d Cir. 1968). Cf. Dottenheim v. Emerson Electric Manufacturing Co., 77 F.Supp. 306 (E.D. N.Y.1948).

14. 133 F.Supp. 300 (S.D.N.Y.1955).

15. 133 F.Supp. at 302, n. 3.

16. Blau v. Mission Corp., 212 F.2d 77 (2d Cir.1954), cert. denied 347 U.S. 1016; Dottenheim v. Murchison, 227 F.2d 737 (5th Cir.1955), cert. denied 351 U.S. 919 (1956); Blau v. Ogsbury, CCH Fed.Sec.L. Rptr. ¶ 90,635 (S.D.N.Y.1953), aff'd 210 F.2d 426 (2d Cir.1954).

17. Truncale v. Blumberg, CCH Fed. Sec.Law Rptr. ¶ 90,470 (S.D.N.Y.1949); cf. McClure v. Borne Chemical Co., 292 F.2d 824 (3d Cir.1961), cert. denied 368 U.S. 939 (1961).

18. Lewis v. McAdam, 762 F.2d 800 (9th Cir.1985).

19. Netter v. Ashland Paper Mills, Inc., 19 F.R.D. 529 (S.D.N.Y.1956); Weisman v. Spector, 158 F.Supp. 789 (S.D.N.Y.1958).

period.[20] Intervention by a security holder in an action brought by the corporation is liberally granted to avoid any possibility of collusion.[21]

Since Section 16(b) permits an action at law or in equity, the plaintiff has an option to demand a jury trial or not; the defendant cannot demand a jury trial if the plaintiff does not, since the failure of the plaintiff to do so indicates his election to have the action tried as an equitable action.[22]

Section 16(b) provides that no action thereunder "shall be brought more than two years after the date such profit was realized." However, the failure of an officer, director or 10% holder to file reports of his transactions in securities as required by Section 16(a) tolls the running of the two-year statute of limitations.[23] It was held in Truncale v. Universal Pictures Co., Inc.[24] that a minority shareholder had no cause of action under New York law against the directors of a corporation for "waste of corporate assets" because they permitted the statute of limitations to run on an action of the corporation under Section 16(b), since the minority shareholder himself had a statutory right of action when the corporation did not sue. This would seem to be a less-than-satisfactory explanation for the decision.

"OFFICER OR DIRECTOR"

The term "officer" has been defined by the SEC as meaning a president, vice-president, treasurer, secretary, comptroller, and any other person who performs functions corresponding to those performed by the foregoing,[25] and the General Counsel of the SEC has ruled that an assistant-treasurer, assistant-secretary or assistant-comptroller is not an officer for this purpose so long as his duties are performed under the supervision of his chief.[26] Although the Second Circuit in dictum has questioned the validity of this rule and contradicted the opinion of the General Counsel,[27] both have been upheld in the actual decisions.[28] An officer of a subsidiary of the issuer has been held not to be subject to Section 16(b), unless he is in fact performing the functions of an officer of the parent corporation.[29]

20. Grossman v. Young, 72 F.Supp. 375 (S.D.N.Y.1947); Benisch v. Cameron, 81 F.Supp. 882 (S.D.N.Y.1948).

21. Park & Tilford, Inc. v. Schulte, 160 F.2d 984 (2d Cir.1947), cert. denied 332 U.S. 761; Pellegrino v. Nesbit, 203 F.2d 463 (9th Cir.1953). However, the order granting leave to intervene may provide that the intervenor shall receive no allowance for attorney's fees for services which duplicate those of counsel for the corporation. Berkey & Gay Furniture Co. v. Wigmore, CCH Fed.Sec.L.Rptr. ¶ 90,376 (S.D. N.Y.1947). An independent action may be maintained for attorneys' fees under Section 16(b) even though the short-swing profits were voluntarily repaid, where it is alleged that investigation by plaintiff's attorney led to that action. Coran v. Snap-on Tools Corp., 408 F.Supp. 1060 (E.D.Wis. 1976).

22. Dottenheim v. Emerson Electric Manufacturing Co., 7 F.R.D. 343 (E.D.N.Y. 1947); Arbetman v. Playford and Alaska Airlines, Inc., 83 F.Supp. 335 (S.D.N.Y. 1949).

23. Grossman v. Young, 72 F.Supp. 375 (S.D.N.Y.1947); Blau v. Albert, CCH Fed. Sec.L.Rptr. ¶ 90,836 (S.D.N.Y.1957); Carr-Consolidated Biscuit Co. v. Moore, 125 F.Supp. 423 (M.D.Pa.1954).

24. 76 F.Supp. 465 (S.D.N.Y.1948).

25. Rule 3b–2.

26. Securities Exchange Act Release No. 2687 (SEC 1940).

27. Colby v. Klune, 178 F.2d 872 (2d Cir.1949).

28. Lockheed Aircraft Corp. v. Rathman, 106 F.Supp. 810 (S.D.Cal.1952); Lockheed Aircraft Corp. v. Campbell, 110 F.Supp. 282 (S.D.Cal.1953).

29. Lee National Corp. v. Segur, 281 F.Supp. 851 (E.D.Pa.1968). However, a person who was the "Executive Vice-President of International Operations" of a corporation and "one of the more active members of the executive committee" did not get anywhere with the argument that he was "merely a figurehead" and should not be liable under Section 16(b). Selas Corpo-

In Merrill Lynch, Pierce, Fenner & Smith, Inc. v. Livingston [30] the Ninth Circuit held that a securities salesman who was given the "honorary" title of vice president was not an officer with access to inside information within the coverage of Section 16(b). The court said that it must look behind the title of the person to ascertain his real duties and that "A person who does not have the title of an officer may, in fact, have a relationship to the company which gives him the very access to insider information that the statute was designed to reach." This dictum would seem to throw the question of who is an "officer" completely at large, in contrast to the rather mechanical approach to this question which has been followed by other courts in the past. This dictum was limited, however, in the subsequent case of National Medical Enterprises, Inc. v. Small [31] to a situation where the person's title "is essentially honorary or ceremonial."

While the Supreme Court in the case of Blau v. Lehman [32] indicated that one person may be "deputed" to act for another on the board of directors, thereby making the principal a "director" for the purposes of Section 16(b), it also made clear that the actual fact of such "deputizing" must be proven by the plaintiff. To what extent, if any, does the court in the *Feder* case broaden this principle?

It has been held that an officer or director is liable under Section 16(b) for short-swing profits even though he only holds such office at the time of the sale and not at the time of the prior purchase.[33] The same result was reached in the *Feder* case where he was only an officer or director at the time of the purchase and not at the time of the sale. The Seventh Circuit indicated in dictum in Allis-Chalmers Manufacturing Co. v. Gulf & Western Industries, Inc.[34] that it would not hold the director or officer liable unless he was an "insider" (i.e., a director or officer) at both ends of the transaction, but so far all of the cases are against that proposition and the Supreme Court reserved judgment on it in footnote 16 to its opinion in the Provident Securities Co. case (infra, p. 1409).

The Second Circuit's attempt in the *Feder* case to invalidate Rule 16a–10, which exempts from liability any transaction which has been exempted from *filing* by a rule of the Commission, was expressly repudiated by the Supreme Court in Reliance Electric Co. v. Emerson Electric Co.[35] Anyway, the instruction to Form 4 referred to would not seem to be an "exemption" from filing; it merely indicated that the officer or director had to continue to file during the month he ceased to be such.[36] Presumably in the absence of this instruction he could have quit filing as soon as he ceased to be an officer or director. In any event, the SEC subsequently amended its rules to require filing with respect to transactions during the six months before a director or officer takes office and

ration of America v. Voogd, 365 F.Supp. 1268 (E.D.Pa.1973).

30. 566 F.2d 1119 (9th Cir.1978).

31. 680 F.2d 83 (9th Cir.1982).

32. 368 U.S. 403 (1962).

33. Adler v. Klawans, 267 F.2d 840 (2d Cir.1959). Followed in Marquette Cement Manufacturing Co. v. Andreas, 239 F.Supp. 962 (S.D.N.Y.1965). It has also been held that an officer or director may be liable for short-swing profits on stock which was registered at the time of the purchase or sale, although not at the time of the matching transaction less than six months earlier. Arrow Distributing Corporation v. Baum-

gartner, 783 F.2d 1274 (5th Cir.1986); Perfect Photo, Inc. v. Grabb, 205 F.Supp. 569 (E.D.Pa.1962); Perfect Photo, Inc. v. Sentiff, 205 F.Supp. 574 (E.D.Pa.1962).

34. 527 F.2d 335 (7th Cir.1975).

35. 404 U.S. 418 (1972), reh. denied 405 U.S. 969. The Court said that "the Commission has used its power to grant exemptions under § 16(b) to exclude from liability any transaction that does not fall within the reporting requirements of § 16(a)" citing Rule 16(a)–10. 404 U.S. at 426.

36. Compare 2 Loss, Securities Regulation 1061 (2d ed. 1961).

for six months after he leaves.[37] Both the Second Circuit [38] and the Third Circuit [39] have held that this does not impose liability upon a director or officer where both ends of the transaction occur *after* he leaves office, even though within six months thereafter and therefore reportable.

"BENEFICIAL OWNER"

Section 16(a) by requiring reports of changes in "beneficial ownership" of securities makes it clear that the liability for a purchase and sale, or sale and purchase, under Section 16(b) may result from transactions in securities of which the officer, director or 10% holder is not the record owner. In 1935 the General Counsel of the SEC ruled that a husband is considered to be the beneficial owner of securities held by his wife "if he has benefits substantially equivalent to those of ownership by reason of any contract, understanding, relationship, agreement or otherwise." [40] However, on January 19, 1966, the SEC issued a release greatly expanding this concept, and stating: "*Generally* a person is regarded as the beneficial owner of securities held in the name of his or her spouse and their minor children. Absent special circumstances such relationship *ordinarily* results in such person obtaining benefits substantially equivalent to ownership. * * * Accordingly, a person *ordinarily* should include in his reports filed pursuant to Section 16(a) securities held in the name of a spouse or minor children as being beneficially owned by him." [41] In a subsequent release the SEC emphasized that it was addressing itself only to the information required to be included in reports under Section 16(a), and stated: "The fact that ownership of securities and transactions in those securities are reported under Section 16(a) * * * does not necessarily mean that liability will result therefrom under Section 16(b)." [42]

In Whiting v. Dow Chemical Co.,[43] which held that purchases by the husband-director could be matched with sales by his wife of shares of the company owned as her separate property to impose Section 16(b) liability, Judge Gurfein stated:

" 'Beneficial owner' is the language of § 16(a) and we have been told to read the words of § 16(b) not literally. In the broader sense, we think the term should be read more expansively than it would be in the law of trusts. For purposes of the family unit, shares to which legal title is held by one spouse may be said to be 'beneficially owned' by the other, the insider, if the ordinary rewards of ownership are used for their joint benefit. These rewards are generally the dividend income as well as the capital gains on sale and the power to dispose of the shares to their children by gift or upon death.

"While we cannot earmark the proceeds of Mrs. Whiting's particular sales as going to household and family support, we know from the findings that the larger part of their joint maintenance came from her estate, the

---

37. SEC Sec.Exch.Act Rel. No. 8697 (Sept. 18, 1969).

38. Lewis v. Varnes, 505 F.2d 785 (2d Cir.1974).

39. Lewis v. Mellon Bank, 513 F.2d 921 (3d Cir.1975).

40. Securities Exchange Act Release No. 175 (SEC 1935). A director, officer or 10% holder is liable for the full amount of the profit realized on a short-swing trans-action even though the securities are the community property of himself and his wife. Walet v. Jefferson Lake Sulphur Co., 202 F.2d 433 (5th Cir.1953), cert. denied 346 U.S. 820.

41. Securities Exchange Act Release No. 7793 (SEC 1966) (Italics added).

42. Securities Exchange Act Release No. 7824 (SEC 1966).

43. 523 F.2d 680 (2d Cir.1975).

bulk of it in Dow stock. We also know that they engaged in joint estate planning. So that while it is true that if they ever separated, Mrs. Whiting would take her Dow shares, it is also true that while they continue to live as a married couple, there is hardly anything Mrs. Whiting gets out of the ownership that appellant does not share." [44]

The SEC has also defined beneficial ownership as including ownership of securities *as trustee* where (a) the trust holds more than 10% of the equity securities in question, or (b) where any ancestor, descendant or spouse of the trustee has a vested beneficial interest in the income or corpus of the trust, including step-parents and step-children and adoptive relationships.[45] For example, the ownership of securities as trustee is considered the beneficial ownership of the trustee if his step-son has a beneficial interest in the trust. The SEC in adopting these rules stated that they were "not to be construed as imposing any obligations or liabilities under Section 16(b). They are designed solely as interpretative and exemptive rules affecting Section 16(a)." [46] Marquette Cement Manufacturing Co. v. Andreas [47] refused to impose liability under Section 16(b) on the basis of these rules. Also, in CBI Industries, Inc. v. Horton [48] the court refused to apply these rules to an action under Section 16(b) but on the clearly erroneous basis that Rule 16a–8 applies only to determine who is a ten-percent shareholder. The court in that case distinguished the *Whiting* case and the *Whittaker* case on the basis that the defendant director did not receive any "direct pecuniary benefit" from the sale by the trust of which he was a co-trustee.

On the other hand, any interest as settlor or beneficiary in a trust where less than 20% in market value of the securities in the trust consist of the equity security in question or where trust transactions in such security are made without prior approval by the settlor or beneficiary, and ownership as beneficiary of a remainder interest in a trust, are not considered beneficial ownership.[49] These rules apply to Section 16(b) as well as Section 16(a).[50]

With respect to securities owned by a corporation of which the officer, director or 10% holder is a shareholder, an opinion of the General Counsel of the SEC indicated that the shareholder would be considered the beneficial owner of the securities held by the corporation if the corporation "merely provides a medium through which one person, or several persons in a small group, invest or trade in securities." [51] In the *Andreas* case [52] the court held, without any discussion, that Mr. Andreas was liable for 19% of the profit made by a corporation of which he owned (through a trust) 19% of the stock, although the corporation also owned and operated a "bowling alley and recrea-

44. See, also, Whittaker v. Whittaker Corp., 639 F.2d 516 (9th Cir.1981), cert. denied 454 U.S. 1031 (1981) in which the court held that a corporate insider who exercised virtually complete control over his mother's affairs by virtue of a power of attorney was the "beneficial owner" of her securities for the purposes of Section 16(b), since he enjoyed "benefits substantially equivalent to those of ownership." Compare Blau v. Potter, CCH Fed.Sec.Law Rptr. ¶ 94,115 (S.D.N.Y.1973).

45. Rule 16a–8(a), (c) and (e).

46. Securities Exchange Act Release No. 4801 (SEC 1953).

47. 239 F.Supp. 962 (S.D.N.Y.1965).

48. 682 F.2d 643 (7th Cir.1982).

49. Rule 15a–8(b) and (f). However, clause (f) of this Rule was amended in 1965 to restrict its applicability solely to the question of determining whether a person is a 10% owner. Securities Exchange Act Release No. 7525 (SEC 1965). Therefore, this portion of the rule no longer applies to exclude from "beneficial ownership" a remainder interest owned by an officer or director or by a person who is otherwise a 10% holder.

50. Rule 16a–10.

51. Securities Exchange Act Release No. 1965 (SEC 1938). See Boston & Maine R. v. Hillman, CCH Fed.Sec.L.Rptr. ¶ 90,813 (S.D.N.Y.1957).

52. Supra, note 47.

tion center" in addition to the equity securities in question, and certainly could not be described as merely a "medium" through which he and his family "invested or traded in securities." The lack of any rationale for this result in that case, however, considerably dilutes its value as a precedent.[53]

See Block and Barton, Section 16(b) of the Exchange Act: An Archaic Insider Trading Statute in Need of Reform, 12 Sec.Reg.L.J. 203 (1984); Darm, Short-Swing Profits in Failed Take-Over Bids—The Role of Section 16(b), 59 Wash.L.Rev. 895 (1984); Tomlinson, Application of Section 16(b) to Tax-Qualified Employee Benefit Plans, 33 Stan.L.Rev. 231 (1981); Husband and Powers, Section 16(b) of the Securities Exchange Act of 1934 and Insider Trading Involving Issuer-Granted Employee Stock Options, 57 Denver L.J. 71 (1979); Deitz, A Practical Look at Section 16(b) of the Securities Exchange Act, 43 Ford. L.Rev. 1 (1974); Bateman, The Pragmatic Interpretation of Section 16(b) and the Need for Clarification, 45 St. John's L.Rev. 772 (1971); Wagner, Deputization under Section 16(b); The Implications of Feder v. Martin Marietta Corporation, 78 Yale L.J. 1151 (1969); Munter, Section 16(b) of the Securities Exchange Act of 1934: An Alternative to "Burning Down the Barn in Order to Kill the Rats", 52 Corn.L.Q. 69 (1966); Shreve, Beneficial Ownership of Securities Held by Family Members, 22 Bus.Law. 431 (1967); 2 Loss, Securities Regulation 1040–58, 1087–90, 1091–95, 1100–1108 (2d ed. 1961).

FOREMOST–McKESSON, INC. v. PROVIDENT SECURITIES CO.

United States Supreme Court, 1976.
423 U.S. 232, 96 S.Ct. 508, 46 L.Ed.2d 464.

MR. JUSTICE POWELL delivered the opinion of the Court.

This case presents an unresolved issue under § 16(b) of the Securities Exchange Act of 1934 (the Act), 48 Stat. 896, 15 U.S.C. § 78p(b). That section of the Act was designed to prevent a corporate director or officer or "the beneficial owner of more than 10 per centum" of a corporation from profiteering through short-swing securities transactions on the basis of inside information. It provides that a corporation may capture for itself the profits realized on a purchase and sale, or sale and purchase, of its securities within six months by a director, officer, or beneficial owner. Section 16(b)'s last sentence, however, provides that it "shall not be construed to cover any transaction where such beneficial owner was not such both at the time of the purchase and sale, or the sale and purchase, of the security involved * * *." The question presented here is whether a person purchasing securities that put his holdings above the 10% level is a beneficial owner "at the time of the purchase" so that he must account for profits realized on a sale of those securities within six months. The United States Court of Appeals for the Ninth Circuit answered this question in the negative. 506 F.2d 601 (1974). We affirm.

---

53. Contra: Popkin v. Dingman, 366 F.Supp. 534 (S.D.N.Y.1973). See, also, Blau v. Mission Corp., 212 F.2d 77 (2d Cir. 1954), cert. denied 347 U.S. 1016. For a case involving an attempt by the officer-director to divert the profits of the transactions from himself to escape Section 16(b) liability, see Mouldings, Inc. v. Potter, 465 F.2d 1101 (5th Cir.1972), cert. denied 410 U.S. 929.

I

Respondent, Provident Securities Co., was a personal holding company. In 1968 Provident decided tentatively to liquidate and dissolve, and it engaged an agent to find a purchaser for its assets. Petitioner, Foremost-McKesson, Inc., emerged as a potential purchaser, but extensive negotiations were required to resolve a disagreement over the nature of the consideration Foremost would pay. Provident wanted cash in order to facilitate its dissolution, while Foremost wanted to pay with its own securities.

Eventually a compromise was reached, and Provident and Foremost executed a purchase agreement embodying their deal on September 25, 1969. The agreement provided that Foremost would buy two-thirds of Provident's assets for $4.25 million in cash and $49.75 million in Foremost convertible subordinated debentures. The agreement further provided that Foremost would register under the Securities Act of 1933 $25 million in principal amount of the debentures and would participate in an underwriting agreement by which those debentures would be sold to the public. At the closing on October 15, 1969, Foremost delivered to Provident the cash and a $40 million debenture that was subsequently exchanged for two debentures in the principal amounts of $25 million and $15 million. Foremost also delivered a $2.5 million debenture to an escrow on the closing date. On October 20 Foremost delivered to Provident a $7.25 million debenture representing the balance of the purchase price. These debentures were immediately convertible into more than 10% of Foremost's outstanding common stock.

On October 21 Provident, Foremost, and a group of underwriters executed an underwriting agreement to be closed on October 28. The agreement provided for sale to the underwriters of the $25 million debenture. On October 24 Provident distributed the $15 million and $7.25 million debentures to its stockholders, reducing the amount of Foremost common into which the company's holdings were convertible to less than 10%. On October 28 the closing under the underwriting agreement was accomplished. Provident thereafter distributed the cash proceeds of the debenture sale to its stockholders and dissolved.

Provident's holdings in Foremost debentures as of October 20 were large enough to make it a beneficial owner of Foremost within the meaning of § 16. Having acquired and disposed of these securities within six months, Provident faced the prospect of a suit by Foremost to recover any profits realized on the sale of the debenture to the underwriters. Provident therefore sued for a declaration that it was not liable to Foremost under § 16(b). The District Court granted summary judgment for Provident and the Court of Appeals affirmed.

Provident's principal argument below for nonliability was based on Kern County Land Co. v. Occidental Petroleum Corp., 411 U.S. 582 (1973). There we held that an "unorthodox transaction" in securities that did not present the possibility of speculative abuse of inside information was not a "sale" within the meaning of § 16(b). Provident contended that its reluctant acceptance of Foremost debentures in exchange for its assets was an "unorthodox transaction" not presenting the possibility of speculative abuse and therefore was not a "purchase" within the meaning of § 16(b).

Although the District Court's pre-Kern County opinion had adopted this type of analysis, 331 F.Supp. 787 (ND Cal.1971), the Court of Appeals rejected it, reasoning that Provident's acquisition of the debentures was not "unorthodox" and that the circumstances did not preclude the possibility of speculative abuse. 506 F.2d, at 604–605.

The Court of Appeals then considered two theories of nonliability based on § 16(b)'s exemptive provision: "This subsection shall not be construed to cover any transaction where such beneficial owner was not such both at the time of the purchase and sale, or the sale and purchase * * *." The first was Provident's argument that it was not a beneficial owner "at the time of * * * sale." After the October 24 distribution of some debentures to stockholders, the debentures held by Provident were convertible into less than 10% of Foremost's outstanding common stock. Provident contended that its sale to the underwriters did not occur until the underwriting agreement was closed on October 28. If this were the case, the sale would not have been covered by § 16(b), since Provident would not have been a beneficial owner "at the time of * * * sale." The Court of Appeals rejected this argument because it found that the sale occurred on October 21 upon execution of the underwriting agreement.

The Court of Appeals then turned to the theory of nonliability based on the exemptive provision that we consider here.[8] It held that in a purchase-sale sequence the phrase "at the time of the purchase," "must be construed to mean prior to the time when the decision to purchase is made." 506 F.2d at 614. Thus, although Provident became a beneficial owner of Foremost by acquiring the debentures, it was not a beneficial owner "at the time of the purchase." Accordingly, the exemptive provision prevented any § 16(b) liability on Provident's part.

II

The meaning of the exemptive provision has been disputed since § 16(b) was first enacted. The discussion has focused on the application of the provision to a purchase-sale sequence, the principal disagreement being whether "at the time of the purchase" means "before the purchase" or "immediately after the purchase." The difference in construction is determinative of a beneficial owner's liability in cases such as Provident's where such owner sells within six months of purchase the securities the acquisition of which made him a beneficial owner. The commentators divided immediately over which construction Congress intended,[10] and they remain divided.[11] The courts of appeals also are in disagreement over the issue.

---

8. Our holding on this issue disposes of this case by precluding any liability on Provident's part. We therefore do not consider whether the Court of Appeals properly rejected Provident's arguments based on Kern County and on the sale not having occurred until October 28.

10. Compare C. Meyer, The Securities Exchange Act of 1934, at 112 (1934) (adopting a "before" construction), with Seligman, Problems Under the Securities Exchange Act, 21 Va.L.Rev. 1, 19–20 (1934) (adopting an "immediately after" construction).

11. Compare, e.g. Munter, Section 16(b) of the Securities Exchange Act of 1934: An Alternative to "Burning Down the Barn in Order to Kill the Rats," 52 Cornell L.Q. 69, 74–75 (1966); Note, Insider Liability for Short-Swing Profits: The Substance and Function of the Pragmatic Approach, 72 Mich.L.Rev. 592, 616–619 (1974); Comment, 9 Stan.L.Rev. 582 (1957) (adopting a "before" construction), with, e.g., 2 L. Loss, Securities Regulation 1060 (2d ed. 1961) (favoring an "immediately after" construction). The weight of the commentary appears to be with the "before the purchase" construction. The ALI Federal Securities

The question of what Congress intended to accomplish by the exemptive provision in a purchase-sale sequence came to a court of appeals for the first time in Stella v. Graham-Paige Motors Corp., 232 F.2d 299 (CA2), cert. denied 352 U.S. 831 (1956). There the Court of Appeals for the Second Circuit without discussion, but over a dissent, affirmed the District Court's adoption of the "immediately after the purchase" construction. That court had been impelled to this construction at least in part by concern over what the phrase "at the time of * * * purchase" means in a sale-repurchase sequence, reasoning.

"If the ['before the purchase'] construction urged by [Graham-Paige] is place upon the exemption provision, it would be possible for a person to purchase a large block of stock, sell it out until his ownership was reduced to less than 10%, and then repeat the process, ad infinitum." 104 F.Supp. 957, 959 (S.D.N.Y.1952).

The District Court may have thought that "before the purchase" seemed an unlikely construction of the exemptive provision in a sale-repurchase sequence, so it could not be the proper construction in a purchase-sale sequence. The Stella construction of the exemptive provision has been adhered to in the Second Circuit, Newmark v. RKO General, Inc., 425 F.2d 348, 355–356 (CA2), cert. denied 400 U.S. 854 (1970); Perine v. William Norton & Co., 509 F.2d 114, 118 (CA2 1974), and adopted by the Court of Appeals for the Eighth Circuit. Emerson Electric Co. v. Reliance Electric Co., 434 F.2d 918, 923–924 (CA8 1970), aff'd on other grounds, 404 U.S. 418 (1972). But in none of the foregoing cases did the court examine critically the legislative history of § 16(b).

The Court of Appeals considered this case against the background, sketched above, of ambiguity in the pertinent statutory language, continued disagreement among the commentators, and a perceived absence in the relatively few decided cases of a full consideration of the purpose and legislative history of § 16(b). The court found unpersuasive the rationales offered in Stella and its progeny for the "immediately after the purchase" construction. It noted that construing the provision to require that beneficial-ownership status exist before the purchase in a purchase-sale sequence would not foreclose an "immediately after the purchase" construction in a sale-repurchase sequence. 506 F.2d, at 614–615. More significantly, the Court of Appeals challenged directly the premise of the earlier cases that a "before the purchase" construction in a purchase-sale sequence would allow abuses Congress intended to abate. The court reasoned that in § 16(b) Congress intended to reach only those beneficial owners who both bought and sold on the basis of inside information, which was presumptively available to them only after they became statutory "insiders." 506 F.2d, at 608–614.[16]

Code (Tentative Draft No. 2, 1973), § 1413(d) and Comment (6), considers the "immediately after the purchase" construction "questionable" on the statutory language and proposes an amendment to codify the result.

16. Shortly before this case was argued the Court of Appeals for the Seventh Circuit reached the same conclusion on somewhat different analysis. Allis-Chalmers Mfg. Co., 527 F.2d, at 347–349. The court apparently would have reached its result even in the absence of the exemptive provision, reasoning that § 16(b) covers no transactions by any § 16(b) insiders who were not insiders before their initial transaction. 527 F.2d, at 347–348. Since we rely on the exemptive provision, we intimate no view on the proper analysis of a case where a director or officer makes an initial transaction before obtaining insider status. See, e.g., Adler v. Klawans, 267

III

A

The general purpose of Congress in enacting § 16(b) is well known. See Kern County Land Co., 411 U.S., at 591–592; Reliance Electric Co. v. Emerson Electric Co., 404 U.S. 418, 422 (1972), and the authorities cited therein. Congress recognized that insiders may have access to information about their corporations not available to the rest of the investing public. By trading on this information, these persons could reap profits at the expense of less well informed investors. In § 16(b) Congress sought to "curb the evils of insider trading [by] * * * taking the profits out of a class of transactions in which the possibility of abuse was believed to be intolerably great." Reliance Electric Co., supra, at 422. It accomplished this by defining directors, officers, and beneficial owners as those presumed to have access to inside information and enacting a flat rule that a corporation could recover the profits these insiders made on a pair of security transactions within six months.

Foremost points to this purpose, and invokes the observation in Reliance Electric Co. that "where alternative constructions of the terms of § 16(b) are possible, those terms are to be given the construction that best serves the congressional purpose of curbing short-swing trading by corporate insiders." 404 U.S., at 424 (footnote omitted). From these premises Foremost argues that the Court of Appeals' construction of the exemptive provision must be rejected because it makes § 16(b) inapplicable to some possible abuses of inside information that the statute would reach under the Stella construction. We find this approach unsatisfactory in its focus on situations that § 16(b) may not reach rather than on the language and purpose of the exemptive provision itself. Foremost's approach also invites an imposition of § 16(b)'s liability without fault that is not consistent with the premises upon which Congress enacted the section.

B

The exemptive provision, which applies only to beneficial owners and not to other statutory insiders, must have been included in § 16(b) for a purpose. Although the extensive legislative history of the Act is bereft of any explicit explanation of Congress' intent, see Reliance Electric Co., supra, at 424, the evolution of § 16(b) from its initial proposal through passage does shed significant light on the purpose of the exemptive provision.

The original version of what would develop into the Act was S. 2693, 73d Cong., 2d Sess. (1934). * * *

The structure of the clause imposing liability in the revised § 15(b) did not unambiguously retain S. 2693's requirement that beneficial ownership precede a purchase-sale sequence. But we cannot assume easily that Congress intended to eliminate the requirement in the revised bill. The legislative history reveals that the requirement was made clear in the hearings, yet no complaint was made about it.

F.2d 840 (2d Cir.1959). Nor do we have occasion here to assess the approach taken by the Court of Appeals for the Seventh Circuit to the exemptive provision. 527 F.2d, at 348 and n. 13. See n. 25, infra.

* * *

The legislative record thus reveals that the drafters focused directly on the fact that S. 2693 covered a short-term purchase-sale sequence by a beneficial owner only if his status existed before the purchase, and no concern was expressed about the wisdom of this requirement. But the explicit requirement was omitted from the operative language of the section when it was restructured to cover sale-repurchase sequences. In the same draft, however, the exemptive provision was added to the section. On this record we are persuaded that the exemptive provision was intended to preserve the requirement of beneficial ownership before the purchase. Later discussions of the present § 16(b) in the hearings are consistent with this interpretation. We hold that, in a purchase-sale sequence, a beneficial owner must account for profits only if he was a beneficial owner "before the purchase."

IV

Additional considerations support our reading of the legislative history.

A

Section 16(b) imposes a strict prophylactic rule with respect to insider, short-swing trading. In Kern County Land Co., 411 U.S., at 595, we noted:

"The statute requires the [statutorily defined] inside, short-swing trader to disgorge all profits realized on all 'purchases' and 'sales' within the specified time period, without proof of actual abuse of insider information, and without proof of intent to profit on the basis of such information."

In short, this statute imposes liability without fault within its narrowly drawn limits.

As noted earlier, Foremost recognizes the ambiguity of the exemptive provision, but argues that where "alternative constructions" of § 16(b)'s terms are available, we should choose the construction that best serves the statute's purposes. Foremost relies on statements generally to this effect in Kern County Land Co., supra, at 595, and Reliance Electric Co., 404 U.S., at 424. In neither of those cases, however, did the Court adopt the construction that would have imposed liability, thus recognizing that serving the congressional purpose does not require resolving every ambiguity in favor of liability under § 16(b). We reiterate that nothing suggests that the construction urged by Foremost would serve better to further congressional purposes. Indeed, the legislative history of § 16(b) indicates that by adding the exemptive provision Congress deliberately expressed a contrary choice. But even if the legislative record were more ambiguous, we would hesitate to adopt Foremost's construction. It is inappropriate to reach the harsh result of imposing § 16(b)'s liability without fault on the basis of unclear language. If Congress wishes to impose such liability, we must assume it will do so expressly or by unmistakable inference.

It is not irrelevant that Congress itself limited carefully the liability imposed by § 16(b). See Reliance Electric Co., supra, at 422–425. Even an insider may trade freely without incurring the statutory liability if, for example, he spaces his transactions at intervals greater than six months. When Congress has so recognized the need to limit carefully the "arbitrary and sweeping coverage" of § 16(b), Bershad v. McDonough, 428 F.2d 693, 696 (CA7 1970), cert. denied 400 U.S. 992 (1971), courts should not be quick to determine that, despite an acknowledged ambiguity, Congress intended the section to cover a particular transaction.

B

Our construction of § 16(b) also is supported by the distinction Congress recognized between short-term trading by mere stockholders and such trading by directors and officers. The legislative discourse revealed that Congress thought that all short-swing trading by directors and officers was vulnerable to abuse because of their intimate involvement in corporate affairs. But trading by mere stockholders was viewed as being subject to abuse only when the size of their holdings afforded the potential for access to corporate information. These different perceptions simply reflect the realities of corporate life.

It would not be consistent with this perceived distinction to impose liability on the basis of a purchase made when the percentage of stock ownership requisite to insider status had not been acquired. To be sure, the possibility does exist that one who becomes a beneficial owner by a purchase will sell on the basis of information attained by virtue of his newly acquired holdings. But the purchase itself was not one posing dangers that Congress considered intolerable, since it was made when the purchaser owned no shares or less than the percentage deemed necessary to make one an insider. Such a stockholder is more analogous to the stockholder who never owns more than 10% and thereby is excluded entirely from the operation of § 16(b), than to a director or officer whose every purchase and sale is covered by the statute. While this reasoning might not compel our construction of the exemptive provision, it explains why Congress may have seen fit to draw the line it did. Cf. Adler v. Klawans, 267 F.2d 840, 845 (CA2 1959).

C

Section 16(b)'s scope, of course, is not affected by whether alternative sanctions might inhibit the abuse of inside information. Congress, however, has left some problems of the abuse of inside information to other remedies. These sanctions alleviate concern that ordinary investors are unprotected against actual abuses of inside information in transactions not covered by § 16(b). For example, Congress has passed general antifraud statutes that proscribe fraudulent practices by insiders. See Securities Act of 1933, § 17(a); Securities Exchange Act of 1934, § 10(b); 3 L. Loss, supra, n. 11, 1423–1429, 1442–1445. Today an investor who can show harm from the misuse of material inside information may have recourse, in particular, to § 10(b) and Rule 10b–5.[29] It also was thought that § 16(a)'s publicity

---

29. Rule 10b–5 has been held to embrace evils that Foremost urges its construction of § 16(b) is necessary to prevent. The Rule has been applied to trading by one who acquired inside information in the course of negotiations with a corporation, such as the negotiations for Provident's purchase of the Foremost debentures. Van Alstyne, Noel & Co., 43 S.E.C. 1080 (1969); 3 L. Loss, supra, n. 11, at 1451– 1452. And a stockholder trading on information not generally known has been held subject to the sanctions of the Rule. Shapiro v. Merrill Lynch, Pierce, Fenner & Smith, Inc., 495 F.2d 228 (CA2 1974); SEC v. Texas Gulf Sulphur Co., 401 F.2d 833 (CA2 1968), cert. denied, 394 U.S. 967 (1969). The liability of insiders who improperly "tip" others, SEC v. Texas Gulf Sulphur Co., 446 F.2d 1301 (CA2), cert.

requirement would afford indirect protection against some potential misuses of inside information. See Hearings on H.R. 7852 and H.R. 8720, supra, at 134–135; H.Rep. No. 1383, 73d Cong., 2d Sess., 13 (to accompany H.R. 9323, 73d Cong., 2d Sess., passed by the House, May 7, 1934, without the present § 16(b)).

* * *

The judgment is

Affirmed.

MR. JUSTICE WHITE joins in the judgment of the Court, and in all but Part IV–C of the Court's opinion.

MR. JUSTICE STEVENS took no part in the consideration or decision of this case.

———

TEN PERCENT HOLDER

While the statute provides that it does not cover any transaction by a 10% holder where he "was not such both at the time of the purchase and sale, or the sale and purchase, of the security involved," Stella v. Graham-Paige Motors Corp.[1] held that "at the time" meant "simultaneously with" rather than before or after. Under this decision, if a person bought 25% of a registered security in one transaction and sold the entire block of 25% in another transaction within six months, he would be liable under Section 16(b) because he was a 10% holder "simultaneous with" both the purchase and sale, although not before the purchase or after the sale. Until 1974 this opinion was contradicted only by a lowly District Court in Arkansas,[2] but then both the Ninth Circuit[3] and the Seventh Circuit[4] disagreed with it and in 1976 the Supreme Court decided the *Provident Securities Co.* case definitively overruling the *Stella* case.[5]

In Reliance Electric Co. v. Emerson Electric Co.[6] the Supreme Court held that where a 10% holder sold an amount of stock sufficient to bring him below the 10% level and then sold the remainder of his holdings, both sales being within six months of a purchase, only the first sale could be matched with the purchase to produce Section 16(b) liability, even though the sales were arranged in this way for the express purpose of avoiding such liability with respect to the second sale. The Court said: "In this case, the respondent, the owner of 13.2% of a corporation's shares, disposed of its entire holdings in two sales, both of them within six months of purchase. The first sale reduced the respondent's holdings to 9.96% and the second disposed of the remainder. The question

denied, 404 U.S. 1005 (1971), may reduce the threat that beneficial owners not themselves represented on the board of directors will be able to acquire inside information from officers and directors. We cite these cases for illustrative purposes without necessarily implying approval.

1. 232 F.2d 299 (2d Cir.1956), cert. denied 352 U.S. 831.

2. Arkansas Louisiana Gas Co. v. Stephens Investment Co., 141 F.Supp. 841 (W.D.Ark.1956).

3. Provident Securities Co. v. Foremost-McKesson, Inc., 506 F.2d 601 (9th Cir. 1974), aff'd 423 U.S. 232 (1976).

4. Allis-Chalmers Manufacturing Co. v. Gulf & Western Industries, Inc., 527 F.2d 335 (7th Cir.1975).

5. In both the Kern County Land Co. case, infra, p. 1418, and Reliance Electric Co. v. Emerson Electric Co., 404 U.S. 418 (1972), reh. denied 405 U.S. 969, previously decided by the Supreme Court, this question had been involved in the lower courts but the cases had been decided on different grounds and the question was not presented to the Supreme Court.

6. Supra, note 5.

presented is whether the profits derived from the second sale are recoverable by the Corporation under § 16(b). We hold that they are not."

The result of the *Provident Securities Co.* case and the *Reliance Electric Company* case may be illustrated as follows: If a person acquires 120,000 shares of a registered security, of which there are 1,000,000 shares outstanding, on May 1; purchases an additional 50,000 shares on July 1; sells 70,001 shares on September 1; and sells all of his remaining 99,999 shares on September 5; he would be liable under Section 16(b) only for any profit resulting from the sale of 50,000 of the shares sold on September 1 as matched with the purchase of 50,000 shares on July 1. The purchase on May 1 cannot be considered since he was not a 10% holder before that purchase and the sale on September 5 cannot be considered since he was not a 10% holder either before or after that sale.

In Chemical Fund, Inc. v. Xerox Corp.[7] a mutual fund purchased more than 10% of an outstanding issue of convertible debentures of Xerox Corp. The debentures were a registered security and an "equity security" as defined in the 1934 Act, but these debentures were convertible only into approximately 2.72% of the Xerox common stock if they had all been converted. While it was in this position, the fund purchased convertible debentures of Xerox and sold common stock of Xerox within a six months period, and the District Court held it liable for the profit computed by matching these transactions. The Second Circuit reversed. Judge Lumbard said:

"Thus the question is: are the Debentures by themselves a 'class of any equity security,' or does the class consist of the common stock augmented, as to any beneficial holder in question, by the number of shares into which the Debentures it owns are convertible? We think that the Debentures are not a class by themselves; the total percentage of common stock which a holder would own following a hypothetical conversion of the Debentures it holds is the test of liability under section 16(b). The history of the legislation, the stated purpose of the Act, and the anomalous consequences of any other meaning all support this conclusion." [8]

After the *Chemical Fund* case the SEC adopted an amendment to Rule 16a–2 on June 6, 1968,[9] which would in effect recognize the result of that case so far as the underlying securities are concerned by providing that for the purpose of determining whether a holder of convertible securities is a 10% holder he will be deemed to be the owner of the underlying securities and all of such underlying securities issuable upon conversion will be deemed to be outstanding. However, the SEC refused to accept the result of that case so far as the convertible securities are concerned by stating that it would continue to regard a person who held more than 10% of the convertibles as a 10% holder, at least for the purpose of Section 16(a): "Although * * * Chemical Fund v. Xerox Corp. * * * [held] that such a class should not be considered a separate class of equity securities for the purposes of determining liabilities for short-swing profits under Section 16(b), the Commission does not believe, in light of the differing purposes of Section 16(a), that that decision was determinative of the obligation to file ownership reports. The Commission, therefore, will continue to take the position that reports are required of persons holding 10 percent of a class of registered securities convertible into equity securities." [10] Although no mention is made of this question, and it was not of course involved in the *Chemical Fund* case, the SEC will also apparently continue to regard a holder

---

7. 377 F.2d 107 (2d Cir.1967).

8. 377 F.2d at 110.

9. Securities Exchange Act Release No. 8325 (SEC 1968).

10. Securities Exchange Act Rel. No. 8202 (SEC 1967).

of more than 10% of the underlying securities as a 10% holder under Section 16(a) even though the conversion of all of the outstanding convertibles would reduce his ownership to less than that figure. The result seems to be that 10% ownership so far as the SEC is concerned will be determined with respect to a holder of convertibles both by assuming no conversion and by assuming total conversion, and will be determined with respect to a holder of underlying securities by assuming no conversion.[11]

Rule 16a–2 also requires that a person be treated as the beneficial owner of stock subject to an option held by him for the purposes of the filing rules under Section 16(a). The court in Colan v. Monumental Corporation [12] held, however, that he would not be considered a "beneficial owner" of the optioned stock for the purposes of liability under Section 16(b).

While a person who falls within Section 16(b) is liable for short-swing profits in "*any* equity security" of the issuer, regardless of whether it is registered or not, in order for the section to apply the corporation must have *some* equity security registered, and in order to be brought within the section as a 10% holder (as distinguished from an officer or director) the person must be a 10% holder of a *registered* security.

Suppose that a corporation has a listed common stock outstanding and also a convertible preferred which is neither listed nor registered under Section 12(g) (because not held by more than 500 persons). A owns 90% of the preferred issue, which is convertible into more than 10% of the common, assuming complete conversion. He purchases and sells preferred within a period of six months. Under the *Chemical Fund* rationale, is he subject to liability under Section 16(b) as a 10% holder of a *registered* security?[13]

Suppose a corporation has outstanding 1,000,000 shares of listed common stock and an outstanding debenture issue which is convertible into 500,000 shares of common stock, although none of it has been converted. A owns 110,000 shares of common stock, and he purchases and sells common stock within a period of six months. Under the *Chemical Fund* rationale, is he subject to liability under Section 16(b) as a *10% holder* of a registered security?

KERN COUNTY LAND CO. v. OCCIDENTAL PETROLEUM CORP.

United States Supreme Court, 1973.
411 U.S. 582, 93 S.Ct. 1736, 36 L.Ed.2d 503.

MR. JUSTICE WHITE delivered the opinion of the Court.

Section 16(b) of the Securities Exchange Act of 1934 * * * provides that officers, directors, and holders of more than 10% of the listed stock of any company shall be liable to the company for any profits realized from any purchase and sale or sale and purchase of such stock occurring within a period of six months. Unquestionably, one or more statutory purchases

---

11. Compare with the *Chemical Fund* case, Ellerin v. Massachusetts Mutual Life Insurance Co., 270 F.2d 259 (2d Cir.1959), in which the court held that two "series" of preferred stock, differing as to dividend rates, redemption prices and sinking fund provisions, nevertheless constituted a single "class" for the purpose of determining whether a person was a 10% holder under Section 16(b).

12. 713 F.2d 330 (7th Cir.1983).

13. Simon v. Sunasco, Inc., CCH Fed. Sec.Law Rptr. ¶ 92,547 (S.D.N.Y.1970), held that the owner was to be regarded as a 10% holder for the purposes of Section 16(b) in this situation, even though the convertible was not registered. Accord: Gold v. Scurlock, 324 F.Supp. 1211 (E.D.Va. 1971).

occurs when one company, seeking to gain control of another, acquires more than 10% of the stock of the latter through a tender offer made to its shareholders. But is it a § 16(b) "sale" when the target of the tender offer defends itself by merging into a third company and the tender offeror then exchanges his stock for the stock of the surviving company and also grants an option to purchase the latter stock that is not exercisable within the statutory six months period? This is the question before us in this case.

I

On May 8, 1967, after unsuccessfully seeking to merge with Kern County Land Company (Old Kern), Occidental Petroleum Corporation (Occidental) announced an offer, to expire on June 8, 1967, to purchase on a first-come, first-served basis 500,000 shares of Old Kern common stock at a price of $83.50 per share plus a brokerage commission of $1.50 per share. By May 10, 1967, 500,000 shares, more than 10% of the outstanding shares of Old Kern, had been tendered. On May 11, Occidental extended its offer to encompass an additional 500,000 shares. At the close of the tender offer, on June 8, 1967, Occidental owned 887,549 shares of Old Kern.

Immediately upon the announcement of Occidental's tender offer, the Old Kern management undertook to frustrate Occidental's takeover attempt. A management letter to all stockholders cautioned against tender and indicated that Occidental's offer might not be the best available, since the management was engaged in merger discussions with several companies. When Occidental extended its tender offer, the president of Old Kern sent a telegram to all stockholders again advising against tender. In addition, Old Kern undertook merger discussions with Tenneco, Inc. (Tenneco), and, on May 19, 1967, the Board of Directors of Old Kern announced that it had approved a merger proposal advanced by Tenneco.[9] Under the terms of the merger, Tenneco would acquire the assets, property, and goodwill of Old Kern, subject to its liabilities, through "Kern County Land Company" (New Kern), a new corporation to be formed by Tenneco to receive the assets and carry on the business of Old Kern. The shareholders of Old Kern would receive a share of Tenneco cumulative convertible preference stock in exchange for each share of Old Kern common stock which they owned. On the same day, May 19, Occidental, in a quarterly report to stockholders, appraised the value of the new Tenneco stock at $105 per share.

Occidental, seeing its tender offer and takeover attempt being blocked by the Old Kern-Tenneco "defensive" merger, countered on May 25 and 31 with two mandamus actions in the California courts seeking to obtain extensive inspection of Old Kern books and records. Realizing that, if the Old Kern-Tenneco merger were approved and successfully closed, Occidental would have to exchange its Old Kern shares for Tenneco stock and would be locked into a minority position in Tenneco, Occidental took other steps to protect itself. Between May 30 and June 2, it negotiated an arrangement with Tenneco whereby Occidental granted Tenneco Corporation, a subsidiary of Tenneco, an option to purchase at $105 per share all of

---

9. Although technically a sale of assets, the corporate combination has been consistently referred to by the parties as a "merger" and will be similarly denominated in this opinion. The only significance of the characterization is the fact that a sale of assets required, under California law, approval of only a majority of the Old Kern shareholders and provided no appraisal rights for dissenters.

the Tenneco preference stock to which Occidental would be entitled in exchange for its Old Kern stock when and if the Old Kern-Tenneco merger was closed. The premium to secure the option, at $10 per share, totaled $8,866,230 and was to be paid immediately upon the signing of the option agreement. If the option were exercised, the premium was to be applied to the purchase price. By the terms of the option agreement, the option could not be exercised prior to December 9, 1967, a date six months and one day after expiration of Occidental's tender offer. On June 2, 1967, within six months of the acquisition by Occidental of more than 10% ownership of Old Kern, Occidental and Tenneco Corporation executed the option. Soon thereafter, Occidental announced that it would not oppose the Old Kern-Tenneco merger and dismissed in a state court suits against Old Kern.

The Old Kern-Tenneco merger plan was presented to and approved by Old Kern shareholders at their meeting on July 17, 1967. Occidental refrained from voting its Old Kern shares, but in a letter read at the meeting Occidental stated that it had determined prior to June 2 not to oppose the merger and that it did not consider the plan unfair or inequitable. Indeed, Occidental indicated that had it been voting, it would have voted in favor of the merger.

* * *

The Old Kern-Tenneco merger transaction was closed on August 30. Old Kern shareholders thereupon became irrevocably entitled to receive Tenneco preference stock, share-for-share in exchange for their Old Kern stock. Old Kern was dissolved and all of its assets including "all claims, demands, rights and choses in action accrued or to accrue under and by virtue of the Securities Exchange Act of 1934 * * *" were transferred to New Kern.

The option granted by Occidental on June 2, 1967, was exercised on December 11, 1967. Occidental, not having previously availed itself of its rights, exchanged certificates representing 887,549 shares of Old Kern stock for a certificate representing a like number of shares of Tenneco preference stock. The certificate was then endorsed over to the optionee-purchaser, and in return $84,129,185 was credited to Occidental's accounts at various banks. Adding to this amount the $8,886,230 premium paid in June, Occidental received $93,905,415 for its Old Kern stock (including the 1,900 shares acquired prior to issuance of its tender offer). In addition, Occidental received dividends totaling $1,793,439.22. Occidental's total profit was $19,506,419.22 on the shares obtained through its tender offer.

On October 17, 1967, New Kern instituted a suit under § 16(b) against Occidental to recover the profits which Occidental had realized as a result of its dealings in Old Kern stock. The complaint alleged that the execution of the Occidental-Tenneco option on June 2, 1967, and the exchange of Old Kern shares for shares of Tenneco to which Occidental became entitled pursuant to the merger closed on August 30, 1967, were both "sales" within the coverage of § 16(b). Since both acts took place within six months of the date on which Occidental became the owner of more than 10% of the stock of Old Kern, New Kern asserted that § 16(b) required surrender of the profits realized by Occidental. * * *

Although traditional cash-for-stock transactions that result in a purchase and sale or a sale and purchase within the six-month, statutory period are clearly encompassed within the purview of § 16(b), the courts have wrestled with the question of inclusion or exclusion of certain "unorthodox" transactions. The statutory definitions of "purchase" and "sale" are broad and, at least arguably, reach many transactions not ordinarily deemed a sale or purchase. In deciding whether borderline transactions are within the reach of the statute, the courts have come to inquire whether the transaction may serve as a vehicle for the evil which Congress sought to prevent—the realization of short-swing profits based upon access to inside information—thereby endeavoring to implement congressional objectives without extending the reach of the statute beyond its intended limits. The statute requires the inside, short-swing trader to disgorge all profits realized on all "purchases" and "sales" within the specified time period, without proof of actual abuse of insider information, and without proof of intent to profit on the basis of such information. Under these strict terms, the prevailing view is to apply the statute only when its application would serve its goals. "[W]here alternative constructions of the terms of § 16(b) are possible, those terms are to be given the construction that best serves the congressional purpose of curbing short-swing speculation by corporate insiders." Reliance Electric Co. v. Emerson Electric Co., supra, at 424. See Blau v. Lamb, 363 F.2d 507 (C.A.2 1966), cert. denied 383 U.S. 1002 (1967). Thus, "[i]n interpreting the terms 'purchase' and 'sale,' courts have properly asked whether the particular type of transaction involved is one that gives rise to speculative abuse." Reliance Electric Co. v. Emerson Electric Co., supra, at 424, n. 4.

In the present case, it is undisputed that Occidental became a "beneficial owner" within the terms of § 16(b) when, pursuant to its tender offer, it "purchased" more than 10% of the outstanding shares of Old Kern. We must decide, however, whether a "sale" within the ambit of the statute took place either when Occidental became irrevocably bound to exchange its shares of Old Kern for shares of Tenneco pursuant to the terms of the merger agreement between Old Kern and Tenneco or when Occidental gave an option to Tenneco to purchase from Occidental the Tenneco shares so acquired.[28]

III

On August 30, 1967, the Old Kern-Tenneco merger agreement was signed, and Occidental became irrevocably entitled to exchange its shares of Old Kern stock for shares of Tenneco preference stock. Concededly the transaction must be viewed as though Occidental had made the exchange on that day. But even so, did the exchange involve a "sale" of Old Kern shares within the meaning of § 16(b)? We agree with the Court of Appeals that it did not, for we think it totally unrealistic to assume or infer from the facts before us that Occidental either had or was likely to have access to inside information, by reason of its ownership of more than 10% of the outstanding shares of Old Kern, so as to afford it an opportunity to reap

---

28. Both events occurred within six months of Occidental's first acquisition of Old Kern shares pursuant to its tender offer. Although Occidental did not exchange its Old Kern shares until December 11, 1967, it is not contended that that date, rather than the date on which Occidental became irrevocably bound to do so, should control. Similarly, although the option was not exercised until December 11, 1967, no liability is asserted with respect to that event, because it occurred more than six months after Occidental's last acquisition of Old Kern stock.

speculative, short-swing profits from its disposition within six months of its tender offer purchases.

It cannot be contended that Occidental was an insider when, on May 8, 1967, it made an irrevocable offer to purchase 500,000 shares of Old Kern stock at a price substantially above market. At that time, it owned only 1,900 shares of Old Kern stock, far fewer than the 432,000 shares needed to constitute the 10% ownership required by the statute. There is no basis for finding that, at the time the tender offer was commenced, Occidental enjoyed an insider's opportunity to acquire information about Old Kern's affairs.

It is also wide of the mark to assert that Occidental, as a sophisticated corporation knowledgeable in matters of corporate affairs and finance, knew that its tender offer would either succeed or would be met with a "defensive merger." If its takeover efforts failed, it is argued, Occidental knew it could sell its stock to the target company's merger partner at a substantial profit. Calculations of this sort, however, whether speculative or not and whether fair or unfair to other stockholders or to Old Kern, do not represent the kind of speculative abuse at which the statute is aimed, for they could not have been based on inside information obtained from substantial stockholdings that did not yet exist. Accepting both that Occidental made this very prediction and that it would recurringly be an accurate forecast in tender-offer situations, we nevertheless fail to perceive how the fruition of such anticipated events would require, or in any way depend upon the receipt and use of inside information. If there are evils to be redressed by way of deterring those who would make tender offers, § 16(b) does not appear to us to have been designed for this task.

By May 10, 1967, Occidental had acquired more than 10% of the outstanding shares of Old Kern. It was thus a statutory insider when, on May 11, it extended its tender offer to include another 500,000 shares. We are quite unconvinced, however, that the situation had changed materially with respect to the possibilities of speculative abuse of inside information by Occidental. Perhaps Occidental anticipated that extending its offer would increase the likelihood of the ultimate success of its takeover attempt or the occurrence of a defensive merger. But again, the expectation of such benefits was unrelated to the use of information unavailable to other stockholders or members of the public with sufficient funds and the intention to make the purchases Occidental had offered to make before June 8, 1967.

The possibility that Occidental had, or had the opportunity to have, any confidential information about Old Kern before or after May 11, 1967, seems extremely remote. Occidental was, after all, a tender offeror, threatening to seize control of Old Kern, displace its management, and use the company for its own ends. The Old Kern management vigorously and immediately opposed Occidental's efforts. Twice it communicated with its stockholders, advising against acceptance of Occidental's offer and indicating prior to May 11 and prior to Occidental's extension of its offer, that there was a possibility of an imminent merger and a more profitable exchange. Old Kern's management refused to discuss with Occidental officials the subject of an Old Kern-Occidental merger. Instead, it undertook negotiations with Tenneco and forthwith concluded an agreement, announcing the merger terms on May 19. Requests by Occidental for inspection of Old Kern records were sufficiently frustrated by Old Kern's management to force Occidental to litigation to secure the information it desired.

There is, therefore, nothing in connection with Occidental's acquisition of Old Kern stock pursuant to its tender offer to indicate either the possibility of inside information being available to Occidental by virtue of its stock ownership or the potential for speculative abuse of such inside information by Occidental. Much the same can be said of the events leading to the exchange of Occidental's Old Kern stock for Tenneco preferred, which is one of the transactions that is sought to be classified a "sale" under § 16(b). The critical fact is that the exchange took place and was required pursuant to a merger between Old Kern and Tenneco. That merger was not engineered by Occidental but was sought by Old Kern to frustrate the attempts of Occidental to gain control of Old Kern. Occidental obviously did not participate in or control the negotiations or the agreement between Old Kern and Tenneco. Cf. Newmark v. RKO General, 425 F.2d 348 (C.A.2), cert. denied 400 U.S. 854 (1970); Park & Tilford v. Schulte, 160 F.2d 984 (C.A.2), cert. denied 332 U.S. 761 (1947). Once agreement between those two companies crystalized, the course of subsequent events was out of Occidental's hands. Old Kern needed the consent of its stockholders, but as it turned out, Old Kern's management had the necessary votes without the affirmative vote of Occidental. The merger agreement was approved by a majority of the stockholders of Old Kern, excluding the votes to which Occidental was entitled by virtue of its ownership of Old Kern shares. See generally Ferraiolo v. Newman, 259 F.2d 342 (C.A.6 1958), cert. denied 359 U.S. 927 (1959); Roberts v. Eaton, 212 F.2d 82 (C.A.2 1954). Occidental, although registering its opinion that the merger would be beneficial to Old Kern shareholders, did not in fact vote at the stockholders' meeting at which merger approval was obtained. Under California law, its abstention was tantamount to a vote against approval of the merger. Moreover, at the time of stockholder ratification of the merger, Occidental's previous dealing in Old Kern stock was, as it had always been, fully disclosed.

Once the merger and exchange were approved, Occidental was left with no real choice with respect to the future of its shares of Old Kern. Occidental was in no position to prevent the issuance of a ruling by the Internal Revenue Service that the exchange of Old Kern stock for Tenneco preferred would be tax-free; and, although various lawsuits were begun in state and federal courts seeking to postpone the merger closing beyond the statutory six months period, those efforts were futile. The California Corporation Commissioner issued the necessary permits for the closing that took place on August 30, 1967.[a] The merger left no right in dissenters to

---

a. [Eds.] This cryptic reference to "various lawsuits" and to the proceedings before the California Commissioner of Corporations conceals a monumental legal battle initiated when Occidental woke up after the shareholders' meeting to the fact that it had a Section 16(b) problem if the sale of assets was consummated within six months of its purchases of stock of Old Kern, although it would seem that it would have been relatively easy for Occidental to have negotiated a postponement of the

closing at the time it made its option deal with Tenneco if it had recognized the problem then. A flurry of lawsuits were filed all over the United States to enjoin the transaction until the six months had passed; an attempt was made to get the California Commissioner of Corporations to deny the permit necessary for the closing on the basis that the transaction was not "fair, just and equitable" to the shareholders of Old Kern, although Occidental had publicly read a letter to the shareholders'

secure appraisal of their stock. Occidental could, of course, have disposed of its shares of Old Kern for cash before the merger was closed. Such an act would have been a § 16(b) sale and would have left Occidental with a prima facie § 16(b) liability. It was not, therefore, a realistic alternative for Occidental as long as it felt that it could successfully defend a suit like the present one. See generally Petteys v. Butler, 367 F.2d 528 (C.A.8 1966), cert. denied 385 U.S. 1006 (1967); Ferraiolo v. Newman, supra; Lyman v. Livingston, 276 F.Supp. 104 (Del.1967); Blau v. Hodgkinson, 100 F.Supp. 361 (S.D.N.Y.1951). We do not suggest that an exchange of stock pursuant to a merger may never result in § 16(b) liability. But the involuntary nature of Occidental's exchange, when coupled with the absence of the possibility of speculative abuse of inside information, convinces us that § 16(b) should not apply to transactions such as this one.

IV

Petitioner also claims that the Occidental-Tenneco option agreement should itself be considered a sale either because it was the kind of transaction the statute was designed to prevent or because the agreement was an option in form but in fact a sale. But there mere execution of an option to sell is not generally regarded as a "sale." See Booth v. Varian Associates, 334 F.2d 1 (C.A.1 1964), cert. denied 379 U.S. 961 (1965); Allis-Chalmers Mfg. Co. v. Gulf Western Industries, 309 F.Supp. 75 (Wis.1970); Marquette Cement Mfg. Co. v. Andreas, 239 F.Supp. 962 (S.D.N.Y.1965). And we do not find in the execution of the Occidental-Tenneco option agreement a sufficient possibility for the speculative abuse of inside information with respect to Old Kern's affairs to warrant holding that the option agreement was itself a "sale" within the meaning of § 16(b). The mutual advantages of the arrangement appear quite clear. As the District Court found, Occidental wanted to avoid the position of a minority stockholder with a huge investment in a company over which it had no control and in which it had not chosen to invest. On the other hand, Tenneco did not want a potentially troublesome minority stockholder that had just been vanquished in a fight for the control of Old Kern. Motivations like these do not smack of insider trading; and it is not clear to us, as it was not to the Court of Appeals, how the negotiation and execution of the option agreement gave Occidental any possible opportunity to trade on inside information it might have obtained from its position as a major stockholder of Old Kern. Occidental wanted out, but only at a date more than six

meeting stating that in its opinion the transaction was the "best deal" that those shareholders could get; and application was made to the Securities and Exchange Commission for a special exemptive rule to relieve Occidental of its potential Section 16(b) liability. In one county in Texas where an injunction action had been filed, Louis Nizer was flown in from New York City to represent Occidental and local counsel for Tenneco wrote a classic brief in which the country bumpkin lawyer took on the city slicker and illustrated each point of his argument with a quotation from one of Mr. Nizer's published literary efforts extolling his own exploits as an attorney. (Occidental and Mr. Nizer of course had the last laugh, when the Second Circuit reversed a $23,500,000 judgment against Occidental and the Supreme Court affirmed.) None of this effort succeeded and the transaction closed on schedule; and then the race by the 16(b) Bar to the courthouse began, initiating six years of litigation over the liability question. If the judgment against Occidental had been affirmed, the result would have been that the public shareholders of Occidental would have been forced to make a gift of $23,500,000 to the public shareholders of Tenneco. Total fees paid to lawyers throughout this fiasco are unknown, but undoubtedly ran into the millions. *Cui bono?*

months hence. It was willing to get out at a price of $105 per share, a price at which it had publicly valued Tenneco preferred on May 19 when the Tenneco-Old Kern agreement was announced. In any event, Occidental was dealing with the putative new owners of Old Kern who undoubtedly knew more about Old Kern and Tenneco's affairs than did Occidental. If Occidental had leverage in dealing with Tenneco, it is incredible that its source was inside information rather than the fact of its large stock ownership itself.

Neither does it appear that the option agreement, as drafted and executed by the parties, offered measurable possibilities for speculative abuse. What Occidental granted was a "call" option. Tenneco had the right to buy after six months, but Occidental could not force Tenneco to buy. The price was fixed at $105 for each share of Tenneco preferred. Occidental could not share in a rising market for the Tenneco stock. See Silverman v. Landa, 306 F.2d 422 (C.A.2 1966). If the stock fell more than $10 per share, the option might not be exercised, and Occidental might suffer a loss if the market further deteriorated to a point where Occidental was forced to sell. Thus, the option, by its very form, left Occidental with no choice but to sell if Tenneco exercised the option, which it was almost sure to do if the value of Tenneco stock remained relatively steady. On the other hand, it is difficult to perceive any speculative value to Occidental if the stock declined and Tenneco chose not to exercise its option. See generally Note, Put and Call Options Under Section 16 of the Securities Exchange Act, 69 Yale L.Rev. 868 (1960); Filer, Understanding Put and Call Options, 96–111 (1959); Leffler, The Stock Market, 363–378 (2d ed. 1957).

The option, therefore, does not appear to have been an instrument with potential for speculative abuse, whether or not Occidental possessed inside information about the affairs of Old Kern. In addition, the option covered Tenneco preference stock, a stock as yet unissued, unregistered, and un-traded. It was the value of this stock that underlay the option and that determined whether the option would be exercised, whether Occidental would be able to profit from the exercise, and whether there was any real likelihood of the exploitation of inside information. If Occidental had inside information when it negotiated and signed the option agreement it was inside information with respect to Old Kern. Whatever it may have known or expected as to the future value of Old Kern stock, Occidental had no ownership position in Tenneco giving it any actual or presumed insights into the future value of Tenneco stock. That was the critical item of intelligence if Occidental was to use the option for purposes of speculation. Also, the date for exercise of the option was over six months in the future, a period that, under the statute itself, is assumed to dissipate whatever trading advantage that might be imputed to a major stockholder with inside information. See Note, Stock Exchanges Pursuant to Corporation Consolidation: A Section 16(b) "Purchase or Sale?," 217 U.Pa.L.Rev. 1034, 1054 (1969); Silverman v. Landa, 306 F.2d 422 (C.A.2 1962). By enshrining the statutory period into the option, Occidental also, at least if the statuto-ry period is taken to accomplish its intended purpose, limited its specula-tive possibilities. Nor should it be forgotten that there was no absolute assurance that the merger, which was not controlled by Occidental, would be consummated. In the event the merger did not close, the option itself would become null and void.

Nor can we agree that we must reverse the Court of Appeals on the ground that the option agreement was in fact a sale because the premium paid was so large as to make the exercise of the option almost inevitable, particularly when coupled with Tenneco's desire to rid itself of a potentially troublesome stockholder. The argument has force, but resolution of the question is very much a matter of judgment, economic and otherwise, and the Court of Appeals rejected the argument. That court emphasized that the premium paid was what experts had said the option was worth, the possibility that the market might drop sufficiently in the six months following execution of the option to make exercise unlikely, and the fact that here, unlike the situation in Bershad v. McDonough, 428 F.2d 693 (C.A.7 1970), the optionor did not surrender practically all emoluments of ownership by executing the option. Nor did any other special circumstances indicate that the parties understood and intended that the option was in fact a sale. We see no satisfactory basis or reason for disagreeing with the judgment of the Court of Appeals in this respect.

The judgment of the Court of Appeals is affirmed.

So ordered.

MR. JUSTICE DOUGLAS, with whom MR. JUSTICE BRENNAN and MR. JUSTICE STEWART concur, dissenting.

* * *

The very construction of § 16(b) reinforces the conclusion that the section is based in the first instance on a totally objective appraisal of the relevant transactions. See Smolowe v. Delendo Corp., supra, at 236. Had the draftsmen intended that the operation of the section hinge on abuse of access to inside information it would have been anomalous to limit the section to purchases and sales occurring within six months. Indeed, the purpose of the six-month limitation, coupled with the definition of an insider, was to create a *conclusive presumption* that an insider who turns a short-swing profit in the stock of his corporation had access to inside information *and* capitalized on that information by speculating in the stock. But, the majority departs from the benign effects of this presumption when it assumes that it is "totally unrealistic to assume or infer from the facts before us that Occidental either had or was likely to have access to inside information * * *." Ante, at 201. The majority abides by this assumption even for that period after which Occidental became a 10% shareholder and then extended its tender offer in order to purchase additional Old Kern shares.

The majority takes heart from those decisions of lower federal courts which endorse a "pragmatic" approach to § 16(b). Many involved the question whether a conversion of one security of an issuer into another security of the same issuer constituted a purchase or a sale. It would serve no purpose to parse their holdings because, as Louis Loss describes, they have a "generalization-defying nature." In 1966 the Securities and Exchange Commission exercised its exemptive power under § 16(b) to adopt Rule 16b–9, which under specified conditions excludes a conversion from the operation of § 16(b). This rule will relieve the courts of much of the burden that has developed from *ad hoc* analysis in this narrow area. But, by sanctioning the approach of these cases, the majority brings to fruition Louis Loss's prophecy that they will "continue to rule us from their graves," for henceforth they certainly will be applied by analogy to the area of mergers and other consolidations.

Thus, the courts will be caught up in an *ad hoc* analysis of each transaction, determining both from the economics of the transaction and the *modus operandi* of the insider whether there exists the possibility of speculative abuse of inside information. Instead of a section that is easy to administer and by its clear-cut terms discourages litigation, we have instead a section that fosters litigation because the Court's decision holds out the hope for the insider that he may avoid § 16(b) liability. In short, the majority destroys much of the section's prophylactic effect. I would be the first to agree that "[e]very transaction which can be reasonably defined as a purchase [should] be so defined, if the transaction is of a kind which can possibly lend itself to the speculation encompassed by Section 16(b)." Ferraiolo v. Newman, 259 F.2d 342, 345 (C.A.6 1958) (Stewart, J.). See also Reliance Electric Co. v. Emerson Electric Co., supra, at 424. Certainly we cannot allow transactions which present the possibility of abuse but do not fall within the classic conception of a purchase or sale to escape the confines of § 16(b). It is one thing to interpret the terms "purchase" and "sale" liberally in order to include those transactions which evidence the evil Congress sought to eliminate; it is quite another to abandon the bright-line test of § 16(b) for those transactions which clearly fall within its literal bounds. Section 16(b), because of the six-month limitation, allows some to escape who have abused their inside information. It should not be surprising, given the objective nature of the rule, if some are caught unwittingly.

* * *

It is this "objective standard" that the Court hung to so tenaciously in Reliance Electric, but now apparently would abandon to a large extent. In my view the Court improperly takes upon itself the task of refashioning the contours of § 16(b) and changing its essential thrust.

* * *

"PURCHASE" AND "SALE"

A "purchase" or "sale" for the purposes of Section 16(b) may occur even though there is not a cash transaction, but an exchange of stock for property or for other stock.[1] However, the courts have experienced considerable difficulty in deciding whether certain types of corporate transactions, involving the exchange of one security for another, should be fitted into these categories.

Conversions. The transaction which has given the courts the most difficulty in deciding whether a purchase and sale has occurred under Section 16(b) is the conversion of a debenture or preferred stock into common stock pursuant to a provision of the articles of incorporation or indenture giving the holder the option of making such a conversion. The earliest case of Park & Tilford, Inc. v. Schulte[2], held that such a transaction was a "purchase" of the common stock issuable upon the conversion, and (while the question was not involved in that case) also indicated quite clearly that it would be a "sale" of the convertible security given up in the transaction. However, this decision has been distin-

---

1. See Booth v. Varian Associates, 334 F.2d 1 (1st Cir.1964), cert. denied 379 U.S. 961 (1965); cf. Blau v. Albert, CCH Fed. Sec.Law Rptr. ¶ 90,836 (S.D.N.Y.1957) (a transfer of shares to a person arranging the purchase, as compensation for his services, is a "sale.")

2. 160 F.2d 984 (2d Cir.1947), cert. denied 332 U.S. 761.

guished to the point where it would not seem to have any value left as a precedent.

In Ferraiolo v. Newman [3] and Petteys v. Butler [4] it was held by the Sixth Circuit and the Eighth Circuit that a conversion of preferred stock into common stock did not involve any "purchase" of the common stock, directly contrary to the holding in the *Schulte* case; but those cases might be distinguishable from the *Schulte* case in that the conversions were "involuntary" because the preferred stock had been called for redemption and the holder was forced to convert or lose a large portion of his investment. There was also a call for redemption in the *Schulte* case, but the court indicated that the Schultes controlled the corporation and therefore were in a position to determine whether the redemption call would be made or not. The case of Blau v. Max Factor & Co.[5] in the Ninth Circuit held that a conversion of Common into Class A common stock, differing only in that the Class A had greater dividend rights, was not a "purchase" of the Class A stock under Section 16(b), although there was nothing "involuntary" about the conversion. Finally, Blau v. Lamb [6] held that a conversion of preferred stock into common stock was not a "sale" of the preferred stock. While the court reserved the question whether it would be a "purchase" of the common stock, it obviously did this only because it did not want to overrule the *Schulte* case by name; it is impossible to reconcile this holding with *Schulte*.

The case of Heli-Coil Corp. v. Webster [7] in the Third Circuit held that a conversion of convertible debentures into common stock involved both a sale of the debentures and a purchase of the common, where the debentures had been purchased less than six months prior to the conversion and some of the common was sold less than six months after the conversion, but that no "profit" was realized on the sale of the debentures because there should be added to their initial purchase price the value of the conversion privilege on the date of the conversion, which necessarily totalled exactly the value of the common stock received on the conversion. This approach, however, had the support of only four of the eight judges deciding that case [8] and has the support of no other case in this area. Therefore, it can probably safely be ignored outside of the Third Circuit.

The SEC on February 17, 1966,[9] amended Rule 16b–9 so as to solve the major problems involved in these cases. That rule provides that a conversion of one security into another pursuant to the terms of the corporate charter or other governing instruments is not to be considered either a purchase or sale for the purpose of Section 16(b), except that the rule does not apply whenever there has been a purchase of the convertible and a sale of the common or a sale of the convertible and a purchase of the common (other than the conversion transaction itself) within a period of six months which includes the date of

---

3. 259 F.2d 342 (6th Cir.1958), cert. denied 359 U.S. 927 (1959).

4. 367 F.2d 528 (8th Cir.1966), cert. denied 385 U.S. 1006 (1967). See, also, Lynam v. Livingston, 276 F.Supp. 104 (D.Del.1967).

5. 342 F.2d 304 (9th Cir.1965), cert. denied 382 U.S. 892.

6. 363 F.2d 507 (2d Cir.1967), cert. denied 385 U.S. 1002.

7. 352 F.2d 156 (3d Cir.1965).

8. Judges McLaughlin and Staley agreed that both a purchase and sale was

involved in the conversion transaction, but thought that a profit was realized on the sale of the debentures as well as on the subsequent sale of the common received on conversion. Judges Hastie and Kalodner thought that no purchase or sale was involved in the conversion transaction and therefore the defendant should not be liable for any amount (since the purchase of the convertible debenture and the sale of the common were separated by more than six months).

9. Securities Exchange Act Release No. 7826 (1966).

conversion. This exclusionary provision means that the differing approaches of the courts will still be applicable (because the rule is irrelevant) in the following types of cases:

No. 1. A purchase of the convertible at a price equivalent to $50 per share for the underlying common stock; a conversion into common stock at a time when the market price is $60 per share; a sale of the common stock for $50 per share; all within a period of six months.

No. 2. A purchase of the convertible at a price equivalent to $50 per share for the underlying common stock; a conversion into common stock at a time when the market price is $40 per share; a sale of the common stock for $50 per share; all within a period of six months.

How would the Second, Third, Sixth, Eighth and Ninth Circuits rule on these two cases without any assistance from Rule 16b–9?

In Gund v. First Florida Banks, Inc.[10] the Eleventh Circuit held that a director who sold convertible debentures and within six months purchased common stock into which the debentures were convertible was liable under Section 16(b). The court pointed out that Rule 16b–9 was not applicable because the debentures had never been converted but simply sold and common stock purchased within six months, which by its express terms makes Rule 16b–9 inapplicable. (The debentures were not converted because the conversion privilege was under water and the director acquired 27,000 more shares of common stock by using the proceeds of the sale to purchase stock than he would have by converting the debentures.) The court upheld the ruling of the district court, however, that the profit recoverable was limited by Rule 16b–6 (see page 1441, below). This ruling was clearly erroneous, since Rule 16b–6 only applies where there is a purchase "pursuant to the exercise of an option or similar right"; even if the conversion privilege were considered a "similar right" to an option, which is highly doubtful, there was no such purchase pursuant to the exercise of any kind of a right in this case.

The courts have generally held that they will not restructure a transaction to create a purchase and sale and therefore liability under Section 16(b) where on the face of the transaction there has been only one or the other. For example, both the Ninth and the Seventh Circuits have held that where selling shareholders sell warrants to underwriters of a public offering, which they have held for more than six months, and the underwriters thereupon exercise the warrants and resell the common stock purchased to the public, there has been no purchase and sale by the selling shareholders, and therefore no liability under Section 16(b), despite the fact that the substance of the transaction may be the same as one where the selling shareholders exercised the warrants and then sold the common stock to the underwriters.[11] (The transactions by the underwriters were exempt by Rule 16b–2.)

Reorganizations. The SEC has impliedly ruled that statutory mergers and consolidations are covered generally by exempting certain of them in Rule 16b–7. That rule provides that where one of the corporations involved in a merger or consolidation (as well as a sale of assets in a "C" reorganization) owns 85% or more of the stock of the other corporation prior to the merger or had 85% or more of the combined assets of all corporations involved in the merger or consolidation, any acquisition or disposition of securities by *its* shareholders in connection with the merger or consolidation is not to be treated as a purchase or sale under Section 16(b). In other words, if there is a "downstairs" merger of

---

10. 726 F.2d 682 (11th Cir.1984).

11. Portnoy v. Texas International Airlines, Inc., 678 F.2d 695 (7th Cir.1982);

Portnoy v. Memorex Corporation, 667 F.2d 1281 (9th Cir.1982).

a corporation into its own subsidiary, or a merger of a "giant" corporation into a "pigmy", and in either case the percentage test is met, the shareholders of the merging corporation have not made a sale of their stock in the merging corporation nor a purchase of the stock received by them in the continuing corporation, for the purpose of Section 16(b). There is a qualification, however, to the effect that the rule does not apply if the person makes both a purchase of a security of a corporation involved in the merger and a sale of a security of any other corporation involved in the merger (other than the merger transaction itself) during a period of six months within which the merger occurs.

There is no exemption in this rule for the shareholders of the continuing corporation, but presumably since they have not exchanged their stock but merely retained that previously owned in the same coroporate entity, there would be no purchase or sale as far as they are concerned anyway. However, an argument can be made that, since their investment has been so transformed as a result of their corporation swallowing a "giant" and issuing an amount of additional stock almost 6 times that previously outstanding, they should be considered to have sold their old stock and acquired new stock for the purpose of Section 16(b), despite the formality of retaining their old certificates.

Where the merger or sale of assets falls outside the terms of this exemptive rule, the *Kern County Land Co.* case holds that it *may be* a sale of the stock of the acquired corporation (and presumably a purchase of stock of the acquiring corporation), but that in the case of such an "unorthodox" transaction it will not be held to be a purchase or sale if there is no "possibility" that the transaction could "lend itself" to the abuses which Section 16(b) was designed to prevent. In American Standard, Inc. v. Crane Co.[12] the Second Circuit held that where an unsuccessful tender offeror was forced to exchange its holdings for those of another company with which the target company had arranged a "defensive merger", that exchange was not a sale of the securities purchased nor a purchase of the securities received in the merger which could be matched with its sale of those securities within six months. The court also held that the tender offeror's original purchases of stock of the target company which disappeared in the merger could not be matched with its sale of the securities received in the merger, although those also were within a period of six months, because they were securities of different issuers.

In Gold v. Sloan [13] the Fourth Circuit held that the receipt of securities in a merger was a purchase as to one officer-director of the acquired corporation who had complete control of the negotiations, but was not a purchase with respect to another director sued in the same case because he was on the outs with the management of the acquired corporation and had no knowledge of the negotiations beyond what was publicly released, even though he cast the deciding vote for the transaction (which was only approved by a 4–3 vote on the board).[14]

A number of cases prior to the *Kern County Land Co.* case had held that a sale of assets for stock in a "C" type reorganization, followed by the distribution of the stock received by the selling corporation to its shareholders, involved a

---

12. 510 F.2d 1043 (2d Cir.1974), cert. denied 421 U.S. 1000.

13. 486 F.2d 340 (4th Cir.1973), cert. denied 419 U.S. 873. In Mueller v. Korholz, 449 F.2d 82 (7th Cir.1971), the Seventh Circuit assumed that a merger was a "purchase" of the stock of the surviving corporation by all shareholders of the merged corporation, although in that particular case it was held that no profit was realized.

14. Compare Morales v. Arlen Realty & Development Corp., 352 F.Supp. 941 (S.D. N.Y.1973); Makofsky v. Ultra Dynamics Corp., 383 F.Supp. 631 (S.D.N.Y.1974).

"purchase" of that stock by those shareholders for the purpose of section 16(b).[15] There would seem little doubt that this type of transaction would be subject to the same analysis as a merger under that opinion, since *Kern County* itself involved a sale of assets and not a merger (see footnote 9 of the Court's opinion). Strangely, however, the Ninth Circuit in the *Provident Securities Co.* case [16] held that a sale of assets for convertible debentures of the acquiring corporation was not an "unorthodox" transaction subject to the *Kern County* rationale. Since the Supreme Court affirmed on other grounds, it expressly pretermitted the question whether this holding was correct.

The cases have generally held that a transaction whereby a hostile tender offeror tenders the shares acquired by him to a "White Knight" or sells them back to the issuer in a "Greenmail" transaction is not an "unorthodox transaction" within the meaning of the *Kern County Land Company* case, since it is merely a voluntary sale for cash.[17] On the other hand, it was held by the Second Circuit that a defeated tender offeror which was forced to accept securities of a rival bidder, when the target company was merged with a subsidiary of the White Knight, was not liable under Section 16(b) under the rationale of the *Kern County Land Company* case, since the exchange of securities was involuntary (the defendant voted against the merger) and there was no possibility of access to inside information in view of the relationship of the defendant to the issuer.[18] There has been a debate in the cases, not yet finally resolved, as to whether the application of the *Kern County Land Company* doctrine requires that the transaction both be "involuntary" (that is, through the legal compulsion of a merger) and an exchange of securities rather than a transaction for cash. However, in Sterman v. Ferro Corporation,[19] the Sixth Circuit upheld the ultimate end-run around potential liability under Section 16(b) by ruling that, where the shareholder sold stock back to the issuer in a greenmail transaction, the issuer simply added on to the purchase price the potential liability under Section 16(b) of the seller and the seller immediately acknowledged such liability and repaid that portion of the consideration back to the issuer, any liability under Section 16(b) had been satisfied. This ploy would of course only work, if at all, where the sale is to the issuing corporation.

Cash-Out Mergers. A cash merger pursuant to which the shareholders of the acquired corporation are simply paid in cash for their shares would seem to be functionally equivalent to a simple purchase for cash (aside from the involuntary nature of the sale as to those who vote against the merger), and it is doubtful whether it would be considered to be an "unorthodox" transaction

---

15. Marquette Cement Manufacturing Co. v. Andreas, 239 F.Supp. 962 (S.D.N.Y. 1965); Stella v. Graham-Paige Motors Corp., 232 F.2d 299 (2d Cir.1956), cert. denied 352 U.S. 831; Blau v. Hodgkinson, 100 F.Supp. 361 (S.D.N.Y.1951). *A fortiori*, an exchange of stock for stock in a "B" reorganization would be a purchase and sale. Booth v. Varian Associates, 334 F.2d 1 (1st Cir.1964), cert. denied 379 U.S. 961; Fistel v. Christman, 135 F.Supp. 830 (S.D.N.Y. 1955). It has also been held that a sale of pledged stock by a bank is a "sale" of the stock by the beneficial owner, even though he has no control over it, for the purposes of Section 16(b). Alloys Unlimited, Inc. v. Gilbert, 319 F.Supp. 617 (S.D.N.Y.1970).

Compare Oliff v. Exchange International Corp., 669 F.2d 1162, CCH Fed.Sec.Law

Rptr. ¶ 97,634 (7th Cir.1980) (a purchase of shares by an estate from a foundation established by the decedent to avoid a stiff tax penalty was a "purchase" under Section 16(b) depite the "involuntary" nature of the transaction).

16. Provident Securities Co. v. Foremost-McKesson, Inc., 506 F.2d 601 (9th Cir. 1974), aff'd 423 U.S. 232.

17. Texas International Airlines v. National Airlines, Inc., 714 F.2d 533 (5th Cir. 1983), cert. denied 465 U.S. 1052, (1984); Super Stores, Inc. v. Reiner, 737 F.2d 962 (11th Cir.1984).

18. Heublein, Inc. v. General Cinema Corp., 722 F.2d 29 (2d Cir.1983).

19. 785 F.2d 162 (6th Cir.1986).

within the *Kern County Land Co.* case. The issuer of the securities is extinguished, however, by such a transaction. Such a transaction is usually carried out with a subsidiary of the acquiring corporation (or a subsidiary of a subsidiary) and the surviving corporation has only one shareholder—its new parent. Despite the fact that several cases have held that a cause of action under Section 16(b) passes to the surviving corporation in any merger transaction, the Seventh Circuit held in the case of Portnoy v. Kawecki Berylco Industries, Inc.[20] that a shareholder of the new parent corporation had no standing to bring an action under Section 16(b), if the surviving corporation failed or refused to do so, since he was not a shareholder of the "issuer." The only "shareholder" with such standing would be the new parent corporation owning 100% of the stock of the surviving corporation, and if it desired such an action it would simply cause the surviving corporation to bring it. In a friendly merger of this sort, it is, of course, unlikely that the new owner of the business is going to sue the officers of its own subsidiary to try to take away from them some portion of what it voluntarily gave them in the transaction. In a hostile takeover environment, this might be done, but the involuntary nature of the entire transaction in that situation might make the *Kern County Land Co.* principle applicable.

Stock Appreciation Rights. The recent popularity of "stock appreciation rights" as a form of executive compensation prompted a number of suits under Section 16(b). This type of plan involves offering to the executives covered by it a cash bonus equal to the increase in value of the stock of the corporation over some period of time, usually in tandem with stock options or with the executive having a choice as to whether to take the cash or to take an equivalent amount of stock. It was alleged in these cases that the election to take cash amounted, constructively, to a purchase of the stock and a simultaneous resale of it to the corporation for cash, thus triggering a short-swing profit equal to the excess of the resale price over the price hypothetically paid (or the entire amount of the cash received). The lower court cases uniformly rejected this contention,[21] and the Commission then made it untenable by amending Rule 16b–3 to exempt such a transaction if the conditions of that Rule are complied with.[22]

Recapitalizations. Roberts v. Eaton,[23] held that a reclassification of common stock into common and preferred by charter amendment was not a "purchase" of the new stock under Section 16(b). The *Roberts* case would seem to indicate that most recapitalizations do not involve any purchase or sale under Section 16(b) since they treat equally all shareholders similarly situated, require shareholder approval and merely continue the shareholders' investment in a different form in the same corporate enterprise. However, the refusal of the court to issue a "blackletter rubric" leaves open the possibility that some recapitalizations might be covered.

Acquisitions not for "value." It has been held that no "purchase" is involved in the issuance by a corporation of "rights" to purchase additional shares to all of its shareholders pro rata nor in the issuance of a stock dividend (although the exercise of the "rights" would obviously involve a purchase).[24]

20. 607 F.2d 765 (7th Cir.1979). Followed in Lewis v. McAdam, 762 F.2d 800 (9th Cir.1985).

21. Matas v. Siess, 467 F.Supp. 217 (S.D.N.Y.1979); Freedman v. Barrow, 427 F.Supp. 1129 (S.D.N.Y.1976); Rosen v. Drisler, 421 F.Supp. 1282 (S.D.N.Y.1976).

22. Sec. Exch. Act Rel. No. 13097 (Dec. 27, 1976).

23. 212 F.2d 82 (2d Cir.1954), cert. denied 348 U.S. 827.

24. Shaw v. Dreyfus, 172 F.2d 140 (2d Cir.1949), cert. denied 337 U.S. 907.

Similarly, it has been held that no purchase or sale is involved in a bona fide gift.[25]

See Tomlinson, Section 16(b): A Single Analysis of Purchases and Sales—Merging the Objective and Pragmatic Analyses, 1981 Duke L.J. 941 (1981); Katz and Lang, Section 16(b) and "Extraordinary" Transactions: Corporate Reorganizations and Stock Options, 49 Notre Dame Law 705 (1974); Weinstock, Section 16(b) and the Doctrine of Speculative Abuse: How to Succeed in Being Subjective Without Really Trying, 29 Bus.Law. 1153 (1974); Davis, Conversions as Purchases and Sales under Section 16(b) of the Securities Exchange Act of 1934, 24 Bus.Law. 1109 (1969); Hamilton, Convertible Securities and Section 16(b): The End of an Era, 44 Tex.L.Rev. 1447 (1966); Lang and Katz, Liability for "Short Swing" Trading in Corporate Reorganizations, 20 Sw.L.J. 472 (1966); 2 Loss, Securities Regulation 1066–84 (2d ed. 1961).

BERSHAD v. McDONOUGH

United States Court of Appeals, Seventh Circuit, 1970.
428 F.2d 693, cert. denied 400 U.S. 992 (1971).

Before SWYGERT, CHIEF JUDGE, CUMMINGS, CIRCUIT JUDGE, and GRANT, DISTRICT JUDGE.[1]

CUMMINGS, CIRCUIT JUDGE. This appeal is from a summary judgment in favor of the plaintiff, a common stockholder in the Cudahy Company of Phoenix, Arizona. Plaintiff brought this action under Section 16(b) of the Securities Exchange Act of 1934 (15 U.S.C. § 78p(b) to recover for Cudahy's benefit the "short-swing" profits coming to defendant from his and his wife's purchase and sale of 272,000 shares of Cudahy common stock.

On March 15 and 16, 1967, defendant Bernard P. McDonough and his wife Alma, who reside in Parkersburg, West Virginia, each purchased 141,363 shares of Cudahy common stock at $6.75 per share, totaling over 10% of the outstanding common stock of Cudahy. Soon after the purchase, McDonough was elected to the Cudahy Board of Directors and named Chairman of the Board. At the same time, Donald E. Martin and Carl Broughton, business associates of McDonough, were elected to the Cudahy Board.

On July 20, 1967, in Parkersburg, West Virginia, Mr. and Mrs. McDonough and Smelting Refining and Mining Co. ("Smelting") entered into a formal "option agreement" granting Smelting the right to purchase 272,000 shares of the McDonoughs' Cudahy stock. Smelting paid $350,000 upon execution of the agreement, which set the purchase price for the shares of $9 per share, or a total of $2,448,000. The option was exercisable on or before October 1, 1967. The 350,000 was to be applied against the purchase price but was to belong to the McDonoughs if Smelting failed to exercise the option. Accompanying this "option" was an escrow agreement under which the McDonoughs' 272,000 shares of Cudahy stock were placed in escrow with their lawyer. They also simultaneously granted Smelting in irrevocable proxy to vote their 272,000 shares of stock until October 1, 1967.

---

25. Shaw v. Dreyfus, supra note 24; Truncale v. Blumberg, 80 F.Supp. 387, 83 F.Supp. 628 (S.D.N.Y.1948).

1. Chief Judge Grant of the United States District Court for the Northern District of Indiana is sitting by designation.

A day or two after the documents were signed, Mr. McDonough and Carl Broughton, his business associate, acceded to the request of Smelting and agreed to resign from the Cudahy Board if Smelting representatives were put on the Board. Both of them resigned as directors on July 25, 1967. About that time, five nominees of Smelting were placed on the Cudahy Board. Smelting subsequently wrote the McDonoughs on September 22, 1967, that it was exercising its option. The closing took place in Parkersburg five days later, with the $2,098,000 balance of the purchase price being paid to the McDonoughs through the escrow agent. From their sales, Mr. and Mrs. McDonough realized a profit of $612,000.

In the court below, defendant contended that under West Virginia law the July 20 agreement constituted an option contract with Smelting, and not a contract for the sale of the Cudahy stock. Graney v. United States, 258 F.Supp. 383, 386 (S.D.W.Va.1966), affirmed per curiam, 377 F.2d 992 (4th Cir.1967), certiorari denied, 389 U.S. 1022. A stock option, he argued, does not qualify as a "sale or contract for sale" for purposes of applying the rule of Section 16(b) of the Securities Exchange Act of 1934 (15 U.S.C. § 78p(b)). The district court, however, took another view of the transaction. In a thoughtful memorandum opinion, the trial judge looked beyond the formal wording of the July 20 "option" and concluded that the transaction between the McDonoughs and Smelting "amounted to a sale or a contract of sale" within the terms of the Securities Exchange Act. Since this event occurred less than six months after the McDonoughs had purchased the Cudahy stock, under Section 16(b) summary judgment for $612,000, together with interest, was entered for plaintiff. We affirm.

Under Section 3(a)(14) of the Act, the "sales" covered by Section 16(b) are broadly defined to include "any contract to sell or otherwise dispose of" any security. See SEC v. National Securities, Inc., 393 U.S. 453, 467, n. 8. Construction of these terms is a matter of federal law (see Tcherepnin v. Knight, 389 U.S. 332, 337–338; Blau v. Lehman, 368 U.S. 403), and "[w]hatever the terms 'purchase' and 'sale' may mean in other contexts," they should be construed in a manner which will effectuate the purposes of the specific section of the Act in which they are used. SEC v. National Securities, Inc., 393 U.S. 453, 467. Applying this touchstone, courts have generally concluded that a transaction falls within the ambit of Section 16(b) if it can reasonably be characterized as a "purchase" or "sale" without doing violence to the language of the statute, and if the transaction is of a kind which can possibly lend itself to the speculation encompassed by Section 16(b). * * *

The phrase "any purchase and sale" in Section 16(b) is therefore not to be limited or defined solely in terms of commercial law of sales and notions of contractual rights and duties. * * * Applicability of this Section may depend upon the factual circumstances of the transaction, the sequence of relevant transactions, and whether the insider is "purchasing" or "selling" the security. Cf. Blau v. Lamb, 363 F.2d 507, 523–524 (2d Cir.1966), certiorari denied, 385 U.S. 1002. By the same token, we conclude transactions subject to speculative abuses deserve careful scrutiny. The insider should not be permitted to speculate with impunity merely by varying the paper form of his transactions. The commercial substance of the transaction rather than its form must be considered, and courts should guard against sham transactions by which an insider disguises the effective transfer of stock. Cf. Blau v. Allen, 163 F.Supp. 702, 705–706 (S.D.N.Y. 1958).

The considerations thus guiding the application of Section 16(b) provide substantial support for coverage of an insider's sale of an option within six months of his purchase of the underlying security. The utility of various stock options as a tool of speculation is well recognized. As noted in Booth v. Varian Associates, 334 F.2d 1, 4 (1st Cir.1964), certiorari denied, 379 U.S. 961:

> "Options, conversions and similar devices have lent themselves quite readily to the abuses uncovered in the Congressional investigation antedating the Act, and in order to give maximum support to the statute courts have attempted to include these transactions by characterizing them as purchases or sales."

The insider's sale of options in his stock is well adapted to speculation and abuse of inside information whether or not the option is subsequently exercised. The sale of the right to purchase the underlying security is itself a means of realizing a profit from that security. The right to purchase stock at a given price under specified circumstances, although clearly not identical to the rights attendant upon ownership of the stock itself, derives from and is dependent upon the value of the underlying security. Sale of such purchase rights provides an easy vehicle for the use of inside information in extracting profits from the stock itself. Where the option is ultimately exercised, moreover, the exact date of exercise may be unimportant to the substance of the transaction from the point of view of the insider-vendor, since he can exploit his position in the corporation by setting the terms of sale in the option. In addition, parties frequently provide that the option price shall be considered a retroactive down payment of the purchase price of the stock sold upon exercise of the option. Under such circumstances, it may be reasonable to hold the parties to their own treatment of the transaction and date the "sale" of the stock at the purchase of the option rather than its exercise. Cf. Booth v. Varian Associates, 334 F.2d 1, 4 (1st Cir.1964), certiorari denied, 379 U.S. 961; Michaely & Lee, Put and Call Options: Criteria for Applicability of Section 16(b) of the Securities Exchange Act of 1934, 40 Notre Dame Law. 239 (1965).

It is unnecessary, however, to rely solely upon these considerations to conclude that the McDonoughs' "sale" of the Cudahy stock to Smelting took place well in advance of the exercise of the option on September 22. The circumstances of the transactions clearly indicate that the stock was effectively transferred, for all practical purposes, long before the exercise of the option. The $350,000 "binder" ostensibly paid for the option represented over 14% of the total purchase price of the stock. Granting the magnitude of the sale contemplated, the size of the initial commitment strongly suggests that it "was not just a binder." Cf. Blau v. Allen, 163 F.Supp. 702, 705 (S.D.N.Y.1958). The extent of that payment represented, if not the exercise of the option, a significant deterrent to the abandonment of the contemplated sale. In addition, the reverse side of the "Option Agreement" contained provisions for the transfer of the Cudahy stock, endorsed in blank, to an escrow agent pending completion of the transaction. At the same time, the McDonoughs delivered an irrevocable proxy to Smelting to vote the 272,000 shares at any regular or special shareholders' meetings. Within a few days, McDonough and one of his associate directors resigned and were replaced by representatives of Smelting's interests, including the Chairman of the Board of Directors of Smelting, and the president and director of that corporation. Significantly, only a few days after the expiration of the six-month period from the McDonoughs' purchase of the Cudahy stock, Smelting formally exercised its option and, on the same day that Smelting mailed its notification, the McDonoughs executed the necessary stock powers.

Defendant finally contends that these facts were insufficient to support the district court's grant of summary judgment in favor of plaintiff. We cannot accept this contention. The question in this case, unlike Blau v. Allen, 163 F.Supp. 702, 705 (S.D.N.Y.1958), involves the determination not of the existence of the sale, but the date to be ascribed to the transfer under Section 16(b). The basic facts in this case are undisputed and far exceed those present in Allen. We conclude that as a matter of law, the sale was effectively accomplished within the six-month period contemplated by Section 16(b). Cf. Booth v. Varian Associates, 334 F.2d 1 (1st Cir.1964), certiorari denied, 379 U.S. 961. Consequently, the motion for summary judgment was properly granted.

Affirmed.

TIME OF THE PURCHASE OR SALE

The general rule has been stated to be that a purchase for the purposes of Section 16(b) occurs when the purchaser incurs "an irrevocable liability to take and pay for the stock,"[1] and conversely a sale would occur when the seller incurs an irrevocable liability to deliver and accept payment for the stock. While this formula is adequate in the ordinary case, there are some situations which raise a question as to its applicability.

Contracts where the amount or price of the stock is to be determined contingent upon future events. In Booth v. Varian Associates[2] there was an agreement in connection with a reorganization entered into in 1959 to issue "contingent shares" based upon a guarantee of the market price of the stock of the acquiring corporation in 1962. The court held that the date of purchase of the contingent shares for the purposes of Section 16(b) was the date of their delivery in 1962 because the price at which the stock was to be purchased was to be determined by the market price at the time of delivery.

How would this ruling apply to a situation where all of the stock of a closely-held corporation is sold to a listed company in a "B" reorganization, with a certain number of shares of the listed company to be delivered at a first closing,

---

1. Blau v. Ogsbury, 210 F.2d 426, at 427 (2d Cir.1954); Stella v. Graham-Paige Motors Corp., 232 F.2d 299 (2d Cir.1956), cert. denied 352 U.S. 831. As to when the obligation becomes "irrevocable" during the course of negotiation and signing of an agreement, see Champion Home Builders Co. v. Jeffress, 490 F.2d 611 (6th Cir.1974), cert. denied 416 U.S. 986; Morales v. Reading & Bates Offshore Drilling Co., 392 F.Supp. 41 (N.D.Okla.1975). In Riseman v. Orion Research, Inc., 749 F.2d 915 (1st Cir. 1984), a director exercised his stock option on the last day of his tenure as a director (which was the last day he *could* exercise it) and delivered a check in payment of the option price, but refused to deliver the required "investment letter" until some time later in an effort to delay the date of purchase and thereby elude liability under Section 16(b). The court held that this did not work.

2. 334 F.2d 1 (1st Cir.1964), cert. denied 379 U.S. 961.

and an additional number of shares to be delivered at a second closing two, three or four years later based upon the earnings of the acquired company, but with the additional delivery to be based on the market price of the stock at the time of the first closing? For example, the formula might be that a number of additional shares would be delivered equal to four years' earnings in excess of a certain amount divided by 25 (the current market price of the stock of the acquiring company). Would the second batch of shares be "purchased" for the purpose of Section 16(b) at the time of the first closing or at the time of the second closing, under the *Booth* case? Here the price at which the stock is to be purchased is fixed at the time of the signing of the contract, but the number to be purchased, and indeed (unless there is a minimum number specified in the contract) whether any at all will be purchased, is entirely dependent upon future events.

In Prager v. Sylvestri [3] Judge Carter refused to follow Booth v. Varian Associates. In that case the defendant sold his company in 1972 in a merger with another corporation which contained an "earned-out" provision. In 1975, he received an additional 105,362 shares under this earn-out provision in addition to those received in the two prior years, representing the maximum specified in the agreement of 300,000 shares. Six weeks after he received the shares earned in 1975, he sold his entire holdings in the company which, at that time, constituted more than 10% of the outstanding shares. The court held that the purchases were made in 1972, not in 1975 when the earn-out shares were received. Therefore, there was no liability under Section 16(b). The court said that the effective date of the merger was the date on which his commitment to purchase became irrevocable and the size of his investment (i.e., the stock of his prior company) was fixed for the purposes of Section 16(b).

Options. Under the formula quoted at the beginning of this note, it would seem quite clear that the obtaining of an option to buy is not a "purchase" under Section 16(b), since it does not impose upon the holder an irrevocable or any other kind of liability to take and pay for the stock but merely a right to acquire it at a determined price during the option period. And all of the employee stock option cases (see infra, p. 1439) have followed this approach, holding that the date of purchase is the date of *exercise* of the option. While theoretically there might be a purchase both at the time of the grant of the option and at the time of its exercise, it seems highly unlikely that Congress intended the same stock to be "purchased" at two different times for the purpose of Section 16(b). From time to time there has been worry that the *grant* of the option might also be a purchase, but no case has ever so held, and the SEC's employee stock option rule [4] exempts such grant.

A few moments thought, however, should be sufficient to demonstrate that this approach is wrong—the economic position which permits a person to profit from short-swing speculation is obtaining the *right* to acquire or dispose of stock at a predetermined price, not whether he has an "irrevocable liability." For example, suppose an officer or director or 10% holder purchases 10,000 shares of stock of his corporation at a price of $20 per share on May 1, on the basis of inside information that the price is temporarily going to rise. On September 1, he has inside information that the price, which has risen to $35 per share, is very shortly going to decline. He would like to sell the 10,000 shares, but he knows that if he does he will have to return the profit to the corporation under Section 16(b) (aside from the undesirable tax consequences). Therefore, he buys a 90–day put on 10,000 shares at a price of $35 per share; on November 15,

3. 449 F.Supp. 425 (S.D.N.Y.1978).

4. Rule 16b–3, as revised following the case of Greene v. Dietz, 247 F.2d 689 (2d Cir.1957). Securities Exchange Act Release No. 6275 (SEC 1960).

when the price has fallen to $15 per share, he exercises the put and sells the stock for $35 per share. By buying the put he has insured his profit of $15 per share minus the cost of the put. If this is all that is required for a person to evade Section 16(b), then the section is a ridiculous farce; but this is the result which would follow from a holding that the date of sale is the date of exercise of the option rather than the date of its acquisition.

Perhaps thoughts such as these, and the disturbing realization that it may have been totally wrong for 30 years in dealing with employee stock options, was what caused the Second Circuit in Miller v. General Outdoor Advertising Co.[5] to refuse to rule on the question whether the acquisition of a put or call was a "purchase" or "sale" for the purposes of Section 16(b), but instead to send the case back for trial in order to develop the "facts." It did not suggest what further "facts" it thought were going to throw any more light on this problem.[6]

The case of Silverman v. Landa,[7] which is sometimes discussed as bearing on this problem, actually has nothing to do with it. The court there held that an insider who *issued* a "straddle" (i.e., a simultaneous put and call) was not liable under Section 16(b) for the price received for the straddle. The *writing* of a put, call or straddle of course has exactly the opposite economic effect as the acquisition of one. The writer of the option has not improved his economic position for speculation but has worsened it (for which naturally he charges a price). Therefore, this case has no bearing on whether the acquisition of a put or call should be treated as a sale or purchase.[8]

On the other hand, as illustrated by the *Bershad* case, the granting of an option may be accompanied by the payment of such a large amount (to be subsequently credited upon the purchase price of the stock if the option is exercised) that the optionee economically has no choice but to exercise; and therefore the granting of the option is the practical equivalent of a sale. Compare the ruling of the Federal Reserve Board that "deep in the money" put and call options written by a broker-dealer are the practical equivalent of an extension of credit and therefore subject to Regulation T.[9] How do you reconcile the *Bershad* case with the *Kern County Land Co.* case, supra, on this point?

Rule 16a–6, as amended on February 23, 1972, requires the reporting of the acquisition or disposition of any put, call or straddle [10] by an insider; but the rule provides that it does not excuse the reporting of the *exercise* of the option also.

---

5. 337 F.2d 944 (2d Cir.1964).

6. In Morales v. Mapco, CCH Fed.Sec. Law Rptr. ¶ 95,094 (N.D.Okla.1975), the court held that the exercise of a warrant by the payment of $9 cash for stock, followed by a simultaneous sale of the stock, was not a "purchase" under Section 16(b); the value of the warrant plus $9 was the economic equivalent of the stock. This court thus became the first one to recognize the economic realities in the option situation.

7. 306 F.2d 422 (2d Cir.1962).

8. Of course, if the put or call is not exercised, but allowed to lapse, then there is a further question as to whether any profit has been "realized."

9. See Gordon & Co., Inc. v. The Board of Governors of the Federal Reserve System, 317 F.Supp. 1045 (D.Mass.1970), where the validity of this ruling was challenged in the court.

10. SEC Sec.Exch.Act Rel.No. 9499 (1972). Employee stock options meeting the conditions specified in Rule 16b–3 are excluded. Prior to this amendment only transferable options were covered by the reporting rule.

"ANY PERIOD OF LESS THAN SIX MONTHS"

Any purchase or sale may be matched under Section 16(b) with any sale or purchase within six months before or after its date, not merely three months before or after such date.[11] A "period of less than six months" means, since the law does not take account of fractions of days, a period commencing at 0001 hours on one day and ending at midnight on the day two days prior to the corresponding date in the sixth succeeding month; e.g., from January 15 through July 13, inclusive, in any year. On the other hand, a purchase at 8:00 a.m. on January 15 followed by a sale at 4:00 p.m. on July 14 would be in a period of exactly six months (since January 15 and July 14 are counted as full days), and therefore not within a period of "less than" six months.[12]

"PROFIT REALIZED"

The amount recoverable with respect to a single transaction in a Section 16(b) action is the difference between the purchase price and the sale price for any purchase and sale occurring within less than six months of each other, disregarding all other transactions. In other words, all such transactions producing profits result in recovery, and any transactions producing losses during the same period may be ignored, subject only to the limitation that a purchase or sale of a given number of shares may be matched only once against a transaction of the opposite character. The leading case of Smolowe v. Delendo Corp.,[13] which established this rule, stated: "Another possibility might be the striking of an average purchase price and an average sale price during the period, and using these as bases of computation. What this rule would do in concrete effect is to allow as offsets all losses made by such trading. * * * [T]his rule seems one not to be favored in the light of the statutory purpose. Compared to other possible rules, it tends to stimulate more active trading by reducing the chance of penalty. * * * Its application to a case where trading continued more than six months might be most uncertain. * * *" [14] The statute itself, of course, precludes any requirement that the particular shares sold must be identified as those purchased, since it applies to a sale preceding a purchase within the six months period.

Employee Stock Options. Employee stock options have been subjected to a very peculiar rule relating to the amount recoverable. If a five-year employee stock option on 1,000 shares is granted on March 1, 1960 at 100% of the market price on that date ($50 per share), and the option is later exercised on February 15, 1965 when the market price is $100 per share, and then the entire 1,000

---

11. Gratz v. Claughton, 187 F.2d 46 (2d Cir.1951).

12. Stella v. Graham-Paige Motors Corp., 132 F.Supp. 100 (S.D.N.Y.1955), rev'd on other grounds 232 F.2d 299 (2d Cir.), cert. denied 352 U.S. 831; Colonial Realty Corp. v. MacWilliams, 381 F.Supp. 26 (S.D.N.Y.1974), aff'd 512 F.2d 1187 (2d Cir.); Morales v. Reading & Bates Offshore Drilling Co., 392 F.Supp. 41 (N.D.Okla. 1975) (citing this passage of the casebook).

13. 136 F.2d 231 (2d Cir.1943), cert. denied 320 U.S. 751. Accord, Gratz v. Claughton, 187 F.2d 46 (2d Cir.1951); Arkansas Louisiana Gas Co. v. Stephens Investment Co., 141 F.Supp. 841 (W.D.Ark.

1956). Regarding the valuation of the consideration, when it is not in cash, see Lewis v. Realty Equities Corporation of New York, 396 F.Supp. 1026 (S.D.N.Y.1975).

14. 136 F.2d at 239. In S. & S. Realty Corp. v. Kleer-Vu Industries, Inc., 575 F.2d 1040 (2d Cir.1978), the Second Circuit held that if a rescission of a stock sale was to be treated as a sale and a repurchase, there was, nevertheless, no recoverable profit, even though the insider who was a party to the transaction avoided a loss as a result of the rescission. The court said: "The word 'recoverable' implies the existence of a tangible asset or a fund. One would be hard put to recover the avoidance of a loss."

shares is sold on June 1, 1965 at $100 per share, the courts have said that the issuer is entitled to recover $50,000 under Section 16(b) if the option was exercisable immediately at the time it was granted. However, if the option was not exercisable until one year after the date of its grant (beginning on March 1, 1961), and the market price on that date was $55 per share, then the amount recoverable would be only the difference between the $100 sale price and $55, or a total of $45,000.[15]

It seems quite clear, or at least it would have seemed quite clear if it had ever been recognized by any court (other than the Oklahoma District Court in the *Morales* case cited in Note 6, above) that if the date of the purchase is taken as March 1, 1960, then the purchase price of $50 is correct but the sale is not within six months; on the other hand, if the date of the purchase is taken as February 15, 1965, then the sale is within six months but what the employee paid for the stock was the cash consideration of $50 plus the value of the option on that date, which was necessarily $50, or a total of $100. What the market price on the date the option became exercisable (in the case of delayed exercisability) has to do with anything has never been satisfactorily explained.

Recognizing the injustice of thus recapturing a long-term gain as a fictitious short-swing profit, the SEC first exempted the exercise of the option (if certain conditions were met) from being a purchase for the purpose of Section 16(b).[16] The validity of this rule was "questioned" in Greene v. Dietz,[17] and later declared invalid in Perlman v. Timberlake.[18] The SEC subsequently amended this rule to eliminate the exemption for the exercise of the option, but continued an exemption for the grant of the option [19] against the possibility that some court might say that the same stock was purchased twice (despite the fact that Blau v. Ogsbury [20] specifically denied that this could be true).

15. Steinberg v. Sharpe, 95 F.Supp. 32 (S.D.N.Y.1950), aff'd 190 F.2d 82 (2d Cir.); Truncale v. Scully, 88 F.Sup. 677 (S.D.N.Y.), aff'd 182 F.2d 1021 (2d Cir.). How this rule would work where (as is quite common) the option becomes exercisable in installments, and several installments have accrued at the time of an exercise, has never been explained. Literally it is impossible to apply it. For example, suppose a 5-year option is granted on July 1, 1960, for 5,000 shares, which is to become exercisable as to 1,000 shares on each anniversary date for three years and as to the final 2,000 shares on the fourth anniversary date. On August 15, 1963, it is exercised as to 1,000 shares, and there is a sale of stock within 6 months before or after that date. The market price was different on each of the dates July 1, 1961, July 1, 1962 and July 1, 1963. Which 1,000 of the 3,000 shares as to which the option was exercisable on August 15, 1963, were in fact purchased? There is absolutely no way of telling, except by making some arbitrary assumption. But that information is essential in order to apply the rule of the *Steinberg* case. In Arrow Distributing Corporation v. Baumgartner, 783 F.2d 1274 (5th Cir.1986), the court held that the rule of the *Steinberg* case was not changed by the fact that the optioned stock was subject to restrictions upon resale. The court followed the rule of the *Steinberg* case, al-

though it noted the criticism of it set forth above.

16. Rule 16b-3, prior to its amendment on June 27, 1960, by Securities Exchange Act Release No. 6275 (SEC 1960). 2 CCH Fed.Sec.Law Rptr. ¶ 26,967.

17. 247 F.2d 689 (2d Cir.1957).

18. 172 F.Supp. 246 (S.D.N.Y.1959). Contra: Continental Oil Co. v. Perlitz, 176 F.Supp. 219 (S.D.Tex.1959). The following cases found it unnecessary to consider the validity of Rule 16b-3 because the insider had relied on it in good faith under Section 23(a) of the Exchange Act before it was declared invalid. Van Aalten v. Hurley, 176 F.Supp. 851 (S.D.N.Y.1959); Emerson Electric Manufacturing Co. v. O'Neill, 168 F.Supp. 804 (E.D.Mo.1958).

19. Rule 16b-3, as amended by Securities Exchange Act Release No. 6275 (SEC 1960). Keller Industries, Inc. v. Walden, 462 F.2d 388 (5th Cir.1972), holds that Rule 16b-3 no longer exempts the acquisition of stock pursuant to a restricted or qualified stock option, after the amendment on June 27, 1960.

20. 210 F.2d 426, at 427 (2d Cir.1954). The problem which would arise if the day of the grant of the option were taken as the date of purchase is that many companies make annual grants of options, and this would preclude any sales at any time

However, the SEC had also adopted another rule, Rule 16b–6, limiting the amount recoverable in the employee stock option cases to an amount equal to the difference between the sale price and the lowest market price within a period of six months before and after the date of the sale. This rule was subsequently held to be valid in Blau v. Hodgkinson [21] and Kornfeld v. Eaton,[22] despite the fact that the section gives the SEC the power to exempt "transactions", not to redefine the measure of damages.[23]

Dividends. The case of Adler v. Klawans [24] held that the following dividends were not recoverable as a part of the "profit realized": dividends declared on stock prior to its purchase by the insider; dividends declared on stock owned by a person before he became an officer or director (even though he need not be such both at the time of the purchase and sale in order to incur liability); and dividends declared on specific certificates which were not sold at a profit (although there need be no matching of specific certificates purchased and sold in order to create liability). However, the case of Western Auto Supply Co. v. Gamble-Skogmo, Inc.[25] seems to be somewhat inconsistent with the last holding of the *Adler* case. That case held that dividends payable on an equivalent number of shares during the interval between the purchase and sale were recoverable as a part of the "profit realized", even though the shares sold were not those purchased and the ones purchased had been immediately disposed of by gift, so that the insider never received any dividends on those shares. However, the cases may be reconcilable, as suggested in the *Western Auto Supply Company* case, by the fact that the dividends involved in the third branch of the *Adler* case were on shares which were later disposed of at a loss and were declared during an interval when no profitable insider trading occurred. Apparently all courts would agree that dividends declared while the owner is an insider on the particular shares sold at a profit are a part of the recoverable profit.

Interest. The case of Blau v. Lehman [26] establishes that interest may be allowable on the recovery under Section 16(b) in the discretion of the court "in response to considerations of fairness."

Tax Consequences of Liability under Section 16(b). The Tax Court has consistently and persistently held that amounts recovered from an officer or director under Section 16(b) can be deducted by him on his tax return as an "ordinary and necessary" business expense; and all of the Circuit Courts to

by an insider so long as he was receiving such annual grants. The problem would be even more serious if the date that the option *became exercisable* were taken as the date of purchase, since many more stock option plans provide that options granted become exercisable in annual pro rata increments during the life of the options.

21. 100 F.Supp. 361 (S.D.N.Y.1951).

22. 327 F.2d 263 (2d Cir.1964).

23. See Rattner v. Lehman, 193 F.2d 564, at 566 (2d Cir.1952): "The Commission may exempt 'transactions'; but it cannot reduce the liability imposed by section 16(b)." In Volk v. Zlotoff, 285 F.Supp. 650 (S.D.N.Y.1968), it was held that a mutual rescission of the exercise of a stock option between an officer and the corporation does not wipe out any Section 16(b) liabili-

ty which arose upon the exercise. In Brenner v. Johnson, 328 F.Supp. 149 (E.D.Wis. 1971), it was held that Rule 16b–9 dealing with convertible securities does not apply to an employee stock option, even if the exercise price is less than 15% of the market price at the time of the exercise.

For cases dealing with the computation of the maximum recovery under Rule 16b–6, see B.T. Babbitt, Inc. v. Lachner, 332 F.2d 255 (2d Cir.1964); Brenner v. Career Academy, Inc., 467 F.2d 1080 (7th Cir. 1972); Sonics International, Inc. v. Johnson, 387 F.Supp. 741 (N.D.Tex.1975); Volk v. Zlotoff, 318 F.Supp. 864 (S.D.N.Y.1970).

24. 267 F.2d 840 (2d Cir.1959).

25. 348 F.2d 736 (8th Cir.1965), cert. denied 382 U.S. 987.

26. 368 U.S. 403 (1962).

which these cases have been appealed by the Internal Revenue Service have consistently and persistently reversed the Tax Court.[27]

See Michaely and Lee, Put and Call Options: Criteria for Applicability of Section 16(b) of the Securities Exchange Act of 1934, 40 Notre Dame L.Rev. 239 (1965); Wheat, Securities Regulation Aspects of Employee Stock Options Under the 1964 Revenue Act, 17 So.Calif.Tax Inst. 151 (1965); Laufer, Effect of Section 16(b) of the Securities Exchange Act on Use of Options by Insiders, 8 N.Y.L.F. 232 (1962); Note, Put and Call Options Under Section 16 of the Securities Exchange Act, 69 Yale L.J. 868 (1960); 2 Loss, Securities Regulation 1062–66, 1075–82 (2d ed. 1961).

27. Cummings v. Commissioner, 506 F.2d 449 (2d Cir.1974); Anderson v. Commissioner, 480 F.2d 1304 (7th Cir.1973).

Part V

THE RACKETEER INFLUENCED AND CORRUPT ORGANIZATIONS ACT

Chapter 22

CIVIL RICO

Statutes and Regulations

Securities Act of 1933, § 17(a).

Securities Exchange Act of 1934, §§ 10(b), 20(a).

Rule 10b-5.

18 U.S.C. §§ 1961-1968; 18 U.S.C. §§ 1341 & 1343; 18 U.S.C. § 1954.

UNITED STATES v. TURKETTE

Supreme Court of the United States, 1981.
452 U.S. 576, 101 S.Ct. 2524, 69 L.Ed.2d 246.

JUSTICE WHITE delivered the opinion of the Court.

Chapter 96 of Title 18 of the United States Code, 18 U.S.C. §§ 1961–1968 (1976 ed. and Supp. III), entitled Racketeer Influenced and Corrupt Organizations (RICO), was added to Title 18 by Title IX of the Organized Crime Control Act of 1970, Pub.L. 91–452, 84 Stat. 941. The question in this case is whether the term "enterprise" as used in RICO encompasses both legitimate and illegitimate enterprises or is limited in application to the former. The Court of Appeals for the First Circuit held that Congress did not intend to include within the definition of "enterprise" those organizations which are exclusively criminal. 632 F.2d 896 (1980). This position is contrary to that adopted by every other Circuit that has addressed the issue.[1] We granted certiorari to resolve this conflict. 449 U.S. 1123 (1981).

1. See United States v. Sutton, 642 F.2d 1001, 1006–1009 (CA6 1980) (en banc), cert. pending, Nos. 80–6058, 80–6137, 80–6141, 80–6147, 80–6253, 80–6254, 80–6272; United States v. Errico, 635 F.2d 152, 155 (CA2 1980); United States v. Provenzano, 620 F.2d 985, 992–993 (CA3), cert. denied, 449 U.S. 899 (1980); United States v. Whitehead, 618 F.2d 523, 525, n. 1 (CA4 1980); United States v. Aleman, 609 F.2d 298, 304–305 (CA7 1979), cert. denied, 445 U.S. 946 (1980); United States v. Rone, 598 F.2d 564, 568–569 (CA9 1979), cert. denied, 445 U.S. 946 (1980); United States v. Swider-

ski, 193 U.S.App.D.C. 92, 94–95, 593 F.2d 1246, 1248–1249 (1978), cert. denied, 441 U.S. 933 (1979); United States v. Elliott, 571 F.2d 880, 896–898 (CA5), cert. denied, 439 U.S. 953 (1978). See also United States v. Anderson, 626 F.2d 1358, 1372 (CA8 1980), cert. denied, 450 U.S. 912 (1981). But see United States v. Sutton, 605 F.2d 260, 264–270 (CA6 1979), vacated, 642 F.2d 1001 (1980); United States v. Rome, supra, at 573 (Ely, J., dissenting); United States v. Altese, 542 F.2d 104, 107 (CA2 1976) (Van Graafeiland, J., dissenting), cert. denied, 429 U.S. 1039 (1977).

I

Count Nine of a nine-count indictment charged respondent and 12 others with conspiracy to conduct and participate in the affairs of an enterprise engaged in interstate commerce through a pattern of racketeering activities, in violation of 18 U.S.C. § 1962(d). The indictment described the enterprise as "a group of individuals associated in fact for the purpose of illegally trafficking in narcotics and other dangerous drugs, committing arsons, utilizing the United States mails to defraud insurance companies, bribing and attempting to bribe local police officers, and corruptly influencing and attempting to corruptly influence the outcome of state court proceedings. * * *" The other eight counts of the indictment charged the commission of various substantive criminal acts by those engaged in and associated with the criminal enterprise, including possession with intent to distribute and distribution of controlled substances, and several counts of insurance fraud by arson and other means. The common thread to all counts was respondent's alleged leadership of this criminal organization through which he orchestrated and participated in the commission of the various crimes delineated in the RICO count or charged in the eight preceding counts.

After a 6–week jury trial, in which the evidence focused upon both the professional nature of this organization and the execution of a number of distinct criminal acts, respondent was convicted on all nine counts. He was sentenced to a term of 20 years on the substantive counts, as well as a 2–year special parole term on the drug count. On the RICO conspiracy count he was sentenced to a 20–year concurrent term and fined $20,000.

On appeal, respondent argued that RICO was intended solely to protect legitimate business enterprises from infiltration by racketeers and that RICO does not make criminal the participation in an association which performs only illegal acts and which has not infiltrated or attempted to infiltrate a legitimate enterprise. The Court of Appeals agreed. We reverse.

II

In determining the scope of a statute, we look first to its language. If the statutory language is unambiguous, in the absence of "a clearly expressed legislative intent to the contrary, that language must ordinarily be regarded as conclusive." Consumer Product Safety Comm'n v. GTE Sylvania, Inc., 447 U.S. 102, 108 (1980). Of course, there is no errorless test for identifying or recognizing "plain" or "unambiguous" language. Also, authoritative administrative constructions should be given the deference to which they are entitled, absurd results are to be avoided and internal inconsistencies in the statute must be dealt with. Trans Alaska Pipeline Rate Cases, 436 U.S. 631, 643 (1978); Commissioner v. Brown, 380 U.S. 563, 571 (1965). We nevertheless begin with the language of the statute.

Section 1962(c) makes it unlawful "for any person employed by or associated with any enterprise engaged in, or the activities of which affect, interstate or foreign commerce, to conduct or participate, directly, or indirectly, in the conduct of such enterprise's affairs through a pattern of racketeering activity or collection of unlawful debt." The term "enterprise" is defined as including "any individual, partnership, corporation, association, or other legal entity, and any union or group of individuals associated in fact although not a legal entity." § 1961(4). There is no restriction upon the associations embraced by the definition: an enterprise includes any union or group of individuals associated in fact. On its face, the definition appears to include both legitimate and illegitimate enterprises within its scope; it no more excludes criminal enterprises than it does legitimate ones. Had Congress not intended to reach criminal associations, it could easily have narrowed the sweep of the definition by inserting a single word, "legitimate." But it did nothing to indicate that an enterprise consisting of a group of individuals was not covered by RICO if the purpose of the enterprise was exclusively criminal.

The Court of Appeals, however, clearly departed from and limited the statutory language. It gave several reasons for doing so, none of which is adequate. First, it relied in part on the rule of *ejusdem generis* an aid to statutory construction problems suggesting that where general words follow a specific enumeration of persons or things, the general words should be limited to persons or things similar to those specifically enumerated. See 2A C. Sands, Sutherland on Statutory Construction § 47.17 (4th ed. 1973). The Court of Appeals ruled that because each of the specific enterprises enumerated in § 1961(4) is a "legitimate" one, the final catchall phrase—"any union or group of individuals associated in fact"—should also be limited to legitimate enterprises. There are at least two flaws in this reasoning. The rule of *ejusdem generis* is no more than an aid to construction and comes into play only when there is some uncertainty as to the meaning of a particular clause in a statute. * * * Considering the language and structure of § 1961(4), however, we not only perceive no uncertainty in the meaning to be attributed to the phrase, "any union or group of individuals associated in fact" but we are convinced for another reason that *ejusdem generis* is wholly inapplicable in this context.

Section 1961(4) describes two categories of associations that come within the purview of the "enterprise" definition. The first encompasses organizations such as corporations and partnerships, and other "legal entities." The second covers "any union or group of individuals associated in fact although not a legal entity." The Court of Appeals assumed that the second category was merely a more general description of the first. Having made that assumption, the court concluded that the more generalized description in the second category should be limited by the specific examples enumerated in the first. But that assumption is untenable. Each category describes a separate type of enterprise to be covered by the statute—those that are recognized as legal entities and those that are not. The latter is not a more general description of the former. The second category itself not containing any specific enumeration that is followed by a general description, *ejusdem generis* has no bearing on the meaning to be attributed to that part of § 1961(4).[4]

---

4. The Court of Appeals' application of *ejusdem generis* is further flawed by the assumption that "any individual, partnership, corporation, association or other legal entity" could not act totally beyond the pale of the law. The mere fact that a given enterprise is favored with a legal existence does not prevent that enterprise from proceeding along a wholly illegal course of conduct. Therefore, since legitimacy of purpose is not a universal characteristic of the specifically listed enterprises, it would be improper to engraft this characteristic upon the second category of enterprises.

A second reason offered by the Court of Appeals in support of its judgment was that giving the definition of "enterprise" its ordinary meaning would create several internal inconsistencies in the Act. With respect to § 1962(c), it was said:

"If 'a pattern of racketeering' can itself be an 'enterprise' for purposes of section 1962(c), then the two phrases 'employed by or associated with any enterprise' and 'the conduct of such enterprise's affairs through [a pattern of racketeering activity]' add nothing to the meaning of the section. The words of the statute are coherent and logical only if they are read as applying to legitimate enterprises." 632 F.2d, at 899.

This conclusion is based on a faulty premise. That a wholly criminal enterprise comes within the ambit of the statute does not mean that a "pattern of racketeering activity" is an "enterprise." In order to secure a conviction under RICO, the Government must prove both the existence of an "enterprise" and the connected "pattern of racketeering activity." The enterprise is an entity, for present purposes a group of persons associated together for a common purpose of engaging in a course of conduct. The pattern of racketeering activity is, on the other hand, a series of criminal acts as defined by the statute. 18 U.S.C. § 1961(1) (1976 ed., Supp. III). The former is proved by evidence of an ongoing organization, formal or informal, and by evidence that the various associates function as a continuing unit. The latter is proved by evidence of the requisite number of acts of racketeering committed by the participants in the enterprise. While the proof used to establish these separate elements may in particular cases coalesce, proof of one does not necessarily establish the other. The "enterprise" is not the "pattern of racketeering activity"; it is an entity separate and apart from the pattern of activity in which it engages. The existence of an enterprise at all times remains a separate element which must be proved by the Government.[5]

Apart from § 1962(c)'s proscription against participating in an enterprise through a pattern of racketeering activities, RICO also proscribes the investment of income derived from racketeering activity in an enterprise engaged in or which affects interstate commerce as well as the acquisition of an interest in or control of any such enterprise through a pattern of racketeering activity. 18 U.S.C. §§ 1962(a) and (b). The Court of Appeals concluded that these provisions of RICO should be interpreted so as to apply only to legitimate enterprises. If these two sections are so limited, the Court of Appeals held that the proscription in § 1962(c), at issue here, must be similarly limited. Again, we do not accept the premise from which the Court of Appeals derived its conclusion. It is obvious that § 1962(a) and (b) address the infiltration by organized crime of legitimate businesses, but we cannot agree that these sections were not also aimed at preventing racketeers from investing or reinvesting in wholly illegal enterprises and from acquiring through a pattern of racketeering activity wholly illegitimate enterprises such as an illegal gambling business or a loan-sharking

---

5. The Government takes the position that proof of a pattern of racketeering activity in itself would not be sufficient to establish the existence of an enterprise: "We do not suggest that any two sporadic and isolated offenses by the same actor or actors *ipso facto* constitute an 'illegitimate' enterprise; rather, the existence of the enterprise as an independent entity must also be shown." Reply Brief for United States 4. But even if that were not the case, the Court of Appeals' position on this point is of little force. Language in a statute is not rendered superfluous merely because in some contexts that language may not be pertinent.

operation. There is no inconsistency or anomaly in recognizing that § 1962 applies to both legitimate and illegitimate enterprises. Certainly the language of the statute does not warrant the Court of Appeals' conclusion to the contrary.

Similarly, the Court of Appeals noted that various civil remedies were provided by § 1964, including divestiture, dissolution, reorganization, restrictions on future activities by violators of RICO, and treble damages. These remedies it thought would have utility only with respect to legitimate enterprises. As a general proposition, however, the civil remedies could be useful in eradicating organized crime from the social fabric, whether the enterprise be ostensibly legitimate or admittedly criminal. The aim is to divest the association of the fruits of its ill-gotten gains. See infra, at 2532–2534. Even if one or more of the civil remedies might be inapplicable to a particular illegitimate enterprise, this fact would not serve to limit the enterprise concept. Congress has provided civil remedies for use when the circumstances so warrant. It is untenable to argue that their existence limits the scope of the criminal provisions.

Finally, it is urged that the interpretation of RICO to include both legitimate and illegitimate enterprises will substantially alter the balance between federal and state enforcement of criminal law. This is particularly true, so the argument goes, since included within the definition of racketeering activity are a significant number of acts made criminal under state law. 18 U.S.C. § 1961(1) (1976 ed., Supp. III). But even assuming that the more inclusive definition of enterprise will have the effect suggested, the language of the statute and its legislative history indicate that Congress was well aware that it was entering a new domain of federal involvement through the enactment of this measure. Indeed, the very purpose of the Organized Crime Control Act of 1970 was to enable the Federal Government to address a large and seemingly neglected problem. The view was that existing law, state and federal, was not adequate to address the problem, which was of national dimensions. That Congress included within the definition of racketeering activities a number of state crimes strongly indicates that RICO criminalized conduct that was also criminal under state law, at least when the requisite elements of a RICO offense are present. As the hearings and legislative debates reveal, Congress was well aware of the fear that RICO "would mov[e] large substantive areas formerly totally within the police power of the State into the Federal realm." 116 Cong.Rec. 35217 (1970) (remarks of Rep. Eckhardt). See also id., at 35205 (remarks of Rep. Mikva); id., at 35213 (comments of the American Civil Liberties Union); Hearings on Organized Crime Control before Subcommittee No. 5 of the House Committee on the Judiciary, 91st Cong., 2d Sess., 329, 370 (1970) (statement of Sheldon H. Eisen on behalf of the Association of the Bar of the City of New York). In the face of these objections, Congress nonetheless proceeded to enact the measure, knowing that it would alter somewhat the role of the Federal Government in the war against organized crime and that the alteration would entail prosecutions involving acts of racketeering that are also crimes under state law. There is no argument that Congress acted beyond its power in so doing. That being the case, the courts are without authority to restrict the application of the statute. See United States v. Culbert, 435 U.S. 371, 379–380 (1978).

Contrary to the judgment below, neither the language nor structure of RICO limits its application to legitimate "enterprises." Applying it also to criminal organizations does not render any portion of the statute superfluous nor does it create any structural incongruities within the framework of the Act. The result is neither absurd nor surprising. On the contrary, insulating the wholly criminal enterprise from prosecution under RICO is the more incongruous position.

Section 904(a) of RICO, 84 Stat. 947, directs that "[t]he provisions of this Title shall be liberally construed to effectuate its remedial purposes." With or without this admonition, we could not agree with the Court of Appeals that illegitimate enterprises should be excluded from coverage. We are also quite sure that nothing in the legislative history of RICO requires a contrary conclusion.

* * *

As a measure to deal with the infiltration of legitimate businesses by organized crime, RICO was both preventive and remedial. Respondent's view would ignore the preventive function of the statute. If Congress had intended the more circumscribed approach espoused by the Court of Appeals, there would have been some positive sign that the law was not to reach organized criminal activities that give rise to the concerns about infiltration. The language of the statute, however—the most reliable evidence of its intent—reveals that Congress opted for a far broader definition of the word "enterprise," and we are unconvinced by anything in the legislative history that this definition should be given less than its full effect.

The judgment of the Court of Appeals is accordingly

Reversed.

JUSTICE STEWART agrees with the reasoning and conclusion of the Court of Appeals as to the meaning of the term "enterprise" in this statute. See 632 F.2d 896. Accordingly, he respectfully dissents.

SEDIMA, S.P.R.L. v. IMREX COMPANY, INC.

Supreme Court of the United States, 1985.
473 U.S. 479, 105 S.Ct. 3275, 87 L.Ed.2d 346.

JUSTICE WHITE delivered the opinion of the Court.

The Racketeer Influenced and Corrupt Organizations Act (RICO), Pub.L. 91–452, Title IX, 84 Stat. 941, as amended, 18 U.S.C. §§ 1961–1968, provides a private civil action to recover treble damages for injury "by reason of a violation of" its substantive provisions. 18 U.S.C. § 1964(c). The initial dormancy of this provision and its recent greatly increased utilization[1] are now familiar history.[2] In response to what it perceived to be misuse of civil RICO by private plaintiffs, the court below construed

---

1. Of 270 district RICO decisions prior to this year, only 3% (nine cases) were decided throughout the 1970s, 2% were decided in 1980, 7% in 1981, 13% in 1982, 33% in 1983, and 43% in 1984. Report of the Ad Hoc Civil RICO Task Force of the ABA Section of Corporation, Banking and Business Law 55 (1985) (hereinafter ABA Report); see also *id.*, at 53a (table).

2. For a thorough bibliography of civil RICO decisions and commentary, see Milner, A Civil RICO Bibliography, 21 C.W. L.R. 409 (1985).

§ 1964(c) to permit private actions only against defendants who had been convicted on criminal charges, and only where there had occurred a "racketeering injury." While we understand the court's concern over the consequences of an unbridled reading of the statute, we reject both of its holdings.

I

RICO takes aim at "racketeering activity," which it defines as any act "chargeable" under several generically described state criminal laws, any act "indictable" under numerous specific federal criminal provisions, including mail and wire fraud, and any "offense" involving bankruptcy or securities fraud or drug-related activities that is "punishable" under federal law. § 1961(1).[3] Section 1962, entitled "Prohibited Activities," outlaws the use of income derived from a "pattern of racketeering activity" to acquire an interest in or establish an enterprise engaged in or affecting interstate commerce; the acquisition or maintenance of any interest in an enterprise "through" a pattern of racketeering activity; conducting or participating in the conduct of an enterprise through a pattern of racketeering activity; and conspiring to violate any of these provisions.[4]

3. RICO defines "racketeering activity" to mean "(A) any act or threat involving murder, kidnapping, gambling, arson, robbery, bribery, extortion, or dealing in narcotic or other dangerous drugs, which is chargeable under State law and punishable by imprisonment for more than one year; (B) any act which is indictable under any of the following provisions of title 18, United States Code: Section 201 (relating to bribery), section 224 (relating to sports bribery), sections 471, 472, and 473 (relating to counterfeiting), section 659 (relating to theft from interstate shipment) if the act indictable under section 659 is felonious, section 664 (relating to embezzlement from pension and welfare funds), sections 891–894 (relating to extortionate credit transactions), section 1084 (relating to the transmission of gambling information), section 1341 (relating to mail fraud), section 1343 (relating to wire fraud), section 1503 (relating to obstruction of justice), section 1510 (relating to obstruction of criminal investigations), section 1511 (relating to the obstruction of State or local law enforcement), section 1951 (relating to interference with commerce, robbery, or extortion), section 1952 (relating to racketeering), section 1953 (relating to interstate transportation of wagering paraphernalia) section 1954 (relating to unlawful welfare fund payments), section 1955 (relating to the prohibition of illegal gambling businesses), sections 2312 and 2313 (relating to interstate transportation of stolen motor vehicles), sections 2314 and 2315 (relating to interstate transportation of stolen property), section 2320 (relating to trafficking in certain motor vehicles or motor vehicle parts), sections 2341–2346 (relating to traf-

ficking in contraband cigarettes), sections 2421–24 (relating to white slave traffic), (C) any act which is indictable under title 29, United States Code, section 186 (dealing with restrictions on payments and loans to labor organizations) or section 501(c) (relating to embezzlement from union funds), (D) any offense involving fraud connected with a case under title 11, fraud in the sale of securities, or the felonious manufacture, importation, receiving, concealment, buying, selling, or otherwise dealing in narcotic or other dangerous drugs, punishable under any law of the United States, or (E) any act which is indictable under the Currency and Foreign Transactions Reporting Act." 18 U.S.C.A. § 1961(1) (Supp.1985).

4. In relevant part, 18 U.S.C. § 1962 provides:

"(a) It shall be unlawful for any person who has received any income derived, directly or indirectly, from a pattern of racketeering activity or through collection of an unlawful debt ∗ ∗ ∗ to use or invest, directly or indirectly, any part of such income, or the proceeds of such income, in acquisition of any interest in, or the establishment or operation of, any enterprise which is engaged in, or the activities of which affect, interstate or foreign commerce. ∗ ∗ ∗

"(b) It shall be unlawful for any person through a pattern of racketeering activity or through collection of an unlawful debt to acquire or maintain, directly or indirectly, any interest in or control of any enterprise which is engaged in, or the activities of which affect, interstate or foreign commerce.

Congress provided criminal penalties of imprisonment, fines, and forfeiture for violation of these provisions. § 1963. In addition, it set out a far-reaching civil enforcement scheme, § 1964, including the following provision for private suits:

"Any person injured in his business or property by reason of a violation of section 1962 of this chapter may sue therefor in any appropriate United States district court and shall recover threefold the damages he sustains and the cost of the suit, including a reasonable attorney's fee." § 1964(c).

In 1979, petitioner Sedima, a Belgian corporation, entered into a joint venture with respondent Imrex Co. to provide electronic components to a Belgian firm. The buyer was to order parts through Sedima; Imrex was to obtain the parts in this country and ship them to Europe. The agreement called for Sedima and Imrex to split the net proceeds. Imrex filled roughly $8,000,000 in orders placed with it through Sedima. Sedima became convinced, however, that Imrex was presenting inflated bills, cheating Sedima out of a portion of its proceeds by collecting for nonexistent expenses.

In 1982, Sedima filed this action in the Federal District Court for the Eastern District of New York. The complaint set out common-law claims of unjust enrichment, conversion, and breach of contract, fiduciary duty, and a constructive trust. In addition, it asserted RICO claims under § 1964(c) against Imrex and two of its officers. Two counts alleged violations of § 1962(c), based on predicate acts of mail and wire fraud. See 18 U.S.C. §§ 1341, 1343, 1961(1)(B). A third count alleged a conspiracy to violate § 1962(c). Claiming injury of at least $175,000, the amount of the alleged overbilling, Sedima sought treble damages and attorney's fees.

The District Court held that for an injury to be "by reason of a violation of section 1962," as required by § 1964(c), it must be somehow different in kind from the direct injury resulting from the predicate acts of racketeering activity. 574 F.Supp. 963 (EDNY 1983). While not choosing a precise formulation, the District Court held that a complaint must allege a "RICO-type injury," which was either some sort of distinct "racketeering injury," or a "competitive injury." It found "no allegation here of any injury apart from that which would result directly from the alleged predicate acts of mail fraud and wire fraud," id., at 965, and accordingly dismissed the RICO counts for failure to state a claim.

A divided panel of the Court of Appeals for the Second Circuit affirmed. 741 F.2d 482 (1984). * * *

II

As a preliminary matter, it is worth briefly reviewing the legislative history of the private treble damages action. RICO formed Title IX of the Organized Crime Control Act of 1970, Pub.L. 91–452, 84 Stat. 922. The

"(c) It shall be unlawful for any person employed by or associated with any enterprise engaged in, or the activities of which affect, interstate or foreign commerce, to conduct or participate, directly or indirectly, in the conduct of such enterprise's affairs through a pattern of racketeering activity or collection of unlawful debt.

"(d) It shall be unlawful for any person to conspire to violate any of the provisions of subsections (a), (b), or (c) of this section."

civil remedies in the bill passed by the Senate, S. 30, were limited to injunctive actions by the United States and became §§ 1964(a), (b), and (d). Previous versions of the legislation, however, had provided for a private treble damages action in exactly the terms ultimately adopted in § 1964(c). See S. 1623, 91st Cong., 1st Sess., § 4(a) (1969); S. 2048, S. 2049, 90th Cong., 1st Sess. (1967).

During hearings on S. 30 before the House Judiciary Committee, Representative Steiger proposed the addition of a private treble damages action "similar to the private damage remedy found in the antitrust laws. * * * [T]hose who have been wronged by organized crime should at least be given access to a legal remedy. In addition, the availability of such a remedy would enhance the effectiveness of title IX's prohibitions." Hearings on S. 30, and related proposals, before Subcommittee No. 5 of the House Committee on the Judiciary, 91st Cong., 2d Sess., 520 (1970) (hereinafter House Hearings). The American Bar Association also proposed an amendment "based upon the concept of Section 4 of the Clayton Act." Id., at 543–544, 548, 559; see 116 Cong.Rec. 25190–25191 (1970). See also H.R. 9327, 91st Cong., 1st Sess. (1969) (House counterpart to S. 1623).

Over the dissent of three members, who feared the treble damages provision would be used for malicious harassment of business competitors, the Committee approved the amendment. H.R.Rep. No. 91–1549, pp. 58, 187 (1970), U.S.Code Cong. & Admin.News 4007. In summarizing the bill on the House floor, its sponsor described the treble damages provision as "another example of the antitrust remedy being adapted for use against organized criminality." 116 Cong.Rec. 35295 (1970). The full House then rejected a proposal to create a complementary treble damages remedy for those injured by being named as defendants in malicious private suits. Id., at 35342. Representative Steiger also offered an amendment that would have allowed private injunctive actions, fixed a statute of limitations, and clarified venue and process requirements. Id., at 35346; see id., at 35226–35227. The proposal was greeted with some hostility because it had not been reviewed in Committee, and Steiger withdrew it without a vote being taken. Id., at 35346–35347. The House then passed the bill, with the treble damages provision in the form recommended by the Committee. Id., at 35363–35364.

The Senate did not seek a conference and adopted the bill as amended in the House. Id., at 36296. The treble damages provision had been drawn to its attention while the legislation was still in the House, and had received the endorsement of Senator McClellan, the sponsor of S. 30, who was of the view that the provision would be "a major new tool in extirpating the baneful influence of organized crime in our economic life." Id., at 25190.

III

The language of RICO gives no obvious indication that a civil action can proceed only after a criminal conviction. The word "conviction" does not appear in any relevant portion of the statute. See §§ 1961, 1962, 1964(c). To the contrary, the predicate acts involve conduct that is "chargeable" or "indictable," and "offense[s]" that are "punishable," under various criminal statutes. § 1961(1). As defined in the statute, racketeering activity consists not of acts for which the defendant has been convicted, but of acts for which he could be. See also S.Rep. No. 91–617, p. 158 (1969): "a racketeering activity * * * must be an act in itself *subject to* criminal sanction" (emphasis added). Thus, a prior conviction requirement cannot be found in the definition of "racketeering activity." Nor can it be found in § 1962, which sets out the statute's substantive provisions. Indeed, if either § 1961 or § 1962 did contain such a requirement, a prior conviction would also be a prerequisite, nonsensically, for a criminal prosecution, or for a civil action by the government to enjoin violations that had not yet occurred.

* * *

The Court of Appeals was of the view that its narrow construction of the statute was essential to avoid intolerable practical consequences.[9] First, without a prior conviction to rely on, the plaintiff would have to prove commission of the predicate acts beyond a reasonable doubt. This would require instructing the jury as to different standards of proof for different aspects of the case. To avoid this awkwardness, the court inferred that the criminality must already be established, so that the civil action could proceed smoothly under the usual preponderance standard.

We are not at all convinced that the predicate acts must be established beyond a reasonable doubt in a proceeding under § 1964(c). In a number of settings, conduct that can be punished as criminal only upon proof beyond a reasonable doubt will support civil sanctions under a preponderance standard. See, e.g., United States v. One Assortment of 89 Firearms, 465 U.S. 354 (1984); One Lot Emerald Cut Stones v. United States, 409 U.S. 232, 235 (1972); Helvering v. Mitchell, 303 U.S. 391, 397 (1938); United States v. Regan, 232 U.S. 37, 47–49 (1914). There is no indication that Congress sought to depart from this general principle here. See Measures Relating to Organized Crime, Hearings on S. 30 et al. before the Subcommittee on Criminal Laws and Procedures of the Senate Committee on the Judiciary, 91st Cong., 1st Sess., 388 (1969) (statement of Assistant Attorney General Wilson); House Hearings, at 520 (statement of Rep. Steiger); id., at 664 (statement of Rep. Poff); 116 Cong.Rec. 35313 (1970) (statement of Rep. Minish). That the offending conduct is described by reference to criminal statutes does not mean that its occurrence must be established by criminal standards or that the consequences of a finding of liability in a private civil action are identical to the consequences of a criminal conviction. Cf. United States v. Ward, supra, 448 U.S., at 248–251. But we need not decide the standard of proof issue today. For even if the stricter standard is applicable to a portion of the plaintiff's proof, the resulting logistical

---

9. It is worth bearing in mind that the holding of the court below is not without problematic consequences of its own. It arbitrarily restricts the availability of private actions, for lawbreakers are often not apprehended and convicted. Even if a conviction has been obtained, it is unlikely that a private plaintiff will be able to recover for all of the acts constituting an extensive "pattern," or that multiple victims will all be able to obtain redress. This is because criminal convictions are often limited to a small portion of the actual or possible charges. The decision below would also create peculiar incentives for plea-bargaining to non-predicate-act offenses so as to ensure immunity from a later civil suit. If nothing else, a criminal defendant might plead to a tiny fraction of counts, so as to limit future civil liability. In addition, the dependence of potential civil litigants on the initiation and success of a criminal prosecution could lead to unhealthy private pressures on prosecutors and to self-serving trial testimony, or at least accusations thereof. Problems would also arise if some or all of the convictions were reversed on appeal. Finally, the compelled wait for the completion of criminal proceedings would result in pursuit of stale claims, complex statute of limitations problems, or the wasteful splitting of actions, with resultant claim and issue preclusion complications.

difficulties, which are accepted in other contexts, would not be so great as to require invention of a requirement that cannot be found in the statute and that Congress, as even the Court of Appeals had to concede, 741 F.2d, at 501, did not envision.

* * *

In sum, we can find no support in the statute's history, its language, or considerations of policy for a requirement that a private treble damages action under § 1964(c) can proceed only against a defendant who has already been criminally convicted. To the contrary, every indication is that no such requirement exists. Accordingly, the fact that Imrex and the individual defendants have not been convicted under RICO or the federal mail and wire fraud statutes does not bar Sedima's action.

IV

In considering the Court of Appeals' second prerequisite for a private civil RICO action—"injury * * * caused by an activity which RICO was designed to deter"—we are somewhat hampered by the vagueness of that concept. Apart from reliance on the general purposes of RICO and a reference to "mobsters," the court provided scant indication of what the requirement of racketeering injury means. It emphasized Congress' undeniable desire to strike at organized crime, but acknowledged and did not purport to overrule Second Circuit precedent rejecting a requirement of an organized crime nexus. 741 F.2d, at 492; see Moss v. Morgan Stanley, Inc., 719 F.2d 5, 21 (CA2 1983), cert. denied sub nom. Moss v. Newman, 465 U.S. 1025 (1984). The court also stopped short of adopting a "competitive injury" requirement; while insisting that the plaintiff show "the kind of economic injury which has an effect on competition," it did not require "actual anticompetitive effect." 741 F.2d, at 496; see also id., at 495, n. 40.

The court's statement that the plaintiff must seek redress for an injury caused by conduct that RICO was designed to deter is unhelpfully tautological. Nor is clarity furnished by a negative statement of its rule: standing is not provided by the injury resulting from the predicate acts themselves. That statement is itself apparently inaccurate when applied to those predicate acts that unmistakeably constitute the kind of conduct Congress sought to deter. See id., at 496, n. 41. The opinion does not explain how to distinguish such crimes from the other predicate acts Congress has lumped together in § 1961(1). The court below is not alone in struggling to define "racketeering injury," and the difficulty of that task itself cautions against imposing such a requirement.

We need not pinpoint the Second Circuit's precise holding, for we perceive no distinct "racketeering injury" requirement. Given that "racketeering activity" consists of no more and no less than commission of a predicate act, § 1961(1), we are initially doubtful about a requirement of a "racketeering injury" separate from the harm from the predicate acts. A reading of the statute belies any such requirement. Section 1964(c) authorizes a private suit by "[a]ny person injured in his business or property by reason of a violation of § 1962." Section 1962 in turn makes it unlawful for "any person"—not just mobsters—to use money derived from a pattern of racketeering activity to invest in an enterprise, to acquire control of an enterprise through a pattern of racketeering activity, or to conduct an enterprise through a pattern of racketeering activity. §§ 1962(a)–(c). If the defendant engages in a pattern of racketeering activity in a manner forbidden by these provisions, and the racketeering activities injure the plaintiff in his business or property, the plaintiff has a claim under § 1964(c). There is no room in the statutory language for an additional, amorphous "racketeering injury" requirement.

A violation of § 1962(c), the section on which Sedima relies, requires (1) conduct (2) of an enterprise (3) through a pattern [14] (4) of racketeering activity. The plaintiff must, of course, allege each of these elements to state a claim. Conducting an enterprise that affects interstate commerce is obviously not in itself a violation of § 1962, nor is mere commission of the predicate offenses. In addition, the plaintiff only has standing if, and can only recover to the extent that, he has been injured in his business or property by the conduct constituting the violation. As the Seventh Circuit has stated, "[a] defendant who violates section 1962 is not liable for treble damages to everyone he might have injured by other conduct, nor is the defendant liable to those who have not been injured." Haroco, Inc. v. American National Bank & Trust Co. of Chicago, 747 F.2d 384, 398 (1984), aff'd, 473 U.S. 479.

But the statute requires no more than this. Where the plaintiff alleges each element of the violation, the compensable injury necessarily is the harm caused by predicate acts sufficiently related to constitute a pattern, for the essence of the violation is the commission of those acts in connection with the conduct of an enterprise. Those acts are, when committed in the circumstances delineated in § 1962(c), "an activity which RICO was designed to deter." Any recoverable damages occurring by reason of a violation of § 1962(c) will flow from the commission of the predicate acts.[15]

14. As many commentators have pointed out, the definition of a "pattern of racketeering activity" differs from the other provisions in § 1961 in that it states that a pattern "*requires* at least two acts of racketeering activity," § 1961(5) (emphasis added), not that it "means" two such acts. The implication is that while two acts are necessary, they may not be sufficient. Indeed, in common parlance two of anything do not generally form a "pattern." The legislative history supports the view that two isolated acts of racketeering activity do not constitute a pattern. As the Senate Report explained: "The target of [RICO] is thus not sporadic activity. The infiltration of legitimate business normally requires more than one 'racketeering activity' and the threat of continuing activity to be effective. It is this factor of *continuity plus relationship* which combines to produce a pattern." S.Rep. No. 91–617, p. 158 (1969) (emphasis added). Similarly, the sponsor of the senate bill, after quoting this portion of the Report, pointed out to his colleagues that "[t]he term 'pattern' itself requires the showing of a relationship. ∗ ∗ ∗ So, therefore, proof of two acts of racketeering activity, without more, does not establish a pattern. ∗ ∗ ∗" 116 Cong.Rec. 18940 (1970) (statement of Sen. McClellan). See also *id.*, at 35193 (statement of Rep. Poff)

(RICO "not aimed at the isolated offender"); House Hearings, at 665. Significantly, in defining "pattern" in a later provision of the same bill, Congress was more enlightening: "criminal conduct forms a pattern if it embraces criminal acts that have the same or similar purposes, results, participants, victims, or methods of commission, or otherwise are interrelated by distinguishing characteristics and are not isolated events." 18 U.S.C. § 3575(e). This language may be useful in interpreting other sections of the Act. Cf. Iannelli v. United States, 420 U.S. 770, 789 (1975).

15. Such damages include, but are not limited to, the sort of competitive injury for which the dissenters would allow recovery. See post, at 3303. Under the dissent's reading of the statute, the harm proximately caused by the forbidden conduct is not compensable, but that ultimately and indirectly flowing therefrom is. We reject this topsy-turvy approach, finding no warrant in the language or the history of the statute for denying recovery thereunder to "the direct victims of the [racketeering] activity," post, at 3303, while preserving it for the indirect. Even the court below was not that grudging. It would apparently have allowed recovery for both the direct and the ultimate harm flowing

This less restrictive reading is amply supported by our prior cases and the general principles surrounding this statute. RICO is to be read broadly. This is the lesson not only of Congress' self-consciously expansive language and overall approach, see United States v. Turkette, 452 U.S. 576, 586–587 (1981), but also of its express admonition that RICO is to "be liberally construed to effectuate its remedial purposes," Pub.L. 91–452, § 904(a), 84 Stat. 947. The statute's "remedial purposes" are nowhere more evident than in the provision of a private action for those injured by racketeering activity. See also n. 10, supra. Far from effectuating these purposes, the narrow readings offered by the dissenters and the court below would in effect eliminate § 1964(c) from the statute.

Underlying the Court of Appeals' holding was its distress at the "extraordinary, if not outrageous," uses to which civil RICO has been put. 741 F.2d, at 487. Instead of being used against mobsters and organized criminals, it has become a tool for everyday fraud cases brought against "respected and legitimate 'enterprises.'" Ibid. Yet Congress wanted to reach both "legitimate" and "illegitimate" enterprises. United States v. Turkette, supra. The former enjoy neither an inherent incapacity for criminal activity nor immunity from its consequences. The fact that § 1964(c) is used against respected businesses allegedly engaged in a pattern of specifically identified criminal conduct is hardly a sufficient reason for assuming that the provision is being misconstrued. Nor does it reveal the "ambiguity" discovered by the court below. "[T]he fact that RICO has been applied in situations not expressly anticipated by Congress does not demonstrate ambiguity. It demonstrates breadth." Haroco, Inc. v. American National Bank & Trust Co. of Chicago, supra, at 398.

It is true that private civil actions under the statute are being brought almost solely against such defendants, rather than against the archetypal, intimidating mobster.[16] Yet this defect—if defect it is—is inherent in the statute as written, and its correction must lie with Congress. It is not for the judiciary to eliminate the private action in situations where Congress has provided it simply because plaintiffs are not taking advantage of it in its more difficult applications.

We nonetheless recognize that, in its private civil version, RICO is evolving into something quite different from the original conception of its enactors. See generally ABA Report, at 55–69. Though sharing the doubts of the Court of Appeals about this increasing divergence, we cannot agree

---

from the defendant's conduct, requiring injury "not *simply* caused by the predicate acts, but also by an activity which RICO was designed to deter." 742 F.2d, at 496 (emphasis added).

The dissent would also go further than did the Second Circuit in its requirement that the plaintiff have suffered a competitive injury. Again, as the court below stated, Congress "nowhere suggested that actual anti-competitive effect is required for suits under the statute." Ibid. The language it chose, allowing recovery to "[a]ny person injured in his business *or property*," § 1964(c) (emphasis added), applied to this situation, suggests that the statute is not so limited.

16. The ABA Task Force found that of the 270 known civil RICO cases at the trial court level, 40% involved securities fraud, 37% common-law fraud in a commercial or business setting, and only 9% "allegations of criminal activity of a type generally associated with professional criminals." ABA Report, at 55–56. Another survey of 132 published decisions found that 57 involved securities transactions and 38 commercial and contract disputes, while no other category made it into double figures. American Institute of Certified Public Accountants, The Authority to Bring Private Treble-Damage Suits Under "RICO" Should be Removed 13 (Oct. 10, 1984).

with either its diagnosis or its remedy. The "extraordinary" uses to which civil RICO has been put appear to be primarily the result of the breadth of the predicate offenses, in particular the inclusion of wire, mail, and securities fraud, and the failure of Congress and the courts to develop a meaningful concept of "pattern." We do not believe that the amorphous standing requirement imposed by the Second Circuit effectively responds to these problems, or that it is a form of statutory amendment appropriately undertaken by the courts.

V

Sedima may maintain this action if the defendants conducted the enterprise through a pattern of racketeering activity. The questions whether the defendants committed the requisite predicate acts, and whether the commission of those acts fell into a pattern, are not before us. The complaint is not deficient for failure to allege either an injury separate from the financial loss stemming from the alleged acts of mail and wire fraud, or prior convictions of the defendants. The decision below is accordingly reversed, and the case is remanded for further proceedings consistent with this opinion.

It is so ordered.

JUSTICE POWELL, dissenting:

I agree with JUSTICE MARSHALL that the Court today reads the civil RICO statute in a way that validates uses of the statute that were never intended by Congress, and I join his dissent. I write separately to emphasize my disagreement with the Court's conclusion that the statute must be applied to authorize the types of private civil actions now being brought frequently against respected businesses to redress ordinary fraud and breach of contract cases.[1]

I

* * *

As the Court of Appeals observed in this case, "[i]f Congress had intended to provide a federal forum for plaintiffs for so many common law wrongs, it would at least have discussed it."[2] 741 F.2d 482, 492 (1984). The Court today concludes that Congress *was* aware of the broad scope of the statute, relying on the fact that some Congressmen objected to the possibility of abuse of the RICO statute by arguing that it could be used "to harass innocent businessmen." H.R.Rep. No. 91–1549, at 187 (1970) (dissenting views of Reps. Conyers, Mikva, and Ryan); 116 Cong.Rec. 35,342 (1970) (remarks of Rep. Mikva).

In the legislative history of every statute, one may find critics of the bill who predict dire consequences in the event of its enactment. A court need not infer from such statements by opponents that Congress *intended* those consequences to occur, particularly where, as here, there is compelling

---

1. The Court says these suits are not being brought against the "archetypal, intimidating mobster" because of a "defect" that is "inherent in the statute." Ante, at 3287. If RICO must be construed as the Court holds, this is indeed a defect that Congress never intended. I do not believe that the statute *must* be construed in what in effect is an irrational manner.

2. The force of this observation is accented by RICO's provision for treble damages—an enticing invitation to litigate these claims in federal courts.

evidence to the contrary. The legislative history reveals that Congress did not state explicitly that the statute would reach only members of the Mafia because it believed there were constitutional problems with establishing such a specific status offense. E.g., id., at 35343–35344 (remarks of Rep. Celler); id., at 35344 (remarks of Rep. Poff). Nonetheless, the legislative history makes clear that the statute was intended to be *applied* to organized crime, and an influential sponsor of the bill emphasized that any effect it had beyond such crime was meant to be only incidental. Id., at 18914 (remarks of Sen. McClellan).

* * *

It has turned out in this case that the naysayers' dire predictions have come true. As the Court notes, ante, at 3287 & n. 15, RICO has been interpreted so broadly that it has been used more often against respected businesses with no ties to organized crime, than against the mobsters who were the clearly intended target of the statute. While I acknowledge that the language of the statute *may* be read as broadly as the Court interprets it today, I do not believe that it *must* be so read. Nor do I believe that interpreting the statutory language more narrowly than the Court does will "eliminate the [civil RICO] private action," ibid., in cases of the kind clearly identified by the legislative history. The statute may and should be read narrowly to confine its reach to the type of conduct Congress had in mind. It is the duty of this Court to implement the unequivocal intention of Congress.

II

The language of this complex statute is susceptible of being read consistently with this intent. For example, the requirement in the statute of proof of a "pattern" of racketeering activity may be interpreted narrowly. Section 1961(5), defining "pattern of racketeering activity," states that such a pattern "requires at least two acts of racketeering activity." This contrasts with the definition of "racketeering activity" in § 1961(1), stating that such activity "means" any of a number of acts. The definition of "pattern" may thus logically be interpreted as meaning that the presence of the predicate acts is only the beginning: something more is required for a "pattern" to be proved. The ABA Report concurs in this view. It argues persuasively that "[t]he 'pattern' element of the statute was designed to limit its application to planned, ongoing, continuing crime as opposed to sporadic, unrelated, isolated criminal episodes," ABA Report, at 72, such as the criminal acts alleged in the cases before us today.

The legislative history bears out this interpretation of "pattern." Senator McClellan, a leading sponsor of the bill, stated that "proof of two acts of racketeering activity, without more, does not establish a pattern." 116 Cong.Rec. 18940 (1970). Likewise, the Senate Report considered the "concept of 'pattern' [to be] essential to the operation of the statute." S.Rep., at 158. It stated that the bill was not aimed at sporadic activity, but that the "infiltration of legitimate business normally requires more than one 'racketeering activity' *and* the threat of continuing activity to be effective. It is this factor of continuity *plus* relationship which combines to produce a pattern." Id. (emphasis added). The ABA Report suggests that to effectuate this legislative intent, "pattern" should be interpreted as requiring that (i) the racketeering acts be related to each other, (ii) they be part of some common scheme, and (iii) some sort of continuity between the acts or a threat of continuing criminal activity must be shown. ABA Report, at 193–208. By construing "pattern" to focus on the manner in which the crime was perpetrated, courts could go a long way toward limiting the reach of the statute to its intended target—organized crime.

The Court concedes that "pattern" could be narrowly construed, ante, at 3285, n. 14, and notes that part of the reason civil RICO has been put to such extraordinary uses is because of the "failure of Congress and the courts to develop a meaningful concept of 'pattern,'" id., at 3287. The Court declines to decide whether the defendants' acts constitute such a pattern in this case, however, because it concludes that that question is not before the Court. Id., at 3287. I agree that the scope of the "pattern" requirement is not included in the questions on which we granted certiorari. I am concerned, however, that in the course of rejecting the Court of Appeals' ruling that the statute requires proof of a "racketeering injury" the Court has read the entire statute so broadly that it will be difficult, if not impossible, for courts to adopt a reading of "pattern" that will conform to the intention of Congress.

The Court bases its rejection of the "racketeering injury" requirement on the general principles that the RICO statute is to be read "broadly," that it is to be "'liberally construed to effectuate its remedial purposes,'" ante, at 3286 (quoting Pub.L.No. 91–452, § 904(a), 84 Stat. 947), and that the statute was part of "an aggressive initiative to supplement old remedies and develop new methods for fighting crime." Ante, at 3286. Although the Court acknowledges that few of the legislative statements supporting these principles were made with reference to RICO's private civil action, it concludes nevertheless that all of the Act's provisions should be read in the "spirit" of these principles. Id., at 3286. By constructing such a broad premise for its rejection of the "racketeering injury" requirement, the Court seems to mandate that all future courts read the entire statute broadly.

* * *

The reference in the report to "predatory activities" was to organized crime. Only a small fraction of the scores of civil RICO cases now being brought implicate organized crime in any way.[3] Typically, these suits are being brought—in the unfettered discretion of private litigants—in federal court against legitimate businesses seeking treble damages in ordinary fraud and contract cases. There is nothing comparable in those cases to the restraint on the institution of criminal suits exercised by government prosecutorial discretion. Today's opinion inevitably will encourage continued expansion of resort to RICO in cases of alleged fraud or contract violation rather than to the traditional remedies available in state court. As the Court of Appeals emphasized, it defies rational belief, particularly in light of the legislative history, that Congress intended this far-reaching result. Accordingly, I dissent.

JUSTICE MARSHALL, with whom JUSTICE BRENNAN, JUSTICE BLACKMUN, and JUSTICE POWELL join, dissenting.

---

3. As noted in the ABA Report, of the 270 District Court RICO decisions prior to this year, only 3% (9 cases) were decided throughout the entire decade of the 1970s, whereas 43% (116 cases) were decided in 1984. ABA Report, at 53a (Table). See ante, n. 1.

The Court today recognizes that "in its private civil version, RICO is evolving into something quite different from the original conception of its enactors." Ante, at 3302. The Court, however, expressly validates this result, imputing it to the manner in which the statute was drafted. I fundamentally disagree both with the Court's reading of the statute and with its conclusion. I believe that the statutory language and history disclose a narrower interpretation of the statute that fully effectuates Congress' purposes, and that does not make compensable under civil RICO a host of claims that Congress never intended to bring within RICO's purview.

I

The Court's interpretation of the civil RICO statute quite simply revolutionizes private litigation; it validates the federalization of broad areas of state common law of frauds, and it approves the displacement of well-established federal remedial provisions. We do not lightly infer a congressional intent to effect such fundamental changes. To infer such intent here would be untenable, for there is no indication that Congress even considered, much less approved, the scheme that the Court today defines.

The single most significant reason for the expansive use of civil RICO has been the presence in the statute, as predicate acts, of mail and wire fraud violations. See 18 U.S.C. § 1961(1). Prior to RICO, no federal statute had expressly provided a private damage remedy based upon a violation of the mail or wire fraud statutes, which make it a federal crime to use the mail or wires in furtherance of a scheme to defraud. See 18 U.S.C. §§ 1341, 1343. Moreover, the Courts of Appeals consistently had held that no implied federal private causes of action accrue to victims of these federal violations. See, e.g., Ryan v. Ohio Edison Co., 611 F.2d 1170, 1178-1179 (CA6 1979) (mail fraud); Napper v. Anderson, Henley, Shields, Bradford & Pritchard, 500 F.2d 634, 636 (CA5 1974) (wire fraud), cert. denied, 423 U.S. 837 (1975). The victims normally were restricted to bringing actions in state court under common-law fraud theories.

Under the Court's opinion today, two fraudulent mailings or uses of the wires occurring within ten years of each other might constitute a "pattern of racketeering activity," § 1961(5), leading to civil RICO liability. See § 1964(c). The effects of making a mere two instances of mail or wire fraud potentially actionable under civil RICO are staggering, because in recent years the Courts of Appeals have "tolerated an extraordinary expansion of mail and wire fraud statutes to permit federal prosecution for conduct that some had thought was subject only to state criminal and civil law." United States v. Weiss, 752 F.2d 777, 791 (CA2 1985) (Newman, J., dissenting). In bringing criminal actions under those statutes, prosecutors need not show either a substantial connection between the scheme to defraud and the mail and wire fraud statutes, see Pereira v. United States, 347 U.S. 1, 8 (1954), or that the fraud involved money or property. Courts have sanctioned prosecutions based on deprivations of such intangible rights as a shareholder's right to "material" information, United States v. Siegel, 717 F.2d 9, 14-16 (CA2 1983); a client's right to the "undivided loyalty" of his attorney, United States v. Bronston, 658 F.2d 920, 927 (CA2 1981), cert. denied, 456 U.S. 915 (1982); an employer's right to the honest and faithful service of his employees, United States v. Bohonus, 628 F.2d

1167, 1172 (CA9), cert. denied, 447 U.S. 928 (1980); and a citizen's right to know the nature of agreements entered into by the leaders of political parties, United States v. Margiotta, 688 F.2d 108, 123–125 (CA2 1982), cert. denied, 461 U.S. 913 (1983).

The only restraining influence on the "inexorable expansion of the mail and wire fraud statutes," United States v. Siegel, 717 F.2d, at 24 (Winter, J., dissenting in part), has been the prudent use of prosecutorial discretion. Prosecutors simply do not invoke the mail and wire fraud provisions in every case in which a violation of the relevant statute can be proved. See United States Attorney's Manual § 9–43.120 (Feb. 16, 1984). For example, only where the scheme is directed at a "class of people or the general public" and includes "a substantial pattern of conduct," will "serious consideration be given to mail fraud prosecution." In all other cases, "the parties should be left to settle their differences by civil or criminal litigation in the state courts." Ibid.

The responsible use of prosecutorial discretion is particularly important with respect to criminal RICO prosecutions—which often rely on mail and wire fraud as predicate acts—given the extremely severe penalties authorized by RICO's criminal provisions. Federal prosecutors are therefore instructed that "[u]tilization of the RICO statute, more so than most federal criminal sanctions, requires particularly careful and reasoned application." § 9–110.200 (March 9, 1984). The Justice Department itself recognizes that a broad interpretation of the criminal RICO provisions would violate "the principle that the primary responsibility for enforcing state laws rests with the state concerned." Ibid. Specifically, the Justice Department will not bring RICO prosecutions unless the pattern of racketeering activity required by 18 U.S.C. § 1962 has "some relation to the purpose of the enterprise." United States Attorney's Manual § 9–110.350 (March 9, 1984).

Congress was well aware of the restraining influence of prosecutorial discretion when it enacted the criminal RICO provisions. It chose to confer broad statutory authority on the Executive fully expecting that this authority would be used only in cases in which its use was warranted. See Measures Relating to Organized Crime: Hearings on S. 30, S. 974, S. 975, et al., Before the Subcomm. on Criminal Laws and Procedures of the Senate Comm. on the Judiciary, 91st Cong., 1st Sess. pp. 346–347, 424 (1969) (hereinafter cited as Senate Hearings). Moreover, in seeking a broad interpretation of RICO from this Court in United States v. Turkette, 452 U.S. 576 (1981), the Government stressed that no "extreme cases" would be brought because the Justice Department would exercise "sound discretion" through a centralized review process. See Brief for Petitioner in No. 80–808, O.T. 1980, p. 25, n. 20.

In the context of civil RICO, however, the restraining influence of prosecutors is completely absent. Unlike the Government, private litigants have no reason to avoid displacing state common-law remedies. Quite to the contrary, such litigants, lured by the prospect of treble damages and attorney's fees, have a strong incentive to invoke RICO's provisions whenever they can allege in good faith two instances of mail or wire fraud. Then the defendant, facing a tremendous financial exposure in addition to the threat of being labelled a "racketeer," will have a strong interest in settling the dispute. See Rakoff, Some Personal Reflections on the Sedima

Case and on Reforming RICO, in RICO: Civil and Criminal 400 (Law Journal Seminars-Press 1984). The civil RICO provision consequently stretches the mail and wire fraud statutes to their absolute limits and federalizes important areas of civil litigation that until now were solely within the domain of the states.

In addition to altering fundamentally the federal-state balance in civil remedies, the broad reading of the civil RICO provision also displaces important areas of federal law. For example, one predicate offense under RICO is "fraud in the sale of securities." 18 U.S.C. § 1961(1). By alleging two instances of such fraud, a plaintiff might be able to bring a case within the scope of the civil RICO provision. It does not take great legal insight to realize that such a plaintiff would pursue his case under RICO rather than do so solely under the Securities Act of 1933 or the Securities Exchange Act of 1934, which provide both express and implied causes of action for violations of the federal securities laws. Indeed, the federal securities laws contemplate only compensatory damages and ordinarily do not authorize recovery of attorney's fees. By invoking RICO, in contrast, a successful plaintiff will recover both treble damages and attorney's fees.

More importantly, under the Court's interpretation, the civil RICO provision does far more than just increase the available damages. In fact, it virtually eliminates decades of legislative and judicial development of private civil remedies under the federal securities laws. Over the years, court have paid close attention to matters such as standing, culpability, causation, reliance and materiality, as well as the definitions of "securities" and "fraud." See, e.g., Blue Chip Stamps v. Manor Drug Stores, 421 U.S. 723 (1975) (purchaser/seller requirement). All of this law is now an endangered species because plaintiffs can avoid the limitations of the securities laws merely by alleging violations of other predicate acts. For example, even in cases in which the investment instrument is not a "security" covered by the federal securities laws, RICO will provide a treble damage remedy to a plaintiff who can prove the required pattern of mail or wire fraud. Cf. Crocker National Bank v. Rockwell International Corp., 555 F.Supp. 47 (ND Cal.1982). Before RICO, of course, the plaintiff could not have recovered under federal law for the mail or wire fraud violation.

Similarly, a customer who refrained from selling a security during a period in which its market value was declining could allege that, on two occasions, his broker recommended by telephone, as part of a scheme to defraud, that the customer not sell the security. The customer might thereby prevail under civil RICO even though, as neither a purchaser nor a seller, he would not have had standing to bring an action under the federal securities laws. See also 741 F.2d 482, 499 (2d Cir.1984) ("two misstatements in a proxy solicitation could subject any director in any national corporation to 'racketeering' charges and the threat of treble damages and attorneys' fees").

The effect of civil RICO on federal remedial schemes is not limited to the securities laws. For example, even though commodities fraud is not a predicate offense listed in § 1961, the carefully crafted private damage causes of action under the Commodity Exchange Act may be circumvented in a commodities case through civil RICO actions alleging mail or wire fraud. See, e.g., Parnes v. Heinold Commodities, Inc., 487 F.Supp. 645 (ND Ill.1980). The list goes on and on.

The dislocations caused by the Court's reading of the civil RICO provision are not just theoretical. In practice, this provision frequently has been invoked against legitimate businesses in ordinary commercial settings. As the Court recognizes, the ABA Task Force that studied civil RICO found that 40% of the reported cases involved securities fraud, 37% involved common-law fraud in a commercial or business setting. See ante, at ___. Many a prudent defendant, facing ruinous exposure, will decide to settle even a case with no merit. It is thus not surprising that civil RICO has been used for extortive purposes, giving rise to the very evils that it was designed to combat. Report of the Ad Hoc Civil RICO Task Force of the ABA Section of Corporation, Banking and Business Law 69 (1985) (hereinafter cited as ABA Report).

Only 9% of all civil RICO cases have involved allegations of criminal activity normally associated with professional criminals. See ante, at ___. The central purpose that Congress sought to promote through civil RICO is now a mere footnote.

In summary, in both theory and practice, civil RICO has brought profound changes to our legal landscape. Undoubtedly, Congress has the power to federalize a great deal of state common law, and there certainly are no relevant constraints on its ability to displace federal law. Those, however, are not the questions that we face in this case. What we have to decide here, instead, is whether Congress in fact intended to produce these far-reaching results.

Established canons of statutory interpretation counsel against the Court's reading of the civil RICO provision. First, we do not impute lightly a congressional intention to upset the federal-state balance in the provision of civil remedies as fundamentally as does this statute under the Court's view. For example, in Santa Fe Industries v. Green, 430 U.S. 462 (1977), we stated that "[a]bsent a clear indication of congressional intent, we are reluctant to federalize the substantial portion of the law of corporations that deals with transactions in securities." Id., at 479. Here, with striking nonchalance, the Court does what it declined to do in *Santa Fe Industries*—and much more as well. Second, with respect to effects on the federal securities laws and other federal regulatory statutes, we should be reluctant to displace the well-entrenched federal remedial schemes absent clear direction from Congress. See, e.g., Train v. Colorado Public Interest Research Group, 426 U.S. 1, 23–24 (1976); Radzanower v. Touche Ross & Co., 426 U.S. 148, 153 (1976).

In this case, nothing in the language of the statute or the legislative history suggests that Congress intended either the federalization of state common law or the displacement of existing federal remedies. Quite to the contrary, all that the statute and the legislative history reveal as to these matters is what Judge Oakes called a "clanging silence," 741 F.2d, at 492.

Moreover, if Congress had intended to bring about dramatic changes in the nature of commercial litigation, it would at least have paid more than cursory attention to the civil RICO provision. This provision was added in the House of Representatives after the Senate already had passed its version of the RICO bill; the House itself adopted a civil remedy provision almost as an afterthought; and the Senate thereafter accepted the House's version of the bill without even requesting a Conference. See infra, at ___.

Congress simply does not act in this way when it intends to effect fundamental changes in the structure of federal law.

II

The statutory language and legislative history support the view that Congress did not intend to effect a radical alteration of federal civil litigation. In fact, the language and history indicate a congressional intention to limit, in a workable and coherent manner, the type of injury that is compensable under the civil RICO provision. As the following demonstrates, Congress sought to fill an existing gap in civil remedies and to provide a means of compensation that otherwise did not exist for the honest businessman harmed by the economic power of "racketeers."

* * *

Putting together these various pieces [of the legislative history], I can only conclude that Congress intended to give to businessmen who might otherwise have had no available remedy a possible way to recover damages for competitive injury, infiltration injury, or other economic injury resulting out of, but wholly distinct from, the predicate acts. Congress fully recognized that racketeers do not engage in predicate acts as ends in themselves; instead, racketeers threaten, burn, and murder in order to induce their victims to act in a way that accrues to the economic benefit of the racketeer, as by ceasing to compete, or agreeing to make certain purchases. Congress' concern was not for the direct victims of the racketeers' acts, whom state and federal laws already protected, but for the competitors and investors whose businesses and interests are harmed or destroyed by racketeers, or whose competitive positions decline because of infiltration in the relevant market. Its focus was on the victims of the extraordinary economic power that racketeers are able to acquire through a wide range of illicit methods. Indeed, that is why Congress provided for recovery only for injury to business or property—that is, commercial injuries—and not for personal physical or emotional injury.

The only way to give effect to Congress' concern is to require that plaintiffs plead and prove that they suffered RICO injury—injury to their competitive, investment, or other business interests resulting from the defendant's conduct of a business, or infiltration of a business or a market, through a pattern of racketeering activity. As I shall demonstrate, this requirement is manageable, and it puts the statute to the use to which it was addressed. In addition, this requirement is faithful to the language of the statute, which does not appear to provide recovery for injuries incurred by reason of individual predicate acts. It also avoids most of the "extraordinary uses" to which the statute has been put, in which legitimate businesses that have engaged in two criminal acts have been labelled "racketeers," have faced treble damage judgments in favor of the direct victims, and often have settled to avoid the destructive publicity and the resulting harm to reputation. These cases take their toll; their results distort the market by saddling legitimate businesses with uncalled-for punitive bills and undeserved labels. To allow punitive actions and significant damages for injury beyond that which the statute was intended to target is to achieve nothing the statute sought to achieve, and ironically to injure many of those lawful businesses that the statute sought to protect. Under such circumstances, I believe this Court is derelict in its failure to interpret the statute in keeping with the language and intent of Congress.

Several lower courts have remarked, however, that a "RICO injury" requirement, while perhaps contemplated by the statute, defies definition. I disagree. The following series of examples, culled in part from the legislative history of the RICO statute, illustrates precisely what does and does not fall within this definition.

First. If a "racketeer" uses "threats, arson and assault to force competitors out of the market and obtain larger shares of the market," House Hearings 106 (statement of Sen. McClellan), the threats, arson and assault represent the predicate acts. The pattern of those acts is designed to accomplish, and accomplishes, the goal of monopolization. Competitors thereby injured or forced out of business could allege "RICO" injury and recover damages for lost profits. So, too, purchasers of the racketeer's goods or services, who are forced to buy from the racketeer/monopolist at higher prices, and whose businesses therefore are injured, might recover damages for the excess costs of doing business. The direct targets of the predicate acts—whether competitors, suppliers, or others—could recover for damages flowing from the predicate acts themselves, but under state or perhaps other federal law, not RICO.

Second. If a "racketeer" uses arson and threats to induce honest businessmen to pay protection money, or to purchase certain goods, or to hire certain workers, the targeted businessmen could sue to recover for injury to their business and property resulting from the added costs. This would be so if they were the direct victims of the predicate acts or if they had reacted to offenses committed against other businessmen. In each case, the predicate acts were committed in order to accomplish a certain end—e.g., to induce the prospective plaintiffs to take action to the economic benefit of the racketeer; in each case the result would have taken a toll on the competitive position of the prospective plaintiff by increasing his costs of doing business.

At the same time, the plaintiffs could not recover under RICO for the direct damages from the predicate acts. They could not, for example, recover for the cost of the building burned, or for personal injury resulting from the threat. Indeed, compensation for this latter injury is barred already by RICO's exclusion of personal injury claims. As in the previous example, these injuries are amply protected by state law damage actions.

Third. If a "racketeer" infiltrates and obtains control of a legitimate business either through fraud, foreclosure on usurious loans, extortion, or acceptance of business interests in payment of gambling debts, the honest investor who is thereby displaced could bring a civil RICO action claiming infiltration injury resulting from the infiltrator's pattern of predicate acts that enabled him to gain control. Thereafter, if the enterprise conducts its business through a pattern of racketeering activity to enhance its profits or perpetuate its economic power, competitors of that enterprise could bring civil RICO actions alleging injury by reason of the enhanced commercial position the enterprise has obtained from its unlawful acts, and customers forced to purchase from sponsored suppliers could recover their added costs of doing business. At the same time, the direct victims of the activity—for example, customers defrauded by an infiltrated bank—could not recover under civil RICO. The bank does not, of course, thereby escape liability. The customers simply must rely on the existing causes of action, usually under state law.

Alternatively, if the infiltrated enterprise operates a legitimate business to a businessman's competitive disadvantage because of the enterprise's strong economic base derived from perpetration of predicate acts, the competitor could bring a civil RICO action alleging injury to his competitive position. The predicate acts then would have enabled the "enterprise" to gain a competitive advantage that brought harm to the plaintiff/competitor. Again, the direct victims of the predicate acts whose profits were invested in the "legitimate enterprise," would not be able to recover damages under civil RICO for injury resulting from the predicate acts alone.

These examples are not exclusive, and if this formulation were adopted, lower courts would, of course, have the opportunity to smooth numerous rough edges. The examples are designed simply to illustrate the type of injury that civil RICO was, to my mind, designed to compensate. The construction I describe offers a powerful remedy to the honest businessmen with whom Congress was concerned, who might have had no recourse against a "racketeer" prior to enactment of the statute. At the same time, this construction avoids both the theoretical and practical problems outlined in Part I. Under this view, traditional state law claims are not federalized; federal remedial schemes are not inevitably displaced or superceded; and, consequently, ordinary commercial disputes are not misguidedly placed within the scope of civil RICO.[2]

III

The Court today permits two civil actions for treble damages to go forward that are not authorized either by the language and legislative history of the civil RICO statute, or by the policies that underlay passage of that statute. In so doing, the Court shirks its well-recognized responsibility to assure that Congress' intent is not thwarted by maintenance of unintended litigation, and it does so based on an unfounded and ill-considered reading of a statutory provision. Because I believe the provision at issue is susceptible of a narrower interpretation that comports both with the statutory language and the legislative history, I dissent.

MOSS v. MORGAN STANLEY, INC.

United States Court of Appeals, Second Circuit, 1983.
719 F.2d 5.

Before MANSFIELD, MESKILL and KEARSE, CIRCUIT JUDGES.

MESKILL, CIRCUIT JUDGE:

This appeal spotlights two issues of significance for the litigation of federal securities fraud claims: (1) whether a shareholder who unwittingly sold stock of a "target" company on the open market prior to public announcement of a tender offer has a cause of action for damages under section 10(b) of the Securities Exchange Act of 1934 (the 1934 Act), and rule 10b-5 promulgated thereunder against a person who purchased "target" shares on the basis of material nonpublic information which he acquired

---

2. The analysis in my dissent would lead to the dismissal of the civil RICO claims at stake here. I thus do not need to decide whether a civil RICO action can proceed only after a criminal conviction. See ante, at 3296–3299.

from the tender offeror's investment adviser; and (2) whether this same unwitting shareholder can recover treble damages under the Racketeer Influenced and Corrupt Organizations Act, 18 U.S.C. §§ 1961 et seq. (1976 & Supp. III 1979) (RICO), on the ground that he was injured by an unlawful "enterprise" conducting a "pattern of racketeering activity" comprised of "fraudulent" securities transactions.

The district court held that the shareholder failed to state a cause of action under both the 1934 Act and RICO. We agree for the reasons stated below.

Affirmed.

BACKGROUND

The chain of events that culminated in this action began in the latter months of 1976 with tender offer discussions between Warner-Lambert Company (Warner) and Deseret Pharmaceutical Company (Deseret). On November 23, 1976 Warner retained the investment banking firm of Morgan Stanley & Co. Incorporated, a subsidiary of Morgan Stanley Inc. (Morgan Stanley), to assess the desirability of acquiring Deseret, to evaluate Deseret's stock and to recommend an appropriate price per share for the tender offer.

One of the individual defendants in this action, E. Jacques Courtois, Jr., was then employed by Morgan Stanley in its mergers and acquisitions department. In that capacity Courtois acquired knowledge of Warner's plan to purchase Deseret stock. On November 30, 1976 Courtois informed defendant Adrian Antoniu, an employee of Kuhn Loeb & Co., of the proposed tender offer and urged him to purchase Deseret stock. Antoniu in turn informed James M. Newman, a stockbroker, that Warner intended to bid for Deseret. Pursuant to an agreement with Antoniu and Courtois, Newman purchased 11,700 shares of Deseret stock at approximately $28 per share for his and their accounts. Newman also advised certain of his clients to buy Deseret stock.

Trading was active in Deseret shares on November 30, 1976, with approximately 143,000 shares changing hands. Michael E. Moss, the plaintiff in this action, was among the active traders, having sold 5,000 shares at $28 per share. On the following day, December 1, 1976, the New York Stock Exchange halted trading in Deseret stock pending announcement of the tender offer. Trading remained suspended until December 7, 1976 when Warner publicly announced its tender offer for Deseret stock at $38 per share. Newman and the other defendants tendered their shares to Warner and reaped a substantial profit.

On August 5, 1982 Moss commenced this action on his own behalf and on behalf of the class of investors who sold stock in Deseret on November 30, 1976. He contended that "members of the class have been substantially damaged in that they sold Deseret stock prior to the public announcement of the Warner tender offer at prices substantially below [those] offered by Warner." J.App. at 11. The amended complaint stated three causes of action: (1) Moss sought to recover damages from Newman for allegedly violating section 10(b) of the 1934 Act and rule 10b–5 thereunder by purchasing Deseret shares with knowledge of the imminent tender offer and without disclosing such information to Deseret shareholders; (2) Moss sought to recover damages from Morgan Stanley on the ground that as a "controlling person" under section 20(a) of the 1934 Act Morgan Stanley should be derivatively liable for Courtois' wrongdoing; and (3) pursuant to RICO, 18 U.S.C. § 1964(c) (1976), Moss sought to recover treble damages from Newman on the ground that he engaged in "at least two acts of fraud in connection with the purchase and sale of securities and as such [his actions represented] a pattern of racketeering activity within the meaning of RICO."[4] J.App. at 11.

* * * Although we disagree with several of the reasons advanced by the district court for dismissing plaintiff's RICO claim, we affirm the judgment dismissing the complaint and awarding costs to both defendants.[6]

DISCUSSION

I. *Section 10(b) Liability*
* * *

[The court's discussion of Rule 10b–5 liability is omitted. See Chapter 15, above, at p. 1051. Eds.]

III. *RICO*

A. *Introduction*

In Count II of the amended complaint, plaintiff Moss alleged that defendant Newman's unlawful purchase and sale of Deseret stock constituted a violation of RICO, 18 U.S.C. § 1962(c) (1976), thereby subjecting him to civil liability under 18 U.S.C. § 1964(c) (1976). The district court dismissed plaintiff's RICO claim on the grounds that the complaint failed to include several allegations "essential" to pleading a RICO claim. We affirm the district court's dismissal of the RICO count, but do not endorse the court's reasons for doing so.

B. *Threshold Defect in the Complaint*

To state a claim for damages under RICO a plaintiff has two pleading burdens. First, he must allege that the defendant has violated the substantive RICO statute, 18 U.S.C. § 1962 (1976), commonly known as "criminal RICO." In so doing, he must allege the existence of seven constituent elements: (1) that the defendant (2) through the commission of two or more acts (3) constituting a "pattern" (4) of "racketeering activity" (5) directly or

---

4. Count 2 also alleged that Morgan Stanley violated RICO. Judge Pollack dismissed the RICO claims against all defendants, but plaintiff appeals only from the dismissal of the claim against Newman.

In Count 3 of the complaint, plaintiff alleged that all of defendants' unlawful acts "constitute[d] violations of the applicable principles of common law fraud" and that defendant Morgan Stanley was "liable under the doctrine of *respondeat superior.*" J.App. at 12. The district court dismissed this count and plaintiff has not appealed.

6. Prior to this civil suit, on February 3, 1981, a 27 count criminal indictment charged Courtois and Newman with committing a series of criminal violations of § 10(b) and rule 10b–5 (including trading on the Deseret tender offer information),

as well as violations of the federal mail fraud and conspiracy statutes. United States v. Courtois, 81 Cr. 53 (S.D.N.Y. filed Feb. 3, 1981), *as superseded,* 82 Cr. 0166 (S.D.N.Y. filed March 1, 1982). Newman was convicted on seven counts of securities fraud, seven counts of mail fraud and one count of conspiracy. He received a one year jail sentence and a fine of $10,000. United States v. Newman, 722 F.2d 729 (2d Cir.1983) (unpublished order affirming conviction), for *cert. denied,* __ U.S. __, 104 S.Ct. 193, 78 L.Ed.2d 170 (1983).

Antoniu cooperated with the government and pled guilty to an Information based on his role in the securities scheme. He was sentenced to a three month term of imprisonment. Courtois, who was indicted with Newman, remains a fugitive from justice.

indirectly invests in, or maintains an interest in, or participates in (6) an "enterprise" (7) the activities of which affect interstate or foreign commerce. 18 U.S.C. § 1962(a)–(c) (1976). Plaintiff must allege adequately defendant's violation of section 1962 before turning to the second burden— i.e., invoking RICO's civil remedies of treble damages, attorneys fees and costs. See Bays v. Hunter Savings Association, 539 F.Supp. 1020, 1023 (S.D.Ohio 1982). To satisfy this latter burden, plaintiff must allege that he was "injured in his business or property *by reason of* a violation of section 1962." 18 U.S.C. § 1964(c) (1976) (emphasis added). Moss' complaint fails to carry either pleading burden.

Section 1962

Plaintiff's complaint fails to allege one of the elements needed to state a violation of section 1962—that defendant Newman engaged in "racketeering activity." Section 1961(5) defines "pattern of racketeering activity" as at least two acts of "racketeering activity" occurring within ten years of each other. 18 U.S.C. § 1961(5) (1976). In turn, section 1961(1)(D) defines "racketeering activity" to include "any offense involving fraud * * * in the sale of securities." 18 U.S.C. § 1961(1)(D) (Supp. III 1979). Plaintiff sought to satisfy both the "pattern" and "racketeering" elements of RICO by alleging that "[d]efendants' actions as set forth herein in this Complaint constitute at least two acts of fraud in connection with the purchase and sale of securities and as such represent a pattern of racketeering activity within the meaning of RICO." J.App. at 11. Thus, the complaint clearly relies on Newman's allegedly "fraudulent" securities transactions with respect to Deseret stock as the predicate acts of "racketeering" that form the "pattern" underpinning plaintiff's RICO claim. Such allegations of fraud would ordinarily satisfy RICO's "racketeering activity" pleading prerequisite.

However, in section I of this opinion, we held that plaintiff Moss' pleadings had failed *as a matter of law* to state a claim that Newman had *defrauded* him in violation of section 10(b) and rule 10b–5. In affirming the district court's grant of Newman's 12(b)(6) motion to dismiss, we dismissed plaintiff's claim of "securities fraud" from the complaint. In addition, the district court's dismissal of plaintiff's section 14(e), rule 14(e)–3 and common law fraud claims was never appealed. Therefore, since the complaint contains no *valid* allegation of "fraud," [14] to underpin the "predicate acts" of "racketeering," it necessarily must fail.

With respect to the sufficiency of the "racketeering" allegations, the district court's decision in Mauriber v. Shearson/American Express, Inc., 546 F.Supp. 391 (S.D.N.Y.1982), is instructive. There the plaintiff alleged that defendant's mismanagement of a discretionary brokerage account violated section 10(b) of the Securities Exchange Act of 1934, 15 U.S.C.

---

14. Although RICO provides that "fraud in the sale of securities" may constitute "racketeering activity," it supplies neither a definition of "fraud" nor a reference to other federal laws contemplated in drafting this "predicate offense."

The district court did not define "RICO fraud" when it dismissed plaintiff's complaint. Similarly, we need not decide this complex and far-reaching question. Fol-

lowing the district court's rejection of plaintiff's 14(e) and common law fraud claims, we put to rest any lingering existence of "fraud" in the instant complaint by rejecting plaintiff's section 10(b) and rule 10b–5 claims. Therefore, as neither common law fraud nor traditional securities fraud underpins plaintiff's RICO claim, we need not delineate RICO's definition of "fraud in the sale of securities."

§ 78j(b) (1976), and RICO, 18 U.S.C. § 1962(c) (1976). In response to defendant's Rule 12(b)(6) motion the district court found that plaintiff had failed to state its section 10(b) fraud claim with sufficient particularity to meet the pleading requirements of Fed.R.Civ.P. 9(b). The court further concluded that:

> [T]he RICO claim must fail for reasons not advanced by defendants. In Count II, the complaint alleges a violation of RICO by vaguely referring back to all of the preceding paragraphs that constitute the Section 10(b) violation. As earlier stated, the securities fraud allegations fail in numerous respects to comply with the specificity requirements of Fed.R. Civ.P. 9(b). *Until such time as plaintiff adequately pleads fraud it will not be known whether a RICO violation is properly alleged.* As a result, Count II of the complaint is dismissed with leave to replead within 20 days of the date hereof.

Id. at 397 (emphasis added); accord Maryville Academy v. Loeb Rhoades & Co., 530 F.Supp. 1061, 1070 (N.D.Ill.1981) (Court notes that "filing the lawsuits is not fraud in connection with a securities transaction; *thus* the filings are not within the scope of racketeering activity under the RICO statute."); see also Van Schaick v. Church of Scientology, 535 F.Supp. 1125, 1138 (D.Mass.1982).

The instant complaint suffers from a defect more fundamental than that found in *Mauriber*. As plaintiff has failed to state a valid claim that defendant Newman's securities transactions were "fraudulent" violations of section 10(b) or rule 10b–5, we cannot now conclude that such acts represent "racketeering activity" sufficient to support his RICO cause of action. Rather, since our dismissal of the securities fraud claim so undercut the existence of any "racketeering activity" in the complaint,[15] we affirm the district court's dismissal of plaintiff's RICO claim.

15. In speaking of plaintiff's RICO claim, the district court apparently believed that "[p]laintiff rests his argument that Newman is liable in treble damages for a violation of RICO on *the mere fact that Newman has been convicted of violating some of the statutes listed in Section 1961.*" 553 F.Supp. at 1363 (emphasis added). Conceivably, Newman's prior convictions for mail fraud, as well as securities fraud (both enumerated as racketeering activities within 18 U.S.C. § 1961(1)), could provide the proof of the predicate acts of "racketeering" that is presently absent from the complaint.

Although the courts have noted that prior convictions for alleged predicate offenses are not preconditions to bringing a RICO civil suit, see, e.g., USACO Coal Co. v. Carbomin Energy, Inc., 689 F.2d 94, 95 n. 1 (6th Cir.1982); United States v. Malatesta, 583 F.2d 748, 757 (1978), aff'd on rehearing, 590 F.2d 1379 (5th Cir.), cert. denied, 444 U.S. 846 (1979); Glusband v. Benjamin, 530 F.Supp. 240, 241 (S.D.N.Y. 1981); see also State Farm Fire and Casualty Co. v. Estate of Caton, 540 F.Supp. 673, 675 (N.D.Ind.1982); Heinold Commodities, Inc. v. McCarty, 513 F.Supp. 311, 313–

14 (N.D.Ill.1979); Parnes v. Heinold Commodities, Inc., 487 F.Supp. 645, 647 (N.D. Ill.1980); Farmers Bank v. Bell Mortgage Corp., 452 F.Supp. 1278, 1280 (D.Del.1978); but see Kleiner v. First National Bank, 526 F.Supp. 1019, 1022 n. 2 (N.D.Ga.1981) ("It may well be that entitlement to the civil remedy of section 1964 should be conditioned upon a criminal conviction or at least an indictment."), a growing number of courts have recognized that a prior criminal conviction on the alleged predicate offense may exert a collateral estoppel effect on the issue of "racketeering activity" in pleading a "civil RICO" claim. See Municipality of Anchorage v. Hitachi Cable, Ltd., 547 F.Supp. 633, 644 (D.Ala.1982) ("Under traditional theories of collateral estoppel, Hitachi's pleas of guilty to the mail and wire fraud counts estop it from denying that it engaged in a pattern of racketeering activity. * * *"); Anderson v. Janovich, 543 F.Supp. 1124, 1127–32 (W.D.Wash.1982); State Farm Fire and Casualty Co. v. Estate of Caton, 540 F.Supp. at 682–83; but see United States v. Malatesta, 583 F.2d at 757 ("Because the United States was not a party in the state proceedings, it is not collaterally estopped

C. *District Court Dismissal of RICO*

We now turn to the remaining rationales offered by the district court to support its dismissal of plaintiff's RICO claim. The district court dismissed the RICO claim on the grounds that plaintiff had failed to allege several elements essential to pleading such a claim. Most notably, the court found that the complaint failed to allege (1) the existence of an "enterprise" and that this "enterprise" was economically independent from defendants' "pattern of racketeering activity," and (2) that the "enterprise," or any of the defendants, had a tie to "organized crime." We do not agree with the district court's assessment that these omissions required dismissal of the complaint.

1. *Civil RICO*

The district court's opinion is replete with expressions of concern about the broad scope of civil RICO. The court began its analysis by noting that "[t]he Racketeer Influenced and Corrupt Organizations Act, part of the Organized Crime Control Act of 1970, was designed in a multifaceted campaign against the pervasive presence of organized crime infiltrated in American business and trade," 553 F.Supp. at 1359, and then cautioned that "[t]he statutory language and recent Supreme Court and Second Circuit precedent, if carefully applied, can be extraordinarily effective in limiting RICO to its intended scope and filtering out many RICO claims that are just efforts to claim treble damages for ordinary violations of criminal or tort laws." Id. at 1360. The court continued, "The sweep of the statute does not embrace ordinary violators charged in common law fraud actions or federal securities law violations as the predicate offenses for RICO relief," id. at 1361, and finally concluded that "there is nothing in the legislative history to suggest that Congress intended to create a private right of action for treble damages for violations of substantive statutes by ordinary business[es] or parties." Id. at 1361.

We sympathize with the district court's concerns. However, it is not the "[judiciary's] role to reassess the costs and benefits associated with the creation of a dramatically expansive * * * tool for combating organized crime." Schact v. Brown, 711 F.2d at 1361 (citing United States v. Turkette, 452 U.S. at 586–87). In this regard we agree with the author of the Note, Civil RICO: The Temptation and Impropriety of Judicial Restriction, 95 Harv.L.Rev. 1101, 1120–21 (1982):

> Courts should not be left to impose liability based on their own tacit determination of which defendants are affiliated with organized crime. Nor should they create standing requirements that would preclude liability in many situations in which legislative intent would compel it. Complaints that RICO may effectively federalize common law fraud and erode recent restrictions on claims for securities fraud are better addressed to Congress than to courts.

from proving in the federal prosecutions [RICO] facts that the state was unable to prove."). See generally Tarlow, RICO: The New Darling of the Prosecutor's Nursery, 49 Fordham L.Rev. 165, 266–67 (1980).

However, we need not examine the collateral estoppel effect of Newman's crimi-nal conviction in this case. Plaintiff's complaint never mentioned the existence of Newman's prior criminal conviction, let alone presented it as proof of "racketeering activities" sufficient to support the RICO claim.

Although we appreciate the concerns motivating the district court to limit RICO's scope, we believe that the court misinterpreted the elements essential to pleading a RICO cause of action.

* * *

3. *The "Enterprise" Element*

The district court recognized that section 1962(c) requires plaintiffs to plead that an "enterprise" exists and that "there must be some nexus between the pattern of racketeering activity and the enterprise." 553 F.Supp. at 1363. We agree. Section 1962(c) states: "It shall be unlawful for any person employed by or associated with any enterprise * * * to conduct or participate, directly or indirectly, in the conduct of such enterprise's affairs through a pattern of racketeering activity * * *." 18 U.S.C. § 1962(c) (1976). "Enterprise" is defined as "any individual, partnership, corporation, association, or other legal entity, and any union or group of individuals associated in fact although not a legal entity." 18 U.S.C. § 1961(4) (1976); see United States v. Turkette, 452 U.S. 576, 581–82 (1981).

Yet, in addition to requiring plaintiff to plead the existence of this "enterprise," the district court required him to allege facts showing that the "enterprise" had an "independent economic significance from the pattern of racketeering activity." 553 F.Supp. at 1363. The district court concluded that because Morgan Stanley's and Newman's alleged "pattern of activity [was] identical to the enterprise * * * the plaintiff completely fails to make out this element [enterprise] of a RICO claim." Id. This conclusion cannot stand in light of our recent decisions in United States v. Mazzei, 700 F.2d 85 (2d Cir.1983), cert. denied, 461 U.S. 945 (1983), and United States v. Bagaric, 706 F.2d 42 (2d Cir.1983).

In United States v. Mazzei we expressly rejected the Eighth Circuit's view that the evidence offered to prove the "enterprise" and "pattern of racketeering" must necessarily be distinct. Id. at 89–90; see Bennett v. Berg, 685 F.2d at 1060; United States v. Anderson, 626 F.2d 1358, 1372 (8th Cir.1980) (enterprise "to encompass only an association having an ascertainable structure which exists for the purpose of maintaining operations directed toward an economic goal that has an existence that can be defined apart from the commission of the predicate acts constituting the 'pattern of racketeering activity.' "), cert. denied, 450 U.S. 912 (1981). Instead, we relied on the Supreme Court's decision in *Turkette* that "proof used to establish the 'pattern of racketeering activity' element 'may in particular cases coalesce' with the proof offered to establish the 'enterprise' element of RICO." United States v. Mazzei, 700 F.2d at 89 (quoting United States v. Turkette, 452 U.S. at 583; see United States v. Bagaric, 706 F.2d at 55. In *Mazzei* a group of individuals—bettors and Boston College basketball players—conspired illegally to shave points in Boston College basketball games in order to maximize their gambling proceeds. The "enterprise" consisted of the Boston College conspirators functioning as a "continuing unit, i.e., during the 1978–79 B.C. basketball season" and the "pattern of racketeering activity" consisted of " 'fixing' nine B.C. basketball games." 700 F.2d at 89. We upheld the propriety of Mazzei's RICO conviction even though the proof offered to establish the existence of these two elements had "coalesced." Id.; see United States v. Bagaric, 706 F.2d at 55 ("We have upheld application of RICO to situations where the enterprise was, in effect, no more than the sum of the predicate racketeering acts.").

In this case the "enterprise" allegedly consisted of Courtois' use of his position at Morgan Stanley to obtain confidential information about imminent tender offers; Antoniu's transmission of tender offer information to Newman; and Newman's use of his brokerage abilities to purchase the "target's" stock. The criminal indictment of these individuals reported that their tender offer "enterprise" existed for approximately two years. J.App. at 60–62. As previously mentioned, the "pattern of racketeering activity" consisted of Newman's purchase and sale of Deseret stock on the basis of the confidential information about the imminent tender offer. We can see no logical or practical basis upon which to distinguish between the enterprise/racketeering relationship of the illegal gamblers in *Mazzei* and the enterprise/racketeering relationship of the securities "schemers" in this case. See also United States v. Errico, 635 F.2d 152, 156 (2d Cir.1980) (a network of jockeys and bettors, who joined together for the single illegal purpose of betting on "fixed" horseraces, constituted an "enterprise" for the purposes of RICO), cert. denied, 453 U.S. 911 (1981). We find that under the standard articulated in *Mazzei,* the district court erred in its characterization of RICO's "enterprise" and "pattern of racketeering activity" elements.

Summary

We affirm the district court's dismissal of plaintiff's complaint on the grounds that (1) under *Chiarella* and *Dirks* plaintiff's inability to show that any defendant owed him a duty of disclosure precluded a violation of section 10(b) or rule 10b–5; (2) as the individual defendants were not held liable for violating the federal securities laws, Morgan Stanley could not be held derivatively liable under section 20(a) of the 1934 Act; (3) because plaintiff failed to state a claim under section 10(b) of the 1934 Act that defendant Newman committed fraud in the sale of securities, the RICO claim—which premises its "pattern of racketeering activity" on the alleged securities fraud—must likewise fail; and (4) since plaintiff failed to allege that his injury was causally connected to defendant's "unlawful" conduct, his civil RICO claim must be dismissed.

Affirmed.

SUPERIOR OIL CO. v. FULMER
United States Court of Appeals, Eighth Circuit, 1986.
785 F.2d 252.

Before HEANEY and BOWMAN, CIRCUIT JUDGES, and WANGELIN,* SENIOR DISTRICT JUDGE.

WANGELIN, SENIOR DISTRICT JUDGE.

This is an appeal from a jury-tried case. The jury found for plaintiff, Superior Oil Company, and against the defendants, Huey Fulmer, James Branch, and Roy Nichols. It returned a verdict on the claim for wrongful conversion in the amount of $145,125.00, on the claim under the Racketeer

---

* THE HONORABLE H. KENNETH WANGELIN, Senior United States District Judge for the   Eastern and Western Districts of Missouri, sitting by designation.

Influenced and Corrupt Organizations Act (RICO) in the amount of $25,000.00, and against defendant Fulmer alone on a compressor rental claim in the amount of $26,397.70. The court trebled the RICO award.

I. BACKGROUND.

Huey Fulmer was an employee for Austral Oil Company (Austral). Austral had developed several oil and gas wells in South Lafayette County, Arkansas, and Fulmer was responsible for the mechanical upkeep and the production at the wells. Fulmer also leased a compressor to Austral to increase pressure in the pipeline and thereby aid the flow of Liquid Petroleum Gas (LPG) to an International Paper Company plant from a well denominated as International Paper Company No. 2 (I.P. No. 2).

I.P. No. 2 consists of an oil/gas well from which a pipeline runs to a separator plant. The oil is then transferred through a pipeline to two storage tanks. The LPG product continues down another pipeline, through a compressor, eventually joining with a pipeline that runs to the International plant. Just prior to the junction of the Superior and International pipelines is a metering device and a six-inch flange. This was the physical arrangement of I.P. No. 2.

When appellee Superior Oil Company (Superior Oil) purchased this operation from Austral, it retained Fulmer as a pumper and also as lessor of the compressor unit. In 1981, Fulmer entered into a partnership with James Branch and Roy Nichols whereby they would install a cryogenic plant on the pipeline to remove the heavier hydrocarbons from the natural gas supply. To that end, they procured a letter of permission from the manager of the International Paper Company (International) mill to put a dryer on the pipeline. Testimony at trial indicated that the letter was addressed to Fulmer as the representative and employee of the appellee and that appellant Fulmer never indicated that the letter was intended for his personal use nor was it meant to convey ownership of LPG products. The mill manager also stated that he understood the purpose of Fulmer's request was to remove water from the gas purchased from I.P. Well No. 2, and that he would have no authority to authorize the installation of a cryogenic unit.

After Branch and Nichols installed the cryogenic plant, Fulmer removed the metering unit from its position near the juncture of the Superior Oil and International pipelines. This unit measured the quantity of gas moving through the pipeline and formed the basis for billing International. Fulmer installed the meter at a point on the pipeline prior to, or "upstream" from, the cryogenic plant. The original position of the meter had been "downstream" from the plant.

The cryogenic unit had the effect of reducing the burning capacity of the LPG product. The contract between Superior Oil and International provided that the LPG product purchased by International have a minimum 1,000 BTU capacity. It also provided that a premium would be paid for BTU capacity above 1,000. Testimony at trial indicated that the cryogenic plant reduced the BTU capacity from 1,170–1,200 BTU to approximately 1,050 BTU.

Among Fulmer's other duties as pumper of the Superior Oil station was to make daily reports regarding the pressure at the wellhead and in the pipeline.

Fulmer regularly reported that there was thirty pounds of pressure at the wellhead. At this pressure level, a well is barely producing and must have a compressor on the pipeline to operate efficiently. After Fulmer's termination, Superior Oil employees found that the actual wellhead pressure was between 300 to 380 pounds. At these pressure levels, a compressor unit is unnecessary. Testimony at trial indicated, however, that the appellant utilized the compressor to increase the pressure in the pipeline to 400 pounds in order to increase the efficiency of the cryogenic unit.

Reported oil production during the time that Fulmer operated the station also differed radically from subsequent events. Under Fulmer's operation, the well produced approximately seventeen barrels of oil for every million cubic feet of gas. When Superior undertook operation of the plant, oil production increased to approximately thirty-five barrels per million cubic feet of gas. This production output has remained constant since that time.

In this regard, relevant testimony indicated that all authorized sales of oil were made to P & O Falco. On several occasions, however, Delton Hanson, an employee of one Dewey Williams, testified that he had gone to I.P. No. 2 and picked up truckloads of oil. Fulmer was present on these occasions, and demonstrated to Hanson how the oil could be obtained without breaking the seals.

Superior was notified by an anonymous letter that Fulmer was stealing LPG product. It notified the Federal Bureau of Investigation (FBI) which investigated the allegations. Fulmer was later arrested and the cryogenic plant was seized by the FBI and placed in Superior Oil's possession. Fulmer's indictment was dismissed and Superior Oil was ordered to return the cryogenic plant. Thereafter, Superior Oil filed a cause of action for a receiver to be appointed in the Chancery Court of Lafayette County, Arkansas. This action was removed to the United States District Court where Superior prevailed.

II. DISCUSSION.

Under Arkansas law, which controls this diversity action, a reviewing court must examine the evidence in the light most favorable to the appellee and must sustain the jury verdict if it is supported by substantial evidence. DeWitt v. Brown, 669 F.2d 516 (8th Cir.1982); Garoogian v. Medlock, 592 F.2d 997, 999–1000 (8th Cir.1979).

The appellants cite as their first point of error that the Court erred in failing to direct a verdict in favor of the appellants on the issue of conversion of LPG products. Essentially, the appellants argue that no conversion of the LPG products occurred because the meter which determined the amount of product sold to the International plant was moved upstream of the cryogenic unit. Thus, the appellants conclude that the appellee suffered no loss through the taking of the LPG product.

We disagree. The contract between Superior Oil and the International specified that the point of delivery of the LPG product was a six-inch flange downstream of the cryogenic unit. Moving the meter unit did not change the contractually mandated point of sale. Thus, whether the meter was upstream or downstream to the cryogenic unit is irrelevant; the LPG product belonged to appellee Superior Oil at the time of its conversion.

* * *

The appellants next allege that the trial court erred in failing to direct a verdict in their favor on the RICO count. We agree. In our view, Superior Oil failed to prove that Fulmer, Branch and Nichols engaged in a "pattern of racketeering activity" as that term is construed in the United States Supreme Court's recent decision in Sedima, S.P.R.L. v. Imrex Co., 473 U.S. 479 (1985). In *Sedima*, the Court held that "[a] violation of § 1962(c), the section on which [Superior Oil] relies, requires (1) conduct (2) of an enterprise (3) through a pattern (4) of racketeering activity." 87 L.Ed.2d at 358–59 (footnote omitted).[1] The definition of a "pattern of racketeering activity" set forth in section 1961(5) states that a pattern "requires at least two acts of racketeering activity, one of which occurred after the effective date of this chapter and the last of which occurred within ten years * * * after the commission of a prior act of racketeering activity." "Racketeering activity" is defined in section 1961(1) to include a wide range of criminal acts, including mail and wire fraud.

Prior to the Supreme Court's decision in *Sedima*, several courts had suggested that a "pattern of racketeering activity" requires "related"[2] predicate acts which have "continuity" in the sense of some prolonged course of conduct, not merely an isolated event.[3]

1. Sections 1962(a) and (b) also share in common the "pattern of racketeering activity" requirements.

2. See, e.g., United States v. Stofsky, 409 F.Supp. 609, 612–14 (S.D.N.Y.1973), aff'd, 527 F.2d 237 (1975), cert. denied, 429 U.S. 819 (1976) ("The racketeering acts must have been connected to each other by some common scheme, plan or motive so as to constitute a pattern and not simply a series of disconnected acts.").

3. See, e.g., United States v. Computer Sciences Corp., 689 F.2d 1181, 1189–90 (4th Cir.1982) (*dicta* stating that, "[w]e express doubt that Congress ever contemplated the extension of the RICO statute to include a situation where one of the predicate offenses, separated in character and by a long time period, could combine with a set of closely related wire fraud and mail fraud claims essentially representing subdivisions of a single ongoing illegal act to meet the predicate requirements of so serious a statute."); Exetor Towers Associates v. Bowditch, 604 F.Supp. 1547, 1554–55 (D.Mass.1985) ("I conclude that the connotations of a 'pattern of racketeering activity,' as that phrase is used in the RICO statute, are not satisfied by proof that, in effectuating the purchase of a single mortgage, the defendants committed two or more predicate acts of mail fraud. To construe the statute as applying in these circumstances would be to give it a sweep so broad as to be inconsistent with manifested congressional objectives. Most substantial business transactions involve two or more uses of the mail during negotiations. To hold that two such uses of the mail, in circumstances otherwise satisfying the prerequisites of proof of an offense under the

mail fraud statute, are sufficient to constitute a 'pattern of racketeering activity' would be to sweep into federal courts, under RICO, the great majority of actions for fraud in commercial transactions. I conclude that the Supreme Court will not read the RICO statute this broadly, whatever may be the precise terms of the limiting formulation it fashions."); Teleprompter of Erie, Inc. v. Erie, 537 F.Supp. 6, 13 (W.D. Pa.1981) (Court holds that the alleged receipt by a councilman of multiple bribes at a single political fundraiser was not a "*series* of unlawful acts sufficient to establish 'a pattern of racketeering activity' within the meaning of RICO."); United States v. Field, 432 F.Supp. 55, 59 (S.D.N.Y.1977) ("The language of the Act, which makes a pattern of conduct the essence of the crime, 'clearly contemplates a prolonged course of conduct.'"); United States v. Moeller, 402 F.Supp. 49, 57–58 (D.Conn. 1975) (dicta stating that, "I would have thought the common sense interpretation of the word 'pattern' implies acts occurring in *different criminal episodes*, episodes that are at least somewhat separated in time and place yet still sufficiently related by purpose to demonstrate a continuity of activity. I would further have thought that the normal canon of narrowly construing penal statutes points toward such an interpretation. Finally, I would have thought that the legislative history made such an interpretation clear."); United States v. White, 386 F.Supp. 882, 883 (E.D.Wis.1974) (Court holds that the term "pattern" was not unconstitutionally vague because "[i]n common usage, the term 'pattern' is applied to a combination of qualities or acts forming a consistent or characteristic ar-

The majority of pre-*Sedima* decisions, however, concluded that a "pattern" of racketeering activity could be proved simply by showing the commission of two acts of "racketeering activity" within the last ten years, see, e.g., Alexander Grant v. Tiffany, 742 F.2d 408, 410 (8th Cir.1984), vacated, ___ U.S. ___, 105 S.Ct. 3550 (1985), on remand, 770 F.2d 717 (8th Cir.1985);[4] United States v. Aleman, 609 F.2d 298 (7th Cir.1979), cert. denied, 445 U.S. 946 (1980); United States v. Parness, 503 F.2d 430 (2d Cir. 1974), cert. denied, 419 U.S. 1105 (1975), even if the two acts occurred on the same day, in the same place, and formed a part of the same criminal episode. *Parness,* 503 F.2d at 441–42.

In *Sedima,* the Supreme Court suggested that it disagreed with this broad construction of "pattern." * * *

Justice Powell's dissent emphasizes that in examining "pattern," "the presence of the predicate acts is only the beginning: something more is required for a 'pattern' to be proved." 105 S.Ct. at 3289. He suggested his agreement with the ABA Civil RICO report: * * *

In short, proof of a "pattern of racketeering activity" "requires more than one 'racketeering activity' and the threat of continuing activity to be effective. It is this factor of *continuity plus relationship* which combines to produce a pattern." *Sedima,* 473 U.S. at 479 n. 14 (quoting S.Rep. No. 91–617, p. 158 (1969)).[7] Superior Oil clearly has proved the "relationship" prong. They proved several related acts of mail and wire fraud in pursuit of the underlying conversion or theft of gas from Superior Oil's interstate pipeline. See *Sedima,* 473 U.S. at 479 n. 14.

Superior Oil has, however, failed to prove the "continuity" sufficient to form a "pattern of racketeering activity." The actions of Fulmer, Branch, and Nichols comprised one continuing scheme to convert gas from Superior Oil's pipeline. There was no proof that Fulmer, Branch, or Nichols had ever done these activities in the past and there was no proof that they were engaged in other criminal activities elsewhere.

---

rangement."); *Stofsky,* 409 F.Supp. at 614 ("In spite of the quantitative nature of the section 1961 definition of 'pattern,' the major concern of Congress * * * was the special danger * * * of a continuity of racketeering activity.").

4. But see United States v. Anderson, 626 F.2d 1358, 1367 (8th Cir.1980), cert. denied, 450 U.S. 912 (1981) ("use of the 'enterprise' element to provide a relationship between the two predicate crimes aids to contain the prohibitions of RICO rather than to expand them to cover purely sporadic criminal activity").

7. The *Sedima* Court also suggested that the courts look to the definition of "pattern" in 18 U.S.C. § 3275(e), in giving meaning to RICO's "pattern of racketeering activity" requirement. This definition construes pattern as a series of related acts which "are not isolated events." Although our research reveals no judicial interpretations of section 3575(e)'s pattern requirement, the legislative history behind this

element indicates that it was intended to isolate the professional, long-term criminal elements in society. See 116 Cong.Rec. 847 (Jan. 22, 1970) (statement of Senator Hruska) (This section is aimed at "the special criminal. That is the kind who will never be rehabilitated * * * because he has participated in a life of illegal conduct."); *Organized Crime Control, Hearings on S. 30 and Related Proposals before Subcomm. No. 5 of the House Comm. on the Judiciary,* 91st Cong., 2d Sess. 130 (1970) (Statement of Senator McClellan) ("If there is a pattern of illegal conduct, in other words, if they are more or less professional criminals engaged in crime, you have the beginning of a special offender situation."); id. at 245 (The "pattern of conduct" requirement would not be "just another bribery count or something of that nature. It would be continuous conduct like that of a major bookie operating over a long period of time.")

Superior Oil attempted to show that Fulmer, Branch, and Nichols intended to engage in similar gas conversion schemes at other locations. Although it may be that proof of a threat of continuing racketeering activities in the future could, in combination with ongoing acts of racketeering, be sufficient to establish a "pattern of racketeering," we find insufficient proof of such a threat here. Instead, the record reveals one isolated fraudulent scheme. On the facts of this case, we agree with the court's conclusion in Northern Trust Bank/O'Hare, N.A. v. Inryco, Inc., 615 F.Supp. 828, 832 (D.C.Ill.1985), that "[i]t is difficult to see how the threat of continuing activity stressed in the Senate Report could be established by a single criminal episode. * * * It places a real strain on the language to speak of a single fraudulent effort, implemented by several fraudulent acts, as a 'pattern of racketeering activity.' " [8]

We also express doubt over whether Superior Oil proved the "enterprise" element of a RICO action. In United States v. Anderson, 626 F.2d 1358, 1365 (8th Cir.1980), cert. denied, 450 U.S. 912 (1981), we held that "[t]he term 'enterprise' must signify an association that is substantially different from the acts which form the 'pattern of racketeering activity'." See also United States v. Turkette, 452 U.S. 576, 583 (1981); Bennett v. Berg, 685 F.2d 1053, 1061–63 (8th Cir.1982), aff'd in part and rev'd in part on other grounds, 710 F.2d 1361 (8th Cir.1983) (en banc), cert. denied, 464 U.S. 1008 (1983); United States v. Bledsoe, 674 F.2d 647, 665 (8th Cir.1982); Bennett v. United States Trust Co. of New York, 770 F.2d 308, 315 (2d Cir. 1985) (post-*Sedima* application of this test). Here, Fulmer, Branch and Nichols entered into a partnership which had the sole purpose of con-

---

8. For other similar post-*Sedima* opinions, see Allington v. Carpenter, 619 F.Supp. 474 (C.D.Cal.1985) (Court dismisses without prejudice a RICO claim based on allegations that the defendants falsely promised high rates of return on loans secured by worthless promissory notes or real estate trust deeds, holding that the commission of three acts of wire fraud in connection with this single and isolated fraudulent scheme comprised merely a single criminal episode rather than a "pattern of racketeering activity."); Professional Assets Management, Inc. v. Penn Square Bank, N.A., 616 F.Supp. 1418 (W.D.Okla. 1985) (Court dismisses RICO action against accounting firm for allegedly fraudulent preparation of a single audit on Penn Square Bank. In dismissing the claim of fraudulent preparation of the audit, the court held that the claim "is not based on a 'pattern' as that term was elaborated in *Sedima* and *Inryco*, but arises from one engagement to perform one audit[.]" Id. at 1421–22. In dismissing a second RICO claim alleging the dissemination of false information, the court held: "Assuming, arguendo, that such a 'scheme' existed and that multiple wire or telephone communications were made in its furtherance, it remains apparent that any statements were merely constituents of a single, unified activity. This is not a situation where several distinct torts or crimes are commit-

ted over the course of an enterprise; here the court finds only a series of related statements that PAM tries to splinter into several elements of a civil RICO cause of action." Id. at 1423.); Rojas v. First Bank National Association, 613 F.Supp. 968, 971 n. 1 (E.D.N.Y.1985) (Dicta stating that a " 'pattern' requires a showing of at least two acts of racketeering activity and the threat of continuing activity. * * * Plaintiffs' allegations, arising out of two discrete transactions with defendant, fall far short of establishing a pattern within the meaning of the RICO statute."); Morgan v. Bank of Waukegan, 615 F.Supp. 836 (N.D.Ill.1985) (Court dismisses RICO complaint alleging that sale of twenty percent interest in certain drugstores was part of a scheme to divest plaintiffs of their investment and their security interest, holding that, even if the allegation of fraud was true, this single scheme failed to demonstrate a "pattern of racketeering activity."); Cullen v. Nassau County Republican Committee, II RICO Law Rptr. 564 (E.D. N.Y.1985) (In a section 1962(c) action alleging that Republican party officials engaged in a pattern of extortion, the court instructed the jury that "[t]o establish a pattern of illegal activity, it is not enough that plaintiffs show at least two crimes of extortion * * * plaintiffs must also show that the crimes constituted part of a larger pattern of criminal activity[.]").

verting and selling the heavier hydrocarbons from Superior Oil's gas pipeline to the International Paper Company. This partnership appears to have had no purpose distinct from the conduct inherent in their conversion scheme. We need not definitively rule on this issue, however, in light of our holding that Superior Oil failed to prove that the appellants engaged in a "pattern of racketeering activity."

Accordingly, we vacate the jury's award on Superior Oil's RICO claim, and dismiss appellee's cross-appeal on the RICO issue.

* * *

* * * In sum, we affirm the wrongful conversion award of $145,125.00 against Fulmer, Branch and Nichols, affirm the fraud award of $26,397.70 against Fulmer, and vacate the $25,000.00 RICO award.

Affirmed in part and reversed in part.

R.A.G.S. COUTURE, INC. v. HYATT
United States Court of Appeals, Fifth Circuit, 1985.
774 F.2d 1350.

Before WISDOM, POLITZ and TATE, CIRCUIT JUDGES.

OPINION

WISDOM, CIRCUIT JUDGE.

This case raises questions concerning the Racketeer Influenced and Corrupt Organizations Act (RICO), 18 U.S.C. §§ 1961–1968, in the wake of the Supreme Court's decision in Sedima, S.P.R.L. v. Imrex Co., 1985, 473 U.S. 479. In *Sedima*, the majority opinion relied heavily on the broad language of the statute. The present case stretches the statutory language to its limit. The complaint minimally complies with the requirements sufficient to support a civil RICO violation: two individual defendants are termed an "enterprise" and two acts of mail fraud they allegedly committed constitute a pattern of "racketeering activity". The district court granted the defendants' motions to dismiss and for summary judgment. We conclude that we are compelled to reverse in the light of the *Sedima* decision and the procedural setting of this case.

I.

The plaintiff, R.A.G.S. Couture, Inc. (R.A.G.S.), filed this suit against the defendants who allegedly attempted to defraud the company. Defendant Mary Hyatt was the president and a stockholder of R.A.G.S., a clothing manufacturer in Louisiana, from April 1982 to March 1983. Her daughter Kellie was a stockholder and employee of the company during that period. Defendant Oren Welborne is alleged by the defendants to own industrial sewing machines that he rented to R.A.G.S. while Hyatt was president. Hyatt, her daughter, and the two other stockholders of the company had a meeting on March 13, 1983, at which Hyatt and her daughter terminated their employment with R.A.G.S. and released their interest in the company. On the same day, Hyatt and Welborne told the two remaining stockholders that the sewing machines used by R.A.G.S. were owned by Welborne and rented to the company. The stockholders allege that Hyatt had previously told them that the company owned the sewing machines. Welborne took possession of the machines on March 14th after signing a statement in which he claimed that he owned all of them.

R.A.G.S. alleges that on March 30, 1983, either Welborne or Hyatt mailed or caused to be mailed to the plaintiff copies of invoices, signed by Hyatt, for repair services performed by Welborne on the sewing machines and for rental fees. The plaintiff maintains that both defendants knew of the mailing. The invoices had various dates from July 1982 to February 1983, but the plaintiff alleges that the invoices were fraudulently prepared by the defendants after March 13, 1983. On August 24, 1983, counsel for Welborne mailed copies of the invoices and a demand for payment to counsel for R.A.G.S.

R.A.G.S. filed suit under the civil provision of RICO, 18 U.S.C. § 1964(c), against Hyatt and Welborne. The gravamen of the plaintiff's complaint is that the defendants combined to defraud R.A.G.S. by submitting false invoices. The plaintiff alleges that it had no contract to rent the sewing machines. Furthermore, the plaintiff contends that Welborne did not service the machines, as the defendants have asserted. R.A.G.S. contends that it is entitled to relief because the defendants formed an enterprise— the association of Hyatt and Welborne—that affects interstate commerce and conducted the affairs of the enterprise "through a pattern of racketeering activity" in violation of 18 U.S.C. § 1962(c). The pattern of racketeering activity consisted of two alleged acts of mail fraud, the mailings on March 30, 1983 and August 24, 1983. The plaintiff seeks damages under § 1964(c) and an order prohibiting the defendants from attempting to defraud the company.

Before trial, each defendant moved to dismiss and for summary judgment. The district court granted the defendants' motions and the plaintiff has appealed.

II.

To prove a violation of 18 U.S.C. § 1962(c) a plaintiff must show that (1) an enterprise existed that affected interstate commerce; (2) the defendant was associated with the enterprise; (3) the defendant participated in the conduct of the enterprise's affairs; and (4) the participation was through a "pattern of racketeering activity." See United States v. Phillips, 5 Cir. 1981, 664 F.2d 971, 1011, cert. denied, 1982, 457 U.S. 1136. The term "enterprise" is defined broadly to include any "group of individuals associated in fact". 18 U.S.C. § 1961(4). A pattern of racketeering activity is "at least two acts" indictable under an enumeration of state and federal criminal laws.

In their motions to dismiss and for summary judgment the defendants asserted that the plaintiff failed to allege or offer any proof of an enterprise that affects interstate commerce or of a "pattern of racketeering activity". The district court granted the motions to dismiss on the grounds that the plaintiff failed to allege a sufficient nexus between the enterprise and interstate commerce. Also, the court dismissed the complaint because the plaintiff failed to allege a "racketeering injury". The parties had not raised this issue. The court granted the motions for summary judgment because it found that the plaintiff had failed to offer proof of two acts of mail fraud and thus could not show a pattern of racketeering activity.

R.A.G.S.'s complaint alleged that Hyatt and Welborne were "associated in fact" and thus constituted an enterprise for purposes of the RICO Act. The district court denied the defendants' motions to dismiss and for summary judgment on this issue. The court found that a material question of fact exists as to whether the defendants formed an association. This ruling is correct in the light of this circuit's broad interpretation of the definition of "enterprise" in 18 U.S.C. § 1962(c). See Alcorn County v. U.S. Interstate Supplies, Inc., 5 Cir.1984, 731 F.2d 1160, 1168.

* * *

C. *Pattern of Racketeering Activity*

The district court granted the defendants' motions for summary judgment on the grounds that there was evidence of only one alleged act of mail fraud and therefore the plaintiff had failed to show a pattern of racketeering activity since "at least two acts" are required by the statute. A summary judgment is appropriate only if there is no genuine issue of material fact and the movant is entitled to judgment as a matter of law. Fed.R.Civ.P. 56. The record must be viewed in the light most favorable to the party opposing the motion.

The law on the subject of mail fraud is well established. A person who participates in a "scheme or artifice to defraud" and causes a use of the mails "for the purpose of executing the scheme" violates 18 U.S.C. § 1341.[6] The test to determine whether a defendant caused the mails to be used is whether the use was reasonably foreseeable. The defendant need not intend to cause the mails to be used. United States v. Toney, 5 Cir.1979, 598 F.2d 1349, 1355, cert. denied, 1980, 444 U.S. 1033.

Two acts of mail fraud were alleged in the complaint. The first was the mailing on March 30, 1983 to R.A.G.S. and the second was the mailing by counsel for Welborne to counsel for R.A.G.S. on August 24, 1983. The plaintiff maintains that either Welborne or Hyatt caused both mailings and that each defendant knew of the mailings. The district court found that there was a material question of fact whether either of the defendants caused the first mailing. If one of the defendants caused the mailing and they both participated in the fraudulent scheme, then both would have committed mail fraud. A defendant need not personally cause the mails to be used; "there need only be sufficient evidence to connect him to the fraudulent scheme involving the use of the mails". United States v. Finney, 5 Cir.1983, 714 F.2d 420, 423.

The district court ruled that the second mailing was not caused by the defendants because it was sent in response to an inquiry from the plaintiff's

---

6. Whoever, having devised or intending to devise any scheme or artifice to defraud, or for obtaining money or property by means of false or fraudulent pretenses, representations, or promises, or to sell, dispose of, loan, exchange, alter, give away, distribute, supply, or furnish or procure for unlawful use any counterfeit or spurious coin, obligation, security, or other article, or anything represented to be or intimated or held out to be such counterfeit or spurious article, for the purpose of executing such scheme or artifice or attempting so to do, places in any post office or authorized depository for mail matter, any matter or thing whatever to be sent or delivered by the Postal Service, or takes or receives therefrom, any such matter or thing, or knowingly causes to be delivered by mail according to the direction thereon, or at the place at which it is directed to be delivered by the person to whom it is addressed, any such matter or thing, shall be fined not more than $1,000 or imprisoned not more than five years, or both.

18 U.S.C. § 1341.

counsel. The court did not determine whether the defendants reasonably could have foreseen the inquiry by the plaintiff's counsel and the response by Welborne's counsel. If these mailings were foreseeable and made in execution of the defendants' alleged scheme to defraud R.A.G.S., then the mailing on August 24th by Welborne's counsel was an act of mail fraud. This is a question of fact inappropriate for resolution before trial.

The defendants argue that even if they committed two acts of mail fraud, these were not sufficient to constitute a "pattern of racketeering activity". They rely on the language of the statute, which requires "at least two acts", and the suggestion in *Sedima* that "while two acts are necessary, they may not be sufficient." 105 S.Ct. at 3285 n. 14. The district court did not consider this issue. We are not persuaded by the defendants' argument. The Supreme Court in *Sedima* implied that two "isolated" acts would not constitute a pattern. Id. In this case, however, the alleged acts of mail fraud are related.

Since there is a material question of fact whether two acts of mail fraud were committed, the summary judgment for the defendants must be reversed.

III.

The scope of the civil RICO statute is breathtaking. An allegation of fraud in a contract action can transform an ordinary state law claim into a federal racketeering charge. It may be unfortunate for federal courts to be burdened by this kind of case, but it is not for this Court to question policies decided by Congress and upheld by the Supreme Court. The broad language of the statute and the *Sedima* decision provide us with clear guidance. Material questions of fact exist that cannot be resolved before trial. The judgment of the district court is therefore REVERSED and the case is remanded for further proceedings.

HAROCO, INC. v. AMERICAN NATIONAL BANK AND TRUST COMPANY OF CHICAGO

United States Court of Appeals, Seventh Circuit, 1984.
747 F.2d 384, aff'd. on other grounds, 473 U.S. 606, 105 S.Ct. 3291, 87 L.Ed.2d 437 (1985).

Before BAUER and CUDAHY, CIRCUIT JUDGES, and KELLAM, SENIOR DISTRICT JUDGE.**

CUDAHY, CIRCUIT JUDGE.

This appeal presents several issues involving civil claims under the federal Racketeer Influenced and Corrupt Organizations ("RICO") statute. 18 U.S.C. §§ 1961–1968. The central issue concerns the type of injury a private civil plaintiff must allege to support a RICO claim under 18 U.S.C. § 1964(c). We must also consider several questions involving the RICO provisions requiring that a "person" conduct or participate in the conduct of the affairs of an "enterprise" through a pattern of racketeering activity,

---

** Honorable Richard B. Kellam, Senior District Judge for the Eastern District of Virginia, is sitting by designation.

as those terms are defined in RICO. 18 U.S.C. § 1962(c). We affirm in part and reverse in part.

I

This is an appeal from the district court's dismissal for failure to state a claim. We shall therefore treat all allegations in the complaint as true and view them in the light most favorable to plaintiffs. The case arises from loans made by defendant American National Bank & Trust Company of Chicago ("ANB") to plaintiffs. Plaintiffs are several businesses, Haroco, Inc., Roman Ceramics, Inc., California Originals, Inc. and Mike Wayne Distilled Products Co. Haroco independently and together with other plaintiffs borrowed several million dollars from ANB between 1979 and 1981. Each loan agreement provided that the rate of interest would be "one per cent over the bank's prime rate," and the prime rate was defined as the "rate of interest charged by the bank to its largest and most creditworthy commercial borrowers for 90–day unsecured commercial loans." The defendants, in addition to ANB, are Ronald J. Grayheck, who is an officer and director of ANB, and Walter E. Heller International Corporation ("Heller International"), which is the parent company of ANB.[1]

Plaintiffs brought this action in March 1983 alleging that defendants had defrauded them in the calculation of the prime rate which determined their own variable interest payments. The only alleged injuries were excessive interest charges resulting from defendants' calculation of the prime rate. Plaintiffs included in their complaint three state law causes of action and two counts based on alleged violations of the federal Racketeer Influenced and Corrupt Organizations ("RICO") provisions in 18 U.S.C. §§ 1961–1968. As we shall explain in more detail below, plaintiffs' RICO claims were predicated on defendants' use of the mails in furtherance of the alleged scheme to defraud plaintiffs by overstating the prime interest rate. Count I of the amended complaint alleged that defendant ANB violated 18 U.S.C. § 1962(c) by conducting ANB's and Heller International's affairs through a pattern of racketeering activity. Count II alleged that defendants Heller International and Grayheck violated section 1962(c) by conducting ANB's affairs through a pattern of racketeering activity.

Defendants moved on three principal grounds to dismiss the RICO counts. First, they argued that plaintiffs failed to allege the requisite causal relationship between their injuries and the RICO violations. Second, defendants argued that plaintiffs failed to allege the requisite relationships between "persons" and the "enterprises," the affairs of which were allegedly conducted through patterns of racketeering activity. Third, defendants argued that plaintiffs had not pleaded the predicate acts of mail fraud with the necessary particularity.

The district court concluded that the plaintiffs had failed to state claims under RICO because they did not allege that they had suffered any injury by reason of a RICO violation in addition to the injuries caused by the alleged mail fraud. The district court held "that a plaintiff's injury to be cognizable under RICO must be caused by a RICO violation and not simply

---

1. According to the complaint, ANB has at all relevant times been either a wholly owned subsidiary of Heller, or a wholly owned subsidiary of American National Corporation, which in turn is a wholly owned subsidiary of Heller.

by the commission of predicate offenses, such as acts of mail fraud." Haroco, Inc. v. American National Bank & Trust Co., 577 F.Supp. 111, 114 (N.D.Ill.1983). The district court therefore dismissed plaintiffs' RICO claims without reaching defendants' other arguments. Because there was no other ground for federal jurisdiction, the district court also dismissed the remaining pendent state law claims.

II

Before proceeding to the specific issues raised on this appeal, we must first sketch RICO's broad civil provisions. This court recently said that the civil RICO provisions are "constructed on the model of a treasure hunt." Sutliff, Inc. v. Donovan Companies, 727 F.2d 648, 652 (7th Cir.1984). We begin the hunt with 18 U.S.C. § 1964(c), which provides the private cause of action:

> Any person injured in his business or property by reason of a violation of section 1962 of this chapter may sue therefor in any appropriate United States district court and shall recover threefold the damages he sustains and the cost of the suit, including a reasonable attorney's fee.

The next step is to examine section 1962, which describes the prohibited conduct. In this case, the most relevant portion of the section provides:

> It shall be unlawful for any person employed by or associated with any enterprise engaged in, or the activities of which affect, interstate or foreign commerce, to conduct or participate, directly or indirectly, in the conduct of such enterprise's affairs through a pattern of racketeering activity or collection of unlawful debt.

18 U.S.C. § 1962(c). We must next turn to section 1961, which provides special statutory definitions for the key terms of section 1962(c). "Racketeering activity" is defined in section 1961(1) in terms of a long list of state and federal crimes, including mail fraud, 18 U.S.C. § 1341. A person commits mail fraud by using the mails for the purpose of executing a scheme or artifice to defraud. 18 U.S.C. § 1341; United States v. Wormick, 709 F.2d 454, 461–62 (7th Cir.1983). A "pattern of racketeering activity," as required by section 1962(c), requires at least two acts of racketeering activity within a ten year period. 18 U.S.C. § 1961(5). The individual acts of racketeering activity, such as the alleged mail fraud in this case, are usually described as the "predicate offenses."

RICO also defines "person" and "enterprise" very broadly. The term "person" includes "any individual or entity capable of holding a legal or beneficial interest in property." 18 U.S.C. § 1961(3). The term "enterprise" includes "any individual, partnership, corporation, association, or other legal entity, and any union or group of individuals associated in fact although not a legal entity." 18 U.S.C. § 1961(4).

RICO's terms are obviously very broad. Because various fraud offenses are included in the definition of "racketeering activity," RICO claims (with their treble-damage provisions) have recently become attractive to many plaintiffs in commercial disputes that otherwise might involve only breach of contract, or securities or state law fraud claims. In cases involving allegations of commercial fraud, for example, it is often possible for a plaintiff to allege two acts of mail fraud, thus constituting a "pattern of racketeering activity," and to allege further that the defendant conducted the affairs of an "enterprise" through that pattern of racketeering activity in violation of section 1962(c). Whether RICO's broad terms should be read literally to permit RICO claims in instances of such "garden variety" fraud has recently been the subject of extended debates in the federal courts. The central issue in this case concerns the type of injury a plaintiff must allege to sustain a RICO claim.

* * *

[The court's discussion of the "racketeering injury" issue is omitted. The case was affirmed on that point without reaching the "enterprise" argument by the Supreme Court. 105 Sup.Ct. 3291 (1985).]

IV

Although the district court's dismissal of the complaint cannot be affirmed based on the elusive racketeering injury requirement, the defendants also contend that the dismissal is supported by other arguments not reached by the district court. These issues involve the necessary relationship between a person and an enterprise under 18 U.S.C. § 1962(c). The defendants correctly observe that we may reach these issues on appeal, at least where the arguments were presented to the district court and where the present record permits resolution of the issues.

Defendant ANB: ANB argues that it cannot be held liable under section 1962(c) in Count I because the requisite relationship between a person and an enterprise is not alleged. Plaintiffs offer two theories to support their RICO claims against ANB. First, they argue that ANB was both the "person" and the "enterprise" under section 1962(c) so that it conducted its own affairs through a pattern of racketeering activity. Second, they argue that ANB was the "person" conducting the affairs of its parent corporation, Heller International.

We turn first to the plaintiffs' contention that the same corporation may be both the liable "person" and the "enterprise" under section 1962(c). There is now a split in the circuits on this question. In United States v. Hartley, 678 F.2d 961, 987–90 (11th Cir.1982), cert. denied, 459 U.S. 1170 (1983), the Eleventh Circuit held that the corporation at the center of a fraudulent scheme could be both the person and the enterprise under section 1962(c). The Fourth Circuit held precisely the opposite in United States v. Computer Sciences Corp., 689 F.2d 1181, 1190–91 (4th Cir.1982), *cert. denied,* 459 U.S. 1105 (1983).[17] Both cases were criminal RICO prosecutions, but the interpretations of 18 U.S.C. § 1962(c) are equally applicable to civil cases.

Discussion of whether the same corporation may be both the liable "person" and the "enterprise" under section 1962(c) has proceeded at two levels—the statutory language and the policies of RICO, and we shall consider both.

---

17. The Eighth Circuit appears to agree with the Fourth Circuit's conclusion that section 1962(c) requires an enterprise distinct from the person. Bennett v. Berg, supra, 685 F.2d at 1061–62 (affirming dismissal of count naming identical defendant and enterprise, but permitting amendment on remand), Bennett v. Berg, supra, 710 F.2d at 1364 & n. 4 (en banc); id, at 1365 (McMillian, J., dissenting in part); Alexander Grant & Co. v. Tiffany Industries, supra, 742 F.2d at 411 n. 6 (Bennett v. Berg held count insufficient precisely because of possibility of identity of enterprise and person). The Ninth Circuit also recently followed *Computer Sciences* on the point. Rae v. Union Bank, 725 F.2d 478, 481 (9th Cir.1984).

In terms of the language, it is clear that a corporation can satisfy the definitions of both "person" and "enterprise" under section 1961. The court in *Hartley* found that there was nothing in the statutory language to prevent the same corporation from being both the liable person and the enterprise. 678 F.2d at 988. By contrast, the Fourth Circuit in *Computer Sciences* concluded that " 'enterprise' was meant to refer to a being different from, not the same as or part of, the person whose behavior the act was designed to prohibit, and, failing that, to punish." 689 F.2d at 1190. Similarly, Judge Shadur concluded in Parnes v. Heinold Commodities, Inc., 548 F.Supp. 20, 23–24 (N.D.Ill.1982), that section 1962(c) contemplates a separate "person" and "enterprise" because the enterprise may very well be the victim of the racketeering activity.

We are persuaded by the Fourth Circuit in *Computer Sciences* and by Judge Shadur in *Parnes* that section 1962(c) requires separate entities as the liable person and the enterprise which has its affairs conducted through a pattern of racketeering activity. See also Addis v. Moser, No. 83 C 6118, slip op. at 9–11 (N.D.Ill. Feb. 15, 1984) (following *Parnes*). We do not doubt that a corporation may satisfy the section 1961 definitions of both "person" and "enterprise," as the court observed in *Hartley*. 678 F.2d at 988. But we focus our attention on the language in section 1962(c) requiring that the liable person be "employed by or associated with any enterprise" which affects interstate or foreign commerce. The use of the terms "employed by" and "associated with" appears to contemplate a person distinct from the enterprise. If Congress had meant to permit the same entity to be the liable person and the enterprise under section 1962(c), it would have required only a simple change in language to make that intention crystal clear. Also, we do not think the general principle of liberal interpretation of RICO can be used to stretch section 1962(c) to reach this situation in the face of the subsection's own limits. See Pub.L. 91–452, section 904, 84 Stat. 947. Cf. Blakey, The Rico Civil Fraud Action in Context, 58 Notre Dame Law 237, 324 n. 181 (1982) (approving of *Hartley* and disapproving of *Computer Sciences,* relying in part on liberal construction clause).

The court in *Hartley* supported its reading of section 1962(c) by also arguing that there is, for RICO purposes, no significant difference between a corporation and an "association in fact," see 18 U.S.C. § 1961(4). The court said there should be no practical difference between a complaint or indictment naming a corporation as the enterprise and one naming an association in fact as the enterprise, with the corporation as a member of the association. 678 F.2d at 989–90. We agree that a corporation and an association in fact can both satisfy the "enterprise" requirement of section 1962(c). See United States v. Turkette, supra, 452 U.S. at 583. However, a corporation and an association in fact differ substantially with respect to the "person" element. Where persons associate "in fact" for criminal purposes, *see id.,* each person may be held liable under RICO for his, her or its participation in conducting the affairs of the association in fact through a pattern of racketeering activity. But the nebulous association in fact does not itself fall within the RICO definition of "person." We doubt that an "association in fact" can, as such, hold any interest in property or even be brought into court. In the association in fact situation, each participant in the enterprise may be a "person" liable under RICO, but the association itself cannot be. By contrast, a corporation obviously qualifies as a "person" under RICO and may be subject to RICO liability. And it is not obvious that the problem can be resolved by merely alleging that the corporation and its employees constitute an association in fact. For these reasons, we are unpersuaded by the comparison to an association in fact.[18]

Discussion of this person/enterprise problem under RICO can easily slip into a metaphysical or ontological style of discourse—after all, when is the person truly an entity "distinct" or "separate" from the enterprise? We are therefore reluctant to base our conclusion on the statutory language without also examining the relevant policies and potential consequences of our conclusion.

At the policy level of the dispute, there are several significant competing arguments. The Eleventh Circuit argued in *Hartley* that where the defendant corporation is the central figure in a criminal scheme, as it was in that case, Congress could not have meant to let the central perpetrator escape RICO liability while subjecting only the sidekicks to RICO's severe penalties. 678 F.2d at 989. Similarly, plaintiffs here argue that Congress intended to make a "deep pocket" (in the person of the corporation) liable where corporate agents engage in a pattern of racketeering activity redounding to the benefit of the corporation. In *Parnes,* Judge Shadur argued that it would make little sense to hold a corporation liable under RICO for the misconduct of lower level employees, at least where it appears that the corporation is a passive instrument or even a victim of the racketeering activity. 548 F.Supp. at 23–24.

In our view, the RICO provisions have already taken into account these competing policies in different situations, and a careful parsing of section 1962 reveals a sensible balance among these policies. We find helpful here Professor Blakey's discussion in The Rico Civil Fraud Action in Context, supra, 58 Notre Dame Law. at 307–25. Blakey points out that under the subsections of section 1962, the enterprise may play the various roles of victim, prize, instrument or perpetrator. The RICO liability of the enterprise should depend on the role played. In our view, the plaintiffs here and the court in *Hartley* are correct when they argue that the corporate enterprise should be liable where it is the perpetrator, or the central figure in the criminal scheme. In that situation, the corporate deep pocket should certainly be subject to RICO liability. At the same time, the defendants here and Judge Shadur in *Parnes* are surely correct in saying that the corporation-enterprise should not be liable when the corporation is itself the victim or target, or merely the passive instrument for the wrongdoing of others.

In our view, the tensions between these policies may be resolved sensibly and in accord with the language of section 1962 by reading subsection (c) together with subsection (a). As we read subsection (c), the "enterprise" and the "person" must be distinct. However, a corporation-enterprise may be held liable under subsection (a) when the corporation is also a perpetrator. As we parse subsection (a), a "person" (such as a corporation-enterprise) acts unlawfully if it receives income derived directly

---

18. We agree with the statement in *Hartley* concerning a corporation's responsibility for the acts of its agents. 678 F.2d at 988 n. 43. However, as we discuss below, those concerns are better addressed in terms of subsection (a) of section 1962. The court in *Hartley* was apparently dealing only with subsection (c). There are significant differences between the two subsections, and we must analyze closely the terms of these carefully drafted provisions.

or indirectly from a pattern of racketeering activity in which the person has participated as a principal within the meaning of 18 U.S.C. § 2, and if the person uses the income in the establishment or *operation* of an enterprise affecting commerce. Subsection (a) does not contain any of the language in subsection (c) which suggests that the liable person and the enterprise must be separate. Under subsection (a), therefore, the liable person may be a corporation using the proceeds of a pattern of racketeering activity in its operations. This approach to subsection (a) thus makes the corporation-enterprise liable under RICO when the corporation is actually the direct or indirect beneficiary of the pattern of racketeering activity, but not when it is merely the victim, prize, or passive instrument of racketeering. This result is in accord with the primary purpose of RICO, which, after all, is to reach those who ultimately profit from racketeering, not those who are victimized by it.[20]

Applying this reading of subsection (c) to the complaint in this case, we conclude that ANB may not be held liable under section 1962(c) for conducting its own affairs through a pattern of racketeering activity. ANB might be held liable under section 1962(a) if it received the proceeds from the alleged racketeering activity and if it also could be held liable as a principal for those acts. However, plaintiffs here have abandoned any claim they might have stated under section 1962(a).[21]

Count I does not fail completely, however, for Count I also alleges that ANB violated section 1962(c) by conducting through a pattern of racketeering activity the affairs of its parent corporation, Heller International. That is a good allegation under section 1962(c). The subsection requires only some separate and distinct existence for the person and the enterprise, and a subsidiary corporation is certainly a legal entity distinct from its parent. Defendants do not challenge this point but argue only that the allegation does not adequately specify either the relationship between ANB and Heller International or the way in which ANB conducted or participated in Heller International's affairs. However, the complaint alleges that ANB is a wholly owned subsidiary of Heller International, and we think it virtually self-evident that a subsidiary acts on behalf of, and thus conducts the affairs of, its parent corporation. We doubt that more detailed allegations on the subject would serve any useful purpose, and we see no reason to require them.

Defendants Grayheck and Heller International: Defendants also contend that the RICO claims against Grayheck and Heller International do not contain sufficiently specific allegations to withstand a motion to dismiss. In Count II of the amended complaint, plaintiffs seek to hold Grayheck and Heller International liable as persons conducting ANB's affairs through a pattern of racketeering activity. *See* 18 U.S.C. § 1962(c).[23] Defendants

---

20. Blakey argues that where the enterprise is an "instrument," it should be civilly, but not criminally, liable to third parties under RICO. 58 Notre Dame Law. at 323–25. We see no statutory grounds for such a distinction between civil and criminal liability. Cf. Bernstein v. Idt Corp., 582 F.Supp. 1079, 1082–84 (D.Del.1984).

21. Paragraph 19 of the complaint appears in part to track the language of section 1962(a), alleging that ANB violated

section 1962 by using in the operation of ANB's business income from a pattern of racketeering activity. In this court the plaintiffs have argued only section 1962(c). Defendants suggested in their brief that plaintiffs had abandoned the section 1962(a) allegation, and plaintiffs have not responded to the suggestion. Plaintiffs have therefore abandoned the point.

23. The claim against Heller International is premised on the theory that Hel-

argue first that the complaint does not allege that Grayheck or Heller International acted with the requisite fraudulent intent. We reject this argument. The complaint is hardly a model of clarity on the intent issue, and it involves a lengthy trail of cross-references. However, at the end of the trail there are sufficient allegations of Grayheck's intent and Heller International's intent as embodied in its agents.

* * *

There can be little doubt that Fed.R.Civ.P. 9(b), which requires that allegations of fraud specify "with particularity" the circumstances of the alleged fraud, applies to fraud allegations in civil RICO complaints. See Moss v. Morgan Stanley, Inc., supra, 719 F.2d at 19. In this case, the complaint adequately specified the transactions, the content of the allegedly false representations, and the identities of those involved. In addition, the identification of the transactions and the description of the alleged scheme to defraud put defendants on fair notice of the time and place of the alleged false representations. See Thornton v. Evans, 692 F.2d 1064, 1082 & n. 41 (7th Cir.1982); Tomera v. Galt, 511 F.2d 504, 508 (7th Cir.1975). See also McGinty v. Beranger Volkswagen, Inc., 633 F.2d 226, 228–29 (1st Cir.1980); Miscellaneous Service Workers v. Philco-Ford Corp., 661 F.2d 776, 782 (9th Cir.1981); Felton v. Walston & Co., 508 F.2d 577, 581–82 (2d Cir.1974). There would have been little point in requiring plaintiffs to expand the complaint by also identifying each notice which included an interest rate. The complaint here therefore satisfies Rule 9(b).

For the foregoing reasons, we affirm the district court's dismissal of the portion of Count I alleging that ANB conducted its own affairs through a pattern of racketeering activity. We reverse the remainder of the district court's dismissal of the complaint and remand for further proceedings not inconsistent with this opinion.

SCHOFIELD v. FIRST COMMODITY CORPORATION OF BOSTON

United States Court of Appeals, First Circuit, 1986.
793 F.2d 28.

Before CAMPBELL, CHIEF JUDGE, and COFFIN and BOWNES, CIRCUIT JUDGES.

COFFIN, CIRCUIT JUDGE. Appellant Rebecca Schofield claims that First Commodity Corporation of Boston (FCCB) fraudulently induced her and her husband to invest all of their liquid assets in trading commodity futures. Her complaint alleged violations of three federal statutes, but the district court held that she failed to state viable claims under two of them, including the Racketeer Influenced and Corrupt Organizations Act (RICO), 18 U.S.C. § 1964(c). The case proceeded to trial on claims under section

---

ler International acted through Grayheck, who is an officer and director of ANB, and perhaps through other unidentified persons. Heller International is alleged to have thereby conducted or participated in the conduct of ANB's affairs through the alleged pattern of racketeering activity. The terms "conduct" and "participate" in section 1962(c) are quite broad, but it is not obvious to us that they extend to a parent corporation's involvement in racketeering activity solely through the actions of an agent of a subsidiary corporation. However, since the defendants have not raised the point and the district court did not pass on it, we shall not consider it in this appeal as a possible basis for affirming a portion of the dismissal.

4b(A) of the Commodity Exchange Act (CEA), 7 U.S.C. § 6b(A)(1982), and a jury awarded appellant $30,000 in damages.

Appellant challenges dismissal of the RICO count, claiming that the district court erred in finding that a RICO "enterprise" may not be held liable for civil damages under section 1962(c) either directly or under principles of *respondeat superior*. In a cross-appeal, FCCB challenges jury instructions on the CEA claims, including the court's refusal to instruct on the theory of ratification. We affirm the district court on all issues.

I.

Section 1962(c) of RICO states:

"It shall be unlawful for any person employed by or associated with any enterprise engaged in, or the activities of which affect, interstate or foreign commerce, to conduct or participate, directly or indirectly, in the conduct of such enterprise's affairs through a pattern of racketeering activity or collection of unlawful debt."

Most courts, including the district court here, have construed the language of this subsection to require that the "person" who engages in the pattern of racketeering activity be an entity distinct from the "enterprise". See United States v. Benny, 786 F.2d 1410, 1415–16 (9th Cir.1986); Bennett v. United States Trust Co. of New York, 770 F.2d 308, 315 (2d Cir.1985), cert. denied, 106 S.Ct. 800 (1986); B.F. Hirsch v. Enright Refining Co., 751 F.2d 628, 633–34 (3d Cir.1984); Haroco v. American National Bank and Trust Co. of Chicago, 747 F.2d 384, 401–402 (7th Cir.1984), aff'd on other grounds, 105 S.Ct. 3291 (1985); Rae v. Union Bank, 725 F.2d 478, 480–81 (9th Cir.1984); Bennett v. Berg, 685 F.2d 1053, 1061–62 (8th Cir.1982), modified, 710 F.2d 1361 (en banc), cert. denied, 464 U.S. 1008 (1983); United States v. Computer Sciences Corp., 689 F.2d 1181, 1190 (4th Cir. 1982), cert. denied, 459 U.S. 1105 (1983); Yancoski v. E.F. Hutton Co., 581 F.Supp. 88, 97 (E.D.Penn.1983); Van Schaick v. Church of Scientology, 535 F.Supp. 1125, 1135–1136 (D.Mass.1982); Parnes v. Heinold Commodities, Inc., 548 F.Supp. 20, 23–24 (N.D.Ill.1982). Although a corporation may be a "person" under the statute, 18 U.S.C. § 1961(3), (4), these courts hold that the statute envisions liability only when there is the specified interaction between two entities; thus, the same corporation may not serve in two roles at the same time. Only one circuit has rejected the separate person/ enterprise distinction. United States v. Hartley, 678 F.2d 961, 988 (11th Cir.1982), cert. denied, 459 U.S. 1170, 1183 (1983). See also, e.g., Gerace v. Utica Veal Co., 580 F.Supp. 1465, 1469 n. 4 (N.D.N.Y.1984); B.F. Hirsch v. Enright Refining Co., 577 F.Supp. 339, 347 (D.N.J.1983), rev'd (on this issue), 751 F.2d 628, 633–34 (3d Cir.1984).

Appellant does not attack head-on the precedent holding that section 1962(c) requires that the person and the enterprise be two separate entities. Instead, she argues that a corporation may be held liable either directly as the section 1962(c) enterprise, or vicariously under principles of *respondeat superior*. We shall address first the theory of direct liability.

Appellant's argument regarding direct liability is as follows. The section 1962(c) "persons" are the FCCB account representatives with whom appellant directly transacted business, and the "enterprise" is FCCB. Thus, the requirement of two separate entities is met. Under the usual construction of section 1962(c), the brokers would be held liable if they conducted FCCB's affairs through a pattern of racketeering. Appellant argues that FCCB, the enterprise, also should be liable if the brokers' actions represented FCCB policy. In other words, in a case in which the enterprise is not a victim, but is an active participant in the racketeering, it also should be subject to liability. Appellant points out that the language in section 1962(c)—"It shall be unlawful"—is impersonal in form, and she suggests that this sentence structure means that the wrongdoing may be committed by the enterprise as well as by the person conducting the enterprise. In addition, she emphasizes Congressional intent that RICO be liberally construed, and the common sense notion that a culpable corporation should not be able to evade liability when its policies are at the heart of the wrongdoing.

Notwithstanding the appeal of appellant's argument as a matter of policy, we must reject it as a matter of law. Appellant is correct that Congress envisioned a broad reading of RICO, Sedima, S.P.R.L. v. Imrex Co., 105 S.Ct. 3275, 3286 (1985). Yet the Supreme Court in interpreting RICO also has made it clear that the words of the statute must be the starting point for any statutory construction. United States v. Turkette, 452 U.S. 576, 580 (1981). It is only by straining the language that we could read section 1962(c) as imposing liability on even a culpable enterprise as well as on the person. Stripped to its essentials, section 1962(c) states that it is unlawful for any person associated with an enterprise to conduct that enterprise through racketeering. The enterprise is mentioned in the section only as the instrument of the person doing the racketeering, and there is no suggestion that the enterprise also may be liable, even if it is a wholly illegitimate operation.

"[The express language of section 1962(c)] quite clearly envisions a relationship between a 'person' and an 'enterprise' as an element of the offense which 1962(c) proscribes and for which 1964(c) would subject the 'person' to treble damages. * * *

"* * * It is only a person, or one associated with an enterprise, not the enterprise itself, who can violate the provisions of the section." Van Schaick v. Church of Scientology of California, 535 F.Supp. 1125, 1136 (D.Mass.1982).

The legislative history surrounding RICO adds to our conviction that section 1962(c) does not extend liability to the enterprise. "[T]he legislative history forcefully supports the view that the major purpose of Title IX [including section 1962(c)] is to address the infiltration of legitimate business by organized crime." United States v. Turkette, 452 U.S. at 591. If the primary purpose of RICO is "to cope with the infiltration of legitimate businesses", id., it is logical that Congress would have designed section 1962(c) so that it reached the criminal but protected the victimized enterprise from liability.

Moreover, an interpretation that insulates the enterprise from liability under section 1962(c) is not, as appellant asserts, inconsistent with the remedial purposes of RICO. Cf. United States v. Turkette, 452 U.S. at 589–90. On this point, we agree with the analysis of the Seventh Circuit in Haroco v. American National Bank and Trust Co. of Chicago, 747 F.2d at 401–402, which found that a culpable enterprise may be held liable under another section of RICO, § 1962(a). That section states, in relevant part:

"It shall be unlawful for any person who has received any income derived, directly or indirectly, from a pattern of racketeering activity or through collection of an unlawful debt in which such person has participated as a principal * * * to use or invest, directly or indirectly, any part of such income, or the proceeds of such income, in acquisition of any interest in, or the establishment or operation of, any enterprise which is engaged in, or the activities of which affect, interstate or foreign commerce."

The language in section 1962(a) does not require a relationship between the person and the enterprise as does section 1962(c), and so it does not require the involvement of two separate entities. Applied to the facts of this case, section 1962(a) would prohibit FCCB, the person, from using ill-gotten gains in FCCB, the enterprise. In contrast, section 1962(c) requires that the culpable person be "employed by or associated with" an enterprise; we think it stretches the language too far to suggest that a corporation can be employed by or associated with itself. This approach to the two subsections

"thus makes the corporation-enterprise liable under RICO when the corporation is actually the direct or indirect beneficiary of the pattern of racketeering activity, but not when it is merely the victim, prize, or passive instrument of racketeering. This result is in accord with the primary purpose of RICO, which, after all, is to reach those who ultimately profit from racketeering, not those who are victimized by it." *Haroco,* 747 F.2d at 402.

* * *

See also Masi v. Ford City Bank and Trust Co., 779 F.2d 397, 401–402 (7th Cir.1985); Bennett v. United States Trust Co. of New York, 770 F.2d at 315 (2d Cir.1985); B.F. Hirsch v. Enright Refining Co., 751 F.2d 628, 633–34 (3d Cir.1984); The Bruss Co. v. Allnet Communication Services, 606 F.Supp. 401, 407 (N.D.Ill.1985).[2]

We think it worth noting that at least one court has taken issue with this manner of resolving the policy concerns behind RICO. In Rush v. Oppenheimer & Co., 628 F.Supp. 1188, 1197 (S.D.N.Y.1985), the court concluded that, in light of the identical terminology in each subsection and the consistent legislative intent to convict only the violator of the predicate acts, and not the infiltrated enterprise, "if it is inappropriate to plead identity in 1962(c), it is then inappropriate to plead it under section 1962(a)". Thus, the court refused to allow a dual corporate role under either subsection. See also Note, Judicial Efforts to Redirect an Errant Statute: Civil RICO and the Misapplication of Vicarious Corporate Liability, 65 Boston U.L.Rev. 561, 595 (1985) (hereinafter "Errant Statute") (questioning the distinction between the two subsections).

2. We recognize that funneling corporate liability into subsection (a) may affect plaintiffs in ways other than simply in the drafting of the complaint under one subsection rather than another. See Note, Judicial Efforts to Redirect an Errant Statute: Civil RICO and the Misapplication of Vicarious Corporate Liability, 65 Boston U.L. Rev. 561, 596–598 (1985). For example, subsection (a) requires a showing of the source of income and proof that funds were channeled into the corporation. It also covers only wrongdoing involving money. But if neither section 1962(a) nor section 1962(c) cover all methods of corporate wrongdoing, it is up to Congress, and not the courts, to expand the scope of the statute. We rely on section 1962(a) only to show that our reading of section 1962(c) does not insulate corporations from *all* liability.

We disagree with this approach to statutory construction, and to construction of RICO, in particular. In a sense, the *Rush* court has interpreted both subsections of section 1962 together; because the language of one is not susceptible to a reading that the enterprise can serve in two roles, it concludes that the other subsection is similarly limited. But we read United States v. Turkette, 452 U.S. 576 (1981), to say that where the language in RICO permits liability against a culpable entity, courts should find that such liability exists. In *Turkette,* the Court rejected the argument that the word "enterprise" as used in RICO referred only to legitimate businesses, observing that the contrary construction would put much organized criminal activity beyond the substantive reach of the statute. Id. at 589. The Court settled on the broader meaning of enterprise despite the unambiguous legislative history showing that Congress' primary concern was the infiltration of *legitimate* enterprises.

Because a narrow reading of section 1962(a) also would insulate much criminal activity, and because the language permits a broader reading, that section must be read to allow corporations to serve both as the RICO person and the RICO enterprise. Section 1962(c), in contrast, does not give us the same flexibility. Its language, requiring a relationship of employment or association between the person and the enterprise and pinpointing liability on the person, simply does not permit us to find liability against the enterprise. Accordingly, we reject appellant's argument that FCCB may be held directly liable under section 1962(c).

We thus turn to appellant's alternative argument that principles of *respondeat superior* operate so as to make FCCB liable under RICO for the fraudulent actions of its brokers. Like the issue of the enterprise/person distinction, the applicability of *respondeat superior* to section 1962(c) has generated conflicting responses from the courts, although again the majority rejects vicarious corporate liability. See, e.g., *Haroco,* 747 F.2d at 401 n. 18 (suggesting vicarious liability may be appropriate under section 1962(a) but not under section 1962(c)); Rush v. Oppenheimer, 628 F.Supp. at 1194–95; *Parnes,* 548 F.Supp. at 24 and n. 9; Dakis v. Chapman, 574 F.Supp. 757, 759–60 (N.D.Cal.1983).[3] The most frequently cited case in support of appellant's proposition is Bernstein v. IDT Corp., 582 F.Supp. 1079, 1083 (D.Del.1984), where the court observed that "the normal rules of agency law apply in the absence of some indication that Congress had a contrary intent". See also Morley v. Cohen, 610 F.Supp. 798, 811 (D.Md.1985).

We agree with the *Bernstein* court's proposition of law, but disagree as to where it leads in this case. The premise of *respondeat superior* is that one who is without fault may be held vicariously liable for the wrongdoing of another. W. Prosser, Law of Torts 458 (4th ed. 1971). As our previous discussion of direct liability reveals, we think the concept of vicarious liability is directly at odds with the Congressional intent behind section 1962(c). Both the language of that subsection and the articulated primary motivation behind RICO show that Congress intended to separate the

---

3. We acknowledge that in some of these cases, the courts have rejected *respondeat superior* only because the corporation was not sufficiently involved in the wrongdoing, suggesting that liability would attach if the corporation actively participated in the prohibited activity. See, e.g., *Parnes,* 548 F.Supp. at 24 and n. 9; *Dakis,* 574 F.Supp. at 759–60. We think even a conditional approach to *respondeat superior* is inconsistent with our prior conclusion on direct liability, and so we choose not to adopt it.

enterprise from the criminal "person" or "persons". Indeed, there is unlikely to be a situation, in the absence of an express statement, in which Congress more clearly indicates that *respondeat superior* is contrary to its intent. But see G. Blakey, The Civil RICO Fraud Action in Context: Reflections on Bennett v. Berg, 58 Notre Dame L.Rev. 237, 308–325 (1982).

* * * *

Appellant apparently concedes that a wholesale adoption of the *respondeat superior* concept would conflict with the primary thrust of section 1962(c). In order to conform to Congress' obvious desire to insulate legitimate businesses from liability, she suggests that we could adopt a modified version of vicarious liability, perhaps requiring some level of *scienter* before imposing liability. For example, *respondeat superior* could be limited to acts of high corporate officials, whose actions may be deemed corporate policy, and thus would reflect corporate intent.

The flaw in this approach is that it is no more than a recasting of the argument for direct liability. In either form, appellant's argument is that corporations at least should be liable when they participate in causing the wrongdoing that RICO punishes. We concede the appeal of this argument, and wholeheartedly agree that corporations should not escape liability when their policies foster the racketeering activity that is at the heart of RICO's prohibitions. But as we now have stated more than once in this opinion, the language of section 1962(c) poses a formidable barrier to holding the enterprise liable under that subsection. We think it inappropriate to use *respondeat superior* to accomplish indirectly what we have concluded the statute directly denies. We therefore hold that the district court correctly dismissed appellant's claim against FCCB under section 1962(c).[4]

* * * *

For the foregoing reasons, the judgment of the district court is affirmed. Each party shall bear its own costs.

THE ELEMENTS OF A RICO CAUSE OF ACTION

The civil liability provisions of the Racketeer Influenced and Corrupt Organizations Act,[1] as all of the above cases emphasize and as all of the justices on the Supreme Court acknowledged, threaten to revolutionize all securities litigation, completely contrary to any discoverable intent of Congress to bring about that result. One of the major problems in connection with the interpretation of the provisions of the RICO statute is the inept draftsmanship of the entire statute. The Seventh Circuit in the *Haroco* case commented that the statute was constructed "on the model of a treasure hunt" and that its provisions lead to "a metaphysical or ontological style of discourse." (In the light of these

---

4. One commentator agrees that vicarious liability principles are inappropriate in the context of RICO, and argues that courts interpreting RICO instead should adopt agency law principles as they traditionally are used to determine direct corporate liability in the tort context. See "Errant Statute", 65 Boston U.L.Rev. 561, 598–605. This commentator asserts that this approach would "simply follow[ ] the statute's verbs. The person held liable un-

der RICO must have invested, participated, acquired or conspired." Id. at 604. What is unclear in this analysis is how the commentator overrides the language in section 1962(c) that forecloses liability against a corporation when it serves only in the role of enterprise, or when it serves in both roles at the same time.

1. 18 U.S.C. §§ 1961–1968; Pub.L. 91–452, 84 Stat. 941 (1970).

comments, the same court surely must have intended to be sarcastic when it referred in Footnote 18 to "these carefully drafted provisions.")

Because of its revolutionary nature, the lower courts before the *Sedima* case were concerned almost exclusively with debating various "gimmicks" invented to confine the scope of the statute, unsupported by anything in the statutory language. The Supreme Court in the *Sedima* case knocked out two of these gimmicks and it seems probable that it will knock out any others which are invented, although one of the five justice majority in *Sedima* has already left the court and one or more others may do so before the next RICO case is considered.

In order to understand the elements of a RICO cause of action, it is necessary to refer to three different sections of that statute. Reference will be made here only to those portions of those three sections which are typically involved in RICO claims arising in ordinary commercial and securities litigation, which have been the cause for the concern of the Bar and the courts with respect to the unwarranted extension of RICO.

A. Section 1964(c) provides that any "person injured in his business or property by reason of a violation of Section 1962" may bring an action in the federal court and "shall recover threefold the damages he sustains" plus his attorney's fees.

B. Section 1962(c) provides that it is "unlawful" for any "person employed by or associated with any enterprise" in or affecting interstate commerce "to conduct or participate, directly or indirectly, in the conduct of such enterprise's affairs through a pattern of racketeering activity. ＊ ＊ ＊"

C. The term "racketeering activity" is defined in Section 1961(1) as meaning the violation of any one of a host of criminal statutes detailed in that section, but the three almost invariably involved in a civil RICO action are:

1. "any act which is indictable" under 18 U.S.C. "section 1341 (relating to mail fraud), [or] section 1343 (relating to wire fraud). ＊ ＊ ＊" and

2. "Any offense involving ＊ ＊ ＊ fraud in the sale of securities ＊ ＊ ＊ punishable under any law of the United States."

Therefore, in order for a plaintiff to recover in a civil RICO action, it is only necessary for him to prove that the defendant (i) violated the mail fraud or the wire fraud statute (these are lumped together because they are virtually identical, except for the means of communication used which invokes their application), or engaged in "fraud in the sale of securities", (ii) that these violations (at least two—see the discussion of "pattern" below) formed a "pattern" of activity, (iii) that the defendant "through" such a pattern of activity conducted or participated in the conduct of an "enterprise's affairs", and (iv) that the plaintiff suffered damages "in his business or property by reason of" the defendant's conduct specified above.

Each of these elements of a RICO cause of action will be examined in greater detail below.

Much of the discussion dealing with RICO, both in the court opinions and the articles in law journals, as the Seventh Circuit observed, tends to become somewhat metaphysical. In order to attempt to bring the discussion down to earth, we will consider two hypothetical cases against which the following discussion relating to the elements of a cause of action under RICO will be tested.

A. *Hypothetical Case No. 1:* Joe Hotshot Salesman is a registered representative working for the nationwide brokerage house of Payne, Hutton & Barney, which is engaged in all aspects of the broker-dealer business. It employs 1500 persons. Joe Hotshot has 150 customers whose accounts he handles, including 50 over which he has discretionary authority to buy and sell securities. Over a period of a year and a half, Joe Hotshot engages in the "churning" of the accounts of three of these customers from whom he holds discretionary authority. Assume that all of the classic elements of a "churning" case, actionable under Rule 10b–5 (see Chapter 11, above), are present with respect to each of these three accounts. One of these customers sues Joe Hotshot Salesman and Payne, Hutton & Barney for treble damages (and attorney's fees) under RICO.

B. *Hypothetical Case No. 2:* Joe Hotshot Salesman is transferred to the investment banking division of Payne, Hutton & Barney and in the course of his duties working for that division he obtains information regarding proposed takeover bids by clients of the firm. Joe Hotshot incorporates a new corporation of which he is the sole owner and has that corporation open a brokerage account with another brokerage firm. Through that corporation he purchases stock of the "target companies" which are to be the subject of a takeover bid on two separate occasions over a period of one year, prior to the public announcement of the tender offer. After that public announcement, he either tenders the securities purchased to the offeror at the tender offer price or sells the securities to arbitrageurs in the market after the announcement of the tender offer and the consequent increase in the market price. He does this in only two instances out of the ten cases in which he obtained such advance knowledge of a proposed tender offer. A person who sold stock of one of the target companies during the time Joe Hotshot was buying brings a class action under RICO on behalf of all such sellers against Joe Hotshot Salesman and Payne, Hutton & Barney to recover treble damages for the amount which the sellers "lost" as a result of not retaining the stock until after the public announcement of the tender offer.

JURISDICTION; VENUE

The RICO statute confers jurisdiction on the federal district courts to entertain civil actions created by that statute, but it does not say whether this jurisdiction is concurrent with that of the state courts or is exclusive. As we have seen above in Chapter 20, page 1337, the 1933 act expressly provides that the jurisdiction of civil actions under that statute is concurrent in the federal and state courts and the 1934 act expressly provides that the jurisdiction of actions under that statute is exclusively in the federal courts. Despite these examples of legislative clarity before them, the draftsmen of the RICO statute ignored the lesson and "no one even thought of the issue." [2]

There is little decisional law on this question as yet, but the California Supreme Court on December 31, 1985, rendered a decision in Cianci v. Superior Court [3] that the state courts have concurrent jurisdiction over civil actions under RICO. In a careful opinion by Justice Mosk, the court noted that the United States Supreme Court cases have established a presumption that the state courts have concurrent jurisdiction over federally created causes of action unless it can be shown from the language of the statute or the legislative history that Congress intended otherwise or there is some "incompatibility" between the provisions or purposes of the federal statute and the granting of

2. Flaherty, Two States Lay Claim To RICO, Natl. L.J. 10 (May 7, 1984), quoting Professor G. Robert Blakey, the self-proclaimed principal draftsman of RICO.

3. 40 Cal.3d 903, 221 Cal.Rptr. 575 (1985).

concurrent jurisdiction to the state courts. The court was unable to find any of these bases for excluding jurisdiction of the state courts over civil RICO claims.

The court said: "In sum, concurrent jurisdiction is consistent with the language of the statute, its legislative history, and its structure and substance, and is therefore supported by Congress's express mandate that RICO 'be liberally construed to effectuate its remedial purposes' (Pub.L. No. 91–452, § 904(a), 84 Stat. 947). Congress, as Professor Blakey has conceded, evidently did not consider the question of jurisdiction, less still resolve it. Whether, as he has argued, Congress would or should have limited jurisdiction to the federal courts is immaterial to the question before us: Congress simply did not so limit jurisdiction, and we are powerless to do what Congress has failed to do. Accordingly, we hold that real parties have not carried their burden of rebutting the presumption of concurrent jurisdiction, and hence that state courts may entertain RICO claims." [4]

Section 1965 of the RICO statute provides that venue of any civil action may be laid in "any district in which * * * [the defendant] resides, is found, has an agent, or transacts his affairs," and that any other parties may be summoned to appear in the same case if "the ends of justice require that other parties residing in any district be brought before the court." Process may be served upon such other parties in any judicial district. In general, process may be served in any judicial district where venue can be established, but not necessarily the same judicial district as one actually selected for the venue of the action.

RACKETEERING INJURY; PRIOR CONVICTION; BURDEN OF PROOF

In the *Sedima* case, the Supreme Court eliminated two efforts which had been made by the lower courts to contain the unbridled scope of RICO as it has developed, and substantially disposed of a third, although making no specific ruling on that issue. The Supreme Court held:

1. In order to maintain a RICO action, there is no need for a prior criminal conviction of the defendant for violation of the "predicate offenses" (those crimes specified in Section 1961(1)), but simply proof in the civil action that the defendant committed them. In the absence of any Congressional action, this holding definitively lays to rest this attempt to limit RICO.

2. There is no requirement in a RICO action that the plaintiff establish any injury other than the injury suffered by him as a direct result of the crimes committed by the defendant which form the so-called "predicate acts" under § 1961(1). The Court said that there is no "requirement that in order to maintain a private action under § 1964(c) the plaintiff must establish a 'racketeering injury,' not merely an injury resulting from the predicate acts themselves." That requirement had been the holding of the lower court in the *Sedima* case and also of some other federal courts, although none of them had been able to offer any intelligible definition of what was meant by "racketeering injury." The majority of the Supreme Court also rejected the position of the minority justices that there had to be shown a "competitive injury" or an "infiltration" or "investment" injury in order for a RICO action to be maintained. The minority justices were willing to accept the fact that such a holding would leave the direct victims of mobster activity without civil redress

---

4. 40 Cal.3d at 916, 221 Cal.Rptr. at 581–582.

under RICO (although there are of course other pre-existing civil remedies available) and generally permit a civil cause of action under that statute only by the indirect victims. The majority of the Supreme Court, however, were unwilling to accept this result, despite the support which the minority found in the "legislative history" for that conclusion.

3. In addition, while making no specific ruling, the majority opinion in the *Sedima* case clearly indicated that the court would not impose any requirement that the plaintiff prove his case "beyond a reasonable doubt" in a civil RICO action on the basis that civil liability under RICO is predicated on criminal conduct. The court said: "We are not at all convinced that the predicate acts must be established beyond a reasonable doubt in a proceeding under § 1964(c). In a number of settings, conduct that can be punished as criminal only upon proof beyond a reasonable doubt will support civil sanctions under a preponderance standard * * * There is no indication that Congress sought to depart from this general principle here * * * That offending conduct is described by reference to criminal statutes does not mean that its occurrence must be established by criminal standards or that the consequences of a finding of liability in a private civil action are identical to the consequences of a criminal conviction."

While the result in the *Sedima* case might have been predictable in the light of the statutory language, the lineup of the justices on the Supreme Court was quite surprising. The three justices considered the most "pro-business" (Burger, Rehnquist and O'Connor) were in the majority which dealt this blow to legitimate enterprises and the three justices who are generally considered to be most "anti-business" (Marshall, Brennan and Blackmun) were among the four dissenters who wanted to limit the scope of RICO. White and Stevens, who have the reputation of being "swing votes", lined up in this case with the majority and Justice Powell, whose vote was perhaps the only one predictable, joined the dissenters.

The explanation for this strange division has to be that the predilection of the majority justices for the "strict construction" of statutes overcame any other bias which they might have had and the "liberal constructionists" in the minority were willing in effect to embellish upon the statute in order to curb the unjustified extension of liability under RICO, which was too much for them to countenance. The loud and clear message which this lineup sends to Congress is that the Supreme Court is not going to extricate it from the mess which it has created by the language used in the RICO statute, and that it will take Congressional action for any effective limitation to be imposed upon the scope of RICO.

The one thing which the majority and the minority agreed upon in the opinions in the *Sedima* case was that civil RICO, as it has developed, was never contemplated or intended by Congress when it enacted the statute.

THE "PREDICATE OFFENSES"

As indicated above, the likely "predicate offenses" which would be alleged to have been committed in our two hypothetical cases are (a) mail fraud or wire fraud or both, depending on the method or methods of communication used, and (b) "fraud in the sale of securities."

A. *Fraud in the Sale of Securities.* There are two very significant differences between the language employed here in RICO and the language in Section 10(b) of the Securities Exchange Act of 1934. That section prohibits certain acts "*in connection with the purchase or* sale of" securities. The language of RICO is much more restrictive—it requires that the "fraud" be *in* the sale of securities, not merely "in connection with," and it says nothing about purchase. Therefore, the so-called "touch test" established by the Supreme Court in Superintendent of Insurance v. Bankers Life and Casualty Co., supra, page 1056, i.e., that the misrepresentation or omission need only be "touching" the securities transaction in order for the "in connection with" requirement to be established, is obviously not applicable under RICO. Furthermore, the situation existing under the securities laws prior to the adoption of Rule 10b–5, that there was no remedy for a fraudulent *purchase* of securities, since Section 17(a) of the Securities Act of 1933 only refers to a "sale of securities", would seem to exist under RICO so far as *this* predicate offense is concerned.

With respect to our Hypothetical Case No. 1, it appears likely that the predicate offense of "fraud in the sale of securities" was present in that case since the churning of the brokerage account involved both purchases and sales; and the sales were made (along with the purchases) for the purpose of inflating the commissions to be earned and not for any legitimate objective of the customer. The meaning of the word "fraud" in the RICO statute has not been addressed by the courts, however, and it is conceivable, although unlikely, that it could be interpreted to require some affirmative misrepresentation in a specific sale, which probably would not occur in the context of a "churning" operation. This interpretation would find some support in the legislative history, since apparently all that Congress considered regarding the intent of this phrase was that it would catch gangsters who sold securities that had been stolen or counterfeited.[5]

With respect to our Hypothetical Case No. 2, it seems clear that the predicate offense of "fraud in the sale of securities" is not present in that case, since the only "fraud", if any, occurred *in the purchase* of the securities, not in their resale. The tender offeror could hardly claim that he was defrauded because someone tendered securities to him at the price which he offered to pay. The offense committed by the defendant, if any, certainly existed before there was any resale of the securities.

The *Moss* case, which deals with an almost identical situation to that set forth in our Hypothetical Case No. 2, illustrates the confusion which descends upon many courts when they start discussing RICO. The court there never mentioned the fact that the RICO statute does not cover any purchase of securities, but kept referring to a "fraudulent securities transaction", as though that were the statutory language. Many other courts have done the same thing in casually referring to this predicate offense. The Second Circuit nevertheless dismissed the RICO claim of the plaintiff, because, they said, his civil cause of action asserted under Rule 10b–5 had to be dismissed under the Supreme Court holding in the *Chiarella* case, supra, page 1027; therefore, there was no allegation of any predicate offense left to form the basis for his RICO claim. The very same court, however, had previously affirmed a *criminal* conviction of the *same defendant* for a violation of Rule 10b–5 on the basis of the very *same facts* alleged in this civil complaint.[6] The court in that prior case had distinguished a criminal action from a civil action and had held that

---

5. American Bar Association, Report of the Ad Hoc Civil RICO Task Force 100–103 (March 28, 1985). This monumental report of over 400 pages collects all of the cases up to March 1985. It will be cited in this Chapter (as "ABA Report") rather than attempting to reproduce all of the citations readily accessible in that report.

6. United States v. Newman, 664 F.2d 12 (2d Cir.1981).

the requirement of *Chiarella* that the defendant owe a fiduciary duty to the plaintiff-sellers did not apply in a criminal context. The court in the *Moss* case does not question the correctness of that prior ruling. Therefore, what it is holding is that there must be a prior existing *civil action* in order for RICO to be applicable, which is of course directly contrary to the language of the statute, which requires only criminal conduct, and that holding cannot be correct. There never has been any private right of action under the mail fraud and wire fraud statutes; such a requirement would read them out of RICO.

The court in the *Moss* case in a footnote says that the plaintiff failed to allege the prior criminal conviction of the defendant and therefore they do not need to consider whether that conviction would collaterally estop the defendant from relitigating the facts adjudicated in that case. But certainly the plaintiff alleged the facts upon which the criminal conviction was based in his cause of action under Rule 10b–5; and he surely incorporated those allegations by reference in his cause of action under RICO. Therefore, dismissing the Rule 10b–5 claim could not simply wipe out the RICO claim if the facts alleged were sufficient to establish a criminal act, whether the plaintiff had to prove those facts or could invoke collateral estoppel based on the prior criminal conviction. On this Motion to Dismiss, which was granted, no question of collateral estoppel was presented to the court.

B. *Mail Fraud and Wire Fraud.* The mail fraud and wire fraud statutes [7] make liable to criminal punishment any person "devising or intending to devise any scheme or artifice to defraud, or for obtaining money or property by means of false or fraudulent pretenses, representations or promises" if he uses the mails or wire, radio or television communication in interstate commerce "for the purpose of executing such scheme or artifice."

The first portion of these wire fraud and mail fraud statutes is, of course, virtually identical to clause (1) of both Section 17(a) of the 1933 Act and Rule 10b–5 ("to employ any device, scheme, or artifice to defraud"). However, the emerging majority view seems to be that there is no civil liability under Section 17(a) [8] (prior to RICO—now, of course, there is treble damage liability, if the other requirements of RICO are met). And the Supreme Court in the *Hochfelder* case, supra, page 936, held that the language of Rule 10b–5 had to be interpreted in the light of the language of Section 10(b) itself ("any manipulative or deceptive device or contrivance", which the Supreme Court indicated were "terms of art" referring primarily to market manipulation), and that to the extent Rule 10b–5 goes beyond that language, it is invalid. This basis is of course not available for limiting the mail fraud and wire fraud statutes or Section 17(a) of the 1933 Act, since that language is a part of the statutes themselves; and violations of those criminal statutes can be "predicate acts" with respect to a civil claim under RICO. This language, "device, scheme or artifice to defraud," was the primary basis for the virtually unlimited expansion of Rule 10b–5 before *Hochfelder* reversed that trend.

It is instructive to compare the scope of the mail fraud and wire fraud statutes with that of Rule 10b–5 as it presently is interpreted:

1. Is it necessary for a "security" to be involved under those statutes? The answer to this question is clearly "no", since those statutes deal with any "scheme to defraud" in connection with anything, and are not limited to securities transactions. Therefore, all of the cases holding that Rule 10b–5 is inapplicable because there is no "security" within the meaning of the 1934 Act (see Chapter 4, supra) are irrelevant under those statutes.

7. 18 U.S.C. §§ 1341 and 1343.   8. See supra, pp. 890 to 892.

2. Does a false or misleading statement have to be transmitted by the mails or the wires in order for those statutes to be applicable? The answer to this question is also clearly "no" under the decisions.[9] The same is true, of course, under Rule 10b–5.[10] In fact, the mail fraud and wire fraud statutes provide that the mere "receipt" of mail in connection with the "scheme" is sufficient to invoke those statutes, and the cases hold that the defendant does not have to cause the mailing or wire transmission if it is "reasonably foreseeable" by him. An intrastate telephone call may not be sufficient to invoke the wire fraud statute (which requires that something be transmitted "*in* interstate commerce"), although it is sufficient as a jurisdictional basis under Rule 10b–5.[11]

3. Do any false or misleading statements have to be made at all by the defendant, if what he did can be labeled a "scheme to defraud." The answer to this question also seems to be "no", since the statute speaks in the alternative of schemes to defraud and false or fraudulent statements. However, the question remains of when "non-disclosure" will be labeled a "scheme to defraud". In United States v. Dowling,[12] the Ninth Circuit held that "non-disclosure can only serve as a basis for a fraudulent scheme when there exists an independent duty that has been breached by the person so charged. This independent duty may exist in the form of a fiduciary duty to third parties, * * * or may derive from an independent explicit statutory duty created by legislative enactment." [13]

United States v. Newman [14] upheld the indictment (and the court later affirmed the conviction) of the defendant for violation of the mail fraud statute (and therefore RICO) in connection with a scheme essentially like that involved in our Hypothetical Case No. 2. The court based this holding both upon the fact that the defendant "misappropriated" confidential information of his employer and breached fiduciary duties to his employer by his "material misrepresentations * * * and non-disclosure" to his employer.[15]

In the *Chiarella* case, the Supreme Court held that there was no violation of Rule 10b–5 in a situation like that because the defendant owed no "fiduciary duty" to the plaintiff class of sellers of stock of the target company, although it reserved the question of whether a violation might be found under the "misappropriation theory" of Chief Justice Burger (because the jury had not been charged on that theory). Many attorneys and scholars believe that the Supreme Court will not ultimately accept this theory under Rule 10b–5, but it would seem to be alive and well under RICO with mail fraud and wire fraud as the predicate offenses. There are many cases holding that breach of a "fiduciary duty" to one's employer is a sufficient basis for a mail fraud or wire fraud conviction.[16]

4. Does the plaintiff have to be a purchaser or seller of securities under the mail fraud and wire fraud statutes, as under Rule 10b–5? The answer to this question is also clearly "no", since no security at all has to be involved in the transaction or transactions which comprise the "scheme." Therefore, the *Blue Chip Stamp* case (supra, page 1096), is clearly inapplicable to a civil RICO

---

9. Pereira v. United States, 347 U.S. 1 (1954); United States v. Haimowitz, 725 F.2d 1561 (11th Cir.1984), cert. denied 469 U.S. 1072 (1984); United States v. Mitchell, 744 F.2d 701 (9th Cir.1984).

10. See supra, pp. 1336–1337.

11. See supra, p. 1336.

12. 739 F.2d 1445 (9th Cir.1984).

13. 739 F.2d at 1449.

14. 664 F.2d 12 (2d Cir.1981), cert. denied 464 U.S. 863 (1983).

15. In the *Moss* case the court in a footnote mentions the fact that Newman had been convicted of mail fraud, but it doesn't even discuss the question of why the facts underlying that conviction wouldn't be a sufficient allegation of "predicate offenses" under the RICO count.

16. ABA Report, 224, 251–254.

action where the predicate offenses are alleged to be mail fraud and wire fraud even though a security is involved in the transactions. There is nothing in RICO itself which could be the basis for such a limitation.

5. What fault is required on the part of the defendant under the mail fraud and wire fraud statutes? There are cases stating that the "fraud" must be intentional,[17] as the Supreme Court held with respect to Rule 10b–5 in the *Hochfelder* case, although the Supreme Court reserved the question whether "recklessness" is sufficient. All of the circuit court decisions since *Hochfelder* have held that it is. (See supra, page 956). But there are also cases under the mail fraud and wire fraud statutes holding that "reckless disregard" of the truth or falsity of a statement is enough.[18] There would appear to be no substantial difference between the fault required with respect to Rule 10b–5 and that required under the mail fraud and wire fraud statutes.

6. In short, virtually all of the limitations which the Supreme Court has imposed upon an action under Rule 10b–5 in recent years are swept aside by RICO where the predicate offenses are mail fraud and wire fraud, if the other requirements for civil liability under RICO are met. These statutes would appear to cover *all* conduct actionable under Rule 10b–5 and a great deal more. In fact, the Fifth Circuit has stated that conduct is actionable under these statutes if it "[departs] from moral uprightness, fundamental honesty, fair play and candid dealings in the general life of members of society" [19]—a prohibition the scope of which would be hard to duplicate in any other criminal law in any civilized jurisdiction.

THE "PATTERN" REQUIREMENT

While RICO defines "racketeering activity" as any one violation of any one of the dozens of criminal laws specified in § 1961(1), in order for there to be any criminal or civil liability under RICO there must be shown, in addition, a "pattern" of such racketeering activity. The statute does not define "pattern" of such activity, but it does say that one is not enough. Section 1961(5) states that such a pattern of racketeering activity "requires at least two acts of racketeering activity" occurring within ten years of each other. The case law has not really grappled with this question, as stated by the Supreme Court in *Sedima*. The majority opinion said: "The 'extraordinary' uses to which RICO has been put appear to be primarily the result of the breadth of the predicate offenses, in particular the inclusion of wire, mail and securities fraud, and the failure of Congress and the courts to develop a meaningful concept of 'pattern.'"

A. *The Supreme Court Dicta in Sedima.* The majority opinion in *Sedima* does comment on this issue of the meaning of the word "pattern". First, the court in effect rebukes those lower courts (and there are many) which have casually assumed in the language they have used (although the issue was usually not involved in the case) that because two criminal acts are necessary to form a pattern, they are sufficient to do so. The court states in Footnote 15: "The implication [of § 1961(5)] is that while two acts are necessary, they may

---

17. United States v. Kreimer, 609 F.2d 126 (5th Cir.1980); United States v. Fuel, 583 F.2d 978 (8th Cir.1978); United States v. Precision Medical Laboratories, Inc., 593 F.2d 434 (2d Cir.1978).

18. United States v. Farris, 614 F.2d 634 (9th Cir.1979); United States v. Dick,

744 F.2d 546 (7th Cir.1984); cf. United States v. Brien, 617 F.2d 299 (1st Cir.1980), cert. denied 446 U.S. 919 (1980) ("conscious avoidance" of knowledge whether statements are false).

19. United States v. Kreimer, 609 F.2d 126, at 128 (5th Cir.1980).

not be sufficient. Indeed, in common parlance, two of anything do not generally form a 'pattern.' The legislative history supports the view that two isolated acts of racketeering activity do not constitute a pattern. As the Senate Report explained: 'The target of [RICO] is thus not a sporadic activity. The infiltration of legitimate business normally requires more than one "racketeering activity" and the threat of continuing activity to be effective. It is this factor of *continuity plus relationship* which combines to produce a pattern.'" How many more than two may be required and what the "relationship" among them must be is not, however, further elucidated in the legislative history or in the Supreme Court's footnote.

Secondly, the majority opinion in the same footnote drops a broad hint to the lower courts that they should use the definition of "pattern" in the Dangerous Special Offenders Act, a part of the same Bill as RICO. The court stated: "Significantly, in defining 'pattern' in a later provision of the same Bill, Congress was more enlightening: 'Criminal conduct forms a pattern if it embraces criminal acts that have the same or similar purposes, results, participants, victims or methods of commission, or otherwise are interrelated by distinguishing characteristics and are not isolated events.' 18 U.S.C. § 3575(e). *This language may be useful in interpreting other sections of the Act.*" (Italics added).

In his separate dissent, Justice Powell also in effect urges the lower courts to use this phrase "pattern of racketeering activity" to find the necessary "rubber" in the statute so as to enable them to accomplish the objective which they all seem to have shared, that is, the restriction of RICO to manageable proportions. Justice Powell stated: "The ABA Report suggests that to effectuate this legislative intent, 'pattern' should be interpreted as requiring that (i) the racketeering acts be related to each other, (ii) they be part of some common scheme, and (iii) some sort of continuity between the acts or a threat of continuing criminal activity must be shown * * * By construing 'pattern' to focus on the manner in which the crime was perpetrated, courts could go a long way toward limiting the reach of the statute to its intended target—organized crime."

Both of these suggested approaches to the definition of "pattern" have some difficulties of interpretation and doubtless would lead to varying results as applied by different courts. For example, in our Hypothetical Case No. 1 dealing with the churning of three accounts by a registered representative, did these criminal acts "have the same or similar purposes [yes], results [presumably yes], participants [yes—only one], victims [no], or methods of commission [yes], or [were they] otherwise * * * interrelated by distinguishing characteristics [perhaps] * * * and not isolated events [depends upon what "isolated" means in this context—isolated how?; isolated from what?]." Were they or were they not therefore a "pattern" within the meaning of § 3575(e)? It is easy to imagine that different courts might give different answers to this question.

Under the ABA–Powell approach, were these separate churning "episodes" related to each other [only in the sense that they were all committed by the same person], were they "part of some common scheme" [who knows?—he may simply have felt an overwhelming urge to "churn", which he couldn't resist, on three separate occasions or he may have decided in his own mind that henceforth he would "churn" every once in a while], and was there "some sort of continuity" between the acts [depends on what "continuity" means—they followed one after the other and perhaps overlapped to some extent] or a threat of continuing criminal activity [one might infer that he would do it again from the fact he'd done it three times—certainly that would be enough to justify a permanent injunction against him under the decided cases]. Were they therefore a "pattern" under the ABA–Powell approach? Again, one can certainly imagine different courts arriving at different answers to this question.

The same questions can be asked regarding our Hypothetical Case No. 2, with virtually the same answers, or lack thereof.

B. *The Conyers Bill.* H.R. 2517 (introduced by Representative Conyers on May 15, 1985) has a slightly different definition of "pattern" which requires that the acts of predicate criminal activity be (i) "separate in time and place", (ii) "interrelated by a common scheme, plan or motive", and (iii) that they not be "isolated events." In our two hypothetical cases, the different predicate acts were separate in time (to some extent) but not separate in place (since they all occurred in the office of the registered representative or employee of Payne, Hutton & Barney); they presumably had the same motive, and were to that extent "interrelated"; and they were or were not "isolated events", depending on how you define "isolated" under this requirement and what they are supposed to be isolated from.

C. Under any of these suggested definitions, would the separate defrauding of different customers in a typical Ponzi scheme (such as those recently carried out by J. David Dominelli and Ronald Rewald) form a "pattern" or not? Would the separate mailings of a false and misleading offering circular in a best efforts underwriting of a real estate syndication over a period of six months to different offerees constitute a "pattern" or not?

It would seem that in order to bring the necessary clarity into this element of an offense under RICO, additional drafting efforts will be necessary. In any event, it would seem that any definition of this one element is not going to be sufficient to stop the harassment of legitimate business enterprises by suits under RICO.

The Eighth Circuit in the *Superior Oil Co.* case struggled to comply with the admonition from the Supreme Court regarding the need to focus on the "pattern" requirement; but the Fifth Circuit in the *Couture* case incorrigibly said again that "two are plenty", even if the two "predicate offenses" are simply two separate mailings in connection with a single indivisible fraudulent scheme.

"ENTERPRISE"

The use of the word "enterprise" in the RICO statute has perhaps produced more confusion in the decisions than any other single aspect of the statute. In trying to determine the meaning of this word in the statute, it certainly is helpful to focus upon the plain dictionary definition of this word, although no court has done so. The Oxford English Dictionary defines the word (as a substantive) as follows: "A design of which the execution is attempted; a piece of work taken in hand, an undertaking; *chiefly,* and now exclusively, a bold, arduous or momentous undertaking." As a verb (which is identified as now being "archaic"), it is defined as meaning "To take in hand (a work), take upon oneself (a condition), attempt or undertake (a war, an expedition, etc.), run the risk of or venture upon (danger)." Webster's New International Dictionary (Second Edition) has substantially the same definition.[20] The OED traces the use of this word as a substantive to 1430 and as a verb to 1485. Neither

---

20. "An attempt or project, esp. one which involves activity, courage, energy, or the like; a bold, arduous, or hazardous attempt; an important undertaking; as, a warlike enterprise." The synonyms given are: "Undertaking, venture, essay, attempt." See, also, Webster's New International Dictionary (Third Edition).

dictionary has any indication that the word has ever meant a person or group of persons, however organized. In those dictionaries a person that carries out an enterprise is an "enterpriser" (or that modern abomination "entrepreneur").

In short, the word signifies an *activity*, and not a person or group of persons, and it has been so understood since Elizabethan times.

The term "enterprise" is not defined in the statute, although § 1961(4) does say that the word "enterprise" *includes* "any individual, partnership, corporation, association, or other legal entity, and any union or group of individuals associated in fact although not a legal entity." Literally, this statement is nonsensical, since an enterprise is not a person or group of persons, whether constituting a legal entity or not. All that this statement really says is that the persons conducting an enterprise under RICO may or may not constitute a legal "entity". The Supreme Court expressly so stated in the *Turkette* case. Apparently misled by this shorthand reference in § 1961(4), the lower courts however, have never asked the question, What is the enterprise?, but only the question: *Who* is the enterprise? This has led to the parsing of words in the statute the like of which has not been seen since the Year Books.

The correct interpretation of the word "enterprise" is made crystal clear, so far as Section 1962(c) is concerned, over which most of the ink has been spilled, by the reference to "conducting" an enterprise. One does not conduct other people; one conducts an activity. (It is true that a "conductor" is generally stated in shorthand fashion to be conducting "the orchestra", but the obvious and necessary meaning of this expression is that he is conducting a "performance of the composition" by the orchestra.)

A. What is the scope of the "enterprise" which must be conducted through illegal means? In our hypothetical cases, if the only enterprise which can be considered under RICO is the entire operation of Payne, Hutton & Barney, then obviously it cannot be proven that the entire enterprise is being conducted through a "pattern of racketeering activity." However, many of the cases have held that where a segment or division of a business or a group of persons working in a larger organization start conducting a portion of its affairs by criminal activities, that segment or portion of the business being so conducted can constitute the "enterprise" for RICO purposes.[21] Almost by definition, then, that "enterprise" is being conducted through a pattern of racketeering activity since the scope of the enterprise has been narrowed to encompass only the criminal activities.

B. Can a single individual constitute an "enterprise", or more accurately, can he be the only participant in the enterprise? This question is of course directly raised by our hypothetical cases, in which we have assumed that only one individual is involved in the dirty work. It would seem that the answer to this question has to be "yes", since the statute flatly says so. It states that an "enterprise" "includes" an individual. Certainly there was no reason for Congress to exempt a "one-man gang" who starts his criminal career alone by operating an extortion racket (see Godfather I), until his business develops enough for him to begin hiring assistants.

C. Does the "enterprise" have to include any activities other than those that constitute the predicate offenses? In the *Turkette* case, the United States Supreme Court answered this question "no." In that case a criminal "family" was indicted for engaging in drug trafficking, committing arson, defrauding insurance companies, and bribing police and judges, and the "enterprise", for the purposes of RICO, was described in the indictment as consisting entirely of those activities. The rather bizarre contention was made that because they

21. ABA Report, 160, n. 254; Ch. 14.

never did anything legal, they were therefore not subject to a RICO prosecution. This was based upon the semi-plausible argument that because Congress was primarily concerned with the infiltration and taking over of legitimate businesses by "organized crime", there had to be involved, at least at one time, some legitimate enterprise other than a purely criminal one. (This, of course, may possibly be true under subsections (a) and (b) of Section 1962, since they deal with the "infiltration" or capture of legitimate "enterprises" by criminal activity.) In rejecting this contention, the Supreme Court pointed out that this would make the worst offenders the least liable to punishment.

D. There have been a large number of cases which have discussed the rather metaphysical issue of whether the "person" who is made liable for conducting an "enterprise" under § 1961(c) must be "distinct" from the enterprise itself.[22] In a sense, of course, the person or persons who commit the predicate crimes are always distinct from the enterprise of committing them— any person must be "distinct" from any enterprise which he conducts, since a person is a *person* and an enterprise is an *activity*. A cat-burglar who makes his living burglarizing wealthy homes and engages in no other productive activity is not identical with his business, since he has other personal and social activities. As Gilbert and Sullivan say, a burglar "when he is not a' burgling" may be a devoted family man who takes good care of his wife and children. Nevertheless, the cat-burglar is certainly conducting an enterprise (in any ordinary sense of the word) "through a pattern of racketeering activity" (if the word "robbery" in the statute includes "burglary", which it might, although historically they have very distinct meanings).[23]

Those cases which say that the "person" who does the dirty work must be distinct from the "enterprise" through which the crimes are committed would seem to be directly contradicting the holding of the United States Supreme Court in the *Turkette* case. In that case, the members of the "family" who carried out the crimes of dope peddling, arson and insurance fraud were not "distinct" from the "enterprise" itself in any meaningful sense (except that noted above, which must always exist); and that was essentially the objection to their being punishable under RICO which the Supreme Court flatly rejected.

Nevertheless, virtually all of the circuit courts which have considered this question have held that there is such a requirement, following the *Haroco* case.[24] These cases may, however, be of little significance if the same requirement doesn't apply under subsection (a) of § 1972, as the *Haroco* and *Schofield* cases say it does not. Section 1962(a) prohibits any person who has received any income from a pattern of racketeering activity from "us[ing] ＊ ＊ ＊ any part of such income ＊ ＊ ＊ in ＊ ＊ ＊ the operation of [,] any enterprise ＊ ＊ ＊." While primarily directed against the "infiltration" of legitimate business by organized crime, this subsection also appears to prohibit organized crime from "infiltrating" itself and to make illegal the continued operation of any business which has already been "infiltrated." However, that provision requires that the person liable must have participated "as a principal" in the pattern of racketeering activity. This must mean as a "primary" actor,[25] and Payne, Hutton & Barney in our hypothetical cases certainly could not be liable

---

22. ABA Report, Ch. 14.

23. Originally, of course, "burglary" referred to a breaking and entering in the nighttime for the purpose of committing a felony; "robbery" referred to a taking of property by force (e.g., by a highwayman— hence, "highway robbery"); and "theft" to a surreptitious purloining of property. Why Congress should have made such common law distinctions, however, would be a mystery.

24. The cases are all cited in the *Schofield* case.

25. Congress can hardly have used the word "principal" in its agency sense, since this would have immunized the actual actor (the "agent") from prosecution under subsection (a).

under subsection (a) (except upon general principles of *respondeat superior*—see below).

Perhaps what the courts which have attempted to make this distinction are really trying to do is to resist those cases holding that the scope of the RICO enterprise under § 1961(c) may be narrowed to fit the criminal activities of a group of persons within a much larger legitimate enterprise, so that the RICO enterprise may be said to be conducted through a "pattern of racketeering activity." If you do that, however, and then say: "Now the enterprise is not distinct from the persons who conduct it and therefore there is no RICO liability", you have simply gone around in a full circle. In any event, this holding would seem to be precluded by *Turkette* and by the statutory provision that an individual may be an "enterprise" all by himself. Whether such a narrowing of the scope of the RICO enterprise is appropriate should be addressed directly. It is probably contrary to what Congress contemplated, although there is certainly support for it in the language of the statute providing that such an "enterprise" may be any group of persons or a single individual.

CONDUCTING AN ENTERPRISE "THROUGH" A PATTERN OF RACKETEERING ACTIVITY

Assuming that racketeering activity has been established, that a "pattern" has been established and that an "enterprise" has been identified, it must further be shown that the enterprise was *conducted through* that pattern of racketeering activity. What does this mean? It would seem that this is the provision by which Congress attempted to limit RICO essentially to "organized crime", without attempting to *define* organized crime. It suggests that the predominant purpose of the enterprise, or at least a major purpose, has to be that of engaging in criminal conduct. The "family" involved in the *Turkette* case are typical of the "mobsters" whom Congress thought it was attacking when it enacted RICO (rather than all banks, brokerages houses and corporations in the country).

Here again, we encounter the crucial question of the scope of the RICO enterprise which must be alleged and be shown to have been conducted through this pattern of racketeering activity. In our two hypothetical cases, is the "enterprise" merely the two or three episodes in which Joe Hotshot Salesman committed crimes; or is it Joe Hotshot Salesman's entire activities as a registered representative, in the vast majority of which he did not engage in any criminal conduct; or is it all of the activities of Payne, Hutton & Barney as a broker-dealer firm? If it is the third, then certainly that enterprise cannot be said to be conducted through any pattern of racketeering activity. If it is the second, then that enterprise also probably cannot be said to have been conducted through any pattern of racketeering activity; rather, the person conducting it simply succumbed to temptation on two or three occasions. The primary purpose of that enterprise can hardly be said to be to engage in criminal conduct, although under this alternative the issue is more debatable. If, however, the "enterprise" is narrowed to include nothing but the criminal activity, then obviously it will be conducted through that criminal activity.

RESPONDEAT SUPERIOR

Assuming that a case has been made by the plaintiff that Joe Hotshot Salesman is liable in treble damages for a violation of RICO, what is the liability of Payne, Hutton & Barney as his employer? It should be noted that this question has nothing to do with the scope of the "enterprise" which has been conducted through a pattern of racketeering activity. An "enterprise" is not made liable by § 1962(c), but only a "person" who conducts the enterprise. Regardless of the scope of the enterprise, the claim here would be that Payne, Hutton & Barney conducted this enterprise *vicariously* through its employee and therefore is liable on the basis of the ordinary rules of *respondeat superior* or otherwise as that person. There are at least four different bases on which such secondary liability might be asserted, varying considerably in scope.

A. *Civil Rules Relating to Respondeat Superior.* Under the ordinary civil rules relating to liability of an employer for acts of the employee, an employer is liable for the wrongful acts of its employee if in committing them he was acting "within the scope of his employment." It would seem to be fairly clear here that Joe Hotshot Salesman in our Hypothetical Case No. 1 was acting within the scope of his employment and therefore Payne, Hutton & Barney would be liable as the employer based simply upon the determination of his wrongful conduct. Liability under our Hypothetical Case No. 2 is much more problematical, since it can be argued that Joe Hotshot Salesman was merely off on a "frolic" of his own, particularly if Payne, Hutton & Barney had rules prohibiting that kind of conduct. He did not intend to share any of his "ill-gotten" gains with the firm. It has apparently been assumed (especially by counsel for plaintiffs) that these ordinary rules of *respondeat superior* would apply in connection with a civil action under RICO, but the *Scholfield* case holds to the contrary.[26] There is certainly nothing in the statute itself, however, which supports this conclusion.[27]

B. *Criminal Liability.* The second possible basis for liability of Payne, Hutton & Barney is the rules relating to the criminal liability of a corporation or other entity which is the employer of an individual or individuals who actually commit the crime. If this were the basis of liability adopted, the test would be whether the employer could itself be convicted of a crime for violation of RICO. While this test may be somewhat more restrictive than those relating to civil liability for torts committed by employees, in some jurisdictions those rules may not differ materially from the rules relating to civil liability, at least for corporate employers.[28] A possible justification for adopting this test would be that while we are dealing here with civil liability, under RICO that civil liability is based upon the commission of crimes by someone.

C. *The Rules Relating to Liability Under Rule 10b–5.* While most courts have applied the doctrine of *respondeat superior* in Rule 10b–5 cases in the same manner as it is applied with respect to any other tort committed by an employee, there are other cases which hold that liability of an employer under Rule 10b–5 can only be based on Section 20(a) of the 1934 Act making liable controlling persons, "unless the controlling person acted in good faith and did not directly or indirectly induce the act or acts constituting the violation." (See supra, pp. 1163–1166.) Some courts have said that in order to establish "good faith" the defendant, particularly a broker-dealer, must show that he carried out whatever duties of supervision of his employees are required under the SEC rules or otherwise. Others have said that "good faith" only implies purity of mind. The difficulty with importing this limitation into vicarious liability under RICO, even if it were the majority view under the 1934 Act, is that it is based upon a specific section of that statute which is not reproduced in RICO.

26. For other cases, see ABA Report, 352–356.

27. See Bernstein v. IDT Corp., 582 F.Supp. 1079, at 1083–1084 (D.Del.1984).

28. ABA Report, 343–348.

D. *Conspiracy.* Finally, subsection (d) of § 1962 makes it unlawful for "any person to conspire to violate any of the provisions of subsections (a), (b) or (c) of this section," and § 1964(c) renders liable any person who has violated any subsection of § 1962. Therefore, if the employer can be found to have "conspired" with its employee to commit the RICO violation, then it will be liable along with him under this subsection. However, since such a finding of conspiracy would presumably require a showing of some involvement of senior executives, or perhaps even the board of directors, of a corporate employer in the actual commission of the crime, it is unlikely that this provision could be used as a basis for liability in a case like those which we have been discussing. Furthermore, since it is a much narrower basis of liability than any of the others mentioned, it would not have practical importance unless all of those are ruled inapplicable in a civil action under RICO, as the court ruled in the *Schofield* case.

DAMAGES

Under § 1954(c), a person "injured in his business or property" may recover the "damages he sustains" as a result of a RICO violation, which will be trebled under the provisions of that subsection. A remarkable thing about this provision is that personal injuries are not compensable. If a person engaged in business refuses to pay "protection money" to the "mob" and is then killed or beaten up and paralyzed for life, neither he nor his family may recover any damages under RICO for that injury, although they may recover single damages under any other existing liability provision of state or federal law for that type of conduct, with the possibility of punitive damages. The minority opinion in *Sedima* emphasized this result under RICO as a reason for holding that *no* direct injuries caused by the predicate acts alone were intended to be the subject of a civil action under RICO, but only the indirect injuries arising from the "pattern" of racketeering activity. The phrase injury "in his * * * property" would seem to be broad enough to include any monetary loss suffered by the plaintiff. In our two hypothetical cases, it would seem that the plaintiff could establish that he suffered such monetary loss as the proximate result of the activities of Joe Hotshot Salesman constituting the criminal violations.

In addition to the ABA Report, see Brickey, Forfeiture of Attorneys' Fees: The Impact of RICO and CCE Forfeitures on the Right to Counsel, 72 Va.L.Rev. 493 (1986); Carey, Civil RICO and the Prior Criminal Conviction Requirement: Has the Second Circuit Drawn the Net Too Tightly, 60 Wash.L.Rev. 461 (1985); Headley, Sedima v. IMREX: Civil Immunity for Unprosecuted RICO Violators?, 85 Colum.L.Rev. 419 (1985); Manogue, Liability for General Business Fraud: Putting a Contract Out on RICO Treble Damages, 45 U.Pitt.L.Rev. 481 (1984); Johnson, Predators' Rights: Multiple Remedies for Wall Street Sharks Under Securities Laws and RICO, 10 J.Corp.L. 3 (1984); Reed and Gill, RICO Forfeitures, Forfeitable "Interests," and Procedural Due Process, 62 N.C.L.Rev. 57 (1983); Tyson and August, The Williams Act After RICO: Has the Balance Tipped in Favor of Incumbent Management, 35 Hastings L.J. 53 (1983); Wexler, Civil RICO Comes of Age: Some Maturational Problems and Proposals for Reform, 35 Rutgers L.R. 285 (1983); Mathews, Civil RICO Cases, 14 Inst. on Sec. Reg. 279 (1983); Glanz, RICO and Securities Fraud, A Workable Limitation, 83 Colum.L.Rev. 1513 (1983).

Part VI

SEC ENFORCEMENT ACTIONS

Chapter 23

SEC ENFORCEMENT ACTIONS

Statutes and Regulations

Securities Act of 1933, §§ 19, 20, 21, 22.

Securities Exchange Act of 1934, §§ 21, 22, 23.

SEC Rules of Practice.

SECURITIES AND EXCHANGE COMMISSION v. WHEELING–PITTSBURGH STEEL CORP.

United States Court of Appeals, Third Circuit, 1981.
648 F.2d 118.

Before: SEITZ, CHIEF JUDGE, and ALDISERT, ADAMS, GIBBONS, ROSENN, HUNTER, WEIS, GARTH, HIGGINBOTHAM and SLOVITER, CIRCUIT JUDGES.

ALDISERT, CIRCUIT JUDGE: This appeal requires us to decide if the district court erred in refusing to enforce a subpoena *duces tecum*, issued by the Securities and Exchange Commission pursuant to § 21(b) of the Securities Exchange Act to Wheeling-Pittsburgh Steel Corporation (W–P) and its president, Dennis J. Carney. The district court determined that W–P failed to meet its burden of proving that the SEC acted in bad faith, district court op., typescript at 14, but concluded that the SEC "has permitted, and at times encouraged, the abuse of its investigating function," id. at 18. Accordingly, the court denied enforcement of the subpoena, and the SEC has appealed. Because we believe that the district court must educe additional testimony and clarify its determinations, we will vacate the order and remand these proceedings for further consideration.

The subpoena was issued to compel Mr. Carney to identify companies involved in reported merger negotiations with Wheeling-Pittsburgh and to provide documents relating to those negotiations. Wheeling-Pittsburgh's basic contention is that the SEC proceedings are tainted because of improper interference by United States Senator Lowell Weicker of Connecticut on behalf of the Colorado Fuel and Iron Company (CF & I), an acknowledged competitor of Wheeling-Pittsburgh, for no legitimate legislative purpose. The district court was persuaded that sufficient improprieties had occurred to deny enforcement of the subpoenas.

Because the district court determined that W–P had not proved bad faith on the part of the SEC, the precise issue before us is whether the court's determination that the SEC allowed its investigatory process to be abused is sufficient under the teachings of United States v. Powell, 379 U.S.

1509

48 (1964), to deny enforcement of the SEC's subpoena. Corollary issues of equal importance are whether we should determine the length of time the refusal to enforce should remain in effect and, if so, an identification of conditions affecting that time period.

I.

Wheeling-Pittsburgh Steel Corporation, a Delaware corporation with offices at Pittsburgh, Pennsylvania, manufactures and sells steel and related products. Its stock is registered pursuant to § 12(b) of the Securities Exchange Act and is listed on the New York Stock Exchange. W-P files annual and other periodic reports with the SEC pursuant to § 13(a) of the Act. Mr. Carney is President and Chief Executive Officer of Wheeling-Pittsburgh.

A.

Beginning in 1977, and for some time thereafter, W-P attempted to obtain loan guarantees from the Economic Development Administration of the United States Department of Commerce (EDA) and the Farmers Home Administration of the United States Department of Agriculture (FmHA). The loans, to be obtained from private lenders, were to be used to install government mandated pollution control equipment at several plants and to construct a rail rolling mill at Monessen, Pennsylvania. The court found that the loan guarantees were critical to the company because the rail rolling mill could not be constructed without pollution control devices required by the Environmental Protection Agency. In addition, the company could not finance the production facility construction without the loan guarantees.

United States Steel Corporation, Bethlehem Steel Corporation, and CF & I also manufacture steel rails and all have opposed loan guarantees to W-P. The district court found that CF & I, a company owned by Crane Company, played a major role in opposing the guarantees, individually and in conjunction with Senator Weicker.

W-P signed loan guarantee agreements with the EDA on August 28, 1979, under which the EDA pledged to guarantee loans totaling $100 million. Of this $100 million, $63.5 million are earmarked to finance partial construction of the mill at Monessen, Pennsylvania, and $36.5 million are to finance the purchase and installation of pollution control equipment at plants in Monessen and Allenport, Pennsylvania. On the same day, FmHA issued conditional commitments (revised and reissued in September, 1979, and further revised in September, 1980) to guarantee six separate loans to W-P totaling $50 million for the purchase and installation of pollution control equipment at plants in Ohio and West Virginia. These guarantees have induced a consortium of private lenders to agree to extend loans to W-P for the purposes contemplated by the guarantees. As of the date of oral argument, W-P had actually received over $50 million in guaranteed loan funds. The balance of almost $100 million represents loans that W-P expects to draw at intervals through the end of 1982. W-P's application for these loan guarantees and the violent opposition thereto by Senator Weicker and CF & I precipitated this law suit.

B.

On December 28, 1978, and January 9, 1979, before the loan guarantee agreements were actually executed, Carney received identical "Letters of Intent" from EDA and FmHA. The letters stated that the agencies "will recommend" respectively to the Assistant Secretary for Economic Development and the Assistant Secretary for Rural Development loan guarantees of $100 million (EDA) and $40 million (FmHA). The "Letters of Intent" were contingent on a number of provisions. The district court determined that "[a] careful examination of these provisions reveals, however, that the conditions involved ministerial matters which offered no major obstacles to receipt of the guarantees." District court op., typescript at 4.

On April 27, 1979, in a "Report on the Annual Meeting of Stockholders," Carney discussed the status of the loan guarantees: "We obtained commitments for federal loan guarantees of $140 million, and for a $10-million direct loan through the State of Pennsylvania. These commitments will enable us to finalize financial arrangements in June through a consortium of insurance companies." Report on the Annual Meeting of Stockholders and Report on Results for the Three Months Ended March 31, 1979 (April 27, 1979), at 10. In the same report, Carney remarked: "We are also exploring future acquisitions being proposed to us by several domestic and foreign firms." Id. at 12. Following the report to shareholders, Carney spoke to news reporters. He related that the turn-around in W–P's financial position had attracted domestic and foreign concerns who were interested in entering business combinations, but "so far none of them looks good." He termed the discussions "preliminary" and declined to elaborate. Wall St.J., April 30, 1979, at 20, col. 6.

In September, 1978, before W–P had received the first "Letter of Intent," CF & I's counsel, Paul R. Hundt, hired Arthur T. Downey, an attorney in Washington, D.C., to assist CF & I in opposing W–P's efforts to obtain the guarantees. That opposition led Downey to meet in February, 1979, with two members of Senator Lowell Weicker's staff. App. at 419–20. Senator Weicker was the ranking minority member of the Subcommittee for State, Justice & Commerce Appropriations of the Senate Committee on Appropriations. That subcommittee was in charge of a supplemental appropriation to the EDA essential to the W–P loan guarantees. The record indicates that between February and October, 1979, Downey met with Timothy Keeney, Weicker's administrative assistant, as many as ten to twenty times. App. at 425.

Downey continued his assault on the W–P loan application by writing to the EDA and the FmHA, suggesting that these agencies compel W–P to withdraw the statements made in the quarterly report concerning "commitments" received from those agencies. He then furnished Keeney with copies of the quarterly report and of his letters to EDA and FmHA. Later, Keeney and Downey met in Downey's office to discuss the W–P quarterly report in preparation for a hearing before Weicker's subcommittee on June 4, 1979.

Weicker publicly attacked the proposed EDA loan guarantee to W–P at the June 4 hearing and thereafter. App. at 215–16. Carney appeared at the June 11, 1979, subcommittee hearing to explain W–P's position. On the evening before the hearing, Downey and various CF & I executives met with Keeney in a hotel in Washington, D.C. App. at 576–79. Carney appeared on June 11, read a prepared statement, and was questioned by various members of the subcommittee. Weicker and Carney engaged in a colloquy over the distinction between a "letter of intent" and a "commitment." Although Carney contended that the terms were substantially synonymous, Weicker expressed the view that use of the term "commitments" in Carney's report to W–P shareholders violated § 10(b) of the Securities Exchange Act of 1934 and Commission Rule 10b–5.

Subsequently, the subcommittee approved the appropriation for the W–P loan guarantee over the opposition of Senator Weicker, who declared that he would take the matter to the floor of the Senate. He later did so, but at the same time opened a new front in his opposition to the W–P loans, soliciting the cooperation of the SEC in his campaign against W–P. Three days after the Senate subcommittee hearing, Weicker had a letter delivered by hand to Stanley Sporkin, head of SEC's Division of Enforcement, requesting an investigation of whether Carney's use of the term "commitments" instead of "letters of intent" in his report to W–P stockholders constituted a violation of the Securities Exchange Act of 1934. App. at 37–38.

Sporkin routed the letter to Richard E. Brodsky of the Division of Enforcement, who then assigned the case to staff attorney Martin Aussenberg. Aussenberg contacted Keeney on June 19. Keeney explained the loan guarantee process to Aussenberg, advised him of W–P's pending application, noted Carney's use of the word "commitments" in the quarterly report, and gave Aussenberg a transcript of the Senate hearings. Keeney also suggested that Aussenberg contact Downey, whom he described as CF & I's attorney. When Aussenberg called Downey later that same day, Downey suggested other potential securities law violations. Downey testified that CF & I was "frustrated" and "exasperated" by its inability to block the loan guarantees and that he provided much of the information as a means of "venting my exasperation." Deposition of Arthur T. Downey (Oct. 9, 1979) at 193, 195, reprinted in App. at 592, 594; see district court op., typescript at 6–7.

While conducting the informal inquiry, Aussenberg received a call from Keeney, who asked what actions the SEC had taken in response to Senator Weicker's letter. Aussenberg refused to disclose any information or even confirm the existence of SEC investigations. In a second call, Keeney notified Aussenberg that Senator Weicker intended to introduce an amendment to the supplemental appropriations bill for the EDA and that the amendment would preclude the FDA from providing federal loan guarantees to corporations under investigation by the SEC. The SEC objected to Weicker's amendment through Aussenberg, and expressed fear that the amendment would compromise the confidentiality of its investigation. On June 25, Senator Weicker introduced the amendment, along with nine others, each of which would have blocked an EDA loan guarantee to W–P. During the Senate debate on Weicker's amendment, he engaged in a heated exchange with Senator John Heinz of Pennsylvania, during which Senator Heinz questioned the motives of Senator Weicker.[3] When the amendment

---

3. See App. at 225–26. The reason for Senator Weicker's peculiar interest in this Pennsylvania-based steel company is not clear. W–P has alleged that Thomas Mel- lon Evans, the chairman of Crane Co., parent company of CF & I, is a neighbor and acquaintance of Senator Weicker. See Answer and Counterclaim for W–P at 7, ¶ 5.

that would have tied loan guarantees to SEC activity was called for a vote, it was defeated by a substantial margin.

The SEC entered an order pursuant to 17 C.F.R. § 202.5(a) on July 31, 1979, directing a private formal investigation into W–P's activities and Carney's statements. The order empowered the Commission officers to issue subpoenas, take testimony, and compel the production of documents. The SEC issued a subpoena *duces tecum* to Carney on August 2, 1979, who appeared for questioning by Aussenberg. Aussenberg's inquiries focused primarily on the loan guarantee process, particularly Carney's use of the word "commitments" in the report of April 27. Carney answered all questions relating to the loan guarantees. During a final phase of the deposition, however, Aussenberg instructed Carney to disclose the names of every company that had approached him, or he had approached, since January, 1979, concerning possible acquisition by or of W–P. Carney refused to divulge names or turn over any documents pertaining to those discussions.

On August 15, 1979, W–P filed a motion for a protective order to enjoin further attempts to obtain information from Carney. On August 17, the SEC filed the present subpoena enforcement action. W–P then voluntarily dismissed its motion for a protective order but in its answer requested an injunction against the investigation. It later withdrew that request. The case was heard before the district court on August 22. The court conducted four additional hearings primarily focusing on two allegations by W–P: that the SEC allowed Senator Weicker and CF & I to abuse its normal discretionary investigative process, and that the SEC acted in bad faith in investigating W–P. The district court treated these allegations separately. It primarily emphasized the abuse of the investigative process and concentrated on the motivation of third parties who may have influenced the SEC investigation.

Although recognizing that the merit of the SEC's charges was not before it, the court expressed skepticism about the reasonableness of the charges, characterizing them as "patently frivolous." District court op., typescript at 19. It determined that the SEC's investigative process had been abused by third parties, and that "[w]ittingly or not, the agency has permitted, and at times encouraged, the abuse of its investigating function." Id. at 18. The court held that it would not "compound the gross lack of judgment by sanctioning such abuse." Id. Yet it concluded that W–P did not meet its burden of proving that the SEC was acting in "bad faith." Id. at 14 (footnote omitted).

The special dichotomy employed by the district court is central to the resolution of this appeal. If the abuse of process contention is considered to be subsumed in the good faith argument, then we believe there is an inconsistency in the district court's determination. Resolution of this inconsistency requires a remand for the purpose of clarification. If the contentions are separate and distinct, the proceedings still must be remanded for development of an adequate record on the abuse of process issue. The district court seems to have concentrated on the abuse by third parties of the agency's process, and did not explain, to our satisfaction, the relationship between the abuse of the agency's process and the abuse of the court's process. This can be rectified by further discovery and testimony. We note that following the October 27, 1979, hearing W–P advised the district court that it would not press its right for discovery if the court denied the SEC's application for enforcement. The following considerations will guide the district court's proceedings on remand.

II.

In asking this court to reverse the district court's refusal to enforce the subpoenas, the Commission argues that the district court exceeded the narrow authority accorded it in administrative subpoena enforcement actions. The implicit premise of the Commission's argument is that the judiciary's role is strictly confined by Supreme Court precedent and that, under these authorities, a court has little flexibility in confronting new situations. Although we agree that courts generally must defer to the agencies and that the scope of judicial inquiry is not expansive, we disagree with the Commission's premise that the Supreme Court has foreclosed incremental development of the law by the courts when we are faced with allegations of egregious abuses.

A.

We begin by noting that although congressional subpoenas are self-executing, McGrain v. Daugherty, 273 U.S. 135 (1927), Congress has entrusted the enforcement of the administrative process for the production of witnesses and papers to the courts. United States v. Friedman, 532 F.2d 928, 936–37 (3d Cir.1976). Since ICC v. Brimson, 154 U.S. 447 (1894), it has been clear that in passing on the application for enforcement of a subpoena the court acts *judicially* in a case or controversy. See In re Grand Jury Proceedings, 486 F.2d 85, 90 (3d Cir.1973) (*Schofield I*). Appellate courts have consistently recognized that whether to enforce an administrative subpoena is a judicial decision, based on the totality of particular circumstances proved on a given record. This court, speaking through Judge Gibbons, has emphasized that "federal courts have never lent their enforcement machinery to an executive branch investigative body in the manner of a rubber stamp." Id.

* * *

Because the courts must not interfere unduly in the administrative process, * * * our primary concern is with the integrity of the judicial process; our examination of the administrative process at this stage is important only to the extent that it bears on the agency's request that the court's process be used to enforce its subpoena. We have some doubt whether the parties correctly perceived the distinction between abuse by an agency of the court's process and abuse by third parties of the administrative process. The court's determination that W–P had failed to demonstrate the SEC's bad faith, though a rejection of the most common basis for attacking an agency subpoena, does not foreclose further inquiry. But if the court directed the further inquiry to the motivations of third parties and their illicit use of the agency's authority to investigate, that inquiry was misdirected. In our view, the inquiries in an adversary enforcement proceeding are limited: a determination that the court's process would or would not be abused by enforcement of the subpoena, and the conclusion that enforcement will be denied or granted. In the case before us, the presence of SEC bad faith is only one of several possible reasons for the ultimate conclusion; a determination that the court's process would be abused if the subpoena were to be enforced is the ultimate conclusion. Similarly, the finding that the SEC knew that *its* process was being abused, that it knowingly did nothing to prevent this abuse, *see* district court op., typescript at 7, 18, and, in addition, that it vigorously pursued the frivolous charges is, like a determination of bad faith, a separate reason for an ultimate conclusion that the *court's* process was being abused.[9] The distinction between the abuse of the SEC's process and abuse of the court's process must always be recognized.

Good jurisprudence advises against statement of universal precepts in single cases, see Walz v. Tax Commission, 397 U.S. 664, 668 (1970), especially when the allegations are as unusual as the ones in this case. But because the allegations in this case are so unusual, they would, if proved, transcend the reason for judicial deference to the SEC. And, given our disposition of this case, we perceive no threat to the efficient functioning of the SEC's investigative process by giving Wheeling-Pittsburgh an opportunity to conduct discovery prior to its attempt to prove its non-frivolous allegations. We conclude, therefore, that neither the reasons nor the language of the Supreme Court administrative summons decisions forecloses us from allowing an inquiry into W–P's allegations of abuse.

B.

Our ultimate inquiry, therefore, is whether enforcement of the administrative subpoena would constitute an abuse of the court's process. One determination that would support such a conclusion that the agency is abusing the court's process is a finding that the agency is acting in "bad faith." In analogous situations, the Supreme Court has defined "bad faith" as a "prosecution * * * brought without a reasonable expectation of obtaining a valid conviction." Kugler v. Helfant, 421 U.S. 117, 126 n. 6 (1975); see also Perez v. Ledesma, 401 U.S. 82, 85 (1971) ("without hope of obtaining a valid conviction"); Cameron v. Johnson, 390 U.S. 611, 619–20 (1968). In this case, W–P has alleged that a politically powerful third party influenced the SEC to bring an action that it ordinarily would not pursue. To determine if W–P has met its burden of alleging abuse of the court's process, we must first examine the relationship of this allegation to the bad faith standard. The examination must not end there, however, because "bad faith" action by the agency represents but one ground for denying the enforcement request.

We do not doubt the usefulness to administrative agencies of information gained from third parties. Nor do we doubt that frequently the motivations of informants are less than altruistic. See United States v. Cortese, 614 F.2d 914, 921 (3d Cir.1980). But we cannot simply avert our eyes from the realities of the political world: members of Congress are requested to, and do in fact, intrude, in varying degrees, in administrative proceedings. * * * An administrative agency that undertakes an extensive investigation at the insistence of a powerful United States Senator

---

9. The distinction between agency bad faith and agency acquiescence in an abuse of its process leading to an abuse of the court's process, though subtle, is significant. "Bad faith" connotes a conscious decision by an agency to pursue a groundless allegation without hope of proving that allegation. See part II B infra. In contrast, an agency could be found to be abusing the court's process if it vigorously pursued a charge because of the influence of a powerful third party without consciously and objectively evaluating the charges. See 17 C.F.R. § 202.–5(a) (1980).

"with no reasonable expectation" of proving a violation and then seeks federal court enforcement of its subpoena could be found to be using the judiciary for illicit purposes. We need not lend the processes of the federal courts to aid such behavior.

The allegations by Wheeling-Pittsburgh and the preliminary submissions before the district court are substantial enough not to be dismissed as a matter of law. Under the SEC's own regulations, it may conduct two types of investigations. A preliminary investigation, in which no process is issued or testimony compelled, is proper whenever "it appears that there may be [a] violation. * * *" 17 C.F.R. § 202.5(a) (1980). A formal investigation, in which process may be used, may be ordered by the Commission if "it appears from information obtained * * * that there is a likelihood that a violation has been or is about to be committed and that the issuance of process may be necessary. * * *" Id. In this case, the Commission issued a formal investigation order on July 26, 1979, and therefore must have found a "likelihood" of a violation. See In re Wheeling-Pittsburgh Steel Corp., File no. HO–1175 (SEC July 31, 1979). This implicit finding by the Commission cannot be squared with the district court's conclusion that the claims of wrongdoing by W–P are "patently frivolous." District court op., typescript at 19.

Although we will not countenance judicial interference with agency decisions to conduct investigations, decisions that are committed entirely to agency discretion, if the district court reaffirms its determination of frivolity after a more thorough review of the evidence, this judicial conclusion would serve as an impressive indication of agency bad faith or harassment, or adoption by the SEC of the animus of a third party who inspired the agency's action originally. See *Cortese,* 614 F.2d at 921. Alternatively, the district court's determination that the SEC knowingly allowed its process to be abused would also be consistent with a finding that the Commission allowed a formal investigation to proceed without first ascertaining the "likelihood" of a violation. See district court op., typescript at 18–19. At all times, of course, the burden is on the respondent of showing an abuse of the court's process, *Powell,* 379 U.S. at 58, and, at least in the context of the Internal Revenue Service's criminal and civil fraud liability, the Court has indicated that the burden of proving bad faith "is a heavy one." *LaSalle National Bank,* 437 U.S. at 316. Nevertheless, these considerations bear on the ultimate question of whether the SEC is pursuing a claim it knows it cannot win, or is in some other manner abusing the court's process.

* * * In these circumstances, we conclude that the proceedings should be remanded for clarification of these issues.

* * *

At bottom, this case raises the question whether, based on objective factors, the SEC's decision to investigate reflected its independent determination, or whether that decision was the product of external influences. The reality of prosecutorial experience, that most investigations originate on the basis of tips, suggestions, or importunings of third parties, including commercial competitors, need hardly be noted. That the SEC commenced these proceedings as a result of the importunings of Senator Weicker or CF & I, even with malice on their part, is not a sufficient basis to deny enforcement of the subpoena. *See Cortese,* 614 F.2d at 921. But beginning an informal investigation by collecting facts at the request of a third party, even one harboring ulterior motives, is much different from entering an order directing a private formal investigation pursuant to 17 C.F.R. § 202.5 (1980), without an objective determination by the Commission and only because of political pressure. The respondents are not free from an informal investigation instigated by anyone, in or out of government. But they *are* entitled to a decision by the SEC itself, free from third-party political pressure, that a "likelihood" of a violation exists and that a private investigation should be ordered. See 17 C.F.R. § 205.2(a). The SEC order must be supported by an independent agency determination, not one dictated or pressured by external forces. If an allegation of improper influence and abdication of the agency's objective responsibilities is made, and supported by sufficient evidence to make it facially credible, respondents are entitled to examine the circumstances surrounding the SEC's private investigation order. The court should be guided by twin beacons: the *court's* process is the focus of the judicial inquiry and the respondent may challenge the summons on any appropriate ground.

V.

Accordingly, for the reasons heretofore stated, the judgment of the district court will be vacated, and the cause remanded for additional proceedings consistent with the foregoing.

Each side to pay its own costs.

ADAMS, CIRCUIT JUDGE, dissenting, with whom CHIEF JUDGE SEITZ and JUDGES ROSENN and HIGGENBOTHAM join.

* * *

SECURITIES AND EXCHANGE COMMISSION v. NATIONAL STUDENT MARKETING CORP.

United States Court of Appeals, District of Columbia Circuit, 1976.
176 U.S.App.D.C. 56, 538 F.2d 404, cert. denied 429 U.S. 1073 (1977).

Before McGOWAN, TAMM, and ROBB, CIRCUIT JUDGES.

Per Curiam: This appeal concerns an affirmative defense asserted in the answer of appellants White & Case and Epley as their Fifteenth Defense to a complaint by the Securities and Exchange Commission.

That defense alleges:

> [T]he Securities and Exchange Commission violated its own rules, procedures, and directives and the United States Constitution by instituting this action without informing * * * [appellants] that they were "prospective defendants or targets" of the Commission investigation prior to the institution of the suit, and without affording * * * [appellants] or their counsel an opportunity to present their contentions to the Commission or the Commission staff as to why they should not be sued.

Amended Answer of Defendants White & Case and Marion Jay Epley, III, to the first Amended Complaint, April 9, 1973, ¶ 50; J.A. at 105.

The Commission moved to strike the Fifteenth Defense as legally insufficient. In response, appellants pointed to an internal, non-public memorandum of September 1, 1970, from the Commission to its senior staff, by which the Commission request[ed] that the staff memoranda to the Commission recommending the particular action set forth separately any arguments or contentions as to either the facts or the law involved in the case which have been advanced by the prospective respondents and which countervail those made by the staff in its memoranda as a basis for the recommendation.

SEC Memorandum to All Division Directors and Office Heads, Re: Procedures Followed in the Institution of Enforcement Proceedings, September 1, 1970; J.A. 1–3. Appellants assert that this language embodies the directive which the Fifteenth Defense alleges the staff to have violated, and that the staff's departure from this procedure constitutes grounds for dismissal of this action.

The district court struck the Fifteenth Defense as legally insufficient, holding that the 1970 Memorandum was not designed for protection of prospective defendants' rights, but later vacated its decision and reinstated the Fifteenth Defense without prejudice to the Commission to renew its motion to strike. The latter order was based on the court's determination to ensure that no evidence relevant to the Commission's intent to issuing the 1970 Memorandum had been overlooked in the earlier ruling.

Appellants then requested production of various documents, including memoranda prepared by individual Commissioners and agency staff members. The Commission responded by producing the only document issued by the Commission itself that referred to the 1970 Memorandum and related to the circumstances of its issuance, a minute of the Commission approving issuance of the 1970 Memorandum and dissemination to the staff. The Commission moved for a protective order respecting 67 other internal Commission documents that fell within the scope of the request and submitted the documents to the court for *in camera* inspection. The Commission contended that these internal documents were protected from disclosure by the intra-governmental privilege and that, in any case, none was relevant to the intent, reason or purpose of the Commission in issuing the 1970 Memorandum. At the same time, the Commission renewed its motion to strike the Fifteenth Defense on March 18, 1975. The district court granted the Commission's motions, concluding that none of the documents contained interpretive material or tended to support petitioners' claim that the 1970 Memorandum constituted a procedural directive or that noncompliance with the discretionary procedure could be a basis for dismissal. This appeal followed.

We affirm the order of the district court, satisfied that the court was correct in concluding that the Commission documents are "protected from disclosure by reason of the privilege for internal governmental memoranda containing advice or opinions," and that the privilege should not be overridden in this instance because "none of the requested documents [examined *in camera*] is relevant to the intent behind the 1970 directive." By way of explanation, the court further stated that none of the documents could indicate agency intent, since internal documents authored by agency staff or individual Commissioners "cannot be considered as an official expression of the will and intent of the Commission." The "great bulk of the documents requested * * * are not 'Commission-authored' but rather * * * consist with few exceptions, of memoranda among individual Commissioners, their legal assistants and Commission staff." Consequently, the court concluded that such documents could not be relied upon as indicators of agency intent.

At best, the documents indicate that there was a practice of notification, at the discretion of the staff, where such notification would not impede the investigation. There is no indication that the practice was regularly followed or that any such policy was ever established by the Commission. Given the novel nature of this cause, we see no procedural infirmity, Constitutional or statutory, in the decision of the staff not to inform the prospective defendants that they were under investigation or to solicit their arguments as to why they should not be sued. Mandating such a procedure would seriously burden the Commission's enforcement procedure, already characterized by adequate due process safeguards. See 15 U.S.C. § 78u (1970). Had the Commission intended to establish a procedural rule which, if breached, would require dismissal of a complaint, we think it would have said so in language far clearer and more direct than that found in the 1970 Memorandum.

For these reasons, we affirm the action of the district court in striking the Fifteenth Defense.

McGOWAN, CIRCUIT JUDGE, dissenting: By reference to what is in the public record of this case, I can conclude only that in 1970 the Commission directed its staff to transmit with all recommendations for the institution of formal proceedings the arguments of the prospective respondents against such action. It is obvious that that policy could not be effectuated without notification being given to persons who were the targets of the staff investigations. That policy, although never publicly revealed, was in effect at the times relevant to this appeal, and on its face does not admit of any exceptions. We know also, however, that in a public release issued in 1972 the Commission characterized the practice it had been following as one permitting persons involved in a staff investigation, *on their request,* to submit to the Commission statements before staff recommendations for formal proceedings would be acted upon; and in that context the Commission stated the obviously correlative proposition that the staff, "in its discretion, may" take the necessary step of notifying investigation targets of the nature of the violations involved and the time available to them for making a submission to the Commission.

But whether the staff did or did not have discretion at the times here in issue does not seem to me determinative of this appeal. For even if discretion existed *vis-a-vis* the Commission, in relation to those under investigation, problems of procedural fair play swarm around the question of how and why that discretion is exercised in a particular case. That is especially true when, as here, professional advisers of clients under investigation are the unknowing targets. And it is not only the interests of those advisers that are affected adversely but that of the clients themselves. Is it seriously to be supposed that the lawyers here involved, if they had been apprised of their target status, would not have immediately withdrawn as counsel for the clients and, indeed, retained counsel for themselves?

I am not prepared to say that the defense in issue should have been stricken by the district court without more exploration on the record of both the authority and the justifications for the staff's proceeding as it did in this case. That exploration can, in my judgment, best be achieved by directing the reinstatement of the defense in question at the present stage of the litigation, and of ventilating its merits or demerits at trial or, at the least, after further opportunity for discovery as to exactly what the Commission's policy was and the standards by which it was being applied generally as well as in this particular instance. As a start in this direction, the district court should make available to defendants the materials examined by it *in camera.*

SECURITIES AND EXCHANGE COMMISSION v. DRESSER INDUSTRIES, INC.

United States Court of Appeals, District of Columbia Circuit, 1980.
202 U.S.App.D.C. 345, 628 F.2d 1368, cert. denied 449 U.S. 993 (1981).

Before WRIGHT, CHIEF JUDGE, and MCGOWAN, TAMM, ROBINSON, MACKINNON, ROBB, WILKEY, WALD, MIKVA, and EDWARDS, CIRCUIT JUDGES.

WRIGHT, CHIEF JUDGE: Dresser Industries, Inc. (Dresser) appeals from a decision of the District Court requiring obedience to a subpoena *duces tecum* issued by the Securities and Exchange Commission (SEC) on April 21, 1978, and denying Dresser's motion to quash the subpoena. The subpoena was issued in connection with an SEC investigation into Dresser's use of corporate funds to make what are euphemistically called "questionable foreign payments," and into the adequacy of Dresser's disclosures of such payments under the securities laws.

The principal issue facing this *en banc* court is whether Dresser is entitled to special protection against this SEC subpoena because of a parallel investigation into the same questionable foreign payments now being conducted by a federal grand jury under the guidance of the United States Department of Justice (Justice). Dresser argues principally that the SEC subpoena abuses the civil discovery process of the SEC for the purpose of criminal discovery and infringes the role of the grand jury in independently investigating allegations of criminal wrongdoing. On November 19, 1979 a panel of this court issued a decision affirming the District Court but, with Judge Robb dissenting, attaching a condition prohibiting the SEC from providing Justice with the information received from Dresser under this subpoena. Because of the importance of this issue to enforcement of the regulatory laws of the United States, this court voted to vacate the panel opinions and rehear the case *en banc.*

I. BACKGROUND

A. *Origin of the Investigations*

Illegal and questionable corporate payments surfaced as a major public problem in late 1973, when several major scandals implicated prominent American corporations in improper use of corporate funds to influence government officials in the United States and foreign countries. The exposure of these activities disrupted public faith in the integrity of our political system and eroded international trust in the legitimacy of American corporate operations abroad.[3] SEC investigation revealed that many corporate officials were falsifying financial records to shield questionable

---

3. The Senate Committee on Banking, Housing, and Urban Affairs reported in May 1977:

Recent investigations by the SEC have revealed corrupt foreign payments by over 300 U.S. companies involving hun-

foreign and domestic payments from exposure to the public and even, in many cases, to corporate directors and accountants. Since the completeness and accuracy of corporate financial reporting is the cornerstone of federal regulation of the securities markets, such falsification became a matter of grave concern to the SEC.[4]

Beginning in the spring of 1974 the SEC brought a series of injunctive actions against certain American corporations. It obtained consent decrees prohibiting future violations of the securities laws and establishing internal corporate procedures for investigation, disclosure, and prevention of illegal corporate payments. However, the problem of questionable foreign payments proved so widespread that the SEC devised a "Voluntary Disclosure Program" to encourage corporations to conduct investigations of their past conduct and make appropriate disclosures without direct SEC coercion. Participation in the Voluntary Disclosure Program would not insulate a corporation from an SEC enforcement action, but the Commission would be less likely to exercise its discretion to initiate enforcement actions against participants. The most important elements of the Voluntary Disclosure Program were (1) an independent committee of the corporation would conduct a thorough investigation into questionable foreign and domestic payments made by the corporation; (2) the committee would disclose the results of this investigation to the board of directors in full; (3) the corporation would disclose the substance of the report to the public and the SEC on Form 8–K; and (4) the corporation would issue a policy statement prohibiting future questionable and illegal payments and maintenance of false or incomplete records in connection with them. Except in "egregious cases" the SEC would not require that public disclosures include specific names, dates and places. Rather, the disclosure might be "generic" in form. Thus companies participating in the Voluntary Disclosure Program would ordinarily be spared the consequences to their employees, property, and business that might result from public disclosure of specific instances of foreign bribery or kickbacks. However, companies participating in the Voluntary Disclosure Program had to agree to grant SEC requests for access to the final report and to the unexpurgated underlying documentations.

B. *The Dresser Investigations*

On January 27, 1976 an attorney and other representatives of Dresser met with members of the SEC staff to discuss a proposed filing. At the meeting Dresser agreed to conduct an internal inquiry into questionable foreign payments, in accordance with the terms of the Voluntary Disclo-

---

dreds of millions of dollars. These revelations have had severe adverse effects. Foreign governments friendly to the United States in Japan, Italy, and the Netherlands have come under intense pressure from their own people. The image of American democracy abroad has been tarnished. Confidence in the financial integrity of our corporations has been impaired. The efficient functioning of our capital markets has been hampered.

S.Rep. No. 114, 95th Cong., 1st Sess. 3 (1977).

4. The history of the SEC's involvement with the questionable and illegal foreign payments is recounted briefly in Report of the Securities and Exchange Commission on Questionable and Illegal Corporate Payments and Practices, submitted to the Senate Committee on Banking, Housing, and Urban Affairs, 94th Cong., 2d Sess. (Comm. Print 1976), reprinted in CCH Federal Securities Law Reports, No. 642 (May 19, 1976) (hereinafter cited as Report).

sure Program. The next day Dresser submitted a Form 8–K describing, in generic terms, one questionable foreign payment. Joint Appendix (JA) 100–102. On November 11, 1976 Dresser filed a second Form 8–K reporting the results of the internal investigation. JA 103–108. On February 10, 1977 the company supplemented this report with a third Form 8–K concerning a questionable payment not reported in the earlier reports. JA 109–113. The reports concerned Dresser's foreign activities after November 1, 1973. All disclosures were in generic, not specific, terms.

As part of its general monitoring program the SEC staff requested access to the documents underlying Dresser's report. On July 15, 1977 Dresser refused to grant such access. The company argued that allowing the staff to make notes or copies might subject its documents to public disclosure through the Freedom of Information Act. Dresser stated that such disclosure could endanger certain of its employees working abroad. During the ensuing discussions with the staff Dresser attempted to impose conditions of confidentiality upon any SEC examination of its documents, but the staff did not agree. Instead, it issued a recommendation to the Commission for a formal order of investigation in the Dresser case.

* * *

Meanwhile, the Department of Justice had established a task force on transnational payments to investigate possible criminal violations arising from illegal foreign payments. Two SEC attorneys participated in the task force. In the summer of 1977 the Justice task force requested access to SEC files on the approximately 400 companies, including Dresser, that had participated in the Voluntary Disclosure Program. Pursuant to Commission authorization the SEC staff transmitted all such files to the Justice task force in August 1977. After its preliminary investigation of the Form 8–K's submitted by Dresser under the Voluntary Disclosure Program, Justice presented Dresser's case to a grand jury in the District of Columbia on January 25, 1978.

Before any summons or subpoena had issued in either the SEC or the grand jury investigation, Dresser filed suit in the Southern District of Texas against the SEC and Justice to enjoin any further investigation of it by either agency. While Dresser's suit was pending in the Southern District of Texas, the District of Columbia grand jury subpoenaed Dresser's documents on April 21, 1978. At roughly the same time the SEC issued a formal order of private investigation, authorizing the staff to subpoena the documents and to obtain other relevant evidence. JA 7–9 (April 11, 1978). Pursuant to that order the staff issued a subpoena *duces tecum,* returnable on May 4, 1978. JA 14–16 (April 21, 1978). This subpoena covered substantially the same documents and materials subpoenaed by the grand jury, and more. Dresser did not respond to the subpoena.

* * *

II. General Principles

A. *Parallel Investigations*

The civil and regulatory laws of the United States frequently overlap with the criminal laws, creating the possibility of parallel civil and criminal proceedings, either successive or simultaneous.[19] In the absence of substantial prejudice to the rights of the parties involved, such parallel proceedings are unobjectionable under our jurisprudence. As long ago as 1912 the Supreme Court recognized that under one statutory scheme—that of the Sherman Act—a transaction or course of conduct could give rise to both criminal proceedings and civil suits. Standard Sanitary Manufacturing Co. v. United States, 226 U.S. 20, 52 (1912). The Court held that the government could initiate such proceedings either "simultaneously or successively," with discretion in the courts to prevent injury in particular cases. * * *

  * * *

The Constitution, therefore, does not ordinarily require a stay of civil proceedings pending the outcome of criminal proceedings. See Baxter v. Palmigiano, 425 U.S. 308 (1976); DeVita v. Sills, 422 F.2d 1172, 1181 (3d Cir.1970). Nevertheless, a court may decide in its discretion to stay civil proceedings, postpone civil discovery, or impose protective orders and conditions "when the interests of justice seem[ ] to require such action, sometimes at the request of the prosecution, * * * sometimes at the request of the defense[.]" United States v. Kordel, supra, 397 U.S. at 12 n. 27 (citations omitted); see Horne Brothers, Inc. v. Laird, 463 F.2d 1268, 1271–1272 (D.C.Cir.1972). The court must make such determinations in the light of the particular circumstances of the case.

Other than where there is specific evidence of agency bad faith or malicious governmental tactics, the strongest case for deferring civil proceedings until after completion of criminal proceedings is where a party under indictment for a serious offense is required to defend a civil or administrative action involving the same matter. The noncriminal proceeding, if not deferred, might undermine the party's Fifth Amendment privilege against self-incrimination, expand rights of criminal discovery beyond the limits of Federal Rule of Criminal Procedure 16(b), expose the basis of the defense to the prosecution in advance of criminal trial, or otherwise prejudice the case. If delay of the noncriminal proceeding would not seriously injure the public interest, a court may be justified in deferring it. See, e.g., United States v. Henry, 491 F.2d 702 (6th Cir.1974); Texaco, Inc. v. Borda, 383 F.2d 607, 608–609 (3d Cir.1967); Silver v. McCamey, 221 F.2d 873, 874–875 (D.C.Cir.1955). * * * In some such cases, however, the courts may adequately protect the government and the private party by merely deferring civil discovery or entering an appropriate protective order. Gordon v. FDIC, 427 F.2d 578, 580–581 (D.C.Cir.1970). The case at bar is a far weaker one for staying the administrative investigation. No indictment has been returned; no Fifth Amendment privilege is threatened; Rule 16(b) has not come into effect and the SEC subpoena does not require Dresser to reveal the basis for its defense.

B. *SEC Investigations*

The case at bar concerns enforcement of the securities laws of the United States, especially the Securities Act of 1933 ('33 Act) and the Securities Exchange Act of 1934 ('34 Act). These statutes explicitly empower the SEC to investigate possible infractions of the securities laws with a

---

19. See generally, Note, Concurrent Civil and Criminal Proceedings, 67 Colum. L.Rev. 1277 (1967).

view to both civil and criminal enforcement, and to transmit the fruits of its investigations to Justice in the event of potential criminal proceedings. The '34 Act provides in relevant part: "The Commission may, in its discretion, make such investigations as it deems necessary to determine whether any person has violated, is violating, or is about to violate any provision of this chapter[.]" Section 21(a) of the '34 Act (1976). This investigative authority includes the power to administer oaths and affirmations, subpoena witnesses, take evidence, and require production of any books, papers, correspondence, memoranda, or other records which the SEC deems relevant or material. Id., Section 21(b). If it determines that a person "is engaged or is about to engage in acts or practices constituting a violation" of the Act, the SEC may bring an action in federal district court to enjoin such acts or practices. Id., Section 21(d). Under the same subsection of the '34 Act the SEC may "transmit such evidence as may be available concerning such acts or practices * * * to the Attorney General, who may, in his discretion, institute the necessary criminal proceedings under this chapter." Id. The '33 Act is to similar effect. See Sections 19(b), 20(a), (b) of the '33 Act.

Effective enforcement of the securities laws requires that the SEC and Justice be able to investigate possible violations simultaneously. Dissemination of false or misleading information by companies to members of the investing public may distort the efficient workings of the securities markets and injure investors who rely on the accuracy and completeness of the company's public disclosures. If the SEC suspects that a company has violated the securities laws, it must be able to respond quickly: it must be able to obtain relevant information concerning the alleged violation and to seek prompt judicial redress if necessary. Similarly, Justice must act quickly if it suspects that the laws have been broken. Grand jury investigations take time, as do criminal prosecutions. If Justice moves too slowly the statute of limitations may run, witnesses may die or move away, memories may fade, or enforcement resources may be diverted. See United States v. Fields, 592 F.2d 638, 646 (2d Cir.1978), cert. denied 442 U.S. 917 (1979). The SEC cannot always wait for Justice to complete the criminal proceedings if it is to obtain the necessary prompt civil remedy; neither can Justice always await the conclusion of the civil proceeding without endangering its criminal case. Thus, we should not block parallel investigations by these agencies in the absence of "special circumstances" in which the nature of the proceedings demonstrably prejudices substantial rights of the investigated party or of the government. See United States v. Kordel, supra, 397 U.S. at 11–13.

     * * *

In essence, Dresser has launched this attack on the parallel SEC and Justice proceedings in order to obtain protection against the bare SEC proceeding, which it fears will result in public disclosure of sensitive corporate documents. The prejudice Dresser claims it will suffer from the parallel nature of the proceedings is speculative and undefined—if indeed Dresser would suffer any prejudice from it at all. Any entitlement to confidential treatment of its documents must arise under the laws pertaining to the SEC; the fortuity of a parallel grand jury investigation cannot expand Dresser's rights in this SEC enforcement action. Thus Dresser's invocation of *LaSalle* [United States v. LaSalle National Bank, 437 U.S. 298 (1978)] can avail the company nothing.

IV. COOPERATION BETWEEN SEC AND JUSTICE

In its initial decision in this case a panel of this court ruled that "the broad prophylactic rule enunciated in *LaSalle* is inappropriate where the SEC and the Justice Department are simultaneously pursuing civil and criminal investigations." Slip opinion at 18. The panel therefore affirmed the District Court and ordered enforcement of the SEC subpoena. Out of a concern that the SEC subpoena might somehow "subvert the limitations of criminal discovery," id., however, the panel, with one judge dissenting, modified the terms of the subpoena enforcement order. It required that "once the Justice Department initiates criminal proceedings by means of a grand jury, the SEC may not provide the Justice Department with the fruits of the Commission's civil discovery gathered after the decision to prosecute." Id. at 22. We affirm the judgment of the District Court and reject the panel's modification.

First, we note that no party to this case had suggested or requested a modification such as that imposed by the panel majority, either in the District Court or in this court. * * *

Second, we note that there is no support for the panel's modification in either the relevant statutes or legislative history. Both the '33 Act and the '34 Act—and other statutes related to securities law enforcement as well—expressly authorize the SEC to "transmit such evidence as may be available * * * to the Attorney General, who may, in his discretion, institute the necessary criminal proceedings under this subchapter." Section 20(b) of the '33 Act; Section 21(d) of the '34 Act. The statutes impose no limitation on when this transmittal may occur. The parties have not cited any portions of the legislative histories of these Acts relevant to this question, nor have we found any. But the SEC and Justice find considerable support for their interpretation in the legislative history of the Foreign Corrupt Practices Act of 1977, 91 Stat. 1494, Title I, 15 U.S.C. §§ 78a, 78m, 78dd–1, 78dd–2, 78ff (Supp. I 1977).

* * *

Congress manifestly did not intend that the SEC be forbidden to share information with Justice at this stage of the investigation. Under the panel majority's theory of the case the SEC would be foreclosed from sharing the fruits of its investigation with Justice as soon as Justice begins its own investigation through a grand jury. Only by waiting until the close of the SEC proceeding before initiating its own grand jury investigation could Justice obtain access to the evidence procured by the SEC. In view of Congress' concern that the agencies share information "at the earliest stage of any investigation in order to insure that the evidence needed for a criminal prosecution does not become stale," S.Rep. No. 114, supra, at 12, and that the agencies avoid "a costly duplication of effort," H.R.Rep. No. 640, supra, at 9, it would be unreasonable to prevent a sharing of information at this point in the investigation.

Third, we note that there is little or no judicial precedent for the panel's modification. * * *

* * *

Finally, we note that the panel's modification would serve no compelling purpose, and might interfere with enforcement of the securities laws by the SEC and Justice. As the Second Circuit has said, the procedure permitting the SEC to communicate with Justice during the preliminary stages of an investigation has "significant advantages." United States v. Fields, supra, 592 F.2d at 646.

Allowing early participation in the case by the United States Attorney minimizes statute of limitations problems. The more time a United States Attorney has, the easier it is for him to become familiar with the complex facts of a securities fraud case, to prepare the case, and to present it to a grand jury before expiration of the applicable statute of limitations. Earlier initiation of criminal proceedings moreover is consistent with a defendant's right to a speedy trial. * * *

Id. The panel's modification would "interfere with this commendable example of inter-agency cooperation," id., to the detriment of securities law enforcement and in contravention of the will of Congress. On the other side of the balance, the panel's concern for preserving the limitations on criminal discovery is largely irrelevant at this stage of the proceedings, as Dresser agrees. Thus this would be an inappropriate situation to impose a "prophylactic" rule against cooperation between the agencies. We believe the courts can prevent any injustice that may arise in the particular circumstances of parallel investigations in the future. We decline to adopt the position of the panel majority.

* * *

The judgments of the District Court are Affirmed.

Concurring Opinion of CIRCUIT JUDGE EDWARDS: I concur in the opinion of the court in this case. I wish to point out, however, that I do not read the court's opinion as expressing any view as to the proper outcome in a case of this sort *once an indictment has issued.* * * * Once an indictment has issued, the policy interest expressed in United States v. LaSalle National Bank, 437 U.S. 298, 312 (1978), concerning the impermissibility of broadening the scope of criminal discovery through the summons authority of an agency, may come into play. I express no opinion as to whether or not the summons authority of a government agency may continue once an indictment has been issued or, if it may, whether protective conditions need be placed on the exercise of that power. These issues raise questions which are not presented here. The resolution of these questions, therefore, must await another day.

SEC INVESTIGATIONS

As indicated in the *Wheeling-Pittsburgh* case, a Commission investigation into a possible violation of the federal securities laws is typically divided into two stages. The first is merely an informal inquiry by the SEC staff into allegations of misconduct or as a result of information coming to the staff through many different sources. At this stage, while the staff investigators may interview prospective witnesses or even prospective defendants, no compulsory process is available, and no one is required to talk to the investigators if he does not wish to do so. In order to progress to the second stage of the investigation, the Commission staff must present to the Commission itself a request for an order instituting a "formal investigation," based upon a showing that there is a "likelihood" that a violation of the securities laws has taken place.

The order of investigation authorizes the staff to issue subpoenas and subpoenas *duces tecum,* and witnesses are examined under oath, with a court reporter present to make a transcript of the testimony. There is no punishment provided for ignoring such a subpoena. If a witness refuses to appear or refuses to answer certain questions, the only recourse of the Commission is to initiate a proceeding in court to enforce compliance with the subpoena as was done in the *Wheeling-Pittsburgh* case. Such contumacy is rarely advisable, since it will infuriate the SEC staff, and they are likely to make life as unpleasant as possible to the person involved during the subsequent course of the proceeding. It may even result in that person being named as a defendant in an injunction action or in a criminal reference to the Justice Department, which might not have occurred if he had been cooperative.

The Commission, and in particular its Enforcement Division under its former director Stanley Sporkin, has established an enviable reputation over many years as one of the most efficient and incorruptible of all of the federal governmental agencies. While there have been many complaints about the vigor with which the Enforcement Division pursued certain investigations and about some of the tactics which it has used, few have ever questioned its integrity. The *Wheeling-Pittsburgh* case must be regarded as at most an isolated aberration in that regard.

Right to Counsel A person who is subpoenaed to testify in a formal investigation has the right to be accompanied and represented by counsel during his testimony. The persons who are being investigated, or who think that they may be "targets" of the investigation, have no right, however, to be represented by counsel during the taking of the testimony of other witnesses. In Securities and Exchange Commission v. Meek,[1] the Tenth Circuit upheld the right of the Commission to refuse to permit such a person to have counsel present at the taking of all of the testimony in the investigation, which was likened to a grand jury investigation where the accused has no right to counsel. And in Securities and Exchange Commission v. Jerry T. O'Brien, Inc.[2] the Supreme Court held that the Commission is not required to notify the target of a non-public investigation regarding the issuance of subpoenas to other witnesses in connection with the investigation, reversing a decision by the Ninth Circuit.

The Commission has always insisted upon the secrecy of its investigations, even after the formal order of investigation has been issued, and the examining attorney on the Commission staff typically warns a witness that he is not permitted to reveal to anyone the testimony that he has given; but there does not appear to be any legal basis upon which the Commission could enforce such a prohibition.[3] The Commission at one time went so far as to take the position that the same attorney could not represent two or more persons who were being called as witnesses, and in particular could not represent a corporation under investigation and its officers and directors being interrogated, since this would permit the attorney to hear the testimony of all of the witnesses who were his clients and to advise each of them what the others had said. The Court of Appeals for the District of Columbia in Securities and Exchange Commission v.

---

1. CCH Fed.Sec.Law Rptr. ¶ 97,323 (10th Cir.1980).

2. 467 U.S. 735 (1984).

3. The secrecy of grand jury proceedings is provided for in Rule 6(e), Federal Rules of Criminal Procedure. There is no similar statutory provision relating to an SEC investigation, although the right of an agency to refuse to release the information acquired in the course of an investigation is recognized in the Freedom of Information Act, subject to certain qualifications. 5 U.S.C. § 552(b)(7).

Csapo[4] held that the Commission had no authority to enforce this so-called "segregation rule", and it no longer makes any serious attempt to impose that restriction.[5] A witness testifying in such an investigation has the right to obtain a copy of the transcript of his own testimony, but the SEC will not ordinarily release such evidence to other persons.[6] A statutory exception prevents the obtaining of such material from the SEC under the Freedom of Information Act.[7]

Wells Submissions. The practice of the Commission (referred to in the *National Student Marketing* case) of normally giving persons who are targeted as potential defendants in an injunction action the opportunity to make a formal presentation to the Commission itself at the time the staff recommends an injunction action arose out of the recommendation in 1972 of an advisory committee known as the Wells Committee, after its chairman.[8] The brief which is thus submitted to the Commission is therefore known as a "Wells submission." Although the Advisory Committee recommended that this practice be made mandatory in all cases by a formal rule, the Commission never adopted that recommendation, although it earlier had given the internal direction to its staff which is quoted in that case.[9]

The persons who are initially "targeted" as potential defendants in the action are named in the order of investigation as those whose activities likely violated the securities laws, but the staff is not limited to those named persons when it makes a recommendation to the Commission as to the institution of an injunction action. It may add other defendants during the course of its investigation. White and Case never knew that it was going to be named as a defendant in the *National Student Marketing* action until the complaint was filed or shortly before that, and was never given an opportunity to make any presentation to the Commission itself as to why it should not be sued. Nevertheless, the staff will normally inform a person that it intends to make a recommendation to the Commission that he be included as a defendant and of his opportunity to make a "Wells submission" if he so desires. This is an opportunity which should not normally be passed up. In many instances, as a result of such submissions, the Commission has refused to include a particular peripheral defendant in the lawsuit, despite the staff recommendation that he be named.

Parallel Proceedings. In a sense, all SEC investigations are "parallel proceedings" from the time of their initiation, since the end result may be either a recommendation to the Commission that it authorize the filing of an injunction action against the alleged violators of the federal securities laws or a reference to the Justice Department recommending that it initiate a criminal prosecution by bringing the matter before a federal grand jury.[10] The examining official of

---

4. 174 U.S.App.D.C. 339, 533 F.2d 7 (1976).

5. This does not mean, of course, that an attorney may not have ethical problems in representing more than one client if their interests conflict. See Trone v. Smith, 621 F.2d 994 (9th Cir.1980); Trone v. Mudge, Rose, Guthrie & Alexander, CCH Fed.Sec.Law Rptr. ¶ 96,799 (S.D.Cal.1978).

6. There is a question regarding the ability of a third party in a lawsuit to subpoena the transcript from the witness once it has been obtained by him. See Peloso, Discovery of SEC Transcripts, 10 Rev.Sec.Reg. 829 (1977).

7. 5 U.S.C. § 552(b)(7).

8. Report of the Securities and Exchange Commission's Advisory Committee on Enforcement Policies and Practices (June 1, 1972), reprinted in Cohen, Demmler and Wells, Changes in Securities Law Enforcement and Litigation 7–87 (1972), summarized in CCH Fed.Sec.Law Rptr. ¶ 79,266 (June 29, 1972).

9. The Commission publicly announced this policy, although not mandatory in all cases, in Sec.Exch.Act Rel. No. 9796, CCH Fed.Sec.Law Rptr. ¶ 97,010 (Sept. 27, 1972).

10. Securities Exchange Act, § 21(d).

the SEC staff routinely gives a type of "Miranda warning" to the witnesses who are summoned to testify, advising them that the investigation possibly may result in criminal prosecution of some persons and advising them of their rights. The witness, of course, has a right to refuse to testify on the basis that his answers might tend to incriminate him; and in a case where it appears that he will probably be prosecuted anyway, this sometimes might be the wisest course of action. In most instances, however, it is fairly apparent that, if any action is taken by the Commission, it will only take the form of an injunction action. In that situation, a target of the investigation is not likely to do himself any good by "taking the Fifth Amendment" since he will eventually have to testify anyway in order to have any hope of defeating the injunction action. But the possibility of a criminal proceeding should never be lost sight of by an attorney representing a person in that position.[11]

More narrowly, the phrase "parallel proceedings" refers to a situation where the SEC investigation is continuing at the same time that the Justice Department is conducting a grand jury investigation with respect to the same matter, either as a result of a reference from the SEC or as a result of its own independent investigation of the same conduct. In Donaldson v. United States [12] and United States v. LaSalle National Bank,[13] the United States Supreme Court held that a summons issued by the Internal Revenue Service after a recommendation for prosecution had been made to the Department of Justice would not be enforced. The court said in the LaSalle National Bank case that "Nothing in § 7602 [of the Internal Revenue Code] or its legislative history suggests that Congress intended the summons authority to broaden the Justice Department's right of criminal litigation discovery or to infringe on the role of the grand jury as a principal tool of criminal accusation." [14] In the Dresser Industries case, however, the Circuit Court for the District of Columbia distinguishes those cases on the ground that different statutory provisions were involved and holds that an SEC subpoena will be enforced after such a reference has been made to the Department of Justice and a grand jury investigation actually commenced. Is there any sound policy basis for this difference in result with respect to investigations conducted by the Internal Revenue Service on the one hand and by the Securities and Exchange Commission on the other?

Section 21(a) Reports. Section 21(a) of the 1934 Act provides, in addition to authorizing the Commission to conduct investigations regarding violations of the statute and the rules and regulations thereunder, that it is authorized "in its discretion, to publish information concerning any such violations." In addition, Section 15(c)(4) of the 1934 Act provides that the Commission may "publish its findings" relating to violations of the provisions of Sections 12, 13, 14 and 15(d) and order any person subject thereto to comply with such provision, but only after notice and opportunity for a hearing. In recent years, the Commission has developed the practice of issuing reports under Section 21(a) which, in effect, constitute adjudications of a violation or probable violation of some provision of the securities laws (not limited to Sections 12, 13 and 15(d) of the 1934 Act) without any formal administrative proceeding and with respect to persons (such as directors of corporations) over whom the Commission then had no administrative jurisdiction to impose any disciplinary action.

---

11. In United States v. Fields, 592 F.2d 638 (2d Cir.1978), cert. denied 442 U.S. 917 (1979), the court refused to dismiss an indictment obtained against the defendant after his attorneys had been led to believe by SEC officials, by conduct which Judge Mansfield called "deceitful and duplici-

tous", that their client's consent to a civil injunction would avoid a criminal reference (which was nevertheless made).

12. 400 U.S. 517 (1971).

13. 437 U.S. 298 (1978).

14. 437 U.S. at 312 (1978).

In the 1984 amendments to the 1934 Act, the SEC secured an amendment to Section 15(c)(4) which added Section 14 (the proxy regulations) to the sections specified in that section and added as persons to whom the Commission may issue an order to comply with the referenced sections "any person [for example, the issuer's lawyer?] who was a cause of the failure to comply due to an act or omission the person knew or should have known would contribute [for example, by issuing in good faith an opinion that a particular filing was not required?] to the failure to comply." There has been some controversy between the securities bar and the staff of the Commission regarding the circumstances under which this particular provision was inserted in the amendatory bill and its exact effect. One thing is certain, however, and that is that the amendment doesn't authorize the SEC to issue such an order to "any person" or to "publish its findings" except after "notice and opportunity for a hearing."

In addition, pursuant to the authority granted in Section 21(a) for the Commission to "require or permit any person to file with it a statement in writing * * * as to all the facts and circumstances concerning the matter to be investigated," the Commission has negotiated with such persons the filing of written statements which amount to public confessions and which frequently contain "undertakings" as to certain remedial action which the sinner agrees to implement, as the price of the Commissioner's not instituting any formal investigation or any injunctive action.

During the time that Commissioner Karmel was on the Commission, she dissented in a number of instances from these actions[15] and asserted that they amounted, in effect, to the creation of a new form of administrative remedy for which there was no statutory basis. In In re Spartek, Inc.[16] Commissioner Karmel stated:

"I object to the use of Section 21(a) as an alternative administrative remedy against persons who allegedly violate the securities laws. In particular, it should not be used to take administrative action against persons not subject to the Commission's jurisdiction under Section 15 of the Exchange Act. I object even more strenuously to the use of Section 21(a) as an enforcement vehicle to publicize facts which do not constitute violations of the securities laws. The Commission has express statutory provisions under which it must proceed to determine whether violations have occurred and what sanctions should be imposed. Once those findings are made, the Commission then may publish information about these violations under Section 21(a) for the purposes enumerated therein. Using Section 21(a) instead of invoking express statutory procedures I believe is improper.

"The Commission could have instituted an injunctive action based on the facts set forth in the opinion of the majority. If the public interest were not sufficient to warrant such action, the matter could have been resolved informally by the filing of adequate definitive proxy materials by Spartek. * * * I recognize there is a strong public policy which favors both the settlement of cases and the utilization of creative procedures by a regulatory agency to fulfill a statutory mandate. Nevertheless, I do not believe that prosecutorial discretion should be exercised by choosing an administrative course not set forth by statute.

---

15. In re Spartek, Inc., Sec.Exch.Act Rel. No. 15567, CCH Fed.Sec.Law Rptr. ¶ 81,961 (1979); In re Compass Investment Group, Sec.Exch.Act Rel. No. 16343, CCH Fed.Sec.Law Rptr. ¶ 82,352 (1979); In re Lifton and Weingrow, Sec.Exch.Act Rel. No. 15665, CCH Fed.Sec.Law Rptr. ¶ 82,015 (1979); In re Vance, Sanders & Co., Sec. Exch.Act Rel. No. 15746, CCH Fed.Sec.Law Rptr. ¶ 82,058 (1979).

16. Supra, note 15.

"If the Commission does not have adequate remedies for handling cases like this under the present law, it should request further authority from the Congress. The implication of new remedies by a government agency is not an appropriate way to vindicate or develop the law."

On March 21, 1979, the Commission issued a release asserting its intention to continue with both of these practices "in appropriate instances." [17]

See Steinberg and Ferrara, Securities Practice: Federal and State Enforcement (1987); Sporkin and Jakoby, SEC Investigations, 18 Rev. of Sec. & Comm. Reg. 45 (1985); Shapiro, Wayward Capitalists (1984); Mathews, Defensive Corporate Tactics for Dealing with SEC Investigations: The Role of Outside Counsel, 61 N.C.L.Rev. 483 (1983); Rowe, Handling an SEC Investigation (P.L.I. 1980); Block and Pickholz, The Internal Corporate Investigation (P.L.I.1980); Mathews, Negotiating SEC Consent Decrees: Targets & Tactics for Settling Civil Injunctive Actions (1979); Mathews, SEC Enforcement and White Collar Crimes (1979); Jacobs, Judicial and Administrative Remedies available to the SEC for Breaches of Rule 10b–5, 53 St. John's L.Rev. 397 (1979); Winter, Representing Witnesses in SEC Formal Investigations, 5 Litigation 24 (1979); Block and Barton, Securities Litigation—Section 21(a): A New Enforcement Tool, 7 Sec.Reg.L.J. 265 (1979); Hazen, Administrative Enforcement, 31 Hastings L.J. 427 (1979); Mathews, A.L.I. Proposed Federal Securities Code: Part XV—Administration and Enforcement, 30 Vand.L.Rev. 465 (1977); Merrifield, SEC Investigations, 34 Bus.Law. 1583 (1977); Mathews, Securities Litigation Under the Federal Securities Laws (P.L.I.1977); Merrifield, Negotiating and Settling Enforcement Actions Under the Securities Laws (P.L.I.1976); Mathews, Enforcement and Litigation Under the Federal Securities Laws (P.L.I.1975).

STEADMAN v. SECURITIES AND EXCHANGE COMMISSION

Supreme Court of the United States, 1981.
450 U.S. 91, 101 S.Ct. 999, 67 L.Ed.2d 69.

JUSTICE BRENNAN delivered the opinion of the Court.

In administrative proceedings, the Securities and Exchange Commission applies a preponderance of the evidence standard of proof in determining whether the antifraud provisions of the federal securities laws have been violated. The question presented is whether such violations must be proved by clear and convincing evidence rather than by a preponderance of the evidence.

I

In June 1971, the Commission initiated a disciplinary proceeding against petitioner and certain of his wholly-owned companies. The proceeding against petitioner was brought pursuant to § 9(b) of the Investment Company Act of 1940 and § 203(f) of the Investment Advisers Act of 1940. The Commission alleged that petitioner had violated numerous provisions of the federal securities laws in his management of several mutual funds registered under the Investment Company Act.

17. Sec.Exch.Act Rel. No. 15664, CCH Fed.Sec.Law Rptr. ¶ 82,014 (1979) (Commissioner Karmel dissenting).

After a lengthy evidentiary hearing before an administrative law judge and review by the Commission in which the preponderance of the evidence standard was employed, the Commission held that between December of 1965 and June of 1972, petitioner had violated antifraud, reporting, conflict of interest, and proxy provisions of the federal securities laws. Accordingly, it entered an order permanently barring petitioner from associating with any investment adviser or affiliating with any registered investment company, and suspending him for 1 year from associating with any broker or dealer in securities.[8]

Petitioner sought review of the Commission's order in the United States Court of Appeals for the Fifth Circuit on a number of grounds, only one of which is relevant for our purposes. Petitioner challenged the Commission's use of the preponderance of the evidence standard of proof in determining whether he had violated antifraud provisions of the securities laws. He contended that, because of the potentially severe sanctions that the Commission was empowered to impose and because of the circumstantial and inferential nature of the evidence that might be used to prove intent to defraud, the Commission was required to weigh the evidence against a clear and convincing standard of proof. The Court of Appeals rejected petitioner's argument, holding that in a disciplinary proceeding before the Commission violations of the antifraud provisions of the securities laws may be established by a preponderance of the evidence. 603 F.2d 1126, 1143 (CA5 1979). See n. 8, supra. Because this was contrary to the position taken by the United States Court of Appeals for the District of Columbia, see Whitney v. Securities and Exchange Commission, 196 U.S.App.D.C. 12, 604 F.2d 676 (1979); Collins Securities Corp. v. Securities and Exchange Commission, 183 U.S.App.D.C. 301, 562 F.2d 820 (1977), we granted certiorari to resolve the conflict. 446 U.S. 917 (1980). We affirm.

II

Where Congress has not prescribed the degree of proof which must be adduced by the proponent of a rule or order to carry its burden of persuasion in an administrative proceeding, this Court has felt at liberty to prescribe the standard, for "[i]t is the kind of question which has traditionally been left to the judiciary to resolve." Woodby v. Immigration and Naturalization Service, 385 U.S. 276, 284 (1966). However, where Congress has spoken, we have deferred to "the traditional powers of Congress to prescribe rules of evidence and standards of proof in the federal courts"[9] absent countervailing constitutional constraints. Vance v. Terrazas, 444 U.S. 252, 265 (1980). For Commission disciplinary proceedings initiated pursuant to * * * [§ 9(b) of the Investment Company Act of 1940 and the

---

8. Petitioner was allowed 90 days in which to sell his stock in Steadman Securities Corporation. Compliance with the Commission's order has been stayed pending completion of judicial review.

Because the Commission imposed severe sanctions on petitioner, the Court of Appeals remanded to the Commission "to articulate carefully the grounds for its decision, including an explanation of why lesser sanctions will not suffice." 603 F.2d 1126, 1143 (CA5 1979).

9. There is no reason to accord less deference to congressionally-prescribed standards of proof and rules of evidence in administrative proceedings than in federal courts. See Woodby v. Immigration and Naturalization Service, 385 U.S. 276, 284 (1966) (ascertaining first that Congress had not legislated a standard of proof for administrative deportation proceedings before determining appropriate standard).

Investment Advisers Act of 1940] we conclude that Congress has spoken, and has said that the preponderance of the evidence standard should be applied.[10]

The securities laws provide for judicial review of Commission disciplinary proceedings in the federal courts of appeals and specify the scope of such review. Because they do not indicate which standard of proof governs Commission adjudications, however, we turn to § 5 of the Administrative Procedure Act (APA), 5 U.S.C. § 554, which "applies * * * in every case of adjudication required by statute to be determined on the record after opportunity for an agency hearing," except in instances not relevant here. 5 U.S.C. § 554. Section 5(c)(2), 5 U.S.C. § 554(c)(2), makes the provisions of § 7, 5 U.S.C. § 556, applicable to adjudicatory proceedings. The answer to the question presented in this case turns therefore on the proper construction of § 7.

The search for Congressional intent begins with the language of the statute. Andrus v. Allard, 444 U.S. 51, 56 (1979); Reiter v. Sonotone Corp., 442 U.S. 330, 337 (1979); 62 Cases of Jam v. United States, 340 U.S. 593, 596 (1951). Section 7(c), 5 U.S.C. § 556(d), states in pertinent part:

> "Except as otherwise provided by statute, the proponent of a rule or order has the burden of proof. Any oral or documentary evidence may be received, but the agency as a matter of policy shall provide for the exclusion of irrelevant, immaterial, or unduly repetitious evidence. A sanction may not be imposed or rule or order issued except on consideration of the whole record or those parts thereof cited by a party and supported by and *in accordance with* the reliable, probative, and *substantial evidence.*" (Emphasis added.)

The language of the statute itself implies the enactment of a standard of proof.

By allowing sanctions to be imposed only when they are "in accordance with * * * *substantial* evidence," Congress implied that a sanction must rest on a *minimum quantity* of evidence. The word "substantial" denotes quantity. The phrase "in accordance with * * * substantial evidence" thus requires that a decision be based on a certain quantity of evidence. Petitioner's contention that the phrase "reliable, probative and substantial evidence" sets merely a standard of *quality* of evidence is, therefore, unpersuasive.[17]

---

10. Because the task of determining the appropriate standard of proof in the instant case is one of discerning Congressional intent, many of petitioner's arguments are simply inapposite. He contends, for example, that as a matter of policy, the potentially severe consequences to a respondent in a Commission proceeding involving allegations of fraud demand that his burden of risk of erroneous factfinding should be reduced by requiring the Commission to prove violations of the antifraud provisions of the securities laws by clear and convincing evidence. This argument overlooks, however, Congress' "traditional powers * * * to prescribe standards of proof * * *." Vance v.

Terrazas, 444 U.S. 252, 265 (1980). It is not for this Court to determine the wisdom of Congress' prescription.

17. Section 7(c), of course, also sets minimum quality of evidence standards. For example, the provision directing agency exclusion of "irrelevant, immaterial, or unduly repetitious evidence," and the further requirement that an agency sanction rest on "reliable" and "probative" evidence mandate that agency decision-making be premised on evidence of a certain level of quality. Thus, while the words "reliable" and "probative" may imply quality of evidence concerns, the word "substantial" implies quantity of evidence.

The phrase "in accordance with" lends further support to a construction of § 7(c) as establishing a standard of proof. Unlike § 10(e), the APA's explicit "Scope of review" provision that declares that agency action shall be held unlawful if "unsupported by substantial evidence," § 7(c) provides that an agency may issue an order only if that order is "supported by and *in accordance with* ∗ ∗ ∗ substantial evidence" (emphasis added). The additional words "in accordance with" suggest that the adjudicating agency must weigh the evidence and decide, based on the weight of the evidence, whether a disciplinary order should be issued. The language of § 7(c), therefore, requires that the agency decision must be "in accordance with" the weight of the evidence, not simply supported by enough evidence " 'to justify, if the trial were to a jury, a refusal to direct a verdict when the conclusion sought to be drawn from it is one of fact for the jury.' " Consolo v. Federal Maritime Commission, 383 U.S. 607, 620 (1966), quoting National Labor Relations Board v. Columbian Enameling & Stamping Co., 306 U.S. 292, 300 (1939). Obviously, weighing evidence has relevance only if the evidence on each side is to be measured against a standard of proof which allocates the risk of error. See Addington v. Texas, 441 U.S. 418, 423 (1979). Section 10(e), by contrast, does not permit the reviewing court to weigh the evidence, but only to determine that there is in the record " 'such relevant evidence as a reasonable mind might accept as adequate to support a conclusion,' " Consolo v. Federal Maritime Commission, supra, 383 U.S., at 620, quoting Consolidated Edison Co. v. National Labor Relations Board, 305 U.S. 197, 229 (1938). It is not surprising, therefore, in view of the entirely different purposes of § 7(c) and § 10(e), that Congress intended the words "substantial evidence" to have different meanings in context. Thus, petitioner's argument that § 7(c) merely establishes the scope of judicial review of agency orders is unavailing.

While the language of § 7(c) suggests, therefore, that Congress intended the statute to establish a standard of proof, the language of the statute is somewhat opaque concerning the precise standard of proof to be used. The legislative history, however, clearly reveals the Congress' intent. The original Senate version of § 7(c) provided that "no sanction shall be imposed ∗ ∗ ∗ except as supported by relevant, reliable, and probative evidence." S. 7, 79th Cong., 1st Sess. (1945). After the Senate passed this version, the House passed the language of the statute as it reads today, and the Senate accepted the amendment. Any doubt as to the intent of Congress is removed by the House Report, which expressly adopted a preponderance of the evidence standard:

"[W]here a party having the burden of proceeding has come forward with a prima facie and substantial case, he will prevail unless his evidence is discredited or rebutted. In any case the agency must decide 'in accordance with the evidence.' Where there is evidence pro and con, the agency must weigh it and decide *in accordance with the preponderance*. In short, these provisions require a conscientious and rational judgment on the whole record in accordance with the proofs adduced." H.R.Rep. No. 1980, 79th Cong., 2d Sess. 37 (1946) (emphasis added).

Nor is there any suggestion in the legislative history that a standard of proof higher than a preponderance of the evidence was ever contemplated, much less intended. Congress was primarily concerned with the elimination of agency decisionmaking premised on evidence which was of poor quality—irrelevant, immaterial, unreliable and nonprobative—and of insufficient quantity—less than a preponderance. See H.R.Rep. No. 1980, supra, at 36–37 and 45; S.Doc. No. 248, supra, at 320–322 and 376–378; n. 21, supra.

The language and legislative history of § 7(c) lead us to conclude, therefore, that § 7(c) was intended to establish a standard of proof and that the standard adopted is the traditional preponderance of the evidence standard.

III

Our view of Congressional intent is buttressed by the Commission's long-standing practice of imposing sanctions according to the preponderance of the evidence. As early as 1938, the Commission rejected the argument that in a proceeding to determine whether to suspend, expel or otherwise sanction a brokerage firm and its principals for, *inter alia*, manipulation of security prices in violation of § 9 of the Securities Exchange Act, a standard of proof greater than the preponderance of the evidence standard was required. In re White, 3 S.E.C. 466, 539–540 (1938). Use of the preponderance standard continued after passage of the APA, and persists today. E.g., In re Cea, 44 S.E.C. 8, 25 (1969); In re Pollisky, 43 S.E.C. 458, 459–460 (1967). The Commission's consistent practice, which is in harmony with § 7(c) and its legislative history, is persuasive authority that Congress intended that Commission disciplinary proceedings, subject to § 7 of the APA, be governed by a preponderance of the evidence standard. See Andrus v. Sierra Club, 442 U.S. 347, 358 (1979); United States v. National Association of Securities Dealers, Inc., 422 U.S. 694, 719 (1975); Skidmore v. Swift & Co., 323 U.S. 134, 140 (1944).

In Vermont Yankee Nuclear Power Corp. v. Natural Resources Defense Council, Inc., 435 U.S. 519, 524 (1978) (footnote omitted), we stated that § 4 of the APA, 5 U.S.C. § 553, established the "maximum procedural requirements which Congress was willing to have the courts impose upon agencies in conducting rulemaking procedures." In § 7(c), Congress has similarly expressed its intent that adjudicatory proceedings subject to the APA satisfy the statute where determinations are made according to the preponderance of the evidence. Congress was free to make that choice, Vance v. Terrazas, supra, 444 U.S. at 265–266, and, in the absence of countervailing constitutional considerations, the courts are not free to disturb it.

Affirmed.

JUSTICE POWELL, with whom JUSTICE STEWART joins, dissenting.

* * *

SEC ADMINISTRATIVE PROCEEDINGS

Ex Parte Proceedings. In most instances where the Commission is authorized to take administrative action against a company or person, this can be done only after notice and an opportunity for hearing given to the person who will be affected by such action; and the proceedings have to be conducted in accordance with the Administrative Procedure Act in the manner of a court trial (although not subject to all of the procedural restrictions of such a trial). However, one remedial action which the Commission is authorized to employ, the suspension of trading in a particular security, may be taken ex parte without any notice or hearing to the company involved or its shareholders, whose ability to sell their stock is for all practical purposes terminated. Section 12(k) of the 1934 Act provides that the Commission "is authorized summarily to suspend trading in any security (other than an exempted security) for a period not exceeding ten days," or to suspend all trading on any national securities exchange for a period not to exceed ninety days, although in the latter case only with the approval of the President.[1] For a period of more than forty years the Commission used this authority to effect a permanent suspension of trading (until lifted by the Commission) in the stock of a particular company, by simply routinely renewing the suspension of trading for another ten days at the end of each ten-day period. In one case the suspension of trading was continued in this fashion for thirteen years.[2]

In Securities and Exchange Commission v. Sloan[3] the United States Supreme Court held that such action by the Commission was unauthorized and illegal where the subsequent suspensions of trading were not based on any new circumstances arising after the initial suspension. Mr. Justice Brennan in his concurring opinion stated that, "the SEC's procedural implementation of its § 12(k) power mocks any conclusion other than that the SEC simply could not care whether its § 12(k) orders are justified. So far as this record shows, the SEC never reveals the reasons for its suspension orders. To be sure, here respondent was able long after the fact to obtain some explanation through a Freedom of Information Act request, but even the information tendered was heavily excised and none of it even purports to state the reasoning of the Commissioners under whose authority § 12(k) orders issue. Nonetheless, when the SEC finally agreed to give respondent a hearing on the suspension of Canadian Javelin stock, it required respondent to state, in a verified petition (that is, *under oath*) why he thought the unrevealed conclusions of the SEC to be wrong. This is obscurantism run riot."[4]

Burden of Proof. Most of the formal administrative proceedings conducted by the Commission are disciplinary proceedings to punish alleged violations of the federal securities laws by persons required to be registered with the Commission and expressly subjected to such administrative sanctions by statute. Such proceedings against registered broker-dealers, investment advisers, registered investment companies and others are required to be conducted, as noted above, pursuant to the provisions of the Administrative Procedure Act. They may result in various types of disciplinary action, ranging from a mere censure to a permanent revocation of the registration of the respondent, thereby preventing him from continuing to engage in the particular business which he has conducted. The hearing is conducted before an Administrative Law Judge as provided by the Administrative Procedure Act and his "recommended decision" is then reviewed by the Commission itself and either adopted or modified or rejected by the Commission (see the *Carter and Johnson* case, supra page 1202). An appeal is available to the Circuit Court of Appeals from the decision of the Commission.[5]

For several years there was a dispute among the circuit courts, now resolved by the Supreme Court in the *Steadman* case, over what "burden of proof" had to be met by the Commission staff in establishing the facts which allegedly constituted "fraud" on the part of the respondent in such a disciplinary

---

1. This latter authority has never been employed by the Commission, although anticipated in tens of thousands or hundreds of thousands of underwriting agreements, which always relieve the underwriters of their obligation to purchase the securities if this happens with respect to the NYSE (or perhaps other exchanges) before the closing.

2. See the concurring opinion of Justice Brennan in Securities and Exchange Commission v. Sloan, infra, note 3.

3. 436 U.S. 103 (1978).

4. 436 U.S. at 124–125.

5. Securities Exchange Act, § 25.

proceeding. The Court of Appeals for the District of Columbia held in Collins Securities Corp. v. Securities and Exchange Commission [6] that the Commission had to prove such a violation by "clear and convincing evidence." The court based this decision on the analogy to the requirement in a civil fraud action that fraud be established by clear and convincing evidence and upon the severity of the sanction (i.e., deprivation of livelihood) which might be imposed by the Commission as a result of such a proceeding. The Supreme Court in the *Steadman* case did not consider it necessary to address the policy grounds for this decision in view of its conclusion that Congress had specified the appropriate burden of proof as being only by a "preponderance of the evidence."

In the decision of the Fifth Circuit [7] which was affirmed by the Supreme Court with respect to the burden of proof, the circuit court did not, however, affirm the imposition of the sanction of permanent disqualification upon the respondent in that proceeding. Rather, it remanded the case to the Commission for further consideration in the light of its holding that where the Commission imposed such a severe sanction it "has an obligation to explain why a less drastic remedy would not suffice," and that it had not sufficiently articulated its reasons in the decision from which the appeal was taken. The court held: "When the Commission imposes the most drastic sanctions at its disposal, it has a duty to articulate carefully the grounds for its decision, including an explanation of why lesser sanctions will not suffice." [8] This holding of the Fifth Circuit was left undisturbed by the Supreme Court, although it did not directly address this question. The effect of this requirement may not be greatly different from requiring that the violations be proved by "clear and convincing evidence." [9]

In addition to the books and articles cited in the preceding note at p. 1531, dealing generally with SEC enforcement actions, see, also, Steinberg, Steadman v. SEC—Its Implications and Significance, 6 Del.J.Corp.L. 1 (1981); Mathews, Litigation and Settlement of SEC Administrative Enforcement Proceedings, 29 Catholic U.L.Rev. 215 (1980); Note, Scope of Review or Standard of Proof— Judicial Control of SEC Sanctions and Steadman v. SEC, 93 Harv.L.Rev. 1845 (1980); Lowenfels, A Lack of Fair Procedures in the Administrative Process: Disciplinary Proceedings at the Stock Exchanges and the NASD, 64 Cornell L.Rev. 375 (1979); Poser, Reply to Lowenfels, 64 Cornell L.Rev. 402 (1979); Prettyman, How to Try a Dispute Under Adjudication by an Administrative Agency, 45 Va.L.Rev. 179 (1959); Timbers and Garfinkel, Examination of the Commission's Adjudicatory Process: Some Suggestions, 45 Va.L.Rev. 817 (1959).

SECURITIES AND EXCHANGE COMMISSION v. CATERINICCHIA

United States Court of Appeals, Fifth Circuit, 1980.
613 F.2d 102.

Before MORGAN, REAVLEY and HATCHETT, CIRCUIT JUDGES.

LEWIS R. MORGAN, CIRCUIT JUDGE.

6. 562 F.2d 820 (D.C.Cir.1977). See, also, Whitney v. Securities and Exchange Commission, 196 U.S.App.D.C. 12, 604 F.2d 676 (1979). In Investors Research Corp. v. Securities and Exchange Commission, 202 U.S.App.D.C. 168, 628 F.2d 168 (D.C.Cir. 1980), cert. denied 449 U.S. 919 (1981), however, the court approved the application of the "preponderance of the evidence" standard because the proceeding was not based on "fraud" and the respondent was only censured.

7. 603 F.2d 1126 (5th Cir.1979).

8. 603 F.2d at 1143.

9. See Note, Scope of Review or Standard of Proof—Judicial Control of SEC Sanctions, 93 Harv.L.Rev. 1845 (1980).

The Securities and Exchange Commission (SEC) appeals from the denial of its motion for a permanent injunction enjoining Trustees Loan and Discount Company (Trustees) and its president, Frank Caterinicchia, from further violations of the antifraud provisions of the federal securities laws. Following an evidentiary hearing, the District Court for the Middle District of Alabama found that defendants' failure to disclose material information relative to the sale and renewal of the company's subordinated commercial notes constituted a violation of section 17(a) of the Securities Act of 1933 and section 10(b) of the Securities Exchange Act of 1934, as implemented by rule 10b–5. However, because the court concluded that there was no likelihood that defendants would resume their misconduct, it declined to grant the requested injunctive relief. Finding no error requiring reversal in this case, we affirm the district court.

I.

Trustees is an Alabama corporation engaged in the business of making small consumer loans. Beginning in 1972, the primary source of funds for these loans was the sale and renewal of the company's eight-month subordinated commercial notes. Before offering its notes for sale, Trustees obtained a ruling from the Alabama Securities Commission exempting the notes from registration under Alabama law. Trustees' decision to sell its notes only to Alabama residents enabled the company to rely upon the intrastate exemption from federal registration provided by section 3(a)(11) of the 1933 Act.

In 1973 Trustees began to advertise its notes in newspapers of general circulation in Montgomery and Birmingham, Alabama. These advertisements advised readers to "earn 9% per year" by purchasing the promissory notes of this "home owned and home operated" corporation. Potential investors who responded to these ads were provided with a brochure which, in essence, promised both a high rate of interest and a high degree of safety. The brochure described the advantages of the notes in these terms:

- High interest return with safety
- Always worth face value of notes plus interest
- Hedge against inflation
- Will keep Alabama's dollars working in Alabama

In addition, the brochure assured investors that

> These notes are backed by the integrity of an Alabama Corporation doing business since 1914 with sound financial management whose reputation is unexcelled in the state.

The brochure furnished to investors contained no information reflecting the financial condition of Trustees. This information would not have been encouraging to investors for, as the defendants concede, the company had sustained operating losses for five of the six years from 1970 through 1975. Moreover, Trustees did not provide investors with financial statements or otherwise inform them of the company's losses even after some purchasers had specifically requested access to such information. The district court concluded that Trustees' failure to inform investors of the company's weak financial condition constituted "material omissions in light of statements made."

Frank Caterinicchia began working for Trustees in October 1973 when he became manager of the company's Birmingham branch office. In 1974 Caterinicchia acquired an option to purchase the common stock of Arthur M. Whitney, then president and majority shareholder of Trustees. In May 1976, shortly after Whitney's death, Caterinicchia purchased a controlling interest in the corporation and was elected as its president and one of its directors.

Simultaneously with Caterinicchia's gaining control of Trustees, the company came under the scrutiny of both the SEC and the Alabama Securities Commission. In a letter dated April 15, 1976, the state securities commission notified Trustees that its notes would no longer be exempt from state registration requirements. In response to this ruling, Trustees stopped the sale of promissory notes on April 16, 1976 at its Montgomery office and on May 7, 1976 at its Birmingham office. In further conversations with Trustees' attorney, the Director of the Alabama Securities Commission stated that because a previous director had approved the sale of these notes, he had no intention of commencing either civil or criminal proceedings against the company. The director made clear, however, that in addition to stopping the sale of new notes, the company should redeem existing notes as they matured and not allow them to be automatically renewed.[1] Although Trustees' counsel advised Caterinicchia that failure to obey the director's ruling would subject him to possible civil and criminal penalties, the company continued to renew the notes of Alabama residents who did not specifically request redemption.

On April 21, 1976, Trustees received a letter from the SEC advising the company of the antifraud provisions of the federal securities laws and seeking information as to whether the company had properly claimed an exemption from the registration provisions of the 1933 Securities Act. In preparing its response to the SEC's inquiry, Trustees discovered that some noteholders had moved out of state after purchasing the company's notes. On advice of counsel, Trustees began to redeem the notes of out-of-state noteholders.[2] However, the company continued to make no disclosure of relevant financial information to the Alabama residents whose notes it was renewing.

On December 16, 1976, a meeting was held between SEC officials and representatives of Trustees. At this meeting the SEC expressed its opinion that Caterinicchia should inform the company's noteholders that Trustees had a history of operating losses and had recently become insolvent. Fearing that disclosure would cause a run on the company, Caterinicchia sought additional time from the Commission in which to rehabilitate the company and make it into a profitable operation. On December 21, 1976, the SEC informed Trustees that it intended to seek injunctive relief against the company and to have the company placed in receivership. On December 28, 1976, Trustees filed a petition for an arrangement under Chapter XI of the Bankruptcy Act. Under this plan and its subsequent amendments, Trustees avoided liquidation through an agreement with its noteholders

---

1. Under the terms of the note agreement, unless the holder requested payment within ten days after the due date, the note would be automatically renewed.

2. In November 1976 Trustees sent a letter to out-of-state noteholders representing that it was redeeming their notes because the company had "extra cash on hand."

and other creditors to extend the time for payment and reduce the interest rate on the notes.

The district court found that defendants' failure to disclose the company's financial condition constituted a violation of the antifraud provisions of the federal securities laws. Nevertheless, the court determined that the SEC had "failed to prove the likelihood of any continuing menace to the public" and, therefore, declined to grant the request for a permanent injunction.

II.

Under section 20(b) of the Securities Act of 1933 and section 21(d) of the Securities Exchange Act of 1934, the SEC may seek an injunction whenever a person is engaged in or "about to engage in" proscribed activity. The district court is required to grant the injunction "upon a proper showing" by the SEC.

In this case the SEC seeks to enjoin future violations of the federal securities laws and does not allege that defendants are currently violating the law. The Fifth Circuit has stated that under these circumstances

The critical question in issuing the injunction and also the ultimate test on review is whether the defendant's past conduct indicates that there is a reasonable likelihood of further violations in the future. To obtain injunctive relief the Commission must offer positive proof of the likelihood that the wrongdoing will recur. SEC v. Commonwealth Securities, Inc., 574 F.2d 90, 99–100 (2d Cir.1978). The Commission needs to go beyond the mere fact of past violations. Id.

SEC v. Blatt, 583 F.2d 1325, 1334 (5th Cir.1978). Accord, SEC v. Monarch Fund, 608 F.2d 938 (2d Cir.1979). Furthermore, the cases recognize that the decision whether to grant or deny injunctive relief is addressed to the sound discretion of the district court and will not be disturbed on appeal except for clear abuse. * * * The burden of showing that the trial court abused its discretion is necessarily a heavy one, SEC v. Manor Nursing Centers, Inc., 458 F.2d 1082, 1100 (2d Cir.1972), particularly in view of the developing judicial attitude toward a closer appellate scrutiny of the issuance of injunctions. SEC v. Blatt, supra, 583 F.2d at 1334 and n. 28, citing SEC v. Commonwealth Chemical Securities, Inc., 574 F.2d 90, 99 (2d Cir.1978).

III.

Initially, the SEC argues that in declining to grant injunctive relief, the district court misunderstood the remedial nature of the statutory provisions involved. As evidence of this misunderstanding, the SEC points out that the court characterized the injunction as an "extraordinary measure" warranted only if a "continuing menace to the public" is demonstrated. In describing the injunctive remedy provided by the securities laws as an "extraordinary measure," argues the SEC, the court failed to appreciate the important distinctions between private actions for injunctive relief and SEC injunctive actions.

We agree that "extraordinary" is an inappropriate adjective in the context of *statutory* injunctive relief.[3] Such relief must be granted whenever either of the statutory conditions, i.e. "engaged in or about to engage in" proscribed activity, are satisfied. We cannot agree, however, that the court reached its judgment by disregarding these statutory bases for injunctive relief. In framing the issues of fact to be determined at trial, the court accurately perceived that the determinative factor in an injunctive action is whether there exists a reasonable likelihood of further misconduct by the defendant. In requiring the SEC to establish that defendants presented a "continuing menace to the public," the court placed no greater burden on the SEC than the statute requires. Furthermore, had the SEC carried the burden of showing that future violations were likely, it is clear that the court would have issued the requested injunction. Thus, the court did not fundamentally misperceive the remedial nature of the statutory injunction as the SEC argues.

The SEC next argues that the three principal factors relied upon by the trial court in denying the injunction do not support its conclusion that future violations are unlikely. First, the SEC asserts that the court assumed that the supervisory control exercised by the bankruptcy court over Trustees' affairs militated against injunctive relief. The SEC then questions the ability of the bankruptcy court to detect violations of the securities laws and notes that, in any event, the supervision would last for only one year. We reject this argument for the simple reason that we do not believe that the bankruptcy court's supervision was an important factor in the trial court's decision to deny injunctive relief. As is evidenced by the Pretrial Order, the court was quite aware that the actual supervision of Trustees' affairs was limited to one year. Furthermore, the court noted in its opinion that Caterinicchia would remain in control of the company and would not be under the direct supervision of the bankruptcy court. In our view, the challenged statement appears in the court's opinion not as an argument against issuing an injunction but as one of the facts necessary to an understanding of the case.

Second, the SEC contends that the court mistakenly attributed significance to defendants' decision to voluntarily cease their violations of the registration provisions of state and federal law. The SEC argues that in focusing on defendants' efforts to comply with the securities *registration* provisions, the court ignored the more important fact that defendants did not cease their *antifraud* violations until the SEC threatened to sue. We disagree. The court was familiar with all the facts in this case and did not overlook defendants' continued refusal to reveal the company's financial condition to investors. Throughout its opinion the court refers to defendants' "omissions" and "misrepresentations" and, at one point, notes that these acts "were done day-to-day over a substantial period of time and were not a single inadvertent act." In essence, the SEC's argument amounts to no more than an assertion that defendants' previous nondisclosure of relevant financial information raises an inference that such misconduct is

---

3. Because the SEC's injunctive power is a creature of statute, the SEC need only establish what the statute requires, i.e., that a person is engaged in or about to engage in prohibited acts or practices. The private plaintiff, on the other hand, must show irreparable harm and inadequate remedy at law before injunctive relief will be granted. See Note, Scienter and Injunctive Relief Under Rule 10b–5, 11 Ga.L.Rev. 879, 880 (1977).

likely in the future. Because the SEC presented no convincing proof of this likelihood, the court was entitled to conclude otherwise. We do not believe the district court abused its discretion in declining to accept the suggested inference.

Finally, the SEC points to the court's conclusion that substantial future violations would be impossible without public newspaper advertisements. The SEC objects that not only can violations occur without such ads, but that, even if the court's assumption were true, the denial of injunctive relief for this reason would place an impossible burden of surveillance on the Commission's limited resources. It is true that the courts have spared the SEC the task of having to keep potential violators under constant scrutiny. It would, therefore, be impermissible to deny an injunction for the reason that the SEC would be able to detect violations as they occurred. However, we do not believe the court committed this error. Reading the opinion as a whole, it is apparent that the court denied the injunction because the SEC had failed to prove that Caterinicchia was a bad character who was likely to continue to engage in unlawful practices if he thought he could get away with it. The comment that these violations would be easily detectable was added as a make-weight and was not intended as a primary rationale for denying injunctive relief.

To summarize, we decline to accept the premise that the court's finding of no reasonable likelihood of future violations was based primarily on the above "factors." We believe the true rationale for the court's decision was its conclusion that defendants' violation of the antifraud provisions resulted from a misguided attempt to protect investors by saving the company from bankruptcy and liquidation. The court was satisfied that defendants would not in the future sell securities without making the disclosures required by federal law. The fact that defendants violated the law in the past does not require a different conclusion. Finding no abuse of discretion, we affirm the district court's denial of injunctive relief.

Affirmed.

IN THE MATTER OF OCCIDENTAL PETROLEUM CORP.

Securities and Exchange Commission.
Exchange Act Release No. 16950 (July 2, 1980).

The Commission deems it appropriate in the public interest following an investigation by its Division of Enforcement that pursuant to Section 15(c) (4) of the Securities Exchange Act of 1934 (the "Exchange Act") proceedings be instituted with respect to Occidental Petroleum Corporation ("Oxy") to determine whether, during the period January 1, 1973 to the present, Oxy failed to make certain required disclosures in various filings submitted to the Commission pursuant to Section 13 of the Exchange Act and the Rules and Regulations promulgated thereunder.

Simultaneously with the institution of these proceedings, Oxy has submitted an Offer of Settlement for the purpose of disposing of the issues raised in these proceedings. Under the terms of its Offer of Settlement, incorporated herein by reference, Oxy, solely for the purpose of these proceedings, without trial or any adjudication, makes certain undertakings, and without admitting or denying any of the matters set forth herein, consents to the issuance of this Order of the Commission. In its Offer of Settlement to dispose of these proceedings, Oxy has made certain undertakings which are accepted by the Commission as detailed herein.

The Commission has determined that it is appropriate and in the public interest to accept the Offer of Settlement of Oxy and the undertakings contained in the Offer of Settlement, and, accordingly, issues this Order.

I

STATEMENT

A. *INTRODUCTION*

Oxy, a California corporation organized in 1920 with headquarters in Los Angeles, California, is engaged in exploring for and developing and producing natural resources, principally oil and gas outside of the United States and coal within the United States; marketing and transporting petroleum and petroleum products; and manufacturing and distributing chemicals of various types. Its securities are registered with the Commission pursuant to Section 12(b) of the Exchange Act and are traded on the New York Stock Exchange and other exchanges. Throughout all times relevant herein Oxy has filed annual and other periodic reports with the Commission pursuant to Section 13(a) of the Exchange Act and the Rules and Regulations promulgated thereunder. For the year ended December 31, 1979, Oxy reported net sales of approximately $9.55 billion and net income of approximately $561.7 million.

Oxy's oil and gas exploration and production operations are conducted throughout the world with the principal operations in Libya, the United Kingdom sector of the North Sea, Peru, Bolivia, the United States and Canada. For the year ended December 31, 1979, as reflected in Oxy's 1979 Annual Report on Form 10–K, all its oil and gas exploration and production operations, including the sale of its shares of oil production in these countries and additional crude oil purchased from Libya, accounted for approximately 42% of Oxy's total revenues, approximately 87% of its operating profit after Libyan taxes but before other income taxes and unallocated interest and corporate expenses, and approximately 39% of identifiable assets.

Oxy's chemical operations are conducted through Hooker Chemical Corporation ("Hooker"), a wholly-owned subsidiary, and its subsidiaries, including Hooker Chemicals & Plastics Corp., acquired by Oxy in 1968. Hooker, with over 18,400 employees, is a major producer of industrial chemicals, plastics, metal finishing chemicals and equipment, and agricultural chemicals and fertilizers. For the year ended December 31, 1979, as reflected in Oxy's 1979 Annual Report on Form 10–K, Oxy's chemical operations accounted for approximately 21% of Oxy's total revenues, approximately 7% of its operating profit and approximately 25% of identifiable assets.

As discussed below, various filings by Oxy with the Commission since January 1, 1975 did not contain certain required disclosures relating to: (1) Oxy's discharge of chemical or toxic wastes ("waste") into the environment; (2) the status of the proposed construction of a hydro-skimming refinery on Canvey Island; (3) the status of Oxy's negotiations with Libya concerning the financial arrangement pursuant to which Oxy operated in Libya; and

(4) signed, undated letters of resignation which were submitted by certain nominees to Oxy's Board of Directors at the request of Dr. Armand Hammer, the Chairman of the Board.

B. ENVIRONMENTAL MATTERS

As a major chemical company with facilities throughout the United States, Oxy's wholly owned subsidiary, Hooker, is subject to compliance with various federal, state and local environmental protection laws and regulations restricting the discharge of pollutants into the environment. Such regulatory restraints have had and have a significant financial impact on Hooker with respect to increased expenditures attributable to compliance with environmental laws and actual or potential liabilities arising from its discharge of pollutants.

Set forth below is a description of the three areas of non-disclosure in Oxy's filings with the Commission with respect to matters regulating the discharge of waste into the environment, or otherwise relating to the protection of the environment, which the Commission, as a result of its investigation, believes should have been disclosed. Oxy did not disclose, in numerous instances, the required information concerning pending or contemplated administrative or judicial proceedings by governmental authorities arising under federal, state, or local law relating to the protection of the environment. In addition, as set forth below, Oxy did not make adequate disclosures in filings with the Commission concerning the effects that compliance with environmental regulations would have upon its capital expenditures and earnings. Finally, Oxy did not disclose certain potential material liabilities resulting from the leaching of wastes into the environment from various chemical disposal sites.

1. Disclosure of Environmental Proceedings Involving Oxy

In 1973, the Commission adopted amendments to its registration and reporting forms with respect to environmental matters which were designed to promote investor protection and at the same time promote the purposes of the National Environmental Policy Act of 1969. One such rule required reporting companies to disclose information relating to administrative or judicial proceedings arising under provisions relating to the protection of the environment and pending or known to be contemplated by governmental authorities.

Since at least 1974, Oxy has been the subject of numerous proceedings instituted by governmental authorities pursuant to federal, state or local governmental regulatory provisions and has frequently been involved in various types of proceedings relating to the environment. From April 1974 through December 1976, Oxy was involved in at least 90 legal proceedings with governmental units relating to the protection of the environment. Approximately three-quarters of these proceedings between 1974 and 1976 were administrative in nature and related to excessive emissions into the air, or the improper discharge of effluents into waterways, or violations of National Pollutant Discharge Elimination System ("NPDES") permits issued to various Oxy facilities. Corrective actions were undertaken by Oxy, and in most cases civil penalties ranging from $250 to $2500 per violation were imposed. Other proceedings between 1974 and 1976 involved administrative and criminal misdemeanor actions against Island Creek Coal Company, a wholly-owned subsidiary of Oxy, principally for the discharge of pollutants into streams in violation of West Virginia pollution control laws, all of which were terminated by settlement or, in the misdemeanor actions, by pleas of *nolo contendere*, resulting in the aggregate in fines or penalties of $19,736.00.

Prior to May 1977, Oxy did not disclose, as required, in any filing with the Commission the existence and nature of these 90 pending or contemplated proceedings relating to discharge of waste into the environment or otherwise relating to the protection of the environment.

* * *

2. *Disclosure of the effects of compliance upon Oxy's capital expenditures and earnings*

As part of the Commission's 1973 amendments to its registration and reporting forms, the Commission required disclosure of "the material effects that compliance with federal, state and local provisions which have been enacted or adopted regulating the discharge of materials into the environment, or otherwise relating to the protection of the environment, may have upon the capital expenditures, earnings and competitive position of the registrant and its subsidiaries."

During the period from 1973 until 1977, as set forth below, Oxy did not make required disclosure in filings with the Commission concerning the effects that compliance with provisions relating to the protection of the environment may have upon Oxy's capital expenditures and earnings.

* * *

3. *Disclosure of Potential Liabilities Resulting From Disposal of Wastes*

Significant property damage and personal injury has occurred near various waste disposal sites of Hooker. By at least 1977, the time varying with respect to specific sites, as discussed herein, Hooker was exposed to material potential liabilities as a result of its ownership and use of these sites. Nevertheless, Oxy only disclosed in certain documents filed with the Commission including, for example, its Annual Report on form 10–K for the period ending December 31, 1977, that "[i]n light of the expansion of corporate liability in the environmental area in recent years * * *, there can be no assurance that Occidental will not incur material liabilities in the future as a consequence of the impact of its operations upon the environment." Oxy did not specifically disclose the amount, or describe the nature or extent, of the potential liabilities of Hooker due to its discharge of substantial amounts of wastes, as set forth below.

From the 1940's to the early 1970's, Hooker utilized essentially four sites in the Niagara Falls area of western New York State for the disposal of certain hazardous chemical wastes. As discussed below, the Niagara Falls disposal sites are the source of potential significant financial claims against Oxy. Claims have been made in presently existing lawsuits in excess of hundreds of millions of dollars as a result of the alleged leaching of wastes from dump sites and into the homes surrounding Love Canal and the waters of the Niagara River, which is a source of drinking water for the Niagara Falls area.

(a) *Love Canal*

Love Canal was used by Hooker as a landfill for the disposal of residues from Hooker's chemical manufacturing processes from 1942 until 1952 prior to the time Oxy acquired Hooker. During that period, Hooker estimates that it may have dumped more than 21,000 tons of various chemical wastes in the site. In 1953, at the request of the Board of Education of the School District of the City of Niagara Falls, Hooker deeded the landfill site to the Board for $1.00. Hooker's deed to the Board contains language with respect to a release from liability and a general description of the prior use of the landfill site.

* * *

By 1977, as a result of Hooker's prior ownership and use of the Love Canal site and problems relating thereto, Oxy was potentially exposed to substantial financial risk. There was no disclosure of the potential liability in Oxy's Annual Report on Form 10–K for the fiscal year ended December 31, 1977. In December 1979, the EPA and Department of Justice commenced an action against Hooker seeking security for remedial action at Love Canal estimated to cost approximately $45 million. In April 1980, the State of New York commenced an action against Hooker and Oxy seeking injunctive relief to abate migration of wastes from the Love Canal site, $250 million damages for environmental injury, $95 million for restitution costs, $270 million in punitive damages, and $20 million actual damages.

* * *

C. *OTHER DISCLOSURE MATTERS*

Oxy failed in various filings with the Commission to disclose the full facts and circumstances surrounding the reasons for the halting of construction in 1975 of a proposed major hydroskimming refinery at Canvey Island, England and the risks and uncertainties concerning its investment there. Moreover, it did not disclose certain matters and risks related to Oxy's dispute with the Libyan government over the interpretation and implementation of the "fair remuneration" arrangements concerning certain operations in Libya. Finally, Oxy did not disclose that signed undated letters of resignation were submitted by certain nominees to Oxy's Board of Directors at the request of Dr. Armand Hammer.

* * *

III

OFFER OF SETTLEMENT

Oxy has submitted an Offer of Settlement to the Commission in which it undertakes that:

A. It will designate a director ("the director") satisfactory to the Commission, who shall:

i. Be responsible for preparing an environmental report (the "report") in which he shall:

a. Recommend procedures to the full Board of Directors to ensure that Oxy will be in a position to disclose, in accordance with the federal securities laws on a complete, timely and accurate basis, all required information relating to environmental matters.

b. Reasonably determine the potential costs which Oxy will be required to incur within the next three years to bring its facilities into compliance with present federal, state and local environmental requirements at its Hooker Chemical Corporation and Island Creek Coal Company domestic facilities.

c. Determine the maximum civil penalties that may be imposed on Oxy pursuant to relevant environmental provisions and identify the factors which may mitigate the risk that the maximum amount of such penalties are likely to be imposed.

d. Describe third party claims, proceedings or litigations regarding the impact of Oxy's operations on the environment and the amount sought thereunder based on alleged claims against the Company.

ii. Assure that any potential liabilities regarding the impact of Oxy's operations on the environment have been identified to the Board of Directors of Oxy and that appropriate disclosure has been made in filings with the Commission as required by the federal securities laws. In the event that the required disclosure concerning such potential liabilities has not been made in such filings, as of the date of the filing of the report with the Commission, pursuant to this Order, the director shall append to the report a list identifying such liabilities, not then the subject of litigation.

iii. Describe the relevant legal, interpretative and/or technological problems in those instances, if any, in which the director is unable to ascertain or determine the matters specified above.

B. The Commission may consult with the director and be provided access to documents received, used or generated in the preparation of the report described above in a manner and with such limitations as are satisfactory to the Commission and Oxy.

C. The director will utilize Oxy's newly elected senior environmental official ("the environmental officer") and an independent consulting firm ("independent consultant"), each of whom will be satisfactory to the Commission, to assist with the development of information for, and the preparation of, the report described above.

D. The environmental officer and the independent consultant, prior to completion and submission of the report as provided in Paragraph G below, can only be dismissed by the director or by a majority vote of the Board of Directors of Oxy upon the recommendation of the director.

E. Oxy will cooperate fully with the director by permitting him to review such documents and interview such employees of Oxy as he deems relevant to the preparation of the report. Furthermore, the director will have authority to retain experts whom he determines are reasonably necessary to complete the Report.

F. It will make appropriate disclosure of a change in its policy that neither Oxy nor any officer, director or employee of the company will request or receive any written or oral agreement, assurance or promise of any kind from any nominee to, or member of, Oxy's Board of Directors as it now is or may in the future be constituted, that such member would resign from the Board of Directors prior to the expiration of the term for which the director was nominated or elected by Oxy, in a filing with the Commission on Form 8-K in advance of requesting or receiving any such agreement, assurance or promise. This provision does not apply to a resignation initiated by a director or a resignation of a director sought or received in connection with the termination of his status as an officer of Oxy, provided that such resignation occurs within ninety (90) days of a request for or receipt of his agreement, assurance or promise to resign. In connection with this undertaking, Oxy has represented that no Oxy director, officer or employee has either sought or received any such agreement, assurance or promise from any current member of Oxy's Board of Directors.

G. Within 10 months of the date of the issuance of this Order, or such later date as the staff of the Commission and Oxy may agree, the director shall complete the report and submit it to the Board of Directors of Oxy.

H. Within 10 days of the submission of the report to the Board of Directors, Oxy will transmit copies thereof to the Commission and, within 30 days of such submission, file with the Commission on Form 8–K a description thereof and a summary of the principal conclusions and recommendations.

I. In connection with the recommendations of the director, the Board of Directors of Oxy will review them within 45 days of their receipt and adopt and implement such of the recommendations as it reasonably believes necessary or appropriate.

J. Within 60 days of the submission of the report to the Board of Directors, Oxy will file with the Commission on Form 8–K a description of the actions taken by the Board of Directors, if any, with respect to the recommendations of the director.

IV

ORDER

In view of the foregoing, the Commission deems it appropriate and in the public interest to accept the Offer of Settlement of Oxy and accordingly, IT IS HEREBY ORDERED that such proceedings be, and they hereby are instituted.

IT IS FURTHER ORDERED THAT Oxy:

1. Comply with the reporting requirements of the Exchange Act.

2. Amend its reports currently on file with the Commission by filing this Order on a Form 8–K within 30 days after the date of entry of this Order.

3. Include in its next quarterly report to shareholders a summary of the contents of this Order.

4. Upon Oxy becoming aware of non-compliance with its undertakings set forth herein, Oxy shall immediately notify the Commission of that fact and unless the Commission otherwise agrees, Oxy shall disclose such non-compliance in a Current Report on Form 8–K within 10 days.

5. Upon the entry of this Order, these proceedings are terminated, provided however, the Commission specifically reserves the right to reopen these proceedings solely to enforce the Commission's Order or if Oxy fails to comply with its undertakings set forth in this Order. If these proceedings are reopened, the only issues in such proceedings shall be Oxy's failure to comply with its undertakings as set forth in this Order or its failure to comply with this Order.

By the Commission.

INJUNCTION ACTIONS

The most frequent action of the Commission to enforce the federal securities laws, other than administrative proceedings to discipline the persons registered with it, takes the form of an action for an injunction in the federal district court to enjoin the persons named as defendants from violating those laws. Section 21(d) of the 1934 Act authorizes the Commission to "bring an action in the proper district court of the United States * * * to enjoin such acts or practices [in violation of the securities laws], and upon a proper showing a permanent or temporary injunction or restraining order shall be granted without bond." Section 27 of the 1934 Act gives the federal district courts "exclusive jurisdiction of violations of this title or the rules and regulations thereunder, and of all suits in equity and actions at law brought to enforce any liability or duty created by this title or the rules and regulations thereunder." In the great majority of such cases, however, there is no actual litigation in court, since a "consent injunction" has been worked out between the attorneys for the defendants and the Commission staff and is entered as a judgment of the court on the same day that the complaint is filed by the Commission.

Although described by some courts as being only a "mild prophylactic", merely requiring that the defendant obey the law in the future, in fact an injunction entered against a person in this area of the law is a severe punishment. There are literally dozens of statutory provisions in both the federal and the state securities laws disqualifying a person who has been subjected to such an injunction from engaging in almost any aspect of the securities business, without the prior consent of the appropriate regulatory agency. This is true whether or not the injunction is entered on the basis of a consent by the defendant and without his admitting any of the allegations in the complaint. Secondly, if the defendant has any money (or any insurance), the entry of the injunction is certain to be followed almost immediately by a number of class actions attempting to recover damages from him on behalf of investors on the basis of the conduct with respect to which the injunction was granted. As Chief Justice Burger stated in the *Aaron* case, supra page 946, an injunction "is a drastic remedy, not a mild prophylactic, and should not be obtained against one acting in good faith."

In Securities and Exchange Commission v. American Board of Trade, Inc.[1] Judge Friendly stated: "We think it appropriate to begin our discussion by emphasizing the gravity of an injunction against violation of the securities laws. * * * Even a more narrowly drawn injunction against defendants who are in the securities business would have serious collateral consequences, as we suggested in S.E.C. v. Commonwealth Chemical Securities, Inc., 574 F.2d 90, 99 (2d Cir.1978), and as a comprehensive article has now abundantly documented, see Andre, The Collateral Consequences of S.E.C. Injunctive Relief: Mild Prophylactic or Perpetual Hazard?, [1981] U.Ill.L.Rev. 625. Fully appreciating the role played by S.E.C. injunctions in the enforcement of the securities laws, as we have done for decades, we nevertheless agree with the statement of the Chief Justice concurring in Aaron v. S.E.C., 446 U.S. 680, 703 (1980) * * *, that at least when defendants are active in the securities field '[a]n injunction is a drastic remedy, not a mild prophylactic. * * *' "[2]

Unlike private litigants seeking damages, at least in some cases (see Chapter 18, above), the Commission is not required to prove that any investor actually relied on the misrepresentations or that the misrepresentations caused any investors to lose money in order to obtain an injunction against future viola-

---

1. 751 F.2d 529 (2d Cir.1984). 2. 751 F.2d at 535–536.

tions. Violations of the anti-fraud provisions of Section 206 of the Investment Advisers Act also do not depend on actual injury to any client.[3]

The Question of "Scienter". In the *Ernst & Ernst* case, supra page 936, the Supreme Court reserved the question whether the requirement of *scienter* (an intent to "deceive, manipulate or defraud"), which it required in the case of a private damage action under Rule 10b–5, would be imposed in connection with an SEC enforcement action. Between the time of the decision of that case and the decision of the *Aaron* case, supra page 946, there was considerable controversy in the lower courts over this issue, some of them answering the question, "Yes", and others, "No." In the *Aaron* case the Supreme Court answered the question: yes and no. Yes, under Rule 10b–5 and under clause (1) of Section 17(a) of the 1933 Act; and No, under clauses (2) and (3) of Section 17(a). Since the Commission can as easily, perhaps more easily, allege a violation of clause (2) or (3) or both of Section 17(a) as it can a violation of clause (1), and all three are identical in language with the three clauses of Rule 10b–5, it would appear that the Commission won this battle. It is true, however, that Section 17(a) does not cover *purchases* of securities, but only sales; therefore, an injunction action alleging misconduct on the part of the defendant in connection with his purchase of securities would require the Commission to show *scienter,* at least if the action is based on Rule 10b–5. But almost all such enforcement actions deal with the sale of securities, rather than their purchase.

Basis for an Injunction. Since an injunction is supposed to be a preventive and not a punitive remedy, the courts have always acknowledged that it is necessary to find a reasonable likelihood of the recurrence of unlawful conduct on the part of the defendant in order to justify the issuance of an injunction, even though the defendant has been found to be guilty of a past violation. However, some courts have tended to agree with the contention of the Commission that proof of one past violation is a sufficient basis upon which to find a likelihood of future violations. There is no doubt that the Commission itself has viewed the injunctive process as one of its "arsenal of weapons" with which it can punish transgressions of the securities laws. But in the last few years this attitude on the part of the courts has begun to change. The Second Circuit stated in Securities and Exchange Commission v. Commonwealth Chemical Securities, Inc.[4] that "the current judicial attitude * * * has become more circumspect" and that "recent decisions have emphasized * * * the need for the SEC to go beyond the mere facts of past violations and demonstrate a realistic likelihood of recurrence."

The factors which the district court should consider in determining whether an injunction should issue have been stated to include "the likelihood of future violations, the degree of scienter involved, the sincerity of defendant's assurances against future violations, the isolated or recurrent nature of the infraction, defendant's recognition of the wrongful nature of his conduct, and the likelihood, because of defendant's professional occupation, that future violations might occur."[5]

---

3. Securities and Exchange Commission v. Blavin, 760 F.2d 706 (6th Cir.1985).

4. 574 F.2d 90, 99–100 (2d Cir.1978).

5. Securities and Exchange Commission v. Universal Major Industries Corp., 546 F.2d 1044, at 1048 (2d Cir.1976), cert. denied 434 U.S. 834 (1977). In Securities and Exchange Commission v. Dimensional Entertainment Corp., 518 F.Supp. 773 (S.D. N.Y.1981), Judge Tenney at first refused to enter an injunction against the defendant

because he was currently serving an eight-year prison term, and therefore was hardly likely to repeat his offenses; but at a subsequent hearing he granted the injunction upon a showing by the SEC that the defendant was likely to be paroled in one year. In Securities and Exchange Commission v. Haswell, 654 F.2d 698 (10th Cir.1981), the Tenth Circuit held that a finding of lack of scienter was alone sufficient to justify the district court's refusal to enter an injunc-

Ancillary Relief. The Commission has sought and obtained in many of its civil injunction actions a variety of ancillary remedies designed to remedy the consequences of past violations or reduce the likelihood of future violations or both. These remedies have included: (1) The appointment of a receiver for the corporation where the affairs of the corporation are in such a condition as a result of past violations that that drastic remedy is considered necessary to protect the rights of investors.[6] In Securities and Exchange Commission v. Wencke[7] the Ninth Circuit held that, in connection with such a receivership, the court has jurisdiction to issue a general stay of all state court actions against the corporation by any persons, even though not involved in any way in the violations of the securities laws, as in a bankruptcy proceeding. (2) An order for the disgorgement of profits made by the defendant to the persons allegedly defrauded by his conduct in violation of the securities laws.[8] In other words, the Commission may assume the role, in connection with an injunction action, of a class action plaintiff for the benefit of the persons who have been damaged as a result of the violations.

The most controversial of these ancillary relief measures have been those designed to give the Commission (or the court) a certain control over the future conduct of the corporation and its business, short of imposing a receivership. Typical of these measures have been: (3) The appointment of "special counsel", who is required to be satisfactory to or approved by the Commission, to make an investigation of the past misdeeds of management and report, not only to the board of directors of the corporation, but also to the Commission (or the court).[9] (4) The election to the board of directors of one or more "independent directors" who are not beholden to the existing management, to control the future conduct of the corporation in specific regards or generally. The Occidental Petroleum case illustrates the latter type of provision. Such independent director or directors are required to be approved by (i.e., in effect nominated by) the Securities and Exchange Commission. Where the board is required to be restructured so that a majority of its members consist of such new directors, the SEC has, in effect, carried out a *coup d'etat,* taking over complete control of the corporation.

While the types of remedies mentioned in the last paragraph have been employed in a large number of cases, this has been done almost invariably pursuant to a consent of the defendant corporation either in a provision of a consent injunction or pursuant to an "undertaking" given by the corporation to the Commission as the price of avoiding further litigation. There is, therefore, virtually no legal authority as to whether the court has the power to impose such a condition upon a corporate defendant at the request of the Commission where the corporation resists. In Securities and Exchange Commission v.

tion against an attorney for alleged violations of the federal securities laws.

6. Los Angeles Trust Deed & Mortgage Exchange v. Securities and Exchange Commission, 285 F.2d 162 (9th Cir.1960), cert. denied 366 U.S. 919 (1961); Securities and Exchange Commission v. Manor Nursing Centers, Inc., 458 F.2d 1082 (2d Cir.1972); Securities and Exchange Commission v. Bartlett, 422 F.2d 475 (8th Cir.1970); Securities and Exchange Commission v. Keller Corp., 323 F.2d 397 (7th Cir.1963).

7. 622 F.2d 1363 (9th Cir.1980).

8. See Securities and Exchange Commission v. Blatt, 583 F.2d 1325, at 1335–

1336 (5th Cir.1978); Securities and Exchange Commission v. Wills, 472 F.Supp. 1250, at 1275–1276 (D.D.C.1978); Securities and Exchange Commission v. E and H Oil Co., Inc., CCH Fed.Sec.Law Rptr. ¶ 97,652 (W.D.La.1980).

9. For problems arising in connection with the appointment of "special counsel", see Handler v. Securities and Exchange Commission, 610 F.2d 656 (9th Cir.1979); Securities and Exchange Commission v. Medic-Home Enterprises, Inc., CCH Fed. Sec.Law Rptr. ¶ 97,291 (S.D.N.Y.1980); Canadian Javelin, Limited v. Lawler, Kent & Eisenberg, 478 F.Supp. 448 (D.D.C.1979).

Falstaff Brewing Corp.,[10] the district court refused to order a restructuring of the board of directors of the corporation and stated that "the court should not, without considerable justification, impose a remedy which would in effect regulate areas traditionally left to internal corporate management."

Collateral Estoppel. If an SEC injunction action is litigated and the court decides that the defendant has committed a violation of the federal securities laws, the United States Supreme Court in Parklane Hosiery Co., Inc. v. Shore [11] held that the defendant would be collaterally estopped from relitigating the same factual issues in a class action brought against him by a private plaintiff involving the same transaction. While other issues or defenses might still be open in the subsequent action, such as the question of reliance by the plaintiffs, the plaintiff is entitled to a partial summary judgment to the effect that the defendant committed the violation asserted by the Commission, as found in the injunction action. This consequence of resisting the SEC injunction action, if the defendant loses, puts extreme pressure on him to settle the SEC action by a consent decree, since he will then not be so precluded from litigating all of the issues with a private plaintiff, so long as there has been no adjudication of any issue in the prior case and he does not admit any of the facts alleged in the complaint in connection with his consent to the injunction. Such a consent typically recites that the defendant "neither admits nor denies" the allegations in the complaint. The Commission in recent years has refused to enter into any such consent decree which recites that the defendant "denies" the allegations which it is making, but that is not necessary in order to avoid the effects of collateral estoppel.

See Steinberg and Ferrara, Securities Practice: Federal and State Enforcement (1987); Ferrara and Nerkle, Overview of an SEC Enforcement Action, 8 Corp.L.Rev. 306 (1985); Dent, Ancillary Relief in Federal Securities Law, 67 Minn.L.Rev. 865 (1983); Steinberg, The Securities and Exchange Commission's Administrative, Enforcement, and Legislative Programs and Policies, 58 Notre Dame L.Rev. 173 (1982); Steinberg, SEC and Other Permanent Injunctions—Standards for Their Imposition, Modification and Dissolution, 66 Cornell L.Rev. 27 (1980); Mathews, The SEC and Civil Injunctions: It's Time to Give the Commission an Administrative Cease and Desist Remedy, 6 Sec.Reg.L.J. 345 (1979); Hazen, Administrative Enforcement: An Evaluation of the Securities and Exchange Commission's Use of Injunctions and Other Enforcement Methods, 31 Hastings L.J. 427 (1979); Pickholz and Brodsky, An Assessment of Collateral Estoppel and SEC Enforcement Proceedings After Parklane Hosiery Co. v. Shore, 28 Am.U.L.Rev. 37 (1978); Ellsworth, Disgorgement in Securities Fraud Actions Brought by the SEC, 1977 Duke L.J. 641 (1977); Farrand, Ancillary Remedies in SEC Civil Enforcement Suits, 89 Harv.L.Rev. 1779 (1976); Berner and Franklin, Scienter and Securities and Exchange Commission Rule 10b-5 Injunctive Actions, 51 N.Y.U.L.Rev. 769 (1976); Mathews, Recent Trends in SEC Requested Ancillary Relief in SEC Civil Injunctive Actions, 31 Bus.Law. 1323 (1976); Malley, Far-Reaching Equitable Remedies Under the Securities Acts and the Growth of Federal Corporate Law, 17 Wm. & Mary L.Rev. 47 (1975); Program of the Committee on Federal Regulation of Securities: SEC Civil Injunctive Actions, 30 Bus.Law. 1303 (1975); Jaeger and Yardley, Equitable Uncertainties in SEC Injunctive Actions, 24 Emory L.J. 639 (1975); Treadway, SEC Enforcement Techniques: Expanding and Exotic Forms of Ancillary Relief, 32 Wash. & Lee L.Rev. 637 (1975); Sporkin, SEC Developments in Litigation and the Molding of Remedies, 29 Bus.Law. 121 (1974);

---

10. CCH Fed.Sec.Law Rptr. ¶ 96,583 (D.D.C.1978), aff'd, 629 F.2d 62 (D.C.Cir. 1980), cert. denied 449 U.S. 1012 (1981).

11. 439 U.S. 322 (1979).

Mathews, S.E.C. Civil Injunctive Actions—I and II, 5 Rev.Sec.Reg. 949, 969 (1973).

TOUCHE ROSS & CO. v. SECURITIES AND EXCHANGE COMMISSION

United States Court of Appeals, Second Circuit, 1979.
609 F.2d 570.

Before: KAUFMAN, CHIEF JUDGE, TIMBERS and GURFEIN, CIRCUIT JUDGES.

TIMBERS, CIRCUIT JUDGE: One of the most urgent problems of our day is the responsibility of the courts and other government bodies to prescribe high standards of conduct for their members and for those who practice before them. An indispensable corollary of this responsibility is the right—indeed, the duty—to discipline those who fail to conform to the high standards of conduct which have been prescribed.

We are called upon today to determine (1) whether the Securities and Exchange Commission ("SEC" or "Commission"), pursuant to one of its Rules of Practice which has been in effect for more than forty years, may conduct an administrative proceeding to determine whether certain professionals—in this case, accountants—should be censured or suspended from appearing or practicing before the Commission because of alleged unethical, unprofessional or fraudulent conduct in their audits of the financial statements of two corporations; and (2) if the Commission is authorized to conduct such an administrative proceeding, whether it should be permitted to conclude it before the accountants resort to the courts. For the reasons below, we hold that both questions must be answered in the affirmative.

I.

On September 1, 1976—more than two and one-half years ago—the SEC, pursuant to Rule 2(e) of its Rules of Practice, 17 C.F.R. § 201.2(e) (1978),[1] entered an order which provided for a public administrative proceeding against the accounting firm of Touche Ross & Co. and three of its former partners, Edwin Heft, James M. Lynch and Armin J. Frankel. The firm and the three partners, all appellants, will be referred to collectively as "Touche Ross" or "appellants".

The proceeding was instituted to determine whether appellants had engaged in unethical, unprofessional or fraudulent conduct in their audits of the financial statements of Giant Stores Corporation and Ampex Corporation.

The Commission's order alleged that Touche Ross and the individual appellants, in examining the companies' financial statements, had failed to follow generally accepted accounting standards and had no reasonable basis

---

1. Rule 2(e) of the SEC's Rules of Practice in relevant part provides:

"(e) *Suspension and disbarment.* (1) The Commission may deny, temporarily or permanently, the privilege of appearing or practicing before it in any way to any person who is found by the Commission after notice of and opportunity for hearing in the matter (i) not to possess the requisite qualifications to represent others, or (ii) to be lacking in character or integrity or to have engaged in unethical or improper professional conduct, or (iii) to have willfully violated, or willfully aided and abetted the violation of any provision of the Federal securities laws (15 U.S.C. 77a to 80b–20), or the rules and regulations thereunder."

for their opinions regarding the financial statements of these companies. The order also recited that, if these allegations were found to be true, they tended to show that Touche Ross and the individual appellants had engaged in improper professional conduct and willfully had violated, and had aided and abetted violations of, §§ 5, 7, 10 and 17(a) of the Securities Act of 1933 and §§ 10(b) and 13 of the Securities Exchange Act of 1934, and rules and regulations thereunder.

In view of the nationwide accounting practice of Touche Ross,[6] the SEC decided that it would be in the public interest to institute a public proceeding and to order a hearing at which Touche Ross would be afforded an opportunity to present a defense to these charges.[7] The Commission then would have been in a position to determine whether the substantive allegations were true and, if so, whether Touche Ross and the individual appellants should be disqualified, either temporarily or permanently, from appearing and practicing before the Commission.

No administrative hearings have ever been held in this case.

On October 12, 1976, Touche Ross commenced the instant action for declaratory and injunctive relief in the Southern District of New York, naming as defendants the Commission and four of its members in their official capacities. By this action, Touche Ross sought a permanent injunction against the on-going administrative proceeding which had been instituted against them by the SEC pursuant to Rule 2(e). Touche Ross also sought a declaratory judgment that Rule 2(e) had been promulgated "without any statutory authority"; that the Rule 2(e) administrative proceeding had been instituted against them "without authority of law"; and, in any event, since the SEC does not constitute an impartial forum for the adjudication of the issues raised in the SEC's Rule 2(e) order, that such administrative proceedings would deny Touche Ross due process of law.

The SEC moved to dismiss the complaint pursuant to Fed.R.Civ.P. 12(b) (6) and 12(b)(1) on the grounds that Touche Ross' complaint failed to state a claim upon which relief could be granted and that the court lacked subject matter jurisdiction over the asserted claims for relief. The crux of the SEC's position in support of its motion to dismiss was that Touche Ross improperly had failed to exhaust administrative remedies.

After a hearing, the district court, Constance B. Motley, District Judge, filed a well-reasoned opinion granting the SEC's motion and ordering that the action be dismissed. [1978 Transfer Binder] Fed.Sec.L.Rep. (CCH) ¶ 96,415 (S.D.N.Y. April 24, 1978). The district court rested its decision on the failure of Touche Ross to exhaust its administrative remedies. It did not reach the substantive question of the validity of Rule 2(e).

From the judgment entered on the district court opinion, this appeal has been taken.

* * *

The absence of the need for agency expertise or discretion has proven decisive in several decisions of our Court which have held that exhaustion was not necessary. * * *

---

6. Touche Ross is a partnership of certified public accountants. There are 525 partners and principals, and approximately 4500 other professional employees. The firm has offices located in 37 states.

7. Rule 2(e)(7) provides that all hearings under Rule 2(e) shall be non-public unless the Commission directs otherwise.

* * *

Similar considerations are present in the instant case. Appellants challenge the legal authorization of the Commission to proceed against them pursuant to Rule 2(e). While the Commission's administrative proceeding is not "plainly beyond its jurisdiction", nevertheless to require appellants to exhaust their administrative remedies would be to require them to submit to the very procedures which they are attacking.

Moreover, the issue is one of purely statutory interpretation. See Consumers Union v. Cost of Living Council, 491 F.2d 1396, 1399 (Temp. Emer.Ct.App.), cert. denied 416 U.S. 984 (1974). Further agency action is unnecessary to enable us to determine the validity of Rule 2(e). There is no need for the exercise of discretion on the part of the agency nor for the application of agency expertise. While the Commission has the power to declare its own rule invalid, it is unlikely that further proceedings would produce such a result. Accordingly, we now turn to the merits of that question.

III.

Section 23(a)(1) of the 1934 Act authorizes the Commission to "make such rules and regulations as may be necessary or appropriate to implement the provisions of this title for which [it is] responsible or for the execution of the functions vested in [it] by this title. * * * "[12] Pursuant to this general rulemaking authority, the Commission adopted and subsequently has amended[13] Rule 2(e) of its Rules of Practice, the relevant part of which is set forth above. See note 1, supra.

The current Rule and its predecessors have been in effect for over forty years. It has been the basis for a number of disciplinary proceedings

---

12. Congress has given the Commission similar rulemaking powers in each of the other statutes which it is responsible for administering. See, e.g., Section 19 of the Securities Act of 1933; Section 20 of the Public Utility Holding Company Act of 1935; Section 319 of the Trust Indenture Act of 1939; Section 38 of the Investment Company Act of 1940; Section 211 of the Investment Advisers Act of 1940.

13. In 1935, shortly after it was created, the Commission promulgated its Rules of Practice. Rule II(1) originally provided that the Commission in its discretion could discipline attorneys or other persons who did not possess the requisite qualifications to represent others before the Commission. See Securities and Exchange Commission, First Annual Report 45–53 (1935). Rule II was amended in 1938 to eliminate the provision that persons wishing to practice before the Commission were required to file applications with the Commission. The disciplinary provision, however, was retained. Securities Act Release No. 1761 (June 27, 1938).

Appellants contend that the enactment in 1965 of 5 U.S.C. § 500, eliminating federal agency practice *admission* require-

ments, demonstrates the intent of Congress to strip the SEC of any authority to discipline professionals practicing before it. The stated purpose of the section was quite to the contrary. It was intended to ensure that persons appearing before the agencies *be represented by attorneys of their choice.* H.R.Rep. No. 1141, 89th Cong., 1st Sess. (1965), reprinted in [1965] 2 U.S.Code Cong. & Ad.News 4170, 4171. Moreover, the statute explicitly provides in § 500(d)(2) that the section "*does not* * * * authorize or limit the discipline, including disbarment, of individuals who appear in a representative capacity before an agency. * * * " (emphasis added). We find nothing in this language to support appellants' contentions. The language, as appellants acknowledge, is "neutral". It neither authorizes nor limits the power of the agencies to discipline professionals who appear or practice before them; that was not the purpose of the section. And there certainly is nothing to suggest that Congress intended to limit disciplinary proceedings to those agencies with specific statutory authorization to do so. See, e.g., 111 Cong. Rec.H. 27193 (Oct. 18, 1965); S.Rep. No. 755, 89th Cong., 1st Sess. 5 (1965).

brought against professionals—including accountants and attorneys—during this forty year period. See, e.g., Touche Ross & Co., Accounting Series Release No. 153, Fed.Sec.L.Rep. (CCH) ¶ 72,175 (1974) (firm waived formal Rule 2(e) proceedings, was censured by Commission, and consented to an order providing remedial sanctions); In the Matter of Myears, Accounting Series Release No. 92, Fed.Sec.L.Rep. (CCH) ¶ 72,114 (1962); In the Matter of Touche, Nevin, Bailey & Smart, Accounting Series Release No. 78, Fed. Sec.L.Rep. (CCH) ¶ 72,100 (1957); In the Matter of Masquelette & Co., Accounting Series Release No. 68, Fed.Sec.L.Rep. (CCH) ¶ 72,087 (1949); In the Matter of Logan, 10 S.E.C. 982 (1942) (accountants disciplined under Rule 2(e)); In the Matter of Ronald H. Freemond, Release No. 33–4736 [1964–1966 Transfer Binder] Fed.Sec.L.Rep. (CCH) ¶ 77,190 (1964); In the Matter of Schwebel, 40 S.E.C. 347 (1960) (attorney permanently disqualified from practice before the SEC under Rule 2(e)).

Although the mere fact that the Rule is of long standing does not relieve us of our responsibility to determine its validity, see SEC v. Sloan, 436 U.S. 103 (1978), it is noteworthy that no court has ever held that the Rule is invalid. Indeed, in SEC v. Ezrine, Civil Action No. 72–3161, [1972–1973 Transfer Binder] Fed.Sec.L.Rep. (CCH) ¶ 93,594 (S.D.N.Y. Aug. 3, 1972), Judge Frankel specifically rejected an attorney's claim that the Commission lacked the power to discipline him, granted the Commission's request for an injunction, and enjoined the attorney from further practice before the Commission. See also Schwebel v. Orrick, 153 F.Supp. 701, 704 (D.D.C.1957) (district court upheld authority of Commission to proceed under Rule 2(e)), affirmed on other grounds 251 F.2d 919 (D.C.Cir.) (denial of injunction affirmed but on ground that appellant failed to exhaust administrative remedies), cert. denied 356 U.S. 927 (1958).

Other courts, although not squarely ruling on the question, nevertheless have intimated that the Commission has the authority to promulgate Rule 2(e) and to discipline professionals who appear before it. See, e.g., SEC v. Csapo, 533 F.2d 7, 12 (D.C.Cir.1976) (Lumbard J.) ("Nothing in our opinion today is intended to limit the right of the SEC to institute itself such disciplinary proceedings. * * *"); Kivitz v. SEC, 475 F.2d 956, 962 (D.C.1973) (Danaher, J.). These decisions, although persuasive, are not binding on this Court. We must examine independently the statutory scheme to determine if the Rule is in accordance with Congressional policy and purpose. See SEC v. Sloan, supra, 436 U.S. at 115–16.

Appellants concede that there is no express statutory prohibition against promulgation of the Rule. They contend, however, that the statutory scheme negates any implied authority that the SEC may discipline accountants pursuant to Rule 2(e). Specifically, they point to § 27 of the 1934 Act, which provides that the district courts "shall have *exclusive* jurisdiction of violations of this chapter." (emphasis added) Viewed in conjunction with other statutory provisions which authorize the SEC to commence proceedings in the district courts to enjoin what the Commission believes to be violations of the Acts, appellants argue that these provisions indicate that Congress intended that only the courts should adjudicate violations of the Acts. Absent express Congressional authorization for the Commission to adjudicate such violations—so the argument goes—the Commission is without power to promulgate its disciplinary Rule.

We reject appellants' argument for several reasons. First, it is clear that the SEC is not attempting to usurp the jurisdiction of the federal courts to deal with "violations" of the securities laws. The Commission, through its Rule 2(e) proceeding, is merely attempting to preserve the integrity of its own procedures, by assuring the fitness of those professionals who represent others before the Commission. Indeed, the Commission has made it clear that its intent in promulgating Rule 2(e) was not to utilize the rule as an additional weapon in its enforcement arsenal, but rather to determine whether a person's professional qualifications, including his character and integrity, are such that he is fit to appear and practice before the Commission. Securities Act Release No. 5088 at 1 (Sept. 24, 1970).

Moreover, an examination of the policies underlying the securities laws indicates that, contrary to appellants' assertions, the Rule is not inconsistent with the Commission's statutory authority. In considering questions of the authority of an agency to promulgate rules or regulations, the Supreme Court has held that if the regulation is in furtherance of a legitimate statutory purpose, the validity of the regulation will be upheld. In Mourning v. Family Publications Services, Inc., 411 U.S. 356 (1973), the Court stated:

"Where the empowering provision of a statute states simply that the agency may 'make * * * such rules and regulations as may be necessary to carry out the provisions of this Act,' we have held that the validity of a regulation promulgated thereunder will be sustained so long as it is 'reasonably related to the purposes of the enabling legislation.'" Id. at 369, quoting from, Thorpe v. Housing Authority of the City of Durham, 393 U.S. 268, 280–81 (1969).

If the powers exercised by the agency constitute a " 'legitimate, reasonable and direct adjunct to the Commission's explicit statutory power' ", Trans Alaska Pipeline Rate Cases, 436 U.S. 631, 655 (1978), quoting from United States v. Chesapeake & Ohio Railway Co., 426 U.S. 500, 512 (1976), then an express grant of authority is not necessary to sustain the validity of the challenged rule or regulation.

In the general rulemaking provisions of the federal securities laws, Congress has provided the Commission with "broad authority" to adopt those rules and regulations necessary for carrying out the agency's designated functions. See e.g. Commercial Capital Corp. v. SEC, 360 F.2d 856, 857 (7 Cir.1966). Congress realized that it could not enact express statutory provisions to deal with every possible evil that might develop. Thus, the wide latitude given to the Commission has been seen as necessary, "in view of the nature of the subject matter, * * * to protect investors against fraud or deception made possible by constantly changing conditions." R.A. Holman & Co. v. SEC, supra, 299 F.2d at 132. Indeed, in discussing the role of the SEC in the enforcement of the Foreign Corrupt Practices Act, Congress implicitly gave its approval to the SEC's use of Rule 2(e) proceedings as a possible alternative to injunctive action or criminal referral. See S.Rep. No. 95–114, 95th Cong., 1st Sess. 12 n. 6 (1977); H.R.Rep. No. 95–640, 95th Cong., 1st Sess. 10 n. 1 (1977).

The chief purpose of the 1933 Act was to "provide investors with full disclosure of material information concerning public offerings of securities in commerce." Ernst & Ernst v. Hochfelder, 425 U.S. 185, 195 (1976). One of the mechanisms designed to implement this policy of full disclosure was the requirement that a registration statement be filed with the Commission before a security could be sold to the public. See SEC v. Arthur Young & Co., 584 F.2d 1018, 1025 n. 51 (D.C.Cir.1978), cert. denied 439 U.S. 1071 (1979). In connection with the filing requirements, the Commission was given broad authority to regulate the contents of the filings, including the authority to prescribe the form and method of preparing financial statements, to define accounting terms, and to require that financial statements be certified by an independent public accountant.

The role of the accounting and legal professions in implementing the objectives of the disclosure policy has increased in importance as the number and complexity of securities transactions has increased. By the very nature of its operations, the Commission, with its small staff and limited resources, cannot possibly examine, with the degree of close scrutiny required for full disclosure, each of the many financial statements which are filed. Recognizing this, the Commission necessarily must rely heavily on both the accounting and legal professions to perform their tasks diligently and responsibly. Breaches of professional responsibility jeopardize the achievement of the objectives of the securities laws and can inflict great damage on public investors. As our Court observed in United States v. Benjamin, 328 F.2d 854 (2 Cir.), cert. denied 377 U.S. 953 (1964), "In our complex society the accountants' certificates or the lawyer's opinion can be instruments for inflicting pecuniary loss more potent than a chisel or a crowbar."

Rule 2(e) thus represents an attempt by the SEC essentially to protect the integrity of its own processes. If incompetent or unethical accountants should be permitted to certify financial statements, the reliability of the disclosure process would be impaired.

These concerns have led courts to reject challenges to the authority of other agencies to discipline attorneys practicing or appearing before them. * * *

* * *

Appellants attempt to distinguish *Goldsmith* [Goldsmith v. Board of Tax Appeals, 270 U.S. 117 (1926)] and *Herman* [Herman v. Dulles, 205 F.2d 715 (D.C.Cir.1953)] from the instant case on the ground that the agencies involved in those cases exercised only "judicial functions", whereas the SEC, according to appellants, is authorized to act only as an enforcement agency.[20] Assuming arguendo the correctness of appellants' restrictive description of the SEC's functions, it is uniformly accepted that many agencies properly combine the functions of prosecutor, judge and jury. Indeed, the Supreme Court has held that a hearing conducted by such a body does not automatically constitute a violation of due process. Withrow v. Larkin, 421 U.S. 35, 47–50 (1975). Accord, Wright v. SEC, 112 F.2d 89, 94 (2 Cir.1940). Appellants nevertheless argue—we think facetiously—that permitting the SEC to discipline attorneys who appear before it would be equivalent to empowering United States Attorneys to disbar lawyers who represent clients in criminal prosecutions in the federal courts. Aside from

---

20. As we are sure appellants' lead counsel recalls, the SEC is a quasi-legislative, quasi-judicial and quasi-executive agency. It has been so recognized throughout the 45 years of its existence.

[Eds.—This is a jibe at Milton V. Freeman, Esq., who argued the case for Touche Ross and who, many years previously, had like Judge Timbers been on the staff of the SEC.]

the obviously inapt analogy, this contention at most merely suggests the possibility that the power to discipline may be abused; it is wide of the mark of suggesting a reason for invalidating the Commission's rule. As the Court stated in Withrow v. Larkin, supra, 421 U.S. at 47:

"The contention that the combination of investigative and adjudicative functions necessarily creates an unconstitutional risk of bias in administrative adjudication has a much more difficult burden of persuasion to carry. It must overcome a presumption of honesty and integrity in those serving as adjudicators; and it must convince that, under a realistic appraisal of psychological tendencies and human weakness, conferring investigative and adjudicative powers on the same individuals poses such a risk of actual bias or prejudgment that the practice must be forbidden if the guarantee of due process is to be adequately implemented."

To summarize: we reject appellants' assertion that the Commission acted without authority in promulgating Rule 2(e). Although there is no express statutory provision authorizing the Commission to discipline professionals appearing before it, Rule 2(e), promulgated pursuant to its statutory rulemaking authority, represents an attempt by the Commission to protect the integrity of its own processes. It provides the Commission with the means to ensure that those professionals, on whom the Commission relies heavily in the performance of its statutory duties, perform their tasks diligently and with a reasonable degree of competence. As such the Rule is "reasonably related" to the purposes of the securities laws. Mourning v. Family Publications Service, Inc., supra. Moreover, we hold that the Rule does not violate, nor is it inconsistent with, any other provision of the securities laws. We therefore sustain the validity of the Rule as a necessary adjunct to the Commission's power to protect the integrity of its administrative procedures and the public in general. Goldsmith v. Board of Tax Appeals, supra.

Accordingly, we hold that the district court properly refused to enjoin the Commission from proceedings against Touche Ross pursuant to Rule 2(e). We affirm the judgment dismissing the action. In view of our holding that Rule 2(e) represents a valid exercise of the Commission's rulemaking power, appellants must exhaust their administrative remedies before the SEC before they attempt to obtain judicial review of their other claims, including their claim that the Commission is acting with bias and will not afford them a fair hearing in accordance with due process.[21]

---

21. Touche Ross chose to remain loyal to its retired partners and to challenge Rule 2(e) in a broadside attack on the right of the Commission to discipline *anyone*. Our opinion today rejects this sally. Nothing in the complaint, or the district court proceedings, or the briefs and oral argument before us purports to raise the question of the extent to which the Commission has the power, in a disciplinary action, to hold Touche Ross and its 525 partners vicariously liable to the extent of permanent revocation of the right to practice for the acts of its erstwhile partners. It may be argued, for example, that the Commission may not proceed against Touche Ross on a theory of *respondent superior* without first establishing that Congress has delegated such authority and that the Commission has, through a rulemaking proceeding, set standards for such an adjudication, including a definition of "willful conduct" by organizations. See generally Fuller, The Forms and Limits of Adjudication, 92 Harv.L.Rev. 353, 373 (1978). We express no view on this question, but it is one that the Commission might want to consider. In any event, since it is far from clear that the Commission will in fact determine to discipline Touche Ross, and since the question was *not* raised before the Commission or this court, the resolution of such issues should await the conclusion of the administrative process.

We affirm the district court's dismissal of the action.

KAUFMAN, CHIEF JUDGE (with whom TIMBERS, CIRCUIT JUDGE, joins) concurring: * * *.

RULE 2(e) AND THE ACCOUNTING AND LEGAL PROFESSIONS

Rule 2(e) of the Rules of Practice of the Securities and Exchange Commission purports to provide for the discipline by the Commission of attorneys and accountants by temporary or permanent suspension from practice before the Commission. The bases specified in the rule for such a suspension or disbarment of an attorney or accountant from practice before the Commission are:

(1) Lack of the "requisite qualifications";

(2) Lack of "character";

(3) Lack of "integrity";

(4) "[U]nethical * * * professional conduct";

(5) "[I]mproper professional conduct";

(6) A "willful violation" of any provision of the federal securities laws or any of the rules or regulations thereunder (including having willfully aided and abetted such a violation);

(7) The suspension or revocation of his license to practice law or accounting by the state authority authorized to take such action;

(8) Conviction of a felony (any felony);

(9) Conviction of a "misdemeanor involving moral turpitude";

(10) The entry of a permanent injunction by a court against him (including a consent decree), prohibiting him from violating or aiding and abetting a violation of the federal securities laws;

(11) A "finding" by any court or by the Commission that he has violated or aided and abetted a violation of the federal securities laws.

For an analysis of these grounds for suspension or disbarment, see Marsh, Rule 2(e) Proceedings, 35 Bus.Law. 987, at 995–1003 (1980).

Several of these grounds for suspension or disbarment have been added in more recent years, but the basic provisions of Rule 2(e) have been in effect since 1935. During the first forty years of its existence, this rule generated very little discussion or controversy. During the last ten years, however, it has become a very serious bone of contention between the Securities and Exchange Commission and the accounting and legal professions. The reasons for this are twofold. First, relatively few proceedings were instituted under this rule by the Commission during the first thirty-five or forty years of its existence. In the last ten years, the Commission has instituted a very large number of such proceedings, with geometrically increasing frequency, some of them against highly respected and prestigious law firms and accounting firms.[1] Secondly, in the earlier period the Commission instituted such proceedings only where the respondent's conduct constituted a direct and egregious interference with the functioning of the processes of the Commission. In the last ten years, the Commission has used this rule as a basis for asserting jurisdiction to regulate the practice of their professions by attorneys and accountants, even where there was no proceeding whatever before the Commission, so long as the alleged

1. See Marsh, Rule 2(e) Proceedings, 35 Bus.Law. 987, at 988–989 (1980).

conduct of the respondent assertedly facilitated in some fashion some violation of the federal securities laws.[2]

The *Touche Ross* case was the first direct challenge of the authority of the Commission to adopt Rule 2(e) and to implement it in the fashion which has been employed in recent years,[3] and the court fully supported the arguments of the Commission that the rule was necessary in order to "protect the integrity of its processes." This alleged necessity arises from the assertion that the Commission "with its small staff and limited resources, cannot possibly examine, with the degree of close scrutiny required for full disclosure, each of the many * * * [documents] which are filed [with it] * * *." Because the Commission is unable to do this, it is asserted that attorneys and accountants must do that job for it and may be punished by the Commission when they fail to perform it adequately. The Ninth Circuit in Davy v. Securities and Exchange Commission[4] followed the *Touche Ross* case in upholding the authority of the SEC to discipline accountants under Rule 2(e). The Court distinguished the *Arthur Young & Co.* case, supra, page 1181, on the basis that that was "an enforcement action" against the accounting firm, and not a disciplinary action under Rule 2(e). Surely, however, the court did not intend to say that the SEC could punish an accountant for conduct which would not be the basis for an injunction. In fact, the conduct of the accountant in the *Davy* case was clearly distinguishable from that of the accountant in the *Arthur Young & Co.* case. The court said that Davy "does not dispute that his audit violated Generally Accepted Auditing Standards and Generally Accepted Accounting Principles."

In the case of In the Matter of Keating, Muething & Klekamp,[5] however, then Commissioner Karmel dissented from the imposition of sanctions under Rule 2(e) on a law firm (even though it had consented to the order), on the basis that the Commission had no statutory authorization to discipline attorneys who practice before it. She said: "When Rule 2(e) is invoked to discipline attorneys for misconduct which does not directly obstruct the administrative process, in my opinion it is done so improperly as a matter of law and as a matter of policy. In the *Emmanuel Fields* case[6] the Commission barred an attorney on the theory that the Commission can regulate the manner in which lawyers counsel clients and render opinions in securities transactions in order to protect investors. A primary rationale for so using Rule 2(e) has been that 'the task of enforcing the securities laws rests in overwhelming measure on the bar's shoulders' and that given 'its small staff, limited resources, and onerous tasks, the Commission is peculiarly dependent on the probity and diligence of the professionals who practice before it.' However, Congress did not authorize the Commission to conscript attorneys to enforce their clients' responsibilities under the federal securities laws. Furthermore, institutional limitations alone cannot justify the creation of a new remedy not contemplated by the Congress.

---

2. Id. at 990–993.

3. Two earlier circuit court cases have casual dicta assuming the validity of Rule 2(e), but in both instances the court *reversed* the action of the Commission being challenged. Securities and Exchange Commission v. Csapo, 174 U.S.App.D.C. 339, 533 F.2d 7 (1976); Kivitz v. Securities and Exchange, 154 U.S.App.D.C. 372, 475 F.2d 956 (1973). The validity of the rule was upheld in two early district court cases. Schwebel v. Orrick, 153 F.Supp. 701 (D.D.C.1957), rev'd on other grounds 251

F.2d 919 (D.C.Cir.), cert. denied 356 U.S. 927 (1958); Securities and Exchange Commission v. Ezrine, CCH Fed.Sec.Law Rptr. ¶ 93,594 (S.D.N.Y.1972) (otherwise unreported).

4. 792 F.2d 1418 (9th Cir.1986).

5. Sec.Exch.Act Rel. No. 15982, CCH Fed.Sec.Law Rptr. ¶ 82,124 (July 2, 1979).

6. Sec.Act Rel. No. 5404, CCH Fed.Sec. Law Rptr. ¶ 79,407 (SEC 1973), aff'd without opinion 495 F.2d 1075 (D.C.Cir.1974).

"I am firmly convinced that such conscription, or the promulgation and enforcement of regulatory standards of conduct for securities lawyers by the Commission, is very bad policy. It undermines the willingness and ability of the bar to exercise professional responsibility and sows the seeds for government abuse of power.

"A person's right to counsel is protected by various common law principles, the Administrative Procedure Act and the Sixth Amendment to the U.S. Constitution. When a prosecutorial agency like the Commission disciplines attorneys acting in a representative capacity, it necessarily impinges upon and interferes with a client's right to counsel. Because of the importance of the right to counsel of persons in their dealings with the government, it seems to me that government agencies, especially those with a prosecutorial function, should exercise caution in taking administrative action against attorneys. Such regulation necessarily gives an advocate pause, whether he is acting as an advisor or an adversary." [7]

It was expected that the *Carter and Johnson* case, supra page 1202, would provide an opportunity for a decision in another circuit court as to the validity of Rule 2(e) and possibly, if it did not agree with the Second Circuit, a review by the United States Supreme Court. The Commission, however, neatly avoided any such test of its power by its failure to impose any sanctions on the respondents in that proceeding (while threatening to do so for similar conduct in the future); but it vigorously reasserted its own opinion that it had full authority to adopt and enforce Rule 2(e). At the same time, the Commission, by redefining what it expects of attorneys under Rule 2(e) fundamentally in terms of adherence to the Canons of Ethics, has apparently attempted to defuse to some extent the controversy between it and the legal profession. Nevertheless, the basic issue remains: Does the Commission have any authority to "conscript attorneys to enforce their clients' responsibilities under the federal securities laws" and to punish the attorneys if they fail to perform this duty to the satisfaction of the Commission?

See Siedel, Rule 2(e) and Corporate Officers, 39 Bus.Law. 455 (1984); Dolin, SEC Rule 2(e) After Carter-Johnson: Toward a Reconciliation of Purpose and Scope, 9 Sec.Reg.L.J. 331 (1982); Gruenbaum, SEC's Use of Rule 2(e) to Discipline Accountants and Other Professionals, 56 Notre Dame Law. 820 (1981); Krane, Attorney Unshackled: SEC Rule 2(e) Violates Clients' Sixth Amendment Right to Counsel, 57 Notre Dame Law 50 (1981); Ferrara, Administrative Disciplinary Proceedings under Rule 2(e), 36 Bus.Law. 1807 (1981); Best, In Opposition to Rule 2(e) Proceedings, 36 Bus.Law. 1815 (1981); Marsh, Rule 2(e) Proceedings, 35 Bus.Law. 987 (1980); Patterson, The Limits of the Lawyers' Discretion and the Law of Legal Ethics, 1979 Duke L.J. 1251; Gross, Attorneys and Their Corporate Clients: SEC Rule 2(e) and the Georgetown Whistle Blowing Proposal, 3 Corp.L.Rev. 197 (1980); Wheat, The Impact of SEC Professional Responsibility Standards, 34 Bus.Law. 969 (1979); Downing and Miller, The Distortion and Misuse of Rule 2(e), 54 Notre Dame Law. 774 (1979); Troger, Reassessing the Validity of SEC Rule 2(e) Discipline of Accountants, 59 Boston U.L.Rev. 968 (1979); Dockery, Attorney Liability Under SEC Rule 2(e): A New Standard, 11 Tex.Tech.L.Rev. 83 (1979); Hoffman, On Learning of a Corporate Client's Crime or Fraud—The Lawyer's Dilemma, 33 Bus.Law. 1389 (1978); Daley and Karmel, Attorneys' Responsibilities: Adversaries at the Bar of the SEC, 24 Emory L.J. 747 (1975); Sonde, Professional Responsibility—A

---

7. See also the dissenting opinions of Commissioner Karmel in In re Richard D. Hodgin, Sec.Exch.Act Rel. No. 16225, CCH Fed.Sec.Law Rptr. ¶ 82,334 (SEC 1979); In re Bernard J. Coven, Sec.Exch.Act Rel. No. 16448 (SEC 1979), 19 SEC Docket, No. 1, p. 12, Jan. 8, 1980.

New Religion, or the Old Gospel? 24 Emory L.J. 827 (1975); Burton, SEC Enforcement and Accountants: Philosophy, Objectives and Approach, 28 Vand. L.Rev. 19 (1975); Fiflis, Current Problems of Accountants' Responsibilities to Third Parties, 28 Vand.L.Rev. 31 (1975); Mathews, Liabilities of Lawyers Under the Federal Securities Laws, 30 Bus.Law. 105 (1975); Gonson, Disciplinary Proceedings and Other Remedies Available to the SEC, 30 Bus.Law. 191 (1975); Bialkin, Sanctions Against Accountants, 8 Rev.Sec.Reg. 823 (1975); Lowenfels, Expanding Public Responsibilities of Securities Lawyers, 74 Colum.L.Rev. 412 (1974); Sonde, The Responsibility of Professionals Under the Federal Securities Laws—Some Observations, 68 Nw.U.L.Rev. 1 (1973); Small, An Attorney's Responsibilities Under Federal and State Securities Laws: Private Counselor or Public Servant?, 61 Calif.L.Rev. 1189 (1973); Karmel, Attorneys' Securities Law Liabilities, 27 Bus.Law. 1153 (1973).

Part VII

TRANSNATIONAL TRANSACTIONS

Chapter 24

TRANSNATIONAL TRANSACTIONS

Statutes and Regulations

Securities Act of 1933, §§ 2(7), 5.

Securities Exchange Act of 1934, §§ 3(a)(17), 30.

LEASCO DATA PROCESSING EQUIPMENT CORP. v. MAXWELL

United States Court of Appeals, Second Circuit, 1972.
468 F.2d 1326.

Before FRIENDLY, CHIEF JUDGE, FEINBERG, CIRCUIT JUDGE, and DAVIS, ASSOCIATE JUDGE.*

FRIENDLY, CHIEF JUDGE:

This case, in which the plaintiffs (hereinafter collectively referred to as Leasco) seek large damages allegedly resulting from the purchase of shares of a British company on the London Stock Exchange, first came to our attention in October, 1971, on Leasco's appeal from a judgment entered by Judge Lasker in the District Court for the Southern District of New York, 319 F.Supp. 1256, dismissing the complaint as against defendant Isidore Kerman, a London solicitor, for lack of jurisdiction over the person. Consideration of the questions presented by that appeal led us to wonder whether, because of the foreign elements in the transaction in suit, the district court had jurisdiction over the subject matter. * * *

I. *The Facts Claimed by Leasco*

The gist of the complaint is that the defendant conspired to cause Leasco to buy stock of Pergamon Press Limited ("Pergamon"), a British corporation controlled by defendant Robert Maxwell, a British citizen, at prices in excess of its true value, in violation of § 10(b) of the Securities Exchange Act and the SEC's sufficiently known Rule 10b-5. According to Leasco, and—as we shall not always repeat—we here state only Leasco's version, the first contact occurred early in 1969 when Maxwell came to Great Neck, N.Y., where Leasco then had its principal office, and proposed to Saul Steinberg, Chairman of Leasco, that Pergamon and Leasco engage in a joint venture in Europe. Maxwell falsely told Steinberg that Pergamon had a computerized typesetting plant in Ireland and gave Steinberg

---

* Of the United States Court of Claims, sitting by designation.

1564

the most recent Pergamon annual report, which contained untruthful and misleading statements of Pergamon's affairs. Steinberg telephoned Maxwell in London to decline the joint venture; Maxwell invited him to come there to discuss areas of possible cooperation.

Steinberg and Robert Hodes, a director of Leasco, met Maxwell at the latter's London office in late April, 1969; Maxwell made various false or exaggerated statements of Pergamon's performance and prospects. When he suggested that Pergamon could acquire Leasco's European operations, Steinberg responded that Leasco would be interested only in acquiring Pergamon and its related companies. Clark, a director of Pergamon, entered the room, Maxwell having left for a short time, and whetted Leasco's interest by falsely touting the profitability of International Learning Systems Company (ILSC). Pergamon was a 50% owner and had an option to acquire the other 50% of ILSC. When Maxwell rejoined the group, he told Steinberg and Hodes that Ladislaus Majhtenyi, an official of Pergamon Press, Inc., an American subsidiary whose stock was traded on the American Stock Exchange, would provide Leasco with all financial data necessary to evaluate the worth of Pergamon and the Maxwell-related companies.

In late April or early May, Michael Gibbs, Leasco's director of corporate planning, met in New York with Majhtenyi. The latter said that the Pergamon and Maxwell operations were very profitable. He added that Pergamon was in the process of acquiring MSI Publishers, Inc. (MSI) and falsely spoke in glowing terms of the profitability of that company's operations in selling Pergamon back issues in Canada, Mexico and South America. This was followed by telephone calls between Maxwell and Steinberg; in some (or perhaps all) of the calls, one (or perhaps both) of the participants were in the United States. Maxwell reported enthusiastically, and falsely, about sales of ILSC encyclopedias in Australia. Expressing surprise at the paucity of information Majhtenyi had given to Gibbs, he said he would meet Steinberg in New York City.

The meeting occurred at a hotel in early May; Maxwell, with Majhtenyi present, made various misrepresentations about the sales and earnings of Pergamon and ILSC. Around May 17 Maxwell mailed a letter from London to Leasco in New York enclosing a dozen documents. Among these were a false report of ILSC's profits; a draft of the 1968 Pergamon annual report, certified by defendant Chalmers, Impey & Co., containing false reports of profits; and a misleading report on Pergamon's affairs, prepared by Whinney, Murray & Co., accountants retained by defendant Robert Fleming & Co. Ltd. (Fleming Ltd.), a London banking firm whose clients were large holders of Pergamon stock and which also acted as financial adviser to Pergamon. Late in the month Maxwell, in London, called Steinberg, in New York; he said that any contract for the takeover would have to be signed before the Pergamon annual meeting on or about June 19. As a result, Gibbs and Schwartz went to London around May 30 and met for four days with Maxwell, Clark, Kerman (a director of Pergamon and Pergamon Press, Inc. and senior partner of a large London firm of solicitors which represented Pergamon and the Maxwell family interests), and others. Many further misrepresentations with respect to Pergamon and ILSC were allegedly made by Maxwell. The meetings were followed by telephone conversations between Maxwell in London and Steinberg in New York, in the course of which Maxwell is claimed to have made further false statements, especially with respect to Pergamon's profits from the sale of back issues. Around the same time Richard Fleming, chairman of Fleming Ltd., and Lawrence Banks, president of its American subsidiary, Robert Fleming, Incorporated (Fleming, Inc.), visited Leasco's offices in New York and told Schwartz and Hodes that Pergamon was far more valuable than the price Leasco was proposing to pay; in effect they also vouched for the correctness of the Whinney Murray & Co. report.

Later Maxwell telephoned from London that the contract would have to be signed on or before June 17. He and Paul DiBiase, a member of Kerman's firm, arrived in New York shortly thereafter. * * * The upshot was an agreement between Leasco and Maxwell signed in New York on June 17, 1969. This provided that, subject to certain conditions, Leasco would offer to acquire each outstanding share of Pergamon for 37 shillings in cash or Leasco debentures plus, in respect of each 10 Pergamon shares tendered, a 5–year warrant to acquire from Leasco one Pergamon share for 42 shillings. Among the conditions were acceptance by not less than 51% of the Pergamon shares and the obtaining of all necessary United Kingdom exchange control permits. The tender offer was to comply with the Code on Take-Overs and Mergers of the City of London and the regulations of the London Stock Exchange. Maxwell agreed to accept the offer and procure the assent of "the Maxwell interests," to recommend acceptance by the Pergamon shareholders, and to use his best efforts to obtain a similar recommendation by the Pergamon board of directors. * * *

Apparently Steinberg and Hodes accompanied Maxwell back to England. There he told them, on June 18, that it would be in Leasco's interest to purchase Pergamon stock on the open market as soon as possible. * * * On June 20 Leasco, acting through the London banking firm of N.M. Rothschild & Sons ("Rothschild") began buying Pergamon shares on the London Stock Exchange. By July 24 it purchased 5,206,210 such shares, expending some $22,000,000; later it learned that some 600,000 of these shares had been secretly sold by one or more of the defendants. The stock was paid for with cash furnished by a wholly-owned subsidiary, Leasco International N.V. (Leasco N.V.), a Netherlands Antilles corporation, which had recently sold to a group headed by two United States underwriters, $40,000,000 of 5% debentures and $20,000,000 of 7% notes for offering only outside the United States and to persons not nationals or citizens thereof or resident or normally resident therein. Both the debentures and the notes were unconditionally guaranteed by Leasco, and the debentures were convertible into its common stock.

Investigation of Pergamon's affairs by Leasco, authorized by the June 17 agreement, caused Leasco's representatives to make further inquiries of Maxwell in England; many of his responses are alleged to have been false and misleading. In early August, Leasco's representatives met with Maxwell, Majhtenyi and others in Elmsford, N.Y.; Leasco was provided with data indicating that previous representations on the subject of sales of back issues had been misleading. As a result of this and other information, Leasco declined to go forward with the tender offer. However, it was left with the $22,000,000 of Pergamon stock acquired on the London Stock Exchange. Leasco seeks damages in that amount, together with exemplary damages.

* * *

II. *Subject Matter Jurisdiction*

One of the few points on which all parties are in accord is that subject matter jurisdiction depends on the applicability of the Securities Exchange Act. Leasco's principal place of business is in New York. Defendants Isthmus Enterprises, Inc., Maxwell Scientific International Inc., and MSI Publishers, Inc. appear to have their principal offices in New York, and this is stated to be true of defendant Robert Fleming, Inc. Plaintiff Leasco World Trade Company (U.K.) Limited, the reason for whose joinder is not apparent, is a British corporation, and most of the defendants are British citizens or corporations. There is thus no jurisdiction under 28 U.S.C. § 1332(a). However, § 27 of the Securities Exchange Act vests the district court with jurisdiction over an action "to enforce any liability created by this title or the rules and regulations thereunder * * *." * * *

It will be useful at the outset to differentiate the problem here present-ed from the point decided in Schoenbaum v. Firstbrook, 405 F.2d 200 (2 Cir.), modified with respect to the issue of liability of one set of defendants, 405 F.2d 215 (2 Cir.1968), cert. denied, 395 U.S. 906 (1969). *Schoenbaum* held § 10(b) to be applicable, *even when the fraudulent acts were all committed outside the United States* and the security was that of a foreign company doing no business in the United States, in a case where "the transactions involve stock registered and listed on a national securities exchange, and are detrimental to the interests of American investors." 405 F.2d at 208. If we treat the matter in terms of the distinctions drawn in the Restatement (Second) of Foreign Relations Law of the United States (1965), *Schoenbaum* raised the problem, considered in § 18, of the circum-stances in which "[a] state has jurisdiction to prescribe a rule of law attaching legal consequences to conduct that occurs outside its territory and causes an effect within its territory * * *" and consequently may be thought to have been meant to do so. If all the misrepresentations here alleged had occurred in England, we would entertain most serious doubt whether, despite United States v. Aluminum Co. of America, 148 F.2d 416, 443–444 (2 Cir.1954), and *Schoenbaum,* § 10(b) would be applicable simply because of the adverse effect of the fraudulently induced purchases in England of securities of an English corporation, not traded in an organized American securities market, upon an American corporation whose stock is listed on the New York Stock Exchange and its shareholders. Cf. Vanity Fair Mills, Inc. v. T. Eaton & Co., 234 F.2d 633 (2 Cir.) cert. denied 352 U.S. 871 (1956). It is true, as Judge L. Hand pointed out in the *Aluminum* case, supra, 148 F.2d at 443, that if Congress has expressly prescribed a rule with respect to conduct outside the United States, even one going beyond the scope recognized by foreign relations law, a United States court would be bound to follow the Congressional direction unless this would violate the due process clause of the Fifth Amendment. However, the language of § 10(b) of the Securities Exchange Act is much too inconclusive to lead us to believe that Congress meant to impose rules governing conduct through-out the world in every instance where an American company bought or sold a security. When no fraud has been practiced in this country and the purchase or sale has not been made here, we would be hard pressed to find justification for going beyond *Schoenbaum.*

On plaintiffs' version of the facts, that issue does not here arise. The instant case deals rather with the problem considered in the Restatement's

§ 17, "Jurisdiction to Prescribe with Respect to Conduct, Thing, Status, or other Interest within Territory." While the black letter seems to require that, in a case like this, not only there should be conduct within the territory but also the conduct relate "to a thing located, or a status or other interest localized, in its territory," Comment A and Illustrations 1 and 2, the latter of which [3] is quite pertinent here, appear to be satisfied if there has been conduct within the territory. Conduct within the territory alone would seem sufficient from the standpoint of *jurisdiction* to prescribe a rule. It follows that when, as here, there has been significant conduct within the territory, a statute cannot properly be held inapplicable simply on the ground that, absent the clearest language, Congress will not be assumed to have meant to go beyond the limits recognized by foreign relations law. Defendants' reliance on the principle stated in Foley Bros. v. Filardo, 336 U.S. 281 (1949), that regulatory statutes will generally not be construed as applying to conduct wholly outside the United States, is thus misplaced. However, it would be equally erroneous to assume that the legislature always means to go to the full extent permitted. This is a question of the interpretation of the particular statute, which we will consider below with specific reference to § 10(b).

* * *

Up to this point we have established only that, because of the extensive acts alleged to have been performed in the United States, considerations of foreign relations law do not preclude our reading § 10(b) as applicable here. The question remains whether we should. Appellants have three lines of defense: they claim (1) that § 10(b) has no application to transactions in foreign securities not on an organized American market; (2) that if it does, it has no application when such transactions occur outside the United States; and (3) that in any event it can have no application when the purchaser is not a citizen of the United States. * * *

* * *

Since Congress thus meant § 10(b) to protect against fraud in the sale or purchase of securities whether or not these were traded on organized United States markets, we cannot perceive any reason why it should have wished to limit the protection to securities of American issuers. The New Yorker who is the object of fraudulent misrepresentations in New York is as much injured if the securities are of a mine in Saskatchewan as in Nevada. Defendants have pointed to nothing in the legislative history which would indicate an intention that the language of § 10(b) should be narrowed so as not to protect him.

We likewise cannot see any sound reason for believing that, in a case like that just put, Congress would have wished protection to be withdrawn merely because the fraudulent promoter of the Saskatchewan mining security took the buyer's check back to Canada and mailed the certificate from there. In the somewhat different yet closely related context of choice of law, the mechanical test that, in determining the *locus delicti*, "The place of wrong is in the state where the last event necessary to make an actor liable for an alleged tort takes place," Restatement of the Conflict of

---

3. X and Y are in State A. X makes a misrepresentation to Y. X and Y go to State B. Solely because of the prior misrepresentations, Y delivers money to X. A has jurisdiction to prescribe a criminal penalty for obtaining money by false pretenses.

Restatement (Second) of the Foreign Relations Law of the United States 45.

Laws § 377 (1934), has given way, in the case of fraud and misrepresentation, to a more extensive and sophisticated analysis. See Restatement (Second) of the Conflict of Laws § 148 (1971).

Our case, however, is not the simple one thus hypothesized. In that instance not only the fraudulent misrepresentation but the issuance of the check and the receipt of the securities occurred in the United States, although the check was deposited and the security mailed in Canada. Here it was understood from the outset that all the transactions would be executed in England. Still we must ask ourselves whether, if Congress had thought about the point, it would not have wished to protect an American investor if a foreigner comes to the United States and fraudulently induces him to purchase foreign securities abroad—a purpose which its words can fairly be held to embrace. While, as earlier stated, we doubt that impact on an American company and its shareholders would suffice to make the statute applicable if the misconduct had occurred solely in England, we think it tips the scales in favor of applicability when substantial misrepresentations were made in the United States.

* * *

[Eds.—The court held that this result was not changed by the fact that the purchase was made through the wholly-owned Netherlands Antilles subsidiary of plaintiff Leasco.]

III. *Jurisdiction over the Person*

Jurisdiction over the person is challenged, thus far unsuccessfully, by defendant Fleming Ltd., and Chalmers, Impey & Co. and, thus far successfully, by defendant Kerman. * * *

Fleming Ltd.

In light of these principles we have little difficulty in upholding the denial of the motion of Fleming Ltd. to dismiss for lack of personal jurisdiction. Richard Fleming, its managing director, and Lawrence Banks, first with him and then representing him, appeared at meetings in the United States and allegedly made misrepresentations concerning the value of Pergamon and the accuracy of the Whinney Murray & Co. report which Fleming Ltd. had commissioned. We thus do not reach the question whether Fleming Ltd. could be considered to be "doing business" in the United States by virtue of the activities of its New York subsidiary in buying and selling securities in the American markets and furnishing other services to Fleming Ltd.

Chalmers, Impey & Co.

We come to an opposite conclusion with respect to Chalmers, Impey & Co. ("Chalmers"). Plaintiffs' attempt to show that Chalmers was doing business in the United States in the spring of 1969 completely failed. * * *

This leaves only the ground elaborated in § 37 of the Restatement (Second) of Conflict of Laws:

A state has the power to exercise judicial jurisdiction over an individual who causes effects in the state by an act done elsewhere with respect to any cause of action arising from these effects unless the nature of the effects and of the individual's relationship to the state makes the exercise of such jurisdiction unreasonable.

The classic illustration is the man who shoots a bullet across a state boundary; a more realistic example is furnished by McGee v. International Life Ins. Co., supra, 355 U.S. 220 (soliciting purchase of insurance policy and sending premium notices by mail from outside the state into the state). But this is a principle that must be applied with caution, particularly in an international context. See Duple Motor Bodies, Ltd. v. Hollingsworth, 417 F.2d 231, 239 (9 Cir.1969) (dissenting opinion); Von Mehren & Trautman, Jurisdiction to Adjudicate: A Suggested Analysis, 79 Harv.L.Rev. 1121, 1127 (1966). At minimum the conduct must meet the tests laid down in § 18 of the Restatement (Second) of Foreign Relations Law, including the important requirement that the effect "occurs as a direct and foreseeable result of the conduct outside the territory." We believe, moreover, that attaining the rather low floor of foreseeability necessary to support a finding of tort liability is not enough to support *in personam* jurisdiction. The person sought to be charged must know, or have good reason to know, that his conduct will have effects in the state seeking to assert jurisdiction over him.

The amended complaint does charge that Chalmers "knew or had good reason to know" that the allegedly false and misleading financial reports it had prepared "would be given by the defendants to plaintiffs as prospective purchasers of Pergamon and that plaintiffs would receive them and rely upon them." But the affidavit of John Ralph Briggs, the Chalmers partner who was in charge of the firm's work on Pergamon, broadly denies this. * * * Leasco did not dispute Briggs' assertions; it relied simply on the fact that Chalmers must have known that its reports on Pergamon would be relied on by anyone interested in buying Pergamon shares. On that basis accountants operating solely in London could be subjected to personal jurisdiction in any country whose citizen had purchased stock of a company they had audited; the same would be true, of course, of accountants operating solely in the United States. Although such worldwide reliance may be, in a sense, foreseeable, it is not sufficiently so to constitute a basis of personal jurisdiction consonant with due process. * * *

Isidore Kerman

The issue with respect to Kerman is closer than either of those previously discussed. As stated above, he was a director of Pergamon and the firm in which he is a senior partner acted as its solicitors, although he states that his partner DiBiase was "generally responsible for handling commercial matters" for it. Admittedly he attended the London meetings over four days in early June, 1969. His affidavit minimized his participation, saying that he attended because he "was a Director of the Company, as well as one of its solicitors and as such was keeping informed of developments of significance to the company and its stockholders." An opposing affidavit by a Leasco officer alleged that Kerman "took an active part" in the meetings and remained silent when, to his knowledge, Maxwell was misrepresenting the facts. Other Leasco officers averred that in the New York negotiations DiBiase did not act simply as a draftsman but "made numerous false and misleading statements to plaintiffs as to the operations and financial condition of Pergamon and its affiliated companies." Steinberg averred "upon information and belief," the source of which was undisclosed, that "Maxwell and DiBiase received from and sent to Kerman many communications respecting the terms of the June 17th Agreement." Kerman responded that there had been no such communications. DiBiase did not submit an affidavit, and Maxwell's affidavit neither mentions nor denies communication with Kerman. On the other hand, Leasco apparently made no effort to subpoena the telephone company or other records that would show whether transatlantic telephone calls were made. Leasco averred that, in addition to his position as director and solicitor, Kerman had an interest as owner of 60,000 Pergamon shares and trustee of Maxwell family trusts owning 600,000 shares, some or all of which may have figured in the purchases on the London Stock Exchange. Kerman denied he was a trustee of any Maxwell family trusts holding Pergamon shares or had any connection with sales by any such trusts; he said nothing with respect to the sale of the 60,000 shares. Leasco urged that if Judge Laskar was not prepared to deny Kerman's motion to dismiss, he should postpone decision until Kerman had answered interrogatories which Leasco intended shortly to serve upon him.

Kerman's conduct in England differs from that of Chalmers (except for the two insignificant episodes after June 18) in that he was at all times well aware that Maxwell was endeavoring to sell Pergamon shares to Leasco. On the other hand, Leasco did not allege that Kerman himself made any misrepresentations; his offense, if offense it was, lay in remaining silent while Maxwell did. Kerman's case may differ also from Chalmers' with respect to his performing acts in the United States. To be sure, the rule in this circuit is that the mere presence of one conspirator, such as Maxwell, does not confer personal jurisdiction over another alleged conspirator. Bertha Building Corp. v. National Theatres Corp., 248 F.2d 833, 836 (2 Cir. 1957), cert. denied, 356 U.S. 936 (1958); H.L. Moore Drug Exchange, Inc. v. Smith, Kline & French Laboratories, 384 F.2d 97 (2 Cir.1967). Neither would the partnership relation between Kerman and DiBiase alone justify a conclusion that DiBiase's acts in New York were the equivalent, for purposes of personal jurisdiction, of acts by Kerman here—as would be apparent if Leasco sought to assert such jurisdiction over other members of the firm. However, the matter could be viewed differently when the relationship was the closer one between a senior partner, especially one who is a director of the client, and a younger partner to whom he has delegated the duty of carrying out an assignment over which the senior retains general supervision. The case for doing this would be materially strengthened by proof that the junior was in frequent communication with the senior.

There were too many unresolved questions of fact to make it proper for the judge to take the important step of dismissing Kerman as a defendant on the basis of the conflicting affidavits before him. * * *

* * *

The orders of Judge Ryan denying the motions to dismiss for lack of subject matter jurisdiction and for lack of personal jurisdiction over Fleming Ltd. are affirmed. His order denying the motion of Chalmers to dismiss for lack of personal jurisdiction is reversed, with instructions to enter an order of dismissal. The order of Judge Laskar dismissing the complaint against Kerman is vacated and the cause remanded for further proceedings consistent with this opinion. * * *

BERSCH v. DREXEL FIRESTONE, INC.

United States Court of Appeals, Second Circuit, 1975.
519 F.2d 974.

FRIENDLY, CIRCUIT JUDGE:

These appeals from orders of Judge Carter in an action in the District Court for the Southern District of New York again bring before us the question of the territorial reach of the federal securities laws with which we have previously dealt in Schoenbaum v. Firstbrook, 405 F.2d 200 (2 Cir.), rev'd on the merits, 405 F.2d 215 (2 Cir.1968) (en banc), cert. denied sub nom., Manley v. Schoenbaum, 395 U.S. 906 (1969), and Leasco Data Processing Equipment Corp. v. Maxwell, 468 F.2d 1326 (2 Cir.1972). Apart from differences in the facts, there is the added complexity that whereas *Schoenbaum* was a derivative action by stockholders of a Canadian corporation and *Leasco* an action by two corporate plaintiffs, the suit here is a class action on behalf of thousands of plaintiffs preponderantly citizens and residents of Canada, Australia, England, France, Germany, Switzerland, and many other countries in Europe, Asia, Africa, and South America.

I. *The Basic Facts.*

The securities transactions giving rise to this litigation go back to 1969. The securities were the common stock of defendant I.O.S., Ltd. (IOS), an international sales and financial service organization principally engaged in the sale and management of mutual funds and complementary financial activities organized under the laws of Canada,[3] having had its main business office in Geneva, Switzerland. It is now in the hands of liquidators appointed in November, 1973, by the Supreme Court of New Brunswick pursuant to the Canadian Winding-Up Act, Revised Statutes of Canada, 1970, ch. W-10.

Prior to 1968 the stock of IOS and its subsidiaries had been held by its organizer, defendant Bernard Cornfeld, his associates, and their employees. Although Cornfeld had always been free to sell his IOS shares, and in fact

---

3. The mutual fund sales business which in 1960 was transferred to I.O.S., Ltd. (S.A.), a Panamanian Company, was founded by Bernard Cornfeld in Paris in 1956. By 1969, in addition to operating more than a dozen mutual fund sales companies throughout the world and a dozen mutual funds of its own, the Company owned ten banks and finance companies, a life insurance company with subsidiaries in six countries, a group of real estate companies, a couple of small publishing enterprises, and a data publishing firm.

[Eds.—The rise and fall of the "offshore empire" of Bernard Cornfeld is chronicled by three London Times reporters in a journalistic *tour de force* titled "Do you Sincerely Want to be Rich?". (Raw, Page and Hodgson, "Do You Sincerely Want to be Rich?", New York, The Viking Press, 1971). From being an obscure salesman of shares of a mutual fund to American NATO personnel stationed in the Paris area in 1956, Cornfeld rose to command a financial empire disposing of total resources exceeding those of the vast majority of governments in the world; then the edifice collapsed, with most of the components ending up in the bankruptcy courts of several nations; and Cornfeld had a sojourn in a Swiss jail (he was reported as saying that the accommodations were not too bad, but the cuisine left a great deal to be desired), until he was finally permitted to post bail and fled the country—all within a period of less than twenty years.]

had disposed of significant amounts of these over the prior nine year period, his employees had been denied the right to sell their holdings and no organized market for IOS shares existed. Within the company the price of the stock was set by a theoretical formula value; the stock was used as a means of partial compensation and was granted to employees as a performance incentive, it being commonly understood by the employees that the company would eventually be taken public and they might then "cash in". A plan was developed wherein each of IOS's principal subsidiaries would first separately be taken public; finally common shares of IOS itself would be sold. In 1968 IOS floated 600,000 shares of one of its principal subsidiaries, IOS Management Ltd., a Canadian registered concern. The shares were offered at $12.50; trading opened at $75; and by March 1969 they had reached a peak of around $180. Subsequent to this sale, no doubt in part due to the success of this offering and more importantly to growing salesman dissatisfaction in light of a successful offering by a recently created competitor, the decision was made to abandon the original plan and to take IOS public as soon as appeared feasible. The planning of this offering was constrained by the framework set out in an Order Accepting Offer of Settlement entered by the SEC on May 23, 1967. Paragraph 4 of this order provided in pertinent part:

> Upon entry of the Order based on this Stipulation, IOS and all its affiliates shall cease all sales of securities to United States citizens or nationals wherever located, except for (i) offers and sales outside of the United States (and its territories, possessions or commonwealth subject to the jurisdiction of the United States) to officers, directors and full-time personnel of IOS and its subsidiaries. * * *

Three separate distributions of IOS common stock were proposed. The largest was to be a primary offering of 5,600,000 newly issued shares underwritten by six of the defendants (hereafter the Drexel Group)—two American banking houses, Drexel Firestone, Inc. and Smith, Barney & Co., having their principal offices in the United States but also having offices in Europe, and four foreign underwriting houses, Banque Rothschild; Hill, Samuel & Co., Limited; Guinness Mahon & Co., Limited; and Pierson, Heldring & Pierson, having their principal offices abroad. The 5,600,000 shares were to be and were in fact sold under a prospectus outside the United States to foreign nationals residing in Europe, Asia and Australia. Prospectuses were printed abroad in English, French, and German and delivered to the purchasers outside the United States. A secondary offering of 1,450,000 shares, underwritten by defendant J.H. Crang & Co., a Toronto investment house (Crang), was made in Canada by a prospectus conforming to the laws of Canada and its provinces; all of these shares were sold in Canada and none was sold to Americans resident there. The third distribution, whence this action springs, was a secondary offering of 3,950,000 shares by defendant Investors Overseas Bank Limited of Nassau, the Bahamas, an IOS subsidiary (IOB). The prospectus stated, as had that of the Drexel Group, that the shares "are not being offered in the United States of America or any of its territories or possessions or any area subject to its jurisdiction" and was "being made to approximately 25,000 persons who are either (1) employees or sales associates of the Company, (2) certain clients presently holding investments in managed funds or other products of the Company, or (3) persons who have had a long-standing professional or business relationship with the Company."

The offerings were made at the same price, $10 per share, and at approximately the same time. Each prospectus referred to the two other offerings. Reference was made to plans to list the IOS stock on various stock exchanges, none of these being in the United States. The Drexel Group and IOB prospectuses were substantially identical. Although the Crang prospectus was somewhat different insofar as compliance with particular Canadian securities regulations was sought, all three contained balance sheets of IOS and various subsidiaries as of December 31, 1968, and income statements for the five years then ended, and a report of defendant Arthur Andersen & Co. (Andersen), an international accounting firm with its principal office in the United States, that, subject to usual qualifications, the statements fairly presented the financial condition of the company as of December 31, 1968, and for the five years then ended. The Drexel and IOB prospectuses stated that the offerings had not been registered under United States securities laws.[12] The offerings were successful in the limited sense of being fully subscribed, but after stabilizing briefly at $14 the price of the shares drifted downward until April 1970 when it collapsed through the $10 level and three weeks later the shares apparently were virtually unsaleable. The plight of the purchasers was further aggravated when control of IOS passed into the hands of Robert L. Vesco, currently a resident of Costa Rica, and a defendant in a substantial number of actions for fraud pending in this circuit.

II. *The Proceedings in the District Court and this Court.*

The complaint in this action alleging violations of the Securities Act of 1933 and the Securities Exchange Act of 1934, and also containing allegations which can be read as charging common law fraud, was filed in December 1971 by Howard Bersch, a United States citizen living in New York, who had purchased 600 shares of IOS common distributed as part of the IOB underwriting. Characterizing the three underwritings as the "IOS Public Offering", Bersch alleged he was bringing the action individually and on behalf of all persons who purchased stock in each of the offerings, estimated to approximate 100,000. The complaint contained the allegations usual when a plaintiff desires designation of his action as a class action under Fed.R.Civ.P. 23(b)(3). It alleged that the underwriters "impliedly represented to the public that IOS was a suitable company for public ownership" when, in part as a result of the refusal of other investment houses to participate, they should have known that it was not. It also contained more particularized charges, e.g., that the prospectuses failed to reveal illegal activities by IOS and its officers which had seriously damaged the company,[15] that the books and records of IOS and its subsidi-

---

12. In a release dated July 9, 1964, S.E.C. Release No. 33–4708 and No. 34–7366, 17 C.F.R. § 231.4708, 1 CCH Fed.Sec. Rep. ¶ 1362, the SEC stated that it has traditionally taken the position that the registration requirements of Section 5 of the Act are primarily intended to protect American investors. Accordingly, the Commission has not taken any action for failure to register securities of United States corporations distributed abroad to foreign nationals, even though use of jurisdictional means may be involved in the offering. It is assumed in these situations that the distribution is to be effected in a manner which will result in the securities coming to rest abroad.

15. An example of this alleged illegal activity was the participation by IOS officers in the smuggling of currency outside of developing countries in violation of their restrictive currency laws. As a result of this activity IOS had been barred from doing business in several of these countries.

aries and affiliates were in such a chaotic condition that it was impossible to determine from them an accurate picture of IOS' financial position, and that during the months preceding the offering various IOS officials, including Cornfeld, had touted IOS' prospects. It charged that the underwriters in the Drexel Group had failed to use due diligence with regard to their prospectus, and that Andersen had failed to observe generally accepted accounting principles in connection with its audit with the result that the financial statements were false and misleading in various respects unnecessary to detail here.

* * *

III. *Subject Matter Jurisdiction in General.*

Appellants vigorously attack the district court's "integration" of the three offerings. They say that the SEC has employed this concept only to prevent evasion of rules exempting from registration offerings of a certain amount or less as in Regulation A, 17 C.F.R. § 230.254, or to no more than a specified number of purchasers, as in SEC Rule 144, 17 C.F.R. § 230.144, but not in a situation like that here presented. They argue that once the integration theory is rejected, there is no subject matter jurisdiction over purchasers in the Drexel offering, in which there was certain United States activity, since there were no American purchasers, no subject matter jurisdiction with respect even to the American purchasers in the IOB offering since defendants engaged in no activities in the United States with respect to that offering, and no subject matter jurisdiction as to the Crang offering since there were neither United States activities nor American purchasers. Plaintiff responds that all this is simply playing on the judge's use of the word "integration", and that what he meant and indeed said was that, for purposes of determining subject matter jurisdiction, the three offerings were sufficiently intertwined that it is unrealistic to fractionate them. For reasons that will appear in the course of our discussion, we do not believe this point to be quite so vital as the parties do. We shall deal with it when its relevance appears.

A few preliminary observations will be helpful. We have no doubt that the activities within the United States, detailed in the judge's thorough factual findings,[24] were sufficient to authorize the United States to impose

---

24. The judge found, among other things, that representatives of IOS, the major underwriters in the Drexel Group, their attorneys and accountants met in New York on numerous occasions to initiate, organize and structure the offering; that a New York law firm was retained to represent the underwriters and had numerous meetings with IOS; that Drexel officials and counsel met with the SEC; that the underwriters retained Price Waterhouse & Co. in New York as accountants to assist in reviewing the operations of IOS and received reports from that firm there; that on one occasion Andersen representatives met in New York with the underwriters to explain why Andersen could not perform a full audit for the period January 1–June 30, 1969, within the time allotted and to discuss the amount of work that Andersen might be able to complete during that peri-

od; that preliminary discussions on underwriting discounts and commissions possibly took place in New York in July and August, 1969; that parts of the prospectus were drafted in New York and read over the telephone to Geneva; that prospective underwriters were shown a draft of the prospectus in New York; and that accounts for the proceeds of the underwriting were opened at the Bank of New York and the proceeds in dollars were to be deposited there pending remittance to IOS. Appellants do not seriously dispute these findings. Their contention is rather that the findings give a distorted picture since the work that was done in New York was mostly preliminary or ancillary to the work done in Europe, that the substantial bulk of the work was done in Europe, that all final action was taken there, and that there was no distribution of prospectuses

a rule with respect to consequences flowing from them wherever they might appear, under the principle stated in Restatement (2d) of the Foreign Relations Law of the United States § 17, "Jurisdiction to Prescribe with Respect to Conduct, Thing, Status, or Other Interest within Territory" (1965),[25] quite apart from the power of the United States to impose rules on the conduct of its own nationals, id. § 30, and see Steele v. Bulova Watch Co., Inc., 344 U.S. 280, 282 (1952). But, as we said in *Leasco,* supra, 468 F.2d at 1334, "it would be * * * erroneous to assume that the legislature always means to go to the full extent permitted." When, as here, a court is confronted with transactions that on any view are predominantly foreign, it must seek to determine whether Congress would have wished the precious resources of United States courts and law enforcement agencies to be devoted to them rather than leave the problem to foreign countries.

The second observation is that, despite the vigorous but opposing contentions of the parties, neither *Schoenbaum* nor *Leasco* is decisive. * * * Plaintiff has not brought himself within the ambit of either case; moreover, neither *Schoenbaum* nor *Leasco* raised the serious problem here presented of the dubious binding effect of a defendants' judgment (or a possibly inadequate plaintiff's judgment) on absent foreign plaintiffs or the propriety of purporting to bind such plaintiffs by a settlement. However, the absence of certain of the elements which led to finding subject matter jurisdiction in those cases does not necessarily preclude a similar conclusion on the different facts presented here. See Travis v. Anthes Imperial Ltd., 473 F.2d 515, 523–24 n. 14 (8 Cir.1973).

Thirdly, the SEC's disclaimer of the applicability of the registration requirements of the 1933 Act, see footnote 12 supra, to public offerings even of the securities of American corporations outside the United States, wherever the offerings may have originated, "so long as the offering is made under circumstances reasonably designed to preclude distribution or redistribution of the securities within or to nationals of the United States," greatly emphasized by appellant Andersen, has only a peripheral bearing. While counsel for the underwriters could justifiably have relied on this policy statement in advising that registration was not here required, they could not have relied on it to advise their clients that the latter were free to engage in fraud, and there is, of course, no suggestion that they did. It is elementary that the anti-fraud provisions of the federal securities laws apply to many transactions which are neither within the registration requirements nor on organized American markets. See *Leasco,* supra, 468 F.2d at 1335–37.

With this background we turn to the three elements a combination of which led the district judge to conclude that subject matter jurisdiction existed with respect not only to the relatively few Americans who had purchased IOS shares but to the many thousands of foreign purchasers

---

or other promotional literature to purchasers within the United States—therefore that any fraudulent misrepresentations were neither made nor relied on in the United States.

25. A state has jurisdiction to prescribe a rule of law.

(a) attaching legal consequences to conduct that occurs within its territory,

whether or not such consequences are determined by the effects of the conduct outside the territory, and

(b) relating to a thing located, or a status or other interests localized, in its territory.

whom plaintiff sought to represent. We think it will be useful to consider the first and third elements on which the court relied before we take up the second.

Assuming that there were no American purchasers and that the underwriting related, for example, to a large foreign industrial company clearly identified with a foreign country rather than with the United States, e.g., Rolls-Royce, Mercedes-Benz or Fiat, we do not believe the activities in the United States, see note 24 supra, would justify an American court in taking jurisdiction in a suit for damages by foreign plaintiffs. The fraud, if there was one, was committed by placing the allegedly false and misleading prospectus in the purchasers' hands. Here the final prospectus emanated from a foreign source—London or Brussels in the case of the Drexel offering, Toronto in the case of the Crang offering, and apparently the Bahamas and Geneva in the case of the IOB offering. Not only do we not have the case where all the misrepresentations were communicated in the nation whose law is sought to be applied as in Illustration 2 of § 17 of the Restatement (2d) of Foreign Relations Law at 45, see *Leasco,* 468 F.2d at 1334 n. 3, or the case where a substantial part of them were, as in *Leasco* itself, but we do not even have the oft-cited case of the shooting of a bullet across a state line where the state of the shooting as well as of the state of the hitting may have an interest in imposing its law. At most the acts in the United States helped to make the gun whence the bullet was fired from places abroad; alternatively proper action in the United States would have prevented the gun's ever being sent abroad. We are indeed holding in IIT v. Vencap, Ltd., decided this day, that Congress did not mean the United States to be used as a base for fraudulent securities schemes even when the victims are foreigners, at least in the context of suits by the SEC or by named foreign plaintiffs. But as we there point out, that holding itself goes beyond any case yet decided, and we see no reason to extend it to cases where the United States activities are merely preparatory or take the form of culpable nonfeasance and are relatively small in comparison to those abroad. We thus conclude that the action and inaction which here occurred in the United States would not of itself confer subject matter jurisdiction with respect to foreign plaintiffs even if we assume *arguendo* that the three underwritings may be considered for this purpose as one.

We turn next to the third ground on which the district court predicated subject matter jurisdiction—the adverse general effect of the collapse of IOS in the United States. This was based on an affidavit by Morris Mendelson, Associate Professor of Finance at the Wharton School of the University of Pennsylvania. Professor Mendelson's principal conclusions were that:

(1) The aftermath of the Drexel offering "was a debacle of monumental proportions which resulted in a deterioration of investor confidence in American underwriters at home and, particularly, abroad," and increased the problems of United States corporations in seeking to raise capital abroad.

(2) "The false and misleading prospectus issued in connection with the Public Offering impaired investors' confidence and trust and contributed to a steep decline in the purchase of United States securities by foreigners" with attendant adverse effects on the balance of payments and the price of American securities generally.

(3) Loss of investor confidence in IOS led to large redemption of shares in the mutual funds controlled by it, notably Fund of Funds Limited, which required the funds to sell substantial parts of their portfolios, mainly United States securities, with consequent depression of prices.

(4) Part of the attraction of American securities to foreigners has been the superior disclosures afforded by SEC registration requirements. The collapse of IOS after the offering undermined this confidence since IOS was "identified as an American company in the minds of investors", the Drexel underwriting was led by an American firm and the accountants, Andersen, were American.

(5) The collapse of IOS after the offering "contributed to a breakdown in the entire structure of building up an offshore investing industry whereby funds of European investors were channeled into American securities markets."

Although appellants attack certain of Professor Mendelson's conclusions as erroneous or exaggerated, we do not doubt that the collapse of IOS after the offering had an unfortunate financial effect in the United States. Nevertheless we conclude that the generalized effects described by Professor Mendelson would not be sufficient to confer subject matter jurisdiction over a damage suit by a foreigner under the anti-fraud provisions of the securities laws.

This branch of plaintiff's arguments goes back to Mr. Justice Holmes' statement in Strassheim v. Daily, 221 U.S. 280, 284–85 (1911), which was relied on by Judge L. Hand in United States v. Aluminum Co. of America, 148 F.2d 416, 443 (2 Cir.1945), and by Chief Judge Lumbard in *Schoenbaum,* supra, 405 F.2d at 206:

> Acts done outside a jurisdiction, but intended to produce and producing detrimental effects within it, justify a state in punishing the cause of the harm as if he had been present at the effect, if the state should succeed in getting him within its power.

See Restatement (2d) of Foreign Relations Law § 18, "Jurisdiction to Prescribe with Respect to Effect within Territory". The statement, however, must be read in context. The indictment at issue in Strassheim v. Daily charged that Daily, in Illinois, had connived with the warden of a Michigan prison to defraud the prison's Board of Control by substituting worn and second-hand machinery for the new machinery that had been ordered, and the Court declined to upset, on a petition for habeas corpus, an order extraditing Daily from Illinois to Michigan. This principle would support subject matter jurisdiction if a defendant, even though acting solely abroad, had defrauded investors in the United States by mailing false prospectuses into this country, see ALI Proposed Federal Securities Code (Draft No. 3, April, 1974) § 1604(a)(1)(A) & Comment (3)(b) at 165–66, or if, as in *Schoenbaum,* the number of shares of a company traded on American exchanges was increased by a sale to insiders without adequate consideration at least when this is imperfectly disclosed, cf. Popkin v. Bishop, 464 F.2d 714 (2 Cir.1972). But it does not support subject matter jurisdiction if there was no intention that the securities should be offered to anyone in the United States, simply because in the long run there was an adverse effect on this country's general economic interests or on American security prices. Moderation is all. * * * These considerations are particularly pertinent in view of the limitations in § 17(a) of the 1933 Act to acts in "the offer or sale of any securities" and in § 10(b) of the 1934 Act to acts "in connection with the purchase or sale of any security." This means to us that there is subject matter jurisdiction of fraudulent acts relating to securities which are committed abroad only when these result in injury to purchasers or sellers of those securities in whom the United States has an interest, not where acts simply have an adverse effect on the American economy or American investors generally. Also we do not think that a combination of the district court's first and third grounds, neither sufficient in itself, supports a result different from that which would be proper if each subsisted alone.

IV. *Subject Matter Jurisdiction—Americans.*

We find it rather strange that this large record, with appendices alone running to more than 1200 pages, leaves us in serious doubt about one simple fact that seemingly could have been established quite readily. That is how plaintiff Bersch came to buy 600 shares of IOS that were part of the 3,950,000 share IOB offering.

* * *

If the record is thus murkey on how Bersch came to subscribe, it is even murkier about how other American residents did. Appellant Andersen repeatedly says that the only information on this is a statement in an affidavit of Bersch:

> I was not the only American residing here who purchased IOS stock. * * * Among the New Yorkers purchasing the IOS securities were: Christine Cullen, Naydyne Nelson, Claire Pipolo, David Ellner, Elliott Adler, Robin Leach, Robert Sutner, Raymond Grant, Simme Arthur, Hyman Feld, and Morten Schiowitz.

But this is simply not so. Much more information is furnished in a series of letters from IOS to the SEC in the fall of 1970. These indicate that sales aggregating 41,936 shares were made to 22 American residents, all having relationships with IOS or its affiliates as employees, lawyers, directors, or consultants. Although Andersen loudly claims that Bersch and other American residents bought the shares when they knew they should not have, we find nothing in the record to support this. The IOB prospectus does not exclude American employees residing in the United States and, as indicated above, * * * the SEC 1967 order does not clearly do so. We note also that several of the subscribers were members of law firms that had represented IOS or its affiliates; it is scarcely to be thought that they would have subscribed for shares which they knew were not intended to and could not lawfully be made available to them.

We see no reason why there would not be subject matter jurisdiction with respect to such persons on the part of defendants IOS and Cornfeld who were responsible for the IOB offering. This type of situation—the dispatch from abroad of misleading statements to United States residents— would be closely analogous to that in which jurisdiction was upheld in Strassheim v. Daily, supra, and in the *Aluminum* case and one which would be considered an appropriate subject of United States jurisdiction under § 18 of the Restatement (2d). To be sure, it may turn out that particular individuals never saw the statements or, because of their knowledge, were not misled. But at the present stage we must assume that there was some mailing of prospectuses into the United States and some reliance on them. The same result should also follow with respect to Andersen; action in the United States is not necessary when subject matter jurisdiction is predicated on a direct effect here and Andersen allowed its report on the 1968 financial statements to be used in the IOB offering as much as in the two others. Subject matter jurisdiction with respect to the Drexel Group defendants is more debatable; this depends on whether their activities, whether in the United States or abroad, can be considered as essential to the carrying out of the IOB offering and thus of the purchases here at issue. On the material before the district judge we think they can properly be, although this would be open to disproof at a trial. Cf. Leasco, 468 F.2d at 1330. Whether the same is true with respect to Crang is more debatable since the IOB offering was far more dependent on the large Drexel offering throughout the world than on the much smaller Canadian offering by Crang, but in view of our approval of the court's holding of lack of in personam jurisdiction over Crang, we need not decide this.

Plaintiff asserts that, in addition to purchases by Americans resident in the United States, there were significant purchases by Americans resident abroad.[42] Whether Congress intended that such persons should be entitled to obtain damages for violation of the securities laws is a different and closer question from that on which we have just ruled. We think the answer would be in the negative if none of the defendants engaged in significant activities within the United States, as defendants, with apparent soundness, claim to be the case with respect to the IOB offering considered alone. Congress surely did not mean the securities laws to protect the many thousands of Americans residing in foreign countries against securities frauds by foreigners acting there, and we see no sufficient reason to believe it would have intended otherwise simply because an American participated so long as he had done nothing in the United States. However, in Judge Carter's view the IOB offer to American citizens residing abroad would not have occurred but for the primary offering which involved the many documented activities of the defendants in the United States. There was enough basis for this to justify a holding of subject matter jurisdiction as regards American citizens residing abroad, with respect to IOS and Andersen. Despite the paucity of physical acts on its part in the United States, the head and front of its alleged offending was its decision to allow its 1968 report to be used in all three prospectuses, including the IOB prospectus, and this must have emanated from its headquarters in the United States. We are of the same view with respect to the Drexel Group. While merely preparatory activities in the United States are not enough to trigger application of the securities laws for injury to foreigners located abroad, they are sufficient when the injury is to Americans so resident. We here assume that, for reasons stated in the preceding paragraph, proof will disclose a significant causal relationship between the Drexel offering and the IOB offering. The case with respect to Crang is weaker but, since we sustain the judge's ruling of lack of *in personam* jurisdiction, we need not reach it. This leaves Cornfeld; the

---

42. In response to inquiries by the SEC with respect to whether, and to what extent, Americans had purchased IOS shares at the "public offering", IOS' counsel admitted that approximately 385 "American persons" were known to have acquired such shares. Since many shares of IOS were held in the form of bearer share warrants, making it impossible to determine the ownership thereof, many additional Americans may have in fact been purchasers.

question of how far the alleged defrauding of American citizens abroad resulted from acts which he did or caused in the United States had best be left for development at a trial. We again invite attention to our observation in *Leasco:*

> We add that if a trial should disclose that the allegedly fraudulent acts of any of the defendants within the United States were nonexistent or so minimal as not to be material, the principles announced in this opinion should be applied to the proven facts: the issue of subject matter jurisdiction persists.

468 F.2d at 1330.

We have thus concluded that the anti-fraud provisions of the federal securities laws:

> (1) Apply to losses from sales of securities to Americans resident in the United States whether or not acts (or culpable failures to act) of material importance occurred in this country; and

> (2) Apply to losses from sales of securities to Americans resident abroad if, but only if, acts (or culpable failures to act) of material importance in the United States have significantly contributed thereto; but

> (3) Do not apply to losses from sales of securities to foreigners outside the United States unless acts (or culpable failures to act) within the United States directly caused such losses.

Other fact situations, such as losses to foreigners from sales to them within the United States, are not before us. We freely acknowledge that if we were asked to point to language in the statutes, or even in the legislative history, that compelled these conclusions, we would be unable to respond. The Congresses that passed these extraordinary pieces of legislation in the midst of the depression could hardly have been expected to foresee the development of off-shore frauds thirty years later. We recognize also that reasonable men might conclude that the coverage was greater, or less, than has been outlined in this opinion and in IIT v. Vencap, Ltd., this day decided. Our conclusions rest on case law and commentary concerning the application of the securities laws and other statutes to situations with foreign elements and on our best judgment as to what Congress would have wished if these problems had occurred to it.

* * *

The order is reversed insofar as it sustains subject matter jurisdiction with respect to all purchasers of IOS securities and is affirmed insofar as it sustains such jurisdiction with respect to purchasers who were American residents or citizens. The cause is remanded with directions to modify the class action determination insofar as this includes purchasers who were not American residents or citizens and to consider whether the action should be allowed to proceed as a class action with respect to one or both such classes, in light of the discussion in this opinion. The stay of mailing and publishing notice of the proposed settlement is made permanent. The order dismissing the complaint against Crang for lack of *in personam* jurisdiction is affirmed. * * *

RESTATEMENT OF THE FOREIGN RELATIONS LAW OF THE UNITED STATES (REVISED) *

American Law Institute.

(1986).

§ 403. Limitations on Exercise of Jurisdiction to Prescribe

(1) Even when one of the bases for jurisdiction under § 402 is present, a state may not exercise jurisdiction to prescribe law with respect to the activities, relations, status, or interests of persons or things having connections with another state or states when the exercise of such jurisdiction is unreasonable.

(2) Whether the exercise of jurisdiction is reasonable or unreasonable is judged by evaluating all the relevant factors, including, where appropriate,

(a) the extent to which the activity (i) takes place within the regulating state, or (ii) has substantial, direct, and foreseeable effect upon or in the regulating state;

(b) the connections, such as nationality, residence, or economic activity, between the regulating state and the persons principally responsible for the activity to be regulated, or between that state and those whom the law or regulation is designed to protect;

(c) the character of the activity to be regulated, the importance of regulation to the regulating state, the extent to which other states regulate such activities, and the degree to which the desirability of such regulation is generally accepted;

(d) the existence of justified expectations that might be protected or hurt by the regulation in question;

(e) the importance of the regulation in question to the international political, legal or economic system;

(f) the extent to which such regulation is consistent with the traditions of the international system;

(g) the extent to which another state may have an interest in regulating the activity; and

(h) the likelihood of conflict with regulation by other states.

(3) When more than one state has a reasonable basis for exercising jurisdiction over a person or activity, but the prescriptions by two or more states are in conflict, each state has an obligation to evaluate its own as well as the other state's interest in exercising jurisdiction in light of all the relevant factors, including those set out in Subsection (2), and should defer to the other state if that state's interest is clearly greater.

* * *

§ 416. Jurisdiction to Regulate Activities related to Securities: Law of the United States

(1) The United States generally has jurisdiction to prescribe with respect to

---

* Copyright, 1986, American Law Institute. All rights reserved. Reprinted by permission.

(a) i) any transaction in securities in the United States to which a national or resident of the United States is a party, and

ii) any offer to enter into a securities transaction, made in the United States by or to a national or resident of the United States;

(b) any transaction in securities

i) carried out, or intended to be carried out, on an organized securities market in the United States, or

ii) carried out, or intended to be carried out, predominantly in the United States, although not on an organized securities market;

(c) conduct, regardless of where it occurs, significantly related to a transaction described in Subection 1(b), if the conduct has, or is intended to have, a substantial effect in the United States;

(d) conduct occurring predominantly in the United States that is related to a transaction in securities, even if the transaction occurs outside the United States; and

(e) investment advice or solicitation of proxies or of consents with respect to securities, carried out predominantly in the United States.

(2) The jurisdiction of the United States to apply its securities laws to transactions or conduct other than those addressed in Subsection (1) depends on whether it is reasonable to do so in the light of § 403, giving particular weight to

(a) whether the transaction or conduct has, or can reasonably be expected to have, a substantial effect on a securities market in the United States for securities of the same issuer or on holdings in such securities by United States nationals or residents;

(b) whether representations are made or negotiations are conducted in the United States; and

(c) whether the party sought to be subjected to the jurisdiction of the United States is a United States national or resident, or the persons sought to be protected are United States nationals or residents.

Comment:

a. Protection of U.S. securities markets and investors. The reach and application of securities legislation of the United States depend on their reasonableness as determined by evaluation under § 403(2) in the light of the principal purpose of the legislation, i.e., to protect U.S. investors as well as the securities markets of the United States and those who buy and sell in those markets. The more direct and substantial the effect of a given transaction on the United States market, or on United States investors, the more reasonable it is for the United States to apply its laws to that transaction. The reasonableness of the exercise of jurisdiction depends not only on the territorial and transactional links of a given activity with the United States but also on the character of the activity to be regulated. See § 403(2)(c). Thus, for instance, exercise of jurisdiction to punish fraudulent or manipulative conduct is entitled to greater weight than are routine administrative requirements. Under this setion, the United States may exercise its jurisdiction to prescribe not only in respect to acts that have had prohibited effects, but also in respect to attempts or conspiracies even if thwarted before they are realized. * * *

* * *

Subsection (1) addresses a category of situations where generally no reasonable expectations would be frustrated by application of United States law, including regulation by the Securities and Exchange Commission and litigation at private initiative. Subsection (1)(a) is addressed to situations in which jurisdiction to prescribe is based on territoriality, supported by links of nationality or residence. Subsections (1)(b) and (d) address situations in which it is generally reasonable for the United States to exercise jurisdiction under § 402(1)(a) (territoriality), even as applied to securities sold outside the United States or to persons who are not U.S. nationals or residents. Subsection (1)(c), addressed to conduct not carried out predominantly in the United States, is based on jurisdiction under § 402(1)(c) (effects); exercise of such jurisdiction is also generally reasonable if there is a showing of substantial effect in the United States, actual or intended.

Subsection (2) addresses other transactions and conduct related to securities, with respect to which exercise of U.S. jurisdiction may or may not be reasonable. As organized securities markets in different states are increasingly connected through electronic and institutional links, the territorial factors drawn on in Subsection (1) may become less relevant, and distinctions under Subsection (2) may become more refined, both through practice of states and through agreements between states. The considerations set forth in Subsection (2) are particular applications of § 403(2), but all of the factors set forth in that section may be relevant.

b. *Private or governmental invocation of jurisdiction.* In general, appropriate weight is to be given to statements and other evidence of national interest, and the reasonableness of the exercise of regulatory jurisdiction by the United States will be evaluated in the same way, whether in litigation initiated by a private party or by an agency of the United States government. * * * As of 1985, however, challenges to exercise of U.S. jurisdiction under the securities laws had come only from private parties and not from foreign states, so that the need to weigh competing or conflicting state interests is less likely in this area than in connection with other assertions of jurisdiction over economic activity having transnational aspects. See Reporters' Note 3.

* * *

REPORTERS' NOTES

1. *Changing approaches to jurisdiction.* Earlier cases involving the application of U.S. securities laws to transnational transactions focused on "subject matter jurisdiction," the existence of minimum contacts to bring a given transaction within the definition of interstate commerce. * * * See, e.g., Schoenbaum v. Firstbrook, 405 F.2d 200 (2d Cir.1968); cert. denied sub nom. Manley v. Schoenbaum, 395 U.S. 906 (1969). Increasingly the courts began to ask whether the minimum contacts were "significant" so as to warrant the conclusion that Congress intended that U.S. law be applied. Leasco Data Processing Equipment Corp. v. Maxwell, 468 F.2d 1326 (2d Cir.1972); Travis v. Anthes Imperial Limited, 473 F.2d 515 (8th Cir.1973). * * * Possible limitations under international law that might be relevant to interpreting the U.S. statutes were generally seen as satisfied by such significant contacts with the United States, citing previous Restatement § 17. However, although the approach indicated, on its face, seemed to concentrate exclusively on the interests of the United States, the interests of other states were taken into account to some extent in evaluat-

ing the facts of the particular case to determine whether the acts or effects in the United States were sufficiently "significant." * * *

2. *Protecting the interests of the United States.* Subsection (1) is addressed to situations in which it would generally be reasonable for the United States to apply its laws. Subsections (1)(a) and (b) provide the clearest case for exercise of jurisdiction by the United States under the criteria of §§ 402–403. Subsection 1(a) addresses activity in the United States that is carried out by a national or resident of the United States, or is directed at U.S. nationals or residents. In Subsection 1(b), the activity is centered in the United States—even if directed from elsewhere—and it is reasonable to impute to anyone engaged in a transaction carried out on an organized securities market in the United States or otherwise predominantly in the United States, regardless of his own nationality or residence, the expectation that United States law will apply. Situations coming under Subsection (1)(c) also engage the interests of the United States in protecting the integrity of its securities markets and other transactions in its territory, but if the conduct occurred outside of the United States—for instance, advice by a foreign securities house given abroad—it would be reasonable to apply U.S. law to that conduct only on the basis of actual or intended effect in the United States in significant measure. Jurisdiction in situations coming under Subsection (1)(d) is, in general, related to the function of protecting United States investors, but even where neither the actors nor the victims are U.S. nationals or residents it is generally not unreasonable for the United States to apply its law on the basis of territoriality to prevent or punish fraudulent conduct. If the persons involved are in the United States only transitorily, for instance if a German and a Japanese businessman meet in New York for convenience and the latter there fraudulently induces the former to make purchases of Japanese securities on the Tokyo Stock Exchange, it might not be reasonable to interpret the U.S. securities laws as applicable, because neither party acted with the expectation that those laws would apply and neither the actors nor the market involved was within the zone of protection of U.S. securities legislation. Compare Leasco Data Processing Equipment Corp. v. Maxwell, 468 F.2d 1326 at 1338 (2d Cir.1972), with Grunenthal GmbH v. Hotz, 712 F.2d 421 (9th Cir.1983).

Comment *a*, drawing on § 403(2)(c), suggests that the case for applying United States law under both Subsections (1) and (2) would be stronger if designed to avert, or to provide a remedy for, fraud than if designed merely to enforce an obligation to file or give notice not directly associated with fraud. Compare *Schoenbaum v. Firstbrook*, Reporters' Note 1, in which the protection of U.S. investors in stock registered on a U.S. stock exchange was held a sufficient basis to support an exercise of U.S. jurisdiction. * * *

* * *

Whether exercise of regulatory jurisdiction by the United States is justified in order to protect residents of the United States against actions taken outside the country depends on the circumstances. For instance, a resident of the United States who deliberately traveled to Canada to trade in Canadian securities under margin rules looser than those applicable in the United States should not later be entitled to protection of United States law in an action against his Canadian vendor/lender. See Kook v. Crang, 182 F.Supp. 388 (S.D.N.Y.1960). In contrast, a fraudulent seller luring unsuspecting American tourists to a Caribbean island with promises of favorable securities deals might properly be held subject to United States law, especially if some form of advertisement or solicitation (though not the fraudulent transaction) had taken place in the United States. Protection of members of U.S. armed forces or their dependents stationed abroad may provide a sufficient jurisdictional link, since these persons are perceived as entitled to special protection by the United States government and its laws and their protection would be likely to involve minimal occasion for conflict with the jurisdiction to prescribe of other states.

3. *Conflict with foreign state interests unlikely.* In contrast to assertion by the United States of jurisdiction to prescribe under the antitrust laws, when not infrequently the United States sought to prohibit what another state favored or required, * * * the experience with the substantive aspects of U.S. securities regulation (as contrasted with transnational discovery efforts, § 437, Reporters' Note 8) has not resulted in state-to-state conflict. In every case cited in the Reporters' Notes to this section (as well as in similar cases not cited), the challenge to the application of U.S. law to a given situation was raised by the person charged with a violation, not by a foreign government. While many states define prohibited conduct with respect to securities differently from the United States, no instance is known in which a transaction challenged under U.S. law—such as misrepresentation or insider trading—was asserted to be mandated by the law of a foreign state. Thus while an international consensus on the substance of securities regulation could not be said to have emerged as of 1985, the likelihood of conflict with regulation by other states, § 403(2)(h) and § 403(3), is slight.

* * *

6. *Proposed Federal Securities Code compared.* A somewhat different approach to securities regulation based on minimum contacts with the United States is taken in § 1905 of the proposed Federal Securities Code (1980) of the American Law Institute. As stated in the introduction to that work, § 1905 was designed to make substantive coverage of the Code quite broad, but always "within the limits of international law." This Restatement seeks to define those limits, including the principle of reasonableness for the exercise of jurisdiction to prescribe and apply a state's law, and the method for applying it. Since the proposed Federal Securities Code calls for vesting maximum power in the Securities and Exchange Commission subject to narrowing the exercise of that power by regulation, this Chapter would also guide the Commission in its rule-making.

* * *

§ 437. Discovery and Foreign Government Compulsion: Law of the United States

(1)(a) Subject to Subsection (1)(c), a court or agency in the United States, when authorized by statute or rule of court, may order a person subject to its jurisdiction to produce documents, objects, or other information relevant to an action or investigation, even if the information or the person in possession of the information is outside the United States.

(b) Failure to comply with an order to produce information may subject the person to whom the order is directed to sanctions, including finding of contempt, dismissal of a claim or defense, or default judgment, or may lead to a determination that the facts to which the order was addressed are as asserted by the opposing party.

(c) In issuing an order directing production of information located abroad, a court or agency in the United States should take into account the importance to the investigation or litigation of the documents or other information requested; the degree of specificity of the request; whether the information originated in the United States; the availability of alternative means of securing the information; and the extent to which non-compliance with the request would undermine important interests of the United States, or compliance with the request would undermine important interests of the state where the information is located.

(2) If disclosure of information located outside the United States is prohibited by a law, regulation, or order of a court or other authority of the state in which the information or prospective witness is located, or of the state of which the prospective witness is a national,

(a) the person to whom the order is directed may be required by the court or agency to make a good faith effort to secure permission from the foreign authorities to make the information available;

(b) sanctions of contempt, dismissal, or default should not ordinarily be imposed on the party that has failed to comply with the order for production, except in cases of deliberate concealment or removal of information or of failure to make a good faith effort in accordance with paragraph (a);

(c) the court or agency may, in appropriate cases, make findings of fact adverse to a party that has failed to comply with the order for production, even if that party has made a good faith effort to secure permission from the foreign authorities to make the information available and that effort has been unsuccessful.

Comment:

a. Discovery as exercise of jurisdiction. Discovery for use in a judicial or administrative proceeding is an exercise of jurisdiction by a state, whether it emanates from an order of a court or from a demand by a party pursuant to a statute or rule of practice. In order to ensure that such exercise of jurisdiction is carried out consistently with the principle of reasonableness (§§ 403, 421), Subsection (1) contemplates that, in civil litigation in the United States affecting foreign interests, courts control discovery practice from the outset of the litigation pursuant to Rule 16 of the Federal Rules of Civil Procedure and comparable State rules. Thus, except as authorized by specific statute or rule of court, * * * requests to produce documents or information located abroad should, as a matter of good practice, be issued as an order by the court, not merely in the form of a demand by a private party. General authorizations to litigants, as under Rule 34 of the Federal Rules of Civil Procedure, should not be construed to support departure from this practice.

Before issuing an order for production of documents, objects, or information located abroad, the court, or where authorized the agency, should scrutinize a discovery request more closely than it would scrutinize comparable requests for information located in the United States. Under Rule 26(b)(1) of the Federal Rules of Civil Procedure, discovery (including requests for documents) may extend to any matter not privileged which is relevant to the subject matter of the action, even if the information sought would be inadmissible at trial, if it appears reasonably calculated to lead to the discovery of admissible evidence. However, the second paragraph of that Rule, added in 1983, calls for imposition by the court of limits on the extent of discovery comparable to those set out in Subsection 1(c). Given the degree of difficulty in obtaining compliance, and the amount of resistance that has developed in foreign states to discover demands originating in the United States, it is ordinarily reasonable to limit foreign discovery to information necessary to the action (typically, evidence not otherwise readily obtainable) and directly relevant and material. Information that could lead to admissible evidence would not ordinarily be subject to discovery under this standard, but a court might in some instances order disclosure of the identity and location of persons who may have knowledge of information meeting the standard, as well as of documents that may lead to such information. Nothing in this section prevents parties from making disclosure of information without court intervention.

b. Grand jury subpoenas and agency demands for information. A grand jury investigating crime may issue a subpoena to a person in the United States requiring production of documents or information located abroad. Such a subpoena does not require prior judicial approval, but its enforcement through civil or criminal contempt may be carried out only through judicial proceedings. Under 28 U.S.C. § 1783, subpoenas directed to persons outside the United States may be issued only by a court, and only to nationals or residents of the United States. * * *

Some federal administrative agencies have authority to issue subpoenas or other orders requiring disclosure of documents and information in connection with administrative hearings or investigations. Whether an agency's authority to require disclosure includes authority to demand production of documents or information located abroad is a matter of interpretation of the governing statutes, in the first instance by the agency itself, in line with the criteria of Subsection (1). General authorization to issue disclosure orders should not ordinarily be construed as implying such authority. In interpreting the governing statutes, a particularly relevant consideration may be whether the subject matter regulated by the agency extends significantly to international commerce or other international matters. * * * Generally, agency orders for production of documents or information also require judicial proceedings for their enforcement.

* * *

Where production of documents or other information in response to a grand jury subpoena or administrative agency demand is resisted on the ground that the documents or information are located abroad, the rules stated in this section govern the court's exercise of authority in determining the obligation of compliance and appropriate sanctions for noncompliance.

* * *

f. Finding contrary to position of non-complying party. In contrast to orders under Subsection (2)(b), a finding under Subsection (2)(c) is not deemed to be a penalty for conduct commanded by a foreign state, but is designed rather, as a form of pressure to induce compliance with justified requests for information. Such a finding does not change the burden of proof; it is appropriate only if there is reason to believe that the information, if disclosed, would be adverse to the non-complying party, and if the court or agency is satisfied that the request was made in good faith, not in the hope that the opposing party's noncompliance would enable the requesting party to establish a fact that it could not establish if all the information were available. Furthermore such a finding is normally made only after prior warning; where practicable, the finding should be made in a tentative form, subject to reopening if the information is produced by a given date.

* * *

h. Good faith and sanctions for non-disclosure. Parties to litigation and targets of investigation (whether criminal or civil) may be required to show that they have made serious efforts before administrative bodies or courts of states with blocking statutes, Reporters' Note 4, to secure release or waiver from a prohibition against disclosure; evidence that parties or targets have actively sought a prohibition against disclosure, or that the information was deliberately moved to a state with blocking legislation, may be regarded as evidence of bad faith and justification for sanctions in accordance with Subsection (2)(b). U.S. courts have divided on the obligations of non-party custodians such as banks and brokers with offices in the United States and foreign states * * *; at a minimum, such custodians may not, without risking sanctions, transfer to a state with secrecy legislation records reflecting transactions based in the United States. Whether and to what extent such intermediaries must apply for waivers or appeal from adverse findings of foreign courts in order to avoid sanctions in the United States is not clear. Whether the U.S. government has an obligation to cooperate with efforts by custodians to secure release of information, for example by disclosing sufficient information from a grand jury investigation to enable a foreign court or other authority to rule on the applicability of an exception to a secrecy law, has not been decided.

REPORTERS' NOTES

1. *International controversy concerning discovery abroad.* No aspect of the extension of the American legal system beyond the territorial frontier of the United States has given rise to so much friction as the request for documents associated with investigation and litigation in the United States. Some 15 states as of 1985 had adopted legislation expressly designed to counter U.S. efforts to secure production of documents situated outside the United States; other states, such as Switzerland, have had bank and business secrecy laws in effect for longer periods and not directed specifically against the United States.

* * *

4. *Blocking statutes.* Blocking statutes are laws designed to take advantage of foreign government compulsion defense (§ 436) by prohibiting the disclosure, copying, inspection or removal of documents located in the territory of the enacting state in compliance with orders of foreign authorities. Some statutes cover all documents, some only certain categories (for instance documents related to merchant shipping or to production of uranium); some statutes are always applicable, some are applicable when invoked by a minister or comparable official, and some are applicable unless a waiver is obtained from the competent official or a (local) court directs that the documents be produced. All blocking statutes appear to carry some form of penal sanction.

* * *

All of the statutes cited were adopted to counter litigation or investigation emanating from the United States. Other blocking statutes not specifically aimed at the United States, notably the Swiss Bank Secrecy and Business Secrets acts, are discussed in notes 5 and 6. See, generally, "Foreign Nondisclosure Laws and Domestic Discovery Orders in Antitrust Litigation," 88 Yale L.J. 612 (1979).

5. *Blocking statutes and the foreign compulsion defense.* While nondisclosure in compliance with a foreign blocking statute could be considered an example of reliance on the sovereign compulsion defense, § 436, both the criteria and the techniques for resolution of inconsistent commands under this section are somewhat different from those addressed in § 436. In particular, restrictions on the production of information are often not absolute, and it is not unreasonable to require persons to whom orders to produce information are addressed to make good faith efforts to secure permission to comply. Further, whereas under § 436 the defense of government compulsion, when applicable, entitles a defendant (civil or criminal) to complete discharge of liability for obeying the law of the state where an act was (or is to be) done, a variety of inferences are permissible under this section in response to failure to comply with reasonable requests for information on the basis of obedience to foreign law. Overall, this section takes the position, consistent with that of most courts in the United States, that when a state has jurisdiction to prescribe and its courts have jurisdiction to adjudicate, adjudication should (subject to generally applicable rules of evidence) take place on the basis of the best information available, and that statutes that frustrate this goal need not be given the same deference by courts of the United States as substantive rules of law at variance with the law of the United States. * * * On the other hand, the degree of friction created by discovery requests, particularly in antitrust cases, and the differing perceptions of the acceptability of American-style discovery under national and international law, suggest some efforts to moderate the application abroad of U.S. procedural techniques, consistent with the overall principle of reasonableness in the exercise of jurisdiction.

6. *Société Internationale v. Rogers* (the *Interhandel* case). The leading U.S. decision on the relation between U.S. discovery and foreign rules of non-disclosure is Société Internationale pour Participations Industrielles et Commerciales, S.A. v. Rogers, 357 U.S. 197 (1958). The case arose out of the vesting by the United States during World War II of assets found by the Alien Property Custodian to be owned or held for the benefit of a German corporation. After the war a Swiss holding company claimed that it had title to the assets, that it had owned them at the time of the vesting, and that as the national of a neutral state it was entitled to return of the property. Having exhausted its administrative remedies, the claimant brought suit in federal district court. The U.S. government moved for an order (as was then required under Rule 34) requiring the claimant to make available for inspection and copying a large number of banking records in a Swiss bank. Claimant asserted that disclosure of these records would be a violation of Article 273 of the Swiss Penal Code (the Business Secrets Law), and Article 47 of the Swiss Banking Law relating to the secrecy of banking records.

The district court found that disclosure would indeed violate Swiss law, that there was no proof of collusion between the claimant and the Swiss government, and further that the claimant had sustained the burden of good faith in its efforts to comply with the production order. Nevertheless, the district court dismissed the complaint, on the ground that Swiss law did not furnish an adequate excuse for claimant's failure to comply with the production order.

The Supreme Court unanimously reversed the order of dismissal. The Court said:

> The findings below, and what has been shown as to petitioner's extensive efforts at compliance, compel the conclusion on this record that petitioner's failure to satisfy fully the requirements of this production order was due to inability fostered neither by its own conduct nor by circumstances within its control. It is hardly debatable that fear of criminal prosecution constitutes a weighty excuse for nonproduction, and this excuse is not weakened because the laws preventing compliance are those of a foreign sovereign. 357 U.S. at 211.

The Court remanded to the district court with instructions to continue the inquiry:

> This is not to say that petitioner will profit through its inability to tender the records called for. . . . It may be that in the absence of complete disclosure by petitioner, the District Court would be justified in drawing inferences unfavorable to petitioner as to particular events. . . . But these problems go to the adequacy of petitioner's proof and should not on this record preclude petitioner from being able to contest on the merits. 357 U.S. at 212–13.

Subsequent U.S. cases have drawn on different aspects of the Supreme Court's opinion. Some have focused on the requirement of good faith in attempting to secure permission to disclose documents covered by foreign secrecy laws * * *; others have focused on the Court's unwillingness to use the ultimate sanction of dismissal in instances of foreign government compulsion; still others have applied the Court's suggestion that inferences unfavorable to the non-producing party may be drawn even if that party is not at fault; and some have stressed the Court's emphasis on a case-by-case approach and reliance on discretion of the district court.

7. *Balancing competing state interests.* Numerous decisions of U.S. courts have expressly engaged in a balancing of interests, both in considering the appropriateness of discovery orders in the face of foreign nondisclosure laws, Subsection (1)(c), and in considering sanctions for noncompliance, Subsection (2)(c). In Ings v. Ferguson, 282 F.2d 149 (2d Cir.1960), the court of appeals declined to enforce a subpoena directed to the New York agencies of two Canadian banks to produce records maintained in Canada, holding that upon "fundmental principles of international comity," the effort to secure the records should be undertaken through letters rogatory, § 473, so that Canadian courts could rule on the question whether disclosure would violate Canadian law. No U.S. governmental interest was involved in the case. In United States v. First National City Bank, 396 F.2d 897 (2d Cir.1968), a federal grand jury in New York investigating a world-wide quinine cartel issued a subpoena to a New York bank requiring production of documents relating to transactions of its customers located both at its head office in New York and at its branch in Frankfurt, West Germany. Citibank complied with the subpoena with respect to the documents located in New York, but refused to comply with respect to the

documents located in Frankfurt. Germany did not have a law, like that of Switzerland, making it a crime to disclose banking records, but Citibank asserted that to comply with the subpoena would subject it to civil liability and economic loss in Germany. After hearing, the district court concluded that the risk of civil liability in Germany if the bank acted pursuant to the order of a U.S. court was "speculative." Finding that the bank had not made a good faith effort to comply with the subpoena, the court adjudged the bank and its relevant officer in contempt. The Court of Appeals for the Second Circuit affirmed, setting the importance of antitrust enforcement to the United States against the bank secrecy doctrine in Germany which, the court observed, seemed not to be imbedded in important public policy or even required by statute. It pointed out that the German government had not raised an objection to enforcement of the subpoena, as it had, for instance, in connection with the Federal Maritime Commission's investigation of international shipping * * *.

* * *

8. *Good faith and sanctions for non-compliance.* In Montship Lines, Ltd. v. Federal Maritime Board, 295 F.2d 147 (D.C.Cir.1961), one of the many cases arising out of the U.S. inquiry into shipping conferences in the 1960's, * * * the Court of Appeals for the D.C. Circuit said it would deal with the defense of foreign prohibition only after the respondents had demonstrated a good faith effort to obtain a waiver of the prohibition from their respective governments. This two-step technique was followed in several succeeding cases. In Federal Maritime Commission v. DeSmedt, 366 F.2d 464 (2d Cir.), cert. denied, 385 U.S. 974 (1966), the Court of Appeals for the Second Circuit upheld a subpoena for shipping documents located in various foreign countries, but when the foreign parties thereafter made the required showing of (i) the applicability of the prohibition; (ii) the good faith effort to secure a waiver; and (iii) the continued refusal of the government concerned to permit disclosure, a motion to hold them in contempt was denied. Federal Maritime Commission v. DeSmedt, 268 F.Supp. 972 (S.D.N.Y.1967). * * *

* * *

In SEC v. Banca della Svizzera Italiana, 92 F.R.D. 111 (S.D.N.Y.1981), the Securities and Exchange Commission, investigating the likelihood of insider trading through a Swiss bank's New York office, demanded disclosure from the bank of the identity of its customer, and when the bank refused on the basis of Swiss bank secrecy laws, the SEC brought suit, naming the bank as defendant. Though there was no assertion that the bank had itself engaged in insider trading, the court imposed sanctions on the bank for nondisclosure, apparently on the basis that the circumstances imposed a duty of inquiry on the bank, the breach of which constituted bad faith.

* * *

EXTRATERRITORIAL APPLICATION OF THE FEDERAL SECURITIES LAWS

A question which has arisen with some frequency in the last few years, and which will undoubtedly assume increasing importance in the future as the world shrinks, is the question of the applicability of the various provisions of the federal securities laws to multinational transactions.

Registration under the 1934 Act. The question first arose with some urgency in connection with the 1964 amendment program which required issuers with more than 500 shareholders to register under Section 12(g) and subjected them to various requirements, including the periodic reporting and insider trading provisions. How would this apply, for example, to a German company doing no business in the United States, with 10,000 shareholders in Germany, but also with 600 shareholders in the United States? And, perhaps more importantly, how could these requirements be enforced if they did apply to such a foreign issuer?

After much argument, Congress refused to include any exemption in the statute for such foreign issuers, but simply dumped the entire problem in the lap of the SEC by authorizing it to exempt any or all of such foreign issuers. The SEC after much soul searching finally adopted Rule 12g3–2(b) which exempts all such foreign issuers if they file with the SEC, in the original language, copies of all reports which they are required to file by the law of their domicile, which they file with any stock exchange on which their securities are listed and which they in fact distribute to their security holders.

Professor Buxbaum has described the result as follows:[1]

"The demand for information adequate to protect American shareholders has been tailored to the convenience of the foreign issuer. The 'registration' need contain only information released by such issuers either voluntarily or under their domestic requirements. In addition, the SEC is willing to police this requirement by relying on apparently harmless administrative sanctions, which involve some unspecified pressures on trading by American dealers.[47] Indeed, the whole weight of regulation has shifted to a mere request for disclosure of the violation, because the SEC does not presently intend to ban trading in the securities of non-complying issuers. On the other hand, dealers who do not disclose an issuer's failure to comply with the registration require- ment may in the future be found guilty of a 'fraudulent device' with attendant administrative and civil sanctions. Further, the SEC plans to publish a 'grey list' of the names of non-complying issuers, on which dealers may rely in advising customers."

Even this minimal disclosure may not always be achieved in practice. The German companies were very excited about this issue when it was debated before Congress and the Commission, since the typical German could hardly entertain the thought of simply refusing to comply with whatever rules were adopted. The Japanese companies, on the other hand, took the position that they would file the required material if such filing were made "voluntary", but not if it were "mandatory" since that would be an affront to their sovereignty. When it was nevertheless made mandatory (in order to secure the exemption from registration, which would be more onerous), the Japanese companies, we are told, then devised a typical Japanese response: They got together and shipped several crates of documents in Japanese to the SEC, but they did not

---

1. Buxbaum. Securities Regulation and the Foreign Issuer Exemption, 54 Cor- nell L.Rev. 358, at 373 (1969).

"47. If on that much. SEC Securities Act of 1933 Release No. 8066 (Apr. 28, 1967), states:

'While no sanction will attach to any broker or dealer by reason of its transac- tions in the securities of an issuer solely because it is listed as neither registered nor exempt, the Commission expects that

brokers and dealers will consider this fact in deciding whether they have a reasonable basis for recommending these securities to customers.'

"Id. at 3.

"In fairness, however, the dissonance between such dealer sanctions and the ultimate aim of investor protection should be noted; the current investor is the victim, not beneficiary, of driving traders out of the market. * * *"

include a list in English of what they had filed, as required by the Rule. Several plaintive letters from the SEC staff saying, "Please send us the list in English of what you have sent us," went unanswered. We do not know how this game of one-upsmanship finally came out; but we suspect that the SEC decided that it could more profitably employ its regulatory efforts in other enterprises.

What the SEC will do with all those Japanese documents, assuming that every company punctiliously files every document required to be filed, and even includes the list in English, is a question we could not attempt to answer. Assuming that some regulatory purpose would be served by such an operation, how the SEC could go about forcing a Japanese company to file, if it refuses to do so, is also a question the answer to which is not self-evident. A stop-trading order with respect to the securities of that company in the United States could only hurt the American investors in those securities, whom the SEC supposedly is trying to protect.

Section 30(b) of the 1934 Act. In Schoenbaum v. Firstbrook [2] an American shareholder of Banff Oil Ltd. brought an action alleging that its parent corporation, Acquitaine, had purchased additional shares in Banff at an unfair price on the basis of inside information regarding the oil explorations of Banff, in violation of Rule 10b–5. Both Banff and Acquitaine were Canadian corporations and the transactions complained about occurred entirely in Canada. The District Court dismissed the action on the basis, among others, that the provisions of the Securities Exchange Act of 1934 did not have any extraterritorial application. However, the Second Circuit reversed on the ground that the listing and trading of Banff's stock on the American Stock Exchange and the involvement of United States investors were sufficient to give the court jurisdiction.

One of the questions involved in the analysis of this problem is the proper interpretation to be given to Section 30(b) of the 1934 Act, which provides:

The provisions of this chapter or of any rule or regulation thereunder shall not apply to any person insofar as he transacts a business in securities without the jurisdiction of the United States, unless he transacts such business in contravention of such rules and regulations as the Commission may prescribe as necessary or appropriate to prevent the evasion of this chapter.

The approaches taken by the Second Circuit in the *Schoenbaum* case and by the Securities and Exchange Commission in its amicus brief filed in that case, not only to the interpretation of Section 30(b) but also to the general problem of the extraterritorial application of the 1934 Act, are discussed in a Note appearing in the Journal of Law and Policy in International Business: [3]

"An analysis of the legislative history underlying Section 30(b) sheds little light in determining what scope it was intended to have. As a result, Section 30(b) has given rise to a number of inconsistent interpretations. More often than not, the courts have interpreted the word "jurisdiction" to mean jurisdiction in a territorial sense, thus equating it with boundaries. The result has been a significant effort by the courts to find some substantial act within the United States to which subject matter jurisdiction may be attached before they can reach the result they feel is justified. Currently the most intensive and

---

2. 405 F.2d 200 (2d Cir.1968), rev'd on rehearing en banc 405 F.2d 215 (2d Cir.), cert. denied 395 U.S. 906 (1969).

3. Note, The International Character of Securities Credit: A Regulatory Problem, 2 Law & Pol.Int.Bus. 147, at 158–164 (1970). Copyright 1970. Reprinted by permission.

most authoritative judicial position on the extraterritoriality of the '34 Act is Schoenbaum v. Firstbrook, which departs from this approach. In applying the '34 Act to extraterritorial conduct, the Second Circuit stated:

> We believe that Congress intended the Exchange Act to have extraterritorial application in order to protect domestic investors who have purchased foreign securities on American exchanges and to protect the domestic securities market from the effects of improper foreign transactions in American securities. In our view, neither the usual presumption against extraterritorial application of legislation nor the specific language of Section 30(b) show Congressional intent to preclude application of the Exchange Act to transactions regarding stocks traded in the United States which are effected outside the United States when extraterritorial application of the Act is necessary to protect American investors.[42]

The Court then went on to consider Section 30(b) in depth. It concluded that the exemption contained in Section 30(b) extended only to persons who transact a business in securities, not to persons who engage in intermittent isolated transactions. In effect, the Court suggested that Section 30(b) contemplates privileged treatment of foreign securities professionals. The Court further indicated that this exemption would be unavailable even to these professional persons unless the transactions in issue were truly outside the jurisdiction of the United States as delineated under the protective approach. The Court concluded that the district court has subject matter jurisdiction over violations of the Securities Exchange Act although the transactions which are alleged to violate the Act take place outside the United States, at least when the transactions involve stock registered and listed on a national securities exchange, and are detrimental to the interests of American investors.[45]

"The SEC's interpretation of the legislative intent with regard to the application of Section 30(b) and the extranational extent of the '34 Act differs somewhat from the *Schoenbaum* approach, although the end result in most situations would be much the same.

"The SEC maintains that the '34 Act is 'generally applicable extraterritorially whenever such application is necessary and appropriate for the protection of American investors and markets.'[46] According to the SEC, however, Congress did not seek to utilize the 'protective' theory to its outermost limits. Rather, it built into each provision of the '34 Act certain jurisdictional prerequisites that, in effect, limited its application.

> There are three different elements that Congress utilized for this purpose, either singly or in combination. The first was the use of the so-called jurisdictional means: the mails, the means or instrumentalities of interstate commerce or the facilities of a national securities exchange. The second was the involvement of a registered security—in 1934, a security listed on a national securities exchange. Finally, some provisions apply only to persons in the securities business. Thus, the operative provisions of the Act either require the presence of one or more of these elements or were tied into other provisions that did require their presence.[47]

"In the SEC's view, whenever a use of this first element, i.e., the jurisdictional means, is involved, it is quite reasonable to apply United States law to a transaction, whether foreign or domestic, because of the direct and immediate interest of the United States in regulating the use of the mails, means and

---

"42. 405 F.2d at 206."

"45. 405 F.2d at 208."

"46. Brief for SEC as Amicus Curiae, at 16, Schoenbaum v. Firstbrook, 405 F.2d 208 (2d Cir.1968)."

"47. Id. at 17."

instrumentalities of interstate commerce [48] and facilities of the national securities exchanges. If the transaction involves only the second element, i.e., a registered security, the SEC states that this may or may not affect national interests sufficiently to require the exercise of jurisdiction. However, the provisions of the '34 Act which apply to registered securities, even if the jurisdictional means are missing, were drafted in such a way that, according to the SEC, 'an effect on significant national interests would almost invariably be present.' [49]

"Thus, the SEC contends that Section 30(b) was intended to be clearly available only for those provisions that are applicable because of the identity of the person involved, i.e., those provisions that apply to brokers, dealers, and contain neither of the other two elements, jurisdictional means or registered security.

The final group of operative provisions of the original version of the Act was applicable to persons in the securities business even in the absence of a registered security or a use of the jurisdictional means. Under these provisions the 'triggering' element was the identity of the person involved in the transaction, not the nature of the transaction itself, and any particular foreign transaction might or might not have a sufficient impact on American interests to justify the direct application of the Act to the transaction irrespective of the participation or nonparticipation of someone in the securities business. In other words, although the United States might have power over a participant in a foreign transaction and thereby be able indirectly to regulate the transaction, the transaction itself might not have a sufficient impact on American interests and therefore not be within the direct legislative jurisdiction of Congress under the Constitution and the law of nations. It was *this problem* to which Section 30(b) was addressed.[50]

"The SEC further maintains that a person who qualifies for the Section 30(b) exemption is not exempt with respect to all his transactions, but only for those particular transactions that occur 'without the jurisdiction of the United States.' [51]

"It should be clear that Congress did not use the phrase 'without the jurisdiction of the United States' as the equivalent of 'without the United States' or 'not within the United States.' Such an interpretation would ascribe no significance to the words 'the jurisdiction of' and would do violence to the accepted canon of statutory construction that, if possible, effect must be given to every word of a statute. E.g., 2 Sutherland, *Statutory Construction* § 4705 (3d ed. Horack 1943). On the other hand, if 'without the jurisdiction of the United States' is read as a shorthand expression for 'neither (1) within the United States; (2) directly or indirectly, by the use of any means or instrumentality of interstate commerce or of the mails, or of any facility of any national securities exchange nor (3) involving a registered security (under provisions of the Act applicable only to registered securities),' it would both give effect to all the words of Section 30(b) and reinforce the apparent statutory purpose of the provision. As we have seen, this purpose was to authorize the Commission to promulgate rules to reach foreign transactions not involving the use of a jurisdictional

---

"48. 15 U.S.C. § 78(c) (1964) defines 'interstate commerce' to include 'trade, commerce, transportation or communication * * * between any foreign country and any State, or between any State and any place or ship outside thereof.' Id. § 78(c) (17)."

"49. Brief for SEC as Amicus Curiae at 19, Schoenbaum v. Firstbrook, 405 F.2d 208 (2d Cir.1968)."

"50. Id. at 20–21."

"51. Id. at 23."

means or a registered security whenever necessary to prevent evasion of the Act and, at the same time, to limit the otherwise universal application of certain provisions of the Act to persons in the securities business in the absence of those elements or such rules. * * * Thus, Section 30(b) is unavailable even to persons in the securities business insofar as they use the jurisdictional means to engage in foreign securities transactions.[52]

"The SEC analysis of the jurisdictional limits of the '34 Act, while somewhat mechanistic in its approach, is significant in its treatment of individual sections of the act as divisible for purposes of jurisdiction. The SEC view appears to recognize that while Congress may have intended some sections of the act to have an extraterritorial reach, this intent may have been lacking with regard to other sections. * * *"

The later case of Roth v. Fund of Funds, Limited [4] dealt with the question whether a Canadian corporation which was domiciled in Switzerland could be held liable under Section 16(b) for short-swing profits in the securities of an American corporation generated by purchases and sales executed on the New York Stock Exchange as a result of orders placed by the defendant from Switzerland. The defendant argued that, because it was engaged in a "business in securities without the jurisdiction of the United States", Section 30(b) immunized it from liability under Section 16(b). The Second Circuit rejected this argument, partially on the basis that the court doubted that the defendant, not being a broker-dealer but a mutual fund, was engaged in "a business in securities" anywhere, but also on the basis that since the orders were executed on the NYSE this particular "business" was not "without the jurisdiction of the United States."

RULE 10b–5

Almost all of the cases, dealing with the question of the extent to which the civil liability provisions of the Federal securities laws apply to transactions some portion or all of which take place outside the territorial boundaries of the United States, have involved an alleged violation of Rule 10b–5, like the *Leasco* case and the *Bersch* case. In analyzing this question it is helpful to distinguish between cases where American residents are suing foreigners (as in Leasco) and where foreigners are suing American residents (as in Bersch). As a preliminary matter, it would seem that the citizenship of the parties would have little, if any, significance. As Judge Friendly has said: "Although the United States has power to prescribe the conduct of its nationals everywhere in the world, see Restatement (2d) of the Foreign Relations Law of the United States, § 30(1)(a) (1965), Congress does not often do so and courts are forced to interpret the statute at issue in the particular case." [5] As to suits by residents of the United States against non-residents, presumably the Equal Protection Clause would prohibit denying relief to the plaintiff merely because he was not a United States citizen.

"**52.** Id. at 23–24."

4. 405 F.2d 421 (2d Cir.1968), cert. denied 394 U.S. 975 (1969).

Compare Wagman v. Astle, 380 F.Supp. 497 (S.D.N.Y.1974), in which Judge Ward held that the court had no jurisdiction over a Canadian resident doing no business in the United States in an action for a violation of Section 16(b) with respect to shares of a Canadian corporation listed on the AMEX, where all of the purchases and sales occurred in Canada.

5. IIT, An International Investment Trust v. Vencap, Ltd., 519 F.2d 1001, at 1016 (2d Cir.1975).

Suits by Residents against Non-residents. As indicated in the *Leasco* case, where an American resident is suing a foreigner for fraud, some significant portion of the transaction or some significant portion of the wrongful conduct must have occurred within the boundaries of the United States in order for the American courts to have jurisdiction.[6] If an American goes abroad and gets himself defrauded by a resident of a foreign country solely by acts committed there, he must seek redress in the courts of the foreign country.[7]

The question may arise as to what constitutes conduct within the United States under this approach. In Travis v. Anthes Imperial Limited [8] a Canadian corporation made an exchange offer to the shareholders of another Canadian corporation which had a small minority of its shareholders residing in the United States, but did not extend the offer to the United States holders because it did not want to register the offering under the 1933 Act. Thereafter, it entered into various communications with the plaintiff shareholders and their counsel in St. Louis regarding their objection to being thus excluded and eventually agreed to purchase their shares for cash. The closing of this transaction was held in St. Louis. The defendants never did anything in the United States, except presumably to have an agent present at the closing of the purchase, but the court held that the directing of communications by mail and telephone to the plaintiffs in the United States, which allegedly contained the misrepresentations and omissions, together with the closing of the purchase here, was sufficient to give the American court jurisdiction. The court said:

" * * * the [trial] court was of the view that the contacts were insignificant because they were initiated by the plaintiffs—i.e., the letters were in response to Travis's inquiries and in most, though not in all cases, the plaintiffs or their representatives telephoned the defendants or their representatives. In our opinion, it is not material who initiated the communications. Instead, the real question is whether the mails or instrumentalities of interstate commerce were used to mislead the plaintiffs. The defendants were not forced in these communications to make misrepresentations to the plaintiffs. We are aware of no case law on this point which is contrary to the view we express here. Further, we believe common sense requires the rejection of the argument that a person could freely communicate a misrepresentation by the mails or an instrumentality of interstate commerce without fear of violating § 10(b) of the Act, if the defrauded party had initiated the communication." [9]

Suits by Non-residents against Residents. In IIT, An International Investment Trust v. Vencap, Limited,[10] decided the same day as the *Bersch* case in an opinion also by Judge Friendly, the facts were extraordinarily complicated and to a large extent obscure. Basically, however, it was alleged that Mr. Richard C. Pistell, who was a United States citizen well known in financial circles but

---

6. For a case quite similar to the Leasco case, see Alco Standard Corp. v. Benalal, 345 F.Supp. 14 (E.D.Pa.1972).

7. In Roman Catholic Archbishop of San Francisco v. Superior Court, 15 Cal. App.3d 405, 93 Cal.Rptr. 338 (1971), the plaintiff Californian traveling in Europe purchased a St. Bernard dog from the monastery Hospice du Great St. Bernard (operated by the Canons Regular of St. Augustine) in Switzerland. When he returned to California and the dog did not arrive, apparently recognizing his inability to obtain service on the other contracting party or presumably subject matter jurisdiction (except in an action based on Swiss

law), he sued the Archbishop of San Francisco, a corporation sole, as the "alter ego" of the Canons Regular of St. Augustine (possibly on the theory that "all those Catholics are alike"). The court didn't think much of his lawsuit. A hearing was granted in this case by the California Supreme Court, but the appeal was dismissed when there was a "compromise agreement of litigants." Perhaps the Archbishop gave him a toy poodle.

8. 473 F.2d 515 (8th Cir.1973).

9. 473 F.2d at 526–27.

10. Supra, note 5.

who was found to be a resident of The Bahamas, organized a Bahamian corporation; sold shares of the corporation to the plaintiff investment trust, organized under the laws of Luxembourg but headquartered in London; and siphoned off the funds thus obtained, through a complicated series of transactions involving a German bank (Handelskredit-Bank) and a Netherlands Antilles corporation (Intercapital N.V.) owned by Pistell and an associate, for the purpose of paying his own personal tax bills for which the IRS had filed a lien against him.

The court held that the mere fact that Pistell was an American citizen would not give the court jurisdiction, nor would the fact that Americans owned approximately .5% of the plaintiff trust's shares and therefore to that extent American investors were injured by the fraud. However, the court held that the alleged fact that certain actions essential to the consummation of the fraud took place in the offices of the attorneys for Mr. Pistell in New York City was a sufficient basis to give the American court jurisdiction. The court said:

"We do not think Congress intended to allow the United States to be used as a base for manufacturing fraudulent security devices for export, even when these are peddled only to foreigners. This country would surely look askance if one of our neighbors stood by silently and permitted misrepresented securities to be poured into the United States. By the same token it is hard to believe Congress meant to prohibit the SEC from policing similar activities within this country; * * * If there would be subject matter jurisdiction over a suit by the SEC to prevent the concoction of securities frauds in the United States for export, there would also seem to be jurisdiction over a suit for damages or rescission by a defrauded foreign individual. Our ruling on this basis of jurisdiction is limited to the perpetration of fraudulent acts themselves and does not extend to mere preparatory activities or the failure to prevent fraudulent acts where the bulk of the activity was performed in foreign countries, such as in *Bersch*. Admittedly the distinction is a fine one. But the position we are taking here itself extends the application of the securities laws to transnational transactions beyond prior decisions and the line has to be drawn somewhere if the securities laws are not to apply in every instance where something has happened in the United States, however large the gap between the something and a consummated fraud and however negligible the effect in the United States or on its citizens." [11]

In IIT, An International Investment Trust v. Cornfeld [12] Judge Friendly again distinguished the *Bersch* case and held that there was subject matter jurisdiction of a suit by the same Luxembourg investment trust which was involved in the *Vencap* case against various residents of the United States in connection with a Eurodollar convertible debenture offering by King Resources Corporation based in Denver (although the debentures were technically issued by a Netherlands Antilles subsidiary of Kings Resources Corporation, as is customary in such transactions—see page 1602, below). The court pointed out that most of the activities relating to the offering were carried out in the United States and that it was an offering of what were essentially American securities, although offered only to foreigners in Europe and elsewhere. The court held that these activities were more than "merely preparatory" within the meaning of the rule adopted in the *Bersch* case. Several other circuit court decisions have held on the basis of the facts there involved that conduct

---

11. 519 F.2d at 1017–18. See, also, Wandschneider v. Industrial Incomes Inc. of North America, CCH Fed.Sec.Law Rptr. ¶ 93,422 (S.D.N.Y.1972).

12. 619 F.2d 909 (2d Cir.1980).

occurring within the United States was a sufficient basis for invoking the jurisdiction of the federal courts.[13]

In addition to this so-called "conduct test", the courts have said that jurisdiction may be based on acts which cause substantial effects within the United States regardless of where those acts occurred.[14] For example, in Des Brisay v. The Goldfield Corp.[15] the Ninth Circuit held that where an American corporation whose shares were listed on the American Stock Exchange acquired a Canadian corporation for stock which was so listed, pursuant to a transaction entered into and carried out in Canada, there was subject matter jurisdiction of an action under Rule 10b–5 by Canadian sellers who were allegedly defrauded. The court said: "The fact that an allegedly improper transaction occurred outside the United States or involved parties other than United States citizens has been held not to defeat subject matter jurisdiction where the securities involved in the transaction were registered and listed on a national exchange, and the effect of the foreign transaction adversely affected buyers, sellers and holders of those securities."

Suits by Foreigners against Foreigners. The courts have refused, however, to entertain suits between two foreign entities involving a dispute over what was essentially or predominantly a foreign transaction.[16] In Fidenas AG v. Compagnie Internationale Pour L'Informatique CII Honneywell Bull, S.A.[17] the Second Circuit quoted with approval the language of Judge Frankel below as follows:

"It is undisputed that all of the parties to this action, both plaintiffs and defendants, are foreign. It is also clear that whatever the scope of the activity within the United States that might emerge from discovery, the essential core of the alleged fraud took place in Switzerland. Any activities in the United States were clearly secondary and ancillary."

The court concluded that it would not devote the "precious resources" of the United States courts to the adjudication of such a controversy.

REGISTRATION UNDER THE 1933 ACT

The registration provisions of the Securities Act of 1933 literally apply whenever the jurisdictional means are used in connection with the offering, which specifically include any instrumentality of commerce "between any foreign country and any state, territory, or the District of Columbia." Therefore, if there is even one sale made in the United States to an American investor in an otherwise foreign public offering, there would seem to be a violation of Section 5 of the 1933 Act, unless some exemption is available.[18] The private offering exemption would not be applicable, since the sale in the United States "involves" the foreign public offering. By the same token, any

13. Continental Grain (Australia) Party Limited v. Pacific Oilseeds, Inc., 592 F.2d 409 (8th Cir.1979); United States v. Cook, 573 F.2d 281 (5th Cir.1978), cert. denied 439 U.S. 836; Securities and Exchange Commission v. Kasser, 548 F.2d 109 (3d Cir.1977), cert. denied 431 U.S. 938.

14. See the Continental Grain case, supra note 13.

15. 549 F.2d 133 (9th Cir.1977).

16. Fidenas AG v. Compagnie Internationale Pour L'Informatique CII Honneywell

Bull, S.A., 606 F.2d 5 (2d Cir.1979); Ogdeninvest, A.G. v. Hessiche Landesbank-Girozentrale, CCH Fed.Sec.Law Rptr. ¶ 96,555 (S.D.N.Y.1978); Recaman v. Barish, 408 F.Supp. 1189 (E.D.Pa.1975).

17. Supra, note 16.

18. Securities and Exchange Commission v. United Financial Group, Inc., 474 F.2d 354 (9th Cir.1973).

sale by a United States corporation of its securities solely to foreign residents would seem literally to require registration under the 1933 Act, since it would almost inevitably require preparation in the United States and the use at some stage of the jurisdictional means. However, at the prodding of a Presidential Task Force, the SEC in 1964 issued a Release stating that such foreign offerings by American corporations did not have to be registered under certain circumstances.[19]

In this Release the Commission stated:

"The registration requirements of the Securities Act apply to any offer or sale of a security involving interstate commerce or use of the mails unless an exemption is available. Since 'interstate commerce' is defined in section 2(7) of the Act to include 'trade or commerce in securities or any transportation or communication relating thereto * * * between any foreign country and any state, territory, or the District of Columbia,' this might be construed to encompass virtually any offering of securities made by a United States corporation to foreign investors. However, the Commission has traditionally taken the position that the registration requirements of section 5 of the Act are primarily intended to protect American investors. Accordingly, the Commission has not taken any action for failure to register securities of United States corporations distributed abroad to foreign nationals, even though use of jurisdictional means may be involved in the offering. It is assumed in these situations that the distribution is to be effected in a manner which will result in the securities coming to rest abroad. On the other hand, a distribution of securities by a United States corporation, through the facilities of Canadian Stock Exchanges may be expected to flow into the hands of American investors [and] may therefore be subject to registration. Similarly, a public offering specifically directed toward American nationals abroad, including servicemen, would be regarded as subject to registration. Apart from such situations, however, it is immaterial whether the offering originates from within or outside of the United States, whether domestic or foreign broker-dealers are involved and whether the actual mechanics of the distribution are effected within the United States, so long as the offering is made under circumstances reasonably designed to preclude distribution or redistribution of the securities within, or to nationals of, the United States.

"Active trading in the United States of the securities subject to the offering during or shortly after the distribution abroad may raise a question whether a portion of the distribution was in fact being made by means of such trading. However, absent such a situation, if a distribution of securities by a United States corporation is made abroad without registration in reliance upon the foregoing interpretation of the Act, dealers may trade in other securities of the same class in the United States without regard to the time limitations of the dealer's exemption in section 4(1) [now section 4(3)].

"The Task Force also suggests that the Commission's statement extend to simultaneous private placements in this country of a security being offered abroad. This specifically concerns the application of the exemption from registration provided by the second clause of section 4(1) [now section 4(2)] of the Act for 'transactions by an issuer not involving any public offering,' the requirements for which were discussed in detail in Securities Act Release No. 4552. Generally, transactions otherwise meeting the requirements of this exemption need not be integrated with simultaneous offerings being made abroad and, therefore, are not subject to the registration requirements of the

19. SEC Sec.Act Rel. No. 4708 (July 9, 1964).

Act solely because a foreign offering is being made concurrently with the American private placement which otherwise meets the standards of the exemption." [20]

This Release facilitated the placement of billions of dollars of debt issues abroad by American corporations, in what were called "Eurobond offerings." The technique was to organize a Netherlands Antilles subsidiary of the American corporation which would make a public offering of debt securities (fully guaranteed by the United States parent) through a European underwriting syndicate (although typically including some American houses with offices in London or on the Continent) primarily to residents of the European Common Market area. The use of the Netherlands Antilles subsidiary had nothing to do with the securities laws—the guarantee would itself be a separate security of which the United States corporation would be the issuer. That was designed to avoid the 30% withholding tax on the interest paid on the debentures to non-resident aliens under Section 1441 of the Internal Revenue Code, as authorized in a ruling of the IRS; the Netherlands Antilles was selected as itself having the most favorable tax laws from the point of view of avoiding any tax on the European holder of the security except those of his own country (if he chose to pay them).

However, in Securities and Exchange Commission v. United Financial Group, Inc.[21] the SEC attempted to strangle its own child by taking the position in litigation that the registration provisions of the 1933 Act applied whenever the jurisdictional means were used, thus repudiating the Release. Because there were one or more American purchasers in that case, the court found it unnecessary to rule on this question. In describing the position taken in the brief of the SEC the court said:

"An alternate theory of jurisdiction advanced by respondent is based solely upon appellants' use of the facilities of interstate commerce. If accepted without qualification, there would be jurisdiction in every case regardless of whether American investors were involved. Such a theory is squarely at odds with appellants' argument of improper extraterritorial application of legislation. Although the 'interstate commerce facilities use' theory may have some merit, it is unnecessary to our decision in this case and we, therefore, express no opinion as to its soundness." [22]

The court also said: "Given our ruling in this case, we also find it unnecessary to render an opinion as to the appropriateness of asserting jurisdiction on the ground of a national interest in protecting this country's reputation abroad or on the ground that the activities of the appellants have an adverse economic impact upon this country's economy." [23]

For consideration of the issues dealt with in this Chapter, see Michaels, Subject Matter Jurisdiction Over Transnational Securities Fraud, 71 Cornell L.Rev. 919 (1986); Kozyris, Corporate Wars and Choice of Law, 1985 Duke L.J. 1 (1985); Evans, Offering of Securities Solely to Foreign Investors, 40 Bus.Law. 69 (1984); Murano, Extraterritorial Application of the Antifraud Provisions of the Securities Exchange Act of 1934, 2 Int'l. Tax & Bus.Law 298 (1984);

---

20. Are the pronouncements in this Release an interpretation of the statute (and a correct interpretation) or merely an act of "administrative grace" by the SEC? Note that the Release says that "the Commission has not taken any action" but it also says that the statute was "primarily intended to protect American investors." Note also that if the statute exempts foreign offerings, the SEC has attempted to read Canada out of the United Nations. Although urged to do so, the SEC has refused to state the principles of this Release in a Rule, which would give protection against civil liability unless and until it were declared invalid.

21. Supra, note 18.

22. 474 F.2d at 357.

23. Ibid.

Symposium, Compelling Discovery in Transnational Litigation, 16 N.Y.U.J.Int'l L. & Policy 957 (1984); Morgenstern, Extraterritorial Application of United States Securities Law: A Matrix Analysis, 7 Hastings Int'l. & Comp.L.Rev. 1 (1983); Thomas, Extraterritoriality in an Era of Internationalization of the Securities Markets, 35 Rutgers L.Rev. 453 (1983); Hearn, Regulation of Off-Shore Investment Companies Through Extraterritorial Application of Rule 10b–5, 1982 Duke L.J. 167 (1982); Miles, Constraints on Broker-Dealers Operating Outside Their Home Country, 4 J.Comp.Corp.L. & Sec.Rev. 36 (1982); Thomas, Internationalization of the Securities Markets, 50 Geo.Wash.L.Rev. 155 (1982); Thomas, Extraterritorial Application of the United States Securities Laws, 7 J. of Corp.L. 189 (1982); Hacker and Rotunda, Extraterritorial Regulation of Foreign Business Under the U.S. Securities Laws, 59 N.C.L.Rev. 643 (1981); Johnson, Application of Federal Securities Laws to International Securities Transactions, 45 Albany L.Rev. 896 (1981); Pozen, Disclosure and Trading in an International Securities Market, 15 Int.Law. 84 (1981); Loss, Extraterritoriality in the Federal Securities Code, 20 Harv.Int.L.J. 305 (1979); Liftin, The Extraterritorial Reach of the Federal Securities Code: An Analysis of Section 1905, 32 Vand.L.Rev. 455 (1979); Extraterritorial Effect of the Registration Requirements of the Securities Act of 1933, 24 Vill.L.Rev. 729 (1979); Casper, Transnational Offerings and the Problem of Integration, 34 U.Miami L.Rev. 47 (1979); Toth, Registration and Regulation of Foreign Securities Businesses, 12 Int.Law. 159 (1978); Tomlinson, Federal Regulation of Secondary Trading in Foreign Securities, 32 Bus.Law. 463 (1977); Pollack, Control of Securities Transactions Overseas—A Comparison and Contrast, 32 Bus.Law. 1405 (1977); Onkelinx, Conflict of International Jurisdiction: Ordering the Production of Documents in Violation of the Law of the Situs, 64 Nw.U.L.Rev. 487 (1969).

Part VIII
STATE SECURITIES REGULATION

Chapter 25

REGULATION AND LIABILITY UNDER STATE SECURITIES LAWS

State Blue Sky Laws

All States regulate in one form or another the distribution of securities. Section 18 of the Securities Act of 1933 expressly preserves such state regulation even though the issue is required to be registered under the federal act. However, these statutes and regulations take a variety of forms ranging from those which impose a minimum degree of regulation to the California system which imposes a very sophisticated system of regulation; the California statute is unique in that it builds upon and attempts to interrelate with the federal securities laws.

The Commissioners on Uniform State Laws have attempted to reduce the confusion and expense incident to the qualification of an issue of securities under these statutes by a proposed Uniform Securities Act, promulgated in 1956. While this act was not adopted without change in very many States, it was "adapted" rather than adopted, in the majority of states.[1] And in 1985, the National Conference of Commissioners on Uniform State Laws promulgated a revised Uniform Securities Act (1985), which has now been recommended for adoption by the various states.[2]

It seems inadvisable, if not impossible, to deal here with state securities regulation in any detail. Although there is considerable similarity in the statutory approach to regulation, as distinguished from the details, it is still necessary to make a "Blue Sky Survey" in connection with each interstate offering of securities, to determine what action, if any, is required to qualify the issue for sale in each jurisdiction where the offering is intended to be made; however, the task has been made easier by the existence of more comprehensible statutes and sources of information regarding the individual statutes and regulations.[3] Thus, the CCH Blue Sky Law Reporter (Loose Leaf) contains the statutes and regulations in all fifty states, the District of Columbia, Guam and Puerto Rico. In some states, treatises have been written, with accompanying forms, which assist the securities lawyer in qualifying an issue in that state.[4] The North American Securities Admin-

---

1. The 1956 Act was drafted by Professor Louis Loss of the Harvard Law School. For the draft and draftsmens' comments, see L. Loss & E. Cowett, Blue Sky Law (1958).

2. Professor Robert B. Titus of the Western New England College School of Law served as the Reporter to the Drafting Committee.

3. See P. Fass & D. Wittner, Blue Sky Practice For Public and Private Limited Offerings (1987). The California Corporate

Securities Law of 1968 was accompanied by the drafting of detailed regulations, which were adopted only after being proposed for public comment pursuant to the California Administrative Procedure Act.

4. See H. Marsh & R. Volk, Practice Under the California Corporate Securities Laws (1986 ed.); Moscow & Makens, Michigan Securities Regulation: A Blue Sky Compendium (1983).

istrators Association (NASAA) has been active in promoting uniformity in the administration of securities regulation among the states and in the development of statements of policy designed to implement the administration of the statutes with respect to novel new investment vehicles.[5] In addition, NASAA is the entity through which the states cooperate with the SEC in promoting greater uniformity in Federal-State securities matters pursuant to Section 19(c) of the Securities Act of 1933.

It is the purpose of this chapter to give the reader an overview of state securities regulation. We begin with an article by the Reporter of the Revised Uniform Securities Act (1985) explaining the scope and objectives of the new proposed act. A recurring issue in state regulation is the extent to which the states should go beyond the disclosure philosophy embodied in the Securities Act of 1933 and impose substantive standards with respect to the nature and terms of an offering—what has been euphemistically called "merit regulation of securities." A recent report of an American Bar Association special subcommittee has studied the supposed merits and demerits of state merit regulation of securities, marshalled the arguments for and against merit regulation and produced an excellent report which "explore[s] the effective limits on merit regulation's function in a joint state-federal system of securities regulation." This report also provides an overview of the various approaches to securities regulation current among the individual states. One who is knowledgeable in federal securities regulation will find considerable similarity between the Securities Act of 1933 and the Uniform Securities Act (1985), although the two acts differ in philosophical approach. Armed with this background, one should be able to comprehend the details of any particular state act and the implementing regulations.

In addition to regulating offers and sales of securities by issuers, these acts also regulate certain secondary issues of securities as well as broker-dealers' activities. In addition, there are also a whole range of conflict of laws issues relating to state jurisdiction over out-of-state sellers to in-state buyers and of in-state sellers to out-of-state buyers. These issues will also be explored. Finally, we will consider some aspects of civil liability under state securities laws.

Excerpt from: ROBERT B. TITUS *

UNIFORM SECURITIES ACT (1985) **

19 Review of Securities & Commodities Regulation 81–88 (1986).

At its 1985 annual meeting, the National Conference of Commissioners on Uniform State Laws ("NCCUSL") approved a revised Uniform Securities Act (1985) (the "1985 Act"), which will be recommended for adoption by individual states over the next several years. Thirty-seven states have adopted, with varying degrees of subsequent amendment, the original Uniform Securities Act (the "1956 Act") drafted by Professor Louis Loss in

---

5. The NASAA Rep. (CCH) is devoted to the activities, policies and positions of the North American Securities Administrators Association.

* Robert B. Titus is Associate Professor of Law at Western New England College School of Law, Springfield, Massachusetts. He served as the Reporter to the Uniform Securities Act Drafting Committee of the National Conference of Commissioners on Uniform State Laws, which prepared the Uniform Securities Act (1985). The views expressed in this article are those of the author and not necessarily those of the National Conference of Commissioners on Uniform State Laws.

** Copyright 1986. Reprinted from the Review of Securities & Commodities Regulation with the permission of the author and Standard & Poor's Corporation.

1956[1] and approved by the NCCUSL in 1958. This article reviews the objectives that supported and directed the drafting of the 1985 Act and the principal changes in state securities law regulation that are proposed by the 1985 Act.

As one would expect when revision is undertaken of an existing uniform act that has proven quite effective, there are no radical changes in the 1985 Act. Indeed, approximately 90 of the 120 different sections and principal subsections in the 1985 Act are in substance the same as their counterparts in the 1956 Act, and perhaps another 10 or 15 codify practices that have become widely accepted under the 1956 Act provisions. Nevertheless, the 1985 Act does propose a number of changes that could have a significant impact upon state securities regulation and practice.

OBJECTIVES

The basic objective of state securities law regulation as expressed in the 1956 Act—the protection of investors[2]—continues to be the driving force behind the 1985 Act. Sections 705(c) of the latter confirms that every action to be taken by a state securities administrator is to be measured against the standard that "the action is * * * in the public interest and appropriate for the protection of investors."[3] Furthermore, as with the earlier Act, the 1985 Act has as an additional purpose "to make uniform the law with respect to the subject of this [Act] among states enacting it and to coordinate the interpretation and administration of this [Act] with the related federal laws and regulations."[4]

Several significant 1985 Act provisions are premised upon additional specific assumptions and objectives. One obvious objective of the NCCUSL Drafting Committee was to incorporate provisions reflecting the various changes in the securities markets and regulatory structure that have occurred since the 1956 Act was promulgated. Many of the revisions in the professional licensing and securities registration provisions are indeed of such a technical or updating nature.

In addition to updating, however, the NCCUSL Drafting Committee of necessity reviewed and discussed, among its membership and with its advisers, the premises underlying the provisions of the 1956 Act. Here, of course, the Committee could draw upon almost 30 years of experience under the 1956 Act, as well as receiving valuable input from state securities regulators, securities practitioners, and various industry groups.

The overwhelming majority of provisions from the 1956 Act were retained, following the maxim, "If it ain't broke, don't fix it."[5] Where significant changes are proposed in the 1985 Act, they are based upon conscious choices. If any underlying premises or assumptions upon which

---

1. The 1956 Act, together with official and draftsmen's commentary, appears in its entirety in Loss and Cowett, *Blue Sky Law* (Little, Brown and Company, 1958). The 1956 Act also is reproduced in 1 Blue Sky L.Rep. (CCH) ¶ 5500 et seq. Except where specific reference is made to a 1956 Act section, all section references in this article are to the 1985 Act provisions. [The 1985 Act appears in 7B U.L.A. (Master Edition) (1985 Cumul.Pocket Part) and 1 Blue Sky L.Rep. (CCH) ¶ 5601 et seq.]

2. See, e.g., § 412(b) of 1956 Act.

3. § 705(c).

4. § 803.

5. An earlier draft revision presented to the NCCUSL in 1983, which made more sweeping revisions of the 1956 Act, was not approved. The most recent Drafting Committee thus understood the NCCUSL's preference for working from the 1956 Act as the accepted base.

the Drafting Committee proceeded are more significant than others, it is probably the three following conclusions:

(1) that investors require greater protection with respect to offerings of securities of unseasoned issuers than with offerings of seasoned companies;

(2) that state securities administrators will be required to undertake a greater share of enforcement activities in the future; and

(3) that the regulatory provisions of the Act should be as efficient as possible, i.e., should impose no greater regulatory costs or burdens on the persons required to comply than are necessary to promote the public interest and protect investors.

REORGANIZATION OF THE ACT

Although approximately three-fourths of the 1956 Act provisions have been substantially retained, the 1985 Act reorganizes the component parts. Following the standard NCCUSL format more closely, the 1985 Act is composed of eight parts, as follows: Definitions (Part I); Licensing of Broker-Dealers, Sales Representatives, and Investment Advisers (Part II); Registration of Securities (Part III); Exemptions from Registration (Part IV); Fraudulent and Other Prohibited Practices (Part V); Enforcement and Civil Liability (Part VI); Administration (Part VII); and Miscellaneous Provisions (Part VIII).[6] A prefatory note and a cross-reference list to the 1956 Act provisions will be included with the final printed version of the 1985 Act, together with section-by-section comments.

The remainder of this article principally will discuss the licensing of professionals (Part II), the securities registration and exemptions (Parts III and IV), and the fraud and enforcement provisions (Parts V and VI).

LICENSING OF PROFESSIONALS

These provisions in the 1985 Act probably involve the least substantive revisions, although numerous technical and updating changes have been made. The general objective of protecting investors has been and continues to be effectuated in the licensing of securities professionals in three specific ways: (1) ensuring, through the licensing process, that the professionals satisfy minimum competency requirements; (2) imposing various post-licensing obligations; and (3) providing appropriate sanctions and remedies when a securities professional is not in compliance with the requirements of the Act.

The licensing and examination procedures of the 1956 Act have basically been carried over into the 1985 Act, as have the post-licensing and sanction provisions.[7] The post-licensing provisions have been modified to reflect, and indeed encourage, the high degree of uniformity and centralization that exists among the federal and state administrators and self-regulatory organizations such as the National Association of Securities

---

6. The sections of the 1956 Act that correspond to these reorganized parts are set forth in the parentheses below:

Part I (401)

Part II (201–204)

Part III (301–306)

Part IV (402–403)

Part V (101–102, 404–405)

Part VI (407–410)

Part VII (406, 411–413)

Part VIII (414–419)

7. See §§ 205–207, 209, and 212–213.

Dealers, Inc. ("NASD"). Among the areas in which uniformity can minimize the costs and burdens of regulatory compliance without jeopardizing investor protection are the financial reporting and record-keeping requirements. Section 209 recognizes this in providing that compliance with the federal securities law requirements shall constitute compliance with respect to the net capital, financial reports, and record-keeping requirements of the 1985 Act.[8]

The requirement for annual renewal of registrations under the 1956 Act[9] has been eliminated; under the 1985 Act, a license once effective remains so until withdrawn, suspended, or revoked.[10] One other gap in previous practice that has been filled concerns licensing of successor firms. Section 210 now authorizes a successor to a licensed professional to utilize the license of the latter for a period of 60 days while the successor's license application is being processed.[11] This will enable the business of a troubled or failing broker-dealer to be continued without interruption by a party assuming the business and accounts of the former.

Three significant changes have been made in the exclusionary and exemptive provisions. In the first instance, the 1985 Act now classifies as broker-dealers or investment advisers those persons who carry on activities typical of such persons but engage in only de minimis transactions in a given state. Under the 1956 Act, such persons were excluded from the respective definitions;[12] under the 1985 Act they are considered broker-dealers or investment advisers, but then are exempted from the applicable licensing requirements.[13] Secondly, a specific exemption from licensing, in addition to the de minimis exemption, has been added for professionals dealing with transient or vacationing customers.[14] Thus, a broker-dealer licensed in Connecticut dealing with an existing customer whose principal place of residence is in Connecticut but who is vacationing in South Carolina at the time of a particular transaction will not be required also to register as a broker-dealer in South Carolina. Lastly, the 1985 Act extends broker-dealer licensing requirements to the so-called secondary dealers in government securities.[15]

One further development should be noted with respect to the licensing of securities professionals. The NCCUSL Drafting Committee chose not to remove the exception from the definition of a "broker-dealer" that has been available for banks and other depository institutions.[16] This does not reflect a determination by the Drafting Committee that depository institutions should not be regulated as broker-dealers when engaging in broker-dealer activities, but rather the view that appropriate resolution of this jurisdictional issue can be achieved only at the federal level. Indeed, early indications are that the issue may become moot because of resolution at the federal level. The likely result of rule 3b–9,[17] promulgated by the SEC last

---

8. § 209(a), (c)(2) and (3), and (d)(2).

9. See § 202 of 1956 Act.

10. § 208(a).

11. § 210(b).

12. See § 401(c) and (f) of 1956 Act.

13. §§ 202 and 204.

14. §§ 202(a)(ii) and 204(1)(ii).

15. § 202(a)(1)(i) and (b). One of the key premises to the exemption from bro-

ker-dealer licensing is the registration and licensing of the broker-dealer *somewhere*, i.e., at either the federal or state level. For many secondary government securities dealers, no one currently fulfills that role.

16. § 101(2)(iii). § 401(c)(3) of the 1956 Act is to the same effect.

17. See Sec.Exch.Act Rel. No. 22205, set out in [1984–85 Transfer Binder] Fed.Sec.L.Rep. (CCH) ¶ 83,800 (July 1,

summer, and analogous rules adopted by various banking agencies,[18] appears to be that most depository institutions will utilize separate subsidiaries to engage in broker-dealer activities. Those subsidiaries will not be entitled to the exemption available to the parent depository institution under section 101, and would be required to be licensed as broker-dealers.[19]

REGISTRATION OF SECURITIES AND EXEMPTIONS FROM REGISTRATION

One major issue that confronted the NCCUSL Drafting Committee concerned the appropriate philosophy to be followed with respect to the registration of securities in order to achieve investor protection, i.e., whether to continue the disclosure philosophy set out in both the 1956 Act and the federal Securities Act of 1933, or also to recommend or include merit regulation, which a substantial minority of states presently follows. That issue, of course, is not new. Numerous commentators and groups have addressed the perceived advantages and disadvantages of merit regulation.[20] During the past few years, several state legislatures have consciously chosen to add or delete merit regulation provisions as part of their state securities laws.[21] The Drafting Committee ultimately concluded that since a substantial number of states follow a merit regulation philosophy, the 1985 Act should recognize that alternative as an appropriate choice for a state legislature. Thus, while the language of the existing Act, to the effect that registration of securities can be denied if "the offering has worked or tended to work a fraud upon purchasers," has been retained in section 306(a)(2)(v), an alternative version of clause (v) can be adopted that would permit denial of registration if the terms of the offering are "unfair, unjust or inequitable."[22]

Once this basic regulatory philosophy issue had been addressed, the next major consideration by the NCCUSL Drafting Committee was the extent to which public offerings by various types of issuers created more or less need for investor protection.

Experience under existing state securities provisions, including the 1956 Act, suggests that offerings by well-established, "seasoned"[23] companies typically do not raise major concerns, with respect to the protection of investors, whether the regulatory philosophy followed is that of disclosure

1985). Rule 3b–9 is effective January 1, 1986.

18. See, e.g., the FDIC's policy statement requiring the securities activities of FDIC-insured banks to be conducted through separate subsidiaries. 49 Fed.Reg. 46,709 (November 28, 1984).

19. § 101(2)(iii) and (3).

20. See, e.g., Warren, Reflections on Dual Regulation of Securities: A Case Against Preemption, 25 B.C.L.Rev. 495 (1984); Makens, Who Speaks for the Investor? An Evaluation of the Assault on Merit Regulation, 13 U.Balt.L.Rev. 435 (1984); and Campbell, An Open Attack on the Nonsense of Blue Sky Regulation, 10 J.Corp.L. 553 (1985).

21. See, as examples of retreat from merit standards, the provision for registration by notification adopted in Illinois for

all federally registered offerings [1A Blue Sky L.Rep. (CCH) ¶ 22,124] and the exception from merit review applicable under Wisconsin law when certain suitability standards are satisfied [3 Blue Sky L.Rep. (CCH) ¶ 64,118(7)].

On the other hand, Maine has recently adopted a revised securities act that includes a merit standard, and legislation in that direction has been introduced in other state legislatures (e.g., New Jersey).

22. § 306(a)(2)(v) (bracketed version).

23. Although the term "seasoned" is not used or defined in any securities statute of which the author is aware, it is used here to refer to a company that has a history both of earnings from continuing operations and of substantial public trading of its securities.

or merit review. That result should not be surprising, in light of the following facts: first, it is very likely that at least one (and possibly several) prior offerings by such an issuer already will have been subject to detailed review at the state securities level; second, that in many cases such issuer is subject to additional qualitative standards (i.e., of a corporate governance nature) imposed by some other body or agency (e.g., a stock exchange) [24]; and third, when there is an active and meaningful market for the shares of an issuer, that marketplace (being the aggregate of many investors' decisions to buy or sell) exerts a disciplinary influence on the issuer.[25] An obvious corollary is that when none of these factors is present—as when a company makes an initial public offering or when its securities have not long been publicly held or traded, i.e., an unseasoned company—investors cannot be assured of comparable protection.

These considerations underlie the significant revisions undertaken in Parts III and IV of the 1985 Act. The Drafting Committee put them into practice in the following fashion:

(1) The most seasoned public companies, those that generally are subject to some comprehensive qualitative standards, can and should be exempt from state securities registration without any significant loss of investor protection.

Consistent with this view, the NCCUSL Drafting Committee approved the continued exemption for securities listed on the New York, American, and Midwest Stock Exchanges (with the important exception of companies making initial public offerings).[26] In addition, recognizing the development during the past decade of the NASD's National Market System ("NMS") as a significant and effective marketplace, the Committee adopted in section 401(b)(8) a parallel exemption for securities of issuers designated as national market system securities. The latter step was taken only after considerable debate and discussion, both in the Committee and at the Conference level. The NASD Board of Governors' proposed corporate governance standards [27] for qualification requirements in addition to the previously approved designation criteria appears to have been enough to convince the NCCUSL to recommend exemption parity for NMS securities.

(2) Other established public companies not subject to such qualitative standards but that meet minimal statutory criteria can and should be accorded expedited registration processing.

To achieve this objective, the NCCUSL Drafting Committee approved, after many drafts, a new "registration by filing" provision in section 302. In order to be eligible for this "super coordination" procedure, an issuer must satisfy certain qualifications relating to its history [28] as well as to the

---

24. See, e.g., the listing requirements of the New York and American Stock Exchanges, as set forth in the NYSE Company Manual and The American Stock Exchange Guide.

25. With an active and meaningful market, an investor can signal his or her displeasure with a particular management or business arrangement by exercise of the "Wall Street rule," i.e., by selling the securities. See, e.g., J. Livingston, The American Stockholder, 60–61, 66–67 (J.B. Lippincott Company: 1958).

26. § 401(b)(7).

27. See, e.g., Sec.Exch.Act Rel.Nos. 22505 and 22506, Fed.Sec.L.Rep. (CCH) ¶ 83,925 (October 4, 1985).

28. To be eligible to use § 302, an issuer must have (1) actively engaged in business operations in the United States for at least 36 consecutive months [302(a)(2)]; (2) registered a class of securities under § 12 of the 1934 Act and been subject to the reporting and proxy requirements for at least 36 months prior to the filing of the

breadth of the existing market for its securities.[29]   In addition, the terms of the offering itself must meet certain criteria.[30]   Once an offering qualifies for this registration procedure, there are two significant consequences as to the status of a state administrator's securities review under the 1985 Act. First, the length of time for review at the state level is shortened to five business days.[31] Second, and probably more significant, effectiveness of that offering cannot be denied upon the so-called "merit" grounds of section 306(a)(2)(v) or (vi).[32] On the other hand, if there are misleading disclosures, if other provisions of the Act have been willfully violated, if the issuer's enterprise includes illegal activities, or if any of the other denial or stop order provisions of section 306(a)(2) are applicable, the state administrator retains the power to deny effectiveness of the offering.[33]

As one might expect, this provision was one of the most widely debated during the course of the Committee's deliberation and drafting efforts.[34] The Committee has gone to great lengths to attach substantial qualifying conditions [35] to ensure that this expedited registration process cannot be used except by persons whose offerings do not raise significant investor protection issues. Although there are no hard data, according to preliminary estimates only a very small percentage of all federally registered offerings probably would be entitled to utilize the procedure.[36]

(3) Other issuers, particularly first-time issuers ("initial public offerings"), should be subject to the full scope of state securities review, including, where applicable, merit review.

registration statement [302(a)(3) and (5)]; and (3) have a total net worth of $4,000,000 (or a total net worth of $2,000,000 and net pretax income from operations in at least two of the three preceding years) [302(a)(4)(i)]. In addition, the issuer must not have (1) failed to pay a dividend or sinking fund installment of preferred stock; (2) defaulted on repayment of indebtedness; or (3) defaulted on the rental of long-term leases if such defaults were material to its financial position as a whole [302(a)(9)].

29. The issuer must: (1) have at least 400,000 units of the class security registered under § 12 of the 1934 Act held by the public (excluding shares of officers and directors and certain other interested persons) [302(a)(4)(ii)], and (2) have, for a period of at least 30 days during the three months preceding the offering, at least four "market makers" in its principal class of equity securities [302(a)(6)].

30. Each of the underwriters must be subject to the Rules of Fair Practice of the NASD or a comparable body, and the offering must be on a "firm commitment" basis [302(a)(7)]; the aggregate commissions to be received by the underwriters shall not exceed 10% of the aggregate public offering price [302(a)(8)]; and, in the case of an equity security, the price at which it is offered to the public shall be at least $5 per share [302(a)(10)]. In addition, the issuer

may not have outstanding warrants and options held by underwriters, executive officers, and directors in an amount exceeding 10% of the total number of shares to be outstanding after the offering [302(a)(5)].

31. § 302(c)(3).

32. § 306(b)(2).

33. § 306(a) and (b).

34. The North American Securities Administrators Association ("NASAA") has voted to oppose adoption of the Act due to concerns, among others, as to "a subordinated state regulatory role," which presumably refers both to the new section 302 and the exemptive provisions regarding exchange listed and NMS securities.

35. Most of the criteria suggested for § 302 eligibility by the NASAA Uniform Securities Act Subcommittee advisers in April 1985 have been incorporated into § 302.

36. The number of public companies eligible to use § 302, excluding those exempt under either § 401(b)(7) or (8), is believed to be relatively small. A review by this author of limited information regarding the nature and number of filings previously made under Pennsylvania's "reporting company" exemption suggests that the percentage of issuers filing 1933 Act registration statements eligible under § 302 would be less than 5%.

All issuers not entitled either to an exemption under sections 401 or 402 or to registration by filing under section 302 will need to register, as they do currently under the 1956 Act, by either coordination [37] or qualification.[38] One important exception made to the previous exchange-listed security exemption was to recommend that initial public offerings (IPO's) be excluded from the exemption.[39] This is consistent with the overall view of the NCCUSL Drafting Committee that investors need greater protection with respect to offerings of unseasoned issuers than they do with seasoned companies.

A number of technical changes have been made in section 305 concerning the provisions generally applicable to the registration of securities. Under the 1933 Act, registration of mutual fund and other investment company shares now allows the registration of an indefinite amount at the time a registration is first filed, to be followed with annual filings and fee payments based upon actual sales within the state.[40] Two other subsections have been added to allow registrants to solve the problem of inadvertent oversales. Section 305(o) and (p) authorize after-the-fact filings of additional fees to reflect the additional shares sold, assuming, of course, that they were sold on the same terms and conditions as the other shares previously registered. Finally, with respect to offerings that also have been registered under the 1933 Act, section 305(k) requires that the 1933 Act prospectus be delivered to each purchaser in accordance with the prospectus delivery requirements applicable under the 1933 Act.[41]

Several changes have been proposed with respect to the exemptions from registration for the securities of certain issuers (now set forth in section 401) and for securities issued in certain transactions (now set forth in section 402). The exemptions for exchange-listed and NMS securities have been discussed above; four other provisions are perhaps worthy of note. The separate previous exemptions [42] in the 1956 Act for banks, thrift institutions, and credit unions have been combined into a single exemption [section 401(b)(2)], with eligibility for exemption turning on a uniform standard, namely, whether or not the deposit or share accounts of the depository institution are insured by a federally created insurance fund. Two other previous exemptions for securities that have been the source of sporadic investor losses over the years were modified slightly. The exemption for nonprofit organizations includes an alternative pre-sale notification procedure that a state legislature can impose if that state has experienced considerable abuses with nonprofit offerings.[43] Similarly, the "commercial paper" exemption of section 402(b)(11) has been revised to include objective criteria for determining what constitutes "commercial paper" within the exemption.[44] Finally, a new exemption has been proposed for "blue chip"

---

37. § 303.

38. § 304.

39. See, e.g., the language in § 401(b)(7) and (8) requiring that quotations have been available for the security so listed or designated and public trading have taken place "prior to the offer or sale . . . in reliance upon [the] exemption."

40. § 305(c).

41. The principal effect of this change is that failure to deliver a copy of whatever prospectus is required under the 1933 Act will also be a violation of this Act when the

state registration is by filing or coordination. See § 605(a).

42. See §§ 402(a)(3), (4), and (6) of the 1956 Act.

43. § 401(b)(10).

44. To be eligible for the exemption, the commercial paper must have a maturity of nine months or less, be issued in denominations of at least $50,000, and receive a rating from a nationally recognized rating organization in one of the three highest categories. § 401(b)(11).

investment companies.[45] The rationale underlying this exemption is similar to that supporting other new provisions in the 1985 Act, viz., that investment companies generally are subject to extensive substantive regulation under the Investment Company Act of 1940, and in addition any company sponsored by an entity that manages an excess of $100,000,000 of assets or that has acted as such a sponsor for at least three years has been subjected to and judged by the discipline of the marketplace.

With respect to exempt transactions, the NCCUSL Drafting Committee's effort was directed in large part to reflecting various developments in securities law generally since the 1956 Act was promulgated. One of the principal areas in which the transactional exemptions have been both broadened and heightened concerns secondary trading. If the capital markets are to function effectively, genuine secondary trading must be possible without further registration requirements. This is reflected in section 402 by the retention of the previous non-issuer transactional exemptions and the addition of a new non-issuer exemption for trading in the securities of companies subject to the reporting requirements of the Securities Exchange Act of 1934.[46] However, to ensure that such secondary transactions are not used as a "back door" for selling unregistered initial public offering securities, both the reporting company exemption in section 402(2) and the manual exemption in section 402(3) require that the applicable qualifications have been satisfied for not less than 90 days before the transaction in question can be effected.

Two provisions in the 1985 Act bear upon limited offerings. At the federal level, most unregistered offerings made today to a limited group of persons or in a limited amount are effected in reliance upon regulation D.[47] The SEC, the practicing bar, and the state securities administrators have expended considerable effort in developing a mutually acceptable provision for handling many regulation D offerings at the state level through the Uniform Limited Offering Exemption (ULOE).[48] The Drafting Committee strongly supports ULOE; the problem was how to accommodate a detailed exemption that includes a variety of footnotes, and that might be revised from time to time, in the 1985 Act. Following a practice used in other uniform acts, in section 403(b) the Committee authorized the state securities administrator to adopt, by rule, a limited offering transactional exemption comparable to ULOE. In addition, the existing limited offering exemption was modified to make it applicable, assuming three general conditions are satisfied,[49] to either typical private placement syndications or to true "limited offerings" (i.e., less than $500,000 during any twelve-month period).[50]

Finally, section 402(17) was added to exempt merger and related transactions. Since mergers, consolidations, and statutory sales of assets are no longer excluded from the definition of sale in section 101(13),[51] an exemp-

---

45. § 401(b)(14).

46. § 402(2) is new; §§ 402(1) and 402(3) through (6) continue the non-issuer transactional exemptions of the 1956 Act.

47. See 17 CFR 230.501 through 230.506.

48. 1 Blue Sky Rep. (CCH) ¶ 5,294.

49. In order to utilize § 402(11), there can exist no general solicitation or advertising and no payments of commissions to anyone other than a licensed or exempt broker-dealer, and there must be no more than 25 purchasers in the state.

50. § 402(11)(i) and (ii).

51. With the change in position announced under the 1933 Act with the promulgation of rule 145, the Drafting Committee concluded that there was no sense viewing mergers, and similar transactions inconsistently at the state level. Accord-

tion from registration has been added to cover those transactions. If the transaction is one in which the securities ultimately to be distributed are registered under the 1933 Act, the exemption is operative without further action. If, on the other hand, the securities to be distributed are not so registered, then a filing of the solicitation material must be made with the state securities administration at least ten days before the transaction is consummated, and the administrator may disallow the exemption within that period if he or she finds it in the public interest to do so.

FRAUD AND ENFORCEMENT PROVISIONS

A basic premise underlying the fraud prohibition provisions of Part V and the enforcement and civil liability provisions of Part VI of the 1985 Act is that the states will assume a greater enforcement role with respect to securities law violations. This premise is based upon at least two assumptions: first, that the states will have access to greater revenues and resources to fund such efforts,[52] and second, that there will be a continuing emphasis on deregulation at the federal level,[53] which will necessitate the states assuming a larger enforcement role. Working from that premise, the Drafting Committee focused on the adequacy of the existing antifraud provisions and of the sanctions and remedies available to state administrators, and the administrative procedures that should govern such activities.

With respect to the antifraud provisions of the 1956 Act, no significant evidence was presented that the coverage of those provisions generally was inadequate, and they have thus been retained substantially as in the previous Act. However, the Committee did determine to add a provision regarding manipulation, consistent with the federal law prohibitions.[54] While a manipulation claim probably could be asserted successfully under the general antifraud prohibition of section 501, the Committee concluded that it would be helpful for enforcement purposes to spell out separately in section 502 the principal elements of a manipulation claim. Subsection 502(b) ensures that the various interpretive rules promulgated at the federal level under the counterpart provisions are to be followed in determining whether particular conduct violates section 502. Section 605(c) further limits any recovery of private damages under section 502 to locally traded securities, i.e., securities other than those traded on a national exchange or in the over-the-counter market.

One of the major improvements in the 1985 Act has been to increase the range of sanctions available to a state administrator. Section 602 now catalogs the various sanctions available, which include granting an administrator the power to: issue a cease and desist order [55]; censure a licensed person [56]; bar or suspend a person from association with a licensed person in the state [57]; impose a civil penalty up to a maximum of $2,500 for a

---

ingly, the former exclusion from the definition of sale for such transactions was dropped.

52. With the advent and use of the Central Registration Depository (CRD) System of the NASD for licensing of professionals at the state level, the states have substantial additional sums available for greater enforcement activities.

53. At the Second Annual SEC–NASAA Conference in Williamsburg, Virginia, in February 1985, SEC Commissioner Mari-

naccio forecast continuing cuts in the SEC's enforcement budget and a resulting need for "state securities administrators [to shoulder] a bigger part of the enforcement load than they have heretofore." 17 Sec.Reg.L.Rep. (BNA) No. 9, at 364 (March 1, 1985).

54. § 502.

55. § 602(a) and (b)(1).

56. § 602(b)(2).

57. § 602(b)(3).

single violation (or \$25,000 for multiple violations)[58], or seek various forms of relief through court action.[59] Several standards have been set forth in section 602(c) and (d) to guide in the imposition of one or more of these sanctions.

In addition, the 1985 Act includes a number of provisions intended to facilitate cooperation among the states and between the states and other regulatory agencies with respect to enforcement and other matters. Section 704 includes a broad list of areas in which a state administrator is authorized to cooperate with other securities agencies or administrators. Section 601 expands the grounds on which subpoenas may be issued to include requests by other state administrators in connection with activities constituting a violation under the laws of the other state if those activities would constitute a violation under the forum state laws had they occurred in the latter state.[60] Finally, section 703 authorizes administrators to share with enforcement agencies in another state information obtained in an investigation if the other state proposes to utilize the information for its own investigation, and has comparable protection to ensure the confidentiality and security of the information.[61]

The criminal penalty provisions included in section 604 of the 1985 Act have been reworked, first, to make willfulness (in the sense of knowingly undertaking the conduct that violates the Act) an element of the criminal provisions, and second, to distinguish between misdemeanors and felonies.

The civil damages remedy under section 410 of the 1956 Act has been substantially retained as section 605(a) of the 1985 Act. As noted above, an express remedy is granted under section 605(c) for manipulations in violation of section 502 with respect to locally traded securities. Subsection (d) of section 605 allows a good faith defense, in the same manner as section 20 of the 1934 Act, to persons otherwise liable under section 605 as "controlling persons." The statute of limitation provisions have been revised to require that a claimant must bring suit within "the earliest of one year after the discovery of the violation, one year after discovery should have been made by the exercise of reasonable care, or 3 years after the act, omission or transaction constituting the violation." [62]

The final major new effort in the 1985 Act provisions concerning civil liability is the attempt in section 607 to establish a self-effectuating mechanism by which a seller who has committed a technical violation of some provision of the Act can avoid civil liability under section 605 by undertaking a rescission and settlement offer. Ordinarily that would require only a statement of the basis on which liability has arisen and an offer meeting the requirements of section 607(a)(1)(iii) and (iv). If, however, the violation consists of a failure to disclose information in violation of section 501(2), then the rescission offer can be effected only if all financial and other information "necessary to correct all material misstatements or omissions" is furnished to the purchaser.[63]

ADMINISTRATIVE AND MISCELLANEOUS PROVISIONS

Part VII of the 1985 Act includes the applicable administrative procedures act provisions. As drafted, Part VII can be used in its entirety if a state currently has in its statutes the Model State Administrative Procedure Act

---

58. § 602(b)(4).

59. §§ 602(b)(5) and 603.

60. § 601(d).

61. § 703(c).

62. § 606.

63. § 607(a)(1)(ii).

(1961)[64] or a reasonable counterpart thereof. If a state has adopted the Model State Administrative Procedure Act (1981),[65] several of the provisions in Part VII will be unnecessary.[66] The obvious purpose of this Part is to ensure that all actions are taken in compliance with recognized due process procedures. Except for certain actions necessarily of an emergency or summary nature, all rules adopted by and contested proceedings initiated by the state securities administrator are intended to be effective only after prior notice, opportunity for hearing, and written findings of fact.[67]

Part VIII is the repository for a variety of miscellaneous provisions. The most important of these is section 801, "Scope of Act," which closely follows its predecessor [68] in the 1956 Act, but adds comparable provisions to reflect more recent technological and market developments in radio, television, cable, and other forms of electronic communication.

CONCLUSION

Only time will show whether the 1985 Act proves as successful as its predecessor, the 1956 Act. The 1985 Act is not a radical departure from the former, but rather builds upon the foundation established by it. There should be little question that the strengthened enforcement and civil liability provisions will make the 1985 Act a more useful vehicle for protecting investors. The shift in regulatory focus suggested by the securities registration and exemption provisions is likely to be a more contested subject, on which there will be a lively difference of views. The several states will undertake an increasing share of the responsibility for protection of investors, and at the same time continue their important role as the testing ground for the efficiency and soundness of specific adaptations and modifications in securities laws. Those who have been involved in drafting the 1985 Act believe that its provisions are based upon sound and reasonable premises and that its implementation will facilitate the achievement of the objectives intended by state securities laws for the past 75 years.

Excerpt from:

REPORT ON STATE MERIT REGULATION OF SECURITIES OFFERINGS *

41 Business Lawyer 785–852 (1986).
By the Ad Hoc Subcommittee on Merit Regulation of the State Regulation of
Securities Committee, American Bar Association.**

The long-standing debate [1] over state blue sky merit regulation of securities offerings recently has assumed a new intensity and practical

---

64. See 14 U.L.A. (Master Edition).

65. See 14 U.L.A. (Master Edition) (1985 Cumul. Pocket Part).

66. In this instance, §§ 705(a) and (d), 706, 710, and 712 of the 1985 Act will be unnecessary, as the 1981 version of the Model State Administrative Procedure Act includes comparable provisions.

67. See § 711.

68. § 414(a)–(f) of the 1956 Act.

* Copyright 1986 by the American Bar Association. All rights reserved. Reprinted with the permission of the American

Bar Association and its Section of Corporation, Banking and Business Law.

** Mark A. Sargent, reporter, is Associate Professor of Law at the University of Baltimore Law School. Cyril Moscow is the subcommittee chairman.

1. Among the more recent articles arguing in support of merit regulation are Hueni, Application of Merit Requirements in State Securities Regulation, 15 Wayne L.Rev. 1417 (1969); Jennings, The Role of the States in Corporate Regulation and Investor Protection, 23 L. & Contemp.Probs. 193 (1958); Makens, Who

significance. The new intensity is reflected not only in increased commentary on the topic [2] but also in the sometimes exaggerated claims of both critics and supporters about merit regulation's value, or lack thereof. The new practical significance of today's debate is demonstrated by the changes that have actually taken place in the regulatory schemes of several states. The most important changes have occurred in Illinois and Louisiana: a 1983 amendment of the Illinois statute eliminated the State Securities Department's merit authority,[3] and a 1985 amendment of the Louisiana statute produced even more far-reaching results.[4] Similar developments have taken place in other states. Attempts to eliminate or at least constrain the merit aspects of the Texas statute failed narrowly in both 1983 and 1985.[5] Amendment in 1983 of the Wisconsin statute reduced the state administrators' merit authority,[6] while new administrative rules in Michigan and other states reflected an attempt to blunt the attack on merit regulation by experimenting with novel techniques of investor protection.[7]

In contrast, the New Jersey legislature recently considered a new securities law that would have granted the state administrator merit review authority.[8] These crosscurrents were strengthened by the "hot issues" market of 1983, which led the industry and some representatives of the bar to challenge merit restraints on initial public offerings (IPOs), and by perceived abuses in the "penny stock" market, which led state administrators and others to resist challenges to merit authority and to expand its

Speaks for the Investor? An Evaluation of the Assault on Merit Regulation, 13 U.Balt.L.Rev. 435 (1984); Tyler, More About Blue Sky, 39 Wash. & Lee L.Rev. 899 (1982). Among the more recent articles critical of merit regulation are Bateman, State Securities Registration: An Unresolved Dilemma and a Suggestion for the Federal Securities Code, 27 Sw.L.J. 759 (1973); Bloomenthal, Blue Sky Regulation and the Theory of Overkill, 15 Wayne L.Rev. 1447 (1969); Campbell, An Open Attack on the Nonsense of Blue Sky Regulation, 10 J.Corp.L. 553 (1985); Mofsky, State Securities Regulation and New Promotions: A Case History, 15 Wayne L.Rev. 1401 (1969); Mofsky & Tollison, Demerit in Merit Regulation, 60 Marq.L.Rev. 367 (1977). The debate over merit regulation did not begin, however, in the 1960s. The relative values of merit and disclosure regulation were debated in the hearings over the Securities Act of 1933. See Warren, Reflections on Dual Regulation of Securities: A Case Against Preemption, 25 B.C.L.Rev. 495, 518 n. 189 (1984). In addition, the early battles over the blue sky laws enacted prior to World War I focused on their merit aspects. See authorities cited infra note 33.

2. Numerous discussions of merit regulation have appeared recently * * *. See, e.g., Bromberg, Texas Securities Act, 46 Tex.B.J. 36 (1983); Dumont, The Case for States to Abolish 'Merit Review' of New Offerings, N.Y.L.J., Nov. 20, 1985, at 1, col. 3; Honig, Massachusetts Securities Regulation: An Evolving Matrix, 27 B.B.J. 10 (1983); Sosin & Fein, The Landmark 1983

Amendments to the Illinois Securities Law, 72 Ill.B.J. 196 (1983); States Stop Playing Detective for Investors, Bus. Week, July 16, 1984, at 131, * * *. The Securities Industry Association (SIA) has added fuel to the fire by urging consideration of federal preemption of state securities regulation. See 15 Sec.Reg. & L.Rep. (BNA) 1737, 1738 (1983).

3. For discussion of the Illinois developments, see Sosin & Fein, supra note 2; Fein & Sosin, Securities Law of 1953, Interpretive Comments (1983 Amendments), Ill.Ann.Stat. ch. 121½, § 137.1 (Smith-Hurd 1984–1985).

4. The Louisiana amendments not only eliminated all merit provisions from the statute but created an exemption for transactions pursuant to a registration statement effective under the Securities Act of 1933. See La.Rev.Stat.Ann. §§ 51:707, 51:709(5) (West 1965 & Supp.1985), 1A Blue Sky L.Rep. (CCH) ¶¶ 28,137, 28,139.

5. See 17 Sec.Reg. & L.Rep. (BNA) 969 (May 31, 1985).

6. For discussion of the Wisconsin developments, see Sargent, The Challenge to Merit Regulation—Part I, 12 Sec.Reg.L.J. 276, 284 (1984).

7. For discussion of developments in Michigan and other states, see Sargent, The Challenge to Merit Regulation—Part II, 12 Sec.Reg.L.J. 367, 371–77 (1985).

8. See 17 Sec.Reg. & L.Rep. (BNA) 1147 (1985). In addition, Maine has recently adopted legislation clarifying and expanding the basis for its merit authority.

scope. The recent adoption of the Revised Uniform Securities Act [9] (RUSA) by the National Conference of Commissioners on Uniform State Laws further confused the matter. RUSA does not attempt to eliminate the merit provisions of the Uniform Securities Act [10] (the Uniform Act), but it has attempted to modestly restrict the administrator's merit authority.[11] This has already produced significant controversy and will continue to do so as RUSA is considered in the individual states.[12]

While the interest in merit regulation thus is very high, the terms of debate have not been well defined. There is, for example, no universally agreed upon definition of merit regulation, nor is there any comprehensive understanding of its theoretical or functional relation to federal or state disclosure review. There is a general understanding that a merit regulator has the authority to deny registration to an offering on the ground that it is substantively unfair or presents excessive investment risk to the investor, but there has been little formal inquiry into merit's goals and assumptions. There is a tendency, furthermore, to generalize about the benefits or costs of merit regulation, with little sensitivity to the lack of a coordinated national approach to securities regulation, to the significant state-to-state variations in merit policy and practice, or to the different functions of merit regulation in transactions as disparate as initial public offerings of corporate stock, tax-advantaged limited partnership syndications, or investment company offerings. The debate also has been flawed by possibly excessive claims from both sides, such as claims that merit regulation has a crucial effect on plant location and job formation decisions,[13] or, conversely, that the existing empirical data "proves" the "value" of merit regulation.[14] The arguments used are mostly anecdotal: administrators cite egregious abuses, and practitioners cite inconsistent and unnecessary regulation of particular issues.

* * * *

9. The text of the Revised Uniform Securities Act [hereinafter cited as RUSA] can be found at 1 Blue Sky L.Rep. (CCH) ¶¶ 5601–5707 (1985).

10. The text of the Uniform Securities Act [hereinafter cited as Uniform Act] can be found at 1 Blue Sky L.Rep. (CCH) ¶¶ 5501–5573 (1957).

11. It does so primarily through a narrow exclusion from merit review for a very small class of "seasoned" issuers (see RUSA § 302, 1 Blue Sky L.Rep. (CCH) ¶ 5632 (1985)) and a new set of limitations on the administrator's ability to require escrow of cheap stock held by promoters (see RUSA § 305(g), 1 Blue Sky L.Rep. (CCH) ¶ 5635 (1985)). RUSA clearly is, however, a merit statute (see RUSA § 306(a)(2)[v]–(vi), 1 Blue Sky L.Rep. (CCH) ¶ 5636 (1985)).

12. For discussion of RUSA and its potential impact on merit regulation, see Hensley, The Development of a Revised Uniform Securities Act, 40 Bus.Law. 721, 732–36 (1985); Sargent, Some Thoughts on

the Revised Uniform Securities Act, 14 Sec.Reg.L.J. 62 (1986). See also infra notes 235–36.

13. See statement of Jack Bailey, executive director of the Iowa Development Commission: "We have lost jobs in Iowa and now we need risk capital to get the state going again. Merit review has flagged those efforts because some companies don't want to put up with it." 15 Sec.Reg. & L.Rep. (BNA) 1882 (Oct. 7, 1983). Bailey added that several Iowa-owned companies have located in other states because of the difficulty of getting approval for stock issues. Id. For a critique of this kind of argument, see Makens, supra note 1, at 449 n. 87.

14. One of the published empirical studies of merit regulation is sometimes described as providing such "proof." See Walker & Hadaway, Merit Standards Revisited: An Empirical Analysis of the Efficacy of Texas Merit Standards, 7 J.Corp.L. 651 (1982). * * *.

A BLUE SKY OVERVIEW—CURRENT STATUS AND HISTORICAL ORIGINS

Today, every American state, the District of Columbia, Guam, and Puerto Rico have some form of blue sky law.[15] Thirty-nine of those jurisdictions have adopted the Uniform Act, although many have done so with significant variations. The Uniform Act and the other blue sky laws represent broadly based schemes of securities regulation; they require the registration or exemption of securities offerings; they impose registration and supervision requirements on securities professionals; they create civil and criminal liabilities for fraud and other violations of the state securities law; and they establish agencies with the authority to administer and enforce these laws.[17] This is the basic framework of blue sky law, although there are some significant variations, such as in the District of Columbia, which regulates broker-dealers but not securities offerings, and in New York, in which the Attorney General has significant antifraud powers but very limited authority to review most securities offerings.

The state statutes, while quite comprehensive in their regulation of issuer offerings, broker-dealers, and securities fraud, do not attempt to cover the entire range of the securities markets. The blue sky laws have minimal impact on the vast majority of trading transactions or on the regulation of the exchanges. Similarly, they do not attempt to regulate the commodities markets, public utility holding companies, proxy solicitations, or (since the U.S. Supreme Court's decision in Edgar v. MITE Corp.[18]) the great majority of tender offers. State regulation is concentrated, therefore, on registering or exempting issuer offerings, on supervising broker-dealers, and sometimes other securities professionals, and on enforcing the antifraud provisions.

The basic similarity among the laws of the fifty-odd blue sky jurisdictions does not mean, however, that blue sky law is a monolith. There are, for example, many differences in the language of the statutes and regulations, in the interpretations of that language, in the substantive conditions for registration and exemption of securities and persons, and in the informal practices of the administrators.[19] More profound differences also distinguish the blue sky laws.

First, some states are more seriously engaged in securities regulation than others. State X may have a statute that gives its administrator the fullest possible range of administrative authority, but if the agency lacks funding, a large and well-trained staff, and support from local prosecutorial and law-enforcement agencies, it will not be able to administer its statute effectively.[20] Conversely, if state Y has all of that support, it will regulate far more actively, even if its statute does not grant the broadest range of

---

15. The securities acts and associated rules and regulations of every American jurisdiction are published by CCH in the Blue Sky Law Reporter. All references in this report to state statutes and rules and regulations will cite to this publication.

17. For more detailed analysis of the Uniform Act, see L. Loss, Commentary on the Uniform Securities Act (1976). For discussion of the funding and operations of the state securities agencies, see Empirical Research Project, Blue Sky Laws and State

Takeover Statutes: New Importance for an Old Battleground, 7 J.Corp.L. 689, 787–802 (1982) [hereinafter cited as ERP].

18. 457 U.S. 624 (1982). * * *

19. For discussion of the practical difficulties created by these many differences, see Gray, Blue Sky Practice—A Morass?, 15 Wayne L.Rev. 1519 (1969).

20. For data demonstrating the differences in funding and staffing, see ERP, supra note 17, at 787–94.

regulatory powers. States vary significantly in this regard. The blue sky world thus is divided between those states that have the practical ability to regulate and those that do not.

Second, the states are also divided between those that have merit review authority and those that do not. Some states lack merit authority and review securities filings only on a full-disclosure basis. These are the "disclosure," as distinguished from the "merit," jurisdictions.[21] Other jurisdictions either do not require securities registration at all [22] or exempt the vast majority of offerings.[23] These can be described as nonregulatory jurisdictions.

Third, the ranks of the merit states are divided. Although a majority of the states have merit language in their statutes,[24] at any given time only ten or so states can be regarded as tough merit states—jurisdictions that frequently and systematically raise objections of merit grounds to the offerings presented for their consideration.[25] Among the merit states, furthermore, distinctions must be drawn between leaders and followers, that is, states that draw independent conclusions about offerings and states that tend to follow the lead of others. These distinctions must be drawn in pencil, however, because changes in law, in personnel, and in funding often cause states that were inactive or followers to become leaders, and vice versa. These changes can often be quite sudden and dramatic. Illinois and Louisiana have recently shifted from strong merit to pure disclosure systems of review as a result of legislative changes. Conversely, Massachusetts suddenly became one of the most rigorous merit states after years of relative inactivity, largely as a result of a change in directors.[26]

State securities regulation as a whole, therefore, does not constitute a single, homogenous, uniform system: major states, such as California [27] and Texas,[28] are strong merit jurisdictions; Illinois now reviews on a disclosure basis only; and New York generally applies an antifraud statute while merit regulating a very narrow spectrum of real estate and theatrical

---

21. Two examples are Illinois and Maryland. For discussion of the Illinois approach, see Sosin & Fein, supra note 2, at 197; Sargent, supra note 7, at 367–71. For discussion of the Maryland approach, see Miller, A Prospectus on the Maryland Securities Act, 23 Md.L.Rev. 289 (1963).

22. See D.C.Code Ann. §§ 2-2601—2-2619 (1981 & Supp.1985), 1A Blue Sky L.Rep. (CCH) ¶¶ 16,101–16,119.

23. See Colo.Rev.Stat. § 11–51–113(2)(n) (1973 & Supp.1984), 1 Blue Sky L.Rep. (CCH) ¶ 13,113 (exempts any offer of securities pursuant to a registration statement filed under the Securities Act of 1933 and any sales of securities pursuant to a registration statement filed under that act); Nev.Rev.Stat. § 90.140 (1983), 2 Blue Sky L.Rep. ¶ 38,125 (requires registration only of "public intrastate" offerings).

24. For a relatively current list, see ERP, supra note 17, at 803–11. This list does not reflect the recent changes in Illinois and Louisiana. The extent of the merit authority conferred by a particular

state statute can, however, be debated. See Honig, Massachusetts Securities Regulation: In Search of the Fulcrum, 13 U.Balt.L.Rev. 469, 474–76 (1984); see also infra note 136.

25. That list as of this writing would include Arizona, California, Iowa, Massachusetts, Michigan, Missouri, Ohio, Oklahoma, Pennsylvania, Texas, and Wisconsin. For an empirical analysis of perceptions of the relative stringency of merit states, see Brandi, Securities Practitioners and Blue Sky Laws: A Survey of Comments and a Ranking of States by Stringency of Regulation, 10 J.Corp.L. 689 (1985).

26. See Honig supra note 24, at 470–71.

27. For discussion of California regulation, see 1 H. Marsh & R. Volk, Practice Under the California Securities Laws §§ 8.01–8.14 (1985).

28. For discussion of Texas regulation, see Walker & Hadaway, supra note 14.

syndications.[30] The practical and conceptual complexities of this nonsystematic regulation are compounded by the simultaneous applicability of state and federal regulation to many different kinds of transactions.

The Securities Act of 1933 (the 1933 Act) contains language expressly saving the blue sky laws from preemption.[31] As a result, issuers planning a securities offering must comply with both state and federal requirements to sell their securities. By statute and rule, some offerings are exempted from state registration requirements because they are adequately regulated federally, while other relatively small or local offerings are exempted from federal registration on the theory that the states should regulate such transactions.[32] These attempts to allocate regulatory responsibilities between the states and the SEC, however, are partial and nonsystematic. Thus, the state-federal system of securities regulation is not a precisely coordinated allocation of regulatory responsibilities but a relatively uncoordinated combination of state and federal agencies with overlapping, and sometimes conflicting, regulatory philosophies and priorities. The blue sky laws function in an uneasy alliance with a complex network of federal securities laws. Perhaps this partnership works, but the existing state-federal regulatory partnership does contain many practical and logical inconsistencies and may not necessarily be the best available system.

This curious combination of overlapping jurisdiction and conflicting regulatory philosophies reflects the historical origins of securities regulation in the United States. The blue sky laws are significantly older than the federal securities laws. They originated in Kansas in 1911 and, prior to World War I, spread rapidly throughout the Midwest, West, and South in response to a perceived increase in securities fraud.[33] These laws were highly paternalistic merit statutes that imposed stringent substantive requirements and allowed very few exemptions from registration. They also established administrative agencies with broad authority to implement and enforce these statutes. As a group, these statutes reflected a complex set of assumptions about the capital markets and government's responsibilities toward them. They reflected, primarily, a strong sense of the ordinary person's vulnerability to securities fraud. The image constantly invoked by the early administrators is that of the unfortunate widow or the naive farmer gulled by persons who "would sell building lots in the blue sky in fee simple." [34]

---

30. For discussion of New York regulation of real estate syndications, see T. DiMeo, Effect of Securities Regulation on Real Estate Transactions 207 (1983). New York's statutory requirements for theatrical syndications are set out at N.Y. Arts & Cultural Affairs Law §§ 23.01–23.23 (McKinney 1983).

31. Securities Act of 1933, § 18, 15 U.S.C. § 77r (1982) ("[n]othing in this subchapter shall affect the jurisdiction of the securities commission * * * of any State * * * over any security or person").

32. For discussion of these rough allocations of regulatory responsibility, see Sargent, State Limited and Private Offering Exemptions: The Maryland Experience in

a National Perspective, 13 U.Balt.L.Rev. 496, 498–505 (1984).

33. For discussion of the historical origins of blue sky law, see M. Parrish, Securities Regulation and the New Deal 5–31 (1970); C. Cowing, Populists, Plungers and Progressives 67–74 (1965); V. Carosso, Investment Banking in America, 156–90 (1970); 1 L. Loss, Securities Regulation 23–67 (2d ed. 1961); L. Loss & E. Cowett, Blue Sky Law 1–13 (1958) * * *.

34. Mulvey, *Blue Sky Law*, 36 Can.L.T. 37 (1916). Mulvey attributes the origin of this term to the state of Kansas, in which the first modern state securities act was adopted. 1911 Kan.Sess.Laws c. 133. * * *

The blue sky laws drew on the sense of victimization associated with populist unrest as they created a regulatory scheme designed to protect the innocent not only from the local confidence men but from the investment bankers, the broker-dealers, and the corporations operating out of eastern financial centers.[36] The blue sky law's preoccupation with fairness, which dates from its earliest days, stemmed from this vivid sense of the disparity in bargaining power between those who issued securities and controlled the securities markets, on the one hand, and public investors on the other.

The resulting tension between the goals of the blue sky laws and the operating assumptions of the eastern financial community soon erupted into full-scale conflict. The assault on the blue sky laws was led by the Investment Bankers Association (IBA), the predecessor to the Securities Industry Association (SIA). This assault took the form of five years of litigation over the constitutionality of the blue sky laws (particularly their merit aspects),[40] leading to the Supreme Court's vindication of their constitutionality in the Blue Sky Cases of 1917.[41] These decisions ultimately led to an accommodation: the blue sky statutes were amended to exempt offerings by exchange-listed issuers, thus insulating many major issuers from merit review, and most eastern states adopted blue sky statutes that merely prohibited fraud and did not require securities registration.

It was in this context that the federal securities legislation of the 1930s was enacted. The dire consequences of the stock market crash of 1929 made it clear that state administrators could not police the securities markets without federal assistance and meaningful self-regulation by the exchanges.[43] Federal securities regulation was needed to control the great number of interstate transactions over which the blue sky administrators had no effective jurisdiction. The blue sky laws also seemed patently unequal to the task of reforming the serious abuses of the trading markets and the stock exchanges. The response to these dilemmas, of course, was enacting the federal securities acts and establishing the SEC.

* * * *

Much about state securities regulation has changed since 1933, as the national economy, trading markets, and population have changed. A key difference is that blue sky administrators now operate in an environment

---

36. This sense of regional polarization was reflected in the persistent conflict between the New York—based Investment Bankers Association and the predominately midwestern blue sky regulators. See M. Parrish, supra note 33, at 21–23; V. Carosso, supra note 33, at 181–90.

40. See cases cited in L. Loss & E. Cowett, supra note 33, at 10 nn. 1–3.

41. Hall v. Geiger-Jones Co., 242 U.S. 539 (1917); Caldwell v. Sioux Fall Stock Yards Co., 242 U.S. 559 (1917); Merrick v. N.W. Halsey Co., 242 U.S. 568 (1917). Constitutional challenges to the blue sky laws still surface occasionally, despite these precedents. See, e.g., North Star Int'l v. Arizona Corp. Comm'n, 720 F.2d 578 (9th Cir.1983) (merit provisions of the Arizona blue sky law do not violate either the commerce or supremacy clauses of the Constitution); Colorado v. Riley, No. 83SA247

(Colo. Nov. 18, 1985) (antifraud provisions of the Colorado blue sky law are not unconstitutionally vague); Carney v. Hanson Oil Co., 690 S.W.2d 404 (Mo.1985) (exemptive provisions of the Missouri blue sky law do not violate either the commerce, supremacy, or equal protection clauses of the Constitution). * * *

43. The exchange-listed exemptions created a significant regulatory dilemma, because they placed exchange-listed issuers beyond the reach of the blue sky administrators, and they deferred to self-regulation at a time when there was little meaningful self-regulation by the exchanges. For discussion of the defects in self-regulation prior to 1934, see J. Seligman, The Transformation of Wall Street: A History of the Securities and Exchange Commission and Modern Corporate Finance 73–100 (1982).

in which their efforts are components of a much larger regulatory mosaic. For example, the National Association of Securities Dealers, Inc. (the NASD) now prohibits its members' participation in the public distribution of any securities in which the underwriting arrangements are unfair and unreasonable,[48] and the NASD[49] and the New York Stock Exchange[50] have adopted rules prohibiting their members from selling securities to customers who do not meet appropriate suitability standards. State administrators' attempts to protect investors through regulation of securities offerings, therefore, are now part of a broader regulatory effort.[51] As a result, greater coordination among the different agencies has become essential. Similarly, state administrators have attempted to deal with problems of interstate or regional fraud through cooperative efforts linking the resources of several blue sky offices and various state and federal law-enforcement agencies.

Another key difference is the proliferation of novel investment opportunities, indeed the development of whole new investment industries, such as the tax-shelter syndication industry. Because of these market developments, state administrators have brought merit regulation to new levels of sophistication and complexity. Their success has placed them in a leading role in the structuring of new investment vehicles.[53] The growth of a unified national securities market, furthermore, has created an even greater need for uniformity. The states have made progress in this direction, building on the widespread adoption of the Uniform Act and making good use of the resources of the North American Securities Administrators Association (NASAA).[54]

Despite these differences, however, much about state securities regulation has remained unchanged. The blue sky administrators continue in the task of protecting the hypothetical ordinary investor, and merit regulation has remained a state preserve. The overlap of the state and federal securities laws has also continued, leading to increasing controversy not only over merit regulation, but also over state accommodation (or lack thereof) to revision of the SEC's exemptive scheme,[55] state regulation of

---

48. NASD Rules of Fair Practice, art. III, § 1, NASD Manual (CCH) ¶ 2151. For a discussion of the NASD and its role in securities regulation, see White, National Association of Securities Dealers, Inc., 28 Geo.Wash.L.Rev. 1250 (1959).

49. NASD Rules of Fair Practice, art. III, § 2, NASD Manual (CCH) ¶ 2152.

50. N.Y.S.E. rule 405, N.Y.S.E. Guide (CCH) ¶ 2405 (the "know your customer rule").

51. Impending changes in information technology may also require a reassessment of the blue sky laws' role in the overall regulatory system. In particular, as information technology improves both the efficacy and equity of the securities marketplace, the need for merit regulation (as well as SEC-mandated disclosure) may diminish, or at least change. For an excellent discussion of developments in information technology and their potential impact on federal securities regulation, see Langevoort, Information Technology and

the Structure of Securities Regulation, 98 Harv.L.Rev. 747 (1985).

53. See Makens, supra note 1, at 445–47.

54. Among NASAA's contributions to the growth of uniformity are the official statements of policy, or guidelines, which can be used by the individual state members in their efforts to regulate the areas covered by the guidelines. The current NASAA guidelines are at 1 Blue Sky L.Rep. (CCH) ¶¶ 5151–5384. [The NASAA guidelines no longer appear in the CCH Blue Sky L.Rep.; they can now be found in a new service, NASAA Reports (CCH), exclusively devoted to the activities, policies and positions of the North American Securities Administrators Association.] For detailed discussion of some of these guidelines, see infra text accompanying notes 154–204. NASAA has also contributed to uniformity by developing uniform forms.

55. For a survey of the pattern of accommodation, see Hainsfurther, Summary

investment companies,[56] and a host of other issues. Such controversies will continue, since they are an inevitable by-product of the structural tension within our state-federal system.

What Is Merit Regulation?

There is no accepted definition of merit regulation. It has been variously defined as "a composite of substantive standards";[57] as a "discretionary power" allowing the administrator "to pass on the investment merits of an issue of securities proposed to be offered to the public";[58] as a device "which attempts to lessen the investment risks for investors in newly promoted firms";[59] and as a "quality-of-issue assessment . . . based on a comparison of regulatory standards to the corresponding values of the issue."[60] Some discussions of merit regulation do not even use the term. For example, a leading article on California securities law avoids the term while describing the law "as an integral part of a broad scheme for correcting some of the inequities and defects which may otherwise arise in the practices of corporation finance."[61] In view of the complexity involved, the difficulty in fixing a definition is understandable and will require analysis on several levels.

*   *   *   *

MERIT REGULATION AND THE ADMINISTRATIVE PROCESS

Registration versus Exemption

The Uniform Act requires all offers and sales of securities within the state to be either registered or exempted from registration.[62] This aspect of the Uniform Act parallels section 5[63] of the 1933 Act, much as the Uniform Act's provisions for exempt securities and exempt transactions parallel parts of sections 3[64] and 4[65] of that federal statute. The Uniform Act also parallels the 1933 Act in its broad definition of "security,"[66] with the result that offerings of interests as disparate as limited partnership units, industrial revenue bonds, franchises, and a broad variety of "investment contracts" may be subject to state registration requirements. The structural similarities between the 1933 Act and the state securities acts, however, do not simplify the task of determining when merit regulation will apply.

Large numbers of offerings that must be registered with the SEC, for example, are exempted from state registration. Offerings by issuers with securities listed on one of the national exchanges have long been treated as

of Blue Sky Exemptions Corresponding to Regulation D, 38 Sw.L.J. 989 (1984). For discussion of the sources of and background to the current problem, see Sargent, supra note 32, at 498–511.

56. See Sargent, State Reglation of Investment Companies—Sources of the Current Controversy, 13 Sec.Reg.L.J. 167 (1985).

57. Makens, supra note 1, at 439.

58. Bateman, supra note 1, at 759 n. 4.

59. Mofsky & Tollison, supra note 1, at 368.

60. Brandi, supra note 25, at 692.

61. Jennings, supra note 1, at 213.

62. Uniform Act § 301, 1 Blue Sky L.Rep. (CCH) ¶ 5531 (1957).

63. 15 U.S.C. § 77e (1982).

64. 15 U.S.C. § 77c (1982).

65. 15 U.S.C. § 77d (1982).

66. Uniform Act § 401(l), 1 Blue Sky L.Rep. (CCH) ¶ 5541 (1957). Some state acts have adopted even broader definitions of security. For discussion of the state variations, see J. Long, 1985 Blue Sky Law Handbook §§ 2.01–2.06 (1984).

offerings of exempt securities,[67] as have secondary distributions of the securities of issuers listed in certain securities manuals.[68] Similar securities exemptions have been provided in recent years in some states for offerings by over-the-counter (OTC) issuers that meet certain blue-chip quality criteria,[69] that are included on the Federal Reserve Margin list,[70] or that are traded on some part of the NASDAQ system.[71] Offerings of these exempt securities thus will receive no merit review, whether they are registered with the SEC or not. The exemptions for exchange-listed issuers and certain OTC-traded issuers thus have the effect of exempting thousands of issuers from the most rigorous aspects of state securities registration.

* * * *

Not all federally exempt offerings, however, are exempted at the state level. There are no exact equivalents in the Uniform Act or in many of its variants to the 1933 Act's section 3(b)[78] limited-offering exemption or section 4(2)[79] private-offering exemption. Intrastate offerings federally exempt under section 3(a)(11)[80] have no matching state exemption. This lack of equivalence did not pose much of a problem until the development of the tax-shelter syndication industry. The revision of the federal exemptive scheme in the 1970s and 1980s led to an increase in the number, size, and complexity of transactions exempt from federal registration. In the absence of coordinated state exemptions, a substantial number of offerings exempt from federal registration remained subject to state registration and hence merit review. The practical difficulties of combining a federal exemption with state registration has led to new pressure for state exemptions coordinating with federal exemptions, such as regulation D.[82] The result has been that numerous states have recently adopted coordinating exemptions;[83] these exemptions have made it possible to reduce the number of state registrations of regulation D offerings. Some regulation D and other federally exempt offerings, however, still have to be state registered and may be subject to merit review.

In sum, offerings by exchange-listed and certain OTC issuers may avoid state registration altogether by virtue of the simple, self-executing securities exemptions. Most IPOs registered with the SEC, however, must be registered in most states and hence will be subject to merit review. An offering exempt from federal 1933 Act registration under section 3(a)(11), statutory section 4(2), regulation A, or regulation D will face an array of options, ranging from registration in every state in which it is offered, to exemption in every such state, to registration in some and exemption in others. Thus the applicability of merit regulation to a federally exempted

---

67. Uniform Act § 402(a)(8), 1 Blue Sky L.Rep. (CCH) ¶ 5542 (1957). See also RUSA § 401(8), 1 Blue Sky L.Rep. (CCH) ¶ 5641 (1985), which provides a parallel exemption for securities listed on the NASDAQ/National Market System.

68. Uniform Act § 402(b)(2)(A), 1 Blue Sky L.Rep. (CCH) ¶ 5542 (1957).

69. See, e.g., the Michigan blue-chip exemption, Mich.Comp.Laws R. 451.818.1 (1979), 1A Blue Sky L.Rep. (CCH) ¶ 32,489.

70. See, e.g., the Pennsylvania Federal Reserve Margin List exemption, Pennsylvania Securities Act of 1972,

Pa.Stat.Ann. tit. 70, § 1–202(f) (Purdon 1965 & Supp.1985), 2 Blue Sky L.Rep. (CCH) ¶ 48,112.

71. See, e.g., the Maryland NASDAQ/National Market System exemption, Md.Admin.Code tit. 02, § 02.04.12 (1957), 1A Blue Sky L.Rep. (CCH) ¶ 30,438.

78. 15 U.S.C. § 77c(b) (1982).

79. 15 U.S.C. § 77d(2) (1982).

80. 15 U.S.C. § 77c(a)(11) (1982).

82. 17 C.F.R. §§ 230.501–06 (1985).

83. See generally Hainsfurther, supra note 55.

offering generally will depend on whether it has to be registered in a merit state.

Kinds of Registration

Registering an offering in a particular state requires consideration of the various registration alternatives. This decision will have certain procedural and timing consequences, but it may also affect the level of merit review applied to the offering.

* * * *

Issuers that have registered an offering with the SEC are most likely, in Uniform Act jurisdictions, to register by coordination.[87] A registration by coordination automatically becomes effective at the moment the federal registration statement becomes effective, provided that no stop order is in effect, that the registration statement has been on file with the administrator for a specified period (usually at least ten days), and that the pricing amendment has been on file for at least two days, or such shorter period as the administrator may permit. Automatic effectiveness, however, does not mean that the offering registered by coordination will avoid merit review. During the waiting period, the administrator can and often does review the offering in light of the applicable merit criteria; indeed, one of the attorney's major tasks in a national public offering is to resolve the problems that arise during that review period. If problems in a particular state cannot be resolved, the application will ordinarily be withdrawn (state stop orders are very rare). Occasionally, the application for registration by coordination will be converted to or withdrawn and resubmitted as an application for registration by qualification. This will give the administrator and the attorney more time to work out the compliance problem, since the timing of state effectiveness under a qualification registration is not tied to SEC effectiveness.

* * * *

If an issuer is unable to use registration by notification (because it does not meet the no-default and earnings criteria) or registration by coordination (because the offering is not registered with the SEC), it will have to rely, in Uniform Act jurisdictions, on registration by qualification.[93] A key difference here is in the timing of effectiveness: there is no automatic effectiveness, and the registration statement becomes effective only when the administrator so orders. * * *

* * * *

Some non-Uniform Act jurisdictions present variations on the basic scheme of notification, coordination, and qualification. California, for example, refers to all forms of registration as "qualification" but then offers three forms of qualification roughly equivalent to the Uniform Act registration techniques: qualification by notification,[98] coordination,[99] and permit.[100] "Qualification by notification" under section 25112 of the California statute is not an exact equivalent of Uniform Act "registration by notification" but rather is a narrow device useful only to 1934 Act report-

---

87. Uniform Act § 303, 1 Blue Sky L.Rep. (CCH) ¶ 5533 (1957).

93. Uniform Act § 304, 1 Blue Sky L.Rep. (CCH) ¶ 5534. * * *

98. Cal.Corp.Code § 25112 (West 1977), 1 Blue Sky L.Rep. (CCH) ¶ 11,143.

99. Cal.Corp.Code § 25111 (West 1977 & Supp.1985), 1 Blue Sky L.Rep. (CCH) ¶ 11,142.

100. Cal.Corp.Code § 25113 (West 1977), 1 Blue Sky L.Rep. (CCH) ¶ 11,144.

ing companies and investment companies registered under the Investment Company Act of 1940 (the 1940 Act) that are registering securities in California but proceeding on an exempt basis federally. Offerings qualified by notification in California will be merit reviewed.

Ohio offers "registration by description" [102] as an alternative to registration by coordination or qualification. It is available to issuers of equity securities that meet certain earnings tests, issuers of certain secured debt interests, issuers of offerings that do not include cheap stock, certain limited offerings, and certain offerings exclusively to existing securityholders. Registration by description requires a less copious registration statement than registration by coordination or qualification and will ordinarily receive a less rigorous merit review.

The New York blue sky law, the Martin Act, is primarily an antifraud statute, and requires only a simple notice filing for most interstate offerings.[103] Real estate offerings, however, are subject to a precommencement filing requirement and may receive a detailed disclosure review.[104] Certain real estate offerings, such as nonspecified property, or blind-pool programs, may also receive a strict merit review.[105]

In short, the form of registration available to a particular offering will partially determine the level of merit review applicable to it. The crucial variable is time. * * *

The Review Process and Merit Safe Harbors

Once a registration statement has been filed, the review process begins. The first level of review may be carried out by a secretary, a clerk, or another nonprofessional—a technical review of the application to determine whether the correct form has been used, the appropriate information provided, and the necessary fees paid. This kind of review is carried out in every state. Many applications contain technical errors serious enough to require withdrawal and resubmission.

If a jurisdiction lacks any merit authority whatsoever, the next and final stage of review is a disclosure review. An example of a pure disclosure statute is the Maryland Securities Act, whose drafters purposely excluded from the Maryland version of the Uniform Act all language creating any kind of merit authority. A recent example of such a statute is the Illinois Securities Law, as amended in 1983. All merit authority has been excised from the Illinois statute, leaving the administrator only the ability to review the adequacy of disclosure and to prohibit or suspend the sale of securities for fraud.

It should be emphasized that jurisdictions with merit authority also have the authority to review the adequacy of disclosure. In fact, many "merit" reviews contain more disclosure comments than substantive comments. A disclosure review by a merit administrator, however, may differ

---

102. Ohio Rev.Code Ann. § 1707.08 (Page 1985), 2 Blue Sky L.Rep. (CCH) ¶ 45,109.

103. See N.Y.Gen.Bus.Law § 359–e(3), (8) (McKinney 1984), 2 Blue Sky L.Rep. (CCH) ¶ 42,111 (requires filing of "State Notice" and "Further State Notice").

104. See N.Y.Gen.Bus.Law § 352–e (McKinney 1984), 2 Blue Sky L.Rep. (CCH)

¶ 42,106 (requires precommencement filing of offering statement or prospectus).

105. See N.Y.Admin.Code tit. 13, § 16.11 (1983), 2 Blue Sky L.Rep. (CCH) ¶ 42,521J (guidelines for nonspecified property real estate syndication offerings).

significantly from an SEC review in that it might focus primarily on disclosure of the facts that generate merit problems. This can create practical difficulties for the attorney responsible for blue sky compliance, since the prospectus is often drafted in accordance with SEC disclosure requirements and not the special concerns of the merit states.[108] The key point, however, is that merit review and disclosure review are interrelated, since the examiner may require extensive disclosure of merit issues, such as conflicts of interest and promoter compensation.

If a jurisdiction has merit authority, the technical review will be followed by a merit review—a review of the substantive terms of the offering and underlying transactions. The statutory basis of a state's merit authority, the kind of transactions it will review, the intensity with which it will review, and its goals all vary. It remains true, however, that full-scale merit review in a jurisdiction with rigorous merit standards may require prolonged and detailed negotiations between the examiner and the issuer's or underwriter's attorney.[109]

* * * *

Withdrawal from certain key states may prove fatal to the offering for two reasons. First, the underwriter may need access to the markets of major population and financial centers, such as California, Texas, Massachusetts, Michigan, Ohio, and Pennsylvania. Second, withdrawing from one or more of those jurisdictions may induce administrators in less well staffed offices in smaller states to object or to request withdrawal of the offering. The level of review in such a follower state may not extend beyond inquiry as to whether the offering has cleared in state X.

The level of merit review may also depend on whether the offering can qualify for one of the merit safe harbors that have proliferated in recent years. A safe harbor from merit regulation is not an exemption from registration. These provisions merely provide that offerings that meet the conditions of the safe harbor will be deemed fair, just, and equitable or will be excused from compliance with one or more of the major merit standards, such as the limitations on cheap stock or the offering price.

Major examples of safe harbor provisions are those available to certain firmly underwritten offerings in California, Washington, West Virginia, and Michigan. The California statutory safe harbor is the oldest and most limited.[112] Adopted in 1968, it provides only that the price at which a security is to be offered shall not be considered unfair whenever the security is being publicly offered for cash pursuant to a 1933 Act registration and the offering is firmly underwritten by an underwriter or syndicate of underwriters all of whom are registered under the 1934 Act. This limited safe harbor provides relief only from merit review of the offering price. It was apparently enacted to prevent administrative reduction of the offering price when the after-market would support a price based on a very high price-earnings multiple.[113]

---

108. This is not to suggest, however, that planning for compliance with blue sky disclosure requirements should be ignored or downplayed. Many problems can be averted if responsibility for blue sky compliance is taken seriously early in the preparation of the registration statement.

109. For discussion of this negotiation process, see Bartell, Merit Regulation and Clearing Strategy, in Blue Sky Laws: A Satellite Program 393 (1985).

112. Cal.Corp.Code § 25140(d) (West 1977), 1 Blue Sky L.Rep. (CCH) ¶ 11,171.

113. For a discussion of § 25140(d), see H. Marsh & R. Volk, supra note 27, at § 8.07[2][a].

The Washington safe harbor, adopted by rule in 1982, is equally narrow but different in focus, since it merely removes the restrictions on amounts of "cheap and promotional shares."[114] It is available to offerings firmly underwritten by fifteen investment banking firms, each of which purchases at least $100,000 of securities, if the amount firmly underwritten is not less than $4 million and the offering price is not less than $5 per share. West Virginia adopted a virtually identical rule in 1983.[115]

Michigan took a similar but more complex approach late in 1983. Under Michigan rule 706.26(2)(a),[116] a corporate equity offering shall not be deemed "on unfair terms" or in violation of the specific Michigan merit criteria (in the absence of unspecified "unusual circumstances") if the offering is firmly underwritten by a qualified underwriter, dilution and promoter's compensation are fully disclosed, and the offering is made in compliance with the NASD Rules of Fair Practice.[117] A "qualified underwriter" means a managing underwriter registered with the New York Stock Exchange or otherwise determined by the administrator to be qualified in light of such factors as the size of the offering and the underwriter's track record, size, and independence.

The Washington, West Virginia, and Michigan provisions are attempts to test the proposition that underwriters, under some circumstances, can be relied upon to ensure that the issuer is relatively stable, to negotiate offering terms reasonably fair to the public investor, to restrain self-dealing by the promoters, and to set a reasonable offering price. Having recognized that this proposition is by no means self-evident, the administrators in these states imposed certain basic conditions. All three of these safe harbors are available only to firmly underwritten offerings, since firmly committed underwriters will presumably take a more cautious approach to the negotiations than a best-efforts or standby underwriter. Similarly, the Washington and West Virginia safe harbors are available only to underwriters that have purchased at least $100,000 of the securities and therefore have an incentive to police the offering. The Michigan "qualified underwriter" concept serves the same purpose. Presumably that kind of reputable, independent underwriter will tend to be involved in offerings appropriate for most public investors. In addition, all three safe harbors require the offering to be of a certain size (Washington and West Virginia, $4 million; Michigan, $1 million), and Washington and West Virginia require a $5 minimum offering price. These provisions are apparently designed to make the safe harbors unavailable to penny stock offerings, some of which are firmly underwritten.

* * * *

SOURCES AND EXTENT OF MERIT AUTHORITY

One of the difficulties in dealing with merit regulation, from the standpoints both of compliance and of evaluating its goals and effects, is understanding the sources and extent of its authority. The authority

---

114. Wash.Admin.Code R. 460–16A–108 (1983), 3 Blue Sky L.Rep. (CCH) ¶ 61,562A.

115. W.Va.Admin.Reg. § 14.15 (1984), 3 Blue Sky L.Rep. (CCH) ¶ 63,485.

116. Mich.Admin.Code R. 451.706.26(2) (a) (1979), 1A Blue Sky L.Rep. (CCH) ¶ 32,467.

117. NASD Rules of Fair Practice, NASD Manual (CCH) ¶¶ 2001–2303. As of this writing, the Rules of Fair Practice are in the process of revision.

conferred by the blue sky statutes and regulations can be either highly general or extremely specific. Furthermore, merit standards can be expressed in written statutes or rules, or they can be unwritten, informal, desk-drawer standards. They can be stated in the form of detailed NASAA statements of policy, which may or may not be applied by individual states, and which when applied may function merely as a set of guidelines or as a compendium of inflexible limits and requirements. Because of this uncertainty, some detailed consideration of the sources and extent of merit authority is essential to an understanding of merit regulation.

General Statutory Standards

Many of the statutes that confer merit authority provide very broad grounds for the administrator's decision to deny, revoke, or suspend the effectiveness of a registration statement. A typical provision would authorize the administrator to take such action if he or she finds that the offering is not "fair, just and equitable." There are numerous minor variations in the statutory statements of such general standards. * * *
* * * *

None of these distinctions seems to make any difference in the actual exercise of the state administrator's authority. * * * [The various formulations appear] to have been absorbed into the mainstream concept of "fair, just and equitable."

Much as these differences in statutory language tell us nothing about differences among the states, these general standards tell us very little about a particular state's regulatory philosophy. Only analysis of a state's implementing regulations and, perhaps more important, the way it applies those regulations, will show what that state's merit authority means.
* * *

Specific Statutory Standards

The Uniform Act [of 1956] itself contains no general fair, just, and equitable standard. Several Uniform Act jurisdictions have refused to follow the Uniform Act in this regard and have inserted some kind of fair, just, and equitable language into their versions of the statute,[128] but those statutes more closely adhering to the Uniform Act contain only a statement of several specific merit criteria.[129] Under section 306(a)(2)(F) of the Uniform Act, the administrator may issue a stop order denying, suspending, or revoking the effectiveness of any registration statement, if he or she finds that "the offering has been or would be made with unreasonable amounts of underwriters' and sellers' discounts, commissions, or other compensation, or promoters' profits or participation, or unreasonable amounts or kinds of options."[130]

In his *Draftsman's Commentary* on section 306(a), Loss explained why no fair, just, and equitable language had been included among the grounds for denial, suspension, or revocation of effectiveness:

128. See, e.g., Mich.Comp.Laws § 451.706(2)(E) (1967), 1A Blue Sky L.Rep. (CCH) ¶ 32,126; Neb.Rev.Stat. § 8–1109.01(2) (1983), 2 Blue Sky L.Rep. (CCH) ¶ 37,111; Wis.Stat. § 551.28(1)(e) (1985), 3 Blue Sky L.Rep. (CCH) ¶ 64,118.

129. See, e.g., Mass.Gen.Laws Ann. ch. 110A, § 305 (West 1980 & Supp.1985), 1A

Blue Sky L.Rep. (CCH) ¶ 31,125; Okla.Stat. tit. 71, § 306 (1965 & Supp. 1985), 2 Blue Sky L.Rep. (CCH) ¶ 46,146; 70 Pa.Cons. Stat.Ann. § 1–208 (Purdon 1965 & Supp. 1985), 2 Blue Sky L.Rep. (CCH) ¶ 48,118.

130. Uniform Act § 306(a)(2)(F), 1 Blue Sky L.Rep. (CCH) ¶ 5536 (1957).

The *standards* in § 306(a) are a cross-section of the existing standards somewhere between the two extremes: the simple "fraud" test exemplified by the Georgia statute and the "fair, just, and equitable" or "sound business principles" language of states like California and formerly Kansas. This is not a mere practical compromise. Administrative flexibility is important in this area, but it must always be balanced against the proper claim of legitimate business to as great a degree of specificity as the public interest will permit.[131] * * *

The Uniform Act, therefore, attempted to achieve a modest reform of the merit regulatory system. The draftsman was apparently uncomfortable with the open-ended character of the general merit standards included in many of the state statutes. He did not propose abandoning the merit philosophy then characteristic of most blue sky laws, however. Apparently, no such fundamental rethinking of the economic goals of state securities regulation was possible if the conference's goal of uniformity was to be achieved. Instead, a lawyerly solution was reached: express adoption of a full-disclosure standard combined with specific articulation of what were deemed the most important merit criteria. This solution was acceptable to some of the states that adopted the Uniform Act and thus can be found in some of the blue sky laws today.[136] Other jurisdictions refused to relinquish their fair, just, and equitable standards and incorporated some kind of fair, just, and equitable language into their versions of the Uniform Act in tandem with the specific standards of section 306(a)(2)(F). RUSA has acknowledged this split among Uniform Act jurisdictions by including, as bracketed, optional language, a provision authorizing the administrator to determine whether the offering is "unfair, unjust or inequitable." [137]

* * * *

[The discussion of the application of merit standards to the issuance of options and warrants, cheap stock, real estate and oil and gas programs, etc. under the various NASAA statements of policy is omitted.]

A WORKING DEFINITION OF MERIT REGULATION

Merit regulation is a complex phenomenon that eludes simple definition. It must be defined, in fact, through analysis of the key merit

---

131. L. Loss, supra note 17, at 83.

136. The Uniform Act's solution of the merit question has created some new questions, so further analysis may be helpful. Since the early 1970s, merit regulation has become increasingly complex and sophisticated. The Central Securities Administrators Council, the Midwestern Securities Administrators Council and NASAA contributed to this process by developing merit guidelines in their statements of policy. Many statements, and some individual states' rules and regulations, however, raise merit concerns that cannot fairly be said to fall within § 306(a)(2)(F).

Examples are restrictions on offering price found in many states. These restrictions may indirectly relate to the § 306(a)(2)(F) reference to "unreasonable amounts of underwriters' and sellers' discounts," but there seems to be little express authority under the Uniform Act for

consideration of this issue. Similarly questionable are some states' use of existing capitalization requirements to indirectly limit the offering price.

* * * *

Some conclusions about the scope and extent of merit authority under the Uniform Act are clear. The statute contemplates a merit authority both specifically stated and limited in extent. The message to the administrator is restraint. The statute contemplates the use of objective merit criteria, rather than reliance on the administrator's sense of what is fair and fitting. A statute that tracks the Uniform Act and contains no fair, just, and equitable language cannot be used to support a regulatory system in which finite, objective merit standards do not predominate.

137. RUSA § 306(a)(2)[(v)], 1 Blue Sky L.Rep. (CCH) ¶ 5636 (1985).

techniques, goals, and assumptions. By analyzing merit regulation in this way, the arguments in its favor can be understood.

Merit Regulatory Techniques

The distinctive aspect of merit regulatory techniques is the administrator's authority to deny registration to any offering that does not meet the applicable substantive standards. Full and timely disclosure to the investor of the offering's failure to meet those standards may not be enough; the administrator has the authority to require the offering or the underlying transaction to be restructured, at the risk of denial of registration. Key examples of this authority are the administrator's right to require escrow of promoter's cheap stock and to require the offering price to be changed as a condition of registration. In short, merit regulation accomplishes its goals through its power to require rewriting of the terms of the relationship among the parties. This power is different in both kind and degree from the SEC's. It contemplates the state acting on behalf of investors as a negotiator of terms.

While this distinction must be recognized, both as a matter of theory and of practice, it should be qualified. Merit problems often are resolved through appropriate disclosure of the facts generating the problems. For example, a merit state may require a highlighted discussion of how cheap stock was acquired and by whom, what those persons can do with it, and what the possible negative effects on the public investor might be. Similarly, detailed discussion of compensation or loans paid to officers may be required, as may be a discussion of voting rights arrangements in a limited partnership. When that happens, merit regulation functions by forcing disclosure of facts the states may regard as more important than the SEC staff does.

Similarly, the SEC staff is perfectly capable of using its disclosure authority to take an egregious offering and "disclose it to death" because the Staff believes that it is just too bad to register. Furthermore, the quasi-merit aspects of SEC disclosure review are more than a question of Staff overreaching. One effect of the necessity to comply with SEC disclosure requirements is that some transactions that could not withstand public scrutiny simply do not happen. The fish-bowl aspect of SEC-mandated disclosure has some marginal influence on what managers and issuers do, and not just on what they say.[214]

In terms of regulatory technique, therefore, state merit regulation and SEC disclosure regulation are not opposites. They represent relative positions on a continuum. It should be reemphasized, however, that the SEC cannot routinely and directly force the kind of substantive restructuring that the states can. But to what ends do the merit states use this powerful regulatory technique? The answer to this question requires a closer look at the link between merit goals and assumptions.

Merit Goals and Assumptions

Fairness

The first goal of merit regulation is to ensure fair treatment of the public investor by the promoters of the corporation. It is really an attempt

---

214. See Ratner, The SEC: Portrait of the Agency as a Thirty-Seven Year Old, 45 St. John's L.Rev. 583, 586–88 (1971).

to systematically define the proper relations of insiders and public investors. This concern with fairness has several aspects.

First is a concern that the offering price be fair. This concern is reflected most obviously in the limits on the price-earnings multiple and on the degree of dilution to the public investor. It is also reflected, however, in the merit concern with cheap stock.

Part of this concern are certain assumptions about the prices of issues subject to merit regulation. For example, a proponent of merit regulation would assume that the public investor is not present at the issuer-underwriter bargaining table and that the interests of the underwriter and the public investor are not coterminous. The underwriter has an incentive to charge as high a price as possible to maximize the value of its discount or commission and hence may not bargain very hard for a price fair to the public investor. Furthermore, the underwriter may not be able to bargain hard, even if it wants to, because in some markets the competition for underwritings leaves underwriters with little leverage. Of course, it must be conceded that underwriters usually cannot set grossly excessive prices. Such prices would cause the issue to go unsold or would create problems with customers who purchased at the high public-offering price and were still holding the securities after the price collapsed in the after-market. One would assume, however, that the partial inconsistency between the underwriter's and the public investor's interests could lead to marginally higher and possibly unfair prices.

Another assumption is that public investors are induced to purchase at unfair prices by market forces beyond their control, such as hot-issue expectations, pressure sales by brokers, and year-end tax-shelter fever. The corollary of this assumption is that SEC-mandated disclosure is unread and useless in such a market environment; only the merit regulator can offset the public investor's inherent disadvantages. Fairness to the investor, therefore, demands that the regulator adjust the offering price so that the security is more likely to be worth what the investor pays for it. This approach assumes that there is an objective, ascertainable investment value for securities that differs from the price investors will pay.

Second is a concern that the promoters and the public be equally subject to the risks of the enterprise. This is really another way of saying that merit regulation attempts to protect the investor from the promoters' attempts to guarantee themselves a significant return while leaving the investor to take his or her chances. There are several different kinds of such promoter overreaching. The most egregious is the promoter who obtains substantial amounts of cheap stock at a minimal price and then bails out at a substantial profit by (i) engaging in a secondary distribution of all or most of his or her stock simultaneously with the IPO; (ii) using the proceeds of the IPO to redeem his or her stock or repay loans; (iii) dumping his or her stock into the secondary market created by the IPO after hot-issue pressure has driven up the price of the stock; or (iv) taking advantage of the dilution of the public investor's equity through liquidation of the issuer. Furthermore, the promoter can augment his or her profits in all of these cases through the use of options. In any event, the public investor is left with the long-term risks of the enterprise, while the promoter has made a substantial front-end profit and may have severed all ties with the issuer.

For limited partnership syndications, there is deep concern with the promoters' ability to use the offering proceeds and cash flow generated by the real estate, oil and gas, or equipment-leasing projects to pay themselves substantial front-end fees and other compensation, thereby hedging (or even eliminating) their own risk, while the public investors bear the risk of the venture with no such hedge. Furthermore, merit regulation attempts to ensure that the offering proceeds be applied to funding the enterprise in amounts sufficient to allow the investor a reasonable opportunity to recoup his or her investment and obtain some return.

Third is a related concern with enhancing the public investor's ability to exercise control over the entity after the offering is completed and throughout the duration of the venture. This goal is realized through requiring corporate stockholders to be assigned certain voting rights and limited partners to be granted rights of approval, inspection rights, meeting rights, and other powers that may not be provided under the limited partnership agreement or the limited partnership act. Such requirements, besides reflecting merit's basic assumptions about the consequences of the separation of ownership and control, also express the conviction that the general corporation statute and the limited partnership act not only fail to redress but exacerbate that imbalance. One commentator on substantive regulation of securities offerings under the California statute described that principle in these terms:

> The theory is that every issue of securities offers an opportunity to create inequities among shareholders and that any general exemption [from registration] would fail to give the protection which the minority or outside shareholders need * * *. Accordingly, rather than relying upon the class or other voting provision in the general corporation statute of the state, the Commissioner is vested with the power to review those transactions as to fairness.[215]

Merit standards for governing public corporations and limited partnerships supplement the substantive law of corporations and limited partnerships in order to establish standards of fairness.

To establish standards of fairness, with respect to both governance and promoter compensation, is perhaps the most deeply felt argument in favor of merit regulation because no other mechanism directly imposes such standards upon issuers, promoters, and underwriters. State corporation and partnership laws are generally enabling rather than regulatory; they are flexible tools that the parties can use to structure their business relationships without significant legal restrictions on their control of the enterprise.[216] Without such legal restrictions, the argument follows, there

---

215. Jennings, supra note 1, at 214.

216. The significance of this is a matter of great debate. Most commentators have argued that state corporation laws provide inadequate protection for shareholders' interests. See, e.g., Cary, Federalism and Corporate Law: Reflections Upon Delaware, 83 Yale L.J. 663 (1974); Folk, Corporation Statutes: 1959–1966, 1966 Duke L.J. 875; Kaplan, Fiduciary Responsibility in the Management of the Corporation, 31 Bus.Law. 883 (1976); Jennings, Federalization of Corporation Law: Part Way or All the Way, 31 Bus.Law. 991 (1976); Schwartz, Symposium-Federal Chartering of Corporations: An Introduction, 61 Geo. L.J. 71 (1972); Seligman, A Brief History of Delaware's General Corporation Law of 1899, 1 Del.J.Corp.L. 249 (1976); Young, Federal Corporate Law, Federalism, and the Federal Courts, 41 Law & Contemp. Probs. 146 (1977). But see R. Winter, Government and the Corporation (1978); Arsht, Reply to Professor Cary, 31 Bus.Law. 1113 (1976); Fischel, The "Race to the Bottom" Revisited: Reflections on

is no effective restraint on the behavior of controlling persons. Underwriters compete for securities to sell and are unlikely to object to less than shocking overreaching by insiders. Lawyers and other professionals involved in securities offerings are retained by the issuer and are not expected to impose their standards of business conduct on the transaction. The SEC does not have authority to regulate the terms of the offering or the organization of the issuer. The argument concludes that, without merit regulation, ever-lower standards of promoter conduct would result in excessive compensation, increased self-dealing transactions, unfair voting arrangements, larger amounts of options in favor of insiders, and overpricing. These problems are exacerbated at times of high speculation, when investors purchase for short-term market gain without concern for the ultimate fairness of the management arrangements or the price.

One answer to this argument is that market mechanisms work effectively to control such behavior by the persons controlling the issuer; if such overreaching were really egregious, then full disclosure of the facts would prevent the issue from being sold, or at least from being sold at a price unfair to the public investor. The merit response to this argument is straightforward: the market does not work well enough to ensure those results, at least for the kinds of issues subject to merit regulation, so administrative intervention is necessary.

In short, the core assumptions are that insistence upon minimum standards by state securities administrators is the only effective restraint on the general deterioration of the quality of securities offerings and the underlying economic structures, and the ultimate goal of the securities regulatory system should be to establish desirable standards for the market as a whole. Recognizing those goals provides the appropriate perspective for evaluating merit regulation: the regulatory system should not be judged solely in terms of its effect on individual offerings or particular kinds of transactions but rather in terms of its overall effect on behavior in the marketplace.

Risk

Although the primary goal of merit regulation may be fairer relations between the promoter and the public investor, merit regulation also has always been concerned with the degree of risk created by investment opportunities. Here, the administrator functions as a kind of public investment adviser, registering only those offerings that provide public investors with what the administrator considers a reasonable possibility of return or restricting the class of offerees to those persons the administrator deems able to bear the risk. While this is an important goal of merit regulation, and perhaps one of its important effects, the merit approach to questions of risk is not well defined.

It is not well defined because there are no express merit standards of appropriate risk. It is not even entirely clear how much authority an administrator has with respect to questions of risk, and it is rare to see an offering denied registration expressly on the ground that it presents excessive risk. Furthermore, merit regulation does not usually focus per se on the major issues determinative of investment risk—the issuer's competitive

Recent Developments in Delaware Corporate Law, 76 Nw.U.L.Rev. 913 (1982); Manning, Thinking Straight About Corporation Law Reform, 41 Law & Contemp. Probs. 3, 15–19 (1977).

position, the marketability of its product or service, the abilities of its management, or the adequacy of its business plan. A notable exception is California, where the Commissioner will consider the abilities of management, the adequacy of the business plan, the marketability of the product, and other business factors.[217] In most other merit jurisdictions, however, substantive regulation tends to focus more on how the pie is divided than on how it is produced in the first place.

To some extent, concern with risk can be understood as an aspect of the primary concern with fairness. One way to reduce the public investor's risk, for example, is to reduce the offering price in the interest of fairness. Another way is to restrict the promoters' ability to use self-dealing behavior to divert the proceeds of the offering from the productive uses of the enterprise into their own pockets.[218] Both of these techniques are used to help the public investor obtain a better return than he or she would if the offering price were too high or if substantial portions of the proceeds were appropriated by the promoters.

The concern with risk, however, is more than a mere by-product of the primary concern with fairness. Some regulators are not reluctant to make a subjective, ad hoc determination that a particular offering presents an unacceptably high risk to the public investor. This determination is usually bound up with more specific determinations about the offering's fairness, but it remains a judgment about risk. When a regulator considers an offering too risky to be allowed into the state's capital markets, he or she will usually take a tougher stand on the specific merit criteria defined in the statute or rules rather than deny the offering on the express ground of excessive risk.

Implicit in this goal of excluding certain risky investment opportunities from a state's capital markets are certain assumptions about who the public investors are and what they need. Merit regulation is primarily designed to protect the average investor—a person relatively unsophisticated, relatively risk averse, long-term in investment perspective, vulnerable to hot-issue hysteria, indifferent to or uninformed by disclosure, excessively dependent on his or her broker, and possibly desperate for a tax shelter. Some administrators tend to assume further that all public-offering issues should present only a degree of risk appropriate to that class of investors. In short, it is often assumed that the needs of the average investor should control the terms of the offering and the associated risk.

Fraud Prevention

Another assumption behind merit regulation is that the antifraud remedies under the state and federal securities laws do not completely protect investors. This assumption involves more than a belief that existing antifraud remedies are ineffective. Merit regulation assumes that

---

217. See 1 H. Marsh & R. Volk, supra note 27, at § 8.14.

218. The most direct restraint on this kind of behavior is the common requirement that the proceeds from the sale of the registered securities be impounded until a specified amount of money has been invested. Uniform Act § 305(g)(2), 1 Blue Sky L.Rep. (CCH) ¶ 5535. Impounding the proceeds prevents use of the initial investors' contributions to compensate the promoters before the offering is completed, and is required in connection with both corporate and limited partnership offerings. For discussion of limitations upon the administrators' ability to impose additional preconditions to the release of proceeds from escrow, see Fred J. Schwaemmle Constr. Co. v. Department of Commerce, 360 N.W.2d 141 (Mich.1984).

investors need protection against more than fraud, that they also need protection against unfairness and excessive risk—problems the antifraud remedies cannot reach. Merit practice also reflects, however, a second assumption: that because even the limited goal of protection against fraud per se is not completely served by the existing fraud remedies, merit regulation plays at least some role in fraud prevention.

Private remedies are regarded as inadequate protection against fraud because they apply retroactively (after the money and the perpetrator are long gone) and are too expensive for most small investors. Similarly, the state administrators' civil and criminal enforcement powers may be inadequate because they usually are applied retroactively, the administrators' resources are limited, and the law-enforcement agencies and state courts often do not understand, or are even unsympathetic to, securities law enforcement. Supporters of merit regulation thus would conclude that the in terrorem effect of the antifraud prohibitions and remedies is substantially less than it should be.

Merit regulation may be seen, therefore, as a means of flushing out and preventing fraud before the damage is done. In this regard, merit regulation's goal is not much different from that of SEC disclosure review, also intended as a prophylaxis against fraud. Supporters of merit regulation would probably maintain, however, that merit review covers a broader range of facts and issues than an SEC disclosure review, that a properly conducted merit review is more likely to find the problems than an SEC review, and that many offerings are never reviewed by the SEC. It may even be argued that merit regulation has the more general prophylactic effect of dissuading the real "bad boys" from even trying to enter a strong merit state's securities markets.

Investor Confidence

A merit advocate would respond to the claim that merit regulation restrains capital formation by arguing the opposite: merit regulation facilitates capital formation by bolstering investor confidence in the securities markets. According to this argument, merit regulation clears from the securities markets investment opportunities that carry an excessively high risk of business failure or that allow the promoters too many advantages over the public investor. The offerings permitted to be sold in a merit jurisdiction thus can be regarded as having met certain minimum quality criteria, promoting greater confidence in the market as a whole.

This argument also assumes that the sense of quality grows as merit standards gradually become industry standards, as the prolonged process of negotiation with merit administrators over the original deals leads to new deals that already reflect their requirements. The goal is to make merit standards more or less normative, as it seems to have been for NASAA in the development of guidelines for real estate and oil and gas syndications. Once that happens, individual offerings will have relatively little trouble complying with merit regulation, and the market as a whole will possess the quality that will encourage public investor participation.

Definition of Merit Regulation and Summary of Its Rationale

The foregoing analysis of goals and assumptions suggests this definition of merit regulation: a regulatory system that authorizes state administrators to deny registration to a securities offering unless the substantive terms of the offering and the associated transactions (i) ensure a fair relation between promoters and public investors, and (ii) provide public investors with a reasonable relation of risk to return. While merit and disclosure regulation should not be regarded as antitheses, merit regulation differs from disclosure regulation in its direct regulation of the internal structure of a securities issuer, of the relations among insiders and outsiders, and of the terms of the offering.

With this definition in mind, the essential arguments in support of merit regulation can be summarized in the following terms.

Private incentives and market forces are in many instances inadequate to ensure that the average investor will be treated fairly by the promoter and that the securities he or she purchases will be priced appropriately. There is a substantial risk of unfair treatment of public investors because they are almost completely unable to affect the structure of the issuer or the terms of the offering and because the promoter tends toward overreaching. Some form of government intervention thus is needed.

Disclosure alone is insufficient. Many offerings presented to the public investor have not been effectively reviewed by the SEC, either because the transaction was exempt or because it was for some other reason not subject to Staff review. Even if subject to review, the disclosure document often is not read by the investor. Even if the investor does read it, it is either incomprehensible or has little effect on the investment decision. And if the prospectus were read and understood, it still would not provide adequate protection because the SEC's disclosure-based system permits transactions unfair in merit terms to proceed, provided that all facts deemed material by the SEC staff are disclosed. As a matter of public policy, transactions defined as unfair to the public investor should not be permitted to go forward. SEC disclosure review, while useful, thus should not be the public investor's sole source of protection.

"Fairness," in all of its manifestations, is a concept capable of reasonable definition and application by conscientious, experienced, and impartial administrators. A continuing process of experimentation and cooperation among the states, NASAA, the SEC, the underwriting community, and the bar will ensure that merit regulation achieves its goal of protecting investors without seriously impeding capital formation.

Merit regulation imposes standards that create a healthy environment for both public and private offerings and for financial transactions generally. Merit restraints on excessive compensation, insider loans, inadequate voting rights, and other abuses establish standards and market norms that benefit the economy and the public generally.

THE LIMITS UPON MERIT REGULATION

The foregoing definition and analysis of merit regulation suggests that it is an ambitious attempt to redefine the relations of promoters and public investors. Merit regulation can be regarded as an expression of the belief that state corporation statutes do not adequately serve the state's interest "of protecting its shareholder against unfair and inequitable share structures loaded in favor of promoters and managers,"[219] and that "a lax corporation statute may be strengthened by a strong 'blue sky' law, and a

---

219. Jennings, supra note 1, at 207.

more regulatory corporation statute can be buttressed by a fair but effective state securities statute."[220] Merit regulation also seems to reflect similar assumptions about the state limited partnership statutes. When the scope of merit regulation's ambitions is viewed in light of its broad applicability to a variety of securities offerings, merit regulation appears to be a significant regulatory effort.

There is, however, no broad consensus on the role that merit regulation can or should play in regulating securities offerings. Some argue that it should play no role. This argument may be based on a perception of theoretical or practical shortcomings peculiar to merit regulation itself. It may also be the corollary of a critique focused on the SEC's disclosure-based regulatory system.[221] This critique would maintain that if SEC-mandated disclosure is of little social benefit, then the states' much more paternalistic intervention into private economic decision making is of even less value. Others argue that merit regulation fills major gaps in securities offerings regulation and that it should play a more important role than it does now, especially in light of the SEC's inability to regulate all aspects of a rapidly growing and diversifying securities industry.[222] We recognize the lack of consensus on these issues, but we also recognize that merit regulation may play a useful, although limited, role with respect to some kinds of offerings by providing a kind of protection for the public investor not provided by the SEC or the private incentives of the promoters and underwriters. To define that role, however, it is important to emphasize that merit regulation is subject to certain inherent structural constraints that limit its effectiveness and utility, that the benefits it attempts to provide may be of limited social and economic value, and that it generates signficant costs.

THE STRUCTURAL CONSTRAINTS UPON MERIT REGULATION

The Tension Between Merit Goals and Merit Practice

Even if it is accepted that the goals of merit regulation are desirable and attainable and that their complete implementation would produce a net social gain, there is tension between merit goals and merit practice. This tension in part results from the ambitious goals of merit regulation, which call upon the administrator not only to determine the fairness of the relationship between the insiders and the public investors but also to decide whether the offering price reflects the value of the security. To perform this task well requires a staff of persons who are both gifted financial analysts and ethical philosophers. It is also a result, however, of the peculiar qualities of the blue sky administrative process itself.

Multiple Jurisdictions

Arguments for merit regulation frequently overlook the most troublesome aspect of this regulatory system. Merit regulation cannot be evaluated solely as abstract regulatory philosophy or on the basis of a single

---

220. Id.

221. Perhaps the leading critic of the SEC's disclosure-based regulatory system is Homer Kripke. See Kripke, The SEC and Corporate Disclosure Regulation in Search of a Purpose (1979), and the numerous commentators cited therein.

222. For discussion of the impact of industry growth and staff cutbacks on the SEC, see Wall St. J., Dec. 16, 1985, at 1, col. 1.

jurisdiction's historical experience. Merit regulation must be evaluated in terms of what it really is: multiple fairness reviews in different jurisdictions. Multiple reviews can produce confusion and frustration. One state will attack an offering on the basis of cheap-stock problems, another on voting rights, and another on insider loans. One state may accept a three-year escrow without conditions, while another will insist upon a five-year escrow with conditions. Practitioners recount tales of being trapped between inconsistent merit standards or disputes between states. For example, a particular voting-rights arrangement may pass through a Michigan review without objection while regarded as anathema in Wisconsin. One state will require rigid adherence to the real estate guidelines' limits on promoter compensation while others will permit considerable flexibility. Several states may decide to resolve one or more merit problems through special disclosures, but they may end up requiring mutually inconsistent or at least different disclosures. In a large jurisdiction like California, in which the state provides sufficient resources and there are many similar securities offerings, a merit regulatory system may work to the satisfaction of most observers, especially when the offering is confined or limited principally to that state. Effective regulation may become less likely, however, when this stringent regulatory technique is applied by multiple jurisdictions to national offerings. An overall assessment of merit regulation, therefore, must take into account the impact of a multiplicity of merit concerns and practices upon national offerings subject to multistate review.

Administrative Weakness

Most of the blue sky offices are understaffed.[223] Many are also subject to significant turnover, especially at the commissioner level. When an agency has frequent commissioner or staff turnover, only the most mechanistic, simplistic merit regulation tends to survive. The problems associated with staff and leadership are common to all regulatory agencies, but they seem worse in this area because the practitioner must deal with numerous agencies and because the merit administrators possess enormous (and practically unreviewable) discretion over what their merit standards are, how and when they are applied, and why. Some administrators operate largely case by case, reacting to individual offerings personally and subjectively and without reliance on published standards. This inconsistency and uncertainty in merit practice seriously undermines the administrators' ability to turn merit goals into reality and to convince the industry of those goals' legitimacy. In addition, these problems generate costs that must be weighed against any social benefits of merit regulation.

Other practical problems arise when specific merit standards become virtual fetishes with certain administrators, leading them to ignore the fundamental question of whether the particular offering, as a whole and in comparison with other deals, is unfair to investors. A typical example may be an administrator's rejection of a real estate syndication in which NASAA guideline limits on general partner compensation are exceeded to some degree, or in which the limited partners' rights to equity participation do not fit the letter of the guidelines but which is sponsored by a general partner with a proven track record of investing the proceeds in excellent

---

223. For data on blue sky office staffing and funding, see ERP, supra note 17, at 787–802.

properties with a reasonable return to the investors. The examiner may have reasons other than mechanical adherence to the guidelines for denying registration, but the decision may be based on such adherence. Such behavior usually results from a combination of inexperience, understaffing, inadequate training, and an attitude of "us against them." It happens more often than it should, and it heightens the tension between merit goals and merit practice.

The problems of inconsistency, unpredictability, uncertainty, and inflexibility seem to be almost unavoidable structural problems, generated by the vast discretion inherent in the regulatory scheme, the inherent difficulties of the multiple review process, and persistent turnover and inadequacy of training among blue sky administrators. Merit regulation can be evaluated, and its role defined, only in light of these realities, and not just in light of its goals.

The Inappropriateness of Merit Regulation to Certain Offerings

Merit regulation is at least potentially applicable to a vast majority of securities offerings, including not only those registered with but also many exempted from SEC registration. A strong argument can be made, however, that applying merit review to many of these offerings is inconsistent with the needs of public investors and generates compliance costs without any real social benefit. This recognition is already roughly built into the exemption structures of the Uniform Act and the other state statutes; the current question is how much further it should be extended.

Exchange-Listed and NASDAQ/National Market System Issuers

The Uniform Act has recognized a broad exception to merit regulation by exempting offerings by issuers listed on the New York and American Stock Exchanges. This exemption, traditional to blue sky law, was originally a concession to the political pressure brought by the Investment Banking Association (which represented issuers listed on the New York Stock Exchange) and by the local exchanges.[225] The present exemption thus could be regarded cynically as a giant loophole driven through the statute by political necessity. That view, however, is misleading.

The present exchange-listed exemption,[226] at least insofar as it applies to established New York or American Stock Exchange issuers, can be justified on at least four grounds. First, the issuer is significantly restrained by these self-regulatory organizations, not only in terms of its internal governance but also of dissemination of information about itself. Second, many of these issuers can meet substantial blue-chip quality criteria. Third, historical experience prior to the adoption of such exemptions in some states showed that new offerings by exchange-listed issuers typically did not require modification to meet applicable substantive standards. The compliance costs thus outweighed any benefit to investors. Fourth, since these issuers are, almost by definition, widely followed by market participants who rapidly circulate the information they disseminate, the trading markets for their securities operate efficiently, producing consensus, or fair, prices for their securities.[227] Since new distributions of securities by these

---

225. See J. Seligman, supra note 43, at 45; M. Parrish, supra note 33, at 27–28.

226. Uniform Act § 402(a)8, 1 Blue Sky L.Rep. (CCH) ¶ 5542 (1957).

227. The literature on the efficient market theory is extensive. For a recent discussion of its impact on securities regulatory policy, see Gilson & Kraakman, The Mechanisms of Market Efficiency, 70

issuers take place in an efficient market, the imposition of legal standards of fairness on the offering's terms is probably superfluous. In essence, the exchange-listed exemption functions similarly to the exclusion from rigorous (or any) SEC disclosure review for subsequent offerings by Form S-2 and Form S-3 issuers, issuers deemed by the SEC to be widely followed and hence operating in an efficient market environment.[229]

These justifications do not pertain (at least with such force), however, to initial public offerings by companies newly listed on one of the exchanges, especially some of the regional exchanges.[230] The exchange-listed exemption only makes sense as applied to established issuers returning to the public market for additional capital. If an exemption for these issuers is appropriate, an exemption for other established issuers also may be appropriate.

A significant number of 1934 Act reporting companies, including many Form S-2 issuers and some Form S-3 issuers, have securities traded over the counter.[231] Many of these issuers could qualify for listing on the New York or American Stock Exchange,[232] but choose to remain OTC for marketing reasons or because of objections to some of the New York Stock Exchange's corporate-governance requirements. These issuers thus may not be subject to the self-regulatory restraints of an organized exchange, but many can satisfy blue-chip criteria and many are operating in an efficient market environment.

Some states already have recognized that merit review may not be needed for offerings by such issuers and have adopted either blue-chip exemptions, which depend on quality criteria, or exemptions for issuers listed under NASDAQ and the National Market System, which seem to depend on efficient market theory. The drafters of RUSA have followed this trend by including within that act both a NASDAQ/National Market

Va.L.Rev. 549 (1984). See also authorities cited, id., at 549 n. 1. Note that earlier arguments using efficient market theory to criticize SEC-mandated disclosure have been qualified by more recent commentators. See Easterbrook & Fischel, Mandatory Disclosure and the Protection of Investors, 70 Va.L.Rev. 669, 715 (1984) ("We cannot say that the existing securities laws are beneficial, but we also are not confident that their probable replacement would be better"); Coffee, Market Failure and the Economic Case for a Mandatory Disclosure System, 70 Va.L.Rev. 717, 752 (1984) ("Economic logic also points to the conclusion that there will be inadequate securities research and verification in the absence of a mandatory disclosure system").

229. For discussion of the efficient market rationale for the SEC's integrated disclosure system and the associated "shelf" registration device, see generally Banoff, Regulatory Subsidies, Efficient Markets, and Shelf Registration: An Analysis of Rule 415, 70 Va.L.Rev. 135 (1984); Fox, Shelf Registration, Integrated Disclosure, and Underwriter Due Diligence: An Economic Analysis, 70 Va.L.Rev. 1005 (1984).

230. See Makens, A State Reglatory Perspective of the Report of the Advisory Committee on Corporate Disclosure to the SEC, 26 U.C.L.A.L.Rev. 147, 152–54 (describing lack of public information about smaller issuers); Walker & Hadaway, supra note 14, at 656–69 (the efficient market theory is not applicable to merit regulated securities). But see Mofsky & Tollison, supra note 1, at 367–68 (in view of the efficient market theory, merit regulation generates more costs than benefits). The implications of the efficient market theory for critical analysis of merit regulation have not yet been fully defined. Additional empirical research and theoretical analysis are badly needed.

231. A key factor in the development of the OTC market has been the development of the NASDAQ/National Market System. For discussion of the historical background, see J. Seligman, supra note 43, at 486–534.

232. See Hensley, The Development of a Revised Uniform Securities Act, 40 Bus.Law. 721, 738 (1985).

System exemption [235] and a short-form, non-merit reviewable registration device for a small class of "seasoned" issuers.[236] This trend, however, has proven controversial, since the administrators, the bar, and the securities industry have been unable to agree on line drawing, that is, how blue-chip does a blue-chip issuer have to be, and which issuers listed under NASDAQ and the National Market System should be allowed exemption. The blue-chip criteria adopted by the states, as well as those proposed by the bar and the industry, vary significantly, reflecting a true lack of consensus on this approach.[237] Similarly, some consensus is needed on how long an issuer should be listed on the NASDAQ/National Market System (or, for that matter, on an exchange) before its offerings should qualify for a securities exemption. The lack of consensus, however, does not obscure the basic point. A substantial class of offerings does not need merit review for the reasonable protection of investors. This report will suggest in part five that greater attention should be devoted to defining appropriate parameters for that class.

Investment Company Offerings

Even clearer evidence of the inappropriateness of merit review is presented by investment company offerings. A strong case can be made that most, if not all, merit regulation of these offerings produces few significant benefits to investors while imposing compliance costs on the industry and hence on the public investor.[238]

The first point to recognize is that little serious merit regulation of investment company offerings actually takes place. Many states have general merit authority and specific merit requirements for investment companies, but they either do not enforce their merit standards or they administer them mechanically. The substance of their merit standards, furthermore, is often highly questionable, since they may reflect antiquated approaches to the problems or they may depart from SEC standards without any well-articulated reason for doing so. This kind of trivial merit regulation is not beneficial, especially when it is the basis for requiring the issuers to go through a registration process that generates enormous filing fees, a tremendous paper burden, and unnecessary liability for oversales.

* * * *

In short, the case for merit regulation of investment company offerings has not been made. As it stands, merit regulation of these offerings, whether trivial or serious, appears wholly inappropriate.

Nonsystematic, Uneven Merit Regulation

Merit regulation affects only a small part of investment activity. First, most securities trading is exempt from state registration, although most securities transactions are trading transactions. Second, the exemptions for government, bank, insurance, and exchange-listed securities and for limited offerings exclude vast numbers of primary issues from regulatory review. Merit regulation thus can provide only a limited degree of investor protection for a limited number of investors, however well it is applied.

---

235. RUSA § 401(8), 1 Blue Sky L.Rep. ¶ 5641.

236. RUSA § 302, 1 Blue Sky L.Rep. ¶ 5632.

237. Compare Cal.Admin.Code tit. 10, R. 260.105.17 (1983), 1 Blue Sky L.Rep.

(CCH) ¶ 11,809, with Tex.Admin.Code tit. 7, § 139.3 (1982), 3 Blue Sky L.Rep. (CCH) ¶ 55,713.

238. See generally Sargent, supra note 56, at 172–78.

Not every state is a merit jurisdiction, and not every jurisdiction with merit authority in its statute exercises that authority regularly. This means that a substantial number of offerings can proceed without any attempt, or at least any serious attempt, to comply with merit regulation. Only those issuers who for marketing reasons must sell in California or Massachusetts or in a few of the other tough states will always have to conform to rigorous merit review. In effect, merit regulation is not a system at all; rather, merit regulation applies to some offerings but not to others, depending entirely on where the offering needs to be sold and not on substantive criteria of risk or fairness. Merit regulation thus will tend to apply to the fifty-state offerings and to the local offerings in merit states. This uneven application casts doubt on the effectiveness of merit regulation.

Furthermore, some merit states' ability to meet their own goals is undermined by the way in which securities denied registration in one state can rapidly, if not instantaneously, flow from nonmerit states into the merit jurisdiction's secondary market through the nonissuer exemption for unsolicited broker-dealer transactions.[242] Merit regulation in that jurisdiction, therefore, results in its citizens being denied the opportunity to purchase at the offering price rather than the possibly higher trading price. The irony is that investors will buy the stock deemed unworthy to be sold in the state but at a higher after-market price.

Another negative consequence of this uneven application is the manner in which it disproportionately increases the influence of the administrators in a few key states. When a new securities product is to be offered to the public, it is often the administrator in one of those states who determines what the shape of the offering will be.[243] While these well-intentioned administrators typically act responsibly, it should be questioned whether the representatives of any one or two states should have this kind of de facto authority. This authority is even more questionable in that it does not result from a conscious decision to allocate regulatory responsibility but from an almost accidental combination of factors: the nonpreemption by the 1933 Act of the existing blue sky statutes, the large number of investors resident in key states such as Texas and California, and the relative rigor of their merit criteria at the time the new product is introduced. In view of all this, it is difficult to conclude that merit regulation, when viewed nationally, represents a coherent regulatory system.

An Inadequate Basis for Risk Analysis

Merit regulation attempts to control investment risk to provide public investors with a reasonable chance of return on their investment. This concern is to some extent merely an aspect of merit regulation's central goal of establishing fair relations between promoters and public investors. For example, merit regulation tries to control investment risk by ensuring that an adequate portion of the proceeds of a real estate limited partnership offering will be devoted to the enterprise and not to compensating the promoters. Similarly, cheap-stock escrow requirements ensure the promot-

---

242. Uniform Act § 402(b)(3), 1 Blue Sky L.Rep. (CCH) ¶ 5542. The same result can also be achieved through rapid listing of an issuer in a securities manual. All nonissuer transactions in the securities of manual-listed issuers are exempt under

Uniform Act § 402(b)(2), 1 Blue Sky L.Rep. (CCH) ¶ 5542.

243. For discussion of this phenomenon, see *PTLP*, supra note 153, at 714; Makens, supra note 1, at 443–47.

ers' continuing commitment to the growth of the enterprise. Other fairness provisions function similarly to control investment risk by controlling the promoter's ability to profit at the expense of the enterprise, and hence of the public investor.

Such provisions may represent a theoretically coherent approach to regulating risk, but there are practical problems of application. Under the real estate and oil and gas guidelines, limitations on sponsor compensation and the use of proceeds were developed without systematic empirical analysis of the effects of actual compensation structures on the programs operations and profitability. Accordingly, it is difficult to conclude that the specific limitations applied in the guidelines are essential to controlling the public investor's risk. An examiner's refusal to approve alternative compensation structures on the simple ground that they are inconsistent with the guidelines thus can seem a knee-jerk response that fails to take into account the economic realities of the offering.[244] This does not mean, of course, that the examiner should ignore the guidelines, or that the guidelines are useless. The guidelines are essential to uniformity, and their use allows the examiners to review large numbers of offerings quickly and efficiently. They are merely guidelines, however, and counsel should have a reasonable opportunity to demonstrate the fairness of departures from their specific provisions.

The lack of an empirical foundation for some of merit regulation's attempts to control risk, however, is not the only problem. A more basic problem is the lack of any systematic basis for fundamental analysis of investment risk. Fundamental analysis requires far more than consideration of the relative positions of insider and outsider and the effect of managerial-compensation arrangements on the eventual return to the investor. It requires analyzing the business as a whole, including its plan of operations, the adequacy of its financing, the qualifications of its management, the condition of its facilities, the marketability of its products, its competitive position within the industry, the potential impact of long-term economic trends, and myriad other factors. It also requires comparison with similar companies in the same industry. Similarly, a fundamental analysis of an oil and gas offering would require consideration of the venture's ability to find and extract oil or gas, and of a real estate offering, would require analysis of the development potential of the properties to be acquired.

To be sure, a merit review will include some fundamental analysis. The real estate and oil and gas guidelines, for example, require consideration of the sponsors' qualifications and track record. Review of the offering price of corporate stock will involve analyzing the corporation's price-earnings multiple and comparing it to other issuers'. A few administrators will go further and financially and economically analyze the business plan, although no state has published guidelines or standards for such analysis. These attempts at fundamental analysis, however, are limited, and the conclusions reached by the administrators, like all conclusions based on fundamental analysis, are debatable. The basic fact remains: merit regulation is not well equipped to analyze many of the basic components of investment risk.

244. See Strahota, supra note 171, at 820.

Two possible conclusions may be derived from this fact. The first is that merit regulation does not achieve its own goal of controlling investment risk. Experience in oil and gas has shown that, even if a program sponsor complies with all of the program guidelines, there is no assurance that that sponsor is more capable of finding oil and gas and producing economic returns for the investor than a noncomplying sponsor. Indeed, while the oil and gas guidelines have been in existence, several public program sponsors have managed to raise substantial investor capital, notwithstanding less than satisfactory prior program performance that sometimes led to financial difficulties. In short, the lack of sophisticated fundamental analysis in the typical merit review significantly limits merit regulation's ability to achieve its own goal of controlling the public investor's risk.

The second possible conclusion is that this problem may be unavoidable. At their current staff level, the state administrators cannot engage in fundamental analysis in any meaningful way. Examiners have neither the training nor the time to engage in fundamental analysis of the great number and variety of offerings that cross their desks. They are capable of weeding out issuers whose plans, financing, and management are grossly inadequate, but they are not in any systematic way capable of doing more. Furthermore, even if resources were vastly expanded to permit a serious attempt at fundamental analysis, it is doubtful that such an effort would make sense. Fundamental analysis is subtle and highly subjective; its administrative exercise multistate would surely generate even more confusion and uncertainty than exists already.

In sum, merit regulation may identify and control certain gross problems generating excessive risks for the public investor, but it cannot be described as a precise and consistently effective device for controlling such risk.

A Tendency Toward Overkill

This report has emphasized that merit regulation is an ambitious attempt to control the fundamental structures of issuers and offerings. The administrators have a significant and (practically speaking) unreviewable discretion to exercise in achieving their goals. This combination of lofty goals and enormous discretion sometimes leads to regulatory overkill, establishing merit standards or requirements designed to remedy specific abuses but that penalize without purpose legitimate ventures.

For example, the current NASAA *Statement of Policy on Cheap Stock,* adopted on April 23, 1983 (the statement),[246] has been the signal failure among NASAA's several statements of policy. It has been adopted by only one state [247] and applied informally by only two.[248] This failure, which is the direct result of the statement's rigid and doctrinaire approach to the

---

246. NASAA Statement of Policy, Cheap Stock, 1 Blue Sky L.Rep. (CCH) ¶¶ 5311–5314 [hereinafter cited as Cheap Stock]. As of this writing, NASAA has proposed certain liberalizing changes to this statement, which may or may not have been adopted by the time this report is published. Even if the statement is amended, discussion of NASAA's approach to cheap stock should still be useful as a case study of merit regulation overkill.

247. See Wis.Admin.Code § SEC 3.04 (1981–1982), 3 Blue Sky L.Rep. (CCH) ¶ 64,524. Apparently the Wisconsin administrator has applied these guidelines flexibly.

248. Massachusetts and Ohio have attempted to apply these guidelines from time to time.

problem of cheap stock, should be regarded as a cautionary tale demonstrating the problems that can be created when merit powers are used unrestrainedly. It also demonstrates how the product of a group of merit regulators working together through NASAA can be so extreme and arbitrary as to undermine the overall credibility of merit regulation.

* * * *

When viewed as a whole, the statement is a dramatic example of regulatory overkill. It was adopted without clear articulation of the problems it attempted to resolve or the policies implicit in its approach; it provides little scope for administrative discretion; it attempts to eliminate all possible abuses through requirements either too broad, too rigid, or wholly misdirected; and it demonstrates a marked insensitivity to its policing efforts' effect on the incentives of legitimate entrepreneurs.

Obviously, not all NASAA statements of policy reflect such an uncompromising and impractical attitude. The statement of policy on cheap stock represents the most egregious example to date, and NASAA has recently proposed amendments that may mitigate some of the problems. This experience does demonstrate, however, that state merit authority can be the basis for an unnecessarily restrictive regulatory scheme. NASAA's failure to secure widespread adoption of the statement shows that most states will take a realistic, balanced approach to such problems, but the tendency toward overkill will remain as a constant undercurrent.

THE LIMITED BENEFITS THAT MERIT REGULATION CAN PROVIDE

One major problem in defining a role for merit regulation is evaluating its supposed benefits. Some of its defenders invoke investor protection almost ritualistically, with little appreciation of the tension between merit goals and merit practice, of how superfluous merit review is for many offerings, and of how uneveningly it is applied. Even if these problems were to disappear, however, the benefits provided by merit regulation, while real, would still be limited.

First, merit regulation often does not protect investors against the true thieves and confidence men.[260] These types usually disregard the state and federal securities laws, seldom worrying about compliance with the registration provisions of the blue sky or the federal securities statutes. Thus merit regulators seldom see their offerings in advance. While theoretically merit review acts as a prophylaxis against fraud in the offerings that are actually reviewed, it does not—indeed cannot—serve that function for most of the egregious frauds. Merit regulation thus is no substitute for a strong system of private antifraud remedies and state and federal enforcement powers.

Second, merit regulation is primarily concerned with the problem of fairness: prohibiting or reducing promoters' self-dealing to ensure that promoters' and public investors' risks are roughly equivalent. The merit regulator's concerns, however, in practice can extend beyond questions of fairness to more basic questions of economic risk. We suggested that merit judgments about economic risk are especially troublesome when made

260. See Bloomenthal, supra note 1, at 1481.

without reference to any articulated standard by persons untrained in fundamental analysis and without business experience.

Merit's problematic regulation of investment risk, however, is more than a question of the occasional administrator engaging in excessively subjective or standardless judgments. The real problem is, once again, structural. As a practical matter, some legitimate start-up companies have difficulty complying with the merit standards of many states. Entrepreneurs are often unable to contribute substantial cash to the enterprise; they reasonably expect control in compensation for their ideas and the commitment to those ideas and thus demand substantial amounts of cheap stock. Venture capitalists, who incur substantial research costs in identifying promising start-up companies and significant transactional costs in preparing those issuers to come to market, expect compensation for those costs in the form of cheap stock and options. Key employees are often compensated with cheap stock or options in lieu of the cash they could normally expect in exchange for their services. Merit concepts of fairness thus contain a structural bias toward the seasoned issuer; the effect is a tendency to exclude riskier enterprises from certain state capital markets. While this may benefit the risk-averse investor, it is of no benefit whatsoever for the investor willing to incur a more substantial risk or who can absorb that risk through a diversified portfolio.

This is not to say that merit regulation is uniformly hostile to high-risk ventures. The California administrators' long experience with new, high-technology ventures has shown that the sophisticated application of merit principles by a well-trained staff can compensate for a structural bias against risk. The California experience is exemplary, but it has not become a model for merit practice elsewhere. Merit regulators need to be more aware of this structural bias and the problems it creates for such ventures.

Third, the merit conception of fairness to the public investor, while laudable, confers mixed blessings upon the public investor. At their best, merit standards can usefully restrain promoters' self-dealing in the form of misallocation of the offering's proceeds to their private uses or front-end loading of promoter compensation, leaving the long-term risk of the enterprise to the investors. Merit regulation thus can be a useful device for controlling egregious overreaching. Furthermore, the mere existence of merit regulation can be used by counsel to persuade their clients not to take excessive compensation. At its worst, however, applying merit conceptions of fairness or risk can amount to little more than arbitrary rewriting of the economic terms of the offering and the underlying transactions. In short, there is a serious question whether the current practice of merit regulation consistently promotes a more equitable relation between insider or outsider, or whether it tends to force all offerings to adopt a predetermined structure.

Finally, the existing empirical studies of merit regulation, which have been cited as establishing its value by comparing the performances of complying and noncomplying issuers, cannot be regarded as providing conclusive evidence of the efficacy or desirability of merit regulation.[261] No

261. The principal empirical studies are Goodkind, Blue Sky Law: Is There Merit in the Merit Requirements?, 1976 Wis.L.Rev. 79 (Wisconsin merit standards), and Walker & Hadaway, supra note 14 (1982) (Texas merit standards).

systematic evidence establishes that merit regulation accomplishes its goals.

THE COSTS OF MERIT REGULATION

Before it can be assumed that the benefits provided by merit regulation produce a net social gain, its costs must be defined and weighed against those benefits. The need for some kind of cost-benefit analysis has been widely acknowledged, but no one has attempted to systematically identify, let alone quantify, the costs of merit regulation.[262] In fact, many of the costs of merit regulation are probably not quantifiable. A few basic observations about its cost, however, can be made.

First, there are compliance costs associated with merit regulation. Some of these costs, of course, are not peculiar to merit regulation but result from having to register with the SEC and in the states. Examples of such costs are filing fees, printing costs, some attorneys' fees, and some accounting fees. These costs would be incurred even if all states were to shift to disclosure review. Other compliance costs, however, are directly attributable to merit regulation.

Among those costs are the attorneys' fees incurred when the issuer or the underwriter has to negotiate with merit administrators to clear an offering in one or more states. These costs can increase when the offering is controversial and negotiations are prolonged.

The burden on the issuer of these direct compliance costs, however, is relatively insignificant, at least in most cases. More significant are the delays sometimes generated by difficulties with merit review. These delays can take different forms. Merit difficulties in key states can sometimes cause a national offering to be postponed, even after SEC registration has been effected. A merit problem in a smaller state may simply delay the offering in that state, since counsel may withdraw the registration by coordination and file a registration by qualification, which would give more time to resolve the problem. These delays are perhaps most likely to occur when a new securities product is about to come to market. In short, merit regulation can produce costs through producing delays.

Although compliance costs and the costs of delay can be important, they are perhaps not the most significant: there are larger and less quantifiable costs. For example, we do not know whether denying access to merit states' securities markets has seriously inhibited potentially successful enterprises from raising capital. Similarly, we do not know whether merit regulation inhibits venture capital investment.

Venture capitalists serve the valuable function of searching for, identifying, and providing the initial financing for potential growth companies. Typically, a venture capitalist makes substantial investments in such an enterprise before it seeks public financing. The venture capitalist thus incurs substantial search and information costs and substantial risks associated with an early commitment to a start-up enterprise. Venture capitalists need substantial incentives to incur such costs and risks. Principal among those incentives is the possibility of obtaining cheap stock and options that can be liquidated or held for long-term appreciation once a

262. Campbell, supra note 1, at 577–79, provides data on the aggregate costs of state securities regulation, but he does not attempt to distinguish the costs attributable to merit regulation per se.

market for the issuer's shares has been established. There is a tension between that incentive and merit restrictions on cheap stock and options. It cannot be said, however, that this tension has actually impeded venture capital investment. Venture capital has found ways to live with merit regulation, even in such heavily regulated states as California and Massachusetts. Furthermore, no one has devised a method of measuring merit regulation's actual effect on venture capitalists' incentive and ability to perform their valuable economic functions. It is thus difficult to conclude that one social cost of merit regulation is a significant negative impact on the behavior of venture capitalists. Because of the theoretical conflict between venture capital incentives and merit principles, however, this question deserves future study.

A question also arises about the effect on the incentives of another key actor in the capital formation process—the private entrepreneur. For many entrepreneurs, the most important payoff is the ability to engage in a secondary distribution, simultaneous with the IPO, of some portion of the stock held by that entrepreneur.[264] These secondary distributions are used to convert an essentially illiquid equity investment into money, to produce a cash return on what may have been a major commitment of ingenuity, time, and energy. A regulatory scheme that inhibits the entrepreneur's ability to obtain that return may diminish a major incentive for entrepreneurial activity.

There is, however, absolutely no empirical evidence on the effect of merit regulation on entrepreneurial incentives. It can even be argued that merit regulation contributes to the stability and ultimate profitability of new ventures. Strong regulatory states, such as California, Massachusetts and Texas, have fostered the development of numerous start-up companies. Because it is by no means clear what effect merit regulation has, either in individual states or nationally, on entrepreneurial incentives, we cannot conclude that it has generated significant social costs by interfering with entrepreneurial activity. As with venture capitalists, however, the potential conflict requires that more thought be given to the problem.

In sum, much work remains in defining the costs of merit regulation. It can be assumed, however, that merit regulation is not, indeed cannot be, without costs, and the reality of those costs must be acknowledged before any judgment about the value of the benefits provided can be made.

* * * *

CONCLUSION

The best approach to merit regulation is recognition, tempered by a healthy skepticism, of its positive goals. The skepticism should result from an awareness of the structural constraints upon merit regulation, the limited benefits it provides, and its costs. We should, however, appreciate how merit regulation can help prevent managerial self-dealing in certain transactions and in the absence of other regulatory or market mechanisms. The problem in defining a role for merit regulation is to determine when skepticism is more appropriate than respect. However, there may be some keys to resolving this problem.

264. See Adamsk, 100 Who Made Millions, Venture, Apr. 1984, at 48.

First, merit regulation can be useful when market forces are inadequate to protect the public investor from promoters' unfair behavior. Thus merit regulation is arguably most appropriate for first-time issuers. Similarly, merit regulation may be useful when a hot-issue market encourages promoter overreaching, and competition for underwritings reduces underwriters' ability to control such activity. Some aspects of merit regulation thus may be useful in the regulation of corporate IPOs.

Second, merit regulation is most justifiable when it is confined to what it does best: promoting a fairer relation between promoters and public investors. It is significantly less justifiable when the administrator functions as a kind of public investment adviser, substituting his or her own judgments about business risk for those of the actors in the marketplace.

Third, merit regulation is useful when it strikes an appropriate balance between ensuring fair treatment of the public investor and diminishing the incentives of entrepreneurs and venture capitalists. It is impossible to define a universal standard for striking this balance, but progress can be made by recognizing that this balance needs to be struck and, more specifically, by reemphasizing one of the basic goals of securities regulation, facilitating capital formation.

Fourth, an overall assessment of merit regulation requires more than consideration of individual states' historical experience. The theory and practice of merit regulation in a particular state may be exemplary; merit regulation is administered, however, interstate. That simple fact means that merit regulation needs to be evaluated not just in view of the investors' needs in individual states but in view of its national impact.

Fifth, whatever the theoretical advantages of merit regulation may be, the current regulatory system, viewed nationally, does not work well. If merit is to make a more positive contribution to regulation of the securities markets, significant reform must be achieved. We strongly urge that NASAA, the states, the SEC, the bar, and the industry explore possible approaches to reform.

Sixth, legislators evaluating their state securities regulatory schemes should realize that the issue is not simply deciding whether or not to implement merit regulation. There are actually a great many more choices. Legislators should first fundamentally determine whether the state can or should adopt a rigorous consumer-protection-oriented regulatory posture toward securities issues. This decision is too important to be decided solely by the administrator on the basis of his or her personal views. If legislators are particularly concerned with specific abuses in connection with penny stocks, tax shelters, Ponzi schemes, or fraudulent commodity programs, they should consider whether these abuses can be remedied without adopting a full-scale merit regulatory system uniformly applicable to all offerings registered in the state. For example, states should first determine whether their existing antifraud remedies and provisions for regulating securities professionals are adequately enforced by an appropriately financed, trained, and supervised blue sky office. If the state's problem is enforcement, then more resources should be devoted to that. It a state determines that its securities laws need revision, it should decide whether the wholesale adoption or expansion of merit authority is the most appropriate solution, or rather committing to SEC-like disclosure review, redefining existing civil or criminal liabilities, expanding the administrator's enforcement powers, imposing greater restraints or closer supervision on securities professionals, constricting existing exemptions, targeting only specific kinds of transactions for detailed merit or disclosure review, or a combination of these regulatory techniques. All of these possibilities should be considered as policymakers evaluate the future role of merit regulation in their states' blue sky laws.

In sum, merit can play a useful, although limited, role in regulating a finite class of transactions in which market forces, private incentives, and federal and state disclosure requirements do not suffice to protect certain investors. Since merit regulation is not without cost, however, and because its benefits are limited, modesty of purpose and flexibility of means should be built into it. The merit states simply cannot—indeed should not—control the structure of governance and the quantum of risk associated with most registered securities offerings. Once that is accepted, merit regulation can begin to function as a less controversial aspect of the state-federal regulatory scheme.

LIMITED OFFERING EXEMPTIONS

Almost all of the States now have some sort of exemption for primary sales (by an issuer or underwriter) based upon the limited number of offerees or of purchasers or shareholders involved. The maximum number of purchasers or shareholders varies from 5 to 40, with the most common number being 35.[1] These limited offering exemptions are of at least seven different varieties. (1) An exemption for an "isolated transaction." (2) An exemption for the offer to or the sale to a specified number of offerees or purchasers within a specified period, usually twelve months. (3) An exemption for a "private offering," as in the Securities Act of 1933. (4) An exemption for a sale if the shareholders of the corporation after the sale do not exceed a specified number. (5) Sales to accredited investors, following the pattern of Regulation D. (6) A limited offering exemption conforming to or patterned on the Uniform Limited Offering Exemption, promulgated by the National Association of Securities Administrators Association (NASAA). (7) A combination of these exemptions.

The "isolated transaction" exemption, which was once the most widespread but has generally been diminished in importance by one or more of the other types is illustrated by the *Tarsia* case. In *Tarsia v. Nick's Laundry & Linen Co.*,[2] the Oregon court held that any two sales by a controlling person or corporation made to not more than two individuals within a reasonable period of time would be deemed to be "isolated sales." On the other hand, some courts said that any two sales within reasonable proximity to each other were not "isolated" from each other and therefore were not entitled to the "isolated transaction" exemption. Elting v. Pickett[3] held that three separate sales in slightly over a month to the same individual constituted "isolated transactions." On the other hand, Gales v. Weldon[4] held that five separate sales and four additional offers over a period of two months did not constitute "isolated transactions." In practice, this exemption proved to be of very limited utility.

1. See Hainsfurther, Summary of Blue Sky Exemptions Corresponding to Regulation D, 38 Sw.L.J. 989 (1984); MacEwan, Blue Sky Regulation of Regulation D Offerings, 18 Rev. of Sec. & Commodities Reg. 103 (1985).

2. 239 Ore. 562, 399 P.2d 28 (1965).

3. 190 Kan. 54, 372 P.2d 261 (1962).

4. 282 S.W.2d 522 (Mo.1955). See Annot., Sales as "Isolated" or "Successive," or the Like Under State Securities Acts, 1 A.L.R.3d 614 (1965).

This type of exemption now most often takes the form, following the Uniform Securities Act, of limiting the number of offerees within a twelve-month period. However, some states limit the number of *purchasers*, rather than offerees.[5] The number to be counted may be all offerees (or purchasers) in a particular offering, or only those "within this State." If the statute contains this phrase from the Uniform Securities Act, then the exemption may be applicable in a particular state even though the offers and sales are part of a nation-wide public offering. In In the Matter of Information Resources Corporation [6] the court held that the maximum number of offerees (10) under the New Jersey statute, which contained this language, was to be determined with respect only to those in New Jersey. The court said: "The Bureau [of Securities] does not allege that the statutory language under consideration is vague or ambiguous. Unambiguous language is presumed to express the legislative purpose, * * * and is not, except in the clearest case, to be given extraterritorial operation. * * * Only eight (at best, nine) of the offers were 'in this State.'"

There may also be an exemption, either alone or as an alternative to the exemption for a limited number of offerees or purchasers, which relates to the number of shareholders of the corporation after the sale. In the *Cann* case [7] the court held that where both such exemptions were in the statute you could in effect add the two together, so that the first 25 purchasers could come under the shareholder exemption and the next 15 under the purchaser exemption. This result seems questionable. The availability of a shareholder exemption is usually subject to conditions.

Under the California Corporate Securities Law of 1968 a sale of common stock by a corporation is exempt if there will be, after the sale, no more than thirty-five shareholders (counting husband and wife as one), subject to certain conditions. These conditions are (a) that there be no advertisement, (b) there be no promotional consideration or selling expenses, (c) that the transfer of the stock be restricted by a legend on the certificate, (d) that, if there is more than one shareholder, the consideration to be received by the corporation be of certain prescribed kinds designed to require equitable contributions by the various shareholders, and (e) that a notice of the issuance of the stock be filed with or mailed for filing to the Commissioner not later than the day on which the stock is issued.[8] However, the utility of this close corporation exemption has been diminished by the subsequent amendment of California Corporations Code § 25102(f) to provide a much less restrictive limited offering exemption.

Until recently a significant "private offering" exemption was included in only a few state statutes. In California, aside from the close corporation exemption of § 25102(h) previously discussed, prior to 1981, a private offering exemption was available only for partnerships and joint venture interests and for evidences of indebtedness.[9] In 1981, however, subdivision (f) was repealed and a new subdivision (f) was reenacted. Subdivision (f) now broadly exempts any security offered and sold to not more than 35 persons in what amounts to a "private offering," or more accurately, a limited offering exemption for all types of securities by all types of issuers.

5. Cann v. M&B Drilling Co., 480 S.W. 81 (Mo.App.1972).

6. 126 N.J.Super. 42, 312 A.2d 671 (App.Div.1973).

7. Note 5 supra.

8. West's Ann.Cal.Corp.Code, § 25201(h). See Marsh & Volk, Practice

Under the California Corporate Securities Law of 1968, at § 4.02 (1969, Supp.1986).

9. West's Ann.Cal.Corp.Code, § 25102(e) (evidences of indebtedness) and (f) (partnership and joint venture interests).

The amendment was passed in anticipation of the adoption by the Securities and Exchange Commission of Regulation D which provides a series of limited offering exemptions expressly designed to complement parallel state limited offering exemptions. Regulation D was adopted specifically for the purpose of enabling small business to raise capital without having to incur the expenses entailed in a 1933 Act registration. In addition, the deregulation movement spurred efforts to promote uniformity in securities regulation at the state and federal level. Rules have been adopted by the California Corporations Commissioner which were formulated with Regulation D in mind in an attempt to achieve a uniform federal-state exemption. Section 25102(f) was a tremendous advance in securities regulation with respect to small issues and became part of a nationwide movement to provide a uniform limited offering exemption applicable at the state level.

Section 19(c)(3)(C) of the Securities Act of 1933, added by the Omnibus Small Business Capital Formation Act of 1980, provides for federal and state cooperation in the development of a uniform exemption from registration for small issuers. In connection with the adoption of Regulation D at the federal level, the North American Securities Administrators Association promulgated the NASAA Uniform Limited Offering Exemption (ULOE); ULOE is designed to coordinate with Regulation D.[10] ULOE is drafted as a rule which a state administrator may adopt pursuant to statutory authority.

The basic ULOE rule provides an exemption from state registration for issuers of securities offered or sold in compliance with Rules 501–503 and 505 of Regulation D, provided the following conditions are met: (1) No commissions or other remuneration shall be paid, unless the recipient is appropriately registered in the state; (2) none of the persons described in Regulation A, Rule 252(c), (d), (e), and (f) are subject to certain specified "bad boy" disqualifying provisions at the state level which are similar to those specified in Rule 252 at the federal level; (3) the issuer shall file a Form D notice with the state administrator; and (4) that in all sales to nonaccredited investors, the issuer and any person acting in its behalf shall have reasonable grounds to believe that the investment is suitable for the purchaser, and that the purchaser or his or her purchaser representative is capable of evaluating the merits and risk of the investment.

It is to be noted that the exemption only extends to offerings under Rules 501–503 and 505; that is the "basic" ULOE. ULOE, however, provides that a state may elect to accept Rule 506 offerings within the ambit of the exemption as a matter of state policy. NASAA did not include Rule 506 as a part of the basic ULOE because of a lack of a dollar limit. This lack of a dollar limit for Rule 506 offerings made the rule available for large unregistered private placements, including abusive, high write-off tax shelter offerings. The exclusion of Rule 506 offerings from the basic ULOE has been criticized by issuers and their counsel, and it is possible that states may reconsider the Rule 506 exclusion in the light of the Tax Reform Act of 1986. That Act contains provisions designed to correct the abuses previously existing in tax sheltered direct participation programs.

More than half of the states have adopted ULOE or have a limited offering exemption that is even less restrictive than ULOE. Thus, some sixteen states have adopted the basic ULOE provisions, and fourteen of these states have also

10. Reprinted in NASAA Rep. (CCH) ¶ 6201; Jennings & Marsh, Selected Statutes, Rules and Forms Under the Federal Securities Laws, following Regulation D.

elected to include the Rule 506 exemption. Thirteen other states have a limited offering exemption less restrictive than ULOE.[11]

The Regulation D–ULOE innovations are a major achievement in federal-state cooperative securities regulation. And it now seems possible that in the next few years most states will have adopted the ULOE exemption or an equivalent. Moreover, these regulations seem to have solved a large number of problems in the administration of a "private offering" or limited offering exemption while providing reasonable investor protection safeguards.

OTHER TRANSACTION EXEMPTIONS

Preincorporation Subscriptions. While a preincorporation subscription is generally included in the definition of a "security" for which registration is required, a number of States exempt the sale of such subscriptions either permanently or temporarily, under certain conditions.[1] These exemptions are apparently based upon a recognition of the need for some preliminary agreements to launch a proposed corporation and the practical difficulty of filing all of the required information in a registration before the financing plans take more definite form. In California, under the 1968 Law, the former temporary exemption relating to preincorporation subscriptions was repealed; it was replaced by an exemption for any non-public offering and any agreement of sale pursuant thereto which conditions issuance of the security and payment of the consideration upon prior qualification whether before or after incorporation.[2] Under this provision, preincorporation subscriptions can no longer be publicly offered without qualification. The Uniform Securities Act (1985) makes the exemption a temporary one, conditioned upon no payment being made, and it also conditions it upon there being no more than 10 preincorporation subscribers.[3]

Postincorporation Subscriptions and Sales to Special Parties. Most of the Blue Sky laws include a "subscription" within the definition of a security and do not offer any exemption for postincorporation subscriptions as distinguished from final sales. This means that the registration of the security must precede the taking of subscriptions, as well as the sale. However, there is authority that if the statute is complied with prior to the delivery of the security and receipt of payment, this will cure any illegality involved in the taking of the subscription prior to registration.[4] On the other hand, under some statutes, the cases have indicated that the lack of a permit at the time the subscription agreement is signed "infects the entire transaction" and that the security issued is "void" even if a permit is obtained prior to issuance and payment.[5]

The California Corporate Securities Law of 1968 exempts any offer (but not a sale) after a registration statement under the Securities Act of 1933 has been filed and before it has become effective (thus permitting oral offers and

11. A periodic ULOE adoption table appears in NASAA Rep. (CCH) ¶ 6401. And see Hainsfurther, note 1 supra; MacEwan, note 1 supra.

1. See Loss & Cowett, Blue Sky Law 375 (1958); Annot., Applicability of Blue Sky Laws to Preincorporation Subscriptions, 50 A.L.R.2d 1103 (1956).

2. West's Ann.Cal.Corp.Code § 25102.

3. Uniform Securities Act (1985) § 402(b)(10).

4. Bauer v. Bond & Goodwin, Inc., 285 Mass. 117, 188 N.E. 708 (1934); Moore v. Moffatt, 188 Cal. 1, 204 P. 220 (1922).

5. See Ogier v. Pacific Oil & Gas Development Corp., 135 Cal.App.2d 776, 288 P.2d 101 (1955); United Bank & Trust Co. v. Joyner, 40 Ariz. 229, 11 P.2d 829 (1932). The Ogier case has clearly been overruled by the California Corporate Securities Law of 1968, § 25503.

circulation of a Preliminary Prospectus during the waiting period without any qualification under state law) and also any private offer and agreement conditioned upon the obtaining of qualification prior to issuance of the security or payment of the consideration.[6]

In many States, and in the Uniform Securities Act,[7] there is also an exemption not only for subscriptions by but also for sales to certain designated persons regarded as sophisticated investors.[8]

SECURITY EXEMPTIONS

All of the State Blue Sky laws exempt some securities from the regulation imposed. For example, the exemption of governmental issues is probably universal,[1] since it would not do to have one state official reviewing the actions of municipal and state finance officials, and frequently of the voters, in authorizing bond issues. United States government issues would of course be beyond the power of any State to regulate. Also, short-term commercial paper has to be exempt, since it would be impossible to impose the type of regulation contemplated by most Blue Sky laws upon the issuance of negotiable instruments in ordinary commercial transactions.[2]

Beyond these obvious categories, most Blue Sky laws also exempt various classes of securities for the reason that their issuance is regulated (or the *company* issuing them is regulated) by another governmental authority, state or federal, in order to avoid a conflict of jurisdiction. Securities which are issued by a carrier and are subject to the approval of the Interstate Commerce Commission under the Interstate Commerce Act cannot be regulated by any State, since the federal government in that statute has pre-empted the field.[3] On the other hand, the Public Utility Holding Company Act of 1935 expressly preserves state jurisdiction, like the Securities Act of 1933, where the state regulation "does not conflict" with that Act or the rules and regulations thereunder.[4]

Frequently, securities issued by certain types of corporations, such as public utilities, insurance companies, or banks, are exempted from the general State Blue Sky law[5] because their issuance and sale is regulated by another branch of the state government, such as the public utility commission, the insurance commissioner or the superintendent of banks.[6] This is merely a matter of distribution of functions within the state government, and does not really affect the scope of the regulation. However, some state statutes exempt securities of public utilities merely because the *rates and charges* of the issuer are subject to

6. West's Ann.Cal.Corp.Code § 25102(a) and (b).

7. Uniform Securities Act (1985), § 402(b)(8).

8. Loss & Cowett, Blue Sky Law 367–368 (1958).

1. Loss & Cowett, Blue Sky Law 353 (1958).

2. Id. at 360–361. Loss and Cowett indicate that five States do not have such an exemption in their statutes, but it is impossible to believe that they actually attempt to apply the Blue Sky law to such commercial transactions.

3. 49 U.S.C.A. § 11301(b)(1) provides that the Interstate Commerce Commission has "exclusive jurisdiction to approve the issuance of securities by a carrier and the assumption of an obligation * * * related to the securities of another person by a carrier." See In re St. Louis Southwestern Ry. Co., 53 F.Supp. 914, 920 (E.D.Mo.1944), aff'd 157 F.2d 337 (8th Cir.1946), cert. denied 330 U.S. 836.

4. Public Utility Holding Company Act, § 21.

5. See, for example, West's Ann.Cal.Corp.Code, § 25100(c), (d), (e), (g), (h) and (i).

6. See, for example, (West's Ann.) Cal.Pub.Util.Code § 818; Cal.Ins.Code, § 827; Cal.Fin.Code, §§ 362, 622, 662.

regulation by some state authority, although not necessarily its issuance of securities. This exemption has been incorporated into the Uniform Securities Act.[7] It is difficult to see what the regulation of the rates and charges of a corporation has to do with protection of the persons who purchase its securities.

Almost all States also exempt securities which are listed on one or more designated stock exchanges (and usually securities senior to those so listed), apparently on the theory that the requirements of the exchange for listing and its policing of the activities of listed companies, plus that of the SEC under the Securities Exchange Act of 1934, are a sufficient guarantee of the quality of such securities. In this respect, these State Blue Sky laws go further than the Securities Act of 1933, which contains no exemption based upon listing and registration under the 1934 Act.

There are many other security exemptions, dealing generally with special types of securities as to which it is felt that regulation under the Blue Sky laws is inappropriate or unnecessary. In this respect, as everywhere in this area, there is great diversity among the various States.

EXEMPTIONS FOR SECONDARY DISTRIBUTIONS

The Federal Securities Act of 1933 applies to a secondary distribution of securities, i.e., a sale of an outstanding block of securities by the owner thereof who is not an "underwriter" for the issuer (as defined in the Securities Act), only if the person making the sale is in a control relationship with the issuer.[1] On the other hand, many of the State Blue Sky laws require registration or qualification for every sale of an outstanding security from one person to another, with various exemptions from this requirement. Those Blue Sky laws which require registration for secondary distributions must have some scheme for exemption of ordinary trading transactions in the market if the regulation is to be workable at all. Usually these take two forms. (1) The "isolated transaction" or limited offering exemption previously discussed. Most States have such an exemption for non-issuer transactions. Of course, if the "isolated transaction" exemption is interpreted narrowly, the exemption is of very limited application.[2] (2) An exemption for securities which are listed on stock exchanges and listed in certain manuals, thus eliminating the need for registration of the great bulk of trading transactions in recognized securities.[3] It should be noted that this sort of exemption, being phrased in terms of a "security" exemption rather than a "transaction" exemption, eliminates the necessity for registration not only of ordinary trading transactions in these securities but also of a large secondary distribution by a syndicate. For example, the distribution of Ford Motor Company stock by the Ford Foundation would be exempt since the stock is listed on the New York Stock Exchange, but on the other hand a similar sale by the Ford Motor Company itself would not be exempt unless the State had an exchange listing exemption for *primary* distributions. Most of them do; but few exempt primary issues merely because the security is listed in some manual.

7. Uniform Securities Act (1985) § 401(a)(5)(iii).

1. See Chapter 9, supra.

2. See Kneeland v. Emerton, 280 Mass. 371, 183 N.E. 155 (1932), and cases cited at 280 Mass. 390, 183 N.E. 164.

3. Loss & Cowett, Blue Sky Law 359–360, 363–365 (1958).

For a survey of the variety of approaches to registration of nonissuer transactions under state law, see Note, Regulation of Nonissuer Transactions Under Federal and State Registration Laws, 78 Harv.L.Rev. 1635 (1965).

The California Corporate Securities Law of 1968 exempts from the requirement of qualification for secondary distributions (a) any sale not made through a broker-dealer in a public offering and not accompanied by the publication of any advertisement, (b) any sale effected by or through a licensed broker-dealer pursuant to an unsolicited offer to buy, and (c) any sale of a security of a corporation which is registered under Section 12 of the Securities Exchange Act of 1934 or under the Investment Company Act of 1940.[4] This exemption, however, does not apply "to such securities offered pursuant to a registration under the Securities Act of 1933 or pursuant to an exemption under Regulation A of that Act if the aggregate offering price of the securities offered under such exemption exceeds fifty thousand dollars ($50,000)." The purpose of this exclusion is to permit the California Commissioner of Corporations to review the Prospectus or Offering Circular in the case of such registered or qualified secondary distributions.

For articles dealing with Blue Sky problems generally and with the laws of particular States, see State Securities Regulation: A Symposium (with bibliography), 13 U.Balt.L.Rev. 435–651 (1984); State Securities Regulation: A Survey, 41 Bus.Law. 1509 (1986); Survey: State Securities Regulation, 40 Bus.Law. 669–759 (1985); Brandi, Securities Practitioners and Blue Sky Laws: A Survey of Comments and a Ranking of States by Stringency of Regulation, 10 J.Corp.L. 689–710 (1985); Warren, Reflections on Dual Regulation of Securities: A Case Against Preemption, 25 B.C.L.Rev. 495 (1984); M. Jennings, Childers & Kudia, Federalism to an Advantage: The Demise of State Blue Sky Laws Under the Uniform Securities Act, 19 Akron L.Rev. 395 (1986); Walker & Hadaway, Merit Standards Revisited: An Empirical Analysis of the Efficacy of Texas Merit Standards, 7 J.Corp.L.Rev. 651 (1982); Tyler, More About Blue Sky, 7 J.Corp.L.Rev. 899 (1982); Campbell, An Open Attack on the Nonsense of Blue Sky Regulation, 10 J.Corp.L. 553 (1985); Levinson, Real Estate Investments, Public Offerings, and the New York Real Estate Syndicate Act, 57 St. John's L.Rev. 662 (1983); Note, California Corporate Securities Law: Small Business Capital Formation and Investor Protection, 13 Pacific L.J. 459 (1982); Note, Florida's Response to the Need for Uniformity in Federal and State Securities Registration Exemption Requirements, 12 Fla.St.U.L.Rev. 309 (1984); Lipsman, Exemptions Under the Texas Securities Act: A Logical Framework for the Practicing Attorney, 22 Hous.L.Rev. 725 (1985); Note, State Securities Regulation: Merit Review of Foreign Equity Offerings, 25 Va.J.Int'l.L. 939 (1985); Note, Compromise Merit Review—A Proposal for Both Sides of the Debate, 60 Wash.L.Rev. 141 (1984). Note, New Montana Exemptions to Securities Registration, 45 Mont.L.Rev. 281 (1984); Note, A Critique of the Vermont Securities Act: Is Vermont's Blue Sky Really Grey?, 11 Vt.L.Rev. 131 (1986); McClard, The Applicability of Local Securities Acts to Multi-State Securities Transactions, 20 U.Rich.L.Rev. 139 (1986); Note, What to Do With Merit Review, 65 Neb.L.Rev. 413 (1986).

With respect to non-issuer transactions, see Note, Regulation of Nonissuer Transactions Under Federal and State Securities Registration Laws, 78

---

4. West's Ann.Cal.Corp.Code §§ 25101(a), (b), (c), 25104(a). Section 25101(a) also exempts those securities which are exempted from registration under Section 12(g) of the 1934 Act by Section 12(g)(2)(G) (i.e., the stock of insurance companies which are subjected to comparable state regulation). The suggestion that Section 12(g), as opposed to listing in a privately-published "manual", be made the basis for exemption from regulation of secondary trading in state blue-sky laws was first made in Gray and Rosen, Section 12(g) and Blue Sky Laws, 20 Bus.Law 1075 (1965). This article did not come to the attention of the California committee drafting the new securities law prior to the introduction of the bill. It arrived at the same idea independently.

Harv.L.Rev. 1635 (1965); Note, Nonissuer Transactions Under the California Securities Law of 1968, 21 Stan.L.Rev. 152 (1968); Note, Secondary Trading in Securities: Labyrinth Beneath the Blue Sky, 1969 Wash.U.L.Q. 41; 1 Marsh & Volk, Practice Under the California Securities Laws, at Ch. 10 (Rev. ed. 1986).

KREIS v. MATES INVESTMENT FUND, INC.
United States Court of Appeals, Eighth Circuit, 1973.
473 F.2d 1308.

Before BRIGHT and STEPHENSON, CIRCUIT JUDGES, and SMITH, DISTRICT JUDGE (sitting by designation).

PER CURIAM: The matter before us is an action for rescission. The plaintiff, Fred P. Kreis, Jr. (hereafter "Kreis"), a citizen and resident of Missouri, bought shares of the defendant Mates Investment Fund, Inc. (hereafter, the "Fund") by mail, relying upon a glowing account thereof published in Barron's National Business and Financial Weekly in the issue dated June 3, 1968.[1] Eventually Kreis became unhappy with his purchase. Hence this action.

The ground of rescission asserted was noncompliance by the Fund with the registration provisions of the Missouri Uniform Securities Act, Chapter 409, RSMo 1969 (hereafter the Act, or the "new" Act).

* * *

It was the holding of the District Court that, upon the facts * * * stipulated, although there was an offer by Kreis to buy the shares of the Fund under Section 409.415(c), there was no acceptance thereof in Missouri and hence that the Act does not apply to the purchase. In addition, it was held that * * * [a] stock dividend of 952 shares was outside the coverage of the Act, being exempt under Section 409.401(j)(6) thereof. The Court thus having concluded that the Fund was not liable to Kreis with respect to the sale of the original 2,178 shares or the stock dividend of 952 shares, did not reach the issue of the liability of Frederick S. Mates, asserted by reason of his being the controlling officer and director of the Fund.

The principal issues on appeal turn on the interpretation of the terms offer and acceptance under the Act. The appellant, Kreis, argues that the Court below erred in holding that the offer to buy the securities was not both made and accepted in Missouri. The appellee Fund asserts that neither the offer nor the acceptance can be deemed to have occurred in Missouri.

The "new" Missouri Uniform Securities Act represents a substantial adoption of the Uniform Securities Act. The portion with which we are here principally concerned is a separate section dealing with what was aptly termed (by the draftsmen of the Uniform Act) to be the "bewildering state of affairs" in the case law governing transactions which crossed state lines. "In order to resolve many uncertainties in this area of conflict of laws, the draftsmen undertook in Section 414 of the Uniform Act [Section 415 of the new Missouri Act] to codify basic rules to determine the applicability of the substantive provisions of the Act to interstate securities transactions and to define the jurisdiction of the courts over nonresidents in actions under the Act."

---

1. This Weekly was at the time published and printed entirely without the State of Missouri. Its circulation in the state was less than one-third of its total circulation. See Section 409.415(c) RSMo 1969.

The Act provides in part as follows:

409.415 "Scope of the act and service of process

(c) *For the purpose of this section,* an offer to sell or to buy is made in this state, whether or not either party is then present in this state, when the offer (1) originates from the state or (2) is directed by the offeror to this state and received at the place to which it is directed (or any post office in this state in the case of a mailed offer); provided, however, if an offer is directed to an offeree in a state other than this state and that offer would be lawful if made in such other state, then for the purposes of this section such offer is not made in this state.

(d) *For the purpose of this section,* an offer to buy or to sell is accepted in this state when acceptance (1) is communicated to the offeror in this state and (2) has not previously been communicated to the offeror, orally or in writing, outside this state; and acceptance is communicated to the offeror in this state, whether or not either party is then present in this state, when the offeree directs it to the offeror in this state reasonably believing the offeror to be in this state and it is received at the place to which it is directed (or at any post office this state in the case of a mailed acceptance)" [emphasis supplied].

It is clear that what the Act is here seeking is to bring both order and predictability into an area in which decisions in the various states heretofore rendered, "defy generalization." Common law contract concepts, where supplanted by the Act, obviously no longer control in the applicable areas.

With respect to offer and acceptance (with which we are particularly concerned) the Act, as quoted above, defines its own terms but solely, it must be stressed, "for the purpose of this section," that is to say for the scope of the applicability of the new Act and service of process thereunder. For these purposes, "an offer to sell or to buy is made in this state * * * when the offer (1) originates from this state * * *." Stopping at this point it would seem clear upon our facts that Mr. Kreis made an offer in Missouri. But the statute contains a proviso (not found in the Uniform Act) and it is this proviso that gives rise to the controversy over the term "offer." The proviso, according to Jensen and Mills [7] in their article in 24 J.Mo.Bar 60 (1968), had its origin in the problem presented (to use their terms) where a Missouri broker offered to sell to a customer in Illinois a security which was registered under the Securities Law of Illinois but not registered in Missouri. As the Act stood without the proviso the Missouri broker would be violating Missouri law. To eliminate the problem the following proviso was added to the new Act:

"* * * provided, however, if an offer is directed to an offeree in a state other than this state and that offer would be lawful if made in such other state, then for purposes of this section such offer is not made in this state."

The issue as to construction arises over the content of the word "offer" in the clause of the proviso stating "if an offer is directed to an offeree in a state other than this state * * *" Does the word offer, so used, mean offer to buy, offer to sell or both?

We turn to the defining section of the Act, Section 409.401(j)(2). There we find the word "offer" defined in terms of an offer to sell and equated to an

---

7. Chairman, and member, respectively, of the Securities Law Subcommittee of the Missouri Bar, which drafted the new Missouri Uniform Securities Act. See 24 J.Mo.Bar at 62 and 63.

"offer to sell." The District Court concluded, under the plain words of such definition, that the word "offer," so used, applies only to offers to sell and not to offers to buy. Such construction, moreover, makes sense not only in the light of what the draftsmen of the Act were seeking to accomplish, supra, but also in the practical realities of the market since offers to buy, as such, would rarely be illegal under any law. We conclude, with the District Court, that "the plaintiff made an offer to buy the Fund shares in Missouri within the meaning of Section 409.415(c)."

With regard to acceptance, again it is to be stressed that the Act does not speak in terms of general contract law, with all of the complexities and subtleties acquired over years of classroom hypothetical questions (can the offer to pay $100 for touching the top of the flagpole be revoked as the offeree's hand reaches out for the touch?), but solely as to "acceptance in this state" and "[f]or the purpose of this section," that is, for scope of coverage under the new Act and service of process. In the subsection devoted to acceptance, Section 409.415(d), the stress is upon communication. Substantially, an offer is accepted here in Missouri when it is "communicated to the offeror in this state" (and has not theretofore been communicated outside the state). And it is "communicated to the offeror in this state" when the offeree directs it to him here and it is received where directed. At that point, for the purpose of the new Act, the offer has been accepted in Missouri.

In construing the above Subsection (d) the appellee urges that the mailing of the confirmation into Missouri "would constitute acceptance in this state only if that confirmation constituted the Fund's 'acceptance' of appellant's offer to buy." But, it goes on, such confirmation was not an acceptance, since acceptance had already been "accomplished by the Fund's performance."

The difficulty with the argument is that it ignores the plain language of the Act. We are concerned with (1) acceptance "in this state" (2) for the purposes of this Act, and, as we have noted, such acceptance turns upon communication. Consequently, whether there has been a prior acceptance under orthodox contracts principles in New York, or whether acceptance is accomplished by the precise contents of some communication relating thereto, is not material to the resolution of the applicability of the new Act to the transaction. For, in either event, it is communication to the Missouri offeror that is the critical requirement. When that takes place the offer "is accepted in this state," provided, of course, that there has been no previous communication "to the offeror, orally or in writing, outside this state."

We note, in passing, that such is also the interpretation stated in Logan's Blue Sky Ways and Byways in Missouri, 25 J.Mo.Bar 460, 464 (1969), in these terms: "Furthermore, the situs of an acceptance is Missouri if it was originally communicated to the offeror in Missouri." The official comments to the Act also support such interpretation. Comment 8 thereof states:

"If the selling dealer in State S merely sends a confirmation or delivers a security into State B, or the buyer in State B sends a check in payment from within State B, the statute of State B does not apply *except when under 414(d) the confirmation or delivery constitutes the seller's acceptance of the buyer's offer to buy.*" (Emphasis supplied.)

Section 414(d), referred to in the quoted Comment is, it will be noted, the acceptance subsection of the Uniform Securities Act, with its stress upon communication "to the offeror in this state."

In view of the stipulated fact that the only communication received by Kreis as to the action taken upon his offer, namely its acceptance in New York, was the written confirmation of the purchase, mailed by the Fund to

Kreis, addressed to him, and received by him, at his home in Missouri, we hold that under the terms of Section 409.415(d) there was acceptance in this state. We need not, then, explore appellant's arguments that the terms of his offer were not exactly complied with, involving thus a rejection, a counter-offer, and the completion of the contract only upon Kreis' acceptance of the allegedly modified terms. Such orthodox contractual complexities have, wisely we think, been discarded by the terms of the Act for purposes of the scope and enforcement thereof.

The appellee, in closing, urges that if we find both offer and acceptance to have taken place in Missouri, we go further and hold that "the Missouri Act would unconstitutionally deprive the Fund of due process of law, through the extraterritorial abrogation of contract rights which arose in New York." So far as our study of this record reveals, no such issue was pleaded below, if argued it is not adequately reflected in the record before us, and it is not touched upon in the trial court's opinion. We thus decline the invitation tendered. Ludwig v. Marion Laboratories, Inc., 465 F.2d 114 (8th Cir.1972). Nor do we rule upon the disposition of the stock dividend, or the value thereof, received by Kreis, such issues not having been reached by the District Court in the light of its liability ruling.

Reversed and remanded for further proceedings not inconsistent with this opinion.

JURISDICTION OF A STATE OVER OUT–OF–STATE SELLERS TO IN–STATE BUYERS

Under the conflict of laws provisions of the Uniform Securities Act, which have been adopted in a number of states including California,[1] the question whether a particular state's Blue Sky Law applies to a transaction involving a sale by an out-of-state seller to one of its residents turns upon the location of the offer and acceptance under the definitions in that statute and whether the transaction involves an offer to sell which is accepted by the buyer or an offer to buy which is accepted by the seller. The location of an offer or acceptance is defined to include *both* the state from which it is transmitted and the state to which it is directed. If an offer to *sell* is made in a state, that gives jurisdiction regardless of where the acceptance may be made. However, if the transaction is initiated by an offer to *buy*, then both the offer and the acceptance must be "in this state" in order for it to have jurisdiction.

Under these provisions, if an out-of-state seller directs an offer to sell (by mail or telephone, or in person) to a buyer in State A, then the jurisdiction of State A attaches at that moment and there may have already been a violation of State A's Blue Sky Law if the issue was not qualified or exempted. However, in the Kreis case the advertisement in the national magazine seen by the plaintiff did not confer jurisdiction because there is an exclusion from the definition of "offer" for this purpose of such an advertisement in a newspaper or magazine "which has had more than two-thirds of its circulation outside this state during the last 12 months" or carried on a radio or television program originating outside the state.

---

1. Uniform Securities Act, § 414; West's Ann.Cal.Corp.Code, § 25008. The language of the Uniform Act was somewhat condensed in California without intending any change of substance. In addition, one minor provision was added dealing with the delivery of a security "in this state" where both the seller and the buyer are domiciled "in this state."

Accordingly, in the Kreis case it was necessary to base jurisdiction upon the offer to buy sent by the plaintiff to the fund in New York and to find that both the offer to buy *and its acceptance* were in Missouri. Since the offer to buy was directed from Missouri and the acceptance was communicated to the plaintiff in Missouri, the court holds that the jurisdiction of Missouri attached even though the acceptance in a contractual sense may have occurred in New York and the contract performed in New York by the issuance of the shares before any communication to the plaintiff in Missouri.

In Robbins v. Pacific Eastern Corporation,[2] decided under the former California Corporate Securities Law, the court held that, where there was clearly an offer made to buyers in California and even a contract of sale made there by acceptance in California (although there was argument over whether it might have later been amended in New York), the California law nevertheless did not apply because the transaction was closed by the actual payment for and delivery of the shares in New York.[3] This case is directly contrary to the Kreis case and would seem to have clearly been overruled by the provisions of the 1968 California statute. However, it might still have some persuasive authority in those states which have not adopted these conflict of laws provisions of the Uniform Securities Act.

It seems clear that this scope of application of state Blue Sky Laws is not subject to any constitutional objection. In Travelers Health Ass'n v. Commonwealth of Virginia State Corporation Commission [4] the Supreme Court upheld the validity under the due process clause of service by mail in a cease and desist proceeding by the State of Virginia upon an out-of-state seller which had communicated only by a mail solicitation with residents of Virginia. The question of whether a state may, under the due process clause and the commerce clause, constitutionally regulate such activities was reached explicitly only by Justice Douglas in his concurring opinion in the Travelers Health Ass'n case. However, the opinion of the other four majority justices would seem to indicate that they would concur in his views. What would be the point of sustaining service of process upon the out-of-state corporation if the whole regulation was constitutionally inapplicable to it? However, the activities of the existing members of the Association in soliciting new business from other Virginia residents may be argued to distinguish this case (although it is unlikely) from one where nothing but a mail solicitation originating out of state is involved. Justice Douglas said: "This device for soliciting business in Virginia may be unconventional and unorthodox; but it operates functionally precisely as though appellants had formally designated the Virginia members as their agents."

---

2. 8 Cal.2d 241, 65 P.2d 42 (1937).

3. The Robbins case was followed in Robinson v. Cupples Container Co., 316 F.Supp. 1362 (N.D.Cal.1970), despite the fact that the statute, which at the time of the Robbins case only declared void securities "issued" without a permit [Cal.Stats.1917, Ch. 532, § 12, p. 679], had been amended before the Robinson case to refer to securities "*sold or* issued" without a permit [Cal.Stats.1947, Ch. 129, § 1, p. 649; codified as former § 26100 of the Cal.Corp.Code].

4. 339 U.S. 643 (1950). See, however, Gaillard v. Field, 381 F.2d 25 (10th Cir.1967), in which the court held that where the solicitation emanated from Oklahoma into California to a California resident, and suit was brought in Oklahoma, the Federal district court in Oklahoma would apply the *Oklahoma* definition of a "security" which resulted in absolving the seller from liability (because the oil and gas interests which he sold were not "securities" under the Oklahoma blue sky law, although they were under that of California). The decision seems clearly wrong—under this theory the seller could have gone to Delaware, which formerly had no blue sky law, and sell from there to residents of every state in the Union without liability.

As to whether or not a particular communication by an out-of-state seller constitutes an "offer", it is clear that this term in the state Blue Sky Laws, as under the 1933 Act, is much broader than the common-law contractual sense of the word. Such definitions commonly include any "solicitation" of a sale, as well as any "attempt to dispose of" the security. Some also proscribe, as did the California statute at the time of the B. C. Turf & Country Club case,[5] any "negotiation" for a sale prior to compliance with the Blue Sky Law. It is not clear to what extent, if at all, "negotiation" covers more ground than "solicitation." Perhaps the latter suggests that the seller has to be the active party, whereas certainly "negotiation" could occur entirely at the instance and urging of the buyer.

This broad scope of the statutes does not cause any great difficulty in the case of a public offering, except occasionally with respect to the distribution of a Preliminary Prospectus. In such an offering the buyer is given no choice as to terms, but is presented with a take-it-or-leave-it proposition. Therefore, the first offer to or solicitation of prospective buyers can be delayed until the issue has been registered. However, a problem may arise when there is a "rights offering" by a corporation which has shareholders in every state in the Union. The corporation mails a warrant to each shareholder offering the right to subscribe to additional shares, which can be exercised by signing an acceptance form and mailing it back to the corporation or its warrant agent. Does the corporation have to go to the expense of qualifying this issue in a state where, for example, only two shareholders holding insignificant amounts of stock reside? If the issue cannot be qualified in a particular state, but the shareholders have pre-emptive rights, the corporation is then faced with the necessity of perhaps violating that state's Blue Sky Law or violating the pre-emptive rights of those shareholders. It is for this reason that many statutes, including the Uniform Securities Act, exempt such rights offerings, but others do not.

If a person violating the Blue Sky Law of a state either stays out of the state entirely or leaves the jurisdiction before the state officials or the buyers of the securities take action, there is a practical problem of bringing him to account for his violations. Some of the state statutes do not contain any provision for substituted service upon a non-resident violating the state Blue Sky law along the lines of the non-resident motorist statutes. Almost all statutes require the filing of a consent to service of process in connection with the registration of securities for sale, but a person who simply ignores the Blue Sky Law does not register and therefore has not filed the consent. However, the Uniform Securities Act, in Section 414(h), contains a provision for substituted service of process similar to one which was upheld in Paulos v. Best Securities Incorporated.[6] Approximately half of the states and the District of Columbia and Puerto Rico now have such a provision in their Blue Sky Laws, most of which have obviously been copied from the Uniform Act; however, many States have adopted large portions of the Uniform Act but have not included this provision.

There would seem to be little doubt of the constitutionality of such a provision in the light of the McGee Case.[7] See Loss & Cowett, Blue Sky Law

---

5. B.C. Turf & Country Club v. Daugherty, 94 Cal.App.2d 320, 210 P.2d 760 (1949). See, also, Intermountain Title Guaranty Co. v. Egbert, 52 Idaho 402, 16 P.2d 390 (1932).

6. 260 Minn. 283, 109 N.E.2d 576 (1961).

7. McGee v. International Life Insurance Co., 355 U.S. 220, 78 S.Ct. 199 (1957).

See Annot., Construction and Application, as to Isolated Acts or Transactions, of State Statutes or Rules of Court Predicating In Personam Jurisdiction over Non-residents or Foreign Corporations Upon the Doing of an Act, or Upon Doing or Transacting Business or "any" Business, Within the State, 27 A.L.R.3d 397 (1969); Loss, Securities Regulation (Supp.1969) 2255–2256.

220–222, 407–409 (1958) (written before the McGee case). It is possible that the courts may take the lead in this regard and authorize substituted service to the full extent constitutionally permissible, without any legislative authorization.[8]

With regard to criminal extradition for a violation of the Blue Sky laws, see L. Loss & E. Cowett, pp. 222–224.

JURISDICTION OF A STATE OVER IN–STATE SELLERS TO OUT–OF–STATE BUYERS

There would seem to be little doubt that a state has jurisdiction, if it chooses to exercise it, over sellers located in that state even though they are selling to out-of-state buyers. There is also no doubt that the definitions in the Uniform Securities Act make that state's Blue Sky Law applicable whenever the seller directs any offers to sell from that state to persons out of the state. This scope of the provisions was justified by the authors of the Uniform Act on the basis that a state should not permit itself to be used as the basis for the manufacture of fraudulent devices for export to other states. However, it would seem that this reasoning overlooked the fact that virtually every state has a Blue Sky Law, and if the state of the buyer's residence undertakes to protect him by requiring qualification of the transaction, the state of the seller's residence certainly has little interest in duplicating that effort (except to give employment to its bureaucrats).

This is the problem which led to the amendment to the Uniform Act in Missouri referred to in the Kreis case, under which an offer to sell directed from Missouri to another state does not give jurisdiction to Missouri if it is lawful (i.e., qualified or exempted) in the other state. The same problem was recognized in California during the drafting of the Corporate Securities Law of 1968. However, the statute was not amended, but it was agreed that the problem would be taken care of by a rule of the Commissioner, which was done prior to the effective date of the statute. That Rule[1] exempts from the qualification requirements of the California statute any offer or sale of a security by a broker-dealer licensed in California to any out-of-state resident if the security is either qualified for sale under the law of the purchaser's residence or is exempt from such qualification under that law.

The California rule does not go as far as the Missouri amendment, since it requires that a California broker-dealer be involved in the transaction. Therefore, it does not extend to a direct private placement by a California-based corporation to out-of-state purchasers. However, the California Commissioner of Corporations has been quite liberal in interpreting the scope of the term "offer" in this situation, and has ruled that various activities in California do not constitute an offer from that state where the transaction is predominantly negotiated in, and is closed in, the foreign state. For example, in one case where a California-based company made a private placement to purchasers in New York through the agency of a New York broker-dealer (and the rule was therefore not applicable because the offer and sale was not by a California-licensed broker-dealer), and the board of the company approved the transaction in California, documents were prepared there for the closing in New York and communications passed back and forth between the California corporation and

---

8. See Long v. Mishicot Modern Dairy, Inc., 252 Cal.App.2d 425, 60 Cal.Rptr. 432 (1967).

1. Rule 260.105.2, California Administrative Code, Title 10.

the New York broker-dealer, the Commissioner nevertheless ruled that the transaction did not have to be qualified in California.[2] He said:

"The Corporate Securities Law of 1968 was enacted for the protection of California investors and for the regulation of broker-dealers, agents, and investment advisers operating in California. Pursuant to Sec. 260.105.2, Title 10, Adm. Code, a sale of securities in California by a broker-dealer licensed under the Corporate Securities Law of 1968, even if the purchaser is a nonresident, is not exempted from the qualification requirements of Sec. 25110 and Sec. 25130, unless the securities are qualified for sale under the law of the purchaser's residence or exempt from such qualification under that law; but a sale made outside the State of California is within the jurisdiction of the state where the sale takes place and that state may take whatever legislative, administrative, or judicial action it deems appropriate for the protection of investors within its borders. The Commissioner of Corporations of the State of California does not interfere with the sovereign power of such other state to regulate a business transaction executed in such other state and subject to regulation by that state in accordance with the dictates of local policy."

JURISDICTION OF A STATE OVER REORGANIZATIONS AND RECAPITALIZATIONS OF MULTI–STATE CORPORATIONS

In Western Air Lines, Inc. v. Sobieski[1] the California District Court of Appeal held that the California Commissioner of Corporations had jurisdiction to require Western Air Lines, a Delaware corporation, to obtain a permit to amend its articles of incorporation to change from cumulative voting to straight voting, where Western had its principal office in California, a substantial portion of its revenues were derived from business done in California and a large portion of its shares were held by California residents (it was unclear whether or not this amounted to more than half, depending upon how you counted "street name" holdings; in any event, the holdings by California residents were much larger than those of the residents of any other single state).

The court emphasized the fact that Western, though incorporated in Delaware, did not engage in business in that state, and had its "commercial domicile" in California;[2] however, the court failed to give guidance as to whether the Commissioner's jurisdiction over reorganizations applied only to "pseudo-foreign" corporations.

The problem involved in the Western Air Lines case is significantly different from those involved in an initial sale of securities in a multi-state transaction.

2. California Commissioner of Corporations, Interpretive Opinion No. 69/65 (July 9, 1969).

1. 191 Cal.App.2d 399, 12 Cal.Rptr. 719 (1961). Upon the remand of this case the Superior Court again held for the plaintiff, Western Air Lines, on the basis that there was no substantial evidence to support the Commissioner's determination that the change from cumulative voting to straight voting was unfair, unjust and inequitable. Upon appeal, the District Court of Appeal again reversed the trial judge and ordered Western Air Lines to restore cumulative voting, Western Air Lines, Inc. v. Schutz-

bank, 258 Cal.App.2d 218, 66 Cal.Rptr. 293 (1968). And see People, ex rel. Sobieski v. Western Air Lines, Inc., 258 Cal.App.2d 213, 66 Cal.Rptr. 316 (1968); Bixby v. Pierno, 4 Cal.2d 130, 93 Cal.Rptr. 234, 481 P.2d 242 (1971).

2. The court cited Southern Pacific Co. v. McColgan, 68 Cal.App.2d 45, 156 P.2d 81 (1945). See also Wheeling Steel Corporation v. Fox, 298 U.S. 193 (1936) (state of commercial domicile may impose a tax upon foreign corporation having only a "paper domicile" in Delaware measured by income derived from its intangible assets).

In the initial sale of securities through a proposed nationwide distribution, if the securities cannot be qualified in a particular state or the promoters do not want to submit to the requirements of that state, it will simply be omitted from the distribution. On the other hand, where there is a proposed change in the rights of existing securities, the change must be made in *all* of the securities of a given class or in none. This raises the theoretical possibility that, where such securities are held by residents of every state in the Union, the change might be blocked by the Blue Sky official in one state where one shareholder lives (assuming that he has jurisdiction) even though it is approved by similar officials in all of the other 49 states. This is purely a theoretical possibility at the moment, regardless of the ruling on the question of jurisdiction, since the only state which effectively regulates such changes is California.

The California statute clearly required a permit for a change in the voting rights of outstanding shares such as that attempted in the Western Air Lines case. However, it then contained no provision indicating to what extent jurisdiction was asserted in this regard over foreign corporations. Thus this case presented both a question of interpretation of the statute and a question of the constitutionality of the statute as interpreted. Two extreme positions could be taken, both of which are manifestly absurd. (1) If a foreign corporation does no business in California but has one shareholder residing in California holding one share, with 100,000 shareholders holding 10,000,000 shares residing elsewhere, the California Commissioner can refuse to permit any change in the rights of all those shares, even if approved by a 100% vote of the shareholders (including the one residing in California), unless he finds that it is "fair, just and equitable." (2) If a corporation does all of its business in California and all of its shareholders reside there, the California Commissioner has no jurisdiction over a proposed change in the rights of its outstanding shares simply because it is incorporated in a foreign state. Somewhere between these extremes must lie both the legislative intent and the constitutionally permissible area of regulation.

The former regulations of the California Commissioner of Corporations referred to by the court in the *Western Air Lines* case as creating a class of "pseudo-foreign" corporations concerned the question of cumulative voting rights. The Commissioner initially issued a proposed regulation to the effect that no stock could be sold in California which did not carry cumulative voting rights. There was of course a great outcry from the brokerage fraternity in California, who knew that they would simply be cut out of the syndicate in every case where the foreign issuer chose not to offer its securities in California rather than comply with this requirement. When the rule was adopted it was revised to "view with disfavor" the absence of cumulative voting rights only in the case of a foreign corporation "whose principal business or principal place of business is located in California."[3] In the case of other foreign corporations, the absence of cumulative voting was only a "negative factor."[4] This meant that it would result in the denial of a permit only if the Commissioner also had some other reason for refusing it. In addition, the absence of cumulative voting had to be disclosed in the prospectus.[5] These provisions were repealed by the new regulations issued under the California Corporate Securities Law of 1968.

The California Corporate Securities Law of 1968 established as a test of the jurisdiction of the California Commissioner of Corporations to regulate recapitalizations and reorganizations the record ownership by California residents of 25% or more of the securities affected by the action. However, securities held

---

3. Former 10 Cal.Adm.Code § 367.1(b).   5. Id., § 844.

4. Id., § 367.1(c).

in "street name" are excluded from the computation because of the practice of national brokerage houses of giving the addresses of their main offices in New York for all street-name certificates; and securities owned directly or indirectly by any one person who controls 50% or more of the outstanding securities of that class also are excluded.[6] In addition, securities listed or approved for listing on any national securities exchange qualifying under West's Ann.Cal.Corp.Code, § 25100(o) are exempt from the jurisdiction of the California Commissioner of Corporations with respect to recapitalizations and reorganizations.

The suggestion has been made that these statutes may violate the supremacy, commerce and full faith and credit clauses of the United States Constitution.[7] We believe, however, that the California legislation asserting jurisdiction over the modification of outstanding securities of foreign corporations where twenty-five percent or more of the securities affected are held by residents of California will withstand an attack based upon those grounds.[8]

A state may require a foreign corporation to obtain a permit under a merit type statute to sell securities on original issue in that state despite objections based on commerce and full faith and credit considerations.[9] Two conditions imposed on foreign corporations under the Corporate Securities Law may be those of cumulative voting and annual election of directors. It has never been contended that imposing such conditions on original issues would violate the commerce clause. Moreover, Section 18 of the Securities Act of 1933 specifically preserves state jurisdiction of any state securities commission in the administration of its securities laws despite registration under the Securities Act of 1933. The modification of outstanding securities by the majority in an unfair reorganization or recapitalization deprives the outside security holders of any choice other than to accept the new securities or exercise any appraisal right. It would seem absurd to permit a corporation to incorporate in Delaware and accept a condition of cumulative voting upon the issuance of shares in California and then allow the corporation to eliminate the provision through charter amendment or through a "phantom" merger.[10]

Moreover, a statute providing for administrative supervision of reorganization or recapitalizations is by no means a novel idea. Under the Interstate Commerce Act, the Interstate Commerce Commission requires a permit for a carrier to change the rights of outstanding securities by way of a charter amendment or otherwise, even though authorized by the law of the state of incorporation; it has been held that the modification entails the issue and sale of a new security.[11] Section 11(e), 6 and 7 of the Public

6. West's Ann.Cal.Corp.Code, § 25103(b), (c) and (d).

7. See, e.g. De Mott, Perspectives on Choice of Law for Corporate Internal Affairs, 48 L. & Contemp. Prob. 161, 180, 183–197 (Summer 1985), discussing West Ann.Cal.Gen.Corp.L. § 2115.

8. West's Cal.Corp.Code Ann. § 25103(b) and (c). See H. Marsh & R. Volk, Practice Under the California Corporate Securities Laws § 7.06 (1986 rev.).

9. See Hall v. Geiger-Jones Co., 242 U.S. 539 (1917) (Ohio); Caldwell v. Sioux Falls Stock Yards Co., 242 U.S. 559 (1917) (South Dakota) and Merrick v. Halsey &

Co., 242 U.S. 568 (1917) (Michigan); L. Loss & E. Cowett, Blue Sky Law (1958).

10. Cf. Pinney v. Nelson, 183 U.S. 145 (1901); (Former California statute applying to any foreign corporation doing business in California proportional liability upon shareholders for all corporate debts held constitutional); Peck v. Noee, 154 Cal. 351, 97 P. 865 (1908); Provident Gold Mining Co. v. Haynes, 173 Cal. 44, 159 P. 155 (1916).

11. United States v. New York, New Haven & Hartford Railroad Co., 276 F.2d 525 (2d Cir.1960) cert. denied 362 U.S. 961 (1960). Cf. Western Air Lines v. Sobieski,

Utility Holding Company Act of 1935 gives the SEC similar powers over reorganizations and recapitalizations and in connection with securities transactions.[12]

As for the obligation of other states to give "full faith and credit" to the General Corporation Law of Delaware, by the same token, Delaware must give full faith and credit to California Corporations Code § 25103(b) and (c) relating to reorganizations and recapitalizations. Marsh states with respect to matters covered by Section 2115 of the California Corporations Code relating to "pseudo-foreign corporations": "As applied to a corporation which has all of its property in the State of California and has a piece of paper lodged in a public office in Delaware and no other relationship whatever to that state, the argument that California must give 'full faith and credit' to the Delaware law becomes ludicrous."[13] The only question under Section 25103(b) and (c) would seem to be whether the twenty-five percent jurisdictional threshold is reasonable under all of the circumstances of the case.

For a general discussion of conflict of laws problems in connection with state securities regulation, see 1 Marsh & Volk, Practice Under the California Securities Laws § 7.06 (1986 ed.); Loss & Cowett, Blue Sky Law 186–210 (1958). See, also, Note, Interstate Scope of the Uniform Securities Act—A Case Analysis, 1974 Wash.U.L.Q. 421; Note, B.C. Turf Revisited—Preliminary Negotiations and the Sophisticated Investor under the California Corporate Securities Law of 1968, 46 So.Cal.L.Rev. 856 (1974); Loss, Conflict of Laws and the Blue Sky Laws, 71 Harv.L.Rev. 209 (1957) (an earlier version of Chapter V of the Loss and Cowett book); Bickford, California Corporate Securities Law of 1968: Some Interpretations, Some Problem Areas, 2 Pac.L.J. 497, 499–507 (1971); Jurisdiction of States under Blue Sky Laws, 17 U.Chi.L.Rev. 382 (1950); Note, 26 Calif.L.Rev. 265 (1938).

For a general discussion of conflict of laws problems in connection with pseudo-foreign corporation statutes, see Wilson v. Louisiana-Pacific Resources, Inc., 138 Cal.App.3d 216, 187 Cal.Rptr. 852 (1982); Marsh's California Corporation Law §§ 25.17–25.20 (2d ed. 1982); Shaffer v. Heitner, 433 U.S. 186 (1977); Allstate Insurance Co. v. Hague, 449 U.S. 302 (1981); Armstrong v. Pomerance, 423 A.2d 174 (Del.1980); Cf. Dynamics Corporation of America v. CTS Corporation, 794 F.2d 250 (7th Cir.1986); De Mott, Perspectives on Choice of Law for Corporate Internal Affairs, 48 L. & Contemp. Prob. 161 (Summer 1985); Kozyris, Corporate Wars and Choice of Law, 1985 Duke L.J. 1; Ratner & Schwartz, The Impact of Shaffer v. Heitner on the Substantive Law of Corporations, 45 Brooklyn L.Rev. 641 (1979); Kirgis, The Roles of Due Process and Full Faith and Credit in Choice of Law, 62 Cornell L.Rev. 94, 139 (1976); Oldham, California Regulates Pseudo-Foreign Corporations—Trampling Upon the Tramp, 17 Santa Clara L.Rev. 85 (1977); Halloran & Hammer, Section 2115 of the New California General Corporation Law—The Application of California Corporation Law to Foreign Corporations, 23 UCLA L.Rev. 1282 (1976); Horowitz, The Commerce Clause as a Limitation on State Choice of Law Doctrine, 84 Harv.L.Rev. 806 (1971); Note, The Pseudo-Foreign Corporation in California, 28 Hastings L.J. 119 (1976).

191 Cal.App.2d 399, 12 Cal.Rptr. 719 (1961). See Note, Protection of Shareholders Interests in Recapitalizations of Publicly Held Corporations, 58 Colum.L.Rev. 1030 (1958).

Company Act, 49 Yale L.J. 1297 (1940); Note, The Rights of Cumulative Preferred Stockholders Under the Public Utilities Holding Company Act, 52 Harv.L.Rev. 1331 (1939).

12. See Note, Recapitalization under Section 11(e) of the Public Utility Holding

13. 3 Marsh's California Corporation Law 238 (2d ed. 1982).

The *Western Air Lines* case is discussed in Reese & Kaufman, The Law Governing Corporate Affairs: Choice of Law and the Impact of Full Faith and Credit 58 Colum.L.Rev. 1118 (1958). See, also, Note, State Regulation of Securities Issued in Corporate Reorganizations: A Cloud in the Blue Sky, 25 Case Wes.Res.L.Rev. 149 (1974); Sobieski, State Blue Sky Jurisdiction Over Foreign Corporations, 14 Hastings L.J. 75 (1962); Small, Changes in Rights, Preferences, Privileges and Restrictions on Outstanding Securities Under the California Corporate Securites Law, 14 Hastings L.J. 94 (1962); Kaplan, Foreign Corporations and Local Corporate Policy, 21 Vand.L.Rev. 433 (1966); 4 Loss, Securities Regulation (Supp.1969) 2246–2251.

CIVIL LIABILITY UNDER STATE BLUE SKY LAWS

Formerly, most of the state Blue Sky laws did not contain extensive or detailed provisions regarding civil liability, but merely declared that securities issued in violation of the qualification requirements (and frequently certain other requirements) were either "void" or "voidable."[1] It has usually been held that securities issued in violation of the registration requirements are voidable at the election of the buyer even in those States where the statute makes no mention at all of civil liability.[2] In recent years, there has been a tendency to enact more detailed civil liability provisions[3] under the influence of the Uniform Securities Act, the civil liability provisions of which are modeled upon Section 12 of the Federal Securities Act of 1933.[4]

Under these various statutes, the issuer is usually held absolutely liable for any violation of the qualification requirements of the Blue Sky Laws, as it is under the 1933 Act.[5] In addition, there may be liability for violating the "conditions" of a qualification which is obtained.[6]

Until the adoption or adaptation of the Uniform Securities Act (1956) by most of the States, virtually no State had any statutory provisions imposing civil liability for "fraud" in the sale of securities; where there were any civil liability provisions at all, they related solely to violation of the qualification requirements. However, the Uniform Securities Act (1956) incorporated a civil liability provision in favor of *buyers* modeled upon Section 12(2) of the 1933 Act. That act also incorporated a copy of Rule 10b–5 in Section 101, but Section 410(h) expressly states that the act does not create any liability other than that specified in the latter section. The comments explain that this is intended to prevent the development of any civil liability based upon the Rule 10b–5 language in Section 101. The state of Washington adopted a number of provisions of the 1956 Uniform Act, including Section 101 [Rule 10b–5], but did not adopt the language excluding civil liability for violation of that section. In Shermer v. Baker, a Washington court held that the Washington version of Section 101 gave rise to a private right of action for violation of that section.[7]

The Shermer case, however, is not authority for the imposition of civil liability under Section 101 in any state which has adopted the entire Uniform

1. 3 Loss, Securities Regulation 1631–1636, and chart at 1662–1666 (2d ed. 1961).

2. Id. at 1661–1669.

3. Compare L. Loss & E. Cowett, Blue Sky Law 147–153 (1958), with 3 Loss, Securities Regulation 1643–1654 (2d ed. 1961).

4. Uniform Securities Act § 410; Uniform Securities Act (1985) § 605.

5. See Weidner v. Engelhart, 176 N.W.2d 509 (N.D.1970).

6. Randall v. California Land Buyers' Syndicate, 217 Cal. 594, 20 P.2d 331 (1933).

7. Shermer v. Baker, 2 Wash.App. 845, 472 P.2d 589 (1970). Accord, Kittilson v. Ford, 93 Wash.2d 223, 608 P.2d 264 (1980).

Act. In Goodman v. Poland[8] the court held that the Maryland Uniform Securities Act does not give any civil cause of action to sellers of securities under Section 101. The plaintiff argued that while the statute said that it did not "create" any other cause of action, that did not prevent the "implication" by the court of a cause of action. The court said: "The trouble with plaintiffs' argument is that it disregards the clear contrary intent of sections 13 and 34. Those sections, which were adopted nearly verbatim from sections 101 and 410 of the Uniform Securities Act, clearly differentiate between the rights accorded thereunder to defrauded buyers and sellers. * * * Moreover, as the Notes of the Commissioners on Uniform State Laws make clear, those sections were specifically designed to avoid the development of an implied cause of action thereunder in favor of a defrauded seller."[9]

The California Corporate Securities Law of 1968[10] establishes the most detailed civil liability provisions of any similar statute. Under Sections 25400 and 25500 (modeled upon Section 9 of the Securities Exchange Act of 1934) any broker-dealer or other person selling or offering for sale or buying or offering to buy a security, who willfully makes a false or misleading statement for the purpose of inducing the purchase or sale of such security by others, is liable to any other person who purchases or sells any security at a price which was affected by such act, for damages equal to the difference between the price paid or received and the price which would have obtained in the absence of the illegal manipulation. Similar liability results from matched orders, transactions effected for the purpose of manipulating the price, tipster sheets, etc.

Under Sections 25401 and 25501, any person who sells or purchases a security by means of any false or misleading statement is liable to the person who purchases the security from him or sells the security to him either for rescission or for damages, unless the defendant proves that the plaintiff knew the facts concerning the untruth or omission or proves that the defendant exercised reasonable care and did not know (or if he had exercised reasonable care would not have known) of the untruth or omission.

Under Sections 25402 and 25502, any "insider" who purchases or sells a security at a time when he knows material information about the issuer which would significantly affect the market price of the security and which is not generally available to the public is liable to the other party to the transaction, unless he has reason to believe that the other party is also in possession of the information or unless the defendant proves that the plaintiff in fact knew the information or that the plaintiff would have purchased or sold at the same price even if the information had been revealed to him. An "insider" is defined as an issuer or any officer, director or controlling person of the issuer or any other person whose relationship to the issuer gives him access, directly or indirectly, to material information about the issuer not generally available to the public. Damages recoverable are the difference between the price paid and the market value which the security would have had if the information known

---

8. 395 F.Supp. 660 (D.Md.1975).

9. Because the Committee drafting the California Corporate Securities Law of 1968 feared that just such an argument would be made, i.e., that implied liabilities are not "created" by the statute but by the common law under the "tort theory" or the "crime theory", it was much more specific in Section 25510 of that statute, which provides: "Except as explicitly provided in this chapter, no civil liability in favor of any private party shall arise against any person by implication from or as a result of the violation of any provision of this law or any rule or order hereunder." In addition, however, the California statute expressly provides civil remedies for sellers as well as buyers; therefore, there should be much less pressure on the courts to invent a remedy than there was under the 1934 Act and will be under the 1956 Uniform Act.

10. West's Ann.Cal.Corp.Code, § 25000 et seq.

to the defendant had been publicly disseminated prior to the transaction and a reasonable time had elapsed for the market to absorb the information.

Under Section 25503, a right of action is given to any person who purchases a security sold in violation of the qualification requirements. However, this section also provides that there is no cause of action under the section if the security is qualified prior to the receipt of any part of the consideration, even though an offer or a contract of sale may have been made before that time, thus abolishing the so-called "infection" doctrine in California under which it was perhaps impossible to avoid civil liability, once an illegal offer had been made prior to qualification, by any means (other than by not carrying out the transaction).

LIABILITY OF DIRECTORS AND OFFICERS FOR VIOLATION OF THE BLUE SKY LAWS

Some of the state Blue Sky laws deal expressly with the question of the liability of directors and officers of a corporation which sells securities in violation of the statute, and such a provision has been included in the Uniform Securities Act.[1] Others make no mention of the liability of directors and officers, but it is generally held that any director or officer who participates or aids in the sale is jointly and severally liable with the corporation for which he is acting.

What is required in order to show participation in the sale by the officer or director? Apparently, under some decisions, a director may become liable merely by participating in the meeting at which the issuance of the securities is approved. In Randall v. California Land Buyers' Syndicate[2] the court said: "The evidence on this phase of the case is that the proposition to exchange the real property for stock was placed before said defendants as directors and the direction for the consummation of the transaction was voted by them." In Davis v. Walker[3] even less was shown. There was no evidence (at least none referred to by the court) to indicate that two of the directors had anything to do with certain violations for which they were held liable, except for the fact that one or the other was a director at the time the transactions occurred. The court reviewed the minutes of three directors' meetings at which they were present and at each of which counsel for the corporation warned the directors that no securities could be sold in Nebraska without the approval of the Department of Banking. There was nothing in these minutes as recited by the court, however, to indicate that they approved the president's going ahead and doing it despite the warning from counsel. While there may be speculation as to the extent of their involvement, on the basis of the evidence it would appear that they were held liable for not *preventing* the president from violating the

---

1. Uniform Securities Act § 605 (1985). See, also, West's Ann.Cal.Corp.Code, § 25504. The latter section reads:

"Every person who directly or indirectly controls a person liable under Section 25501 or 25503, every partner in a firm so liable, every principal executive officer or director of a corporation so liable, every person occupying a similar status or performing similar functions, every employee of a person so liable who materially aids in the act or transaction constituting the violation, and every bro-

ker-dealer or agent who materially aids in the act or transaction constituting the violation, are also liable jointly and severally with and to the same extent as such person, unless the other person who is so liable had no knowledge of or reasonable grounds to believe in the existence of the facts by reason of which the liability is alleged to exist."

2. 217 Cal. 594, 20 P.2d 331 (1933).

3. 170 Neb. 891, 104 N.W.2d 479 (1960).

Nebraska Blue Sky law after receiving these warnings. Should more than this be required for liability? If so, what? See, also, Moerman v. Zipco, Inc.,[4] interpreting the Connecticut Blue Sky Law.

DEFENSES OF PARI DELICTO, WAIVER, ESTOPPEL, RATIFICATION, ETC.

In certain instances, courts will deny a buyer of securities sold in violation of the Blue Sky Laws a right to recover from the seller, because of the buyer's conduct. Various phrases are used to explain this result, such as *pari delicto,* estoppel, waiver and the like. In Hargiss v. Royal Air Properties, Inc.[1] three shareholders formed a corporation and when it fell upon evil days, one of them, who also happened to be the president, sued the corporation for a violation of the California Corporate Securities Law in the issuance of stock to him. The court said:

> "On the other hand, if the trial court took the view that the transactions involved violations of Corporations Code sections 25102 or 25153 or both, it is difficult to understand how plaintiff could avoid the position of being in pari delicto. He was the original moving spirit in the entire enterprise. Everything done prior to April 12, 1957, was under his guidance and direction. At his own insistence he was president of defendant [corporation]. If there were violations he was the one who urged them. These facts are all uncontradicted. * * * As was said in Domenigoni v. Imperial Live Stock etc. Co., 189 Cal. 467, 475, 209 P. 36, 39, in discussing an erroneous finding by the trial court,
>
> " 'But it does not follow that the plaintiff was entitled to any relief. The entire transaction was an attempt to circumvent the law. The notes and agreements were each of them made in violation thereof and are therefore against the policy of the law, as he claims, and void. He was a party to them and is equally guilty with the defendant. In such a case the court will give no relief even if the point is not raised by either party.'
>
> * * * *
>
> "Under the facts presented in the case here at bar it is apparent that if plaintiff had the right to recover, then Heathman and Peister [the other two shareholders] had the same right. No outside investors are involved. Nothing in the evidence shows any greater equities in favor of plaintiff than exist in favor of Heathman and Peister. If any recovery should be had by plaintiff it should be had through an action for dissolution and accounting as between the partners so that all may be treated with equality. To allow plaintiff to recover a separate judgment under the circumstances here present would work a gross inequity to the other partners. If plaintiff is innocent of any conspiracy to violate the Corporate Securities Act, then the evidence certainly could not be said to convict the other partners. The finger of suspicion in that respect, if it points at all, points most strongly at plaintiff."

Compare Holmberg v. Marsden,[2] Russek v. Tomark Jet Components, Inc.,[3] and Popper v. Havana Publications, Inc.,[4] where the doctrine of *pari delicto* or

---

4. 430 F.2d 362 (2d Cir.1970).

1. 206 Cal.App.2d 406, 23 Cal.Rptr. 678 (1962).

2. 39 Cal.2d 592, 248 P.2d 417 (1952).

3. 152 Cal.App.2d 131, 312 P.2d 737 (1957).

4. 122 So.2d 247 (Fla.Ct.App.1960).

estoppel was successfully invoked by the defendants, with Smith v. Turner,[5] Schvaneveldt v. Noy-Burn Milling & Processing Corp.[6] and Randall v. California Land Buyers' Syndicate,[7] where its applicability was denied.[8]

See Symposium: The Operation and Effectiveness of Blue Sky Legislation, 15 Wayne L.Rev. 1401 (1969); Bordwine, Civil Remedies under the Texas Securities Laws, 8 Houston L.Rev. 657 (1971); Hodge, Civil Liability under the Mississippi Securities Act, 43 Miss.L.J. 597 (1972); Note, Regulation of Insider and Tippee Trading in Minnesota, 59 Minn.L.Rev. 223 (1974); Toll, Civil Remedies of Purchasers of Securities under New Hampshire Law, 15 N.H.B.J. 123 (1974); Note, Underdevelopment of Securities Fraud in North Carolina Courts and the Potential Effects of the North Carolina Securities Act of 1975, 53 N.C.L.Rev. 1104 (1975).

With respect to officer and director liability, see Note, Director and Officer Liability under Blue Sky Laws: A Need for Revision, 5 Ga.L.Rev. 128 (1970); Note, Personal civil liability of corporate officers and directors in case of sale of bonds or stock in violation of statutory requirements, 144 A.L.R 1356 (1943); Dahlquist, Regulation and Civil Liability Under the California Corporate Securities Act: III, 34 Calif.L.Rev. 543, 562–563 (1946); 3 Loss, Securities Regulation 1681–1682 (2d ed. 1961).

For discussions of the doctrine of *pari delicto* and the like, see Bateman Eichler Hill Richards, Inc. v. Berner, 472 U.S. 299, 105 S.Ct. 2622 (1985), supra page 1300; Loss & Cowett, Blue Sky Law 166–170 (1958); 3 Loss, Securities Regulation 1676–1680 (2d ed. 1961); Dahlquist, Regulation and Civil Liability Under the California Corporate Securities Act: IV, 34 Calif.L.Rev. 695, 697–701 (1946); Note, Denying Purchasers the Assertion of Illegality under Blue Sky Laws, 42 Va.L.Rev. 205 (1956).

---

5. 238 Cal.App.2d 141, 47 Cal.Rptr. 582 (1965).

6. 10 Utah 2d 1, 347 P.2d 553 (1959).

7. 217 Cal. 594, 20 P.2d 331 (1933).

8. On the statute of limitations in the Blue Sky area, see 3 Loss, Securities Regulation 1639–1643 (2d ed. 1961); Dahlquist, Regulation and Civil Liability Under the California Corporate Securities Act: IV, 34 Calif.L.Rev. 695, 701–710 (1946). In the California Corporate Securities Law of 1968, there is established a four-year statute of limitations (or one year after discovery by the plaintiff of the facts constituting the violation, whichever is earlier) for violations of the "fraud" sections (dealing with false or misleading statements or nondisclosure). West's Ann.Cal.Corp.Code, § 25506. There is a two-year statute of limitations (or one year after discovery by the plaintiff, whichever is earlier) for violations of the requirements for qualification of the sale of securities. Id., § 25507.

INDEX

BRIBERY
Contracts, securing contracts, jurisdiction, 1348
Foreign countries, enforcement, 1520
Racketeer influenced and corrupt organizations, 1444

BROKERS
Bankruptcy exemption, 439
Government securities, registration, 545
Licenses, state laws, 1608
Registration, 43
  Activities during waiting period, 90
  Revocation, 54
Repurchase of securities, limitation, 815
Sales, shelf shareholders, 492
Trading activities, regulation, 597
Transactions, 476

BURDEN OF PROOF
Racketeer influenced and corrupt organizations, 1496
Securities and exchange commission, enforcement, 1536

BURIED FACTS DOCTRINE
Civil liability, 1023

BUSH TASK GROUP
Regulation of financial services, 23

BUSINESS COMBINATIONS
Registration and disclosure, 408

BUSINESS JUDGMENT RULE
Trading in securities, 749

BUSINESS TRUSTS
Issuer, defined, 299

BYRNES CASE
Prospectus, preregistration distribution, 99

CARDIFF CASE
Takeovers, 704
Tender offers, 704

CARTER & JOHNSON CASE
Persons liable, 1202

CARTER HAWLEY HALE STORES CASE
Takeovers, tender offer regulations, 658

CASHOUT MERGER
Short-swing profits, 1431

CATERINICCHIA CASE
Securities and exchange commission, enforcement actions, 1537

CERTIFICATES OF DEPOSIT
Issuer, defined, 299
Securities, definitions, 256

CHANGE OF CIRCUMSTANCES
Sales, registration, 506

CHARITABLE ORGANIZATIONS
Exempt securities, 294
Securities Exchange Act of 1934, exemptions, 540

CHASINS CASE
Damages, dealers, fiduciary duties, 644

CHIARELLA CASE
Takeovers, disclosure, civil liability, 1027

CHICAGO BOARD OF OPTIONS EXCHANGE
Generally, 3

CHINESE CONSOLIDATED BENEVOLENT ASSOCIATION CASE
Registration, underwriters, 456

CHURNING
Generally, 639

CIVIL ACTIONS
Racketeer influenced and corrupt organizations, 1470

CIVIL LIABILITY
Generally, 832
Blue sky laws, 1670
Conduct creating liability, 969
Fault, evidence, 901
State laws, 1614

CLASS ACTIONS
Disclosure, damages, 1370
Fraud,
  Materiality, 1262
  Persons liable, 1131
Persons entitled to sue, 1093
Registration, fraud, conduct creating liability, 969

CLEARING AGENCIES
Registration, 43

CLOSE CORPORATIONS
Insiders, purchases, persons entitled to sue, 1126

COLLATERAL ESTOPPEL
Securities and exchange commission, enforcement actions, 1552

COLLEGES AND UNIVERSITIES
Exempt securities, 294
Securities Exchange Act of 1934, exemptions, 540

COMFORT LETTER
Merger and consolidation, persons liable, 1188

COMMERCIAL PAPER
Defined, securities, 220
Participation, definition of securities, 290

EXCESSIVE TRADING
Brokers, churning, 639
Commissions, 635

EXCHANGE NATIONAL BANK CASE
Notes, definition of securities, 244

EXCHANGE OF PROPERTY
Bankruptcy exemptions, 433
Fraud, conduct creating liability, 973
Persons liable, 1168
Reorganization, 399

EXEMPLARY DAMAGES
Generally, 1393
Racketeer influenced and corrupt organizations, 1508

EXEMPTIONS
Bankruptcy, 432
Brokers, transactions, 479
Dealers, transactions, 477
Integration of exemptions, 440
Interstate offerings, 378
Limited offering exemptions, 328
Registration, 40
    State laws, 1609
    State merit regulations, 1624
Reorganizations, 427
    Exchange of property, 399
Sales, 1652
Securities, 293
    Defined, 220
    Securities Act of 1934, 539
Underwriters, controlling persons, distributions, 467

EXPENSES AND EXPENDITURES
Going public, underwriters compensation, 139
Registration, statement, 139

EXTORTION
Racketeer influenced and corrupt organizations, 1464

FALSE STATEMENTS
Fraud, generally, this index

FARMERS COOPERATIVES
Exempt securities, 294

FAULT
Civil liability, evidence, 901

FEDER CASE
Short-swing profits, liability, 1395

FEDERAL BANKING LAWS
Generally, 21

FEDERAL RESERVE SYSTEM
Generally, 21

FEDERAL SECURITIES CODE
Generally, 171

FIDUCIARY RELATIONSHIP
Brokers, 652
Dealers, 652
Disclosure, civil liability, 1035

FINANCIAL STATEMENTS
Banks, civil liabilities, 873
Persons liable, 1181

FINES AND PENALTIES
Racketeer influenced and corrupt organizations, 1450
Securities and exchange commission, powers and duties, 53
State laws, 1614

FIXED PRICE OFFERINGS
Stock exchanges, 577

FORCED SELLER
Persons entitled to sue, 1124

FORECLOSURE
Racketeer influenced and corrupt organizations, 1464

FOREIGN COMMERCE
Racketeer influenced and corrupt organizations, 1444

FOREIGN COUNTRIES
Bribery,
    Enforcement, 1520
    Jurisdiction, 1348
Transnational transactions, 1564, 1582

FOREMOST-MCKESSON CASE
Short-swing profits, 1409

FORFEITURES
Racketeer influenced and corrupt organizations, 1450

FOUNDATIONS
Private offering exemptions, 300

FOUR (ONE AND A HALF) PHENOMENON
Resale, 522

FRANCHARD CORPORATION CASE
Real estate development, syndication arrangements, disclosure, 154
Registration, disclosure, 154

FRANCHISES
Securities, defined, 291

FRATERNAL ORGANIZATIONS
Exempt securities, 294
Securities Exchange Act of 1934, exemptions, 540

FRAUD
Blue sky laws, civil liability, 1670
Class actions, materiality, 1262
Commodity exchanges, damages, 857
Damages, this index

FRAUD—Cont'd
Dealers, excessive trading to generate commissions, 631
Defenses, 1288
Disclosures, voluntary disclosure, 190
Exempt securities, 293
Jurisdiction, 1336
Merit regulation, definitions, 1636
Persons entitled to sue, 1093
Persons liable, 1131
Purchases, civil liability, 1087
Racketeer influenced and corrupt organizations, 1444
Sales, civil liability, 1087
Securities, contribution, 146
Securities Act of 1933, 63
Securities and exchange commission, powers and duties, 53
Securities Exchange Act of 1934, 539
Shares and shareholders, continuous offerings, 611
State laws, 1614
Takeovers, conduct creating liability, 969
Trading activities, 615
Work product, immunity, 1351

FRAUD ON THE MARKET
Reliance, 1282

FREE–RIDING AND WITHHOLDING
Sales, maximum dollar figure, 620

FRUSTRATED SELLER
Persons entitled to sue, 1125

FULBRIGHT CASE
Production of documents and things, 1339

FUNGIBILITY CONCEPTS
Sales, registration, 506

FUTURE EVENTS
Prices, short-swing profits, 1436

FUTURES TRADING
 Generally, 3
Fraud, damages, 857

GAF CORPORATION CASE
Tender offiers, 693

GAMBLING
Racketeer influenced and corrupt organizations, 1464

GENERAL HOST CORPORATION CASE
Tender offers, compliance with statute, 716

GILLIGAN CASE
Sales, unregistered securities, 498

GIVE–UPS
Stock exchanges, commissions, 560

GLASS–STEAGALL ACT
Generally, 20, 22

GLOBUS CASE
Contribution, joint tort-feasors, 146
Registration, judgments and decrees, contribution, 126

GOING PRIVATE
Rules and regulations, 827
Treasury stock, purchases, 822

GOING PUBLIC
Back door, 448
Practice and procedure, 123
Registration, 122
Structure of the offering, 124, 125

GOLDBERG CASE
Civil liability, 1066

GOLDEN PARACHUTES
Generally, 807

GORDON CASE
Stock exchanges, regulation, 547

GOVERNMENT BONDS
Market structure, 3

GOVERNMENT SECURITIES
Exemptions, 1656

GOVERNMENT SECURITIES ACT OF 1986
Generally, 545

GRAND JURY
Transnational transactions, 1588

GRANDFATHER RIGHTS
Exempt securities, 293

GREEN CASE
Minority stockholders, elimination, 1059

GREEN MAIL
Takeover bids, 803
Tender offers, 683
Trading in securities, 763

GREENFIELD CASE
Civil liability, conduct creating liability, 992

GROUP LEGAL THERAPY
Tender offers, 701

GUILD FILMS COMPANY CASE
Registration, underwriters, 460

GUN JUMPING
Registration, 69

HANSON TRUST CASE
Tender offers, voting rights, 667

HARD SELL TACTICS
Persons liable, 1145

HARDSHIP
Discovery, 1350

SECURITIES ACT OF 1933—Cont'd
Section 5, limited offering exemptions, 374

SECURITIES ACT RELEASE NO. 312
Reorganization, court approval, 422

SECURITIES ACT RELEASE NO. 646
Reorganization, 400

SECURITIES ACT RELEASE NO. 2029
Reorganization, 403

SECURITIES ACT RELEASE NO. 3844
Generally, 72

SECURITIES ACT RELEASE NO. 4434
Controlling persons, sales, 495
Resale, controlling persons, 538

SECURITIES ACT RELEASE NO. 4968
Generally, 92

SECURITIES ACT RELEASE NO. 5009
Generally, 78

SECURITIES ACT RELEASE NO. 5101
Generally, 80

SECURITIES RELEASE ACT NO. 5180
Generally, 82

SECURITIES ACT RELEASE NO. 5316
Business combinations, 408
Resale of securities issued in bankruptcy, 533

SECURITIES ACT RELEASE NO. 5450
Interstate offerings, exemptions, 385
Resale under Rule 147, 538

SECURITIES ACT RELEASE NO. 5463
Reclassification, 415
Resale of securities in connection with acquisition, 534

SECURITIES ACT RELEASE NO. 5487
Private offering exemptions, 315

SECURITIES ACT RELEASE NO. 6389
Limited offering exemptions, 330

SECURITIES ACT RELEASE NO. 6455
Limited offering exemptions, 346

SECURITIES ACT RELEASE NO. 6499
Shelf registration, 199

SECURITIES EXCHANGE ACT RELEASE NO. 16385
Tender offers, 676

SECURITIES EXCHANGE ACT RELEASE NO. 23611
Shelf distribution, 484

SECURITIES AND EXCHANGE ACT OF 1934
Generally, 40

SECURITIES AND EXCHANGE ACT OF 1934—Cont'd
Civil liability, 832
Summary of rule, 81
Trading in securities, 539

SECURITIES AND EXCHANGE COMMISSION
Generally, 37
Disclosure, 152
Divisions, 49
Enforcement actions, 1509
Going public, review of registration statement, 133
Offices, 55
Organization, 48
Powers and duties, 50
Registration, review of statement, 132
Rules and regulations, 51

SECURITIES EXCHANGES
Stock Exchanges, generally, this index

SECURITIES MARKETS
Regulation, 547

SECURITY RATINGS
Disclosure, 119

SEDIMA, S.P.R.L. CASE
Racketeer influenced and corrupt organizations, 1448

SENTENCE AND PUNISHMENT
Racketeer influenced and corrupt organizations, 1450

SETOFF AND COUNTERCLAIM
Prospectus, preregistration delivery, damages, 105

SETTLEMENT
Compromise and Settlement, generally, this index

SHARES AND SHAREHOLDERS
Additional shares, issuance, 785
Cooperative apartments, definition of security, 230
Defenses, 1288
Defined, securities, 220
Deprivation of preemptive rights, civil liability, 837
Integration of offerings, 445
Market structure, 3
Persons entitled to sue, 1094
Preferred Stock, generally, this index
Securities, definitions, 260
Shelf shareholders, offerings by underwriters and dealers, 488
Speculative shares, disclosure, 150
Valuation, fraud, defenses, 1288

SHARK REPELLENTS
Takeover bids, 804
Tender offers, 683

TREASURY STOCK
Key employees, private offering exemptions, 303
Purchases, 818

TREBLE DAMAGES
Racketeer influenced and corrupt organizations, 1448, 1508

TRUST INDENTURE ACT OF 1939
Generally, 45

TRUST RECEIPTS
Exempt securities, 294

TRUSTS AND TRUSTEES
Exempt securities, 294
Limited offering exemptions, 350
Participation certificates, market structure, 3

TSC INDUSTRIES CASE
Proxies, materiality of evidence, 1241

TWO–TIER TENDER OFFERS
Generally, 712

UNDERWRITERS
Agreement, 134
Compensation, 586
Controlling persons, distributions, 465
Defined, 453
Fault, civil liability, 913
Going public, selection, 123, 124
Persons entitled to sue, 1128
Persons liable, 1180
Reclassification, 413
Registration, indemnification, 143
Resale, registration, 453
Securities, 31

UNDERWRITING AGREEMENT
Going public, 135

UNDERWRITING PROCESS
Investment, 25

UNIFORM SECURITIES ACT
Generally, 1605

UNITED STATES AUTOMATIC MERCHANDISING COMPANY CASE
Continuous offerings, registration, 606

UNITED STATES SECURITIES
Exemptions, 1656

UNIVERSAL CAMERA CORPORATION CASE
Disclosure,
Registration, 148
Traditional standards, 148

USURY
Racketeer influenced and corrupt organizations, 1464

VALUE ASSURANCE PLAN
Takeovers, defenses, 797

VENTURE CAPITAL
Private offering exemptions, 318
Stock exchanges, restrictions, 592

VENUE
Generally, 1336
Racketeer influenced and corrupt organizations, 1495

VEXATIOUS LITIGATION
Generally, 1102

VICARIOUS LIABILITY
Persons liable, 1159

VOLUME
Conditions, repurchase of securities, 814

VOTING RIGHTS
Takeovers, tender offers, 667

VOTING TRUST RECEIPTS
Issuer, defined, 299

WAGES
Compensation and Salaries, generally, this index

WAITING PERIOD
Registration, 84
Identifying statement, 88

WAIVER
Blue sky laws, defenses, 1673
Brokers, wait and see investors, 633

WARRANTS
Reorganization, 396

WEALTH
Promises of quick wealth, persons liable, 1145

WHEAT REPORT
Reorganization, 405
Sales, registration, 506

WHEELING PITTSBURGH STEEL CO. CASE
Securities and Exchange Commission, enforcement actions, 1509

WHITE KNIGHT
Hostile tender offer, shark repellent, 805
Tender offers, 683

WILLIAMS ACT
Civil liability, 841
Takeovers, fraud, 843
Tender offers, 660

WITHDRAWAL RIGHTS
Tender offers, trading and securities, 779

†